Pratt&
Kulsrud

Dear Student,

We are excited you decided to take a course in a field we have dedicated our life to teaching. We understand this is likely your first in-depth exposure to the study of taxation and do not necessarily share our passion for taxes. Indeed, if you're like most, taxation is probably a subject that you have been dreading. So, in every edition we have been very careful to match our enthusiasm and experience with the expectations of the first-time student. What you will discover is a unique and proven pedagogy. At first glance, the tax law appears to be an endless maze of boring rules and regulations. However, we try to make sense of the complexity. Throughout the text, we explain the rationale underlying the rule. We have found that students who understand the reason for the rule also have an easier time in learning how the rule applies. It's a simple but effective approach. This technique has helped thousands of students we have taught not only to learn more about taxes but have fun doing it.

Since staying current on the latest tax laws and regulations is important, we continue, as we have with every edition, to highlight the changes. We wait to the last possible moment to go to press so as not to miss any key changes. In addition, at our website **www.prattkulsrud. com** you will see we continue to supplement the book with updates for new legislation and other current developments that affect the taxation of individuals, corporations, partnerships, estates, and trusts.

Finally, if you find yourself in need of additional learning tools, you will find at our website an online study guide. With its chapter review, study guide questions and true-false/multiple-choice questions, the study guide is an excellent companion to the text.

We wish you the very best in your course and your career.

Cordially,

Jim Pratt & Bill Kulsrud

Pratt & Kulsrud

James W. Pratt
William N. Kulsrud

Contributing Authors

Hughlene A. Burton, Ph.D., C.P.A.
University of North Carolina at Charlotte

Christine C. Cheng, Ph.D.
Louisiana State University

Marguerite R. Hutton, Ph.D., C.P.A.
Western Washington University

Robert W. Jamison, Ph.D., C.P.A.
Indiana University

William N. Kulsrud, Ph.D., C.P.A.
Indiana University

Nathan Oestreich, Ph.D., C.P.A.
San Diego State University

James W. Pratt, D.B.A., C.P.A.
University of Houston

Roby B. Sawyers, Ph.D., C.P.A.
North Carolina State University

Edward J. Schnee, Ph.D., C.P.A.
University of Alabama

Steven C. Thompson, Ph.D., C.P.A.
Texas State University

INDIVIDUAL TAXATION

2018 EDITION

VAN-GRINER

Individual Taxation

2018 Edition

James W. Pratt
William N. Kulsrud

Printed in the United States of America
10 9 8 7 6 5 4 3 2 1
ISBN: 978-1-61740-434-4

Van-Griner Publishing
Cincinnati, Ohio
www.van-griner.com

CEO: Mike Griner
President: Dreis Van Landuyt
Project Manager: Maria Walterbusch
Customer Care Lead: Julie Reichert

Pratt 434-4 Sp17
179370
Copyright © 2018

Preface

Welcome to the 2018
Pratt & Kulsrud Taxation Series

Proven Approach

Our focus has always been one that blends Code and context. We try to decipher the law and explain it in a way students can appreciate and understand. Then, we incorporate thousands of examples to provide students with the right amount of context. Because students are more likely to remember the rules when they're set in a historical perspective, we try to provide the underlying rationale whenever it makes sense. Students not only learn the "what" of the tax law, but they better understand the "how" and the "why" as well. As tax professionals and authors, we have been explaining the fundamentals of the statutory law clearly and efficiently for over 35 years, helping to better prepare our students for what awaits them in their careers. Interestingly, even the IRS has used our book for their training programs!

Our logical approach to teaching tax is tried and true—we follow the organization of the Code as well as the 1040. We start with an overview of the tax formula, and then, in the chapters that follow, we systematically examine each component of the computation: income, exclusions, deductions, credits, and property transactions. If you're looking for a topic, it's easy to find!

Thorough and Flexible

The sheer number of rules and regulations makes it nearly impossible to cover all the material in the course time allotted. Do you want to cover the ABLE accounts, 529 Plans, MACRS, 1231, AMT, UNICAP, EITC, DPAD, IRAs, PTINs, and more? Maybe yes—and maybe no. While other books may channel you into covering a specific set of topics, we cover all topics and let you decide which topics best meet the needs of your students. Regardless of your approach, the content you need is in our books, so you can tailor your syllabus to meet your requirements. It's all in there, so cover (and cut) what you want. We also offer custom options and can create a unique book that suits your particular course, department, or curriculum. Ask us about our custom options.

Self-Checks

Today's students want immediate feedback. They want to confirm they understand what they've read. To help them, we've created Check Your Knowledge questions and placed them immediately following core blocks of material, so students can quickly determine how well they understand the concepts they've just covered. There is no log-in, no clicking, no searching! Each question requires students to fully grasp the applicable tax laws before they can answer it correctly. In addition, we've classroom tested these questions to ensure they address all the key issues.

Quick References for Form 1040 Topics

We also have a tool that both instructors and students should like, our Quick References for Form 1040. Immediately preceding the inside back cover, you will find a Form 1040. For each line, we have inserted a page number in the text where the item for this line is discussed. These references should help instructors find where we cover various topics and help students understand how a particular topic translates to the form as well aiding them when preparing tax return problems.

Tax Return Problems and the Software to do Them

Most students like to do tax returns, and we provide an assortment of problems and problem styles that allows students to deepen their experience with this core competency. Do you like end-of-semester comprehensive tax-return problems that require students to use multiple concepts and understand them in detail? Each edition of our book has three new comprehensive problems that provide variety and depth. In case you missed it, we recently added a comprehensive problem devoted solely to property transactions (e.g., Sections 1231, 1245, and 1250). Or maybe cumulative problems are more your style? The end of each chapter includes problems that require students to draw on material covered in previous chapters. We also have what we call continuous problems. We start with a basic fact pattern and, with each new chapter, add additional facts that apply the principles in that chapter. To support these continuous problems, we include a variety of tax documents—such as a W-2, 1099, or K-1—populated with data just like it would be in the real world.

To enhance the real-world simulation, each new book includes H&R Block™ software. This software is perfect for the continuous tax return problems. Students can build problem solutions, adjust for new and additional facts, and test the way different data affects outcomes. And to ensure students truly understand, we include follow-up questions that require students to explain how the software arrived at a particular answer. For example, a question might ask how a self-employment tax figure was calculated or what difference an extra $100,000 of income would make.

As We Go to Press

This textbook has been revised to reflect tax law changes and significant judicial and administrative developments during the past year. As we go to press, Congress is considering various proposals that may lead to significant and immediate changes in the tax law. Should any of these proposals be enacted, we will continue our long-standing policy of posting these changes to the Pratt & Kulsrud instructor website, **www.prattkulsrud.com.**

For the Student

A *Study Guide to Accompany Individual Taxation 2018* is available online at **www.prattkulsrud.com.** Written by the authors, the Study Guide provides in-depth chapter reviews, study exercises, and true-false/multiple-choice questions. These materials may be used in students' initial study of the chapter content, and also in their review. The Study Guide is only available online.

Enhanced and Updated Support for Instructors

Instructor Website. The 2018 edition continues with its one-stop instructor resource website. At **www.prattkulsrud.com** you will find access to all of these items. To register for access, visit the site and complete the registration form.

- **Solutions Manual.** Solutions to end-of-chapter discussion questions and computational problems are included in this manual. Specific pages and examples from the text are referenced, as are supporting statutory and administrative authorities, when appropriate.

- **Instructor's Resource Guide and Test Bank.** This guide contains answers to the tax research questions found in the text as well as solutions to the tax return problems, complete with filled-out forms. In addition, the Instructor's Guide includes a test bank of more than 750 objective questions (true-false and multiple choice), whose answers reference specific pages and examples in the text.

- **PowerPoint® Slides.** Designed for classroom use, there are slides for each chapter's principal topics. In addition, there are slides containing solutions for many problems. These solution slides typically are animated so that parts of the solution can be revealed however the instructor desires.

- **Lecture Outlines.** These outlines provide additional background on various subjects contained in the chapters as well as useful tips on how to teach the topics.

- **Legislative Updates.** Page-specific updates, tax law changes, and inflation adjustments are posted on a regular basis to the Pratt & Kulsrud website: **www.prattkulsrud.com.**

Instructor's Resources

Instructor ancillaries—including the Solutions Manual, Instructor's Resource Guide and Test Bank, PowerPoint Slides, and Lecture Outlines—are provided online at our website. Moreover, if you have any questions, any problems, any comments, you can contact Professor Kulsrud directly at wkulsrud@iupui.edu. How many other textbooks encourage you to contact the authors! These resources give instructors the ultimate tool for preparing and customizing lectures, presentations, and exams. The test bank files are provided in Microsoft® Word so they can be modified easily for your use.

Additional Offerings from the Pratt & Kulsrud Taxation Series

The series includes new editions of

Corporate, Partnership, Estate and Gift Taxation
2018 Edition
ISBN 978-1-61740-432-0

Areas of taxation essential to the education of individuals pursuing careers in taxation or tax-related fields are emphasized. The first eight chapters are devoted to the tax problems of regular corporations and their shareholders. Two chapters consider the taxation of partnerships and partners, and two chapters examine S corporations. These chapters are followed by two separate chapters examining the special problems of international taxation and state and local taxation, areas of growing importance. Another chapter discusses Federal estate and gift taxation. And two additional chapters contain related topics for the income taxation of estates, trusts and beneficiaries, and the major aspects of family tax planning. The scope of this text is intentionally broad to accommodate a variety of uses and to provide flexibility for instructors designing advanced tax courses. Includes H&R Block™ desktop software.

Federal Taxation
2018 Edition
ISBN 978-1-61740-433-7

To offer maximum flexibility in your course, the text not only focuses on the Federal income taxation of individuals, but also covers additional topics, such as the income taxation of regular corporations and shareholders; the taxation of partnerships and S corporations; Federal estate and gift taxation; the income taxation of estates, trusts, and beneficiaries; and the major aspects of family tax planning. Includes H&R Block™ desktop software.

Acknowledgments

The editor and author team would like to thank particularly Silvia F. Hinkley, James Motter of Indiana University, Jeff McGowan of Trine University, Susan Megaard of Eastern Washington University, Leonard Goodman of Rutgers University, Brigitte Muehlmann of Babson University, and Ramon Fernandez of St. Thomas University for their comments and suggestions. In addition, the editors and authors would like to acknowledge Van-Griner's Project Manager, Maria Walterbusch, who has gone beyond the call of duty in helping us compile this year's book. Her work on this edition has led to a strong revision that will benefit both students and instructors.

Brief Contents

Contents

Part 3   Deductions and Losses

Chapter 7   Overview of Deductions and Losses   7-1

Part 6   Employee Compensation and Taxation of Business Forms

Appendices

Index

Quick References

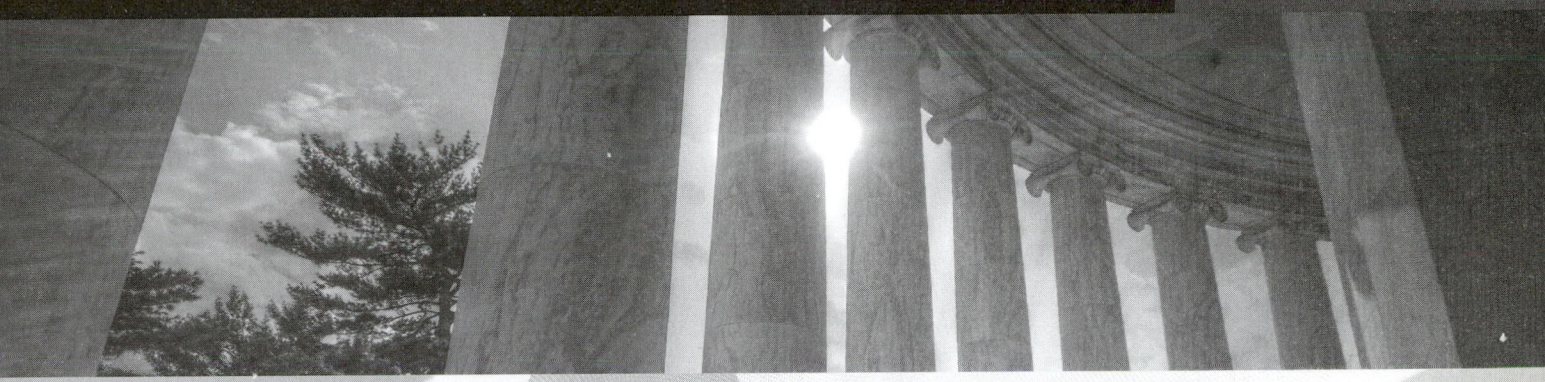

Introduction to the Federal Tax System

1

An Overview of Federal Taxation

Learning Objectives

Upon completion of this chapter you will be able to:

LO.1 Explain what a tax is and distinguish it from other types of government charges.

LO.2 Trace the historical development of our Federal income tax system.

LO.3 Explain the key terms used to describe most taxes.

LO.4 Identify the different types of Federal taxes found in the United States.

LO.5 Describe the estate tax and the gift tax and their relationship.

LO.6 Explain the differences in the employment taxes levied on employees versus those levied on self-employed individuals.

LO.7 Identify some of the more common social and economic goals of our Federal tax system.

Chapter Outline

Introduction

The United States has developed what is perhaps the most sophisticated and complex national tax systems in the world today. So why does it matter? The answer is simple but not necessarily obvious. Taxes are important because, believe it or not, they impact virtually everything Americans do. Taxes are everywhere. Think about life's major decisions. Planning on getting married? For tax purposes, it may be better to remain single. But then again, depending on your incomes, it may be better to be married. Having kids or thinking adoption? The tax system rewards parents with a host of deductions and credits that reduce the cost having children as well as incentives to adopt or to be a foster parent. Saving for college? Income from a 529 investment is never taxed if used for education. Taking a job? Taxes are reduced for job seeking expenses and there's another tax break if that job requires a move. Buying a house or renting? The tax law subsidizes the cost of home ownership but offers nothing to renters. Thinking about saving for retirement? Look before leaping since some investments are taxed differently than others. Where to retire? Florida has no income tax. Arizona does. And what about dying? The final act might be taxed. Dying in some states like Illinois or New York triggers a death tax. For others, there is no exit charge.

Of course, taxes also impact business decisions since taxes are just another cost of doing a business—for many businesses, taxes are their major cost. And, like any cost, with some attention, their cost can be reduced. It starts when the business begins. What form should the new business take? Someone said that corporate income is taxed twice. Maybe a partnership or LLC would be better. What about acquiring the operating assets? Should the company buy or lease the equipment? What about location? Should the business be located in Kansas City, Missouri or Kansas City, Kansas? They are just two places separated by a river but maybe one state has a friendlier tax system than its neighbor. What about shifting production to Ireland? The corporate tax rate for Irish companies is far less than the U.S. rate.

As the examples above suggest, the tax law has a long arm, reaching, touching, and affecting Americans and their businesses in many of their personal and business decisions. Moreover, taxes are not a one time phenomenon. Their impact is recurring. At a minimum, they are an annual event. However, the more prudent approach is to understand that taxes are not something to think about only once a year. But rather, they are an ongoing consideration. Arguably, for every decision, some thought should be given to the tax implications. For this reason, the primary purpose of this book is to help build a *tax awareness* (i.e., ability to recognize tax problems, pitfalls, and planning opportunities). Such an awareness is not only an important attribute of accountants and lawyers—it enables all who have it to make better decisions.

THE NATURE OF A TAX

LO.1

Explain what a tax is and distinguish it from other types of government charges.

The Supreme Court of the United States has defined a *tax* as "an exaction for the support of the Government."[1] Thus, what a tax does is to provide a means by which the government derives a majority of the revenues necessary to keep it in operation. A tax is not merely a source of revenue, however. As discussed in a later section of this chapter, taxes have become a powerful instrument that policymakers use to attain social as well as economic goals.

A tax normally has one or more of the following characteristics:

1. There is no *direct relationship* between the exaction of revenue and any benefit to be received by the taxpayer. Thus, a taxpayer cannot trace his or her tax payment to an Army jeep, an unemployment payment, a weather satellite, or any of the myriad expenditures that the Federal government authorizes.

2. Taxes are levied on the basis of *predetermined criteria*. In other words, taxes can be objectively determined, calculated, and even planned around.

---

[1] *U.S. v. Butler,* 36-1 USTC ¶9039, 16 AFTR 1289, 297 U.S. 1, 70 (USSC, 1936). An explanation of case citations such as this is presented in Chapter 2.

3. Taxes are levied on a *recurring* or *predictable* basis. Most taxes are levied on an annual basis, although some, like the estate tax, are levied only once.

4. Taxes *may be distinguished* from regulations or penalties. A regulation or penalty is a measure specifically designed to control or stop a particular activity. For instance, at one time Congress imposed a charge on the products of child labor. This charge was specifically aimed at stopping the use of children in manufacturing and thus was a regulation rather than a tax, even though it was called a "tax." Also, taxes can be distinguished from licenses and fees, which are payments made for some special privilege granted or services rendered (e.g., marriage license or automobile registration fee).

The major types of taxes imposed by taxing authorities within the United States (e.g., income, employment, and wealth transfer taxes) are discussed later in this chapter. As will be noted, one or more of the above characteristics can be found in each of these various taxes.

Development of U.S. Taxation

The entire history of the United States, from its beginnings as a colony of England to the present day, is entwined with the development of Federal taxation. From its infancy until well into the current century, the United States Federal tax system closely paralleled the tax laws of its mother country, England.[2]

LO.2
Trace the historical development of our Federal income tax system.

EXCISE AND CUSTOMS DUTIES

Shortly after the colonies won independence and became the United States of America, tariffs became the Federal government's principal revenue-raising source.[3] At the time of its adoption in 1789, the U.S. Constitution gave Congress the power to levy and collect taxes. Promptly exercising this authority, Congress passed as its first act the Tariff Act of 1789, which imposed a system of duties (called excise taxes) on imports.

FEDERAL INCOME TAX

As time passed and the Federal government enlarged the scope of its activities, it became more and more apparent to political leaders that they would need to identify additional sources of revenue to supplement the tariff system. Congress enacted the first Federal income tax in 1861 to finance the vastly increased expenditures brought on by the Civil War. The income tax was reasonably successful. However, when the Civil War came to an end so did the need for additional revenues as well as need for an income tax. The tax was repealed officially in 1872. With the repeal of the income tax, the burden of financing government once again was placed on a system of tariffs and duties.

But the tariff system had its opponents. Many believed that a tax system that relied on tariffs protected capitalists by protecting their products from competition from imports. They also argued that tariffs increased the prices of goods, and consequently, the burden of taxation was disproportionately imposed on the poor and middle class. As a result, the allure of an income tax—reducing tariffs and increasing the tax burden on the affluent—did not die, particularly among populist politicians. From 1872 to 1894, Congress introduced more than sixty bills to restore the income tax. This effort culminated in the reenactment of the income tax in 1894. However, less than a year later, the Supreme Court ultimately held that it was unconstitutional.[4]

Shortly thereafter, in 1909, Congress was able to enact an income tax on corporations. Interestingly, this tax was found to be constitutional on other grounds.[5] More importantly, with the passage of the corporate income tax, Congress proposed an amendment to the

---

[2] The states in turn have developed their own systems of taxation which often parallel—but sometimes diverge from—the Federal tax system.

[3] A tariff is a duty imposed on an importer. Since it is a cost of the product being imported, it usually is passed on to the consumer as part of the product's price. Thus, the higher the

tariff imposed on a product, the higher must be its price if importation is to be profitable.

[4] *Pollock v. Farmers' Loan and Trust Co.*, 3 AFTR 2602, 157 U.S. 429 (USSC, 1895).

[5] *Flint* v. *Stone Tracy Co.*, 3 AFTR 2834, 220 U.S. 107 (USSC, 1911).

Constitution that would allow it to levy a tax on *all* incomes. This effort resulted in the passage of the Sixteenth Amendment on February 25, 1913, which provided that

> The Congress shall have the power to lay and collect taxes on incomes from whatever source derived, without apportionment among the several States, and without regard to any census or enumeration.

Without hesitation, Congress enacted the Revenue Act of 1913 on October 3, 1913 and made it retroactive to March 1, 1913.

Because of special exemptions and the progressive tax rates of the 1913 income tax law, it too was challenged as a denial of due process of law as guaranteed by the Fifth Amendment to the Constitution. In 1916 the Supreme Court upheld the validity of the new income tax law in *Brushaber v. Union Pacific Railroad Co.*[6] Although many changes have taken place, the United States has not been without a Federal income tax since 1913.

As historical conditions changed and the Federal government's need for additional revenues increased, Congress exercised its income taxing authority by the passage of many separate pieces of legislation that resulted in greater complexity in the Federal income tax law. Each new revenue act was a reenactment of a previous revenue act with added amendments. This process created great confusion for those working with the law, since it could be necessary to research more than 100 separate sources to determine exactly what law was currently in effect. In addition, the reenactment of a statute sometimes suggested that any intervening interpretation of that statute (law) by the courts or the Treasury was approved by Congress, although no such Congressional approval was expressly stated. Congress resolved the confusion in 1939 with its systematic arrangement of all tax laws into the Internal Revenue Code of 1939, a permanent codification that required no reenactment.

The 1939 Code was revised in 1954 and again in 1986. Thus, today's governing Federal tax law is the *Internal Revenue Code of 1986*. The 1986 Code has been amended by significant tax changes made since 1986, and it will continue to be amended to incorporate changes in the tax law as those changes are enacted.

TAX LAW ADMINISTRATION

The administration of the tax laws in the United States is the responsibility of the Internal Revenue Service or as it is commonly called, the IRS. The IRS is 1 of 10 bureaus of the Department of the U.S. Treasury. Its head is referred to as the Commissioner of the IRS and is appointed by the President with the consent of the Senate. The Commissioner is in charge of leading an agency that in 2015 had more than 78,000 employees and a budget of over $11 billion.

The IRS serves as the nation's tax collection agency and administers the tax laws that are enacted by Congress. In fiscal year 2015, the IRS collected almost $3.3 trillion in revenue and processed almost 250 million tax returns. It's annual report for 2015 estimates that it spent just 35 cents for each $100 it collected!

The IRS is routinely criticized and held responsible for what many see as an unfair and unwieldy tax system. However, in reality, the IRS only implements the laws that Congress writes. Arguably, if the public wants to blame anyone, it should blame its elected officials!

FEDERAL TAXES AS A SOURCE OF REVENUE

Among sources of revenue, only the Federal income tax can claim a dominant role in providing the funds with which the U.S. government operates. The chart in Exhibit 1-1 illustrates the role of the Federal income tax in funding the federal government in fiscal year 2016.[7] Of the total tax collections, excluding "contributions" to Social Security, Medicare and unemployment and borrowing, about 86% come from individual and corporate income

---

[6] 240 U.S. 1 (USSC, 1916).

[7] See Instructions to Form 1040 (2016), p. 102 Internal Revenue Service

taxes. Observe the limited role of excise taxes, including estate and gift taxes. Note also that the proposed budget shows an operating deficit of about $438 billion ($3.250 trillion of expenditures − $3.688 trillion of revenues = $438 billion deficit). Interestingly, from 1900–2015, there have been only 32 years during which the Federal government has operated at a surplus![8]

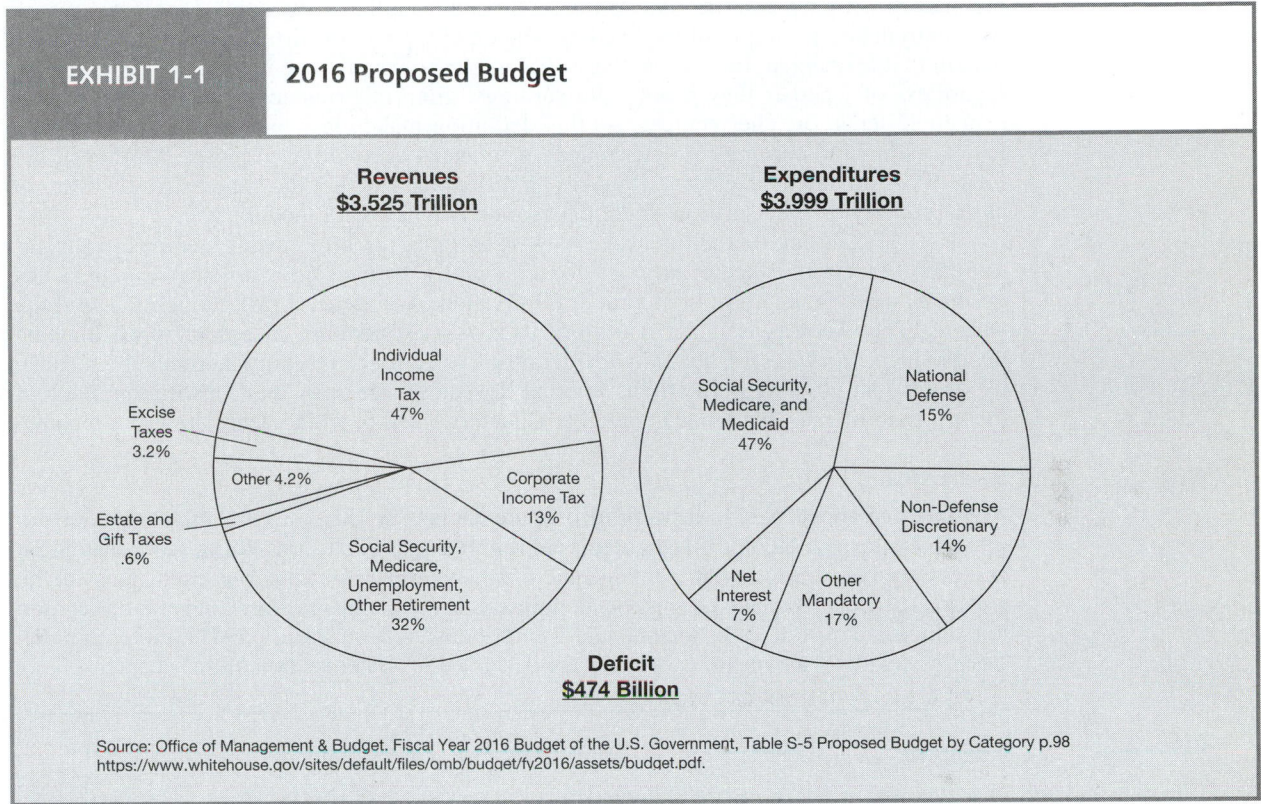

EXHIBIT 1-1	2016 Proposed Budget

Revenues
$3.525 Trillion

- Individual Income Tax 47%
- Excise Taxes 3.2%
- Other 4.2%
- Estate and Gift Taxes .6%
- Corporate Income Tax 13%
- Social Security, Medicare, Unemployment, Other Retirement 32%

Expenditures
$3.999 Trillion

- Social Security, Medicare, and Medicaid 47%
- National Defense 15%
- Non-Defense Discretionary 14%
- Net Interest 7%
- Other Mandatory 17%

Deficit
$474 Billion

Source: Office of Management & Budget. Fiscal Year 2016 Budget of the U.S. Government, Table S-5 Proposed Budget by Category p.98
https://www.whitehouse.gov/sites/default/files/omb/budget/fy2016/assets/budget.pdf.

KEY TAX TERMS

Before examining the various types of Federal taxes in more detail, the reader must first become familiar with basic tax terminology. Some of the more common terms are briefly presented below.

LO.3

Explain the key terms used to describe most taxes.

Tax Base

A tax base is that amount upon which a tax is levied. For instance, in the case of Federal income taxation, the tax base is *taxable income*. Taxable income is the taxpayer's total income less exclusions, deductions, and exemptions that might be available to a particular taxpayer. In the case of the Federal wealth transfer taxes, the tax base is the fair market value of the property transferred by gift or at death *reduced* by certain exclusions, exemptions, or deductions allowed by Congress.

[8] See Table 1.1—Summary of Receipts, Outlays, and Surpluses or Deficits: 1789–2020 at http://www.whitehouse.gov/omb/budget/Historicals.

Income

The computation of taxable income begins with a determination of the taxpayer's income. This is not always as simple as it may seem. For tax purposes, the definition of income is extremely broad. This was made clear in a landmark court case that concerned whether punitive damages awarded to one company for fraud and antitrust violations by another company were income for tax purposes. In this case, the Supreme Court explained that income for tax purposes includes "all accessions to wealth."[9] Under this approach—a now well-entrenched principle of the tax law—income consists of virtually every conceivable benefit that is realized. In essence, these "accessions to wealth" are income for tax purposes regardless of whether they result from earnings, gifts, inheritances, capital gains, prizes, cancelled debts, or other sources. As this definition make clear, income for tax purposes is not confined to earnings as determined for financial accounting purposes. Moreover, the form of the income is irrelevant. It makes no difference whether the benefits received are in cash, property or even services that are performed on behalf of the taxpayer.

Notwithstanding this all-inclusive view of income, not all items of income are subject to Federal taxation. Whether they are taxed generally depends upon whether Congress has *exempted* a particular form of income from taxation. As a general rule, Congress—and the various Federal courts assigned to interpret its laws—consider *any* increment to wealth to be taxable income *unless* it is *excluded* by definition (e.g., loans received that must be repaid), by specific statutory authority in the Internal Revenue Code or by the Constitution. Each of these possibilities is examined in detail in Chapters 5 and 6, which deal with gross income.

Exclusion

As suggested above, certain items of income are not taxable (i.e., they are nontaxable and not included in taxable income). These items are referred to as exclusions. Since the Constitution grants Congress the authority to tax income *from whatever source derived,* exclusions are the creations of Congress. For various social, political, or economic reasons, Congress has chosen to exclude many sources of income and wealth transfers from taxation. The more common Congressional objectives for exclusions are discussed in a later section of this chapter.

Example 1

This year N received a $14,000 graduation gift from her aunt. N does not have to include this amount in determining taxable income because Congress has specifically excluded gifts from income. If N had received the $14,000 in exchange for rendering services to her aunt, or if N had received the $14,000 for appearing on a television game show, then in both cases she would have to include (report) the amount in income subject to taxation.

Example 2

Refer to *Example 1* above. If N's aunt transfers $14,000 to N in the current year as a graduation gift, and this is the only gift made by the aunt to N in the current year, this transfer will not be subjected to the Federal gift tax. Congress has provided an annual exclusion from gift taxation of $14,000 per donee in 2017.

---

[9] *Glenshaw Glass v. U.S.,* 55-1 USTC ¶9308, 47 AFTR 162, 348 U.S. 426 (USSC, 1955).

Deduction

A deduction is a reduction in the gross (total) amount that must be included in the taxable base. For instance, when an individual taxpayer incurs expenses such as medical expenses, interest on a home mortgage, or property taxes, he or she generally will be allowed to deduct these expenses to arrive at taxable income for Federal tax purposes. Similarly, corporations are allowed to deduct most of their costs of doing business to determine corporate taxable income. It is *extremely important* to note, however, that deductions are said to be a matter of legislative grace. In other words, unless Congress has specifically authorized a particular deduction, the expense will not be deductible.

Example 3

Shortly after graduation from college, Tim and Jennifer were married. They immediately bought a home where they have lived for the last five years. The home cost $200,000. This year the couple sold their home for $190,000. They may not take a deduction for the $10,000 loss (a permanent reduction in wealth) in determining taxable income *because* Congress has not authorized a deduction for this particular type of loss.

Most deductions available to individual taxpayers and to other taxable entities (i.e., corporations, estates, and trusts) are discussed in detail in Chapters 7 through 12 of this text.

Tax Rates

A tax rate is some percentage applied to the tax base to determine a taxpayer's liability. Tax rate structures usually are either proportional or progressive. A *proportional* tax rate is one that remains at a constant percentage regardless of the size of the tax base. A *progressive* tax rate structure is one in which an increasing percentage rate is applied to increasing increments of the tax base. A *regressive* tax rate structure is one in which a decreasing percentage rate is applied to increasing increments of the tax base.

Example 4

B has taxable income of $5,000 and pays a tax of $500, or 10% of the tax base. C's tax base is $10,000 and the tax on this amount is $1,000, or 10 percent. If the same constant rate of 10% is applied to any amount of tax base, the tax is proportional. In other words, if the rate remains the same regardless of increases or decreases in the base, the rate is proportional. Most sales taxes are proportional.

Example 5

R has a tax base of $10,000 and pays a tax of $500 on the first $5,000, and a tax of $1,000 on the next $5,000. The total tax of $1,500 was calculated by applying a 10% rate to the first $5,000 increment of the tax base and then applying a 20% rate to the excess tax base over $5,000. Since a higher percentage rate is applied as the tax base increases, this is a progressive rate structure. In other words, if the rate increases as the base increases, the rate is progressive. The federal income tax and most state income taxes are progressive.

The 2017 Federal income tax rate schedules for individual taxpayers appear on the inside back cover of this text for ready reference. The income tax rates for corporations, estates, and trusts are presented on the inside back cover of the text. The Federal gift and estate tax rates are reproduced in Appendix A-3 at the back of the text. A glance at either of these sources will reveal the progressive nature of the Federal tax system.

Marginal, Average, and Effective Tax Rates

It is not surprising that tax rates receive a great deal of attention. Since taxes have such a significant impact on taxpayer's lives, everyone has an interest in—as well as an opinion about—tax rates. Are tax rates too high or too low? Are they too progressive or too flat? In any dialogue regarding tax rates, it is important to understand the terminology and distinguish between three different tax rate concepts: the marginal rate, the average rate and the effective tax rate. To put it another way, when politicians talk about raising or lowering tax rates, it is important to understand exactly what rate they are talking about.

Marginal Tax Rates. The marginal tax rate of any tax rate structure is that percentage at which the next unit of the tax base will be taxed. For example, in the case of the income tax, if a taxpayer earns an additional dollar of income, the marginal rate would be the rate that applied to that dollar. The marginal tax rates of the Federal income tax rate structure for single and married taxpayers for 2017 and the amounts of income to which they apply are shown below:

Tax Rate	Single Taxpayers Taxable Income	Married Taxpayers Taxable Income
10%	$ 0 – $ 9,325	$ 0 – $ 18,650
15	9,325 – 37,950	18,650 – 75,900
25	37,950 – 91,900	75,900 – 153,100
28	91,900 – 191,650	153,100 – 233,350
33	191,650 – 416,700	233,350 – 416,700
35	416,700 – 418,400	416,700 – 470,700
39.6	Over $418,400	Over $470,700

Note the progressive or graduated nature of the rate structure. There are currently seven marginal tax rates for individuals, starting at 10% and climbing to a high of 39.6 percent. Each of these rates applies to a range of income known as a tax bracket. It is not uncommon to hear people say they are in a particular tax bracket. If a single person says he is in the "25% bracket," it simply means that his taxable income is at a level ($37,950 – $91,900 in 2017) such that the next dollar of income is taxed at 25 percent. While the tax rates for married taxpayers are the same as those for singles, they generally apply to different brackets of income. For the 10% and 15% rates, the married brackets are exactly twice the size of those for single taxpayers but vary thereafter until the top rate is reached. The potential for implicit tax "penalties" for being married or single, depending on a couple's income, who earns it and other factors, is discussed in Chapter 4.

Over the years, the tax rates and ranges of income to which they apply have varied dramatically. The first income tax that applied in 1913 had seven rates, ranging from 1 to 7 percent. In contrast, in 1962 there were 23 brackets, beginning at a rate of 22% and ending at 91 percent! No doubt rates and brackets will continue to change as Congress deems it necessary to balance the budget, raise revenues or to provide a tax cut. A typical tax computation using the current tax rate schedule is illustrated below.

Example 6

H, an unmarried taxpayer, has taxable income of $67,000 for 2017. Referring to tax rate Schedule X on the inside back cover of this text, an unmarried taxpayer with taxable income of $67,000 has a tax of $12,488.75 as computed below.[10] H's marginal tax rate is 25 percent.

2017 tax on $37,950	$ 5,226.25
Plus: Tax on income above $37,950: ([$67,000 – $37,950 = $29,050] × 25%)	7,262.50
Tax liability	$12,488.75

---

[10] For preparing tax returns, the IRS has prescribed rules for rounding. Round amounts of 50 cents or more up to the next whole dollar. For example, if the actual amount is $100.50, enter $101.00. Round amounts of less than 50 cents down to the next whole dollar. For example, an actual amount of $200.43 is rounded down to $200.00. If adding two or more amounts to figure the amount to enter on a line, include cents when adding the amounts and round off only the total. Thus the tax in the example above would be $12,489. See *2016 Instructions to Form 1040*, p. 20.

A taxpayer's knowledge of his or her marginal tax rate is essential in any tax-planning effort to minimize taxes. Without such knowledge, the tax impact of an additional dollar of the tax base or an additional dollar deduction cannot be determined.

Example 7

Refer to *Example 6*. H, age 40, is considering depositing $5,000 in a special savings vehicle for retirement referred to as an Individual Retirement Account. Contributions to such accounts are deductible and any income earned on the contributions are non-taxable until they are distributed. His immediate tax savings would be $1,250 (the 25% marginal tax rate × the $5,000 income not taxed). Similarly, if H had a 33% marginal tax rate and wanted to know the after-tax amount of a proposed $10,000 increase in salary, he would simply multiply $10,000 by 67% (100% − 33%). In such case, the after-tax value of the $10,000 salary increase would be $6,700.

Many individuals, including those who are highly educated, do not understand the marginal tax rate concept. All too often one hears the expression, "I can't afford to earn more because it will throw me into a higher tax bracket and I will keep less than I do now after taxes." This theoretically cannot occur unless the marginal tax rate exceeds 100 percent.

While the rates above normally are used to compute an individual's tax liability, a lower rate can apply. An individual's gains from the sale of so-called capital assets (e.g., corporate stocks) held for more than a year receive preferential treatment. Such gains, referred to as long-term capital gains, usually are taxed at 15 percent. Gains from sales of capital assets that are held for a year or less, short-term capital gains, are taxed at an individual's ordinary rates.

Corporate tax rates, like individual rates, are progressive (see inside back cover). The rates run from 15 percent to 35 percent. Corporations with taxable incomes less than $75,000 may take advantage of the lower rates. When taxable income exceeds the $75,000 threshold, corporations generally face marginal rates of 34% up to $10,000,000 of taxable income and 35% for taxable incomes exceeding the $10,000,000 mark. The long-term capital gains of a corporation receive no preferential treatment and are taxed at regular rates.

Average Tax Rates. The average rate is computed by dividing the taxpayer's tax liability by the tax base. For the income tax, the average tax rate is simply the tax divided by taxable income (tax ÷ taxable income).

Example 8

K, an unmarried taxpayer, has 2017 taxable income of $85,000 and pays a tax of $16,989. Although her marginal tax rate is 25 percent, K's average tax rate is only 19.99% ($16,989 ÷ $85,000).

Average tax rates are a bit misleading in that they seem to suggest that all units of the tax base (e.g., all dollars of income) are treated equally. But as seen above, in a progressive tax rate system where marginal rates increase as income increases, some dollars of income are taxed higher than others. The average tax rate is just that, an average. While providing some insight about the overall rate structure, average rates say little about the true impact of a tax on the taxpayer. For this information, effective tax rates are the preferred statistic.

Effective Tax Rates. The effective tax rate is computed by dividing the tax by some broader measure other than the tax base, often some quantity reflecting taxpayer's ability to pay. For example, for the income tax, the effective tax rate is normally determined by dividing the tax by total economic income (tax ÷ total economic income).

> ### Example 9
>
> Assume the same facts as in *Example 8* except that K's total economic income is $100,000, the $15,000 difference between total income and taxable income being attributable to exclusions and deductions (e.g., interest on tax-exempt bonds and the personal exemption). In such case, K would pay taxes at an effective rate of 16.99% [$16,989 ÷ $100,000].

Marginal rates are often confused with average rates and effective rates. For example, in decrying the harshness of the income tax, people often point to their marginal rate and declare that they are paying that percent (e.g., 25%) of their income to the government. A comparison of *Examples 8* and *9* above reveals that this clearly is not the case. Although the taxpayer has a marginal tax rate of 25% the average rate is 19.99% and the effective rate is only 16.99%, obviously much lower than the marginal rate.

While effective tax rates provide meaningful information about a taxpayer's tax burden, it is not without problems, the most difficult of which is that there is no uniform definition of total economic income or the amount that will serve as the denominator in the formula. Any use of effective tax rates must recognize this potential weakness. In practice, however, the denominator for any particular purpose such as financial reporting or economic studies is usually well-defined from the outset. As a result, effective tax rates (ETRs) usually provide a relatively straightforward measure of the percentage of income siphoned away by taxes. For this reason, ETRs are of great interest not only to individual taxpayers but also businesses, governments (U.S. and foreign), investors, analysts, academics, public interest groups and others.

One of the most common uses of the ETR concept can be found in financial reporting. Since taxes have a significant impact on a company's earnings, management, investors, creditors, and other users of financial statements are particularly interested in the company's ETR. Due to the importance of taxes on a company's net income, generally accepted accounting principles—specifically ASC 740 and its interpretations—require public companies to provide additional disclosures, a detailed footnote, regarding the impact of income taxes on financial statement income (book income).[11] This information includes the company's ETR. In this context, ETR generally is the percentage of taxes paid on pre-tax book income (tax ÷ pre-tax book income). Although a corporation's statutory U.S. tax rate is normally a flat 35 percent, the ETR usually differs. For example, the footnotes to the financial statements of Microsoft reported an ETR of 21% in 2014 and 19% in 2015.

Differences between the statutory rate and an ETR occur because book income may be higher or lower than taxable income. For example, interest income from municipal bonds is included in book income but is excluded from taxable income. Similarly dividend income is fully included in book income but corporations normally pay taxes on only 30% of their dividends. On the expense side, book income includes fines and penalties and life insurance premiums on key executives but taxable income does not allow deductions for such costs. In addition, book income includes income from foreign subsidiaries but is not included in a corporation's consolidated taxable income (until it is repatriated or paid back to the U.S. usually through dividend payments). The substantial difference between the U.S. statutory rate and the ETR for multinational companies like Microsoft, Google, Apple, Amazon, Starbucks, Walmart, Pfizer, and many more normally results because foreign earnings are taxed at foreign rates that are much lower than U.S. tax rate. For example, the Irish corporate tax rate in 2017 was only 12.5% and that is high compared to some tax havens such as Bermuda or the Cayman Islands. Corporations take advantage of these lower rates through a number of tax planning techniques such as locating manufacturing or distribution facilities in the low tax country.

The ETR is a useful tool since it provides a snapshot of whether a business is or is not paying taxes and if so, how much. In addition, the ETR provides a criterion for determining how well a business is managing its tax liability relative to other firms in the same industry or businesses as a whole.

---

[11] See *Accounting for Income Taxes,* Statement of Financial Accounting Standards No. 109, Financial Accounting Standards Board, 1992. For financial statement purposes, FAS 109 requires income tax expense to be based on financial statement income rather than actual taxable income. Thus actual taxes paid may differ significantly from the reported amount. The ETR provides a picture of the taxes actually paid relative to book income rather than taxable income.

Tax Credits

A tax credit is a dollar-for-dollar offset against a tax liability. A credit is quite different from a deduction, since it directly reduces the tax liability itself, whereas a deduction simply reduces the base amount subject to the tax.

Example 10

T is a single taxpayer with a 28% marginal tax rate. An additional $100 tax deduction would reduce T's tax by $28 (28% × $100). If the $100 qualified as a tax credit, however, T would have a $100 tax reduction—the equivalent of a $357 tax deduction at a marginal tax rate of 28% ($357 × 28% = $100).

Tax credits are discussed in detail in Chapter 13 of this text.

Withholding and Estimated Tax Payments

A critical feature of the income tax is its requirement for taxpayers to pay their tax as income is earned. The so-called pay-as-you-go system became a permanent part of the tax law with the enactment of the Current Tax Payment Act of 1943.[12] Faced at that time with the overwhelming revenue needs of World War II, the Treasury Department was able to convince Congress that collection at the source and withholding were necessary to "the very existence of the income tax." Treasury portrayed its withholding proposal as providing taxpayers "a way of meeting their tax obligations with a maximum of convenience and a minimum of hardship." Perhaps more important, Treasury viewed the system as a "way to collect some money from people who would not otherwise make any report on income." As one Treasury official testified "[W]e cannot get those fellows unless we have the collection-at-the-source method."

Almost 75 years after the adoption of pay-as-you-go, its withholding requirements make paying taxes—just as Treasury hoped back in 1943—simple and convenient. No doubt, the system could not function without collection at the source. That said, withholding has led to a problem that few thought about at its creation, refund fraud. More and more, dishonest individuals are stealing identities and using them to file false tax returns. These phony returns are completed so as to obtain refunds of taxes that honest taxpayers have paid during the year. During the last several years, the IRS has reported that refund fraud is increasing at an alarming rate.

Pay-as-you-go is made easy because the law requires all employers to withhold taxes from the pay of their employees. The tax withheld is based on the employee's income and other information that the employee provides to the employer. All employers must have employees complete Form W-4 Employee's Withholding Allowance Certificate (see Appendix B). On the W-4, employees indicate (1) the number of withholding allowances claimed (each allowance reduces the amount withheld); (2) the rate for withholding, single or the lower rate for marrieds, and (3) any additional amount that should be withheld. Much as many would like, employees cannot simply specify a particular amount of withholding. If an employee fails to provide his or her employer a properly completed Form W-4, the employer must withhold federal income taxes from the employee's wages as if he or she were single and claiming no withholding allowances.

For taxpayers who do not pay tax through withholding such as self-employed individuals, or who do not pay enough tax through withholding, the alternative is the payment of estimated taxes throughout the year. Payments normally must be made on April 15, June 15, September 15, and January 15 of the following year. As discussed in Chapter 4, taxpayers who fail to pay the required amount of taxes during the year on the dates above, may be required to pay a penalty.

Withholding is not limited to salaries and self-employment income. Taxes may also be withheld from other types of income such as interest, dividends, retirement income (e.g., pensions), bonuses, commissions, and gambling winnings. In each case, the amount withheld is paid to the IRS in the taxpayer's name.

---

[12] See Twight, "Evolution of Federal Income Tax Withholding: The Machinery of Institutional Change," 14 *Cato Journal* 3 (Winter, 1995) p. 359.

Major Types of Taxes

LO.4

Identify the different types of Federal taxes found in the United States.

Taxing authorities within the United States have a wide array of taxes that they use to raise revenues or attempt to effect social, political, or economic change. As someone once said, the motto for the IRS should be, we have what it takes to take what you have! Indeed, the average individual will feel the impact of quite a number of taxes during his or her lifetime. Although the principal thrust of this text is aimed at the Federal income and wealth transfer taxes, some of the other types of taxes merit a brief introduction.

INCOME TAXES

An income tax is generally a tax on some portion of a taxpayer's income as that term is defined for tax purposes. The income tax is imposed annually based on the taxpayer's taxable income for the year. In addition to the Federal government, most states and some local governments impose a tax on income.

When most people think about taxes, they tend to think of the federal income tax and rightfully so. It is without doubt, the most visible and productive tax in the U.S. As noted earlier in Exhibit 1-1, the individual income tax was budgeted to provide 47% of the Federal government's 2016 revenues. Of all the sources providing revenues to the Federal government, the individual income tax is the largest. In contrast, the corporate income tax was budgeted to provide only 13% of the Federal government's projected revenues in 2016.[13]

The Federal government imposes an income tax on individuals, corporations, estates, and trusts. Usually, a final tax reckoning (reporting and paying taxes due) is made at the end of each year. On every April 15, millions of Americans brave the annual ritual of filing what most know as an income tax return. On that return, taxpayers report their taxable income for the previous year and compute the tax on such income. The amount of tax that is actually due depends on how much tax was paid during the year. In order to ensure that the tax due is collected, Congress has created a pay-as-you-go requirement. Basically, this process requires employers to withhold and remit to the Federal government income taxes on wages paid to employees. Individuals with income from sources other than wages, and most other taxable entities, are required to make estimated tax prepayments during the year.[14] When individuals file their tax returns, their withholding and estimated tax payments are compared to their total tax due to determine whether the taxpayer owes additional tax or has paid too much during the year and is entitled to a refund.

Application of the Federal income tax to individuals is discussed in Chapters 3 and 4. Computation of a corporation's Federal income tax is explained in Chapter 19. The Federal income taxation of a business operated in either the partnership or corporate form is also examined in Chapter 19. For now, the procedures for determining the Federal income tax liability of corporate and individual taxpayers are reduced to computational formulas presented in Exhibits 1-2 and 1-3. The components of these formulas are introduced and discussed in greater detail in Chapter 3.

---

[13] Such heavy reliance on the income tax as a source of government revenues is peculiar to the United States. Most Western European nations have turned to a Value-Added Tax (VAT). A VAT is a system of taxing the increment in value of goods as they move through the production and manufacturing process to the market place. The VAT operates very much like a national sales tax and has occasionally been proposed, though unsuccessfully, for the United States.

[14] This procedure was developed by Congress during World War II to accelerate annual tax payments needed to finance the war effort. The process served so well to increase compliance with, and facilitate administration of, the Federal income tax law that Congress chose not to abandon it at the close of the war.

EXHIBIT 1-2	Tax Formula for Corporate Taxpayers	

Income (from whatever source)	$xxx,xxx
Less: Exclusions from gross income	− xx,xxx
Gross income	$xxx,xxx
Less: Deductions	− xx,xxx
Taxable income	$xxx,xxx
Applicable tax rates	xx%
Gross tax	$ xx,xxx
Less: Tax credits and prepayments	− x,xxx
Tax due (or refund)	$ xx,xxx

EXHIBIT 1-3	Tax Formula for Individual Taxpayers	

Income (from whatever source)		$xxx,xxx
Less: Exclusions from gross income		− xx,xxx
Gross income		$xxx,xxx
Less: Deductions for adjusted gross income		− xx,xxx
Adjusted gross income		$xxx,xxx
Less: 1. The larger of:		
a. Standard deduction	$x,xxx	
or	or	− x,xxx
b. Total itemized deductions	$x,xxx	
2. Personal and dependency exemptions ×		
exemption amount		− x,xxx
Taxable income		$xxx,xxx
Applicable tax rates (from tables or Schedules X, Y, or Z)		xx%
Gross tax		$ xx,xxx
Less: Tax credits and prepayments		− x,xxx
Tax due (or refund)		$ xx,xxx

Most states—43 in 2017—impose some sort of income tax.[15] Generally, state income taxes are designed to operate much like the Federal income tax. For example, most states use Federal adjusted gross income or Federal taxable income (see Exhibit 1-3) as the starting point in the calculation of state taxable income. States then make various modifications, adding or subtracting certain items. Some states allow a deduction for Federal income taxes, while others exclude income that is subject to Federal income taxation. Interest income from Federal government obligations (e.g., U.S. Treasury Bonds) is not subject to state income taxation, and interest income from state and local government obligations generally is not subject to either Federal or state income taxation. Most states have developed their own set of rates, exemptions, and credits; however, the filing date for the state income tax return generally coincides with the due date of the taxpayer's Federal income tax return.[16] Almost all states have a tax withholding procedure that mirrors the Federal system.

WEALTH TRANSFER TAXES

Unlike Federal and state income taxes, wealth transfer taxes are not significant revenue producers. For example, Federal transfer tax revenues for 2016 represented less than 1% of Federal government revenues.[17] Historically, the primary function of wealth transfer taxes has been to *hinder* the accumulation of wealth by family units. Thus, the goal of wealth redistribution generally underlies the design of estate and gift tax systems. Indeed, those who wish to give away their wealth while they are alive or when they die may pay a tax on the margin of 40% to do so.

The estate tax and its partner, the gift tax, are both excise taxes on the transfers of property. The estate tax, enacted in 1916, is imposed on the amount of a decedent's *net* wealth (fair market value of total assets less debts and expenses) that passes to his or her heirs at death. Absent any other rule, the estate tax easily could be avoided by giving away property before death. For this reason, Congress enacted a tax on gifts in 1932. The gift tax is imposed on the value of property transferred during an individual's life. As explained below, only a relatively small percentage of taxpayers are affected by the gift or estate tax since they apply only when the transfer of wealth is substantial. Currently, the taxes generally are triggered in 2017 only when cumulative transfers—those made during life and at death—exceed $5,490,000 ($10,980,000 for married couples). Despite their limited application, for those to whom the taxes do apply, the cost can be significant. For this reason and the fact that there are a number of income tax issues related to the gift and estate tax, it is important to have a basic understanding of how they work.

Prior to 1977, the gift tax and estate tax were two separate taxes. Taxable gifts made during life generally did not impact the estate tax calculation. However, in 1976, the gift tax and estate tax were combined into what is conceptually a unified transfer tax. The taxes are unified in the way that the taxes are calculated. As an individual makes taxable gifts during life, the gift tax is computed on a cumulative basis. To calculate the tax on current year gifts, the donor must add all taxable gifts made in prior years to the current gifts, calculate the gross tax on the sum of the lifetime transfers, and then subtract gift taxes assessed on the prior years' gifts. The remainder is the current year gift tax. When the individual dies, the estate tax is computed in a similar manner by adding all prior taxable gifts to the taxable estate, applying the appropriate rate and subtracting any prior gift taxes assessed. It is sometimes useful to think of the transfer at death as the final gift. Note that in both cases, the addition of prior taxable gifts does not result in the gifts being taxed twice but only raises the marginal rate at which the current transfers are taxed. Like the Federal income tax rate structure, the gift tax and the estate tax rates are progressive.

---

[15] States *not* currently imposing an income tax on individuals are Alaska, Florida, Nevada, South Dakota, Texas, Washington, and Wyoming. Tennessee and New Hampshire impose an income tax on an individual's dividend and interest income. Every state imposes either a corporate income tax or a tax on the privilege of conducting business within the state's boundaries. See subsequent discussion of franchise taxes.

[16] For individuals and partnerships, the due date of the Federal income tax return is the fifteenth day of the fourth month following the close of the tax year. For corporate taxpayers, the due date of the Federal return is the fifteenth day of the *third* month following the close of the tax year.

[17] Office of Management and Budget, 2016 *Fiscal Year Budget.*

As noted above, the estate and gift tax do not apply to most taxpayers. For starters, to eliminate the vast administrative problems that would result if the gift tax were imposed on all gifts (e.g., birthday presents), the tax only applies to transfers that exceed a certain threshold. In 2017, this amount is $14,000. Technically, individuals are entitled to an exclusion of $14,000 per donee per year. The exclusion enables an individual to make an unlimited number of gifts as long as they do not exceed $14,000 per donee in one year. For married couples, these rules permit a husband and wife to give $28,000 a year to a particular donee (e.g., a child) tax free. In addition to the annual exclusion, gifts to a spouse, charity, or transfers for educational or medical purposes normally are not taxable.

Provisions also exist to ensure that only transfers of substantial wealth are subject to tax. For gift tax purposes, gifts in excess of amounts excluded are not subject to tax until the cumulative amount of all taxable gifts made during a person's lifetime exceeds a certain level. As adjusted annually for inflation, the threshold for 2017 is $5,490,000. Once cumulative taxable gifts (those in excess of the annual exclusion) exceed this amount, a tax is imposed at a marginal rate of 40 percent.

The Federal Estate Tax

A decedent's estate tax liability is based on his or her net wealth and whether he or she leaves it to a surviving spouse or charity. The procedure for computing the Federal estate tax liability is illustrated in Exhibit 1-4 and is explained below.

The first step in computing the estate tax is to identify the decedent's gross estate. A decedent's gross estate includes the value of *all* property owned at date of death, wherever located. This includes the proceeds of an insurance policy on the life of the decedent if the decedent's estate is the beneficiary, or if the decedent had any ownership rights[18] in the policy at time of death. Property is generally included in the gross estate at its *fair market value* as of the date of death.[19]

LO.5
Describe the estate tax and the gift tax and their relationship.

EXHIBIT 1-4	Computation of Federal Estate Tax Liability		
Gross estate.			$x,xxx,xxx
Less the sum of:			
Expenses, indebtedness, and taxes.	$ xx,xxx		
State death taxes	x,xxx		
Losses	x,xxx		
Charitable bequests	xx,xxx		
Marital deduction.	xxx,xxx	– xxx,xxx	
Taxable estate			$ xxx,xxx
Plus: Taxable gifts made after December 31, 1976			+ xx,xxx
Total taxable transfers			$ xxx,xxx
Tentative tax on total transfer			$ xxx,xxx
Less the sum of:			
Gift taxes paid on post-1976 taxable gifts	$ x,xxx		
Estate tax credit	xx,xxx		
Other tax credits	x,xxx	– xx,xxx	
Estate tax liability.			$ xx,xxx

---

[18] Ownership rights in a life insurance policy include the power to change the policy's beneficiary, the right to cancel or assign the policy, and the right to borrow against the policy.

[19] For further discussion of the valuation of a decedent's gross estate, see *Corporate, Partnership, Estate and Gift Taxation,* 2018 Edition, Chapter 15.

The taxable estate is the gross estate reduced by deductions allowed for funeral and administrative expenses, debts of the decedent, certain taxes and losses, state death taxes, and charitable gifts made from the decedent's estate. It is important to note that there is no limit imposed on the charitable deduction. If an individual is willing to leave his or her entire estate for public, charitable, or religious use, there will be no taxable estate.[20] Finally, an *unlimited* marital deduction is allowed for the value of property passing to a surviving spouse. Thus, if a married taxpayer leaves all of his or her property to the surviving spouse, no Federal estate tax will be imposed on the estate. On the death of the surviving spouse, the couple's wealth may be subject to taxation.

Under current Federal estate tax laws, taxable gifts made after 1976 are added to the taxable estate to arrive at total taxable transfers. A tentative estate tax is then computed on the base amount. All gift taxes paid on post-1976 gifts, as well as certain tax credits, are subtracted from this tentative tax in arriving at the Federal estate tax due, if any. Most estate tax credits have a single underlying purpose—to reduce or eliminate the effect of multiple taxation of a single estate. Estate taxes paid to the various states or foreign countries on property owned by the decedent and located within their boundaries are examples of estate tax credits. However, the major credit available to reduce the Federal estate tax has been the *unified credit*. The unified credit protects all but the wealthiest of taxpayers from the estate and gift tax. For 2017 the credit is $2,141,800 (indexed annually for inflation) and has the effect of eliminating the tax on taxable transfers of $5,490,000 or less. The credit is unified in the sense that it can be used to offset gift taxes during the taxpayer's life. However, any credit used for gift tax purposes is not available at death.

Example 11

In 2017, D died owning Google stock worth $5,490,000. D had never made a taxable gift. D was not married and had no deductions. In such case, the taxable estate and total taxable transfers would be $5,490,000, and there would be no estate tax computed as follows:

Taxable estate and total taxable transfers................	$5,490,000
Gross estate tax (see Appendix A-3)	$2,141,800
Estate tax credit....................................	(2,141,800)
Tax due	$ 0

Note how the estate tax credit operates to exempt $5,490,000 of total taxable transfers from tax. For this reason, it is commonly said that taxpayers have an estate tax exemption equal to $5,490,000.

---

[20] For Federal income tax purposes, an individual's charitable contribution deduction may be subject to several limitations. Chapter 11 for more details.

Portability of the Unused Unified Credit

Beginning in 2011, taxpayers can take advantage of the so-called portability rule.[21] This rule provides that any unified credit that remains unused as of the death of a spouse who dies after 2010 is portable; that is, the unused amount is generally available for use by the surviving spouse as an addition to the surviving spouse's exemption. In 2017, portability effectively allows a married couple to exempt up to about $10,890,000 from the estate tax.

Example 12

H and W are husband and wife. H died in in 2011 when the available exemption for estate taxes was $5,000,000. His estate used $3,000,000 of that exemption to eliminate H's estate tax. As a result, $2,000,000 of his exemption was unused. In 2017, W died. W's exemption amount is $7,490,000 (her $5,490,000 + the unused amount of her last deceased husband of $2,000,000). In effect, the couple is able to exempt $10,490,000 from estate taxes ($3,000,000 when H died and $7,490,000 when W died).

If a surviving spouse is predeceased by more than one spouse, the amount of unused credit that is available for use by such surviving spouse is limited to the unused exclusion of the last such deceased spouse.

Example 13

H and W are married. H dies and his unused exclusion is $4,900,000. W remarried NH, a new husband. NH died and his unused exclusion is $2,000,000. By what amount can W increase her exemption? She can use only the unused amount of her last spouse, $2,000,000 (and not the $4,900,000 of her first spouse). The rule may discourage W from remarrying in this case.

The unused exclusion amount is available to a surviving spouse only if the executor of the estate of the deceased spouse files an estate tax return on which such amount is computed and makes an election on such return that such amount may be used. The election is irrevocable. The election cannot be made unless that estate tax return is filed on a timely basis as extended. Thus, even if a decedent normally is not required to file an estate tax return, a return is now necessary simply to preserve the unused exclusion amount.

The Federal Gift Tax

The purpose of the federal gift tax is to prevent a taxpayer's avoidance of the federal estate tax simply by giving away his or her property prior to death. The procedure for computing the federal gift tax liability is presented as a formula in Exhibit 1-5. To arrive at taxable gifts for the year, the taxpayer's total gifts may be reduced by the annual exclusion and by the deductions allowed for property transferred to a spouse or charity. The annual exclusion is $14,000 per donee in 2017. The annual exclusion is allowed *each year* even if the donor has made gifts in the prior years to the same donee.

---

[21] § 2010(c).

EXHIBIT 1-5	Computation of Federal Gift Tax Liability

Fair market value of all gifts made in the current year.		$xxx,xxx
Less the sum of:		
Annual exclusions ($14,000 per donee in 2017)	$xx,xxx	
Marital deduction	xx,xxx	
Charitable deduction	x,xxx	– xx,xxx
Taxable gifts for current year		$xxx,xxx
Plus: Taxable gifts made in prior years.		+ xx,xxx
Taxable transfers to date.		$xxx,xxx
Tentative tax on total transfers to date		$ xx,xxx
Less the sum of:		
Gift taxes computed at current rates on prior years' taxable gifts.	$ x,xxx	
Unified credit.	x,xxx	– x,xxx
Gift tax due on current gifts		$ xx,xxx

Example 14

T, a widower, wanted his son, daughter-in-law, and their five children to share his wealth. On December 25, 2017 he gave $14,000 to each family member. He repeats these gifts in 2018. Although T has transferred $196,000 [$14,000 × 7 (number of donees) × 2], he has not made taxable gifts in either 2017 or 2018.

Another unique feature of the Federal gift tax involves the *gift-splitting* election available to a married donor. If a donor makes the election on his or her current gift tax return, one-half of all gifts made during the year will be considered to have been made by the donor's spouse. The election is valid *only if* both spouses *consent* to gift-splitting.

Example 15

H and W are married. In 2017 H makes two gifts of $100,000 each to his son and daughter. W makes a gift of $5,000 to the daughter only. H and W elect gift-splitting on their 2017 gift tax returns. As a result, H will report a gift to the son of $50,000 and a gift to the daughter of $52,500 (½ of [$100,000 + $5,000]), and will claim two $14,000 gift tax exclusions. W will report exactly the same gifts and claim two annual exclusions. Without gift-splitting, H would still be entitled to $28,000 of exclusions, but W could only claim an exclusion of $5,000 for her gift to the daughter. Thus, by electing to split gifts, a married donor can, in effect, make use of any annual exclusions not needed by his or her spouse. More importantly, if taxable gifts are made under a gift-splitting arrangement, H can use his unified credit and W can use her lifetime credit to reduce the tax liability.

The marital and charitable deductions for Federal gift tax purposes are the same as for the Federal estate tax—*unlimited.* Thus, if a taxpayer gives his or her spouse a $2,000,000 anniversary present or transfers $100,000 to his or her church, a taxable gift has not been made.

If taxable gifts have been made for the current year, the cumulative computational procedure of the gift transfer tax must be applied.

Example 16

In 2000, X made his first taxable gift of $100,000 (after the exclusion). The tax (before credits) on this amount was $23,800. X made a second taxable gift of $85,000 in 2017. The tax (before credits) on the second gift is $26,200, computed as follows:

2000 taxable gift	$100,000
2017 taxable gift	+ 85,000
Cumulative gifts	$185,000
Tax on cumulative taxable gifts of $185,000	$ 50,000
2000 taxable gift	− 23,800*
Tax on 2017 gift	$ 26,200

* See the estate and gift transfer tax rate schedules in Appendix A. Note that the current year's tax rate is used to compute the tax reduction for the 2000 gift.

Note that the cumulative system of wealth transfer taxation *and* the progressive rate schedule cause a higher tax on the 2017 gift, even though the 2017 gift was $15,000 *less* than the 2000 gift.

The tentative tax liability in the above example is reduced by the unified credit available for the gift tax, $2,141,800 in 2017 (same as the estate tax). The gift tax credit is the only credit available to offset the federal gift tax liability.

The unified credit for the gift tax is the same as that for the estate tax, $2,141,800 and is equivalent to an exemption of $5,490,000. In applying the credit, it is important to understand that whatever amount is used in one year reduces the amount of the credit available in future years or at death. In other words, if a taxpayer makes no taxable gifts during his or her lifetime, the entire unified credit of $2,141,800 in 2017 is available to reduce any estate taxes that otherwise may be due at the taxpayer's death (see Example above). In contrast, if the taxpayer uses all $2,141,800 of the unified credit to reduce gift taxes, such amount is not available at death.

The $5,490,000 exemption (effectively about $10,980,000 for married couples), protects most individuals from the estate and gift tax.[22] However, for high wealth individuals, gifts can produce substantial savings. For example, a gift of income producing property (e.g., dividend paying stock or rental real estate) to children who may be in lower tax brackets not only reduces the income tax that might be paid but also removes all of the accumulated income from the donor's estate. In addition, a gift of property that is appreciating or will increase in value (e.g., land, stock, art, life insurance), removes all of the appreciation from the estate by transferring ownership of the property.

---

[22] According to a survey by the SpectremGroup, the number of persons in the U.S. that had a net worth of $1 million or more (excluding the value of their primary residence) rose 16% in 2009 to 7.8 million. The increase in those with $5 million in net worth was 17% to 980,000. See www.spectrem.com press release March 9, 2010.

State and Local Transfer Taxes

As a practical matter, most people will not pay the federal estate tax due to the generous exemption. However, individuals in 20 states and the District of Columbia must be concerned with some type of state death tax.[23] For example, Washington, Oregon, Minnesota, Illinois, New Jersey, Delaware, Maryland, New York, Connecticut, Rhode Island, Vermont, Maine, Hawaii, and the District of Columbia impose estate taxes. Massachusetts is typical. Its exemption is $1,000,000 with a top rate of 16 percent. While a Massachusetts resident with an estate of $5,490,000 would not pay a federal estate tax, the state estate tax would be about $439,000.

Six states (Nebraska, Iowa, Kentucky, Pennsylvania, New Jersey, and Maryland) impose an inheritance tax on the right to receive property at death. The amount of an inheritance tax payable usually is directly affected by the degree of kinship between the recipient and the decedent. The inheritance tax typically provides an exemption from the tax, which increases as the relationship between the recipient (e.g., surviving spouse, children, grandchildren, parents, etc.) and the decedent becomes closer. In addition, as the relationship becomes closer, the transfer tax rates decrease. Thus, the more closely related one is, the smaller the inheritance tax will be. Generally, little, if any, inheritance tax exemption is available for transfers to unrelated recipients, and the highest rate is imposed.

Example 17

The Nebraska inheritance tax is similar to most inheritance taxes. For example, transfers to a surviving spouse and charities are totally exempt. In contrast, the exemption for immediate relatives such as parents, grandparents, siblings, and children is $40,000. The exemption for more remote relatives such as aunts and uncles is $15,000 and for all others is $10,000. The rates follow a similar pattern: 1% for immediate relatives, 13% for remote relatives and 18% for all others.

Any inheritance or estate taxes imposed by a state are deductible in computing the Federal taxable estate.

While many states impose some type of death tax, only a few states have a gift tax. In those states where there is no gift tax, wholesale avoidance of any state death tax is prohibited by certain special rules. For example, a state law may require that transfers made within one year of death to be included in the death tax base.

EMPLOYMENT TAXES

LO.6

Explain the differences in the employment taxes levied on employees versus those levied on self-employed individuals.

When most people think about taxes, they usually think about the federal income tax. However, focusing solely on the federal income tax misses an important fact. The federal income tax is not the largest tax bill for most Americans. The largest federal tax for most Americans is the tax paid for "social insurance" programs such as Social Security and Medicare. Along with these, federal and state governments provide programs to provide benefits to eligible workers who are unemployed through no fault of their own.

While most do not commonly think of the Social Security, Medicare and unemployment programs as a form of insurance, in reality they are. They mirror insurance found in the private sector in that they provide benefits upon the occurrence of certain insured events. By paying for Social Security, individuals are insuring that they will receive a number of benefits but most importantly a stream of income after they retire. Similarly, by paying for Medicare, individuals are ensuring that they will have health insurance once they reach the age of 65. Finally, payments related to unemployment insure that employees who are out of work receive a temporary replacement for lost wages until they can find another job. Just like insurance purchased in the private sector only those that contribute to the program are entitled to its benefits. In this regard, Social Security and Medicare are funded through employment taxes, often called payroll taxes. Unemployment benefits are funded through unemployment taxes paid by employers (and in some states, employees).

---

[23] It is not uncommon for the decedent's will to provide that his or her estate pay any inheritance tax imposed on the recipient of property from the estate.

The Federal government and most states impose some form of employment tax on either self-employed individuals, employees,[24] or employers. The most common form of state employment tax is levied on wages, with the proceeds used to finance the state's unemployment benefits program. State unemployment taxes are imposed on employers who have employees working within the state's boundaries, but only if the employees would be eligible for unemployment benefits from the state. Most states' unemployment taxes are based on the same taxable wage base as that used for the Federal unemployment tax (see discussion below), and employers are allowed to take state unemployment taxes paid as a credit against the Federal unemployment tax liability.

The Federal government imposes two types of taxes on employment—a Social Security tax and an unemployment tax. The Federal Insurance Contribution Act (FICA) imposes a tax on self-employed individuals, employees, and employers. The FICA tax is paid by both an employee and his or her employer if the employee is eligible for Social Security and Medicare health insurance benefits. Although subject to a different tax rate, self-employed individuals are required to pay FICA taxes on net earnings from self-employment. The Federal Unemployment Tax Act (FUTA) imposes a tax *only* on the employer. Self-employed individuals are not eligible for unemployment benefits and thus are not subject to the FUTA tax. The tax base and rate structure of both these Federal employment taxes are presented below.

FICA Taxes

FICA taxes, often referred to as Social Security and Medicare taxes, have a long history. Both taxes help pay for a variety of federal programs that assist individuals in times of need such as old-age, disability, death and illness. Social Security was enacted in 1935 to pay a guaranteed source of income to retired workers normally when they reach age 65. However, the age to receive full Social Security benefits is slowly increasing to 67 for those born in 1960 and later.

Since 1935 the Act has been modified many, many times, providing more and more benefits. For example, major additions occurred in 1956 and 1960 when the Act was amended to extend benefits for most disabled workers and their families. The programs established by these amendments are now collectively known as the Old Age, Survivors and Disability Insurance (OASDI) programs. In addition to these programs, Congress addressed problems of health care for the aged with the creation of Medicare Health Insurance in 1965. Medicare helps pay hospital and medical expenses for persons who have reached age 65. In 2006, Medicare was amended to help pay for prescription drugs.

The Social Security and Medicare programs are paid for primarily through taxes on wages and self-employment income. These taxes are commonly referred to as employment taxes. Taxes to pay for Social Security benefits were first collected in 1937 at a rate of 1% on the first $3,000 of wages or a maximum of $30! In 1966, tax collections began for Medicare at a rate of 0.35% on the same wage base as for Social Security. At that point, 1966, the total tax for the two components of FICA, Social Security and Medicare, was 4.2% (3.85 + 0.35) on wages of $6,600 or a maximum of $2,772. Since those early days both the tax rates as well as the base have slowly increased.

The rates stopped climbing in 1990 when they reached what they are currently: 6.2% for Social Security and 1.45% for Medicare. However, as explained below, in 2013, Congress increased the Medicare contribution for high income taxpayers.

The wage base for Social Security is adjusted for inflation every year and in 2017 is $127,200. Until 1992, the wage base for Medicare was the same as for Social Security but starting in 1993 the base for Medicare became unlimited and remains unlimited today. Many believe that it is only a matter of time before the Social Security base also will become unlimited.

---

[24] The term "employee" is used to identify persons whose work effort, tools, place of work, and work time periods are subject to the supervision and control of another (the employer). A person who provides his or her own tools and who has the *right* to exercise control over when, where, and for whom services are rendered (i.e., an independent contractor) generally is classified as self-employed rather than as an employee. See Chapter 8 for a discussion of the importance this classification has in the deductions allowed to individuals for Federal income tax purposes.

In 2010, Congress enacted and President Obama signed into law the *Patient Protection and Affordable Care Act,* as amended by the *Health Care and Reconciliation Act of 2010* (the Affordable Care Act). To help pay for the cost of the Affordable Care Act, the law provided for an increase in the Medicare tax on *employees* (i.e., but *not* on employers). Beginning in 2013, the rate increases by 0.90 percentage points on wages in excess of $200,000 or $250,000 in the case of those filing joint returns (i.e., at these levels, the rate increases from 1.45% to 2.35%). Unlike the Social Security wage base, the $200,000 and $250,000 amounts are not adjusted for inflation. With the creation of the additional Medicare tax, the portion of wages received in connection with "employment" in excess of the thresholds are subject to a total Medicare tax rate (combined employer and employee portions) of 3.8% (i.e., 1.45% by the employer, and 2.35% (1.45% + 0.90%) by the employee). A similar increase applies to self-employed persons. The additional Medicare tax for both employees and self-employed individuals is computed on Form 8959.

Employees and Employers

To summarize the current state of employment taxes, FICA taxes normally are imposed at the combined rate of 7.65% (6.2% Social Security + 1.45% Medicare) on each dollar of an employee's wages up to $127,200 in 2017. The Medicare tax of 1.45% continues to apply to each additional dollar of wages. To emphasize, there is no maximum amount on the Medicare component of the FICA tax because the 1.45% Medicare tax is applicable to *all* compensation. In addition, 0.9% is added to the Medicare tax when wages exceed $200,000 or $250,000 for joint filers. The effect of these rules on employees is to impose a total Medicare tax of 2.35% (1.45% + 0.9%) on amounts over the thresholds of $200,000 and $250,000. The employer normally is required to pay a matching amount of FICA taxes for each employee (i.e., the same tax rates on each employee's wage base up to the same limits).[25] However, the employer is not required to match the additional Medicare tax of 0.9% paid by the employee. The rates for employers and employees are summarized below.

Employment Tax	Employer Rates	Employee Rates	Wage Base
Social Security	6.2%	6.2%	$127,200 (2017)
Medicare.	1.45%	1.45%	Unlimited
Additional Medicare tax. .		0.9%	> $200,000 > $250,000 (joint returns)

Example 18

During 2017 employee E earns wages of $70,000. As a result, E will pay $5,355 (7.65% × $70,000) FICA taxes, and her employer must pay the same amount as an employment tax.

Example 19

During 2017 employee F earns wages of $240,000. F is married and her spouse did not work during the year. F will pay $11,366 FICA taxes, and her employer must pay the same amount as an employment tax. It is important to note that the 1.45% Medicare tax has no ceiling amount. The calculation is as follows:

Social Security portion = 6.2% × $127,200 limit	$ 7,886
Plus: Medicare portion = 1.45% × $240,000	+ 3,480
Total FICA taxes.	$11,366

---

[25] Employers are allowed a tax deduction for all payroll taxes.
See Chapter 7 for a discussion of business deductions.

Example 20

H and W are married and file a joint return. H receives $210,000 of wages, while W has wages of $35,000. The employer of H is required to *withhold* an additional 0.9% Medicare tax on the last $10,000 of his taxable wages of $210,000 (i.e., 0.9% × $10,000 = $90) since the taxpayer had more than $200,000 of wages. Withholding is required even though the couple will *not* owe the additional 0.9% Medicare tax at all because as joint filers their combined wages and self-employment income do not exceed $250,000. The $90 of tax withheld will be a tax credit against any other type of tax that the couple might ultimately owe (e.g., income, alternative minimum tax, self employment tax, etc.). As discussed below, this is similar to the situation where an employee might have multiple jobs and the various employers have collectively withheld excess employment or income tax.

Example 21

Harry and Wilma are married. They earned wages of $175,000 and $125,000, respectively. Neither would have the additional Medicare tax withheld by their employers. Even though their combined wages of $300,000 exceeds the $250,000 mark for joint filers, neither the separate wages of Harry nor the separate wages of Wilma exceeded the $200,000 threshold. Nevertheless, they would still owe $450 (0.9% × [$300,000 − $250,000 = $50,000]) in additional Medicare taxes when they file their Form 1040 for 2017.

An employer is required to withhold the proper amount of both Federal income taxes and FICA taxes from each employee's wages paid during the year. The employer is then required to remit these withheld amounts plus the employer's matching FICA taxes for each employee to the IRS on a regular basis, usually weekly or monthly.[26] Employers also are required to file Form 941, Employer's Quarterly Federal Tax Return, by the end of the first month following each quarter of the calendar year (e.g., by April 30, 2017 for the quarter ended March 31, 2016) and pay any remaining amount of employment taxes due for the previous quarter.[27]

In some instances, an employee who has had more than one employer during the year may have paid *excess* FICA taxes for the year and will be entitled to a Federal income tax credit or refund for the excess. This credit for excess Social Security is claimed on Line 71 of Form 1040 (2016).

Example 22

During 2017 E earned $100,000 from his regular job and $50,000 from a part-time job. E's full-time employer withheld $7,650 ($100,000 × 7.65%) and E's part-time employer withheld $3,825 ($50,000 × 7.65%). Each employer made matching contributions and paid the withheld amount and the employer's match to the IRS. Since E has paid a total of $11,475 ($7,650 + $3,825) of FICA taxes and the maximum amount due for 2017 is $10,061 ([$127,200 × 6.2% = $7,886] + [$150,000 × 1.45% = $2,175]), E will be entitled to a tax credit or refund of the $1,414, the difference between the $11,475 he paid and the $10,061 that is due. Note that the $1,414 simply represents the FICA taxes withheld on E's wages in excess of the $127,200 maximum amount subject to the 6.2% Social Security rate in 2017 ($150,000 − $127,200 = $22,800 × 6.2% = $1,414).

---

[26] The frequency of these payments depends on the total amount of Federal income taxes withheld and the FICA taxes due on the employer's periodic payroll. The amount of Federal income and FICA taxes to be withheld from each employee's wages, and the reporting and payment requirements are specified in Circular E, *Employer's Tax Guide,* a free publication of the Internal Revenue Service.

[27] Because of significant penalties for underpayment of these Federal employment taxes, most employers exercise great care to make payments on a timely basis. See Circular E for a discussion of these penalties and due dates.

Self-Employed Taxpayers

Like employees, self-employed individuals are normally required to pay FICA taxes on their self-employment income (commonly known as self-employment tax or the SE tax). The Social Security portion of the self-employment tax rate is 12.4% and the Medicare portion is normally 2.9 percent. These rates are *twice* the FICA tax rates imposed on an employee's wages. In 2017 the ceiling amount for the Social Security portion of the SE tax is $127,200, the same as for employees. As a result, taxpayers with self-employment income not exceeding this amount will pay an SE tax of 15.3% on their self-employment income. However, the 2.9% Medicare tax continues to apply for every additional dollar of self-employment income over the base. In addition, like employees, self-employed individuals must pay an additional Medicare tax of 0.9% where total wages and self-employment income exceed $200,000 ($250,000 for joint filers). These rates are summarized below.

Self-Employment Tax	Rates (%)	Self-Employment Income Base*
Social Security	12.4%	$127,200 (2017)
Medicare	2.9	Unlimited
Additional Medicare Tax . .	0.9	> $200,000 > $250,000 (joint returns)

* The 12.4% and 2.9% components of the Medicare tax are based on 92.35% of self-employment income while the additional 0.9% Medicare tax applies to 100% of every dollar of self-employment income over the thresholds

The SE tax is computed as part of Form 1040 on Schedule SE. (See Appendix B for this form.) The additional Medicare tax is computed on Form 8959 (the same form used by employees). Note that a taxpayer is not required to pay self-employment taxes unless he or she has self-employment income of $400 or more.[28]

Self-Employment Income

Self-employed persons do not receive wages. Employees receive wages. The equivalent of wages for a self-employed person is self-employment income. Self-employment income is generally the trade or business income earned by an individual as an independent contractor, a sole proprietor or a general partner in a partnership. Self-employment income does not include income passive in nature or investment income such as interest, dividends or rents. Nor does it include gains from the sale of property (other than sales of inventory or property customarily held for sale to customers). Note that self-employment income is a "net" concept so expenses related to producing the income may be subtracted in reaching the base.

The most common type of self-employment income is that received for providing services *other than in an employee capacity*. For example, it includes income earned by accountants, tax preparers, doctors, dentists, veterinarians, engineers, lawyers and consultants as long as they are independent contractors, sole proprietors, or general partners. But self-employment income is not limited to income earned by professionals. It also includes income earned by such persons as farmers, fisherman, contractors, subcontractors, massage therapists, graphic designers, hair stylists, salesmen, and freelance writers. Income from odd jobs also counts as self-employment income such as income from babysitting and child care, mowing lawns, driving a taxi, painting, tutoring, selling handicrafts, operating a bed and breakfast, or serving on a board of directors. In all cases, the services must have been performed as an independent contractor, sole proprietor or partner to be considered self-employment income.

Whether an individual is an independent contractor or an employee depends on the facts in each case. An individual is normally considered an independent contractor if the payer has the right to control or direct only the result of the work and not how it will be done. Unfortunately, this is a dreadfully controversial area. As might be expected, payers, wanting to avoid payment of a 7.65% employment tax, are inclined to call a worker an

---

[28] Technically, self-employment income is defined as "net earnings from self-employment." Because the amount of net earnings from self-employment is 92.35% of self-employment income, there is no self-employment tax unless the taxpayer's self-employment income is $433 ($400/92.35%) or more. See §§ 1401 and 1402(b).

independent contractor. Similarly, they avoid paying unemployment taxes or workman's compensation. Contractors also are not entitled to overtime pay nor are they protected under anti-discrimination laws or wrongful termination statutes. A company may even be able to avoid liability if, for example, a delivery truck driver who is a contractor were to injure someone in an accident.[29]

Conversely, the government, hoping to ensure the collection of employment and income taxes, wants to classify the worker as an employee. To dissuade employers from misclassification, the government imposes severe penalties if the employer intentionally classifies a worker as an independent contractor when it is clear he or she is an employee.

In most cases, an independent contractor's self-employment income is reported to the taxpayer on Form 1099. Just like an employer that must provide an employee with a Form W-2 reporting wages earned, businesses must give a Form 1099 to any "independent contractor" who provides $600 or more of services to the business during the year. Generally a payer is not required to provide a Form 1099 to a corporation but there are a number of exceptions. For example, businesses must always give attorneys a Form 1099 regardless of the form of business in which the attorneys perform their services. Note that while the reporting threshold for a payer is $600, an individual is not required to pay self-employment tax unless his or her total self-employment income is $400 or more.

Calculation of Self-Employment Tax

As a general rule, the self-employment tax is 15.3% of self-employment income. However, in computing the amount of a taxpayer's self-employment income subject to tax, a special adjustment is required as explained in the following example.

Example 23

S is a sole proprietor who prepares tax returns. This year his income from operations net of all expenses *except* the self-employment tax related to such income is $10,000. To arrive at the correct measure of *net* income for the sole proprietorship, the taxpayer must reduce the $10,000 by the portion of the self-employment tax that represents a cost of doing business. This is analogous to an employer whose labor expenses include the 7.65% FICA tax on an employee's wages (i.e., the employer's matching share of FICA). A self-employed person incurs a similar cost and that cost is one-half of the individual's self-employment tax. Consequently, to determine the self-employment tax base, the individual's self-employment income of $10,000 is reduced by one-half of the hypothetical self-employment tax on the $10,000 or $765 ($10,000 × 7.65% [15.3% × ½]). This results in self-employment income subject to tax of $9,235 ($10,000 − $765). The actual self-employment tax is $1,412.96 (15.3% × $9,235).

Following the approach above, in computing the amount subject to tax for each of the self-employment tax bases (both the 12.4% and the 2.9%), the taxpayer always reduces net earnings from self-employment by an amount equal to one-half the combined 15.3% tax rate times net earnings from self-employment (i.e., 7.65% × net earnings from self-employment).[30] This approach also applies to the computation of the additional Medicare tax. Note that this adjustment applies only in the computation of the amount of the self-employment tax bases. However, consistent with the theory above, a self-employed individual is entitled to an actual deduction for one-half of the self-employment tax as a business expense in computing adjusted gross income. For this purpose, the additional Medicare tax of 0.9% is not deductible. Using the facts of the example above, the actual deduction would be $706.48 (½ × actual self-employment tax of $1,412.96). Observe that the actual deduction in computing adjusted gross income is $706.48 and not the $765 used to compute the self-employment tax bases. Examples of these calculations are given below.

---

[29] Misclassification can result not only in additional taxes but other penalties. See Zetlin, "Employee or Contractor?," *INC.* (September, 1, 2008) http://www.inc.com/magazine/20080901/employee-or-contractor.html.

[30] § 1402(a)(12).

Each component of the self-employment tax required to be paid is computed as follows:

1. Compute the base for the 12.4% and 2.9% components. Multiply net earnings from self-employment by one-half of the self-employment tax rate, 7.65% (½ × 15.3%) and subtract that amount to reach a tentative tax base of 92.35% (100% − 7.65%) of the original amount.[31]

2. Apply the limitation for 12.4% component. Compare the result in Step 1 with the maximum base amount for the Social Security portion of the self-employment tax ($127,200 in 2017) and select the smaller amount.

3. Compute the Medicare and Social Security tax components. Multiply the amount in Step 1 by the Medicare rate of 2.9% and the amount in Step 2 by the Social Security rate of 12.4 percent.

4. Compute the additional Medicare tax. Multiply the excess of 100% of self-employment over the threshold ($200,000 or $250,000 for joint filers) by 0.9 percent.

5. Add the amounts of the separate components from Steps 2 and 3. This is the amount of self-employment tax required to be paid.

Example 24

Individuals C and D have net earnings from self-employment for 2017 of $50,000 and $150,000, respectively. Self-employment taxes for C and D are determined as follows:

Self-Employment Tax Computation	C		D	
Social Security (12.4% portion)				
Net earnings from self-employment........	$ 50,000		$150,000	
− (½ × 15.3% = 7.65%) of net earnings......	(3,825)		(11,475)	
SE tax base (92.35% net earnings)*	$ 46,175		$138,525	
Smaller of SE tax base above or maximum wage base ($127,200 in 2017)..........	$ 46,175		$127,200	
× 12.4%	× 12.4%		× 12.4%	
Social Security tax		$5,726		$15,773
Medicare (2.9% portion)				
Net earnings from self-employment........	$ 50,000		$150,000	
− (½ × 15.3% = 7.65%) of net earnings......	(3,825)		(11,475)	
SE tax base (92.35% net earnings)**.......	$ 46,175		$138,525	
× 2.9%	× 2.9%		× 2.9%	
Medicare tax		1,339		4,017
Total self-employment tax.................		$7,065		$19,790
Deduct ½ SE tax for AGI		$3,533		$ 9,895

 * Not to exceed wage base less wages received

** No reduction for wages

C will be allowed to deduct $3,533 (one-half of $7,065 self-employment tax paid) for income tax purposes, and D will be allowed to deduct $9,895 (one-half of $19,790). Although both will receive a benefit from the income tax deduction, note that only C has received any benefit from the so-called second deduction in arriving at his self-employment tax base for the Social Security component. Because D's reduced net earnings for self-employment are still greater than the maximum tax base for the Social Security component, she is required to pay the maximum amount of this component of the self-employment tax for 2017 (i.e., $127,200 × 12.4% = $15,773).

---

[31] Note that the steps can be combined simply by multiplying the individual's net earnings from self-employment by 100% − one-half the current combined self-employment tax rate (i.e., 100% − 7.65% = 92.35%).

Example 25

For 2017, S, single, had self-employment income of $300,000. Only $277,050 (92.35% × $300,000) is potentially subject to the 12.4% and 2.9% components. The self-employment income subject to the additional Medicare tax of 0.9% applies to $77,050 ($277,050 – $200,000 threshold for single individuals). The total tax is computed as follows:

Social Security tax ($127,200 in 2017 × 12.4%)	$15,773
Medicare tax ($277,050 × 2.9%)	8,034
Additional Medicare tax ([$277,050 – $200,000 = $77,050] × 0.9%)	+ 693
Total self-employment tax	$24,500

S is entitled to a deduction for AGI of 50% of the 12.4% and 2.9% components of the tax of $11,903 (50% × [$15,773 + $8,034 = $23,807]). No deduction is allowed for the additional Medicare tax paid of $693. S reports his self-employment taxes (Social Security and Medicare taxes of $23,807) on Schedule SE of Form 1040 and the deduction of $11,903 on line 17 of page 1 of Form 1040. The additional Medicare tax is reported on Form 8959.

In some instances, a self-employed individual may also earn wages subject to FICA withholding while working as a full or part-time employee. In such a case, the maximum earnings base subject to the Social Security component of the self-employment tax is reduced by the wages earned as an employee.

Example 26

During 2017 T received wages of $101,800 and had self-employment income of $50,000. In computing T's self-employment tax, the maximum taxable base for the Social Security tax is reduced by the wages paid because T's employer has already withheld the appropriate FICA amount on these wages.

	Social Security
Maximum tax base	$127,200
Less: Wages subject to FICA tax	(101,800)
Reduced maximum tax base	$ 25,400
Net earnings from self-employment	$ 50,000
Subtract: 7.65% of net earnings from self-employment	(3,825)
	$ 46,175
Smaller of reduced maximum tax base or amount determined above	$ 25,400
Times: Social Security tax rate	× 12.4%
Tax on Social Security component	$ 3,150
Social Security tax	$ 3,150
Plus: Medicare tax ($46,175 × 2.9%)	+ 1,339
Equals: T's self-employment tax	$ 4,489

T will also have an income tax deduction of $2,245 (one-half of the $4,489 self-employment taxes paid).

For purposes of the additional Medicare tax of 0.9 percent, self-employed individuals who have combined wages and self-employment income in excess of the thresholds, compute the amount on which they are liable for the additional tax by reducing the $200,000/$250,000 threshold by any wages earned.

Example 27

In 2017, J, a single filer, has $130,000 in wages and $145,000 in self-employment income. His wages are not in excess of the $200,000 threshold for single filers, so he is not liable for the additional Medicare tax on these wages. However, he is liable for the additional Medicare tax on his self-employment income. For this calculation, only 92.35% of self-employment income is used or $133,908 (92.35% × $145,000) In calculating the additional Medicare tax on self-employment income, the $200,000 threshold for single filers is reduced by J's $130,000 in wages, resulting in a reduced self-employment income threshold of $70,000 ($200,000 − $130,000). J is liable to pay the additional Medicare tax on $63,908 of self-employment income ($133,908 in self-employment income less the reduced threshold of $70,000). The additional tax would be $575 (0.9% × $63,908). If J had wages exceeding $200,000, all of his self-employment income would be subject to the additional 0.9% Medicare tax.

FUTA Taxes

A Federal unemployment tax is imposed on employers who pay wages of $1,500 or more during any calendar quarter in the calendar year, or who employ at least one individual on each of some 20 days during the calendar year or previous year.[32] Certain exceptions are made for persons employing agricultural or domestic workers.

FUTA tax revenues are used by the Federal government to augment unemployment benefit programs of the various states. The current FUTA tax rate is 6% of the first $7,000 of wages paid during the year to each covered employee. This translates into a *maximum* FUTA tax of $420 (6% × $7,000) *per employee* per year. Since most states also impose an unemployment tax on employers, a credit is allowed against an employer's FUTA tax liability for any similar tax paid to a state. Currently, the maximum FUTA tax credit allowed for this purpose is 5.4% of the covered wages (i.e., maximum of $378 ($7,000 × 5.4%) per employee). Thus, the maximum FUTA tax paid is normally $42 ($420 − $378, or 0.6% × $7,000) per employee.

All employers subject to FUTA taxes must file Form 940, Employer's Annual Federal Unemployment Tax Return, on or before January 31 of the following year. If the employer's tax liability exceeds certain limits, estimated tax payments must be made during the year.[33] Most states require an employer to file unemployment tax returns and make tax payments quarterly.

EXCISE TAXES

The purpose of an excise tax is to tax certain privileges as well as the manufacture, sale, or consumption of specified commodities. Federal excise taxes are imposed on the sale of specified articles, various transactions, occupations, and the use of certain items. This type of tax is not imposed on the profits of a business or profession, however. The major types of excise taxes are as follows:

1. Occupational taxes;

2. Facilities and services taxes;

3. Manufacturers' taxes; and

4. Retail sales of products and commodities taxes.

---

[32] § 3306(a)(1).   [33] See instructions in Circular E, *Supra*, Footnote 27.

Occupational Taxes

Some businesses must pay a fee before engaging in their business. These types of businesses include, but are not limited to, liquor dealers, dealers in medicines and dealers in firearms.

Facilities and Services Taxes

The person who pays for services and facilities must pay the tax on these items. The institution or person who furnishes the facilities or services must collect the tax, file returns, and turn over the taxes to the taxing authorities. A few of the common services subject to the facilities and services excise tax include air travel, hotel or motel lodging, and telephone service.

Manufacturers' Taxes

As a rule, certain manufactured goods are taxed at the manufacturing level to make collection easier. Most of these items are of a semi-luxurious or specialized nature, such as sporting goods or firearms. This excise tax applies to the sale or use by the manufacturer, producer, or importer of specified articles. The taxes may be determined by quantity of production (e.g., pounds or gallons) or by a percentage of the sales price. When sales price is used as an index, the tax is based on the sales price of the manufacturer, producer, or importer.

Retail Sales of Products and Commodities Taxes

This excise tax applies to the retail sale or use of diesel fuel, special motor fuels, and fuel used in noncommercial aviation. The tax is collected from the person buying the product by the seller, and the seller must file and pay the tax unless the buyer purchased it tax-free.

State Excise Taxes

Many states and local governments also have excise taxes. They vary in range of coverage and impact, but most parallel the Federal excise taxes. For instance, most states have an excise tax on gasoline, liquor, and cigarettes, as does the Federal government.

ADDITIONAL TYPES OF TAXES

Many other types of taxes are used to augment state, local, and Federal income, employment, excise, and wealth transfer taxes. The three levels of government have never been reluctant to exercise their imagination in creating and developing new ways of supplementing governmental revenues. A few of the other more common types of taxes are briefly explained below.

Franchise Tax

A franchise tax is a tax on the privilege of doing business in a state or local jurisdiction. The measure of the tax generally is the net income of the business or the value of the capital used within the taxing authority's jurisdiction.

Sales Tax

A sales tax is imposed on the gross receipts from the retail sale of tangible personal property (e.g., clothing, automobiles, and equipment) and certain services. Each state or local government determines the tax rate and the services and articles to be taxed. The seller will collect the tax from the consumer at the time of the sale, and then periodically remit the taxes to the appropriate taxing authority. Often a state or local government allows the seller to retain a nominal percentage of the collected taxes to compensate for the additional costs incurred by the seller in complying with the tax requirements.

Use Tax

A use tax is a tax imposed on the use within a state or local jurisdiction of tangible property on which a sales tax was not paid. The tax rate normally equals that of the taxing authority's sales tax.

Doing-Business Penalty

This penalty tax is imposed on a business that has not obtained authorization from the state or local government to operate within its border. Usually, a business must pay a fee for a state charter or some other kind of license as permission to enter business within the state.

Real Property Tax

A real property tax is a tax on the value of realty (land, buildings, homes, etc.) owned by nonexempt individuals or organizations within a jurisdiction. Rates vary with location. This type of tax normally supports local services, such as the public school system or the fire department, and is levied on a recurring annual basis.

Tangible Personal Property Tax

This tax is levied on the value of tangible personalty located within a jurisdiction. Tangible personalty is property not classified as realty and includes such items as office furniture, machinery and equipment, inventories, and supplies. The tax normally must be paid annually, with each local jurisdiction determining its own tax rate and the items to tax.

Intangible Personal Property Tax

This tax is imposed on the value of intangible personalty (i.e., stocks, bonds, and accounts and notes receivable) located within a jurisdiction. The tax generally is paid annually, with each local jurisdiction setting its own tax rate and items to be taxed.

Goals of Taxation

LO.7

Identify some of the more common social and economic goals of our Federal tax system.

In subsequent chapters, the specific provisions that must be followed to compute the Federal income tax will be discussed in detail. Some may view this discussion as a hopeless attempt to explain what seems like an endless barrage of boring rules—rules that, despite their apparent lack of "rhyme or reason," must be considered if the final tax liability is to be determined. The frustration that students of taxation often feel when studying the rules of Federal tax law is not completely unfounded. Indeed, a famous tax scholar, Boris Bittker, once commented on the increasing intricacy of the tax law, saying, "Can one hope to find a way through a statutory thicket so bristling with detail?"[34] As this statement suggests, many provisions of the law are, in fact, obscure and often appear to be without purpose. However, each provision of the tax law originated with some goal, even if no more than to grant a benefit to some Congress person's constituency. A knowledge of the goals underlying a particular provision is an important first step toward a comprehension of the provision. An understanding of the purpose of the law is an invaluable tool in attacking the "statutory thicket." In studying taxation, it becomes apparent that many provisions have been enacted with similar objectives. The following discussion reviews some of the goals of taxation that often serve as the reasons behind the rule.

Economic Objectives

At first glance, it seems clear that the primary goal of taxation is to provide the resources necessary to fund governmental expenditures. At the Federal level, however, this is not entirely true. As many economists have pointed out, any taxing authority that has the power to control the money supply—as does our Federal government—can satisfy its revenue needs by merely creating money. Nevertheless, complete reliance on the Treasury's printing press to provide the needed resources is not a viable alternative. If the government's expenditures were financed predominantly with funds that it created rather than those obtained through taxation, excess demand would result, which in turn would cause prices to rise, or inflation. Thus, taxation in serving a revenue function also operates along with other instruments of policy to attain a stable price level.

---

[34] Boris I. Bittker and Lawrence M. Stone, *Federal Income Taxation,* 5th Ed. (Boston: Little, Brown & Co., 1980).

Although Congress can create its own resources, revenue objectives often can explain a particular feature of the law. Consider the personal and dependency exemption deductions, the purpose of which is to free from tax the income needed to maintain a minimum standard of living. Although the cost of living has risen substantially over the years, Congress has been reluctant to increase the amount of these exemptions. The exemption deduction was set at $600 from 1948 to 1969. It slowly crept to $1,000 in 1979 where it essentially stayed until Congress started requiring inflation adjustments in 1985. In effect, the deduction has changed very little over the years, despite significant increases in the price level during this time. The reluctance to alter the exemption amount derives primarily from the potential impact on revenues. A slight increase in the exemption without a corresponding increase in revenues from other sources would result in a tremendous revenue loss because of the number of exemptions taxpayers claim—approximately 269 million in 2005. For similar reasons, Congress has refrained, until recently, from adjusting the tax rate schedules to compensate for inflation, since to do so would significantly reduce its inflow of resources. In 1985, however, both the personal and dependency exemption amount, the standard deduction *and* the individual tax rate schedules were adjusted (indexed) for the increase in the Consumer Price Index that occurred during the previous year.

Revenue considerations also can explain why tax accounting methods sometimes differ from those used for financial accounting. Prior to 1954, an accrual basis taxpayer could neither defer taxation of prepaid income nor deduct estimates of certain expenses, such as the expected costs of servicing warranty contracts. In 1954, the treatment of such items was changed to conform with financial accounting principles that permit deferral of income and accrual of expenses in most situations. The expected revenue loss attributed to this change was $50 million. Within a year after the change, however, the Treasury requested that Congress repeal the new provisions retroactively because estimates of the revenue loss were in excess of several billion dollars. In short, Congress responded and, as a result, the treatment of prepaid income and certain accruals for tax and financial accounting purposes differs—a difference attributable to revenue considerations.

The role of Federal taxation in carrying out economic policy extends beyond the realm of revenue raising and price stability. Taxation is a major tool used by the government to attain satisfactory economic growth with full employment. The title of the 1981 tax bill is illustrative: *The Economic Recovery Tax Act of 1981* (ERTA). As the title suggests, a major purpose of this legislation was directed toward revitalizing the health of the economy. ERTA significantly lowered tax rates to spur the economy out of a recession. Its objective was to place more *after-tax* income in the hands of taxpayers for their disposal. By so doing, it was hoped that taxpayers would consume more and thus increase aggregate demand, resulting in economic growth.

Congress also has used the tax structure to directly attack the problem of unemployment. In 1977, employers were encouraged to increase employment by the introduction of a general jobs tax credit, which effectively reduced the cost of labor. In 1978, Congress eliminated the general jobs credit and substituted a targeted jobs credit. This credit could be obtained only if employers hired certain targeted groups of individuals who were considered disadvantaged or handicapped. This credit was expanded in 1983 to stimulate the hiring of economically disadvantaged youth during the summer. The credit was further refined and is now referred to as the work opportunity credit. As the credit for jobs suggests, Congress believes that major economic problems can be solved using the tax system.

A subject closely related to economic growth and full employment is investment. To stimulate investment spending, Congress has enacted numerous provisions. For example, accelerated depreciation methods—the modified accelerated cost recovery system (MACRS)—may be used to compute the deduction for depreciation, thus enabling rapid recovery of the taxpayer's investment.

Congress encourages certain industries by granting them favorable tax treatment. For example, the credit for research and experimental expenditures cited above clearly benefits those engaged in technology businesses. Other tax provisions are particularly advantageous for other groups such as builders, farmers, and producers of natural resources. Special incentives also are available for manufacturers. As will become clear in later chapters, the income tax law is replete with rules designed to encourage, stimulate, and assist various enterprises as Congress has deemed necessary over the years.

SOCIAL OBJECTIVES

The tax system is used to achieve not only economic goals but social objectives as well. Some examples are listed below:

1. The deduction for charitable contributions helps to finance the cost of important activities that otherwise would be funded by the government.

2. The deduction for interest on home mortgages subsidizes the cost of a home and thus encourages home ownership.

3. The work opportunity credit noted above exists to fight unemployment problems of certain disadvantaged groups of citizens.

4. Larger standard deductions are granted to taxpayers who are 65 or over, or who are blind, to relieve their tax burden.

5. Deductions for contributions to retirement savings accounts encourage individuals to provide for their future needs.

These examples are representative of the many provisions where social considerations provide the underlying rationale.

The above discussion is but a brief glimpse of how social and economic considerations have shaped our tax law. Interestingly, most of the provisions mentioned have been enacted in the past 25 years. During this time, Congress has relied increasingly on the tax system as a means to strike at the nation's ills. Whether the tax law can be used successfully in this manner is unclear. Many believe that attacking such problems should be done directly through government expenditure programs—not through so-called *tax expenditures*. A *tax expenditure* is the estimated amount of revenue lost for failing to tax a particular item (e.g., scholarships), for granting a certain deduction (e.g., charitable contributions), or for allowing a credit (e.g., work opportunity credit). The concept of tax expenditures was developed by noted tax authority Stanley S. Surrey. While Assistant Secretary of the Treasury for Tax Policy during 1961–1969, Surrey and his supporters urged that certain activities should not be encouraged by subsidizing them through reduced tax liabilities. They argued that paying for government-financed activities in such a roundabout fashion makes their costs difficult if not impossible to determine. In addition, they asserted that such expenditures are concealed from the public eye as well as from the standard budgetary review process.[35] Others, however, argued that the tax system could be used effectively for this purpose. Whether either view is correct, Congress currently shows no apparent signs of discontinuing use of the tax system to influence taxpayers' behavior.

OTHER OBJECTIVES

Although social and economic goals provide the rationale for much of our tax law, many provisions can be explained in terms of certain well-established principles of taxation. These principles are simply the characteristics that "good" taxes exhibit. Most tax experts agree that a tax is good if it satisfies the following conditions:[36]

1. The tax is *equitable* or fair;

2. The tax is *economically efficient* (i.e., it advances a goal where appropriate and otherwise is as neutral as possible);

3. The tax is *certain* and not arbitrary;

4. The tax can be administered by the government and complied with by the taxpayer at a *low cost* (i.e., it is *economical* to operate); and

5. The tax is *convenient* (i.e., administration and compliance can be carried out with the utmost simplicity).

These five qualities represent important principles of taxation that must be conformed with in pursuing social and economic goals. As discussed below, these criteria have greatly influenced our tax law.

---

[35] The annual U.S. budget now contains a projection of annual tax expenditures.

[36] These qualities were first identified by Adam Smith. See *The Wealth of Nations,* Book V, Chapter II, Part II (New York: Dutton, 1910).

Equity

A tax system is considered equitable if it treats all persons who are in the same economic situation in the same fashion. This aspect of equity is referred to as *horizontal equity*. In contrast, *vertical equity* implies that taxpayers who are not in the same situation will be treated differently—the difference in treatment being fair and just. There are two major obstacles in implementing the equity concept as explained. First, there must be some method to determine when taxpayers are in the same economic situation. Second, there must be agreement on reasonable distinctions between those who are in different situations. The manner in which these obstacles are addressed explains two significant features of our tax system.

As indicated above, the first major difficulty in implementing the equity concept is identification of some technique to determine when taxpayers are similarly situated. For tax purposes, it is well settled that similarity is measured in terms of a taxpayer's *ability to pay*. Hence, taxpayers with equal abilities to pay should pay equal taxes. To the dismay of some tax policymakers, however, there is no simple, unambiguous index of an individual's ability. A taxpayer's ability to pay is the composite of numerous factors including his or her wealth, income, family situation, health, and attitude. Clearly, no one measure captures all of these factors. This being so, tax specialists generally have agreed that the best objective measure of ability to pay is income. This agreement, that income is a reasonable surrogate for ability to pay and thus serves the equity principle, explains in part why the primary tax used by the Federal government is an *income* tax.

The second obstacle in implementing the equity concept concerns the treatment of taxpayers who are differently situated. In terms of income, the problem may best be explained by reference to two taxpayers, A and B. If A's income (e.g., $100,000) exceeds B's (e.g., $20,000), it is assumed that A has more ability to pay and thus should pay more tax. The dilemma posed is not whether A and B should pay differing amounts of tax, but rather, what additional amount may be fairly charged to A. If a proportional tax of 5% is levied against A and B, A pays $5,000 (5% of $100,000) and B pays $1,000 (5% of $20,000). While application of this tax rate structure results in A paying $4,000 more than B absolutely, A pays the same amount in relative terms; that is, they both pay the *same* five percent. Those charged with the responsibility of developing Federal tax policy have concluded that paying more tax in absolute terms does not adequately serve the equity goal. For this reason, a progressive tax rate structure is used, requiring relatively more tax to be paid by those having more income. With respect to A and B above, this structure would require that A pay a greater percentage of his income than B.

The equity principle explains (at least partially) not only the basic structure of our predominant tax device—an income tax and its progressive tax rate structure—but also explains many other provisions in our law. In fact, some of the factors mentioned earlier that affect a taxpayer's ability to pay are recognized explicitly by separate provisions in the Code. For example, a taxpayer may deduct medical expenses and casualty losses—items over which the taxpayer has little or no power—if such items exceed a certain level. Similarly, a taxpayer's family situation is considered by allowing exemption deductions for dependents whose support is the taxpayer's responsibility.

There are many other specific situations where the equity principle controls the tax consequences. For example, fairness dictates that taxes should not be paid when the taxpayer does not have the *wherewithal to pay* (i.e., the money to pay the tax). This is true even though the transaction results in income to the taxpayer.

Example 28

Upon the theft of valuable machinery, LJM Corporation received a $20,000 insurance reimbursement. Assuming the machinery had a cost (adjusted for depreciation) of $5,000, LJM has realized a $15,000 gain ($20,000 – $5,000). Although the corporation has realized a gain, it also has lost the productive capacity of the machinery. If LJM reinvests the entire $20,000 proceeds in similar assets within two years of the theft, the gain is not taxed but rather deferred. This rule derives from Congressional belief that equity would not be served if taxes were levied when the taxpayer did not have the wherewithal to pay. In addition, the taxpayer's total economic situation has not been so materially altered as to require recognition of the gain.

Administrative Concerns

The final three qualities of a good tax—certainty, economy, and simplicity—might be aptly characterized as administrative in nature. Numerous provisions exist to meet administrative goals. Some of these are so obvious as to be easily overlooked. For example, the certainty requirement underlies the provision that a tax return generally is due each April 15, while economy of collection is the purpose, at least in part, for withholding. Similarly, provisions requiring the taxpayer to compute the tax using tables provided by the IRS are motivated by concerns for simplicity.

Perhaps the most important aspect of the administrative principles is that they often conflict with other principles of taxation. Consequently, one principle must often be adhered to at the expense of another. For example, our tax system could no doubt be more equitable if each individual's ability to pay was personally assessed, much like welfare agents assess the needs of their clients. However, this improvement could be obtained only at a substantial administrative cost. The administrative principle is first in importance in this case, as well as in many others.

A Prelude to Tax Planning

Although taxes affect numerous aspects of our lives, their impact is not uncontrollable. Given an understanding of the rules, taxes can be managed with considerable success. Successful management, however, is predicated on good tax planning.

Tax planning is simply the process of arranging one's actions in light of their potential tax consequences. It should be emphasized that the tax consequences sometimes turn on how a particular transaction is structured—that is, *form* often controls taxation.

Example 29

Z is obligated to make monthly payments of interest and principal on a note secured by his home. During the year, he was short of cash so his mother, B, who lives with Z, made the payments for him. Even though B made the payments directly, she may not deduct the interest expense because interest is deductible only if it relates to a debt for which the taxpayer is personally liable. Moreover, her son cannot deduct the expense since he did not make payment. Note that the deduction could have been obtained had the payment been structured properly. If Z had received a gift of cash from his mother and then made payment, he could have claimed the interest deduction. Alternatively, if B had been jointly liable on the note, she could have deducted the interest payments she made.

In the example above, note that regardless of how the transaction is structured, the result is the same *except for* the tax ramifications. By merely planning and changing the form of the transaction, tax benefits are obtained. Before jumping to the conclusion that form always governs taxation, a caveat is warranted. Courts often are obliged to disregard form and let substance prevail. Notwithstanding the form versus substance difficulty, the point to be gained is that the pattern of a transaction often determines the tax outcome.

The obvious goal of most tax planning is the minimization of the amount that a person or other entity must transfer to the government. The legal minimization of taxes is usually referred to as tax avoidance. Although the phrase "tax avoidance" may have a criminal connotation, there is no injustice in legally reducing one's taxes. The most profound statement regarding the propriety of tax avoidance is found in a dissenting opinion authored by Judge Learned Hand in the case of *Commissioner v. Newman* Judge Hand wrote:[37]

> Over and over again courts have said that there is nothing sinister in so arranging one's affairs so as to keep taxes as low as possible. Everybody does so, rich or poor, and all do right, for nobody owes any public duty to pay more than the law demands: taxes are enforced exactions, not voluntary contributions. To demand more in the name of morals is pure cant.

---

[37] 159 F.2d 848 (CA-2. 1947).

This statement is routinely cited as authority for taking those steps necessary to reduce one's taxes. It should be emphasized that tax planning and tax avoidance involve only those actions that are legal. Tax evasion is the label given to illegal activities that are designed to reduce the tax liability.

The objective of most tax planning is simple: pay less tax. More formally, the objective is to structure proposed transactions so as to maximize the present value of the tax savings or alternatively minimize the present value of any tax costs. The planning effort for Federal income taxation (the principal area covered in this text) requires an understanding of the answer to *four* basic questions regarding the flow of cash and cash equivalents into and out of various tax entities. These questions concern the amount, character, and timing of income, deductions and credits, and recognition (reporting) of these items. The answers depend on four variables:

1. The *tax entity* (which legal entity carries out the transaction, i.e., receives or transfers the cash or cash equivalents, and whether the entity is considered a taxpayer separate from its owners or simply a conduit through which items of income, gain, loss deduction or credit flow to the owners);

2. The *time* when the tax consequences of the transaction are reported (as determined by the entity's accounting period and methods);

3. The *jurisdiction* where the transaction is governed (which country, state or city); and

4. The *character* of the item of income, gain, loss or deduction resulting from the transaction (e.g., whether it arises from business or investment).

The tax entities recognized for Federal tax purposes, and the tax planning questions, are presented in Exhibit 1-6.

Tax planning efforts often involve deferring the recognition of income or shifting the incidence of its tax to a lower tax bracket entity (e.g., from parents to children), or accelerating, deferring, or shifting deductions and credits to tax periods or among tax entities with higher or lower tax rates. Keeping this overall scheme of tax minimization in mind, many of the subsequent chapters of this text conclude with a discussion of tax planning considerations.

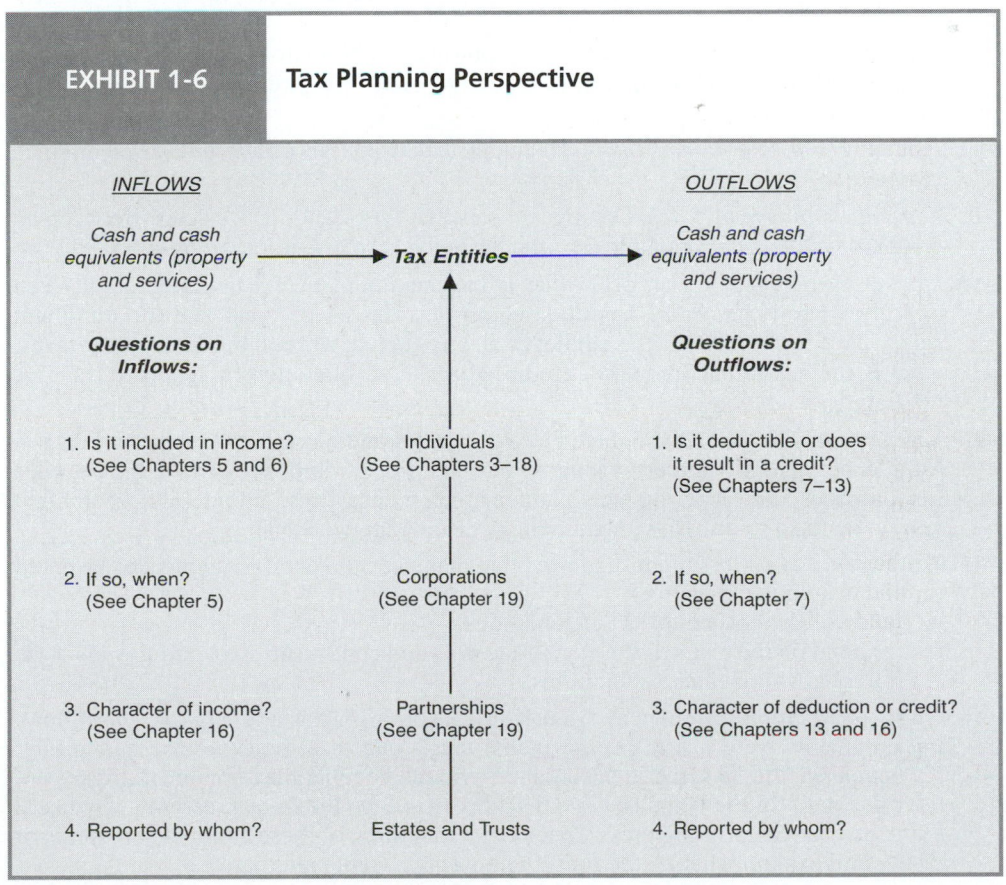

EXHIBIT 1-6	Tax Planning Perspective

INFLOWS — OUTFLOWS

Cash and cash equivalents (property and services) → **Tax Entities** → Cash and cash equivalents (property and services)

Questions on Inflows:

1. Is it included in income? (See Chapters 5 and 6)

2. If so, when? (See Chapter 5)

3. Character of income? (See Chapter 16)

4. Reported by whom?

Individuals (See Chapters 3–18)

Corporations (See Chapter 19)

Partnerships (See Chapter 19)

Estates and Trusts

Questions on Outflows:

1. Is it deductible or does it result in a credit? (See Chapters 7–13)

2. If so, when? (See Chapter 7)

3. Character of deduction or credit? (See Chapters 13 and 16)

4. Reported by whom?

Problem Materials

DISCUSSION QUESTIONS

1-1 *Tax Bases.* Describe the tax bases for the Federal income tax and for each of the Federal wealth transfer taxes.

1-2 *Tax Rates.* Distinguish between a proportional tax rate structure and a progressive tax rate structure. What is the significance of the marginal tax rate under either a proportional or a progressive rate structure?

1-3 *Progressive, Proportional, and Regressive Taxes.* The media often refer to sales taxes as regressive. Similar comments are made when discussing Social Security taxes (FICA). Are the media correct? Include in your comments an explanation of the different types of tax rate structures.

1-4 *Deduction versus Credit.* Distinguish between a deduction and a credit. If a credit is allowed for 20% of an expenditure in lieu of a deduction for the total expenditure, under what circumstances should you prefer the credit? The deduction?

1-5 *Individual versus Corporate Taxable Income.* Based on the tax formulas contained in Exhibits 1-2 and 1-3, what are the significant differences in computing a corporation's taxable income as opposed to computing an individual's taxable income?

1-6 *Withholding Taxes at Source.* What do you believe is the principal reason that Congress continues the pay-as-you-go requirements of employers withholding Federal income taxes from the wages paid their employees?

1-7 *Marital Deduction.* Describe the marital deduction allowed for Federal estate and gift taxes. How might an individual use this deduction to avoid all Federal wealth transfer taxes?

1-8 *Estate Tax Credit.* How is the estate transfer tax credit applied in determining taxable wealth transfers?

1-9 *Annual Gift Tax Exclusion.* What is the amount of the annual Federal gift tax exclusion? If a widow were interested in making gifts to her daughter and seven grandchildren, how much could she transfer to them in any given year before incurring a taxable gift?

1-10 *Gift-Splitting Election.* What is the gift-splitting election allowed for Federal gift tax purposes? How might the marital deduction be used to explain why Congress allows this election?

1-11 *Estate versus Inheritance Taxes.* Distinguish between an estate and an inheritance transfer tax.

1-12 *Federal Employment Taxes.* Distinguish between FICA and FUTA taxes. Between an employee and his or her employer, who bears the greater burden of these taxes?

1-13 *Unemployment Taxes.* For 2017 what is the maximum FUTA tax an employer can expect to pay if he or she has three employees during the year and the minimum salary paid is $10,000? If the employer also is subject to state unemployment taxes, what is the maximum amount of credit he or she will be allowed against the FUTA tax liability?

1-14 *Sales versus Use Tax.* Distinguish between a sales and a use tax. Assume you live in State A but near the border of State B and that State A imposes a much higher sales tax than does State B. If you were planning to purchase a new automobile, what might you be tempted to do? How might State A discourage your plan?

1-15 *Tax Expenditures.* It is often suggested that many of our social problems can be cured through use of tax incentives.
   a. Discuss the concept of tax expenditures.
   b. Expand on the text's discussion of the pros and cons of tax expenditures vis-a-vis direct governmental expenditures.

1-16 *Goals of Taxation.* In a recent discussion concerning what a fair tax is, the following comments were made: (1) the fairest tax is one that someone else has to pay; (2) people should be taxed in accordance with the benefits they obtain (i.e., taxes are the price paid for the benefit); (3) a head tax would be the fairest; and (4) why tax at all?—just use the printing press. Discuss the first three of these comments in terms of equity and explain whether the fourth represents a viable alternative.

PROBLEMS

1-17 *Marginal Tax Rates.* T, a single taxpayer, has taxable income of $45,000 for 2017. If T anticipates a marginal tax rate of 15% for 2018, what income tax savings could she expect by accelerating $1,000 of deductible expenditures planned for 2018 into the 2017 tax year?

1-18 *Tax Rate Schedules and Rate Concepts.* An examination of the tax rate schedules for single taxpayers for 2017 (see the inside cover of the text) indicates that the tax is a "given dollar amount" plus a percentage of taxable income exceeding a particular level.
  a. Explain how the "given dollar amounts" are determined.
  b. Assuming the taxpayer has a taxable income of $50,000 and is single, what is his tax liability for 2017?
  c. Same facts as (b). What is the taxpayer's marginal tax rate?
  d. Same facts as (b). What is the taxpayer's average tax rate?
  e. Assuming the taxpayer has tax-exempt interest income from municipal bonds of $30,000, what is the taxpayer's effective tax rate?

1-19 *Tax Equity.* Taxpayer R has income of $20,000. Similarly, S has income of $20,000. Each taxpayer pays a tax of $1,000 on his income.
  a. Discuss whether the tax imposed is equitable. Include in your discussion comments concerning horizontal and vertical equity.
  b. Assume S has a taxable income of $40,000 and pays a tax of $2,000 on his income. Discuss whether the tax imposed is equitable in light of this new information.

1-20 *Tax Fairness.* R and S both own homes in Houston. Both have an appraised value of $200,000 and, consequently, both R and S pay $5,000 in real property taxes. Explain why such a tax may be considered fair by some and unfair by others.

1-21 *Understanding Tax Rate Concepts.* Indicate whether the following statements are true or false and, if false, explain why.
  a. Tax-exempt income would cause the taxpayer's average tax rate to increase.
  b. Tax-exempt income would cause the taxpayer's marginal tax rate to decrease.
  c. Tax-exempt income would cause the taxpayer's effective tax rate to decrease.

1-22 *Understanding Tax Rate Concepts.* Indicate whether the following statements are true or false and, if false, explain why.
  a. From a technical point of view, sales taxes are progressive.
  b. From a popular point of view, sales taxes are regressive.
  c. From a popular point of view, sales taxes are proportional.
  d. From a technical point of view, there are no regressive taxes in the United States.

1-23 *Think Tax.* From a tax perspective, a transaction that may make sense for one taxpayer may be complete nonsense for another. Consider two married taxpayers, H and W who have taxable income of $600,000 per year and L and M who have taxable income of $70,000 per year. Both plan on buying interest-paying bonds with a face value of $1,000, either State of Indiana bonds paying 6% tax-exempt interest or AT&T bonds paying eight percent taxable interest. Assume the bonds are in all other respects equivalent (e.g., price, risk, etc.). Show (with calculations) why it would make perfect sense for H and W to buy the Indiana bonds but it would be foolish for L and M to buy the Indiana bonds.

1-24 *Identifying Tax Expenditures.* Indicate whether the following would be considered a tax expenditure.
  a. Tax deduction allowed for payment of gasoline purchased by a taxicab driver who owns and operates his own taxicab business.
  b. Deduction for charitable contributions made by individual taxpayers.
  c. Postponement of taxation of income earned on an individual's savings in an Individual Retirement Account until such income is distributed (ignore the time value of money).
  d. Straight-line depreciation of an office building used in a trade or business.
  e. Tax credit for purchase of electric automobile.
  f. Deduction for interest paid on a home mortgage.

1-25 *Advantages and Disadvantages of Tax Expenditures.* Indicate whether the following would be considered an advantage or disadvantage of a tax expenditure.
  a. Administrative costs less than other forms of government financial assistance.
  b. Beneficiaries easily identified.
  c. Only those entitled to financial assistance receive it.
  d. Costs and budgetary effects readily assessed.
  e. Benefits (e.g., from deductions) rise and fall without direct approval from the government.
  f. Less palatable to beneficiaries.
  g. Effect on tax system.

1-26 *Taxable Gifts.* M made the following cash gifts during 2017:

To her son	$50,000
To her daughter	50,000
To her niece	10,000

  a. If M is unmarried, what is the amount of taxable gifts she has made in 2017?
  b. If M is married and her husband agrees to split gifts with her, what is the total amount of taxable gifts made by M and her husband for 2017?

1-27 *Taxable Estate.* R dies in 2017. R made taxable gifts during his lifetime in 1990, 1991, 1993, 1997, and 1999 but paid no Federal transfer taxes due to the unified transfer tax credit in effect in those years. What effect will these taxable gifts have on determining the following:
  a. R's Federal taxable estate?
  b. The rates imposed on the Federal taxable estate?

1-28 *Estate Tax Computation.* T died on January 4, 2017. He owned the following property on his date of death:

Cash	$12,000,000
Stocks and bonds	700,000
Residence	800,000
Interest in partnership	350,000
Miscellaneous personal property	25,000

Upon T's death, he owed $80,000 on the mortgage on his residence. T also owned a life insurance policy. The policy was term life insurance which paid $200,000 to his mother upon his death. Its value immediately before his death was $0. T had all of the incidents of ownership with regard to the policy.

During his life, T had made only one gift. He gave a diamond ring worth $30,000 (it was an old family heirloom) to his daughter in 1995. No gift taxes were paid on the gift due to the annual exclusion (gift-splitting was elected and the annual exclusion was $10,000) and the unified transfer tax credit in effect for that year. The ring was worth $50,000 on his date of death.

T's will contained the following provisions:
  a. To my wife I leave all of the stocks and bonds.
  b. To my alma mater, State University, I leave $50,000 to establish a chair for a tax professor in the Department of Accounting in the School of Business.
  c. The residue of my estate is to go to my daughter.

Compute T's estate tax before any credits other than the Federal estate tax credit.

1-29 *Inheritance Taxes.* This year Bob died, leaving $500,000 to his heirs. His state of residence imposes an inheritance tax. Indicate whether the following statements are true or false and, if false, explain why. Consider using the Internet to find information on how the inheritance tax laws of your state operate.

    a. The amount of the inheritance tax is $0 since Bob's estate does not exceed the 2017 taxable threshold of $5,490,000.

    b. Assume Bob is single. The amount of inheritance tax due from Bob's estate, like the Federal estate tax, is the same regardless of whom he names as the beneficiaries.

    c. Assume Bob is married. The amount of inheritance tax due from Bob's estate— like the Federal estate tax—is zero if he leaves the entire amount to his surviving spouse or children.

    d. Any inheritance tax paid by Bob's estate may be used to reduce any Federal estate tax his estate owes.

1-30 *Excess FICA Taxes.* During 2017 E earned $90,000 of wages from employer X and $50,000 of wages from employer Y. Both employers withheld and paid the appropriate amount of FICA taxes on E's wages.

    a. What is the amount of excess taxes paid by E for 2017?

    b. Would it make any difference in the amount of E's refund or credit of the excess of FICA taxes if he was a full-time employee of each employer for different periods of the year, as opposed to a full-time employee of X and a part-time employee of Y for the entire year?

1-31 *Self-Employment Tax.* During 2017 H had earnings from self-employment of $50,000 and wages of $98,000 from employer X. Employer X withheld and paid the appropriate amount of FICA taxes on H's wages. Compute H's self-employment tax liability for 2017. What is the amount of H's income tax deduction for the self-employment taxes paid?

1-32 *Additional Medicare Tax.* Matt and Jennifer are married and file a joint return. During 2017, Matt received wages of $130,000. Jennifer received wages of $140,000. Both of their employers withheld the proper amount of Social Security and Medicare taxes. Since the employers of both Matt and Jennifer withheld the proper amount of Social Security and Medicare taxes will they owe any additional employment tax (Social Security and Medicare)? If so, how much?

1-33 *Self Employment Tax and the Additional Medicare Tax.* In 2017, Al, single, had self-employment income of $270,000.

    a. Compute Al's self-employment tax and the amount of his deduction for self-employment taxes.

    b. Same as (a) except Al had $90,000 of wages and self-employment income of $120,000.

1-34 *Tax Awareness.* Assume that you are currently employed by Corporation X in state A. Without your solicitation, Corporation Y offers you a 20% higher salary if you will relocate to state B and become its employee. What tax factors should you consider in making a decision as to the offer?

1-35 *Think Tax: The Jurisdiction Variable.* Global Corporation is in the business of producing, distributing, and selling women's clothing all over the world. It plans to manufacture a new line of garments to sell primarily in the U.S. To do this, it will use three subsidiaries. It will have a company produce the clothing in Ireland. The Irish company will sell the clothing to another subsidiary in Bermuda. The Bermuda company will sell the items to third subsidiary in the U.S. that will market and sell the items to clothing stores throughout the U.S. The corporate tax rates that will apply to any income earned in the three countries are: Ireland 12.5 percent, Bermuda 0 percent, and the U.S. 35 percent. The clothing will cost about $10 to manufacture in Ireland and it will sell for $90 in the U.S. How might Global minimize the amount of tax it will pay on the sales of the clothing?

2

Tax Practice and Research

Learning Objectives

Upon completion of this chapter you will be able to:

LO.1 Describe the basic features of tax practice: compliance, planning, litigation, and research.

LO.2 Identify typical career paths in taxation.

LO.3 Understand the difference between primary and secondary authority.

LO.4 Understand the composition of statutory authority.

LO.5 Describe the process in which Federal tax law is enacted and subsequently modified or evaluated by the judiciary.

LO.6 Understand the organization of the Internal Revenue Code.

LO.7 Identify the various types of administrative authority.

LO.8 Understand the judicial system as it relates to tax matters.

LO.9 Explain secondary authority.

LO.10 Evaluate the relative strength of various tax authorities.

LO.11 Understand the importance of communicating the results of tax research.

LO.12 Explain the key penalties that influence positions taken on tax returns.

LO.13 Understand the rules of conduct that must be followed by those who perform tax services.

LO.14 Appreciate the role of ethics in tax practice and the responsibilities of tax practitioners.

Chapter Outline

Introduction

Before discussing the rules and regulations that must be applied to determine the taxpayer's tax liability, one should have an appreciation of the nature of tax practice and how to go about finding answers to tax questions. This chapter lays the necessary foundation by first exploring exactly what it is that tax professionals do and the rules of conduct that they must observe while doing it. The chapter concludes by identifying the various sources of tax law and how they may be accessed and used to solve tax questions.

Tax Practice in General

There are four aspects of tax practice: compliance, planning, litigation, and research. Although these may be thought of as discrete areas, as a practical matter, tax professionals are normally involved in all four.

Tax Compliance

LO.1

Describe the basic features of tax practice: compliance, planning, litigation, and research.

Tax compliance encompasses all of the activities necessary to meet the statutory requirements of the tax law. This largely involves the preparation of the millions of tax returns that must be filed by individuals and other organizations each year. Interestingly, the reliance of individuals on professional return preparation is rather a recent phenomenon. There was a time when most individuals prepared their own returns and H&R Block was unheard of. However, the ever-increasing complexity of the tax law has made professional assistance almost a necessity and in fact created a tax preparation industry. In 2011, 55% of all the individual tax returns filed were completed by a paid preparer.[1] Tax preparation services are typically performed by Certified Public Accountants (CPAs), attorneys, enrolled agents (individuals who have passed a two-day examination given by the IRS), and commercial tax return preparation services. Until recently, there were no special requirements to be met to become a tax return preparer. Consequently, anyone willing to try his or her hand at mastering the tax law—as well as any shysters who thought there was a buck to be made—could hang out a shingle. Indeed, the amount of preparer fraud has grown increasingly worse over the last few years. However, in an attempt to address the problems, the IRS introduced-sweeping changes in the rules governing tax return preparers. Before looking at these rules, it should be emphasized that only CPAs, attorneys, and enrolled agents are authorized to practice before the IRS and are therefore able to represent taxpayers beyond the initial audit.

Tax Return Preparers

After an extensive review that included significant public input, the IRS made fundamental changes in how it regulates the tax return preparation industry. In 2010, the IRS began implementing new regulations and procedures that it believed better served taxpayers, tax administration and the tax professional industry.[2] The new requirements became effective on January 1, 2011. But, the new rules did not last long. In 2014 in *Loving v. IRS*,[3] the Court of Appeals affirmed a lower court ruling that the IRS did not have the authority to enforce the tax return preparer rules. In answer, the IRS created a new voluntary program described below. In the meantime, in early December of 2015, Congress introduced the *Tax Return Preparer Competency Act* primarily designed to eliminate scam artists and help protect taxpayers from identify theft and fraud. If enacted, the new law would override the *Loving* decision and give the IRS broad authority to regulate all aspects of tax practice. Under the proposal, tax return preparers would be required to pass a competency exam, attend annual continuing education classes (at least 15 hours per year) and submit to a background check. Preparer tax identification numbers (PTINs) would also be required (as they are currently). However, the AICPA responded to the bill, saying that it went too far in its regulation efforts. At this point, Congress has not acted but it appears that it is just a matter of time before legislation will be enacted.

PTIN Requirements. One part of the IRS overhaul that still remains is a requirement concerning preparer tax identification numbers, or so-called PTINs. All tax return preparers

---

[1] See SOI Tax Stats—Tax Stats at a Glance, https://www.irs.gov/uac/soi-tax-stats-tax-stats-at-a-glance

[2] See § 6019 and Reg. § 1.6019-2.

[3] 2014-1 USTC 50,175, 113 AFTR 2d 2014-867, 742 F.3d 1013 (CA-DC, 2014).

who are compensated for preparing, or assisting in the preparation of, all or substantially all of a federal tax return must be registered and have a PTIN. The preparer's PTIN must be disclosed on the return. Prior to the new rules, preparers could use either their Social Security number or their PTIN but this option no longer exists. Only the PTIN can be used.

The PTIN requirement applies to virtually anyone who prepares or assists in the preparation of a return. The rule extends to attorneys, certified public accountants, and enrolled agents who are compensated for preparing returns. Note that the IRS has indicated that students who have internships with accounting firms and who prepare returns, regardless of their simplicity, must have a PTIN. In contrast, individuals who volunteer and prepare returns as part of the IRS' VITA program (voluntary income tax assistance program) need not have PTINs.

Preparers can obtain a PTIN, using Form W-12 or an online sign-up system available through the following website: www.IRS.gov/taxpros. PTINs must be renewed annually. The cost for both a new PTIN or renewal for the 2017 filing season is $50. All applicants must be at least 18 years old.

Competency Testing. Prior to the decision in *Loving*, individuals seeking a PTIN were required to pass a competency test covering the Form 1040 series returns. However, one ramifications of *Loving* was the elimination of the competency test requirement.

Continuing Education. As originally constructed, paid preparers (other than CPAs, attorneys and enrolled agents) had to meet a continuing education responsibility. The *Loving* decision ended this requirement. However, in its place the IRS created a voluntary education program.[4] The new approach referred to as the Annual Filing Season Program (AFSP) covers tax return preparers who are not attorneys, CPAs, or enrolled agents. The stated purpose of the program is to recognize the efforts of non-credentialed return preparers who aspire to a higher level of professionalism. The program requires 18 hours of continuing education, including a six hour tax annual update course with a test. Upon completion, the IRS would give the individual an Annual Filing Season Program—Record of Completion. Participants who successfully complete the program are included in a public database of return preparers found on the IRS website. The database entitled Directory of Federal Tax Return Preparers with Credentials and Select Qualifications contains the name, city, state, zip code, and credentials of all attorneys, CPAs, enrolled agents, enrolled retirement plan agents, and enrolled actuaries with a valid PTIN, as well as all AFSP—Record of Completion holders. In 2015, the IRS launched a public education campaign to encourage taxpayers to select return preparers carefully and seek those with professional credentials or other select qualifications. One of the benefits of those participating AFSP will be somewhat greater rights to represent clients whose returns they prepare. The education requirement does not apply to attorneys, certified public accountants, enrolled agents, enrolled actuaries, or enrolled retirement plan agents since all of these are already subject to education requirements to maintain their credentials.

As might be imagined, the day-to-day tasks of those working in the tax compliance area typically surround preparation of a tax return. They collect the appropriate information from the taxpayer and then analyze and evaluate such data for use in preparing the required tax return or other tax filing. But tax compliance goes far beyond merely placing numbers in boxes. In many cases, completion of the return requires tax research to determine the appropriate treatment of a particular item. Preparation of a return may also uncover tax planning opportunities that can be shared with the client to obtain future savings. In addition, tax compliance involves representation of the taxpayer before the IRS during audits and appeals.

Tax Planning

Perhaps the most rewarding part of tax practice is tax planning and the sense of satisfaction one gets from helping clients minimize their tax liability. As explained in the previous chapter, tax planning is simply the process of arranging one's financial affairs in light of their potential tax consequences. Unlike the weather, taxpayers often have some degree of control over their tax liability, and it is the job of the tax adviser to help the taxpayer whenever possible. A great deal of tax planning is simply an outgrowth of the tax compliance process. Well-trained tax professionals often recognize a situation where a little planning could have brought a more favorable result. In these so-called *closed fact* situations, it is typically too late to do anything until the opportunity once again presents itself, typically the next year. On the other hand, taxpayers about to embark on a transaction—an *open fact* situation—may engage a tax adviser to determine the tax consequences and how to structure the transaction to obtain the most beneficial outcome.

---

[4] Rev. Proc. 2014-42, 2014-29 IRB 192 (2014).

Tax Litigation

As might be expected, taxpayers and the IRS do not always agree on the tax treatment of a particular item. Many disputes and controversies are settled during an appeals process within the IRS itself. Others, however, are ultimately resolved in a court of law. In most cases, tax litigation is conducted only by licensed attorneys. However, CPAs and others, including the taxpayer himself, can represent the taxpayer in certain situations. In addition, accountants often assist legal counsel and provide litigation support.

Tax Research

Many tax practitioners believe that tax research is the most interesting part of their professional work. Tax research is simply the process of obtaining information and synthesizing it to answer a particular tax question. Regardless of the area of tax practice—compliance, planning, or litigation—tax research plays an important part.

Tax research generally involves identifying tax issues, finding relevant information on the issues, and assessing the pertinent authority to arrive at a conclusion. Unfortunately, the law is not so straightforward that the answer to every tax question is readily available. Consequently, being able to do the research is an important skill for anyone involved in tax. For example, a decorator that works out of her home may want to know whether the cost of maintaining a home office can be deducted in computing taxable income. It may seem that a common problem like this could be easily resolved, but it is often much more difficult than might be imagined. To answer this question, the tax adviser may be required to sift through mounds of information—rules, regulations, IRS pronouncements, and court cases—in order to determine the proper treatment. Even if an answer seems apparent, the dynamic nature of the tax law often requires the practitioner to constantly update his or her research to ensure that it is current and has not been changed by some recent development.

Taxation as a Professional Career

LO.2

Identify typical career paths in taxation.

The need for tax advisory services has grown almost exponentially in recent years. The growth is not surprising given the growth in the tax law. In recent years, there have been tax law changes virtually every year. During this time Congress has turned to the tax system again and again to attack not only the country's economic ills but its social problems as well. The end result is a tax law, both Federal and state, that is forever changing and quite complex. Consequently, individuals and organizations have increasingly needed to call upon tax specialists to help them cope with the law. These demands on the tax profession have created tremendous opportunities for those interested in careers in taxation.

The tax specialists of today wear a number of hats. They act as tax consultants as well as business advisers. They help individuals and business owners with tax compliance, keep them informed of changes in the tax law, and assist them in personal financial planning. Tax advisers not only consult on Federal and state income tax matters; they also prepare sales, payroll, and franchise tax returns. Industry and government also employ tax specialists who are involved in planning and compliance. Here are some examples of activities in which the tax specialist might be involved:

- A husband and wife want to transfer their business to their children. Should they sell the business to the kids or would they be better off just giving it to them? A tax specialist can compare the income tax consequences of a sale to that of a gift or bequest and help design the best plan in light of the couple's wishes.

- A taxpayer wants to sell her corporation. Should she sell the stock or cause the corporation to sell its assets? A tax specialist can explain the tax and nontax factors affecting the decision.

- An individual and his son are forming a new business. Should it be operated as a corporation, an S corporation, a partnership, or a limited liability company? A tax specialist can help with the analysis.

- A corporation is planning on opening operations in a foreign country. A tax specialist can help reorganize the company to help minimize U.S. and foreign taxes.

- A corporation is considering the establishment of a retirement plan. A tax adviser who specializes in employee benefits can provide information regarding the tax considerations.

- A taxpayer is seeking a divorce. A tax specialist can explain the tax consequences.

- A corporation and its subsidiaries are thinking about filing a consolidated tax return. The tax specialist can assist the taxpayer in filing such a return, preparing estimated tax payments, or reviewing a corporation's tax returns.

- The IRS wants to deny the taxpayer a deduction for meals and entertainment. The tax specialist might represent an individual during the IRS examination or present oral and written arguments before an IRS appeals conference and (if qualified) before the U.S. Tax Court.

In these and similar matters, the tax specialist is often an important member of the client's professional advisory team and works with other high-caliber individuals to minimize client costs. For example, if a business owner is seeking estate planning advice, the team typically includes the individual's attorney, accountant, life insurance agent, and tax adviser.

Thousands of men and women enjoy successful careers in taxation. They are highly respected as professionals and are well compensated for their work. Those in tax rarely find their jobs boring or dull. Tax work, particularly once one has paid one's dues and built a firm foundation, is interesting and challenging. Moreover, working in a tax department along with other professionals with like interests can be a vastly rewarding personal experience. Tax professionals also serve the public good by raising the standard of tax practice and administration and by working with other groups to improve the tax system.

Sources and Applications of Tax Law

As stated at the outset of this chapter, before delving into the rules and regulations of taxation, it is important at a minimum to have an appreciation of not only the nature of tax practice but also the sources of the tax law and how they can be used for solving questions. The second half of this chapter identifies the various components of the tax law, explains how they can be accessed, and reviews the basic methods of tax research.

Primary versus Secondary Authority

Without doubt, the most important task of a tax professional is answering tax questions. Indeed, tax professionals spend much of their careers—much of their daily lives—determining the tax treatment of some transaction. Unfortunately, the tax law does not provide clear-cut definitive answers to all questions. There is no certainty in these matters. Consequently, in these *gray* areas, the job of the tax professional is not to find the perfect solution but rather to reach an answer that is defensibly or authoritatively correct. In this regard, the type of authority is critical.

LO.3
Understand the difference between primary and secondary authority.

In legal matters, like taxation, all "authority" is classified as either primary authority or secondary authority. The distinction is important because in tax controversies, as in any legal dispute, courts normally are obligated to follow primary authority and not secondary authority.

Primary authority generally refers to the written laws passed by the legislative branch of government (e.g., Congress). Primary authority also includes "official" interpretations of these laws. These interpretations include those issued by either the executive branch (e.g., the Treasury Department including the IRS) or the judicial branch (the courts). In short, primary authority generally has some official source that courts normally are obligated to follow.

Secondary authority is generally anything other than primary authority. Secondary authority essentially consists of any information that is not issued by the executive, legislative or judicial branches of government. It could be a scholarly article written by a professor or practicing attorney or a book or a treatise. Courts are not required to follow secondary authority. However, courts as well as lawyers and tax professionals often use secondary authority to support their arguments that are rooted in primary authority.

Primary authority and secondary authority are broad classifications of the various types of authority. As might be expected, there are different types of authority within each group. These different types of authority are discussed in detail below.

Authoritative Sources of Tax Law

Primary authority can be classified into two broad categories: (1) the law, and (2) official interpretations of the law. The law consists primarily of the Constitution, the laws enacted by Congress (the Acts of Congress), and tax treaties. In general, these sources are referred to as the *statutory* law. Most statutory law is written in general terms for a typical situation. Since general rules, no matter how carefully drafted, cannot be written to cover variations on the normal scheme, interpretation is usually required. The task of interpreting the statute is one of the principal duties of the Internal Revenue Service (IRS) as representative of the Secretary of the Treasury. The IRS annually produces thousands of documents that explain and clarify the law. To no one's surprise, however, taxpayers and the government do not always agree on how a particular law should be interpreted. In situations where the taxpayer or the government decides to litigate the question, the courts, as final arbiters, are given the opportunity to interpret the law. These judicial interpretations, administrative interpretations, and the statutory law are considered in detail below.

Statutory Law

LO.4

Understand the composition of statutory authority.

The Constitution of the United States provides the Federal government with the power to tax. Disputes concerning the constitutionality of an income tax levied on taxpayers without apportionment among the states were resolved in 1913 with passage of the Sixteenth Amendment. Between 1913 and 1939, Congress enacted revenue acts that amounted to a complete rewrite of all tax law to date, including the desired changes. In 1939, due primarily to the increasing complexity of the earlier process, Congress codified all Federal tax laws into Title 26 of the *United States Code,* which was then called the *Internal Revenue Code of 1939.* Significant changes in the Federal tax laws were made during World War II and the postwar period of the late 1940s. Each change resulted in amendments to the 1939 Code. By 1954, the codification process had to be repeated in order to organize all additions to the law and to eliminate obsolete provisions. The product of this effort was the *Internal Revenue Code of 1954.* After 1954, Congress took great care to ensure that each new amendment to the 1954 Code was incorporated within its organizational structure with appropriate cross-references to any prior provisions affected by a new law. In 1986, Congress again made substantial revision in the tax law. Consistent with this massive redesign of the 1954 Code, Congress changed the title to the *Internal Revenue Code of 1986.* Like the 1954 Code, the 1986 Code is subject to revisions introduced by a new law. Recent changes incorporated into the 1986 Code include those made by the *Protecting Americans From Tax Hikes Act of 2015.*

The legislative provisions contained in the Code are by far the most important component of tax law. Although the steps necessary to enact a law are generally well known, it is important to review this process with a special emphasis on taxation. Much of the job of the tax professional is to determine how a particular rule works or how it applies. What did Congress intend when it wrote the rule? For this reason, it is critical to understand how a law is created or more specifically, the legislative process.

THE MAKING OF A TAX LAW

LO.5

Describe the process in which Federal tax law is enacted and subsequently modified or evaluated by the judiciary.

Who writes the tax laws? The short answer is Congress—and not the IRS. Article I, Section 7, Clause 1 of the Constitution provides that the House of Representatives of the U.S. Congress has the basic responsibility for initiating revenue bills.[5] The Ways and Means Committee of the House of Representatives must consider any tax bill before it is presented for vote by the full House of Representatives. On bills of major public interest, the Ways and Means Committee holds public hearings where interested organizations may send representatives to express their views about the bill. The first witness at such hearings is usually the Secretary of the Treasury, representing the President of the United States. In many cases, proposals for new tax legislation or changes in existing legislation come from the President as a part of his political or economic programs.

---

[5] Tax bills do not originate in the Senate, except when they are attached to other bills.

After the public hearings have been held, the Ways and Means Committee usually goes into closed session, where the Committee prepares the tax bill for consideration by the entire House. The members of the Committee receive invaluable assistance from their highly skilled staff, which includes economists, accountants, and lawyers. The product of this session is a proposed bill that is submitted to the entire House for debate and vote.

After a bill has been approved by the entire House, it is sent to the Senate and assigned to the Senate Finance Committee. The Senate Finance Committee may also hold hearings on the bill before its consideration by the full Senate. The Senate's bill generally differs from the House's bill. In these situations, both versions are sent to the Joint Conference Committee on Taxation, which is composed of members selected from the House Ways and Means Committee and from the Senate Finance Committee. The objective of this Joint Committee is to produce a compromise bill acceptable to both sides. On occasion, when compromise cannot be achieved by the Joint Committee or the compromise bill is unacceptable to the House or the Senate, the bill "dies." If, however, compromise is reached and the Senate and House approve the compromise bill, it is then referred to the President for his or her approval or veto. If the President vetoes the bill, the legislation is "killed" unless two-thirds of both the House and the Senate vote to override the veto. If the veto is overridden, the legislation becomes law.

When a bill is signed into law by the President it is sent to the Office of the Federal Register to be assigned a "public law number." For example, the Tax Reform Act of 1986 is designated P.L. 99-514 and is explained in the following diagram.

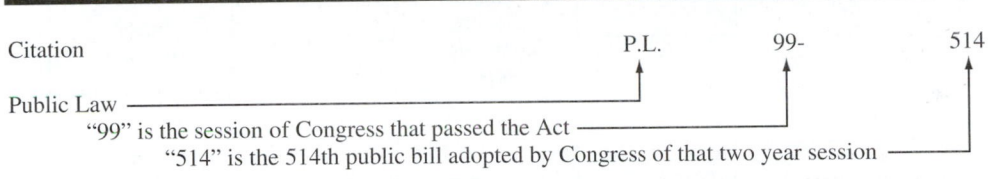

References to the various laws are often made using their public law numbers. Unfortunately, the public law number does not indicate the year in which the bill was enacted. However, the legislative session in which a public law was enacted can be determined using the following formula:

For laws enacted before 2000:   (Session number × 2) – 112 = Second year of session + 1,900
For laws enacted after 1999:   (Session number × 2) – 212 = Second year of session + 2,000

Using this formula, the Tax Reform Act of 1986, P.L. 99-514 was enacted during the 1985–1986 legislative session [(99 × 2 = 198) – 112 = 86]. The Tax Relief and Health Care Act of 2006 was P.L. 109-432. Using the formula reveals that this Act was enacted during the 2005–2006 legislative session [(109 × 2 = 218) – 212 = 6 + 2,000 or 2,006]. Note that if the public law number is 106 or higher the legislative session occurred in 2000 or later.

COMMITTEE REPORTS

At each stage of the legislative process, various documents are generated that may be useful in assessing the intent of Congress. One of the better sources of Congressional intent is a report issued by the House Ways and Means Committee. This report contains the bill as well as a general explanation. This explanation usually provides the historical background of the proposed legislation along with the reasons for enactment. The Senate Finance Committee also issues a report similar to that of the House. Because the Senate often makes changes in the House version of the bill, the Senate's report is also an important source. Additionally, the Joint Conference Committee on Taxation issues its own report, which is sometimes helpful. Two other sources of intent are the records of the debates on the bill and publications of the initial hearings.

Committee reports and debates appear in several publications. Committee reports are officially published in pamphlet form by the U.S. Government Printing Office as the bill proceeds through Congress. The enacted bill is published in the *Internal Revenue Bulletin* and the *Internal Revenue Cumulative Bulletin*. The debates are published in the *Congressional Record*. In addition to these official government publications, several commercial publishers make this information available to subscribers.

The diagram below illustrates the normal flow of a bill through the legislative process and the documents that are generated in this process.

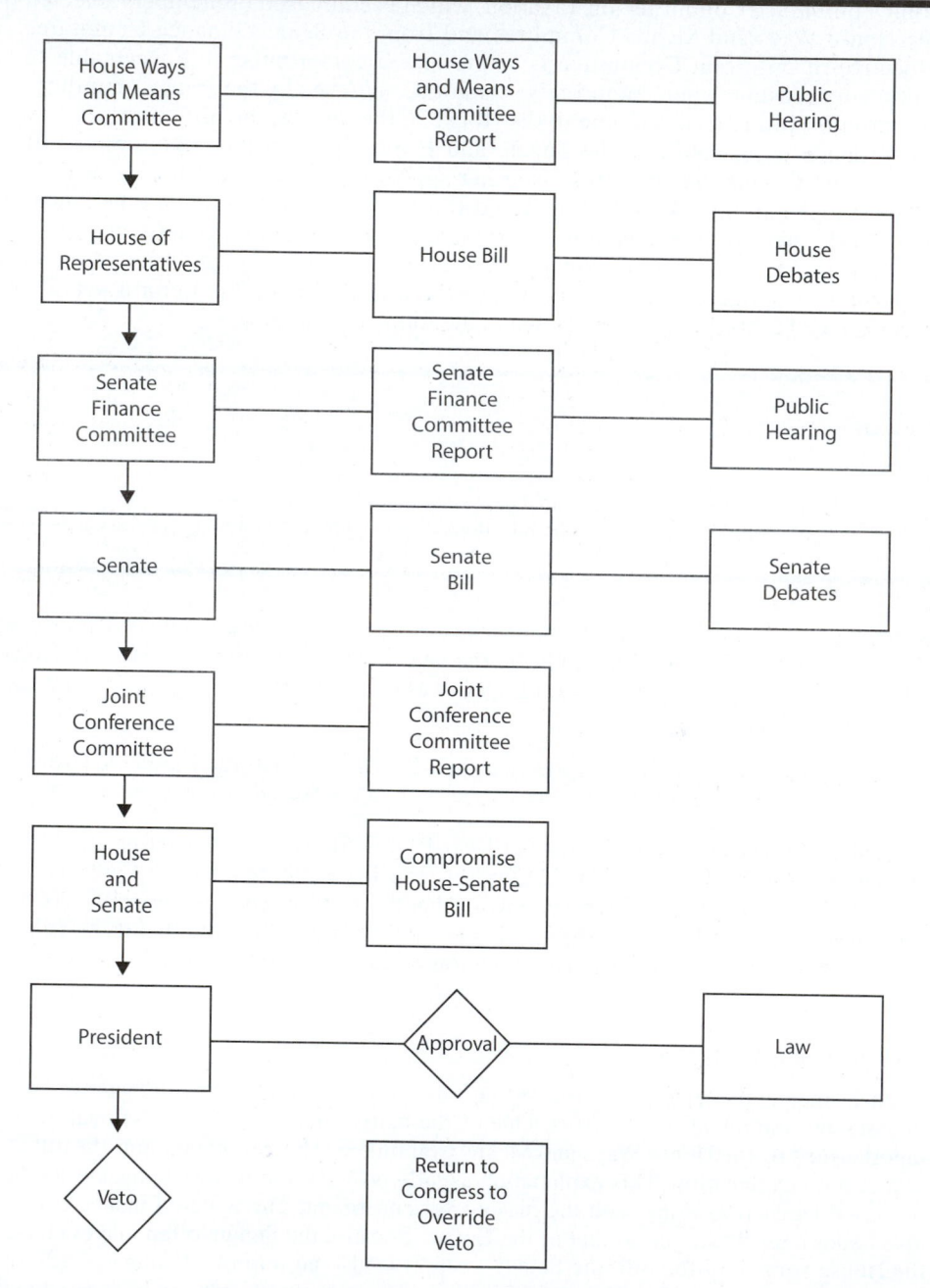

Organization of the Internal Revenue Code

Once a tax bill becomes tax law, it is incorporated into the existing structure of the U.S. federal laws known as the *United States Code*. As mentioned above, the *U.S. Code* is the collection of all laws enacted by Congress. Laws concerning the same subject matter (e.g., taxation) are consolidated in a single "title." As shown in Exhibit 2-1, there are 50 titles. Tax laws are incorporated directly into Title 26 entitled *Internal Revenue Code*.[6]

LO.6
Understand the organization of the Internal Revenue Code.

EXHIBIT 2-1	United States Code		

Title Number	Title Name	Title Number	Title Name
Title 1	General Provisions	Title 26	Internal Revenue Code
Title 2	The Congress	Title 27	Intoxicating Liquors
Title 3	The President	Title 28	Judiciary and Judicial Procedure
Title 4	Flag and Seal, Seat of Government, …	Title 29	Labor
Title 5	Government Organization and Employees	Title 30	Mineral Lands and Mining
Title 6	Domestic Security	Title 31	Money and Finance
Title 7	Agriculture	Title 32	National Guard
Title 8	Aliens and Nationality	Title 33	Navigation and Navigable Waters
Title 9	Arbitration	Title 34	Navy (repealed)
Title 10	Armed Forces	Title 35	Patents
Title 11	Bankruptcy	Title 36	Patriotic Societies and Observances
Title 12	Banks and Banking	Title 37	Pay and Allowances of the Uniformed Services
Title 13	Census	Title 38	Veterans' Benefits
Title 14	Coast Guard	Title 39	Postal Service
Title 15	Commerce and Trade	Title 40	Public Buildings, Property, and Works
Title 16	Conservation	Title 41	Public Contracts
Title 17	Copyrights	Title 42	The Public Health and Welfare
Title 18	Crimes and Criminal Procedure	Title 43	Public Lands
Title 19	Customs Duties	Title 44	Public Printing and Documents
Title 20	Education	Title 45	Railroads
Title 21	Food and Drugs	Title 46	Shipping
Title 22	Foreign Relations and Intercourse	Title 47	Telegraphs, Telephones, and Radiotelegraphs
Title 23	Highways	Title 48	Territories and Insular Possessions
Title 24	Hospitals and Asylums	Title 49	Transportation
Title 25	Indians	Title 50	War and National Defense

Title 26 (the Internal Revenue Code) is further divided as follows:

Title 26 of the United States Code (referred to as the Internal Revenue Code)

    Subtitle A—Income Taxes

        Chapter 1—Normal Taxes and Surtaxes

            Subchapter A—Determination of Tax Liability

                Part I—Tax on Individuals

                    Sections—1 through 5

---

[6] All future use of the term Code or Internal Revenue Code refers to the *Internal Revenue Code of 1986*, as amended.

EXHIBIT 2-2	Internal Revenue Code: Subtitles, Chapters, and Subchapters

Subtitle	Subject	First Code Section
Subtitle A	Income Taxes	§ 1
Subtitle B	Estate and Gift Taxes	§ 2001
Subtitle C	Employment Taxes	§ 3101
Subtitle D	Miscellaneous Excise Taxes	§ 4001
Subtitle E	Alcohol, Tobacco, and Certain Other Excise Taxes	§ 5001
Subtitle F	Procedure and Administration	§ 6001
Subtitle G	The Joint Committee on Taxation	§ 8001
Subtitle H	Financing of Presidential Election Campaigns	§ 9001
Subtitle I	Trust Fund Code	§ 9501

Chapters in Subtitle A	Name	First Code Section
1	Income Taxes	§ 1
2	Tax on Self-Employment Income	§ 1401
3	Withholding of Tax on Nonresident Aliens and Foreign Corporations	§ 1441
4	[Repealed]	
5	[Repealed]	§ 1491
6	Consolidated Returns	§ 1501

Selected Subchapters of Chapter 1	Name	Code Sections
A	Determination of Tax Liability	§§ 1–59B
B	Computation of Taxable Income	§§ 61–291
C	Corporate Distributions and Adjustments	§§ 301–385
D	Deferred Compensation, etc.	§§ 401–436
E	Accounting Periods and Methods of Accounting	§§ 441–483
F	Exempt Organizations	§§ 501–530
G	Corporations Used to Avoid Income Tax on Shareholders	§§ 531–565
H	Banking Institutions	§§ 581–597
I	Natural Resources	§§ 611–638
J	Estates, Trusts, Beneficiaries, and Decedents	§§ 641–692
K	Partners and Partnerships	§§ 701–777
L	Insurance Companies	§§ 801–848
M	Regulated Investment Companies and Real Estate Investment Trusts	§§ 851–860L
N	Tax Based on Income From Sources Within or Without the United States	§§ 861–999
O	Gain or Loss on Disposition of Property	§§ 1001–1111
P	Capital Gains and Losses	§§ 1201–1298
S	Tax Treatment of S Corporations and Their Shareholders	§§ 1361–1379

Exhibit 2-2 reveals the contents of the various subdivisions. As a practical matter, virtually all of a tax practitioner's work is done in Subtitle A, Chapter 1, which deals with income taxes. Note that subtitles are further divided into chapters, subchapters, parts, subparts, and finally the most important element: sections.

The most critical portions of the Internal Revenue Code are its "sections." The sections contain the laws—often referred to as provisions or rules—that a taxpayer must follow to determine taxable income and ultimately the final tax liability. For example, the starting point in determining taxable income is gross income and Code Section 61 provides the definition of gross income as follows: income. Section 61 appears below.

> *Section 61: Gross Income Defined*
>
> (a) *General definition. Except as otherwise provided in this subtitle (A), gross income means all income from whatever source derived, including (but not limited to) the following items:*
>
> > (1) *Compensation for services, including fees, commissions, fringe benefits, and similar items;*
> >
> > (2) *Gross income derived from business;*
> >
> > (3) *Gains derived from dealings in property;*
> >
> > (4) *Interest;*
> >
> > (5) *Rents;*
> >
> > .
> > .
> > .
> >
> > (14) *Income in respect of a decedent; and*
> >
> > (15) *Income from an interest in an estate or trust.*

The ability to use the Internal Revenue Code is essential for all individuals who have any involvement with the tax laws.

When working with the tax law, it is often necessary to make reference to, or *cite,* a particular source with respect to the Code. The *section* of the Code is the source normally cited. A complete citation for a section of the Code would be too cumbersome. For instance, a formal citation for § 1 of the Code would be "Subtitle A, Chapter 1, Subchapter A, Part I, Section 1." In most cases, citation of the section alone is sufficient. Sections are numbered consecutively throughout the Code so that each section number is used only once. Currently the numbers run from §§ 1 through 9833. Not all section numbers are used, so that additional ones may be added by Congress in the future without the need for renumbering.[7]

Citation of a particular Code section in tax literature ordinarily does not require the prefix "Internal Revenue Code" because it is generally understood that, unless otherwise stated, references to section numbers concern the Internal Revenue Code of 1986 as amended. However, since most Code sections are divided into subparts, reference to a specific subpart requires more than just its section number. Section 170(a)(2)(B) serves as an example.

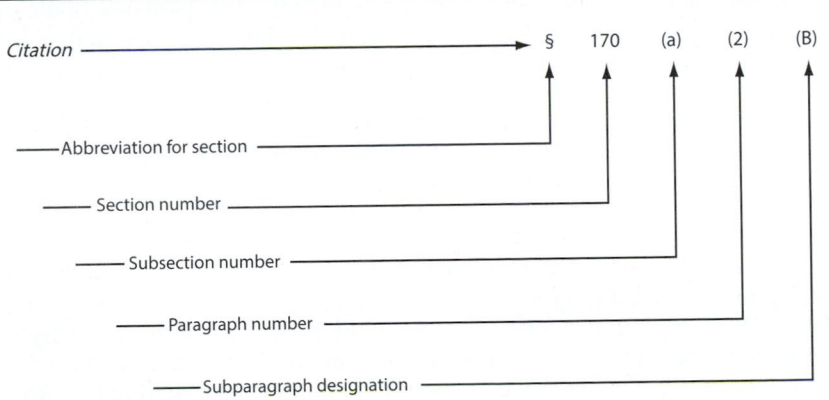

All footnote references used throughout this text are made in the form given above. In most cases, the "§" or "§§" symbols are used in place of the terms "section" or "sections," respectively.

---

[7] It is interesting to note that when it adopted the 1954 Code, Congress deliberately left section numbers unassigned to provide room for future additions. Recently, however, Congress has been forced to identify new sections by alphabetical letters following a particular section number. See, for example, Sections 280, 280A, 280B, and 280C of the 1986 Code.

Single-volume or double-volume editions of the Internal Revenue Code are published after every major change in the law. Private publishing companies such as Commerce Clearing House, Inc. (CCH) and the Research Institute of America (RIA) publish these editions as well as a wealth of other tax information. All of this tax information is included in so-called tax services—massive tax libraries—compiled and published by these companies and others. The major tax services, all available electronically, are discussed in a later section of this chapter.

TAX TREATIES

The laws contained in tax treaties represent the third and final component of the statutory law. Tax treaties (also referred to as tax conventions) are agreements between the United States and other countries that provide rules governing the taxation of residents of one country by another. For example, the tax treaty between the United States and France indicates how the French government taxes U.S. citizens residing in France and vice versa. Tax treaties, as law, have the same authority as those laws contained in the Code.[8] Treaty provisions may override provisions of the Internal Revenue Code under certain circumstances.[9] For this reason, persons involved with an international tax question must be aware of tax treaties and recognize that the Code may be superseded by a tax treaty.

Administrative Interpretations

LO.7

Identify the various types of administrative authority.

After Congress has enacted a tax law, the Executive branch of the Federal government has the responsibility for enforcing it. In the process of enforcing the law, the Treasury interprets, clarifies, defines, and analyzes the Code in order to apply Congressional intention of the law to the specific facts of a taxpayer's situation. This process results in numerous administrative releases, such as regulations, rulings, procedures and other pronouncements discussed below.

REGULATIONS

Regulations are the Treasury's official interpretation of the Internal Revenue Code. In contrast to a Revenue Ruling (discussed below), which is an interpretation of the law as it applies to a specific set of facts, a regulation provides a general interpretation. To illustrate, consider the problem of a couple who discovered $4,467 of old currency in a piano seven years after they purchased it at an auction for $15.[10] Is this taxable income? Note that the definition of gross income contained in § 61 above provides little guidance, indicating only that "income is income from whatever source derived." However, a regulation explaining what constitutes gross income, Reg. § 1.61-14, indicates that buried treasure is to be included in income. Other regulations concerning gross income discuss in detail the treatment of such items as dividends, interest, and rents. The major purpose of the regulations is to interpret, explain, clarify, and elaborate on the various provisions of the Internal Revenue Code. When researching a tax question, the tax professional always examines both the Code and the Regulations.

Code § 7805(a) authorizes the Secretary of the Treasury to "prescribe all needful rules and regulations for the enforcement" of the tax law. Section 7805(b) provides authority to the Secretary to prescribe the extent, if any, to which any ruling or regulation relating to the tax laws will be applied without retroactive effect. In most cases the Secretary delegates the power to write the regulations to the Commissioner of the Internal Revenue Service. In practice, this means that the regulations are written by the technical staff of the IRS or by the office of the Chief Counsel of the IRS, an official who is also an assistant General Counsel of the Treasury Department.

---

[8] See Code § 7852(d)(1).

[9] § 7852(d)(2).

[10] *Ermenegildo Cesarini v. U.S.*, 69-1 USTC ¶9270, 23 AFTR 2d 69-997, 296 F Supp 3 (DC-OH, 1969).

Final and Proposed Regulations

Regulations are issued in the form of *Treasury Decisions* (often referred to as TDs), which are published in the *Federal Register* and sometimes later in the *Internal Revenue Bulletin*. The *Federal Register* is the official publication for regulations and legal notices issued by the executive branch of the Federal government. The *Federal Register* is published every business day. Before a TD is published in final form, it must be issued in proposed form, a *proposed regulation,* for a period of at least 30 days before it is scheduled to become final.

Upon publication, interested parties have at least 30 days to comment on proposed regulations. In addition, public hearings are often scheduled. In theory, at the end of this comment period, the Treasury responds in any one of three ways; it may withdraw the proposed regulation, amend it, or leave it unchanged. In the latter two cases, the Treasury normally issues the regulation in its final form as a TD, published in the *Federal Register.* The final version of any given regulation is quite frequently significantly different from the proposed version.

Afterwards, the new regulation is included in Title 26 of the *Code of Federal Regulations.* In fact, however, proposed regulations sometimes remain in proposed form for many years. Proposed regulations do not have the force of law and are not the Treasury's official position on a particular issue.

Temporary Regulations

The National Office of the Treasury issues temporary regulations as the need arises. Often such regulations are issued in response to substantive changes in the tax law when tax practitioners, in particular, need immediate guidance in applying a new or revised statute. Such regulations usually deal with immediate filing requirements or details regarding a mandated accounting method change. Temporary regulations are effective immediately without the comment period. This is true even though temporary regulations normally are also issued as proposed regulations which are subject to the comment period. Temporary regulations expire three years after issuance and are given the same respect and precedential value as final regulations.

The primary purpose of the regulations is to explain and interpret particular Code sections. Although regulations have not been issued for all Code sections, they have been issued for the great majority. In those cases where regulations exist, they are an important authoritative source on which one can usually rely. Regulations can be classified into three groups: (1) legislative; (2) interpretive; and (3) procedural.

Legislative Regulations

Occasionally, Congress will give specific authorization to the Secretary of the Treasury to issue regulations on a particular Code section. For example, under § 1502, the Secretary is charged with prescribing the regulations for the filing of a consolidated return by an affiliated group of corporations. There are virtually no Code sections governing consolidated returns, and the regulations in effect serve in lieu of the Code. In this case and others where it occurs, the regulation has the force and effect of a law, with the result that a court reviewing the regulation usually will not substitute its judgment for that of the Treasury Department unless the Treasury has clearly abused its discretion.[11]

Interpretative Regulations

Interpretative regulations explain the meaning of a Code section and commit the Treasury and the Internal Revenue Service to a particular position relative to the Code section in question. In contrast to legislative regulations, procedural regulations are issued under the

---

[11] *Anderson, Clayton & Co. v. U.S.,* 77-2 USTC
¶9727, 40 AFTR2d 77-6102, 562 F.2d 972 (CA-5, 1977),
Cert. den. at 436 U.S. 944 (USSC, 1978).

general authority of § 7805 that authorizes Treasury to provide interpretations and guidance as necessary. This type of regulation is binding on the IRS but not on the courts, although it is "a body of experience and informed judgment to which courts and litigants may properly resort for guidance."[12] Interpretive regulations have considerable authority and normally are invalidated only if they are inconsistent with the Code or are unreasonable.

For many years, taxpayers and the government have disagreed over the level of deference that courts should give to regulations. In other words, how much authoritative weight should courts give to the rules that Treasury writes? The Supreme Court's recent decision in *Mayo Foundation* seems to have resolved this issue.[13]

Mayo involved a long-running controversy between the IRS and the medical community over whether medical residents are "students" and therefore exempt from employment taxes. After losing a number of cases on this issue, Treasury revoked a 50 year old regulation favorable to Mayo and the students and replaced it with one saying that anyone who works more than 40 hours a week cannot qualify for the student exemption. The primary concern of the case was the authoritative value that should be given the new regulation and whether it was valid at all. According to the *Mayo* court, all regulations should be analyzed using the standards developed in *Chevron,* a non-tax case.[14]

The *Chevron* approach involves a two step inquiry. The first step asks whether Congress has directly addressed the precise question at issue. If Congress has made its intent clear, then the regulation must give effect to Congress' stated intent. If Congressional intent is not clear, the second inquiry is whether the regulation is a reasonable construction of the statute. In this case, the Court concluded that the statute that Congress had written to address the issue (the definition of a student) was unclear. So it turned to the second *Chevron* inquiry: Was the regulation a reasonable interpretation of the ambiguous statute? The Court believed it was reasonable and held against the taxpayer.

The effects of *Mayo* appear to be far reaching. Most importantly, courts now must apply the two-part test of *Chevron* in evaluating regulations. Moreover, the *Mayo* court made it clear that the authority of a regulation did not depend on whether the regulation was issued at the specific direction of Congress or under the general rulemaking authority granted to the Treasury Department. Whether a regulation is legislative or interpretive now appears irrelevant. Finally, the court indicated that the history of a regulation, such as whether it represents a reversal of Treasury policy or whether it was issued because the government was losing cases, is not a consideration in determining whether the regulation is valid. According to some, the immediate effect of *Mayo* will cause challenges to regulations to ignore history and whether the regulation is legislative or interpretive and center on substance.

Procedural Regulations

Procedural regulations cover such areas as the information a taxpayer must supply to the IRS and the internal management and conduct of the IRS in certain matters. Those regulations affecting vital interests of the taxpayers are generally binding on the IRS, and those regulations stating the taxpayer's obligation to file particular forms or other types of information are given the effect of law.

Citation for Regulations

Regulations are arranged in the same sequence as the Code sections they interpret. Thus, a regulation begins with a number that designates the type of tax or administrative, definitional, or procedural matter and is followed by the applicable Code section number. For example, Treasury Regulation Section 1.614-3(f)(5) below is as an illustration of how regulations are cited throughout this text.

---

[12] *Skidmore v. Swift and Co.,* 323 U.S. 134 (USSC, 1944).

[13] *Mayo Foundation for Medical Education and Educational Research v. U.S.,* 2011-1 USTC ¶50,143, 107 AFTR 2d 2011-341, 131 S.Ct. 704 (USSC, 2011).

[14] *Chevron USA v. Natural Resources Defense Council, Inc.,* 467 U.S. 837 (USSC, 1984).

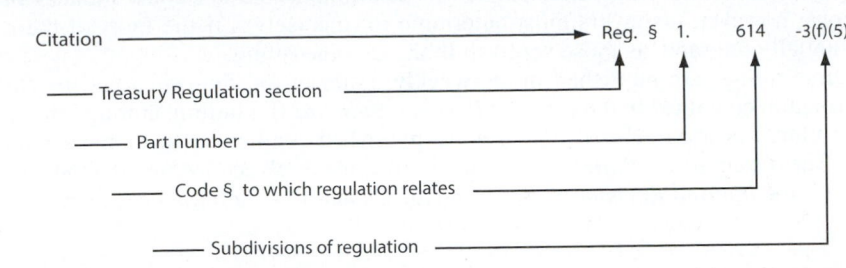

If a regulation is proposed, the word "Prop." is added prior to the word "Treas." or more simply, Prop. Reg. An example is Prop. Reg. § 1.280A-1. Similarly, for a temporary regulation the word "Temp." is usually added and the letter "T" follows the number of the regulation such as Temp. Reg. § 1.67-4T.

The part number of a Treasury regulation is used to identify the general area covered by the regulation as follows:

Part Number	Law Subject
1	Income Tax
20	Estate Tax
25	Gift Tax
31	Employment Tax
48–49	Excise Tax
301	Procedural Matters

The various subdivisions of a regulation are not necessarily related to a specific subdivision of the Code.

Treasury often issues temporary regulations when it is necessary to meet a compelling need such as shortly after enactment of a major change in the tax law. These temporary regulations have the same binding effect as final regulations until they are withdrawn or replaced.

Temporary regulations should not be confused with proposed regulations. The latter have no force or effect.[15] Nevertheless, proposed regulations provide insight into how the IRS currently interprets a particular Code section. For this reason, they should not be ignored.

REVENUE RULINGS

Revenue rulings also are official interpretations of the Federal tax laws and are issued by the National Office of the IRS. Revenue rulings do not have quite the authority of regulations, however. Regulations are a direct extension of the law-making powers of Congress, whereas revenue rulings are an application of the administrative powers of the Internal Revenue Service. In contrast to rulings, regulations are usually issued only after public hearings and must be approved by the Secretary of the Treasury.

Unlike regulations, revenue rulings are limited to a given set of facts. For example, in Rev. Rul. 97-9, the IRS addressed whether the provision that concerns medical expenses, § 213, allowed a deduction for the costs of controlled substances such as marijuana when used for medical care. The ruling evaluated § 213 as it applied to this specific set of facts and held that because such purchases were in violation of Federal law they were not deductible.

---

[15] Federal law (i.e., the Administrative Procedure Act) requires any federal agency, including the Internal Revenue Service, that wishes to adopt a substantive rule to publish the rule in proposed form in order to give interested persons an opportunity to comment. Proposed regulations are issued in compliance with this directive.

Taxpayers may rely on revenue rulings in determining the tax consequences of their transactions; however, taxpayers must determine for themselves if the facts of their cases are substantially the same as those set forth in the revenue ruling.

Revenue rulings are published in the weekly issues of the *Internal Revenue Bulletin*. The information contained in the *Internal Revenue Bulletins* (including, among other things, revenue rulings) is accumulated and usually published semiannually in the *Cumulative Bulletin*. The *Cumulative Bulletin* reorganizes the material according to Code section. Citations for the *Internal Revenue Bulletin* and the *Cumulative Bulletin* are illustrated below.

REVENUE PROCEDURES

Revenue procedures are statements reflecting the internal management practices of the IRS that affect the rights and duties of taxpayers. Occasionally they are also used to announce procedures to guide individuals in dealing with the IRS or to make public something the IRS believes should be brought to the attention of taxpayers. For example, each year the IRS announces how certain amounts, such as those for the personal exemption and standard deduction, are adjusted for inflation (e.g., Rev. Proc. 2016-55 increased the standard deduction amount from $12,600 in 2016 to $12,700 in 2017).

Revenue procedures are published in the weekly *Internal Revenue Bulletins* and bound in the *Cumulative Bulletin* along with revenue rulings issued in the same year. The citation system for revenue procedures is the same as for revenue rulings except that the prefix "Rev. Proc." is substituted for "Rev. Rul."

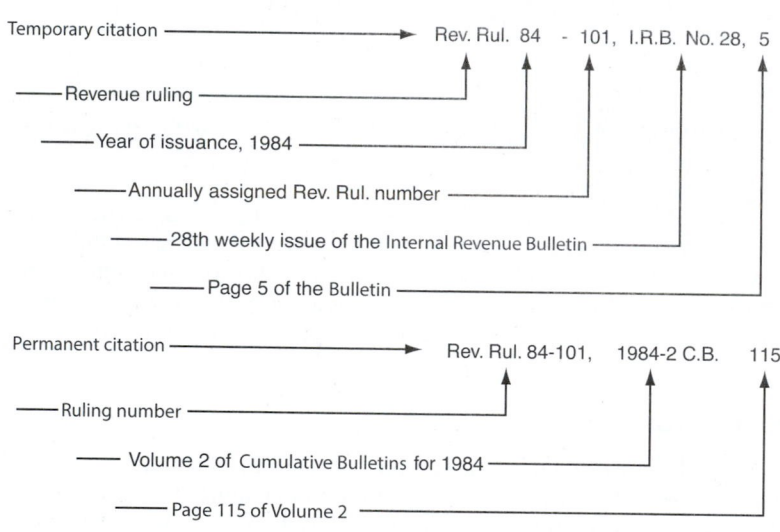

LETTER RULINGS

The term *letter ruling* actually encompasses three different types of rulings: private letter rulings, determination letters, and technical advice memoranda. These items are not published in an official government publication but are available from commercial sources.

Private Letter Ruling

Taxpayers who are in doubt about the tax consequences of a contemplated transaction can ask the National Office of the IRS for a ruling. Generally, the IRS has discretion about whether to rule or not, and it has issued guidelines describing the circumstances under which it will rule.[16]

Unlike revenue rulings, private letter rulings apply only to the particular taxpayer asking for the ruling and are thus not applicable to taxpayers in general. Section 6110(j)(3)

---

[16] See Rev. Proc. 2017-1, I.R.B. 2017-1 for a description of the areas in which the IRS has refused to issue advanced rulings. Note, also, that the IRS is required to charge taxpayers a fee for letter rulings, opinion letters, determination letters, and similar requests. A sense of the various fees charged can be found in Rev. Proc. 2017-1, IRB 2017-1, (Appendix A). See § 6591.

specifically states that "unless the Secretary otherwise establishes by regulations, a written determination may not be used or cited as a precedent." Recently, however, the IRS has expanded the list of authorities constituting "substantial" authority for § 6662 purposes to include private letter rulings. As discussed in the previous section, § 6662 imposes an accuracy-related penalty equal to 20% of the underpayment unless the taxpayer can cite "substantial authority" for his or her position.

For those requesting a ruling, the IRS's response might provide insurance against surprises. As a practical matter, a favorable ruling should preclude any controversies with the IRS on an audit of that transaction, at least with respect to the matters addressed in the private letter ruling. During the process of obtaining a private letter ruling, the IRS often recommends changes in a proposed transaction to assist the taxpayer in achieving the tax result he or she wishes. Since 1976, the IRS has made individual private letter rulings publicly available after deleting names and other information that would tend to identify the taxpayer. Private letter rulings are published by both CCH and RIA.

Determination Letter

A determination letter is similar to a private letter ruling, except that it is issued by the office of the local IRS district director, rather than by the National Office. Unlike private letter rulings, determination letters usually relate to completed transactions. Like private letter rulings, they are not published in any official government publication but are available commercially. In most instances, determination letters deal with issues and transactions that are not overtly controversial. Obtaining a determination letter in order to ensure that a pension plan is qualified is a typical use of a determination letter.

Technical Advice Memorandum

A technical advice memorandum ("tech advice") is typically requested by an IRS agent during an audit. The request is normally made to the National Office when the agent has a question that cannot be answered by sources in his or her local office. The technical advice memorandum only applies to the taxpayer for whose audit the technical advice was requested and cannot be relied upon by other taxpayers. Technical advice memoranda are available from private publishers but are not published by the government.

Citations for letter rulings and technical advice follow a multi-digit file number system. IRS Letter Ruling 200434039 serves as an example.

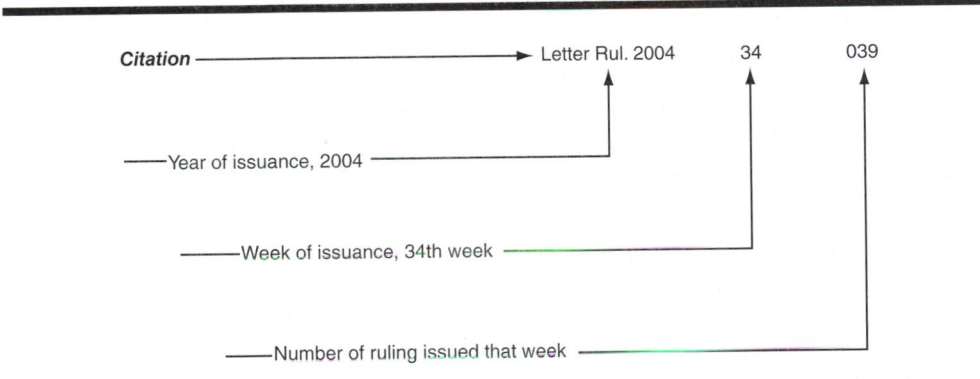

Judicial Interpretations

Although Congress passes the tax law and the Executive branch of the Federal government enforces and interprets it, under the American system of checks and balances, it is the Judiciary branch that ultimately determines whether the Executive branch's interpretation is correct. This provides yet another source of tax law—court decisions. It is therefore absolutely essential for the student of tax as well as the tax practitioner to have a grasp of the judicial system of the United States and how tax cases move through this system.

Before litigating a case in court, the taxpayer must have exhausted the administrative remedies available to him or her within the Internal Revenue Service. If the taxpayer has not exhausted his or her administrative remedies, a court will deny a hearing because the claim filed in the court is premature.

LO.8
Understand the judicial system as it relates to tax matters.

All litigation begins in what are referred to as *courts of original jurisdiction,* or *trial courts,* which "try" the case. There are three trial courts: (1) the Tax Court; (2) the U.S. District Court; and (3) the U.S. Court of Federal Claims. Note that the taxpayer may select any one (and only one) of these three courts to hear the case. If the taxpayer or government disagrees with the decision by the trial court, either party has the right to appeal to either the U.S. Court of Appeals or the U.S. Court of Appeals for the Federal Circuit, whichever is appropriate in the particular case. If a litigating party is dissatisfied with the decision by the appellate court, it may ask for review by the Supreme Court, but this is rarely granted. The judicial system is illustrated and discussed on the following page.

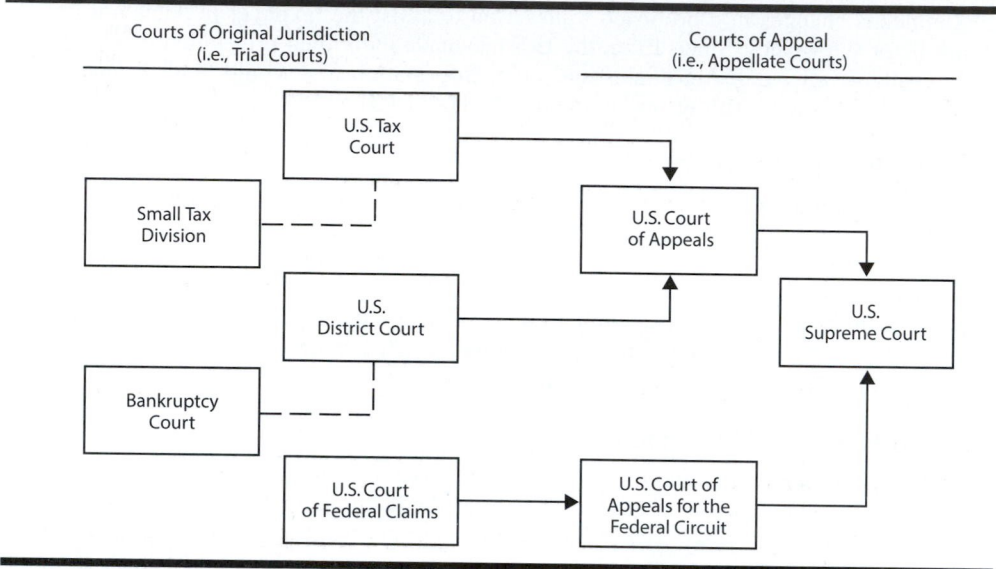

TRIAL COURTS

U.S. Tax Court

The Tax Court, as its name suggests, specializes in tax matters and hears no other types of cases. The judges on the court are especially skilled in taxation. Usually, prior to being selected as a judge by the President, the individual was a practitioner or IRS official who was noted for his or her expertise. This Court is composed of 19 judges who "ride circuit" throughout the United States (i.e., they travel and hear cases in various parts of the country as can be seen in the map contained in Exhibit 2-3). Occasionally, the full Tax Court hears a case, but most cases are heard by a single judge who submits his or her opinion to the chief judge, who then decides whether the full court should review the decision.

Besides its expertise in tax matters, two other characteristics of the Tax Court should be noted. Perhaps the most important feature of the Tax Court is that the taxpayer does not pay the alleged tax deficiency before bringing his or her action before the court. The second facet of the Tax Court that bears mentioning is that a trial by jury is not available.

U.S. District Courts

For purposes of the Federal judicial system, the United States is divided into 11 geographic areas called circuits, which are subdivided into districts. For example, the second circuit, which is composed of Vermont, Connecticut, and New York, contains the District Court for the Southern District of New York, which covers parts of New York City. Other districts may include very large areas, such as the District Court for the State of Arizona, which covers the entire state. A taxpayer may take a case into the District Court for the district in which he or she resides, but only after the disputed tax deficiency has been paid. The taxpayer then sues the IRS for a refund of the disputed amount. The District Court is a court of general jurisdiction and hears many types of cases in addition to tax cases. This is the only court in which the taxpayer may obtain a jury trial. The jury decides matters of fact but not matters of law. However, even in issues of fact, the judge may, and occasionally does, disregard the jury's decision.

U.S. Court of Federal Claims

The United States Court of Federal Claims hears cases involving certain claims against the Federal government, including tax refunds. The Court is made up of 16 judges and usually meets in Washington, D.C. A taxpayer must pay the disputed tax deficiency before bringing an action in this court, and may not obtain a jury trial. Appeals from the U.S. Court of Federal Claims are taken to the U.S. Court of Appeals for the Federal Circuit.

The chart below illustrates the position of the taxpayer in bringing an action in these courts.

Small Claims Cases

When the amount of tax and penalties or a claim for refund are $50,000 per year or less, the taxpayer may elect to submit the case to the division of the Tax Court hearing small claims cases, called the Small Tax Division of the Tax Court. This procedure allows a taxpayer to obtain a decision with a minimum of formality, delay, and expense. However, the taxpayer loses the right to appeal the decision. The Small Tax Division is administered by the chief judge of the Tax Court, who is authorized to assign small claims cases to special trial judges. These cases receive priority on the trial calendars, and relatively informal rules are followed whenever possible. The special trial judges' opinions are published on these cases, but the decisions are not reviewed by any other court or treated as precedents in any other case.

Bankruptcy Court

Under limited circumstances, it is possible for the bankruptcy court to have jurisdiction over tax matters. The filing of a bankruptcy petition prevents creditors, including the IRS, from taking action against a taxpayer, including the filing of a proceeding before the Tax Court if a notice of deficiency is sent after the filing of a petition in bankruptcy. In such cases, a tax claim may be determined by the bankruptcy court.

	U.S. Tax Court	*U.S. District Court*	*U.S. Court of Federal Claims*
Jurisdiction	Nationwide	Specific district in which court is sitting	Nationwide
Subject Matter	Tax cases only	Many different types of cases, both criminal and civil	Claims against the Federal government, including tax refunds
Payment of Contested Amount	Taxpayer does not pay deficiency, but files suit against IRS Commissioner to stop collection of tax	Taxpayer pays alleged deficiency and then files suit against the U.S. government for refund	Taxpayer pays alleged deficiency and then files suit against the U.S. government for refund
Availability of Jury Trial	No	Yes	No
Appeal Taken to	U.S. Court of Appeals	U.S. Court of Appeals	U.S. Court of Appeals for the Federal Circuit
Number of Courts	1	95	1
Number of Judges per Court	19	1	16

APPELLATE COURTS

U.S. Courts of Appeals

Which appellate court is appropriate depends on which trial court hears the case. Taxpayer or government appeals from the District Courts and the Tax Court are taken to the U.S. Court of Appeals that has jurisdiction over the court in which the taxpayer lives. Appeals from the U.S. Court of Federal Claims are taken to the U.S. Court of Appeals for the Federal

Circuit, which has the same powers and jurisdictions as any of the other Courts of Appeals except that it only hears specialized appeals. Courts of Appeals are national courts of appellate jurisdiction. With the exceptions of the Court of Appeals for the Federal Circuit and the Court of Appeals for the District of Columbia, these appellate courts are assigned various geographic areas of jurisdiction as shown in the map in Exhibit 2-3 and in the table below.

Court of Appeals for the Federal Circuit (CA-FC)	*District of Columbia Circuit (CA-DC)*	*First Circuit (CA-1)*		
U.S. Court of Federal Claims	District of Columbia	Maine Massachusetts New Hampshire Puerto Rico Rhode Island		

Second Circuit (CA-2)	*Third Circuit (CA-3)*	*Fourth Circuit (CA-4)*	*Fifth Circuit (CA-5)*	*Sixth Circuit (CA-6)*
Connecticut New York Vermont	Delaware New Jersey Pennsylvania Virgin Islands	Maryland N. Carolina S. Carolina Virginia W. Virginia	Louisiana Mississippi Texas	Kentucky Michigan Ohio Tennessee

Seventh Circuit (CA-7)	*Eighth Circuit (CA-8)*	*Ninth Circuit (CA-9)*	*Tenth Circuit (CA-10)*	*Eleventh Circuit (CA-11)*
Illinois Indiana Wisconsin	Arkansas Iowa Minnesota Missouri Nebraska N. Dakota S. Dakota	Alaska Arizona California Guam Hawaii Idaho Montana Nevada Oregon Washington	Colorado New Mexico Kansas Oklahoma Utah Wyoming	Alabama Florida Georgia

Taxpayers may appeal to the Courts of Appeal as a matter of right, and the Courts must hear their cases. Very often, however, the expense of such an appeal deters many from proceeding with an appeal. Appellate courts review the record of the trial court to determine whether the lower court completed its responsibility of fact finding and applied the proper law in arriving at its decision.

District Courts must follow the decision of the Appeals Court for the circuit in which they are located. For instance, the District Court in the Eastern District of Missouri must follow the decision of the Eighth Circuit Court of Appeals because Missouri is in the Eighth Circuit. If the Eighth Circuit has not rendered a decision on the particular issue involved, then the District Court may make its own decision or follow the decision in another Circuit.

The Tax Court is a national court with jurisdiction throughout the entire country. Prior to 1970, the Tax Court considered itself independent and indicated that it would not be bound by the decisions of the Circuit Court to which its decision would be appealed. In *Golsen*,[17] however, the Tax Court reversed its position. Under the *Golsen rule*, the Tax Court now follows the decisions of the Circuit Court to which a particular case would be appealed. Even if the Tax Court disagrees with a Circuit Court's view, it will decide based upon the Circuit Court's view. On the other hand, if a similar case arises in the jurisdiction of another Circuit Court that has not yet ruled on the same issue, the Tax Court will follow its own view, despite its earlier decision following a contrary Circuit Court decision.

The U.S. Courts of Appeals generally sit in panels of three judges, although the entire court may sit in particularly important cases. They may reach a decision that affirms the lower court or that reverses the lower court. Additionally, the Appellate Court could send the case back to the lower court (remand the case) for another trial or for rehearing on another point not previously covered. It is possible for the Appellate Court to affirm the decision of the lower court on one particular issue and reverse it on another.

---

[17] *Jack E. Golsen.* 54 T.C. 742 (1970).

EXHIBIT 2-3   **United States Tax Court: Places of Trial and U.S. Courts of Appeals**

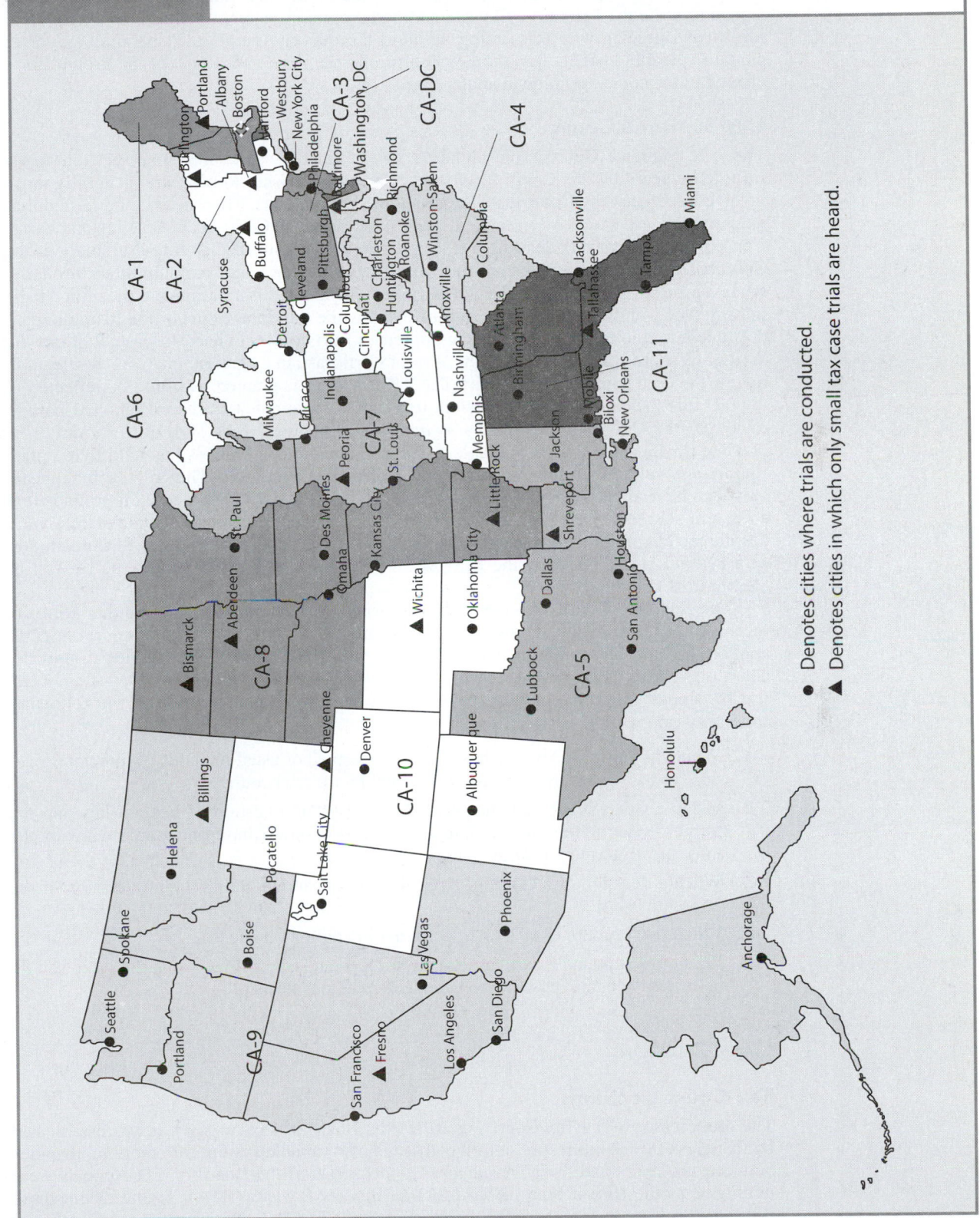

● Denotes cities where trials are conducted.
▲ Denotes cities in which only small tax case trials are heard.

Generally, only one judge writes a decision for the Appeals Court, although in some cases no decision is written and an order is simply made. Such an order might hold that the lower court is sustained, or that the lower court's decision is reversed as being inconsistent with one of the Appellate Court's decisions. Sometimes other judges (besides the one assigned to write the opinion) will write additional opinions agreeing with (concurring opinion) or disagreeing with (dissenting opinion) the majority opinion. These opinions often contain valuable insights into the law controlling the case, and often set the ground for a change in the court's opinion at a later date.

U.S. Supreme Court

The U.S. Supreme Court is the highest court in the U.S. judicial system. No one has a *right* to be heard by this Court. It only accepts cases it wishes to hear, and generally those involve issues that the Court feels are of national importance. There is no minimum dollar amount for these cases. As a practical matter, the Supreme Court hears very few tax cases. Consequently, taxpayers desiring a review of their trial court decision find it solely at the Court of Appeals. Cases that are appealed to the Supreme Court are submitted through a request process known as the "Writ of Certiorari." Certiorari is a Latin word meaning "to be informed of." Thus the Writ of Certiorari informs the Supreme Court of the losing party's desire to have the case reviewed. If the Supreme Court decides to hear the case, it grants the Writ of Certiorari; if not, it denies the Writ of Certiorari. In a citation, the Court's refusal to review the case is indicated by "cert. den." If certiorari is granted, it would be reflected in the fact that the court issued a decision. It is important to note that there is another path to review by the U.S. Supreme Court—*by appeal*—as opposed to by Writ of Certiorari. This "review by appeal" may be available when a U.S. Court of Appeals has held that a state statute is in conflict with the laws or treaties of the United States. The "review by appeal" may also be available when the highest court in a state has decided a case on grounds that a Federal statute or treaty is invalid, or when the state court has held a state statute valid despite the claim of the losing party that the statute is in conflict with the U.S. Constitution or a Federal law. Review by the U.S. Supreme Court is still discretionary, but a Writ of Certiorari is not involved.

The Supreme Court, like the Courts of Appeals, does not conduct another trial. Its responsibility is to review the record and determine whether or not the trial court correctly applied the law in deciding the case. The Supreme Court also reviews the decision of the Court of Appeals to determine if the court used the correct reasoning.

In general, the Supreme Court hears cases only when one or more of the following conditions apply:

1. When the Court of Appeals has not used accepted or usual methods of judicial procedure or has sanctioned an unusual method by the trial court;

2. When a Court of Appeals has settled an important question of Federal law and the Supreme Court feels such an important question should have one more review by the most prestigious court of the nation;

3. When a decision of a Court of Appeals is in apparent conflict with a decision of the Supreme Court;

4. When two or more Courts of Appeals are in conflict on an issue; or

5. When the Supreme Court has already decided an issue but feels that the issue should be looked at again, possibly to reverse its previous decision.

CASE CITATION

Tax Court Decisions

The predecessor to the Tax Court was called the Board of Tax Appeals. It was established by Congress in 1924 in response to the absence of a suitable system for resolving disputes between taxpayers and the government. The decisions of the Board of Tax Appeals were published as the *United States Board of Tax Appeals Reports* (BTA). To the extent these decisions concern laws that are still in effect, most believe that they have the same authority of Tax Court decisions. BTA cases are cited as follows:

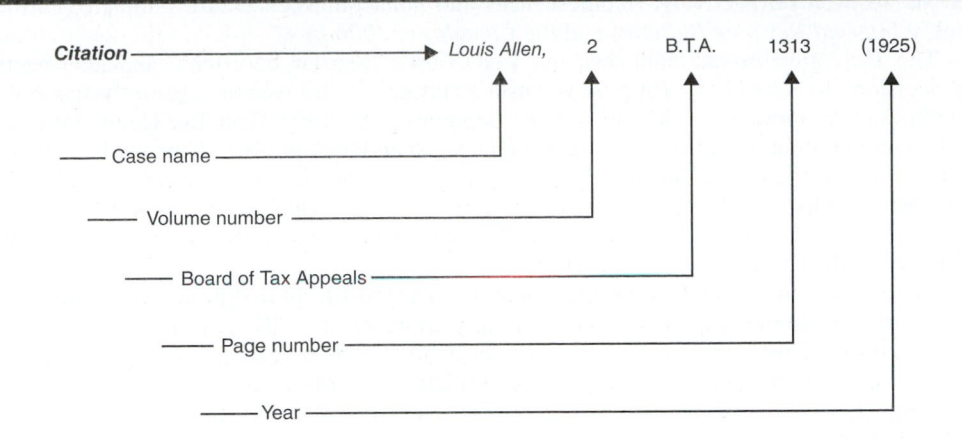

The Tax Court renders two different types of decisions with two different citation systems: Regular decisions and Memorandum decisions.

Tax Court *Regular* decisions address new issues that the court has not yet resolved. In contrast, decisions that concern the application of already established principles of law are called *Memorandum* decisions. The United States government publishes Regular decisions in *United States Tax Court Reports* (T.C.). Tax Court Regular decisions are cited as follows:

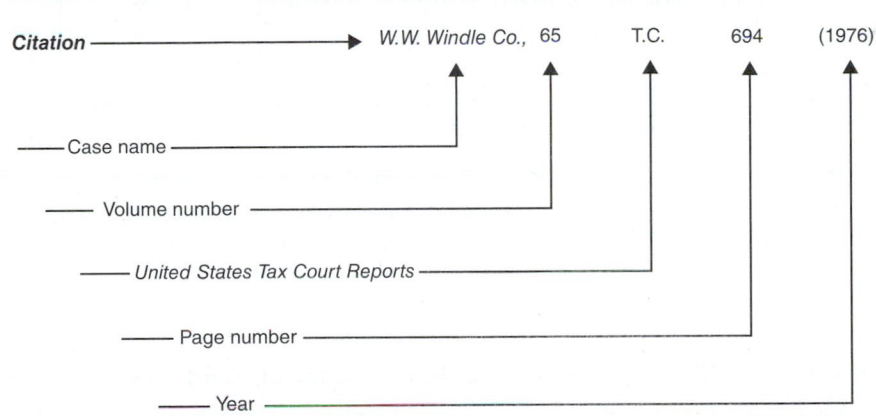

Like revenue rulings and the *Cumulative Bulletins,* there is a time lag between the date a Tax Court Regular decision is issued and the date it is bound in a *U.S. Tax Court Report* volume. In this case, the citation appears as follows:

Temporary Citation:

W.W. Windle Co., 65 T.C. —————————, No. 79(1976).

Here the page is left out, but the citation tells the reader that this is the 79th Regular decision issued by the Tax Court since Volume 64 ended. When the new volume (65th) of the Tax Court Report is issued, then the permanent citation may be substituted for the old one. Both CCH and RIA have tax services that allow the researcher to find these temporary citations.

The IRS has adopted the practice of announcing whether it agrees or disagrees with a decision issued by a court by announcing its acquiescence or nonacquiescence. Until 1991, this practice was limited to certain Regular decisions of the Tax Court. At that time, however, the IRS began to acquiesce or nonacquiesce to other cases where it thought it would be useful.[18] The IRS may withdraw its acquiescence or nonacquiescence at any time and

---

[18] The IRS's acquiescence is symbolized by "A" or "Acq." and its nonacquiescence by "NA" or "Nonacq."

may do so even retroactively. Acquiescences and nonacquiescences are published in the weekly *Internal Revenue Bulletins* and the *Cumulative Bulletins*.

The U.S. government publishes the Tax Court's Regular decisions, and also posts the decisions to its website (http://www.ustaxcourt.gov). The website currently has both Regular and Memorandum decisions since September 25, 1995. The Tax Court does not publish memorandum decisions. However, both CCH and RIA publish them. CCH publishes the memorandum decisions under the title *Tax Court Memorandum Decisions* (TCM), while RIA publishes these decisions as *Tax Court Reporter and Memorandum Decisions* (T.C. Memo). In citing Tax Court memorandum decisions, some authors prefer to use both the RIA and the CCH citations for their cases.

Decisions of the Small Claims division of the Tax Court were first published on the U.S. Tax Court Web site as U.S. Tax Court Summary Opinions in 2001. All of these decisions appear with the caveat that such cases may not be treated as precedent for any other case.

In an effort to provide the reader the greatest latitude of research sources, this dual citation policy has been adopted for this text. The case of *Alan K. Minor* serves as an example of the dual citation of Tax Court memorandum decisions.

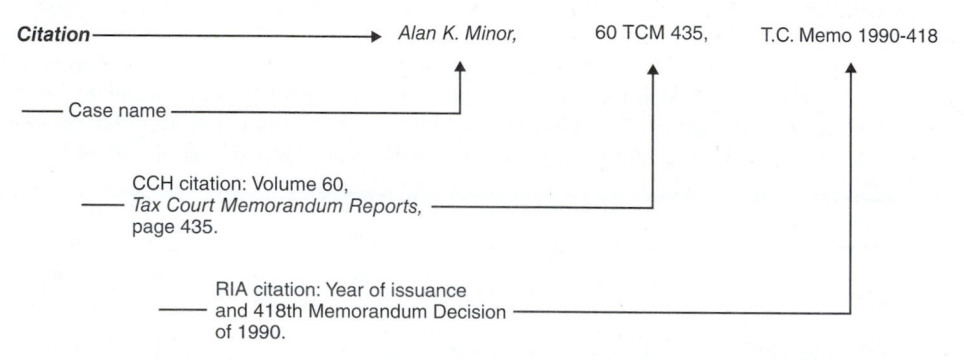

As noted above, Tax Court Summary Opinions can be found at the website of the Tax Court or through RIA and CCH. All use the same form of citation. For example, the decision in Richard Bradley on January 21, 2006 would be cited as follows:

Richard Bradley, T.C. Summary Opinion, 2006–61

Citations for U.S. District Court, Court of Appeals, and Claims Court

Commerce Clearing House, Research Institute of America, and West Publishing Company all publish decisions of the District Courts, Courts of Appeals, and the Court of Federal Claims. When available, all three citations of a case are provided in this text.[19] CCH publishes the decisions of these courts in its *U.S. Tax Cases* (USTC—not to be confused with the *U.S. Tax Court Reports*) volumes, and RIA offers these decisions in its *American Federal Tax Reports* (AFTR) series.[20] West Publishing Company reports these decisions in either its *Federal Supplement Series* (F. Supp.—District Court decisions), or its *Federal Second Series or Federal Third Series* (F.2d or F.3d—Court of Federal Claims and Courts of Appeals decisions).

The citation of the U.S. District Court decision of *Cam F. Dowell, Jr. v. U.S.* is illustrated for each of the three publishing companies as follows:

CCH Citation:

Cam F. Dowell, Jr. v. U.S., 74-1 USTC ¶9243, (D.Ct. Tx., 1974)

Interpretation: This case is reported in the first volume of the *U.S. Tax Cases,* published by CCH for calendar year 1974 (74-1), located at paragraph (¶) 9243, and is a decision rendered in 1974 by a U.S. District Court located in Texas (Tx.).

---

[19] When all three publishers have not printed the case, only the citations to the cases published are provided.

[20] Until the acquisition of Prentice Hall by RIA, Prentice Hall published cases under its own name. Accordingly, researchers needing cases from before 1993 will often encounter Prentice Hall as publisher of these reporters now carried under RIA's name.

RIA Citation:

Cam F. Dowell, Jr. v. U.S., 33 AFTR2d 74-739, (D.Ct. Tx., 1974)

Interpretation: Reported in the 33rd volume of the second series of the *American Federal Tax Reports* (AFTR2d), published by RIA for 1974, and located at page 739.

West Citation:

Cam F. Dowell, Jr. v. U.S., 370 F.Supp. 69 (D.Ct. Tx., 1974)

Interpretation: Located in the 370th volume of the *Federal Supplement Series* (F.Supp), published by West Publishing Company, and located at page 69.

The multiple citation of the U.S. District Court case illustrated above appears as follows:

Cam F. Dowell, Jr. v. U.S., 74-1 USTC ¶9243, 33 AFTR2d 74-739, 370 F.Supp. 69 (D.Ct. Tx.,1974)

Decisions of the Court of Federal Claims (Ct. Cls.), the Courts of Appeals (e.g., CA-1, CA-2, etc.), and the Supreme Court (USSC) are published by CCH and RIA in the same reporting source as District Court decisions (i.e., USTCs and AFTRs). Court of Federal Claims and Court of Appeals decisions are reported by West Publishing Company in its *Federal Second Series* (F.2d) or *Federal Third Series* (F.3d). West also publishes the *Federal Appendix* (Fed. Appx.) which includes opinions not selected by the Courts of Appeals for publication in the Federal reporters. Supreme Court decisions are published by West Publishing Company in its *Supreme Court Reports* (S.Ct.), and the U.S. Government Printing Office publishes Supreme Court decisions in its *Supreme Court Reports* (U.S.).

An example of the multiple citation of a Court of Appeals decision follows:

Citation:

Millar v. Comm., 78-2 USTC ¶9514, 42 AFTR2d 78-5246, 577 F.2d 212 (CA-3, 1978)

A multiple citation of a Supreme Court decision would appear as follows:

Citation:

Fausner v. Comm., 73-2 USTC ¶9515, 32 AFTR2d 73-5202, 413 U.S. 838 (USSC, 1973)

Note that in each of the citations above, the designation "Commissioner of the Internal Revenue Service" is simply abbreviated to "Comm." In some instances, the IRS or U.S. is substituted for Comm., and older cases used the Commissioner's name. For example, in *Gregory v. Helvering*, 293 U.S. 465 (USSC, 1935), Mr. Helvering was the Commissioner of the Internal Revenue Service at the time the case was brought to the Court. Also note that the citation contains a reference to the Appellate Court rendering the decision (i.e., CA-3, or USSC) and the year of issuance.

Exhibits 2-4 and 2-5 and summarize the sources of case citations from various reporter services.

EXHIBIT 2-4	**Reporters of Tax Court Decisions**		
Reporter	*Abbr.*	*Type*	*Publisher*
Tax Court Reports	TC	Regular	Government Printing Office
Tax Court Memorandum Decisions	TCM	Memorandum	Commerce Clearing House
Tax Court Memorandum Decisions	TC Memo	Memorandum	Research Institute of America

		EXHIBIT 2-5	Reporters of Decisions Other than Tax Court

Reporter	Abbr.	Courts Reported	Publisher
Supreme Court Reports	U.S.	Supreme Court	Government Printing Office
Supreme Court Reporter	S.Ct	Supreme Court	West Publishing
Federal Supplement	F. Supp	District Courts	West Publishing
Federal Reporter	F. F.2d F.3d	Cts. of Appeals and Ct. of Fed. Cls.	West Publishing
Federal Appendix	Fed. Appx.	Cts. of Appeals Unreported cases	West Publishing
American Federal Tax Reports	AFTR2d	Ct. of Fed. Cls. Cts. of Appeals, and Supreme Ct.	Research Institute of America
United States Tax Cases	USTC	Same as AFTR and AFTR2d	Commerce Clearing House

Secondary Sources

LO.9

Explain secondary authority.

The importance of understanding the sources discussed thus far stems from their role in the taxation process. As mentioned earlier, the statutory law and its official interpretations constitute the legal authorities that set forth the tax consequences for a particular set of facts. These legal authorities, sometimes referred to as *primary authorities,* must be distinguished from so-called *secondary sources* or *secondary authorities.* The secondary sources of tax information consist mainly of books, periodicals, articles, newsletters, and editorial judgments in tax services. When working with the tax law, it must be recognized that secondary sources are unofficial interpretations—mere opinions—that have no legal authority.

Although secondary sources should not be used as the supporting authority for a particular tax treatment (except as a supplement to primary authority or in cases where primary authority is absent), they are an indispensable aid when seeking an understanding of the tax law. Several of these secondary materials are discussed briefly below.

TAX SERVICES

"Tax service" is the name given to a set of organized materials that contains a vast quantity of tax-related information organized so as to make it useful and accessible to tax practitioners. In general, a tax service is a paper or electronic compilation of some or all of the following: the Code, regulations, court decisions, IRS releases, and explanations of these primary authorities by the editors. As the listing of contents suggests, a tax service is invaluable since it contains, all in one place, a wealth of tax information, including both primary and secondary sources. The major tax services are all available on the Internet. Moreover, these materials are updated constantly to reflect current developments—an extremely important feature given the dynamic nature of tax law. The major tax services follow:

Publisher	Name of Publication
Commerce Clearing House	Standard Federal Tax Reporter—Income Taxes
Research Institute of America	United States Tax Reporter and Federal Tax Coordinator—2nd Series
The Bureau of National Affairs, Inc.	Tax Management Portfolios—U.S. Income

Commerce Clearing House, Research Institute of America, and other publishers issue daily online updates that include newly released cases, regulations, rulings and other tax developments that many practitioners and scholars find helpful in keeping up with current events in the tax field. The Bureau of National Affairs publishes the *Daily Tax Bulletin,* a comprehensive daily journal of late-breaking tax news that often reprints entire cases or regulations of particular importance. *Tax Notes,* published by Tax Analysts, is a weekly publication addressing legislative and judicial developments in the tax field. *Tax Notes* is particularly helpful in following the progress of tax legislation through the legislative process.

TAX PERIODICALS

In addition to these services, there are a number of quality publications (usually published monthly) that contain articles on a variety of important tax topics. These publications are very helpful when new tax acts are passed, because they often contain clear, concise summaries of the new law in a readable format. In addition, they serve to convey new planning opportunities and relay the latest IRS and judicial developments in many important subspecialities of the tax profession. Some of the leading periodicals include the following:

ATA Journal of Legal Tax Research

Estate Planning

Journal of Corporate Taxation

Journal of Partnership Taxation

Journal of Real Estate Taxation

Journal of Taxation

Tax Law Journal

Tax Law Review

Taxes—The Tax Magazine

The International Tax Journal

The Review of Taxation of Individuals

The Tax Advisor

The Tax Executive

The Tax Lawyer

Trusts and Estates

In addition to these publications, many law journals contain excellent articles on tax subjects.

Several indexes exist that may be used to locate a journal article. Through the use of a subject index, author index, and in some instances a Code section index, articles dealing with a particular topic may be found. Three of these indexes follow:

Title	Publisher
Index to Federal Tax Articles	Warren, Gorham and Lamont
Federal Tax Articles	Commerce Clearing House
The Accountant's Index	American Institute of Certified Public Accountants

In addition, the *United States Tax Reporter,* published by RIA, contains a section entitled "Index to Tax Articles."

Tax Research

Having introduced the sources of tax law, the remainder of this chapter is devoted to working with the law—or more specifically, the art of tax research. Tax research may be defined as the process used to ascertain the optimal answer to a question with tax implications. Although there is no perfect technique for researching a question, the following approach normally is used:

1. Obtain all of the facts.
2. Diagnose the problem from the facts.
3. Locate the authorities.
4. Evaluate the authorities.
5. Derive the solution and possible alternative solutions.
6. Communicate the answer.

Each of these steps is discussed below.

OBTAINING THE FACTS

Before discussing the importance of obtaining all the facts, the distinction between closed fact research and open- or controlled-fact research should be noted. If the research relates to a problem with transactions that are complete, it is referred to as closed-fact research and normally falls within the realm of tax practice known as tax compliance. On the other hand, if the research relates to contemplated transactions, it is called controlled- or open-fact research and is an integral part of tax planning.

In researching a closed-fact problem, the first step is gathering all of the facts. Unfortunately, it is difficult to obtain all relevant facts upon first inquiry. This is true because it is essentially impossible to understand the law so thoroughly that all of the proper questions can be asked before the research task begins. After the general area of the problem is identified and research has begun, it usually becomes apparent that more facts must be obtained before an answer can be derived. Consequently, additional inquiries must be made until all facts necessary for a solution are acquired.

DIAGNOSING THE ISSUE

Once the initial set of facts is gathered, the tax issue or question must be identified. Most tax problems involve very basic questions such as these:

1. Does the taxpayer have gross income that must be recognized?
2. Is the taxpayer entitled to a deduction?
3. Is the taxpayer entitled to a credit?
4. In what period is the gross income, deduction, or credit reported?
5. What amount of gross income, deduction, or credit must be reported?

As research progresses, however, such fundamental questions can be answered only after more specific issues have been resolved.

Example 1

R's employer owns a home in which R lives. The basic question that must be asked is whether use of the home constitutes income to R. After consulting the various tax sources, it can be determined that § 61 requires virtually all benefits to be included in income unless another provision specifically grants an exclusion. In this case, § 119 allows a taxpayer to exclude the value employer-provided of housing if the housing is on the employer's premises, the lodging is furnished for the convenience of the employer, and the employee is required by the employer to accept the housing. Due to the additional research, three more specific questions must be asked:

1. Is the home on the employer's premises?
2. Is the home provided for the employer's convenience?
3. Is R required to live in the home?

As the above example suggests, diagnosing the problem requires a continuing refinement of the questions until the critical issue is identified. The refinement that occurs results from the awareness that is gained through reading and rereading the primary and secondary authorities.

Example 2

Assume the same facts as in *Example 1*. After determining that one of the issues concerns whether R's home is on the business premises, a second inquiry is made of R concerning the location of his residence. (Note that as the research progresses, additional facts must be gathered.) According to R, the house is located in a suburb, 25 miles from his employer's downtown office. However, the house is owned by the employer, and hence R suggests that he lives on the employer's premises. He also explains that he often brings work home and frequently entertains clients in his home. Having uncovered this information, the primary authorities are reexamined. Upon review, it is determined that in *Charles N. Anderson*,[21] the court indicated that an employee would be considered on the business premises if the employee performed a significant portion of his duties at the place of lodging. Again the question must be refined to ask: Do R's work and entertainment activities in the home constitute a significant portion of his duties?

LOCATING THE AUTHORITIES

Identification of the critical issue presented by any tax question begins by first locating, then reading and studying the appropriate authority. Locating the authority is ordinarily done using a tax service. With the issue stated in general terms, the subject is found in the index volume and the location is determined. At this point, the appropriate Code sections, regulations, and editorial commentary may be perused to determine their applicability to the question.

Example 3

In the case of R above, the problem stated in general terms concerns income. Using an index, the key word, *income,* could be located and a reference to information concerning the income aspects of lodging would be given.

Once information relating to the issue is identified, the authoritative materials must be read. That is, the appropriate Code sections, regulations, rulings, and cases must be examined and studied to determine how they relate to the question. As suggested above, this process normally results in refinement of the question, which in turn may require acquisition of additional facts.

EVALUATING THE AUTHORITY

After the various authorities have been identified and it has been *verified* that they are applicable, their value must be appraised. This evaluation process, as will become clear below, primarily involves appraisal of court decisions and revenue rulings.

LO.10
Evaluate the relative strength of various tax authorities.

The Code

The Internal Revenue Code is the final authority on most tax issues since it is the Federal tax law as passed by Congress. Only the courts can offset this authority by declaring part of the law unconstitutional, and this happens rarely. Most of the time, however, the Code itself is

---

[21] USTC ¶9136, 19 AFTR2d 318, 371 F.2d 59
   (CA-6, 1966).

only of partial help. It is written in a style that is not always easy to understand, and it contains no examples of its application. Accordingly, to the extent the Code can be understood as clearly applicable, no stronger authority exists, except possibly a treaty. But in most cases, the Code cannot be used to solve a tax problem without further support.

Treasury Regulations

As previously discussed, the regulations are used to expand and explain the Code. Because Congress has given its authority to make laws to the Executive branch's administrative agency—the Treasury—the regulations that are produced are a very strong source of authority, second only to the Code itself. Normally, the major issue when a regulation is under scrutiny by a Court is whether the regulation is consistent with the Code. If the regulations are inconsistent, the Court will not hesitate to invalidate them. In completing a research project, the tax professional should always discuss the Code and the applicable regulations.

Judicial Authority

The value of a court decision depends on numerous factors. On appraising a decision, the most crucial determination concerns whether the outcome is consistent with other decisions on the same issue. In other words, consideration must be given to how other decisions have evaluated the one in question. An invaluable tool in determining the validity of a case is a *citator.* A tax citator provides an alphabetical listing by last name of virtually all tax cases and other administrative pronouncements (e.g. rulings). After the name of each case, there is a record of other decisions that have cited (in the text of their facts and opinions) the first case. The list of cases is organized by type of court and then by year. Exhibit 2-4 provides sample entries from the citators published by RIA and CCH for the Supreme Court's decision in *Indianapolis Power and Light Co.*

Example 4

Refer to Exhibit 2-6 and the sample entries from the RIA and CCH citators. Observe that the Supreme Court's decision in *Indianapolis Power and Light Co. (IPL)* was cited (mentioned) in a number of cases at various levels as well in several rulings. For instance, the *IPL* decision was cited by the Supreme Court in *Banks II,* by the Ninth Circuit in *Westpac-Pacific Foods* and by the Tax Court in *Tampa Bay Devil Rays, Ltd.* Similarly, *IPL* was cited in *Rev. Proc. 91-31* and *Rev. Rul. 2003-39.*

It is important to note that tax citators often use abbreviations for subsequent case history. For example, the abbreviations *aff'g* and *aff'd* mean "affirming" and "affirmed" and indicate that an appeals court has upheld the decision in question. Similarly, *rev'g* and *rev'd* mean "reversing" and "reversed" and indicate that a trial court's decision was overturned. Finally, *rem'g* and *rem'd* mean "remanding" and "remanded" and indicate that the case has been sent back to a lower court for reconsideration.

The validity of a particular decision may be assessed by examining how the subsequent cases viewed the cited decision. For example, subsequent cases may have agreed or disagreed with the decision in question, or distinguished the facts of the cited case from those examined in a later case. In this regard, note how the RIA citator provides a notation, indicating the relationship between the cited and citing cases. For example, the *Banks II* decision is shown as having "cited favorably" the IPL decision. The CCH citator does not provide this information.

Another important factor that must be considered in evaluating a court decision is the level of the court that issued it. Decisions issued by trial courts have less value than those issued by appellate courts. And, of course, decisions of the Supreme Court are the ultimate authority.

A court decision's value rises appreciably if the IRS agrees with its result. As discussed earlier, the IRS usually indicates whether it acquiesces or does not acquiesce to Regular Tax Court decisions. The position of the Service may also be published in a revenue ruling.

EXHIBIT 2-6	Tax Citators: RIA and CCH

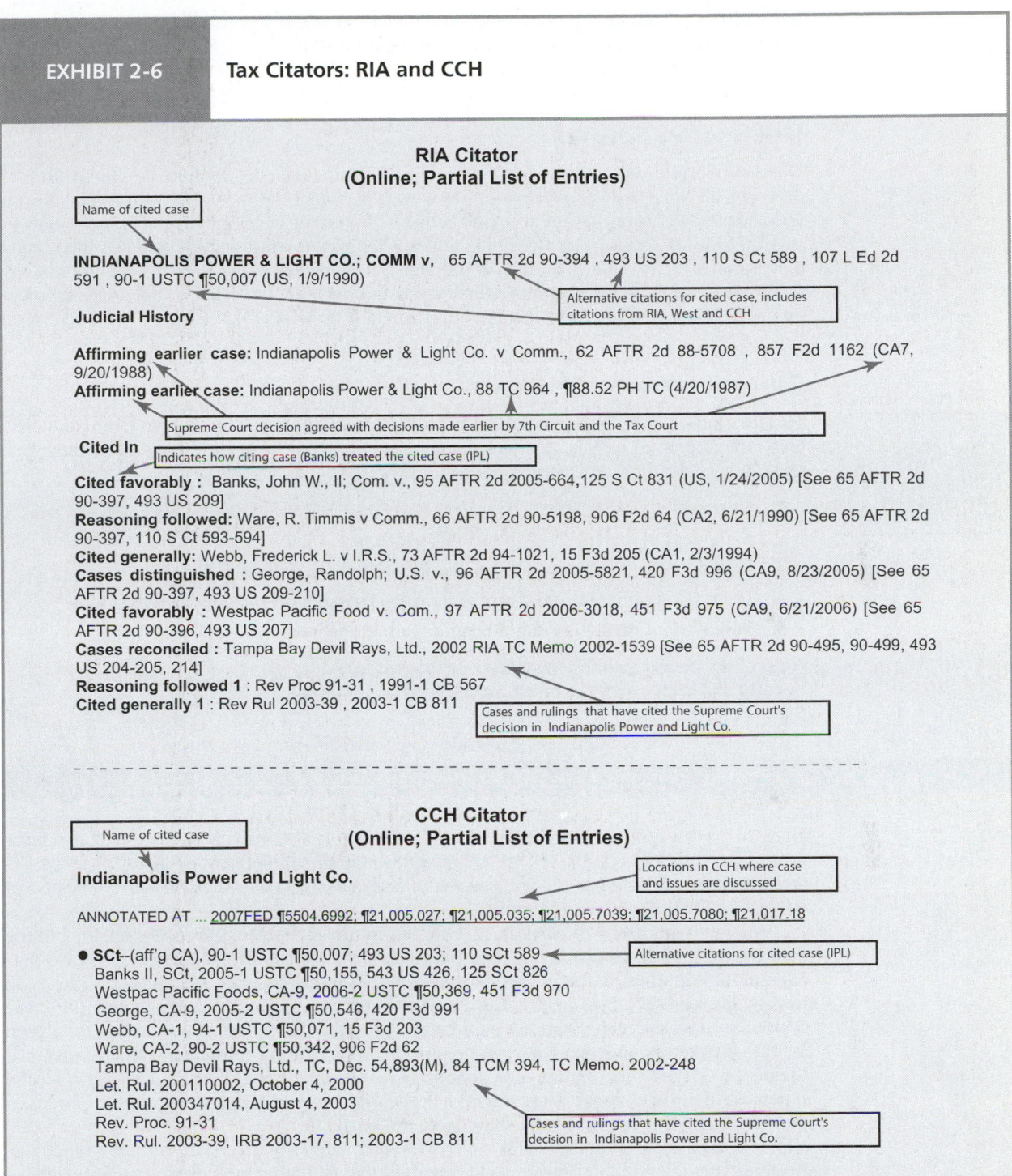

RIA Citator
(Online; Partial List of Entries)

Name of cited case

INDIANAPOLIS POWER & LIGHT CO.; COMM v, 65 AFTR 2d 90-394 , 493 US 203 , 110 S Ct 589 , 107 L Ed 2d 591 , 90-1 USTC ¶50,007 (US, 1/9/1990)

Alternative citations for cited case, includes citations from RIA, West and CCH

Judicial History

Affirming earlier case: Indianapolis Power & Light Co. v Comm., 62 AFTR 2d 88-5708 , 857 F2d 1162 (CA7, 9/20/1988)
Affirming earlier case: Indianapolis Power & Light Co., 88 TC 964 , ¶88.52 PH TC (4/20/1987)

Supreme Court decision agreed with decisions made earlier by 7th Circuit and the Tax Court

Cited In

Indicates how citing case (Banks) treated the cited case (IPL)

Cited favorably : Banks, John W., II; Com. v., 95 AFTR 2d 2005-664,125 S Ct 831 (US, 1/24/2005) [See 65 AFTR 2d 90-397, 493 US 209]
Reasoning followed: Ware, R. Timmis v Comm., 66 AFTR 2d 90-5198, 906 F2d 64 (CA2, 6/21/1990) [See 65 AFTR 2d 90-397, 110 S Ct 593-594]
Cited generally: Webb, Frederick L. v I.R.S., 73 AFTR 2d 94-1021, 15 F3d 205 (CA1, 2/3/1994)
Cases distinguished : George, Randolph; U.S. v., 96 AFTR 2d 2005-5821, 420 F3d 996 (CA9, 8/23/2005) [See 65 AFTR 2d 90-397, 493 US 209-210]
Cited favorably : Westpac Pacific Food v. Com., 97 AFTR 2d 2006-3018, 451 F3d 975 (CA9, 6/21/2006) [See 65 AFTR 2d 90-396, 493 US 207]
Cases reconciled : Tampa Bay Devil Rays, Ltd., 2002 RIA TC Memo 2002-1539 [See 65 AFTR 2d 90-495, 90-499, 493 US 204-205, 214]
Reasoning followed 1 : Rev Proc 91-31 , 1991-1 CB 567
Cited generally 1 : Rev Rul 2003-39 , 2003-1 CB 811

Cases and rulings that have cited the Supreme Court's decision in Indianapolis Power and Light Co.

CCH Citator
(Online; Partial List of Entries)

Name of cited case

Indianapolis Power and Light Co.

Locations in CCH where case and issues are discussed

ANNOTATED AT ... 2007FED ¶5504.6992; ¶21,005.027; ¶21,005.035; ¶21,005.7039; ¶21,005.7080; ¶21,017.18

• **SCt**–(aff'g CA), 90-1 USTC ¶50,007; 493 US 203; 110 SCt 589

Alternative citations for cited case (IPL)

  Banks II, SCt, 2005-1 USTC ¶50,155, 543 US 426, 125 SCt 826
  Westpac Pacific Foods, CA-9, 2006-2 USTC ¶50,369, 451 F3d 970
  George, CA-9, 2005-2 USTC ¶50,546, 420 F3d 991
  Webb, CA-1, 94-1 USTC ¶50,071, 15 F3d 203
  Ware, CA-2, 90-2 USTC ¶50,342, 906 F2d 62
  Tampa Bay Devil Rays, Ltd., TC, Dec. 54,893(M), 84 TCM 394, TC Memo. 2002-248
  Let. Rul. 200110002, October 4, 2000
  Let. Rul. 200347014, August 4, 2003
  Rev. Proc. 91-31
  Rev. Rul. 2003-39, IRB 2003-17, 811; 2003-1 CB 811

Cases and rulings that have cited the Supreme Court's decision in Indianapolis Power and Light Co.

Rulings

The significance of revenue rulings lies in the fact that they reflect current IRS policy. Since agents of the IRS are usually reluctant to vary from that policy, revenue rulings carry considerable weight.

Revenue rulings are often evaluated in court decisions. Thus, a tax service should be used to determine whether relevant rulings have been considered in any decisions. By examining the Court's view of the ruling, possible flaws may be discovered.

The IRS must adhere to private letter rulings issued to the taxpayer as long as the transaction is carried out in the manner initially approved. Variation from the facts on which the ruling was based permits the Service to revise its position. As mentioned earlier, a private letter ruling applies only to the particular taxpayer to whom it was issued. It does not apply to other taxpayers. However, such a ruling should prove helpful to any other taxpayer faced with a substantially identical fact pattern.

DERIVING THE SOLUTION

Once all the relevant authorities have been evaluated, a conclusion must be drawn. Before deriving the final answer or answers, however, an important caveat is warranted: the researcher must ensure that the research reflects all current developments. The new matters section of a tax service can aid in this regard. The new matters section updates the textual discussion with any late-breaking developments. For instance, the section will contain any new cases, regulations, or pronouncements of the Internal Revenue Service that may bear on the discussion of the topic covered in the main text.

COMMUNICATING THE FINDINGS

LO.11

Understand the importance of communicating the results of tax research.

The final product of the research effort is a memorandum recording the research and a letter to the interested parties. Although many formats are suitable for the memorandum, one technique typically used is structured as follows:

1. Description of the facts.
2. Statement of the issues or questions researched.
3. Report of the conclusions (brief answers to the research questions).
4. Discussion of the rationale and authorities that support the conclusions.
5. Summary of the authorities consulted in the research.

A good tax memorandum is essential. If the research findings are not communicated intelligently and effectively, the entire research effort is wasted.

Rules of Tax Practice: Responsibilities and Ethics

Over the past several years there has been a great deal of attention focused on ethics in business. The world of taxation has not escaped this attention. Unethical behavior of taxpayers and tax preparers has always been a serious concern of the tax system, primarily because of its reliance on voluntary compliance.

Anyone who has ever filed an income tax return recognizes the potential for bilking the system. It is as easy as under reporting income or overstating deductions. What is perhaps more important is that it can be done with so little risk. The current audit rate is so low—approximately 1 percent—that many dishonest taxpayers think they can exploit the system with little chance that they will ever get caught. That the tax system has long been an easy mark was underscored years ago in testimony given before the House Ways and Means Oversight Subcommittee by practitioners convicted of tax fraud for illegal refund schemes. In his testimony, Barry Becht, a 36-year-old former tax return preparer, explained that, before he was convicted and sent to Federal prison in 1993, he had "helped" over 4,000 clients reduce their tax liabilities by over $750,000 simply by overstating their deductions. Another convicted felon, Frazier Todd, reported that he had gained more than $500,000 in only two years using electronic filing schemes. Shortly after college and with the help of a few courses on computers, accounting, and business, Todd had set up a tax-preparation service near public housing in Atlanta. There he was able to strike deals with low-income taxpayers who allowed him to use their names and Social Security numbers to falsify wage statements (W-2 forms). He then proceeded to file returns electronically, which enabled him to obtain a refund before the IRS discovered that the returns were phony. More recently, in 2015, Linda Mary Anderson of Coyote Accounting was charged with filing false returns that collectively claimed more than $63 million in false income and withholdings in less than two tax seasons in 2009 and 2010. Unfortunately, the stories above are just a few examples from a long list of fraudulent preparers that is growing at an alarming rate.[22]

---

[22] For more of the same, see *Accounting Today,* a free online newsletter that periodically publishes its   "Tax Fraud, Blotter" containing "some of our favorite recent tax fraud cases."

As might be expected, governments everywhere have long been concerned about the amount of tax that goes uncollected. In the U.S., the IRS tries to measure it. Periodically, it issues a report on the so-called "tax gap," which generally is the amount of unpaid taxes (income, payroll, and excise) due to cheating and fraud. The most recent report was released in April, 2016 and it was for years 2008–2010.[23] For this period, the annual tax gap averaged $458 billion. To put this in perspective, this is just less than 20 percent of the total tax liability or 18.3% of the estimated $2.496 trillion of taxes for the three year period. The IRS expects to collect $52 billion of these amounts through late payments, audits and enforcement actions.

To safeguard the system, encourage compliance, and promote ethical behavior, the government has adopted a number of mechanisms. Among these is an intricate set of penalties that can be applied to both taxpayers and tax return preparers. These penalties cover a variety of violations, such as failure to file and pay taxes on a timely basis, negligence in preparing the tax return, and outright fraud. While the penalties are usually monetary in nature, criminal penalties—such as the jail sentences given to Mr. Becht and Mr. Todd—may result if the taxpayer goes beyond these civil offenses and purposefully attempts to evade tax. The failure-to-file and failure-to-pay penalties—penalties that typically result not because taxpayers are trying to deceive the government but simply because they are late in filing and paying their taxes—are discussed in Chapter 4. The focus in this chapter is on the responsibilities of taxpayers and tax return preparers in filing returns and the major penalties that may be imposed with respect to positions taken on returns.

TAXPAYER PENALTIES

In a 1985 IRS survey, one out of every five people reported that they cheated on their tax return. In the same survey, 41% said they believed that their fellow taxpayers also cheated. Similarly, Professor Peggy Hite found in a 1993 survey of Indiana residents that 40% of the individuals asked indicated that they definitely would not voluntarily report prize income, such as money won in a lottery or similar contests and sweepstakes.[24] Another 30% were somewhat wishy-washy in their answers, suggesting that, depending on the circumstances, they also would not report the income.

> **LO.12**
> Explain the key penalties that influence positions taken on tax returns.

More recently, in a 2014 survey of taxpayer attitudes,[25] the IRS asked, "[D]o you agree it is every American's civic duty to pay their fair share of taxes?" The vast majority, 94% of those surveyed, responded that they agree. Surprisingly, only 71% completely agreed. When asked specifically about cheating, only 86% said it is not at all acceptable to cheat. The obvious conclusion is that the remaining 14% believes some cheating is permissible. In fact, the survey reported that about 11% believed a little cheating here and there or as much as possible is acceptable.

These surveys confirm what everyone suspects. Taxpayers cheat. But anyone thinking about cheating should understand that cheating can be quite expensive.

The IRS has over 140 penalties in its arsenal that it could apply. In their simplest form, these penalties provide that as long as taxpayers do not cheat and make a good faith effort—try like a reasonable and prudent person would to determine their tax liability, they have no reason to worry. But in reality the ethical problems created by the tax system for taxpayers and tax preparers can be difficult to resolve. Unfortunately, the law rarely provides clear-cut answers, leaving taxpayers wondering what they should do.

As an illustration, consider two taxpayers, both with bad backs, who bought $5,000 hot tubs on the hope that they might have some therapeutic value. Can the taxpayers deduct their costs as a medical expense? Even if they researched the question every day of the week for a month, the answer may not be clear. Should the fact that the answer is not clear preclude them from deducting their expenses? Some taxpayers might be inclined to simply abandon the issue, pay the tax and never worry about it again. But others might believe that there is some support for their position and want to take the deduction. So assume in this case taxpayer A deducts the expense and taxpayer B deducts not only the cost of the tub

[23] https://www.irs.gov/uac/the-tax-gap.

[24] "Nearly 1 in 3 Would Cheat on Taxes," *The Indianapolis Star*, April 7, 1994, B1.

[25] IRS Oversight Board 2014 Taxpayer Attitude Survey https://www.treasury.gov/irsob/reports/Pages/default.aspx.

but, banking on the audit lottery, also deducts the entire cost of the house on the grounds that it serves as a rehabilitation facility. What happens if both returns are audited and the agent rejects the deductions of both taxpayers? Obviously the system of punishment should fit the crime. And this is what Congress has attempted to do by creating a penalty system that fairly treats taxpayers who in good faith believe that their position has validity but at the same time discourages taxpayers from taking frivolous positions, hoping that the audit lottery will never pick their number.

As the penalty discussion below will reveal, the tax law has its own way of dealing with taxpayers who stray too far from the correct position. While the system is complex, it is somewhat analogous to the way a mother treats her teenage son who is apt to stay out beyond his 12 o'clock curfew. If the son is a few minutes late, there will probably be no penalty if he has a reasonable explanation. On the other hand, if he gets home two hours late, the penalty will probably be severe unless he called to say he would be late. But if he never called, punishment is a virtual certainty unless his story is truly believable and backed by witnesses. And, of course, if her son lies, he will be grounded forever. Although the rules for breaking curfew are not completely analogous to those for taxpayers that take erroneous positions on returns, the comparison may be useful. If a taxpayer takes an incorrect position with respect to a *small* amount, there will be no penalty as long as there is a *reasonable basis* for the position. On the other hand, if the tax dollars involved are *substantial,* a penalty is normally imposed unless the taxpayer has *substantial authority* for the position or, alternatively, has disclosed the position and has a reasonable basis for it. Of course, if the taxpayer commits blatant fraud, the penalties could be quite harsh. These ethical standards for taxpayers are embedded in two types of penalties: accuracy-related penalties and penalties for fraud.

ACCURACY-RELATED PENALTIES

What happens if a waiter simply fails to report all of his tips? What if a 70-year-old grandmother fails to file her return believing that senior citizens do not have to pay tax? And what if the taxpayer deducts the cost of his daughter's wedding as business entertainment? As might be expected, the IRS does not treat such transgressions lightly. If the taxpayer's behavior can be characterized as negligent, a penalty in addition to the regular tax may be imposed. In 1989, Congress consolidated several existing penalties relating to negligence into a so-called accuracy-related penalty. The accuracy-related penalty is generally 20% of the portion of the tax underpayment. The principal accuracy-related penalties include:[26]

- Negligence or disregard of rules and regulations,

- Substantial understatement of income tax,

- Substantial valuation misstatement.

Note that these penalties do not stack on top of each other. The IRS must pick which one it wants to assess.

Negligence Penalty (Insubstantial)

The negligence penalty, as an accuracy-related penalty, is 20% of the portion of the tax underpayment that is attributable to negligence or disregard of the rules and regulations.[27] For example, assume a taxpayer forgets to report $1,000 that he received for consulting during the year. If the taxpayer is in the 28% tax bracket, the underpayment is $280 and the penalty would be $56 (20% × $280). Note that when the day of reckoning comes, the taxpayer will be required to pay the underpayment, interest on the underpayment from the original due date, and the penalty, if any. The taxpayer may also owe interest on the penalty. Interest on the penalty generally starts to run when the taxpayer has been notified of the penalty, usually sometime after the audit. Under § 6601(e)(2)(B) interest must be paid on the failure-to-file penalty, accuracy-related penalties, and the fraud penalty.

---

[26] § 6662.   [27] § 6662(c).

Negligence is generally defined as any failure to do what a reasonable and ordinarily prudent person would do under the circumstances. To avoid the negligence penalty, the taxpayer must make a reasonable attempt to comply with the law. The negligence penalty is usually imposed when the taxpayer fails to report income or claims large amounts of unsubstantiated expenses. For example, a waitress who fails to report her cash tips would probably get hit with the penalty, as would the businessperson who claims thousands of dollars of business entertainment expenses with little or no substantiation—a specific requirement for travel and entertainment expenses. A taxpayer is automatically considered negligent and liable for the 20% penalty if he or she fails to report any type of income for which there is an information return filed by the party paying the income (e.g., Form 1099). In other situations, determination of whether the penalty should be imposed is in the hands of the auditor. It is important to note, however, that taxpayers who intentionally attempt to deceive the government are normally not subject to the negligence penalty but rather the more severe fraud penalty discussed below.[28]

For most taxpayers, the most important aspect of the negligence penalty concerns its relationship to positions taken on returns.

Example 5

This year D graduated with a marketing degree from Rutgers University and immediately took a job with a publishing company as a sales representative. The company did not provide her with an office, so she worked out of her home. After talking with her boss at work, she found out that he deducted his home office expenses as business expenses on his return. Knowing little about tax, she followed her boss's lead and deducted $3,000 of expenses related to her home office. Two years later D's return was audited and the agent informed her that he planned to deny her deduction for the home office expenses. Assuming the agent is correct, another issue is raised: Should the negligence penalty apply since D has taken an incorrect position on the return?

Prior to 1994, the taxpayer could avoid the negligence penalty as long as the position was not frivolous and it was disclosed on the return. But that approach inspired taxpayers to play the audit lottery. For example, aggressive taxpayers might take a questionable deduction, disclose it, then hope that they would never be audited. Even if they got caught, there was little risk of punishment since disclosure protected them against a negligence penalty in every situation except where the position was frivolous or patently improper. In other words, as long as the position was nonfrivolous—that is, the taxpayer had some basis on which to argue the disclosed position (e.g., a merely arguable or merely colorable claim)—the negligence penalty could be avoided.[29] Believing that the ethical standard set by this rule was far too low, the Revenue Reconciliation Act of 1993 changed the rules. Under the current approach, taxpayers are forced to be more cautious about the positions they take on their returns.

The basic negligence penalty can be assessed unless the taxpayer has a *reasonable basis* for the position taken on the return regardless of whether it is disclosed on the return. What the current approach means to taxpayers is that in situations where the potential tax understatement is insubstantial they can ethically take a position that is contrary to the rules and regulations without fear of the negligence penalty as long as there is a reasonable basis for believing that if the matter were litigated, the taxpayer would prevail against the IRS. Of course, the critical issue here is what constitutes a reasonable basis.

Although any definition of a "reasonable basis" would be subject to debate, the regulations do provide some guidance. According to the regulations, the reasonable basis standard is met if the return position is "arguable, but fairly unlikely to prevail in court."[30]

---

[28] In 2008 and 2009, three well known politicians ran afoul of the tax law: Congressman Charles Rangel, Chairman of the House Ways and Means Committee which is charged with writing the tax law; Timothy Geithner, Secretary of the Treasury and overseer of the IRS; and Tom Daschle, former Senate majority leader from South Dakota and nominee to head the office of Health and Human Services who withdrew his nomination in light of his tax woes. Rangel and Daschel failed to report income while Geithner did not pay his self-employment taxes. Interestingly, the IRS waived the penalties! See "Rangel Rule Would Give a Free Pass on Penalties," AccountingWeb at http://www.accountingweb.com/topic/tax/rangel-rule-would-give-taxpayers-free-pass-penalties.

[29] Reg. §§ 1.6662-3(b)(3) and 1.6694-2(c)(2).

[30] § 6662(d).

Practitioners generally interpret this to mean that a position has a reasonable basis if it has at least a 20% chance of succeeding (without regard to the possibility that it might not be discovered at all). Apparently, this represents a slight increase in the level of support required by the nonfrivolous standard for disclosed positions under prior law. In the final analysis, however, the standard leaves a great deal to be desired. The regulations do provide one additional insight that may be useful: the "too good to be true" rule. This rule indicates that the reasonable basis standard is not met if the taxpayer fails to make a reasonable attempt to determine the correctness of a position that seems too good to be true.

Substantial Understatement Penalty

The substantial understatement penalty, like the negligence penalty, is an accuracy-related penalty that is 20% of the portion of the underpayment of tax due to any substantial understatement of income tax.[31] The understatement is considered substantial if it exceeds the larger of (1) 10% of the correct tax or (2) $5,000.

Taxpayers can avoid the substantial understatement penalty due to an erroneous position on a return in two ways: the taxpayer has either (1) substantial authority for the position or (2) a reasonable basis for the position and it is adequately disclosed on the return. In essence, the major difference between the substantial understatement penalty and the negligence penalty concerns the level of authority required to avoid penalty for an erroneous *undisclosed* position. In effect, Congress is telling taxpayers that if the risky position they are taking involves a substantial amount of tax and they are *unwilling to disclose* the position, the degree of support they must have is greater than simply a reasonable basis. The substantial understatement penalty applies to undisclosed positions unless the taxpayer has *substantial authority* for the position. It is unclear what the substantial authority requirement calls for, but it seems that it is somewhat more stringent than the 1 in 3 test of the realistic possibility of success standard discussed below but less demanding than the more-likely-than-not requirement, a more than 50% chance, related to certain positions taken with respect to certain tax shelter investments. For purposes of the substantial authority analysis, only materials published by Congress, the IRS, and the courts are relevant. Note, however, that IRS publications are not considered authority for this purpose.[32] Conclusions suggested by tax professionals in treatises, legal periodicals (which provide the basis of many arguments), or the like are not to be considered.[33]

As noted above, the degree of support necessary to avoid the substantial understatement penalty drops down a notch if the taxpayer is willing to disclose the position. The substantial understatement penalty can be avoided if the taxpayer makes *adequate disclosure* and has a *reasonable* basis for his position. What constitutes adequate disclosure is clearer than what constitutes a reasonable basis. Disclosure is considered adequate if the position is explained on a special form intended just for this purpose, specifically Form 8275 or 8275-R, or on the return in accordance with rules issued by the IRS each year.[34] In effect, when the tax dollars involved are material, taxpayers must meet a much higher standard—substantial authority—than is normally applied unless they are willing to disclose the position.

Substantial Valuation Misstatement

The tax law often requires taxpayers and tax return preparers to provide valuations for certain items. For example, taxpayers are generally entitled to a deduction for the fair market value of property given to qualified charitable organizations. What happens if a taxpayer in the 30% bracket gives a work of art that he says is worth $6,000 when its value is really closer to $2,000? The answer is that he has saved $1,200 ($4,000 × 30%) if he wins the audit lottery. But if the IRS does catch him, the taxpayer may face an accuracy-related penalty for substantial valuation misstatement. A 20% penalty is imposed on the underpayment of tax attributable to the misstatement.[35] The taxpayer avoids the penalty, however, if the

---

[31] § 6662(d)(2)(B). A corporate taxpayer has a substantial understatement if the amount of the understatement exceeds the lesser of (1) 10% of the tax required to be shown on the return for the tax year (or, if greater, $10,000), or (2) $10 million.

[32] See *Alvan L Bobrow*, T.C. Memo. 2014-21.

[33] Reg. § 1.6692-4(d)(3)(iii).

[34] Reg. § 1.6694-2(c)(3).

[35] § 6662(e). The penalty is 40% if the claimed value is 200% or more of the correct value.

misstatement does not exceed 150% of the correct value or if the amount of tax underpayment attributable to the misstatement is less than $5,000 ($10,000 for corporations). Thus the taxpayer above, who overstated the correct value by 300 percent, would still escape the valuation penalty since the amount of tax attributable to the misstatement, $1,200, is less than the $5,000 threshold. However, the taxpayer could still be subject to the negligence or the substantial understatement penalties.

Summary of Penalties for Inaccurate Returns

There is a great deal of confusion over penalties concerning erroneous positions on tax returns and what one can do to avoid them. Nevertheless, Exhibit 2-7 summarizes the three accuracy-related penalties discussed above and what defenses are available to the taxpayer. After a great deal of studying, it may become clear that the likelihood of a penalty depends on three factors: the amount of the potential understatement, whether the taxpayer has disclosed the position adequately, and the level of support that there is for the position. As a rule, if the tax dollars are not significant, a reasonable basis protects the taxpayer from penalty. On the other hand, if the tax dollars are substantial, the taxpayer is protected only if there is substantial authority or if there is disclosure with reasonable basis. Exhibit 2-8 summarizes the various standards of compliance and ranks them according to their level of certainty. Note that in all cases the taxpayer can avoid the penalties by showing that there was *reasonable cause* for the position taken or that he or she acted in *good faith*. Obviously, these are both purely subjective determinations based on the individual facts and circumstances.

EXHIBIT 2-7	The 20% Penalty for Inaccurate Returns and Defenses: § 6662

1. Negligence (insubstantial)
   - Defined: Reasonable attempt to comply with the tax laws
   - Defenses:
     - Reasonable basis (disclosure is unnecessary)
     - Exercise of reasonable care in preparing tax return
     - Reasonable cause and good faith

2. Substantial understatement
   - Defined: Understatement greater than 10% of tax or $5,000, whichever is larger
   - Defenses:
     - Understatement does not exceed threshold
     - Disclosure with reasonable basis
     - No disclosure with substantial authority
     - Reasonable cause and good faith

3. Substantial valuation misstatement
   - Defined: Misstatement more than 150% of correct valuation
   - Defenses:
     - Misstatement does not exceed threshold
     - Amount of underpayment of tax is less than $5,000
     - Reasonable cause and good faith

EXHIBIT 2-8	Standards of Compliance Required to Avoid Penalties

1. Frivolous position
   - Defined: Patently improper
     - No protection for frivolous positions
2. Not frivolous position
   - Defined: Not patently improper, merely arguable
     - Pre-1994: Protection against negligence with disclosure
     - Post-1993: Apparently no protection
3. Reasonable basis
   - Defined: Arguable but fairly unlikely to prevail in court
     - Protects against insubstantial negligence
     - Protects against substantial understatement if position disclosed
4. Realistic possibility of success
   - Defined: More than one in three chances for success
     - Protects against insubstantial negligence without disclosure
     - Protects against substantial negligence with disclosure
5. Substantial authority
   - Defined: Supporting authorities are substantial (Congress, IRS, or court cases)
     - Protects against insubstantial and substantial negligence without disclosure (except tax shelter items)
6. More-likely-than-not
   - Defined: Greater than 50% chance of prevailing against the IRS if the matter were litigated
     - Protects against insubstantial and substantial negligence without disclosure related to certain positions taken with respect to certain tax shelter investments
7. Reasonable cause and good faith
   - Defined: Facts and circumstances determination
     - Protects normally against all penalties

ECONOMIC SUBSTANCE DOCTRINE

It is not surprising that some taxpayers—both individuals and businesses—go to great lengths, often concocting intricate transactions, to avoid paying taxes. Some schemes are the ingenious creation of a company's legal or accounting department, sometimes with the aid of tax professionals at big name accounting or law firms. Some are the outrageous products of charlatan promoters. Others fall somewhere in between. Interestingly, many of these plans actually adhere to the letter of the law, meeting all of the statutory and administrative requirements. Nevertheless, courts often deny taxpayers the tax benefits of these otherwise "legal" transactions if they lack so-called *economic substance*. A transaction is said to lack economic substance if it did not result in a meaningful change to the taxpayer's economic position other than reducing federal income taxes. In short, if the transaction was solely for tax purposes, it will be disregarded. This principle is referred to as the "economic substance doctrine."

The economic substance doctrine is just one of several judicial theories that have been used to attack tax avoidance schemes. Another theory is the "business purpose doctrine." This principle says that the transaction must be motivated by business considerations and reducing taxes is *not* a business purpose. In other situations, where the alleged activity never took place or what took place was merely a facade, the court often asserts that the events were a "sham transaction" and disregards the outcome. Similarly, the court may disallow the tax benefits by invoking the "substance over form" principle. This well-known doctrine stands for the proposition that the tax results of an arrangement should be based on the underlying substance rather than a simple evaluation of the formal steps by which the arrangement was undertaken. Yet another weapon in the court's arsenal is the "step transaction" doctrine. This doctrine treats what are purportedly separate steps as a single transaction if the steps are integrated, interdependent, and focused toward a particular result. The purpose of each of these doctrines is to test the transactions and sort out those that are primarily or solely motivated by tax savings from those that have a substantial business purpose or economic motive.

In 2010, Congress created § 7701(o)(1) that effectively enacts into law the economic substance doctrine and its variations. Section 7701 imposes a significant penalty for transactions that fail its tests.

Under § 7701(o), a transaction has economic substance only if it (1) changes in a meaningful way (apart from federal taxes) the taxpayer's economic position and (2) the taxpayer has a substantial purpose for entering the transaction (other than for federal income taxes). This is a two prong test where the taxpayer must meet both tests for the transaction to be honored. The law does allow an exception for personal transactions of individuals. Individuals will be subject to the economic substance doctrine only for transactions entered in connection with a trade or business or an activity entered into for the production of income.

For transactions not meeting the two-part test, there is a penalty based on the underpayment of taxes resulting from the transaction. If the transaction is disclosed, the penalty is 20% of the underpayment. For undisclosed transactions, the penalty is doubled to 40 percent.

The impact of § 7701(o) is yet to be determined. Few commentators believe that many tax professionals will lose sleep wondering whether even the most common transactions have economic substance. However, the provision is quite broad, and many legitimate business transactions, if tested for economic substance, could fail the statutory tests. Because of the uncertainty and because of the strict liability penalty, it does seem that taxpayers will face increased tax risk with respect to some transactions and, in some cases, will be deterred from engaging in transactions that otherwise would have been undertaken.

Uncertain Tax Positions: Financial Accounting Reporting

Part of the difficulty encountered in tax practice is uncertainty. For many transactions, the tax treatment may not be clear. In such case, companies, as might be expected, usually take positions that reduce their tax liability. For example, a company may exclude income that it may believe is tax-exempt or take a tax credit that it believes is appropriate. Similarly, a company may not file a tax return in a particular state because it believes it is not required. These positions normally have a sound legal basis and are taken in good faith. However, given the complexities and varying interpretations of the tax law, these positions may not ultimately prevail. Consequently, uncertainty exists regarding the actual benefit a company will derive from a position taken on its tax return. This has an impact not only on a company's tax return but also its financial statements.

Over time, the Financial Accounting Standards Board (FASB) became concerned about the accounting for uncertainty in income taxes and how it was reported for financial accounting purposes. In June 2006, the FASB issued FASB Interpretation (FIN) No. 48, *Accounting for Uncertainty in Income Taxes* (now contained in Accounting Standards Codification Topic 740). FIN 48 or ASC 740 was created primarily as a mechanism to provide greater transparency for uncertain tax positions and greater uniformity in the financial reporting of tax issues.

FIN 48 requires companies to identify their uncertain tax positions and determine the likelihood that they will or will not survive audit, appeals and litigation. Once that is determined, FIN 48 forces companies to disclose and create a reserve for uncertain tax positions that are more likely than not to occur. Basically, FIN 48 contains a two step-process that must be applied to all tax positions: recognition and measurement. First, a tax position is recognized for financial accounting purposes only if it is "more likely than not" (i.e., greater than 50%) that the position will be sustained upon examination by a taxing authority. Second, if the tax position is recognized, the effect is measured. Using probability techniques, measurement determines what amount of a tax position will be sustainable upon a potential examination or settlement. Finally, FIN 48 requires certain disclosures to be footnoted in the financial statements. In short, it has completely changed the way companies account for uncertainty with respect to tax positions.

Uncertain Tax Positions: Tax Reporting

It was not long after the issuance of FIN 48 that the government decided it deserved similar treatment. In 2010, the IRS created Schedule UTP that requires certain companies to report *on their tax returns* their uncertain positions. Generally, a corporation that is required to file a corporate income tax return, Form 1120 (and certain others) must attach Schedule UTP if it meets the following requirements:

1. The corporation has assets that equal or exceed $10 million;
2. The corporation or a related party issued *audited* financial statements; and
3. The corporation has one or more tax positions that must be reported on Schedule UTP.

Schedule UTP requires the reporting of an income tax position taken by the corporation on its tax return if it recorded a reserve for that tax position in audited financial statements or did not record a reserve because the corporation expects to litigate the position.

Fraud

When the taxpayer attempts to defraud the government, the tax law imposes a minimum penalty equal to 75% of the amount of underpayment attributable to the fraud.[36] *In addition,* the taxpayer may also be subject to the criminal penalties for fraud. Criminal penalties can be as high as $100,000 ($500,000 for corporate taxpayers) and imprisonment for up to five years. Despite these penalties, it appears that some taxpayers continue to play the audit lottery, including some rich and famous tax felons:[37]

- Leona Helmsley, New York hotel magnate, who will forever be remembered for her offhand comment to her housekeeper, "we don't pay taxes; only the little people pay taxes." Helmsley, convicted in 1992 for deducting millions of dollars of personal expenses, including renovations to her personal residence, was fined more than $7 million and sentenced to four years in prison (served 18 months).

- Pete Rose, baseball player and all-time leader in hits (4,256). Rose failed to report income from memorabilia shows and gambling and served five months in prison.

- Spiro Agnew, vice-president during the Nixon era. Agnew, who failed to report income from bribes, was fined $10,000 and had a three-year suspended sentence.

- Chuck Berry, famous rock and roll star of Johnny B. Goode fame. Berry underreported his income by $110,000 in 1979 and served four months in prison.

- Aldo Gucci, famous designer. Gucci pleaded guilty to $7 million of tax fraud in 1989 and was sentenced to one year in jail and fined $30,000.

- Al Capone, racketeer and mobster. Capone, convicted of tax evasion in 1931, was fined $50,000 and served eight years of a ten-year sentence, then retired to his Miami estate.

- Willie Nelson, country and western singing star. Nelson ran up his tax bill to over $32 million. He served no time in prison, but part of the bill was paid from part of his ranch, which was seized by the IRS.

- Richard Hatch, winner in the debut season of reality show "Survivor." Hatch failed to report $1,000,000 and pay taxes on the winnings. He reportedly asked an accountant to prepare two tax returns, one with the winnings and the other without, and chose to file the latter. Hatch was found guilty of tax evasion and was sentenced in 2006 to serve 51 months in prison.

---

[36] § 6663.

[37] See in part "Famous Faces from IRS Hall of Shame," *Sacramento Bee,* March 29, 1994. Metro Final Scene, D3.

Civil fraud has not been clearly defined, but it requires more than simply negligent acts or omissions by the taxpayer. There is a fine line between fraud and negligence (to which a lesser penalty applies, as explained above). Fraud does not occur by accident. It is a willful and deliberate attempt to evade tax. For example, consider a taxpayer who is entitled to a deduction of $19,000. What penalty applies if he transposed the digits and claimed a deduction of $91,000? Fraud occurs only if it can be shown that the taxpayer knew that the amounts reported on the return were false. In this regard, the IRS must prove this to be true by a "preponderance of evidence." Thus for the transposition error above, the fraud penalty can be upheld if the IRS can carry its burden of proof and show that the taxpayer intentionally transposed the numbers. Lacking this, the negligence or substantial understatement penalty would probably be assessed. Note that before the *criminal* fraud penalty can be imposed, the IRS must show that the taxpayer intentionally tried to evade tax "beyond a shadow of any reasonable doubt." All of those in the "hall of shame" above found that this is not an impossible task. As a practical matter, the penalty imposed—negligence, civil, or criminal fraud—depends on the severity of the offense and the ability of the IRS to carry the burden of proof.

Example 6

Dr. Bradford Calloway paid his children, all of whom were under 12 years of age, $11,000 for performing various tasks relating to his business. The kids did such chores as mail sorting, trash collecting, and answering the telephone. Although expenses incurred in carrying on a business such as these are normally deductible, the IRS did not believe that children that age could perform work worth that much money for any business. The Tax Court agreed with the IRS, and the judge added a fraud penalty, explaining that "We find it inherently incredible that Calloway, an intelligent and educated professional man, would pay a total of $11,138.56 for such services, performed by small children on a part-time basis, or that he could seriously believe that such payments represented reasonable and deductible compensation for services rendered in his medical practice … particularly in the face of his accountant's contrary advice."[38]

TAX PREPARER PENALTIES

Understanding the penalty structure becomes doubly hard when a tax preparer is involved. What are the responsibilities of tax preparers when the client is unscrupulous or simply wants to take an aggressive position? As a practical matter, it is not the totally dishonest taxpayer that presents difficulties for tax return preparers. Most practitioners can easily walk away from such engagements. The more perplexing and more common problems concern situations where the client wants the preparer to take an aggressive position on issues for which the answer is unclear. Similarly, taxpayers may want to pursue a particular position because they view the law as arbitrary or capricious or they are not receptive to the preparer's response. These situations often present an ethical dilemma for the preparer. What side should the practitioner take? Should the preparer sign the return if he or she disagrees with the taxpayer? First, it needs to be emphasized that the tax practitioner is being paid to be an advocate for the client, not an independent third party hired to provide an unbiased or neutral opinion. It is the job of the tax expert to explain the relevant considerations and possible consequences, including positions that may be contrary to the law but which may be defensible. That done, it is not the right of the practitioner to impose his or her own set of moral values on the client. The final decision is to be made by the client after reviewing the alternatives provided. If the practitioner believes that the client's actions violate his or her personal code of ethics, the practitioner should withdraw from the engagement.

LO.13

Understand the rules of conduct that must be followed by those who perform tax services.

---

[38] A. J. Cook, *A. J.'s Tax Court* (St. Luke's Press, 1987), p. 96.

Beyond the basic preparer-client relationship, there are a number of other forces at work that affect whether the preparer signs the return containing a risky position. First, even if an answer to a particular question does exist, the costs of uncovering it probably cannot be recovered from the client. Second, given the small percentage of tax returns that are audited, there is only a slight chance that either the taxpayer or preparer will ever come face to face with the IRS. Third, preparers, like most people, want to please their customers and find it hard to just say no. When these dynamics are present, they make it relatively easy for practitioners to resolve an issue in favor of the client, notwithstanding the lack of reasonable support for the position. This is particularly true when the practitioner knows that the unprincipled competitor down the street will do whatever the client wants and at a cheaper price. On the other hand, the practitioner's sense of public duty, concern about his or her personal and professional reputation, and possible legal liability may cause him or her to be something less than an advocate for the client. As might be expected, the practitioner's proper role in these situations is not clearly defined. There are, however, in addition to the preparer's own personal code of ethics, some guidelines that a preparer generally must follow in carrying on a tax practice.

Individuals who prepare tax returns are subject to a variety of rules regulating their professional conduct. The rules governing tax practice are contained in Treasury Circular 230 and various provisions of the Internal Revenue Code. In addition, CPAs and attorneys engaged in tax practice must also follow the rules of conduct imposed by their professional organizations: the American Institute of Certified Public Accountants (AICPA) and the American Bar Association (ABA). The general rules of conduct prescribed by the AICPA for all CPAs concern a variety of matters such as independence, integrity, objectivity, advertising, contingent fees, and responsibilities of the accountant when undertaking an engagement—but none of these are directly related to tax practice. Acknowledging that individuals engaged in tax practice have ethical concerns beyond those covered in the general rules of conduct, the AICPA has developed Statements on Standards for Tax Services (SSTSs). These statements, currently seven in number, provide additional guidelines for professional conduct of CPAs in tax practice. Similarly, the ABA Standing Committee on Ethics and Professional Responsibility has also issued certain opinions regarding an attorney's conduct when practicing before the IRS.

Tax Return Positions

As might be imagined, the rules and applicable penalties concerning practitioner conduct as set forth by Circular 230, the Internal Revenue Code, the AICPA, and the ABA deserve a chapter devoted solely to these topics. In essence, however, the most important penalty for those preparing returns is that contained in § 6694(a). Section 6694(a) provides that a penalty of $1,000 (or if greater, 50% of the income from preparing the return) is imposed on the preparer of a tax return if any part of an understatement of the liability on a return is due to an unreasonable position taken on the tax return and the return preparer knew (or reasonably should have known) of the position.[39] If the position is properly disclosed on the return, the penalty does not apply if there was a reasonable basis for the position.[40] If the position is not disclosed, the penalty applies unless there is substantial authority for the position. As noted earlier, substantial authority includes the Internal Revenue Code, Regulations (final, temporary, and proposed), court cases, tax treaties, and administrative pronouncements (Revenue Rulings, Revenue Procedures, Private Letter Rulings, Technical Advice Memoranda, Notices, and similar documents). If the position is with respect to a tax shelter investment, the threshold for authority is raised, and the penalty is imposed unless it was reasonable to believe that the position would "more likely than not" be sustained on its merits if the position were litigated. The preparer penalty is not imposed in any case if it is shown that there is reasonable cause for the understatement and the preparer acted in good faith. Note that the penalty applies to any paid preparer regardless of whether the person is a CPA, enrolled agent, friend, or relative. If the preparer is compensated, the penalty could apply.[41]

---

[39] The penalty increases to the greater of $5,000 or 50% of the income derived from preparation of the return if it is attributable to willful or reckless conduct. See § 6694(b).

[40] Disclosure must be made on Form 8275 or, when the position is contrary to a Regulation, Form 8275-R. See Reg. § 1.6694-2(c)(3)(i).

[41] See § 7701(a)(36) for a definition of preparer.

> **Example 7**
>
> T purchased a computer this year that he uses in his job as a financial planner. His friends at the office say that he can deduct it. His accountant, P, explained that it might be deductible but only if T can demonstrate that the computer's use is for his employer's convenience and not his own. If the position is disclosed, neither P nor T will be subject to penalty if there is a reasonable basis for the position. If the position is not disclosed, then normally substantial authority must exist to avoid penalty.

At first glance, it would appear that the size of penalty imposed by the IRS, $1,000, is so small that it would do little to dissuade preparers from taking whatever position a client wishes. What may not be apparent, however, is the significance of this standard *and* its violation should a disgruntled client end up suing the preparer for malpractice. In a civil action against a preparer, the courts, both judges and juries, typically rely on expert testimony to assess whether the preparer should be held liable. In such case, it is not too hard to imagine a judge or jury believing that the preparer was negligent once an expert has explained that the preparer has already been penalized under § 6694(a). Even if the preparer is ultimately exonerated, the costs to defend such action could be substantial. Moreover, failing to observe such a standard could ultimately cost the practitioner the loss of his or her professional license to practice as a CPA or attorney. In short, it is not the size of the penalty that the practitioner fears but the other consequences that the penalty may trigger.

> **Example 8**
>
> T, a CPA, has prepared the tax return for D&G Home Products for the past 15 years. It is normally a week-long job and worth well over $10,000 to T's practice. He also does the monthly preparation of financial statements worth another $20,000 per year. This year G spent more than $100,000 on a Super Bowl excursion for its customers. In preparing the return, D&G insists that it should be able to deduct all of the expenses, but T has some reservations. T understands there have been some recent changes in the law in this area but does not have time to adequately research the issue, and, even if he did, he doubts whether he could charge for the time spent. He also knows that this is a lucrative engagement and he wants to continue the relationship with the client. Finally, T recognizes that it is highly unlikely that the return will ever be audited. Consequently, T decides to sign the return and worry about it only if a problem arises. But what happens if the return is audited, the position is overturned, and a preparer penalty is assessed on the grounds that the return contained an undisclosed position that did not have substantial authority supporting it. While the penalty would be monetarily small, the real concern is the effect of the reversal on the client. D&G may have a short memory once it is forced to pay the tax, interest, and perhaps a substantial understatement penalty and interest on the penalty. It may not remember conversations with T and his admonitions. In the end, the corporation may feel that it was misled and sue T for malpractice and thousands of dollars. In such a proceeding, D&G may have the upper hand since it has been determined by a court of law that the position was unrealistic under that standards of § 6694(a) and T has therefore failed to meet his ethical responsibilities.

The decision that all practitioners ultimately face with every return they prepare is whether they can in good faith sign the tax return as preparer. Under the current rules, preparers normally will be reluctant to sign if the return contains an undisclosed position that does not have substantial authority.[42]

---

[42] Prop. Reg. § 10.34.

In addition to the $1,000 penalty, the tax law provides a number of other penalties to encourage ethical conduct by preparers. For example, a penalty of $1,000 per return is imposed where the preparer willfully attempts to understate the liability of the taxpayer or where the preparer understates the taxpayer's liability by reckless or intentional disregard of the rules or regulations.[43] The law also contains a number of criminal penalties for preparers with fines of up to $10,000 and imprisonment for up to three years.[44]

Other Guidelines for CPAs

LO.14

Appreciate the role of ethics in tax practice and the responsibilities of tax practitioners.

In 2000, the AICPA issued the Statements on Standards for Tax Services (SSTS) that are enforceable ethical standards that apply to all AICPA members. The SSTSs are intended to complement other standards of tax practice, including Circular 230 and the statutory penalty provisions. There are currently seven statements. SSTS No. 1 concerns tax positions taken on returns. The remaining statements generally fall into one of two categories: (1) return preparation issues (SSTS Numbers 2, 3, and 4) and (2) issues that arise after a return is filed (SSTS Numbers 5 and 6). Statement Number 7 addresses the form and content of advice given to taxpayers. These statements are summarized below.

- *SSTS No. 1: Tax Return Positions.* As revised in 2010, this Standard explains that CPAs must observe the level of support for tax positions expected by the applicable taxing authority. However, the minimum level of support required for an undisclosed tax position recommended by a CPA is a good-faith belief that there is at least a realistic possibility of the position's being sustained administratively or judicially on its merits if challenged. This level of support applies if the taxing authority has no standards or has less rigorous standards than the realistic-possibility standard. Obviously, the CPA must adhere to the taxing authority's standards if they are higher than the realistic-possibility standard. According to the standard, a CPA may recommend a position for which there is a reasonable basis of support if the CPA advises the client to disclose the position.

- *SSTS No. 2: Answers to Questions on the Return.* When there are questions on a return that have not been answered, the CPA should make a reasonable effort to obtain appropriate answers from the taxpayer and provide the answers to the questions on the return. The significance of the question in terms of the information's effect on taxable income or loss and tax liability may be considered in determining whether the answer to a question may be omitted. However, omission of an answer is not justified simply because the answer may prove to be disadvantageous to the taxpayer.

- *SSTS No. 3: Certain Procedural Aspects of Preparing Returns.* In preparing or signing a return, a CPA may, without verification, rely in good faith on information furnished by the taxpayer or a third party. However, the CPA cannot ignore the implications of information furnished, and should make reasonable inquiries if the information appears to be incorrect, incomplete, or inconsistent either by itself or on the basis of other facts known to the CPA. When preparing the current return, the CPA should make use of returns from prior years wherever feasible. If the tax law or regulations impose conditions with respect to the tax treatment of an item (e.g., substantiating documentation), the CPA should make appropriate inquiries to determine if the conditions are met. In addition, when preparing a return, the CPA should consider relevant information known to the CPA from the tax return of another taxpayer, but should also consider any legal limitations relating to confidentiality.

- *SSTS No. 4: Use of Estimates.* Unless it is prohibited by the Internal Revenue Code or other tax rule, a CPA may prepare returns involving the use of the taxpayer's estimates, if under the circumstances, exact data cannot be obtained in a practical manner. When estimates are used, they should be presented in such a manner as to avoid the implication of greater accuracy than that which exists. The CPA should be satisfied that estimated amounts are reasonable under the circumstances.

- *SSTS No. 5: Departure from Positions Previously Concluded in an Administrative Proceeding or Court Decision.* A CPA may recommend a tax return position that differs from the way an item was previously treated in an IRS examination, IRS appeals conference, or a court decision for that taxpayer, unless the taxpayer is bound to a

---

[43] § 6694(b).   [44] See §§ 7206, 7207, and 7216.

specific treatment for the item in the later year (such as by a formal closing agreement). The CPA should still follow the realistic possibility standard in recommending tax return positions, discussed above.

- *SSTS No. 6: Knowledge of Error (Return Preparation and Administrative Proceeding).* A CPA should advise the taxpayer promptly upon learning of an error in a previously filed return, or upon learning of a taxpayer's failure to file a required return. The advice of the CPA may be oral, and should include a recommendation of the measures to be taken. The CPA is not obliged to inform the IRS and may not do so without the permission of the taxpayer, except where required by law. If the CPA is requested to prepare the current year's return and the taxpayer has not taken appropriate steps to correct an error on a prior year's return, the CPA should consider whether to withdraw from preparing the return and whether to continue a professional or employment relationship with the taxpayer.

    When the CPA represents a taxpayer in an administrative proceeding regarding a return with an error known to the CPA that has resulted or may result in more than an insignificant effect on the taxpayer's tax liability, the CPA should notify the taxpayer and recommend corrective measures to be taken. The recommendations may be given orally. The CPA is not obligated to inform the IRS or other taxing authority, and may not do so without the taxpayer's permission, except where required by law. However, the CPA should request permission from the taxpayer to disclose the error to the IRS. Absent such permission, the CPA should consider withdrawing from the engagement.

- *SSTS No. 7: Form and Content of Advice to Taxpayers.* In providing tax advice to a taxpayer, the CPA must use judgment to ensure that the advice reflects professional competence and appropriately serves the taxpayer's needs. There is no standard format nor standard guidelines to be used in giving written or oral advice to a taxpayer. A CPA should assume that tax advice provided to a taxpayer will affect the manner in which items are reported on the taxpayer's tax returns, so should follow the realistic possibility and reasonable basis standards from Statement Number 1 or that of the applicable taxing authority. Finally, the CPA has no obligation to communicate with a taxpayer when subsequent developments affect prior advice, unless the CPA is assisting the taxpayer in implementing procedures or plan associated with the advice, or there is a specific agreement for subsequent communications.

The above discussion is just a brief introduction to the penalties and rules of practice that serve to define the proper conduct for taxpayers and preparers. In reality, there are a number of other penalties and rules that may apply in certain situations.[45] Nevertheless, this introduction may provide a sense of what are the most common ethical problems facing tax practitioners. Moreover, it underscores the importance of being able to find authoritative answers for questions, the subject of the next section.

 CHECK YOUR KNOWLEDGE

Review Question I

The system of penalties provides an escape for taxpayers if the positions taken on their returns meet certain standards. In effect, meeting a certain standard enables the taxpayer to avoid a penalty. Practitioners generally associate a probability of success rate for each standard. What probabilities would you assign?

Frivolous	_____
Substantial authority	_____
Nonfrivolous	_____
More-likely-than-not	_____
Reasonable basis	_____
Realistic possibility of success	_____

---

[45] For a more complete discussion, see the related text, *Corporate Partnership, Estate and Gift Taxation, 2017 Edition,* Chapter 19.

None of these probabilities other than *realistic possibility of success* have been quantified by the law. However, practitioners would typically rank the standards in the following order with the associated probabilities of success. Although the probabilities might vary from firm to firm and practitioner to practitioner, the order would remain the same.

1.	More-likely-than-not	> 50%
2.	Substantial authority	≥ 40
3.	Realistic possibility of success	≥ 33
4.	Reasonable basis	≥ 20
5.	Nonfrivolous	≥ 5
6.	Frivolous	< 5

Review Question 2

Pete Hartman operates an accounting practice in northern Virginia just outside of Washington. One of his long-time clients is Jim Anderson. Last year the IRS audited Jim's 2009 tax return, and he ultimately had to pay additional taxes as well as interest on that amount. Jim now wants to deduct a portion of this interest as a business expense. He reasons that because business expenses are deductible and the interest was directly attributable to back taxes on business income, the deduction should be allowed. There has also been another development this year. Jim's daughter has been diagnosed to have dyslexia. The problem is not to enroll his daughter in a private school that is better equipped to provide the additional help she needs. The tuition for the school is $20,000, and Jim wants to deduct the cost as a medical expense. After some research, Pete believes that both positions are somewhat risky. Jim has asked Pete about the downside risk of taking this position on his return. Pete estimates that taking the deduction for the interest will reduce Jim's tax liability of $30,000 about $1,000. If he were to claim only the medical expense deduction by itself, it would reduce his tax liability by about $6,000. Try to answer the following questions:

a. What is the maximum penalty that Jim might pay if he deducts only the interest and it is considered erroneous but not fraudulent?

Jim would be subject to an accuracy-related penalty (negligence), which is 20% of the amount of the underpayment due to the overstatement of deductions. In this case, the penalty would be $200 (20% × $ 1,000). In addition, Jim would owe the additional $1,000 in tax plus interest on the underpayment *and* interest on the penalty.

b. True-False. Jim will not be subject to penalty with respect to the interest deduction as long as his position has a reasonable basis even if he does not specifically disclose the position on the return since the amount of tax at stake is not substantial.

True. The negligence penalty will not be assessed as long as the taxpayer has a reasonable basis for the position regardless of whether the position is disclosed on the tax return.

c. True-False. Jim will not be subject to penalty with respect to the tuition deduction as long as his position has a reasonable basis even if he does not specifically disclose the position on the return.

False. In this situation, Jim's $6,000 understatement would be considered substantial since it exceeds the larger of $5,000 or 10% of the correct tax, $3,000 (10% × $30,000). When the understatement in question is substantial, the substantial understatement penalty applies. This penalty can be avoided only if the taxpayer has substantial authority for his position *or* he discloses the position and such position has reasonable basis. Here Jim will not have disclosed the position, so a reasonable basis for the position will not suffice.

d. Jim has indicated that he does not want to flag either position. Pete would not be subject to a preparer penalty with respect to the tuition deduction if the position is *not* disclosed as long as the position:

(1) has a reasonable basis
(2) is nonfrivolous
(3) has a realistic possibility of success
(4) has a more-likely-than-not chance of prevailing
(5) all of the above

The answer is (4). To avoid the $1,000 preparer penalty of § 6694(a), an undisclosed position must be supported with substantial authority. However, if the position is disclosed, the preparer penalty will not apply as long as it there is a reasonable basis for the position.

e. Pete understands that the SSTS indicate that he is not supposed to sign the return where there is an undisclosed position unless the position has a realistic possibility of success. However, he has no real idea whether the chances are 20 percent, 30 percent, 40 percent, or whatever based on what he has found. Can Pete sign a return containing a position for which there is no reasonable basis without violating the AICPA statements if he discloses the position?

Yes. The SSTS provide that a practitioner can sign any return as long as the position is disclosed and it is not frivolous.

Problem Materials

DISCUSSION QUESTIONS

2-1 *Taxpayer Penalties.* In reviewing his last year's return, T noticed that he had inadvertently deducted the entire cost of a new air-conditioning system. Such cost should have been capitalized and depreciated.

    a. T wants to know what penalties, if any, might be assessed if his return is audited and the IRS uncovers his mistake.

    b. What should T do?

2-2 *Tax Positions.* R operates a small accounting practice in Columbus, Ohio. While preparing the return for his long-time client C, he found out that C wants to deduct the cost of lawn care for her home. C is a landscape architect who recently started using a room at her home as an office. She feels that this is clearly a business expense. During the interview she seemed to have a point. "What if my clients came to my house and the yard was less than picture perfect? It would kill my business," she explained. R has reviewed the proposed regulations on the home office deduction, and they specifically state that lawn care is not deductible. Nevertheless, he understands C's point. R just cannot say no, and he is thinking about preparing the return and deducting a portion of lawn care allocable to C's home office.

    a. Assume the position is erroneous and is not disclosed. Will C be subject to any penalty? Explain.

    b. Assume the position is erroneous and is disclosed. Will C be subject to any penalty? Explain.

2-3 *Avoiding Preparer Penalties.* H recently quit a national public accounting firm and purchased the practice of a local accountant. Her first busy season with this new set of clients has been eye-opening. Some of the taxpayers have been taking very questionable positions on certain recurring items. Somewhat paranoid, H is now quite concerned about incurring penalties. What can she do to guard against possible preparer penalties?

2-4 *Knowledge of Error.* Last March, P put the finishing touches on the tax return of one of his most prized clients, Great Buy Corporation. When preparing the monthly financial statement for June, P noticed that $30,000 of sales somehow got left off of the return. What should P do?

2-5 *Knowledge of Error.* This year P got a new client from the firm down the street, Dewey, Cheatham and Howe. After reviewing the client's prior year return, he found, as he had expected, an error in the way Dewey had computed depreciation. What should P do?

2-6 *Making a New Tax Law.* Describe the Congressional process of making a tax bill into final law.

2-7 *Legislative versus Interpretative Regulations.* Explain the difference between a legislative Treasury Regulation and an interpretative Regulation.

2-8 *Proposed versus Final Regulations.* Distinguish between proposed and final Regulations. How would either type of Regulation involving Code § 704 be cited?

2-9 *Revenue Rulings and Revenue Procedures.* Distinguish between a Revenue Ruling and a Revenue Procedure. Where can either be found in printed form?

2-10 *Private versus Published Rulings.* Distinguish between a private letter ruling and a Revenue Ruling. Under what circumstances would a taxpayer prefer to rely on either of these sources?

2-11 *Technical Advice Memoranda.* What are Technical Advice Memoranda? Under what circumstances are they issued?

2-12 *Trial Courts.* Describe the trial courts that hear tax cases. What are the advantages or disadvantages of litigating a tax issue in each of these courts?

2-13 *The Appeals Process.* A taxpayer living in Indiana has exhausted her appeals within the IRS. If she chooses to litigate her case, trace the appeals process assuming she begins her effort in each of the following trial courts:
  a. The U.S. Court of Federal Claims
  b. The U.S. District Court
  c. The U.S. Tax Court
  d. The Small Tax Division of the U.S. Tax Court

2-14 *Tax Court Decisions.* Distinguish between a Regular Tax Court decision and a Memorandum decision.

2-15 *Authority of Tax Law Sources.* Assume that you have discovered favorable support for your position taken in a controversy with an IRS agent in each of the sources listed below. Which of these has the greater weight of authority? Rank them from strongest to weakest.
  a. A decision of the U.S. District Court having jurisdiction over your case if litigated
  b. Treasury Regulation
  c. The Internal Revenue Code
  d. A decision of the Supreme Court
  e. A decision of the Court of Appeals
  f. A decision of the Small Claims Court
  g. A decision of the U.S. Tax Court
  h. A private letter ruling issued to another taxpayer
  i. A Revenue Ruling
  j. A tax article in a leading periodical

2-16 *Tax Services.* What materials are generally found in leading tax services? Which does your library have?

YOU MAKE THE CALL

2-17 T is the owner of a small CPA firm that has developed a very good auditing and tax practice over the years. Recently, while visiting the home of S, his best client (revenues of about $50,000 annually for audit and tax services), T learned some very disturbing information about S's business practices. During a tour of her home, S accidentally revealed that some very expensive personal entertainment equipment acquired this year had been charged to her corporation (cost of approximately $100,000). S stated that everyone she knew charged personal assets to their business accounts and that it appeared to be generally accepted practice. She said she hoped T would not mind.

When T returned to his office, he immediately checked S's 2013 corporate income tax return and found that depreciation had been taken on the $100,000 cost of assets listed simply as "Equipment." Of course, T never suspected the assets were for personal use in S's home.

What should T do? This client is too good to lose, but T is worried about the consequences of allowing this type of behavior to continue.

PROBLEMS

2-18 *Interpreting Citations.* Interpret each of the following citations:
   a. Reg. § 1.721-1(a).
   b. Rev. Rul. 60-314, 1960-2 C.B. 48.
   c. Rev. Proc. 86-46, 1986-2 C.B. 739.
   d. Rev. Rul. 98-36, I.R.B. No. 31, 6.
   e. § 351.

2-19 *Citation Abbreviations.* Explain each of the abbreviations below.
   a. B.T.A.
   b. Acq.
   c. D. Ct.
   d. CA-9
   e. F.Supp.
   f. NA.
   g. Ct. Cls.
   h. USTC
   i. AFTR
   j. *Cert. Den.*
   k. *aff'g* and *aff'd*
   l. *rev'g* and *rev'd*
   m. *rem'g* and *rem'd*

2-20 *Interpreting Citations.* Identify the publisher and interpret each of the following citations:
   a. 41 TCM 289.
   b. 71-1 USTC ¶9241 (CA-2, 1971).
   c. 236 F. Supp. 761 (D. Ct. Va., 1974).
   d. T.C. Memo 1977-20.
   e. 48 T.C. 430 (1967).
   f. 6 AFTR2d 5095 (CA-2, 1960).
   g. 589 F.2d 446 (CA-9, 1979).
   h. 277 U.S. 508 (USSC, 1928).

2-21 *Citation Form.* Record the following information in its proper citation form.
   a. Part 7, subdivision (a)(2) of the income tax Regulation under Code § 165
   b. The 34th Revenue Ruling issued March 2, 1987, and printed on page 168 of the Cumulative Bulletin
   c. The 113th letter ruling issued the last week of 1986

2-22 *Citation Form.* Record the following information in its proper citation form.
   a. A 1982 U.S. Tax Court case in which Roger A. Schubel sued the IRS Commissioner for a refund, published in volume 77 on pages 701 through 715 as a Regular decision.
   b. A 1974 U.S. Tax Court case in which H. N. Schilling, Jr. sued the IRS Commissioner for a refund, published by (1) Commerce Clearing House in volume 33 on pages 1097 through 1110 and (2) Research Institute of America (Prentice Hall) as its 246th decision that year.
   c. A 1966 Court of Appeals case in which Boris Nodiak sued the IRS Commissioner in the second Circuit for a refund, published by (1) Commerce Clearing House in volume 1 of that year at paragraph 9262, (2) Prentice Hall in volume 17 on pages 396 through 402, and (3) West Publishing Company in volume 356 on pages 911 through 919.

TAX RESEARCH PROBLEMS

2-23 *Using a Citator.* Use either the Commerce Clearing House or Research Institute of America Citator in your library and locate *Richard L. Kroll, Exec. v. U.S.*
   a. Which Court of Appeals Circuit heard this case?
   b. Was this case heard by the Supreme Court?
   c. James B. and Doris E. Wallach are included in the listing below the citation for Kroll. In what court was the Wallach case heard?

2-24 *Using a Citator.* Using any available citator, locate the case of *Corn Products v. Comm.,* 350 U.S. 46. What effect did the decision in *Arkansas Best v. Comm.* (58 AFTR2d 86-5748, 800 F.2d 219) have on the precedential value of the *Corn Products* case?

2-25 *Locating Court Cases.* Locate the case of *Robert Autrey, Jr. v. United States,* 89-2 USTC ¶9659, and answer the following questions.
   a. What court decided the case on appeal?
   b. What court originally tried the case?
   c. Was the trial court's decision upheld or reversed?

2-26 *Locating Court Cases.* Locate the case of *Fabry v. Commissioner,* 111 T.C. 305, and answer the following questions.
   a. What court tried the case?
   b. Identify the various types of precedential authority the judge used in framing his opinion.

2-27 *Locating Court Cases.* Locate the cited court cases and answer the questions below.
   a. *Stanley A. and Lorriee M. Golanty,* 72 T.C. 411 (1979). Did the taxpayers win their case?
   b. *Hamilton D. Hill,* 41 TCM 700, T.C. Memo ¶71,127 (1971). Who was the presiding judge?
   c. *Patterson (Jefferson) v. Comm.,* 72-1 USTC ¶9420, 29 AFTR2d 1181 (Ct. Cls., 1972). What was the issue being questioned in this case?

2-28 *Completing Citations.* To the extent the materials are available to you, complete the following citations:
   a. Rev. Rul. 98-60, _____ C.B. _____.
   b. *Lawrence W. McCoy,* _____ T.C. _____ 1962.
   c. *Reginald Turner* _____ TCM _____ T.C. Memo 1954-38.
   d. *RCA Corp. v. U.S.,* _____ USTC _____ (CA-2, 1981).
   e. *RCA Corp. v. U.S.,* _____ AFTR2d _____ (CA-2, 1981).
   f. *RCA Corp. v. U.S.,* _____ F.2d _____ (CA-2, 1981).
   g. *Comm. v. Wilcox,* _____ S. Ct. _____ (USSC, 1946).
   h. _____, 79-1 USTC ¶9139 (USSC, 1979).
   i. _____, 34 T.C. 842 (1960).
   j. *Brian E. Knutson,* 60 TCM 540, T.C. Memo _____
   k. *Samuel B. Levin v. Comm.,* 43 AFTR2d 79-1057 (_____).

2-29 *Examination of Tax Sources.* For each of the tax sources listed below, identify at least one of the tax issues involved. In addition, if the source has a temporary citation, provide its permanent citation (if available).
   a. *Battelstein Investment Co. v. U.S.,* 71-1 USTC ¶9227, 27 AFTR2d 71-713, 442 F.2d 87 (CA-5, 1971).
   b. *Joel Kerns,* 47 TCM, _____ T.C. Memo 1984-22.
   c. *Patterson v. U.S.,* 84-1 USTC ¶9315 (CA-6, 1984).
   d. *Webster Lair,* 95 T.C. 484 (1990).
   e. *Thompson Engineering Co., Inc.,* 80 T.C. 672 (1983).
   f. *Towne Square, Inc.,* 45 TCM 478, T.C. Memo 1983-10.
   g. Rev. Rul. 85-13, I.R.B. No. 7, 28.
   h. Rev. Proc. 85-49, I.R.B. No. 40, 26.
   i. *William E Sutton, et al. v. Comm.,* 84 T.C. _____ No. 17.
   j. Rev. Rul. 86-103, I.R.B. No. 36, 13.
   k. *Hughes Properties, Inc.,* 86-1 USTC ¶9440, 58 AFTR2d 86-5062, _____ U.S. _____ (USSC, 1986).
   l. Rev. Rul. 98-27, I.R.B. No. 22, 4.

2-30 *Office in the Home.* T comes to you for advice regarding the deductibility of expenses for maintaining an office in his home. T is currently employed as an executive vice president for Zandy Corporation. He has found it impossible to complete his job responsibilities during the normal forty-hour weekly period. Although the office building in which he works is open nights and weekends, the heating and air-conditioning systems are shut down at night (from 6 p.m.) and during the entire weekend. As a result, T has begun taking work home with him on a regular basis. The work is generally done in the den of T's home. Although T's employer does not require him to work at home, T is convinced that he would be fired if his work assignments were not completed on a timely basis. Given these facts, what would you advise T about taking a home-office deduction?

Partial list of research aids:

Section 280A.

Proposed Reg. § 1.280A.

M.G. Hill, 43 TCM 832, T.C. Memo 1982-143.

2-31 *Journal Articles.* Refer to *Problem 2-30.* Consult an index to periodicals (e.g., AICPA's *Accountants Index;* Warren, Gorham, and Lamont's *Index to Federal Tax Articles;* or CCH's *Federal Tax Articles*) and locate a journal article on the topic of tax deductions for an office in the home. Copy the article. Record the citation for the article (i.e., author's name, article title, journal name, publication date, and first and last pages of the article) at the top of your paper. Prepare a two-page summary of the article, including all relevant issues, research sources, and conclusions. Staple your two-page summary to the article. The grade for this exercise will be based on the relevance of your article to the topic, the accuracy and quality of your summary, and the quality of your written communication skills.

2-32 *Deductible Medical Expenses.* B suffers from a severe form of degenerative arthritis. Her doctor strongly recommended that she swim for at least one hour per day in order to stretch and exercise her leg and arm muscles. There are no swimming pools nearby, so B spent $15,000 to have a swimming pool installed in her back yard. This expenditure increased the fair market value of her house by $5,000. B consults you about whether she can deduct the cost of the swimming pool on her individual tax return. What do you recommend?

Hint: You should approach this problem by using the tax service volumes of either Commerce Clearing House or Research Institute of America. Both tax services are organized according to Code Sections, so you should start with Code § 213. You will find the Code Sections on the back binding of the volumes. Research Institute of America has a very extensive index, so look under the term "medical expenses."

2-33 *Deductible Educational Expenses.* T is a CPA with a large accounting firm in Houston, Texas. He has been assigned to the international taxation group of his firm's tax department. As a result of this assignment, T enrolls in an international tax law course at the University of Houston Law School. The authorities of the University require T to enroll as a regular law student; and, theoretically, if he continues to attend courses, T will graduate with a law degree. Will T be able to deduct his tuition for the international tax law course as a business expense?

Hint: Go to either the RIA or CCH tax service and use it to find the analysis of Code § 162. When you have found the discussion of § 162, find that part of the subsection dealing with educational deductions. Read the appropriate Regulations and then note the authorities listed after the Regulations. Read over the summaries provided and then choose those you think have the most relevance to the question asked above. Read these cases and other listed authorities, and formulate a written response to the question asked in light of these cases and other authorities Finally, for the authorities you choose, go to the RIA or CCH Citator and use it to ensure that your authorities are current.

3

Taxable Entities; Tax Formula; Introduction to Property Transactions

Learning Objectives

Upon completion of this chapter you will be able to:

LO.1 Identify the entities that are subject to the Federal income tax.

LO.2 Explain the basic tax treatment of individuals, corporations, partnerships, S corporations, and fiduciary taxpayers (trusts and estates).

LO.3 Understand the basic tax formulas to be followed in computing the tax liability for individuals and corporations.

LO.4 Define many of the basic terms used in the tax formula such as gross income, adjusted gross income, taxable income, exclusion, deduction, and credit.

LO.5 Identify other taxes, including the alternative minimum tax and the net investment income tax.

LO.6 Calculate the gain or loss on the disposition of property and explain the tax consequences, including the special treatment of capital gains and losses.

Chapter Outline

Introduction

The amount of income tax ultimately paid by any taxpayer is determined by applying the many rules comprising our income tax system. This chapter examines some of the fundamental features of this system. They are:

- *Taxable Entities*—those entities that are subject to taxation and those that are merely conduits.

- *Tax Formulas*—the mathematical relationships used to compute the tax for the various taxable entities.

- *Property Transactions*—the tax treatment of sales, exchanges, and other dispositions of property.

This chapter, in covering the essentials, provides a bird's-eye view of the entire income tax system. For many, this may be sufficient. This one chapter may contain enough tax law and have more than enough detail for some. Nevertheless, it is just part of the picture. Many of the details as well as the conceptual basis for some of these provisions are left to later chapters. This can be frustrating to those who want more or know that more exists, but the major purpose of this chapter is to establish the basic framework in which the implications of any particular transaction on taxable income can be assessed. To this end, the chapter gives not only a brief description of what is taxable and what is deductible but also a glimpse of such complex topics as the passive loss rules and the alternative minimum tax. Remember, the goal is not necessarily to provide a detailed discussion of all the rules but to provide a foundation so that problems, pitfalls, and opportunities can be recognized.

THE TAXABLE ENTITY

LO.1

Identify the entities that are subject to the Federal income tax.

The income tax is imposed on the income of some type of entity. Unfortunately, there is no uniform agreement on what is the theoretically correct unit of taxation. There are a variety of legal, economic, social, and natural entities that Congress could select: individuals (natural persons), family units, households (those living together), sole proprietorships, partnerships, corporations, trusts, estates, governments, religious groups, nonprofit organizations, and other voluntary or cooperative associations. Despite the disagreement over which of these or other entities are the proper choices, Congress has provided that only certain entities are responsible for actually paying the tax. According to the Code, individuals, most corporations, and fiduciaries (estates and trusts) are taxable entities. Other entities, such as sole proprietorships, partnerships, and so-called "S" corporations, are not required to pay tax on any taxable income they might have. Instead, the taxable income of these entities is passed through or allocated to their owners, who bear the responsibility for paying any tax that may be due. For this reason, these entities are often referred to as flow-through entities or conduits. Exhibit 3-1 summarizes the various types of entities.

EXHIBIT 3-1	Types of Entities
Taxpaying Entities	*Flow-Through Entities or Conduits*
Individuals	Sole proprietorships
C corporations (regular corporations)	Partnerships and limited liability companies
Trusts	S corporations
Estates	

> ### Example 1
>
> R and S are equal partners in a partnership that had taxable income of $50,000 in the current year. The partnership does not pay tax on the $50,000. Rather, the income is allocated equally between R and S. Thus, both R and S will report $25,000 of partnership income on their individual returns and pay the required tax regardless of whether they received distributions from the partnership.

In the following sections, the general tax treatment of the taxable entities—individuals, corporations, and fiduciaries—is explained along with the treatment of flow-through entities, sole proprietorships, partnerships and "S" corporations. The specific tax treatment of entities other than individuals is discussed separately in later chapters. However, it should be emphasized that many of the tax rules applying to one entity also apply to other entities. These similarities are pointed out as the various rules are discussed.

Taxable Entities

INDIVIDUAL TAXPAYERS

The primary target for the income tax is the *individual* taxpayer. For 2015, about 149 million individual returns were filed (Forms 1040, 1040A, and 1040 EZ), and these were responsible for about 54% of the total tax revenue collected by the federal government. This amount easily exceeded the second and third place finishers, employment taxes (31%) and corporate income taxes (12%).[1] These statistics leave little doubt about the importance of the individual income tax in the United States.

LO.2

Explain the basic tax treatment of individuals, corporations, partnerships, S corporations, and fiduciary taxpayers (trusts and estates).

Citizens and Residents of the United States

Section 1 of the Internal Revenue Code provides that a tax is imposed on the taxable income of all individuals. As might be expected, the term *individual* generally applies to U.S. citizens. However, it also includes persons who are *not* U.S. citizens but who are considered residents, so-called *resident aliens.* Thus, if Prince Harry decides to move to New York to escape the tabloids of London, he could be subject to U.S. taxes even though he is not a U.S. citizen. The same could be said for a Japanese citizen working for Honda in Marysville, Ohio or a Canadian citizen who lives and works in Detroit. Whether these people are residents requires application of a complicated test.[2] The key point to remember is that foreign citizens who are not merely visiting but stay for an extended period must worry about the need for filing.[3] As discussed below, the tax would be levied on both their U.S. income and any foreign income.

Foreign Taxpayers

Individuals who are not U.S. citizens and who do not qualify as residents may be subject to U.S. tax. These persons, referred to as *nonresident aliens,* are taxed on certain types of income that are received from U.S. sources.[4] If the income is derived from a trade or business carried on in the United States, that income is taxed in the same way as it is for a citizen or resident. Most other income earned in the United States is taxed at a flat rate of 30 percent. However, there are a number of special rules that must be observed.

Age

It should be noted that the age of an individual is not a factor in determining if he or she is a taxpaying entity. Whether the individual is eight years old or eighty years old, he or she is still subject to tax on any taxable income received. Contrary to the belief of some people, a child's income is taxed to the child and not the parent. As explained later, age may have an impact on *both* the method of computing the tax and the amount of tax owed; it does not, however, impact the individual's status as a taxpayer.

---

[1] *2015 IRS Data Book,* Table 1 Collections, by Type of Tax and Table 2 Number of Returns and Other Forms Filed, by Type of Return, Fiscal Years 2014–2015.

[2] See § 7701(b) for a definition of the "substantial presence test" that is used to determine if an individual is a resident alien and subject to U.S. tax.

[3] Reg. § 1.871-2(b).

[4] § 871.

Worldwide Income

The Federal income tax on individuals applies not only to domestic (U.S.) source income, but also to income from foreign sources. In other words, a U.S. citizen is subject to U.S. taxation on his or her worldwide income regardless of where he or she lives (e.g., Rhode Island or Rome) or the source of the income (e.g., Connecticut or Copenhagen). It is therefore possible to have foreign source income taxed by more than one country (e.g., the foreign country and the United States). Several provisions exist to prevent or minimize double taxation, however. For example, U.S. citizens and residents living abroad may claim either the foreign tax credit (a direct reduction in the tax)[5] or deduct such taxes.[6]

In lieu of claiming a credit or deduction for foreign taxes, a U.S. citizen who works and lives in a foreign country may exclude from his or her U.S. income certain amounts of income earned abroad.[7] The foreign earned income exclusion is adjusted annually for inflation and for 2017 is $102,100. An individual qualifies for the exclusion if he or she maintains his or her tax home in a foreign country (i.e., his or her principal place of business is in the foreign country) and he or she is either a bona fide resident of a foreign country or is physically present in a foreign country for 330 days in any 12 consecutive months. To ensure that the taxpayer's taxable income (i.e., the amount not excluded) is taxed at the rate that the taxpayer would have paid without the exclusion, a special computation is required. The tax is determined by first calculating the amount of income tax on total income without the exclusion and then subtracting the tax on the amount of foreign earned income that is excluded. The result is the amount of the federal income tax liability.

Example 2

R, a U.S. citizen, is a construction supervisor who was temporarily assigned to work in Paris, France. R lived in Paris all of 2017 except for two weeks when he came back to the United States to visit relatives. From his French job, he earned $112,100 in 2017. Because R's tax home is in a foreign country and he was present in the foreign country for at least 330 days during 12 consecutive months, he meets the physical presence test and may exclude $102,100 of his $112,100 salary. The remaining $10,000 plus any other income, such as dividends and interest, are subject to tax. In this case, his final tax liability generally would be the difference between the tax on $112,100 and the tax on $102,100, effectively taxing the $10,000 at the rate at which it would have been taxed without the exclusion.

In addition to the relief measures mentioned above, taxpayers may exclude, subject to certain limitations, allowances (in-kind or cash) for foreign housing. Also, tax treaties often exist that deal with the problem of double taxation by the United States and foreign countries.

State Income Taxes

While virtually the entire focus of this text is on the federal income tax, state income taxes cannot be ignored. All but seven states have a state income tax imposed on individuals. The seven that do not have an income tax are: Alaska, Florida, Nevada, South Dakota, Texas, Washington, and Wyoming. However, the income taxes of New Hampshire and Tennessee extend only to interest and dividends. Thus the vast majority of all individuals must pay not only federal income taxes but also state and local income taxes.

As might be expected, states that impose an income tax do not necessarily follow the federal rules. Each has its own unique method to compute taxable income. Of the 41 states with an income tax, 25 begin their calculation with federal adjusted gross income, 8 use federal taxable income as the starting point, and 3 use the federal income tax liability as the basis for their tax. To make matters more challenging, some states conform with the methods allowed for federal tax purposes (e.g., depreciation) while others do not. As might be imagined, the world of state and local taxes can become quite complex.

The important concept to grasp here is not how the various state laws work but whether they apply to the taxpayer at all. Those working in tax must not overlook the possibility that

---

[5] § 901.

[6] § 164(a).

[7] § 911(a).

a taxpayer may be responsible not only for federal taxes but for state or local taxes as well. For example, consider a professional football player, say Peyton Manning of the Denver Broncos who lives in Denver and files a Colorado income tax return. If he plays a game in Philadelphia, must he file a state income tax return for Pennsylvania and perhaps another return for the city of Philadelphia? Similarly, if a staff accountant working for a national accounting firm in Chicago is assigned temporarily to an audit in Denver, must he pay income taxes in Colorado? If a son is a professor at Michigan State but is a shareholder in his father's S corporation that operates a farm in Iowa, must the son pay Iowa taxes? At this juncture, the answer is not as important as asking the question!

CORPORATE TAXPAYERS

Section 11 of the Internal Revenue Code imposes a tax on all corporations. The corporate income tax applies to both domestic corporations and foreign corporations that operate a trade or business in the United States.[8] However, the federal tax treatment of a corporation differs depending on whether it is a "C" corporation (a regular corporation) or an "S" corporation. For tax purposes, a corporation is treated as a C corporation unless it is eligible and elects to be treated as an S corporation. C corporations, like individuals, are treated as separate taxable entities. On the other hand, S corporations normally are not separate taxable entities but are treated as conduits, passing their income and losses through to their shareholders (as discussed below). It should be emphasized that this difference—C or S—is made only for tax purposes. For all other purposes (e.g., liability), the applicable state laws make no distinction.

The overall income tax treatment of corporations is quite similar to that of individuals. In fact, all of the basic rules governing income, exclusions, deductions, and credits apply to individuals as well as C corporations and, for that matter, fiduciaries. For example, the general rule concerning what is deductible, found in § 162, allows *all* taxpayers a deduction for trade or business expenses. Similarly, § 103 provides that *all* taxpayers are allowed to exclude interest income from state and local bonds. Although many of the general rules are the same for both individuals and corporations, there are several key differences.

The most obvious difference can be seen by comparing the corporate and individual formulas for determining taxable income as found in Exhibits 3-2 and 3-3. The concepts of adjusted gross income and itemized deductions found in the individual tax formula are conspicuously absent from the corporate formula. Other major differences in determining taxable income involve the treatment of particular items, such as dividend income and charitable contributions. These and other differences are discussed in detail in Chapter 19. It should be emphasized once again, however, that most of the basic rules apply whether the taxpayer is a corporation or an individual.

EXHIBIT 3-2	Tax Formula for Corporate Taxpayers

Total income (from whatever source)	$xxx,xxx
Less: Exclusions from gross income	− xx,xxx
Gross income	$xxx,xxx
Less: Deductions	− xx,xxx
Taxable income	$xxx,xxx
Applicable tax rates	xx%
Gross tax	$ xx,xxx
Less: Tax credits and prepayments	− x,xxx
Tax due (or refund)	$ xx,xxx

LO.3
Understand the basic tax formulas to be followed in computing the tax liability for individuals and corporations.

[8] § 882(a). See Chapter 19 for more details.

EXHIBIT 3-3	**Tax Formula for Individual Taxpayers**

Income (from whatever source)			$xxx,xxx
Less:	Exclusions from gross income		− xx,xxx
Gross income			$xxx,xxx
Less:	Deductions *for* adjusted gross income		− xx,xxx
Adjusted gross income			$xxx,xxx
Less:	1. The larger of:		
	a. Standard deduction	$x,xxx	
	or	*or*	− x,xxx
	b. Total itemized deductions	$x,xxx	
	2. Number of personal and dependency		
	exemptions × exemption amount		− x,xxx
Taxable income			$xxx,xxx
	Applicable tax rates (from Tables or Schedules X, Y, or Z)		xx%
Gross income tax			$ xx,xxx
Plus:	Additional taxes (e.g., self-employment tax, alternative		
	minimum tax, recapture of tax credits)		+ x,xxx
Less:	Tax credits and prepayments		− x,xxx
Tax due (or refund)			$ xx,xxx

One difference in the taxation of individuals and corporations that is not apparent from the basic formula, but which should be noted, concerns the tax rates that each uses in computing the tax liability (see the inside back cover of the text). A comparison of the individual and corporate tax rates shows a somewhat similar progression: 10 to 35 percent for individuals and 15 to 39 percent for corporations. But note that the rates apply at quite different levels of income.

Perhaps the most critical aspect of corporate taxation that is generally not shared with any other taxable entity concerns the potential for double taxation. When a corporation receives income and subsequently distributes that income as a dividend to its shareholders, the effect is to tax the income twice: once at the corporate level and again at the shareholder level. Double taxation can occur because the corporation is not allowed to deduct any dividend payments to its shareholders. As one might suspect, many have questioned the equity of this treatment, arguing that it penalizes those who elect to do business in the corporate form. Note, however, that this treatment is consistent with the fact that the corporation is considered a separate legal entity. Moreover, it is often argued that the corporation and its owners in reality do not bear the burden of the corporate tax. According to the argument, corporations are able to shift the tax burden either to consumers by charging higher prices or to employees by paying lower wages. In addition, those who reject the double tax theory often note that closely held corporations, whose owners may also be employees of the business, are able to avoid double taxation to the extent they can characterize any corporate distributions as deductible salary payments rather than nondeductible dividends. Whether in fact double taxation does or does not occur, it appears that this feature, which has been part of the U.S. tax system since its inception, is unlikely to change in the immediate future.

Example 3

J owns all of the stock of ZZ Inc., a C corporation. This year ZZ reported taxable income of $1,000,000 before considering any distributions to J. Assume that ZZ is in the 34% marginal tax bracket while J is in 39.6% bracket. J plans on withdrawing $600,000 from the corporation. Ignoring payroll taxes, is J better off if he causes the corporation to distribute $600,000 as a qualifying dividend or $600,000 as a salary?

Taxpaying Entities	ZZ Inc.	J	Total
Taxable income before distributions to J..........	$1,000,000		
Distributions to J nondeductible dividend........	—	$600,000	
Taxable income	$1,000,000	$600,000	
Tax rate	× 34%	× 20%	
Total tax.................................	$ 340,000	$120,000	$460,000

Distribution Treated as a Salary			
Taxable income before distributions to J..........	$1,000,000		
Distributions to J deductible salary.............	(600,000)	$600,000	
Taxable income	$ 400,000	$600,000	
Tax rate	× 34%	× 39.6%	
Total tax.................................	$ 136,000	$237,600	$373,600
Savings			$ 86,400

As calculated above, J saves $86,400 by withdrawing the $600,000 as a salary rather than as a dividend. The savings result because $600,000 of the total income is taxed twice when it is distributed as a dividend (once at the corporate level and again at the individual level) but only once when the distribution is treated as a salary because the corporation is allowed to deduct the salary payment as a business expense. Note that ignoring the net investment income tax the qualifying dividend is taxed at a maximum rate of 20% (2017).

Special rules apply to the formation of a corporation, corporate dividend distributions, and distributions made to shareholders in exchange for their stock. Penalty taxes also may be assessed against corporations that try to shelter income from high personal tax rates by accumulating it in the corporation, rather than making dividend distributions. These topics and others related to the income taxation of corporations and their owners are discussed in Chapter 19.

FIDUCIARY TAXPAYERS

A *fiduciary* is a person who is entrusted with property for the benefit of another, the *beneficiary*. The individual or entity that acts as a fiduciary is responsible for managing and administering the entrusted property, at all times faithfully performing the required duties with the utmost care and prudence.

Two types of fiduciary relationships are the trust and the estate. The trust is a legal entity created when the title of property is transferred by a person (the *grantor*) to the fiduciary (the *trustee*). The trustee is required to implement the instructions of the grantor as specified in the trust agreement. Typically, the property is held in trust for a minor or some other person until he or she reaches a certain age or until some specified event occurs.

An estate is also recognized as a legal entity, established by law when a person dies. Upon the person's death, his or her property generally passes to the estate, where it is administered by the fiduciary until it is distributed to the beneficiaries. Both trusts and estates are treated as taxpaying entities.

The Code specifically provides for a tax on the taxable income of estates and trusts.[9] Determining the tax for such entities is very similar to determining the tax for individuals, with one major exception.[10] When distributions are made to beneficiaries, the distributed income is generally taxed to the beneficiary rather than to the estate or trust.[11] In essence, the trust or estate is permitted to reduce its taxable income by the amount of the distribution—acting as a *conduit*, since the distributed income flows through to the beneficiaries.

Example 4

T is the trustee of a trust established for the benefit of A and B. The trust generated $4,000 of income subject to tax for the current year and no distributions were made to either A or B during the year. The trustee files an annual fiduciary tax return for the year and pays the tax based on the $4,000 taxable amount.

Example 5

Assume that for the next year the trust in *Example 4* had $10,000 of income subject to tax and that distributions of $2,000 each were made to A and B. The trustee files an annual trust return for the year and pays a tax based on $6,000 ($10,000 taxable income − $4,000 distributions). A and B each include $2,000 in their income tax returns for the year.

Distributions made by a trust or estate from its corpus (also called the trust property or principal), including undistributed profits from prior years, generally are not taxable to the beneficiary.[12] This is because these distributions are part of a gift or inheritance or have been taxed previously. Similarly, the trust or estate is not entitled to deductions for these nontaxable distributions.[13]

Flow-Through Entities

SOLE PROPRIETORSHIPS

LO.2

Explain the basic tax treatment of individuals, corporations, partnerships, S corporations, and fiduciary taxpayers (trusts and estates).

The first of the nontaxpaying, flow-through entities is the sole proprietorship. A sole proprietorship is commonly defined as an unincorporated business owned by one individual. The definition includes essentially all individuals who are in business for themselves. Indeed, while they may not think of themselves as proprietors, individuals who are self-employed (e.g., doctors, lawyers, accountants, consultants, plumbers, carpenters) as well as independent contractors are taxed as sole proprietorships. In addition, for tax purposes, a single member limited liability company (SMLLC) that does not elect to be treated as a corporation is disregarded as an entity separate from its owner and is treated as a sole proprietorship.

The tax treatment of sole proprietorships differs somewhat from that of financial accounting. For financial accounting purposes, the business activities of the proprietor are treated as distinct from other activities of the owner. The sole proprietorship is considered a

[9] §§ 1(e) and 641(a).

[10] § 641(b).

[11] §§ 651 and 661.

[12] § 662.

[13] § 661. For further information on the income taxation of fiduciaries, see *Corporate, Partnership, Estate and Gift Taxation*, 2018 Edition, Chapter 16.

totally independent accounting entity for which separate records and reports are maintained. For tax purposes, a similar approach applies except the sole proprietorship is not a separate taxable entity. For this reason, it does not file its own tax return. Instead, the income and deductions from operating a proprietorship are summarized and reported on Schedule C of the owner's personal income tax return along with other tax items (See Appendix B for Form 1040 and Schedule C).

Although some might not consider a sole proprietorship as a "flow-through" entity in the same sense that partnerships and S corporations are, they clearly function in much the same way. In essence, a sole proprietorship serves as a conduit through which its net income or loss flows through to the individual. Any item of income or deduction of the proprietorship that might receive some type of special treatment had the owner received or paid it directly—rather than running it through the business—is not included on the Schedule C but is reported separately on the owner's personal return (e.g., interest income, capital gains, charitable contributions). Distributions or withdrawals that an owner receives from a proprietorship are not considered salary or other income since all of the proprietorship income is included on the individual's return regardless of whether it is distributed. Therefore, a proprietor's "draw" is ignored.

Example 6

K is employed as a law professor at State University, where she earns a salary of $102,000. K also operates a part-time consulting practice as a sole proprietorship. She maintains a separate checking account for the business. The business earned net income of $30,000 this year before considering $50 of interest earned on the money in the business' checking account, a $100 charitable contribution drawn on the business account to the United Way and a withdrawal of $18,000. How are the activities reported?

The sole proprietorship does not file a separate return and pay tax. Instead, K reports the sole proprietorship's income of $30,000 on her Schedule C. This amount is subsequently combined with her salary of $102,000 and other income and deductions on her return to compute her taxable income. She then pays both the income and self-employment taxes required. The $50 of interest income is not considered part of the proprietorship income but is aggregated with other interest income that K might have and is reported separately (Schedule B). The same approach is used for the charitable contribution. The contribution is treated as if K had made it personally and would be deducted as an itemized deduction on Schedule A if K itemizes. The $18,000 withdrawal is ignored since it represents either part of her original investment in the business or income that is currently or previously reported on Schedule C.

It is easy to dismiss sole proprietorships in a world dominated by multinational corporations. Indeed IRS statistics bare this out, indicating that in 2012, proprietorships accounted for only 10.32% of the net income reported by businesses. Nevertheless, based on returns filed for that year, proprietorships cannot be ignored. The number of proprietorship returns (nonfarm) far exceeded the number for corporations and partnerships: 23.55 million proprietorships (71.89% of total returns for C and S corporations, partnerships and nonfarm proprietorships) versus 1.62 million C corporations (4.94%), 4.21 million S corporations (12.83%) and 3.39 million partnerships (10.34%).[14]

PARTNERSHIPS

A partnership is a conduit for Federal income tax purposes. This means that the partnership itself is not subject to Federal income tax and that all items of partnership income, expense, gain, loss, or credit pass through to the partners and are given their tax effect at the partner level.[15] The partnership is required to file an information return (Form 1065) reporting the results of the partnership's transactions and how those results are divided among the partners. Each partner's share of the various items are reported to the partner on Schedule K-1.

---

[14] *The Statistics of Income Tax Stats—Integrated Business Data*   [15] § 701.
   https://www.irs.gov/uac/SOI-Tax-Stats-Integrated-Business-
   Data Table 1: Selected Financial Data on Businesses.

Using this information, the partners each report their respective shares of the items on their own tax returns.[16] Because partners pay taxes on their shares of the partnership income regardless of whether it is distributed, distributions made by the partnership generally are not taxable to the partners.[17]

Example 7

For its current calendar year, EG Partnership had taxable income of $18,000. During the year, each of its two equal partners received cash distributions of $4,000. The partnership is not subject to tax, and each partner must include $9,000 in his annual income tax return, despite the fact that each partner actually received less than this amount in cash. The distributions normally are not taxable since they represent previously taxed income. The partnership must file an annual information return reporting the results of its operations and the effect of these operations on each partner.

A characteristic of a partnership (as well as an S corporation or sole proprietorship) that deserves special emphasis is the treatment of losses. If a business is typical, it will take several years of operation before it can be declared a profitable venture. Until that time, expenses normally exceed revenues and the result is a net loss. In the case of a conduit entity such as a partnership, that net loss flows through to the owners, who are generally allowed to offset it against any other income they may have. In contrast, if a regular C corporation sustains a loss, referred to as a net operating loss, or NOL, the shareholders do not benefit from that loss directly. A C corporation is allowed, like individuals, to use the loss to offset taxable income of prior or subsequent years. Generally, losses are carried back two years and forward 20 years. For example, the taxpayer would first carry back the loss to the second prior year and offset it against any taxable income. In such case, the taxpayer would file a claim for a tax refund. Any remaining loss is carried to the first prior year. Any remaining loss is carried forward for 20 years. The key point to remember is that the losses of a partnership flow through and thus may provide immediate benefit, whereas those of a C corporation do not flow through and can be used only if the corporation has income in other tax years.

In some respects, the partnership is treated as a separate entity for tax purposes. For example, many tax elections are made by the partnership,[18] and a partnership interest generally is treated as a single asset when sold.[19] On the other hand, transactions between the partners and partnership are sometimes treated as if the partner was an independent third party and sometimes special rules apply.[20] For example, an individual partner who performs services for the partnership in his or her role as a partner is generally not considered an employee for tax purposes. Payments for the performance of such services are not considered salaries or wages. Consequently, the payments are not subject to withholding or employment taxes and are not reported to the partner at the end of the year on Form W-2. Instead, these so-called "guaranteed payments" are reported to the partner on a Schedule K-1 and are subject to self-employment taxes. Consistent with this approach, a partner does not qualify for the favorable tax treatment of certain employee fringe benefits (see Chapter 6). In addition, a partner's share of any trade or business income of the partnership is generally subject to self-employment taxes. These and other controlling provisions related to the Federal income tax treatment of partnerships are introduced in Chapter 19.

---

[16] § 702(a).

[17] § 731(a).

[18] § 703(b).

[19] § 741 states that the sale or exchange of an interest in a partnership shall generally be treated as the sale of a capital asset.

[20] § 707(a).

ELECTING SMALL BUSINESS CORPORATIONS: "S" CORPORATIONS

The Internal Revenue Code allows certain closely held corporations to elect to be treated as conduits (like partnerships) for Federal income tax purposes. The election is made pursuant to the rules contained in Subchapter S of the Code.[21] For this reason, such corporations are referred to as *S corporations*. Not all corporations are eligible to elect S status. The only corporations that qualify are those that have 100 or fewer shareholders and meet certain other tests.

If a corporation elects S corporation status, it is taxed in virtually the same fashion as a partnership. Like a partnership, the S corporation's items of income, expense, gain, or loss pass through to the shareholders to be given their tax effect at the shareholder level. Salaries and wages of shareholders who work for the corporation and other employees are reported on a Form W-2 and are subject to withholding of income taxes and FICA (that is matched by the employer corporation). Although employees generally qualify for favorable treatment of fringe benefits, shareholder-employees owning 2% or more of the corporation's stock do not. As a result, the value of any fringe benefits, such as medical insurance coverage, is taxable as compensation to the employee-shareholder (who is allowed to deduct it). Distributions from an S corporation, like those from partnerships, normally are nontaxable since they usually represent previously taxed income.

The S corporation files an information return (Form 1120S) similar to that of a partnership, reporting the results of the corporation's transactions and how those results are allocated among the shareholders. The individual shareholders report their respective shares of the various items on their own tax returns. Chapter 19 contains an introductory discussion of the taxation of S corporations and their shareholders.

LIMITED LIABILITY COMPANIES

All 50 states and the District of Columbia have passed legislation creating a relatively new form of business entity: the limited liability company (LLC). What is this new creature and how is it taxed? Perhaps the best characterization of an LLC is that it is a cross between a partnership and a corporation. LLCs are created under state law by filing articles of organization. The owners of an LLC are called members and can be individuals, partnerships, regular corporations, S corporations, trusts, or other LLCs. Although some states allow single-member LLCs, two or more members usually form the entity. Like a corporation, an LLC can act on its own behalf and sue and be sued. Also like a corporation, members generally possess limited liability except that they may be liable for their own acts of malpractice in those states that allow professionals to form LLCs.

The tax law does not specifically address the tax treatment of an LLC. Initially, this omission caused some uncertainty as to whether an LLC should be taxed as a corporation or a partnership. To eliminate this confusion, the Treasury issued the so-called check-the-box regulations.[22] Under these rules, an LLC with two or more owners is treated as a partnership for tax purposes unless it elects to be treated as a corporation (i.e., the LLC is a partnership unless it checks the box on Form 8832 to be treated as a regular C corporation). An LLC with only one member is disregarded and treated as a sole proprietorship, unless it elects to be treated as a corporation.

The treatment of LLCs for self-employment tax purposes has also produced some confusion. As noted above, in the case of a partnership, a partner's share of partnership income is generally self-employment income subject to self-employment taxes. However, this rule is true only for general partners. Historically, limited partners have been treated differently on the theory that their role is similar to that of an investor rather than someone who is actively involved in the business. Consequently, a limited partner's share of partnership income has been viewed more similar to investment income (e.g., dividends and interest) than business income. Section 1402(a)(13) reflects this line of reasoning, providing that a limited partner's share of partnership income is not subject to self-employment tax. However, based

---

[21] §§ 1361 through 1379.

[22] Reg. § 301.7701-3.

on this approach, it was not clear whether a member of an LLC was to be treated like a limited partner, in which case the LLC's income would escape employment taxes. Hoping to eliminate this potential loophole, proposed regulations created new rules to test limited partners as well as LLC members. Under the proposed regulations, a limited partner or LLC member must treat his or her share of income as self-employment income if any of the following tests are met:[23]

1. The individual has personal liability for the debts of or claims against the business by reason of being a partner. This rule should rarely apply to a member of an LLC.

2. The individual has authority to contract on behalf of the entity.

3. The individual participates in the entity's trade or business for more than 500 hours during the year.

4. Substantially all of the activities of the entity involve the performance of services in the fields of health, law, engineering, architecture, accounting, actuarial science, or consulting.

Although these proposals provide needed guidance, they were heavily criticized. As a result, Congress intervened in 1997, passing legislation that postponed their implementation.[24] Since that time there has been no further action and the treatment of LLCs for purposes of self-employment taxes is still unresolved.

TAX-EXEMPT ORGANIZATIONS

Since inception, U.S. tax laws have exempted from federal income taxation charitable and religious organizations as well as a variety of nonprofit associations. The vast majority of tax-exempt organizations obtain their tax exempt status from § 501(c)(3). Under this provision, corporations that are organized and operated exclusively for religious, charitable, scientific, literary, or educational purposes are exempt, assuming certain requirements are met. It is often said that these so-called § 501(c)(3) organizations are twice blessed since not only are they exempt from tax but contributions they receive are deductible.

Although tax-exempt entities usually do not pay tax, there are exceptions. If a nonprofit organization conducts a business unrelated to the purpose for which its exemption was granted, any income resulting from that business would be subject to tax. The tax is referred to as the unrelated business income tax (UBIT).[25] The UBIT rules are designed to prevent unfair competition that would otherwise arise between taxable and nontaxable entities that carry on the same business. If the tax-exempt entity is organized as a corporation, its tax on unrelated business taxable income is computed in the same manner as a regular corporation. Also note that if unrelated business income comprises a substantial portion of the organization's income, it could lose its tax-exempt status.

Example 8

HHH Corporation is a nonprofit organization that operates a health agency. It collects dues from all of its members that number over 50,000. The dues income is nontaxable. Each month it e-mails a monthly newsletter to its members. Recently, several companies expressed interest in advertising in its newsletter. Would the advertising income be considered unrelated business income?

Yes. Even though the corporation is a nonprofit organization, the advertising income would be taxable since the sale of ads is sufficiently commercial in nature to constitute a business activity that is carried on regularly (e.g., monthly). Moreover, if the advertising income comprised a substantial portion of the organization's income, it could lose its tax-exempt status.

[23] Prop. Reg. § 1.1402(a)-2(h).

[24] See § 935 of the Tax Reform Act of 1997.

[25] These rules can be found in §§ 511 through 514.

Example 9

The Mudville Little League Baseball Organization is a tax-exempt organization. Every spring it holds a car wash to raise money for its operation. Is the income subject to tax?

No. The income from the car wash is exempt because the activity is not regularly carried on as a business.

As the examples might suggest, whether an otherwise tax-exempt organization has unrelated taxable income is often unclear. The point to grasp at this level is that even those organizations that might seem exempt—churches, universities, foundations and the like—may produce taxable income and, if the amount is substantial, they may lose their tax-exemption.

 ## CHECK YOUR KNOWLEDGE

Review Question 1

Section 1 of the Internal Revenue Code imposes a tax on all individuals. If taken literally, this would mean that the United States taxes not only Oprah Winfrey but also the Prime Minister of Russia, Vladimir Putin and singer-songwriter Sir Elton John. Are these foreign citizens subject to U.S. tax?

The U.S. income tax generally applies to the worldwide income of U.S. citizens and resident aliens. As a result, it would not apply to Mr. Putin and Mr. John since they are not citizens and do not live in the United States. The key question for an alien is whether the individual could be considered a resident. Whether a foreign citizen is considered a resident is normally based on the period of time he or she is present in the United States. For this purpose, an alien who is a mere transient (e.g., a foreigner who vacations in the United States) is not a resident.

Although foreign citizens such as Putin and John usually are not subject to U.S. tax, they can be. Nonresident aliens are taxed on their income from U.S. sources. Based on this rule, income earned from a job or a business in the United States is subject to U.S. tax. In addition, nonresident aliens who receive investment income from U.S. sources, such as dividends on U.S. stocks, normally must pay U.S. taxes on such income.

Review Question 2

Child actors and actresses have made millions of dollars from their movie appearances.

a. Must these children file their own returns and report the income, or do their parents simply include it on their return?

Although there are some special rules that can apply, parents normally do not report the income of their children on their return. A child is treated as a taxable entity, separate and distinct from his or her parents. Consequently, if a child's income exceeds the filing requirement threshold, he or she must usually file a return.

b. Do you think there could be any advantage derived from the fact that a child is a separate taxpayer?

Besides all of the other things that children are—both good and bad—they can also be mini-tax shelters. Since they are separate taxpayers, they have their own set of tax rates and other tax characteristics. Therefore, to the extent that parents are able to shift income from the parents' high bracket to the child's low bracket (and still control the use of the income), taxes can be saved. These opportunities and some limitations that restrict such schemes are discussed more fully in Chapter 4 and Chapter 5.

Review Question 3

After all these years, Bob decided to start his own business: Bob's Bar and Grill. He has even convinced his wife, Jane, to help. Bob has everything ready but still must decide what form the business should take. Originally, he did not even think about it. Bob simply thought he would operate the business as a sole proprietorship.

a. If Bob does pursue this course, will he need to file a separate return for the business?

A sole proprietorship is not considered a separate taxable entity. Instead, all of the information related to the proprietorship is included on the individual's personal tax return. The results of operation are summarized on Schedule C. The net profit or loss is transferred from Schedule C to page 1 of Form 1040. In addition, since such income is also subject to self-employment tax, the net profit is also transferred to Schedule SE, where the special computation is made. It is important to note that either Bob or Jane can be the proprietor—but not both. If Jane is to be the proprietor, she must own the business. If Jane wishes to compensate Bob, she can pay him a salary or wages. However, if Bob and Jane both wish to be owners, they must use another form of business.

b. After Bob and Jane talked to their attorney, it was clear that they did not want to be a general partnership (where each and every partner is liable for partnership obligations) or a sole proprietorship. Why?

Typically, individuals want to protect their personal assets from the liabilities of risky ventures. While insurance may provide some protection, most individuals want the added safety of limited liability that only the corporate or LLC form offers. A *limited* partnership allows some partners protection, but this business form requires that there must be at least one *general* partner (who would have unlimited liability).

c. At first Bob and Jane thought they would be a corporation. But according to their accountant, this new thing called an LLC allows business owners to achieve what he believes is tax nirvana. What is all the fuss about LLCs? Can you not get the same thing with S corporations? What do you think? How are LLCs taxed? What form of business organization seems best for Bob and Jane's business?

The beauty of an LLC is that all of the owners have limited liability yet the entity is usually taxed like a partnership. As a result, all of the income, as well as any loss, flows through to the partners. The significance of this treatment is twofold. First, if any loss occurs, it can be used to offset any other income Bob and Jane may have. If a C corporation is chosen, early losses do not provide any benefit until the business starts to make money. The NOL carryback feature for corporations is useless, because the business is brand new. Moreover, if it is like most businesses, Bob and Jane's operation will experience losses—at least until the clientele develop a love for Bob's cooking. The second attraction of an LLC is the fact that its income avoids the double tax that can occur with C corporations. But why opt for an LLC? Is not this same treatment available with an S corporation? In this regard, the LLC is virtually identical to an S corporation, but there are many differences that some argue make the LLC more attractive. The only difference that can be gleaned from the discussion above is that an S corporation is limited to 100 shareholders while a partnership or LLC can have an unlimited number of owners. This may be irrelevant for Bob and Jane but could be extremely important for some businesses (e.g., a large public accounting firm). Another difference concerns the type of owner allowed. For example, an S corporation can generally have only individuals (and no nonresident aliens) as shareholders, but there are no restrictions on the type of partner or member that a partnership or an LLC can have. This too may be unimportant for Bob and Jane but there are still other considerations too technical to touch on here.

As a practical matter, prior to the advent of the LLC, most advisers would have suggested that Bob and Jane choose to be an S corporation. Since 1986 S corporations have generally been the most popular form of conducting business—at least when there were no more than the maximum shareholders allowed—because they were the only form of business that offered limited liability to all of its owners and a single level of tax. But the advent of the LLC changes all of this. As time passes, it will be interesting to see if LLCs become more popular than S corporations. In any event, they provide yet one more option for the business owner to select.

Computing an income tax liability is normally uncomplicated, requiring only a few simple mathematical calculations.[26] These steps, referred to as the tax formula, are shown in Exhibits 3-2 and 3-3. The tax formula is presented here in two forms: the simpler general formula that establishes the basic concepts as applicable to corporate taxpayers (Exhibit 3-2) and the more complex formula for individual taxpayers (Exhibit 3-3). The formulas in Exhibits 3-2 and 3-3 are useful references while studying the various aspects of Federal income tax law in the subsequent chapters. To make such reference easier, both formulas are reproduced on the inside back cover of the text.

The tax formula for each type of entity is incorporated into the Federal income tax forms. Exhibit 3-2 may be compared with Form 1120 (the annual income tax return for corporations) and Exhibit 3-3 with Form 1040 (the return for individuals). These forms are included in Appendix B at the back of the text.

Examination of the two formulas reveals the importance of tax terms such as *gross income, deductions, and exemptions.* Each of these terms and countless others used in the tax law have very specific meanings. Indeed, as later chapters will show, taxpayers often have been involved in litigation solely to determine the definition of a particular term. For this reason, close attention must be given to the terminology used in taxation.

LO.3
Understand the basic tax formulas to be followed in computing the tax liability for individuals and corporations.

ANALYZING THE TAX FORMULA

Income

The tax computation begins with a determination of the taxpayer's total income, both taxable and nontaxable. As the formula in Exhibit 3-3 suggests, income is defined very broadly to include income from any source.[27] The list of typical income items in Exhibit 3-4 illustrates its comprehensive nature. A specific definition of income is developed in Chapter 5.

LO.4
Define many of the basic terms used in the tax formula such as gross income, adjusted gross income, taxable income, exclusion, deduction, and credit.

EXHIBIT 3-4	Partial List of Items Included in Gross Income

Alimony and separate maintenance payments	Income in respect of a decedent
Annuities	Interest
Awards	Pensions and other retirement benefits
Bonuses	Prizes and gambling or lottery winnings
Commissions	Pro rata share of income of a partnership
Debts forgiven to debtor by a creditor	Pro rata share of income of an S corporation
Dividends from corporations	Punitive damages
Employee expense reimbursements	Rewards
Fees and other compensation for personal services	Royalties
Gains from illegal transactions	Salaries and wages
Gains from transactions in property	Social Security benefits (zero or a portion)
Gross profit from sales	Tips and gratuities
Hobby income	Trade or business income
Income from an interest in an estate or trust	Unemployment compensation
Income from rental operations	

[26] §§ 1 and 63.   [27] § 61(a).

EXHIBIT 3-5	Partial List of Exclusions from Gross Income

Amounts received from employer-financed health and accident insurance to the extent of expenses

Amounts received from health, accident, and disability insurance financed by the taxpayer

Amounts received under qualified educational assistance plans

Certain specified employee fringe benefits

Child support payments received

Contributions by employer to employer-financed accident and health insurance coverage

Dependent care assistance provided by employer

Gifts and inheritances

Improvements by lessee to lessor's property

Interest on most state and local government debt

Meals and lodging furnished for the convenience of one's employer

Personal damage awards (physical injury or sickness)

Premiums paid by employer on group-term life insurance (for coverage up to $50,000)

Proceeds of life insurance paid on death

Proceeds of borrowing

Qualified transportation plan benefits

Scholarship and fellowship grants (but only for tuition, fees, books, and supplies)

Social Security benefits (within limits)

Veteran's benefits

Welfare payments

Exclusions

Although the starting point in calculating the tax is determining total income, not all of the income identified is taxable. Over the years, Congress has specifically exempted certain types of income from taxation, often in an attempt to accomplish some specific goal.[28] In tax terminology, income exempt from taxation and thus not included in a taxpayer's gross income is referred to as an "exclusion." Exhibit 3-5 shows a sample of the numerous items that can be excluded when determining gross income. Exclusions are discussed in detail in Chapter 6.

Gross Income

The amount of income remaining after the excludable items have been removed is termed *gross income.* When completing a tax return, gross income is usually the only income disclosed, because excluded income normally is not reported.

Example 10

E is divorced and has custody of her only child. E's income for the current year is from the following sources:

Salary	$34,000
Alimony from former spouse	12,000
Child support for child	6,000
Interest from First Savings and Loan	1,200
Interest on U.S. Government Treasury Bonds	1,600
Interest on State of Texas Bonds	2,000
Total	$56,800

Even though E's total income is $56,800, her gross income for tax purposes is only $48,800 because the child support and the interest income from the State of Texas are excluded. All the other items are included in gross income. Note that the interest from the Federal government is taxable, even though interest from state and local governments is generally excluded from gross income.

---

[28] See Chapter 6 for a discussion of the social and economic reasons for excluding certain items of income from taxation.

Deductions

Deductions are those items that are subtracted from gross income to arrive at taxable income. The deductions normally allowed may be classified into two major groups:

1. *Business and Production-of-Income Expenses*—deductions for expenses related to carrying on a business or an income-producing activity, such as an investment.[29]

2. *Certain Personal Expenses*—deductions for a few expenses of individual that are primarily personal in nature, such as charitable contributions and medical expenses.[30]

Observe that the Code allows a deduction only for business or investment expenses. Personal expenses—other than a handful of special items—are not deductible. As someone once said, the Code's treatment of deductions is relatively simple: the costs of earning a living are deductible but the costs of living are not. The problem is determining into which category the expense falls.

A trade or business is an activity that is entered into for profit and involves significant taxpayer participation, either personally or through agents. It typically involves providing goods or services to customers, clients, or patients. If the activity qualifies as a trade or business, all the costs normally associated with operating the business are generally deductible. In most cases, it is easy to determine whether a taxpayer is engaged in a trade or business, but not always. For example, consider a taxpayer who travels around the world looking for antiques and incurs $10,000 of travel expenses but ultimately sells one item for a $100 profit. In this situation, the taxpayer might argue that he has a $9,900 loss from the activity that he should be able to offset against other income. On the other hand, it could easily be argued that the taxpayer was not really trying to make a profit. In such case, the IRS may deny the taxpayer's deduction. In these and similar situations, the determination of whether the taxpayer is truly in a trade or business must be based on all the facts and circumstances.

Note also that the tax law assumes that an individual who is employed is in the business of providing services. This is an extremely important assumption since it enables employees to deduct their business expenses (e.g., professional dues, subscriptions, and similar costs).[31]

Although business expenses are deductible, the line between a deductible business expense and a nondeductible personal expense is not always clear. For this reason, the Code often contains additional rules or requires certain conditions to be met to ensure that the expense is truly for business. For example, the Code addresses the personal element of business meals and entertainment that are not reimbursed by limiting the deduction to only 50% of their cost. Similarly, expenses related to education, travel, transportation, moving or a home office are not deductible unless they meet a laundry list of requirements. Most of these special rules are discussed in detail in Chapter 8.

The rental of real estate is generally not considered to be a trade or business, unless the tenants are transient (i.e., stay for short periods of time, as in a hotel or motel) or there are extraordinary services provided to tenants (e.g., a nursing home). Nevertheless, the expenses (e.g., repairs, utilities) are normally deductible as expenses related to an income-producing activity and are classified as deductions for adjusted gross income.

As might be expected, Congress is quite cautious in granting deductions. There are rules, rules, and more rules that try to ensure that only true business expenses are deductible. The tax law is particularly concerned about deduction of losses (i.e., the excess of deductions over revenues) from activities in which the taxpayer has an interest. The problem became particularly acute in the 1970s and 1980s, when certain activities were designed primarily to generate tax losses (tax shelter limited partnerships and rental real estate were the biggest culprits). In an attempt to eliminate widespread abuse, Congress enacted the so-called *passive loss* rules in 1986. These highly complex rules generally limit the deduction of losses from activities, including rental real estate, in which the taxpayer is a mere investor and does not materially participate. For example, an individual's share of a net loss from a partnership in which the partner was a mere investor would be a passive loss, deductible only to offset passive income. The passive loss rules are covered in detail in Chapter 12.

---

[29] §§ 162 and 212.

[30] §§ 170 and 213.

[31] See Reg. § 1.162-6 and *David J. Primuth*, 54 T.C. 374 (1970).

Classifying Deductions

A comparison of the general tax formulas used by corporations and by individuals reveals some differences in the treatment of deductions. For a corporate taxpayer, all deductions are subtracted directly from gross income to arrive at taxable income. In contrast, the individual formula divides deductions into two groups:[32] One group of deductions is allowed to reduce gross income, resulting in what is referred to as adjusted gross income (AGI), while a second group is subtracted from AGI. As explained more fully below, the first group of deductions is generally composed of certain business expenses and other special items. The deductions in this group are referred to as deductions *for* adjusted gross income. The second group of expenses consists of two categories of allowable deductions: (1) deductions *from* adjusted gross income, and (2) deductions for personal and dependency exemptions. Deductions from adjusted gross income, normally referred to as *itemized deductions,* may be deducted only if they exceed a stipulated amount known as the *standard deduction* (e.g., in 2017, $6,350 for single taxpayers and $12,700 for married taxpayers filing jointly). The deduction for any personal and dependency exemptions claimed (e.g., $4,050 per exemption in 2017) is deductible regardless of the amount of other deductions.

Dividing deductions into two groups is done primarily for administrative convenience. Congress substantially reduced the number of individuals who claim itemized deductions because such deductions need to be reported only if they exceed the taxpayer's standard deduction. This reduction in the number of tax returns with itemized deductions significantly reduced the IRS audit procedures involving individual taxpayers. In recent years, only about 35% of taxpayers have itemized their deductions. Since corporate taxpayers have only business deductions, no special grouping was needed and thus the term *adjusted gross income* does not exist in the corporate formula.

Adjusted Gross Income

The amount of an individual taxpayer's adjusted gross income (AGI) serves two primary purposes. First, it is simply a point of reference used for classifying deductions: deductions are classified as either for or from AGI. Second, the calculation of many deductions, credits and other tax items is made with reference to AGI. For example, medical expenses and personal casualty losses may be deducted only if they exceed 10% of AGI. In addition, recent changes in the tax law make AGI even more important for some taxpayers. As explained below, most itemized deductions and the deduction for exemptions are reduced if adjusted gross income exceeds certain levels.

Example 11

This year proved to be very difficult for T; his divorce became final, and shortly thereafter he became very sick. For the year, he earned $45,000 and paid $5,000 in alimony to his ex-wife and $10,000 for medical expenses that were not reimbursed by insurance. T's AGI is $40,000 ($45,000 − $5,000) because alimony is a deduction for AGI. As computed below, T's medical expense deduction is limited to $6,000 because he is allowed to deduct only the amount that exceeds 10% of his AGI.

Medical expenses (unreimbursed)		$10,000
Adjusted gross income	$40,000	
Times	× 10%	
Threshold	$ 4,000	(4,000)
Deductible medical expenses		$ 6,000

Deductions for Adjusted Gross Income

Code § 62 specifically lists the deductions that are subtracted from gross income to determine AGI. This listing is a potpourri of items, as illustrated in Exhibit 3-6. Over the years, this group of deductions has gone by various names. For example, practitioners often refer to this category of deductions as being "above the line"—the line being AGI.

---

[32] § 62.

Some commentators and authors label these as deductions from gross income. For years, the Form 1040 listed these deductions as "adjustments" to income, although this label is no longer used (see Form 1040 in Appendix B). This text will use the "deduction for" terminology. Classification of a deduction as one for AGI is significant for numerous reasons, as explained fully in Chapter 7. The most important of these reasons, however, is that unlike itemized deductions, deductions for AGI need not exceed a minimum level before they are subtracted when computing taxable income.

EXHIBIT 3-6	List of Deductions for Adjusted Gross Income

Alimony and separate maintenance payments paid

Attorney fees and court costs related to unlawful discrimination cases

Certain deductions of life tenants and income beneficiaries of property

Certain portion of lump-sum distributions from pension plans subject to the special averaging convention

Certain required repayments of supplemental unemployment compensation benefits

Contributions to health savings accounts

Contributions to pension, profit sharing, and other qualified retirement plans on behalf of a self-employed individual

Contributions to the retirement plan of an electing Subchapter S corporation on behalf of an employee/shareholder

Deduction for domestic production activities

Deductions attributable to property held for the production of rents and royalties (reported on Schedule E)

Educator expenses up to $250

Individual retirement account contributions (within limits)

Losses from the sale or exchange of property

Moving expenses

One-half of any self-employment tax

Penalties for premature withdrawal of deposits from time savings accounts

Reforestation expenses

Reimbursed trade or business expenses of employees (only if the employee adequately accounts to the employer under an accountable plan in which case neither the reimbursement nor the expense is reported (see Chapter 8; see also expenses of statutory employees)

State and local official's deductible expenses

Statutory employee's deductions (life insurance salespersons, traveling salespersons and certain others report income and deductions on Schedule C; see Chapters 7 and 8)

Student loan interest

Trade or business deductions of self-employed individuals (including deductions claimed on Schedule C and unreimbursed expenses of qualified performing artists)

Tuition payments up to $4,000 for some students (extended through 2017)

Itemized Deductions and the Standard Deduction

Itemized deductions are all deductions other than the deductions for AGI and the deduction for personal and dependency exemptions.[33] While deductions for AGI are deductible without limitation, itemized deductions are deducted only if their total exceeds the taxpayer's standard deduction. For example, if in 2017 T has total itemized deductions of $5,000 and his standard deduction amount is $6,350, he normally would claim the standard deduction in lieu of itemizing deductions. In contrast, if T's itemized deductions were $7,000, he would no doubt elect to itemize in order to maximize his deductions.

---

[33] § 63.

The standard deduction was introduced along with the concept of adjusted gross income and deductions *for* and *from* AGI as part of the overall plan to eliminate the need for every taxpayer to list or itemize certain deductions on his or her return. As suggested above, by allowing the taxpayer to claim some standard amount of deductions in lieu of itemizing each one, the administrative problem of verifying the millions of deductions that otherwise would have been claimed has been eliminated. The standard deduction also simplifies return preparation since most individuals no longer have to determine the amount of most of the deductions to which they are entitled. For this reason, the amount of the standard deduction is theoretically set at a level that equals or exceeds the average person's expenditures for those items qualifying as deductions from AGI. Consequently, the great majority of taxpayers claim the standard deduction in lieu of itemizing deductions.

The deduction is the sum of the following components:

1. Basic standard deduction.
2. Increase for individuals who are age 65 or over and/or blind.

Basic Standard Deduction

The basic amount of each taxpayer's standard deduction differs depending on his or her filing status.[34] The amounts for each filing status are adjusted annually for inflation. For 2016 and 2017, the amounts are shown below.

	Standard Deduction Amount		Age 65 or Blind
Filing Status	2016	2017	2017
Single	$ 6,300	$ 6,350	$ 1,550
Unmarried head of household	9,300	9,350	1,550
Married persons filing a joint return (and surviving spouse)	12,600	12,700	1,250
Married persons filing a separate return	6,300	6,350	1,250

Additional Standard Deduction for Elderly or Blind Taxpayers

Congress has long extended some type of tax relief to the elderly and blind to take into account their special circumstances. As shown above, an unmarried taxpayer who is either legally blind or age 65 at the close of the taxable year is allowed to increase his or her basic standard deduction by an additional $1,550 (2017).[35] If an unmarried taxpayer is *both* blind and 65 or older, he or she is allowed to increase the standard deduction by $3,100 ($1,550 × 2). If a taxpayer is married, the increase for each status in 2016 is only $1,250. Thus, for a married couple where both are age 65 and blind, the maximum increase on a joint return would be $5,000 (4 × $1,250) for a standard deduction of $17,700 ($12,700 + $5,000).

> **Example 12**
>
> In 2017, S, single, celebrated her sixty-fifth birthday. Instead of using the basic standard deduction of $6,350 for single taxpayers in 2017, S will be allowed a standard deduction of $7,900 ($6,350 basic standard deduction + $1,550 additional standard deduction).
>
> If S were married filing a joint return for 2017, the standard deduction amount allowed would be $13,950 ($12,700 + $1,250). If both S and her husband were 65 or older, the standard deduction would be $15,200 ($12,700 standard deduction + [2 × $1,250 = $2,500 additional standard deduction]).

Both age and blindness are determined at the close of the taxable year. Guidelines are provided for determining whether an individual is legally blind.[36] An individual is

---

[34] § 63(c) contains the standard deduction amounts for 1988. The amounts for subsequent years are adjusted for inflation and announced by the IRS annually. Filing status is discussed in Chapter 4.

[35] § 63(f).

[36] §§ 151(d) and 151(d)(3). A taxpayer is legally blind if he or she cannot see better than 20/200 in the better eye with corrective lenses, or the taxpayer's field of vision is not more than 20 degrees. A statement prepared by a physician or optometrist must be attached to the return when a taxpayer is less than totally blind. Reg. § 1.151-1(d)(2).

considered to have attained age 65 on the day *preceding* his or her sixty-fifth birthday.[37] Thus, if a taxpayer's sixty-fifth birthday is on January 1, 2018, he or she is considered to be 65 on December 31, 2017.

Limitations on Use of Standard Deductions

Not all individuals are entitled to the full benefit of the standard deduction.[38] For example, a married person filing a separate return is not allowed a standard deduction if his or her spouse itemizes. This prevents a married couple from increasing their total deductions by having one spouse claim all of the itemized deductions and the other spouse claiming the standard deduction. Nonresident aliens are also denied use of the standard deduction. In addition, the standard deduction is limited for an individual who is claimed as a dependent on another tax-payer's return. This limitation is discussed in Chapter 4.

Itemized Deductions

As explained above, itemized deductions simply are those deductions that are not deductible for AGI. The majority of itemized deductions are for selected personal, family and living expenses that Congress believed should be allowed for various policy reasons. These include medical expenses; state and local property, income and sales taxes; home mortgage interest; charitable contributions; and casualty and theft losses. A partial list of itemized deductions is provided in Exhibit 3-7. In addition to these, a special subset of itemized deductions, so-called "miscellaneous itemized deductions" are allowed as discussed below. Finally, as explained in Chapter 11, itemized deductions of high income taxpayers are reduced as income exceeds certain thresholds.

EXHIBIT 3-7	Partial List of Itemized Deductions

Medical expenses unreimbursed (amount in excess of 10% of AGI):
  Prescription drugs and insulin
  Medical insurance premiums
  Fees of doctors, dentists, nurses, hospitals, etc.
  Medical transportation
  Hearing aids, dentures, eyeglasses, etc.
Investment interest (to extent of investment income)
Casualty and theft losses (amount in excess of 10% of AGI)
Wagering losses (to the extent of wagering income)
Certain state, local, and foreign taxes:
  State, local, and foreign income taxes
  State, local, and foreign real property taxes
  State and local personal property taxes
  State and local sales taxes
Mortgage interest on personal residences (limited)
Mortgage insurance on personal residences
Charitable contributions (not to exceed 50% of AGI)
Miscellaneous itemized deductions (amount in excess of 2% of AGI):
  Costs of preparation of tax returns
  Fees and expenses related to tax planning and advice
  Investment counseling and investment expenses
  Certain unreimbursed employee business expenses (including travel and transportation, professional dues, subscriptions, continuing education, union dues, and special work clothing)

---

[37] Reg. § 1.151-1(c)(2).   [38] See § 63(c)(6) for this exception and others.

3-22   Chapter 3   *Taxable Entities; Tax Formula; Introduction to Property Transactions*

Miscellaneous Itemized Deductions. Itemized deductions are also allowed for a group of other expenses referred to as *miscellaneous itemized deductions*. Miscellaneous itemized deductions include the deductions for unreimbursed employee business expenses (e.g., dues to professional organizations, subscriptions to professional journals, travel and others that are not reimbursed under an accountable plan), tax return preparation fees and related costs, and certain investment expenses (e.g. safety deposit boxes, investment advice).[39] The classification of an expense as a miscellaneous itemized deduction is extremely important because a limitation is imposed on their deduction. Only the portion of miscellaneous itemized deductions exceeding 2% of adjusted gross income is deductible. Congress imposed this limitation in hopes of simplifying the law. The 2% floor is intended to relieve taxpayers of the burden of recordkeeping (unless they expect to incur substantial expenditures) and relieve the IRS of the burden of auditing these expenditures.

Example 13

R, single, is employed as an architect. This year his wages were $50,000. His itemized deductions for the year were interest on his home mortgage, $7,000; charitable contributions, $900; tax return preparation fee, $300; and unreimbursed professional dues, $800. R's total itemized deductions are computed as follows:

Miscellaneous itemized deductions:	
Tax return preparation fee	$ 300
Professional dues	800
Total miscellaneous itemized deductions	$ 1,100
AGI limitation (2% × $50,000)	(1,000)
Total deductible miscellaneous itemized deductions	$ 100
Other itemized deductions:	
Interest on home mortgage	7,000
Charitable contributions	900
Total itemized deductions	$ 8,000

Because R's itemized deductions of $8,000 exceed the standard deduction for single persons, $6,350 (2017), he will deduct the entire $8,000. Note that only $100 of R's miscellaneous itemized deductions are deductible, whereas all of his other itemized deductions are deductible.

Exemptions

Congress has always recognized the need to insulate from tax a certain amount of income required by the taxpayer to support himself and others. For this reason, every individual taxpayer is entitled to a basic deduction for himself and his dependents. This deduction is called an *exemption*. For 2017, an individual taxpayer is entitled to a deduction of $4,050 for each *personal* and *dependency* exemption.[40] *Personal exemptions* are those allowed for the taxpayer. Generally, every taxpayer is entitled to claim a personal exemption for himself or herself. However, taxpayers *cannot* claim a personal exemption on their own return if they can be claimed as a dependent on another taxpayer's return.[41] If husband and wife file a joint return, they are treated as two taxpayers and are therefore entitled to claim two personal exemptions. *Dependency exemptions* may be claimed for qualifying individuals who are supported by the taxpayer.[42] The deduction for personal and dependency exemptions is phased out for high-income taxpayers. All the special rules governing deductions for exemptions are discussed in detail in Chapter 4.

---

[39] An employee's business expenses are treated as reimbursed under § 62 only if the employee adequately accounts for the expense to his or her employer (e.g., submits documentation) under the accountable plan rules. In such case the employee reports neither income nor expense and the expense is essentially the employer's. Otherwise the employee reports the income and claims the expense as a miscellaneous itemized deduction. See Reg. § 1.62-2 and Chapter 8.

[40] § 151(d)(1). For 1989 the exemption was $2,000. For years *after* 1989, the amount has been indexed for inflation.

[41] § 151(d)(2).

[42] § 152.

Taxable Income and Tax Rates

After all deductions have been identified, they are subtracted from gross income to arrive at taxable income. Taxable income is the tax base to which the tax rates are applied to determine the taxpayer's gross tax liability (i.e., the tax liability before any credits or prepayments).

The tax rate schedule to be used in computing the tax varies, depending on the nature of the taxable entity. For example, one set of tax rates applies to all regular corporations (see inside back cover of text). In contrast, individuals use one of four tax rate schedules (see inside front cover) depending on their filing status, of which there are four. These are

1. Unmarried individuals (i.e., single) but not surviving spouses or heads of household.
2. Heads of household.
3. Married individuals filing jointly and surviving spouses.
4. Married individuals filing separately.

These tax rate structures are all graduated with seven rates: 10, 15, 25, 28, 33, 35, and 39.6 percent. Although the rates in each schedule are identical, the degree of progressivity differs. For example, in 2017 the 28% marginal rate applies to single taxpayers when income exceeds $91,200, but this rate does not apply to married individuals filing jointly until income exceeds $153,100. Filing status and rate schedules are discussed in Chapter 4.

Example 14

H and W are married and file a joint return for 2017. They have AGI of $151,000, two dependents, and itemized deductions of $30,800. Their taxable income is $104,000, computed as follows:

Adjusted gross income.		$ 151,000
Minus: Itemized deductions.	$30,800	
Personal exemptions ($4,050 × 4)	+16,200	− 47,000
Equals: Taxable income		$ 104,000

The tax for a married couple filing jointly on this amount computed using the rate schedules is $17,477.50 as shown below.

Tax on $75,900.	$10,452.50
Plus: Tax on excess at 25% ([$104,000 − $75,900 = $28,100] × 0.25).	+ 7,025.00
Equals: Total tax	$17,477.50

Credits

Unlike a deduction, which reduces income in arriving at taxable income, a credit is a direct reduction in tax liability. Normally, when the credit exceeds a person's total tax, the excess is not refunded—hence, these credits are referred to as *nonrefundable* credits. In some instances, however, the taxpayer is entitled to receive a payment for any excess credit. This type of credit is known as a *refundable* credit.

EXHIBIT 3-8	**Partial List of Tax Credits**

Child and dependent care credit	Earned income credit
Child tax credit	Foreign tax credit
Credit for adoption expenses	Hope scholarship credit
Credit for increasing research activities	Lifetime learning credit
Credit for producing fuel from a nonconventional source	Low income housing credit
Credit for rehabilitating certain buildings	Welfare to work credit
Credit for the elderly	Work opportunity credit

Credits have frequently been preferred by Congress and theoreticians because they affect all taxpayers equally. In contrast, the value of a deduction varies with the taxpayer's marginal tax rate. However, credits often have complicated rules and limitations. A partial list of tax credits is included in Exhibit 3-8.

Prepayments

Attempting to accelerate the collection of revenues for the war effort in 1943, Congress installed a "pay-as-you-go" system for certain taxes. Under this system, income taxes are paid in installments as the income is earned.

Prepayment, or advance payment, of the tax liability can be made in several ways. For individual taxpayers, the two most common forms of prepayment are Federal income taxes withheld from an employee's salaries and wages and quarterly estimated tax payments made by the taxpayer. Certain corporate taxpayers must make quarterly estimated tax payments as well. Quarterly estimated tax payments are required for taxpayers who have not prepaid a specified level of their anticipated Federal income tax in any other way, and there are penalties for failure to make adequate estimated prepayments.

These prepayments serve two valuable purposes. As suggested above, prepayments allow the government to have earlier use of the tax proceeds. Secondly, prepayments reduce the uncertainty of collecting taxes since the government, by withholding at the source, gets the money before the taxpayer has a chance to put it to a different use. In effect, the government collects the tax while the taxpayer has the wherewithal (ability) to pay the tax.

Other Taxes

LO.5

Identify other taxes, including the alternative minimum tax and the net investment income tax.

There are several types of other taxes that must be reported and paid with the regular Federal income tax. A partial list of these taxes is included in Exhibit 3-9. Two deserve special mention.

EXHIBIT 3-9	Partial List of Other Taxes

Alternative minimum tax
Net investment income tax
Self-employment tax
Social Security tax on tip income not reported to employer
Tax on premature withdrawal from an Individual Retirement Account
Tax from recapture of investment credit
Uncollected employee F.I.C.A. and R.R.T.A. tax on tips

Self-Employment Tax. As explained in Chapter 1, self-employed individuals as well as general partners in partnerships are, like employees, required to pay FICA taxes (commonly known as self-employment taxes). Since the tax is paid on income from sole proprietorship and partnership businesses carried on by individual partners, it is convenient for the IRS to collect this tax along with the income tax on Form 1040. The individual calculates the tax on Schedule SE and claims the income tax deduction for one-half of the self-employment tax paid on page 1 of Form 1040.

Alternative Minimum Tax. In 1969 there was an outcry by the media and others that the rich did not pay their fair share of taxes. Indeed, the House Ways and Means Committee Report indicated that in 1964 over 1,100 returns with adjusted gross incomes over $200,000 paid an average tax of 22 percent. Moreover, it reported that there were a significant number of cases where taxpayers with economic income of $1 million or more paid an effective tax amounting to less than 5% of their income. As might be expected, faced with such facts

Congress decided to take action. However, instead of risking the wrath of their constituents by simply repealing the various loopholes that enabled these taxpayers to avoid taxes, Congress elected to take a politically cautious approach: a direct tax on the loopholes. In effect, the taxpayer simply added up all of the loopholes and paid a flat tax on them. As a result, the minimum tax was born. The whole thrust of this new tax was to ensure that all individuals paid a minimum tax on their income. It currently applies to all taxpayers, individuals, corporations, and fiduciaries.

Over the years, the minimum tax evolved into a monster and was adorned with its current name, the alternative minimum tax (AMT). Despite the changes and increased complexity, it remains basically the same. The mathematical steps for computing the AMT are relatively simple:

$$
\begin{array}{l}
\text{Regular taxable income} \\
\underline{\pm\ \text{Adjustments and preferences}} \\
\text{Alternative minimum taxable income} \\
\underline{-\ \text{Exemption (subject to phase-out)}} \\
\text{Tax base} \\
\underline{\times\ \text{Rate}} \\
\text{Tentative alternative minimum tax} \\
\underline{-\ \text{Regular tax}} \\
\text{Alternative minimum tax}
\end{array}
$$

As the formula above illustrates, the taxpayer starts with taxable income and then adds certain income that is excluded for regular tax purposes and adds back certain deductions that are normally allowed. These modifications to regular taxable income are referred to as *preference items* and *adjustments*. In this regard, it is important to recognize that the AMT effectively functions as an entirely separate system with its own rules. For example, while most interest from state and local bonds is not taxable, such interest is taxable for AMT purposes if the bonds are used to fund some private activity such as a downtown mall. Similarly, deductions that are usually allowed for regular tax purposes, such as exemptions, miscellaneous itemized deductions, and state and local taxes, are not allowed in computing the AMT. In effect, there are two rules for some items: one rule for regular tax purposes and another for AMT purposes. After taking into account all of the special adjustments required under this alternative system, the new result is called alternative minimum taxable income. This amount is then reduced by an allowable exemption to arrive at the tax base. The exemption is reduced by 25% for each dollar by which AMTI exceeds certain levels. Both the exemption amounts and the thresholds at which the exemption phase-outs begin are adjusted annually for inflation. These amounts are shown below. A two-tier rate structure (adjusted annually for inflation) is then applied to the tax base (26% on the first $186,300 (2017) and 28% on the excess). The product is referred to as the tentative AMT. This amount is compared to the regular tax, and the taxpayer pays the higher. Technically, the excess of the tentative AMT over the regular tax is the AMT, but the bottom line is that the taxpayer pays the higher amount.

Alternative Minimum Tax Exemption Amounts and Phase-Out Thresholds

	2017 Exemptions	2017 Exemption Thresholds	
		Phase-Out Begins	Phase-Out Complete
Unmarried individuals	$54,300	$120,700	$337,900
Married filing jointly or surviving spouse . . .	84,500	160,900	498,900
Married filing separately	42,250	80,450	249,450

Example 15

H and W are married with four children. For 2017, they filed a joint return, reporting gross income of $400,000 and regular taxable income of $180,000. Various adjustments required under the AMT were $40,550. Using the 2017 AMT exemption and 2017 regular tax rates, the couple must pay an AMT, computed as follows:

Regular taxable income	$180,000
± Adjustments	40,550
Alternative minimum taxable income	$220,550
− Exemption ($84,500 − $14,913 [25% × ($220,550 − $160,900 = 59,650)])	(69,588)
Tax base	$150,963
× Rate	× 26%
Tentative alternative minimum tax	$ 39,250
− Regular tax (2017 rates)	(37,285)
Alternative minimum tax	$ 1,966

Note that the AMT is only $1,966, but the taxpayer must pay a total of $39,250 (regular tax of $37,285 + AMT of $1,966).

There is not a good rule of thumb as to when the AMT is triggered. For the vast majority of taxpayers it is simply not an issue. These individuals are not subject to the tax since they have low to moderate taxable incomes with few adjustments, causing them to fall below the exemption amounts. It is typically high-income taxpayers who have substantial adjustments, and other taxpayers who are successful in avoiding the regular tax, that fall prey to the AMT. Obviously the key lies in the nature of the adjustments. For now it is sufficient to say that beyond the few preferences and adjustments mentioned above there are several more such as those relating to depreciation, depletion, and stock options. Full coverage of the AMT is deferred until Chapter 13. Nevertheless, even at this early juncture it is important to recognize that the AMT exists and often alters what appears to be very favorable tax treatment for some items. More importantly, the net of the AMT has started catching far more taxpayers than Congress ever intended.

Net Investment Income Tax (§ 1411 Tax). One component of the healthcare legislation enacted in 2010 was the creation of a special tax on investment income.[43] This tax is 3.8% on the net investment income of high income taxpayers. The tax applies only to individuals, estates and trusts. Technically, the tax is 3.8% of the lesser of

- Net investment income or

- The excess of modified AGI (MAGI) over a threshold amount shown below (note that these amounts are not adjusted for inflation).

Filing Status	Modified AGI Threshold Amount
Married filing jointly and surviving spouses . . .	$250,000
Married filing separately	125,000
Single	200,000
Head of household	200,000
Estates and trusts.	11,650

---

[43] § 1411 is included in Chapter 2A of the Internal Revenue Code, entitled "Unearned Income Medicare Contribution." For this reason, it is often confused with the Medicare withholding tax on wages. However, the § 1411 surtax raises general revenues that are unrelated to the Medicare Trust Fund.

Example 16

S, single, has modified AGI of $230,000, including $12,000 of interest and $8,000 of dividend income. His net investment income tax would be $760 (3.8% × lesser of his net investment income of $20,000 or his excess MAGI of $30,000 [$230,000 MAGI – $200,000 threshold for single taxpayers]). Had his MAGI been $205,000, the base would be limited to $5,000 ($205,000 – $200,000) and his tax would be $190 (3.8% × $5,000 excess MAGI). Note that the effect of the tax for high income taxpayers is the equivalent of paying Medicare taxes on their investment (1.45% + 1.45% + 0.9% = 3.8%; see explanation of employment taxes in Chapter 1).

The net investment income tax (NIIT) must be paid along with an individual's income tax, just like self-employment taxes and the alternative minimum tax. It is reported on Form 8960 and shown as an "Other Tax" on page two of Form 1040. Like the other taxes, the NIIT must be considered in determining the required estimated tax payments during the year as discussed in Chapter 4.

The critical factor in determining whether someone is subject to the NIIT is MAGI. For this purpose, MAGI is AGI without the exclusion for foreign earned income. For taxpayers who do not have foreign earned income, MAGI is simply AGI. As a practical matter, the NIIT tax applies to relatively few taxpayers since it is triggered only at high levels of income.

Net investment income is generally investment income reduced by deductions properly allocable to that income. Investment income includes the following:

- Interest, dividends, annuities, royalties, rents (unless these items are derived in the ordinary course of business).

- Gains from the sale of stocks, bonds, mutual funds (as well as capital gain distributions).

- Gain from the sale of investment real estate, including gain from the sale of a vacation home.

- Gain on the sale of a personal residence that exceeds the applicable exclusion of $250,000 ($500,000 for a husband and wife).

- Income from a trade or business that is a passive activity and from a trade or business of trading in financial instruments or commodities is included in investment income.

Net investment income does not include the following:

- Tax-exempt interest income (e.g., from municipal bonds).

- Wages or self-employment income.

- Unemployment benefits.

- Gambling winnings.

- Alimony.

- Cancellation of debt income.

- Taxable distributions from retirement plans and individual retirement accounts (traditional).

- Distributions from Roth individual retirement accounts.

- Social Security benefits.

Although the items directly above are not considered net investment income, such income may increase AGI which could cause the taxpayer's AGI to exceed the "applicable threshold" of either $200,000 or $250,000 which in turn causes any net investment income to be subject to the 3.8% surtax.

Examples of properly allocable deductions include investment interest expense, investment advisory and brokerage fees, expenses related to rental and royalty income, and properly allocable state and local income taxes.

This brief overview of the NIIT suggests that its rules are relatively straightforward. However, appearances can be deceiving. The recently issued proposed regulations on § 1411 provide over 159 pages of proof to the contrary. In creating the new tax, Congress has created an entirely new and separate tax regime. Like the alternative minimum tax, the net investment income tax runs parallel to the income tax and taxpayers and tax practitioners must be alert to avoid unwelcome surprises.

 CHECK YOUR KNOWLEDGE

Review Question I

It's time for "Tax Jeopardy." Here are the answers; supply the questions.

a. The type of expenses all taxpayers can deduct.

What are business expenses? Around tax time, there is a single question that can be heard reverberating across the land: What can I deduct? The answer is business expenses. All taxpayers are allowed to deduct the ordinary and necessary expenses incurred in carrying on a trade or business. The vast majority of all deductions fall into this category. Note also that this rule allows the deduction of employee business expenses. In addition, taxpayers are entitled to deduct expenses related to investment activities (e.g., investment advice or repairs and maintenance on rental property).

b. The type of expenses taxpayers normally cannot deduct.

What are personal expenses? Although business expenses are deductible, personal expenses normally are not deductible. For example, the costs of food, shelter, clothing, and personal hygiene cannot be deducted. However, there are some exceptions.

c. Five notable exceptions to the rule that personal expenses are not deductible. (**Hint:** They are all reported on Schedule A of Form 1040, found in Appendix B of this book.) What are the following?

1. Medical expenses (but only if they exceed 10% of AGI)

2. Taxes

- State and local income or sales taxes but not both
- Real estate taxes
- Personal property taxes

3. Interest

- Home mortgage interest
- Student loan interest (maximum of $2,500)
- Investment interest (but only to the extent of investment income)

4. Charitable contributions

5. Casualty and theft losses

d. The type of business expenses that are deductible as itemized deductions.

What are unreimbursed employee business expenses? For example, if an employee pays for a business meal and his or her employer reimburses the cost of the meal, the expense is deductible in arriving at AGI if the employer includes the reimbursement in the employee's gross income. Technically, if the employee adequately accounts to the employer under the accountable plan rules, the employee has no income for the reimbursement nor any deduction for the expense (see Chapter 8). However, when the expense is not reimbursed, it is allowable only as a miscellaneous itemized deduction subject to the 2% floor. Other common examples of employee business expenses that are frequently deductible as miscellaneous itemized deductions are unreimbursed professional expenses (e.g., subscriptions, dues, license fees), union dues, and special clothing (when deductible).

e. The only type of tax-exempt income reported on the return. (**Hint:** See page 1 of Form 1040.)

What is tax-exempt interest income (reported on line 8b of page 1 of Form 1040)?

f. Something the individual tax formula has that the corporate tax formula does not have.

What is AGI? What is the standard deduction? What are exemptions?

g. A benefit received by the elderly and blind.

What is the increased standard deduction for taxpayers who are age 65 or over or who are blind?

h. Deductions that are deductible for individuals even if the taxpayer does not itemize deductions.

What are deductions for AGI? In addition, deductions for exemptions are permitted regardless of whether the taxpayer itemizes. However, exemption deductions are not deductions for AGI.

i. A deduction that may be claimed by virtually all individual taxpayers.

What is the exemption deduction, or the standard deduction? As explained above, however, certain persons are not entitled to a standard deduction. For example, a married person filing a separate return must itemize if his or her spouse does. In addition, as fully explained in Chapter 4, taxpayers cannot claim a personal exemption on their own return if they can be claimed as a dependent on another taxpayer's return.

j. A loss from this activity may not be deductible.

What are losses from rental real estate and any other activity in which the taxpayer does not materially participate? Before losses from an activity can be deducted (e.g., a loss that passes through from a partnership or a loss from renting a duplex), they must run through the gauntlet of tests prescribed by the passive loss rules covered in Chapter 12.

k. A separate tax intended to close loopholes.

What is the alternative minimum tax?

Review Question 2

Mabel, single, just reached the age of 65 and was somewhat relieved because she remembered hearing of the tax she would save as a 65-year-old senior. What tax savings can Mabel *expect?*

Perhaps none. The only benefit for being 65 years old is an additional standard deduction ($1,550 for unmarried taxpayers for 2017). If Mabel itemizes her deductions rather than claiming the standard deduction, she receives no benefit. If she does not itemize, her standard deduction for 2017 is $7,900 (the basic standard deduction of $6,350 plus the extra $1,550).

Review Question 3

Dick and Jane just learned that they are expecting their first child. What tax benefits can they expect after Junior is born?

Many. First are the dependency exemption deduction ($4,050 for 2017) and the child tax credit ($1,000 for 2017). In addition, Dick and Jane can look forward to a credit for any job-related child care expenses that they pay.

Review Question 4

Are deductions of a sole proprietor deductible *for* or *from* adjusted gross income? (**Hint:** See lines 23 through 27 on Page 1 of Form 1040 and Schedule C in Appendix B of this book.)

The trade or business expenses of a sole proprietor or someone who is self-employed are deductible for AGI. Note that these are not shown as one of the deductions for AGI on Page 1 of Form 1040. Instead, they are netted against the sole proprietor's income on Schedule C, and this net profit is included in the taxpayer's total income reported on Page 1 of Form 1040.

Review Question 5

A sole proprietor's income generally is subject to self-employment tax. Is the deduction for one-half of the self-employment tax deducted for or from adjusted gross income? Is it reported on Schedule C or Form 1040?

This is a deduction for AGI and is reported as a deduction for AGI on page 1 of Form 1040 (and not Schedule C).

Introduction to Property Transactions

The tax provisions governing property transactions play a very important part in our tax system. Obviously, their major purpose is to provide for the tax treatment of transactions involving a sale, exchange, or other disposition of property. However, the basic rules covering property transactions can also impact the tax liability in other indirect ways. For example, the amount of the deduction granted for a charitable contribution of property may depend on what the tax result would have been had the property been sold rather than donated. As this example suggests, a basic knowledge of the tax treatment of property transactions is helpful in understanding other facets of taxation. For this reason, an overview of property transactions is presented here. Chapters 14, 15, 16, and 17 examine this subject in detail.

The tax consequences of any property transaction may be determined by answering the following three questions:

1. What is the amount of gain or loss *realized?*
2. How much of this gain or loss is *recognized?*
3. What is the *character* of the gain or loss recognized?

Each of these questions is considered in the following sections.

GAIN OR LOSS REALIZED

LO.6

Calculate the gain or loss on the disposition of property and explain the tax consequences, including the special treatment of capital gains and losses.

A realized gain or loss results when a taxpayer sells, exchanges, or otherwise disposes of property. In the simple case where property is purchased for cash and later sold for cash, the gain or loss realized is the difference between the purchase price and the sale price, adjusted for transaction costs. The determination of the realized gain or loss is more complicated when property other than cash is received, when liabilities are involved, or when the property was not acquired by purchase. As a result, a more formal method for computing the gain or loss realized is used. The formulas for computing the gain or loss realized are shown in Exhibits 3-10, 3-11, and 3-12. As these exhibits illustrate, the gain or loss realized in a sale or other disposition is the difference between the *amount realized* and the *adjusted basis* in the property given up.

EXHIBIT 3-10	Computation of Amount Realized
	Amount of money received (net of money paid)
Plus:	Fair market value of any other property received
	Liabilities discharged in the transaction
Less:	Selling expenses
	Liabilities incurred
Equals:	**Amount realized**

EXHIBIT 3-11	Determination of Adjusted Basis

Basis at time of acquisition:

        For purchased property, use cost

        Special rules apply for the following methods of acquisition:

          Gift

          Bequest or inheritance

          Nontaxable transactions

Plus: Capital improvements, additions

Less: Depreciation and other capital recoveries

Equals: **Adjusted basis in property**

EXHIBIT 3-12	Computation of Gain or Loss Realized

        Amount realized from sale or other disposition

Less: Adjusted basis in property (other than money) given up

Equals: **Gain or loss realized**

Amount Realized

The amount realized is a measure of the economic value received for the property given up. It generally includes the amount of any money plus the fair market value of any other property received, reduced by any selling costs.[44] In determining the amount realized, consideration must also be given to any liabilities from which the taxpayer is relieved or which the taxpayer incurs. From an economic standpoint, when a taxpayer is relieved of debt, it is the same as if cash were received and used to pay off the debt. In contrast, when a taxpayer assumes a debt (or receives property that is subject to a debt), it is the same as if the taxpayer gave up cash. Consequently, when a sale or exchange involves the transfer of liabilities, the amount realized is increased for the net amount of any liabilities discharged or decreased for the net amount of any liabilities incurred.

Adjusted Basis

The adjusted basis of property is similar to the concept of "book value" used for accounting purposes. It is the taxpayer's basis at the time of acquisition—usually cost—increased or decreased by certain required modifications.[45] The taxpayer's basis at the time of acquisition, or original basis, depends on how the property was acquired. For purchased property, the taxpayer's original basis is the property's cost. When property is acquired by gift, inheritance, or some form of tax-deferred exchange, special rules are applied in determining the original basis. Once the original basis is ascertained, it must be increased for any capital improvements and reduced by depreciation and other capital recoveries. The adjusted basis represents the amount of investment that can be recovered free of tax.

---

[44] § 1001(b).   [45] §§ 1011 through 1016.

Example 17

This year, L sold 100 shares of M Corporation stock for $41 per share for a total of $4,100. He received a settlement check of $4,000, net of the broker's sales commission of $100. L had purchased the shares several years ago for $12 per share for a total of $1,200. In addition, he paid a sales commission of $30. L's realized gain is $2,770, computed as follows:

Amount realized ($4,100 − $100)	$4,000
Less: Adjusted basis ($1,200 + $30)	−1,230
Gain realized	$2,770

Example 18

This year T sold his office building. As part of the sales agreement, T received $20,000 cash, and the buyer assumed the mortgage on the building of $180,000. T also paid a real estate brokerage commission of $7,000. T originally acquired the building for $300,000 in 1991, but since that time had deducted depreciation of $230,000 and had made permanent improvements of $10,000. T's gain realized is computed as follows:

Amount realized:		
Cash received	$ 20,000	
Liability assumed by buyer	+180,000	
Selling expenses	− 7,000	
		$193,000
Less: Adjusted basis:		
Original cost	$300,000	
Depreciation claimed	−230,000	
Capital improvements	+ 10,000	
		− 80,000
Gain realized		$113,000

GAIN OR LOSS RECOGNIZED

The gain or loss *realized* is a measure of the economic gain or loss that results from the ownership and sale or disposition of property. However, due to special provisions in the tax law, the gain or loss reported for tax purposes may be different from the realized gain or loss. The amount of gain or loss that affects the tax liability is called the *recognized* gain or loss.

Normally, all realized gains are recognized and included as part of the taxpayer's total income. In some instances, however, the gain recognition may be permanently excluded. For example, an individual is generally allowed to exclude up to $250,000 of gain realized on the sale of a personal residence ($500,000 for married taxpayers). Other gains may be deferred or postponed until a subsequent transaction occurs.

Example 19

M exchanged some land in Oregon costing $10,000 for land in Florida valued at $50,000. Although M has realized gain of $40,000 ($50,000 − $10,000), assuming certain requirements are satisfied, this gain will not be recognized, but rather postponed. This rule was adopted because the taxpayer's economic position after the transaction is essentially unchanged. Moreover, the taxpayer has not received any cash or wherewithal with which she could pay any tax that might result.

Chapter 15 contains a discussion of the more common types of property transactions in which the recognition of an individual taxpayer's realized gains are postponed.

Any loss realized must be specifically allowed as a deduction before it is recognized. Individuals generally are allowed to deduct *three* types of losses. These are

1. Losses incurred in a trade or business (e.g., an uncollectible receivable of an accrual basis taxpayer).

2. Losses incurred in an activity engaged in for profit (e.g., sale of investment property such as stock at a loss).

3. Casualty and theft losses.

Losses in the first two categories generally are deductions for adjusted gross income. Casualty and theft losses from property used in an individual's trade, business, or income-producing activity also are allowed as deductions for adjusted gross income. However, casualty and theft losses from personal use property are classified as itemized deductions and are deductible only to the extent they exceed $100 per casualty or theft and 10% of AGI. Other than casualty and theft losses, all other losses from dispositions of personal use assets are *not* deductible. For example, if a taxpayer sold his personal residence for a loss, the loss would not be deductible. The rules governing the deductibility of losses in the first three categories are covered in Chapter 10. The special rules governing the deduction of "capital" losses are introduced below and covered in greater detail in Chapter 16.

CHARACTER OF THE GAIN OR LOSS

From 1913 through 1921, all includible income was taxed in the same manner. Since 1921, however, Congress has provided special tax treatment for "capital" gains or losses. As a result, in determining the tax consequences of a property transaction, consideration must be given to the character or nature of the gain or loss—that is, whether the gain or loss should be classified as a *capital* gain or loss or an *ordinary* gain or loss. Any *recognized* gain or loss must be characterized as either an ordinary or a capital gain or loss.

Capital Gains and Losses

Although capital gains and losses arise in numerous ways, they normally result from the sale or exchange of a *capital asset.* Any gain or loss due to the sale or exchange of a capital asset is considered a capital gain or loss.

Capital assets are defined in § 1221 of the Code as being anything *other* than the following:

1. Inventory, or other property held primarily for sale to customers in the ordinary course of a trade or business.

2. Depreciable property or real property used in a trade or business of the taxpayer.

3. Trade accounts or notes receivable.

4. Certain copyrights, literary, musical, or artistic compositions, and letters or memoranda held by the person whose personal efforts created them, and certain specified other holders of these types of property.

5. U.S. government publications acquired other than by purchase at the price at which they are sold to the general public.

The term *capital assets,* therefore, includes most passive investments (e.g., stocks and bonds) and most personal use assets of a taxpayer. However, property used in a trade or business is not a capital asset but is subject to special tax treatment, as discussed later in this chapter.

Treatment of Capital Gains

Except for a short period between 1913 and 1922, the tax law consistently has taxed gains from the sale of certain "capital assets" at rates that are substantially lower than those that apply to other income. Most recently, the special advantage is justified on the grounds that it encourages greater investment and savings. Regardless of the rationale, the hard fact is that the rules necessary to carry out the objective create an incredible layer of complexity to the tax laws. To illustrate, simply consider that capital gains qualifying for special treatment could now be taxed at one of five different rates (28, 25, 20, 15, 10, or 0 percent). Moreover, capital gains, both short-term and long-term are subject to the 3.8% tax on net investment income discussed previously.

Holding Period. The exact treatment of a capital gain or loss depends primarily on how long the taxpayer held the asset or what is technically referred to as the taxpayer's *holding period*. The holding period is a critical element in determining which of the rates will apply. As might be expected, the longer the holding period is, the lower the applicable tax rate will be. A *short-term* gain or loss is one resulting from the sale or disposition of an asset held *one year or less*. A *long-term* gain or loss occurs when an asset is held for *more than one year*.

Netting. After classifying capital gains and losses as either short-term or long-term, taxpayers must subdivide the long-term group into additional subgroups. However, this introductory discussion postpones the discussion of these subgroups until Chapter 16. At this stage, the analysis assumes that there are just two types of capital gains or losses: short-term capital gains and losses (STCGs and STCLs) and long-term capital gains (LTCGs and LTCLs). The effect of the rules is to require taxpayers to assign their capital gains and losses into two different groups and net the amounts to determine the net gain or loss in each group as shown below.

	Short-Term	Long-Term
Holding period (months) . . .	≤ 12	> 12
Gains.	$xx,xxx	$xx,xxx
Losses	(xxx)	(x,xxx)
Net gain or loss	????	????

Applicable Capital Gains Rates

Generalizations about the treatment of capital gains and losses are difficult because the actual treatment can be determined only after the various groups (i.e., the four groups above) are combined, or netted, to determine the overall net gain or loss during the year. Suffice it to say here that the treatment of the net gains of each group—*before any netting between groups*—can be summarized as follows:

1. A net short-term capital gain (NSTCG) generally receives no special treatment and is taxed as ordinary income at the taxpayer's regular tax rate (up to 39.6%).

2. A net long-term capital gain (NLTCG) is taxed at a maximum rate of 15%. However, if the taxpayer's taxable income *including* the net 15% gain would be taxed at 15% or less, a special rule applies. In this case, the net gain in this group is taxed at a rate of 0 percent. For example, if a joint filer has $60,000 of ordinary taxable income and $9,000 of NLTCG, his total taxable income normally is taxed at no greater than a 15% rate. Therefore, the NLTCG is taxed at a 0% rate. On the other hand, if the taxpayer's taxable income including the NLTCG is in the 39.6% bracket, the NLTCG is taxed at a 20% rate.

Example 20

This year, T, who is in the 35% tax bracket, reported the following capital gains and losses.

	Short-Term	Long-Term
Gains	$10,000	$10,000
Losses.	(4,000)	(3,000)
	$ 6,000	$ 7,000

T has a NSTCG of $6,000 and a NLTCG of $7,000. No further netting of these transactions occurs. T's NSTCG of $6,000 receives no special treatment and is taxed as ordinary income. T's NLTCG is taxed at 15 percent.

Dividends Taxed at Capital Gain Rates

Since 2003 most dividends received are taxed at the same rate that historically has been reserved for long-term capital gains rates.[46] The qualifying dividend is not subject to the capital gain and loss netting process. As a result, the dividends are subject to capital gains tax rates regardless of whether the taxpayer has other capital gains or losses. The dividend rates mirror the general rates for LTCGs of 0, 15, or 20 percent.

Example 21

During 2017, T, single, sold stock she had held for several years. She sold 100 shares of L for a $500 long-term capital loss and 200 shares of G for a $3,200 long-term capital gain. T also received qualified dividends of $370 for the year. T is single and has no dependents. Assume her taxable income including the above transactions is $94,971. Observe that T's NLTCG and her dividends are taxed at a favorable 15% rate since the income would otherwise be taxed at a rate of 28 percent.

Gain on G stock	$ 3,200
Loss on L stock	(500)
Net capital gain	$ 2,700
Dividend income	370
Amount subject to capital gains rate	$ 3,070
S's taxable income is taxed as follows:	
Amount subject to capital gains rate	$ 3,070
Amount treated as ordinary income ($94,971 – $3,070)	$91,900
S's tax is calculated as follows:	
Tax on ordinary income of $91,900 (see inside front cover)	$18,714
Tax on gains and dividends at 15% ($3,070 × 15%)	461
Total tax	$19,175

Treatment of Capital Losses

While capital gains receive favorable treatment, such is not the case with capital losses. As can be seen in *Example 20*, capital losses are first netted with capital gains within the same group. A net capital loss from a particular group can then be combined with net capital gains from the other group. As a general rule, the long-term gains and losses are netted together before considering any short-term items. If after netting all of the groups together, the taxpayer has an overall net capital loss, the loss is deductible up to an annual limit of $3,000. The deductible capital loss is a deduction for adjusted gross income. Any losses in excess of the annual $3,000 limitation are carried forward (retaining the character as either long-term or short-term) to the following year where they are treated as if they occurred in such year. In effect, an unused capital loss can be carried over for an indefinite period.

---

[46] § 1(h)(11).

Example 22

During the year, B reported the following capital gains and losses.

	Short-Term	Long-Term
Gains	$10,000	$5,000
Losses	(18,000)	(4,000)
	$ (8,000)	$1,000

B's only other taxable income included his salary of $50,000. He had no other deductions for AGI. After netting all of his gains and losses, B has a net capital loss of $7,000. B may deduct only $3,000 of the net capital loss in determining his AGI. Therefore, his AGI is $47,000 ($50,000 – $3,000). The unused capital loss of $4,000 ($7,000 – $3,000) is carried forward to future years when it is treated as if it arose in the subsequent year. In such case, the loss can be used against other capital gains or ordinary income just as it was this year.

Details of capital gain and loss treatment, including the treatment of the various subgroups of LTCGs, and the capital loss carryover rules are discussed in Chapter 16.

Corporate Taxpayers

The taxation of capital gains for corporate taxpayers differs somewhat from that for individuals. Most important, the capital gains of a corporation normally receive no special treatment but are taxed as ordinary income. In addition, the capital losses of a corporation can never offset ordinary income but can be carried back three and forward five years to offset other capital gains. If the capital losses of the corporation are not used by the end of the five year carryover period, they are lost. There are a number of other differences which are considered in a full discussion of a corporation's capital gains and losses in Chapter 19.

TRADE OR BUSINESS PROPERTY

Surprisingly, real and depreciable property used in a trade or business are not capital assets, but are subject to several special provisions. Nevertheless, gain on the sale of these assets may ultimately be treated as capital gain while losses may be treated as ordinary losses. These rules are quite complex and considered in Chapter 17.

CHECK YOUR KNOWLEDGE

Try the following true-false questions.

Review Question 1

An individual always receives preferential treatment for his or her capital gains.

False. An individual can receive special treatment only for long-term capital gains. Short-term capital gains are treated just like ordinary income.

Review Question 2

J invests in the stock market. This year she realized a $1,000 short-term capital gain and an $8,000 capital loss from stock she held for two years. She will report a $1,000 short-term capital gain and carry over the $8,000 long-term capital loss.

False. She first nets the short-term gain of $1,000 against her $8,000 long-term capital loss, resulting in an overall long-term capital loss of $7,000. She may deduct $3,000 of this loss as a deduction for AGI. The remaining loss is carried over to the following year as a long-term capital loss. Next year it will be treated as if she had realized a long-term capital loss of $4,000.

Review Question 3

K makes $500,000 a year and plays the stock market. So far this year she has realized a long-term capital gain of $3,000. It is now December 31. Should K sell stock and recognize a $3,000 capital loss?

Who knows? If she recognizes a $3,000 loss, the loss is offset against the gain and therefore reduces income that would have been taxed at a 20% rate. This would produce a tax benefit from the loss of only $600 ($3,000 × 20%). If she waits and uses the loss against ordinary income, it will produce a tax benefit of $1,188 (39.6% × $3,000), or $588 ($1,188 – $600) more. However, if she postpones the loss until some subsequent year hoping to use it to offset income taxed at a higher rate, she will lose the time value of the $600. Moreover, this analysis ignores the § 1411 tax of 3.8% on net investment income for taxpayers with income over $200,000 ($250,000 for joint filers).

Review Question 4

A corporation normally receives no special treatment for its long-term capital gains.

True. The long-term capital gains of a corporation normally are treated in the same manner as ordinary income.

Review Question 5

John Doe is the typical American taxpayer. He is married, has a dog and two kids. He also owns two cars: a brand new Ford and a 1996 Chevrolet. He bought the Ford for $17,000 and the Chevy for $10,000. Both of the cars were used for personal purposes. This year John and his family moved to New York and decided they did not need the cars, so he sold them. He sold the Chevy for only $3,000. The story on the Ford was different. The Ford happened to be a Mustang convertible, and because Mustangs were in demand and were on back order, a car nut was willing to give him $19,000, a $2,000 premium for not having to wait. How will these sales affect John's taxable income? Explain whether the taxpayer has a gain or loss, its character, and in the case of a loss whether it is deductible for or from AGI.

John reports a capital gain of $2,000. The first step is to determine John's gain or loss *realized*. In this case, the determination is simple. On the sale of the Chevy, John realized a loss of $7,000 ($3,000 – $10,000), and on the sale of the Mustang he realized a gain of $2,000 ($19,000 – $17,000). The second step is to determine whether he *recognizes* the gain and loss realized. John must recognize the gain. As a general rule, all income is taxable unless the taxpayer can point to a specific provision that specifically exempts the income from tax. In this case, there is no exclusion. On the other hand, the $7,000 loss is not deductible. Although all income is normally taxable, only those items specifically authorized are deductible. Only three types of losses are deductible: (1) losses incurred in carrying on a trade or business; (2) losses incurred in an activity engaged in for profit (e.g., investment losses); and (3) casualty and theft losses. In this case, the loss on the sale of the Chevy is purely personal, and therefore no deduction is allowed. Thus John is not allowed to net the loss against the gain but must report only the gain of $2,000. While this may seem like a surprising result, understand that tax is a one-way street: as a general rule, all income is taxable and only those expenses and losses specifically allowed are deductible. The final step is determining the character of the gain, that is, whether the gain is capital gain or ordinary income. In order for a taxpayer to have a capital gain, there must be a sale or exchange of a capital asset. The Code defines a capital asset as essentially everything but inventory and real or depreciable property used in a trade or business. In this case, the car is not used in business and it does not represent inventory, so it is a capital asset. As a result, John reports a capital gain of $2,000.

Review Question 6

Indicate whether the following assets are capital assets.

a. 2,000 boxes of Frosted Flakes held by a grocery store.

b. A crane used in the taxpayer's bungee-jumping business.

c. A warehouse owned by Wal-Mart.

d. IBM stock held for investment.

e. The personal residence of Jane Doe.

The Code generally defines a capital asset as essentially everything but inventory, business receivables, and real or depreciable property used in a trade or business. Based on this definition, the Frosted Flakes are not a capital asset since they are held as inventory by the grocery; the crane is not a capital asset since it is depreciable property used in a business; and the warehouse is not a capital asset since it is real property used in a business. The personal residence and IBM stock are both capital assets since they are neither inventory nor property used in a trade or business.

Tax Planning Considerations

CHOICE OF BUSINESS FORM

One of the major decisions confronting a business from a tax perspective concerns selecting the form in which it conducts its operations. A taxpayer could choose to operate a business as a sole proprietorship, a partnership, a limited liability company, an S corporation, or a regular C corporation. Each of these entities has its own tax characteristics that make it more or less suitable for a particular situation. The following discussion highlights a number of the basic factors that should be considered.

Perhaps the most important consideration in choosing a business form is the outlook for the business. A business that expects losses will typically opt for a business form different from the one that expects profits. A key advantage of a conduit entity (i.e., partnership or S corporation) applies in years in which a business suffers losses. Like income, losses flow through to the owners of the entity and generally can be used to offset other income at the individual level. In contrast, losses suffered by a regular C corporation are bottled up inside the corporate entity and can benefit only the corporation. Losses of a regular corporation generally are carried back two years and carried forward 20 years to offset income that the corporation has in prior or subsequent years.

A profitable business may also benefit from choosing the proper form of organization. To illustrate, consider a business that is generating taxable income of $1 million per year. If the taxpayer conducts the business as a sole proprietorship or through one of the conduit entities, the top tax rate applied to the income is 39.6 percent. If a C corporation is used to operate the business, the top rate is 35 percent. However, for many corporations—those with taxable incomes not exceeding $10 million—the top rate is 34 percent. Moreover, tax savings may also be generated at lower levels of income. This possibility can be seen in the tax rate schedules for corporations and individuals. A quick comparison reveals that the first $50,000 of income of a corporate taxpayer is taxed at a 15% rate, whereas married taxpayers filing jointly receive the benefits of a 15% (or lower) rate on a maximum of $75,900 (for 2017). Obviously, the tax-wise individual might try to structure the activities so that the best of both worlds could be obtained. Consider a business that produces taxable income of $90,000. If a corporation is used, the company could pay a deductible salary of $50,000 to the owner (assuming it is a reasonable amount), leaving $40,000 of taxable income in the corporation. By so doing, the maximum tax rate paid on the income would be 15 percent. Had the business been operated as a sole proprietorship or an S corporation, $14,100 ($90,000 − $75,900), the amount of taxable income in excess of $75,900, would have been taxed at a 25% rate (married filing jointly) or 10 percentage points higher. This may seem appealing, but it is a very simplistic analysis and leaves vital elements out of the equation. For example, this scheme completely ignores the problem of double taxation; it assumes that the taxpayer will be able to withdraw the $34,000 ($40,000 − $6,000 corporate income tax) left in the corporation at a later time in a deductible fashion so as to avoid the second tax. Unfortunately, doing so is not as easy as it may appear, and this plan as well as any other requires careful analysis. Suffice it to say here, however, that careful planning at the outset of a new business can save the taxpayer substantial taxes in the future.

A possible disadvantage of partnerships and S corporations concerns the treatment of certain fringe benefits. As explained in Chapter 6, the Code contains a host of fringe benefits that generally are deductible by the employer and nontaxable to the employee. For example, a corporation is entitled to deduct the costs of group-term life insurance provided to an employee, and the benefit (i.e., the payment of the premiums) is not treated as taxable compensation to the employee but is tax-free. Note that if the employee purchases the insurance directly, it is purchased with compensation that has been previously taxed. As a result, the employee acquires the benefit with after-tax dollars. The favorable tax treatment of fringe benefits is generally available only to employees of a business. Unfortunately, partners and shareholders in S corporations who work in the business are not considered employees for this purpose and consequently cannot obtain a number of the tax-favored fringe benefits. In contrast, shareholders in regular C corporations who work in the business are treated as employees and are therefore able to take advantage of the various benefits. Consideration should also be given to payroll and self-employment taxes.

ITEMIZED DEDUCTIONS VERSUS STANDARD DEDUCTION

A typical complaint of many taxpayers is that they have insufficient deductions to itemize and therefore cannot benefit from any deductions they have in a particular year. Nevertheless, with a little planning, not all of those deductions will be wasted. Taxpayers in this situation should attempt to bunch all their itemized deductions into one year. By so doing, they may itemize one year and claim the standard deduction the next. By alternating each year, total deductions over the two-year period are increased. This could be accomplished simply by postponing or accelerating the payment of expenses. Cash basis taxpayers have this flexibility because they are entitled to deduct expenses when paid.

Example 23

Marie, a widow age 61, sold her home and moved to an apartment. Due to the sale of the house, she anticipates that the only itemized deduction she would have in the future would be charitable contributions to her church as follows.

	2017	2016
Charitable contributions	$6,350	$6,350

If the pattern above continues, Marie will not receive any tax benefit from her charitable contributions since they do not exceed the standard deduction for single taxpayers, $6,350 (2017). However, what would happen if Marie simply shifted the payment of the charitable contributions from one year to the other by paying it either earlier or later. In such case, total itemized deductions in one year would be $12,700 ($6,350 + $6,350) and she could itemize, while in the other year she could claim the standard deduction. As a result, she would obtain total deductions over the two-year period of $19,050 ($12,700 charitable deduction + $6,350 standard deduction), or $6,350 ($19,050 − $12,700) more than if she merely claimed the standard deduction in both years.

EMPLOYEE BUSINESS EXPENSES

Most employee business expenses are typically paid by the employer, either through direct payment or reimbursement according to the accountable plan rules. Under these rules, employees must "adequately account" to their employers for their expenses by submitting a record, with receipts and other substantiation and return in excess advance or allowance, if any.[47] When this is done, it is as if the employee had no expense at all. Essentially, it is the employer's deduction. This approach, as set forth in the Regulations, is equivalent to treating the expenses as deductible for AGI.[48] Note that the net effect on AGI is zero.

On the other hand, if an employer requires employees to incur some business expenses, the employee can claim them only to the extent he or she itemizes and has miscellaneous itemized deductions in excess of 2% of AGI. The result is the same if an employee does not adequately account for an expense under the accountable plan rules. The amount received from the employer is included in gross income and the expense is reported as a miscellaneous itemized deduction. When this occurs, the employee may receive little or no tax benefit from the expenses.

---

[47] Regs. § 1.62-2 and § 1.162-17. See also Chapter 8.   [48] § 62(b) and Reg. § 1.62-2.

In reviewing the employee's compensation package, employers might consider changing their reimbursement policies. If an employer adopts more generous reimbursement policies in lieu of compensation increases, the employees may benefit.

Example 24

E, single, is an employee with gross income of $50,000. She typically has annual employee business expenses of $1,000 that are not reimbursed. Since E does not itemize, she derives no tax benefit from the expenses.

If, instead of the above arrangement, E received a salary of $49,000 and the $1,000 of expenses were reimbursed, she would be in the same economic position before tax. However, she would pay $250 ($1,000 × 25% marginal tax on her salary) less in Federal income taxes.

Problem Materials

DISCUSSION QUESTIONS

3-1 *Taxable Entities.* List the classes of taxable entities under the Federal income tax. Identify at least one type of entity that is not subject to the tax.

3-2 *Double Taxation.* It has been stated that corporate earnings are subject to double taxation by the Federal government. Elaborate.

3-3 *Fiduciary.* In some regards, the fiduciary is a conduit for Federal income tax purposes. Explain.

3-4 *Partnership and S Corporation Returns.* The partnership and S corporation tax returns are often referred to as information returns only. Explain.

3-5 *Income from Partnerships.* Y is a general partner in the XYZ Partnership. For the current calendar year, Y's share of profits includes his guaranteed compensation of $55,000 and his share of remaining profits, which is $22,000. What is the proper income tax and payroll tax (F.I.C.A. or self-employment tax) treatment of each of the following to Y for the current calendar year?
   a. The guaranteed compensation of $50,000.
   b. The remaining income share of $22,000.

3-6 *Income from S Corporations.* K is the president and chief executive officer of KL, Inc., an S corporation that is owned equally by individuals K and L. K receives a salary of $83,000, and her share of the net income, after deducting executive salaries, is $50,000. What is the proper income tax and payroll tax (F.I.C.A. or self-employment tax) treatment of each of the following to K for the current calendar year?
   a. The salary, assuming it is reasonable in amount.
   b. The net income of $50,000 that passes through to K.
   c. The $3,600 that the company paid for group employee medical insurance for K and her family.

3-7 *Tax Formula.* Reproduce the tax formula for individual taxpayers in good form and briefly describe each of the components of the formula. Discuss the differences between the tax formula for individuals and that for corporations.

3-8 *Gross Income.* How is gross income defined in the Internal Revenue Code?

3-9 *Deductions.* Distinguish between deductions *for* and deductions *from* adjusted gross income.

3-10 *Standard Deduction.* What is the standard deduction? Explain its relationship to itemized deductions. Which taxpayers are entitled to additional standard deductions?

3-11 *Itemized Deductions.* List seven major categories of itemized deductions. How and when are these reduced? Is the standard deduction reduced? If so, under what circumstances?

3-12 *Employee Business Expenses.* Expenses incurred that are directly related to one's activities as an employee are trade or business expenses. True or False?

3-13 *Additional Standard Deduction.* H and W are married and are 74 and 76 years of age, respectively. They also paid real property taxes on their home of $1,500. The couple does not itemize. Assuming they have gross income of $40,000 for 2017 and file a joint return, determine their taxable income.

3-14 *Exemptions.* Differentiate between personal exemptions and dependency exemptions. Which taxpayers are denied a personal exemption?

3-15 *Credits.* There are numerous credits that are allowed to reduce a taxpayer's Federal income tax liability. List at least four such credits.

3-16 *Credits.* Credits of equal amount affect persons in different tax brackets equally, whereas deductions of equal amount are more beneficial to taxpayers in higher tax brackets. Explain.

3-17 *Prepayments.* What is meant by the concept of "wherewithal to pay" for tax purposes? How do prepayments of an individual's income taxes in the form of withholding and quarterly estimates represent the application of this concept?

3-18 *Alternative Minimum Tax.* What is the alternative minimum tax? Explain what is meant by *alternative* and *minimum* in this context.

3-19 *Amount Realized.* What is meant by "the amount realized in a sale or other disposition"? How is the amount realized calculated?

3-20 *Adjusted Basis.* Describe the concept of adjusted basis. How is the basis in purchased property determined?

3-21 *Gain or Loss Realized.* Reproduce the formula for determining the gain or loss realized in a sale or other disposition of property.

3-22 *Gain or Loss Recognized.* Differentiate between the terms "gain or loss realized" and "gain or loss recognized."

3-23 *Losses.* Which losses are deductible by individual taxpayers?

3-24 *Capital Assets.* Define the term "capital asset."

3-25 *Holding Period.* The determination of the holding period is important in determining the treatment of capital gains and losses. What is the difference between a long-term holding period and a short-term holding period?

3-26 *Capital Gains.* Briefly explain the favorable treatment given to capital gains and when such treatment applies.

3-27 *Capital Losses of Individuals.* There are "limitations" on the capital loss deduction for individuals. Identify these limitations.

3-28 *Capital Losses of Corporations.* What is the limitation on the deduction for capital losses of a corporate taxpayer?

3-29 *Carryover of Excess Capital Losses.* Excess capital losses of individuals may be offset against gains for other years. Specify the carryover and/or carryback period for such excess losses.

YOU MAKE THE CALL

3-30 Shortly after Murray began working in the tax department of the public accounting firm of Dewey, Cheatham, and Howe, he was preparing a tax return and discovered an error in last year's work papers. In computing the gain on the sale of the taxpayer's duplex, the preparer had failed to increase the amount realized by the $50,000 mortgage assumed by the buyer. Apparently, the mistake was overlooked during the review process. Upon discovering the mistake, Murray went to his immediate supervisor, Norm (who actually prepared last year's return), and pointed out the error. Norm, knowing that the client would probably flip if he found out he had to pay more tax, told Murray "let's just wait and see if the IRS catches it. Forget it for now." What should Murray do?

PROBLEMS

3-31 *To Whom Is Income Taxed?* In each of the following separate cases, determine how much income is to be taxed to each of the taxpayers involved:

    a.   Alpha Partnership is owned 60% by W and 40% by P, who agree to share profits according to their ownership ratios. For the current year, Alpha earned $12,000 in ordinary income. The partnership distributed $3,000 to W and $2,000 to P.

    b.   Beta Trust is managed by T for the benefit of B. The trust is required to distribute all income currently. For the current year, Beta Trust had net ordinary income of $5,500 and made cash distributions to B of $7,000.

    c.   Gamma Inc., a C corporation, is owned and operated by its two equal owners, H and K. This year the corporation reported earned income—before any distributions to its owners—of $24,000. On May 4, the corporation declared a dividend, distributing $1,350 to H and $1,350 to K.

3-32 *Selecting a Form of Doing Business.* Which form of business—sole proprietorship, partnership, S corporation, limited liability company, or regular corporation—is each of the following taxpayers likely to choose? An answer may include more than one business form.

    a.   Edmund and Gloria are starting a new business that they expect to operate at a net loss for about five years. Both Edmund and Gloria expect to have substantial incomes during those years from other sources.

    b.   Robin would like to incorporate her growing retail business for nontax reasons. Because she needs all of the net profits to meet personal obligations, Robin would like to avoid the corporate "double tax" on dividends.

3-33 *Income from C Corporations.* M is the president and chief executive officer of MN, Inc., a corporation that is owned solely by M. During the current calendar year, MN, Inc. paid M a salary of $80,000, a bonus of $22,000, and dividends of $30,000. The corporation's gross income is $350,000, and its expenses excluding payments to M are $225,000.

    a.   Compute the corporation's taxable income and determine its gross income tax. See inside back cover for corporate tax rates.

    b.   Assuming M's only other income is interest income of $12,500, determine M's AGI.

    c.   Does this situation represent double taxation of corporate profits? Explain.

3-34 *Income from Partnerships.* J is a one-fourth partner in JKLM Partnership. The partnership had gross sales of $880,000, cost of sales of $540,000, and operating expenses excluding payments to partners of $145,000 for the current calendar year. Partners' compensation for services of $90,000 ($45,000 to J) were paid, and distributions of $120,000 ($30,000 to J) were made for the year.

    a.   Determine the partnership's net income for tax reporting purposes.

    b.   Determine the amount of income J must report from the partnership for the year.

    c.   Determine how much of the income in (b) is self-employment income.

3-35 *Income from Fiduciaries.* G created a trust for the benefit of B to be managed by T. For the current year, the trust had gross income of $45,000, income-producing deductions of $1,900, and cash distributions to B of $12,500.

    a.   Determine the taxable income of the trust.

    b.   Assuming B's only other income is interest of $22,300, determine B's AGI.

3-36 *Tax Treatment of Various Entities.* Office Supplies Unlimited is a small office supply outlet. The results of its operations for the most recent year are summarized as follows:

Gross profit on sales	$95,000
Cash operating expenses	43,000
Depreciation expense	16,500
Compensation to owner(s)	20,000
Distribution of profit to owner(s)	5,000

In each of the following situations, determine how much income is to be taxed (i.e., to be included along with any other income in calculating taxable income) to each of the taxpayers involved.

a. The business is a sole proprietorship owned by T.
b. The business is a partnership owned by R and S with an agreement to share all items equally. S is guaranteed a salary of $20,000 (see above).
c. The business is a corporation owned equally by U and K. K is employed by the business and receives a salary of $20,000 (see above).

3-37 *Gross Income.* The following represent some of the more important items of income for Federal tax purposes. For each, indicate whether it is fully includible in gross income, fully excludable from gross income, or partially includible and partially excludable.

a. Alimony received from a former spouse.
b. Interest from state and local governments.
c. Money and other property inherited from a relative.
d. Social Security benefits.
e. Tips and gratuities.
f. Proceeds of life insurance received upon the death of one's spouse.

3-38 *Classifying Deductions.* The following represent some of the more important deductions for Federal tax purposes. For each, indicate whether it is deductible for AGI or as an itemized deduction.

a. Alimony paid to one's former spouse.
b. Charitable contributions.
c. Trade or business expenses of a self-employed person.
d. Expenses of providing an apartment to a tenant for rent.
e. Interest incurred to finance one's principal residence.
f. Reimbursed trade or business expenses of an employee.
g. Unreimbursed business expenses of an employee.

3-39 *Determining Adjusted Gross Income and Taxable Income.* Fred and Susan are married and file a joint income tax return. Neither is blind or age 65. They have two children whom they support, and the following income and deductions for 2017:

Gross income	$57,200
Deductions for AGI	1,200
Total itemized deductions	8,900
Credits and prepayments	3,050

Determine Fred and Susan's AGI and taxable income for the calendar year 2017.

3-40 *Tax Formula.* The following information is from the 2017 joint income tax return of Gregory and Stacy Jones, both of good sight and under 65 years of age.

Gross income	$67,800
Adjusted gross income	58,950
Taxable income	29,250
Number of personal exemptions	2
Number of dependency exemptions	2

Determine the amount of the Jones's deductions for AGI and the amount of their itemized deductions.

3-41 *Tax Formula.* Complete the following table of independent cases for Zac Williams for 2017. Zac is 31 years old and is single.

	A	B	C
Gross income	$50,000	$???	$???
Deductions for AGI	(???)	(8,000)	(7,000)
Adjusted gross income (AGI)	$42,000	$78,000	???
Itemized deductions	(???)	(4,650)	(7,350)
Standard deduction	(???)	(???)	(???)
Exemptions	2	1	1
	(???)	(???)	(???)
Taxable income	$25,400	$???	$65,950

3-42 *Worldwide Income Subject to Tax.* T, a U.S. citizen, has income that was earned outside the United States. The income was $20,000, and a tax of $2,000 was paid to the foreign government. Determine the general treatment of this income and the tax paid under the following circumstances:

a. The tax paid was on income earned on foreign investments, and the U.S. tax attributable to this income is $2,800.

b. Same as (a), except the U.S. tax attributable to this income is $1,800.

c. Same as (a), except the income is from services rendered while absent from the United States for 13 successive months.

3-43 *Alternative Minimum Tax.* L is single, has no dependents, and uses the cash method and the calendar year for tax purposes. The following information was derived from L's records for 2017:

Taxable income (regular income tax)	$74,200
AMT adjustments and preferences	70,200

Although L has substantial gross income and deductions, she does not itemize. Calculate L's regular income tax using the tax rates for 2017 and her alternative minimum tax, if any.

3-44 *Asset Classification.* For each of the assets in the list below, designate the appropriate category using the symbols given:

> C – Capital asset
> T – Trade or business asset (§ 1231)
> O – Other (neither capital nor § 1231 asset)

a. Personal residence.
b. Stock in Xerox Corporation.
c. Motor home used for vacations.
d. Groceries held for sale to customers.
e. Land held for investment.
f. Land and building held for use in auto repair business.
g. Trade accounts receivable of physician's office.
h. Silver coins held primarily for speculation.

3-45 *Gain or Loss Realized.* During the current year, W disposed of a vacant lot which he had held for investment. W received cash of $12,000 for his equity in the lot. The lot was subject to a $32,000 mortgage that was assumed by the buyer. Assuming W's basis in the lot was $23,000, how much is his realized gain or loss?

3-46 *Adjusted Basis.* M owns a rental residence that she is considering selling, but she is interested in knowing her exact tax basis in the property. She originally paid $39,000 for the property. M has spent $8,000 on a new garage, $2,500 for a new outdoor patio deck, and $4,500 on repairs and maintenance. M has been allowed depreciation on the unit in the amount of $7,500. Based on this information, calculate M's basis in the rental residence.

3-47 *Gain or Loss Realized, Adjusted Basis.* This year S sold her rental house. She received cash of $6,000 and a vacant lot worth $30,000. The buyer assumed the $36,000 mortgage loan outstanding against S's property. S had purchased the house for $52,000 four years earlier and had deducted depreciation of $12,000. How much are S's amount realized, her adjusted basis in the house sold, and her gain or loss realized in this transaction?

3-48 *Capital Gain and Loss.* Individual D is in the 35% tax bracket. This year he executed the following transactions.

Transaction	Sales Price	Adjusted Basis	Holding Period
Sale of 100 shares of XYZ.	$2,000	$1,000	15 months
Sale of land held for investment	9,000	3,000	19 months
Sale of silver held for speculation	5,000	7,000	23 months
Sale of personal jewelry	4,000	6,000	60 months

Determine the tax consequences (e.g., gain, loss, applicable tax rates) of these transactions.

3-49 *Excess Capital Loss.* This year, T, an individual taxpayer, had a short-term capital gain of $4,000 and a capital loss of $9,000 from stock he held for four years. How much is T's allowable capital loss deduction for the year? What is the treatment of the short-term gain?

3-50 *Individual's Tax Computation.* Richard Hartman, age 29, single with no dependents, received a salary of $62,670 in 2017. During the year, he received $1,300 interest income from a savings account and a $1,500 gift from his grandmother. At the advice of his father, Richard sold stock he had held as an investment for five years, for a $3,000 gain. He also sustained a loss of $1,000 from the sale of land held as an investment and owned for four months. Richard had itemized deductions of $9,250. For 2017 compute the following for Richard:

   a. Gross income.
   b. Adjusted gross income.
   c. Taxable income.
   d. Income tax before credits and prepayments (use the appropriate 2017 tax rate schedule located on the inside front cover).
   e. Income tax savings that would result if Richard made a deductible $2,000 contribution to a qualified Individual Retirement Account.

3-51 *Tax Treatment of Income from Entities.* The G family—Mr. G, Mrs. G, and G Jr.—owns interests in the following successful entities:

1. X Corporation is a calendar year regular corporation owned 60% by Mr. G and 15% by G Jr. During the year, it paid salaries to Mr. G of $80,000 to be its president and to G Jr. of $24,000 to be a plant supervisor. The company earned a net taxable income of $75,000, and paid dividends to Mr. G and G Jr. in the amounts of $42,000 and $10,500, respectively.

2. Mrs. G owned a 60% capital interest in a retail outlet, P Partnership. The partnership earned a net taxable income of $60,000 and made distributions during the year of $72,000. The profit and the distributions were allocated according to relative capital interests.

3. Mr. G and G Jr. each own 25% interest in H Corporation, an electing S Corporation. The corporation is a start-up venture and generated a net tax loss of $28,000 for the calendar year. No dividend distributions were made by H. Both Mr. G and G Jr. have bases in their H Corporation stock of $30,000.

4. G Jr. is the sole beneficiary of G Trust created by Mrs. G's father. The trust received dividends of $16,000 and made distributions of $4,500 to G Jr.

    Determine the amount of income or loss from each entity that is to be reported by the following:

    a. Mr. and Mrs. G on their joint calendar year tax return
    b. G Jr. on his calendar year individual return
    c. X Corporation
    d. P Partnership
    e. H Corporation
    f. G Trust

3-52 *Comprehensive Taxable Income Computation.* Indy Smith, single, is an anthropology professor at State University. The tax records that he brought to you for preparation of his return revealed the following items.

Income:

Salary from State University	$68,450
Part-time consulting	5,000
Dividend income	1,250
Reimbursement of travel to Denver by State University	200

Expenses:

Interest on personal residence	$ 9,800
Travel expenses related to consulting	1,000
Tax return preparation fee	500
Safe deposit box to hold bonds	50
Travel and lodging to present academic paper in Denver related to his teaching position	450

In addition, Indy claims a dependency exemption for his father for whom he provides 60% support (including 60% of housing costs). Compute Indy's final tax liability for calendar year 2017.

3-53 *Comprehensive Taxable Income Computation.* Eli and Lilly have been happily married for 30 years. Eli, 67, is a research chemist at Pharmaceuticals Inc. Lilly, 64, recently retired but stays busy managing the couple's investments, including a duplex. The majority of the couple's income is derived from Eli's employment, from which he received a salary of $95,000 this year. Other income includes interest on corporate bonds of $5,600 and interest on State of Illinois bonds of $1,000. In addition, rents collected from the duplex were $10,000 while rental expenses (e.g., maintenance, utilities, depreciation) were $6,000. During the year, the company transferred Eli to a new division located in nearby suburb about 55 miles north of his old office. As a result, the couple decided to move so that Eli would not have such a long commute. They paid deductible moving expenses of $2,000. The couple also paid the following expenses: unreimbursed medical expenses, $7,400; interest on the home mortgage, $11,300; property taxes on the home, $3,000; charitable contributions, $4,000; and rental of safe deposit box, $100. Determine the couple's taxable income for 2017.

3-54 *Alternative Minimum Tax.* H and W are married and filed a joint return for 2017. The couple has five children between the ages of 3 and 13. Their records for the current year reveal the following:

Salary income (their only income).	$165,000
State and local taxes (property and income)	40,000
Miscellaneous itemized deductions (after 2% of AGI limitation)	$5,000

Using the 2017 tax rates, compute the alternative minimum tax, if any.

3-55 *Losses.* This year, B and J formed a partnership to operate a bar and grill. B was the brains behind the venture and J supplied the bulk of the financing. B contributed $30,000 to the partnership, receiving a 30% interest while J contributed $70,000 for a 70% interest. B received 30% of the profits and losses and J received 70 percent. During the year, B worked his fingers to the bone, running the business. J did little, sitting back and watching his investment. For the year, the partnership reported a $30,000 loss (revenues $60,000, deductible expenses $90,000). Can B and J use their share of the loss as a deduction to offset other income they might have on their own individual tax return (Form 1040) such as the salary income of their spouses? Explain.

3-56 *Net Investment Income Tax.* Jack and Diane are married. Jack is an attorney and this year earned $120,000. Diane is a partner with a local public accounting firm. She earned $140,000. For the current year, the couple reported adjusted gross income of $260,000. Their income included interest of $8,000.
   a. What is the amount of their net investment income tax for the year?
   b. Same as (a) above except the couple's adjusted gross income was $255,000.

3-57 *Net Investment Income Tax.* Which of the following items would have an impact on the amount, if any, of the net investment income tax that a taxpayer might have to pay?
   a. The taxpayer's marital status.
   b. The taxpayer's salary.
   c. The taxpayer's share of income from a partnership; the taxpayer does not actively participate in the partnership.
   d. Rental income from a duplex the taxpayer owns.
   e. Repairs and maintenance expenses on the duplex.
   f. Sale of Google stock held for three months.
   g. Gain on the sale of the taxpayer's personal residence.
   h. Distribution from an individual retirement account (e.g., a Roth IRA).
   i. Income earned from performing services in Japan.

3-58 *Issue Identification.* Fred Stevens is the CIO (chief information officer and head of the information technology) for Global Solutions. GHI has operations all over the world. Normally, Fred works in his hometown, Boston, but for all of 2016, the company assigned Fred to a special project in London, England. Fred and his wife just returned from London and he wants to talk to you about this year's tax return. He will be coming over to your office later today. Fred noted that he had the income shown below.

Salary income.	$300,000
Interest on First National Bank of Boston savings account.	10,000

His salary represented a substantial increase over the prior year. Based on this information, what points would you want to make regarding his tax liability for 2017?

TAX RETURN PROBLEMS

■ *CONTINUOUS TAX RETURN PROBLEMS* See Appendix I, Part 1.

TAX RESEARCH PROBLEM

3-59 *Using the Internal Revenue Code.* Locate a copy of the *Internal Revenue Code of 1986.* Read §§ 61 through 65, 67, 151, and 152. Read the titles of §§ 71 through 135, 161, and 162.
   a. Describe how Congress defined "gross income."
   b. Why is the "exemption deduction" properly called a deduction from adjusted gross income?
   c. A taxpayer is self-employed and incurs an ordinary and necessary expense in his business endeavor. What is the authority for deducting the expense? Why is it considered a deduction *for* adjusted gross income?
   d. A taxpayer pays alimony to her former husband. Within limits, it is deductible *for* adjusted gross income. Why?

4

Personal and Dependency Exemptions; Filing Status; Determination of Tax for an Individual; Filing Requirements

Learning Objectives

Upon completion of this chapter you will be able to:

LO.1 Identify the types of exemptions that may be claimed.

LO.2 Explain the requirements to claim an exemption for dependents.

LO.3 Describe the child tax credit.

LO.4 Apply the rules to determine the taxpayer's filing status.

LO.5 Compute the tax liability of an individual taxpayer using the tax rate schedules and the tax tables.

LO.6 Explain the special approach used in computing the tax liability of certain children.

LO.7 Describe the filing requirements for individual taxpayers.

LO.8 Explain when taxes must be paid and the penalties that apply for failure to pay on a timely basis.

LO.9 Describe the statute of limitations as it applies to the filing of tax returns.

Chapter Outline

Introduction

As seen in Chapter 3, numerous factors must be considered in the determination of an individual's net tax liability. Beginning in this chapter and continuing through Chapter 18, a detailed examination of these factors is conducted. This chapter is devoted to five particular concerns of individual taxpayers:

1. Personal and dependency exemptions;
2. Child tax credit;
3. Filing status;
4. Calculation of the tax liability using the tax rate schedules and tax tables; and
5. Filing requirements.

Personal and Dependency Exemptions

LO.1

Identify the types of exemptions that may be claimed.

Since the inception of the income tax, policymakers have recognized the need to protect from tax some minimum amount of income that could be used for the support of the taxpayer and those who depend on him. The device used to accomplish this objective is the deduction allowed for exemptions. There are two types of exemptions for which deductions are allowed: personal exemptions and exemptions for a child or other dependent.[1] Taxpayers may deduct the *exemption amount* for each of their exemptions. The exemption amount for 2016 and 2017 is $4,050.[2] Each type of exemption is discussed below.

PERSONAL EXEMPTIONS

There are *two* types of personal exemptions:

1. Exemption for the taxpayer.
2. Exemption for the taxpayer's spouse.

Each individual taxpayer normally is entitled to one personal exemption. When a *joint return* is filed by a married couple, *two* personal exemptions may be claimed. This occurs not because one spouse is the dependent of the other, but because the husband and wife are each entitled to his or her own personal exemption. If a married individual files a *separate return,* however, a personal exemption may be claimed for his or her spouse only if the spouse has no gross income and is not claimed as a dependent of another taxpayer.[3]

Disallowance of Personal Exemption

A taxpayer is denied a personal exemption if he or she qualifies as a dependent of another taxpayer (see discussion below).[4] This rule prevents two taxpayers (e.g., a child and his or her parent) from benefiting from two exemptions for the same person.

Example 1

J is 21 years of age and a full-time college student. J receives a partial scholarship and works part-time, but the majority of his support is received from his parents. Assuming J is eligible to be claimed as a dependent on his parents' return, he is not entitled to a personal exemption deduction on his own return. This rule applies *regardless* of whether J's parents actually claim an exemption for him.

---

[1] §§ 151(a), 151(b), and 151(c).

[2] Since 1985 the exemption amount has been increased to reflect price level changes based on changes in the consumer price index. The exact amount is announced by the IRS in the fall of the preceding year. For instance, the exemption amount for 2018 will be announced by December 15, 2017. §§ 1(f) and 151(d)(3). If the exemption amount had been adjusted for inflation since 1948, when it was $600, it would have been about $6,009 for 2016 (calculated using the Bureau of Labor Statistics inflation calculator based on the Consumer Price Index, http://www.bls.gov/data/inflation_calculator.htm). Also see Steurle, "Decline in the Value of the Dependent Exemption," 62 *Tax Notes* 109 (October 4, 1993).

[3] § 151(b).

[4] § 151(d)(2).

EXEMPTIONS FOR DEPENDENTS

For as long as most remember, an individual qualified as a taxpayer's dependent if he or she met one set of rules. Ironically, in an attempt toward simplicity in 2005, Congress added a second set of rules under which an individual might be considered a dependent. Section 152 now defines a dependent as either:

LO.2
Explain the requirements to claim an exemption for dependents.

1. A qualifying child, or
2. A qualifying relative.

EXEMPTION FOR QUALIFYING CHILD

An individual is considered a *qualifying child* and can be claimed as a dependent of the taxpayer if he or she satisfies all of the following tests.[5]

1. *Relationship Test.* The individual and the taxpayer must meet one of the following relationship tests:
    *   Natural child, stepchild, adopted child, certain foster children.
    *   A sibling or step-sibling.
    *   A descendant of one of the above.

    Note that the scope of these rules goes far beyond the conventional definition of a taxpayer's "child." For example, a taxpayer's brother or sister is considered his or her child as are his nieces or nephews. Similarly, a taxpayer's "children" include a grandchild as well as great grandchildren and other descendants.

2. *Residence Test.* The "child" must have the *same principal place of abode* (i.e., residence) as the taxpayer for more than one-half of the taxable year. Temporary absences are permissible if due to special circumstances such as education, illness, business, vacation, or military service. Note that a child could live more than half of the taxable year with more than one person where several people, including the child, live together. For example, the child could live with his mother, grandmother, and grandfather. Thus this test could be met with respect to more than one person.

3. *Age Requirement.* The "child" must also meet one of the conditions concerning age:
    *   Has not reached age 19 by the close of the taxable year.
    *   Has not reached age 24 *and* is considered a full-time student at a qualifying educational institution. For this purpose, "full-time" is whatever is considered full-time under the rules and regulations of the institution. The individual must meet the full-time condition for any part of five calendar months during the calendar year.
    *   Is permanently and totally disabled at any time during the year. The age limitation does not apply to these individuals.
    *   The qualifying child must be younger than the taxpayer.

4. *Joint Return Test.* The "child" must not have filed a joint return with his or her spouse except to claim a refund (i.e., the tax due was zero before prepayments).

5. *Citizenship or Residency Test.* The "child" must be a U.S. citizen, resident or national, or a resident of Canada or Mexico.

6. *Not Self-Supporting Test.* To be a "qualifying child" the "child" may not be self-supporting; that is, the child must not have provided more than one-half of his or her own support. For this purpose, scholarships received from an educational institution are not considered an amount spent on support.

---

[5] § 152(c).

Tie Breaker Rules

Application of the tests above could result in an individual being a "qualifying child" for more than one taxpayer. For example, if a 10-year-old child lived with his father, grandmother, and uncle in the same residence during the year, the father, grandmother, or uncle could potentially claim the child as a dependent since the child meets the relationship, age and residence test with respect to each. Such a situation is not surprising in an age when family structures are often unconventional due to divorce and remarriage, absentee parents, childbearing by unmarried individuals, and multi-generational households. When a child is a qualifying child for more than one taxpayer and the parties cannot agree as to who will claim an exemption, the following tie-breaker rules apply:[6]

- If only one of the taxpayers is the child's parent, the parent claims the exemption for the child.

- If both taxpayers are the child's parents and they do not file a joint return, the parent with whom the child resided for the longest period of time during the tax year claims the exemption for the child. Note that this tie-breaker rule must be used. The parents cannot agree between themselves as to whom will claim the exemption.

- If the child resides with both parents for the same period of time during the tax year and the parents do not file a joint return, the parent with the highest adjusted gross income claims the exemption for the child.

- If none of the taxpayers are the child's parent, the taxpayer with the highest adjusted gross income for the tax year claims the exemption for the child.

Example 2

For the current year, M and D, mom and dad, provide a home in which they live with their son, P, and P's daughter, G. P is unmarried, 23 years of age and a full-time student. P earned $6,000 for the year, which is less than 50% of his total support. M and D may claim an exemption for P—he is their qualifying child since he meets all of the tests (age, residence, and relationship). Under the tie-breaking rules, P, as parent, would be able to claim an exemption for his daughter G; however, P cannot claim G as a dependent because P is, himself, a dependent. In this case, M and D could claim an exemption for their granddaughter G because she is a qualifying child with respect to them.

EXEMPTION FOR QUALIFYING RELATIVE

The second type of dependent is a *qualifying relative*—generally a relative or member of the taxpayer's household that depends on the taxpayer for support. In contrast to the definition for qualifying children, this term permits exemptions for a broader class of individuals but only if the taxpayer provides for their support and the prospective dependent meets an income test.

Technically, an individual is considered a *qualifying relative* only if he or she is *not* a qualifying child and meets the following requirements each of which is discussed in detail below.[7]

1. *Support Test.* The taxpayer must provide more than 50% of the dependent's total support.

2. *Gross Income Test.* The dependent's gross income must be less than the exemption amount.

---

[6] § 152(c)(4).   [7] § 152(d).

3. *Relationship or Member of the Household Test.* The dependent must be a relative of the taxpayer or a member of the taxpayer's household for the entire taxable year.

4. *Joint Return Test.* The dependent must not have filed a joint return with his or her spouse.

5. *Citizenship or Residency Test.* The dependent must be a U.S. citizen, resident or national, or a resident of Canada or Mexico.

Although an individual could conceivably be a qualifying relative and a qualifying child, the Code makes it clear that in such case the individual is treated as a qualifying child, and therefore, he or she cannot be claimed as a dependent by someone under the qualifying relative rules.

Support Test for Qualifying Relative

To satisfy the support requirement, the taxpayer must provide more than half of the amount spent for the dependent's total support.[8] Total support includes not only amounts expended by others on behalf of the dependent but also any amounts spent by the dependent. Note that only the amount *actually spent* for support is relevant. Income and other funds available to the dependent for spending are ignored unless they are spent.

Example 3

During the year, C paid $10,000 to maintain her father, F, in a nursing home that provides all of his needs. No other amounts were spent for his support. C made these payments, even though her father could afford them since he has cash in the bank and tax-exempt bonds valued at $200,000. Although F has funds available for providing his own support, they are not considered in applying the support test because the funds were not spent. Consequently, the support test is satisfied.

Support is generally measured by the cost of the item to the individual providing it. However, when support is provided in a noncash form, such as the use of property or lodging, the amount of support is the fair market value or fair rental value.

What constitutes an item of support is not always clear. If, for example, a child receives a stereo or car, are these items considered support, or do only necessities qualify? The Regulations provide some guidance as to the nature of support, indicating that it includes food, shelter, clothing, medical and dental care, education, recreation, and transportation.[9]

EXHIBIT 4-1	**Partial List of Support Items**
Automobile	Lodging
Care for a dependent's pet	Medical care
Charitable contributions by or on behalf of dependent	Medical insurance premiums
Child care	Singing lessons
Clothing	Telephone
Dental care	Television
Education	Toys
Entertainment	Transportation
Food	Utilities
Gifts	Vacations

---

[8] § 152(d)(1)(c).   [9] Reg. § 1.152-1(a)(2)(i).

Support is not limited to these items, however. Examination of the numerous cases and rulings reveals a hodgepodge of qualifying expenditures as well as some that are not. For example, the costs for boats, life insurance, and lawn mowers are not considered support. Additionally, the value of any services performed for the dependent by the taxpayer is ignored.[10] Exhibit 4-1 presents a sampling of those items that constitute support.

The determination of support also is complicated by several items accorded special treatment. For example, scholarships and fellowships received by the taxpayer's child or stepchild are not considered support items. Accordingly, such amounts are not treated as being provided by either the taxpayer or the dependent.[11]

Example 4

J was the recipient of an athletic scholarship that covered 100% of her tuition, books, supplies, room, and board. In addition, J was paid a small cash allowance. J's parents also provided her with $4,000 cash to be used for clothing, entertainment, and miscellaneous expenses.

The scholarship package, which was related to J's continued scholastic activity, was valued at $19,500 per year. Nevertheless, assuming the other four tests are met, J's parents are entitled to a dependency exemption, since the scholarship is not included in her support and she is not self-supporting.[12]

Although Social Security benefits generally are not taxable income to the recipient, they are considered as support provided by the person covered by Social Security. Thus, Social Security benefits are included in determining support to the extent they are spent for support.[13] State welfare payments are considered provided by the state, and therefore are not treated as provided by the parent or any other taxpayer. This is true even though the parent is entrusted to oversee the prudent expenditure of the funds.[14]

Example 5

F received support during the current year from various sources, including amounts contributed by his son, S. The amounts spent toward F's support were provided as follows:

F's Social Security benefits	$ 7,500
Taxable interest income	900
Amount provided by S	4,100
Total	$12,500

S is not entitled to a dependency exemption for F because he did not provide more than 50% of F's total support ($4,100 is not greater than 50% of $12,500).

---

[10] *Markarian v. Comm.,* 65-2 USTC ¶9699, 16 AFTR2d 5785, 352 F.2d 870 (CA-7, 1965).

[11] Reg. § 1.152-1(c). Note that G.I. Bill benefits are not treated as scholarships and therefore are included as support items provided by the recipient.

[12] Any part of a scholarship providing benefits other than tuition, fees, and supplies, is *includible* in the recipient's gross income to the extent of those benefits. See Chapter 6 for a discussion of taxable scholarships.

[13] Reg. § 1.152-1(a)(2)(ii).

[14] See Rev. Rul. 71-468, 1971-2 C.B. 115 and *N. Williams,* T.C. Memo 1996-126. A similar result was reached related to state payments for the care of a mentally retarded child. See *Trail,* T.C. Memo 1993-221, *aff'd* at 73 AFTR2d ¶ 94-931 (CA-5, 1994).

Example 6

This year K received Social Security benefits of $8,000. Amounts spent toward K's support were provided as follows:

K's Social Security benefits spent.....................	$ 2,500
Taxable interest income spent.......................	600
Amount provided by K's brother, B	4,000
Total	$ 7,100

Assuming the other tests are met, B may claim K as a dependent since he provided more than one-half of her support expenditures ($4,000 is > 50% of $7,100).

In many instances, an individual who is not self-supporting is supported by more than one taxpayer. Generally, no dependency exemption is allowed for such persons because no *one* individual provides more than 50% of the total support provided. However, an exemption may be allowed under what is referred to as a "multiple support agreement."

Multiple Support Agreements

A dependency exemption for a qualifying relative may be assigned to a taxpayer under a multiple support agreement if all of the following tests are met:[15]

1. No one person contributed over half the support of the individual.
2. Over half the support was provided by a group, all of whose members are qualifying relatives of the individual.
3. The citizenship, joint return, and gross income requirements are met by the individual.
4. The dependency exemption is assigned by agreement to a group member *who contributed more* than 10% of the total support.
5. Each of the members contributing more than 10% signs a declaration that he or she will not claim the exemption on Form 2120 (see Appendix B), which is then filed with the return of the taxpayer claiming the exemption.

Example 7

M, single, received her support of $12,000 for this year from the following sources:

	Amount	Percentage
Social Security benefits..	$ 4,000	33.33%
Taxable interest income	800	6.67
From D, M's daughter	4,700	39.17
From S, M's son	1,500	12.50
From G, M's grandchild	1,000	8.33
	$12,000	100.00%

Together, D, S, and G contribute more than 50% of M's support for the year ($7,200 > 50% of $12,000). If a multiple support agreement is executed, either D or S may claim the exemption deduction. G is not eligible since he did not contribute more than 10% of the total support. Also, note that S may claim M as a dependent even though D provided more of M's support.

---

[15] § 152(c).

Gross Income Test for Qualifying Relative

The second test that must be met before an individual is considered a qualifying relative concerns his or her gross income. The individual's gross income cannot exceed the exemption amount ($4,050 for 2017).[16] In applying this test, the technical definition of "gross income" must be heeded.[17] It does not include items that are excluded from income. Accordingly, a person whose only sources of income are excluded from gross income (e.g., Social Security and municipal bond interest) may qualify as a dependent. Note also that gross income is not always synonymous with includible gross receipts. Regulation § 1.61-3 indicates that gross income for a merchandising business generally means the total sales less the cost of goods sold *plus* any income from investments or other sources. The importance of this distinction between gross receipts and gross income is demonstrated in the following example.

Example 8

For 2017, T provides 60% of the support for his single brothers, F and R. F's only income is from the sale of fireworks. During the year, he sold fireworks costing $4,000 for $6,500. R's only income is derived from rental property. During the year, he collected rents of $4,200 while incurring expenses of $1,700 for repairs, maintenance, and interest. Although F and R each earned $2,500 (F: $6,500 − $4,000 = $2,500; R: $4,200 − $1,700 = $2,500), F's gross income was $2,500, while R's was $4,200. As a result, T can only claim an exemption for F, since F's *gross income* of $2,500 was less than the $4,050 exemption amount for 2017.

Relationship or Member of Household Test for Qualifying Relative

The third of the five hurdles that must be cleared before an individual can be claimed as a dependent concerns the individual's relationship to the taxpayer. Regardless of the amount of support that the taxpayer provides for another person, no exemption is allowed unless the prospective dependent is properly related to the taxpayer.[18] Apparently the authors of the dependency rules believed that the tax law should not grant an exemption unless there is some obligation on the part of the taxpayer to support an individual. Such an obligation normally exists between relatives or others who are members of the taxpayer's household. Therefore, to qualify as a dependent, an individual must satisfy one the qualifying relationship tests below. All of these are *familial* (i.e., related by blood, marriage, or adoption) except one. These are

1. A child or descendant of a child (other than one who would be considered a "qualifying child" under the tests discussed earlier).

2. A brother, sister, stepbrother, or stepsister.

3. The father or mother, or an ancestor of either (e.g., a grandparent).

4. A stepfather or stepmother.

5. A niece or nephew.[19]

6. An aunt or uncle.[20]

7. A son-in-law, daughter-in-law, father-in-law, mother-in-law, brother-in-law, or sister-in-law.

---

[16] § 151(c)(1)(A). Under prior law, this test did not apply to a taxpayer's child who was less than 19 or less than 24 and a full-time student.

[17] See Chapters 5 and 6 for discussion of "gross income."

[18] § 152(a).

[19] A niece or nephew must be a daughter or son of a brother or sister of the taxpayer. § 152(a)(6).

[20] An aunt or uncle must be a sister or brother of the father or mother of the taxpayer. § 152(a)(7). For example, the person married to your mother's sister would be her brother-in-law, but he would not qualify as your uncle for purposes of this definition. Technically, such a person would be your "uncle-in-law," a relationship not defined in Code § 152.

8. Any person who lives in the taxpayer's home and is a member of the taxpayer's household for the entire *taxable* year. Although such persons are not legally related to the taxpayer (i.e., a familial relative), they are treated the same as one who satisfies one of the legal relationships as long as they live with the taxpayer the entire taxable year; for this purpose, temporary absences due to illness, school, vacation, business, or military service are ignored; in addition, a person cannot be claimed as a dependent if the relationship with the taxpayer violated local law (e.g., cohabitation).[21]

A relationship created by marriage does not cease upon divorce or the death of the spouse. Thus, for tax purposes, a divorce would not terminate an individual's relationship with his or her mother-in-law.[22] Additionally, if a dependent dies before the close of the tax year, the taxpayer may still claim a dependency exemption.

Example 9

This year F provided all the support for several individuals, none of whom had income in excess of the exemption amount. Each person and his or her status as a relative is shown below:

1. S, F's 25-year-old son, living in Los Angeles and attending UCLA. S is a relative; a son is a familial relative and such persons need not live in the home.

2. B, F's 29-year-old brother who moved in with F on November 1 after leaving the military. B is a relative; a brother is a familial relative and such persons need not live in the home.

3. C, F's 27-year-old cousin who moved in with F on October 1 after being unemployed for 10 months. C is not a relative; a cousin is not considered a familial relative and, thus, qualifies only if he lives with the taxpayer the entire taxable year.

4. BL, the brother of F's former wife. BL is a relative; BL is F's brother-in-law, a familial relative; such a relationship continues to exist whether F is divorced or his wife dies.

5. Z, a friend who has been living with F since December 1 of the prior year. Z is considered a relative. A person who lives with the taxpayer the *entire* taxable year qualifies as a relative even though such person is not related by blood or marriage.

Joint Return Test

The dependent must not have filed a joint return with his or her spouse. This requirement is discussed further below.

Citizenship or Residency Test

The dependent must be a U.S. citizen, resident or national, or a resident of Canada or Mexico. Additional exceptions exist as noted below.

PROVISIONS COMMON TO ALL DEPENDENCY EXEMPTIONS

Although there are several important differences in the definitions of a qualifying child and a qualifying relative there are some rules common to both types of dependents. Each of these is considered in greater detail below.

---

[21] § 152(d)(2)(h).   [22] Reg. § 1.152-2(d).

No Joint Return

A taxpayer normally cannot claim a dependency exemption for a married individual if such person files a joint return.[23] This is true for both a qualifying child and a qualifying relative. This rule appears to reflect a presumption that married taxpayers usually rely on themselves for support rather than others. Note, however, that if a joint return is filed solely for a refund (i.e., the tax is zero and all withholding is refunded), the return is ignored and the individual may be claimed as a dependent (assuming the other tests are met).[24] Also observe that the test is met as long as a joint return is *not* filed. If the married individual files a separate return, he or she may still be claimed as a dependent. In certain situations, parents of newlyweds and others may find it beneficial for their child to file a married, separate return.

Example 10

B and C were married on December 21, 2017. B, a budding 25-year-old attorney, earned $48,000 for the year. C, age 23, is a full-time graduate student. Because C was fully supported by her parents, she was eligible to be claimed as a dependent on her parents' return. However, C's parents may not claim C as a dependent if B and C elect to file a joint return. The family must determine whether they are better off if: (1) B and C file a joint return and C claims her exemption on their joint return; or (2) B and C each file married filing separately and they relinquish C's exemption to her parents. A partial analysis would suggest the first alternative is far superior. If a joint return is filed, all of B's income would be taxed at 15% or less (see inside front cover of text for rates). Alternatively, the filing of separate returns would cause a substantial portion of B's taxable income to be taxed at 25 percent. In this case, it would appear that the additional tax caused by filing separate returns would more than offset any savings to be derived from shifting the exemption to C's parents.

Example 11

D and E were married on December 28, 2017. During 2017, D, age 22, attended State University full time. In addition, she worked part-time, earning $10,500 for the year. E, age 21, was also a full-time student, fully supported by his parents. E had no income. In this case, E's parents are entitled to claim an exemption for E even if D and E elect to file a joint return. The joint return requirement would not be violated because the couple owes no tax (the couple's standard deduction eliminates their taxable income). Consequently, under the IRS view, they would be filing merely to obtain a refund of any withholding and not filing an actual return.

It should be emphasized that the fact that a person files his or her own tax return does not bar another taxpayer (who otherwise meets all the necessary tests) from claiming him or her as a dependent. This is true as long as the dependent does not file a joint return for any reason other than to claim a refund of the entire amount of taxes withheld. Otherwise, the joint return test would not be met and the dependency exemption would be denied.

Citizenship or Residency Test

A dependent must be a citizen or national (e.g., an American Samoan) of the United States or a resident of the United States, Canada, or Mexico. In addition, an adopted child of a citizen qualifies, even though not a resident, if he or she was a member of the taxpayer's household for the entire taxable year. For example, if a taxpayer's employment results in his relocation to London where he adopts a British child, this rule enables the taxpayer to claim the child as a dependent even though the child is not a U.S. citizen or resident.

Taxpayer Not a Dependent

A person who is a dependent cannot claim others as dependents. For example, if a child is a dependent of his or her parents, the child cannot claim his or her own children as dependents.

---

[23] § 151(c)(2).   [24] Rev. Rul. 54-567, 1954-2 C.B. 108.

Social Security Number

In order to claim an exemption for a dependent, the taxpayer must list the dependent's Social Security number on the tax return. If the number is not listed or is listed incorrectly, the exemption may be disallowed and a $50 penalty may be imposed. More importantly, the taxpayer's filing status (head of household, surviving spouse) or child credit could be affected. Since it usually takes about two weeks to obtain a Social Security number, obtaining one by the extended due date of the return normally does not present a problem.[25]

COMPARING QUALIFYING CHILDREN AND QUALIFYING RELATIVES

While the tests for determining whether an individual is a qualifying child or a qualifying relative—and therefore qualifies as a dependent—are similar, there are some important differences.

- Qualifying children include only children or siblings or a descendant of either while qualifying relatives include virtually all relatives (except cousins) as well as individuals who are unrelated if they live in the taxpayer's home for the entire taxable year.

- Qualifying relatives must meet a gross income test while a qualifying child does not.

- Qualifying children must meet an age requirement while qualifying relatives do not.

- Qualifying relatives must meet a support test while qualifying children do not (although they cannot provide more than half of their support).

Exhibit 4-2 also provides a brief comparison of the two provisions.

EXHIBIT 4-2	Qualifying Child versus Qualifying Relative	
Test	*Qualifying Child*	*Qualifying Relative*
Relationship	Yes *(child and siblings, their descendants)*	Yes *(familial and certain nonrelatives)*
Residence	Yes *(> ½ taxable year)*	No *(but see support)*
Age	Yes *(< 19; < 24 and full-time student)*	No *(but see income)*
Tie-breaker	Yes *(parent first)*	No *(but see multiple support agreement)*
Support	No *(not self supporting)*	Yes *(> ½ spent)*
Income	No	Yes *(but not child if < 19; < 24 and full-time student)*
Joint return	Cannot file joint return	Cannot file joint return
Citizenship	Yes	Yes

CHILDREN OF DIVORCED OR SEPARATED PARENTS

If a married couple with children is divorced or separated, special rules may apply in determining who claims exemptions for the children.[26] These rules operate when the couple is

- Legally separated under a decree of divorce or separate maintenance;

- Separated under a written separation agreement; or

- Lived apart at all times during the last six months of the calendar year.

In these situations, if over half of a child's support is provided by one parent or collectively by both parents and the child is in custody of one or both parents for more than half of the year, the parent with custody for the greater portion of the year may claim the exemption. Thus, the custodial parent ordinarily receives the exemption regardless of the amount paid by either parent.

[25] The year that this requirement became effective, the number of exemptions dropped 7 million below what had been expected, resulting in about $2.8 billion in additional tax revenue. Interestingly, more than 48% of the drop was attributable to single taxpayers. See IRS Pub. 1500 (August 1991).

[26] § 152(e).

In certain situations, the divorced couple may be better served if the noncustodial parent claims the exemption. Consequently, if the conditions above are met, the custodial parent may surrender his or her right to the exemption to the noncustodial parent. To accomplish this, the release must be evidenced in a signed declaration that the custodial parent will not claim the exemption. For this purpose, the custodial parent must complete Form 8332. The custodial parent then transfers the form to the noncustodial parent who must attach the form or statement to his or her return.

PHASE-OUT OF PERSONAL AND DEPENDENCY EXEMPTIONS

Beginning in 1989, Congress began reducing the benefits that high-income taxpayers receive from their personal and dependency exemptions. Although this reduction was allowed to expire in 2010, it was restored for 2013 and beyond. Currently, taxpayers must reduce their deduction for personal and dependency exemptions by 2% for each $2,500 or fraction thereof ($1,250 for married persons filing separate returns) by which a taxpayer's AGI exceeds an applicable threshold.[27] These thresholds depend on the taxpayer's filing status, and the amounts are adjusted annually for inflation. For 2017, the phase-out begins at $313,800 for joint filers and a surviving spouse; $287,650 for heads of household; $261,500 for single filers and $156,900 for married taxpayers filing separately. These thresholds at which the phase-out begins are summarized below. Note that these are at the same level as those for the 3% cutback of itemized deductions discussed in Chapters 3 and 11.

Exemption Phase-Out Thresholds

Filing Status	Threshold AGI
Single individuals (not surviving spouse nor head of household)	$261,500
Married filing jointly or surviving spouse	313,800
Head of household	287,650
Married filing separately	156,900

The reduction in the exemption deduction is computed as follows:

$$\frac{AGI - Threshold}{\$2,500 \ (or \ \$1,250)} = Factor \ (round\text{-}up) \times 2 \ percentage \ points = Percentage \ reduction$$

Note that if AGI exceeds the threshold by more than $122,500, all of the exemptions are lost.

Example 12

H and W are married with four children. They are entitled to claim six exemptions. In 2017, their AGI is $354,800. The reduction in the couple's exemption deduction is computed as follows:

AGI	$354,800
Threshold	(313,800)
Excess	$ 41,000

$$\frac{\$41,000}{\$2,500} \quad 16.4 \ rounded \ to \ 17 \times 2 = 34\%$$

H and W are required to reduce their exemption deduction by 34 percent. The exemption amount for 2017 is $4,050. Assuming the total exemption deduction is $24,300 ($4,050 × 6), the deduction is reduced by $8,262 (34% × $24,300) to $16,038 ($24,300 − $8,262). In effect, the couple receives only 66% of their normal exemption deduction. Had the couple's AGI exceeded $433,800 ($311,300 + $122,500), their total deduction for exemptions would be eliminated ([$433,801 − $311,300 = $122,501]/$2,500 = 49.0004, rounded up to 50 × 2 = 100% reduction).

---

[27] § 151(d).

CHILD TAX CREDIT

Although most credits are covered in Chapter 13, the child tax credit is addressed briefly here because it is so closely tied with exemptions.[28] Under § 24, the amount of the child tax credit is $1,000 for each *qualifying child*.[29] For example, if a taxpayer had four children, the potential credit would be $4,000 ($1,000 × 4). The definition of a qualifying child for purposes of the child credit piggybacks on the uniform definition of a child used in determining a taxpayer's dependency exemption (discussed earlier in this chapter). In other words, a *qualifying child* for the child credit is a *qualifying child* as that expression is defined for determining a taxpayer's dependents but with certain modifications. A qualifying child for the child credit is any person who meets the following conditions.

LO.3

Describe the child tax credit.

- The individual is a *qualifying child* as defined in § 152 relating to dependents (age, relationship, residence tests).

- The individual has not attained the age of 17 by the close of the calendar year.

- The individual is a U.S. citizen.

To summarize, a taxpayer normally can claim the $1,000 credit for each child under age 17. Also note that as mentioned above, if a divorced or separated taxpayer waives his or her right to an exemption, the child credit is also waived and transferred to the noncustodial spouse.

Example 13

M and D are the proud parents of a 16-year-old daughter, C. The parents file jointly, reporting gross income of $39,975 for 2017. After claiming a standard deduction of $12,700 and three exemptions of $4,050 each, their taxable income is $15,125. Their tax on $15,125 (using the tax rate schedules) is $1,513. In computing their final tax, the couple may claim the child tax credit for C since she is a qualifying child and is less than 17 years old. After claiming their child tax credit of $1,000 for C, the couple's gross income tax before prepayments is $513.

Phase-Out of Credit

Like many other tax benefits, the child tax credit is phased out for high income taxpayers. Specifically, the allowable credit is reduced by $50 for each $1,000 (or fraction thereof) of AGI in excess of specified thresholds. The thresholds are $75,000 for unmarried taxpayers and $110,000 for married taxpayers filing jointly ($55,000 for those filing separately).[30]

Example 14

R and S have two daughters, L and M (both under age 17). R and S are married and file jointly. They reported AGI of $117,100 for 2017. The child tax credit for two qualifying children is generally $2,000, but R and S must reduce their credit by $400 ($50 × 8, since $117,100 exceeds $110,000 by $7,000 and a fraction) to $1,600.

---

[28] § 24.

[29] §§ 24(c)(1)(C) and 32(c)(3)(B).

[30] § 24(b). For purposes of this phase-out, adjusted gross income is increased by the amount of the foreign earned income exclusions under §§ 911, 931, and 933.

Refundable Child Tax Credit

As a general rule, most credits are limited to the taxpayer's tax liability for the year. For example, if the taxpayer's tax liability before the child credit is $5,000 and the child credit is $3,000, the taxpayer's regular tax usually would be reduced to $2,000. If the taxpayer's regular tax liability before the credit is $3,000 and the child credit is $4,000, the credit would reduce the tax to zero and *normally* the $1,000 balance of the credit would not be used and the taxpayer would not receive a refund of the unused credit. However, the law permits a portion of the unused child credit to be refunded. In other words, in the situation above, all or a portion of the unused credit of $1,000 would be refunded. The amount of the refundable credit depends on several variables, including the number of children, the taxpayer's earned income, other credits and some additional factors. The actual calculation of the amount of refundable credit can be found in Chapter 13 in the discussion of refundable credits.

 # CHECK YOUR KNOWLEDGE

Try these nine true-false questions concerning exemptions. If the statement is false, explain why. Assume all tests are met unless otherwise implied.

Review Question 1

All individuals are entitled to claim a personal exemption.

False. An individual who may be claimed as a dependent on another taxpayer's return cannot claim a personal exemption. This prohibits two different taxpayers from claiming two separate exemptions for the same person.

Review Question 2

Certain people who are normally considered relatives (e.g., cousins) do not qualify as relatives for purposes of the exemption tests.

True. A cousin is not a familial relative.

Review Question 3

An individual, such as a cousin, can qualify as a "relative" even though he or she is not a familial relative.

True. An individual who lives in the taxpayer's home the entire taxable year is treated as a relative even though such person and the taxpayer would not be "related" under the statutory definition.

Review Question 4

T takes care of his mom. He satisfies the support test if he provides more than 10% of her total support.

False. A taxpayer must generally provide more than 50% of an individual's support in order to claim the individual as a dependent. However, an individual who provides more than 10% of a person's support may be able to claim a dependency exemption under a multiple support agreement.

Review Question 5

In determining whether T provides more than 50% of his mom's support, her savings of over $100,000, and any earnings from them, are not counted except to the extent they are actually spent.

True. Funds available for an individual's support are ignored in applying the support test. Only amounts spent (or the value of support items provided, such as lodging) are considered.

Review Question 6

T's mom has no income other than Social Security benefits of $5,000 and interest from City of Duluth bonds of $6,000. T may claim an exemption for her mom.

True. A dependency exemption normally cannot be claimed for an individual if such person's gross income exceeds the exemption amount. For this purpose, gross income includes only income that is subject to tax. In this case, T's mom's income from Social Security is excluded as is the interest from the municipal bonds.

Review Question 7

T's 25-year-old son lives with him. This year he earned $5,000 from his paper route. T may not claim an exemption for his son.

True. T's son is not a qualifying child since he fails the age test (not less than 19 nor a full-time student less than 24). He also is not a qualifying relative because he fails the gross income test since he earns more than the exemption amount.

Review Question 8

In the case of a divorced couple with children, the custodial parent normally receives the exemption for the children even if the noncustodial parent provides all of the child support.

True. The custodial parent is entitled to the exemption unless he or she releases it to the noncustodial parent. This treatment generally follows from the uniform definition of a qualifying child that requires a child to have lived with the taxpayer for more than one-half of the taxable year.

Review Question 9

H and W are married with three children ages 15, 16, and 17. The couple can normally claim a child tax credit of $3,000.

False. The child tax credit is generally available for dependent children less than 17 years old. Therefore the couple can usually claim a credit of $2,000 ($1,000 × 2).

Filing Status

EVOLUTION OF FILING STATUS

The tax rates that are applied to determine the taxpayer's tax liability depend on the taxpayer's filing status. From 1913 to 1948, there was only one set of tax rates that applied to individual taxpayers. During this period, each taxpayer filed a separate return, even if he or she were married. For example, if both a husband and wife had income, each would file a separate return, reporting their respective incomes. This system, however, proved inequitable due to the differing state laws governing the ownership of income (or property).

LO.4

Apply the rules to determine the taxpayer's filing status.

In the United States, the rights that married individuals hold in property are determined using either the common law or community property system. There are nine community property states: Arizona, California, Idaho, Louisiana, Nevada, New Mexico, Texas, Washington, and Wisconsin.[31] In a community property state, income generated through the personal efforts of either spouse is generally owned *equally* by the community (i.e., the husband and wife). In common law states, income belongs to the spouse that earns the income. The differing treatments of income by community property and common law states produced the need for a special rate schedule for married taxpayers.

Married Status

The category of married couples filing jointly and its unique rate schedule were added to the law because of an inequity that existed between married couples in community property states and non-community property jurisdictions (separate or common law property states). As noted above, earnings derived from personal services performed by married persons in community property states generally are owned jointly by the two spouses. Accordingly, both husband and wife in a community property state would file returns showing one-half of their earned income, even though only one may have been employed. Note that the total income of the couple would be split equally between the husband and wife regardless of who earned the income. If a couple in a non-community property state relied on one spouse's earnings, the employed spouse filed a return showing the entire amount of those earnings.

---

[31] In Alaska, property is separate property unless both parties agree to make it community property.

Since the tax rates are progressive, a married couple in a non-community property state would bear a larger tax burden than one in a community property state if only one spouse was employed outside the home or one spouse earned substantially more than the other. To eliminate this inequity, Congress elected to grant the benefits of income splitting to all married couples. This was accomplished by authorizing a new tax schedule for married persons filing jointly. A joint return results in the same amount of tax as would be paid on two "married, filing separate" returns showing half the total income of a married couple.

Example 15

L and M are married and reside in California with their two children. L is an accountant and M works in the home. Under state law, L's salary of $70,000 is owned equally by L and M. Each may file a separate return and report $35,000 of the salary.

Example 16

S and T are married and reside in Ohio with their two children. S is an executive with a major corporation and T works in the home. S earns a salary of $70,000. If S were to file a separate return, she would report the entire $70,000 salary on that return. Since the tax rate schedules for individuals are progressive, S would pay a higher tax than the total paid by L and M in *Example 15*. Consequently, the total tax burden on S and T would be greater than that on L and M. By filing a joint return, S and T are placed in a position equivalent to that of L and M.

Head-of-Household Status

Introduction of the joint return in 1948 was not viewed by the public as merely a solution to a problem caused by differing state laws. Many saw it as a tax break for those who had family obligations. As a result, single parents and other unmarried taxpayers with dependents tried to persuade Congress that they should be entitled to some tax relief due to their family responsibilities. Their arguments were based on the fact that they suffered a greater tax burden than single-earner married couples. In 1957, a tax reduction was allowed in the form of a new tax rate schedule for taxpayers who qualify as a *head of household*. The rates were designed to be lower than the original rates that applied to all taxpayers, but *higher* than the rates for married persons filing jointly.

Single Status

The most recent change in the overall tax rate structure was the addition of a separate tax rate schedule for single persons. This change was made because on the same amount of income a single person was paying a higher rate of tax than married persons filing jointly and heads of households. The reduced rates for single taxpayers still are higher than those for a head of household, but lower than those in the original rate structure. As a result of this final change, the original tax rate structure that once applied to all taxpayers now applies only to married persons filing separately.

Summary

The Federal income tax on individuals is now based on four tax rate schedules. Taxpayers must file under one of the following classifications, listed in order from lowest to highest in tax rates:

1. Married filing jointly (including surviving spouses)
2. Head of household
3. Single
4. Married filing separately

The 2017 tax rate schedules for these classifications are reproduced on the inside front cover of this text.[32]

MARRIED INDIVIDUALS

Marital status is determined on the last day of an individual's taxable year. A person is married for tax purposes if he or she is married under state law, regardless of whether he or she is separated or in the process of seeking a divorce.[33]

Joint Return

A husband and wife who are married on the last day of the taxable year may choose to file a return using the rates for married persons filing jointly.[34] This is commonly referred to as a joint return. Alternatively, the spouses could choose to file separate returns as discussed below.

If a joint return is filed, both the husband and wife are jointly and severally (individually) liable for any tax, interest or penalties related to *that* joint return. As a result, one spouse may be held liable for paying the entire tax, even though the other spouse earned all the income. For this reason, a spouse should be cautious in signing a joint return. However, under the *innocent spouse rule,* a spouse will not be held liable for tax and penalties attributable to misstatements by the other spouse in two instances. The first provision allows relief if the innocent spouse establishes that he or she did not know and had no reason to know of the understatement and it is inequitable to hold him or her liable for the deficiency. The second provision limits the liability of a spouse to only the portion of the deficiency properly allocable to him or her if he or she is no longer married to, is legally separated from, or is no longer living with the spouse with whom the joint return was filed.[35]

Surviving Spouse

To provide relief in those situations where a spouse dies and the surviving spouse must continue to support the couple's children, the law permits use of the joint return rates for a short period. A so-called *surviving spouse* may use the lower rates in the first and/or second taxable year after the year of his or her spouse's death. Technically, a taxpayer qualifies as a surviving spouse if he or she meets two tests. First, the spouse must have died within the two taxable years preceding the current taxable year. Second, the taxpayer must provide over half the cost of maintaining a home in which he or she and a *dependent* son, stepson, daughter, or stepdaughter live.[36] In determining whether the child is a dependent, the following modifications are made when applying the qualifying child or qualifying relative tests:

- For purpose of determining whether the child is a dependent under the "qualifying relative" standard, the gross income test is ignored.

- In applying either test, the fact that the individual files a joint return is ignored.

- In applying either test, the fact that a dependent is ineligible to have dependents is ignored.

Remarriage terminates surviving spouse status. Of course, a joint return can be filed with the new spouse.

Example 17

H and W were married and had two children, S and D. In 2017, H died. After H's death, W continued to provide a home and all the support of S and D. As a result, W is entitled to claim S and D as dependents. For the year of death, 2017, W normally will file a joint return with her deceased husband, H. In the following two years, 2018 and 2019, W may file as a surviving spouse since she provides a home for a dependent child. As a surviving spouse, she may use the same rates as married persons filing jointly. In subsequent years, W may file as a head of household if she meets all the other requirements.

---

[32] The 2017 tax tables had not been issued by the IRS at the date of publication of this text. However, the 2017 tax tables are reproduced in Appendix A.

[33] Special rules apply to a taxpayer whose spouse dies during the year. See §§ 7703(a)(1) and 6013(a)(2).

[34] Special rules apply if one spouse is a nonresident alien (e.g., a U.S. citizen is married to a French citizen and they are living in France). See § 6013(a)(1) and (g)(1).

[35] § 6015(b) and (c).

[36] § 2(a).

Separate Returns

Normally, it will be advantageous for married persons to file a joint return because it is simpler to file one return than it is to file two, and the tax will be as low or lower than the tax based on the rules for married persons filing separately. In some situations, a taxpayer may prefer to file a separate return. For example, a person may wish to avoid liability for the tax on the income—especially any unreported income—of his or her spouse. Similarly, a husband and wife who are separated and are contemplating divorce may wish to file separate returns.

Separate returns may be to the taxpayers' advantage in other circumstances. Although rare, use of the separate rate schedules may result in a lower total tax than by using the rates applicable to a joint return. Filing of separate returns may also prove beneficial when the filing of a joint return would prevent another taxpayer (e.g., a parent) from claiming a dependency exemption deduction for either the husband or the wife (*see Example 10 above*). State income tax laws may also make filing separately beneficial.[37]

Head-of-Household

Head-of-household rates may be used if the taxpayer satisfies two conditions. First, the taxpayer must be unmarried (and not a surviving spouse) or considered unmarried (i.e., an abandoned spouse) on the last day of the tax year. Second, the taxpayer must provide more than one-half of the cost of maintaining as his or her home a household which is the principal place of abode for more than one-half the year of:

1. A qualifying child, or
2. A dependent familial relative.[38]

As might be expected, the same individuals that are considered "relatives" for exemption purposes generally qualify as relatives when applying the head-of-household rules (e.g., children, grandchildren, parents, grandparents). However, there is an exception. Even though a person who is not truly related to the taxpayer but who lives in the taxpayer's home for the entire taxable year is treated as a relative for purposes of the dependency exemption, such is not the case here. In order for the taxpayer to qualify for head-of-household status, the individual living in the home must be a familial relative.[39] Exhibit 4-3 gives a listing of those who are normally considered relatives for purposes of meeting both the head-of-household and dependency rules. Note that they are all the same except for the nonfamilial relative.

An individual normally enjoys head of household status *only* if he or she is the taxpayer's dependent *and* lives in the taxpayer's household. Two exceptions exist to this general rule.

1. A parent must be a dependent but need not live in the taxpayer's home; however, the taxpayer still must pay more than half of the cost of keeping up a home for his or her mother or father.

For example, the taxpayer qualifies if he or she paid more than half the cost of the parent's living in a nursing home and the parent is a dependent.

2. An *unmarried qualifying child* of the taxpayer need not be a dependent. For this purpose, a person is considered a qualifying child if he or she meets the relationship test, the age test, and the residence test, even if the taxpayer does not claim an exemption for the person.

---

[37] If a couple files separate returns, they are allowed to switch to a joint return within three years of filing. However, a couple that chooses to file a joint return cannot later switch to separate after the due date of the return. See § 6013(b).

[38] § 2(b)(1).

[39] §§ 2(b)(3), 152(a)(9), and 152(c).

	EXHIBIT 4-3	**Relatives for Dependency and Head-of-Household Tests**

Relative	For Dependency Exemption	For Head-of-Household Test
Qualifying child.	Yes	Yes
Familial relative	Yes	Yes
Other individuals—person who lives in taxpayer's home entire taxable year.	Yes	No

Example 18

D, an unmarried individual, lives in Seattle and pays more than half of the cost of maintaining a home in Reno for her dependent parents. Although her parents do not live with her in Seattle, D qualifies for the head-of-household rates.

Example 19

R is divorced and maintains a household for herself and her 10-year-old daughter. Although R is the custodial parent, she allows her former husband to claim the exemption for the child. R still qualifies for the head-of-household rates.

Example 20

M is divorced. At the beginning of the year, M's son, S, started medical school and moved in with his mom to save money. M pays all of the cost of maintaining the home and also provides more than one-half of S's support. S is 25 years old and earned $46,000 during the year. M cannot claim head of household because S is neither a qualifying child nor a qualifying relative. S is not a qualifying child because he is too old. To be a qualifying child, S must be less than 19 or a full-time student less than 24. S is also not a qualifying relative since his income is too high (i.e., $46,000 exceeds the amount of the personal exemption).[40]

It should be noted that a person for whom a dependency exemption is claimed solely under a multiple support agreement (e.g., the taxpayer did not provide over half the cost of maintaining the home) is not considered a qualifying relative and the agreement *cannot* qualify the taxpayer as a head of household. In addition, a nonresident alien cannot be a head of household.[41]

Costs of Maintaining a Home

In determining whether a taxpayer qualifies for head-of-household status, it is necessary to determine whether he or she pays more than half of the cost of maintaining a home for the taxable year. This determination must also be made for surviving spouse filing status. The costs of maintaining the home include the costs for the mutual benefit of the occupants and

---

[40] Prior to 2005, M would have qualified for head of household treatment since the child of a taxpayer was not required to be a dependent.

[41] *Supra,* footnote 37.

include such expenses as property taxes, mortgage interest, rent, utilities, insurance, repairs, upkeep, and *food* consumed on the premises. The cost of maintaining a home does not include clothing, educational expenses, medical expenses, or transportation.[42]

Abandoned Spouse Provision

Without a special provision, an individual whose spouse has simply abandoned him or her might be forced to file using the high rates for married individuals filing separately. Aware of this problem, Congress has provided that a married individual who files a separate return may file as head of household if he or she qualifies as an *abandoned spouse*. To qualify, the individual must provide more than half the cost of maintaining a home that houses him or her and a child for whom a dependency exemption deduction is *either* claimed or could be claimed by the taxpayer except for the fact that the exemption was assigned to the non-custodial parent.[43] The child must live in the home with the taxpayer for more than half the taxable year and the taxpayer's spouse must not live in the home at any time during the last six months of the year. If each of these requirements is met, an abandoned spouse qualifies as a head of household.

Example 21

M and N are married with six children. In October, M stormed out of the house, saying he would never return. N was hopeful that M would return and consequently had not taken action to obtain a divorce by the end of the year. Although M and N are eligible to file a joint return, M indicated that he would not. Consequently, N's filing status is married filing separately. She does not qualify as an abandoned spouse since her husband lived in the home during the last six months of the year. In the following year, however, N could qualify and file as head of household.

Single

Single filing status is defined by exception. A single taxpayer is anyone who is unmarried and does not qualify as a head of household or surviving spouse. Even though single rates are somewhat lower, they may not be used by married persons filing separately.[44]

Marriage Tax Penalty

A well-known tax phenomenon faced by couples contemplating marriage is the possibility of a marriage tax penalty. Whether matrimony is for better or for worse on the couple's tax return depends on a number of factors, such as how much each earns as well as whether either individual brings dependents into the marriage.

Joint filing originally was intended as a benefit to married couples. Prior to 1969, the joint return schedule was designed to tax one-half of total marital income at the tax rates applicable to single individuals. The resultant tax was then doubled to produce the married couple's tax liability. Note that this procedure produces a perfect split of a single earner's income between two spouses so that it is taxed at a lower marginal rate. While this approach is quite beneficial for married taxpayers, single taxpayers felt that they were paying an unjustifiable "singles penalty." To illustrate, consider the situation of a single taxpayer with taxable income of $24,000. In 1965, this taxpayer owed $8,030 of income tax, with the last dollar of income taxed at a 50% marginal tax rate. A married couple with the same 1965 taxable income owed only $5,660 (more than $2,000 less) and faced a marginal tax rate of only 32 percent.

In 1969 Congress attempted to alleviate the singles penalty by enacting a new (and lower) rate schedule for single taxpayers. While this action did reduce (but not eliminate) the singles penalty, it also created a marriage penalty for certain individuals as shown in the example below.

---

[42] Reg. § 1.2-2(d).

[43] § 2(c) and § 7703(b). An adopted child of the taxpayer is considered a son or daughter for this test.

[44] Single filing status is referred to in Code § 1(c) as "Unmarried Individuals (Other Than Surviving Spouses and Heads of Households)."

Example 22

H is currently single and his only source of income is his salary of $150,000. He is considering marrying his girlfriend, W. As shown below, for 2017 his tax as a single taxpayer after considering his standard deduction and one exemption is $32,070. If H marries W and W has no taxable income, their tax on a joint return with its wider brackets and double the standard deduction and exemption amounts would be $23,778 or $8,292 less ($32,070 − $23,778). Observe that in this situation where there is one earner, there is a singles penalty. In other words, for the same amount of income ($150,000), those who are single pay more than those who are married. But now consider what happens if W also has a $150,000 salary, the same as H. If W and H remain single, they both will pay a tax of $32,070 for a combined total of $64,140. However, if they marry, their combined taxable income remains the same at $300,000 (2 × $150,000) but their tax on a joint return is $67,353 or $3,213 more. Here, where there are two high-income earners both with about the same income, there is a marriage tax penalty.

Filing Status	2017 H One Earner Single	2017 H & W One Earner Married	2017 H & W Two Earners Married
Gross income of H	$150,000	$150,000	$150,000
Gross income of W	—	—	$150,000
Gross income	$150,000	$150,000	$300,000
Standard deduction	$ (6,350)	$ (12,700)	$ (12,700)
Exemption(s)	$ (4,050)	$ (8,100)	$ (8,100)
Taxable income.	$139,600	$129,200	$279,200
Tax	$ 32,070	$ 23,778	$ 67,353

	H Single	H & W Married	H & W Married
Tax.	$ 32,070	$ 23,778	$ 67,353
Tax for two singles (2 × $32,070).			$ (64,140)
Singles penalty ($32,070 − $23,778)		$ 8,292	
Marriage penalty ($67,353 − $64,140).			$ 3,213

As a general rule, if a couple marries and only one spouse has income (or there is a large disparity between their incomes), marriage will be beneficial due to the splitting effect (i.e., the married, one earner effect above). In contrast, if a couple marries and they have similar incomes, there may be a marriage tax penalty (i.e., the married, two earners effect above).

Tax Reform and the Marriage Penalty

One of the goals of changes made in 2001 was to reduce the marriage tax penalty. The specific provisions are summarized as follows:

- The standard deduction for a married couple was increased to an amount which is exactly double that for a single individual.

- The tax brackets were adjusted in a way to reduce the marriage penalty. First, the 10% bracket for married couples ($18,650 in 2017) is double that for single individuals ($9,325 in 2017). Next, the 15% bracket was adjusted to an amount which is double that for single taxpayers. Note, however, that the higher tax brackets were not adjusted and remain in the same proportions that they were before for married persons compared to unmarried persons (retaining an element of marriage penalty). Absent these changes, the married rates would be 167% of the single rates.

EXHIBIT 4-4	Determination of Filing Status

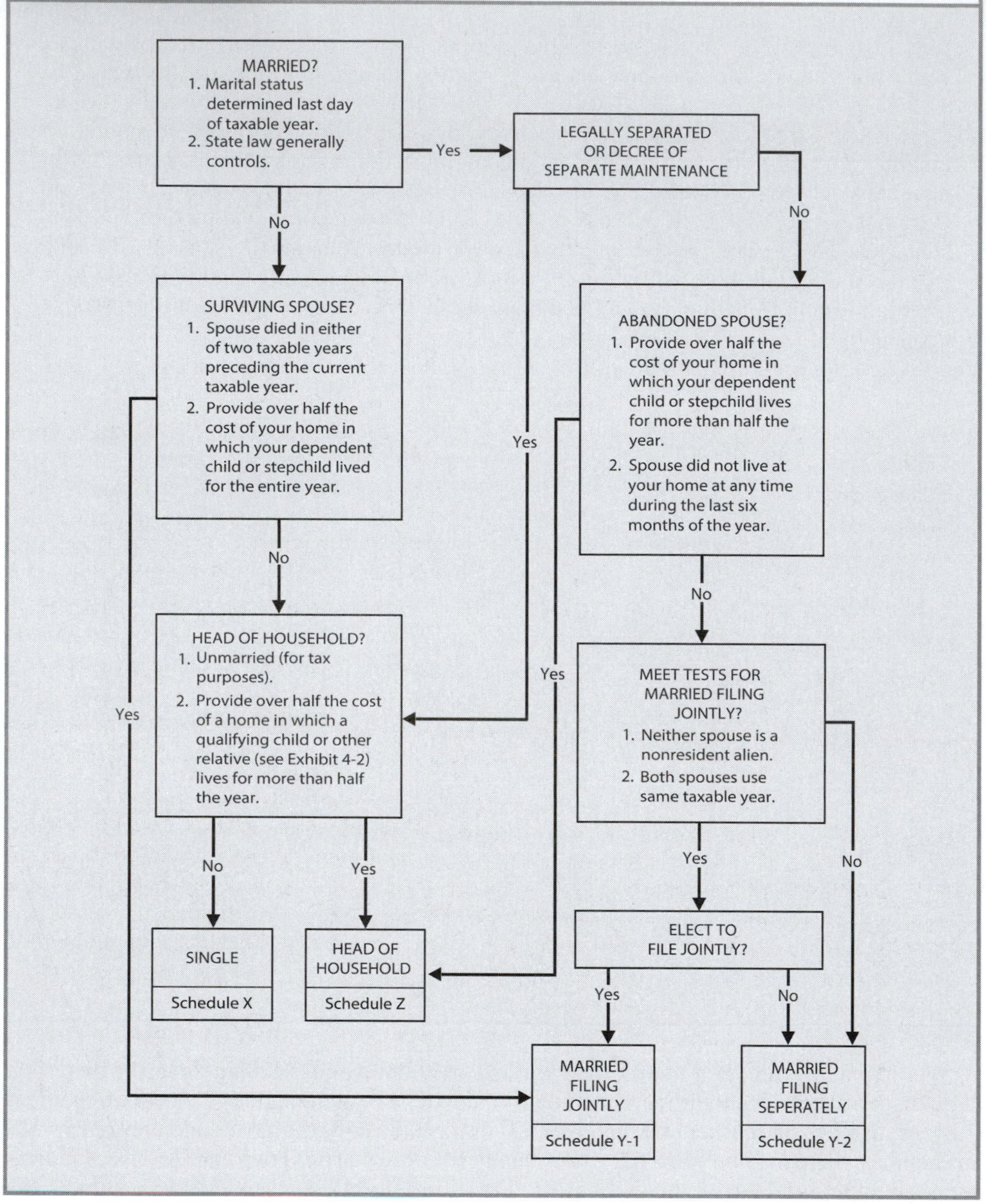

MARRIED?
1. Marital status determined last day of taxable year.
2. State law generally controls.

→ Yes →

LEGALLY SEPARATED OR DECREE OF SEPARATE MAINTENANCE

No ↓

No ↓

SURVIVING SPOUSE?
1. Spouse died in either of two taxable years preceding the current taxable year.
2. Provide over half the cost of your home in which your dependent child or stepchild lived for the entire year.

ABANDONED SPOUSE?
1. Provide over half the cost of your home in which your dependent child or stepchild lives for more than half the year.
2. Spouse did not live at your home at any time during the last six months of the year.

Yes

No ↓

No ↓

HEAD OF HOUSEHOLD?
1. Unmarried (for tax purposes).
2. Provide over half the cost of a home in which a qualifying child or other relative (see Exhibit 4-2) lives for more than half the year.

Yes

MEET TESTS FOR MARRIED FILING JOINTLY?
1. Neither spouse is a nonresident alien.
2. Both spouses use same taxable year.

Yes

Yes ↓

No →

No ↓   Yes ↓

ELECT TO FILE JOINTLY?

Yes   No

SINGLE	HEAD OF HOUSEHOLD
Schedule X	Schedule Z

MARRIED FILING JOINTLY	MARRIED FILING SEPERATELY
Schedule Y-1	Schedule Y-2

 CHECK YOUR KNOWLEDGE

Review Question 1

List the available rate schedules in the order of their progressively (highest to lowest tax rates).

Married filing separately, single, head of household, and married filing jointly (including surviving spouses).

Review Question 2

H died in 2015, survived by his wife, W, and two young children, S and D. What rate schedule may W use in 2017 assuming she has not remarried?

She should be able to file as a surviving spouse and use the joint return rate schedule for the two taxable years after her husband's death (2016 and 2017). A taxpayer qualifies as a surviving spouse if his or her spouse has died in either of the two taxable years preceding the current year (i.e., 2015 or 2016 in this case) and he or she provides over half the cost of a home in which he or she and a dependent child live. In this case, H died in 2015, and it appears that W provides a home in which she and her dependent children live.

Review Question 3

Q, divorced, is alive and well in Los Angeles. She has a 19-year-old daughter who attends school full-time at Arizona State. Q provides all her daughter's support, including payment of her dorm bill each month. Can Q file as a head of household? What additional questions must be asked before this question can be answered?

An individual can normally file as a head of household if he or she provides over *one-half* the cost of maintaining a home in which a qualifying child or a dependent familial relative lives for more than *one-half* of the taxable year. In this case, it is not completely clear whether the half-and-half test is met. As a general rule, the relative must live in the home of the taxpayer one-half of the year. Here Q's daughter may only live in Q's home during the summer months, and it would therefore appear that Q could not qualify. However, temporary absences due to special circumstances such as those due to education, business, vacation, and military service are ignored. Since the daughter's absence is temporary, the test is satisfied. Note that Q's daughter need not be a dependent since this requirement is relaxed in the case of an unmarried child of the taxpayer.

Computation of Tax for Individual Taxpayers

Once filing status and taxable income have been determined, the tax computation for most individuals is fairly straightforward. The gross tax is computed using the tax tables or the tax rate schedules. This amount is then reduced by any tax credits available to the taxpayer and any tax prepayments in arriving at the tax due or the refund. Children under age 19 with unearned income and all persons claimed as dependents are subject to special rules in the computation of their income tax. In addition, special rules must be followed in computing the tax if the taxpayer has a net long-term capital gain.

> **LO.5**
> Compute the tax liability of an individual taxpayer using the tax rate schedules and the tax tables.

Tax Tables

The vast majority of individuals must determine their tax using *tax tables,* which are provided by the IRS along with the instructions for preparing individual income tax returns. The tables are derived directly from the rate schedules to simplify compliance and reduce taxpayer errors. The tax for any particular range of taxable income is determined by using the midpoint of the range and the appropriate rate schedule. For example, the tax in the 2016 tables for a single taxpayer with taxable income of $23,010 is $2,990 (see Exhibit 4-5 for an excerpt and Appendix A-2 for the complete 2016 Tax Tables). The $2,990 amount is actually the tax computed on $23,025, using the tax rate schedules for 2016 (see Appendix A-1 for the 2016 tax rate schedules). The tables cover taxpayers in each filing status with taxable incomes less than $100,000. A taxpayer who qualifies generally is required to use the tax tables.[45] While the tax rate schedules for 2017 were released in December 2016, the tax tables for 2017 will not be available until late 2017.

---

[45] § 3.

EXHIBIT 4-5   **Excerpts From Tax Tables for 2016**

If line 43 (taxable income) is—		And you are—			
At least	But less than	Single	Married filing jointly *	Married filing separately	Head of a household
		Your tax is—			

21,000

At least	But less than	Single	Married filing jointly *	Married filing separately	Head of a household
21,000	21,050	2,690	2,226	2,690	2,491
21,050	21,100	2,698	2,234	2,698	2,499
21,100	21,150	2,705	2,241	2,705	2,506
21,150	21,200	2,713	2,249	2,713	2,514
21,200	21,250	2,720	2,256	2,720	2,521
21,250	21,300	2,728	2,264	2,728	2,529
21,300	21,350	2,735	2,271	2,735	2,536
21,350	21,400	2,743	2,279	2,743	2,544
21,400	21,450	2,750	2,286	2,750	2,551
21,450	21,500	2,758	2,294	2,758	2,559
21,500	21,550	2,765	2,301	2,765	2,566
21,550	21,600	2,773	2,309	2,773	2,574
21,600	21,650	2,780	2,316	2,780	2,581
21,650	21,700	2,788	2,324	2,788	2,589
21,700	21,750	2,795	2,331	2,795	2,596
21,750	21,800	2,803	2,339	2,803	2,604
21,800	21,850	2,810	2,346	2,810	2,611
21,850	21,900	2,818	2,354	2,818	2,619
21,900	21,950	2,825	2,361	2,825	2,626
21,950	22,000	2,833	2,369	2,833	2,634

22,000

At least	But less than	Single	Married filing jointly *	Married filing separately	Head of a household
22,000	22,050	2,840	2,376	2,840	2,641
22,050	22,100	2,848	2,384	2,848	2,649
22,100	22,150	2,855	2,391	2,855	2,656
22,150	22,200	2,863	2,399	2,863	2,664
22,200	22,250	2,870	2,406	2,870	2,671
22,250	22,300	2,878	2,414	2,878	2,679
22,300	22,350	2,885	2,421	2,885	2,686
22,350	22,400	2,893	2,429	2,893	2,694
22,400	22,450	2,900	2,436	2,900	2,701
22,450	22,500	2,908	2,444	2,908	2,709
22,500	22,550	2,915	2,451	2,915	2,716
22,550	22,600	2,923	2,459	2,923	2,724
22,600	22,650	2,930	2,466	2,930	2,731
22,650	22,700	2,938	2,474	2,938	2,739
22,700	22,750	2,945	2,481	2,945	2,746
22,750	22,800	2,953	2,489	2,953	2,754
22,800	22,850	2,960	2,496	2,960	2,761
22,850	22,900	2,968	2,504	2,968	2,769
22,900	22,950	2,975	2,511	2,975	2,776
22,950	23,000	2,983	2,519	2,983	2,784

23,000

At least	But less than	Single	Married filing jointly *	Married filing separately	Head of a household
23,000	23,050	(2,990)	2,526	2,990	2,791
23,050	23,100	2,998	2,534	2,998	2,799
23,100	23,150	3,005	2,541	3,005	2,806
23,150	23,200	3,013	2,549	3,013	2,814
23,200	23,250	3,020	2,556	3,020	2,821
23,250	23,300	3,028	2,564	3,028	2,829
23,300	23,350	3,035	2,571	3,035	2,836
23,350	23,400	3,043	2,579	3,043	2,844
23,400	23,450	3,050	2,586	3,050	2,851
23,450	23,500	3,058	2,594	3,058	2,859
23,500	23,550	3,065	2,601	3,065	2,866
23,550	23,600	3,073	2,609	3,073	2,874
23,600	23,650	3,080	2,616	3,080	2,881
23,650	23,700	3,088	2,624	3,088	2,889
23,700	23,750	3,095	2,631	3,095	2,896
23,750	23,800	3,103	2,639	3,103	2,904
23,800	23,850	3,110	2,646	3,110	2,911
23,850	23,900	3,118	2,654	3,118	2,919
23,900	23,950	3,125	2,661	3,125	2,926
23,950	24,000	3,133	2,669	3,133	2,934

24,000

At least	But less than	Single	Married filing jointly *	Married filing separately	Head of a household
24,000	24,050	3,140	2,676	3,140	2,941
24,050	24,100	3,148	2,684	3,148	2,949
24,100	24,150	3,155	2,691	3,155	2,956
24,150	24,200	3,163	2,699	3,163	2,964
24,200	24,250	3,170	2,706	3,170	2,971
24,250	24,300	3,178	2,714	3,178	2,979
24,300	24,350	3,185	2,721	3,185	2,986
24,350	24,400	3,193	2,729	3,193	2,994
24,400	24,450	3,200	2,736	3,200	3,001
24,450	24,500	3,208	2,744	3,208	3,009
24,500	24,550	3,215	2,751	3,215	3,016
24,550	24,600	3,223	2,759	3,223	3,024
24,600	24,650	3,230	2,766	3,230	3,031
24,650	24,700	3,238	2,774	3,238	3,039
24,700	24,750	3,245	2,781	3,245	3,046
24,750	24,800	3,253	2,789	3,253	3,054
24,800	24,850	3,260	2,796	3,260	3,061
24,850	24,900	3,268	2,804	3,268	3,069
24,900	24,950	3,275	2,811	3,275	3,076
24,950	25,000	3,283	2,819	3,283	3,084

25,000

At least	But less than	Single	Married filing jointly *	Married filing separately	Head of a household
25,000	25,050	3,290	2,826	3,290	3,091
25,050	25,100	3,298	2,834	3,298	3,099
25,100	25,150	3,305	2,841	3,305	3,106
25,150	25,200	3,313	2,849	3,313	3,114
25,200	25,250	3,320	2,856	3,320	3,121
25,250	25,300	3,328	2,864	3,328	3,129
25,300	25,350	3,335	2,871	3,335	3,136
25,350	25,400	3,343	2,879	3,343	3,144
25,400	25,450	3,350	2,886	3,350	3,151
25,450	25,500	3,358	2,894	3,358	3,159
25,500	25,550	3,365	2,901	3,365	3,166
25,550	25,600	3,373	2,909	3,373	3,174
25,600	25,650	3,380	2,916	3,380	3,181
25,650	25,700	3,388	2,924	3,388	3,189
25,700	25,750	3,395	2,931	3,395	3,196
25,750	25,800	3,403	2,939	3,403	3,204
25,800	25,850	3,410	2,946	3,410	3,211
25,850	25,900	3,418	2,954	3,418	3,219
25,900	25,950	3,425	2,961	3,425	3,226
25,950	26,000	3,433	2,969	3,433	3,234

26,000

At least	But less than	Single	Married filing jointly *	Married filing separately	Head of a household
26,000	26,050	3,440	2,976	3,440	3,241
26,050	26,100	3,448	2,984	3,448	3,249
26,100	26,150	3,455	2,991	3,455	3,256
26,150	26,200	3,463	2,999	3,463	3,264
26,200	26,250	3,470	3,006	3,470	3,271
26,250	26,300	3,478	3,014	3,478	3,279
26,300	26,350	3,485	3,021	3,485	3,286
26,350	26,400	3,493	3,029	3,493	3,294
26,400	26,450	3,500	3,036	3,500	3,301
26,450	26,500	3,508	3,044	3,508	3,309
26,500	26,550	3,515	3,051	3,515	3,316
26,550	26,600	3,523	3,059	3,523	3,324
26,600	26,650	3,530	3,066	3,530	3,331
26,650	26,700	3,538	3,074	3,538	3,339
26,700	26,750	3,545	3,081	3,545	3,346
26,750	26,800	3,553	3,089	3,553	3,354
26,800	26,850	3,560	3,096	3,560	3,361
26,850	26,900	3,568	3,104	3,568	3,369
26,900	26,950	3,575	3,111	3,575	3,376
26,950	27,000	3,583	3,119	3,583	3,384

27,000

At least	But less than	Single	Married filing jointly *	Married filing separately	Head of a household
27,000	27,050	3,590	3,126	3,590	3,391
27,050	27,100	3,598	3,134	3,598	3,399
27,100	27,150	3,605	3,141	3,605	3,406
27,150	27,200	3,613	3,149	3,613	3,414
27,200	27,250	3,620	3,156	3,620	3,421
27,250	27,300	3,628	3,164	3,628	3,429
27,300	27,350	3,635	3,171	3,635	3,436
27,350	27,400	3,643	3,179	3,643	3,444
27,400	27,450	3,650	3,186	3,650	3,451
27,450	27,500	3,658	3,194	3,658	3,459
27,500	27,550	3,665	3,201	3,665	3,466
27,550	27,600	3,673	3,209	3,673	3,474
27,600	27,650	3,680	3,216	3,680	3,481
27,650	27,700	3,688	3,224	3,688	3,489
27,700	27,750	3,695	3,231	3,695	3,496
27,750	27,800	3,703	3,239	3,703	3,504
27,800	27,850	3,710	3,246	3,710	3,511
27,850	27,900	3,718	3,254	3,718	3,519
27,900	27,950	3,725	3,261	3,725	3,526
27,950	28,000	3,733	3,269	3,733	3,534

28,000

At least	But less than	Single	Married filing jointly *	Married filing separately	Head of a household
28,000	28,050	3,740	3,276	3,740	3,541
28,050	28,100	3,748	3,284	3,748	3,549
28,100	28,150	3,755	3,291	3,755	3,556
28,150	28,200	3,763	3,299	3,763	3,564
28,200	28,250	3,770	3,306	3,770	3,571
28,250	28,300	3,778	3,314	3,778	3,579
28,300	28,350	3,785	3,321	3,785	3,586
28,350	28,400	3,793	3,329	3,793	3,594
28,400	28,450	3,800	3,336	3,800	3,601
28,450	28,500	3,808	3,344	3,808	3,609
28,500	28,550	3,815	3,351	3,815	3,616
28,550	28,600	3,823	3,359	3,823	3,624
28,600	28,650	3,830	3,366	3,830	3,631
28,650	28,700	3,838	3,374	3,838	3,639
28,700	28,750	3,845	3,381	3,845	3,646
28,750	28,800	3,853	3,389	3,853	3,654
28,800	28,850	3,860	3,396	3,860	3,661
28,850	28,900	3,868	3,404	3,868	3,669
28,900	28,950	3,875	3,411	3,875	3,676
28,950	29,000	3,883	3,419	3,883	3,684

29,000

At least	But less than	Single	Married filing jointly *	Married filing separately	Head of a household
29,000	29,050	3,890	3,426	3,890	3,691
29,050	29,100	3,898	3,434	3,898	3,699
29,100	29,150	3,905	3,441	3,905	3,706
29,150	29,200	3,913	3,449	3,913	3,714
29,200	29,250	3,920	3,456	3,920	3,721
29,250	29,300	3,928	3,464	3,928	3,729
29,300	29,350	3,935	3,471	3,935	3,736
29,350	29,400	3,943	3,479	3,943	3,744
29,400	29,450	3,950	3,486	3,950	3,751
29,450	29,500	3,958	3,494	3,958	3,759
29,500	29,550	3,965	3,501	3,965	3,766
29,550	29,600	3,973	3,509	3,973	3,774
29,600	29,650	3,980	3,516	3,980	3,781
29,650	29,700	3,988	3,524	3,988	3,789
29,700	29,750	3,995	3,531	3,995	3,796
29,750	29,800	4,003	3,539	4,003	3,804
29,800	29,850	4,010	3,546	4,010	3,811
29,850	29,900	4,018	3,554	4,018	3,819
29,900	29,950	4,025	3,561	4,025	3,826
29,950	30,000	4,033	3,569	4,033	3,834

Example 23

William W. Bristol was single for 2016 and had no dependents. His only income was wages of $27,410 and taxable interest from First National Bank of $400. Since his itemized deductions totaled only $1,650, he claims the $6,300 standard deduction allowed for single taxpayers in 2016. Federal income tax of $2,820 was withheld from his salary. His taxable income and tax for 2016 are calculated as follows:

Salary			$ 27,410
Taxable interest			+ 400
Equals:	Adjusted gross income		$ 27,810
Less:	Standard deduction for 2016	$6,300	
	Personal exemption for 2016	4,050	– 10,350
Equals:	Taxable income		$ 17,460
Tax on Taxable Income from Tax Table for 2016 (See Appendix A)			$ 2,158
Less:	Income tax withheld		– 2,820
Equals:	Tax due or (refund)		$ (662)

A completed Form 1040EZ for William W. Bristol, based on the information in this example, is shown in the Appendix at the end of the chapter.

Example 24

Clyde F. and Delia C. Cooper were married during all of 2016 and had income from the following sources:

Salary, Clyde		$ 33,445
Federal income tax withheld	$ 1,170	
Part-time salary, Delia		23,600
Federal income tax withheld	780	
Interest from City Savings		950
Interest from U.S. Government Treasury bond		750

Clyde and Delia are the sole support for their two children, Gary and Debra, ages 2 and 7. During 2016, they paid job-related child care expenses of $3,500 ($1,500 for Gary and $2,000 for Debra) and made deductible contributions of $4,000 to their Individual Retirement Accounts ($2,000 each). Their itemized deductions for the year do not exceed their standard deduction for 2016 of $12,600. They file a joint return. The Coopers' taxable income and tax for 2016 are calculated as follows:

Salary ($33,445 + $23,600)		$ 57,045
Plus: Taxable interest ($950 + $750)		+ 1,700
Less: Contributions to IRAs		– 4,000
Equals: Adjusted gross income		$ 54,745
Less: Standard deduction for 2016	$12,600	
Exemptions for 2016 ($4,050 × 4)	16,200	– 28,800
Equals: Taxable income		$ 25,945
Tax on Taxable Income for 2016 (See Tax Tables for 2016 in Appendix A)		$ 2,961
Less: Child care credit (0.20 × $3,500)		– 700
Child tax credit (2 × $1,000)		– 2,000
Equals: Net tax		$ 261
Less: Income tax withheld ($1,170 + $780)		– 1,950
Equals: Tax due or (refund)		$ (1,689)

A completed Form 1040A using this information is included in the Appendix at the end of the chapter.

TAX RATE SCHEDULES

Taxpayers who are unable to use the tax tables must use the tax rate schedules in computing their income tax. These schedules contain the rates provided in § 1 of the Internal Revenue Code. The 2016 tax rate schedules are included, along with the 2016 tax tables, in Appendix A. The 2017 tax rate schedules are summarized in Exhibit 4-6. The tax rate schedules for 2017 also are reproduced on the inside back cover of this text.

EXHIBIT 4-6	Individual Tax Rate Schedules for 2017

2017 Tax Rates Single

If Taxable Income Is				
Over	But Not Over	The Tax Is	% on + Excess	Of the Amount Over
$ 0	$ 9,325	$ 0.00	10%	$ 0
9,325	37,950	932.50	15%	9,325
37,950	91,900	5,226.25	25%	37,950
91,900	191,650	18,713.75	28%	91,900
191,650	416,700	46,643.75	33%	191,650
416,700	418,400	120,910.25	35%	416,700
418,400		121,505.25	39.6%	418,400

2017 Tax Rates Married Filing Jointly

If Taxable Income Is				
Over	But Not Over	The Tax Is	% on + Excess	Of the Amount Over
$ 0	$ 18,650	$ 0.00	10%	$ 0
18,650	75,900	1,865.00	15%	18,650
75,900	153,100	10,452.50	25%	75,900
153,100	233,350	29,752.50	28%	153,100
233,350	416,700	52,222.50	33%	233,350
416,700	470,700	112,728.00	35%	470,700
470,700		131,628.00	39.6%	470,700

2017 Tax Rates Head of Household

If Taxable Income Is				
Over	But Not Over	The Tax Is	% on + Excess	Of the Amount Over
$ 0	$ 13,350	$ 0.00	10%	$ 0
13,350	50,800	1,335.00	15%	13,350
50,800	131,200	6,952.50	25%	50,800
131,200	212,500	27,052.50	28%	131,200
212,500	416,700	49,816.50	33%	212,500
416,700	444,550	117,202.50	35%	416,700
444,550		126,950.00	39.6%	444,550

2017 Tax Rates Married Filing Separate

If Taxable Income Is				
Over	But Not Over	The Tax Is	% on + Excess	Of the Amount Over
$ 0	$ 9,325	$ 0.00	10%	$ 0
9,325	37,950	932.50	15%	9,325
37,950	76,550	5,226.25	25%	37,950
76,550	116,675	14,876.25	28%	76,550
116,675	208,350	26,111.25	33%	116,675
208,350	235,350	56,364.00	35%	208,350
235,350		65,814.00	39.6%	235,350

A typical example illustrating the use of the tax rate schedules is given below.

Example 25

R, single, has taxable income of $192,650 for 2017. R's gross tax liability is $46,973.75, computed using the rate schedules as follows:

Tax on $191,650	$46,643.75
Plus: Tax on income above $191,650 ([$192,650 – $191,650 = $1,000] × 33%).	+ 330.00
Tax liability	$46,973.75

Tax Reform and the Tax Rates

One of the major changes made during the Obama administration in 2013 was the increase of the tax rates for high income individuals. Before the change, there were six brackets: 10, 15, 25, 28, 33, and 35 percent. The new law added a seventh bracket of 39.6 percent. Note that all of the tax brackets (i.e., their widths) are adjusted for inflation annually.

SPECIAL TAX COMPUTATION RULES

Unfortunately, the computation of the income tax is not always as straightforward as shown in *Example 25* above. For certain individuals, special rules must be followed.

Persons Claimed as Dependents

As one might deduce from the brief introduction to tax rates, one of the most fundamental principles of tax planning concerns minimizing the marginal tax rate that applies to the taxpayer's income. The significance of this principle is easily understood when it is recognized that Federal marginal tax rates have at times exceeded 90 percent. Even with the reduction of marginal rates to their current levels, minimizing the tax rate can provide benefits.

LO.6
Explain the special approach used in computing the tax liability of certain children.

Historically, one of the most popular techniques to minimize the tax rate has been to shift income to a taxpayer in a lower tax bracket such as a child. As discussed in Chapter 5, this could be accomplished most easily by giving the child income-producing property. For example, a parent might establish a savings account for a child. In this way, the income would be taxed to the child at his or her low rate rather than the parents' high rate. In addition, this strategy—absent any special rules—takes advantage of the standard deduction available to a child.

Congress has long recognized the tax-saving potential inherent in such plans. For this reason, it is not surprising that it has taken steps to limit the opportunities. These are

1. **Personal Exemption.** A taxpayer who can be claimed as a dependent on another taxpayer's return is not entitled to a personal exemption. This rule effectively prohibits all children from claiming a personal exemption. Observe that *without this rule,* a child could currently receive up to $4,050 (2017) of income tax-free due to the exemption.

2. **Standard Deduction.** The standard deduction available to a taxpayer who can be claimed as a dependent on another taxpayer's return is limited to the *greater* of $1,050 or $350 plus his or her earned income—but not to exceed the standard deduction amount ($6,350 for single taxpayers in 2017). Without this rule, a child could receive unearned income such as interest of up to $6,350 tax-free.

3. Kiddie Tax. As explained further below, the investment income (technically referred to as unearned income) of most children is generally taxed as if the parent received it to the extent it exceeds $2,100.[46] Absent this provision, affectionately known as the *kiddie tax,* a parent could shift up to $37,950 of taxable income to the child in 2017, who would pay taxes at a rate of 15% or less.

The effect of these provisions is to severely limit the success of any schemes designed to shift income to children.

Example 26

V, age 15, lives at home and may be claimed as a dependent on her parents' return. Several years ago, V's grandfather died, leaving her with a tidy sum to help send her to college. For 2017 V received interest income of $3,225. Her taxable income is computed as follows:

Adjusted gross income		$3,225
Less: Standard deduction	$1,050	
Personal exemption	+ 0	−1,050
Taxable income		$2,175

Note that, in computing V's taxable income, her standard deduction is limited to $1,050 (the larger of $350 plus her earned income, $350, or $1,050 in 2017). The limitation is imposed because she is eligible to be claimed as a dependent on another taxpayer's return. For the same reason, she is not allowed to claim her own personal exemption deduction. In addition, a portion of her income is subject to the kiddie tax as explained below.

Example 27

Assume the same facts in *Example 26,* except that V also earns $2,000 from a part-time job. V's taxable income is determined as follows:

Adjusted gross income:		
Earned income	$2,000	
Interest income	+3,225	$5,225
Less: Standard deduction ($2,000 earned income + $350)	$2,350	
Personal exemption	+ 0	−2,350
Taxable income		$2,875

As in *Example 26,* because V is a dependent, she is not allowed to claim her personal exemption deduction, nor may she claim the full standard deduction of $6,350 (2017). Note, however, that her standard deduction has increased because of her earned income. Her standard deduction is now $2,350 (the *larger* of $350 plus her earned income of $2,000, or $1,050 in 2017). In effect, V is able to shelter income from tax with the standard deduction to the extent it is earned from personal services (plus another $350).

---

[46] § 1(g). The annual threshold is adjusted for inflation and is twice the standard deduction for dependents.

Kiddie Tax

The *kiddie tax* generally extends to children who at the close of the taxable year are either under 19 or are full-time students under the age of 24. However, the kiddie tax does not apply to children ages 18 through 24 if they are is self-supporting (i.e., earned income exceeds one-half of the amounts spent on his or her support). For example, a 21-year old student is normally subject to the kiddie tax. However, if the student provides more than half of his or her own support, the kiddie tax does not apply (even though he is a full-time student less than 24). For this purpose, scholarships received by a child are not included in the individual's total support. In addition, the kiddie tax does not apply if the child files a joint return or has no living parents.

The kiddie tax rules are triggered only when the affected child has *net unearned income.* For this purpose, unearned income generally includes investment income such as dividends, interest, capital gains, rents, royalties, and income received from a trust. Net unearned income is unearned income in excess of $2,100 in 2017.[47] This threshold is adjusted annually for inflation. In short, most "children" who have unearned income exceeding the annual threshold, $2,100 in 2017, must compute their tax using a special procedure. The effect of this calculation is that the first $1,050 of unearned income is offset by the standard deduction and the second $1,050 of unearned income is taxed at the child's rates (currently 10%). Any unearned income exceeding $2,100 is taxed at the parents' top rates.

Example 28

J is 18 years old. In 2017, he received interest income from a savings account and earned income from his paper route. The table below shows several sample calculations of J's taxable income assuming various amounts of earned and unearned income. In addition. the amount taxed at his rates and his parents' rates is computed.

	A	B	C	D
Unearned income......................	$2,150	$ 500	$2,150	$3,200
Earned Income	400	750	700	6,500
Total.................................	$2,550	$1,250	$2,850	$9,700
Standard deduction:				
Greater of $1,050 or earned income + $350 not to exceed $6,350 (2017) standard deduction................	–1,050	–1,100	–1,050	–6,350
Personal exemption	—	—	—	—
Taxable income (a)......................	$1,500	$ 150	$1,800	$3,350
Taxed at parents' rates:				
Unearned income > $2,100 (b).............	$ 50	$ 0	$ 50	$1,100
Taxed at child's rates [(a) – (b)].............	$1,450	$ 150	$1,750	$2,250

In case B, there is no net unearned income because J's unearned income was less than $2,100 (2017). J has net unearned income in cases A, C, and D. In each case, the amount taxed at his parents' rate is the amount by which the child's unearned income exceeded $2,100 (2017). Any other income is taxed at the regular rates for the child.

---

[47] § 1(i)(4).

When the child has net unearned income, the tax must be computed as if such income had been the parents' income. The child is required to pay the tax computed using his or her parents' rates except in rare cases where the tax computed in the normal manner is greater (in which case the higher tax must be paid). The tax computation cannot be completed until the parents' taxable income is known.

Although the thrust of the kiddie tax is to tax income that would be taxed at a 10 or 15 percent rate at a higher rate, determination of the child's actual tax is somewhat complicated.[48] The tax is computed on Form 8615 using the following approach:

Taxable income from parents' return.	$ xxx
Plus: Net unearned income of child (children).	+ xxx
Equals: Total income taxed at parents' rate.	$ xxx
Tax on total income taxed at parents' rate	$ xxx
Less: Tax on parents' income	− xxx
Equals: Parental tax on child's net unearned income	$ xxx
Plus: Tax on child's remaining taxable income at child's rate	+ xxx
Equals: Total tax on child's taxable income	$ xxx

The first step in this process requires the calculation of the parental tax. This is accomplished by combining the income of the parents with the net unearned income of the child and then calculating the total tax on this combined income as if the parents had reported all the income. Then, by subtracting the tax on the parents' income (from the parents' return), the amount of tax that the parents would have paid on the child's net unearned income is determined. This *parental tax* is, therefore, the tax that the parents would have paid on the net unearned income had they reported it directly.

The final part of the calculation involves determining the tax on the child's remaining taxable income at the child's tax rate of 10% (or higher). This tax is added to the parental tax to arrive at the child's total tax.

In those situations where the parents are divorced, the parental tax is computed using the taxable income of the custodial parent (or joint income if he or she has remarried). Where the parents file separate returns, the tax is computed using the greater of the parents' two taxable incomes.

In computing the tax on the parent *including* the child's net unearned income, such income is not considered when computing any of the parents' deductions or credits (e.g., the deduction for miscellaneous itemized deductions, which is limited to the amount that exceeds two percent of adjusted gross income).

Where there is more than one child under 19 with net unearned income, the parental tax must be computed using the net unearned income of all children. As shown below, the tax so computed is then allocated pro rata based on each child's relative contribution to total net unearned income.

$$\frac{\text{Child's net unearned income}}{\text{All children's net unearned income}} \times \text{Parental tax} = \text{Child's share of parental tax}$$

---

[48] If the child has dividend income or long-term capital gains, such income continues to be taxed at the favorable rates at the parents' level. See Form 8615.

Example 29

In 2017, T, age 15, received $5,500 in interest from a savings account. Similarly, his sister, V, age 6, had $2,700 of interest income. T and V both have net unearned income in excess of the $2,100 threshold for 2017. T's net unearned income is $3,400 ($5,500 – $2,100) while V's is $600 ($2,700 – $2,100). Since both T and V are under 19 and have net unearned income in excess of the threshold, their tax must be computed in the special manner. The children's parents had AGI of $120,000. In addition, due to special medical problems of the father, they incurred $17,000 of medical expenses. The couple also has other itemized deductions of $10,000. T's tax is computed as follows:

1. Tax on parents computed in the normal manner:

Adjusted gross income.	$120,000
Deductions:	
Medical expenses ($17,000 – [10% × $120,000 = $12,000])	– 5,000
Other itemized deductions.	– 10,000
Exemptions (4 × $4,050)	– 16,200
Taxable income computed in the normal manner	$ 88,800
Tax ($10,452.50 + 25% [$88,800 – $75,900 = $12,900])	$ 13,678

2. Tax on parents including net unearned income of all children:

Parents' taxable income computed in the normal manner	$ 88,800
Net unearned income of children:	
(T's $3,400 + V's $600)	+ 4,000
Taxable income including net unearned income.	$ 92,800
Tax ($10,452.50 + 25% [$92,800 – $75,900 = $16,900])	$ 14,678

3. Parental tax:

Tax on parents including net unearned income	$ 14,678
– Tax on parents computed in the normal manner.	– 13,678
= Parental Tax	$ 1,000

4. T's share of parental tax ($1,000 × [$3,400 ÷ $4,000]) = ... | $ 850 |

5. Tax on T excluding net unearned income:

Interest income	$ 5,500
– Net unearned income (T's interest income).	– 3,400
– Standard deduction (as limited for dependents)	– 1,050
– Exemption deduction (none for dependents)	– 0
Taxable income excluding net unearned income.	$ 1,050
Tax (10% × $1,050).	$ 105

6. Total tax on T:

Tax on T excluding net unearned income.	$ 105
+ Parental Tax	+ 850
= T's total tax	$ 955

The total parental tax of $1,000 is the product of the net unearned income of $4,000 ($3,400 + $600) and the parents' marginal tax rate of 25 percent. Note that the parents' medical expense deduction is computed without net unearned income of the children (i.e., the percentage limitation is based on $120,000 rather than $124,000).

Election to Report Child's Income on Parents' Return

In order to simplify the return filing process, parents may elect to include on their own return the unearned income of a child if certain conditions are satisfied.[49] Note that this is contrary to the normal procedure where the child files his or her own return and pays the tax computed with respect to the parents' rates. Parents of a child can make the election if all of the following requirements are met:

- The child's gross income is only from interest and dividends.

- The child's gross income in 2017 is more than $1,050 and less than $10,500.

- Estimated taxes have not been paid using the name and Social Security number of the child.

- The payer of the income has not withheld taxes from the payment (no "backup withholding").

From an administrative view, it appears that the election clearly would be beneficial since it eliminates the hassle of filing returns for the children. However, there is a cost. If the election is made, the parent(s) must also pay an additional tax for each child equal to the lesser of $100 (10% of the standard deduction) or 10% of the child's gross income over $1,000 (the standard deduction). In addition, inclusion of the child's income, increases the parents' AGI and therefore may reduce the deductions and credits that are phased out based on AGI.

DETERMINATION OF NET TAX DUE OR REFUND

Once the tax is determined using the tax tables, tax rate schedules, or the special tax computation procedures described above, it is reduced by the amount of any credits or prepayments. The primary prepayments are the Federal income tax withheld from the taxpayer's salary or wages by an employer, quarterly estimated tax payments, and the estimated tax paid when an extension of time to file a return is requested. Estimated tax payments and extensions of time to file are discussed later in this chapter.

Numerous credits are allowed in computing the Federal income tax. The credit most frequently encountered on an uncomplicated income tax return is the child care credit. This and other credits are discussed in detail in Chapter 13.

 CHECK YOUR KNOWLEDGE

Review Question I

What are the top and bottom tax rates for individuals?

For 2017, the lowest rate is 10% and the highest rate is 39.6% (on taxable incomes over $470,700 for married filing jointly, $418,400 for single or $444,550 for head-of-household).

Review Question 2

Several years ago Grandma gave her grandchild K, now 17, $20,000 to be used for her college education. All of the money was invested in stock. This year K's dad, acting on her behalf, sold some of the stock for a $6,100 short-term capital gain. K's parents are in the 35% tax bracket.

a. Compute K's taxable income and K's tax.

Income (unearned)	$6,100
Standard deduction:	
Greater of $1,050 or $350 plus earned income	(1,050)
Exemption.	0
Taxable income	$5,050

K's personal exemption and standard deduction are limited since she can be claimed as a dependent on her parent's return. Consequently, she is not entitled to an exemption,

---

[49] § 1(g)(7). The parents use Form 8814 for this purpose. If the child file his or her own return, the child uses Form 8615 to compute the tax. Per this provision, the

threshold, $10,000, is 10 times the amount of the child's standard deduction of $1,000.

and her standard deduction is $1,050 since she has no earned income. K is also subject to the kiddie tax since she is less than 19. In computing K's tax, the amount of unearned income in excess of $2,100 is $4,000 ($6,100 − $2,100), which must be taxed at her parents' rates while the remainder is taxed at her rates. Thus her tax is $1,505 ([35% × $4,000] + [$1,050 × 10% = $105]).

b. Assume there were no kiddie tax. How much unearned income could be shifted to a dependent child and taxed at the child's 15% or lower rate rather than the parents' rate?

The 10% bracket for single taxpayers 2017 extends from taxable income of $1 to $9,325 and the 15% bracket extends from $9,326 to $37,950 for single taxpayers. Plus, another $1,050 escapes tax all together due to the child's standard deduction.

Filing Requirements

An individual normally must file a Federal income tax return. While tax protesters often assert that there is no law that demands the filing of a return, Section 6012(a) says otherwise. According to its language, "returns with respect to income taxes … shall be made by … every individual having for the taxable year gross income that equals or exceeds … the exemption amount plus … the basic standard deduction." So there it is. The law clearly requires individuals to file returns if their gross income exceeds a certain level.

LO.7
Describe the filing requirements for individual taxpayers.

As § 6013 indicates, a low income taxpayer need not file a return for the year if his or her gross income is less than the *total* of his or her standard deduction (including the additional amount for the elderly but not the blind) *plus* personal exemptions (but not dependency exemptions).[50] These taxpayers generally are not liable for any Federal income tax. The filing requirement is based on gross income, so taxpayers who have gross incomes exceeding specified thresholds *must* file even if they owe no Federal income tax. A partial list of filing requirements for 2017 and how they are computed is illustrated in Exhibit 4-7.

In addition to the general requirement for filing (gross income is at least as much as the taxpayer's standard deduction + personal exemptions), certain individuals *must* file returns. These include:

1. Any taxpayer who has self-employment income of $400 or more;

2. An individual who is claimed as a dependent on another taxpayer's return *and* who has unearned income at least equal to his or her minimum standard deduction (i.e., generally $1,050 (2017), but increased by the additional amount for elderly or blind taxpayers)[51]

3. Any person who receives any advance payments of earned income credit.

EXHIBIT 4-7	**Gross Income Filing Requirements for 2017**			
	Personal Exemption +	*Standard Deduction* +	*Elderly Standard Deductions* =	*2017 Gross Income*
Single person < 65	$4,050	$ 6,350	—	$10,400
Single person ≥ 65	4,050	6,350	$1,550	11,950
Head of household < 65	4,050	9,350	—	13,400
Head of household ≥ 65	4,050	9,350	1,550	14,950
Married filing jointly, both < 65	8,100	12,700	—	20,800
Married filing jointly, both ≥ 65	8,100	12,700	2,500	23,300
Married filing separately	4,050			4,050
Surviving spouse < 65	4,050	12,700	—	16,750
Surviving spouse ≥ 65	4,050	12,700	1,250	18,000
Dependents				Special Rules

[50] § 6012(a)(1).

[51] § 6012(a)(1)(C)(i). As stated earlier, certain children under the age of 19 are not required to file a tax return *if* their parents *elect* to include the child's income on their return and pay the appropriate additional tax.

FORMS FOR FILING: FORMS 1040, 1040A, AND 1040EZ

Individuals normally must compute and report their taxable income annually on forms provided by the IRS. There are a number of tax forms available from which to select. Of course, the object is to choose the one that is most advantageous, not necessarily the one that is easiest to fill out. Virtually all tax forms can be downloaded from the IRS website (www.irs.gov).

The basic form that can be used by any taxpayer is Form 1040. The "1040" can handle both simple and complex situations. Complicated returns often require many forms and schedules in addition to Form 1040. (See Exhibit 4-8 below and Appendix B for the multitude of forms that may be needed.) However, to make the filing process easier for taxpayers with uncomplicated situations, the IRS provides two simplified versions of Form 1040: Form 1040EZ and Form 1040A.

Form 1040EZ is the simplest return to complete. Unfortunately, the most difficult task related to this "easy" return may be determining whether it can be used. It generally is available only for taxpayers whose filing status is single or married filing jointly, who have no dependents and are under age 65. Taxpayers who want to file as head of household, married filing separately, or as a surviving spouse cannot use Form 1040EZ. As far as income is concerned, taxable income cannot exceed $100,000. Moreover, the type of income is generally limited to wages, salaries, tips, unemployment compensation, and no more than $1,500 of interest. Deductions are also limited. The only allowable deductions are the personal exemption and the standard deduction. Taxpayers cannot claim any deductions for AGI or itemized deductions. Still other rules may bar the use of Form 1040EZ.

Form 1040A accommodates returns that are a bit more complex than Form 1040EZ but less complicated than those that require Form 1040. Form 1040A has some of the same restrictions as Form 1040EZ. Taxable income must be less than $100,000 and itemized deductions are not allowed. However, it does allow any filing status. The types of income are more extensive, including ordinary dividends, capital gains distributions from mutual funds, pension and annuity income, IRA distributions, and taxable Social Security benefits. Taxpayers can also claim deductions for IRA contributions, student loan interest, tuition and fee payments, and expenses that educators pay for supplies for their own classrooms.

Not to be forgotten in this medley of forms are the special ones that exist for nonresident aliens. Generally, nonresident aliens who have a business in the U.S. or who have U.S. source income on which the taxes owed were not paid through withholding generally must file Form 1040NR or 1040NR-EZ.

Example 30

Scott S. Allen, a salesman, and Mia R. Allen, a nurse, are married and file a joint return for 2016. They are the sole support of their three children: Jim, Emily, and Noah (all under age 17). Their records provide the following:

Salaries and wages, Scott		$ 32,875
Federal income tax withheld	$ 1,700	
Salaries and wages, Mia		44,900
Federal income tax withheld	2,400	
Interest income—Mercantile National Bank		3,000
Itemized deductions are as follows:		
Unreimbursed prescription drugs.		200
Hospitalization insurance.		700
Unreimbursed fees of doctors, hospitals, etc.		2,100
Real estate taxes on residence		1,200
State income taxes paid.		3,400
Interest paid on original home mortgage.		8,900
Charitable contribution—First Church		1,500
Preparation of prior year's tax return		275

The Allens' AGI is $80,775 ($32,875 + $44,900 + $3,000 interest income) since there were no deductions for AGI. The deductible amount of their itemized deductions is $15,000, summarized as follows:

Medical expenses exceeding $8,078 ($3,000 < [10% × $80,775 = $8,078])	$	0
Deductible taxes ($1,200 + $3,400)		4,600
Qualifying home mortgage interest		8,900
Charitable contributions		1,500
Miscellaneous itemized deductions exceeding $1,616 ($275 < [2% × $80,775 = $1,616]). . .		0
Total itemized deductions		$ 15,000

The Allens' taxable income, gross tax, and tax refund for 2016 are computed below:

Adjusted gross income			$ 80,775
Less:	Itemized deductions	$ 15,000	
	Personal and dependency exemptions ($4,050 in 2016 × 5).	+ 20,250	– 35,250
Equals: Taxable income.			$ 45,525
Gross Tax (from 2016 Tax Table).			$ 5,901
Less:	Prepayments ($1,700 + $2,400).		– 4,100
	Child tax credit (3 × $1,000)		– 3,000
Equals: Tax due or (refund).			$ (1,199)

The Allens' completed 2016 tax return is shown in the Appendix at the end of the chapter. It consists of a Form 1040 plus Schedules A and B.

The more common tax forms and schedules used by individual taxpayers are listed in Exhibit 4-8. Copies of these forms are contained in Appendix B at the end of the text.

EXHIBIT 4-8	**List of Common Forms and Schedules Used by Individual Taxpayers**

Form 1040	U.S. Individual Income Tax Return

Accompanying Schedules:

Schedule A	Itemized deductions
Schedule B	Interest and dividend income
Schedule C	Profit (or loss) from business or profession
Schedule D	Capital gains and losses
Schedule E	Supplemental income schedule (rents, royalties, etc.)
Schedule F	Farm income and expenses
Schedule R	Credit for the elderly
Schedule SE	Computation of self-employment tax

Accompanying Forms:

Form 2106	Employee business expenses
Form 2210	Underpayment of estimated tax by individuals
Form 2441	Credit for child and dependent care expenses
Form 3800	General business credit
Form 3903	Moving expense adjustment
Form 4562	Depreciation
Form 4684	Casualties and thefts
Form 4797	Supplemental schedule of gains and losses
Form 6251	Alternative minimum tax computation
Form 6252	Computation of installment sale income
Form 8582	Passive activity losses
Form 8615	Computation of tax for children under age 19 who have investment income of more than $1,900
Form 8814	Parents' election to report child's interest and dividends

Other Common Forms:

Form 1040A	U.S. Individual Income Tax Return
Form 1040EZ	Income tax return for single filers with no dependents
Form 4868	Application for automatic extension of time to file

DUE DATES FOR FILING RETURNS

LO.8
Explain when taxes must be paid and the penalties that apply for failure to pay on a timely basis.

The day on which a Federal return must be filed with the IRS depends upon the type of return required. Generally, tax returns must be filed on or before the due dates provided below. (**Note:** Congress recently changed some of the due dates; the following dates are for taxable years ending after December 31, 2015.[52]

---

[52] § 6072(a).

Type of Tax Return	Due Date	Extended Due Date	Extension Form
Individual Form 1040, 1040-A, or 1040-EZ	15th day of the 4th month after year-end (April 15 for calendar year individuals)	6-month extension from original due date (October 15 for calendar year individuals)	Form 4868
Partnership Form 1065 and S Corporation Form 1120-S	15th day of 3rd month after close of tax year (March 15 for calendar year entities)	6-month extension from original due date (September 15 for calendar year entities)	Form 7004
C Corporation Form 1120 (Calendar Year-End)	April 15	September 15	Form 7004
C Corporation Form 1120 (Year-End Other Than 12/31 or 6/30)	15th day of 4th month after close of tax year	6-month extension from original due date	Form 7004
C Corporation Form 1120 (6/30 Year-End)	September 15	April 15	Form 7004
Trust Form 1041	April 15	September 15	Form 7004
Estate Form 1041	15th day of 4th month after close of tax year	5½-month extension from original due date (September 30 for calendar year estates);	Form 7004
Estate Tax Return Form 706	9 months after date of death	6-month extension from original due date	Form 4768
Gift Tax Return Form 709	April 15	6-month extension from original due date (October 15)	Form 4868; Form 8892 to make tax payment

Any return that is mailed via the U.S. Postal Service is deemed to be delivered when mailed, so any return postmarked on or before the above due dates is timely filed. If any of these due dates fall on Saturday, Sunday, or a legal holiday, the return must be filed on the succeeding day that is not a Saturday, Sunday, or legal holiday.

Extension of Time to File

The Internal Revenue Code provides extensions of time for filing returns. The extension must be requested on or before the due date of the return. Currently, there is an *automatic* six-month extension for filing the individual income tax return (Form 1040). Thus the extended due date for calendar year individuals is October 15. If the taxpayer desires to use the six-month extension, he or she simply fills out Form 4868 and mails it to the IRS by the original due date along with a check covering the estimated balance due. It should be noted that an extension of time to file is not an extension of time to pay. There is *no extension of time to pay the tax due.*[53] The penalty for failing to pay the tax due is discussed below.

The extensions for other taxpayers are designed so that the extended due date is normally one month before the extended due date for individuals. To illustrate, consider the returns of calendar year partnerships and S corporations. Their returns are due on March 15, and the extended due date for these returns is six months later on September 15. Note that their extended due is one month before the extended due date for individual returns of October 15. This approach attempts to ensure that individuals will have the information from these flow through entities that is necessary to prepare their personal returns. The extended due dates for the various returns are shown above.

Interest on Underpayments and Overpayments

As might be expected, when payments or refunds of tax are late, interest comes into play.[54] If a taxpayer fails to pay the amount of tax owed by the due date of the return, § 6601 allows the government to charge interest. To encourage payment, the rate is three percentage points higher than the Federal short-term rate. For the quarter October 1–December 31, 2016, the annual interest rate charge on such a deficiency for individuals is

---

[53] Reg. § 1.6081-4(a).

[54] See § 6601(a) for underpayments, § 6611(a) for overpayments, and § 6621(a)(2) for interest rates.

4% (1% + 3%), compounded daily on the unpaid balance. Interest is generally charged from the day the tax is due (e.g., the due date of the return) and continues until the tax is paid.

On the other hand, the IRS does not pay interest to taxpayers for holding their money all year if they have too much withheld or paid too much in estimated tax. However, the Code does require the IRS to pay the taxpayer interest on an overpayment if it sends a refund more than 45 days from the filing deadline for the return. If a return is filed before it is due, the IRS still has 45 days from the deadline, usually April 15. If the return is filed after the deadline of April 15 (e.g., the taxpayer obtained an extension), the 45-day period begins the date the return is filed. The rate is the same as that on underpayments.

PENALTIES

Around April 15, it is not uncommon to hear procrastinating taxpayers ask what happens if they neither file their returns nor pay their taxes on time. When either of these occurs, taxpayers not only have to pay interest but also penalties. There are three types of penalties that may apply:[55]

1. A penalty for *failure to file a return* by the due date;
2. A penalty for *failure to pay* at least 90% of the *tax* by the due date; and
3. A penalty for *failure to pay estimated taxes* during the course of the year.

If the taxpayer owes nothing or is entitled to a refund, these penalties do not apply even if he or she does not file a return. On the other hand, if the taxpayer has an amount due, any one or all three of these penalties could be imposed. In addition, since these penalties are technically additions to and part of the total tax liability, any interest that must be paid effectively includes *interest on the penalties*. Finally, if the taxpayer wants to obtain a refund, there are time limits for claiming it. Each of these possibilities is discussed below.

Failure-to-File

When taxpayers complete their tax return and discover they owe Uncle Sam more than they expected, they don't celebrate. It's like going to the dentist and finding out you have a cavity. In both cases, there is this temptation not to act: don't file or don't get the filling. We know what happens when the cavities aren't fixed but what happens when taxpayers do not file.

Taxpayers who do not file their returns by the due date (e.g., April 15) or fail to obtain a proper extension on such date are subject to the *failure-to-file penalty*. Under § 6651, the penalty is 5% of the amount of tax due for each month the return is not filed.[56] The penalty cannot exceed a maximum of 25% (e.g., 5% × 5 months). For this purpose, any fraction of a month is counted as a full month. To illustrate how harsh this rule can be, consider a taxpayer who owes $10,000 and his return is postmarked one day late. Even though the return is only one day late, the failure-to-file penalty is 5% for an entire month on the amount due or $500 (5% × 1 month × $10,000 amount due)!

To deal with the administrative costs of handling small penalties, a minimum failure-to-file penalty exists. If the return is more than 60 days late, the minimum penalty is the lesser of $205 or 100% of the tax due.[57] For example, a taxpayer who owes $300 and files her return on June 16 would normally owe a penalty of $45 (5% × 3 months × $300) but the minimum penalty is $205 (the lesser of $205 or the tax due of $300).

Taxpayers who fail to file their returns may not be penalized in certain situations. The penalty is not imposed if the failure was due to reasonable cause and not willful neglect. In addition, since the penalty is based on the amount due no penalty results if there is no amount due. Because of this rule taxpayers who are entitled to a refund are not penalized for filing late since there is no amount due.

Failure-to-Pay Penalty

Filing a return is not enough to avoid penalty. Section 6651 also imposes a *failure-to-pay* penalty if a taxpayer does not pay at least 90% of the total tax on or before the due date

---

[55] Technically, the Internal Revenue Code does not refer to these as penalties but as "additions to the tax." See §§ 6651 and 6654.

[56] § 6651(a)(1). If the failure to file is fraudulent, the penalty is 15% per month up to a maximum of 75 percent. § 6551(f).

[57] § 6651(a)(1). Prior to enactment of the *Trade Facilitation and Enforcement Act of 2015*, the minimum penalty was $135.

of the return.[58] In other words, the IRS does not assess a penalty if an extension of time to file is properly obtained and the tax due is less than 10% of the total tax shown on the return (i.e., gross tax after credits but before any withholding and estimated tax payments). The penalty can also be avoided if the failure is due to reasonable cause and not willful neglect. If the taxpayer does not meet either test, the *failure-to-pay* penalty is one-half of 1% (0.5% or 0.005) per month (or any fraction of a month) up to a maximum 25% of the amount due.[59] Note that if the taxpayer files an extension and pays 90% of the tax by the due date, the taxpayer must still pay interest on any tax due but avoids both the failure-to-pay and failure-to-file penalties. For those taxpayers who cannot pay their tax bill, the IRS offers an installment payment plan.

Example 31

As the time approached for filing his tax return, W was too busy to file. Accordingly, on April 15 he requested an automatic extension of time to file until October 15. W estimated that his total tax would be $6,000, and he had prepaid taxes of $5,300 in the form of withholding. Therefore, when he filed his request for an extension, he paid $700 ($6,000 − $5,300). By filing a timely extension, he is treated as filing a return and avoids the failure-to-file a return penalty. When he finally did file his return on June 15, W's earlier estimate proved wrong and the return showed a total tax of $7,000 and a tax due of $1,000 ($7,000 total tax due − $6,000 [$5,300 withholding + $700 payment with the extension]). W is required to pay a penalty for failure-to-pay since the total paid by the due date, $6,000 is less than 90% of the tax due, $6,300 (90% × $7,000). The amount of the penalty is based on the total amount due that was unpaid on April 15, $1,000 ($7,000 − $6,000 paid) and not the amount short of the 90% requirement ($300). In addition, assuming the current rate of interest on underpayments is 10 percent, W must pay interest of about $17 ($1,000 amount due at 10% annually, compounded daily until June 15 for 61 days).

Interaction of Failure-to-Pay and Failure-to-File Penalties. When both the failure-to-file and failure-to-pay penalties apply, the penalty for failure-to-file is reduced by the amount of the penalty for failure to pay.

Example 32

K forgot to file her Federal tax return for 2017. When she finally filed the return on November 1 (7 months late), her return showed a gross tax of $8,000 and a tax due after withholding of $2,000. If the current rate of interest on underpayments is 3 percent, K must pay not only her tax due of $2,000 but also a failure to pay penalty of $70, a failure to file penalty of $450 and interest on the tax and penalties of $33, for a total of $2,553, as computed below.

Tax due		$2,000
Penalties:		
Failure to pay ($2,000 × 0.005 × 7)		70
Failure to file:		
Failure-to-file penalty ($2,000 × 0.05 × 5)	$500	
Reduced by failure-to-pay penalty ($2,000 × 0.005 × 5).	(50)	450
Total tax and penalties.		$2,520
Interest on tax and penalties ($2,500 × 3% × 199/365)		33
Total due		$2,553

Note that the minimum failure-to-file penalty is not triggered here since the penalty of $450 computed in the normal manner exceeds the minimum penalty of $205 (2017) (the lesser of the total tax due, $2,000, or $205).

---

[58] § 6651(a)(2); Although the Code requires the taxpayer to pay 100% of the tax, the regulations provide an exemption from the penalty where the tax owed is less than 10% of the tax due. See Reg. § 301.6651-1(c)(3) and (4).

[59] § 6651(a)(2).

Failure to Pay Estimated Tax Payments

The last of the three "late" penalties is the penalty for failure to pay estimated taxes.[60] This penalty should be distinguished from the *failure-to-file* and *failure-to-pay* penalties that begin to run as of the due date of the return. The estimated tax penalty applies if the taxpayer fails to pay sufficient taxes *during the year*. In essence, the law sets forth a series of intermediate due dates for estimated tax payments during the tax year.

The estimated tax penalty is a product of the "pay-as-you-go" system for collection of taxes. Under this system, taxpayers are required to prepay Federal income taxes periodically during the year. Prepayments are made through withholding from certain types of income (e.g., salary and wages) and by making estimated tax payments. Failure to make adequate payments during the year results in a penalty that is computed much like interest.

As a practical matter, estimated tax penalties do not affect the vast majority of individuals. For those receiving only salaries and wages, withholding is usually sufficient to cover the required payments. However, those taxpayers with other income may need to make up the shortfall by making estimated tax payments. Regardless of the causes, if the amount of taxes paid during the year is insufficient, the penalty may apply.

Imposition of the Estimated Tax Penalty. Individual taxpayers avoid the estimated tax penalty if total prepayments (estimated taxes and withholding) equal or exceed the *required annual payment,* which is the lesser of[61]

1. 90% of the tax shown on the return, or
2. 100% of the tax shown on the return for the individual for the preceding year. If AGI in the prior year exceeded $150,000, the payment must be 110% of the prior year's tax.
3. The annualized income installment

For this purpose, the tax due includes the self-employment tax as well as the alternative minimum tax and certain other taxes. If the total amounts paid are less than the amount due, an *underpayment* exists and the penalty must be calculated and paid as explained below. However, there is no estimated tax penalty if the underpayment is less than $1,000.[62]

Example 33

For 2016, T, a single individual, reported an adjusted gross income of $165,000, a taxable income of $140,000, and a tax liability (after credits) of $40,000. In 2017 his tax liability is $60,000. Under the general rules T must have paid the lesser of 90% of the current year's tax, $54,000, or 100% of last year's tax, $40,000, to avoid the underpayment penalty. However, because T's adjusted gross income exceeded $150,000 in the prior year, 2016, he is subject to the 110% rule regarding his estimated tax payments for the current year, 2017. As a result, he can avoid underpayment penalties with respect to 2017 only if he pays the lesser of the following:

1. 90% of the current year's tax of $60,000 . . . . $54,000
2. 110% of last year's tax of $40,000   44,000

Thus, if T pays at least $44,000 on a timely basis during 2017, he will not be subject to any penalty for failing to pay estimated taxes.

The required payment is due in four equal installments or 25% on each due date. Although it is convenient to say that the payments are made on a quarterly basis, this is not quite the case. For calendar year taxpayers, the amounts are due on April 15, June 15, September 15, and January 15.

Whether the payments are adequate is determined at the end of each "quarter." For this purpose, withholding is treated as if one-fourth of the total amount withheld is paid on each of the payment dates unless the taxpayer can establish otherwise. At the end of each quarter, the payments to date are compared to the amount required to be paid. If the proper amount has not been paid, an underpayment exists and a penalty must be paid.

---

[60] § 6654.

[61] § 6654(d).

[62] § 6654(e)(1).

The penalty is assessed on the amount of the underpayment at the same rate as the interest that is charged on tax deficiencies. This penalty is separate from the failure-to-pay penalty as well as the interest which is charged. As noted earlier, interest and the failure-to-pay penalty apply to underpayments of tax due as of the due date of the return (e.g., April 15, 2018). In contrast, the estimated tax penalty is charged from the date each estimated tax installment was due (e.g., April 15, June 15, September 15 of 2017, and January 15, 2018) until the tax is paid (or, if the tax is paid late, the due date of the return).

Example 34

For 2016 and 2017 G's gross tax was $12,000 and $16,000, respectively. G's withholding for 2017 was $6,500 and his estimated tax payments were $1,500 on April 15 and June 15 and $500 on September 15 and January 15. Assume the underpayment rate is 3%. G's underpayment penalty is computed like interest on the underpayment.

		Payment Due Date		
	4/15	6/15	9/15	1/15
(1) 90% of current year's tax (90% × $16,000 × percentage due)	$ 3,600	$ 3,600	$ 3,600	$ 3,600
(2) 100% of prior year's tax (100% × $12,000 × percentage due)	$ 3,000	$ 3,000	$ 3,000	$ 3,000
(3) Required installment Lesser of (1) 90% or (2) 100%	$ 3,000	$ 3,000	$ 3,000	$ 3,000
Payments to date:				
Withholding	$ 1,625	$ 1,625	$ 1,625	$ 1,625
Estimated tax payments	+ 1,500	+ 1,500	+ 500	+ 500
Total actual payments to date	$ 3,125	$ 3,125	$ 2,125	$ 2,125
Overpayment from previous period	—	125	250	—
(4) Total deemed paid	$ 3,125	$ 3,250	$ 2,375	$ 2,125
Applied to previous balance				(625)
Available				$ 1,500
(5) (4) − (3) Overpayment (underpayment)	$ 125	$ 250	$ (625)	$ (1,500)
(6) Period outstanding/365				
9/15/15 through 1/15/16			×122/365	
1/15/16 through 4/15/16				× 90/365
(7) Annual underpayment rate 2017			× 3%	× 3%
(5) × (6) × (7) penalty			$ 6	$ 11

G's required payment for each installment is $3,000 (the lesser of the amounts determined using the 90% and 100% rules). His payments for the first installment are adequate and actually exceed the amount due, resulting in an overpayment of $125 ($3,125 − $3,000). The $125 overpayment is applied to his second installment for a total payment of $3,250, resulting in a $250 ($3,125 + $125 − $3,000) overpayment. For the third installment, his payments of $2,375 ($2,125 + $250 of overpayments from the previous installments) are insufficient, producing an underpayment of $625 ($3,000 − $2,125 − $250). His payments for the fourth installment of $2,125 are first applied to the outstanding underpayment of $625. The penalty on the $625 underpayment is computed like interest, 3% underpayment rate on $625 for a period from 9/15/15 to 1/15/16 or 122 days for a total of about $6 (3% × 122/365 × $625). The balance of the payments on 1/15/16 of $1,500 ($2,125 − $625) is applied to the fourth installment of $3,000, resulting in another underpayment of $1,500. Assuming this amount is paid with the filing of the return, it is outstanding for 90 days (1/15/16 to 4/15/16), creating a second penalty of about $11 (3% × 90/365 × $1,500). Note that while the underpayment penalty is computed like interest, no deduction is allowed.

The penalty for failure to make adequate estimated tax payments is calculated on Form 2210 (see Appendix for a sample form). Unless a taxpayer can reduce the penalty by applying the annualized income installment or otherwise, he or she may simply let the IRS calculate this penalty and assess a deficiency for it. In addition, the IRS may waive the underpayment penalty in the event of a casualty or unusual circumstances where it might be inequitable to impose the additional tax. The IRS may also waive the penalty for retired taxpayers who are at least age 62 or disabled where the underpayment was due to reasonable cause rather than willful neglect.

Annualized Income Installment

If income for a year is earned disproportionately during the year, the taxpayer may be able to avoid penalty for one or more of the first three payments under the *annualized income installment* method.[63] Under this method, no penalty is imposed when the payment to date exceeds the tax which would be due on the income for the months preceding the payment date determined on an annualized basis.

Example 35

F, a calendar year individual, is engaged in a seasonal business that earns most of its income during the fourth quarter. F is able to demonstrate that the income was earned as follows:

	Payment Due Date			
	4/15	6/15	9/15	1/15
Months preceding payment	3	5	8	12
Net income earned for the months preceding the payment	$10,000	$18,000	$25,000	$50,000
Annualized amount (Net income × [12/months to date])	$40,000	$43,200	$37,500	$50,000

To apply this exception, the tax on the annualized income is determined. There is an underpayment only if the estimated tax payments are less than the appropriate portion of the tax on the annualized income.

The required payment for April 15 is the fraction 3 months ÷ 12 months times the tax on $40,000. If the tax on $40,000 is $8,000, F has no underpayment for the first payment so long as she paid $2,000 ($8,000 × 3/12) or more. If she had paid less, the underpayment would be the amount by which $2,000 exceeded the payments. A similar process would be followed for each quarter.

To apply the annualized income installment calculations, a taxpayer completes a worksheet that accompanies the Form 2210. If this method is used to the benefit of the taxpayer for one payment, it must be used for *all* four payments.

Other Penalties

As mentioned in Chapter 2, many other penalties exist to ensure proper compliance with the tax laws. For example, the Code provides for an accuracy-related penalty of 20% of the amount of understatement due to negligence or intentional disregard of the rules (e.g., failing to report income), or substantial valuation misstatements.[64] In addition, severe penalties, both civil and criminal, exist for fraud.[65]

---

[63] § 6654(d).

[64] § 6653(a)(1).

[65] § 6653(b).

CLAIM FOR REFUND

The vast majority of taxpayers actually overpay their taxes and are entitled to a refund. For example, the IRS reported in 2014 that of the 143 million returns filed about 114.9 million (about 80%) claimed a refund.[66] On average, this represented a refund of about $3,393 per return. While most people routinely file their returns and receive their refund checks, others procrastinate. Unfortunately, some people assume it makes no difference how late they file if they wish to recover a refund. That can be a costly mistake. As a general rule, the Code requires taxpayers to file a tax return to claim a refund within two years of paying the tax, *deemed* to be April 15 in most cases.[67] Taxpayers who file a timely return, but subsequently realize that they overpaid, have a bit longer—three years from the due date of the return.

Example 36

With April 15, 2015 just a day away, C made a few quick calculations and determined his tax was about $12,000. Knowing that he had $14,000 withheld and did not owe any tax, C did not file a return. C continued to put off filing a return until one day he received a letter from the IRS. In the letter dated November 2017, the IRS explained that based on information available to it C owed a tax of $1,500. In response, C finally filed a correct return on May 1, 2018, showing that he did in fact owe $12,000 in tax and the government should refund him his overpayment of $2,000 ($14,000 − $12,000). C is not entitled to any of the $2,000 refund. Since C did not file a timely return on April 15, 2015, the time for filing a refund claim expired two years from the date the tax was paid, April 15, 2017. By procrastinating, C lost his entire refund. Had he filed a timely return, the date for claiming the refund would have been three years after the return was filed or April 15, 2018.

The two-year rule applies if the taxpayer did not file a return.[68] If a return was filed, a claim for a refund can be filed by the later of three years from the date of filing the original return (April 15 if filed before such date), or two years from the time the tax was paid. In situations where a return has been filed, the claim for refund usually arises from the filing of an amended individual income tax return (i.e., Form 1040X—see Appendix).

Example 37

K filed a timely return for 2016 on March 12, 2017. The total tax on the return was $5,500, and after withholding of $4,700, K owed $800. K's return was audited and she was required to pay a deficiency of $200 on June 3, 2018. K may file a claim for refund for any part of the tax of $5,700 ($5,500 on the original return plus the additional tax of $200) until April 15, 2020 (three years from the date filed). A claim for up to $200 could be filed up until June 3, 2020 (two years from the date the $200 was paid).

[66] Individual Income Tax Returns 2014, Publication 1304, Statistics of Income, IRS, Washington D.C.

[67] See § 6511 and § 6513.

[68] *Comm. v. Lundy,* 116 116 S. Ct. 647, 77 AFTR2d 406, 96-1 USTC 50,035 (USSC, 1996).

EXHIBIT 4-9	**Interest and Penalties**

Description	Violation	Amount
Interest on underpayments and refunds	Insufficient payment on due date; applies to tax and penalties	3% + Federal short-term rate until paid
Failure to file	Tax return or extension not filed by due date	5% per month of amount due (maximum 25%) if more than 60 days late, minimum penalty is smaller of $135 or 100% of tax due
Failure to file (fraud)	Tax return or extension not filed by due date because of fraud	15% per month of amount due (maximum 75%)
Failure to pay tax	Fail to pay 90% of tax due on due date	0.5% per month of amount due (maximum 25%)
Failure to pay estimated taxes	Failure to pay 25% of required annual payment on 4/15, 6/15, 9/15, or 1/15	3% + Fed short-term rate until paid
Accuracy related	Negligence or disregard of rules or regulations	20% of tax underpayment
Fraud		75% of tax underpayment
Claim for refund	Filed later than two years after tax paid or three years after return filed	Loss of refund

STATUTE OF LIMITATIONS

Even in the administration of the Federal tax laws, all things must finally come to an end. As the U.S. Supreme Court has stated:

> Congress has regarded it as ill advised to have an income tax system under which there would never come a day of final settlement and which required both a taxpayer and the Government to stand ready forever and a day to produce vouchers, prove events, and recall details of all that goes into an income tax contest.[69]

Accordingly, there are certain time periods within which the IRS must take action *against* a taxpayer. If the Service does not take action within the prescribed time period, it is *barred* from pursuing the matter further. Technically the period in which an action must be commenced is called the statute of limitations. If the statute of limitations runs (expires) without any action on the part of the IRS, then the government is prohibited from assessing additional taxes for the expired periods.

Under the general rule, the IRS has three years from the date a return is filed to assess an additional tax liability against the taxpayer. If the tax return is filed before its due date, the three-year period for assessment begins *on* the due date.

---

[69] *Rothensies v. Electric Storage Battery Co.,* 47-1 USTC ¶9106, 35 AFTR 297, 329 U.S. 296, 301 (USSC, 1946).

> ### Example 38
>
> R, a calendar year taxpayer, files a 2017 income tax return (due April 15) on March 8, 2018. The IRS will be prevented from assessing R additional taxes for 2017 any time after April 15, 2021.

> ### Example 39
>
> Refer to *Example 38*. If R files a 2017 income tax return on October 15, 2018, the IRS may assess additional taxes for 2017 at any time through October 15, 2021.

There are several important exceptions to the three-year time period for assessing additional taxes. First, if the taxpayer has filed a false or a fraudulent return with the intention to *evade* the tax, then the tax may be assessed (or a proceeding may be initiated in court without assessment) at *any time* in the future. Similarly, if the taxpayer fails to file a return, the statute of limitations will not begin to run. Interestingly, a willful failure to file, a negligent failure to file, or an innocent failure to file are all treated the same. Thus, under any of these circumstances there is no limit to the time in which the IRS may make an assessment or begin a court proceeding against the taxpayer.

In the case of a *substantial omission of income* from a tax return, the statute of limitations is extended to six years. A substantial omission is defined as an omission of income in excess of 25% of the gross income *reported* on the return.[70] If the omission of gross income was committed with the intent of evading the tax, however, the assessment period would be unlimited.

> ### Example 40
>
> T, a calendar year taxpayer, unintentionally failed to include $8,000 of dividends in his 2016 tax return filed on April 15, 2017. If the $8,000 omitted is more than 25% of the gross income reported on T's 2016 return, the IRS may assess an additional income tax liability against him at any time until after April 15, 2023.

The periods within which assessments must be made are summarized in Exhibit 4-10, which follows.

EXHIBIT 4-10	Periods within Which Assessments Must Be Made
Circumstances of Return	*Period of Assessment*
Normal return had been filed	Three years from date of filing or due date, whichever is later
Return filed with substantial omission of gross income	Six years from date of filing or due date, whichever is later
No return is filed	No time limit
False or fraudulent return	No time limit

---

[70] § 6501(e).

INDEXATION AND THE FEDERAL INCOME TAX

Inflation has significant effects on a progressive tax rate structure stated in terms of a *constant* dollar. Taxpayers whose *real* incomes remain constant will have increasing levels of income, stated in terms of *nominal* dollars. Accordingly, their incomes will *creep up* into higher tax brackets. As an illustration, assume a taxpayer who earned $100,000 in 2007 is entitled to an annual raise at least equal to any increase in the Consumer Price Index (approximately four percent increase in 2007). Although his 2008 salary will creep up to $104,000, his before tax income in terms of 2007 prices remains at $100,000. At first glance, the taxpayer is as well off in 2008 as he was in 2007. Note, however, that the salary increase will be taxed at his marginal tax bracket, in which case he would have less after-tax income in real terms in 2008 than he had in 2007. Over time, this *bracket creep,* as it has been labeled, results in a larger portion of the taxpayer's earnings being paid to the Federal government. In effect, unlegislated tax increases occur.

For many years, Congress simply ignored the bracket creep phenomenon, choosing instead to allow the hidden tax increases to occur. As might be expected, this was a very palatable approach to politicians, particularly considering the alternative. The concerns of the few who objected were mollified in part by tax reduction packages enacted in 1981 and 1986. Both the Economic Recovery Tax Act of 1981 and the Tax Reform Act of 1986 directly reduced tax rates. These specific tax rate adjustments have since been followed by a permanent remedy for bracket creep: indexation.

Congress began adding the concept of indexation to the tax law in 1985. In 1986 it specified the amounts of the standard deduction, exemption amounts, and tax brackets for 1987 and 1988 (and the exemption amount for 1989). Thereafter, each of these amounts and many others have been annually adjusted for price level changes as measured by the Consumer Price Index.[71]

 CHECK YOUR KNOWLEDGE

Review Question 1

Z, age 16, earned $2,500 from umpiring baseball games and refereeing soccer matches during the year. Z—rather Z's parents—wants to know whether he is required to file a tax return since this was his only income.

A taxpayer normally is not required to file a return if his or her income is less than the sum of the personal exemption amount and the standard deduction. However, this general rule does not apply to an individual who can be claimed as a dependent on another return since he or she is not entitled to claim a personal exemption and the standard deduction may be limited. In this case, all of Z's income is earned income and is therefore offset by his standard deduction of $2,850 (in 2017 the greater of $1,050 or $2,850 ($350 + earned income of $2,500). Consequently, it seems that there is no need for him to file a return. However, even though he is not subject to the income tax, he still must consider self-employment taxes (assuming the income is self-employment income). A return is required if a taxpayer has self-employment income of at least $400. As a result, Z must file a return.

---

[71] See §§ 1(f), 1(g)(4), 639(c)(4), and 151(d)(3).

Review Question 2

After spending three years on the auditing staff of a large accounting firm, Norm took a job as controller of a small construction company. On the first day of the job, Norm looked around his new office and noticed a bunch of tax forms on the corner of his desk. One looked like the 1040 for his boss, and the others were corporate and partnership returns related to the company. At first he panicked. But then he realized that it was only the end of February and he had until April 15 to figure out what needed to be done. Should Norm relax?

Doubtful. Although returns for calendar year individuals and partnerships are normally due on April 15, the returns for C corporations or S corporations are due on March 15.

Review Question 3

As always, April 15 arrived and T had not even begun to prepare his tax return. Not to worry, he thought. He could simply file for an extension.

a. Assume T does not file for an extension and files his return late. Are there any penalties?

   Maybe. A failure-to-file and a failure-to-pay penalty may be imposed. Both penalties apply only if there is a tax due. If T is entitled to a refund, there is no penalty. The failure-to-file penalty is 5% per month on the balance due, not to exceed 25 percent.

b. How long is the extension?

   An automatic extension of six months until October 15 is available.

c. Is an extension for time to file the return also an extension of time to pay the tax?

   No. If T does not pay a sufficient amount of his tax by April 15, he faces penalties and interest imposed on the balance due.

d. Assuming T's gross tax liability before withholding is $10,000, how much must he pay by April 15 in order to avoid penalty?

   T must pay 90% of the gross tax, or $9,000, by April 15. Otherwise, a penalty of ½ of 1% per month is imposed (up to a maximum of 25%) on the entire underpayment from the due date of the return (April 15).

e. Assume that T's net tax due for the year is $10,000 and he never files a return or a proper extension. What is the maximum failure-to-file and failure-to-pay penalty that can be assessed (ignore any potential fraud penalty and interest)?

   The maximum failure-to-file and failure-to-pay penalty in this case is $4,750 (47.5% × $10,000). The failure-to-file penalty is 5% per month up to a maximum of 25% reduced by 0.5% per month for any month in which the failure-to-pay penalty also applies. Thus, the maximum failure-to-file penalty when the failure-to-pay penalty also applies is 22.5% ([5 × 5% = 25%] − [5 × 0.05 = 2.5%]). The maximum failure-to-pay penalty is 0.5% per month up to a maximum of 25 percent. Adding the two penalties together produces a maximum penalty for failure to file the return and failure to pay the tax of 47.5% (22.5% + 25%) of the amount due.

f. If T fails to pay his tax and he is subject to penalties, how does interest work? Must he pay interest on just the tax due or on both the tax and the penalties?

   He pays interest not only on the tax due but also on the penalties since the penalties are considered an additional tax.

Review Question 4

Penalties for failing to file a return and failing to pay at least 90% of the tax due by the due date must be distinguished from penalties for failure to adequately make estimated tax payments during the year (underpayment penalties). Try the following true-false questions concerning estimated tax payments.

a. T finally filed her 2016 tax return and is now worrying about 2017. As a general rule, an individual taxpayer must pay 22.5% of her 2017 tax (even though she has no idea what it will be) 15 days after the end of each quarter (i.e., April 15, July 15, October 15, and January 15).

False. Although it is true that the taxpayer must normally pay 90% of the current tax due during the year (or 22.5% per installment), the installments are due on April 15, June 15, September 15, and January 15. Notwithstanding the fact that these payments are not truly paid on a quarterly basis, most people refer to them as "quarterly" estimated tax payments.

b. In lieu of paying 90% of their current tax liability, individual taxpayers may avoid the underpayment penalty by paying 90% of last year's tax liability.

False. Penalty can be avoided if the taxpayer pays 90% of the current year's tax or 100% of last year's tax. However, the 100% rule is increased to 110% if the taxpayer's adjusted gross income in the prior year exceeded $150,000.

c. T earns a salary but also does some tinkering in the stock market. In October she realized that she should have paid estimated taxes throughout the year given what her income was going to be. Asking her employer to withhold an extra $36,500 in taxes during October, November, and December will help solve T's estimated tax problems for April, June, and September.

True. Withholding is treated as being paid ratably throughout the year. Therefore the additional $36,500 is not simply applied to the later due dates. Instead, T is treated as having paid $100 per day each day of the year. For example, she is treated as having paid an additional $10,500 (105 × $100) on April 15.

Review Question 5

T filed her 2016 tax return on March 15, 2017. The IRS is barred from assessing a deficiency after:

a. March 15, 2019
b. March 15, 2020
c. March 15, 2021
d. April 15, 2020
e. April 15, 2021

The answer is (d). The statue of limitations runs out on April 15, 2020, three years from the later of the due date, April 15, 2017, or the date of filing, March 15, 2017.

Appendix

TAX RETURN ILLUSTRATIONS

The following pages provide realistic examples of uncomplicated tax returns for individual taxpayers. The information from *Examples 23, 24,* and *30* of this chapter is used.

Department of the Treasury—Internal Revenue Service

Form 1040EZ

Income Tax Return for Single and Joint Filers With No Dependents (99)   **2016**

OMB No. 1545-0074

Your first name and initial	Last name	Your social security number
William W	Bristol	187	52	9034

If a joint return, spouse's first name and initial	Last name	Spouse's social security number

Home address (number and street). If you have a P.O. box, see instructions.
651 South Hampton   Apt. no.

▲ Make sure the SSN(s) above are correct.

City, town or post office, state, and ZIP code. If you have a foreign address, also complete spaces below (see instructions).
Blue Springs, MO 64015

Presidential Election Campaign
Check here if you, or your spouse if filing jointly, want $3 to go to this fund. Checking a box below will not change your tax or refund. ☐ You ☐ Spouse

Foreign country name	Foreign province/state/county	Foreign postal code

Income

Attach Form(s) W-2 here.

Enclose, but do not attach, any payment.

1 Wages, salaries, and tips. This should be shown in box 1 of your Form(s) W-2. Attach your Form(s) W-2. — **1** 27,410 00

2 Taxable interest. If the total is over $1,500, you cannot use Form 1040EZ. — **2** 400 00

3 Unemployment compensation and Alaska Permanent Fund dividends (see instructions). — **3**

4 Add lines 1, 2, and 3. This is your **adjusted gross income.** — **4** 27,810 00

5 If someone can claim you (or your spouse if a joint return) as a dependent, check the applicable box(es) below and enter the amount from the worksheet on back.

☐ You   ☐ Spouse

If no one can claim you (or your spouse if a joint return), enter $10,350 if **single**; $20,700 if **married filing jointly**. See back for explanation. — **5** 10,350 00

6 Subtract line 5 from line 4. If line 5 is larger than line 4, enter -0-. This is your **taxable income.** ▶ **6** 17,460 00

Payments, Credits, and Tax

7 Federal income tax withheld from Form(s) W-2 and 1099. — **7** 2,820 00

8a **Earned income credit (EIC)** (see instructions) — **8a**

b Nontaxable combat pay election. 8b

9 Add lines 7 and 8a. These are your **total payments and credits.** ▶ **9** 2,820 00

10 **Tax.** Use the amount on **line 6 above** to find your tax in the tax table in the instructions. Then, enter the tax from the table on this line. — **10** 2,158 00

11 Health care: individual responsibility (see instructions)   Full-year coverage [X] — **11** 0 00

12 Add lines 10 and 11. This is your **total tax.** — **12** 2,158 00

Refund

Have it directly deposited! See instructions and fill in 13b, 13c, and 13d, or Form 8888.

13a If line 9 is larger than line 12, subtract line 12 from line 9. This is your **refund.** If Form 8888 is attached, check here ▶ ☐ — **13a** 662 00

▶ b Routing number [X][X][X][X][X][X][X][X] ▶ c Type: ☐ Checking ☐ Savings

▶ d Account number [X][X][X][X][X][X][X][X][X][X][X][X][X][X][X][X][X]

Amount You Owe

14 If line 12 is larger than line 9, subtract line 9 from line 12. This is the **amount you owe.** For details on how to pay, see instructions. ▶ **14**

Third Party Designee

Do you want to allow another person to discuss this return with the IRS (see instructions)? ☐ **Yes.** Complete below. [X] **No**

Designee's name ▶   Phone no. ▶   Personal identification number (PIN) ▶ [   ]

Sign Here

Under penalties of perjury, I declare that I have examined this return and, to the best of my knowledge and belief, it is true, correct, and accurately lists all amounts and sources of income I received during the tax year. Declaration of preparer (other than the taxpayer) is based on all information of which the preparer has any knowledge.

Joint return? See instructions.

Keep a copy for your records.

Your signature   Date   Your occupation Restaurant Manager   Daytime phone number (816) 229 – 1207

Spouse's signature. If a joint return, **both** must sign.   Date   Spouse's occupation   If the IRS sent you an Identity Protection PIN, enter it here (see inst.) [   ]

Paid Preparer Use Only

Print/Type preparer's name   Preparer's signature   Date   Check ☐ if self-employed   PTIN

Firm's name ▶   Firm's EIN ▶

Firm's address ▶   Phone no.

For Disclosure, Privacy Act, and Paperwork Reduction Act Notice, see instructions.   Cat. No. 11329W   Form **1040EZ** (2016)

Form **1040A**	Department of the Treasury—Internal Revenue Service **U.S. Individual Income Tax Return** (99) **2016**	IRS Use Only—Do not write or staple in this space.

Your first name and initial	Last name	OMB No. 1545-0074
Clyde F	Cooper	**Your social security number** 234	56	7890
If a joint return, spouse's first name and initial	Last name	**Spouse's social security number**
Delia C	Cooper	345	67	8901

Home address (number and street). If you have a P.O. box, see instructions.   Apt. no.
1234 Fine Street

▲ Make sure the SSN(s) above and on line 6c are correct.

City, town or post office, state, and ZIP code. If you have a foreign address, also complete spaces below (see instructions).
Tulsa, OK 74105

Presidential Election Campaign
Check here if you, or your spouse if filing jointly, want $3 to go to this fund. Checking a box below will not change your tax or refund.   ☐ You   ☐ Spouse

Foreign country name	Foreign province/state/county	Foreign postal code

Filing status
Check only one box.

1 ☐ Single
2 ☒ Married filing jointly (even if only one had income)
3 ☐ Married filing separately. Enter spouse's SSN above and full name here. ▶
4 ☐ Head of household (with qualifying person). (See instructions.) If the qualifying person is a child but not your dependent, enter this child's name here. ▶
5 ☐ Qualifying widow(er) with dependent child (see instructions)

Exemptions

If more than six dependents, see instructions.

6a ☒ **Yourself.** If someone can claim you as a dependent, **do not** check box 6a.
b ☒ **Spouse**

c **Dependents:**			
(1) First name Last name	**(2)** Dependent's social security number	**(3)** Dependent's relationship to you	**(4)** ✔ if child under age 17 qualifying for child tax credit (see instructions)
Gary Cooper	777-99-6451	Son	☒
Debra Cooper	564-99-8765	Daughter	☒
			☐
			☐
			☐
			☐

Boxes checked on 6a and 6b — **2**
No. of children on 6c who:
• lived with you — **2**
• did not live with you due to divorce or separation (see instructions)
Dependents on 6c not entered above
Add numbers on lines above ▶ — **4**

d   Total number of exemptions claimed.

Income

Attach Form(s) W-2 here. Also attach Form(s) 1099-R if tax was withheld.

If you did not get a W-2, see instructions.

7	Wages, salaries, tips, etc. Attach Form(s) W-2.	7	57,045	00
8a	**Taxable** interest. Attach Schedule B if required.	8a	1,700	00
b	**Tax-exempt** interest. **Do not** include on line 8a. 8b			
9a	Ordinary dividends. Attach Schedule B if required.	9a		
b	Qualified dividends (see instructions). 9b			
10	Capital gain distributions (see instructions).	10		
11a	IRA distributions. 11a	11b Taxable amount (see instructions).	11b	
12a	Pensions and annuities. 12a	12b Taxable amount (see instructions).	12b	
13	Unemployment compensation and Alaska Permanent Fund dividends.	13		
14a	Social security benefits. 14a	14b Taxable amount (see instructions).	14b	
15	Add lines 7 through 14b (far right column). This is your **total income.** ▶	15	58,745	00

Adjusted gross income

16	Educator expenses (see instructions). 16			
17	IRA deduction (see instructions). 17	4,000	00	
18	Student loan interest deduction (see instructions). 18			
19	Tuition and fees. Attach Form 8917. 19			
20	Add lines 16 through 19. These are your **total adjustments.**	20	4,000	00
21	Subtract line 20 from line 15. This is your **adjusted gross income.** ▶	21	54,745	00

For Disclosure, Privacy Act, and Paperwork Reduction Act Notice, see separate instructions. Cat. No. 11327A   Form **1040A** (2016)

Form 1040A (2016)   Clyde F & Delia C Cooper   234 – 56 – 7890   Page **2**

Tax, credits, and payments	22	Enter the amount from line 21 (adjusted gross income).		22	54,745	00
	23a	Check if: ☐ **You** were born before January 2, 1952, ☐ Blind / ☐ **Spouse** was born before January 2, 1952, ☐ Blind } Total boxes checked ▶ 23a				
	b	If you are married filing separately and your spouse itemizes deductions, check here ▶ 23b ☐				

Standard Deduction for—
• People who check any box on line 23a or 23b **or** who can be claimed as a dependent, see instructions.
• All others:
Single or Married filing separately, $6,300
Married filing jointly or Qualifying widow(er), $12,600
Head of household, $9,300

	24	Enter your **standard deduction**.		24	12,600	00
	25	Subtract line 24 from line 22. If line 24 is more than line 22, enter -0-.		25	42,145	00
	26	**Exemptions.** Multiply $4,050 by the number on line 6d.		26	16,200	00
	27	Subtract line 26 from line 25. If line 26 is more than line 25, enter -0-. This is your **taxable income.** ▶		27	25,945	00
	28	**Tax,** including any alternative minimum tax (see instructions).	28	2,961	00	
	29	Excess advance premium tax credit repayment. Attach Form 8962.	29			
	30	Add lines 28 and 29.		30	2,961	00
	31	Credit for child and dependent care expenses. Attach Form 2441.	31	700	00	
	32	Credit for the elderly or the disabled. Attach Schedule R.	32			
	33	Education credits from Form 8863, line 19.	33			
	34	Retirement savings contributions credit. Attach Form 8880.	34			
	35	Child tax credit. Attach Schedule 8812, if required.	35	2,000	00	
	36	Add lines 31 through 35. These are your **total credits.**		36	2,700	00
	37	Subtract line 36 from line 30. If line 36 is more than line 30, enter -0-.		37	261	00
	38	Health care: individual responsibility (see instructions). Full-year coverage ☐		38	0	00
	39	Add line 37 and line 38. This is your **total tax.**		39	261	00

If you have a qualifying child, attach Schedule EIC.

	40	Federal income tax withheld from Forms W-2 and 1099.	40	1,950		
	41	2016 estimated tax payments and amount applied from 2015 return.	41			
	42a	**Earned income credit (EIC).**	42a			
	b	Nontaxable combat pay election. 42b				
	43	Additional child tax credit. Attach Schedule 8812.	43			
	44	American opportunity credit from Form 8863, line 8.	44			
	45	Net premium tax credit. Attach Form 8962.	45			
	46	Add lines 40, 41, 42a, 43, 44, and 45. These are your **total payments.** ▶		46	1,950	00

Refund

Direct deposit? See instructions and fill in 48b, 48c, and 48d or Form 8888.

	47	If line 46 is more than line 39, subtract line 39 from line 46. This is the amount you **overpaid.**		47	1,689	00
	48a	Amount of line 47 you want **refunded to you.** If Form 8888 is attached, check here ▶ ☐ 48a			1,689	00
	▶ b	Routing number XXXXXXXX ▶ c Type: ☐ Checking ☐ Savings				
	▶ d	Account number XXXXXXXXXXXXXXXXX				
	49	Amount of line 47 you want **applied to your 2017 estimated tax.**	49			

Amount you owe

	50	**Amount you owe.** Subtract line 46 from line 39. For details on how to pay, see instructions. ▶		50		
	51	Estimated tax penalty (see instructions).	51			

Third party designee

Do you want to allow another person to discuss this return with the IRS (see instructions)? ☐ **Yes.** Complete the following. ☒ **No**

Designee's name ▶ _____   Phone no. ▶ _____   Personal identification number (PIN) ▶ _____

Sign here

Joint return? See instructions. Keep a copy for your records.

Under penalties of perjury, I declare that I have examined this return and accompanying schedules and statements, and to the best of my knowledge and belief, they are true, correct, and accurately list all amounts and sources of income I received during the tax year. Declaration of preparer (other than the taxpayer) is based on all information of which the preparer has any knowledge.

Your signature	Date	Your occupation Professional Model	Daytime phone number
Spouse's signature. If a joint return, **both** must sign.	Date	Spouse's occupation Programmer	If the IRS sent you an Identity Protection PIN, enter it here (see inst.)

Paid preparer use only

Print/type preparer's name	Preparer's signature	Date	Check ▶ ☐ if self-employed	PTIN
Firm's name ▶			Firm's EIN ▶	
Firm's address ▶			Phone no.	

Form **1040A** (2016)

Form **2441**

Department of the Treasury
Internal Revenue Service (99)

Child and Dependent Care Expenses

▶ Attach to Form 1040, Form 1040A, or Form 1040NR.

▶ Information about Form 2441 and its separate instructions is at www.irs.gov/form2441.

1040
1040A
1040NR
2441

OMB No. 1545-0074

20**16**

Attachment
Sequence No. **21**

Name(s) shown on return
Clyde F & Delia C Cooper

Your social security number
234 – 56 – 7890

Part I   **Persons or Organizations Who Provided the Care**—You **must** complete this part.
(If you have more than two care providers, see the instructions.)

1	(a) Care provider's name	(b) Address (number, street, apt. no., city, state, and ZIP code)	(c) Identifying number (SSN or EIN)	(d) Amount paid (see instructions)
	Happy Trails Preschool	2391 Bronco Street Tulsa, OK 74105	44-5678656	3,500 00

Did you receive **dependent care benefits?**

No ────▶ Complete only Part II below.

Yes ────▶ Complete Part III on the back next.

Caution: If the care was provided in your home, you may owe employment taxes. If you do, you cannot file Form 1040A. For details, see the instructions for Form 1040, line 60a, or Form 1040NR, line 59a.

Part II   **Credit for Child and Dependent Care Expenses**

2   Information about your **qualifying person(s)**. If you have more than two qualifying persons, see the instructions.

(a) Qualifying person's name		(b) Qualifying person's social security number	(c) **Qualified expenses** you incurred and paid in 2016 for the person listed in column (a)
First	Last		
Gary	Cooper	777-99-6451	1,500 00
Debra	Cooper	564-99-8765	2,000 00

3   Add the amounts in column (c) of line 2. **Do not** enter more than $3,000 for one qualifying person or $6,000 for two or more persons. If you completed Part III, enter the amount from line 31 . . . .   **3**   3,500 00

4   Enter your **earned income.** See instructions **4**   33,445 00

5   If married filing jointly, enter your spouse's earned income (if you or your spouse was a student or was disabled, see the instructions); **all others**, enter the amount from line 4 .   **5**   23,600 00

6   Enter the **smallest** of line 3, 4, or 5 . . . .   **6**   3,500 00

7   Enter the amount from Form 1040, line 38; Form 1040A, line 22; or Form 1040NR, line 37 . . . . .   **7**   54,745 00

8   Enter on line 8 the decimal amount shown below that applies to the amount on line 7

If line 7 is:			If line 7 is:		
Over	But not over	Decimal amount is	Over	But not over	Decimal amount is
$0—15,000		.35	$29,000—31,000		.27
15,000—17,000		.34	31,000—33,000		.26
17,000—19,000		.33	33,000—35,000		.25
19,000—21,000		.32	35,000—37,000		.24
21,000—23,000		.31	37,000—39,000		.23
23,000—25,000		.30	39,000—41,000		.22
25,000—27,000		.29	41,000—43,000		.21
27,000—29,000		.28	43,000—No limit		.20

8   X . 20

9   Multiply line 6 by the decimal amount on line 8. If you paid 2015 expenses in 2016, see the instructions **9**   700 00

10   Tax liability limit. Enter the amount from the Credit Limit Worksheet in the instructions. **10**   2,961 00

11   **Credit for child and dependent care expenses.** Enter the **smaller** of line 9 or line 10 here and on Form 1040, line 49; Form 1040A, line 31; or Form 1040NR, line 47 . . . . .   **11**   700 00

For Paperwork Reduction Act Notice, see your tax return instructions.   Cat. No. 11862M   Form **2441** (2016)

Form **1040**	Department of the Treasury—Internal Revenue Service (99)		

Form 1040 Department of the Treasury—Internal Revenue Service (99)

U.S. Individual Income Tax Return **2016** OMB No. 1545-0074 | IRS Use Only—Do not write or staple in this space.

For the year Jan. 1–Dec. 31, 2016, or other tax year beginning _____ , 2016, ending _____ , 20 ___ **See separate instructions.**

Your first name and initial	Last name	Your social security number
Jeremy S	Allen	123 45 9875

If a joint return, spouse's first name and initial	Last name	Spouse's social security number
Shelly R	Allen	456 85 2447

Home address (number and street). If you have a P.O. box, see instructions. | Apt. no.
8473 Smithson Place

▲ **Make sure the SSN(s) above and on line 6c are correct.**

City, town or post office, state, and ZIP code. If you have a foreign address, also complete spaces below (see instructions).
Boring, OR 97832

Foreign country name | Foreign province/state/county | Foreign postal code

Presidential Election Campaign
Check here if you, or your spouse if filing jointly, want $3 to go to this fund. Checking a box below will not change your tax or refund. ☐ You ☐ Spouse

Filing Status

Check only one box.

1. ☐ Single
2. ☒ Married filing jointly (even if only one had income)
3. ☐ Married filing separately. Enter spouse's SSN above and full name here. ▶
4. ☐ Head of household (with qualifying person). (See instructions.) If the qualifying person is a child but not your dependent, enter this child's name here. ▶ _____
5. ☐ Qualifying widow(er) with dependent child

Exemptions

6a ☒ **Yourself.** If someone can claim you as a dependent, **do not** check box 6a . . . . .
b ☒ **Spouse** . . . .

Boxes checked on 6a and 6b	2

c **Dependents:**

(1) First name Last name	(2) Dependent's social security number	(3) Dependent's relationship to you	(4) ✓ if child under age 17 qualifying for child tax credit (see instructions)
William Allen	789 65 4321	Son	X
Susan Allen	456 65 9879	Daughter	X
Gregory Allen	321 72 9741	Son	X
			☐

No. of children on 6c who:
• lived with you **3**
• did not live with you due to divorce or separation (see instructions) ___

Dependents on 6c not entered above ___

If more than four dependents, see instructions and check here ▶ ☐

d Total number of exemptions claimed . . . .

Add numbers on lines above ▶ **5**

Income

Attach Form(s) W-2 here. Also attach Forms W-2G and 1099-R if tax was withheld.

If you did not get a W-2, see instructions.

7	Wages, salaries, tips, etc. Attach Form(s) W-2	7	77,775	00
8a	**Taxable** interest. Attach Schedule B if required	8a	3,000	00
b	**Tax-exempt** interest. **Do not** include on line 8a . . .	8b			
9a	Ordinary dividends. Attach Schedule B if required	9a		
b	Qualified dividends	9b			
10	Taxable refunds, credits, or offsets of state and local income taxes	10		
11	Alimony received	11		
12	Business income or (loss). Attach Schedule C or C-EZ	12		
13	Capital gain or (loss). Attach Schedule D if required. If not required, check here ▶ ☐	13		
14	Other gains or (losses). Attach Form 4797	14		
15a	IRA distributions . 15a	b Taxable amount . .	15b		
16a	Pensions and annuities 16a	b Taxable amount . .	16b		
17	Rental real estate, royalties, partnerships, S corporations, trusts, etc. Attach Schedule E	17		
18	Farm income or (loss). Attach Schedule F	18		
19	Unemployment compensation	19		
20a	Social security benefits 20a	b Taxable amount . .	20b		
21	Other income. List type and amount _____	21		
22	Combine the amounts in the far right column for lines 7 through 21. This is your **total income** ▶	22	80,775	00

Adjusted Gross Income

23	Educator expenses	23		
24	Certain business expenses of reservists, performing artists, and fee-basis government officials. Attach Form 2106 or 2106-EZ	24		
25	Health savings account deduction. Attach Form 8889 .	25		
26	Moving expenses. Attach Form 3903	26		
27	Deductible part of self-employment tax. Attach Schedule SE .	27		
28	Self-employed SEP, SIMPLE, and qualified plans . .	28		
29	Self-employed health insurance deduction	29		
30	Penalty on early withdrawal of savings	30		
31a	Alimony paid b Recipient's SSN ▶	31a		
32	IRA deduction	32		
33	Student loan interest deduction	33		
34	Tuition and fees. Attach Form 8917	34		
35	Domestic production activities deduction. Attach Form 8903	35		
36	Add lines 23 through 35	36		
37	Subtract line 36 from line 22. This is your **adjusted gross income** . . . . . . ▶	37	80,775	00

For Disclosure, Privacy Act, and Paperwork Reduction Act Notice, see separate instructions.   Cat. No. 11320B   Form **1040** (2016)

Form 1040 (2016)   Jeremy S & Shelly R Allen   123 – 45 – 9875   Page **2**

Tax and Credits	38	Amount from line 37 (adjusted gross income)	38	80,775 00
	39a	Check if: ☐ **You** were born before January 2, 1952, ☐ Blind. ☐ **Spouse** was born before January 2, 1952, ☐ Blind. } **Total boxes** checked ▶ 39a		
	b	If your spouse itemizes on a separate return or you were a dual-status alien, check here▶ 39b ☐		
Standard Deduction for— • People who check any box on line 39a or 39b **or** who can be claimed as a dependent, see instructions. • All others: Single or Married filing separately, $6,300 Married filing jointly or Qualifying widow(er), $12,600 Head of household, $9,300	40	**Itemized deductions** (from Schedule A) **or** your **standard deduction** (see left margin) . .	40	15,000 00
	41	Subtract line 40 from line 38	41	65,775 00
	42	**Exemptions.** If line 38 is $155,650 or less, multiply $4,050 by the number on line 6d. Otherwise, see instructions	42	20,250 00
	43	**Taxable income.** Subtract line 42 from line 41. If line 42 is more than line 41, enter -0- . .	43	45,525 00
	44	**Tax** (see instructions). Check if any from: **a** ☐ Form(s) 8814 **b** ☐ Form 4972 **c** ☐ _____	44	5,901 00
	45	**Alternative minimum tax** (see instructions). Attach Form 6251	45	
	46	Excess advance premium tax credit repayment. Attach Form 8962	46	
	47	Add lines 44, 45, and 46 . . . . ▶	47	5,901 00
	48	Foreign tax credit. Attach Form 1116 if required . . .	48		
	49	Credit for child and dependent care expenses. Attach Form 2441	49		
	50	Education credits from Form 8863, line 19	50		
	51	Retirement savings contributions credit. Attach Form 8880	51		
	52	Child tax credit. Attach Schedule 8812, if required . . .	52	3,000 00	
	53	Residential energy credits. Attach Form 5695	53		
	54	Other credits from Form: **a** ☐ 3800 **b** ☐ 8801 **c** ☐ _____	54		
	55	Add lines 48 through 54. These are your **total credits**	55	3,000 00
	56	Subtract line 55 from line 47. If line 55 is more than line 47, enter -0- . . . . . . ▶	56	2,901 00
Other Taxes	57	Self-employment tax. Attach Schedule SE	57	
	58	Unreported social security and Medicare tax from Form: **a** ☐ 4137 **b** ☐ 8919 . .	58	
	59	Additional tax on IRAs, other qualified retirement plans, etc. Attach Form 5329 if required . .	59	
	60a	Household employment taxes from Schedule H	60a	
	b	First-time homebuyer credit repayment. Attach Form 5405 if required	60b	
	61	Health care: individual responsibility (see instructions) Full-year coverage ☒	61	0 00
	62	Taxes from: **a** ☐ Form 8959 **b** ☐ Form 8960 **c** ☐ Instructions; enter code(s) _____	62	
	63	Add lines 56 through 62. This is your **total tax** . . . . ▶	63	2,901 00
Payments If you have a qualifying child, attach Schedule EIC.	64	Federal income tax withheld from Forms W-2 and 1099 . .	64	4,100 00	
	65	2016 estimated tax payments and amount applied from 2015 return	65		
	66a	**Earned income credit (EIC)**	66a		
	b	Nontaxable combat pay election 66b _____			
	67	Additional child tax credit. Attach Schedule 8812	67		
	68	American opportunity credit from Form 8863, line 8	68		
	69	Net premium tax credit. Attach Form 8962	69		
	70	Amount paid with request for extension to file	70		
	71	Excess social security and tier 1 RRTA tax withheld	71		
	72	Credit for federal tax on fuels. Attach Form 4136 . . .	72		
	73	Credits from Form: **a** ☐ 2439 **b** ☐ Reserved **c** ☐ 8885 **d** ☐ _____	73		
	74	Add lines 64, 65, 66a, and 67 through 73. These are your **total payments** . . . . . ▶	74	4,100 00
Refund Direct deposit? See instructions.	75	If line 74 is more than line 63, subtract line 63 from line 74. This is the amount you **overpaid**	75	1,199 00
	76a	Amount of line 75 you want **refunded to you.** If Form 8888 is attached, check here . ▶ ☐	76a	1,199 00
	▶ b	Routing number X X X X X X X X X ▶ **c** Type: ☐ Checking ☐ Savings		
	▶ d	Account number X X X X X X X X X X X X X X X X X		
	77	Amount of line 75 you want **applied to your 2017 estimated tax** ▶ 77		
Amount You Owe	78	**Amount you owe.** Subtract line 74 from line 63. For details on how to pay, see instructions . . ▶	78	
	79	Estimated tax penalty (see instructions)	79		

Third Party Designee	Do you want to allow another person to discuss this return with the IRS (see instructions)? ☐ **Yes.** Complete below. ☒ **No**
	Designee's name ▶ _____ Phone no. ▶ _____ Personal identification number (PIN) ▶ ☐☐☐☐☐

Sign Here
Joint return? See instructions.
Keep a copy for your records.

Under penalties of perjury, I declare that I have examined this return and accompanying schedules and statements, and to the best of my knowledge and belief, they are true, correct, and accurately list all amounts and sources of income I received during the tax year. Declaration of preparer (other than taxpayer) is based on all information of which preparer has any knowledge.

Your signature	Date	Your occupation Registered Nurse	Daytime phone number
Spouse's signature. If a joint return, **both** must sign.	Date	Spouse's occupation Air Traffic Control	If the IRS sent you an Identity Protection PIN, enter it here (see inst.) ☐☐☐☐☐☐

Paid Preparer Use Only	Print/Type preparer's name	Preparer's signature	Date	Check ☐ if self-employed	PTIN
	Firm's name ▶			Firm's EIN ▶	
	Firm's address ▶			Phone no.	

SCHEDULE A
(Form 1040)

Department of the Treasury
Internal Revenue Service (99)

Itemized Deductions

▶ Information about Schedule A and its separate instructions is at *www.irs.gov/schedulea.*
▶ **Attach to Form 1040.**

OMB No. 1545-0074

2016

Attachment
Sequence No. **07**

Name(s) shown on Form 1040

Jeremy S & Shelly R Allen

Your social security number

123 – 45 – 9875

Medical and Dental Expenses	**Caution:** Do not include expenses reimbursed or paid by others.			
	1 Medical and dental expenses (see instructions)	**1**	3,000 00	
	2 Enter amount from Form 1040, line 38 **2** | 80,775 00			
	3 Multiply line 2 by 10% (0.10). But if either you or your spouse was born before January 2, 1952, multiply line 2 by 7.5% (0.075) instead	**3**	8,078 00	
	4 Subtract line 3 from line 1. If line 3 is more than line 1, enter -0-		**4**	0 00
Taxes You Paid	5 State and local **(check only one box):**			
	a ☒ Income taxes, **or**	**5**	3,400 00	
	b ☐ General sales taxes			
	6 Real estate taxes (see instructions)	**6**	1,200 00	
	7 Personal property taxes	**7**		
	8 Other taxes. List type and amount ▶ _____	**8**		
	9 Add lines 5 through 8		**9**	4,600 00
Interest You Paid	10 Home mortgage interest and points reported to you on Form 1098	**10**	8,900 00	
	11 Home mortgage interest not reported to you on Form 1098. If paid to the person from whom you bought the home, see instructions and show that person's name, identifying no., and address ▶			
Note: Your mortgage interest deduction may be limited (see instructions).	_____	**11**		
	12 Points not reported to you on Form 1098. See instructions for special rules	**12**		
	13 Mortgage insurance premiums (see instructions)	**13**		
	14 Investment interest. Attach Form 4952 if required. (See instructions.)	**14**		
	15 Add lines 10 through 14		**15**	8,900 00
Gifts to Charity	16 Gifts by cash or check. If you made any gift of $250 or more, see instructions	**16**	1,500 00	
If you made a gift and got a benefit for it, see instructions.	17 Other than by cash or check. If any gift of $250 or more, see instructions. You **must** attach Form 8283 if over $500 . . .	**17**		
	18 Carryover from prior year	**18**		
	19 Add lines 16 through 18		**19**	1,500 00
Casualty and Theft Losses	20 Casualty or theft loss(es). Attach Form 4684. (See instructions.)		**20**	
Job Expenses and Certain Miscellaneous Deductions	21 Unreimbursed employee expenses—job travel, union dues, job education, etc. Attach Form 2106 or 2106-EZ if required. (See instructions.) ▶ _____	**21**		
	22 Tax preparation fees	**22**	275 00	
	23 Other expenses—investment, safe deposit box, etc. List type and amount ▶ _____	**23**		
	24 Add lines 21 through 23	**24**	275 00	
	25 Enter amount from Form 1040, line 38 **25** | 80,775 00			
	26 Multiply line 25 by 2% (0.02)	**26**	1,616 00	
	27 Subtract line 26 from line 24. If line 26 is more than line 24, enter -0-		**27**	0 00
Other Miscellaneous Deductions	28 Other—from list in instructions. List type and amount ▶ _____		**28**	
Total Itemized Deductions	29 Is Form 1040, line 38, over $155,650?			
	☐ **No.** Your deduction is not limited. Add the amounts in the far right column for lines 4 through 28. Also, enter this amount on Form 1040, line 40.	}	**29**	15,000 00
	☐ **Yes.** Your deduction may be limited. See the Itemized Deductions Worksheet in the instructions to figure the amount to enter.			
	30 If you elect to itemize deductions even though they are less than your standard deduction, check here . . . . ▶ ☐			

For Paperwork Reduction Act Notice, see Form 1040 instructions.   Cat. No. 17145C   Schedule A (Form 1040) 2016

SCHEDULE B
(Form 1040A or 1040)

Department of the Treasury
Internal Revenue Service (99)

Interest and Ordinary Dividends

▶ **Attach to Form 1040A or 1040.**
▶ **Information about Schedule B and its instructions is at *www.irs.gov/scheduleb*.**

OMB No. 1545-0074

2016

Attachment
Sequence No. **08**

Name(s) shown on return
Jeremy S & Shelly R Allen

Your social security number
123 – 45 – 9875

Part I **Interest** (See instructions on back and the instructions for Form 1040A, or Form 1040, line 8a.) **Note:** If you received a Form 1099-INT, Form 1099-OID, or substitute statement from a brokerage firm, list the firm's name as the payer and enter the total interest shown on that form.	**1**	List name of payer. If any interest is from a seller-financed mortgage and the buyer used the property as a personal residence, see instructions on back and list this interest first. Also, show that buyer's social security number and address ▶ Mercantile Bank		Amount	
			1	3,000	00
	2	Add the amounts on line 1	**2**	3,000	00
	3	Excludable interest on series EE and I U.S. savings bonds issued after 1989. Attach Form 8815 .	**3**		
	4	Subtract line 3 from line 2. Enter the result here and on Form 1040A, or Form 1040, line 8a . . . . ▶	**4**	3,000	00

Note: If line 4 is over $1,500, you must complete Part III.

Part II **Ordinary Dividends** (See instructions on back and the instructions for Form 1040A, or Form 1040, line 9a.) **Note:** If you received a Form 1099-DIV or substitute statement from a brokerage firm, list the firm's name as the payer and enter the ordinary dividends shown on that form.	**5**	List name of payer ▶		Amount	
			5		
	6	Add the amounts on line 5. Enter the total here and on Form 1040A, or Form 1040, line 9a . . . . ▶	**6**		

Note: If line 6 is over $1,500, you must complete Part III.

Part III **Foreign Accounts and Trusts** (See instructions on back.)		You must complete this part if you **(a)** had over $1,500 of taxable interest or ordinary dividends; **(b)** had a foreign account; or **(c)** received a distribution from, or were a grantor of, or a transferor to, a foreign trust.	Yes	No
	7a	At any time during 2016, did you have a financial interest in or signature authority over a financial account (such as a bank account, securities account, or brokerage account) located in a foreign country? See instructions		X
		If "Yes," are you required to file FinCEN Form 114, Report of Foreign Bank and Financial Accounts (FBAR), to report that financial interest or signature authority? See FinCEN Form 114 and its instructions for filing requirements and exceptions to those requirements		
	b	If you are required to file FinCEN Form 114, enter the name of the foreign country where the financial account is located ▶		
	8	During 2016, did you receive a distribution from, or were you the grantor of, or transferor to, a foreign trust? If "Yes," you may have to file Form 3520. See instructions on back		X

For Paperwork Reduction Act Notice, see your tax return instructions.   Cat. No. 17146N   Schedule B (Form 1040A or 1040) 2016

DISCUSSION QUESTIONS

4-1 *Exemptions.* Distinguish between personal and dependency exemptions.

4-2 *Dependency Exemption for a Qualifying Child.* List the requirements that must be met in order for one to claim a dependency exemption for a *qualifying child.*

4-3 *Relationship.* In addition to a natural child, which other *children* are included in the definition of a *qualifying child?*

4-4 *Tie-Breaking.* Determine who gets the dependency exemption for D in each of the independent cases below. Assume that the parties cannot agree if more than one person could claim the exemption. Also assume that any tests that are not addressed (e.g., citizenship) are met. F's other support (> $3,000) is provided by S.
   a.   Q provides a home in which she lives with her daughter, C, and C's son, D. C is 25 years of age and has gross income of $6,500 for the current year.
   b.   R provides a home in which she lives with her son, E, and E's son, D. E is 18 years of age and has gross income of $6,500 for the current year.
   c.   S provides a home in which she lives with her daughter, F, and F's daughter, D. F is 25 years of age and has gross income of $3,000 for the current year.

4-5 *Tests for Dependency Exemptions.* List and briefly describe the five tests that must be met before a taxpayer is entitled to a dependency exemption for an individual other than a qualifying child. Must all five tests be met?

4-6 *Support.* Describe the concept of support, including examples of support items.

4-7 *Support—Special Items.* With respect to the support test, discuss the treatment of each of the following items: athletic scholarships, Social Security survivors' benefits paid to an orphan, and aid to dependent children paid by the state government.

4-8 *Gross Income Test.* Explain the gross income test. Must all dependents for whom a dependency exemption is claimed meet this test?

4-9 *Gross Income Test—Dependency Exemption.* M provides more than half of the support for her father, F, who is single for tax purposes. F's other support is in the form of interest income of $5,000 and Social Security benefits of $9,000.
   a.   May M claim a dependency exemption for supporting F in the current year?
   b.   Would your answer differ if F's interest income were only $1,500?

4-10 *Relationship Test—Dependency Exemption.* Assuming Q provides more than 50% of their support and the dependent meets the gross income, relationship, and citizenship tests, which of the following relatives may be claimed as a dependent?
   a.   Widow of Q's deceased son
   b.   Q's husband's brother
   c.   Daughter of Q's husband's brother
   d.   Q's mother's brother
   e.   Q's grandmother's brother
   f.   Q's great grandson

4-11 *Joint Return Test—Dependency Exemption.* K and L were married in 2017 and elected to file a joint return. K had interest income of $5,000 and a salary of $30,000 for the year. L had interest income of $2,250 and received the remainder of her support from her mother and K.
   a.   If L's mother provided more than 50% of L's support, can she claim a dependency exemption for L?
   b.   If not, under what circumstances could the exemption be claimed?

4-12 *Eligibility.* This year P, 25, was accepted to medical school. P is a single parent. To save money, she and her one-year-old baby, B, moved in with P's mom and dad, M and D. The four lived together from May through December. May anyone claim an exemption for B? If so, whom?

4-13 *Community Property Law.* How does the treatment of earned income differ between a community property state and a non community property (i.e., separate property) state for Federal income tax purposes? Why?

4-14 *Filing Status, Tax Schedules.* List the four sets of rate schedules that apply to individual taxpayers. Refer to them by filing status and schedule designation (e.g., Schedule Z). Which taxpayers must use the rate schedules rather than the tax rate tables?

4-15 *Determination of Marital Status.* Married taxpayers are subject to a separate set(s) of tax rates. When is marital status determined? What authority (state or federal) controls marital status?

4-16 *Exceptions—Marital Status.* In certain instances, a person who is married may use the rates for unmarried persons. In another instance, a single person may use the rates for married persons filing jointly. Elaborate.

4-17 *Head of Household—Requirements.* What are the specific requirements for head-of-household status? List at least ten relatives who may qualify the taxpayer for head-of-household filing status.

4-18 *Head of Household—Divorced Parents.* May a divorced parent with custody of a child qualify as a head of household even though his or her former spouse is entitled to the dependency exemption for the child? Explain.

4-19 *Head of Household—Taxpayer's Home.* Must the person who qualifies a taxpayer as a head of household (i.e., the taxpayer's child or other dependent) live in the taxpayer's home? Are there any exceptions to this rule?

4-20 *Costs of Maintaining Home.* Which of the following expenses are included in determining the cost of a home when determining whether a taxpayer qualifies as a head of household?
a. Food consumed on the premises
b. Transportation for a dependent to and from school
c. Clothing for a dependent
d. Property taxes on residence
e. Rent paid on residence

4-21 *Spouses Living Apart.* M is married and lives with her dependent son, S. M receives child support sufficient to provide 65% of S's support from S's father, who lived in a nearby city for the entire year. M provides more than one-half of the cost of providing the home in which she and S live.
a. What is M's filing status and what is the number of exemption deductions that she may claim?
b. How would your answers differ if M agreed to let S's father claim the dependency exemption for S?

4-22 *Tax Tables.* Are taxpayers required to use the tax tables? Which taxpayers are ineligible to use the tables?

4-23 *Limited Standard Deduction.* W is 16 years old, single, and claimed as a dependent by his parents. His 2017 AGI is $6,250, and he claims the standard deduction. Given W's taxable income below, what is the character of his income, earned or unearned?
a. Taxable income $5,200
b. Taxable income $3,700
c. Taxable income $350

4-24 *Kiddie Tax.* G is 13 years old and claimed as a dependent by her parents. G's top marginal tax rate is 10% and her parents' is 25 percent. Calculate G's taxable income and the rate at which it will be taxed in the following instances:
a. Interest of $1,100
b. Interest of $2,200
c. Interest of $900 and wages of $5,000
d. Interest of $3,500 and wages of $500

4-25 *Filing Requirements.* Which individuals are exempted from filing a Form 1040 (or equivalent Form 1040A or Form 1040EZ)?

4-26 *Due Date.* P is a calendar year taxpayer with taxable income of $45,000 and a tax due of $350 for the current year.

    a. When is P's tax return due if P is an individual?

    b. Assume P is a corporation and uses a fiscal year ending June 30, when is its annual income tax return due?

4-27 *Extensions.* Q is a calendar year individual taxpayer with taxable income of $25,000 and a tax refund of $150 for the current year.

    a. If Q is unable to file on time, she may request an automatic extension of time to file her tax return. How long is the maximum extension period?

    b. If Q is unable to complete her return by the extended due date and she has an appropriate reason, how long of an additional extension can she request?

    c. How much is Q's penalty if she fails to file an extension?

4-28 *Due Dates for Estimated Tax Payments.* R is a calendar year taxpayer whose estimated tax liability for the current year is $4,000. What are the amounts and the due dates of R's estimated tax payments?

4-29 *Amount of Estimated Tax Payments.* H is a calendar year taxpayer who estimates his Federal income tax to be $5,500 and his self-employment tax to be $4,500 for 2017. For 2016, H's Federal income tax was $4,950, and his self-employment tax was $3,975. What is the amount of estimated tax that H must pay on each due date to avoid a penalty for failure to make adequate estimated tax payments?

4-30 *Penalties and Interest.* J is a calendar year individual whose gross tax for 2016 is $10,000. J had taxes of $5,750 withheld and made estimated tax payments of $500 each due date. She submitted $1,350 along with her request for an automatic extension on April 15, 2017. The remaining $900 was paid when J's tax return was filed on July 9. J's 2017 tax totaled $9,950.

    a. Does J owe a penalty for failure to file for her 2016 tax return?

    b. Does J owe a penalty for failure to pay for her 2016 tax return? If so, for what period?

    c. Does J owe a penalty for failure to make adequate estimated tax payments for her 2016 tax return? If so, over what period?

    d. Does J owe interest on any of the amounts paid? If so, for what period?

4-31 *Statute of Limitations.* What is the importance of the Federal statute of limitations to the taxpayer? To the IRS? Generally, how long is the statute of limitations on tax matters?

4-32 *Six-Year Statute of Limitations.* Under what circumstances will the regular three-year statutory period for assessments be extended to six years?

4-33 *Scope of the Income Tax.* H and W are married with two children, ages 10 and 7. Like many Americans, they wonder about whether they are required to pay income taxes. Assuming they file a joint return, claim the standard deduction and all available credits, answer the following questions.

    a. What is the maximum amount of income (e.g., salary and wages) that the couple may have and still have a zero income tax liability?

    b. Using your answer above, what is the amount of employment taxes that the couple would be required to pay?

PROBLEMS

4-34 *Exemption and Child Tax Credit Phase-Out.* H and W are married with two children, ages 3 and 5. Compute the couple's deduction for exemptions and the child tax credit for the year 2017, assuming they file a joint return and have adjusted gross income as follows:

    a. $115,500

    b. $220,000

    c. $350,000

4-35 *Exemptions.* In each of the following situations determine the proper number of personal and dependency exemptions available to the taxpayer. Unless otherwise implied, assume that all tests are satisfied.

    a. R's mother, age 85, lives in his home. R figures that including the value of the lodging, he provides support of about $6,000. The remainder of her support is paid for with her Social Security benefits of $4,000.

    b. This year D sent his father, F, monthly checks of $200, or $2,400 for the year. F used these checks along with $2,300 of rental income ($4,400 of rents less $2,100 of expenses) to pay all of his support.

    c. H and W are married with one daughter, D, age 7. D models children's clothing and earned $4,000 of wages this year. D also has a trust fund of $50,000 established by her grandparents. All of D's wages were saved and none were used to pay for her support. Similarly none of the funds of the trust were used to pay for D's support.

    d. Professor and Mrs. Smith participated in the foreign exchange student program at their son's high school. In December of 2016 a student, Hans, arrived from Germany, spent the spring of 2017 with the Smiths, then returned to Germany.

    e. B and C are happily married with one son, S. S, age 20, is a full-time student at the University of Cincinnati. S worked as a painter during the summer to help put himself through school. He earned wages of $4,000, $2,500 of which was used to pay for his room and board at school and $1,500 for miscellaneous living expenses (e.g., gas for his car, dates, laundry, etc.). He lived with his parents during the summer. The value of their support including meals and lodging was $5,000. He also received a National Merit Scholarship, which paid for his tuition of $8,000.

4-36 *Personal and Dependency Exemptions.* In each of the following situations determine the proper number of personal and dependency exemption deductions available to the taxpayer.

    a. A is single and 44 years of age. He provides full support for his mother, who is 67 and lives in a small retirement community in A's hometown.

    b. D and K are married and file a joint return for the year. D is 67 years of age and K is 62. They have no dependents.

    c. E and O are married and file a joint return for the year. They provide all the support for their two younger children for the entire year. E and O also provided all the support for their oldest child (age 19) for the eight months she was a fulltime student. After graduating from high school, she accepted a job that paid $3,000 in salary. Nevertheless, her parents contributed more than one-half of her support for the entire year.

4-37 *Married Dependents.* In November of this year Jim Jenkins married his college sweetheart, Kate Brown. Jim was 27 and Kate was 25. Jim had graduated two years ago. Kate was in graduate school and had one more year left. The majority of Kate's support this year was provided by her parents. Jim earned $16,250 during the year while Kate received $1,100 of interest from her savings account. Assume Kate's parents are in the 25 (2017) percent tax bracket and would give the couple any tax savings to be derived from claiming Kate as a dependent.

    a. May Kate's parents claim an exemption for Kate if the couple files a joint return?

    b. Would the couple be better off filing separate returns (and thus receiving any taxes saved by Kate's parents) or filing a joint return? Show all computations you must make to determine your answer.

4-38 *Multiple Support Agreements.* G's support is provided as follows:

Social Security benefits	$3,600
Taxable interest income	800
Support from:	
A, G's oldest son—Cash for trip to Europe.	1,600
B, G's daughter—Fair value of lodging and cash	2,300
C, G's youngest son—Cash	+ 700
Total.	$9,000

   a. Who is entitled to a dependency exemption for G in the absence of any agreement as to who gets the deduction?

   b. Who may claim a dependency exemption for G under a multiple-support agreement?

   c. How would your answer to (b) differ if A contributed $650 instead of $1,600?

4-39 *Children of Divorced Parents.* For each of the following, determine whether M or F is entitled to the dependency exemption in 2017 for their only child, S. M and F were divorced in 2014 and M has custody, except when F has visitation privileges. Together, M and F provide 100% of S's support.

   a. M was granted the dependency exemption under the divorce decree. F pays child support for the year totaling $1,500. Total support expenditures for S are $5,600.

   b. No mention of the dependency exemption was made in the divorce decree. F pays child support for S of $3,400, and the total support for S is $6,500.

   c. F paid child support of $2,800 for the year. M signed Form 8332, indicating that she will not claim a dependency exemption for S. The total support for S for the year was $5,500.

4-40 *Filing Status and Standard Deduction.* Determine the most beneficial filing status and the standard deduction for each of the following taxpayers for 2017:

   a. M is a 54-year-old unmarried widow whose spouse died in 2014. During all of 2017 M's 15-year-old son, for whom she claims a dependency exemption, lives with her.

   b. S is a 67-year-old bachelor who lives in New York City. S pays more than half the cost of maintaining a home in Tampa, Florida for his 89-year-old mother. He is entitled to a dependency exemption under a multiple-support agreement executed by his brother, his sister, and himself.

   c. R is a widower whose wife died in 2016. R maintained a household for his three dependent children during 2017 and provided 100% of the cost of the household.

   d. J is divorced and has custody of his 9-year-old child. J provides more than half the cost of the home in which he lives with his child, but his ex-wife is entitled to the dependency exemption for the child for the current year.

4-41 *Head of Household.* Indicate whether the taxpayer would be entitled to file using the head-of-household rate schedule.

   a. Y is divorced from her husband. She maintains a home in which she and her 10-year-old son live. Her ex-husband pays child support to her that she uses to provide all of the support for the child. In addition, Y has relinquished her right to claim her son as a dependent to her former spouse.

   b. C is divorced from his wife. He provides 75% of the support for his mother, who lives in a nursing home. His mother receives $5,000 of interest income annually.

   c. J's grandson, G, had a falling-out with his parents and moved in with him early this year. J did not mind because he had grown lonely since his wife died three years ago. G is 17 years old and earned $5,000 this year as a part-time grocery clerk. G's total support was $12,000.

   d. B's wife died four years ago and he has not remarried. Last year his 26-year old daughter, D, graduated from Arizona State University and moved to Hawaii with the intention of living there permanently. Unfortunately, D was unable to earn enough money to make ends meet and had to rely on checks from dad. B paid for D's own apartment and provided the majority of her support.

   e. M's wife died last year. This year he maintains a home for himself and his 25-year-old daughter, E, who is temporarily away from home while attending graduate school in a nearby city. While going to school, E rents an apartment but then returns home during the summer and on holidays. M not only pays for all of the costs associated with his home but also the E's cost of living in the apartment. E earned $8,000 as a teaching assistant. Nevertheless, M provided the majority of E's support.

   f. F's husband died this year. She continues to provide a home for her two children, ages 6 and 8.

4-42 *Dependent's Personal Exemption and Standard Deduction.* K is 16 years old and is claimed as a dependent on her parents' income tax return. She earned wages of $2,800 and collected interest of $1,450 for the year. What is the amount of K's taxable income for the year?

4-43 *Dependent's Personal Exemption and Standard Deduction.* B is 20 years old and is claimed as a dependent on his sister's tax return. B earned $3,000 from a part-time job during the year. What is B's taxable income?

4-44 *Tax Tables.* S earned a salary during 2017 of $56,015. She is single, claims the standard deduction, and has no dependents for the year. Her only other income was taxable interest income of $560. Determine S's taxable income and her Federal income tax. (**Note:** Use the 2017 amounts for the standard deduction and personal exemption but use the 2016 tax table. This tax table computation is for 2016 because the 2017 tax tables will not be available until late 2017. See Appendix for the 2016 tax tables.)

4-45 *Tax Rate Schedules.* W and T were married and filed a joint return for 2017. Their adjusted gross income for the year was $141,950. Their total itemized deductions were $18,000 and they were entitled to three personal and dependency exemptions. Neither W nor T is 65 or older and both have good sight. Determine W and T's taxable income and their Federal income tax liability before prepayments and credits for 2017.

4-46 *Kiddie Tax.* For each situation below compute the child's taxable income and the amounts that would be taxed at the child's and parents' rates for the 2017 tax year.
   a. When J's rich uncle died, he left her GM corporate bonds. This year J received $3,050 of interest from these bonds, her only income. J is seven years old and her parents claim an exemption for her.
   b. L, age 13, works in his father's music store on weekends. During the year, he earned $1,200 from this job. In addition, L had $2,500 of interest income attributable to a gift from his grandfather. L's father claims an exemption for him.
   c. Same as (b) except L's earned income was $6,600 and interest income was $2,850.

4-47 *Computation of the Kiddie Tax.* G's great aunt gave her a certificate of deposit that matures in ten years when she is 21. The certificate pays interest of $4,050 annually. G's parents file a joint return. Their 2017 taxable income is $131,500. Compute G's tax.

4-48 *Failure-to-File Penalty.* T, overwhelmed by other pressing concerns, simply forgot to file his tax return for 2016 until July 20, 2017. When filed, T's 2016 return showed a tax due before withholding and estimated taxes of $10,000.
   a. Will T be penalized for failure to file his return if the total income taxes withheld by his employer were $11,000?
   b. If T's employer withheld $9,000, what is the failure to file penalty?

4-49 *Failure-to-Pay Penalty.* On April 13, 2018, R, a calendar year taxpayer, sat down to prepare his 2017 tax return. Realizing that he did not have time to get it done, he decided to file for an extension. R's tax liability for the previous year, 2016, was $8,000. During 2017 R's employer withheld $2,500 and R paid estimated taxes of $500. R estimates that his final gross tax liability for 2017 will be $12,000.
   a. If R obtains an extension to file his 2017 return, when is his return due?
   b. What amount must R pay by April 15 to avoid a failure to-pay penalty?
   c. R completed and filed his return on July 20, 2018. Unfortunately, his initial estimate of his tax was low and his final tax (before withholding and estimated tax payments) was $15,000. Assuming R paid the amount determined in (b) above, what is the amount of the failure-to-pay penalty, if any?

4-50 *Estimated Taxes.* K sells pharmaceuticals for ELI Inc. He receives a salary plus a percentage commission on sales over a certain threshold. In the current year, 2017, K's tax liability before prepayments was $20,000. His 2016 tax liability was $12,000. In each year his AGI was less than $150,000.
   a. What is the lowest required tax installment (including withholding) that K can make and avoid the penalty for underpaying his taxes during the year? (Ignore the annualized income installment.)
   b. Assume that K paid estimated taxes of $1,000 on each due date. In addition, K's employer withheld a total of $3,000 during the year. K filed and paid the balance of his liability on April 15, 2018. Assume the applicable interest rate charged on underpayments for each period in 2017 is 10 percent. Compute K's penalty, if any, for failure to pay estimated taxes. Compute the penalty for the first installment only.
   c. Assume that K works solely for commissions and that he had no income through March 31, 2017 because he decided to take a winter vacation. Income for the remainder of the year was sufficient to generate a tax liability before prepayments of $20,000. What implications do these facts have on the calculation of the underpayment penalty for 2017?

4-51 *Penalties for Inadequate Estimated Tax Payments.* Z is a calendar year individual whose gross tax for 2017 is $40,000. Z had taxes of $8,000 withheld and did not make estimated tax payments. Z's tax due was paid with his timely filed return on April 15, 2018. His 2016 tax was $35,000 on adjusted gross income of $148,000. Assume the penalty rate is 10 percent.

   a. Calculate the amount of estimated taxes and withholding that must be made for the year to avoid the penalty for underestimate of tax.

   b. Same as (a) above, except Z's adjusted gross income for 2016 was $160,000.

4-52 *Penalties and Interest.* Y filed her tax return for 2016 on April 15, 2017. Upon discovering an inadvertent error, Y filed an amended return and submitted additional tax of $1,250.

   a. Does Y owe a penalty for failure to pay? If so, how much?

   b. Does Y owe interest on the $1,250 paid with the amended return? If so, how much?

4-53 *Statute of Limitations.* T, a calendar year taxpayer, filed her 2016 Federal income tax return on January 29, 2017 and received a tax refund check for overpaid 2016 taxes on May 17, 2017.

   a. Assuming that T did not file a false return or have a substantial omission of income, what is the last date on which the IRS may assess an additional income tax liability against her for the 2016 tax year?

   b. If T unintentionally had a substantial omission of income from her 2016 return, what is the last day on which the IRS may assess her an additional 2016 income tax liability?

   c. If T had never bothered to file her 2016 tax return, what is the last day on which the IRS may assess her an additional 2016 income tax liability?

TAX RETURN PROBLEMS

■ *CONTINUOUS TAX RETURN PROBLEMS* See Appendix I, Part 1.

■ *ADDITIONAL TAX RETURN PROBLEMS*

4-54 *Form 1040EZ.* Samuel B. White was single for 2016 and had no dependents. Sam's only income was wages of $21,150 and taxable interest of $465. Federal income tax of $930 was withheld from Sam's salary.

      Calculate Sam's Federal income tax and his tax due or refund for 2016. A Form 1040EZ may be completed based on this information. Supply fictitious occupation, Social Security number, and address. (**Note:** Use the 2016 tax forms since the 2017 forms may not be available.)

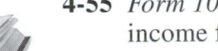

4-55 *Form 1040A.* Charles D. and Alice A. Davis were married during all of 2016 and had income from the following sources:

Salary, Charles	$47,100
Federal income tax withheld	1,425
Part-time salary, Alice	16,700
Federal income tax withheld	880
Interest from home savings	320
Interest from U.S. Government Bonds	430

Charles and Alice provide the sole support of their two children (both under age 17). During the year, they paid job-related child care expenses of $2,200. Their itemized deductions for the year are insufficient for them to itemize, but a deductible $2,000 was deposited in each of their individual retirement accounts.

      Calculate the Federal income tax and the tax due (or refund) for Mr. and Mrs. Davis, assuming they file a joint return. Use the 2016 amounts for exemptions and the standard deduction. Also use the 2016 tax tables since the 2017 tables may not be available. A Form 1040A may also be completed. Supply fictitious information for the address, occupations, Social Security numbers, and children's names. (**Note:** Use 2016 tax forms since the 2017 forms may not be available.)

4-56 *Form 1040.* William A. Gregg, a high school educator, and Mary W. Gregg, a microbiologist, are married and file a joint income tax return for 2016. Neither William nor Mary is over 50 years old, and both have excellent sight. They provide the sole support of their three children: Barry, Kimberly, and Rachel (all under age 17). The following information is from their records for 2016:

Salaries and wages, William	$34,550
Federal income tax withheld	$2,320
Salaries and wages, Mary	44,800
Federal income tax withheld	4,360
Interest income—Home Savings and Loan	690
Interest income—City Bank	220
Tax-exempt interest income—State of Texas	1,400
Itemized deductions as follows:	
Hospitalization insurance	320
Unreimbursed fees of doctors, hospitals, etc.	740
Unreimbursed prescription drugs	310
Real estate taxes on residence	1,350
State income taxes paid	2,440
State sales taxes paid	720
Interest paid on original home mortgage	8,430
Charitable contribution—Faith Church	1,720
Charitable contribution—State University	200
Quarterly estimated federal taxes paid	3,500

Calculate the 2016 Federal income tax and the tax due (or refund) for the Greggs assuming they file a joint return. Form 1040, along with Schedules A and B, may be completed. Supply fictitious information for the address and Social Security numbers. (**Note:** Use 2016 tax forms since the 2017 forms may not be available.)

TAX RESEARCH PROBLEMS

4-57 *Nonresident Alien Spouse.* C is a citizen of the United States who resides indefinitely in Europe. C is married to N, a citizen of Greece. C has $32,000 of gross income subject to United States tax and would like to file jointly with N. Can C accomplish this goal? If so, what steps are necessary? How is the income of N treated?

Code § 6013(g) and Reg. § 1.6013-6.

4-58 Much to Ted's surprise, his employer, a major hotel chain, asked him to manage the company's premier resort property in Cabo San Lucas, Mexico for the entire calendar year. Ted accepted and was paid $110,000 in compensation for the assignment, visiting the U. S. for only two weeks during the year. Ted's only other income is interest income of $20,000. Ted is single, claims the standard deduction and has no dependents. He is a U. S. citizen. Calculate Ted's tax due and refund assuming he uses the foreign earned income exclusion rather than the foreign tax credit. Ted's tax paid to Mexico was $8,500.

Research aid:

Code §§ 901 and 911(a).

Gross Income

5

Gross Income

Learning Objectives

Upon completion of this chapter you will be able to:

LO.1 Define income for tax purposes and explain how it differs from the definitions given to it in accounting or economics.

LO.2 Explain the concept of the taxable year and identify who is eligible to use fiscal years.

LO.3 Apply the cash and accrual methods of accounting to determine the tax year in which items are reported.

LO.4 Determine the effect of a change in accounting method.

LO.5 Describe some of the special rules governing the treatment of prepaid income, interest income, interest free loans, and income from long-term contracts.

LO.6 Identify which taxpayer is responsible for reporting income and paying the taxes on such income.

Chapter Outline

Introduction

Determination of the final income tax liability begins with the identification of a taxpayer's gross income. Before that can be done, however, one obviously must understand what constitutes *income* for tax purposes. The primary purpose of this chapter is to examine the income concept and thus provide some general guidelines regarding what is and what is not subject to taxation. As a practical matter, income is normally easy to spot. Salary, interest, dividends, rents, gains from the sales of property, and most other items that one customarily thinks of as income are in fact income for tax purposes. In fact, these represent the bulk of all income that is reported. But what if a taxpayer is lucky enough to receive an inheritance, a gift, or a scholarship? Are these taxable? What about court-awarded damages? And if a taxpayer borrows $1,000, is there income? What happens if Publishers Clearing House gives you $10 million? Is the IRS as happy as you are? And how do hurricane victims treat their government aid? Is their relief taxable? The list of possible income items goes on and on. Fortunately, these items are more the exception than the rule. In any event, newcomers to tax should understand that there are no hard and fast rules that can be applied to every conceivable situation. The Supreme Court clearly stated the problem in a case concerning the income status of embezzled funds:

> In fact, no single conclusive criterion has yet been found to determine in all situations what is sufficient gain to support the imposition of an income tax. No more can be said in general than that all relevant facts and circumstances must be considered.[1]

Notwithstanding the Court's observations, three important generalizations developed in this chapter are:

1. "Income" is broadly construed for tax purposes to include virtually any type of gain, benefit, or profit that has been realized.

2. Although the scope of the income concept is broad, certain types of income are excepted from taxation by statute, administrative ruling, or judicial decree.

3. Taxpayers who realize income may not be required to recognize and report it immediately but may be able to postpone recognition until some time in the future.

To sum up, there are three basic questions to address concerning income:

1. Did the taxpayer have income?

2. If the taxpayer had income, was it realized?

3. If the taxpayer has realized income, must it be recognized now or is it permanently excluded or perhaps temporarily deferred and reported at some future date?

The first part of this chapter examines the concept of income. Once one is sensitive to the concept of income, consideration must be given to *if and when* the income must be reported as well as *who* must report it. The latter part of the chapter focuses on the timing of income recognition and the identification of the reporting entity.

---

[1] *Comm. v. Wilcox,* 46-1 USTC ¶9188, 34 AFTR 811, 327 U.S. 404 (USSC, 1946).

The definition of income found in the Internal Revenue Code reflects the language of the constitutional amendment empowering Congress to impose taxes on income.[2] Section 61(a) of the Code defines *gross income* as follows:

> *Section 61. Gross Income Defined.*
>
> (a) *General definition. Except as otherwise provided in this subtitle, gross income means all income from whatever source derived, including (but not limited to) the following items:*
>
> (1) *Compensation for services, including fees, commissions, fringe benefits, and similar items;*
>
> (2) *Gross income derived from business;*
>
> (3) *Gains derived from dealings in property;*
>
> (4) *Interest;*
>
> (5) *Rents;*
>
> (6) *Royalties;*
>
> (7) *Dividends;*
>
> (8) *Alimony and separate maintenance payments;*
>
> (9) *Annuities;*
>
> (10) *Income from life insurance and endowment contracts;*
>
> (11) *Pensions;*
>
> (12) *Income from discharge of indebtedness;*
>
> (13) *Distributive share of partnership gross income;*
>
> (14) *Income in respect of a decedent; and*
>
> (15) *Income from an interest in an estate or trust.*

Despite the statute's detailed enumeration of income items, the list is not comprehensive. The items specified are only a sample of the more common types of income. Taxable income includes many other economic benefits not identified above.

As a practical matter, Code § 61 furnishes little guidance for determining whether a particular benefit should be treated as income. The statute provides no criteria or factors that could be used for assessment. For example, the general definition does not provide any clue as to whether a gift or an inheritance constitutes taxable income. Similarly, the statute is not helpful in determining whether income arises upon the discovery of buried treasure. These and similar issues, as will be seen, are often answered by reference to other, more specific, sections of the Code. On the other hand, many questions cannot be resolved by reference to the statute or the regulations. In situations where clear statutory guidance is absent, the difficult task of ascertaining how far the definitional boundary of income extends falls to the courts. To this end, the courts have utilized the meanings given income in both economics and accounting to mold a workable definition of income for tax purposes.

ECONOMIC CONCEPT OF INCOME

Economists define income as the amount that an individual could have spent for consumption during a period while remaining as well off at the end of the period as at the beginning of the period. This concept of income may be expressed mathematically as the sum of an individual's consumption during the period plus the change in the individual's net worth between the beginning and end of the period.[3] Note that an increase in net worth is actually savings. Thus income can be defined as $I = C + S$ where I is income, C is consumption and S is savings.

LO.1

Define income for tax purposes and explain how it differs from the definitions given to it in accounting or economics.

---

[2] See Chapter 1.

[3] The economic definition of income given here is often referred to as the Haig-Simons definition as derived from the following works: Robert M. Haig, "The Concepts of Income—Economic and Legal Aspects," *The Federal Income Tax* (New York: Columbia University Press, 1921); Henry C. Simons, *Personal Income Taxation* (Chicago: University of Chicago Press, 1921).

Example 1

K's records revealed the following assets and liabilities as of December 31, 2017 and 2018:

	12-31-2017	12-31-2018
Assets (fair market value)	$100,000	$140,000
Liabilities	(20,000)	(30,000)
Net worth	$ 80,000	$110,000

During the year, K spent $25,000 on rent, food, clothing, entertainment, and other items. From an economic perspective, K's income for 2018 is $55,000 determined as follows:

Consumption	$25,000
Change in net worth ($110,000 – $80,000)	30,000
Economic income	$55,000

There are two key aspects of an economist's definition. The first is the emphasis on a change in net worth. According to the economist, a taxpayer has income under any circumstances that cause his or her net worth to increase. Note that this view is extremely broad. Taxpayers who receive an inheritance, are the beneficiaries of a life insurance policy, discover buried treasure, or have their debts cancelled have all had an increase in net worth and would therefore have income using this definition. Some may object to this comprehensive approach. It is nevertheless consistent with § 61, which states that income includes *all* income regardless of its source.

The second and perhaps more critical aspect of the economist's definition from a tax perspective is the notion that consumption and the change in net worth must be computed using market values on an accrual basis rather than on a realization basis. For example, economists include in income any increase in the value of an individual's shares of stock during the period, even though the shares are not sold and the individual does not *realize* the increase in value. In addition, economists would include in income the rental value of one's car or home, as well as the value of food grown for personal use, since such items constitute consumption. Gifts and inheritances would also be considered income by an economist since these items would affect an individual's net worth. Although the economist's approach to income is theoretically sound, it has significant drawbacks from a practical view.

For practical application, the meaning given to income must be objective to minimize controversies. The economist's reliance on market values to measure net worth and consumption violates this premise. Few assets have readily determinable and accurate values. Valuation of most assets would be a subjective determination. For example, an individual may be able to value shares of stock by referring to an active publicized market, but how is the value of a closely held business or work of art to be computed? The difficulty in making such valuations would no doubt lead to countless disputes and administrative hassles. These practical problems of implementing the economic concept of income have caused the courts to adopt a different interpretation.

It should be pointed out, however, that the economist's approach to measuring income—the so-called net worth method—is sometimes used when the IRS decides that the taxpayer's records do not adequately reflect income.[4] Application usually occurs where the taxpayer has not maintained records, or has falsified or destroyed any records that were kept. In these situations, the IRS reconstructs income by determining the change in net worth during the year and adding estimated living expenses.

Before leaving the economist's definition of income, a final observation is warranted. Over the years, some have argued that the income tax does not encourage savings and, therefore, the U.S. should switch to a consumption tax such as a national retail sales tax. Observe, however, that a similar result could be obtained under the current income tax law if taxpayers were given a deduction for savings. This can be demonstrated mathematically by simply manipulating the terms of the income equation above:

---

[4] *Holland v. U.S.*, 54-2 USTC ¶9714, 46 AFTR 943, 348 U.S. 121 (USSC, 1954). Net worth, however, is to be determined using the tax basis in assets and not their fluctuating market values [*S. Bedeian*, 54 T.C. 295 (1970)].

$$I = C + S$$

$$C = I - S$$

In recent discussions of tax reform, it is not surprising that this concept has surfaced. Only time will tell what changes will be made.

ACCOUNTING CONCEPT OF INCOME

The principle of realization distinguishes the accountant's concept of income from that of the economist. Under this principle, accountants recognize income when it is *realized*. Income is generally considered realized when (1) the earnings process is complete, and (2) an exchange or transaction has taken place.[5] Normally, some type of *conversion* occurs that substantially changes the taxpayer's relationship to the asset. To illustrate, consider a taxpayer who discovers oil on his property. He may have "income" in the economic sense (at least to the extent that the value of his property and his net worth have increased). But he has not realized that increase in net worth and does not have income in the accounting sense until he converts his discovery into another asset (e.g., he sells the property or the oil). Observe that these two criteria provide the objective determination of value traditionally believed necessary for the work that accountants perform. As a result, accounting income usually does not recognize changes in market values of assets during a period (as would economic income) unless such changes have been realized.

INCOME FOR TAX PURPOSES: THE JUDICIAL CONCEPT

The landmark decision of the Supreme Court in *Eisner v. Macomber* in 1918 provided the first glimpse of how the concept of income would be interpreted for tax purposes.[6] In this case, the court embraced the realization principle of accounting, indicating that income must be *realized* before it can be taxed. As later decisions suggested, the primary virtue of the realization principle is not that it somehow yields a better or more theoretically precise income figure. Rather, it provides an objective basis for measuring income, eliminating the problems that would arise if income were determined using subjective valuations. In short, the realization principle is a well-entrenched part of the tax law because it makes the law so much easier to administer.

A second issue addressed by the *Eisner* decision concerned the scope of the income concept. How far did it reach? Did income include gifts, scholarships, court-awarded damages, a personal secretary, and other types of benefits? In essence, the Court again followed the accounting approach, stating that income was restricted to gains realized from property or personal services.

Hence, finding a $10 bill, receiving a prize or award, or profiting from a cancelled debt would not have been taxable under *Eisner,* since the benefits were obtained without any effort by the taxpayer. Later decisions, however, expanded the concept of income by rejecting the notion that only gains derived from capital or labor are recognized. The courts have taken what is often referred to as an "all-inclusive" approach; that is, *all* gains are presumed to be taxable except those specifically exempted. The Supreme Court's opinion in *Glenshaw Glass Co.* provides the definition of income that is perhaps most commonly accepted today.[7] This case involved the treatment of punitive damages awarded to Glenshaw Glass for fraud and antitrust violations of another company. In holding that such awards were income, the Court stated:[8]

> Here we have instances of undeniable accessions to wealth, clearly realized, and over which the taxpayer has complete dominion. The mere fact that the payments were extracted from wrongdoers as punishment for unlawful conduct cannot detract from their character as taxable income to the recipients.

Thus, income for tax purposes is construed to include any type of gain, benefit, profit, or other increase in wealth that has been realized and is not exempted by statute. Note that the

---

[5] "Basic Concepts and Accounting Principles Underlying Financial Statements of Business Enterprises," *Accounting Principles Board Statements No. 4* (New York: American Institute of Certified Public Accountants, 1970), ¶134.

[6] 1 USTC ¶32, 3 AFTR 3020, 252 U.S. 189 (USSC, 1920).

[7] 55-1 USTC ¶9308, 47 AFTR 162, 348 U.S. 426 (USSC, 1955).

[8] *Ibid.*

courts have adopted key elements of both the economic and accounting definition of income: income is any increase in the taxpayer's *net worth* (i.e., wealth) that has been *realized*. Also note that, even though it all sounds very technical and precise, the rule, like so many rules in taxation, may be difficult to apply in a given situation. For example, if a tenant paints the walls of her apartment or plants some gladiolus in the garden, has the landlord realized income? Arriving at a solution for this and any particular set of facts can be quite frustrating, but one can generally take heart that these are rare and, moreover, a common sense approach generally works: if it seems as if the taxpayer is better off, there is probably income.

It should be emphasized that even though a taxpayer may have "income" that has in fact been realized, this by itself does not guarantee that it will be taxed. In tax parlance, the question still remains as to whether the taxpayer must "recognize" the income (i.e., report the income for tax purposes). There are *three* relatively common exceptions to the general rule that all income must be recognized immediately:

1. *Excluded Income.* Income that has been realized need not be recognized if it is specifically exempted from taxation by virtue of some provision in the Code. For example, as discussed in Chapter 6, interest income from state and local bonds is specifically excluded under § 103 while gifts and inheritances (which obviously increase net worth) are excluded under § 102. In these cases, the income permanently escapes tax and normally creates a difference between taxable income and financial accounting income. It should be noted that, notwithstanding the Code's all-inclusive concept of income, the tax base is far from comprehensive because of the numerous exclusions and exemptions that have crept into the law over the years.[9]

2. *Accounting Methods.* A taxpayer may be able to defer recognition of income to a subsequent year by following some particular method of accounting (e.g., the installment sales method or the completed contract method).

3. *Nontaxable Exchanges.* Income realized on a sale or exchange may be deferred under a special nonrecognition rule. For example, a taxpayer who swaps one parcel of land costing $10,000 for another parcel worth $50,000 is not required to recognize the $40,000 gain under the like-kind exchange rules. The theory underlying nonrecognition in this and similar situations is that the taxpayer has not liquidated his investment to cash but has continued it, albeit in another form. In effect, the law is willing to defer the tax until such time when the taxpayer does in fact convert the asset to cash and has the wherewithal to pay the tax. It is important to note, however, that in these and similar cases, the gain is only *deferred;* it does not escape tax permanently as is the case with excluded income.

In summary, income for tax purposes can generally be defined as any increase in wealth (net worth) or consumption that has been realized. In addition, such income normally must be recognized unless it is specifically excluded or postponed due to an accounting rule or deferral provision. A list of some of the common types of income—both taxable and nontaxable—can be found in Exhibit 3-3 and Exhibit 3-4 in Chapter 3.

Before leaving this subject, one final observation should be made. It is important to understand that this definition of gross income is the same for all types of taxpayers. In other words, § 61 and its many interpretations not only applies to individual taxpayers but also applies equally to business entities such as C corporations, S corporations, partnerships, and LLCs as well as trusts and estates.

Refinements of the Gross Income Definition

As one might imagine, in the early years of the tax law, when there were few specific rules, people found it easy to take the position that Congress never intended to tax their particular type of "income." To support such contentions, taxpayers, never lacking for imagination, often concocted ingenious arguments explaining why they should escape tax. In one

---

[9] For an excellent discussion of the concept of income and the notion of a comprehensive tax base see Boris Bittker, "A Comprehensive Tax Base as a Goal of Income Tax Reform," 80 *Harvard Law Review* 925 (1967).

memorable case, a taxpayer who received a gift (gifts are specifically excluded from income) argued that the income from the gifted property was also exempt since the income was merely an extension of the gift. Unfortunately, the court did not accept this gift-that-keeps-on-giving theory and taxed the income. But this was typical of the development of the tax law. As the courts dealt with this and other income issues, their decisions set a number of precedents that shaped and refined the concept of income. Because of their significance, some of the principles established by early court decisions were given statutory effect; that is, the rule evolving from the decision was subsequently enacted as part of the law, or codified. For example, § 102(b) now provides that income from gifted property is not part of the gift and is fully taxable.

Other court rulings have been incorporated into the Regulations either directly or by way of reference. Several of these rulings, however, have not found their way into the Code or Regulations. Nevertheless, they provide authoritative guidance for the determination of taxable income. This section examines three major principles that are relevant to the income concept. These concern:

1. *Form of Benefit.* Must income be realized in a particular form, such as cash, before it becomes taxable?

2. *Return of Capital.* Does gross income mean gross receipts or net gain after allowance for a tax-free recovery of the taxpayer's capital investment?

3. *Indirect Economic Benefits.* Are benefits provided by an employer (such as a company car) taxable where they are not intended as compensation?

FORM-OF-BENEFIT PRINCIPLE

Many taxpayers erroneously believe that income need be reported only when cash is received. The Regulations clearly state, however, that gross income includes income realized in any form.[10] Thus, income is not limited to receipts of cash but also extends to receipts of property, services, and *any other economic benefits.* For example, taxpayers may realize income when their debts are cancelled or they purchase property at a price less than its fair market value—a so-called *bargain purchase.* In situations where income is received in a form other than cash, a cash-equivalent approach is adopted.[11] Under this method, the measure of income is its fair market value at the time of receipt.

Example 2

Several years ago on the television show *60 Minutes,* a segment was devoted to what the commentators implied was a tax travesty. In truth, it was a sad tale. According to the story, a generous employer who wanted to reward his employees for their long years of service gave them stock in the company. At that time, the stock had a value of about $100 per share. The employees, as one might guess, were extremely pleased. Unfortunately, a sudden turn of events caused the value of the shares to plummet. By the close of the year, the stock was practically worthless. Some employees still holding the stock were upset but accepted their misfortune graciously. On April 15, however, those still holding the stock found themselves in tax shock. What was the problem? As may be apparent from the discussion of the form-of-benefit principle, the employees were required to report compensation income equal to the value of stock at the time of receipt, $100 per share. This meant that many employees had to report thousands of dollars of income even though the stock was currently worthless. They had income without any way to pay the tax. Although the employees might be able to claim a deduction for worthless stock, it might not provide total relief since such loss would be a capital loss, the deduction of which is limited.

---

[10] Reg. § 1.61-1(a).   [11] Reg. § 1.446-1(a)(3).

> ### Example 3
>
> Borrower B owed Lender L $10,000, evidenced by a note payable due in six months. If L allows B to cancel the note for a payment of $9,000, B must normally recognize gross income of $1,000.

RETURN OF CAPITAL DOCTRINE

The return of capital doctrine is best illustrated by a simple loan transaction. When a taxpayer lends money and it is later repaid, no income is recognized since the repayment represents merely a *return of capital* to the taxpayer. Although there is no statutory provision to this effect, it is a well-recognized rule. Moreover, the taxpayer's net worth has not increased (one asset, a receivable, has simply been replaced by another, cash). However, any interest on the loan that is paid to the taxpayer would be income.

Sale or Disposition

The application of the return of capital doctrine is not limited to loans. One of the first refinements made to the income concept concerned the use of the return of capital principle to determine the income from a sale of property. In 1916 the Supreme Court held that the total proceeds received on a sale were not to be treated as income.[12] Rather, the portion of the proceeds representing the taxpayer's capital (i.e., adjusted basis) could be recovered tax free. Thus, it is the return of capital doctrine that allows the taxpayer to determine the income upon a sale or disposition of property by reducing the amount realized (cash + the fair market value of other receipts such as property) by the adjusted basis of the property. Using this approach—now contained in § 1001(a)—the taxpayer's income on dispositions of property is limited to the *gain* realized.

> ### Example 4
>
> R sold XYZ stock for $10,000. He purchased the stock for $6,000. R's realized gain is $4,000 ($10,000 amount realized − $6,000 adjusted basis) rather than the gross amount of the sales price, $10,000, since the return of capital doctrine permits him to recover his $6,000 investment tax free.

The return of capital doctrine also stands for the important proposition that gross income is not the same as gross receipts. This is reflected in Regulations, which provide that in the manufacturing, merchandising, or mining business, *gross income* means total sales less costs of goods sold.[13]

Damages

The return of capital doctrine may also apply to amounts awarded for injury inflicted upon the taxpayer.

> ### Example 5
>
> In *Edward H. Clark,* the Clarks overpaid their taxes by about $19,000 due to a mistake made by an attorney in the preparation of their return. The attorney subsequently reimbursed the Clarks for the overpayment.[14] The Court allowed the Clarks to exclude

---

[12] *Doyle v. Mitchell Bros.,* 1 USTC ¶17, 3 AFTR 2979, 247 U.S. 179 (USSC, 1918). See also *Southern Pacific Company v. Lowe,* 1 USTC ¶19, 247, 3 AFTR 2989, 247 U.S. 330 (USSC, 1918).

[13] Reg. § 1.61-3(a).

[14] 40 BTA 333 (1939); See also Rev. Rul. 81-277, 1981-2 CB 14.

> the reimbursement since there was no economic gain but merely a recovery of their capital. In *Inaja Land Co., Ltd.,* the taxpayer received payments from the city of Los Angeles to compensate it for damages caused by the city's diversion of polluted waters into the taxpayer's fishing area.[15] The court granted an exclusion on the return of capital theory but required the taxpayer to reduce its basis in the property by the amount received.

Section 104, discussed in detail in the following chapter, specifically excludes from income the amount of any damages awarded for personal physical injury or physical sickness on the grounds that the amount received represents a return of the personal capital destroyed. In many cases, amounts are also awarded to penalize the party responsible for the wrongdoing. These so-called punitive damages are normally taxable.[16] Similarly, where the damages awarded represent reimbursement for lost profits, the amounts are considered taxable since they are merely substitutions for income.[17]

Example 6

After ten consecutive losing seasons as head football coach at Trample University and a swing at his offensive line coach, Coach F was fired. Shortly thereafter, F developed an ulcer, which forced him to have surgery. It was subsequently determined that the operation had been improperly performed. F sued the university for lost wages and the court awarded him $25,000. The $25,000 is fully taxable since it represents a substitution of income. F also sued the surgeon for $300,000 for malpractice and won. If the $300,000 represents damages awarded for physical injury, the amount is excluded under § 104. However, if the award represents punitive damages, it is taxable.

Damages awarded to businesses are generally subject to the same tests applied to individuals. Awards or settlements for antitrust violations or patent infringements are examples of substitutions for income and thus are taxable. This is true for both actual and punitive damages. Compensation for damages to property are taxable to the extent that amounts received exceed the adjusted basis of the assets. Where the award is for damages to the goodwill of the business, the entire amount is usually taxable since the taxpayer normally does not have any recoverable basis in the goodwill.[18]

Example 7

M left her car running and ran inside the bank to make a deposit. When she came back, she stopped in shock as she watched her car plunge through the front of a furniture store. The furniture store ultimately received $50,000 in damages for property for which it had a basis of $35,000. The store realized a gain of $15,000. This gain must be recognized unless certain special rules concerning involuntary conversions discussed in Chapter 15 are followed.

Other Considerations

The scope of the return of capital doctrine extends beyond situations involving damages and simple sales transactions. Numerous Code sections are grounded on this principle, and often contain detailed rules for ascertaining how a receipt should be apportioned between capital and income. For example, amounts received under a life insurance policy are not

---

[15] 9 T.C. 727, (1947).

[16] § 104(a)(2); but see § 104(c) for an exception if only punitive damages can be awarded.

[17] *Phoenix Coal Co. v. Comm.,* 56-1 USTC ¶9366, 49 AFTR 445, 231 F.2d 420 (CA-2, 1956).

[18] *Raytheon Production Corp. v. Comm.,* 44-2 USTC ¶9424, 32 AFTR 1155, 144 F.2d 100 (CA-1, 1944).

taxable on the theory that the proceeds—at least in part—represent a return of the taxpayer's premium payments.[19] Similarly, where the taxpayer purchases an annuity (i.e., an investment which makes a series of payments to the investor in the future), the return of capital doctrine provides that each payment is in part a tax-free return of capital.[20] In addition, somewhat intricate provisions exist to determine whether a corporate distribution represents a distribution of earnings (i.e., a dividend) or a tax-free return of the taxpayer's investment.[21] The special rules governing life insurance, annuities, and dividends are covered in detail in Chapter 6.

INDIRECT ECONOMIC BENEFITS

Another refinement to the otherwise all-inclusive definition of gross income concerns certain benefits provided by employers for employees. Early rulings and decisions exempted benefits conferred to employees that did not represent compensation and were provided for the convenience of the employer. For example, in 1919, the IRS ruled that lodging furnished seamen aboard ship was not taxable.[22] Similarly, in 1925, the Court of Claims held that the value of quarters provided an Army officer was not includible in income.[23] Explanations offered for exempting the lodging from income emphasized that the employee was granted the benefit solely because the employer's business could not function properly unless an employee was furnished that benefit on the employer's premises. The Court also observed that the benefits were not designed as a form of compensation for the employee, but rather were an outgrowth of business necessity. These early holdings established the view that certain benefits an employee receives indirectly from his or her employer are nontaxable. Current law grants an exclusion only if the employee can demonstrate that the benefit served a business purpose of the employer other than to compensate the employee.[24]

Example 8

In the following situations an employee is permitted to exclude the benefit received under the rationale discussed above.

1. An employer provides the employee with a place to work and supplies tools and machinery with which to do the work. Similarly, an employee is not taxed when his or her secretary types a letter.

2. An employer provides tuition-free, American-style schools for its overseas employees.

3. An employer provides an executive with protection in response to threats made by terrorists.

4. An employer requires its employees to attend a convention held in a resort in Florida and pays the travel costs of the employees.

It is often difficult to determine whether a particular benefit represents compensation or, alternatively, serves the business needs of the employer. For example, free parking places and similar fringe benefits provided by an employer could arguably fall into either category, depending upon the circumstances. After many years of controversy concerning the taxation of fringe benefits, Congress addressed the problem in 1984. To emphasize that fringe benefits are taxable, Congress modified the listing of typical income items found in § 61 to specifically include "fringe benefits and similar items." However, several exceptions exempting certain benefits still exist. These exceptions are discussed in Chapter 6 concerning exclusions.

---

[19] § 101.

[20] § 72.

[21] §§ 301 and 316.

[22] O.D. 265, 1 C.B. 71 (1919).

[23] *Jones v. U.S.,* 1 USTC ¶129, 5 AFTR 5297, 60 Ct. Cls. 552 (1925). Section 119, discussed in Chapter 6, currently provides specific rules that must be satisfied before meals and lodging may be excluded.

[24] *George D. Patterson v. Thomas,* 61-1 USTC 9310, 7 AFTR2d 862, 289 F.2d 108 (CA-2, 1960).

✓ CHECK YOUR KNOWLEDGE

Review Question 1

After exploring the cavernous pits of his patient's mouth, Dr. Will Floss, a dentist, concluded that the gentleman had to have a root canal. Floss explained to the patient the nature of the work and that it could very well be the first in a series of expensive steps required to put his teeth back in working order. He estimated the total cost at $5,000. At that moment, the patient, a wily floor-covering dealer, immediately recalled Floss's need for new carpeting. As a result, he suggested that he would be happy to make a deal: carpeting, pad, and installation in exchange for the dental work. The two agreed, the teeth were repaired, and the carpeting was installed. Is there a tax problem here?

The issue is whether either party must report income. Many individuals think that barter transactions, exchanges of property for services or property other than cash, are not taxable. However, taxpayers who believe bartering escapes the eye of the tax collector are in for a rude awakening by the IRS. Barter transactions are fully taxable under the form-of-benefit principle. It makes no difference whether the taxpayer's net worth is increased by cash or property. In either case, the taxpayer is better off and must recognize income. Here the dentist recognizes income equal to the value of the services rendered, $5,000, and the carpet salesman has revenue equal to the value of services received.

Review Question 2

Several years ago, Intel Corporation, a leading manufacturer of computer chips in the United States, sued another chip manufacturer, American Micro, for using its patented technology. The courts awarded Intel millions of dollars for the infringement. Another situation, perhaps more well-known, was the McDonald's coffee debacle. In this case, a jury awarded 79-year-old Stella Liebeck of Albuquerque, New Mexico $200,000 in compensatory damages and another $2.7 million in punitive damages for severe burns she suffered when she spilled McDonald's coffee in her lap. (Liebeck and McDonald's ultimately settled for unknown amounts out of court.) In a comparable story, Theresa Burke and more than 8,000 other women employees of the Tennessee Valley Authority claimed unlawful discrimination in the payment of salaries on the basis of sex. The TVA had increased the salaries in certain male-dominated pay schedules, but not in certain female-dominated pay schedules. Moreover, the TVA lowered salaries in the latter. The female employees asked for and were awarded back pay, costs, and attorney's fees. Burke and the other women each received amounts in settlement according to a formula based on their length of service and rates of pay. What tax treatment might be proposed for these taxpayers?

The basic question in all of these situations is the same: Does Intel, Liebeck, or Burke have taxable income? The key is recognizing that the amounts received may be taxable or nontaxable depending on the application of the return of capital doctrine and perhaps other provisions of the Code. The problem that Intel faces is demonstrating that the award for the patent infringement is not merely a replacement of lost income. It would appear that the corporation would have a difficult time overcoming a long string of cases that indicates that patent infringement awards are taxable. Nevertheless, there is no certainty in these matters without knowledge of all of the facts and a great deal of research. On the other hand, Liebeck probably had an easier time excluding her compensatory damages for her physical injury since they represent a return of her personal capital. However, the treatment of the punitive damages, although clearly taxable now, was not as clear under prior law. And what about Ms. Burke? It would seem that the knife could cut either way. On the one hand, the amounts received reimbursed her for back pay and arguably should be taxable as a substitution of income. On the other hand, the amounts could be viewed as a nontaxable reimbursement for a personal injury, sexual discrimination. If this seems difficult, it was. The courts struggled with the issue. The Sixth Circuit Court of Appeals held that the amounts were not taxable, but that decision was reversed by the Supreme Court. In 1996, Congress clarified the treatment, providing in § 104 that emotional distress does not constitute physical injury or physical sickness, thereby making damages from sex or age discrimination taxable.

Review Question 3

There is little doubt that the CEOs of Chrysler and GM, receive the use of a company car. The same can probably be said for the owners of every car dealership in the country as well as their salespeople. (If only accountants could receive such a deal!) Assume that each individual can drive the car for only 3,000 miles, after which he or she must evaluate the experience then exchange the old car for a new one and do it all over again. This is a nice arrangement: use a Jeep Grand Cherokee one month and a Chrysler Town and Country Van the next. Great benefits, but what are the tax consequences?

Once again the question concerns income. Is the value of the use of the company car taxable? Can the taxpayers argue that their use (including all personal trips) is not compensation but simply an incidental benefit that they must endure in order to evaluate the car? Does the indirect benefit rule apply? Is there a special provision that exempts fringe benefits of this nature? In a long line of cases, it has been established that the value of a car provided by an employer is compensation to the extent of the employee's personal use. The twist on the basic fact pattern—the required evaluation—may, however, suggest a different conclusion. The fringe benefit rules enacted in 1984 and discussed more fully in Chapter 6 do allow an exclusion for certain full-time automobile salespeople who use demonstration vehicles in the sales area in which the automobile dealer's sales office is located. Note that this rule applies only to salespeople. Thus an owner or executive would not qualify for an exclusion under this exception unless he or she also is considered a salesperson. There may be another escape hatch for executives and other management personnel, however, buried in the Regulations concerning product testing.[25] These Regulations allow the employee to exclude the benefit if the employee receives goods for testing and evaluation if a laundry list of requirements is met. The key point to remember here is not necessarily knowing the specific answer to this question but recognizing that an important theory exists—the indirect benefit doctrine—that is a valuable weapon on which the taxpayer can sometimes rely to avoid taxation of what at first glance has all the characteristics of taxable income.

Reporting Income: Tax Accounting

Once the taxpayer has realized an item of taxable income, he or she must determine *when* the income should be reported. This determination, however, requires an understanding of the nature of accounting periods and accounting methods that may be used for tax purposes. This section examines some of the fundamental rules of tax accounting and how they govern the timing of income recognition.

ACCOUNTING PERIODS

LO.2
Explain the concept of the taxable year and identify who is eligible to use fiscal years.

Taxable income is usually computed on the basis of an annual accounting period commonly known as the taxable year.[26] There are two types of taxable years: a calendar year and a fiscal year. A calendar year is a 12-month period ending on December 31, whereas a fiscal year generally is any period of 12 months ending on the last day of any month other than December.[27] Any taxpayer may use a calendar year. Fiscal years may be used only by taxpayers who maintain adequate books and records. A taxpayer filing his or her *first* return may adopt either a calendar year or a fiscal year without IRS consent simply by filing a return. After adoption, however, any change does require IRS consent.[28]

Income from Partnerships, S Corporations, and Fiduciaries

Reporting income derived from an interest in a partnership, an S corporation, or an estate or trust presents a special problem. As explained in Chapter 3, income realized by a partnership or an S corporation is not taxable to either of these because they are not treated as separate taxable entities. Rather, the partnership or S corporation merely serves as a conduit

---

[25] Reg. § 1.132-5(n).

[26] § 441(a) and (b).

[27] Reg. § 1.441-1(d) and (e). The taxpayer may elect to end the tax year on a particular day of the week rather than a date, resulting in a tax year that varies in length between 52 and 53 weeks. See Reg. § 1.441-2.

[28] A request for a change is made on Form 1128. The initial selection of, or a change in, tax year may result in a short tax year, in which case the tax may have to be computed on an annualized basis. See §§ 442 and 443.

through which the income flows. Consequently, partners or S shareholders report their distributive shares of the entity's income in their taxable year within which (or with which) the partnership or S corporation tax year ends. Partners or S shareholders must report their share of the income regardless of the amounts distributed to them.

Example 9

DEF Company, a fiscal year taxpayer, is a partnership owned equally by D, E, and F. For the taxable year ending September 30, 2017, the company had net income of $90,000. During the 12-month period ending on September 30, 2017, D withdrew $15,000 from his capital account. For his year ending December 31, 2017, D must report his share of partnership income, $30,000 (of $90,000), even though he only received a distribution of $15,000. Note that any income earned by the partnership from October 2017 through December 2017 is not reported until D files his 2018 tax return, which is normally due on April 15, 2019.

Income realized by a trust or an estate is generally taxed to the beneficiaries to the extent it is actually distributed or required to be distributed. Income that is not taxed to the beneficiaries is taxed to the estate or trust.

Limitation on Fiscal Years

One effect of allowing fiscal years for reporting is to enable certain taxpayers to *defer* the taxation of income. For instance, in *Example 9* above, the choice by the partnership to use a fiscal year creates an opportunity for D. Note that D's share of the partnership's income for October 2017 through December 2017 is not reported until D files his 2018 tax return, which is normally filed on April 15, 2019. A small corporation that primarily provides personal services could obtain a similar deferral.

Example 10

G&H Inc., a law firm, is a regular C corporation owned by two attorneys, G and H. The corporation reports using a fiscal year ending on January 31. During 2017 the corporation paid G and H small salaries. Just before the close of its taxable year ending January 31, 2018, the corporation paid a bonus to G and H equal to its taxable income. By deducting the bonus, the corporation reports no income for its taxable year ending January 31, 2018, and G and H defer reporting the bonus until they file their 2018 tax return on April 15, 2019.

In 1986, Congress felt that the use of fiscal years to create deferral of income as shown above was improper. As a result, provisions were enacted that restrict the use of fiscal years by partnerships, S corporations, and so-called personal service corporations (i.e., corporations where the principal activity is the performance of services, substantially all of which are performed by employees who are also the owners of the business). Although certain exceptions enable these entities to use a fiscal year on a limited basis, as a general rule, these taxpayers normally must use the calendar year.[29]

Annual Accounting and Progressive Rates

The use of an annual accounting period in combination with other features of the taxation process causes numerous difficulties. For example, consider the effect of the tax system's use of both an annual accounting period and a progressive tax rate structure. Each year the taxpayer computes his or her taxable income for that period and applies a progressive rate structure to the income of that year. If income varies from one year to the next, taxes paid on the *total* income of those two years are likely to exceed the total taxes that would have resulted had the taxpayer earned the income equally each year. The problems that occur with so-called income-bunching are illustrated below.

---

[29] §§ 441(i), 444, 706(b), and 1378.

Example 11

Taxpayer R is a salesperson whose income is derived solely from commissions. Taxpayer S earns a salary. Both taxpayers are single. In 20X1 and 20X2 R's taxable income was $80,000 and $20,000 respectively, while S had taxable income of $50,000 each year. The tax effect on R and S (rounded to the nearest dollar and using the 2017 tax rate schedules) is as follows:

	R (Single)		S (Single)	
	Taxable Income	Tax	Taxable Income	Tax
20X1	$ 80,000	$15,739	$ 50,000	$ 8,239
20X2	20,000	2,534	50,000	8,239
Total	$100,000	$18,273	$100,000	$16,478

Note that although R and S have the same total income of $100,000 for the two-year period, R's total tax bill of $18,273 exceeds S's bill of $16,478 by $1,795.

As the above example demonstrates, the use of an annual accounting period may create inequities. Here R could reduce his tax bite if he could defer some of his income from one year to the next so as to split his income between years as equally as possible. Occasionally, Congress has responded by enacting special provisions. For example, where a taxpayer has a loss during the year, the net operating loss rules allow the taxpayer to utilize the loss by permitting it to be carried back or forward to profitable years.[30] Without these carryback and carryover provisions, the taxpayer would receive no benefit from any losses realized. Unfortunately, Congress has not always acted. Gamblers can deduct their losses but only to the extent of their winnings. So if they have winnings in one year and losses in another, they are out of luck.

ACCOUNTING METHODS

LO.3

Apply the cash and accrual methods of accounting to determine the tax year in which items are reported.

Once a tax year is identified, the taxpayer must determine in which period a transaction is to be reported. The year in which a particular item becomes part of the tax calculation is not a trivial matter. The time of recognition can make a substantial difference in the taxpayer's total tax liability not only because of the time value of money but also because factors affecting the tax calculations may change from year to year. For instance, tax rates may go up or down from one year to the next. Such change does not necessarily take an act of Congress. A taxpayer may simply marry, divorce, incorporate, or change from a taxable to tax-exempt entity. In such case, deferral of income to the low-rate year and acceleration of deductions to the high-rate year could produce significant savings. Similarly, Congress may completely revise the treatment of an item. For example, in 1993 Congress raised the top tax rate from 31 to 39.6 percent, eliminated the deduction for business club dues, dropped the amount of the deduction for business meals and entertainment from 80 to 50 percent, eliminated the deduction for certain moving expenses, increased the Medicare tax, increased the amount of Social Security benefits that are subject to tax, and raised the amount of business equipment that may be expensed from $10,000 to $17,500. Changes like these have become an annual rite in the tax area, consequently making timing critical.

The rules that determine when a particular item is reported are generally referred to as accounting methods. The Code identifies four permissible methods of accounting:[31]

1. The cash receipts and disbursements method.
2. The accrual method.
3. Any other method permitted by the Code (e.g., a method for a specific situation such as the completed contract method or the use of LIFO to value inventories).[32]
4. Any combination of the three methods above permitted by the Regulations.

---

[30] § 172. See Chapter 10 for a discussion of the net operating loss rules.

[31] § 446(c).

[32] Reg. § 1.446-1(c)(1)(iii).

The term *accounting method* is not limited to the overall method of accounting used by the taxpayer (e.g., the cash or accrual method). It generally includes the treatment of *any particular item* if such treatment affects *when* the item will be reported. For example, the use of LIFO to value inventories would be considered an accounting method since the use of this method determines when the cost of a product will become part of cost of goods sold.

It should be emphasized that the taxpayer is not required to adopt one overall method of accounting. For example, a taxpayer with inventories generally must use the accrual method to account for inventories and related sales. However, the same taxpayer could use the cash method to report interest income or other items. This approach (referred to as the *hybrid method*) is completely acceptable as long as the taxpayer applies the same methods consistently.

Taxpayers are generally allowed to select the methods of accounting they wish to use. In all cases, however, the IRS has the right to determine if the method used *clearly reflects income*, and, if not, to make the necessary adjustments.[33] For example, assume that each year a taxpayer changes the way it computes the amount of overhead that it capitalizes as part of inventory (e.g., on the basis of direct labor hours one year, machine hours the next). In such case, the IRS might require the taxpayer to use one method consistently so that income would not be distorted from year to year but would be clearly reflected.

Tax Methods versus Financial Accounting Methods

At first glance, many people—particularly accountants—would no doubt conclude that a method of accounting that conforms with generally accepted accounting principles (GAAP) would be regarded as clearly reflecting income.[34] Although this is ordinarily true, it is not always the case.[35] Conflicts sometimes exist because the objectives of the income tax system differ from that of financial accounting. The primary goal of financial accounting is to provide useful information to management, shareholders, creditors, and other interested parties. In contrast, the goal of the income tax system is to ensure that revenues are fairly collected. Due to these different goals, the tax law may disregard fundamental accounting principles. Perhaps the most obvious example can be found in the tax law's allowance of the cash method of accounting. Despite its failure to properly match revenues and expenses, the cash method is normally tolerated because from an administrative view it is simple and objective. Such administrative concerns often dictate a different approach for tax purposes. For example, an accrual basis taxpayer is often required to report prepaid income when received rather than when earned. Although this practice violates the matching principle, it ensures that the tax is imposed when the taxpayer has the cash to pay it.

The operation of differing objectives can also be seen in the use of estimates. One of the major responsibilities of financial accountants is to ensure that financial statement users are not misled. This demand normally encourages accountants to be conservative, which in turn may cause them to understate rather than overstate income. Although the government does not want taxpayers to overstate income, it certainly does not want to endorse principles that would tend toward understatement. Thus, the tax law generally does not allow taxpayers to estimate future expenses such as bad debts or warranty costs and deduct them currently, as is the case with financial accounting. Instead, the deduction is allowed only when there is objective evidence that a cost has been incurred. The government frowns on estimates of expenses, presumably because taxpayers would tend to overstate them.

Reporting of prepaid income and the treatment of estimated expenses are just two examples of where financial accounting principles deviate from tax accounting. The key point to recognize is that a particular item may be treated one way for financial accounting purposes and another way for tax purposes. As a practical matter, this may mean that two sets of books are maintained, or what is perhaps more likely, one set based on financial accounting principles to which adjustments must be made to arrive at taxable income.

CASH METHOD OF ACCOUNTING

General Rule

Virtually all individuals—as well as many corporations, partnerships, trusts, and estates—use the cash method of accounting. Its prevalence is no doubt attributable to the fact that it is

---

[33] § 446(b).

[34] Reg. § 1.446-1(a)(2).

[35] For an excellent example, see *Thor Power Tool Co.*, 79-1 USTC ¶9139, 43 AFTR2d 79-362, 439 U.S. 522 (USSC, 1979).

easy to use. Under the cash method, taxpayers simply report items of income and deduction in the year in which they are received or paid.[36] In effect, the cash method allows taxpayers merely to refer to their checkbooks to determine taxable income.

In using the cash method, items of income need not be in the form of cash but need only be capable of valuation in terms of money. Under this rule, sometimes termed the *cash equivalent doctrine,* the taxpayer reports income when the equivalent of cash is received.[37] Thus, where property or services are received, the fair market value of these items serves as the measure of income.

Due to the cash equivalent doctrine, reporting of income arising from notes and accounts receivable differs. Notes received by a cash basis taxpayer are usually considered property and hence constitute income equal to the value of the note.[38] Where a promise to pay is *not* evidenced by a note (e.g., credit sales resulting in accounts receivable), income is normally not recognized by a cash basis taxpayer until payment is received.[39] This treatment results because unsupported promises to pay normally are not considered as having a fair market value.

Constructive Receipt Doctrine

Taxpayers using the cash method of accounting have substantial control over income recognition since they may control the timing of the actual receipt of cash. If the requirement calling for *actual* receipt were strictly adhered to, the cash basis taxpayer could easily frustrate the purpose of progressive taxation. For example, taxpayers could select the year with the lowest tax rate and simply cash their salary or dividend checks or redeem their interest coupons in that year. To curtail this practice, the doctrine of constructive receipt was developed. Under this principle, a taxpayer is *deemed* to have received income even though such income has not actually been received. It should be noted that there is no corresponding doctrine for deductions (i.e., there is no constructive payment doctrine).

The constructive receipt doctrine is currently expressed in Regulation § 1.451-2(a) as follows:

> Income, although not actually reduced to the taxpayer's possession, is constructively received by him in the taxable year in which it is credited to his account, set apart for him or otherwise made available so that he could have drawn upon it during the taxable year if notice of intention to withdraw had been given. However, income is not constructively received if the taxpayer's control of its receipt is subject to substantial limitations or restrictions.

As the Regulation indicates, the taxpayer is treated as having received income when three conditions are satisfied:

1. The taxpayer has control over the amount without substantial limitations and restrictions.
2. The amount has been set aside or credited to the taxpayer's account.
3. The funds are available for payment by the payer (i.e., the payer's ability to make payment must be considered).

Some of the common situations to which the rule is applied are illustrated in the following examples.

Example 12

B refereed a basketball game on Saturday night, December 31, 2017 and did not receive the check for his services until after the banks had closed. He cashed the check on January 3, 2018. B must report the income in 2017. In the case of a check, a taxpayer is deemed to have received payment in the year the check is received rather than when it is cashed.[40]

---

[36] Reg. § 1.446-1(c)(1)(i).

[37] Reg. § 1.446-1(a)(3).

[38] *A.W. Wolfson,* 1 B.T.A. 538 (1925).

[39] *Bedell v. Comm.,* 1 USTC ¶359, 7 AFTR 8469, 30 F.2d 622 (CA-2, 1929).

[40] *C.F. Kahler,* 18 T.C. 31 (1952).

Example 13

T mailed a check on December 29, 2017, which S received in January 2018. S is not in constructive receipt of the check since it was not available to him for his immediate use and enjoyment. However, if S requested that T mail him the check so that he receives it in 2018, or if S could have received the check by merely appearing in person and claiming it, S would be deemed to have received the payment in 2017.

Example 14

When G made a deposit on January 15, 2018, the bank updated her passbook on December 31, 2017 to show that $200 of interest was credited to her account for the last quarter of 2017. G withdrew the interest on January 31. G must report the interest in 2017. Interest credited to the taxpayer's account is taxable when credited, regardless of whether it is in the taxpayer's possession, assuming that it may be withdrawn.[41]

Example 15

B Corporation mailed dividend checks dated December 20 on December 28, 2017. R, a shareholder in B, received her check on January 4, 2018. R reports the dividend income in 2018 as long as the payer customarily pays dividends by mail so that the shareholder receives it after the end of the year.[42]

Example 16

R's secretary received several checks for services that R had performed. Payments received by a taxpayer's agent are considered constructively received by the taxpayer.[43]

Example 17

A taxpayer who agrees not to cash a check until authorized by the payer has not constructively received income if the payer does not have sufficient funds in the bank to cover the check.[44]

Limitations on the Use of the Cash Method

As a method of accounting, the cash method's principal advantage lies in its simplicity and objectivity. If a taxpayer uses the cash method, taxable income is easily computed merely by referring to cash receipts and disbursements. Moreover, the amount of taxable income computed in this manner is incontrovertible—it is not open to question or dispute and is readily verifiable. Unlike the accrual method, whether income has been "earned" or expenses have been "incurred" are simply not issues under the cash method.

[41] Reg. § 1.451-2(b).

[42] Ibid.; S.L. Avery, 4 USTC ¶1277, 13 AFTR 1168, 292 U.S. 210 (USSC, 1934). See also H.B. McEuen v. Comm., 52-1 USTC ¶9281, 41 AFTR 1169, 196 F.2d 127 (CA-5, 1952).

[43] T. Watson, 2 TCM 863 (1943).

[44] A.V. Johnston, 23 TCM 2003, T.C. Memo 1964-323.

On other counts, the cash method scores poorly, ranking a distant second to the accrual method. From an accounting perspective, the cash method is entirely inappropriate since income and expense are recognized without regard to the taxable year in which the economic events responsible for the income or expense actually occur. Similarly, when some parties to a transaction use different methods of accounting, there may be a mismatching of income and deductions. For example, an accrual basis corporation could accrue expenses payable to a cash basis individual. In such case, the corporation could obtain deductions without ever having to make a disbursement and, moreover, without the individual taxpayer recognizing any offsetting income.

While the above are clearly shortcomings, the major flaw found in the cash method is that it is easily abused. Taxpayers have often secured benefits by merely timing their transactions appropriately: recognizing income in one year, deductions in the next, or what is more likely, deductions in years in which the taxpayer is in a high tax bracket and income in years in which the taxpayer is in a low tax bracket.

To attack these problems, Congress has limited the use of the cash method of accounting. The following entities are normally prohibited from using the cash method:[45]

1. Regular C corporations;
2. Partnerships that have regular C corporations as partners (other than certain personal service corporations described below); and
3. *Tax shelters,* generally defined as any enterprise (other than a regular C corporation) in which interests have been offered for sale in any offering required to be registered under Federal or State security agencies.

Despite these general restrictions, Congress believed that the simplicity of the cash method justified its continued use in certain instances. For example, Congress felt that it would be costly for small businesses to switch to the accrual method. Similarly, it recognized that the accrual method would create undue complexity for farming businesses if such a method were required to account for growing crops and livestock. In addition, Congress believed that personal service corporations, which have traditionally used the cash method, should be allowed to continue their use. Accordingly, the following entities are allowed to use the cash method.[46]

1. Any corporation or partnership whose average annual *gross receipts* for *all* preceding years do not exceed $5 million. This test is satisfied for any prior year only if the average annual gross receipts[47] for the three-year period ending with such year does not exceed $5 million. Once this average *exceeds* $5 million, the corporation cannot use the cash method for the following year.
2. Certain farming businesses.
3. Qualified personal service corporations. A regular C corporation is qualified if substantially all of the activities consist of performing services in eight fields, including health, law, engineering, architecture, accounting, actuarial science, performing arts, or consulting, *and* at least 95% of its stock is held by the employees who are providing such services.[48]

Example 18

Dr. C and Dr. D, both heart surgeons, own 100% of the stock of Cardiac Care Corporation. The corporation provides the latest in diagnostic testing and treatments, including open heart surgery and rehabilitation. Because all of the corporations' services are in the area of health and more than 95% of the stock is owned by the doctors who are providing the services, the corporation may use the cash method of accounting.

[45] § 448(a).

[46] § 448(b).

[47] Gross receipts include total sales (net of returns and allowances but not reduced by costs of goods sold) and amounts received for services, interest, rents, royalties, and annuities. For sales of capital assets and real or depreciable property used in trade or business, gross receipts are reduced by the taxpayer's adjusted basis in such property. See Temp. Reg. § 1.448-1T(f)(2)(iv).

[48] § 448(d)(2).

Example 19

C's Video Rentals, a regular C corporation, started business in 20X1. Since that time it has grown to 20 locations and had annual gross receipts as follows:

Year	Gross Receipts	Average Annual Gross Receipts*
20X1.........	$ 4,000,000	$4,000,000
20X2.........	2,000,000	3,000,000
20X3........	6,000,000	4,000,000
20X4........	10,000,000	6,000,000

$$*\text{Current} + \text{Prior two years} \over 3 \text{ (or if less, years in existence)}$$

It initially adopted the cash method in 20X1. It was able to use the cash method through 20X4 because the average annual gross receipts for all prior years did not exceed $5 million. Note that although its gross receipts were $6,000,000 in 20X3, its *average annual* gross receipts for that year were only $4,000,000 ([$4,000,000 + $2,000,000 + $6,000,000] ÷ 3). Consequently, the cash method could be used for 20X4. It will be denied use of the cash method for 20X5 since the average annual gross receipts for 20X4 exceed $5 million ([$2,000,000 + $6,000,000 + $10,000,000] ÷ 3 = $ 6,000,000).

It should be noted that the above exceptions do not apply to tax shelters. Any enterprise considered a tax shelter must use the accrual method. In addition, as discussed below, if the taxpayer maintains inventories, special rules apply.

Accounting for Inventory

As noted above, most businesses—other than large C corporations—are permitted to use the cash method. However, an important exception exists for taxpayers with inventories. According to the longstanding rule of Regulation § 1.471-1 "[I]n order to reflect taxable income correctly, inventories … are necessary in every case in which the production, purchase, or sale of merchandise is an income producing factor." Regulation § 1.446-1(c)(2) adds that in any case in which it is necessary to use an inventory the accrual method of accounting must be used with regard to purchases and sales. … In short, if a business sells "inventory," taxpayers must capitalize the cost of inventory purchases and can expense such costs only when the item is sold. Just as important, if not more so, businesses with inventories also must accrue and recognize income at the time of sale—regardless of when the cash is received. Both halves of the accrual requirement are significant since both affect the amount of income that the taxpayer ultimately reports in a particular year.

The reasoning behind the regulatory scheme requiring inventories is anchored in the matching principle that ensures income will be clearly reflected. The rationale was eloquently stated by the Appellate Court in *Knight-Ridder Newspapers Inc.,* a case involving whether a cash-basis corporation should inventory its costs of newsprint and ink.[49]

---

[49] 84-2 USTC ¶9827, 54 AFTR 2d 84-6120, 743 F.2d 781
(CA-11, 1984).

According to accounting wisdom the income realized from the sale of merchandise is most *clearly measured* by matching the cost of the merchandise with the revenue from its sale. In order to achieve such matching of revenue and cost, it is necessary to keep an inventory account reflecting the costs of merchandise, raw materials, and manufacturing expenses. These costs are not deducted immediately when paid but are deferred until the year when the resulting merchandise is sold.

To make the matching complete, the taxpayer must report income on the accrual method. That method helps to ensure that income from the sale (like the inventory costs) is reflected in the year of the sale. For example, if the sale is made on credit, the accrual method nevertheless treats the income as accrued and reflects it when the sale occurs. The prophetic skills of the accrual shaman permit it to recognize both income and deductions in the same year.

By contrast, the primal cash method is unable to achieve such a mystical joinder [matching] of inventory deductions and credit sale income. To be sure, the cash method could theoretically operate in tandem with inventories. The beast could conceivably close its eyes to deductions until the year of the sale. It could never learn, however, to prophesy future cash payments. If there were a credit sale, the beast could not grasp income and deductions simultaneously in its rugged paw. The goal of matching costs and revenues would fail.

While the inventory rule seems relatively simple and necessary to guarantee the clear reflection of income of a cash basis taxpayer, it is has led to a great deal of controversy. These issues are discussed in further detail in Chapter 10.

ACCRUAL METHOD OF ACCOUNTING

Taxpayers using the accrual method of accounting report income in the year in which it is considered earned under the so-called *all-events test.* Under this test, income is earned when all the events have occurred that fix the right to receive such income and the amount of income can be determined with reasonable accuracy.[50] As the courts have consistently observed in cases involving the all-events test, the "objective is to determine at what point in time the seller acquired an unconditional right to receive payment under the contract."[51]

Example 20

Sellco Corporation manufactures a special machine used in a process to convert oranges into orange juice. On December 15, 2017, Sellco sold a machine to B Inc. According to the terms of the sales agreement, B was given a 30-day period for testing and acceptance. As of the end of 2017, B had not indicated its acceptance. Sellco would not accrue the income from the sale in 2017 because it did not have an unconditional right to receive the income. The first prong of the all-events test, a fixed right to receive income, is not met. The sale was contingent on satisfaction of certain conditions—test and acceptance—and since these conditions had not been met at the close of 2017 the sale was not completed and Sellco had no right to the income. If B subsequently rejected the machine, this would clearly mean delay or a complete loss of the sale.[52]

In most situations involving a sale of merchandise, the right becomes fixed when the goods are shipped, when the product is delivered or accepted or when title passes, as long as the method is consistently used.[53]

[50] Reg. § 1.451-1(a).

[51] *Hallmark Cards, Inc. v. CIR,* 90 T.C. 26, 33 (1988).

[52] See *Webb Press Co. v. CIR,* 3 BTA 247 (1925) (acq.).

[53] *Lucas v. North Texas Lumber Co.,* 2 USTC ¶484, 8 AFTR 10276, 281 U.S. 11 (USSC, 1929). See also Reg § 1.446-1(c)(1)(ii).

> ## Example 21
>
> In *Hallmark Cards,* the greeting card giant, a calendar year accrual basis taxpayer, shipped Valentine cards before year end but deferred income from the sales to the next year. Early shipment was necessary to deal with production and shipping problems related to supplying cards in a timely manner to its customers (more than 20,000 retailers at over 35,000 locations). Contracts with the customers specified that title and risk of loss passed to customers on January 1. The IRS argued that Hallmark must accrue the income when the cards were shipped since it had a fixed right to the income, thus meeting the all-events test. Despite the fact that the items had been delivered to customers prior to year end, the Court held that Hallmark was *not* required to accrue the income upon shipment. The Court explained that "passage of title and risk of loss to buyer" did not occur under the contract until January 1 allowing Hallmark to postpone recognition since it did not have a fixed right to the income.[54]

As the two examples above illustrate, the terms of the agreement are critical in determining whether the taxpayer has an unconditional right to the income. Other facts may also be important such as doubts concerning whether the receivable can be collected or disputes or other uncertainties relating to the amount of the liability. If the agreement requires a particular act, such as submitting a bill, and such act is viewed as simply ministerial, the requirement may be ignored in determining whether the taxpayer has a "right" to the income.

> ## Example 22
>
> In 1996, in *Charles Schwab Corp.,* the discount securities broker asserted that its commission income accrued on the settlement date.[55] However, the Tax Court ultimately agreed with the government that the income should be accrued on the trade date. According to the Court, the broker's "essential service" was "execution of trades," and the subsequent settlement activities were merely "of a ministerial nature."

Normally, the accrual method *must* be used in accounting for sales, purchases, and inventories if inventories are an income-producing factor. However, the taxpayer who must use the accrual method in this instance may still account for other items of income and expense using the cash method. The accrual method, as noted earlier, must be used by regular C corporations and partnerships with C corporations as partners unless one of several exceptions is satisfied.

There are several special rules relating to the accrual method of accounting that create inconsistencies. For example, dividends normally would accrue under the all-events test on the date of record. However, an exception exists so that dividends are reported when received.[56] Other exceptions exist that are discussed later in this chapter.

CHANGES IN ACCOUNTING METHODS

Taxpayers are given great freedom in the accounting methods they may use initially. However, once a particular method has been adopted (e.g., when it is first used to account for an item), it may not be changed unless consent is granted by the IRS. This is true when the taxpayer is switching from an erroneous method to a permissible method as well as one permissible method to another permissible method. Taxpayers seeking a change must apply for permission by filing Form 3115, Application for Change in Accounting Method, anytime during the tax year when the change is to become effective.[57] The IRS does not rubber-stamp these requests. Permission is granted only if the taxpayer is willing to make any adjustments required by the IRS. Under § 481, the IRS is authorized to require adjustments if a change in method would result in the omission of income or the duplication of deductions.

LO.4
Determine the effect of a change in accounting method.

---

[54] *Supra*, Footnote 51, *Hallmark Cards, Inc. v. CIR,* 90 T.C. 26, 33 (1988).

[55] *Charles Schwab Corp. v. CIR,* 107 T.C. 282 (1996).

[56] Reg. § 1.451-2(b), *Tar Products Corp. v. Comm.,* 42-2 USTC ¶9662, 29 AFTR 1190, 130 F.2d 866 (CA-3, 1942).

[57] Some changes may be made automatically without consent, thereby avoiding the user fee for filing Form 3115.

Example 23

T, Inc. operates a consulting company. It has always used the cash method to account for its income from services. In 2017, it decided that it should switch to the accrual method. At the end of 2016, T's outstanding receivables were $10,000. If T were allowed to switch to the accrual method and no adjustment were required, the $10,000 would escape taxation. The $10,000 would not be taxed in 2016 since T was on the cash basis in that year and no collections were made. Similarly, the $10,000 would not be taxed in 2017 because T is on the accrual method in that year and the income did not accrue in 2017 but rather 2016. Thus, without an adjustment, the $10,000 of income would be omitted from both the 2016 and 2017 returns, never to be taxed.

Accounting for the Adjustment

Taxpayers are normally required to report any adjustment attributable to a change in method in the year of the change and pay any additional tax due (or receive a refund).[58] In certain situations, this may create a severe hardship for the taxpayer (e.g., the required inclusion of several years' income in a single year). Moreover, taxpayers may be reluctant to change from an erroneous method of accounting to a correct method and simply wait for the IRS to detect their mistake. However, § 481(c) allows the IRS to alter this approach. The IRS has used this authority to develop a system that encourages taxpayers to switch from an erroneous method they may be using to a correct method.[59]

Under the revised approach of Revenue Procedure 97-27, the treatment of the adjustment depends primarily on whether the taxpayer voluntarily or involuntarily changes the accounting method. If the change is voluntary, the adjustment is spread over a four-year period (the year of the change and the three subsequent years). If the change is involuntary (e.g., the taxpayer is under examination and is not allowed under the rules of Revenue Procedure 97-27 to make a change) and the adjustment is positive, the entire adjustment is included in the earliest tax year under examination. However, a taxpayer may elect to use a one-year adjustment period if the entire adjustment is less than $25,000.

Example 24

J has operated a small hardware store as a sole proprietorship since 2006. In August, 2019 the IRS audited J's 2017 tax return and determined that J had failed to use the accrual method of accounting for inventories. Instead, J had expensed all of his inventory as it was acquired. Consequently, the IRS required J to change his method of accounting. Based on a physical count and valuation of his inventory, the IRS determined that J had understated his income in prior years by $300,000. Assuming J is not allowed to voluntarily change his accounting method during the examination, he must report all $300,000 in income in 2017. Had J voluntarily made the change prior to examination or had he qualified under the special relief provisions to voluntarily make the change while under examination, he could have spread the adjustment over four years: $75,000 of income in 2017—the year of the change—and $75,000 in each of the three following years, 2018, 2019, and 2020.

Example 25

During 2017, R asked for and obtained permission to change from the cash method to the accrual method. This change resulted in a negative income adjustment of $19,000. Because this adjustment is less than the $25,000 threshold, R can take into account the entire adjustment in 2017.

---

[58] *Ibid.*

[59] Rev. Proc. 97-27, 1997-1, C.B. 680, as modified by Rev. Proc. 2002-19, 2002-1 C.B. 696.

Changes in accounting method are not to be confused with correction of errors. Errors such as mathematical mistakes or the improper calculation of a deduction or credit can be corrected by the taxpayer without permission of the IRS by simply filing an amended return. Alternatively, the IRS may discover the mistake and require the taxpayer to make a correction. However, if the statute of limitations has run on a return containing an error, no correction can be made. In these cases, the taxpayer's income is forever over- or understated, as the case may be.

 ## CHECK YOUR KNOWLEDGE

Review Question 1

On Sunday, December 31, 1961 in Green Bay, Wisconsin, Paul Hornung, All-American quarterback from Notre Dame, star of the Green Bay Packers and later a sports analyst, won a Corvette for being the most valuable player in the NFL championship game.[60] After the game, the editor of *Sport* magazine, the sponsor of the award, gave nothing to Hornung to evidence his ownership of the car, which was being held at a dealership in New York. Hornung picked up the car on January 3, 1962 in New York. What are the tax concerns here?

There is little question that Hornung must report income (although that was uncertain in 1961). The important issue to be resolved is when. Was Hornung in constructive receipt of the car that snowy afternoon in December 1961? Although Hornung, wanting to report the income in 1961, argued that he had received the car, the court disagreed. In a decision that should be mandatory reading for its witty analysis, the court explained that the basis of constructive receipt is unfettered control over the date of actual receipt. In this case, the facts indicated that Hornung did not have such control. He did not receive the car or even the keys or title to the car in 1961. Moreover, the car was in a dealership that was not only 1,000 miles away but was also closed. In addition, the car had not been set aside for Hornung's use and delivery was not solely up to him. Accordingly, the doctrine of constructive receipt was inapplicable.

Review Question 2

Mr. Mike, an accountant, is the proud owner of Maggie, a West Highland terrier. Shortly after Mike acquired Maggie, he discovered the need to take her to get the appropriate shots. It did not take long for Mike to pick a vet. He elected to use one of his long-time clients for whom he prepares tax returns, Nonhuman Companion Inc. that operates a chain of veterinary clinics throughout Arizona and California. Mike's visit to the vet was the first time he had actually been to his client's office. While there, he noticed that the clinic provided not only veterinarian and kennel services but also a great variety of food, toys, and pet paraphernalia for sale. To his best recollection, the corporation used the cash method of accounting. Is this the correct method?

There are two rules concerning accounting methods that come into play here. First, a corporation is normally required to use the accrual method of accounting. However, several exceptions may apply. The accrual requirement is waived if the corporation is an S corporation or its average annual gross receipts are less than $5 million for all preceding tax years. If neither of these exceptions applies, the corporation could possibly use the cash method if it is considered a personal service corporation, since it provides services in the health field. Interestingly, the IRS has addressed this question and ruled that veterinarian services fall within the definition of "personal" services (i.e., health services). Nevertheless, there could be a concern that "substantially all the activities" do not consist of performing "health" services. The second rule that operates in this situation concerns accounting for inventory. A business normally must use the accrual method to account for inventory even if it otherwise qualifies to use the cash method. The IRS has held that a partnership that provided veterinary services was required to switch from the cash method to the accrual method when more than 50% of the partnership's receipts were from merchandise (pet food, supplies, and drugs).[61]

---

[60] *Paul v. Hornung,* 47 T.C. 428 (1967).   [61] Technical Advice Memorandum 9218008.

Review Question 3

X Inc., an accrual basis calendar year taxpayer, filed a lawsuit against the U.S. government for breach of contract. X was awarded a judgment of $100,000 by the Court of Appeals for the Fifth Circuit for the alleged breach in 2016. The income was fully taxable. The government tried to appeal the decision to the Supreme Court, filing a petition for writ of certiorari. The writ and appeal were denied in 2017. No appropriation was made by the U.S. government for payment of the claim during 2016. When should X report the income?

X should accrue the income if the all-events test is met. The test is met when X has an unconditional right to the income. Here, the taxpayer's right to the income is not fixed until the Supreme Court denied the government's appeal in 2017. Such a condition is not simply ministerial in nature. In determining whether X's right was fixed, the fact that Congress did not make an appropriation for the payment of such sum in 2016 is irrelevant since the judgment became an acknowledged liability of the government in 2017.[62]

Review Question 4

In light of the decision in *Hallmark Cards,* Greetings Inc., an accrual basis calendar year taxpayer changed the terms of its contracts for sales of Valentine cards this year so that passage of title and risk of loss to buyer did not occur under the contract until January 1. In the past, Greetings had accrued the income when the cards were shipped. Indicate whether the following statements are true or false and if false explain why.

a. Greetings' change in the terms of its contracts constitutes a change in accounting method.

b. Greetings must seek permission from the IRS to change its method.

c. Any omission of income that results in Greetings' change must be reported in the year of the change.

Statements (a) and (b) are true. Any change which affects the time when income will be reported is considered a change in accounting method and permission must be obtained from the IRS to ensure there is not an omission of income or duplication of deduction. In this case, the change shifts incomes it normally reports in one year to the next year. Statement (c) is false. Assuming Greetings receives permission to change, it is normally permitted to spread the income adjustment over four years.

Accounting for Income: Special Rules

CLAIM OF RIGHT DOCTRINE

LO.5

Describe some of the special rules governing the treatment of prepaid income, interest income, interest-free loans, and income from long-term contracts.

Occasionally income may be received before the taxpayer's rights to such income have been clearly established. The tax difficulty posed in these instances concerns whether the taxpayer should report the income currently or wait until the proper claims to the income have been identified. For these situations, the courts have established a rule of law termed the *claim of right doctrine.* Under this rule, if a taxpayer actually or constructively *receives* income under a claim of right (i.e., the taxpayer claims the income is rightfully his or hers) and such income is not restricted in use, it must be included in gross income.[63] In other words, earnings received must be included in income if the taxpayer has an *unrestricted claim,* notwithstanding the possibility that the income may be subsequently relinquished if the taxpayer's claim is later denied.

---

[62] Rev. Rul. 70-151, 1970-1 C.B. 116.

[63] *North American Oil Consolidated v. Burnet,* 3 USTC ¶943, 11 AFTR 16, 286 U.S. 417 (USSC, 1932).

Example 26

Television station WXYZ received $100,000 from KLM Company to air the firm's commercials during a local talk show in the month of December. During this month, the ratings dropped sharply when the star of the show quit. Shortly thereafter, KLM contacted the station, indicating that it wanted to discontinue its sponsorship and requesting return of $75,000 of the payment. In view of their interpretation of the agreement, the station continued to air the firm's commercials and retained the $100,000. KLM brought suit to recover the $75,000. Under the claim of right doctrine, WXYZ must include the entire $100,000 in income even though it may have to repay the amount or a portion thereof to KLM. The amount is included because WXYZ received the money and could use the amount without restriction.

The claim of right doctrine applies to both cash and accrual basis taxpayers. As previously discussed, income is usually reported by an accrual basis taxpayer only when all the events have occurred that fix the taxpayer's right to receive such income. However, in the case of contested income, the taxpayer's rights to such amounts have not been fixed, and under the all events test he or she would not report it. The all-events test notwithstanding, the claim of right doctrine carves out an exception to this rule for contested income the taxpayer has *received*. An accrual basis taxpayer who *receives* contested income under a claim of right without restrictions on its use must report the amount in income even though his or her rights to the income have not been fixed.[64] Alternatively, if the accrual basis taxpayer has *not received* the contested income, it will not be included because his or her rights thereto have not been fixed.[65] Thus, an *accrual basis* taxpayer's reporting of contested income depends on whether or not the taxpayer has received it.

Example 27

RST, Inc, an accrual basis taxpayer, shipped parts to MNO Corporation and sent MNO a bill for $25,000. MNO used the parts and reported that they did not perform according to specifications. If MNO had paid the $25,000 and subsequently sued to recover the purchase price, RST would be required to include the $25,000 in income since the amount was received and the claim of right doctrine applies (i.e., RST has an unrestricted claim to the income). On the other hand, if MNO had not paid the $25,000, RST would not be required to accrue the income because the amount was *not* received and the all-events test has not been satisfied (i.e., RST's rights to the income have not been fixed).

The claim of right doctrine has been used in many differing instances to cause the inclusion of income in the year received. Some examples where the rule has been applied to make the income taxable are

1. Contingent legal fees that must be returned upon a reversal by an appellate court;[66]

2. Illegal income and gains (e.g., embezzled amounts);[67] and

3. Bonuses and commissions that were improperly computed and had to be subsequently repaid.[68]

The claim of right doctrine does not apply where the taxpayer receives the income but recognizes an obligation to repay.[69] For example, a landlord would not be required to report the receipt of a tenant's security deposit as income because the deposit must be repaid upon the tenant's departure if the apartment unit is undamaged.

---

[64] *Ibid.*

[65] Reg. § 1.446-1(c)(1)(ii).

[66] *Michael Phillips v. Comm.*, 56-2 USTC ¶10,067, 50 AFTR 718, 238 F.2d 473 (CA-7, 1956).

[67] *James v. U.S.*, 61-1 USTC ¶9449, 7 AFTR2d 1361, 366 U.S. 213 (USSC, 1961).

[68] *U.S. v. Lewis*, 51-1 USTC ¶9211, 40 AFTR 258, 340 U.S. 590 (USSC, 1951).

[69] *Comm. v. Turney*, 36-1 USTC ¶9168, 17 AFTR 679, 82 F.2d 661 (CA-5, 1936).

In those situations where the taxpayer repays an amount that previously had been included in income, a deduction is allowed. Section 1341 provides a special rule for computing the deduction, which ensures that the tax benefit of the deduction is the equivalent to the tax paid on the income in the prior year.

PREPAID INCOME

Over the years, a web of exceptions and special rules have developed regarding the reporting of prepaid income by an *accrual basis taxpayer.* Absent these rules, the accrual basis taxpayer (in accordance with the all-events test) would defer recognition of prepaid income until it becomes earned, as is the case in financial accounting. For tax purposes, however, accrual basis taxpayers often report prepaid income in the year received. This treatment normally results from application of the claim of right doctrine, which requires income recognition when the taxpayer receives earnings under an unrestricted claim. For example, accrual basis taxpayers must report prepaid rental income when received (not when earned) since the taxpayer accepts the money under a claim of right without restrictions on its use. Unfortunately, no general rule is completely reliable to determine when prepaid income must be reported. Rather, the reporting procedure depends on the type of income received. As discussed below, special rules exist for prepaid income from rents, interest, services, warranties, goods, dues, subscriptions, and similar items. Note, however, these rules apply to *accrual basis* taxpayers only. A *cash basis* taxpayer reports all of these prepaid items of income in the year the cash is received.

Prepaid Interest, Rents, and Royalties

Several types of advance payments are included in income when received without question. For example, prepaid interest is income when received.[70] Prepaid rent and lump-sum payments, such as bonuses or advance royalties received upon execution of a lease or other agreement, are also income when received.[71] As subsequently explained, however, the term *rent* does not include payments for the use or occupancy of rooms or space where their use is ancillary to the services provided to the user of the property (e.g., hotels, motels, and convalescent homes are not considered as having received rents).[72] Because of the significant service element, these prepayments are reported using the rules applying to prepaid service income. Prepaid rents must be distinguished not only from services but also from lease or security deposits. Amounts received from a lessee that are refundable provided the lessee complies with the terms of the lease are not income since the lessor recognizes an obligation to repay.[73] The deposits become income only when the lessor becomes entitled to their unrestricted use upon the lessee's violation of the agreement.

Prepaid Service Income

Over the years, the treatment of advance payments for services—prepaid service income—has been quite controversial. Disputes between the IRS and taxpayers began when the IRS argued that the claim of right doctrine required accrual basis taxpayers to report prepayments for services as income in the year received. The IRS took this approach notwithstanding the fact that the taxpayer had not performed the services. After a great deal of litigation, the government relented and permitted limited deferral in certain circumstances. These rules were revised in 2004, with the issuance of Rev. Proc. 2004-34.[74]

Rev. Proc. 2004-34 now permits two acceptable methods of accounting for advanced payments for services. These are a "full-inclusion method" and a "deferral method." The full-inclusion option is the easiest and the least desirable: All of the payments are

---

[70] *Franklin Life Insurance v. U.S.,* 68-2 USTC ¶9459, 22 AFTR2d 5180, 399 F.2d 757 (CA-7, 1968).

[71] *South Dade Farms, Inc. v. Comm.,* 43-2 USTC ¶9634, 31 AFTR 842, 138 F.2d 818 (CA-5, 1943); *W.M. Scott,* 27 B.T.A. 951.

[72] Rev. Proc. 2004-34, 2004-22 I.R.B. 991.

[73] *Clinton Hotel Realty Corp. v. Comm.,* 42-2 USTC ¶9559, 29 AFTR 758, 128 F.2d 968 (CA-5, 1942).

[74] Rev. Proc. 2004-34, 2004-22 IRB 991 (effective for tax years ending after 5/5/04) superseding Rev. Proc. 71-21, 1971-2 C.B. 549.

reported in the year of receipt regardless of how the payments are reported for financial accounting purposes. In contrast, under the deferral method, taxpayers generally must report advanced payments as income in the year of receipt to the extent the payments are included in the revenues of the taxpayer's financial statements.[75] The balance of the advanced payments are deferred and reported as income in the following year. Thus, book income normally equals taxable income in the first year but may differ in subsequent years. This technique, unlike the previous approach, permits at least one year of deferral regardless of the length of the contract.

Example 28

Murray Inc.—a calendar-year, accrual-method taxpayer—is in the business of providing ballroom dance lessons. On October 29 of year 1, Murray received $4,800 for a 48-month contract under which Murray would provide up to 96 lessons. Murray provides 8 lessons in year 1, 48 lessons in year 2, and 40 lessons in year 3. In its audited financial statements, the company reports the income as the lessons are provided. Therefore, for financial accounting purposes, Murray reports $400 ($4,800 × 8/96) in year 1. Similarly, under the deferral method of Rev. Proc. 2004-34, Murray would also report $400 of income for tax purposes since this procedure permits deferral equal to that reported for financial statement purposes. In year 2, for financial statement purposes, Murray would report $2,400 (48/96 × $4,800) based on the number of lessons provided. However, in year 2 for tax purposes, Murray would report the remaining balance of the advanced payment, $4,400, as income.

The advance payment rules allowing limited deferral for prepaid service income also apply to prepaid rental income if the occupancy or use of property is ancillary to the provision of services to the user of the property.[76] According to the procedure, advance payments for the use of hotel rooms or other quarters, booth space at a trade show, campsite space at a mobile home park, and recreational or banquet facilities are not considered rents but rather services. Note that this treatment permits hotels, motels, and the like to enjoy the deferral provision as outlined above for services.

Advance Payments for Goods

Normally, an accrual basis taxpayer reports advance payments for sales of merchandise when they are earned (e.g., when the goods are shipped). This treatment enables the taxpayer to defer recognition of the prepayments. However, this approach is allowed only if the taxpayer follows the same method of reporting for financial accounting purposes.[77]

Example 29

C Corporation, a calendar year taxpayer, manufactures kitchen appliances. In late December 2017, it received $50,000 for kitchen appliances that it will produce and ship in May 2018. The corporation may postpone recognition of the income until 2018, assuming that such income is also reported on the financial accounting income statement in 2018.

---

[75] If "applicable" financial statements (a certified audited financial statement used for credit purposes, reporting to shareholders, or any other substantial nontax purpose) have not been prepared, the amount of the payment earned is reported in the first year. Rev. Proc. 2004-34 (4.06), 2004-22 I.R.B. 991.

[76] Rev. Proc. 2004-34 identifies other types of prepayments that do and do not qualify as an advanced payment for which limited deferral is permitted.

[77] Reg. § 1.451-5(b). See Reg. § 1.451-4(c)(1) for certain situations where the prepayments must be reported earlier.

Long-Term Contracts

Section 460 contains special rules for the reporting of income from long-term contracts. A long-term contract is defined as any contract for the manufacture, building, installation, or construction of property that is not completed within the same taxable year in which it was entered into. However, a *manufacturing* contract is still not considered long-term unless it also involves either (1) the manufacture of a unique item not normally carried in finished goods inventory (e.g., a special piece of machinery), or (2) items that normally require more than 12 months to complete. If a manufacturing contract does not qualify as a long-term contract, deferral may still be available under the rules regarding advance payments for goods discussed above. Note that contracts for services normally do not qualify for treatment as long-term contracts.

The tax law has long allowed taxpayers who enter into a long-term contract to use the percentage of completion method or the completed contract method (subject to certain limitations) to account for advance payments.[78] The percentage of completion method requires the taxpayer to recognize a portion of the gross profit on the contract based on the estimated percentage of the contract completed. In contrast, the completed contract method allows the taxpayer to defer income recognition until the contract is complete and acceptance has occurred. When available, taxpayers usually opt to use the completed contract method in order to postpone recognition of income. In some extreme cases, however, taxpayers have been able to postpone income for many years on the claim that the contract was not complete.

Over the years, Congress became concerned about the opportunities for deferral as well as the potential for abuse. Consequently, it took various steps, slowly but surely limiting the use of the completed contract method. These actions culminated with the virtual repeal of the method in 1989. As a result, long-term contracts currently entered into normally must be accounted for using the percentage of completion method.[79] However, there are two situations where the completed contract method can still be used. These include[80]

1. *Home construction contracts.* Contracts in which 80% of the costs are related to buildings containing four or fewer dwelling units. Special rules apply to contracts if the buildings contain more than four units (i.e., so-called residential construction contracts).[81]

2. *Contracts of small businesses.* Construction contracts that are completed within two years of commencement and are performed by a contractor whose average annual gross receipts for the three preceding tax years do not exceed $10 million.

When using the percentage of completion method, the portion of the total contract price reported during the year and matched against current costs is computed as follows:

$$\text{Total contract price} \times \frac{\text{Direct and allocable indirect costs incurred this period}}{\text{Total estimated costs of contract}}$$

Note that if less than 10% of the contract's costs have been incurred, the taxpayer may elect to defer reporting until the year in which the 10% threshold is reached.[82]

Example 30

In October 2017, W Corporation entered into a contract to build a hotel to be completed by May 2019. The contract price was $1 million. The company's estimated total costs of construction were $800,000. W's average annual gross receipts exceed $10 million, and, therefore, it is required to use the percentage of completion method. Total costs incurred during 2017 were $600,000. In 2018, the contract was completed at a total cost of $840,000. The income reported in 2017 and 2018 is computed below:

[78] Reg. § 1.451-3.
[79] § 460(a).
[80] § 460(e).
[81] A 70% of completion method may be used for certain residential construction contracts.
[82] § 460(b)(5).

	2017	2018
Revenue recognized	$ 750,000*	$ 250,000
Current costs	(600,000)	(240,000)
Total	$ 150,000	$ 10,000

$$\frac{*600,000}{$800,000} = 75\% \times \$1,000,000$$

Any contract for which the percentage of completion method is used is subject to the special *look-back* provisions.[83] Under these rules, once the contract is complete, annual income is recomputed based on final costs rather than estimated costs. Interest is then paid to the taxpayer if there was an overstatement of income. Conversely, the taxpayer must pay interest if income was understated.

Example 31

Same facts as in *Example 30,* above. Based on total actual costs of $840,000, W's 2017 income should have been $114,000, computed as follows:

	2017
Revenue recognized	$714,000*
Current costs	(600,000)
Total	$114,000

$$\frac{*600,000}{$840,000} = 74.1\% \times \$1,000,000$$

Because the contract was in reality only 71.4% complete and not 75% complete, W overstated income in 2017 by $36,000 ($150,000 − $114,000). Consequently, the IRS is required to pay the taxpayer interest on the overpayment of the related tax.

Prepaid Dues and Subscriptions

Amidst much controversy concerning the reporting of prepaid income, Congress provided specific rules for the reporting of prepaid dues and subscriptions. Section 455 permits the taxpayer to elect to recognize prepaid subscription income (amounts received from a newspaper, magazine, or periodical) ratably over the subscription period. Section 456 provides that taxpayers may elect to report prepaid dues ratably over the membership period.

INTEREST INCOME

The period in which a taxpayer recognizes interest income usually follows the basic tax accounting rules for cash and accrual basis taxpayers. In some cases, however, these taxpayers must observe special provisions that may cause reporting to vary from the normal pattern.

General Rules

As a general rule, cash basis taxpayers recognize interest income when received, while accrual basis taxpayers recognize the income when it is earned. As previously noted, both accrual and cash basis taxpayers that receive interest before it is earned (prepaid interest) must report the income when it is received.

---

[83] § 460(b)(2). The look back rule is elective if the cumulative income (loss) determined using estimated contract price and cost is within 10% of actual.

Example 32

T operates a small business that manufactures pottery dishes. When one of her customers was unable to pay her bill, T accepted a $10,000 note, dated October 1, 2017, payable with 6% interest on October 1, 2018. Assuming T is a cash basis taxpayer, she will report $600 of interest income ($10,000 × 6%) when received in 2018. If T uses the accrual method, she would include $150 ($10,000 × 3/12 × 6%) in her gross income for 2017 and $450 ($10,000 × 9/12 × 6%) when received in 2018. Had the customer paid all of the interest, $600, in 2017 as a showing of good faith, T would report the entire $600 in 2017 regardless of whether she is a cash or accrual basis taxpayer.

In many instances, a taxpayer will purchase an interest-bearing instrument between payment dates. When this occurs, it is assumed that the purchase price includes the interest accrued to the date of the purchase. Thus, when the buyer later receives the interest payment, the portion accrued to the date of purchase is considered a nontaxable return of capital that reduces the taxpayer's basis in the instrument. On the other hand, the seller must include as interest income the amount accrued to the date of the purchase, regardless of the seller's method of accounting.

Example 33

S owned a $1,000, 12% AT&T bond that paid interest semiannually on November 1 and May 1. He purchased the bond at par several years ago. On September 1, 2017, S sold the bond for $1,540 including $40 of the accrued interest ($1,000 × 12% × 4/12). S must report $40 of interest income accrued to the date of sale. In addition, S will report a capital gain of $500 ($1,540 − $40 interest − $1,000 basis). The result is the same if S is a cash or accrual basis taxpayer.

Example 34

Assume B purchased for $1,540 the bond that S sold in the example above. On November 1, B receives an interest payment of $60 ($1,000 × 12% × 6/12). B treats the interest accrued to the date of purchase, $40, as a nontaxable return of basis. Thus, B's basis is reduced to $1,500 ($1,540 − $40). The remaining $20 of interest is included in B's gross income.

In practice, the broker's statement normally reflects the interest accrued to the date of the sale or purchase.

Discount

When accounting for interest income, any discount relating to the debt instrument—the excess of the face value of the obligation over the purchase price—must be considered. Discount typically results when the rate at which the instrument pays interest is less than the market rate. In such case, the discount essentially functions as a substitute for interest. Consistent with this view, the tax law attempts to ensure that the discount is treated as interest income and is normally reported currently. Special provisions have been introduced over the years to clarify the reporting of the discount income as well as to prohibit taxpayers from converting the discount income into capital gain.

Example 35

During 2015, T purchased a $10,000, 8% corporate bond for $8,000, or a $2,000 discount. In 2017 the bond matured and the taxpayer redeemed the bond for its par value of $10,000. The redemption is treated as an exchange, and the taxpayer recognizes a long-term capital gain of $2,000 ($10,000 redemption price − $8,000 basis). In this case, the taxpayer has converted the discount of $2,000, which from an economic view is ordinary interest income, to capital gain. Moreover, the taxpayer has deferred the reporting of such income from the time it accrues to the time the bond is sold. To eliminate this opportunity, the discount generally must be amortized and included in gross income as it accrues. These rules are discussed in greater detail in Chapter 16.

The tax treatment of discount depends in part on when it arises. The discount often occurs at the time the instrument is issued. For example, certain instruments such as U.S. Savings Bonds, Treasury bills, and so-called zero coupon bonds do not bear interest and are usually *issued* at discounts. Other debt obligations that do bear interest (such as corporate bonds) also may be issued at a discount, usually if the coupon rate is set lower than the current rate. Discount could also result after the instrument is issued. For example, where interest-bearing instruments are issued at par, discount may arise upon a subsequent purchase. The specific treatment of discount is examined below.

Non-Interest-Bearing Obligations Issued at a Discount

Buy bonds America! Over the years, this has been a familiar cry of the federal government when it needs public support or simply wants to encourage investment. There have been Liberty Bonds, War Bonds, Build America Bonds, and perhaps the most familiar, Savings Bonds. Does the interest from these bonds receive any special tax treatment? When is the interest income reported?

The Code provides special rules for non-interest-bearing obligations that are issued at a discount and redeemable for a fixed amount that increases over time. The instruments to which these rules would normally apply are Series E and EE U.S. Savings Bonds. Series E Bonds were issued between 1941 and 1980, having maturities up to 40 years. Beginning in 1980, these bonds were replaced by Series EE Bonds. Beginning in 2001, Series EE Bonds are inscribed with the special legend "Patriot Bonds" inspired by the tragedy of September 11, 2001. Series EE bonds earn 90% of five-year Treasury security yields. Bonds issued before May 2005 do not pay interest but were sold at a discount (half their face value). Bonds issued in May 2005 or later are issued at face value. Currently, the bonds are available in denominations ranging from $50 through $10,000. They generally have maturities of 30 years. The bonds are normally redeemable at any time up until the final maturity date at a price that increases with the passage of time. No interest payments are made while the bond is held. For bonds issued before May 2005, the holder's interest income is represented by the difference between the redemption price and purchase price. For bonds issued after April 2005, interest is simply added to the bond every month. Note, however, that Series EE savings bonds stop increasing in value after 20 years. Bonds issued after May 1, 2005 have a fixed rate of interest. The interest rates are revised each year in May and again in November. For example, for bonds issued in November 2016 through April 2017, the rate was 0.1%.

Interest on Series EE savings bonds is fully taxable for federal income tax purposes. However, the interest income is exempt from state income tax. Obviously, this is an important factor in determining the potential return on an investment in these bonds.

As far as when the income is reported, there are two options. Taxpayers may elect to include in income the annual increase in the redemption price of the bond.[84] In essence, this election allows a cash basis taxpayer to use the accrual method with respect to these bonds. If income is not reported on an annual basis, the taxpayer reports the entire difference between the redemption and issue prices as income when the bond is redeemed.

---

[84] § 454(a).

Example 36

S purchased Series EE Bonds with a face value of $10,000 at a cost of $8,000. The redemption price of the bonds increases during the year by $100. If S elects to report the income annually, she will include $100 in her gross income each year. Alternatively, S could wait until she redeems the bond to report the income. For example, if S later redeemed the bonds for $9,500, she would report $1,500 income (the difference between the redemption price of $9,500 and her cost of $8,000) at the time of redemption.

If S chooses not to report the income and later dies, an individual who inherits the bonds has several options: (1) hold the bond and continue to receive interest until the bond matures or (2) cash in the bond and report any income that may have been accrued while the holder was alive. It is not unusual for an heir to cash in the bonds and then be shocked by the fact that an income tax is due (after he or she spends the inheritance)!

The taxpayer may make the election to report the interest annually at any time. When the election is made, all interest previously deferred on all Series E and EE Bonds must be reported. This procedure effectively allows the taxpayer to choose the year in which the interest income is to be reported. However, once the election is made, it applies to *all* Series E and EE Bonds subsequently acquired. Should the taxpayer desire to change to reporting the income at redemption, consent from the IRS is required.[85]

As discussed in Chapter 6, certain taxpayers who cash in Series EE Bonds and use the proceeds for educational expenses may be able to exclude the interest.

Government Obligations

Special rules also govern the treatment of the discount arising upon the purchase of short-term government obligations such as Treasury bills.[86] Typically, a taxpayer purchases a short-term Treasury bill at a discount and redeems it for par value shortly thereafter. In this instance, Code § 454(b) applies to cash basis taxpayers to ensure that the gain on the redemption—in effect, the discount—is treated as ordinary interest income. Specifically, any gain realized by cash basis taxpayers from the sale or redemption of non-interest-bearing obligations issued by governmental units that have a fixed maturity date that is one year or less from the date of issue is always ordinary income. This ordinary income is reported *in the year* of sale or redemption. In contrast, accrual basis taxpayers are required to amortize the discount (i.e., include it in income) on a *daily* basis under Code § 1281(a).

Example 37

On December 1, 2016, B, a cash basis calendar year taxpayer, purchased a $10,000 non-interest-bearing Treasury bill. She purchased the bill at 97 ($9,700) and redeemed the bill on March 1, 2017 at par. B recognizes a $300 gain ($10,000 − $9,700) on the redemption, and the entire gain is treated as ordinary income in 2017. The same result would occur if B had *sold* the Treasury bill for $10,000 on January 15, 2017. Note that if B were an accrual basis taxpayer, the $300 discount would have been included in income on a daily basis. Consequently, a portion of the income would be reported in 2016 and the remainder in 2017.

Original Issue Discount

When interest-bearing obligations such as corporate bonds are *issued* at a discount, a complex set of provisions operates to prevent taxpayers from not only deferring the discount income but also converting it to capital gain as depicted in *Example 35*. These rules apply only to discount that arises when the bonds are originally issued. This discount is technically referred to as *original issue discount* (OID) and is determined as follows:

---

[85] As of September 1, 2004, investors are no longer able to exchange EE/E bonds for HH bonds.

[86] Special rules also apply to Treasury Inflation-Protection Bonds (TIPs) and Treasury Inflation-Indexed Securities.

Redemption price	$x,xxx
− Issue price	− xxx
= Original issue discount	$x,xxx

The thrust of the provisions is to require the holder of the bond to amortize the discount into income during the period the bond is held. A complete discussion of the treatment of OID is provided in Chapter 16.

 ## CHECK YOUR KNOWLEDGE

Review Question 1

For financial accounting purposes, prepaid income is generally reported as it is earned. Does the same treatment apply for tax purposes? Explain the treatment of prepaid interest, rents, royalties, services, and advance payments for goods.

As a general rule, prepaid income must be reported when received. This is obviously true for cash basis taxpayers and surprisingly true for accrual basis taxpayers. The unusual treatment for accrual basis taxpayers stems from the claim of right doctrine, which requires recognition of income whenever the amount has been received and the taxpayer does not recognize an obligation to repay. This treatment applies to prepaid interest, rents, and royalties. It does not apply to prepaid service income (including prepaid rents if the property's use is secondary to the services provided) where the reporting follows that for books in the first year with the balance reported in the second year. It also does not apply to advance payments for goods, which are normally reported in the same manner as they are for financial accounting purposes (the normal accrual method).

A close look at the reporting requirements for prepaid income reveals that cash basis taxpayers report prepaid income when it is received and this approach is consistent with the cash method of accounting. In contrast, accrual basis taxpayers report—subject to certain exceptions—prepaid income as if they were on the cash basis. The table below summarizes the law's schizophrenic approach to prepaid income and—as seen in Chapter 7—prepaid expenses.

	Prepaid Income	Prepaid Expenses
Cash basis taxpayer	Report in year received *Consistent with cash method*	Deduct over appropriate period *Treat as if on accrual basis*
Accrual basis taxpayer	Report in year received *Treated as if on cash basis*	Deducted over appropriate period *Consistent with accrual method*

Review Question 2

After the changes made during the 1980s, some commentators pronounced the use of the completed contract method dead. Is this true? Are there any circumstances under which the completed contract method can be used?

The completed contract may be dead for large construction companies that build mammoth projects such as airplanes, stadiums, dams, office towers, and the like. But it is alive and well for the majority of construction companies. The completed contract method may be used by any home builder (regardless of size) and small construction companies (those with average annual gross receipts of less than $10 million).

Review Question 3

During the autumn of 1986, it became clear that the Reagan administration and Congress planned to cut tax rates from a top rate of 50% to something around 28 percent. As a result, the papers and financial press were filled with planning ideas. Some advisers suggested that people who had cash sitting in money market accounts should buy Treasury bills. Why?

An investment in Treasury bills allows the taxpayer to defer the interest until the bonds are redeemed. Consequently, many advisers suggested purchasing Treasury bills at a discount during the fall of 1986 with the idea of redeeming them when income tax rates dropped in 1987.

Identification of the Taxpayer

LO.6

Identify which taxpayer is responsible for reporting income and paying the taxes on such income.

A final consideration in the taxation of income concerns identification of the taxpayer to whom the income is taxed. Generally, this is not a mind-boggling task. The person who receives the income usually must pay the tax. As discussed below, however, receipt or non-receipt of income does not always govern who must report it.

INCOME FROM PERSONAL SERVICES

In the famous case of *Lucas v. Earl,* the Supreme Court was required to determine whether Mr. Earl was taxable on earnings from personal services despite a legally enforceable agreement made with his wife in 1901 that the earnings would be shared equally.[87] At the time of this decision, such agreements effectively split income between a husband and wife; this resulted in a reduced tax liability since each individual was treated as a separate taxable entity and a progressive income tax rate structure existed. The Court eliminated the usefulness of this technique, however, by holding that the income is taxable to the taxpayer who earns it. Thus, anticipatory assignments of income that one has a *right* to receive are an ineffective device to escape taxation. In explaining what has become the assignment of income doctrine, the Court gave birth to the well-known *fruit of the tree* metaphor. According to Justice Holmes, the fruit (income) must be attributed to the tree from which it grew (Mr. Earl's services).

Section 73 directly addresses the treatment of a child's earnings. This provision indicates that amounts received for the services of a child are included in the *child's* gross income. Thus, a parent or a guardian who collects income earned by a child would not report the income; rather the income would be reported by the child since he or she earned it. As discussed in Chapter 4, however, the *unearned* income of a child under age 19 (or under age 24, if a full-time student) may be reported on his or her parents' tax return and taxed at the parents' rates.

INCOME FROM PROPERTY

The assignment of income doctrine also applies when income from property is received. Under this rule, income from property is included in the gross income of the taxpayer who owns the property. This principle was derived from another famous case, *Helvering v. Horst.*[88] In this case, Mr. Horst clipped the interest coupons from bonds he owned and gave them to his son, who later collected them. The Supreme Court held Mr. Horst taxable since he owned and controlled the source of income (i.e., the bonds). Accordingly, income from property can be effectively assigned only if the taxpayer relinquishes ownership of the property.

UNEARNED INCOME OF CHILDREN

Perhaps the most fundamental principle in tax planning concerns minimizing the marginal tax rate that applies to the taxpayer's income. The significance of this principle is easily understood when one realizes that Federal marginal tax rates have at times exceeded 90 percent. Although the current disparity between the top and bottom rates, 29.6% (39.6% − 10%), is not as great as in some years, the potential for significant tax savings still exists.

Minimizing the tax rate is normally accomplished by shifting income to a lower bracket taxpayer. As discussed above, the assignment of income doctrine makes it virtually impossible for taxpayers to shift income arising from services. Opportunities do exist, however, for shifting income through transfers of property. The most popular technique in this regard has traditionally involved transferring income-producing property to a child. In this manner, not only is the tax rate applying to the income reduced, but the income also stays within the family unit, normally to be used as the parent directs.

As part of the tax overhaul in 1986, Congress took steps to reduce tax avoidance opportunities available through income shifting to a child. This was accomplished by enacting a special provision affectionately referred to as the "kiddie" tax.[89] The thrust of this rule—as

---

[87] 2 USTC ¶496, 8 AFTR 10,287, 281 U.S. 111 (USSC, 1930).

[88] 40-2 USTC ¶9787, 24 AFTR 1058, 311 U.S. 112 (USSC, 1940).

[89] § 1(i).

explained in Chapter 4—is to tax the *unearned* income of a child under the age of 19 (or less than 24 if a full-time student) as if it were the parents' income and thus at the parents' rates. By limiting the tax to unearned rather than earned income, Congress was taking direct aim at parents and others who shifted income by making gifts of property. Accordingly, shifting techniques based on gifts of property such as bonds and rental property that produce unearned income (e.g., interest and rents) are now severely limited.

INTEREST-FREE AND BELOW-MARKET LOANS

To be successful in shifting income to another, the assignment of income doctrine generally requires that the taxpayer transfer the income-producing property itself, not merely the income from the property. Thus, shifting income requires a completed gift of the property. Taxpayers, however, are understandably reluctant to forever relinquish ownership and control of the property. For this reason, taxpayers have attempted to design techniques that enable them to retain ownership of the property yet shift income.

Prior to 1984, a popular method of shifting income from one family member to another, or from a corporation to its shareholders (or employees), used interest-free loans. Under the typical arrangement, a father who was in the 50% tax bracket would make a loan to his son who was in a far lower bracket. Upon receipt of the loan, the son would invest the funds. As a result, any income earned on the investment would be taxed to the son at a lower rate than would have been paid had the father received the income directly. This arrangement could secure substantial tax savings, particularly if there was a great disparity between the tax rates of the two family members.

The success of this tax-saving technique was attributable to the terms of the loan agreement. These terms required the son to repay the loan on demand *without interest.* Had the father charged interest, he would still have income attributable to the amount loaned, and no income shifting would have occurred. By not charging interest, however, the interest income that the father would have earned was successfully shifted to the son and tax savings resulted. In addition, the interest that was not charged, a valuable benefit for the son, was not considered a taxable gift. Moreover, this arrangement was extremely appealing because it did not require the father to part with the property forever. Since he had only loaned the funds to his son, he could demand repayment of the funds at any time.

The IRS viewed interest-free loans as a tax avoidance device designed to circumvent the assignment of income rules. After much controversy, Congress eliminated this opportunity in 1984 by enacting Code § 7872, which imputes interest income to the lender where the actual interest is considered inadequate.

Treatment of Below-Market Loans

In general, § 7872 applies to loans when the interest charged is below the current market rate of interest. As pictured below, when such a loan is made, the treatment is determined *assuming* that the borrower pays the "foregone interest" to the lender at the market rate, which the lender is then deemed to transfer back to the borrower:[90]

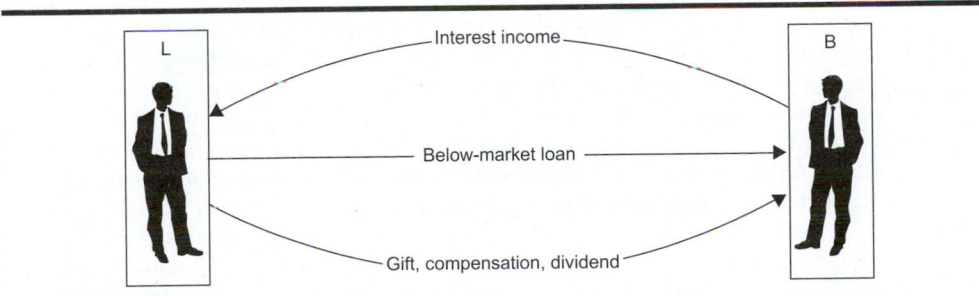

This hypothetical scenario results in the following tax consequences:

1. The borrower may be allowed a deduction for the interest hypothetically paid to the lender, while the lender reports the fictitious payment as *interest income.*

---

[90] See § 7872(e)(2) for definition of foregone interest.

2. The lender treats the hypothetical payment to the borrower as either compensation, dividend, or gift depending on the nature of the loan. The borrower treats the payment as either compensation, dividend, or gift as the case may be. In determining the character of the lender's hypothetical payment, the Code classifies loans into three types based on the relationship between the lender and the borrower.

- *Gift loans*—those where the forgone interest is in the nature of a gift;
- *Compensation-related loans*—those made by an employer to an employee or an independent contractor; and
- *Corporation-shareholder loans*—those made by a corporation to a shareholder.[91]

The thrust of these rules is to treat the borrower as having paid the foregone interest, which is funded by the lender through compensation, dividends, or gift.

Example 38

Lender L loaned $500,000 to Borrower B payable on demand without interest. Assume the foregone interest is $15,000. Thus, the interest hypothetically paid by B and which must be imputed to L is $15,000. The following table shows the effect on L and B, assuming the loan is

1. A gift loan.
2. A compensation-related loan.
3. A corporation-shareholder loan.

	Lender L				Borrower B			
	Interest Income	Gift Made	Comp. Expense	Dividend Paid	Interest Expense	Gift Received	Comp. Income	Dividend Received
(1)	$15,000	$15,000			$(15,000)	$(15,000)		
(2)	15,000		$(15,000)		(15,000)		$15,000	
(3)	15,000			$15,000	(15,000)			$15,000

The first situation reveals the effects where the interest forgone by the lender is considered a gift (e.g., loans between family members). In this case, income shifting is prohibited since L does not avoid taxation on the income from the loan. Rather, he or she is deemed to receive an interest payment from B on the amount loaned. In addition, L is treated as having made a taxable gift to B of $1,000 ($15,000 gift – $14,000 annual exclusion in 2017). On the other hand, B is entitled to exclude the $15,000 gift from income. B's hypothetical interest payment may or may not be deductible, depending on whether it is treated as investment interest, business interest, or personal interest (see Chapter 11 for a discussion of interest).

The second situation assumes that the loan is made by an employer to an employee, and, thus, the hypothetical payment by the lender is considered compensation. In this case, the lender is treated as having received interest income that is offset by a deduction for compensation expense to B. Note, however, that if B is an employee, L would be responsible for employment taxes and withholding. The effect on the borrower, B, depends on whether the hypothetical interest payment is deductible. If so, there generally will be no effect since such deduction offsets B's compensation income.

The third situation demonstrates the undesirable consequences that a corporation encounters when its deemed payment is considered a dividend rather than compensation. This problem would normally arise where the loan is made to an individual who is both a shareholder and an employee of the corporation. In this situation, like the second situation above, L (a corporation) has income from the deemed payment. In contrast to the second situation, however, L receives no offsetting deduction since dividend payments are not deductible. The effect on B again depends on whether the hypothetical interest is deductible.

---

[91] In this regard, Prop. Reg. § 1.7872-4(d)(2) indicates that a payment to a shareholder-employee is presumed to be a dividend if the corporation is (1) closely held and such person owns more than 5% of its stock, or (2) publicly held and such person owns one-half of 1% of the stock.

These provisions govern not only the treatment of gift, compensation-related, and corporate shareholder loans, but also any other type of below-market loan designed to achieve tax avoidance or affect the tax liability of the lender or the borrower.

Example 39

During the year, J joined a country club. The club requires each member to loan the club $10,000 without interest. Assuming interest rates are currently 8 percent, the club is effectively receiving annual dues of $800 from each member. More important from the member's standpoint, the dues are paid with tax-free dollars.

Had J received the $800 directly, she would be required to pay taxes. By making the loan to the club, she has effectively converted taxable income to tax-exempt income. Under Code § 7872, however, this arrangement would not be effective since J would be treated as having received the $800 income and would have no offsetting deduction for the payment to the club.

Exempt Loans

To restrict the application of § 7872 to predominantly abusive situations, Congress carved out several exceptions to the rules described above. Under the first exception, § 7872 does not apply to *gift* loans as long as the loans outstanding during the year do not exceed $10,000 *and* the borrower does not use the loan proceeds to purchase or carry income-producing assets. Without this latter requirement, income of small amounts could still be shifted. The effect of this provision is to exempt small loans where income shifting is absent.

Congress also granted compensation-related and corporation-shareholder loans an exemption from the onerous rules of § 7872 if they do not exceed $10,000. The exemption does not apply to these loans, however, if tax avoidance is one of the principal purposes of the loan.

Interest Income Cap

Another special rule imposes a limit on the amount of imputed interest income for loans between individuals. Generally, if the amount of outstanding loans does not exceed $100,000 and their principal purpose is not tax avoidance, the deemed interest payment by the borrower to the lender is limited to the borrower's investment income. This rule follows from the theory that the amount of income shifted by the lender is limited to that which the borrower actually earns. In addition, to enable loans where tax avoidance is obviously not a motive, the lender is treated as having no imputed interest income if the borrower's investment income does not exceed $1,000. However, the lender is still deemed to have made a gift of the forgone interest.

Example 40

L has a son, B, who earns a salary and has $800 investment income. During the year, L loaned B $90,000 without interest to purchase a home. Interest imputed at the IRS rate is $15,000. L has no imputed interest income since the loan is less than $100,000 and investment income is less than $1,000. However, L is charged with a taxable gift of $1,000 ($15,000 – $14,000 exclusion (2017)). Note that if B had $7,000 of investment income, L also would have been charged with interest income of $7,000.

Loans to Qualified Continuing Care Facility

Older individuals who must enter a continuing care facility may be required to make an interest free or below-market-rate loan to the facility as a condition of admission. Absent any special rule, the § 7872 requirement to impute interest would saddle these individuals with taxable interest income without cash. Section 7872(g) creates an important exception, exempting loans made to "qualified continuing care facilities" if the contractual provisions meet certain requirements.

INCOME FROM COMMUNITY PROPERTY

In the United States, the rights that married individuals hold in property are determined using either the common law or community property system. The community property system developed in continental Europe and was adopted in several states having a French or Spanish origin. The ten states currently recognizing the community property system are Alaska, Arizona, California, Idaho, Louisiana, Nevada, New Mexico, Texas, Washington, and Wisconsin. However, Alaska is an opt-in community property state; that is, the property is considered separate property unless a couple agrees to treat it as community property. The remaining 40 states use the common law system, which originated in England.

The community property system categorizes property into two types: separate property, which is considered belonging separately to one of the spouses, and community property, which is considered owned equally by each spouse. In general, separate property consists only of those assets owned before marriage or acquired by gift or inheritance while married. All property acquired during a marriage except by gift or inheritance is community property.

Income from separate property may be community property or separate property depending on the state of jurisdiction. In Texas, Louisiana, and Idaho, income from separate property is community property. Accordingly, for Federal tax purposes each spouse is responsible for one-half of the income. In the other seven states, income from separate property is separate property and must be reported by the person owning the property. Income from personal services is generally treated as belonging to the community. The following example illustrates how these differing rules must be taken into account.

Example 41

A husband and wife elect to file separate returns. The husband received a $30,000 salary and $1,000 of dividends on stock he had purchased prior to the couple's marriage. The husband also receives $500 of taxable interest from a certificate of deposit that he had purchased in his own name while married. The wife's income would vary depending on the state in which she lived:

	Texas	Arizona	Common Law States
Salary	$15,000	$15,000	$0
Dividends	500	0	0
Interest	250	250	0
Wife's income	$15,750	$15,250	$0

Community Income Where Spouses Live Apart

The treatment of community income can create financial problems, particularly where spouses live apart during the year and are later divorced before the end of the taxable year. For example, consider R and S, who were married but lived apart during the first half of the year before their divorce became final. Under these circumstances, the property settlement should consider the accrued tax liability that arises due to any community income. Accounting for the liability may be difficult or impossible, however, if one of the spouses has abandoned the other. In such cases, the abandoned spouse becomes liable for the tax on income earned by a spouse who cannot be located to share the financial responsibility. To eliminate these difficulties, special provisions were enacted.

Section 66 provides that a spouse will be taxed only on the earnings attributed to his or her personal services if during the year the following requirements are satisfied:

1. The two married individuals live apart at all times.
2. The couple does not file a joint return with each other.
3. No portion of the earned income is transferred between the spouses.

This rule only applies to income from personal services and not income from property.

Example 42

M and N, residents of Texas, decided in November 2015 to obtain a divorce, which became final on March 31, 2017. N earns $2,000 each month and M is unemployed. N has a savings account that yielded $200 of taxable interest during the first three months of 2017. Assuming the two live apart during all of 2017 and none of the earned income is transferred between them, N will report all of the $6,000 ($2,000 × 3) attributable to her personal services and $100 of the interest. M will report his $100 share of the taxable interest.

 CHECK YOUR KNOWLEDGE

Review Question 1

In 1960 18-year-old Randy Hundley signed a contract to play baseball for the Chicago Cubs.[92] The contract provided for a bonus of $110,000 (a grand sum in those days) to be paid over a five-year period at a rate of $22,000 per year: $11,000 to Randy and $11,000 to his father, Cecil. The payment to Randy's father was pursuant to an oral agreement the two had made when Randy was 16. According to the agreement, Cecil, a former semiprofessional baseball player and coach, acted as Randy's coach and business manager in exchange for 50% of any bonus that Randy might receive if he should obtain a baseball contract.

At about the same time that the Cubs were striking a deal with Hundley, the Philadelphia Phillies reached an agreement with Richie Allen, another future star.[93] According to this arrangement, Allen was to receive a $70,000 bonus: $30,000 paid to him over five years and $40,000 paid to his mother. How should the bonuses be treated? Should they both be treated the same?

The question in both cases is whether the child has effectively split the income between himself and his parent or merely made an anticipatory assignment of income. If the latter is true, all of the income would be taxed to the child and none to the parent. In both cases, the IRS argued that the payment to Randy's father and Richie's mother should be treated as being first made to the child and then followed by a nondeductible gift. Despite the similarity of the cases, the Court believed that the services provided by Hundley's father were instrumental in his son's success, whereas Allen's mother made no tangible contribution. As a result, Hundley was allowed to deduct the payment to his father as a business expense and, therefore, split the income between them. In contrast, no deduction was allowed to Allen and he was required to pay taxes on the entire bonus.

Review Question 2

M wants to shift income to her 19-year-old daughter (who is not a student) so that it will be taxed at the daughter's 10% rate rather than at M's 39.6% rate. M plans on loaning her daughter $10,000 interest-free for this purpose. Will her plan to shift income to the daughter work?

As a general rule, interest-free loans can no longer be used successfully to shift income, since interest income must be imputed to the lender. In this case, M would be treated as having received an interest payment from her daughter, thus defeating the entire plan. At first blush, some might believe that because the loan is less than $10,000, the de minimis rule operates and M is not required to impute interest; this is a typical misconception. It is true that imputation is not required if the loan is less than $10,000, but only if the borrower does not invest the loan amount in income-producing property. Of course, if the borrower does not invest in income-producing property there is no income and nothing is shifted. Therefore, the $10,000 de minimis rule does not create any opportunity. In this particular case, the $100,000 rule also would come into play. This exception provides that the maximum amount of interest to be imputed to the lender is equal to the net investment income of the borrower (zero, if net investment income is less than $1,000). This provision does provide a small opportunity.

[92] *Cecil Randolph Hundley, Jr.*, 48 T.C. 339 (1967).   [93] *Richard A. Allen*, 50 T.C. 466 (1968).

If the daughter invests the $10,000 to produce $900 of interest income, no income would be imputed to M and $900 would be successfully shifted. M would be treated as having made a gift of $900 to her daughter, but there would be no gift tax because of the annual exclusion of $14,000 in 2017.

Tax Planning

TIMING INCOME RECOGNITION

The proper timing of income recognition can reap great benefits for the taxpayer. As a general rule, postponement of income recognition is wise since the tax on such income is deferred. The major advantage of tax deferral is that the taxpayer has continued use of the real funds that otherwise would have been used to pay taxes. Deferral of the tax is in essence an interest-free loan from the government.

When considering deferral, attention must be given to the marginal tax rates that may apply to the income. For example, taxpayers often postpone income until their retirement years, when they are usually in a lower tax bracket. Although deferral may be wise in this situation, it may be unwise where tax rates rise by operation of law or because of the taxpayer's increase in earnings. Ideally, the taxpayer should attempt to level out taxable income from one year to the next and equalize the tax rate that applies annually (to avoid the situation of R in *Example 11* and duplicate that of S).

The opportunities for most individuals to postpone income are limited, in part due to the constructive receipt doctrine. Techniques do exist, however:

1. Installment sales of property enable the taxpayer not only to avoid the bunching of income in a single year but also to defer the tax.

2. Income on Series E and EE bonds, Treasury bills, and certain certificates of deposit may be deferred until they are redeemed.

3. Investments in Individual Retirement Accounts (IRAs), Keogh plans, and qualified retirement plans are all made with before-tax dollars (since these contributions are deductible), and earnings on these investments are not taxed until they are withdrawn.

4. Deferred compensation arrangements may be suitable, as in the case of a professional athlete, celebrity, or executive. (See Chapter 18.)

INCOME-SPLITTING TECHNIQUES

As stressed earlier, the most fundamental rule in tax planning concerns minimizing the marginal tax rate that applies to the taxpayer's income. Minimizing the applicable rate is usually accomplished through use of some type of income splitting or shifting technique.

Example 43

Mr. and Mrs. J pay taxes at a rate of 35% in 2017. The couple helps support Mr. J's 67-year-old retired mother, M, by giving her $5,000 annually. Such gifts do not entitle the couple to claim M as a dependent. In providing M's support through gifts, the couple is using after-tax dollars. That is, the couple would have to earn $7,692 to provide M with $5,000 in support [$7,692 − (35% of $7,692) = $5,000]. Instead, the couple could transfer income-producing property to M to provide the needed support. By so doing, the income would not be subject to tax because M could utilize her own exemption and standard deduction. In 2017, M may claim an exemption deduction of $4,050 and a standard deduction of $7,900 ($6,350 regular + $1,550 addition for unmarried 65 years of age or over) for total deductions of $11,950. Providing support in this manner would be far less expensive than making outright gifts of $5,000 annually. Although this arrangement requires the couple to give up the property permanently (since any type of reversionary interest would cause the income to be taxed back to the couple), in many family situations, M would probably give the property back when she no longer needs it or when she dies. In addition, other techniques are available that can circumvent the problem of permanently departing with the property.

The above example illustrates how income can be shifted successfully. However, when income is to be shifted to children, the taxpayer must contend with the "kiddie" tax.

The "kiddie" tax clearly limits opportunities for shifting unearned income to children. However, it does not eliminate them. Recall that the "kiddie" tax generally applies to children less than 19 or those that are full-time students less than 24. However, the "kiddie" tax does not apply until unearned income exceeds $2,100 (in 2017). Consequently, for a child subject to the kiddie tax, the first $1,050 of unearned income bears no tax because of the standard deduction, and the next $1,050 is taxed at the child's rates. Although the "kiddie" tax severely curtails the amount of tax that could otherwise be saved through shifting income to children, taxpayers attempting to shift modest amounts of income are not affected.

For taxpayers wanting to shift more unearned income to their children, other techniques are available. One way of coping with the "kiddie" tax is by making investments with income that is deferred until the child is no longer subject to the tax. For example, the taxpayer could give a child Series EE savings bonds. The income from these bonds can be deferred by not electing to report the accumulated interest until after the child has turned 24 (or 19 if he or she is not a student). Interest thereafter would be reported annually. Similarly, discount bonds—those *without* original issue discount—could be purchased. In this case, the interest is not reported until the bond is sold.

The "kiddie" tax applies to unearned income and not earned income. As a result, earned income can be successfully shifted by paying the child for performing some task. Of course, shifting does not occur unless the payment is deductible by the parent. Such payments, when made by a parent directly to a child under 18, have the added benefit of not being subject to Social Security taxes.

EXCLUDED ECONOMIC INCOME

In arranging one's affairs, it should be observed that certain "economic" income does not fall within the definition of income for tax purposes and thus can be obtained tax-free.

Example 44

R inherited $100,000 that she plans to invest in either a condominium or corporate stocks. The condominium in which she is interested is the one in which she currently lives and rents for $9,000 annually. In lieu of buying the condominium, she could continue to rent and invest the $100,000 in preferred stocks paying dividends of 10% annually, or $10,000 of income per year. Assume R pays taxes on the dividends at a marginal rate of 15 percent. The return after taxes on the preferred stock will be 8.5 percent, or $8,500. The return from the investment in the condominium is represented by the rent that she does not pay of $9,000, that is nontaxable. In effect, the condominium pays a dividend-in-kind (i.e., shelter) that is tax-exempt. Thus, R would obtain a higher yield on her investment by purchasing the condominium. Note that income for tax purposes does not include the value of the condominium which would be considered income in the economic sense because the use of the condominium's shelter represents consumption. This same type of analysis applies to all types of investments in consumer goods that provide long term benefits, such as washers and refrigerators.

DISCUSSION QUESTIONS

5-1 *Economic versus Tax Concept of Income.* It has been said that the income tax discriminates against the person who lives in a rented home as compared with the person who owns his or her own residence. Comment on the truth of this assertion and why such discrimination may or may not be justified.

5-2 *Net Worth Method.* Explain the circumstances in which the economist's approach to measuring income might be used for tax purposes and what specific steps might be taken to implement such an approach.

5-3 *What Is Income?* Listed below are several items that may or may not constitute income for purposes of economics and income taxes. Indicate whether each item would be considered income for each of these purposes, including comments on why differences, if any, might exist.

   a. Beef raised and consumed by a cattle rancher.

   b. Interest received on state or local bonds.

   c. Air transportation provided by an airline to one of its flight attendants.

   d. Appreciation of XRY stock from $1,000 to $6,000 during the year.

   e. Proceeds collected from an insurance company for a casualty loss and reinvested in similar property.

   f. A loan obtained from a friend.

   g. $105 received from sale of stock purchased one year ago for $100; inflation during the past year averaged five percent.

   h. A gift received as a Christmas present.

5-4 *Cash Equivalent Doctrine.* A financial newsletter recently reported the many advantages that may be obtained from belonging to a barter club or organization. Would tax benefits be included among these advantages (e.g., no taxable income realized on the exchange of services)?

5-5 *Return of Capital Doctrine—General.* Explain the return of capital doctrine and discuss three situations in which the doctrine operates.

5-6 *Indirect Benefits.* A, an assistant manager for a department store, often is required to work overtime to help mark down merchandise for special sales. On these occasions, her employer pays the cost of her evening meal. Does the meal constitute income? Explain.

5-7 *Annual Accounting Period-Planning.* Briefly explain the notion of "income bunching" and why it is a problem.

5-8 *52-53 Week Year.* At first glance, it may appear that the "52-53 week" taxable year is one of those accounting practices that has no real world application. Using the Internet, determine if any well-known company uses the 52-53 week accounting period as its taxable year.

5-9 *Relationship between Tax and Financial Accounting Methods.* Does conformity with generally accepted accounting principles satisfy the requirement of § 446(c) that income must be clearly reflected? Explain, including some illustrations where income for tax purposes will differ from that for financial accounting purposes.

5-10 *Cash Basis Taxpayer's Receipt of Notes.* Does a cash basis taxpayer recognize income when a note is received or when collections are made?

5-11 *Constructive Receipt Doctrine.* Discuss the planning opportunities related to the cash method of accounting and how these are affected by the constructive receipt doctrine.

5-12 *Accrual Method of Accounting.* Address the following questions:

   a. When does a taxpayer using the accrual method of accounting normally report income?

   b. Under what circumstances is an accrual basis taxpayer treated like a cash basis taxpayer for purposes of reporting income?

5-13 *Change in Accounting Method.* T Corporation is considering altering the way in which it accounts for a particular item.
  a. If T wishes to make the change, how should it proceed?
  b. Explain the § 481 adjustment and how T must account for it.

5-14 *Changing Accounting Methods: Procedures.* F files the tax returns for his three-year-old son, S. Up until this year, F had always reported the interest on S's Series EE savings bonds annually. F now wishes to report the interest income when the bonds are redeemed (e.g., when the child reaches age 18). Can F change the way he reports the interest? If so, how?

5-15 *What Is an Accounting Method?* This year, T hired a new accountant, A. As part of A's routine review procedures, A determined that T's previous accountant had improperly computed the gross profit percentage to be used in recognizing income on an installment sale. Based on the previous accountant's calculation, 40% of each year's receipts were to be included in income, whereas according to A's calculation the proper percentage was 50 percent. Explain what A should do upon finding the discrepancy.

5-16 *Claim of Right.* Consider the questions below.
  a. Is the application of the claim of right doctrine limited to situations that involve only contested income? Explain.
  b. Explain the difference between the claim of right and constructive receipt doctrines.

5-17 *Prepaid Rent.* In light of the tax treatment, if landlords of apartment complexes had a choice, should they characterize an initial $500 payment from their tenants as a security deposit or as a payment of the last month's rent in advance? Explain.

5-18 *Prepaid Services.* Identify several types of services where the accrual basis provider will not be permitted to defer any prepayments of income related to such services. Explain.

5-19 *Long-Term Contracts.* Indicate which method of accounting for long-term contracts—completed contract or percentage of completion—the taxpayer may use in the following situations. Assume each contract is considered a long-term contract unless otherwise implied.
  a. A contract to build an office building. The taxpayer's annual gross receipts for the past five years have exceeded $11 million.
  b. A contract to build a home to be finished next year. The taxpayer's annual gross receipts for the last five years have exceeded $11 million.
  c. A contract to build a high-rise apartment complex containing 135 units. The contractor's average gross receipts are $11 million.
  d. A contract to manufacture 15,000 seats for a football stadium. The taxpayer has several contracts for this type of seat. Average gross receipts are $12 million.
  e. A contract to manufacture a special part for NASA's space shuttles. Average annual gross receipts were $12 million.

5-20 *Taxpayer Identification—Family Trusts.* In recent years, many taxpayers have fallen victim to vendors of the so-called family trust tax shelter. Under this arrangement the taxpayer signs a contractual agreement entitling the trust to all of the taxpayer's income which is subsequently distributed to the beneficiaries of the trust. Explain how this arrangement is supposed to save taxes and why it fails.

5-21 *Income Reporting by Partnerships and S Corporations.* Absent special rules, explain how partners and shareholders in S corporations might defer the reporting of income by having their respective entities select fiscal years for reporting rather than calendar years.

5-22 *Income from Community Property.* Under what circumstances will knowledge of the community property system be relevant? Is it necessary for persons residing in common law states to understand the community property system?

5-23 *Planning—Timing Income Recognition.* Although it is generally desirable to defer income recognition and the related taxes. when would acceleration of income be preferred?

5-24 *Planning—Income Splitting.* How might R, who operates a shoe store as a sole proprietorship, reduce the taxes that are imposed on his family using income-splitting techniques?

5-25 *"Kiddie" Tax.* R has been advised that due to changes in the tax law over the years he can no longer save taxes by shifting income to his children.
   a. Explain the origin of such advice.
   b. What techniques currently exist to shift income successfully to children and other low-bracket family members?

YOU MAKE THE CALL

5-26 In the last episode in the adventures of Dr. Will Floss, the tax-evading dentist identified earlier in this chapter, he was found exploring the cavities of his patient's mouth. As may be remembered, Dr. Floss had just made a deal with a patient whereby he exchanged a root canal for some carpet complete with pad and installation. Floss's accountant, Al, was faced with a dilemma. After dumping his records on Al's desk, Floss had proudly proclaimed that it was another great year. Al could remember his exact words: "Made over $250,000 but reported only $100,000. Not bad," said Floss. "Am I glad I talked to Dr. Moller!" Unfortunately, Al had to lower the boom on Floss's plan, explaining to him that he was required to report his barter income. However, Floss has stated flatly that he will not report the income. "If Moller doesn't report his, I'm not reporting mine," insists Floss. What should Al the accountant do about his client Floss and his friend Moller? If Floss goes to another accountant, does Al have any responsibilities?

PROBLEMS

5-27 *What Is Income?* In each of the following situations indicate whether taxable income should be recognized.
   a. Q purchased an older home for $30,000. Shortly after its purchase, the area in which it was located was designated a historical neighborhood, causing its value to rise to $50,000.
   b. R, a long-time employee of XYZ Inc., purchased one of the company's cars worth $7,000 for $3,000.
   c. I borrowed $10,000 secured by property that had an adjusted basis of $3,000 and a fair market value of $15,000.
   d. S, a 60% shareholder in STV Corporation, uses a company car 70% of the time for business and 30% for personal purposes. The rental value of the car is $350 per month.

5-28 *What Is Income?* In each of the following situations indicate whether taxable income should be recognized.
   a. Ima Rich discovered oil on her farm, causing the value of her land to increase by $100 million.
   b. While jogging, Lucky found an iPad valued at $500.
   c. This year Mr. Landlord agreed to lease his lake cottage to Renter for $1,000 during the summer. After living there for two weeks, Landlord and Renter agreed that Landlord would only charge $700 if Renter made certain improvements.
   d. Mr. Kahn Artist borrowed $100,000, $25,000 each from F, U, L, and Z. He gave them each a one-year note bearing interest at a rate of 25 percent. At the end of the year, Mr. Artist borrowed $200,000 from Patsy, promising to pay her back in one year plus 30% interest. She couldn't resist and gave him the money. Mr. Artist used part of the $200,000 from Patsy to pay the interest due to F, U, L, and Z. Artist also convinced them to extend the original notes for another year. Near the end of the year, Patsy discovered from her cousin Abe that Artist had no intention of repaying any of the loans.

5-29 *What Is Income?* In each of the following situations indicate whether taxable income should be recognized.
   a. L sued her former employer for sex discrimination evidenced in his compensation policy. She was awarded $100,000, $39,000 of which represented reimbursement for mental anguish.
   b. M, a sales clerk for a department store, purchased a microwave oven from the store's appliance department. The store has a policy allowing employees a 10% discount. This discount results in $45 savings to M.
   c. R received a bottle of perfume and a case of grapefruit from her boss at the annual Christmas party. The items were valued at $25.

5-30 *Constructive Receipt.* When would a cash basis taxpayer recognize income in the following situations? Assume the taxpayer reports on a calendar year.
   a. R, a traveling salesperson, was out of town on payday, December 31. He picked up his check when he arrived back on January 3.
   b. C owns a bond with interest coupons due and payable on December 31. C clipped the coupons and redeemed them on January 7.
   c. R is an officer and controlling shareholder in XYZ Corporation. In December the corporation authorized bonuses for all officers. The bonus was paid in February of the following year.

5-31 *Constructive Receipt.* For each of the following situations, indicate whether the taxpayer has constructively received the income.
   a. R received a bonus as top salesperson of the year. He received the check for $25,000 at 10 p.m. on December 31 at a New Year's Eve party. All the banks were closed.
   b. On January 3, D received the check for January's rent of her duplex. The envelope was postmarked December 31.
   c. On December 25, C Corporation rewarded its top executive, E, with 100 shares of stock for a job well done. E was unable to find a buyer until March 15 of the following year.
   d. Immediately after receiving her check on December 31, Z went to her employer's bank to cash it. The bank would not cash it since the employer's account was overdrawn.

5-32 *Constructive Receipt.* For each of the following situations, indicate whether the taxpayer has constructively received the income.
   a. X Corporation declared a dividend on December 15 and mailed dividend checks on December 28. R received her check for $250 on January 4.
   b. F owns a small apartment complex. His son, S, lives in one of the units and manages the complex. Several tenants left their January rent checks with S during the last week of December. S delivered the checks to his father in January.
   c. This year, the cash surrender value of L's life insurance policy increased by $500. In order to obtain the value, L must cancel the policy.

5-33 *Changes in Accounting Method.* JB and his sons have operated a small "general store" in Backwoods, Idaho, since 2013. This year, JB hired a new accountant, who immediately told him he should be using the accrual method to account for his inventories and related sales and receivables. The receivables were primarily attributable to sales of seed to farmers as well as appliances. JB has always used the cash method of accounting, reporting all of his income when he receives it and deducting all costs when paid. According to the accountant, as of the close of the current year, JB had $70,000 in receivables outstanding (none of which had been reported in income), inventory of $130,000 (all expensed), and outstanding accounts payable for recent purchases of inventory of $20,000.
   a. If the IRS audits JB and requires him to change his method of accounting, what is the adjustment amount and when will JB report it?
   b. Same as (a) except JB voluntarily changes his method of accounting prior to the audit.
   c. If JB changes to the accrual method of accounting to account for inventories and sales, may he continue to report other items of income (e.g., interest income) and expense (e.g., supplies) using the cash method?

5-34 *Advanced Payments for Goods.* HIJ Furniture, an accrual basis company for both tax and financial accounting purposes, normally does not sell the items displayed in its showrooms, nor does it keep those items in stock. Instead, it obtains partial payment from the customer and orders the items directly from the manufacturer. During the current year, HIJ collected $60,000 with respect to furniture sales still on order at the close of the year. (The partial payments collected by HIJ do not exceed their cost for the items ordered.) Must HIJ report any of the $60,000 as income this year?

5-35 *Percentage of Completion.* THZ Corporation is a large construction company. This year it contracted with the city of Old York to build a new performing arts center for a price of $5,000,000. Estimated total costs of the project were $4,000,000. Annual costs incurred were as follows:

2018	$2,000,000
2019	500,000
2020	+1,000,000
Total	$3,500,000

a. What method(s) of accounting may the corporation use to report income from the project?

b. How much income would be reported each year under the percentage of completion method?

c. Would any interest be due to (or from) the IRS as a result of this contract? If so, compute for the first year only, assuming the taxpayer is in the 34% tax bracket and the interest rate is 10 percent.

5-36 *U.S. Savings Bonds.* This year S purchased U.S. Government Series EE Bonds for $700. The redemption value of the bonds at the end of the year was $756. What options are available to S with respect to reporting the income from the bonds?

5-37 *Contested Income.* In 2017, GLX Company, an accrual basis taxpayer, received $10,000 for supplying running shoes to T for sale in his sporting goods store. During 2017, T claimed the shoes had defective soles and requested GLX to refund the $10,000 payment.

a. Must GLX report any of the $10,000 as income in 2017?

b. Had GLX not received payment in 2017, would your answer in (a) change?

5-38 *Deposits and Prepaid Rents.* Q owns several duplexes. From each new tenant she requires a $150 security deposit and $300 for the last month's rent. The deposit is refundable assuming the tenant complies with all the terms of the lease. During the year, Q collected $1,000 in deposits and $2,400 of prepaid rents for the last month of occupancy. In addition, she refunded $400 to previous tenants but withheld $300 due to damages. How much must Q include in income assuming she is an accrual basis taxpayer?

5-39 *Prepaid Service Income: Accrual Method.*

a. LL Corporation, a calendar year and accrual basis taxpayer, is engaged in the lawn care business, providing fertilizer treatments. It sells one-, two-, and three-year contracts. Each contract provides that the customer will receive four treatments (fall, winter, spring, and summer). An analysis of its customer contracts revealed that it received $200,000 during the fall for a one-year contract. Each of these customers will receive one treatment in 2017 and three treatments in 2018. In its financial accounting statements, the company reports the income as services are performed. What amount of income must the corporation report in 2017 and 2018?

b. Same as (a) above except the contracts are for two years. The customers will receive one treatment in 2017, four treatments in 2018 and three treatments in 2019.

c. A professional basketball team that reports on the calendar year and uses the accrual method collected $700,000 in pre-season ticket sales in August and September of 2017. Of its 41-game home season, 15 games were played *prior to the end* of the year. In its financial statements, the organization reports the income as the games are played. What amount must be included in income in 2017?

d. A posh resort hotel in Florida reports on the calendar year and uses the accrual method. During 2017, it collected $10,000 in advance payments for rooms to be rented during January and February 2018. What amount of income must be included in 2017 and 2018?

5-40 *Income from Transferred Property.* E's grandmother owns several vending machines on campus. To help him through college, she allows E to collect and keep all the receipts from the machines. During the year, E spent approximately two hours a month to collect $5,000. Who must report the income and what is the amount to be included?

5-41 *Partnership Income.* QRS, a partnership, had taxable income of $120,000 for the fiscal year ended September 30, 2017. For the first quarter ending December 31, 2017, taxable income was $30,000. During 2017, Q, a partner with a 30% interest in profits and losses, withdrew $1,000 per month for a total of $12,000. What is Q's taxable income from QRS for 2017?

5-42 *Reporting Interest Income.* On November 1, 2016, G received a substantial inheritance and promptly made several investments. Indicate in each of the following cases the amount of interest income that he must report and the period in which the income is properly reported, assuming that G uses (1) the cash method of accounting, or (2) the accrual method of accounting. G reports using the calendar year.

a. G purchased a $10,000, 90-day U.S. Treasury bill at 99. The bill matured on January 30, 2017, when G redeemed it at par.

b. G purchased $100,000 of AFN Inc. 10% bonds for $95,000. The bonds were issued at par in 2009. The bonds pay interest semiannually on March 1 and September 1. On March 1, 2017, G received an interest payment of $5,000.

5-43 *Interest-Free Loans.* This year Dr. W, an orthopedic surgeon, and her husband, H, an attorney, established a trust for their five-year-old daughter, D. In conjunction with setting up the trust, the couple loaned the trust $200,000 payable on demand without interest. Assuming the interest that should have been charged under the applicable rate was $23,000, explain the effect of the loan on all of the parties.

5-44 *Shareholder Advances.* In 2006, J started ACC Corporation, a construction company. J owns all of the stock of the corporation and is also its president. Like many owners of closely-held corporations, J pretty much treats the corporation's checkbook as his own. He often asks the bookkeeper to make out checks to him that he ostensibly uses for business purposes. Over time, J does repay the amounts used for personal purposes, or turns in receipts for amounts used for business. In the meantime, the bookkeeper charges these checks to a special account titled "J Suspense." Upon the accountant's review this year, he noted that the account showed a balance of $15,000 (indicating an amount due from J). Explain the tax consequences.

5-45 *Interest-Free Loans.* F is chief executive officer of CVC Corporation and has taxable income in excess of $200,000 annually. During the year, he loaned his 20-year-old son, S, $30,000, payable on demand without interest. S promptly invested the $30,000 and earned $1,200, which was his only income during the year.

a. Assuming the interest that should have been charged under applicable rate is $3,000, compute the effect of the loan on the taxable income of both F and S.

b. Would F be able to shift income to his son if he had made a loan of only $9,000?

5-46 *Code § 7872: Exceptions.* For each of the following independent cases, indicate the income and gift tax consequences for both the lender and the borrower.

a. J loaned his 25-year-old son, K, $8,000 interest-free, which K used to purchase a car. K had $400 investment income from a savings account for the year.

b. Same as (a) except K decided to invest the money in a certificate of deposit yielding $800 of interest income producing a total net investment income of $1,200 for the year.

c. G loaned her 29-year-old daughter, D, $50,000 interest-free to help her acquire a franchise for a fast-food restaurant. All of D's funds were invested in the business and consequently she had no investment income for the year.

d. P Corporation loaned its sole shareholder, Q, $150,000 interest-free.

e. Same as (d) except Q owns no stock in P but is simply a key employee.

5-47 *Cash Method Eligibility.* Given the facts below, indicate whether the taxpayer may use the cash method for 2017 in the following situations.

    a. Sweatshirt Corporation, a publicly traded corporation: annual gross receipts for 2014 and previous years were $1 million annually; gross receipts for 2015 were $3 million; and for 2016, $8 million.

    b. Dewey, Cheatham, and Howe, a national public accounting firm, operated as a partnership. Annual gross receipts for the past five years have exceeded $50 million.

    c. McSwane, McMillan, and McClain, Inc., an architectural firm, operated as a regular C corporation. Annual gross receipts for the past two years have exceeded $7 million. McSwane, McMillan, and McClain own all of the stock and perform services for the firm.

    d. Buttons and Bows, Inc., an S corporation.

    e. A trust established for John Doe.

    f. Plantation Office Park, a publicly traded limited partnership: annual gross receipts have never exceeded $2 million. The partnership is a tax shelter.

5-48 *Accrual Method of Accounting.* Frank's Casing Crew and Rental Tools Inc. uses the accrual method of accounting and reports using the calendar year. The corporation sells oil pipes, leases equipment used in oil fields, and provides crews necessary to operate the leased equipment. The company's customers are primarily large oil companies. The company's contracts provide that payment is due when it sends the customer an invoice that includes all supporting documentation (i.e., job tickets, equipment tickets, and third party charges). In 2017, the company finished several jobs but did not invoice the customers until after year-end because it had not yet received a third party's invoice. When should the corporation report the income from these contracts?

5-49 *Accrual Method of Accounting.* N Corporation operates a chain of coffee shops in various locations throughout Indiana. It uses the accrual method of accounting and reports using the calendar year. In 2018, its expenses exceeded its revenue resulting in a net operating loss (NOL). Like federal law, Indiana's state law, permits corporations to carry back an NOL to prior years where it can be used to offset such year's taxable income, enabling the corporation to obtain a refund of previously paid Indiana state income taxes. (Note that state income taxes are deductible business expenses so a recovery of such expenses is taxable income.) The Indiana Department of Revenue has the right to examine any refund claim before determining whether to allow the claim and the refund amount. In 2019, the corporation filed the proper forms to carry back the NOL, seeking a refund of part of the state income taxes it had paid in previous years. In 2020, N received a refund of $100,000. When should N report the income?

5-50 *Accrual Method of Accounting.* Giant Corp. operates retail stores throughout the country. It uses the accrual method of accounting and reports using the calendar year. Each store offers film processing. Customers wanting film developed put the film in an order envelope and place the envelope in a drop box. Finished prints are produced primarily by Giant's own processing labs but also unrelated labs. The labs develop the film using highly specialized equipment and a complex chemical process, normally returning the finished prints within two days of when their couriers pick up the film. The finished prints are held for customer pick-up at the stores. Customers are not required to buy the prints unless they are completely satisfied. Store employees review the unsold prints on hand every 30 days and remind customers by phone or mail that their prints are available. Finished prints that are unclaimed after 120 days or customer rejects are discarded. Giant owns the finished prints until either a customer purchases them or they are discarded. Only a small percentage of customers do not purchase the finished prints. Upon audit, the IRS asserted that Giant should have to report the income when the stores receive the finished prints. Indicate whether the agent is correct or incorrect and explain the reasons for your answer.

5-51 *Shifting Income to Children.* Mr. and Mrs. D wish to shift income to their seven-year-old son, C, to be used for his college education. Explain whether the following would serve their goals or, alternatively, how they affect any technique designed to shift income.

a. Paying C an allowance for making his bed and picking up his clothes.
b. Paying C for helping to wash cars at his dad's car wash.
c. Buying C Series EE Savings Bonds.
d. Arranging to have Mrs. D's employer pay C part of her salary.
e. The Social Security rules.
f. The rules governing personal exemptions.

TAX RETURN PROBLEMS

■ *CONTINUOUS TAX RETURN PROBLEMS* See Appendix I, Part 1.

CUMULATIVE PROBLEM

5-52 David K. Gibbs, age 37, and his wife, Barbara, age 33, have two children, Chris and Ellen, ages 2 and 12. David is employed as an engineer for an oil company, and his wife recently completed a degree in accounting and will begin working for a public accounting firm next year. David has compiled the following information for your use in preparing his tax return for 2016.

1. For the current year, David received a salary of $70,000. His employer withheld Federal income taxes of $9,000 and the appropriate amount of FICA taxes.
2. At the annual Christmas party, he received a card indicating that he would receive a bonus of $3,000 for his good work during the year. The bonus check was placed in his mailbox at work on December 30. Since David was out of town for the holidays, he did not pick up the bonus check until January 2.
3. A bond issued by AM&T Inc. was sold on May 30, 2016 for $9,700, $700 of which represented interest accrued to the date of the sale. The Gibbs had purchased the bond (issued at par value of $10,000 on March 1, 2005) in 2012 for $10,000.
4. The couple has a $500 U.S. Savings Bond, which they purchased for $300 and gave to their daughter several years ago. The proper election to report the income from the bond annually was made. The bond's redemption value increased $30 this year.
5. David was an instant winner in the state lottery and won $50.
6. The Gibbs sold 100 shares of stock in JB Corporation for $10,000 on May 1, 2016. They had purchased the stock on June 1, 2009 for $14,000.
7. During the year, Barbara prepared a number of tax returns for which she received $5,000. Her only deductible expense incurred in performing these services was $100 for some tax software.
8. The couple's itemized deductions were medical expenses of $7,468, interest on their home mortgage of $8,500, state income taxes $3,750, property taxes on their home of $5,000, and charitable contributions of $2,000.

Compute Mr. and Mrs. Gibbs' Federal income tax liability (or refund) for 2016. If a tax return is required by your instructor, prepare Form 1040, including Schedules A and B.

TAX RESEARCH PROBLEMS

5-53 During the year, J, a college accounting professor, received complimentary copies of various textbooks from numerous publishers. J gives some of these books to students and the school library. J also keeps some of the books for his personal use and reference. A few times during the year J sold an unwanted text to a wholesale book dealer who periodically checked with him and other professors for texts. Must J report any income related to receipt of these books?

5-54 R recently became a member of a religious order. As a member, she was subject to the organization's complete control. The organization often required its members to terminate their employment in order to work in other jobs consistent with the organization's philosophy. For example, the organization supplied personnel to missions, hospitals, and schools. The organization also requires all members to take an oath of poverty and pay over all their earnings to it. Members' living expenses are paid for by the organization out of its own funds. Is R taxed on her earnings?

5-55 In each of the following cases, indicate who is responsible for reporting the income.
   a. Dr. A instructed the hospital for which he worked to pay his salary to his daughter C.
   b. R, a famous entertainer, agreed to perform at a concert gratuitously (without fee) for the benefit of a charitable organization.
   c. In a contest for the best essay on why education is important, T, age 25, won the right to designate a person under 17 to receive $1,000.

5-56 M owed her good friend, F, $20,000. In addition, M planned on making a charitable contribution to her church of $10,000. Instead of using cash to pay her friend and to make the contribution, M is considering transferring stock to each in the appropriate amount. The stock is currently worth $100 per share. M had purchased the 300 shares of stock several years ago for $6,000 ($20 per share). Will M realize any income if she transfers the stock rather than paying cash?

5-57 Sam Sellit is a salesperson for Panoramic Pools of St. Louis, a construction company that builds and sells prefabricated swimming pools. Over the past several years, Sam has progressed to become the top salesperson for the St. Louis franchise. Sam has done so well that he is considering purchasing his own franchise and starting a company in San Antonio. This year he contacted the home office in Pittsburgh about the possibility of opening up his own shop. The vice president in charge of expansion, Greg Grow, suggested that the two of them meet at the company's annual meeting of franchisees in Orlando. Greg knew that Sam, although not a franchisee, would be attending because he was the top salesperson in the St. Louis office, and the company invites the top salesperson from each office as well as his or her spouse to attend the meeting.

While at the four-day meeting (Tuesday through Friday) in Orlando, Sam and his wife, Sue, met with Greg and discussed the potential venture. In addition, Greg allowed Sam and Sue to attend the parts of the meeting that were only for franchisees so that they could get a glimpse of how the company operated. Of course, while they were in Orlando, Sam and his wife visited all of the tourist attractions. On Tuesday, there were no meetings scheduled and everyone spent the day at Disney World and Epcot Center. On Thursday afternoon, no meetings were scheduled and the couple went with Greg and his wife to Sea World. Sam attended meetings for several hours on Friday while his wife played golf. The couple stayed over through Sunday and continued their sightseeing activities.

The company picked up the tab for the couple's trip, reimbursing Sam $3,500 which included the costs of air fare, meals, lodging, and entertainment. What are the tax consequences to Sam?

5-58 Large Corporation manufactures computers. Its total sales of computers last year were well over $100 million. With each computer it offers a three-year warranty, covering parts and labor. The company estimates the future costs of warranty work related to current-year sales and defers the recognition of income until such time that it expects the warranty work will be done. Currently, the corporation reports 60% of the warranty income in the year of sale because the majority of warranty work occurs shortly after the computer has been sold. Thirty percent of the warranty income is reported in the second year of the warranty, and the remaining 10% is reported in the last year of the warranty. The company's estimates were based on sophisticated statistical techniques. Such techniques have produced estimates that appear extremely accurate based on the past ten years of data. No insurance is purchased to cover the warranty risk. Upon audit this year, the IRS agent indicated that the company cannot defer the warranty income and assessed a large tax deficiency. Advise the taxpayer as to whether it should pay the additional tax or pursue the matter in court.

5-59 Several years ago, R started his own delivery company, RT Haulers Inc. (RTH). The corporation is an accrual basis taxpayer. The corporation grew quickly, in part because of the excellent service that it was able to offer. Historically, the company has accrued its income when its services were completed. If the customer objected to the manner in which the services were performed (e.g., late delivery, damaged goods), RTH gave the client a credit against any future services that it might provide. RTH is now considering changing its agreements with customers to provide for a seven day acceptance period during which the customer could reject the services, in which case the customer would not have any obligation to pay. Advise the client regarding when its income should be reported, specifically addressing how the change in terms might impact the reporting of future service revenues.

5-60 Basinger Hauling is a trucking company that does business primarily on the west coast and in Mexico and Canada. Its headquarters are in Portland, Oregon. The company generally pays its drivers a specific rate, depending on a variety of factors such as miles driven, load weight, weather, unloading, fuel costs and the like. The company treats eight percent of each driver's compensation as a reimbursement for meals and lodging. Consequently, the company does not pay employment taxes (Social Security and Medicare) on the portion considered a reimbursement and does not include the reimbursement on the driver's W-2 form, reporting the amount representing wage income. Advise the client regarding this practice.

6

Gross Income: Inclusions and Exclusions

Learning Objectives

Upon completion of this chapter you will be able to:

LO.1 Explain the important distinction between taxable and nontaxable income.

LO.2 Explain the tax treatment of common items of investment income: dividends, interest, and annuities.

LO.3 Identify various types of employee compensation and fringe benefits and explain their tax treatment.

LO.4 Explain the treatment of gifts, inheritances, alimony, and child support.

LO.5 Describe the treatment created for unique items of income such as life insurance, debt cancellation, prizes, awards scholarships, and government transfers.

Chapter Outline

Introduction

LO.1

Explain the important distinction between taxable and nontaxable income.

While the tax law makes it clear that any type of gain, benefit, profit, or other increase in wealth is potentially taxable, in reality not all income is within the grasp of the IRS. As a practical matter, there are a number of special rules that must be observed before the final treatment of any particular benefit can be determined. For example, Congress has specifically exempted several types of income from tax such as interest on state and local bonds, scholarships, gifts, and inheritances. In addition, special provisions exist that clarify the treatment of a long list of possible income items such as annuities, alimony, and employee benefits. Because of these rules, the concept of income is not quite as comprehensive as perhaps suggested in Chapter 5. As a result, any particular item initially identified as "income" might ultimately fall into one of the following three categories:

- Taxable (i.e., totally includible);
- Nontaxable (i.e., excluded in full);
- Taxable in part and nontaxable in part.

The fact that some income does escape tax provides a huge opportunity. For this reason, tax advisers go to great lengths to identify methods that will convert taxable income into nontaxable income. In some cases, it may be as simple as changing a label or altering the nature of the payment. Regardless of how it is done, the benefits can be significant. For example, assume an employee pays federal and state income taxes at a combined rate of 30 percent. If a $1.00 of the employee's taxable compensation can be converted to a nontaxable fringe benefit of $1.00, it is the equivalent of giving the employee $1.42 ($1/[1 − 30%]), a significant increase in after-tax income. Think of the advantage that can be obtained if this principle is applied on a grand scale to an employer with thousands of employees! The magic of exclusions is the subject of this chapter.

This chapter examines the more frequently encountered sources of income. To provide some order and logic to the presentation, the various sources of income are grouped and discussed as follows:

- Investment income (dividends, interest, annuities);
- Employee compensation and fringe benefits;
- Personal transfers (gifts, inheritances, alimony);
- Transfers by unrelated individuals (life insurance, prizes, scholarships);
- Business income;
- Miscellaneous items.

Investment Income

As shown in Exhibit 6-1, the vast majority of the income reported by individuals comes in some form of employee compensation such as salaries and wages (69.44% of all reported income for 2011). However, as Exhibit 6-1 also shows the income of many individuals is also likely to contain some type of investment income.

Common examples of investment income—sometimes referred to as unearned income:

- Dividends;
- Interest;
- Annuities;
- Rents.

EXHIBIT 6-1	Major Sources of Income 2014		

Type of Income	Percent of Returns Showing	Percent of All Income Reported
Salaries and wages.	82.86% *	69.44%
Taxable interest	29.16	0.96
Pensions, annuities, individual retirement accounts (taxable) . . .	29.82	9.17
Dividends	18.61	2.61
Qualified dividends	12.31	1.97
Net long-term capital gain (Form 1040, Schedule D)	8.48	7.22
Business or profession net income	3.89	3.83
Social Security benefits (taxable)	12.80	2.67
Net capital loss (Form 1040, Schedule D).	5.11	–0.18
Partnership and S corporation income (net income – net loss) . .	8.25	5.98
Unemployment compensation.	5.01	0.34
Tax-exempt interest.	3.90	0.64
Rent and royalty net income (including farms).	4.69	1.15
Business or profession net loss.	3.89	–0.59
Rent and royalty net loss (including farms)	3.14	–0.48
Farm net income less loss.	1.20	–0.08
Estate or trust net income less loss	0.43	0.31

* Item/([Adjusted Gross Income less deficit] or 9,771,035,412)
  Preliminary estimates based on samples taken from 148,606,578 individual returns filed in 2014.
  Source: Statistics of Income, 2014 Individual Income Tax Returns, Table 1.4, Fall 2014. Publication 1304 Internal Revenue Service, Washington, D.C.

For the most part, these income items present little problem for taxpayers. Each is usually fully taxable as ordinary income. In addition, to make reporting and compliance easier, those who pay dividends, interest, and annuities during the taxable year normally must report such payments to both the taxpayer and the IRS on the appropriate Form 1099. Nevertheless, special rules often apply in determining not only the amount of income that must be reported but also when it must be reported. In addition, for those with modified AGI exceeding $200,000 ($250,000 for joint filers), these items are subject to the § 1411 tax on net investment income of 3.8% discussed in Chapter 3. The treatment of each is discussed below.

LO.2

Explain the tax treatment of common items of investment income: dividends, interest, and annuities.

DIVIDENDS

Today it is not uncommon for even the smallest investor to own stock in a corporation or an interest in a mutual fund. Those who do are likely to obtain part of their investment return in the form of dividends. As shown in Exhibit 6-1, about 19% of all return reported dividend income. One of the high-profile debates surrounding the Jobs and Growth Tax Relief Reconciliation Act of 2003 concerned the taxation of dividends. The original proposal of the administration called for the complete exclusion for dividends in order to address the potential problem of double taxation. However, the final legislation did not adopt such a sweeping measure. Instead, the Act reduced the tax rates imposed on dividends to what they are for capital gains. Currently, the rate is normally 15% but drops to 0% for taxpayers whose income falls in the 10 or 15 percent ordinary income tax brackets and rises to 20% for those in the 39.6% bracket. In addition, for those with modified AGI exceeding $200,000 ($250,000 for joint filers), dividends are subject to the § 1411 tax on net investment income of 3.8 percent.[1]

---

[1] § 1(h)(11).

The reduced rate generally applies to so-called *qualified dividends*. Qualified dividends include dividends paid with respect to stock of all domestic corporations. For domestic stock, it makes no difference whether it is publicly traded or closely held. In addition, the reduced rate generally applies to dividends from foreign corporations but only if the stock is readily tradable on an established U.S. securities market. Also, to secure the special rate the taxpayer must hold the stock for more than 60 days during a 120 day window that begins 60 days before the stock goes ex-dividend. This requirement helps prevent taxpayers from exploiting the preferential treatment for dividends. To illustrate the possible injustice, consider a taxpayer who buys a stock a few days before the ex-dividend date, receives a $1,000 dividend and then sells the stock. Assuming the value of the stock drops in direct proportion to the amount of the dividend, a sale immediately after the ex-dividend date would produce a $1,000 short-term capital loss. It appears that the $1,000 dividend is offset by the $1,000 loss and the net effect is zero. However, the dividend is taxed at 15% and the loss may offset ordinary income that is taxed at 35 percent. In such case, the taxpayer is better-off by $200 ($350 − $150). The holding period rule requires taxpayers to be at risk for at least 61 days if they want to use this scheme.[2]

Note that this change represents a major philosophical shift that has little precedent in tax history. Dividends received by individuals have historically been taxed as ordinary income with little or no special treatment. Although a small exclusion for dividends once existed, dividends have otherwise been treated the same as ordinary income. It should also be observed that there is no special treatment for interest income.

Corporate Dividends

The vast majority of all distributions made by corporations to their shareholders are considered dividends and are fully taxable as ordinary income. Technically, however, a distribution made by a corporation is treated as a *dividend* only to the extent that it is out of the corporation's current or accumulated *earnings and profits,* or *E&P* as it is commonly called.[3] Amounts not considered dividends because the distribution exceeds E&P are treated as nontaxable returns of capital to the extent of the shareholder's basis in the stock. In effect, the nondividend portion of the distribution is applied to and reduces the basis of the stock. Should the return of capital distribution exceed the shareholder's basis, the excess is capital gain. In applying these rules, all distributions by corporations are deemed to be distributions of E&P to the extent thereof.

Example 1

C, Inc. distributes $100,000 to shareholders when its current E&P is $60,000 and it has no accumulated E&P. T, a 10% shareholder, has a basis in C, Inc. stock of $3,000. T receives $10,000, of which $6,000 (10% × $60,000) is from C's current E&P. Thus, T has a $6,000 taxable dividend; the $3,000 equal to his basis in the stock is a nontaxable return of investment, and the remaining $1,000 is capital gain. T's basis in the stock after the distribution will be zero.

As noted above, for individual taxpayers dividends are fully taxable as ordinary income but are taxed at favorable rates.[4]

Dividends received by corporate taxpayers are treated differently than dividend received by individuals. As explained in Chapter 3, in order to prevent multiple taxation of dividends, corporate taxpayers are entitled to a special dividends-received deduction. This special deduction (discussed more fully in Chapter 19) normally entitles the corporation to deduct 70% of the dividend received.[5] The favorable tax rates, 15 or 0 percent, do not apply to dividends received by a corporation.

---

[2] The holding period is extended for preferred stock. For other special rules see § 1(h)(11).

[3] §§ 301 and 316.

[4] Special rules apply to the rare distribution of noncash property (e.g., land). See §§ 301(b) and (d).

[5] § 243 through 246. Generally, the deduction is a percentage of the dividends received from a domestic corporation determined as follows: (1) 70% when the stock ownership percentage (SOP) is less than 20 percent, (2) 80% when the SOP is 20% or more but less than 80 percent, and (3) 100% when the SOP is 80% or more.

The most critical variable in determining the treatment of a corporate distribution is the amount of the corporation's earnings and profits. The actual computation of E&P can be quite complex but the theory underlying it is relatively simple. The calculation attempts to measure the amount the corporation can pay out without impairing its capital account. In this regard, it is quite similar to the financial accounting concept of retained earnings. However, the two are not identical. Current E&P generally represents taxable income as adjusted for certain specified items.[6] Accumulated E&P is the sum of current E&P reduced by distributions. Using this information, a corporation determines the amount of its distribution that is considered a dividend (e.g., 60%) and reports this information to the shareholder on Form 1099-DIV or similar statement.

Mutual Fund Dividends

Millions of taxpayers now invest in stocks, bonds, and other securities indirectly through mutual funds. Mutual funds typically buy and sell investments realizing gains and losses as well as collect earnings from investments such as interest on bonds or dividends on stock.[7] Like corporations, mutual funds make distributions. However, the treatment of these distributions differs somewhat from regular corporate dividends in that they are generally characterized to reflect the nature of the income realized by the mutual fund. Mutual fund distributions are normally characterized as either *ordinary dividends* or *capital gain dividends*.[8] Ordinary dividends represent the individual's share of the fund's earnings from its own investments such as interest or dividends as well as any short-term gains the fund may realize. An individual reports all ordinary dividends as dividend income. The mutual fund designates the portion that represents "qualified dividend" income which is taxed at favorable rates. Capital gain dividends represent the capital gains and losses actually realized by the mutual fund during the year. All capital gain dividends are treated as *long-term* capital gains. Corporate taxpayers are entitled to the dividends-received deduction for ordinary dividends but not capital gain dividends. Each fund reports the information regarding its distributions to its shareholders on Form 1099-DIV.

A few funds retain their capital gains, in which case they are required to pay tax on such amounts. Nevertheless, these gains are allocated to the shareholders who must include them in income as capital gain.[9] In such case, shareholders may claim a credit for any tax paid by the fund and increase their basis in their shares for the amount included in income less the tax paid.

Other "Dividends"

There are a number of other distributions that taxpayers receive that are often called dividends. Technically, however, these are not "dividends" in the tax sense but receive special treatment. Some of these are listed below.

1. In some instances, earnings on deposits with banks, credit unions, investment companies, and savings and loan associations are referred to as dividends when they actually possess all the characteristics of interest. These dividends are reported as interest.[10]

2. Mutual insurance companies distribute amounts referred to as dividends to owners of unmatured life insurance policies. These dividends are treated as a nontaxable return of a portion of the insurance premium paid.[11]

3. Cooperatives distribute patronage dividends to cooperative members. These dividends are treated as a return of part of the original price paid for items purchased by members.[12]

4. As noted above, dividends from regulated investment companies (mutual funds) that represent gains on sales of investments from the fund are treated as long-term capital gains.[13]

---

[6] E&P is not defined in the Code. See § 312 and the related regulations.

[7] Funds are taxed like trusts, deducting income distributed and paying tax on income retained. Distributed income generally retains its character as either ordinary income or capital gain.

[8] Reg. § 1.852-4(a) and (b).

[9] § 852(b)(3)(D).

[10] Reg. § 1.61-7(a).

[11] § 316(b)(1).

[12] § 1385(b).

[13] § 1382(b).

Stock Dividends

From time to time, a corporation may make a distribution of its own stock. These so-called stock dividends are normally declared as a means to reduce the selling price of the stock or as simply a gesture of goodwill to the shareholders. As a practical matter, when a corporation distributes its own stock, it is not distributing an asset of the business; indeed, the corporation's assets remain completely intact and only the number of shares outstanding changes. From the shareholder's point of view, assuming all shareholders receive their proportionate shares of the stock distributed, they have essentially received nothing because their interest in corporate assets remains unchanged. Since the effect is to leave both the corporation and the shareholder in the same economic position as they held prior to the distribution, the stock dividend—a misnomer in this case—is nontaxable.[14] On the other hand, if the distribution is structured so that the shareholder's interest does change (e.g., the shareholder can elect to take stock or cash), the stock distribution is taxable.[15]

If the distribution of stock is nontaxable, the only responsibility of the shareholder is to determine the basis of the "new" and the "old" stock. Note that only the shareholder's per-share basis is altered. Total basis for all of the stock owned remains the same. Technically, the shareholder must allocate a portion of the basis of the original stock to the distributed stock. The basis is allocated between the old and the new in proportion to the relative values of the old and new stock on the date of the distribution.[16] When the old shares are identical to the new shares (e.g., a common on common stock dividend), the basis for each share is determined simply by dividing the basis of the old stock by the total number of shares held by the shareholder after the distribution. The holding period of the old shares carries over to the new shares.[17]

Example 2

V owns 100 shares of Z common with a basis of $2,200 ($22 per share). He receives 10 shares of Z common as a stock dividend. If V did not have the right to receive cash or other assets in lieu of the stock, he has no taxable income from this transaction and his $2,200 basis is allocated among the 110 shares of common for a $20 per share basis ($2,200 ÷ 110).

Example 3

Q owns 100 shares of S common with a basis of $2,200. She receives 10 shares of S preferred as a stock dividend. The market value is $4,000 ($40 per share) for common and $1,000 ($100 per share) for preferred. If Q did not have the right to receive cash or other assets in lieu of the stock, she has no taxable income since her proportionate interest did not change. Her basis for the preferred stock is $440 [$1,000 ÷ ($4,000 + $1,000 = $5,000 total value) = 20% × $2,200] and her basis for the common stock is $1,760 [either ($2,200 − $440) or ($4,000 ÷ $5,000) × $2,200].

INTEREST

The second most common item of income appearing on individual tax returns is interest (see Exhibit 6-1). More than 35% of all returns filed in 2011 reported some type of taxable interest. As a general rule, interest income is taxable. This is true regardless of its source (a bank, business, friend, or relative) or the form of the interest-bearing instrument (savings account, bond, or note). However, there are two notable exceptions to this rule: (1) the exclusion for interest on certain state and local government obligations, and (2) the exclusion for interest on educational savings bonds. In addition, interest income is subject to the special 3.8% tax on net investment income for taxpayers with modified AGI exceeding $200,000 ($250,000 for joint filers).

---

[14] § 305(a).

[15] § 305(b).

[16] § 307(a).

[17] § 1223(5).

Interest on State and Local Government Obligations

From the inception of the Federal income tax law, interest on obligations of a state, a territory, a U.S. possession, or any of their political subdivisions has been *nontaxable*.[18] Although such income is nontaxable, it still must be reported (Form 1040, line 8b). In that regard about 4% of all returns in 2014 reported some tax-exempt interest. It should be emphasized that interest on obligations of the federal government, such as interest on U.S. Treasury bonds, is fully taxable for federal tax purposes.

From time to time and even currently this exclusion has been criticized as an unwarranted loophole. Critics often characterize this exclusion as simply a tax shelter existing primarily for the rich. In truth, however, this treatment stems from an uncertainty about whether taxing this interest would be unconstitutional and also from political pressure exerted by the affected governments.[19] The exclusion is exceedingly beneficial to these governments because it means they can pay a lower interest rate and still attract investors, especially those investors who are subject to taxes at the highest marginal rates.

Example 4

K Corporation invests $10,000 in corporate bonds that pay 13% annually and $10,000 in state bonds that pay 9% annually. If K, Inc.'s marginal tax rate is 34 percent, its after-tax earnings on the corporate bonds are less than its earnings on the state bonds.

	Corporate Bonds	State Bonds
Annual interest income	$1,300	$900
Federal income tax (34%)	442	0
After-tax income	$ 858	$900

If the corporation's marginal tax rate is 15 percent, however, its after-tax earnings for the corporate bonds increase to $1,105 ($1,300 − $195).

A break-even point between taxable and nontaxable rates of return may be calculated with the following formula:

$$\text{Taxable interest rate} \times (1 - \text{Marginal tax rate}) = \text{Tax-free rate}$$

Applying the numbers in the example above when K, Inc.'s tax rate is 34 percent, the break-even point for the taxable bond is

$$13\% \times (1 - 0.34 = 0.66) = 8.58\%$$

Thus, at the 34% marginal tax rate, a 13% taxable return is equal to an 8.58% tax-exempt return.

The formula can be converted to compute the break-even point for the tax-exempt bond as follows:

$$\text{Tax-free rate} \div (1 - \text{Marginal tax rate})$$

or

$$9\% \div (1 - 0.34 = 0.66) = 13.6\%$$

Thus, at the 34% marginal tax rate, a 9% tax-exempt return is equal to a 13.6% taxable return.

---

[18] § 103(a); § 103(c).

[19] The constitutional issue now seems to be moot. See *South Carolina v. Baker,* 109 S.Ct. 1355 (1988) where the Supreme Court noted that there was no constitutional prohibition barring the Federal government from taxing such interest. See also *National Life Insurance Co.,* 1 USTC ¶314, 6 AFTR 7801, 277 U.S. 508 (USSC, 1928), where the Supreme Court originally indicated that Federal taxation of *interest* paid by state and local governments was unconstitutional.

EXHIBIT 6-2	Comparison of Taxable versus Tax-Free Investments					

	If Your Tax-Free Investment Is Yielding					
	4.50%	5.00%	5.50%	6.00%	6.50%	7.00%
Marginal Tax Bracket	*Your Taxable Equivalent Yield Is*					
15%	5.29%	5.88%	6.47%	7.06%	7.65%	8.24%
25%	6.00%	6.67%	7.33%	8.00%	8.67%	9.33%
28%	6.25%	6.94%	7.64%	8.33%	9.03%	9.72%
33%	6.72%	7.46%	8.20%	8.96%	9.70%	10.45%
35%	6.92%	7.69%	8.46%	9.23%	10.00%	10.77%
40%	7.50%	8.33%	9.16%	10.0%	10.83%	11.67%

A comparison of the effective yield on tax-free versus taxable investments is provided in Exhibit 6-2. Given current market conditions, the effective yield on tax-exempt securities will be difficult to match with taxable investments. For example, if a taxpayer is in the 28% bracket and the current yield on tax-exempt securities is five percent, the after-tax return on taxable securities would be greater as long as the yield exceeded 6.94 percent.

Over the years, Congress has reacted to the criticism that this exclusion subsidizes the wealthy (i.e., those subject to the highest tax rates) and has also reacted to the increasing number and complexity of financial offerings developed by state and local governments. Originally, these governments sold securities to fund public projects. More recently, however, bonds have been issued to fund business construction and other industrial development projects. When this occurs, a governmental unit retains ownership of the facilities and leases them to a business. Because the interest rate on these bonds is lower than it would be on bonds issued by the corporation, the negotiated lease payments can be lower. Congress has curtailed the tax-exempt status of these so-called industrial development bonds. With certain specified exceptions, interest on industrial development bonds is taxable income.[20]

In addition to the limitations imposed on industrial development bonds, there are still other restrictions intended to curb the use of state and local bonds to finance business activities. For example, tax-exempt bonds can no longer be issued to finance airplanes, gambling facilities, liquor stores, health clubs, sky boxes, or other luxury boxes. Nor can the bonds be issued to finance the acquisition of farmland or existing facilities, with certain exceptions.

Gain on Sale of Tax-Exempt Bonds

It should be noted that any exclusion on state and local obligations is for *interest* income received by the bondholder. Thus, *gain* on the sale of tax-exempt securities that does not represent interest is taxable income.[21]

Example 5

On January 1 of the current year N purchased at par a $30,000, 10-year tax exempt municipal bond, yielding 8 percent. On September 30 of the following year, she sold the bond for $32,000 plus accrued interest of $800. Although the accrued interest is tax-exempt, N must report $2,000 of capital gain ($32,000 − $30,000) subject to tax of up to 15 percent.

---

[20] § 103(b).

[21] *Willcuts v. Bunn*, 2 USTC ¶640, 9 AFTR 584, 282 U.S. 216 (USSC. 1931). (See Footnote 17.)

Educational Savings Bonds

In 1988, Congress took steps to help taxpayers finance the rising costs of higher education by offering a special tax break for those who save to meet such expenses. Code § 135 generally provides that accrued interest on Series EE savings bonds issued after 1989 is exempt from tax when the accrued interest and principal amount of such bonds are used to pay for *qualified educational expenses* of the taxpayer or the taxpayer's spouse or dependents (but only if these relationships are satisfied in the year of the redemption). For this purpose, qualified education expenses include those for tuition or fees to attend college or certain schools offering vocational education. Costs that otherwise qualify must be reduced by any scholarships or fellowships that may be received, as well as any employer-provided assistance.

The interest exclusion is allowed only to the extent that the taxpayer uses the proceeds of the bond redemption to pay qualified educational expenses during the year that he or she redeems a bond. If the redemption proceeds received during the year exceed the amount of education expenses paid during the same year, the amount of the interest exclusion must be reduced proportionately. The amount of the exclusion may be computed as follows:

$$\frac{\text{Qualified educational expenses paid during the year}}{\text{Total redemption proceeds of qualified bonds during the year}} \times \text{Accrued interest} = \text{Exclusion}$$

Example 6

Mr. and Mrs. T purchased Series EE savings bonds in 2017 for $4,000. On June 2, 2027 they cashed in the bonds and received $10,000, $6,000 representing accrued interest and $4,000 representing their original investment. Three months later on September 2, they paid tuition of $9,000 for their dependent daughter, D, who attends a private university. In November, D received a scholarship of $1,000 for being an outstanding accounting major. Only $8,000 ($9,000 tuition – $1,000 scholarship) of D's expenses are considered qualified educational expenses. Since this amount represents only 80% ($8,000/$10,000) of the total redemption proceeds, Mr. and Mrs. T may exclude only 80% of the $6,000 accrued interest, or $4,800.

Note that to qualify for the exclusion, the savings bonds need not be transferred directly to the educational institution. The exclusion applies to interest on *any* post-1989 Series EE savings bond that is realized during the taxable year as long as the taxpayer pays sufficient qualified educational expenses during the same taxable year.

The special exclusion is designed to benefit only those who have moderate incomes. To achieve this objective, the exclusion is gradually reduced once the taxpayer's AGI (as determined in the taxable year when the bonds are redeemed) reaches a certain level. The 2017 income level at which the phase-out begins depends on the taxpayer's filing status as shown below.

Filing Status	Phase-Out Range Modified AGI*
Single (including heads of household)...................................	$ 78,150 – $ 98,150
Married filing jointly..	$117,250 – $147,250

*Adjusted annually for inflation

The reduction of the exclusion otherwise allowed is computed as follows:

$$\frac{\text{Excess AGI}}{\$15,000\ (\$30,000\ \text{for joint returns})} \times \text{Otherwise excludable interest} = \text{Reduction}$$

Married taxpayers filing separately are not eligible for the exclusion. Taxpayers who are married must file a joint return to secure the exclusion.

Example 7

Mr. and Mrs. B have an AGI, after proper modifications, of $127,250, before the exclusion. As a result, the amount of any interest that would otherwise be nontaxable must be reduced by one third:

$$\frac{(\$127{,}250 \text{ AGI} - \$117{,}250 \text{ threshold} = \$10{,}000)}{(\$147{,}250 - \$117{,}250 = \$30{,}000 \text{ phase-out range})}$$

Assume the couple redeemed qualified bonds this year with accrued interest of $10,000. Only 90% of the proceeds of the bonds (i.e., interest and principal) were spent on qualifying education expenses. They could exclude $6,000 of the interest, computed as follows:

Excludable interest (90% × $10,000)	$ 9,000
Exclusion phase-out (1/3 × $9,000)	− 3,000
Amount of interest excluded.	$ 6,000

Note that the exclusion would not be available to the couple if their AGI in the year they redeemed the bonds exceeded the phase-out range (e.g., $147,250 for 2017).

Without any special provision, taxpayers with high incomes might try to circumvent the income limitation to obtain the exclusion. For example, a father earning an income of $150,000 might give $10,000 to his 10-year-old daughter who would then be instructed to buy the bonds. When the daughter started college, she would redeem the bonds to pay for her tuition. Absent any restrictions, the daughter could secure 100% of the available exclusion since she would have little or no income. To prevent such schemes, the exclusion is available only for bonds that are *issued* to individuals who are at least 24 years old. In addition, the exclusion is available only to the original purchaser of the bond or his or her spouse. This rule prohibits gifts of qualified bonds.

Example 8

Mr. and Mrs. C have an AGI of $150,000. Assume they currently hold qualified Series EE bonds with $10,000 of accrued interest. To avoid the income limitation, the bonds are given to Mr. C's father, GF, who has little income. This year, GF cashes the bonds in and pays for his grandson's tuition. The payment is sufficient to qualify the grandson as GF's dependent. Even though the redemption proceeds are used to pay for education expenses of the taxpayer's dependent, no exclusion is available for the interest since GF was not the original purchaser of the bond. Had GF originally purchased the bonds for his grandson, the exclusion would be allowed (assuming his grandson is his dependent).

ANNUITIES

An annuity is a type of investment contract normally between an individual and an insurance company. In its simplest form, the annuity contract requires the insurance company to pay a fixed amount of money to be paid to the purchaser (the annuitant) beginning at a particular date (the starting date) and continue at specific intervals for either a certain period of time or for life. Annuities are quite common in a number of situations. For example, retirees often receive their retirement benefits (i.e., their pensions) in the form of an annuity. In this case, employees and employers contribute to a retirement fund while the individual is employed. Upon retirement, the employee is usually given the choice of receiving his or her pension in the form of a lump-sum distribution or the accumulations are used to buy an annuity. The annuity option is often selected. Annuities are also a popular investment among elderly taxpayers. These taxpayers, often fearing that they may outlive their assets, purchase an annuity that will provide a steady stream of income until they die. Indeed, the aging of the population—the graying of America—is making annuities far more popular than ever before.

When the annuity is purchased by an individual, the insurance company invests the amount received and the investment income increases the value of the account. Under the terms of the contract, the individual has the right to cancel the annuity. When this occurs, the insurance company pays the individual the value of the investment normally reduced by penalties for early cancellation referred to as surrender charges. These charges can run as high as ten percent of the amount withdrawn and are an important consideration when investing in an annuity. In most cases, however, insurance companies allow withdrawals of a certain percentage of the account annually without having to pay any surrender charge. The tax treatment of these withdrawals is discussed below.

The income earned on the investment is tax-deferred. This means the income is taxable but not during the current year when it is earned. Instead, the income is taxable at some future date when the annuitant receives cash payments. Until then, the income is automatically reinvested in full, without payment of Federal income taxes, to earn tax-deferred income. Observe that the income is not taxed currently because the individual has not received it either directly or constructively. It is not treated as constructively received since it is not available unless the taxpayer cancels the policy—a substantial restriction on its use.

The tax deferral feature of annuities make them particularly attractive for persons considering retirement. Annuity payments are commonly scheduled to begin on retirement when the recipients' marginal tax rates are lower. Because of the lower rates, these individuals usually pay less total taxes in addition to receiving the benefits from tax deferral.

Taxation of Annuities

The taxation of annuities reflects the cost recovery principle. As discussed in Chapter 5, the portion that is a return of capital is nontaxable.[22] Determination of the portion that represents income and the portion that is a nontaxable return of capital generally depends on whether the amounts are received before or after the starting date for periodic payments.

Amounts Received before Starting Date. Cash withdrawals, including loans, before the annuity starting date are normally taxable to the extent of the earnings accumulated in the account. Amounts in excess of the earnings are treated as a nontaxable return of capital until the taxpayer's cost has been completely recovered. Additional amounts are taxable.[23]

Early Withdrawals of Annuities. To discourage investors from withdrawing funds before the starting date, a 10% penalty is assessed on the deferred income. The penalty is waived if the taxpayer has reached age 59½ or is disabled.[24]

Example 9

When S was 50, he purchased an annuity from an insurance company for $10,000. The annuity was to start when S became 65. At age 55, he requested and received an $8,000 distribution from the account. At the time of the distribution, the annuity had grown by $7,000 and had a total cash value of $17,000. Since the withdrawal is before the starting date and before he reached age 59½ the distribution is taxable to the extent of the accumulated earnings and a 10% penalty is imposed. Of the $8,000 received, $7,000 ($17,000 − $10,000) is attributable to earnings and taxable and the remaining $1,000 is a nontaxable return of capital. The penalty imposed is $700 (10% × the income recognized of $7,000).

---

[22] § 72(b)(1).

[23] Special rules may apply depending on the type of annuity. See Pension and Annuity Income, IRS Publication 575 (Revised 2016) p. 15.

[24] See § 72(q)(2). The penalty provision does not apply to contracts issued before August 14, 1982.

Amounts Received on or after Starting Date. The treatment of periodic payments beginning on or after the starting date differs from that for amounts received before the starting date. In these situations, the portion that is a return of capital is the product of the exclusion ratio (investment in the contract ÷ expected return) and the amount received as shown in the following formula:

$$\frac{\text{Investment in the contract}}{\text{Expected return from the contract}} \times \text{Amount received currently} = \text{Excluded portion}$$

The taxable portion is the amount received currently less the portion that is a return of capital (i.e., the excluded portion). When the annuity will be received over a stipulated number of years, the expected return from the contract is the amount to be received each year (or month) multiplied by the number of years (or months) payments are to be received.

Example 10

W invests $20,000 in a single-premium deferred annuity. At the end of 15 years, W elects to receive the $20,000 principal plus interest over the next ten years. She receives $7,000 in the current year and will receive $7,000 each of the following nine years. W's nontaxable return of capital each year is $2,000 computed as follows:

$$\frac{\$20,000}{\$7,000 \times 10 \text{ years} = \$70,000} \times \$7,000 = \$2,000$$

W's taxable income each year is $5,000 ($7,000 − $2,000).

Example 11

Refer to *Example 10*. If W receives only three payments in the first year totaling $1,750 ($7,000 × 3/12), the computation remains the same except the amount received currently is $1,750 (instead of $7,000). Consequently, her nontaxable return of capital in the first year is $500 ([$20,000 ÷ $70,000] × $1,750) and her taxable income is $1,250 ($1,750 − $500).

Note that the solution to *Example 10* is the same if W had simply divided the $20,000 principal by the 10 years (and to *Example 11* if W adjusted the annual amount to months). This is not true, however, when the annuity payments are received over the individual's life. For these situations, the Regulations provide several tables based on contract payment terms and the annuitant's age.[25] These tables must be used by those taxpayers making post-June 1986 contributions to the annuity contract. A portion of these tables is reproduced in Exhibit 6-3.

When the payments will be received over the life of the annuitant, the expected return from the contract is the amount to be received each year multiplied by the multiple that corresponds to the annuitant's age in the table. It also is important to note that the portion of any annuity payment to be excluded from gross income cannot *exceed* the unrecovered investment in the contract immediately before the receipt of the payment.[26] In other words, the exclusion ratio remains the same until the investment is fully recovered at which time subsequent receipts are fully taxable. In addition, if the annuitant dies before the entire investment is recovered, the amount of the *unrecovered investment* is allowed as a *deduction* on his or her final tax return.[27] The deduction is not a miscellaneous itemized deduction subject to the 2% floor.

---

[25] Reg. § 1.72-9.

[26] § 72(b)(2). For annuities beginning before July 2, 1986, the exclusion ratio remains the same for life regardless of whether the investment is recovered and no deduction is allowed for any unrecovered investment.

[27] § 72(b)(3).

EXHIBIT 6-3	Ordinary Life Annuities—One Life—Expected Return Multiples

Age	Multiple	Age	Multiple	Age	Multiple
21	60.9	58	25.9	95	3.7
22	59.9	59	25.0	96	3.4
23	59.0	60	24.2	97	3.2
24	58.0	61	23.3	98	3.0
25	57.0	62	22.5	99	2.8
26	56.0	63	21.6	100	2.7
27	55.1	64	20.8	101	2.5
28	54.1	65	20.0	102	2.3
29	53.1	66	19.2	103	2.1
30	52.2	67	18.4	104	1.9

Example 12

T, 65 years old, purchased a single-premium immediate life annuity on January 1, 2017 for $11,400. It will pay $100 a month for the rest of her life (i.e., annual payment of $1,200). From Exhibit 6-3, her multiple is 20.0. T's nontaxable return of capital each year is $570 computed as follows:

$$\frac{\$11,400}{\$1,200 \times 20 = \$24,000} \times \$1,200 = \$570$$

T's taxable income is $630 ($1,200 − $570). The $570 is considered a return of capital until T recovers her $11,400 investment. Note that if she lives 21 years, the total amount she excludes is limited to $11,400 ($570 × 20 years = $11,400). Thus, T's taxable income for year 21 is the entire $1,200 received. In contrast, if she lives just 15 years, the total amount she excludes is $8,550 ($570 × 15 years), and the unrecovered amount of $2,850 ($11,400 − $8,550) is allowed as a deduction on T's final tax return.

As noted above, employers with qualified pension or profit-sharing plans Chapter 18 purchase annuity contracts for their employees' retirement. The taxable income to the employee is dependent on the employee's total *after-tax* investment in the annuity. After-tax funds generally exclude contributions, for example, to certain Individual Retirement Accounts (when individuals are allowed a deduction for the contribution) and to qualified employer retirement plans (since these contributions are made from amounts that are excluded from gross income in the current year). Investments that are not from after-tax funds are ignored in determining the individual's capital investment in the annuity. In some situations, employees may not have invested any after-tax funds in the employer's plan. Consequently, their basis in the annuity contract is zero and all amounts are included in gross income when received by them. In all other instances, calculations for return of capital and taxable income are identical to the procedure outlined in the above paragraphs.

Simplified Treatment for Annuities from Qualified Plans

As a general rule, the method above must be used for purchased commercial annuities and certain other annuities. However, many, if not most annuities, come from retirement plans. The method to be used for an annuity from a qualified retirement plan depends on when the annuity started. If the annuity payments started before November 19, 1996, the method above must be used. For annuities starting after November 18, 1996, a simplified method must be used.[28]

A taxpayer using the simplified method will find the computations less onerous than those previously described for computing the exclusion ratio under § 72. Under this method, the total number of monthly annuity payments expected to be received is based on the distributee's age at the annuity starting date. Consequently, the life expectancy tables (such as Exhibit 6-3) can be ignored. Instead, Exhibit 6-4 is used, and is applicable whether the annuity is single life or joint and survivor type.[29]

EXHIBIT 6-4	Monthly Payments Table

Age of Distributee	Number of Payments
55 and under	360
56–60	310
61–65	260
66–70	210
71 and over	160

The portion of each monthly annuity payment that is nontaxable is determined using the following formula:

$$\frac{\text{Investment in the contract}}{\text{Number of monthly payments}} = \text{Nontaxable return of capital}$$

Example 13

On January 1 of this year, H, an employee, retired at the age of 65. He started receiving retirement benefits in the form of a joint and 50% survivor annuity to be paid for the joint lives of H and W (his spouse), who is 60. H contributed $52,000 (after-tax contributions) to the plan and will receive a retirement benefit of $2,000 a month. Upon H's death, W will receive a survivor retirement benefit of $1,000 each month. The nontaxable portion of each monthly annuity payment to H is calculated as follows:

$$\frac{\$52,000 \text{ investment}}{260 \text{ payments (see Exhibit 6-4)}} = \$200 \text{ nontaxable return of capital}$$

Should H die prior to receiving his entire investment of $52,000, W will likewise exclude $200 from her $1,000 monthly payment. As explained earlier, after 260 annuity payments have been made, any additional payments will be fully taxable. Should both H and W die prior to receiving 260 payments, a deduction is allowed in the amount of the unrecovered investment in the last income tax return.

---

[28] § 74(d). The simplified method cannot be used by (1) those 75 or older on the starting date whose annuity payments are guaranteed for at least five years and (2) annuities from a nonqualified plan such as a private annuity.

[29] A single life annuity pays a fixed amount at regular intervals for the remainder of one person's life. A joint and survivor annuity pays a fixed amount at regular intervals to one individual for life, and on his or her death, the payments continue over the life of a designated person such as a spouse or child.

529 Plans: Qualified Tuition Programs

To help families fund the increasing costs of higher education, Congress created several tax-favored savings arrangements. The most popular plans are contained in § 529 that was enacted in 1996. Interestingly, the annual 529 Plan Awareness Survey from the financial services firm of Edward Jones in 2016 indicated that only about 28% of Americans can correctly identify what a 529 plan is! Unfortunately, this means that about 72% of the country cannot. In its fifth year of monitoring college savings awareness, the survey found that only 28% of Americans identified a 529 plan as a college savings tool from among four potential options, and this was down six percentage points from 34% in 2015. There are actually two types of 529 plans: (1) prepaid tuition plans and (2) savings plans. Every state has either a prepaid tuition or a savings plan and some states have both. Similar to Educational Savings Bonds, the income from these savings programs is nontaxable if used for higher education expenses.

Prepaid Tuition Plans

Under a prepaid tuition plan, an individual buys tuition credits or certificates that can be redeemed to pay tuition at a later date. States typically offer a "units" plan that allows parents to buy units of tuition (e.g., a set number of credit hours or a certain percentage of the college's tuition). Some states offer "contract" plans that permit the purchase of contracts for one to five years of tuition. Individuals normally are allowed to contribute to either arrangement in a lump sum or in installments. There is no deduction allowed for such purchases.

Without special treatment, the difference between cost of the tuition credits and the value of the credits when used would represent taxable income. However, § 529 permits taxpayers to exclude this benefit.

Example 14

Shortly after H and W had their first son, S, they decided to start saving for his college education. Betting that the costs of tuition would continue to increase, they opted for a prepaid tuition plan. They purchased 15 hours of college credit from their alma mater, State University, at a cost of $200 per hour. This year S began his freshman year at State when the cost of tuition was $350 per hour. H and W used the prepaid credits to pay for the first semester's tuition. Although H and W have income of $150 ($350 – $200) per credit, it is nontaxable.

At first glance, it would appear that prepaid tuition plans enable parents to freeze the cost of future tuition to the price currently charged by the institution. In other words, parents could buy tomorrow's tuition at today's prices. While this may have been the original intent of such plans, it is now a misconception. In most states, the price paid for tuition does not reflect current prices but includes some additional premium that is often substantial. For this reason, such plans, like any investment, must be evaluated carefully.

Depending on its terms, the plan may also permit prepayment of fees, books, supplies, equipment and room and board. Prepaid tuition plans can be offered only by eligible educational institutions which include colleges and universities as well as proprietary and vocational institutions (e.g., trade schools). Prepaid tuition plans are not restricted to those residing in the state where the university is located. For example, an individual living in Illinois can invest in a prepaid tuition plan offered by the state of Florida. If a child does not attend the school at which the plan was established, all is not lost. The contributions may be withdrawn without a tax penalty, assuming the funds are used at another school. If not, the 10% penalty would apply to any earnings. However, the plan itself may charge some type of administrative fee and may or may not pay interest. It should be mentioned that many private universities, nearly 300 (2016), have joined together so that any tuition prepaid can be used at any member college (see Private College 529 Plan at *www.privatecollege529.com*).

529 College Savings Plans

A 529 savings plan (or simply a 529 plan as it is commonly called) is much different than a prepaid tuition plan. A 529 plan is simply a tax favored savings account for any person that the donor wants to name as a beneficiary. Contributions are made to 529 accounts where they normally can be invested in one or more mutual funds offered by the plan. Contributions are not deductible for federal income tax purposes. However, some states allow a deduction or a credit. The amount that can be contributed is not limited by the tax law but only by the plan itself, and these amounts can be substantial. For example, in 2016 the plan for Indiana state universities, CollegeChoice, allows contributions of up to $298,770 for one individual. In addition, Indiana provides a 20% credit of contributions but not to exceed $1,000 per year. Earnings attributable to the account are nontaxable. In other words, contributions to the plan grow tax-free for as long as money stays in the plan. Distributions from the account are nontaxable to the extent they are used to pay for qualified higher education expenses. Section 529(e)(3) defines qualified expenses as those for tuition, books, supplies, equipment required for enrollment or attendance and certain expenses incurred for special needs beneficiaries. Expenses for room and board also qualify if the student attends at least half-time. However, the amount cannot exceed that normally charged for housing owned or operated by the university. After changes in 2015, computer equipment and related expenses (including computer software and even internet access) qualify. Amounts withdrawn which are not considered qualified are subject to 10% penalty. In addition, as explained in Chapter 8, taxpayers may utilize the qualified tuition deduction to deduct the amount of a distribution from a qualified tuition plan that is used for qualified expenses and is not attributable to earnings (e.g., amounts contributed).

Example 15

This year, F withdrew $1,000 from a qualified tuition plan to pay her undergraduate tuition at State University. F does not claim a credit for the amount spent. If the $1,000 consists of $800 of contributions to the plan and $200 of earnings, a qualified tuition deduction for the $800 of contributions may be claimed for AGI by F. Furthermore, the $200 of earnings is excluded from F's income.

What happens if there is a downturn in the market and the plan drops in value? If this occurs—as it did in the market crash of 2008—the contributor can deduct a loss but only if the account is liquidated; that is, everything in the account must be withdrawn. If the total withdrawals are less than the amount the individual contributed (i.e., the basis for the account), a deduction is allowed for the difference. Unfortunately, the loss is deductible only as a miscellaneous itemized deduction. In addition, the funds cannot be reinvested too soon. If the distributions are rolled over to another 529 account for that or another related beneficiary within 60 days of their withdrawal, there is not a taxable transaction and no deduction would be allowed.

In a 529 plan, the named beneficiary has no rights to the funds. The donor has complete control, deciding when withdrawals are taken and for what purpose. Most plans allow the donor to reclaim the funds at any time desired, no questions asked. However, as noted above, the earnings portion of the "non-qualified" withdrawal are subject to income tax and an additional 10% penalty tax. Amounts contributed can be withdrawn at any time without penalty.

In situations where an account balance is not used (e.g., student did not finish, qualified expenses did not exhaust the account balance), the unused amount can be rolled over without penalty to an account for another member of the taxpayer's family.

Gift and Estate Tax Considerations

Contributions to either a prepaid tuition plan or a 529 savings plan are considered gifts and, therefore, could be subject to the gift tax if they exceed the annual exclusion of $14,000 (2017). However, for purposes of contributions to 529 plans, a taxpayer may elect to on the gift tax return, Form 709, have a contribution to a plan treated as if it had been made ratably over five years. In so doing, the amount may come under the annual exclusion. For example, a contributor could give $70,000 in 2017 to a plan and treat the transfer as if he or she had made gifts of $14,000 per year over the next five years. A gift tax return must be filed for amounts contributed in excess of the exclusion. If the contributor should die before the five-year period has elapsed, the balance is included in his or her estate.

Example 16

In 2017 G made a $70,000 contribution to Indiana University's qualified tuition plan for the benefit of her grandson. She elected to treat the transfer as being made over a five-year period. In 2019, G died. In 2017, 2018, and the year of death, G may exclude $14,000 annually. The remaining $28,000 ($70,000 − [3 × $14,000 = $42,000]) would be included in her gross estate.

The current gift tax law also permits an unlimited exclusion for tuition paid on someone's behalf if it is paid directly to an educational institution. This latter rule is not extended to payments made to qualified prepaid tuition plans. Consequently, only the basic $14,000 (2017) exclusion applies. For example, this prohibition bars a grandmother from prepaying a grandchild's tuition for four years and quickly removing substantial amounts from her estate tax-free.

The law also clarifies the estate tax treatment of amounts accumulated in prepaid tuition plans. Such amounts are not included in an individual's taxable estate (i.e., neither the estate of the parent nor that of the student). Traps: accounts owned by grandparents or noncustodial parents can count against a child's aid calculations after distributions are made. Also, money from a 529 account cannot be used for expenses that are also used to claim tax credits. Clients who want to receive a tax break on 529 withdrawals must wait until a student has incurred enough qualified education expenses to withdraw funds.

Interaction with Education Credits

As discussed in Chapter 13, there are two credits related to education: (1) the American Opportunity Tax Credit (AOTC) credit available for the first four years of college, and (2) the Lifetime Learning Credit for undergraduate, graduate, and other educational courses. Interestingly, the statute makes it clear that taxpayers receiving qualified tuition plan distributions are also eligible to claim either the AOTC or Lifetime Learning Credit for a taxable year as long as the income portion of the distributions is not used for the same expenses for which a credit is claimed.

ACHIEVING A BETTER LIFE EXPERIENCE (ABLE) ACCOUNTS

In 2014, Congress enacted § 529A to create tax-favored savings accounts that help address the financial challenges faced by individuals with disabilities—an estimated 36 million people, about 12% of the U.S. population. The plans are referred to as Achieving a Better Life Experience Accounts or ABLE accounts for short. ABLE accounts are quite similar to 529 plans. The critical aspects of ABLE accounts are identified below.

- ABLE accounts can only be created for eligible individuals. To be eligible, individuals must be blind or disabled, must have become so before turning 26, and generally must be entitled to benefits under the Supplemental Security Income (SSI) or Social Security Disability Insurance (SSDI) programs. Apparently, individuals over 26 could establish such accounts if they can document that the onset of the disability occurred before age 26.

- Each eligible person is limited to one ABLE account. An account can be created and contributions made by the individual with the disability or others. Such individual is considered the owner of the account.

- Total annual contributions that can be made by all individuals to any one ABLE account cannot exceed the amount of the annual gift tax exclusion, ($14,000 in 2015). Noncash contributions are not allowed.

- Contributions are not deductible. Therefore, they are made with after-tax dollars.

- Earnings attributable to the amounts in the account are exempt from federal taxation. Thus contributions and income can be accumulated, invested, and grown without tax.

- Distributions from ABLE accounts are nontaxable to the extent they are used for disability-related expenses. These expenses include education; housing; transportation; employment training and support; medical and dental care, as well as other health, prevention, and wellness costs; assistive technology and personal support services; financial management and administrative services; legal fees; and other IRS-approved expenses.

- Distributions that are not used for qualified expenses are subject to income tax plus a 10% penalty on a pro rata portion of the earnings. Note, however, distributions that represent contributions to the account are not taxable. For this reason, a special calculation must be made to determine the amount taxable in those situations where distributions exceed qualified expenses.

- ABLE accounts can generally be rolled over into another ABLE account for the same individual or into an ABLE account for a sibling who is also an eligible individual.

- Like 529 plans, each state is responsible for establishing and operating an ABLE program. Plans generally have multiple saving options and caps on the total amounts that can be contributed.

- ABLE accounts are subject to the so-called Medicaid payback provision. Upon the death of an eligible individual or when the person is no longer disabled, any amounts remaining in the account are to be repaid to the government for services provided during that person's lifetime. In other types of arrangements used for disabled persons such as special needs trusts, there is no requirement to repay Medicaid.

- Any remaining amounts that are not repaid to Medicaid would be distributed to the decedent's estate or a designated beneficiary. Distributions of the earnings to the estate or beneficiaries would be subject to the income tax, but not to any type of penalty.

- Like 529 plans, amounts in ABLE accounts are not included in the individual's gross estate for estate tax purposes. Amounts transferred to an ABLE account are not considered gifts nor are any distributions.

Employee Compensation and Other Benefits

By far the most important source of income for individual taxpayers is compensation from their employment. As seen earlier in Exhibit 6-1, preliminary statistics from 2011 indicate that salaries and wages represent more than 72% of all income reported on returns. While the bulk of employee compensation consists of salaries and wages, compensation includes all payments received for personal services such as commissions, bonuses, tips, vacation pay, severance pay, jury fees, and director's fees.[30] In addition, employers typically provide a variety of fringe benefits for their employees such as health and life insurance, child care, discounts on merchandise or services, parking, and contributions to retirement plans.

Although most forms of compensation are taxable, Congress has exempted certain benefits (e.g., health insurance, group-term life insurance), hoping the exclusion would encourage employers to provide such benefits for their employees. It is important to emphasize that these benefits are typically exempt not only from income tax but also from Social Security and Medicare taxes. The power of the exclusion feature is shown in the following example.

LO.3
Identify various types of employee compensation and fringe benefits and explain their tax treatment.

Example 17

T recently began working for B Corporation, which provides each of its employees with a number of fringe benefits. Among these benefits is payment of the premium on a health insurance policy for T and his family at an annual cost of $2,000 (a nontaxable fringe benefit). However, T may elect to receive $2,000 in cash instead. Assume that T's marginal tax rate is 15% and that he would buy the health insurance in any event. The table below compares the two options.

	Salary	Premium Payment
Amount	$2,000	$2,000
Income tax (15% × $2,000)	(300)	—
FICA (7.65% × $2,000)	(153)	—
After tax	$1,547	$2,000

Observe that T is much better off if he elects to have the employer pay for his health care. Electing the cash option would leave T with $453 less to pay for a similar insurance policy. Moreover, the employer is probably able to secure a better insurance rate than T could individually.

As the above example demonstrates, structuring a compensation package to include nontaxable fringe benefits provides a significant advantage to an employee. In effect, the employee is able to secure a particular benefit with before-tax or pre-tax rather than after-tax dollars. Employers also benefit because not only can they deduct the cost of the benefit just like cash compensation but they normally reduce their compensation cost since they are not required to pay Social Security, Medicare, or unemployment taxes on such amounts.

Exhibit 6-5 provides a listing of the common examples of compensation grouped by whether they are ordinarily taxable or nontaxable.

---

[30] § 61(a)(1) and Reg. § 1.61-2(a). See Chapter 18 for the treatment of stock received for services.

EXHIBIT 6-5	Taxable and Nontaxable Employee Compensation

Generally Included in Gross Income	*Generally Excluded from Gross Income*
Salaries, wages	Premiums paid on
Commissions	• Group-term life insurance (up to $50,000 coverage)
Bonuses	• Health, accident, disability, or long-term care insurance
Garnished wages	Life insurance proceeds
Tips	Meals and lodging if for employer's convenience
Director's fees	Adoption assistance
Jury fees	Educational assistance plans (undergraduate and graduate)
Severance pay	Child or dependent care
Reimbursements for	Benefits otherwise deductible by the employee (i.e., working condition fringe benefits)
• Business transportation and travel	
• Business entertainment	Qualified employee discounts
• Indirect moving expenses	No-additional cost services
• Educational expenses	De minimis benefits
Employer gifts	Parking
Employer awards	Use of company facilities or services
	Qualified retirement planning services
	Supper money
	Tuition reduction by educational institutions

Most employee fringe benefit plans must meet rigid rules to enable the employer to deduct contributions to the plans and for employees to exclude these amounts. Basically, the plans must (1) not discriminate in favor of highly compensated employees, (2) be in writing, (3) be for the exclusive benefit of the employees, (4) be legally enforceable, (5) provide employees with information concerning available plan benefits, and (6) be established with the intent that they will be maintained indefinitely. In addition, several eligibility and benefit tests provide detailed rules that must be met to ensure that employer costs are nontaxable income for employees. Additional employment benefits involving stock option, profit-sharing, and pension plans are discussed in Chapter 18.

REIMBURSEMENT OF EMPLOYEE EXPENSES

Employers often reimburse employees for their business-related expenses. Commonly reimbursed items include expenses for transportation, out-of-town travel, entertainment, and moving expenses. Such reimbursements are generally considered taxable. However, the employee usually has an offsetting expense that is deductible for AGI, so the effect on the tax return is usually a wash.[31] This is not always the case, however. If the employee is over-reimbursed or reimbursed for nondeductible expenses, there is a net increase in AGI. The effects of under-reimbursements and other aspects of reporting reimbursed expenses is considered in Chapter 8.

EMPLOYER GIFTS

Although § 102(a) allows taxpayers to exclude gifts from gross income, amounts transferred from an employer to an employee in the form of cash or other property are not excludable as a gift.[32] In effect, employers are prohibited from disguising compensation as a nontaxable gift. Consequently, employers interested in providing nontaxable benefits must look to other

---

[31] This is only true if the reimbursement is made pursuant to an "accountable plan." See Chapter 8 for a complete discussion.

[32] § 102(c). See *Lisa B. Williams* 2005-1 USTC 50,163, 95 AFTR 2d 2005-764, 120 Fed. Appx. 289 (CA-10, 2005).

sections of the Code that offer exclusions. For example, as discussed below, an employee can exclude certain employee achievement awards (e.g., Fitbit for productivity) and certain insignificant or de minimis fringe benefits such as inexpensive holiday gifts (e.g., a turkey at Thanksgiving).[33]

EMPLOYER AWARDS

It is quite common for an employer to award an employee for some type of achievement. An employee might receive a gold watch for many years of faithful service, a gift certificate for low absenteeism, or a free dinner for a great idea dropped in the suggestion box. For many years, employees argued that such awards were gifts rather than compensation and, therefore, were not taxable. Congress finally addressed this problem in two ways. As discussed above, the rules governing gifts were amended to make it clear that employers generally cannot make nontaxable gifts to employees. At the same time, Congress created a special rule allowing employees to exclude awards from their employer if certain conditions are met.

Employer awards to employees, other than de minimis fringe benefits (discussed later in this chapter), are generally treated as taxable compensation. However, § 74 allows an exclusion for a so-called employee achievement award.[34] An employee achievement award is defined as an item of tangible personal property (e.g., a television or watch) transferred to the employee for (1) length-of-service or (2) safety achievements.

There is a laundry list of requirements that must be met to ensure that the awards are not simply disguised compensation. To start, no exclusion is available for cash payments or their equivalents. This is understandable since cash looks like regular compensation. However, a gift certificate is permissible but only if it allows the employee to acquire tangible personal property (e.g., gift card to buy something at Amazon).[35] Tangible personal property is generally property that is movable like a plaque or golf clubs. Intangibles such as vacations, travel, meals, tickets to the theater or sporting events, stocks, bonds, or other securities do not qualify.

To avoid the look of compensation, the award must be given as part of a meaningful presentation. Also, no exclusion is available for a length-of-service award if it or a similar award is made within the individual's first five years of employment with the employer. Length of service awards can be made to the same individual once every five years. In addition, safety awards cannot have been made to more than 10% of a company's eligible employees. All employees are considered to be eligible except those in managerial, professional, and clerical positions.[36]

Awards that pass through the gauntlet of tests are deductible by the employer and nontaxable to the employee if the amount does not exceed certain statutory limits. The cost of property—the golf clubs or watch—normally cannot exceed $400 per employee per year for length-of-service and safety awards. If the employer maintains a qualified written plan that does not favor highly compensated employees and that has an average annual benefit of no more than $400 per employee, then the per employee maximum is raised to $1,600. Excess costs are taxable income to the extent of the *greater* of (1) the nondeductible cost to the employer due to the limitations, or (2) the property's market value in excess of the limitations. This taxable income must be reported on the employee's Form W-2.

Example 18

R, Inc. pays $525 ($640 market value) J for a brooch that it awards to L in recognition of her 15 years of service to the company. No other awards are given to L during the year. R's deduction is limited to $400, and L has taxable income of $240 (the greater of $525 − $400 = $125 and $640 − $400 = $240). The $240 will appear on L's Form W-2 as taxable income.

---

[33] § 132(e).

[34] §§ 74(c) and 274(j).

[35] Prop. Reg. § 1.274-8(c)(2) also makes taxable such items as vacations, meals, lodging, event tickets, and securities.

[36] See §§ 74(c) and 274(j).

SOCIAL SECURITY BENEFITS

When most taxpayers collect Social Security benefits, these benefits can be excluded from gross income. This treatment can be traced to an early IRS ruling that granted the exclusion with little explanation in 1941.[37] Interestingly, the exclusion was allowed notwithstanding the fact that there was no statutory authority for it. In 1984, however, Congress apparently felt that this gracious treatment, while proper for those whose primary source of income was Social Security, was not appropriate for higher-income taxpayers. As a result, it created § 86 to address its concern.

Under the 1984 legislative formula, the Social Security benefits of most taxpayers continued to be nontaxable. However, upper-income taxpayers could have as much as 50% of their Social Security benefits taxed. Note that the effect of this provision is to tax these amounts—at least that portion representing the taxpayer's contributions—twice; first when included as gross wages and second when included as Social Security benefits are received. On the other hand, the portion received representing the contribution by the employer and any earnings on the amounts contributed are not taxable at all.

The treatment created in 1984 continued until 1993 when the Clinton administration, with the backing of Congress, increased the amount that could be taxed from 50 to 85 percent.[38] The thrust of the current rules is quite simple. As long as income remains below a certain threshold, Social Security benefits are completely nontaxable. But as income increases, the amount of Social Security that may be taxed increases. Unfortunately, the actual calculation of the amount that must be included in gross income is unduly cumbersome. The effect of the revised provisions is to establish two income thresholds:

	Married Filing Jointly	Married Filing Separately	Unmarried Taxpayers
Modified AGI threshold #1	$32,000	$0	$25,000
Modified AGI threshold #2	44,000	0	34,000

Notice that in determining whether a taxpayer's level of income warrants taxation of his or her Social Security benefits, an expanded notion of income referred to as *modified adjusted gross income* is used. Modified adjusted gross income is generally computed as follows:

	Adjusted gross income
+	½ of Social Security benefits
+	Tax-exempt income
+	Foreign earned income exclusion
	Modified AGI

Taxpayers whose modified AGI is less than the first threshold ($32,000 for married filing jointly) are not taxed on their Social Security benefits. Those whose modified AGI falls between the two thresholds ($32,000 – $44,000 for married filing jointly) must include the lesser of one-half of their Social Security benefits or one-half of the excess of their modified AGI over the specified threshold. For those taxpayers whose modified AGI *exceeds* the first threshold (e.g., $32,000 for married filing jointly), the calculation can be made using the following schedules:

---

[37] Rev. Rul 70-217,1970-1 C.B. 12.   [38] § 86.

Married Filing Jointly

If Modified AGI Over:	But Not Over:	Amount Taxed
$32,000	$44,000	Step 1: Lesser of (1) 50% of benefits, or (2) 50% × (Modified AGI − $32,000)
$44,000		Step 2: Lesser of (1) Step 1 amount, not to exceed $6,000, + 85% × (Modified AGI − $44,000), or (2) 85% of benefits

Unmarried Taxpayers

If Modified AGI Over:	But Not Over:	Amount Taxed
$25,000	$34,000	Step 1: Lesser of (1) 50% of benefits, or (2) 50% × (Modified AGI − $25,000)
$34,000		Step 2: Lesser of (1) Step 1 amount, not to exceed $4,500, + 85% × (Modified AGI − $34,000), or (2) 85% of benefits

Example 19

George and Mildred, happily married for 45 years, received the following income:

Dividend income	$50,000
Social Security benefits	16,000

Here the couple's modified AGI is $58,000 ($50,000 + [50% × $16,000 = $8,000]). Because the couple's $58,000 modified AGI exceeds the second threshold of $44,000, the 85% rule is triggered. Their taxable Social Security is $13,600, computed as follows:

Step 1 Amount	
Lesser of (1) or (2)	
(1) 50% × Social Security of $16,000	$ 8,000
(2) 50% × ($58,000 − $32,000 = $26,000)	$13,000
Step 1 amount	$ 8,000

Step 2 Amount	
Lesser of (1) or (2)	
(1) Step 1 amount ($8,000), not to exceed $6,000, +	$ 6,000
85% × ($58,000 − $44,000 = $14,000)	11,900
	$17,900
(2) 85% × benefits of $16,000	$13,600
Step 2 amount and taxable Social Security benefits	$13,600

Example 20

Assume the same facts as in *Example 19* above except that dividend income amounts to \$30,000. Because the couple's \$38,000 modified AGI (\$30,000 + [50% × \$16,000]) falls below the second threshold (\$44,000), their taxable Social Security is \$3,000, computed as follows:

Lesser of		
50% × Social Security of \$16,000	\$8,000	
or		
50% × (\$38,000 – \$32,000 = \$6,000)	\$3,000	
Step 1 amount and taxable Social Security benefits		\$3,000

As indicated above, the base or threshold amount is zero for married filing separately. Consequently, married taxpayers who elect to file separately automatically expose Social Security benefits to taxation.

Taxpayers whose Social Security benefits are subject to taxation should give consideration to shifting money out of municipal bonds and into other investment vehicles such as growth stocks that do not pay dividends or into Series EE U.S. savings bonds, which generally do not produce taxable income until they are redeemed.

UNEMPLOYMENT BENEFITS

In any dynamic economy, the forces at work often leave individuals without a job. For example, in the United States, weekly unemployment claims during 2008 surged, ranging from about 300,000 to 750,000. During 2008 and 2009, the unemployment rate was 4.9% in January of 2008 and reached 10.2% by October 2009. While the rate has declined from these levels, the rate was still about 4.6% as of this writing (December, 2016). In order to help those workers who have lost their jobs through no fault of their own, Congress created the unemployment insurance system as part of the Social Security Act in 1935. Under this system, employers, not employees, are subject to Federal and State unemployment taxes, which they are entitled to deduct as ordinary business expenses. These taxes are then used to provide benefits for the unemployed, thus allowing them a period of time that they can seek a new job without major financial distress.

Prior to 1979, unemployment benefits received were not taxable. In 1979, however, Congress reversed direction and opted to tax such benefits. Apparently it believed that the exclusion might actually reduce the incentive to work, making unemployment more, rather than less, attractive. Currently, unemployment benefits received under a government program are fully taxable.[39]

EMPLOYEE INSURANCE

Over the years, Congress has created several exclusions for employer-provided life, health, accident, and disability insurance. The continuation for these exclusions can generally be found in the Congressional desire to ensure that all individuals are adequately protected against unforeseen hardships. As a result, it is quite common for employers to provide some type of group insurance for employees. Premiums for insurance coverage may be paid by the employer only, by the employee only, or by both the employer and employee under some shared cost arrangement. Generally, employer-paid premiums for health, accident, and disability insurance are deductible business expenses and are excluded from the employee's gross income. On the other hand, life insurance premiums paid by the employer generally are included by the employee and deductible by the employer. As may be expected, however, there are exceptions.

---

[39] § 85(a).

Life Insurance Premiums and Proceeds

Employer-paid life insurance premiums are nontaxable by an employee but *only* for the first $50,000 of *group-term life insurance* protection.[40] Premiums paid by an employer for any other type of life insurance are fully included in each employee's gross income. In order to qualify as group insurance, the employer's plan generally must not discriminate. The employer must provide coverage for all employees with a few permitted exceptions based on their age, marital status, or factors related to employment. Examples of employment-related factors are union membership, duties performed, compensation received, and length of service.[41] Acceptable discrimination, however, is limited by the Regulations. Thus, employers may establish eligibility requirements that exclude certain types of employees, such as those who work part-time, who are under age 21, or who have not been employed at least six months. But omitting older employees or those with longer service records generally is not permitted.

When group-term insurance protection exceeds $50,000, the employee generally must include in income the premium attributable to the amount of coverage over $50,000. The actual amount to be included is set forth in the Regulations rather than actual premiums paid. The taxable amount for each $1,000 of insurance in excess of $50,000 is based on the employee's age as of the last day of his or her tax year. These amounts (which were recently lowered by the Treasury) are shown in Exhibit 6-6.[42]

EXHIBIT 6-6	Imputed Costs of Excess Group-Term Life Insurance	
	Includible Income per $1,000	
Employee's Age	*Monthly*	*Annually*
Under 25	$0.05	$ 0.60
25 to 29	0.06	0.72
30 to 34	0.08	0.96
35 to 39	0.09	1.08
40 to 44	0.10	1.20
45 to 49	0.15	1.80
50 to 54	0.23	2.76
55 to 59	0.43	5.16
60 to 64	0.66	7.92
65 to 69	1.27	15.24
70 and over	2.06	24.72

Source: Reg. § 1.79-3, effective July 1, 1999.

---

[40] § 79(a)(1). The $50,000 limit is eliminated for retired employees who are disabled.

[41] Reg. §§ 1.79-0 and 1.79-1(a)(4).

[42] Reg. § 1.79-3. Beginning in 1988, the cost of group-term life insurance that an employee must include in his or her gross income must also be treated as wages for Social Security withholding purposes.

Example 21

BC, Inc. provides all full-time employees with group-term insurance. Records for three of the employees show the following information. All three were employed by BC for the full year.

Employee	Age	Insurance Coverage	Coverage in Excess of $50,000
D	56	$80,000	$30,000
E	38	62,000	12,000
F	35	40,000	0

D's taxable income is $154.80 ($5.16 × $30,000 ÷ $1,000). E's taxable income is $12.96 ($1.08 × $12,000 ÷ $1,000). F has no taxable income from group-term life insurance, since the coverage does not exceed $50,000.

As explained further within, regardless of whether life insurance is provided by the employer, proceeds received by a beneficiary on the death of the insured ordinarily are excludable from gross income.[43]

Health Insurance Benefits

As a general rule, all medical insurance benefits are excluded from income regardless of who pays the premiums.[44] Any reimbursement of medical costs simply reduces the amount of medical expenses that can be itemized (as deductions from AGI—discussed in Chapter 11).[45] However, in some instances the expenses are paid in one year but reimbursement is not received until a later year. Taxpayers have a choice when this occurs. One, they may anticipate the reimbursement and not deduct any of the reimbursable expenses. This decision means the reimbursement is nontaxable when received. Alternatively, these taxpayers may choose to itemize all medical costs in the year paid even though reimbursement is expected. This decision means the reimbursement is included in gross income when received to the extent a *tax benefit* was obtained for the prior year's deduction.[46] Since only the amount of medical expenditures that exceeds 10% of AGI provides a tax benefit (i.e., reduces an individual's taxable income), it is possible that part of the reimbursement is nontaxable.

Example 22

J, age 50 and single, paid medical expenses of $17,000 in 2017. However, her insurance company reimbursed her for the entire amount with two checks, $11,000 in 2017 and $6,000 in 2018. J's 2017 AGI was $50,000, and her other itemized deductions exceeded her standard deduction for the year. If J chooses to deduct *all* of the unreimbursed medical expenses in 2017, her itemized deduction is $6,000 ($17,000 − $11,000 reimbursed in 2017) but her tax benefit is only $1,000 ($6,000 − [10% × $50,000 AGI = $5,000]). Thus, only $1,000 of the $6,000 reimbursement received in 2018 is included in her gross income. Alternatively, if J, knowing that ultimately she will be fully reimbursed, decides to forgo the deduction in 2017, she has no taxable income in 2018. In this case, J's decision depends in part on (1) her marginal tax rates for both years, and (2) the present value to her of the tax deferral for one year.

If medical coverage is financed by the employer, any reimbursement in excess of medical expenses incurred by an employee for himself or herself, a spouse, and dependents is included in gross income.[47] These excess amounts, however, are not included if the premiums were paid by the individual.

---

[43] § 101(a)(1).

[44] § 106.

[45] §§ 105(b) and 213.

[46] § 111(a).

[47] § 105(b).

Many businesses finance their own medical benefit plans from company funds (instead of through insurance). These companies must establish plans that do not discriminate in favor of certain officers, shareholders, or highly paid employees. If the plan is discriminatory, individuals in these three categories must report taxable income equal to any medical reimbursement they received that is not available to other employees.[48] Thus, the purpose is to encourage businesses to extend medical coverage to all of their employees.

Qualified Long-Term Care Benefits

Under prior law, benefits received under long-term care insurance policies were not necessarily excluded. Current law makes it clear that insurance contracts for long-term care that provide services for chronically-ill individuals and meet a number of other requirements are considered an accident and health insurance contract. As a result, taxpayers can exclude benefits received under such policies. However, the amount of the exclusion from gross income for 2017 is the greater of $360 per day or the actual cost of the care.[49]

Qualified long-term care services generally include necessary diagnostic, preventive, therapeutic, curing, treating, mitigating and rehabilitative services, and maintenance or personal care services that are required by a chronically-ill individual and provided pursuant to a plan of care prescribed by a licensed health care practitioner.[50] A chronically-ill individual is generally a person who is unable to perform at least two activities of daily living (e.g., eating, toileting, transferring, bathing, dressing, and continence) for a period of at least 90 days due to a loss of some type of functional capacity.

Example 23

In 2017, L, 93, broke her hip and was confined to a nursing home for 30 days. The nursing home charged L $200 per day for a total of $6,000. L's long-term care insurance policy pays 90% of the amount charged by the home after a 10-day waiting period. In October, L received an insurance reimbursement of $3,600 (90% × [$200 × 20 days]). L may exclude the entire $3,600 received since it is less than the maximum allowable exclusion of $7,200 (20 days × $360 per day in 2017). In addition, she can deduct the unreimbursed amount of $2,400 ($6,000 − $3,600) as a medical expense subject to the 7.5% of AGI limitation (see Chapter 11).

Employees normally can exclude from income the value of employer-provided coverage under a long-term care plan. However, there is no exclusion if the coverage is provided through a cafeteria plan. Furthermore, long-term care services cannot be reimbursed on a tax-free basis under a flexible spending account.

Accident and Disability Insurance Benefits

As a general rule, all amounts received under an *employer-financed* accident or disability plan are taxable, with few exceptions. However, when payments are for permanent loss or use of a function or member of the body or for permanent disfigurement of the employee, employee's spouse or dependent, they are nontaxable.[51] Moreover, to be excludable, the payments must be computed with reference to the *nature* of the injury, and not on the *time* the employee is absent from work (i.e., a wage substitute).

Example 24

G lost two fingers while making repairs to her automobile. She received $20,000 from her employer-provided accident insurance policy. The $20,000 is nontaxable to G because the payment was solely for loss of a function or member of the body.

---

[48] § 105(h).

[49] § 7702B(d)(4).

[50] § 7702B(c).

[51] §§ 105(a) and (c).

In contrast with employer-financed disability plans, all disability income is *nontaxable* if the taxpayer paid for the disability coverage.[52] Consequently, those employees with long-term disabilities may incur substantial tax costs if their disability income is received from employer-financed plans.

Example 25

After graduation from high school, R was employed by WW Manufacturing Company. The company's employee benefits included disability insurance. R's disability insurance premiums averaged $250 annually. After 15 years with WW, R became seriously ill. The illness left him permanently disabled. After a three-month wait, required by the insurance company, R began receiving $800 monthly disability income. Whether the $800 is taxable income depends on who paid the $250 annual premium on the disability policy. If WW paid the premium, the $800 monthly disability income is taxable income. If R paid the premium, the $800 is nontaxable. If R paid a portion of the premium, for example 40 percent, then that portion, $320 (40% × $800), is nontaxable, and the remaining $480 is attributable to the employer's contribution and is, therefore, taxable income.

EMPLOYER-PROVIDED MEALS AND LODGING

As explained in Chapter 5, early rulings and decisions exempted certain benefits given to employees when they did not serve as compensation but rather were for the "convenience of the employer." A classic example of this principle can be found in the working relationship between many apartment owners and their managers. Typically, owners require their managers to live on the premises without charge so that they are immediately available should they be needed. While this is an obvious benefit to employees, the tax law allows employees to exclude the value of the housing because in this case it is not primarily a means of compensation but serves some overriding purpose of the employer. In 1954, Congress codified this principle for meals and lodging in § 119.

Under § 119, the value of meals and lodging provided by an employer to an employee and the employee's spouse and dependents is excluded from income if:

1. Provided for the *employer's convenience;*

2. Provided on the employer's *business premises;* and

3. In the case of lodging, the employee is *required* to occupy the quarters in order to perform employment duties.[53]

Generally, meals and housing furnished to employees without charge are considered to be for the employer's convenience if a substantial noncompensatory business purpose exists.[54] The regulations provide some guidance in this regard, indicating that meals are usually considered noncompensatory if there are insufficient eating facilities in the vicinity of the employer's premises (e.g., an employee working on an oil rig in the North Sea) or the employee must be available for emergency calls during the meal period (a 911 operator). The regulations also specifically provide that meals provided to wait staff, and other food service employees are noncompensatory. Beyond the examples in the regulations, there are numerous court decisions on the subject. For example, the Tax Court found that there were substantial business reasons to provide meals and lodging to the manager of a motel who is on 24-hour call.[55] But, if the employee has the option to receive other compensation instead, the value of the meals and lodging is included in income.[56]

---

[52] § 104(a)(3) and Reg. § 1.104-1(d).

[53] § 119(a)(2) and Reg. § 1.119-1(b).

[54] Reg. §§ 1.119-1(a)(2) and (b).

[55] *J.B. Lindeman,* 60 T.C. 609 (1973), acq.

[56] Reg. § 1.119-1(c)(2).

Employee Compensation and Other Benefits

Example 26

Z is a warden at a state prison in Northern Arizona. She must be on duty from 8:00 a.m. until 5:00 p.m. Monday through Friday. Z is given the choice of residing at the prison free of charge (value of $12,000 per year), or of residing elsewhere and receiving a cash allowance of $1,000 per month in addition to her regular salary. If she elects to reside at the prison, the value to Z of the lodging furnished by the prison will be taxable because her residence at the prison is not required in order for her to perform properly the duties of her employment.

Nontaxable meals and lodging must be furnished on the employer's premises. The term *business premises* has been interpreted to be either the primary place of business (e.g., the hotel, restaurant, or construction site) or elsewhere as long as it is near the place of business and where a significant portion of the business is conducted.[57] However, employer-owned housing located two blocks from the primary place of business, a motel, was disallowed because it was not considered to be on the employer's premises.[58] This contrasts with employer-owned housing located across the street from the primary place of business, a hotel, that was held to be on the premises.[59] Apparently, taxpayer success in this second case was based on the amount of business conducted in the home rather than its location.

Over the years, there has been a great deal of controversy about application of the exclusion where the employer did not provide the meals but rather reimbursed the employee for his or her meal cost. The landmark case in the area is *Kowalski,* which dealt with a New Jersey state trooper who was given meal allowances under the condition that he eat in his assigned duty area and remain on call.[60] In denying the exclusion, the Supreme Court explained that it applied only to meals in kind and not to cash reimbursements. Despite the apparent clarity of this decision, controversy still arises over this issue.

Interestingly, the *Kowalski* court indicated in a footnote that its decision was not intended to address the treatment of so-called supper money, the term used to describe meal money given to employees who are required to work overtime. The IRS had historically allowed taxpayers to exclude such amounts.[61] This exclusion, as discussed later in this chapter, is now preserved in the Regulations as a de minimis fringe benefit. These rules specifically allow taxpayers to exclude supper money which is provided to overtime workers on an occasional basis.[62]

Example 27

F Inc., a furniture retailer, has an exhibit each year at the local home show convention. Three of F's employees are asked to put in 12-hour days during the week-long convention. To help ease their burden, F provides each of the three employees $8 per day to cover the cost of their dinner. The $56 ($8 × 7 days) each employee receives is considered "supper money" and is therefore excluded as a de minimis fringe benefit.

In addition, § 119 explains that meals provided to all employees will be excludable if provided to more than one-half of all employees for the convenience of the employer. This rule is important for employers as well since it enables employers to deduct all of such costs (e.g., the cost of a company cafeteria) and avoid employment taxes that otherwise would apply.

CHILD AND DEPENDENT CARE ASSISTANCE

A touchy issue over the years has been the treatment of child care expenses. Arguably, a taxpayer should be extended some tax relief because such costs are inevitable if he or she is to be gainfully employed. Currently, the tax law underwrites the cost of child care under these

---

[57] Rev. Rul. 71-411, 1971-2 C.B. 103.

[58] *Comm. v. Anderson,* 67-1 USTC ¶9136, 19 AFTR2d 318, 371 F.2d 59 (CA-6, 1966), cert. denied.

[59] *J.B. Lindeman,* 60 T.C. 609 (1973), acq.

[60] *Kowalski v. Comm.,* 77-2 USTC ¶9748, 40 AFTR2d 6128, 434 U.S. 77 (USSC, 1977).

[61] O.D. 514, 2 C.B. 90 (1920).

[62] Reg. § 1.132-6.

circumstances in two ways. Employees who receive reimbursements for their child care expenses or whose employer provides child care in kind (e.g., a daycare facility) may exclude up to $5,000 annually.[63] In addition, the law allows gainfully employed individuals a limited credit for their child care expenses (20–35 percent of $3,000–$6,000 of expenses depending on the taxpayer's income and the number of children).[64] While this might suggest that the taxpayer may be able to secure two benefits, the law effectively prohibits this by reducing any expenses that qualify for the credit by the amount of any benefits that are excluded. In order to claim either the exclusion or the credit, a laundry list of special rules must be followed. These are discussed in connection with the child care credit in Chapter 13.

Example 28

J routinely drops off her two young children at a daycare facility provided by her employer. This year the value of the service is worth about $5,000. J normally may exclude the full $5,000 from income. Had J paid $5,000 for child care which her employer reimbursed, she could also exclude the $5,000. However, in such case, the amount of her qualifying expenses for purposes of the child care credit would be zero ($5,000 expense − $5,000 exclusion). Alternatively, J could report the $5,000 as income and claim a credit equal to 20–35 percent of the maximum allowable expenses of $6,000.

ADOPTION ASSISTANCE PROGRAMS

For many, one of life's biggest events is starting a family. In some cases, this may involve adoption. Rough estimates (apparently there is no single source that keeps track) indicate that the number of adoptions per year is about 135,000. Experts say that this number would be even larger if adoption were not so expensive. Costs for an adoption vary widely but for a newborn expenses may run from $35,000 to $50,000. However, the tax law provides several measures that help reduce this cost. Perhaps, the most important of these is a nonrefundable credit. Individuals can claim a credit for qualified adoption expenses for each child they adopt. The credit is adjusted annually for inflation and is $13,570 in 2017. Thus, if a couple adopted two children, they would be eligible for two credits or $27,140. In some cases, an employer may pay or provide reimbursement of the adoption expenses. In this case, § 137 provides an employee an exclusion equal to the same amount as the credit or $13,570 per child.

Qualified adoption expenses are reasonable and necessary adoption fees, court costs, attorney's fees and other expenses that are directly related to the legal adoption of an eligible child. An eligible child is an individual who (1) has not attained age 18 as of the time of the adoption, or (2) is physically or mentally incapable of caring for himself or herself. Both the credit and the exclusion begin to phase out for taxpayers with modified AGI above $203,540 and is not available once modified AGI reaches $243,540.

Adoption expenses paid or reimbursed by an employer under an adoption assistance program may not also be taken into account in determining the adoption credit. This prevents a taxpayer from getting a double benefit (i.e., a credit for expenses that the taxpayer never paid). A taxpayer may, however, satisfy the requirements of the adoption credit and the exclusion with different expenses paid or incurred by the taxpayer and the employer, respectively. It is worth noting here that when the adoption involves a "special needs" child, the full credit may be claimed even if there were no adoption expenses incurred. Further discussion of the credit can be found in Chapter 13 on nonbusiness credits.

FOSTER CARE PAYMENTS

Unfortunately, there are times when parents are unable, unwilling or unfit to care for a child. In these situations, the child is usually placed in foster care—a temporary home where adults, the foster parents, care for the child until he or she can be reunited with his or her biological parents or perhaps adopted. Foster care can be informal or arranged through the courts or a social service agency. Although the goal for children in foster care is usually reunification with their parents, this may change to adoption if this is seen as in the child's best interest.

---

[63] § 129(a)(1).   [64] § 21.

In the U.S., the predominant form of foster care is still ordinary people serving as foster parents. Foster home licensing requirements vary from state to state but are generally overseen by the state's Department of "Social Services" or "Human Services." At the close of 2014, the Children's Bureau reported that there were about 415,000 children in foster care.

Foster parents (and other foster care providers such as foster homes) are responsible for directly providing the shelter, food, clothing, supervision, and other personal incidentals necessary for the safety and well-being of children in their care. To assist them in meeting the child's needs, child welfare agencies offer foster parents a payment. The amounts paid are set by each state (i.e., each state has its own reimbursement rate) and the rates vary primarily by age and the level of care a child requires. For example, the reimbursement rate for younger children with special needs will likely be higher than the rate for an older children without special problems. In addition to a basic amount, states usually provide separate allowances for certain expenses (birthdays, holidays). The amounts paid to the foster care providers vary widely by state but the basic rate is about $20–$25 per day or $600–$750 per month.

For many years, these payments were nontaxable but only to the extent of the expenses incurred by the foster parents.[65] However, in 1983, Congress enacted § 131 to exempt all qualified foster payments. Generally, most foster care payments qualify as long as the state has a foster program; the payments are made by the state or a state licensed agency; and the child is living in the foster parents' home.

Example 29

Last year, 8-year old Louisa lost both parents due to a terrible accident. She had no living relatives and the state of Indiana put her in a temporary foster care facility. This year the Department of Child Services placed her in the care of Mr. and Mrs. Smith. Louisa lives in the couple's home where she has her own room, which previously served as a guest bedroom. For the year, the Smiths received an $8,000 payment from the state based on a standard per diem amount. The Smith's out of pocket costs for food and clothing and other incidentals were $5,000. The Smiths may exclude the entire $8,000 because it meets the requirements for qualified foster payments. The payment was paid under a state plan, paid by a state agency and paid to the Smiths for caring for a "placed" child in their own home. The exclusion of the entire $8,000 is available even though the only additional costs the Smiths incurred were $5,000.

The phrase "foster care" usually suggests an image of a child who is placed with a family, unrelated to them, for temporary care. While that is a correct impression, recent changes made the exclusion of § 131 much broader. If an individual provides non-skilled medical support services or care for a person living in his or her home and such person has physical, mental or emotional issues, payments from the state or a certified Medicaid provider are excluded. Observe that under this approach, there is no requirement that care be given to a qualified foster child. Thus, taxpayers who care for family members and receive payments from a state or Medicare can receive the same tax-free treatment allowed for care of unrelated foster children.[66]

Example 30

Same facts as *Example 29* above except Louisa is Mrs. Smith's 89 year-old mother, who is fighting dementia. The Smiths have decided to care for her in their own home instead of placing her in a nursing home, which promised to be expensive, time-consuming and probably exhausting. The state would pay a small wage to Mrs. Smith to take care of her mother. Under the IRS's current approach, Mrs. Smith could exclude the wages even though her mother is related to her.

[65] Rev. Rul. 77-280, 1977-2 CB 14.   [66] Notice 2014-7, 2014-4 IRB 445.

In addition to the exclusion for qualified foster payments, there are other tax aspects of providing foster care that foster parents or those thinking of becoming foster parents should understand. Some of these are quite beneficial. For example, if the payments received actually exceed the costs of care as in the *Example 29* above, the excess is nontaxable. Note also that reimbursements include an amount for housing and, therefore, cover a fixed cost the foster parents have with or without a child. See *Example 29* above.

A common question of foster parents is whether they can claim a dependency exemption for the foster child. As discussed in Chapter 4, a foster child is considered a qualifying child so an exemption should normally be available. If the child is a dependent, the foster parents should qualify for the child tax credit of $1,000 for each child, the child and dependent care credit, and possibly the earned income credit (although the payments received are not considered earned income). In addition, a single foster parent may qualify for head-of-household filing status.

EDUCATIONAL ASSISTANCE PLANS

Employers often assist their employees in furthering their education by providing them with financial assistance. To encourage such initiatives, Congress enacted § 127. This provision grants an annual exclusion of up to $5,250 for employer-provided educational assistance (i.e., tuition, fees, books, supplies and equipment). The exclusion applies to reimbursements or direct payment of expenses related to both undergraduate and graduate level courses.

SECTION 132 FRINGE BENEFITS

In 1984, Congress attempted to tackle what was a growing controversy over fringe benefits. During that time, more and more employers were finding innovative ways to reward their employees with benefits that many aggressive taxpayers argued were nontaxable fringe benefits. Congress responded to these potential abuses by inserting a clause in the definition of gross income in § 61, stating that all fringe benefits were taxable. At the same time, however, § 132 was added and it not only sanctioned the exclusion for certain benefits that historically had escaped tax, but also created guidelines for evaluating others. It should be emphasized that the amendment to include fringe benefits as income reinforces the principle that *all* benefits are taxable unless the Code specifically excludes them. Unfortunately, this concept apparently was lost on Senator Tom Daschle who was nominated to be Secretary of Health and Human Services in 2009. During his vetting, it came to light that he had failed to report the value of a car and driver provided by his employer as income in the amounts of $73,031, $89,129, and $93,096 in 2005, 2006, and 2007, respectively. In addition, he omitted more than $80,000 of income from consulting!

An overview of the nontaxable fringe benefits now provided under § 132 is given in Exhibit 6-7. These additional employee benefits include the following:

1. Working condition fringe benefits.
2. No-additional-cost services.
3. Qualified employee discounts.
4. De minimis fringe benefits.
5. On-premises athletic facilities.
6. Qualified transportation fringe benefits.
7. Qualified moving expense reimbursement.
8. Qualified retirement planning services.

Furthermore, employees of educational institutions receive special treatment under § 117 for reduction in tuition costs.

Working Condition Fringe Benefits

This exclusion provides that fringe benefits are nontaxable to the extent that employees could deduct the costs if they reimbursed their employer or otherwise paid the costs.[67] For example, if an accounting firm paid $100 for an employee's membership dues to the AICPA and $50 for a subscription to the *Wall Street Journal*, the employee could exclude the amounts since such costs could be deducted by the employee as routine business expenses had he or she paid them directly. Similarly, many businesses furnish some of their employees with company-owned automobiles. Expenses related to the business usage of the cars are deductible by employers and are excluded from income by the employees. In contrast, personal use of the cars, which includes commuting between the employees' home and work, is taxable compensation (unless it is nontaxable under the de minimis rule discussed later in this section).[68] This income is reported as other compensation, and thus not subject to withholding taxes.[69] If, however, employees reimburse their employers for all personal use of the automobiles, there is no auto-related taxable compensation. These benefits need not be provided to all employees (i.e., they may be reserved for officers, owners, and highly paid employees).

EXHIBIT 6-7	Nontaxable Fringe Benefits under § 132	
Type of Benefit	*Conditions*	*Examples*
No additional cost service—§ 132(b)	Company incurs no substantial additional cost Service sold in normal course of business Same-line-of-business limitations Reciprocal agreements allowed Must be nondiscriminatory	Airplane tickets Hotel rooms Telephone services
Qualified employee discount—§ 132(c)	Offered for sale in normal course of business Same-line-of-business limitation Merchandise discounts limited to employer's gross profit Service discounts limited to 20% of normal price Must be nondiscriminatory Not applicable to investment property or real estate	Retail items
Working condition fringes—§ 132(d)	Nontaxable to extent employee would have deducted the cost had he or she paid for the property or service	Company car Club memberships Professional dues and subscriptions Seminar expenses

De minimis fringes—§ 132(e)	Benefits are so small that accounting for them is unreasonable or administratively impractical	Employee picnics
		Cocktail parties
		Holiday gifts
		Occasional use of:
		   Copying machine
		   Typing services
		   Meals
		   Coffee and donuts

---

[67] Such costs would have been deductible as business expenses under § 162 or as depreciation under § 167. § 132(d); Reg. § 1.132-5.

[68] § 61(a)(1) and Reg. § 1.61-2(d)(1).

[69] Reg. § 1.6041-2 and Ltr. Rul. 8122017. Although not subject to withholding taxes, this income is subject to Social Security taxes.

Qualified transportation fringes—§ 132(f)	Valuation of parking: amount a person would pay in an arm's-length transaction to obtain parking at the same site
	Available only to employees—not "partners" and "independent contractors"
		Up to $255 (2017) per month
		  Transit passes and
		  Vanpooling combined
		Up to $255 per month:
		  Parking

Qualified bicycle commuting reimbursement	Reimbursements by an employer for employee expenses related to a bicycle used regularly for commuting	Up to $20 per month
		  Bicycle tires
		  Repairs, storage

Moving expense reimbursement—§ 132(g)	Reimbursements or payments by an employer to an employee for qualified moving expenses (i.e., those that would be deductible under § 217)	Moving expenses in connection with
		  Beginning employment
		  Changing job locations

Athletic facilities—§ 132(j)(4)	Located on employer's premises Operated by employer Substantially all use is by employees, spouses, and children	Tennis court Golf course Gym Pool

Qualified retirement planning services—§ 132(m)(1)	Any retirement planning services provided to an employee/spouse by an employer maintaining a "qualified" employer plan (i.e., pension plans)	Advice and information on retirement income planning
		Does not apply to
		  Tax preparation
		  Accounting services
		  Legal or brokerage services

In addition to the above exclusions, the working condition fringe allows an exclusion for payments made for education by an employer if the employee could have deducted the cost as a business expense under § 162 (e.g., the education enabled the taxpayer to improve his skills used in his business and was not necessary to meet the minimum education requirement imposed by the job). This rule supplements the exclusion for employer-provided educational assistance of $5,250 but only in those cases where the educational costs would have been deductible had they been paid by employee. For example, if an employee could meet the tests for deducting the expenses related to a graduate degree (e.g., an M.B.A.), financial assistance provided by an employer could be excluded.

No-Additional-Cost Services

Some employers allow employees to use company facilities or services without charge or for a minimal maintenance fee. For example, an airline may allow its employees to fly stand-by for free because it loses nothing since the seat would have otherwise not been used. In this and similar situations, § 132(b) permits the employee to exclude the benefit as long as the company incurs *no substantial additional cost* as a result of the employee's usage. However, unlike the working condition fringe benefit, the exclusion is not allowed if the benefit discriminates in favor of officers or other highly compensated employees.

There are literally thousands of benefits that could qualify as no-additional-cost services. They range from use of company meeting rooms to free tickets in the entertainment industry for seats that would otherwise be empty. Note that the exclusion is limited to services sold in the normal course of business in which the employee works. For example, the value of a hotel room is nontaxable if used by an employee (and/or a spouse or dependent children) who works in the employer's hotel business. It is taxable, however, if the employee works for another line of business of an employer with diversified interests such as hotels and auto rentals. Those employees identified with more than one line of business (e.g., an accountant) may exclude the benefits received from all of them. The exclusion is extended to benefits provided under a written reciprocal agreement by another employer that is in the same line of business.[70] Thus, the hotel employee has nontaxable income for free use of a hotel room provided by another company that has a qualified reciprocal agreement with the employer.

---

[70] § 132(i). The line of business limitation is relaxed in certain instances if a special excise tax is paid.

Qualified Employee Discounts

It is common practice for companies to allow employees to purchase inventory items at a discount. For example, a department store may allow its employees to purchase merchandise at the selling price less a stipulated discount. Such discounts seldom result in taxable income unless they discriminate in favor of highly compensated employees.[71] The exclusion, however, is not available for discounts on investment property or on residential or commercial real estate.

The rules governing nondiscrimination, the requirement that items must be offered for sale in the normal course of business and line of business, and the rules governing coverage of spouses and dependent children discussed above for nontaxable services also pertain to nontaxable discounts. In contrast with services, however, discounts under reciprocal agreements are taxable income. The merchandise discount exclusion is limited to the employer's normal profit (i.e., the discount may not exceed the employer's gross profit). In the case of employer services, the discount may not exceed 20% of the price charged to customers. Any discount beyond that amount is taxable income to the employee.

Example 31

V, an employee of an auto mechanic business, has her automobile repaired by the company. Accounting records show the following information for the parts and service necessary to repair V's car:

	Normal Selling Price	Firm's Cost	V's Cost
Parts.....................	$200	$120	$112
Service	90	81	70

V's taxable income for the parts is $8 ($120 − $112) and for the service is $2 ([$90 − $70 = $20] − [$90 × 20% = $18]).

De Minimis Fringe Benefits

Exclusion of employee benefits also extends to items of minimal value such as the occasional use of a company's photocopy machines, other equipment, or typing services; annual employee picnics, cocktail parties, or occasional lunches; and inexpensive holiday gifts such as a turkey at Thanksgiving. No dollar amount is specified in determining what qualifies as de minimis. Section 132(e) simply states that a fringe is de minimis if the value of these benefits is so small that accounting for them is unreasonable or administratively impractical. The exclusion also covers discounts on food served in an eating facility provided by an employer *if* (1) the facility is located on or near the employer's business premises, (2) its revenue equals or exceeds its direct operating costs, and (3) the nondiscriminatory rules discussed above are met.[72] In addition, as noted earlier, supper money—cash meal allowances—given occasionally to employees who are required to work overtime may be excluded as a de minimis fringe benefit.

Note also that meals provided on the employer's premises for the convenience of the employer (and excluded from an employee's income under Code § 119) are considered a de minimis fringe benefit under Code § 132. As a result, employers can deduct the entire cost of the provided meals and they are not subject to the 50% disallowance rule that normally applies for meals and entertainment (see Chapter 8).

---

[71] § 132(c) See "Reg § 1.132-4(g) and reference to § 4977.   [72] § 132(e)(2).

Employer-Provided Transportation Benefits

It is not unusual for employers to reimburse employees for their costs of commuting to and from work. When Congress finally addressed the treatment of such benefits in 1984, it grandfathered the practice of excluding certain reimbursements. Thus was born the "qualified transportation fringe." The law is structured so that the benefit available to those who use mass transit is equivalent to that for those who drive personal vehicles. The components of this exclusion and their amounts in 2017 are given below:[73]

- Commuting to work in a qualified commuter vehicle (i.e., a vehicle that seats at least six people, excluding the driver such as a van) and transit passes, subway tokens, vouchers; maximum total exclusion for both when summed is $255 (2017) per month.

- Qualified parking (parking on or near the employers premises); maximum exclusion of $255 (2017) per month.

- Qualified bicycle commuting reimbursement (e.g., reimbursements for costs relating to using a bicycle for commuting such as the cost of the bicycle, repairs, and storage); maximum exclusion is $20 per month.

Amounts received in excess of these limits are included in gross income for both income and employment tax purposes.

Example 32

For each month in 2016, Employer R provides a transit pass valued at $300 to Employee E. E does not reimburse R for any portion of the pass. Because the value of the monthly transit pass exceeds the statutory limit of $130 per month for 2017 by $170, D is subject to both income and employment taxes on the $170 excess.

Note that if an employer offers cash in lieu of free parking, those who elect to take cash are taxed while those who opt for parking are not. Also note that in determining whether an amount can be excluded, any payments made by the employee to the employer must be considered. Payments by employees for qualified transportation fringes must also be considered in determining if the value of the benefit exceeds the statutory limit.

Example 33

Employer P provides qualified parking with a value of $270 per month to its employees. However, P charges the employees $30 per month. Because the net benefit of $240 ($270 − $30) is less than the monthly exclusion amount in 2017 of $255, no amount is includible in the employee's gross income.[74]

Qualified Moving Expense Reimbursement

Section 132 also excludes reimbursements received by employees for qualified moving expenses. These expenses, as discussed in Chapter 8, are those that would be deductible such as the cost of the moving van and transportation to the new location.[75]

On-Premises Athletic Facilities

Section 132 also authorizes an exclusion for the value of the use of athletic facilities provided on the employer's premises primarily for current or retired employees, their spouses, and their dependent children. Facilities that qualify for the exclusion include gyms, golf courses, swimming pools, tennis courts, and running and bicycle paths. Resorts are not qualifying facilities. Although the athletic facility must be located on premises owned or

---

[73] Rev Proc 2016-55, 2016-45 IRB ____.   [75] § 132(g).

[74] Notice 94-3. p. 15.

leased by the employer, it need not be located on the employer's business premises. Because the nondiscrimination rules are not applicable to on-premises athletic facilities, they may be made available to executives only.[76]

Employer-Provided Retirement Advice

In order to help employees adequately prepare for retirement, § 132 provides that "qualified retirement planning services" are an excludable fringe benefit.[77] The exclusion is granted for retirement planning services provided to an employee and his or her spouse by an employer that maintains a qualified pension plan. For example, General Motors might pay a financial planning firm to meet with their employees regarding retirement planning. The exclusion is not intended to apply to services that may be related to tax preparation, accounting, legal, or brokerage services. In an earlier ruling, the IRS concluded that financial counseling services provided to family members of terminally ill employees and survivors of deceased employees were taxable income.[78] Presumably, the value of such services would not be taxable under current fringe benefit rules.

Qualified Tuition Reduction by Educational Institutions

A common and extremely valuable fringe benefit offered by educational institutions to their employees is a tuition reduction or tuition waiver. For example, a child of a university faculty member might pay only a portion of the tuition normally charged to other students. Since 1984, § 117(d) has blessed these arrangements and granted an exclusion for a "qualified tuition reduction." Such reductions qualify only if they are offered by a nonprofit educational institution and do not discriminate in favor of highly compensated employees. Therefore, most plans offer benefits not only to faculty but also to all other employees of the institution (e.g., advisors, librarians, secretaries, maintenance personnel). This exclusion is available to the employee, a spouse, and dependent children and is extended to these individuals even if the employee is retired, disabled, or deceased.[79]

As a general rule, the exclusion applies only to tuition waivers for undergraduate education. However, the exclusion also is extended to tuition waivers for graduate students if they are engaged in teaching or research (e.g., teaching or research assistants).[80]

It should be emphasized that the regulations indicate that only the benefit in excess of the portion representing reasonable compensation for the graduate student's services can be excluded. Moreover, the amount received for services cannot be excluded solely because all candidates for the degree are required to perform such services.

> ### Example 34
>
> F is a doctoral student at State University. As part of her doctoral program she is required to teach one of the basic accounting courses each semester. For her efforts, she receives free tuition worth $17,000. Assuming other adjunct professors receive $3,000 for providing like services, F may only exclude $14,000. She must report $3,000 because it represents compensation for services.

MILITARY PERSONNEL

Military personnel are employees subject to most of the same provisions as nonmilitary employees. As a result, all compensation is normally taxable. However, the character and tax treatment of some military benefits differ from those of nonmilitary employee benefits. Examples of taxable compensation are active duty and reservist pay, reenlistment bonuses, lump-sum severance and readjustment pay, and retirement pay. Examples of nontaxable benefits are allowances for subsistence, uniforms, and quarters; extra allowances for housing and living costs while on permanent duty outside the United States, and family separation allowances caused by overseas duty; moving and storage expenses; compensation received by *enlisted* service members (up to the highest monthly enlisted pay plus any

[76] § 132(j)(4) and Reg. § 1.132-1T(e)(5).

[77] § 132(a)(7).

[78] Letter Ruling 199929043.

[79] § 117(d)(1).

[80] § 117(d) is subject to the compensation limitation in 117(c).

hostile fire or imminent danger pay received for commissioned officers) for active duty in an area designated by the President as a combat zone (e.g., Iraq); and all pay while a prisoner of war or missing in action.[81] Benefits provided to military veterans by the Veterans Administration also are nontaxable. Examples of these are allowances for education, training, and subsistence; disability income; pensions paid to veterans or family members; and grants for specially equipped vehicles and homes for disabled veterans. In addition, bonuses paid from general welfare funds by state governments to veterans are nontaxable.

Military deployed in combat zones, qualified hazardous duty areas, or certain contingency operations may deposit up to $10,000 of their pay into a special Department of Defense savings account during a single deployment. Interest accrues on the account at an annual rate of 10% and compounds quarterly. Although federal income earned in hazardous duty zones is tax-free, interest accrued on earnings deposited into these accounts is taxable.

REPARATIONS TO HOLOCAUST VICTIMS

Over the years, countries and businesses that benefited from forced labor or property confiscation during the Holocaust have made restitution payments to those who suffered and returned property to the rightful owners. To ensure that the victims, their heirs and estates receive the full benefit of the payments undiminished by taxes, Congress granted an exclusion for reparation payments received after January 1, 2000. In addition, confiscated property that is returned is deemed to have a basis equal to its fair market value.[82]

Personal Transfers between Individuals

LO.4

Explain the treatment of gifts, inheritances, alimony, and child support.

While the bulk of all income is derived from the fruits of one's labor or invested capital, there are a number of items that still have significance for which special rules exist. Among these are the provisions covering the treatment of certain transfers between individuals, specifically gifts, inheritances, child support, and alimony. With the exception of alimony, each of these is nontaxable. In each case, the recipient does not include the amount in income and the payer is not entitled to a deduction.

GIFTS AND INHERITANCES

Section 102 excludes the value of property received as a gift, bequest, devise, or inheritance from gross income.[83] This exclusion is normally justified on the theory that there is merely a redistribution of the donor's or decedent's after-tax income.

While gifts are nontaxable, it is not always easy to determine whether an amount received represents a gift or compensation. The problem was clearly revealed in the landmark case of *Comm. v. Duberstein*.[84] In this case, Duberstein, a businessman from Dayton, Ohio, provided the names of potential customers to Berman, an entrepreneur from New York City. The names proved to be very valuable to Berman and, to show his appreciation, he gave Duberstein a Cadillac. Although Berman's company deducted the cost of the car on its tax return as a business expense, Duberstein considered the Cadillac a gift and therefore nontaxable. The issue was ultimately reviewed by the Supreme Court, which announced its now famous distinction between gifts and compensation. According to the court, a gift is made out of a detached and disinterested generosity and not as a reward for past services or made in expectation of future services. Based on the Court's view, Berman intended the car to be remuneration for services rendered and consequently ruled that Duberstein had taxable compensation.

The exclusion for gifts does not extend to income earned on the property.[85] For example, the value of bonds inherited or received as a gift is nontaxable, but any interest income earned on the bonds by the new owner is taxable unless specifically exempted by the Code (e.g., interest on tax-exempt bonds issued by a municipality).

---

[81] The TRA of 1986 consolidated existing military benefits and provided the Treasury with the authority to expand the list.

[82] § 803(a), Economic Growth and Tax Relief Reconciliation Act of 2001, P.L. 107-16.

[83] § 102(a).

[84] 60-2 USTC ¶9515, 5 AFTR2d 1626, 363 U.S. 278 (USSC, 1960).

[85] Reg. § 1.102-1(a). Amounts paid out of an estate or trust may be taxable under certain circumstances. However, the end result should protect the exclusion for the gift or inheritance. See § 663.

Since a gift is excluded the donee normally has no reporting responsibility. However, in the case of a gift or inheritance from a foreign donor, the government is concerned that it may be compensation rather than a gift. For this reason, individuals who receive a gift or inheritance of more than $100,000 from a nonresident alien or a foreign estate must file Form 3520. Annual Return to Report Transactions With Foreign Trusts and Receipt of Certain Foreign Gifts. Penalties for failing to report such gifts can be severe (greater of 35% of the reportable amount or $10,000).

ALIMONY AND SEPARATE MAINTENANCE

As may be clear by now, virtually nothing is left untouched by the tax law and that includes the area of matrimonial disputes. Indeed, given the divorce rate in the United States (generally thought to be between 40 and 50 percent of first marriages), it should not be surprising that a thriving part of many tax practices relates to the tax consequences of divorce and separation. This is due in part to the fact that a major element in the dissolution of many marriages is the financial arrangement of the settlement.

Typically, a divorcing couple must first split up their property and establish separate households. Under most state laws, each spouse is entitled to the property he or she brought into the marriage and an equal share of property accumulated during the marriage. In addition to the property settlement, the divorce decree may require one of the spouses to pay support for the children (i.e., child support), and in many cases make support payments—normally referred to as alimony or separate maintenance payments—to the ex-spouse. For tax purposes, the obvious questions concern the treatment of the property settlement, child support, and alimony. The general rules governing these transfers are quite straightforward:

- *Property Settlement.* The division of the property (i.e., the transfer of property from one spouse to the other in exchange for the release of that spouse's marital claim) is a nontaxable event.[86] Neither spouse has income for the property received or a deduction for the property transferred. Consistent with this approach, the basis of the property received by either spouse under the property settlement remains the same, leaving any built-in gain or loss unchanged.[87]

- *Alimony.* Amounts designated as alimony (or equivalent payments) are considered a mere reallocation or sharing of the payer's income and, therefore, are taxable to the recipient and deductible by the payer.[88]

- *Child Support.* Amounts paid for child support, often covered in a separate agreement, are nontaxable to the recipient (regardless of how the money is used) and non-deductible to the payer.

Example 35

H and W are divorced, and W was awarded custody of their only child. Pursuant to the divorce decree, this year H transferred his various investments in stock to W worth $24,000 (basis to H of $16,000). In addition, H paid W $18,000 in alimony and $10,000 in child support. Neither H nor W is affected by the transfer of stocks. H's basis of $16,000 carries over to W so that her basis is also $16,000. Thus the built-in appreciation of $8,000 shifts to W. H is entitled to deduct all $18,000 of the alimony as a deduction for AGI while W must report the $18,000 as taxable income. H is not entitled to deduct the $10,000 paid as child support, but W is allowed to exclude the $10,000 from income.

Due to the drastically different tax treatments of these transfers, characterization of a particular payment as alimony, child support, or part of the property settlement is obviously crucial in structuring a divorce settlement. As might be expected, without some rules and coordination, a paying spouse might want to call something alimony while the recipient

---

[86] § 1041(b)(2). Prior to 1985, transfers between spouses were taxable. See *U.S. v. Thomas Crawley Davis,* 62-2 USTC S ¶9509, 9 AFTR2d 1625, (USSC, 1962).

[87] § 1041(b)(2).

[88] § 215(a) and § 71(a)(1).

spouse may feel that it is either child support or part of the property settlement. Moreover, the two parties, despite their failure in marriage, may be able to work out a financial arrangement that works well for both but unfairly reduces the government's rightful share. To help eliminate controversy, a number of special rules must be observed when dealing in this area. In this regard, these rules normally do not apply to divorces occurring before 1985.[89]

Alimony

Prior to 1942, there was no specific statute governing the treatment of alimony or child support. Before that time, recipients of alimony relied on a 1917 decision by the Supreme Court that held that alimony did not fall within the definition of income and, consequently, the recipient avoided tax.[90] However, from the payer's perspective, the payments were not deductible since there was no provision that authorized the deduction. In some cases, this treatment could produce an inequitable result. For example, consider a taxpayer who earns $150,000 and is required to pay alimony of $100,000 to his ex-wife. Assuming the taxpayer pays taxes at a rate of 50 percent, he would have only $75,000 after-tax to meet his $100,000 alimony obligation! Because alimony seriously reduced the taxpayer's ability to pay, Congress believed it was more appropriate to view the payments of alimony as simply a splitting of the payer's income. Consequently, the law was changed to make payments of alimony deductible by the payer and taxable to the recipient.

Under current law, payments qualify as alimony or separate maintenance only if six conditions are met:[91]

1. They are made in *cash;*
2. They are made as a result of a divorce or separation under a *written decree* of separate maintenance or support;
3. They are *required* under a decree or a written instrument incident to a divorce or separation;
4. The spouses or court do *not* elect that they be designated as not qualifying as alimony;
5. The husband and wife do not live together nor do they file a joint return together; and
6. Payments cease with the death of the *recipient.*

Payments meeting these requirements, however, are not treated as alimony if the divorce or separation agreement clearly states they are not alimony for Federal income tax purposes. Note that this provision gives the parties a great deal of flexibility in structuring the divorce.

As noted above, payments only qualify as alimony if they are in cash. However, the payments need not be made directly to the ex-spouse.[92] Specifically, the following types of payments qualify as alimony:

1. Payments made in cash, checks, and money orders payable on demand.
2. Payments of cash by the ex-husband to the ex-wife's creditors in accordance with the terms of the divorce or separation instrument such as payments of the ex-wife's mortgage (i.e., on house ex-wife owns), taxes, rent, medical and dental bills, utilities, tuition, and other similar expenses.
3. Premiums paid by the ex-husband for term or whole life insurance on the ex-husband's life made pursuant to the terms of the divorce or separation instrument, provided the ex-wife is the owner of the policy.
4. Payments of cash to a third party on behalf of the ex-wife, if they are made at the written request of the ex-wife, such as a contribution to a charitable organization.

However, the following *do not* qualify as alimony or separate maintenance payments:[93]

1. Assets transferred as a part of the property settlement, such as a home, car, stocks and bonds, life insurance policies, annuity contracts, etc.
2. Any payments to maintain property owned by the ex-husband and used by the ex-wife, including mortgage payments, real estate taxes, insurance premiums, and improvements. Such payments increase the ex-husband's equity in the property.

---

[89] These rules apply to a pre-1985 divorce decree *only if* both parties expressly agree. Ltr. Rul. 8634040.

[90] *Gould vs. Gould,* 1 USTC ¶13, 3 AFTR 2958, 245 U.S. 151 (USSC, 1917).

[91] § 71(a) and (b) and Reg. § 1.71-1.

[92] Temp. Reg. § 1.71-1T(b).

[93] Temp. Reg. § 1.71-1T(b), Questions 5 and 6.

3. Fair rental value of residence owned by ex-husband but used exclusively by ex-wife.
4. Repayment by the ex-husband of a loan previously made to him by his ex-wife as part of the general settlement.[94]
5. Transfers of services (i.e., professional or otherwise).[95]
6. Voluntary payments not required by the divorce or separation agreement.
7. Payments made prior to a divorce or separation.

Example 36

Dick and Jane are divorced. The divorce decree requires Dick to (1) transfer his half of their home to Jane; (2) help support Jane by paying her $2,400 per year until she remarries or dies; and (3) pay Jane $50,000 over a period of 12 years. This year Dick paid Jane the following:

1. $1,000, voluntarily made prior to their separation or divorce.
2. $2,400 as support (i.e., separate maintenance), made in accordance with the divorce agreement.
3. His half of their home worth $150,000, transferred in accordance with the divorce agreement.
4. $6,000 of the $50,000 to be paid over 12 years.

Dick's alimony is $8,400 ($2,400 + $6,000). The $1,000 payment is not alimony because it was paid voluntarily and before any divorce or separate maintenance agreement was made. The $150,000 transfer of his half of their home is not alimony since it is a property settlement. Since Jane has taxable alimony of $8,400, Dick has a deduction for AGI of $8,400.

Limitations on Front Loading

Absent some limitations, *both* spouses might be better off if what is really a property settlement is treated as deductible alimony. To illustrate, consider the following example.

Example 37

H and W are in the process of negotiating the terms of their divorce. It is anticipated that after the divorce, H will be in the 50% bracket while W will pay taxes at a rate of 20 percent. If H pays $10,000 to his wife and the amount is *not* considered alimony, the after-tax cost of the payment to the husband is $10,000 while the after-tax benefit to the wife is $10,000. On the other hand, if the payment is considered deductible alimony, H could increase the payment to W to $20,000 and it would have the same $10,000 after-tax cost as the first payment. However, in such case, W would receive $16,000 after-tax, $6,000 more even though she has to pay taxes. As a result, both H and W are inclined to characterize any payment that is made as alimony.

As the above example illustrates, depending on the tax rates of the parties, a divorcing couple may be inclined to characterize a payment as alimony regardless of its actual substance. This is particularly true for the spouse required to make the payments since the value of the alimony deductions up front is normally far greater than their value if deferred to later years.

---

[94] Reg. § 1.71-1(b)(4).   [95] Temp. Reg. § 1.71-1T(b), Question 5.

When an arrangement like this might provide an advantage, the divorce agreement normally calls for large "alimony" payments for the first few years followed by smaller payments later. As a practical matter, however, the large payments made initially that are purportedly alimony are in all likelihood simply part of what is a disguised property settlement. To prevent this so-called front loading, Congress created special rules.[96]

The front loading rules are triggered when there is a significant drop in alimony in either the second or third year after the divorce. If such a drop occurs, the alimony is *recaptured,* that is, the payment is no longer treated as alimony. As a result, the payer must include the amount in income and the recipient who previously reported the payment as income is entitled to a deduction. Unfortunately, the actual calculation of the amount to be recaptured is quite cumbersome.

Alimony paid in the first and second years must be recaptured in the third year if, during this three years, alimony payments decreased by more than $15,000. Amounts recaptured are included in gross income by the payor and deductible by the payee in arriving at AGI. To compute the recapture, the years must be considered in reverse order. Thus, the recapture formula for the second post-separation year is (1) total payments made in the second year less (2) payments made in the third year less (3) $15,000. The recapture formula for the first year is similar with one exception. In the second step, an *average* is computed of the second-year payments (less excess payments for that year, determined in the preceding computation above) plus the third-year payments.

Example 38

Alimony payments by W to H for the first three years after divorce are $25,000, $20,000, and $15,000. Since payments did not decrease by more than $15,000, no recapture is required. Both W's deductions for AGI and H's taxable income are $25,000 the first year, $20,000 the second year, and $15,000 the third year.

Example 39

Alimony payments by M to F for the first three years after divorce are $50,000, $20,000, and $0. Since payments decrease by more than $15,000, recapture is required in the third year. As computed below, the recapture for the second year is $5,000 and for the third year is $27,500.

Drop from Year 2 to Year 3:

Total payments made in second year.	$20,000
− Payments made in third year	0
Drop from Year 2 to Year 3	$20,000
− $15,000 allowance	(15,000)
Year 3 recapture amount	$ 5,000

Drop from Year 1 to Year 2:

Total payments made in first year	$50,000
− (Year 2 + Year 3 payments − Year 3 recapture)/2	(7,500)*
Drop from Year 1 to Year 2	$42,500
− $15,000 allowance	(15,000)
Recapture amount	$27,500

*($20,000 + $0 − $5,000 = $15,000)/2 = $7,500

M's deduction for AGI and F's taxable income are $50,000 the first year and $20,000 the second year. In the third year, the recaptures exceed payments: Thus, M's taxable income and F's deduction for AGI is $32,500 ($5,000 + $27,500).

---

[96] § 71(f).

The recapture rules do not apply for post-1984 divorce instruments if payments:

1. Cease because of the death of either spouse during the three-year period;
2. Cease because the payee remarries during the three-year period;
3. Are made under a support agreement, and thus do not qualify as alimony; or
4. Are a fixed portion of income to be paid for at least three years and based on revenues from a business, from property, or from employee or self-employment compensation.

Child Support

If there are children, it is reasonable to assume that a portion of the husband's payments will be for their care and support. Amounts that qualify as child support are nondeductible personal expenses for the husband and nontaxable income to the wife.[97] Funds qualify as child support *only* if

1. A specific amount is fixed or is contingent on the child's status (e.g., reaching a certain age);
2. Paid solely for the support of minor children; and
3. Payable by decree, instrument, or agreement.

If all three requirements are not met, the payments are treated as alimony with no part considered to be child support.[98] All other factors are irrelevant to the issue. For example, the intent of the parties involved, the actual use of the funds, and state or local support laws have no bearing on whether payments qualify as child support. Also, even though state law may be to the contrary, a minor child is anyone under age 21.[99]

Example 40

A divorce decree states that B is to pay $300 per month as alimony and support of two minor children. The agreement also states that the payments will decrease by one-third (1) if the former spouse dies or remarries, and (2) as each child reaches 21 years of age. This type of agreement meets the contingency rule for child support. Consequently, $100 per month qualifies as alimony and $200 per month qualifies as child support.

Once child support is established, no payments are considered to be alimony until all past and current child support payments are made.[100]

Example 41

A divorce decree states that H is to pay $100 per month as alimony and $200 per month as support of two minor children. The first payment was due October 1. H paid $150 in October, $300 in November, and $350 in December. These payments are allocated between child support and alimony as follows:

	Payment	Child Support	Alimony
October	$150	$150	$ 0
November	300	250	50
December	350	200	150
Total	$800	$600	$200

The above allocation is made even if H or state law stipulates that payments are to cover alimony first.

---

[97] Reg. § 1.71-1(e).

[98] See § 71(c)(2) and Temp. Reg. § 1.71-1T, Questions 16 and 17. Also, see *Arnold A. Abramo,* 78 T.C. 154 (1983) acq. and

Comm. v. Lester, 61-1 USTC ¶9463, 7 AFTR2d 1445,366 U.S. 299 (USSC, 1961).

[99] *W.E. Borbonus,* 42 T.C. 983 (1964).

[100] Reg. § 1.71-1(e).

LO.5

Describe the treatment created for unique items of income such as life insurance, debt cancellation, prizes, awards scholarships, and government transfers.

The last section clearly revealed that the income concept can be quite broad and could, without special rules, encompass benefits normally derived from personal relationships. This section discusses a hodgepodge of provisions that are loosely associated in that the benefits are received from unrelated or third parties. These include life insurance, prizes and awards, scholarships, cancellation of debts, and government transfer payments.

LIFE INSURANCE PROCEEDS AND OTHER DEATH BENEFITS

Life Insurance

Since its inception the tax law has contained an exclusion for life insurance proceeds received by a beneficiary after an insured person's death.[101] Congress apparently wanted to encourage individuals to buy life insurance to provide adequate resources for their survivors and, at the same time, provide tax-free funds in a time of need.

Many life insurance policies allow the beneficiary to take the life insurance proceeds in either a lump-sum payment or installments. The exclusion applies in either situation. However, the beneficiary is entitled to exclude only the face amount of the policy. Any excess (e.g., investment earnings while the proceeds were left with the insurance company) are taxable.

Example 42

This year W's husband, H, died. Under the terms of a life insurance policy, W is to receive $500,000. Alternatively, W can elect to receive $55,000 per year for the next 10 years. If W takes the lump sum payment, she can exclude the entire $500,000. If she elects to take the installment payout of $55,000 annually, $50,000 of each payment is a nontaxable return of the life insurance proceeds, but the remaining $5,000 is taxable income ($55,000 − [$500,000/10]).

Although life insurance proceeds are normally nontaxable, there are several special rules that should be observed.

Cashing-In the Policy before Death. Some life insurance policies, notably whole-life, enable the holder to cash the policy in before the taxpayer's death. Any amount received in excess of the premiums paid is taxable. No loss is recognized if the premiums paid exceed the amount received. The 1996 tax legislation provides, however, tax-favored treatment for accelerated death benefits.

Over the past several years, many terminally-ill individuals (e.g., AIDS patients) have surrendered their life insurance policies or sold the policies to a third party in exchange for the death benefits. These death benefits would then be used to pay for medical and other expenses. Although life insurance benefits that are payable on account of death are normally nontaxable, the treatment of accelerated death benefits, often referred to as "viatical settlements," was somewhat unclear. Congress clarified their treatment by adding Code § 101(g). This section provides that accelerated death benefits (i.e., surrender of the policy to the insurer for a lump sum or sale to a third party) generally may be excluded if the individual is chronically or terminally ill. While the exclusion for terminally ill individuals is unlimited, the exclusion for a chronically ill individual (who is not also terminally ill) is restricted to the amount of long-term care services actually incurred.

An individual is considered terminally ill if he or she has been certified by a physician as having an illness or physical condition that can reasonably be expected to result in death in 24 months or less. A chronically-ill individual is generally a person who is unable to perform at least two activities of daily living (e.g., eating, toileting, transferring, bathing, dressing, and continence) for a period of at least 90 days due to a loss of functional capacity.

---

[101] § 101(a)(1). Insurance proceeds are also taxable if the policy is an investment contract with little or no *insurance risk* or the owner of the policy does not have an *insurable interest* in the insured. In addition to the insured, a spouse, dependents, business partners, and in some instances, creditors and employers are considered to possess the requisite insurable interest.

> ### Example 43
>
> C is 60 years old and has smoked two packs of cigarettes a day since he was a young man. Three years ago, C was diagnosed with lung cancer. His condition recently took a turn for the worse and his physician now expects that C will live less than a year. C owns a life insurance policy with a face value of $150,000. In order to pay for his medical expenses and home nursing care, C has elected to surrender the policy to his insurance provider for a lump sum of $130,000. Because C is expected to die in 24 months or less, the accelerated death benefit of $130,000 is excluded from his gross income.

Substitute for Taxable Income. In some instances, life insurance is used to protect a creditor against a bad debt loss on the death of the insured. However, the fact that the debt is offset by life insurance proceeds on the death of the insured does not cause otherwise taxable income to be nontaxable. For example, amounts equal to unreported interest due on the debt are taxable interest income.[102] Similarly, proceeds offsetting debt that was previously written off as uncollectible, or proceeds representing gain not previously reported, are included in gross income.[103]

Transfer for Valuable Consideration. If a policy is transferred to another party in exchange for valuable consideration, any *gain* from the proceeds on the insured's death is taxable income.[104] Gain is defined as the insurance proceeds less the owner's basis. Basis is the total purchase price plus all premiums paid by the subsequent owner after the transfer.

> ### Example 44
>
> XY Corporation purchased a $15,000 life insurance policy from S, the insured, for $7,300. The corporation made five annual premium payments of $600 each on the policy. S died at the end of the fifth year and XY collected $15,000 insurance. Since XY's basis in the policy is $10,300 ([$600 × 5 payments] + $7,300), its taxable income is $4,700 ($15,000 − $10,300).

There are four exceptions to *Example 44*. All gain is nontaxable if the purchaser is (1) a partner of the insured, (2) a partnership in which the insured is a partner, (3) a corporation in which the insured is a shareholder or officer, or (4) the insured.[105]

EMPLOYEE DEATH BENEFITS

Upon the death of an employee, it is not uncommon for employers to provide the employee's family with some type of compensation for their loss. These amounts are fully taxable to the beneficiaries and cannot be excluded as gifts.

PRIZES AND AWARDS

The tax law provides no escape for those fortunate enough to receive prizes and awards. Prizes and awards are fully taxable. This is true regardless of the reason for the award. While this was not always the case, since 1986 winners of the Nobel Prize are taxed the same as those who win the lottery. Similarly, winners of sweepstakes, employer service awards, contests, door prizes, and raffles held by charitable organizations have taxable income to the extent the fair market value of the winnings exceeds the cost of entering the contests.[106]

---

[102] *Landfield Finance Co. v. Comm.*, 69-2 USTC ¶9680, 24 AFTR2d 69-5744, 418 F.2d 172 (CA-7, 1969), aff'g. 69-1 USTC ¶9175, 23 AFTR2d 69-601, 296 F. Supp. 1118 (DC, 1969).

[103] *St. Louis Refrigerating & Cold Storage Co. v. Comm.*, 47-2 USTC ¶9298, 35 AFTR 1477, 162 F.2d 394 (CA-8, 1947), aff'g. 46-2 USTC ¶9320, 34 AFTR 1574, 66 F. Supp. 62 (DC, 1946) and Rev. Rul. 70-254, 1970-1 C.B. 31.

[104] § 101(a)(2).

[105] § 101(a)(2)(B).

[106] Reg. § 1.74-1(a)(2). For the determining the value of property won, see *Lawrence W. McCoy*, 38 T.C. 841(1962), acq. and *Reginald Turner*, 13 TCM 462, T.C. Memo. 1954-38.

Taxpayers who have won a prize or award may avoid taxation if they immediately transfer the prize or award to charity. Although this may seem unnecessary given that taxpayers are entitled to a charitable contribution deduction, the deduction is generally limited to 50% of the taxpayer's AGI. Consequently, if the taxpayer received a $100,000 award that he or she wanted to donate to charity, an outright contribution might not necessarily offset the income. This treatment is available only for prizes and awards that are made in recognition of religious, charitable, scientific, educational, artistic, literary, or civic achievements, but only if:

1. The recipient was selected without any direct action on his or her part to enter the contest or proceeding;

2. The recipient is not required to perform substantial future services as a condition of receiving the prize or award; and

3. The prize or award is given by the payor to a governmental unit or tax-exempt organization as designated by the recipient.[107]

When these rules are met, the award has no impact on the winner's tax liability; it is neither taxable income nor a deductible charitable contribution.

Example 45

After twenty years of medical research at the MNO Institute, E gained an international reputation for her computer studies of protein structures. As a result, she was recently awarded the Nobel Prize in Medicine. E gave the award, which amounted to $375,000, to the American Cancer Society. Because all of the conditions for exclusion are satisfied, the $375,000 prize is excludable from E's gross income.

SCHOLARSHIPS AND FELLOWSHIPS

Although scholarships and fellowships are considered to be prizes and awards, Congress has elected to specifically exempt them from the above provisions in order to promote and lower the cost of education. To this end, § 117 generally allows an exclusion of scholarships and fellowships for those individuals who are candidates under the following conditions:

*   The individual is a candidate for a degree (either undergraduate or graduate).

*   The degree granting organization is a qualified educational institution, that is, the organization has a faculty, curriculum, and an organized student body (e.g., obtaining a degree at correspondence schools would not qualify).

*   The amount received is a scholarship. It must aid the individual in his or her pursuit of study or research and not represent compensation for services.

*   The amounts received are used for tuition and related expenses, including fees, books, supplies, equipment, and other expenses that are required for either enrollment or attendance (but not room and board).

Example 46

C holds a Ph.D. in chemistry from the University of Michigan. This year the Gemini Foundation, a nonprofit research institution, awarded C a post-doctoral fellowship of $30,000 to do research for a semester at the University of Texas with a noted scientist. C must include the fellowship as taxable income since he is not a candidate for a degree.

---

[107] § 74(b).

As a practical matter, most scholarships easily meet these requirements. A few potential difficulties should be mentioned, however.

It should be emphasized that amounts received for room and board cannot be excluded; however, they are considered earned income for purposes of determining the individual's standard deduction, which should facilitate an offsetting deduction.

Example 47

J, a junior majoring in engineering at Private University, was awarded a $10,000 scholarship during the current year. She used the funds to pay the following school-related expenses: tuition $6,000, technology fee $100, athletic fee $25, books $875, room and board $2,500, and notebooks, pencils, and other supplies, $100. J used the remaining $400 to purchase a set of software products (word processor, spreadsheet, database, presentation) that several of her professors said would be useful in their courses. J must report $2,900 of taxable income, representing the room and board of $2,500, and the equipment that was not required of $400. Assuming J had no other sources of income, her standard deduction would be equal to her earned income, which in this case is the $2,900 spent on room and board and the suggested equipment. As a result, J's standard deduction would offset her $2,900 of taxable income.

In some situations, amounts that are characterized as scholarships may be considered compensation for services rendered or to be rendered. In such case, the amounts received are taxable even if a current employment relationship does not exist. For example, a scholarship that was awarded a beauty contest winner was considered taxable, since much like an employee, she participated in a televised pageant and was expected to perform promotional services in the future.[108]

Note, however, that amounts received by an employee may qualify for exclusion under an educational assistance plan or as a working condition fringe benefit, as discussed earlier in this chapter. Similarly, employees of educational institutions, including graduate students engaged in teaching or research activities, are entitled to exclude any tuition reductions. In addition, amounts paid for education that are related to the taxpayer's employment may be deductible if certain conditions are met, as described in Chapter 8.

CANCELLATION OF INDEBTEDNESS

When taxpayers borrow money, they do not report income. This follows from the assumption that they will repay the loan in which case there is no increase in their net worth. On the other hand, if a lender reduces or cancels a taxpayer's debt, there is a corresponding increase in net worth. In such case, the taxpayer is normally required to include the amount of debt forgiveness in gross income.[109] The lender is usually required to report the amount of canceled debt to both the taxpayer and the IRS on Form 1099-C Cancellation of Debt. However, in certain situations the taxpayer may be able to exclude this so-called cancellation of debt income. Some of these include:

- The cancellation represents a gift or bequest (e.g., a father forgives his son's debt).

- The cancellation occurs when the taxpayer is insolvent or bankrupt.

- The cancellation represents a renegotiation of the purchase price.

- The cancellation of student loans.

- The cancellation is of debt related to the taxpayer's principal residence.

---

[108] Rev. Rul. 68-20, 1968-1 C.B. 55.   [109] § 61(a)(12).

Bankruptcy or Insolvency

If the taxpayer is *solvent* at the time a debt is cancelled, there is normally no exclusion and income must be recognized to the extent of the debt forgiveness. On the other hand, if the taxpayer is *bankrupt* or *insolvent* (liabilities exceed the value of the assets), the IRS does not add to the taxpayer's financial woes with more taxable income but provides a reprieve under § 108.

When a debt is cancelled pursuant to a bankruptcy proceeding, there is no taxable income.[110] However, the taxpayer is required to reduce certain tax attributes that normally would produce tax savings in the future. For example, the taxpayer must reduce any net operating loss carryovers by the amount of debt forgiveness. As a result, the taxpayer would lose the benefit of deducting the NOL in the future. In this sense, the income is not truly excluded but rather deferred. However, any debt reduction that exceeds the attributes identified below is ignored entirely, and the related income forever escapes tax. The attributes that must be reduced are

1. Net operating losses (NOLs) and any NOL carryovers.
2. General business credit carryovers.
3. Minimum tax credit.
4. Capital losses (current and carryovers).
5. Basis of the taxpayer's property (generally depreciable realty).
6. Passive activity loss and credit carryovers.
7. Foreign tax credit carryovers.

While the attributes normally must be reduced in the order shown, the taxpayer may elect to reduce the basis of property first (i.e., shift number 5 to number 1). By so doing, the taxpayer gives up a deferred deduction (i.e., the depreciation related to the property) for perhaps an immediate deduction (e.g., an NOL as soon as income is produced).

If the taxpayer is not bankrupt when the debt is cancelled, but insolvent, the approach is generally the same as shown above.[111] However, to the extent the taxpayer becomes solvent, taxable income results. Thus, an insolvent taxpayer reduces the attributes identified above until solvency results and the balance is included in gross income.

Example 48

XYZ Inc. has assets of $375,000, liabilities of $500,000, and an NOL carryover of $100,000. If creditors forgive $90,000 of debt, none of the forgiveness will generate taxable income because, as shown below, XYZ is insolvent both before and after the debt cancellation. XYZ would be required to reduce the NOL carryover by $90,000 (from $100,000 to $10,000).

	Before	After
Total assets	$ 375,000	$ 375,000
Total liabilities	(500,000)	(410,000)
Insolvent	$(125,000)	$ (35,000)

If, on the other hand, the creditors forgive $140,000 of debt, XYZ will be solvent after the cancellation (i.e., $375,000 − $360,000 = $15,000). Consequently, the firm would report $15,000 of the forgiveness as taxable income in such case. In addition, XYZ would reduce the NOL carryover by $100,000 to zero.

---

[110] § 108(a)(1)(A).   [111] § 108(a)(1)(B).

Qualified Real Property Business Indebtedness

As explained above, if a business's debt is cancelled, the taxpayer normally must recognize income unless the business is bankrupt or insolvent. To provide relief to those engaged in the real estate business (other than corporations), Congress created a special exception. Under § 108, a taxpayer may elect to exclude the income resulting from the cancellation of indebtedness incurred or assumed in connection with real property used in a trade or business (*qualified real property business indebtedness*). This is true even though the taxpayer is neither bankrupt nor insolvent. The cancellation of debt income does not escape tax, however. The taxpayer must reduce the basis of the depreciable property for any income that is excluded. As a result, the taxpayer forgoes future deductions. The maximum amount of exclusion may not exceed the excess of the outstanding principal amount of the debt over the fair market value of the property.

Example 49

During 2008 T acquired an office building in Houston for $800,000. He borrowed $700,000 of the purchase price by giving First Bank of Houston a note payable with interest at a rate of 14 percent. The note was secured by the building. By 2016 the value of the building had dropped to $400,000. At that time, the balance on the note was $600,000. Instead of foreclosing and taking the property, the bank agreed it would be better to leave the real estate in the hands of T and renegotiate the terms of the note so that T could handle the payments. As a result, the bank reduced the principal of the note from $600,000 to $400,000. T may elect to exclude the cancellation of debt income of $200,000, but he must reduce the basis of the property by $200,000.

Seller Reduction of Purchaser's Debt

Another situation where § 108 allows the taxpayer to exclude cancellation of debt income relates to sales where the seller provides the financing for the buyer. If the seller/lender cancels the debt, the buyer may exclude the benefit but must reduce the basis of the property.[112] In effect, the Code treats the transaction as a renegotiation of the purchase price. Note that the result is identical to that discussed above for qualified real property business indebtedness. This rule does not apply if the buyer is bankrupt or insolvent.

Example 50

Several years ago, B purchased an apartment building from S for $1,000,000. B gave S $200,000 cash and signed a note payable to S for the $800,000 balance. The note was secured by the building. B has recently fallen on hard times and may default on the note, which has a current balance of $700,000. S, not wanting to become a landlord again and not sure that he could find another buyer, reduced the note's principal to $400,000. Since S provided the financing and B is solvent, B may exclude the $300,000 cancellation of debt income but must reduce his basis in the building by $300,000.

Cancellation of Debt on a Principal Residence

One of the devastating effects of the recent recession is the foreclosure of millions of homes—over 2.3 million in 2012 alone. Unfortunately, affected individuals not only could lose their home but also face a tax bill for cancellation of indebtedness. However, beginning in 2007, income realized as a result of modification of the terms of a mortgage (e.g., a restructuring) or a foreclosure on a principal residence can be excluded. The taxpayer's basis in the residence must be reduced by the amount of the exclusion. Note that the taxpayer

---

[112] § 108(e)(5)(A).

need not be bankrupt or insolvent to take advantage of this rule. The provision generally applies to debt of up to $2,000,000 ($1,000,000 for married filing separately) used to acquire, construct or improve the taxpayer's principal residence. When the debt was the result of a refinancing, the amount of the exclusion is limited to the amount of debt that was refinanced. The rule does not apply to home equity loans or debt forgiven related to a second home, a credit card loan, a car loan, or any other type of loan. The exclusion is claimed on Form 982.

Example 51

Several years ago, R purchased a residence for $115,000, paying $10,000 and financing the balance. R lost his job and was no longer able to make payments on the mortgage that at the time had a balance of $100,000. After discussions with the holder of the mortgage, the debt was reduced to $80,000. Although R is neither bankrupt nor insolvent, he can exclude the $20,000 cancellation of debt income. Had the lender foreclosed on the home and sold it for $80,000 in complete satisfaction of the $100,000 debt, the $20,000 of forgiveness also can be excluded. Note also that a foreclosure is generally treated as a sale for the amount of cancelled debt. In this case, R is not allowed to deduct the loss on the sale of his home of $35,000 ($80,000 − $115,000). In contrast, if R had realized a gain (i.e., the amount of cancelled debt exceeded his basis of $115,000), the exclusion for gain on the sale of a residence normally will apply.

Cancellation of Student Loans

Code § 108(f) allows individuals to exclude from income the amount of certain student loans that have been cancelled. This exclusion normally applies only if the loan is issued by the government and the forgiveness is contingent on the student's fulfilling a public service work requirement.

GOVERNMENT TRANSFER PAYMENTS

Many government transfer payments are excluded from income. For example, earlier discussion in this chapter revealed that all or a portion of Social Security benefits are excluded from income. Since medicare benefits are considered to be Social Security, they also are nontaxable. Supplementary medicare payments received as reimbursement of medical expenses deducted in a prior year are taxable, however, to the extent the taxpayer received a *tax benefit* in that year.[113]

Worker's compensation received as a result of a work-related injury is excluded from income.[114] Similar to the typical accident insurance policy discussed earlier in this chapter, worker's compensation provides the injured employee with a fixed amount for the permanent loss or use of a function or member of the body. For example, an individual who loses a hand, fingers, or hearing in a work-related accident receives a nontaxable amount, according to a schedule of payments. This exclusion is extended to compensation received by the survivors of a deceased worker. Other worker's compensation benefits are taxable unless the requirements for accident or health plans, previously discussed, are met.

Both state and Federal government transfer payments that are classified as public assistance (e.g., food stamps) or paid from a general welfare fund (e.g., welfare payments) are nontaxable.[115] Among others, these include payments to foster and adoptive parents, to individuals who are blind, to victims of crimes, for disaster relief, (e.g., hurricane or flood relief) to reduce energy costs for low-income groups, and for urban renewal relocation payments.[116]

---

[113] Rev. Rul. 70-341, 1970-2 C.B. 31.

[114] § 104(a)(1).

[115] Rev. Rul. 71-425 1971-2 C.B. 76.

[116] See generally § 139. Rev. Ruls. 78-80, 1978-1 C.B. 22; 74-153, 1974-1 C.B. 20; 77-323, 1977-2 C.B. 18; 74-74, 1974-1 C.B. 18; 76-144, 1976-1 C.B. 17; 78-180, 1978-1 C.B. 136; and 76-373, 1976-2 C.B. 16.

Benefits to participants in government programs designated to train or retrain specified groups are frequently nontaxable. Whether these benefits are nontaxable or not is dependent upon the primary purpose of the programs. Thus, if the objective of the program is to provide unemployed or under-employed individuals with job skills that enhance their employment opportunities, amounts received are nontaxable.[117] But, if the primary purpose is to provide compensation for services, participants are government employees with taxable wages.[118]

Most government transfer payments to farmers are included in income.[119] For example, gross income from farming includes government funds received for trees, shrubs, seed, and certain conservation expenditures, and for reducing farm production.[120] If materials are received instead of cash, their fair market value is taxable income. In addition, taxpayers receiving government funds under qualifying conservation cost-sharing plans may elect to exclude the reimbursement of capital improvements. However, the capitalized cost of the projects must be reduced by the excluded amount.[121]

Business Gross Income

The amount to be included in gross income for proprietorships, partnerships, and corporations is total revenues plus net sales less cost of goods sold. This same concept is applicable even if the business conducted is illegal or if the activities do not qualify as a trade or business but constitute a hobby. Many of the other includible and excludable business gross income items are discussed earlier in this chapter. Additional income items peculiar to business that deserve discussion are classified as (A) generally includible in, or (B) generally excludable from, gross income.

A. *Generally Includible in Gross Income*

- Agreement not to compete

- Goodwill

- Business interruption insurance proceeds

- Damages awarded

- Lease cancellation payments

B. *Generally Excludable from Gross Income*

- Leasehold improvements (unless made in lieu of rent)

- Contributions to capital

AGREEMENT NOT TO COMPETE AND GOODWILL

The sale of a business often contains an agreement that the seller will not compete with the buyer in the same or similar business within a particular area or distance. In such case, the seller must treat any amount assigned to the agreement as ordinary income. The purchaser may amortize (deduct) this amount over 15 years on a straight-line basis regardless of its useful life.

When the net selling price of the business exceeds the fair market value of all identifiable net assets, the business generally is considered to possess *goodwill*. That is, its potential value exceeds its net assets because of the business name, location, reputation, or other intangible factor. Goodwill is considered a capital asset and, consequently any amounts

---

[117] Rev. Ruls. 63-136, 1963-2 C.B. 19; 68-38, 1968-1 C.B. 446; 71-425, 1971-2 C.B. 76; and 72-340, 1972-2 C.B. 31.

[118] Rev. Rul. 74-413, 1974-2 C.B. 333.

[119] Reg. § 1.61-4(a)(4).

[120] *R.L. Harding*, 29 TCM 789, T.C. Memo. 1970-179 and Rev. Rul. 60-32, 1960-1 C.B. 23.

[121] See § 126 and Temp. Reg. § 16A.126-1.

received for goodwill are normally treated as capital gain. As provided in the Revenue Reconciliation Act of 1993, acquired goodwill can be amortized ratably over a period of 15 years. If the contract includes a single amount for both goodwill *and* a noncompetition agreement, the entire amount is treated as goodwill. In negotiating the sale, the seller should consider the tradeoffs involved in an allocation of the sales price between the covenant not to compete and goodwill. As a general rule, a seller will normally prefer to allocate more of the sales price to assets that produce capital gain, such as goodwill, than to those that produce ordinary income, such as a covenant not to compete.

Example 52

On January 1 of the current year, Ralph purchased all of the assets of Ed's Bowling Alley (a sole proprietorship) for $500,000. Included in the purchase contract is $60,000 allocable to goodwill and $45,000 to a covenant that prohibits Ed from opening another bowling alley in the next five years. Ed will report $60,000 as a long-term capital gain (taxed at no more than 15%) and the $45,000 as ordinary income. On the other hand, Ralph may amortize the amount paid for goodwill over 15 years (i.e., $60,000 ÷ 15 years = $4,000 per year), and the amount paid for the covenant not to compete over 15 years, notwithstanding it has a useful life of only five years ($45,000 ÷ 15 = $3,000 per year).

BUSINESS INTERRUPTION INSURANCE PROCEEDS

Some businesses carry insurance policies that provide for the loss of the use of property and of net profits sustained when the business property cannot be used because of an unexpected event such as fire or flood. The Regulations state that the insurance proceeds are included in gross income regardless of whether they are a reimbursement for the loss of the use of property or of net profits.[122] Similarly, insurance proceeds that are to reimburse the business for overhead expenses during the period of interruption are taxable.[123]

Example 53

Jordan Manufacturing, Inc. (JMI) was the victim of arson during the current year. The fire destroyed the main office building and the company's warehouse and its contents. JMI received a check for $1.5 million from its insurance company covering the projected lost profit for six months during which operations at JMI ceased. Since the profits which were not generated would be taxed, the payment representing the lost profit is fully included in JMI's gross income.

DAMAGES AWARDED

Cash may be awarded by the courts or by insurance companies for damages suffered by businesses because of patent infringement, cancellation of a franchise, injury to a business's reputation (see later discussion concerning professional reputation), breach of contract, antitrust action, or unfair competition. The treatment of the damages depends on whether they are compensatory (i.e., those amounts making the taxpayer whole) or punitive (i.e., those amounts that serve as a penalty). Punitive damages are fully taxable.[124] On the other hand, compensatory awards may be used *first* to offset any litigation expenses or other expenditures in obtaining the award.[125] *Second,* funds that represent a recovery of capital when damages

---

[122] Reg. § 1.1033(a)-2(c)(8).

[123] Rev. Rul. 55-264, 1955-1 C.B. 11.

[124] *Comm. v. Glenshaw Glass Co.,* 55-1 USTC ¶9308, 47 AFTR 162,348 U.S. 426 (USSC, 1955).

[125] *State Fish Corp.,* 49 T.C. 13 (1967), mod'g. 48 T.C. 465 (1967).

are awarded because of a loss in value to a business's goodwill or other assets are used to off-set or write down the capitalized asset costs.[126] Remaining damages generally are considered to be a reimbursement for a loss of profits and are included in gross income.[127] An exception to the latter classification occurs when compensatory damages are awarded in an antitrust suit. While the punitive damages in these cases are taxable, the compensatory damages are taxable only to the extent that losses sustained by the business resulted in a tax benefit.[128]

Example 54

Several years ago, Good Corporation contracted with Bad Corporation to build a condominium project. Good later identified defects in the construction and sued Bad. This year the court awarded Good $1,000,000; $750,000 for compensatory damages and $250,000 for punitive damages. Good incurred legal fees of $150,000. Good must treat the $250,000 punitive damages as ordinary taxable income. The compensatory damages are first reduced by the costs incurred to secure the award, $150,000. The remaining $600,000 is used to reduce the basis of the property, and any excess would be taxable.

LEASE CANCELLATION PAYMENTS

Early termination of lease agreements may result in a lease cancellation payment. Either a lessor or a lessee may receive these payments, depending on which party cancelled the lease. In *Hort,* the Supreme Court held that lease cancellation funds received by a lessor are a substitute for rent.[129] Consequently, these receipts are taxable income. Amounts received by a lessee on cancellation of a lease are considered proceeds from the sale of the lease.[130] Thus, the gain is included in gross income. Whether the gain is ordinary or capital depends on the use of the property (see discussion in Chapter 16).

Example 55

Alice owns a 50-unit apartment complex in Manhattan. Nancy, who rents one of Alice's units, has decided to purchase her own house. Consequently, Nancy paid Alice $1,100 in return for cancelling her lease. Alice must treat the payment as a substitute for rental income and, therefore, must include the amount as ordinary income.

Example 56

This year Alice decided to convert her 50-unit apartment complex into a medical clinic for use by physicians and dentists. She paid one of her tenants $2,000 to cancel the lease. Because the lease agreement represents a capital asset to the tenants (i.e., the lease on a residence is a personal asset), the tenant will treat the $2,000 as capital gain.

---

126 *Farmers' and Merchants Bank of Cattletsburg, Ky. v. Comm.,* 3 USTC ¶972,11 AFTR 619,59 F.2d 912 (CA-6, 1932) and *Thomson v. Comm.,* 69-1 USTC ¶9199,23 AFTR2d 69-529,406 F.2d 1006 (CA-9, 1969).

127 *Durkee v. Comm.,* 1950-1 USTC ¶9283,35 AFTR 1438, 162 F.2d 184 (CA-6, 1947), *rem'g.* 6 T.C. 773 (1946).

128 § 186 and Reg. § 1.186-1.

129 *Hort v. Comm.,* 41-1 USTC ¶9354, 25 AFTR 1207, 313 U.S. 28 (USSC, 1941).

130 § 1241.

LEASEHOLD IMPROVEMENTS

A lessee often makes improvements to leased real estate. These may range from minor improvements up to the construction of a building on the leased land. If these improvements are made in lieu of rent payments, they are included in the lessor's gross income.[131] Otherwise, the lessor has no taxable income either at the time the improvements are made or at the time the lease is terminated, even if the improvements substantially increase the property's value.[132] The lessor's only taxable income from these improvements will occur indirectly on the sale of the property to the extent the improvements result in a higher net selling price.

Example 57

For the past 10 years W had leased land to X. During the current year the lease expired and W became the owner of a three-stall garage (FMV $19,000) that X had constructed on the property seven years previously. Assuming the improvements were not made in lieu of rent, the FMV of the garage is not currently included in W's gross income.

Under § 110, a retail tenant that receives cash or rent reductions from the lessor of retail space does not include such amounts in income if the cash (or equivalent) is used for qualified construction or improvement to the space. In order to qualify for the exclusion, the tenant must have a short-term lease (i.e., a lease of retail space for 15 years or less). The amount excluded cannot exceed the amount spent by the tenant for the improvement.

From time to time, lessors will make improvements on their property in order to attract lessees. If a lessor abandons a leasehold improvement in the year the lease terminates, the lessor is allowed a deduction equal to the landlord's adjusted basis of the improvement [§ 168(i)(8)]. This rule does not apply where the improvement is demolished in which case the landlord simply increases the basis of the property (§ 280B).

CONTRIBUTIONS TO CAPITAL

Cash or other property received by a business in exchange for an ownership interest are nontaxable transactions for the business. These transfers are treated as contributions to capital and not income.[133] Contributions to capital that are not in exchange for an ownership interest also are nontaxable.

Miscellaneous Items

As noted throughout this chapter, gross income includes *all* income unless specifically exempted. Although this chapter is not intended to discuss every income item, some additional items are classified for discussion purposes as miscellaneous.

FEES RECEIVED

Ordinarily, fees received for services performed are included in gross income. Thus, fees paid to corporate directors, jurors, and executors are reported as miscellaneous gross income. However, if executor fees are paid regardless of whether the taxpayer performs any services, they may qualify as nontaxable gifts.[134]

---

[131] Reg. § 1.109-1.

[132] § 109.

[133] §§ 118 and 721.

[134] Rev. Rul. 57-398, 1957-2 C.B. 93.

ASSET DISCOVERY, WINDFALL RECEIPTS

Cash, treasure or other assets found by a taxpayer are taxable income even if found accidentally, with no effort expended in discovering them.[135] For example, taxpayers were held to have taxable income equal to cash found in a used piano they had purchased.[136] Reg. § 1.61-14 provides that "treasure trove" constitutes gross income for the year in which it is reduced to the taxpayer's undisputed possession.

GAMBLING WINNINGS

Winnings from gambling are fully taxable. This includes winnings from any kind of contest, lotteries, raffles, bingo, horse races, slot machines, card games and similar sources. On the other hand, gambling losses are deductible only to the extent of current year winnings and only then as an itemized deduction (but not a miscellaneous itemized deduction).[137] However, if a taxpayer is considered a professional gambler, gambling losses are deductible for AGI. Professional gamblers are also subject self-employment taxes on their net income. Losses that exceed winnings die at the end of the taxable year and do not create a net operating loss that can be carried over to other years, even if the taxpayer is luckier in the other years.

ILLEGAL INCOME, INCOME FROM UNLAWFUL ACTIVITIES

The long arm of the government also taxes income from illegal activities. At first glance, it might seem that the taxpayer does not realize income since the income must be returned or repaid. However, if property is obtained illegally and the taxpayer does not recognize an obligation to repay, the benefit is taxable. Courts have held that profits from a wide array of unlawful activities are taxable, including theft, bank robbery, sale of narcotics, illegal sale of liquor, bribes, a kidnapper's ransom and many more. Costs incurred to obtain the illegal income may be deductible. In addition, a deduction is allowed if and when the wrongdoer reimburses the victim for the loss.

CAR POOL RECEIPTS

One type of earned income is nontaxable. Vehicle owners operating car pools for fellow commuters may exclude all the revenues received.[138] Car pool expenses are *personal* commuting expenses, and therefore are not deductible. If, however, the car pool activities are sufficient to qualify a taxpayer as being in a trade or business, all revenues are taxable. How much activity constitutes a trade or business is a question of fact not easily answered, but in this type of situation, the definition of trade certainly requires considerably more activity than a single automobile or small van making one round trip daily.

INCOME TAX REFUNDS

All state and local income tax refunds are nontaxable except to the extent the taxpayer received a *tax benefit* in a prior year.[139] A corporation receives a tax benefit for all business expenses, including state and local income taxes, unless the corporation incurs a net operating loss for the year of deduction. State and local income taxes paid by individuals, however, provide a tax benefit only if the taxpayer itemized these deductions in the year paid. There is no tax benefit for the expense if the standard deduction was used instead of itemized deductions. The tax benefit and the amount of the refund that must be included generally is limited to the excess of itemized deductions over the standard deduction. For example, assume that in 2017, a taxpayer's total itemized deductions, including state income taxes

[135] Rev. Rul. 53-61, 1953-1 C.B. 17.

[136] *Cesarini v. Comm.*, 70-2 USTC ¶9509, 26 AFTR2d 70-5107. 428 F.2d 812 (CA-6, 1970).

[137] See § 165(d) and Chapter 10. See *Groetzinger,* 87-1 USTC ¶9191, 59 AFTR2d 87-532, 771 F.2d 269 (USSC, 1987).

[138] Rev. Rul. 55-555, 1955-2 C.B. 20.

[139] § 111(a).

of $3,000, exceeded the standard deduction by $1,000. If next year the taxpayer, receives a refund of the $3,000 taxes, the maximum amount included is limited to $1,000. In addition, the taxable amount of a state and local income tax refund is affected by the amount of state and local sales tax that the taxpayer could have otherwise deducted. Taxpayers are entitled to deduct the larger of state and local income taxes or state and local sales taxes (see Chapter 11). Taxpayers do not receive refunds of sales taxes, only state income taxes. For this reason, the amount of the any state income tax refund is taxable only to the extent that the state income taxes deducted exceeded the amount of state sales tax that the taxpayer could have otherwise deducted.[140]

Example 58

John and Lori Hansen are married and live in Indiana. The couple filed a joint return for 2017. Their total itemized deductions, including state income taxes withheld by their employers of $7,000, amounted to $14,500 in 2017. The couple could have deducted state and local sales taxes of $6,000 but deducted the state and local income taxes since the $7,000 amount was larger. The standard deduction that the couple could have claimed for 2017 was $12,700. On June 12, 2018, the Hansens received a refund from the State of Indiana for $3,000 as a result of overpaying their 2017 Indiana income taxes. In determining the tax benefit that the couple received and the amount of the refund that is taxable, the law takes the view that it was the deduction for state income taxes that enabled them to itemize. For this reason, the initial tax benefit from the state income taxes is $1,800 ($14,500 itemized deductions – $12,700 standard deduction). However, the Hansens could have deducted the $6,000 of sales taxes and there would not have been a refund in which case there would be not be any taxable income. Consequently, the tax benefit is further limited to $1,000 ($7,000 state income tax – $6,000 state sales tax). Therefore, they must include only $1,000 of the refund in gross income on their 2017 Federal income tax return.

TEMPORARY LIVING COSTS

If an individual receives insurance proceeds to cover temporary living costs incurred because the principal residence was destroyed or damaged by fire, flood, or other casualty, the funds are nontaxable to the extent they are offset by *extra* living costs.[141] These funds also may be excluded if the government prevented the individual from using an undamaged residence because of the existence or threat of a casualty. Extra living costs are limited to those additional costs actually incurred for temporarily housing, feeding, and transporting the taxpayer and members of the household. Typical qualifying costs are hotel or apartment rent and utilities, extra costs for restaurant meals, and additional transportation necessitated by having to live outside the immediate area of the residence.

DAMAGES AWARDED TO INDIVIDUALS

More and more often people are suing or being sued. Each year millions of lawsuits are filed in state and federal courts. Most of these cases have financial implications. Some of these are settled out of court while others go on. In many situations, individuals receive damages compensating them for their loss (compensatory damages) and, in some, damages are awarded to penalize or punish the wrongdoer (punitive damages). Section 104(a) provides the treatment of compensatory and punitive damages.

---

[140] But see *Marrita Murphy* 2006-2 USTC, ¶50,476, 98 AFTR 2d 2006-6088, 460 F3d 79, (CA-DC, 2006) where the appellate court recently held that this provision was unconstitutional.

[141] § 123.

Compensatory Damages

For many years, Section 104(a)(2) provided that damages awarded on account of personal injuries and sickness were nontaxable. Historically, the treatment was justified on the grounds that the amounts received represent a return of human capital. According to the theory, injured parties are no better off since the damages merely restored them to their original state. However, controversies arose in applying this exclusion to certain awards such as those involving age, sex, and race discrimination. Taxpayers artfully argued that these awards were related to personal injuries, hoping to qualify for an exclusion. The seriousness of the situation could be seen in a class action suit brought by hundreds of IBM employees that had been laid off who argued for the exclusion of their severance pay on the grounds that such payments were made in part to allay future claims of discrimination.

To address these concerns, § 104 was amended in 1996 to make it clear that only damages awarded on account of physical injury and sickness are not taxable.[140] In addition, § 104 explains that *emotional distress* is not considered a physical injury or sickness unless such distress had its origins from physical injury or sickness. Emotional distress includes physical symptoms such as insomnia, headaches or stomach disorders that may result from such emotional distress. According to the Committee Reports, this rule bars an exclusion for any damages received based on a claim of employment discrimination or injury to reputation (e.g., slander or libel) accompanied by a claim of emotional distress. Thus it appears that awards made due to employment discrimination based on age, sex, race, or similar factors would be fully taxable. The fact that the individual suffered emotional distress that produced physical symptoms would not enable the taxpayer to qualify for the exclusion. However, the law does explain that damages actually used to pay for medical expenses related to emotional distress are nontaxable.

Example 59

In July of 2015 K filed a sex discrimination lawsuit against Statewide University after being denied promotion to associate professor with tenure. In November of 2017 the parties entered into an out-of-court settlement pursuant to which the university awarded K $80,000 in lost wages, $5,000 for medical expenses related to emotional distress and $40,000 of punitive damages. Of the $125,000 she received, only the $5,000 payment for medical expenses would be excluded from K's gross income. Amounts allocated to lost wages and punitive damages are taxable.

Punitive Damages

Historically, punitive damages normally have been taxable. At times, however, courts have reached differing opinions about the treatment of punitive damages related to cases involving damages awarded for physical injury or sickness. One theory allowed the taxpayer to exclude punitive damages related to physical injury or sickness since the compensatory damages were nontaxable. The other theory took the view that all punitive damages were taxable. Section 104(a)(2) now makes it clear that all punitive damages are taxable even if they are related to physical injury or sickness.

Tax Planning

INVESTMENTS

Tax-planning strategy must be viewed in terms of each taxpayer's own financial position. When considering investments, both the after-tax return and the risk involved must be evaluated. Before-tax income frequently is lower for tax-exempt and tax-deferred investments than it is for taxable investments with the same degree of risk. Consequently, tax-exempt investments should be most attractive to those in the higher tax bracket. They may not be beneficial to those in the lower bracket. Tax-deferred investments should be most attractive to those expecting a lower tax bracket when the deferral period ends. In addition, investors must consider whether any gains will be taxed as ordinary income or capital gains (see Chapter 16), and whether capital gains will be needed to offset capital losses.

Taxpayers have a variety of investment opportunities available to them. In order to arrive at informed investment decisions, comparative evaluations are necessary. However, such evaluations must be viewed with caution. The very nature of this type of analysis means that tentative assumptions must be made about the future. For example, when comparing a possible stock purchase with an annuity purchase, assumptions must be made about (1) future cash flows for the two investments, (2) future marginal tax rates, and (3) the discount rate to be used in determining the present value of the expected cash flows. A decision should never be based on a simple nonmathematical tax comparison of the total of annual dividends plus capital gains for the stock, as opposed to the total deferred ordinary income for the annuity. A tax adviser should always remember that while taxation is a very important factor, it is just one of several that must be considered.

On the death of an insured person, life insurance companies ordinarily allow beneficiaries to receive the proceeds in one lump sum, or in installments for a stipulated period or over the beneficiary's life. Tax concerns aside, some beneficiaries may elect to leave the proceeds with the insurance company simply because they like the security of receiving a periodic payment from an established financial institution. Each installment contains a ratable portion of the proceeds plus interest. This interest is taxable income. Thus, life insurance proceeds received in installments are treated the same as annuities.

Example 60

M is the sole beneficiary of her husband's $60,000 life insurance policy. She elects to receive the proceeds in monthly installments for 10 years. Her monthly installment is $500 plus interest on the unpaid principal. In the current year, she receives $6,000 plus $3,700 interest. Her taxable interest income is $3,700.

One feature of life insurance that has enticed many investors over the years is its tax-free cash build-up. Taxpayers have taken advantage of this by borrowing against the policy—in effect receiving use of the income without having to pay tax on it. To discourage the purchase of life insurance as a tax-sheltered investment vehicle, special rules have been established. As a result, taxpayers must closely scrutinize the type of insurance they purchase with respect to its tax treatment. Under the revised rules, a taxpayer who receives amounts before age 59½, including loans, from certain single premium and other investment-oriented life insurance contracts (modified endowment contracts) is treated as receiving income first and then a recovery of basis. In addition, the recipient is subject to an additional 10% income tax on the amounts received that are includible in gross income. This provision affects only "modified endowment contracts" entered into on or after June 21, 1988.

An investor who desires nontaxable income may choose to purchase assets such as

1. Qualifying state and local government bonds to obtain the full interest income exclusion.
2. Stocks in companies with net income for accounting purposes, but no earnings and profits for tax purposes, to obtain the full exclusion for distributions that are treated as a return of capital.

Investors who wish to defer income may choose to

1. Purchase Series E or EE bonds and report interest that accrues when the bonds are redeemed.
2. Purchase annuities (or to elect that life insurance proceeds be received as annuities) to obtain the deferral of all interest income until received.
3. Purchase assets that are expected to appreciate, such as stocks, real estate, and collectables, to obtain the deferral of all appreciation until it is realized.

If the taxpayer does not dispose of the assets, the deferral becomes permanent. That is, no one recognizes the income and the assets are inherited at their market values, including the deferred income.

EMPLOYEE BENEFITS

Company fringe benefits can provide employees with tax consequences that range from excellent savings to actual disadvantages. From a tax viewpoint, the best fringe benefits are those that are deductible by the employer and convert otherwise taxable income to nontaxable income for the recipient. For example, most employee benefits that are provided in lieu of additional salary convert taxable compensation to nontaxable benefits.

Example 61

W is a new employee of Z Corporation. Her compensation package is $20,000. However, she may choose to receive (a) $20,000 salary and no benefits, or (b) $19,000 salary and Z will pay premiums of $600 for medical insurance and $400 for group-term life insurance. If W chooses the first option, she has $20,000 taxable income, but if she selects the second option, she has $19,000 taxable income.

Another very valuable type of fringe benefit is one that is nontaxable income if provided by the employer but is a nondeductible expenditure if paid by the employee. Most fringe benefits are of this type. These include premiums paid for group-term life insurance up to $50,000, qualifying meals and lodging on the premises, supper money, company parking, use of company facilities, and employee discounts. All of these benefits are deductible costs by the employer but nontaxable income to the employee when the necessary requirements discussed in this chapter are met. If, however, the employees pay these costs instead of the employer, there is no tax deduction for them.

A third type of fringe benefit includes expenditures that are deductible expenses, when paid by individuals, but are subject to restrictions. For example, health insurance premiums are deductible for employees who itemize their deductions but *only* to the extent that all qualifying medical expenditures exceed 7.5% of AGI (see Chapter 11). Thus, employer-paid health insurance represents different tax savings to different employees.

Example 62

L's compensation includes a salary of $30,000 plus employer-paid health insurance premiums of $600. L's taxable income is $30,000 since the $600 is nontaxable. If the company policy is changed so that L pays the $600 health insurance premiums and the company increases his salary to $30,600, the tax effect on L depends on his individual tax situation.

1. If L does not itemize medical expenses, he has taxable income of $30,600 salary and no deduction for the $600.

2. If L itemizes deductions and his medical expenditures before the health insurance premiums exceed 7.5% of AGI, he still has taxable income of $30,600 salary but now has a deduction of $600.

Assume L has a 25% marginal tax rate. In the first situation, his tax benefit from employer-paid health insurance premiums is $150 ($600 × 25%). In the second situation, L appears to receive no tax benefit when his company pays the health insurance premiums. However, his AGI is $600 higher when L pays the premium. Since medical expenses equal to 7.5% of AGI are not deductible, this increases the nondeductible portion by $45 ($600 × 7.5%). Thus, at the 25% tax rate, his tax increases by $11.25 ($45 × 25%).

Some employer-provided benefits can be a disadvantage to employees. Recall, for example, that disability income is taxable if the premiums were paid by the employer but nontaxable if they were paid by the individual. The best tax-planning advice when employers pay disability insurance premiums is for employees to convince employers to provide another benefit and let employees pay their own disability premiums.

Considerable leeway in tax planning is available to those employees who are allowed to select their own fringe benefits. Simply looking at the cost of each benefit to the company, however, is inadequate. Each employee should carefully evaluate personal needs and the tax effect of each desirable benefit before selection is made.

EMPLOYEE VERSUS SELF-EMPLOYED

The tax advantages of many fringe benefits are available only if an employer/employee relationship exists. For example, sole proprietors are not considered employees of their proprietorships so many fringe benefits are not available to them. Similarly, partners in partnerships and members of LLCs are not considered employees and, therefore, some benefits are not available to them. In contrast, owners of C corporations can be employees of the corporation and are entitled to fringe benefits. This situation creates an incentive to operate some businesses as corporations rather than as proprietorships or partnerships or LLCs.

One of these fringe benefits, employer-furnished meals and lodging, has been of interest to closely held businesses for years. Farming represents a particularly good example of a business that requires someone to be available on the property 24 hours a day. When the working owner lives on the farm, a business deduction plus an employee exclusion for the cost of meals and lodging provided to the farmer can be significant.

Example 63

A farm owned by M has the following information for the current year:

Gross income	$130,000
Cost of food consumed by M	2,000
Cost of lodging used by M	4,200
Salary to M	20,000
Other farm expenses	85,000

If the farm is a proprietorship, net farming income is $25,000 ($130,000 − $20,000 − $85,000) and M has an AGI of $45,000 ($25,000 + $20,000).[142] Similar results occur if the farm is a partnership, except M will report only his share of the $25,000. In contrast, if the farm is a corporation, net income is $18,800 ($130,000 − $2,000 − $4,200 − $20,000 − $85,000) and M has an AGI of $20,000. Thus, M, the proprietor, has $45,000 AGI compared with a combined income of $38,800 ($18,800 + $20,000) for the M Corporation and M, the employee.

Although the above example seems to result in a tax advantage for the corporate farm, such a conclusion is over-simplified. Other tax factors are important. For example, corporate net income is taxed to the corporation currently and again as dividend income to shareholders when distributed to them (see Chapter 19). Another important factor is that individuals and corporations are subject to different tax rates. Also, if farming losses occur, the results may be very unfavorable with a corporate entity. The important point to remember is that the tax advantage achieved with the corporation for meals and lodging (and other employee benefits) is just one of the necessary ingredients when evaluating whether a business should be incorporated.

---

[142] Technically, a proprietor's salary is not a farming expense but is shown in the example for comparison purposes.

Thus, net income is $45,000 ($130,000 − $85,000) and M's AGI is $45,000.

DIVORCE

Insufficient attention usually is given to tax planning during separation and divorce. Of course, favorable tax results are easier to accomplish when the individuals are parting amicably, but good results still can occur amid animosity. The more disparate the husband's and wife's tax brackets, the greater the benefits to be achieved. This is because payments classified as alimony or separate maintenance are deductible by the payor and are taxable income to the recipient. In contrast, all other asset transfers are neither deductible expenses nor taxable income.

Example 64

H and W are divorced. H's marginal tax rate is 35% while W's is 15 percent. Every $10 of alimony costs H $6.50 after taxes ($10 paid – $3.50 tax savings [$10 × 35%]) and is worth $8.50 to W after taxes ($10 received – $1.50 tax due [$10 × 15%]). Thus, H pays $6.50 for W to receive $8.50. If W requires $425 after taxes each month, she must receive $500 if the payments qualify as alimony ($500 – [$500 × 15% = $75]) or $425 if they do not. On the surface, it seems that H would rather pay $425 a month than $500 but $500 in alimony results in an after-tax cost of $325 ($500 – [$500 × 35% = $175]) for a monthly savings of $100 ($425 – $325). Naturally, the closer the two marginal rates, the less there is in tax savings.

Problem Materials

DISCUSSION QUESTIONS

6-1 *Basic Concepts.* Determine whether each of the following statements is true or false. If false, rewrite the statement so that it is true. Be prepared to explain each statement.
  a. Receipts are included in gross income only if specifically listed in the Code.
  b. Tax returns show (1) gross receipts from all sources, less (2) excludable income, which equals (3) taxable income.
  c. Interest earned on tax-exempt municipal bonds is nontaxable income regardless of whether it is received by an individual or by a corporation.

6-2 *Investment—Stocks versus Bonds.* C has $10,000 to invest but is uncertain whether to purchase H, Inc. stocks or tax-exempt bonds issued by the State of Illinois. List the relevant types of information that C must obtain or estimate in order to make a mathematical calculation of her after-tax return on the two investments she is considering.

6-3 *Investments—Bonds.* D, Inc. bonds are selling for $1,000 each with an interest rate of 7 percent. Tax-exempt bonds issued by the State of Kentucky are selling for $1,000 each with an interest rate of three percent. Which bond provides a taxpayer with the higher after-tax return when the marginal tax rate is
  a. 35 percent?
  b. 15 percent?

6-4 *Investment Income.* Indicate whether the following statements are true or false and if false, explain why the statement is false.
  a. A dividend received by an individual taxpayer is taxed as ordinary income and, consequently, could be taxed at the highest marginal tax rate.
  b. Whether a distribution from a C corporation is a dividend, return of capital, or capital gain depends on the amount of the corporation's retained earnings.
  c. This year C received a distribution from a C corporation with respect to his stock. If the distribution results in capital gain, B's basis in his stock will be zero.
  d. A distribution from a mutual fund may consist of dividend income as well as capital gains.
  e. During the year, E received interest from a U.S. Treasury bond. The interest is tax-exempt.
  f. STK Corporation declared a dividend in August. Shareholders could elect to take cash or an equivalent amount of stock. Shareholders who elected to take stock do not have taxable income.

6-5 *Distributions from 529 Savings Plans.* During the year, G withdrew $18,000 from a 529 plan for his daughter. He used the most of the money to pay for the following costs associated with her first year of college: tuition $10,000, fees $1,000, apartment rental $3,000, computer $1,600, books $400, appliances and furniture $505, and bedding $200. How will the $18,000 be treated?

6-6 *ABLE Accounts.* H and W are married and have an autistic child, age seven. Explain how an ABLE account is treated for tax purposes and how it may be beneficial for the family.

6-7 *Employee Benefits.* Z, Inc. owns and operates several businesses, including six hotels and two real estate agencies. R, an employee of Z, spends three nights free of charge in one of Z's hotels in Indiana. Is the value of the lodging nontaxable to R, assuming the information below? Explain.
  a. R works for one of the real estate agencies.
  b. R tends bar in one of the hotels in Maine.
  c. R is a tax accountant in Z's corporate headquarters where the tax records of all of Z's businesses are maintained.

6-8 *Employee Benefits—Comparison.* Compare the tax treatment for each of the items listed below assuming they are paid by (1) the employer, or (2) the employee.
  a. Parking in the company lot during working hours.
  b. Health insurance premiums.
  c. Disability insurance premiums.
  d. Meals eaten in the company cafeteria when the employee must remain on the premises for job reasons.

6-9 *Employee Benefits—Meals and Lodging.* Employer-provided meals and lodging that qualify as nontaxable income can be an exceedingly valuable employee benefit.
  a. When do employer-provided meals and lodging qualify as nontaxable income?
  b. List at least 10 types of occupations in which employer-provided lodging and/or meals could qualify for the exclusion. Explain why these occupations are appropriate for the exclusion.

6-10 *Employee Benefits.* Over the years, the list of employee benefits that qualify as deductible expenses by the employer and nontaxable income for the employee has expanded. Assume Congress is interested in further expanding the list of benefits available for this special tax treatment. Prepare a list for Congress of at least three items not discussed in this chapter that would provide many employees with valuable benefits. Explain why these three would be logical additions.

6-11 *Gifts.* How can gifts to family members reduce the family's income tax liability?

6-12 *Alimony and Child Support.* A husband and wife who are obtaining a divorce disagree whether certain periodic payments should be classified as alimony or child support.
  a. What difference does it make how the payments are classified?
  b. What if the agreement states the payments are for both alimony and child support without making a specific distinction in dollar allocation between the two?
  c. List three types of compromise offers that could be made by the husband to reach an allocation that might satisfy both the husband and wife. Explain the tax consequences of each of the three possible solutions.

6-13 *Alimony.* A husband (H) and wife (W) are obtaining a divorce. He agrees to pay alimony of $25,000 in each of the two years after the divorce to enable her to attend graduate school. No alimony will be paid after the second year.
  a. What are his deductible and her taxable amount of alimony for each of the two years, and what are the tax effects in year three?
  b. How could the payment schedule be restructured to maximize his deductions?
  c. How could the payment schedule be restructured to minimize her taxable income?

6-14 *Prizes and Awards.* Contest winners must report the value of prizes won as taxable income.
  a. What arguments could the taxpayer use to convince the IRS and the courts that the values of the prizes are less than their retail selling prices?
  b. Are any prizes or awards ever nontaxable? Explain.

6-15 *Scholarships and Fellowships.* CPA firms are interested in encouraging practical research that explores accounting issues with an objective of developing better accounting methods for the profession. Assume the XY firm decides to establish a fund that will support individual research efforts. Recipients of these grants will be selected based on the quality of their past work and on a written proposal of a specific research project to be completed with funds from the XY firm. Do recipients of these grants have taxable or nontaxable income? Explain.

6-16 *Goodwill versus Agreement Not to Compete.* A preliminary agreement covering the sale/purchase of a dental practice includes an allocation of $40,000 to goodwill and the agreement that the seller will not practice dentistry within a five-mile radius for five years.
- **a.** What are the tax consequences of this $40,000 allocation?
- **b.** What advice should a tax adviser give the seller?
- **c.** What advice should a tax adviser give the buyer?

6-17 *Damages Awarded.* As the result of a newspaper article, V claims his character was damaged beyond repair, he lost his job, and he incurred medical expenses for psychiatric care. His lawsuit requested that the court award him the following amounts: $500,000 for personal injury due to slander; $30,000 in lost wages; and $5,000 for psychiatric care.
- **a.** What are the tax consequences to V if he is awarded the $535,000?
- **b.** V decides to accept an out-of-court settlement of $150,000. The newspaper and its insurer are willing to allocate the $150,000 in any manner that V requests. How should V have the amount allocated?

PROBLEMS

6-18 *Basic Concepts.* Calculate the amount to be included in gross income for the following taxpayers.
- **a.** T is self-employed as a beautician. Her records show

Receipts:	
Services	$21,000
Product sales	3,000
Expenditures:	
Cost of products sold	1,800
Cost of supplies used	2,600
Utilities	2,400
Shop and equipment rent	3,600
Other expenses	1,000

- **b.** R owns rental property. His records show

Gross rents	$ 6,000
Depreciation expense	4,200
Repair expense	2,100
Miscellaneous expense	300

- **c.** S is an employee with the following tax information:

Gross salary	$15,000
Social Security (FICA) taxes withheld (rounded for simplicity)	1,000
Federal income tax withheld	2,200
Health insurance premiums withheld	500
Net salary received in cash	11,300
Employer's share of Social Security taxes	1,000

6-19 *Investments—Cash Dividends.* Three years ago, Z purchased 50 shares of L common stock for $6,000. Although Z is married, the stocks are recorded in his name alone. The current market value of these shares totals $7,200. He and Mrs. Z file a joint return and neither of them owns any other stock. Mr. Z wants to know what effect each of the following totally separate situations has upon (1) his taxable income and (2) his basis in each share of stock.

  a. L distributes a cash dividend and Z receives $330.

  b. L distributes cash as a return of capital and Z receives $330.

6-20 *Investments—Stock Dividends.* A, who is single, purchased 100 shares of N Corporation common stock four years ago for $12,000. The stock has a current fair market value of $14,400. A asks how each of the following separate situations affects her (1) taxable income and (2) basis in each share of stock.

  a. N distributes common stock as a dividend and A receives ten shares.

  b. N distributes nonconvertible preferred stock as a dividend and A receives 10 shares. The preferred stock has a current fair market value of $100 per share.

6-21 *Investments—Cash Dividends.* D, Inc. had accumulated earnings and profits at January 1 of the current year of $20,000. During the taxable year, it had current earnings and profits of $10,000. On December 31 of the current year, D, Inc. made a cash distribution of $40,000 to its sole shareholder, G. G paid $25,000 for his stock three years ago.

  a. How will G treat the $40,000 he received on December 31?

  b. Assume G sold all of his stock for $36,000 on January 1 of the following year. Compute his capital gain.

6-22 *Investments—Interest.* Mr. K died at the beginning of the year. Mrs. K received interest during the year from the following sources:

Interest from U.S. Treasury bond	$ 900
Corporate bonds	1,100
Bank savings account	200
Personal loan to a friend	500
City of Maryville bonds (issued to build a new high school)	600
Employer's share of Social Security taxes	1,000

Mrs. K also sold the City of Maryville bonds for a gain of $300. In addition to the above, Mrs. K was the beneficiary of her husband's $50,000 life insurance policy. She elected to receive the $50,000 proceeds plus interest over the next 10 years. She receives $7,500 in the current year and will receive a like amount each of the following nine years. Compute Mrs. K's taxable income for the year.

6-23 *Educational Savings Bonds Requirements.* H and W have twin sons, S and T, and two daughters, D and E. The couple purchased Series EE savings bonds, hoping to take advantage of the interest exclusion for their children's education. This year, they cashed in some of the bonds, receiving $5,000. Of this amount, $2,000 represented interest. For each of the following independent situations, indicate how much, if any, of the exclusion is allowed this year.

  a. D enrolled at Michigan State University and paid tuition of $4,000. To help defray some of these expenses, she used an academic scholarship of $1,000.

  b. While on her way to the first day of class, D fell and broke her leg. She withdrew from classes and received all of her money back.

  c. S is 25 and entered the Ph.D. program at the University of Texas this year. As a teaching assistant, he receives a salary of $7,000 during the year. His parents paid $1,000 of his tuition.

  d. H and W paid for all of T's tuition to attend Arizona State University. The couple's AGI for this year was $110,000. When the couple purchased the particular bonds used to pay for T's tuition, their AGI was $55,000.

  e. E, 22, redeemed bonds this year, receiving $5,000. E used all of the proceeds to pay for her tuition. She received the bonds as a gift from her parents last year. E's AGI for this year is $3,000.

6-24 *Investments—Annuities.* P is single, 65 years old, and retired. On August 1, 2006 he purchased a single-premium deferred life annuity for $40,000 using after-tax funds. This year, P received $5,000 in annuity benefits. He will receive a like amount each year for the rest of his life. (**Note:** In answering the following questions, use the information in Exhibit 6-3 of this chapter.)
   a. Calculate P's taxable income from the annuity for the current year.
   b. Calculate P's taxable income from the annuity for year five.
   c. Calculate P's taxable income from the annuity for year 22.
   d. Assume P lives just 15 more years. Calculate the deduction that would be allowed on P's final tax return.
   e. Assume the annuity was purchased by P and his employer jointly. P contributed $12,000 in after-tax funds, and the employer contributed $28,000. Calculate P's taxable income from the annuity for the current year.

6-25 *Annuities.* A, age 62, retired after 30 years of service as an employee of the XYZ Corporation. He started receiving retirement benefits in the form of a single life annuity on January 1 of the current year. A's total after-tax contributions to the plan amounted to $39,000, and his retirement benefit is $1,500 per month.
   a. Determine A's nontaxable portion of each monthly payment, assuming he elects the simplified safe-harbor method.
   b. Assume A lives another 25 years. Will there be a time period in which A will be required to fully include the monthly payments in gross income? If so, when?

6-26 *Annuities: Early Withdrawal.* Several years ago, Lois, a widow, inherited $100,000 from her brother and used it to purchase an annuity. Under the terms of the annuity, when she turn 60 years of age she will receive $600 per month for the rest of her life. Answer the following questions related to the annuity.
   a. When Lois was 57, she lost her job. As a result, she is thinking about withdrawing $10,000 from her annuity account. At the time, the earnings accumulated on the annuity were $4,000. She has asked you whether this would be wise. How would you respond? In so doing, explain the treatment of the withdrawal.
   b. Would your answer in (a) change if Lois simply borrowed the funds?
   c. How would your response in (a) change if Lois was 63?

6-27 *529 Savings Plan.* Z is a dependent beneficiary of a 529 savings plan established by her parents. During the current year, Z received a $20,000 distribution and used it to pay $20,000 for tuition at a private university. Z's parents contributed $60,000 to the plan and earnings from investments total an additional $20,000.
   a. How much of the $20,000 distribution may Z exclude from gross income?
   b. Assume Z elects to join the work force rather than attend college and the entire $80,000 accumulated in the plan is distributed to Z's parents. How much is included in the parent's gross income?

6-28 *529 College Savings Plan.* V, who is divorced, transfers $45,000 to Eastern University's 529 savings plan for the benefit of his son, W, in 2017. W received no other gifts during 2017.
   a. Compute V's taxable gift for 2017 (assume no election was made).
   b. Assume V elects to treat the contribution as a gift made over five years. Does V owe any gift taxes?
   c. Assume V dies in 2020. How much of the $45,000 contribution made in 2017 will be included in V's gross estate?

6-29 *Investments—Life Insurance.* L is 65 years old and retired. Her husband died early in the year. L was the beneficiary of his $20,000 life insurance policy. L elected to receive $5,200 annually for five years rather than receive a single payment of $20,000 immediately. Calculate L's taxable income from the first payment.

6-30 *Social Security Benefits.* X, who is single and retired, has the following income for the current year:

Taxable interest.	$12,000
Dividend income.	10,000
Tax-exempt bond interest.	8,000
Social Security benefits.	7,200

    a   Compute the taxable portion of X's Social Security benefits.

    b. Assume the above information remains the same, except X's taxable interest amounted to $10,000. Compute the taxable portion of his Social Security benefits.

6-31 *Group-Term Life Insurance.* E, age 55, is Vice President of QRS, Incorporated. His salary for the year amounted to $75,000. Employees at QRS receive group-term life insurance coverage equal to twice their annual salaries. Determine E's taxable income from his group-term life insurance protection for the year.

6-32 *Employee Benefits.* Determine the (1) deductible employer amount, and (2) taxable employee amount for each of the following employer-provided benefits.

    a. Reimbursement of expenses paid by an employee to entertain a client of the business, $200.

    b. Bonus paid an employee when a sales quota was met, $300.

    c. Watches given employees at Christmas, $18 each.

    d. The company provides free parking on its premises for its employees. The fair value of this parking is $500 per month, as evidenced by the fact that a commercial parking lot located across the street from the company's property charges $500 per month to park in its lot.

    e. Supper money of $15 paid to an employee for each of 10 nights that she worked past 6 p.m., $150.

6-33 *Employee Benefits.* Determine the (1) deductible employer amount, and (2) taxable employee amount for each of the following employer-provided benefits.

    a. Premiums of $700 paid on $70,000 of group-term life insurance for a 52-year-old woman employee.

    b. Ten percent employee discounts are allowed on the retail price of all merchandise purchased from the employer. During the year, sales to employees totaled $18,000 ($20,000 retail price – $2,000 discount) for merchandise that cost the employer $14,000. The employer reported the $18,000 as sales and the $14,000 as cost of goods sold.

    c. The employer company reimburses employees who use public transportation, such as a bus or train, to get to work. The maximum amount the company is willing to reimburse an employee for this expense is $200 per month.

    d. The employer has a small room that contains a refrigerator, a microwave, a beverage machine, and a table where a few employees can eat. Each day the employer puts out donuts and coffee for the employees at a cost of about $3,000 per year.

6-34 *Employee Benefits—Medical Insurance.* F's $400 annual health insurance premium is paid by his employer. During the year, F received $870 reimbursement of medical expenses; $650 for this year's expenses and $220 for last year's expenses. Determine F's taxable income from the reimbursement in the current year if:

    a. F never itemizes any medical expenses.

    b. F deducted medical expenses from his AGI this year of $900 and last year of $450.

6-35 *Tax Benefit Rule.* During 2017 K had adjusted gross income of $60,000. A list of itemized deductions available to K in preparing her 2017 return is shown below:

State income taxes paid	$2,250
Property taxes on residence	600
Charitable contributions	400
Interest paid on residence	3,700

K is single. In 2018, she received a state income tax refund of $1,000. The standard deduction for single taxpayers in 2017 was $6,350. What amount of the state tax refund, if any, must she include in her gross income for 2018?

6-36 *Fringe Benefits versus Compensation.* P is a 46-year-old professor at Z University, a private school in the Midwest. P is married and has triplets who are freshmen at Z University. Among others, P is provided with the following fringe benefits during the current year:

- Group-term life insurance coverage of $75,000.

- Premium cost to Z University is $300.

- Tuition reduction of $30,000 for the triplets.

  a. How much does the group-term life insurance cost Professor P? Assume his marginal tax bracket is 31 percent.
  b. Would P be equally well off if the university simply paid him an additional $300 in compensation to cover the term insurance?
  c. Is the tuition reduction for the triplets taxable?
  d. Assuming tuition remains constant, how much will Professor P save in tuition payments by remaining on the faculty at Z University until the triplets graduate?
  e. What would be the result for the current year if the university increased Professor P's salary by $30,000 a year to pay for the triplets' tuition?

6-37 *Unemployment Compensation and Disability Income.* Mr. and Mrs. B are married filing jointly. Mrs. B was permanently disabled the entire year and Mr. B was unemployed part of the year. Both are 68 years old. Their receipts for the year were

Disability income—Mrs. B.	$ 6,200
Social Security income—Mrs. B.	1,000
Salary—Mr. B	16,500
Unemployment compensation—Mr. B	4,500

Calculate their taxable income for the year, assuming the disability insurance premiums were paid
  a. Entirely by Mrs. B.
  b. Entirely by Mrs. B's employer.

6-38 *Damages Awarded and Disability Income.* D works for the XYZ Tool and Die Shop. On March 1, 2017 a stamping press that D was operating malfunctioned, resulting in the loss of the index finger on his right hand. D, claiming the machine was not properly maintained, sued XYZ for the following damages:

Medical expenses during D's one-week stay in the hospital	$ 8,000
Loss of D's finger	50,000
Punitive damages	5,000
Total	$63,000

On April 1, 2018 the court awarded D $63,000.
  a. Assuming D did not deduct the $8,000 of medical expenses he incurred in 2017, what portion of the $63,000 settlement is included in D's gross income in 2018?
  b. D did not return to work for three months. During this time period, he received $3,000 in disability income payments. Assuming D paid the annual premium on the disability insurance, how much of the $3,000 is taxable income to D?

6-39 *Meals and Lodging.* Mr. and Mrs. G own and operate a small motel near Big Mountain resort area. Their only employees are two maids and one cook. The rest of the work is done by Mr. and Mrs. G. In order to be on 24-hour call, they live in a home next to the motel. The home is owned by the business. Both Mr. and Mrs. G eat most of their meals in the motel restaurant. Answer the questions below assuming the business is (1) a corporation, or (2) a partnership.
  a. Are any of the costs for the meals and lodging deductible by either the business or Mr. and Mrs. G?
  b. Is the value of the meals and lodging included in Mr. and Mrs. G's gross income?
  c. Answer the questions in (a) and (b) again, but assume Mr. and Mrs. G paid the business for all their meals in the restaurant and for rent of the home.

6-40 *Adoption Assistance.* R and L are married and file a joint return. R is the controller of a tool and die firm and is paid a salary of $140,000. L is a grade school teacher and earns $27,500. Other income received during the current year includes $1,000 in interest on State of Ohio bonds owned by R and $2,500 in dividends on Chevron stock that L owns. R and L, who have no children of their own, incurred $15,000 in qualified adoption expenses (i.e., adoption fees, attorney fees, and court costs) to adopt a two-year-old "special needs" child. These expenses were paid for by R's employer under the company's adoption assistance program.
  a. Determine R and L's AGI for the current year.
  b. Same as (a) except the couple adopted two children?

6-41 *Transportation Fringes.* How much is includible in the employee's gross income in each of the following scenarios?
  a. Employee A receives a transit pass each month from Employer X valued at $95.
  b. Employer Y provides free parking each month to employee B valued at $300.
  c. Employer Z provides parking each month to employee C valued at $250. Employee C pays Employer Z $40 per month for this parking fringe.
  d. Employer Q reimburses employee R $15 a month for storage of his bike while at work.

6-42 *Employer-Provided Parking.* Employer G operates a factory in a rural area in which no commercial parking is available. G provides ample parking for its employees on the business premises, free of charge.
  a. What guidance does the Internal Revenue Service provide for determining the value of free parking?
  b. Given the facts presented above, what value would the IRS place on the free parking provided by Employer G?

6-43 *Military Compensation.* After graduating from high school last year, K, who is single, joined the U.S. Air Force. Her military compensation for 2017 is

	Cash	Market Value
Salary	$50,000	
Military housing		$2,500
Computer training on the job		1,800
Uniforms		800
Meals on the base		3,600
Reimbursement of moving expenses	500	

Calculate K's taxable income for the year.

6-44 *Inheritances.* In each of the following independent situations, determine how much, if any, the taxpayer must include in gross income.
  a. At the beginning of this year, a taxpayer inherited rental property valued at $87,000 from his grandmother. Rental income from the property after the transfer of title totaled $6,000, and rental expenses were $5,200.
  b. A taxpayer inherited $50,000 from her employer. She was his housekeeper for ten years and was promised she would be provided for in his will if she continued employment with him until his death.
  c. A taxpayer lent $15,000 to a friend. To protect the loan, the taxpayer had his friend make him beneficiary on her $20,000 life insurance policy. Six months later the friend died and the taxpayer received $20,000 from the insurance company.

6-45 *Gifts.* In each of the following independent situations, determine how much, if any, the taxpayer must include in gross income.
  a. A taxpayer often visits her uncle in a nursing home. In addition, she manages his investment portfolio for him. To show his gratitude, he has given her stock valued at $5,000. He has also implied that if she continues these activities, he will transfer other shares of stock to her.
  b. A taxpayer saved a child's life during a fire. The child's parents gave him land valued at $5,000 to show their gratitude. They paid $2,200 for the land several years ago.
  c. Taxpayer's employer gave him $1,200 in recognition of his 20 years of service to the company. The employer deducted the $1,200 as a business expense.

6-46 *Awards.* In each of the following independent situations, determine how much, if any, the taxpayer must include in gross income.

a. The taxpayer, a professional basketball player, was voted as the outstanding player of the year. In addition to the honor, he received an automobile with a sticker price of $16,000. He drove the car for six months and sold it for $12,000. The taxpayer's employer also gave him a gold watch worth $1,200. He wears the watch. Both donors deducted their respective costs for the automobile and the watch as business expenses. The costs of the automobile and watch were $13,500 and $800, respectively.

b. The taxpayer was selected by the senior class as the most outstanding classroom teacher. The high school presented her with a $1,000 check in recognition of her significant accomplishments. She used the money to take a well-earned vacation to Cancun.

c. M, Inc. gave T a watch in recognition of her 20 years of service to the company. The watch cost the employer $400.

6-47 *Child Support and Alimony.* Determine the effect on AGI for the husband (H) and wife (W) in each of the following *continuous* situations. H and W are divorced and do not live in a community property state. They have three children.

a. H pays W $400 per month as alimony and support of the three children.

b. W discovers her attorney did not word the agreement correctly. H and W sign a statement that the *original* agreement is retroactively amended to hold that H pays $100 per month as alimony to W and $300 per month as support of the three children. All other language remains unchanged. What is the effect of this change on future and past payments?

c. Assume the original agreement contained the wording in (b) above. In the first year, H makes only 10 of the 12 payments for a total of $4,000. In the second year, H pays the $800 balance due for the prior year and makes all 12 payments of $400 each on time.

d. On their divorce, W was awarded an automobile. H is required to pay the loan outstanding on the car, $94 per month for 20 months. During the year, H pays $94 for 12 months. This includes $130 interest and $998 loan principal.

e. H owns the home in which W and the children live free of charge. H's mortgage payments are $360 per month for the next 20 years. During the year, his expenses on the home are $2,900 interest, $800 property taxes, $340 insurance, $280 loan principal, and $218 repairs. The rental value of the home is $425 per month.

f. In addition to the monthly alimony and support payments above, H is to pay W $30,000 over a period of 11 years. H pays $2,500 of this amount the first year and $3,600 the second year.

g. H inherits considerable property. As a result, he voluntarily increases the alimony to $150 and child support to $450 per month. He makes 12 payments of $600 each during the year.

h. Part of the child support was for his 21 year old daughter.

6-48 *Alimony.* Determine the effect on AGI for the husband (H) and wife (W) in each of the three years. W is to pay H alimony of $100,000 as follows:

Year	Amount
1	$56,000
2	26,000
3	18,000

6-49 *Divorce—Property Settlement.* Husband (H) and wife (W) are divorced this month. The divorce agreement states that all jointly owned property will be transferred as follows:

	Cost	Market Value	Transferred to
Home	$35,000	$65,000	W
Investments	3,000	5,000	W
Cash	7,000	7,000	H and W equally

W will occupy the home and H will rent an apartment. Determine the recognized gain or loss and the basis of the assets to H and W after the transfer. Explain.

6-50 *Divorce—Property Settlement.* H and W, who live in Michigan (a common law state), decided to end their troubled 30-year marriage. Pursuant to the divorce decree, the following assets are transferred from H to W on March 1, 2017:

	Basis to H	Market Value
Stocks (purchased by H on April 10, 2011).	$300,000	$400,000
Land (purchased by H on June 2, 2008)	200,000	500,000

In addition to the above, H transferred a life insurance policy on his life with a face value of $200,000 to W, who assumed responsibility for the annual premium. W sold the stocks for $500,000 on November 1, 2017 and the land for $550,000 on December 1, 2017. H died on December 20, 2017.

    a. Determine W's gain on the sale of the stocks and land in 2017.

    b. Are any of the life insurance proceeds taxable to W? Explain.

6-51 *Accelerated Death Benefits.* T, a wife and mother of three, was diagnosed with throat cancer. Due to the complications from chemotherapy treatments, she resigned from her teaching position at a private university in Chicago on June 1. Having been certified by her medical doctor on July 7 as terminally ill, T is considering selling her life insurance policy with a face value of $200,000 to a viatical "settlement provider" (VSP) for a lump sum.

    a. Assuming T has paid $15,000 in premiums, how much must she include in her gross income if she sells her policy to VSP for $150,000 on August 1?

    b. Does your answer change if T lives longer than 24 months from the date of certification?

    c. If T dies eight months later, how much must VSP include in its gross income? (Assume VSP paid additional premiums of $10,000 after purchasing the policy.)

6-52 *Employee Fringe Benefits.* For each of the following independent situations, indicate whether the fringe benefit the employee receives is taxable or nontaxable. Explain your answer.

    a. C is a ticket agent for North Central Airways. The airline has a nondiscriminatory policy that allows its employees to fly without charge on a standby basis only. The last week in July, C took a vacation and flew from Kansas City to San Francisco. The value of the round-trip ticket was $400.

    b. Assume that C [in part (a) above] also stayed, without charge, for the entire week at a hotel in San Francisco that North Central Airways owns. The value of a week's stay in the hotel was $2,000.

    c. Assume in part (a) above that C was unable to obtain an empty seat on North Central the last week in July. Consequently, utilizing the qualified reciprocal arrangement that North Central has with South Shore Airlines, C flew free to San Francisco on South Shore. The value of the round-trip ticket was $400.

    d. M is a sales clerk for J-mart department store. The store has a nondiscriminatory policy whereby its employees may purchase inventory items at a discount. In June, M purchased a microwave oven for $250 that J-mart sells to its customers for $300. J-mart's gross profit rate is 20 percent.

    e. F is a CPA and works for a public accounting firm. On F's behalf, the firm paid $375 in subscription fees for three professional accounting journals.

    f. Officers of the XYZ Corporation are provided free parking space in a public parking garage located across the street from the firm's office building. The monthly cost of the parking space to XYZ is $300 for each officer.

6-53 *Unrelated Party Transfers.* In each of the following independent situations, determine how much, if any, the taxpayer must include in gross income.

  a. Taxpayer has been very active as a volunteer hospital worker for many years. In the current year, the city named her as the Outstanding Volunteer of the Year. She later discovered that she was nominated for the award by two nurses at the hospital. The honor included a silver tray valued at $400. In addition, the two nurses collected $700 from hospital personnel and gave her a prepaid one-week vacation for two people.

  b. Taxpayer, an undergraduate degree candidate, was selected as one of five outstanding sophomore students in accounting by the Institute of Management Accountants. Selection was based on an application submitted by eligible students. The winner received $15,000. Although there was no stipulation of how the money was to be used, the award was given with the expectation that the money would be used for tuition, books, and fees in the student's junior and senior years.

  c. Taxpayer won the bowling league award for the highest total score over a five week period. Taxpayer received a trophy valued at $65 and $100 cash.

  d. Taxpayer purchased church raffle tickets in her eight-year-old son's name and gave the tickets to him. One of the tickets was drawn. The prize was a $600 color television.

  e. Taxpayer receives a $20,000 grant from the National Association of Chiefs of Police to conduct a research study on crowd control. The grant stipulates that the research period is for eight months and that $8,000 of it is for travel and temporary living costs.

  f. An accounting student accepted an internship with a CPA firm and is paid $3,000. The stated purpose of the internship is to provide students with a basic understanding of how accounting education is applied. It is believed this understanding will help students in remaining course work and later job selection. Although the faculty believes internships would benefit all students, only 40% of the accounting majors participate in the program.

6-54 *Businesses.* In each of the following independent situations, determine how much, if any, the taxpayer must include in gross income.

  a. A taxpayer sold a beauty shop operated as a proprietorship for $60,000. The assets were valued as follows: tangible assets, $45,000; agreement not to compete, $10,000; and goodwill, $5,000. The seller's basis for the tangible assets is $45,000 but there is no basis for the other two assets.

  b. The building in which a drug store is located is damaged by fire. The store had to be closed for two weeks while repairs were made. As a result, the insurance company paid the store $50,000 for lost profits during the period and $15,000 to cover overhead expenses.

  c. E, Inc. leases land to V, Inc. The agreement states that the lease period is for five years and the annual lease payment is $1,000 per month. Under the terms of the lease, V immediately constructs a storage building on the land for $40,000. E receives $12,000 from V each year for three years. At the end of the third year, V cancels the lease and pays a cancellation penalty of $6,000. At this time, the building's market value is $30,000. Thus, in the third year, E received $18,000 cash and a building worth an additional $30,000. Determine E's taxable income from the lease for each of the three years.

  d. A corporation accepted $100,000 from an insurance company as an out-of-court settlement of a lawsuit for patent infringement.

6-55 *Debt Cancellation.* DEF, Inc. is in the van conversion business. Due to stiff competition and a declining economy in the region served by DEF, the company has incurred significant operating losses during the past year. As of December 31 of the current year, DEF's financial statements reflect the following pertinent information:

Total assets.	$ 750,000
Total liabilities.	1,000,000
Tax attributes	3,000
Adjusted basis of depreciable assets.	300,000
NOL carryover.	100,000
Capital loss carryover.	25,000

In an attempt to rescue the company from going out of business, DEF's suppliers have agreed to forgive $180,000 of indebtedness.

a. Assuming DEF is not in bankruptcy proceedings, what are the tax consequences to the corporation resulting from the cancellation of the debt?

b. Would your answer to part (a) change if DEF makes an election under Code § 108(b)(5)?

c. Would your answer to part (a) change if the $180,000 of debt is cancelled under bankruptcy proceedings?

d. Assume that the facts in the problem remain the same, except that DEF has total assets of $1 million and total liabilities of $750,000. What impact does the cancellation of $180,000 in debt now have on DEF?

6-56 *Debt Cancellation: Principal Residence.* Five years ago, J and his wife decided that it was time to quit renting and buy a new home. They had little cash. Nevertheless they shopped around and found the perfect home. Although it was beyond their price range, they could afford it by virtue of an ultra low-interest rate. Thus they bought the home for $110,000, paying $10,000 down and financing the remaining $100,000 with an adjustable rate mortgage. This year the rate was adjusted in accordance with the terms of the agreement. As a result, J was no longer able to make his mortgage payments. J considered refinancing to get a lower fixed rate but this was not an option. There was a steep penalty for refinancing. Moreover, the value of the home had actually dropped and no one was willing to refinance a mortgage that was more than the value of their home. Fortunately, the bank did not want to become the owner of the home given the current market and agreed to reduce the debt to $90,000. What are the tax consequences to J?

6-57 *Miscellaneous Items.* In each of the following independent situations, determine how much, if any, the taxpayer must include in gross income.

a. A taxpayer's round trip mileage to and from work is 50 miles. Five fellow employees live near him and pay to ride with him. The taxpayer's records for the current year show $3,900 receipts and $3,120 automobile expenses.

b. While walking across campus, a taxpayer found a diamond ring. She notified the authorities on campus and paid $10 for an ad in the lost-and-found section of the newspaper. When six weeks went by with no response, she had the ring appraised. It was valued at $1,200. After six more weeks with no response, she sold the ring for $850.

c. A taxpayer was injured on the job and was out of work for most of the year. He received the following government benefits during the year: $800 in food stamps; $1,500 worker's compensation for the injury; and $1,800 in welfare payments.

d. A taxpayer sued her neighbor for malicious slander. The court awarded her $30,000 for personal injury due to indignities suffered as a result of the slander; $3,500 in lost income; and $200 reimbursement for medical expenses incurred. The taxpayer does not itemize deductions.

6-58 *Miscellaneous Income Items.* In each of the following scenarios, determine the amount (if any) and type of income to be included in gross income by the recipient:

    a. Denise acquired all of the net assets of Mary's CPA firm. Mary operated the practice as a sole proprietorship. The purchase price includes $20,000 allocable to goodwill and $15,000 allocable to a covenant not to compete for five years.

    b. Ernie rents an apartment from Doug. Because Ernie is being transferred to another city by his employer, he paid Doug $800 to cancel his lease.

    c. Mary Ann owns an apartment complex in Jacksonville, Florida. In an effort to convert the apartment into an office building, she pays Jean, one of her tenants, $900 to cancel the apartment lease.

6-59 *Miscellaneous Fringe Benefits.* In each of the following independent situations answer true if the ending sentence is correct and false if the ending sentence is incorrect.

    a. During the current year, A withdraws $2,000 from a qualified tuition plan (i.e., 529 plan) to pay his undergraduate tuition at Ivy Tech. Of the $2,000 received, $1,600 represents contributions to the plan and $400 represents earnings.

    b. B is employed at the Tire Rack Company. She works the day shift and her two children, ages 3 and 4, stay at the company's daycare facility. The current year's value of this service is approximately $4,000.

    c. C works for Ever Green, Inc. During the evenings C attends State University where she is working on her undergraduate degree in Marketing. During the current year Ever Green paid C's tuition ($3,000) and her textbooks ($800) out of the company's nondiscriminatory educational assistance program.

    d. D is an employee of Night Line, Inc. where he is covered under the company's qualified pension plan. During the current year D, who is 64 years old, and his wife attended several seminars related to retirement planning that were sponsored by Night Line. The value of this service is approximately $1,500.

6-60 *The U.S. System of Adoption and Foster Care.* As noted in the text, reports estimate that there were 415,000 children in foster care in 2014 while there are about 135,000 adoptions per year.

    a. Explain how the current system of income taxation attempts to encourage adoption and foster care.

    b. Assume you are a newly elected member of Congress and one of your promises was to introduce legislation that would improve the federal approach to foster care and adoption. What changes to the tax system might you make (assume any change must be revenue neutral)?

TAX RETURN PROBLEMS

■ *CONTINUOUS TAX RETURN PROBLEMS* See Appendix I, Part 1.

CUMULATIVE PROBLEM

6-61 H, age 45, and W, age 43, are married with two dependent children: M, age 18, and N, age 19. Both are full-time students at a local university. H, who is president of a local bank, is paid a salary of $125,000. He also is the sole proprietor of a jewelry store that had a net profit for 2016 of $75,000. W, a registered nurse at a large hospital, is paid a salary of $50,000. In addition to the above income, H and W received the following during 2016:

a. $3,000 cash dividend on ABC, Inc. stock, which they own jointly. They paid $25,000 for the stock three years ago and it has a current market value of $40,000. ABC, Inc. has $300,000 of current and accumulated E&P.

b. $750 in interest on State of Michigan bonds that H owns.

c. $7,000 in interest on corporate bonds that H and W purchased two years ago at face value for $100,000.

d. W received a check for $400 from her employer in recognition of her outstanding service to the hospital during the past 10 years.

e. The bank provides H with $90,000 of group term life insurance protection. The bank provides all full-time employees with group term insurance.

f. 1,000 shares of XYZ common as a stock dividend. Prior to the distribution, H and W owned 9,000 shares of common with a basis of $15,000. H and W did not have the right to receive cash or other assets in lieu of the stock.

g. Because W must be available should an emergency arise, she is required to eat her lunches in the hospital cafeteria. The value of the free meals provided by her employer during 2016 was $1,100.

h. H's grandfather passed away in February 2016, leaving H a 400-acre farm in southern Illinois valued at $500,000. H rented the land to F, a neighboring farmer, for $13,000.

i. In order to drain off the excess surface water from 10 acres, F (see (h) above) installed drainage pipe at a cost of $1,500.

j. W sold 50 shares of DEF stock for $100 per share. She bought the stock four years ago for $1,800.

k. H received a dividend check for $280 from the MNO Mutual Life Insurance Company. H purchased the policy in 2003, and W is the primary beneficiary.

l. H and W's only itemized deductions were interest on their home mortgage, $18,000; property taxes on their home, $4,000; and charitable contributions, $6,000.

m. The hospital withheld $11,000 of Federal income taxes on W's salary and the appropriate amount of FICA taxes. The bank withheld $30,000 in Federal income taxes from H's salary and the appropriate amount of FICA taxes. Furthermore, H's quarterly estimated tax payments for 2016 total $35,000.

Part I: Computation of Federal Income Tax. Calculate H and W's 2016 Federal income tax liability (or refund) assuming they file a joint return.

Part II: Tax Planning Ideas. H and W are very concerned about the amount of Federal income tax they now pay. Because they want to send M and N on to graduate school, they have come up with the following strategies, which they hope will reduce their family's total tax liability.

1. In 2017 M and N will begin working at the jewelry store two nights a week and on Saturdays throughout the school year and 20 hours a week during the summer months. Each child will be paid $4,500 for services during the year.

2. On January 1, 2017 H and W will sell their corporate bonds for $100,000 and invest the cash proceeds in Series EE savings bonds. H and W will use the bonds to pay for M and N's qualified educational expenses.

3. On January 1, 2017 H and W will gift their stock in ABC, Inc. to M and N equally.

4. Beginning in 2017 H will instruct the farmer who is leasing his Illinois farm to pay the $13,000 in rent directly to M and N (i.e., $6,500 each).

H and W have asked for your opinion concerning the above strategies. For each idea, explain why it will or will not reduce the family's total tax liability. Assuming H and W implement only the strategies that will reduce taxes, how much will the family save in taxes in 2017 compared to 2016. (**Note:** Calculate the 2017 tax using the tax law and rates applicable to 2016 and assume all other data from Part I above is the same.)

TAX RESEARCH PROBLEMS

6-62 *Divorce.* J and M are obtaining a divorce after ten years of marriage. They have two children. A draft of the divorce agreement and property settlement between them states that they will have joint custody of the children. They plan to live in the same general area and each child will live half of each year with each parent. Since J's AGI is $40,000 and M's $15,000, he will pay her $100 per month for each child ($2,400 per year) and $500 per month for her support. The $500 ceases on his or her death, her remarriage, or when her AGI equals his. In addition, J agrees to continue to pay premiums of $50 per month on his life insurance policy payable to her. All jointly owned property will be distributed as follows:

	Basis	Market Value	Transfer to
Home...............	$50,000	$80,000	M
Furnishings...........	20,000	15,000	M
Investments...........	10,000	30,000	J

Each will keep his or her individually owned personal items and an automobile. This is an amicable divorce and they both request your advice. Their objective is to maximize total tax benefits without making too many changes to the agreement. Use tax-planning techniques when possible in responding to the following questions.

a. Who will be able to claim the children as dependents?

b. What is each one's filing status for the current year if neither one remarries?

c. Does the $500 per month qualify as alimony? Does the $50 per month qualify as alimony?

d. J expects to make the $500 and $50 payments for three months while legally separated before the divorce. What are the tax effects during this period?

e. What is the tax effect of the distribution of jointly owned property to J and to M?

f. What tax planning advice could you give to J and M that would decrease their combined tax liability?

6-63 *Meals and Lodging.* H and W are married with three children. The children are 8, 10, and 15 years old. H and W are purchasing a 500-acre farm, which they will manage and operate themselves. In addition, they will employ one full-time farmer year round and several part-time people at peak times. H will be responsible primarily for management of the operations, the crops, and the dairy herd and other farm animals. W will be responsible primarily for the garden, the chickens, providing meals for the family and farm hands, and maintaining the family home. The children are assigned farm chores to help their parents after school and on weekends.

The taxpayers prefer to operate the farm as a partnership but, after all factors are considered, are willing to incorporate the farm if it seems to provide greater benefits. Presently, they ask for detailed information about the residence on the farm and the groceries that will be purchased to feed them and their employees on the farm. Some of their specific questions are listed below.

a. What are the benefits and requirements covering meals and lodging provided by the business?

b. Is it possible to meet the requirements and obtain all or at least some of the benefits if the farm is operated as a proprietorship or partnership, or must it be operated as a corporation?

c. If full benefits are obtained, are any adjustments required for the children, for personal entertainment and meals shared with friends and relatives in the farm home, or any other personal use? If any adjustments are required, which ones, and are they made at cost or market value?

d. If full benefits are obtained, exactly what qualifies? For example, do all groceries qualify, including supplies that are not eaten, such as freezer bags to store frozen foods from the garden, soap, and bathroom supplies? Do all expenses for the home qualify, such as utilities, insurance, and repairs?

e. Should the business or should H and W own the home?

f. Is it acceptable for H and W to purchase the food and be reimbursed by the business?

6-64 *Discharge of Indebtedness.* T, who is single, purchased a new home in 1979 from the XYZ Construction Co. for $55,000. She received a 7.25% mortgage from the Federal Savings and Loan Association (FS&L). Currently, the home's fair market value is approximately double its original purchase price. Since interest rates have risen significantly in recent months, FS&L wants to rid itself of the low 7.25% mortgage. Lending to others at a much higher interest rate would clearly enhance FS&L's profits. Consequently, during the current year FS&L sent a letter to T offering to cancel the mortgage (which had a remaining principal balance of $35,000) in return for a payment of $29,000. T took advantage of the prepayment opportunity, thus receiving a discount equal to the difference between the remaining principal balance of $35,000 and the amount paid by T of $29,000, or $6,000.

    a. Although T is pleased she no longer has a monthly mortgage payment, she is concerned about the possible tax consequences resulting from the discharge of indebtedness. T has come to you for your advice.

    b. Assume that the fair market value of T's residence has declined to $25,000 due to the construction of a nearby land fill operation. Does this fact change your answer?

6-65 *Compensatory Damages.* T. J. Taxpayer, CLU, has owned an insurance agency in Santa Rosa, California since 1981. As an independent agent, he represented five companies selling auto, home, commercial, and life insurance. Because of his excellent reputation in the community, T. J. has built a very successful agency. Last year, T. J. applied for an agency license from the American Life Insurance Co. in order to broaden his life insurance business. In reviewing his application, American requested a credit report from Federal Credit. Federal Credit provided copies to American Life as well as other insurance companies.

    The credit report contained numerous false accusations. In addition to questioning Taxpayer's integrity, the report stated that T. J. seldom returned phone calls from clients and lacked understanding of basic insurance practices and concepts. As a result, American Life denied T. J. a license to sell its life insurance. Because the report adversely affected his ability to work with existing clients and to attract new business, T. J.'s profits declined considerably.

    T. J. sued Federal Credit for libel, claiming that the credit report was issued with intent to damage his business or professional reputation. The jury found that Federal Credit had committed libel and awarded him $100,000 in compensatory damages. T. J. has heard conflicting comments from various sources about whether the $100,000 is taxable and comes to you for help. What advice would you give T. J. Taxpayer concerning the taxability of the $100,000?

6-66 *Sex Discrimination.* Alice Johnson has worked for the AMAX Corporation for ten years. In March 2012, after talking with various company employees, Alice came to the realization that there was a significant pay differential between men and women. In fact, she discovered that the corporation had modified its compensation package in 2011 whereby the salaries of employees in certain male-dominated pay schedules were increased but those in certain female-dominated pay schedules were either unchanged or reduced.

    As a result, Alice Johnson brought suit (under Title VII of the Civil Rights Act of 1964) in District Court against the AMAX Corporation alleging unlawful discrimination in the payment of wages based upon gender. Alice sought back pay from the company in the amount of $10,000 to eliminate the discrimination. Rather than incur substantial costs in litigating the issue, AMAX reached an out-of-court settlement with Alice on January 15, 2014. The settlement requires AMAX to pay Alice back pay of $8,000 and to develop gender-neutral pay schedules.

    Is the $8,000 subject to tax?

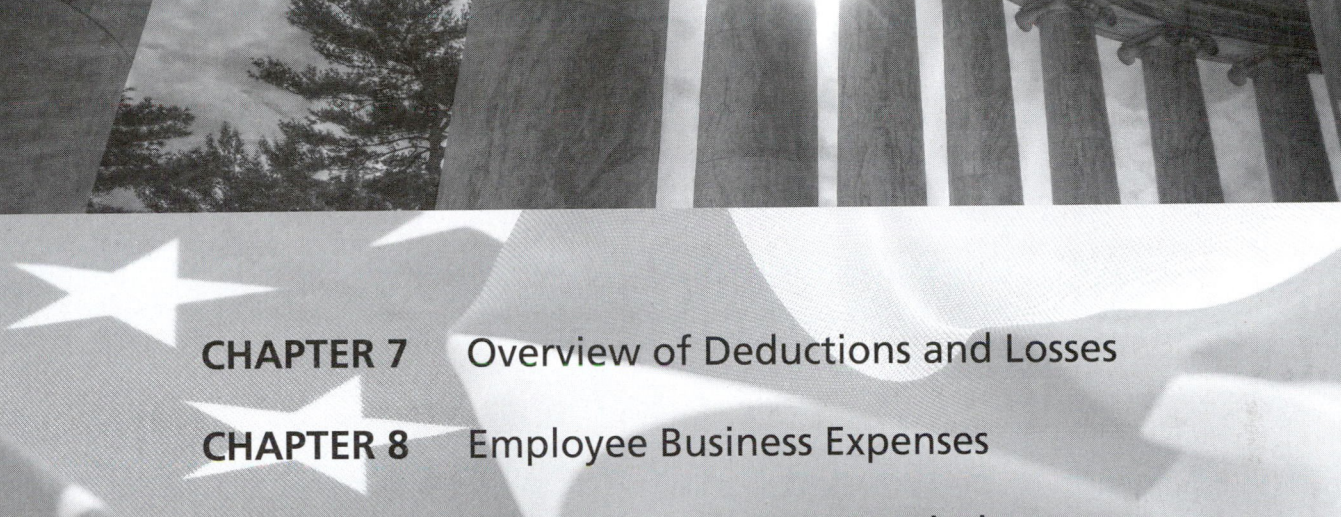

PART 3

Deductions and Losses

DEDUCTIONS!

Overview of Deductions and Losses

7

Learning Objectives

Upon completion of this chapter you will be able to:

LO.1 Recognize the general requirements for deducting expenses and losses.

LO.2 Define the terms *ordinary, necessary,* and *reasonable* as they apply to business deductions.

LO.3 Recognize tax accounting principles with respect to deductions and losses.

LO.4 Describe the importance of properly classifying expenses as deductions for or from adjusted gross income.

LO.5 Classify expenses as deductions for or from adjusted gross income.

LO.6 Explain the proper treatment of employee business expenses.

LO.7 Recognize statutory, administrative, and judicial limitations on deductions and losses.

LO.8 Explain tax planning considerations for optimizing deductions.

Chapter Outline

Introduction

As explained in Chapter 3, the income tax is imposed on taxable income, a quantity defined as the difference between gross income and allowable deductions.[1] The concept of gross income was explored in Chapters 5 and 6. This chapter and the following four chapters examine the subject of deductions.

There is little doubt that when it comes to taxation, the questions asked most frequently concern deductions. What is deductible? Can this expense be deducted? How much can I deduct? This is a familiar refrain around taxpaying time, and rightfully so, since any item that might be deductible reduces the tax that otherwise must be paid. Many of the questions concerning deductions are easily answered by merely referring to the basic criteria. On the other hand, many items representing potential deductions are subject to special rules. The purpose of this chapter is to introduce the general rules that are in fact used for determining the answer to that age-old question: Is it deductible?

DEDUCTION DEFINED

In the preceding chapters, the definition given for income was described as being "all-inclusive" (i.e., gross income includes *all* items of income except those specifically excluded by law). Given this concept of income, it might be assumed that a similarly broad meaning is given to the term deduction. Deductions, however, are defined narrowly. Deductions are only those *particular* expenses, losses, and other items for which a deduction is authorized.[2] The significance of this apparently meaningless definition is found in the last word—"authorized." *Nothing is deductible unless it is allowed by the Code.* It is a well-established principle that before a deduction may be claimed the taxpayer must find some statutory provision permitting the deduction. The courts consistently have affirmed this principle, stating that a taxpayer has no constitutional right to a deduction. Rather, a taxpayer's right to a deduction depends solely on "legislative grace" (i.e., Congress has enacted a statute allowing the deduction).[3]

Although a taxpayer's deductions require statutory authorization, this does not mean that a particular deduction must be specifically mentioned in the Code. While several provisions are designed to grant the deduction for a specific item, such as § 163 for interest expense and § 164 for taxes, most deductions are allowed because they satisfy the conditions of some broadly defined category of deductions. For example, no specific deduction is allowed for the advertising expense of a restaurant owner, but the expense may be deductible if it meets the criteria required for deduction of *business expenses.*

The remainder of this chapter examines those provisions authorizing several broad categories of deductions: § 162 on trade or business expenses, § 212 on expenses of producing income, and § 165 on losses. In addition to these deduction-granting sections, several provisions that expressly deny or limit deductions for certain items are considered. The rules provided by these various provisions establish the basic framework for determining whether a deduction is allowed. Once the deductibility of an item is determined, an additional problem exists for individual taxpayers—the deduction must be classified as either a deduction *for* adjusted gross income or a deduction *from* adjusted gross income (itemized deduction). The classification process is also explained in this chapter.

---

[1] § 63.

[2] § 161.

[3] *New Colonial Ice Co. v. Helvering,* 4 USTC ¶1292, 13 AFTR 1180, 292 U.S. 435 (USSC, 1934).

Given that the taxpayer can deduct only those items that are authorized, what deductions does Congress in fact allow? The central theme found in the rules governing deductions is relatively straightforward: those expenses and losses incurred in business and profit-seeking activities are deductible while those incurred in purely personal activities are not. The allowance for business and profit-seeking expenses stems in part from the traditional notion that income is a *net* concept. From a conceptual perspective, income does not result until revenues exceed expenses. It generally follows from this principle that it would be unfair to tax the revenue from an activity but not allow deductions for the expenses that produced it.

LO.1
Recognize the general requirements for deducting expenses and losses.

In light of the Code's approach to deductions, many commentators have aptly stated that the costs of *earning* a living are deductible while the costs of living are not. Although this is a good rule of thumb, it is also an over-generalization. As will become clear, the Code allows deductions not only for the costs of producing income, but also for numerous personal expenses such as interest on home mortgages, property taxes, medical expenses, and charitable contributions. To complicate matters further, the line between personal and business expenses is often difficult to draw. For this reason, the various rules governing deductions must be examined closely.

GENERAL RULES: CODE §§ 162 AND 212

Two provisions in the Code provide the authority for the deduction of most expenses: § 162 concerning trade or business expenses and § 212 relating to expenses for the production of income. Numerous other provisions of the Code pertain to deductions. These other provisions, however, normally build on the basic rules contained in §§ 162 and 212. For this reason, the importance of these two provisions cannot be overstated.

Section 162(a) on trade or business expenses reads, in part, as follows:

> *Section 162. Trade or business expenses.*
>
> *(a) In general. There shall be allowed as a deduction all the ordinary and necessary expenses paid or incurred during the taxable year in carrying on any trade or business, including:*
>
> > *(1) a reasonable allowance for salaries or other compensation for personal services actually rendered;*
> >
> > *(2) expenses (including amounts expended for meals and lodging other than amounts which are lavish or extravagant under the circumstances) while away from home in the pursuit of a trade or business;*
> >
> > *(3) rentals or other payments required to be made as a condition to the continued use or possession, for purposes of the trade or business, of property to which the taxpayer has not taken or is not taking title or in which he has no equity.*

Although § 162(a) specifically enumerates three items that are deductible, the provision's primary importance lies in its general rule: ordinary and necessary expenses of carrying on a trade or business are deductible.

Section 212 contains a general rule very similar to that found in § 162. Section 212, in part, reads as follows:

> *Section 212. Expenses for the production of income.*
>
> *(a) In the case of an individual, there shall be allowed as a deduction all the ordinary and necessary expenses paid or incurred during the taxable year—*
>
> > *(1) for the production of income.*
> >
> > *(2) for the management, conservation, or maintenance of property held for the production of income ....*

Production of income expenses are normally those related to investments, such as rental property (e.g., repairs and maintenance, depreciation, management fees), investment advisory fees, and safe deposit box rentals.

An examination of the language of §§ 162 and 212 indicates that a deduction is allowed under either section if it meets *four* critical requirements. The expense must have all of the following properties:

1. It must be related to carrying on a trade or business or an income-producing activity.
2. It must be ordinary and necessary.
3. It must be reasonable.
4. It must be paid or incurred during the taxable year.

It should be emphasized, however, that satisfaction of these criteria does not ensure deductibility. Other provisions in the Code often operate to prohibit or limit a deduction otherwise granted by §§ 162 and 212. For example, an expense may be ordinary, necessary, and related to carrying on a business, but if it is also related to producing tax-exempt income, § 265 prohibits a deduction. This system of allowing, yet disallowing, deductions is a basic feature in the statutory scheme for determining deductibility.

RELATED TO CARRYING ON A BUSINESS OR AN INCOME-PRODUCING ACTIVITY

The Activity

Whether an expense is deductible depends in part on the type of activity in which it was incurred. A deduction is authorized by § 162 only if it is paid or incurred in an activity that constitutes a trade or business. Similarly, § 212 permits a deduction only if it is paid or incurred in an activity for the production or collection of income. The purpose of each of these requirements is to deny deductions for expenses incurred in an activity that is *primarily personal* in nature. For example, the costs incurred in pursuing what is merely a hobby, such as collecting antiques or racing automobiles, normally would be considered nondeductible personal expenditures. Of course, this assumes that such activities do not constitute a trade or business.

The Code does not provide any clues as to when an activity will be considered a trade or business or an income-producing activity and not a personal activity. Over the years, however, one criterion has emerged from the many court cases involving the issue. To constitute a trade or business or an income-producing activity, the activity must be *entered into for profit*.[4] In other words, for the taxpayer's expenses to be deductible, they must be motivated by his or her hope for a profit. For this reason, taxpayers who collect antiques or race automobiles can deduct all of the related expenses if they are able to demonstrate that they did so with the hope of producing income. In such case, they would be considered to be in a trade or business. If the required profit motive is lacking, however, expenses of the activity generally are not deductible except to the extent the activity has income.

As may be apparent, the critical question in this area is what inspired the taxpayer's activities. The factors to be used in evaluating the taxpayer's motivation, along with the special provisions governing activities that are not engaged in for profit—the so-called hobby loss rules—are considered in detail later in this chapter.

A profit motive is the only requirement necessary to establish existence of an *income-producing* activity. However, the courts have imposed an additional requirement before an activity qualifies as a *trade or business*. Business status requires both a profit motive and a sufficient degree of taxpayer involvement in the activity to distinguish the activity from a passive investment. No clear guidelines have emerged indicating when a taxpayer's activities rise to the level of carrying on a business. The courts, however, generally have permitted business treatment where the taxpayer has devoted a major portion of time to the activities or the activities have been regular or continuous.[5]

---

[4] *Doggett v. Burrett,* 3 USTC ¶1090, 12 AFTR 505, 65 F.2d 192 (CA-D.C., 1933).

[5] *Grier v. U.S.,* 55-1 USTC ¶9184, 46 AFTR 1536, 218 F.2d. 603 (CA-2, 1955).

Example 1

C owns six rental units, including several condominiums and townhouses. He manages his rental properties entirely by himself. His managing activities include seeking new tenants, supplying furnishings, cleaning and preparing the units for occupancy, advertising, and bookkeeping. In this case, C's involvement with the rental activities is sufficiently continuous and systematic to constitute a business.[6] If the rental activities were of a more limited nature, they might not qualify as a trade or business. The determination ultimately depends on the facts of the particular situation.[7]

Example 2

H owns various stocks and bonds. Her managerial activities related to these securities consist primarily of maintaining records and collecting dividends and interest. She rarely trades in the market. These activities are those normally associated with a passive investor, and accordingly would not constitute a trade or business under § 162 (they would be considered an income-producing activity under § 212).[8] On the other hand, if H had a substantial volume of transactions, made personal investigations of the corporations in which she was interested in purchasing, and devoted virtually every day to such work, her activities could constitute a trade or business.[9] Again, however, the answer depends on the facts.

Distinguishing between §§ 162 and 212

Prior to enactment of § 212, many investment-related expenses were not deductible because the activities did not constitute a business. The enactment of § 212 in 1942, allowing for the deduction of expenses related to production or collection of income, enabled the deduction of investment-oriented expenses. This expansion of the deduction concept to include so-called nonbusiness or investment-related expenses eliminates the need for an activity to constitute a business before a deduction is allowed. As a result, the issue of deductibility (*assuming* the other requirements are met) is effectively reduced to a single important question: Is the expense related to an activity engaged in for profit?

It may appear that the addition of § 212 completely removed the need for determining whether the activity resulting in the expense constitutes a business or is merely for the production of income. However, the distinction between business and production of income expenses remains important. For example, the classification of the expense as a deduction *for* or *from* adjusted gross income may turn on whether the expense is a trade or business expense or a production of income expense. Production of income expenses (other than those related to rents or royalties) are usually miscellaneous itemized deductions that can be deducted only to the extent they *exceed* two percent of adjusted gross income. In contrast, most business expenses are deductions for adjusted gross income and are deductible in full.

---

[6] *Edwin R. Curphey,* 73 T.C. 766 (1980).

[7] *Ibid.*

[8] *Higgins v. Comm.,* 41-1 USTC ¶9233, 25 AFTR 1160, 312 U.S. 212 (UCSC, 1941).

[9] *Samuel B. Levin v. U.S.,* 79-1 USTC ¶9331, 43 AFTR2d 79-1057, 597 F.2d 760 (Ct. Cls., 1979). But see *Joseph Moller v. U.S.,* 83-2 USTC ¶9698, 52 AFTR2d 83-633 (CA-FC, 1983) where, for purposes of the home office deduction, the court held that the taxpayer's management of his substantial investment portfolio could not be a trade or business regardless of how continuous, regular, and extensive the activities were. But see Chapter 16 and discussion of traders in securities and § 475(f).

Example 3

Refer to *Example 2.* In the first situation, where H is considered a passive investor, her investment related expenses (e.g., subscriptions to stock advisory services and investment newsletters) would be miscellaneous itemized deductions and deductible only to the extent they exceed 2% of adjusted gross income. In the second situation, however, the same type of expenses would be deductions for adjusted gross income since H's trading activities qualify as a trade or business.

Another reason for ascertaining whether the activity constitutes a business relates to the use of the phrase "trade or business" in other Code Sections. The phrase "trade or business" appears in at least 60 different Code Sections, and the interpretation given to this phrase often controls the tax treatment. For example, whether an activity is an active business or a passive investment affects the tax consequences related to losses (deductible or limited), bad debts (short-term capital loss versus ordinary loss), property sales (capital gain or loss versus ordinary gain or loss), expenses for offices in the home (deductible versus nondeductible), and limited expensing of depreciable property (allowed versus disallowed).[10]

The Relationship

Before an expense is deductible under §§ 162 or 212, it must have a certain relationship to the trade or business or income-producing activity. The Regulations require that business expenses be directly connected with or pertain to the taxpayer's trade or business.[11] Similarly, production of income expenses must bear a reasonable and proximate relationship to the income-producing activity.[12] Whether an expenditure is directly related to the taxpayer's trade or business or income-producing activity usually depends on the facts. For example, the required relationship for business expenses normally exists where the expense is primarily motivated by business concerns or arises as a result of business, rather than personal, needs.[13]

Example 4

While driving from one business to another, T struck a pedestrian with his car. He paid and deducted legal fees and damages in connection with the accident that were disallowed by the IRS. The Court found that the expenses were not directly related to, nor did they proximately result from, the taxpayer's business. The accident was merely incidental to the transportation and was related only remotely to the business.[14]

Whether a particular item is deductible often hinges on whether the expense was incurred for business or personal purposes. Consider the case of a law enforcement officer who is required to keep in top shape to retain his employment. Is the cost of a health club membership incurred for business or personal purposes? Similarly, can a disc jockey who obtains dentures to improve his speech deduct the cost as a business expense? Unfortunately, many expenses—like these—straddle the business-personal fence and the final determination is difficult. In both of the cases above, the Court denied the taxpayers' deductions on the theory that such expenses were inherently personal.

Another common question concerns expenses paid or incurred prior to the time that income is earned. In the case of § 212 expenses, it is not essential that the activity produce income currently. For example, expenses may be deductible under § 212 even though there is little likelihood that the property will be sold at a profit or will ever produce income.[15] Deductions are allowed as long as the transaction was entered into for profit.

---

[10] See §§ 165, 166, 1221, 280A, and 179.

[11] Reg. § 1.162-1(a).

[12] Reg. § 1.212-1(d).

[13] *U.S. v. Gilmore,* 63-1 USTC ¶9285, 11 AFTR2d 758, 372 U.S. 39 (USSC, 1963).

[14] *Julian D. Freedman v. Comm.,* 62-1 USTC ¶9400, 9 AFTR2d 1235, 301 F.2d. 359 (CA-5, 1962); but see *Harold Dancer,* 73 T.C. 1103 (1980), where the Tax Court allowed the deduction when the taxpayer was traveling between two locations of the *same* business. Note how the subtle change in facts substantially alters the result!

[15] Reg. § 1.212-1(b).

> **Example 5**
>
> B purchased a vacant lot three years ago as an investment. During the current year she paid $200 to have it mowed. Although the property is not currently producing income, the expense is deductible since it is for the conservation or maintenance of property held for the production of income.

ORDINARY AND NECESSARY EXPENSES

The second test for deductibility is whether the expense is ordinary and necessary. An expense is *ordinary* if it is normally incurred in the type of business in which the taxpayer is involved.[16] This is not to say that the expense is habitual or recurring.[17] In fact, the expense may be incurred only once in the taxpayer's lifetime and be considered ordinary. The test is whether other taxpayers in similar businesses or income-producing activities would customarily incur the same expense.

LO.2

Define the terms *ordinary, necessary,* and *reasonable* as they apply to business deductions.

> **Example 6**
>
> P has been in the newspaper business for 35 years. Until this year, his paper had never been sued for libel. To protect the reputation of the newspaper, P incurred substantial legal costs related to the libel suit. Although the taxpayer has never incurred legal expenses of this nature before, the expenses are ordinary since it is common in the newspaper business to incur legal expenses to defend against such attacks.[18]

It is interesting to note that the "ordinary" criterion normally becomes an issue in circumstances that are, in fact, unusual. For example, in *Goedel*,[19] a stock dealer paid premiums for insurance on the life of the President of the United States, fearing that his death would disrupt the stock market and his business. The Court denied the deduction on the grounds that the payment was not ordinary but unusual or extraordinary.

A deductible expense must be not only ordinary, but also *necessary*. An expense is necessary if it is appropriate, helpful, or capable of making a contribution to the taxpayer's profit-seeking activities.[20] The necessary criterion, however, is rarely applied to deny a deduction. The courts have refrained from such a practice since to do so would require overriding the judgment of the taxpayer.[21] The courts apparently feel that it would be unfair to judge *currently* whether a previous expenditure was necessary at the time it was incurred.

It should be emphasized that not all necessary expenses are ordinary expenses. Some expenses may be appropriate and helpful to the taxpayer's business but may not be normally incurred in that particular business. In such case, no deduction is allowed.

> **Example 7**
>
> W was an officer in his father's corporation. The corporation, unable to pay its debts, was adjudged bankrupt. After the corporation was discharged from its debts, W decided to resume his father's business on a fresh basis. To reestablish relations with old customers and to solidify his credit standing, W paid as much of the old debts as he could. The Supreme Court held that the expenses were necessary in the sense that they were appropriate and helpful in the development of W's business. However, the Court ruled that the payments were not ordinary because people do not usually pay the debts of another.[22]

---

[16] *Deputy v. DuPont,* 40-1 USTC ¶9161, 23 AFTR 808, 308 U.S. 488 (USSC, 1940).

[17] *Dunn and McCarthy, Inc. v. Comm.,* 43-2 USTC ¶9688, 31 AFTR 1043, 139 F.2d 242 (CA-2, 1943).

[18] *Welch v. Helvering,* 3 USTC ¶1164, 12 AFTR 1456, 290 U.S. 111 (USSC, 1933).

[19] 39 B.T.A. 1 (1939).

[20] *Supra,* Footnote 18. See also *Comm. v. Heininger;* 44-1 USTC ¶9109, 31 AFTR 783, 320 U.S. 467 (USSC, 1943).

[21] *Supra,* Footnote 18.

[22] *Supra,* Footnote 18.

REASONABLE EXPENSES

The third requirement for a deduction is that the expense be reasonable in amount. An examination of § 162(a) reveals that the term "reasonable" is used only in conjunction with compensation paid for services (e.g., a reasonable allowance for salaries). The courts have held, however, that reasonableness is implied in the phrase "ordinary and necessary."[23] In practice, the reasonableness standard is most often applied in situations involving salary payments made by a closely held corporation to a shareholder who also is an employee. In these situations, if the compensation paid exceeds that ordinarily paid for similar services—that which is reasonable—the excessive payment may represent a nondeductible dividend distribution.[24] Dividend treatment of the excess occurs if the amount of the excessive payment received by each employee closely relates to the number of shares of stock owned.[25] The distinction between reasonable compensation and dividend is critical because characterization of the payment as a dividend results in double taxation (i.e., it is taxable to the shareholder-employee and not deductible by the corporation).

Example 8

B and C own 70 and 30% of XYZ Corporation, respectively. Employees in positions similar to that of B earn $60,000 annually while those in positions similar to C's earn $20,000. During the year, the corporation pays B a salary of $130,000 and C a salary of $50,000. The excessive payment of $100,000 ([$130,000 + $50,000] − [$60,000 + $20,000]) is received by B and C in direct proportion to their percentage ownership of stock (i.e., B's salary increased by $70,000 or 70% of the excessive payment). Because the payments are in excess of that normally paid to employees in similar positions and the excessive payment received by each is closely related to his stockholdings, the excessive payment may be treated as a nondeductible dividend.

Some of the factors used by the IRS when considering the reasonableness of compensation are:[26]

1. Duties performed (i.e., amount and character of responsibility).
2. Volume and complexity of business handled (i.e., time required).
3. Individual's ability and expertise.
4. Number of available persons capable of performing the duties of the position.
5. Corporation's dividend policies and history.

PAID OR INCURRED DURING THE TAXABLE YEAR

Sections 162 and 212 both indicate that an expense is allowable as a deduction only if it is "paid or incurred during the taxable year." This phrase is used throughout the Code in sections concerning deductions. Use of both terms, "paid" and "incurred," is necessary because the year in which deductions are allowable depends on the method of accounting used by the taxpayer.[27] The term *paid* refers to taxpayers using the cash basis method of accounting while the term *incurred* refers to taxpayers using the accrual basis method of accounting. Accordingly, the year in which a deduction is allowed usually depends on whether the cash or accrual basis method of accounting is used. Each of these methods is discussed in detail in a later section.

---

[23] *Comm. v. Lincoln Electric Co.,* 49-2 USTC ¶9388, 38 AFTR 411, 176 F.2d 815 (CA-6, 1949).

[24] Reg. § 1.162-7(b)(1).

[25] Reg. § 1.162-8.

[26] Internal Revenue Manual 4233, § 232.

[27] § 461(a).

EMPLOYEE BUSINESS EXPENSES

The definition of *trade or business* also includes the performance of services as an employee. In other words, an employee is considered to be in the business of being an employee.[28] As a result, the ordinary and necessary expenses incurred by an employee in connection with his or her employment are deductible under § 162 as business expenses (rather than § 212 that primarily relates to expenses related to investment activities). Examples of deductible employee expenses include union dues, dues to trade and professional societies, subscriptions to professional journals, small tools and supplies, and medical exams required by the employer. Work clothes such as uniforms and protective clothing (hard hats, surgical masks, welder's gloves) also qualify. Similarly, theatrical clothing, costumes and accessories are deductible. Cleaning and maintenance of such items are also allowed. Note, however, uniforms and clothing must be required as a condition of employment and not suitable for everyday use).[29] Expenses such as travel, entertainment, and education may also be deducted as employee business expenses under certain conditions explained in Chapter 8. As explained later in this chapter, employee business expenses—other than those that are reimbursed—are considered miscellaneous itemized deductions and thus are deductible only to the extent they exceed 2% of AGI.

Accounting for Deductions

LO.3
Recognize tax accounting principles with respect to deductions and losses.

Identifying the taxable year in which a taxpayer can claim a deduction is extremely important for a number of reasons. No doubt the most important of these is the time value of money. Taxpayers normally want to claim their deductions and obtain the accompanying tax savings as soon as possible. In contrast, the government is concerned about zealous taxpayers who, in its view, prematurely deduct their expenses. When an expense is deductible generally depends on whether the taxpayer uses the cash or accrual method of accounting. However, the natural friction between taxpayers and the government over when an expense should be deducted has led to a somewhat confusingly intricate set of rules filled with exceptions. Interestingly, the effects of the various exceptions often make the accrual method look like the cash method and vice versa.

CASH METHOD OF ACCOUNTING

General Rule

For those taxpayers eligible to use the cash method (as discussed in Chapter 5), expenses are deductible in the taxable year when the expenses are actually paid.[30] However, there are numerous exceptions to this rule that are designed to restrict the flexibility a cash basis taxpayer would otherwise have in reporting deductions. Without these restrictions, a cash basis taxpayer could choose the year of deductibility simply by appropriately timing the cash payment. Before examining these restrictions, it is important to understand when the taxpayer is considered to have paid the expense.

Time of Payment

Determining when a cash basis taxpayer has paid an expense usually is not difficult. A cash basis taxpayer "pays" the expense when cash, check, property, or service is transferred. Neither a promise to pay nor a note evidencing such promise is considered payment. Consequently, when a cash basis taxpayer buys on credit, no deduction is allowed until the debts are paid. However, if the taxpayer borrows cash and then pays the expense, the expense is deductible when paid. For this reason, a taxpayer who charges expenses to a credit card is deemed to have borrowed cash and made payment when the charge is made. Thus, the deduction is claimed when the charge is actually made and not when the bank makes payment or when the taxpayer pays the bill.[31] If the taxpayer uses a "pay-by-phone" account,

---

[28] See *Lloyd U. Noland, Jr. v. Comm.* 59-2 USTC ¶9600, 4 AFTR 2d 5031, 269 F2d 108, (CA-4, 1959) holding that "every person who works for compensation is engaged in the business of earning his pay, and that expense which is essential to the continuance of his employment is deductible ..."

[29] Rev. Rul. 70-474, 1970 C.B. 35.

[30] Reg. § 1.446-1(a)(1).

[31] Rev. Rul. 78-39, 1978-1 C.B. 73.

the expense is deductible in the year the financial institution paid the amount as reported on a monthly statement sent to the taxpayer.[32] When the taxpayer pays by mail, payment is usually considered made when the mailing occurs (i.e., dropping it in the post-office box).[33]

Restrictions on Use of Cash Method

Under the general rule, a cash basis taxpayer deducts expenses when paid. Without restrictions, however, aggressive taxpayers could liberally interpret this provision to authorize not only deductions for routine items, but also deductions for capital expenditures and other expenses that benefit future periods (e.g., supplies, prepaid insurance, prepaid rent, and prepaid interest). To preclude such an approach, numerous limitations have been imposed.

Inventories. One of the more fundamental restrictions applying to cash basis taxpayers concerns inventories. For example, if no limitation existed, a cash basis owner of a department store could easily reduce or eliminate taxable income by increasing purchases of inventory near year-end and deducting their cost. To prevent this possibility, the Regulations require taxpayers to use the accrual method for computing sales and costs of goods sold if inventories are an income-producing factor.[34] In such cases, inventory costs must be capitalized, and accounts receivable and accounts payable (with respect to cost of goods sold) must be created. The taxpayer could continue to use the cash method for other transactions, however. It is also important to note that there are two relief provisions for small business owners that allow them to elect out of the accrual method and the requirement to account for inventories. As discussed in Chapter 10, taxpayers with average gross receipts of no more than $1 million, and certain taxpayers with average annual gross receipts of more than $1 million and up to $10 million may use the cash method of accounting even when inventory is an income producing factor.[35]

Capital Expenditures. Provisions of both the Code and the Regulations limit the potential for deducting capital expenditures. As discussed later in this chapter, Code § 263 specifically denies the deduction for a capital expenditure; such costs as those for equipment, vehicles, and buildings normally are recovered through depreciation, as discussed in Chapter 9. Special rules exist requiring taxpayers to capitalize certain costs as part of their inventory under the uniform capitalization rules of § 263A. The "unicap" rules are discussed in Chapter 10.

The Regulations—at least broadly—deal with other expenditures that are not capital expenditures per se but that do benefit future periods. According to the Regulations, any expenditure resulting "in the creation of an asset having a useful life which extends *substantially beyond the close of the taxable year* may not be deductible when made, or may be deductible only in part."[36] In this regard, the courts agree that "substantially beyond" means a useful life of more than one year.[37] Perhaps the simplest example of this rule as so interpreted concerns payments for supplies. Assuming the supplies would be exhausted before the close of the following tax year, a deduction should be allowable when payment is made.

Prepaid Expenses in General

One of the most troublesome issues related to both the cash and accrual methods of accounting concerns prepaid expenses. If prepayments are made for regularly recurring expenses and the payments result in the creation of an asset having a life extending substantially beyond the taxable year of payment, the treatment historically has not always been clear. Unfortunately, the *one-year rule* described above was not necessarily applied to all expenses uniformly.

12-Month Rule. The problems with prepaid expenses became acutely apparent in *U.S. Freightways Corporation.*[38] Here an accrual basis calendar-year trucking company claimed a deduction for permits, licenses and fees paid in order for its trucks to operate legally in certain locations. In 1993, the company paid $4,308,460 for licenses, many of which expired in 1994 rather than 1993. Similarly, in 1993, the company paid premiums of $1,090,602 for liability and property insurance for the 1-year period from July 1, 1993 to June 30, 1994.

---

[32] Rev. Rul. 80-335, 1980-2 C.B. 170.

[33] See Rev. Rul. 73-99, 1973-1 C.B. 412 for clarification of this general rule.

[34] Reg. § 1.446-1(c)(2).

[35] Rev. Proc. 2000-22, Rev. Proc. 2001-10, and Rev. Proc. 2002-28. See full discussion of inventory in Chapter 10.

[36] Reg. § 1.446-1(a)(1).

[37] *Martin J. Zaninovich,* 69 T.C. 605, rev'd in 80-1 USTC ¶9342, 45 AFTR2d 80-1442, 616 F.2d 429 (CA-9, 1980).

[38] 2001-2 USTC 50,731, 88 AFTR2d 2001-6703, 270 F3d 1137 (CA-7, 2001).

Relying on the one-year rule, the corporation expensed all of the prepayments. However, the government denied the deduction, asserting that the 12-month rule existed solely for cash basis taxpayers and did not apply to accrual basis taxpayers. The Seventh Circuit disagreed and extended the rule to accrual basis taxpayers.

To address the confusion resulting from *U.S. Freightways* and similar cases, the government issued Regulations in 2004 to address the capitalization of intangibles.[39] Among these lengthy provisions is the government's own 12-month rule. Under these Regulations, taxpayers—both cash and accrual—are entitled to claim an immediate deduction for prepaid expenses (e.g. prepaid insurance) if the rights or benefits do not extend beyond the earlier of

- 12 months after the first date on which the taxpayer realizes the benefit, or
- The end of the taxable year following the year in which payment was made.

This rule generally is consistent with prior law that enables cash basis taxpayer to claim deductions for prepaid expenses for supplies, service and other non-capital expenditures. It should be emphasized that the rule applies to both cash and accrual taxpayers. However, as discussed below, accrual taxpayers must meet the all events and economic performance tests before a deduction can be claimed. Specific items are discussed below.

Prepaid Insurance and Prepaid Rent

Prepayments of insurance and rent follow the 12-month rule. If the 12-month rule does not apply, the prepayment cannot be deducted when paid and must be amortized over the term for which the insurance is provided or the term of the lease.[40]

Example 9

On December 1, 2017, Blue Inc., a cash basis taxpayer, paid a $12,000 insurance premium to obtain a property insurance policy with a one-year term that begins on February 1, 2018. Although the policy is only for one year, the payment does not meet the 12-month rule since the benefit attributable to the $12,000 payment extends beyond the end of the taxable year following the taxable year in which the payment was made. The corporation must capitalize the payment and amortize it over the policy period. Thus the corporation's deduction is $0 in 2017, $11,000 in 2018 and $1,000 in 2019.

Example 10

Same facts as above except the policy has a term beginning on December 15, 2017. The 12-month rule applies since the benefit does not extend more than 12 months beyond December 15, 2017 (the date when the benefit is first realized by the corporation) nor beyond the close of the tax year following the year in which the payment was made (December 31, 2018). Thus the corporation may deduct the entire $12,000 prepayment in the year paid, 2017.

Example 11

WRK Inc., a cash basis taxpayer, leases space at a monthly rate of $2,000. In December of 2017, the corporation prepays its rent for the first six months of 2018 in the amount of $12,000. The corporation may deduct the entire $12,000 in 2017 since the benefits received for the prepayment do not extend beyond 12 months. (Note as discussed below accrual basis taxpayers would be required to amortize this expense over the term because the economic performance test delays deduction until the property is used.)

---

[39] Reg. § 1.263-(a)(4).   [40] See Reg. 1.263(a)-4(f)(8) Ex. 1, 2, and 10.

Other Prepayments

Perhaps the Service's current view of the proper treatment of most prepayments is best captured in a ruling concerning prepaid feed. In this ruling, the taxpayer purchased a substantial amount of feed prior to the year in which it would be used.[41] The purchase was made in advance because the price was low due to a depressed market. The IRS granted a deduction for the prepayment because there was a business purpose for the advanced payment, the payment was not merely a deposit, and it did not materially distort income. Based on this ruling and related cases, prepayments normally should be deductible if the asset will be consumed by the close of the following year, there is a business purpose for the expenditure, and there is no material distortion of income.

Prepaid Interest

The Code expressly denies the deduction of prepaid interest. Prepaid interest must be capitalized and deducted ratably over the period of the loan.[42] The same is true for any costs associated with obtaining the loan. The sole exception is for "points" paid for a debt incurred by the taxpayer to purchase his or her *principal* residence. In this regard, the IRS has ruled that points incurred to refinance a home must be amortized over the term of the loan.[43] However, an Appeals Court case allowed a taxpayer to deduct the amount of points paid on refinancing a home. The proceeds were used to pay off a three-year, temporary loan that was made to allow the borrower time to secure permanent financing for the home.[44] The court stated that, since the temporary loan was merely an integrated step in securing permanent financing for the taxpayer's residence, the points were deductible currently.

Example 12

K desires to obtain financing for the purchase of a new house costing $100,000. The bank agrees to make her a loan of 80% of the purchase price, or $80,000 (80% of $100,000) for thirty years at a cost of two points (two percentage "points" of the loan obtained). Thus, she must pay $1,600 (2% of $80,000) to obtain the loan. Assuming it is established business practice in her area to charge points in consideration of the loan, the $1,600 in points (prepaid interest) is deductible. However, if the house is not the principal residence of the taxpayer, then the prepaid interest must be deducted ratably over the 30-year loan period.

ACCRUAL METHOD OF ACCOUNTING

An accrual basis taxpayer deducts expenses when they are incurred. For this purpose, an expense is considered incurred when the all events test is satisfied and economic performance has occurred.[45]

All Events Test

Two requirements must be met under the all-events test: (1) all events establishing the existence of a liability must have occurred (i.e., the liability is fixed); and (2) the amount of the liability can be determined with reasonable accuracy. Therefore, before the liability may be accrued and deducted it must be fixed and determinable.

---

[41] Rev. Rul. 79-229, 1979-2 C.B. 210. See also, *Kenneth Van Raden,* 71 T.C. 1083 (1979), aff'd in 81-2 USTC ¶9547, 48 AFTR2d 81-5607, 650 F.2d 1046 (CA-9, 1981).

[42] § 461(g).

[43] Rev. Rul. 87-22, 1987-1 C.B. 146. See also Rev. Proc. 94-27, 1994-1 I.R.B. 15.

[44] *James R. Huntsman,* 90-2 USTC ¶50,340, 66 AFTR2d 90-5020, 905 F.2d 1182 (CA-8, 1990). In an *Action on Decision* issued on February 11, 1991, the IRS ruled that although it will not appeal the *Huntsman* decision, it will not follow this decision outside the Eighth Circuit.

[45] § 461(h).

> **Example 13**
>
> In *Hughes Properties, Inc.,* an accrual basis corporation owned a gambling casino in Reno, Nevada that operated progressive slot machines that paid a large jackpot about every four months.[46] The increasing amount of the jackpot was maintained and shown by a meter. Under state gaming regulations, the jackpot amount could not be turned back until the amount had been paid to a winner. In addition, the corporation had to maintain a cash reserve sufficient to pay all the guaranteed amounts. At the end of each taxable year, the corporation accrued and deducted the liability for the jackpot as accrued at year-end. The IRS challenged the accrual, alleging that the all events test had not been met, and that the amount should be deducted only when paid. It argued that payment of the jackpot was not fixed but contingent, since it was possible that the winning combination may never be pulled. Moreover, the Service pointed out the potential for tax avoidance: the corporation was accruing deductions for payments that may be paid far in the future, and thus—given the time value of money—overstated the amount of the deduction. The Supreme Court rejected these arguments, stating that the probability of payment was not a remote and speculative possibility. The Court noted that not only was the liability fixed under state law, but it also was not in the interest of the taxpayer to set unreasonably high odds, since customers would refuse to play and would gamble elsewhere.

The all events test often operates to deny deductions for certain estimated expenditures properly accruable for financial accounting purposes. For example, the estimated cost of product guarantees, warranties, and contingent liabilities normally may not be deducted—presumably because the liability for such items has not been fixed or no reasonable estimate of the amount can be made.[47] However, the courts have authorized deductions for estimates where the obligation was certain and there was a reasonable basis (e.g., industry experience) for determining the amount of the liability.

Economic Performance Test

The condition requiring *economic performance* was introduced in 1984 due to Congressional fear that the all events test did not prohibit so-called premature accruals. Prior to 1984, the courts—with increasing frequency—had permitted taxpayers to accrue and deduct the cost of estimated expenditures required to perform certain activities *prior* to the period when the activities were actually performed. For example, in one case, a strip-mining operator deducted the estimated cost of backfilling land that he had mined for coal.[48] The court allowed the deduction for the estimated expenses in the current year even though the back filling was not started and completed until the following year. According to the court, the liability satisfied the all-events test since the taxpayer was required by law to backfill the land and a reasonable estimate of the cost of the work could be made. A similar decision involved a taxpayer that was a self-insurer of its liabilities arising from claims under state and Federal worker's compensation laws.[49] Under these laws, the taxpayer was obligated to pay a claimant's medical bills, disability payments, and death benefits. In this situation, the taxpayer was allowed to accrue and deduct the estimated expenses for its obligations even though actual payments would extend over many years. In Congress' view, allowing the deduction in these and similar cases prior to the time when the taxpayer actually performed the services, provided the goods, or paid the expenses, overstated the true cost of the expense, because the time value of money was ignored. Perhaps more importantly, Congress recognized that allowing deductions for accruals in this manner had become the foundation for many tax shelter arrangements. Accordingly, the economic performance test was designed to defer the taxpayer's deduction until the activities giving rise to the liability are performed.

---

[46] *Hughes Properties, Inc.,* 86-1 USTC ¶9440, 58 AFTR2d 86-5015, 106 S. Ct. 2092 (USSC, 1986).

[47] *Bell Electric Co.,* 45 T.C. 158 (1965).

[48] *Paul Harrold v. Comm.,* 52-1 USTC ¶9107, 41 AFTR 442, 192 F.2d 1002 (CA-4, 1951).

[49] *Crescent Wharf & Warehouse Co. v. Comm.,* 75-2 USTC ¶9571, 36 AFTR2d 75-5246, 518 F.2d 772 (CA-5, 1975).

The time at which economic performance is deemed to occur—and hence the period in which the deduction may be claimed—depends on the nature of the item producing the liability. A taxpayer's liabilities commonly arise in three ways, as summarized below.

1. *Liability of Taxpayer to Provide Property and Services.* When the taxpayer's liability results from an obligation to provide goods or services to a third party (e.g., perform repairs), economic performance occurs when the taxpayer provides the goods or services to the third party.

2. *Liability for Property or Services Provided to the Taxpayer.* When the taxpayer's liability arises from an obligation to pay for services, goods, or the use of property provided to (or to be provided to) the taxpayer (e.g., consulting, supplies, and rent), economic performance occurs when the taxpayer receives the services or goods or uses the property. Note that in this case, economic performance occurs when the taxpayer *receives* the consideration bargained for, while in the situation above it occurs when the taxpayer *provides* the consideration. Under a special rule, a taxpayer may treat services or property as being provided when the taxpayer makes *payment* to the person providing the services or property *if* the taxpayer can reasonably expect the person to provide the services or property within 3½ months after the date of payment.[50]

3. *Liabilities for which Payment Represents Economic Performance.* There are a number of liabilities for which economic performance is deemed to occur only when the taxpayer actually makes payment. This rule for so-called "payment liabilities" effectively places the taxpayer on the cash basis for these liabilities. These include the following:

   - Refunds and rebates.
   - Awards, prizes, and jackpots.
   - Premiums on insurance.
   - Provision of work to the taxpayer under warranty or service contracts.
   - Taxes.
   - Liabilities arising under a worker's compensation act or out of any tort, breach of contract, or violation of law, including amounts paid in settlement of such claims.

Example 14

In 2017 C, an accrual basis corporation, contracted with P, a partnership, to drill 50 gas wells over a five-year period for $500,000. Absent the economic performance test, C could accrue and deduct the $500,000 fee in 2017 because the obligation is fixed and determinable. However, because economic performance has not occurred (i.e., the services have not been received by C), no deduction is permitted in 2017. Rather, C may deduct the expense when the wells are drilled.

Example 15

Same facts as above. Although P is obligated to perform services for C for $500,000 over the five-year period (i.e., the obligation is fixed and determinable), P cannot prematurely accrue the cost of providing these services because economic performance has not occurred. Deduction is permitted only as the wells are drilled.

---

[50] Reg. § 1.461-4(d)(6)(ii).

Example 16

C Corporation, a calendar year, accrual method taxpayer, owns several casinos across the country. Each contains progressive slot machines. These machines provide a guaranteed jackpot that increases as money is gambled through the machine until the jackpot is won or until a maximum predetermined amount is reached. On July 1, 2017, the guaranteed jackpot amount on one of C's slot machines reaches the maximum predetermined amount of $100,000. On February 1, 2018, the $100,000 jackpot is won by B. Although the all-events test is met in 2017 when the amount of the liability becomes fixed (i.e., guaranteed) and determinable, economic performance does not occur for prizes until payment is actually made. As a result, C is not allowed to accrue the deduction in 2017 but must wait and claim the expense when it pays the jackpot in 2018. (Note this rule reverses the decision in *Hughes Properties, Inc*. However, the deduction may still be allowed under the recurring item exception discussed below.)

Note that even though payment of an expense may make it ripe for accrual, other rules may require deferral of the deduction.

Example 17

On December 10, 2017, T Inc., an accrual basis calendar year taxpayer, paid a painting contractor $15,000 to paint the interior of its office building. T anticipated that the painting would be completed by February 15 of 2018. Since the painting services are to be provided within 3½ months after the date of payment, economic performance is deemed to have occurred when the payment is made and T may deduct the $15,000 expense in 2017.

Example 18

Kidco Products Corporation, a calendar year, accrual method taxpayer, manufactures car seats for children. On July 1, 2017 it purchased an insurance policy from INS Inc. for $360,000 under which INS must satisfy any liability arising during the next three years for any claims attributable to defects in the manufacturing. Although economic performance occurs when Kidco pays the premium, it has created an asset with a life that extends substantially beyond 2017. Under cash-basis principles, such expenses cannot be deducted currently but must be amortized. Consequently, Kidco should amortize the insurance premium over the term of the policy, deducting $60,000 ($360,000/36 × 6 months) in 2017 and the remaining $300,000 over the next 30 months.

Example 19

WNDE Corporation leases space at a monthly rate of $2,000. In December of 2017, the corporation prepays its rent for the first six months of 2018 in the amount of $12,000. If WNDE is a cash basis taxpayer, it could deduct the $12,000 in 2017 under the 12-month rule (see *Example 10* above). However, if WNDE uses the accrual method, economic performance for the rent does not occur until the corporation uses the property and, therefore, it cannot use the 12-month rule but must deduct the rental expense over the period it uses the property, 2018.

Economic Performance and Recurring Item Exception

To prohibit the disruption of normal business and accounting practices, certain recurring expenses are exempted from the economic performance rules. The expense may be accrued and deducted under the recurring item exception if all of the following conditions are met.[51]

1. The all-events test is satisfied.

2. Economic performance does in fact occur within eight and one-half months after the close of the taxable year or the filing of the return if earlier.

3. The item is recurring in nature, and the taxpayer consistently treats such items as incurred in the taxable year.

4. The item is immaterial or accrual in the earlier year results in a better match against income than accruing the item when economic performance occurs.

The recurring item exception does not apply to liabilities arising under a worker's compensation act or out of any tort, breach of contract, or violation of law.

Example 20

M Inc., a C corporation, uses the accrual method and reports on the calendar year. M, manufactures and sells automobile mufflers. Under the terms of an agreement with D Corporation, one of its distributors, D is entitled to a discount on future purchases (i.e., a rebate) from M based on the amount of purchases made by D from M during any calendar year. During 2017, purchases by D entitled it to future rebates of $20,000. M paid $12,000 of the rebate in January 2018 and the remaining $8,000 in November 2018. M filed its 2017 tax return on April 15, 2018. Although the all events test has been met in 2017 (i.e., the fact of the liability is fixed and the amount can be determined with reasonable accuracy), no deduction is allowed until economic performance occurs. Normally, economic performance for rebates is deemed to occur when the rebate is paid. Therefore, the expense would usually be deductible by M in 2018. However, under the recurring item exception M should be able to accrue $12,000 of the $20,000 in 2017 because all of the conditions are met: (1) the all events test is met, (2) economic performance occurs in a timely manner (i.e., the January payment occurs before the earlier of the filing of the tax return or 8½ months after the close of the year), (3) the item is recurring, and (4) accrual in the earlier year results in a better match against income. The remaining $8,000 is not eligible for the recurring item exception because economic performance (payment of the $8,000 liability) did not occur until November, which is beyond both the filing of the return and the 8½-month window ending on October 15.

Real Property Taxes

The addition of the economic performance test and the recurring item exception posed a problem for a great number of taxpayers who incur real property taxes.

---

[51] § 461(h)(3).

Example 21

Oldco Corporation uses the accrual method and reports on the calendar year. It owns a warehouse in a state where the lien date (i.e., the date on which the corporation technically becomes liable) for real property taxes for 2017 is January 1, 2018. Payment is due in two installments, 40% due on June 1 and the remaining 60% due on December 1. Shortly after the close of 2017, the corporation received its bill for its 2017 taxes of $100,000, paying $40,000 on June 1, 2018 and $60,000 on December 1, 2018. For financial accounting purposes, the corporation accrues the entire $100,000 expense in 2017. For tax purposes, however, economic performance for taxes does not occur until payment is made. Therefore, accrual normally is not allowed until the payment is made (2018) unless the recurring item exception applies. In this case, the recurring item exception would apply. However, the corporation could deduct only the portion paid by the earlier of the filing of its tax return or September 15 (8½ months after the close of the taxable year). If the corporation delayed filing its return until the extended due date, October 15, it could accrue and deduct on its 2017 tax return the $40,000 paid on June 1. However, if it filed its return by April 15, none of the taxes could be accrued under the recurring item exception.

Recognizing the problem illustrated *Example 18* above, Code § 461(c) was created. Under this provision, taxpayers can elect to accrue real property taxes ratably over the period to which the taxes relate. Note that if the taxpayer makes the election, the treatment for tax purposes is consistent with that for financial accounting.

Example 22

Same facts as *Example 21*. If the corporation makes the election under § 461(c), it may accrue and deduct the entire $100,000 in 2017 because all of the taxes related to such period.

RELATIONSHIP TO FINANCIAL ACCOUNTING

As may be apparent from the discussion above, the rules for accruing expenses for tax accounting purposes do not necessarily produce the same result as those for financial accounting. Differences often occur, particularly in the treatment of estimated expenses. As noted in Chapter 5, such differences are justified given the differing goals of financial and tax accounting. Financial accounting principles adopt a conservative approach in measuring income to ensure that income is not overstated and investors are not misled. Accordingly, financial accounting embraces the matching principle that encourages the accrual of estimated expenditures. In contrast, the objective of the income tax system is to ensure that taxable income is objectively measured so as to minimize controversy. Consistent with this view, the tax law allows a deduction only when a liability is actually fixed and economic performance has occurred. Estimates of future expenses are not sufficient to warrant a deduction for tax purposes (unless the recurring item exception should apply). Note, however, that these different accounting techniques produce differences only in *when* the expense is taken into account. The total amount of expense to be accounted for is not affected. Common examples of these so-called timing differences include:

- *Depreciation.* As discussed in Chapter 9, depreciation for tax purposes differs substantially from that for financial accounting purposes. Although the total amount of depreciation is often the same in both cases, the amount expensed in any one period may differ significantly.

- *Bad Debts.* For tax purposes, bad debts normally may be deducted only in the year they actually become worthless. In contrast, financial accounting permits use of the reserve method, which allows an estimate of future bad debts related to current year sales to be charged against current year income. The tax treatment of bad debts is discussed fully in Chapter 10.

- *Vacation Pay.* For financial accounting purposes, vacation pay accrues as it is earned by the employees. For tax purposes, however, vacation pay may be accrued and deducted only if it is paid within 2½ months following the close of the taxable year.

- *Warranty Costs.* For financial accounting purposes, warranty costs are normally estimated and matched against current year sales. For tax purposes, no deduction is allowed until the warranty work is actually performed (unless the recurring item exception applies).

Timing differences should be distinguished from permanent differences. As seen throughout this text, there are a number of situations in which an expense for financial accounting purposes is not allowed as a deduction for tax purposes. For example, fines and penalties are expenses that must be taken into account in determining financial accounting income, as are expenses related to tax-exempt income. However, tax deductions for such costs are not allowed. Similarly, expenses for business meals and entertainment may be fully expensed for financial accounting but only 50% of such costs can be deducted for tax purposes.

The rules governing the accrual of deductions are summarized in Exhibit 7-1.

EXHIBIT 7-1	**Requirements for Accrual of Deduction**

Requirements:
- All events test is met
  - All events have occurred that fix the fact of the liability
  - The amount of the liability can be determined with reasonable accuracy
- Economic performance has occurred as follows:

Event Producing Liability	Time When Economic Performance Occurs	Example
Taxpayer obligated to provide goods or services to a third party	When the taxpayer provides the property or services	Taxpayer to perform repairs, warranty work
Goods or services provided or to be provided to the taxpayer	When taxpayer actually receives the goods or services	Taxpayer buys supplies, contracts for consulting
Property provided or to be provided to the taxpayer	When taxpayer uses the property	Taxpayer rents property
Obligations to pay refunds, rebates, awards, prizes, insurance, warranty or service contracts, taxes	When taxpayer makes payment	Refunds, rebates, etc.
Claims under worker's compensation, tort, breach of contract	When taxpayer makes payment	Taxpayer incurs product liability
Real property taxes	When taxpayer makes payment unless he or she elects special accrual rule	Real estate taxes

Deductions for Losses

The general rules concerning deduction of losses are contained in § 165. This provision permits a deduction for any loss sustained that is not compensated for by insurance. The deductions for losses of an individual taxpayer, however, are limited to:

1. Losses incurred in a trade or business.
2. Losses incurred in a transaction entered into for profit.
3. Losses of property not connected with a trade or business if such losses arise by fire, storm, shipwreck, theft, or some other type of casualty.

Note that personal losses—other than those attributable to a casualty—are not deductible. For example, the sale of a personal residence at a loss is not deductible.

Before a loss can be deducted, it must be evidenced by a closed and completed transaction. Mere decline in values or unrealized losses cannot be deducted. Normally, for the loss to qualify as a deduction, the property must be sold, abandoned, or scrapped, or become completely worthless. The amount of deductible loss for all taxpayers cannot exceed the taxpayer's basis in the property. Special rules related to various types of losses are discussed in Chapter 10.

Classification of Expenses

Once the deductibility of an item is established, the tax formula for individuals requires that the deduction be classified as either a deduction *for* adjusted gross income or a deduction *from* adjusted gross income (itemized deduction).[52] In short, the deduction process requires that two questions be asked. First, is the expense deductible? Second, is the deduction for or from adjusted gross income (AGI)? Additional aspects of the first question are considered later in this chapter. At this point, however, it is appropriate to consider the problem of classification.

The classification process arose with the introduction of the standard deduction in 1944. The standard deduction was introduced to simplify filing for the majority of individuals by eliminating the necessity of itemizing primarily personal deductions such as medical expenses and charitable contributions. In addition, the administrative burden of checking such deductions was eliminated. Although these objectives were satisfied by providing a blanket deduction in lieu of itemizing actual expenses, a new problem arose. The standard deduction created the need to classify deductions as either deductions that would be deductible in any event (deductions for AGI), or deductions that would be deductible only if they exceeded the prescribed amount of the standard deduction (deductions from AGI).

IMPORTANCE OF CLASSIFICATION

Improper classification can produce a number of undesirable results. No doubt the most important of these is that itemized deductions may be deducted only to the extent they exceed the standard deduction. For this reason, a taxpayer whose itemized deductions do not exceed the standard deduction would lose a deduction if a deduction for AGI is improperly classified as a deduction from AGI. This would occur because deductions for AGI are deductible without limitation.

LO.4

Describe the importance of properly classifying expenses as deductions for or from adjusted gross income.

Another reason for properly classifying deduction concerns the limitations and restrictions that exist for certain itemized deductions. Miscellaneous itemized deductions—defined below—are allowed only to the extent that they exceed 2% of AGI. Similarly, high income taxpayer must reduce their total itemized deductions by 3% of their AGI in excess of certain levels, generally $261,500 in 2017 ($313,800 for joint filers). Consequently, improperly classifying a deduction as an itemized deduction could render the deduction either partially or totally nondeductible.

Adjusted gross income for Federal income tax purposes also serves as the tax base or the starting point for computing taxable income for many state income taxes. Several states do not allow the taxpayer to itemize deductions. Consequently, misclassification could result in an incorrect state tax liability.

Still another reason for properly classifying expenses concerns the self-employment tax. Under the Social Security and Medicare programs, self-employed individuals are required to make an annual contribution based on their net earnings from self-employment. Net earnings from self-employment include gross income from the taxpayer's trade or business less allowable trade or business deductions attributable to the income. Failure to properly classify a deduction as a deduction for AGI attributable to self-employment income results in a higher self-employment tax.

---

[52] § 62.

DEDUCTIONS FOR AGI

LO.5

Classify expenses as
deductions *for* or *from*
adjusted gross income.

The deductions for AGI are specifically identified in Code § 62. It should be emphasized, however, that § 62 merely classifies expenses; it does *not* authorize any deductions.
Deductions *for* AGI are:

1. Trade or business deductions except those expenses incurred in the business of being
   an employee (e.g., expenses of a sole proprietorship or self-employment normally are
   reported on Schedule C of Form 1040).

2. Trade or business deductions of a "statutory employee," generally including traveling
   salespersons, full-time life insurance salespersons, agent-drivers, commission-drivers
   and homeworkers. Statutory employees (discussed in detail in Chapter 8) generally
   report both their income (i.e., wages) and their business expenses on Schedule C much
   like a sole proprietor.

3. Three categories of employee business deductions:

   • Expenses that are reimbursed by an employee's employer (and the reimbursement
     is included in the employee's income);[53]

   • Expenses incurred by a qualified performing artist (see below); and

   • Expenses incurred by an official of a state or local government who is compensated
     on a fee basis.

4. Losses from sale or exchange of property (investment losses).

5. Deductions attributable to rental or royalty income.

6. Educator expenses (up to $250 of supplies for K–12 teachers).

7. Deductions for reservists, performing artists, fee-basis government officials.

8. Deductions for certain tuition and fees.

9. Student loan interest expense.

10. Deduction for certain legal expenses.

11. Deductions for contributions to Individual Retirement Accounts or retirement plans
    for self-employed individuals.

12. Deductions for alimony payments (but not child support).

13. Deductions for penalties imposed for premature withdrawal of funds from a savings
    arrangement.

14. Deduction for 50% of self-employment tax paid by self-employed persons.

15. Deduction for contributions to Health Savings Accounts (HSAs).

16. Moving expenses.

17. Deduction for self-employed taxpayers for 100% of payments of medical insurance
    premiums for the coverage of the taxpayer, spouse and any dependents.

18. Certain other deductions.

All of the above are deductible for AGI, while all other deductions are from AGI (i.e., itemized deductions).

---

[53] Reimbursements must be made under an "accountable plan."
Chapter 8 discusses in detail the proper reporting for these
reimbursements.

ITEMIZED DEDUCTIONS

As seen above, only relatively few expenses are deductible for AGI. The predominant expenses in this category are the deductions incurred by taxpayers who are self-employed (i.e., those carrying on as a sole proprietor). All other expenses are deductible from AGI as itemized deductions.

Itemized deductions fall into two basic categories: those that are *miscellaneous itemized deductions* and those that are not. The distinction is significant because miscellaneous itemized deductions are deductible only to the extent they exceed two percent of AGI. Miscellaneous itemized deductions are all itemized deductions *other than* the following:

1. Interest.
2. Taxes.
3. Casualty and theft losses.
4. Medical expenses.
5. Charitable contributions.
6. Gambling losses to the extent of gambling gains.
7. Deduction where annuity payments cease before investment is recovered.
8. Certain other deductions.

The miscellaneous itemized deductions category is comprised primarily of *unreimbursed* employee business expenses, investment expenses, and deductions related to taxes such as tax preparation fees. Examples of these (assuming they are not reimbursed by the employer) include

1. Employee travel away from home (including meals and lodging).
2. Employee transportation expenses.
3. Outside salesperson's expenses (unless those individuals qualify as a "statutory employee" in which case they are allowed to report their income [i.e., wages] and expenses on a separate Schedule C and avoid the two percent of AGI limitation).
4. Employee entertainment expenses.
5. Employee home office expenses.
6. Union dues.
7. Professional dues and memberships.
8. Subscriptions to business journals.
9. Job-seeking expenses (in the same business) or employment-seeking expenses.
10. Education expenses.
11. Investment expenses, including expenses for an investment newsletter, investment advice, and rentals of safety deposit boxes.
12. Tax preparation fees or other tax-related advice including that received from accountants or attorneys, tax seminars, and books about taxes.

With respect to item 12 above, expenses related to tax preparation and resolving tax controversies normally are reported as miscellaneous itemized deductions. However, the IRS allows taxpayers who own a business, farm, or rental real estate or have royalty income to allocate a portion of the total cost of preparing their tax return to the cost of preparing Schedule C (trade or business income), Schedule E (rental and royalty income), or Schedule F (farm income) and deduct these costs "for" AGI.[54] The same holds true for expenses incurred in resolving tax controversies, including expenses relating to IRS audits or business or rental activities.

---

[54] Rev. Rul. 92-29, 1992-1 C.B.20.

SELF-EMPLOYED VERSUS EMPLOYEE

LO.6

Explain the proper treatment of employee business expenses.

Under the current scheme of deductions for and from AGI, an important—and perhaps inequitable—distinction is made based on whether an individual is an employee or self-employed. As seen above, employees generally deduct all unreimbursed business expenses as itemized deductions. In contrast, self-employed taxpayers (i.e., sole proprietors or partners) deduct business expenses for AGI. At first glance, the difference appears trivial, particularly for those taxpayers who itemize their deductions. Recall, however, that an employee's business expenses are treated as miscellaneous itemized deductions and thus are deductible only to the extent that these and all other miscellaneous itemized deductions collectively exceed 2% of the taxpayer's AGI. Due to this distinction, deductibility often depends on the employment status of the taxpayer.

Example 23

T is an accountant. During the year she earns $70,000 and pays dues of $200 to be a member of the local CPA society. These were her only items of income and expense. If T practices as a self-employed sole proprietor (e.g., she has a small firm or partnership), the dues are fully deductible for AGI. However, if T is an employee, none of the expense is deductible since it does not exceed the 2% floor of $1,400 (2% × $70,000). If T's employer had reimbursed her for the expense and included the reimbursement in her income, the expense would have been completely deductible, totally offsetting the amount that T must include in income. If T is employed, but at the same time does some accounting work on her own, part-time, the treatment is unclear.

The logic for the distinction based on employment status is fragile at best. According to the committee reports, Congress believed that it was generally appropriate to disallow deductions for employee business expenses because employers reimburse employees for those expenses that are most necessary for employment. In addition, Congress felt that the treatment would simplify the system by relieving taxpayers of the burden of record keeping and at the same time relieving the IRS of the burden of auditing such deductions.

Reimbursed Expenses

The classification and treatment of an employee's deductible business expenses can vary depending on whether they are reimbursed. If the employee is not reimbursed, the unreimbursed business expenses are deductible as miscellaneous itemized deductions. If the employee is reimbursed and he or she properly accounts to the employer according to the "accountable plan" rules, neither the amount of the reimbursement nor the expense is reported on the return.[55] The accountable plan rules, which are discussed in detail in Chapter 8, generally require employees to substantiate their expenses (e.g., provide documentation such as receipts). If the accountable plan rules are not followed or a plan does not exist, the reimbursement is treated as wages subject to employment taxes and the expense is deducted as a miscellaneous itemized deduction.

Example 24

Professor K is employed by State University in the finance department. The department has a policy of reimbursing up to $150 for each faculty member's costs of subscribing to finance journals. During the year, K spent $175 on subscriptions. He submitted the receipt for $150 of his expenses and was reimbursed by his employer. Assuming the employer's reimbursement policy meets the accountable plan requirements and K has adequately accounted for the expense, the $150 reimbursement is not included in K's wages and K claims no deduction. K may deduct the remaining $25 as a miscellaneous itemized deduction. In this situation, there is no effect on AGI. The transaction is a "wash" economically for K and is, therefore a "wash" on K's tax return.

---

[55] See Reg. § 1.62-2. Note also that the employer is not required to file an information return when there is an accountable plan.

Example 25

Same as above except the plan did not meet the accountable plan standard. In this case, the employer would include the reimbursement of $150 in K's wages (e.g., his W-2) and K could deduct the $150 of expenses along with the other $25 as miscellaneous itemized deductions. Of course, if K does not itemize or his miscellaneous itemized deductions do not exceed the 2% floor, he would not benefit from the deduction. Observe that in this situation where the accountable plan rules are not met, the transaction is not a "wash" from a tax point of view. The amount K receives is reduced by employment taxes on the $150 and he may or may not be able to deduct the $150 of his subscriptions.

Expenses of Performing Artists

Most employee business expenses were relegated to second-class status in 1986 as they became subject to the 2% limitation. However, one group of employees, the struggling performing artists, escaped this restriction. These actors, actresses, musicians, dancers, and the like are technically employees but exhibit many attributes of the self-employed. They often work for several employers for little income yet incur relatively large unreimbursed expenses as they seek their fortunes. For these reasons, "qualified performing artists" are permitted to deduct their business expenses *for* AGI. To qualify, the individual must perform services in the performing arts as an employee for at least two employers during the taxable year, earning at least $200 from each. In addition, the individual's AGI before business deductions cannot exceed $16,000. Lastly, the artist's business deductions must exceed 10% of his or her gross service income, otherwise they too are considered miscellaneous itemized deductions.

Example 26

Z is an actress. This year she worked in two Broadway productions for two different employers, earning $7,000 from each for a total of $14,000. Her expenses, including the fee to her agent, were $2,000. She may deduct all of her expenses for AGI.

Self-Employed or Employee?

The above discussion illustrates the importance of determining whether an individual is self-employed or is treated as an employee. However, whether an individual is self-employed or is an employee is often difficult to determine. An employee is a person who performs services for another individual subject to that individual's direction and control.[56] In the employer-employee relationship, the right to control extends not only to the result to be accomplished but also to the methods of accomplishment. Accordingly, an employee is subject to the will and control of the employer as to both what will be done and how it will be done. In the case of the self-employed person, the individual is subject to the control of another only as to the end result, and not as to the means of accomplishment. Generally, physicians, lawyers, dentists, veterinarians, contractors, and subcontractors are not employees. An insurance agent or salesperson may be an employee or self-employed, depending on the facts. The courts have developed numerous tests for differentiating between employees and self-employed persons. Each of the following situations would suggest that an employer-employee relationship exists.[57]

1. Complying with written or oral instructions (an independent contractor need not be trained or attend training sessions).

2. Regular written or oral reports on the work's status.

---

[56] Reg. § 31.3401(c)-1(a).

[57] Rev. Rul. 87-41, 1987-1 C.B. 296. This Revenue Ruling actually contains 20 questions.

3. Continuous relationship—more than sporadic services over a lengthy period.

4. Lack of control over the place of work.

5. No risk of profit or loss; no income fluctuations.

6. Regular payment—hourly, weekly, etc. (an independent contractor might work on a job basis).

7. Specified number of hours required to work (an independent contractor is master of his or her own time).

8. Unable to delegate work—hiring assistants not permitted.

9. Not independent—does not work for numerous firms or make services available to general public.

Limitations on Deductions

LO.7

Recognize statutory, administrative, and judicial limitations on deductions and losses.

Some provisions of the Code specifically prohibit or limit the deduction of certain expenses and losses despite their apparent relationship to the taxpayer's business or profit-seeking activities. These provisions operate to disallow or limit the deduction for various expenses unless such expenses are specifically authorized by the Code. As a practical matter, these provisions have been enacted to prohibit abuses identified in specific areas. Several of the more fundamental limitations are considered in this chapter.

HOBBY EXPENSES AND LOSSES

As previously discussed, a taxpayer must establish that he or she pursues an activity with the objective of making a profit before the expense is deductible as a business or production of income expense. When the profit motive is absent, the deduction is governed by § 183 on activities not engaged in for profit (i.e., hobbies). Section 183 generally provides that hobby expenses of an individual taxpayer or S corporation are deductible only to the extent of the gross income from the hobby. Thus, the tax treatment of hobby expenses substantially differs from profit-seeking expenses if the expenses of the activity exceed the income, resulting in a net loss. If the loss is treated as arising from a profit-motivated activity, then the taxpayer ordinarily may use it to reduce income from other sources.[58] Conversely, if the activity is considered a hobby, no loss is deductible. Note, however, that hobby expenses may be deducted to offset any hobby income.

Profit Motive

The problem of determining the existence of a profit motive usually arises in situations where the activity has elements of both a personal and a profit-seeking nature (e.g., auto racing, antique hunting, coin collecting, horse breeding, weekend farming). In some instances, these activities may represent a profitable business venture. Where losses are consistently reported, however, the business motivation is suspect. In these cases all the facts and circumstances must be examined to determine the presence of the profit motive. The courts have held that the taxpayer simply is required to pursue the activity with a bona fide intent of making a profit. The taxpayer, however, need not show a profit. Moreover, the taxpayer's expectation of profit need not be considered reasonable.[59] The Regulations set out nine factors to be used in ascertaining the existence of a profit motive.[60] Some of the questions posed by these factors are:

1. Was the activity carried on in a businesslike manner? Were books and records kept? Did the taxpayer change his or her methods or adopt new techniques with the intent to earn a profit?

2. Did the taxpayer attempt to acquire knowledge about the business or consult experts?

---

[58] The limitations imposed on losses from passive activities should not be applicable in this situation since the taxpayer materially participates in the activity. See discussion in Chapter 12 and § 469.

[59] Reg. § 1.183-2(a).

[60] Reg. § 1.183-2(b).

3. Did the taxpayer or family members devote much time or effort to the activity? Did they leave another occupation to have more time for the activity?

4. Have there been years of income as well as years of loss? Did the losses occur only in the start-up years?

5. Does the taxpayer have only incidental income from other sources? Is the taxpayer's wealth insufficient to maintain him or her if future profits are not derived?

6. Does the taxpayer derive little personal or recreational pleasure from the activity?

An affirmative answer to several of these questions suggests a profit motive exists.

Presumptive Rule

The burden of proof in the courts is normally borne by the taxpayer. Section 183, however, shifts the burden of proof to the IRS in hobby cases where the taxpayer shows profits in any three of five consecutive years (two of seven years for activities related to horses).[61] The rule creates a presumption that the taxpayer has a profit motive unless the IRS can show otherwise. An election is available to the taxpayer to postpone IRS challenges until five (or seven) years have elapsed from the date the activity commenced. Making the election allows the taxpayer sufficient time to have three profitable years and thus shift the burden of proof to the IRS. This election must be filed within three years of the due date of the return for the taxable year in which the taxpayer first engages in the activity, but not later than 60 days after the taxpayer has received notice that the IRS proposes to disallow the deduction of expenses related to the hobby. The election automatically extends the statute of limitations for each of these years, thus enabling a later challenge by the IRS. It should be emphasized that this presumptive rule only shifts the burden of proof. Profits in three of the five (or two of seven) years do not absolve the taxpayer from attack.

Example 27

T enjoys raising, breeding, and showing dogs. In the past, she occasionally sold a dog or puppy. In 2016 T decided to pursue these activities seriously. During the year, she incurred a loss of $4,000. T also had a loss of $2,000 in 2017. If T made no election for any of these years (i.e., within three years of the start of the activity), the IRS may assert that T's activities constitute a hobby. In this case, the burden of proof is on T to show a profit motive, since she has not shown a profit in at least three years. If T made an election, then the IRS is barred from assessing a deficiency until five years have elapsed. Five years need to elapse to determine whether T will have profits in three of the five years and, if so, shift the burden of proof to the IRS in any litigation that may occur. If an election is made, however, the period for assessing deficiencies for all years is extended until two years after the due date of the return for the last taxable year in the five-year period.[62] In T's case, an election would enable the IRS to assess a deficiency for 2016 and subsequent years up until April 15, 2023, assuming T is a calendar year taxpayer. If an election were not made, the statute of limitations would normally bar assessments three years after the return is due (e.g., assessments for 2016 would be barred after April 15, 2020).

Deduction Limitation

If the activity is considered a hobby, the related expenses are deductible to the extent of the activity's gross income as reduced by *otherwise allowable deductions*.[63] Otherwise allowable deductions are those expenses relating to the hobby that are deductible under other sections of the Code regardless of the activity in which they are incurred. For example, property taxes are deductible under § 164 without regard to whether the activity in which they are incurred is a hobby or a business. Similarly, interest on debt secured

---

[61] § 183(d).

[62] § 183(d)(4).

[63] § 183(b). On classification of the deductions, see Rev. Rul. 75-14, 1975-1 C.B. 90 and Senate Finance Committee Report on H.R. 3838, S. Rep. No. 99-313 (5/29/86), p. 80, 99th Cong., 2nd. Sess.

by the taxpayer's principal or secondary residence is deductible regardless of the character of the activity. Consequently, any expense otherwise allowable is deducted *first* in determining the gross income limitation. Any other expenses are deductible to the extent of any remaining gross income (i.e., other operating expenses are taken next, with any depreciation deductions, taken last). Otherwise allowable deductions are fully deductible as itemized deductions, while other deductible expenses are considered miscellaneous itemized deductions and are deductible only to the extent they exceed 2% of AGI (including the hobby income).

Example 28

R, an actor, enjoys raising, breeding, and racing horses as a hobby. His AGI excluding the hobby activities is $68,000. He has a small farm on which he raises the horses. During the current year, R won one race and received income of $2,000. He paid $2,300 in expenses as follows: $800 property taxes related to the farm and $1,500 feed for horses. R calculated depreciation with respect to the farm assets at $6,500. As a result, R has a net loss from the activity of $6,800 ($2,000 − $2,300 − $6,500). If the activity is *not* considered a hobby but rather a trade or business, R would report the loss on Schedule C and assuming it is not a passive loss, he could use it to offset his other income. However, if the activity is considered a hobby and R itemizes deductions, he would compute his deductions as follows:

Gross income		$2,000
Otherwise allowable deductions:		
Taxes	(800)	$ 800
Gross income limitation	$1,200	
Feed expense:		
$1,500 limited to remaining gross income		1,200
Total		$2,000

Note that because depreciation is taken last, there is no deduction for this item.

R would include $2,000 in gross income, increasing his AGI to $70,000. Of the $2,000 in deductible expenses, the property taxes of $800 are deductible in full as an itemized deduction. The remaining $1,200 is considered a miscellaneous itemized deduction. In this case, none of the $1,200 is deductible since this amount does not exceed the 2% floor of $1,400 (2% of $70,000). No deduction is allowed for the remaining feed expense of $300 ($1,500 − $1,200) due to the gross income limitation.

Example 29

Assume the same facts as in *Example 28* except that R's expense for property taxes is $2,400 instead of $800. In this case, because the entire $2,400 is deductible as an otherwise allowable deduction and exceeds the gross income from the hobby, none of the feed expense is deductible. Thus, R would include $2,000 in gross income and the $2,400 of property taxes would be fully deductible from AGI.

PERSONAL LIVING EXPENSES

Just as the Code specifically authorizes deductions for the costs of pursuing income—business and income-producing expenses—it denies deductions for personal expenses. Section 262 prohibits the deduction of any personal, living, or family expenses. Only those personal expenditures expressly allowed by some other provision in the Code are deductible.

Some of the personal expenditures permitted by other provisions are medical expenses, contributions, qualified residence interest, and taxes. Normally, these expenses are classified as itemized deductions. These deductions and their underlying rationale are discussed in Chapter 11.

The disallowance of personal expenditures by § 262 complements the general criteria allowing a deduction. Recall that the general rules of §§ 162 and 212 permit deductions for ordinary and necessary expenses *only where a profit motive exists*. As previously seen in the discussion of hobbies, however, determining whether an expense arose from a personal or profit motive can be difficult. Some of the items specifically disallowed by § 262 follow:

1. Expenses of maintaining a household (e.g., rent, utilities).
2. Losses on sales of property held for personal purposes.
3. Amounts paid as damages for breach of promise to marry, attorney's fees, and other costs of suits to recover such damages.
4. Premiums paid for life insurance by the insured.
5. Costs of insuring a personal residence.

Legal Expenses

Legal expenses related to divorce actions and the division of income-producing properties are often a source of conflict. Prior to clarification by the Supreme Court, several decisions held that divorce expenses incurred primarily to protect the taxpayer's income-producing property or his or her business were deductible.[64] The Supreme Court, however, has ruled that deductibility depends on whether the expense arises in connection with the taxpayer's profit-seeking activities. That is, the *origin* of the expense determines deductibility.[65] Under this rule, if the spouse's claim arises from the marital relationship—a personal matter—then no deduction is allowed. Division of income-producing property would only be incidental to or a consequence of the marital relationship.

Example 30

R pays legal fees to defend an action by his wife to prevent distributions of income from a trust to him. Because the wife's action arose from the marital relationship, the legal expenses are nondeductible personal expenditures.[66]

Legal expenses related to a divorce action may be deductible where the expense is for advice concerning the tax consequences of the divorce.[67] The portion of the legal expense allocable to counsel on the tax consequences of a property settlement, the right to claim children as dependents, and the creation of a trust for payment of alimony are deductible.

Contingent Attorney Fees

Over the years, there has been a great deal of controversy regarding the treatment of contingent attorney fees incurred in securing a damages award. To illustrate, assume a taxpayer receives an award of fully taxable punitive damages of $10 million and the attorney is to receive a contingent fee of 40% of that amount or $4 million. In this situation, the taxpayer typically asserted that the fees represent a splitting of the income and, therefore, he or she should be taxed only on the net amount received or $6 million. Conversely, the government argued that the full $10 million is included in gross income and the $4 million of attorney fees were a miscellaneous itemized deduction subject to the two percent limitation and the three percent cutback. But more importantly, since the attorney fees were classified as miscellaneous itemized deductions, they were not allowed in computing the alternative minimum tax (AMT). As a result, an AMT often resulted. In effect, the taxpayer paid tax on $10 million when he or she had only received $6 million.

---

[64] *F.C. Bowers v. Comm.*, 57-1 USTC ¶9605, 51 AFTR 207, 243 F.2d 904 (CA-6, 1957).

[65] *Supra*, Footnote 13, Also, compare *Comm. v. Tellier*, 66-1 USTC ¶9319, 17 AFTR2d 633, 383 U.S. 687 (USSC, 1966) with *Boris Nodiak v. Comm.*, 66-1 USTC ¶9262, 17 AFTR2d 396, 356 F.2d 911 (CA-2, 1966).

[66] *H.N. Shilling, Jr.*, 33 TCM 1097, T.C. Memo 1974-246.

[67] Rev Rul. 72-545, 1972-2 C.B. 179.

Congress addressed this problem in 2004. Attorney's fees and court costs incurred for certain legal actions are deductible for AGI. This rule applies to most legal actions, but not necessarily all.[68] Apparently, certain types of tort actions, such as defamation, would not fall within the statute unless they occur within the employment context. By classifying these expenses as deductions for AGI, the AMT problem is eliminated since the AMT limitations generally apply only to certain itemized deductions.

CAPITAL EXPENDITURES

A capital expenditure is ordinarily defined as an expenditure providing benefits that extend beyond the close of the taxable year. It is a well-established rule in case law that a business expense, though ordinary and necessary, is not deductible in the year paid or incurred if it can be considered a capital expenditure.[69] Normally, however, a capital expenditure may be deducted ratably over the period for which it provides benefits. For example, the Code authorizes deductions for depreciation or cost recovery, amortization, and depletion where the asset has a determinable useful life.[70] Capital expenditures creating assets that do not have a determinable life, however, generally cannot be deducted. For example, land is considered as having an indeterminable life and thus cannot be depreciated or amortized. The same is true for stocks and bonds. Expenditures for these types of assets are recovered (i.e., deducted) only when there is a disposition of the asset through sale (e.g., cost offset against sales price), exchange, abandonment, or other disposition.

As a general rule, assets with a useful life of one year or less need not be capitalized. For example, the taxpayer can write off short-lived assets with small costs such as supplies (e.g., stationery, pens, pencils, calculators), books (e.g., the Internal Revenue Code), and small tools (e.g., screwdrivers, rakes, and shovels).

Goodwill

Like land, goodwill is an example of an asset that does not have a determinable useful life. Because of this indeterminate life, for many years acquired goodwill was treated as a capitalized asset that could not be depreciated. The only way a taxpayer could receive a current tax benefit from acquired goodwill was to identify components separate and apart from goodwill that had an ascertainable value and limited useful life (e.g., client files and subscription lists). If a taxpayer was successful in establishing the requisite valuation and limited life for a goodwill component, the taxpayer could depreciate the cost of the intangible asset over its useful life using the straight-line method (known as amortization). However, in practice, taxpayers often faced challenges by the IRS, and many attempts to depreciate goodwill components were unsuccessful.

Congress enacted Code § 197 to reduce the uncertainty surrounding the depreciation of goodwill and its identifiable components. Effective August 10, 1994, the cost of acquiring intangible assets (including acquired goodwill) may, at the election of the taxpayer, be amortized over a 15-year period. If the election is not made, the cost of acquiring goodwill and related intangibles must be capitalized and no amortization will be allowed.

Example 31

B has decided to purchase a newspaper business in a small town for $100,000. It can be determined that $80,000 of the purchase price is allocable to the assets of the business and $20,000 is attributable to goodwill (subscription lists and other intangibles). B may be able to recover all $100,000 of the cost through deductions for depreciation and amortization.

---

[68] See § 62(a)(20).

[69] *Supra,* Footnote 18.

[70] §§ 167, 168, 169, 178, 184, 188, and 611 are examples.

Capital Expenditures versus Repairs

The general rule of case law disallowing deductions for capital expenditures has been codified for expenditures relating to property. Code § 263 provides that deductions are not allowed for any expenditures for new buildings or for permanent improvements or betterments made to increase the value of property.[71] Additionally, expenditures substantially prolonging the property's useful life, adapting the property to a new or different use, or materially adding to the value of the property are not deductible.[72] Conversely, the cost of incidental repairs that do not materially increase the value of the property nor appreciably prolong its life, but maintain it in a normal operating state, may be deducted in the current year.[73] For example, costs of painting, inside and outside, and papering are usually considered repairs.[74] However, if the painting is done in conjunction with a general reconditioning or overhaul of the property, it is treated as a capital expenditure.[75]

Example 32

L operates his own limousine business. Expenses for a tune-up such as the costs of spark plugs, points, and labor would be deductible as routine repairs and maintenance since such costs do not significantly prolong the car's life. In contrast, if L had the transmission replaced at a cost of $1,800, allowing him to drive it for another few years, the expense must be capitalized.

Over the years, there has been substantial controversy concerning what constitutes a capital expenditure. Hoping to resolve the issue, the government released final regulations in 2013. As might be imagined, the rules are voluminous and quite complex. For this reason, they are not discussed in this text.[76]

Acquisition Costs

As a general rule, costs related to the acquisition of property must be capitalized. For example, freight paid to acquire new equipment or commissions paid to acquire land must be capitalized. In addition, Code § 164 requires that state and local general sales taxes related to the purchase of property be capitalized. The costs of demolition or removal of an old building prior to using the land in another fashion must be capitalized as part of the cost of the land.[77] Costs of defending or perfecting the title to property, such as legal fees, are normally capitalized.[78] Similarly, legal fees incurred for the recovery of property must be capitalized unless the recovered property is investment property or money that must be included in income if received.[79] Taxpayers must also capitalize costs for work performed before the property is placed in service (e.g., refinish floors, patch holes, repair steps, paint the interior and exterior).[80]

INDOPCO and the Long-Term Benefit Theory

Interestingly, one of the most important and widely debated tax developments to occur in recent years concerns the capital expenditure area. The controversy stems from a Supreme Court decision involving the treatment of costs incurred by a target company as part of a friendly takeover. In 1977, Unilever approached one of its suppliers, INDOPCO, about the possibility of a takeover to which INDOPCO agreed. During the acquisition process, INDOPCO paid an investment banking company, Morgan Stanley, about $2.2 million for advice and a fairness opinion and another $500,000 to its own legal counsel for services related to the takeover. The IRS ultimately denied deduction of the expenses (as well as amortization) on the grounds that the expenses were capital in nature. In 1992, the Supreme

---

[71] § 263(a).

[72] Reg. § 1.263(a)-1(b).

[73] Reg. § 1.162-4.

[74] *Louis Allen,* 2 BTA 1313 (1925).

[75] *Joseph M. Jones,* 57-1 USTC ¶9517, 50 AFTR 2040, 242 F.2d 616 (CA-5, 1957).

[76] See Reg. § 1.162-3 (materials and supplies); Reg. § 1.162-4 (repairs and maintenance); Reg. § 1.263(a)-1 (capital expenditures).

[77] § 280B.

[78] Reg. § 1.263(a)-2.

[79] Reg. § 1.212-1(k).

[80] Reg. § 1.263(a)-2(d)(1) and (2) Ex. 10.

Court concurred with the IRS, believing that INDOPCO would receive long-term benefits from the acquisition, including the opportunity for synergy with Unilever and the future availability of Unilever's financial and business resources.[81]

The effect of the INDOPCO decision would not be so great if it were confined to costs incurred as part of a friendly takeover. However, the IRS has used the broad language of the court to capitalize any expense to which it can associate any long-term benefit. In this regard, it is important to understand that the Supreme Court indicated that the long-term benefits need not be associated with any specific identifiable asset. As long as the expenditure leads to the permanent betterment of the business as a whole, capitalization may be in order. For example, the IRS has used this approach to deny a deduction for the costs of removing asbestos insulation from equipment if the removal is part of a general plan of rehabilitation, despite the fact that the expense did not extend the life of the asset.[82] Instead, the taxpayer was required to capitalize the expenditure on the grounds that the firm would derive long-term benefits from safer working conditions and reduced risk of liability. In short, the INDOPCO decision has increased the tension between taxpayers and the IRS in the capital expenditure arena.

Over time, the intensity of the controversy and the level of uncertainty produced by INDOPCO escalated to an intolerable level. In response to the criticism, the IRS issued final regulations in 2004 to reign in the scope of INDOPCO and its "long-term-benefit" theory.[83] Like the capitalization regulations for expenditures related to tangible property, these regulations for intangibles are extensive. There are over 50 pages and more than 80 examples all aimed at resolving whether a particular cost related to an intangible should be capitalized. Although a full discussion of these regulations is beyond the scope of this text, they are required reading whenever a taxpayer incurs an expense related to an intangible. Specifically, the regulations address amounts paid to

- *Acquire* an intangible (e.g., purchase a customer list, lease, patent, copyright, franchise, trademark, trade name, assembled workforce, or goodwill; most of these must be amortized over 15 years under § 197).

- *Create* an intangible (e.g., costs for prepaid items such as prepaid rents and insurance, membership privileges such as membership in a trade association, rights from governmental agencies such as the exclusive rights obtained from the local government by a cable television company to serve a particular region, contract rights and contract terminations such as the rights to renew or renegotiate, licenses, and covenants not to compete).

- *Create* or enhance a separate and distinct intangible.

- *Facilitate* the acquisition or creation of an intangible (e.g., legal expenses for negotiating commercial property lease, drafting agreements).

- *Facilitate* the acquisition of a trade or business, a change in the capital structure of a business entity, and certain other transactions (e.g., legal expenses to issue debt, payments to investment banker and outside legal counsel for evaluating alternative investments, performing due diligence, structuring the transaction, preparing SEC filings, and obtaining necessary regulatory approvals, hostile takeover defenses).

These regulations should bring to a close a period of great uncertainty that was not envisioned when the Supreme Court decided the INDOPCO case in 1992.

Environmental Remediation Costs

Under Code § 198 which took effect on August 5, 1997, a taxpayer may elect to treat certain environmental remediation expenditures that would otherwise be chargeable to a capital account as deductible in the year paid or incurred. To qualify for this special treatment, the expense must be incurred in connection with the abatement or control of hazardous

[81] *INDOPCO, Inc. v. Comm.*, 92-1 USTC ¶50,113, 69 AFTR2d 92-694, 503 U.S. 79 (USSC, 1992).

[82] *Norwest Corporation*, 108 T.C. No. 15 (1997).

[83] Reg. § 1.263(a)-4 and -5.

substances at a qualified contaminated site. As noted above, prior to the enactment of this provision, the IRS took the view that costs incurred to clean-up the environment were controlled by the long-term benefit theory of INDOPCO and were capital expenditures for which no deduction was allowed. The effect of § 198, then, is to override the IRS's reliance on the long-term benefit theory to deny deductions with respect to environmental remediation costs.

Elections to Capitalize or Deduct

Various provisions of the Code permit a taxpayer to treat capital expenditures as deductible expenses, as deferred expenses, or as capital expenditures. For example, at the election of the taxpayer, expenses for research and experimentation may be deducted currently, treated as deferred expenses and amortized over at least 60 months, or capitalized and included in the basis of the resulting property.[84]

BUSINESS INVESTIGATION EXPENSES AND START-UP COSTS

Another group of expenses that arguably may be considered capital expenditures are those incurred when seeking and establishing a new business, such as costs of investigation and start-up. Business investigation expenses are those costs of seeking and reviewing prospective businesses prior to reaching a decision to acquire or enter any business. Such expenses include the costs of analysis of potential markets, products, labor supply, and transportation facilities. Start-up or pre-opening expenses are costs that are incurred after a decision to acquire a particular business and prior to its actual operations. Examples of these expenses are advertising, employee training, lining up distributors, suppliers, or potential customers, and the costs of professional services such as attorney and accounting fees.

For many years, the deductibility of expenses of business investigation and start-up turned solely on whether the taxpayer was "carrying on" a business at the time the expenditures were incurred. Notwithstanding some modifications, the basic rule still remains: when the taxpayer is in the same or similar business as the one he or she is starting or investigating, the costs of investigation and start-up are wholly deductible in the year paid or incurred.[85] The deduction is allowed regardless of whether the taxpayer undertakes the business.[86] However, this rule often forces taxpayers to litigate to determine whether a business exists at the time the expenses are incurred. Prior to the enactment of § 195, if the taxpayer could not establish existence of a business, the expenditures normally were treated as capital expenditures with indeterminable lives.[87] As a result, the taxpayer could only recover the expenditure if and when he or she disposed of or abandoned the business.

In 1980 Congress realized that the basic rule not only was a source of controversy but also discouraged formation of new businesses. For this reason, special provisions permitting deduction of these expenses under certain conditions were enacted.[88] Before examining these provisions, it should be emphasized that the traditional rule continues to be valid. Thus, if a taxpayer can establish that the investigation and start-up costs are related to a similar existing business of the taxpayer, a deduction is allowed.

Example 33

S owns and operates an ice cream shop on the north side of the city. A new shopping mall is opening on the south side of the city, and the developers have approached her about locating a second ice cream shop in their mall. During 2017 S pays a consulting firm $1,000 for a survey of the potential market on the south side. Because S is in the ice cream business when the expense is incurred, the entire $1,000 is deductible regardless of whether she undertakes the new business.

---

[84] § 174. See §§ 175 and 180 for other examples.

[85] *The Colorado Springs National Bank v. U.S.,* 74-2 USTC ¶9809, 34 AFTR2d 74-6166, 505 F.2d 1185 (CA-10, 1974).

[86] *York v. Comm.,* 58-2 USTC ¶9952, 2 AFTR2d 6178, 261 F.2d 421 (CA-4, 1958).

[87] *Morton Frank,* 20 T.C. 511 (1953).

[88] § 195(a).

Amortization Provision

Section 195 sets out the treatment for the start-up and investigation expenses of taxpayers who are *not* considered in a similar business when the expenses are incurred *and* who actually enter the new business. Eligible taxpayers may elect to deduct up to $5,000 of business investigation and start-up expenses in the tax year in which the business begins. If the § 195 expenses exceed $5,000, the excess must be amortized over the 180-month period (15 years) beginning with the month in which the business begins.[89] If the expenses exceed $50,000, the $5,000 allowance is reduced one dollar for each dollar in excess of $50,000. Expenses for research and development, interest payments, and taxes are not considered start-up expenditures.[90] Thus, these costs are not subject to § 195 and may be deducted under normal rules.

Example 34

J, a calendar year, cash basis taxpayer, recently graduated and received $10,000 from his uncle as a graduation gift. J paid an accountant $1,200 in June to review the financial situation of a small restaurant he desired to purchase. In December, J purchased the restaurant and began actively participating in its management. J may deduct the entire $1,200 for the current year since it does not exceed $5,000.

Example 35

S, a famous bodybuilder, has decided to build his first health spa. While the facility is being constructed, a temporary office is set up in a trailer next to the site. The office is nicely decorated and contains a small replica of the facility. S hired a staff who will manage the facility but at this time are calling prospective customers. Elaborate brochures have been printed. All of these costs, including the salaries paid to the staff, the printing of the brochures, and the costs of operating the trailer such as depreciation and utilities, are start-up costs. Assuming the total start-up costs were less than $50,000, the taxpayer could expense the first $5,000 and amortize the balance over 180 months.

Example 36

Same facts as above except S incorporated and the corporation incurred $23,000 of start-up and investigation expenses. The corporation was formed in July of this year and adopted the calendar year. In this case, the corporation could deduct $5,000 immediately and amortize the remaining balance of $18,000 over 15 years (180 months) beginning in July. This would result in amortization of $100/month for 180 months. The deduction for start-up and investigation expenses for 2017 would be $5,600 computed as follows:

First-year allowance	$5,000
Amortization ($18,000/180 = $100/month × 6 months)	600
Total deduction in first year	$5,600

In 2018, the corporation would continue to amortize the remaining expenses, resulting in a deduction of $1,200 ($100/month × 12).

---

[89] § 195 expenses incurred prior to October 23, 2004 are amortized over 60 months.

[90] § 195(c)(1).

Example 37

In March, 2017 LMN, LLC was formed and incurred start-up and investigation expenses of $52,000. LMN's immediate expensing allowance of $5,000 must be reduced one dollar for each dollar of § 195 expense exceeding $50,000. In this case, the allowance is reduced by $2,000 ($52,000 – $50,000) to $3,000. Thus LMN may deduct $3,000 plus amortization of the remaining $49,000, resulting in a deduction of $5,720 computed below.

First-year allowance ($5,000 – [$52,000 – $50,000 = $2,000])		$3,000
Amortization:		
Total expense.	$52,000	
First-year allowance.	(3,000)	
Amortizable balance	$49,000	
Amortization ($49,000/180 = $272/month × 10 months).		2,720
Total § 195 expense deduction in first year		$5,720

Note that if LMN had incurred $55,000 or more of § 195 expenses, the $5,000 immediate write-off would be reduced to zero and all $55,000 of the expenses would be amortized over 180 months.

As suggested above, the taxpayer must enter the business to qualify for amortization. Whether the individual is considered as having entered the business normally depends on the facts in each case.

If the taxpayer (who is not in a similar, existing business) does not enter into the new business, the investigation and start-up expenses generally are not deductible. The Tax Court, however, has held that a taxpayer may deduct costs as a loss suffered from a transaction entered into for profit if the activities are sufficient to be considered a "transaction."[91] The IRS has interpreted this rule to mean that those expenditures related to a *general search* for a particular business or investment are not deductible.[92] Expenses are considered general when they are related to whether to enter the transaction and which transaction to enter. Once the taxpayer has focused on the acquisition of a *specific* business or investment, expenses related to an unsuccessful acquisition attempt are deductible as a loss on a transaction entered into for profit.

Example 38

L, a retired army officer, is interested in going into the radio business. He places advertisements in the major trade journals soliciting information about businesses that may be acquired. Upon reviewing the responses to his ads, L selects two radio stations for possible acquisition. He hires an accountant to audit the books of each station and advise him on the feasibility of purchase. He travels to the cities where each station is located and discusses the possible acquisition with the owners. Finally, L decides to purchase station FMAM. To this end, he hires an attorney to draft the purchase agreement. Due to a price dispute, however, the acquisition attempt collapses. The expenses for advertising, auditing, and travel are not deductible since they are related to the taxpayer's general search. The legal expenses are deductible as a loss, however, since they occurred in the taxpayer's attempt to acquire a specific business.

---

[91] *Harris W. Seed,* 52 T.C. 880 (1969).   [92] Rev. Rul. 77-254, 1977-2 C.B. 63.

Job-Seeking Expenses

The tax treatment of job-seeking expenses of an employee is similar to that for expenses for business investigation. If the taxpayer is seeking a job in the same business in which he or she is presently employed, the related expenses are deductible as miscellaneous itemized deductions subject to the 2% floor.[93] The deduction is allowed even if a new job is not obtained. No deduction or amortization is permitted, however, if the job sought is considered a new trade or business or the taxpayer's first job.

Example 39

B, currently employed as a biology teacher, incurs travel expenses and employment agency fees to obtain a new job as a computer operator. The expenses are not deductible because they are not incurred in seeking a job in the profession in which she was currently engaged. Moreover, the expenses are not deductible even though B obtained the new job. However, the expenses would be deductible if she had obtained a new job in her present occupation.

PUBLIC POLICY RESTRICTIONS

Although an expense may be entirely appropriate and helpful, and may contribute to the taxpayer's profit-seeking activities, it is not considered necessary if the allowance of a deduction would frustrate sharply defined public policy. The courts established this long-standing rule on the theory that to allow a deduction for expenses such as fines and penalties would encourage violations by diluting the penalty.[94] Historically, however, the IRS and the courts were free to restrict deductions of any type of expense where, in their view, it appeared that the expenses were contrary to public policy—even if the policy had not been clearly enunciated by some governmental body. As a result, taxpayers were often forced to go to court to determine if their expense violated public policy.

Recognizing the difficulties in applying the public policy doctrine, Congress enacted provisions specifically designed to limit its use.[95] The rules identified and disallowed certain types of expenditures that would be considered contrary to public policy. Under these provisions no deduction is allowed for fines, penalties, and illegal payments.

Fines and Penalties

A deduction is not allowed for any fine or similar penalty paid to a government for the violation of any law.[96]

Example 40

S is a salesperson for an office supply company. While calling on customers this year, he received parking tickets of $100. None of the cost is deductible because the violations were against the law.

Example 41

Upon audit of T's tax return, it was determined that he failed to report $10,000 of tip income from his job as a maitre d', resulting in additional tax of $3,000. T was also required to pay the negligence penalty for intentional disregard of the rules. The penalty—20% of the tax due—is not deductible.

---

[93] Rev. Rul. 75-120, 1975-1 C.B. 55, as clarified by Rev. Rul. 77-16, 1977-1 C.B. 37.

[94] *Hoover Motor Express Co., Inc. v. U.S.*, 58-1 USTC ¶9367, 1 AFTR2d 1157, 356 U.S. 38 (USSC, 1958).

[95] S. Rep. No. 91-552, 91st Cong., 1st Sess. 273-75 (1969). Note, however, that the Tax Court continues to utilize the doctrine despite Congress's attempt to restrict its use—see *R. Mazzei,* 61 T.C. 497 (1974).

[96] § 162(f).

Example 42

This year the Federal Drug Administration fined C Inc., a drug manufacturing company, $5,000,000 for failure to maintain adequate quality control. The fine is not deductible because the practices were in violation of Federal law.

Fines include those amounts paid in settlement of the taxpayer's actual or potential liability.[97] In addition, no deduction is allowed for two-thirds of treble damage payments made due to a violation of antitrust laws.[98] Thus, one-third of this antitrust "fine" is deductible.

Illegal Kickbacks, Bribes, and Other Payments

The Code also disallows the deduction for four categories of illegal payments:[99]

1. Kickbacks or bribes to U.S. government officials and employees if illegal.

2. Payments to governmental officials or employees of *foreign* countries if such payments would be considered illegal under the U.S. Foreign Corrupt Practices Act.

Example 43

R travels all over the world, looking for unique items for his gift shop. Occasionally when going through customs in foreign countries, he is forced to "bribe" the customs official to do the necessary paperwork and get him through customs as quickly as possible. These so-called grease payments to employees of foreign countries are deductible unless they violate the Foreign Corrupt Practices Act. In general, such payments are not considered to be illegal.

---

3. Kickbacks, bribes, or other illegal payments to any other person if illegal under generally enforced U.S. or state laws that provide a criminal penalty or loss of license or privilege to engage in business.

4. Kickbacks, rebates, and bribes, although legal, made by any provider of items or services under Medicare and Medicaid programs.

Those kickbacks and bribes not specified above would still be deductible if they were ordinary and necessary. The payment, however, may not be necessary and thus will be disallowed if it controverts public policy.

Kickbacks generally include payments for referral of clients, patients, and customers. However, under certain circumstances, trade discounts or rebates may be considered kickbacks.

Example 44

M, a life insurance salesperson, paid rebates or discounts to purchasers of policies. Since such practice is normally illegal under state law, the rebate is not deductible.[100]

---

[97] § 162(g).

[98] Reg. § 1.162-21(b).

[99] § 162(c).

[100] *James Alex*, 70 T.C. 322 (1978).

Expenses of Illegal Business

The expenses related to an illegal business are deductible.[101] Similar to the principle governing taxation of income from whatever source (including income illegally obtained), the tax law is not concerned with the lawfulness of the activity in which the deductions arise. No deduction is allowed, however, if the expense itself constitutes an illegal payment as discussed above. In addition, Code § 280E prohibits the deduction of any expenses related to the trafficking in controlled substances (i.e., drugs).

LOBBYING AND POLITICAL CONTRIBUTIONS

Although expenses for lobbying and political contributions may be closely related to the taxpayer's business, Congress has traditionally limited their deduction. These restrictions usually are supported on the grounds that it is not in the public's best interest for government to subsidize efforts to influence legislative matters.

Lobbying

Prior to 1962, no deduction was permitted for any type of lobbying expense. In 1962, however, Congress altered its position slightly with the addition of § 162(e), which carved out a narrow exception for certain lobbying expenses. This provision allowed a deduction for the expenses of appearing before or providing information to governmental units on legislative matters of *direct interest* to the taxpayer's business. Similarly, a deduction was permitted for expenses of providing information to a trade organization of which the taxpayer was a member where the legislative matter was of direct interest to the taxpayer and the organization. The portion of dues paid to such an organization attributable to the organization's allowable lobbying activities was also deductible. Beginning in 1994, however, these rules for deducting lobbying expenses are even more restrictive. Lobbying expenditures are now deductible only if incurred for the purpose of influencing legislation at the *local* level. Therefore, the expense of influencing national and state legislation (including the costs of hiring lobbyists to represent the taxpayer in these matters) is not deductible. This prohibition is extended to the costs of any direct communication with executive branch officials in an attempt to influence official actions or positions of such official.

The taxpayer must have a direct interest in the local legislation before lobbying expenses may be deducted. Although the definitional boundaries of the term "direct" are vague, a taxpayer is considered as having satisfied the test if it is reasonable to expect that the local legislative matter affects or will affect the taxpayer's business. However, a taxpayer does not have a direct interest in the nomination, appointment, or operation of any local legislative body.[102]

The deduction for lobbying *does not* extend to expenses incurred to influence the general public on legislative matters, elections, or referendums.[103] Expenses related to the following types of lobbying are not deductible:

1. Advertising in magazines and newspapers concerning legislation of direct interest to the taxpayer.[104] However, expenses for "goodwill" advertising presenting views on economic, financial, social, or similar subjects of a general nature, or encouraging behavior such as contributing to the Red Cross, are deductible.[105]

2. Preparing and distributing to a corporation's shareholders pamphlets focusing on certain legislation affecting the corporation and urging the shareholders to contact their representatives in Congress.[106]

---

[101] See *Max Cohen v. Comm.*, 49-2 USTC ¶9358, 176 F.2d 394 (CA-10, 1949) and *Neil Sullivan v. Comm.*, 58-1 USTC ¶9368, AFTR2d 1158, 356 U.S. 27 (USSC, 1958).

[102] Reg. § 1.162-20(b).

[103] § 162(e)(2).

[104] Rev. Rul. 78-112, 1978-1 C.B. 42.

[105] Reg. § 1.162-20(a)(2).

[106] Rev. Rul. 74-407, 1974-2 C.B. 45, as amplified by Rev. Rul. 78-111, 1978-1 C.B. 41.

Example 45

T owns a restaurant in Austin, Texas. Legislation has been introduced by the City Council to impose a sales tax on food and drink sold in Austin, to be used for funding a dome stadium. T places an ad in the local newspaper stating reasons why the legislation should not be passed. He goes to the City Council and testifies on the proposed legislation before several committees. He pays dues to the Austin Association of Restaurant Owners organization, which estimates that 60% of its activities are devoted to lobbying for local legislation related to restaurant owners. T may deduct the cost of travel and 60% of his dues since the local legislation is of direct interest to him. He may not deduct the ad since it is intended to influence the general public.

Political Contributions

No deduction is permitted for any contributions, gifts, or any other amounts paid to a political party, action committee, or group or candidate related to a candidate's campaign.[107] This rule also applies to indirect payments, such as the payments for advertising in a convention program and admission to a dinner, hall, or similar affair where any of the proceeds benefit a political party or candidate.[108]

EXPENSES AND INTEREST RELATING TO TAX-EXEMPT INCOME

Section 265 sets forth several rules generally disallowing deductions for expenses relating to tax-exempt income. These provisions prohibit taxpayers from taking advantage of the tax law to secure a double tax benefit: tax-exempt income and deductions for the expenses that help to produce it. The best known rule prohibits the deduction for any *interest* expense or nonbusiness (§ 212) expense related to tax-exempt *interest* income.[109] Without this rule, taxpayers in high tax brackets could borrow at a higher rate of interest than could be earned and still have a profit on the transaction.

Example 46

D, an investor in the 25% tax bracket with substantial investment income, borrows funds at 9% and invests them in tax-exempt bonds yielding 7 percent. If the interest expense were deductible, the after-tax cost of borrowing would be 6.75% ([100% − 25% = 75%] × 9%). Since the interest income is nontaxable, the after-tax yield on the bond remains 7 percent, or 0.25 percentage points higher than the effective cost of borrowing. Section 265, however, denies the deduction for the interest expense, thus eliminating the feasibility of this arrangement. It should be noted, however, that business (§ 162) expenses (other than interest) related to tax-exempt interest income may be deductible.

If the income that is exempt is not interest, none of the related expenses are deductible.[110]

Example 47

A company operating a baseball team paid premiums on a disability insurance policy providing that the company would receive proceeds under the policy if a player were injured. Because the proceeds would not be taxable, the premiums are not deductible even though the expenditure would apparently qualify as a business expense.[111] Note, however, that such expenses would enter into the calculation of net income for financial accounting purposes.

---

[107] § 162(e).

[108] § 276.

[109] § 265(2).

[110] § 265(l).

[111] Rev. Rul. 66-262, 1966-2 C.B. 105.

As a practical matter, it would appear difficult to determine whether borrowed funds (and the interest expense) are related to carrying taxable or tax-exempt securities. For example, an individual holding tax-exempt bonds may take out a mortgage to buy a residence instead of selling the bonds to finance the purchase price. In such case, it could be inferred that the borrowed funds were used to finance the bond purchase. Generally, the IRS will allow the deduction in this and similar cases unless the facts indicate that the primary purpose of the borrowing is to carry the tax-exempt obligations.[112] The facts must establish a *sufficiently direct relationship* between the borrowing and the investment producing tax exempt income before a deduction is denied.

Example 48

K owns common stock with a basis of $70,000 and tax-exempt bonds of $30,000. She borrows $100,000 to finance an investment in an oil and gas limited partnership. The IRS will disallow a deduction for a portion of the interest on the $100,000 debt because it is presumed that the $100,000 is incurred to finance all of K's portfolio including the tax-exempt securities.[113]

Example 49

R has a margin account with her broker. This account is devoted solely to the purchase of taxable investments and tax-exempt bonds. During the year, she buys several taxable and tax-exempt securities on margin. A portion of the interest expense on this margin account is disallowed because the borrowings are considered partially related to financing of the investment in tax-exempt securities.[114]

Business Life Insurance

Absent a special rule, premiums paid on insurance policies covering officers and employees of a business might be deductible as ordinary and necessary business expenses. However, to ensure that the taxpayer is not allowed to deduct expenses related to tax-exempt income (i.e., life insurance proceeds), a special provision exists. Under § 264, the taxpayer is not allowed any deduction for life insurance premiums paid on policies covering the life of any officer, employee, or any other person who may have a financial interest in the taxpayer's trade or business, if the taxpayer is the *beneficiary* of the policy. Thus, premiums paid by a business on a key-person life insurance policy where the company is beneficiary are not deductible. Note that this differs from the financial accounting treatment, where the premiums would be considered routine operating costs that should be expensed in determining net income. In contrast, payments made by a business on group-term life insurance policies where the employees are beneficiaries are deductible.

RELATED TAXPAYER TRANSACTIONS

Without restrictions, related taxpayers (such as husbands and wives, shareholders and their corporations) could enter into arrangements creating deductions for expenses and losses, and not affect their economic position. For example, a husband and wife could create a deduction simply by having one spouse sell property to the other at a loss. In this case, the loss is artificial because the property remains within the family and their financial situation is unaffected. Although the form of ownership has been altered, there is no substance to the transaction. To guard against the potential abuses inherent in transactions between related taxpayers, Congress designed specific safeguards contained in § 267.

---

[112] Rev. Proc. 72-18, 1972-1 C.B. 740, as clarified by Rev. Proc. 74-8, 1974-1 C.B. 419, and amplified by Rev. Rul. 80-55, 1980-2 C.B. 849.

[113] *Ibid.*

[114] *B.P. McDonough v. Comm.*, 78-2 USTC ¶9490, 42 AFTR2d 78-5172, 577 F.2d 234 (CA-4, 1978).

Related Taxpayers

The transactions that are subject to restriction are only those between persons who are considered "related" as defined in the Code. Related taxpayers are:[115]

1. Certain family members: brothers and sisters (including half-blood), spouse, ancestors (i.e., parents and grandparents), and lineal descendants (i.e., children and grandchildren).

2. Taxpayer and his or her corporation: an individual and a corporation if the individual owns either directly or *indirectly* more than 50% of the corporation's stock.[116]

3. Personal service corporation and an employee-owner: a corporation whose principal activity is the performance of personal services that are performed by the employee-owners (i.e., an employee who owns either directly or indirectly *any* stock of the corporation).

4. Certain other relationships involving regular corporations, S corporations, partnerships, estates, trusts, and individuals.

In determining whether a taxpayer and a corporation are related, the taxpayer's direct and indirect ownership must be taken into account for the 50% test. A taxpayer's indirect stock ownership is any stock that is considered owned or "constructively" owned but not actually owned by the taxpayer. Section 267 provides a set of constructive ownership rules, also referred to as *attribution rules,* indicating the circumstances when the taxpayer is considered as owning the stock of another. Under the constructive ownership rules, a taxpayer is considered owning indirectly:[117]

1. Stock owned directly or indirectly by his or her family as defined above.

2. His or her proportionate share of any stock owned by a corporation, partnership, estate, or trust in which he or she has ownership (or of which he or she is a beneficiary in the case of an estate or trust).

3. Stock owned indirectly or directly by his or her partner in a partnership.

In using these rules, the following limitations apply: (1) stock attributed from one family member to another *cannot* be reattributed to members of his or her family, and (2) stock attributed from a partner to the taxpayer *cannot* be reattributed to a member of his or her family or to another partner.[118]

Example 50

H and W are husband and wife. HB is H's brother. H, W, and HB own 30, 45, and 25% of X Corporation, respectively. H is considered as owning 100% of X Corporation, 30% directly and 70% indirectly (25% through HB and 45% through W, both by application of attribution rule 1 above). W is considered as owning 75% of X Corporation, 45% directly and 30% indirectly through H by application of attribution rule 1 (note that HB's stock cannot be attributed to H and reattributed to W). HB is considered as owning 55% of X Corporation, 25% directly and 30% indirectly through H by application of attribution rule 1 and the reattribution limitation.

---

[115] § 267(b).

[116] A partner and a partnership in which the partner owns more than a 50% interest are treated in the same manner. See § 707(b).

[117] § 267(c).

[118] § 267(c)(5).

Losses

The taxpayer is not allowed to deduct the loss from a sale or exchange of property directly or indirectly to a related taxpayer (as defined above).[119] However, any loss disallowed on the sale may be used to offset any gain on a subsequent sale of the property by a related taxpayer to an unrelated third party.[120]

Example 51

A father owns land that he purchased as an investment for $20,000. He sells the land to his daughter for $15,000, producing a $5,000 loss. The $5,000 loss may not be deducted because the transaction is between related taxpayers. If the daughter subsequently sells the property for $22,000, she will then realize a $7,000 gain ($22,000 sales price − $15,000 basis). However, the gain may be reduced by the $5,000 loss previously disallowed, resulting in a recognized gain of $2,000 ($7,000 realized gain − $5,000 previously disallowed loss). If the daughter had sold the property for only $19,000, the realized gain of $4,000 ($19,000 − $15,000) would have been eliminated by the previous loss of $5,000. The $5,000 loss previously disallowed is used only to the extent of the $4,000 gain. The remaining portion of the disallowed loss ($1,000) cannot be used. Had the father originally sold the property for $19,000 to an outsider as his daughter subsequently did, the father would have recognized a $1,000 loss ($19,000 sales price − $20,000 basis). Note that the effect of the disallowance rule does not increase the basis of the property to the related taxpayer by the amount of loss disallowed.

The results of these transactions are summarized below.

Original sale between related parties:

Sales price	$ 15,000
Adjusted basis	(20,000)
Disallowed loss	$ (5,000)

Subsequent sale:

	1	2
Sales price	$ 22,000	$19,000
Adjusted basis	(15,000)	(15,000)
Realized gain (loss)	$ 7,000	$ 4,000
Usage of disallowed loss	(5,000)	(4,000)
Recognized gain	$ 2,000	$ 0

Example 52

S owns 100% of V Corporation. She sells stock with a basis of $100 to her good friend T for $75, creating a $25 loss for S. T, in turn, sells the stock to V Corporation for $75, thus recouping the amount he paid S with no gain or loss. The $25 loss suffered by S, however, is not deductible because the sale was made *indirectly* through T to her wholly owned corporation.

Unpaid Expenses and Interest

Prior to enactment of § 267, another tax avoidance device used by related taxpayers involved the use of different accounting methods by each taxpayer. In the typical scheme, a taxpayer's corporation would adopt the accrual basis method of accounting while the taxpayer reported on a cash basis. The taxpayer could lend money, lease property, provide services, etc. to the corporation and charge the corporation for whatever was provided. As an accrual basis taxpayer, the corporation would accrue the expense and create a deduction. The cash basis

---

[119] § 267(a)(1).   [120] § 267(d).

individual, however, would report no income until the corporation's payment of the expense was actually received. As a result, the corporation could accrue large deductions without ever having to make a disbursement and, moreover, without the taxpayer recognizing any offsetting income. The Code now prohibits this practice between "related taxpayers" as defined above. Code § 267 provides that an accrual basis taxpayer can deduct an accrued expense payable to a related cash basis taxpayer *only* in the period in which the payment is included in the recipient's income.[121] This rule effectively places all accrual basis taxpayers on the cash method of accounting for purposes of deducting such expenses.

Example 53

B, an individual, owns 100% of X Corporation, which manufactures electric razors. B uses the cash method of accounting while the corporation uses the accrual basis. Both are calendar year taxpayers. On December 27, 2017 the corporation accrues a $10,000 bonus for B. However, due to insufficient cash flow, X Corporation was not able to pay the bonus until January 10, 2018. The corporation may not deduct the accrued bonus in 2017. Rather, it must deduct the bonus in 2018, the year in which B includes the payment in his income.

Example 54

Assume the same facts as above, except that B owns only a 20% interest in X. In addition, X is a large law firm in which B is employed. The results are the same as above because B and X are still related parties: a personal service corporation and an employee-owner.

PAYMENT OF ANOTHER TAXPAYER'S OBLIGATION

As a general rule, a taxpayer is not permitted to deduct the payment of a deductible expense of another taxpayer. A deduction is allowed only for those expenditures satisfying the taxpayer's obligation or arising from such an obligation.

Example 55

As part of Q's rental contract for his personal apartment, he pays 1% of his landlord's property taxes. No deduction is allowed because the property taxes are the obligation of the landlord.

Example 56

P is majority stockholder of R Corporation. During the year, the corporation had financial difficulty and was unable to make an interest payment on an outstanding debt. To protect the goodwill of the corporation, P paid the interest. The payment is not deductible, and P will be treated as having made a contribution to the capital of the corporation for interest paid.

---

[121] § 267(a)(2).

An exception to the general rule is provided with respect to payment of medical expenses of a dependent. To qualify as a dependent for this purpose, the person needs only to meet the relationship, support, and citizen tests.[122] If the taxpayer pays the medical expenses of a person who qualifies as a dependent under the modified tests, the expenses are treated as if they were the taxpayer's expenses and are deductible subject to limitations applicable to the taxpayer.

SUBSTANTIATION

The Code requires that taxpayers maintain records sufficient to establish the amount of gross income, deductions, credits, or other matters required to be shown on the tax return.[123] As a practical matter, record keeping requirements depend on the nature of the item. With respect to most deductions, taxpayers may rely on the "*Cohan* rule."[124] In *Cohan*, George M. Cohan, the famous playwright, spent substantial sums for travel and entertainment. The Board of Tax Appeals (predecessor to the Tax Court) denied any deduction for the expenses because the taxpayer had no records supporting the items. On appeal, however, the Second Circuit Court of Appeals reversed this decision, indicating that "absolute certainty in such matters is usually impossible and is not necessary."[125] Thus, the Appeals Court remanded the case to make some allowance for the expenditures. From this decision, the "*Cohan* rule" developed, providing that a reasonable estimation of the deduction is sufficient where the actual amount is not substantiated. In 1962, however, Congress eliminated the use of the *Cohan* rule for travel and entertainment expenses and established rigorous substantiation requirements for these types of deductions. Substantiation for other expenses, however, is still governed by the *Cohan* rule. Despite the existence of the *Cohan* rule, records should be kept documenting deductible expenditures since estimates of the expenditures may be substantially less than actually paid or incurred.

Tax Planning Considerations

MAXIMIZING DEDUCTIONS

LO.8
Explain tax planning considerations for optimizing deductions.

Perhaps the most important step in minimizing the tax liability is maximizing deductions. Maximizing deductions obviously requires the taxpayer to identify and claim all the deductions to which he or she is entitled. Many taxpayers, however, often overlook deductions that they are allowed because they fail to grasp and apply the fundamental rules discussed in this chapter. To secure a deduction, the taxpayer needs only to show that the expense paid or incurred during the year is ordinary, necessary, and related to a profit-seeking activity. Notwithstanding the special rules of limitation that apply to certain deductions, most deductions are allowed because the *taxpayer* is able to recognize and establish the link between the expenditure and the profit-seeking activity. The taxpayer is in the best position to recognize that an expenditure relates to his or her trade or business, not the tax practitioner. Practitioners typically lack sufficient insight into the taxpayer's activities to identify potential deductions. Thus, it is up to the taxpayer to recognize and establish the relationship between an expenditure and the profit-seeking activity. Failure to do so results in the taxpayer's paying a tax liability higher than what he or she is required to pay.

The taxpayer should maximize not only the absolute dollar amount of deductions, but also the value of the deduction. A deduction's value is equal to the product of the amount of the deduction and the taxpayer's marginal tax rate. Because the taxpayer's marginal rate fluctuates over time, the value of a deduction varies depending on the period in which the deduction is claimed. When feasible, deductions should normally be accelerated or deferred to years when the taxpayer is in a higher tax bracket. In timing deductions, however, the time value of money also must be considered. For example, in periods of inflation, the deferral of a deduction to a high-bracket year may not always be advantageous, since a deduction in the future is not worth as much as one currently.

[122] § 213(a)(1).
[123] Reg. § 1.6001-1(a).
[124] *Cohan v. Comm.,* 2 USTC ¶489, 8 AFTR 10552, 39 F.2d 540 (CA-2, 1930).
[125] *Ibid.*

An individual taxpayer's timing of itemized deductions is particularly important in light of the standard deduction and the floor on miscellaneous itemized deductions. Many taxpayers lose deductions because their deductions do not exceed the standard deduction in any one year. These deductions need not be lost, however, if the taxpayer alternates the years in which he or she itemizes or uses the standard deduction. For example, in those years where the taxpayer itemizes, all tax deductible expenditures from the prior year should be deferred while expenditures of the following year should be accelerated. By so doing, the taxpayer bunches itemized deductions in the current year to exceed the standard deduction. In the following year, the taxpayer would use the standard deduction. Itemized deductions are considered in detail in Chapter 11.

Maximizing deductions also requires shifting of deductions to the taxpayer who would derive the greatest benefit. For example, if two sisters are co-obligors on a note, good tax planning dictates that the sister in the higher tax bracket pay the deductible interest expense. In this case, either sister may pay and claim a deduction.

TIMING OF DEDUCTIONS

In the previous section, the importance of maximizing the absolute amount of deductions was emphasized. However, because of the time value of money it is equally important to consider the timing of deductions.

Example 57

R, who pays Federal, state, and local taxes equal to 50% of his income, makes a cash expenditure of $10,000. If the $10,000 is deductible immediately, R will realize a tax benefit of $5,000 ($10,000 × 50%). Moreover, because the tax savings were realized immediately, the present value of the benefit is not diminished. On the other hand, if R is not able to deduct the $10,000 for another five years, the benefit of the deduction is substantially reduced. Specifically, assuming the annual interest rate is 10 percent, the present value of the $5,000 tax savings decreases to $3,105 ($5,000 × [1 ÷ (1 + 0.10)5]), a decrease of almost 38 percent.

As the above example illustrates, accelerating a deduction from the future to the present can substantially increase its value. Awareness of the provisions permitting acceleration of deductions allows taxpayers to arrange their affairs so as to reap the greatest rewards. For example, a taxpayer may choose an investment that the tax law allows him or her to deduct immediately rather than an investment that must be capitalized and deducted through depreciation over the asset's life.

EXPENSES RELATING TO TAX-EXEMPT INCOME

Although expenses related to tax-exempt income are not deductible, expenses related to tax-deferred income are deductible.[126] For example, income earned on contributions to Individual Retirement Accounts is not taxable until the earnings are distributed (usually at retirement). If the taxpayer borrows amounts to contribute to his or her Individual Retirement Account, interest paid on the borrowed amounts may be deductible (if the general rules for deductibility are met) because the income to which it relates is only tax-deferred, not tax-exempt.

"POINTS" ON MORTGAGES

"Points" paid to secure a mortgage to acquire or improve a principal residence normally are deductible in the year paid or incurred. In some cases, however, the points are not paid out of independent funds of the taxpayer but are withheld from the mortgage proceeds. For example, where a lender is charging two points on a $50,000 loan, or $1,000 (2% of $50,000),

[126] *Hawaiian Trust Co., Ltd. v. U.S.,* 61-1 USTC ¶9481, 7 AFTR2d 1553, 291 F.2d 761 (CA-9, 1961). See also Letter Rul. 8527082 (April 2, 1985).

the $1,000 is withheld by the lender as payment while the remaining $49,000 ($50,000 − $1,000) is advanced to the borrower. The Tax Court has ruled that in these situations, the taxpayer has not prepaid the interest (as represented by the points) and thus must amortize the points over the term of the loan.[127] To avoid this result and obtain a current deduction, the taxpayer should pay the points out of separate funds rather than having them withheld by the lender. This requirement will be met if the cash paid by the borrower up to and at the closing (including down payments, escrow deposits, earnest money, and amounts paid at closing) is at least equal to the amount deducted for points.[128] In this regard, the IRS has ruled that points paid by the seller on behalf of a borrower will be treated as paid directly from the funds deposited by the borrower.[129] Thus, the borrower will be entitled to a deduction. However, in determining the basis of the residence, the borrower must subtract the amount of seller paid points from the purchase price.

HOBBIES

Several studies suggest that the factor on which the hobby/business issue often turns is the manner in which the taxpayer carries on the activity.[130] For business treatment, it is imperative that the taxpayer have complete and detailed financial and nonfinancial records. Moreover, such records should be used in decision making and in constructing a profit plan. The activity should resemble a business in every respect. For example, the taxpayer should maintain a separate checking account for the activity, advertise where appropriate, obtain written advice from experts and follow it, and acquire some expertise about the operation.

Although the taxpayer is not required to actually show profits, profits in *three* of *five* consecutive years create a substantial advantage for the taxpayer. Where the profit requirement is satisfied, it is presumed that the activity is not a hobby and the IRS has the burden of proving otherwise. For this reason, the cash basis taxpayer might take steps that could convert a loss year into a profitable year. For example, in some situations it may be possible to accelerate receipts and defer payment of expenses. However, the taxpayer should be cautioned that arranging transactions so nominal profits occur has been viewed negatively by the courts.

Problem Materials

DISCUSSION QUESTIONS

7-1 *General Requirements for Deductions.* Explain the general requirements that must be satisfied before a taxpayer may claim a deduction for an expense or a loss.

7-2 *Deduction Defined.* Consider the following:
   a. It is often said that income can be meaningfully defined while deductions can be defined only procedurally. Explain.
   b. The courts are fond of referring to deductions as matters of "legislative grace." Explain.
   c. Although deductions may only be defined procedurally, construct a definition for a deduction similar to the "all inclusive" definition for income.
   d. Will satisfaction of the requirements of your definition ensure deductibility? Explain.

7-3 *Business versus Personal Expenditures.* Consider the following:
   a. If the taxpayer derives personal pleasure from an otherwise deductible expense, will the expense be denied? Explain.
   b. Name some of the purely personal expenses that are deductible, and indicate whether they are deductions for or from AGI.

7-4 *Business versus Investment Expenses.* Two Code sections govern the deductibility of ordinary and necessary expenses related to profit-motivated activities. Explain why two provisions exist and the distinction between them.

---

[127] *Roger A. Schubel,* 77 T.C. 701 (1982).

[128] Rev. Proc. 92-12, 1992-3, I.R.B. 27.

[129] Rev. Proc. 94-27, 1994 I.R.B. 15, 6.

[130] See, for example, Burns and Groomer, "Effects of Section 183 on the Business Hobby Controversy," *Taxes* (March 1980) pp. 195–206.

7-5 *An Employee's Business.* Is an employee considered as being in trade or business? Explain the significance of your answer.

7-6 *Year Allowable.* The year in which a deduction is allowed depends on whether the taxpayer is a cash basis or accrual basis taxpayer. Discuss.

7-7 *Classification of Expenses.* F is a self-employed registered nurse and works occasionally for a nursing home. G is a registered nurse employed by a nursing home. Their income, exemptions, credits, etc. are identical. Explain why a deductible expense, although paid in the same amount by both, may cause F and G to have differing tax liabilities.

7-8 *Above- and Below-the-Line Deductions.* At a tax seminar, F was reminded to ensure that he properly classified his deductions as either above- or below-the-line. After the seminar, F came home and scrutinized his Form 1040 to determine what the instructor meant and why it was important. Despite his careful examination of the form, F could not figure out what the instructor was talking about or why it was important. Help F out by explaining the meaning of this classification scheme.

7-9 *Performing Artists.* V hopes to become a movie star someday. Currently, she accepts bit parts in various movies, waiting for her break. What special tax treatment may be available for V?

7-10 *Classification of Deductions.* J and K are both single, and each earns $30,000 of income and has $2,000 of deductible expenses for the current year. J's deductions are for AGI while K's deductions are itemized deductions.
   a. Given these facts, and assuming that the situation of J and K is identical in every other respect, will their tax liabilities differ? Explain.
   b. Same as (a) except their deductions are $7,000.

7-11 *Constructive Distributions.* D owns all of the stock of DX Inc., which manufactures record jackets. Over the years, the corporation has been very successful. This year, D placed his 16- and 14-year-old sons on the payroll, paying them each $10,000 annually. The boys worked on the assembly line a couple of hours each week. Explain D's strategy and the risks it involves.

7-12 *Disguised Distributions.* E owns all of the stock of EZ Inc., which operates a nursery. During the past several years, the company has operated at a deficit and E finally sold all of his stock to C. C drew a very low salary before he could turn things around. Now the business is highly profitable, and C is paying himself handsomely. As C's tax adviser, what counsel if any should be given to C?

7-13 *Income and Expenses of Illegal Business.* B is a bookie in a state where gambling is illegal. During the year, he earned $70,000 accepting bets. His expenses included those for rent, phone, and utilities. In addition, he paid off a state legislator who was a customer and who obviously knew of his activity.
   a. Discuss the tax treatment of B's income and expenses.
   b. Same as (a) except B was a drug dealer.

7-14 *Permanent and Timing Differences.* Financial accounting and tax accounting often differ in the manner in that certain expenses are treated. Identify several expenditures that, because of their treatment, produce permanent or timing differences.

7-15 *Capital Expenditures.* Can a cash basis taxpayer successfully reduce taxable income by purchasing supplies near year-end and deducting their cost?

7-16 *Independent Contractor versus Employee.* Briefly discuss the difference between an independent contractor (self-employed person) and an employee and why the distinction is important.

7-17 *Hobby Expenses.* Discuss the factors used in determining whether an activity is a hobby and the tax consequences resulting from its being deemed a hobby.

7-18 *Public Policy Doctrine.* A taxpayer operates a restaurant and failed to remit the sales tax for August to the city as of the required date. As a result, he must pay an additional assessment of 0.25% of the amount due. Comment on the deductibility of this payment.

7-19 *Constructive Ownership Rules.* Explain the concept of constructive ownership and the reason for its existence.

7-20 *Expenses Relating to Tax-Exempt Income.* Discuss what types of expenses relating to tax exempt income may be deductible.

7-21 *Substantiation.* Explain the Cohan rule.

PROBLEMS

7-22 *General Requirements for Deduction.* For each of the following expenses identify and discuss the general requirement(s) (ordinary, necessary, related to business, etc.) upon which deductibility depends.

   a.   A police officer who is required to carry a gun at all times lives in New York. The most convenient and direct route to work is through New Jersey. The laws of New Jersey, however, prohibit the carrying of a gun in the car. As a result, he must take an indirect route to the police station to avoid New Jersey. The indirect route causes him to drive ten miles more than he would otherwise. The cost of the additional mileage is $500. (**Note:** Commuting expense from one's home to the first job site generally is a nondeductible personal expense.)

   b.   The current president of a nationwide union spends $10,000 for costs related to reelection.

   c.   The taxpayer operates a lumber business. He is extremely religious and consequently is deeply concerned over the business community's social and moral responsibility to society. For this reason, he hires a minister to give him and his employees moral and spiritual advice. The minister has no business background although he does offer solutions to business problems.

   d.   The taxpayer operates a laundry in New York City. He was recently visited by two "insurance agents" who wished to sell him a special bomb policy (i.e., if the taxpayer paid the insurance "premiums," his business would not be bombed). The taxpayer paid the premiums of $500 each month.

7-23 *Accrual Basis Deductions.* In each of the situations below assume the taxpayer uses the accrual method of accounting and indicate the amount of the deduction allowed.

   a.   R sells and services gas furnaces. As part of his sales package, he agrees to turn on and cut off the buyer's furnace for five years. He normally charges $80 for such service, which costs him about $50 in labor and materials. Based on 2017 sales, R sets up a reserve for the costs of the services to be performed, which he estimates will be $9,000 over the next five years.

   b.   At the end of 2017, XYZ, a regular corporation, agreed to rent office space from ABC Leasing Corp. Pursuant to the contract, XYZ paid $10,000 on December 1, 2017 for rent for all of 2018.

   c.   RST Villas, a condominium project in a Vermont ski resort, reached an agreement with MPP Pop-Ins providing that MPP would provide maid services in 2018 for $20,000. RST transferred its note payable for $20,000 at the end of 2018 to MPP on December 1, 2017.

7-24 *Economic Performance.* KKO Printing, a calendar year, accrual method taxpayer, leases a number of copying machines. As part of the lease, it typically purchases a one-year maintenance contract covering service on the machines. On July 20, 2017, KKO paid $6,000 for a one-year service contract that runs from July 1, 2017 through June 30, 2018. Ignoring the recurring item exception, when may KKO deduct the expense?

7-25 *Recurring Items.* M Corporation is an accrual basis taxpayer and uses the calendar year for both financial accounting and tax purposes. The corporation manufactures car stereo equipment and provides a one-year warranty. Based on an analysis of its sales for 2017, it estimates that its warranty expense for equipment sold in 2017 will be $500,000. For financial accounting purposes, M plans to accrue the expense in 2017. The corporation is in the process of finishing its 2017 tax return, which it plans on filing by the extended due date, September 15, 2018. According to the company's latest figures, as of August 31, it had incurred $200,000 in parts and labor costs in honoring warranties on 2017 sales. How should the corporation treat the $500,000 estimated warranty cost on its 2017 tax return?

7-26 *Accrual of Real Property Taxes.* M Inc. owns a chain of hamburger restaurants located all across the country. In one state where the company has several outlets, it paid real property taxes of $12,000 for the period October 1, 2016 through September 30, 2017 on January 10, 2018. M is an accrual basis taxpayer and uses a calendar year-end for reporting.

   a. When is M entitled to a deduction for the real estate taxes assuming it has not made an election under § 461(c) and the recurring item exception does not apply?

   b. Same as (a) except the M makes an election under § 461(c).

7-27 *Accrual versus Cash Method of Accounting.* D operates a hardware store. For 2017, D's first year of operation, D reported the following items of revenue and expense:

Cash receipts	$140,000
Purchase of goods on credit	90,000
Payments on payables	82,000

By year-end, D had unsold goods on hand with a value of $25,000.

   a. Using the cash method of accounting, compute D's taxable income for the year.

   b. Using the accrual method of accounting, compute D's taxable income for the year.

   c. Which method of accounting is required for tax purposes? Why?

7-28 *Prepaid Interest.* In each of the following cases, indicate the amount of the deduction for the current year. In each case, assume the taxpayer is a calendar year, cash basis taxpayer.

   a. On December 31, P, wishing to reduce his current year's tax liability, prepaid $3,000 of interest on his home mortgage for the first three months of the following taxable year.

   b. On December 1 of this year, T obtained a $100,000 loan to purchase her residence. The loan was secured by the residence. She paid two points to obtain the loan bearing a 6% interest rate.

   c. Same as (b) except the loan was used to purchase a duplex, which she will rent to others. The loan was secured by the duplex.

7-29 *Prepaid Rent.* This year F, a cash basis taxpayer, secured a ten-year lease on a warehouse to be used in his business. Under the lease agreement he pays $12,000 on September 1 of each year for the following twelve months' rental.

   a. Assuming F pays $12,000 on September 1 for the next 12 months' rental, how much, if any, may he deduct? How would your answer change if F were an accrual basis taxpayer?

   b. In order to secure the lease, F also was required to pay an additional $12,000 as a security deposit. How much, if any, may he deduct?

7-30 *Prepaid Expenses.* D, a cash basis taxpayer, operates a successful travel agency. One of her more significant costs is a special computer form on which airline tickets are printed as well as stationery on which itineraries are printed. Typically, D buys about a three-month supply of these forms for $2,000. Knowing that she will be in a lower tax bracket next year. D would like to accelerate her deductions to the current year.

   a. Assuming that D pays $12,000 on December 15 for forms that she expects to exhaust before the close of next year, how much can she deduct?

   b. Same as above except D purchases the larger volume of forms because D's supplier began offering special discounts for purchases in excess of $3,000.

7-31 *Expenses Producing Future Benefits.* B took over as chief executive officer of Pentar Inc., which specializes in the manufacture of cameras. As part of his strategy to increase the corporation's share of the market, he ran a special advertising blitz just prior to Christmas that cost more than $1,000,000. The marketing staff estimates that these expenditures could very well increase the company's share of the market by 10% over the next three years. Speculate on the treatment of the promotion expenses.

7-32 *Capital Expenditure or Repair.* This year, Dandy Development Corporation purchased an apartment complex with 100 units. At the time of purchase, it had a 40% vacancy rate. As part of a major renovation, Dandy replaced all of the carpeting and painted all of the vacant units. Discuss the treatment of the expenditures.

7-33 *Identifying Capital Expenditures.* K, a sole proprietor, made the following payments during the year. Indicate whether each is a capital expenditure.
   a. Sales tax on the purchase of a new automobile.
   b. Mechanical pencil for K.
   c. Mops and buckets for maintenance of building.
   d. Freight paid on delivery of new machinery.
   e. Painting of K's office.
   f. Paving of dirt parking lot with concrete.
   g. Commissions to leasing agent to find new office space.
   h. Rewiring of building to accommodate new equipment.

7-34 *Hobby Expenses—Effect on AGI.* C is a successful attorney and stock car racing enthusiast. This year she decided to quit watching the races and start participating. She purchased a car and entered several local races. During the year, she had the following receipts and disbursements related to the racing activities:

Race winnings	$3,000
Property taxes	2,800
Fuel, supplies, maintenance	1,000

Her AGI exclusive of any items related to the racing activities is $100,000.
   a. Indicate the tax consequences assuming the activity is not considered to be a hobby.
   b. Assuming the activity is treated as a hobby, what are the tax consequences?
   c. Assuming the activity is deemed a hobby and property taxes are $4,000, what are the tax consequences?
   d. What is the critical factor in determining whether an activity is a hobby or a business?
   e. What circumstances suggest the activity is a business rather than a hobby?

7-35 *Hobby-Presumptive Rule.* In 2016 R, a major league baseball player, purchased a small farm in North Carolina. He grows several crops and maintains a small herd of cattle on the farm. During 2016 his farming activities resulted in a $2,000 loss, which he claimed on his 2016 tax return, filed April 15, 2017. In 2017 his 2016 return was audited, and the IRS proposed an adjustment disallowing the loss from the farming activity, asserting that the activity was merely a hobby.
   a. Assuming R litigates, who has the burden of proof as to the character of the activity?
   b. Can R shift the burden of proof at this point in time?
   c. Assume R filed the appropriate election for 2016 and reported losses of $3,000 in 2017 and profits of $14,000 in 2018, $5,000 in 2019, and $6,000 in 2020. What effect do the reported profits have?

7-36 *Hobby Losses and Statute of Limitations.* Assume the same facts as in *Problem 7-35*. When does the statute of limitations bar assessment of deficiencies with respect to the 2016 tax return?

7-37 *Investigation Expenses.* H currently operates several optical shops in Portland. This year he traveled to Seattle and Tacoma to discuss with several doctors the possibility of locating optical shops adjacent to their practices. He paid travel costs to Seattle of $175 and to Tacoma of $200. The physicians in Seattle agreed to an arrangement and H incurred $500 in legal fees drawing up the agreement. The physicians in Tacoma did not agree, and H did not pursue the matter further.

   In the following year, H decided to enter the ice cream business. He sent letters of inquiry to two major franchisers of ice cream stores and subsequently traveled to the headquarters of each. He paid $400 for travel to Phoenix for discussions with P Corporation and $500 for travel to Santa Fe for discussions with S Corporation. He also paid an accountant $2,400 to evaluate the financial aspects of P and $3,000 for S. H decided to acquire a franchise from S Corporation. He paid an attorney $800 to review the franchising agreement.

a. Discuss the tax treatment of H's expenses associated with the attempt to expand his optical shop business.

b. Discuss the tax treatment of the expenses incurred in connection with the ice cream business, assuming H acquires the Y franchise and begins business.

c. Same as (b). Discuss the treatment of these costs if H abandons the transaction after being informed that there is no franchise available in his city.

7-38 *Investigation Expenses.* P incurred significant expenses to investigate the possibility of opening a Dowell's Hamburgers franchise in Tokyo, Japan. Her expenditures included hiring a local firm to perform a feasibility study, travel, and accounting and legal expenses. Her 2017 expenditures total $25,000. With respect to this amount:

a. Assuming this was P's first attempt at opening a business of her own, how much may she deduct in 2017 if she decides not to acquire the franchise?

b. Assuming this was P's first attempt at opening a business of her own, how much may she deduct in 2017 if she decides to acquire the franchise?

c. Assuming P was already in the fast-food business (she owns a Dowell's franchise in Toledo, Ohio), how much may she deduct in 2017 to acquire the franchise?

7-39 *Capital Expenditures.* Consider the following:

a. A corporate taxpayer reimbursed employees for amounts they had loaned to the corporation's former president, who was losing money at the racetrack. Comment on the deductibility of these payments as well as those expenditures discussed in *Example 7* of this chapter (relating to payments of debts previously discharged by bankruptcy) in light of the rules concerning capital expenditures.

b. How are expenditures such as land and investment securities recovered?

c. How are the costs of expenditures for goodwill recovered?

d. Distinguish between a capital expenditure and a repair.

7-40 *Classification of Deductions.* M works as the captain of a boat. His income for the year is $20,000. During the year, he purchased a special uniform for $100. Indicate the amount of the deduction and whether it is for or from AGI for the following situations:

a. M's boat is a 50-foot yacht, and he operates his business as a sole proprietorship (i.e., he is self-employed).

b. M is an employee for Yachts of Fun Inc.

c. M is an employee for Yachts, which reimbursed him $70 of the cost (included in his income on Form W-2).

7-41 *Computing Employee's Deductions.* T is employed as a supervisor in the tax department of a public accounting firm in Manhattan. She took the job after working on the tax staff at a commercial tax preparation firm. She lives in a condominium on the upper east side. Every day she takes the subway to and from work. She loves living in New York. T's total income for the year consisted of compensation of $80,000 and alimony of $2,100. This year she incurred the following expenses:

AICPA dues	$ 400
New York State Society of CPAs dues	315
State of New York CPA license	345
Subscriptions to tax journals	225
Continuing education course on new tax law	600
New business suits	700
Cleaning of suits	389
Legal fee for preparation of will ($230 related to tax planning)	1,500
Legal fee to collect alimony	250
Job hunting expenses (resumes and employment agency fee)	150
Subway expenses	456
Safe deposit box (holds investment documents)	90
Annual fee on brokerage account	130
Qualified residence interest	8,100
Real estate taxes	3,700

T's employer reimbursed her $100 for the AICPA dues (included in her income).

a. Compute T's taxable income.

b. Assuming T expects her expenses to be about the same for the next several years, what advice can you offer?

7-42 *Computing Employee's Deductions.* Z, single, is employed as a nurse at a local hospital. Z's records reflect the following items of income and expense for 2017:

Gross wages	$20,000
Expenses:	
Employee travel expenses, not reimbursed	1,100
Cost of commuting to and from work,	
reimbursed (included in gross wages)	520
Charitable contributions	700
Interest and taxes on personal residence	3,900
Nurse's uniform, reimbursed (included in gross wages)	250

a What is Z's AGI?
b. What is Z's total of itemized deductions?

7-43 *Interest.* Mr. E operates a replacement window business as LLC. He uses the cash method of accounting. On November 1, 2017 he secured a loan in order to purchase a new warehouse to be used in his business. Information regarding the loan and purchase of the warehouse is shown below. All of the costs indicated were paid during the year.

Term	20 years
Loan origination fee	$ 2,000
Points	6,000
One year's interest paid in advance	20,000
Legal fees for recording mortgage lien	500

What amount may E deduct in 2017?

7-44 *Insurance.* Hawk Harris owns and operates the Waterfield Mudhens, a franchise in an indoor soccer league. Both Hawk and the corporation are cash basis, calendar year taxpayers. During 2017 the corporation purchased the following policies:

Policy Description	Cost	Date Paid
Two-year fire and theft effective 12/1/2017	$2,400	12/15/2017
One-year life insurance policy on Jose Greatfoot, star forward; the corporation is beneficiary; effective 11/1/2017	1,000	11/1/2017
One-year group-term life insurance policy covering entire team and staff; effective 1/1/2018	9,000	11/15/2017
One-year policy for payments of overhead costs should the team strike and attendance fall; effective 11/1/2017	3,600	9/1/2017

In addition to the policies purchased above, the corporation is unable to get insurance on certain business risks. Therefore, the corporation has set up a reserve—a separate account—to which it contributes $5,000 on February 1 of each year. How much may the corporation deduct for 2017?

7-45 *Life Insurance.* The Great Cookie Corporation is owned equally by F and G. Under the articles of incorporation, the corporation is required to purchase the stock of each shareholder upon his or her death to ensure that it does not pass to some undesirable third party. To finance the purchase, the corporation purchased a life insurance policy on both F and G, naming the corporation as beneficiary. The annual premium is $5,000. Can the corporation deduct the premiums?

7-46 *Business Life Insurance.* L, 56, has operated her sole proprietorship successfully since its inception three years ago. This year she has decided to expand. To this end, she borrowed $100,000 from the bank, which would be used for financing expansion of the business. The bank required L to take out a life insurance policy on her own life that would serve as security for the business loan. Are the premiums deductible?

7-47 *Public Policy—Fines, Lobbying, etc.* M is engaged in the construction business in Tucson. Indicate whether the following expenses are deductible.
   a. The Occupational Safety and Health Act (OSHA) requires contractors to fence around certain construction sites. M determined that the fences would cost $1,000 and the fine for not fencing would be only $650. As a result, he did not construct the fences and paid a fine of $650.
   b. M often uses Mexican quarry tile on the floors of homes that he builds. To obtain the tiles, he drives his truck across the border to a small entrepreneur's house and purchases the materials. On the return trip he often pays a Mexican customs official to "expedite" his going through customs. Without the payment, the inspection process would often be tedious and consume several hours. This year he paid the customs officials $200.
   c. M paid $100 for an advertisement supporting the administration's economic policies, which he felt would reduce interest rates and thus make homes more affordable. In addition, he paid $700 for travel to Washington, D.C. to testify before a Congressional Committee on the effects of high interest rates on the housing industry. While there, he paid $100 to a political action committee to attend a dinner, the proceeds from which went to Senator Q.

7-48 *Limitations on Business Deductions.* This is an extension of *Problem 7-22(d).* In that problem, you are asked to determine if the case contains expenditures that are ordinary, necessary, and reasonable under the provisions of Code § 162. Assume the positive criteria of § 162 are met (i.e., the expenditures are ordinary, necessary, and reasonable). Are there any additional provisions in § 162 that will cause the expenditures to be disallowed?

7-49 *Related Taxpayers—Sale.* E sold stock to her son for $8,000. She purchased the stock several years ago for $11,000.
   a. What amount of loss will E report on the sale?
   b. What amount of gain or loss will the son report if he sells the stock for $12,000 to an unrelated party?
   c. If the son sells for $10,000?
   d. If the son sells for $4,000?

7-50 *Related Taxpayers—Different Accounting Methods.* G, a cash basis, calendar year taxpayer, owns 100% of XYZ Corporation. XYZ is a calendar year, accrual basis taxpayer engaged in the advertising business. G leases a building to the Corporation for $1,000 per month. In December, XYZ accrues the $1,000 rental due. Indicate the tax treatment to XYZ and G assuming the payment is
   a. Made on December 30 of the current year; or
   b. Made on April 1 of the following year.
   c. Would your answers above change if G owned 30% of XYZ?

7-51 *Constructive Ownership Rules.* How much of RST Corporation's stock is B considered as owning?

Owner	Shares Directly Owned
B.	20
C, B's brother	30
D, B's partner	40
E, B's 60-percent-owned corporation	100
Other unrelated parties.	10

7-52 *Expenses of Another Taxpayer.* B is the only child of P and will inherit the family fortune. P, who is in the 28% tax bracket, is willing to give B and his wife $500 a month. Comment on the advisability of P paying the following directly in lieu of making a gift.

   a. Medical expenses of B, who makes $20,000 during the year; P (the father) provides 55% of B's support.

   b. Interest and principal payments on B's home mortgage, on which B and his wife are the sole obliges.

   c. Same as (b) except that P is also an obligee on the note.

7-53 *Losses.* This year was simply a financial disaster for Z. Indicate the effects of the following transactions on Z's taxable income. Ignore any limitations that may exist.

   a. After the stock market crash, Z sold her stock and realized a loss of $1,000.

   b. Z sold her husband's truck for $3,000 (basis $2,000) and her own car for $5,000 (basis $9,000). Both vehicles were used for personal purposes.

   c. Z's $500 camera was stolen.

   d. The land next to Z's house was rezoned to light industrial, driving down the value of her home by $10,000.

7-54 *Planning Deductions.* X, 67, is a widow, her husband having died several years ago. Each year, X receives about $30,000 of interest and dividends. Because the mortgage on her home is virtually paid off, her only potential itemized deductions are her contributions to her church and real estate taxes. Her anticipated deductions are

Year	Contribution
2017	$3,000
2018	4,000
2019	2,000

What tax advice can you offer X?

7-55 *Timing Deductions.* T currently figures that Federal, state, and local taxes consume about 30% of his income at the margin. Next year, however, due to a tax law change his taxes should increase to about 40% and remain at that level for at least five or six years. Assuming T buys a computer for $4,000 and he has the option of deducting all of the cost this year or deducting it ratably through depreciation over the next five years, what advice can you offer?

7-56 *Classification and Deductibility.* In each of the following independent situations, indicate for the current taxable year the amounts deductible *for* AGI, *from* AGI, or *not deductible* at all. Unless otherwise stated, assume all taxpayers use the cash basis method of accounting and report using the calendar year.

   a. M spent $1,000 on a life insurance policy covering her own life.

   b. G is an author of novels. His wife attempted to have him declared insane and have him committed. Fearing the effect that his wife's charges might have on him and his book sales, G paid $11,000 in legal fees, resulting in a successful defense.

   c. Taxpayer, a plumber employed by XYZ Corporation, paid union dues of $100.

   d. Q Corporation paid T, its president and majority shareholder, a salary of $100,000. Employees in comparable positions earn salaries of $70,000.

   e. L operates a furniture business as a sole proprietorship. She rents a warehouse (on a month-to-month basis) used for storing items sold in her store. In late December, L paid $2,000 for rental of the warehouse for the month of January.

   f. M is a self-employed security officer. He paid $100 for uniforms and $25 for having them cleaned.

   g. N is a security officer employed by the owner of a large apartment complex. He pays $350 for uniforms. In addition, he paid $95 for having them cleaned. His employer reimbursed him $175 of the cost of the uniforms (included in his income on Form W-2).

   h. K owns a duplex as an investment. During the year, she paid $75 for advertisements seeking tenants. She was unable to rent the duplex, and thus no income was earned this year.

   i. P paid $200 for subscriptions to technical journals to be used in his employment activities. Although P was fully reimbursed by his employer, his employer did not report the reimbursement in P's income.

7-57 *Classification and Deductibility.* In each of the following independent situations, indicate for the current taxable year the amounts deductible *for* AGI, *from* AGI, or *not deductible* at all. Unless otherwise stated, assume all taxpayers use the cash basis method of accounting and report using the calendar year.

a. O paid the interest and taxes of $1,000 on his ex-wife's home mortgage. The divorce agreement provided that he could claim deductions for the payments.

b. P paid an attorney $1,500 in legal fees related to her divorce. Of these fees, $600 is for advice concerning the tax consequences of transferring some of P's stock to her husband as part of the property settlement.

c. R paid $10,000 for a small warehouse on an acre of land. He used the building for several months before tearing it down and erecting a hamburger stand.

d. H and his wife moved into the city and no longer needed their personal automobiles. They sold their Chevrolet for a $1,000 loss and their Buick for a $400 gain.

e. C is employed as a legal secretary. This year he paid an employment agency $300 for finding him a new, higher-paying job as a legal secretary.

f. X operates his own truck service. He paid $80 in fines for driving trucks that were overweight according to state law.

g. T, an employee, paid $175 to an accountant for preparing her personal income tax returns.

7-58 *Classification and Deductibility.* In each of the following independent situations, indicate for the current taxable year the amounts deductible for AGI, from AGI, or not deductible at all. Unless otherwise stated, assume all taxpayers use the cash basis method of accounting and report using the calendar year.

a. B sold stock to his mother for a $700 loss. B's mother subsequently sold the stock for $400 less than she had paid to B.

b. Same as (a) but assume the mother sold the stock for $500 more than she had paid to B.

c. D operates three pizza restaurants as a sole proprietorship in Indianapolis. In July he paid $1,000 in air fares to travel to Chicago and Detroit to determine the feasibility of opening additional restaurants. Because of economic conditions, D decided not to open any additional restaurants.

d. T owns and operates several gun stores as a sole proprietorship. In light of gun control legislation, he traveled to the state capital at a cost of $80 to testify before a committee. In addition, he traveled around the state speaking at various Rotary and Kiwanis Club functions on the pending legislation at a cost of $475. T also placed an advertisement in the local newspaper concerning the merit of the legislation at a cost of $50. He pays dues to the National Rifle Association of $100.

e. D is employed as a ship captain for a leisure cruise company. He paid $1,000 for rent on a warehouse where he stores smuggled narcotics, which he sells illegally.

f. M, a plumber and an accrual basis taxpayer, warrants his work. This year he estimates that expenses attributable to the warranty work are about 3% of sales, or $3,000.

g. G, a computer operator, pays $75 for a subscription to an investment newsletter devoted to investment opportunities in state and municipal bonds.

7-59 *Employee Business Expenses: Planning.* J is employed as a salesman by Big-Time Business Forms Inc. He is considering the purchase of a new automobile that he would use primarily for business. Are there any tax factors that J might consider before purchasing the new car?

TAX RETURN PROBLEMS

■ *CONTINUOUS TAX RETURN PROBLEMS* See Appendix I, Part 1.

CUMULATIVE PROBLEMS

7-60 Tony Johnson (I.D. No. 456-23-7657), age 45, is single. He lives at 5220 Grand Avenue, Brooklyn, NY 10016. Tony is employed by RTI Corporation, which operates a chain of restaurants in and around New York City. He has supervisory responsibilities over the managers of four restaurants. An examination of his records for 2016 revealed the following information.

1. During the year, Tony earned $33,000. His employer withheld $2,200 in Federal income taxes and the proper amount of FICA taxes. Tony obtained his current job through an employment agency to which he paid a $150 fee. He previously was employed as a manager of another restaurant. Due to the new job, it was necessary to improve his wardrobe. Accordingly, Tony purchased several new suits at a cost of $600.
2. On the days that Tony works, he normally eats his meals at the restaurants for purposes of quality control. There is no charge for the meals, which are worth $2,000.
3. He provides 60% of the support for his father, age 70, who lived with Tony all year and who has no income other than Social Security benefits of $7,000 during the year. Tony provided more than one-half of the cost of maintaining the home.
4. Dividend income from Chevron Corporation stock that he owned was $350. Interest income on savings was $200.
5. Tony and other employees of the corporation park in a nearby parking garage. The parking garage bills RTI Corporation for the parking. Tony figures that his free parking is worth $1,000 annually.
6. Tony subscribes to several trade publications for restaurants at a cost of $70.
7. During the year, he paid $200 to a bank for a personal financial plan. Based on this plan, Tony made several investments, including a $2,000 contribution to an individual retirement account, and also rented for $30 a safety deposit box in which he stores certain investment related documents.
8. Tony purchased a new home, paying three points on a loan of $70,000. He also paid $6,000 of interest on his home mortgage during the year. In addition, he paid $650 of real property taxes on the home. He has receipts for sales taxes of $534.
9. While hurrying to deliver an important package for his employer, Tony received a $78 ticket for violating the speed limit. Because his employer had asked that he deliver the package as quickly as possible, Tony was reimbursed $78 for the ticket, which he paid.

Compute Tony's taxable income for the year. If forms are used for the computations, complete Form 1040 and Schedule A.

7-61 Wendy White (I.D. No. 526-30-9001), age 29, is single. She lives at 1402 Pacific Beach Ave., San Diego, CA 92230. Wendy is employed by KXXR television station as the evening news anchor. An examination of her records for 2016 revealed the following information.

1. Wendy earned $150,000 in salary. Her employer withheld $40,000 in Federal income taxes and the proper amount of FICA taxes.
2. Wendy also received $10,000 in self-employment income from personal appearances during the year. Her unreimbursed expenses related to this income were: transportation and lodging, $523; meals, $120; and office supplies, $58.
3. Wendy reports the following additional deductions: home mortgage interest, $6,250; charitable contributions, $1,300; state and local income taxes, $3,100; and employment-related expenses, $920.

Compute Wendy's taxable income for 2016 and her tax due (including any self-employment tax). If forms are used for the computations, complete Form 1040, Schedule A, Schedule C, and Schedule SE.

TAX RESEARCH PROBLEMS

7-62 T and two associates are equal owners in LST Corporation. The three formed the corporation several years ago with the idea of capitalizing on the fitness movement. After a modest beginning and meager returns, the corporation did extremely well this year. As a result, the corporation plans on paying the three individuals salaries that T believes the IRS may deem unreasonable. T wonders whether he can avoid the tax consequences associated with an unreasonable compensation determination by paying back whatever amount is ultimately deemed a dividend.

   a. What would be the effect on T's taxable income should he repay the portion of a salary deemed a dividend?

   b. Would there be any adverse effects of adopting a payback arrangement?

Partial list of research aids:

    Oswald, 49 T.C. 645.

    Rev. Rul. 69-115, 1969-1 C.B. 50.

7-63 C, a professor of film studies at State University, often meets with her doctoral students at her home. In her home, C has a room that she uses solely to conduct business related to the classes she teaches at the university. In the room she and her students often review the movies the students have made to satisfy requirements in their doctoral program. Can C deduct expenses related to her home office?

7-64 R moved to St. Louis in 2016 and purchased a home. After living there for a year, his family had grown and required a much larger home. On August 1, 2017 they purchased their dream house, which cost far more than their first home. Shortly before he closed on the new residence, he put his first house on the market to sell. After two months had passed, however, he had received no offers. Fearing that he would be unable to pay the debt on both homes, R decided to rent his old home while trying to sell it. Surprisingly, he was able to rent the house immediately. However, in order to secure the party's agreement to rent monthly, he was required to perform a few repairs costing $500. Seven months after he had rented the home, R sold it. During the rental period, R paid the utilities and various other expenses. R has come to you for your advice on how these events in 2017 would affect his tax return.

7-65 In November 2017 B, employed as a life insurance salesperson for PQR Insurance Company in Newark, New Jersey, purchased a personal computer for use in his work. B has come to you for help in deciding how to handle this purchase on his 2017 tax return. He, of course, wants to expense the full price of the computer under Code § 179. B relates the following salient information to you with respect to this purchase:

1. B files a joint return with his wife, L. They have a combined AGI of $65,000 before considering this item. They have sufficient qualified expenditures to itemize deductions on Schedule A, but they have no miscellaneous itemized deductions.
2. B paid $3,000 for the laptop computer, which will be used 100% for business use.
3. B bought the computer to analyze client data. He figures this will help him increase his sales because he can analyze the results of various insurance options at the client's home or office (all personalized, of course).
4. PQR does not provide B with company-owned computing equipment. In fact, they refused to pay for B's computer because the expense of providing computers for all of PQR's agents would be too great.

How should B treat this purchase on his 2017 tax return?

7-66 On January 28, 2017 S comes to you for tax preparation advice. She has always prepared her own return, but it has become somewhat complicated and she needs professional advice.

During your initial interview, you discover that S is a teacher at a high school in Chicago, Illinois. She is also the coach of the golf team. In 2015 S decided she wanted to be a professional golfer. So, when she was 32 years old, she began a part-time apprenticeship program with the Professional Golfers' Association of America (PGA), where she was an unpaid assistant to the pro at a local country club. Then, in 2016 she became a member of the PGA and began her professional career.

S has not made much money as a professional golfer. In fact, her expenses exceeded her income in both 2015 and 2016 ($4,000 loss in 2015; $3,500 loss in 2016). Believing she was actively engaged in a trade or business (she kept separate records for her golf activities, practiced about 10 hours each week, and worked with a pro whenever she could), S deducted her golf-related expenses on Schedule C and reported her losses from this activity on her prior returns.

The IRS has challenged S's 2015 and 2016 loss deductions, calling them nondeductible "hobby" losses. Is the IRS correct in this matter? Would she win if the matter is taken to court? What planning steps can S take to ensure that any future losses are deductible trade or business losses?

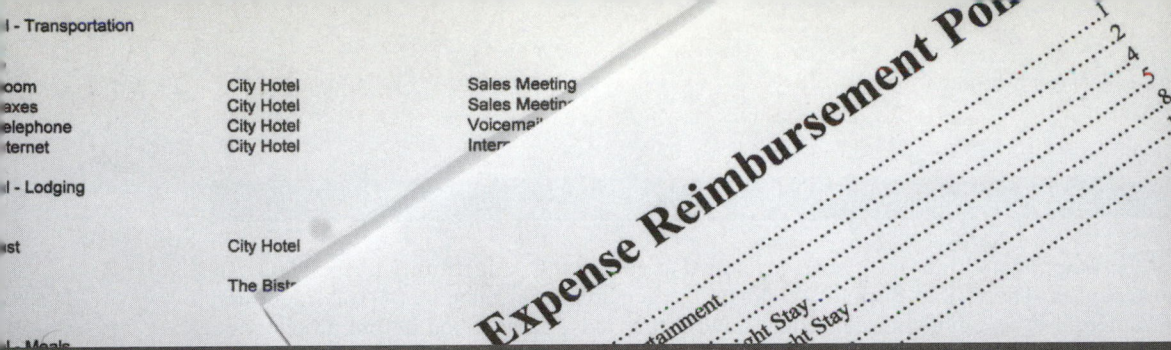

8

Employee Business Expenses

Learning Objectives

Upon completion of this chapter you will be able to:

LO.1 Discuss the rules governing the deduction of several common expenses incurred by employees and self-employed persons.

LO.2 Recognize when educational expenses are deductible.

LO.3 Explain the rules concerning the deduction of moving expenses.

LO.4 Describe when expenses of maintaining a home office are deductible.

LO.5 Distinguish between deductible transportation expenses and nondeductible commuting costs.

LO.6 Understand the differences between deductible travel expenses and deductible transportation costs.

LO.7 Determine when entertainment expenses can be deducted.

LO.8 Describe the 50% limitation on the deduction of meals and entertainment.

LO.9 Explain the special record-keeping requirements for travel and entertainment expenses.

LO.10 Discuss the two types of reimbursement arrangements: accountable and nonaccountable plans.

Chapter Outline

Introduction

LO.1

Discuss the rules governing the deduction of several common expenses incurred by employees and self-employed persons.

Over the years, many rules have been developed to govern the deductibility of specific business expenses. These rules normally augment the general requirements of § 162 (identified in Chapter 7) by establishing additional criteria that must be satisfied before a deduction may be claimed. As a practical matter, the primary purpose of many of these rules is to prohibit taxpayers from deducting what are in reality personal expenditures. For example, consider a taxpayer who uses a room at home to work or a taxpayer who takes a customer to lunch. In both cases, the expenses incurred very well may be genuine business expenses and deductible under the general criteria. On the other hand, such expenses could simply be *disguised* personal expenditures. As these examples suggest, some of the expenses that are likely to be manipulated are those often incurred by employees in connection with their employment duties. Such common employee expenses as those for travel and entertainment, education, moving, and home offices have long been the source of controversy. Of course, such costs are incurred by a self-employed person as well as by employees and raise similar problems. This chapter examines the special provisions applicable to these items.

Education Expenses

Historically, the tax law has viewed most education expenses as personal and, therefore, not deductible. For example, an art appreciation course for the taxpayer's cultural enrichment is purely personal in nature. Consequently, its cost is not deductible.[1] Similarly, no deduction is granted for expenses of a college education as a business expense on the theory that they are costs of preparing the taxpayer to enter a new business—not the costs of carrying on a business. Therefore, such general education expenses are nondeductible capital expenditures for which no amortization is allowed. Other education expenses, however, such as those incurred by an accountant to attend a seminar on a new tax law, are considered essential costs of pursuing income and are deductible like other ordinary and necessary business expenses. To ensure that deductions are permitted only for education expenses that serve current business objectives and are not personal or capital in nature, special tests must be met.

LO.2

Recognize when educational expenses are deductible.

The Regulations allow a deduction if the education expenses satisfy *either* of the following conditions *and* are not considered personal or capital in nature, as discussed below.[2]

1. The education maintains or improves skills required of the taxpayer in his or her employment or other trade or business.

2. The education meets the express requirements imposed by either the individual's employer or applicable law, and the taxpayer must meet such requirements to retain his or her job, position, or rate of compensation.

Education expenses that meet either of these conditions are still not deductible if they are considered personal or capital expenditures under either of the following two tests:[3]

1. The education is necessary to meet the minimum educational requirements of the taxpayer's trade or business.

2. The education qualifies the taxpayer for a new trade or business.

REQUIREMENTS FOR DEDUCTION

Maintain Skills

For the expense to qualify under the first criterion, the education must be related to the taxpayer's present trade or business and maintain or improve the skills used in such business. The taxpayer must be able to establish the necessary connection between the studies pursued and the taxpayer's current employment. For example, a personnel manager seeking an M.B.A. degree was allowed to deduct all of her education expenses when she ingeniously related each course taken to her job (e.g., a computer course enabled her to be more

---

[1] As discussed below, beginning in 2002, § 222 permits a deduction for qualified expenses.

[2] Reg. § 1.162-5(a).

[3] Reg. §§ 1.162-5(b)(2) and (3).

effective in acquiring information from and communicating with computer personnel).[4] In contrast, the Tax Court denied the deductions of a research chemist's cost of an M.B.A., indicating that courses such as advanced business finance, corporate strategy, and business law were only remotely related to the skills needed for his job.[5]

Refresher and continuing education courses ordinarily meet the skills maintenance test.

Example 1

T repairs appliances. To maintain his proficiency, he often attends training schools. The costs of attending such schools are deductible because the education is necessary to maintain and improve the skills required in his job.

Required by Employer or Law

Once the minimum education requirements are met to obtain a job, additional education may be required by the employer or by law to retain the taxpayer's salary or position. Costs for such education are deductible if they do not qualify the taxpayer for a new trade or business.

Example 2

This year, R took a new job as a high school instructor in science. State law requires that teachers obtain a graduate degree within five years of becoming employed. Expenses for college courses for this purpose are deductible even though they lead to a degree since such education is mandatory under state law.

New Trade or Business

If education prepares the taxpayer to enter a new trade or business, no deduction is permitted. In this regard, a mere change of duties usually is not considered a new business.[6] For example, a science teacher may deduct the cost of courses enabling him or her to teach art since the switch is a mere change in duties. The taxpayer becomes qualified for a new occupation if the education enables the taxpayer to perform substantially different tasks, regardless of whether the taxpayer actually uses the skills acquired.

Example 3

R was hired as a trust officer in a bank several years ago. His employer now requires that all trust officers must have a law degree. R may not deduct the cost of obtaining a law degree because the degree qualifies him for a new trade or business.[7] No deduction is allowed even though it is required by his employer and R does not actually engage in the practice of law.

Minimum Education

Expenses of education undertaken to gain entry into a business or to meet the minimum standards required in a business are not deductible. These standards are determined in light of the typical conditions imposed by the particular job. For example, the Tax Court denied a $21,000 deduction for the cost of a Northwestern University "MBA" because the degree not only enabled the taxpayer to meet the minimum education requirements for her position at Merrill Lynch and Raymond James but also prepared her for a new trade or business.[8]

[4] Frank S. Blair, III, 41 TCM 289, T.C. Memo 1980-488.

[5] Ronald T. Smith, 41 TCM 1186, T.C. Memo 1981-149.

[6] Reg. § 1.162-5(b)(3).

[7] Reg. § 1.162-5(b)(3)(ii) Ex. 1.

[8] Will M. McEuen III, TC Summary Opinion 2004-107. See also Daniel Allemeir TC Memo 2005-207 and Veronica L. Foster, TC Summary Opinion 2008-22.

In contrast, is a recent case, concerning a senior assistant controller for a Marriott hotel.[9] In addition to his accounting responsibilities, the taxpayer managed a team of employees, which involved hiring, training and giving performance reviews. While at Marriott, he decided to return to school part-time to improve his leadership skills. To this end, he enrolled in the Executive MBA program at Brigham Young University and commuted from Los Angeles to attend classes in Salt Lake City. While in the program, his employment was abruptly terminated. However, he continued to pursue his degree and was hired after graduation to perform duties in his new job similar to those at Marriott. He deducted $18,879 for tuition, commuting and other expenses. The IRS disallowed the deduction on the theory that: (1) the taxpayer did not carry on his trade or business during the year in question because he was unemployed for part of the year; (2) the education was just a general degree that did not maintain or improves his skills; and (3) the degree qualified him for a new trade or business. But the Tax Court disagreed, believing the taxpayer's facts refuted the government's contention. The case is significant because it was the first to address an executive MBA and good for MBAs who are unemployed because they are MBA students.

The minimum education requirement also operates to prohibit the deduction of such expenses as those for a review course for the bar or C.P.A. exam and fees to take such professional exams.[10] Similarly, education expenses related to a pay increase or promotion may not be deductible under this rule if the increase or promotion was the primary objective of the education. However, as discussed below, a special provision allows a deduction for qualified tuition expenses.

TRAVEL AS A FORM OF EDUCATION

Prior to 1986, travel in and of itself was considered a deductible form of education when it was related to a taxpayer's trade or business. For example, an instructor of Spanish could travel around Spain during the summer to learn more about the Spanish culture and improve her conversational Spanish. In such case, the travel cost would have been deductible since it was related to the taxpayer's trade or business. In 1986, Congress became concerned that many taxpayers were using this rule to deduct what were essentially the costs of a personal vacation. Moreover, Congress believed that any business purpose served by traveling for general education purposes was insignificant. To eliminate possible abuse, no deduction is allowed simply because the travel itself is educational.[11] Deductions are allowed for travel only when the education activity otherwise qualifies and the travel expense is necessary to pursue such activity. For example, a deduction for travel would be allowed where a professor of French literature travels to France to take courses that are offered only at the Sorbonne.

TYPES AND CLASSIFICATION OF EDUCATION DEDUCTIONS

Education expenses normally deductible include costs of tuition, books, supplies, typing, tutors, transportation, and travel (including meals, lodging, and similar expenses). Typical education expenses are for college or vocational courses, continuing professional education programs, professional development courses, and similar courses or seminars.

The costs of transportation between the taxpayer's place of work and school are deductible. If the taxpayer goes home before going to school, however, the expense of going from home to school is deductible, but only to the extent that it does not exceed the costs of going directly from work. The cost of transportation from home to school on a nonworking day represents nondeductible commuting.

Unreimbursed educational expenditures of an employee are treated as miscellaneous itemized deductions subject to the 2% floor. In contrast, if an employer reimburses an employee for such expenses under an *accountable plan* (discussed later in this chapter), the reimbursement is excludable from gross income and the employee does not claim a deduction (thus nothing appears in the employee's W-2 nor on the tax return). Any reimbursement not made under an accountable plan must be included in the employee's gross income, and qualifying deductions must be treated as miscellaneous itemized deductions. Finally, education expenses incurred by a self-employed person are deductible *for* AGI.

---

[9] *Alex Kopaigora,* TC Summary Opinion 2016-35.

[10] Rev. Rul. 69-292, 1969-1 C.B. 84.

[11] § 274(m)(2).

DEDUCTION FOR QUALIFIED TUITION AND RELATED EXPENSES

The general rules governing the deduction of education expenses normally prohibit tax-payers from deducting the costs of obtaining a college education since such expenses are considered personal (i.e., incurred to meet minimum education requirements). However, to help subsidize the increasing cost of higher education, Congress created a special provision. Section 222 allows a deduction for *qualified tuition and related expenses* incurred in connection with enrollment or attendance at an *eligible educational institution*. Normally, the amount of the deduction is $4,000 and is available to all taxpayers since it may be claimed for AGI. However, the deduction can be reduced or eliminated depending on the taxpayer's filing status and adjusted gross income as follows:

AGI Joint Returns	AGI Other Taxpayers	Amount of Deduction
$ 0–$130,000	$ 0–$65,000	$4,000
$130,001–$160,000	$65,001–$80,000	$2,000
>$160,000	>$80,000	$ 0

Note that there is no phase-out of the deduction, but rather a cliff effect. For example, if a single parent's AGI increases $1 from $65,000 to $65,001, the deduction drops from $4,000 to $2,000.

The deduction can be claimed for expenses of the taxpayer, the taxpayer's spouse, and the taxpayer's dependents. Consistent with this approach, the law prohibits taxpayers who are eligible to be claimed as dependents from claiming the deduction. In addition, married taxpayers must file jointly in order to claim the deduction. Finally, to prohibit a double benefit, the deduction is not allowed if the taxpayer or any other person claims the American Opportunity (Hope Scholarship) credit or the Lifetime Learning credit (see below) with respect to that individual for that particular year. In contrast, the deduction can be claimed in the same year a student takes a tax-free distribution from a § 529 plan or an educational savings account as long as the same expenses are not used for both benefits.[12]

Only qualified tuition and related expenses may be deducted. This definition normally encompasses the tuition and fees charged by most universities. It should be noted, however, that fees for course-related books, supplies, and equipment normally do not qualify unless—according to the IRS—the fees must be paid *to the institution* as a condition of enrollment or attendance. For example, a student activity fee, a special technology or lab fee charged by a university should qualify. On the other hand, qualified expenses do not include the cost of: insurance, medical expenses (including student health fees), room and board, transportation, or similar personal, living, or family expenses. This is true even if the fee must be paid to the institution as a condition of enrollment or attendance. In addition, qualified tuition and related expenses generally do not include expenses that relate to any course of instruction or other education that involves sports, games or hobbies, or any noncredit course unless the course is part of the student's degree program. Note that both undergraduate and graduate courses qualify and it makes no difference whether the course is part of a program that leads to a degree.

Only qualified expenses paid to *eligible educational institutions* are deductible. An eligible education institution is defined as any accredited post secondary institution that offers credit toward a bachelor's degree, an associate's degree or other recognized post-secondary credential. Thus tuition for most colleges and universities as well as junior colleges qualify. Some vocational institutions (e.g., trade schools) and proprietary for-profit organizations may qualify as well.

---

[12] See *Tax Benefits for Higher Education*, IRS Publication 970 (Rev. 2016, pp. 39 and 60).

Example 4

In August 2017, Mr. and Mrs. Smith paid the tuition for their son's attendance at State University to obtain a graduate degree in accounting. Tuition was $1,900. In December 2017, the Smiths paid the tuition for the second semester of $2,300. The second semester began in January 2018. Mr. and Mrs. Smith have an AGI of $125,000. The son is a graduate student and, consequently, the expenses do not qualify for the Hope Scholarship credit discussed below. In addition, because their AGI exceeds $125,000, the couple is not entitled to claim the Lifetime Learning credit. While the credits are not available, a deduction is allowed since the expenses are paid during the year and are for education for such year or education that begins within three months after the close of the year. The deduction is limited to $4,000 and may be claimed for AGI.

Example 5

This year R started law school. He is a part-time student and has a part-time job. He paid tuition of $12,000 for the year. He may deduct $4,000 of the tuition for AGI. Alternatively, he could elect to use the Lifetime Learning credit of $2,000 ($10,000 maximum qualified expenses × 20%). However, as noted above, he can either deduct the expenses or claim the credit but not both. If his marginal rate was 25 percent, the $4,000 deduction would be worth only $1,000 so in this case, he would be better off claiming the credit.

RELATIONSHIP TO EDUCATION CREDITS AND QUALIFIED PREPAID TUITION

In addition to the deduction for education expenses, the Code provides other benefits for education related expenses. There are two credits related to education: (1) the American Opportunity Tax Credit (formerly referred to as the Hope Scholarship Credit), and (2) the Lifetime Learning credit. Special benefits are also extended to Educational Savings Accounts and Qualified Tuition Programs (§ 529 plans). These credits and tax-favored savings arrangements, discussed in detail in Chapters 13 and 18, are designed to help middle America fund the ever-increasing cost of higher education.

The American Opportunity Tax Credit (AOTC) and the Lifetime Learning credit are both available for education expenses paid on behalf of the taxpayer, the taxpayer's spouse, or a dependent. For 2017, the AOTC is 100% of the first $2,000 of education expenses and 25% of the next $2,000 of expenses for each student. Thus the maximum credit is $2,500 ([100% × $2,000 = $2,000] + [25% × $2,000 = $500]) per year per student. The AOTC generally can be claimed only for the first four years of post-secondary education (e.g., college).

The Lifetime Learning credit can be claimed for 20% of up to $10,000 of qualified tuition and fees annually. Thus the maximum credit per taxpayer return would be $2,000. In contrast to the AOTC, the Lifetime Learning is available for virtually any type of education for an unlimited number of years.

For any one particular student, a taxpayer could elect *either* the AOTC or a Lifetime Learning credit but not both. Note that the AOTC is per child and not per taxpayer. The Lifetime Learning credit is per return. As noted above, if the taxpayer elects either credit, the deduction is not allowed. Both credits are phased out based on the taxpayer's AGI and filing status as shown below. See Chapter 13 for a complete discussion.

AGI Phase-Out Ranges for Education Credits 2017		
	Joint Filers	*All Others*
American Opportunity Tax Credit . .	$80,000–$90,000	$160,000–$180,000
Lifetime Learning Credit	$112,000–$132,000	$ 56,000–$ 66,000

The tax law also provides favorable treatment for two savings arrangements: (1) Educational Savings Accounts (Coverdell Accounts described in § 530) and (2) Qualified Tuition Programs (so-called § 529 plans). Contributions to these plans are not deductible. However, income on amounts contributed are nontaxable when earned. In addition, amounts distributed from the plans are nontaxable if such amounts are used for certain expenses for higher education. As noted above, to prevent a double benefit, taxpayers cannot deduct qualified education expenses that have been used to figure the tax-free portion of a distribution from an education savings account or a 529 plan.[13]

It is important to note that the law prevents taxpayers from trying to double dip; that is, the law specifically prohibits taxpayers from claiming both a deduction and a credit for the same education expenses. For example, if a CPA spends $300 to attend a continuing education course, he could claim a deduction of $300 as a business expense under § 162, qualified tuition under § 222, or as the basis for the Lifetime Learning credit of $60. Observe, however, that due to limitations, differing phase-out amounts, definitions of qualifying expenditures, and the interaction with other educational provisions such as the exclusion for educational assistance of § 127 and the working condition fringe benefit rules of § 132, a single expense could be covered by multiple provisions and results in mind-boggling complexity.

Example 6

J recently completed his undergraduate degree at the University of Texas and took a job with a brokerage firm in Dallas. The firm agreed to reimburse him for a portion of the cost of an M.B.A. program. In January, J enrolled as a part-time student in the M.B.A. program at a local university. This year he paid tuition of $22,250 and the firm reimbursed him $8,250 of this amount. In addition, J withdrew $1,000 from an Educational Savings account to help pay the tuition. He paid for the remaining $13,000 from a student loan.

Under the educational assistance rules of § 127 (see Chapter 6), J could exclude $5,250 reimbursement for the coursework (both undergraduate and graduate courses qualify) and neither he nor his employer would be required to pay FICA or Medicare taxes on this amount. J also could exclude $1,000 withdrawn from the Educational Savings Account since it was used for qualified higher education expenses. Note that J could not deduct the amount for which he was reimbursed or the withdrawal since both were excluded. The treatment of the remaining $16,000 ($22,250 − $5,250 − $1,000) is not clear. In order to exclude the $3,000 balance reimbursed by his employer as a working condition fringe benefit under § 132, the expense must qualify as a deductible business expense under § 162. The IRS might take the position that none of the remaining amount paid is deductible under § 162 since J has not met the minimum education requirement of the brokerage firm and, therefore, the $3,000 reimbursement would not qualify for exclusion. In any event, J could deduct $4,000 as a qualified tuition expense under § 222. (Observe, that to exclude the $3,000 reimbursement as a working condition fringe under § 132, the item must be deductible under § 162—not § 222.) J could utilize the Lifetime Learning credit instead of the deduction. If it is assumed that he could not exclude the additional reimbursement under § 132 and he did not deduct *any* amount under § 222, he could claim a Lifetime Learning credit of $2,000 (20% × up to $10,000). Whether J utilizes the amount paid as a basis for claiming the credit or as a deduction under § 222 depends on any phase-outs and his tax bracket. However, he cannot use the expenses for claiming both the deduction and the credit. Also note that the new § 222 deduction is a deduction for AGI and not a miscellaneous itemized deduction subject to the 2% floor.

---

[13] The reduction is normally equal to the amount of earnings that are nontaxable because they were used to pay qualified education expenses. However, for 529 plans, the amount representing the recovery of contributions to the program that are used for education expenses could be deducted subject to the $4,000 limitation. See Footnote 12.

DEDUCTION FOR EXPENSES OF PRIMARY AND SECONDARY SCHOOL TEACHERS

In 2002, the Bush administration reached out to the teaching profession by creating a special deduction. The deduction originated from a 1996 National Education Association study which found that the average kindergarten–12th grade teacher spent approximately $400 per year out of their personal funds for unreimbursed classroom supplies (e.g., a first grade teacher may incur expenses for the decoration of his or her classroom). Although such expenses were deductible, because they were miscellaneous itemized deductions, it was unlikely that most teachers could deduct such expenses. In supporting the deduction, President Bush asserted that if a businessperson could deduct a meal, "a teacher certainly ought to be able to deduct the cost of pencils or a Big Chief tablet." To this end, the Code allows a small deduction for unreimbursed business expenses incurred in connection with books, supplies, computer equipment (including related software and services), other equipment and supplementary materials used in the classroom.[14] And, in 2016, the list of eligible expenses is expanded to include expenses that teachers incur in participating in professional development courses that relate to what they teach. The amount of the deduction is adjusted annually for inflation and is $250 for 2017.[15] Note also that the deduction is for AGI and, therefore, all qualifying teachers benefit. A qualifying teacher is defined as an "eligible educator" who for at least 900 hours during a school year is a kindergarten through 12th grade teacher, instructor, counselor, principal, or aide. The educator is eligible only if he or she works at a school that provides elementary or secondary education (kindergarten through 12th grade). Expenses in excess of the limitation are deductible as miscellaneous itemized deductions subject to the 2% floor.

 ## CHECK YOUR KNOWLEDGE

For each of the following situations, indicate whether the expenditures are deductible as education expenses.

Review Question 1

Last June, D graduated magna cum laude from the University of Virginia. This fall he entered Johns Hopkins Medical School, paying tuition of thousands of dollars.

The costs of medical school are not deductible under § 162 as business expenses for two reasons. First, the education is necessary to meet the minimum educational requirements to become a doctor. Second, the education qualifies the taxpayer to carry on a new trade or business. Nevertheless, D could deduct a portion under § 222 as qualified tuition or claim the Lifetime Learning credit, but not both.

Review Question 2

H, a practicing tax accountant, is taking a series of correspondence courses to become a certified financial planner.

As may be clear by now, very little is black or white in the tax law; here is yet another case. The IRS would probably take the position that the expenses are not deductible because the education qualifies the taxpayer to carry on a new trade or business. From the accountant's perspective, however, the course work simply improves or maintains the skills that he is already using in his business. It would appear that the education does not necessarily enable the taxpayer to do anything that he could not do before except to hold himself out as a certified financial planner. The accountant would deduct the expense. In addition, the Lifetime Learning credit and qualified tuition deduction may also be available if the courses are taken at an eligible educational institution (e.g., as part of a university sponsored program).

---

[14] § 62(a)(2)(D). *The Protecting Americans from Tax Hikes Act of 2015* made this provision permanent in 2015.

[15] Rev. Proc. 2016-55, 2016-45 IRB, 10/25/2016

Review Question 3

Ms. McClain, an elementary school teacher, took a sabbatical to Ireland, where she studied the art of storytelling.

Whether her expenses are deductible ultimately depends on the facts and circumstances. As noted above, changes made in 1986 aimed to eliminate deductions for travel that were primarily personal in nature. In this case, the taxpayer appears to be pursuing that which might not be available at home. Assuming she spent a reasonable amount of time studying and researching, the expense would be deductible. In contrast, consider an architect who travels all over Europe simply taking pictures of classic architectural styles that he may incorporate in his work. Without more, a court would probably view his trip as merely a disguised vacation and deny a deduction for his travel expenses. As in the previous question, the Lifetime Learning credit and qualified tuition deduction may also be available if the courses are taken at an eligible educational institution (e.g., as part of a university sponsored program).

Moving Expenses

LO.3
Explain the rules concerning the deduction of moving expenses.

For many years, moving expenses were viewed as nondeductible personal expenses. In 1964, however, Congress revised its position, believing that moving expenses necessitated by the taxpayer's employment should be regarded as a deductible cost of earning income. To this end, Code § 217 was enacted, expressly authorizing a deduction for moving expenses. Section 217 allows self-employed individuals and employees to deduct moving expenses incurred in connection with beginning employment or changing job locations. To ensure that the deduction is allowed only for moves required by the taxpayer's employment, the taxpayer must satisfy *both* a distance test and a time test in order to qualify for the deduction.

DISTANCE REQUIREMENT

The thrust of § 217 is to allow a taxpayer to deduct moving expenses only if there is a change in job location *and* the new location is sufficiently far away that it essentially requires the taxpayer to uproot and move his or her residence. This idea is captured in a somewhat misleading 50-mile distance test. The taxpayer does not satisfy the requirement simply by moving 50 miles to a new residence in connection with a new job location. If this were the case, the taxpayer could meet the requirement by simply moving his office down the hall and at the same time moving his residence 50 miles. Instead, the distance test is constructed to determine if the taxpayer's commute to the new job site *without the move* would have increased at least 50 miles. Technically, the condition is satisfied if the distance between the old residence and the new job site is at least 50 miles greater than the distance between the old residence and the old job site. Note that both distances are measured from the taxpayer's *former residence*. Thus, if the taxpayer's old commute was four miles, the new commute (absent a move) would have to be at least 54 miles (54 − 4 = 50) before the test is satisfied.

Example 7

During the year, R was promoted to district sales manager, requiring her to move from Tucson to Phoenix. To determine whether the 50-mile test is met, the distances shown below must be compared.

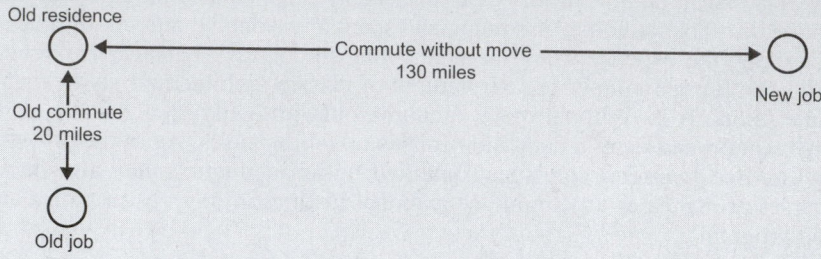

Since the distance between R's old residence and new job (AC = 130 miles) exceeds the distance between R's old residence and old job (AB = 20 miles) by at least 50 miles (130 − 20 = 110), the distance requirement is satisfied. In this case, it is quite clear that if the taxpayer had not moved, her commute would have increased significantly (110 miles). Consequently, § 217 grants her a deduction for the costs of moving her residence to a place where the commute is more reasonable. In applying the test, note that the location of the new residence is irrelevant.

If the taxpayer has no old job site, the distance test is satisfied if the new job site is 50 miles from the old residence.[16]

TIME TEST

If taxpayers were not required to maintain employment at the new job site for a minimum amount of time, they could move from place to place, taking temporary jobs in each location to justify the deduction of what in effect are personal travel expenses. To prohibit this possibility, the second test generally requires the taxpayer to work for a *sustained period* of time upon arrival at the new job location. This condition is met if the taxpayer is a *full-time* employee in the area of the new job location for at least 39 weeks during the 12-month period immediately following arrival.[17] Alternatively, the taxpayer may satisfy the test by being an employee or self-employed on a *full-time* basis for at least 78 weeks during the 24-month period after arrival. Note, however, that—like the first test—39 of these 78 weeks must be during the first 12-month period. In either case, the taxpayer need not work for the same employer or for 39 weeks in a row. The time requirement is waived if the taxpayer dies, becomes disabled, is involuntarily dismissed, or is transferred by the new employer.[18]

Example 8

N, an accountant, left his job in Boston to take a new job with a firm in Orlando. After working for the firm for eight months, he became dissatisfied and quit to open his own practice as a sole proprietor. Due to the poor economy, N closed the business after six months and moved to Denver. N may not deduct his expenses of moving to Orlando. Since he was employed for only 32 weeks (eight months) during the 12-month period after arrival in Orlando, he does not meet the 39-week test for employees. Similarly, he does not meet the alternative 78-week test since he was employed or self-employed only 56 weeks (14 months) of the 24-month period in Orlando after his arrival. Whether the costs of moving to Denver are deductible depends on whether either of the tests can be satisfied.

---

[16] § 217(c)(1).

[17] § 217(c)(2).

[18] § 217(d).

In many instances, taxpayers do not know by the end of the tax year whether they will be able to satisfy the time test. Accordingly, the law permits the taxpayer to claim the deduction on the assumption that the test will be satisfied. If the test is subsequently failed, the taxpayer must increase income in the year of failure by the amount of the previous deduction. In lieu of claiming the deduction prior to satisfaction of the test, the taxpayer may wait until the test is satisfied and file an amended return for the year of the moving expense.

DEDUCTIBLE MOVING EXPENSES

For many years, taxpayers were allowed to deduct a variety of moving expenses. These included not only direct expenses such as the cost of moving the taxpayer's personal belongings and the cost of traveling to the new location but also a limited amount of indirect expenses. For example, a taxpayer could deduct expenses for house-hunting trips, temporary living at the new location, and expenses related to disposing of the taxpayer's former residence. In 1993, however, Congress eliminated the deduction for all indirect moving expenses. Currently, only the following direct moving expenses are deductible. They are[19]

1. Costs of moving household goods and personal belongings; and
2. Costs of traveling from the old location to the new location.

Costs of Moving Household Goods and Personal Belongings

This category of direct moving expenses includes the following:[20]

- Packing, crating, and transporting the taxpayer's personal possessions (e.g., the cost of hiring a moving company or renting a truck).

- Storage and insurance of goods and personal effects while "in-transit" (i.e., any consecutive 30-day period after the day the items are moved from the former home and before they are delivered to the new home).

- Connecting and disconnecting utilities required by the moving of the taxpayer's appliances.

- Moving a pet or shipping a car.

- Losses on dispositions of club memberships, expenses of refitting rugs and drapes, mortgage prepayment penalties (perhaps deductible as interest), and similar expenses are not deductible.

Costs of Traveling

Once the taxpayer's furniture and other items are out the door, the taxpayer's household must follow. Only the costs of moving a taxpayer's family members (including pets) are deductible. Those for such nonfamily members as servants, chauffeurs, governesses, or nurses do not qualify. The following travel expenses are deductible:

- *Transportation costs.* The taxpayer may use actual expenses (i.e., the costs of oil, gasoline, tolls, and parking—but not those for general repairs or maintenance) or 17 cents per mile in 2017.[21]

- *Lodging expenses.* The taxpayer may deduct the costs of lodging incurred in traveling to the new location. No deduction is allowed for any meal expenses related to the move.[22]

Nondeductible Expenses

As noted above, in 1993 Congress eliminated the deduction for so-called "indirect" moving expenses. As a result, expenses for the following are no longer deductible:

- House-hunting trips.

- Temporary living at the new job location (e.g., an apartment or motel).

---

[19] §§ 217(b)(1)(A) and (B).

[20] Reg. § 1.217-2(b)(3).

[21] Notice 2016-79, 2016-52 IRB ___.

[22] § 217(b)(1)(B).

- Sale, purchase, or lease of a residence (e.g., appraisals, attorney's fees, points, or payments to a lessor to cancel a lease).

- Meals.

Example 9

During the year, K, who was employed as a professional basketball player in Oklahoma City, became a free agent and moved to San Francisco to play with the Golden State Warriors. Although he had lived in Oklahoma City for several years, K decided to move permanently to San Francisco. Prior to the move, K made several trips to San Francisco to look for a new home. After finding just the right one, he hired a moving company to pack and move all of his personal belongings. During the summer, he drove to San Francisco. Upon arrival, however, complications arose and he was not able to move in immediately. He ended up staying at a hotel for three weeks before he was able to take possession. K incurred the following expenses in making the move:

Costs of traveling to San Francisco to look for a house	$ 900
Costs of moving van (including costs of $500 for packing and crating).	15,000
Costs of storage in San Francisco	1,000
Transportation costs (2,000 miles @ 17 cents per mile in 2017)	340
Three-week hotel stay (meals and lodging).	3,000
Real estate commission on sale of former residence	30,000

K is allowed to deduct only the direct expenses related to the move: the van, storage, and transportation, for a total of $16,340 ($15,000 + $1,000 + $340). The indirect expenses, house-hunting, temporary living, and selling expenses are not deductible. However, K may treat the costs of selling his home as a reduction in the amount realized on the sale of the home, decreasing any gain realized or increasing any loss realized. Note that if K's new employer reimburses K for any of the expenses, he must include the reimbursement in income.

CLASSIFYING AND REPORTING THE MOVING EXPENSE DEDUCTION

Moving expenses of an employee or a self-employed person are deductible for AGI. All moving expenses are reported on Form 3903.

In many cases, the employer will either pay the moving expenses directly or reimburse the employee for such expenses. When the latter occurs, the employee excludes the payment from gross income as a qualified fringe benefit under § 132. However, the exclusion is allowed only to the extent that the moving expenses meet the requirements for deductibility. It is not unusual for the employer to pay for a number of moving expenses that are not deductible (e.g., house-hunting and temporary living expenses); in such case, these amounts are included in the employee's W-2 as other income. Similarly, no exclusion is allowed for any moving expenses actually deducted by the employee in the prior year.

 ### CHECK YOUR KNOWLEDGE

Review Question 1

After 15 years with the firm, J was finally promoted to partner. The substantial raise that came along with the promotion enabled him to build the house of his dreams. The new home is nestled in the woods near Lake Lemon, 60 miles from his old condo in the city. His new commute is 58 miles. Will J be able to deduct his moving expenses?

No. The distance requirement focuses on what would have happened to the taxpayer's commute had he not moved. As a general rule, J's commute absent the move must have increased by at least 50 miles. In other words, the distance between the old home and the *new job site* must exceed the distance between the old home and the *old job site* by at least 50 miles.

Note that in order to satisfy this requirement there normally must be a change in job location. In this case, his commute without the move does not increase since the job location did not change. Therefore, his moving expenses are not deductible.

Review Question 2

Mitch's three grueling years in law school finally paid off. This year he graduated from Harvard and took a job with a firm in Memphis for $80,000 a year. He does not itemize his deductions. Can he deduct any of his moving expenses?

Yes. Deduction of moving expenses normally requires the taxpayer to change job sites. However, if the taxpayer is not currently employed and has no former job site, the distance test is met if the new job site is at least 50 miles from the taxpayer's old residence. Also note that because moving expenses are deductible for AGI, Mitch can claim the deduction even though he does not itemize.

Review Question 3

Grandma and Grandpa retired this year and moved from Detroit to Florida at a cost of $15,000. Both took part-time jobs at a local fast-food restaurant. Can they deduct their moving expenses?

No. In order to meet the time test, the taxpayer must be employed on a *full-time* basis for 39 weeks of the 12-month period immediately following arrival at the new location.

Review Question 4

Indicate whether the following moving expenses are deductible.
   a. Rental of moving truck.
   b. Boxes to pack household items.
   c. Brake job for car while en route to new location.
   d. 53.5 cents per mile for each mile driven to the new job location.
   e. Meals on the three-day, 900-mile trip to the new location.
   f. Trip to look for a new house after the new job was secured but before the move.

Only (a) and (b) are deductible. Unusual costs incurred in traveling to the new location such as repairs are not deductible. In lieu of deducting actual transportation expenses, 17 cents per mile (2017) is allowed. Meals and house-hunting trips are not deductible.

Home Office Expenses

It is currently estimated that more than 39 million Americans—39% of the labor force—work at home either full or part time. However, simply working at home does not automatically enable a taxpayer to write off the costs of owning or renting. Very narrow standards must be met before a deduction is permitted.

   At one time, expenses relating to use of a portion of the taxpayer's home for business purposes were deductible without limitation when they were merely appropriate and helpful in the taxpayer's business. In 1976, however, Congress felt that the appropriate and helpful test was insufficient to prevent the deduction of what were really personal expenses. For example, under the helpful test, a university professor who was provided an office by his employer could convert personal living expenses into deductions by using a den or some other room in his residence for grading papers. In such a situation, it was unlikely that any additional expense was incurred due to the business use. To prevent the deduction of disguised personal expenses, Congress enacted § 280A, severely limiting the deduction of expenses related to the home. Section 280A generally disallows deduction of any expenses related to the taxpayer's home except those otherwise allowable, such as qualified residence interest and taxes, and those for *certain* business and rental use (the exception for rental use is discussed in Chapter 12).

REQUIREMENTS FOR DEDUCTIBILITY

LO.4

Describe when expenses of maintaining a home office are deductible.

Under the business use exception, a deduction is allowed for a home office if a portion of the home is "exclusively" used on a "regular" basis for any of three types of business use:[23]

1. As the principal place of business for *any* business of the taxpayer;

2. As a place of business used regularly by patients, clients, or customers in meeting or dealing with the taxpayer in the normal course of his or her trade or business; or

3. In connection with the taxpayer's trade or business when the office is located in a separate structure.

Beyond these basic requirements applicable to all taxpayers, there is one additional test that must be met if the taxpayer is an employee. Employees are entitled to claim a home office deduction only if the home office is for the *convenience of the employer*. Each of these prerequisites is considered below.

Exclusive Use

Under prior law, a taxpayer might write off his whole kitchen just because he opened his briefcase there. The exclusive use requirement was intended to put an end to such shenanigans. A deduction is allowed only when the space in the home is devoted solely to business use. The authors of § 280A apparently did not believe a deduction should be allowed where the space was used for both personal and business purposes. The exclusive use requirement does not mean that the home office must be physically separated from the remainder of the home. It is not necessary that the portion of the room be marked off by a permanent partition. It is sufficient if the home office activities are confined to a particular space in a room that is used only for business purposes.[24] To what extent, if any, the IRS will permit personal activities to be carried on in the home office (e.g., making personal phone calls, reading for pleasure, taking care of investments as well as business) is not clear. In any event, the taxpayer should be reminded that the key word is *exclusive*. Two exceptions to the exclusive use test, storage and daycare use, are discussed below.

Regular Use

Section 280A also requires the home office to be used on a regular basis. Fortunately, the Code and Regulations have not adopted precise rules that require the taxpayer to punch a time clock every time he or she steps into the home office. Currently, there is no requirement to keep track of the hours spent in the office. The little guidance that does exist on the issue can be found in IRS publications. The Service does not specifically define *regular* but does explain that occasional or incidental use does not meet the regular use test even if that part of the home is used for no other purpose.[25]

Convenience of the Employer

As noted above, if the taxpayer is an employee, he or she must jump one additional hurdle before claiming the home office deduction. An employee must work at home for the *convenience of the employer*. To meet this condition, the home office must be more than appropriate and helpful. The Tax Court has suggested that satisfaction of this test requires the taxpayer to show that he or she was unable to do the work performed at home at the employer's office.[26] For example, the Second Circuit has held in *Weissman* that this standard is met if the employer does not provide the employee with space to properly perform his or her employment duties.[27] In this case, a college professor who shared an office and did extensive research at home satisfied the test because in the Court's view the home office was necessitated by lack of suitable working space on campus.

---

[23] § 280A(c).

[24] *George Weightman*, 42 TCM 104, T.C. Memo 1981-301.

[25] § 280A(c)(1). See *Business Use of Your Home*, IRS Publication 587 (2016), p. 3.

[26] *Robert Chauls*, 41 TCM 234, T.C. Memo 1980-471.

[27] *Weissman v. Comm.*, 85-1 USTC ¶9106, 55 AFTR2d 85-539, 751 F.2d (CA-2, 1984). The convenience test is also used in § 119 relating to exclusion of meals and lodging and § 280F on employee use of listed property. See Chapters 6 and 9.

Principal Place of Any Business

A taxpayer satisfies the first business use test if the home office is the principal place of business for *any* business of the taxpayer. Most taxpayers, as employees, fail this test since their only business is that of being an employee and the principal location of that business is at the employer's office. This rule is not foolproof, however. In one decision, the court held that the principal place of business of a taxpayer employed as a concert musician was his home practice room rather than where he gave performances.[28] In contrast, employees who have a *second* business (e.g., selling cosmetics or vitamins) or self-employed persons who operate these activities out of their home normally satisfy the first business use test as long as they can show that the home is in fact the principal place of business.

For years, taxpayers and the IRS squabbled over when a home office constituted a taxpayer's *principal* place of business.[29] The leading case was the Supreme Court's 1993 decision in *Nader E. Soliman*.[30] Soliman was an anesthesiologist who worked for three hospitals. However, none of the hospitals provided him an office so he spent 10 to 15 hours a week at his home office doing his billing and scheduling. To Soliman's chagrin, the IRS denied his deductions for his home office expenses. Upon review, the Tax Court was more sympathetic, allowing the deductions on the grounds that the home office was essential to Soliman's business, he had spent substantial time there, and there was no other location available to perform the office function of the business. Although the Fourth Circuit agreed with the Tax Court, the Supreme Court did not. The high court stated that it is not sufficient that the work done in the home office is essential to the business. The court explained that to satisfy the principal place of business test, the home office must be the most important place of business as compared to all the other locations where the taxpayer carries on business. In determining whether the home office is the *most important place of business,* the court identified two factors that should be considered: (1) the relative importance of the functions performed at each of the business locations, and (2) the amount of time spent at each location. In this case, the court believed that the hospital, where Soliman performed his services and treated patients, was his most important place of business.

As might be expected, a huge backlash erupted after the *Soliman* decision since it operated to deny the home office deduction to millions of taxpayers. Most affected were those who performed essential business functions in their homes but who spent most of their time at the locations of their clients and customers (e.g., salespeople, consultants, repair people, personal trainers, caterers, etc.). In response, Congress acted in 1997 to restrict the scope of *Soliman*. Although the tests of *Soliman* can still apply, the taxpayer may now meet the principal place of business test if both of the following conditions are met:

1. The office is used by the taxpayer to conduct *administrative and management activities* of a trade or business; and

2. There is no other fixed location of the trade or business where the taxpayer conducts *substantial* administrative and management activities of the trade or business.

Under current law, taxpayers who manage or administer their businesses out of a home office may claim a deduction even if the taxpayer conducts substantial non-administrative or nonmanagement business activities at a fixed location of the business outside the home. For example, this approach allows taxpayers like the doctor in *Soliman* a deduction for their home office expenses even though they conduct significant activities away from home at a fixed location (e.g., surgery at a hospital). Similarly, outside salespeople who spend the majority of their time calling on customers can claim the deduction if they use their home office to conduct administrative activities such as receiving orders, setting up appointments, or writing-up orders. In some cases, taxpayers may have an office available to perform administrative activities but opt to perform these tasks at home. In such case, the test is still met assuming the taxpayer does not actually perform substantial management or administrative activities at the other location. At all times, however, it must be emphasized that in the case of an employee, the *convenience of the employer test* must still be met. For this reason, an *employee* may be denied the deduction of expenses for a home office used for administrative activities if suitable space is available for performing such duties at the employer's office.

[28] *Drucker v. Comm.*, 83-2 USTC ¶9550, AFTR2d 83-5804 (CA-2, 1983); but see *Popov v. Comm.*, T.C. Memo 1998-374.

[29] For example, see *Rudolph Baie*, 74 T.C. 105 (1980).

[30] *Comm. v. Soliman*, 93-1 USTC ¶50,014 (USSC, 1993), rev'g *Nader E. Soliman*, 94 T.C. 20 (1990).

Example 10

T is a manufacturer's representative. He promotes the products of several companies, selling to both wholesalers and retailers all over the state of Ohio. None of the companies he represents provide him an office, so he maintains an office at home. T spends an average of 30 hours a week visiting customers and 12 hours a week working in his home office. Under the *Soliman* rule, T would not be allowed to deduct the costs of maintaining a home office since his clients' premises would be his most important place of business.[31] Using the revised approach, however, T could claim the deduction since he conducts management activities in the home and there is no other fixed location where he conducts substantial management activities related to his business.

It should be emphasized that taxpayers who cannot qualify for the home office deduction under the principal place of business test may still find relief if they meet one of the other—more liberal—tests discussed below (i.e., regularly meet with clients or separate structure tests).

Trade or Business

No deduction is permitted for home office expenses if the activities to which they relate do not constitute a business.[32]

Example 11

B, an engineer, regularly uses a room in his home exclusively for evaluating his investments. No deduction is permitted since the activity does not constitute a business.

Meeting Place

The second exception for business use is less restrictive than the first. Under this exception, the home office qualifies if clients regularly meet with the taxpayer there. Interestingly, in *John W. Green,* the taxpayer ingeniously argued that this exception should be satisfied where he regularly received phone calls in his home office. Although a majority of the Tax Court agreed with the taxpayer, the decision was reversed on appeal. The Appellate Court believed that the statute required that the taxpayer *physically* meet with clients in the home office.[33]

Separate Structure

The third exception for business use is the least restrictive of the three. If a separate structure is the site of the home office, it need be used only in connection with the taxpayer's work (e.g., a converted detached garage or barn).

AMOUNT DEDUCTIBLE: GENERAL METHOD

If the taxpayer qualifies for the home office deduction, an allocable portion of expenses related to the home may be deducted. The allocation of expenses generally must be based on square footage. Typical expenses include utilities, depreciation, insurance, security systems, repairs (e.g., furnace repair), interest, taxes, and rent. It should be emphasized that the home office deduction is limited to the gross income from the home business as reduced by allowable deductions. This computation is very similar to that for determining deductible hobby expenses. The taxpayer may deduct expenses equal to the extent of gross income reduced by (1) expenses allowable without regard to the use of the dwelling unit (e.g., interest—assuming it is a primary or secondary residence—and taxes), and (2) business or rental expenses incurred in carrying on the activity other than those of the home office (e.g., supplies and secretarial expenses).[34] Any home office expenses that are not deductible due to this limitation may be

[31] Notice 93-12, 1993-1 C.B. 202; see also, Rev. Rul. 94-24, 1994-1 C.B. 87 for how the IRS will apply the *Soliman* tests.

[32] S. Rep. No. 94-938, 94th Cong., 2d Sess. 147-49 (1976).

[33] 78 T.C. 428 (1982).

[34] See § 280A(c)(5).

carried over and used to offset income from the business which led to the deduction, even if the taxpayer does not use the unit in the business in subsequent years.

When the taxpayer is self-employed (i.e., a sole proprietor), all of the taxpayer's expenses, including those attributable to the home office, are deductible for AGI. In contrast, if the taxpayer is an employee, the *otherwise allowable* expenses (e.g., interest and taxes) are deductible in full as itemized deductions. The other business expenses, including the home office expenses, are considered miscellaneous itemized deductions and are subject, along with other miscellaneous itemized deductions, to the 2% floor. All expenses for business use of a home office must be reported on Form 8829 (see Appendix B for a sample form).

Example 12

K maintains a qualifying home office. During this year, she earned only $2,000 from the home office activities. Her expenses included the following: interest and taxes allocable to the home office, $600; secretarial services, miscellaneous supplies and postage, $900; and expenses directly related to the home office including insurance, utilities, and depreciation, $1,700. K's potential deduction is $2,000 computed as follows:

Gross income		$2,000
Otherwise allowable deductions:		
Interest and taxes	(600)	$ 600
Other business expenses	(900)	900
Gross income limitation	$ 500	
Home office expenses:		
$1,700 limited to remaining gross income		500
Total potential deduction		$2,000

Whether the $2,000 of deductible expenses are deductible for or from AGI depends on whether K is self-employed or an employee. If K is self-employed, the entire $2,000 is deductible for AGI. If the taxpayer is an employee, the $600 of interest and taxes allocable to the home office are deductible as itemized deductions. The remaining $1,400 is considered a miscellaneous itemized deduction subject (along with other miscellaneous itemized deductions) to the 2% floor. The home office expenses that are not deductible this year, $1,200 ([$600 + $900 + $1,700 = $3,200] − $2,000), may be carried over to the following years to be offset against future home office income.

AMOUNT DEDUCTIBLE: SIMPLIFIED OPTIONAL METHOD

The IRS provides a simplified option for computing the amount of the home office deduction.[35] This safe harbor rule is much like the standard mileage rate for business automobiles discussed below. The optional method allows a uniform deduction of $5 for each square foot of the home used for business up to a maximum of 300 square feet. If the square footage is less than 300, the lower amount is used to compute the deduction. The maximum deduction is $1,500 ($5 × 300). In addition, the taxpayer must follow the special rules below.

- Interest and taxes related to the home office are deductible in full as itemized deductions on Schedule A. Such amount does not reduce gross income for purposes of computing the maximum home office deduction. No special allocation is made (e.g., between Schedule C for self-employed taxpayers and Schedule A).

- If the deductible amount as based on square footage exceeds gross income from the home office activity, the excess is not deductible and cannot be carried over.

---

[35] Rev. Proc. 2013-13 2013-6 IRB 478.

- No depreciation is allowed and consequently, the basis of the home is not reduced. If the regular method (rather than the optional method) is used and the home is subsequently is sold at a gain, the gain realized (which is normally excluded) must be recognized to the extent of any depreciation allowable. In contrast, if the optional method is used, this depreciation recapture rule does not apply.

- The taxpayer can choose to use either the simplified method or the regular method for any taxable year. The taxpayer may switch methods from one year to the next.

- Classification of the deduction based on square footage depends on how the home office is used. If the taxpayer operates a sole proprietorship or is self-employed, the deduction would be claimed on Schedule C. If the home office is used in connection with the taxpayer's employment, the expense would be an unreimbursed employee business expense and treated as a miscellaneous itemized deduction subject to the 2% floor. In any event, the interest and taxes are deductible as itemized deduction on Schedule A.

- No recordkeeping is required, which may be a big advantage for many taxpayers.

Example 13

T is a CPA. In addition to having a small tax practice, he provides continuing education programs for tax practitioners. Income from these activities for the year is $45,000. T uses a room in his home for the tax preparation business and to create materials used in his programs. The room qualifies as a home office. The size of the room is 400 square feet and represents 10% of the size of his home. His adjusted basis of the room is $10,000. T's expenses directly related to his business for the year include the following:

Supplies	$ 1,000
Advertising	600
Journal subscriptions	800
Postage	100
Total	$ 2,500

The expenses related to his home for the year are shown below.

Mortgage interest	$ 9,000
Real property taxes	3,400
Homeowner's insurance	1,500
Utilities	2,600
Repairs	700
Total	$17,200

For the current year, T elected to compute his home office deduction using the simplified option. In filing his Form 1040 for the year, T deducts his mortgage interest of $9,000, and property taxes of $3,400 as itemized deductions on Schedule A. His deduction for his home office is $2,000 ($5 × 400 square feet) and is reported along with his other business expenses of $2,500 on Schedule C. The other home office expenses (insurance, utilities and repairs) are not deductible. In addition, T may not deduct any depreciation with respect to his home office and the depreciation is deemed to be zero. Consequently, his basis in the room is unchanged and continues to be $10,000. The gross income limitation does not limit T's home office deduction since it does not exceed $42,500 ($45,000 gross income − $2,500 business deductions). Note that in determining the gross income limitation the mortgage interest and real property taxes are ignored.

DAYCARE AND STORAGE USE

The home office rules for taxpayers who use their home as a daycare center or as a place to store inventory or product samples of a home-based business receive special attention from the Code. In both cases, the normal rules apply except that the exclusive use test is relaxed.

Daycare Use

If a portion of the taxpayer's home doubles as both a living space and a daycare center it would appear that no deduction would be allowed since the exclusive use test would not be satisfied. When the home is used as a daycare center, however, the exclusive use test does not apply.[36] Instead, the expenses attributable to the room are prorated between personal and daycare use based on the number of hours of use per day. Thus, if the taxpayer uses a family room for daycare 40% of the time, 40% of the expenses allocable to that room would be deductible. A portion of the home qualifies for this special treatment if the taxpayer uses the home to provide daycare services for children, individuals over age 65, or those who are physically or mentally incapable of taking care of themselves.

Storage Use

If the taxpayer regularly uses part of the home to store product samples or goods sold at retail or wholesale *and* the home is the sole fixed location of that business, expenses related to the storage space are deductible.[37] More important, the space need not be used exclusively for this purpose. However, the space should be a specific area (e.g., a particular part of a basement or closet).

RESIDENTIAL PHONE SERVICE, CELLPHONES, SMARTPHONES, AND INTERNET SERVICE

For many years, taxpayers who used their home phone for business or income-producing purposes deducted a portion of the basic charge for local service on the grounds that it was business-related. In 1988, however, Congress saw the issue differently. Apparently, in 1988, it believed that the cost of basic phone service to a taxpayer's residence would have been incurred in any event—without regard to any business that the taxpayer might otherwise conduct. As a result, a taxpayer may not deduct any charge (including taxes) for local phone service for the *first* phone line provided to any residence.[38] The taxpayer may still deduct the costs of long-distance phone calls or optional phone services such as call waiting or call forwarding, when such costs are related to business. In addition, taxpayers may deduct the costs of additional phone lines into the home that are used for business (e.g., a separate line for a fax machine or modem).

However, the world has come a long way since 1988. As of October 2014, the Pew Center for Research reported that 90% of American adults had cellphones and 64% had smartphones. And, they are not just using them for personal purposes. In the world of business, cellphones and smartphones have become just as vital as land lines, if not more so. So it's not surprising that the tax law allows employees and self-employed individuals to deduct the cost of using their high-tech phones for business. If the phone is used *exclusively for business,* the initial cost of the phone as well as monthly bills are fully deductible. For employees, the deduction would be a miscellaneous itemized deduction while self-employed individuals would claim the deduction on Schedule C, resulting in a deduction for AGI. As explained more fully in Chapter 9, taxpayers normally are required to depreciate the cost of their phone over seven years unless they use it more than 50% for business in which case they may be able to deduct the business percentage all in one year under § 179.

---

[36] § 280A(c)(4).

[37] § 280A(c)(2).

[38] § 262(b).

Of course, the difficulty is determining and substantiating the amount of business use. For many, cellphones have become inextricably woven into their daily lives. That makes separating deductible business use from nondeductible personal use difficult, if not impossible. In that regard, itemized phone bills that provide call-time can help. One failsafe solution is to have two phones, one for business and the other for personal purposes. But, few want to go to that extreme. Nevertheless, if the IRS asks, there is no doubt that it will want records to support the deduction! Perhaps, the only hope for the taxpayer is there's an app out there that can sort this all out!

Like cellphone costs, fees paid to internet service providers for internet access are deductible to the extent the internet is used for business purposes. In one recent case, the Tax Court allowed a deduction for 70% of such costs even thought only 33% of the taxpayer's home qualified for the home office deduction.[39]

 ## CHECK YOUR KNOWLEDGE

Review Question 1

Indicate whether the following taxpayers would be allowed to deduct expenses attributable to a home office.

a. T is on the tax staff of a public accounting firm. From time to time, he brings home returns and does a little work in his home office. In addition, he does most of his technical reading in the home office.

T would not be allowed a deduction since he does not meet the principal place of business or convenience of the employer tests. He fails the first of these tests since his principal place of business is his employer's office. He fails the convenience of the employer test since the employer provides him an office and he could do at the office what he does at home. His work at home appears to be for his own convenience.

b R is a decorator. She works out of an office in her home. She spends about 10 hours per week visiting her client's homes and another 10 visiting businesses that carry furniture and home accessories. The remainder of her 40-hour week is spent at her home office doing sketches, ordering, keeping books, and the like.

R may deduct her home office expenses since she conducts management activities in the home and there is no other fixed location used by her to perform substantial management activities related to her business.

c. J operates a floral shop in town. He grows the plants for his shop in a greenhouse behind his home.

Even though the principal place of J's business is arguably at J's shop, J would still qualify for the deduction under the separate structure exception.

Review Question 2

With the kids starting college, income from their regular jobs was not enough, so this year N and her husband started a small blind and drapery operation. They run it out of an office in their home. N orders the fabric and sews the drapes while her husband installs. In their first year of business, the couple had gross income of $2,000. Interest and taxes allocable to the home office were $600. Various supplies and equipment, including a file cabinet, table, Rolodex, sewing machine, and scissors, cost $1,000. Depreciation, utilities, insurance, and similar expenses allocable to the home office were $900. According to their friend Norm, they should be able to deduct all $1,900 since they are all ordinary and necessary business expenses. Is Norm correct? How much can they deduct?

Norm is only partially right. Section 280A limits the deduction of home office expenses. Home office expenses are essentially deductible to the extent of net income from the business before taking into account the home office expenses (other than the interest and taxes). The home office expenses cannot create a loss from the activity. As a result, the couple can deduct $400 ($2,000 – $1,000 – $600), and the couple's net income from the business after the home office deductions is zero. Note that § 280A limitations do not apply to the $1,000 of expenses for items directly used in the business. These costs relate directly to the business (rather than the home) and, therefore, are fully deductible (or depreciable, as explained in Chapter 9).

---

[39] See *Lauren E. Miller,* TC Summary Opinion 2014-74 where an estimate of internet use sufficed.

If there ever was a contest for the most popular tax deduction or at least the one that arouses the most attention, it would be easy to pick the winner. Virtually everyone who tumbles out of bed each morning and makes the daily trip to work has the same question at tax time: Can I deduct the costs of getting there and getting back? In a world where commuting is routine for millions of taxpayers, it would seem that the answers would be clear-cut. But this is not necessarily the case.

Before examining the deduction for transportation expenses, the distinction between transportation expenses and travel expenses should be explained. In tax jargon, transportation and travel are not synonymous. Travel expenses are broadly defined to include not only the costs of transportation but also related expenses such as meals, lodging, and other incidentals when the taxpayer is in a travel status. As discussed below, the taxpayer is in travel status when he or she is *away from home overnight* on business.[40] In contrast, transportation expenses are defined narrowly to include only the actual costs of transportation—expenses of getting from one place to another while in the course of business when the taxpayer is *not* away from home overnight.[41] Transportation expenses normally occur when the taxpayer goes and returns on the same day. The most common transportation expense is the cost of driving and maintaining a car, but the term also includes the cost of traveling by other forms of transportation such as bus, taxi, subway, or train.[42]

Example 14

M is an architect in Cincinnati. At various times during the year, he drove to Cleveland to inspect one of his projects. He often ate lunch and dinner in Cleveland before returning home. M is allowed to deduct only the costs of transportation. The costs of the meals are not deductible since he was not away from home overnight. Had he spent the night in Cleveland and returned the next day, the costs of meals and lodging as well as transportation would be deductible.

The deduction for transportation is allowed under the general provisions of §§ 162 and 212. Therefore, to qualify for deduction, the transportation expense must be ordinary, necessary, and related to the taxpayer's trade or business or income-producing activity. Personal transportation, of course, does not qualify for deduction. Like many other expenses, however, the boundary between business and personal transportation is often difficult to identify. Some of the common problem areas are discussed below.

DEDUCTIBLE TRANSPORTATION VERSUS NONDEDUCTIBLE COMMUTING

The cost of transportation or commuting between the taxpayer's home and his or her place of employment may appear to be a necessary business expense. It is settled, however, that commuting expenses generally are nondeductible personal expenses. This rule derives from the presumption that the commuting expense arises from the taxpayer's *personal preference* to live away from the place of business or employment. The distance is irrelevant.[43] Moreover, this presumption persists even though there often is no place to live within walking distance of employment, much less one that is suitable or within the taxpayer's means. The fact that the taxpayer is forced to live far away from the place of employment is irrelevant and does not alter the personal nature of the expenses.

LO.5
Distinguish between deductible transportation expenses and nondeductible commuting costs.

---

[40] § 162(a)(2).

[41] Reg. § 1.62-1(g).

[42] *Ibid.*

[43] *Roger A. Green*, TC Summary Opinion 2008-80.

Example 15

In *Sanders v. Comm.*, the taxpayers were civilian employees working on an Air Force base.[44] Despite the fact that they were not allowed to live on the base next to their employment and could only live elsewhere and commute, the transportation costs were not deductible. The Court found it impossible to distinguish between these expenses and those of a suburban commuter, both being personal in origin.

Example 16

In *Tauferner v. Comm.*, the taxpayer worked at a chemical plant that was located 20 miles from any community due to the dangers involved.[45] The taxpayer was denied deductions for his commuting even though he lived in the nearest habitable spot. Arguably, the nature of his job—not personal convenience—produced additional transportation costs. Nevertheless, the Court did not believe that such hardship changed the personal character of the expenses.

While the costs of commuting normally are not deductible, there are several exceptions. These exceptions are discussed below.

Commuting with Tools and Similar Items

The fact that the taxpayer hauls tools, instruments, or other equipment necessary in pursuing business normally does not cause commuting expenses to be deductible. The Supreme Court has ruled that only the *additional* expenses attributable to carrying the tools are deductible.[46] The IRS determines the taxpayer's "additional expenses" by applying the so-called "same mode" test.[47] Under this test, a deduction is allowed for the extra cost of commuting by one mode with the tools over the cost of commuting by the same mode without the tools. Thus, a carpenter who drives a truck would not be allowed a transportation deduction simply by loading it with tools since carrying the tools created no additional expense. The fact that tools may have caused the carpenter to drive a truck, which is more expensive than some other type of transportation, is irrelevant under the IRS view. The courts, however, have rejected this test in certain cases.[48]

Example 17

M plays third trumpet in the Dallas orchestra. During the year, his employer indicated that they did not need the third trumpet and that M would have to switch to his second instrument, the tuba, to retain his job. If, in order to transport the tuba, M had to change from driving to work in a small car costing $3 per day to driving to work in a van costing $5 per day, the IRS would not allow a deduction for the additional cost. Under the same mode test, the cost of driving the van with the tuba is the same as without the tuba. The courts, however, may allow a deduction for the $2 increase in cost. On the other hand, if M rented a trailer to carry the tuba at a cost of $2 per day, the IRS would allow the deduction because the cost of driving the van with the tuba is now $2 more than without the tuba.

The IRS view on the treatment of local transportation is summarized in Exhibit 8-1.

---

[44] 71-1 USTC ¶9260, 27 AFTR2d 71-832, 439 F.2d 296 (CA-9, 1971).

[45] 69-1 USTC ¶9241, 23 AFTR2d 69-1025, 407 F.2d 243 (CA-10, 1969).

[46] *Fausner v. Comm.*, 73-2 USTC ¶95-15, 32 AFTR2d 73-5202, 413 U.S. 838 (USSC, 1973).

[47] Rev. Rul. 75-380, 1975-2 C.B. 59.

[48] *J.F. Grayson*, 36 TCM 1201, T.C. Memo 1977-304. See also *H.A. Pool*, 36 TCM 93, T.C. Memo 1977-20.

Commuting between Two Jobs

The transportation cost of going from one job to a second job is deductible.[49] The deduction is limited to the cost of going *directly* from one job to the other.

EXHIBIT 8-1	When Are Local Transportation Expenses Deductible?

Home: The place where you reside. Transportation expenses between your home and your main or regular place of work are personal commuting expenses.

Regular or main job: Your principal place of business. If you have more than one job, you must determine which one is your regular or main job. Consider the time you spend at each, the activity you have at each, and the income you earn at each.

Temporary work location: A place where your work assignment is realistically expected to last (and does in fact last) one year or less. Unless you have a regular place of business, you can only deduct your transportation expenses to a temporary work location outside your metropolitan area.

Second job: If you regularly work at two or more places in one day, whether or not for the same employer, you can deduct your transportation expenses of getting from one workplace to another. If you do not go directly from your first job to your second job, you can only deduct the transportation expenses of going directly from your first job to your second job. You cannot deduct your transportation expenses between your home and a second job on a day off from your main job.

Source: *Travel, Entertainment, Gift and Car Expense,* IRS Publication 463 (Rev. 2016), p. 14.

[49] *Supra*, Footnote 44.

Example 18

R works for X Corporation on the morning shift and for Y Corporation on its afternoon shift. The distances he drives are diagrammed below.

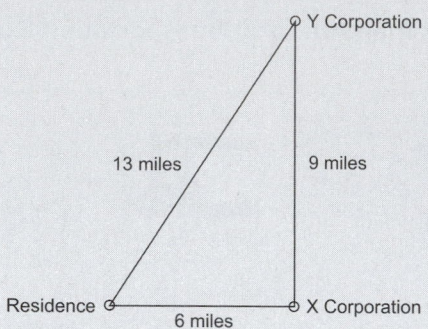

If R leaves X and goes home to eat lunch before going to Y, he actually drives 19 miles to get to Y, or 10 more miles than if he had driven directly (19 − 9). However, only the cost of driving directly, 9 miles, is deductible.

Commuting to a Temporary Assignment

Individuals are often assigned to work at a location other than where they regularly work. When a taxpayer commutes to a *temporary work location,* the commuting expenses are deductible transportation costs if either of the following tests are satisfied:

1. The temporary assignment is *within* the general area of the taxpayer's employment and he or she otherwise has a *regular* place of business (e.g., an office);[50] or

2. The temporary assignment is *outside* the general area of the taxpayer's employment (i.e., his or her tax home).[51]

Example 19

C is an auditor for a public accounting firm that has its office in downtown Chicago. C works about 30% of the time in her employer's office, and the remaining 70% is spent at various clients' offices around the city. C may deduct the costs of commuting between her residence and a client's office because the client's office is a temporary work location and C otherwise has a regular place of business (i.e., her employer's office).

Example 20

M is a carpenter. He works for a construction company that builds houses in subdivisions in various areas of Houston. Most of his assignments are located within about 25 miles of downtown Houston. During the year, M worked at two different locations, one on the north side of Houston and the other on the west side. Although M is assigned to temporary work locations, he is not allowed to deduct any of his commuting expenses because he does not otherwise have a regular place of business.

[50] Rev. Rul. 99-7, 1999-1 C.B. 361.   [51] *Ibid.*

Example 21

Assume the same facts as above except that M was temporarily assigned to a job in Galveston, 60 miles from Houston. He drove to Galveston daily and returned home in the evenings. Under these circumstances, M may deduct the cost of driving the entire 120-mile round trip from his home to Galveston. Observe that when the temporary assignment is beyond the general vicinity of employment, the taxpayer need not have a regular place of business.[52] The following diagram illustrates this approach.

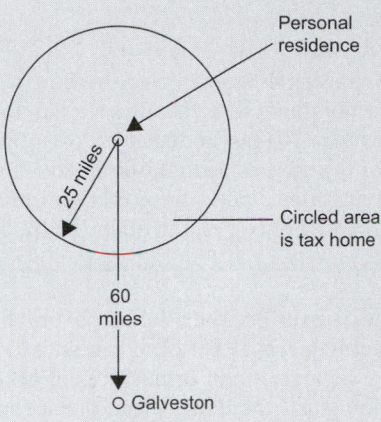

The IRS draws an important distinction between temporary and regular work locations. A work location is temporary if employment at the location is realistically expected to last and does in fact last for one year or less.[53] In contrast, a work location is considered a *regular* place of business if—as one might expect—the taxpayer performs services there on a regular basis. According to the IRS, a taxpayer may have more than one regular place of business even though he or she does not perform services at that location every week or on a set schedule. When the taxpayer commutes to these different locations on a "regular" basis, the costs of commuting would not be deductible because such locations are not temporary.

Example 22

Dr. T, a podiatrist, has an office on both the north side and south side of Indianapolis. In addition, she performs services at a clinic and a hospital with which she is associated. T may not deduct the costs of transportation between her residence and these various locations because each is considered a regular place of business and not a temporary work location. As discussed below, however, the costs of going between two business locations (e.g., a clinic and a hospital) are deductible.

Transportation between Job Sites

While the transportation costs between a taxpayer's home and the first and last job sites generally are considered nondeductible commuting expenses, transportation costs between two job sites are deductible.[54] Accordingly, once the taxpayer arrives at the first job site any business travel thereafter usually is deductible.

---

[52] See *Estate of David B. Lease, Deceased,* TC Summary Opinion 2008-11.

[53] *Ibid.*

[54] Rev. Rul. 55-109, 1955-1 C.B. 261 and Rev. Rul. 99-7, 1999-1 C.B. 361.

> ### Example 23
>
> R is employed as a tax accountant and works primarily in his employer's office downtown. R drives 34 miles round-trip from his home to the office. After arriving at work one day, R drove 6 miles to a client's office and returned to his employer's office. In this case, R may deduct the cost of driving 12 miles.

> ### Example 24
>
> Assume R drives 17 miles to work in the morning. In the afternoon, he drives 15 miles to a client's office where he conducts some business. From the client's office he drives 9 miles home. In this situation, R may deduct the cost of driving 15 miles because transportation between two job sites is deductible. In addition, it appears that he may deduct the cost of driving 9 miles since transportation between the taxpayer's residence and a temporary work location (i.e., the client's office) is deductible.

Although transportation expenses between the taxpayer's home and work normally are not deductible, the rule concerning travel between job sites creates a favorable exception for taxpayers who maintain a separate trade or business at home. For these taxpayers, the transportation from the first job site—the home—and the second job site in the same trade or business would be deductible.

> ### Example 25
>
> V is a landscape engineer and works out of his home, which qualifies as the taxpayer's principal place of business under the home office rules. Transportation costs from his home to a client's place of business are deductible since the expenses are incurred in traveling from his principal place of business to a job site.[55]

OTHER TRANSPORTATION EXPENSES

Certain other transportation expenses are deductible, including the following.

- Transportation expenses related to income-producing activities (in contrast to business activities) are deductible under § 212. Expenses are deductible for AGI if related to rental or royalty income while expenses connected with other investment activities are deductible as miscellaneous itemized deductions subject to the 2% floor.

- Transportation expenses related to medical treatment and charitable activities may be deductible as itemized deductions (see Chapter 11).

COMPUTING CAR EXPENSES

Deductions relating to driving and maintaining a car may be computed using actual expenses or a standard mileage rate (automatic mileage method). Under either method, if the car is used for both business and personal purposes, only the car expenses attributable to business or income production are deductible.

---

[55] See *Edwin R. Curphey,* 73 TC 766 (1980), *Raymond Garner,* 42 TCM 1181, T.C. Memo 1981-542, *Joe J. Adams,* 43 TCM 1203, T.C. Memo 1982-223, *Charles Walker,* 101 T.C. 36 (1993) and Rev. Rul. 94-47, 1994-2 C.B. 18. See also *Bogue v. Comm.* 2013-1 USTC ¶50,354, 111 AFTR 2d 2013-2179, 522 Fed. Appx. 169 (CA-3, 2013) aff'g T.C. Memo 2011-164 where separate structures enabled him to claim the home office deduction but did not qualify the taxpayer's home as his principal place of business for purposes of deducting transportation expenses.

Actual Expenses

Actual car expenses normally deducted include the costs for gas, oil, repairs, insurance, depreciation, interest on loans to purchase the car (other than that of an employee), taxes, licenses, garage rent, parking fees, and tolls. Calculating actual expenses usually requires determining the portion of the nondeductible expenses attributable to personal use. Under the actual expense method, the total actual expense is allocated based on mileage.

Example 26

R, self-employed, drove 20,000 miles during the year: 16,000 on business and 4,000 for personal purposes. Total actual expenses were as follows:

General expenses:	
Gas...	$1,200
Maintenance (oil, repairs)...............................	200
Insurance	1,100
Interest expense	600
Depreciation...	1,900
Total	$5,000

Other business expenses:	
Tolls incurred on business trips.......................	$ 10
Parking fees when calling on clients	90
Total	$ 100

Since R used the car 80% (16,000 ÷ 20,000) for business, he may deduct 80% of the general expenses, $4,000 (80% × $5,000). He also may deduct the entire $100 cost for the parking and tolls since they were incurred for business purposes, for a total deduction of $4,100. Note that the nonbusiness portion of the interest expense would not be deductible, assuming it is not attributable to a loan secured by his first or second home. If R were an employee, *none* of the interest would be deductible because business interest of an *employee* is not deductible.

Standard Mileage Rate

The automatic mileage method allows a deduction of 53.5 cents per mile (2017) for *all* business miles driven during the year.[56] The business portion of expenses for interest (if self-employed), state and local property taxes, parking, and tolls also may be added to the amount computed using the mileage rate. Other expenses such as depreciation, insurance, and maintenance are built into the mileage rate and cannot be added.

Example 27

Same facts as in *Example 26*. R's deduction using the standard mileage rate would be $9,140, as computed below.

Business mileage (16,000 × $0.535).....................	$8,560
Interest ($600 × 80%)	480
Parking and tolls......................................	100
Total	$9,140

Note that in arriving at the deduction, gas, maintenance, insurance, and depreciation are not added to the amount computed using the standard rate since they are built into the rate. Conversely, interest (if self-employed), parking, and tolls are added since they are not included in the rate.

---

[56] Notice 2016-79, 2016-2 IRB ___.

Taxpayers who lease their cars may also use the standard mileage rate. If a taxpayer elects to use the rate for a leased car, it must be used for the entire lease period.[57]

The standard mileage rate may be used *only* if it is adopted in the first year the car is placed in service. In addition, the following conditions must be satisfied:[58]

1. The car must not be one of two or more cars being used simultaneously in a business, such as in a fleet operation. When a taxpayer alternates in using different cars on different occasions, the cars are treated as one and the mileage is combined.

2. The car must not be for hire, such as a taxi.

3. Additional first-year depreciation or depreciation using an accelerated method must not have been claimed in a prior year.

If these conditions are met, the taxpayer may switch methods from year to year. However, use of the standard mileage method precludes the taxpayer from using the Modified Accelerated Cost Recovery System (MACRS) for computing depreciation in a subsequent year, and depreciation must be computed under one of the alternative methods (e.g., straight-line).[59] Note that selecting the actual method in the first year generally *prohibits* the taxpayer from ever using the standard mileage rate for that automobile.

Taxpayers who use the standard mileage rate are required to reduce the adjusted basis of their automobiles just as if they had claimed depreciation. The rate per mile varies by year as shown below.[60]

Year	Depreciation per Mile		Year	Depreciation per Mile
2017	25¢		2008–2009	21¢
2015–2016	24¢		2007	19¢
2014	22¢		2005–2006	17¢
2012–2013	23¢		2003–2004	16¢
2011	22¢		2001–2002	15¢
2010	23¢		2000	14¢

CLASSIFICATION OF TRANSPORTATION AND TRAVEL EXPENSES

The *unreimbursed* transportation and travel expenses of an employee are treated as miscellaneous itemized deductions subject to the 2% floor. In contrast, if an employee is reimbursed for such expenses under a qualified arrangement known as an *accountable plan* (discussed later in this chapter), the reimbursement is excludable from gross income. Any reimbursement not made under such a plan must be included in the employee's gross income, and any qualifying deductions must be treated as miscellaneous itemized deductions. If the expenses are incurred by a self-employed person, the expenses are deductible for AGI. An employee reports the expenses on Form 2106, a copy of which is reproduced in the last section of this chapter.

Travel and transportation expenses related to property held for the production of income are also considered miscellaneous itemized deductions unless the income is rents or royalties, in which case the deductions would be for AGI. In addition, the deduction for meals may be limited to 50% of their cost. This limitation is discussed in detail with entertainment expenses later in this chapter.

Travel Expenses

LO.6

Understand the differences between deductible travel expenses and deductible transportation costs.

Section 162 of the Code provides for the deduction of travel expenses while "away from home" in the pursuit of a trade or business.[61] A similar deduction is allowed for travel expenses connected with income-producing activities not constituting a business.[62] The definition of travel expenses is not as narrow as that of transportation expenses. Travel expenses

---

[57] Prop. Reg. § 1.274-5(g).

[58] *Ibid.*

[59] *Supra*, Footnote 52.

[60] For previous rates see *Travel, Entertainment, Gift and Car Expenses*, IRS Publication 463 (Rev. 2016) p. 24.

[61] *Supra*, Footnote 38.

[62] §§ 212(1) and (2).

include not only the costs of transportation but also the costs of meals (but limited to 50% of actual costs, as discussed later), lodging, cleaning and laundry, telephone, and other similar expenses related to travel.[63] Whether these additional expenses such as meals and lodging are deductible depends on whether the taxpayer is considered "away from home."

AWAY-FROM-HOME TEST

The taxpayer must be *away from home* before travel expenses are deductible. The "away from-home" test poses two questions: for what period does the taxpayer need to be away from home, and where is the taxpayer's home for tax purposes? With respect to the first question, the Supreme Court has ruled that the away-from-home test generally requires the taxpayer to be away from home *overnight*.[64] Later interpretations of this decision have indicated that the taxpayer will be considered to be "overnight" when it is reasonable for the taxpayer to stop for needed sleep or rest. A trip where the taxpayer leaves and returns the same day is not travel and, consequently, only the transportation cost would be deductible. Meals eaten during the trip, lodging, etc., would not be deductible.

The second and more critical aspect of the away-from-home test concerns the determination of the taxpayer's *tax home*. The IRS and the Tax Court have defined the term *tax home* to mean the business location of the taxpayer or the general vicinity of the taxpayer's employment, regardless of the location of the taxpayer's personal residence.[65] The Court of Appeals in several circuits, however, has held that "home" should be interpreted in the normal fashion (i.e., as the place where the taxpayer normally maintains his or her residence;[66] see Example 29). The interpretation problems usually arise when taxpayers live in one location but also conduct substantial business at another location where they often stay because it is impractical to return to the residence. To illustrate, consider a construction worker who lives with his family in Milwaukee but obtains a job to work on the construction of a nuclear power plant near Chicago. During the week, he stays in a motel in Chicago and eats his meals. The issue here is the location of the taxpayer's tax home. If the taxpayer normally works in Chicago, the IRS would take the position that the taxpayer's tax home is in Chicago and deny the deductions for meals and lodging. On the other hand, if the taxpayer normally works in Milwaukee and takes a job in Chicago, he may be able to secure a deduction for his Chicago expenses if he could demonstrate that the Chicago job is only a *temporary* assignment. The IRS permits taxpayers to deduct travel expenses incurred away from the principal place of business if an assignment away from home is temporary and not indefinite. Under § 162(a), assignments in a single location lasting a year or more are not temporary but indefinite.[67] Consequently, if a taxpayer anticipates an assignment to last more than a year or it actually exceeds one year, none of the taxpayer's travel expenses are deductible (not even those for the first 12 months).

Example 28

D is employed as an engineer, living and working in Kansas City. D's employer assigned her to a job in El Paso that D expected to complete in five months. In reality, D lived and worked in El Paso for ten months before completing the job and returning to Kansas city. Because she realistically expected the assignment to last for one year or less and it in fact did not exceed this period, D may deduct her travel expenses for the entire ten months. What would be the result if at the end of four months it became clear that D's stay in El Paso would exceed a year? In such case, the IRS takes the position that she would be able to treat the first four months as temporary and deduct her expenses for those months. However, the expenses for the remainder of the job assignment would not be deductible.

---

[63] Reg. § 1.162-2(a).

[64] *U.S. v. Correll*, 68-1 USTC ¶9101, 20 AFTR2d 5845, 389 U.S. 299 (USSC, 1967).

[65] G.C.M. 23672, 1943 C.B. 66, superseded by Rev. Rul. 74-291, 1974-1 C.B. 42.

[66] For example, see *Rosenspan v. U.S.*, 71-1 USTC ¶9241, 27 AFTR2d 71-707, 438 F.2d 905 (CA-2, 1971).

[67] *Supra*, Footnote 49 and Rev. Rul 93-86, 1993-2 C.B. 71. Federal employees providing services related to investigating or prosecuting a Federal crime are not subject to this rule. See § 162(a), last sentence.

> ### Example 29
>
> In *Joseph Cornelius*,[68] Mr. Cornelius, a computer system administrator, lived and worked in Austin, Texas. In 2001, his employer closed its Austin office and he became unemployed. Subsequently, he was offered work by a systems company on an "as needed" basis and was immediately assigned to work on a client in Boulder, Colorado. The assignment lasted from March 2002 to April 2003. While in Boulder, he stayed in a hotel and shared a condominium. After Boulder, he took another assignment in New Jersey that lasted from April 2003 to July 2005. While in New Jersey he lived in a hotel and shared an apartment. During the time he was on both assignments, he continued to rent his apartment in Austin and periodically returned to visit family and friends. On his 2002 and 2003 tax returns, Mr. Cornelius deducted expenses for meals and lodging while on assignment on the theory that he was away from home on business temporarily. However, upon audit, the IRS denied the deductions and assessed deficiencies of $16,445 and $19,420 for the two years in question. At trial, the Court understood how Mr. Cornelius could believe his assignments to be "temporary," as that word is commonly used. Still, it denied the deductions since both assignments exceeded a year and by law could not be considered temporary. Moreover, deductions for traveling back and forth between Austin and Boulder and Austin and New Jersey were treated as being for personal purposes and disallowed.

If the taxpayer has no principal place of employment, the tax home is normally his regular place of abode.[69] However, if the taxpayer has no permanent place of residence, the courts have consistently denied the taxpayer's deductions for meals and lodging since there is no "home" to be away from. This rule has been applied to itinerant construction workers and salespeople whom the courts view as being *at home* wherever their work may take them.[70]

The purpose of the away-from-home provision is to reduce the burden of the taxpayer who, because of business needs, must maintain two places of abode and consequently incurs additional and duplicate living expenses. The rule is based on the principle that a taxpayer normally lives and works in the same general vicinity. Thus, when taxpayers choose to live in an area other than where they work, the resulting expenses normally are considered personal. This rule often is difficult to apply in particular situations. For this reason, the deduction of travel expenses ultimately depends on the facts.

> ### Example 30
>
> C works at a testing laboratory in a remote mountain area of New Mexico, 70 miles from his home. His residence, however, is the closest place to the laboratory to live. C normally commutes to work but sometimes stays at the testing facilities' quarters overnight when he works overtime. In this situation, the IRS would not allow a deduction for travel expenses since C's tax home is at the testing laboratory, and when staying there he is not away from home. Some Appellate Courts, however, may permit the deduction for meals and lodging since he is away from his residence.[71]

[68] TC Summary Decision 2008-42.

[69] Criteria exist for determining whether a taxpayer has a regular place of abode. See Rev. Rul. 73-529, 1973-2 C.B. 37.

[70] *George H. James v. U.S.*, 62-2 USTC ¶9735, 10 AFTR2d 5627, 308 F.2d 204 (CA-9, 1962).

[71] For example, see *Lee E. Coombs*, 79-2 USTC ¶9719, 45 AFTR2d 80-444, 608 F.2d 1269 (CA-9, 1979).

COMBINED BUSINESS AND PLEASURE TRAVEL

As discussed above, travel costs are deductible only while away from home in pursuit of business or income-producing activities. When traveling away from home, however, taxpayers often combine business with pleasure with the hope that they can deduct what is really a personal vacation. With an eye to this possibility, the Regulations provide special guidance as to how much can be deducted in this situation. The rules governing combined business and pleasure travel differ depending on whether the taxpayer is traveling inside or outside of the United States.

Domestic Travel

The taxpayer who travels within the United States (all 50 states and the District of Columbia) may deduct *all* of the costs of travel to and from the destination if the trip is *primarily* for business.[72] If the trip is primarily for business, the taxpayer will not lose all or even a part of the deduction merely because he or she takes a personal side-trip or extends the trip for a short vacation. However, the costs of any personal side-trips are not allowed. Travel which is primarily for personal purposes is not deductible even though some business is conducted. Note that the taxpayer either deducts *all* of the *to-and-from* travel expenses or deducts *none* of them—there is no allocation. Of course, any travel expenses (e.g., meals and lodging) directly related to business upon arriving at the destination qualify.

Example 31

F, a CPA, flew from Dallas to Denver to attend a conference. The air fare was $500. Meals and lodging for the three days she attended were $150 and $230, respectively. Upon conclusion of the meeting, F drove to the mountains and skied for two days before returning home. The travel to the mountains, including meals and lodging, cost $600. F may deduct all of the air fare, $500, because costs of transportation are fully deductible without allocation when the trip is primarily for business. In addition, F may deduct 50% of the meal costs, $75 (50% × $150), and $230 for lodging because these travel expenses are directly related to business. The expenses of $600 for the ski trip are nondeductible personal expenses.

Example 32

Assume the same facts as in *Example 30,* except that F skied for five days. Here the trip may be treated as primarily personal thus preventing any deduction of the $500 air fare. Fifty percent of the expenses for meals and all of the lodging costs while at the convention on business are still deductible.

Obviously the most troublesome question concerning domestic travel is whether the nature of the trip is primarily business or pleasure. The Regulations, Rulings, and reported decisions offer little guidance—saying only that the answer depends on the facts and circumstances in each case. Among the factors normally considered, the amount of time devoted to business as compared to personal activities is often decisive. Another factor emphasized is the type of location where the business occurs (e.g., a resort hotel or a more businesslike setting). As might be expected, the IRS casts a doubtful eye on deductions for meetings in resort areas, believing that the alleged business trip is merely a disguised vacation. In this regard, Congress took action concerning travel expenses related to nonbusiness conventions (e.g., investment and tax seminars), completely disallowing their deduction after 1986.[73] However, if it can be clearly shown that the expenses were incurred for *business* purposes, the deduction is not disallowed merely because the meeting occurs at a resort.

---

[72] Reg. § 1.162-2(b)(1).

[73] § 274(h)(7). For an interesting case, see *Carl Jones,* 131 TC 3 (2008), where the taxpayer was denied travel deductions incurred to take a course on day trading.

> ### Example 33
>
> This year, Dr. H, a surgeon, attended a week-long course on arthroscopic surgery in Miami. His wife accompanied him and attended a seminar on personal financial planning. H may deduct his costs of transportation as well as the travel expenses incurred after arriving in Miami because the expenses are related to business. None of his wife's expenses are deductible because they relate not to her trade or business but to investments and taxes.

Travel Expense of Spouse and Dependents

The IRS has always taken a dim view of taxpayers who combine business travel with pleasure and in the process deduct the cost of taking their families with them. For years, the Service attacked this abuse with a longstanding regulation that denied the deduction of a family member's travel expenses unless the taxpayer could demonstrate that the family member's presence served a bona fide business purpose.[74] Apparently this ammunition was incapable of adequately policing the problem. Consequently, Congress provided the IRS more help with new legislation in 1994.[75] Currently, no deduction is allowed for any travel expenses paid or incurred with respect to a spouse, dependent, or other individual accompanying the taxpayer (or an officer or employee of the taxpayer) on business unless (1) the individual is an employee of the person paying or reimbursing the expenses, (2) the travel of such individual has a bona fide business purpose, and (3) such expenses are otherwise deductible. The rule does not apply to deductible moving expenses.

> ### Example 34
>
> T is the owner and president of TDI Corporation, which owns seven car dealerships in and around Des Moines. This year General Motors held a meeting for all of its dealers in Maui, and T took his wife and 18-year-old daughter. TDI reimbursed T for all of his traveling expenses including those of his wife and daughter. TDI is not allowed to claim a deduction for the travel expenses of T's wife and daughter unless they are both employees of the company and it can establish that their presence had a bona fide business purpose. Note that T and TDI may be able to overcome the first requirement by employing both his wife and daughter. Satisfying the second test is more difficult. In this regard, the regulations provide that performance of incidental services does not cause a family member's expenses to qualify. The courts, however, have allowed a deduction for a spouse's expenses when the facts have shown that the spouse's presence enhanced the image of the taxpayer or the spouse acted as a business assistant.[76]

Foreign Travel

When the taxpayer travels outside the United States, the travel expenses must satisfy more stringent requirements for deduction. Generally, the costs of transportation to and from the foreign destination and other travel expenses must be allocated between business (or income-producing activities) and personal activities. If the travel is *primarily* business, the costs of transportation are fully deductible without allocation if *one* of the following conditions is satisfied:[77]

1. *Travel outside the United States does not exceed one week* (seven consecutive days). In counting the days out of the United States, the day of departure from the United States is excluded while the day of return to the United States is included. (For example, leaving on Sunday and returning on the following Sunday is exactly seven days.)

---

[74] Reg. § 1.162-2(c); Rev. Rul. 55-57, 1955-1 C.B. 315.

[75] § 274(m).

[76] See *Fraser Wilkins*, 72-2 USTC ¶9707, 30 AFTR2d 72-5639, 348 F. Supp. 1282 (D.Ct. Neb., 1972); *Pierre C. Warwick*, 64-2 USTC ¶9864, 14 AFTR2d 5817, 236 F. Supp. 761 (D.Ct. Va., 1974).

[77] § 274(c); Reg. § 1.274-4.

2. *More than 75% of the days on the trip were devoted to business.* A day is treated as a business day if during any part of the day the taxpayer's presence is required at a particular place for a business purpose. Moreover, the day is considered a business day even though the taxpayer spends more time during normal working hours on nonbusiness activity than on business activity. Weekends, holidays, or other "standby" days that fall between the taxpayer's business days are also considered business days. However, such days are not business days if they fall at the end of the taxpayer's business activities and the taxpayer merely elects to stay for personal purposes. The day of departure and the day of return are both treated as business days.

3. Taxpayer has no substantial control over arranging the business trip.

4. Personal vacation is not a major consideration in making the trip.

If the travel is not primarily for business or fails to satisfy one of the above conditions, an *allocation* of the to-and-from travel expenses must be made. In such cases, the deductible travel expenses are determined by the following allocation formula:

$$\frac{\text{Business days on trip}}{\text{Total days on trip}} \times \frac{\text{Total to-and-from}}{\text{travel expenses}} = \frac{\text{Deductible to-and-from}}{\text{travel expenses}}$$

A deduction for the to-and-from travel expenses is not allowed if the trip is primarily personal. However, travel costs (e.g., meals and lodging) directly related to business upon arriving at the destination are deductible.

Example 35

B, an executive, arranged a trip to Japan primarily for business. He left Chicago for Tokyo on July 1 and returned on July 20. During his trip, he spent 15 days on business (including the two travel days) and five days sight-seeing. His air fare was $1,000 and his lodging plus 50% of the meal costs totaled $100 per day. Unless B can show that a personal vacation was not a major consideration for the trip, he must allocate his expenses because none of the other conditions are satisfied. In such case, B may deduct $2,250 ([15 business days ÷ 20 total days = 75%] × $3,000 total expenses). If B had returned July 8 or spent one less day sight-seeing, no allocation would be required since he would have been out of the United States less than a week or would have spent more than 75% of his time on business activities.

Luxury Water Travel

When lawmakers lowered the boom on entertainment and meal expenses in 1986, they also took a swipe at unhurried business people who travel by cruise ships, ocean liners, and other luxury water transportation. As a general rule, deductions for transportation by water are limited to *twice* the highest per diem amount allowed to Federal employees while away from home but serving in the 48 contiguous states.[78] The rate for travel from September 1, 2016 through September 30, 2016 was $760. If meal or entertainment expenses are not separately stated, they are not subject to the 50% limitation discussed later in this chapter.

Example 36

To conduct a business meeting in London, T traveled by ocean liner, taking five days at a total cost of $3,000. If the per diem rate for luxury water travel is $760 per day, T's deduction is limited to $3,800 ($760 × 5).

---

[78] § 274(m)(1). For rates see Travel, Entertainment, Gift and Car Expenses, IRS Publication 463 (Rev. 2016) p. 9.

FOREIGN CONVENTIONS

Notwithstanding the restrictions imposed on deductions related to foreign travel, substantial abuse existed until 1976. Most of this abuse involved travel to foreign conventions, seminars, cruises, etc., which if properly scheduled amounted to government-subsidized vacations. To eliminate this possibility, specific safeguards were enacted. Currently, no deduction is allowed for travel expenses to attend a convention, seminar, or similar meeting *outside* of North America *unless* the taxpayer establishes the following:[79] (1) the meeting is directly related to the active conduct of his or her trade or business, and (2) it is as reasonable to hold the meeting outside North America as within North America. North America includes the United States, its possessions, Canada, Mexico, the Trust Territory of the Pacific Islands, Bermuda, and qualifying Caribbean countries.

Example 37

B, a professor of international business, traveled to Spain to present a paper on tax incentives for exports at the International Accounting Convention. Since it is as reasonable to hold an international meeting in Spain as in North America, and presentation of the paper is directly related to B's business, she may deduct her travel expenses subject to the normal rules for travel outside the United States.

CRUISE SHIPS

No deduction is allowed for the cost of attending a meeting conducted on a cruise ship unless the following requirements are met:[80] (1) The ship is a vessel registered in the United States and it sails *only* between ports in the United States or its possessions; (2) the meeting is directly related to the taxpayer's business; and (3) certain detailed information regarding the cruise is submitted with the return. For qualifying cruises, the maximum deduction is $2,000 per calendar year for each taxpayer. An employer, however, may deduct the cost of sending an individual to a foreign convention or on any type of cruise if the amount is included in the employee's income.

 ## CHECK YOUR KNOWLEDGE

Review Question 1

Try the following true-false questions. F is director of sales for QVS in Los Angeles but chooses to live 90 miles away in Santa Barbara. Each day he drives to and from work. Once in a while he will leave the office to call on a customer and then return. F may not deduct his cost to commute but can deduct the cost of driving to make calls.

True. As a general rule, commuting is not deductible regardless of the distance traveled. However, the cost of going from one job site to another site is deductible.

Review Question 2

A taxpayer must have a regular work location in order to deduct the costs of commuting to a temporary work assignment outside his tax home.

False. In order to deduct the cost of commuting to a work location *within* the taxpayer's tax home, the taxpayer must have a regular place of business. The same requirement does not apply to commuting outside the taxpayer's tax home.

---

[79] See §§ 274(h)(1), (3), and (6).   [80] § 274(h)(2).

Review Question 3

The costs of depreciation and insurance for an automobile vary significantly depending on the type of car and driver. Consequently, these items are not reflected in the standard mileage rate; however, the taxpayer can add the appropriate amount of depreciation and insurance expense to the amount computed using the standard rate in computing deductible automobile expenses.

False. Depreciation and insurance are included in the rate.

Review Question 4

T is the district manager for Mississippi Catfish, a fast-food chain with more than 100 stores. He lives in New Orleans. On Monday he traveled to Baton Rouge and returned the same day. On Tuesday he traveled to Houston, spent the night, and returned on Wednesday. T may deduct the costs of lunch both in Baton Rouge and in Houston.

False. In order to deduct the costs of meals and lodging, the taxpayer must be in a travel status (i.e., away from home overnight). Thus T cannot deduct the cost of lunch on his day trip to Baton Rouge. He is allowed to deduct the cost of his lunch while in Houston since he was there overnight.

Review Question 5

This year, Dr. F, an ophthalmologist, attended a four-day meeting of his professional organization in Cancun. He remained another three days to lie on the beach and fish. Dr. F may deduct 4/7 of his airfare.

False. If the trip is primarily for business, the taxpayer is allowed to deduct all of the transportation costs to and from the destination.

Entertainment Expenses

Perhaps no single deduction has created as much controversy as that for entertainment expenses. The difficulty lies in the fact that there is no simple way to distinguish entertainment expenses incurred out of business necessity from those incurred for personal purposes. The problem is the "dual personality" of entertainment. Entertainment can be purely for fun and amusement. Or it can be used to break the ice with a potential customer, to relax, or to create an engaging atmosphere for closing the sale or getting the contract. Over the years, Congress and various administrations have continually struggled to devise the proper test that would prohibit taxpayers from deducting what might be a personal expenditure.

The Kennedy administration was the first to have some success in limiting the entertainment deduction. In 1961, President Kennedy recommended abolishing the deduction for entertaining customers at parties, nightclubs, etc., as well as disallowing the deduction for country club dues. Although Kennedy's suggestions were not enacted, Congress did move to make it more difficult to deduct entertainment expenses with the enactment of Code § 274. This provision—discussed below—still stands as the major hurdle that must be overcome before entertainment expenses may be deducted. Under § 274, entertainment expenses must not only satisfy the normal criteria for business and income-producing expenses but also several additional requirements, including certain record keeping standards. Despite these additional conditions, the so-called *Kennedy rules* still were viewed by many to be inadequate.

President Carter's administration ventured into the battle over entertainment deductions in 1977, blasting the taxpayer's right to deduct the cost of what is now the infamous "three-martini lunch." The Carter attacks were generally unsuccessful, however. It was not until President Reagan's term that the entertainment deduction was drastically curtailed. Present law now presumes that virtually every entertainment and meal expense contains a personal element that is not deductible. As discussed below, only 50% of the cost of allowable meals and entertainment is currently deductible.

DEDUCTION REQUIREMENTS

LO.7

Determine when
entertainment expenses
can be deducted.

To be deductible, an entertainment expense must survive the gauntlet of tests applied to all potential deductions by § 162 and then pass the special requirements of § 274. Section 162 first demands that the expense must be reasonable, ordinary, and necessary, and incurred in carrying on a trade or business.

Example 38

D is a sales representative of M Corporation, a manufacturer of cookware. Twice a month, she takes buyers from the leading retail department stores to lunch where they discuss the corporation's new products. Business meals are customary, appropriate, and helpful in commissioned sales and thus are deductible.

As a practical matter, most entertainment expenses satisfy the ordinary and necessary tests with little difficulty. It is the additional requirements of § 274 that provide the greatest obstacles.

The restrictions contained in § 274 apply to any expense related to an activity customarily considered to provide entertainment, amusement, or recreation.[81] The provision applies to expenses for entertaining guests such as those for the following: food, liquor, sporting events, movie and theater productions, social, athletic and country clubs, yachts, hunting and fishing trips, and company-provided vacations. Business gifts also are governed by this provision.[82] It should be emphasized that expenses ostensibly for other purposes also are subject to the requirements of § 274 if they are of an entertaining nature.

Example 39

A national magazine desiring publicity often sends the company president flying in a hot air balloon emblazoned with the corporation's logo. Although the expense is for advertising, § 274 applies since the activity constitutes entertainment.

As might be expected, when the IRS questions the taxpayer about his or her deductions for entertainment, the auditor does not ask whether the taxpayer had a good time. Unfortunately, the agent is concerned with whether the taxpayer has satisfied either of two principal tests. Under § 274, no deduction is allowed unless the taxpayer can adequately substantiate that the entertainment expense is *either* "directly related to" or "associated with" the taxpayer's business or falls within one of ten exceptions.

Directly-Related-To Expenses

The Regulations set forth what the taxpayer must establish for an entertainment expenditure to be considered *directly related* to the taxpayer's business or income-producing activity. Expenses are treated as directly related under the so-called *general test* if the taxpayer shows all of the following:[83]

1. More than a general expectation of deriving some income or other specific benefit (other than goodwill) existed as a result of making the expenditure; no resulting benefit must be shown, however.

2. Business was actually discussed or engaged in during the entertainment.

3. The combined business and entertainment was principally characterized by business.

---

[81] § 274(a)(1).

[82] § 274(d).

[83] Reg. § 1.274-2(c)(3).

Business Benefit

Prior to the enactment of § 274, entertainment deductions were liberally granted where they were shown to promote the customer's goodwill. Section 274 rejects this prior standard. Under current law, the taxpayer must have more than just a general expectation of deriving some income or some specific business benefit. Although this standard is hardly the epitome of clarity, it is clear that the likelihood of a benefit must be greater than a remote possibility.

Example 40

T, an insurance salesperson, sees his old college chum, C, in a bar. T buys his buddy a few drinks and then takes him to a ball game, using an extra ticket T has. Before the night is over, T mentions that if C ever needs insurance he should give T a call. In this case, T's prospect of a business benefit is slight, too distant, and thus not directly related. It simply creates goodwill, which is insufficient to obtain a deduction. However, T may be able to benefit from hindsight. If C later calls him about insurance, T could rightfully claim the deduction.

Actively Engage in Business

Under the general test, the taxpayer must actually discuss or engage in business. This means that at some point during the entertainment—at halftime, during the intermission, between innings—the taxpayer must forsake the merriment of the moment and get down to business, negotiating, dealing, or bargaining with respect to a bona fide business transaction. Since this is obviously difficult to police, the Regulations have given the IRS two helpful presumptions.[84] First, it is presumed that no business can take place if the taxpayer is not present. If the taxpayer is at home mowing the lawn while the client is enjoying the game using tickets given to him by the taxpayer, the implication is that no business can take place. (In such case, the taxpayer may be able to deduct the cost of the tickets as a business gift as discussed below.) Second, it is presumed that no business can take place where there are substantial distractions. The Regulations insist that such distractions are present at night clubs, sporting events, social gatherings, cocktail lounges, theaters, and wherever the taxpayer meets with a group including not only business associates but others. Despite these presumptions, a deduction is still allowed if the taxpayer can establish to the contrary that he or she actively engaged in the discussion of business. As a practical matter, most taxpayers take advantage of this latitude, claiming the deduction and hoping that they will never be called upon to justify it.

Principal Character Is Business. During the entertainment, business must predominate. This does not mean that the taxpayer must spend more time on business than enjoying the activity. It does mean that the business aspects must be more than incidental. As above, the Regulations rest on the rebuttable presumption that the primary character of certain activities—those on a hunting or fishing trip, a yacht or pleasure boat—is not business.

The Regulations also specify several other situations where the entertainment expense will be considered directly related. For example, entertainment is directly related if it is provided in a clear business setting—a setting where the guest recognizes the taxpayer's business motive (e.g., a hospitality room provided by a book publisher at a convention of accounting professors).[85] Expenditures for entertainment provided for those who render services for the taxpayer also are regarded as directly related. For example, a vacation trip awarded by a manufacturer to the retailer selling a number of its products qualifies.[86]

---

[84] Reg. § 1.274-2(c)(7).

[85] Reg. § 1.274-2(d)(4).

[86] Reg. § 1.274-2(d)(5).

Associated-With Expenses

It is often difficult to qualify the entertainment under the directly-related-to test, generally due to the presumption regarding distractions or simply because the taxpayer could not squeeze in any business during the show or game. However, the entertainment may still qualify for deduction if it satisfies the *associated-with test*. Entertainment expenses are considered *associated with* the taxpayer's business if the entertainment is immediately before or after a substantial business discussion.[87] The key distinction between associated-with and directly-related-to expenses concerns when the business activity occurs. The associated-with test allows the business to occur immediately preceding or following the entertainment while the directly-related-to standard requires business during the entertainment. Note that to satisfy the "immediately preceding or following" requirement it is sufficient that the entertainment merely takes place on the same day as business. In some cases, the entertainment may be on the day before or after the business activity.

Example 41

B operates a chain of sporting goods stores in Dallas. Before school begins each fall, he invites area coaches to one of his stores, where he presents his new lines of equipment. Immediately afterward, he takes them to a Cowboys football game. B may deduct the costs of tickets to the game since there was substantial business activity immediately before the entertainment. Note that due to the distractions presented by the game no deduction would be permitted if B merely took the coaches to the game and discussed business there.

Business Meals

For many years, taxpayers were allowed to deduct the cost of meals with business associates regardless of whether they satisfied the directly-related-to or associated-with requirements. More importantly, the costs could be deducted even if business was not discussed. The effect of these rules was to allow a deduction for entertaining that created goodwill. In 1986, Congress believed that this favorable treatment was no longer justified and therefore tightened the rules.

Currently, expenses for meals, like other entertainment expenses, are not deductible unless they satisfy the directly-related-to or associated-with tests.[88] Under these criteria, the business meal is not deductible unless there is a substantial and bona fide business discussion either before, after, or during the meal.[89] In addition, the taxpayer or an employee of the taxpayer normally must be present at the meal.[90] For example, if the taxpayer merely reserves a table for dinner at a restaurant for a customer, but neither the taxpayer nor one of his or her employees attends the dinner, no deduction is allowed. For purposes of this rule, an independent contractor who performs significant services for the taxpayer such as an attorney or accountant is considered an employee.

A common question regarding the deduction for business meals concerns the costs of the taxpayer's own meals. From a purely theoretical view, the cost would presumably be a nondeductible personal expense since the taxpayer has to eat in any event. In *Richard A. Sutter,* the Tax Court took just such a view in disallowing a taxpayer's deduction for his own meals at business lunches.[91] The Court said:

> We think the presumptive nondeductibility of personal expenses (the taxpayer's meals) may be overcome only by clear and detailed evidence as to each instance that the expenditure in question was *different from or in excess* of that which would have been made for the taxpayer's personal purposes (emphasis supplied).

---

[87] *Supra,* Footnote 76; Reg. § 1.274-2(d).

[88] An individual who is away from home on business and eats alone need not satisfy these tests.

[89] §§ 274(a) and (b).

[90] § 274(k)(1)(B).

[91] 21 T.C. 170 (1953).

Despite the Court's holding, the IRS has been quite gracious. The Service permits the taxpayer to deduct the *entire cost* of his or her own meal except in abusive situations where it is evident that a substantial amount of personal expenditures are being deducted.[92] Where abuse is apparent, the IRS would invoke the *Sutter* rule and allow a deduction only to the extent it exceeds the amount the taxpayer would normally spend.

Another common question concerns the costs of entertaining those who are not directly involved in the business activities to which the entertainment relates. The portion of any entertainment expense attributable to the customer's and the taxpayer's spouses is deductible where the purpose is business rather than personal or social.[93] For example, when the taxpayer entertains a business client and it is impractical to entertain the client without the spouse, the expenses of both the taxpayer's spouse and the client's spouse are deductible. Any expenses of other persons not closely connected with those who attended the business discussion are not deductible.

ENTERTAINMENT FACILITIES

For many years, the costs of owning and maintaining such status symbols as airplanes, luxury skyboxes, yachts, and hunting and fishing lodges could be subsidized by deducting them as entertainment expenses. Typically, taxpayers would deduct expenses like depreciation, utilities, maintenance, insurance, and salaries (e.g., that of the yacht's captain) that were allocable to business usage of the property. In 1978, however, Congress imposed severe restrictions. Currently, costs such as those listed above that are related to *any entertainment facility* are not deductible.[94] Additional special rules apply to expenses incurred in using a luxury skybox.[95]

These rules governing entertainment facilities do not prohibit the deduction of out-of-pocket expenses incurred while at the entertainment facility. Expenses for such items as food or beverage would be deductible, assuming they meet the directly-related-to or associated-with tests. In addition, the various exceptions of § 274 discussed below may enable an employer to deduct expenses connected with entertainment facilities. For example, an employer may deduct the costs of vacation condominiums, swimming pools, tennis courts, and similar facilities if such entertainment facilities are provided primarily for employees.[96]

Club Dues

For years, the tax law contained an exception to the facility rule that allowed taxpayers to deduct their dues or fees paid for a membership in country clubs, etc., if the club was primarily used for business. In the never-ending attack on entertainment expenses, Congress eliminated the deduction for club dues in 1993. Currently no deduction is allowed for the cost of membership in any club organized for business, pleasure, recreation, or any other social purpose.[97] The new rule extends not only to country club dues but to all types of clubs, including luncheon, social, athletic, airline, and hotel clubs. The prohibition does not apply to dues paid to civic organizations, such as the Kiwanis or Rotary Club, or to professional organizations, such as the bar association, as long as the principal purpose of the organization is not entertainment. Note that specific expenses incurred at a club such as a business meal continue to be deductible to the extent that they satisfy any other applicable requirements.

---

[92] Rev. Rul. 63-144, 1963-2 C.B. 129.

[93] Reg. § 1.274-2(d)(4).

[94] § 274(a)(1)(B); Reg. § 1.274-2(e)(2).

[95] § 274(l)(2).

[96] § 274(e)(5).

[97] § 274(a)(3).

EXCEPTIONS TO DIRECTLY-RELATED-TO AND ASSOCIATED-WITH TESTS

In certain innocent situations, entertainment and meal expenses need not meet either the directly-related-to or associated-with requirements. These include expenses for the following:[98]

1. Food and drink furnished on the business premises primarily for employees (e.g., costs of a holiday office party).

2. Recreational or social activities, including facilities primarily for employees (e.g., a summer golf outing, a company health club, an annual picnic).

3. Entertainment and meal expenses for an employee if the employee reports their value as taxable compensation (e.g., a company-provided vacation for the top salesperson).

4. Entertainment and meal expenses at business meetings of employees, stockholders, and directors (e.g., refreshments at a directors' meeting).

5. Costs of items made available to the general public (e.g., soft drinks at a grand opening, free ham to the first 50 customers).

6. Costs of entertainment and meals sold to customers (e.g., costs of food sold at an event).

FIFTY PERCENT LIMITATION ON ENTERTAINMENT AND MEAL EXPENSES

LO.8

Describe the 50% limitation on the deduction of meals and entertainment.

Opponents of the deduction for entertainment and meal expenses have long argued that, despite their business relationship, such expenses are inherently personal and should not be deductible. These same critics typically declare that business persons should not be able to live high-on-the-hog at the expense of the government. In 1986 the critics got their way, cutting the deduction to 80% of the actual cost. In 1993, they did it again, slashing the deduction even further.[99]

Currently, § 274(n) generally limits the amount that can be deducted for meals and entertainment to 50% of their actual cost. In effect, 50% of the cost is disallowed. For employees whose entertainment expenses are *not reimbursed,* the 50% limitation is applied before the 2% floor for itemized deductions.

Example 42

B, an employee, pays $3,000 for business entertainment for which he is not reimbursed. B's AGI is $50,000 for the year and he has no other miscellaneous itemized deductions. B's deduction is $500, computed as follows:

Total unreimbursed entertainment expenses	$3,000
Less 50% reduction (50% × $3,000)	(1,500)
Miscellaneous itemized deductions	$1,500
Less 2% of AGI (2% × $50,000)	(1,000)
Itemized deduction	$ 500

Expenses subject to the 50% limitation include the costs of taxes, tips, and parking related to a meal or an entertainment activity. In contrast, the costs of transportation to and from the activity are not subject to limitation.

---

[98] § 274(e)(1) through (9).

[99] § 274(n). Taxpayers subject to the hours of work limitations of the Department of Transportation (e.g., pilots and flight attendants, truck operators) and workers at remote seafood processing facilities (e.g., Alaskan whale boat captains) may deduct a greater portion.

Example 43

B is the agent of G, who recently signed a lucrative contract with the Milwaukee Bucks. After successfully negotiating G's contract, B and G took a cab to a local restaurant where they toasted their success. After dinner, they walked to a nearby nightclub. For the night, B spent $207 for the following:

	Limited Expenses	Other
Meal	$120	
Tax	12	
Tips	30	
Cover charge	38	
Cab	0	$7
Total	$200	$7

The cost of the cab ride, $7, is not subject to limitation and thus can be deducted in full. Of the remaining $200, only $100 is deductible (50% of $200).

It should be emphasized that the percentage reduction rule applies to meals while away from home overnight on business as well as the traditional quiet business meal. The 50% limitation does not apply in several situations, thus allowing the taxpayer to deduct the meal or entertainment in full. These exceptions are discussed below.

Reimbursed Expenses

When the taxpayer is reimbursed for the meal or entertainment, the limitation is imposed on the party making reimbursement, not the taxpayer.[100]

Example 44

N, a sales representative for Big Corporation, took a customer to lunch after he secured a large order. He paid $30, for which he was totally reimbursed. The corporation can deduct only $15 (50% of $30). Technically, N would report $30 in income and may deduct the entire $30 as a deduction for AGI. However, in practice, if the reimbursement is made in accordance with an accountable plan (discussed later in this chapter), nothing is included in the employee's W-2 and he would not claim any deduction. In such case, nothing would appear on N's tax return.

If an employee has a reimbursement or expense allowance arrangement with the employer, but under the arrangement the full amount of business expenses is not reimbursed, special problems arise. These problems are considered along with record keeping requirements later in this chapter.

Excludable Fringe Benefit

The 50% limitation does not apply where the food or beverage provided is excludable as a de minimis employee fringe benefit (e.g., holiday turkeys, hams, fruitcakes, etc., given to employees, subsidized cafeterias, or to meals provided on the employer's premises for the convenience of the employer).[101]

---

[100] §§ 274(n)(2) and 274(e)(3).   [101] § 274(n)(2)(B).

Code § 274(e) Exceptions

The percentage reduction rule generally is not imposed on entertainment and meal costs which are exempted from the directly-related-to and associated-with tests noted above.[102] For example, there is no reduction required for the deductible costs of an annual employee Christmas party, summer golf outings, or company-provided vacations treated as compensation. Similarly, the costs of promotional items made available to the general public (e.g., 100 baseball tickets given by a radio to the first 100 callers) or the salaries of comedians paid by a nightclub are not subject to the 50% limitation.

Charitable Sporting Event

The costs of tickets to a sporting event are not subject to the reduction rule if the event is related to charitable fund-raising.[103] Specifically, the event must be organized for the primary purpose of benefiting a tax-exempt charitable organization, must contribute 100% of the proceeds to the charity, and must use volunteers for substantially all work performed in putting on the event. For example, the cost of tickets to attend a golf or tennis celebrity tournament sponsored by the local chapter of the United Way would normally satisfy these requirements and would be fully deductible. Tickets for high school, college, or other scholastic events (e.g., a football game or theater tickets) do not qualify for this exception on the grounds that volunteers do not do all the work (e.g., coaches, their assistants, and other paid individuals provide substantial work such as coaching and recruiting).

LIMITATIONS ON DEDUCTIONS FOR TICKETS

In the entertainment fracas of 1986, lawmakers also struck a blow at the deductible costs of tickets. This deduction is limited to the face value of the ticket (e.g., 50% of the normal ticket price).[104] This rule is aimed at amounts paid to a ticket scalper in excess of the regular price of the ticket. Such excess is not deductible. The rule also makes nondeductible any fee paid to a ticket agency for arranging tickets. Note, however, that this rule does not apply to tickets to qualified charitable fundraisers.

BUSINESS GIFTS

In hopes that their generosity will someday be rewarded, taxpayers often make gifts to customers, clients, and others with whom they have a business relationship. Such business connected gifts are deductible under the general rules of § 162. Under prior law, taxpayers wanting to create goodwill could shower their business associates with gifts and deduct these instruments of goodwill. Moreover, the recipient of such bounty could arguably exclude the presents. Currently, § 274(b) curbs such practice by limiting the deduction for business gifts to $25 per donee per year.[105] For this purpose, the following items *are not* considered gifts:

1. An item costing $4 or less imprinted with the taxpayer's name (e.g., pens).
2. Signs, display racks, or other promotional materials to be used on the business premises of the recipient.

Incidental costs such as engraving, mailing, and wrapping are not considered part of the cost of an item for purposes of the $25 limit. However, husband and wife are treated as *one* recipient for purposes of the $25 limitation.

---

[102] § 274(n)(2).

[103] § 274(n)(2)(C).

[104] § 274(l)(1).

[105] § 274(b).

Example 45

J, a saleswoman of hospital supplies, computes her deduction for business gifts during the year in the following manner.

Description of Gift	Amount	Deduction
H, head of purchasing at St. Jude hospital:		
Perfume	$10	
Solar calculator	30	
Total	$40	$25
Dr. Z:		
Box of golf balls	$18	
Gift wrap	2	
Total	$20	20
Total business gift deduction		$45

Assuming J is an employee, she may deduct the $45 as a miscellaneous itemized deduction.

Employee Achievement Awards

When a business expresses its gratitude for an employee's performance with a gift, special rules allow amounts greater than $25 to be transferred. The effect of these rules is to allow an employer to make and deduct gifts of up to $1,600 to an employee who is allowed to *exclude* the amount of the gift. The Code generally allows an employer to deduct up to $400 per employee for an *employee achievement award*.[106] An employee achievement award is defined as an item of tangible personal property (e.g., a television or watch, but not cash) transferred to the employee for *length of service* or for *safety* achievement. To help ensure that such awards are not merely disguised compensation, the award must be transferred as part of a meaningful presentation. When the employer has a qualified plan in effect—a nondiscriminatory written plan where the average annual award to all employees does not exceed $400—an exclusion and deduction of up to $1,600 for a particular award is allowed.

Travel and Entertainment Record Keeping Requirements

Travel and entertainment expenses (including business gifts) are not deductible unless the taxpayer properly substantiates the expenses.[107] The *Cohan* rule permitting a deduction for an unsupported but reasonable estimation of an expense does not apply in regard to travel and entertainment.[108]

Section 274(d) specifically requires the taxpayer to substantiate each of the following five elements of an expenditure for travel or entertainment:

1. Amount.
2. Time.
3. Place.
4. Business purpose.
5. Business relationship (for entertainment only).

LO.9

Explain the special record-keeping requirements for travel and entertainment expenses.

---

[106] § 274(j). For a more complete discussion, see Chapter 6.

[107] § 274(d).

[108] Reg. § 1.274-5T(a)(4).

In most cases, each item must be supported by adequate records such as a diary, account book, or similar record, *and* documentary evidence including receipts or paid bills. Where adequate records have not been maintained, the taxpayer's personal statement will suffice—but only if there is other corroborating evidence, such as the testimony of the individual who was entertained.[109] Congress has indicated that oral evidence would have the least probative value of any evidence and has also authorized the IRS to ask certain additional questions concerning substantiation on the return (see Part II, lines 19–21 of Form 2106, discussed below). In addition, the legislative history makes it clear that the IRS and the courts will invoke the negligence and fraud penalties in those cases where the taxpayer claims tax benefits far in excess of what can be justified.

A receipt is necessary only for lodging expenses and any other expenses of $75 or more. Cancelled checks, without other evidence, may not be sufficient. In the well-known blizzard case of 1975, the importance of properly substantiating each element of the expense was made clear.[110] In this case, the taxpayer did not keep a diary or other record of his substantial travel and entertainment expenses, but he presented the District Court with over 1,700 bills, chits, and memos, as well as 20 witnesses. The District Court allowed the deduction holding that the virtual "blizzard" of bills, etc., met the required tests. The Appellate Court, however, disagreed, indicating that the District Court did not determine whether the elements of each expense were substantiated. Lacking sufficient information on the specific purpose of each expenditure, deductions were denied. A written statement of the purpose is unnecessary, however, where the business purpose or business relationship is obvious from other surrounding facts.

In lieu of substantiating the *amount* of meals and lodging expenses while away from home on business, employees and self-employed individuals may elect to compute the deduction using a standard daily allowance rate. For example, in 2017 the standard meal and incidental expense rate (M&IE rate) is usually $51 per day and is reduced by the 50% limit on meals. The standard lodging rate is $91 per day. These rates vary depending on location and time of year. For example, for 2017 the lodging rate in Indianapolis is $161 per day (includes $54 M&IE) while in Manhattan it is $375 for December of 2017 (includes $74 M&IE).[111]

CHECK YOUR KNOWLEDGE

Review Question 1

P, the public defense attorney of South City, occasionally takes all of his staff to lunch. Q, an attorney in private practice, occasionally takes all of her staff to lunch. Can P and Q deduct the costs of the meals?

Too bad, P. This question illustrates the relatively rare situation when the taxpayer's entertainment expenses may fail the ordinary and necessary criterion or perhaps be considered lavish or extravagant. Q, the attorney in private practice, would have no trouble deducting her expenses. However, the IRS denied (with the Tax Court's support) a public defender's deduction since public defenders do not commonly take their staffs to lunch!

---

[109] Reg. § 1.274-5(c)(3).

[110] *Cam F. Dowell, Jr. v. U.S.*, 75-2 USTC ¶9819, 36 AFTR2d 75-6314, 522 F.2d 708 (CA-5, 1975), *vac'g. and rem'g.*

74-1 USTC ¶9243, 33 AFTR2d 74-739, 370 F. Supp. 69 (D.Ct. Tex., 1974).

[111] See U.S. General Services Administration at http://www.gsa.gov/portal/category/104711.

Review Question 2

To illustrate the problems with entertainment expenses, consider the case of Danville Plywood Corporation,[112] a custom manufacturer of plywood. In 1981, Danville sponsored a four-day excursion for 116 people to the Super Bowl in New Orleans. The so-called Super Bowl Sales Seminar cost $103,444 including tickets, airfare, food, and lodging. On its 1981 tax return, the corporation claimed a deduction for the entire amount, euphemistically calling it "advertising expense." The list of attendees included 55 customers, 37 of their spouses, and two of their children. The remainder consisted of a few employees of the corporation and their spouses, as well as the owner, a few of his friends, and two of his children. According to the corporation, the goal of the seminar was to have discussions with the customers over a period of days in order to ascertain how Danville could do a better job as well as cut down on the travel expenses its salespeople incurred on customer visits. In the past, customers had rarely participated in plant visits so the corporation thought some type of sales meeting held in conjunction with a sporting event might boost attendance. In preparation for the trip, the company instructed its employees regarding some new products and provided other information that they were to share with the customers during the Super Bowl or a side trip to the French Quarter. The company also arranged a display showing some of its products in an area adjacent to the lobby of the hotel where everyone stayed. However, when Danville invited its guests, the letter made no reference to business meetings of any kind, nor did the company reserve rooms where business could be conducted. The corporation did hold a dinner in the hotel for all of its guests, but other individuals were also present. Danville had sponsored a similar trip to the 1980 Super Bowl and had deducted about $98,000. Was Danville able to deduct the expenses of all of the attendees?

Unfortunately, Danville got sacked on this play and none of the costs were deductible. In denying the deduction, the court emphasized that the expenses not only had to meet the tests of § 162 (i.e., ordinary and necessary business expenses) but also had to pass the rigorous requirements of § 274. The court found little difficulty in concluding that these tests were not met. It found incredible the corporation's attempt to deduct not only the expenses of the president's children but also those of the customers, explaining that their presence did not serve a bona fide business purpose. The court felt similarly about the president's friends as well as the spouses of both the customers and the employees. With respect to the customers and employees, it noted that there was little if any business discussed—a few idle conversations at most. Moreover, the letters to the customers never mentioned the possibility of business discussions or meetings. Nor were meeting rooms reserved for such purpose. In addition, the court believed that such trips were not commonplace in the industry. Based on these observations, the court concluded that the central focus of the trip was entertainment, not business. Unfortunately, it appears that Danville could have won this contest if it had a better game plan. For example, the deduction may have been secured if only the company's correspondence had properly explained the business nature of the weekend and it had actually conducted a business meeting in a separate room devoted to such purpose. No doubt, it also did not sit well with the IRS that the corporation was so aggressive that it deducted the expenses of the children and the friends. Simply bypassing these deductions may have saved the day.

Review Question 3

Although there appears to be one test after another that taxpayers must meet before they deduct entertainment expenditures, there are some basic requirements. Describe them.

The entertainment must be either directly related or associated with business. This means that a taxpayer must discuss business either before, after, or during the entertainment activity.

---

[112] *Danville Plywood Corp. v. U.S.* 65 AFTR 2d 90-982, 899 F2d 3, 90-1 USTC ¶50,161 (CA-FC, 1990) aff'g 63 AFTR 2d 89-1036, 16 Cl Ct 584, 89-1 USTC ¶9248 (Cl Ct, 1989). Contrast with *Townsend Industries, Inc. v. U.S.* 92 AFTR 2d 2003-6096 342 F3d 890 (CA-8, 2003) rev'g 90 AFTR 2d 2002-6588 (Southern D. Ct. IA, 2002), where a fishing trip for employees had "a bona fide business purpose" for the trip and it enabled informal conversation about employer's business.

Review Question 4

D, an attorney in Indianapolis, is an avid Hoosier fan. Somehow he managed to obtain season tickets to the IU basketball games. From time to time, he is unable to attend a game, so he calls a client and surprises him or her with a pair of tickets. Can D deduct the cost of the tickets for his clients?

D can continue to make his friends happy. As a general rule, no deduction is allowed unless the taxpayer or his representative (e.g., an employee) is present, since business cannot take place. However, D could deduct up to $25 as a business gift.

Review Question 5

E runs an advertising firm and is constantly taking people to lunch. Just yesterday he took the ad director at Channel 12 to dinner at his favorite gourmet restaurant. They both had drinks, salad, prime rib, dessert, and coffee: a total of $30 each. When E eats alone, he typically eats a value meal at the local fast-food place. Can E deduct the cost of his client's meal? Can he deduct the entire cost of his own meal or only the amount in excess of what he normally spends?

E can eat, drink, and be merry. As long as E and his friend discussed business in between bites or the meal followed or preceded a business meeting, he can deduct the entire $60 subject to the 50% limitation.

Review Question 6

This year F was admitted to the partnership of her accounting firm. Not only was F required to contribute $50,000 to the partnership but she was also required to join a country club. She joined the plush Meridian Lakes Country Club at a cost of $25,000. In addition, she must pay monthly dues of $300. Assuming F uses the club exclusively for business, can she deduct the membership and dues?

Sorry, F, but it is the price of being a partner. The Code denies a deduction for the costs of both the membership and the club dues.

Review Question 7

True or False: Taxpayers are generally allowed to deduct only 50% of their unreimbursed travel and entertainment expenses.

False. Do not be fooled. A typical mistake is to lump travel and entertainment together. Only meals and entertainment expenses are subject to the 50% rule. Travel (other than meals) is not subject to the limitation.

Review Question 8

G&H, a public accounting firm, provides continuing education for its tax staff at a resort in Florida. During the week, the employees spend hour upon hour in seminars devoted to the tax law. The firm pays for the meals and lodging of the participants. Is G&H entitled to deduct the entire costs of the meals or only 50 percent?

The 50% limitation normally applies to the costs of all meals and entertainment. However, the limitation does not apply if any of the various exceptions contained in § 274(e) apply. One of these concerns business meetings of employees. Consequently, the firm is allowed to deduct 100% of the meal costs.

Review Question 9

This year the School of Business at X University created an annual award of $100 given to three staff members (e.g., secretaries) for outstanding performance during the year. The School's bookkeeper is uncertain as to whether taxes are to be withheld on such awards. How should the awards be handled?

Unfortunately, what appears to be an award of $100 is probably closer to $60 since the award is fully taxable and both income and employment taxes must be withheld. No exclusion is available since the award is given in cash and is not for length of service or safety.

SOLE PROPRIETORS AND SELF-EMPLOYED PERSONS

Sole proprietors and self-employed persons are not treated as separate taxable entities. Rather, their income and expenses are compiled and reported simply as a part of their individual return. This information is reported on Schedule C or C-EZ of Form 1040. Page 1 of Schedule C appears below. An examination of Schedule C reveals that it is relatively straightforward and self-explanatory. The net income or loss as reported on line 31 of Schedule C is transferred to Page 1 of Form 1040 and is added to the taxpayer's income. The net income or loss on Schedule C also is used in the computation of self-employment tax. Accordingly, the net amount on Schedule C must also be transferred to Schedule SE.

STATUTORY EMPLOYEES

Before examining the reporting requirements for employees, attention must be given to a subset of workers commonly referred to as *statutory employees*. These are individuals who work in four occupational groups (described below) and are not otherwise employees under the usual common law tests. Rather, under a specific statutory provision, they are treated as employees for purposes of FICA (and sometimes FUTA) and are subject to favorable rules concerning the reporting of their income and deductions.[113] Statutory employees include:[114]

- Life insurance salespersons who work full-time for a single life insurance company selling life insurance or annuity contracts.

- Traveling salespersons who work full-time for one person to solicit orders for merchandise from customers for resale or supplies for use by the customers in their businesses (e.g., a manufacturers representative, salesmen that regularly call on customers and get paid a commission).

- Agent-drivers or commission-drivers that distribute meat, vegetable, fruit or bakery products, beverages (other than milk), or laundry or dry cleaning services (e.g., a delivery man that distributes bakery products).

- Individuals who work off the premises of the person for whom the services are performed (e.g., at home or the home of another) according to furnished specifications on material provided and the products are returned to the principal (e.g., garment workers who make clothing, quilts, bedspreads, and similar items at home and return them to the person for whom they performed the work; people who address envelopes at home or provide typing or transcribing services).[115]

To be considered statutory employees, these individuals also must perform all of the work (no delegation of a significant portion), have no substantial investment in facilities (vehicles excluded) and have a regular and recurring relationship with the business for which they are providing services.

---

[113] § 3121(d).

[114] See reference in § 3509(d)(3) concerning withholding to the workers identified in § 3121(d)(3).

[115] For an example of the reach of this rule, see *Laverne S. VanZant* TCS 2007-195.

SCHEDULE C
(Form 1040)

Department of the Treasury
Internal Revenue Service (99)

Profit or Loss From Business
(Sole Proprietorship)

▶ Information about Schedule C and its separate instructions is at *www.irs.gov/schedulec.*
▶ Attach to Form 1040, 1040NR, or 1041; partnerships generally must file Form 1065.

OMB No. 1545-0074

2016

Attachment
Sequence No. **09**

Name of proprietor

Social security number (SSN)

A Principal business or profession, including product or service (see instructions)

B Enter code from instructions
▶

C Business name. If no separate business name, leave blank.

D Employer ID number (EIN), (see instr.)

E Business address (including suite or room no.) ▶
City, town or post office, state, and ZIP code

F Accounting method: **(1)** ☐ Cash **(2)** ☐ Accrual **(3)** ☐ Other (specify) ▶

G Did you "materially participate" in the operation of this business during 2016? If "No," see instructions for limit on losses . ☐ Yes ☐ No

H If you started or acquired this business during 2016, check here . . . . ▶ ☐

I Did you make any payments in 2016 that would require you to file Form(s) 1099? (see instructions) . . . . ☐ Yes ☐ No

J If "Yes," did you or will you file required Forms 1099? . . . . ☐ Yes ☐ No

Part I   Income

1	Gross receipts or sales. See instructions for line 1 and check the box if this income was reported to you on Form W-2 and the "Statutory employee" box on that form was checked . . . . ▶ ☐	**1**
2	Returns and allowances	**2**
3	Subtract line 2 from line 1	**3**
4	Cost of goods sold (from line 42)	**4**
5	**Gross profit.** Subtract line 4 from line 3	**5**
6	Other income, including federal and state gasoline or fuel tax credit or refund (see instructions)	**6**
7	**Gross income.** Add lines 5 and 6 . . . . ▶	**7**

Part II   Expenses. Enter expenses for business use of your home **only** on line 30.

8	Advertising	**8**	18	Office expense (see instructions)	**18**
9	Car and truck expenses (see instructions)	**9**	19	Pension and profit-sharing plans .	**19**
10	Commissions and fees .	**10**	20	Rent or lease (see instructions):	
11	Contract labor (see instructions)	**11**	a	Vehicles, machinery, and equipment	**20a**
12	Depletion	**12**	b	Other business property . . .	**20b**
13	Depreciation and section 179 expense deduction (not included in Part III) (see instructions)	**13**	21	Repairs and maintenance . . .	**21**
			22	Supplies (not included in Part III) .	**22**
			23	Taxes and licenses	**23**
			24	Travel, meals, and entertainment:	
14	Employee benefit programs (other than on line 19) . .	**14**	a	Travel	**24a**
15	Insurance (other than health)	**15**	b	Deductible meals and entertainment (see instructions)	**24b**
16	Interest:		25	Utilities	**25**
a	Mortgage (paid to banks, etc.)	**16a**	26	Wages (less employment credits) .	**26**
b	Other	**16b**	27a	Other expenses (from line 48) . .	**27a**
17	Legal and professional services	**17**	b	**Reserved for future use** . . .	**27b**

28	**Total expenses** before expenses for business use of home. Add lines 8 through 27a . . . . ▶	**28**	
29	Tentative profit or (loss). Subtract line 28 from line 7	**29**	
30	Expenses for business use of your home. Do not report these expenses elsewhere. Attach Form 8829 unless using the simplified method (see instructions). **Simplified method filers only:** enter the total square footage of: (a) your home: _____ and (b) the part of your home used for business: _____ . Use the Simplified Method Worksheet in the instructions to figure the amount to enter on line 30	**30**	
31	**Net profit or (loss).** Subtract line 30 from line 29.		
	• If a profit, enter on both **Form 1040, line 12** (or **Form 1040NR, line 13**) and on **Schedule SE, line 2.** (If you checked the box on line 1, see instructions). Estates and trusts, enter on **Form 1041, line 3.** • If a loss, you **must** go to line 32.	**31**	
32	If you have a loss, check the box that describes your investment in this activity (see instructions).		
	• If you checked 32a, enter the loss on both **Form 1040, line 12,** (or **Form 1040NR, line 13**) and on **Schedule SE, line 2.** (If you checked the box on line 1, see the line 31 instructions). Estates and trusts, enter on **Form 1041, line 3.** • If you checked 32b, you **must** attach **Form 6198.** Your loss may be limited.	**32a** ☐ All investment is at risk. **32b** ☐ Some investment is not at risk.	

For Paperwork Reduction Act Notice, see the separate instructions.   Cat. No. 11334P   Schedule C (Form 1040) 2016

Statutory employees report their income and expenses in a unique manner. They receive a Form W-2 that reports their wages or commissions. In recognition of their special treatment, box 13 of the W-2 for "Statutory Employee" is checked. The wages or commissions earned by the statutory employee that are reported on the W-2 are subject to FICA taxes but withholding of income taxes is optional. More significant is the manner in which a statutory employee reports the W-2 income and related expenses. They are not considered employees subject to the normal rules governing the reporting of deductions.[116] Even though a statutory employee receives a W-2, he or she reports that income and the related expenses on Schedule C. The net amount is not subject to self-employment taxes as is normally the case since the employer withheld FICA. By reporting the expenses in this fashion, a statutory employee effectively deducts these expenses for AGI and avoids the need to itemize deductions as well as the floor on miscellaneous itemized deductions (MIDs). Avoiding classification as MIDs is extremely important in light of the alternative minimum tax (AMT), which denies deductions for MIDs, making the taxpayer more vulnerable to the AMT (see Chapter 13).

Although statutory employee status provides substantial benefits, unfortunately employers do not always cooperate. Sometimes they are reluctant to check the magic box on the W-2, making the individual reluctant to claim the benefits of being a statutory employee for risk of an audit. Nevertheless, this is not a choice the employer has and it seems that the statutory employee should be able to report the W-2 correctly.

EMPLOYEES

Both the treatment and reporting of an employee's business expenses vary significantly depending on whether the expenses are reimbursed. As explained in Chapter 7, employee business expenses that are *not* reimbursed are treated as miscellaneous itemized deductions, and are therefore deductible only to the extent that total miscellaneous itemized deductions exceed 2% of AGI. On the other hand, expenses reimbursed under an accountable plan (discussed below) are *not deductible* by the employee, *but* the reimbursement is excludable from his or her gross income. In such case, there is no effect on the taxpayer's return. This latter treatment normally applies to most employee expense accounts, including those arrangements where the employer reimburses an employee for a particular expense as well as those where the employer gives the employee a fixed allowance (e.g., a per diem amount such as $15 per day for meals and $25 per day for lodging). It should be emphasized, however, that even though an expense may appear to be reimbursed in the normal sense, it may not be treated as reimbursed for determining whether the expense is deductible from AGI or the reimbursement is excludable from gross income.

Accountable and Nonaccountable Plans

Since 1989, an employee's business expenses are treated as reimbursed only if his or her employer has a reimbursement or allowance arrangement that qualifies as an *accountable plan*. An arrangement generally qualifies as an accountable plan if the employee properly substantiates the expenses to the employer, and, in the case of advances or allowances, is required to return to the employer any amount in excess of that which is substantiated.[117] If the arrangement does not meet the accountable plan requirements, it is considered a *nonaccountable plan*. As might be expected, the tax treatment of payments under the two different plans differs drastically.

Reimbursements or advances made under an accountable plan are treated far more favorably than those under a nonaccountable plan. Amounts paid under an accountable plan are normally excluded from gross income, not reported on the employee's Form W-2, and are exempt from employment taxes (i.e., Social Security and unemployment). In contrast, reimbursements and advances made under a nonaccountable plan must be reported in the employee's gross income, included on Form W-2, and are subject to employment taxes.

> **LO.10**
>
> Discuss the two types of reimbursement arrangements: accountable and nonaccountable plans.

---

[116] Statutory employees are not considered employees for purposes of § 62 that identifies the deductions that are for AGI See IRS acknowledgement in Rev. Rul. 90-93, 1990-2 CB 33 concerning a full-time life insurance salesman.

[117] Reg. § 1.62-2(b).

More importantly, the expenses for which the employee is reimbursed under a nonaccountable plan must be claimed as miscellaneous itemized deductions subject to the 2% floor. In contrast, in the case of an accountable plan, consistent with the fact that the reimbursement is not included in income, the expense is not deducted—at least in the normal sense. Instead, the expense, like the reimbursement, is not reported. As the IRS puts it, there is "no deduction since [the employee's] expenses and reimbursements are equal." In effect, the employer claims the deduction rather than the employee.

Under either plan, the employee normally summarizes employee business expenses on Form 2106 (shown on pp. 8-54 and 8-55). When this form is properly completed, expenses not considered reimbursed flow to Schedule A and are deducted as miscellaneous itemized deductions. The reporting of employee business expenses is summarized in Exhibit 8-2, which follows.

Under an accountable plan, an employee who substantiates his or her expenses and returns any excess reimbursement reports neither the reimbursements nor the expenses because there is a complete wash. (See Exhibit 8-2, Item 1.) *However,* if the employee fails to return any excess reimbursement, a different accounting is required. In this case, the excess reimbursement is treated as *if* paid under a nonaccountable plan. Therefore, the employer must report the *excess* in the employee's Form W-2 as well as pay the related employment taxes. On the other side, the employee must include the excess in gross income. (See Exhibit 8-2, Item 3).

Example 46

R is a sales representative for C Corporation and has an expense account arrangement. Under this arrangement, R fills out an expense report every two weeks, documenting all of his expenses, and submits it for reimbursement. This year R submitted travel expenses of $5,000, all of which were reimbursed. Assuming this is an accountable plan and R has properly substantiated expenses of $5,000, there is nothing included on his Form W-2 and none of the expenses are reported on his return. In effect, there is no effect on R because the reimbursement and expenses wash. (See Exhibit 8-2, Item 1.)

Example 47

Assume the plan in *Example 44* was not properly structured and did not require R either to substantiate his expenses or to return any excess reimbursement. In this case, the arrangement would be a nonaccountable plan. Consequently, the $5,000 reimbursement would be included as income in R's Form W-2 and he could deduct the $5,000 as a miscellaneous itemized deduction. In this case, the income and deduction do not necessarily wash (e.g., if R does not itemize), and R ends up with taxable income that economically he does not have. (See Exhibit 8-2, Item 4. The Form 2106 shown on pp. 8-54 and 8-55 reveals how this information would be reported.)

As the above examples illustrate, most employers should opt to establish reimbursement arrangements that meet the accountable plan requirements so that employees are not unduly penalized. Nevertheless, as noted above, even if the employer has an accountable plan, the employee must still substantiate any expenses and return any reimbursements in excess of the expenses substantiated to avoid unfavorable treatment.

Substantiation

A plan generally satisfies the substantiation requirement if the employee meets the normal rules for substantiation of expenses. For example, travel and entertainment expenses must be substantiated under the special rules of § 274(d) discussed earlier in this chapter. Note that an employee whose reimbursement is based on some type of fixed allowance (e.g., a per diem for meals and lodging or a mileage allowance) is *deemed* to have substantiated the amount of his or her expenses up to the amount set by the IRS for per diem, mileage, or other expense allowances.[118]

---

[118] See Regs. §§ 1.62-2(e)(2) and 1.274-5(g).

EXHIBIT 8-2	Reporting Travel, Transportation, Meal, and Entertainment Expenses and Reimbursements		
Type *of Reimbursement or Other Expense Allowance Arrangement*	**Employer** *Reports on Form W-2*	**Employee** *Shows on Form 2106*	**Employee** *Claims on Schedule A*
1. **Accountable** *Adequate accounting and excess returned*	*Not reported*	*Not shown*	*Not claimed*
2. *Per diem or mileage allowance (up to government rate)* *Adequate accounting and excess returned*	*Not reported*	*All expenses and reimbursements only if excess expenses are claimed. Otherwise, form is not filed.*	*Expenses the employee can prove and which exceed the reimbursements received*
3. *Per diem or mileage allowance (exceeds government rate)* *Adequate accounting up to the government rate only and excess not returned*	*Excess reported as wages in Box 1. Amount up to the government rate is reported only in Box 13—it is not reported in Box 1.*	*All expenses, and reimbursements equal to the government rate, only if expenses in excess of the government rate are claimed.[1] Otherwise, form is not filed.*	*Expenses the employee can prove and which exceed the government rate[2]*
4. **Nonaccountable** *Adequate accounting or return of excess either not required or required but not met*	*Entire amount is reported as wages in Box 1[3]*	*All expenses[1]*	*Expenses the employee can prove[2]*
5. *No reimbursement*	*Normal reporting of wages, etc.*	*All expenses[1]*	*Expenses the employee can prove[2]*

[1] These amounts are subject to income tax withholding and to all employment taxes such as FICA and FUTA.

[2] Any allowable expense is carried to line 20 of Schedule A and deducted as a miscellaneous itemized deduction.

[3] These amounts are subject to the applicable limits including the 50% limit on meals and entertainment expenses and the two percent of adjusted gross income limit on the total miscellaneous itemized deductions.

Source: Travel, Entertainment, Gift and Car Expense, IRS Publication 463 (Rev. 2016), p. 32.

Generally, the only expense substantiation for such plans is the number of business miles traveled and the number of days away from home spent on business. Due to this rule, employees who receive allowances within the IRS guidelines will have no reimbursements in excess of their substantiated expenses and, therefore, will not have any excess to return.

Example 48

K works as an accountant for a public accounting firm in Tampa. This year she attended a continuing education course in Jacksonville. The firm gives its employees a meal allowance of $12 per diem, which is within the IRS guidelines. K attended the course for five days. When she returned from the trip, she submitted her expense report requesting reimbursement for meals of $60 (5 × $12). In reality, K, wanting to save as much as she could, spent only $40 on meals. Although K has actually received $20 more than she spent ($60 − $40), she does not have to return the excess because she is deemed to have substantiated expenses of $60.

If an employee has expenses that the employer did not reimburse, the employee should file Form 2106 to claim a deduction for the unreimbursed expenses. Proper completion of this form results in the unreimbursed expenses being claimed as miscellaneous itemized deductions on Schedule A. (See Exhibit 8-2, Item 2.)

Example 49

Under an accountable plan, T is reimbursed 40 cents per mile for all business miles driven. For the year, he received $1,000. After consulting his records, T determined that his actual expenses exceed 40 cents per mile for a total of $1,200. None of the reimbursement is included on T's Form W-2 because this is an accountable plan and the allowance does not exceed the government rate. T should report the $1,200 of expenses on lines 1–6 of Form 2106. The $1,000 reimbursement is entered on line 7 and subtracted from the $1,200 expense amount to leave $200. The $200 (the amount for which T did not receive a reimbursement) flows through to Schedule A and is treated as a miscellaneous itemized deduction. (See line 10 of Form 2106 and Exhibit 8-2, Item 2).

Example 50

J's employer pays her a flat $100 per month to cover her car expenses. The employer does not have an accountable plan. Thus the employer must include the $100 as income in J's Form W-2, and J may deduct her car expenses as miscellaneous itemized deductions. (See Exhibit 8-2, Item 4.)

In certain instances, the employer may give the employee a per diem allowance that exceeds the Federal government allowable rate (e.g., 60 cents per mile instead of the allowable standard mileage rate). In such cases, special reporting rules apply.[119] Similarly, special allocation rules must be observed when the amount of the reimbursement covers only a portion of the employee's expenses.[120]

---

[119] *Supra*, Footnote 106, p. 11.   [120] Reg. § 1.62-1(f).

MOVING EXPENSES

Upon retirement, many individuals move to another location. Normally, the moving expenses would not be deductible. If the taxpayer can obtain a *full-time* job at the new location, however, the costs of moving become deductible. In this regard, the taxpayer must be sure to satisfy the 39- or 78-week test.

TRAVEL AND ENTERTAINMENT EXPENSES

The rules governing deductions for combined business and pleasure travel permit some vacationing on business trips without jeopardizing the deduction. As long as the trip is primarily for business, the entire cost of traveling to the business/vacation destination is deductible. Although the expenses of personal side-trips are not allowed, these expenses may be incidental to the major costs of getting to the desired location. For example, a taxpayer living in New York can deduct a major portion of the cost of a vacation in Florida—the cost of getting there—by properly scheduling business in Miami. In those situations where vacation time exceeds time spent on business, the taxpayer must be prepared to establish that the trip would not have been taken *but for* the business need.

When traveling, the taxpayer may also be able to deduct the expenses of a spouse if a business purpose for the spouse's presence can be established. Even where a spouse's travel expenses are clearly not deductible, only the *incremental* expense attributable to the spouse's presence is not allowed. When an automobile is used for transportation, there is no incremental expense. In the case of lodging, the single room rate would be fully deductible and only the few extra dollars added for a double room rate, if any, would not be deductible.

The importance of adequate records for travel and entertainment expenses cannot be over-emphasized. However, the *actual* cost of travel expenses need not be proved when a per diem or a fixed mileage allowance arrangement exists between the employee and the employer. In these situations, the other elements of the expense—time, place, and business purpose—must still be substantiated by the employer and employee. Moreover, the taxpayer must substantiate the cost of travel where the employee is "related" to the employer (an employee is considered related when he or she either owns more than 10% of a corporate employer's stock or is the employer's spouse, brother, sister, ancestor, or lineal descendant). Notwithstanding the relaxation of the substantiation requirements for travel costs, it is advisable to maintain receipts and other records to substantiate the other elements of the expenditure.

The taxpayer should get in the habit of contemporaneously recording the required elements for each expenditure. Although a bothersome task, this must be done to secure deductions for travel and entertainment expenses. *Each* element of each expenditure must be established.

With respect to vehicle expenses, the taxpayer cannot simply deduct the expenses and hope that he or she will never be asked to produce evidence supporting the deduction. Form 2106 (Part II, Line 21) specifically asks whether the taxpayer has proper written evidence. Thus, failure to maintain such documentation would mean that the taxpayer could not answer this question in the affirmative, increasing the probability of audit. Of course, indicating that such evidence exists when it in fact does not could subject the taxpayer to negligence or fraud penalties.

Form **2106**	**Employee Business Expenses**	OMB No. 1545-0074
Department of the Treasury Internal Revenue Service (99)	▶ Attach to Form 1040 or Form 1040NR. ▶ Information about Form 2106 and its separate instructions is available at *www.irs.gov/form2106*.	**2016** Attachment Sequence No. **129**

Your name	Occupation in which you incurred expenses	Social security number

Part I   Employee Business Expenses and Reimbursements

Step 1   Enter Your Expenses

		Column A Other Than Meals and Entertainment		**Column B** Meals and Entertainment	
1	Vehicle expense from line 22 or line 29. (Rural mail carriers: See instructions.) **1**				
2	Parking fees, tolls, and transportation, including train, bus, etc., that **didn't** involve overnight travel or commuting to and from work . . **2**				
3	Travel expense while away from home overnight, including lodging, airplane, car rental, etc. **Don't** include meals and entertainment. . **3**				
4	Business expenses not included on lines 1 through 3. **Don't** include meals and entertainment **4**				
5	Meals and entertainment expenses (see instructions) **5**				
6	**Total expenses.** In Column A, add lines 1 through 4 and enter the result. In Column B, enter the amount from line 5 . . . . . . **6**				

Note: *If you weren't reimbursed for any expenses in Step 1, skip line 7 and enter the amount from line 6 on line 8.*

Step 2   Enter Reimbursements Received From Your Employer for Expenses Listed in Step 1

7	Enter reimbursements received from your employer that **weren't** reported to you in box 1 of Form W-2. Include any reimbursements reported under code "L" in box 12 of your Form W-2 (see instructions). **7**				

Step 3   Figure Expenses To Deduct on Schedule A (Form 1040 or Form 1040NR)

8	Subtract line 7 from line 6. If zero or less, enter -0-. However, if line 7 is greater than line 6 in Column A, report the excess as income on Form 1040, line 7 (or on Form 1040NR, line 8) **8**				
	Note: *If **both columns** of line 8 are zero, you can't deduct employee business expenses. Stop here and attach Form 2106 to your return.*				
9	In Column A, enter the amount from line 8. In Column B, multiply line 8 by 50% (0.50). (Employees subject to Department of Transportation (DOT) hours of service limits: Multiply meal expenses incurred while away from home on business by 80% (0.80) instead of 50%. For details, see instructions.) **9**				
10	Add the amounts on line 9 of both columns and enter the total here. **Also, enter the total on Schedule A (Form 1040), line 21** (or on **Schedule A (Form 1040NR), line 7**). (Armed Forces reservists, qualified performing artists, fee-basis state or local government officials, and individuals with disabilities: See the instructions for special rules on where to enter the total.) . ▶ **10**				

For Paperwork Reduction Act Notice, see your tax return instructions.   Cat No. 11700N   Form **2106** (2016)

Part II	**Vehicle Expenses**			

Section A—General Information (You must complete this section if you are claiming vehicle expenses.)

			(a) Vehicle 1	(b) Vehicle 2
11	Enter the date the vehicle was placed in service	11	/ /	/ /
12	Total miles the vehicle was driven during 2016	12	miles	miles
13	Business miles included on line 12	13	miles	miles
14	Percent of business use. Divide line 13 by line 12	14	%	%
15	Average daily roundtrip commuting distance	15	miles	miles
16	Commuting miles included on line 12	16	miles	miles
17	Other miles. Add lines 13 and 16 and subtract the total from line 12	17	miles	miles
18	Was your vehicle available for personal use during off-duty hours?		☐ Yes	☐ No
19	Do you (or your spouse) have another vehicle available for personal use?		☐ Yes	☐ No
20	Do you have evidence to support your deduction?		☐ Yes	☐ No
21	If "Yes," is the evidence written?		☐ Yes	☐ No

Section B—Standard Mileage Rate (See the instructions for Part II to find out whether to complete this section or Section C.)

22	Multiply line 13 by 54¢ (0.54). Enter the result here and on line 1	22	

Section C—Actual Expenses

			(a) Vehicle 1	(b) Vehicle 2
23	Gasoline, oil, repairs, vehicle insurance, etc.	23		
24a	Vehicle rentals	24a		
b	Inclusion amount (see instructions)	24b		
c	Subtract line 24b from line 24a	24c		
25	Value of employer-provided vehicle (applies only if 100% of annual lease value was included on Form W-2—see instructions)	25		
26	Add lines 23, 24c, and 25.	26		
27	Multiply line 26 by the percentage on line 14	27		
28	Depreciation (see instructions)	28		
29	Add lines 27 and 28. Enter total here and on line 1	29		

Section D—Depreciation of Vehicles (Use this section only if you owned the vehicle and are completing Section C for the vehicle.)

			(a) Vehicle 1	(b) Vehicle 2
30	Enter cost or other basis (see instructions)	30		
31	Enter section 179 deduction and special allowance (see instructions)	31		
32	Multiply line 30 by line 14 (see instructions if you claimed the section 179 deduction or special allowance).	32		
33	Enter depreciation method and percentage (see instructions)	33		
34	Multiply line 32 by the percentage on line 33 (see instructions)	34		
35	Add lines 31 and 34	35		
36	Enter the applicable limit explained in the line 36 instructions	36		
37	Multiply line 36 by the percentage on line 14	37		
38	Enter the **smaller** of line 35 or line 37. If you skipped lines 36 and 37, enter the amount from line 35. Also enter this amount on line 28 above	38		

Form **2106** (2016)

DISCUSSION QUESTIONS

8-1 *Requirements for Education Expenses.* J has been told that, as a practical matter, most education expenses are considered nondeductible personal expenses. Under what conditions, if any, may J deduct expenses for education?

8-2 *Education: Degrees, Promotion, and Employer Assistance.* Y is currently employed as the manager of a fast-food restaurant, earning $29,000. In order to improve her upward mobility in the company, Y decides that she should go to college and earn her degree.
   a. Can Y deduct any of the cost of obtaining her bachelor's degree in business?
   b. Same as above, except Y already has her bachelor's degree and now decides to take courses which could lead to her receiving an M.B.A.
   c. What is the effect on Y if her employer pays for her education costs this year of $6,000? Answer for both a bachelor's degree and an M.B.A.

8-3 *Expenses of Education.* F, vice president of sales for a large corporation, is in the executive M.B.A. program at the University of Michigan. F lives in Chicago and travels to Ann Arbor and Detroit to take certain courses.
   a. F's employer reimburses F for the tuition, which is $30,000 per year. Explain how F will treat the reimbursement and the expense. What if F was not reimbursed?
Indicate whether the following expenses incurred by F would be deductible:
   b. Meals and lodging when he stays overnight.
   c. Transportation costs from Chicago and back.
   d. Books.
   e. Secretarial fees for typing term projects.
   f. Copying expenses.
   g. Value of vacation time used to take classes.
   h. Tutor.

8-4 *Qualifying Educational Expenses.* Indicate whether education expenses would be deductible in the following situations:
   a. J is currently an elementary school teacher. State law requires beginning teachers to have a bachelor's degree and to complete a master's degree within five years after first being hired. This year he took two courses toward the master's degree.
   b. R is a full-time engineering student and has a part-time job as an engineer with a firm that will employ him as an engineer when he graduates.
   c. C is an airline pilot and is presently taking lessons to become a helicopter pilot.
   d. H retired from the finance department of the Army and now is getting his M.B.A. He plans to get a job with a financial institution.

8-5 *Moving Expenses.* Address the following:
   a. What two tests must be satisfied before moving expenses may be deducted?
   b. What moving expenses are deductible?
   c. Are moving expenses deductible *for* or *from* adjusted gross income?

8-6 *Moving Expenses: Real Estate Commissions.* B's employer transferred him during the year. As a result, B sold his home in North Dakota and moved to New York, where he lives in an apartment. He does not plan to move into a new home. B's real estate commissions were $6,000. B has asked how he should treat the real estate commissions.

8-7 *Home Office Expenses.* The enactment of the restrictive rules related to home office deductions caused many commentators to conclude that the home office deduction had been essentially eliminated. Which particular requirement(s) of § 280A prompted such a conclusion?

8-8 *Computing Car Expenses.* Briefly answer the following:
   a. With respect to a business car, can the taxpayer claim depreciation in addition to the expense determined using the standard mileage rate?
   b. Can a taxpayer switch to the automatic mileage method after using MACRS to compute depreciation? If so, when does the car become fully depreciated?

8-9 *Transportation versus Travel.* Explain the distinction between transportation expenses and travel expenses.

8-10 *U.S. Travel versus Foreign Travel.* Compare and contrast the rules governing travel in the United States to those rules governing travel outside of the United States.

8-11 *Limitations on Entertainment and Meals.* T is employed by KL Publishing Corporation. He is a sales representative with responsibility for college textbook sales in Alabama, Florida and Georgia. T lives in Atlanta. For each of the following situations, indicate whether T's or the corporation's deduction for entertainment or meals would be limited, and if so, how?

    a. T flew to Birmingham on a Tuesday night. After checking in at the hotel, he caught a cab to his favorite restaurant where he ate by himself. The cost of the meal was $20, including a $1 tax and a $3 tip. The cost of the cab ride was $10. The next day he called on a customer.

    b. Same as (a), except that T's employer reimbursed him under an accountable plan for all of his costs.

    c. Same as (a), but further assume that T's AGI for the year was $30,000 and that he has other miscellaneous itemized deductions of $700.

    d. At the year-end Christmas party for employees, the corporation gave T a 10 pound, honey-baked ham, costing $40. The cost of the party (excluding the ham), which was held at a local restaurant, was $300.

    e. During the annual convention of college marketing professors in New Orleans, the corporation rented a room in the convention hotel for one night and provided hors d'oeuvres. The room cost $200 while the food and drink cost $1,000.

8-12 *Statutory Employees.* L was an education consultant for ALS. Her duties required her to visit schools, collect data and input the data into a software template provided by ALS. Upon completion, she e-mailed the information to ALS. Is she a statutory employee? Regardless of your answer, explain the benefits of being so classified.

8-13 *Entertainment Expenses.* Distinguish between entertainment expenses that are considered "directly related to" the taxpayer's business and those that are "associated with" the taxpayer's business.

8-14 *Business Meals.* Can the taxpayer deduct the cost of his or her own meal when he or she pays for the lunch of a customer and no business is discussed?

8-15 *Entertainment Facilities.* Under what circumstances are expenses related to an entertainment facility deductible?

8-16 *Substantiation of Travel and Entertainment Expenses.* What information must the taxpayer be prepared to present upon the audit of his or her travel and entertainment expenditures? Does the taxpayer need to maintain records if he or she has a per diem arrangement with the employer?

8-17 *Foreign Convention.* Dr. B recently learned that a world famous plastic surgeon will be making a presentation concerning her area of expertise at a convention of physicians in Switzerland. If B attends, can she deduct the costs of airfare, meals, lodging, and registration? Explain.

8-18 *Cruise Ship Seminars.* The American Organization of Dental Specialists is offering a seven-day seminar on gum disease aboard a cruise ship. Dr. D, a dentist. would like to attend. If D attends, can he deduct his expenses?

8-19 *Reporting Reimbursements.* R is regional sales manager for a large steel manufacturing corporation. His job requires him to travel extensively to call on customers and salespeople. As a result, he incurs substantial expenses for airfare, hotel, meals, and entertainment, for which he is reimbursed. Under what conditions may R simply ignore reporting the reimbursements and the expenses for tax purposes?

8-20 *Reporting Employee Business Expenses.* T is a salesperson for Classy Cosmetics Inc. During the year, she incurred various business expenses for which she was reimbursed under an accountable plan. Discuss the problems T encounters when reporting the reimbursements and expenses in the following situations, assuming an adequate accounting was made.

    a. T was reimbursed $3,800 for expenses totaling $3,000.

    b. T was on a per diem of $25 per day for lodging and $15 per day for meals. She received $2,000 under the per diem arrangement for expenses totaling $2,200.

8-21 *Per Diem Arrangement.* Al was recently hired by a public accounting firm as a staff accountant. When Al is out of town on business (e.g., staff training or an audit at a client's place of business), the firm gives him $12 a day for dinner. Al normally spends $5 and banks the rest. What are the tax consequences?

8-22 *Substantiation Requirements.* Indicate whether each of the following is required in order to properly substantiate a deduction:
a. Purpose of an entertainment expenditure.
b. Date of entertainment expenditure.
c. Receipt for business meal with client, which cost $15.
d. Receipt for lodging at Motel Cheap, which cost $12.
e. Description of what the taxpayer wore on the day he lunched with client.
f. Diary detailing information normally required for substantiation of entertainment expenses.
g. Canceled check for $12 for tickets to baseball game that was attended with customer.
h. Social Security number of client entertained.

YOU MAKE THE CALL

8-23 The unfortunate experience of Danville Plywood Corporation and its deduction for the Super Bowl trip described earlier in this chapter raises another issue. The corporation booked what clearly seemed to be entertainment expenses as advertising expenses, perhaps with the hope that the expense would be forever buried. Assume that you were the accountant on the job, noted this, and proposed a reclassification entry to the client who objected. What action should you take?

PROBLEMS

8-24 *Education Expenses.* Indicate the amount, if any, of deductible education expenses in each of the following cases. Comment briefly on your answer and state whether the deduction is deductible *for* or *from* adjusted gross income:
a. C is employed as a plumber, but is training to become a computer programmer. During the year, he paid $500 for tuition and books related to a college course in programming.
b. E is a licensed nurse. During the year, she spent $300 on courses to become a registered nurse.
c. R paid a $1,000 fee to take the C.P.A. exam and $3,000 for a C.P.A. review course. R currently is employed by a public accounting firm.
d. R is an IRS agent. This year, he began taking courses toward a law degree emphasizing tax. Tuition and books cost for the year cost $20,000.
e. H is a high school instructor teaching European history. On a one-year sabbatical leave from school, he traveled to Europe, taking slides which he planned on using in his classes. The trip cost $7,000, including $1,000 for meals.

8-25 *Moving Expenses.* In May of the current year. M found a new job, forcing him to move from Tulsa to Seattle. On June 1, the moving company picked up all of M's possessions. M and his family stayed in a hotel on June 1, left the morning of June 2, and arrived in Seattle on June 4. They incurred the following expenses.
1. Airfare and meals for him and his wife while traveling to Seattle to look for a new house, $260 and $50 respectively. They failed to find a home. Consequently, they moved into an apartment, from which they continued their search.
2. Lodging in Tulsa on the day they moved out of their house, $70.
3. Expenses on the way to Seattle included meals, $80, and lodging, $100.
4. Mileage to Seattle, 2,000 miles.
5. Car repair on trip to Seattle, $175.
6. Moving van, $4,000.
7. Storage charges for furniture that would not fit in the apartment: $3 per day for the period June 5–July 31.
8. Temporary living expenses for period June 5–July 31: apartment, $10 per day; meals, $20 per day; and cleaning and laundry, $25.
9. Realtor's commission on sale of old home. $1,000.
Compute M's moving expense deduction (Form 3903 may be helpful).

8-26 *Home Office.* In each of the following independent situations, indicate whether the taxpayer is entitled to deduct expenses related to the home office:

  a. C, a dermatologist employed by a hospital, also owns several rental properties. He regularly uses a bedroom in his home solely as an office for bookkeeping and other activities related to management of the rental properties.

  b. R, an attorney employed by a large law firm, frequently brings work home from the office. She uses a study in her home for doing this work as well as paying bills, sorting coupons and conducting other personal activities.

  c. M is a research associate employed by the Cancer Research Institute. His duties include designing and carrying out experiments, reviewing data, and writing articles and grant proposals. His employer furnishes M a laboratory but due to insufficient space cannot provide an office for him. Thus, for about three hours each day, M uses a portion of his bedroom (where he and his wife sleep) to do the writing, reviewing, and other related activities.

  d. T is a self-employed tax consultant. He has an office downtown and a home office. He occasionally meets with his clients in the home office since it is often more convenient for the clients to meet there.

  e. S, an artist, converted a detached garage to a studio for painting. She sells her paintings at her own gallery located in town.

  f. D has four toddlers. Since her home is virtually a nursery already, she decided to turn her family room into a daycare center.

8-27 *Home Office.* R is considering purchasing a home priced somewhat over her budget. Her brother has suggested that converting a room to a home office would enable her to deduct a substantial part of the costs related to the home, thus making the purchase feasible. R is a sales manager for X Corporation, which transfers its middle management employees frequently.

    Comment on the following advice given to R by her brother:

  a. Establishing a home office is an effective method for reducing the costs of home ownership by the amount of the tax benefits received.

  b. There are no disincentives for claiming the home office deduction.

8-28 *Home Office Computations.* T is employed as a law professor at State University. Outside of her university work she occasionally provides legal services. T does all her work for these outside pursuits in her home office. Income and expenses relating to these were:

Income:	
Fees for services	$2,000
Expenses:	
Depreciation on home office furniture and computer.	400
Miscellaneous supplies, books, etc.	500
Expenses attributable to home office:	
Depreciation	500
Insurance and utilities	700
Taxes.	300
Interest	700

  a. Using the general method, determine the tax consequences resulting from T's part-time activities.

  b. Using the optional simplified method, determine the tax consequences resulting from T's part-time activities. Assume that the square footage used for the home office is 120 square feet.

8-29 *Deductible Moving Expenses.* Indicate whether the following expenses qualify as deductible moving expenses:
   a.   Costs of meals and lodging while en route to new location.
   b.   Insurance on household and personal effects being transported—an option provided by the moving company.
   c.   Costs of driving the family car to new location.
   d.   Costs of storing items that would not fit in apartment at the new location; the apartment served as a temporary residence until a home was purchased.
   e.   Costs of new carpeting and wallpaper to prepare old home to be sold.
   f.   Real estate commission on sale of former residence.
   g.   Loss on sale of residence.
   h.   Payment of six months' rent to settle lease obligation at old location; the lease had six more months to run.
   i.   Cost of appraisal of new home required as part of loan application.

8-30 *Moving Expenses: Time Test.* On September 1, 2017, L left her former employment in Indianapolis to seek her fortune in Cincinnati. Indicate whether L could deduct the cost of her moving expenses to Cincinnati under the following conditions.
   a.   L found a teaching job with the public school system for which she worked ten months, September through June. After school was out, L took a three-month vacation. She then decided to leave Cincinnati and move to Atlanta.
   b.   Same as (a) except L found a job as a tutor and was considered self-employed.
   c.   L moved to take a new position as product manager with P&G Corporation. After working three months, she and her new employer had a falling out over what she considered unethical advertising. She quit her job and moved to New York.

8-31 *Moving Expenses: Distance Test.* P is an accountant for L Corporation. This year, his employer moved from its downtown Manhattan location to a new office in New Jersey. As a result, P decided to move to be closer to the office.
   a.   Assuming P did not change jobs, is he allowed to deduct any moving expenses?
   b.   Regardless of your answer to (a), indicate whether P satisfies the distance test in light of the following information:

   • Old office building to new building: 60 miles

   • Old home to new home: 65 miles

   • New home to old office: 51 miles

   • Old home to old office: 30 miles

   • New home to new office: 15 miles

   • Old home to new office: 58 miles

8-32 *Standard Mileage Rate.* R, self-employed, leases her car. She elects to compute her deduction for car expenses using the standard mileage rate. Indicate whether the following expenses may be deducted in addition to expenses computed using the standard rate:
   a.   Depreciation
   b.   Interest on car loan
   c.   Insurance
   d.   Parking while calling on customers
   e.   Parking tickets incurred while on business
   f.   Major overhaul
   g.   Personal property taxes on car
   h.   Tolls

8-33 *Transportation Expenses.* Indicate the amount, if any, deductible by the taxpayer in each of the following cases. (Ignore the floor on miscellaneous itemized deductions.)

   a. R works in downtown Denver, but chooses to live in the mountains 90 miles away. During the year, he spent $2,700 for transportation expenses to and from work.

   b. Q, a high school basketball coach, liked to scout his opposition. On one Friday afternoon, he left school and drove 40 miles to attend the game of the team he played next. On the way, he stopped for a meal ($5). He watched the game and returned home.

   c. R, a carpenter, commutes to work in a truck. He drives the truck in order to carry the tools of his trade. During the year, R's total transportation costs were $5,000. R estimates that his costs of transportation without the tools would have been $4,000, since he otherwise would have taken public transportation.

   d. G, an attorney, works downtown. She is on retainer, however, with a client who has offices two miles from her home. G often stops at the client's office before going to work. The distance between these locations is as follows: home to office, 20 miles; home to client, 2 miles; and client to office, 22 miles. During the year, G drove directly to work 180 days and via the client's office 50 days.

8-34 *Transportation to Temporary Assignments.* For each of the following cases, indicate the number of business miles driven by the taxpayer. (Ignore the floor on miscellaneous itemized deductions.)

   a. K is employed as a salesperson for Midwest Surgical Supply Company. The company's offices are in downtown Chicago. K's sales territory is the northwest side of Chicago and the adjacent suburbs. During Monday through Thursday, K drives directly from her residence to call on various customers. She sees each customer about once a month. On Friday of each week, she goes directly from her home to her office downtown to turn in orders, attend the weekly sales meeting, and do any other miscellaneous work. A portion of K's trip diary appears below.

		Odometer Reading		
Date	Destination	Begin	End	Mileage
3-17	Springmill Clinic	470	482	12
	Dr. J	482	485	3
	Home	485	500	15
3-18	Office	500	530	30
	Home	530	560	30

   b. F, an electrician, works for EZ Electrical. He lives and works in the Los Angeles area. For 200 days of this year, he was assigned to do the wiring on a 30-story office building in downtown Los Angeles. His mileage from his home to the building was 20 miles. For 50 days during the year, he was assigned to a job in San Diego. Most of F's assignments are 20 miles closer than San Diego. F commuted 70 miles from his home to San Diego. Although the company's headquarters are in downtown Los Angeles, F goes there only on rare occasions.

8-35 *Travel Expenses.* Indicate the amount, if any, deductible by the taxpayer in each of the following situations. (Ignore the floor on miscellaneous itemized deductions.)

   a. P, a steelworker, obtained a job with XYZ Corporation to work on a nuclear reactor 200 miles from his residence. P drove to the site early on Monday mornings and returned home late Friday nights. While at the job site he stayed in a boarding house. P anticipates that the job will last for eight months. During the year, he traveled 4,000 miles in going to and from the job. Other expenses while away from home included the following: meals, $1,000; lodging, $900; and laundry, $75.

   b. Same as (a), except P anticipates the job to last for more than a year.

   c. W plays professional football for the Minnesota Vikings. He has an apartment in St. Paul but he and his wife's permanent personal residence is in Tucson. During the season, W usually stays in St. Paul. In the off-season he returns to Tucson. Expenses for the year include travel between St. Paul and Tucson, $2,000; apartment in St. Paul, $1,800; meals while in St. Paul, $900.

   d. R took a trip to New York primarily for business. R's husband accompanied her. She spent two weeks on business and one week sight-seeing in the city. Her train fare was $400 and meals and lodging cost $30 and $50 per day, respectively. R's husband incurred similar expenses.

   e. L flew from Cincinnati to Chicago for $300 round-trip. She spent one day on business and four days shopping and sight-seeing. Her meals and lodging cost $30 and $50 per day, respectively.

8-36 *Car Expense Computation.* E, a salesperson for T Corporation, incurred the following expenses for transportation during the year:

Gas and oil	$1,200
Repairs	200
Insurance	700
Interest on car loan	400
Depreciation	2,000
License	100

In addition, he spent $70 on parking while calling on customers. E drove the car 20,000 miles during the year, 18,000 for business.

   a. Compute E's deduction, assuming the standard mileage rate is elected.

   b. Compute E's deduction, assuming he claims actual expenses.

8-37 *Travel outside of the United States.* S, an executive for an automotive company, traveled to Paris this year for business meetings with a European subsidiary. Prior to the trip, she thought that the meetings presented an ideal opportunity for her to vacation in Paris as well as to conduct business. For this reason, she scheduled the trip. S's airfare to Paris was $1,000 and her daily meals and lodging were $30 and $50 respectively. Given the additional facts below, indicate the amount, if any, of the deduction that S may claim.

   a. S's trip was primarily business. She spent two days on business (including travel days) and four days sight-seeing.

   b. Her itinerary revealed the following:

Thursday May 1:	Depart New York, arrive Paris
Friday, May 2:	Business 9–11 a.m.; remainder of day sight-seeing in Paris
Saturday and Sunday, May 3–4:	Tour French countryside
Monday and Tuesday, May 5–6:	Business 9–5
Wednesday–Sunday, May 7–11:	Tour Germany
Monday, May 12	Business 9–5
Tuesday, May 13:	Depart Paris, arrive New York

   c Same as (a) except the travel was to Paris for the International Car Exposition, a foreign convention.

   d. Same as (a) except the business meetings took place on a luxury liner cruising the Caribbean.

   e. Same as (a) except S had no control over arranging the trip.

   f. Same as (a) except the trip was primarily personal.

8-38 *Entertainment Expenses.* R is president of X Corporation, a company that manufactures and distributes office supplies. During the year, he and the company incurred various expenses relating to entertainment. In each of the following situations, indicate the amount of the deduction for entertainment expenses. Briefly explain your answer and classify the deduction as either *for* or *from* adjusted gross income. (Assume all the substantiation requirements are satisfied.)

  a. R and his wife took a potential customer and his wife to a night club to hear a popular singer. Tickets for the event cost $10 each. R was unable to discuss any business during the evening.

  b. After agreeing in the afternoon to supply S's company with typing paper, R took S to a baseball game that evening. Tickets were $8 each. X Corporation reimbursed R $16 for the tickets under an accountable plan.

  c. R and S, a client, went to lunch at an expensive restaurant. R paid the bill for both his meal, $30, and S's meal, $40. No business was discussed during lunch.

  d. X Corporation purchased a vacation condominium for use primarily by its employees. Expenses relating to the condominium, including depreciation, maintenance, utilities, interest, and taxes, were $7,000.

  e. R joined an exclusive country club this year. The membership fee, which is not refundable, was $1,000. In addition, R paid annual dues of $3,600. During the year, R used the club 100 days, 70 days for entertainment directly related to business and 30 days for personal use.

  f. R gave one of the company's best customers a $100 bottle of wine.

  g. X Corporation gave one of its retailers 1,000 golf balls ($1 each) to distribute for promotional purposes. X Corporation's name was imprinted on the balls.

8-39 *Convention and Seminar Expenses.* Dr. F, a pediatrician, is employed at a hospital located in Chicago. He also operates his own practice. During the year, he attended the following seminars and conventions. In each case, he incurred expenses for registration, travel, meals, and lodging. Indicate whether such expenses would be deductible assuming he attended.

  a. "The Care and Feeding of Newborns," a seminar in Honolulu sponsored by the American Family Medical Association.

  b. While Dr. F was attending the meeting above, his wife attended a concurrent seminar entitled "Tax Planning for Physicians and their Spouses."

  c. "The Economics of a Private Practice: Make Your Investment Count," sponsored by the American Management Corporation in Chicago.

  d. "Investing and Inside Information," sponsored by the National Association of Investment Specialists in Orlando.

CUMULATIVE PROBLEM

8-40 George (445-42-5432) and Christina Campbell (993-43-9878) are married with two children, Victoria, 7, and Brad, 2. Victoria and Brad's Social Security numbers are 446-75-4389 and 449-63-4172, respectively. They live at 10137 Briar Creek Lane, Tulsa, OK 74105. George is the district sales representative for Red Duck, a manufacturer of sportswear. His principal job is to solicit orders of the company's products from department stores in his territory, which includes Oklahoma and Arkansas. The company provides no office for him. Christina is a maker of fine quilts which she sells in selected shops in the surrounding area. The couple uses the cash method of accounting and reports on the calendar year. Their records for the year reveal the following information:

  1. George received a salary of $65,000 and a bonus of $5,000. His employer withheld Federal income taxes of $5,000 and the proper amount of FICA taxes.

  2. Christina's income and expenses of her quilting business, Crazy Quilts, include

Quilt sales.	$7,000
Costs of goods sold.	600
Telephone (long-distance calls)	100

Christina makes all of the quilts at home in a separate room that is used exclusively for her work. This room represents 10% of the total square footage of their home. Expenses related to operating the entire home include utilities, $2,000; and insurance, $500. Depreciation attributable solely to the home office is $800. Christina computes her deduction relating to use of her car using actual expenses, which included gas and oil, $900; insurance, $300; and repairs, $100. The car is fully depreciated. Her daily diary revealed that, for the year, she had driven the car a total of 20,000 miles, including the following trips:

Trip Description	Miles
Home to sales outlets and return	10,000
Between sales outlets	2,000
Miscellaneous personal trips	8,000

3. George incurs substantial expenses for travel and entertainment, including meals and lodging. He is not reimbursed for these expenses. This is the second year that George has used the standard mileage rate for computing his automobile expenses. During the year he drove 50,000 miles; 40,000 of these were directly related to business. Expenses for parking and tolls directly related to business were $90. Total meal and lodging costs for days that he was out of town overnight were $600 and $1,200, respectively. Entertainment expenses were $400.

4. This is George's second marriage. He has one child, Ted (age 11), from his first marriage to Hazel, who has custody of the child. He provides more than 50% of the child's support. The 2007 divorce agreement between George and Hazel provides that George is entitled to the exemption for Ted. George paid Hazel $4,800 during the year, $1,600 as alimony, and the remainder as child support. Ted's Social Security number is 122-23-3221.

5. The couple's other income and expenses included the following:

Dividends (IBM stock owned separately by George)	$ 400
Interest on redeemed Treasury bills	700
Interest on City of Reno bonds	566
Interest paid on home mortgage	10,000
Real property taxes on home	900
Safety deposit box fee	50
State income taxes	4,000

6. Both taxpayers elect to give to the Presidential campaign fund.

Compute the couple's tax liability for the year. If forms are used, complete Form 1040 for the year, including Schedules A, B, C, SE, and Form 2106. Ignore any alternative minimum tax.

TAX RESEARCH PROBLEMS

8-41 *Travel Away from Home.* M is a traveling salesperson who lives with his family in Cincinnati. His sales territory consists of Indiana, Illinois, and Kentucky. Most of his business, however, is in the Louisville area. For this reason, he normally travels to Louisville weekly and spends three or four days there living in a hotel. He also spends considerable time traveling throughout his territory. M completes the paperwork and other tasks incidental to his work at his home in Cincinnati. M's wife has a good job in Cincinnati and consequently M has never considered moving to Louisville. May M deduct the costs of traveling between his residence in Cincinnati and Louisville (including the costs of meals and lodging while in Louisville)?

8-42 *Business Gifts.* R is product manager for a large pharmaceutical company. At the annual Christmas party, he handed out $50 gifts (checks from his personal account) to each of the 10 employees that work in his division under his supervision. R's group had been highly successful during the year and he felt that each person contributed to the division's profitability. He also gave his secretary $100. What amount, if any, may R deduct?

9

Capital Recovery: Depreciation, Amortization, and Depletion

Learning Objectives

Upon completion of this chapter you will be able to:

LO.1 Explain the concept of cost recovery and the various cost recovery methods used for tax purposes, including depreciation, amortization, and depletion.

LO.2 Describe the requirements that must be met to claim deductions for depreciation.

LO.3 Calculate depreciation for tax purposes, using the modified cost recovery system.

LO.4 Describe the special election under § 179, allowing immediate expensing of certain property.

LO.5 Identify the restrictions on depreciation of listed property, including automobiles, trucks, computers, and other items.

LO.6 Distinguish amortization from depreciation and identify assets subject to amortization.

LO.7 Determine the current depletion deduction for various assets.

LO.8 Explain the options available in selecting the appropriate tax treatment of research and experimentation expenditures.

LO.9 Explain the tax treatment of certain expenditures incurred in farming and ranching activities.

Chapter Outline

Introduction

LO.1

Explain the concept of cost recovery and the various cost recovery methods used for tax purposes, including depreciation, amortization, and depletion.

The concept of capital recovery originated with the basic premise that income does not result until revenues exceed the capital expended to produce such revenues. For example, consider the situation where a taxpayer purchases an asset at a cost of $1,000 and subsequently sells it. Generally, the sale produces no income unless the asset is sold for a price exceeding $1,000. This result derives from the principle that the taxpayer first must *recover* his or her $1,000 of capital invested (basis) before he or she can be considered as having income. Here, the recovery occurs as the taxpayer offsets the basis of the asset against the amount realized on the sale. This same principle operates when an asset, instead of being sold and providing a readily identifiable benefit, provides benefits indirectly (e.g., a machine used for many years as part of a process to manufacture a product). In this case, the cost of the asset or the capital invested is *recovered* by offsetting (deducting) the asset's cost against the revenues the asset helps to produce. Thus, in the absence of a sale or other disposition of an asset, capital recovery usually occurs when the taxpayer is permitted to deduct the expenditure. Certain capital expenditures such as research and experimental costs are recovered in the year of the expenditure since the tax law allows immediate deduction. For other types of capital expenditures, the taxpayer is allowed to deduct or recover the cost over the years for which the asset provides benefits.

This chapter examines the various cost allocation methods allowed by the Code. These are depreciation, amortization, and depletion. Although each of these methods relates to a process of deducting the cost of an asset over time, different terms for the same process are used because each method relates to a different type of property. Depreciation concerns tangible property, where tangible property is defined as property that has a physical existence (i.e., property capable of being touched such as plant, property, and equipment). There are two types of tangible property: real property and personal property. Real property (or realty) is land and anything attached to the land such as buildings, curbs, streets, fences, landscaping, and other improvements. Personal property (or personalty) is property that is not realty and is usually movable. The concept of personal property should be distinguished from property that a person owns and uses for his or her benefit—usually referred to as personal-use property. Amortization concerns intangible property, where intangible property is property that has no physical existence but exists only in connection with something else (e.g., goodwill of a business, stock, patents, and copyrights). Finally, depletion concerns natural resources such as oil, gas, coal, gold, silver, copper, and other minerals.

In addition to the cost recovery methods mentioned above, this chapter discusses the tax treatment of other capital expenditures such as those for research and experimentation, and certain expenses of farmers.

Depreciation and Amortization for Tax Purposes

GENERAL RULES FOR DEPRECIATION DEDUCTIONS

LO.2

Describe the requirements that must be met to claim deductions for depreciation.

The Code allows as a depreciation deduction a reasonable allowance for the exhaustion, wear and tear, and obsolescence of property that is either used in a trade or business or held for the production of income.[1] This rule makes it clear that not all capital expenditures for property are automatically eligible for depreciation. Rather, like all other expenditures, only those that satisfy the initial hurdles can be deducted.

---

[1] § 167(a).

Exhaustion, Wear and Tear, and Obsolescence

Only property that wears out or becomes obsolete can be depreciated. As normally construed, this requirement means that depreciation is allowed only for property that has a *determinable life*.[2] Property such as land that does not wear out and that has no determinable life cannot be depreciated. Similarly, works of art cannot be amortized or depreciated since they normally have an indefinite life. In contrast, intangible assets with definite lives, such as patents, copyrights, and licenses that cover a fixed term, can be amortized.

Business or Income-Producing Property

Like other expenses, no deduction is allowed for depreciation unless the property is used in a trade or business or an income-producing activity. Property used for personal purposes cannot be depreciated. For example, self-employed individuals may have a portion of their home dedicated as a home office, or use their car for both personal and business purposes. In many instances, however, a single asset may be used for *both* personal purposes and profit-seeking activities. In these cases, the taxpayer is permitted to deduct depreciation on the portion of the asset used for business or production of income.

Example 1

N is a salesperson who uses his car for both business and personal purposes. He purchased the car this year for $18,000. During the year, N drove the car 50,000 miles: 40,000 miles for business and 10,000 miles for personal purposes. Under these circumstances, 80% (40,000 ÷ 50,000) of the cost of the car is subject to depreciation in the current year. Note that the business-use percentage may vary from year to year. If so, the depreciation allowed each year will vary accordingly.

Property held for the production of income, even though not currently producing income, may still be depreciated. For example, a duplex held out for rental that is temporarily vacant may still be depreciated for the period during which it is not rented. Similarly, if the taxpayer's trade or business is suspended temporarily, rather than indefinitely, depreciation can be continued despite the suspension of activity.

Depreciable Basis

The basis for depreciation is the adjusted basis of the property as used for computing gain or loss on a sale or other disposition.[3] This is usually the property's cost. Where property used for personal purposes is *converted* to use in business or the production of income, the basis for depreciation purposes is the lesser of the fair market value or the adjusted basis at the time of conversion.[4] This ensures that no deduction is claimed for declines in value while the property was held for personal purposes.

Example 2

R purchased a home computer for $1,000 while attending college. He used it solely for personal purposes. After graduation, R went into the consulting business and began using the computer for business purposes. At the time he converted the computer to business use, its value was $400. R may compute depreciation using a basis of $400 (the lesser of the adjusted basis, $1,000, or its value, $400, at the time of conversion).

---

[2] Reg. §§ 1.167(a)-2 and 1.167(a)-3.

[3] § 167(g).

[4] Reg. § 1.167(g)-1.

Commencement of Depreciation

The date on which depreciation begins can be quite important. Depreciation may not begin until an asset is *placed in service*. This is not necessarily the time when the asset is purchased. According to the Regulations, an asset is placed in service when it is in a "state of readiness and availability for the assigned function" of the activity.[5] For those assets acquired for a new business, the depreciation period starts when the business begins.

Example 3

In 1981, William and Lois Walsh[6] leased a building and immediately began making substantial repairs and improvements to prepare it to open as a restaurant. Although the restaurant did not open until 1982, the couple claimed depreciation deductions in 1981 that were denied by the IRS. At trial, the taxpayers asserted that their restaurant business began in 1981 when they acquired assets for use in the restaurant and executed a lease for the premises. Although the taxpayers purchased the assets in 1981, the court denied the taxpayers' 1981 depreciation deductions. According to the court, the restaurant had not yet begun to function as a going concern and to perform those activities for which it was organized. For this reason, the assets had not been placed in service until the restaurant opened in 1982.

HISTORICAL PERSPECTIVE

Prior to 1981, taxpayers could compute depreciation using either of two approaches: (1) the facts-and-circumstances method or (2) the Class Life System. Depreciation methods such as straight-line, declining balance, and sum-of-the-years'-digits were available for most assets under each system. The facts-and-circumstances method enabled taxpayers to choose useful life and salvage value estimates for depreciable assets based on their experience and judgment of all surrounding facts and circumstances. There were no predetermined or prescribed guidelines. Conflicts often arose between taxpayers and the IRS over useful life selections because taxpayers were motivated to employ short useful lives in order to maximize the present value of tax savings from depreciation deductions.

As an alternative to the facts-and-circumstances system, the Class Life System became part of the law in 1971. It was developed primarily to minimize IRS-taxpayer conflicts over useful life estimates. The system prescribed depreciable life ranges for numerous categories of assets. For example, office furniture and fixtures could be depreciated using lives from 8 years to 12 years under the Class Life System.[7] Taxpayers electing this system were not challenged by the IRS. However, IRS-taxpayer conflicts were not eliminated because many taxpayers continued to employ the facts-and-circumstances system, seeking depreciable lives that were shorter than those available with the Class Life System.

In 1981, the facts-and-circumstances system and Class Life System were all but eliminated for assets placed in service after 1980. In the Economic Recovery Tax Act of 1981 (ERTA), Congress substantially revised the method for computing depreciation by enacting Code § 168 and the Accelerated Cost Recovery System (ACRS). Altered several times since 1981, the current version of this system is known as the Modified Accelerated Cost Recovery System (MACRS). An alternative to MACRS, called the Alternative Depreciation System (ADS), is also available.

A major benefit of MACRS and ADS is the elimination of previous areas of dispute between taxpayers and the IRS. Under these systems, the taxpayer is required to choose from a small set of predetermined options regarding depreciable life and depreciation method. Salvage value is ignored in all cases. Thus, depreciation calculations are more uniform for all taxpayers.

It should be emphasized, however, that some assets may not be depreciated using either of these systems. For this reason, the facts-and-circumstances approach and the Class Life System have continuing validity in certain instances.

---

[5] Reg. §§ 1.46-3(d)(1) and 1.167(a)-11(e)(1)(i).

[6] *William J. Walsh*, TC Memo 1988-242.

[7] Rev. Proc. 77-10, 1977-1 C.B. 548.

Modified Accelerated Cost Recovery System

AN OVERVIEW OF MACRS

Once it is determined that property is eligible for depreciation, the amount of the depreciation deduction must be computed. Under current law, taxpayers are required to calculate depreciation for most property using the Modified Accelerated Cost Recovery System (MACRS) or what is sometimes referred to as the General Depreciation System or GDS. As suggested earlier, MACRS is a radical departure from traditional approaches to depreciation. Under MACRS, useful lives for assets are termed *recovery periods* and are prescribed by statute. Regardless of the effects of nature and outside forces, each asset is deemed to have a particular useful life of 3, 5, 7, 10, 15, 20, 27.5, or 39 years. In addition, salvage value is ignored under MACRS. By assuming there is no salvage value, taxpayers can depreciate the basis of each asset to zero. With these rules, possibilities for abuse using unrealistic values for useful life and salvage value are essentially eliminated. Finally, certain assumptions—so-called *accounting conventions*—exist regarding how much depreciation is allowed for the year of acquisition and disposition (e.g., a half-year or something more or less).

> **LO.3**
> Calculate depreciation for tax purposes, using the modified cost recovery system.

The basic machinery of MACRS that is used to compute depreciation can be summarized as follows:

1. The system establishes eight classes or categories of property (e.g., three-year property, five-year property, seven-year property, etc.).
2. For each class of property, a specific useful life and depreciation method are prescribed (e.g., for three-year property the useful life is three years and either the 200% declining-balance or straight-line method must be used).

To actually compute depreciation, taxpayers must first determine when the asset is placed in service, whether the property is subject to MACRS, then—based on the property's classification—determine the applicable method, recovery period, and accounting convention. These elements of the depreciation calculation are discussed below.

PROPERTY SUBJECT TO MACRS

Taxpayers generally must use MACRS to compute depreciation for all *tangible* property, both real and personal, new or used.[8] MACRS is not used to amortize *intangible* assets such as patents or copyrights, which are amortized using the straight-line method. In addition, MACRS may not be used with respect to the following property:[9]

1. Property depreciated using a method that is not based on years (e.g., the units-of production or income forecast methods).
2. Automobiles if the taxpayer has elected to use the standard mileage rate (such an election precludes a depreciation deduction).
3. Property for which special amortization is provided and elected by the taxpayer in lieu of depreciation (e.g., amortization of pollution control facilities).
4. Certain motion picture films, video tapes, sound recordings, and public utility property.
5. Any property that the taxpayer—or a party related to the taxpayer—owned or used (e.g., leased) prior to 1987.

As a practical matter, MACRS is mandatory for all tangible property. But as explained below, the taxpayer has several alternatives under MACRS, including the option to elect out entirely and use the Alternative Depreciation System. In addition, in lieu of depreciation, the taxpayer may be allowed to expense a portion of the cost of certain assets placed in service during the year. Observe, however, that there are no elections available enabling the taxpayer to use the facts-and-circumstances method typically used for financial accounting purposes. Exhibit 9-1 identifies the depreciation methods and accounting conventions available under the MACRS and ADS systems.

---

[8] § 168(a).   [9] § 168(f).

EXHIBIT 9-1	**Depreciation Methods and Accounting Conventions under MACRS and ADS**			
8 MACRS Property Classes	*Modified Accelerated Cost Recovery System (MACRS): Use MACRS Property Class Life*	*Alternative Depreciation System (ADS): Use ADS Life*	*Accounting Convention**
3-year, 5-year, 7-year, 10-year**	Choices: 200% DB, 150% DB, or SL***	SL	Half-year or mid-quarter
15-year, 20-year	Choices: 150% DB or SL	Choices: 150% DB or SL	Half-year or mid-quarter
Residential rental real estate	27.5 years SL	40 years SL	Mid-month
Nonresidential real estate	39 years SL	40 years SL	Mid-month

Notes:

* Taxpayers do *not* have the option of choosing either the half-year or mid-quarter convention. As explained later in this chapter, either the half-year or mid-quarter convention is *required* depending on the timing of asset purchases during the year.

** Under certain conditions, Code § 179 allows taxpayers to expense (rather than depreciate) the cost of most 3-, 5-, 7-, and 10-year assets (i.e., depreciable tangible personal property). In 2017, the limit on the amount expensed is $510,000.[10]

*** Abbreviations:
DB = declining balance; SL = straight-line

CLASSES OF PROPERTY

As indicated in Exhibit 9-1, all property subject to MACRS is assigned to one of eight classes.[11] Classification is important because the recovery periods, methods, and accounting conventions to be used in calculating depreciation can vary among the different classes of property. Property is assigned to a particular class based on its *class life* as prescribed in Revenue Procedure 87-56.[12] This Revenue Procedure, an excerpt of which is provided in Exhibit 9-2, specifies not only the class lives of various assets but also the recovery periods to be used for both MACRS and ADS. Note that the "General Depreciation System" column of Exhibit 9-2 pertains to MACRS. Exhibit 9-3 provides examples of property in each of the eight MACRS property classes.

In examining Exhibit 9-2, it is important to emphasize that many classes of assets and their descriptions are omitted. Only by examining Revenue Procedure 87-56 can one truly appreciate its scope. Nevertheless, it is impossible to identify the useful life of every asset. For this reason, as can be seen in Exhibit 9-2, Revenue Procedure 87-56 divides assets into two major categories: *Specific Depreciable Assets Being Used in All Business Activities* (such as computers and automobiles) and *Depreciable Assets Used in the Following Activities*. Thus if a particular asset is not assigned a recovery period its life is determined by the activity in which it is used.

Example 4

FunSpot Inc. operates a chain of bowling alleys all over New Jersey. During the year, it purchased furniture, computers, automatic pin-setters, bowling balls, and shoes. In determining the recovery period of these assets, the only assets to which a specific life has been assigned are the furniture (Asset Class 0.11, 7 years) and the computers (Asset Class 0.12, 5 years). The life of the pin-setters, bowling balls, and shoes would be determined based on the activity in which they are used (Asset Class 80.0, 7 years).

---

[10] The Protecting Americans from Tax Hikes Act of 2015 permanently extends the § 179 expensing limitation to $500,000 and indexes the $500,000 amount for inflation in $10,000 increments. For 2017, the expensing limitation was increased to $510,000.

[11] § 168(e).

[12] 1987-2 C.B. 674, as modified by Rev. Proc. 88-22, 1988-1 C.B. 785. For class lives, see *How to Depreciate Property*, IRS Publication 946, (Rev. 2013) p. 98.

EXHIBIT 9-2	**Excerpt from Revenue Procedure 87-56**

Asset Class	Description of Assets Included	Class Life (in years)	Recovery Periods (in years) General Depreciation System	Recovery Periods (in years) Alternative Depreciation System
SPECIFIC DEPRECIABLE ASSETS BEING USED IN ALL BUSINESS ACTIVITIES, EXCEPT AS NOTED				
00.11	**Office Furniture, Fixtures, and Equipment** Includes furniture and fixtures that are not structural components of a building. Includes such assets as desks, files, safes, and communications equipment. Does not include communications equipment that is included in other classes	10	7	10
00.12	**Information Systems:** Includes computers and their peripheral equipment	6	5	5
00.13	**Data Handling Equipment, Except Computers** Includes only typewriters, calculators, adding and accounting machines, copiers, and duplicating equipment	6	5	6
00.21	**Airplanes (Airframes and Engines), Except Those Used in Commercial or Contract Carrying of Passengers or Freight, and All Helicopters (Airframes and Engines)**	6	5	6
00.22	**Automobiles, Taxis**	3	5	5
00.23	**Buses**	9	5	9
00.241	**Light General Purpose Trucks** Includes trucks for use over the road (actual unloaded weight less than 13,000 pounds)	4	5	5
00.242	**Heavy General Purpose Trucks** Includes heavy general purpose trucks, concrete ready mix trucks, and ore trucks, for use over the road (actual unloaded weight 13,000 pounds or more)	6	5	6
DEPRECIABLE ASSETS USED IN THE FOLLOWING ACTIVITIES				
01.1	**Agriculture** Includes machinery and equipment, grain bins, and fences but no other land improvements, that are used in the production of crops or plants, vines, and trees; livestock; the operation of farm dairies, nurseries, greenhouses, sod farms, mushroom cellars, cranberry bogs, apiaries, and fur farms; the performance of agriculture, animal husbandry, and horticultural services	10	7	10
01.11	**Cotton Ginning Assets**	12	7	12
01.21	**Cattle, Breeding or Dairy**	7	5	7
01.4	**Single-Purpose Agricultural or Horticultural Structures**	15	10	15
15.0	**Construction** Includes assets used in construction by general building, special trade, heavy and marine construction contractors, operative and investment builders, real estate subdividers and developers, and others except railroads	6	5	6
20.1	**Manufacture of Grain and Grain Mill**	17	10	17
27.0	**Printing, Publishing, and Allied Industries**	11	7	11

EXHIBIT 9-2   **Excerpt from Revenue Procedure 87-56 (Continued)**

Asset Class	Description of Assets Included	Class Life (in years)	Recovery Periods (in years)	
			General Depreciation System	Alternative Depreciation System
36.0	Manufacture of Electronic Components, Products, and Systems	6	5	6
37.11	Manufacture of Motor Vehicles	12	7	12
39.0	Manufacture of Athletic, Jewelry, and Other Goods:			
	Includes assets used in the production of jewelry; musical instruments; toys and sporting goods; motion picture and television films and tapes; pens, pencils, office and art supplies, brooms, brushes, caskets, etc.	12	7	12
45.0	Air Transport	12	7	12
48.2	Radio and Television Broadcastings:			
	Includes assets used in radio and television broadcasting, except transmitting towers.	6	5	6
48.42	CATV-Subscriber Connection and Distribution Systems.	10	7	10
79.0	Recreation:			
	Includes assets used in the provision of entertainment services on payment of a fee or admission charge, as in the operation of bowling alleys, billiard and pool establishments, theaters, concert halls, and miniature golf courses. Does not include amusement and theme parks and assets which consist primarily of specialized land improvements or structures, such as golf courses, sports stadia, race tracks, ski slopes, and buildings which house the assets used in entertainment services.	10	7	10
80.0	Theme and Amusement Parks	12.5	7	12

EXHIBIT 9-3   **Examples of MACRS Property**

MACRS Property Class	Examples
3 years	Special tools, race horses, tractors, and property with a class life of 4 years or less
5 years	Automobiles, trucks, computers and peripheral equipment (such as printers, external disk drives, and modems), typewriters, copiers, R&E equipment, and property with a class life of more than 4 years and less than 10 years
7 years	Office furniture, fixtures, office equipment, most machinery, property with a class life of 10 years or more but less than 16 years, and property with no assigned class life
10 years	Single-purpose agricultural and horticultural structures, assets used in petroleum refining and manufacturing of tobacco and certain food products, and property with a class life of 16 years or more but less than 20 years
15 years	Land improvements (such as sidewalks, roads, parking lots, irrigation systems, sewers, fences, and landscaping), service stations, billboards, telephone distribution plants, and property with a class life of 20 years or more but less than 25 years; any qualified leasehold improvement property, qualified restaurant property and qualified retail improvement property (see §§ 168(e)(6), (7) and (8))
20 years	Municipal sewers and property with a class life of 25 years or more
27.5 years	Residential rental real estate, including apartment buildings, duplexes, etc.
39 years	Nonresidential real estate, including office buildings, warehouses, factories, and farm buildings

CALCULATING DEPRECIATION

Under MACRS, depreciation is a function of *three* factors: the recovery period, the depreciation method, and the accounting convention.

Recovery Periods

As seen in Exhibit 9-1, recovery periods run various lengths of time depending on the class of property.[13] In examining the different classes, several features should be observed. First, certain property is assigned to a class without regard to its class life. The most notable example of this is cars, which are assigned to the five-year class (see asset class 00.22 in Exhibit 9-2). Note also that the current structure provides different recovery periods for real property, depending on whether it is residential (27.5 years) or nonresidential (39 years) real estate. As a result, when a building is used for both residential and nonresidential purposes (e.g., a multilevel apartment building with commercial space on the bottom two floors) it must be classified as one or the other. For this purpose, realty qualifies as residential real estate if 80% of the gross rents are for the dwelling units.[14] In addition, special rules generally provide a much shorter life of 15 years for buildings that house restaurants, certain improvements to retail space and other qualified leasehold improvements. This latter group includes much of the property in shopping malls and strip centers, and is obviously an important segment of the economy. For this reason, the shorter depreciation lives are an important factor in determining whether a business should buy or lease the space it needs.

Depreciation Method

The depreciation method to be used—like the recovery period—varies depending on the class of the property. A closer look at Exhibit 9-1, however, reveals that the variation is actually between real and personal property. Real property is depreciated using the straight-line method, while personal property is depreciated using either straight-line or a declining balance method. If a declining-balance depreciation method is elected, a switch to straight-line is made in the first year in which a larger depreciation would result. *Example 5* illustrates this procedure, and the IRS depreciation tables presented later in this chapter incorporate the switch to straight-line.

Accounting Conventions

For assets placed in service or disposed of during the year, an assumption is made regarding the amount of depreciation that is allowed for the year (e.g., a half-year).[15] These assumptions are referred to as depreciation or accounting conventions. The conventions apply only in the years of acquisition and disposition. The applicable convention generally depends on the type of property: realty or personalty. As discussed further below, they are listed below:

Type of Property	Convention
Real property	Mid-month convention
Tangible personal property	Half-year convention
Tangible personal property	Mid-quarter convention

Half-Year Convention

The half-year convention applies to all property *other than* nonresidential real property and residential rental property. From a practical perspective, the half-year convention applies to *all depreciable tangible personal property.* Under the half-year convention, one-half year of depreciation is allowed regardless of when the asset is placed in service or sold during the year (e.g., ½ × the annual depreciation as normally computed).[16] Since only one-half year's depreciation is allowed in the first year, the recovery period is effectively extended one year so that the remaining one-half may be claimed.

[13] § 168(c).
[14] § 168(e)(2).
[15] § 168(d).
[16] § 168(d)(4).

Example 5

On March 1, 2017 T purchased a car to be used solely for business for $10,000. It was his only acquisition during the year. The car had an estimated useful life of four years and an estimated salvage value of $2,000. Although these estimates might be used for financial accounting purposes, under MACRS, salvage value is ignored and T is required to use the recovery period, depreciation method, and accounting convention prescribed for five-year property, the class to which cars are assigned under MACRS. T elects to compute his depreciation using the 200% declining-balance method (switching to straight-line where appropriate), a five-year recovery period, and the half-year convention. The 200% declining-balance rate would be 40% (200% × straight-line rate, 15 or 20 percent). The declining balance method would be used through 2020, when a switch to straight-line maximizes the depreciation deduction. Due to the half-year convention, the cost is actually recovered over six years rather than the five-year recovery period. Depreciation would be computed as follows:

Year	Depreciation Method	Basis for Depreciation Computation	Rate	Depreciation
2017	200% DB	$10,000	20%*	$ 2,000
2018	200% DB	8,000	40%	3,200
2019	200% DB	4,800	40%	1,920
2020	200% DB	2,880	40%	1,152**
2021	SL	1,730	1.0/1.5	1,152***
2022	SL	1,730	0.5/1.5	576
				$10,000

* Half-year allowance (40% × ½ = 20%).

** Note that straight-line depreciation is the same ($2,880 × 2/5).

*** Declining-balance depreciation would have been $692 ($1,730 × 40%); since straight-line depreciation over the remaining 1.5 years is $1,152 and greater than $692, the switch to straight-line is made.

Example 6

Same facts as above except T sold the property on December 20, 2019. In computing depreciation for personal property in the year of sale or disposition, the half-year convention must be used. Thus, depreciation for 2019 would be $960 ($4,800 × 40% × ½).

To simplify the computation of depreciation, the IRS provides optional tables as shown in Exhibit 9-4 to Exhibit 9-7.[17] The percentages (or rates) shown in the tables are the result of combining the three factors used in determining depreciation—method, rate, and convention—into a single, composite percentage to be used for each class of property.[18]

---

[17] Rev. Proc. 87-57, 1987-2 C.B. 687.

[18] Depreciation percentages in the tables are rounded to one-hundredth of a percent for recovery property with a recovery period of less than 20 years, and one-thousandth of a percent for all other property. See Rev. Proc. 87-57 *Supra*.

Example 7

The depreciation rates shown in Exhibit 9-4 for 5-year property for the year that it is placed in service and for the following year is determined as follows:

Year 1

Straight-line rate (1/5)	20%
× Declining-balance rate	× 200%
200% declining-balance rate	40%
× Half-year allowance	× ½
Depreciation rate per table	20%

Year 2

Basis of asset remaining (100% − 20%)	80%
× 200% declining-balance rate	× 40%
Depreciation rate per table	32%

EXHIBIT 9-4	**MACRS Accelerated Depreciation Percentages Using the Half-Year Convention for 3-, 5-, and 7-Year Property**

	Property Class		
Recovery Year	3-Year	5-Year	7-Year
1	33.33%	20.00%	14.29%
2	44.45	32.00	24.49
3	14.81	19.20	17.49
4	7.41	11.52	12.49
5		11.52	8.93
6		5.76	8.92
7			8.93
8			4.46

Source: Rev. Proc. 87-57, Table 1. Appendix C of this book has additional depreciation tables.

EXHIBIT 9-5	MACRS Depreciation Percentages for Residential Rental Property

	Recovery Year					
Month Placed in Service	1	2	3–26	27	28	29
1	3.485%	3.636%	3.636%	3.636%	1.970%	0.000%
2	3.182	3.636	3.636	3.636	2.273	0.000
3	2.879	3.636	3.636	3.636	2.576	0.000
4	2.576	3.636	3.636	3.636	2.879	0.000
5	2.273	3.636	3.636	3.636	3.182	0.000
6	1.970	3.636	3.636	3.636	3.485	0.000
7	1.667	3.636	3.636	3.637	3.636	0.152
8	1.364	3.636	3.636	3.637	3.636	0.455
9	1.061	3.636	3.636	3.637	3.636	0.758
10	0.758	3.636	3.636	3.637	3.636	1.061
11	0.455	3.636	3.636	3.637	3.636	1.364
12	0.152	3.636	3.636	3.637	3.636	1.667

Source: IRS Publication No. 534. Appendix C of this book has additional depreciation tables.

EXHIBIT 9-6	MACRS Depreciation Percentages for Nonresidential Real Property Placed in Service after May 12, 1993

	Recovery Year		
Month Placed in Service	1	2–39	40
1	2.461%	2.564%	0.107%
2	2.247	2.564	0.321
3	2.033	2.564	0.535
4	1.819	2.564	0.749
5	1.605	2.564	0.963
6	1.391	2.564	1.177
7	1.177	2.564	1.391
8	0.963	2.564	1.605
9	0.749	2.564	1.819
10	0.535	2.564	2.033
11	0.321	2.564	2.247
12	0.107	2.564	2.461

Source: IRS Publication No. 534. Appendix C of this book has additional depreciation tables.

EXHIBIT 9-7	MACRS Accelerated Depreciation Percentages Using the Mid-Quarter Convention for 3- and 5-Year Property			

| | | Quarter Placed in Service | | |
Recovery Year	1	2	3	4
3-Year Property:				
1	58.33%	41.67%	25.00%	8.33%
2	27.78	38.89	50.00	61.11
3	12.35	14.14	16.67	20.37
4	1.54	5.30	8.33	10.19
5-Year Property:				
1	35.00	25.00	15.00	5.00
2	26.00	30.00	34.00	38.00
3	15.60	18.00	20.40	22.80
4	11.01	11.37	12.24	13.68
5	11.01	11.37	11.30	10.94
6	1.38	4.26	7.06	9.58

Source: Rev. Proc. 87-57. Appendix C of this book has additional depreciation tables.

In studying *Example 7* above, note how the table percentage for the second year, 32 percent, is derived. This percentage takes into account the requirement of the declining-balance method that the annual rate must be applied to the cost of the asset less previous depreciation (i.e., the second-year percentage of 32% is the product of the annual rate of 40% and the balance of the asset not yet depreciated, 80% [100% − 20%]). Similarly, the percentages given for declining-balance methods also incorporate a switch to the straight-line method whenever the straight-line rate would yield a higher depreciation amount. Because these various considerations are already reflected in the tables, depreciation is computed by simply applying the appropriate percentage to the *unadjusted basis* of the property. The general formula for computing depreciation can be expressed as follows.

Unadjusted basis of the property × Recovery percentage = Annual depreciation

Example 8

Same facts as in *Example 5* where T purchased a business car for $10,000. Depreciation computed using the table in Exhibit 9-4 would be the same as above, computed as follows:

Year	Unadjusted Basis	×	Accelerated Recovery Percentage	Annual Depreciation
2017	$10,000		20.00%	$ 2,000
2018	10,000		32.00	3,200
2019	10,000		19.20	1,920
2020	10,000		11.52	1,152
2021	10,000		11.52	1,152
2022	10,000		5.76	576
			100.00%	$10,000

The basic steps necessary to compute annual depreciation using MACRS are:

1. Identify the *depreciable basis* of the asset (generally its cost): $10,000 in *Example 8*.

2. Determine the MACRS *property class:* five-year property in *Example 8*.

3. Identify the *depreciation convention* (either half-year or mid-quarter for personal property; mid-month for real estate): half-year convention in *Example 8*.

4. Determine the *recovery period* and *method*. See Exhibit 9-1 for a summary of the available choices: five-year 200% declining balance in *Example 8*.

5. Locate the *appropriate table* based on the depreciation convention, recovery period, and method: Exhibit 9-4 for the five-year property (car) in *Example 8*. (Note the depreciation convention is already reflected in the table percentages for the year of acquisition, but *not* for the year of disposition.)

6. Choose the *table percentages* relating to the recovery period of the asset: five-year property percentages for *Example 8* (i.e., 20 percent, 32 percent, etc.).

7. Multiply the table percentages by the depreciable (cost) basis of the asset to *compute annual depreciation* amounts: $10,000 multiplied by 20% provides $2,000 of depreciation for 2017 in *Example 8*.

When using the depreciation tables, a special adjustment must be made if there is a disposition of the property before its cost is fully recovered. As noted above, under the half-year convention the taxpayer is entitled only to a half-year of depreciation in the year of disposition. Therefore, where the half-year convention applies and the property is used for only a portion of the disposition year, only one-half of the amount of depreciation determined using the table is allowed.

Example 9

Same facts as *Example 8* except the taxpayer sold the property on December 1, 2019. Since the taxpayer did not hold the property the entire taxable year and the half-year convention is in effect, only one-half of the amount of depreciation using the table is allowed. Therefore, depreciation for 2019 would have been $960 ($10,000 × 19.2% × ½). Note that this is the same result as obtained in *Example 6* above.

Mid-Month Convention

This convention applies only to real property (i.e., nonresidential real property and residential rental property).[19] Under the mid-month convention, one-half month of depreciation is allowed for the month the asset is placed in service or sold and a full month of depreciation is allowed for each additional month of the year that the asset is in service.[20] For example, if a calendar year taxpayer places a building in service on April 3, the fraction of the annual depreciation allowed is 8.5/12 (half-month's depreciation for April and eight months' depreciation for May through December).

Example 10

The first-year depreciation rate for residential rental realty that is placed in service in April is determined as follows:

Straight-line rate (1/27.5)	3.636%
× Mid-month convention	× 8.5/12
Depreciation rate per table	2.576%

Due to the mid-month convention, the recovery period must be extended one month to claim the one-half month of depreciation that was not claimed in the first month. For example, the entire cost of residential rental property is recovered over 331 months (27½ years is 330 months + 1 additional month to claim the half-month of depreciation not claimed in the first month). As a result, depreciation deductions are actually claimed over either 28 or 29 years depending on the month in which the property was placed in service. This can be seen by examining the composite depreciation percentages for real property reflecting the mid-month convention given in Exhibit 9-5 and Exhibit 9-6.

Example 11

S purchased a duplex as an investment for $110,000 on July 17, 2017. Of the $110,000 cost, $10,000 is allocated to the land. The estimated useful life of the duplex is 30 years—the same period as her mortgage—and the estimated salvage value is $15,000. Despite these estimates, under MACRS salvage value is ignored and S is required to use the recovery period, depreciation method, and convention prescribed for residential rental property, the class to which the duplex is assigned. Therefore, S uses a 27.5-year life, the straight-line method, and the mid-month convention. Using the table in Exhibit 9-5, depreciation for the first year would be $1,667 ($100,000 × 1.667%).

When using the depreciation tables, an adjustment must be made if there is a disposition of the real property before its cost is fully recovered. This adjustment is similar to that required where the half-year convention applies, but not identical. In the year of disposition, the taxpayer may deduct depreciation only for those months the property is used by the taxpayer. In addition, under the mid-month convention, the taxpayer is entitled to only a half-month of depreciation for the month of disposition.

Example 12

Same facts as *Example 11* except the taxpayer sold the duplex on May 22, 2018. Depreciation for 2018 would be $1,363 ($100,000 × 3.636% × 4.5/12).

---

[19] § 168(d)(2).   [20] § 168(d)(4)(B).

Mid-Quarter Convention

The mid-quarter convention applies only to *personal property*. However, it applies only if more than 40% of the aggregate bases of all personal property placed in service during the taxable year is placed in service during the last three months of the year.[21] Property placed in service and disposed of during the same taxable year is not taken into account. Also not taken into account is any amount immediately expensed under § 179 (discussed below) or property used for personal purposes. If the 40% test is satisfied, the mid-quarter convention applies to *all* personal property placed in service during the year (regardless of the quarter in which it was actually placed in service).

Example 13

K Company, a calendar year taxpayer, acquired and placed in service the following assets:

Assets	Acquisition Date	Cost
Office furniture...	March 28, 20X1	$20,000
Machinery	October 9, 20X1	80,000
Warehouse...	February 1, 20X2	90,000

Of the total *personal* property placed in service during the year, more than 40% ($80,000 ÷ [$20,000 + $80,000]) occurred in the last quarter (i.e., October through December). As a result, K must use the mid-quarter convention for computing the depreciation of both the furniture and the machinery.

When applicable, the mid-quarter convention treats all personal property as being placed in service in the middle of the quarter of the taxable year in which it was actually placed in service.[22] Therefore, one-half of a quarter's depreciation—in effect one-eighth ($\frac{1}{2} \times \frac{1}{4}$) or 12.5% of the annual depreciation—is allowed for the quarter that the asset is placed in service or sold. In addition, a full quarter's depreciation is allowed for each additional quarter that the asset is in service. For example, personal property placed in service on March 3 would be treated as having been placed in service in the middle of the first quarter and the taxpayer would be able to claim $3\frac{1}{2}$ quarters—3.5/4 or 87.5 percent—of the annual amount of depreciation. The percentages of the annual depreciation allowed under the mid-quarter convention for a year in which an asset is placed in service are

	Quarter Placed in Service			
	1 January–March	2 April–June	3 July–September	4 October–December
Percentage of annual depreciation allowed	87.5%	62.5%	37.5%	12.5%

The above chart illustrates that where an asset is placed in service in the first quarter and the mid-quarter convention applies, the taxpayer is allowed to deduct 87.5% of the annual depreciation. In contrast, for personal property placed in service during the fourth quarter only 12.5% of the annual depreciation may be deducted. Note that the recovery period must be extended by one year so that the balance of the depreciation not claimed in the first year may be deducted. Composite depreciation percentages to be used for 3-year and 5-year property where the mid-quarter convention applies are provided in Exhibit 9-7. Appendix C has depreciation tables for all categories of personal property under the mid-quarter convention.

---

[21] § 168(d)(3).   [22] *Ibid.*

Example 14

In 2017 T, a calendar year taxpayer, purchased five trucks to use in his business at a cost of $20,000 each. These purchases were his only acquisitions of personal property during the year. Four of the trucks were purchased in December while the other truck was purchased in January. Since more than 40% of the property placed in service during the year was placed in service in the last quarter ($80,000 ÷ $100,000 = 80%), the mid-quarter convention applies in computing depreciation. Thus, the depreciation allowed on the truck purchased in January would be limited to 87.5% of a full year's depreciation, and the depreciation allowed on the four trucks purchased in December would be limited to 12.5% of a full year's depreciation. Since a full year's depreciation would be 40% of cost (straight-line rate of 20% per year × 200% declining-balance = 40%), the depreciation for the January purchase would be limited to 35% of cost (40% × 87.5%), or $7,000 (35% × $20,000). Similarly, the depreciation for the December purchases would be limited to 5% of cost (40% × 12.5%), or $4,000 (5% × $80,000). Total depreciation under the mid-quarter convention is limited to $11,000 ($4,000 + $7,000). These amounts are easily computed using the tables in Exhibit 9-7.

Note that had the mid-quarter convention not applied, the depreciation percentage would have been 20%—reflecting the half-year allowance for five-year property (40% × ½ = 20%), or $20,000 ($100,000 × 20%). Due to the timing of the acquisitions, T's depreciation for the year is reduced by $9,000 ($20,000 − $11,000).

When using the depreciation tables, a special adjustment must be made if there is a disposition of the property before its cost is fully recovered. This adjustment is similar to that for the half-year and mid-month conventions. As noted above, under the mid-quarter convention, the taxpayer is entitled to only one-half of a quarter's depreciation—in effect one-eighth (½ × ¼) or 12.5% of the annual depreciation—for the quarter that the asset is sold. In addition, a full quarter of depreciation is allowed for each quarter that the asset is in service. For example, if property was sold on August 2, the taxpayer could claim 2½ quarters—2.5/4 or 62.5 percent—of the annual amount of depreciation. The percentages of annual depreciation allowed under the mid-quarter convention for the year an asset is sold are:

	Quarter Property Sold			
	1	2	3	4
	January–March	April–June	July–September	October–December
Percentage of annual depreciation allowed	12.5%	37.5%	62.5%	87.5%

Example 15

Same facts as in *Example 14* above, except the truck acquired in January 2017 was sold on August 9, 2019. Since T did not hold the property the entire taxable year and the mid-quarter convention is in effect, only 62.5% of the amount of depreciation using the table is allowed. Therefore, using the table in Exhibit 9-7, T's depreciation for this truck would have been $1,950 ($20,000 × 15.6% × 62.5%).

OTHER METHODS

The accelerated depreciation methods prescribed by MACRS are normally desirable since they allow taxpayers to recover their costs more rapidly than the straight-line method. However, there may be circumstances where the slower-paced straight-line method may be more advantageous. For example, if the taxpayer is currently in the 10 or 15% tax bracket, he or she may want to defer depreciation deductions to years when he or she is in a higher tax bracket. By doing this, the taxpayer may be able to maximize the present value of the tax savings from depreciation deductions (depending upon the taxpayer's discount rate).

Perhaps a more common reason for using straight-line depreciation concerns the alternative minimum tax (AMT). As discussed briefly in Chapter 3 and in detail in Chapter 13, the AMT is an alternative system for computing the tax, using certain modifications. For AMT purposes, depreciation is generally computed using a method slower than MACRS (e.g., 150% rather than 200% declining balance). This difference can lead to an AMT liability. To avoid this, taxpayers often elect to use a straight-line method for regular tax purposes. If a taxpayer elects to use the straight-line method in lieu of the accelerated method, two different approaches are available: straight-line under MACRS, or straight-line under ADS.

MACRS Straight-Line

Although it may seem inconsistent, the *Modified Accelerated Cost Recovery System* offers taxpayers a straight-line method of depreciation.[23] If the taxpayer so elects, the straight line method is used in conjunction with all of the other rules that normally apply under MACRS; that is, the taxpayer simply uses the straight-line method (in lieu of the accelerated method) along with the applicable recovery period and accounting convention. The depreciation percentages to be used where the taxpayer elects the straight-line method are contained in Exhibit 9-8 (half-year convention property) for 3-, 5-, and 7-year property. Appendix C has straight-line depreciation tables for all categories of personal property under the half-year convention. The depreciation percentages for the straight-line method when the mid-quarter convention applies can be found in Revenue Procedure 87-57.[24]

Example 16

On June 1, 2017 L purchased 5-year property (to which the half-year convention applies) for $50,000. Using the table in Exhibit 9-8, depreciation for the year would be $5,000 ($50,000 × 10%). Depreciation for 2018 would be $10,000 (20% × $50,000). If L sold the property on January 22, 2019, depreciation would be $5,000 ($50,000 × 20% × ½).

---

[23] § 168(b)(3)(C).   [24] 1987-2 C.B. 687.

EXHIBIT 9-8	MACRS and ADS Straight-Line Depreciation Percentages Using the Half-Year Convention for 3-, 5-, and 7-Year Property

| | Property Class | | |
Recovery Year	3-Year	5-Year	7-Year
1	16.67%	10.00%	7.14%
2	33.33	20.00	14.29
3	33.33	20.00	14.29
4	16.67	20.00	14.28
5		20.00	14.29
6		10.00	14.28
7			14.29
8			7.14

Source: Rev. Proc. 87-57.

Appendix C has additional depreciation tables.

The election to use the straight-line method is made annually by class (recall the straight-line method must be used for realty). For example, if in 2017 the taxpayer makes the election for 7-year property, *all* 7-year property placed in service during the year must be depreciated using the straight-line method. The election does not obligate the taxpayer to use the straight-line method for any other class. Similarly, the taxpayer need not use the straight-line method for such class of assets placed in service in the following year.

EXHIBIT 9-9	Alternative Depreciation System Recovery Periods

General Rule: Recovery period is the property's class life unless
1. There is no class life (see below), or
2. A special class life has been designated (see below).

Type of Property	Recovery Period
Personal property with no class life	12 years
Nonresidential real property with no class life	40 years
Residential rental property with no class life	40 years
Cars, light general-purpose trucks, certain technological equipment, and semiconductor manufacturing equipment	5 years
Computer-based telephone central office switching equipment	9.5 years
Railroad track	10 years
Single-purpose agricultural or horticultural structures	15 years
Municipal wastewater treatment plants, telephone distribution plants	24 years
Low-income housing financed by tax-exempt bonds	27.5 years
Municipal sewers	50 years

Alternative Depreciation System

The Alternative Depreciation System (ADS) is an option for taxpayers.[25] This system is similar to MACRS in two ways: salvage value is ignored, and the same averaging conventions must be followed. The major differences between MACRS and ADS are the longer recovery periods provided by ADS for most assets and in some cases, slower rates of depreciation. The recovery period to be used for ADS is normally the property's class life. The class life—which is usually longer than the MACRS life—is used unless no class life has been prescribed for the property or a specific class life has been designated in Code § 168. For example, as shown in Exhibit 9-2, the ADS class life for copiers (asset class 00.13) is six years, whereas the MACRS life is five years. Thus, depreciation under ADS would be computed using a six-year life, whereas depreciation for MACRS would be computed using a five-year life. The recovery periods to be used for ADS are summarized in Exhibit 9-9.

Taxpayers electing ADS for real property are restricted to straight-line depreciation. Thus, an office building (nonresidential real property) would be depreciated using straight-line and a 40-year recovery period under ADS. The ADS depreciation percentages for real property are found in Exhibit 9-10.

EXHIBIT 9-10	ADS Straight-Line Depreciation Percentages for Real Property Using the Mid-Month Convention		

| Month Placed in Service | Recovery Year | | |
	1	2–40	41
1	2.396%	2.500%	0.104%
2	2.188	2.500	0.312
3	1.979	2.500	0.521
4	1.771	2.500	0.729
5	1.563	2.500	0.937
6	1.354	2.500	1.146
7	1.146	2.500	1.354
8	0.938	2.500	1.562
9	0.729	2.500	1.771
10	0.521	2.500	1.979
11	0.313	2.500	2.187
12	0.104	2.500	2.396

Source: Rev. Proc. 87-57, Table 13.

In contrast, either straight-line or 150% declining balance depreciation may be chosen for depreciable tangible personal property. The ADS straight-line depreciation percentages for such property, which in fact have class lives of three, five, and seven years, are the same as those for MACRS straight-line and can be found in Exhibit 9-8.

Taxpayers have as many as four options for depreciating personal property—straight line or accelerated depreciation over the MACRS recovery period, or straight line over a longer ADS recovery period. Accelerated depreciation options are 200% or 150% declining balance. For example, the ADS option for a copier consists of straight-line over six years. The MACRS alternatives allow for a five-year write-off using either 200% or 150% declining balance or straight line. Which of these four choices would be best for depreciating the copier? In general, the taxpayer should select the depreciation method that maximizes the present value of tax savings from depreciation deductions. For taxpayers who expect their future marginal tax rate to either remain constant or decline, the fastest depreciation method over the shortest time period will maximize the present value of tax savings from depreciation.

---

[25] § 168(g).

The mechanics of the election to use ADS—except for real property—are identical to those of MACRS discussed above. Except for real property, the taxpayer may elect to use ADS on a class-by-class, year-by-year basis.[26] For realty, the election is made on a property-by-property basis. In addition, the taxpayer *must* use ADS straight-line for depreciating the following:[27]

- Certain "listed property" that is not used predominantly for business (see discussion below).

- Foreign use property (i.e., property used outside the U.S. more than half of a taxable year).

- Property leased to a tax-exempt entity.

- Property leased to foreign persons (unless more than 50% of the income is subject to U.S. tax).

- Property financed by the issuance of tax-exempt bonds (i.e., tax-exempt bond-financed property).

ADS is also used for computing depreciation for purposes of the alternative minimum tax (discussed in Chapter 13) and a corporation's earnings and profits (discussed in Chapter 19).

Leasing and Leasehold Improvements

There are an estimated 30 million businesses in the U.S. and, while the exact number is unknown, there is little doubt that a large percentage of these choose to lease rather than buy the space they require. For companies that choose to lease, they normally must customize the space to suit their needs.

Consider the typical strip mall and its row of stores, a nail salon, dry cleaners, liquor store, drug store, florist, restaurant, bank, dental office, and more. Each business has unique requirements. The restaurant needs a kitchen and walk-in freezer. The bank needs a vault and drive-through window while a dental office needs partitions, and so on. Then, a few years pass and the space needs reconfiguring, sprucing up and as a result, more work is done. These customizations or alterations are referred to as leasehold improvements. They may include painting, installing walls, changing the flooring, putting in customized light fixtures and changing whatever their business needs demand.

Leasehold improvements can be made either by landlords, who may do so to increase the marketability of their rental units, or by the tenants themselves. In these situations, the lessor or lessee is entitled to recover any investment in the improvement.[28] In addition, the landlord and the tenant may incur a number of expenses—leasehold acquisition expenses—when entering a lease and these expenses are subject to special treatment.

Leasehold Acquisition Costs

Both the landlord and the tenant may incur leasehold acquisition expenses. Such costs include commissions to the real estate agent that helped find the property and close on the lease, attorney's fees for drawing up the lease, lease signing bonuses, and appraisal costs. They may also include inspection fees. Once the amount of acquisition costs is determined, these costs must be capitalized and amortized over the life of the lease.[29] If a lease contains renewal options, the question arises as to whether the acquisition costs should be amortized over the initial term of the lease or over the initial term plus the periods of renewal. Under § 178, renewal periods are ignored as long as 75% of the lease costs are for the initial term rather than the renewal.

[26] § 168(g)(7).

[27] § 168(g)(1).

[28] See generally § 168(i)(8)(A).

[29] Rev. Rul. 70-408, 1970-2 CB 68 (broker's commission); Rev. Rul. 73-421, 1973-2 CB 33 (other expenses). See also Elavitch and Schachat, "Income Tax Issues for Lessors and Lessees," *William & Mary Annual Tax Conference.* Paper 130; http://scholarship.law.wm.edu/tax/130.

Example 17

Spinning Inc. operates indoor cycling facilities throughout Los Angeles. This year, the company arranged to lease space at various locations from an owner of several strip centers. Spinning paid $10,000 to acquire the leases with an initial term of 5 years. The lease also contains two options to renew for periods of 2 years each. The accountant for Spinning wants to know whether to amortize the $10,000 over 5 years or the extended term of 9 years. Of the $10,000 cost, $8,000 was paid for the initial 5-year term. Since at least 75 percent of the cost was attributable to the initial term, the entire acquisition cost of $10,000 is amortized over 5 years at a rate of $2,000 per year. If only $7,000 of the $10,000 cost had been attributable to the initial term, the 75 percent threshold would not be met and the amortization period would include the two renewal terms of 2 years each for a total of 9 years. Consequently, the amortization of the $10,000 would be $1,111 per year ($10,000/9 years).

Unfortunately, the amount paid for a renewal is not always apparent so the apportionment to the intial term and the resulting amortization period may be subject to question by the government.

Leasehold Improvements

The cost of any leasehold improvement made by a lessor or lessee is usually depreciated in the normal manner without regard to the actual term of the lease.[30] Lessors and lessees are allowed to depreciate improvements they make for tenants such as interior walls over 39 years for nonresidential real estate and 27.5 years for residential real estate. This is true even if the lease term is less than these periods. They must use the straight-line method. If the improvement is tangible property, the shorter MACRS lives may be used.

What happens to the unrecovered costs of lessor-owned improvements should a termination of the lease occur? The lessor is treated as having disposed of the property and would recognize a loss. Any unrecovered cost at the end of the lease term would increase the taxpayer's basis for determining gain or loss.

Qualified Leasehold Improvements. In 2004, the rules governing depreciation of leasehold improvements were changed to encourage the improvement of leased nonresidential real property. For the most part, this is the property typically found in shopping centers, malls and strip centers—obviously a large component of the economy. Instead of the normal 39-year recovery period, the special rules provide a 15-year recovery period (using a half-year or mid-quarter convention rather than the mid-month convention). This shorter recovery period generally is available to lessors and lessees making structural improvements to the interior portion of the property for three specifically defined situations.[31]

- *Qualified Leasehold Improvement Property* is generally any improvement to an interior portion of a building that is nonresidential real property and placed in service more than three years after the date the building was first placed in service. The improvement must be made pursuant to a lease.

- *Qualified Restaurant Property* is generally any building or an improvement to a building if more than 50 percent of the building's square footage is devoted to the preparation, seating and consumption of prepared meals.

- *Qualified Retail Improvement Property* is any improvement to an interior portion of a building, which is nonresidential real property and placed in service more than three years after the date the building was first placed in service. Retail establishments that qualify include those open to the public and primarily in the business of selling goods (tangible personal property) to the general public and not services. Examples of these retail establishments include grocery stores, clothing stores, hardware stores, and convenience stores.

As noted in the discussion of § 179 and bonus depreciation later in this chapter, these qualified leasehold improvements are eligible for the special treatment offered by these provisions.

---

[30] § 168(i)(8)(A)

[31] See § 168(b)(3)(G),(H) and (I); § 168(e)(3)(E)(iv),(v) and (ix); § 168(e)(6),(7) and (8).

> ### Example 18
>
> Infinitely Better is a high-end restaurant, serving steaks and seafood. This year it plans to open a new location in leased space in an old downtown building in Chicago. To provide the right ambiance for its unique dining experience, it had to create the right décor. It added walls, painted the entire interior, installed custom light fixtures, constructed a bar, made some changes to the plumbing, and built a walk-in freezer in the back. In addition, it added new signage to the exterior. All of the changes are leasehold improvements. However, the signage improvement must be depreciated over 39.5 since it is for the exterior. In contrast, because the improvements to the interior are for qualified restaurant property, Infinitely can take advantage of the limited expensing of § 179, additional first-year depreciation and straight-line depreciation over 15 years.

CHANGES IN DEPRECIATION

There are many situations where the taxpayer incorrectly computes depreciation, resulting in too much or too little depreciation. For example, a corporation may discover it mistakenly classified an asset initially and the wrong recovery period was used. Similarly, the IRS may change the recovery period of an asset. In 2003, the Service ruled that the life of canopies at gas stations that protect the pumps and customers from inclement weather are 5-year rather than 15-year property.[32] When the taxpayer is entitled to additional depreciation, the IRS permits a change in accounting method and the taxpayer may deduct all of the unclaimed depreciation for years that are closed by the statute of limitations as well as open years. This is normally done through a § 481(a) adjustment that reduces income in the year of the change (a single year adjustment).[33] If the adjustment increases the taxpayer's income, the increase is normally spread over four years.

 ## CHECK YOUR KNOWLEDGE

Review Question 1

Indicate whether the following statements concerning tax depreciation are true or false.

a. During the year, Mr. L purchased a computer that he uses to track how his stocks and bonds are doing. L can depreciate the computer even though it is not used in a trade or business.

True. An asset generally may be depreciated to the extent that it is used in a trade or business or an income-producing activity. Since the computer is used to monitor investments, an income-producing activity, it is depreciable. Thus if L uses the computer 30% of the time to monitor his stocks and bonds and 70% for playing solitaire (i.e., personal use), 30% of the cost of the computer could be depreciated.

b. Land and goodwill are never depreciable or amortizable since neither has a determinable life.

False. Assets without a determinable life normally cannot be depreciated or amortized. Under normal circumstances, neither of these assets would be considered as having a determinable life and, therefore, neither could be depreciated. However, § 197 of the Code creates a specific exception to this rule for goodwill, allowing taxpayers to amortize goodwill over 15 years. Land normally is not depreciable.

---

[32] Rev. Rul. 2003-54, 2003-23 I.R.B. 982.

[33] Rev. Proc. 96-31, 1996-1 C.B. 714. But see *Brookshire Brothers Holding, Inc.,* 320 F.3d 507 (CA-5, 2003) where the court held that it was not a change in accounting method and the government was barred from reducing depreciation in closed years. See also *Green Forest Manufacturing Inc.,* T.C. Memo 2003-75.

c. This year Z Corporation purchased a new car to be used in its business. For financial accounting purposes, the company computed depreciation assuming the car had an estimated useful life of three years and an approximate salvage value of $1,000. In computing depreciation for tax purposes, the company will also use a three-year life and a salvage value of $1,000.

False. The computation of tax depreciation ignores the asset's actual useful life and salvage value. For tax purposes, a car is deemed to have a five-year life and salvage value is always ignored. Note that because different depreciation methods are used annual depreciation for financial accounting will normally differ from tax depreciation.

Review Question 2

In November of this year, Park and Ride Inc., a calendar year taxpayer, purchased five new vans to use in its limousine service for $100,000. In February, the company closed on the acquisition of a new maintenance facility. Indicate whether the following are true or false.

a. Assuming the cost of the maintenance facility was $50,000, the corporation must use the mid-quarter convention to depreciate the facility.

False. The mid-quarter convention applies only to personal property and not realty. The mid-month convention must be used in computing depreciation for realty. The mid-quarter convention must be used for the vans.

b. Assuming the cost of the maintenance facility was $500,000, the corporation must use the *half-year* convention in depreciating the vans.

False. The mid-quarter convention applies if more than 40% of the *personal property* placed in service during the year is placed in service during the last three months. For purposes of making this calculation, only personal property—the vans—is considered and the realty (i.e., the maintenance facility) is ignored. Moreover, any personal property that is expensed under § 179 (discussed below) is also ignored. In this case, all of the personal property was placed in service during the last quarter of the year and, therefore, the corporation must use the mid-quarter convention.

Review Question 3

During the year, C Corporation purchased equipment that qualifies as five-year property. Due to other purchases of personal property during the year, the mid-quarter convention must be used in computing depreciation. Compute the first- and second-year depreciation rates that should be used assuming the asset was placed in service in February. Check your answers by using the table in Exhibit 9-7.

The depreciation rates are 35% for the first year and 26% for the second year, which are computed as follows:

Year 1:

Straight-line rate (1/5)	20%
× Declining-balance rate	× 200%
200% declining-balance annual rate	40%
− Mid-quarter percentage	× 87.5%
Depreciation rate per table	35%

Year 2:

Basis of asset remaining (100% − 35%)	65%
× 200% declining-balance annual rate	× 40%
Depreciation rate per table	26%

Review Question 4

On February 15 of this year, K Corporation purchased a warehouse for $250,000 ($50,000 allocable to the land). For financial accounting purposes, the building is treated as having a 40-year life and a salvage value of $20,000.

a. Compute the depreciation deduction for the year.

Depreciation for the year is $4,494 as computed below. Note that the useful life and the salvage value that are used for financial accounting purposes are irrelevant for tax purposes.

Unadjusted basis of the building	$200,000
× Recovery percentage for month placed in service (February).	×2.247%
Depreciation	$ 4,494

b. Assuming the corporation sold the building on March 10 of the following year, compute the depreciation deduction for the year.

Unadjusted basis of the building	$200,000
× Recovery percentage for second year	×2.564%
× Mid-month convention in year of disposition	× 2.5/12
Depreciation	$ 1,068

Review Question 5

Fit-for-Life fitness centers plans to expand. What is the major tax advantage of leasing rather than buying space for its operations?

Under current law, leasehold improvements can be depreciated over 15 years while nonresidential real estate such as a free-standing building must be depreciated over 39 years.

Limited Expensing Election: Code § 179

When Congress introduced ACRS in 1981, it also created § 179. This provision allows taxpayers (other than estates or trusts) to *elect* to treat the cost of qualifying property as a currently deductible expense rather than a capital expenditure subject to depreciation. Initially, the maximum amount that could be expensed under § 179 was $5,000. However, over the years, Congress has tinkered with the amount and also provided for a phase-out once acquisitions exceed a certain level. Currently, both the expensing limitation and the phase-out threshold are adjusted annually for inflation. For 2017, the expensing limitation is $510,000 and, as explained below, this amount begins to phase-out when acquisitions exceed $2,030,000. Note that this measure was intended primarily to stimulate investment; however, its corollary effect was to eliminate the need for maintaining depreciation records where the taxpayer's annual acquisitions were not substantial.

> **LO.4**
>
> Describe the special election under § 179, allowing immediate expensing of certain property.

There are two limitations that may restrict the amount that the taxpayer may otherwise expense:

1. *Acquisitions of Eligible Property Exceeding $2,030,000 in 2017.* When the aggregate cost of *qualifying* property placed in service during the year exceeds $2,030,000 in 2017, the $510,000 amount must be reduced $1 for each $1 of cost in excess of $2,030,000. For example, taxpayers purchasing $2,050,000 of property could expense up to $490,000 [$510,000 – ($2,050,000 – $2,030,000 = $20,000)] of the cost while taxpayers purchasing in excess of $2,540,000 ($2,030,000 + $510,000) could not benefit from § 179 at all. Of course, any portion of the cost that is inelgible for § 179 treatment may still be depreciated.

2. *Taxable Income Limitation.* The § 179 deduction cannot exceed the amount of taxable income derived from all of the taxpayer's trades or businesses (including wage income).[34] Any amount not deductible due to this limitation is carried over indefinitely to following years to be used against future taxable income. Note, however, that the $510,000 (2017) maximum amount that can be expensed in subsequent years is not increased by the carryover amount. Also observe that the taxpayer could avoid this limitation by simply choosing to depreciate the amount with the rest of the asset's cost.

As explained later in this chapter, additional limitations on the use of § 179 apply in the case of luxury automobiles, sports utility vehicles (SUVs), and "listed" property.

In applying § 179, the taxpayer may elect to expense all or a portion of an asset so long as the total amount expensed does not exceed the dollar limitation. If only a portion of an asset is expensed, the remaining portion is subject to depreciation.

Example 19

T Inc. purchased 7-year property for $560,000. If T elects to expense $510,000 (the maximum amount for 2017), its deduction would be $517,145 computed as follows:

Original cost	$ 560,000	
– Expensed portion	– 510,000	$510,000
Remaining depreciable basis	$ 50,000	
× Depreciation percentage	× 14.29%	
Depreciation deduction	$ 7,145	+ 7,145
Total deduction		$517,145

Eligible Property

Only so-called § 179 property that satisfies certain requirements is eligible for expensing. To qualify, the property may be new or used and generally must be:[35]

1. Tangible depreciable property other than buildings or their structural components (except qualified real property);

2. Qualified real property defined as qualified leasehold property, qualified restaurant property, or qualified retail improvement property (see § 179(f) and discussion on qualified leasehold improvements earlier);

3. Property used in a trade or business, as distinguished from property held for the production of income; and

4. Property acquired by purchase from someone who is generally not a "related party" under § 267 (e.g., gifted or inherited property usually does not qualify nor would property acquired from a spouse or parent or the taxpayer's corporation if he or she owns more than 50 percent of the stock).

Certain property is designated as *ineligible* for expensing:

1. Property used predominantly to furnish lodging or in connection with furnishing lodging unless the business is a hotel or motel that provides accommodations used primarily by transients. Presumably, this rule prohibits taxpayers who provide long-term rentals (e.g., apartments, duplexes, etc.) from expensing such items as furniture and appliances.

2. Property that is primarily used by a tax-exempt organization; and

3. Property used outside the U.S. (but there are a number of exceptions).

---

[34] Taxable income is computed with § 1231 gains and interest from working capital but not deductions allowable for § 179, one-half of self-employment tax, net operating loss carrybacks or carryforwards and deductions suspended under other Code sections (e.g., passive losses, partnership, or S corporation losses limited for lack of basis). Note that taxable income presumably reflects depreciation for the § 179 property without considering § 179. [See § 179(b)(3)(C) and Reg. § 1.179-2(c)(1) and -(2)(c)(5)].

[35] §§ 179(d)(1) and (2).

Recapture for § 179 Expensing

Without any special rule, taxpayers could use an asset in business for a short period (e.g., one day), expense it for tax purposes, then convert it to nonbusiness use. To prohibit this possible abuse, a special rule applies. If the property is converted to *nonbusiness* use *at any time,* the taxpayer must *recapture* the benefit derived from expensing.[36] For this purpose, a sale does not trigger recapture. Recapture requires the taxpayer to *include* in income the difference between the amount expensed and the MACRS deductions that would have been allowed for the actual period of business use.

Example 20

On January 1, 2015 F purchased a computer for $5,000. He used it for business for one year, then gave it to his teenage son as a graduation present and bought himself another computer. F may expense the entire $5,000 cost of the computer. However, in 2016 he must recapture and include in income the difference between the expensed amount and the deduction computed under MACRS, $4,000 ($5,000 expensed – MACRS deduction of $1,000 [$5,000 × 20%]). Note that the net effect in this case is to allow F a deduction equal to what he otherwise could have claimed under MACRS, $1,000.

ADDITIONAL FIRST-YEAR (BONUS) DEPRECIATION

When the economy struggles, Congress often turns to a tool that it hopes will provide the necessary stimulation: additional first-year or so-called bonus depreciation. The theory is that the greater write-offs will attract new investment and help put the economy back on its feet. As can be seen in the table below, the amount of the additional first-year depreciation has varied over the years. Under the current law, for property placed in service from January 1, 2012 through December 31, 2017, the bonus depreciation is 50 percent of the adjusted basis of new qualified property.[37] As discussed further below, bonus depreciation is in addition to any amount expensed under § 179 and regular depreciation.[38]

Effective Dates for Bonus Depreciation

Start Date	End Date	Bonus Amount
9/11/2001	5/5/2003	30%
5/6/2003	12/31/2004	50%
1/1/2008	9/8/2010	50%
9/9/2010	12/31/2011	100%
1/1/2012	12/31/2017	50%
1/1/2018	12/31/2018	40%
1/1/2019	12/31/2019	30%

---

[36] § 179(d)(10).

[37] § 168(k)

[38] Bonus depreciation can be used for purposes of the alternative minimum tax but not in computing the earnings and profits of a corporation.

Qualified Property

Section 168(k)(2) provides that qualified property is generally all newly acquired depreciable property other than buildings. Only new property qualifies. Used property does not qualify. In other words, to qualify under the current rules, the property's first or original use must commence with the taxpayer after December 31, 2011 and before January 1, 2020. For this purpose, capital expenditures incurred to recondition or rebuild property meet this requirement. In contrast, the cost of reconditioned or rebuilt property acquired by the taxpayer is considered used property and does not qualify. Technically, qualified property includes the following:

- Property eligible for MACRS depreciation with a recovery period of 20 years or less (business and investment property);

- Qualified improvement property generally defined as any improvement to an interior portion of a building which is nonresidential real property if placed in service after the date such building was first placed in service. This includes qualified restaurant property and qualified retail improvement property. See the discussion of qualified leasehold improvements earlier;

- Certain water utility property (as defined in Code § 168(e)(5));

- Computer software (except software acquired in connection with the acquisition of a business unless such software is available to the general public and is not substantially modified).

In light of these rules, certain property is not eligible. Bonus depreciation cannot be used for residential and nonresidential real estate since the lives of these properties (27.5 and 39 years respectively) exceed 20 years. Intangibles are not subject to MACRS and, thus, do not qualify for the additional allowance. Section 197 intangibles such as goodwill, covenants not to compete, and customer lists acquired in connection with the purchase of a business also would not be eligible. In addition, property that must be depreciated using the alternative depreciation system (ADS) does not qualify. As discussed below, under the special depreciation limitations of § 280F for so-called listed property (e.g., automobiles and computers), ADS is required if qualified business used does not exceed 50 percent. Similarly, ADS must be used for tangible property (e.g., a machine) used predominantly outside of the U.S. However, if the taxpayer merely elects to use ADS for certain property, bonus depreciation can still be claimed. In addition, it should be emphasized that bonus depreciation and limited expensing under § 179 is available for certain qualified leasehold improvements.

Computation of Bonus Depreciation

Taxpayers may claim bonus depreciation for all *qualified* property. In addition, taxpayers may claim both bonus depreciation and § 179 expensing. When both amounts are claimed for the same property, the bonus depreciation is equal to 50% (2017) of the adjusted basis of the property *after the reduction for the amount expensed under § 179*. The effect is to reduce the amount of bonus depreciation that may be claimed since the basis is smaller. Regular depreciation is computed after the basis of the property is reduced by both the § 179 amount and the 50% additional allowance.

Example 21

On March 1, 2017, X Inc. purchased a number of items, including two heavy-duty machines. Each machine cost $175,000. After using part of its § 179 amount on other property, it elected to expense $125,000 of the cost of one machine under § 179 and take advantage of the additional 50% bonus depreciation for both machines. The machinery is 5-year property. Regular depreciation, § 179 expense and bonus depreciation for the first year would be computed as shown below.

	Machine #1		Machine #2	
Adjusted basis	$175,000		$175,000	
Section 179 expensed portion . .	(125,000)	$125,000	—	
Remaining depreciable basis . . .	$ 50,000		$175,000	
Additional allowance	× 50%		× 50%	
Bonus depreciation	$ 25,000	25,000	$ 87,500	$ 87,500
Remaining depreciable basis . . .	$ 25,000		$ 87,500	
Regular depreciation	× 20%		× 20%	
Regular depreciation	$ 5,000	5,000	$ 17,500	17,500
Total deduction		$155,000		$105,000

A comparison of the *bonus depreciation* for both machines reveals different amounts deducted even though the costs of the machines were the same. This occurs because of the special ordering rule. The rule requires that the property's basis for computing bonus depreciation must first be reduced by any amount expensed under § 179.

The full amount of bonus depreciation may be claimed regardless of whether the mid-quarter convention applies. Note also that a taxpayer may elect *not* to claim the additional 50% allowance. This may be done simply by computing depreciation in the normal fashion.

Bonus Depreciation and § 179 Compared

Bonus depreciation and § 179 expensing allowance are subject to special limitations that are similar but not identical. Bonus depreciation:

- Is not limited to the taxable income from the business;

- Does not phase-out based on the amount of property placed in service during the year;

- Is allowed for investment property and § 179 applies only to business property;

- Can be claimed on purchases from related parties while § 179 cannot;

- Can be used by estates and trusts which are not allowed to elect § 179;

- Cannot be used for used property while § 179 can.

LIMITATIONS FOR AUTOMOBILES

Over the years, Congress has become more and more concerned about taxpayers who effectively use the benefits of the tax law to reduce the cost of what are essentially personal expenses. A good illustration concerns automobiles. For example, a taxpayer may justify the purchase of a luxury rather than standard automobile on the grounds that the government is helping to defray the additional cost through tax deductions and credits allowed for the purchase. In 1984 Congress enacted Code § 280F to reduce the benefits of depreciation and limited expensing for certain automobiles and other properties that are often used partially for personal purposes. In addition, the record keeping requirements for travel and entertainment were tightened and extended to certain property used for personal purposes.

Section 280F addresses the concern for vehicles with three different sets of rules for three different categories of vehicles. The three categories are (1) passenger automobiles, light-duty trucks and vans; (2) "heavy" vehicles (e.g., those weighing more than 6,000 pounds); and (3) qualified nonpersonal vehicles.

LO.5

Identify the restrictions on depreciation of listed property, including automobiles, trucks, computers, and other items.

Passenger Automobiles, Vans, and Light-Duty Trucks. A passenger automobile is defined as any four-wheeled vehicle manufactured primarily for use on public streets, roads, and highways that weighs 6,000 pounds or less unloaded.[39] This definition not only covers most cars but also includes light duty trucks and vans. However, it does not extend to many vehicles used in farming or ranching such as tractors and combines since they are not designed primarily for use on public roads. Also excluded from the passenger automobile classification are vehicles used for hire such as taxis, rental cars and trucks, as well as ambulances and hearses used for business purposes.

For passenger automobiles, trucks and vans, § 280F imposes a cap on the amount of annual depreciation and first-year expensing deductions. The *maximum* depreciation and/or § 179 expense is shown in Exhibit 9-11 for automobiles and Exhibit 9-12 for trucks and vans. At the time of this writing, the IRS had not released the inflation adjusted amounts for 2017.

EXHIBIT 9-11	Section 280F Depreciation Limits for Autos		
	Limits for Autos Based on Year Placed in Service		
	2012–2016	2011	2010
First year of service	$3,160*	$3,060*	$2,960
Second year of service	5,100	4,900	4,900
Third year of service	3,050	2,950	2,950
Thereafter	1,875	1,775	1,775

* Increase by $8,000 to $11,160 ($11,060 in 2011) if the taxpayer claims bonus depreciation as extended through 2019

The depreciation and § 179 limits for a particular auto are determined by the year the auto is placed in service by the taxpayer. The annual limits for autos placed in service in 2016 are found in the 2016 column in Exhibit 9-11.[40] For example, in 2016 the deduction for depreciation and § 179 expensing cannot exceed $3,160 for the year placed in service and $5,100 for the second year of service. If the taxpayer used bonus depreciation in 2009–2016, the first year deduction amounts for passenger vehicles as well trucks and vans are increased by $8,000. However, the later year amounts remain the same.

The 2016 limitations under § 280F restrict the annual depreciation amounts for autos costing $15,800 or more (assuming 200% declining-balance depreciation was claimed). The $15,800 amount reflects the $3,160 first-year depreciation limitation ($15,800 × 20% = $3,160 regular depreciation for five-year property).

When the car is used less than 100% of the time for business—including the portion of time the car is used for production of income purposes—the maximum amounts given above must be reduced proportionately.

Example 22

T purchased a car for $20,000 in 2016. She used it 60% of the time for business purposes and 20% of the time traveling to her rental properties. Depreciation and limited expensing may not exceed $2,528 (80% × $3,160) for the first year, $4,080 (80% × $5,100) for the second year, and so on. If bonus depreciation is claimed in 2016, depreciation and limited expensing would be limited to $8,928 (80% × [$3,160 + $8,000 = $11,160]) for the first year and remains the same $4,080 (80% × $5,100) for the second year.

[39] § 280F(d)(5), Reg. § 1.280F-6(c) and Ann. 85-15, 1985-4 IRB. 43.

[40] Rev. Proc. 2016-23, 2016-16 IRB (4/1/2016); at the time of this writing, the official limitations for 2017 had not been released by the IRS. However, based on the inflation factors that were available, the depreciation caps for vehicles for 2017 should be the same as they were for 2016.

If the property's basis has not been fully deducted by the close of the normal recovery period (i.e., typically the extended recovery period of six years), a deduction for the *unrecovered basis* is allowed in subsequent years. Deductions for the property's unrecovered basis are limited to $1,875 (2016) annually until the entire basis is recovered.

Example 23

On December 1, 2016, R purchased a new automobile for $18,000. He uses it 100% for business. R's regular depreciation for the first year is initially $3,600 but is limited to $3,160 as shown below:

Original cost	$18,000
Depreciation percentage	× 20%
Depreciation before limitation	$3,600
Limitation	$3,160

The calculation of regular depreciation for the first year and subsequent years is summarized below.

   In examining the schedule below, note that the recovery period is extended from six to eight years due to the limitations. Also, understand that the unadjusted depreciable basis used for computing depreciation is $18,000 for each year even though only $3,160 (2016) of the depreciation was deducted in the first year.

	1 2016	2 2017	3 2018	4 2019	5 2020	6 2021	7 2022	8 2023
Unadjusted basis.........	$18,000	$18,000	$18,000	$18,000	$18,000	$18,000	$18,000	$18,000
Depreciation percentage...	20.00%	32.00%	19.20%	11.52%	11.52%	5.76%		
MACRS depreciation	$ 3,600	$ 5,760	$ 3,456	$ 2,074	$ 2,074	$ 1,037	$ 1,875	$ 1,875
Limit	3,160	5,100	3,050	1,875	1,875	1,875	1,875	1,875
Deduction	3,160	5,100	3,050	1,875	1,875	1,037	1,875	128
Cumulative depreciation...	3,160	8,260	11,310	13,185	15,060	16,097	17,872	18,000
Adjusted basis..........	14,840	9,740	6,690	4,815	2,940	1,903	128	0

Trucks, Vans, and SUVs. Responding to criticisms that the limitations for passenger automobiles did not fairly reflect the higher price that must be paid for trucks and vans, the IRS created a separate set of limitations for these vehicles as shown in Exhibit 9-12.

   For this purpose, a vehicle qualifies as a truck or van if it is built on a truck chassis. Since most sport utility vehicles (SUVs) are built on a truck chassis these higher limits would apply, assuming these vehicles do not have a gross vehicle weight exceeding 6,000 pounds. If the weight exceeds 6,000 pounds, special rules apply as discussed below.

EXHIBIT 9-12	Section 280F Depreciation Limits for Trucks and Vans			
Year	2016	2015	2014	2013
1	$3,560*	$3,460*	$3,360*	$3,360*
2	5,700	5,600	5,400	5,300*
3	3,350	3,350	3,250	3,150
Thereafter	2,075	1,975	1,975	1,875

*Increase by $8,000 ($11,560 in 2016) if the taxpayer claims bonus depreciation.

Leasing. Without any special rule, the taxpayer could lease a car and circumvent the limitations on depreciation since the restrictions would appear to apply only to the deduction for depreciation and not lease payments. For instance, in *Example 21* above, the taxpayer might lease the car for $400 per month and claim a deduction of $4,800 for the year—far in excess of the amount allowed for depreciation after the first year. To prohibit this possibility, lessees may deduct the amount of the lease payment (applicable to business or income-producing use)—but must *include* certain amounts in income to bring their deductions for use of the car in line for owners. In practice, these inclusion amounts are not actually added to income but simply reduce the deduction for the lease payment.

The amount that the taxpayer must include in income is generally based on the automobile's fair market value and is determined in the following manner.[41]

1. Using the value of the automobile for the taxable year in which the auto is first used under the lease, identify the annual inclusion amount from the table found in Exhibit 9-13. Note that for the last year of the lease, the dollar amount for the preceding year is used unless the lease term begins and ends in the same year.

2. Prorate the dollar amount for the number of days of the lease term included in the taxable year.

3. Multiply the prorated dollar amount by the business and investment use for the taxable year.

EXHIBIT 9-13	Dollar Amounts for Passenger Automobiles (that are not trucks or vans) with a Lease Term Beginning in Calendar Year 2016*

Fair Market Value of Passenger Automobile		Tax Year during Lease				
Over	Not Over	1	2	3	4	5 & Later
$ 19,000	$19,500	6	13	20	23	27
19,500	20,000	7	15	23	27	30
20,000	20,500	8	17	26	30	35
20,500	21,000	9	19	29	33	39
21,000	21,500	10	21	31	38	42
21,500	22,000	11	23	34	41	47
22,000	23,000	12	26	39	46	53
23,000	24,000	14	30	44	54	60
24,000	25,000	16	34	50	60	69
25,000	26,000	17	38	56	67	78
26,000	27,000	19	42	62	74	85
27,000	28,000	21	46	68	81	93
28,000	29,000	23	50	73	89	101
29,000	30,000	25	53	80	95	110
30,000	31,000	26	58	85	102	118
31,000	32,000	28	62	91	109	126
32,000	33,000	30	65	98	116	134
33,000	34,000	32	69	103	123	142
.						
.						
.						
240,000	And over	411	902	1,340	1,607	1,854

Source: Rev. Proc. 2016-23, 2016-16 IRB (4/1/2016). This table extends to values of $240,000 and up. A separate table exists for trucks and vans.

*At the time of this writing, the IRS had not released the inflation adjusted amounts for 2017.

---

[41] § 280F(c) and Reg. § 1.280F-7(a). Note that these limitations do not apply to cars leased for 30 or fewer days or to lessors who regularly engage in the auto-leasing business.

Taxpayers who lease trucks and vans do not use the tables above for passenger automobiles but must use separate tables designed specifically for these two categories.

Example 24

On April 1, 2016, M, a calendar year taxpayer, signed a three-year lease on a new passenger automobile with a value of $27,800. For 2016 and 2017, M used the car exclusively in his business. During 2018 and 2019, his business use dropped to 40 percent. The amounts that M must include in income for 2016 through 2019 are computed as follows:

Tax Year	Dollars Amount	Proration	Business Use	Inclusion Amount
2016	$ 21	275/365	100%	$16
2017	46	365/365	100%	46
2018	68	365/365	40%	27
2019	68	90/365	40%	17

Observe that dollar amounts are based on the value of the car in the first year of the lease. Subsequent declines in the car's value are ignored. Also note that in computing the inclusion amount for 2019, the $68 amount for the preceding year (2018) is used instead of $81 per the table because the lease did not begin and end in the same year.

Heavy Vehicles and Certain SUVs. The second category of vehicles receiving special treatment is so-called "heavy vehicles." As noted above, a truck or van—including an SUV or minivan—is *not* treated as a passenger automobile subject to annual depreciation limits if it has *a gross vehicle weight* (GVW) of more than 6,000 pounds. Without special limitations, taxpayers could use § 179 to expense in 2017 up to $510,000 of the cost of a heavy vehicle. As a result, the vehicle's GVW is critical since it determines whether greater deductions may be allowed. For this purpose, "GVW" is the weight of the vehicle plus its maximum load.[42] The GVW loaded weight is the sum of (1) the weight of the vehicle, (2) government-determined weights for passengers who can ride in the vehicle, and (3) a government determined weight based on the cubic feet of the cargo area. The GVW is typically printed on a label on the inside of the driver's door. Note that the GVW should be distinguished from the curb weight which is the unloaded amount.

This unique exception for heavy vehicles was created for taxpayers who need to use large vehicles in their businesses such as farmers, construction workers, and others—but not white-collar professionals. As note above, with limited expensing up to $510,000 in 2017, taxpayers would be able to deduct the entire cost of a qualified SUV. For example, the taxpayer could expense the entire cost of a Jeep Grand Cherokee, Porsche Cayenne or a BMW X5 that weigh about 7,000 pounds and could cost more than $100,000, assuming they were used entirely for business. Believing that many of these SUVs were in reality luxury automobiles, Congress decided to close what had become the so-called SUV loophole.

As revised, the expensing rules of § 179 now limit the first-year write-off for vehicles considered SUVs. The maximum amount that can be expensed in the first year is limited to $25,000.[43] Taxpayers may still claim regular depreciation and bonus depreciation (until 2020) for the balance. Note that the $25,000 amount is not reduced for personal use (as are the other limitations as seen in *Example 20*).

The $25,000 allowance is available only for an SUV. For this purpose, an SUV is defined as any four-wheeled vehicle that is primarily designed or that can be used to carry passengers over public streets, roads, or highways and that has a loaded GVW of more than 6,000 pounds and not more than 14,000.[44] Heavier vehicles, weighing 14,000 pounds or more (e.g., refrigerated trucks), are not subject to the $25,000 limitation. Similarly, to ensure that the $25,000 limitation does not apply to heavy pickup trucks, vans, and small buses [and thereby allowing the taxpayer to expense up to $510,000 (2017) of their cost], the following vehicles are not considered SUVs.[45]

---

[42] PLR 9520034.

[43] § 179(b)(5)(A).

[44] § 179(b)(5)(B). Note that the vehicle cannot be subject to the limitations of § 280F. In this regard, § 280F(d)(5) provides that it does not apply to vehicles rated at GVW of more than 6,000 pounds. However, the provision notes that in the case of a truck or van (including an SUV), the GVW is the loaded weight rather than the unloaded GVW. From a planning perspective, an individual who is planning to use a vehicle for business purposes should consider purchasing a "heavy" SUV, which will qualify for greater deductions.

[45] § 179(b)(5)(B)(ii).

- A vehicle designed to have a seating capacity of more than nine persons behind the driver's seat.

- A vehicle equipped with a cargo area of at least six feet in interior length which is an open area or is designed for use as an open area but is enclosed by a cap and is not readily accessible directly from the passenger compartment.

- A vehicle having an integral enclosure, fully enclosing the driver compartment and load carrying device, and does not have seating rearward of the driver's seat.

- A vehicle having no body section protruding more than 30 inches ahead of the leading edge of the windshield.

Note that the exceptions would permit deductions for large pick-up trucks weighing more than 6,000 pounds under the cargo area exception or because it has no seats behind the driver. Similarly, cargo vans should qualify under the exception.

Example 25

In 2017, T purchased a Mercedes-Benz GLE 350 for $65,000. The SUV has a GVW (i.e., loaded weight) exceeding 6,000 pounds and is used 100% for business. In such case, the § 179 deduction is limited to $25,000, bonus depreciation is $20,000 (50% × [$65,000 − $25,000 = $40,000]) and regular depreciation would be $4,000 (20% × [$65,000 − $25,000 − $20,000 = $20,000]) for a total deduction of $49,000 ($25,000 + $20,000 + $4,000). If T were in the 39.6% tax bracket, the deduction would save him $19,404. Moreover, if T is subject to self-employment tax, the deduction would reduce that liability as well (e.g., 15.3% rate). Note that the § 179 deduction is limited to $25,000 and there is no limit on depreciation since the SUV is not a passenger automobile because it weighs more than 6,000 pounds.

Example 26

Same facts as in *Example 25* except the SUV is used 80% of the time for business. There is no reduction for the $25,000 allowance as is required for the luxury automobile limitations. Thus the § 179 amount is still $25,000. However, depreciation must be adjusted for personal use. The depreciable basis would be 80% of the $65,000 cost or $52,000. The taxpayer could expense $25,000 and claim bonus depreciation of $13,500 (50% × [$52,000 − $25,000 = $27,000]) and regular depreciation of $2,700 (20% × [$52,000 − $25,000 − $13,500 = $13,500]) for a total depreciation deduction of $41,200 ($25,000 + $13,500 + $2,700).

Below is a list of some SUVs with loaded GVWs more than 6,000 pounds:

Audi Q7	Dodge Durango	Infiniti QX80	Mercedes-Benz GLE 350
BMW X5, X6	Ford Expedition	Jeep Grand Cherokee	Nissan Armada NV
Cadillac Escalade	Ford Explorer	Land Rover Range Rover	Porsche Cayenne
Chevrolet Suburban	Hummer H2	Lexus LX 570	Toyota Land Cruiser
Chevrolet Tahoe	GMC Acadia	Lincoln MKT	Toyota Sequoia
Chevrolet Traverse	GMC Yukon	Lincoln Navigator	Volkswagen Touareg

Qualified Nonpersonal Use Vehicle (*De Minimis* Personal Use). The third category of vehicles subject to special rules is that for qualified nonpersonal use vehicles. These vehicles are not subject to the limitations of § 280F. A qualified nonpersonal use vehicle is any vehicle which, by reason of its nature (i.e., design or modification), is not likely to be used more than a *de minimis* amount for personal purposes.[46] Typical modifications are installation of permanent shelving or painting the vehicle to display advertising or a company's name. This category includes a wide variety of vehicles including:

- Police and fire vehicles
- Delivery trucks with seating only for the driver
- Flatbed trucks
- School buses
- Ambulances and hearses used as such
- Cranes and forklifts
- Qualified moving vans (generally those used by professional moving companies)
- Vehicles weighing over 14,000 pounds

The normal rules for depreciation, bonus depreciation, and limited expensing under § 179 apply to qualified nonpersonal vehicles.

LIMITATIONS FOR PERSONAL USE

Section 280F also restricts the amount of depreciation that may be claimed for so-called listed property that is not used predominantly—more than 50 percent—for business. If the property is not used more than 50% *for business* in the year it is placed in service, the following restrictions are imposed:[47]

1. Limited expensing under § 179 is not allowed.
2. MACRS may *not* be used in computing depreciation. Property not qualifying must be depreciated using the straight-line method of ADS and the asset's class life (except in the case of certain property such as automobiles and computers, where the life to be used is specifically prescribed as five years).

Note that these restrictions are imposed if the property is not used primarily for business in the *first* year. Subsequent usage in excess of 50% does not permit the taxpayer to amend the earlier return or later use accelerated depreciation or limited expensing. On the other hand, if qualified usage initially exceeds 50% but subsequently drops to 50% or below, benefits previously secured must be relinquished. The recapture of these benefits is discussed below. Exhibit 9-14 identifies the depreciation methods available for listed property.

---

[46] Reg. § 1.274-5(k)(2).   [47] § 280F(b).

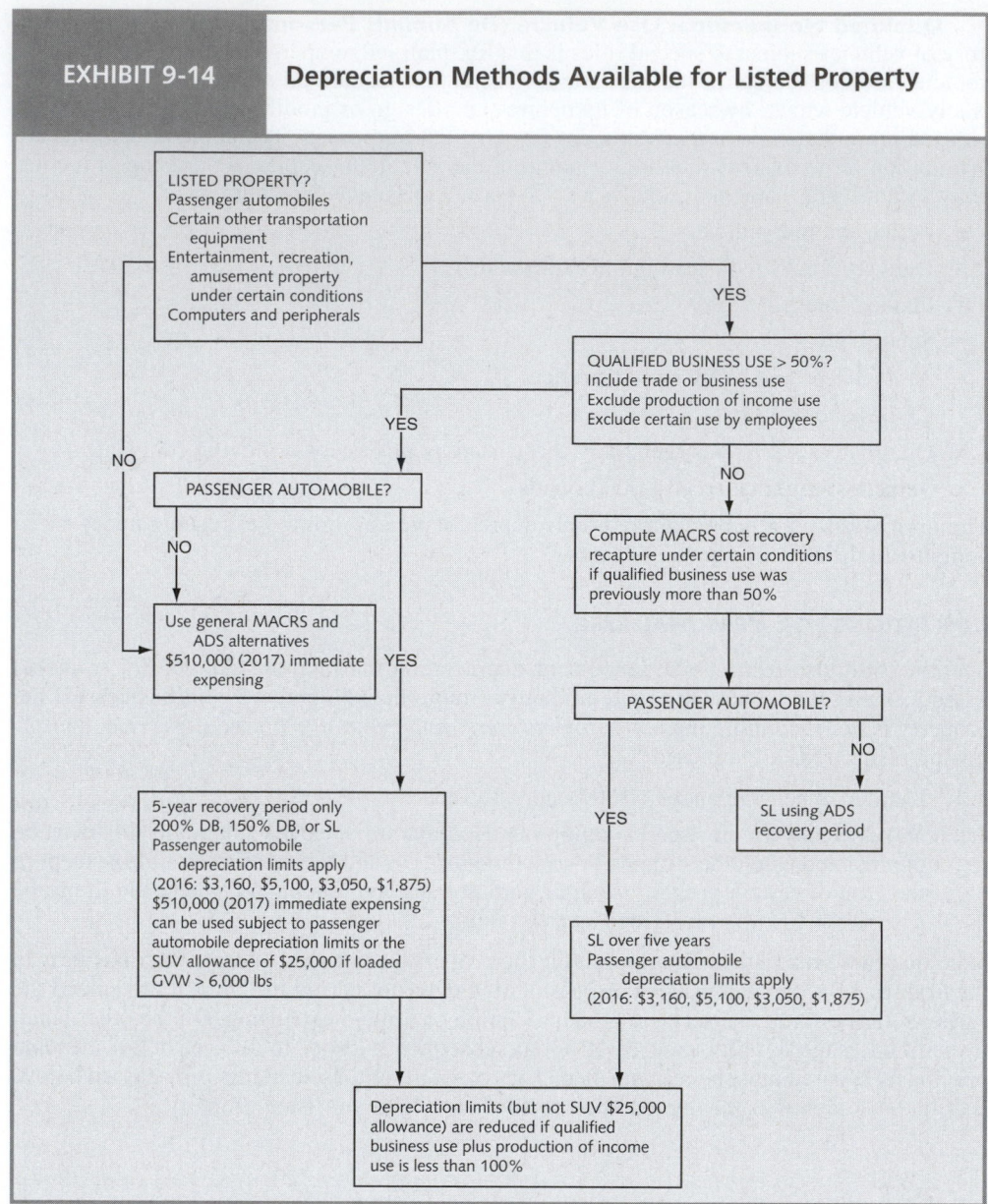

EXHIBIT 9-14   **Depreciation Methods Available for Listed Property**

These restrictions apply only to *listed property*. Listed property includes the following:[48]

1. Passenger automobiles (as defined above).

2. Any other property used as a means for transportation (e.g., motorcycles and trucks).

3. Any property generally used for purposes of entertainment, recreation, or amusement (e.g., yacht, photography equipment, video recorders, and stereo equipment) *unless* used exclusively at a regular business establishment (e.g., at the office or at a home office) or in connection with the taxpayer's principal trade or business.

4. Any computer or peripheral equipment *unless* used exclusively at a regular business establishment.

---

[48] § 280F(d)(4).

> ### Example 27
>
> K, self-employed, purchased a car for $20,000 in 2016. She uses her car 40% of the time for business and the remaining time for personal purposes. Since the property is a car, the limitations on depreciation are first reduced in light of the personal usage. In the first year, depreciation would initially be limited to $1,264 ($3,160 (2016) maximum allowed in 2016 × 40% business use). In addition, since the car is listed property and is not used more than 50% for business, K must use ADS to compute depreciation. Therefore, depreciation in the first year is $800 ($20,000 cost × 40% business use = $8,000 × 10% ADS rate).

Qualified Business Use. In determining whether the property is used more than 50% for business, only *qualified business use* is considered.[49] Generally, qualified business use means any use in a trade or business of the taxpayer.[50] Thus, for this test *only,* use in an activity that does not constitute a trade or business is ignored (e.g., use of a computer to monitor the taxpayer's investments does not count toward the 50% threshold since the activity is not a business).[51] Additionally, an employee's use of his or her own property in connection with employment is not considered business use unless it is for the *convenience of the employer* and is *required as a condition of employment.*[52] In this regard, it is important to note that if the employee's use is not qualified, the employee is treated as having no business use and, therefore, no deduction would be allowed.

While the Code does not provide definitions for the convenience and condition tests, the Regulations do provide some guidance. According to the Regulations, these two requirements generally have the same meaning for § 280F as they have for § 119 relating to the exclusion for meals or lodging.[53] Given this interpretation, a mere statement by the employer expressly requiring the employee to use the property is insufficient. Conversely, the employer need not explicitly require the employee to use the property. Rather, the property is considered required only if it enables the employee to properly perform the duties of his or her employment.

> ### Example 28
>
> T is employed by X, a newspaper company, to deliver papers in a rural area where the homes are widely scattered. The company does not provide T with a car and does not require T to own a car for employment. Since the car enables T to properly perform his duties and is for the convenience of X, T's use should qualify for purposes of the 50% test even though he is not explicitly required to own a car.

> ### Example 29
>
> J is a budget analyst in the accounting department of a large construction firm. She owns a personal computer that is identical to the one she uses at work. Instead of staying late at the office, J occasionally brings home work for which she uses her computer. J's use of her computer for her work is not qualified business use. See Reg. § 1.280F-6 Ex. 5.

The IRS takes a very narrow view regarding what satisfies the convenience-of-the employer and condition-of-employment tests. In a letter ruling, the Service held that a professor's use of her home computer for writing related to her research—which was required for continued employment—did not satisfy the tests.[54] Although the Service agreed that the use

---

[49] § 280F(b)(1) and (2).

[50] § 280F(d)(6).

[51] Reg. § 1.280F-6(a)(1) and (d)(2).

[52] § 280F(d)(3).

[53] Reg. § 1.280F-6(a)(2).

[54] Letter Ruling 8615024. But see *Thomas C. Cadwallader* and *Judy C. Douglas v. Comm.,* 90-2 USTC ¶50,597, 67 AFTR 2d 91-301, 919 F2d 1273, (CA-7, 1990) aff'g 57 TCM 1030, TC Memo 1989-356 (1989).

of the computer was related to her work, it found no evidence that employees who did not use home computers were professionally disadvantaged. The Service also felt that her employer did not explicitly require use of the home computer before she was hired. Apparently, the Service will require taxpayers to demonstrate that the work could not properly be performed without the computer or at least that they will be professionally disadvantaged if they do not use the computer. In addition, under the IRS view, taxpayers will be obliged to show that use of the computer was mandatory and not optional.

The reach of this and other rulings goes farther than it first appears. As brought out by the Service, a literal interpretation of the statute indicates that if an employee does not satisfy the convenience-of-the-employer and condition-of-employment tests, *none* of the employee's use is treated as business use. This view does *not* mean that the employee is merely relegated to using ADS for depreciation. Rather, with no business use, the employee is prohibited from claiming any deductions relating to the listed property.

Example 30

R is employed as a high school teacher. As part of his job, he periodically prepares report cards for his students, including a short narrative regarding their work. The school does not provide him a computer to use for these tasks. Consequently, he uses his own personal computer 40% of the time to do this work. Assume R's use would be considered qualified business use (i.e., used for the convenience of the employer and necessary for him to perform his duties properly). Although the use is otherwise qualified, it does not exceed the 50% threshold. As a result, because he is an employee and did not use the computer (listed property) more than 50% for business, he is treated as having not used it for business at all and no depreciation or § 179 expensing is allowed.

In those cases where qualified business use exceeds 50 percent, any usage for the production of income or other business purposes is included in determining the percentage of the asset that may be depreciated using MACRS. Similarly, if business use is 50% or less, the usage for production of income or other nonqualified business purposes is still included in determining the percentage of the asset that may be depreciated using ADS. Note that depreciation is still allowed where the 50% test is not met, assuming there is business or investment usage.

Example 31

V, a financial consultant, operates her business as an independent contractor. She purchased a car for $20,000. She uses the car 25% of the time for business and 55% for production of income activities (e.g., managing her rental properties) that do not qualify as a business. V must use ADS since business usage is only 25 percent. Although the time spent for the production of income cannot be counted toward the 50% test, it may be considered in the depreciation computation. Thus, V's depreciation would be $1,600 ($20,000 × [55% + 25%] × 10%). It should be noted that where the listed property is an automobile, the limitations on depreciation also apply. Here the depreciation limitation in 2016 is $2,528 ([55% + 25%] × $3,160); note that the production of income usage is considered in making the proper reduction; thus it does not restrict the amount of the depreciation deduction. Had the usage percentages been reversed (i.e., 55% for business), the depreciation and limited expensing deduction would still have been limited to $2,528.

Employer-Provided Cars. The qualified business use rules directly address the problems of the company-owned car and other company-owned property used by employees. In the case of automobiles, employers often provide company-owned cars to their employees principally for use in the employer's business. Normally, however, the employee also uses the car for personal purposes if only to commute to work. In these situations, the employer is normally entitled to depreciate the entire automobile while the employee must include the value of the personal use as compensation. For these and other situations such as the use of company airplanes and chauffer services, the regulations provide several alternative treatments.[55]

Recapture Provisions. Absent a special rule, individuals could easily expense assets that are purchased primarily for personal use. For example, an individual might purchase a computer, camera, or SUV (all listed property), use it more than 50% in the first year, expense it under § 179, and then convert it to personal use in the next year. To prohibit this abuse, if the use of listed property drops to 50% or lower after the first year, the benefits of MACRS and limited expensing must be recaptured.[56] The taxpayer must recompute the depreciation in the prior years using ADS and include in income the excess of the depreciation actually claimed over the ADS amounts. Depreciation in future years is computed using the straight-line method.

Example 32

In 20X1 G purchased a car for $10,000 and used it entirely for business. Depreciation for 20X1 was $2,000 ($10,000 × 20%). In 20X2 G's business usage dropped to 40 percent. Since G's business usage is no longer greater than 50 percent, he must recapture the benefits of accelerated depreciation. Depreciation using the straight-line method in 20X1 would have been $1,000 ($10,000 × 10%). Thus, G must include $1,000 ($2,000 original depreciation—$1,000 straight-line depreciation) in income in 20X2. Depreciation for 20X2 and all subsequent years must be computed using the straight-line method.

Recordkeeping Requirements. Not only has Congress severely restricted tax benefits for listed property, it also has imposed strict record keeping requirements for such property. The substantiation rules contained in Code § 274(d), which were formerly reserved solely for travel and entertainment expenses, now extend to expenses related to "listed property." For listed property, the taxpayer is required to substantiate the following:[57]

1. The amount of each expenditure related to the property, including the cost of acquisition, maintenance, and repairs.

2. The date of the use of the property.

3. The amount of each business or investment use as well as total use (the number of miles—in the case of a car or other means of transportation—or the amount of time that the property was used for other listed property [e.g., a computer]).

4. The purpose of the use of the property.

In those cases where the overall use of the property for a taxable year can be definitely determined without entries, nonbusiness use need not be recorded. For example, in the case of a car, total miles can be determined by comparing the odometer readings at the beginning and the end of the taxable year. Consequently, the taxpayer needs to make entries only for business and investment use.

---

[55] For inclusion and valuation rules of employer provided property see Reg § 1.61-21(b) through (e).

[56] § 280F(b)(2).

[57] Temp. Reg. § 1.274-5T(b)(6).

✔ CHECK YOUR KNOWLEDGE

Review Question 1

This year Y purchased new property. Indicate whether the following questions are true or false.

a. Assuming the property is a duplex that Y rents to others, she may not expense any of the cost.

True. Only eligible property may be expensed. As a general rule, only personal property such as machinery and equipment are eligible. Buildings are normally not eligible.

b. Assuming the property is machinery costing $550,000, Y may expense $530,000 in 2017, and the $20,000 balance may be carried over to the following years to be expensed to the extent the maximum amount is not used in such years.

False. Y may expense $510,000 in 2017, and the balance is subject to depreciation as well as bonus depreciation in 2017.

c. Assuming the property is a $20,000 passenger automobile that is used 70% for business, Y may deduct $14,000.

False. Depreciation and expensing for automobiles are limited. The maximum amount of depreciation or expense claimed in the year the automobile is placed in service is limited in 2016 to $2,212 ($3,160 × 70%).

d. Assuming the property is a $40,000 car that is used 30% for business, Y may deduct $948 ($3,160 in 2016 × 30%).

True. If the property is listed property and qualified business use does not exceed 50 percent, the taxpayer is not allowed to expense any of the car and must use straight-line depreciation. Therefore, Y's potential deduction is $1,200 ($40,000 × 30% × 10%) but is limited to $938. If Y were an employee, no depreciation or § 179 expensing is allowed since qualified business use does not exceed 50 percent.

e. If the property is listed property, such as a passenger automobile or a computer, and the property is not used more than 50% of the time for business, the restrictions of § 280F do not affect the total amount of cost deducted but simply alter the time when it is deducted.

True. The total depreciation is not changed. If the property is restricted and qualified business use does not exceed 50 percent, the taxpayer is simply forced to use the straight-line method in lieu of the accelerated methods of MACRS and the expensing allowance of § 179 that are normally available. However, if Y is an employee, Y is deemed to have no business use and no deduction would be allowed.

OTHER CONSIDERATIONS

Anti-Churning Rules

In some cases, a taxpayer's depreciation deductions under MACRS would be higher than those that the taxpayer may currently have. For this reason, Congress believed that some taxpayers would engage in transactions that might enable them to secure the advantages of MACRS.

Example 33

In 1980 H acquired an apartment building as an investment that she chose to depreciate using the straight-line method over 35 years. H made this decision because the use of accelerated depreciation caused a portion of any gain from the subsequent sale of such property to be treated as ordinary income rather than favorable capital-gain. With the elimination of favorable capital-gain treatment in 1986, there no longer was any disincentive to use the accelerated method. Therefore, H created a plan to benefit from the change. She sold the property to her son, who immediately leased it back to her. The rental payments to be paid by H were structured in light of the higher depreciation deductions (27.5-year life instead of 35 years) that her son would be able to take as the new owner of the property.

Sales, exchanges, and other dispositions of assets such as that illustrated above are referred to as "churning" transactions—exchanges of used property solely to obtain the benefits of MACRS.

The thrust of the anti-churning rules is to preclude the use of MACRS for property placed in service prior to the enactment of either version of MACRS, unless the property is transferred in a transaction where not only the owner changes but also the user.[58] In the example above, the anti-churning rules prohibit H's son from using MACRS since ownership did not truly change.

There are three sets of rules designed to police churning. For practical purposes these provisions should be given close review whenever the taxpayer is involved in a leasing or nontaxable transaction. For example, a taxpayer would typically be subject to the antichurning rules in the following situations:

1. Sale followed by immediate leaseback.
2. Like-kind exchange.
3. Formation and liquidation of a corporation or partnership, including transfers of property to and distributions from these entities.

Property Leased to Tax-Exempt Entities

For a variety of reasons, tax-exempt entities, such as schools, hospitals, or government organizations, lease property from taxable entities rather than purchase it. One incentive for this type of transaction is that the taxable entity can benefit from depreciation deductions, whereas the tax-exempt entity cannot. Thus, a tax plan might be devised under which a taxable lessor and a tax-exempt lessee "share" the tax benefits of the depreciation deductions. This would be accomplished through discounted lease payments. The taxable lessor would be willing to accept discounted lease payments "in exchange" for receiving all of the tax benefits from depreciation deductions. To reduce the incentive for this type of tax plan, depreciation of "tax-exempt use property"—most property leased to a "tax-exempt entity"—must be depreciated using ADS with special rules to determine the applicable recovery period.[59] This rule applies regardless of the tax planning motives of the lessor and lessee. The result of the rule is to lower the present value of the tax savings from the depreciation deductions. There are several types of leasing transactions that are exempted from the rule. For example, the rule does not apply to "short-term leases."

Amortization

As previously discussed, MACRS does not apply to intangible property. Therefore, intangibles are subject to the rules existing prior to enactment of ACRS and MACRS. Generally, intangibles are amortized using the straight-line method over their estimated useful life. Special amortization and depreciation rules apply to certain expenditures, however.

LO.6
Distinguish amortization from depreciation and identify assets subject to amortization.

GOODWILL AND COVENANTS NOT TO COMPETE

As mentioned in Chapter 6, buyers of a going concern often pay an amount in excess of the fair market value of the concern's tangible assets. This excess purchase price normally is attributable to intangible assets such as goodwill and/or a covenant not to compete. The tax treatment for such intangible assets was changed dramatically by the Revenue Reconciliation Act of 1993 for acquisitions occurring after August 10, 1993. Acquisitions taking place on or before August 10, 1993 continue to be treated under prior law, which held that goodwill could not be amortized because it was considered as having an unlimited life. Thus, recovery of a taxpayer's basis in goodwill could occur only when the business was subsequently sold or abandoned. In contrast, a covenant not to compete usually has an ascertainable life because the seller typically agrees to refrain from conducting similar business or some other activity for a certain number of years. As a result, prior law held that any cost attributable to the covenant may be amortized over the appropriate period using the straight-line method.

---

[58] § 168(e)(4).   [59] § 168(g)(1)(C).

Under prior law, taxpayers attempted to allocate the purchase price to assets other than goodwill since goodwill could not be amortized. In this regard, accountants were quite creative, assigning the purchase price to a variety of intangibles such as covenants not to compete, favorable contracts, customer lists, accounting control systems, and a long list of other items. As long as the taxpayer was able to establish that the intangible was separate and distinct from goodwill and had a determinable useful life, the taxpayer was entitled to amortize the cost. For example, a taxpayer might allocate a substantial portion of the purchase price of a business to a covenant not to compete and amortize the cost over three years, producing a significant benefit where otherwise there would be no benefit at all if the cost were allocated to goodwill.

Post-August 10, 1993 Acquisitions

As might be expected, the IRS did not sit idly by and allow taxpayers to do as they pleased. In case after case, the IRS challenged the taxpayer's allocation, and there was a great deal of controversy and litigation. To put an end to the disputes and clear up the uncertainty, Congress enacted § 197. Effective for acquisitions after August 10, 1993 all "§ 197 intangibles" must be amortized over 15 years. (A taxpayer may elect to have the rules of § 197 apply to intangibles acquired after July 15, 1991.) Much like MACRS, § 197 forces the taxpayer to use the 15-year period even if the useful life is actually more or less than 15 years. Section 197 intangibles include a number of items such as goodwill, going-concern value, covenants not to compete, information bases such as customer or subscription lists, know-how, customer-based intangibles, governmental licenses and permits (e.g., liquor licenses, taxicab medallions, landing or takeoff rights, regulated airline routes, television or radio licenses), franchises, trademarks, and trade names.

To further prohibit the deduction of an intangible obtained as part of an acquisition, special rules govern disposition. No loss is allowed on the disposition of an intangible if the business retains other intangible assets acquired in the same or a series of related transactions. Instead, any remaining basis is reallocated among the bases of other § 197 intangibles. Although losses are not recognized, the same treatment does not apply to gains.

If § 197 intangibles are sold at a gain, the gain is recognized. The tax character of the entire gain is ordinary income if the intangible is held one year or less. Gains from sales of intangibles held more than one year are treated as gains from sales of § 1245 property. As explained in Chapter 17, gains from dispositions of § 1245 property are "recaptured" and treated as ordinary income up to the amount of amortization on the intangible deducted through the time of sale. Any excess gain is a § 1231 gain.

Example 34

Buyer allocates $150,000 to intangible assets in a purchase. Under § 197 Buyer would claim $10,000 per year for 15 years as an amortization deduction. The deduction would not be affected by breaking the $150,000 into separate portions for goodwill, a covenant not to compete, or any other specifically identified intangibles.

Assume that the purchase occurred on January 1, 2017. Buyer will claim a $10,000 deduction every year for 15 years through 2031. Assume that Buyer allocates $105,000 to goodwill and the remaining $45,000 to a covenant not to compete that would expire on January 1, 2020. From 2017 through 2019, Buyer claims an annual amortization deduction of $3,000 ($45,000/15) on the covenant and $7,000 ($105,000/15) on the goodwill. Note that the covenant not to compete is amortized over 15 years regardless of its economic life. On January 1, 2020, Buyer will have an unrecovered basis of $36,000 on the covenant, which has expired ($45,000 − $9,000 amortization [$3,000 amortization per year for three years]). However, Buyer must add the $36,000 unrecovered basis to the basis of goodwill and continue to deduct $10,000 per year as amortization of the goodwill.

A number of anti-churning rules exist to prohibit taxpayers from creating and amortizing goodwill and going-concern value. Other intangibles are not covered by these rules.

FIVE-YEAR ELECTIVE AMORTIZATION

To accomplish certain economic and social objectives, Congress has enacted various optional five-year (60-month) amortization procedures from time to time over the last 40 years. During certain periods, a five-year amortization election (in lieu of regular depreciation) has been available for expenditures made in connection with childcare facilities (§ 188), pollution control facilities (still an option under § 169), railroad rolling stock (§ 184), and rehabilitation of low-income housing [§ 167(k)]. In 2006, Congress passed legislation allowing five-year amortization of costs of creating or acquiring musical works or copyrights (§ 167(g)).

Depletion

A taxpayer who invests in natural resources that are exhausted over time is entitled to recover his or her capital investment. Depletion is the method of recovering this cost and is similar to depreciation.[60] Depletion usually is claimed for investments in oil, gas, coal, copper, and other minerals. Land is not subject to depletion.

LO.7
Determine the current depletion deduction for various assets.

To qualify for depletion, the taxpayer must have an economic interest in the mineral deposits.[61] Typically, both the owner of the land who leases the property and the operator to whom the land is leased have the requisite interest since they both receive income from the severance or extraction of the minerals.

COMPUTING THE DEPLETION DEDUCTION

Taxpayers generally are permitted to compute their depletion deduction using either the cost or percentage (statutory) depletion method. The taxpayer computes both cost and percentage depletion and is required to claim the higher amount.[62]

Cost Depletion

Using cost depletion, the taxpayer recovers the actual investment (adjusted basis in the natural resource) as the mineral is produced. The following formula is used:[63]

$$\text{Annual cost depletion} = \frac{\text{Unrecovered adjusted basis}}{\text{Estimated recoverable units}} \times \text{Number of units sold during the year}$$

This formula generally matches the cost of the investment against the revenues produced.

Example 35

A coal producer, T, paid $150,000 to acquire the mineral rights in a property that contains coal. He estimates that 90,000 tons of coal are recoverable from the property. During the year, 58,000 tons of coal were produced and 30,000 were sold. T's cost depletion would be $50,000 computed as follows:

$$\frac{\$150,000 \text{ basis}}{90,000 \text{ units}} \times 30,000 \text{ units sold} = \$50,000 \text{ depletion}$$

Similar to depreciation, total cost depletion can never exceed the taxpayer's adjusted basis in the property.

---

[60] § 611.

[61] Reg. § 1.611-1(b).

[62] § 613(a); Reg. § 1.611-1(a).

[63] Reg. § 1.611-2(a).

Percentage Depletion

For large oil and gas producers, cost depletion is the only depletion method allowed. However, both cost depletion and percentage depletion are available to small "independent" oil and gas producers as well as royalty owners.[64] Both cost depletion and percentage depletion are also allowed for *all* producers of certain types of minerals (e.g., gold, silver, gravel).

Under the percentage depletion method, the taxpayer's depletion deduction is computed *without reference* to the taxpayer's cost of the investment. Rather, percentage depletion is based on the amount of income derived from the property.[65] For this reason, the taxpayer may deduct percentage depletion in excess of the adjusted basis of the investment. Thus, the taxpayer is entitled to a deduction for percentage depletion as long as the property continues to generate income.

To compute percentage depletion, a percentage specified in the Code (see Exhibit 9-15) is applied to the *gross* income from the property. The resulting product is the amount of percentage depletion unless limited. For oil and gas properties, percentage depletion is generally limited to the taxpayer's *taxable* income before depletion. Percentage depletion is limited to 50% of the taxpayer's taxable income from mineral properties. Gross income is the value of the natural resource when severed from the property before any processing. Taxable income from the property is the difference between income and operating expenses including overhead.

EXHIBIT 9-15	Summary of Various Percentage Depletion Rates

Natural Resource	Percentage Rate
1. Gravel, sand, and other items	5
2. Shale and clay used for sewer pipes; or brick and clay, shale, and slate used for lightweight aggregates	7.5
3. Asbestos, coal, sodium chloride, etc.	10
4. Gold, silver, oil and gas, oil shale, copper, and iron ore from deposits in the United States	15
5. Sulfur and uranium and a series of minerals from deposits in the United States	22
6. Metals, other than those subject to 22% or 15% rate	14

---

[64] § 613A(c).   [65] § 613.

Example 36

Assume the same facts in *Example 35* and that the 30,000 tons of coal sold were sold for $10 per ton (gross income of $300,000). Further, operating expenses for the coal operation were $260,000. Percentage depletion is computed as follows:

Gross income	$300,000
× Statutory percentage for coal	× 10%
Percentage depletion before limitation	$ 30,000

Taxable income limitation:	
Gross income	$300,000
− Operating expenses	−260,000
Taxable income before depletion...........................	$ 40,000
× Limitation percentage	× 50%
Percentage depletion limit	$ 20,000
Percentage depletion allowable	$ 20,000

In this situation, T would use cost depletion of $50,000 as computed in *Example 33* because it exceeds allowable percentage depletion.

Example 37

Assume the same facts in *Example 36* except that barrels of oil are being produced, rather than tons of coal. Cost depletion computations are the same as in *Example 33*. Percentage depletion is computed as follows:

Gross income	$300,000
× Statutory percentage for oil.............................	× 15%
Percentage depletion before limitation	$ 45,000
Gross income	$300,000
− Operating expenses	−260,000
Taxable income before depletion...........................	$ 40,000
Percentage depletion limit................................	$ 40,000
Percentage depletion allowable............................	$ 40,000

T would use cost depletion of $50,000 (computed in *Example 33*) rather than percentage depletion of $40,000 because cost depletion is larger.

Whether percentage or cost depletion is used, the taxpayer must reduce the property's basis (but not below zero) by the amount of depletion claimed. Note that once the basis of the property is reduced to zero, only percentage depletion may be claimed (when the taxpayer is permitted to take percentage depletion), and *no* adjustment is made to create a negative basis.

Research and Experimental Expenditures

LO.8

Explain the options available in selecting the appropriate tax treatment of research and experimentation expenditures.

At first glance, it may appear that the proper tax treatment for research and development expenses requires their capitalization as part of a project's cost. This approach seems appropriate since these costs normally yield benefits only in future periods. Under this theory, the capitalized costs could be recovered over the period during which the project provides benefits or when the project is disposed of or abandoned. Upon closer examination, however, it becomes apparent that this approach is fraught with problems. Since it is difficult to establish any direct relationship between costs of research and development and the actual period benefited, it may be impossible to determine the appropriate period for recovery. For example, establishing a useful life for a scientific discovery that has numerous applications and which continually contributes to later research would be guesswork at best. A similar problem exists for unsuccessful efforts. Although a particular effort may not prove fruitful, it may at least indicate what does not work and thus lead to other, perhaps successful, research. As such, it is not clear whether the costs should be written off or capitalized as part of the subsequent project.

Due to the administrative difficulties inherent in these determinations, the IRS historically granted research and experimental costs favorable treatment by generally allowing the taxpayer to deduct the expenses as incurred or to capitalize the expenses and amortize them over whatever period the taxpayer desires. Although this approach encountered difficulties in the courts, Congress eliminated the problems with enactment of special provisions in 1954.

RESEARCH AND EXPERIMENTAL EXPENDITURES DEFINED

The Code provides separate rules for research and experimental costs.[66] It should be emphasized that the provisions apply to research and *experimental* costs, not to research and *development* costs. The term *experimental* was used instead of *development* to limit the special treatment to laboratory costs.[67] Qualified costs generally include those incident to the development or improvement of a product, a formula, an invention, a plant process, an experimental or pilot model, or similar property. Research and experimental costs do *not* include expenditures for ordinary testing or inspection of materials or products for quality control, efficiency surveys, management studies, consumer surveys, advertising, or promotion. Costs of obtaining a patent, such as legal fees, qualify. However, the costs of acquiring an existing patent, model, or process are not considered research and experimental costs. Expenditures for depreciable property do not qualify but the depreciation allowable on the property is eligible for special treatment.

ALTERNATIVE TAX TREATMENTS

Three alternative methods may be used to account for research and experimental expenditures. The expenses may be deducted as they are paid or incurred, deferred and amortized, or capitalized. Immediate deduction usually is the preferred method since the present value of the tax benefit is greater using this method. Deferral may be preferable in two instances, however. If the taxpayer's income is low in the current year, the tax benefit of the deduction might be increased by deferring the deduction to high-income years when the taxpayer is in a higher marginal tax bracket. Deferral also may be better if an immediate deduction creates or adds to a net operating loss since such losses may be carried over and used only for a limited period of time. The general rule for selecting the best alternative is to choose the one that maximizes the present value of the tax savings from the research and experimental expenditures.

---

[66] § 174.   [67] Reg. § 1.174-2(a).

Expense Election

The taxpayer can elect to deduct all research and experimental expenditures currently.[68] Note, however, that expenditures for depreciable property cannot be expensed currently.[69] If the taxpayer adopts this method in the first tax year in which research and experimental expenses are incurred, the method must be used for all such expenditures in all subsequent years, unless permission is secured to change methods of part or all of the expenditures.[70] The IRS does not need to approve the method the taxpayer adopts initially. Consent is required, however, if the taxpayer wishes to change methods.

Deferral Option

Research and experimental expenditures may be deferred and amortized at the election of the taxpayer.[71] The expenses must be amortized ratably over a period not less than 60 months beginning in the period in which benefits from the expenditures are first realized. It should be emphasized that costs of depreciable property are not deferred expenses; rather, the depreciation expense must be capitalized and amortized over 60 months. Also, if the taxpayer elects to defer the expenditures and a patent is subsequently obtained, the cost must be amortized over the life of the patent, 20 years (17 before June 8, 1995). If the deferral method is initially elected, the taxpayer must use this method for all future expenses in subsequent tax years unless permission to change methods is obtained.[72]

Election to Capitalize

A taxpayer who does not elect either to amortize research and experimental expenditures over 60 months or to deduct them currently must capitalize them. Capitalizing the expenditure increases the basis of the property to which the expense relates. No deduction is permitted for the capital expenditure until the research project is considered worthless or abandoned. A disposition of the research project such as a sale or an exchange enables the taxpayer to offset the capitalized expenditures—the basis of the project—against any amount realized.

Example 38

L Corporation, a drug manufacturer, is an accrual basis, calendar year taxpayer. During 2017 the corporation performed research to improve various cold and flu medications. On December 1, 2017 a new cold and flu product line was successfully introduced on the market. In connection with this project, L incurred the following costs:

Lab equipment (5-year property)	$ 50,000
Salaries	90,000
Laboratory materials	5,000

If L Corporation elects to expense the research and experimental costs, it may deduct $105,000 in 2017 as follows:

MACRS depreciation on lab equipment (20% of $50,000)	$ 10,000
Salaries	90,000
Laboratory materials	+ 5,000
Total deductions	$105,000

---

[68] § 174(a).

[69] § 174(c).

[70] § 174(a)(2).

[71] § 174(b).

[72] § 174(b)(2).

Note that only the depreciation on the lab equipment may be deducted as a research and experimental cost, not the entire cost of the equipment. If L Corporation elects to defer the expense, its monthly amortization beginning December 1, 2017 would be

$$\frac{\$105{,}000}{60} = \$1{,}750$$

Alternatively, L could capitalize all the expenses as an asset (including the $10,000 of depreciation) and receive no deduction until a later disposition or abandonment.

OTHER RELATED PROVISIONS

Several other provisions exist relating to the treatment of research and experimental expenditures, such as a tax credit for research and experimentation. Congress made the provision of the tax credit for research and experimentation permanent when it passed the Protecting Americans From Tax Hikes (PATH) Act of 2015. Generally, the credit is 20% of the current year's expenditures after adjustments (see Chapter 13).[73] Taxpayers electing the credit are generally required to reduce their research and experimentation expenses by 50% of the credit for purposes of computing the amount to either be expensed, deferred, or capitalized.[74] Special rules also exist for contributions of research property by corporations (see Chapter 11).[75]

Expenses of Farmers and Ranchers

LO.9

Explain the tax treatment of certain expenditures incurred in farming and ranching activities.

Special provisions exist for certain types of expenditures incurred by those engaged in farming and ranching. The rules examined below generally differ from the treatment of expenses that normally would be considered capital expenditures subject to depreciation.

EXPENSES RELATED TO LIVESTOCK

Costs of acquiring animals used for breeding, dairy, work, or sport are treated as capital expenditures and are depreciable under MACRS unless such animals are primarily held for sale and would be appropriately included in inventory. If a farmer raises his or her own livestock, however, expenses incurred such as feed normally can be deducted as paid, assuming the taxpayer uses the cash basis method of accounting.[76] This rule is in sharp contrast to that applying to other self-production costs. Costs incurred by farmers and others in constructing their own equipment and buildings must be capitalized and depreciated.

SOIL AND WATER CONSERVATION, FERTILIZER, LAND CLEARING

Farmers often incur expenses for soil and water conservation. Examples of these expenses are the costs of leveling or terracing the soil to control the flow of water, irrigation and drainage ditches, ponds, dams, eradication of brush, and planting windbreaks. Although normal tax rules would require these expenses to be capitalized, Code § 175 permits a deduction when such expenses are paid or incurred as long as such expenses are consistent with a conservation plan approved by the Soil Conservation Service of the Department of Agriculture. To encourage these practices and still restrict the availability of this benefit, the Code requires that the taxpayer be engaged in the business of farming. In addition, the annual deduction for these expenses is limited to 25% of the taxpayer's gross income from farming. This limitation prohibits a taxpayer from using the deductions to reduce nonfarm income. Expenditures exceeding this limitation may be carried over to subsequent years.

---

[73] § 41.

[74] § 280C(c).

[75] § 170.

[76] Reg. § 1.162-12.

Like soil and water conservation expenditures, Code § 180 provides that the cost of fertilizer, lime, and other materials used to enrich farmland can be deducted in the year paid or incurred by those engaged in the business for farming. There is no limitation imposed on the amount of the deduction.

Taxpayers engaged in the farming business must capitalize expenses of clearing land in preparation for farming. These expenses include any cost of making the land suitable for farming such as those for removing and eradicating brush or tree stumps and the treating or moving of earth. Routine brush clearing and other ordinary maintenance related to the land may be expensed, however.

DEVELOPMENT EXPENSES

Expenses incurred in the development of farms and ranches prior to the time when production begins may be capitalized or expensed at the election of the taxpayer.[77] Examples of these expenses are costs of cultivation, spraying, pruning, irrigation, and management fees.

The expensing of development and other farm-related costs prior to the period in which the farm begins to produce income provides an attractive device for high-bracket taxpayers—who have no interest in farming—to shelter their income from other nonfarm sources. These and other tax advantages offered by farming in the 1960s brought such an influx of "urban cowboys" to the farming industry that several farm groups protested and demanded protection. Congress first responded to these groups in 1969. Currently, this provision prohibits the immediate expensing of any amount attributable to the planting, cultivation, maintenance, or development of any citrus or almond grove. Any of these development costs that are incurred in the first four years of the grove's life must be capitalized.

Congress adopted additional safeguards in 1976. Section 447 generally requires that corporations (and partnerships having a corporate partner) engaged in the business of farming must use the accrual method of accounting. Since this provision was intended to protect small farmers and family-owned farms, the following are not treated as corporations: (1) S corporations; (2) family-owned corporations (at least 50% of the stock is owned by family members); and (3) any corporation that did not have gross receipts exceeding $1 million in any prior year. In addition, farming syndicates may deduct the costs of feed, seed, fertilizer, and similar farm supplies only as they are actually used.[78] A farming syndicate generally is defined to include partnerships and S corporations where the sale of their interests is specifically regulated by state or local securities laws, or more than 35% of their losses during any period are allocated to limited partners or persons who do not actively participate in the management of the business.

In 1986 the prohibition against the deduction of prepaid farming expenses was extended to all farmers that prepay more than 50% of their expenses such as feed, seed, and fertilizer.[79] Farmers cannot deduct such expenses until the items are consumed or used. Several exceptions exist, however.

Tax Planning Considerations

DEPRECIATION AND AFTER-TAX CASH FLOW

Many taxpayers, when analyzing an investment, fail to consider the tax aspects. For example, a taxpayer who looks solely to the cash flow projections of investing in a rental property might overlook the effect of depreciation. The depreciation deduction does not require an outlay of cash, but does produce a tax benefit.

---

[77] *Ibid.*

[78] § 464.

[79] § 464(f).

Example 39

In January of the current year, L purchased a duplex for $80,000, which she rented to others. Of the $80,000 purchase price, $70,000 was allocable to the building and $10,000 was allocable to the land. L financed the purchase with a $5,000 down-payment and a mortgage calling for monthly payments of interest and principal of $400. During the year, L rented the property for $7,000. Expenses for the year were as follows:

Mortgage interest	$ 4,000
Taxes	1,200
Insurance	500
Maintenance and utilities	300
Depreciation (MACRS: $70,000 × 3.485%)	2,440
Total expenses	$ 8,440

The net taxable loss from the real property would be

Rental income	$ 7,000
Less: Rental expenses	− 8,440
Net taxable loss	$ 1,440

Note that the taxable loss contains depreciation expense of $2,440, a noncash expenditure. Assuming L is in the 28% tax bracket, the net cash flow from the project would be computed as follows:

Cash inflow:			
Rental income			$ 7,000
Tax saving from loss ($1,440 × 28%)			403
Total cash inflow			$ 7,403
Cash outflow:			
Total expenses		$ 8,440	
Less: Depreciation		− 2,440	
		$ 6,000	
Debt service:			
Mortgage payments ($400 × 12)	$ 4,800		
Less: Interest (included in expenses above)	− 4,000	+ 800	
Total cash outflow			(6,800)
After-tax cash flow			$ 603

Therefore, L has a positive cash flow of $603 on the project notwithstanding the taxable loss that she suffered of $1,440.

Under certain circumstances, limitations are imposed on the deduction of losses from rental property. These limitations are discussed in Chapter 12.

ACCELERATING DEPRECIATION WITH COST SEGREGATION

Prior to 1981, some taxpayers used a technique called "component depreciation" to accelerate real estate depreciation deductions. These taxpayers separated the costs of their depreciable buildings into various components with useful lives shorter than the rest of the building. For example, structural components such as wiring, plumbing, and roofing were depreciated over periods of 10 or 15 years rather than the much longer periods typically associated with the useful life of the building shell.

While the introduction of ACRS and MACRS prohibited component depreciation, it did not eliminate a similar but different technique referred to as "cost segregation." In 1997, the Tax Court, in a the seminal case on cost segregation, *Hospital Corporation of America (HCA),* permitted HCA for purposes of depreciation to segregate the costs of components constituting real property (§ 1250 property) and tangible personal property (§ 1250 property).[80] As a result, HCA was able to depreciate a long list of improvements as 5-year property rather than 39-year property, producing huge tax savings. Shortly after the *HCA* decision, the IRS grudgingly acquiesced and announced that cost segregation did not constitute component depreciation.[81] As a result, this subtle distinction permitted what has become the widespread use of cost segregation.

The importance of cost segregation cannot be overemphasized. Consider the benefits of reclassifying $100,000 of property from a 39- to a 5-year recovery period. Depreciation as 39-year property using the required straight-line method produces an annual deduction of about $2,600 per year for 39 years. In contrast, depreciation as five-year property using double declining balance results in the entire cost being deducted over six years ($20,000, $32,000, $19,200, $11,500, $11,500, and $5,760). Reclassifying $100,000 from 39- to 5-year property produces about $16,000 in net-present-value savings, assuming a 5% discount rate and a 35% marginal tax rate. It is no wonder that a whole niche business involving cost segregation has developed.

Examples of assets that taxpayers should segregate from the cost of the building and depreciate over five or seven years include movable partitions, computers, separate fire protection systems, manufacturing equipment, and built-in desks and cabinets. Properties reclassified from 39- to 5-year property in *HCA* included carpeting, vinyl wall and floor coverings, electrical distribution system, and a number of other items. A rule of thumb for identifying these separate depreciable assets is to assess whether the items would be removed if the business were to relocate. If so, the removable assets can have their own depreciation schedules.

Land improvements represent another set of costs that should be separated since they can be depreciated over 15 years. These include parking lots, landscaping, sewers, and irrigation systems.

To segregate costs successfully, taxpayers or their advisers should work closely with building contractors to document the costs of fast-depreciating assets. Early involvement with the contractor or architect could even lead to building designs that maximize the number of separate depreciable assets while not reducing the productive use of the building.

---

[80] 109 TC 21 (1997).

[81] AOD 1999-008 9/08/1999 and Announcement 99-116, 1999-52 I.R.B. 763. See also Reg. § 1.446-1T and CCA 199921045.

GOODWILL AMORTIZATION RULE BENEFITS BUYERS AND SELLERS

Prior to August 10, 1993 the goodwill portion of the cost of acquiring a business provided no tax benefit to the buyer until the buyer later sold the business because the basis assigned to goodwill could not be amortized. Now that goodwill can be amortized over 15 years, its value is greater because the present value of a series of tax deductions received throughout a 15-year period is higher than the present value of a single deduction received many years in the future (assuming constant or declining marginal tax rates over time). Buyers and sellers will share this increase in value as they negotiate purchase/sale prices of their businesses.

Typically, buyers and sellers have some flexibility regarding the allocation of purchase price between goodwill (a capital asset that produces capital gain for the seller) and other intangibles. Two factors encourage increased allocations to goodwill. First, the seller will recognize capital gain income instead of ordinary income (assuming the allocation choice is between goodwill and a covenant not to compete). Second, for buyers concerned about earnings per share, goodwill may be preferable to payments for a covenant not to compete due to the treatment of goodwill under generally accepted accounting principles (GAAP). Under GAAP, goodwill normally is not amortized unless it is found to be impaired. Thus, as long as there is no reduction in the value of goodwill, no amortization is required. In contrast, the covenant may be amortized over its economic life. Buyers not concerned about GAAP should be indifferent between allocations to goodwill versus a covenant not to compete because *all* intangibles are amortizable over 15 years for tax purposes. Thus, at best, increased allocations to goodwill could benefit both buyers and sellers of businesses. At worst, increased goodwill allocations will neither help nor harm buyers or sellers.

Problem Materials

DISCUSSION QUESTIONS

9-1 *Requirements for Depreciation.* Provide the basic requirements that must be satisfied before property may be depreciated.

9-2 *Return of Capital Doctrine.* What is the basic premise from which the concept of capital recovery originates?

9-3 *Conversion to Business Property.* When personal use property is converted to business use property, the basis of the converted property for tax purposes is recorded as the lesser of the fair market value of the property at the time of conversion or the adjusted basis at the time of conversion. Does this requirement make sense? Why or why not?

9-4 *Depreciation and Amortization: Eligible Property.* Indicate whether a taxpayer could claim deductions for depreciation or amortization of the following property:
  a.   Land used in the taxpayer's farming business.
  b.   A duplex—the taxpayer lives in one-half while he rents the other half out.
  c.   The portion of the taxpayer's residence that she uses as a home office.
  d.   The taxpayer's former residence, which he listed for rental temporarily until he is able to sell it. The residence was listed in late November and was not rented as of the end of the taxable year.
  e.   A mobile home that the taxpayer initially purchased and used while he was in college and this year began renting to several students.
  f.   The costs attributable to goodwill and a covenant not to compete.
  g.   An automobile used for business. The taxpayer accounts for his deductible car expenses using the standard mileage rate.

9-5 *Definitions: Cost Allocation Methods and Types of Property.* Explain the terms depreciation, amortization, and depletion. Include in your discussion an explanation of tangible and intangible property as well as personal and real property.

9-6 *Depreciation Systems.* Briefly describe the depreciation systems (e.g., MACRS) for computing tax depreciation that one may encounter in practice. In addition, identify a benefit derived from the uniformity imposed by MACRS property recovery periods.

9-7 *Ineligible Property.* What types of property are not depreciated using MACRS? How can the taxpayer avoid MACRS?

9-8 *Depreciation Methods and MACRS Statutory Percentages.*
    a. Indicate the first-year depreciation percentage applicable to office furniture and show how it is determined.
    b. Same as (a) except the property is an apartment building.

9-9 *MACRS and Straight-Line Depreciation.* Assuming a taxpayer desires to use the straight-line method of depreciation, what alternatives, if any, are available?

9-10 *Alternative Depreciation System.* Typically, all depreciation is computed using MACRS. However, Code § 168 also establishes an alternative depreciation system (ADS). As a practical matter, when will use of ADS be most likely?

9-11 *Depreciating Recovery Property.* During the year, X purchased land and a building for a total of $500,000 and furniture for the building for $100,000. He intends to lease the building. Indicate whether the following factors are taken into account in computing the depreciation of these assets.
    a. Each asset's useful life as estimated by the taxpayer in light of industry standards.
    b. Salvage value.
    c. The month in which the property was placed in service.
    d. The use of the building by the lessee.
    e. The taxpayer is a corporation.
    f. The property is used for investment rather than business use.
    g. The acquisition cost of the building including the land.
    h. The lessee.

9-12 *Half-Year Convention.* Indicate whether the following statements are true or false regarding the half-year convention.
    a. Depreciation can be claimed for the *entire* year if the asset has been in service for more than six months.
    b. The half-year convention applies to *all* property placed in service during the year.
    c. The half-year convention applies *both* in the year of acquisition and the year of disposition of the asset.
    d. The convention must be considered when expensing an asset under Code § 179.

9-13 *Acquiring a Business.* L has worked as a salesperson in the outdoor advertising business for ten years. This year he decided to go into business for himself. To this end he purchased all of the assets of Billboards Unlimited Corporation for $2 million. The value of the tangible assets such as the office building, furniture, and equipment was $1.4 million. Explain how L will recover the cost of his investment.

9-14 *Luxury Cars.* Indicate whether the following statements are true or false. If false, explain why.
    a. W purchased a new car used solely for business for $12,000. The limitations imposed by Code § 280F on deductions related to automobiles do not alter what W could claim in the year of acquisition.
    b. P Corporation is a distributor of hospital supplies. During the year, it purchased a $20,000 car for its best salesperson. Section 280F does not alter the total amount of depreciation deducted while P owns the car. Section 280F alters only the timing of the depreciation deductions.

9-15 *Leasing and Luxury Automobiles.* D is a manufacturer's representative for several different companies. His sales territory covers all of Indiana, Kentucky, and Ohio. Recently, he decided it was time to get rid of his old car, which had just passed the 100,000-mile mark. Many of his friends have told him that he should lease his next car rather than buy it. Assuming D plans on using the car exclusively for business, briefly discuss the tax factors that should be considered in making the decision.

9-16 *Listed Property.* Indicate whether the following statements are true or false. If false, explain why.

   a. J is a part-time photographer. This year she purchased a camera that cost $1,000. Thirty percent of her usage was for business while the remainder was personal. J may use the accelerated depreciation recovery percentages of MACRS.

   b. P, a proprietor of a lighting store, purchased computer equipment for $10,000 which he uses 50% of the time for business. Under Code § 280F, the maximum deduction for depreciation and limited expensing in the first year is $500, while without § 280F the deduction would be $5,000.

   c. C purchased computer equipment that he uses 60% of the time for managing his investments and 35% of the time in connection with a mail-order business he operates out of his home. C may claim straight-line depreciation deductions based on 95% of the cost of the asset.

   d. G is employed as a research consultant for RND Corporation, a research institute. G uses the company's computer at the office but often takes home work, which she does on her home computer. G's use of her home computer for work done for her employer is considered qualified business use.

   e. T is a college professor who uses a computer, for which he properly claims deductions, to write textbooks in his home office. It is unnecessary for T to maintain records on business usage of the computer.

9-17 *Employer-Provided Automobiles.* WS Corporation, a large clothing manufacturer, provides a company car for each of its salespeople. Identify the issues that must be addressed.

9-18 *Amortization.* How are the costs of patents, copyrights, and goodwill recovered?

9-19 *Leasing Restrictions.* Address the following:

   a. Construct a numerical example illustrating why a tax-exempt entity would rather lease than buy.

   b. R acquired a ten-year ground lease on three acres on which it constructed a small office building. Explain how R will recover its cost of the building.

9-20 *Depreciation—Allowed or Allowable.* R inherited her mother's personal residence in 1991 and converted it to rental property. Her basis for depreciation was $100,000. The residence had an estimated useful life of 30 years. This year, R sold the residence for $170,000. During the time R held the property, she never claimed a deduction for depreciation on the residence. What amount of gain will R report upon the sale?

9-21 *Salvage Value.* How is salvage value used in computing the depreciation deduction using MACRS?

9-22 *Depreciable Basis and Limited Expensing.* Explain how the taxpayer's depreciable basis may be affected by the amount expensed under the limited expensing election of § 179.

9-23 *Anti-Churning Rules.* Explain the purpose of the anti-churning rules and when they normally will apply.

9-24 *Cost Segregation.* Answer the following:

   a. Why would a business want a cost segregation study?

   b. May the taxpayer use component depreciation? Explain.

9-25 *Mid-Quarter Convention.* T Company, a calendar year taxpayer, purchased $300,000 of equipment on December 3 of this year.

   a. Under what circumstances will the mid-quarter convention apply in computing depreciation of the equipment?

   b. Assume that T can purchase the equipment at any time during the year. How will T time the acquisitions if it wants to maximize the firm's depreciation deductions for the year?

9-26 *Determining Recovery Periods: Special Considerations.* During the year, the WJ LLC opened a gas station that also had a convenience food store. The controller is trying to determine how these new items should be depreciated for tax purposes.

   a. After reading *Iowa 80 Group and Subs v. U.S.* 95 AFTR 2d 2005-2367, 371 F. Supp. 2d 1036 (D.Ct. Southern District of Iowa, 2004), explain the alternatives that might be available and how the court ruled. For fun, see http://iowa80truckstop.com/.

   b. What happened in *Iowa 80* on appeal?

   c. What can you conclude about using the standard procedures for determining depreciation outlined in this chapter?

9-27 *Leasehold Acquisition Costs and Leasehold Improvements.* Fourth National Bank of Baton Rouge is opening a new branch. From a tax perspective, why might it lease space for the expansion rather than buy the land and construct a building?

9-28 *Depletion.* Address the following:

   a. Briefly describe how cost and percentage depletion are computed and determine which is used in a particular year.

   b. Assuming the taxpayer has completely recovered her depletable cost basis (e.g., her basis is zero), is she entitled to further depletion deductions?

9-29 *Farming Expenses.* N plans on stepping down from his position as president of a large energy company in five years. At that time, he and his wife would like to move to the country where they would retire and perhaps operate a small dairy farm. N has spotted some land through which a sparkling creek runs. His accountant has suggested that he purchase the land now and begin to operate it despite initial losses. Explain the rationale behind the accountant's advice.

PROBLEMS

9-30 *Depreciation of Converted Personal-Use Property.* F purchased a mobile home to live in while at college. The home cost $50,000. When he graduated, he left the home in the trailer park and rented it. At the time he converted the home to rental property, it had a fair market value of $15,000.

   a. What is F's basis for depreciation?

   b. F now lives 75 miles away from his alma mater. Can he deduct the cost of traveling back to check on his rental property (including those trips on which he also attended a football game)?

9-31 *MACRS Accelerated Depreciation.* In 2017 T, a calendar year taxpayer, decided to move her insurance business into another office building. She purchased a used building for $700,000 (excluding the land) on March 15. T also purchased new office furniture for the building. The furniture was acquired for $200,000 on May 1. Compute MACRS depreciation. Ignore first-year expensing and bonus depreciation. MACRS depreciation tables are located in the Appendix.

   a. Compute T's depreciation deduction for 2017.

   b. Compute T's depreciation deduction for 2018.

   c. Assuming that T sold the office building and the furniture on July 20, 2019, compute T's depreciation for 2019.

   d. Answer (a), (b), and (c) above assuming that the furniture was purchased on October 20.

9-32 *Mid-Quarter Convention.* Q Corporation anticipates purchasing $300,000 of office furniture and fixtures (seven-year property) next year. This will be Q's only personal property acquisition for the year. Q Corporation management is willing to purchase and place the property in service any time during the year to accelerate its depreciation deductions. In addition, management wants to depreciate the property as rapidly as possible. MACRS depreciation tables are located in the Appendix. Ignore limited expensing.

    a. Compute depreciation for the first two years of ownership assuming *all* of the property is purchased and placed in service on February 2.

    b. Compute depreciation for the first two years of ownership assuming *all* of the property is purchased and placed in service on December 6.

    c. Compute depreciation for the first two years of ownership assuming $177,000 (59%) of the property is purchased and placed in service on February 2 and $123,000 (41%) is purchased and placed in service on December 6.

    d. Based on the results of (a) through (c) above, what course of action do you recommend for Q Corporation?

9-33 *MACRS Straight-Line Depreciation.* G Corporation operates a chain of fast-food restaurants. On February 7, 2017 the company purchased a new building for $1,000,000 (excluding the land). In addition, on May 5, 2017 G purchased a used stove for $5,000 and refrigeration equipment for $30,000 (both seven-year property). G does not elect to use the limited-expensing provision. The company does elect to compute depreciation using the straight-line method under MACRS. MACRS depreciation tables are located in Appendix. Ignore limited expensing and bonus depreciation.

    a. Why might G elect to use the straight-line method?

    b. Assuming G elects to use the straight-line method and a seven-year recovery period for depreciating the stove applies, can it use MACRS accelerated recovery percentages for the refrigeration equipment? For the building?

    c. Compute G's depreciation for the stove and building in 2017 assuming it elects the straight-line method for the seven-year property.

    d. Compute the depreciation for the stove and building in 2018.

    e. If G does not dispose of either the stove or building, what is the final (i.e., last year's) depreciation deduction for the stove and the building?

    f. Assuming G disposes of both the stove and the building on October 18, 2018, what is the depreciation for each of these assets in 2018?

9-34 *ADS Depreciation.* P retired several years ago to live on a small farm. To supplement his income, he cuts wood and sells it in the nearby community. This year he purchased a used light duty truck to haul and deliver the wood. He used the truck 20% of the time for business. Assuming the truck cost $9,000, compute P's depreciation for the year.

9-35 *Leasing.* Lexico plans to expand its business this year. It is planning on leasing some vacant space in a strip center on the outskirts of Happyville called Hometown Shops. It is in the process of negotiating a 10-year lease for 5,000 square feet of space. Indicate whether the following questions are true or false and, if false, explain why the statement is false.

    a. In order to secure the lease, Lexico will pay a real estate broker a fee of $5,000 for finding the property and negotiating the lease and another $1,000 to an attorney to draw up the lease. The lease will be for a period of 10 years. Lexico must amortize the acquisition costs over 39 years.

    b. Assume in (a) above that as part of the negotiations, Lexico has the right to renew the lease for an additional 5 years. The renewal period has no effect on the amortization.

    c. Assume that several years from now, Lexico terminates the lease. It's unamortized lease acquisition costs are totally deductible.

    d. Lexico plans to build several interior walls within the space. Hometown Shops is a well-established center built in 2011. Lexico can depreciate the walls over 15 years.

    e. Same as (d) except Hometown Shops was opened this year and Lexico will operate a restaurant where the meals are consumed primarily in the facility.

    f. Lexico decided to open another location in another strip center, called the Downtown Professional Center. This is brand new space. Lexico will operate a child-care center, which will emphasize learning. Lexico can depreciate any improvements over 15 years.

9-36 *Section 179 Election.* Although K is currently a systems analyst for 3L Corporation, her secret desire is to write a best-selling novel. To this end, she purchased a computer for $3,000 this year. She used the computer only for writing her novel. Can she deduct the entire cost of her computer this year even though she has not yet received any income from the novel? Next year?

9-37 *Limitations on § 179 Expensing.* In each of the following situations, indicate whether T may elect to use the limited-expensing provisions of § 179. Assume the acquisition qualifies unless otherwise indicated.

    a. T is a corporate taxpayer.

    b. This year, T purchased a $600,000 building and $50,000 of equipment.

    c. T suffered a net operating loss of $40,000 this year before consideration of the § 179 deduction.

    d. T placed the asset in service on the last day of the taxable year.

9-38 *Limited-Expensing Election: Eligible Property.* For each of the following assets, indicate whether the taxpayer may elect to expense a portion or all of the asset's cost.

    a. A $40,000 car used 75% of the time for business purposes and 25% of the time for personal purposes.

    b. A home computer used by the taxpayer to maintain records and perform financial analyses with respect to her investments.

    c. An apartment building owned by a large property company.

    d. A roll-top desk purchased by the taxpayer's father, who gave it to the taxpayer to use in her business.

9-39 *Limited-Expensing Election Calculations.* N, a single taxpayer, purchased used copying equipment to use in his business. He purchased the equipment on June 3 of 2017 for $610,000. N elects to expense the maximum amount allowable with respect to the equipment.

    a. What portion of the cost of the equipment may N expense for this year?

    b. Is bonus depreciation available for the equipment in 2017?

    c. Compute N's depreciation deduction for the current year, assuming bonus depreciation is not available.

    d. Answer parts (a) and (c) assuming that the cost of the equipment was $2,050,000.

9-40 *Leasing Automobiles.* On May 27, 2016, J signed a three-year lease on a new Cadillac with a list price of $30,000. His lease payments are $500 a month beginning on June 15. Assuming J is self-employed and uses the car exclusively for business, how does the lease affect his taxable income in 2016 and 2017?

9-41 *Section 280F Calculations.* In the current year, H purchased a new automobile for $30,000. The § 179 immediate expensing election is not made, and the taxpayer has elected out of the additional first year bonus depreciation for this asset class for this year. Use the most current limits from Exhibit 9-11 in responding to the questions below.

    a. Assuming the car is used solely for business, prepare a depreciation schedule illustrating the amount of annual depreciation to which H is entitled assuming he holds the car until the entire cost is recovered.

    b. Assume the same facts as (a) except the car is used 80% of the time for business and 20% of the time for personal purposes. Compute the current year's depreciation deduction.

    c. Same as (b) except the car is used 70% of the time for business, 10% of the time for production of income activities, and 20% of the time for personal purposes.

    d. Same as (a) except the car is used 40% of the time for business and 60% of the time for personal purposes.

9-42 *SUV Limitations.* On March 7, 2016, C, an attorney, purchased an SUV for $40,000. The SUV had a gross vehicle weight exceeding 6,000 pounds. She expects to use the vehicle 80% of the time for business. C wishes to maximize her deductions related to the vehicle. Ignore bonus depreciation.

a.   Compute C's depreciation and § 179 expense for 2016.

b.   Same as (a) except the SUV cost $30,000.

c.   Assume C plans to purchase a pickup truck rather than the SUV. She plans to buy a pickup truck that is available in three body styles (regular cab, extended cab, and crew cab) and three bed lengths (5.5-foot, 6.5-foot, and 8-foot). The truck has a gross vehicle weight exceeding 6,000 pounds. What tax advice may be appropriate, assuming C plans to use the truck like the SUV?

d.   Would the answer to (a) change if the vehicle weighed more than 14,000 pounds? If so, how?

9-43 *Section 280F Calculations.* M purchased a new automobile for $30,000. The first year expensing election is not made. The car is used solely for business. M is in the 25% tax bracket. The present value factors for a 10% discount rate are as follows: year 1, 0.91; 2, 0.83; 3, 0.75; 4, 0.68; 5, 0.62; 6, 0.56; 7, 0.51; 8, 0.47; 9, 0.42; 10, 0.39; 11, 0.35; 12, 0.32; 13, 0.29; 14, 0.26; 15, 0.24; 16, 0.22; 17, 0.20.

a.   Prepare a depreciation schedule.

b.   Compute the total tax savings M will receive throughout the recovery period from depreciation deductions.

c.   Using an after-tax discount rate of 10 percent, compute the present value of tax savings from depreciation deductions under § 280F.

d.   Using an after-tax discount rate of 10 percent, compute the present value of tax savings from depreciation deductions under MACRS as if § 280F were repealed.

e.   Compare the results of (b) and (c) above. What impact does discounting have in assessing the tax benefits of depreciation?

f.   Compare the results of (c) and (d) above. What is the discounted after-tax cost of the § 280F limitations for this taxpayer?

9-44 *Research and Experimental Expenditures.* ABC Corporation is developing a new process to develop film. During the year, the company had the following expenditures related to research and development:

Salaries	$60,000
Laboratory equipment (5-year property).	30,000
Materials and supplies	10,000

Compute ABC's deduction for research and experimental expenditures under each of the alternative methods.

9-45 *Depletion.* DEF Company produces iron ore. It purchased a property for $100,000 during the year. Engineers estimate that 50,000 tons of iron ore are recoverable from the property. Given the following information, complete DEF's depletion deduction and undepleted cost basis for each year.

Year	Units Sold (tons)	Gross Income	Taxable Income before Depletion
1	15,000	$300,000	$124,000
2	20,000	400,000	50,000
3	10,000	250,000	90,000

9-46 *Depletion.* Assume the same facts in *Problem 9-41* except that barrels of oil are being produced rather than tons of iron ore. Compute DEF's depletion deduction and undepleted cost basis for each year.

CUMULATIVE PROBLEMS

9-47 David and Lauren Hammack are married with one child, Jim, age 12. The couple lives at 2006 Rolling Drive, Indianapolis, IN 46222. David is a product manager for G&P Corporation, a food company. Lauren operates a clothing store as a sole proprietorship (employer identification number 35-1234567). The couple uses the cash method of accounting except where the accrual method is required. They report on the calendar year.

David earned a salary of $60,000 during the year. G&P also provides health insurance for David and his family. Of the total insurance premium, the company paid $750. Income taxes withheld from David's salary were $7,000. The couple paid $9,000 in estimated taxes in four equal installments during the year. Last year's tax liability was $5,000.

Lauren's father died on June 20. As a result, Lauren received $40,000 as beneficiary of a life insurance policy on her father. In addition, her father's will provided that she receive all of his shares of IBM stock. The stock was distributed to her in October when it was worth $30,000.

On August 1 of this year, the couple purchased a six-month Treasury Bill for $9,700. They redeemed it on February 1 of the following year for its face value, $10,000. In addition, the couple purchased a previously issued AT&T bond with the face value of $1,000 for $890 on June 1. The bond pays interest at 6% per year on January 1 and July 1. On July 1 they received an interest payment of $30, which was also reported on Form 1099-INT, sent to them shortly after year-end. The couple plans on reporting any accrued market discount in taxable income when they sell or redeem the bond, in some future year.

Each year, Lauren travels to Paris to attend the annual fashion shows for buyers. When scheduling her trip for this year, Lauren decided to combine business with pleasure. On Thursday, March 6, Lauren departed for Paris, arriving on Friday morning. Friday afternoon was devoted to business discussions with several suppliers. Since the shows began on Monday, she spent the weekend touring Paris. After attending the shows Monday through Wednesday, she returned to Indianapolis on Thursday, arriving late that night. The cost of her round-trip air fare to Paris was $500. Meals were $30 per day and lodging was $100 per day for Friday through the following Wednesday.

In addition to running her own shop, Lauren teaches an M.B.A. course in retailing at the local university. She received a $5,400 salary for her efforts this year. The university withheld $429 in FICA and Medicare, but did not make additional tax withholdings related to the salary. The school is ten miles from her office. Normally, she goes home from her office to get dinner before she goes to the school to teach (16 miles from her home). According to her log she made 80 trips from home to school. In addition, the log showed that she had driven 20,000 miles related to her clothing business. She uses the standard mileage rate to compute her automobile expenses.

Lauren's records, which she maintains for her business using the cash method of accounting, reveal the following additional information:

Sales	$120,000
Cost of goods sold	(50,000)
Gross profit	$ 70,000
Advertising	6,000
Insurance	1,400
Rent	9,000
Wages	15,000
Employment taxes	2,000

The insurance included (1) a $200 premium paid in September for coverage of her car from October through March of the following year; and (2) a $1,200 payment for fire insurance for June 1 through May 31 of the following year. Similarly, rent expense includes a $4,500 payment made on November 1 for rent from November through April. She has a five-year lease requiring semiannual rental payments of $4,500 on November 1 and May 1.

During the year, David purchased a new automobile for $30,000, which he uses 60% of the time for business (i.e., "qualified business usage" is 60%). His actual operating expenses, excluding depreciation, were $3,000.

In addition to the information provided earlier in this problem, the couple paid the following amounts during the year:

State income taxes	$5,500
County income taxes	500
Real estate taxes	2,400
Mortgage interest on their home	3,600
Charitable contributions	2,000

David and Lauren's Social Security numbers are 445-54-5565 and 333-44-5789, respectively. Their son Jim's Social Security number is 464-57-4681.

Compute David and Lauren's tax liability for the year. Make all computations (including any special elections required) to minimize the Hammacks' tax liability based on current tax law. If a tax return is to be prepared for this problem, complete the following forms: 1040 (including Schedules A, C, and SE), and 2106. There is no alternative minimum tax liability. (**Note:** If the § 280F limitations apply to any auto depreciation, you should use the most current numbers from Exhibit 9-11.)

9-48 Michelle Kay purchased a small building on February 1 of the current year for $650,000. In addition, she paid $15,000 for land. Ms. Kay obtained a $640,000 mortgage for the acquisition. She and five of her employees use the property solely to store and sell a variety of gift items under the business name of "Michelle's Gifts." The following information pertains to the business:

Sales	$950,000
Cost of goods sold	627,000
Wages for employees ($20,000 each)	100,000
Payroll taxes for five employees	?
Depreciation	?
Advertising	25,000
Mortgage interest	60,000
Legal services	20,000
Real estate taxes	4,000
Fire insurance	3,000
Meals and entertainment	2,500

During the year, Ms. Kay purchased the following assets for the business. She wants to depreciate all business assets as rapidly as the law allows.

	Cost	Month/Day of Acquisition
Personal computer	$14,000	March 31
Printer for computer	2,000	April 2
Office furniture and fixtures	20,000	April 29
Machinery (7-year property)	30,000	May 12

Michelle Kay was divorced from Benjamin Kay two years ago. The divorce decree stipulates that Benjamin Kay would receive the dependency exemption for their son, Eric (now 12 years old), even though Eric lives full-time with Ms. Kay in a home she maintains. During the year, Ms. Kay provided 25% of Eric's support and Mr. Kay provided 75 percent. Ms. Kay received $15,000 of alimony and $10,000 of child support from Mr. Kay during the year. Ms. Kay's Social Security number is 333-46-2974. Her address is 567 North Hollow Drive, Grimview, IL 48124. For business purposes, her employer ID number is 66-2869969. She uses the cash method of accounting for all purposes.

Unrelated to her business, Ms. Kay paid the following amounts during the year:

Estimated federal income taxes.	$16,000
State income taxes	3,500
County income taxes	1,500
Real estate taxes.	2,000
Mortgage interest on her home	5,600
Charitable contributions	2,900
Deductible contribution to individual retirement account (**Note:** This is a deduction for AGI It is one of the "adjustments to income" on page 1 of Form 1040.).	2,000
Health insurance for Ms. Kay	1,000

Compute Ms. Kay's tax liability for the year based on current tax law. (**Hint:** Ms. Kay's adjusted gross income is less than $100,000.) If a tax return is to be prepared for this problem, complete the following forms: 1040 (including Schedules A, C, and SE) and 4562. There is no alternative minimum tax liability. For grading purposes, attach a sheet to Schedule C showing supporting calculations for payroll taxes.

TAX RESEARCH PROBLEMS

9-49 *Depreciation.* S is a land developer. During the year, he finished construction of a complex containing a new shopping mall and office building. To enhance the environment of the complex, substantial landscaping was done including the planting of many trees, shrubs, and gardens. In addition, S acquired a massive sculpture that served as the focal point of the complex. S also purchased numerous pictures, which were hung in the shopping center and office building. Can S claim depreciation deductions for any of the items noted above?

9-50 *Amortization.* During the year, the metropolis of Burnsberg accepted bids from various cable television companies for the right to provide service within its city limits. The accepted bid was submitted by Cabletech Inc. in the amount of $500,000. For this amount, the city granted the company a license to operate for 10 years. The terms of the agreement further provided that the company's license would be renewed if the city was satisfied with the services provided. May Cabletech amortize the cost of the license?

10

Certain Business Deductions and Losses

Learning Objectives

Upon completion of this chapter you will be able to:

LO.1 Determine when a deduction is allowed for a bad debt.

LO.2 Understand the different tax treatment for business and nonbusiness bad debts.

LO.3 Explain what constitutes a deductible casualty or theft loss.

LO.4 Compute the amount of the deduction for casualty and theft losses.

LO.5 Determine the net operating loss deduction and explain how it is treated.

LO.6 Explain the basic tax accounting requirements for inventories.

LO.7 Identify the costs that must be capitalized as part of inventory and the role of the uniform capitalization rules in making this determination.

LO.8 Explain how inventory costs are assigned to costs of goods sold using the FIFO and LIFO assumptions.

LO.9 Explain the special deduction related to domestic production activities.

Chapter Outline

The rules governing the treatment of expenses and losses discussed in Chapter 7 set forth the general requirements that must be met if the taxpayer wishes to claim a deduction. As already seen, the basic test—whether the item was incurred in carrying on business or profit-seeking activities—is often just the initial hurdle in obtaining a deduction. Other provisions in the Code may impose additional conditions or limitations that must be considered. This chapter examines some of the special rules that relate to certain business losses and expenses of the taxpayer, including the provisions for bad debts, casualty losses, the net operating loss deduction, and inventories.

Bad Debts

LO.1

Determine when a
deduction is allowed
for a bad debt.

Loans are made for a variety of reasons. Some are made in connection with the taxpayer's trade or business while others are made for purely personal purposes. People also make loans hoping to make a profit. Regardless of the motive, with the extension of credit comes the possibility—as every lender knows—that the loan will never be repaid. When the borrower, in fact, cannot repay the loan, the taxpayer has what is termed a *bad debt* and may be entitled to a deduction. For tax purposes, a bad debt is considered a special form of loss subject to the specific rules of Code § 166. This provision governs the treatment of all types of bad debts: those that arise from the sale of goods or services such as accounts receivable, as well as those resulting from a direct loan of money. Moreover, § 166 applies regardless of the form of the debt (e.g., a secured or unsecured note receivable or a mere oral promise to repay).[1]

TREATMENT OF BUSINESS VERSUS NONBUSINESS BAD DEBTS

The tax treatment of a bad debt vastly differs depending on whether it is a *business* or *nonbusiness* bad debt. Business bad debts generally may be deducted without limitation. In contrast, nonbusiness bad debts are deductible only as *short-term* capital losses and are therefore subject to the limitation on deductions of capital losses (i.e., to the extent of capital gains plus $3,000).[2] Congress provided this distinctive treatment for nonbusiness bad debts in part to ensure that investments cast in the form of loans are handled in virtually the same manner as other investments that become worthless. As a general rule, an investment in a company's stock or bonds that becomes worthless also receives capital loss treatment.

Another difference between business and nonbusiness bad debts concerns the method allowed to claim a deduction. For some debts, it may be apparent that a portion of the loan will become uncollectible but determination of the exact amount must await final settlement. In the case of a nonbusiness bad debt, there is no deduction for partial worthlessness.[3] A deduction is postponed until the ultimate status of the debt is determined.

Example 1

R loaned his neighbor $5,000 in 2016. During 2017 his neighbor declared bankruptcy, and it is estimated that R will recover no more than 20 cents on the dollar or a maximum of $1,000 from the debt. Although R can establish that he has a bad debt of at least $4,000 ($5,000 − $1,000), no deduction is permitted in 2017 since the debt is nonbusiness, and it is partially worthless. If in 2018 R settles for $500, he will realize a

---

[1] Notes issued by a corporation (with interest coupons or in registered form) that are considered capital assets in the hands of the taxpayer are treated as worthless securities, as discussed in Chapter 12.

[2] § 166(d)(1)(B). See Chapter 16 for a detailed discussion of capital gains and losses.

[3] Reg. § 1.166-5(a)(2).

> loss of $4,500. Assuming he has no capital gains or other capital losses, he may deduct $3,000 of this loss as a *short-term* capital loss and carry over the remaining $1,500 ($5,000 − $3,000 − $500) to the following year. On the other hand, if the debt had arisen from R's *business,* R could deduct $4,000 in 2017 based on his estimate of the uncollectible amount, and the $500 remainder of the loss in 2018, all against ordinary income.

Because of their significantly different treatments, the determination of whether a particular debt is a business or nonbusiness bad debt has produced substantial controversy.

Business Bad Debts

Business bad debts are defined as those that arise in connection with the taxpayer's trade or business.[4] To qualify, the loan must be closely related to the taxpayer's business activity. Simply making a loan to a business associate does not make the loan business-related; it must support the business activity. Common business bad debts include the following:

LO.2
Understand the different tax treatment for business and nonbusiness bad debts.

1. Uncollectible accounts receivable (for accrual basis taxpayers only).
2. Loans to suppliers to ensure a reliable source of materials.
3. Loans to customers, clients, and others to preserve business relationships or nurture goodwill.
4. Loans to protect business reputation.
5. Loans or advances to employees.
6. Loans by employees to protect their employment.
7. Loans made by taxpayers in the business of making loans.

It is important to note that C corporations are not subject to the nonbusiness bad debt rules.[5] All loans made by a C corporation are deemed to be related to its trade or business. Thus, any bad debt of a corporation is considered to be a *business* bad debt.

Nonbusiness Bad Debts

A nonbusiness bad debt is defined as any debt other than one acquired in connection with the taxpayer's trade or business.[6] From a practical perspective, nonbusiness bad debts are simply those that do not qualify as business bad debts.

The most common nonbusiness bad debts are losses on personal loans, such as those made to friends or relatives. As suggested above, however, nonbusiness bad debt treatment also extends to loans that are made to make a profit and that essentially function as investments. For example, a loan to an acquaintance to start a new business is in effect an investment and thus a nonbusiness debt. Similarly, a loan to a business to protect an investment in such enterprise would be considered a nonbusiness debt. For instance, an investor may loan funds to a struggling corporation in which he owns stock, hoping that the infusion of cash might sustain it and save the original investment.

Although the dividing line between business and nonbusiness bad debts usually is clear, controversy typically arises in several common situations. One troublesome area involves taxpayers who frequently make loans to make a profit but who do not make such loans their full-time occupation. In such cases, the Service takes the view that the taxpayers are not in the business of making loans and thus any bad debts are not business bad debts. These situations can become even more difficult when the taxpayer devotes substantial time and energy to establishing and developing the business.

---

[4] § 166(d)(2).   [6] § 166(d)(2).

[5] § 166(d)(1).

> ### Example 2
>
> In *Whipple v. Comm.*, Whipple had made sizable cash advances to the Mission Orange Bottling Co., one of several enterprises that he owned.[7] He spent considerable effort related to these enterprises but received no type of compensation, either salary, interest, or rent. When these advances subsequently became worthless, Whipple deducted them as a business bad debt. The Supreme Court held that the loans made by the shareholder to his closely held corporation were nonbusiness bad debts even though Whipple had worked for the company. According to the Court:
>
> > Devoting one's time and energies to the affairs of a corporation is not of itself, and without more, a trade or business of the person so engaged. Though such activities may produce income, profit or gain in the form of dividends—this return is distinctive to the process of investing—as distinguished from the trade or business of the taxpayer himself. When the only return is that of an investor, the taxpayer has not satisfied his burden of demonstrating that he is engaged in a trade or business.

Despite the Court's holding in *Whipple,* taxpayers have achieved limited success where they have shown that they were in the business of organizing, promoting, and financing businesses.

The other prominent area of controversy concerns a situation common to many new struggling corporations: loans made to corporations by employees who are also shareholders. Here, the issues are similar to that above. Is the taxpayer making the loan to protect an investment or to protect his or her job (i.e., the business of being an employee)? When employee-shareholders have been able to show that a loan was made to protect their jobs rather than their investment, they have been able to secure business bad debt treatment.

Although the deduction is normally unlimited, in the case of an employee, the loss is considered an employee business expense and therefore treated as a miscellaneous itemized deduction subject to the 2% floor.[8]

GENERAL REQUIREMENTS

To be deductible, the debt must not only be partially or totally worthless but must also represent a bona fide debt and have a basis.[9]

Bona Fide Debt

A debt is considered bona fide if it arises from a true debtor-creditor relationship. For this relationship to exist, there must be a promise to repay a fixed and determinable sum, and the obligation must be enforceable under local law.

The question of whether there is valid debtor-creditor relationship usually arises when it appears that the taxpayer made the loan with little expectation of being repaid. This is typically the case when there is a close relationship between the taxpayer and the borrower. For example, loans to relatives or friends are likely to be viewed as nondeductible gifts rather than genuine debts. Such treatment is most likely where the lender makes little attempt to enforce repayment of the loan—a common occurrence when the borrower is a child or parent. In a similar fashion, advances to a closely held corporation that are not repaid may be considered nondeductible contributions to capital. On the other hand, loans made by a corporation may be something other than what they purport to be. For example, a loan to a shareholder may be treated as a disguised dividend distribution while a loan to an employee could be considered compensation.

---

[7] 63-1 USTC ¶9466,11 AFTR2d 1454, 373 U.S.193 (USSC, 1963).

[8] *Graves v. Comm.,* 2007-1 USTC ¶50,252, 99 AFTR 2d 2007-950, 220 Fed. Appx. 601 (CA-9, 2007). Note that miscellaneous itemized deductions are not deductible for purposes of the alternative minimum tax in which case the taxpayer may not benefit from the deduction.

[9] Reg. §§ 1.166-1(c) and (e).

To determine whether a bona fide debtor-creditor relationship exists requires an assessment of all of the facts and circumstances related to the debt. Besides the relationship of the parties, factors typically considered are (1) whether the debt is evidenced by a note or some other written instrument (in contrast to a mere oral promise to repay that has not been reduced to writing); (2) whether the debt is secured by collateral; (3) whether the debt bears a reasonable interest rate; and (4) whether a fixed schedule for repayment has been established.

Basis

A taxpayer may deduct a loss from a bad debt only if he or she has a basis in the debt.[10] For this reason, cash basis taxpayers who normally do not report income until it is received are not entitled to deductions for payments they cannot collect. Their loss is represented by the unrecovered expenses incurred in providing the goods or services. Conversely, accrual basis taxpayers who engage in credit transactions usually report income as it is earned. Accordingly, they may deduct bad debts for those amounts previously included in income. Uncollectible loans (as distinguished from accounts receivable) made by either cash or accrual basis taxpayers may be deducted, assuming the taxpayer has a basis for the loan.

Example 3

R is an orthodontist and uses the cash method of accounting. This year he completed some dental work for B for $3,000, which he never collected. In addition, he loaned $1,000 to a material supplier who left the country. Assuming both debts are worthless, R may deduct only the loan to the supplier for $1,000. No deduction is allowed for the uncollected $3,000 since R does not report the amount as income until he collects it and, therefore, has no basis in the debt. However, any expenses incurred in doing the dental work (i.e., materials. etc.) are deductible.

Worthlessness

Whether a debt is worthless ultimately depends on the facts. The Regulations indicate that a taxpayer does not have to undertake legal action to enforce payment or obtain an uncollectible judgment with respect to the debt to prove its worthlessness.[11] It is sufficient that the surrounding circumstances suggest that legal action would not result in recovery. Among the circumstances indicating a debt's worthlessness are the debtor's bankruptcy or precarious financial position, consistent failure to pay when requested, or poor health or death. As noted above, a *business* bad debt need not be totally worthless before a deduction is allowed. When events occur which suggest that the debt will not be recoverable in full, a deduction for partial worthlessness is granted.

DEDUCTION METHODS

As a general rule, deductions for bad debts must be claimed using the specific charge-off method.[12] This method—often called the direct write-off method—allows a deduction only in the year when the debt actually becomes worthless. The reserve method, which allows deductions for estimated bad debts and is typically used for financial accounting purposes, was repealed for all businesses except certain financial institutions and service businesses by the Tax Reform Act of 1986.

The direct write-off method provides some flexibility in accounting for business bad debts. When the facts indicate that a specific debt is *partially* worthless, the portion considered uncollectible may be deducted, but only if such portion is actually written off the taxpayer's books for financial accounting purposes.[13] Any remaining portion of the debt

---

[10] Reg. §§ 1.166-1(d) and (e).

[11] Reg. §§ 1.166-2(a) and (b).

[12] § 166(a).

[13] Reg. § 1.166-3(a).

that later becomes worthless can be deducted in subsequent years. Using this approach, taxpayers need not wait until the debt becomes totally worthless before any deduction is claimed. Alternatively, taxpayers can wait until the debt becomes totally worthless and claim the entire deduction at that time. Note that when the debt is totally worthless (in contrast to partially worthless), there is no requirement that the debt actually be written off the taxpayer's books.

Example 4

K Company is a major supplier of lumber to homebuilders. One of its customers, which owed the company $10,000, fell on hard times in 2017 and declared bankruptcy. Because this event suggests that the debt is partially worthless, a deduction is permitted. K estimated that it would recover $7,000 of the debt, and therefore claimed a $3,000 bad debt deduction in 2017. The $3,000 amount was also charged off the taxpayer's books as required. In 2019 K Company actually received $1,000 and deducted the remainder of the loss, $6,000 ($10,000 − $3,000 previously deducted − $1,000 actually received). Alternatively, K may opt to claim no deduction for 2017 and deduct the entire $9,000 loss in 2019. Note that when the debt becomes totally worthless in either case, the taxpayer is not required to write the debt off its books for financial accounting purposes. The company should take heed, however. If the IRS later determines that the debt is partially worthless, no deduction would be allowed since the debt was not written off on the books.

Experience Method for Service Businesses

Although the 1986 Act ostensibly eliminated the reserve method of accounting for bad debts, it provided an equivalent—but not identical—technique for service businesses. If a business uses the *accrual method* to account for income from services, the business is not required to accrue any amount that, *based on experience,* it knows will not be collected.[14] Businesses can take advantage of this exception only if they do not charge interest or a late charge on the amount billed. The experience method is available only for businesses that (1) have average annual gross receipts of less than $5,000,000 or (2) perform services in the following eight areas: health, law, engineering, architecture, accounting, actuarial science, performing arts, or consulting.

As a practical matter, the actual use of this technique may be limited, since most service businesses are allowed and often do use the cash method rather than the accrual method of accounting. Service businesses usually are exempt from the rule requiring use of the accrual method,[15] falling under the exceptions for sole proprietorships, S corporations, qualifying partnerships, personal service corporations, or taxpayers with gross receipts that generally do not exceed $5 million.

 CHECK YOUR KNOWLEDGE

Review Question 1

Over the years Dr. D has done extremely well financially and has made a number of investments. Several years ago, her good friend T started a small amusement park with such attractions as a water slide and a miniature golf course. Needing some venture capital, T convinced D to lend the new business $50,000, which he would repay to D in three years with 15% interest. This year the note came due and T was unable to repay because his business had failed. How will D treat the bad debt?

D's loan did not arise during the ordinary course of business but rather was in the nature of an investment. Therefore, the debt is considered a nonbusiness bad debt and is deductible as a short-term capital loss (limited annually to $3,000 plus capital gains).

---

[14] § 448(d)(5).

[15] Subject to certain exceptions, § 448 requires corporations, partnerships with corporate partners, or tax shelters to use the accrual method of accounting.

Review Question 2

T worked for P Corporation for 25 years. When the company began struggling this year, she worked without pay. The company finally went out of business this year, owing T six months of back pay. Does T have a business or nonbusiness bad debt?

Neither. Although most taxpayers would believe that they have a deductible loss, such is not the case. As a cash basis taxpayer, which T no doubt is, no deduction is allowed because she has no basis in her debt. Had she reported the income (i.e., had she been on the accrual basis), the IRS would be happy to allow a bad debt deduction.

Review Question 3

At the close of current year, Z Corporation, a lumber company, estimated that based on current year sales about $30,000 of its accounts receivable would be uncollectible. Therefore, in accordance with generally accepted accounting principles, the company adjusted its reserve account, charging bad debt expense for $22,000. May Z claim a $22,000 bad debt deduction for tax purposes?

For most businesses, the reserve method is not permitted for tax purposes. Since 1986 the law has generally required the use of the direct write-off method. Under this method, a taxpayer can claim a deduction for a bad debt only when the debt actually becomes totally or partially worthless. This requirement is relaxed for service businesses that are allowed to use a method based on their experience. Consequently, since Z is not a service business, it is not allowed to deduct $22,000 but only the amount that represents debts that are actually worthless.

Casualty and Theft Losses

GENERAL RULES

Unfortunately, as everyone knows, disaster may strike at any moment. Hurricanes hit, volcanoes erupt, and rivers overflow. Thieves steal, and people are mugged. The list of possible calamities is endless. Luckily, Congress has recognized that when such events occur they may seriously impair a taxpayer's ability to pay taxes. For this reason, taxpayers are generally allowed to deduct losses arising from casualty or theft. The special rules governing this deduction are the subject of this section.

The Code generally provides that an individual's losses arising from casualty or theft are deductible regardless of the activity in which the losses are incurred. An individual's casualty and theft losses related to profit-seeking activities may be deducted under the general rules, which provide that losses incurred in a trade or business or a transaction entered into for profit are deductible.[16] In addition, § 165(c)(3) expressly allows a deduction for losses related to property used for *personal* purposes where the loss arises from fire, storm, shipwreck, theft, or other casualty.

A deduction is allowed only for casualty losses related to property owned by the taxpayer; no deduction is allowed for damages the taxpayer may be required to pay for inflicting harm upon the person or property of another.[17] Further, the casualty must damage the property itself. A casualty that indirectly reduces the resale value of the property normally does not create a deductible loss (e.g., a mud slide near the taxpayer's residence).[18] Any expenses of cleanup, or similar expenses such as repairs to return the damaged property to its condition prior to the casualty, are usually deductible as part of the casualty loss. Incidental expenses that arise from the casualty, such as the cost of temporary housing or a rental car, are considered personal expenses and are not deductible as part of the casualty loss.

---

[16] §§ 162 and 212.

[17] *Robert M. Miller,* 34 TCM 528, T.C. Memo 1975-110.

[18] *Pulvers v. Comm.,* 48 T.C. 245, aff'd. in 69-1 USTC ¶9272, 23 AFTR2d 69-678, 407 F.2d 838 (CA-9, 1969).

CASUALTY AND THEFT DEFINED

Casualties

LO.3

Explain what constitutes a deductible casualty or theft loss.

The Code permits a deduction for losses arising not only from fire, storm, or shipwreck, but also from other casualties. While the terms *fire, storm,* and *shipwreck* are easily construed and applied, such is not the case with the phrase "other casualty." Interpretation and application of this phrase is a continuing subject of conflict. The courts and the IRS generally have agreed that to qualify as a casualty the loss must result from some *sudden, unexpected, or unusual event, caused by some external force.*[19] Losses deductible under these criteria include those resulting from earthquakes, floods, hurricanes, cave-ins, sonic booms, and similar natural causes.[20] On the other hand, losses resulting from ordinary accidents or normal everyday occurrences (e.g., breakage due to dropping) are not considered unusual and consequently are not deductible.[21] Similarly, no deduction is allowed for losses due to a gradual process, since such losses are not sudden and unexpected.[22] For this reason, losses suffered because of rust, corrosion, erosion, disease, insect infestation, or similar types of *progressive deterioration,* generally are not deductible. Unfortunately, the casualty criteria are vague, and the taxpayer may be forced to litigate to determine if his or her loss is sufficiently sudden or unusual to qualify. For example, the IRS has ruled that termite damage does not occur with the requisite swiftness to be deductible.[23] The courts, however, have found the necessary suddenness to be present in several termite cases and have allowed a deduction for the resulting losses.[24]

Thefts

Losses of business or personal property due to theft are deductible. The term *theft* includes, but is not limited to, larceny, embezzlement, and robbery.[25] If money or property is taken as the result of kidnapping, blackmail, threats, or extortion, it also may be a theft. Seizure or confiscation of property by a foreign government does not constitute a casualty or theft loss but may be deductible if incurred in profit-seeking activities.[26] Losing or misplacing items is not considered a theft but may qualify as a casualty if it results from some sudden, unexpected, or unusual event.[27]

Example 5

H slammed a car door on his wife's hand, dislodging the diamond from her ring, never to be found. The Tax Court held that the loss was deductible as an "other" casualty.[28]

LOSS COMPUTATION

LO.4

Compute the amount of the deduction for casualty and theft losses.

The loss computation is the same whether the casualty or theft relates to property connected with profit-seeking activities or personal use.[29] As explained below, however, limitations on the amount of deductible loss may differ depending on the property's use.

The *amount* of the loss is the difference between the fair market value immediately before the casualty and the fair market value immediately after the casualty as reduced by any insurance reimbursement. Of course, when the property is completely destroyed or stolen, the loss is simply the fair market value of the property as reduced by any insurance reimbursement. Although appraisals are the preferred method of establishing fair market values, costs of repairs to restore the property to its condition immediately before the casualty may be sufficient under certain circumstances.[30] Note that the appraisal costs are deductible as miscellaneous itemized deductions as a cost of preparing the tax return.

---

[19] *Matheson v. Comm.,* 2 USTC ¶830,10 AFTR 945, 54 F.2d 537 (CA-2, 1931).

[20] *Your Federal Income Tax,* IRS Publication 17 (Rev. Nov. 96), p. 190.

[21] *Diggs v. Comm.,* 60-2 USTC ¶9584, 6 AFTR2d 5095, 281 F.2d 326 (CA-2, 1960).

[22] *Supra,* Footnote 18.

[23] Rev. Rul. 63-232, 1963-2 C.B. 97.

[24] *Rosenberg v. Comm.,* 52-2 USTC ¶9377, 42 AFTR 303, 198 F.2d 46 (CA-8, 1952).

[25] Reg. § 1.165-8(d).

[26] *W.J. Powers,* 36 T.C. 1191 (1961).

[27] Rev. Rul. 72-592, 1972-2 C.B. 101.

[28] *John P. White,* 48 T.C. 430 (1967).

[29] Reg. § 1.165-7(a).

[30] Reg. § 1.165-7(a)(2)(ii).

For many years, a controversy existed concerning the deductibility of insured casualty losses for which taxpayers chose not to file a claim. The problem typically arises when taxpayers avoid filing a claim for fear that their insurance coverage may be cancelled or its cost may increase. When this occurs, the Treasury is effectively acting as an insurance company, partially subsidizing the taxpayer's loss. In 1986 Congress eliminated the controversy for *nonbusiness* property by providing that no deduction is permitted for casualty losses of insured property unless a timely insurance claim is filed.[31]

The amount of the deductible loss generally is limited to the lesser of the property's adjusted basis or fair market value (decline in value if a partial casualty).[32] The lesser of these two amounts is then reduced by any insurance reimbursements. There are two exceptions to this general rule, however. First, for property used in a trade or business or for the production of income that is *completely* destroyed or stolen, the deductible loss is the property's adjusted basis reduced by insurance reimbursements. Second, losses to property *used for personal* purposes are deductible only to the extent they exceed a $100 floor. The $100 floor does not apply to property used in a trade or business or for the production of income. The $100 floor applies to each event, not each item. Further, if spouses file a joint return, they are subject to a single $100 floor. If spouses file separately, each one is subject to a $100 floor for each casualty.[33]

In 1982, Congress added a further limitation on the deduction for casualty or theft losses of property used for personal purposes. In addition to the $100 floor on personal losses, only total losses (after reduction by the $100 floor) in excess of 10% of adjusted gross income are deductible.[34] This limitation does not apply to property used in a trade or business or an income-producing activity. The computation of the casualty and theft loss deduction is summarized in Exhibit 10-1. Individuals deduct their personal casualty and theft losses as an itemized deduction. Since this deduction is already limited it is not subject to the 3%-cutback rule.

EXHIBIT 10-1	Computation of Casualty and Theft Loss Deduction

Smaller of:

    1. Decline in value; or

    2. Adjusted basis*

Less:

    • Insurance reimbursement

    • $100 floor/casualty if personal

    • 10% of AGI if personal

Equals: Deductible casualty loss

*Adjusted basis, not decline in value, is used used if business or income property is completely destroyed or stolen.

Example 6

R had four casualties during the year:

Casualty	Property	Adjusted Basis	Fair Market Value Before Casualty	Fair Market Value After Casualty
1. Accident	Business car	$ 3,000	$ 9,000	$ 5,000
2. Robbery	Ring	500	800	0
	Suit	95	75	0
3. Tornado	Residence	50,000	60,000	57,000
4. Fire	Business computer	3,000	4,000	0

---

[31] § 165(h)(4)(E).

[32] Reg. § 1.165-7(b)(i).

[33] Reg. § 1.165-7(b)(4)(iii).

[34] § 165(h)(2). The 10% floor is waived for losses in federally declared disasters (§ 165(h)(3)).

R received a $600 insurance reimbursement for his loss on the residence. The deductible loss for each casualty is as follows:

1. The loss for the business car is $3,000 [lesser of the decline in value $4,000 ($9,000 − $5,000) or the adjusted basis of $3,000]. The deduction is *for* AGI unless it is related to R's business as an employee, in which case the deduction would be an itemized deduction.

2. The loss for the ring and suit is $475. The loss for the ring is $500 [lesser of decline in value of $800 ($800 − $0) or the adjusted basis of $500]. The loss for the suit is $75 [lesser of decline in value of $75 ($75 − $0) or the adjusted basis of $95]. The total loss attributable to the robbery is $575 ($500 + $75). This loss must be reduced by the $100 floor to $475 ($575 − $100). Note that the $100 floor is applied to the event, not to each item of loss. The loss, subject to the ten percent overall limitation, is deductible *from* AGI.

3. The loss on the residence is $2,300 [lesser of decline in value of $3,000 ($60,000 − $57,000) or the adjusted basis of $50,000, reduced by the insurance reimbursement of $600 and the $100 floor]. The loss, subject to the ten percent overall limitation, is deductible *from* AGI. Assuming R's AGI is $20,000, $775 is deductible ($2,300 + $475 − $2,000 [10% × $20,000]).

4. The loss for the computer is $3,000. Since the computer is used for business and is completely destroyed, the loss is the adjusted basis of the property regardless of its fair market value. The loss is deductible *for* AGI.

CASUALTY GAINS AND LOSSES

When the claims for some casualties are settled, the insurance reimbursement may exceed the taxpayer's adjusted basis for the property resulting in a gain. As discussed in Chapter 15, the Code provides some relief in this case, permitting the taxpayer to postpone recognition of the gain if the insurance proceeds are reinvested in similar property. When the gain must be recognized, however, Code § 165(h) sets forth special treatment.

Under § 165(h), all gains and losses arising from a casualty unrelated to business or a transaction entered into for profit—*personal casualty gains and losses*—must first be netted. For this purpose, the personal casualty loss is computed after the $100 floor but before the 10% limitation. If personal casualty gains exceed personal casualty losses, each gain and each loss is treated as a gain or loss from the sale or exchange of a capital asset. The capital gain or loss would be long-term or short-term depending on the holding period of the asset. In contrast, if losses exceed gains, the net loss is deductible as an itemized deduction to the extent it exceeds 10% of the taxpayer's AGI.

Example 7

This year T had three separate casualties involving personal use assets.

| | | Adjusted | Fair Market Value | |
Casualty	Property	Basis	Before Casualty	After Casualty
1. Accident	Personal car	$ 12,000	$ 8,500	$ 6,000
2. Robbery	Jewelry	1,000	4,000	0
3. Hurricane	Residence	60,000	80,000	78,000

T received insurance reimbursements as follows: (1) $900 for repair of the car; (2) $3,200 for the theft of her jewelry; and (3) $1,500 for the damages to her home. If T does not elect (under § 1033) to purchase replacement jewelry, her personal casualty gain exceeds her personal casualty losses by $300, computed as follows:

1. The loss for the car is $1,500 ([lesser of $2,500 decline in value or the $12,000 adjusted basis = $2,500] − $900 insurance recovery − $100 floor).

2. The loss from the residence is $400 ([lesser of $2,000 decline in value or the $60,000 adjusted basis = $2,000] − $1,500 insurance recovery − $100 floor).

T must report each separate gain and loss as a gain or loss from the sale or exchange of a capital asset. The classification of each gain and loss as short-term or long-term depends on the holding period of each asset.

Example 8

Assume the same facts as in *Example 7* except the loss for the personal car was not insured. In this case the loss on the car is $2,400 and the personal casualty losses exceed the gain by $600 ($2,400 + $400 − $2,200). T must treat the $600 net loss as an itemized deduction subject to the limitation of 10% of AGI.

Year Deductible

A casualty loss usually is deductible in the taxable year in which the loss occurs.[35] A theft loss is deductible in the *year of discovery*. If a claim for reimbursement exists and there is a reasonable prospect of recovery, the loss must be reduced by the amount the taxpayer *expects* to receive.[36] If later receipts are less than the amount originally estimated and no further reimbursement is expected, an amended return is *not* filed. Instead, the remaining loss is deductible in the year in which no further reimbursement is expected. If the casualty loss deduction was reduced by the $100 floor in the prior year, the remaining loss need not be further reduced. However, the remaining loss is subject to the 10% limitation of the later year.

Example 9

G's diamond bracelet was stolen on December 4, 2017. Her loss was $700 before taking into account any insurance reimbursement. She expects the insurance company to reimburse her $400 for the loss. In 2017 G may deduct $200 ($700 loss less the expected reimbursement of $400 and reduced by the $100 floor) subject to the 10% limitation for 2017. If G actually receives only $300 in the following year, she may deduct an additional $100 (the difference between the expected reimbursement of $400 and the $300 received) subject to the 10% limitation for 2018. If the reimbursement was greater than that expected, the excess is included in gross income.

A special rule exists for the reporting of casualty losses sustained within an area designated by the President as a "disaster area." This rule permits the taxpayer to accelerate the tax relief provided for casualty losses by electing to deduct the disaster loss in the taxable year immediately preceding the year of the disaster loss.[37]

Example 10

F, a calendar year taxpayer, suffered a loss in a "disaster area" from a flood on March 4, 2017. F may elect to deduct the loss on his 2016 return. If he has not filed the 2016 return by the casualty date, he may include the loss on the original 2016 return. If the 2016 return has been filed prior to the casualty, an amended return or refund claim is required. Alternatively, F could claim the loss on his 2016 return.

---

[35] Reg. § 1.165-7(a).

[36] Reg. § 1.165-1(d)(2)(i).

[37] § 165(i).

✓ CHECK YOUR KNOWLEDGE

Review Question 1

While acting like a couch potato and channel surfing one rainy day, S felt a drop on the end of his nose. Then, all of a sudden, water started gushing out of the ceiling. S later determined that squirrels had eaten a hole in his roof. Can S claim a casualty loss deduction for any damage caused by the squirrels? What must S demonstrate before he can claim a casualty loss deduction?

In order to claim a deduction for an "other casualty," S must establish that the damage is sudden, unexpected, and unusual. As can be imagined, these standards are often difficult to apply. In this case, the IRS has ruled that no deduction was allowed since it is common knowledge that squirrels are destructive and because the roof holes caused by the rodents were not unexpected or unusual.[38]

Review Question 2

In 2011 B purchased a music box as a Christmas present for his wife at a cost of $1,000. This year the box was stolen. It turned out that the music box was an antique worth more than $5,000. Because of the deductible on his homeowner's insurance policy, B received only $400 for his loss.

a.   Before considering *any* limitation, what is the amount of B's casualty loss deduction?

   In the case of a casualty of personal use property, a taxpayer is generally allowed to deduct the lesser of the property's value or basis as reduced by any insurance reimbursement. As a result, B is allowed to deduct a loss of $600 ($1,000 – $400).

b.   After B found out that his loss in the eyes of the tax law was only $600, he went crazy. He said it was ridiculous to allow a deduction of only $600 when in fact his economic loss was really $4,600 ($5,000 – $400). Is B right or wrong?

   B's belief that he has a $4,600 loss rather than a $600 loss is based on the value of the property. It is true that he has had an economic loss of $4,600, but he never had to recognize the increase in value from $1,000 to $5,000 as income for tax purposes. Therefore, the loss is measured from his basis.

c.   Answer (a) assuming the music box had been worth only $700.

   In this case, the deduction would be $300 ([lesser of fair market value, $700, or basis, $1,000] – $400). Note that B would probably believe this is unfair since he paid $1,000 for the box and was reimbursed only $400. However, the starting point for measuring the loss is the value; Congress did not want to allow a deduction for the loss in value that is not attributable to the casualty since to do so would allow the taxpayer to deduct a personal expense.

d.   Even though B has a casualty loss, he will probably not receive any tax relief. Why?

   Despite the loss, the deduction for *personal* casualty losses is subject to two limitations. The amount of the casualty (as measured above) must exceed the $100 floor per casualty and 10% of the taxpayer's AGI. After the 10% floor was added to the law in 1982, reported casualty loss deductions fell by 97 percent. Because of this limitation, a personal casualty loss must be almost catastrophic before a taxpayer receives any tax relief.

e.   Answer (a) and (c) assuming that B was in the business of selling music boxes.

   If the property is used in a trade or business, the taxpayer is entitled to a deduction equal to the basis of the property reduced by an insurance reimbursement. Consequently, in (a), where the box is worth $5,000 and has a basis of $1,000, the deduction would be $600 (adjusted basis $1,000 – insurance reimbursement $400). The same rationale provided for the solution in (b) above applies here. The deduction is limited since the taxpayer has never recognized the appreciation as income. In (c),

---

[38] Ltr. Rul. 8133097.

where the box is worth $700 and has a basis of $1,000, the taxpayer is also allowed a deduction for $600 (rather than $300 as was the case when the property was used for personal purposes). Note that even though the value of the property is less than its basis, the business taxpayer is allowed to deduct the entire basis in the property. This treatment is allowed since the taxpayer would have been able to deduct the $1,000 in any event because the property is used in a trade or business. For example, the taxpayer would be able to claim a deduction when the property was sold or if the property was depreciable, through depreciation.

Review Question 3

Checkers Pizza delivers. This year one of its cars was stolen. Does the $100 floor and 10% of AGI limitation apply in determining the amount of its casualty loss?

The $100 floor and 10% rule do not apply to casualties of property used in a trade or business or an income-producing activity. These limitations apply only to casualties of personal use property.

Review Question 4

During 2017, the Smiths' house was destroyed by a hurricane. As a result, the Smiths moved into a motel until their home was rebuilt six months later. The cost of their motel stay was $2,700. May the couple deduct the $2,700 cost as a casualty loss?

No deduction is allowed. This is considered an incidental personal expense and is not deductible as part of the casualty loss.

Net Operating Losses

LO.5
Determine the net operating loss deduction and explain how it is treated.

As someone once said, life is not always a bed of roses. This chapter, at least in part, is a testimonial to that. Debts do go bad, lightning may strike, and casualties can happen. Perhaps taxpayers can take some consolation in that in each of these cases, the government shares in the taxpayer's misfortune and provides some relief. Unfortunately, this section also dwells on the negative. For some taxpayers, income does not always exceed deductions. Businesses are not always profitable and catastrophic events may give rise to large expenses. In those lean or rotten years, the taxpayer may actually have a negative taxable income, usually referred to as a loss. When this happens, as might be expected, the taxpayer to his or her joy does not have to pay taxes. More importantly, the taxpayer may be able to use the loss to reduce his or her tax in a previous or subsequent year. This section examines this possibility.

In a year during which the taxpayer's deductions exceed gross income, the taxpayer is allowed to use the excess deductions to offset taxable income of prior or subsequent years.[39] Technically, the excess of deductions over income, as modified for several complex adjustments, is referred to as the taxpayer's *net operating loss* (NOL).[40] The Code generally permits the taxpayer to carry back the NOL 2 years and forward 20 years to redetermine taxable income.[41]

Allowance of the net operating loss deduction reduces the inequity that otherwise exists due to the use of an annual reporting period and a progressive tax rate structure. For example, consider a situation involving two taxpayers, R and S, who over a two-year period have equivalent taxable incomes of $100,000 each. R earned $50,000 each year while S earned $300,000 in the first year and had a loss of $200,000 in the second year. Without the NOL provisions, S would *not* be able to offset his $200,000 loss against his $300,000 income and consequently would pay a substantially greater tax than R. Such a result clearly would

[39] § 172.

[40] § 172(C).

[41] § 172(b)(1). Pre-1998 NOLs are carried back three and forward 15 years. NOLs arising in 2001 and 2002 and those of a small business attributable to federally declared disasters may be carried back 5 rather than 2 years. For an NOL arising in 2008 and 2009, businesses may elect to carry it back either 3, 4, or 5 years, instead of the normal 2-year carryback period.

be unfair since both taxpayers had identical taxable incomes over the two-year period. The NOL provision partially eliminates this inequity by allowing a loss in one year to offset income in other years.

Carryback and Carryforward Years

As mentioned above, under the general rules, an NOL resulting in the current year is carried back 2 years and forward 20 years. The loss is first carried back to the second prior year (i.e., the earliest year first) and taxable income is recomputed for that year. If any loss remains after reducing that year's tax liability to zero, the remaining loss is carried to the first prior year. If a loss still remains, the taxpayer carries it forward to the first year after the loss and so on up to the 20th year following the loss year. For example, a loss occurring in 2017 would be applied to taxable income of these years as follows: 2015, 2016, 2018, 2019, …, 2037, 2038.[42]

The taxpayer may *elect* to forego the carryback period and carry forward the loss instead.[43] The election is made simply by attaching a statement to the tax return for the year to indicate the taxpayer's intention of forgoing the carryback period. This election must be made by the due date of the return (including extensions) in which the net operating loss is reported. The election *cannot* be subsequently claimed or revoked by filing an amended return. This election normally is appropriate only where the taxpayer expects future profits. If future profits are anticipated, the taxpayer must determine whether carrying the loss back or forward will yield the greater tax benefit. This decision is often difficult since the taxpayer may be unable to predict the future with any certainty.

When the taxpayer carries the loss back to a prior year, the loss deduction is claimed on an amended return for the earlier year (Form 1040X). For this purpose, the statute-of-limitations period for returns of the earlier years normally is extended to three years after the due date (including extensions) of the return in which the loss was originally reported.[44] Alternatively, the loss may be claimed using Form 1045 (Form 1139 for corporations) for a so-called quick refund. This form must be filed *after* the return of the loss year is filed and *within* one year after the *close* of the loss year. If the taxpayer fails to file Form 1045, an amended return (Form 1040X) may still be filed.

Example 11

B, a calendar year taxpayer, reported a loss for 2017. He filed his 2017 return April 15, 2018. Under normal conditions, B must file an amended return for 2015 (the year to which the loss is carried) by April 15, 2019 (three years after April 15, 2016, the due date for the 2015 return). The Code, however, extends the period for filing an amended return for 2015 until April 15, 2021, three years after the due date of the return for the loss year. Alternatively, B may claim the loss using Form 1045 by filing the form before December 31, 2018, one year after the close of the loss year.

Where the taxpayer carries the loss forward, the loss deduction is claimed on the subsequent year's normal return (Form 1040).

If the taxpayer has losses occurring in two or more years, the loss occurring in the earliest year is used first. When the loss from the earliest year is absorbed, the losses from later years may be claimed.

---

[42] Subject to certain limitations, taxpayers who have an NOL for any tax year ending after December 31, 2007, and beginning before Jan. 1, 2010 may elect to carry the NOL for 2, 3, 4, or 5 years. See § 172(b)(1)(H)(ii).

[43] § 172(b)(3)(c).

[44] § 6511(d)(2).

NET OPERATING LOSS COMPUTATION

The term *net operating loss* (NOL) is defined as the excess of the deductions allowed over gross income, computed with certain modifications.[45] The purpose of the modifications is twofold. First, the net operating loss provisions are designed to permit a taxpayer a deduction for his or her true *economic* loss. Thus, certain artificial deductions that do not require cash outlays (such as the deductions for personal and dependent exemptions) are added back to negative taxable income. Second, the net operating loss provisions were enacted to provide relief only in those cases where there is a business or casualty loss. As a practical matter, a net operating loss is caused by one of the following:

- Loss from operating a sole proprietorship (e.g., a loss on Schedule C).

- Loss from rental operations in which the taxpayer actively participates subject to certain limitations.

- Share of an S corporation or partnership loss.

- A casualty or theft loss.

Since the NOL provisions generally allow only for the carryback or carryforward of losses attributable to business or casualty, restrictions are imposed on the amount of nonbusiness expenses that may be deducted in computing the NOL. As will be seen, it is these limitations on the deduction of nonbusiness expenses and losses that make the computation of the NOL deduction so complex.

The net operating loss deduction of an individual taxpayer is computed by making the following modifications in computing taxable income:[46]

1. Any net operating loss deduction carried forward or carried back from another year is not allowed.

2. The deduction for personal and dependent exemptions is not allowed.

3. Deductions for capital losses and nonbusiness expenses are limited as explained below.

To determine the extent of any deduction for capital losses and nonbusiness expenses, gross income must be classified into *four* categories: (1) capital gains from business; (2) other income from business; (3) capital gains not from business; and (4) other income not from business. With income so classified, the following rules are applied with respect to nonbusiness expenses and capital losses in the following order:[47]

1. Nonbusiness capital losses may be deducted to the extent of any nonbusiness capital gains; thus, any excess is added back to taxable income.

2. Nonbusiness expenses may be deducted to the extent of any nonbusiness income, including any excess of nonbusiness capital gains over nonbusiness capital losses (as determined in Step 1); thus, any excess is added back to taxable income.

3. Business capital losses may be deducted to the extent of any business capital gains; any excess business capital losses may be deducted to the extent of any excess of nonbusiness capital gains over nonbusiness capital losses and nonbusiness expenses (as determined in Step 2).

A general formula for computing the NOL deduction is set forth in Exhibit 10-2. As may be surmised from the previous discussion and the formula, the critical first step when actually calculating the deduction is classifying income and deductions and gains and losses as either business or nonbusiness. Exhibit 10-3 identifies and classifies the most common items appearing on tax returns.

---

[45] *Supra*, Footnote 39.

[46] § 172(d)(1) through (4).

[47] § 172(d)(4).

EXHIBIT 10-2	**Computation of Net Operating Loss**

Taxable loss shown on return

Add back:
- Exemptions

- Nonbusiness deductions
    Less:
        Nonbusiness ordinary income
        Nonbusiness net capital gain

- Nonbusiness capital losses
    Less:
        Nonbusiness capital gains

- Business capital losses
    Less:
        Nonbusiness net capital gains
        Less: (nonbusiness deductions − nonbusiness income)

Equals: Net operating loss deduction

EXHIBIT 10-3	**Calculation of Net Operating Loss Deduction: Classification of Business and Nonbusiness Income and Expenses**

Business Income

Salaries and wages
Schedule C income
Rental income
Farm income
Partnership and S corporation income if not passive
Gains from sale of business assets

Nonbusiness Income

Interest income
Dividends
Pension income
Annuity income
Partnership and S corporation income if passive
Gain from sale of capital assets not used in business (such as stocks)

Business Deductions

Schedule C expenses
Rental expenses
Farm expenses
Partnership and S corporation loss if not passive
Casualty or theft losses (business and personal)
Loss on sale of § 1244 stock
Miscellaneous itemized deductions for business
Moving expenses

Nonbusiness Expenses

Standard deduction
Itemized deductions including medical, interest, taxes, contributions
Partnership and S corporation loss if passive
IRA contribution
Contribution to self-employed retirement plan
Alimony

Example 12

In 2017 G quit his job and opened a car repair shop. G's filing status is married, filing jointly, and he reported the following income and deductions for the year:

Income

Business income	$ 40,000
Salary from previous job	10,000
Business capital gains—long term	7,000
Business capital losses—long term.......................	(2,000)
Nonbusiness capital gains—long term....................	5,000
Nonbusiness capital losses—long term	(3,000)
Interest income on nonbusiness investments.............	1,000

Expenses

Business expenses.......................................	70,000
Casualty loss on personal car...........................	5,100
Interest on home mortgage..............................	8,000

Taxable income is computed as follows:

Net business loss ($40,000 – $70,000)			$(30,000)
Salary			10,000
Interest earned			1,000
Net long-term capital gain.............................			7,000
Adjusted gross income (loss)			$(12,000)
Less: Itemized deductions.............................			
Casualty loss.......................................	$5,000*		
Mortgage interest paid	8,000		(13,000)
Less: Personal exemptions ($4,050 × 2)			(8,100)
Taxable income (loss)			$(33,100)

* $5,100 – $100 floor. Note that the 10% limitation does not apply since AGI is a negative number.

Following Exhibit 10-2, G's NOL for 2017 is computed as follows:

Taxable income (loss)			$(33,100)
Modifications			
Add back:			
Personal exemptions			8,100
Excess nonbusiness expenses:			
Mortgage interest	$8,000		
Nonbusiness income:			
Interest.....................................	$1,000		
Nonbusiness net capital gain ($5,000 – $3,000).......	+2,000	(3,000)	5,000
Net operating loss for 2017			$(20,000)

Computation of the real dollar loss or economic loss results in a similar deduction:

Business loss.......................................	$(30,000)
+ Salary	10,000
+ Business capital gains	5,000
– Casualty loss.....................................	(5,000)
Net operating loss..................................	$(20,000)

Note that the nonbusiness income (capital gains of $2,000 and interest income of $1,000) is not considered in this computation of economic loss since it is offset by nonbusiness expenses.

RECOMPUTING TAXABLE INCOME FOR YEAR TO WHICH NET OPERATING LOSS IS CARRIED

Once the net operating loss deduction is computed, it is carried to the appropriate year and used in the recomputation of taxable income for that year. The net operating loss deduction is a deduction *for* AGI. As a result, the deduction may have an effect on the amount of the deduction for certain items such as medical expenses, which are based on the taxpayer's AGI. All expenses based on AGI except charitable contributions must be *recomputed* in determining the revised taxable income.[48] The net operating loss deduction also may have an effect on any tax credits originally claimed. For example, if a year 2019 net operating loss deduction completely eliminates the taxable income of 2017, any credit originally claimed in 2017 becomes available for use in another year.

After the effect on the tax of the earliest year is computed, the amount of any loss remaining to be carried forward must be determined. In other words, a computation is required to determine how much of the net operating loss is absorbed in the year to which it is carried and how much may be carried to subsequent years. Although this calculation is somewhat similar to that explained above, additional nuances exist making the computation somewhat complex. For this reason, further reference should be made to the Regulations and Form 1045.

 CHECK YOUR KNOWLEDGE

During 2017, T opened his own computer store, specializing in sales of multimedia. He operated the business as an S corporation. Upon his first crack at computing his taxable income for the year, T determined that he had a negative taxable income of $15,000.

Review Question 1

Assuming T has a net operating loss for the year, how is it treated?

An NOL is generally carried back 2 years and forward 20 years. The 2017 loss is carried back to the second prior year (i.e., the earliest year, 2015), where taxable income is recomputed and a refund claim is filed. If any loss remains after reducing the taxable income of 2015 to zero, the loss is carried forward to the first prior year (i.e., 2016). If a loss still remains, T may carry it forward for up to 20 years, after which any remaining loss expires and is lost. Alternatively, T may elect not to carry the loss back but to carry the loss forward for 20 years. Carrying forward the loss may make more sense if he expects to be in a tax bracket in the future that is higher than past years. In such case, the loss would produce greater benefit.

Review Question 2

A review of T's tax return reveals that his negative taxable income of $15,000 includes several items of income and deductions. For example, his only income other than that related to his business was interest and dividends of $5,000. Indicate whether the following deductions would be allowed in computing T's NOL deduction and, if so, how much could be used.

    a. Personal exemption.

    b. Dependency exemption.

    c. Net loss from S corporation operations (sales less operating expenses).

    d. Casualty loss to personal residence from earthquake damage.

    e. Interest expense on the mortgage on his personal residence of $7,000.

    f. Net capital loss $8,000 ($3,000 offsets ordinary income and $5,000 carried over).

In computing his NOL deduction, T must make certain adjustments to negative taxable income to arrive at the taxpayer's true economic loss that the law allows to be carried over. No deduction is allowed for personal or dependency exemptions since these are artificial deductions. Thus, the exemption deduction must be added back to negative taxable income. The net loss from his business (i.e., the S corporation) does reduce taxable income in calculating the NOL, so there is no adjustment. The casualty loss is also allowable in computing the NOL. Nonbusiness expenses such as mortgage interest and taxes are considered personal expenses and can be deducted only to the extent of nonbusiness income. So, only $5,000

---

[48] Reg. § 1.172-5(a)(3)(ii).

of the $7,000 expense is deductible, requiring an addback of $2,000. Finally, a capital loss can generally be used only to offset capital gains. Thus, the $3,000 deduction attributable to the capital loss is not allowed and must be added back.

Gambling Losses and Deductions

As discussed in Chapter 6, winnings from gambling are fully taxable. However, under § 165(d), gambling losses are deductible only to the extent of current year winnings and only then as an itemized deduction (but not a miscellaneous itemized deduction). Losses that exceed winnings expire at the end of the taxable year and do not create a net operating loss that can be carried over to other years, even if the taxpayer is luckier in the other years. The treatment of a professional gambler is considered in Chapter 7.

Inventories

As might be expected, taxpayers who buy or produce merchandise for subsequent sale are not allowed to deduct the costs of the merchandise *at the time* the goods are produced or purchased. Instead, such costs normally must be capitalized (i.e., inventoried) and deducted when the goods are sold. The following example illustrates what might occur if taxpayers were not required to capitalize the costs of inventory.

Example 13

C Corporation began business in 2017 and purchased 10,000 gizmos at $10 each for a total of $100,000. In 2017 the corporation sold 6,000 gizmos for $120,000. In 2018 the corporation made no further purchases and sold the remaining 4,000 gizmos for $80,000. Gross profit reported with and without inventories is computed below:

	No Inventories		Inventories	
	2017	2018	2017	2018
Sales..........................	$120,000	$80,000	$120,000	$80,000
Cost of good sold:				
Beginning inventory...................	—	—	—	$40,000
+ Purchases......................	$100,000	—	$100,000	—
− Ending inventory.................	—	—	(40,000)	—
Costs of goods sold (4,000 @ $10)........	$100,000	—	$ 60,000	$40,000
Gross profit........................	$ 20,000	$80,000	$ 60,000	$40,000

Although the total income for the two-year period is the same under either method ($100,000), when it is reported differs significantly. The use of inventories produces higher income and higher taxes in the first year because only the costs of goods actually sold are deducted.

As the preceding example shows, the lack of inventories causes a mismatching of revenues and expenses and with it the possibility of widely fluctuating incomes. Without inventories, the income reported in any one year would in most cases represent a distorted picture—not a clear reflection—of how well the firm was doing. Perhaps what is more crucial, at least from the Treasury's point of view, is that taxpayers would be able to postpone the payment of taxes if inventories were not required. Note in *Example 13* that absent inventories, the taxpayer is able to defer $40,000 ($60,000 − $20,000) of income and the corresponding tax from 2017 to 2018. Congress recognized these possibilities at an early date and in 1918 took corrective action that is still intact today. Currently, Code § 471 provides the following:

LO.6

Explain the basic tax accounting requirements for inventories.

Whenever in the opinion of the Secretary the use of inventories is necessary in order clearly to determine the income of any taxpayer, inventories shall be taken by such taxpayer on such basis as the Secretary may prescribe as conforming as nearly as may be to the best accounting practice in the trade or business and as most clearly reflecting income.

With the enactment of § 471, Congress delegated its rulemaking authority concerning inventories to the IRS. The IRS has responded with a number of regulations indicating when inventories are necessary as well as what methods are acceptable for tax purposes.

The Regulations require taxpayers to maintain inventories whenever the production, purchase, or sale of merchandise is an income-producing factor.[49] As a practical matter, this means virtually all manufacturers, wholesalers, and retailers must keep track of inventories while service businesses are usually exempt. Note that inventories are required regardless of the taxpayer's method of accounting. Cash basis taxpayers must account for inventories as do accrual basis taxpayers. However, the mandatory use of the accrual method for purchases and sales does not prohibit taxpayers from using the cash method to account for other items such as advertising costs or interest income.[50]

EXCEPTIONS TO THE INVENTORY REQUIREMENT

While the inventory rule seems relatively straightforward, it has led to a significant amount of controversy. To understand the problem, it is necessary to recall that where inventory exists, the taxpayer not only must capitalize inventory costs, it also must accrue income from credit sales. The difficulty stems from the requirement that only those items representing merchandise *inventory* must be capitalized. In contrast, under Regulation § 1.162-3 materials and supplies that are considered *incidental* to the primary function of the business may be expensed currently. In contrast, *nonincidental* materials and supplies can be deducted only as they are consumed—much like inventory. Therefore, according to these rules, if a taxpayer can successfully argue that items are merely incidental materials or supplies, the items can be expensed immediately and the taxpayer may defer recognition of income from their sale until cash is received. On the other hand, if the IRS can prove that the items are inventory, the items must be capitalized and the income from their sale must be accrued. Note how much is at stake in the definition of inventory. If the items are considered incidental, the taxpayer wins the entire battle: deductions now and income in the future. If the items are nonincidental, the IRS secures a partial victory in that nonincidental items cannot be deducted immediately but only as they are consumed; however, income is still deferred. But if the items are considered inventory, the IRS has won the entire war since such characterization not only prevents an immediate write-off of the items' costs but also forces the taxpayer to accrue income currently. The difficulty is that there is no clear definition of inventory.

The problem is particularly acute with service providers. In *Wilkinson-Beane,* a mortuary provided funeral services, including supplying the caskets.[51] The taxpayer did not separately bill for the caskets but merely charged a flat fee for the services. Consistent with this approach, the taxpayer did not treat the caskets as inventory even though the costs represented 15.1% of total cash receipts. Unfortunately for the taxpayer, the court held that the caskets must be capitalized and any income forthcoming from the services to be accrued. A different approach was taken in the recent decision in *Osteopathic Medical Oncology and Hematology P.C.*[52] In this situation, the taxpayer provided chemotherapy treatment for cancer patients. In so doing, it used certain drugs. The IRS argued that the drugs were inventory and, therefore, the taxpayer could not expense the drugs and had to report the income when the treatments were provided (rather than when the cash was received—usually much later). However, the Tax Court sided with the taxpayer, ruling that the drugs were not inventory but rather an indispensable and inseparable part of the service of treating patients.

Due to the growing controversy about the definition of inventory and the ensuing problems, the government reacted. In 2000, the IRS began to relax its position on the mandatory use of inventories and at the same time the mandatory use of the accrual method. In a series of Revenue Procedures, the IRS has carved out two major exceptions, allowing taxpayers with inventories to escape the clutch of the accrual method. As may be grasped from the

---

49 Reg. § 1.471-1 and Reg. § 1.446-1(a)(4)(i).

50 Reg. § 1.446-1(c)(1)(iv).

51 70-1 USTC ¶9173, 25 AFTR 2d 70-418 420 F.2d 352 (CA-1, 1970).

52 113 T.C. 376.

discussion above, the exceptions are of huge importance primarily because they permit the taxpayers—at least small businesses—to defer income.

1. *Gross Receipts of $1,000,000 or Less.* Taxpayers with average annual gross receipts of $1,000,000 or less are not required to use the accrual method for inventories. This does not mean that taxpayers can simply expense inventory purchases. Instead, as discussed above, the items must be accounted for as nonincidental materials and supplies and expensed as they are used or consumed. While the treatment of inventory *costs* is essentially the same whether the costs are treated as inventory or nonincidental materials and supplies, the treatment of *income* significantly differs. Taxpayers who fall under this exception need not recognize accounts receivable income until they collect the receivables. In other words, they may defer the recognition of income until they receive payment for the merchandise.[53]

2. *Gross Receipts Less than $10,000,000.* The above rule carves out a special exception only for small businesses: taxpayers with gross receipts of $1,000,000 or less. *Revenue Procedure 2002-28* extends the same rule discussed above to taxpayers with average annual gross receipts exceeding $1,000,000 but less than $10,000,000 but only if their principal business activity is providing services or is not in certain industries, including manufacturing, wholesale, retail and information industries (e.g., newspapers, books, periodicals, database publishers, and sound recording industries) or they meet certain other exceptions. These businesses also need not use the accrual method for purchases and sales but inventory must be accounted for as nonincidental materials and supplies and expensed as they are used or consumed. Note that this rule does not override § 448 discussed above. Farming businesses, C corporations having gross receipts exceeding $5,000,000 and partnerships with a tainted C corporation partner do not qualify for this exception. This rule should benefit small businesses primarily in service businesses.[54]

Example 14

Golf Accessories Inc. (GAI) sells a variety of items for golfers, such as golf balls, tees, headcovers, ball marks, towels, clothing, training tapes and devices. The company sells direct to the public through its Internet site as well as to golf shops around the country. It has average annual gross receipts (e.g., sales) of $700,000. GAI began the year with $80,000 of merchandise on hand. During the year it purchased $300,000 of new merchandise, and at the end of the year had $70,000 on hand. Sales during the year were $650,000 but at the end of the year it had $40,000 of receivables outstanding. It also collected $15,000 of the receivables outstanding from the prior year. Because GAI averages gross receipts of less than $1,000,000 it need not use the accrual method to account for purchases and sales. As a result, it has revenues of $625,000 ($15,000 + $650,000 − $40,000) and costs of good sold of $310,000 ($80,000 + $300,000 − $70,000). Note that under the exception GAI is able to defer the $40,000 of income from the uncollected receivables until it is collected next year—a very valuable benefit. Also note that the inventory costs were still capitalized and could not be expensed until the items were sold or consumed.

Example 15

Same facts as above except GAI Inc. had average annual gross receipts of $4,000,000. Under these revised circumstances, the company would not qualify for the first exception since its gross receipts exceed $1,000,000. Moreover, it also would not qualify for the second exception even though its gross receipts are less than $10,000,000 since it is in one of the prohibited businesses of retail and wholesale trade.

---

[53] Rev. Proc. 2000-22, 2000-1 C.B. 1008 *modified and superseded* by Rev. Proc. 2001-10, I.R.B. 2001-2, 272. Note that Rev. Proc. 2001-10 eliminated the book conformity requirement.

[54] Rev. Proc. 2002-28, 2002-18 I.R.B. 2002-18, 815 clarifying and implementing Notice 2001-76, I.R.B. 2001-52, 613. See Rev. Proc. 2002-28 for exceptions where the principal business activity is the provision of services or fabrication or modification of or property to meet customer specifications.

Example 16

Same facts as in *Example 14* above except that GAI Inc. had average annual gross receipts of $8,000,000 and provided heating and air conditioning services. GAI meets the requirements of the second exception in that it is in the business of providing services and its gross receipts are less than $10,000,000. It would appear that GAI could avoid use of the accrual method and defer income from credit sales. However, if GAI is a C Corporation, it must still use the accrual method in accounting for purchases and sales because its gross receipts exceed $5,000,000.

INVENTORY ACCOUNTING IN GENERAL

A close reading of § 471 reveals that Congress has given the IRS two criteria to be followed in determining what inventory accounting methods are acceptable for tax purposes: (1) the method should conform as nearly as possible to the best accounting practice used in the taxpayer's trade or business; and (2) the method should clearly reflect income. Because of these requirements, the tax rules for inventory are quite similar to those used for financial accounting. Nevertheless, it is important to recognize that the IRS is the ultimate authority on determining what method represents the "best accounting practice" as well as what method most clearly reflects income. Consequently, as will be seen, taxpayers are sometimes required to adopt methods that vary from generally accepted accounting principles and cause differences between book income and taxable income.

There are three steps that must be followed in accounting for inventories and computing costs of goods sold: (1) identifying what costs (e.g., direct and indirect) are to be inventoried or capitalized; (2) evaluating the costs assigned to the ending inventory and determining whether reduction is necessary to reflect lower replacement costs (i.e., lower of cost or market); and (3) allocating the costs between ending inventory and costs of goods sold (e.g., specific identification, FIFO, LIFO). Each of these steps is discussed below.

COSTS TO BE INVENTORIED: UNICAP RULES

LO.7

Identify the costs that must be capitalized as part of inventory and the role of the uniform capitalization rules in making this determination.

The first step in determining costs of goods sold and ending inventory is identifying the costs that should be capitalized as part of inventory. Without guidance, taxpayers no doubt would be inclined to expense as many costs as possible. However, over the years, the IRS with help from Congress has established strict guidelines concerning what can be deducted currently (i.e., period costs) and what must be capitalized (i.e., product costs). The most recent development in this continuing debate was the enactment of the *uniform capitalization rules* (unicap) in 1986. As discussed below, the unicap provisions narrow further what the taxpayer is able to treat as a period cost.

As a general rule, the costs that must be capitalized depend on whether the taxpayer manufactures the goods (e.g., a producer of razor blades) or purchases the items for later resale (e.g., a wholesaler or a retailer such as a department store). When merchandise is bought for resale, the taxpayer must capitalize as a cost of inventory the invoice price less trade discounts plus freight and other costs of acquisition. Cash discounts may be deducted from the inventory cost or reported as a separate income item. In addition, certain retailers and wholesalers are subject to the unicap rules that require capitalization of particular indirect costs as discussed below. For manufactured items, inventory cost includes costs of raw materials, direct labor, and certain indirect costs. The unicap rules apply to all manufacturers.

Many of the problems concerning inventory involve the treatment of indirect costs. Various methods have been devised to account for these costs. For example, under the *prime costing* method only the costs of direct materials and direct labor are capitalized; all indirect costs are expensed. Another method, often advocated by cost accountants, is the *variable* or *direct costing* approach. This method capitalizes only those costs varying with production and expenses all fixed costs. Despite the acceptance of these methods for managerial and internal reporting, the IRS has outlawed their use.

Determining which costs should be included in inventory has been a continuing source of irritation in the tax law. Prior to 1973, questions were often resolved on a case-by-case method, resulting in confusion and inconsistency. In 1974, the IRS addressed the problems by issuing regulations requiring all manufacturers to use the *full absorption costing method*.[55] The full absorption method requires the capitalization of direct costs of material and labor as well as the capitalization of certain indirect expenses. However, retailers and wholesalers were not subject to the full absorption rules, and, therefore, were not required to capitalize any indirect costs. The full-absorption rules seemed to work but apparently not well enough and were essentially replaced in 1986 by the enactment of § 263A containing *the uniform capitalization rules* (UNICAP).

The UNICAP rules attempt to provide standard guidelines regarding the capitalization of expenditures for all types of taxpayer and all types of activities. The UNICAP rules apply to *all* manufacturers. In addition, they apply to any retailers and wholesalers (resellers) if their average annual gross receipts for the past three years exceed $10 million. For tax purposes, the UNICAP rules generally replace the full-absorption costing method. However, in practice, many manufacturers continue to use the full-absorption method modified to meet the UNICAP requirements. UNICAP requires more expenses to be capitalized than full-absorption so it is sometimes referred to as the super-absorption method. To be clear, for covered taxpayers, UNICAP requirements must be met and traditional full-absorption methods often used for financial accounting purposes do not meet these standards unless modified.

Section 263A requires the capitalization of direct material, direct labor costs, and, most important, any indirect costs that, in the words of the Regulations, "directly benefit or are incurred by reason of the performance of a production or resale activity."[56] The effect of these rules is to require taxpayers to capitalize many costs that they may have otherwise deducted. The Regulations require covered taxpayers to categorize all costs into three categories and treat them as follows:

Category	*Treatment*
1. Production and resale activities	Capitalize
2. General administration	Do not capitalize (expense)
3. Mixed service costs (benefit both production/resale and administration)	Allocate between production and administration

As seen in the more detailed breakdown in Exhibit 10-4, the Regulations classify costs as (1) those that benefit only production and resale activities (must capitalize); (2) those that benefit only policy and management functions (do not capitalize); (3) those that benefit both production and resale activities and policy and management functions, referred to as mixed service costs (capitalized by using any reasonable basis to allocate costs between production and policy functions). In addition, interest expense is subject to special rules. Taxpayers are required to develop reasonable bases for cost allocations. In this regard, the Regulations provide several straightforward allocation techniques.[57]

A threshold question with respect to UNICAP (as well as the special deduction for domestic production activities discussed below) is whether a taxpayer is a manufacturer. If the taxpayer is a manufacturer, § 263A applies regardless of the size of the taxpayer's business. If the taxpayer is not a manufacturer, § 263A only applies if the taxpayer's average gross receipts are greater than $10 million. In this regard, gross receipts includes those from all sources, not merely gross receipts from the sale of inventory. Because of the differing treatment between the two groups, a major concern is whether the manufacturing activities of a business are sufficient to cause it to be treated as a manufacturer. For example, are businesses that assemble some products that they sell considered manufacturers? Is a grocery store that uses a portion of its space to prepare foods for consumption on the premises or for takeout considered a manufacturer? As these examples suggest, a clear distinction between manufacturers and resellers does not always exist.

---

[55] Reg. § 1.471-11. Absorption costing is currently used for financial statement purposes.

[56] Reg. § 1.263A-1T(b)(2)(ii).

[57] For example, see Reg. § 1.263A-3(d) for a discussion of the simplified resale method and the same method used in conjunction with the historic absorption ratio.

EXHIBIT 10-4	Capitalizable Costs for Uniform Capitalization

Direct Costs	*Unicap*
Direct material	C
Direct labor	C

Indirect Costs	
Repairs/maintenance (equipment and facilities)	C
Utilities (equipment and facilities)	C
Rent (equipment and facilities)	C
Indirect labor	C
Indirect material and supplies	C
Small tools and equipment	C
Quality control and inspection	C
Taxes other than income taxes	C
Depreciation and depletion for books	C
Depreciation and depletion: excess tax	C
Insurance (facilities, contents, equipment)	C
Current pension costs	C
Past service pension costs	C
Bidding expenses—successful bids	C
Engineering and design	C
Warehousing, purchasing, handling, and general and administrative related to such functions	C

Policy and Management	
Marketing, selling, advertising, and distribution	E
Bidding expenses-unsuccessful bids	E
Research and experimental expenses	
Losses	E
Depreciation on idle equipment or facilities	E
Income taxes	C
Strike costs	E

Interest	*

Mixed Service Costs	
Administrative/coordination of production or resale	C
Personnel department	C
Purchasing department	C
Materials handling and warehousing	C
Accounting and data servicing departments	C
Data processing	C
Security services	C
Legal department providing services to production	C
Overall management and policies	E
General business planning	E
Financial accounting	E
General financial planning	E
General economic analysis and forecasting	E
Internal audit	E
Shareholder and public relations	E
Tax department	E

C: Capitalize
E: Expense currently

*Capitalized if the produced property has a life of 20 years or more, if the property has an estimated production period of more than two years, or if the production period exceeds one year and the cost exceeds $1 million. Does not apply to property acquired for resale.

ALLOCATING INVENTORIABLE COSTS

After total product costs for the year have been identified, these costs along with the cost of beginning inventory must be allocated between the goods sold during the year and ending inventory. If each item sold could be identified (e.g., a car or jewelry) or all items had the same cost, there would be little difficulty in determining the cost of items sold and those still on hand. As a practical matter, these conditions rarely exist. Consequently, the taxpayer must make some assumptions regarding which costs should be assigned to costs of goods sold. Like financial accounting, the tax law does not require the cost flow assumption to be consistent with the physical movement of goods. There are several acceptable approaches for allocating costs: specific identification, first-in first-out (FIFO), last-in first-out (LIFO), and weighted averaged.

> **LO.8**
> Explain how inventory costs are assigned to costs of goods sold using the FIFO and LIFO assumptions.

Example 17

K Corporation's inventory records revealed a beginning inventory of 300 units acquired at a cost of $3 per unit. This year the corporation purchased 400 units for $4 per unit, and it sold 500 units for $5,000. Gross profit using FIFO and LIFO are computed below:

	FIFO	LIFO
Sales (500 units @ $10)	$5,000	$5,000
Costs of goods sold:		
Beginning inventory (300 @ $3)	$ 900	$ 900
Purchase (400 @ $4)	1,600	1,600
Goods available	$2,500	$2,500
Ending inventory:		
FIFO (200 @ $4)	(800)	
LIFO (200 @ $3)		(600)
Costs of goods sold	$1,700	$1,900
Gross profit	$3,300	$3,100

If K uses FIFO it is assumed that goods are used in the order that they are purchased (i.e., the first goods in are the first goods to be sold). Thus, the ending inventory consists of the most recent purchases, $800 (200 at $4 per unit). The effect of FIFO is to assign the oldest costs to costs of goods sold. In contrast, LIFO assumes that the last goods purchased are the first sold. As a result, under LIFO the most recent costs are assigned to costs of goods sold and the oldest costs to ending inventory. Thus, ending inventory under LIFO is $600 (200 at $3).

The preceding example illustrates the principal advantage of LIFO. In periods of rising prices, LIFO matches current costs against current revenue. From a financial accounting perspective, it can be reasoned that this produces a better measure of current income since both revenues and costs are stated on a comparable price basis, thereby reducing the inflationary element of earnings.[58] From a tax perspective, LIFO appears preferable because taxable income is typically lower and the corresponding tax is reduced. In effect, taxable income is not "overstated" by fictitious gains. Interestingly, LIFO became part of the tax law in 1939 for just this reason—to help businesses reduce the "paper profits" that conventional methods were yielding and that were being taxed at wartime rates of close to 80 percent.

---

[58] Arguably, income results only to the extent that the sales price exceeds what it will cost to buy a replacement item for the merchandise sold. LIFO approximates this approach.

It must be noted, however, that the advantage of LIFO is lost to the extent that sales in any one year exceed purchases (see *Example 17* above). In this case, the lower prices of goods purchased in previous periods are charged to costs of goods sold. This dipping into the past LIFO layers creates inventory profits, the specific problem that LIFO was designed to address. In a worst case scenario, a company that adopted LIFO in 1942 might unexpectedly liquidate all of its LIFO layers, matching 1942 costs with 2017 revenues. This would no doubt lead to an unforeseen tax liability with little "real" income to pay the tax. This is a significant risk when LIFO is used. At the same time, it may represent an opportunity. Companies may be able to create income, if desirable, by liquidating LIFO layers (e.g., to absorb an expiring net operating loss).

DOLLAR VALUE LIFO

As a practical matter, applying the LIFO procedure to specific goods can be quite cumbersome and costly. In contrast to the simple one-item example above, most firms have hundreds or thousands of individual inventory items, and the number of units purchased and sold each period may amount to hundreds of thousands or more. Pricing each separate unit at the oldest costs and properly accounting for the liquidation of any LIFO layers might be a recordkeeping nightmare. Moreover, the major advantage of LIFO could be lost if old LIFO layers had to be liquidated because a specific item was discontinued or replaced. To address the problems of specific-goods LIFO, variations of LIFO have been developed. Perhaps the most widely used version of LIFO is the dollar-value method.

The dollar-value method reaches the desired result—eliminating the inflationary element of earnings attributable to inventory—in a unique way. Ending inventory is priced using the prices at the time LIFO was originally adopted (base-year). This value is then compared to beginning inventory to determine if there is a real increase or decrease in the pool of dollars invested in inventory. If there is no real change (i.e., ending inventory at base-year prices is the same as beginning inventory at base-year prices), the effect is to charge costs of goods sold with an amount reflecting current prices. On the other hand, if there is a real increase in inventory in terms of base-year dollars, the increase is valued at current prices and added to beginning inventory as a separate LIFO layer to determine ending inventory.

Example 18

T Corporation had an ending inventory on December 31, 2016 of 10,000 units at a cost of $20,000. During the year, T sold the original units and purchased another 10,000 units for $24,000. On December 31, 2017 ending inventory valued at current prices was $24,000. In such case, costs of goods sold would be $20,000, computed as follows:

Beginning inventory	$20,000
Purchases	24,000
Ending inventory	(24,000)
Costs of goods sold	$20,000

But what if, as the facts suggest, prices have increased by 20 percent? If so, the real amount invested in inventory has not changed ($24,000 ÷ 120% = $20,000). Consequently, valuing ending inventory at current-year prices of $24,000 (as above) effectively assigns the oldest costs of $20,000 to costs of goods sold, resulting in an inflationary profit of $4,000. Dollar-value LIFO eliminates this artificial gain—the objective of LIFO—by restating ending inventory at base-year prices. In this case, ending inventory would be restated at $20,000 ($24,000 ÷ 120%). This restatement would yield a cost of goods sold of $24,000, and would properly match current-year costs against current-year revenues.

The important difference between dollar-value and specific-goods LIFO is that increases and decreases in inventory are measured in terms of dollars rather than physical units. This approach allows goods to be easily combined into pools and effectively treated as a single unit. Consequently, the likelihood of liquidating LIFO layers is reduced.

Although there are various methods of dollar-value LIFO, the most frequently used is the *double-extension method.*[59] The steps to be used in applying the double-extension method are summarized in Exhibit 10-5 and applied to the following example.

EXHIBIT 10-5	Double-Extension Dollar-Value LIFO Computation of Ending Inventory

Step 1: *Extension #1.* Value ending inventory at current-year prices (actual cost of most recent purchases, average cost, or other acceptable method).

Step 2: *Extension #2.* Value ending inventory at base-year prices.

Step 3: Compute current-year quantity increase or decrease by comparing beginning and ending inventories at base-year prices.

Ending inventory at base-year price (Step 2)
− Beginning inventory at base-year price

Current-year quantity increase (decrease) at base-year price

Step 4: Calculate current-year price index.

$$\text{Index} = \frac{\text{Ending inventory at current-year price (Step 1)}}{\text{Ending inventory at base-year price (Step 2)}}$$

Step 5: Compute the quantity increase or decrease to be added to or subtracted from beginning inventory.

a. For a quantity increase: convert the increase measured at base-year prices (Step 3) to current year's prices using the current-year price index (Step 4).

Quantity increase at base-year price (Step 3) × Index (Step 4) = New LIFO layer

b. For a quantity decrease: a current-year decrease consumes the layer(s) of inventory in LIFO fashion (i.e., the decrease must be subtracted from the most recently added layer). Previous layers are peeled off at the prices at which they were added.

Step 6: Ending LIFO inventory is the beginning inventory increased by the new LIFO layer [Step 5(a)] or decreased by any liquidation of LIFO layers [Step 5(b)].

Example 19

In 2017 T Corporation elected to value inventories using double-extension dollar-value LIFO. Beginning inventory for 2016 consisted of the following:

Date	Pool Items	Ending Quantity	Current Cost per Unit	Total at Current Cost
1-1-2017	A	3,000	$3	$ 9,000
	B	4,000	6	24,000
Total base-year cost				$33,000

[59] Taxpayers may use the link-chain method or certain simplified procedures. See Code §§ 472(f) and 474 and the applicable regulations.

Inventory information for 2017–2019 and the computation of ending inventory using the steps in Exhibit 10-5 are shown below.

Steps 1 and 2: Double extend ending inventory.

Date	Pool Items	Ending Quantity	Current Cost Per Unit	Total at Current Cost	Base-Year Cost Per Unit	Total at Base-Year Cost
				Ending Inventory at Current-Year Prices		Ending Inventory at Base-Year Prices
12-31-2017	A	2,000	$ 4	$ 8,000	$ 3	$ 6,000
	B	5,000	7	35,000	6	30,000
				$ 43,000		$ 36,000
12-31-2018	A	6,000	$ 5	$ 30,000	$ 3	$ 18,000
	B	7,000	9	63,000	6	42,000
				$ 93,000		$ 60,000
12-31-2019	A	4,000	$ 6	$ 24,000	$ 3	$ 12,000
	B	5,000	10	50,000	6	30,000
				$ 74,000		$ 42,000

Step 3: Determine quantity increase (decrease) at base-year price.

	2017	2018	2019
Ending inventory base-year price	$ 36,000	$ 60,000	$ 42,000
Beginning inventory base-year price	(33,000)	(36,000)	(60,000)
Quantity increase at base-year price	$ 3,000	$ 24,000	$ (18,000)

Step 4: Calculate current-year price index.

$$\text{Index} = \frac{\text{Ending inventory at current-year price}}{\text{Ending inventory base-year price}}$$

	2017	2018	2019
	$ 43,000	$ 93,000	Decrease: use index at which units were added
	$ 36,000	$ 60,000	
	1.19	1.55	1.55

Step 5: Compute quantity increase (decrease) to adjust beginning inventory.

	2017	2018	2019
Quantity increase at base-year price	$ 3,000	$ 24,000	$(18,000)
× Index	× 1.19	× 1.55	× 1.55
= Increase or decrease to beginning inventory	$ 3,570	$ 37,200	$(27,900)

Step 6: Compute ending inventory.

	2017	2018	2019
Base-year	$ 33,000	$ 33,000	$ 33,000
2017 layer	3,570	3,570	3,570
2018 layer	0	37,200	9,300*
Total ending inventory	$ 36,570	$ 73,770	$ 45,870

*$37,200 – $27,900 = $9,300

THE LIFO ELECTION

Taxpayers may elect to use LIFO by filing Form 970 with the tax return for the year in which the change is made. Unlike most other changes in accounting method, prior approval by the IRS is not required. Conversely, the LIFO election cannot be revoked unless consent is obtained. As explained below, the lower of cost or market procedure may not be used with LIFO. Consequently, in the year LIFO is elected, all previous write-downs to market must be restored to income. For many years, the IRS required that all of the income due to the change had to be reported in the year of the change. In 1981, Congress expressed its disfavor with this view and enacted Code § 472(d). This provision allows the taxpayer to spread the adjustment equally over three years, the year of the change and the two following years. Nevertheless, if substantial write-downs have been made, there may be a considerable cost to elect LIFO.

Another ramification of the LIFO election concerns the *conformity requirement*. Under § 472(c), taxpayers who use LIFO for tax purposes must also use LIFO in preparing financial reports to shareholders and creditors. Failure to comply with this rule terminates the LIFO election and requires the taxpayer to change the method of accounting for inventory. As a result, taxpayers not conforming may be forced to give back any income tax savings previously obtained with LIFO.

The conformity requirement appears to have stifled the use of LIFO, presumably because during periods of rising prices it produces lower income and earnings per share than other inventory methods. This is true notwithstanding the tax savings that are available with LIFO and the relaxation of the rule over the years. The Regulations now permit the taxpayer to disclose income using an inventory method other than LIFO if the disclosure is made in the form of a footnote to the balance sheet or a parenthetical on the face of the balance sheet.[60] No comparative disclosures are allowed on the face of the income statement.

LOWER OF COST OR MARKET

In certain instances, the value of an inventory item may have dropped below the cost allocated to such items. When this occurs, financial accounting has traditionally abandoned the historical cost principle and allowed businesses to write-down their inventories to reflect the decline in value. The tax law has adopted a similar approach. Under the Regulations, taxpayers may value inventory at either (1) cost, or (2) the lower of cost or market.[61] However, the lower of cost or market approach may not be used if the LIFO method is used. Note that the lower of cost or market procedure deviates from the normal rule that losses are not deductible until they are realized.

In the phrase the *lower of cost or market,* "market" generally means replacement cost, or in the case of manufactured products, reproduction cost. When the rule is applied, the value of each similar item must be compared to its cost, and the lower is used in computing ending inventory.

Example 20

J's inventory records reveal the following:

Item	FIFO Cost	Market	Lower of Cost or Market
A.......	$ 3,100	$ 3,500	$ 3,100
B.......	5,100	3,000	3,000
C.......	6,000	7,500	6,000
	$14,200	$14,000	$12,100

If J elects to value inventories at cost, the inventory value is $14,200. Alternatively, if the lower of cost or market approach is elected, the inventory is valued at $12,100. This value is used because unsimilar items cannot be aggregated for tax purposes. For financial accounting purposes, J could combine the various items. Consequently, a difference may arise between book and taxable income.

---

[60] Reg. § 1.472-2(e). [61] Reg. § 1.471-2(c).

The approach used above is that prescribed in the Regulations for normal goods. Note that these rules only allow a write-down to replacement cost. What if the firm believes that it will ultimately sell the item for less than what it would cost to replace it? Financial accountants refer to estimated sales price less costs of disposition as net realizable value. For tax purposes, a write-down below this value is allowed only for what are often referred to as "subnormal" goods.[62]

Subnormal goods are those items in inventory that cannot be sold at normal prices because of damage (e.g., a dent in a file cabinet), imperfections (e.g., a thousand sweatshirts with the logo improperly spelled), shop wear, changes of style, odd or broken lots, and so on. The Regulations allow the taxpayer to value these "subnormal" goods at a bona fide selling price less direct costs of disposition. However, this lower value is acceptable *only* if the goods are actually offered for sale at such price 30 days after the inventory date (e.g., cars with severe hail-damage are actually on the lot with a sales price slashed below replacement cost within 30 days of when inventory is taken).

Example 21

In the landmark decision of *Thor Power Tool Co.*,[63] the taxpayer manufactured power tools consisting of 50 to 200 parts. Thor followed the common practice of producing additional parts at the same time it manufactured the original tool. This practice helped the company to avoid expensive retooling and special production runs as replacement parts were actually required. When accounting for these spare parts, the company initially capitalized their costs and—consistent with GAAP—subsequently wrote them down to reflect the decline in their expected sales price. The Supreme Court ultimately denied the write-down because Thor could not show that the parts (i.e., the excess inventory) were a subnormal good, and even if they had, the company had not actually offered the parts for sale at the lower price. The effect of this decision is to prohibit companies from writing down the value of slow-moving inventory.

Qualified Production Activities Deduction

LO.9

Explain the special deduction related to domestic production activities.

Over the years, Congress has adopted a number of measures that it hoped would attract, create and maintain manufacturing jobs in the U.S. For the most part, these provisions were designed to encourage businesses to increase its exports. Most of these approaches, however, resulted in a permanent reduction of U.S. tax and were held to constitute an illegal export subsidy under the U.S. trade agreements with the World Trade Organization. Congress addressed the problem with a different tactic in the *American Jobs Creation Act of 2004* (Jobs Act) with the creation of § 199.

In short, the law now provides direct tax breaks for domestic production activities. The focus has shifted to what companies are doing in the United States, not what they are exporting or moving overseas. Section 199 allows taxpayers to claim a special deduction relating to production and manufacturing activity undertaken in the U.S. and Puerto Rico, regardless of whether the items are exported. Eligible taxpayers may claim a deduction equal to 9% of the taxpayer's *qualified production activities income* (QPAI) or if less, the taxpayer's taxable income (modified AGI in the case of an individual). For taxpayers that qualify, the § 199 deduction (also known as the domestic production activities deduction or DPAD for short) is a huge benefit. As seen below, it basically allows eligible taxpayers to exclude 9% of their net income. The deduction is reported on Form 8903.

All taxpayers are entitled to the deduction (C corporations, S corporations, partnerships, sole proprietorships, estates, and trusts). Passthrough entities such as S corporations and partnerships do not actually claim the deduction but provide the information required to compute it as a footnote on Schedule K-1. For individual taxpayers, the deduction is for

---

[62] See Reg. § 1.471-2(c). Note that reduction of net realizable value by an allowance for a normal profit margin is not allowed for tax purposes.

[63] 79-1 USTC ¶9139, 43 AFTR2d 79-362, 439 U.S. 522 (USSC, 1979).

AGI but is not deductible in computing self-employment tax. The effect of the deduction is to reduce a corporation's effective tax rate by about 3% (35% × 9% = 3.15%) and an individual's rate as much as 3.6% (39.6% × 9%).

LIMITATIONS ON DEDUCTION

There are two critical limitations impacting the deduction. QPAI cannot exceed the taxable income limitation and the § 199 deduction itself cannot exceed 50% of the employer's wages.

Taxable Income Limitation

As noted above the deduction is generally 9% of QPAI or if smaller, the taxpayer's taxable income. For individual taxpayers, AGI with certain modifications is substituted for taxable income. The taxable income limitation normally applies when a taxpayer has current losses from activities other than production sufficient to offset production income or no current income because of a carryback or carryforward of losses. In such case, the taxpayer receives no benefit from the manufacturing deduction, either currently or by an increase in its NOL carryback or carryforward.

For pass-through entities, the taxable income limitation is determined at the owner or beneficiary level. Therefore, partnerships, S corporations, trusts and estates must separately state the amount of QPAI that flows through to the owners or beneficiaries.

W-2 Wages Limitation

The § 199 deduction itself cannot exceed 50% of the W-2 wages of the employer for the taxable year. W-2 wages are defined as the sum of wages and elective deferrals [e.g., contributions to § 401(k) plans that must be reported on Form W-2]. Fiscal year taxpayers use the W-2 wages for the calendar year that ends within the taxpayer's fiscal year Wages include production and non-production employees, as well as key executive officers and staff, in-house counsel, and research and marketing staff. Only wages that are related to domestic production gross receipts are considered in computing the limitation. In addition, in a concession to the film industry, any compensation for services performed in the U.S. by actors, directors and producers is considered W-2 wages.

Example 22

H and W are married and file a joint return. Each owns and operates a separate business. H has a tax practice with 10 employees. W's business manufactures handcrafted baskets, pottery, ceramics and matching accessories. W's business has about 25 employees directly involved in production and 10 others including herself that are involved in administration, accounting, marketing and similar support functions. Without a special rule, W could count the wages paid by H to his employees in determining the wage limitation. However, § 199 makes it clear that in determining the wage limitation, only the wages related to domestic production gross receipts are considered. Thus only the wages paid to W's employees are taken into account since the wages paid to H's employees are not related to production activities. Also note that the wages of not only those involved directly in the manufacturing process are counted but also those paid to support personnel. Finally observe that the result would be the same if both activities were carried on within a single C or S corporation or partnership.

With respect to partnerships, S corporations and other flow-through entities, the partners, S shareholders and beneficiaries are treated as having paid qualified wages in an amount equal to that owner's allocable share of the wages paid by the entity.

Wages do not include the Schedule C earnings of sole proprietors or the Schedule F earnings of farmers. In addition, wages do not include payments made to partners in partnerships for services rendered (so-called guaranteed payments). In light of this rule, it would appear that "one-person" sole proprietorships do not qualify for the deduction because the income from such businesses is not paid to the owner in the form of wages. This may encourage "one-person" operations to be conducted in the form of an S corporation that pays its owner/sole-employee wages.

Example 23

Red Flag Inc. manufactures and sells flags. For 2017, it has qualified production activities income (QPAI) of $2,000,000 and taxable income of only $500,000 due to losses from rental activities. The § 199 deduction normally would be $180,000 (9% × $2,000,000) but due to the taxable income limitation the deduction is limited to $45,000 (9% × $500,000 taxable income). The deduction is limited to 9% of the lesser of QPAI or taxable income. Moreover, the deduction cannot exceed 50% of wages paid.

Example 24

Organic Farms Inc. has QPAI and taxable income of $10,000,000 in 2019. Organic's W-2 wage expense for the year is $1,500,000. The normal deduction would be $900,000 (9% of $10,000,000) but is limited to $750,000 (50% × wages of $1,500,000).

Example 25

Carl's Custom Cabinets operates as a single member LLC. Carl produces all of the cabinets himself and has no employees. The LLC reports Schedule C net income of $100,000. The amount of the § 199 deduction is zero since Carl's LLC paid no wages. If the $100,000 net income included a $20,000 payment to an independent contractor, the deduction would still be zero since he paid no W-2 wages. The same result would occur if Carl's business was engaged in farming rather than cabinetry.

QUALIFIED PRODUCTION ACTIVITIES INCOME (QPAI)

QPAI and the § 199 deduction are computed in the following manner:

	Domestic production gross receipts
−	Allocable costs of goods sold
−	Directly allocable deductions
−	Ratable allocation of other deductions not directly allocable to another class of income
=	Qualified production activities income (QPAI) not to exceed taxable income
×	9%
=	Qualified production activities deduction not to exceed 50% of W-2 wages

The starting point for computing QPAI is "domestic production gross receipts" (DPGR). DPGR means the gross receipts derived from specified production activities carried on in the U.S. (or Puerto Rico), including the following:[64]

1. Any lease, rental, license, sale, exchange, or other disposition of:
   - *Qualifying production property* (QPP) that is manufactured, produced, grown or extracted by the taxpayer in whole or in significant part within the U.S.[65] According to the Regulations, the qualifying activities also include constructing, building, installing, manufacturing, developing, or improving property. QPP includes tangible personal property, computer software and certain sound recordings. Production includes farming, food storage, and food processing.

---

[64] § 199(c)(4). For purposes of § 199, the term United States includes Puerto Rico (§ 199(d)(8)). Thus DPGR attributable to activities in Puerto Rico qualify.

[65] A 20% safe harbor exists (e.g., if 20% of costs of good sold are U.S. costs (e.g., screen printing t-shirt purchased from China) 100% of the sales price is DPGR.)

- Certain *qualified films* (e.g., motion pictures, video tapes, live or delayed television programming) produced by the taxpayer, including copyrights, trademarks, and other intangibles created in production of the film.
- Electricity, natural gas, and potable (drinking) water produced in the U.S.

2. Construction performed in the U.S. (including not only erection but also substantial renovation of residential or nonresidential buildings); and

3. Engineering or architectural services performed in the U.S. for construction projects in the U.S.

Example 26

XBX Corporation sells a CD-ROM disk in a plastic case that contains a video game to be played on a computer. XBX also provides technical support. The CD-ROM and the case are tangible personal property but the computer game on the disk is considered computer software. If the disk was manufactured in China, the case was manufactured in Mexico and the software was developed in California, the proceeds of the sale must be allocated between qualified DPGR (the software) and nonqualified gross receipts (the CD-ROM and the case). Note also that computer software qualifies even though it might not be be operated on a computer (e.g., a video game for a video game player (e.g., Playstation, Xbox, Gameboy)). In addition, observe that in selling the game the company has also sold a service (technical support), the price of which is embedded in the total price of the item. Receipts from services do not qualify as DPGR. A special de minimis rule permits the taxpayer to ignore the receipts attributable to the services if they are less than five percent of the receipts received from the property.

Example 27

Same facts as in *Example 26* except the game may be played on demand online for a fee. According to the Regulations, such fees are not considered qualified DPGR. As might be expected, businesses question whether such interpretation is appropriate since the software is produced in the same way but simply delivered differently.[66]

Note that the definition of DPGR is quite broad, extending the benefits of § 199 to a wide variety of activities. In fact, some of these activities normally are not associated with manufacturing. For example, § 199 blesses receipts from engineering and architectural services, farming (including timber, lumber from the timber and logs for homeowners), ranching, publishing and related advertising, motion picture production, television production, musical recording production, traditional or cable broadcasting, home construction, the writing of machine-readable computer code and meat packing. However, § 199 identifies certain gross receipts that do not qualify, including those from the:

1. Sale of food and beverages prepared by the taxpayer at a retail establishment (e.g., restaurants); but, wholesale sales of such prepared items do qualify.

2. Construction services that are cosmetic in nature such as painting do not qualify.

3. Transmission or distribution of electricity, natural gas, or potable (drinkable) water.

4. Property leased, licensed, or rented by the taxpayer for use by any related person.

---

[66] In today's "online" world, it is not surprising that the treatment of software and licensing fees is somewhat controversial. See Reg. § 1.199-3(i)(6)(ii) regarding the treatment of receipts from certain online banking services. See also Generic Legal Advice Memorandum AM 2014-008 (Nov. 21, 2014), holding that receipts allocable to an "App" that enabled a bank's customers to conduct online banking did not qualify as DPGR where the App could not perform any function without being connected to the Internet. Similarly, CCA 201446022 concluded that receipts from production and distribution of multichannel video programming subscription packages were not qualified films.

De Minimis 5% Rule

One major simplification addresses the calculation of DPGR where the taxpayer has receipts from both qualifying and nonqualifying activities (e.g., U.S. and foreign production or manufacturing and services). If the taxpayer earns less than 5% of total gross receipts from nonqualifying activities (including interest, dividends, royalties and all other nonqualifying receipts), it may treat all of its gross receipts as domestic production gross receipts and no allocation is required. The reverse is also true. If less than 5% of total gross receipts are from domestic production activities, all of the taxpayer's gross receipts may be treated as non-DPGR. This rule enables taxpayer to avoid the complex provisions of § 199. In this regard, it should be emphasized that § 199 is not optional.

DPGR: Item-by-Item Determination

In many cases, a product represents the combination of several components only some of which may be qualified property (e.g., manufactured in the U.S). For example, televisions, cars, computers or similar products may consist of components manufactured in the U.S. or elsewhere. In these situations, DPGR must be determined on an item-by-item basis and not by division, product line or transaction.[67] Generally this requires that the taxpayer drill down and perform an analysis of each component of the property to determine its origin even though doing so can be unduly burdensome and costly. This approach is often referred to as the "shrinkback rule" because the taxpayer must "shrink back" the product to the largest component that does qualify. The government believes that if this approach was not used, taxpayers might otherwise receive benefits for gross receipts that do not qualify.

Example 28

Since 1930 CH Inc. has operated a shoe manufacturing business in Maine. Historically, everything was "made in the U.S.A." However, last year, CH hired a new CEO who brought in new ideas, including changes in the company's traditional manufacturing practices. Under the new approach, the company continues to manufacture leather and rubber soles but imports the shoe's uppers (the parts of the shoe above the sole). CH manufactures shoes for sale by sewing or otherwise attaching the soles to the imported uppers. In determining CH's DPGR from the shoe sales, the gross receipts from the sale of the entire shoe would not qualify. However, under the shrinkback rule, the soles would be considered the item and the sales receipts allocable to the soles would qualify as DPGR. Similarly, under this "shoelace" rule, if the taxpayer imported the entire shoe and added a U.S. shoelace, only the sales price attributable to the shoelace qualifies.

Expense Allocation

After DPGR is determined, allocable costs are subtracted to arrive at QPAI. How expenses are allocated can significantly change the calculation of QPAI and thus the size of the allowable deduction. As may be seen in the formula, if a taxpayer is in a "manufacturing" business, the taxpayer's QPAI theoretically will equal its taxable income. Indeed, for many businesses, particularly small ones, this should be the case. For example, if a company only manufactures envelopes in the U.S., its taxable income and QPAI should be the same, since all of its taxable income relates to manufacturing. This also would be the case for a contractor that only builds homes in the U.S. Similarly, an architectural firm whose sole source of income is from providing architectural services should have identical amounts of taxable income and QPAI. On the other, because this is often not the case, the key to calculating the correct deduction amount is a proper allocation of items of gross receipts, expense, losses, and deductions for determining QPAI.

The Regulations contain three methods for allocating expenses. Two of these are simplified methods for small businesses while the third applies to all other taxpayers (or small businesses if they choose).

---

[67] Reg. § 1.199-3(d)(1).

1. *Small Business Simplified Overall Method.* Taxpayers with gross receipts less than $5 million may allocate all costs, including costs of goods sold, based on gross receipts. This also applies to taxpayers with gross receipts less than $10 million if they are eligible to use cash-method of accounting.

2. *Simplified Deduction Method.* Taxpayers with less than $25 million gross receipts may allocate non-costs of good sold expenses based on gross receipts.

3. *Section 861 Method.* This method uses the principles relating to determining the source of taxable income for purposes of the foreign tax credit (i.e., whether taxable income derives from activities within or outside the United States). The § 861 method is mandatory for taxpayers with greater than $25 million gross receipts; it is voluntary for other taxpayers.

Example 29

G Inc. manufactures razor blades in a plants in Columbus, Ohio and Munich, Germany. The blades from both factories are sold all over the world. Gross receipts from the sales of blades from the Columbus operation qualify as DPGR for purpose of calculating the production deduction since they are derived from the sale of qualifying production property—tangible personal property (the razor blades)—that is manufactured by the taxpayer, G, entirely in the U.S. Note that all of the gross receipts qualify as domestic notwithstanding the fact that a portion could be attributable to sales in foreign countries (e.g., Canada and Mexico).

Example 30

Same facts as above. For the current year, the company reported taxable income of $4,000,000. Total wages for all employees were $6,000,000. The company's records reveal the additional information below. Based on this information the production deduction is $360,000 computed as follows:

Qualifying domestic production gross receipts		$15,000,000
Allocable costs:		
Costs of good sold	$4,000,000	
Directly allocable expenses	3,000,000	
Indirect expenses	1,000,000	
Total allocable costs		(8,000,000)
Qualified production activities income		$ 7,000,000
Taxable income before the production deduction		$ 4,000,000
Lesser of QPAI $7,000,000 or taxable income $4,000,000 . . .		$4,000,000
Rate		× 9%
Tentative production deduction		$ 360,000
Wage limitation (50% × $6,000,000 wages)		$3,000,000
Production deduction (lesser of tentative production deduction or wage limitation)		$360,000

Note that the production deduction is permitted for AMT purposes. However, the taxable income limitation is based on AMTI rather than taxable income.

DPAD Difficulties

Unfortunately, the artificial simplicity of the examples above masks the many obstacles that make application of § 199 troublesome. To appreciate the difficulty, simply consider the basic requirements that must be met in order to secure the deduction: *qualified property must be manufactured, produced, grown, or extracted by the taxpayer in whole or in significant part within the U.S.* At the start, § 199 provides no definition of manufacturing or production. Does assembly of vacuum cleaners or conversion of orange concentrate into orange juice constitute production? What about mixing water and concentrate to produce soft drinks or French Vanilla coffee? When McDonald's sells a hamburger is it providing a service or is it combining inputs to manufacture a product? While the Regulations address some of these issues, many still exist and new ones continually arise.

Still another complication involves the complexity in distinguishing between qualified and nonqualified gross receipts and the problem of allocating expenses between them. The already famous "Starbucks footnote" found in the Conference Report acknowledges the difficulty.

Example 31

Coffee Inc. operates a chain of coffee shops all over the world. It buys coffee beans and roasts and packages them at its own central processing facility. It distributes the packages of roasted coffee to its own retail stores which the stores brew for selling to customers. In addition, the stores sell the packaged coffee directly to consumers and to other retail stores. How are the gross receipts from a single sale of coffee classified? How much is attributable to the qualifying production activity, the roasting of the beans, and how much is attributed to the nonqualifying activity, the processing in the retail establishment. An even more daunting question concerns how the various costs of operating the company are to be allocated between these activities. According to the footnote, only the sales receipts attributable to the off-site roasting function can be taken into account in computing QPAI. The balance of the receipts is not qualified. Note also that the rule creates an incentive for a company like Starbucks to increase the amount that its factory charges its retail store in order to increase the amount of factory gross receipts and thus increase the deduction.

There are many other issues worthy of consideration but are beyond the scope of this overview. The Regulations provide guidance on how to solve some of these problems but not all. In any event, it should be emphasized that § 199 can have a major impact not simply on the accounting systems that must be designed to capture the required information but also on how a company structures itself and conducts its business.

Tax Planning Considerations

CASUALTY AND THEFT LOSSES

Much of the controversy surrounding casualty losses results from insufficient documentation of the loss. For this reason, taxpayers should give careful attention to accumulating the evidence necessary to establish the deduction. Such evidence would include, where appropriate, pictures, eyewitnesses, police reports, and newspaper accounts. The taxpayer also should gather evidence regarding the value of the property damaged or destroyed. In situations where an item is not repaired or replaced, an appraisal may be the only method of adequately valuing the loss.

In some cases, a taxpayer may suffer a casualty loss and in seeking insurance reimbursement incur appraisal costs. Even if the casualty loss is not deductible due to the 10% limitation, the appraisal costs are deductible as a cost of preparing the tax return and are therefore claimed as a miscellaneous itemized deduction.

Taxpayers often measure the amount of their casualty losses by the amount paid for repairs that are necessary to bring the property back to its condition before the casualty. This method of measuring may be inappropriate, however, if the repairs do not restore the property to its same condition before the casualty. In such case, an additional loss representing the decline in value should be claimed.

The rules for determining the deductible casualty loss have important implications for the amount of insurance that a taxpayer should maintain.

Example 32

T purchased a home in Boston for $70,000 15 years ago. This year, the home burned to the ground and the taxpayer received a $70,000 reimbursement from the insurance company. The cost of rebuilding the house was $200,000. Although T's economic loss was $130,000 ($200,000 − $70,000), none of the loss is deductible as a casualty loss. The casualty loss deduction is the *lesser* of the decline in value, $200,000, or the taxpayer's adjusted basis, $70,000, less the insurance reimbursement. Since the insurance reimbursement of $70,000 completely offset T's basis, there is no deductible loss.

BAD DEBTS

It is not uncommon for family members or friends to make loans to each other that are never repaid. This often occurs when a son or daughter is embarking on a business venture in which a parent is willing to invest. If the taxpayer wishes to claim a deduction if the debt is not paid, steps should be taken upon making the loan to ensure that the loan is not considered a gift. For example, the taxpayer should document the transaction in such a way that it is clear that both parties intend that repayment of the loan will occur. The best method of documenting the parties' wishes is to have a formal note drafted. Such a note would lend support to the argument that a debtor-creditor relationship existed between the parties. The note also should have a definite payment schedule, and each payment should be made on time. Collateral could be included as well. In addition, the note should call for a reasonable amount of interest. Failure to charge adequate interest could cause the imputed interest rules discussed in Chapter 5 to operate.

Example 33

Several years ago, F loaned his friend K $10,000 to start a chocolate chip cookie business. The business struggled along, requiring K to ask F for another $5,000, which he gladly loaned her. The business failed after six months. If F documented the loans and sought repayment, he may claim a deduction for a nonbusiness bad debt. If he failed to do so, any deduction may be disallowed.

NET OPERATING LOSSES

When a taxpayer suffers a net operating loss, a decision must be made whether to carry the loss back or elect to carry it forward only. Due to the time value of money, a carryback is usually more advantageous since an immediate tax refund can be obtained. However, this gain must be weighed against the future benefits to be obtained by a carryforward. If the taxpayer expects to be in a higher tax bracket in the future, the present value of the higher savings may be greater than the value of an immediate refund.

Problem Materials

DISCUSSION QUESTIONS

10-1 *Business versus No-Business Bad Debts.* R is employed as the chief executive officer of XYZ Corporation. Believing the company's future to be bright, he has acquired 75% of XYZ's stock. During the year, R loaned XYZ $10,000. Explain the tax consequences assuming XYZ is unable to repay all or a portion of the loan.

10-2 *Bad Debt Requirements.* Under what circumstances, if any, is a cash basis taxpayer allowed to claim a deduction for a bad debt? An accrual basis taxpayer?

10-3 *Identifying Bad Debts.* For each of the following situations, indicate whether the taxpayer would be able to claim a deduction for a bad debt.
   a. Several years ago, F advanced $30,000 to his wholly owned corporation, which was experiencing financial difficulties. Last year he loaned it another $10,000. No notes were executed and no payments have been made. During the current year, the company declared bankruptcy.
   b. E quit his old job as a salesperson to become a sales manager for K Corporation this year. As part of his arrangement with K, he was to receive a $10,000 bonus if the company reached $1 million in sales for the year. Sales for the year were $900,000, and K Corporation did not pay E a bonus.
   c. B and C each own 50% of ABC Incorporated. Over the years, ABC made loans to C. When C died he was penniless. He owed the company $20,000.

10-4 *Is There a Bad Debt?* Several years ago, R's son, S, got into the restaurant business. R loaned S $10,000 to help him get the business going. No note was signed nor was any interest charged. The business was initially a huge success but as time passed, it began having financial problems. This year the son's business failed.
   a. Can R claim a bad debt deduction? If so, is the debt a business or non-business bad debt and how much is the deduction?
   b. Same as (a) except R obtained a signed note from his son.

10-5 *Bad Debt of Related Party.* H loaned her son $10,000 to enter the car repair business. If the son subsequently abandons the business and does not repay the loan, what are the tax consequences to H?

10-6 *Casualty Losses.* Explain the rationale underlying the rules (lower of basis or value with certain exceptions) for computing the amount of the deduction for a casualty loss.

10-7 *Casualty Losses.* During the year, R had various losses. Explain whether each of the following would qualify as a casualty loss.
   a. Loss of stove due to electrical fire.
   b. Damage to water pipes from freezing temperatures in Southern California.
   c. Loss of tree from Dutch elm disease.
   d. Ruined carpeting from clogged sewer line.
   e. Hole in his suit from cigarette ashes he dropped; ruined shirt from pen leaking.
   f. Damage to both his and his neighbor's car while R's son drove R's car.
   g. The costs of cleaning up and repairing a home as a result of hurricane Matthew in 2016.
   h. Luggage and contents seized by a foreign government during a European vacation.

10-8 *Theft Loss Calculation.* If taxpayers could plan their taxes to account for thefts of their own personal use property (e.g., theft of their stereo and television), would they want the burglar to take all the property at once or take some property the first time and return for more later?

10-9 *Net Operating Losses in General.* Comment on each of the following:
   a. The purposes of the net operating loss deduction.
   b. The rationale underlying the complex calculation of the net operating loss deduction.
   c. How a net operating loss occurring in 2017 is utilized (i.e., the carryover process).

10-10 *Inventoriable Costs: § 263A.* HHG operates a chain of retail appliance stores. The company has grown tremendously over the past several years. It expects that its gross receipts will exceed $10 million this year. What are the implications of this growth for the company's method of accounting for inventories?

10-11 *LIFO versus FIFO.* During the 1970s, there was a tremendous shift from the FIFO method of inventory to LIFO. Nevertheless, not every company shifted to the LIFO method. Discuss why some might shift to LIFO although others might not.

10-12 *DPAD.* Straight Flight manufactures the top selling golf ball used by both professional and amateur golfers. The balls are manufactured in Georgia.
   a. What benefit will the company receive if its sales qualify for the domestic production activities deduction (i.e., the § 199 deduction)?
   b. Assuming that receipts from sales of the golf balls qualify for the benefits of § 199, why is the allocation of its indirect costs (e.g., overhead costs such as utilities, compensation of management and other personnel, office equipment rental, desktop computers, cell phones, advertising, security, etc.) important?
   c. The company also sells a line of golf clubs under the brand name Zing (put zing in your swing). Management is considering outsourcing the production of its clubs to Thailand. What would you advise in light of the requirements to qualify for the § 199 deduction?

PROBLEMS

10-13 *Treatment of Bad Debts.* AAA Computer Company, an accrual basis corporation, installed a new computerized accounting system for a customer and billed him $1,500 in June, 2017. When aging its accounts receivable at year-end, the company found that the customer was experiencing financial difficulties.
   a. Assuming the company estimated that only $1,000 of the account would be collected, what is the amount of the bad debt deduction, if any, that it can claim in 2017?
   b. Would the answer to (a) change if the debt were a non-business bad debt?
   c. In 2018 the company actually collected $200 and the remainder of the debt was worthless. What is the amount of the bad debt deduction, if any, that it can claim in 2018?

10-14 *Bad Debts and Accounting Methods.* Dr. D, a dentist, performed a root canal for a patient and charged him $300. The patient paid $100, then left town, never to be seen again. What is the amount of bad debt deduction, if any, that D may claim assuming that she is a cash basis taxpayer?

10-15 *Uncollectible Loan.* Several years ago, L loaned his old high-school friend B $5,000 to help him start a new business. Things did not go as well as B planned, and late in 2017 B declared bankruptcy. L expects to collect 40 cents on the dollar. In 2018 all of B's affairs were settled and L received $1,000. What are the tax consequences to L in 2017 and 2018?

10-16 *Personal Casualty.* When the waters of the Mississippi began to overflow their banks and flood the surrounding area, M was forced to leave her home and head for higher ground. On December 2, she returned to her home to find that it had been vandalized as well as damaged from the flood. After cleaning up, she determined that the following items had been stolen or damaged:

Item	Adjusted Basis	FMV Before	FMV After	Insurance Reimbursement
Fur coat	$6,000	$7,000	$0	$7,000
Computer.	4,000	3,000	0	Uninsured
Couch.	1,200	800	See below	500
Van.	7,000	5,000		

The couch had been damaged and M had it reupholstered for $700. The insurance company reimbursed her for the amounts shown on December 27. Under M's insurance policy, the company did not reimburse her for loss on the car until 45 days had passed. M expected to recover $4,000 but, after several delays, finally received a check for $2,000 on April 25, 2018. While she was waiting for reimbursement for her van, she rented a car at a total cost of $700. Although M received value for the coat, she did not replace it. In addition to the losses shown above, her real estate broker advised that even though her house had not been damaged by the flood, the value had dropped by $20,000 since it was evident that it was located in an area prone to flooding.

a. Compute M's casualty loss deduction, assuming her AGI in 2017 was $18,000 and in 2018, $20,000.

b. Assume the loss occurred on January 2, 2018 and the location was officially designated a disaster area by the President. Explain when the loss could be deducted.

10-17 *Casualty Loss: Business and Investment Property.* H is a private detective. While sleuthing this year, his car was stolen. The car, which was used entirely for business, was worth $7,000 and had an adjusted basis of $12,000. H received no insurance reimbursement for his car. Also this year, his office was the victim of arson. The fire destroyed only a painting that had a basis of $1,500 and was worth $3,000. H received a reimbursement of $800 from his insurance company for the painting. H suffered yet another misfortune this year as his rental property was damaged by a flood, the first in the area in 70 years. Before the casualty, the property—which had greatly appreciated in value—was worth $90,000 and afterward only $40,000. The rental property had an adjusted basis of $30,000. He received $20,000 from the insurance company, the maximum amount for which homes in a flood plain could be insured. Compute H's casualty loss deduction assuming his AGI is $30,000. Can a casualty loss create a net operating loss?

10-18 *Casualty Gains and Losses.* This year, C's jewelry, which cost $10,000, was stolen from her home. Luckily, she was insured and the insurance company reimbursed her for its current value, $19,000. In addition, while she was on vacation all of her camera equipment was stolen. The camera equipment had cost her $3,500 and was worth $3,100. She received no reimbursement since she carried a large deductible on such items. C's AGI for the year was $15,000.

a. What is the effect of the casualty losses on C's taxable income?

b. Same as above except the jewelry was worth $11,000.

10-19 *Casualty and Theft Loss Computation.* In each of the following cases, compute the taxpayer's casualty loss deduction (before percentage limitations) and indicate whether it is deductible *for* or *from* adjusted gross income.

    a. While G was at the theater, his house (adjusted basis $60,000, fair market value $80,000) was completely destroyed by fire. The fire also completely destroyed both his skiing equipment (cost $300, fair market value $90) and a calculator (adjusted basis $110, fair market value $80) used for business. He was reimbursed for $30,000 with respect to the house.

    b. B owned a duplex which she rented. A tornado demolished the roof but did not damage the remainder of the duplex. The duplex's value before the tornado was $45,000 and after the tornado was $40,000. B's adjusted basis in the property was $30,000. The President declared the entire city a "disaster area."

    c. Assume the same facts in (b) except that instead of B's duplex being partially damaged it was her personal cabin cruiser, and she received a $2,000 reimbursement from the insurance company.

    d. L backed his car out of the garage and ran over his 10-speed bicycle (cost $400, fair market value $300). The bicycle is worthless.

10-20 *NOL Items.* Indicate whether the following items can create a net operating loss for an individual taxpayer.

    a. Business capital loss
    b. Non-business bad debt
    c. Casualty loss
    d. Interest expense on mortgage secured by primary residence
    e. Employee business expenses
    f. Contribution to Individual Retirement Account
    g. Alimony
    h. Personal exemption

10-21 *Items Considered in Computing an NOL.* Indicate whether the following items are considered in computing the net operating loss deduction for an individual.

    a. Salary
    b. Capital gain on the sale of investment property
    c. Interest income
    d. Interest on a mortgage on a primary residence

10-22 *Net Operating Loss Computation.* R, a single taxpayer, operates a bicycle shop. For the calendar year 2017 he reports the following items of income and expense:

Gross income from business	$150,000
Business operating expenses	210,000
Interest income from investments	7,000
Casualty loss	4,000
Interest expense on home mortgage	9,000
Long-term capital gains (nonbusiness)	3,000
Long-term capital loss (nonbusiness)	5,000
Long-term capital gains (business)	1,000

The casualty loss represented the uninsured theft of R's personal auto worth $4,100 ($9,000 adjusted basis).

    a. Compute R's net operating loss for 2017.

    b. Assuming R carries the loss back to 2015, when must the corrected return for 2015 be filed?

10-23 *Net Operating Loss Computation.* V, married with two dependents, owns a hardware store. For the current year, her records reveal the following:

Gross income from business	$180,000
Business operating expenses	230,000
Royalties from investment	6,000
Nonbusiness expenses	9,000
Long-term capital gain (nonbusiness)	5,000
Long-term capital gain (business)	3,000
Long-term capital loss (business)	3,500

What is V's net operating loss?

10-24 *Valuing Inventories.* Chapters Inc., a large publishing house, prints a variety of titles, some of which are best sellers and others of which are duds. Because it is very difficult for Chapters to estimate with any accuracy which books will be successful, and because the marginal cost of printing an additional book is small, it typically prints 5,000 more copies than it expects to sell. Books that are not sold within a year of release are stored. The company's experience has shown that 95% of the books stored are never sold. Consequently, the company writes off any excess copies once they are delivered to storage. This practice appears permissible for financial accounting purposes. Can the same procedure be used for tax purposes?

10-25 *Applying Lower of Cost or Market.* Fitness Galore specializes in selling physical fitness equipment. The company's inventory at the close of this year revealed the following:

Merchandise	Cost	Replacement Cost
Weight machines	$40,000	$43,000
Stationary bicycles	10,000	8,000
Stair climbers	24,000	27,000

a   Compute the company's inventory assuming it uses the lower of FIFO cost or market.

b.   Assume the company adopts LIFO next year. Explain the tax consequences.

10-26 *Double Extension Dollar-Value LIFO.* Unwound Sound has recently engaged a CPA to evaluate its inventory procedures and determine if it should change from using FIFO to LIFO to account for inventories. The company's inventory records for 2016 and 2017 are shown below. Assume that the company had adopted double-extension dollar-value LIFO in 2016, and compute the ending inventory for

a.   2016

b.   2017

	1-1-2016		12-31-2016	
Inventory Pool	Units	Cost per Unit	Units	Cost per Unit
Records	5,000	$2	3,000	$2
Tapes	4,000	3	6,000	4
Compact discs	2,000	6	5,000	7

	12-31-2017	
Inventory Pool	Units	Cost per Unit
Records	2,000	$3
Tapes	3,000	5
Compact discs	4,000	7

10-27 *LIFO Pooling.* As shown in *Problem 10-25* above, the inventory of Unwound Sound consists of records, tapes, and compact discs. Over the last 15 years, the components of the company's inventory have changed dramatically. Whereas once the company only carried records, now it also carries tapes and CDs. Unwound Sound expects that in the very near future it will discontinue selling records. Assuming the company uses LIFO, explain the advantages of having one single pool containing all three items rather than three different pools.

10-28 *Accounting for Inventories.* VE Trucking Inc., an S Corporation and a cash-basis tax-payer, buys and transports sand and gravel for its customers, primarily contractors and developers. The contractors and developers use the materials in the construction of foundations for streets, houses, buildings and other construction projects. Normally, a customer contacts VE and orders a load of sand or gravel which VE subsequently buys from another source. VE then picks up the materials and delivers them to the customer's job site. VE bills the customer a flat sum, representing the costs of the materials and transportation. To determine the amount of the charge, the total cost is marked up for a reasonable profit. Because VE acquires and delivers the sand and gravel to its customers during the same business day, it does not possess any sand and gravel at the beginning or end of its business day. VE has been very profitable over the past ten years, averaging annual earnings of about $4,000,000 on annual revenues of about $15,000,000.

    a. Must VE use the accrual method? If so, will the accrual method have any impact given that VE has no materials at the beginning and end of each business day?

    b. Same as (a) except VE has average annual gross receipts of $8,000,000.

    c. Same as (b) except VE is a C corporation.

    d. Same as (a) except VE has average annual gross receipts of $700,000.

10-29 *Production Deduction.* For each of the following situations, explain how the facts affect application and determination of the § 199 deduction related to qualified production activities.

    a. BAH is a strategic management and technology consulting firm that provides advisory services to companies around the world.

    b. AMZ Inc. sells books and other products over the Internet throughout the world. All of its products that are purchased for resale are manufactured or produced by U.S. companies in the U.S.

    c. MSFT Inc. distributes software written by its employees.

    d. Forget-Me-Not offers an app that it advertises as a "convenient and secure way to store and manage your passwords." The app costs $3 per month. For this price, it will backup a customer's passwords in one location and sync passwords over multiple devices.

    e. RYL Inc., located in Detroit, is a construction company that primarily builds residential homes. It also is in the business of selling and assembling prefabricated steel buildings used primarily by businesses. The materials for these metal buildings are supplied by another corporation. RYL simply pours the foundation and bolts the materials in place. In addition, RYL's engineers and architects provide consulting services. One of RYL's subsidiaries is in the remodeling business.

    f. CSC is currently a single member limited liability company operated by Jim Smith. The LLC has seven employees. It is in the advertising business, producing commercials for television, radio, the Internet, and print media.

    g. PNA Inc. operates several restaurants in Houston. Its menu consists primarily of soup and sandwiches. The company's baked products such as bread and cookies are also popular. In fact, PNA has its own central baking operation that produces bread and other pastry items that are sold to some of the finest restaurants in the area.

10-30 *Domestic Production Gross Receipts.* OMG owns and operates grocery stores throughout Chicago. In addition to its retail outlets, it has its own bakery, ice-making, meat-processing, and egg-farming businesses. Answer the following questions concerning the company's domestic production gross receipts (DPGR).

    a. OMG is primarily a reseller. Will it qualify for the § 199 deduction?

    b. Many OMG stores have their own bakery that bakes bread, cakes, and similar items that are sold at the store to its retail customers. Do the receipts qualify as DPGR?

    c. Many stores have contracts to provide fresh baked goods daily to area restaurants. Would receipts from sales to these wholesale customers qualify as DPGR?

    d. Many of the baked goods sold to retail customers at OMG stores such as bread are baked off-site at a central baking facility and transported to their stores. Would receipts from sales to its retail customers qualify as DPGR?

    e. In some instances, dough may be made or bread may be partially baked at a central baking facility and then transported to the stores for final baking. Would receipts from sales to its retail customers qualify as DPGR?

    f. OMG has a construction division that builds the company's stores as well as strip malls in which the stores are located and serve as anchors. It leases the space in the strip malls to other businesses. Does OMG have any qualifying DPGR from these activities?

TAX RESEARCH PROBLEMS

10-31 R has had several minor automobile accidents in the last two years. During the current year, R demolished his car (value, $7,000; adjusted basis, $8,000) when he ran into a telephone pole. He used the car solely for business. R decided not to report the accident to the insurance company and claim his reimbursement because he believes his insurance rates will be raised if he does. Will R's deduction of his unreimbursed casualty loss be allowed?

10-32 T, a cash basis taxpayer, paid a swimming pool contractor, C, the sum of $10,000 in advance for improvements that C agreed to make to T's personal residence. C performed part of the contract and then ceased activity, leaving much of the work uncompleted. T seeks advice concerning whether she may claim a deduction for a bad debt.

10-33 Ten years ago Mac and Beth left the stress of city life and moved to a beautiful home near Davenport overlooking the Mississippi River. Mac took a job as a dealer at a local riverboat gambling casino while Beth became a full-time mom. The couple was happily raising their four children until 2016, the year of the great flood. Their home, although several miles from the river, suffered thousands of dollars of water damage. Other homes in their small subdivision that were on somewhat lower ground had far worse damage. Mac and Beth and their neighbors were quite shocked that this could happen to them since they lived in an area where it had not flooded for over 100 years. But then some were calling this the 100-year flood. After cleaning up, several of the owners decided to move, not willing to take any more chances. Unfortunately, those people who were able to sell their homes sold them for far less than what they thought they were worth, presumably because they lived in what was now perceived as a flood-prone area. Although Mac was not planning on selling his home, he did decide it was time to refinance his mortgage, the second time in 18 months. As part of the process, he got an appraisal that revealed that the value of his home had dropped substantially from the last time it was appraised. In 2011, when he refinanced for the first time, it appeared that he had made a great investment since he had purchased the house for $150,000 and the house was appraised at a value of $225,000. However, the most recent appraisal revealed that the house was worth only $120,000. What is the amount of the couple's casualty loss deduction, if any?

10-34 In 1988, Michael Malone, a professor of computer science and a specialist in digital technology, realized that it was only a short time before the computer would change the way people lived. Although he was 49 and quite happy with his $70,000 annual salary, he decided that this was an opportunity he just could not pass up. In 1986, he formed a new corporation, investing virtually all of his accumulated wealth, $200,000, in exchange for 51% of its stock. Three other individuals contributed additional cash for the remaining 49% of the stock. In the first few years of operation, the corporation was immensely successful. In 1988 Mike retired from the university and turned all of his attention to the business. All went well. In fact, things went so well that, by 1995, Mike turned over the supervision of everyday operations to several trusted employees; he began spending more time at the golf course and less time at the office. He was completely content working 20 hours a week and drawing an annual salary of $70,000. That income combined with his pension from the university of $20,000 a year was more than enough to keep him happy. During 2014, however, the competition in the computer business became fierce and the corporation had cash flow problems. As a result, Michael loaned the corporation $150,000 to keep it afloat. Unfortunately, the corporation was not able to survive and declared bankruptcy in 2017. How should Michael treat the worthless loan?

11

Itemized Deductions

Learning Objectives

Upon completion of this chapter you will be able to:

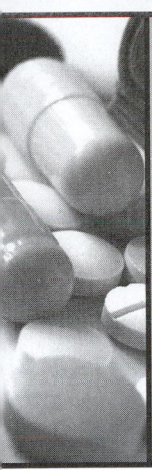

LO.1 Identify the personal expenses that qualify as itemized deductions.

LO.2 Explain the rules regarding deductible medical expenses and compute the medical expense deduction.

LO.3 Distinguish between deductible taxes and nondeductible fees or other charges.

LO.4 Explain the rules regarding deductible state income taxes.

LO.5 Distinguish between currently deductible and nondeductible interest expenses.

LO.6 Explain the requirements for the deductibility of charitable contributions and compute the contribution deduction.

LO.7 Identify the personal expenditures that qualify as either miscellaneous itemized deductions or other itemized deductions.

Chapter Outline

Introduction

LO.1

Identify the personal expenses that qualify as itemized deductions.

The last four chapters have focused primarily on the deductions allowed for expenses incurred in operating a trade or business. However, deductions of an individual taxpayer are not confined to these alone. This chapter examines the short list of personal expenses that individuals can deduct, popularly known as itemized deductions.

Normally, personal expenses are not deductible. Section 262 makes that clear by bluntly providing that "no deduction shall be allowed for personal, living or family expenses." Nevertheless, for various policy reasons, Congress has opted to create a few exceptions. The effect is to create three broad categories of deductions: (1) business expenses, (2) investment or nonbusiness expenses and (3) itemized deductions for certain personal expenses. There are six types of itemized deductions and they are reported on Schedule A of Form 1040 (see Appendix B-9). They include

- Medical and dental expenses

- Taxes

- Interest

- Charitable contributions

- Casualty and theft losses (discussed in Chapter 10)

- Miscellaneous investment and employee business expenses

Before considering these deductions in detail, several important observations are necessary. As noted in Chapter 3, these personal expenses are only deductible if they exceed the available standard deduction. In addition, it should be emphasized that a particular type of expense (e.g. interest) does not necessarily receive the same treatment in all situations. More often than not, the expense is treated differently depending on whether it is for business, investment, or is personal in nature. For example, the deductibility of interest expense generally depends on whether it is related to a loan that was used to make a business, investment, or personal expenditure. In contrast, real property taxes are deductible regardless of whether the property is used for business, investment, or personal purposes. The character of the expense may also affect the deduction's classification. Generally trade or business expenses (other than the unreimbursed expenses of an employee) and expenses related to producing rents or royalties are deductions for AGI and can be deducted regardless of whether a taxpayer itemizes. In contrast, the expenses discussed in this chapter are *itemized deductions* which may or may not be subject to the 2% floor and are only deducted when the taxpayer's itemized deductions exceed the available standard deduction (or the taxpayer is ineligible for the standard deduction). Moreover, itemized deductions of high-income taxpayers may be reduced by a special phase-out rule.

Medical Expenses

INTRODUCTION

LO.2

Explain the rules regarding deductible medical expenses and compute the medical expense deduction.

In 1942, during World War II, Congress added medical expenses to the small list of personal expenses that an individual may be able to deduct. Its purpose was to provide relief to taxpayers who suffered extraordinary medical costs beyond their control. Congress believed that such economic hardships reduced the taxpayers' ability to pay taxes and warranted relief. For this reason, the deduction is available only if a taxpayer's unreimbursed medical expenses, including those of a spouse and dependents, are greater than a certain amount based on a percentage of the taxpayer's income. That amount, sometimes referred to as the floor that must be exceeded, has varied over the years but is currently 10% of AGI.

WHAT MEDICAL EXPENSES ARE DEDUCTIBLE?

Section 213 generally allows a deduction for the costs of medical care defined as amounts paid for the following:

- Diagnosis, cure, mitigation, treatment, or prevention of physical or mental defects or illness[1]

- Payments to affect any structure or function of the body[2]

- Certain medicines and drugs[3]

- Transportation primarily for and essential to medical care[4]

- Qualified long-term care services[5]

- Insurance premiums for medical expenses and long-term care[6]

Partial lists of deductible and nondeductible medical expenses are presented in Exhibits 11-1 and 11-2.[7] Note that the deductibility of fees for medical care depends upon the nature of the services rendered and not on the qualification, experience or title of the person performing them. The most obvious medical expense is for visits to a family doctor, but as the list shows, medical services include the costs of surgeons, eye doctors, dentists as well as chiropractors, podiatrists, osteopaths, psychiatrists, and more. Note that payments to Christian Science practitioners and psychotherapists are deductible even though the practitioner is not licensed, certified, or perhaps not qualified. In addition, the services, operations, treatment or drugs must be legal. In this regard, cost of foreign medical expenses (blood pressure medications from Canada or hip replacement in Belgium) qualify even though their cost may be much less than what is normally paid in the U.S.

EXHIBIT 11-1	Partial List of Deductible Medical Expenses[7]

Fees paid for doctors, surgeons, dentists, osteopaths, ophthalmologists, optometrists, chiropractors, chiropodists, podiatrists, psychiatrists, psychologists, and Christian Science practitioners

Fees paid for hospital services, therapy, nursing services (including nurse's meals while on duty); ambulance hire; and laboratory, surgical, obstetrical, diagnostic, dental, and X-ray services

Meals and lodging provided by a hospital during medical treatment, or by a center during treatment for alcoholism or drug addiction

Medical and hospital insurance premiums

Medicines and drugs, but only if prescribed by doctor (includes vitamins, iron, and pills or other birth control items)

Special foods and drinks prescribed by doctor, but only if for the treatment of an illness

Special items, including braces for teeth, dentures, artificial limbs, eyeglasses, contact lenses, hearing aids, crutches, wheelchairs, and guide dogs for the blind or deaf

Smoking cessation programs

Transportation expenses for needed medical care, including air, bus, boat, railroad, and taxi fares

---

[1] § 213(d)(1)(A) and Reg. § 1.213-1(e)(1)(i).

[2] *Supra,* Footnote 1.

[3] § 213(d)(3) and Reg. § 1.213-1(e)(2).

[4] § 213(d)(1)(B) and Reg. § 1.213-1(e)(1)(iv).

[5] § 213(d)(1)(C) and§ 7702B(c).

[6] § 213(d)(1)(D) and Reg. § 1.213-1(e)(4).

[7] See *Your Federal Income Tax,* IRS Publication 17 (Rev. 2015), p. 147.

A frequent question regarding the medical expense deduction concerns the costs of plastic surgery. For many years, most plastic surgery was deductible since it affected a part of the body. But in 1990 Congress eliminated the deduction for the costs of cosmetic surgery or similar procedures.[8] Cosmetic surgery is defined as any procedure that is directed at improving the patient's appearance and does not meaningfully promote the proper function of the body or prevent or treat disease. Thus, the costs of face lifts, liposuction, hair transplants, and similar elective procedures to improve the taxpayer's physical appearance are not deductible. However, deductions are allowed for procedures necessary to address a congenital deformity, a personal injury arising from an accident or trauma, or a disfiguring disease.

Another item currently in the news is medicinal marijuana. While 28 states have legalized marijuana for medical use, it is still considered a controlled substance for federal law and its procurement is illegal. Consistent with its treatment of other controlled substances (e.g. laertrile), the IRS takes the position that the expense is not deductible.[9]

EXHIBIT 11-2	**Partial List of Nondeductible Expenditures**[10]

Accident insurance premiums

Bottled water

Care of a normal and healthy baby by a nurse*

Controlled Substances (e.g., marijuana, laetrile, etc.)

Cosmetic surgery (with limited exceptions)

Diaper service

Funeral and burial expenses

Health club dues

Household help*

Illegal operation or treatment

Maternity clothes

Social activities, such as dancing lessons, for the general improvement of health, even though recommended by doctor

Toothpaste, toiletries, cosmetics, etc.

Trip for general improvement of health

Vitamins for general health

* Note: A portion of these expenditures may qualify as expenses for the child or dependent care tax credit allowed under § 21. See Chapter 13 for further discussion of this credit.

WHOSE EXPENSES ARE DEDUCTIBLE?

Taxpayers may deduct their own medical expenses as well as those for a spouse and dependents.[11] As long as the relationship between the taxpayer and the other party—a spouse or dependent—existed at the time the expense was paid or incurred, the test is met.[12]

Expenses for a spouse. Suppose a taxpayer was not married when the medical expenses were incurred but were paid after he or she married. Or the expenses were incurred while a couple was married but were paid after one died or after they divorced. As indicated above, an individual is considered someone's spouse if they were married at the time the medical services were rendered or at the time the expenses were paid.[13]

[8] § 213(d)(9).

[9] Rev. Rul. 97-9, 1997-1 CB 77.

[10] *Supra*, Footnote 7.

[11] See §§ 213(a) and 213(d)(1).

[12] Reg. § 1.213-1(e)(3).

[13] Reg. § 1.213-1(e)(3). A spousal relationship does not exist if the taxpayer is legally separated from his or her spouse under a decree of separate maintenance because the two parties are not considered married (See § 143(a)).

> **Example 1**
>
> Jennifer had some dental work done at a cost of $4,000 before she married Dan. After they got married, Dan paid for Jennifer's $4,000 bill. If they file a joint return, the couple would include the medical expenses both paid, including Dan's payment of Jennifer's $4,000 expense. If Dan filed separately, he could include the $4,000 expense in figuring his medical expense deduction even though it was Jennifer's expense.

> **Example 2**
>
> Fred's wife, Wilma, died early in 20X2. The expenses of her last illness were substantial and Fred ended up paying the final installment of $15,000 in 20X4. Fred may deduct the $15,000 on his separate return or a return with a new spouse since the expenses were incurred while he and his former wife were married.

Expenses for a Dependent. A taxpayer also may deduct the medical expenses for the care of a dependent. For this purpose, the definition of a dependent is quite generous. Specifically, individuals are considered dependents under the qualifying relative test even if they fail the gross income requirement (i.e., their gross income exceeds the exemption amount) or they file a joint return with their spouses.[14] This approach allows taxpayers to claim a deduction for medical expenses paid for someone who normally is not a dependent such as an elderly parent or sibling as long as they pay more than 50% of the cost of their support or by virtue of a multiple support agreement. This can be quite beneficial as the example below illustrates.

> **Example 3**
>
> T's 75 year-old mother, M, is in poor health. This year her only income year was interest of $10,000. To help her out, T paid all of her medical expenses, which was more than half of her support. However, T cannot claim his mother as a dependent (i.e., a qualifying relative) since her gross income exceeded the exemption amount of $4,050 in 2017. Normally, a taxpayer can deduct medical expenses paid on behalf of another only if that person is a dependent. While technically M is not a dependent for whom an exemption can be claimed, for purposes of the medical expense rules, the gross income test is waived. Thus T is allowed to deduct the medical expenses paid on behalf of his mother if he itemizes his deductions and his total medical expenses, including those of his mother, exceed 10% of his AGI. The result would be the same even if M filed a joint return or T was a party to a multiple support agreement.

Medical expenses for children of divorced parents are deductible by the parent who pays for them, regardless of which parent is entitled to the dependency exemption. Additionally, if a taxpayer is entitled to a dependency exemption under a multiple support agreement, the taxpayer will be allowed to deduct any medical expenses which he or she actually pays on behalf of the claimed dependent.[15]

---

[14] See Reg. § 1.213-1(a)(3)(i) and Chapter 4 for a discussion of the dependency tests.

[15] See § 213(d)(5) and Reg. § 1.213-1(a)(3)(i). Medical expenses taken into account under § 21 in computing a credit for the care of certain dependents are not allowed to be treated as deductible medical expenses. See § 213(e) and Reg. § 1.213-1(f) and Chapter 13 for a discussion of the tax credit allowed under § 21.

WHEN DEDUCTIBLE

In computing the medical expense deduction for a given tax year, the taxpayer is allowed to take into account *only* those medical expenses *actually paid* during the taxable year, regardless of when the illness[16] or injury that occasioned the expenses occurred, and regardless of the method of accounting used by the taxpayer in computing his or her taxable income (i.e., cash or accrual).[17] Consequently, if the medical expenses are incurred but not paid during the current tax year, the deduction for such expenses will not be allowed *until* the year of payment. The IRS has ruled, however, that the use of a bank credit card to pay for medical expenses *will* qualify as payment in the year of the credit card charge regardless of when the taxpayer actually repays the bank.[18]

The *prepayment* of medical expenses does not qualify as a current deduction unless the taxpayer is required to make the payment as a condition of receiving the medical services.[19] Accordingly, the IRS has ruled that a taxpayer's nonrefundable advance payments required as a condition for admission to a retirement home or institution for future lifetime medical care are deductible as expenses in the year paid.[20]

Example 4

As a prerequisite for prenatal care and the delivery of her child, M prepays $3,150 to her doctor on November 15, 2017. Even though much of the prenatal care and the delivery of the child does not occur until 2018, M will be allowed to treat the prepayment as a medical expenditure in 2017.

Example 5

This year, Al, 75, moved to an assisted living facility, Sunset Senior Living, (see Exhibit 11-3) where he planned to spend the rest of his life. As part of the agreement with Sunset, he paid $100,000 to receive lifetime care, including accommodations meals and medical care. Sunset allocated 30% of the fee to medical expenses based on its prior expenses. Al is allowed to deduct $30,000 as medical expenses (30% × $100,000) notwithstanding the fact that it is for future services.

DEDUCTION LIMITATIONS

The medical expense deduction was created by Congress with the stated social objective of providing individual taxpayers relief from a heavy tax burden during a period of medical emergency and thereby encouraging the maintenance of a high level of public health. However, as noted earlier, the deduction was designed to provide relief for only those expenditures in excess of a normal or average amount. Currently, the medical expense deduction is allowed only to the extent medical expenditures exceed 10% of the taxpayer's AGI. For 2013 through 2016, the floor was 7.5% if the taxpayer or the taxpayer's spouse had reached age 65 by the end of the tax year. This limitation ensures that only extraordinary medical costs will result in a deduction.

In addition to the percentage limitation imposed on the medical expense deduction, it is important to note that most of the everyday type of expenditures incurred by an individual for items incident to his or her general health and hygiene are excluded from the definition of qualifying medical expenses. For example, medicine and drug expenditures are deductible only if they are for insulin and *prescribed* drugs.[21] Over-the-counter medicines and drugs such as aspirin, cold remedies, skin lotions, and vitamins are not deductible. Other nondeductible expenditures are listed in Exhibit 11-2.

---

[16] *Supra,* Footnote 7.

[17] Reg. § 1.213-1(a)(1).

[18] Rev. Rul. 78-39, 1978-1 C.B. 73.

[19] See *Robert S. Basset,* 26 T.C. 619 (1956). Absent such a prohibition, a taxpayer could maximize the tax benefits of medical deductions simply by timing the year of payment.

[20] Rev Rul. 75-303, 1975-2 C.B. 87.

[21] § 213(b) and Reg. § 1.213-1(b)(2)(i).

Example 6

F had AGI of $50,000 for 2017 and paid the following medical expenses:

Doctors	$ 500
Dentist	600
Hospital	1,300
Medical insurance premiums	6,000
Medicines and drugs:	
Prescription drugs	300
Nonprescription medicines	150

Assuming F is not reimbursed for any of the medical expenditures during 2017, her medical expense deduction is computed as follows:

Medical insurance premiums	$6,000
Fees paid doctors and dentist	1,100
Hospital costs	1,300
Prescription drugs only	300
Total medical expenses taken into account	$8,700
Less: 10% of $50,000 (AGI)	−5,000
Allowable medical deduction for 2017	$3,700

SPECIAL ITEMS AND EQUIPMENT

The term *medical care* includes not only the diagnosis, treatment, and cure of disease, but the mitigation and prevention of disease as well. Thus, a taxpayer's expenditures for special items such as contact lenses, eyeglasses, hearing aids, artificial teeth or limbs, and ambulance hire would also qualify as medical expenditures.[22] Similarly, the cost of special equipment (e.g., wheelchairs and special controls or other equipment installed in an auto for use by a physically handicapped person) purchased *primarily* for the prevention or alleviation of a physical or mental defect or illness will be allowed as medical deductions. If the purchase of special equipment qualifies as a medical expenditure, the cost of its operation and maintenance is also a deductible medical expense.[23]

Capital expenditures generally are not deductible for Federal income tax purposes (i.e., depreciation is allowed only for property or equipment used in a taxpayer's trade or business or other income-producing activity). However, if a capital expenditure would otherwise qualify as a medical expense (i.e., it is incurred primarily for medical care), it will not be disqualified as a deduction. If the capital expenditure is for the permanent improvement or betterment of property such as the taxpayer's home, *only* the amount of the expenditure which *exceeds* the increase in value of the property improved will qualify as a medical expense.[24]

Example 7

After suffering a heart attack, T is advised by his physician to install an elevator in his residence rather than continue climbing the stairs. If the cost of installing the elevator is $18,000 and the increase in the value of his residence is determined to be only $7,000, the difference of $11,000 will be deductible by T as a medical expense in the year paid. Annual operating costs (i.e., utilities) and maintenance of the elevator also qualify as deductible medical expenses.

---

[22] Reg. § 1.213-1(e)(1)(ii). The IRS has ruled that the costs to acquire, train, and maintain a dog that assists a blind or deaf taxpayer are deductible medical expenses (see Rev. Rul. 55-216, 1955-1 C.B. 307 and Rev. Rul. 68-295, 1968-1 C.B. 92). In the Committee Reports for the Technical and Miscellaneous Revenue Act of 1988, Congress indicated its approval of this IRS position and stated that similar costs incurred with respect to a dog *or* other service animal used to assist individuals with *other physical disabilities* would also be eligible for the medical expense deduction.

[23] *Supra*, Footnote 7.

[24] Reg. § 1.213-1(e)(1)(iii).

In two specific situations, any increase in value of the improved property is ignored (or deemed to be zero) for purposes of measuring the medical expense deduction. First, if permanent improvements are made to property *rented* by the taxpayer, the *entire* costs are deductible (subject to the 10% floor).[25] Likewise, the entire cost of certain home-related capital expenditures incurred by a physically handicapped individual qualifies as a medical expense. Qualifying costs include expenditures for (1) constructing entrance or exit ramps to the residence; (2) widening doorways at entrances or exits to the residence; (3) widening or otherwise modifying hallways and interior doorways to accommodate wheelchairs; (4) railings, support bars, or other modifications to bathrooms to accommodate handicapped individuals; (5) lowering of or other modifications to kitchen cabinets and equipment to accommodate access by handicapped individuals; and (6) adjustment of electrical outlets and fixtures.

SPECIAL CARE FACILITIES

Expenses paid for emergency room treatment or hospital care of the taxpayer, his or her spouse, or dependents qualify for the medical deduction.[26] However, the deductibility of expenses for care in an institution other than a hospital depends upon the medical condition of the individual *and* the nature of the services he or she receives. If the *principal reason* an individual is in an institution (such as a nursing home or special school) is the availability of medical care, the *entire cost* of the medical care qualifies as a medical expenditure. This includes the cost of meals and lodging as well as any tuition expenses of special schools.[27]

Example 8

T enrolled his dependent son, S, in a special school for children with hearing impairments. If the principal reason for S's attendance at the school is his medical condition *and* the institution has the resources to treat or supervise training of the hearing impaired, the entire cost of S's attendance at the school qualifies as a medical expense. This includes tuition, meals and lodging, and any other costs that are incidental to the special services furnished by the school.

If an individual's medical condition *is not* the principal reason for being in an institution, only that part of the cost of care in the institution which is attributable to medical care will qualify as a medical expense.[28]

Example 9

T placed her dependent father, F, in a nursing home after F suffered a stroke and partial paralysis. Of the $6,000 total nursing home expenses, only $2,500 is attributable to the medical care and nursing attention furnished to F. If F is not in the nursing home for the principal reason of the medical and nursing care, only $2,500 will be deductible by T.

---

[25] Rev. Rul. 70-395, 1970-2 C.B. 65.

[26] This includes the cost of meals and lodging incurred as an in-patient of a hospital. See Reg. § 1.213-1(e)(1)(v).

[27] Reg. § 1.213-1(e)(1)(v)(a). See also *Donald R. Pfeifer,* 37 TCM 817, T.C. Memo 1978-189; *W.B. Counts,* 42

T.C 755 (1963); Rev. Rul. 78-340, 1978-2 C.B. 124; and Rev. Rul. 58-533, 1958-2 C. B. 108.

[28] Reg. § 1.213-1(e)(1)(v)(b). This *excludes* meals and lodging and any other expenses not directly attributable to the medical care or treatment.

THE COSTS OF LONG-TERM CARE, ASSISTED LIVING, AND MORE

As life expectancy increases and the population ages, more and more people need long-term care. Costs of long-term care include expenses not only for medicine and medical treatment but also a variety of services. Many of these help the individual to perform the basic personal tasks of everyday life, tasks that most take for granted. For example, someone may require help getting dressed; taking the right medications at the right time and in the correct amount; taking a shower; combing their hair, going to the bathroom; preparing meals; managing money, driving to the grocery or the drug store or walking anywhere. Long term care is not intended as a cure but is chronic care that a person may need for life. A person may receive the care at home, a nursing home or another long term care facility (see discussion in Exhibit 11-3). According to one government report, 41% of long term care is provided to people under age 65 who need help taking care of themselves. This may due to a car accident, a sports injury, or disabling events such as strokes, brain tumors or diseases such as Parkinson's or multiple sclerosis.[29]

For many years, it was unclear whether the cost of long-term care qualified as a medical expense. The IRS often challenged such costs as personal and denied their deduction. However, in 1996, the definition of medical expenses was broadened to include so-called qualified long-term care services that are provided to a chronically ill individual.[30]

Qualified long-term care services generally include necessary diagnostic, preventive, therapeutic, curing, treating, mitigating and rehabilitative services, and maintenance or personal care services that are (1) required by a chronically-ill individual and (2) are provided according to a plan of care prescribed by a licensed health care practitioner. A person is considered chronically ill only if, within the previous 12 months, a licensed health care practitioner has certified that the person (1) cannot perform at least two activities of daily living (e.g., eating, toileting, transferring, bathing, dressing, and continence) for a period of at least 90 days due to a loss of functional capacity or requires substantial supervision to be protected from threats to health and safety due to severe cognitive impairment. Most of these services are likely to be provided by an assisted living facility. Exhibit 11-3 provides a brief description of what are considered the major types of long-term care living arrangements.

Example 10

D's 90-year-old mother, M, suffers from Alzheimer's disease and had to move to assisted living (not a nursing home). Her doctor certified that she could not bathe, dress or feed herself due to the disease and authorized a personal aide to help her. When M bathed, her aide helped her in and out of the bathtub. The aide also prepared M's daily medications. The help provided to M by her aide would qualify as a qualified long-term care service. M is considered a chronically ill individual since she cannot perform three activities of daily living (bathing, feeding, and dressing) for at least 90 days due to her dementia. In addition, as required, the services were prescribed by her doctor.

The amount deductible for insurance premiums is subject to limitations, but also is adjusted annually for inflation. The limits for 2017 are as follows:

Age before Close of Tax Year	Limitation
40 or less	$ 410
More than 40 but less than 50	770
More than 50 but less than 60	1,530
More than 60 but less than 70	4,090
More than 70	5,110

Amounts paid to relatives for long-term care services normally are not eligible for deduction unless such person is a licensed professional with respect to the services that he or she is providing.

---

[29] https://www.ltcfeds.com/start/aboutltc_whatis.html.   [30] § 7702B(c).

In addition, § 7702B allows an income exclusion for long-term care benefits received by an individual. For 2017, the exclusion from gross income is the greater of $360 per day or the actual cost of the care.

EXHIBIT 11-3	**Medical Expenses for Long-Term Care**

There are several different types of long-term care and housing arrangements. The costs of these can be significant and in many cases result in medical expenses far exceeding 10% of the individual's AGI, an AGI that is typically lower for elderly individuals. Moreover, if a caregiver (e.g., a child) bears some of these costs, he or she may be able to deduct the costs as explained above. The tax treatment generally varies depending on the type of services that these arrangements provide. Many make the mistake that only the costs of nursing homes are deductible but the costs of other arrangements may be deductible. This exhibit provides an overview. The terminology is useful in appreciating the tax treatment.

Independent Living: communities that cater to seniors who are very independent with few, if any, medical problems and need only limited assistance. Residents live in fully equipped (e.g., full kitchen) private apartments and rent covers utilities, maintenance, 1 to 3 restaurant-style, chef prepared meals in a community dining room. They provide exercise programs, weekly social activities (cards, bingo, movies, pickle-ball), transportation for shopping, medical, and offsite activities. These are also known as retirement communities, retirement homes, or senior housing. Generally, there is no fee or cost associated with medical care that is deductible. But see discussion below on fees for assisted living that may be present in some independent living arrangements.

Assisted Living: housing for the elderly and those unable to live safely by themselves. According to a national study of long-term care providers, there are more than 700,000 seniors living in over 22,000 assisted living facilities nationwide. These facilities routinely provide lifestyle activities, and transportation as well as assistance with medications and activities of daily living (e.g., bathing or eating). Residents live in private apartments which include a limited kitchen area but three meals per day normally are provided in a central dining room. Staff is available 24 hours per day for additional safety (e.g., falls, black-outs, other emergencies). Most assisted living communities provide licensed nursing services onsite. Assisted living is a "private pay" environment not covered by Medicare and Medicaid. For a one-bedroom apartment the median cost is about $3,500 per month. Most costs are not deductible. However, if the resident is chronically ill and in the facility primarily for medical care according to a certified care plan from a licensed health care practitioner, then the room and board may be considered part of the medical care and the cost may be deductible, just as it would be in a hospital. The individual must be unable to perform at least two activities of daily living, such as bathing, dressing, or eating. In addition, if an individual is receiving substantial medical care, is in a special needs unit, or is in dementia or care (e.g., cannot live safely by themselves due to Alzheimer's disease) some costs would be deductible. If the resident is in the assisted living facility for custodial and not medical care, the costs are deductible only to a limited extent. Residents who are not chronically ill and do not qualify for the deduction of long-term care costs may still deduct the portion of their expenses that are attributable to medical care, including entrance or initiation fees or annual or monthly fees. The assisted living facility is responsible for providing residents with information as to what portion of fees is attributable to medical costs.

Home Health Care: Living support and care at various levels provided at home by licensed or unlicensed workers as well as designated family members. Home health care is primarily private pay, but Medicare and Medicaid will reimburse some forms of "medically necessary" home health services provided by licensed practitioners for people meeting eligibility requirements. Private pay is accepted and will cover a wider variety of medical and non-medical services.

Nursing Homes: Provide around-the-clock nursing care from licensed nurses for the frail elderly who require a high level of medical care and assistance. Many nursing homes now provide short-term rehabilitative stays for those recovering from an injury (e.g., falls), illness or surgery. Long-term care residents generally have high care needs and complex medical conditions that require routine skilled nursing services. Residents typically share a room and are served meals in a central dining area unless they are too ill to participate. Activities are also available. Some facilities have a separate unit for Alzheimer's residents. Nursing homes are primarily used for medical care, and medical care is always deductible.

MEDICAL TRAVEL AND TRANSPORTATION

Expenses paid for transportation to and from the office of a doctor or dentist or to a hospital or clinic usually are deductible as medical expenses. This includes amounts paid for bus, taxi, train, and plane fares, as well as the out-of-pocket expenses for use of the taxpayer's personal vehicle (i.e., gas and oil, parking fees, and tolls). If the taxpayer uses his or her personal automobile for medical transportation and does not want to calculate actual expenses, the IRS allows a deduction. For 2017, the deduction is 17 cents a mile *plus* parking fees and tolls paid while traveling for medical treatment.[31]

Travel costs include *only* transportation expenses and the cost of lodging. For these expenses to qualify as a medical deduction, a trip beyond the taxpayer's locale *must* be "primarily for and essential to medical care."[32] Meal costs are deductible only if provided by a hospital or similar institution as a necessary part of medical care. Thus, meals consumed while en route between the taxpayer's home and the location of the medical care are not deductible.

If an individual receives medical treatment as an outpatient at a clinic or doctor's office, the cost of lodging while in the new locality may be deductible—but not the cost of meals. The cost of lodging will qualify as a medical expense if (1) the lodging is not lavish or extravagant under the circumstances; and (2) there is no significant element of personal pleasure, recreation, or vacation in the travel away from home. If deductible, the amount of lodging costs includible as a medical expense may not exceed *$50* for *each night* for each individual.[33] It is important to note that travel costs of a companion (including parents or a nurse) are included as medical expenses if the individual requiring medical treatment could not travel alone, or if the companion rendered medical treatment en route.[34] Thus, the lodging costs of such a person while in the new locality should also be treated as a part of any medical expenses (subject to the $50 per night per person limitation).

Example 11

At the advice of a doctor, T travels with his three-year-old daughter, D, from Lincoln, Nebraska to Houston, Texas. D has a rare blood disease and a hospital in Houston is the nearest facility specializing in treatment of her disorder. The transportation costs and lodging for both T and his daughter while en route to and from Houston are deductible. If they stay at a nearby hotel while D receives treatment as an outpatient, the costs of lodging (but not meals) incurred in Houston—up to $100 per night—are also deductible.

MEDICAL INSURANCE COSTS AND REIMBURSEMENTS

Amounts paid for medical care insurance for the taxpayer, his or her spouse, and dependents qualify as medical expenses. If premiums are paid under an insurance contract which offers coverage beyond medical care (e.g., coverage for loss of life, limb, or sight, or loss of income), only the portion of the premiums paid that is attributable to medical care is deductible. To be deductible, however, the medical care portion of the premiums paid must either be separately stated in the contract itself, or included in a separate bill or statement from the insurer.[35]

---

[31] Notice 2016-79, 2016-169 IRB 918.

[32] See § 213(d)(2), Reg. § 1.213-1(e)(1)(iv), and *Comm. v. Bilder,* 62-1 USTC ¶9440, 9 AFTR2d 1355, 369 U.S. 499 (USSC, 1962).

[33] § 213(d)(2).

[34] See Rev. Rul. 75-317, 1975-2 C.B. 57.

[35] Reg. § 1.213-1(e)(4). Participants in the Federal Medicare program are entitled to treat as medical care insurance premiums the amounts withheld for voluntary doctor-bill insurance.

Taxpayers receiving reimbursements for medical expenses in the *same year* in which the expenses were paid must reduce any medical expense deduction to a net amount. However, if the reimbursement is for medical expenses in a prior year, the income tax treatment of the reimbursement depends upon whether the taxpayer claimed a medical expense deduction for the year in which the expenses were actually paid. If no medical expense deduction was taken in the year in which the expenses were paid (e.g., taxpayer used the standard deduction or total medical expenses did not exceed the required percentage of AGI), any reimbursement for such expenses will not be included in gross income. If the taxpayer claimed a deduction for the medical expenses in the prior year, however, the reimbursement must be included in gross income to the extent of the *lesser* of: (1) the previous medical expense deduction, or (2) the excess of the taxpayer's itemized deductions over his or her standard deduction. The inclusion in gross income of all or a part of the reimbursement is in accordance with the tax benefit rule.

Example 12

T had AGI of $30,000 for 2017. During the year, T paid the following medical expenses:

Hospitalization insurance premiums	$ 2,650
Doctor and dental bills	800
Eyeglasses	175
Medical transportation	25
Total medical expenses	$ 3,650

T's medical expense deduction is computed as follows:

Total medical expenses	$ 3,650
Less: 10% of $30,000 AGI	– 3,000
Medical expense deduction for 2017	$ 650

T's itemized deductions (including the $650 medical expense deduction) for 2017 exceeded his standard deduction by $1,500. In 2018, T received $400 as a reimbursement from his insurance company. T must include the *entire* $400 in gross income for 2018. If T had received the $400 reimbursement in 2017, his medical expense deduction would have been limited to $250.

Example 13

Assume the same facts as in *Example 12* except that the medical expense reimbursement was $900 instead of $400. If the reimbursement was received in 2018, T would be required to include only $650 in gross income—the amount of the medical expenses included in his itemized deductions. If the amount by which T's itemized deductions exceeded his standard deduction was *less* than $650 for 2017, he would include in gross income for 2018 only so much of the reimbursement represented by the prior year's itemized deductions in excess of the standard deduction amount. However, if T had used the standard deduction in 2017, none of the $900 reimbursement would be included in 2018 gross income because T received no tax benefit in 2017.

The situations illustrated in *Examples 12* and *13* occur quite often because taxpayers are *not required* to reduce a current year's medical expense deduction by *anticipated* insurance reimbursements. Notice that this can result in a taxpayer receiving reimbursements early in the next tax year and not being required to pay income taxes on the reimbursement until April 15 of the following year.

HEALTH SAVINGS ACCOUNTS AND MEDICAL SAVINGS ACCOUNTS

Over the years, Congress has taken several steps to make health care more affordable. Chief among these was the creation of Health Savings Accounts (HSAs).[36] These accounts enable individuals to pay for unreimbursed medical expenses on a before tax basis. For those familiar with flexible spending accounts for medical expenses (now used by many employers and their employees), HSAs are virtually identical without the use it or lose it rule. For those familiar with Individual Retirement Accounts, HSAs are quite similar.

Example 14

In 2017, H set up an HSA for his family. H can contribute up to $6,750 to the HSA and claim the amount as a deduction for AGI. Any amounts withdrawn from the account that are used to pay for medical expenses are nontaxable. As a result, income funneled through HSAs to pay medical expenses is never subject to tax. Amounts not withdrawn from the HSA can earn income and such income normally is not taxable as long as it remains in the account or is withdrawn to pay medical expenses. In order to obtain this favorable tax treatment, H has a health insurance policy that meets several requirements. The policy has a high "deductible," meaning that he must pay for the first $2,600 of medical expenses incurred by his family (i.e., the individual must report medical expenses to the plan and pay $2,600 before the insurance starts paying). The policy also limits the total costs that H could incur to $13,100 thus providing his family with catastrophic protection. Most importantly for H, because the plan has such a high deductible, the cost of the plan is much less than most and he is able to afford coverage that he otherwise might not be able obtain.

Congress first introduced the forerunner of HSAs in 1996 as an experiment, restricting both the number that could be created and those who were eligible to use them. After a lukewarm reception, a bipartisan effort expanded the concept and created HSAs which debuted in 2004. HSAs are becoming an important tool in the fight against the rising costs of health care.[37] The plans are intended to hold down costs by giving consumers a tax incentive to shop for the best price for health services and to forgo procedures they do not need. At this point, it is difficult to determine whether this theory will work. However, recent reports suggest that there is growing interest in HSAs as more and more employers are offering them to their employees in lieu of traditional plans.[38] As interest in HSAs grow, interest in MSAs has dropped. For this reason, the following discussion focuses on HSAs.

Section 223 permits individuals to deduct for AGI a limited amount of contributions to an HSA. Similarly, § 106(b) allows individuals to exclude limited contributions to such accounts made on their behalf by their employers. Amounts contributed to the HSA may be invested and the earnings are nontaxable. Distributions from the account are nontaxable as long as they are used for medical expenses that normally would be deductible under § 213 other than those for health insurance.

Note that no deduction is allowed for expenses paid for with dollars out of the HSA. However, the deduction for amounts *contributed* and the exclusion for amounts distributed essentially provide the same benefit. The end result of these rules effectively enables an individual to pay for medical expenses not covered by insurance with dollars that have never been subject to tax. Observe that if the taxpayer pays for unreimbursed medical expenses using dollars that do not come from the HSA, they normally are not deductible due to the 10% limitation. In such case, the payments are effectively made with after-tax dollars.

---

[36] See §§ 220 and 223.

[37] MSAs are available only to employees of certain small businesses and to self-employed persons and the number of MSAs were restricted. HSAs are available to all individuals and the required health plan is far more flexible.

[38] Individuals covered by other medical insurance plans are not eligible for HSAs.

Example 15

Assume M is in the 30% tax bracket with an AGI of $60,000. He is covered by health insurance that pays for most but not all of his medical expenses. During the year, M contributed $1,000 to an HSA. Later during the year he withdrew the entire $1,000 to pay for medical expenses related to knee surgery that were not covered by his insurance. As shown by the following analysis (ignoring exemptions and the standard deduction and assuming M itemized deductions), by using an HSA, M saves $300, the tax that otherwise would have been paid on the amounts used to pay for the unreimbursed medical expenses.

	Employee Pays	HSA Pays	
Income	$60,000	$60,000	
Deduction for contribution to HSA	0	(1,000)	
Adjusted gross income	$60,000	$59,000	
Medical expense deduction ($1,000 – [10% × $60,000])	0	0	
Income	$60,000	$59,000	
Tax @ 30%	(18,000)	(17,700)	
Cost of medical expense	(1,000)	0	(HSA pays)
After-tax income	$41,000	$41,300	

Another advantage of contributions provided by an employer to an HSA is that they are not subject to FICA or FUTA taxes.

Penalty for Distributions Not Used for Medical Expenses

If the taxpayer withdraws amounts from the HSA and uses them for something other than qualified medical expenses before age 65 (or death or disability), a penalty equal to 20% of the amount withdrawn is imposed. Amounts withdrawn after age 65 are not subject to penalty but will be taxed as ordinary income to the extent they are not used to pay for medical expenses.

Eligible Individuals

HSAs may be established only by eligible individuals. A person is eligible if he or she is:

- Covered under a high deductible health plan (HDHP). A HDHP is a plan that for 2017 has an annual deductible of at least $1,300 and an annual limitation on out-of-pocket expenses (other health care premiums) not greater than $6,550. These limits are doubled to $2,600 and $13,100 for family coverage.[39]

- Not covered by any other health care plan that is not an HDHP.

- Not eligible for Medicare (i.e., has not reached the age of 65).

- Not claimed as a dependent on another person's tax return.

---

[39] Rev. Proc. 2016-28, 2016-20 IRB 852.

Deductible Contributions

In 2017, annual contributions to HSA are generally limited to $3,400 for singles and $6,750 for families. Individuals from age 55–64 are entitled to make "catch-up" contributions up to $1,000.

EXHIBIT 11-4	Health Savings Accounts High Deductible Health Plan (HDHP) Requirements and Contribution Limitations 2017		
		Individual	*Family*
	Minimum deductible.	$1,300	$ 2,600
	Maximum out-of-pocket expenses	6,550	13,100
	Maximum contribution deduction.	3,400	6,750

Treatment of HSAs at Death

If the taxpayer dies before using the amount in the HSA, the treatment of the balance for both income tax and estate tax purposes depends on who is the beneficiary of the account.[40]

- *Surviving spouse as beneficiary.* If the surviving spouse is the beneficiary, the surviving spouse has no income and treats the account as his or her own.

- *Beneficiary other than surviving spouse.* If the surviving spouse is not the beneficiary but another person is the beneficiary (e.g., a son or daughter), the account stops being an HSA, and the beneficiary must include in taxable income the fair market value of the HSA in the year of the owner's death. Such person would be able to exclude from gross income the amount of any qualified medical expenses for the decedent that are paid by the beneficiary within one year after the date of death as well as deduct any estate taxes that may be paid that are attributable to such amounts.

- *Estate.* If no beneficiary is named or the estate is the beneficiary, the value of the HSA is included on the decedent's final income tax return; however, such amount is not reduced by final medical expenses of the decedent paid after death.

Upon death, any balance in the HSA is included in the decedent's gross estate subject to estate taxes. Such amount would be subject to estate taxes unless it passes to the surviving spouse and therefore, qualifies for the marital deduction.

Recordkeeping and Filing Requirements

Taxpayers with HSAs must file Form 8889 with their Form 1040 if there was any activity in the HSA during the year. Activity includes both distributions (e.g., to pay medical expenses) as well as contributions by the taxpayer or spouse or the employer of either. In addition, HSA owners must keep records sufficient to show that (1) any distributions were used exclusively for qualified medical expenses; (2), the qualified medical expenses had not been previously paid or reimbursed from another source; and (3) the medical expenses had not been taken as an itemized deduction in any year.

---

[40] § 223(f)(8).

HEALTH INSURANCE COSTS OF SELF-EMPLOYED TAXPAYERS

Self-employed individuals are allowed to treat the amounts paid for health insurance on behalf of a self-employed individual, his or her spouse, and dependents as a deductible business expense.[41] A more-than-two-percent owner-employee of S Corp. stock can deduct 100% of the amount paid for medical insurance for himself, spouse and dependents [§ 162(l)(5)]. The deduction is allowed in determining AGI (i.e., a deduction *for* AGI) rather than being treated as an itemized medical expense deduction subject to the 10% floor. No deduction is allowable to the extent it *exceeds* the taxpayer's net earnings from self-employment.[42] Thus, the deduction cannot create a loss. More important, the deduction does not reduce the income base for which the taxpayer is liable for self-employment taxes.

Example 16

K, a self-employed individual, paid $2,600 for health insurance for himself, his wife, and their two children. K had no employees during the year. K is entitled to deduct the entire $2,600 in determining AGI, provided the deduction does not exceed his net earnings from self-employment, and his AGI before the deduction is at least $2,600.[43]

Absent a special rule, self-employed individuals who are also employees might be tempted to opt out of an employer-provided medical insurance plan. By so doing, the 10% floor on medical expenses could be avoided and taxpayers could deduct a portion of what normally would be nondeductible premium payments. To prevent this course of action, the deduction is not allowed if a self-employed individual or spouse is eligible to participate in a health insurance plan of an employer.[44]

Personal Casualty and Theft Losses

As discussed in Chapter 10, Congress has provided for a deduction of losses related to property used for *personal* purposes where the loss arises from fire, storm, shipwreck, or other casualty, or theft.[45] Like the medical expense deduction, the deduction for personal casualty and theft losses is designed to provide relief for only extraordinary losses. Thus, an individual taxpayer's deduction for personal casualty and theft losses is allowed only to the extent such losses exceed $100 per occurrence *and* the sum of all losses (after reduction by the $100 floor) for a given tax year exceeds 10% of the taxpayer's AGI. These deduction limitations were discussed and illustrated in Chapter 10.

YEAR DEDUCTIBLE

A personal casualty loss is generally deductible in the taxable year in which the loss occurs. Recall, however, that a theft loss is deductible only in the year of discovery. If a claim for insurance reimbursement (or any other potential recovery) exists and there is a reasonable prospect of recovery, the loss must be reduced by the amount *expected* to be received.[46] If later receipts are *less* than the amount originally estimated and no further reimbursement is expected, an amended return is not filed. Instead, the remaining loss is deductible in the year in which no further reimbursement is expected. Most important, if the casualty loss deduction claimed in the prior year was reduced by the $100 floor and exceeded the 10% AGI limitation, the remaining loss is not further reduced. However, the remaining loss is subject to the 10% limitation of the later year.[47]

---

[41] § 162(l).

[42] § 162(l)(2)(A).

[43] § 162(l)(3).

[44] § 162(l)(2)(B).

[45] § 165(c)(3) Special rules apply to casualties and thefts occurring in Federally declared disaster areas.

[46] Reg. § 1.165-1(d)(2)(i).

[47] See *Example 9* of Chapter 10.

REPORTING CASUALTY LOSSES

Individual taxpayers are required to report and compute casualty losses on Form 4684,[48] which is to be filed with Form 1040. The casualty loss deduction, if any, is reported with other itemized deductions on Schedule A, Form 1040.

Code § 164 is the statutory authority that permits taxpayers to deduct several types of taxes for Federal income tax purposes. If the taxes are related to an individual taxpayer's trade or business or income-producing activity, the deduction is generally allowed in arriving at AGI. However, both the IRS and the courts have taken the position that state, local, and foreign *income* taxes are deductible by an individual taxpayer *from* his or her AGI—even though it could be argued that such taxes are related to his or her trade or business. Likewise, if *property* taxes are related to personal use property (e.g., residence, car, etc.), such taxes are generally deductible only if the individual itemizes his or her deductions. If taxes are deductible by taxpayers other than individuals, the deductions simply reduce gross income to taxable income.[49]

The types of taxes specifically allowed as deductions under § 164 are

1. State, local, and foreign real property taxes;
2. State and local personal property taxes;
3. State and local general sales taxes;
4. State, local, and foreign income, war profits, and excess profit taxes; and
5. The generation-skipping transfer tax.[50]

The generation-skipping transfer tax is imposed on income distributions from certain trusts. Discussion of this tax is beyond the scope of this text. However, each of the other types of deductible taxes is discussed in detail below.

GENERAL REQUIREMENTS FOR DEDUCTIBILITY

A tax is deductible *only* if (1) it is imposed on the taxpayer's income or property; and (2) it is paid or incurred by the taxpayer in the taxable year for which a deduction is being claimed. Even if these two requirements are met, deductions for certain Federal, state, and local taxes are expressly denied. Exhibit 11-5 contains a list of nondeductible taxes.

In addition to the nondeductible taxes listed in Exhibit 11-5, deductions for *fees* (whether or not labeled as taxes) paid by taxpayers usually are denied *unless* the fees are incurred in the taxpayer's trade or business or for the production of income. Fees paid or incurred in connection with a trade or business, if ordinary and necessary, are deductible as business expenses under § 162. Similarly, fees related to the production of income generally are deductible expenses under § 212.[51]

LO.3

Distinguish between deductible taxes and nondeductible fees or other charges.

---

[48] See Appendix B for a sample of this form.

[49] See the later section in this chapter entitled "Reporting Deductions for Taxes."

[50] § 164(a).

[51] See Chapter 7 for a discussion of the requirements that must be met in order to deduct business and nonbusiness expenses of this nature.

EXHIBIT 11-5	Nondeductible Taxes[52]

Nondeductible federal taxes:

    Federal income taxes (including those withheld from an individual's pay)

    Social Security or railroad retirement taxes withheld from an individual by his or her employer (includes self-employment taxes)

    Social Security and other employment taxes paid on the wages of the taxpayer's employee who performed domestic or other personal services

    Federal excise taxes or customs duties unless they are connected with the taxpayer's business or income-producing activity

    Federal estate and gift taxes

Nondeductible state and local taxes:

    Motor vehicle taxes (unless they qualify as *ad valorem* taxes on personal property)

    Inheritance, legacy, succession, or estate taxes

    Gift taxes

    Per capita or poll taxes

    Cigarette, tobacco, liquor, beer, wine, etc. taxes

The IRS distinguishes a "tax" from a "fee" by looking to the *purpose* of the charge.[53] If a particular charge is imposed upon the taxpayer for the purpose of *raising revenue* to be used for public or government purposes, the IRS will consider the charge to be a tax. However, if the charge is imposed because of either *particular acts or services* received by the taxpayer, such charge will be considered as a *fee*. Thus, fees for driver's licenses, vehicle registration and inspection, license tags for pets, hunting and fishing licenses, tolls for bridges and roads, parking meter deposits, water bills, sewer and other service charges, and postage fees are not deductible *unless* related to the taxpayer's trade or business, or income-producing activity.[54]

Since most individual taxpayers use the cash receipts and disbursements method of accounting for tax purposes, the following discussion of income and property tax deductions concentrates on cash-basis taxpayers and the requirement that taxes be *paid* in the year of deduction. Bear in mind throughout this discussion, however, that accrual method taxpayers are allowed a deduction for taxes in the tax year in which the obligation for payment becomes fixed and determinable (i.e., the all-events test is met).

INCOME TAXES

LO.4

Explain the rules regarding deductible state income taxes.

Most state, local, or foreign income taxes paid or accrued by a taxpayer are deductible in arriving at taxable income. For individual taxpayers, however, a deduction for state and local income taxes is allowed only if the taxpayer itemizes his or her deductions. Furthermore, as explained below, in lieu of deducting state and local income taxes, taxpayers can deduct state and local sales taxes (i.e., deduct either but not both).

Although the income taxes may be related solely to the individual's business income (e.g., income from a sole proprietorship or partnership), or income from rents and royalties, these taxes are considered personal in nature. Since income taxes paid to a foreign country or a U.S. possession may either be deducted as an itemized deduction or claimed as a credit against the U.S. income tax, an individual who does not itemize deductions should elect to claim foreign income taxes as credits.[55]

---

[52] See § 275, Reg. § 1.164-2, and *Your Federal Income Tax,* IRS Publication 17 (Rev. 2015), pp. 147-151.

[53] See § 275 and Reg. § 1.164-2.

[54] *Your Federal Income Tax,* IRS Publication 17 (Rev. 2015), pp. 147-151.

[55] § 27.

Cash-basis taxpayers are allowed to deduct state and local income taxes *paid* during the taxable year, including those taxes imposed on interest income that is exempt from Federal income taxation. Amounts considered paid during the taxable year include:

1. State and local income or foreign taxes withheld from an individual's salary by his or her employer;
2. Estimated payments made by the taxpayer under a pay-as-you-go requirement of a taxing authority; and
3. Payments made in the current year on an income tax liability of a prior year.

Example 17

During 2017, Z, a cash basis taxpayer, had $1,500 of Illinois state income taxes withheld by her employer. In 2017, she paid the remaining $450 in state income taxes due on her 2016 Illinois tax return, and also paid $300 in estimated state income tax payments during 2017. If Z itemizes her deductions for Federal income tax purposes, she is entitled to a $2,250 ($1,500 + $300 + $450) state income tax deduction for 2017.

If a cash basis taxpayer receives a refund of state, local, or foreign income taxes in the current year, the refund must be included in the current year's gross income to the extent a deduction in an earlier tax year provided a tax benefit.[56]

Example 18

Assume the same facts as in *Example 17*. While preparing her 2017 Illinois state income tax return in early 2018, Z determined she had overpaid the state tax liability by $375. She received a refund of the entire overpayment on August 10, 2018. If Z claimed the total $2,250 state income taxes paid as a deduction on her 2017 Federal income tax return and her itemized deductions exceeded the standard deduction amount by at least $375, she must include the entire refund in gross income on her 2018 Federal income tax return.

In determining the amount of the refund that must be included in income, the IRS further explains that the amount is limited to the excess of the tax deducted for the year over the state and local sales taxes that the taxpayer chose not to deduct for that same year.[57]

Example 19

In preparing his 2016 income tax return, H elected to deduct $12,000 of state income tax instead of $11,000 of state sales tax. During 2017, H received a refund of his state income tax of $2,500. The amount of state income tax refund that H must include in gross income for 2017 is $1,000 ($12,000 – $11,000) since he could have deducted the state sales tax.

---

[56] § 111. Special rules apply when married taxpayers file separate state or Federal income tax returns. See *Taxable and Nontaxable Income*, IRS Publication 525 (Rev. 2015), p. 23–26.

[57] These basic rules for inclusion must be modified in several other situations. For example, when a taxpayer receives a state income tax refund for 2016 and the last estimated tax payment of the 2016 state taxes was made in 2017, the portion of the refund attributable to the 2017 payment reduces the deduction for state income taxes.

DEDUCTION FOR STATE AND LOCAL GENERAL SALES TAX

Taxpayers are currently allowed to deduct state and local sales and use taxes instead of state and local income taxes.[58] The sales tax deduction was eliminated in 1986 but was resurrected in 2004 when states without income taxes but high sales taxes wanted equitable treatment. Congress made the provision permanent in 2015.

The sales tax deduction is classified as an itemized deduction but not a miscellaneous itemized deduction. It is subject to the itemized deduction cutback discussed in a later part of this chapter. In addition, the deduction for state and local sales and use taxes is not allowed for alternative minimum tax purposes.

Only "general" sales taxes are deductible. Section 164(b)(5)(B) defines a general sales tax as a tax imposed at one rate with respect to the sale at retail of a broad range of classes of item. In determining whether a tax is a "general" sales tax, the fact that it does not apply to food, clothing, medical supplies, and motor vehicles, or applies at a different rate is disregarded. If other items are taxed at a different rate, such taxes are not deductible. If the rate of tax on a motor vehicle exceeds the general rate, the excess is disregarded. If the amount of the general sales tax is separately stated, to the extent it is paid by the consumer, the amount is treated as a tax imposed on and paid by the consumer.

Taxpayers may deduct their actual sales taxes as substantiated by accumulated receipts or use IRS-published tables. These tables are contained in Appendix A of this text. The tables take into account the number of exemptions, "available" income (AGI increased by any tax-exempt income such as Social Security and tax-exempt interest) and rates of state and local general sales taxation. Since sales tax rates vary from state to state (and even by localities within a state), there are 51 different tables for the 50 states and the District of Columbia. The tables extend to available income as high as $200,000.

The tables include only general *state* sales taxes and do not include any additional *local sales taxes*. Another table may be used to determine the amount of local sales taxes that may be added to the table amount. In addition to the amount determined using the tables, taxpayers may add the taxes on cars, motorcycles, motor homes, recreational vehicles, sport utility vehicles, trucks, vans, and off-road vehicles, aircraft, boats, homes (including mobile and prefabricated), or home-building materials, if the tax rate was the same as the general sales tax rate. Tax commentators have suggested that the sales taxes on other high-priced unusual purchases such as expensive furniture, high-definition plasma televisions or the like arguably could be added. However, the IRS limits the additions to those noted above.[59] Special rules apply when a taxpayer lives in more than one state during the year. A portion of the tables appears below.

2016 Optional State and Certain Local Sales Tax Tables

Income At least	But less than	Exemptions 1	2	3	4	5	Over 5	Exemptions 1	2	3	4	5	Over 5	Exemptions 1	2	3	4	5	Over 5
		Alabama			1	4.0000%		Arizona			2	5.6000%		Arkansas			2	6.5000%	
$0	$20,000	223	255	277	294	309	329	231	250	262	271	279	290	314	344	364	378	391	407
$20,000	$30,000	337	384	416	441	462	492	378	408	428	444	456	473	500	549	580	604	624	651
$30,000	$40,000	397	452	489	518	543	577	460	496	520	538	553	574	602	660	698	727	751	783
$40,000	$50,000	449	510	552	584	611	650	532	573	601	622	640	664	690	757	801	834	862	899
$50,000	$60,000	496	562	608	643	673	715	598	644	675	699	718	745	771	846	895	932	962	1004
$60,000	$70,000	538	609	658	697	729	774	658	709	743	769	790	820	844	926	980	1021	1054	1100
$70,000	$80,000	577	653	705	746	780	828	715	770	806	834	857	889	912	1001	1059	1104	1140	1189
$80,000	$90,000	613	693	748	792	827	878	768	827	866	896	921	955	976	1072	1134	1181	1220	1273
$90,000	$100,000	647	732	789	835	872	925	818	881	923	955	981	1017	1037	1138	1204	1255	1296	1352
$100,000	$120,000	693	782	844	892	932	988	887	954	999	1034	1062	1101	1118	1228	1299	1353	1398	1459
$120,000	$140,000	753	849	915	966	1009	1070	977	1051	1100	1138	1169	1212	1225	1345	1423	1483	1532	1599
$140,000	$160,000	808	910	980	1036	1081	1146	1062	1142	1195	1236	1270	1317	1325	1455	1540	1605	1657	1730
$160,000	$180,000	860	967	1041	1100	1148	1217	1141	1227	1284	1328	1364	1414	1418	1558	1649	1718	1774	1852
$180,000	$200,000	908	1021	1099	1160	1211	1283	1217	1308	1369	1416	1454	1507	1507	1656	1752	1826	1886	1969
$200,000	$225,000	959	1077	1159	1223	1277	1352	1297	1394	1458	1508	1549	1605	1600	1758	1861	1939	2003	2091
$225,000	$250,000	1014	1138	1223	1291	1347	1426	1383	1486	1555	1608	1651	1712	1701	1868	1978	2061	2129	2223
$250,000	$275,000	1065	1195	1284	1355	1413	1496	1465	1574	1647	1703	1749	1812	1796	1973	2089	2177	2249	2348
$275,000	$300,000	1114	1249	1342	1415	1477	1563	1545	1659	1736	1794	1843	1910	1887	2074	2196	2288	2364	2468
$300,000	or more	1409	1573	1687	1777	1852	1958	2027	2176	2275	2351	2413	2500	2439	2681	2839	2959	3057	3192

---

[58] See § 165(b)(5). According to the IRS, the sales tax deduction was claimed on approximately 11.2 million tax returns filed in 2006.

[59] § 164(b)(5)(H).

> ### Example 20
>
> A family of four living in Arkansas has available income of $51,800 for 2016. If the election is made to claim a deduction for their general sales taxes rather than state and local income taxes, the family will be allowed a deduction of $1,072 ($932 from the Optional State Sales Tax Table above + $140 from the Local Sales Tax Tables located in Appendix A of this text). If the taxpayers paid a sales tax of $450 on a new truck purchased in 2016, the sales tax table amounts would be increased to $1,522 ($1,072 + $450). Note that the 2016 Optional Sales Tax Tables were used here because the 2017 tables were not available at the publication date of this text.

Since the addition of the sales tax deduction in 2004, the taxpayers in the seven states that do not impose an income tax—Alaska, Florida, Nevada, South Dakota, Texas, Washington, and Wyoming—have an additional itemized deduction. As a result, taxpayers in these states, who may not have been able to itemize their deductions, now may be able to itemize. For taxpayers in the other 43 states, which levy at least some form of state or local income tax, they will be forced to make a decision about whether an election should be made.

PROPERTY TAXES

Personal property taxes paid to a state, local, or foreign government are deductible *only* if they are *ad valorem* taxes.[60] *Ad valorem* taxes are taxes imposed on the *value* of property. Quite often, state and local taxing authorities impose a combination tax and fee on personal property. In such cases, only that portion of the charge based on value of the property will qualify as a deductible tax.[61]

> ### Example 21
>
> State A imposes an annual vehicle registration charge of 60 cents per hundredweight. X, a resident of the state, paid $24 for the registration of his personal automobile. Since this charge is not based on the value of the auto, it is not considered a tax and no deduction is allowed.

> ### Example 22
>
> State B imposes an annual vehicle registration charge of 1% of value plus 50 cents per hundredweight. Y, a resident of the state, owns a personal use automobile having a value of $10,000 and weighing 4,000 pounds. Of the $120 ([1% × $10,000] + [$0.50 × 40 hundredweight]) total registration charge paid by Y, only $100 would be deductible as a personal property tax.

Real property (real estate) taxes are generally deductible only if imposed on property owned by the taxpayer and paid or accrued by the taxpayer in the year the deduction is claimed. If real property taxes are imposed on jointly held real estate, each owner may claim his or her portion of the taxes. For example, if cash basis, married taxpayers file separate Federal income tax returns and real property taxes are imposed on jointly held real estate, each spouse may claim *half* of the taxes paid.

---

[60] § 164(b)(1) and Reg. § 1.164-3(c).

[61] § 164(b)(2)(E). States known to include some *ad valorem* tax as part of auto and boat registration fees are Arizona, California, Colorado, Indiana, Iowa, Maine, Massachusetts, Nevada, New Hampshire, Oklahoma, Washington, and Wyoming.

If real estate is sold during the year, the deduction for real estate taxes *must be apportioned* between the buyer and seller according to the number of days in the year each held the property, regardless of which party actually paid the property taxes.[62] The taxes are apportioned to the seller up to (but not including) the date of sale, and to the buyer beginning with the date of sale.

Example 23

The real property tax year in Colorado County is April 1 to March 31. X, the owner on April 1, 2017 of real property located in Colorado County, sells the real property to Y on June 30, 2017. Y owns the real property from June 30, 2017 through March 31, 2018. The real property tax is $730 for the county's tax year April 1, 2017 to March 31, 2018. For purposes of § 164(a), $180 (90 ÷ 365 × $730 = $180 taxes for April 1, 2017 through June 29, 2017) of the real property tax is treated as imposed on X, the seller. The remaining $550 (275 ÷ 365 × $730 = $550 taxes for June 30, 2017 through March 31, 2017) of such real property tax is treated as imposed on Y, the purchaser.[63]

When both buyer and seller of real property are cash-basis taxpayers and only one of the parties *actually* pays the real property taxes for the period in which both parties owned the property, *each* party to the transaction is entitled to deduct the portion of the real property taxes based on the number of days he or she held the property. As a practical matter, real property taxes are usually allocated during the closing process, and the details are provided in the closing statement for real property sales. A taxpayer need only acquire the closing statement to ascertain the proper allocation and how the sales price has been affected by the allocation.

Unless the actual real property taxes are apportioned between buyer and seller as part of the sale/purchase agreement, adjustments for the taxes must be made to determine the amount realized by the seller, as well as the buyer's cost basis of the property.[64] The treatment of the adjustments depends upon which party actually paid the real estate taxes.

Example 24

Assume that buyer and seller are both cash basis, calendar year taxpayers, and real estate taxes for the entire year are to be paid at the end of the year. Real property is sold on October 1, 2017 for $30,000, and B, the buyer, pays the real estate taxes of $365 on December 31, 2017. The real estate taxes attributable to and deductible by B are $92 (92 ÷ 365 × $365). The remaining $273 ($365 – $92) of the taxes will be apportioned to and deductible by S, the seller. As a result of this apportionment, the seller must increase the amount realized from the sale to $30,273, and the buyer will have an adjusted cost basis for the property of $30,273.

Example 25

Assume the same facts as in *Example 24,* except that the real property taxes are payable in advance for the entire year and that S, the seller, paid $365 in January 2017. The real estate taxes are apportioned in the same manner, and the buyer, B, will be entitled to deduct $92. However, B must adjust his cost basis of the property to $29,908 ($30,000 purchase price – $92 taxes paid by seller). The seller, S, is entitled to deduct $273 of the taxes and reduce his amount realized from the sale to $29,908.

---

[62] § 164(d) and Reg. § 1.164-6(b).

[63] Reg. § 1.164-6(b)(3) Ex. 1.

[64] Reg. § 1.164-6(d); Reg. § 1.1001-1(b); and Reg. § 1.1012-1(b). A similar result should occur if buyer and seller are using different accounting methods.

Real property taxes assessed against local benefits of a kind tending to increase the value of the property assessed (e.g., special assessments for paved streets, street lights, sidewalks, drainage ditches, etc.) are not deductible.[65] Instead, the property owner simply adds the assessed amount paid to his or her cost basis of the property. However, if assessments for local benefits are made for the purpose of maintenance or repair, or for the purpose of meeting interest charges with respect to such benefits, they are deductible.[66] If an assessment is in part for the cost of an improvement and in part for maintenance, repairs or for interest charges, only *that* portion of the tax assessment relating to maintenance, repairs, or interest charges will be deductible. Unless the taxpayer can show the allocation of the amounts assessed for the different purposes, *none* of the amount paid is deductible.[67]

REPORTING DEDUCTIONS FOR TAXES

Deductible state and local taxes are reported on different forms depending on the taxpaying entity claiming the deduction. Corporations report their deductions for these taxes on Form 1120. Fiduciaries (trusts and estates) report deductible taxes on Form 1041. Partnerships and S corporations report deductible taxes on Forms 1065 and 1120S, respectively. Individuals report deductible taxes on Form 1040, but the particular schedule used depends upon whether the taxes are business expenses or personal itemized deductions.

An individual's deduction for taxes (other than income taxes) related to his or her trade or business is reported on Schedule C of Form 1040 (Schedule F for farmers and ranchers). Deductible taxes (other than income taxes) related to rents and royalties are reported on Schedule E. All other deductible taxes, including state and local general sales taxes or state and local income taxes on business income or income from rents or royalties, are reported by an individual taxpayer on Schedule A of Form 1040.

Interest Expense

Interest expense is an amount paid or incurred for the use or forbearance of money.[68] Under the general rule of Code § 163(a), all interest paid or accrued on indebtedness within the taxable year is allowed as a deduction. As with most general rules in the tax law, however, there are limitations imposed on the deduction of certain interest expense as well as the complete disallowance of deductions for interest related to certain items. These restrictions are discussed below.

LIMITATIONS ON DEDUCTIONS OF INTEREST EXPENSE

Prior to 1987, interest expense for most taxpayers was totally deductible. As part of the tax reform package of 1986, however, Congress substantially limited the deduction for interest. Congress became concerned that by allowing a deduction for all interest expense the tax system encouraged borrowing and, conversely, discouraged savings. This problem was exacerbated by the fact that the "economic" income arising from the ownership of housing and other consumer durables is not subject to tax. For example, when a taxpayer purchases a residence, the return on the investment—the absence of having to pay rent for the item—is not subject to tax. Had the taxpayer invested in assets other than housing or other durables, the return (e.g., interest or dividends) would have been fully taxable. In those situations where the investment is financed by borrowing, allowing a deduction is equivalent to allowing a deduction for expenses related to tax-exempt income—which is expressly prohibited under Code § 265. The net result of this system is to provide an incentive to consume rather than save.

LO.5
Distinguish between currently deductible and nondeductible interest expenses.

[65] § 164(c)(1), Reg. § 1.164-2(g), and Reg. § 1.164-4(a).

[66] § 164(c)(1) and Reg. § 1.164-4(b)(1).

[67] Reg. § 1.164-4(b)(1).

[68] *Old Colony Railroad v. Comm.,* 3 USTC ¶880, 10 AFTR 786, 284 U.S. 552 (USSC, 1936).

In rethinking the approach to interest in 1986, Congress believed that it would not be advisable to impute income on investments in durables and tax it. However, Congress did feel that it was appropriate and practical to address situations where consumer expenditures are financed by borrowing. Accordingly, Congress enacted rules that prohibit the deduction for personal interest (other than certain home mortgage interest and interest on certain education loans). As a result, interest expenses on personal auto loans, credit card purchases, etc. are no longer deductible.

In eliminating the deduction for personal interest, Congress effectively established *six* categories of interest expense, each of which is subject to its own special set of rules. The different categories of interest expense are (1) personal interest, (2) qualified residence interest, (3) trade or business interest, (4) investment interest, (5) passive-activity interest, and (6) qualified student loan interest. As explained in detail below, interest (other than qualified residence interest) is classified according to how the loan proceeds are *spent*. Consequently, taxpayers are required to determine the nature of an expenditure from loan proceeds before the amount of the interest deduction can be determined.

Personal Interest

Today, taxpayers are not allowed to deduct any *personal interest*. Personal interest is defined as all interest arising from personal expenditures *except* the following:[69]

1. Interest incurred in connection with the conduct of a trade or business (other than the performance of services as an employee);

2. Investment interest;

3. Qualified residence interest;

4. Interest taken into account in computing the income or loss from passive activities;

5. Interest on qualified education loans; and

6. Interest related to payment of the estate tax liability where such tax is deferred.

The effect of these rules is to severely limit the deduction for interest on consumer debt. For example, if a taxpayer borrows $3,000 from the bank and uses it to take a Caribbean cruise, none of the interest on the loan is deductible. Similarly, interest and finance charges would not be deductible on the following:

1. Automobile loans;

2. Furniture and appliance loans;

3. Credit card debt;

4. Life insurance loans;

5. Loans from qualified pension plans [including § 401(k) plans]; and

6. Delinquent tax payments and penalties.

It should be emphasized that interest incurred by an *employee* in connection with his or her trade or business is treated as consumer interest and is not deductible. In contrast, interest incurred by a self-employed person in his or her trade or business is fully deductible.

Example 26

K is a salesperson for a cosmetics company. Her job involves calling on department stores all over the state of Ohio and soliciting their orders. She uses her car entirely for business. Interest on her car loan for the year was $2,000. Since K is an employee, none of the interest is deductible.

---

[69] § 163(h)(1).

Example 27

R is a real estate agent working for Bungalow Brokers. All of his compensation is based on the number of homes he sells during the year. He uses his car entirely for business. Under the employment tax rules (§ 3508), real estate agents and direct sellers are not considered employees where their remuneration is determined by sales. Since R would not be considered an employee, all of the interest on his car loan would be deductible.

Example 28

P is a reporter for the *News-Gazette*. She purchased a notebook computer for $1,000, charging it on her bank credit card. She uses the computer entirely for business. Finance charges attributable to the purchase are $25. Even though the finance charges are incurred in connection with P's business, they are not deductible since she is an employee.

Qualified Residence Interest

The elimination of the deduction for personal interest in 1986 did not extend to interest on most home mortgages. As a general rule, interest on any debt *secured* by a taxpayer's first or second home is deductible. The interest is normally deductible whether the interest is on an original, second, or refinanced mortgage. Moreover, the interest is deductible regardless of how the taxpayer uses the money as long as the debt is *secured* by a mortgage on his or her primary or secondary residence. Unfortunately, tucked behind these seemingly simple rules are several complex restrictions.

Qualifying Indebtedness. Technically, only "qualified residence interest" is deductible. There are two types of qualified residence interest:[70]

1. Interest on *acquisition indebtedness:* Interest on debt that is incurred in acquiring, constructing, or improving a qualified residence *and* that is secured by such residence.

2. Interest on *home equity indebtedness:* Interest on debt secured by a qualified residence to the extent that the debt does not exceed the property's fair market value reduced by its acquisition debt.[71]

Note that in both cases, the crucial element in determining whether the interest qualifies is whether the debt is secured by a residence. Unsecured debt and debt secured by other property does not qualify even though the debt proceeds may be used to acquire a personal residence.

Example 29

J borrowed $50,000 from her pension plan and $10,000 from her father to buy a new home. None of the interest on the debt is deductible because neither of the debts is secured by the residence. This is true even though the borrowed amounts were used to buy a residence.

Also observe that in the case of both acquisition and home equity debt, the debt must be secured by a *qualified* residence. A qualified residence is the taxpayer's principal home and one other residence of the taxpayer.[72] This rule effectively allows taxpayers to deduct the interest on only two homes: their first home and a second of their choosing. A taxpayer with more than two homes must designate which is the second home when the return is filed. Different homes can be selected each year.

---

[70] § 163(h)(3).

[71] Interest relating to home equity loans is not deductible for purposes of the alternative minimum tax unless the loan proceeds are used for improvements. See § 56(e).

[72] § 163(h)(4).

Example 30

After winning the New York State lottery, T retired from her job and purchased a home in Tampa, Florida. She also purchased a motor home and a condominium in Vail, Colorado. All purchases were debt-financed and secured by the property. Within certain dollar limitations, T can treat the interest paid on her home in Tampa *and* the interest paid on *either* the motor home *or* the condominium as qualified residence interest.

Example 31

Assume the same facts as above except that T converted the condominium into rental property at the advice of her tax accountant. In this case, the condominium will not qualify as T's secondary residence for the purpose of the qualified residence interest deduction.[73]

In determining the deductibility of interest on a second home, special rules must be considered if the taxpayer *rents* it out. These rules are examined in conjunction with vacation homes discussed later in this chapter. If the second home is not rented out, no personal use is actually needed in order to meet the qualified residence test.

Congress also took steps to ensure that a taxpayer could not convert nondeductible interest into qualified residence interest simply by pitching a tent on the property and calling it a second home (e.g., vacant land or a car). In determining whether the debt is incurred with respect to a qualified residence, the term *residence* includes a vacation home, condominium, mobile home, boat, or recreational vehicle as long as the property contains basic living accommodations (i.e., sleeping space, toilet, and cooking facilities).

Limitations on Deductible Amount. To prevent taxpayers from taking undue advantage of the deductibility of home mortgage interest, Congress imposed limits on the maximum amount of debt qualifying under either definition. The aggregate amount of debt that can be treated as acquisition indebtedness for any taxable year cannot exceed $1 million ($500,000 in the case of a married individual filing a separate return),[74] whereas the aggregate amount of debt that will be treated as home equity indebtedness for any taxable year cannot exceed $100,000 ($50,000 if married and filing separately).[75] Collectively, the total amount of debt in any one year on which the interest paid or accrued will be treated as qualified residence interest cannot exceed $1.1 million.

Example 32

During the current year, T purchases a principal residence in Boston for $900,000 and a vacation home in Tampa for $500,000. Mortgages secured by both properties total $1.3 million. T may treat *only* the interest paid on $1 million of acquisition indebtedness as qualified residence interest. In addition, he may treat $100,000 of the loans as home equity indebtedness and, therefore, the related interest is deductible as qualified residence interest. Whether interest on the balance of the debt, $200,000, is deductible depends on how the funds are used.

---

[73] This does not mean that a taxpayer's interest expense on rental property is not deductible. As discussed later, however, losses from rental property (including interest expense) may be subject to deduction limitations.

[74] Any qualified residence indebtedness incurred before October 14, 1987—whether it is acquisition debt, home equity debt, or a combination of both—is to be treated as acquisition debt and is not subject to the $1 million limitation. If the property is later refinanced, however, the new indebtedness is subject to this limitation. § 163(h)(3)(D).

[75] § 163(h).

> ### Example 33
>
> C purchased his present residence several years ago at a cost of $1.9 million. The present balance on his home mortgage is $800,000 and the property is valued at $2.5 million. This year, C borrowed $300,000 secured by a second mortgage on his home. Even though the total indebtedness does not exceed $1.1 million, C may deduct the interest on the $800,000 unpaid acquisition indebtedness and the interest on only $100,000 of the home equity mortgage. Any excess interest paid during the year will be treated as personal interest.

It is important to note that the interest paid on qualifying home equity indebtedness is allowed as a deduction *regardless* of how the taxpayer uses the loan proceeds. Thus, the obvious reason for the $100,000 limit on qualifying home equity debt is to impose a limit on the amount of an interest deduction the taxpayer may claim on loan proceeds used for personal purposes.

> ### Example 34
>
> K purchased her present residence 10 years ago at a cost of $70,000. The present balance on her home mortgage is $40,000 and the property is appraised at a value of $150,000. This year, K borrowed $80,000 secured by a second mortgage on her home. She used the loan proceeds to purchase new clothes and a new automobile, and to take a vacation to Hawaii. The interest on the $80,000 loan is deductible since it is qualified residence interest. The fact that K used the loan proceeds for personal purposes is irrelevant. Also note that K's original cost of $70,000 is not used to limit the amount of her $80,000 home equity loan.

Refinancing. As mortgage interest rates rise and fall, homeowners often refinance their original home loans to get a better rate. During the past 25 years, refinancing has been quite common as the rates on 30-year fixed mortgages have been as high as about 18% in 1982 and as low as about 2.75% in 2013. Any attempt to refinance acquisition indebtedness should be undertaken with caution. A qualifying residence's acquisition debt is *reduced* by principal payments and *cannot be increased* unless the loan proceeds are used for home improvements. Thus, the acquisition debt can be refinanced only to the extent that the principal amount of the refinancing does not exceed the principal amount of the acquisition debt immediately before the refinancing.[76] The interest paid on any excess refinanced debt will not be treated as acquisition indebtedness. However, any excess may be treated as home equity indebtedness. As noted above, the total qualifying indebtedness (acquisition and home equity) cannot exceed the value of the residence.

> ### Example 35
>
> In 1970, G purchased her California bungalow for $25,000. The house is now worth $350,000. G paid off the mortgage on the home several years ago. This year, G mortgaged her house for $120,000 and subsequently loaned the money to her grandson to enable him to buy his first home. None of the loan qualifies as acquisition debt because the balance of acquisition debt refinanced was zero. However, G may deduct interest on $100,000 of the loan, which qualifies as home-equity debt.

---

[76] § 163(h)(3)(B).

> ### Example 36
>
> R purchased his present residence in 2004 for $250,000 and borrowed $210,000 on an 11% mortgage secured by the property. In 2017, R refinanced the balance of his mortgage, $190,000, by securing a new mortgage of $230,000 at five percent. Unless R used the additional loan proceeds to substantially improve the residence, only $190,000 of the new mortgage constitutes acquisition indebtedness, and the corresponding interest is therefore deductible. In addition, the $40,000 balance of the debt may be treated as home-equity debt. In such case, the interest on the entire $230,000 mortgage would be deductible as qualified residence interest.

Qualified Mortgage Insurance

Many individuals who purchase homes are required to buy mortgage insurance. The insurance is intended to provide funds to pay off the mortgage balance or help meet the payments on a mortgage as they fall due in the case of the individual's death or disability. Mortgage insurance is typically required when the loan has a loan to value ratio of 80% or greater (i.e., the down payment is less than 20% of the home's value). Such insurance is often called private mortgage insurance (PMI) for conventional loans, because a private institution rather than the federal government backs the loan.

Under the Tax Relief and Health Care Act of 2006, taxpayers were allowed to deduct premiums paid for qualified mortgage insurance.[77] As of this writing, this provision is schedule to expire at the end of 2016. Premiums on mortgage insurance provided by VA, FHA, RHA, and private mortgage insurance normally qualify. In addition, the insurance qualifies only if it is on acquisition indebtedness on a qualified residence.

The deduction is subject to phase-out. The phase-out begins when the taxpayer's AGI exceeds $100,000 and is complete once AGI is greater than $110,000. For example, a taxpayer with $1,500 of qualified premiums and AGI of $103,000 will be limited to a deduction of $1,050 ($1,500 – [$3,000/$10,000 × $1,500 = $450]).

Trade or Business Interest

While the taxpayer normally cannot deduct interest of a personal nature, interest related to a trade or business expenditure is totally deductible. Perhaps the most common example of business interest is that arising from loans used to acquire fixed assets such as buildings and equipment that are used in the business. Business interest also includes that attributable to loans used to acquire an interest in an S corporation or a partnership in which the taxpayer materially participates. Recall, however, that interest incurred in connection with performing services as an employee is not considered business interest, and thus is considered nondeductible personal interest.

As explained below, the fact that a business incurs interest expense does not necessarily mean that such interest is classified as business interest. If interest expense incurred by a business arises from an investment considered unrelated to the business, it will not be business interest (e.g., a closely held corporation purchases stock on margin).

Investment Interest

The fourth category of interest expense subject to limitation is investment interest. This limitation is imposed on taxpayers, other than regular corporations, who have paid or incurred interest expense to purchase or carry investments.[78] Common examples include interest on loans to purchase unimproved land and interest incurred on margin accounts used to purchase stocks and other securities. Congress imposed the investment interest limitation to eliminate what it perceived was an unfair advantage to certain wealthy investors.

---

[77] § 163(h)(4)(E)(i).   [78] § 163(d).

For example, consider the taxpayer who borrows to acquire or carry investments that produce little or no income currently but pay off handsomely when the investment is sold. This is commonly the hoped-for result with investments in such assets as growth stock or land. Without any restrictions, the taxpayer would be able to claim an immediate deduction for interest expense yet postpone any income recognition until the property was ultimately sold. Moreover, the income that the taxpayer would realize on the sale would normally be favorable capital gain. Congress apparently felt that this mismatching of income and expense was unwarranted and reacted by limiting the taxpayer's deduction for investment interest to the taxpayer's current investment income.

Before examining the investment interest limitation, the definition of investment interest should be clarified. *Investment interest* is generally any interest expense on debt used to finance property held for investment. It does not include, however, qualified residence interest or any interest related to a passive activity. As discussed in Chapter 12, interest related to a passive activity is allocated to the passive activity and is taken into account in computing the activity's income or loss. As a result, such interest is effectively limited by the passive-loss rules. Note, however, that any interest incurred by a passive activity that is related to its portfolio income (i.e., interest and dividend income) would normally be considered investment interest subject to the investment interest limitation. Because rental activities are usually treated as a passive activity, interest expense allocable to a rental activity is normally subject to the passive-loss rules.

The annual deduction for investment interest expense is limited to the taxpayer's *net investment income,* if any, for the tax year.[79] Any investment interest that exceeds the limitation and is disallowed may be carried forward until it is exhausted. Operationally, the disallowed interest is carried forward to the subsequent year, where it is combined with current year interest and is once again subject to the net investment income limitation. (Note that a sale of the financed property does not trigger the allowance of any disallowed interest.)

Net Investment Income. Net investment income is the excess of the taxpayer's investment income over investment expenses. For this purpose, *investment income* is generally defined as the gross income from property held for investment. Common examples of investment income include

1. Interest;
2. Royalties;
3. Ordinary income from the recapture of depreciation or intangible drilling costs under §§ 1245, 1250, and 1254;
4. Portfolio income under the passive loss rules; and
5. Income from a trade or business in which the taxpayer did not materially participate (but which is not a passive activity, e.g., a working interest in an oil or gas property).

Note that income from rental property and income from a passive activity (other than portfolio income) are not considered investment income. As noted above, any interest expense incurred in rental or passive activities is allocated to those activities and is used in computing the passive income or loss of such activity.[80] For example, mortgage interest on rental property would be deductible only to the extent of passive income. It is also important to note that qualified dividends (i.e., those taxed at a rate of 15%) and a net long-term capital gain from the disposition of an asset producing investment income (e.g., stocks or bonds) normally is not included in investment income. However, a taxpayer currently facing a limitation on the deduction for investment interest expense because of a limited amount of investment income may elect to include all or a part of the dividends or gain as investment income. Basically, such an election results in the dividends or the net capital gain being taxed as ordinary income in order to increase the electing taxpayer's ordinary deduction for investment interest expense.

---

[79] § 163(d)(1).

[80] § 163(d)(4)(E). See Chapter 12 for a detailed discussion of the passive loss rules.

Investment expenses are generally all those deductions (except interest) that are directly connected with the production of the investment income. Any investment expenses that are considered miscellaneous itemized deductions are considered only to the extent they exceed the 2% floor. For this purpose, the 2% floor is first absorbed by all other miscellaneous expenses.

Example 37

G's records for 2017 revealed the following information:

Salary	$ 40,000
Dividends and interest	3,500
Share of partnership income:	
Partnership ordinary income	700
Portfolio income:	
Dividends.	50
Interest	80
Rental income from duplex	15,000
Rental expenses	(14,000)
Adjusted gross income	$ 45,330
Qualified residence interest	$ 8,000
Real estate taxes on home	4,000
Property tax on land held for investment	1,000
Miscellaneous itemized deductions:	
Safety deposit box rental	50
Financial planner	1,500
Fee to maintain brokerage account	100
Unreimbursed employee business expenses	725

G is a limited partner in the partnership and thus treats the partnership as a passive activity. G also paid $7,700 of interest expense on the land held for investment. G's net investment income is computed as follows:

Investment income:		
Dividends and interest	$3,500	
Partnership income:		
Portfolio income:		
Dividends.	50	
Interest.	80	
Total investment income		$ 3,630
Investment expenses:		
Property tax on land	$1,000	
Safe deposit box rental	50	
Financial planner	1,500	
Fee to maintain brokerage account	100	
Miscellaneous itemized deductions disallowed		
2% floor (2% × $45,330)	$ 907	
Unreimbursed employee business expenses	(725)	
Investment expenses classified as		
miscellaneous itemized deductions disallowed	(182)	
Total investment expenses		(2,468)
Net investment income		$ 1,162

For 2017, G may deduct $1,162 of investment interest expense. The balance of $6,538 ($7,700 – $1,162) is carried over to the next year, 2018, and is treated as if it were paid in 2017. There is no limit on the carryover period. Note that in computing investment expenses, only investment expenses exceeding the 2% floor are allowed. In computing the disallowed portion, investment expenses are deemed to come last. Also note that rental income is not considered investment income.

Passive Activity Interest

Deductions attributable to so-called *passive activities* (e.g., those in which a taxpayer does not participate in a material fashion) are subject to special rules. Interest expense incurred by a passive activity itself (e.g., a limited partnership), or by investment in a passive activity, is treated as a deduction relating to the passive activity and is limited by the passive loss rules.[81] The passive activity loss rules are discussed in Chapter 12.

Interest on Student Loans

One of several measures enacted by Congress to help taxpayers finance the cost of higher education concerns the treatment of interest on student loans. As noted earlier, without a special rule, interest paid on loans to help pay college tuition and the like would be nondeductible personal interest. Currently, § 221 authorizes a deduction for interest on qualified educational loans. The maximum amount of interest that can be deducted annually is limited to $2,500.

If the interest qualifies for deduction, it is deductible *for* AGI. Therefore taxpayers are not required to itemize in order to benefit from the deduction.

Student Loan Interest Deduction Phase-Out. Like many relief provisions, the deduction for interest on qualified educational loans is not extended to high-income taxpayers. To accomplish this objective, the maximum deduction is phased out once the taxpayer's AGI (computed with certain modifications) exceeds $135,000 (2017) for joint returns ($65,000 (2017) for other returns).[82] The reduction occurs over a $30,000 income range for married filing jointly ($15,000 for all others), producing a complete phase-out as follows:

$$\text{Reduction of deductible portion of student loan interest} = \text{Deductible amount of interest (\$2,500 maximum in 2017)} \times \frac{\text{Modified AGI} - \text{Threshold}}{\text{Income range}}$$

	Modified AGI Phase-Out Begins (2017)	Modified AGI Phase-Out Complete (2017)
Married filing jointly	$135,000	$165,000
Other taxpayers	65,000	80,000

For this purpose, modified AGI is AGI before the exclusions for (1) foreign earned income and housing; (2) income from American Samoa, Guam and the Northern Mariana Islands; and after the exclusions for (1) Series EE savings bonds interest used to pay for education; (2) employer provided adoption benefits; (3) Social Security; (4) the deduction for contributions to IRAs; and (5) the deduction for losses on passive activities.

Example 38

In 2017, S, single, graduated from Notre Dame with a law degree. During the year, she paid student loan interest of $5,000 and reported AGI before consideration of the interest of $71,000. Since S's AGI exceeds the $65,000 threshold for single taxpayers by $6,000 (40% of the $15,000 range), the maximum allowable deduction is reduced in 2017 to $1,500 ($2,500 − [$6,000/$15,000 × $2,500 = $1,000]). Therefore, S may deduct $1,500 of the $5,000 interest for AGI.

Only interest on qualified education loans is deductible. Such loans are defined as any debt (other than a loan from a related party) incurred to pay qualified educational expenses for the taxpayer, the taxpayer's spouse, or other individuals who were the taxpayer's dependents at the time the debt was incurred. No deduction is allowed for interest paid by the taxpayer if the taxpayer is claimed as a dependent on another's return. For example, a child who pays interest on his student loans could not deduct the interest if his parents claim an exemption for him. Married taxpayers must file a joint return to claim the deduction.

---

[81] § 163(d)(3)(B).

[82] These amounts are adjusted annually for inflation. For 2017 thresholds, see Rev. Proc. 2016-55, 2016-45 IRB ___.

Interest is deductible only if the education is furnished to an eligible student. An eligible student is generally one who is enrolled in a degree, certificate, or other program leading to a recognized credential at an eligible institution of higher education. In addition, the student must have been attending at least half-time (i.e., one-half of the normal full-time work load for the course of study that the student is pursuing).

Qualified educational expenses include the costs of attendance at an eligible educational institution. They include tuition, fees, room and board, and related expenses, such as books and supplies. Such amounts must be reduced by any amounts excluded under § 127 concerning employer educational assistance plans, § 135 concerning interest excluded on Series EE bonds, or § 530 excluding distributions from education IRAs (see discussion in Chapter 6).

CLASSIFICATION OF INTEREST EXPENSE

The different rules for different types of interest expense force taxpayers to classify and allocate their interest expense among appropriate categories. The classification procedure established by the Treasury is very straightforward in principle. Under the Temporary Regulations, interest is generally classified according to how the loan proceeds are spent—that is, the character of the expenditure determines the character of interest.[83] The type of collateral that may secure the loan is irrelevant in the classification process—except in the case of the qualified residence interest which is deductible regardless of how loan proceeds are spent.[84]

Example 39

This year, T pledged IBM stock held as an investment as collateral for a loan which he uses to purchase a personal car. Any interest expense on the loan is considered nondeductible personal interest since the debt proceeds were used for personal purposes. The fact that the debt is secured by investment property is irrelevant. If the loan were secured by T's primary residence, the interest could be deductible as qualified residence interest.

The classification scheme demands that the taxpayer trace how any loan proceeds were used. To simplify this task, specific rules exist for debt proceeds that are (1) deposited in the borrower's account, (2) disbursed directly by the lender to someone other than the borrower, or (3) received in cash.

Proceeds Deposited in the Borrower's Account

In most cases, taxpayers borrow money, deposit it in an account, and write checks for various expenditures. Since money is fungible (that is, one dollar cannot be distinguished from another) it would be impossible without special rules to determine how the loan proceeds were spent, and therefore, how the related interest should be allocated. The Temporary Regulations create such rules.[85]

The first presumption created by the Regulations concerns the treatment of interest on funds that have not been spent. To the extent borrowed funds are deposited and not spent, interest attributable to such a period is considered *investment interest* regardless of whether the account bears interest income.[86]

---

[83] Temp. Reg. § 1.163-8T.

[84] Temp. Reg. § 1.163-8T(c)(1). For purposes of the alternative minimum tax, however, qualified housing interest is deductible only if the debt is spent on the residence. See Chapter 13 for further discussion.

[85] Temp. Reg. § 1.163-8T(c)(4).

[86] *Ibid.*

Example 40

On November 1, K borrowed $1,000 which she intends to use to fix up her boat. She deposited the $1,000 in a separate account. No expenditures were made during the remainder of the year. In this case, K is subject to the interest allocation rules since the interest expense is considered attributable to an investment, and is therefore, investment interest.

Example 41

Same as above except K makes several personal expenditures during the next three months. Interest must be allocated between investment interest and personal interest.

Example 42

A borrows $100,000 on January 1 and deposits it in a separate account where it remains until April 1 when he purchases an interest in a limited partnership for $20,000. On September 1, R purchases a new car for $30,000. Interest expense attributable to the $100,000 is allocated in the following manner:

	Debt Proceeds		
Period	Investment Interest	Passive Interest	Personal Interest
1/1–3/31	$100,000		
4/1–8/31	80,000	$20,000	
9/1–12/31	50,000	20,000	$30,000

Commingled Funds

In most situations, a taxpayer has one account in which all amounts are deposited. When this occurs, all expenditures from the account after the loan is deposited are deemed to come first from the borrowed funds.

Example 43

On October 1, B borrowed $1,000 to purchase a snowplow attachment for the front of his truck. He plans to make some extra money this winter by plowing driveways and parking lots. B deposited the $1,000 in his only checking account. On October 20, he bought the attachment for $1,500. Prior to October 20, he wrote $700 in checks for groceries and other personal items. Of the $1,000 loan, $700 is deemed to have been spent for personal items while the remaining $300 is allocated to the snow plow. Consequently, B may deduct only the interest expense on $300.

If proceeds from more than one loan are deposited into an account, expenditures are treated as coming from the borrowed funds in the order in which they were deposited (i.e., first-in, first-out).

Example 44

Dr. T has a personal checking account with a current balance of $3,000. On November 1, T obtained a $1,000 one-year Loan (Debt A) from her bank, which it credited to her personal account. She planned to use the loan to purchase a small copier for her dental practice. After shopping, T determined she would need additional funds. Therefore, on November 30 she obtained another $1,000 loan (Debt B). On December 12, T wrote a check for $800 to pay for her husband's Christmas present, a diamond ring. On December 19, she wrote a check for $2,100 to purchase the copier. These transactions are summarized as follows:

Date	Transaction	
11/1	Borrowed (Debt A)	$1,000
11/30	Borrowed (Debt B)	1,000
12/12	Purchased ring	(800)
12/19	Purchased copier	(2,100)

For purposes of determining the deduction for the interest on the loan, $800 of Debt A is deemed to be used for personal purposes (i.e., the ring purchase) and $200 toward the copier. All of Debt B is used for the copier. Thus, interest attributable to $800 of Debt A is nondeductible personal interest while that attributable to $200 is totally deductible. All of the interest on Debt B is deductible business interest. This may be summarized as follows:

	11/1 Debt A $1,000		*11/30 Debt B $1,000*		
Expenditure	*Personal*	*Business*	*Personal*	*Business*	*Other*
$ 800 ring	$800				
2,100 copier		$200		$1,000	$900

Thirty-Day Rule

In lieu of allocating the debt proceeds in the above manner, an alternative method is available. A borrower can elect to treat any expenditure made from any account within 30 days before or 30 days after debt proceeds are deposited in any account of the borrower as having been made from the proceeds of that loan.[87]

Example 45

C borrowed and deposited $5,000 in his checking account on December 1. On December 23, he wrote a check for $6,000 for his estimated income taxes. On December 29, he wrote a check for $5,000 for furniture for his business. Under the normal allocation rule, the entire $5,000 proceeds from the debt would be considered spent for personal purposes. Under the 30-day rule, however, C may treat the $5,000 as used to purchase the furniture since the proceeds were spent within 30 days of deposit. Also note that if C actually purchased the furniture for his business in November, he could still elect to treat that expenditure as being made from the December 1 loan proceeds regardless of which checking account (business or personal) was used to deposit the loan proceeds or from which the expenditure was made.

---

[87] See Temp. Reg. § 1.163-8T(c)(5)(i) as modified by Notice 89-35, 1989-1 CB 675.

Loan Proceeds Received Indirectly

In many transactions, a borrower incurs debt without receiving any loan proceeds directly. For example, if the taxpayer borrowed $100,000 from a bank to purchase a building, the bank typically disburses the $100,000 directly to the seller rather than to the borrower. Similarly, the borrower may purchase the building and assume the seller's $100,000 mortgage. In this and similar situations, the borrower is treated as having received the proceeds and used them to make the expenditure for the property, services, or other purpose.[88]

Loan Proceeds Received in Cash

When the borrower receives the loan proceeds in cash, the taxpayer may treat any cash expenditure made within 30 days before or 30 days after receiving the cash as made from the loan.

Debt Repayments, Refinancings, and Reallocations

Loans that are used for several purposes present a unique problem when a portion of the loan is repaid. In this case, repayments must be applied in the following order:[89]

1. Personal expenditures;
2. Investment expenditures and passive activity expenditures (other than rental real estate in which the taxpayer actively participates);
3. Rental real estate expenditures;
4. Former passive activity expenditures; and
5. Trade or business expenditures.

Example 46

R borrows $10,000, $6,000 of which is used to purchase a personal automobile and $4,000 of which is used to invest in land. On June 1 of this year she paid $7,000 on the loan. Of the $7,000 repayment, $6,000 reduces the portion of the loan allocated to personal expenditures and the remaining $1,000 reduces the portion allocated to investment.

If the taxpayer refinances an old debt, interest on the new debt is characterized in the same way as that on the old debt.

Example 47

Last year, S borrowed $10,000 at an annual interest rate of 14 percent. He used $8,000 to purchase a new boat and $2,000 to purchase a computer to use in his business. This year, he borrowed $6,000 from another bank at 10% to pay off the balance of the old loan. At the time the original loan was paid off, $4,000 of the $6,000 balance was allocated to the boat purchase and $2,000 was allocated to the computer purchase. The new debt will be allocated in the same manner as the old debt.

If the taxpayer borrows to finance a business asset, the debt must be recharacterized whenever the asset is sold or the nature of the use of the asset changes.

---

[88] Temp. Reg. § 1.163-8T(c)(3).   [89] *Ibid.*

Example 48

Several years ago B, a traveling salesperson, borrowed $12,000 to buy a car that he used entirely for business. This year, B gave his car to his wife who uses it solely for personal use. The loan and interest thereon must be reclassified.

Computation and Allocation of Interest Expense

The special rules governing the taxpayer's deduction for interest expense do not affect its computation. Interest is computed in the normal manner. However, allocation of the interest expense among the different categories does present certain difficulties. As a general rule, interest expense accruing on a debt for any period is allocated in the same manner as the debt. Interest which accrues on interest—that is, compound interest—is allocated in the same manner as the original interest.[90]

Example 49

On January 1, R borrowed $100,000 at an interest rate of 10 percent, compounded semiannually. She deposited the loan in a separate account and on July 1 used the funds to purchase a yacht. On December 31, R paid the accrued interest of $10,250, computed as follows:

Period	Principal	×	Rate	×	Time	=	Interest
1/1–6/30	$100,000	×	10%	×	6/12	=	$ 5,000
7/1–12/31	105,000	×	10%	×	6/12	=	5,250
							$10,250

Under the allocation rules, R's loan is classified as an investment loan from January 1 through June 30 and, therefore, the interest accruing for that period of $5,000 is investment interest. In addition, the interest expense which accrues on this $5,000 from July 30 through December 31 of $250 ($5,000 × 10% × 612) is considered investment interest for a total of $5,250. This $250 of "compound interest" accruing from July 31 through December 31 is allocated to the investment category even though the original loan has been assigned to a new category for the same period. The remaining $5,000 of interest expense accruing from July 1 through December 31 ($100,000 × 10% × 612) is personal interest.

To simplify the allocation of interest expense, the taxpayer may use a straight-line method. Using this technique, an equal amount of interest is allocated to each day of the year. For this purpose, the taxpayer may treat a year as consisting of twelve 30-day months.

Example 50

Assume the same facts as in *Example 49* above, except that R elects to allocate the interest expense on a straight-line basis, treating the year as consisting of twelve 30-day months. As a result, interest expense of $5,125 (180/360 × $10,250) would be investment interest while the remaining $5,125 of interest expense would be personal interest.

---

[90] Temp. Reg. § 1.163-8T(c)(2).

WHEN DEDUCTIBLE

The taxpayer's method of accounting generally controls the timing of an interest expense deduction. Accrual method taxpayers generally may deduct interest over the period in which the interest accrues, regardless of when the expense is actually paid. However, cash-basis taxpayers must *actually* pay the interest before a deduction is allowed. Many situations arise in which the "actual payment" requirement imposed on cash-basis taxpayers delays the timing of a deduction. Other situations concern measurement of the amount of interest actually paid. The most common of these situations are briefly discussed below.

Interest Paid in Advance

If interest is paid in advance for a time period that extends beyond the end of one tax year, *both* accrual method and cash-basis taxpayers generally are required to spread the interest deduction over the tax years to which it applies.[91] An important exception is made for cash basis individual taxpayers who are required to pay interest "points" in connection with indebtedness incurred to *purchase* or *improve* the taxpayer's principal residence (i.e., taxpayer's home).[92] The term *points* is often used to describe charges imposed on the borrower under such descriptions as "loan origination fees," "premium charges," and "maximum loan charges." Such charges usually are stated as a percentage (point) of the loan amount. If the payment of any of these charges is *strictly* for the use of money *and* actual payment of these charges is made out of *separate funds* belonging to the taxpayer, an interest deduction is allowed in the year of payment.[93]

Example 51

R borrowed $15,000 from State Bank to make improvements on his home. The loan is payable over a 10-year period, and the bank charged R a loan origination fee of $300 (two points). If R pays the $300 charge from separate funds, it is currently deductible as an interest expense (assuming R itemizes his deductions). However, if the $300 charge is added to the amount of the loan, R has not currently paid interest. Instead, R will be required to treat the charge as note-discount interest (see discussion below).

Note-Discount Interest

Taxpayers often sign notes calling for repayment of an amount greater than the loan proceeds actually received. This occurs when the creditor subtracts (withholds) the interest from the face amount of the loan and the taxpayer receives the balance, or when the face amount of the note simply includes add-on interest. In either case, cash-basis taxpayers are not allowed a deduction until the tax year in which the interest is actually paid. Accrual-method taxpayers are allowed to deduct the interest over the tax years in which it accrues.

Graduated Payment Mortgages

A creature of the high interest rate mortgage markets, graduated payment mortgages provide for increasing payments in the early years of the mortgage until the payments reach some level amount. Under these plans, the payments in the early years are less than the amount of interest owed on the loan. The unpaid interest is added to the principal amount of the mortgage and future interest is computed on this revised balance. As should be expected, cash-basis taxpayers may deduct *only* the interest actually paid in the current year; the increases in the principal balance of the mortgage are treated much the same as note-discount interest.

---

[91] § 461(a).

[92] § 461(g).

[93] See *Roger A. Schubel,* 77 T.C. 701 (1982), and *James W. Hager,* 45 TCM 123, T.C. Memo 1982-663. Note, however, that this interest deduction is subject to the rules regarding qualified residence interest.

Installment Purchases

Individual taxpayers who purchase personal property or pay for educational services under a contract calling for installment payments in which carrying charges are separately stated but the interest charge cannot be determined are allowed to *impute* an interest expense. The imputed expense is allowed whether or not a payment is actually made during the tax year, and is computed at a rate of 6% of the *average unpaid balance* of the contract during the year.[94] The average unpaid balance is the sum of the unpaid balance outstanding on the first day of each month of the tax year, divided by 12 months. Credit card and revolving charge account finance charges are generally much greater than six percent. Fortunately, these charges are usually stated separately at a *predetermined* interest rate (e.g., finance charge of 10% of unpaid monthly balance). Recall, however, that this type of interest expense is generally personal interest and thus nondeductible!

WHERE REPORTED

Like the deductions for taxes, the appropriate tax form or schedule on which deductible interest is reported depends upon the entity entitled to the deduction and the nature of the indebtedness to which the interest relates. A corporation's deductible interest is reported on its annual tax return Form 1120. Estates and trusts report interest deductions on Form 1041; partnerships and S corporations claim interest deductions on Forms 1065 and 1120S, respectively. Individuals claiming a deduction for interest expense must report the amount on the appropriate schedule of Form 1040. If the interest is related to business indebtedness—and the business is self-employment—the individual will claim his or her deduction on Schedule C (Schedule F for farmers and ranchers). Interest on debt incurred in connection with the production of rents or royalties is reported on Schedule E. Deductible interest on indebtedness incurred for personal use must be reported as an itemized deduction on Schedule A (with the exception of qualifying student loan interest which is deductible for AGI). However, any individual who has refinanced his or her home, or is otherwise subject to the limitations imposed on qualified residence interest, should see IRS Publication 936 for instructions in computing the home mortgage interest deduction.

An individual's current deduction for investment interest expense should be calculated on Form 4952 (see Appendix B), and any disallowed deduction reported as a carryover amount. The deductible amount from Form 4952 should be transferred to and claimed as a deduction on the individual's Schedule E, Form 1040, if the interest relates to the production of royalties; otherwise, the deductible amount is reported on Schedule A. Partnerships and S corporations are not allowed to deduct investment interest expense in determining income or loss. Instead, these conduit entities are required to set out and separately report each partner's or shareholder's share of *both* investment interest expense *and* net investment income for the current year. Each partner or shareholder must claim his or her deduction subject to the previously described limitations. Recall, however, that a partner that is a regular corporation will not be subject to the investment interest expense limitation.

Charitable Contributions

To encourage the private sector to share in the cost of providing many needed social services, Congress allows individuals, regular corporations, estates, and trusts deductions for charitable contributions (or gifts) of money or other property to certain qualified organizations. Partnerships and S corporations are not allowed to deduct charitable contributions. Instead, these conduit entities pass the contributions through to the partners and shareholders who must claim the deduction on their own Federal income tax returns.[95]

Code § 170 contains the rules regarding deductions for charitable contributions made by individuals and regular corporations. Code § 642(c) sets forth the rules regarding the amount and timing of charitable contribution deductions claimed by estates and trusts. The rules related to the measurement, timing, and qualification of contribution deductions claimed by individuals and corporations are discussed below. A discussion of the percentage limitations imposed on current deductions by individual taxpayers is also included. The specific rules regarding limitations imposed on a corporation's annual charitable contribution deduction are discussed in Chapter 19.

---

[94] § 163(b)(1).   [95] See §§ 702(a)(4) and 1366(a)(1).

DEDUCTION REQUIREMENTS

Individual taxpayers are allowed a deduction for contributions of cash or other property *only if* the gift is made to a qualifying donee organization. Individual taxpayers normally are required to actually pay cash or transfer property before the close of the tax year in which the deduction is claimed.

Substantiation

Congress has established strict substantiation requirements to prevent abuse. These include the following.

- For a single cash contribution of less than $250 (e.g., cash or check), no deduction is allowed unless the taxpayer has some type of bank record such as a cancelled check, credit card statement, or receipt from the charity verifying the contribution. Note that this rule applies to any contribution of money, regardless of amount. Consequently, dropping $10 in the church collection plate or the Salvation Army bucket is not deductible (unless there is verification).[96]

- A contribution of $250 or more is not deductible unless the taxpayer substantiates the contribution by a contemporaneous written acknowledgment of the contribution from the donee organization.[97] No acknowledgement is required for separate contributions of less than $250 each even if the sum of the contributions to the charity during the year equals $250 or more (e.g., separate bags of clothing to Goodwill, none of which have a value of at least $250). The charity's acknowledgement must state the amount of cash and a description (but not the value) of the donated property. The acknowledgement also must indicate whether the charity provided any goods or services in consideration for the contribution, and, if so, the value of such goods or services.[98] To qualify as contemporaneous, the donors must have the receipt (e.g., thank-you letter) by the time their tax return is filed. No acknowledgement is required if, after subtracting the value of the goods and services, the charitable gift is less than $250. For example, if a $500 contribution to a university entitles the taxpayer to purchase tickets for athletic events and this right is valued at $300, the charitable gift is $200 ($500 − $300) and it therefore falls below the $250 threshold and an acknowledgement is not required.

- A charitable contribution for clothing and household goods is permitted only if the items are "in good used condition or better." In this regard, the IRS is authorized to deny deductions for items of minimal value (e.g., used socks and underwear). Unfortunately, the law provides no guidance as to what is good condition for used items.[99]

- For contributions of automobiles, boats, airplanes, and other vehicles, if the claimed value exceeds $500, the donor must include with the return proper acknowledgement. Moreover, should the charity sell the vehicle, the deduction may not exceed the amount received by the charity.[100]

- Form 8283 must be filed for all noncash gifts of more than $500. In some cases, an appraisal must be attached (e.g., contributions of art or privately traded stock).

LO.6

Explain the requirements for the deductibility of charitable contributions and compute the contribution deduction.

[96] Section 170(f)(17), introduced by the Pension Protection Act of 2006. As a result of these requirements, taxpayers are likely to make more contributions by check.

[97] § 170(f)(8).

[98] See *Durden,* 103 TCM 1762,T.C. Memo 2012-40, denying deductions for contributions of more than $25,000 to church where church's initial acknowledgment did not state that no goods and services were provided; a second acknowledgement corrected this omission two years later but

was dismissed because not contemporaneous. Whether the contributions were made and their amount was not disputed!

[99] See § 170(f)(16) and other limitations applying to such items as "taxidermy property," conservation easements and certain other property.

[100] § 170(f)(12)(A). See *NHUSS Trust,* 90 TCM 374, T.C. Memo 2005-236, where the taxpayer presented an appraisal of $19,750 for a donated van that the donee sold six weeks after the gift for $6,900.

Qualifying Donees

To be deductible, contributions of cash or other property must be made to or for the use of one of the following:[101]

1. A state, a U.S. possession, a political subdivision of a state or possession, the United States, or the District of Columbia, if the contribution is made solely for public purposes;

2. A community chest, corporation, trust, fund, or foundation that is organized or created in, or under the laws of, the United States, any state, the District of Columbia, or any possession of the United States *and* is organized and operated exclusively for religious, charitable, scientific, literary, or educational purposes or for the prevention of cruelty to children or animals;

3. A war veterans' organization;

4. A nonprofit volunteer fire company or civil defense organization;

5. A domestic fraternal society operating under the lodge system, but only if the contribution is to be used for any of the purposes stated in Item 2 above; and

6. A nonprofit cemetery company, if the funds are to be used solely for the perpetual care of the cemetery as a whole, and not for a particular lot or mausoleum crypt.

If the taxpayer has not been informed by the recipient organization that it is a qualifying donee, he or she may check its status in the *Cumulative List of Organizations* (IRS Publication 78). This publication contains a frequently updated listing of organizations which have applied to and received tax-exempt status from the IRS. To be a qualifying donee, however, the organization is not required to be listed in this publication.

Disallowance Possibilities

Direct contributions to needy or worthy individuals are not deductible. In addition, contributions to qualifying organizations must not be restricted to use by a specific person; if so, deductions generally are disallowed.

Example 52

F contributed cash of $10,000 to his son, S. S is a missionary for a church that is a qualified organization, and the gift proceeds were used exclusively by S to further the charitable work of the church. F is not entitled to a charitable contribution deduction since the gift was not made to a qualifying donee. Similarly, F would be denied a deduction if he made the gift to the church but restricted the use of the funds only for his missionary son.[102]

A taxpayer's contribution to a qualified organization that is motivated by the taxpayer's expectation and receipt of a significant economic benefit will not be deductible as a charitable contribution. The receipt of an unexpected and indirect economic benefit as a result of the gift should not disqualify the taxpayer's deduction, however.

Example 53

T donated two parcels of land to a nearby city for use as building sites for new public schools. The location of the building sites was such that the city had to construct two access roads through the taxpayer's remaining undeveloped land in order to make use of the gifted property. Construction of the access roads significantly enhanced the value of T's remaining acreage, and as a result, his charitable contribution deduction may be denied.[103]

---

[101] See § 170(c).

[102] *White v. U.S.,* 82-1 USTC ¶9232, 49 AFTR2d 82-364, 514 F. Supp. 1057 (D.Ct. Utah, 1981). For a similar result, see *Babilonia v. Comm.,* 82-2 USTC ¶9478, 50 AFTR2d 82-5442 (CA-9, 1982).

[103] See *Ottawa Silica Co. v. U.S.,* 83-1 USTC ¶9169, 51 AFTR2d 83-590, 699 F.2d 1124 (CA-Fed. Cir., 1983) where, under similar circumstances, the taxpayer's claimed contribution deduction was disallowed.

Apparently, because Congress does not believe that the benefit received by a taxpayer is of great significance, 80% of the amount paid by a taxpayer to a college or university that either directly or indirectly entitles the taxpayer to purchase tickets to the institution's athletic events is allowed as a deduction.[104] However, any amount actually paid for the tickets will not be deductible.

LIMITATIONS ON DEDUCTIONS

Unlike the requirement that an individual's medical expenses and casualty losses *exceed* some minimum percentage of AGI (referred to as the *floor* amount) *before* any deductions are allowed, deductions for charitable contributions are subject to *ceiling* limitations (i.e., not to *exceed* a percentage of AGI). Generally, an individual's current deduction for charitable contributions is limited to 50% of the taxpayer's AGI. A 30% ceiling limitation is imposed on an individual's contributions of *certain appreciated property,* and a 20% overall limitation is imposed on an individual's contributions to *certain qualifying organizations.*

Under the general rule, the amount of a taxpayer's charitable deduction (before any percentage limitation) is the *sum* of money *plus* the fair market value of any property other than money which is contributed to a qualifying donee. However, both the gift of property to certain organizations and the gift of certain types of property other than money may result in a deduction of an amount *less than* the property's fair market value. These exceptions to the general rule are explained below, followed by a discussion of the various percentage limitations imposed on an individual's deduction for charitable contributions.[105]

Contributions Other than Money or Property

No charitable contribution deduction is allowed for the value of time or services rendered to a charitable organization.[106] Likewise, no deduction is allowed for any "lost income" associated with the rent-free use of a taxpayer's property by a qualifying charity. However, *unreimbursed* (out-of-pocket) *expenses* incurred by the taxpayer in rendering services to a charitable institution or allowing rent-free use of property by such an organization *qualify* as charitable contributions.[107] For example, a taxpayer is allowed a deduction for the cost and upkeep of uniforms required to be worn while performing the charitable services, but only if the uniforms are not suitable for everyday use. Similarly, a taxpayer is generally allowed to deduct amounts paid for transportation to and from his or her home to the place where the charitable services are performed.[108] This includes the costs for gasoline, oil, parking, and tolls incurred by a taxpayer using his or her own vehicle in connection with the charitable services. In lieu of deducting the actual expenses for gasoline and oil, a taxpayer is allowed to use a standard mileage rate in calculating the cost of using an automobile in charitable activities. In 2017, the rate is 14 cents per mile.[109] In either case, no deduction is allowed for insurance, depreciation, or the costs of general repairs and maintenance. Note also that the donor must adequately substantiate these expenditures and the charity must provide a written statement that describes the taxpayer's services and whether the organization provided any goods or services in consideration for the unreimbursed expenses and, if so, the amount.

---

[104] See § 170(m).

[105] Regular corporations are subject to an overall limitation of 10% of taxable income, determined without regard to certain deductions. See Chapter 19 for more details.

[106] Reg. § 1.170A-1(g).

[107] *Ibid.*

[108] The Tax Reform Act of 1986 added § 170(k) to the Code to disallow a deduction for travel expenses related to charitable services where there is a significant element of personal pleasure, recreation, or vacation in such travel.

[109] See § 170(j) and Notice 2016-79, 2016-169 IRB 265; this rate is set by statute and is not adjusted annually for inflation.

Example 54

T is the scoutmaster of a local troop of the Boy Scouts of America. During the current year, T incurred the following expenses in rendering his services to this charitable organization:

Cost and upkeep of uniforms.	$ 80
Gasoline and oil expenses	200
Parking and tolls	30
Estimated value of rent-free use of den in home	1,000
Estimated value of services (500 hours @ $50 per hour)	25,000
Total	$26,310

T is entitled to a $310 charitable contribution deduction for his out-of-pocket expenses ($80 + $200 + $30) incurred in rendering the charitable services as a scoutmaster. No deduction is allowed for the estimated value of his services or the rent-free use of his home.

Example 55

Assume the same facts as in *Example 54,* except that T drove his automobile 3,000 miles in connection with the charitable services. If he did not keep records of the actual expenses for gasoline and oil, T could use the standard mileage rate of 14 cents per mile. In this case, he will be allowed to deduct $530 ([3,000 miles × $0.14 per mile (2017) for charitable use of auto = $420] + $30 for parking and tolls + $80 related to uniforms).

Fair Market Value Determination

The IRS defines fair market value as "the price at which the property would change hands between a willing buyer and a willing seller, neither being under any compulsion to buy or sell and both having reasonable knowledge of relevant facts."[110] Determination of this amount usually means the taxpayer must make an educated guess or incur the cost of an independent appraisal. Since the IRS requires that the taxpayer attach a statement to his or her return when a deduction exceeding $500 is claimed for a charitable gift of property (Form 8283, Noncash Charitable Contributions), many taxpayers seek independent appraisals to support their claimed deductions. Independent appraisals are *required*—and the donee must *attach* a summary of the appraisal to his or her return—if the claimed value of the contributed property exceeds $5,000.[111] Appraisal fees are not deductible as contributions. However, they are deductible by individuals as miscellaneous itemized deductions (subject to the 2% floor).[112]

Ordinary Income Property

The term *ordinary income property* is used to describe any property which, if sold, would require the owner to recognize gain *other than* long-term capital gain. For example, ordinary income property includes a donor/taxpayer's property held primarily for sale to customers in his or her trade or business (i.e., inventory items), a work of art created by the donor, a manuscript prepared by the donor, letters and memoranda prepared by or for the donor, and

---

[110] Reg. § 1.170-1(c)(1).

[111] § 6050L. A donee charity that sells or otherwise disposes of such property within two years of the donation *must* report the disposition (and amount received, if any) to the IRS and the donor.

[112] Under § 212(3), individuals are allowed to deduct expenses associated with the determination of their tax liability. This includes appraisal fees paid in valuing property contributions.

a capital asset held by the taxpayer for not more than one year (i.e., short-term capital gain property). Musical compositions can be treated as capital assets for purposes of determining the character of the gain or loss on a sale or exchange but are considered ordinary income property for purposes of determining the amount of the contribution. Thus a contribution of song by the composer would normally result in a deduction equal to the song's basis which is usually little or nothing.[113] The term also includes property which, if sold, would result in the recognition of ordinary income under any of the depreciation recapture provisions.[114]

The charitable deduction (without regard to any percentage limitations) for the gift of ordinary income property is equal to the property's fair market value *reduced* by the amount of ordinary income that would be recognized if the property had been sold at its fair market value (this amount is often called the *ordinary income potential*).[115]

Example 56

F donated 100 shares of IBM stock to his church on December 15, 2017. F had purchased the stock for $9,000 on August 7, 2017 and it was worth $12,000 on the date of the gift. Since F would have recognized a short-term capital gain if the stock had been sold on December 15, 2017 (i.e., holding period not more than one year), the stock is ordinary income property. As a result, F's charitable contribution deduction is limited to $9,000 ($12,000 fair market value – $3,000 ordinary income potential).

In most cases, the charitable deduction for ordinary income property will be limited to the taxpayer's adjusted basis in the property since its fair market value is reduced by the *unrealized appreciation* in value (fair market value – adjusted basis), which would not result in long-term capital gain if the property were sold. There are, however, three important instances when this would not be the case. First, the charitable deduction for *any property* which, if sold, would result in a *loss* (i.e., adjusted basis > fair market value) is limited to the property's fair market value.

Example 57

J donated 1,000 shares of Intel stock to the University of Alabama that he purchased several years ago for $40,000 but that were now worth only $15,000. J may claim a charitable contribution deduction only for the stock's fair market value of $15,000. Note that the property does not qualify as either capital gain property or ordinary income property (since he would have recognized a capital loss on the sale). J would have been better off had he sold the property, recognized the loss and donated the proceeds from the sale.

Second, any depreciable property held by the taxpayer for more than one year and used in his or her trade or business is *§ 1231 property*. The amount of gain from the sale of such property that exceeds any depreciation recapture is referred to as "§ 1231 gain." Potential § 1231 gains are treated as long-term capital gains for purposes of measuring a taxpayer's charitable contribution deduction.[116] As such, any unrealized appreciation in the value of property that is attributable to § 1231 gain will not be considered ordinary income potential for purposes of the limitation described above.

[113] See §§ 170(e)(1)(A) and 1221(b)(3).

[114] See § 170(e)(1), Reg. §§ 1.170A-4(b)(1) and (b)(4).

[115] § 170(e)(1). For an application of this rule, see *William Glen*, 79 T.C. 208 (1982).

[116] § 170(e)(3).

The remaining exception entitles C corporations to increase their deduction for contributions of certain ordinary income items by one-half of the unrealized ordinary income in the property. The enhanced deduction, which is limited to twice the property's basis, is available for contributions of the following:[117]

- Contributions of inventory or depreciable property used in business that is used by the charitable organization for the care of children, the ill, or the needy. For example, gifts of drugs and medical supplies by pharmaceutical companies to a charity would qualify. Gifts of food inventory (by any entity) and book inventory to schools also qualify but are subject to additional rules.

- Contributions of "scientific property or apparatus" constructed or assembled by the taxpayer that is held as inventory and is donated within two years of its manufacture to an educational institution for use in research or for research training in physical or biological sciences. For example, a computer manufacturer's contribution of computers to a university for use in research or by its students in computer science courses would qualify.

- Contributions of computer software, computers, peripheral equipment, and fiber optic cable for computer use to a school, organizations formed to support elementary and secondary education, and certain public libraries.

Example 58

ELI Corporation manufactures insulin and gives $1,000,000 of the drug (basis $700,000) to hospitals around the country to be used for charitable purposes. Normally, the deduction would be limited to the property's adjusted basis of $700,000. However, because the hospitals will use it for the care of children and those who are needy, the deduction is $850,000 ($700,000 + $150,000 [50% × ($1,000,000 − $700,000 = $300,000 unrealized ordinary income)]). If the basis had been $100,000, the tentative deduction would be $550,000 ($100,000 + $450,000 [50% × $900,000]) but it would be limited to $200,000 (2 × adjusted basis of $100,000).

Capital Gain Property

Any property which, if sold by the donor/taxpayer, would result in the recognition of a long-term capital gain or § 1231 gain is *capital gain property*.[118] A taxpayer is generally allowed to claim the fair market value of such property as a contribution deduction. There are two important exceptions to this rule, however. *First,* if capital gain property is contributed to or for the use of a private nonoperating foundation (as defined in § 509(a) such as the Gates Foundation), the donor must *reduce* the contribution deduction by the *entire* amount of any long-term capital gain or § 1231 gain that would be recognized if the property were sold at its fair market value.[119] In effect, this exception treats the contribution of capital gain property to private nonoperating foundations exactly like contributions of ordinary income property, since the donor must reduce the contribution deduction to the basis of the property.

Example 59

G donates land worth $10,000 to a private nonoperating foundation on November 17, 2017. G had purchased the land for $4,000 on August 23, 2013. G's charitable contribution deduction must be reduced to $4,000 ($10,000 fair market value − entire $6,000 appreciation).

---

[117] Reg. § 1.170A-4(b)(4).

[118] § 170(e)(1).

[119] § 170(e)(1)(B)(ii). An exception is provided for contributions of publicly traded stock to private foundations. Taxpayers making such contributions are allowed to deduct the full fair market value of such stock.

It is important to note that this limitation *generally* does not apply to donations of capital gain property to public charities.

Example 60

Assume the same facts as in *Example 59*, except that G donated the land to her alma mater, State University (a public charity). G's charitable contribution would be $10,000 because the reduction requirement applies only to contributions to private foundations.

The *second* exception to the general rule that taxpayers are allowed to claim a deduction for the fair market value of contributed capital gain property involves contributions of tangible personalty.[120] If tangible personalty is contributed to a public charity (i.e., a university, museum, church, etc.) and the property is put to an *unrelated use* by the donee organization, the charitable contribution must be reduced by the entire amount of the property's unrealized appreciation in value (i.e., to the property's basis). For purposes of this limitation, the term *unrelated use* means that the property could not be used by the public charity in its activities for which tax-exempt status had been granted. For example, if antique furnishings are donated to a local museum that either stores, displays, or uses the items in its office in the course of carrying out its functions, the use of such property is a related use.[121] Thus, if the taxpayer can reasonably anticipate that the tangible personalty donated to the charitable organization will be put to a related use, this limitation will not be applicable.[122]

Example 61

This year J contributed a painting to the local university. He had purchased the painting in 2004 for $10,000, and it was appraised at $60,000 on the date of the gift. The painting was placed in the university's library for display and study by art students. J's charitable contribution will be measured at $60,000 (the painting's fair market value) since the property was not put to an unrelated use. This is true even if the university later sells the painting.

Example 62

During the year R donated her gun collection to the YWCA (a public charity). R had paid $8,000 for the collection 10 years ago, and the guns were appraised at $18,000 on the date of the gift. The YWCA immediately sold the collection for $18,000 to a local gun dealer. Although the property had appreciated by $10,000, R's charitable contribution must be reduced to $8,000 (the property's basis) since the property was not (and most likely could not be) put to a related use.

Fifty Percent Limitation

An individual's deduction for contributions made to public charities may not exceed 50% of his or her AGI for the year.[123] This "ceiling" deduction limitation applies to contributions made to the following types of public charities:[124]

1. A church or a convention or association of churches;
2. An educational organization that normally maintains a regular faculty and curriculum;

---

[120] As described in Chapter 9, tangible personalty is all tangible property *other than* realty (i.e., land, buildings, structural components).

[121] Reg. § 1.170A-4(b)(3). Under § 170(e)(7), if tangible personal property worth more than $5,000 is contributed and later sold by the charity, the donor may be required to include certain amounts in income.

[122] Reg. § 1.170A-4(b)(3)(ii).

[123] § 170(b) and Reg. § 1.170A-8(b).

[124] § 170(b)(1).

3. An organization whose principal purposes or functions are providing medical or hospital care (hospitals) or medical education or medical research (medical schools);

4. An organization that receives support from the government and is organized and operated exclusively to receive, hold, invest, and administer property for the benefit of a college or university;

5. A state, a possession of the United States, or any political subdivision of any of the foregoing, or the United States or the District of Columbia;

6. An organization that normally receives a substantial part of its support from a government unit (described in Item 5 above) or from the general public; and

7. Certain types of private foundations discussed below.

Private foundations are organizations that, by definition, do not receive contributions from the general public. Examples of well-known private foundations include the Ford, Carnegie, Cullen, and Mellon Foundations. For charitable deduction purposes, private foundations are classified as either operating or nonoperating foundations. Contributions to *all* private operating foundations are subject to the 50% ceiling limitation.[125] The 50% limit also applies to contributions to certain private, nonoperating foundations if the organizations:

1. Distribute the contributions they receive to public charities and private operating foundations *within* two and one-half months following the year the contributions were received; or

2. Pool all contributions received into a common fund, and distribute *both* the income and the principal from the fund to public charities.

An individual's contributions of cash and ordinary income property to public charities, private operating foundations, and the above described nonoperating foundations that exceed the 50% limitation are carried forward and deducted in subsequent years. The carryover rules are discussed in a later section of this chapter. Contributions of capital gain property *and* contributions to private nonoperating foundations (other than those described above) are subject to *either* the 30% or 20% limitation. These limitations are discussed below.

Thirty Percent Limitation

There are *two* situations in which the 30% limitation may apply. The first situation involves the following types of contributions:

1. Contributions for the *use* of any charitable organization;

2. Contributions to veterans' organizations, fraternal societies, and not-for-profit cemetery companies; *and*

3. Contributions to most private nonoperating foundations.

The annual deduction for these contributions is limited to the *lesser of*

1. Thirty percent of AGI, *or*

2. An amount equal to 50% of AGI, *reduced* by contributions qualifying for the 50% limitation.[126]

---

[125] See § 4942(j) for the requirements for classification as a private operating foundation. For all practical purposes, an operating foundation is recognized as a public charity.

[126] See § 170(b)(1)(C).

Example 63

R has AGI of $50,000 for the current year and contributes $5,000 cash to his church and $20,000 cash to the Veterans of Foreign Wars. R's deduction for the contribution to his church will not be limited because it does not exceed 50% of AGI (i.e., $5,000 < $25,000). However, only $15,000 of the contribution to the veterans' organization will be allowed as a deduction for the current year because this donation is subject to the 30% limitation.

Contribution to church		$ 5,000
Plus:	Lesser of	
(1)	30% × $50,000 = $15,000	
	or	
(2)	50% × $50,000 = $25,000, reduced by $5,000 gift to church = $20,000	
		15,000
Total contribution deduction		$20,000

Example 64

Assume the same facts in *Example 63*, except that the contribution to the church was $20,000 and the contribution to the veterans' organization was $8,000. Again, the contribution to the church will not be limited because it does not exceed 50% of AGI. However, the contribution to the veterans' organization will be limited to $5,000, computed as follows:

Contribution to church		$20,000
Plus:	Lesser of	
(1)	30% × $50,000 = $15,000	
	or	
(2)	50% × $50,000 = $25,000, reduced by $20,000 gift to church = $5,000	
		5,000
Total contribution deduction		$25,000

Note that it is not the 30% of AGI. Limitation that causes R's contribution to the veterans' organization to be limited. Instead, it is the fact that the overall limitation on the annual contribution deduction amount is 50% of AGI, and the contribution to the public charity is considered first.

The *second* situation in which the 30% limitation may apply involves contributions of capital gain property. The annual deduction allowed for contributions of capital gain property that have not been reduced by the unrealized appreciation will generally be limited to 30% of the taxpayer's AGI.[127] As in the first situation discussed above, these contributions subject to the 30% limit are considered only after the amount of contributions allowed under the 50% limitation has been determined. Contributions in excess of the 30% limit can be carried forward and deducted in subsequent years.

---

[127] § 170(b)(1)(C)(i).

Example 65

K has AGI of $30,000 for the 2017 tax year. The only contribution made by K in 2017 consisted of stock worth $10,000, which she had purchased for $4,000 in 2013. The stock was given to her church. Although the contribution does not exceed 50% of her AGI, K's deduction is limited to $9,000 (30% × $30,000 AGI) since the stock is capital gain property. The $1,000 excess contribution can be carried over to subsequent years.

Example 66

Assume the same facts as in *Example 65,* except that K's 2017 AGI is $40,000 and she also gave $14,000 cash to her church. In this case, her deduction for the gift of the stock is limited to $6,000 (50% × $40,000 AGI = $20,000 – $14,000 cash contribution) since the 50% overall limitation is applied before the 30% limitation. The remaining $4,000 ($10,000 fair market value of stock – $6,000 deduction allowed) will be carried forward to subsequent years.

When capital gain property has been contributed, the 30% limitation can be avoided if the taxpayer *elects* to reduce his or her claimed deduction for the capital gain property by the property's unrealized appreciation.[128] This may result in a larger deduction in the current year since the reduced amount will be subject to a higher ceiling limitation (i.e., 50% of AGI rather than 30%). It is important to note that this election, if made, applies to all contributions of capital gain property made during the year.

Example 67

T has AGI of $50,000 for the current year and contributes stock worth $23,000 to the United Way (a public charity). T had purchased the stock for $19,000 two years earlier. Assuming this is T's only contribution for the current year, he can either claim his deduction subject to the 30% limitation and carry over any excess, or *elect* to reduce the claimed deduction by the capital gain property's unrealized appreciation and forgo any carryover. T's deduction choices are

1. $15,000 current deduction (30% × $50,000 AGI) and $8,000 ($23,000 – $15,000) contribution carryover; or

2. $19,000 current deduction ($23,000 – $4,000 unrealized appreciation) and no carryover.

Obviously, the decision to reduce a current deduction by the property's unrealized appreciation *or* to claim the deduction subject to the 30% limit and carry over any excess amount will depend on several factors. Among the factors to be considered are:

1. The difference between the capital gain property's fair market value and its adjusted basis to the taxpayer (i.e., unrealized appreciation);

2. The taxpayer's current marginal income tax bracket compared to his or her anticipated future marginal tax rates; and

3. The taxpayer's expected remaining life and anticipated future contributions.

---

[128] § 170(b)(1)(C)(iii).

Twenty Percent Limitation

The 50% ceiling limitation imposed on an individual's annual charitable contribution deduction is an "overall" limitation. The 30% limitation applies to most contributions of capital gain property and to contributions of cash and ordinary income property contributed to nonqualifying private nonoperating funds. However, a more severe restriction is imposed on deductions for contributions of capital gain property to such private nonoperating foundations. In addition to the required *reduction* of the contribution by any unrealized appreciation in value, the deduction allowed for contributions to *private charities* (i.e., organizations not included in the seven categories listed earlier) is limited to the *lesser of:*

1. Twenty percent of AGI or
2. An amount equal to 50% of AGI, and reduced by contributions qualifying for the 50% and 30% limitations, including any amount in excess of the 30% limitation.[129]

Like excess contributions to public charities, any contributions to private nonoperating foundations that exceed the 20% limitation are carried forward and deductible subject to the 20% limit, in subsequent years.[130]

Example 68

D contributed $8,000 to his church (a public charity) and land worth $15,000 to a private nonoperating foundation in 2017. D had purchased the land for $11,000 in 2012. His AGI for the year is $20,000. D's contribution deduction for 2017 is $10,000 ($8,000 contribution to church + $2,000 of the eligible $11,000 contribution to private foundation [$15,000 market value − $4,000 unrealized "appreciation" = $11,000]). The deduction allowed for the contribution to the private foundation is limited to the *lesser of:*

1. $4,000 (20% × $20,000 AGI); or
2. $2,000 ([50% × $20,000 AGI = $10,000] − $8,000 contribution qualifying for the 50% limitation).

Note that D's total contribution deduction of $10,000 does not exceed 50% of his current adjusted gross income. If D had contributed $10,000 or more to his church, *none* of the $11,000 contribution to the private foundation would have been allowed. In either case, the excess contributions can be carried over to subsequent years.

CONTRIBUTION CARRYOVERS

An individual's contributions that exceed either the 20% limitation, the 30% limitation, or the 50% overall limitation may be carried over for five years.[131] All excess contributions due to the 20 and 30 percent limitations will *again* be subject to these limitations in the carryover years.[132] Although contribution carryovers are treated as having been made in the year to which they are carried, contributions *actually* made in the carryover year must be claimed before any carryover amounts are deducted.[133]

---

[129] § 170(b)(1)(B)(i).

[130] § 170(d)(1).

[131] § 170(d)(1)(A) and Reg. § 1.170A-10(a).

[132] Reg. § 1.170A-10(b)(2).

[133] Reg. § 1.170A-10(c)(1).

> ### Example 69
>
> In 2017, D contributes $10,000 cash to State University (a public charity). Her AGI for 2017 is $15,000. D's contribution deduction for 2017 is limited to $7,500 (50% × $15,000 AGI) and she may carry over the remaining $2,500 to 2018. If she does not make contributions in 2018 that exceed the 50% limitation, D can claim the $2,500 carryover as a deduction. If the contributions actually made in 2018 exceed 50% of D's 2018 AGI, she must carry over the 2018 excess contributions *and* the $2,500 carryover from 2017.

> ### Example 70
>
> Assume the same facts as in *Example 69,* except that D's contribution was a capital gain property worth $10,000 instead of cash. Her 2017 deduction would be limited to $4,500 (30% × $15,000 AGI) and she would have a $5,500 contribution carryover. Since this carryover resulted from the 30% limitation, it will be subject to the 30% limit in any carryover year. Thus if D has adjusted gross income of $10,000 and does not make contributions in 2018, she can claim a deduction of $3,000 (30% × $10,000 AGI) and carry over the remaining $2,500.

All charitable contribution carryovers are applied on a first-in, first-out basis in determining the amount of any carryovers deductible in the current year.[134] Since such carryovers will expire if not deducted within five succeeding tax years, taxpayers obviously should limit actual contributions until the carryovers are used.

Miscellaneous Itemized Deductions

LO.7

Identify the personal expenditures that qualify as either miscellaneous itemized deductions or other itemized deductions.

As discussed in Chapter 7, two major changes regarding miscellaneous itemized deductions were introduced into the tax laws in 1986. Perhaps the most significant change involves the inclusion in this category of all *unreimbursed* employee business expenses. Prior to 1987, an employee's unreimbursed travel and transportation expenses were allowed as deductions in arriving at adjusted gross income. Since 1986, *both* unreimbursed employee expenses *and* those not reimbursed under an accountable plan must be treated as miscellaneous itemized deductions.[135] Additionally, an employee's unreimbursed costs for business entertainment and meals (whether or not incurred in connection with travel) must first be reduced by a 50% disallowance since only 50% of these costs qualify for deduction.[136] It is also important to remember that interest on any indebtedness to finance an employee's business expenses is treated as *nondeductible* personal interest expense.

The second major change involves the introduction of a deduction *floor* on the total of all expenses in this category similar to the approach taken for medical and casualty loss deductions. After 1986, miscellaneous itemized deductions are deductible only to the extent they *exceed* 2% of AGI.[137] The obvious intent of this change in the law is to limit the number of taxpayers who will be able to deduct miscellaneous itemized deductions—and thereby reduce the administrative cost of policing such deductions. Exhibit 11-6 contains a partial list of items qualifying as miscellaneous itemized deductions.

[134] Reg. § 1.170A-10(b)(2).

[135] Reg. § 1.62-2.

[136] § 274(n).

[137] § 67(a).

Example 71

T has $40,000 of adjusted gross income in 2017. His unreimbursed employee business expenses and other miscellaneous itemized deductions include:

Unreimbursed business travel expenses...............	$ 90
Subscription to *The Wall Street Journal*	110
Professional dues	250
Safe deposit box rental	50
Tax return preparation fee.........................	250
Total	$750

Since T's total miscellaneous itemized deductions of $750 do not exceed $800 (2% × $40,000 AGI), he will not be able to claim any deduction for these expenses.

EXHIBIT 11-6	Partial List of Miscellaneous Itemized Deductions

Reimbursed employee expenses under

    A nonaccountable plan

Unreimbursed employee expenses for

    Travel away from home (lodging and 50% of meals)
    Transportation expenses
    Entertainment expenses (after 50% reduction)
    Home office expenses
    Outside salesperson's expenses
    Professional dues and memberships
    Subscriptions to business journals
    Uniform costs, cleaning, and maintenance expenses
    Union dues

Investment expenses for

    Investment advice
    Investment newsletter subscriptions
    Management fees charged by mutual funds
    Rentals of safe deposit boxes

Qualifying education expenses

Job seeking expenses (in the same business)

Tax determination expenses for

    Appraisal costs incurred to measure deductions for medical expenses (capital improvements), charitable contributions, and casualty losses
    Tax return preparation fees
    Tax advice, tax seminars, and books about taxes

OTHER ITEMIZED DEDUCTIONS

The final category of itemized deductions includes certain personal expenses and losses that cannot be classified in any of the other categories discussed thus far. Some of the items in this category—referred to as "Other Miscellaneous Itemized Deductions"—are discussed in other chapters.

1. Unrecovered investment in an annuity where the taxpayer's death prevents recovery of the entire investment. As discussed in Chapter 6, this deduction is allowed on the taxpayer's final tax return.

2. Impairment-related work expenses of persons with disabilities.

3. Amortizable premium on bonds purchased before October 23, 1986. Amortization of bond premium is discussed in Chapter 16.

4. Gambling losses to the extent of gambling winnings.

It is important to note that each of these items may be subject to its own unique set of limitations (e.g., gambling losses). Unlike miscellaneous itemized deductions, however, these deductions *are not* subject to the 2% limit.

THREE PERCENT CUTBACK ON ITEMIZED DEDUCTIONS

In the *American Tax Relief Act of 2012,* the Obama administration succeeded in convincing Congress that the tax benefit of itemized deductions of high-income individuals should be reduced. To do so, Congress resurrected the so-called 3% cutback rule (sometime referred to as the 3% reduction or phase-out) that had existed from 1990 through 2009. Under § 68, individuals must reduce their total itemized deductions (other than medical expenses, casualty and theft losses, investment interest, and gambling losses) by 3% of their AGI in excess of certain levels. These AGI levels are the same as those used for the phase-out of personal exemptions, differing based on filing status. The thresholds are adjusted annually for inflation and those for 2017 are shown below.

Filing Status	2017 Threshold AGI
Single individuals (not surviving spouse or head of household)	$261,500
Married filing jointly or surviving spouse	313,800
Head of household	287,650
Married filing separately	156,900

The total reduction cannot exceed 80% of the deductions. This limitation ensures that taxpayers subject to the cutback rule can deduct at least 20% of their so-called 3% deductions. Consequently, a taxpayer's itemized deductions are never completely phased out. The itemized deductions that are subject to the cutback rule are identified in Exhibit 11-7 below. Again, it is important to note that a taxpayer's medical expenses, investment interest expense, casualty and theft losses, and gambling losses are not subject to this limitation.

EXHIBIT 11-7	Itemized Deductions Subject to Cutback Rule

Taxes paid, including:

    State, local, and foreign income taxes

    State and local general sales taxes

    State, local, and foreign real property taxes

    State and local personal property taxes

    Mortgage interest on personal residences

    Charitable contributions

    Miscellaneous itemized deductions (in excess of 2% of AGI)

Example 72

Z, single, had AGI of $411,500 for 2017. His itemized deductions were: medical expenses ($1,200 after the limitation), real estate taxes paid ($3,000), state income taxes ($7,400), home mortgage interest ($10,300), charitable contributions ($2,500), and miscellaneous itemized deductions ($800 after the 2% limitation). The amount of itemized deductions that Z may deduct for the current year is computed as follows:

Itemized deductions subject to cutback:

Taxes paid ($3,000 + $7,400)	$ 10,400	
Home mortgage interest	10,300	
Charitable contributions	2,500	
Miscellaneous itemized deductions	800	
Deductions subject to 3% cutback rule		$24,000
Tentative cutback:		
Adjusted gross income	$ 411,500	
Threshold amount (single taxpayers in 2017)	(261,500)	
Excess AGI	$ 150,000	
Times: 3%	× 3%	
Tentative cutback	$ 4,500	
Cutback limit:		
Itemized deductions subject to cutback	$ 24,000	
Times: 80%	× 80%	
Maximum cutback	$ 19,200	
Cutback: Lesser of tentative cutback or maximum cutback		(4,500)
Amount deductible after 3% cutback		$19,500
Plus: Itemized deductions not subject to cutback (medical expenses)		1,200
Total deduction for itemized deductions		$20,700

Example 73

Assume the same facts as in the *Example 72* above, except that Z's AGI was $961,500.

Total itemized deductions subject to cutback		$24,000
Tentative cutback:		
Adjusted gross income	$ 961,500	
Threshold amount	(261,500)	
Excess AGI	$ 700,000	
Times: 3%	× 3%	
Tentative cutback	$ 21,000	
Cutback limit:		
Itemized deductions subject to cutback	$ 24,000	
Times: 80%	× 80%	
Maximum cutback	$ 19,200	
Cutback: Lesser of tentative cutback or maximum cutback		(19,200)
Amount deductible after 3% cutback		$ 4,800
Plus: Itemized deductions not subject to cutback (medical expenses)		+ 1,200
Total deduction for itemized deductions		$ 6,000

Note that Z's tentative cutback ($21,000) exceeds the maximum cutback ($19,200). Thus, Z is allowed to deduct at least 20% ($24,000 × 20% = $4,800) of the itemized deductions subject to the cutback rule. As the examples show, relatively few taxpayers will suffer drastic cutbacks in their itemized deductions. However, those taxpayers with AGI above the annual threshold amount will find that they face another complexity in computing their itemized deductions.

As can be seen from the above examples, relatively few taxpayers will suffer drastic cutbacks in their itemized deductions. However, those taxpayers with AGI above the annual threshold amount will find that they face another complexity in computing their itemized deductions.

Tax Planning Considerations

MAXIMIZING PERSONAL DEDUCTIONS

Each year the taxpayer must choose between taking the standard deduction and itemizing actual deductions. If the standard deduction is chosen, then legitimate itemized deductions are lost. If the taxpayer chooses to itemize actual deductions, then the standard deduction is lost. One technique used to minimize the loss of personal deductions is to shift actual itemized deductions from one year to another (to the extent allowed by law) so that they are high in one year and low in the next.

Example 74

S is single and has itemized deductions that are expected to be constant in 2017 and 2018 as follows:

Mortgage interest	$ 400
Dental expense (deductible portion)	1,400
State and local taxes	350
Charitable contributions	+1,350
Total	$3,500

Assume for purposes of illustration, the standard deduction for both years is $4,000. S cannot itemize actual deductions in 2017 or 2018 because actual deductions are less than the standard deduction. Over the two-year period, S will deduct $8,000 for personal expenses by claiming the standard deduction. However, if S were able to shift $1,000 of elective dental expenses from 2018 into 2017, and also accelerate the 2018 charitable contribution into 2017, then she would receive a greater tax benefit in the two-year period for personal expenses. After shifting the expenses, deductions in each year would be:

	2017	2018
Mortgage interest	$ 400	$ 400
Dental expense (deductible portion)	2,400	400
State taxes	350	350
Charitable contributions	2,700	0
Total	$5,850	$1,150

Although actual personal expenses still total $7,000 over the two-year period, S now has itemized deductions of $5,850 in 2017 and a standard deduction of $4,000 in 2018. During the two-year period S will deduct $9,850 for personal expenses and will receive $1,850 more in deductions than if personal expenses had not been shifted.

MEDICAL EXPENSES

The dependency exemption under a multiple support agreement should be assigned to the taxpayer who pays the medical expenses of the dependent. The medical expenses are deductible only by the family member entitled to the dependency exemption and only if that family member actually pays on behalf of the claimed dependent. Medical expenses paid by other family members on behalf of the dependent will not be allowed as deductions.

Often expenditures incurred in the care of an ill or handicapped child may qualify for either a medical expense deduction or for the child care credit (discussed in Chapter 13). When this happens, the tax liability should be computed under each alternative to determine which is more advantageous. Usually the choice depends on the taxpayer's marginal tax rate as compared to the credit percentage rate. The choice will also depend on the 10% threshold and whether the taxpayer is itemizing or taking the standard deduction.

Example 75

In 2017, T and W spend $2,000 for care of their handicapped child. The $2,000 qualifies both as a medical expense and for the child care credit. T and W have other medical expenses that exceed the 10% threshold amount. T and W file a joint tax return, and their marginal tax rate is 33 percent. The applicable percentage for the child care credit is 20 percent. If T and W are able to itemize deductions, they will receive a $660 tax benefit ($2,000 × 33%) for claiming the expenditure as a medical expense, whereas they will receive only a $400 tax benefit ($2,000 × 20%) if they claim the expenditure for the child care credit. If T and W are not able to itemize deductions or if they cannot exceed the 10% medical expense threshold amount, then the expenditure should be claimed for the child care credit.

CHARITABLE CONTRIBUTIONS

When a taxpayer makes noncash donations of property having a fair market value lower than the adjusted tax basis, it may be more advantageous to sell the property and donate the proceeds. If the property is held for investment, the sale will yield a deductible capital loss in addition to the charitable deduction. No loss will result, however, if the property itself is donated. To recognize a loss when selling depreciated property, the property must be held for investment or business use rather than for personal use.

Example 76

T owns 100 shares of X Corporation stock that he bought for $5,000 several years ago. The stock currently has a fair market value of $2,000. If T donates the stock to a qualified charity, he will only be entitled to a $2,000 charitable deduction. If T sells the stock and donates the $2,000 proceeds to a qualified charity, he will be entitled to a $3,000 capital loss as well as a $2,000 charitable deduction.

MISCELLANEOUS DEDUCTIONS

Because certain miscellaneous itemized deductions are deductible only to the extent that they aggregately exceed 2% of the adjusted gross income, it is important that expenses that can be properly classified into another, nonlimited category be identified and separated. For example, if a taxpayer supplements his or her regular salary with self-employed consulting income, it may be proper to deduct some of the cost of professional publications, professional journals, and educational expenses on Schedule C rather than as a miscellaneous itemized deduction.

Some unreimbursed employee business expenses that are not presently deductible because of the 2% limit might be converted into deductible reimbursed employee business expenses by agreement with the employer.

> **Example 77**
>
> K incurs $500 of unreimbursed employee business expenses each year for subscriptions to professional journals. Her miscellaneous itemized deductions do not exceed the 2% limit; she is therefore unable to deduct any of this expense. K's employer agrees, as part of next year's compensation increase, to reimburse her for this $500 of employee business expenses. In effect, K is using pre-tax dollars for the professional subscriptions and the result is equivalent to $500 of increased wages offset by a fully deductible $500 of employee business expenses.

Problem Materials

DISCUSSION QUESTIONS

11-1 *Medical Expenses and Dependency Status.* Under what circumstances is a taxpayer entitled to deduct medical expenses attributable to other people?

11-2 *Medical Expenses.* F and M are the divorced parents of three minor children. M, the custodial parent, has proposed to F that the current child-support payments be increased in order to pay the expected dental costs of having braces put on their oldest son's teeth. F's tax advisor has suggested that F agree to pay these costs directly to the dentist rather than increasing the support payments. From a tax perspective, why has F's advisor made this suggestion?

11-3 *Medical Expenses.* K and her two brothers currently provide more than half the support of their mother. For the past several years, they have taken turns claiming a dependency exemption deduction for their mother under a multiple support agreement. This year, K will be entitled to the exemption, and her mother needs money for cataract surgery and new eyeglasses. K's accountant has suggested that she can double up on the tax benefits by directing her share of her mother's support toward these expenses. How is this possible?

11-4 *Medical Expenses.* For the past several years, L's total itemized deductions have barely exceeded his standard deduction amount, and this pattern is not expected to change in the near future. L is currently faced with elective surgery to repair a hernia, and the procedure is not covered under his health insurance policy. Strictly from a tax perspective, and assuming that this ailment is not life threatening, what advice would you give to L concerning the timing of the surgery?

11-5 *Prepaid Medical Expenses.* What is the requirement imposed on taxpayers who wish to deduct prepaid medical expenses? What potential abuse is prevented by this requirement?

11-6 *Medical Deductions—Percentage Limitation.* The only medical expenditures made by taxpayer T during 2017 were for prescription drugs costing $4,100 and new eyeglasses costing $400. If T has adjusted gross income of $30,000 for the year and itemizes his deductions, how much, if any, medical expense deduction will he be allowed?

11-7 *Medical Travel Expenses.* W resides in Gary, Indiana and suffers from chronic bronchitis. At the advice of her doctor, W spends three months each year in Flagstaff, Arizona. Under what circumstances would W be entitled to claim the costs incurred for these trips as deductible medical expenses? If deductible, which costs?

11-8 *Casualty Losses.* Taxpayer F has adjusted gross income of $20,000 during the current year and he asks you the following questions regarding the deductibility of damages to his home caused by a recent hurricane. (**Hint:** See Chapter 10 for discussion of limitations on casualty loss deductions.)

    a. If F does not have home insurance, how much must his loss be before any deduction is available?

    b. If F repairs the damage himself, what amount can he deduct for the value of his time?

    c. If the area in which he resides is declared a disaster area, what options are available to F as to when and how to claim a deduction for the casualty loss?

11-9 *Taxes versus Fees.* What is the distinction between a deductible tax and a fee? If an individual taxpayer paid appraisal fees in connection with the determination of his personal casualty loss and charitable contribution deductions, would these payments be deductible?

11-10 *Deductible Income Taxes.* Which income taxes are deductible by an individual taxpayer? Does it make any difference whether the taxes are paid directly by the taxpayer as opposed to being withheld from his or her salary and paid by an employer to the appropriate taxing authority?

11-11 *Filing Status and State Income Taxes.* If married taxpayers file separate state or Federal income tax returns, how is the Federal tax deduction for state income taxes determined?

11-12 *State and Local Sales Tax Deduction.* Your brother has called you for advice concerning the deductibility of the $1,460 state sales taxes that he paid on the purchase of his new Ford F250 truck. What other information would you need from you brother to properly answer his question?

11-13 *Personal Property Taxes.* What is an *ad valorem* tax? What difference does it make to a taxpayer if he or she pays a tax on non-business property and the tax is based on weight or model year as opposed to value?

11-14 *Real Estate Tax Apportionment.* How are real estate taxes apportioned between the buyer and seller in the year real property is sold? What effect does the apportionment have on the seller if the buyer pays the real estate taxes for the entire year?

11-15 *Special Tax Assessments.* Under what circumstances can a property owner claim a deduction for a special tax assessment?

11-16 *Personal Interest.* What is the current limitation imposed on the deductions of personal interest? What impact do you suppose this restriction might have on debt-financed consumer purchases?

11-17 *Deductible Interest.* Your neighbor has come up with an excellent tax plan and he asks you for advice on structuring his scheme. He plans to give each of his five children a $10,000 promissory note, due in 20 years and bearing interest at 10% per year. The interest will be paid annually and he plans to claim a $5,000 interest expense deduction. Do you see any flaws in this plan? What advice would you give to your neighbor?

11-18 *Classifying Interest Expenses.* The local bank has just introduced a new loan program entitled "Home Equity Credit Line" under which individuals can either borrow funds or finance credit card purchases based on the equity they have in their homes. What is the tax incentive offered by this arrangement?

11-19 *Investment Interest Expense.* What is the investment interest expense limitation? Which taxpayers are not subject to this limitation? What is the purpose of the limitation?

11-20 *Types of Interest Expense.* D is a spender, not a saver. In fact, he spends money he doesn't even have. This year he borrowed more than $50,000 and paid interest of close to $7,000. D was shocked when his accountant told him that only certain types of interest were deductible.
   a. Identify the different types of interest expense and explain the treatment of each.
   b. How will D classify the interest expense that he paid?

11-21 *Charitable Contribution Requirements.* What are the basic requirements imposed on an individual taxpayer's deduction for charitable contributions?

11-22 *Contributions of Ordinary Income Property.* What is ordinary income property? Does this contribution deduction limitation apply to all taxpayers? Explain.

11-23 *Contributions of Capital Gain Property.* Under what circumstances must a taxpayer reduce his or her contribution deduction by the unrealized appreciation in value of capital gain property donated to a qualifying charity? How might this limitation be avoided?

11-24 *Contribution Deduction Percentage Limitations.* What are the percentage limitations imposed on an individual taxpayer's annual charitable contribution deduction? In what order must these percentage limitations be applied to current contributions?

11-25 *Contribution Carryovers.* Which excess contributions may be carried forward by an individual taxpayer? For how many years? In determining the amount of his or her contribution deduction for the current year, how must the taxpayer treat the carryovers from prior years?

11-26 *Miscellaneous Itemized Deductions.* E's employer has offered her the option of a $50 monthly pay raise or a reimbursement plan to cover her current subscriptions to professional journals ($200) and her dues to professional organizations ($350). E files a joint return with her husband, and they expect their adjusted gross income to be $50,000 for the upcoming year. Assuming that their only miscellaneous itemized deductions are from E's subscriptions and professional dues, is this a good offer? Explain.

PROBLEMS

11-27 *Medical Expense Deduction.* R, an unmarried taxpayer, has adjusted gross income of $60,000 for 2017. During the year, he paid the following amounts for medical care: $900 for prescription medicines and drugs, $8,000 for hospitalization insurance, and $4,400 to doctors and dentists. R filed an insurance reimbursement claim in December 2017 and received a check for $1,200 on January 24, 2018.

    a. Assuming R itemizes deductions, determine the deduction allowed for the medical expenses paid in 2017.

    b. What effect does the insurance reimbursement have on R's deduction for 2017? How should the reimbursement be treated in 2017 if R's itemized deductions for 2017 (including the medical expense deduction) were $4,500 greater than his standard deduction?

    c. How should the reimbursement be treated in 2018 if R's itemized deductions for 2017 were $400 greater than his standard deduction?

11-28 *State Income Taxes.* During 2017, K paid $500 in estimated state income taxes. An additional $400 in state income taxes was withheld from her salary by K's employer and remitted to the state. K also received a $200 refund check during 2017 for excess state income taxes paid in 2016. She had claimed a deduction for $750 of state income taxes paid in 2016. K uses the cash method of accounting and has adjusted gross income of $50,000 for the year.

    a. If K itemizes her deductions, how much may she claim as a deduction for state income taxes on her 2017 Federal tax return?

    b. If K's itemized deductions for 2016 were $1,900 greater than her standard deduction, how must the $200 refund be treated for Federal income tax purposes?

11-29 *General Sales Tax Deduction.* Rob and Lisa are married and file a joint return for 2016. They have three dependent children ages 7, 9, and 12 and the family lived in Orlando Florida for the entire year. For each of the questions below, assume that the couple has AGI of $87,900 and no other available income.

    a. Using the 2016 optional sales tax tables located in Appendix A of this text, determine the couple's state sales tax deduction for 2016.

    b. How would your answer in (a) above change if Rob and Lisa also paid $1,250 sales tax on the purchase of a new car and an additional $350 on the purchase of new furniture?

    c. Assume that the family lived in Georgia rather than Florida for the entire year. Also assume that Rob and Lisa paid $3,200 in state income taxes in 2016. How does this additional information change your answer to (b) above?

11-30 *Real Estate Tax Apportionment.* S sells her home located in Blue Springs, Missouri, on March 1, 2017. Blue Springs assesses real property taxes at the beginning of each calendar year for the entire year, and the property tax becomes a personal liability of the owner of real property on January 1. The tax is payable on April 1, 2017. Buyer B paid $80,000 for the home on March 1, 2017 and also paid the $1,200 real estate taxes on April 1. Both S and B are cash basis, calendar year taxpayers.

    a. How much of the $1,200 in real estate taxes is deductible by S? What adjustment must S make to the amount she realized from the sale?

    b. How much of the $1,200 in taxes is deductible by B? How will he treat any of the taxes paid which are attributable to S?

11-31 *Interest Expense Limitations.* Indicate in each of the following cases the amount of interest expense, if any, that the taxpayer is allowed to deduct.

    a. During the year, H used his bank credit card to purchase a new tablet computer for his teenage daughter. Finance charges for the year were $70.

    b. Over the years, G has consistently borrowed against her insurance policies because of their low rates. This year, she paid interest of $1,100 on the loans.

    c. D has three residences. His principal residence is in Newark, New Jersey. On the Newark home, he has a mortgage of $300,000 on which he paid interest of $18,000 for the year. He also owns a summer home in Martha's Vineyard, a beautiful island off the southern coast of Massachusetts. He has a $200,000 mortgage on his summer home and this year paid $10,000 of interest. His third residence is a condominium in Aspen, Colorado on which he has a $120,000 mortgage. This year he paid $8,000 of interest expense on the condominium's mortgage.

    d. B owns a home in Denver that she purchased in 2005 for $95,000. The current balance on B's mortgage loan is $60,000 and the property is worth $150,000. During the year, B obtained a second mortgage on her home, receiving $20,000 which she used to pay off her two outstanding car loans. Interest on the first mortgage was $4,000 while interest on the second mortgage was $1,000.

    e. M is a heavy trader of stocks and bonds, using his margin account frequently. This year, interest expense charged on his margin purchases was $5,200. M's investment income was $2,400.

    f. R is an employee of a television repair shop. He uses his own truck solely for business, making customer service calls. During the year, he paid $1,450 interest on a loan on his truck.

11-32 *Investment Interest Expense.* R, a cash basis, single taxpayer, paid $17,000 of investment interest expense during 2017. R uses the calendar year for tax purposes and reports the following investment income: $1,500 interest income, and $3,500 dividends.

    a. How much of the investment interest expense is deductible by R in 2017?

    b. What must R do with any investment interest expense deduction which is disallowed for 2017?

11-33 *Investment Interest Expense Limitation.* L is an engineer. This year, she borrowed $300,000 and purchased 40 acres south of Houston. For the year, L paid interest of $30,000 on the loan. Her tax records revealed the following additional information:

Income:	
Salary	$50,000
Qualifying dividends	8,000
Share of partnership income:	
Ordinary loss	(3,000)
Portfolio income:	
Interest	1,000
Rental income	8,000
Expenses:	
Rental expenses	7,000
Qualified residence interest	10,000
Property tax on land	5,000
Investment publications	400
Professional dues, licenses, and subscriptions	1,100

The items noted concerning the partnership result from L's limited partnership interest in Country Homes, a real estate development. The rental income is derived from a four-unit apartment complex that is currently filled with tenants with one-year leases. The related rental expenses include $2,000 of interest expense on the debt to acquire the apartments. Compute L's deduction for investment interest expense this year, assuming that she includes the qualifying dividends in the calculation of net investment income.

11-34 *Interest Expense—Note Discount.* Taxpayer T signed a note for $2,000 on August 30, 2017, agreeing to pay back the loan in 12 equal installments beginning September 30, 2017. The 12% interest charge ($2,000 × 12% = $240) was subtracted from the face amount of the note and T received $1,760, all of which was used to purchase furniture for his business. T uses the calendar year as his taxable year.

a. If T is a cash-basis taxpayer and he makes the four payments scheduled for 2017, what is his deduction for interest on the note in 2017? In 2018?

b. Would your answers to (a) change if T were an accrual method taxpayer? Explain.

11-35 *Charitable Contributions.* Determine the amount of the charitable deduction (without regard to percentage limitations) allowed in each of the following situations:

a. Rent-free use of building for three months allowed for the United Way fund drive. The building normally rents for $900 per month, and the owner paid $1,100 for utilities during this period.

b. Gift of General Motors stock valued at $9,000 to State University. Taxpayer purchased the stock five months ago for $11,000.

c. Donation of stamp collection valued at $4,000 to local museum for display to the general public. Taxpayer had paid $1,000 for the stamps many years ago.

d. Gift of paintings to local hospital to be placed on the walls of a remodeled floor. The paintings were painted by the donor and were appraised at $20,000.

e. Donation of Civil War relics to American Heart Association to be sold at its current fund-raising auction. Taxpayer paid $1,000 for the relics ten years ago and an expert appraiser valued them at $7,000 on the day of the gift.

11-36 *Contribution Deductions—Percentage Limitations.* J contributed $10,000 to the University of Southern California and a long-term capital asset worth $10,000 (basis of $5,000) to a private non-operating foundation during 2017. Assuming his adjusted gross income for the year is $24,000, answer the following:

a. What is the amount of J's contribution deduction for 2017?

b. How must any excess contributions be treated?

c. If J had come to you for advice before making the gifts, what advice would you have offered?

11-37 *Contribution Deductions—Percentage Limitations.* During 2017 R donated land to her church (a public charity) to be used as a building site for a new chapel. R had purchased the land as an investment in 2009 at a cost of $10,000. The land was appraised at a fair market value of $30,000 on the date of the gift. Assuming R's adjusted gross income for 2017 is $60,000, answer the following:

a. If R made no additional charitable contributions during 2017, what is the amount of her contribution deduction for the year?

b. If R contributed cash of $20,000 to her church in addition to the land, what is the amount of her charitable contribution deduction for 2017?

c. Calculate the amount of R's excess contributions from (a) and (b) and explain how these amounts are to be treated.

11-38 *Contribution Deductions—Percentage Limitations.* T, a single taxpayer, had adjusted gross income of $20,000 for 2017. During the year, T contributed cash of $1,000 and Xerox Corporation stock worth $10,000 to his church (a public charity). T inherited the stock during 2014 when it was valued at $8,000.

a. Calculate T's total contribution deduction for 2017.

b. How must any excess contributions be treated?

c. If T does not anticipate being able to itemize his deductions in any future years, what might he do in 2017 to increase his current contribution deduction?

11-39 *Miscellaneous Itemized Deductions.* R, single, has the following miscellaneous itemized deductions for the current year:

Unreimbursed employee business expenses	$1,350
Professional dues and subscriptions	650
Job-seeking expenses	800
Tax return preparation fee	250
Safe-deposit box rental (for stocks and bonds)	50

Assume that R itemizes his deductions for the current year.

a. What is the amount of R's deduction for the above items if his adjusted gross income is $70,000 for the current year?

b. What is the amount of R's deduction for these items if his adjusted gross income is $100,000 for the current year?

11-40 *Calculating Itemized Deductions.* Robert and Jean Snyder have an adjusted gross income of $30,000 for 2017. Their expenses for 2017 are

Prescription drugs	$ 300*
Medical insurance premiums	900
Doctor and dental bills paid	1,400*
Eyeglasses for Robert	185
Hospital and clinic bills paid	450*
Property taxes paid on home	900
State income taxes paid:	
Remaining 2016 tax liability	125
Withheld from wages during year	1,850
State and local sales taxes paid:	
Amount paid on new automobile	800
Amount paid on new wide screen television	280
Personal property taxes paid	100
Interest on home mortgage**	4,750
Interest paid on personal auto loan	1,100
Interest paid on credit card purchases	400
Interest paid on E.F. Hutton margin account***	120
Cash contributions to church	2,000
Fair market value of Hightech Corp. stock contributed to church (purchased for $1,000 three years ago)	5,000
Labor union dues paid by Robert	200
Qualifying education costs paid by Jean	300
Safe deposit box rental (for stocks and bonds)	50
Fee paid accountant for preparation of 2017 state and Federal tax returns	350

* These amounts are net of insurance reimbursements received during 2017.

** This mortgage was created at the time the home was purchased.

*** This investment interest expense is related to the production of $1,500 of net investment income.

The Snyders drove their personal automobile 500 miles for medical and dental treatment and an additional 1,000 miles in connection with charitable services performed for their church. Assuming Robert and Jean are both under age 40, lived in Virginia for the entire year, and plan to file a joint income tax return, determine their total itemized deductions. If a tax form is used for the computations, complete Schedule A (Form 1040).

11-41 *Three-Percent Cutback Rule.* H and W are married and file a joint return for the current year. They have the following itemized deductions (before any percentage limitations) for the year:

Medical and dental expenses	$8,000
Real estate taxes on home	3,500
Deductible interest on home mortgage	9,000
State income taxes paid	5,500
Charitable contributions	4,000
Miscellaneous itemized deductions	2,500

Determine H and W's itemized deductions, assuming the following levels of AGI for the current year.
a. $100,000
b. $413,800
c. $813,800

TAX RESEARCH PROBLEM

11-42 Sam Simpson transferred stock, real estate, and his principal residence to his former wife, Shirley, under the terms of the property settlement agreement. In exchange, Shirley agreed to pay Sam $250,000 down and another $750,000 at 10% per year for 10 years. Can Shirley deduct any of the interest she expects to pay over the next 10 years? Explain.

12

Deductions for Certain Investment Expenses and Losses

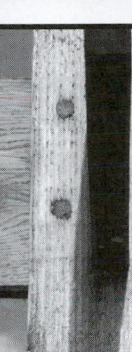

Learning Objectives

Upon completion of this chapter you will be able to:

LO.1 Discuss the basic rules governing the deduction of investment expenses.

LO.2 Describe the structure of a tax shelter.

LO.3 Explain the at-risk rules.

LO.4 Explain the passive loss rules.

LO.5 Understand the special treatment for interest expense related to a passive activity.

LO.6 Discuss the restrictions imposed on deductions related to vacation homes.

Chapter Outline

Introduction

LO.1

Discuss the basic rules governing the deduction of investment expenses.

Since 1942 Congress has generally allowed taxpayers to deduct expenses and losses incurred in connection with investment activities. As explained in Chapter 7, Code § 212 currently authorizes the deduction of investment-oriented expenses. This provision specifically allows a deduction for expenses incurred for the production or collection of income or for the management, conservation, or maintenance of property held for the production of income. Deductible investment expenses typically include such items as fees paid to rent a safety deposit box to hold securities, cost of financial advice, and travel expenses incurred in managing property. Expenses incurred in operating rental property such as those for maintenance, depreciation, utilities, and insurance are also deductible under § 212. Similarly, deductions for interest expense incurred by taxpayers to finance their investments also are deductible under § 212, although certain restrictions apply (as discussed in Chapter 11). Most important, the law generally allows the deduction of losses flowing through to the taxpayer from investments in partnerships and S corporations. Specific investment expenses incurred by the taxpayer are normally classified as miscellaneous itemized deductions and are subject to the two percent limitation and the deduction cutback. However, expenses related to property held for the production of rents or royalties are deductible *for* AGI. In addition, losses flowing from a partnership or S corporation are generally deductible for AGI.

For many years, the general rules adequately governed the deduction of most investment expenses and losses. In time, these rules became insufficient to police growing abuse. As a result, Congress enacted special provisions to restrict investment-type deductions where it found the general rule to be lacking. This chapter examines four additional measures: the at-risk rules, the passive activity limitations, the restrictions on the deduction for interest expense related to passive activities, and the provisions related to the rental of vacation homes.

Introduction to Tax Shelters

Historically, the tax law has generally allowed taxpayers to use deductions from one activity to offset the income of another. Similarly, most credits could be used to offset tax attributable to income from any of the taxpayer's activities.

Example 1

R earns $50,000 annually working as vice president of marketing at Plentiful Products, Inc. Over the years, he has accumulated a modest portfolio of stocks which generates dividends of about $10,000 a year. In addition, he is a 10% limited partner in a partnership that owns an apartment complex consisting of 200 units. During the year, the apartment complex had operating expenses that exceeded rental income, creating a $100,000 loss. Prior to 1987, R could use his share of the loss, $10,000, to offset his other income, both salary and dividends. Assuming R's marginal tax rate was 30 percent, the loss produced tax savings of $3,000.

The above example illustrates the essentials of what is now a well-publicized phenomenon: under prior law, an individual could reduce his or her tax liability—even eliminate it—by investing in "tax shelters" that produced losses which could be offset against other income. The attraction of such losses for taxpayers wishing to avoid taxes was so great that the tax shelter business grew into a thriving industry.

A tax shelter is simply an investment which takes advantage of certain tax rules to enhance its rate of return. Like any investment, there is an outlay of cash (or credit) for something that hopefully will yield income year after year and produce gain on its disposition. The ultimate reward or potential loss is usually commensurate with the risk that the investor is willing to assume. It is the tax treatment of the various pieces of the investment that converts an ordinary investment to a potential tax shelter. For example, in the broadest sense, an investment in municipal bonds may be considered a type of tax shelter because the return paid on the investment—the interest—is tax exempt. In the real world, however, the term *tax shelter* is usually not associated with tax-exempt bonds—tax-favored probably would be a more appropriate label. The words "tax shelter" typically conjures up images of complex investments that—as in *Example 1*—throw off losses to "shelter" the investor's other income.

STRUCTURE OF A TAX SHELTER

In the heyday of the industry, a tax shelter was organized as a limited partnership. From a tax perspective, the partnership form is the perfect structure for the shelter because it is not a separate taxable entity. Instead, a partnership acts as a conduit, enabling the tax benefits produced by the activity to flow through to the investing partners. Operating losses from the partnership's business flow through to the partners who may be able to offset the losses against their other income. Long-term capital gains realized by the partnership flow through, retaining their favorable character to be reported by the partners on their own returns. Special credits generated by the partnership's activity (e.g., the rehabilitation and low-income housing credits) might pass through to the partners to be used to reduce the tax on other taxable income. Observe the vital role that the flow-through characteristic of a partnership plays in a tax shelter. Such results could not be obtained with a C corporation. A C corporation, which is a separate taxable entity, pays taxes on its own income which may be taxed again when distributed to the shareholders as a dividend. More important, at least in a tax shelter sense, the losses of a C corporation can only be used by the corporation to offset its own income and, therefore, produce no benefits to the investing shareholders. For these reasons, tax shelters are not organized as C corporations. Indeed, it is not surprising that as tax shelters became more popular, the IRS tried to halt their growth by arguing that tax shelters posing as limited partnerships were not really partnerships but—because of their limited liability and their close resemblance to a corporation—were corporations. However, the government had little success with this theory and had to devise other techniques to eliminate the perceived abuse.

Promoters of tax shelters historically used limited partnerships—rather than general partnerships—as the vehicle of choice. The promoter, the one who put the deal together and got a fee for his efforts, normally acted as the general partner. To lure an investor, the promoter had to limit an individual's exposure to risk. By structuring the investment as a "limited" partnership, individuals could invest and limit the possibility of financial loss to the amount of their investment. Any liability in excess of that borne by the limited partners was the responsibility of the general partner. This ceiling on an individual's exposure was an extremely attractive feature in the promotion of tax shelters, paving the way for otherwise wary investors to make a financial commitment to the activity.

ELEMENTS OF A TAX SHELTER

Most tax shelters are constructed to offer three basic benefits: tax deferral, conversion of ordinary income into capital gain, and leverage. Each of these characteristics on its own can produce significant benefits. But when the three are combined into a single package, the result is almost too good to be true.

Deferral

Deferral is one of the most important tools in tax planning. Postponing the time at which taxes must be paid is the equivalent of an interest-free loan from the government. To illustrate, consider a taxpayer who can defer the payment of $10,000 of taxes for a five-year period. Assuming an after tax rate of return of ten percent, the present value of the tax payment is only $6,210 [$10,000 × (1/(1.10)^5)]. In this case, postponing payment of tax saves $3,790, a decrease of almost 38 percent!

A typical tax shelter achieves deferral through a mismatching of revenues and expenses. Mismatching occurs because of the timing of income and deductions. Normally a tax shelter produces deductible expenses prior to the period in which the investment produces income in sufficient amounts to offset the deductions. In the appropriately structured tax shelter, taxpayers may be able to use these excess deductions, in effect losses from the shelter, to offset income from other sources thus producing immediate benefits. Most tax shelters were built around this same modus operandi: Deduct expenses now while the gain accrues and is not taxed until later. This approach, "deduct now, pay later," is still the foundation of many current tax planning ideas.

Example 2

R, S, and T formed a partnership for the purpose of breeding cattle. Each contributed $15,000 for a one-third interest. The partnership uses the cash to purchase a herd of cattle consisting primarily of cows, heifers, and a few bulls. The partnership's only cash expenses during the year were the costs for breeding and maintaining the cattle totaling $45,000. No income was produced since none of the cattle were sold. Assuming the partnership uses the cash method of accounting and ignoring depreciation, the partnership has a loss of $45,000 which is allocated equally among R, S, and T. As a result, R, S, and T each have a $15,000 deduction for the losses attributable to their investment in the partnership, and this loss—prior to 1987—could be offset against income from other sources. Assuming each is in the 50% tax bracket (federal, state, and local), each saves taxes of $7,500 ($15,000 × 50%).

(**Note:** While a 50% tax rate might seem high today, that has not always been the case. From 1965–1986, the top federal rate was 70 percent. Even in 2016, a taxpayer living in New York City could pay a combined rate of almost 50% [35% federal + 8.82% state + 3.876% city = 47.696%].)

Note in the above example that the tax savings occur because the cash method of accounting results in a mismatching of expenses and revenues. Had the partnership been required to use the accrual method or simply prohibited from deducting the expenses until the partnership *sold* the cattle, revenue and expenses would have been properly matched—at least in the financial accounting sense—and no tax savings would result (unless the cattle are later sold at a loss). It also should be emphasized that the taxes saved in this situation are not permanently avoided but only *deferred* until the future when the cattle are sold.

Example 3

Refer to the situation in *Example 2* where expenses during the first year of operations were $45,000, producing a $45,000 deductible loss. Now assume that the cattle that were born and raised are sold for $45,000 on the first day of the next accounting period. If there were no other expenses, the partnership would have income of $45,000, each partner reporting $15,000. Since each partner is in the 50% tax bracket each pays taxes of $7,500. Note that the taxes paid in this period are the same as the taxes saved in the prior period. Thus, the taxpayer has not escaped $7,500 in taxes; nevertheless, the taxpayer has benefited since he deferred payment of the tax for one year. In addition, the taxpayer has benefited even though he had no gain or loss on the transaction as a whole ($45,000 income was equal to the $45,000 cost of breeding and raising). Of course, whether the taxpayers are happy with the result depends on the return that they could have otherwise received had the $45,000 been invested elsewhere.

The cattle example typifies the classic tax shelter but there were many more. Taxpayers could invest in partnerships created to explore for oil and gas, produce a movie or broadway show, buy art masters from which lithographs and prints could be made, or lease equipment (e.g., railroad boxcars, barges, cable TV systems, houseboats, executive jets, and any other item someone might be willing to rent). Perhaps the shelter of all shelters is real estate. Here the partnership buys an office or apartment building for which current depreciation deductions can be claimed even though the value of the building is holding or increasing. Despite their differences, all tax shelters had one common thread: claim deductions this year for expenses that add value that will not be taxed until next year.

While deferral is a huge advantage, the opportunities increase dramatically when the element of conversion can be added to the mix.

Conversion

The second element of the successful tax shelter involves conversion. Conversion is a two-step process. The first step concerns the treatment of deductions arising from the tax shelter activity. These expenses are deductible and reduce ordinary operating income that would otherwise be taxed at ordinary tax rates. The second step is where the conversion takes place. When the tax shelter activity is sold, any gain on the sale is taxed as long-term capital gain, which is taxed at the far more favorable capital gain rates.

Example 4

Recall *Example 3* where the cattle were purchased, bred and raised at a cost of $45,000. Assume now that the cattle are sold after they were held for more than two years—the holding period necessary for cattle if gain is to qualify for long-term capital gain treatment. Given this additional fact, the $45,000 gain would be treated as long-term capital gain and thus each partner would (using the tax rates in effect today) pay taxes at a capital gains rate of 20 percent, producing a tax of $3,000 (20% × $15,000) for each of the partners. Contrast the tax paid on the gain, $3,000, with the $7,500 of taxes saved from deducting the costs (50% × $15,000 share of the loss = $7,500). Most important, note that there was no real economic gain on the transaction: the cattle cost $45,000 to raise and then were sold for $45,000. However, because of the difference between the tax rates applying to ordinary income and capital gains, each partner is better off by $4,500 ($7,500 − $3,000). Note that in the previous example the $7,500 of taxes initially saved by each partner were entirely recouped by the government when the cattle were sold. In this situation, however, the government recoups only $3,000 of the original savings because the ordinary income was converted to capital gain. Thus, in this case, the taxpayer has not only benefited from deferral—deductions now, income later—but also earned $4,500 from the conversion of ordinary income into capital gain.

Leverage

The third element of most tax shelters is leverage. In physics, a strategically placed lever provides a mechanical benefit, enabling people to lift more than they would be able to with their own physical strength. The principle is the same in the world of finance. In investing, borrowing money enables an individual to obtain a larger return than otherwise could be obtained. For example, assume an individual purchases land for $100,000, $10,000 of her own money and $90,000 borrowed from a lender. If the investment is sold a year later for $120,000, there has been a 20% return on the total $100,000 investment. But for the individual investor, after paying back the lender $90,000 and $10,000 for the use of the money (i.e., interest), the $20,000 remaining means that she has doubled her money, a return of 100 percent! In tax terminology, the term *leverage* means that by borrowing money, a taxpayer can obtain a disproportionately large benefit from a small investment. The most common use, sometimes referred to as "tax leverage" concerns depreciation. For example, a tax shelter partnership might purchase a railroad boxcar for $25,000 down and finance the balance with a $75,000 note (i.e., the leverage). The law allows depreciation on the entire $100,000 not just the $25,000—creating much larger depreciation deductions than could have been obtained had depreciation been allowed only on the amount not borrowed.

Example 5

Assume the same facts as in the previous examples concerning the cattle breeding tax shelter except that the partnership acquired the original herd using an initial investment of $5,000 each—$15,000 total—and $30,000 of funds borrowed from the bank for which the partners are personally liable. Note the result when the taxpayer leverages a small investment with borrowed funds: Each taxpayer receives a deductible loss providing a tax saving of $7,500 ($45,000 deduction × 1/3 = $15,000 × 50%) which is more than his $5,000 original investment!

Note in the example above that by using leverage the taxpayers are able to generate $45,000 of deductions for an investment of only $15,000. In the language of tax shelters, this means that the taxpayers got a 3:1 write-off, $3 of deduction for each $1 invested. If the taxpayer is in the 50% tax bracket, a $3 deduction produces a benefit of $1.50 in tax savings at a cost of $1—clearly a miracle. When tax shelters were at the peak of their popularity, some investments boasted far greater benefits, 5:1, 10:1, and higher.

While the principle of leverage can work miracles, it can also spell disaster. If a tax-payer invests in a tax shelter where the write-off is 10:1, this means that the deal is highly leveraged—a large amount is being borrowed. If the investment goes sour, the lender still must be repaid. In such cases, the cost of the deductions could result in a severe financial loss. However, tax shelter promoters usually solved this problem by using a magical tool: *nonrecourse financing.*

A nonrecourse note is a loan for which the borrower bears no liability for the debt. If the borrower defaults on the loan, the lender can foreclose on the property (i.e., the collateral). However, if the funds derived from foreclosure and sale of the property are not sufficient to satisfy the loan obligation, the lender is out of luck—there is no recourse against the borrower. In a partnership, if the financing for the tax shelter activity was provided using nonrecourse debt (e.g., an office building or other real estate), the investing partners were only liable for the debt to the extent of their investment. As might be imagined, promoters took advantage of this phenomenon. In the most outrageous deals, the promoter would overstate the value of the investment and then act as the banker, providing the financing, all nonrecourse. The investors' cash investment would cover any real costs of the promoter and the nonrecourse financing simply served to create deductions.

Example 6

P put together a limited partnership to create deductible losses for the investors. Ten doctors invested $10,000 each for a partnership interest. The partnership used the $100,000 to buy a building from P for $1,000,000. The partnership signed a nonrecourse note to P for $900,000, payable with interest only for 20 years and a balloon payment of $900,000 at the end of the term. Before consideration of depreciation, operation of the office building broke even. The partnership proceeded to depreciate the property (a noncash expenditure), producing net losses that could be passed through and deducted by the partners. At the end of 20 years, the partnership might default on the note. In this case, P would take back his property and each partner would have received essentially $100,000 of deductions at a cost of $10,000. If the partners were in the 50% tax bracket, the deductions would be worth $50,000 and the arrangement would have provided a terrific return on the partners' investments. On the other side of the deal, P would pocket the $100,000 for his trouble. Note that the value of the building could have been whatever the partnership wanted to set, $1 million, $1.5 million, $2 million, or whatever, since the debt was nonrecourse and no one was ever going to pay!

In order to prevent what it considered the harmful and excessive use of tax shelters, Congress took action—albeit indirect—with enactment of the at-risk rules in 1976 and the passive loss rules in 1986. Perhaps fearing that it would alienate certain constituencies, Congress opted not to eliminate or limit the provisions on which shelters are built (e.g., special benefits for low-income housing and rehabilitation of old and historic buildings). Instead, the new legislation, placed limitations on the losses created by these special provisions.

At-Risk Rules

LO.3

Explain the at-risk rules.

As can be seen in *Example 6,* the linchpin that held many tax shelters together was non-recourse financing. From the outset, the government believed that investors should not be entitled to deductions unless they actually incurred a cost—something that was not necessarily present when a tax shelter was structured with nonrecourse financing. Consequently, to eliminate the possibility of artificial deductions, as part of the Tax Reform Act of 1976, Congress enacted § 465 and the so-called at-risk rules. Section 465 generally limits the deductions of individuals and closely held businesses to the amount which they could actually lose from the investment—the amount at-risk. Consequently, to secure the deduction, investors generally must commit personal funds to the venture's activities or be personally liable for debt incurred by the venture in carrying on its activities. The at-risk rules were subsequently amended in the Revenue Act of 1978 and the Tax Reform Act of 1986.

Initially, the at-risk rules were limited to four specific types of activities: (1) holding, producing, or distributing motion picture films or tapes; (2) farming; (3) leasing personal property; and (4) oil and gas exploration and development. As the list suggests, all of these were ripe for sheltering income. In 1978, legislation extended the rules to cover all other activities with one blatant omission: real estate. Real estate was added in 1986 but a huge exception was created in 1987. This exception essentially allowed real estate ventures to escape the at-risk limitations when they were financed using funds from a third-party commercial lender. Consequently, as the law currently reads, the at-risk rules apply to all trade or business or the production of income activities operated by individuals and closely held businesses. Real estate placed in service before 1987 (e.g., an office building or an apartment complex) is exempt as is a separate activity that involves the leasing of equipment by a closely held C corporation. It is important to realize that the at-risk rules cover *any* trade or business or investment activity. Unlike the passive loss rules discussed below, they are not limited to those investments that produce portfolio income or loss, or to those that produce passive income or loss.

AT-RISK COMPUTATION

Under § 465(a), the at-risk provisions limit the deduction of losses incurred in an activity to the amount *at-risk* in the activity at the close of the tax year. Any loss in excess of the amount at-risk cannot be deducted in the current year but can be carried forward and used when there is an increase in the amount at-risk. The following formula can be used to compute the amount at-risk (see Form 6198):

	Beginning at-risk balance
+	Contributions of cash and property (adjusted basis)
+	Increases in recourse debt (taxpayer is personally liable and the lender has no interest in the venture)
+	Increases in debt for which the taxpayer has pledged property which is not used in the activity as security
+	Increases in qualified nonrecourse debt related to realty
+	Income (taxable and tax-exempt)
–	Cash or property withdrawals or distributions
–	Nondeductible expenses related to tax-exempt income
–	Decreases in qualified nonrecourse debt related to realty
–	Decreases in recourse debt (T/P personally liable)
–	Losses
=	Amount at-risk

Observe that the calculation attempts to measure the amount of the taxpayer's economic investment that could be lost from the activity. Accordingly, a taxpayer's at-risk basis includes cash and other assets committed to the activity. Similarly, adjustments are made for income that is retained within the activity and not distributed since such amounts represent additional investments that might be lost. In addition, the at-risk amount includes amounts borrowed for use in the activity for which the taxpayer is personally liable for repayment—recourse debt—as well as amounts borrowed for which the taxpayer has pledged property as security (other than property used in the activity). Finally, as discussed further below, Congress appeased the real estate industry by including in the amount at-risk certain nonrecourse debt related to the holding of real property. Note that while the taxpayer's at-risk basis increases as these items increase, conversely, the at-risk amount is reduced as these items decrease (e.g., amounts are withdrawn, losses are incurred, recourse debt is reduced).

Example 7

In 2017, G started a business, designing web pages and providing connections to the Internet. He operated the business as a sole proprietorship. His first step was to purchase a server from a computer manufacturer for $100,000. He gave the company $10,000 cash and agreed to pay the manufacturer $90,000 over the next 10 years. In addition, he put up 20 shares of stock that he owned in his father's business worth $20,000 as collateral. The company agreed to accept the stock and equipment as security for the loan. G also borrowed $150,000 from the local bank. The bank required S to sign a note for the loan for which he is personally liable for repayment. During 2017, he contributed another $50,000 of his own money to keep the business running. For 2017 the business turned a small profit of $30,000 and G left the money in the business for working capital. G's at-risk basis includes, the $50,000 of his own money contributed to the business, the $10,000 used to purchase the equipment, the $20,000 of stock that he pledged to secure the equipment loan, the debt of $150,000 for which he is personally obligated, and the $30,000 of income that he left in the business for a total of $260,000. It does not include the $90,000 to be paid to the manufacturer since the note is nonrecourse and the property is used in the business. Note that the pledged property is included since the property is not used in the business as is the case with the equipment.

In the second year of operations, 2017, the business turned sour and produced a loss of $10,000. In addition, G withdrew $50,000 for personal use. He also made a $20,000 payment on the principal of the loan. Since G's at-risk basis is $260,000 the loss is not limited and G may use the loss to offset his other income (assuming he satisfies the passive loss rules discussed later in this chapter). G must adjust his beginning at-risk basis of $260,000 by reducing it for the loss of $10,000, the distribution of $50,000 and the $20,000 payment of the debt, leaving an at-risk basis of $180,000.

While the at-risk rules went a long way to eliminate abusive tax shelters, one industry was able to escape—real estate. After much controversy, the real estate lobby convinced Congress to provide relief for real estate deals to the extent that they used arm's length, third-party commercial financing (e.g., savings and loan provides loan and charges interest at a reasonable market rate). Consequently, a taxpayer's at-risk amount includes so-called qualified nonrecourse financing. Section 465(b)(6) sets forth the specific requirements.

1. The financing is secured by the real property used in the activity.

2. No person is personally liable for the debt (nonrecourse debt).

3. The amounts are borrowed from a person who is regularly engaged in the lending business (e.g., a commercial lender such as a bank or savings and loan or a federal, state, or local governmental unit).

4. The lender is not related to the taxpayer. Note that financing made by a lending institution that has an equity interest in the venture is permissible if the loan is commercially reasonable and similar to those made to unrelated parties.

5. The lender is not the seller of the property or the promoter of the deal (i.e., receives a fee for the taxpayer's investment) or related to the seller or promoter.

Example 8

J was one of 10 investors to contribute $100,000 to Silver Queen Partnership. Each investor received a 10% partnership interest. The partnership used the cash and $900,000 borrowed from First National Bank to purchase an office building for $1,900,000. The debt was secured by a mortgage on the building and was payable over 20 years with interest at 7 percent, the current market rate. None of the partners were personally liable on the obligation. This year J's share of the partnership's loss was $200,000. J's at-risk amount is $190,000, including the $100,000 cash contribution and 10% of the $900,000 nonrecourse loan. The loan is considered qualified nonrecourse financing since it was borrowed from an unrelated commercial lender and not the seller. Although J's share of the loss is $200,000, her deduction is limited to the amount she has at-risk, $190,000, and the balance is carried over. Her at-risk basis is reduced to zero and she may not deduct the $10,000 carryover until her amount at-risk increases.

Despite the at-risk rules, wily tax shelter promoters were able to structure investments that could avoid them. As might be expected, many of these deals involved real estate since real estate was effectively exempt if the financing was properly structured. To the chagrin of Congress, the tax shelters industry continued to grow. Perhaps one of the most revealing testimonials of the popularity of tax shelters can be found on the cover of the February 1986 issue of *Money* magazine. The cover pictured three highly successful individuals, and indicated that each had made more than a million dollars but paid no taxes. In light of this and other similar reports, it is not surprising that taxpayer confidence in the fairness of the tax system had badly eroded. Many taxpayers had come to believe that tax was paid only by the naive and the unsophisticated. This belief, in turn, was leading to noncompliance and providing incentives for expansion of the tax shelter market, often diverting investment capital from productive activities to those principally or exclusively servicing tax avoidance goals. Consequently, Congress took aim at tax shelters again in 1986 and enacted yet another hurdle to be cleared before losses could be deducted: the passive loss rules of § 469. These rules go beyond the at-risk provisions, placing far-reaching restrictions on when deductions, losses, and credits of a passive activity can be used to offset the income of another activity. Although these restrictions were designed principally for losses from a limited partnership interest, they also limit losses from rental activities, as well as losses from any trade or business in which the taxpayer does not materially participate.

Passive-Activity Loss Limitations

GENERAL RULE

The thrust of § 469 is to divide a taxpayer's income into three types: (1) wages, salaries, and other income from activities in which the taxpayer materially participates (e.g., income from an S corporation that the taxpayer owns and operates); (2) portfolio income (e.g., interest, dividends, capital gains and losses); and (3) passive income—the sort deemed to be produced by most tax shelters and rental activities. Expenses related to passive activities can be deducted only to the extent of income from *all* such passive activities. Any excess expenses of these passive activities—the passive activity loss— may not be deducted against portfolio income or wages, salaries, or any other income from activities in which the taxpayer materially participates. Losses that cannot be used are held in suspension and carried forward to be used to offset passive income of future years.[1] Suspended losses from a passive activity can be used in full to offset portfolio or active income *only* when the taxpayer disposes of his or her entire interest in the activity. Upon disposition, any current and suspended losses (including any loss realized on the disposition) are used to offset income in the following order:[2]

1. Any gain on the disposition of the interest.
2. Any *net* income from all passive activities (after taking into account any suspended losses).
3. Any other income or gain (i.e., active and portfolio income).

Observe that this special ordering rule requires the taxpayer to use up the suspended losses against gain on the disposition and any passive income (net of any passive losses) before offsetting such losses against active or portfolio income. Without this rule, a taxpayer would use all of the suspended loss against active income, thus freeing up the passive gain on the disposition to absorb other passive losses.

LO.4

Explain the passive loss rules.

---

[1] Suspended losses are carried forward to the following year, where they are treated as if they were incurred in such year. Temp. Reg. § 1.469-1T(f)(4)(B). Special limitations apply to farm losses of noncorporate taxpayers that receive subsidies (§ 461(j)).

[2] § 469(g). To date, Regulations have not been issued on dispositions, leaving many unanswered questions. See Erickson, "Passive Activity Disposition," *The Tax Adviser* (May 1989), p. 338. See TAM 9742002 where the taxpayer did not have to offset current and suspended losses from sold activities with passive income from only those activities that produced net incomes.

Example 9

T owned and operated her own construction company as a sole proprietorship. For the year, the company had net income of $120,000. T has a substantial portfolio that produced dividends of $15,000 and a short-term capital loss from the sale of stock of $7,000. In addition, her investment in LP1, a limited partnership, produced a passive loss. T's share of the loss was $30,000. Her investments in LP2 and LP3, two other limited partnerships, generated passive activity income. T's share of the income was $5,000. Under the capital gain and loss provisions, T may deduct $3,000 of the capital loss and carry over the remaining $4,000. The $30,000 passive loss is deductible only to the extent of passive income, which is $5,000. In effect, income and loss from the passive activities are netted, and the net loss attributable to LP1, $25,000, is carried over to the following year.

Example 10

Same facts as above. T held on to her investment in LP1 until this year, when she sold her entire interest, producing a gain of $40,000. Total suspended losses attributable to her investment in LP1 were $70,000. Net income from LP2 was $30,000 for the year while LP3 produced a net loss of $10,000. T may deduct the entire $70,000 loss: $40,000 against the gain, $20,000 against the net passive income from LP2 and LP3 ($30,000 − $10,000), and $10,000 against any other income.

As a practical matter, many taxpayers will have investments in several passive activities, some that produce income and some that produce losses. If the taxpayer has losses from more than one activity, the suspended loss for *each* activity must be determined in the event that the taxpayer subsequently disposes of one of the activities. The suspended loss of each activity is determined by allocating the total loss disallowed for the year, including any suspended losses, pro rata among the loss activities using the following formula:[3]

$$\text{Total disallowed loss for year} \times \frac{\text{Loss for this activity}}{\text{Total losses from all activities with losses}} = \frac{\text{Suspended loss}}{\text{for this activity}}$$

Note that this fraction simply represents the percentage of losses attributable to a particular activity. For example, if a loss from a particular activity represents 10% of all losses, 10% of the disallowed loss is allocated to such activity and carried over to the following year. Alternatively, it could be said that the particular activity absorbs 10% of any passive income. In effect, each loss activity absorbs this fraction of any passive income from other activities.

---

[3] Temp. Reg. § 1.469-1T(f)(2).

Example 11

T owns an interest in three passive activities: A, B, and C. For 2017, activity B reports income of $2,000 while activities A and C report losses of $10,000, $6,000 from A and $4,000 from C. T is allowed to deduct the passive losses from A and C to the extent of the passive income from B. Thus he may deduct $2,000 of the losses. The remaining loss of $8,000 cannot be used to offset T's income from other sources (e.g., wages, dividends, or interest income) but must be suspended and carried forward to the following year. The suspended loss of $8,000 must be allocated between the loss activities pro rata. Since 60% ($6,000/$10,000) of the net loss was attributable to A, the suspended loss for A is $4,800 (60% × $8,000). Similarly, the suspended loss for C is $3,200 ([$4,000/$10,000] × $8,000). Alternatively, the loss activities could be viewed as absorbing the passive income. Using this approach, the suspended losses would be computed somewhat differently but with the same result.

	A	C	Total
Loss for the year......................................	$ (6,000)	$ (4,000)	$ (10,000)
Loss absorbed:			
$2,000 × ($6,000/$10,000)	1,200	—	1,200
$2,000 × ($4,000/$10,000)	—	800	800
Suspended loss......................................	$ (4,800)	$ (3,200)	$ (8,000)

These losses are carried over and treated as if they were a deduction in the following year.

Example 12

Assume the same facts as in *Example 11*. The income and loss for 2018 of the three activities is shown below.

Activity	Current Net Income (Loss)	Carryforward from Prior Years	Total
A	$ (5,200)	$ (4,800)	$(10,000)
B	12,000	—	12,000
C	(1,800)	(3,200)	(5,000)
Total	$ 5,000	$ (8,000)	$ (3,000)

The total passive loss disallowed in 2018 is $3,000. The $3,000 disallowed loss is allocated among the activities with total losses (taking into account both current operations and losses suspended from prior years) as follows:

Activity	Total Disallowed Loss	×	Percentage of Total Loss	=	Allocable Portion of Loss
A	$3,000	×	$10,000/($10,000 + $5,000)	=	$2,000
C	3,000	×	5,000/($10,000 + $5,000)	=	1,000

In making the allocation, the disallowed loss is allocated based on an activity's net loss *including* suspended losses (e.g., $10,000 for A) rather than the loss that actually occurred in the current year (e.g., $5,200 for A).

Example 13

J has three passive activities: R, S, and T. The suspended losses and current income and losses for each activity for 2017 are shown below. In addition, J sold activity S for a $10,000 gain in 2017. Because there has been a complete disposition of S, J is able to deduct all of the suspended losses for S as shown below.

	R	S	T
Suspended loss..................................	$ (9,000)	$(12,000)	$(15,000)
Current income (loss)............................	(5,000)	(6,000)	(7,000)
Total..	$(14,000)	$(18,000)	$(22,000)
Gain on disposition of S		10,000	
Excess loss of S deducted against other income		$ (8,000)	

J must first offset the suspended and current losses of $18,000 from activity S against the $10,000 gain on the sale of S. The next step is to offset the $8,000 balance of losses against any net passive income for the year. In this case, the activities have no income, and thus none of the loss is absorbed by passive income. At this point, the remaining loss of $8,000 is no longer considered passive and can be used to offset any active or portfolio income that J may have.

Example 14

K has three passive activities: X, Y, and Z. The suspended losses and current income and losses for each activity for 2017 are shown below. In addition, in 2017, K sold activity Y for a $21,000 gain. K is able to deduct all of the suspended losses of Y as shown below.

	X	Y	Z
Suspended loss.......................................	$ (7,000)	$(10,000)	$(18,000)
Current income (loss)...............................	(8,000)	(6,000)	8,000
Total..	$(15,000)	$(16,000)	$(10,000)
Gain on disposition of Y...........................	0	21,000	0
	$(15,000)	$ 5,000	$(10,000)
Loss absorbed:			
$5,000 × ($15,000/$25,000)	3,000		
$5,000 × ($10,000/$25,000)			2,000
Suspended loss.....................................	$(12,000)		$ (8,000)

K must first offset Y's current and suspended losses of $16,000 against the $21,000 gain on the sale. Note that the balance of the gain ($5,000) is considered passive income that can be combined with the net losses (the sum of current income or loss and suspended losses) from the other passive activities for the year.[4]

Rules similar to those for passive losses apply to tax credits produced by passive activities (e.g., the low-income housing credit, rehabilitation credit, research credit, and jobs credit). Passive credits can be used *only* to offset any tax attributable to passive income. Any unused credit may be carried forward to the next taxable year to offset future taxes arising from

---

[4] § 469(g)(1)(A) and Temp. Reg. § 1.469-2T(c)(2)(i)(A)(2).

passive income. In contrast to passive losses, however, credits being carried over are not fully triggered when a passive activity is sold. In the year of disposition, like any other year, the credit can be used only if there is tax attributable to passive income (including gain on the sale of the activity). If the credit cannot be used, it can continue to be carried over to offset tax from other passive activities. However, the credit is subject to its own rules concerning carryover and expiration.

Example 15

T invested in a limited partnership that rehabilitated a historic structure. In 2017, T sold his interest, realizing a gain of $5,000. At that time, T had suspended losses of $20,000 and credits of $10,000. T is able to use $5,000 of the losses to offset the gain and the other $15,000 to offset other active or portfolio income. None of the credit can be used, however, because there is no income from the passive activity. Had T sold the property for a gain of $50,000, he would have had $30,000 of passive income. Assuming T is in the 28% tax bracket, he could have used $8,400 ($30,000 × 28%) of the credit. The remaining credit of $1,600 may be carried over to offset tax that may arise from passive income.

TAXPAYERS SUBJECT TO LIMITATIONS

The passive loss rules apply to individuals, estates, trusts, personal service corporations, and certain closely held C corporations.[5] Partnerships and S corporations are not subject to the limitations per se. However, their activities flow through to the owners who are subject to limitation.

The passive loss rules generally do not apply to regular C corporations. Presumably, their immunity is based on the theory that individuals generally do not benefit from losses locked inside the corporate form. Congress, however, did not want taxpayers to be able to circumvent the passive loss rules merely by incorporating. Absent a special rule, a taxpayer could utilize corporate immunity to shelter income derived from personal services. Taxpayers would simply incorporate as a personal service corporation and acquire tax shelter investments at the corporate level. The losses produced by the tax shelters would offset not only the service income but also income from any investments made at the corporate level. Consequently, the passive loss rules apply to *personal service corporations* (PSC). A PSC is one where the principal activity is the performance of personal services and such services are primarily performed by employees who own stock in the corporation either directly or indirectly.[6] Common examples of personal service corporations are professional corporations such as those of doctors, accountants, attorneys, engineers, actors, architects, and others where personal services are performed.

Without additional restrictions, any taxpayer—not just one who derives income from services—could incorporate his or her portfolio and offset the investment income with losses from tax shelters. To prohibit this possibility, the passive loss rules also apply in a limited fashion to all closely held C corporations (i.e., a regular C corporation where five or fewer individuals own more than 50% of the stock either directly or indirectly). Note that some personal service corporations that might escape the tests above may still be subject to the rules due to their status as closely held corporations. A closely held corporation may not use passive losses to offset its portfolio income. However, such corporations may offset losses from passive activities against the income of any active business carried on by the corporation.[7]

---

[5] § 469(a)(2).

[6] A PSC is defined in § 469(j)(2) by reference to § 269 to include any service. An employee-owner is one who owns

any stock during the year either directly or constructively under § 318 with certain modifications.

[7] § 469(e)(2).

Example 16

R and his two brothers own Real Rustproofing Corporation. For 2016, the corporation suffered a loss from operations of $10,000. In addition, it received interest income from short-term investments of working capital of $20,000. The corporation also had a passive loss from a real estate venture of $30,000. In determining taxable income, the passive activity limitation rules apply since the corporation is closely held (i.e., five or fewer individuals own more than 50%). As a result, none of the loss can be deducted since the loss cannot offset portfolio income of the corporation and the corporation did not have any income from operations. Had the corporation had $50,000 of operating profit, the entire loss could be deducted since passive losses can be used by a closely held corporation to offset active income—but not portfolio income.

PASSIVE ACTIVITIES

Assuming the taxpayer is subject to the passive activity rules, the most important determination is whether the activity in which the taxpayer is engaged is *passive.* The characterization of an activity as passive generally depends on the level of the taxpayer's involvement in the activity, the nature of the activity, or the form of ownership. Section 469(c) provides that the following activities are passive:

1. Any activity (other than a working interest in certain oil and gas property) that involves the conduct of a trade or business in which the taxpayer *does not materially participate;* and

2. *Any* rental activity regardless of the level of the taxpayer's participation.

Given these definitions, several questions must be addressed to determine whether a particular endeavor of the taxpayer is a passive activity.

1. What is an activity?
2. Is the activity a rental or nonrental activity?
3. What is material participation?

Unfortunately, none of these questions are easily answered. An exceedingly complex set of Regulations exists that, in large measure, creates intricate definitions designed to prohibit wily taxpayers from deducting their passive losses. The basic rules are considered below.

DEFINITION OF AN ACTIVITY

The definition of an activity serves as the foundation for the entire structure of the passive loss rules. Virtually all of the important determinations required in applying the passive loss rules are made at the activity level. Perhaps the most significant of these concerns the taxpayer's level of participation. As discussed later in this chapter, if the taxpayer participates for more than 500 hours per year in a nonrental activity, he or she is deemed to materially participate in the activity, and the activity is therefore not passive. As the following example illustrates, this 500-hour test requires an unambiguous definition of an activity.

Example 17

Mr R. Rock owns and operates 10 restaurants in 10 different cities. In addition, in each of those 10 cities he owns and operates 10 movie theaters. R spends 80 hours working in each restaurant during the year for a total of 800 hours. R spends 70 hours working in each movie theater for a total of 700 hours. If *each* restaurant and each movie theater are treated as separate activities, it would appear that R would not be treated as a material participant in any one of the businesses because he devoted only a minimum amount of his time during the year, 80 or 70 hours, to each. On the other hand, if all the restaurants are aggregated and deemed a *single activity,* R's total participation in all the restaurants, 800 hours would, in fact, be considered material. A similar conclusion could be reached for the movie theaters. In addition, if the restaurants are adjacent to the movie theaters (or in fact are concession stands in the theaters), it might be appropriate to treat the restaurant operation and the movie theater operation as a single activity.

The definition of an activity is not only important for the material participation test, but it is also significant should there be a disposition. As noted above, a complete disposition of an activity enables a taxpayer to deduct any suspended losses of the activity.

Example 18

Same facts as in *Example 17* above. Also assume that there are suspended losses for each restaurant. If each restaurant is treated as a separate activity, a sale of one of the restaurants would enable R to deduct the suspended loss for that restaurant. In contrast, if the restaurant is not considered a separate activity, none of the loss would be recognized on the tax return for the year of sale.

Examples 17 and *18* demonstrate not only the importance of the definition of an activity but also the problems inherent in defining what constitutes an activity.

The authors of § 469 obviously anticipated the difficulty in defining an activity and therefore provided no working definition in the Code. As a result, the formidable task of defining an activity fell in the laps of those who write the Regulations. Defining an activity would not be difficult if all taxpayers were engaged in a single line of business at one location. As a practical matter, this is not always the case. Some taxpayers, such as Mr. Rock in *Example 17,* are involved in several lines of business at multiple locations. Consequently, any definition of an activity had to consider such situations. In fixing the scope of an activity, the Treasury feared that a narrow definition would allow taxpayers to generate passive income at will that could be used to offset passive losses. For example, if Mr. Rock were able to treat each restaurant as a separate activity, he could easily manipulate his participation at each restaurant to obtain passive or active income as he deemed most beneficial. To combat this problem, the IRS initially designed a broad definition that generally required a taxpayer to aggregate various endeavors into a single activity. By establishing a broad definition that treats several undertakings as a single activity, the IRS made the material participation test easier to meet, resulting in active rather than passive income. Unfortunately, the initial definition was quite complicated, as evidenced by the Temporary Regulations, which contained 196 pages of intricate rules and examples devoted to the subject.[8] In a refreshing change of direction, however, the IRS allowed these Temporary Regulations to expire, creating a far simpler approach all contained in only four pages![9]

Appropriate Economic Unit

Under the final regulations, taxpayers are required to treat one or more trade or business activities or one or more rental activities as a single activity if the activities constitute an *appropriate economic unit* for measuring gain or loss.[10] Whether two or more activities constitute an appropriate economic unit (AEU) is determined by taking into account all of the relevant facts and circumstances. Five factors are to be given the greatest weight in making the determination. These are as follows:

1. Similarities and differences in *types* of business;
2. The extent of common control;
3. The extent of common ownership;
4. Geographical location; and
5. Interdependencies between activities (e.g., they have the same customers or same employees, are accounted for with a single set of books, purchase or sell goods between themselves, or involve products or services that are normally provided together).

A taxpayer may use *any* reasonable method of applying the relevant facts and circumstances.

---

[8] Temp. Reg. § 1.469-4T(a)(2).

[9] Reg. § 1.469-4.

[10] Reg. § 1.469-4(c)(1).

> ### Example 19
>
> C operates several businesses as a sole proprietor. These include a bakery and a movie theater at a shopping mall in Santa Fe and a bakery and a movie theater in Albuquerque. Reasonable groupings, depending on the facts and circumstances, may be as follows:
>
> - A single activity
> - A movie theater activity and a bakery activity
> - A Santa Fe activity and an Albuquerque activity
> - Four separate activities

Consistency Requirement

To ensure that taxpayers do not bounce from one grouping to another to fit their needs, a consistency requirement is imposed. Once the activities have been grouped in a particular manner, the grouping may not be changed unless the original grouping was clearly inappropriate or there has been a material change in the facts and circumstances that makes the original grouping inappropriate.[11] For instance, in *Example 19* above, once one of the groupings is selected, the taxpayer is required to continue using the grouping unless a material change in the facts and circumstances makes it clearly inappropriate.

In addition, to prevent a taxpayer from misusing the facts-and-circumstances approach, the IRS has the power to regroup activities if the taxpayer's grouping fails to reflect one or more appropriate economic units and one of the primary purposes of the taxpayer's grouping is to circumvent the passive loss rules.[12]

Activities Conducted through Conduit Entities

As a practical matter, many taxpayers will conduct activities through a partnership or an S corporation. In this case, the grouping is done at the partnership or S corporation level. Partners and S corporation shareholders then determine whether they should aggregate the entity activities with those they conduct directly or through other partnerships or S corporations.[13]

Grouping of Rental and Nonrental Activities

Rental activities and nonrental activities normally may *not* be grouped together and treated as a single activity. This rule is consistent with the basic provision that all rental activities are passive regardless of the taxpayer's participation. Therefore, it makes sense that rental and nonrental activities should not be aggregated. The practical significance of the rule is to prohibit taxpayers from sheltering active income with passive rental losses. Nevertheless, the Regulations do carve out an exception, allowing aggregation of rental and nonrental activities whenever either activity is *insubstantial* in relation to the other or the owners of the business activity have the same proportionate ownership interest as they have in the rental activity (e.g., 40% in one and 40% in the other).[14]

---

[11] Reg. § 1.469-4(g). In Notice 2008-64, 2008-31 IRB 268, the IRS proposed that taxpayers should be required to report any changes in groupings on the return.

[12] Reg. § 1.469-4(h).

[13] Reg. § 1.469-4(j).

[14] Reg. § 1.469-4(d).

Example 20

PB&K, an accounting firm, operates its practice out of an office building that it owns. The firm occupies two floors of the building and leases the other three floors to third parties. This year, 90% of the firm's income is from its accounting practice and 10% is from rental of the office space. Because the rental operation is insubstantial in relation to the nonrental operation, the rental and nonrental operations are aggregated into a *single nonrental* activity. Note that in this case any net loss on the rental activity is effectively combined with the income of the accounting operation.

Example 21

H and W, husband and wife, equally own Sliders, an S corporation that owns and operates 25 restaurants throughout the Midwest. Sliders is quite profitable. Several years ago, the company decided it should buy an airplane to enable it travel easily to its various locations. On the advice of their attorney, H formed Airmax, a single member LLC that purchased and leases out the plane. Sliders rents the plane on a long-term basis from Airmax. The S corporation pays the LLC a fair rent for use of the plane but because of depreciation and interest, the LLC annually reports a net rental loss from its operations. The LLC does not provide any services with respect to providing the plane so it is considered a rental activity and therefore is deemed to be passive. Absent any special rule, H would not be able to offset the losses of Airmax against the income from Sliders. However, under the Regulations, H may elect to group the LLC rental activity and the S corporation restaurant business as a single activity. This grouping election is permitted because the LLC and the S corporation have identical ownership. Alternatively, had there not been identical ownership, H may have been able to group the airplane leasing activity with the restaurant business assuming the rental activity is insubstantial to the restaurant activity.

It should also be noted that the rental of real property and the rental of personal property cannot be grouped unless the personal property is provided in connection with the real property.[15]

Example 22

T owns a small apartment building with eight units that he rents completely furnished. In addition, the building contains a small room with coin-operated laundry facilities. As a general rule, the laundry rental and apartment rental cannot be aggregated because the rental of real property cannot be grouped with the rental of personal property. In this case, however, the rental income and laundry income can be grouped since the personal property is provided in connection with the real property.

Rental and nonrental operations normally must be separated because they are subject to different rules. For example, rental activities are always passive, whereas nonrental activities are passive only if the taxpayer does not materially participate in such activities. In addition, owners of rental real estate are normally entitled to deduct up to $25,000 of rental losses annually without limitation, whereas there is no comparable rule for nonrental activities. Although rentals and nonrental activities are usually separated, certain exceptions may allow aggregation. As discussed above, if either activity is insubstantial to the other, aggregation can occur or if the owners own the same proportionate interest in each activity, they may be grouped.

---

[15] Reg. § 1.469-4(e).

RENTAL VERSUS NONRENTAL ACTIVITIES

Under the general rule described above, all rental activities are deemed to be passive, *regardless* of whether the taxpayer materially participates. Congress adopted this view based on the belief that there is seldom any significant participation in rental activities. Therefore, it created a presumption that all rental activities would be passive. For this purpose, a rental activity is defined as any activity whereby a taxpayer receives payments that are principally for the use of property owned by the taxpayer (e.g., apartments or equipment).

Observe that this blanket rule effectively classifies many rental activities as passive even though an owner might render significant services in connection with the rental. For example, renting video tapes would be considered passive under the general rule even though the owner might perform substantial services. This approach would be unfair to those who participate yet suffer losses. Moreover, the rule creates a huge planning opportunity for those seeking passive income given that many rental businesses are profitable. Recognizing these problems, the authors of the Regulations identified six situations where what is normally a rental is to be treated as a nonrental activity.[16]

1. *1–7 Days Rental.* The activity is not a rental if the average rental period is seven days or less. Under this exception, short-term rentals of such items as cars, hotel and motel rooms, or videocassettes are not considered rental activities.

2. *8–30 Days Rental.* The activity is not a rental if the average rental period is 30 days or less and significant services are performed by the owner of the property. In determining whether *significant services* are provided, consideration is given to the type of service performed and the value of the services relative to the amount charged for the use of the property. In this regard, the Regulations indicate that telephone service and cable television are to be ignored as are those services commonly provided in connection with long-term rentals of commercial and residential property (e.g., janitorial services, repairs, trash collection, cleaning of common areas, and security services provided by landlords of shopping malls and centers). Unfortunately, the Regulations provide few other clues as to what constitutes significant services.

Example 23

T owns and rents a resort condominium in Florida. He provides telephone, cable, trash removal, cleaning of the common areas, and daily maid and linen service. The cost of the maid and linen services is less than 10% of the amount charged to tenants occupying the apartments. In determining whether significant services are provided, the telephone, cable, trash, and cleaning services are disregarded. Moreover, according to the Regulations, the maid and linen services would not be considered significant in this case. Because there are no significant services under the Regulations' view, the activity would be considered a rental (*assuming* the average rental use exceeds seven days) and, therefore, a passive activity.

---

3. *Extraordinary Services.* The activity is not a rental if extraordinary personal services are provided by the owner of the property. Services are considered extraordinary if the use of the property is merely incidental to the services performed.

Example 24

Nathan Hale Military Academy, a private college preparatory school, provides housing for its students. The school's rental of such facilities would be considered incidental to the educational services provided and thus be treated as a nonrental activity.

---

4. *Incidental Rentals.* The activity is not a rental activity if the rental of the property is merely incidental to the nonrental activity.

---

[16] Temp. Reg. § 1.469-1T(e)(3)(ii).

The Temporary Regulations identify two situations when this rule applies.[17]

- *Investment Property.* An activity is not considered a rental if the rental property is held primarily for investment. Two tests must be met. First, the principal purpose for holding the property must be for the expectation of gain from appreciation due to market changes and not due to improvements to the property. Second, the gross rental income from the property is insignificant; that is, the rent must be less than two percent of the lesser of (1) the unadjusted basis of the property or (2) the fair market value of the property.

Example 25

S owns land that she is holding for future appreciation. She purchased the land for $500,000 and it is currently worth $800,000. To defray the costs of holding the land, she leases it to a rancher for grazing his cattle. The rent is $9,000 per year. Since the rent is less than $10,000 (2% of the lesser of the basis of the property $500,000 or its fair market value of $800,000), the two percent test is met. Because S is holding the property primarily as an investment and her rental income is insignificant (it is less than the two percent threshold), the rental is considered incidental and would not be automatically treated as a rental activity for purposes of the passive loss rules. On the other hand, if S bought the land intending to build a shopping center on it, the rental would not be considered incidental since the land is not considered held primarily for appreciation. In such case, the activity is deemed to be a rental.

- *Property Normally Used in a Trade or Business.* A rental is not considered a rental activity if the property is normally used by the taxpayer in a business and occasionally is rented to others when it is not needed in the business. The property qualifies as business property only if (1) the property is used in the business during the current year (or two of the last five) and (2) the 2% test is met (i.e., gross rental income from the property is less than 2% of the lesser of the unadjusted basis of the property or the fair market value of the property).

Example 26

P, a farmer, owns land that he uses for farming. This year a nearby country club, Roaring Fork Golf and Country Club, is hosting the U.S. Open. P rented a portion of his land to the club to be used for a parking lot for the month of June for $3,000. The allocable cost of the land is $200,000 and it is currently worth $500,000. The rental income is considered incidental and not passive since the property is normally used in P's farming business and the $3,000 rent is less than $4,000 (2% of the lesser of the basis of the property $200,000 or its fair market value of $500,000). The result would be the same if P had rented the property to another farmer or for some other purpose.

---

5. *Nonexclusive Use.* The activity is not a rental activity if the taxpayer customarily makes the property available during defined business hours for the nonexclusive use of various customers. For example, this exception would apply to a golf course that sells annual memberships but which is also open to the public on a daily basis.

6. *Property Made Available for Use in a Nonrental Activity.* The activity is not a rental activity if the taxpayer owns an interest in a partnership, S corporation, or joint venture to which the property is rented. For example, if T rents equipment to a partnership in which he is a partner, the rental is treated as a nonrental activity.

---

[17] Temp. Reg. § 1.469-1T(e)(3)(vi)(B).

Similarly, rental of property to a C corporation in which the taxpayer materially participates is not considered a rental.

Example 27

Mr. F, an attorney, owns and operates F&H Corporation, a law firm. This year F and his wife leased a building that they owned jointly to F&H Inc. The corporation was the sole tenant. Mr. F would like to treat the rent as passive and use it to absorb the couple's passive activity losses. Unfortunately, the regulations provide that rental to a C corporation in which the taxpayer materially participates is a nonrental activity. Therefore, the amounts received for leasing the building are not considered passive income.[18]

As noted above, any activity constituting a "rental" is a passive activity. Note, however, that those activities not classified as rentals (i.e., nonrental activities) may still be considered passive. Whether a *nonrental* activity is a passive activity depends on whether the taxpayer has materially participated in the activity.

MATERIAL PARTICIPATION

Material participation serves a crucial role in the application of the passive loss rules. It is the criterion that distinguishes between "passive" and "active" nonrental activities. The Code provides that an individual meets the material participation test only if he or she is involved in the operation of the activity on a regular, continuous, and substantial basis. Without further guidance, applying this nebulous criterion would essentially be left to the subjective interpretation of the taxpayer. However, the Regulations establish objective standards that look to the actual number of hours spent in the activity.

Under the regulatory scheme, a taxpayer materially participates in an activity if he or she meets any of seven tests.[19]

1. *More Than 500 Hours.* An individual materially participates if he or she spends more than 500 hours in the activity during the taxable year. Apparently the authors of the Regulations believed that this threshold (e.g., about 10 hours per week) appropriately distinguished those who truly were involved in the business from mere investors. Note that the work of a spouse is counted if it is work typically done by owners. For example, if B owned an S corporation that suffered losses (e.g., a football team), he would materially participate if he devoted more than 500 hours to the activity. However, if he spent only 300 hours and hired his wife as a receptionist who spent 250 hours, the test is not met because her work is not normally done by owners.

2. *Substantially All of the Participation.* The individual and his or her spouse materially participate if they are the sole participants or their participation constitutes substantially all of the participation of all individuals (including nonowners and nonemployees) who participate in the activity. This test, as well as the next, takes into account the fact that not all businesses require 500 hours to operate during the year. For example, if S operates a snow removal service by himself and spends only 50 hours in the activity this year because of light snow, the test is met because he was the sole participant.

3. *More Than 100 Hours and Not Less Than Anyone Else.* An individual materially participates if he or she participates for more than 100 hours and no other individual spends more time on the activity. For example, assume that S, above, occasionally hires E to help him remove snow. If S spent 160 hours and E 140, S qualifies because he spent more than 100 hours and not less than anyone else. Had S spent only 60 and E 40, S arguably would not qualify under either this or the previous test.

---

[18] See *Remy Fransen, Jr.,* 99-2 USTC ¶50,882 (CA-5, 1999), aff'g 98-2 USTC ¶50,776 (D.C., E.D. La., 1998) where the Court upheld the validity of Reg. § 1.469-2(f)(6), recharacterizing the activity as active and not passive. See also *Schwalbach,* 111 T.C. No. 9 (1998).

[19] Temp. Reg. § 1.469-5T(a).

4. *Participation in Several Activities.* An individual materially participates if his or her total participation in all *significant participation activities* (SPAs) exceeds 500 hours. A "significant participation activity" is defined as a trade or business in which the taxpayer participates more than 100 hours, but fails the other six tests for material participation. Thus a taxpayer must spend more than 100 hours in each activity and greater than 500 in all. The rule derives from the view that an individual who spends more than 500 hours in several different activities should be treated the same as those who spend an equivalent amount of time on a single activity.

Example 28

T spends 140 hours overseeing his car wash, 160 hours supervising his quick-lube operation, and 499 hours managing his gas station. Each activity qualifies as a SPA because T spends more than 100 hours in each. More importantly, T is treated as materially participating in each because the total hours in all SPAs exceeds 500. However, if T spent two more hours in his gas station, then he would not be a material participant in either the car wash or quick-lube business. This occurs because the gas station would no longer be a SPA since the activity by itself satisfies the more-than-500-hours test. As a result, T's total hours in all SPAs, 300 (160 + 140), would not exceed the 500-hour benchmark. Obviously, this is a strange result.

The Regulations provide what at first glance is a curious treatment of SPAs. As expected, losses from SPAs failing to meet the 500-hour test are passive and generally not deductible. However, income from SPAs failing to meet the 500-hour test is *not* passive. Note that the IRS obtains the best of both worlds when a taxpayer is unable to combine his or her SPAs to get over the 500-hour threshold: passive loss but not passive income. This "heads I win, tails you lose" approach was designed to prevent taxpayers from creating passive income that could be used to absorb passive losses by spending small amounts of time in unrelated activities that are profitable.[20]

---

5. *Prior Participation.* An individual materially participates if he or she has materially participated (by tests 1 through 4) in an activity for five of the past ten years. This test prevents the taxpayer from moving in and out of material participation status. For example, D and son are partners in an appliance business that D started 30 years ago. D has essentially retired, leaving the day-to-day operations to his son. Without a special rule, D could tailor his participation year by year to obtain passive or nonpassive income as fits his needs.

6. *Prior Participation in a Personal Service Activity.* An individual materially participates in a personal service activity if he or she has materially participated in the activity for at least three years. Like the previous test, this rule eliminates the flexibility those working for personal service businesses have in tailoring their participation to obtain passive or nonpassive income as they need. For example, if a general partner in a law firm retired and converted her interest to a limited partnership interest, she would still be treated as a material participant in that law firm.

7. *Facts and Circumstances.* An individual materially participates if, based on the facts and circumstances, he or she participates in the activity on a regular, continuous, and substantial basis.

---

[20] See Reg. § 1.469-2T(f)(2).

Rental Real Estate Exception

An extremely important exception to the passive activity rules is carved out in § 469(i) for rental real estate activities of the small investor. In many cases, the rental real estate held by a taxpayer is a residence that is used part-time, was formerly used, or may be used by the taxpayer in the future. Relief was provided for this type of rental real estate because it is often held to provide financial security to individuals with moderate incomes. In such a case, these individuals share little common ground with the tax shelter investors. The relief is provided solely to individuals and certain trusts and estates. Regular C corporations are ineligible.

Under the exception, a taxpayer who *actively* participates (in contrast to materially participates) may deduct up to $25,000 of losses attributable to rental real estate annually. The $25,000 allowance is reduced by 50% of the excess of the taxpayer's AGI over $100,000. This relationship may be expressed as follows:

Reduction in $25,000 allowance = 50% (AGI – $100,000)

Based on this formula, high-income taxpayers (i.e., those with AGI of $150,000 or more) cannot take advantage of this provision. AGI for this purpose is computed without regard to contributions to individual retirement accounts, taxable Social Security, and any net passive losses that might be deductible. Any portion of the rental loss that is not deductible may be carried over and deducted subject to the same limitations in the following years.

Example 29

L moved to a new home this year. Instead of selling his old home, L decided to rent it out to supplement his income. For the year, rents were $3,000 while expenses including maintenance, depreciation, interest, utilities, and taxes were $10,000. L's AGI is $40,000. L may deduct the $7,000 loss for AGI. Had L's AGI been $140,000, he could have deducted only $5,000 and carried over $2,000 to the following year. This computation is illustrated below.

Loss allowance		$ 25,000
Phase-Out:		
AGI	$ 140,000	
Threshold	(100,000)	
Excess AGI	$ 40,000	
Rate	× 50%	
Phase-Out		(20,000)
Maximum loss allowed		$ 5,000

It should be emphasized that the taxpayer can use this exception only if the property is considered rental real estate. It cannot be used for losses from rental of personal property. More important, the real estate is not considered a "rental" activity where the rental period is either 1 to 7 days or between 8 and 30 days and significant services are performed.[21] For example, consider the typical investor who owns a vacation condominium. If the average rental of the condominium is 1 to 7 days, the condominium is not considered rental property and the $25,000 exception does not apply. The result is the same if the average rental period is between 8 and 30 days and significant services are provided. Note that even though the $25,000 exception is not available in either case, all is not necessarily lost. In both situations, the condominium is treated as a nonrental activity. In such case, the taxpayer will be able to deduct all losses if there is material participation.[22]

---

[21] For an excellent discussion of this topic and issue see Bomyea and Marucheck, "Rental of Residences," *The Tax Adviser* (September 1990), p. 543.

[22] See *Steven D. Rapp,* T.C. Memo 1999-249, 78 TCM 175 and *Walter A. Barniskis,* T.C. Memo 1999-258, 78 TCM 226.

> ## Example 30
>
> M lives in Orlando, where she practices law. M owns a condominium, which she rents out on a daily basis to tourists. M runs ads in the local newspaper, makes arrangements for the rental, and cleans the unit as needed. In this case, it appears that the activity is not a rental business because of the short-term rental. As a result, the $25,000 exception for rentals does not apply. However, M still may be able to deduct a loss. Since the property by definition is not a rental activity due to the short-term rental period, it is—by default—a nonrental activity. Accordingly, the loss would be deductible if she materially participates in the activity. For example, if M spent more than 100 hours in the activity and more than anyone else or met any of the other six material participation tests, the loss would be deductible.

As noted above, the Code draws a distinction between material and active participation. The primary difference concerns the taxpayer's degree of involvement in operations. For example, a taxpayer is actively involved if he or she participates in management decisions such as approving new tenants, deciding on rental terms, approving capital or repair expenditures, or if he or she arranges for others to provide services such as repairs. In all cases, the taxpayer is not treated as actively participating in the activity if less than a 10% interest is owned. On the other hand, the taxpayer is not presumed to actively participate if the interest is 10% or more. The above standard still must be satisfied.

Real Estate Professional Exception

Under the basic rules described above, taxpayers who are engaged in the rental real estate business (e.g., owners of warehouses, shopping centers, or office buildings) cannot deduct losses from such business activities since the law presumes that virtually all long-term rental real estate activities are passive. Note that this treatment occurs regardless of the amount of time and energy spent by the taxpayer in such activities. The level of the taxpayer's participation is irrelevant. After much debate, however, Congress finally agreed in 1994 that the passive loss rules were aimed at passive investors in real estate and not those who were in the real estate business. For this reason, it took steps to enable these individuals to deduct losses arising from these activities. This special relief is granted only if the individual can pass certain tests that effectively establish that he or she is truly in the real estate business.

Generally, an individual can take advantage of the exception for real estate professionals if he or she spends more than half of their working hours in the real estate business and the number of hours spent exceeds 750. Technically an individual is *eligible* to deduct losses from rental real estate if both of the following conditions are met:[23]

1. Services representing more than 50% of the total personal services performed by the individual in all trades or businesses during the tax year are performed in *real property trades or businesses* in which the taxpayer materially participates during the year. For this purpose, real property trades or businesses include real property development, redevelopment, construction, acquisition, conversion, rental, operation, management, leasing, and brokerage. In the case of a closely held C corporation, this test is met if more than 50% of the gross receipts of such corporation are derived from real property businesses in which the corporation materially participates.

2. The individual performs more than 750 hours of services in *real property trades or businesses in which he or she materially participates.*

If a joint return is filed, the special relief is available if either spouse separately satisfies the requirements. Note that for this purpose, the couple *cannot* aggregate their hours.

---

[23] § 469(c)(7). For an interesting example, see *Edward C. Hanna* T.C. Summary Opinion 2006-57.

Observe that satisfaction of these two tests merely opens the door for possible deduction of losses. In order to treat the losses as nonpassive, the taxpayer must still meet the material participation requirements (e.g., spend more than 500 hours in the activity). For this purpose, each activity is normally treated as a separate activity. However, the taxpayer may elect to aggregate such activities.[24] In most cases, it would seem that those who are eligible and who elect to aggregate their real property businesses should be able to meet the material participation tests. It should also be emphasized that personal services as an *employee* in a real property business are not treated as performed in the real property business unless the individual owns at least 5% of the business.

Example 31

G graduated from the Vanderbilt law school in 1983 and has been practicing his trade ever since. Over the years, however, he has accumulated a number of properties. As a result, he is increasingly spending more time being a real estate magnate and less time being a lawyer. Currently, he owns, operates, and manages a small shopping center and several duplexes. Each of these rental activities produces a loss, primarily due to depreciation. According to G's detailed diary of how he spends his time, he worked 40 hours a week for 50 weeks during the year for a total of 2,000 hours. Assuming G elects to aggregate his interests in each of the rental real estate activities and treat them as a single activity, the majority, 1,100 hours, was devoted to his real estate ventures. The other 900 hours related to his law practice. In this case, G meets both tests that enable him to treat the rental operations as nonrental activities: (1) more than 50% of his personal services were performed in real property businesses, and (2) his 1,100 hours of service in these businesses exceeded the 750-hour threshold. Although the rental taint is removed, this does not necessarily mean G is allowed to deduct the losses. He must still satisfy the material participation tests. Whether this final requirement is met depends on whether G elects to aggregate all of the activities. If so, his 1,100 hours of participation is greater than the 500 hours required and he would be entitled to deduct all of the losses.

RECHARACTERIZED PASSIVE INCOME

As is evident throughout the passive loss Regulations, the IRS was concerned that taxpayers might create passive income which could be used to absorb otherwise nondeductible passive losses. Nowhere is this more evident than in the recharacterization rules. In certain situations, income that is characterized under the general rules as passive is recharacterized under a special rule and treated as active. An example of the type of recharacterization that can occur was discussed earlier in connection with SPAs. As noted in that discussion, income from SPAs that fail to meet the 500-hour test would normally be treated as passive, but under the special recharacterization rule it is treated as active. There are several other situations when this might occur. Consequently, before it can be concluded that income is passive, the recharacterization rules must be considered. These rules operate to convert the following types of income to nonpassive (i.e., active) or portfolio income rather than passive income.[25]

1. *Significant Participation Activities:* Income from "significant participation activities" that fail to meet the 500-hour test is nonpassive.

2. *Rental of Nondepreciable Property:* Income from rental activities is active if less than 30% of the basis of the property rented is depreciable (e.g., rental of land). This rule makes not only rental income nonpassive but also gain on a sale of the activity or property used in it. However, losses are passive.

---

[24] The aggregation election is made by filing a statement with the taxpayer's *original* income tax return for the taxable year pursuant to Reg. § 1.469-9(g). The statement must contain a declaration that the taxpayer is a qualifying taxpayer for the taxable year and is making the election pursuant to § 469(c)(7). Merely, aggregating the rental operations on Schedule E is not sufficient. For an excellent example of what not to do, see *Karl Jahina, et ux. v. Commissioner,* TC Summary Opinion 2002-150.

[25] Temp. Reg. § 1.469-2T(f).

3. *Developer Sales of Rental Property:* Rental income, including gain on the sale of rental property, if (1) gain on the sale is included in income during the taxable year; (2) rental of the property commenced less than 24 months before the date of disposition; and (3) the taxpayer performed sufficient services that enhanced the value of the rental property.

4. *Self-Rented Property:* Income from rental of property to an activity in which the taxpayer materially participates, other than related C corporations.

5. *Licensing of Intangible Property:* Royalty income from a pass-through entity that the taxpayer acquired after the entity created the intangible property.

6. *Equity-Financed Lending Activity:* Income from the trade or business of lending money if certain conditions are satisfied.

Example 32

Dr. S owns a dental practice that he operates through a corporation, Family Dentistry, Inc. He also has substantial passive losses derived from two rental properties, an apartment and shopping center. Hoping to generate some passive income to absorb such losses, he purchased a building and leased it to his corporation for $25,000 this year. The corporation uses the building to house the doctor's dental practice. The self-rental rule treats the rental income received by Dr. S as portfolio income since S materially participates in the corporation to which the property is rented.[26]

In a similar move, S and his brother, B, formed an LLC to establish a trailer park. The LLC purchased the land for $300,000 and made depreciable improvements on the land of $100,000. Any rental income derived from the park is treated as portfolio income rather than passive income since the basis of the depreciable property (unadjusted for depreciation) is less than 30% of the basis of all the property used in the rental activity ($100,000/$400,000 = 25%). Any gain on the sale of the partnership interest would also be treated as portfolio income. Note that this recharacterization rule is usually triggered when the bulk of the rental property's cost is in the land rather than the improvements.

Passive-Activity Interest Expense

One aspect related to the passive loss rules that requires special attention is the treatment of interest expense. As discussed in Chapter 11, Congress has imposed severe limitations on the deduction of interest. Interest expense incurred by a taxpayer to finance an investment in a passive activity is subject to the passive loss rules and is not considered investment interest. Similarly, interest expense incurred by an activity that is considered passive (e.g., a partnership if the taxpayer is a limited partner) is subject to the passive loss rules.[27]

LO.5
Understand the special treatment for interest expense related to a passive activity.

Example 33

In 2017, Dr. P borrowed $50,000 and invested it by acquiring an interest in a limited partnership that produces movies. Interest on the loan for the year is $5,000. P can deduct the interest only to the extent of any passive income that he may have.

[26] *Krukowski*, 114 T.C. 366 (2000).   [27] § 163(d)(3)(B).

> **Example 34**
>
> Assume the partnership above incurs interest expense related to loans obtained to acquire equipment used in its operations. For the partnership, the interest is treated as a normal deduction and is used in arriving at the partnership's net income or loss from operations. For 2017, the partnership suffered a net loss including deductions for interest expense. Dr. P is allowed to deduct his share of the loss only to the extent he has passive income from other activities.

 CHECK YOUR KNOWLEDGE

Try the following true-false questions.

Review Question 1

This year T's tax records revealed that he had income consisting of a salary of $90,000, dividends of $10,000, and a capital gain from the sale of stock of $5,000. In addition, he received a Schedule K-1 from a partnership in which he is a limited partner. According to the K-1, his share of the partnership's loss for the year was $50,000. T can deduct $15,000 of this loss (i.e., to the extent of his passive dividend and capital gain income).

False. While a taxpayer is entitled to deduct passive losses to the extent of passive income, passive income does not include dividends, interest, capital gains, and the like, which are considered portfolio income.

Review Question 2

A passive loss that cannot be deducted in the current year is generally suspended. The suspended loss is deductible only in the year in which the property to which the loss relates is sold, since the sale affirms the fact that the taxpayer has actually suffered an economic loss.

False. The above is true for the most part, but suspended passive losses are not frozen to thaw only when the taxpayer sells his or her interest. Passive losses that cannot be deducted in a particular year are carried over to the following year and treated as if they occurred in that subsequent year. Accordingly, the suspended loss can be deducted to the extent that the taxpayer has passive income in the following year. In addition, the taxpayer is allowed to deduct the suspended losses whenever the property to which the loss relates is sold.

Review Question 3

A capital gain from the sale of stock in an S corporation in which the taxpayer does not materially participate is considered portfolio income.

False. Capital gains are normally considered portfolio income, but when such gain arises from the sale of the taxpayer's interest in a passive activity, it is treated as passive income.

Review Question 4

The passive loss rules do not apply to regular C corporations since the losses do not flow through and are not available to the individual shareholders.

False. The passive loss rules do apply to personal service corporations and closely held corporations (i.e., corporations where five or fewer individuals own more than 50% of the stock). Personal service corporations must play by the same rules applicable to individuals. Closely held corporations, however, are allowed to offset passive losses against income from operations *other than* portfolio income.

Review Question 5

Moe, Larry, and Curly pooled all of their savings to start a new restaurant, Stooges. Stooges is operated as an S corporation, and its stock is owned equally by the threesome. In its first year, the restaurant produced a loss. Depending on the circumstances, Moe may be able to deduct his share of the loss this year while Larry and Curly may not be able to deduct their shares.

True. Whether a deduction is allowed for the loss depends on whether the taxpayer materially participates in the activity. Moe may be actively involved on a daily basis, and Larry and Curly may be passive investors. In such a case, only Moe would be able to deduct the loss currently.

Review Question 6

D operates a small bed-and-breakfast motel. Most of his customers rent rooms for one or two days. D's operation is not considered a rental activity for purposes of the passive-loss rules.

True. An activity is not considered a rental for purposes of the passive-loss rules if the average period of customer use is seven days or less.

Review Question 7

T owns a duplex and rents it out. She normally signs six-month leases with her tenants. Any loss related to the rental is considered a passive loss and is not deductible regardless of T's participation.

True. This activity is considered a rental since the average period of customer use exceeds 30 days and T does not provide any extraordinary services. Losses on long-term rental real estate are normally not deductible except to the extent of passive income unless the taxpayer can qualify under one of two exceptions. First, she is permitted to deduct up to $25,000 of losses from rental real estate if she actively participates and her adjusted gross income is less than $150,000. In addition, a special exception allows individuals who spend more than 50% of their time in real property businesses and more than 750 hours in such businesses to treat the activities as nonrental and deduct any losses if they materially participate in such activities.

Review Question 8

Several years ago, Q purchased an interest in a limited partnership. This year his share of the partnership's loss was $10,000. Assuming Q's adjusted gross income is $80,000, he may deduct the loss since it is less than $25,000.

False. The loss would be treated as a passive loss since Q does not materially participate in the partnership activity. The de minimis exception that enables a taxpayer to deduct up to $25,000 of passive losses annually applies only to losses from rental real estate activities in which the taxpayer actively participates.

Review Question 9

B opened her first Planet Jupiter Cafe five years ago in Aspen. Now she has five restaurants, each located in a different resort. Since each store is located in a separate city, she must treat each store as a separate activity.

False. A taxpayer is required to treat one or more activities as a single activity if the activities constitute an appropriate economic unit (AEU). The Regulations give the taxpayer a great deal of flexibility in determining what constitutes an AEU. Thus, the taxpayer could treat each as a separate activity, combine all and treat as a single activity, or use some other grouping that may be appropriate under the Regulations.

Review Question 10

B is a college professor who recently got involved in a mail-order smoke alarm business. This year he spent about 100 hours in the activity, taking orders and arranging to fill them. B materially participates in the business.

True. Under the general rule, a taxpayer is considered a material participant if he or she spends more than 500 hours in the activity during the year. Although B does not meet the general rule, he does meet an alternative test; that is, his participation constitutes substantially all of the participation in the activity. Therefore the activity is not a passive activity.

Review Question 11

G owns two businesses, a convenience grocery store and a dry cleaners. For the last several years, the grocery has not done as well as G had hoped and she has lost money. This year, G did not play as much golf as usual and spent about 400 hours trying to turn the business around. She spent about 300 hours at the cleaners. Each business has a number of full-time employees. G may offset any loss attributable to the grocery store against the profits from her dry cleaners.

True. The restaurant and the dry cleaners are considered significant participation activities since G spends more than 100 hours in each. If the total participation in all SPAs exceeds 500 hours, the taxpayer is deemed to materially participate in each of the activities. In this case, the total participation in all SPAs exceeds the 500-hour threshold, and G is therefore deemed to materially participate in each of the activities. Thus, she can use the loss in the grocery activity to offset the income from the cleaning business.

Review Question 12

Same as above, except G spends 100 hours at the cleaners, 300 hours at the grocery, and the remaining time at the beach. G may offset any loss attributable to the grocery against the profits from her dry cleaners.

False. In this case, G's combined participation in the SPAs does not exceed 500 hours. This is the "heads we win, tails you lose" situation: the loss is passive, the income is nonpassive, and the two cannot be combined.

Review Question 13

J borrowed $100,000 to purchase an interest in the Lockwood Limited Partnership, which operates several apartment complexes. This year J paid $8,000 interest on the loan to acquire his interest. In addition, J's share of the partnership's losses was $10,000. J has no passive income. The loss is a passive loss and cannot be deducted, but the interest is treated as investment interest and is deductible to the extent of J's investment income.

False. J simply treats the $8,000 of interest expense as another operating expense of the partnership, increasing the loss from $10,000 to $18,000. None of the loss, including the interest, is deductible.

Rental of Residence (Vacation Home Rentals)

LO.6

Discuss the restrictions imposed on deductions related to vacation homes.

Section 280A imposes restrictions on the deduction of expenses related to rental of a residence if the taxpayer is considered as using the residence primarily for personal purposes rather than for making a profit. These restrictions are aimed at the perceived abuse existing in the area of vacation home rental. Prior to the enactment of § 280A, many felt that personal enjoyment was the predominant motive for purchasing a vacation home. Any rental of the vacation home served merely to minimize the personal expense of ownership and not to produce income.

Basic Rules

In 1976, Congress prescribed an objective method for ascertaining the purpose of the rental activity as well as the amount of the deduction. According to this approach, the expenses incurred by the taxpayer in owning and operating the home (e.g., interest, taxes, maintenance, utilities, and depreciation) must first be allocated between personal use and rental use. The deductibility of the expenses allocated to each then depends on whether the home is considered the taxpayer's *residence or rental property.* This latter determination is made based on the owner's personal use and the amount of rental activity.[28]

1. *Nominal Rentals:* If the residence is rented out fewer than 15 days, all rental income is excluded from gross income and no deduction is allowed for rental expenses. Otherwise allowable deductions, such as those for qualified residence interest, real estate taxes, and casualty losses may be deducted *from* AGI.

---

[28] §§ 280A(c)(5) and 280A(d) through (g).

2. *Used as a "Residence":* If the taxpayer uses the vacation home for more than 14 days or 10% of the number of days the property is actually rented out, whichever is greater, the home is treated as his or her residence and deductions are restricted as explained below. A typical taxpayer caught by this rule is the owner of a vacation home who uses it for more than two weeks and rents it out to defray the cost.

   a. *Expenses Allocable to the Rental Use:* These expenses are deductible to the extent of gross income less otherwise allowable deductions. Any deductions in excess of gross income can be carried over and deducted to the extent of any future income. These expenses are deductible *for* AGI since they are related to rental use. Note that the passive-loss rules do not apply since the property is used as a residence and not a rental.

   b. *Expenses Allocable to Personal Use:* Since these expenses are considered personal, they may be deducted only if they are specifically authorized by the Code. Allocable property taxes are deductible without limitation as an itemized deduction since such expenses are fully deductible regardless of the activity in which they are incurred. Interest expense *may* be deductible as an itemized deduction. Allocable interest is normally qualified residence interest since the home—*in this case*—is considered the taxpayer's residence (e.g., because it is used more than 14 days). However, if the home is not the primary or secondary residence of the taxpayer (e.g., the taxpayer has several vacation homes), no deduction would be available. The other operating expenses are not deductible.

3. *Used as "Rental Property":* If the taxpayer does not use the property extensively (i.e., more than the greater of 14 days or 10% of the number of days rented out), then the property is effectively treated as rental property.

   a. *Expenses Allocable to the Rental Use:* These expenses are deductible subject only to the restrictions on passive losses. If the property's average rental period is either (1) 1–7 days or (2) 8–30 days *and* significant services are provided, the property is not rental property under the passive loss rules. Thus, the treatment of any loss depends on whether the taxpayer materially participates in this "nonrental activity." If the taxpayer materially participates, any loss would not be passive and would therefore be fully deductible. If the property is considered a rental (e.g., perhaps under the facts-and-circumstances test or if the rental is 8–30 days and no significant services are provided) and the taxpayer is considered as having met the active participation standard, the taxpayer may qualify for the rental exception under the passive loss rules. This would allow the taxpayer to deduct up to $25,000 in losses annually. Any deductions would be for AGI.

   b. *Expenses Allocable to Personal Use:* As noted above, since these expenses are personal, they may be deducted only if they are specifically authorized by the Code. In this case, property taxes would continue to be fully deductible. On the other hand, none of the interest expense would be deductible as qualified residence interest since the vacation home is not considered a "residence" (because the taxpayer did *not* use it more than 14 days). However, the excess interest expense would be treated as investment interest and could be deducted to the extent of investment income. Other operating expenses would not be deductible.

This treatment is summarized in Exhibit 12-1.

For purposes of the owner use test, the number of days a unit is rented out does not include any day the unit is used for personal purposes. The unit is generally treated as used for personal purposes on any day where the owner or a member of his or her family uses it for any portion of the day for personal purposes or the unit is rented at less than a fair rental.[29] A day on which the taxpayer spends at least two-thirds of the time at the unit (or if less than two-thirds then at least eight hours) on repairs is not counted as a personal day. This is true even though individuals who accompany the taxpayer do not perform repairs or maintenance.[30]

---

[29] § 280A(d)(2).   [30] Prop. Reg. § 1.280A-1(e)(4) and § 280A(d)(2).

| EXHIBIT 12-1 | Vacation Homes—Summary of § 280A Rules | |

Character of Vacation Home	Residence	Rental property
Characterization:		
Personal use exceeding the greater of:	Yes	No
1. 14 days, or		
2. 10% of days rented out		
Expenses allocable to rental use:	Limited to gross income by § 280A	Limited by passive-loss rules
		Rental exception may apply
Expenses allocable to personal use:		
Taxes	Deductible	Deductible
Interest	Qualified residence interest	Investment interest
Other	Not deductible	Not deductible

Example 35

In 1985, Floyd Toups and his wife purchased a vacation home for $120,000. The unit was one of 155 individually owned "cottages" located at Callaway Gardens, a favorite vacation resort in Pine Mountain, Georgia, about 70 miles south of Atlanta. The units were marketed and managed by a development company that received 50% of the net rental income for its services. Each owner was entitled to rent-free use of the cottage for no more than 14 days during the year. On their 1988, 1989, and 1990 returns, the Toupses took the position that the cottage, which was generating losses, was a *nonrental* activity since the average period of customer use of the cottage was seven days or less, and accordingly the Toupses deducted the losses on their Schedule C on the grounds that they materially participated in the activity. However, the IRS disagreed and assessed deficiencies exceeding $3,000 for each year. In the Tax Court, the Toupses attempted to justify their position, explaining that they had spent 341 hours each year in activities related to the rental of the unit. They listed 13 activities, which they believed supported their claim. According to the couple they (1) provided funds for the purchase; (2) prepared an annual budget; (3) prepared a cash flow analysis; (4) provided a rental agency for renting their unit; (5) marketed the resort and rental of the cottage; (6) met with other owners; (7) established rental rates for the cottages with other owners; (8) inspected the cottage and common areas at least twice a year; (9) reviewed monthly reports received from the rental agent; (10) reviewed other correspondence from the rental agent; (11) reviewed advertising brochures about the resort received from the rental agent; (12) received and deposited net revenues received from the rental; and (13) issued checks for expenses of the cottage. The Tax Court agreed that the property was not "rental property" under the passive-loss rules and, therefore, did not qualify for the $25,000 allowance available for rental real estate. Unfortunately, the court did not agree with the taxpayers' claim that they materially participated in the activity. The court found that the activities of the taxpayer did not constitute material participation because they were not involved in the day-to-day operation of their cottage or in its management. The activities of the taxpayers were considered to be activities of an investor, and therefore their losses were passive.[31]

---

[31] *Floyd A. and Joanna Toups,* 66 T.C.M. 370, T.C. Memo 1993-359.

EXHIBIT 12-2	Vacation Homes—Expense Allocation Rules

Type of Expense	Personal Use	Rental Use
Directly related (advertising, brokers' fees)	None allocated	Gross rental receipts – Directly related expenses *Sch. E* Gross rental income
Otherwise allowable (qualified residence interest, taxes, etc.)	Itemized deduction*	– Otherwise allowable *Sch. E* Limit on indirect rental expenses
Indirect (maintenance, depreciation, utilities, etc.)	Not deductible	– Indirect expenses Sch. E**

* Interest allocated to personal use:
   (1) if the property is treated as a residence, deductible as qualified residence interest;
   (2) if not a residence, the interest may be deductible as investment interest to the extent of investment income.
       Taxes allocated to personal use are fully deductible in either case.

** Indirect expenses allocated to rental use:
   (1) if the property is treated as a residence, such expenses are limited to remaining rental income;
   (2) if not a residence but a rental, passive loss rules apply unless not considered a rental (i.e., average customer use does not exceed seven days);
   (3) if rental for passive loss purposes, limited to passive income and $25,000 allowance may be available;
   (4) if not a rental for passive activity purposes, loss deductible if materially participate

ALLOCATION OF EXPENSES

As discussed above, the treatment of expenses incurred in operating a vacation home varies depending on whether the expenses are allocated to rental or personal use. Consequently, the critical first step in applying the vacation home rules is allocation of the expenses. Once expenses are properly allocated between rental and personal use, the appropriate limitations can be applied.

Vacation home expenses can be classified as either direct and indirect. Direct expenses are those that are *not* related to the general operation or maintenance of the unit but which are incurred to obtain tenants.[32] For example, advertising, brokers' fees, office supplies, and depreciation on office equipment used in the rental activity are considered directly related to the rental. These direct expenses reduce gross rental receipts to arrive at gross rental income. All other expenses are considered indirect expenses—including otherwise allowable deductions such as interest and taxes—and must be allocated *between* personal and rental use.

In allocating the expenses between personal and rental use, two different methods are used. Under the so-called *Bolton* approach, otherwise allowable deductions such as interest and taxes are assumed to *accrue daily* regardless of use.[33] Consequently, the fraction for allocating these items to the rental use was:

$$\text{Otherwise allowable deduction} \times \frac{\text{Number of rental days}}{365} = \text{Portion attributable to rental use}$$

In contrast, expenses such as utilities, maintenance, and depreciation are considered a *function of use*. As a result, the fraction used for allocating these items to the rental use was:

$$\text{Operating expenses} \times \frac{\text{Number of rental days}}{\text{Rental} + \text{Personal days}} = \text{Portion attributable to rental use}$$

The method of allocating expenses and their treatment is summarized in Exhibit 12-2 top.

Note that the court's approach in *Bolton* (which uses a denominator of 365 rather than total personal and rental days used) allocates less interest and taxes to the rental portion and, therefore, more to the residential or personal portion. This approach enables the taxpayer to

---

[32] Prop. Reg. § 1.280A-3(d)(2).

[33] *Dorance D. Bolton*, 77 T.C. 104 (1982), aff'd. at 82-2 USTC ¶9699, 51 AFTR2d 83-305 (CA-9, 1982).

deduct a larger amount of expenses allocable to the rental. At the same time, this method increases the amount of the itemized deduction for interest and taxes. The end result is that a larger deduction can be secured using the *Bolton* approach. Unfortunately, the IRS continues to oppose *Bolton* so taxpayers must proceed with caution.[34] The example below follows *Bolton*.

Example 36

A owns a condominium in a ski resort. During the year, A uses the condominium as a secondary residence for 30 days and rents it out for 90 days. The condominium is not used the remainder of the year. During the year, A's rental agent, R, collected rents of $5,000. The agent's standard fee was 30% of rents; therefore the charge was $1,500 and R sent Form 1099 to A showing net rental income of $3,500. Total expenses for the entire year include maintenance and utilities of $1,000, interest of $6,200, taxes of $1,100, and $2,000 depreciation on the entire cost of the unit.

A's use for 30 days is more than 14 days, the greater of 14 or 9 days (10% of the 90 days rented). Therefore, the unit is treated as a residence. For this reason, expenses attributable to the rental are deductible to the extent of gross income as reduced by otherwise allowable deductions (the interest and taxes). Deductions are computed and deducted in the *following order:*

Gross rental receipts	$5,000
Deduct directly related expenses (brokerage fee).	−1,500
Gross rental income	$3,500
Deduct allocable portion of otherwise allowable deductions:	
Interest and taxes ($7,300 × [90 ÷ 365])	−1,800
Gross income limitation	$1,700
Deduct allocable portion of deductions other than those otherwise allowable and depreciation:	
Utilities and maintenance ($1,000 × 90 ÷ [30 + 90])	− 750
Gross income limitation	$ 950
Deduct allocable portion of depreciation:	
Depreciation ($2,000 × 90 ÷ [30 + 90]) = $1,500 but limited to $950 balance of gross income	− 950
Net income.	$ 0

All of the above deductions are *for* AGI. The balance of interest and taxes not allocated to the rental use, $5,500 ($7,300 − $1,800), is deductible if the taxpayer itemizes deductions. Note that the interest in this case is qualified residence interest since the unit is treated as A's residence. The deduction for maintenance and utilities is not limited by gross income since all of these expenses attributable to the rental activity are deductible. The $250 ($1,000 − $750) remaining balance of maintenance and utilities would not be deductible in any case since it represents the expenses attributable to personal use. Of the remaining depreciation balance of $1,050 ($2,000 − $950), $550 ($1,500 − $950) attributable to the rental is not deductible due to the gross income limitation but may be carried over to subsequent years. The other $500 of depreciation is not deductible since it is the portion attributable to personal use. Also note that only the $950 of depreciation allowed is treated as a reduction in the basis of A's condominium.

---

[34] § 280A(e). The IRS continues to take the position that all expenses should be allocated based on use. See *Residential*   *Rental Property,* IRS Publication 527 (2016), p. 17 on dividing expenses.

Example 37

Assume the same facts as in *Example 36*, except that A used the condominium for 10 days rather than 30. Also assume that the rental is on a three-month basis to locals and no services are provided. In such case, the condominium would be treated as rental property rather than as a residence since A stayed less than 14 days. In addition, the $25,000 rental exception of the passive loss rules would apply since there is a long-term rental and no significant services are provided. A's deduction would be computed as follows:

Gross rental receipts	$ 5,000
Deduct directly related expenses (brokerage fee)	– 1,500
Gross rental income	$ 3,500
Deduct allocable portion of otherwise allowable deductions ($7,300 × 90 ÷ 365)	– 1,800
Deduct allocable portion of utilities and maintenance ($1,000 × 90 ÷ [90 + 10])	– 900
Deduct allocable portion of depreciation ($2,000 × 90 ÷ [90 + 10])	– 1,800
Loss	$ (1,000)

In this case, a loss is created that may offset any other income of the taxpayer under the $25,000 rental loss exception. In contrast to *Example 36* above, however, the balance of the interest expense, $5,500 ($7,300 – $1,800), would not be deductible as qualified residence interest since the property does not qualify as a residence. Nevertheless, the taxpayer may be able to deduct the amount as investment interest to the extent of any net investment income that he or she may have from other investments. Lacking investment income, the taxpayer would be better off using the condominium more, in order that he could qualify it as a second residence and deduct the interest. The balance of the other expenses would not be deductible.

The vacation home rules, as discussed above, could operate to eliminate legitimate deductions for those taxpayers who convert their personal residence for rental during the year. In these cases, the owner usually uses the residence for more than 14 days and thus deductions are limited. However, § 280A(d) provides relief for taxpayers in these situations. The provision accomplishes this goal by not counting as personal use days any days of personal use during the year immediately before (or after) the rental period begins (or ends). This rule, often referred to as the *qualified rental period exception*, applies only if the rental period is at least a year (or if less than a year, the house is sold at the end of the rental period).

Example 38

B lived in her home from January through July. In August, she moved into a condominium and decided to convert her old home to rental property. B was able to find a tenant who leased the old home for a year. Under the normal rules of § 280A, B's deductions related to the old home would be limited to gross income since her personal use exceeded 14 days. The relief measure of § 280A(d) removes this limitation because the seven months of personal use preceding the one-year rental period are not counted as personal use days. As a result, B would treat the lease as a rental activity and could deduct expenses subject to the passive loss rules, possibly qualifying for the $25,000 exception.

CHECK YOUR KNOWLEDGE

Review Question 1

During the Olympics held in Atlanta during 1996, many Georgians left town and rented their homes out for the two weeks the games were in town. It was rumored that some of the mansions were rented for more than $100,000 during this time. How would these temporary landlords treat the income?

Under § 280A, if the home is rented out for less than 15 days, all of the rental income is excluded and none of the expenses allocable to the rental period are deductible. Consequently, these temporary landlords received a real windfall because they were allowed to exclude all of the income.

Review Question 2

T owns a condominium in Vail. This year his rental agent was able to rent it out for 100 days (most guests stayed for six days). Unfortunately, he was able to use the condo for personal purposes for only one week in January because of a skiing accident in which he broke his shoulder. Interest expense and taxes allocable to the personal use were $500. The net loss attributable to the rental during the remainder of the year was $4,000. What amount can T deduct? Is the property considered rental property subject to the passive loss rules?

Since the personal use was nominal (i.e., not more than the greater of ten percent of the number of days rented or two weeks), the property is not considered a residence. Moreover, it is not considered rental property under the passive loss rules since the average rental period was less than eight days. Thus, it is considered a nonrental activity with the treatment dependent on whether T materially participates in the activity. Since he does not materially participate, the loss is a passive loss and is not deductible unless he has other passive income. The interest attributable to the period of personal use is not qualified residence interest since the unit did not qualify as a residence. Instead the interest is treated as investment interest and is deductible to the extent of investment income.

Review Question 3

W owns a condominium in St. John in the Caribbean. She rented it out for seven months (one month at a time) during the year but used it personally for the entire month of January. Can W treat the activity as a rental activity and take advantage of the $25,000 *de minimis* exception that would allow her to deduct a loss from the property?

No. If a taxpayer uses a home for more than two weeks or 10% of the number of days the unit is rented, she treats the home as a residence. In this case, the taxpayer used the home 31 days for personal purposes, thereby exceeding the threshold and converting the property to a residence. Any interest is deductible as qualified residence interest, assuming this is a first or second home. On the other hand, rental expenses can be deducted only to the extent of rental income. The excess expenses may be carried over and deducted in subsequent years to the extent the unit generates income. The passive loss rules do not apply, and the $25,000 allowance is not available.

Problem Materials

DISCUSSION QUESTIONS

12-1 *Tax Shelters and the Solution.* In 1982, T purchased for $10,000 an interest in Neptune III, a limited partnership created by Dandy Development Company to finance and build a 25-story office building in downtown Houston. T, who was in the 50% tax bracket, hoped that this investment would significantly cut her taxes.
  a. Explain the features of the investment that during that period made such investments attractive and might produce the benefits desired by T.
  b. Explain what steps Congress took in 1986 to eliminate the benefits of investments in such activities as Neptune III. Comment in some detail on the approach used by Congress to accomplish its objective.
  c. What steps might you have suggested had you been advising Congress on the restriction of tax shelter?

12-2 *Effect of Code § 469.* D owns and operates several ski rental shops in Vail, Aspen, Beaver Creek, and Steamboat Springs. Over the years, the shops have had their ups and downs, with profits in some years, losses in others. Recently, D has spent less and less time at the shop, letting his employees do most of the work.
   a. What is the significance should the business be characterized as a passive activity?
   b. Should D worry about his business being treated as a passive activity? When is an activity considered passive?
   c. Does the fact that D's business is a rental operation have any bearing on the nature of the activity?
   d. What are the aggregation or grouping rules and why might they be important in D's case?

12-3 *Taxpayers Subject to § 469.* Dr. R has been quite successful over the years. She left St. James hospital in 2004 and started her own sports medicine practice, The Sports Institute Inc., a regular C corporation. After building this operation into a thriving practice, she branched out. In 2013, she and a good friend opened their own restaurant, The Diner, a partnership. In 2016, her college roommate persuaded R to invest and buy stock in a new venture, Compatible PCS, a corporation that manufactured personal computers. Compatible PCS was owned by R and three other individuals and operated as a regular C corporation until this year, when it converted to S status. Dr. R's other investments include a single family house that she rents out, a limited partnership interest in an oil and gas operation, and a limited partnership interest in a business that develops land into shopping centers. Explain how R is affected by the passive loss rules.

12-4 *Definition of an Activity and Planning.* D owns several businesses, including an indoor soccer facility, a gas station adjacent to the soccer facility (he bought it with the intention of someday expanding the soccer facility), and a fast-food restaurant across the street from the soccer facility. Within the soccer facility, he has rented space to a local soccer retail store. He also rents space in the facility to another company, which operates a small bar and restaurant. In any one year, each business may be profitable or may have losses. For simplicity, assume each business is operated as a sole proprietorship.
   a. Assuming one of the businesses is profitable, would D prefer passive or active income?
   b. Assuming one of the businesses has losses, would D prefer a passive or active loss?
   c. Discuss the passive loss rules, how they might apply to D, and what planning might be considered. Identify as many questions as possible that might be asked in determining how the passive loss rules apply to D.

12-5 *Aggregating Activities.* Aggregation of activities may be required for purposes of the material participation tests.
   a. Explain the general rules concerning aggregation and their purpose.
   b. Explain when this rule is beneficial and when it is detrimental for the taxpayer.

12-6 *Rental Activities and Material Participation.* T owns a 10-unit apartment complex. He not only manages the apartments but also performs all of the routine maintenance and repairs as well as keeping the books. Most of the leases that he signs with tenants are for one year. This year the complex produced a loss of $30,000. How will T treat the loss, assuming his adjusted gross income from other sources is $90,000?

12-7 *Recharacterization.* Briefly explain the purpose of the recharacterization rules and why they must not be overlooked when dealing with passive activities.

12-8 *Credits from a Passive Activity.* P is considering rehabilitating a home in a historic neighborhood. She hopes to qualify for both the rehabilitation credit and the low income housing credit.
   a. Assuming she qualifies, explain how she will compute the amount of credit that she may claim.
   b. P's accountant has explained the limitations that apply to losses and has indicated to P that any losses on the rental that are denied currently will ultimately be allowed once P sells the property. Can the same be said of credits?

12-9   *Grouping Activities.* Urged by their accountants to reduce their tax liability, a group of orthopedic surgeons invested in real estate that produced passive losses. Prior to 1986, these losses did in fact serve as tax shelters. After 1986, however, the passive loss rules significantly restricted the tax benefits of the investments. Consequently, the accountants prodded the doctors to form a partnership to acquire and operate X-ray equipment. The doctors do not participate in the X-ray partnership, and, therefore, any income produced by the partnership is passive income. Most of the income from operation of the partnership is derived from services provided to the doctors themselves. Will this scheme successfully produce passive income that can be used to absorb passive losses?

12-10   *Interest Expense.* This year Dr. Z purchased a 20% interest in a partnership that is building an office building in downtown Dallas. To finance the acquisition, he used his line of credit at the bank and borrowed $100,000. As a result, he paid $10,000 in interest during the year.

    a.   How will Dr. Z treat the interest expense?

    b.   After the building was completed, the partnership secured permanent financing. This year the partnership paid mortgage interest of $700,000, of which $14,000 represented Dr. Z's allocable share. How will Dr. Z treat the interest?

PROBLEMS

12-11   *Identifying Activities.* For each of the following situations, indicate the number of activities in which the taxpayer participates.

    a.   S owns and operates an ice cream store in Southwoods Mall. He is also a camera buff and owns a camera shop in the same mall.

    b.   T owns a small "strip" shopping center that houses 10 businesses, including T's own video store. This year T received $40,000 in income from renting out space in the shopping center and grossed $60,000 from her video store.

    c.   O owns five greeting card stores spread all around Denver.

    d.   P owns 10 gas stations throughout the state of Georgia. Each station not only sells gas but also sells groceries. Seven of the stations derive 60% of their income from gas sales and 40% from food sales. Two of the stations derive 55% of their income from food sales and 45% from gas sales. One station also provides auto repair services and derives one-third of its income from each operation.

    e.   E owns a beer distributorship and ten liquor stores throughout Minneapolis. Sixty percent of the distributorship sales are to the liquor stores.

12-12   *Combining Activities.* T owns a 70% interest in each of three partnerships: a radio station (WAKO), a minor league baseball team (the Harrisville Hippos), and a video and film company (Dynamite Productions) that produces short subjects for television, including advertisements. In any particular year, one business may be profitable while another may be unprofitable. Each business is at a different location. Each business also prepares its own financial statements and has its own management, although T participates extensively in the management of all three partnerships. Any financing needed for the three partnerships is usually obtained from Second National, a local bank. The radio station broadcasts all of the Hippo games, and the production company often prepares material for local television spots on the Hippos. Occasionally, some employees in one partnership assist the other partnership in periods of peak activity or emergency. Explain how the passive loss rules apply to T in this case.

12-13   *Material Participation.* During the week, A is a mild-mannered reporter for the local paper. On the weekends, he is a partner with his brother-in-law, B, in a small van conversion operation in Elkhart. The two typically work seven or eight hours on most Saturdays during the year. This year, the partnership suffered a loss of $10,000.

    a.   How will A treat the loss?

    b.   What planning might you suggest?

12-14 *Participation Defined.* Three recent Purdue graduates—C, D, and E—formed their own lawn treatment company. Each of the three participates on a part-time basis because each is otherwise employed on a full-time basis. In this, their first year of operations, C spent 40 hours, D spent 70 hours, and E contributed 80 hours. E's wife also kept the books for the partnership. Explain whether C, D, and E satisfy the material participation test.

12-15 *Material Participation.* F is an accountant with a large C.P.A. firm. She also has an interest in two partnerships: a night club and a family-owned drugstore. F maintains the accounting records for each partnership, spending 200 hours working for the night club and 400 hours for the drugstore.
    a. How will F treat any losses that the partnerships might have?
    b. How will F treat any income that the partnerships might have?

12-16 *Material Participation.* In 2005, H started his own replacement window business, Sting Construction, an S corporation. Up until 2014 H had been the sole shareholder. In 2014 he sold 90% of his stock to J and K, who continued the business. From time to time, H still provides advice to J and K. This year, H spent 300 hours working for the company. J and K each devoted 1,500 hours to the business. Unfortunately, the corporation suffered a loss this year because of a downturn in the economy. How will H treat the loss?

12-17 *Rental or Nonrental Activities.* Indicate whether the following are rental or non-rental activities.
    a. P owns an airplane. She has an arrangement with a flying club at a small airport to lease the plane out on a short-term basis to its students. Most of the time the plane is rented for two to three hours.
    b. Q owns a condominium in Aspen that he rents out during the year. The average stay is one week. Q has arranged to provide daily maid and linen service for the unit. In addition, his monthly condominium fee pays for maintenance of the common areas.
    c. S and his wife, T, own White Silver Sands, a posh resort on the coast of Florida. As part of its package, the resort provides everything a vacationer could want (daily maid service; free use of the golf, tennis, and pool facilities; an on-site masseuse; etc.). The average stay is two weeks.
    d. Z owns a duplex near the University of Texas that she normally rents out to students on a long-term basis. The average stay is nine months. Z provides typical landlord services such as repairs and maintenance.
    e. B owns Quiet Quarters, a retirement home for the elderly. The home's staff includes a physician and several nurses.
    f. C owns and operates Body Beautiful, a fitness club. The club has over 1,000 members who have use of the club daily from 6 a.m. to 11 p.m.
    g. D owns a 200-acre parcel of land on the outskirts of Lubbock. The land is worth $700,000 (basis $200,000). During the year, D leased the land to a local car enthusiast who used it as a raceway. D collected rents of $5,000.

12-18 *Passive Activities.* G is the head chef for Half-Way Airlines, making a salary of $70,000 a year. In addition, his portfolio income is about $20,000 a year. Over the years, G has made numerous investments and has been a participant in many ventures. Indicate whether the passive activity rules would apply in each of the following situations:
    a. A $10,000 loss from G's interest in Flimsy Films, a limited partnership. G is a limited partner.
    b. A $5,000 loss from G's interest as a shareholder in D's Bar and Grill, an S corporation. G and his wife operate the bar. Each spent 300 hours working there in the current year.
    c. G and his friend, F, are equal partners in a partnership that produces and markets a Texas-style barbecue sauce. G leaves the management of the day-to-day operations to F. However, G spent 130 hours working in the business during the current year. For the year, the partnership had income of $15,000. Assume that this is G's only investment.

    d. Same as (c) except G has an ownership interest in three other distinctly different activities (e.g., construction and consulting). He spends 130 hours in each of the four activities.

    e. G is a 10% partner in a restaurant consulting firm. The firm operates the business on the bottom floor of a three-story building it owns. The firm leases the other two floors to a law firm and a real estate company. The consulting side of the business reported a $100,000 profit from consulting, $5,000 in interest income, and had a loss from the rental operation.

    f. G is the sole owner of Try, Inc., a regular C corporation that produces G's special salad dressing. The corporation had an operating profit of $4,000. In addition, Try, Inc. had interest income of $5,000 and a $7,000 loss from its investment in a real estate limited partnership in which it was a limited partner.

12-19 *Passive-Activity Limitations.* M is a successful banker. Two years ago, M's 27-year-old son, J, asked his dad to become his partner in opening a sporting goods store. M agreed and contributed $50,000 for a 50% interest in the partnership. J operates the store on his own, receiving little advice from his father. Information regarding M's financial activities reveals the following for the past two years:

Year	Salary	Interest Income	Partnership Income (Loss)
2017	$100,000	$20,000	$(40,000)
2018	100,000	20,000	12,000

All parties are cash basis, calendar year taxpayers. Answer the following questions.
    a. How did M's investment in the partnership affect his AGI in 2017?
    b. How did M's investment in the partnership affect his AGI in 2018?
    c. Would your answer to (b) change if the partnership had a loss in 2018 and the income shown was from M's interest as a limited partner in a real estate venture?
    d. On January 1, 2019, M sold his interest in the partnership to his son for a $40,000 gain. What effect?

12-20 *Passive-Activity Limitations: Rental Property.* L, single, is the chief of surgery at a local hospital. During the year, L earned a salary of $120,000. L owns a four-unit apartment building that she rents out unfurnished. The current tenants have one-year leases, which expire at various times. This year, the property produced a loss of $30,000 due to accelerated depreciation. L is actively involved in the rental activity, making many of the decisions regarding leases, repairs, etc.
    a. How much of the loss may L deduct?
    b. Would the answer to (a) change if L materially participated?

12-21 *Rental Real Estate.* M and H are real estate moguls. Together they have created a number of partnerships that own more than 50 shopping malls as well as a few office buildings, apartments, and warehouses. Most of their lease agreements with their mall tenants are tied to the tenant's gross receipts. Unfortunately, with the downturn in the economy, several of the mall projects have produced substantial losses. How will M and H treat their share of the losses?

12-22 *Suspended Losses.* When tax shelter activity was at its highest, G was one of its biggest proponents. Currently, she still owns an interest in several limited partnerships. She is now considering what she should do in light of the passive loss rules. To help her make this decision, she has put together her best guess as to the performance of her investments over the next two years. These are shown below.

Activity	2017	2018
X	$(7,000)	$(2,000)
Y	(3,000)	(9,000)
Z	6,000	1,000

a Determine the amount of suspended loss for each activity at the end of 2017 and 2018.

b. Assume the same facts as in (a) above, except assume that in 2018 G sells the Y activity for a $4,000 gain. Explain the effect of the disposition on any suspended losses G might have, including the amount of suspended losses to be carried forward to 2019.

12-23 *Characterizing Income.* Indicate whether the income in the following situations is passive or non-passive:

a. Ten years ago, T purchased a strip of land for $300,000. Shortly thereafter, he built an office building on the land for $100,000. He currently leases the entire building to a large corporation on a ten-year lease for $90,000 annually. This year he sold the building for $700,000.

b. Q owns a real estate development business that she operates as an S corporation. In 2016, she purchased a vacant lot for $100,000. Q proceeded to put in roads, sewers, and other amenities at a cost of $50,000. Shortly thereafter, she contracted for the construction of a warehouse at a cost of $1 million. Upon completion of the building in September 2016, Q began leasing the space. It was completely leased by June 2017. In December 2018, she sold the property for $2 million.

c. T owns 100% of the stock of Z Corporation, an S corporation that operates a construction company. This year T purchased and leased a crane to the corporation. T received total rents of $10,000.

d. X operates a travel agency and an office supply store to which she devotes 300 and 100 hours, respectively. The travel agency produced a profit of $10,000 while the office supply business sustained a loss of $40,000.

12-24 *Rental versus Nonrental Activities.* Identify rental activities that would not be considered "rental activities" for purposes of the passive loss rules.

12-25 *Vacation Home Rental.* S owns a condominium in Florida, which he and his family use occasionally. During the year, he used the condominium for 20 days and rented it for 40 days. The remainder of the year, the condominium was vacant. S compiled the following information related to the condominium for the entire year:

Rental income	$1,000
Expenses:	
Interest on mortgage.	3,650
Maintenance.	900
Depreciation	6,000

a Compute the tax effect of the rental activity on S.

b. Assuming S only used the condominium personally for ten days, compute the tax effect.

c. Assuming S only rented the condominium for 14 days, compute the tax effect.

12-26 *Vacation Home-Personal Use Days.* Indicate the number of personal use days in each of the following situations:

a. Saturday morning, March 3, S drove to Vail to replace a water heater in his vacation home. He arrived in Vail at 9 a.m. and skied until late afternoon, when he retired to his condominium at 6 p.m. After dinner, he worked on replacing the water heater until midnight, when he went to sleep. The following morning he awoke and went skiing until 5 p.m., when he returned home.

b. Same as (a) except S's wife and family accompanied him. S's family also skied but did not perform any repairs or maintenance related to the vacation home.

c. T owns a duplex, which he rents. On February 1 of this year, the one-year lease of the tenant living upstairs expired and she moved. Unable to rent the upstairs unit, T moved in on December 1 and remained through the end of the year.

12-27 *Participation in Real Estate.* When D reached age 60 several years ago, he decided to cut back on the number of hours he devoted to his dental practice. He figured that the income from a mini-warehouse, a trailer park, and a duplex that he owned would sufficiently supplement the income that he derived from his practice. Unfortunately, this year all of these rental activities produced losses. Assuming D has no passive income, indicate whether each of the following statements is true or false. If false, explain why.

a.   D is not allowed to deduct the losses since rental real estate activities are considered passive regardless of the taxpayer's participation.

b.   D is allowed to deduct the losses if most of his working hours are spent managing the real estate properties.

c.   Assuming D works 700 hours managing the properties and his wife spends 200 hours helping him, the couple will be able to deduct the losses on their joint return.

12-28 *At-Risk Computation.* Ajax Construction builds apartments and condominiums. It has developed a unique construction technique. It created forms in the shape of a U in which concreted is poured. The U forms are then inverted and set on top of each other to form the walls and floors of a building. A crane is needed to hoist a U out of the concrete forms and stack it on top of another U. The owners of Ajax Construction, A and B, formed the AB Partnership to purchase the crane and other heavy equipment that would be rented to Ajax and other parties. The partnership is formed on January 1, 2017 by equal partners A and B who each contribute $100,000. The AB Partnership reports on a calendar year and is engaged in activities subject to § 465. The following transactions occurred during 2017 and 2018:

7/01/2017	AB Partnership borrows $120,000 from a bank using a recourse note.
10/01/2017	AB Partnership acquires equipment at a cost of $400,000 by giving a nonrecourse note to the vendor.
12/01/2017	AB Partnership reduces the recourse note balance to $30,000 and the nonrecourse note balance to $380,000.
12/31/2017	AB Partnership reports a taxable loss of $420,000 for 2017.
12/31/2017	Partners A and B each withdraw $40,000 from the partnership.
4/01/2018	Partners A and B each contribute $50,000 to the partnership.
12/31/2018	AB Partnership reports taxable income of $120,000.

a   Compute partner A's amount at risk on 12/31/2017.

b.   Compute partner A's amount at risk on 12/31/2018.

12-29 *At-Risk: Real Estate.* Kingsmill is a limited partnership. The partnership has three equal partners and it deals exclusively in rental real estate. S is the only general partner. On January 1, all three capital accounts were zero. No changes in the accounts occurred during the year. The partnership incurred losses of $75,000 during the year. As of the close of the year, the partnership had liabilities in the form of $20,000 of accounts payable and a $30,000 nonrecourse mortgage obtained from a commercial lender.

a.   What losses can the partners claim as deductions on their returns for the year?

b.   Would the result be the same if the partnership were engaged in equipment leasing rather than rental real estate?

PART 4

Alternative Minimum Tax and Tax Credits

CHAPTER 13   The Alternative Minimum
Tax and Tax Credits

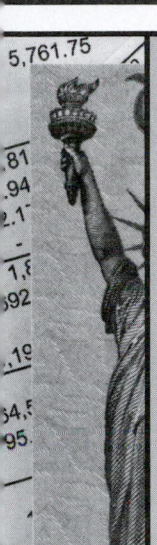

13

The Alternative Minimum Tax and Tax Credits

Learning Objectives

Upon completion of this chapter you will be able to:

LO.1 Explain the tax policy reasons underlying the Alternative Minimum Tax (AMT) system.

LO.2 Understand the conceptual framework of the AMT system and the computation of the AMT.

LO.3 Determine the applicable AMT rate and exemption.

LO.4 Understand AMT adjustments and preferences.

LO.5 Complete Form 6251, Alternative Minimum Tax—Individuals.

LO.6 Explain the difference between a credit and a deduction and why credits are often considered more fair.

LO.7 Distinguish between nonrefundable tax credits subject to dollar limitations and refundable tax credits, which have no such limitations.

LO.8 Understand the components of the general business credit and be able to calculate the amount of credit allowable with respect to separate components.

LO.9 Identify and calculate the nonbusiness tax credits, including the child tax credit, the dependent care credit, the educational tax credits, the earned income credit, and the minimum tax credit.

Chapter Outline

Introduction

As may be abundantly clear at this point, the U.S. tax system is replete with rules whose purpose is not simply to raise revenue but also to shape the behavior of its citizens.[1] These so-called tax incentives—*or tax preferences*—are sprinkled throughout the Code, and they come in several forms. There are exclusions, deductions, and credits that stimulate economic activity and/or modify social behavior. For example, accelerated depreciation stimulates the acquisition of machinery and equipment, and percentage depletion boosts investment in natural resources. Research is encouraged through a quick write-off as well as a credit. There are also credits to attract investment in low-income housing and the rehabilitation of old buildings. Still other credits exhort taxpayers to use certain fuels, buy electric cars, and hire certain people. Even more tax benefits await those who invest in empowerment zones, enterprise communities, and small corporations.

Unfortunately, using the Code to solve some of the country's ills has created problems of its own. As the number of tax preferences began to grow, astute tax advisers and promoters saw an opportunity. They began to structure business and investment deals—all perfectly legal—that took advantage of the favorable treatment extended to particular investments. In fact, tax professionals did their jobs so well that it was not unusual to find wealthy individuals with large economic incomes who paid little or no income tax. Indeed, in 1966, it was determined that 154 individuals with adjusted gross incomes in excess of $200,000 were able to completely escape tax by using the various incentives. Although the revenue lost from these high-income, no-tax individuals was slight, concerns started to surface. By the late 1960s, Congress recognized that an increasing number of people were losing faith in the system, believing that it was unfairly tipped in favor of the rich. Finally, amidst cries that only the poor and middle class paid taxes, the Johnson administration responded.

In 1969, legislation was enacted to guarantee that all wealthy individuals paid at least some amount of Federal income tax. The method adopted, however, was circuitous. Instead of repealing the tax preferences that created the opportunities, Congress chose to add another layer of taxation: the minimum tax. Since 1969, the minimum tax has come a long way, steadily growing in scope and importance. The first part of this chapter takes a look at these complex provisions.

The second part of this chapter is devoted to the world of credits. Over the years, Congress has established a number of credits that attempt to accomplish a variety of objectives. In addition to the business credits noted above, there are also several credits reserved for individuals. For example, there are credits to aid individuals with child care, help the elderly and disabled, encourage individuals to get off welfare and go to work and to conserve energy. Each of the common credit provisions is discussed below.

---

[1] See "Goals of Taxation" discussion in Chapter 1.

POLICY OBJECTIVES

Since its enactment in 1969, the minimum tax has gone through a virtual metamorphosis. Substantial revisions occurred in 1976, 1978, 1981, and 1982, and a complete overhaul took place in 1986. Throughout, however, the rationale behind the tax has remained virtually unchanged. The policy underlying the minimum tax was well-summarized in the following excerpt from the Senate Finance Committee Report on the Tax Reform Act of 1986:

LO.1

Explain the tax policy reasons underlying the Alternative Minimum Tax (AMT) system.

Reasons for Change

The committee believes that the minimum tax should serve one overriding objective: to ensure that no taxpayer with substantial economic income can avoid significant tax liability by using exclusions, deductions, and credits. Although these provisions may provide incentives for worthy goals, they become counterproductive when taxpayers are allowed to use them to avoid virtually all tax liability. The ability of high-income individuals and highly profitable corporations to pay little or no tax undermines respect for the entire tax system and, thus, for the incentive provisions themselves. In addition, even aside from public perceptions, the committee believes that it is inherently unfair for high-income individuals and highly profitable corporations to pay little or no tax due to their ability to utilize various tax preferences.[2]

Guided by these goals, Congress revised the AMT to ensure that the tax liability is at least a minimum percentage of a broad-based concept of income, less related expenses and certain personal or unavoidable expenditures. The intent of the legislation is to increase tax levies on certain wealthy taxpayers.

Under the current AMT rules, taxpayers must make a completely separate tax calculation to determine the *tentative minimum tax;* if the tentative minimum tax is greater than the regular tax liability, the taxpayer will have to pay the higher amount. The upshot of these rules is that the separate tax calculations force taxpayers to keep a separate set of books just to compute the AMT.

OVERVIEW OF AMT

The AMT applies to all of the separate taxable entities: individuals, estates, trusts, and regular C corporations. Partnerships and S corporations are not subject to the AMT per se; but if either has items of AMT significance, such items flow through to the partners or shareholders, who must consider them in calculating their own AMT. Consequently, these flow-through entities, like any other taxpayer, cannot ignore the AMT. The Taxpayer Relief Act of 1997 significantly impacted the AMT system. One ramification is discussed here and the others have been integrated with their related rules discussed later in this chapter. In an attempt at simplification, the new law exempts "small corporations" from the AMT for taxable years beginning after December 31, 1997.[3] For this purpose, a small corporation is one that has less than $5,000,000 in average annual gross receipts for the first three-taxable year period (or portion thereof) of the corporation beginning after December 31, 1993. Subsequent to the first three-taxable year period the corporation's average gross receipts for all three-taxable-year periods ending before the current taxable year cannot exceed $7,500,000.[4]

---

[2] Senate Finance Committee Report. H.R. 3838, Page 518, U.S. Government Printing Office, May 29, 1986.

[3] § 55(e).

[4] See § 448 and Chapter 5. This test is the same as the one applied in determining whether a corporation must use the accrual method of accounting. Note that once a corporation is classified as a small corporation, special rules apply when the gross receipts exceed $7,500,000 because the corporation will lose its status as a small corporation [§ 55(e)].

EXHIBIT 13-1	The Alternative Minimum Tax Formula

Start with:	Regular taxable income	$ xxx,xxx
Plus/Minus:	AMT adjustments (see Exhibit 13-3)	± xx,xxx
Equals:	AMT adjusted taxable income	$ xxx,xxx
Plus:	Sum of tax preference items (see Exhibit 13-5)	+ xx,xxx
Equals:	Alternative minimum taxable income (AMTI)	$ xxx,xxx
Less:	Exemption amount (adjusted for phase-out).	− xx,xxx
Equals:	AMT base (taxable excess)	$ xxx,xxx
Times:	AMT rate	× xx%
Equals:	Gross alternative minimum tax	$ xx,xxx
Less:	AMT foreign tax credit	− x,xxx
Equals:	Tentative minimum tax (TMT)	$ xx,xxx
Less:	Regular tax liability.	− x,xxx
Equals:	Alternative minimum tax (AMT)	$ xx,xxx

LO.2

Understand the conceptual framework of the AMT system and the computation of the AMT.

The basic formula for computing the AMT, like the basic formula for determining taxable income, is relatively uncomplicated. As can be seen from Exhibit 13-1, the calculation starts with the taxpayer's final taxable income computed in the normal fashion.[5] This amount, regular taxable income, is increased by any *tax preferences* and further modified—increased or decreased—by certain *adjustments* (see Exhibit 13-3 and 13-5 for a list and brief explanation). The resulting amount is termed *alternative minimum taxable income* (AMTI). However, AMTI is not the amount subject to tax. AMTI is further reduced by an *exemption* to arrive at the tax base or "taxable excess." The appropriate rate is then applied to produce the gross AMT. This amount is reduced by an available AMT foreign tax credit to yield the *tentative minimum tax*. Finally, the tentative minimum tax (TMT) is compared to the regular tax and the taxpayer pays the higher. Technically, the excess of the tentative minimum tax over the regular tax is the AMT, but as can be seen from the formula, the effect is to require the taxpayer to pay the higher amount.[6] It is important to observe that, in computing the AMT, the regular tax is just that; it does not include the net investment income tax, self-employments taxes or any other taxes. Also note that the general business tax credits normally cannot be used to reduce the TMT.[7] This can be quite a surprise for taxpayers who have a large general business credit that wipes out their regular tax liability but does nothing to shield them from the AMT. Lastly, to prevent more individual taxpayers from paying the AMT, all nonrefundable personal credits can be used to reduce the AMT (as well as the regular tax).[8]

---

[5] § 55(b)(2).

[6] § 55(a).

[7] The empowerment zone credit can offset 25% of the tentative minimum tax as authorized by § 38(c)(2)(A).

[8] The credits include the following: credit for the elderly and disabled, adoption expense credit, child tax credit, credit for interest paid or accrued on certain home mortgages of low-income persons, credit for higher education expenses (the American Opportunity Tax Credit), credit for elective deferrals and IRA contributions (saver's credit), non-business energy property credit for energy-efficient improvements to a principal residence, residential energy efficient property credit for photovoltaic, solar hot water, and fuel cell property added to a residence, and first-time home buyer credit for the District of Columbia.

The last issue that is not revealed in the AMT formula concerns some Congressional largess. In an attempt to protect taxpayers from being taxed under both the regular tax system and the AMT system, Congress introduced the minimum tax credit. As explained later, the minimum tax credit provision essentially allows the alternative minimum tax paid in one year to be used (with some modifications) as a credit in subsequent years against the taxpayer's regular tax liability.

Example 1

K is single and has taxable income of $92,500. In computing her regular taxable income, she utilized regular tax incentives that resulted in $55,000 of AMT adjustments (including her personal exemption) and $35,000 of AMT tax preference items. K's alternative minimum taxable income is $182,500 ($92,500 + $55,000 + $35,000).

As might be suspected, it is not the AMT formula that causes problems. The difficulty lies in the determination of the various adjustments and preferences that must be computed to arrive at AMTI. The next several sections examine each of the items entering into the AMT calculation.

AMT RATES AND EXEMPTIONS

Tax Rates

The AMT has its own set of tax rates. Corporations pay a flat rate of 20 percent. In contrast, individuals, estates and trusts are subject to a two rate structure of 26% and 28%. Like the regular tax rate schedules, the AMT brackets are adjusted annually for inflation. The tax rate structure for 2017 is shown below.

LO.3
Determine the applicable AMT rate and exemption.

AMT Rates for Joint Returns, Unmarried Individuals, Estates, and Trusts for 2017

If the AMT Base Is: Over—	But Not Over—	Tax Liability Is + % on Excess	Of the Amount Over—
$ 0	$187,800	26%	$ 0
187,800	0	$48,828 + 28%	187,800

In addition, to help ensure that taxpayers are not snared by the AMT due to the lower rates on capital gains, Congress conformed the AMT and regular tax. The lower rates for unrecaptured § 1250 gain (25%) and long-term capital gains (15%) now apply for AMT purposes.[9] In contrast, the rate for corporate taxpayers is a flat 20 percent.

AMT Exemption

In order to shield taxpayers with small amounts of tax preferences from the AMT, the Code provides an exemption.[10] As shown in Exhibit 13-2, the exemption amount varies depending on the entity and, in the case of an individual, his or her filing status. The exemption amounts are adjusted annually for inflation.

The exemption provides little or no protection for high income taxpayers. Presumably, Congress did not want high income taxpayers to benefit from the exemption. Consequently, the law provides that the exemption is reduced as the taxpayer's income increases. Specifically, the exemption amount for each taxpayer is reduced (but not below zero) by 25 cents for each $1 of AMTI exceeding a certain threshold. These thresholds are identified in Exhibit 13-2. Note that the phase-out rule completely eliminates the exemption as AMTI increases beyond a certain amount. For example, the $84,500 exemption for married taxpayers is completely eliminated when AMTI reaches $498,900 [($498,900 − $160,900 = $338,000) × 0.25 = $84,500]. The various points at which the phase-out is complete are also shown in Exhibit 13-2.

---

[9] § 55(b)(3).   [10] § 55(d).

EXHIBIT 13-2	Alternative Minimum Tax Exemptions and Phase-Out Levels for 2017		

Taxpayer	Exemption Amount	Phase-Out Begins	Phase-Out Complete
	2017	2017	2017
Married filing jointly or surviving spouse . . .	$84,500	$160,900	$498,900
Unmarried individuals[11]	54,300	120,700	337,900
Married filing separately	42,250	80,450	249,450
Estates and trusts.	24,100	80,450	176,850
C corporations.	40,000	150,000	310,000

Example 2

Assume the same facts as in *Example 1*. Since K is single, her initial AMT exemption in 2017 is $54,300. However, because K's AMTI of $182,500 exceeds the $120,700 threshold for single individuals by $61,800, her exemption amount must be reduced by $15,450 ($61,800 × 0.25). Thus, the allowable exemption for the year is $38,850 ($54,300 −15,450). Based on a regular taxable income of $92,500 her regular tax is $18,882 and her AMT is $18,467, computed as follows:

Regular taxable income	$ 92,500
Plus: AMT adjustments	+ 55,000
AMT adjusted taxable income	$ 147,500
Plus: AMT preference items.	+ 35,000
AMTI	$ 182,500
Less: exemption [$54,300 − 25% ($182,500 − $120,700 = $61,800)]	− 38,850
AMTI base	$ 146,650
Times: AMT rate	× 26%
Gross AMT.	$ 37,349
Less: AMT foreign tax credit	− 0
Tentative AMT	$ 37,349
Less: regular tax liability	− 18,882
AMT.	$ 18,467

[11] § 59(j). The exemption amount for children subject to the "kiddie tax" is earned income plus $7,500. The phase-out range is the same as that for single individuals. Rev. Proc. 2016-55, 2016-45 IRB 707.

ADJUSTMENTS AND TAX PREFERENCE ITEMS IN GENERAL

Once taxable income is determined, the search for AMTI can begin. As noted above, there are two types of modifications that must be made to regular taxable income to arrive at AMTI: adjustments and preferences. Although both of these modifications serve a similar purpose (i.e., provide a more "realistic" measure of the taxpayer's economic income), they are not identical. *Preferences* generally require only an add-back to income. For example, one tax preference item requires the taxpayer to add back certain private activity bond income that was excluded from regular tax gross income under § 103. In contrast, *adjustments* generally call for the complete substitution of some special AMT treatment for the regular tax treatment. For instance, instead of using the regular tax rules to compute depreciation, the taxpayer must use the slower-paced methods for the AMT. Note that, when this occurs, depreciation for regular tax purposes may be more or less than AMT depreciation, resulting in either a positive or a negative adjustment. In short, AMT adjustments may increase or decrease taxable income whereas preferences only increase taxable income.

Another important distinction between adjustments and preferences concerns their effect on the taxpayer's basis in property. Adjustments, such as those for AMT depreciation, usually cause the property's basis for AMT purposes to differ from that for regular tax purposes. Consequently, when the taxpayer later disposes of the property, gain or loss for AMT purposes will normally not be the same as the gain or loss reported for regular tax purposes.[12] As might be imagined, this system effectively requires the taxpayer to maintain a separate set of records for AMT purposes. These separate records are used to compute the annual adjustments as well as the adjustment when the asset is subsequently sold. Note that adjustments can generally be thought of as timing differences between regular taxable income and AMTI. In early years the adjustment normally produces an increase in AMTI. In later years, however, the trend reverses and a negative adjustment is required, actually reducing AMTI.

Although adjustments affect a property's basis, preferences do not. This approach makes accounting for preferences somewhat easier than it is for adjustments. In many cases, only a side calculation is necessary to determine the preference. The preference amount is then simply added to taxable income in the determination of AMTI. Generally, tax preference items are analogous to permanent differences between the regular tax and the minimum tax.

AMT ADJUSTMENTS

AMT adjustments can be classified into four groups. As shown in Exhibit 13-3, not all adjustments apply to all taxpayers; some apply to all taxpayers while others apply only to individuals or only to corporations.[13] In addition, there are special adjustments concerning losses from tax shelters. Although all of the adjustments are listed in Exhibit 13-3, only the more common adjustments are discussed below.

AMT ADJUSTMENTS APPLICABLE TO ALL TAXPAYERS

Depreciation

For AMT purposes, depreciation of property *placed in service after 1986* must be computed using the Alternative Depreciation System (ADS) with an exception for personal property discussed below.[14] This substitution of ADS for the taxpayer's normal method (e.g., MACRS) creates a difference between AMT depreciation and regular tax depreciation, and an adjustment must be made. The amount of the AMT adjustment is merely the difference between regular tax and AMT depreciation, which may be positive or negative as illustrated below.

[12] § 56(b)(1)(F).

[13] § 56.

[14] § 56(a)(1).

EXHIBIT 13-3	AMT Adjustments

Applicable to All Taxpayers		Brief Explanation
§ 56(a)(1)	Depreciation	Use ADS or 150% DB
§ 56(a)(2)	Mining exploration and development costs	Capitalize and amortize over 10 years
§ 56(a)(3)	Income reported on the completed contract method	Use percentage completion
§ 56(a)(4)	Alternative tax net operating loss deduction	Recompute with AMT rules
§ 56(a)(5)	Pollution control facilities	MACRS with straight line method
§ 56(a)(6)	Gains or losses on asset dispositions	Differing AMT basis
§ 56(a)(7)	Alcohol fuel credit	Do not include as income

Applicable Only to Individuals		
§ 56(b)(1)(A)	Itemized deductions	No taxes, misc. itemized deductions; adjust interest, adjust medical
§ 56(b)(1)(E)	Standard deduction	Not allowed
§ 56(b)(1)(E)	Personal dependent exemptions	Not allowed
§ 56(b)(1)(D)	Income tax refunds	Do not include
§ 56(b)(2)	Circulation and research expenditures	Capitalize and amortize
§ 56(b)(3)	Incentive stock options	Include spread (FMV – option price)

Applicable Only to Corporations		
§ 56(c)	ACE (adjusted current earnings)	Add 75% (ACE – AMTI)

Specialized Tax Shelter Loss Adjustments		
§ 56(b)	Passive activity losses	Recompute with AMT rules
§ 56(a)	Farm shelter losses	Deduct in following year, if income

EXHIBIT 13-4	Allowable Depreciation Methods for AMT and Regular Tax Purposes for Property Placed in Service after 1998

Method	Depreciable Life	Regular Tax	AMT	AMT-ACE
200% DB	Recovery period	✓		
150% DB	Recovery period	✓	✓	✓
Straight line	Recovery period	✓		
Straight line	Class life	✓	✓	✓

As discussed in Chapter 9, depreciation under ADS is computed using the straight-line method, the appropriate convention, and the ADS life (the class life for personal property and 40 years for real property). While this same approach generally applies for AMT purposes, there is an exception for tangible personal property. For personal property placed in service after 1998, Congress simplified the depreciation system and the AMT adjustments by allowing the MACRS recovery periods to be used for AMT purposes. The 150% declining-balance method does not apply to assets for which the taxpayer has elected the straight-line method for regular tax purposes. The allowable methods of depreciation for regular tax and AMT purposes are shown in Exhibit 13-4. The exhibit reveals that there are four methods of depreciation available for regular tax purposes, two of which are also suitable for AMT purposes. Two observations should be made that are not obvious from this table. The first concerns realty: note that even though the straight-line method must be used for both AMT and regular tax purposes, an adjustment is still necessary since the AMT class life is longer than the normal recovery period (40 years versus 27.5 or 39 years).[15] The second concerns avoidance of the AMT adjustment. Observe that the taxpayer can avoid the AMT adjustment by electing regular tax depreciation, which uses a slower rate (150% declining-balance or straight-line).[16]

Example 3

T placed an asset costing $100,000 in service on February 5, 2017. Assume the asset is "three-year property" and has an ADR class life of three years. The effect on the minimum tax is computed below assuming that the 150% declining-balance method was used for AMT purposes.

	2017	2018	2019	2020
Regular tax deduction (200%)	$ 33,330	$ 44,450	$ 14,810	$ 7,410
AMT deduction (150%)	– 25,000	– 37,500	– 25,000	– 12,500
Effect of adjustment on AMTI	$ 8,330	$ 6,950	$(10,190)	$ (5,090)
	Increase	Increase	Decrease	Decrease

Note that in the first two years regular depreciation exceeds what is allowed for AMTI—requiring the taxpayer to increase AMTI—a positive adjustment. In the third year, however, the trend reverses itself, and AMT depreciation is greater than what was actually deducted for regular tax purposes. Consequently, the taxpayer is allowed to decrease AMTI—a negative adjustment. Also note that the differences in regular and AMT depreciation cause the property's basis for AMT purposes to be different from the regular tax basis. Accordingly, if the property is sold, the amount of gain or loss for AMT and regular tax purposes may differ.

Recognizing the burdensome task of maintaining one set of depreciation books for each tax system, Congress took steps to coordinate the two. As shown in Exhibit 13-4, taxpayers may eliminate the AMT adjustment by electing the appropriate method for regular tax purposes.[17] For example, the taxpayer could, for regular tax purposes, elect to use the 150% declining balance method, which would be the same as AMT depreciation. Alternatively, if the taxpayer elects to use the ADS life and the straight-line method for regular tax purposes, that same method must be used for the AMT. Either approach eliminates the AMT adjustment.

Example 4

Assume the same facts as in *Example 3* above, except T elects to use the 150% modification. In this case, the need for an AMT adjustment is eliminated, as shown below.

	2017	2018	2019	2020
Regular tax depreciation (150%, ADS life)	$ 25,000	$ 37,500	$ 25,000	$ 12,500
AMT depreciation (150%, ADS life)	– 25,000	– 37,500	– 25,000	– 12,500
AMT adjustment	$ 0	$ 0	$ 0	$ 0

---

[15] § 168(g)(2)(C)(iii).

[16] The Tax Reform Act of 1997 allows AMT depreciation to be computed using the same recovery periods as are used for regular tax purposes. For property placed in service prior to 1999, the AMT required tangible personal property to be depreciated over the longer Alternative Depreciation System class life of the property. See § 56(a)(1)(A)(i).

[17] §§ 168(g)(7) and 56(a)(1)(A)(ii).

Section 179 Limited Expensing

Given the elaborate scheme to curtail accelerated depreciation deductions for AMT purposes, it is surprising that the election to expense property under § 179 does not give rise to an AMT adjustment. Currently, first-year § 179 expensing deductions are allowed for both AMT and regular tax purposes.[18]

Section 168(k) Bonus Depreciation

Bonus depreciation deductions are allowed for both AMT and regular tax purposes.

Mining Exploration and Development Costs

For regular tax purposes, mining exploration and development costs related to mineral property are currently expensed. For AMT purposes, however, such costs must be capitalized and amortized ratably over a 10-year period.[19]

Long-Term Contracts

As explained in Chapter 5, for regular tax purposes, taxpayers normally must use the percentage of completion method to account for long-term contracts. However, the Code carves out two exceptions. The completed contract method may be used to account for home construction contracts and by small contractors who have gross receipts less than $10 million. AMT treatment is similar, but it is not identical. For AMT purposes, there is no exception for small contractors. Consequently, the percentage of completion method must be used for computing AMTI in all cases except in accounting for home construction contracts.[20]

Pollution Control Facilities

While taxpayers are permitted to amortize expenditures related to pollution control facilities over 60 months for regular tax purposes, the AMT requires use of ADS.[21]

Alternative Tax Net Operating Loss (ATNOL) Deduction

An ATNOL is allowed as a deduction for minimum tax purposes.[22] The procedure for computing the ATNOL parallels its cousin, the regular tax NOL, but the ATNOL must be determined taking into consideration all of the AMT adjustments and tax preference items. In addition, the amount of the ATNOL is *limited* to 90% of the AMTI determined without regard to this deduction. An election to forgo the NOL carryback period for regular tax purposes is likely to control the treatment for the ATNOL.[23]

AMT ADJUSTMENTS APPLICABLE ONLY TO INDIVIDUALS

All of the adjustments applicable only to individual taxpayers are listed in Exhibit 13-3. Each of these is discussed below. But first it is important to note that the IRS, while routinely taking the position that the AMT and the regular tax system are two distinct and separate systems, has issued regulations governing the computation of AMTI for noncorporate taxpayers. These regulations provide that, in determining the AMTI of noncorporate taxpayers, all references to the taxpayer's AGI or modified AGI in determining the amount of items of income, exclusion, or deduction in the AMT system must be treated as references to the taxpayer's modified AGI as determined for regular tax purposes.[24] For example, in the AMT system the medical expense deduction is subject to a 10% limitation just as the regular tax medical expense deduction is limited to a 7.5% limitation. The important but apparently inconsistent point is that the limitation for the AMT system is not subject to 10% of AMTI

---

[18] See Footnote 2, *supra,* page 552, note 5.

[19] §§ 616 and 617; but see Footnote 52, *infra,* for the election under § 59(e) that allows taxpayers to avoid an AMT adjustment with respect to these expenditures.

[20] § 56(a)(3).

[21] § 169 and § 56(a)(5).

[22] § 56(a)(4).

[23] *Branum v. Comm.,* 94-1 USTC ¶50, 163, (CA-5, 1994).

[24] Reg. § 1.55-1(e).

(as it should be if the AMT were a separate system), but rather the regulation specifies that the AMT limitation will be subject to 10% of the taxpayer's regular tax system AGI. The purported goal of the regulations is to reduce the complexity and to ease the record keeping burdens that are imposed on noncorporate taxpayers under a completely separate and parallel system that would require a computation of a separate adjusted gross income for alternative minimum tax purposes.

Itemized Deductions

For the most part, itemized deductions allowed for regular tax purposes are also allowed for AMT purposes (sometimes referred to as alternative minimum tax deductions, or ATIDs). However, there are several important exceptions and modifications. These adjustments differ from those above (e.g., depreciation) in that they serve to increase the tax base as permanent adjustments instead of merely altering the timing of the item.

Two itemized deductions are totally disallowed for AMT purposes:[25]

1. Miscellaneous itemized deductions (MIDs). For example, unreimbursed employee business expenses and tax preparation expenses are not allowed for the AMT.[26]

2. Itemized deductions related to the payment of any tax. For example, state, local, and foreign income taxes and real and personal property taxes are not allowed as deductions for AMT purposes.

In computing the itemized deductions allowed for AMT purposes, the limitations for regular tax purposes normally apply (e.g., the 10% limitation on personal casualty losses and medical expenses or the 50% limitation for charitable contributions).[27] In addition, as noted below, special rules exist for medical expenses and interest.

ATIDs generally include the following:[28]

1. Interest expense, but only for
   a. Qualified housing interest.
   b. Investment interest expense to the extent of net investment income.
2. Charitable contributions.
3. Medical expenses, but *only in excess* of 10% of taxpayer's regular tax AGI.
4. Theft, casualty, and wagering losses.
5. Estate tax deductions resulting from reporting income in respect of a decedent under § 691.
6. Impairment-related work expenses.
7. Bond premium amortization deductions.

The above list is self-explanatory with the exception of the amount of interest that will be allowed as an ATID. Several new terms and concepts regarding the deduction for interest were developed and incorporated into the alternative minimum tax system. *Qualified housing interest* is interest paid or accrued on indebtedness incurred after June 30, 1982, in acquiring, constructing, or substantially rehabilitating property that is a principal residence (within the meaning of Code § 121) or qualified dwelling, including a secondary residence.[29] For indebtedness incurred *before* July 1, 1982, a deduction can be taken for interest paid or accrued on a debt that, at that time, was secured by a qualified dwelling without regard for the purpose or use of the proceeds of the indebtedness. The essence of these rules is that interest on second mortgages on homes—home equity loans—established after 1982 is not deductible for AMT purposes as qualified housing interest *unless* the proceeds are used to improve the principal residence.

---

[25] § 56(b)(1)(A).

[26] Beginning in 1998, employee business expenses relating to service as an official of a state or local government or political subdivision thereof are deductible for AGI provided the official is compensated on a fee basis. Thus, these expenses become deductible for the AMT system.

[27] In future years, however, any deduction phase out under § 68 will not apply for AMT purposes. See § 68 and § 56(b)(1)(F).

[28] See § 67(b) for a complete list of itemized deductions that are allowed as ATIDs. Also note that a standard deduction is not allowed for AMT purposes.

[29] A qualified dwelling is a house, apartment, condominium, or mobile home (not used on a transient basis). Qualified dwelling for AMT is a narrow definition and differs from that of Code § 280A(f)(1), which broadly defines a dwelling unit as a house, apartment, condominium, mobile home, boat, or similar property.

When interest rates fall, taxpayers often refinance their homes, and a question arose about the interest paid on a loan (new loan) the proceeds of which were used to pay off the original qualified housing indebtedness (old loan). The TRA of 1986 resolved the issue by allowing an interest expense deduction for AMT purposes on the new loan used to refinance the principal residence, but only to the extent that the new loan does not exceed the outstanding balance of the old loan.[30]

Investment interest expense is allowed as an ATID, but only to the extent of qualified *adjusted* net investment income.[31] The adjustment in computing the net investment income is required for AMT purposes as a result of including a portion of the tax-exempt interest income from specified private activity bonds (SPAB) as a tax preference item that increases the AMTI (see *Example 10* for details relating to the tax-exempt income preference item). If exempt interest income from SPABs is included as a preference item for AMT purposes, the interest expense incurred with respect to it will be allowed as a deduction for AMT purposes. These adjustments for tax-exempt income and its related interest expenses are also allowed in computing the "adjusted" net investment income for AMT purposes.

Circulation and Research Expenditures

For regular tax purposes, § 173 allows newspapers, magazines and other periodicals to immediately deduct circulation expenditures (i.e., costs incurred to establish, maintain, or increase circulation). However, for AMT purposes, circulation expenditures must be capitalized and amortized over a three year period. The same rule applies to research and experimental expenditures, except the amortization period is ten years.[32] However, the Revenue Reconciliation Act of 1989 repealed the AMT adjustment for research expenses of individuals who materially participate in the activity in which research expenses are incurred.[33] As with other adjustments that create a disparity between basis for regular tax and basis for AMT, *separate records must be maintained* to determine the allowable amortization deduction in subsequent years or the gain or loss on disposition or abandonment.

Gains from Incentive Stock Options (ISOs)

For regular tax purposes, the bargain element of ISOs (i.e., the difference between the fair market value of the stock and the option price) is *not* required to be included in income either at the time the option is granted or when the option is exercised.[34] However, an income adjustment may be required for the AMT. Assuming the stock acquired is not subject to substantial risk of forfeiture, the adjustment to AMTI is equal to the amount by which the value of the share at the time of exercise exceeds the option price. If the stock is disposed of in the option year, however, this income adjustment is not required because the income attributable to the bargain element will be reported under the regular tax system in the same year.

Example 5

D receives an incentive stock option to purchase 1,000 shares of her employer's stock at $50 per share. Three years after the receipt of the option, D exercises her option when the stock is selling for $70 per share. When D exercises the option, she has an AMT adjustment of $20,000 ($70,000 – $50,000).

Since the AMT adjustment amount computed above increases the AMTI, an upward basis adjustment in the stock of an equal amount is allowed for AMT purposes. This disparity in the stock's basis for regular tax and the AMT requires an *extra set of books* to determine the amount of gain recognized upon a subsequent disposition of the stock for AMT purposes.

---

[30] § 56(e)(1). See the Tax Reform Act of 1986.

[31] See Chapter 11 for a discussion of the investment interest deduction limitation.

[32] § 56(b)(2)(A)(ii). See Footnote 52, *infra,* for an optional tax accounting method for research and experimental expenditures.

[33] § 56(b)(2)(D). The repeal is effective for taxable years beginning after December 31, 1990.

[34] See Chapter 18 for a discussion of ISOs and § 83.

Example 6

Assume the same facts as in *Example 5* and that D holds the stock until it further increases in value to $85,000. If D sells the stock for $85,000, she has a $35,000 gain for regular tax purposes ($85,000 – $50,000). However, for AMT purposes, the gain is $15,000 ($85,000 – AMT basis of $70,000). To reflect the difference in the regular tax and AMT gain, D makes a negative adjustment to AMTI of $20,000 ($35,000 regular tax gain – $15,000 AMT gain) which potentially reduces her tentative AMT in the year of the sale.[35]

Standard Deduction Not Allowed

Individuals are not permitted to take into account the standard deduction in computing the alternative minimum taxable income.[36]

Personal Exemptions

Personal exemptions authorized under § 151 are not allowed as deductions in computing the AMTI.[37]

Adjustment to Income for Tax Refunds

Generally, taxpayers who itemize deductions must report a refund of a prior year's state or local income tax as gross income in the year of receipt.[38] However, since itemized deductions for all tax expenditures are not allowed for AMT purposes, the refund or recovery in *all cases* is excluded from AMTI.

ADJUSTMENT APPLICABLE ONLY TO CORPORATIONS

The only adjustment applicable solely to corporate taxpayers[39] is the adjustment based on a corporation's adjusted current earnings—commonly referred to as the *ACE adjustment*.[40] The ACE adjustment, like the minimum tax itself, was the Congressional response to what seemed an increasingly frequent phenomenon: corporations were reporting substantial earnings for financial accounting purposes yet paying little or no income tax. Curiously, this occurred despite the existence of the AMT. To address the problem, Congress created the ACE adjustment. This special adjustment is designed to ensure that all corporations pay some minimum tax on economic income.

In theory, the ACE adjustment is relatively simple. It requires a corporation to compare its economic income to taxable income to determine the amount of economic income, if any, that escaped tax. Part of this elusive income is then included in the corporation's AMTI. Technically, the ACE adjustment is equal to 75% of the difference between *adjusted current earnings* and AMTI.[41] In this calculation, adjusted current earnings essentially serve as

---

[35] Taxpayers that have exercised ISOs, properly reported the income for AMT purposes and paid an AMT in the year of exercise, traditionally have looked to the minimum tax credit to reduce the regular tax imposed on the gain from the sale of the stock for regular tax purposes. The AMT rules were designed so that the gain in the regular tax system makes the regular tax larger than the tentative minimum tax and allows the minimum tax credit to reduce the regular tax imposed in excess of the tentative minimum tax. This approach works when the stock appreciates in value but it is flawed if the stock is disposed of after it has decreased in value. There may not be a gain on the disposition in the regular tax system and the taxpayer will not benefit from the minimum tax credit. This situation has been addressed by Congress and is discussed later in this chapter under the refundable minimum tax credit rules.

[36] § 56(b)(1)(E).

[37] *Ibid.*

[38] See § 56(b)(1)(D) and Chapter 6 for an exception based on the tax benefit rule.

[39] Recall, however, that small corporations are exempt from the AMT system. *See supra*, Footnote 3.

[40] This adjustment *does not* apply to certain corporations, including S corporations, regulated investment companies, real estate investment trusts, or real estate mortgage investment conduits. § 56(g)(6).

[41] § 56(g)(1).

a substitute for economic income. The actual computation of adjusted current earnings is quite technical. It begins with AMTI, to which a laundry list of adjustments are made.[42] A discussion of the various adjustments is beyond the scope of this text. Suffice it to say that their collective purpose is to yield the corporation's economic income so its true ability to pay tax can be determined.

Example 7

T Corporation has AMTI of $200,000 without regard to the ACE adjustment. T's adjusted current earnings are determined to be $400,000. T's regular income tax liability is $41,750. T has an ACE adjustment of $150,000, AMTI of $350,000, a tentative AMT of $70,000, and AMT of $28,250, computed as follows:

AMTI before ACE	$ 200,000
Plus: ACE adjustment ([$400,000 − $200,000] × 75%)	+ 150,000
AMTI	$ 350,000
Less: Exemption amount (completely phased out)	− 0
AMTI base	$ 350,000
Times: AMT rate	× 20%
Gross AMT	$ 70,000
Less: AMT foreign tax credit	− 0
Tentative AMT	$ 70,000
Less: Regular tax liability	− 41,750
AMT	$ 28,250

This portion of the alternative minimum tax system has been crafted to make certain the AMT is imposed on corporate taxpayers having an economic ability to pay.

SPECIAL TAX SHELTER LOSS ADJUSTMENTS

Certain losses that may be deductible for regular tax are *denied* for purposes of the AMT. Specifically, tax shelter farm losses and passive-activity losses allowed as deductions for regular tax purposes must be recomputed under the AMT system, taking into account all of the AMT tax accounting rules.[43] Clearly, a separate set of books will be required for each activity. The amount of the AMT adjustment required by the statute is the difference between the loss allowed for the regular tax system and the loss allowed under the AMT system.

Tax Shelter Farm Losses

Noncorporate taxpayers and personal service corporations are not allowed to deduct losses from a tax shelter farm activity in computing AMTI.[44] For the AMT system, the disallowed loss will be treated as a deduction allocable to such activity in the *first* succeeding taxable year, and will be allowed to offset income from that activity in any succeeding year. Under this rule, each farm is treated as a separate activity. In the year that the taxpayer disposes of his or her entire interest in any tax shelter farm activity, the amount of previously disallowed loss related to that activity is allowed as a deduction for the year under the AMT system.

Passive-Activity Losses

As discussed in Chapter 12, there are limitations on the use of losses from passive activities to offset other income of the taxpayer for regular tax purposes.[45] For AMT purposes, similar rules apply, except for AMT purposes a loss generated from a passive activity must

---

[42] § 56(g)(4).

[43] These rules are specified in §§ 56 and 57.

[44] § 58(a).

[45] See Chapter 12 for a discussion of passive losses.

be recomputed to reflect the AMT rules. This means that depreciation, certain intangible drilling and development costs, certain percentage depletion, and other adjustments and preferences must be reflected in computing the loss for AMT purposes.[46] Because of the differences in the treatment of such items, the amount of suspended losses relating to an activity may differ for minimum tax and regular tax purposes and may require that two sets of books be kept in order to track the passive-loss carryover on each activity.[47]

Example 8

C has $200,000 of salary income, $50,000 of gross income from passive activities, and $170,000 of deductions from passive activities for the current year. C's passive activity loss is $120,000 for regular tax purposes. Because the recomputed expenses for AMT purposes are only $130,000, the passive-activity loss is $80,000 for AMT purposes. For regular tax purposes, the taxpayer has taxable income of $200,000 and a suspended passive loss in the amount of $120,000 ($170,000 passive deductions – $50,000 passive income). For minimum tax purposes, the taxpayer has AMTI of $200,000 and a suspended passive loss of $80,000 ($130,000 – $50,000).

As illustrated in the example above, the recomputed passive loss using the AMT rules can be significantly different from the regular tax passive loss with respect to an activity. In fact, in some situations it is possible to have a regular tax passive-loss amount *and* an AMT passive income amount on the same activity!

Example 9

Assume that taxpayer C in the example above had passive-activity deductions of $80,000 for regular tax purposes and $40,000 for minimum tax purposes. C would have regular taxable income of $200,000 and a suspended passive loss of $30,000 ($80,000 – $50,000) for regular tax purposes. For AMT purposes, C has alternative minimum taxable income of $210,000 ($200,000 salary + [$50,000 – $40,000]) and no suspended passive loss for minimum tax purposes.

TAX PREFERENCE ITEMS

Since tax preference items are required to be identified and computed for both corporate and noncorporate taxpayers, all the current preference items are listed in Exhibit 13-5; however, only the most common items are explained below.[48]

EXHIBIT 13-5	AMT Tax Preference Items

Percentage depletion in excess of cost basis on certain mineral properties

Certain intangible drilling and development costs

Specified tax-exempt interest

Exclusion for gain on sale of certain small business stock

---

[46] § 58(b).

[47] P.L. 99-514, Tax Reform Act of 1986, Conference Committee Report, Act § 701.

[48] § 57 sets forth all of the tax preference items and the specifics of each calculation.

Excess Depletion

The amount of the preference item is the excess (if any) of the percentage depletion claimed for the taxable year over the adjusted basis of the property at the end of the taxable year (determined without regard to the depletion deduction for the taxable year).[49] This computation must be made for each unit of property.

Intangible Drilling and Development Costs

In general, the amount of the tax preference is equal to the intangible drilling costs (IDC) incurred and deducted on productive oil, gas, and geothermal wells reduced by the sum of

1. The amount allowed as if the IDCs had been capitalized and amortized over a ten-year period, and

2. Sixty-five percent of the net income for the year from these properties.[50]

If the intangible drilling and development costs are capitalized and amortized in accord with special rules contained in § 59(e), they are not treated as a preference item.[51]

Private Activity Bond Interest

This preference item pertains to interest income on specified private activity bonds (SPABs) issued after August 7, 1986.[52] A bond is considered a *private activity bond* if 10% of the proceeds of the issue is used for private business use in any trade or business carried on by any person that is not a governmental unit. Where interest income on SPABs is includible in AMTI under the above rule, the regular tax rule of Code § 265 (denying deductions for expenses and interest relating to tax-exempt income) does not apply, and expenses and interest incurred to carry SPABs are deductible for minimum tax purposes.

Example 10

In computing his AMTI, P included $10,000 of otherwise tax-exempt interest income on SPABs as a preference item. In addition, he incurred $900 of interest expense on a loan in order to purchase the bonds. Section 265 prohibits a deduction of this $900 for regular tax purposes, but it is deductible for minimum tax purposes.

Gain on the Sale of Qualified Small Business Stock

As explained in detail in Chapter 16, the Revenue Reconciliation Act of 1993 created a special incentive to encourage taxpayers to invest in the stock of qualified small businesses (i.e., stock of a C corporation with gross assets of $50 million or less at the time the stock was issued and that was held by the original owner for more than five years prior to sale). Under this special rule, a taxpayer is entitled to exclude 50% of the gain on the sale of the stock. However, what Congress gives with the right hand it takes away with the left. Seven percent of this exclusion (or 3.5% of the entire gain) is treated as a tax preference item.[53]

---

[49] § 57(a)(1). This preference was repealed for certain independent producer and royalty interest owners of oil and gas properties for taxable years beginning after 1992.

[50] § 57(a)(2)(E)(ii). The CNEPA of 1992 repealed this preference item for taxpayers (other than certain integrated oil and gas companies) for years beginning after December 31, 1992. However, the repeal of the excess IDCs preference "may not result in more than a 40% reduction in the amount of the taxpayer's AMTI computed as if the present-law excess IDC preference had not been repealed."

[51] Code § 59(e) was enacted to provide relief to taxpayers that are subject to the AMT, but through proper planning

want to maximize the regular tax deductions and at the same time minimize the impact of the AMT. This section provides an election to capitalize "qualified expenditures" and deduct them ratably over a 10-year period (three years in the case of circulation expenditures, 60 months in the case of IDCs). Qualified expenditures include IDCs, circulation, research and experimentation, and mining exploration and development costs.

[52] § 57(a)(5)(C)(iv).

[53] § 57(a)(7).

Example 11

On October 31, 2017, J sold qualified small business stock and recognized a gain of $80,000. Only 50% of the gain, $40,000, is subject to regular tax, and the remaining $40,000 is excluded. For AMT purposes, J has a tax preference of $2,800 (7% × $40,000).

ALTERNATIVE MINIMUM TAX COMPUTATIONS

Before the alternative minimum tax calculations can be made, the taxpayer's current taxable income and Federal income tax liability must be determined. As shown in Exhibit 13-1, a taxpayer's AMT liability is the excess of the tentative minimum tax over the regular tax liability. These computations are illustrated in *Example 12,* where the taxpayer's regular tax liability is determined. The same facts are then used to compute the ATIDs in *Example 13* and the taxpayer's AMT liability in *Example 14.*

LO.5

Complete Form 6251, Alternative Minimum Tax—Individuals.

Example 12

T is a married and files a joint return. For 2017, his taxable income and regular tax liability were computed as follows:

Income:		
Salary	$88,000	
Interest	12,000	
Adjusted gross income		$100,000*
Itemized deductions:		
Medical expenses ($12,000 total – [10% of $100,000 AGI])	$ 2,000	
Real property taxes on home........................	12,000	
Real property taxes on beach front property	8,000	
Personal property taxes............................	4,000	
Residence interest	20,000**	
Investment interest on beach front property ($12,000 total, but limited to)	4,000***	
Charitable contributions	10,000	
Casualty loss ($13,000 total – [10% of AGI])	3,000	
Miscellaneous itemized deductions ($11,000 total – [2% of AGI]) ..	9,000	
Total itemized deductions		– 72,000
Personal exemptions (2 × $4,050 in 2017)		– 8,100
Taxable income..		$ 19,900
Regular tax		$ 1,990

* Although not required to be included in his taxable income, T exercised an incentive stock option for $20,000 when the fair market value of the stock was $80,000.

** Residence interest includes $20,000 of qualified housing interest (interest on mortgage to acquire home) and $2,000 of interest on a home equity loan to buy a boat.

*** The beach front property was acquired as a speculative investment and was 90% debt-financed. Recall that interest on investment indebtedness is allowed as a deduction under § 163(d) to the extent of net investment income. Net investment income = $12,000 interest – $8,000 property taxes = $4,000. Thus the $12,000 interest expense deduction is limited to $4,000.

Example 13

Refer to *Example 12*. T's 2017 alternative tax itemized deductions (ATIDs) and the resulting AMT adjustments are determined as follows:

	Allowed ATIDs for AMT	Allowed Itemized Deductions for Regular Tax	AMT Adjustments
Medical expenses (in excess of 10% of AGI)	$ 2,000	$ 2,000	$ 0
Itemized deductions for taxes (not allowed)	0	24,000	24,000
Qualified housing interest.	18,000	18,000	0
Home equity loan.	0	2,000	2,000
Other qualified interest (limited to net investment income = $12,000)	12,000	4,000	(8,000)
Casualty losses	3,000	3,000	0
Charitable contributions	10,000	10,000	0
Miscellaneous itemized deductions (not allowed)	0	9,000	9,000
Totals	$ 45,000	$ 72,000	$ 27,000

The computations for ATIDs are similar to those in *Example 12* for itemized deductions except:

1. Deductions for state and local taxes are not allowed,
2. The miscellaneous itemized deductions are not allowed,
3. The interest on the home equity loan to purchase the boat is not allowed, and
4. In the calculation of net investment income, the real property taxes of $8,000 on the beach front property are not deductible for AMT purposes, which increases net investment income from $4,000 to $12,000. This allows additional investment interest of $8,000 to be deducted.

The differences between the ATIDs allowed for AMT purposes and the itemized deductions allowed for regular tax purposes result in AMT adjustments. These adjustments are added back to T's regular taxable income to arrive at AMT adjusted taxable income and are reported on Form 6251, Computation of Alternative Minimum Tax for Individuals.

Example 14

Refer to *Examples 12 and 13*. T's AMT for 2017 is computed as follows:

Regular taxable income		$ 19,900
Plus:	Net adjustment for itemized deductions	+ 27,000*
	Net adjustment for exercise of ISO	+ 60,000**
	Adjustment for personal exemptions	+ 8,100
AMT adjusted taxable income		$115,000
Plus:	Tax preference items	+ 0
Alternative minimum taxable income (AMTI)		$115,000
Less:	Exemption amount 2017 (married filing jointly)	− 84,500
AMT base (taxable excess)		$ 30,500
Times:	AMT rate	× 26%
Gross alternative minimum tax		$ 7,930
Less:	AMT foreign tax credit	− 0
Tentative minimum tax		$ 7,930
Less:	Regular tax liability (married filing jointly)	− 2,953
AMT liability for 2017		$ 5,877

*	Regular tax itemized deductions	$72,000
	ATIDs allowed for AMT	(45,000)
	Disallowed itemized deductions increase in the AMTI	$27,000
**	Stock FMV when ISO exercised	$80,000
	Option price	(20,000)
	Excess is AMT adjustment that increases AMTI	$60,000

Since the tentative minimum tax of $7,930 *exceeds* his $2,953 regular tax liability (computed in *Example 12*), T must pay the difference of $5,877 for 2017 because of the alternative minimum tax. Note that T must pay a total of $7,930 in taxes for 2017 ($2,953 regular income tax + $5,877 alternative minimum tax).

The previous example illustrates an unfortunate consequence of the AMT. The historical tax benefits of home ownership (e.g., deductibility of interest and real property taxes) are either decreased or totally eliminated by the AMT. Although Congress continues to support the objectives of these incentives, their use by individuals to reduce substantially their income tax liability was never the intent of the law.

Example 14 also illustrates the reach of the AMT. Due to the decrease in regular tax rates for lower and middle income taxpayers and the limitations on ATIDs and deductions for exemptions, it is possible that many unsuspecting individuals (like T) will be subject to the AMT.[54] Consequently, tax planning to avoid or minimize the AMT is becoming more important for a growing number of taxpayers.

A completed Form 6251, based on the facts from *Examples 12, 13,* and *14,* is contained in Exhibit 13-6. The 2016 form is used because the 2017 form was not available at the publication date of this text.

---

[54] *N. Holly v. Comm.,* T.C. Memo 1998-55.

EXHIBIT 13-6	Form 6251 Alternative Minimum Tax for Individuals

Form 6251

Department of the Treasury
Internal Revenue Service (99)

Alternative Minimum Tax—Individuals

▶ Information about Form 6251 and its separate instructions is at www.irs.gov/form6251.
▶ Attach to Form 1040 or Form 1040NR.

OMB No. 1545-0074

2016

Attachment
Sequence No. **32**

Name(s) shown on Form 1040 or Form 1040NR
Mr. T

Your social security number
324 – 91 – 0070

Part I   Alternative Minimum Taxable Income (See instructions for how to complete each line.)

pre-exemptions ($19,900 + $8,100 = $28,000)

1	If filing Schedule A (Form 1040), enter the amount from Form 1040, line 41, and go to line 2. Otherwise, enter the amount from Form 1040, line 38, and go to line 7. (If less than zero, enter as a negative amount.)	**1**	28,000 00
2	Medical and dental. If you or your spouse was 65 or older, enter the **smaller** of Schedule A (Form 1040), line 4, **or** 2.5% (0.025) of Form 1040, line 38. If zero or less, enter -0-	**2**	
3	Taxes from Schedule A (Form 1040), line 9	**3**	24,000 00
4	Enter the home mortgage interest adjustment, if any, from line 6 of the worksheet in the instructions for this line	**4**	2,000 00
5	Miscellaneous deductions from Schedule A (Form 1040), line 27.	**5**	9,000 00
6	If Form 1040, line 38, is $155,650 or less, enter -0-. Otherwise, see instructions	**6**	( )
7	Tax refund from Form 1040, line 10 or line 21	**7**	( )
8	Investment interest expense (difference between regular tax and AMT)	**8**	– 8,000 00
9	Depletion (difference between regular tax and AMT)	**9**	
10	Net operating loss deduction from Form 1040, line 21. Enter as a positive amount	**10**	
11	Alternative tax net operating loss deduction	**11**	( )
12	Interest from specified private activity bonds exempt from the regular tax	**12**	
13	Qualified small business stock, see instructions	**13**	
14	Exercise of incentive stock options (excess of AMT income over regular tax income)	**14**	60,000 00
15	Estates and trusts (amount from Schedule K-1 (Form 1041), box 12, code A)	**15**	
16	Electing large partnerships (amount from Schedule K-1 (Form 1065-B), box 6)	**16**	
17	Disposition of property (difference between AMT and regular tax gain or loss)	**17**	
18	Depreciation on assets placed in service after 1986 (difference between regular tax and AMT)	**18**	
19	Passive activities (difference between AMT and regular tax income or loss)	**19**	
20	Loss limitations (difference between AMT and regular tax income or loss)	**20**	
21	Circulation costs (difference between regular tax and AMT)	**21**	
22	Long-term contracts (difference between AMT and regular tax income)	**22**	
23	Mining costs (difference between regular tax and AMT)	**23**	
24	Research and experimental costs (difference between regular tax and AMT)	**24**	
25	Income from certain installment sales before January 1, 1987	**25**	( )
26	Intangible drilling costs preference	**26**	
27	Other adjustments, including income-based related adjustments	**27**	
28	**Alternative minimum taxable income.** Combine lines 1 through 27. (If married filing separately and line 28 is more than $247,450, see instructions.)	**28**	115,000 00

Part II   Alternative Minimum Tax (AMT)

29	Exemption. (If you were under age 24 at the end of 2016, see instructions.)		

IF your filing status is . . .	AND line 28 is not over . . .	THEN enter on line 29 . . .
Single or head of household	$119,700	$53,900
Married filing jointly or qualifying widow(er)	159,700	83,800
Married filing separately	79,850	41,900

2017 Exemption

If line 28 is **over** the amount shown above for your filing status, see instructions.

29		**29**	84,500 00
30	Subtract line 29 from line 28. If more than zero, go to line 31. If zero or less, enter -0- here and on lines 31, 33, and 35, and go to line 34	**30**	30,500 00
31	• If you are filing Form 2555 or 2555-EZ, see instructions for the amount to enter. • If you reported capital gain distributions directly on Form 1040, line 13; you reported qualified dividends on Form 1040, line 9b; **or** you had a gain on both lines 15 and 16 of Schedule D (Form 1040) (as refigured for the AMT, if necessary), complete Part III on the back and enter the amount from line 64 here. • **All others:** If line 30 is $186,300 or less ($93,150 or less if married filing separately), multiply line 30 by 26% (0.26). Otherwise, multiply line 30 by 28% (0.28) and subtract $3,726 ($1,863 if married filing separately) from the result.	**31**	7,930 00
32	Alternative minimum tax foreign tax credit (see instructions)	**32**	
33	Tentative minimum tax. Subtract line 32 from line 31	**33**	7,930 00
34	Add Form 1040, line 44 (minus any tax from Form 4972), and Form 1040, line 46. Subtract from the result any foreign tax credit from Form 1040, line 48. If you used Schedule J to figure your tax on Form 1040, line 44, refigure that tax without using Schedule J before completing this line (see instructions)	**34**	2,053 00
35	**AMT.** Subtract line 34 from line 33. If zero or less, enter -0-. Enter here and on Form 1040, line 45	**35**	5,877 00

For Paperwork Reduction Act Notice, see your tax return instructions.   Cat. No. 13600G   Form **6251** (2016)

MINIMUM TAX CREDIT

Although the second half of this chapter is devoted entirely to credits, it is perhaps best to cover credits related to the AMT at this point. The first of these is the credit for the AMT.

One significant feature of the AMT system is that many taxpayers are required to pay the AMT on income from certain investments long before they would have had to pay the regular income tax on the same income. For example, taxpayers with substantial investments in depreciable personal property are *denied* the tax reduction benefits of MACRS for purposes of computing the AMT.[55] Likewise, a taxpayer who exercises an ISO must recognize income for AMT purposes to the extent the fair market value of the stock exceeds its option price, but for regular income tax purposes the taxpayer does not recognize income until the stock acquired with the ISO is sold. Without some form of relief, a taxpayer could be subject to the AMT in one year and the regular tax in a later year on the same item.

In order to limit the possibility of double taxation under the two tax systems, Congress introduced an AMT credit. Basically, the AMT paid in one year may be used as a credit against the taxpayer's *regular* tax liability in subsequent years. The credit may be carried forward indefinitely until used; however, the credit cannot be carried back nor can it be used to offset any future AMT liability.[56]

Example 15

In 2016, J paid an alternative minimum tax, and his AMT credit after making the appropriate adjustments was $20,000. In 2017, J's regular tax liability before considering the minimum tax credit, is $45,000 and his *tentative* minimum tax is $40,000. Since J's regular tax exceeds his tentative minimum tax, there is no AMT for 2017. In computing his final tax liability, J is entitled to use the minimum tax credit against his regular tax liability but only to the extent that it does not create an AMT (i.e., bring his regular tax liability below his tentative minimum tax). Consequently, he may use $5,000 of the credit, reducing his regular tax liability to $40,000, as shown below. The remaining $15,000 of the minimum tax credit may be carried forward indefinitely.

Regular tax liability		$45,000
Minimum tax credit:		
Limitation:		
Regular tax	$ 45,000	
Tentative minimum tax	− 40,000	
Allowable minimum tax credit		− 5,000
Total tax due		$40,000

Note that the minimum tax credit effectively converts the AMT from a permanent out-of-pocket tax to a prepayment of regular tax to the extent the AMT is attributable to deferral or timing preferences and adjustments rather than to exclusion items.[57]

For noncorporate taxpayers, the minimum tax credit is generally the difference between the AMT actually paid and the amount of AMT that would have been paid if only exclusion items were taken into account. The exclusion items are listed below.

1. Itemized deductions or standard deduction.
2. Personal exemptions.
3. Percentage depletion treated as a preference.
4. Tax-exempt interest treated as a preference.
5. The preference amount computed on the sale of the § 1202 stock.

---

[55] Recall that depreciable personal property placed in service after 1986 must be depreciated using either the 150% declining balance or the ADS straight-line method over the asset's class life for AMT purposes.

[56] § 53(a). See next section for discussion of AMT refundable credit.

[57] § 53(d)(1)(B)(iv) authorizes corporate taxpayers to use the entire minimum tax liability as the minimum tax credit.

Example 16

J is married and files a joint return. For this year, she reported taxable income of $88,200 and claimed the standard deduction. In computing her taxable income, J excluded $44,400 of tax-exempt interest from SPABs, which creates a $44,400 AMT preference item. In addition, she claimed a $100,000 deduction for research expenses from an activity in which she does not materially participate, which creates a $90,000 AMT adjustment for research and experimental expenditures. Assume J has $100,000 of passive activity income that absorbed the research deductions for regular tax purposes. J's minimum tax credit for 2017 to be carried forward is $28,762, as computed below.

The amount of AMT actually required to be paid is $33,149, determined as follows:

Regular taxable income		$ 88,200
Plus:	AMT adjustment for research expenses	+ 90,000
	AMT adjustment for personal exemptions	+ 8,100
	AMT adjustment for standard deduction	+ 12,700
	AMT preference item for SPAB income	+ 44,400
AMTI		$ 243,400
Less:	Exemption amount 2017 ($84,500 – $20,625 phase-out [$243,400 – $160,900 = $82,500 × 0.25])	– 63,875
AMT base		$ 179,525
Tentative minimum tax ($179,525 × 26%)		$ 46,677
Less:	Regular tax liability for 2017	– 13,528
AMT liability for current year		$ 33,149

The amount of AMT that would have been required to be paid if only exclusion items were taken into account is determined as follows:

Regular taxable income		$ 88,200
Plus:	AMT adjustment for personal exemptions	+ 8,100
	AMT adjustment for standard deduction	+ 12,700
	Tax preference item for SPAB income	+ 44,400
AMTI		$ 153,400
Less:	Exemption amount ($84,500 – $0 phase-out [$153,400 – $160,900 = $0 × 0.25])	– 84,500
	AMT base	$ 68,900
Times:	AMT rate	× 26%
Tentative AMT		$ 17,914
Less:	Regular tax liability for 2017	– 13,528
AMT using only exclusions		$ 4,387

The minimum tax credit is computed as follows:

AMT liability for current year	$ 33,149
AMT using only exclusion items	– 4,387
Minimum tax credit	$ 28,762

The $28,762 minimum tax credit may be carried forward and used to offset (reduce) the regular tax liability in subsequent years.

 **CHECK YOUR KNOWLEDGE**

Review Question 1

After completing his tax return for the year, C has a regular tax liability of $30,000, a tentative minimum tax of $45,000, and an alternative minimum tax of $15,000. How much does C actually owe the IRS?

C owes $45,000 in taxes, consisting of a regular tax liability of $30,000 and an AMT liability of $15,000.

Review Question 2

True-False. Jack is a professional golfer, earning more than $800,000 on the tour this year. After deducting expenses, taxable income for the year is $500,000. He and his wife are entitled to a $84,500 (2017) exemption in computing their alternative minimum tax liability.

False. The exemption phases out once their AMTI exceeds $160,900 and is completely phased out when AMTI reaches $498,900. Based on the size of his earnings, it would appear that his AMTI exceeds $498,900 so that the exemption would provide no benefit.

Review Question 3

True-False. In determining AMTI, the taxpayer begins with taxable income and then adds back all of the deductions allowed by so-called loopholes. There are no negative adjustments.

False. Although the effect of the AMTI is to fill in the loopholes, *adjustments* may be positive or negative (e.g., when AMT depreciation exceeds regular tax depreciation). All tax preference items are positive.

Review Question 4

True-False. Steelco Corporation acquired several new copying machines for its offices and depreciated them under MACRS, using the 200% declining-balance method and a five-year recovery period. For AMT purposes, Steelco must use the straight-line method and a six-year class life. (**Hint:** See Revenue Procedure 87-56 and Exhibit 9-2.)

False. Steelco may use the recovery period of five years, but is only allowed to use 150% declining-balance in computing depreciation for personal property for AMT purposes.

Review Question 5

Fred and Ethel are married with two children. Fred is a partner in a public accounting firm. Ethel recently retired as a traveling salesperson for an athletic shoe manufacturer. After completing their return, Fred and Ethel realized that they may have to pay the alternative minimum tax. Indicate whether an adjustment is required for AMT purposes for the following items that the couple reported for regular tax purposes.

 a. Personal exemptions for Fred and Ethel.
 b. Dependent exemptions for their children.
 c. Social Security benefits that were nontaxable, $10,000.
 d. Contribution to individual retirement account, $2,000.
 e. Fred's membership dues to the Indiana CPA Society reimbursed by his employer, $200.
 f. Straight-line depreciation on their newly acquired duplex, which they are currently renting out, $6,000.
 g. State income taxes, $10,000.
 h. Property taxes on their personal residence, $4,000.
 i. Tax-exempt interest from City of Indianapolis bonds used to finance its downtown mall, $2,000 (the bonds were issued after August 7, 1988).
 j. State income tax refund, $500.
 k. Interest on the mortgage on their personal residence, $22,000.

l. Interest on a second mortgage on their residence (proceeds used to add a porch), $3,600.

m. Ethel's unreimbursed travel and entertainment expenses related to her employment, $1,000.

n. Alimony to Fred's ex-wife, Luci, $4,000.

An adjustment is required for (a) and (b) (exemptions not allowed), (f) (40- versus 39-year life), (g) and (h) (taxes), (i) (private activity bond), (j) (no AMT income for tax refunds), and (m) (miscellaneous itemized deduction). No adjustment is required for (c), (d), (e) (reimbursed employee business expense deductible for AGI), (k) (qualified housing interest), (l) (home equity loan used for improvement to house is qualified housing interest), or (n) (no adjustment required).

Review Question 6

GHI Construction Corporation, a calendar year taxpayer, specializes in building warehouses. Its annual gross receipts average about $8 million. The corporation began work on a building in November 2016 and finished construction in February 2017. The contract was approximately 40% complete as of the close of the year. For regular tax purposes, the corporation uses the completed contract method. Consequently, it reported all of the income from the contract, $100,000, in 2017.

a. What is the amount of the AMT adjustment for 2016, if any?

b. Assume that the AMT adjustment is $40,000 and the AMT attributable to the above contract was $8,000 (20% × $40,000), and that GHI paid this amount as AMT when it filed its 2016 tax return. In 2017, GHI reported the entire $100,000 profit for regular tax purposes and paid $34,000 of regular tax on this contract. Is the $40,000 of profit earned in 2016 taxed twice, once under the AMT system when it is included as a $40,000 adjustment in 2016 and once under the regular tax system when it is included in the $100,000 reported in 2017?

No. The AMT paid in 2016 ($8,000) may be credited against the regular tax in 2017 ($34,000) so the amount actually paid in 2017 is $26,000. The minimum tax credit ensures that the income is not taxed twice. Note that in this case the AMT effectively operates to accelerate the income tax paid on a portion of the $100,000 profit.

Income Tax Credits

LO.6

Explain the difference between a credit and a deduction and why credits are often considered more fair.

One reason tax credits are popular is that a credit is viewed as providing a more equitable benefit than a comparable deduction. This is because a credit is a direct reduction of the tax liability, while a deduction merely reduces the amount of taxable income. This difference is illustrated in *Example 17*.

Example 17

Hi is in the 35% tax bracket, and Lo is in the 15% tax bracket. A credit of $100 is worth the *same* to both taxpayers since it reduces the tax liability of each by $100. On the other hand, a deduction of $100 provides a *different* benefit for each: $35 (35% × $100) for Hi and only $15 (15% × $100) for Lo.

The results from *Example 17* can be generalized for tax policy as (1) all taxpayers receive the *same dollar benefit* from credits, regardless of marginal tax rates; (2) taxpayers with higher marginal tax rates benefit more from tax deductions than do those with lower marginal rates; and (3) taxpayers receive more benefit from tax credits than from tax deductions of the same amount. In addition, the argument has been made that credits are of more benefit to those with lower incomes. This is based on the reasoning that the $100 tax saved has more relative value for those with low incomes than it has for those with high incomes. However, this line of reasoning is questionable since taxable income is just one inexact measure of a person's economic situation.

In recent years, Congress has increased the number of tax credits significantly. Most credits have been enacted into law to achieve a specified social, economic, or political goal. These goals range from encouraging taxpayers to engage in scientific research (the research credit) and the conservation of energy (energy tax credits) to providing compensatory tax reductions for those individuals who may carry greater burdens than others (credits for the elderly and for individuals with low earned incomes).

OVERVIEW OF TAX CREDITS

All credits can be classified into two categories: nonrefundable and refundable. Nonrefundable credits can be used only to the extent of the taxpayer's regular tax liability as that amount is defined in § 26. In other words, nonrefundable credits are normally limited to the taxpayer's tax liability. They cannot be used to reduce the amount of tax owed to less than zero (i.e., produce a refund). In contrast, refundable credits are more like tax payments. As their name suggests, if a refundable credit exceeds the amount of tax owed, the excess is refunded to the taxpayer. For example, if the taxpayer's regular tax liability is $2,000 and the taxpayer has a nonrefundable credit of $5,000, the tax owed would be reduced by $2,000 to zero and the taxpayer would not be entitled to a refund. However, if the $5,000 credit were refundable, the $2,000 tax would be eliminated and the taxpayer would receive a refund of $3,000.

In applying credits, nonrefundable credits are accounted for first followed by refundable credits. The order that the credits are taken into account is important as illustrated in the example below.

LO.7

Distinguish between nonrefundable tax credits subject to dollar limitations and refundable tax credits, which have no such limitations.

Example 18

H and W are married and have a regular tax liability before considering any credits of $3,000. The couple qualifies for a $1,000 credit for child care expenses (a nonrefundable credit) and a $5,000 earned income credit (a refundable credit). The table below illustrates the importance of ordering. If the nonrefundable child care credit is applied first, the couple receives a refund of $3,000. If the refundable earned income credit is applied first, the refund is only $2,000 since the child care credit is not refundable.

Nonrefundable Credit Applied First		*Refundable Credit Applied First*	
Regular tax liability before credits	$ 3,000	Regular tax liability before credits	$ 3,000
Child care credit (nonrefundable)	(1,000)	Earned income credit (refundable) . . .	(5,000)
Remaining tax	2,000	Remaining tax (refund).	(2,000)
Earned income credit (refundable) . . .	(5,000)	Child care credit (nonrefundable)	—
Tax due (refund).	$ (3,000)	Tax due (refund).	$ (2,000)

The order of nonrefundable credits is also important. To illustrate, consider two nonrefundable credits: the credit for child care and the foreign tax credit. Both can be used only to the extent of the tax liability. However, any foreign tax credit that cannot be used may be carried forward or back and utilized in other tax years. In contrast, any child care credit that is not used in the current year is lost and provides no tax benefit. The Code provides the order in which the credits are used.[58]

Available Credits

Exhibit 13-7 provides a long, long list of credits, most of which are contained in §§ 27 through 54. Technically these are all contained in subparts of Part IV—Credits Against Tax which is contained in Subchapter A of the Code.

- Subpart A consists of nonrefundable individual tax credits

- Subpart B contains certain other nonrefundable credits

- Subpart C contains the refundable credits

- Subparts D and E consists of 13 separate credits, which are combined to form the "general business credit"

- Subpart G contains the minimum tax credits discussed earlier in this chapter

- Subpart H contains the credit to holders of clean renewable energy bonds

A quick look at the Exhibit reveals that Congress has gone wild on credits. While some of the credits have widespread applicability, many apply to a very limited group of taxpayers. Due to the magnitude and relative importance of the business credits, they are examined first. A discussion of the tax credits available only to individual taxpayers immediately follows.

GENERAL BUSINESS CREDIT

LO.8

Understand the components of the general business credit and be able to calculate the amount of credit allowable with respect to separate components.

As shown in Exhibit 13-7, the general business credit actually consists of a number of separate credits that are commonly available to business. Each of these credits is computed under its own set of rules. The various credits are then combined to determine the current year's total general business credit. The credits are combined in order to determine an overall limitation on the amount of credit that can be used to offset the taxpayer's tax liability.

In order to prevent taxpayers from using business credits to avoid paying all income taxes, the general business credit is generally limited to $25,000 *plus* 75% of the net regular tax liability in excess of $25,000.[59] It should also be recalled that the business credits normally are not allowed to offset the AMT. Generally, credits that are unused because of these limits can be carried back one year and then forward 20 years, applied on a first-in, first-out basis.[60]

Example 19

In 2017, F has a potential general business credit of $92,000 and a net regular tax liability of $100,000. The maximum allowable business credit for 2017 is $81,250 ($25,000 + [75% × $75,000 = $56,250]). The unused credit of $10,750 ($92,000 − $81,250) is carried back 1 year and forward 20 years.

The rules for computing the separate components of the general business credit beginning with the investment tax credit, are explained in the following sections.

---

[58] Nonrefundable credits are to be used to reduce the regular tax liability in the following order: §§ 21, 22, 25A, 25, 25B, 24, 27, 23, 29, 30, 30A, 38, and 53. The order in which credits are absorbed can be pieced together by reading §§ 25(e), 23(b), 25B(g), and 53(c).

[59] The "net regular tax liability" is the § 26 tax liability reduced by nonrefundable credits. Under § 38(c)(1), married taxpayers filing separate returns are limited to $12,500 plus 75% of the tax liability in excess of $12,500 [§ 38(c)(4)].

[60] § 39(a). Note when the general business credit is limited and two or more components of the credit are applicable, § 38(d) specifies ordering rules to determine the credits utilized currently and those subject to the carryback and carryover rules.

EXHIBIT 13-7	Table of Tax Credits

	Code Section	Specific Credit	Termination Date
Subpart A:	§ 21	Child and Dependent Care Credit	None
(Nonrefundable)	§ 22	Credit for the Elderly	None
	§ 23	Credit for Adoption Expenses	None
	§ 24	Child Tax Credit	None
	§ 25	Credit for Interest on Certain Home Mortgages	None
	§ 25A	American Opportunity and Lifetime Learning Credits	None
	§ 25B	IRA Contribution Credit	None
	§ 25C	Residential Energy Property Credit	12/31/2016
	§ 25D	Residential Alternative Energy Credit	12/31/2021
	§ 25F	Employer Provided Childcare Credit	None
Subpart B:	§ 27	Possession and Foreign Tax Credit	None
(Nonrefundable)	§ 30B	Alternative Motor Vehicle Credit	12/31/2016
	§ 30C	Alternative Motor Vehicle Hydrogen Refueling Property Credit	12/31/2016
	§ 30D	New Qualified Plug-In Electric Drive Motor Vehicles	Special Rule
Subpart C:	§ 31	Credit for Taxes Withheld on Wages	None
(Refundable)	§ 32	Earned Income Credit	None
	§ 33	Credit for Taxes Withheld at Source on Nonresident Aliens and Foreign Corporations	None
	§ 34	Credit for Certain Uses of Gasoline and Special Fuels	None
	§ 35	Health Insurance Credit	None
Subpart D:	§ 38	General Business Credit (including)	
(Nonrefundable)		1. Alcohol Fuels Credit (§ 40)	12/31/2016
		2. The Biodiesel Fuel Credit (§ 40A)	12/31/2016
		3. Research Credit (§ 41)	None
		4. Low-Income Housing Credit (§ 42)	None
		5. Enhanced Oil Recovery Credit (§ 43)	None
		6. Disabled Individual Access Credit (§ 44)	None
		7. Renewable Electricity Production (§ 45)	12/31/2016
		8. Indian Employment Credit (§ 45A)	12/31/2016
		9. Employer Social Security Credit (§ 45B)	None
		10. Credit for Clinical Testing of Certain Drugs (§ 45C)	None
		11. New Markets Tax Credit (§ 45D)	12/31/2019
		12. Small Employer Pension Plan Start-Up Costs (§ 45E)	None
		13. Employer Provided Child Care Credit (§ 45F)	None
		14. Railroad Track Maintenance Credit (§ 45G)	12/31/2016
		15. Credit for production of low sulfur diesel fuel (§ 45H)	None

Code Section	Specific Credit	Termination Date
Cont. Subpart D: § 38 (Nonrefundable)	General Business Credit (including)	
	16. Credit for producing oil and gas from marginal wells (§ 45I)	None
	17. Credit for production from advanced nuclear power facilities (§ 45J)	None
	18. Credit for producing fuel from a non-conventional source (§ 45K)	None
	19. New Energy Efficient Home Credit (§ 45L)	12/31/2016
	20. Energy Efficient Appliance Credit (§ 45M)	12/31/2014
	21. Mine Rescue Team Training Credit (§ 45N)	12/31/2016
	22. Agricultural Chemical Security Credit (§ 45O)	12/31/2012
	23. Differential Wage Payment Credit (§ 45P)	None
	24. Carbon Dioxide Sequestration (§ 45Q)	None
	25. Employee Health Insurance Expenses of Small Employers (§ 45R)	None
	25. Rehabilitation Credit (§ 47)	None
	26. Energy Credit (§ 48)	12/31/2019
	27. Qualifying Advanced Coal Project Credit (§ 48A)	None
	28. Qualifying Gasification Project Credit (§ 48B)	None
	29. Work Opportunity Credit (§ 51)	12/31/2019
	30. Empowerment Zone Employment Credit (§ 1396)	12/31/2016
Subpart G: § 53	Credit for Prior Year Minimum Tax Liability	None

INVESTMENT CREDIT

In 1962, Congress enacted the investment tax credit in hopes of stimulating the economy by encouraging taxpayers to purchase certain assets—generally tangible personal property used in a trade or business. Although application of the provision became quite difficult, the essence of the law was simple. It allowed a credit equal to a particular percentage of the cost of the property. For example, taxpayers who purchased equipment at a cost of $100,000 might be entitled to a credit equal to 10% of the cost, or $10,000—but only as long as they met a host of requirements.

Since its enactment, the investment tax credit has had a tortuous history, in the law one year and out the next. It most recently was part of the Code in 1985 before it fell victim to the Tax Reform Act of 1986. Under current law, the IC is made up of two distinct parts: (1) the credit for rehabilitation expenditures and, (2) the energy credit. Each part of the IC is computed separately under its own specific rules. The actual amount of each part of the IC is the function of two factors: the taxpayer's basis in property qualifying for the credit, and the rate of the credit. The two components of the IC—the rehabilitation and energy credits—are discussed below.[61]

---

[61] Credits for qualifying advanced coal projects and for qualifying gasification projects were added to the energy credit in 2005 but are of limited application and are not discussed in this chapter.

Tax Credit for Rehabilitation Expenditures

The Economic Recovery Tax Act of 1981 created a special credit designed to discourage companies from moving from older, economically distressed locations (e.g., inner cities) to newer areas and at the same time encourage the restoration and preservation of older buildings. The so-called rehabilitation credit contained in § 47 provides significant subsidies to real estate developers who renovate, restore or reconstruct old buildings. The credit is generally 10% to 20% of the costs of rehabilitation.

The rehabilitation credit is available only for substantial *rehabilitation expenditures* related to *commercial buildings* placed in service before 1936 and *certified historic structures*.[62] Rehabilitation expenditures are considered substantial if they exceed the greater of (1) the property's basis or (2) $5,000. Qualifying expenditures do not include the purchase price of the building.

To prevent destruction of these buildings, the following additional requirements must be met if the building is not a historic structure.

1. Fifty percent or more of the existing external walls of the buildings is retained in place as external walls;

2. Seventy-five percent or more of the external walls of the building is retained in place as internal or external walls; and

3. Seventy-five percent or more of the existing internal structural framework of the building is retained in place.

If these requirements are met, the credit is available for qualified expenditures on non-residential real property and residential rental property but only if it is a certified historic structure.[63] Expenditures for additions and improvements also qualify. However, if the rehabilitation credit is taken, the property *must* be depreciated under the straight-line method over the MACRS recovery period (27.5 years for residential property and 39 years for non-residential property) or the alternative depreciation system (40 year recovery period).[64] As explained further below, for purposes of depreciation, the basis of the property must be reduced by the amount of the credit.

The rate of rehabilitation credit is as follows:

Rate	Type of Structure
10%	Commercial building originally placed in service prior to 1936
20%	All certified historic structures[65]

Example 20

On January 3, 2017, R purchased a commercial building that was constructed in 1920. In addition to the $300,000 of the purchase price allocated to the building, the entire core of the building is renovated at a cost of $600,000. R's rehabilitation credit is $60,000, computed as follows:

Qualified investment	$600,000
Rate of credit	× 10%
Current credit (before limitations)	$ 60,000

In some instances, rehabilitation expenditures also qualify for the energy investment credit (discussed below). When this occurs, taxpayers *must choose* between the two credits because both credits cannot be claimed for the same expenditure.[66]

---

[62] § 47(a).

[63] While § 47(c)(2)(A)(i)(III) indicates that qualified expenditures include those for residential rental property, the IC normally prohibits the credit for property used to furnish lodging. However, certified historic structures are exempt from this rule under § 50(b)(2)(C).

[64] § 47(c)(2)(B).

[65] § 47(c)(3).The designation as a certified historic structure is made by the Secretary of the Interior.

[66] § 48(a)(2).

Energy Investment Credit

Recognizing the need for energy conservation, Congress added the *energy credit* provisions to the Code. The objective of this credit is to encourage taxpayers to decrease energy consumption or change the type of energy used.

The credit is 10% for qualified microturbine property and 30% for solar energy property, qualified fuel cell property and qualified small wind energy property.[67] "Energy property" for which the credit is allowed includes subject to a number of limitations:

- Equipment that uses solar energy to generate electricity, to heat or cool (or provide hot water for use in) a structure, to provide solar process heat and in certain cases to illuminate a room.

- Equipment used to produce, distribute, or use energy from a geothermal deposit.

- Qualified fuel cell property or qualified microturbine property.

- Qualified small wind energy property.

Example 21

S is the owner of a deluxe print shop. In March 2017, S installed four solar panels to heat water to be used in a photographic development process. The panels, pumps, valves, storage tanks, control system, and installation cost a total of $80,000. S's energy tax credit is $8,000.

Qualified investment	$80,000
Rate of credit	× 30%
Current credit (before limitations)	$24,000

Basis Reduction of Qualified Property

At one time, taxpayers were allowed to take the full investment credit, including any applicable energy tax credit and still depreciate their entire cost basis of qualifying property. However, in 1986, Congress decided that this treatment was too generous with respect to rehabilitation property and required the basis of the property to be reduced by the amount of credit taken with respect to the property.[68] A similar rule requires that the basis of energy property be reduced by *one-half* of the amount of the credit taken on such energy property.[69]

Example 22

Refer to the facts in *Example 20,* where R's rehabilitation credit is $60,000. R purchased the property for $300,000 and incurred $600,000 of rehabilitation expenditures. R's basis in the rehabilitated property is $840,000 ($300,000 + $600,000 − $60,000).

Example 23

Refer to the facts in *Example 21,* where S's energy tax credit is $24,000. S purchased the solar property for $80,000. S's basis in the energy property is $68,000 ($80,000 − [$24,000 × 50%]).

---

[67] § 48.

[68] § 50(c)(1). Note that for determining the amount and character of gain on the disposition of the property, the downward basis adjustment is treated as a deduction allowed for depreciation. Accordingly, the amount of the basis adjustment will be subject to the § 1245 depreciation recapture rules discussed in Chapter 7.

[69] § 50(c)(3).

The investment credit calculations discussed here provide the background for computing the recapture of IC on early dispositions required by the Code.[70] The amount of IC recapture should be an economic consideration in planning the disposition of any asset upon which the IC was claimed.

Investment Credit Recapture

When taxpayers place qualified investment property into service, they claim the full amount of IC regardless of how long they intend to use the property. However, if an asset ceases to be qualified property during a five-year period (due to a sale or other disposition, or a change in the purpose or use of the asset), taxpayers are required to recapture a portion of the "unearned" IC. The recapture percentages illustrated in Exhibit 13-8 must be used to calculate the amount of unearned credit that is recaptured as an additional tax in the year of early disposition.[71] As a general rule, 20% of the credit is "earned" for each full year the property is held. For example, a qualified rehabilitation property placed in service on December 20, 2016 qualified for the rehabilitation credit in 2016 and was taken on the taxpayer's return for the year. However, none of the credit was *earned* until December 21, 2017. On that date, 20% of the credit allowed in 2016 was earned and thus no longer subject to recapture.

EXHIBIT 13-8	Investment Tax Credit Recapture Percentages[72]

If Qualified Property Ceases to Be Qualified Property:	The Recapture Percentage Is:
Before one full year, after placed in service	100%
After one year, within two full years	80
After two years, within three full years	60
After three years, within four full years	40
After four years, within five full years	20

Example 24

Assume that the commercial building (acquired on January 3, 2017) in *Example 20* was sold by R on September 1, 2018. The IC recapture is computed as follows:

Property	IC Claimed	×	Recapture Percentage	=	Amount Recaptured
Commercial building	$60,000	×	80%	=	$48,000

This amount is reported on Form 4255 and is treated as an additional tax imposed on the taxpayer in the year in which an early disposition occurs. Because the building's basis was originally decreased by the entire credit claimed, its basis is increased by the amount of the recapture for purposes of computing the gain or loss to be recognized on the sale.[73]

In addition to sales and exchanges (including like-kind exchanges), dispositions generally include gifts, dividend distributions from corporations, cessation of business usage, and involuntary conversions.[74]

---

[70] § 50(a).

[71] The recaptured IC is an "other tax" on Form 1040 but is not a tax in computing nonrefundable tax credits allowed under § 26. See § 50(a)(5)(C).

[72] § 50(a)(1)(B).

[73] § 50(c)(2). A similar rule applies to energy property, but only one-half of the amount of recapture is added to the basis of the property.

[74] Reg. § 1.47-2.

The recapture rules do not apply to transfers by reason of death or to assets transferred in certain corporate acquisitions.[75] The recapture rules also will not apply to transfers of property between spouses, even if the transfer is made incident to divorce.[76] Finally, property is not treated as ceasing to be qualified property when a mere change in the form of conducting the trade or business occurs, so long as the property continues to be qualified property in the new business and the taxpayer retains a substantial interest in this trade or business.[77]

Investment Credit Carryovers

Like the other components of the general business credit, the IC allowed in tax years beginning after December 31, 1997 but not utilized because of the tax liability limitation can be carried forward for 20 years. Finally, in determining the extent to which an investment credit is used in a taxable year, the regular investment credit is deemed to be used *before* the rehabilitation credit and the energy credit.[78]

WORK OPPORTUNITY CREDIT

For many years, Congress has tried to spur employment by granting businesses a tax credit for hiring new workers that otherwise had a hard time finding employment. Since 1979, businesses have been able to claim the credit if they hire individuals from certain targeted groups. The targeted groups have been most recently redefined to include:[79]

- Recipients of a state law providing assistance for needy families with minor children

- Qualified veterans

- Qualified ex-felons

- High-risk youth

- Vocational rehabilitation referrals

- Qualified summer youth employees

- Qualified food stamp recipients

- Qualified SSI recipients

- A long term family assistance recipient

- Unemployed veterans

- Disconnected youth

- Qualified long-term unemployment recipient (e.g., unemployed for 27 weeks)

To be eligible, each individual must obtain certification from a designated local agency, specifying that the individual meets the established criteria and therefore qualifies as a member of one of the targeted groups.

The work opportunity credit is not the only tax incentive for hiring. Another credit encourages employers to hire workers who live in certain economically depressed areas designated as empowerment zones. This credit is discussed later in this chapter.

Amount of Credit

The work opportunity tax credit is 40% of the first $6,000 of first-year wages paid to a qualified individual.[80] Thus, the maximum credit for each new employee is normally $2,400 but can be as high as $9,600 for certain groups. Note that, without any restriction, the employer would be able not only to claim a credit for the wages paid to the employee but also to deduct those wages. However, employers who elect to take the credit must reduce their wage expense by the amount of the credit; this eliminates the potential windfall. Note also that, as part of the general business credit, the § 38 rules limiting the amount of the credit ($25,000 + 75% of the tax liability in excess of $25,000) are applicable, as are the one-year carryback and 20-year carryover rules.

---

[75] § 50(a)(4).

[76] § 50(a)(5)(B).

[77] § 50(a)(4) and Reg. § 1.47-3(f).

[78] See § 38(d).

[79] §§ 51(d) and 51(c)(4) This provision is set to expire for years beginning after 2019.

[80] See § 51(i) for other limitations based on the number of hours worked.

Special Rule for Qualified Summer Youth Employees

Employers are allowed to claim the jobs credit for wages paid for the summer employment of teenagers that are members of economically disadvantaged families. These individuals must be 16 or 17 years of age on the hiring date and must not have worked previously for the employer. To qualify for the credit, the services must be attributable to any 90-day period between May 1 and September 15. The summer youth employment credit is 40% of the first $3,000 of eligible wages, for a maximum credit of $1,200 per youth.[81] If a summer youth employee continues to work after the 90-day period, his or her wages may qualify for the general targeted jobs credit previously discussed. However, certification of this employee as a member of a second target group must be determined as of the date of the second certification rather than on the basis of the employee's original certification as a qualified summer youth employee. In addition, the $6,000 wage limit for the targeted job credit must be reduced by the qualified summer wages.

Example 25

On July 29, 2017, the owners of a farm hired 10 youths that were certified as qualified summer employees to help harvest crops. The owners paid the youths $150 a week for eight weeks (through September 22). The amount of targeted jobs credit in 2017 without regard to additional certifications is $4,200, computed in the following manner:

Qualifying wages ($150 × 10 youths × 7 weeks)	$10,500
Percent of credit	× 40%
Amount of credit	$ 4,200

The wage expense deduction attributable to the youths' salaries would be $7,800, computed as follows:

Total wages paid ($150 × 10 youths × 8 weeks)	$12,000
Reduced by allowable credit	− 4,200
Allowable wage expense	$ 7,800

Note that the eighth week does not qualify for the credit since it occurs after the September 15 cutoff date.

Special Rules for a Long Term Family Assistance Recipient

For individuals that receive assistance for more than 18 months under certain state funded programs, the credit amount for the first year of employment is up to 40% on the first $10,000 of wages. Also, an additional 50% credit is available for wages paid up to $10,000 in the second year of employment. The maximum credit per new employee over the two year period is $9,000.[82]

---

[81] § 51(d)(12)(B).   [82] 51(e).

ALCOHOL FUEL CREDIT

The fourth component of the general business credit is the alcohol fuel credit. To foster the production of gasohol, § 40 provides a credit for alcohol and alcohol-blended fuels applies to fuel sales and uses before January 1, 2017. The alcohol fuel credit is computed and reported on Form 6478. Generally, the credit is $0.45 per gallon of alcohol used in a qualified alcohol mixture or as a straight alcohol fuel.[83] Although taxpayers are entitled to a credit, they must include an amount equal to the credit claimed in income.[84]

RESEARCH AND EXPERIMENTAL (R&E) CREDIT

The fifth component of the general business credit is the research credit—commonly referred to as the R&E credit. Created in 1981 and amended several times since, the R&E credit provisions generally allow taxpayers a credit equal to 20% of their *incremental* expenditures that constitute either (1) qualified research expenditures or (2) basic research payments.[85] The method for identifying what qualifies as an incremental expenditure is considered in detail below, as are the types of qualifying research. First, however, the relationship of the R&E credit and the deduction for R&E must be addressed.

Impact of R&E Credit on Current Deductions

The research credit is the second part of Congress's two-prong approach for stimulating research. The first part of this plan, as might be recalled from Chapter 9, allows taxpayers either to deduct research and experimental expenditures immediately or capitalize the expenditures and amortize them over 60 months. As might be expected, taxpayers are not allowed to have their research cake and eat it too—they must reduce their R&E deduction for the amount of R&E credit determined for the year.[86] For those taxpayers who normally expense R&E costs, this means that their deduction for R&E is simply smaller. For those taxpayers who capitalize and amortize the costs, the amount capitalized is reduced. Note that if the credit is not utilized by the taxpayer within the 20-year carryover period, a deduction equal to the amount of the expiring credit is allowed in the year following the expiration of the tax credit carryover period.[87]

Without additional rules, the cutback of the deduction for the credit could prove unduly harsh for taxpayers subject to the AMT, which generally does not allow the use of credits. For this reason taxpayers are allowed to *elect* to claim a reduced credit.[88] This election effectively enables the taxpayer to trade a credit that is not allowed to reduce the AMT for a deduction that could be used to reduce the AMT.

Qualified Research Expenditures

The R&E credit is allowed for both in-house research and contract (outside) research. *Qualified research expenditures* are those incurred in carrying on a trade or business for in-house research expenses (e.g., wages, supplies, rental of equipment, overhead) and 65% of *contract research expenses* (those paid to any person other than an employee of the taxpayer for qualified research).[89] To be eligible for the credit, the expenditures must meet the same criteria that must be met for their deduction. As a general rule, these criteria extend special treatment only for research and development in the experimental or laboratory sense. This includes (1) the development of an experimental or pilot model, plant process, formula, invention, or similar property, and (2) the improvement of such types of property already in existence.[90] In addition, the expenditures must be technological in nature *and* must relate

---

[83] § 40. A similar credit applies to small ethanol producers. Section 40 expires after 12/31/2016. However, this provision is one that Congress has repeatedly extended for many years and may do so again in 2017.

[84] § 87.

[85] § 41(a).

[86] § 280C(c).

[87] § 196. The deduction allowed is 50% of the expired R&E credits attributable to taxable years beginning before 1990.

[88] § 280C(c)(3).

[89] § 41(b)(4). The trade or business requirement may be met by certain start-up companies even though they are not currently in business.

[90] Reg. § 1.174-2(a).

to establishing a new or improved function, or improving the performance, reliability, or quality of a product.[91] Finally, the credit is *denied* for certain expenditure items,[92] including

1. Research undertaken outside the United States.
2. Research conducted in the social sciences or humanities.
3. Ordinary testing or inspection of materials or products for quality control.
4. Market and consumer research.
5. Research relating to style, taste, cosmetic, or seasonal design.
6. Advertising and promotion expenses.
7. Management studies and efficiency surveys.
8. Computer software for internal use of the taxpayer.
9. Research to locate and evaluate mineral deposits, including oil and gas.
10. Acquisition and improvement of land and of certain depreciable or depletable property used in research (including the annual depreciation deduction).

Amount of Credit

The 20% credit is extended only to taxpayers who increase their research activities. As shown in the formula in Exhibit 13-9, this is accomplished by allowing a credit only for qualified research expenditures for the current year that exceed the taxpayer's base amount.[93] The base amount is a fixed percentage of the taxpayer's average gross receipts for the four previous years.[94] As a result, those taxpayers who continually increase their research benefit the most from this special incentive.

The fixed-base percentage is computed differently for firms with a history of doing research than for firms that do not have such a history. For taxpayers reporting both qualified research expenses and gross receipts during each of at least three years from 1984 to 1988, the "fixed-base percentage" is the ratio that its total qualified research expenses for the 1984 to 1988 period bears to its total gross receipts for this period, subject to a maximum ratio of 16 percent. "Start-up companies" and those taxpayers not meeting the R&E expenditures and gross receipt requirements above are assigned a fixed-base percentage of 3% for the first five years in which qualified research expenditures are incurred.[95]

EXHIBIT 13-9	Calculation of R&E Credit

R&E Credit = 20% × (Qualified R&E expenditures – Base amount)

Base amount = Fixed-base percentage × Average gross receipts for four previous years

$$\text{Fixed-base percentage*} = \frac{\text{Total research expenses (1984–1988)}}{\text{Total gross receipts}}$$

* Subject to special rules for start-up companies and limited to a maximum of 16 percent.

[91] § 41(d)(1)(B).

[92] § 41(d)(4).

[93] § 41(a)(1).

[94] § 41(c).

[95] Special rules apply to start-up companies after the sixth taxable year in which they incur qualified research expenditures. See § 41(c)(3)(B).

Example 26

R Corporation reported the following research expenditures and gross receipts:

	1986	1987	1988
Research expenditures	$ 90,000	$100,000	$ 110,000
Gross receipts	700,000	900,000	800,000

	2013	2014	2015	2016	2017
Research expenditures	$120,000	$130,000	$ 140,000	$ 150,000	$ 180,000
Gross receipts	700,000	800,000	1,000,000	1,100,000	1,200,000

R Corporation's R&E credit for 2017 is computed as follows:

1. Fixed-base percentage = $300,000/$2,400,000 = 0.125
2. Base amount = 0.125 × $3,600,000/4 = $112,500
3. Qualified R&E expenditures for 2017 = $180,000
4. R&E credit = 20% × ($180,000 − $112,500) = $13,500

Note that R's fixed-base percentage is based on the research activity and gross receipts during 1984–1988, whereas the average annual gross receipts number is based on receipts for the four previous years, 2013–2016 ($700,000 + $800,000 + $1,000,000 + $1,100,000 = $3,600,000). Also note that in 2017, R must reduce its current deduction for research expenditures by $13,500, or if the deferred asset method of accounting is used, the $180,000 R&E costs must be reduced to $166,500 ($180,000 − $13,500) before being capitalized and amortized over a period of not less than 60 months.

Basic Research Expenditures

The second category of expenditures qualifying for the research credit is the *incremental* amount of *basic research payments* made to universities and other qualified organizations.[96] Basic research means any original investigation for the advancement of scientific knowledge not having a specific commercial objective. The term "basic research payment" means any amount paid in cash during the taxable year by a corporation to a qualified organization for basic research, but only if such payment is made pursuant to a written agreement and the basic research is to be performed by the qualified organization. Qualified organizations include educational institutions, certain scientific research organizations, and certain grant organizations.

The R&E credit applies to the *excess* of corporate cash expenditures in a year over the qualified organization base period amount. The qualified organization base period amount is the *sum* of (1) the minimum basic research amount, plus (2) the maintenance-of-effort amount. The *maintenance-of-effort amount* prevents the corporation from shifting its historical charitable contribution to any qualifying educational organization over to a creditable basic research payment. It is an amount equal to the *average* nondesignated university contributions paid by the corporation during the base period, increased by the cost of living adjustment for the calendar year over the amount of nondesignated university contributions paid by the taxpayer during that year. Any portion of the basic research payment that does not exceed the qualified organization base period amount will be treated as contract research expenses for computing the incremental qualified research expenditures discussed above under "qualified research expenditures" above.[97]

---

[96] § 41(e)(2).   [97] § 41(e)(1)(B).

Alternative Incremental Credit

For taxable years beginning after June 30, 1996, a taxpayer may make an election to compute the research credit utilizing three tiers of reduced fixed base percentages and reduced credit rates.[98] This election may be beneficial for companies that have average gross receipts increasing at a faster rate than the increases in qualified research expenditures. This election is mentioned here only to round out the discussion of this credit but further analysis of the election is beyond the scope of this text.

Alternative Simplified Credit for Qualified Research Expenses

The Tax Relief and Health Care Act of 2006 allows taxpayers, at their election, to compute the research credit under a third method. This method is referred to as the alternative simplified credit. Under this approach, a taxpayer can claim an amount equal to 12% of the amount by which qualified research expenses exceed 50% of the average qualified research expenses for the three preceding tax years. If the taxpayer has no qualified research expenses for any of the preceding three tax years, then the credit is equal to six percent of the qualified research expenses for the current tax year. As with the alternative incremental credit, an election to calculate the research credit using the alternative simplified credit is effective for all succeeding tax years unless revoked with the consent of the IRS.[99]

Credit Limitations

As part of the general business credit, the tax liability limitation ($25,000 + 75% of the tax liability in excess of $25,000) applies, as do the one-year carryback and 20-year carryover rules. Additional limitations are imposed in an effort to prevent the research credit from being exploited by tax shelter promoters. For individuals with ownership interests in unincorporated businesses (i.e., partners of a partnership), trust or estate beneficiaries, or S corporation shareholders, any allowable pass-through of the credit cannot exceed the *lesser of* (1) the individual's net regular tax liability limitation discussed earlier, or (2) the amount of tax attributable to the individual's taxable income resulting from the individual's interest in the entity that earned such credit.

The final unique characteristic of the R&E credit is applicable to changes in business ownership. Special rules apply for computing the credit when a business changes hands, under which qualified research expenditures for periods prior to the change of ownership generally are treated as transferred with the trade or business that gave rise to those expenditures.[100]

LOW-INCOME HOUSING CREDIT

The next component of the general business credit is the low-income housing credit. Under § 42, this credit is available for low-income housing that is constructed, rehabilitated, or acquired after 1986. The credit is claimed over a 10-year period, with an annual credit of approximately 9% of the qualifying basis of low-income units placed in service. If federal subsidies are used to finance the project, the credit is limited to approximately 4 percent.[101] For property placed in service after 1987, the exact percentage is determined by the IRS on a monthly basis. The percentages for any month are calculated to yield, over a 10-year credit period, amounts of credit that have a present value equal to (1) 70% of the qualified basis of new buildings that are not federally subsidized for the tax year, and (2) 30% of the qualified basis of existing buildings and new buildings that are federally subsidized.[102]

> **Example 27**
>
> In January 2017, H, an individual, constructed and placed in service a qualified low-income housing project. The qualified basis of the project was $1 million. The 70% present value credit for buildings placed in service in January 2017 is 7.54 percent.[103] Thus, the annual credit that H could claim is $75,400.

---

[98] § 41(c)(4). These percentages were increased for years beginning after 2006.

[99] § 41(c)(5).

[100] § 41(f)(3).

[101] § 42(b)(1).

[102] § 42(b)(2)(B). A formula for making such computations is provided in Rev. Rul. 88-6, 1988-1 C.B. 3.

[103] Rev. Rul. 2016-2, 2016-4 IRB 284.

Each year, the sum of allowed low-income housing credits is subject to a nationwide cap. The cap amount is allotted among all of the states so that each state will have a cap on the amount of low-income housing credits it can authorize. A credit allocation from the appropriate state credit authority must be received by the owner of the property eligible for the low-income housing credit. The credit is available on a per-unit basis; thus, a single building may have some units that qualify for the credit and some that do not. In order to qualify, a low-income housing project must meet a host of exacting criteria throughout a 15-year compliance period.[104]

DISABLED ACCESS CREDIT

Another component of the general business credit is the disabled access credit. This credit was established in 1994 primarily as a relief measure for those businesses that are required under the Americans with Disabilities Act of 1990 to make improvements that make existing facilities accessible to the disabled. Under Code § 44, an eligible small business can elect to take a nonrefundable tax credit equal to 50% of the amount of the eligible access expenditures for any taxable year that exceed $250 but do not exceed $10,250. An eligible small business is defined as one having gross receipts for the preceding taxable year that did not exceed $1,000,000, or having no more than 30 full-time employees during the preceding taxable year. Eligible access expenditures are defined as amounts paid or incurred by an eligible small business to comply with applicable requirements of the Disabilities Act. Eligible access expenditures generally include amounts paid or incurred for the following:

1. Removing architectural, communication, physical, or transportation barriers that prevent a business from being accessible to, or usable by, individuals with disabilities.

2. Providing qualified interpreters or other effective methods of making aurally delivered materials available to individuals with hearing impairments.

3. Providing qualified readers, taped texts, and other effective methods of making visually delivered materials available to individuals with visual impairments.

4. Acquiring or modifying equipment or devices for individuals with disabilities.

5. Providing other similar services, modifications, materials, or equipment.

In cases where the eligible business is being conducted as a partnership or an S corporation, the dollar limitations are applied at both the entity and the owner level. Any portion of the unused general business credit attributable to the disabled access credit may not be carried back to any taxable year ending before 1990.

Example 28

J, a sole proprietor, had gross receipts of $700,000 last year and incurred $5,250 of eligible access expenditures this year. J's disabled access credit for this year is $2,500 ([$5,250 − $250] × 50%).

As is the case with other components of the general business credit, the depreciable basis of assets acquired subject to the credit using access expenditures must be reduced by the amount of credit claimed with respect to those expenditures. Alternatively, any current deduction attributable to the access expenditures must be reduced by the amount of credit claimed.[105]

---

[104] See §§ 42(g) and 42(l).   [105] § 44(c)(7).

EMPOWERMENT ZONE EMPLOYMENT CREDIT

To help rebuild distressed urban and rural areas, Congress has created several tax incentives. The hope is that these incentives will encourage businesses to locate in these areas and hire individuals who live there. The goal is carried out in § 1396, which authorizes the Secretary of Housing and Urban Development and the Secretary of Agriculture to identify 95 *enterprise communities* and 29 *empowerment zones* where the tax benefits will be offered. The regions must meet certain criteria concerning population, size (urban areas cannot exceed 20 square miles and rural areas cannot exceed 1,000 square miles), and poverty (a minimum rate of 20%).[106]

Businesses that operate within the designated areas are entitled to a variety of benefits. Perhaps the most important of these is the empowerment zone employment credit (EZEC). All employers located in an empowerment zone are entitled to a 20% credit for the first $15,000 of wages paid to full-time as well as part-time employees who are residents of the empowerment zone. The maximum credit per employee is $3,000 per year. If an employer is entitled to both a work opportunity credit (WOC) and an EZEC, the first $6,000 of wages paid qualify for the higher WOC of 40 percent, and the next $9,000 qualify for the EZEC of 20 percent. Thus, the payment of $15,000 of wages could enable the employer to claim a credit as high as $4,200 ($6,000 × 40% = $2,400) + ($9,000 × 20% = $1,800). Of course, the employer's deduction for wages must be reduced by the amount of credits allowed.

Like the WOC, the EZEC is part of the general business credit and is consequently subject to the tax liability limitation as well as the carryback and carryover rule. Unlike the WOC, the EZEC can offset 25% of the employer's AMT liability.

CREDIT FOR EMPLOYER-PROVIDED CHILD-CARE

To encourage employers to provide quality child care for its employees, Congress established a special credit in 2002. The credit is considered a part of the general business credit.

Under § 45F, employers may claim a credit equal to 25% of the cost of qualified child care expenditures and 10% of qualified child care resource and referral expenditures. The maximum total amount of credit is limited to $150,000 per year. Like the rehabilitation expenditures and energy credits, the basis of any property is reduced by the amount of credit claimed. Similarly, any other deduction or credit must be reduced by the amount of credit claimed.

Expenditures qualifying for the 25% credit include the costs of (1) building, acquiring, rehabilitating or expanding property that is used as part of a *qualified child care facility* of the taxpayer for its employees, (2) operating such facilities, and (3) a contract with a qualified child care facility. A qualified child care facility is a facility whose principal use is to provide child care assistance and meets the requirements of all applicable laws and regulations of the state and local government in which it is located, including the licensing requirements applicable to a child care facility. The definition does not include a facility which is the principal residence of the taxpayer, any employee of the taxpayer, or the operator of the facility. Thus daycare centers will be qualified only if they are separate and distinct from the operator's personal residence.

The 10% credit is available for expenses incurred in providing child-care resource and referral services. Usage of a facility cannot favor high-income earners, and at least 30% of the children in the center must be children of employees. Finally, if the facility is no longer used as a child care center or there is a disposition of the taxpayer's interest (e.g., the taxpayer sells the property), § 45F(d)(2) requires the taxpayer to recapture (i.e., pay back to the government) a percentage of the tax savings from prior years as shown below.

If the Recapture Event Occurs in Years	Percentage Recapture
1–3	100%
4	85
5	70
6	55
7	40
8	25
9–10	10
11	0

---

[106] §§ 1391(a), 1391(d)(1)(A), 1391(g), and 1396. This provision is set to expire for years beginning after 12/31/2017, however this provision is one that Congress has repeatedly extended for many years and may do so again in 2017.

OTHER COMPONENTS OF THE GENERAL BUSINESS CREDIT

There are several other credits that make up the general business credit:

- *Enhanced Oil Recovery Credit.* This is a special credit directed at owners of oil and gas properties requiring secondary or tertiary methods of production.

- *Renewable Electricity Production Credit.* Section 45 provides a credit for taxpayers who produce electricity from qualified wind energy or certain other renewable resources.

- *Indian Employment Credit.* Added by the RRA of 1994 to encourage the hiring of Native Americans, the Indian employment credit (authorized in § 45A) generally entitles employers conducting businesses located on Indian reservations to claim a credit of 20% for up to $20,000 of wages and insurance benefits paid to employees who are members of an Indian tribe and who work and live on the reservation. This credit is set to expire after 2017, but may be extended.

- *Employer Social Security Credit.* This credit represents a relief measure (or perhaps a peace offering) for the restaurant industry, which presumably was detrimentally impacted by the 1994 cut in the deduction for business meals from 80 to 50 percent. Section 45B allows employers operating food and beverage establishments to claim a credit against their income tax liability for their FICA obligation (7.65%) on tips in excess of those treated as wages for purposes of satisfying the minimum wage provisions. To prevent a double benefit, no deduction is allowed for any FICA taxes taken into account in determining the credit.

- *Orphan Drug Credit.* To encourage pharmaceutical companies to seek treatments and cures for rare diseases, Congress enacted § 45C. This provision contains a special credit for qualified clinical testing expenses for certain drugs. The credit is equal to 50% of the qualified clinical testing expenses for the taxable year.

- *Credit for Pension Plan Start-Up Costs of Small Employers.* Small employers with no more than 100 employees receive a tax credit for some of the costs of establishing new retirement plans. The credit equals 50% of the start-up costs incurred to create or maintain a new employee retirement plan. The credit is limited to $500 in any tax year and it may be claimed for qualified costs incurred in each of the three years beginning with the tax year in which the plan becomes effective [Code § 45E(b)].

- *Alternative Motor Vehicle Credit.* Perhaps the credit of greatest interest to individuals is that for purchases of personal or business automobiles. Section 30D offers the so-called qualified plug-in vehicle credit for the purchase of electric vehicles (i.e., vehicles that draw propulsion energy from a battery). The amount of the credit depends on the size of the battery. It could be as low as $2,500 and as high as $7,500. Virtually all manufactures produce a qualified vehicle. Examples include the Tesla, Chevrolet Volt, Toyota Prius and the Nissan Leaf. Purchasers of qualified vehicles can continue to claim the credit until the manufacturer has sold 200,000 qualified vehicles for use in the United States. Once a manufacturer's U.S. sales reach 200,000 qualified vehicles, the credit for all qualified vehicles produced by the manufacturer will begin to phase-out over a one year period.

  Section 30B offers another incentive to purchase energy efficient cars. The credit is only available to the original purchaser. The alternative motor vehicle credit is only available for purchases of qualified fuel cell motor vehicles:

  - *Fuel Cell Vehicle (FCV).* The credit can be as much as $12,000 for vehicles powered by fuel cells. However, the cost of these vehicles can be well over $100,000. FCVs are propelled by electric motors that are somewhat like batteries. Fuel cells create their own electricity through an electrochemical reaction between hydrogen and oxygen taken from the air.

In addition to those credits that make up the general business credit, there are still other credits available to business, but they are of limited applicability and are not discussed in this text. The foreign tax credit available to both businesses and individuals, is discussed briefly below.

GENERAL BUSINESS CREDIT CARRYOVER RULES

Recall that the carryback period is one year and the carryforward period is 20 years for business credits incurred in years beginning after 1997. If the business credit carryover cannot be used within the stipulated time period, the credit expires. Without special rules, this would be a double loss for taxpayers who claimed the full investment tax credit percentages or other credits and who decreased the basis of property for MACRS computations. Not only have they lost the credit but they also were unable to depreciate the full cost of the assets. Because of this possibility, taxpayers are allowed to take a deduction equal to the amount of the previous reductions from basis stipulated by the expired IC or other credits. This deduction may be taken in the year *following* the expiration of the tax credit carryover period.[107]

> ### Example 29
>
> Q originally claimed an IC of $10,000 and reduced the basis in the assets by $5,000. After the expiration of the carryforward period, an unused IC of $3,000 expires. In the first taxable year after the expiration of the credit carryover period, Q may deduct $1,500 (½ of $3,000). This amount equals the original decrease in basis for the expired investment credit.

FOREIGN TAX CREDIT

The new emphasis on the global economy and global investing is making the treatment of foreign income and foreign taxes a concern for far more taxpayers than ever before. As explained in Chapter 3, U.S. citizens (including U.S. corporations) and resident aliens must pay U.S. taxes on their worldwide income: income earned in the United States as well as income from foreign sources. In many cases, they pay not only U.S. taxes but also foreign taxes on the same income. To alleviate the burden of two taxes on the same income, § 27 generally allows taxpayers to claim a credit for income taxes paid or accrued to a foreign country. Alternatively, taxpayers may elect to claim a deduction for the taxes. Also note that if the taxpayer elects to use the $102,100 (2017) earned income exclusion (see Chapter 3), any foreign taxes paid on such income cannot be claimed as a credit.

Although the taxpayer is normally allowed a credit for any foreign taxes paid, the amount of the credit may be limited in some cases. As a general rule, the credit for the foreign taxes cannot exceed the U.S. tax that would otherwise be paid on the same income. For example, assume a U.S. taxpayer earns $10,000 while living abroad and pays a foreign tax on such income of $3,000. If the U.S. tax on such income is only $2,000, the taxpayer's credit is limited to $2,000, and she consequently pays a foreign tax of $3,000 and no U.S. tax because her $2,000 U.S. tax liability is reduced to zero by the $2,000 FTC. Note that, without the limitation, the United States could effectively lose $1,000 of taxes on other U.S. income that it would otherwise receive. As this example illustrates, the limitation is generally triggered when the foreign tax rate exceeds the U.S. tax rate. The actual limitation is computed using the following formula:

$$\frac{\text{Foreign source taxable income}}{\text{Worldwide taxable income*}} \times \text{U.S. tax before credits} = \text{Foreign tax credit limitation}$$

* U.S. source taxable income + Foreign source taxable income + Personal exemptions

Any unused foreign tax credits may be carried back two years and carried forward five years. However, the credits may be carried over only to years where the foreign tax credit limitation has not been exceeded.

---

[107] § 196.

Example 30

This year Mr. and Mrs. T took their financial consultants' advice on global investing. As a result, they received $10,000 of dividends from several foreign stocks. The couple's taxable income including the dividends was $92,400, producing a tax before credits of $15,160. The maximum foreign tax credit would be computed as follows:

$$\frac{\$10,000}{\$92,400 + \$7,600 = \$100,000} \times \$15,160 = \$1,516$$

One caveat should be pointed out before leaving the foreign tax credit. Although the above rules normally apply, taxpayers must be careful. Not only are the rules complex (they are applied separately to different classes of income), but tax treaties with a particular country may provide special rules for income earned in that country by U.S. citizens. Such treaties must be examined when dealing with foreign income.

Nonbusiness Credits

LO.9

Identify and calculate the nonbusiness tax credits, including the child tax credit, the dependent care credit, the educational tax credits, the earned income credit, and the minimum tax credit.

In addition to the numerous business credits discussed thus far, there are several nonbusiness credits available to individual taxpayers only. These credits include (1) the child tax credit, (2) the child and dependent care credit, (3) the Hope (the American Opportunity Tax Credit) and Lifetime learning credits, (4) the credit for adoption expenses, (5) the credit for the elderly, (6) the credit for interest on certain home mortgages, and (7) the earned income credit and other refundable credits. Each of these credits is discussed below.

CHILD TAX CREDIT

Section 24 currently allows most taxpayers to claim a special credit of $1,000 for each qualifying child. As a general rule, the credit is nonrefundable. Importantly, however, a portion of the credit may be refundable. The refundable child tax credit is discussed later in this Chapter along with other refundable credits.

In order to be considered a qualifying child, the individual in question must meet the following conditions:

- The individual must be the child of the taxpayer. For this purpose, a stepson or stepdaughter or an eligible foster child qualifies as a child. Descendants of these individuals are also treated as a qualifying child.

- The child must not have attained the age of 17 before the close of the taxable year.

- The taxpayer is eligible to claim a dependency exemption for the child.

- The child is a citizen, or a national of the U.S., or a resident of the U.S.

Like many of the other tax relief provisions contained in the Code, the benefits of the credit are not extended to wealthy individuals. To accomplish this policy objective, the credit is reduced by $50 for each $1,000 (or part thereof) of adjusted gross income (computed with certain modifications) exceeding the levels of income shown in Exhibit 13-10 on the next page.

		Phase-Out Ends When Modified AGI Exceeds			
EXHIBIT 13-10	**Child Tax Credit Phase-Out**				

Taxpayer	Phase-Out Begins When Modified AGI Exceeds	One Child	Two Children	Three Children	Four Children
Single	$ 75,000	$ 94,000	$ 114,000	$134,000	$154,000
Married filing jointly	110,000	129,000	149,000	169,000	189,000
Married filing separately	55,000	74,000	94,000	114,000	134,000

Modified AGI is AGI determined before any exclusion for foreign earned income and foreign housing costs and income from certain possessions. These thresholds are not indexed for inflation. In order to claim the credit, the taxpayer must disclose the TIN of each qualifying child on the return and the taxable year of the taxpayer must include a 12-month period.

Example 31

H and W are married with three children. At the close of 2017, the children, X, Y, and Z, were ages 12, 16, and 18 respectively. H and W claim a dependency exemption for each of the children. This year H and W reported adjusted gross income of $114,200. H and W may claim a child credit for X and Y since they are both dependents and did not attain the age of 17 before the close of the year. The amount of the credit is limited to $1,750 determined as follows:

Tentative credit for each child.....................................		$1,000
Qualifying children...		× 2
Total credit before phase-out		$2,000
Reduction:		
Adjusted gross income	$114,200	
Threshold for joint return	(110,000)	
Excess adjusted gross income	$ 4,200	
Reduction ([$4,200/$1,000 = 4.2 rounded up to 5] × $50)		(250)
Child credit allowed for children....................................		$1,750

The amount of the child tax credit that can be claimed by a taxpayer for any taxable year shall not exceed the excess of the sum of the § 26 regular tax liability plus the AMT over the sum of the credits allowed by the Child and Dependent Care Credit (§ 21), the Credit for the Elderly (§ 22), the Credit for Interest on Certain Home Mortgages (§ 25), Residential Energy Credit (§ 25C) and the foreign tax credit (§ 27). The nonrefundable portion of the child tax credit may be claimed against both regular and AMT tax liability.

CHILD AND DEPENDENT CARE CREDIT

The emergence of the working wife and two-earner couples during the post-World War II era produced a new tax issue. The dilemma concerned the treatment of the costs for the care of children and other dependents. The question posed was whether taxpayers who were forced to pay such costs in order to work should be entitled to deduct them as business expenses. Early court cases denied a deduction for these expenses on the grounds that they were personal in nature. In the court's view, the expenses stemmed from a personal choice by married couples to employ others to discharge their domestic duties, a purely personal expense. Congress, however, became sensitive to the issue in the late 1960s and responded with a limited deduction in 1971. After several alterations and amendments, the deduction received a complete makeover and was converted into a credit in 1976—a far better deal for those who did not itemize. It now appears that, almost 20 years after its creation, the credit is a permanent part of the tax law, presumably justified as both a relief measure for those who have differing abilities to pay and as a stimulant that reduces the costs of entering the work force.

As the statute is now drawn, taxpayers are able to claim a credit for a portion of their child and dependent care expenses if they meet two requirements: (1) the taxpayer maintains a household for a qualifying individual and (2) the expenses—so-called *employment-related expenses*—are incurred to enable the taxpayer to be gainfully employed.[108] Each of these requirements and the computation of the credit are discussed below.

Qualifying Individual

What many believe is simply a credit for child care actually has a far broader scope. True to its name, the *child and dependent care credit* is available not only to those who have children but also to those who take care of other dependents, such as an aging parent or other relative. A taxpayer (or in the case of divorced parents, only the custodial parent) can claim the credit only if he or she maintains a household for one of the following individuals:[109]

- A dependent under the age of 13 (e.g., taxpayer's child).

- An incapacitated dependent.

- An incapacitated spouse.

Note that the year in which a dependent turns 14 is an important factor in determining the applicability of the credit. First, if the individual becomes 13 during the year, he or she normally qualifies only for the part of the year he or she was under 13. Second, once the individual reaches age 14, expenses do not qualify unless the individual is incapable of self-care.

Employment-Related Expenses

Only certain expenses that enable the taxpayer to be gainfully employed or *seek* gainful employment qualify for the credit.[110] The work can be either full-time or part-time, but it must be work. Volunteer work for a nominal salary does not constitute gainful employment. For example, expenses for a baby-sitter while the taxpayer works at a church or hospital do not qualify. Note, however, that expenses incurred when one spouse works and the other attends school on a full-time basis are eligible.

Only certain types of expenses qualify as employment-related expenses. The expenses generally must be for the care of the qualifying individual (e.g., the cost of a baby-sitter). In this regard, the costs of household services qualify if the expenses are attributable at least in part to the care of a qualifying individual. Thus the IRS generally takes the position that the costs of a maid, nanny, or cook can qualify, but not those of a gardener or chauffeur. Eligible expenses normally do not include amounts paid for food, clothing, or entertainment. Similarly, the costs of transportation to a place for care do not qualify unless the qualifying individual is incapacitated. In addition, educational expenses incurred for a child in the first or higher grade level do not qualify. Observe, however, that the costs of pre-school or nursery school are eligible for the credit.

---

[108] § 21.

[109] §§ 21(b)(1) and 21(e)(5).

[110] § 21(b)(2).

As a general rule, expenses for services both inside and outside the home qualify for the credit. However, there are several notable exceptions for the outside services:

- Care provided by a dependent care facility (e.g., a daycare center) qualifies only if the facility provides care for more than six individuals.[111]

- Services outside the home for qualifying individuals other than a dependent under 13 (e.g., nursing home services for a spouse or an over-13-year-old dependent who is incapable of self-care) are eligible only if the individual spends at least eight hours a day in the employee's household.[112]

- Overnight camps do not qualify (day camps, however, can qualify).[113]

A final note on eligible expenses concerns payments made to relatives. Can the credit be claimed if the taxpayer simply pays his mother to baby-sit while he works? Payments to individuals do qualify as long as the individual is not a dependent of the taxpayer.[114] Thus payments to a child's grandparents would probably qualify since the grandparents normally are not dependents. Conversely, payments to a child's older brothers or sisters normally would not qualify since such individuals would be dependents. However, payments to the taxpayer's child can qualify if the child is not a dependent and is at least 19 years of age.

Computation of the Credit

The credit is generally computed by multiplying the applicable percentage times employment-related expenses. A general formula for the calculation is shown in Exhibit 13-11.

Applicable Percentage

The applicable percentage begins at 35% but is reduced (but not below 20%) by one percentage point for each $2,000 (or fraction thereof) that the taxpayer's adjusted gross income exceeds $15,000. For example, the rate for a taxpayer with an AGI of $17,001 is 33 percent, one point reduction for the first $2,000 over $15,000 and another point reduction for the fractional part of the next $2,000. Based on this scheme, taxpayers with adjusted gross incomes exceeding $43,000 have a rate of 20 percent.[115]

EXHIBIT 13-11	Computations of the Child and Dependent Care Credit

Employment-related expenses
Lesser of:
   1. Amount paid,
   2. Earned income or imputed earned income if full-time student or incapacitated spouse, or
   3. $3,000 (if one qualifying individual) or $6,000 (if more than one).
× Applicable percentage (20–35%)

= Child and dependent care credit

---

[111] § 21(b)(2)(C).

[112] § 21(b)(2)(B).

[113] Last sentence of § 21(b)(2)(A).

[114] § 21(e)(6).

[115] § 21(a)(2).

Limitations on Employment-Related Expenses

The Code imposes several limitations on the amount of expenses eligible for the credit. The first limitation simply sets a maximum dollar amount of expenses that may be taken into account in computing the credit. These amounts are based on the number of qualifying individuals: $3,000 for one qualifying individual and $6,000 for two or more individuals.[116] Thus, the maximum credits would be $1,050 (35% × $3,000) and $2,100 (35% × $6,000). As explained below, however, these amounts may be reduced. The computation of the credit requires a three-step approach, as illustrated in the following example.

Example 32

F is a widower and maintains a household for his two small children. He incurs $5,000 of employment-related expenses and reports AGI of $27,300 for the current year. F's child care credit is determined as follows:

Step 1:	Determining the applicable percentage:	
	Adjusted gross income	$27,300
	Less: Ceiling on 35% rate	(15,000)
	Adjusted gross income over $15,000 limit	$12,300
	Divide by $2,000 and round up: ($12,300 ÷ $2,000) = 6.15% round up to 7%	
	Maximum rate	35%
	Percentage reduction	(7%)
	Allowable percentage	28%
Step 2:	Determine the allowable employment-related expenses:	
	Lesser of $5,000 paid or $6,000 limit	$ 5,000
Step 3:	Determine the dependent care credit:	
	Allowable employment-related expenses	$ 5,000
	Times: Applicable percentage	× 28%
	Dependent care credit	$ 1,400

Earned Income Limitation

In addition to the $3,000 and $6,000 limitations, employment-related expenses are limited to the individual's earned income for the year.[117] For this purpose, earned income generally includes such items as salaries, wages, and net earnings from self-employment, but not investment income such as dividends and interest.

The earned income limitation is a bit more cumbersome for married couples. If an individual is married, a joint return is required to claim the credit, and the amount of the exclusion may not exceed the lesser of the taxpayer's earned income or the earned income of the taxpayer's spouse.[118] In addition, in determining the lesser earned income for married couples, special rules apply if one spouse is either a *full-time student*[119] or an incapacitated person. The student or incapacitated spouse will be deemed to have earned income of $250 a month if there is one qualified dependent or $500 a month if there are two or more qualified dependents for each month a taxpayer is incapacitated or is a full-time student. This deemed income does not increase AGI when determining the applicable percentage. These rules are illustrated in the following example.

---

[116] § 21(c).

[117] § 21(d)(1).

[118] §§ 21(e)(2) and 21(d)(2).

[119] § 21(d)(2). For this purpose, a full-time student is defined exactly the same as for the dependency test (i.e., for at least five months, partial months count as full months).

Example 33

B and G are married, have one dependent child, age nine, incur employment-related expenses of $2,700, and have AGI of $22,500 for the current taxable year. G is employed full-time and earns $27,000 a year. B returned to graduate school and was a full-time student for 10 months during the year. He was not employed during the year.

Step 1: The applicable percentage is determined to be 31%
(35% – [$22,500 – $15,000 = $7,500 ÷ $2,000 =
3.75 percent, rounded up to 4%]).

Step 2: The allowable employment-related expenses are $2,500.
This is determined by the lesser of three amounts:
(1) the $2,700 spent, (2) the $3,000 limit, and (3) B's deemed
earned income of $2,500 ($250 for one dependent × 10 months).

Step 3: Determine the dependent care credit:

Allowable employment-related expenses.	$2,500
Applicable percentage (35% – 4%)	× 31%
Dependent care credit	$ 775

Filing Requirements for the Child and Dependent Care Credit

In order to claim the credit for taxable years beginning after 1996, married couples must file a joint return and the taxpayer ID numbers of *both* the daycare service provider and of the child must be disclosed on the return.

Relationship to Other Credits

The child and dependent care credit is nonrefundable and is used to offset the tax liability determined under § 26. It is the *first* credit to be used in reducing an individual's tax liability, and there is no carryover or carryback available for unused credits.

Relationship to Dependent Care Assistance Programs

Congress has addressed the problem of child and dependent care in two ways: the child care credit and the exclusion for dependent care assistance. As mentioned in Chapter 6, since 1981 employers have been allowed to establish qualified dependent care assistance plans.[120] These plans allow employers a current deduction for contributions to the plans and allow employees to exclude from gross income up to $5,000 of payments (e.g., reimbursements) received under the plan to the extent that the expenses would qualify as employment-related expenses for purposes of the child and dependent care credits. If the taxpayer elects to exclude a reimbursement for care, the limit on the amount of employment-related expenses that qualify for the credit ($3,000 or $6,000) is reduced dollar for dollar by the amount excluded.[121] Whether the taxpayer is better off using the exclusion or the credit requires careful analysis of the taxpayer's situation, and some tax planning may be in order.

---

[120] See § 129 and the discussion in Chapter 6.   [121] § 21(c).

Example 34

H and W are married with two children. H works full-time as an accountant, and he estimates his earnings for the year will be $50,000. W is employed part-time and estimates her earnings will be $20,000 for the year. H and W estimate that they will incur $4,000 of qualified employment-related expenses for the year. H and W are in the 28% tax bracket.

At the beginning of H's employer's plan year, H has a decision to make. He can elect to have $1,000 excluded from his gross income in accordance with his employer's qualified dependent care assistance plan, which will be distributed to him as a reimbursement for qualified expenses, or he can elect to have the $1,000 included in his gross income as part of his salary. If the couple elects not to exclude the reimbursement, the child care credit is $800 (20% × $4,000), and they must pay taxes of $280 on the $1,000 of income, a net benefit of $520 ($800 − $280). On the other hand, if the couple elects to exclude the reimbursement, they pay no income tax on the $1,000 reimbursement, and their credit and net benefit is $800, computed as follows:

Employment-related expenses.	$4,000
Dollar limit: Maximum allowable expenses for two individuals	$6,000
Reduction for employer-provided dependent care excluded from income	(1,000)
Limit on expenses eligible for credit.	$5,000
Amount of credit (20% × lesser of $4,000 or $5,000).	$ 800

Note that only the dollar limit eligible for the credit is reduced by the excluded income. The employment-related expenses total of $4,000 is still eligible for the credit.

EDUCATION CREDITS

A major thrust of the Tax Reform Act of 1997 was to provide tax incentives to help reduce the cost of higher education and life-long learning. The law added six different provisions directed at this policy objective. Unfortunately, these rules often conflict and can be quite complex.

Taxpayers planning for the cost of educational programs or college degrees now must consider the following tax incentives:

- The exclusion for interest on Series E bonds.[122]

- The deductibility of certain interest on student loans.[123]

- Participation in qualified state tuition programs (529 plans).[124]

- Distributions from regular IRAs to pay educational expenses.[125]

- Establishing an education IRA.[126]

- The American Opportunity Tax Credit.[127]

- The Lifetime Learning Credit.[128]

---

[122] See § 135 and Chapter 6.

[123] § 222. With respect to tax incentives directed toward students, also see § 117 (exclusion for scholarships and fellowships) and § 127 (employer paid educational expenses).

[124] § 529.

[125] § 72(t).

[126] § 530.

[127] § 25A and § 25A(i).

[128] *Ibid.*

Section 25A contains two credits, the American Opportunity Credit (originally known as the Hope Scholarship Credit) and the Lifetime Learning Credit, that are directly aimed at subsidizing the costs of pursuing undergraduate and graduate degrees as well as vocational training. While there are two credits, for any one particular student, a taxpayer could elect either the American Opportunity Credit or a Lifetime Learning Credit but not both. Like most of the other tax incentives created in 1997, these credits are phased out at specific income levels and, therefore, are not available to high income or wealthy taxpayers. The following discussion first looks at each credit individually and then at requirements common to each credit.

American Opportunity Tax Credit

The American Opportunity Tax Credit (AOTC) was created in 2009 out of Congressional desire to enable all students to continue to pursue their education once they have completed high school. The credit is allowed for qualified tuition and certain related expenses for post-secondary education furnished to an eligible student. Taxpayers may elect to claim a credit for 100% of the first $2,000 of qualifying expenses and 25% of the next $2,000 of expenses for each student. Thus the maximum credit is $2,500 per year per student (e.g., the taxpayer whose triplets enroll at the local state college could claim a maximum credit for the year of $7,500). The AOTC is allowed for each of the first four years of a student's post-secondary education in a degree or certificate program. In addition, 40% of the credit is refundable unless the taxpayer could be subject to the kiddie tax (i.e., the child is a full-time student less than 24 and whose earned income does not exceed one-half his or her support).[129]

The credit is available only for expenses paid on behalf of the taxpayer, the taxpayer's spouse, or a dependent. In the case of a dependent's expenses, the eligible student is not entitled to claim a credit if he or she is claimed as a dependent by the parent or another taxpayer. Instead, if a parent or other taxpayer claims a student as a dependent, any qualified tuition and related expenses paid by the student are treated as paid by the parent and the parent benefits from the credit![130]

The credit is generally available only for expenses paid during the taxable year for education that begins during such year. For this purpose, education that begins during the first three months of the next year is treated as having started in the previous year. This special three-month rule allows a credit for prepaid expenses. Observe that these rules require careful planning to take advantage of the full credit. Because the credit is tied to the taxable year rather than the typical academic year (i.e., a year that begins with the fall semester and ends with the spring semester), taxpayers may lose some of the credit's benefits without taking advantage of the prepayment privilege.

Example 35

H is a typical high school graduate who enrolled for the 2016 fall semester of a local two-year community college. He plans to finish in the spring semester of 2018. The school charges $2,000 tuition per semester. Assuming H elects to claim the credit in 2016 and 2017, he can claim a total credit for the two years of $4,500 ($2,000 for fall 2016 + $2,500 for spring and fall of 2017). In such case, he does not benefit from the entire $5,000 ($2,500 per year) credit available. In order to avoid this result, H should prepay his 2017 tuition in December of 2016. Since prepayments qualify for the credit as long as the education occurs within the first three months of the following year, he would be eligible for the full $2,500 credit in 2016. He should also prepay in 2017 his tuition for the spring 2018 semester so that he will have paid at least $4,000 in 2017.

Note that qualifying expenses paid with loan proceeds are eligible for both credits in the year the expenses are paid, not when the loan is repaid.

---

[129] § 25A(i)(5).   [130] § 25A(g)(3).

Eligible Student

Expenses qualify for the credit only if they are for an eligible student. An eligible student is one who is enrolled in a program leading to a degree, certificate or other recognized educational credential at an eligible education institution. In addition, the student must carry one-half the load that a normal full-time student carries for at least one academic period per year. For example, if a student goes part-time during the spring semester (i.e., presumably one academic period) and carries one-half the full time load, his expenses for the summer and fall semesters will qualify even if he takes less than one-half the full time load during these later periods. Note also that the credit is not available for students that have been convicted of a federal or state felony offense consisting of the possession or distribution of a controlled substance.

Qualified Tuition and Expenses

Qualified tuition and related expenses include tuition and fees required for the enrollment or attendance at an eligible institution. Expenses also include course materials. However, expenses that do not directly relate to the student's education such as student activity fees, athletic fees, insurance expenses, transportation, or other expenses unrelated to an individual's academic course of instruction do not qualify for either credit. Similarly, expenses related to courses involving sports, games, or hobbies do not qualify unless such course is part of the individual's degree program. In addition, neither the AOTC nor the Lifetime Learning Credit is available for expenses incurred for room and board.

For both the AOTC and the Lifetime Learning Credit, the amount of qualifying expenses must be reduced by amounts covered by excludable scholarships or educational assistance plans.[131] However, amounts withdrawn from a qualified prepaid tuition plan and used to pay eligible expenses qualify for the credit.

Eligible Institutions

Only expenses paid to eligible institutions qualify for the credit. While most colleges and universities would be considered eligible, other providers of courses may also qualify. Technically, an eligible institution includes accredited post-secondary educational institutions offering credit toward a bachelor's degree, an associate's degree, or another recognized post-secondary credential. Certain proprietary institutions and post-secondary vocational institutions also are eligible. The bright line test is whether the institution is eligible to participate in Department of Education student aid programs.

Phase-Out for High Income Taxpayers. The AOTC (like the Lifetime Learning Credit discussed below) is not extended to high income taxpayers. To accomplish this objective, the total maximum credit allowed for all eligible students is phased out once the taxpayer's modified adjusted gross income exceeds certain thresholds. For 2017, the thresholds for the AOTC differ from those for the Lifetime Learning Credit. For the AOTC, the phase-out begins at $160,000 for joint returns and $80,000 for other returns. The reduction occurs over a $20,000 *income range* for joint filers and $10,000 for other taxpayers. If the taxpayer is married, a joint return must be filed to claim the credits. The formula for determining the phase-out and the levels at which a complete phase-out occurs is shown below.

---

[131] § 25(g)(2).

EXHIBIT 13-12	Phase-Out of AOTC and the Lifetime Learning Credit for 2017

$$\text{Reduction of total allowable credits} = \text{Allowable credits} \times \frac{\text{Modified AGI}^* - \text{Threshold}}{\text{Income range}}$$

Credit	Taxpayer	Modified AGI* Phase-Out Begins	Modified AGI* Phase-Out Complete
AOTC	Married filing joint	$160,000	$180,000
	Other taxpayers	80,000	90,000
Lifetime Learning	Married filing joint	$112,000	$132,000
	Other taxpayers	56,000	66,000

* Modified AGI is AGI increased by income earned outside the U.S. which normally is excluded under § 911. The income phase-out threshold amounts are indexed annually for inflation. See Rev. Proc. 2016-55, 2016-45 IRB 707.

Example 36

M, a single mother, has modified AGI of $81,000. In 2017, M's daughter, D, begins studying for her bachelor's degree as a full-time student at City University. On September 1, M pays $5,000 in qualified tuition for D's first semester. Without the income limitations, M would be entitled to the maximum AOTC of $2,500 (100% of $2,000 plus 25% of $2,000). However, taking into account the income limitations, M's credit is reduced as shown below.

$$\text{Reduction of total allowable credits} = \$2,500 \times \frac{\$81,000 - \$80,000}{\$10,000} = \$250$$

Thus, M is entitled to a $2,250 ($2,500 − $250) credit.

Lifetime Learning Credit

In addition to the AOTC, § 25A creates the Lifetime Learning Credit. This credit can be claimed for 20% of qualified tuition and fees incurred during the taxable year on behalf of the taxpayer, the taxpayer's spouse, or any dependents. Up to $10,000 of qualified tuition and fees per taxpayer return are eligible for the credit (i.e., the maximum credit per return is $2,000). For any one particular student, a taxpayer could elect either the AOTC or a Lifetime Learning Credit but not both. As noted above, the Lifetime Learning Credit is phased-out as show in Exhibit 13-12.

In contrast to the AOTC, a taxpayer may claim the Lifetime Learning Credit for a unlimited number of taxable years. Also in contrast to the AOTC, the maximum amount of the Lifetime Learning Credit that may be claimed on a taxpayer's return is not related to the number of students in the taxpayer's family. The key variable is the amount of qualified expenses incurred during the year and not the number of eligible individuals.

Qualified Tuition and Related Expenses for Lifetime Learning Credit

Qualified tuition and fees for purposes of the Lifetime Learning Credit are defined in the same manner as for the AOTC but with several important additions. As noted above, the AOTC is available only for four taxable years and ceases after the year the student has completed four years of post-secondary education. In contrast, the Lifetime Learning Credit—true to its name—applies not only to these same expenses but also such expenses incurred in any taxable year during the taxpayer's lifetime. For example, the Lifetime Learning Credit would be applicable to expenses incurred in obtaining an undergraduate degree (all four years or whatever is required) or a graduate degree (e.g., a law degree, a medical degree, an M.B.A., and similar graduate degrees). In addition, the definition of qualified tuition and expenses is expanded for the Lifetime Learning Credit to include any course of instruction at an eligible educational institution to acquire or improve job skills of the taxpayer. Thus expenses need not be incurred in a degree program but could be simply a continuing education course (e.g., a C.P.A. takes a course on the new tax law). Note, however, that for the course to qualify it must be provided by a qualifying educational institution (e.g., one that is eligible to participate in student aid programs of the Department of Education).

Like the AOTC, the amount of qualifying expenses for the Lifetime Learning Credit must be reduced by amounts covered by scholarships or educational assistance plans (assuming such amounts are excludable from gross income). Expenses taken into account for the AOTC cannot be taken into account for the Lifetime Learning Credit.

These credits are automatically available to the taxpayer unless the taxpayer elects not to take the credit with respect to the qualified tuition and related expenses of an individual for any taxable year. Previously, the taxpayer had to elect to claim the credit.[132]

Interaction of AOTC, Lifetime Learning Credit, Education IRAs and Series EE Savings Bonds

Special rules exist to prohibit the taxpayer from obtaining multiple benefits from the credits and nontaxable withdrawals from education individual retirement accounts. For each eligible student in each taxable year, the taxpayer must elect one of the three tax benefits: (1) the AOTC, (2) the Lifetime Learning Credit, or (3) the exclusion from gross income for withdrawals from education IRAs. The election is separate for each student. Thus a parent could elect the AOTC for one child, the Lifetime Learning Credit for another child, and the exclusion for IRA withdrawals for a third child. Any educational expenses taken into account for purposes of the credits or the IRA withdrawal cannot again be taken into account in determining the exclusion for interest on Series EE savings bonds that are used to pay for educational expenses.

CREDIT FOR ADOPTION EXPENSES

To encourage adoptions, § 23 provides for a nonrefundable credit for qualified adoption expenses. Qualified adoption expenses are reasonable and necessary adoption fees, court costs, attorney's fees, travel expenses (including meals and lodging) while away from home and other expenses that are directly related to the legal adoption of an eligible child. An eligible child is an individual (1) who has not attained age 18 as of the time of the adoption, or (2) who is physically or mentally incapable of caring for himself or herself. No credit is allowed for expenses incurred (1) in violation of state or federal law, (2) in carrying out any surrogate parenting arrangement, or (3) in connection with the adoption of a child of the taxpayer's spouse. The maximum credit is adjusted annually for inflation and is $13,570 for 2017. Thus, if a couple adopted two children, they would be eligible for two credits or $27,140. However, the credit is phased out ratably for taxpayers with modified adjusted gross income above $203,540, and is fully phased out at $243,540 of modified AGI. For these purposes modified AGI is computed by increasing the taxpayer's AGI by the amount otherwise excluded from gross income of citizens or residents living abroad.

---

[132] § 25A(e), as amended by the 2001 Tax Act, makes the credits applicable to the taxpayer unless the taxpayer *elects out* of the credit provisions.

The $13,570 (2017) limit is a per child limit, not an annual limitation. If adoption expenses are paid during a tax year before the tax year in which the adoption is final, the credit is allowed in the year after the year of the payment. If the expenses are paid during the year in which the adoption becomes final, the credit is allowed in the year the adoption becomes final. If adoption expenses are paid after the tax year in which the adoption is final, the credit is allowed for the tax year in which the expense is paid. See a summary of these rules in Exhibit 13-13 below.

These rules are modified slightly for an adoption of a foreign child. If the adopted individual is not a U.S. citizen or a resident, the credit for expenses paid before or in the year of the adoption are claimed when the adoption becomes final. Payments made after the adoption becomes final, are claimed in the year paid. These rules are summarized in Exhibit 13-13 below.

EXHIBIT 13-13	**Adoption Credit: Taxable Year for Claiming**	

	When to Claim the Credit	
Qualifying Expenses Paid In:	Domestic Adoption	Foreign Adoption
Any year before the year the adoption becomes final	Year **after** the payment	Year adoption becomes final
Year the adoption becomes final	Year the adoption becomes final	Year adoption becomes final
Any year after the adoption becomes final	Year of payment	Year of payment

Example 37

H and W are married and are in the process of adopting a C who is a U.S. citizen. In 2015, they paid qualified adoption expenses (travel expenses) of $2,000. The couple would claim a credit for these 2015 expenses of $2,000 in the following year, 2016. In 2016, they paid additional qualified expenses (attorney fees) of $3,000 for which a credit would be claimed in the following year. The adoption became final in 2017 and they paid an adoption fee of $9,000. The total expenses eligible for credit in 2017 is the sum of the previous year's expenses, $3,000 and the $9,000 of expenses paid this year (the year the adoption became final), a total of $12,000. However, the credit would be limited to in 2017 to $11,579 ($13,570 maximum − $2,000 claimed in 2016). If C had been a foreign child, the credit for any expenses paid before and during the year of adoption are claimed in the year of adoption or a credit of $13,570 in 2017.

> ### Example 38
>
> Same facts as above except, the couple's only expenses were $10,000 in the year the adoption became final, 2017, and $5,000 in 2018. Also assume that the maximum credit for 2018 increased to $14,000. In this case, they would claim a credit of $10,000 in 2017 and a credit in 2018 of $4,000 ($14,000 the new limit − $10,000 claimed in 2017). The result would be the same if C was a foreign child.

When the adoption credit is attributable to amounts chargeable to a capital account (e.g., the costs of constructing an elevator at the taxpayer's house to accommodate a wheelchair that is required as a condition of the adoption), the taxpayer is not allowed additional basis in the house to the extent of the adoption credit allowed. An ordering rule specifies that qualified adoption expenditures not chargeable to a capital account (the legal fees) are allowed for the credit before any amounts that are chargeable to a capital account.

A unique set of rules apply to the adoption of a child with special needs.[133] "Special needs" include the child's ethnic background, age, or membership in a minority or sibling group, or the presence of such factors such as medical conditions or physical, mental or emotional handicaps. In the case of a special needs child, the full $13,570 (2017) is allowed as an adoption credit regardless of whether the taxpayer has paid or incurred any qualified adoption expenses. The credit for a special needs child is only allowed if the adoption becomes final and the credit is only allowed in the year in which the adoption becomes final.

The adoption credit may be claimed not only by married taxpayers but also those who are single or who file head of household. However, married couples must file a joint return to claim the credit. The credit is claimed on Form 8839.

Recall that this credit can be used to offset the tentative minimum tax. However, it is not a refundable credit.

Interaction with the Exclusion for Qualified Adoption Expenses

A companion but separate $13,570 (2017) exclusion from gross income is also available to employees for qualified adoption expenses paid by the employer in accordance with a qualified adoption assistance program.[134]

Adoption expenses paid or reimbursed under an adoption assistance program may not be taken into account in determining the adoption credit. A taxpayer may, however, satisfy the requirements of the adoption credit *and* the exclusion with different expenses paid or incurred by the taxpayer and the employer, respectively. For example, in the case of an adoption that costs $14,000 with $7,000 of expenses paid by the taxpayer and $7,000 paid by the taxpayer's employer under an adoption assistance program, the taxpayer may qualify for the adoption credit and the exclusion.

CREDIT FOR THE ELDERLY AND PERMANENTLY DISABLED

A nonrefundable tax credit is available to certain taxpayers who are either 65 years of age or older or are permanently and totally disabled.[135] The credit is 15% of an individual's earned and investment income that does not exceed the taxpayer's appropriate § 22 amount.[136] The maximum § 22 amount is

1. $5,000 for single individuals.
2. $5,000 for a joint return where only one spouse is at least 65 years old.
3. $7,500 for a joint return where both spouses are 65 years or older.
4. $3,750 for a married individual filing separately.

---

[133] § 23(a)(3).

[134] § 137.

[135] Limited rules apply to taxpayers who are under 65 years old if they are certain governmental retirees subject to the

Public Retirement System and elect to have this section apply [see § 22(c)].

[136] § 22(a).

The maximum amount from above is then reduced by excludable pension and annuity income received during the year, including Social Security and railroad retirement benefits, and by one-half of the taxpayer's AGI that exceeds:

1. $7,500 for unmarried individuals.
2. $10,000 if married filing jointly.
3. $5,000 if married filing separately.

Example 39

P is single, 65 years old, and has AGI of $8,300 from interest and dividends. During the taxable year, she also received Social Security of $1,500. Her credit for the elderly is computed as follows:

Maximum § 22 amount		$ 5,000
Less: Social Security received	$1,500	
50% of AGI over $7,500 ($8,300 – $7,500 = $800 × 50%)	+ 400	(1,900)
Section 22 amount available for credit		$ 3,100
Multiply by rate		× 15%
Amount of credit		$ 465

There are a number of additional special rules, and because these rules are quite complicated, individuals are allowed to file their return with a request that the IRS compute their tax liability and tax credit. However, few people are able to take advantage of the credit for the elderly since Social Security receipts commonly exceed the maximum § 22 amount.

The credit for the elderly or permanently disabled is limited to the § 26 tax liability reduced by the child and dependent care credit. Like the child and dependent care credit, this credit is nonrefundable and may not be carried back or forward.

CREDIT FOR INTEREST ON CERTAIN HOME MORTGAGES

In order to help provide financing for first-time home buyers, Congress has created several special programs. One of these allows state and local governments to issue mortgage credit certificates (MCCs).[137] Taxpayers who receive such certificates are allowed to claim a nonrefundable credit for a specified percentage of interest paid on mortgage loans on their principal residence. Each certificate must specify the principal amount of indebtedness that qualifies for the credit as well as the applicable percentage rate of the credit. The credit percentage may differ with each certificate but must be between 10 and 50 percent. If the credit exceeds 20 percent, the maximum credit is limited to $2,000. The amount of the taxpayer's interest deduction must be reduced by the amount of the credit claimed during the year. Any credit that cannot be used may be carried over for three years.

[137] § 25.

Example 40

R and his wife, W, bought a new home this year. To finance the purchase, R applied for and received from the state an MCC. The certificate specifies that the rate is 15% and the maximum loan amount is $70,000. The couple purchased a house for $75,000 and obtained a loan of $65,000 from a bank. For the year, R and W paid interest of $5,000 on the loan. They may claim a credit of $750 ($5,000 × 15%). They also may deduct interest of $4,250 ($5,000 − $750).

While the credit can provide a significant benefit, it is not available to everyone. Under the MCC program, state and local governments are limited in the volume of credits they may dispense and in the individuals to whom they may be issued. Taxpayers are eligible to receive a certificate only if they meet certain narrowly defined criteria. For example, the purchaser's income cannot generally exceed 115% of the area's median gross income, the price of the home cannot exceed 90% of the average purchase price of homes in the area, and the homes may be available only in targeted areas. Still other constraints exist that restrict the credit's use.

ADDITIONAL NONREFUNDABLE CREDITS

There are several other nonrefundable credits which are discussed briefly below.

- *Savers Credit.* Section 25B allows low and middle-income taxpayers a nonrefundable tax credit of up to $2,000 of qualified retirement savings contributions. This credit is discussed in Chapter 18.

- *Non-Business Energy Property Credit.* Section 25C allows individuals to claim annual nonrefundable credits for amounts spent to make energy improvements to their homes. The credit is generally 30% of amounts paid for "qualified energy efficient improvements" and "residential energy property expenditures." The credit is available for expenses for such items as insulation, exterior doors and windows (including skylights), and properly coated metal as well as certain energy efficient heating and air conditioning units. However, the total non-business energy credits claimed by taxpayers since 2005 cannot exceed $500 ($200 for windows). Thus for 2017, the maximum credit is $500 reduced by the taxpayer's total nonbusiness energy credits from 2007 through 2016. Expenses must be made on or in connection with a dwelling unit located in the U.S., owned and used by the taxpayer as his principal residence and originally placed in service by the taxpayer. Currently, the credit is available for expenditures made before 2017.

- *Residential Energy Efficient Property (REEP) Credit.* Section 25D also allows individuals annual nonrefundable credit for the purchase of property for their homes that is energy efficient. Qualifying property includes certain photovoltaic property (i.e., property that uses solar power to generate electricity in a home), solar-powered water heaters and certain fuel cell property. Each of the credits is generally 30% of the cost of the property subject to certain limitations. The credit is set to expire in 2021.

Refundable credits are those credits that are recoverable even though an individual has no income tax liability in the current year. They are treated as payments of taxes. Included in this category are the credit for taxes withheld at the source (§ 31), the earned income credit (§ 32), the credit for tax withheld at the source on nonresident aliens and foreign corporations (§ 33), the gasoline and special fuels credit (§ 34) and the AMT refundable credit (§ 53(e)).

Refundable credits may be used to offset all taxes imposed by the Code, including penalty taxes. This result is accomplished by combining all the refundable credits and accounting for them after all the nonrefundable credits have been used to offset the § 26 tax liability.

TAX WITHHELD AT THE SOURCE

The first and most important of the refundable credits is styled "Credit for Tax Withheld on Wages" and obviously includes the amount withheld by an employer as a tax on wages earned.[138] However, the credit has broader application with respect to certain taxes withheld by the payor at the source of payment, including

1. Tax on pensions and annuities withheld by the payor.
2. Overpaid FICA taxes (where a taxpayer has two or more employers in the same year).
3. Amounts withheld as backup withholding in cases where the taxpayer fails to furnish a taxpayer identification number to the payor of interest or dividends.[139]
4. Quarterly estimated tax payments.

EARNED INCOME CREDIT

In 1975, Congress introduced the earned income credit to eliminate some of the disincentives that discouraged low-income taxpayers with children from working.[140] The credit was specifically designed to alleviate the increasing burden of Social Security taxes. In many cases, income taxes were not a concern for these low-income taxpayers since they were protected by personal and dependent exemptions as well as the standard deduction. However, these low-income taxpayers were not exempt from Social Security taxes. Consistent with its purpose, the credit is refundable (e.g., the taxpayer would receive the credit amount even if he or she is not required to pay income taxes since it is viewed as a refund of the Social Security taxes). In its present form, the credit may apply even if the taxpayer does not have children.

Computation of the Credit

The credit is based on the taxpayer's earned income. *Earned income* consists of wages, salaries, tips, and other employer compensation plus earnings from self-employment included in gross income for the taxable year.[141] Earned income does not include pension and annuity income even if provided by an employer for past services. Amounts received similar to compensation that are excluded are not treated as earned income. For example, excludable dependent care benefits, the value of meals and lodging furnished for the convenience of the employer, excludable educational assistance benefits and salary deferrals (contributions to a § 401(k) plan) are not included in earned income.

---

[138] §§ 31(a) and 3401.

[139] §§ 31(c) and 3406.

[140] § 32(a).

[141] § 32(c)(2)(B)(vi). Taxpayers may elect to treat combat zone compensation excluded under § 112 as earned income.

The initial credit is computed by multiplying the earned income of the taxpayer (limited by a ceiling amount) by a statutory percentage; however, this initial credit amount is phased out as the taxpayer's income increases above a phase-out amount. As can be seen from Exhibit 13-14, the maximum amounts of earned income that qualify for the credit as well as the statutory credit percentages vary depending on the number of children the taxpayer has.[142] Observe that the credit for an individual with no children is essentially designed to give the taxpayer back the FICA taxes on the first $6,670 wages (7.65% rate × $6,670 = $510). The maximum credits for eligible individuals for 2017 are shown in Exhibit 13-14.

As noted above, the credit begins to phase out once the taxpayer's income increases above the phase-out amount. The credit is reduced if *either* the earned income or the AGI of the taxpayer exceeds certain specified amounts shown in Exhibit 13-15.[143]

The phase-out is computed by multiplying the applicable phase-out rate by the excess of AGI or earned income (whichever is greater) over the phase-out amounts. The credit can be computed using the following formula:

Maximum credit:
  Applicable percentage × Earned income (not to exceed the ceiling amounts)
− Reduction:
  Applicable percentage × (Larger of earned income or AGI − Phase-out amount)
= Earned income credit

EXHIBIT 13-14	**Earned Income Credit (2017) Credit Percentages and Maximum Credits**		

Number of Qualifying Children	Credit Percentage	Ceiling on Earned Income	Maximum Credit
0	7.65%	$ 6,670	$ 510
1	34.00	10,000	3,400
2	40.00	14,040	5,616
3 or more	45.00	14,040	6,318

EXHIBIT 13-15	**Earned Income Credit: Phase-Outs (2017)**				

Qualifying Children	Phase-Out Percentage	Other than Joint Filers		Joint Filers	
		Threshold Phase-Out Starts At	Completed Phase-Out Level	Threshold Phase-Out Starts At	Completed Phase-Out Level
0	7.65%	$ 8,340	$15,010	$13,930	$20,600
1	15.98	18,340	39,617	23,930	45,207
2	21.06	18,340	45,007	23,930	50,597
3 or more	21.06	18,340	48,340	23,930	53,930

For example, the maximum 2017 earned income credit for an unmarried taxpayer with one child is $3,400 ($10,000 × 34%). This credit is completely eliminated when the taxpayer's modified AGI or earned income exceeds $39,617 (15.98% × [$39,617 − $18,340 = $21,277] = $3,400). The levels at which the credit is completely phased out are shown in Exhibit 13-14.

Example 41

D and M are married, file a joint return for 2017, and maintain a household for their dependent son, who is three years old. D has earned income of $23,000 and M has none. The couple own investments that produce $3,340 of includible income for the year and have an AGI of $24,530 ($23,000 + $1,530). The earned income credit is computed as follows:

Maximum credit (34% × $10,000)	$3,400
Less: Reduction for AGI over $23,930 ($24,530 − $23,930 = $600 × 15.98%)	− 96
Earned income credit	$3,304

To help taxpayers compute the credit, the IRS provides a worksheet and an earned income credit table to aid taxpayers in determining the correct amount of the earned income credit. The worksheet and table are included with the instructions for completing Form 1040 and Form 1040A.[144]

As a refundable credit, qualified individuals may receive tax refunds equal to their earned income credit even in years when they have no tax liability.[145]

Example 42

Y has earned income and AGI of $10,000, has three exemptions (including two qualified children), and files as head of household. As a result, she has no income tax liability for the year. However, she is entitled to a tax refund equal to the earned income credit of $4,000 ($10,000 × 40%) plus any taxes (other than FICA taxes) withheld from her wages. She may also qualify for a refundable child tax credit (see the next section and *Example 42*).

Eligibility Requirements

Because the earned income credit was a mechanical calculation under the former rules, some wealthy taxpayers inadvertently qualified for the earned income credit in years in which they reported a small amount of earned income. To preclude such taxpayers from taking advantage of the earned income credit, a major change was made. The earned income credit is now disallowed for taxpayers that have too much investment income. Taxpayers are not allowed to claim the earned income credit if they have more than $3,450 (2017) of disqualified income.[146] The definition of disqualified income includes

- Interest
- Dividends
- Tax-exempt interest
- The net income from rents or royalties not derived in ordinary course of a trade or business
- Capital gain net income
- The excess of aggregate passive income over aggregate passive losses

---

[144] § 32(f) Note that the earned income credit table prepared annually by the IRS reflects the credit based on a midpoint of each $25 increment of an income range.

[145] The taxpayer is required to reduce his or her earned income credit by the amount of the alternative minimum tax imposed on that individual.

[146] For the amount of excessive investment income see § 32(i) and Rev. Proc. 2016-55, 2016-45 IRB 707.

Finally, in an attempt to cut down on fraud and abuse relating to this credit, the taxpayer identification number required to be disclosed on the return means a Social Security number issued to an individual by the Social Security Administration.

Until 1993, the earned income credit was available only to taxpayers who had children. In a major change, the RRA of 1993 extended the earned income credit to certain individuals without children. In so doing, the law significantly broadened the availability of the credit. In either situation, if the taxpayer is married a joint return must be filed as a requirement to obtain the EIC.[147] The eligibility requirements for taxpayers with and without children are set forth below.

Taxpayers without Children

Taxpayers without a qualifying child are eligible to claim the credit if the taxpayer meets three conditions:[148]

1. The taxpayer (or the spouse of the taxpayer) must be at least 25 years old and not more than 64 years old at the end of the taxable year.
2. The taxpayer is not a dependent in the same year the credit is claimed.
3. The taxpayer has a principal residence in the United States for more than one-half of the taxable year.

Taxpayers with Children

Taxpayers are entitled to claim the credit if they have a qualifying child. The child need not be a dependent but must meet the following tests:

1. *Relationship.* The individual must be a child, stepchild, foster child, a legally adopted child of the taxpayer, or a descendant of any such individual. A married child does not meet this test unless the taxpayer can claim the child as a dependent.
2. *Age.* The child must be either (1) less than 19 years old at the close of the calendar year, (2) less than 24 years old and a full-time student at the close of the calendar year, or (3) permanently and totally disabled any time during the year.
3. *Residency.* The child must share the same principal place of abode as the taxpayer for more than one-half of the taxable year, and that abode must be located in the United States.

Assuming all of the above requirements are met and the taxpayer properly identifies the child on the return (i.e., name, age, taxpayer identification number), the credit is allowed.

REFUNDABLE CHILD TAX CREDITS

The basic child tax credit is generally limited to the taxpayer's regular tax and is nonrefundable. However, the amount exceeding the tax may be refundable. This refundable portion is referred to as the "additional child tax credit."

One of the principal policy goals of the CTC for low-income taxpayers is to offset not only the taxpayer's regular income tax but also the employee's share of FICA (or for those who are self-employed, one-half of the taxpayer's self-employment tax). To accomplish this goal, a portion of the child tax credit was made refundable.

The amount of the refundable child tax credit for 2017 is generally the lesser of:

1. The unused portion of the basic child tax credit or
2. 15% of the taxpayer's earned income in excess of $3,000.

For purposes of computing earned income, combat pay excludable from gross income under § 112, is treated as earned income.

---

[147] § 32(d).　　　　　　　　　　　　　　[148] § 32(c)(1)(A)(ii).

Example 43

T had earned income for the year of $8,000. She had one qualifying child and no tax liability. As a result, her unused child tax credit would be $1,000 since she had no tax liability. The earned income limitation under the 15% rule would be $750 (15% × $5,000 ($8,000 − $3,000 threshold)). Thus T would have an additional child tax credit that is refundable of $750.

Taxpayers with three or more children may use an alternative to the 15% rule. They may calculate the refundable portion of the credit using the excess of their Social Security taxes (i.e., the taxpayer's share of the FICA taxes and one-half of self-employment taxes) over the earned income credit.

Example 44

D, a single parent, has two dependent children. She earns a salary in 2017 of $23,400. The CTC is the only nonrefundable personal tax credit that D may claim.

Income	$23,400
Standard deduction for head of household (2017)	(9,350)
Personal exemptions ($4,050 in 2017)	(12,150)
Taxable income	$ 1,900
Tax on $1,900	$ 190
Earned income credit ($5,616 − [21.06% × ($23,400 − $18,340 = $5,060)])	$ 4,550
FICA paid (7.65% × $23,400)	$ 1,790

The refundable portion of the CTC is the lesser of:

1.	The unused portion of the CTC ($2,000 − $190)	$ 1,810	
	or		
2.	15% rule ($3,060 [15% × (23,400 earned income − 3,000 = $20,400)]) . .	$ 3,060	
	Refundable portion of the child tax credit		$ 1,810

Note that in determining the unused portion of the CTC, the CTC is claimed before the earned income credit.

D's total tax refund is computed as follows:

Tax liability		$ 190
Less: CTC		(190)
Tax liability before refundable credits		$ 0
Less: Refundable credits		
Additional CTC	$1,810	
EIC	4,550	(6,360)
Total refund		$ 6,360

Example 45

H and W have three children, file a joint return, and have earned income of $36,100. For 2017 their tax liability is $330 as computed below. The CTC is the only nonrefundable personal credit that H and W may claim.

Income.	$36,100
Standard deduction (2017).	(12,700)
Personal exemptions ($4,050 in 2017 × 5).	(20,250)
Taxable income.	$ 3,150
Tax on $3,150	$ 315
Earned income credit:	
(Maximum $6,318 – Phase-Out $2,563 [21.06% × ($36,100 – $23,930 = $12,170)])	$ 3,755
FICA paid (7.65% × $36,000)	$ 2,754

The refundable portion of the CTC is the lesser of:

1.	Unused CTC ($3,000 – $315).	$ 2,685
	or	
2.	15% rule ($4,965 [15% × ($36,100 – $3,000)])	$ 4,965
	Refundable portion of the child tax credit.	$ 2,685

Since H and W have at least three children, they should compute the excess of their FICA taxes ($2,762) over their EIC ($3,755) and compare it to $2,685. In this case, there is no excess and H and W will be able to treat $2,685 as the additional child tax credit (i.e., the refundable portion of their CTC). Thus their nonrefundable CTC is $315 ($3,000 – $2,685).

H and W's total refund is $6,440, computed as follows:

Tax liability		$ 315
Less: CTC		(315)
Tax liability before refundable credits		$ 0
Less: Refundable credits		
CTC.	$2,685	
EIC.	3,755	
		(6,440)
Total refund		$ 6,440

OTHER REFUNDABLE CREDITS

Three other refundable credits are allowed. Code § 33 allows as a credit the amount of tax withheld at the source for nonresident aliens and foreign corporations. Code § 34 provides an income tax credit for the amount of excise tax paid on gasoline, where the gasoline is used on a farm, for other nonhighway purposes, by local transit systems, and by operators of intercity, local, or school buses. Finally, Code § 35 provides that an overpayment of taxes resulting from filing an amended return will be treated as a refundable credit.

DISCUSSION QUESTIONS

13-1 *Alternative Minimum Tax.* It has been said that a taxpayer must maintain a second set of books to comply with the AMT system. Why is the extra set of books necessary?

13-2 *Alternative Minimum Tax.* The AMT requires taxpayers to keep an extra set of books for several adjustment items. What action can a taxpayer take to minimize the recordkeeping requirements with respect to depreciation deductions?

13-3 *Alternative Minimum Tax.* Assume a taxpayer has a regular tax liability of $25,000, a tentative AMT of $28,000, and an AMT of $3,000 for the current year. How much does the taxpayer actually owe the IRS?

13-4 *Alternative Minimum Tax.* A taxpayer has an AMT liability of $50,000 and a general business credit of $50,000. He is not concerned about paying the AMT because he thinks the general business credit can be used to offset the AMT. Is he correct? What if the taxpayer were a corporation?

13-5 *Alternative Minimum Tax.* Is it safe to assume that only wealthy individuals who have low taxable incomes are subject to the alternative minimum tax? Are any taxpayers whose marginal rates exceed 26% subject to the alternative minimum tax? Explain.

13-6 *Alternative Minimum Tax.* G will be subject to the alternative minimum tax in 2017 but not in 2018. G's property tax on her residence is due November 15, 2017. If she defers payment of the property tax until 2018, she must pay a 5% penalty. When should G pay the property tax? Explain.

13-7 *Alternative Minimum Tax.* Some interest expense can be taken as an itemized deduction for regular tax purposes but different rules control the interest expenses allowable as an AMT itemized deduction. Explain the differences in these rules and note which rules are more restrictive.

13-8 *Alternative Minimum Tax.* Is the § 179 (first-year expensing) deduction allowed as a deduction for the AMT system?

13-9 *Credits versus Deductions.* Assume taxpayers have a choice of deducting $1,000 for AGI or taking a $250 tax credit for the current year. Which taxpayers should choose the deduction? Why?

13-10 *Rehabilitation and Energy Credits.* A taxpayer purchased an old train station, which was placed in service in 1935, for $20,000. He plans to tear the building down and erect a new office building for $100,000. Will any of this qualify for the rehabilitation or energy investment credit? What tax advice could you give the taxpayer for his consideration in maximizing these credits?

13-11 *Rehabilitation and Energy Credit.* When a taxpayer claims a rehabilitation credit, what impact does the credit have on the basis of the property for cost recovery purposes? What is the impact on the basis when a business energy credit is claimed? What if the disabled access credit is claimed?

13-12 *IC Recapture.* Explain two possible consequences if a taxpayer claims an investment credit on property and then makes an early disposition of the property.

13-13 *Minimum Tax Credit.* If a taxpayer pays an AMT in the current year, what consequences does that payment have on the AMT liability that may be owed in subsequent years? What impact does the payment of the AMT in the current year have on the regular tax liability in subsequent years?

13-14 *Dependent Care Credit.* A husband and wife both work and employ a babysitter to watch the children during their work hours. How much of the babysitter's salary qualifies for the child and dependent care credit if:

    a. The babysitter performs cooking and cleaning services while she is watching the children.

    b. The babysitter also performs services around the house including gardening, bartending, and chauffeuring.

13-15 *Earned Income Credit.* A husband and wife with AGI and earned income of $7,000 maintained a household for their son but were unable to claim him as a dependent because he was 20 years old and earned $3,500. Can the son or his parents qualify for the earned income credit? Explain.

13-16 *Research Credit.* An entrepreneur works in a garage during 2016 doing research for a new patent. He spends $15,000 on the research in 2016. In January 2017, he forms an S corporation and applies for the patent, which is granted in 2017. How much credit for research expenditures will the taxpayer be allowed and in what year?

13-17 *Work Opportunity Credit.* The purpose of the work opportunity credit is to encourage the employment of certain groups of people with high unemployment rates. The credit has not quite achieved the desired objectives. What changes should be made to the present credit to increase its effectiveness?

PROBLEMS

13-18 *Alternative Minimum Tax—Computation.* T is single and has taxable income of $56,550 and a regular tax liability of $10,168 for the current year. T uses the standard deduction for regular tax purposes and has $60,000 of positive adjustments (excluding the adjustment for the standard deduction) for AMT purposes.

    a. Determine T's tentative minimum tax and her AMT.

    b. Determine the amount that T actually has to pay the IRS this year.

13-19 *Alternative Minimum Tax—Computation.* V and W are married and file a joint return for the current year. They have no other dependents and they take the standard deduction. V and W's taxable income is $94,250 and their regular tax liability is $15,623. They have $60,000 of AMT preference items and $32,050 of AMT positive adjustments. Determine V and W's tentative AMT and their AMT liability.

13-20 *AMT and Qualified Small Business Stock.* T is an avid investor, always looking for that one stock that will make him rich and famous. On January 4, 1999, BC Corporation, a fast food chain, went public, and T thought this could be the one. He purchased 10,000 shares of stock for $100,000. One of the benefits from buying this initial offering was that BC's stock was eligible for treatment as qualified small business stock. After enduring the ups and downs of the market, T sold 5,000 shares of the stock for $250,000 on January 9, 2017.

    a. Determine the gain recognized on the sale of the BC stock and the amount included in T's regular taxable income.

    b. Determine the amount of tax preference or adjustment, if any, that T must take into account in computing his alternative minimum tax.

13-21 *Alternative Minimum Tax—Computation.* B is single and reports the following items of income and deductions for the current year:

Salary	$ 50,000
Net long-term capital gain on sale of investment property	200,000
Medical expenses	17,500
Casualty loss	4,500
State and local income taxes	15,000
Real estate taxes	20,000
Charitable contributions (all cash)	15,000
Interest on home mortgage	12,000
Interest on investment loans (unimproved real property)	10,000

B made the election to treat $10,000 of the net long-term capital gain as investment income. The only additional transaction during the year was the exercise of an incentive stock option of her employer's stock at an option price of $12,000 when the stock was worth $100,000. Compute B's tax liability and AMT, if any.

13-22 *Alternative Minimum Tax.* Refer to the facts in *Problem 13-22* and assume B holds the stock acquired by exercising her ISO for two years and sells it for $105,000. Determine the amount of gain that must be reported for regular tax purposes and the gain that must be reflected in the AMT calculations in the year the stock was sold.

13-23 *Alternative Minimum Tax—Cost Recovery Adjustment.* In 2017, T placed a light-duty truck in service at a cost of $40,000. T uses the applicable MACRS method of depreciation for all his assets and does not elect the § 179 first-year expensing option. Identify and calculate the minimum tax adjustment that must be made for AMT purposes.

13-24 *Alternative Minimum Tax—Cost Recovery.* Refer to the facts in *Problem 13-23,* but assume the truck that was placed in service this year at a cost of $40,000 was a heavy-duty truck. Identify and calculate the minimum tax adjustment that must be made for AMT purposes in 2017.

13-25 *Alternative Minimum Tax—Cost Recovery Adjustment.* In January 2017, A purchases residential rental property for $200,000, excluding the cost of the land. For regular tax purposes, the 2017 depreciation on the building is $6,970. For AMT purposes, depreciation is $4,792. Determine the AMT adjustment for cost recovery for 2017 and 2018.

13-26 *Alternative Minimum Tax—Computation.* O is married to G and they file a joint return for 2017. O and G have AGI of $70,000. One of the deductions from gross income was $50,000 of percentage depletion. Cost depletion on their gold mine was zero because the cost basis of the property was reduced to zero by prior years' depletion deductions. They do not itemize deductions. Determine O and G's tax liability.

13-27 *Alternative Minimum Tax.* T is an unmarried entrepreneur. In 2007, he purchased several rental properties and leased them to tenants on long-term leases. In 2017, T has $100,000 of rental losses on his real estate activities in which he actively participates and income of $100,000 from his brokerage business. T also has a $25,000 general business credit carryover from 2016. Determine T's tax liability for 2017, assuming he does not itemize his deductions.

13-28 *Minimum Tax Credit.* Refer to the facts in *Problem 13-21* and determine the minimum tax credit, if any, that is available to offset the regular tax liability in 2018.

13-29 *General Business Credit—Limited by Tax Liability.* K's tax liability before credits is $35,000. She earned a general business credit of $40,000. Determine K's tax liability after credits and any general business credit carryback or carryforward that may exist.

13-30 *Energy Credit.* In May of the current year, J invested $60,000 in a solar system to heat water for a production process.
  a. Determine the amount of business energy credit available to J.
  b. Determine the basis of the energy property that J must use for cost recovery purposes.

13-31 *Rehabilitation Credit.* During the current year, T incurred $300,000 of qualified rehabilitation expenditures with respect to 75-year-old property. Prior to these expenditures, T had a $100,000 cost basis in the depreciable building.
  a. Determine the amount of rehabilitation credit available to T.
  b. Determine the basis of the rehabilitated property that T must use for cost recovery purposes.

13-32 *Rehabilitation Credit—Computation.* During the current year, K incurred $200,000 of qualified rehabilitation expenditures with respect to property constructed in 1930. The entire block where his property is located has been designated as a Certified Historical District.
  a. Determine the amount of credit allowable to K if his structure is recognized as a historical structure.
  b. Assuming that K paid $180,000 for his building in the current year and that he would claim MACRS depreciation, calculate his adjusted basis in the building at the end of the year. Assume that the property was placed in service in July of the current year.

13-33 *IC Recapture.* Assume D claimed a business energy credit of $30,000 for property placed in service on December 18, 2014 and that D sold this property on January 7, 2017. Determine the amount, if any, of IC recapture that D should report as an additional tax in 2017.

13-34 *IC Recapture.* Assume L claimed rehabilitation credit of $80,000 on property placed in service on February 18, 2014 and that L exchanged this rehabilitated property for like-kind property (a § 1031 exchange) on March 17, 2017. Determine the amount of IC recapture that L should report as an additional tax in 2017, if any.

13-35 *Research and Experimentation Credit.* M, a sole proprietor, has been in business only two years but is very successful. He has average annual gross receipts of $150,000 for this period and incurred $40,000 in qualified R&E expenses this year.
   a. Determine M's R&E credit for the current year.
   b. Determine the current deduction for R&E expenditures that M is entitled to, assuming he elects to deduct R&E expenditures currently.

13-36 *Disabled Access Credit—Computation.* P Corp. had gross receipts of $500,000 last year and incurred $9,000 of eligible access expenditures to build a wheelchair ramp this year.
   a. Determine P's disabled access credit.
   b. Determine the basis of the wheelchair ramp that will be eligible for cost recovery deductions.

13-37 *Child Tax Credit.* H and W are married with three children. At the close of 2017, the children, A, B, and C, were ages 2, 6, and 8, respectively. H and W claim a dependency exemption for each of the children. This year H and W reported adjusted gross income of $125,000. Determine the allowable child tax credit for H and W.

13-38 *Child Tax Credit.* M is a single mom raising one child, age 16, at home. M may claim a dependency exemption for her child. This year M earned $70,000 as salary and had investment income of $12,500. Determine the allowable child tax credit for M.

13-39 *Dependent Care Credit.* V and J are married and file a joint return for the current year. Because they both work, they had to pay a babysitter $5,200 to watch their three children (ages 7, 8, and 9). V earned $17,000 and J earned $21,200 during the year. They do not have any other source of income nor do they claim any deductions for adjusted gross income. Determine the allowable dependent care credit for V and J.

13-40 *Dependent Care Credit.* M and B are married, have a son three years old, and file a joint return for the current year. They incurred $500 a month for daycare center expenses. During the year, B earned $23,000 but M did not work outside the home. They do not have any other source of income nor do they claim any deductions for adjusted gross income. Determine the allowable dependent care credit for the year if:
   a. M enrolled as a full-time student in a local community college on September 6 of the current year.
   b. M was in school from January through June, and from September through December of the current year.

13-41 *Dependent Care Credit.* C is a single parent raising a son who is eight years old. During the current year, C earned $19,500 and paid $3,000 to a sitter to watch her son after school. Determine C's dependent care credit for the current year.

13-42 *Hope Scholarship Credit.* D is a single dad and has modified AGI of $52,000. This year D's son begins studying for his bachelor's degree as a half-time student at Arapahoe County Community College. On September 1, D pays $2,500 in qualified tuition for his son's first semester. Determine the amount of Hope credit available to D.

13-43 *Hope Scholarship Credit.* H and W are married and have twins who are attending the State University as freshmen this year. State University is on the semester system and charges $1,000 tuition per semester. H and W pay State University $2,000 this year. H and W have adjusted gross income of $83,000.
   a. Determine the allowable Hope Scholarship credit for H and W.
   b. If H and W ask your advice in terms of maximizing the Hope Scholarship credit, what advice would you give them?

13-44 *Earned Income Credit.* R is 43, divorced, and maintains a household for his 7-year-old dependent daughter. R was laid off last year and his unemployment benefits have run out. This year, he worked at part-time jobs earning $5,500. He has no other sources of income.

    a. Determine R's allowable earned income credit.

    b. Determine R's tax payment due or his refund, assuming that nothing was withheld from his wages and that he did not make any quarterly estimated tax payments.

13-45 *Earned Income Credit.* S, who is 24 and a single parent, maintains a household for her three-year-old dependent daughter and her ten-month-old son. S earned $16,000 during this calendar year. S has no other source of income and does not itemize her deductions.

    a. Determine S's allowable earned income credit.

    b. Determine S's tax payment due or her refund, assuming that $200 was withheld from her wages and that she did not make any quarterly estimated tax payments.

13-46 *Additional Child Tax Credit.* H and W have four children and earned $24,000 this year. H and W paid $1,836 in FICA taxes but neither had any income tax withheld from their wages. Determine the amount of refund they should receive from the IRS.

13-47 *Integrative Credit Problem.* J, who is 32 and a single parent, maintains a household for his six-year-old dependent son. J earned $20,000 and paid $3,000 in child care payments during the calendar year. J did not have any Federal income tax withheld from his check. Determine the amount of J's refund from the IRS, if any, or the amount that J must pay the IRS, if required.

13-48 *Credit for the Elderly.* P and D are 66 years old, married, and file a joint return. The only sources of income they have are dividend income of $14,000 and Social Security of $2,500.

    a. Determine the allowable credit for the elderly for the current year.

    b. Determine the tax payable or refund due, assuming that no withholding was made on the dividends and that no quarterly estimated payments were made.

CUMULATIVE PROBLEM

13-49 R and S, married and the parents of two children ages ten months and six years, file a joint return. R is a college professor of civil engineering and teaches at State University. R applied for a one-year visiting professorship with International Engineering Corporation (IEC) and was selected for the position. The visiting professor position was available from July 1 to May 31 of the following year and required R to relocate his family from Detroit to Los Angeles at a total cost of $6,500 during the last week in June. IEC reimbursed R only $5,000 for these expenses. R rented his Detroit home for the last six months of the calendar year at a net loss of $6,000 for regular tax purposes. Due to the longer life of the residential real property for AMT purposes, and therefore a smaller cost recovery deduction, the net loss for AMT purposes was only $4,000.

    S was employed by the government and was able to get a temporary transfer to Los Angeles. S earned $12,000 for the calendar year. During the calendar year, R and S paid $6,000 in child care expenses.

    R and his family incurred expenses of $2,500 a month to rent a furnished apartment (assume $1,000 a month was attributable to R and $1,000 a month was attributable to S) for the last six months of the calendar year. R and his family incurred expenses of $800 a month for food during the last six months of the year (assume 25% of the food is specifically attributable to R and that 25% is attributable to S). In addition, R incurred transportation expenses, parking fees, and laundry expenses of $2,500, and he spent $1,200 on lunches on work days during the last half of the year. S incurred transportation expenses of $500 and took her lunch to work with her. R earned $25,000 from State University for teaching half of the calendar year and $60,000 from IEC for practicing half of the year. Together, R and S had $12,000 of Federal income tax withheld from their paychecks.

During the year, R and S also incurred the following expenses:

Unreimbursed medical expenses...........................	$17,000
Charitable contribution of stock to State University (adjusted basis $1,000).................................	5,000
State and local income taxes..............................	4,000
Real estate taxes on lake property	3,000
Real estate taxes on principal residence (one-half year)	2,000
Interest on principal residence (one-half year)	4,800

The couple also had these additional income items:

State tax refund from previous year	$ 1,500
Interest income from private activity bonds	7,000

R and S have a minimum tax credit carryover from last year of $5,000. Determine R and S's tax liability for the year.

TAX RESEARCH PROBLEMS

13-50 *Rehabilitation Credit.* Taxpayer S, a real estate developer, rehabilitated an old commercial building and was entitled to an investment credit based on the rehabilitation expenses incurred. Prior to placing the new offices into service, S is approached by P, who is interested in purchasing the building. As an inducement to get P to buy the property, S offers to transfer the IC to P. That is, S agrees not to claim the credit on his tax return with the expectation that P can claim the credit instead. Will P be allowed to take credit on her tax return in the year she places the office building into service?

13-51 *Dependent Care Credit.* B is a single parent and his child is enrolled in a public school. The school administrators have scheduled a supervised trip to Dearborn, Michigan for one full week for the students to see Greenfield Village and the Henry Ford Museum. Total trip cost per student is $800. If B pays for his child to make the trip, will he be entitled to a child care credit for the expenditures? If so, how much of the costs will qualify?

13-52 *Alternative Minimum Tax.* This year T was the victim of his company's restructuring and downsizing. Midway through the year his employer, ABC Corporation, offered him early retirement on the condition that he would provide consulting services when needed. The offer proved so lucrative that T accepted. T ended up working for the company for the first six months of the taxable year and earned $50,000 during this period. Prior to his retirement he exercised an incentive stock option he had received several years earlier. At the time he exercised the option, the market price of the stock was $140,000 and the purchase price under the option was $50,000. After he retired, T began a new business of building toys for disabled children. He materially participated in the business and incurred a loss of $60,000, which he properly reported on Schedule C of his Form 1040 tax return. T is married and files a joint return with his wife. The couple paid $18,000 in qualified housing interest and $6,000 in real estate taxes, and made a $25,000 cash contribution to Children's Hospital during the year. Determine T's regular tax liability and AMT, if any.

13-53 *Child Care Credit.* K recently divorced and decided to go back to school full-time to get her Masters of Taxation at Central University. She has a four-year-old child who attends nursery school at a cost of $4,000 per year. As a single parent, K finds it difficult just to get by. However, she maintains her home using her alimony payments, some dividend and interest income, and her child support. She also works as a volunteer for ten hours a week at the library and receives $15 per week. This year she attended school for 11 months. Is K eligible for the child care credit?

Property Transactions

5

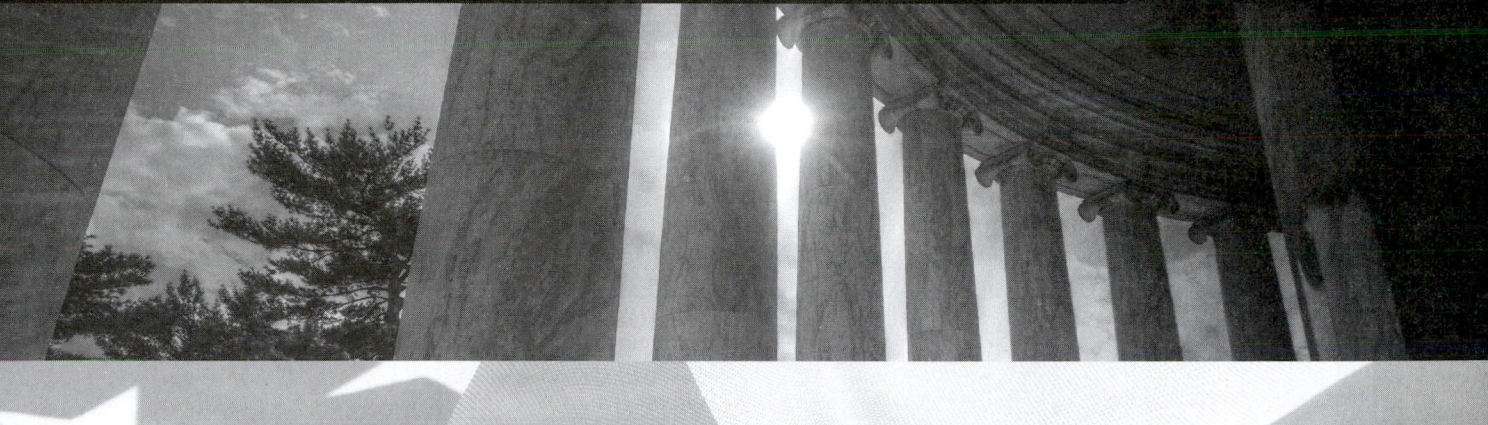

14

Property Transactions: Basis Determination and Recognition of Gain or Loss

Learning Objectives

Upon completion of this chapter you will be able to:

LO.1 Explain the basic computation used to determine gain or loss realized from the disposition of property.

LO.2 Understand the general rule concerning when a gain or loss realized is recognized.

LO.3 Compute the amount realized from a sale or other disposition.

LO.4 Understand how the adjusted basis of property is determined.

LO.5 Identify the most common types of adjustments to basis of property.

LO.6 Understand how liabilities affect the amount realized and adjusted basis.

LO.7 Define an installment sale and identify taxpayers eligible to use the installment method of reporting gain.

LO.8 Compute the amount of gain required to be recognized in the year of installment sale and the gain to be reported in any subsequent year.

LO.9 Explain the limitations imposed on certain installment sales, including:

- The imputed interest rules.
- Related-party installment sales.
- Gain recognition on the disposition of installment obligations.
- Required interest payments on deferred Federal income taxes.

LO.10 Identify various transactions in which loss recognition is prohibited.

Chapter Outline

Section 61(a)(3) of the Code provides that gross income includes gains derived from dealings in property. Similarly, § 165 allows a deduction, subject to limitations, for losses incurred in certain property transactions. The term *dealings in property* includes sales, exchanges, and other types of acquisitions or dispositions of property. This chapter examines the determination of the amount of gains and losses from dealings in property. Specific rules regarding gain recognition are addressed, as are the gain-deferral possibilities associated with certain installment sales. Various limitations on the deductibility of losses also are addressed.

Other topics dealing with property transactions are examined in the next three chapters. Chapter 15 deals with certain nontaxable exchanges. Chapter 16 covers the special treatment accorded gains and losses from sales or exchanges of capital assets. The unique rules governing the disposition of property used in a trade or business, including depreciable property, are examined in Chapter 17.

Determination of Gain or Loss

INTRODUCTION

LO.1

Explain the basic computation used to determine gain or loss realized from the disposition of property.

Determining the gain or loss realized in a property transaction is usually a simple computation. It is the mathematical difference between the amount realized in a sale or other disposition and the adjusted basis of the property surrendered (see Exhibit 14-1). The amount realized is a measure of the consideration received in the transaction. It represents the economic value *realized* by the taxpayer.

Sale or other disposition essentially refers to any transaction in which a taxpayer realizes benefit in exchange for property. It is not necessary that there be a sale transaction or that cash be received for gain or loss to be realized by the taxpayer surrendering property other than cash.

The adjusted basis of purchased property is generally cost, plus or minus certain adjustments. Computing gain or loss realized is similar to determining gain or loss for accounting purposes, and adjusted basis is similar in concept to book value. However, the adjusted basis of a property will not always be, and frequently is not, equal to its book value for accounting purposes.

EXHIBIT 14-1	Computation of Gain or Loss Realized

	Amount realized (see Exhibit 14-3)
−	Adjusted basis
=	Gain or loss realized

In effect, the adjusted cost, or adjusted basis, of a given property is the amount that can be recovered tax-free upon its disposition. For example, if property is sold for exactly its cost, as adjusted, there is no gain or loss realized. This concept is referred to as the *recovery of capital* or *recovery of basis* principle. If a taxpayer receives more than the adjusted basis in exchange for property, gain is realized only to the extent of that excess. The adjusted basis is recovered tax-free. The following examples illustrate this concept:

Example 1

K transferred 30 acres of land to ZX Company for $42,000 cash. K had purchased the 30 acres five years earlier for $35,000, which is his adjusted basis. As a result of this "sale or other disposition," K has a realized gain of $7,000 ($42,000 – $35,000). His $35,000 basis in the land is recovered tax-free.

Example 2

In 2015, L purchased 300 shares of W Corporation stock for $3,600 cash, including brokerage fees. When the market outlook for W Corporation's product began to weaken in 2017, L sold her shares for $3,100. The broker deducted a commission of $48 and forwarded $3,052 cash to her. L has a realized loss on this transaction of $548 ($3,052 – $3,600) in 2017.

Example 3

R transferred 200 shares of C Corporation stock worth $4,000 and $2,000 cash for an auto he will use for personal purposes. The C Corporation stock had been purchased two years earlier for $4,600. R realizes a loss of $600 ([$6,000 – $2,000] – $4,600) on the "sale or other disposition" of the stock.

GENERAL RULE OF RECOGNITION

Any gain or loss realized must be recognized unless some provision of the Internal Revenue Code provides otherwise. A *recognized gain* is reported on a tax return. For example, a gain on the sale of stock generally is recognized in full in the year of sale (i.e., the gain is reported on a tax return, included in gross income, and considered in determining the tax liability for the year). In determining taxable income, the recognized gain is either offset against losses for the year or included in the computation of taxable income.[1]

A *recognized loss* also is generally given its full tax effect in the year of realization. Depending on the type of loss, it may be either offset against gains or deducted against other forms of income in determining taxable income. Some losses, however, are not deductible[2] and others are limited.[3] For example, losses on the sale of property used for personal purposes are disallowed. Certain other losses are deferred to later tax years. Some examples of nontaxable exchanges are listed in Exhibit 14-2.

LO.2
Understand the general rule concerning when a gain or loss realized is recognized.

---

[1] Capital gains must be offset by capital losses, and only net capital gains are included in taxable income. See the discussion of capital gains and losses in Chapter 16.

[2] Losses on certain sales to related parties are disallowed under § 267, and losses on the sale of personal use property are not allowed under § 165(c).

[3] The deduction for capital losses is limited under § 1211(b).

EXHIBIT 14-2	Partial List of Nontaxable Exchanges	

Types of Transaction	Action Required	Tax Result
Casualty, theft, condemnation (involuntary conversion)	Reinvest in similar property	Gain may be deferred see Chapter 15 and § 1033
Like-kind exchange	Exchange directly for like-kind property	Gain or loss is deferred* see Chapter 15 and § 1031
Formation of a corporation or subsequent stock issues	Transfer property in exchange for stock by controlling shareholders	Gain or loss is deferred* see § 351
Corporate reorganizations	Examples include mergers, consolidations, divisions, recapitalizations	Gain or loss is deferred* see § 368
Partnership formation	Transfer property in exchange for a partnership interest	Gain or loss is deferred* see § 721

* When gain or loss is deferred, the deferral is only until the replacement property is sold or otherwise transferred (i.e., the deferred gain or loss is recognized along with any subsequent gain or loss when the replacement property is sold).

COMPUTING AMOUNT REALIZED

LO.3

Compute the amount realized from a sale or other disposition.

The amount realized from a sale or other disposition of property includes the amount of money received plus the fair market value of any other property received in a transaction. Other property includes both tangible and intangible property.

Example 4

P received $20,000 and a motor home worth $80,000 in exchange for a sailing yacht that she had used for personal enjoyment. P's amount realized on the disposition of the yacht is $100,000 ($20,000 + $80,000).

The amount realized also includes any debt obligations of the buyer, and if the contract provides for inadequate interest or no interest, interest must be imputed and the sales price reduced accordingly.

Example 5

Y sold his vintage Dodge automobile to C for $10,000 and a note payable from C to Y for $15,000 plus interest compounded monthly at 9 percent. Y's amount realized in this transaction is $25,000, the down payment plus the value of C's note.

Example 6

Z sold a parcel of real estate for $100,000. Her basis in the land was $60,000. The sales contract called for $10,000 to be paid upon transfer of the property and the remaining $90,000 to be paid in full two years later.

Since no interest was provided for in the contract, interest must be imputed on the buyer's $90,000 obligation (in this case, 9% interest, compounded semiannually, is used).[4] Accordingly, the sales price is reduced to $85,471 ($10,000 cash down payment + $75,471 [the discounted present value of the $90,000 payment in two years]). Z will report an amount realized of $85,471 and a gain realized of $25,471 ($85,471 − $60,000 basis). When Z collects the $90,000, she must report interest income of $14,529 ($90,000 face value − $75,471 present value on date of sale).

The amount realized also includes the amount of any existing liabilities of the seller discharged in the transaction. Specifically, it includes any debts assumed by the buyer and any liabilities encumbering the property transferred that remain with the property in the buyer's hands.[5] Exhibit 14-3 illustrates the computation of *both* the amount realized and the gain or loss realized from the sale or other disposition of property.

Example 7

B purchased a rental house for $40,000 in 2010. She paid $8,000 down and signed a mortgage note for the balance. During the years she owned the property, B deducted depreciation totaling $16,000 and made principal payments on the note of $4,000, leaving a mortgage balance of $28,000.

During 2017, B sold the house for $62,000. The buyer paid $34,000 cash and assumed the $28,000 mortgage liability. B's amount realized is $62,000 ($34,000 cash + $28,000 relief of liability), and her adjusted basis is $24,000 ($40,000 cost reduced by $16,000 depreciation). Her gain realized is therefore $38,000 ($62,000 amount realized − $24,000 adjusted basis).

EXHIBIT 14-3	Computation of Amount Realized and Gain or Loss Realized

Amount realized:		
	Amount of money received..	$xxx,xxx
Add:	Fair market value of other property received.........................	+ x,xxx
	Liabilities discharged:	
	Liabilities assumed by the buyer	+ xx,xxx
	Liabilities encumbering the property transferred	+ x,xxx
Less:	Selling expenses	− xx,xxx
	Amount of money given up	− x,xxx
	Liabilities incurred:	
	Liabilities assumed by the taxpayer	− xx,xxx
	Liabilities encumbering the property received	− x,xxx
Equals:	Amount realized...	$xxx,xxx
Less:	*Adjusted basis* in property other than money given up	− xx,xxx
Equals:	*Gain or loss realized*...	$xxx,xxx

---

[4] The actual rate is determined with reference to current market rates and is announced periodically by the IRS. For transactions involving $2.8 million or less, the rate cannot exceed 9% compounded semiannually.

[5] Reg. § 1.1001-2. Also, see the following discussion of the effect of liabilities in property transactions.

Any expenses of selling the property reduce the amount realized. Selling costs include many costs, paid by the seller, associated with offering a property for sale and transacting the sale. For example, selling costs include advertising expenses, appraisal fees, sales commissions, legal fees, transfer taxes, recording fees, and mortgage costs of the buyer paid by the seller.

Basis Determination Rules

LO.4

Understand how the adjusted basis of property is determined.

The adjusted basis of property may be determined in several ways, depending on how the property is acquired and whether any gain or loss is being deferred in the transaction. Various methods of acquiring property and their specific basis determination rules are discussed below.

PROPERTY ACQUIRED BY PURCHASE

Cost Basis

In a simple purchase transaction, basis is the cost of the property acquired. Cost is the amount of money paid and the fair market value of any other property transferred in exchange for a given property.[6] The cost basis includes any payments made by the buyer with borrowed funds and any obligations (i.e., promissory notes) of the buyer given to the seller or any obligations of the seller assumed by the buyer in the exchange.[7]

Any costs of acquiring property are included in basis. For stock and securities, commissions, transfer taxes, and other acquisition costs are included. For other property, many types of acquisition costs, including commissions, legal fees related to purchase, recording fees, title insurance, appraisals, sales taxes, and transfer taxes, are added to basis.[8] Any installation and delivery costs also are part of basis.

Example 8

C purchased a new machine for his auto repair business during the year. He paid $16,500 for the machine, $8,500 of which was made possible by a bank loan. In addition, C paid state sales taxes of $660, delivery charges of $325, and installation charges of $175. C's cost basis in the equipment is $17,660 ($16,500 purchase price + $660 sales taxes + $325 delivery charges + $175 installation charges).

Periodic operating costs such as interest and taxes are generally deducted in the year paid. However, a taxpayer may elect to *capitalize* (i.e., include in basis) certain taxes and interest related to unproductive and unimproved real property or related to real property during development or improvement rather than take a current tax deduction.[9]

Example 9

T purchased a small parcel of unimproved land near a lake known for its excellent fishing. She uses the property as a weekend retreat and plans someday to build a log cabin. T annually pays $750 for local property taxes but does not itemize deductions. T should elect to capitalize the property taxes paid each year as a part of her basis in the land.

---

[6] Reg. § 1.1012-1(a).

[7] § 1001 and *Crane v. Comm.*, 47-1 USTC ¶9217, 35 AFTR 776, 331 U.S. 1 (USSC, 1947).

[8] § 1012 and Reg. § 1.1012-1(a).

[9] § 266 and Reg. § 1.266-1(b)(1).

Identification Problems

Generally, the adjusted basis of property sold or otherwise transferred is easily traced to the acquisition of the property and certain subsequent events. However, identification of cost may be difficult if a taxpayer has multiple homogeneous assets. For example, if a taxpayer owns identical shares of stock in a corporation that were acquired in more than one transaction and sells less than his or her entire investment in that stock, it is necessary to identify which shares are sold. For tax purposes, the owner must use the *first-in, first-out* (FIFO) method of identification if it is impossible to identify which shares were sold. Specific identification of the shares sold is appropriate if the shares can be identified.[10]

Example 10

K purchased the following lots of G Corporation stock:

50 shares	Purchased 1/10/2014	Cost $5,500
75 shares	Purchased 8/15/2014	Cost $9,000
40 shares	Purchased 6/18/2016	Cost $4,600

K sold 60 shares of her G Corporation stock in 2017 for $8,700. Unless she can specifically identify the shares sold, her basis will be determined using the FIFO method. Therefore, her basis in 50 shares sold is $5,500 and her basis in 10 shares sold is $1,200 (10 shares × $120 [$9,000 ÷ 75 shares]). Her total gain is $2,000.

Example 11

Assuming the same facts in *Example 10,* the gain would be different if K could specifically identify the shares sold. If she directed her broker to deliver to the buyer the shares purchased on 8/15/2014, referring to them by certificate number and date of purchase, her gain would be $1,500 ($8,700 sale price – $7,200 [$120 basis per share × 60]).

PROPERTY ACQUIRED BY GIFT

Generally, the basis of property received by gift is the same as the basis was to the donor.[11] This basis is *increased* by that portion of the gift tax paid by the donor, which is attributable to the appreciation in the property's value, if any, up to the date of the gift. A property's taxable value is its fair market value on the date of gift reduced by any gift tax exclusion, marital deduction or charitable deduction taken on the gift. The appreciation is measured by the difference between the taxable value of the property and the donor's adjusted basis in the property immediately before the gift.[12] The appropriate increase in basis for a given property is determined using the following formula:[13]

$$\frac{\text{Fair market value date of gift} - \text{Donor's basis date of gift} = \text{Appreciation}}{\text{Taxable gift}} \times \text{Gift taxes paid}$$

In making the adjustment for the gift tax, the amount of increase cannot exceed the amount of the tax. Also observe that there is an adjustment for gift tax only if the property had appreciated in the donor's hands at the time of the gift.

---

[10] Reg. § 1.1012-1(c).

[11] § 1015(a).

[12] See § 1015(d)(6) and Reg. § 1.1015-5(c)(3). For gifts made before 1977, the entire amount of the gift taxes paid could be used for the gift tax adjustment, but the adjusted basis could not exceed the property's taxable value at the time of the gift.

[13] See § 1015(d)(2) and Reg. § 1.1015-5(c)(3) Ex. 1. If there is more than one gift on the annual gift tax return, the gift tax is allocated among the gifts proportionately based on the amount of the taxable gift.

Example 12

On March 7, 2014, Ann received 10 acres of undeveloped land as a gift from her Uncle Carl. On the date of the gift, the land had a value of $114,000 and Carl's adjusted basis in the land was $84,000. On his gift tax return, Carl reported a taxable gift of $100,000 (fair market value $114,000 − annual exclusion $14,000) and paid gift taxes of $41,000. Since Ann received the land, she has held it for investment. Now she is thinking about selling the property. If Ann sells the property, her basis in the land, including an adjustment for gift taxes, is $96,300 as determined below.

Appreciation at date of gift:	
Fair market value of property	$114,000
Adjusted basis	(84,000)
Appreciation	$ 30,000
Donee's basis calculation:	
Donor's adjusted basis	$ 84,000
Gift tax attributable to appreciation	
Gift tax $41,000 × ($30,000 appreciation at date of gift/$100,000 taxable gift)	12,300
Donee's adjusted basis	$ 96,300

If Ann sells the land for $156,300, her taxable gain would be $60,000 ($156,300 − $96,300). If Ann sells the land for $76,300, her deductible loss would be $20,000 ($76,300 − $96,300). Note that since the property had appreciated as of the date of the gift, the basis for determining gain and loss is the same.

Loss Limitation Rule

If the fair market value of the property *at the time of the gift* is less than the donor's basis (i.e., it has a built-in loss), special rules must be applied to determine the basis for the donee. The special rule is designed to prevent shifting of the loss to the taxpayer (e.g., a family member), who would obtain the greatest benefit. Perhaps the clearest expression of the rules in this case is as follows: the basis for *determining gain* is the donor's basis, while the basis for *determining loss* is the lower of either (1) the donor's basis or (2) the property's fair market value at the date of the gift.[14] Due to the way the rule for determining loss is stated, the donee will not recognize any gain or loss if the property is disposed of for any amount that is *less than* the donor's basis *but greater than* the value of the property at the date of the gift. These rules are illustrated in the following examples.

Example 13

S received 200 shares of X Corporation stock as a gift from his uncle. The stock had a basis to the uncle of $32,000 and a fair market value on the date of the gift of $29,000. Gift taxes of $1,400 were paid on the transfer.

    This year, S sold all of the shares for $24,000. His loss realized on the sale is $5,000 ($24,000 sale price − $29,000 fair market value at date of gift). Note that S was not permitted to add any of the $1,400 gift taxes to his basis since such adjustments are allowed only if the taxable value is more than the donor's basis on the date of the gift (i.e., the property appreciated in the donor's hands).

---

[14] § 1015(a). It also should be noted that total depreciation claimed using the gain basis for computation cannot exceed the property's fair market value at date of gift. Reg. § 1.167(g)-1.

> ### Example 14
>
> Assuming the same facts as in *Example 13,* if S's stock had been sold for $36,000, his realized gain would have been $4,000 ($36,000 sales price – $32,000 gain basis). There is no adjustment for gift taxes paid because the property did not appreciate in the donor's hands.

> ### Example 15
>
> Assuming the same facts as in *Example 13,* if S had sold his stock for $31,000 he would not realize gain or loss on the sale. His basis for gain is $32,000 (the donor's basis) and his basis for loss is limited to $29,000 (fair market value on the date of the gift). Since the $31,000 sales price does not exceed the gain basis and is not less than his loss basis, neither gain nor loss is realized on the sale.

Application of these special rules illustrates *three* important points. First, *any gain* realized by the donee on a subsequent sale of the property is limited to the amount of gain that the donor would have realized had he or she sold it at the donee's sales price. Second, *any loss* allowed on a subsequent sale of the property is limited to the decline in the property's value that occurs while owned by the donee. Third, although the payment of a gift tax may be required as a result of the gift, the donee is not allowed to adjust the donor's basis in the property by any gift taxes paid because there is no appreciation in value of the property in the donor's hands (i.e., the taxable value of the property at the time of the gift is less than the donor's basis).

PROPERTY ACQUIRED FROM A DECEDENT

The adjusted basis of property acquired from a decedent generally is its fair market value on the date of the decedent's death.[15] This also is the value used in determining the taxable estate for estate tax purposes.[16] The fiduciary (executor or administrator) of the estate may, however, *elect* to value the estate for estate tax purposes six months after the date of death.[17] This election is available only if (1) the estate is required to file a Federal estate tax return (Form 706), and (2) the alternate valuation reduces *both* the gross estate and the Federal estate tax.[18] If the fiduciary elects to use this alternate valuation date, the fair market value on the later date must also be used as the income tax basis to the heir or estate.[19]

> ### Example 16
>
> D inherited some gold jewelry from his grandmother several years ago. The fair market value of the jewelry on the date of her death was $4,000 and its adjusted basis to the grandmother was $3,050. If D sells the jewelry this year for $4,350, his realized gain will be $350 ($4,350 sale price – $4,000 basis).

> ### Example 17
>
> If D, from the previous example, sells the jewelry for $3,000, he will have a realized loss of $1,000 ($3,000 – $4,000).

---

[15] § 1014(a).

[16] § 2031(a).

[17] § 2032(a).

[18] § 2032(c).

[19] § 1014(a)(2).

Exceptions to this basis rule are provided for *income in respect of a decedent* under § 691[20] and for certain property acquired by the decedent by gift. Income in respect of a decedent (often referred to as IRD) includes all items of income that the decedent had earned or was entitled to as of the date of death, but which were not included in the decedent's final income tax return under his or her method of accounting. For example, if a cash basis individual performed all the services required to earn a $3,000 consulting fee but had not collected the fee before his or her death, the $3,000 would be income in respect of a decedent. All IRD items are includible in the decedent's gross estate at fair market value for Federal estate tax purposes. Whoever receives the right to collect these items of income must report them in the same manner as the decedent would have been required to report them had he or she lived to collect the income. As a result, IRD items generally are fully included in the gross income of the recipient when received.[21]

If appreciated property was acquired by the decedent by gift within one year before his or her death and the property passes *back* to the donor or the donor's spouse, the recipient's adjusted basis is the decedent's adjusted basis.[22]

Example 18

H transferred a parcel of lake-front real estate to his elderly grandmother when the property had an adjusted basis to H of $3,000 and a fair market value of $40,000. No gift taxes were paid on the transfer.

H's grandmother died three months after the gift and left the lake-front property to H in her will. H's basis in the property is $3,000 (the rules used for gifted property apply rather than those for inherited property). If his grandmother had lived for more than a year after the gift was made, H's basis would have been determined under the general rule for property acquired from a decedent.

Another exception is provided in the case of real property subject to special use valuation for Federal estate tax purposes. In such cases, the basis to the heir is the special value used for estate tax purposes. This special use valuation applies only to certain real property used in a trade or business and held by the heir more than 10 years.[23]

PROPERTY ACQUIRED IN A NONTAXABLE EXCHANGE

Most nontaxable exchanges provide deferral, rather than permanent nonrecognition of gain or loss. The mechanism for such deferral is typically an adjustment to the basis in some replacement property.[24] This adjustment is a reduction in basis in the case of a deferred gain and an increase in basis in the case of a deferred loss.

The specific rules for determining the basis of property acquired in nontaxable transactions, along with the requirements of each nontaxable transaction, are discussed in various parts of this text. Several such transactions are discussed in the next chapter. The following example illustrates one such transaction:

Example 19

T exchanged a five-acre residential lot for a 100-acre tract of farmland. He realized a $70,000 gain on the exchange because the farmland was worth $90,000 and his basis in the residential lot was $20,000. Since T met all the requirements for nonrecognition of gain in a like-kind exchange under § 1031, his basis in the farmland is $20,000 ($90,000 fair market value − $70,000 deferred gain).

---

[20] § 1014(c).

[21] § 691(a)(1).

[22] § 1014(e).

[23] § 2032A(b).

[24] See, for example, § 1031(d), dealing with like-kind exchanges.

PROPERTY CONVERTED FROM PERSONAL USE TO BUSINESS USE

Losses on the disposition of personal use properties are clearly not deductible. Absent some provision to the contrary, business owners could simply convert personal use assets to business use before disposing of them in order to generate business deductions for losses on their sale. Accordingly, when property is converted from personal use to trade or business use, its basis is limited for determining realized loss and for depreciation purposes. For each of those purposes, fair market value on the date of conversion is used as the property's basis if it is less than its adjusted basis.[25]

Example 20

J owned a single-family home that had been her personal residence for five years. When J discontinued use of the house as her residence, she converted it to rental property. J's original basis in the property was $90,000, and the property was worth $70,000 on the date of conversion. J must determine any depreciation using the fair market value of $70,000, since it is less than her $90,000 adjusted basis. If the property is later sold, J's *gain basis* will be the original $90,000 adjusted basis reduced by the depreciation allowed after the conversion. Her *loss basis* will be the lower fair market value on the date of conversion, $70,000, reduced by the allowed depreciation. Note that if J was hoping to deduct her loss of $20,000 on the property by converting it to business use, she is out of luck since the basis for loss is $70,000. Also observe the similarity to the basis rules that would have applied if J had received the residence as a gift (see *Examples 13, 14,* and *15*).

PROPERTY CONVERTED FROM BUSINESS USE TO PERSONAL USE

Once property is converted from business use to personal use, it is treated as personal use property. Any loss on the disposition of such property would, therefore, be disallowed; and, in the event that the property was subsequently converted back to business use, the limitations discussed above would apply.

Example 21

W has a photocopier used exclusively for business. The copier cost $4,000 and depreciation of $1,800 has been allowed, making its basis $2,200. If W converts the copier to personal and family use and later sells it for $500, no loss will be deductible. Of course, if W had immediately sold the copier at a loss rather than converting it to personal use, he would have a business loss.

---

[25] Reg. § 1.167(g)-1.

ADJUSTMENTS TO BASIS

LO.5

Identify the most common types of adjustments to basis of property.

Regardless of the method used in determining a property's basis initially, certain adjustments are made to that basis. Generally, the adjustments can be broken down into three groups. Basis is *increased* by *betterments* or *improvements*[26] and *reduced* by *depreciation allowed* or *allowable*[27] and by *other capital recoveries.*[28]

Depreciation reduces basis regardless of whether it is actually deducted by the taxpayer. The *allowable depreciation* is determined using the straight-line method if no method is adopted by the taxpayer.[29]

Various types of *capital recoveries* also reduce a property's adjusted basis. The following are some of the specific items that reduce basis:

1. Certain dividend distributions that are treated as a return of basis.[30]
2. Deductible losses with respect to property, such as casualty loss deductions.[31]
3. Credits for rehabilitation expenditures related to older commercial buildings and certified historic structures.[32]

Numerous other events have an impact on a property's adjusted basis. Many of them are discussed in the remaining chapters of this text, which deal with specific types of transactions.

Exhibit 14-4 summarizes the rules for determining a property's adjusted basis.

EXHIBIT 14-4	**Determination of Adjusted Basis**	
Method of Acquisition	*Basis*	*Exceptions*
General Rule		
Acquired by purchase	Purchase cost	See special rules
Special Rules		
Acquired by gift	Donor's basis + gift tax paid adjustment, if any	If fair market value at date of gift is less than donor's basis use fair market value to determine loss
Acquired from a decedent	Fair market value at date of death (or alternate valuation date, if elected)	1. Income in respect of a decedent 2. Property given to the decedent by the donor/heir within one year of decedent's death 3. Property subject to special § 2032A
Converted from personal use	Adjusted basis before conversion	For determining loss and depreciation, use fair market value date of conversion if lower than original adjusted basis
Acquired in a nontaxable exchange	Fair market value less any gain not recognized or plus any loss deferred	

Note: The basis as determined under any of the above methods is subject to adjustments as provided by other provisions of the Code. Basis is increased by betterments or improvements and reduced by depreciation allowed or allowable and by other capital recoveries.

---

[26] § 1016(a)(1).

[27] § 1016(a)(2).

[28] See following examples.

[29] § 1016(a)(2). But see Rev. Proc. 2004-11, 2004-1 C,B. 211 as amended by Rev. Proc. 2007-4 IRB which allows a taxpayer to claim in the year of sale any depreciation allowable that had not been claimed in prior years.

[30] § 1016(a)(4).

[31] See Reg. § 1.1016-6 and Rev. Rul. 74-206, 1974-1 C.B. 198.

[32] See §§ 46(a), 48(q), and 1016(a)(22).

Effect of Liabilities on Amount Realized and Adjusted Basis

Liabilities can affect not only the seller's amount realized but also the buyer's adjusted basis. As noted above, the amount realized in a sale or other disposition of property includes the amount of any liabilities of the seller assumed by the buyer plus any liabilities encumbering the transferred property that remain with the property.[33] In addition, the amount realized from a transaction is reduced by any liabilities assumed by the seller plus any liabilities encumbering property received in the transaction that remain with the property. Similarly, the basis of any property received includes the portion of the cost represented by the liabilities assumed by the seller or encumbering the property.[34]

> **LO.6**
> Understand how liabilities affect the amount realized and adjusted basis.

Example 22

B exchanges a vacant lot with an adjusted basis of $20,000 for a mountain cabin worth $75,000. B's vacant lot has a fair market value of $50,000 and is subject to a $15,000 mortgage. The mountain cabin B receives is subject to a mortgage of $40,000. B assumes the $40,000 mortgage on the mountain cabin and the other party to the exchange assumes the $15,000 mortgage on the vacant lot.

B's amount realized on this exchange is $50,000 ($75,000 fair market value of cabin received + $15,000 mortgage on vacant lot assumed by the other party − $40,000 mortgage on the mountain cabin assumed by B). If this exchange does not qualify for tax deferral, B has a realized and recognized gain of $30,000 ($50,000 amount realized − $20,000 adjusted basis of the vacant lot given up); and his basis in the mountain cabin is $75,000 (i.e., its fair market value).

Example 23

D, the other party to the exchange in *Example 22,* had an adjusted basis in her mountain cabin of $65,000. D's amount realized on the exchange is $75,000 ($50,000 fair value of vacant lot received + $40,000 mortgage assumed by B − $15,000 mortgage on the vacant lot). If the exchange does not qualify for tax deferral, D has a realized and recognized gain of $10,000 ($75,000 amount realized − $65,000 adjusted basis in the mountain cabin given up); and her basis in the vacant lot is $50,000 (i.e., its fair market value).

The amount realized on a sale or exchange of property is affected by liabilities even though neither the buyer nor the seller is personally obligated for payment.[35] The rationale for such treatment is that the owner benefits from the nonrecourse liabilities as owner of the property because his or her basis in the property, or some other property, is properly increased because of the liability.[36]

Concepts Related to Realization and Recognition

SALE OR OTHER DISPOSITION

Realization of gain or loss occurs upon any sale or other disposition of property. Whether such an event has occurred generally is not difficult to ascertain. A typical sale or exchange obviously constitutes a sale or other disposition, but other transactions in which the taxpayer

---

[33] Reg. § 1.1001-2(a)(1).

[34] *Crane v. Comm.,* 47-1 USTC ¶9217, 35 AFTR 776, 331 U.S. 1 (USSC, 1947). Such liabilities are not included if they are contingent or not subject to valuation. Rev. Rul. 78-29, 1978-1 C.B. 62.

[35] *Ibid.*

[36] See *Tufts v. Comm.,* 83-1 USTC ¶9328, 51 AFTR2d 1983-1132, 461 U.S. 300 (USSC, 1983) for an excellent discussion of nonrecourse liabilities and their impact on basis.

surrenders property other than cash also may be so classified. The timing of such realization is determined according to the taxpayer's method of accounting. Under the accrual method, realization generally occurs when a transaction is closed and the seller has an unqualified right to collect the sales price.[37] Under the cash method, the taxpayer realizes gain or loss upon the receipt of cash or cash equivalents.[38] In any case, a sale is consummated and realization occurs if beneficial title or possession of the burdens and benefits of ownership are transferred to the buyer.[39]

Transactions Involving Certain Securities

Generally, a sale or other disposition occurs any time a taxpayer surrenders property in exchange for some consideration. Accordingly, if a taxpayer exchanges securities of one type for securities of another type, a taxable event has occurred.[40]

Example 24

F exchanged X Corporation 12% bonds with a face value of $100,000 for Z Corporation 9% bonds with a face value of $120,000. Each group of bonds was worth $105,000 at the time of the exchange. If the X Corporation bonds that F exchanged had a basis of $100,000, he has a $5,000 gain on the exchange.

Several exceptions to this scheme do exist. In some instances, the exchange of *substantially identical* bonds of state or municipal governments has been declared a nontaxable transfer.[41] The condition of being substantially identical is usually determined in terms of rate of return and fair market value. If the bonds received do not meet this test, the exchange may be taxable.[42]

It is clearly established that converting bonds into stock under a conversion privilege contained in the bond instrument does not result in the recognition of gain.[43] Similarly, the conversion of stock into some other stock of the same corporation pursuant to a right granted under the stock certificate does not result in recognition of gain or loss.[44]

Transfer Related to Taxpayer's Debt

When property is transferred to a creditor, the transfer may or may not be a disposition. The mere granting of a lien against property to secure a loan is not a disposition.[45] The transfer of property in satisfaction of a liability, however, is a taxable disposition.[46] Similarly, the loss of property in a foreclosure sale[47] and the voluntary transfer of mortgaged property to creditors in satisfaction of debt[48] are dispositions of property.

Example 25

M purchased a commercial property for $20,000, paying $4,000 down and signing a note secured by a mortgage for the $16,000 difference. Three years later, when

---

[37] See *Alfred Scully,* 20 TCM 1272, T.C. Memo 1961-243 (1961), and Rev. Rul. 72-381, 1972-2 C.B. 581.

[38] See, for example, *Comm. v. Union Pacific R.R. Co.,* 36-2 USTC ¶9525, 18 AFTR 636, 86 F.2d 637 (CA-2, 1936).

[39] *Ibid.*

[40] Rev. Rul. 60-25, 1960-1 C.B. 283, and Rev. Rul. 78-408, 1978-2 C.B. 203.

[41] *Motor Products Corp. v. Comm.,* 44-1 USTC ¶9308, 32 AFTR 672, 142 F.2d 449 (CA-6, 1944), and Rev. Rul. 56-435, 1956-2 C.B. 506.

[42] See *Emery v. Comm.,* 48-1 USTC ¶9165, 36 AFTR 741, 166 F.2d 27 (CA-2, 1948), and Rev. Rul. 81-169, 1981-25

I.R.B. 17. Also, see *Mutual Loan and Savings Co. v. Comm.,* 50-2 USTC ¶9420, 39 AFTR 1034, 184 F.2d 161 (CA-5, 1950) for an example of nonrecognition where the state Supreme Court held the new bonds with a lower interest rate to be a mere continuation of the original issue.

[43] Rev. Rul. 57-535, 1957-2 C.B. 513.

[44] Ltr. Rul., 2-23-45, ¶76,130 P-H Fed. 1945.

[45] See *Dorothy Vickers,* 36 TCM 391, T.C. Memo 1977-90.

[46] *Carlisle Packing Co.,* 29 B.T.A. 514 (1933), and Rev. Rul. 76-111, 1976-1 C.B. 214 (1976).

[47] *O'Dell & Sons Co., Inc.,* 8 T.C. 1165 (1947).

[48] *Estate of Delman,* 73 T.C. 15 (1979).

M had reduced the balance on the note to $7,000, the lender accepted 300 shares of T Corporation stock in satisfaction of the obligation. The T Corporation stock had a fair market value of $7,000 and an adjusted basis to M of $5,000. By transferring the stock to satisfy the liability, there is a disposition of the stock and M has a $2,000 realized gain. Note that this result is the same as if M had sold the stock for $7,000 cash and paid the balance on the note.

Example 26

K purchased a warehouse for use in her business for $30,000, paying $5,000 down and signing a nonrecourse note (K is not personally liable) secured by a mortgage lien for the $25,000 difference. Over a three-year period, K's business suffered a decline and as a result she was able to make payments of only $3,000 on the note. During the same three-year period, K deducted depreciation of $12,000, thereby reducing her basis in the warehouse to $18,000.

After the three years, K reduced the size of her business substantially and voluntarily transferred the warehouse to the lender. Upon the transfer, K's amount realized from the discharge of the remaining indebtedness is $22,000 ($25,000 original note – $3,000 payments). Since her basis in the warehouse was $18,000, K has a $4,000 realized gain on the disposition of the property.

Abandonment

The abandonment of property used in a business or income-producing activity, whether depreciable or not, results in realization of loss to the extent of the property's adjusted basis. A loss deduction is allowed if the taxpayer takes action that demonstrates that he or she has no intention of retrieving the property for use, for sale, or other disposition in the future.[49]

Example 27

While working in a logging operation, R's truck became unoperational, and it was clear that the cost of having the truck moved to a repair site exceeded its value. R abandoned the truck with no intention of seeking its return. If R has a $2,500 adjusted basis in the truck, he is entitled to an abandonment loss deduction of $2,500.

Demolition

No deduction is allowed for expenses related to the demolition of a building or for a loss where the adjusted basis of the building exceeds any salvage value. Both the cost of the demolition and any disallowed loss are added to the basis of the land on which the building stood.[50]

Example 28

T purchased a rezoned commercial lot with a small house for $75,000. The structure was worth $2,000. In order to expedite construction of a new car wash, T simply razed the house at a cost of $1,500. No deduction is allowed for the loss of the house or the razing cost, and T's basis in the vacant lot is $76,500 ($73,000 lot + $2,000 house + $1,500 demolition costs).

---

[49] Reg. §§ 1.165-2 and 1.167(a)-8.   [50] § 280B.

Spousal Transfers

The transfer of property to one's spouse while married or upon dissolution of the marriage does not constitute a taxable event. This is true even if the transfer is in exchange for the release of marital rights under state law or for other consideration. This rule applies to *any* transfer made to one's spouse during the marriage or within *one year* after the marriage is terminated. It also applies to later transfers to a former spouse if the transfers are made incident to the divorce (e.g., under a provision of the divorce decree).[51] In a consistent manner, the basis of the transferred property for the transferee (recipient) is the same as the transferor's basis.[52]

Note that this nonrecognition provision applies to all transfers between spouses—including the sale of property at a fair market price. Also, the transferor is required to provide the transferee with records needed to determine the basis and holding period of the property.[53]

Example 29

H and W divorced this year. Under the terms of their agreement, H received stock with a basis of $16,000 and a value of $10,000. W received the house with a basis of $80,000, valued at $96,000 and subject to a mortgage of $60,000. No gain or loss is recognized by either party regardless of who owned the property before the transfer. H and W have bases in their separate properties of $16,000 and $80,000, respectively.

Example 30

Under an option provided in their divorce agreement, W (from the previous example) sold the house to H six months later (subject to the mortgage obligation) for $36,000. W still recognizes no gain and H's basis in the residence is $80,000.

Gift or Bequest

A transfer of property by gift or bequest generally does not constitute a sale or other disposition. Accordingly, there is no gain or loss recognized by the donor or decedent, respectively. An exception exists, however, in the case of a sale of property at a price below its fair market value. In such a *part-gift* and *part-sale,* the donor recognizes gain *only* to the extent the sales price exceeds the adjusted basis of the property transferred.[54]

Example 31

M sold her personal automobile to her brother for $4,000. She had a basis of $12,000 in the auto which was worth $6,000 on the date of sale. M has made a gift of $2,000 in this part-sale/part-gift transaction and she recognizes no gain or loss.

Example 32

Assume the same facts above, except that M's basis in the auto had been reduced to $3,000 from depreciation deductions allowed in prior years. Although M has still made a $2,000 gift in this transaction, she must now recognize a $1,000 gain on the sale ($4,000 amount realized − $3,000 adjusted basis).

---

[51] §§ 1041(a) and (c).

[52] § 1041(b)(2).

[53] Temp. Reg. § 1.1041-1T(e).

[54] Reg. § 1.1015-4(d).

If the donee/buyer pays some cash and assumes debt of the donor/seller, or takes the property subject to encumbrances, the amount of the liabilities must be included by the donor/seller in the amount realized from the transaction.[55] Even if no cash changes hands, the part-gift and part-sale rules apply if there are liabilities associated with the transfer. Accordingly, if the donee assumes liabilities that exceed the donor's basis in the transferred property, the donor has taxable gain to the extent the liabilities exceed such basis.[56] Also, the donee/purchaser will take as his or her basis in the property acquired the *greater* of the basis under the gift rules or the purchase (cost) basis.

Example 33

F gave a duplex rental unit to her grandson for his 18th birthday so he could develop property management skills. The duplex had a basis to F of $22,000 and a fair market value on the date of the gift of $40,000. The property was subject to a mortgage of $25,000, for which the grandson is now responsible. F has an amount realized on the gift transaction of $25,000 (transfer of the mortgage). Since the adjusted basis of the duplex was $22,000, F has a $3,000 taxable gain. If no gift taxes were paid, the grandson's basis in the duplex will be $25,000, the greater of the basis under the gift rules ($22,000) or the purchase (cost) basis.

Example 34

If the property in the previous example had been subject to a mortgage of only $8,000, the general rule would have applied, and F would not have recognized gain or loss. The exception only applies when the discharged liabilities exceed the adjusted basis of the gifted property. Note also that the grandson's basis in the duplex would be $22,000, the same basis F had in the property.

Transfer of Property to Charities

The transfer of property to a charity generally is not treated as a sale or other disposition. Accordingly, no gain or loss is realized or recognized. However, an exception is provided for *bargain sales* of property to charities that result in a charitable contribution deduction to the seller. In such a case, the adjusted basis of the transferred property must be allocated between the sale portion and the contribution portion based on the fair market value of the property—and any resulting gain must be recognized.[57]

Example 35

P sold land to her church for $30,000. P had an adjusted basis in the land of $25,000. The land was appraised at $50,000 at the time of the bargain sale. P is entitled to a charitable contribution deduction of $20,000 ($50,000 fair market value − $30,000 sale price). She also has taxable gain of $15,000 on the sale ($30,000 amount realized − the $15,000 pro rata share of the adjusted basis allocable to the sale portion ([$30,000 sale price ÷ $50,000 fair market value] × $25,000 basis).

---

[55] *Reginald Fincke*, 39 B.T.A. 510 (1939).

[56] *Levine Est. v. Comm.*, 80-2 USTC ¶9607, 46 AFTR2d, 80-5349, 634 F.2d 12 (CA-2, 1980).

[57] § 1011(b); Reg. § 1.1011-2(a).

A charitable contribution of encumbered property is also treated as a bargain sale. The amount realized includes the amount of cash and the fair market value of any other property received plus the amount of the liabilities transferred. Accordingly, the property's adjusted basis must be allocated between the sale portion (represented by the amount realized) and the contribution portion.[58] This is true even if no cash or other property is received by the taxpayer.[59]

Example 36

E made a gift of land to his alma mater. The land had a fair market value of $50,000 and was subject to a $22,000 mortgage which was assumed by the university. If the land is a long-term capital asset, E is entitled to a charitable contribution deduction of $28,000 ($50,000 fair market value reduced by the $22,000 mortgage).[60]

Additionally, E's $20,000 adjusted basis in the property must be allocated between the contribution of $28,000 and the amount realized of $22,000. The basis allocated to the sale portion is $8,800 ($20,000 basis × [$22,000 amount realized ÷ $50,000 fair market value]). The result of the bargain sale is a taxable gain to E of $13,200 ($22,000 amount realized − $8,800 allocated basis).

ALLOCATIONS OF PURCHASE PRICE AND BASIS

Properties purchased in a single transaction are often sold separately. In such a situation, the total basis must be allocated between the various items in order to determine gain or loss on the independent sales. Generally, relative fair market values at the time of acquisition are used to allocate the total basis among the various properties.[61] Similarly, allocation is necessary when a single sale involves properties acquired at different times in separate transactions. It may be necessary to allocate the sales price to individual assets; in such a situation, the relative fair market values on the date of sale are used for the allocation. Generally, an allocation in the sale agreement between buyer and seller will sufficiently establish the relative values unless it is shown that such assigned values were arbitrary or unreasonable.[62]

Example 37

T purchased a commercial lot in 2010 for $30,000 and built a warehouse on the site in 2011 at a cost of $60,000. During the six years he used the warehouse in his business, T deducted depreciation of $32,000. The property was sold this year for $110,000. T must allocate the $110,000 sale price between the building and the land to determine the gain or loss on each. If $40,000 is allocated to the land and $70,000 is allocated to the building based on relative fair market values, T has a gain of $10,000 ($40,000 − $30,000) and $42,000 ($70,000 − [$60,000 − $32,000]), respectively, on the properties.

Sale of a Business

When a business operated as a sole proprietorship is sold, the sale is treated as a sale of each of the individual assets of the business. Accordingly, allocations of sales price and basis must be made to the individual assets of the business.[63] The various gains and losses have separate impact, according to their character, on the taxable income of the owner.

---

[58] See Reg. § 1.1011-2(a).

[59] *Winston Guest,* 77 T.C. 9 (1981) and Rev. Rul. 81-163, 1981-1 C.B. 433.

[60] See Chapter 11 for a discussion of charitable contributions involving long-term capital gain property.

[61] See, for example, *Fairfeld Plaza, Inc.,* 39 T.C. 706 (1963), and Rev. Rul. 72-255, 1972-1 C.B. 221.

[62] See *John B. Resler;* 38 TCM 153, T.C. Memo 1979-40.

[63] See Rev. Rul. 55-79, 1955-1 C.B. 370, and *Williams v. McGowan,* 46-1 USTC ¶9120, 34 AFTR 615, 152 F.2d 570 (CA-2, 1945).

Example 38

F has owned and operated a dress shop for 12 years. F's increased interest in her grandchildren and in fishing prompted her to sell the shop and retire. The sales agreement with the buyer allocated the total sales price to the individual assets as follows:

	Value per Sales Agreement	F's Adjusted Basis
Inventory	$16,000	$18,000
Furniture and fixtures	14,000	6,000
Leasehold and leasehold improvements	20,000	3,000
Goodwill	0	0
Total	$50,000	$27,000

F has a $2,000 loss on the sale of inventory, and gains on the furniture and fixtures of $8,000 and on the leasehold and improvements of $17,000, each of which has its separate impact on taxable income.

The sale of an interest in a partnership or in a corporation that operates a business is generally treated as the sale of such interest, rather than of the underlying assets. Therefore, no allocation is necessary and gain or loss is recognized on the sale of the interest. For each type of entity, major exceptions to this treatment exist and are discussed in a later chapter.[64]

Installment Sale Method

The general rule of Federal taxation is that all gains or losses are recognized in the year of sale or exchange. This rule could place a severe burden on taxpayers who sell their property for something other than cash, particularly deferred payment obligations. Without some relief, taxpayers would be required to pay their tax liability before obtaining the sale proceeds with which they could pay the tax. If the tax is substantial, a requirement to pay before sufficient cash collections occur might necessitate the sale of other assets the taxpayer wished to retain.

Because of the potential hardship placed on taxpayers from reporting gain without the corresponding receipt of cash, Congress enacted the installment sale method of reporting in 1926. The installment method has been significantly modified over the years, with each modification further restricting *both* the types of gains and the taxpayers eligible for its use. The eligibility requirements are discussed below.

LO.7

Define an installment sale and identify taxpayers eligible to use the installment method of reporting gain.

GENERAL RULES

The installment method is used to report *gains*—not losses—from qualifying installment sales of property. An *installment sale* is defined as any sale of property whereby the seller will receive at least one payment after the close of the tax year in which the sale occurs. Unfortunately, not all gains from installment sales qualify for installment reporting.

Ineligible Sales

The installment method cannot be used for reporting gains from sales of the following:[65]

1. Property held for sale in the ordinary course of the taxpayer's trade or business (e.g., inventories).
2. Stocks or securities that are traded on an established securities market.

In addition, the portion of any gain from the sale of depreciable property that must be reported as ordinary income under the depreciation recapture rules is not eligible for installment reporting. These rules are discussed in Chapter 17.

---

[64] See Chapter 19 for an introduction to both corporate and partnership taxation.

[65] § 453(b), (i), and (l). See § 453(l)(2) for certain limited exceptions.

Mandatory Reporting Requirement

Generally, gains from eligible sales *must* be reported under the installment method regardless of the taxpayer's method of accounting.[66] Thus, the installment method is considered to be *mandatory* rather than elective. However, Congress recognized the fact that for some taxpayers the installment method of reporting would not be the relief measure that it was intended to be. Consequently, taxpayers are allowed to *elect out* of the installment method simply by reporting the entire gain in the year of sale.[67]

ELECTION OUT OF INSTALLMENT REPORTING

There are various reasons why a taxpayer might wish to elect not to use the installment method of reporting gain from the sale of property. Such reasons might include the following:

1. The taxpayer's income in the year of sale is quite low and income is expected to be higher in subsequent years.

2. The taxpayer might have a large capital loss with which to absorb the capital gain in the year of sale.

3. The taxpayer might have an expiring net operating loss.

4. It might be necessary for the taxpayer to report the gain in order to utilize a tax credit carryover.

5. The burden of complying with the installment sale rules might outweigh the advantage of the installment reporting of the gain.

If a taxpayer *elects not to use* the installment method for a given sale, the amount of gain must be computed under his or her usual method of accounting (i.e., cash or accrual) and reported in the year of sale.[68] A cash basis taxpayer must use the fair market value of any installment obligation received in determining the amount realized from the installment sale.[69] On the other hand, an accrual basis taxpayer must account for an installment obligation at its *face value* in computing the amount realized.[70]

Example 39

S, a cash basis taxpayer, sold land to B on May 15, 2017. S received $100,000 cash and a note from B payable in five equal annual installments of $80,000 (i.e., face value), bearing a 9% interest rate. The note has a value of $300,000 and S has a $75,000 basis in the land. If S elects not to use the installment method, his gain to be reported in 2017 is computed as follows:

Amount realized:	
Cash received	$100,000
FMV of installment obligations	300,000
	$400,000
Less: Basis of land	(75,000)
Gain to be reported in 2017	$325,000

In addition to the interest income that S will recognize when the installment payments are collected, he must recognize additional income on the collection of each installment payment as follows:

Amount realized (installment payment)	$ 80,000
Less: Basis in each installment ($300,000 FMV of note ÷ 5 installments)	(60,000)
Ordinary income to be reported	$ 20,000

---

[66] § 453(a).

[67] See § 453(d) and Temp. Reg. 15a.453-1(d)(2)(ii).

[68] *Ibid.*

[69] § 1001(b).

[70] Rev. Rul. 79-292. 1979-2 C.B. 287.

Example 40

Assume the same facts as in *Example 39,* except that S is an accrual basis taxpayer. His gain to be reported in the year of sale is computed as follows:

Amount realized:	
Cash received	$100,000
Face value of installment obligations	400,000
	$500,000
Less: Basis in land	(75,000)
Gain to be reported in 2017	$425,000

In this case, S will not be required to report any income other than the interest received as each of the payments are collected because his basis in each installment obligation is $100,000 (i.e., its face amount).

GAIN REPORTED UNDER THE INSTALLMENT METHOD

The following *six* factors must be taken into account by a taxpayer using the installment method of reporting gain:

1. The gross profit on the sale.
2. The total contract price.
3. The gross profit percentage.
4. The payments received in the year of sale.
5. The gain to be reported in the year of sale.
6. The gain to be reported in the following years.

LO.8

Compute the amount of gain required to be recognized in the year of installment sale and the gain to be reported in any subsequent year.

Determining Gross Profit

A taxpayer's gross profit is nothing more than the total gain that will be reported (excluding interest) from the installment sale. It is determined by subtracting the *sum* of the seller's adjusted basis and expenses of sale from the selling price:[71]

Selling price	$xxx,xxx
Less: Adjusted basis in property plus selling expenses	– xx,xxx
Gross profit on sale	$ xx,xxx

Determining the Total Contract Price

The total contract price is the total amount of cash (excluding interest) that the seller expects to collect from the buyer over the term of the installment sale. It is usually equal to the selling price less any liabilities of the seller that are transferred to the buyer. However, if the liabilities assumed by the buyer *exceed* the seller's adjusted basis in the property and the selling expenses, the excess must be treated as a *deemed payment* received in the year of sale. Because a deemed payment is treated as cash collected in the year of sale, it must be added to the contract price.[72]

---

[71] Temp. Reg. § 15a.453-1(b)(2)(v).

[72] § 453A(a)(2) and Temp. Reg. § 15a.453-1(b)(2)(ii).

Determining Gross Profit Percentage

The taxpayer's gross profit percentage is the percentage of each dollar received that must be reported as gain. It is equal to the gross profit divided by the total contract price.[73]

$$\frac{\text{Gross profit}}{\text{Total contract price}} = \text{Gross profit percentage}$$

Determining Payments Received in Year of Sale

Payments received in the year of sale include the following:[74]

1. Money received at the time of closing the sale, including any selling expenses *paid* by the buyer.

2. Deemed payments (i.e., excess of seller's liabilities transferred over the property's adjusted basis plus selling expenses).

3. The fair market value of any third-party obligations received at the time of closing and the fair market value of any other property received.

4. Installment payments received in the year of sale, excluding interest income.

Gain Reported in Year of Sale

Gain reported in the year of sale is computed as follows:

$$\frac{\text{Gross profit}}{\text{Total contract price}} \times \text{Payments received} = \text{Recognized gain}$$

Gain Reported in Following Years

Gain to be reported in the years following the year of sale equals the taxpayer's gross profit percentage multiplied by the principal payments received on the purchaser's note in that year.

Example 41

T sold a 70-acre tract of land that she had held as an investment on March 1, 2017. The facts concerning the sale are as follows:

Sales price:			
	Cash payment	$120,000	
	Mortgage assumed by buyer	200,000	
	Buyer's notes payable to T	480,000	$800,000
Less:	Selling expenses	$ 50,000	
	T's basis in land	250,000	(300,000)
Gross profit on sale			$500,000

The contract price is $600,000 ($800,000 sales price − $200,000 debt assumed by buyer). Assuming the $120,000 payment is the only payment received in 2017, T's gain to be reported for the year is computed as follows:

$$\frac{\$500,000 \text{ (gross profit)}}{\$600,000 \text{ (contract price)}} \times \$120,000 = \$100,000 \text{ gain to be recognized}$$

As T collects the remaining $480,000 of the total contract price, she will report the remaining $400,000 gross profit from the sale (i.e., $480,000 × 5/6 gross profit percentage = $400,000).

Example 42

Assume the same facts as in *Example 41*, except that T's basis in the land is only $100,000. In this case, the gross profit on the sale is $650,000 ($800,000 − [$50,000 + $100,000]). T's payments received in the year of sale are computed as follows:

Cash payment		$120,000
Plus: deemed payment received:		
Mortgage assumed by buyer	$200,000	
Less: Selling expense	(50,000)	
T's basis in land	(100,000)	50,000
Total payments received in 2017.		$170,000

The total contract price is $650,000 ($800,000 selling price − $200,000 mortgage transferred + $50,000 excess of mortgage assumed over T's basis in property and selling expenses). T's gain to be reported in 2017 is computed as follows:

$$\frac{\$650,000 \text{ (gross profit)}}{\$650,000 \text{ (contract price)}} \times \$170,000 \text{ payments} = \$170,000$$

Note that the excess of the mortgage transferred over T's basis in the land and the selling expenses (i.e., the deemed payment) causes the gross profit percentage to become 100 percent. This adjustment to *both* the total contract price and the payments received in the year of sale must be made to ensure that the entire gain from the sale is ultimately reported by the seller. As a result, all payments received by T in subsequent years (excluding interest) will be reported as gain from the sale ($650,000 total gross profit − $170,000 gain reported in year of sale = $480,000 gain to be reported in subsequent years [$480,000 buyer's notes × 100%]).

LIMITATIONS ON CERTAIN INSTALLMENT SALES

As mentioned earlier, the installment sales provisions have been modified over the years to limit or stop perceived taxpayer abuse of what was intended to be simply a relief from immediate taxation of all gain from deferred payment sales. These modifications have created the following problem areas:

1. Imputed interest rules.
2. Related-party rules.
3. Gain recognition on dispositions of installment note.
4. Required interest payments on deferred taxes.

Each of these problem areas is discussed below.

Imputed Interest Rules

Without some limitation, a taxpayer planning a deferred payment sale of a capital asset could require the buyer to pay a higher sales price in return for a lower than prevailing market rate of interest on the deferred payments, thereby converting into capital gain what would have been ordinary (interest) income. The imputed interest rules were designed to prevent just such a scheme. Under these rules, any deferred payment sale of property with a selling price exceeding $3,000 must provide a *reasonable* interest rate.[75] Thus, in a deferred payment sale

LO.9

Explain the limitations imposed on certain installment sales, including:

■ The imputed interest rules.

■ Related-party installment sales.

■ Gain recognition on the disposition of installment obligations.

■ Required interest payments on deferred Federal income taxes.

---

[75] See §§ 483 and 1274.

providing little or no interest, the selling price must be *restated* to equal the sum of payments received on the date of the sale and the discounted present value of the future payments. The difference between the face value of the future payments and this discounted value (i.e., the imputed interest) generally must be reported as interest income under the accrual method of accounting, regardless of the taxpayer's regular accounting method.[76]

  If the sales contract does not provide for interest equal to the *applicable Federal rate* (AFR), interest will be imputed at that rate.[77] The AFR is the interest rate the Federal government pays on borrowed funds, and the actual rate varies with the terms of the loan. Loans are divided into short-term (not over three years), mid-term (over three years but not over nine years), and long-term (over nine years).[78]

Example 43

S, a cash basis taxpayer, sold land held as an investment on July 1, 2017 for $1 million cash and a non-interest-bearing note (face value of $4 million) due on July 1, 2019. At the time of the sale, the short-term AFR was 10% (compounded semiannually). Because the sales contract did not provide for interest of at least the AFR, the selling price must be restated and interest must be imputed at 10% (compounded semiannually).

Sale price:

Cash payment.	$1,000,000
Present value of $4,000,000 note due July 1, 2019 (0.8227 × $4,000,000)	3,290,800
Recomputed sale price	$4,290,800

S must use this recomputed sale price in determining the total contract price, gross profit percentage, gain to be reported in the year of sale, and gain to be reported (excluding interest) when the $4 million deferred payment is received. In addition, S must report $164,540 of imputed interest income in 2017, computed as follows:

Period	Present Value	×	10% Compounded Semiannually	=	Imputed Interest
7/1/2017 to 12/31/2017	$3,290,800	×	0.05	=	$164,540

S must also compute and report her imputed interest for 2018 and 2019. When the $4 million note payable is collected on July 1, 2019, S will report only the gain on the sale remaining after that portion reported in 2017.

Related-Party Sales

Generally, installment sales between related parties are subject to the same rules as other such sales *except* (1) when the related-party purchaser resells the property before payment of the original sales price;[79] and (2) when the property sold is depreciable property.[80] The primary purpose of the *resale* rule is to prevent a related-party seller from deferring his or her gain on the first sale while the related-party purchaser enjoys the use of proceeds from its resale.

---

[76] See §§ 1272(a), 1273(a), and 1274(a). Also see §§ 483 and 1274(c) for various exceptions to this requirement.

[77] § 1274(d)(1).

[78] These three Federal rates are published monthly by the IRS.

[79] § 453(e).

[80] § 453(g).

Example 44

M plans to sell a capital asset (basis $40,000) to B, an unrelated party, for $200,000. Instead of selling the asset to B, she sells it to her son, S, for $10,000 cash and a $190,000 note due in five years and bearing a reasonable interest rate. Shortly after his purchase, S sells the asset to B for $200,000.

Without the resale rule, M would report a gain of $8,000 in the year of sale, computed as follows:

$$\frac{\$200,000 - \$40,000}{\$200,000} \times \$10,000 = \$8,000$$

M would have a deferred gain of $152,000 ($160,000 gross profit − $8,000 gain reported in year of sale). More importantly, S would have a cost basis of $200,000 in the asset and report no gain on the subsequent resale to B. The net result of the two transactions is a $152,000 deferred gain and the immediate use of the sales proceeds by a family member.

Under the resale rule, any proceeds collected by the related-party purchaser on the subsequent sale are treated as being collected by the related-party seller. Consequently, M must report her $152,000 deferred gain when S resells the property, even though she has not yet collected the $190,000 note.

For purposes of the resale rule, the term related party includes the spouse, children, grandchildren, and parents of the seller.[81] Any controlled corporation, partnership, trust, or estate in which the seller has an interest is also considered related under these rules.[82] It is also important to note that the resale rule does not apply when the second sale occurs (1) more than two years after the first sale, or (2) after the death of the related-party seller.[83]

The installment method is generally not allowed to be used to report a gain on the sale of depreciable property to an entity controlled by the taxpayer.[84] This rule is designed to prevent a related-party seller from deferring gain on a sale that will result in the purchaser's being able to use a higher (cost) basis to claim depreciation deductions. For this purpose, a *controlled entity* is a partnership or corporation in which the seller owns a more than 50% direct or indirect interest. Indirect ownership includes any interest owned by the seller's spouse and certain other family members.[85] It is important to note that this rule is based on a presumption that the related-party installment sale is motivated by tax avoidance. Thus, the related-party seller can use the installment method of reporting the sale if he or she can establish that tax avoidance *was not* the principal motive of the transaction. This makes such a sale subject to a facts and circumstances review and approval of the Internal Revenue Service.

Dispositions of Installment Obligations

After deciding to report a deferred payment sale under the installment method, rather than *electing out,* sellers ordinarily collect the payments in due course and report the remaining gain in full. However, if this process is interrupted by a sale, gift, or other transfer of some or all of the installment obligations, rules require that any unreported gain be reported at the time of the transfer. Consequently, if an installment obligation is satisfied at other than its face value or is distributed, transmitted, sold, or otherwise disposed of, the taxpayer is generally required to recognize gain or loss.

The amount of gain or loss is the difference between the obligation's basis and *either* the amount realized, if the obligation is satisfied at an amount other than its face value because it is sold or exchanged, *or* its fair market value when distributed, transmitted, or disposed of, if the transfer is not a sale or exchange.[86] The obligation's basis is its face amount less the amount of gain that would have been reported if the obligation had been satisfied in full.[87]

---

[81] §§ 453(f) and 267(b).

[82] §§ 453(f) and 318(a).

[83] § 453(e)(2).

[84] *Supra,* Footnote 80.

[85] §§ 1239(b) and (c).

[86] § 453B(a).

[87] § 453B(b).

Taxable dispositions include most sales and exchanges. Also included are gifts, transfers to trusts, distributions by trusts and estates to beneficiaries, distributions from corporations to shareholders, net proceeds from the pledge of an installment obligation, and cancellation of the installment obligation.

The obvious purpose of the disposition rules is to prevent the seller from *either* shifting the income to another taxpayer (e.g., by gift) *or* enjoying the use of the sales proceeds prior to gain recognition (e.g., by pledging an installment obligation for borrowed funds). However, there are several exceptions to the requirement of immediate gain recognition. Transfers of installment obligations upon the death of the seller, transfers incident to divorce, transfers to or distributions from a partnership, certain transfers to controlled corporations, and certain transfers incident to corporate reorganization are among the exceptions to these rules.[88]

Required Interest Payments on Deferred Taxes

Another rule designed to reduce the benefits of installment reporting for certain taxpayers is the requirement to pay interest to the government on the deferred taxes. This rule applies if *two conditions* are met. First, the taxpayer must have outstanding installment obligations from the sale of property (other than farming property) for more than $150,000. Second, the outstanding obligations from such sales must exceed $5 million at the close of the tax year.[89] Only the deferred taxes attributable to the installment obligations in *excess* of $5 million are subject to this annual interest payment. The interest must be calculated using the tax underpayment rate in § 6621.

Example 45

T has $9 million of installment obligations outstanding on December 31, 2017. These obligations arose from the sale of a vacant lot located in the downtown area of Chicago. T's gross profit percentage on the installment sale was 40 percent. Assuming the underpayment rate in § 6621 is 10% and T's 2017 marginal tax rate is 35 percent, the required interest payment on the deferred taxes is computed as follows:

Outstanding installment obligations	$9,000,000
Less: Amount not subject to rule	(5,000,000)
Excess installment obligations	$4,000,000
Times: Gross profit percentage	× 40%
Deferred gross profit	$1,600,000
Times: T's marginal tax rate	× 35%
Deferred Federal income taxes	$ 560,000
Times: § 6621 underpayment rate	× 10%
Required interest payment	$ 56,000

Because taxpayers are allowed to have up to $5 million of installment obligations outstanding without being subject to the required interest payment rule, it is apparent that only those taxpayers with one or more substantial installment sales need be concerned with this rule.

REPORTING GAIN ON INSTALLMENT SALES

Taxpayers reporting gain on the installment sale method should attach Form 6252, Computation of Installment Sale Income, to the tax return for the year of sale and each subsequent year in which a payment is collected. A sample of this form is contained in Appendix B.

---

[88] See § 453B(c), (d), and (g).   [89] § 453A.

Various limitations exist regarding gain and loss recognition in certain property transactions. Several such limitations have already been discussed. Recall that any losses on the sale of personal use assets are disallowed. Similarly, losses on the sale of property acquired by gift are limited to the decline in its value subsequent to the transfer by gift. This results because the basis for determining loss is the fair market value on the date of gift, if that fair market value is less than the donor's basis (which would otherwise be the donee's basis).[90] Likewise, a loss on the disposition of property that has been converted from personal use to business use is limited to the decline in its value subsequent to the conversion. In determining any loss on such a disposition, the adjusted basis is the lesser of the taxpayer's adjusted basis or the fair market value on the date of conversion.[91]

There are several other limitations on the deductibility of losses arising from sales or other dispositions of property. As discussed in Chapter 7, losses incurred in sales between related taxpayers are not deductible. Also, certain losses incurred from the sale of stock or securities will not be allowed as a deduction.

LO.10
Identify various transactions in which loss recognition is prohibited.

Wash Sales

A *wash sale* occurs when a taxpayer sells stock or securities at a loss and reinvests in substantially identical stock or securities within 30 days before or after the date of sale. Any loss realized on such a wash sale is not deductible.[92] In essence, a taxpayer who has a wash sale has not had a *change* in economic position—thus the transaction resulting in a loss is ignored for tax purposes. The loss is, however, taken into consideration in determining the adjusted basis in the new shares.[93]

Example 46

C, a calendar year taxpayer, owns 400 shares of X Corporation stock (adjusted basis of $9,000), all of which he sells for $5,000 on December 28, 2017. On January 7, 2018, C purchases another 400 shares of X Corporation stock for $5,500. C's realized loss of $4,000 in 2017 will not be deductible because it resulted from a wash sale. Instead, his basis in the 400 shares purchased in 2018 is increased to $9,500 ($5,500 purchase price + $4,000 disallowed loss).

The *numbers* of shares purchased and sold are not always the same. When the number of shares reacquired is less than the number sold, the deduction for losses is disallowed only for the number of shares purchased.[94]

Example 47

Assume the same facts as in *Example 46*, except that C purchased only 300 shares of X Corporation stock for $4,125. Because C replaced only 300 of the shares previously sold at a loss, only 75% (300 ÷ 400) of the $4,000 realized loss is disallowed. Consequently, C will report a $1,000 loss ($4,000 × 25%) in 2017 and will have a basis of $7,125 ($4,125 purchase price + $3,000 disallowed loss) in the 300 shares purchased.

When the number of shares repurchased is greater than the number of shares sold, none of the loss is deductible and the basis in a number of shares equivalent to the number of shares sold is affected by the disallowed loss.[95]

---

[90] § 1015(a).
[91] Reg. § 1.165-9(b).
[92] § 1091(a).
[93] § 1091(d).
[94] Reg. § 1.1091-1(c).
[95] Reg. § 1.1091-1(d).

Any loss also will be disallowed if the "substantially equivalent" stock or securities are acquired by certain related parties. For example, the U.S. Supreme Court held that the wash sale provisions apply if replacement stock is acquired by a taxpayer's spouse *and* they file a joint return for the tax year of the loss.[96]

SALES BETWEEN RELATED PARTIES

The Code places numerous limitations on gain or loss recognition from transactions between certain related parties. The purpose of such restrictions is to prevent related taxpayers from entering into various property transactions solely for the tax reduction possibilities. For example, a father could sell land to his daughter at a loss, deduct the loss, and the property would still remain within the family unit. Similarly, a taxpayer could sell depreciable property to her spouse and report a long-term capital gain on their joint return. For many years thereafter, she and her husband could claim ordinary deductions for depreciation on this higher basis. To control such potentially abusive situations, Congress enacted Code §§ 267 and 1239.

Section 267 disallows deductions for any losses that result from the sale or exchange of property between related parties.[97] Such losses may, however, be used by the related purchaser to offset any gain realized from a subsequent disposition of the property.[98] For purposes of § 267, related parties include the following:[99]

1. Members of an individual's family—specifically, brothers and sisters (including by half blood), spouses, ancestors (i.e., parents and grandparents), and lineal descendants (i.e., children and grandchildren).

2. A corporation owned more than 50% in value by the taxpayer (directly or indirectly).

3. Two corporations owned more than 50% in value by the taxpayer (directly or indirectly) if either corporation is a personal holding company or a foreign personal holding company in the tax year of the transaction.

4. Various partnership, S corporation, grantor, fiduciary, and trust relationships with regular corporations and individual taxpayers.

Example 48

M sells stock (adjusted basis of $10,000) to her daughter, D, for its fair market value of $8,000. D sells the stock two years later for $11,000. M's $2,000 loss is disallowed as a deduction. However, D's realized gain of $3,000 ($11,000 sales price − $8,000 cost basis) is reduced by the $2,000 previously disallowed loss, and she will report only $1,000 of gain.

Note the similarity between the results in *Example 48* and the situation that would result if D had received the stock as a gift from M. First, D's basis for gain would be $10,000 (M's basis) if the stock had been received as a gift; its subsequent sale for $11,000 would have resulted in the same $1,000 recognized (reported) gain. Although the disallowance of a loss deduction might discourage many related-party transactions, some taxpayers prefer to sell rather than give property to a related party in order to avoid paying state or Federal gift taxes.

Section 1239 provides that any gain realized from the sale of depreciable property between specified related parties will be taxed as ordinary income.[100] In effect, this statute precludes the possibility that any gain on the sale might be taxed as a long-term capital gain since the sale results in a higher basis in the depreciable property to a related party. Furthermore, recall that such related-party sales of depreciable property are not eligible for installment sale treatment.[101] Transactions subject to § 1239 treatment are discussed in Chapter 19.

---

[96] *Helvering v. Taft,* 40-2 USTC ¶9888, 24 AFTR 1976, 311 U.S. 195 (USSC, 1940).

[97] § 267(a)(1).

[98] § 267(d).

[99] See §§ 267(b) and (c).

[100] § 1239(a).

[101] § 453(g).

GIFT VERSUS BEQUEST

In devising a plan for transferring wealth from one family member to another, several considerations related to the income tax, the transfer taxes, and the wishes of the parties involved must be evaluated. If there is a desire to transfer properties, there are relative advantages and disadvantages to lifetime transfers as opposed to testamentary transfers (transfers by will). Some of the specific factors that should be considered are as follows:

1. The income tax rate of each individual (decedent and heirs) relative to the estate and gift tax rates.

2. Whether the property is highly appreciated. If so, a testamentary transfer may be preferred since the property's basis to the heirs or the estate will be its fair market value at date of death or alternate valuation date. If the property is gifted, its basis will be the donor's basis increased by a fraction of any gift taxes paid. If the property has declined in value, only the *original owner* (donor) can benefit from any tax loss by disposing of the property to an unrelated party, due to the basis for determination of loss under § 1015(a).

3. Whether the property is expected to appreciate rapidly in the foreseeable future. If so, a current gift might be considered because the amount subject to gift taxes would be the current market value. If the property were held until death, the higher fair market value at that time would be used in calculating estate taxes. This action is, of course, speculative in nature.

4. Whether the transferee is likely to hold the property for a long period of time. If so, the basis considerations are not as important as they would be if the property were to be sold immediately upon its receipt.

5. Whether the property is income-producing property. If the property produces income, and the owner (donor) is in a high income tax bracket, a lifetime transfer could result in the profits being taxed at a lower tax rate to another family member. If the donee is in a significantly lower income tax bracket, substantial income tax savings can be accomplished.

These factors, as well as the health of the parties involved and other personal considerations, must all be considered. It is possible that the personal factors will outweigh the tax factors, or that significant amounts of taxes cannot be saved.

CHARITABLE TRANSFERS INVOLVING PROPERTY OTHER THAN CASH

Taxpayers who are considering making major charitable transfers and who have property other than cash that they would consider transferring must consider both the effects of any gain or loss if property is sold and the effects of any allowable charitable deduction. If a property has declined in value, its owner may benefit from selling the property and deducting the loss and later contributing the cash proceeds to the charity.

Planning can be even more important when the property is appreciated, since in certain instances a charitable deduction is allowed equal to the fair market value of the property. This is true when the property is long-term capital gain property that is used in the exempt function of the charity, is intangible, or is real estate (see Chapter 11). In such a case, the taxpayer will avoid paying tax on the property's unrealized appreciation and still receive full benefit from the charitable deduction.

CHANGES IN THE USE OF PROPERTY

A taxpayer who converts business property to personal use when its value is less than its adjusted basis should consider selling the asset in order to trigger a deduction for the loss. Also, a taxpayer who buys property that he or she intends to use in a business should think carefully before using the asset for personal purposes. For example, a taxpayer who purchases a new auto and drives it for personal purposes for two years before converting it to business use must use the fair value upon conversion—if less than adjusted basis—in determining both depreciation and any loss on disposition.

SALES TO RELATED PARTIES

Care must be exercised to avoid the undesirable effects of transactions between related parties. If a loss on the sale of property to a related party is disallowed, the tax benefit of a loss deduction is permanently lost unless the value of the property subsequently increases. The only way to generate a tax deduction for the loss is for the original owner to sell the property to an unrelated party. Also, characterizing gain on the sale of depreciable property as ordinary income under § 1239 should normally be avoided.

USE OF INSTALLMENT SALES

Installment sale treatment provides an excellent opportunity for deferring the tax on gain (other than depreciation recapture) when a taxpayer is willing to accept an installment obligation in exchange for property. Actually, installment reporting may provide such attractive tax deferral and tax savings possibilities that the taxpayer is induced to accept an installment obligation, even though he or she would not do so otherwise. In short, this is a tax variable that must be considered by a prudent taxpayer in planning sales of property.

A taxpayer may benefit in at least two ways from the installment method. First, benefits accrue from the deferral of the tax. The time value of money works to the taxpayer's benefit, assuming the sales contract provides for a fair rate of interest. The second benefit from installment reporting is the spreading of the gain over more than one tax year. If the gain on a sale is unusual and moves the taxpayer into a higher tax bracket, spreading the gain over several years tends to allow the overall gain to be taxed in lower tax brackets.

It is important to remember, however, that taxpayers may face several limitations on certain installment sales. First, if a reasonable interest rate is not provided in the deferred payment sale, the seller will be required to impute interest at the appropriate Federal rate. Second, a taxpayer unaware of the rules relating to related-party sales may find that he or she is required to report all the gain on such a sale long before the actual collection of cash from the installment obligations. Third, taxpayers with installment obligations must be informed of the rules requiring immediate gain recognition on certain dispositions of such obligations. These rules include treating borrowed funds as collections on the installment notes if such notes are used as collateral for a loan. Finally, taxpayers with significant amounts of installment obligations outstanding at the end of a particular tax year (i.e., in excess of $5 million) may find that the required interest payment on the deferred income taxes is greater than the interest currently being collected.

Problem Materials

DISCUSSION QUESTIONS

14-1 *Realization versus Recognition.* In a few sentences, distinguish realization from recognition.

14-2 *Return-of-Capital Principle.* What is the return-of-capital principle?

14-3 *Computing Amount Realized.* Reproduce the formula for computing the amount realized in a sale or exchange.

14-4 *Impact of Liabilities.* What impact do liabilities assumed by the buyer or liabilities encumbering property transferred have on the amount realized? How are they treated if both parties to the transaction incur new liabilities?

14-5 *Cost Basis.* How does one determine cost basis for property acquired? How is this basis affected if property other than money is transferred in exchange for the new property?

14-6 *Gift Basis.* Reproduce the formula for the general rule for determining basis of property acquired by gift.

14-7 *Gift Basis Exception.* When does the general rule for determining basis of property acquired by gift *(Question 14-6)* not apply?

14-8 *Basis of Inherited Property.* The basis of property acquired from a decedent is generally fair market value at date of death. What are the two exceptions to this rule (do not include property subject to special-use valuation)?

14-9 *Basis Adjustments.* List the three broad categories of adjustments to basis.

14-10 *Transfers Pursuant to Divorce.* In general, do transfers of property in a divorce action result in the realization of gain or loss? Under what circumstances might gain recognition be required?

14-11 *Part-Sale/Part-Gift.* When does a bargain sale to a donee (part-gift) result in gain to the donor? Does the assumption of the donor's liabilities by the donee have any impact? Explain.

14-12 *Bargain Sales.* How is a bargain sale of property to a charitable organization treated for tax purposes?

14-13 *Allocating Sales Price.* Allocations are generally necessary when a sole proprietorship is sold as a unit. What method is normally used for such allocation? What impact does the sales agreement have if it allocates the price to the individual assets?

14-14 *Installment Sales Method—General Rules.* What is the purpose of the installment sale method of reporting gains? Is it an elective provision? How does one elect out of the installment sale method? What sales do not qualify for installment sale treatment?

14-15 *Installment Sales Method—Key Terms.* Explain how each of the following factors related to an installment sale is determined.
    a. Gross profit on deferred payment sale
    b. Total contract price
    c. Gross profit percentage
    d. Payments received in the year of sale
    e. Gain to be reported in the year of sale

14-16 *Imputed Interest Rules.* Under what circumstances must a taxpayer impute interest income from an installment sale? How is the applicable Federal rate (AFR) determined?

14-17 *Related-Party Installment Sales.* Under what circumstances will a taxpayer be faced with the related-party installment sale rules? Explain how a resale of the property by the related party purchaser before the seller has collected the balance of the installment obligation affects the seller.

14-18 *Dispositions of Installment Obligations.* Your neighbor has $30,000 of installment obligations from a recent sale of land held for investment. He asks you for advice concerning his planned gift of these obligations to his children to be used for their future college expenses. An examination of Form 6252 attached to his most recent tax return reveals a gross profit percentage of 60% and a reasonable market rate of interest related to these installment obligations. What tax advice would you give regarding this plan?

14-19 *Wash Sale.* What is a wash sale? How is a wash sale treated for tax purposes?

14-20 *Timing of Recognition.* Under what circumstances is a realized gain actually recognized? What event generally controls the timing of gain recognition?

PROBLEMS

14-21 *Sale Involving Liabilities.* C sold a cottage in which his basis was $32,000, for cash of $12,000 and a note from the buyer worth $28,000. The buyer assumed an existing note of $30,000 secured by an interest in the property.
    a. What is C's amount realized in this sale?
    b. What is C's gain or loss realized on this sale?

14-22 *Exchange Involving Liabilities.* D exchanged a mountain cabin for a leisure yacht and $30,000 cash. The yacht was worth $25,000 and was subject to liabilities of $10,000, which were assumed by D. The cabin was subject to liabilities of $32,000, which were assumed by the other party.

a. How much is D's amount realized?

b. Assuming D's basis in the cabin was $42,000, what is his gain or loss realized?

14-23 *Identification of Stock Sold.* T purchased the following lots of stock in Z Corporation:

50 shares	1/12/2008	Cost $1,200
100 shares	2/28/2013	Cost $3,000
75 shares	10/16/2014	Cost $2,500

T sold 75 shares on January 16, 2017 for $2,800. His only instruction to his broker, who actually held the shares for T, was to sell 75 shares.

a. How much gain or loss does T recognize on this sale?

b. How could this result be altered?

14-24 *Sale of Property Acquired by Gift.* J received 1,000 shares of Exxon stock as a gift from her grandmother in 2013, when the stock was worth $50,000. The stock had a basis to the grandmother of $10,000, and gift taxes of $16,000 were paid on the $40,000 taxable value of the gift.

a. How much gain does J recognize when she sells the stock for $80,000 (net of commissions) during the current year?

b. What would be your answer if the sale price were $35,000 (net of commissions)?

c. What would be your answer if the sale price were $19,000 (net of commissions)?

14-25 *Sale of Property Acquired by Gift.* In 2014, F gave his son, S, 100 shares of IBM stock, which at that time were worth $30,000. F paid a gift tax on the transfer of $5,000. Assuming F had purchased the stock in 2010 for $40,000, what are the tax consequences to S if he sells the stock for the following amounts?

a. $25,000

b. $37,000

c. $45,000

14-26 *Sale of Inherited Property.* D inherited two acres of commercial real estate from her grandmother, who had a basis in the property of $52,000, when it had a fair market value of $75,000. For estate tax purposes, the estate was valued as of the date of death, and estate and inheritance taxes of $8,250 were paid by the estate on this parcel of real estate.

a. How much gain or loss will be realized by D if she sells the property for $77,000?

b. What would be your answer if the sale price were $66,000?

14-27 *Basis of Inherited Property.* H inherited a parcel of real estate from his father. The property was valued for estate tax purposes at $120,000, and the father's basis was $45,000 immediately before his death. H had given the property to his father as a gift six weeks before his death. The proper portion of the gift taxes paid by H are included in his father's basis.

a. What is H's basis in the real estate?

b. What would be your answer if H had given the property to his father two years before his father's death?

14-28 *Basis of Converted Property.* K converted his 2011 sedan from personal use to business use as a delivery vehicle in his pizza business. The auto had an adjusted basis to K of $4,200 and a fair market value on the date of the conversion of $2,400. K properly deducted depreciation on the auto of $900 over two years before the auto was sold.

a. How much is K's gain or loss if he sells the auto for $800?

b. What would be your answer if the auto were sold for $3,500?

14-29 *Part-Sale/Part-Gift.* G sold a personal computer to his son for $2,000. The computer was worth $3,000, and G had a basis in the unit of $2,200. G has made a gift of $1,000 in this part-sale/part-gift.

a. How much gain, if any, must G recognize on this sale?

b. Would your answer differ if G's basis had been $1,700?

14-30 *Bargain Sale to Charity.* F sold a parcel of land to the city to be used as a location for a new art museum. The land had a market value of $70,000 and was sold for $40,000. F's adjusted basis in the property was $35,000. How much is F's charitable contribution deduction on this transfer? How much gain does F recognize on this sale?

14-31 *Installment Sale.* On July 1, 2017, G sold her summer cottage (basis $70,000) for $105,000. The sale contract provided for a payment of $30,000 at the time of sale and payment of the $75,000 balance in three equal installments due in July 2018, 2019, and 2020. Assuming a reasonable interest rate is charged on this deferred payment sale, compute each of the following:
a. Gross profit on the sale
b. Total contract price
c. Gross profit percentage
d. Gain to be reported (excluding interest) in 2017
e. Gain to be reported (excluding interest) in 2018
f. Gain to be reported in 2017 if G elects not to use the installment method

14-32 *Imputed Interest on Installment Sale.* On January 1, 2017, S sold a 100-acre tract of land for $200,000 cash and an $800,000 non-interest-bearing note due on January 1, 2020. On the date of sale, the land had a basis of $400,000. Assuming the applicable Federal rate is ten percent compounded semiannually, calculate the following:
a. Gain, excluding interest, to be reported in 2017
b. The imputed interest to be reported by S for 2017
c. Gain, excluding interest, to be reported in 2020

14-33 *Wash Sale.* R purchased 500 shares of Y Corporation common stock for $12,500 on August 31, 2016. She sold 200 shares of this stock for $3,000 on December 21, 2017. On January 7, 2018, R purchased an additional 100 shares of Y Corporation common stock for $1,600.
a. What is R's realized loss for 2017?
b. How much of the loss realized can R report in 2017?
c. What is R's adjusted basis in the 100 shares purchased on January 7, 2018?

14-34 *Related-Party Sale.* J sold 2,000 shares of T Corporation stock, in which he had an adjusted basis of $3,000, to his brother, F, for $1,200.
a. How much of the realized loss is recognized (reported) by J?
b. How much gain or loss to F if he subsequently sells the stock for $1,000? For $2,000?

14-35 *Property Settlements.* H was divorced from W this year. H was required to transfer stock, which was his separate property, to W in satisfaction of his obligation for spousal support. The stock was worth $57,000 and had an adjusted basis to H of $29,000.
a. How much gain, if any, does H recognize on the transfer?
b. How much gain or loss does W recognize? What is her basis in the property received?

14-36 *Property Tax Allocation.* J purchased a rental property during the current year for $45,000 cash. He was required to pay all of the property taxes for the year of sale, and under the law of the state $47 is allocable to the period before J purchased the property (see Chapter 11).
a. How much is J's property tax deduction if the total payment made during the tax year of acquisition is $700?
b. What is J's adjusted basis in the property?

14-37 *Sales of Inherited Properties.* Each of the following involves property acquired from a decedent. None of the properties include income in respect of a decedent. Determine the gain or loss for each.

Case	Decedent's Basis	Death Taxes Paid	Fair Market Value(*)	Sales Price
A	$3,000	$600	$4,000	$6,000
B	6,000	600	4,000	5,000
C	6,000	400	4,000	3,000

*Date of decedent's death.

14-38 *Nontaxable Dividends.* M owned 300 shares of X Corporation common stock, in which her basis was $6,000 on January 1, 2017. With respect to her stock, during 2017 M collected dividends of $600 and tax-free distributions of $400. What is M's basis in the stock as of December 31, 2017?

TAX RESEARCH PROBLEMS

14-39 *Gain Realized from Transferred Debt.* H owns a small office building and commercial complex, which he purchased for $175,000 in 2011. H invested $20,000 and signed a nonrecourse note secured by an interest in the property for the difference. The note provided for 9% interest, compounded annually and payable quarterly. After six years, H decided his property was not as good an investment as he had originally thought. He found a buyer who offered him $1,000 cash for the property, subject to the existing liabilities. H eventually accepted the offer and sold the property. During the six years he owned the property, H made timely interest payments and no payments of principal. He was allowed depreciation deductions of $34,000, using the straight-line method of depreciation and a 39-year recovery period.

Required:
1. How much is H's gain or loss realized on this sale?
2. Would your answer differ if H's building was only worth $150,000 and instead of selling the building he had voluntarily transferred it to the obligee on the note?

Partial list of research aids:

> Reg. § 1.1001-2.
>
> *Crane v. Comm.*, 47-1 USTC ¶9217, 35 AFTR 776, 331 U.S. 1 (USSC, 1947).
>
> *Tufts v. Comm.*, 83-1 USTC ¶9328, 51 AFTR2d 1983-1132, 461 U.S. 300 (USSC, 1983).
>
> *Millar v. Comm.*, 78-2 USTC ¶9514, 42 AFTR2d 78-4276, 577 F.2d 212 (CA-3, 1978).

14-40 *Bargain Sale to Charity.* K sold a mountain cabin for $55,000 to State University (her alma mater) for use in an annual fund-raising auction. The cabin was worth $85,000. K had purchased the cabin five years earlier as an investment for $40,000, and no depreciation has been allowed.

Required:
1. What is K's charitable contribution deduction and her gain or loss realized on this bargain sale?
2. Would your answers differ if the property were a painting instead of a mountain cabin?

Research aids:

> Section 170(e)(1).
>
> Section 1011(b).
>
> Reg. §§ 1.170A-4(a)(2) and (c)(2).
>
> Reg. § 1.1011-2.

15

Nonrecognition Transactions

Learning Objectives

Upon completion of this chapter you will be able to:

LO.1 Understand the rationale for deferral of gains and losses on certain property transactions.

LO.2 Explain how gain or loss deferral is accomplished through basis adjustments.

LO.3 Explain the tax consequences of a like-kind exchange of business or investment property.

LO.4 Describe how the nonrecognition rules apply to involuntary conversions of property.

LO.5 Apply the nonrecognition rules to the sale of a principal residence.

LO.6 Identify other common nonrecognition transactions.

LO.7 Recognize tax planning opportunities related to the more common types of gain-deferral transactions available to individual taxpayers.

Chapter Outline

Introduction

"If I could show you a perfectly legal way to pyramid your wealth to $1 million without paying tax, would you be interested?" Although this sounds like it came straight out of the con artist's guide to tax scams, its source is far more reputable.[1] More important, the assertion is entirely true. If a taxpayer is able to make the right investments—obviously a big if—the Internal Revenue Code is willing to lend a helping hand. The key to this wonderland without taxes can be found in the provisions that allow taxpayers to postpone or permanently exclude gains they realize on certain transactions. This is the subject of this chapter.

By now, the basic recipe for determining the tax treatment of any sale or exchange is fairly familiar. Whenever a taxpayer disposes of property, three questions must be addressed: (1) what is the gain or loss *realized,* (2) how much of this realized gain or loss is *recognized,* and (3) what is its character. This chapter focuses on the second of these questions, examining a handful of property transactions—such as the sale of a residence or a like-kind exchange—where all or at least a portion of the gain or loss realized is not recognized.

LO.1

Understand the rationale for deferral of gains and losses on certain property transactions.

As a general rule, any gain or loss realized on a sale or other disposition of property must be recognized unless an exception is specifically provided. For the most part, this means taxpayers must include all of their realized gains and losses in determining their taxable income. However, there are a number of transactions that the Code has singled out for *nonrecognition.* In many cases, the property sold or exchanged is replaced with new property. To illustrate, consider R who trades in an old business car for a new one. When this occurs, any gain or loss realized is usually not taxed—at least immediately—on the theory that R's economic situation has not changed sufficiently to warrant taxation. Nonrecognition is deemed appropriate since R has not converted his investment to cash but has continued it, albeit in another form (the new car). In substance, R's investment has remained intact and his economic situation is essentially the same after as it was before the transaction. To put it another way, the underlying assumption of these nonrecognition provisions is that the new property is substantially a continuation of the old investment still unliquidated. For these situations, Congress is willing to allow a taxpayer to postpone the tax (or perhaps defer the deduction for a loss) until such time when the taxpayer does in fact convert the asset to cash and has the wherewithal to pay the tax.

LO.2

Explain how gain or loss deferral is accomplished through basis adjustments.

When the recognition of a gain or loss is deferred, it is normally recognized later, when the replacement property from the deferred transaction is sold in a taxable transaction. This deferral is usually achieved by building the gain or loss not recognized into the basis of the replacement property.

Example 1

D exchanged a vacant lot in San Jose that had been held for investment for unimproved farmland near Fresno. The city lot had cost $35,000 fifteen years earlier and had not been improved. Both the city lot and the rural property were worth $120,000. D recognizes no gain on the exchange and his basis in the farmland is $35,000.[2] Of course, if D later sells the farm for $130,000, his recognizable gain will be $95,000, the gain on the farm of $10,000 plus the gain deferred from the city lot of $85,000.

It is important to observe that nonrecognition can take one of two forms: permanent exclusion or temporary deferral. The world of permanent exclusions, first introduced in Chapter 6, is relatively small. It includes such items as interest paid on state and local government bonds, insurance proceeds paid on account of death, gifts, inheritances, scholarships, child support, and a number of fringe benefits. On the other side of the ledger, losses and expenses that are personal in nature (other than casualty losses) are generally disallowed. Note that if nonrecognition is permanent, the gain or loss never affects taxable income.

---

[1] Robert J. Bruss, "Real Estate Exchange Provides a Way to Build Net Worth," *The Palm Beach Post,* February 19, 1989, p 57H.

[2] See discussion of § 1031 following.

One instance in which the permanent exclusion of gain is allowed in property transactions is upon the sale of one's principal residence. This benefit, which was widely expanded by the *Taxpayer Relief Act of 1997,* allows a taxpayer who has owned and used his or her residence for two years to simply avoid tax on part or all of any gain.

Example 2

F, an elderly widow, sold her personal residence of 30 years for $292,000 (basis $121,000) and moved into a rented unit in a retirement community. Under Code § 121, F is allowed to exclude her gain of $171,000 from gross income. Since the gain is excluded, F will never be required to pay tax on the gain from that residence.[3]

Types of Nonrecognition Transactions

There are several types of nonrecognition transactions blessed by the Internal Revenue Code. Three are discussed in detail in this chapter. Like-kind exchanges are covered first followed by involuntary conversions and finally the sale of a personal residence.

Like-Kind Exchanges

Section 1031 of the Code provides that a taxpayer may exchange certain types of property *in kind* without the recognition of a taxable gain or loss. Specifically, no gain or loss is recognized when property is exchanged *solely* for other property that is of like-kind.

LO.3

Explain the tax consequences of a like-kind exchange of business or investment property.

Example 3

E traded in his automobile that was worth $4,500 and was used entirely for business purposes and also paid $15,000 cash for a new auto worth $19,500. E's basis in the old was $8,200, based on an original cost of $16,000 less depreciation of $7,800. E recognizes no gain or loss on the transaction since it is a qualifying like-kind exchange. His basis in the new auto is $23,200 ($8,200 basis of trade-in + $15,000 cash paid).

If property other than like-kind property—commonly called *boot*—is received in the exchange, a gain may be recognized.[4] Losses, however, are never recognized.

In order for a transaction to qualify as a nontaxable exchange, it must meet four separate requirements:

1. Both the property exchanged and the property received must be held for business or investment purpose.
2. Both the items exchanged and received must not be specifically excluded from § 1031 treatment.
3. The properties are like-kind.
4. There must be an exchange.

Each of these requirements is discussed below.

---

[3] See discussion of § 121 following.　　　　[4] § 1031(b).

QUALIFIED PROPERTY

Holding Purpose

In order to qualify for like-kind exchange treatment, properties both given up and received must be held by the taxpayer for either business or investment purposes. A qualified exchange may, however, involve the transfer of investment property for trade or business property, or vice versa.[5] No personal use properties qualify.

It is important to note that it is the taxpayer's purpose for holding the property that is critical. The purposes or plans of the other party to the exchange are irrelevant. For example, if the taxpayer held the property exchanged for business or investment, the taxpayer has met the holding-purpose requirement even if the other party plans to sell the property, has a contract to sell it before the exchange, or is helped by the taxpayer in finding a buyer.

Excluded Properties

Certain properties are specifically excluded from like-kind exchange treatment. These are:[6]

- Inventory or other property held primarily for sale.

- Stocks, bonds, or notes.

- Other securities or evidences of indebtedness.

- Partnership interests.

- Interest in trusts (e.g., the beneficiary's interest).

- Livestock of different sexes.

Whether an item is inventory (i.e., held primarily for sale to customers in the ordinary course of a trade or business) is discussed in Chapter 16. Several courts have interpreted the phrase *held for sale* to include any property that is acquired in an exchange only to be resold shortly thereafter.[7]

Example 4

K exchanged a parcel of real estate held for investment for another parcel and immediately offered the parcel received for sale. The parcel was sold on the installment basis. Since K held the new property for sale rather than for use in a trade or business or for investment, the entire gain realized on the exchange must be recognized at the time of the exchange.

LIKE-KIND PROPERTY

The term like-kind is not defined in the Code. However, the Regulations provide that "the words like-kind have reference to the nature or character of the property and not to its grade or quality."[8] This interpretation has been applied to allow exchanges of realty for realty and personalty for personalty. Exchanges of realty for personal property (nonrealty) or vice versa, are not considered exchanges of like-kind property and are fully taxable.

---

[5] Reg. § 1.1031(a)-1(a).

[6] § 1031(a)(2) and § 1031(e).

[7] *Ethel Black,* 35 T.C. 90 (1960); *George M. Bernard,* 26 TCM 858, T.C. Memo. 1967-176.

[8] Reg. § 1.1031(a)(1)(A).

Real Estate

Generally, any exchange of realty for realty will meet the like-kind test. It is immaterial whether the real property is improved or unimproved.[9] No distinction is made between improved or unimproved, productive or unproductive, or similar differences since these relate to the grade or quality of the property and are to be specifically ignored. The IRS has ruled that a lease of real property with a remaining term of at least 30 years will be treated as real property for purposes of determining whether a like-kind exchange has occurred.[10] Accordingly, a realized loss from the exchange of property that had declined in value for a lease interest in that property with a life of 30 years or more resulted in a nondeductible (nonrecognized) loss.[11] Recall that condemned real estate in an involuntary conversion is also subject to the like-kind test.

Tangible Depreciable Personalty

In determining the meaning of "like-kind" for personalty, the IRS, with some support, has adopted a much narrower interpretation than its view toward realty.[12] This stems from the fact that personalty includes a far greater variety of assets than realty. From the Service's perspective, adoption of a lenient "like-kind" test for personalty would enable exchanges that violate the spirit of § 1031 (e.g., a car for a horse, a railroad boxcar for an airplane). As noted earlier, deferral is granted on the theory that the taxpayer's economic position has not changed sufficiently to warrant taxation. In the government's opinion, this principle would be seriously undermined if taxpayers were permitted to exchange any type of personalty. Thus, a restrictive approach is understandable. Unfortunately, this approach (i.e., determining whether replacement property represents a continuing interest or a conversion to a wholly new endeavor) is very subjective and difficult to implement.

Notwithstanding support for its position, the IRS became concerned about what it believed could be endless debate over what personalty was like-kind. Consequently, the government issued new Regulations in 1991.[13] These Regulations put taxpayers on alert that the government would continue to take its narrow view of whether one item of personalty is considered the equivalent of another, but, at the same time, offered safe harbors that would provide the taxpayer with some certainty.

Under the current Regulations, personal property qualifies for § 1031 treatment if the properties are either

1. Like-kind or
2. Like-class.

The definition of "like-kind" remains the same, nebulous as it may be. In contrast, the *like-class* definition offers a more practical approach to determine if properties have the requisite similarity. The like-class definition utilizes a two class system: (1) General Asset Classes and (2) Product Classes. If the properties are within the same General Asset Class or the same Product Class, they are considered like-class and, therefore, like-kind for § 1031 purposes. Note that if the properties meet the like-class standard, they are considered like-kind regardless of whether the exchanged properties would be considered like-kind under general § 1031 standards. The like-class system is significant in that it provides taxpayers the certainty they need before engaging in a transaction. This is particularly true given the absence of authority on like-kind characterizations for personal property.

The General Asset Classes are identified and defined in Revenue Procedure 87-56. There are 13 classes of assets, as shown in Exhibit 15-1. If two assets fall in the same class, they are considered like-class. For instance, a computer, printer, monitor, and modem used in a trade or business would qualify as like-class properties since they are all part of the

---

[9] Reg. § 1.1031(a)-1(b). It is also important to note that § 1250 may supersede § 1031 and cause the recognition of gain. Effectively, § 1250 property (generally depreciable realty) must be acquired in an amount at least as great as the § 1250 recapture potential—§ 1250(d)(4)(C). See Chapter 17 for a discussion of § 1250 recapture of depreciation.

[10] Rev. Rul. 76-301, 1976-2 C.B. 241.

[11] *Century Electric Co. v. Comm.*, 51-2 USTC ¶9482, 41 AFTR 205, 192 F.2d 155 (CA-8, 1951).

[12] In *California Federal Life Insurance Co.*, 50 AFTR 2d 82-5271, 680 F2d 85, 82-2 USTC ¶9464 (CA-9, 1982), aff'g 76 TC 107 (1981) the courts upheld the government's argument that Swiss francs and U.S. double-eagle gold coins were not like-kind. In explaining its holding, the Ninth Circuit noted that it was Congressional concern for lenient interpretation of the like-kind standard that prompted it to amend § 1031 to say that livestock of different sexes are not like-kind. According to the Ninth Circuit, in so acting, Congress was suggesting that personal property was to be accorded different treatment.

[13] Reg. § 1.1031(a)-2(b)(1).

information systems class (General Asset Class 0.12). Note that these classes are quite narrow. For example, an automobile and a light-duty truck would not be considered like-class since they are not in the same Class. Recall, however, that these classes serve only as safe harbors in which taxpayers have guaranteed like-kind treatment.[14]

If a General Asset Class is not provided for a particular asset, the Product Classes are to be used to determine if the exchanged properties are like-class. Observe that it is possible—but not likely—that the properties may be in two different General Asset Classes but in the same Product Class. In such case, the items are not like-class since the Product Classes cannot be used if the properties can be found in the General Asset Classes which were designed by the government.

Assets are within the same Product Class if they have the same four-digit product code as listed in the *North American Industrial Classification System* (NAICS) *Manual* published by the Department of Commerce.

EXHIBIT 15-1	General Asset Classes: Revenue Procedure 87-56	
Asset Class		**Class Number**
1.	Office furniture, fixtures, and equipment	0.11
2.	Information systems (computers and peripheral equipment)	0.12
3.	Data handling equipment, except computers	0.13
4.	Airplanes and helicopters (airframes and engines), except those used in commercial or contract carrying of passengers or freight	0.21
5.	Automobiles, taxis	0.22
6.	Buses	0.23
7.	Light general-purpose trucks	0.241
8.	Heavy general-purpose trucks	0.242
9.	Railroad cars and locomotives	0.25
10.	Tractor units for use over the road	0.26
11.	Trailers and trailer-mounted containers	0.27
12.	Vessels, barges, tugs, and similar water-transportation equipment, except those used in marine construction	0.28
13.	Industrial steam and electric generation and/or distribution systems	0.4

As noted above, if the property does not qualify as like-class under the safe harbors created by the Regulations, it may still be treated as like-kind. The IRS historically has allowed like-kind exchange treatment for personal property when the properties were substantially the same. The courts have ruled that livestock used in a trade or business, but not held for sale, may qualify as like-kind. However, the Code does explain that livestock of different sexes are not like-kind.[15] While it may be obvious that a bull is not a cow, the treatment of bullion-type coins (e.g., decorative gold coins) has created a great deal of controversy. For some investors, collecting and trading gold and silver coins is a popular investment strategy. The IRS has ruled that an exchange of gold bullion held for investment for silver bullion held for the same purpose is not a like-kind exchange since gold and silver are intrinsically different minerals.[16] On the other hand, bullion-type coins of different countries constitute like-kind property.[17] Currency exchanges are not like-kind exchanges. Similarly, legal tender coins (currency) are not of like-kind with bullion-type noncurrency coins.[18]

[14] PLR 200450005 provides that sport utility vehicles (SUVs) and passenger automobiles are like-kind. Note, however, that for depreciation purposes heavy SUVs are not subject to the depreciation limitations applicable to passenger automobiles under § 280F.

[15] § 1031(e). Apparently, if male calves could be exchanged for female calves, a breeding herd of females could be built up more quickly and sold for capital gain treatment.

[16] Rev. Rul. 82-166, 1982-2 C.B. 190.

[17] Rev. Rul. 76-214, 1976-1 C.B. 218.

[18] Rev. Rul. 79-143, 1979-1 C.B. 264; *California Federal Life Insurance Co. v. Comm.*, 82-2 USTC ¶9464, 50 AFTR2d 82-5271, 680 F.2d 85 (CA-9, 1982), aff'g. 76 T.C. 107 (1981). It is interesting that the Revenue Ruling states that U.S. gold coins are currency, while the courts in these cases state that they are more like "other property" than "money."

Intangibles

The like-class rules apply only to tangible depreciable personalty. There are no like classes for intangible personal property. Whether intangibles such as patents and copyrights are like-kind depends on the nature of the property to which the rights relate. For example, copyrights on two novels are like-kind; but a copyright on a novel and a copyright on a song are not like-kind.[19] Similarly, the IRS has ruled that the contracts of professional athletes are like-kind.

Multiple Property Exchanges

In some cases an exchange may involve more than one property. When this occurs, as in an exchange of one business for another, the Regulations provide a somewhat complex set of rules. The effect of these rules is that the various assets are matched with those of the same kind or class. Note that if two businesses are exchanged, the IRS guidelines provide that the goodwill and going concern values of similar businesses are not considered like-kind properties."[20]

Property outside the United States

Generally, real property located outside the U.S. is not like-kind with respect to real property located within the U.S. Similarly, personal property used predominately outside the U.S. is not like-kind with respect to personalty used predominantly within the U.S. In determining where property is predominately used, the two years before the exchange are considered for the property given up and the two years after the exchange are considered for the property received.[21]

RECEIPT OF PROPERTY NOT OF A LIKE-KIND (BOOT)

As a general rule, an exchange is nontaxable only if property is exchanged *solely* for like-kind property. But in many cases, taxpayers wanting to make an exchange do not have like-kind property of equal values. Consequently, one of the parties typically throws in cash or some other non-like-kind property—commonly called *boot*—to equalize the values exchanged. Fortunately, the receipt of boot does not totally disqualify the transaction. Instead, § 1031(b) provides that the taxpayer must recognize any gain realized to the extent of any boot received. For these purposes, boot includes any money received in the exchange *plus* the fair market value of any property that is either nonqualified or not like-kind. Under § 1031(c), the receipt of boot does not cause the recognition of any realized losses in such an exchange.[22]

Example 5

J transferred a vacant lot held as an investment and worth $8,000 to another party in exchange for a similar lot worth $6,000. J received $2,000 cash in addition to the new lot. J's basis in her old lot was $5,500. J's realized gain is $2,500 ($8,000 amount realized − $5,500 basis). If she holds the new lot as an investment, J still must recognize gain on this exchange in the amount of $2,000 because she received *cash boot* of $2,000.

---

[19] Reg. § 1.1031(a)-2(c)(3) Ex. 1 and 2.

[20] Reg. § 1.1031(a)-2(c)(2).

[21] § 1031(h).

[22] If a note is received as boot, the gain may be reported using the installment sales rules. See § 453(h)(6) and (7).

Example 6

If J's basis in the property given up in the prior example had been $6,500, her realized gain would have been $1,500 ($8,000 amount realized − $6,500 basis). Although she received $2,000 of boot, J's recognized gain is $1,500 (recognized gain is *never* more than the realized gain).

Example 7

If J's basis in the vacant lot exchanged in the previous two examples had been $9,000, she would have a realized loss of $1,000 and a recognized loss of zero. Losses in like-kind exchanges are never recognized.

Liabilities as Boot

In many exchanges, a taxpayer transfers property encumbered by indebtedness (e.g., land subject to a mortgage) or has liabilities assumed as part of the exchange agreement. When a taxpayer is relieved of a liability, the tax law takes the view that such relief is the equivalent of receiving cash and paying off the liability. In essence, the party assuming the liability is treated as having paid cash for the property. Consistent with this view, any liabilities from which the taxpayer is relieved in a like-kind exchange are treated as boot received (or boot paid in the case of the party assuming the debt).[23] Note that without these rules, taxpayers could mortgage property shortly before the exchange, receive cash, and then transfer the property along with liability without having to recognize any gain. The treatment of liability relief as boot thwarts such plans.

Example 8

Wanting to move his business out of the city, R exchanged his downtown warehouse encumbered by a mortgage of $200,000 for a new suburban building worth $700,000. R's basis in the warehouse was $600,000. As a result, R realized a gain of $300,000 ($700,000 + $200,000 = $900,000 amount realized − $600,000 basis). Although R received only the building, the relief of the $200,000 liability is treated as boot received. Therefore, R must recognize a gain of $200,000.

Relief and Assumption of Liabilities

If both parties to the exchange assume a liability (e.g., the taxpayer is relieved of a liability of $100,000 but also incurs a liability of $90,000), the process becomes a bit more confusing. In this case, the taxpayer first nets the assumption and the relief. If the taxpayer has net relief (i.e., net decrease in liabilities), such amount is treated as boot received, which in turn may trigger gain recognition.[24] If the taxpayer has net incurred (i.e., net increase in liabilities), such amount is treated as boot paid and no gain is recognized. Note that liabilities are the only type of boot paid or received that can be netted. Other types of boot are not netted. But what if a taxpayer receives cash and incurs liabilities? Can the taxpayer offset any cash received (and the gain that goes with it) by any liabilities incurred? And what if a taxpayer is relieved of liabilities? Can the taxpayer offset any liability relief by giving cash? The Regulations have addressed these possibilities. A taxpayer cannot offset boot received by liabilities incurred. However, liability relief can be offset by boot given (since the taxpayer could presumably pay off the debt with the boot, thereby reducing the liability relief).[25] These various situations are addressed in the next three examples.

---

[23] § 1031(d).

[24] See Reg. §§ 1.1031(b)-1(c) and 1.1031(d)-2. It is important to note that liabilities incurred in anticipation of a like-kind exchange will not qualify for this netting treatment. See Prop. Reg. § 1.1031(b)-1(c).

[25] Reg. § 1.1031(d)-2 Ex. 2.

Example 9

S exchanged a tractor worth $11,000 for a similar tractor worth $9,000, both held for use in his landscaping business. The tractor given up was subject to a secured obligation of $8,000 and S incurred a liability secured by the new tractor of $6,000. S's basis in the tractor given up was $6,500, his cost of $13,500 less depreciation allowed of $7,000. S's realized gain on this exchange is $4,500, computed as follows:

Fair market value of property received	$ 9,000
Plus: Liabilities encumbering the property transferred	+ 8,000
Less: Liabilities assumed by tax payer	− 6,000
Amount realized	$11,000
Less: Adjusted basis of property given up	− 6,500
Gain realized	$ 4,500

S's recognized gain is $2,000 since his net liability relief ($8,000 liability relief − $6,000 liability assumed) is treated as boot.

Example 10

Use the facts in *Example 9,* but assume that instead of receiving a $9,000 tractor and incurring a $6,000 liability, S received a tractor worth $7,500 and paid $4,500 cash. S's realized gain is $4,500 computed as follows:

Fair market value of property received	$ 7,500
Plus: Liabilities encumbering the property transferred	+ 8,000
Less: Amount of money given up	− 4,500
Amount realized	$11,000
Less: Adjusted basis of property given up	− 6,500
Gain realized	$ 4,500

S's recognized gain is $3,500, the amount of his liability relief ($8,000) less the other boot paid ($4,500 cash).

Example 11

If S had received a tractor worth $3,000 and incurred no liabilities and paid no cash in the transaction, his realized gain is still $4,500, computed as follows:

Fair market value of property received	$ 3,000
Plus: Liabilities encumbering the property transferred	+ 8,000
Amount realized	$11,000
Less: Adjusted basis of property given up	− 6,500
Gain realized	$ 4,500

The amount of boot received is $8,000, the amount of his liability relief. The recognized gain is $4,500, since the gain is recognized to the extent of boot received, but never more than the gain realized.

BASIS IN PROPERTY RECEIVED

Exhibit 15-2 presents two ways of computing the basis of property received in a like-kind exchange. The first method (Method 1), prescribed by the Code, is based on the notion that the like-kind property received in the exchange is merely a continuation of the taxpayer's investment in the like-kind property given up. Thus, the basis of the property received should be the same as the property given up—a so-called *substituted* basis. This basis is *increased* by any gain recognized and by any additional consideration given or to be paid in the future, or *decreased* by the fair market value of any boot received and by any liabilities transferred.[26] The second method is derived from the basis determination method used for replacement property in involuntary conversions and sales of principal residences. Under this method, the fair market value of the like-kind property received (i.e., its cost if purchased) is *reduced* by a deferred gain or *increased* by deferred loss in determining its basis. This adjustment is made so that if the newly acquired property is later sold, any realized gain or loss that is not recognized (deferred amount) from the previous like-kind exchange will be automatically considered in the computation of the realized gain or loss. Under either method, the basis of any boot received is its fair market value.

EXHIBIT 15-2	Basis of Property Received in a Like-Kind Exchange

Method 1		
Adjusted basis of property given up		$xxx,xxx
Plus: Gain recognized	$xx,xxx	
Boot paid	x,xxx	
Liabilities assumed by the taxpayer.	xx,xxx	
Liabilities encumbering the property received	xx,xxx	+ xx,xxx
		$xxx,xxx
Less: Boot received	$xx,xxx	
Liabilities assumed by the other party (transferee)	xx,xxx	
Liabilities encumbering the property transferred	xx,xxx	− xx,xxx
Basis of property received.		$xxx,xxx
Method 2		
Fair market value of like-kind property received		$xxx,xxx
Less: Deferred gain (realized gain – recognized gain)		− xx,xxx
Plus: Realized loss (deferred).		+ xx,xxx
Basis of property received.		$xxx,xxx

---

[26] § 1031(d).

Example 12

J operates a charter flight business out of Ft. Lauderdale. This year he put together a deal with one of his flying buddies whereby he traded his old plane, with a basis of $40,000, for another smaller plane worth $53,000 and a hangar to park it in, worth $7,000. J's realized gain is $20,000 ([$53,000 + $7,000 = $60,000] – $40,000). Since the hangar is realty, it is treated as boot. Thus, J must recognize a gain of $7,000 (lesser of the gain realized or boot received). The basis of the boot received, the hangar, is its fair market value of $7,000. J's basis in the new plane is $40,000, computed as follows:

Method 1

Adjusted basis of property given up	$ 40,000
Plus: Gain recognized	7,000
Less: Boot received	– 7,000
Basis of property received	$ 40,000

Method 2

Fair market value of like-kind property received	$ 53,000
Less: Deferred gain ($20,000 – $7,000)	– 13,000
Basis of property received	$ 40,000

At first glance, the basis calculations may not make sense. In the substituted basis computation, the basis of the new property is initially the same as the property given up, $40,000. However, any gain recognized, in this case $7,000, must be added to ensure that upon subsequent sale of the property such gain is not taxed again. The sum of these two amounts ($40,000 + $7,000 = $47,000) represents the basis for the like-kind property and the boot received. A portion of this total is then allocated to the boot by subtracting the value of the boot, $7,000. In effect, the basis assigned to the boot is its $7,000 value, leaving the remaining $40,000 to be assigned to the like-kind property. Note how a subsequent sale of the like-kind property for its $53,000 value would cause the taxpayer to recognize the previously postponed gain of $13,000 ($53,000 – $40,000). This same result is accomplished in a much more obvious manner in the second calculation, where the deferred gain is simply subtracted from the value of the property. The following example is a comprehensive review of the like-kind exchange rules.

Example 13

E exchanged a rental house for T's rental condominium. E's house was worth $36,000 and her adjusted basis was $27,000. The house was not subject to any liabilities. T's condominium was worth $82,000 and was subject to a mortgage of $54,000. T also transferred $8,000 worth of Alpha Corp. stock to E in order to equalize the transaction. T's adjusted basis in his condominium and the Alpha stock were $64,000 and $5,600, respectively. The gains realized by E and T are computed as follows:

E

Fair market value of property received	
Rental condominium (like-kind property)	$ 82,000
Alpha Corp. stock (boot received)	+ 8,000
	$ 90,000
Less: Liabilities (mortgage) assumed by taxpayer	− 54,000
Amount realized	$ 36,000
Less: Adjusted basis of rent house given up	− 27,000
Gain realized	$ 9,000

T

Fair market value of rental house received		$ 36,000
Plus: Liabilities discharged (assumed by E)		+ 54,000
Amount realized		$ 90,000
Less: Adjusted basis of properties given up:		
Rental condominium	$64,000	
Alpha Corp. stock (boot paid)	5,600	− 69,600
Gain realized		$ 20,400

E's gain recognized is $8,000, the amount of boot (stock) received. The amount of boot received by T is $54,000 (the amount of liabilities discharged), which is reduced by his boot paid of $8,000 (fair market value of Alpha stock). Therefore, T's net liabilities discharged are $46,000. T's recognized gain, however, is $20,400, since recognized gain never exceeds realized gain. T's recognized gain consists of $2,400 ($8,000 fair market value − $5,600 basis) for the taxable exchange of the Alpha stock, and the remaining $18,000 is attributable to the exchange of his house.

    E and T's bases in their like-kind property received are determined as follows:

		E's Condominium	T's House
Adjusted basis of like-kind property given up		$27,000	$64,000
Plus:	Gain recognized	+ 8,000	+20,400
	Boot paid	+ 0	+ 5,600
	Liabilities assumed	+54,000	+ 0
Less:	Boot received	− 8,000	− 0
	Liabilities discharged	− 0	−54,000
Basis of property received		$81,000	$36,000

E's basis in the Alpha Corp. stock is $8,000, its fair market value.[27] E and T could have computed their bases in the like-kind property received by using the alternative method (Method 2) discussed previously.

	E	T
Fair market value of like-kind property received:		
Rental house		$36,000
Rental condominium	$82,000	
Less: Deferred gain	– 1,000	– 0
Basis of like-kind property received.	$81,000	$36,000

EXCHANGE REQUIREMENT

Generally, the determination of whether an exchange has occurred is not difficult. All that is required is a reciprocal transfer of qualifying properties. An exchange of one real estate investment for another would normally qualify. Similarly, a trade-in of a business auto along with some cash for another auto is a qualifying exchange. However, an argument can be made for collapsing seemingly independent transactions that might appear to be an exchange in substance.[28]

Example 14

B, a traveling salesperson, "sold" his business auto to a car dealership for $3,200 cash. Shortly thereafter, he purchased another auto from the same dealer for $12,000 cash. The IRS could collapse the *two* transactions (sale and purchase) between the same parties in *one* like-kind exchange. Thus, if B's basis in the old vehicle was $6,000, his loss would be disallowed, and his basis in the new auto would be $14,800 ($12,000 fair market value of new auto + $2,800 deferred loss).

Three-Corner Exchanges

It is not always easy for two parties with properties of equal value, both of which are suitable to the other party, to get together. Even so, it may be possible for a taxpayer who cannot find an exchange partner to qualify for like-kind treatment through a three-corner exchange.

Several forms of multiple-party exchanges have qualified for like-kind exchange treatment. The IRS has ruled that when three property owners entered into an exchange in which each gave up and received qualifying property, like-kind exchange treatment was appropriate.[29] However, a three-corner exchange must be part of a single, integrated plan.[30]

Example 15

X, Y and Z each own rental property. They exchange the properties as follows: X gets Y's property, Y gets Z's property, and Z gets X's property. X, Y, and Z pay or receive boot in order to equalize the difference in the values of the properties.

This three-party transaction qualifies as a like-kind exchange under § 1031. Each party receiving boot must recognize gain up to the amount of the boot received.

---

[27] Reg. §§ 1.1031(d)-1(c) and 1.1031(d)-1(d).

[28] Rev. Rul. 61-119, 1961-1 C.B. 395.

[29] Rev. Rul. 57-244, 1957-1 C.B. 247; Rev. Rul. 73-476, 1973-2 C.B. 300.

[30] Rev. Rul. 75-291, 1975-2 C.B. 332; Rev. Rul. 77-297, 1977-2 C.B. 304.

Perhaps a more common situation involves a taxpayer who is willing to "sell" property but does not want to recognize gain. In this situation, the interested buyer purchases like-kind property identified by the "seller" and then exchanges it for the seller's property.

Example 16

C owned rental property worth $70,000 (adjusted basis of $34,000), which she was willing to dispose of only if she could do so without recognizing any gain. B wanted to purchase C's property, but in order that C might defer her potential gain of $36,000, he agreed to purchase another rental property of equal value that was suitable to C. As long as she receives no boot, C would recognize no gain and her basis in the replacement property would be $34,000 ($70,000 fair market value of property received – $36,000 deferred gain). B will not qualify for § 1031 treatment since he purchased the property specifically for the exchange and thus never held it for business use or investment.[31] However, B will not have any realized gain or loss as a result of the transaction since his amount realized of $70,000 (fair market value of rental property received from C) is equal to his cost basis of the property given up.

Delayed Exchanges

The property to be accepted by the taxpayer in a like-kind exchange need not be received *simultaneously* with the transfer of his or her property. Delayed exchanges are popularly referred to as *Starker* exchanges, after a 1979 case in which a taxpayer transferred significant real property in exchange for a promise by a corporation to deliver the replacement property over five years.[32] These exchanges qualify currently for tax deferral only if specific timing requirements are met. In order to qualify for nonrecognition treatment, the property to be acquired must be:

1. Identified within 45 days after the date the taxpayer surrenders the property; and

2. Received within 180 days of the transfer, but no later than the due date (including extensions) of the tax return for the year of transfer.[33]

Example 17

R has agreed to purchase any real property worth $120,000 that is acceptable to S if S will immediately transfer his commercial parking lot, which is adjacent to R's store, to R. S agrees to the plan. S later identifies a duplex worth $120,000 and directs R to purchase it for him. This delayed exchange will qualify under § 1031 if the duplex is specified as the replacement property within 45 days and is transferred to S within 180 days of the transfer of the parking lot to R. Note how the taxpayer has effectively sold the property for $120,000 cash and then reinvested the cash without having to pay tax.

Delayed exchanges are frequently expedited by an escrow company that holds money that is to be used to purchase a property for the transferor. It is possible that a property would be identified within 45 days but, due to circumstances beyond the taxpayer's control, cannot be acquired. To prevent this misfortune, the taxpayer may identify one or more additional properties within the 45-day period to be acquired if the acquisition of the first property cannot be completed.[34]

---

[31] *Biggs v. Comm.*, 81-1 USTC ¶9114, 47 AFTR2d 81-484, 632 F.2d 1171 (CA-5, 1980).

[32] *Starker v. U.S.*, 79-2 USTC ¶9541, 44 AFTR 2d 79-5525, 602 F.2d 1341 (CA-9, 1979).

[33] § 1031(a)(3).

[34] Reg. § 1.1031(k)-1. Also see Rev. Proc. 2000-37, 2000 I.R.B. 40, where the IRS provides a safe harbor for exchanges that occur through an intermediary in a reverse order.

Related-Party Exchanges

For many years, related parties used a clever device to reduce gain on the sale of appreciated property. At the heart of the scheme were the substituted basis rules applied in like-kind exchanges. These rules effectively enabled the taxpayer to create a high basis for what otherwise was low-basis property that the taxpayer planned to sell.

Example 18

T owns all of the stock of D Corporation, which is planning to sell 100 acres of land for $700,000 (basis $100,000). Accordingly, D anticipates that it will recognize a gain of $600,000. To minimize the gain on the sale, however, T transfers one of his real estate investments worth $700,000 (basis $500,000) to the corporation in exchange for the land and subsequently sells the land. T's gain on the sale of the land is only $200,000 ($700,000 − $500,000) since the like-kind exchange rules enabled him to substitute the higher basis of his realty, $500,000, as the basis for the land.

To put an end to the so-called basis-swapping illustrated in *Example 18,* Congress created a special rule. If a taxpayer exchanges property with a *related party* and either taxpayer disposes of the transferred property within two years, the like-kind exchange rules do not apply to the original exchange and any deferred gain must be recognized in the year of the subsequent disposition.[35] For this purpose, the definition of a related party is the same as that used for the loss disallowance rules of §§ 267 and 707(b)(1), which generally includes the taxpayer's family (spouse, brothers, sisters, ancestors, lineal descendants) and certain entities (e.g., corporations and partnerships) in which the taxpayer owns more than a 50% interest.

Example 19

Assume the same facts as in *Example 18* above. Under current law T's plan would not work since T and his corporation are considered related parties and he sold the property within two years of the exchange. As a result, both T and D must recognize their deferred gains on the original exchange in the year of the sale. T recognizes a gain of $200,000 ($700,000 − $500,000) and D recognizes a gain of $600,000 ($700,000 − $100,000). T recognizes no gain on the sale itself because his basis in the land is now treated as $700,000 (i.e., his cost) since the original transaction became taxable. Note that T's plan would have worked had T been patient and sold the land more than two years after the exchange.

TREATMENT MANDATORY

Like-kind exchange treatment is mandatory. Therefore, no gain or loss is recognized on any transaction that meets the like-kind exchange requirements even if the taxpayer desires otherwise. Since the provision applies to losses as well as gains, like-kind treatment may work to the disadvantage of a taxpayer, and it may be to his or her benefit to avoid exchange status.

Example 20

This year B swapped her rental property in Malibu worth $200,000 (basis $230,000) for rental property in Vail worth $175,000 and cash of $25,000. B has realized a loss of $30,000 ($200,000 − $230,000). Although she received boot of $25,000, none of the loss is recognized. In this case, B would probably be better off selling the Malibu property and purchasing the Vail property so that she could recognize her loss.

---

[35] § 1031(f).

HOLDING PERIOD

The holding period of like-kind property received in a § 1031 exchange includes the holding period of the property given up on the exchange.[36] However, the holding period of any property received as boot in a § 1031 exchange *begins* on the date of its receipt. In effect, when boot received is property other than money (or liability relief), it is treated as if the taxpayer received money (equal to the property's fair market value) and used it to purchase the property. Consequently, the property's holding period starts on the day of the exchange *and* the basis of the property is its fair market value.

 CHECK YOUR KNOWLEDGE

Review Question 1

This year H retired. He decided to continue to live in Chicago but wanted to get rid of his rental property (fair market value $240,000, basis $140,000) and buy a condominium in Florida. H is now entertaining an offer to sell the property to a real estate mogul who loves the property and is hot to buy. What would you advise?

Without good advice, most taxpayers would sell the property, recognize a $100,000 gain, and pay a capital gains tax of up to $25,000, leaving them with as little as $72,000 to invest. There is a much better approach. H is a perfect candidate for a delayed like-kind exchange. He could "sell" the property and have the buyer transfer the funds to an escrow agent, who would hold the money while H identifies the property in Florida he wants. He must do this within 45 days after the sale. As long as he closes on the new property within 180 days of the transfer (but no later than the due date of the return for the year of the transfer, including extensions), the like-kind exchange provisions will apply and H does not have to recognize the gain!

Review Question 2

At the outset of this chapter, it was indicated that there is a way to pyramid one's wealth to $1 million without ever having to pay tax. How could this be done?

The first step is to make wise investments (typically real estate). If the investor desires to sell after the property has appreciated, he or she may "sell" the property using the delayed like-kind exchange technique just as H did in the previous question. The effect is to invest in replacement property without having to pay any tax. If H can continue to invest successfully, he never has to pay tax along the way to $1 million (and beyond). Note that H does not necessarily have to find a property of equal value, assuming the amount escrowed is reinvested in like-kind property. As long as all of the cash is used and none passes to H, he does not recognize any gain. Thus, H could effectively use the property as a down payment for new property and use additional leverage to accelerate the process.

Note that the property must be qualifying property. Since like-kind exchange treatment does not apply to stocks and bonds, this scheme would not work with respect to stock market investments.

Review Question 3

True-False. This year D swapped her billiard parlor building for a bowling alley building. The transaction qualifies as a like-kind exchange.

True. Although the properties are not considered similar or related in use according to the functional use test applied to involuntary conversion rules, the two investments are considered like-kind property since they are both realty.

---

[36] § 1223(1).

Review Question 4

True-False. During the year, E exchanged her personal residence for a rental house. The swap qualifies as a like-kind exchange.

False. The properties exchanged must be held for productive use or investment. In this case, E is not holding her home for investment, and therefore the exchange is taxable.

Review Question 5

True-False. Under the like-kind exchange rules, a taxpayer must receive cash before any gain realized is recognized.

False. Although this may appear to be true, the taxpayer is taxed whenever boot is received. Any property other than the like-kind property received is treated as boot. For example, the boot could take the form of stock, a note, or even liability relief.

Review Question 6

True-False. This year, F swapped her investment land for a friend's land and $10,000 of cash. As a result, F realized a $20,000 loss. F may recognize a loss of $10,000.

False. Losses are never recognized on a like-kind exchange even if the taxpayer receives boot.

Review Question 7

True-False. G sold her rental property in Galveston for $100,000 and realized a $25,000 gain. Two months later, she used the $100,000 plus an additional $50,000 to purchase another rental property on Padre Island for $150,000. G does not recognize gain since she has not liquidated her investment but continued it in another rental property.

False. Although G seems to have met the spirit of the law, there must, as a general rule, be a direct exchange in order to qualify for nonrecognition under the like-kind exchange provisions. Note that G could have postponed the gain had she taken advantage of the delayed like-kind exchange rules or had she simply had the buyer of her property buy the Padre Island property and then done an exchange.

Review Question 8

During the year, Fred traded one of his buddies a tractor used solely in his construction business for another tractor for the same use. On the date of the trade, the old tractor had an adjusted basis of $3,000. He received in exchange $500 in cash and a smaller tractor with a fair market value of $2,800. Fred should recognize a gain on the exchange of

  a. $800
  b. $500
  c. $300
  d. $0
  e. None of the above

The answer is (c). Fred realized a gain of $300 ([$2,800 + $500 = $3,300] − $3,000). Since he received boot of $500, he must recognize the lesser of the gain realized, $300, or the boot received, $500.

Review Question 9

Assuming the same facts as above, the basis of the new tractor to Fred would be

  a. $3,300
  b. $3,000
  c. $2,800
  d. $2,300
  e. None of the above

The answer is (c), as determined below.

Method 1

Adjusted basis of property given up	$3,000
Plus: Gain recognized	300
Less: Boot received	− 500
Basis of property received.	$2,800

Method 2

Fair market value of like-kind property received	$2,800
Less: Deferred gain	− 0
Basis of property received.	$2,800

Involuntary Conversions

LO.4

Describe how the nonrecognition rules apply to involuntary conversions of property.

Most of the time, taxpayers intend to sell, exchange or even abandon their property. But occasionally, they lose their property from casualty or theft or are forced to sell their property because of some type of condemnation proceeding. When an *involuntary conversion* like this occurs, the taxpayer usually receives some form of compensation such as insurance proceeds or a condemnation award. In some cases, the compensation may actually cause the taxpayer to realize a gain from the "loss." Without any special rule, the tax resulting from this gain could produce a real hardship since the taxpayer typically uses the compensation received to acquire a replacement property. Recognizing that taxpayers may not have the wherewithal to pay the tax in this situation—which was totally beyond their control—Congress provided some relief. Special rules allow taxpayers to defer any gain realized from an involuntary conversion if they acquire qualified replacement property within a specified period of time.

> ### Example 21
>
> J operates a fishing boat in Miami. Unfortunately, the boat was totally destroyed when Hurricane Charley hit the Florida coast. J's basis in the boat was $40,000 (cost of $60,000 less depreciation of $20,000). Luckily, J was insured. He filed an insurance claim and received $75,000 based on the fair market value of the boat. As a result, he realized a gain of $35,000 ($75,000 − $40,000). J may defer the entire gain if he reinvests at least $75,000 in similar-use property within the allowable period.

INVOLUNTARY CONVERSION DEFINED

An involuntary conversion is defined in the Code as the compulsory or involuntary conversion of property "as a result of its destruction in whole or in part, theft, seizure, or requisition or condemnation or threat or imminence thereof."[37] The terms *destruction* and *theft* have the same basic meaning as when they are used for casualty and theft losses. The IRS has ruled, however, that the destruction of property for purposes of § 1033 need not meet the *suddenness* test, which has been applied to casualty loss deductions.[38]

Typical involuntary conversions involve accidents, natural disasters, and other events beyond the control of the taxpayer. This has been found to include damages caused by other parties such as poisoning of cattle by contaminated feed and destruction of crops and soil by chemicals.[39] In each case, the taxpayer was allowed to defer recognition of gain upon the receipt of damages by reinvesting in qualified property.

---

[37] § 1033(a).

[38] Rev. Rul. 59-102, 1959-1 C.B. 200.

[39] Rev. Rul. 54-395, 1954-2 C.B. 143 and Ltr. Rul. 9615041.

Seizure, Requisition, or Condemnation

It is not as simple to determine what qualifies as a "seizure, or requisition or condemnation" as it is to identify theft or destruction. The property must be taken without the taxpayer's consent and the taxpayer must be compensated.[40]

Not all types of forced dispositions will qualify. For example, the courts have found that a foreclosure sale[41] and a sale after continued insistence by a Chamber of Commerce[42] did not constitute involuntary conversions. Similarly, the IRS has ruled that the condemnation of rental properties due to structural defects or sanitary conditions does not constitute an involuntary conversion since the sale was made to avoid making property improvements necessary to meet a housing ordinance.[43] Generally, a transfer must be made to an authority that has the power to actually condemn the property, and the property must be taken for a public use.

In the case of the conversion of part of a single economic unit, § 1033 applies not only to the condemned portion, but also to the part not condemned if it is *voluntarily sold*. When a truck freight terminal was rendered virtually useless because the adjoining parking lot for the trucks was condemned, a single economic unit was found to exist and § 1033 applied to the sale of the terminal as well as the condemnation of the parking area.[44] In a similar situation when a shopping center was partially destroyed by fire and the owner chose to sell the entire shopping center rather than reconstruct the destroyed portion, the IRS ruled that no conversion existed with respect to the remaining portion since the undamaged portion could still be used and the damaged portion repaired. The fire insurance proceeds, but not the sale proceeds, qualified for deferral under § 1033.[45]

Threat or Imminence of Condemnation

The possibility of a condemnation may very well cause a taxpayer to sell property before the actual condemnation occurs. For example, a farming corporation may discover that its property is being considered as the site for a new airport and sell the property. Section 1033 extends deferral to these *voluntary* sales to someone other than the condemning authority if they are due to the *threat or imminence* of condemnation. It should be emphasized that newspaper reports, magazine articles, or rumors that property is being considered for condemnation are not sufficient.[46] Threat or imminence exists only after officials have communicated that they intend to condemn the property and the owner has good reason to believe they would.

Example 22

LSA Corporation has owned a department store in downtown Indianapolis for more than 50 years. The property has a value of about $2 million and a basis of only $400,000 (since the building is completely depreciated). Recently, the corporation learned that the city fathers, in an attempt to revive the downtown area, plan to build a new mall that may result in the condemnation of the building. Fearing that interest rates may rise before the city gets around to condemning the property, the corporation sold the building to another investor, who wanted to try to preserve the building as a historic structure. The corporation quickly used the sales proceeds to build another store in a nearby suburb. Unfortunately, the corporation's sale may not qualify for deferral since it has not been officially notified that the building will be condemned. The threat or imminence does not exist merely because the city is considering plans that may lead to condemnation. Nevertheless, the corporation may be able to produce evidence that clearly suggests otherwise.

---

[40] See, for example, *Hitke v. Comm.*, 62-1 USTC ¶9114, 8 AFTR2d 5886, 296 F.2d 639 (CA-7, 1961).

[41] See *Cooperative Publishing Co. v. U.S.*, 40-2 USTC ¶9823, 25 AFTR 1123, 115 F.2d 1017 (CA-9, 1940), and *Robert Recio*, 61 TCM 2626, T.C. Memo. 1991-215.

[42] *Davis Co.*, 6 B.T.A. 281 (1927), acq. VI-2 C.B. 2.

[43] Rev. Rul. 57-314, 1957-2 C.B. 523.

[44] *Harry Masser*, 30 T.C. 741 (1958), acq. 1959-2 C.B. 5; Rev. Rul. 59-361, 1959-2 C.B. 183.

[45] Rev. Rul. 78-377, 1978-2 C.B. 208, distinguishing Rev. Rul. 59-361. See also Footnote 98.

[46] Rev. Rul. 58-557, 1958-2 C.B. 402.

As noted above, the sale to a third party after the threat exists is permissible.[47] If the third party realizes gain when the property is later sold to the condemning authority, the new transaction may also qualify for involuntary conversion treatment if the proceeds are reinvested in qualified property after the condemnation of the property, even though the threat existed before the property was acquired.[48]

Example 23

T has owned and operated a successful automobile dealership for many years. This year he received legal notice from the City of New Orleans indicating that it planned to condemn his showroom and car lot for use as the site of a new convention center in approximately five years. As a result, T began searching for an acceptable new location. After finding a suitable location, T sold the old property to a person who could use it for just four or five years.

T's sale and reinvestment qualifies for involuntary conversion treatment and his gain can be deferred so long as all other requirements are met. When the property is finally purchased by the city, the new owner can also qualify for involuntary conversion treatment if he or she realizes a gain and the proceeds are reinvested in qualifying property within the replacement period.

REPLACEMENT PROPERTY

To qualify for deferral of gain on an involuntary conversion, the taxpayer must reinvest in property that is *similar or related in service* or *use* to the property that is converted.[49] The IRS and taxpayers often disagree as to what qualifies as replacement property. It is clear, however, that the new property must replace the converted property, and therefore, property that was already owned by the taxpayer will not qualify.[50]

Generally, the replacement property must serve the same functional use as that served by the converted property. This *functional use* applies to owner-users. It test requires that the character of service or use be the same for both properties. For example, a light-duty truck must be replaced by a light-duty truck and a dental chair must be replaced by another dental chair. As the example below, demonstrates, interpretation of this rules is not always straightforward.

Example 24

N owned and operated a bowling alley for many years. This year the bowling alley burned down, and N replaced it with a billiard parlor. The billiard parlor is not qualified replacement property since the services provided by each are not functionally equivalent. Although they both provide recreational services, the IRS believes bowling balls and billiard balls are not the same.[51]

When tangible trade or business personalty is destroyed in a Presidentially declared disaster area, the taxpayer is given more flexibility. The destroyed property may be replaced with *any* tangible trade or business personalty.[52]

A different and more liberal test applies to involuntary conversions of rental properties. This so-called *taxpayer use* test requires that the replacement property be used by the taxpayer/lessor as rental property regardless of the lessee's use.[53]

---

[47] *Creative Solutions, Inc. v. U.S.,* 63-2 USTC ¶9615, 12 AFTR2d 5229, 320 F.2d 809 (CA-5, 1963); Rev. Rul. 81-180, 1981-2 C.B. 161.

[48] Rev. Rul. 81-181, 1981-2 C.B. 162.

[49] § 1033(a).

[50] § 1033(a)(1)(A)(i).

[51] Rev. Rul. 76-319, 1976-2 C.B. 242.

[52] § 1033(h).

[53] Rev. Rul. 71-41, 1971-1 C.B. 223.

> ### Example 25
>
> Several years ago J purchased 30 acres of land and built a large warehouse that he leased to an appliance store. This year the warehouse site was condemned, and J used the proceeds to purchase a gas station that he currently leases to an oil company. The gas station is qualified replacement property since both properties are rental properties. The fact that the tenants use the properties for different purposes is irrelevant. From the owner's perspective each property is being used in the same way.

Control of Corporation

The replacement property in an involuntary conversion may be controlling stock in a corporation owning property that is "similar or related in use or service."[54] Control consists of owning at least 80% of all voting stock plus at least 80% of all other classes of stock.[55]

Condemned Real Estate

Congress provided special relief in the situation where real property is condemned by an outside authority. A more liberal interpretation of "similar or related in use" is allowed for the replacement of condemned real property if it is held by the taxpayer for use in a trade or business or for investment. The Code provides that the *like-kind* test shall be applied.[56] This is the test used for § 1031 like-kind exchanges. As explained later in this chapter, these rules allow nonrecognition whenever a taxpayer exchanges real estate for real estate regardless of the real estate's use. Thus, if the taxpayer's unimproved real estate (e.g., raw land) is condemned and replaced with improved real estate (e.g., shopping center), deferral would be granted.

Conversion of Livestock

Section 1033 includes certain special provisions related to sales of livestock. Livestock sold because of disease[57] or solely because of drought, flood, or other weather-related conditions[58] are considered involuntarily converted. Furthermore, if livestock are sold because of soil contamination or environmental contamination and it is not feasible for the owner to reinvest in other livestock, then other farm property, including real property, will qualify as replacement property.[59]

Property Acquired from a Related Party

Congress was concerned that the replacement property would conveniently be acquired from a related party. In order to prevent this, C corporations, partnerships with C corporations as partners, and other taxpayers deferring gains in excess of $100,000, will not be allowed the deferral under § 1033 if the replacement is purchased from a related party. For this purpose, a related party includes certain close family members and most entities where there is more than 50% control.[60]

REPLACEMENT PERIOD

The taxpayer is entitled to deferral only if reinvestment in the replacement property occurs within the proper time period. The replacement period usually begins on the date of disposition of the converted property; but in the case of condemnation or requisition, it begins at the earliest date of threat or imminence of the requisition or condemnation. The replacement period ends on the last day of the second taxable year after the year in which a gain is first realized,[61] but may be extended by the IRS if the taxpayer can show reasonable cause for

---

[54] § 1033(a)(2)(A).

[55] § 1033(a)(2)(E)(i).

[56] § 1033(g)(1). The similar or related in use test must be applied if the real property is destroyed or the replacement property is stock in a controlled corporation.

[57] § 1033(d).

[58] § 1033(e).

[59] § 1033(f).

[60] § 1033(i).

[61] § 1033(a)(2)(B).

being unable to replace within the specified time limit.[62] In the case of condemned real property used in a trade or business or held for investment, the replacement period is extended. The extension is one year, causing the replacement period to remain open until the end of the third taxable year after the first year in which gain is first realized.[63] These time periods are diagrammed below.

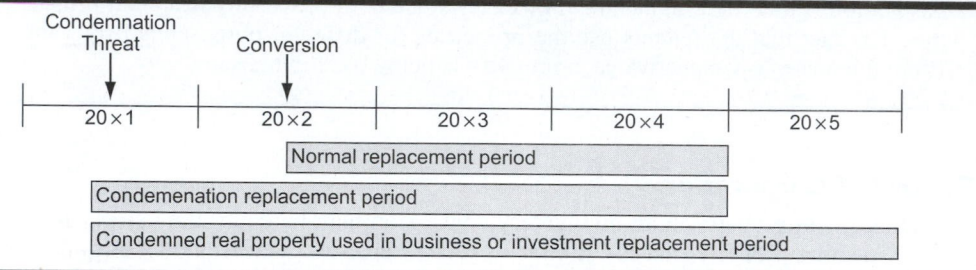

Example 26

E's rental house was condemned for public use by the county during 2017. Her basis in the residence was $32,000 and the county paid her $46,000. E's replacement period begins the day of the condemnation, or threat thereof. The replacement period normally ends at the close of the second taxable year after the year of the conversion. However, in the case of realty that has been held for productive use in business or for investment and which has been condemned, the replacement period is extended to the close of the third taxable year. In this case, the replacement period ends on December 31, 2020.

Example 27

If the residence in the previous example had been used as E's personal residence, the replacement period would end on December 31, 2018. As noted above, the replacement period is extended only for real estate held for productive use in a trade or business or for investment, so the usual two-year rule applies.

Earlier reference was made to specific provisions dealing with replacement property upon the destruction of one's principal residence. A special reinvestment period is also provided. When the destruction is in a Presidentially declared disaster area, the reinvestment period is extended to the last day of the fourth year following the year in which gain is first realized.[64]

Example 28

U's principal residence was destroyed in an earthquake. U's insurance policy included limits of $100,000 for the residence, $40,000 for contents, and an additional $20,000 for U's prized musical instruments. U realized gains on the residence and musical instruments and a small loss on the contents. The region affected by the earthquake was declared a disaster area by the President and U's insurer paid the maximum amounts under the policy. U may defer his gain on the structure and musical instruments by reinvesting $120,000 in similar (residence or contents) property. The reinvestment must take place by the end of U's fourth taxable year after receiving the insurance settlement.

---

[62] Reg. § 1.1033(a)-2(c)(3).

[63] § 1033(g)(4).

[64] § 1033(h)(1)(B).

ELECTION REQUIRED

As a general rule, taxpayers are allowed to elect whether or not they want to defer any gain realized from an involuntary conversion. The election is made simply by not reporting any of the deferred gain on the tax return for the year in which the gain is realized. However, deferral of gain is mandatory if the property is converted directly into property that is similar or related in use.[65]

Example 29

G owned 100 acres of land next to an airport. He had farmed the land for 25 years. All of that changed this year when the city condemned G's land to expand the airport. Pursuant to the condemnation agreement, the city transferred similar farmland to G. In this case, nonrecognition is mandatory since there was a direct conversion into similar property. Had the city paid G for the land, G would have had the option to elect deferral or recognize any gain realized.

The return for the year of conversion must include detailed information relating to the involuntary conversion,[66] and if the taxpayer has not yet reinvested when the return is filed, he or she is required to notify the IRS when replacement property has been acquired or that no replacement will occur.[67] If after an election has been made under § 1033 *and* the taxpayer fails to reinvest all of the required amount within the allowable period, the tax return for the year (or years) in which gain was realized must be *amended to include the recognized gain* and the tax deficiency must be paid.[68]

Statute of Limitations

The statute of limitations is extended for involuntary conversions when the taxpayer elects to defer his or her gain but has not replaced the property by the time the return for the year of the conversion is filed. The IRS may audit the transaction and assess a deficiency any time within three years after the taxpayer notifies the IRS that he or she has replaced the converted property or has failed to replace the property triggering the recognition of gain.[69]

AMOUNT OF GAIN RECOGNIZED

No gain is recognized by an electing taxpayer on an involuntary conversion if the amount reinvested in replacement property equals or exceeds the amount realized from the converted property (i.e., the taxpayer does not "cash out" on the transaction). If the amount reinvested is less than the amount realized, the taxpayer has "cashed out" on the transaction and *must* recognize gain to the extent of the amount *not* reinvested (see Exhibit 15-3).[70] No gain is recognized in a direct conversion.[71]

The *amount reinvested* is the *cost* of the replacement property. The property may not have been acquired by gift, inheritance, or any other method resulting in other than a cost basis.[72] The cost basis would include the amount of any debt incurred in the purchase.

The taxpayer will determine his or her basis in property acquired in an involuntary conversion by taking into consideration the deferred gain. In the case of a direct conversion, the basis of the replacement property is the same as the basis in the converted property. In conversions into money and other property, the basis in the replacement property is its cost *reduced* by the amount of gain realized but not recognized (see Exhibit 15-3).[73]

---

[65] § 1033(a).

[66] Reg. § 1.1033(a)-2(c)(2).

[67] Reg. § 1.1033(a)-2(c)(5).

[68] Special rules extend the statute of limitations.
   § 1033(a)(2)(C): Reg. § 1.1033(a)-2(c)(5).

[69] § 1033(a)(2)(C).

[70] § 1033(a)(2)(A).

[71] § 1033(a)(1).

[72] Reg. § 1.1033(a)-2(c)(4).

[73] § 1033(b); Reg. § 1.1033(b)-1.

EXHIBIT 15-3	Involuntary Conversion: Computation of Recognized Gain and Basis of Replacement Property

1. Gain realized

                Amount realized (net proceeds)

      Less: Adjusted basis

                Gain (loss) realized

2. Gain recognized

                Amount realized

      Less: Cost of replacement property

                Gain recognized (not to exceed gain realized)*

3. Basis of replacement property

                Cost of replacement property

      Less: Gain not recognized

                Adjusted basis of replacement property

* If this amount is negative, the taxpayer has reinvested more than the amount realized and no gain is recognized.

Example 30

M owned a rented industrial equipment warehouse that was adjacent to a railway. The warehouse was destroyed by fire on January 15, 2017, and M received $240,000 from her insurance carrier on March 26, 2017. Her basis in the warehouse was $130,000. M constructed a wholesale grocery warehouse on the same site since the predicted demand for such space was superior to equipment storage. The new warehouse was constructed at a cost of $280,000 and was completed May 7, 2018.

    Leased (rental) property is subject to the more liberal *taxpayer use* test, rather than the *functional use* test that is applied to other properties. Therefore, the new warehouse meets the similar or related in use test since it is rental property to M.

    As calculated below, M reports no gain on her 2017 return since she reinvested a sufficient amount within the reinvestment period, which ends December 31, 2019. She is required to give the IRS the details of the conversion with her 2017 return and provide a description of the replacement property when it is completed. The basis in the replacement property is $170,000 (cost of $280,000 – the gain not recognized of $110,000).

Amount realized	$ 240,000
Less: Adjusted basis.	(130,000)
Gain (loss) realized	$ 110,000
Amount realized	$ 240,000
Less: Cost of replacement property	(280,000)
Gain recognized (not to exceed gain realized).	0
Cost of replacement property	$ 280,000
Less: Gain not recognized	(110,000)
Adjusted basis of replacement property	$ 170,000

Example 31

Assume the same facts as in *Example 30,* except that M reinvested $200,000. In this case she would be required to recognize a gain since she did not reinvest all of the insurance proceeds of $240,000. As a result, her recognized gain would be $40,000 and her basis in the replacement property would be $130,000, calculated as follows:

Amount realized	$ 240,000
Less: Cost of replacement property	− 200,000
Gain recognized (not to exceed gain realized)	$ 40,000
Cost of replacement property	$ 200,000
Less: Gain not recognized ($110,000 − $40,000)	− 70,000
Adjusted basis of replacement property	$ 130,000

Conversion of Personal Residence

Section 1033 also applies to the involuntary conversion of a principal residence. Taxpayers that qualify may elect to exclude the gain under § 121 instead of, or along with, § 1033 for the involuntary conversion of a personal residence.[74]

 ## CHECK YOUR KNOWLEDGE

Over the last several years, Rock and Roller Blades Inc. opened two new roller skating rinks to capitalize on the in-line skating craze. In February 2017, however, one of the rinks was destroyed by fire. At that time, the building had a basis of $300,000. The insurance proceeds awarded to the company amounted to $360,000.

Review Question 1

If the corporation uses the insurance proceeds to build a new indoor soccer facility, will the soccer facility be considered qualified replacement property?

Probably not. In order to qualify for deferral, the replacement property must be similar to or related in service or use to the converted property. This generally means that the replacement property must provide the same functional use as the converted property. Based on the IRS ruling that a billiard parlor is not functionally equivalent to a bowling alley, it would appear that a soccer facility does not provide the same services as a roller rink.

Review Question 2

By what date must the calendar year corporation invest in qualified replacement property?

The corporation must reinvest by the close of the second taxable year following the year in which the conversion takes place, in this case December 31, 2018. The extended replacement period for business or investment realty only applies if the property is condemned.

Review Question 3

Assuming the corporation immediately erects another roller rink at the cost of $390,000 and elects to defer any gain realized, the company's gain (or loss) recognized will be
  a. $60,000
  b. $30,000
  c. $90,000
  d. $0
  e. $30,000 loss
  f. None of the above

---

[74] § 121(d)(4).

The answer is (d). As shown in the following computations, the corporation is allowed to defer the entire gain realized since it reinvested all of the insurance proceeds.

Amount realized	$ 360,000
Less: Adjusted basis	− 300,000
Gain (loss) realized	$ 60,000
Amount realized	$ 360,000
Less: Cost of replacement property	− 390,000
Gain recognized (not to exceed gain realized)	0

Review Question 4

Same facts as in Question 3. The basis of the replacement property is
  a. $300,000
  b. $390,000
  c. $370,000
  d. $0
  e. $360,000
  f. None of the above

The answer is (f). The basis is $330,000, determined as follows:

Cost of replacement property	$390,000
Less: Gain not recognized	− 60,000
Adjusted basis of replacement property	$330,000

Sale of a Personal Residence

LO.5

Apply the nonrecognition rules to the sale of a principal residence.

While one's home may be one's castle, in the United States it is also a tax shelter. The tax law contains several provisions that encourage home ownership. Two of these, the deductions for interest and property taxes, were discussed in Chapter 11. A third, considered in detail below, concerns the sale of a residence. The effect of these provisions, whether intended or not, is to provide what is clearly a tax bonanza. If an individual sells a residence, any gain may be totally excluded from income up to $250,000 ($500,000 for certain married persons filing jointly) if the taxpayer qualifies under § 121. Gain in excess of the limit will generally be recognized.

Example 32

T sold his principal residence for $400,000 on July 22, 2017. He has lived in the home since 2004. His basis in the property was $225,000 and his realized gain on the sale is $175,000 ($400,000 − $225,000). T may exclude all of the $175,000 in gain from his taxable income.

COMPUTATION OF BASIS OF RESIDENCE AND GAIN OR LOSS REALIZED

The calculation of the gain recognized on the sale of the house begins in the normal fashion. It starts with the sales price, which is then reduced by selling expenses to determine the amount realized. The sales price is usually easy to determine. Selling expenses are generally those costs paid to bring about the sale of the property. Although they are not directly deductible, they do reduce the potential gain. A few of the more common selling expenses incurred when selling a home are

Realtor's commission	Inspection fees (termites, radon, etc.)	Transfer taxes
Advertising	Legal fees	Mortgage title insurance
Surveys	Title fees (abstracts, certificate, opinion)	Escrow fees
Buyer's points paid by the seller		

Gain or Loss Realized

The amount of the gain or loss realized is merely the difference between the amount realized and the adjusted basis. In computing the basis of the home, improvements the owner has made should be included. These include anything that adds value to the house and prolongs its useful life. Some of these are

Additions (rooms, porch, deck)	Flooring (carpeting, tile, vinyl)	Curtains
Roof, siding, insulation	Fences	Well
Appliances, attic fan, grill	Air conditioning, furnaces, water heaters	Mailbox, house numbers
Landscaping, sprinkling system	Alarm system	Septic system
Garage	Basketball goal post	Sewer assessment
Basement improvement	Solar or geothermal heating	Smoke detector
Shed	Driveway, walks	

Gain or Loss Recognized

The next concern, and no doubt the most important, is the determination of the amount of the gain or loss to be recognized. Losses are not subject to any special provision. Accordingly, since a personal residence is not held for either trade or business or investment purposes, any realized loss is not deductible.[75] While losses are not deductible, gains receive far more favorable treatment. As explained below, if certain requirements are met, most homeowners will be able to exclude all or at least part of their gain.

SECTION 121 EXCLUSION OF GAIN

On the sale of a principal residence, § 121 generally allows a taxpayer to exclude any gain realized up to a maximum of $250,000 ($500,000 for married taxpayers). Any realized gain in excess of this threshold is taxable as capital gain. This relief provision applies to taxpayers of all ages and as frequently as every two years. To obtain this special treatment, taxpayers must meet several requirements as discussed below.

Principal Residence

The exclusion applies only to the sale of the taxpayer's *principal* residence. Most taxpayers have one residence, and if they move, they simply change their principal residence. However, it is sometimes difficult to determine which residence is the *principal residence* for taxpayers with multiple residences. This is a facts and circumstances determination. Some of the factors to be considered are the amount of time each residence is used, the taxpayer's place of employment, where other family members live, the addresses used (for things like tax returns, driver's licenses, car and voter registration, bills and correspondence), and the location of banks, religious organizations and recreational clubs.[76]

The exclusion only applies if the property is a *residence*. A residence not only includes a conventional home but also a condominium, a cooperative apartment, a mobile home, and a fully equipped recreational vehicle (e.g., plumbing, kitchen, sleeping facilities) not withstanding that it is a means of transportation.[77] The residence also includes the land on which the residence sits and any gain attributable to the land is eligible for exclusion.[78] Land adjacent to the home qualifies if it is regularly used by the owner as part of the residential property, and it is sold along with the home or within two years before or after the sale of the home.[79]

It is not that uncommon for the seller of a home to also sell property that is technically not part of the residence such as furniture, lawn equipment, pool table, hot tub, or similar property. Unless such personalty is treated as a fixture under local law it is not considered part of the residence and, therefore, is not eligible for the exclusion. In most cases, however, sales of such items would result in nondeductible losses.

---

[75] § 165(c).

[76] Reg. § 1.121-1.

[77] See Reg. § 1.121-1(b)(1) and (e)(2), § 280A(f)(1)(A); Prop Reg § 1.280A-1(e)(7), Ex. (2) and *Ronald Haberkorn* 75 T.C. 259 (1980). See also *Richard Dougherty,* T.C. Memo 1994-597, T.C. Memo ¶94597 where a 32-foot charter cruiser that berthed six was considered a home.

[78] But see where a taxpayer who moved his house and sold the land was not entitled to the exclusion for the land. See also IRS Publication 523 (2016) p. 5.

[79] Reg. § 1.121-1(b)(3).

Ownership and Use Tests

The § 121 exclusion is applicable to the sale of a residence only if the residence was *owned* by the taxpayer and *used* as his or her principal residence for at least two of the five years preceding its sale.[80] Observe that the five year window permits taxpayers to use the exclusion even though the property is not owned or used by the taxpayer at the time of the sale. The taxpayer merely needs to meet both tests at some time during the five year period.

The ownership and use requirements are two separate tests. Normally, the period of ownership is not an issue.[81] However, whether the taxpayer *uses* the property as a *principal residence* for the requisite two years during the five-year window can be a bit more troubling. Whether this test is met depends on the fact and circumstances. In this regard, recall that an individual can only have one principal residence at any given time.

Example 33

Y purchased a home in Miami during 1999 and lived in it until she took a new job in Orlando on April 30, 2013. From May 1, 2013 until the Miami house was sold on May 1, 2017, it was used by Y only on occasional days off since she lived in a rented apartment in Orlando. In determining whether the exclusion is available, Y has met the ownership test because she owned it for two of the five years prior to its sale. However, she may fail the use test if she did not use the house as her principal residence for two of the five years before its sale. If so, she did not meet both tests and she does not qualify for the § 121 exclusion.

If, taking into account all facts and circumstances, the house, and not the apartment, is Y's principal residence, she qualifies. She would need to demonstrate that she lived in the house, with only temporary visits to the apartment.

In applying the use test, short temporary absences, such as for vacation or other seasonal absence are counted as periods of use. For this purpose, temporary rental of the property is ignored.

Example 34

T purchased his home in South Bend in 2009. He used the house as his principal residence until January 31, 2015, when he moved to Chicago. Upon moving, T rented his house to tenants until April 18, 2017, when he sold it. T is eligible for the exclusion because he owned and used the house as his principal residence for at least two of the five years preceding the sale.

Example 35

B owned and used her house in Houston as her principal residence from 1991 to the end of 2011. On January 4, 2012, she moved to Denver. Shortly thereafter, B's son moved into the house in March 2012 and used the residence until it sold on July 1, 2017. B may not exclude gain from the sale because she did not use the property as her principal residence for at least two years out of the five years preceding the sale. Use by the son is not counted as the mother's use.

---

[80] § 121(a).

[81] See Reg. § 1.121-1(c)(3) allowing the exclusion where the residence is owned by grantor trusts and disregarded entities such as a single member LLC.

Maximum Exclusion

Generally, the maximum amount excludable with respect to any sale or exchange is $250,000. However, this amount may be doubled to $500,000 for married taxpayers filing joint returns. In such cases, the ownership requirement only needs to be met by one spouse. So if either spouse meets the ownership test and both spouses meet the use test, the $500,000 exclusion applies.[82] However, if only one spouse satisfies the use test, the exclusion is allowable, but limited to $250,000 (or the sum of the amount excludable by each spouse individually).

Example 36

H and W sold their jointly owned and occupied family residence on June 3, 2017, for $650,000. Their basis in the property, that they had owned for thirty years, was $125,000, so their gain was $525,000. If H and W file a joint return for their calendar year 2017, they may exclude $500,000 of the gain and must recognize a long-term capital gain of $25,000.

Example 37

Q purchased a home for use as her principal residence in 1995. On March 31, 2014, Q was transferred by her employer, so she moved away, rented an apartment and left her residence unused. When Q sells the residence at a gain of $200,000 on March 1, 2017, she may exclude the entire gain. During the five years preceding the sale—March 1, 2012 to February 28, 2017—Q *owned* the property for all five years and *used* it as her principal residence for 25 months (i.e., more than the requisite two years).

Example 38

L purchased a residence for use as his principal residence for $123,000 on July 12, 2015. Presented with an attractive offer on the property, L sold the residence on February 2, 2017 for $198,000 (net of selling costs). L must report a long-term capital gain of $75,000 since L does not meet the two of five year tests.

Example 39

F purchased a new personal residence in 1993 for $40,000 and lived in it until June 30, 2005. The house was rented out until January 1, 2009, with depreciation of $8,500 being claimed. On January 2, 2009, F moved back into the house and occupied it as her principal residence until February 5, 2017, when it was sold for $290,000. Since F owned and lived in the home for at least two of the five years preceding the sale, she may exclude up to $250,000 of gain (see subsequent discussions of "depreciation recapture" and "rental and other nonqualified use" after 2008).

---

[82] § 121(b)(1) and (2).

FREQUENCY LIMITATION: ONE SALE EVERY TWO YEARS

The benefits of the § 121 exclusion are so great that without some prohibition taxpayers might utilize the provision in unintended ways. One could easily envision a taxpayer selling one principal residence and excluding the gain, buying and selling another residence and excluding the gain, and continuing this pattern, using the exclusion as a tax shelter. To restrict this possibility, the Code imposes a limitation on the frequency with which the exclusion may be used. The exclusion cannot be used for sales occurring within two years of its last use. In other words, the law allows the exclusion for one sale every two years. To ensure that this rule does not unfairly penalize taxpayers who may be forced to sell their homes before the two-year period has elapsed, special rules concerning sales for unforeseen circumstances exist and are discussed below.[83]

Example 40

M purchased a residence for use as her principal residence for $70,000 on January 2, 2013, and lived in it until March 15, 2014. On March 16, 2014, M rented the original residence and purchased and moved into another residence costing $85,000. Upon retiring, M sold the original residence for $90,000 on December 1, 2015, and excluded most of her gain on the sale (see subsequent discussion of depreciation recapture). Even though M would otherwise be eligible to exclude any gain on the sale of the other residence on March 16, 2016, due to this one sale every two years rule, M will not be eligible until December 2, 2017 (see subsequent discussion related to electing out of § 121).

EXCEPTIONS TO OWNERSHIP, USE, AND FREQUENCY TESTS

At times, taxpayers may be forced to sell their homes due to events beyond their control. For example, an individual may be forced to take a job in another location or move because of health reasons. In these and similar situations, taxpayers may run afoul of the ownership and use requirement or the frequency limitation. Without relief, any realized gain on the sale of the house would be *fully* taxable notwithstanding the fact that there was nothing the taxpayer could do to avoid the sale. Recognizing this problem, § 121 provides some relief.[84] Taxpayers who fail the two-year ownership and use requirement or the one-sale-every-two-year rules may qualify for a *portion* of the exclusion if the sale were due to unforeseen circumstances. In many cases the reduced exclusion would be more than sufficient to offset any appreciation that occurred.

Computation of the Reduced Exclusion

The portion of the exclusion allowed is the percentage of the required 24 months for which the taxpayer satisfies the ownership and use test or if lower the number of months used since the last sale.[85]

$$\begin{matrix} \text{Exclusion} \\ (\$250{,}000 \text{ or } \$500{,}000) \end{matrix} \times \frac{\text{Lesser of time owned and used or time since last sale}}{24 \text{ months}} = \begin{matrix} \text{Reduced} \\ \text{exclusion} \end{matrix}$$

---

[83] § 121(b)(3).

[84] § 121(c).

[85] § 121(c)(1).

> ### Example 41
>
> H and W have one son, S, who was recently diagnosed to have a rare disease. After living in their home only six months, the couple sold their home in Kansas City and moved to Memphis to obtain special treatment only available at St. Jude's Children's Research Hospital. H and W do not meet the ownership and use test since they did not own and use the home as their principal residence for two of the five years prior to the sale. However, because the sale is due to unforeseen circumstances, they qualify for a reduced exclusion of $125,000 ([6/24 = 25%] × $500,000).

This rule is often misconstrued. Taxpayers are *not* entitled to a portion of the exclusion just because they meet the ownership and use test for a few months. For example, if a taxpayer owns and uses the home for only 8 of the 24 months required, he or she is *not* automatically entitled to one-third of the exclusion. The reduced exclusion is granted only if the sale is due to unforeseen circumstances. If a taxpayer simply decides to sell before meeting the tests (e.g., because of market conditions) and without cause, the entire gain is taxable.

The Code provides that the reduced exclusion is available only if due to:[86]

- Change in place of employment.
- Health concerns.
- Unforeseen circumstances.

Change in Place of Employment. Under a safe harbor provided by the Regulations, the reduced exclusion is available due to a change in employment if the new place of business is at least 50 miles farther from the old residence than was the old job.[87] This is the same test that must be met to deduct moving expenses (the taxpayer's new commute without the move would exceed the old commute by more than 50 miles). If the taxpayer was not employed and moves to obtain employment, the distance between the new job and the residence sold must be at least 50 miles.

The tests regarding employment can be met by the

- Taxpayer.
- Taxpayer's spouse.
- Member of the taxpayer's household.
- Co-owner of the residence.

Health Reasons. A reduced exclusion is also allowed for sales due to health reasons (i.e., the sale enables the taxpayer "to obtain, provide, or facilitate the diagnosis, cure mitigation, or treatment of diseases, illness, or injury").[88] If a physician recommends a change of location for health reasons, the test should be met. In contrast, sales that are merely beneficial to the general health or well-being of an individual do not qualify.

Unforeseen Circumstances. If an event occurs that could not reasonably have been anticipated *before* purchasing the residence, the reduced exclusion can be used. According to the Regulations, unforeseen circumstances include[89]

- Involuntary conversion of the residence.
- Natural or man-made disasters.
- Acts of war or terrorism resulting in a casualty to the residence.
- Death.
- Unemployment so as to qualify for unemployment compensation.

[86] § 121(c)(2).

[87] Reg. § 1.121-3(c)(2).

[88] Reg. § 1.121-3(d).

[89] Reg. § 1.121-3(e).

- Change in employment or self-employment status that results in the taxpayer's inability to pay housing costs and reasonable basic living expenses for the taxpayer's household.

- Divorce.

- Multiple births resulting from the same pregnancy.

If a safe harbor is not met, the reduced exclusion may still be available.[90] The Regulations identify a number of other factors to be considered.

Example 42

F purchased a personal residence on March 15, 2016 for $125,000. F must have been living right—he was transferred by his employer to his favorite city, received a big raise, and sold his house in two weeks time for $200,000 (on September 15, 2017). Even though F did not meet the two-of-five-year test, he may exclude his entire $75,000 gain. Because the sale was related to a change of place of employment, F can exclude up to $187,500 ($250,000 × [18 months/24 months]).

Effects of Marriage

In applying the two-of-five-year test, a widow or widower (who has not remarried) selling a residence is treated as having owned and occupied a residence for the period of time it was owned and occupied by his or her deceased spouse.[91]

EXHIBIT 15-4	Section 121 Exclusion Basics

Taxpayer Qualifies If

- The residence was *owned* and used as a *principal residence* for two of the five years preceding the sale.

    and

- No gain was excluded under § 121 in a qualifying sale made within the two years preceding the sale.

Maximum Amount Excluded

- Generally $250,000

- $500,000 for married taxpayers filing jointly if either spouse meets the ownership test and both spouses meet the use test.

- A fraction of these amounts is allowed if the sale is related to a change in the taxpayer's work location, health, or other qualifying unforeseen circumstances.

Example 43

R married S on November 27, 2015, and moved into a home that had been owned and occupied by S since 2002. S died on March 15, 2016, leaving the residence to R. Since R is deemed to have owned and lived in the residence since 2002, she qualifies for the $250,000 exclusion when the residence is sold on February 12, 2017.

---

[90] In PLR 200403049, the IRS found that hostilities between the taxpayers and their neighbors concerning a household member released from rehabilitation qualified as unforeseen circumstances for purposes of § 121.

[91] § 121(e)(1) and (2).

Homes owned by one spouse before marriage or held as separate property during a marriage could also present problems in applying the two of five year rule. To prevent inequities, if a property is transferred to a spouse or former spouse in a transaction that is tax-free under § 1041 (e.g., in a divorce), the transferee is deemed to have owned the residence for the period of time it was owned by the transferor. Recall from Chapter 14 that § 1041 applies to any transfer of property between spouses. It would apply to a transfer by gift, a sale or exchange between spouses acting at arm's length, a transfer in exchange for the relinquishment of property or marital rights, and any exchange otherwise governed by another nonrecognition provision of the Code.

Example 44

D lived in a residence owned as separate property by his spouse, E, for the duration of their four-year marriage. Upon their divorce, D received the residence. Fifteen months after the divorce, D married G and sold the residence (on December 24, 2017), realizing a gain of $280,000. D lived in the residence four years and is deemed to have owned the residence all of the five years preceding the sale. He may, therefore, exclude gain of $250,000 and recognize long-term capital gain of $30,000. D and G cannot exclude $500,000 since G does not meet the residential use test with respect to the residence.

When a spouse dies, the exclusion normally would be limited to that for single taxpayers, $250,000. However, the law provides relief in these situations. A surviving spouse (who has not remarried) qualifies for the $500,000 exclusion if the following conditions are satisfied:

1. All the requirements for the larger exclusion were met at the time of death (i.e., at least one spouse meets the two year ownership test and both spouses meet the two year use test), and

2. The sale occurs within two years of the date of death.

Recall from Chapter 14 that if the property was inherited from the deceased spouse, the basis in the inherited portion is its fair market value at the time of death. Accordingly, there may be little or no gain.

Incapacitated Taxpayers

A taxpayer who purchases a residence and is soon forced to move to a rest home or similar facility may never be able to meet the time requirement for the § 121 exclusion. Fortunately, if a person in this situation lives in the residence for at least one year, he or she will be treated as having lived in that residence during any period of time that he or she has lived in a licensed facility for incapacitated individuals.[92] Thus, anyone who purchases a home, lives in it one year, and spends at least a year in a rest home while still owning the home will meet all the tests for § 121.

Involuntary Conversions

For purposes of § 121, an involuntary conversion of a qualifying residence is treated as the sale of that residence.[93] Thus, a person who meets the ownership and use tests can exclude at least a portion of any gain from the destruction, theft, or condemnation of his or her residence. Involuntary conversions are discussed in detail later in this chapter.

Depreciation Recapture

In some situations, a residence qualifying for the § 121 exclusion may have been used as a rental property or business property (e.g., the taxpayer had a home office). In such case, the taxpayer may have depreciated the property. To be able to depreciate a property, resulting in a basis reduction, and subsequently exclude any gain is too good to be true. Realizing this, Congress requires that the gain be recognized to the extent of any depreciation allowed after May 6, 1997.[94]

---

[92] § 121(d)(9).

[93] § 121(d)(5)(A).

[94] § 121(e)(6).

Example 45

P purchased a home for use as a residence in 2005 for $60,000 and made improvements costing $18,000 in 2013. On June 30, 2016, P retired, moved out and converted the house to rental property. Between that date and the day the property was sold for $200,000, September 30, 2017, P claimed depreciation of $3,600, making the basis in the property $74,400 [$60,000 + $18,000 − $3,600]. P's realized gain is $125,600 ($200,000 − $74,400). P must recognize $3,600 of the gain and may exclude the remaining $122,000 under § 121.

Example 46

Assume the same facts as in the prior example, except the sales price is $77,000. P's gain is $2,600 ($77,000 − $74,400). Since the gain realized is less than the depreciation claimed after May 6, 1997, none of the gain may be excluded under § 121. P must, therefore, recognize a $2,600 gain (i.e., the lesser of the gain realized or the depreciation claimed).

When only a portion of a dwelling was used for business purposes, including use as an office in the home, gain is recognized only to the extent of the depreciation recapture that is required.[95] Any additional gain qualifies for the exclusion, subject to the dollar limitation.

Example 47

B purchased a residence for use as his principal residence for $125,000 in 1993. After the children moved out, he converted a bedroom (ten percent of the residence) to a business office. Depreciation of $1,350 was claimed over three years before the residence was sold during the current year for $375,000. The total gain realized is $251,350 ($375,000 − [$125,000 − $1,350]). One way to look at the sale would be to treat the sale as that of two separate properties.

	Business 10%	Personal 90%
Sales price.	$ 37,500	$ 337,500
Adjusted basis.	(11,150)*	(112,500)
Gain	$ 26,350	$ 225,000

* $125,000 × 10% − $1,350

Fortunately, the IRS chose not to require this two separate sales approach, and B is required to recognize gain of only $1,350. The remaining gain of $250,000 ($251,350 − $1,350) qualifies for exclusion since B owned and occupied the residence for the required period.

Rental and Other Nonqualified Use

Before 2009, individuals who owned rental property could convert it to a personal residence by moving in and living there for two years. By so doing, they would be able to exclude all or a portion of their gain on a subsequent sale.

---

[95] Temp. Reg. § 1.121-2.

Example 48

J, a resident of Illinois, purchased a vacation home in Florida in 1998 for $120,000. After many years of renting it out, he moved into the home on December 19, 2006 and made it his personal residence. At the time of conversion, he had deducted depreciation of $20,000 on the property. After living in the home for the required two years, he sold the residence on December 29, 2008 for $210,000. J realized a gain of $110,000 [$210,000 − (120,000 − $20,000 = $100,000)]. He recognized gain of $20,000 due to the depreciation recapture rule. Prior to 2009, the remaining $90,000 was excluded under § 121.

To eliminate the possible exclusion of the gain by moving into a property for two years before it is sold (as described above), § 121 was amended in 2008. Currently, any gain allocable to periods of nonqualified use after 2008 is not eligible for exclusion. The portion of the gain attributable to nonqualified use is computed as follows:

$$\text{Gain realized (net of depreciation)}^{96} \times \frac{\text{Aggregate periods of nonqualified use}}{\text{Total time owned}} = \text{Taxable gain}$$

The key factor in determining the amount of gain that could be taxed is the taxpayer's nonqualified use. Nonqualified use is generally any period during which the property is not used as the principal residence of the taxpayer or spouse (or former spouse). For this purpose, the numerator does not include nonqualified use prior to 2009. On the other hand, the denominator is the total time owned, including that before 2009. Periods during which the property is vacant or used by relatives are considered periods of nonqualified use. Note also that if the property appreciates in value after a taxpayer makes the property his or her principal residence, the gain is still potentially taxable even though the appreciation occurred while the taxpayer used the property as a personal residence.

Example 49

B, single, was a long-time resident of Cincinnati. On January 1, 2013, he purchased a condominium in South Carolina for $400,000. He used the condo as rental property for two years. He claimed $20,000 of depreciation deductions, reducing his basis in the home to $380,000. On January 1, 2015, B moved to South Carolina and moved into the condo converting it to his principal residence. After living there for three years, on January 1, 2018 B sold the condo for $700,000 and moved out. His gain realized would be $320,000 [$700,000 − ($400,000 − $20,000 = $380,000)]. The $20,000 of gain attributable to the depreciation is included in income.[97] Of the remaining $300,000 gain (the amount remaining after depreciation recapture), 40% of the gain (2 years/5 years), or $120,000 is allocated to nonqualified use and is taxable as long-term capital gain. The remaining 60% of the gain, $180,000, is attributable to qualified use and can be excluded.

Example 50

R bought an investment property on January 1, 2007 and rented it until January 1, 2010 when he began occupying it as his principal residence for the next four years. He sold the property on January 1, 2016, realizing a gain. The two years prior to January 1, 2009 are disregarded for determining nonqualified use (but included for purposes of the ownership test). Thus he has one year of nonqualified use (disregard 2007 and 2008) and eight years of total ownership. Thus, 11.11% (1/9) of the gain (after accounting for depreciation) is taxable.

---

[96] § 121(b)(4)(D) provides that the gain potentially ineligible for the exclusion is the gain remaining after applying depreciation recapture rule.

[97] Gain attributable to the depreciation would be taxed at a maximum rate of 25% (unrecaptured straight-line depreciation on § 1250 property). See Chapter 17.

Although the above examples measure use in terms of years, the IRS requires taxpayers to keep track of their use and its type in terms of days.

The nonqualified use rule was aimed at taxpayers who purchase rental property, rent the property out and then convert it to a personal residence. That is, the rule is designed for taxpayers who formerly used their residence as rental property. For this reason, nonqualified use that occurs after the taxpayer's last use of the property as a principal residence and is within five years prior to the sale is disregarded. This rule allows homeowners to move out of their principal residence and convert it to nonqualified use property (e.g., rental) and still be eligible for the full exclusion assuming the other requirements of § 121 are met.

Example 51

T purchased a home in Nantucket on June 1, 2013. She used it as her personal residence for two years until June 1, 2015 and then converted it to rental property. On June 1, 2018, she sold the home. The rental use is disregarded (i.e., it is not non-qualified use) since it occurred after T had used it as her residence and within five years prior to the sale. While she would be required to recognize income to the extent of any depreciation deducted, the remaining gain would be eligible for the exclusion. Note that the special rule gives taxpayers up to three years to sell the home after moving out without lossing the benefit of this exclusion. Had T sold her home on June 1, 2018, she would not have qualified for the exclusion because she did not use it as her personal residence for 2 of the last 5 years.

In identifying nonqualified use, certain periods when the homeowner did not live in the residence are ignored. These include absences due to government service (e.g., service in the military, intelligence community, or U.S. Foreign Service), change of employment, health conditions and other unforeseen circumstances.

Example 52

Before shipping off to military duty in Europe, H purchased a home in Maryland. He rented the property for the five years that he was stationed overseas. The rental use is not considered nonqualified use since it was attributable to military service.

Sale after a Like-Kind Exchange

The $250,000 or $500,000 exclusion is so attractive that without certain restrictions, it could be easily abused. For example, owners of rental property might be interested in exchanging a rental property for another rental property in a tax-deferred exchange (see subsequent coverage in this chapter), later converting the replacement property to a principal residence, and then (after at least two years) selling the replacement property and taking advantage of the exclusion. This possibility remains, but the § 121 exclusion will not apply to a property unless five years have passed since the like-exchange occured.

Example 53

B owned a duplex that he rented to college students. He purchased it for $240,000 in 1995. Depreciation of $98,000 was claimed, reducing B's basis to $142,000. On November 16, 2013, B exchanged the duplex for a residential property worth $450,000 that was used as rental property. In October 2014, the tenant moved out and B moved into the residence. Under the general rule, B would qualify for the § 121 exclusion in October 2016. However, the special rule for like-kind exchange property applies. As a result, B will not qualify until November 16, 2018 (five years after the exchange).

If B sells the property, after November 15, 2018, for $490,000, the gain realized is $348,000 ($490,000 − [$240,000 − $98,000]). B can exclude up to $250,000. B must recapture the depreciation and apply the nonqualified use rule for the 34 months in 2012–2014. However, if the sale had occurred earlier, none of the gain is excludable.

Interaction of §§ 121 and 1031

Occasionally, a like-kind exchange may involve property that not only qualifies for tax-deferral under the like-kind exchange provisions of § 1031 but also qualifies for the residence exclusion of § 121. For example, a taxpayer may have used a house as a principal residence from 2007 through 2015, rented out the house from 2016 through 2017 and then exchanged the house for cash and new property that will be rented. The IRS has provided guidance for the tax consequences of such exchanges, allowing taxpayers to exclude any otherwise excludable gain and to generally defer any other excess gain.[98]

Electing Out

Taxpayers may find themselves in a position where they may have two or more residence sales within a two year period. However, as noted above, the exclusion cannot be used within two years of its last use. In such case, a taxpayer normally wants to apply the exclusion to the sale producing the most gain. Section 121 provides such flexibility by allowing a taxpayer to elect not to have § 121 apply to an otherwise qualifying sale. The election is made by reporting the gain on the tax return for the year of the sale.[99] Presumably (unless future guidance provides otherwise) the election can be made on an amended return.

Example 54

S purchased her first residence in Chicago on May 1, 2010. She lived there until she was transferred by her employer to Phoenix on August 1, 2014. She did not immediately sell her Chicago residence but decided to rent it to an old friend. In Phoenix, she purchased a second residence which she occupied beginning on September 1, 2014. On December 15, 2016, S sold the second residence in Phoenix, realizing a gain of $5,000. Then on January 31, 2017, she sold her original Chicago residence at a gain of $177,000 ($2,000 of which is attributable to depreciation allowed). Only $175,000 can qualify for exclusion due to the depreciation claimed.

Both residences meet the two of five years ownerships and use tests. If S excludes the $5,000 gain from the second residence in 2016, she cannot exclude the $175,000 gain from the original residence in 2017 because of the one sale every two years rule. It would, therefore, be in her best interest to elect out of the benefits of § 121 exclusion with respect to the $5,000 gain, in order to take advantage of the § 121 exclusion with respect to the $175,000 gain. This would be done by including the $5,000 gain in her 2016 income.

 CHECK YOUR KNOWLEDGE

Review Question 1

True-False. Helen excluded $250,000 of gain from the sale of her primary residence which was sold on August 4, 2015. Helen cannot exclude her $23,000 gain from the sale of another primary residence on November 1, 2017, even though she has owned and used this home for more than two years.

False. Since more than two years transpired from the first sale to the second sale, Helen qualifies to exclude gain on both sales. The fact that the sale was in the second tax year after the original sale is not determinative.

Review Question 2

True-False. Mick purchased a residence on March 1, 2013 and lived in it until July 31, 2014. He rented it from August 1, 2014 until June 30, 2016 (claiming depreciation of $7,000), and then lived in it again from July 1, 2016 until it was sold on June 1, 2017. Mick cannot exclude any of his gain of $40,000 under § 121.

---

[98] Rev. Proc. 2005-14 IRB No. 2005-7.   [99] See § 121(f) and I.R.S. Publication 523, p.2.

False. Mick qualifies for the § 121 exclusion because he lived in the residence more than two years during the five years preceding the sale (i.e., June 1, 2012 to May 31, 2017). Specifically, he lived there 28 (17 + 11) months. However, Mick can only exclude $33,000, since the first $7,000 of the $40,000 gain must be recognized due to the depreciation claimed. Mick must also recognize a fraction of the remaining $33,000 of gain due to nonqualified use for 11 months (11 months nonqualified use/51 months total use × $33,000 = $7,118).

Review Question 3

Lin purchased a residence on June 1, 2016, for $235,000. On December 1, 2017, she sold the residence for $295,000, so she could move to a nearby city where she was transferred by her employer. How much gain, if any, may Lin exclude under § 121?

All $60,000. Even though Lin did not meet the two of five years ownership and use requirements, she qualifies for a reduced exclusion limit since the sale is related to a change in the place of employment. The reduced limit if $187,500 ($250,000 × [18 months/24 months]).

Review Question 4

J and K were married on June 1, 2016, and K moved into the home that J had owned and occupied for ten years. On September 1, 2017, J and K sold the residence, recognizing a gain of $295,000. How much of the gain may J and K exclude on their joint return for 2017?

Only $250,000. In order to qualify for the increased $500,000 exclusion, both husband and wife must have used the residence for two of the five years preceding the sale. K only lived there for 15 months.

Review Question 5

After living together for ten years, L and M finally married on June 1, 2016. After their marriage, the couple continued to live in L's home. L never retitled the property and held it separately primarily for estate planning purposes. On September 1, 2017, L sold the residence, recognizing a gain of $360,000. How much of the gain may L and M exclude on their joint return for 2017?

All $360,000. In order to qualify for the increased $500,000 exclusion, only one spouse must have owned the residence for two of the preceding five years, but both husband and wife must have used the residence for two of the five years. They must file a joint return, but there is no requirement that the property be jointly owned or that they be married during the two years that they lived there.

Other Nontaxable Transactions

CHANGES IN FORM OF DOING BUSINESS

LO.6

Identify other common nontaxable transactions.

Several provisions in the Internal Revenue Code are intended to allow mere changes in the form of carrying on a continuing business activity without the recognition of gain or loss. Section 721, for example, allows the transfer of property to a partnership in exchange for a partnership interest without the recognition of taxable gain or loss. Section 351 allows a similar treatment when property is transferred to a corporation solely in exchange for its stock by persons possessing control, and § 355 provides for nontaxability in certain corporate reorganizations. These specific topics are addressed in subsequent chapters.

CERTAIN EXCHANGES OF STOCK IN SAME CORPORATION

No gain or loss is recognized by the shareholder who exchanges common stock for common stock or preferred stock for preferred stock in the same corporation under § 1036. The exchange may be voting stock for nonvoting stock, and it is immaterial whether the exchange is with another shareholder or with the issuing corporation.[100] If the exchange is not solely in kind, the rules of § 1031(b) (applicable to like-kind exchanges) are applied to determine the amount of any gain recognized.[101]

---

[100] Reg. § 1.1036-1(a).   [101] Reg. § 1.1036-1(b).

CERTAIN EXCHANGES OF U.S. OBLIGATIONS

Gain may be deferred in the case of certain exchanges of U.S. obligations between the taxpayer and the U.S. Government. Section 1037 applies to exchanges of bonds of the government issued under Chapter 31 of Title 31 (the Second Liberty Bond Act). The Treasury regulations for § 1037 discuss the application of this section.

REPOSSESSION OF REAL PROPERTY

Section 1038 provides that the seller of real property will recognize a gain on the repossession of real property only to the extent the sum of the money and other property besides the repossessed realty received exceeds the gain from the transaction previously reported. This provision applies only to repossessions to satisfy debt obligations received in exchange for the sold property (e.g., foreclosure for nonpayment of mortgage). Such purchase-money obligations must be secured by an interest in the property. If any part of these obligations has previously been deducted as a bad debt, the amount of such deductions is included in income in the year of the repossession.

CERTAIN EXCHANGES OF INSURANCE POLICIES

Section 1035 allows the deferral of gain on the exchange of a life insurance contract for another insurance policy. Additionally, it allows certain exchanges involving annuity contracts and endowment contracts.

Tax Planning Considerations

CURRENT RECOGNITION VERSUS DEFERRAL

A basic concept in tax planning, as discussed in earlier chapters, is the deferral of tax payments. Each of the provisions discussed in this chapter (as it relates to gains) is a perfect example of such a deferral. A taxpayer is usually better off by deferring any gain—unless he or she expects to be in a much higher effective tax bracket in the later year when the deferred gain would be recognized. Of course, a taxpayer is *always* better off if he or she can avoid tax altogether, as is the case under § 121. However, if a loss is deferred under § 1031, taxes are accelerated. Thus, if the adjusted basis of business or investment property being disposed of exceeds its fair market value, the nonrecognition treatment of § 1031 should be avoided.

LO.7

Recognize tax planning opportunities related to the more common types of gain-deferral transactions available to individual taxpayers.

CURRENT GAIN RESULTING IN FUTURE REDUCTIONS

In each case of deferred gain, the mechanism is a reduced basis in the replacement property. If this replacement property is depreciable property, the depreciation deductions will also be smaller. It may be advantageous to report a large gain *currently* if the tax cost is low, and reap the benefit of the larger depreciation deductions in later years.

Example 55

W plans to dispose of a building that would result in capital gain if sold, and acquire similar property in a different location. W could defer gain by arranging an exchange, but his basis in the new property would be low. W also has a large capital loss carryforward that he has been deducting at the rate of $3,000 per year.

If W sells the property, the gain would offset the capital loss carryforward and he would pay no tax. His basis in the new building would be its cost, resulting in larger future depreciation deductions.

IMPORTANCE OF CAPITAL BUDGETING IN DECISION MAKING

In any decision of whether to defer taxes when subsequent tax years are affected, capital budgeting techniques are appropriate in making the decision. When considering possible investment opportunities, a taxpayer must *compare* current investment requirements and tax effects with the future returns from the investment and their tax effects. Some form of present-value analysis will help the taxpayer to make a sound decision. A similar analysis should be applied in deciding the appropriateness of entering into any nontaxable (tax-deferred) transaction.

Problem Materials

DISCUSSION QUESTIONS

15-1 *Principal Place of Residence.* V lived in Milwaukee and worked in Chicago for many years. Finally, V rented an apartment in Chicago, where she stayed on week-nights. Weekends and holidays were spent in Milwaukee. Where is V's *principal* place of residence for purposes of § 121?

15-2 *Section 121 Exclusion.* List the two principal requirements that must be met before one can qualify for the § 121 exclusion upon the sale of a residence.

15-3 *Limit on Amount of Exclusion.* What is the maximum amount of gain that can be excluded under § 121?

15-4 *Loss on Sale of Personal Assets.* Y sold his principal residence and realized a $12,000 loss. What is the proper tax treatment of this loss?

15-5 *Depreciation Recapture.* P owned and used a house as her principal residence for 10 years. She moved out and rented it for two years before selling it this year for a $50,000 gain. Depreciation of $4,000 was claimed. How is this sale reported by P on her current year return?

15-6 *Conversion of Residence.* Y purchased a property to be used as a rental on September 15, 2010. Y moved into this house on May 1, 2017 in hopes that it would qualify for the § 121 exclusion.
  a.   Can the residence eventually qualify for the § 121 exclusion?
  b.   If so, how long must Y live in it before the gain can qualify for the exclusion?
  c.   Can the entire gain be excluded?

15-7 *Two-of-Five-Year Test.* F sold her primary residence on June 2, 2017, and excluded her $22,500 gain. She purchased and moved into another primary residence on August 5, 2017. On what date can F first qualify for the § 121 exclusion with respect to the second residence?

15-8 *Frequency Limitation.* G sold a qualifying residence on June 2, 2015, and excluded his $22,500 gain on his calendar year 2015 return. G had previously purchased and moved into another residence on December 7, 2014. On what date may G first qualify for the § 121 exclusion with respect to the second residence?

15-9 *Sale Due to Unanticipated Events.* S purchased her dream home on April 17, 2016 for $120,000. Then, much to her surprise, she was given a promotion and transferred by her employer. So she sold the home on January 2, 2017, for $170,000.
  a.   Does S qualify for the exclusion of gain under § 121?
  b.   If so, what is the maximum amount S can exclude?
  c.   Under what other circumstances might S be able to qualify for this partial exclusion?

15-10 *Conversion of Rental Property.* R lives in the suburbs of Miami. Several years ago, he bought a condo on the beach. He rented the condo out for several years. During this time, the property appreciated substantially. He is now considering selling his suburban home, converting the condo into his personal residence and then selling it to take advantage of the exclusion for gains on the sale of a personal residence. What advice would you give R?

15-11 *Marriage and § 121.* D gave E a one-half interest in D's home of 10 years as a wedding gift. E moved into the home after the wedding. Eighteen months later, on December 2, 2017, the residence was sold at a gain of $314,500. How much of the gain may be excluded by D and E on their joint return for 2017?

15-12 *Divorce and § 121.* F and G lived in a home that was F's separate property during the duration of their five-year marriage. Upon their divorce, G received title to the property. How much, if any, of the $200,000 gain may G exclude upon the sale of the house one year later?

15-13 *Death of a Spouse and § 121.* X and Y were married on November 14, 2017, after which Y moved into the home that had been owned and occupied by X for more than 30 years. Upon X's death, Y inherited the home that had cost $40,000 and was worth $300,000. How much gain must Y recognize when she sells the home one year after X's death for $315,000?

15-14 *Condemnation.* What is required in order to have "threat or imminence" of condemnation?

15-15 *Frequency Limitation.* How does the concept of "similar or related in service or use" differ between an owner/user of property and an owner/lessor?

15-16 *Replacement Period.* B's beauty salon was destroyed by fire on April 21, 2017. The building was covered by current value insurance, and B realized a gain of $70,000. When must B reinvest in order to defer this gain under § 1033?

15-17 *Making the § 1033 Election.* How does a taxpayer elect to defer gain under § 1033 in involuntary conversions?

15-18 *Interaction of §§ 121 and 1033.* G and H had an amount realized of $800,000 and a gain of $520,000 in 2017 on the insurance recovery from the fire that totally destroyed their residence of ten years. May the taxpayers use both the residence exclusion and the involuntary conversion rules to avoid gain recognition?

15-19 *Ineligible Property.* Property "held for sale" is not eligible for like-kind exchange treatment. Elaborate.

15-20 *Real Property under § 1031.* K proposes to exchange a downtown office building she holds as rental property for a 450-acre ranch in Virginia that she would operate as a horse ranch. Will this transaction qualify for like-kind exchange treatment?

15-21 *Personal Property under § 1031.* What constitutes personal property of "like-kind"?

15-22 *Boot.* What is the meaning of "boot" in § 1031 like-kind exchanges?

15-23 *Liabilities.* Are liabilities discharged always treated as boot received in a like-kind exchange under § 1031? Explain.

15-24 *Basis of Property Received.* How is the basis in the property received in a like-kind exchange under § 1031 determined? What is the basis in any boot received?

15-25 *§ 1031 Elective or Mandatory.* Is like-kind exchange treatment elective with the taxpayer? If not, how could such treatment be avoided if the taxpayer was so inclined?

15-26 *Holding Period.* In the current year, R received a rental house and 300 shares of IBM common stock in exchange for a vacant lot he had held as an investment since April 16, 2010. When does the holding period for the rental house begin? For the IBM stock?

PROBLEMS

15-27 *Calculation of Gain Realized.* M, single. purchased a residence on May 1, 2003 for $195,000. M lived in the residence from May 1, 2003 to June 1, 2007 when he began renting it. He rented it from June 2, 2007 through November 30, 2011. He once again lived there from December 1, 2011, until it was sold on May 6, 2017. The following information was derived from M's records:

Purchase closing costs.	$ 1,450
Depreciation claimed while the property was rented	12,250
Addition of family room (January 2010)	23,500
Painting of interior (April 2012).	4,200

The property sold for $289,000, and M incurred realtor's commissions of $16,340 and other closing costs of $2,300. The depreciation claimed was $12,250.
   a.   How much is M's basis in the residence at the time of the sale?
   b.   How much is M's gain realized on the sale?
   c.   How much is M's gain recognized?
   d.   How would the answer to (c) differ if any of the rental period had been after December 31, 2008?

15-28 *Section 121 Exclusion.* P and Q, who are married, sold their residence of 19 years on February 12, 2017. The house had cost $120,000 and improvements of $22,000 had been made. The house sold for $750,000. Selling costs of $37,500 were incurred and deferred maintenance costs of $4,500 were paid weeks before the sale. P and Q have taxable income not including this gain of $70,000 on their joint return for the year.
   a.   How much is P and Q's gain realized on this sale?
   b.   How much of that gain, if any, must be recognized? How will it be taxed?

15-29 *Section 121 Exclusion.* Four years ago C bought a sail boat for $225,000. Immediately after the purchase he moved in and it became his principal residence. He keeps the sail boat in a slip near Sarasota but often sails off for weeks at a time. This year he decided to sell the boat. In preparation for sale, he made improvements costing $22,300 and repairs totaling $32,000. He sold the boat for $345,000. How is this sale treated on C's income tax return for the calendar year of sale?

15-30 *Section 121 Exclusion with Depreciation.* V owned a house that cost $200,000 in which she lived from July 1, 2000 until June 30, 2014. From July 1, 2014 until September 30, 2017, the home was rented, and depreciation of $8,000 was claimed. How will the sale of the residence for $325,000 on October 1, 2017 be treated?

15-31 *Limitation on Amount Excluded.* In each of the following situations, determine the maximum amount that may be excluded under § 121.
   a.   H and W sold their home on October 31, 2017. The home was owned as separate property and lived in by W for six years. H lived in the home since they were married three years ago.
   b.   K owned a rental property which she rented to J for several years. Upon marrying J on June 1, 2016, K moved into the house. The house was sold on August 1, 2017, and J and K file a joint return for 2017.
   c.   L, an unmarried individual, purchased and moved into a residence on March 15, 2016 for $650,000. On June 16, 2017, L sold the residence for $825,000 because she was transferred to a new work location.

15-32 *Sale of Principal Residence—Costs.* U received and accepted an offer to purchase her principal residence for $78,000 on March 12 and completed the sale on May 8 (all in the current year). She later purchased a replacement residence. Specify whether each of the following is properly classified as a nondeductible expense, a selling expense, an addition to the basis of the residence that was sold, or none of these.
   a.   New garage built during February of the current year at a cost of $12,500 because the city requires that every residence that is sold in the subdivision have a garage.
   b.   Real estate transfer taxes of $780 assessed by the city government.
   c.   Steam cleaning of carpets for $125 on April 22 and paid for upon completion.
   d.   Painting interior of residence completed and paid for in February.
   e.   Commissions of $4,680 paid to listing and selling real estate brokers.

15-33 *Sale Due to Unanticipated Events.* Q purchased a new residence on April 17, 2015 for $720,000. Upon receiving a very lucrative offer of employment, Q moved to another city and sold the residence on January 17, 2017, for $1,000,000. How much gain must Q recognize on this sale?

15-34 *Sale of Principal Residence.* During the current year, H and W ended their stormy marriage of 20 years. They had jointly owned a residence valued at $330,000 with a basis of $95,000. As part of their divorce settlement, H sold his interest in the home to W for $165,000. Assuming that there were no selling costs or fixing-up expenses, answer the following:
   a. How much gain must H recognize?
   b. What is W's basis in the residence?

15-35 *Rental Use.* K purchased a house for $200,000 on May 1, 2003. She rented the house to tenants from May 1, 2003 to May 1, 2014 and deducted depreciation of $50,000. On May 1, 2014, she moved into the home and used it as her residence until May 1, 2015 when she sold the home for $400,000.
   a. What is the amount of gain recognized on the sale of the home?
   b. What if she had sold the home on April 29, 2016?

15-36 *Involuntary Conversion.* The business office of K, a real estate broker, was destroyed by fire on August 22, 2017.
   a. By what date must K reinvest to avoid recognizing gain from the insurance proceeds received as a result of the fire?
   b. What type of property must K purchase to avoid recognition?
   c. Would your answers differ if, rather than being destroyed by fire, the office building had been condemned by the state for highway right of way?

15-37 *Involuntary Conversion.* L owned a leased warehouse that was totally destroyed by fire on October 31, 2017. The building had a basis to L of $45,000 and his insurance paid the replacement cost of $75,000. L completed construction of a new warehouse on the same land on December 2, 2019 at a cost of $80,000.
   a. How much gain must L recognize on this conversion?
   b. What is L's basis in the replacement warehouse?
   c. Summarize L's reporting requirements.
   d. How would your answers to parts (a), (b), and (c) differ if L had invested only $65,000 in the replacement property?

15-38 *Involuntary Conversion.* Complete the following table involving certain involuntary conversions in which the taxpayer elects to defer gain. The property is converted into cash and the cash is invested in qualifying replacement property in each case. Each case is independent of the others.

Case	Amount Realized	Adjusted Basis	Amount Reinvested	Gain Recognized	Basis in Replacement
A	$3,000	$1,600	$1,200	$	$
B	3,000	1,300	1,400	$	$
C	6,000	4,000	5,500	$	$
D	7,500	3,400	7,900	$	$
E	8,400	9,000	8,700	$	$

15-39 *Involuntary Conversion Replacement Period.* For each of the following involuntary conversions, state the beginning and ending dates of the permissible replacement period.
   a. The city of Knoxville announced plans to condemn D's rental property on March 15, 2016 and completed condemnation proceedings on June 12, 2017 for $330,000.
   b. Same facts as in part (a), except that the property was D's principal residence.
   c. A fire destroyed G's bike shop on November 7, 2016. G received an insurance settlement on April 12, 2017.

15-40 *Involuntary Conversion—Condemned Real Estate.* The city of Orange Grove condemned T's automobile parts warehouse for use as a community park. Plans to condemn the property were announced on June 14, 2016, instituted on December 12, 2016, and completed on May 1, 2017. T's basis in the warehouse was $235,000, and the condemnation award was $366,000.

a.   Describe the type of property with which T must replace this warehouse in order to qualify for involuntary conversion treatment.

b.   Specify the reinvestment period during which T must reinvest in order to qualify for involuntary conversion treatment.

c.   Determine the amount of gain that T must recognize and T's basis in the replacement property, which costs $387,000.

15-41 *Involuntary Conversion—Destroyed Residence.* B's residence and contents were totally destroyed when a nearby gas main burst. The gas company paid B $90,000 for the building (with a basis of $65,000) and $35,000 for the contents as follows:

	Fair Value	Adjusted Basis
Clothing, personal effects.	$10,000	$22,000
Furniture and fixtures	8,000	16,500
Appliances, utensils, etc..	7,000	11,000
Art collection	10,000	4,500

a.   What requirements must be met for B to defer all of his gain under § 1033?

b.   How would your answer differ if the loss had been caused by a fire which was a Presidentially declared disaster and the payments were made by B's insurer (the art collection was not separately listed in the insurance policy)?

15-42 *Like-Kind Exchange.* F traded in an automobile that was used 100% of the time for business for a new auto for the same use. F had fully depreciated the old auto. The auto received was worth $12,000 and F paid $5,000 cash in addition to giving up her old auto.

a.   How much gain must F recognize on the trade-in?

b.   What is F's adjusted basis in the new auto?

15-43 *Like-Kind Exchange.* T transferred his farmland (100% business) to V in exchange for a parcel of unimproved urban real estate held by V as an investment. The farm was valued at $400,000 and was subject to a mortgage obligation of $260,000. T's basis in the farm was $340,000. The urban real estate was valued at $450,000 and was subject to a mortgage of $310,000.

a.   How much gain must T recognize on this exchange?

b.   What is T's basis in the urban real estate received?

15-44 *Like-Kind Exchange.* Refer to *Problem 15-43*. Assume that V had a basis of $360,000 in the urban real estate transferred to T.

a.   How much gain must V recognize on the exchange?

b.   What is V's basis in the farm property received?

15-45 *Like-Kind Exchange.* B exchanged undeveloped land worth $245,000 with C for developed land worth $225,000 and DEF corporation stock worth $20,000. B's adjusted basis in the land was $176,000. C's adjusted bases in the land and stock were $243,000 and $17,500, respectively.

a.   How much gain or loss must B recognize in this exchange, and what are his bases in the land and stock received?

b.   How much gain or loss must C recognize in this exchange, and what is her basis in the land received?

15-46 *Like-Kind Exchange.* F exchanged undeveloped land worth $45,000 with G for land worth $42,000 and a personal automobile worth $3,000. F's adjusted basis in the land was $36,000. G's adjusted bases in the land and automobile were $39,500 and $2,500, respectively.

a.   How much gain or loss must F recognize in this exchange, and what are his bases in the land and automobile received?

b.   How much gain or loss must G recognize in this exchange, and what is her basis in the land received?

15-47 *Like-Kind Exchange: Installment Reporting.* D entered into an agreement on December 15, 2016 under which he will immediately receive an apartment complex worth $300,000 and an installment obligation of the buyer for $200,000 with interest at 12% annually. D is to give up another apartment complex in which he has a basis of $320,000.

a. What is the minimum gain that D must recognize on this exchange in 2016?

b. How much gain must D report when he receives his first principal installment of $20,000 (plus accrued interest) in 2017?

15-48 *Like-Kind Exchanges.* Complete the following table for exchanges that qualify for like kind exchange treatment under § 1031.

Case	Adjusted Basis of Property Given Up	FMV of Property Received	Cash Boot Received	Cash Boot Paid	Gain or Loss Recognized	Basis of Property Received
A	$3,000	$2,500	$ 0	$ 0	$_____	$_____
B	5,000	5,000	0	1,000	$_____	$_____
C	4,000	6,000	1,000	0	$_____	$_____
D	7,000	5,900	600	0	$_____	$_____
E	5,000	4,000	2,500	0	$_____	$_____
F	3,000	3,200	200	0	$_____	$_____
G	4,000	3,600	500	0	$_____	$_____

TAX RESEARCH PROBLEM

15-49 *Exchange of Businesses.* T has owned and operated a taxi service (T's Taxi) for many years, but he now wishes to move to a new city. If T sells his business, he will have a substantial gain. Through a business broker, T has arranged to exchange his business for a limousine service (U's Limos) in the other city. In order to strike the deal, U insists that T sign a covenant-not-to-compete that U and T value at $25,000. The balance sheets (representing fair market values) of the two businesses are as follows:

	T's Taxi	U's Limos
Automobiles.	$700,000	$750,000
Computers and data handling equipment.	60,000	30,000
Covenant-not-to-compete	25,000	0
Goodwill.	65,000	60,000
Totals	$850,000	$840,000

In order to equalize the transaction, U will pay T $10,000 cash. T's bases are as follows: in the automobiles, $675,000; in the computers, etc., $65,000; and in the covenant and goodwill, $0. T has asked you to determine the tax effect of this proposed exchange before he completes it.

Property Transactions: Capital Gains and Losses

Learning Objectives

Upon completion of this chapter you will be able to:

LO.1 Discuss the rationale for preferential treatment of capital gains.

LO.2 Explain the conditions that must be met to obtain capital gain treatment.

LO.3 Define a capital asset and use this definition to distinguish capital assets from other types of property.

LO.4 Explain the holding period rules for classifying a capital asset transaction as either short-term or long-term.

LO.5 Apply the capital gain and loss netting process to a taxpayer's capital asset transactions and explain their treatment.

LO.6 Explain the differences in tax treatment of the capital gains and losses of a corporate taxpayer versus those of an individual taxpayer.

LO.7 Identify various transactions to which capital gain or loss treatment has been extended.

LO.8 Discuss the tax treatment of investments in corporate bonds and other forms of indebtedness.

Chapter Outline

Introduction

LO.1

Discuss the rationale for preferential treatment of capital gains.

The final piece of the property transaction puzzle concerns the treatment of the taxpayer's recognized gains and losses. In the infancy of the tax law, solving this puzzle was relatively easy. Taxpayers who sold or otherwise disposed of property needed only to determine their gain or loss realized and how much, if any, they had to recognize. The actual treatment of the gain or loss recognized—or more precisely, the rate at which it was taxed—was identical to that for other types of income. The simplicity of treating all income and loss the same was short-lived, however, lasting a mere eight years, from 1913 to 1921. Since 1921, the taxation of property transactions has been complicated by the additional need to determine not only the amount of the taxpayer's gain but also its character. Virtually all of this complication can be traced to one source: Congress's desire to provide some type of preferential treatment for capital gains.

Whether capital gains should be taxed more leniently than wages and other types of income is the subject of what seems to be a never-ending debate. When the first income tax statute was enacted, there was nothing in the definition of income to indicate that gains on dealings in property were taxable. Seizing on the omission, taxpayers relied on somewhat abstract tax theory and ingeniously argued that a gain on a sale of property (e.g., a citrus grove) was not the same as income derived from such property (e.g., sale of the fruit) and should not be taxed at all. Moreover, taxpayers who sold property and reinvested in similar property argued that they had not altered their economic position and that taxation was therefore not appropriate. While detractors cried "nonsense!" champions of favorable treatment offered additional justification, explaining that capital gain is often artificial, merely reflecting increases in the general price level. Perhaps the most defensible argument can be found in the Ways and Means Committee Report that accompanied the Revenue Act of 1921. As the following quotation shows, Congress believed that the progressive nature of the tax rates was unduly harsh on capital gains, particularly when the rate (at that time) could be as high as 77 percent.

> The sale of … capital assets is now seriously retarded by the fact that gains and profits earned over a series of years are under present law taxed as a lump sum (and the amount of surtax greatly enhanced thereby) in the year in which the profit is realized. Many of such sales … have been blocked by this feature of the present law. In order to permit such transactions to go forward without fear of a prohibitive tax, the proposed bill … adds a new section [providing a lower rate for gains from the sale or dispositions of capital assets].[1]

Although the top rate is currently much lower than it has been historically, the bunching effect is still cited as one of the major justifications for lower rates for capital gains. Proponents also reason that taxing capital gains at low rates encourages taxpayers to make riskier investments and also helps stimulate the economy by encouraging the mobility of capital. Without such rules, taxpayers, they believe, would tend to retain rather than sell their assets.

Of course, opponents of special treatment are equally vocal in their objections to the benefits extended capital gains. They reject the proposition that capital gain should not be taxed. They maintain that income is income regardless of its form. Opponents also doubt the stimulus value of preferential treatment and complain about the uneven playing field that such treatment creates. Finally, opponents offer one argument for which there is no denial. As will become all too clear in this and the following chapter, the special treatment reserved for capital gains and losses creates an inordinate amount of complexity in the tax law.

---

[1] House Rep. No. 350, 67th Cong. 1st Sess., pp. 10–11, as quoted in Seidman, *Legislative History of the Income Tax Laws, 1938–1961,* 813 (1938).

Despite the various objections, Congress has generally sided with those in favor of preferential treatment. But, as history shows, there is little agreement on exactly what that treatment should be. For historians, a summary of the treatment of capital gains over the years is contained in the footnote below.[2]

Beginning in 2013, the tax rates that normally apply to long-term capital gains (LTCGs) depend on the top tax rate applying to the taxpayer's ordinary taxable income. The rate on LTCGs is 0% if the gains fall into the 10% or 15% brackets. If the gains fall into the 25, 28, 33, or 35 percent bracket, the LTCG rate is 15 percent. For taxpayers whose gains cause their taxable income to exceed $400,000 ($450,000 for joint filers and $425,000 for heads of household), the LTCG rate is 20 percent. The rate for most dividends is the same as that for LTCGs. The rates for 2017 are summarized below:

Ordinary Income Bracket	LTCG Rate
0–15.0%	0%
25–35.0	15
39.6	20

The current rates applying to capital gains, like their predecessors, can produce substantial savings. The table below illustrates the benefit of the 15% capital gains rate.

Ordinary Rate	Capital Gains Rate	Differential Rate	Percentage Savings
39.6%	20%	19.6%	49.49%
33.0	15	18.0	54.55
28.0	15	13.0	46.43
25.0	15	10.0	40.00
15.0	0	15.0	100.00
10.0	0	10.0	100.00

The § 1411 surtax on investment income can erode the benefit of these capital gains rates for higher income taxpayers. As discussed in Chapter 3, § 1411 imposes an additional tax on net investment income of 3.8% for high income taxpayers (those with modified adjusted gross income exceeding certain thresholds: $250,000 for joint filers or surviving spouses, $125,000 for married individuals filing separate returns, and $200,000 in any other case). When this surtax applies, the overall rate for those with taxable incomes over $441,000 ($466,950 for joint filers) increases to 23.8% (20% + 3.8%).

As is apparent from the table above, capital gain treatment is extremely desirable. But as the remainder of this chapter explains, this favorable treatment is not extended to just any gain. The taxpayer must jump through a few hoops, turn a couple of cartwheels, and clear innumerable hurdles before he or she reaches the pot of gold at the end of the capital gains rainbow.

General Requirements for Capital Gain

A gain or loss is considered a capital gain or loss and receives special treatment only if each of several factors is present. The asset being transferred must be a *capital asset* and the disposition must constitute a *sale or exchange*. In addition, the exact treatment of any net gain or loss can be determined only after taking into consideration the *holding period* of the property transferred. Each of these factors is discussed below.

LO.2

Explain the conditions that must be met to obtain capital gain treatment.

---

[2] From 1922 to 1933, taxpayers could pay a flat 12.5% tax on their capital gains. From 1934 to 1937, the treatment changed, allowing an exclusion for capital gains ranging from 20 to 80 percent, depending on how long the asset was held. In 1942, the exclusion was replaced by a deduction equal to 50% of the gain. The 50% deduction—increased in 1978 to 60%—made capital gains the most popular game in town from 1942 to 1986, a period of about 45 years. In 1986, when Congress lowered the top rate on ordinary income to 28 percent, favorable capital gain treatment was repealed. The period for low rates on ordinary income was only temporary, as Congress raised the top rate to 31% in 1991 and 39.6% in 1993. The increase prompted Congress to resurrect favorable treatment for capital gains, providing that the gains of an individual would be taxed at a maximum rate not to exceed 28 percent. From 2003 to 2012, capital gains could be taxed at one of four different rates (28, 25, 15, 10, or 0 percent), depending on a number of circumstances.

Capital Assets

DEFINITION OF A CAPITAL ASSET

LO.3

Define a capital asset and use this definition to distinguish capital assets from other types of property.

In order for a taxpayer to have a capital gain or loss, the Code generally requires a sale or exchange of a *capital asset*. Obviously, the definition of a capital asset is crucial. Sales involving property that qualifies as a capital asset are eligible for a reduced tax rate while sales of assets that have not been so blessed may not be as lucky.

The Internal Revenue Code takes a roundabout approach in defining a capital asset. Instead of defining what a capital asset is, the Code identifies what is not a capital asset. Under § 1221, all assets are considered capital assets unless they fall into one of five excluded classes. The following are *not* capital assets:

1. Inventory or property held primarily for sale to customers in the ordinary course of a trade or business.

2. Accounts and notes receivable acquired in the ordinary course of a trade or business for services rendered or from the sale of inventory.

3. Depreciable property and land used in a trade or business.

4. Copyrights, literary, musical,[3] or artistic compositions, letters or memoranda, or similar property held by the creator, or letters or memoranda held by the person for whom the property was created; in addition, such property held by a taxpayer whose basis is determined by reference to the creator's basis (e.g., acquired by gift), or held by the person for whom it was created.

5. Publications of the United States Government that are received from the Government by any means other than purchase at the price at which they are offered to the public, and which are held by the taxpayer who received the publication or by a transferee whose basis is found with reference to the original recipient's basis (e.g., acquired by gift).

Before looking at some of these categories, one should appreciate the statutory scheme and the rationale behind it.

As noted above, the Code starts with the very broad premise that all property held by the taxpayer is a capital asset. Thus the sale of a home, car, jewelry, clothing, stocks, bonds, inventory, and plant, property, and equipment used in a trade or business would produce, *at least initially,* capital gain or loss since all assets are by default capital assets. However, § 1221 goes on to alter this general rule with several significant exceptions. It specifically excludes from capital asset status inventory, property held for resale, receivables related to the sales of services and inventory, and certain literary properties. As may be apparent, the purpose of these exclusions, as the Supreme Court has said, "is to differentiate between the 'profits and losses arising from the everyday operation of business' on the one hand … and 'the realization of appreciation in value accrued over a substantial period of time' on the other."[4] In essence, the statute is generally drawn to deny capital gain treatment for income from regular business operations. Income that is derived from the taxpayer's routine personal efforts and services is also treated as ordinary income and in effect receives the same treatment as wages, interest, and all other types of income.

Based on the above analysis, it might seem strange that § 1221 also excludes from capital asset status a class of assets that most people would consider capital assets: the fixed assets of a business (depreciable property and land used in a business). Although it is true that these assets are not "pure" capital assets, as will be seen in Chapter 17, these assets can, if certain tests are met, sneak in the back door and receive capital gain treatment. Also observe that this rule does not exclude intangibles from capital asset treatment even though they may be amortizable. For example, goodwill is a capital asset even though it may be amortized.

One final note, it should be emphasized that the classification of an asset as a capital asset may affect more than the character of the gain or loss on its sale. For example, the amount of a charitable contribution deduction also may be affected in certain instances. For example, generally the amount of a charitable contribution of property is its value but only if

---

[3] Beginning May 18, 2006 taxpayers may elect to treat musical compositions or copyrights in musical works as capital assets but only for sales or exchanges of such items and not charitable contributions. See § 1221(b)(3).

[4] *Malat v. Riddell,* 66-1 USTC ¶9317, 17 AFTR2d 604, 383 U.S. 569 (USSC, 1966).

its sale would have produced long-term capital gain. Otherwise the amount of the contribution is normally the adjusted basis of the property. For this reason, whether the contributed property is a capital asset is critical. For example, authors and artists can deduct only the adjusted basis of art objects or manuscripts (usually little or nothing) because such assets are not capital assets.[5]

INVENTORY

The inventory exception has been the subject of much litigation and controversy. Whether property is held primarily for sale is a question of fact. The Supreme Court decided in *Malat v. Riddell*[6] that the word "primarily" should be interpreted as used in an ordinary, everyday sense, and as such, means "principally" or of "first importance." As a practical matter, such interpretations provide little guidance. In many cases, it simply boils down to whether the court views the taxpayer as a "dealer" in the particular property or merely an investor. Unfortunately, the line of demarcation is far from clear.

The determination of whether an item is inventory or not frequently arises in the area of sales of real property. In determining whether a taxpayer holds real estate, or a particular tract of real estate, primarily for sale, the courts seem to place the greatest emphasis on the frequency, continuity, and volume of sales.[7] Other important factors considered by the courts are subdivision and improvement,[8] solicitation and advertising,[9] purpose and manner of acquisition,[10] and reason for and method of sale.[11]

COPYRIGHTS, ARTISTIC WORKS, LETTERS, AND SIMILAR ITEMS

Should authors and artists be entitled to favorable capital gains treatment on the sale of their works? Should the sale of game show formats like Jeopardy or scripts for television or radio programs produce capital gain to their creators? Prior to 1950, sales of such works were granted lucrative tax treatment even though the property was attributable to the creator's personal efforts.[12] However, amidst growing concerns about the extension of low rates to such transactions, Congress reacted. Section 1223(3) now bars capital asset status to "a copyright, a literary, musical, or artistic composition, a letter or memorandum, or similar property" if the property was created by the taxpayer's personal efforts. In the case of letters, memoranda, and similar property, the disqualification also applies to the person for whom the work was prepared or produced.[13] In addition, a person receiving these items by gift from the creator or the person for whom the work was created is denied capital gain treatment.

The term similar property includes theatrical productions, radio programs, newspaper cartoon strips, manuscripts, diaries, corporate archives, financial records and other property eligible for copyright protection.[14] It is important to emphasize, however, that this provision does not include patents, inventions or other designs that may be protected only under patent law. Thus inventors get favorable capital gain for their creative genius!

Surprisingly, in 2006, Congress created an exception to this rule, allowing taxpayers to elect to treat musical compositions or copyrights in musical works sold as capital assets. This exception extends favorable capital gain treatment to the creators of musical compositions (i.e., song writers). This election is available for compositions or copyrights sold or exchanged in a taxable year beginning after May 17, 2006. It should be noted that musical compositions are not treated as capital assets for purposes of the charitable contributions rules. Thus the deduction for contributions of compositions is not the value, but rather the basis of the property, which is usually little or nothing.

---

[5] See § 170(e)(1) and Chapter 11 for a discussion of these charitable contribution limitations.

[6] *Supra*, Footnote 2.

[7] See, for example, *Houston Endowment, Inc. v. U.S.,* 79-2 USTC ¶9690, 44 AFTR2d 79-6074, 606 F.2d 77 (CA-5, 1979) and *Reese v. Comm.,* 80-1 USTC ¶9350, 45 AFTR2d 80-1248, 615 F.2d 226 (CA-5, 1980).

[8] See, for example, *Houston Endowment, Inc.,* and *Biedenharn Realty Co., Inc. v. U.S.,* 76-1 USTC ¶9194, 37 AFTR2d 76-679, 526 F.2d 409 (CA-5, 1976).

[9] See, for example, *Houston Endowment, Inc.*

[10] See, for example, *Scheuber v. Comm.,* 67-1 USTC ¶9219, 19 AFTR2d 639, 371 F.2d 996 (CA-7, 1967), and *Biedenharn Realty Co., Inc. v. U.S.*

[11] See, for example, *Voss v. U.S.,* 64-1 USTC 9290, 13 AFTR2d 834, 329 F.2d 164 (CA-7, 1964).

[12] For examples, see *Julius H. Marx* 29 T.C. 88 (1957) and *Jack Benny* 25 T.C. 197 (1955).

[13] This expansion was added in 1969 to prevent public officials (e.g., Presidents, Congressmen) from deducting the value of the memorabilia they had collected in office and then contributed to libraries, universities and museums.

[14] Reg. § 1.1221-1(c)(1) and (2).

Example 1

J is an amateur artist who loved to paint desert landscapes. This year she sold one of her paintings through an art dealer in Santa Fe for $2,000. J has ordinary income on the sale because artistic compositions such as paintings are not capital assets. The result would be the same had J painted the picture for her daughter, D, and D sold the picture. Even though D did not paint the picture herself, it was prepared for her and capital asset status is denied for both the creator and the one for whom it was prepared.

Example 2

B returned from a trip around the world and decided to write a book. This year she died and her son, S, inherited the manuscript which he sold several years later for a gain of $10,000. S would have long-term capital gain because the manuscript is a capital asset since S's basis is not determined in reference to B's basis but is automatically fair market value as of the date of death.

FEDERAL PUBLICATIONS

Publications of the U.S. government (e.g., the Congressional Record) that are given to a taxpayer by the government are not capital assets. This provision was enacted in 1976 primarily to prohibit Presidents, Congressmen, Cabinet members, and others from securing charitable contribution deductions for gifts to libraries and museums of items that they collected while working for the government. By denying capital asset treatment for these items, the amount of the contribution is limited to the taxpayer's basis rather than its value.[15] As a result, little or no deduction is available for the contributions.

DISPOSITION OF A BUSINESS

The treatment of the sale of a business depends on the form in which the business is operated and the nature of the sale. If the business is operated as a sole proprietorship, the sale of the proprietorship business is not, as one taxpayer argued, a sale of a single integrated capital asset.[16] Rather, it is treated as a separate sale of each of the assets of the business. Accordingly, the sales price must be allocated among the various assets and gains and losses determined for each individual asset. Any gain or loss arising from the sale of inventory items and receivables would be treated separately as ordinary gains and losses. Gains and losses from the sale of depreciable property and land used in the business would be subject to special treatment discussed in Chapter 17 and may qualify for capital gain treatment. Finally, gains and losses from capital assets would of course be treated as capital gains and losses.

If the business is operated in the form of a corporation or partnership, the sale could take one of two forms: (1) a sale of the owner's interest (e.g., the owner's stock or interest in the partnership) or (2) a sale of all the assets by the entity followed by a distribution of the sales proceeds to the owner. An owner's interest—stock or an interest in a partnership—is a capital asset. Consequently, a sale of such interest normally produces capital gain or capital loss (although there are some important exceptions for sales of a partnership interest). On the other hand, a sale of assets by the entity would be treated in the same manner as the sale of a sole proprietorship, a sale of each individual asset.

---

[15] See § 170(e)(1). The addition of this rule overturned the holding in Rev. Rul. 75-342 1997-2 CB 341 that such assets were capital assets.

[16] *Williams v. McCowan*, 46-1 USTC ¶9120, 34 AFTR 615, 152 F.2d 570 (CA-2, 1945); Rev. Rul. 55-79, 1955-1 C.B. 370.

 **CHECK YOUR KNOWLEDGE**

Review Question I

Lois Price operates an office supply store, Office Discount, and owns the property listed below. Indicate whether each of the following assets is a capital asset. Respond yes or no.

   a. Refrigerator in her home used solely for personal use
   b. The building that houses her business
   c. A picture given to her by a well-known artist
   d. 100 shares of Chrysler Corporation stock held as an investment
   e. Furniture in her office
   f. A book of poems she has written
   g. The portion of her home used as a qualifying home office
   h. 1,000 reams of paper held for sale to customers
   i. Internally generated goodwill of the business

The following are capital assets: (a), (d), and (i). The other assets are not capital assets, including inventory (h), real or depreciable property used in a trade or business (b), (e), and (g), literary or artistic compositions held by the creator (f), or property received by gift from the creator (c). Note that the Code does not exclude intangible assets from capital assets status. For example, internally generated (i.e., not previously purchased) goodwill that is sold as part of a sale of a business is treated as a capital asset.

Review Question 2

Slam-Dunk Corporation manufactures collapsible basketball rims in Houston, Texas. Because of its tremendous growth, Mr. Slam and Ms. Dunk, the owners of the company, brought in a highly skilled executive to manage it, the famous Sam Jam. As part of the employment agreement, the company agreed to buy Sam's house if it should terminate his contract. Slam and Dunk did not get along with Sam and his creative management techniques. Consequently, the corporation dismissed Sam after two years and purchased his house at Sam's original cost of $300,000. Needing the cash, the corporation decided to unload the house immediately. Unfortunately, in the depressed housing market of Houston, the corporation sold the house for only $200,000. Explain the tax problems associated with the sale by the corporation. What important issue must be resolved and why?

In this situation, the corporation has realized a loss of $100,000. The critical issue is determining whether the loss is an ordinary or capital loss. The treatment, as explained below, is quite different. If the loss is ordinary, the corporation may deduct the entire loss in computing taxable income. In contrast, if the loss is a capital loss, the corporation can deduct the loss only to the extent of any capital gains that it has during the year or a three-year carryback and five-year carryforward period. The determination turns on the definition of a capital asset.

Sale or Exchange Requirement

Before capital gain or loss treatment applies, the property must be disposed of in a "sale or exchange." In most cases, determining whether a sale or exchange has occurred is not difficult. The requirement is met by most routine transactions and as a practical matter is often overlooked. Nevertheless, there are a number of situations when a sale or exchange does not actually occur but the Code steps in and creates one, thus converting what might have been ordinary income or loss to capital gain or capital loss. Several of these are considered below.

WORTHLESS AND ABANDONED PROPERTY

When misfortune strikes, leaving the taxpayer with worthless property, the taxpayer normally has a loss equal to the adjusted basis of the property. Note, however, that the loss in these situations does not technically arise from a sale or exchange, leaving the taxpayer to wonder how the loss is to be treated.

Worthless Securities

The Code has addressed this problem with respect to worthless securities (e.g., stocks and bonds). In the event that a qualifying security becomes worthless at any time during the taxable year, the resulting loss is treated as having arisen from the sale or exchange of a capital asset on the last day of the taxable year.[17] Losses from worthlessness are then treated as either short-term or long-term capital losses depending on the taxpayer's holding period.

Example 3

After receiving a hot tip, N bought 200 shares of Shag Carpets, Inc. for $2,000 on November 1, 2016. Just three months later, on February 1, 2017, N received a shocking notice that the company had declared bankruptcy and her investment was worthless. Because of the worthlessness, N is treated as having sold the stock for nothing on the last day of her taxable year, December 31, 2017. Because the sale is deemed to occur on December 31, 2017 (and not February 1), N is treated as if she actually held the stock for more than a year. As a result, she reports a $2,000 long-term capital loss.

The sale or exchange fiction applies only to qualifying securities. To qualify, the security must be (1) a capital asset and (2) a security as defined by the Code. Under § 165, the term *security* means stock, stock rights, and bonds, notes, or other forms of indebtedness issued by a corporation or the government. When these rules do not apply (e.g., property other than securities), the taxpayer suffers an ordinary loss. Whether a security actually becomes worthless during a given year is a question of fact, and the burden of proof is on the taxpayer to show that the security became worthless during the year in question.[18]

Worthless Securities in Affiliated Corporations

The basic rule for worthless securities is modified for a corporate taxpayer's investment in securities of an affiliated corporation. If securities of an affiliated corporation become worthless, the loss is treated as an ordinary loss and the limitations that normally apply if the loss were a capital loss are avoided.[19] A corporation is considered affiliated to a parent corporation if the parent owns at least 80% of the voting power of all classes of stock and at least 80% of each class of nonvoting stock of the affiliated corporation. In addition, to be treated as an affiliated corporation for purposes of the worthless security provisions, the defunct corporation must have been truly an operating company. This test is met if the corporation has less than 10% of the aggregate of its gross receipts from passive sources such as rents, royalties, dividends, annuities, and gains from sales or exchanges of stock and securities. This condition prohibits ordinary loss treatment for what are really investments.

Example 4

Toy Palace Corporation is the parent corporation for more than 100 subsidiary corporations that operate toy stores all over the country. Each subsidiary is 100% owned by Toy Palace. This year the store in Chicago, TPC Inc., declared bankruptcy. As a result, Toy Palace's investment in TPC stock of $1 million became totally worthless. Toy Palace is allowed to treat the $1 million loss as an ordinary loss since TPC was an affiliated corporation (i.e., Toy Palace owned at least 80% of TPC's stock and TPC was an operating corporation). Observe that without this special rule, Toy Palace would have a $1 million capital loss that it could deduct only if it had capital gains currently or within the three-year carryback or five-year carryforward period.

---

[17] § 165(g).

[18] *Young v. Comm.*, 41-2 USTC ¶9744, 28 AFTR 365, 123 F.2d 597 (CA-2, 1941). Code § 6511(d) extends the statute of limitations from three years to seven years because of the difficulty of determining the specific tax year in which stock becomes worthless.

[19] § 165(g)(3).

Abandoned Property

While the law creates a sale or exchange for worthless securities, it takes a different approach for abandoned business or investment property. When worthless property (other than stocks and securities) is abandoned, the abandonment is not considered a sale or exchange.[20] Consequently, any loss arising from an abandonment is treated as an ordinary loss rather than a capital loss, a much more propitious result. Note, however, that the loss is deductible only if the taxpayer can demonstrate that the business or investment property has been truly abandoned and not simply taken out of service temporarily.

CERTAIN CASUALTIES AND THEFTS

Still another exception to the sale or exchange requirement involves *excess* casualty and theft gains from the involuntary conversion of *personal use assets.* As discussed in Chapter 10, § 165(h) provides that if personal casualty or theft gains *exceed* personal casualty or theft losses for any taxable year, each such gain and loss must be treated as a gain or loss from the sale or exchange of a capital asset. Each separate casualty or theft loss must be reduced by $100 before being netted with the personal casualty or theft gains.

Example 5

T had three separate casualties involving personal-use assets during the year:

| | | | Fair Market Value | |
Casualty	Property	Adjusted Basis	Before Casualty	After Casualty
1. Accident	Personal car	$12,000	$ 8,500	$ 6,000
2. Robbery	Jewelry	1,000	4,000	0
3. Hurricane	Residence	60,000	80,000	58,000

T received insurance reimbursements as follows: (1) $900 for repair of the car; (2) $3,200 for the theft of her jewelry; and (3) $21,500 for the damages to her home. Assuming T does not elect (under § 1033) to purchase replacement jewelry, her personal casualty gain exceeds her personal casualty losses by $300, computed as follows:

1. The loss for the car is $1,500 ([lesser of $2,500 decline in value or the $12,000 adjusted basis = $2,500] – $900 insurance recovery – $100 floor).

2. The gain for the jewelry is $2,200 ($3,200 insurance recovery – $1,000 adjusted basis).

3. The loss from the residence is $400 ([lesser of $22,000 decline in value or the $60,000 adjusted basis = $22,000] – $21,500 insurance recovery – $100 floor).

T must report each separate gain and loss as a gain or loss from the sale or exchange of a capital asset. The classification of each gain and loss as short-term or long-term depends on the holding period of each asset.

It is important to note that this exception *does not* apply if the personal casualty losses exceed the gains. In such case, the *net* loss, subject to the 10% limitation, is deductible *from* AGI. Recall, however, that casualty and theft losses are among those itemized deductions that are not subject to the deduction cutback rule imposed on high-income taxpayers. (See Chapter 11 for a discussion of this cutback rule.)

---

[20] Reg. § 1.165-2 and 1.167(a)-8.

> ### Example 6
>
> Assume the same facts in *Example 5* except the insurance recovery from the hurricane damage to the residence was only $11,500. In this case, the loss from the hurricane is $10,400 ($22,000 − $11,500 − $100), and the personal casualty losses exceed the gain by $9,700 ($1,500 + $10,400 − $2,200). T must treat the $9,700 net loss as an itemized deduction subject to the 10% of AGI limitation, but not subject to the cutback rule.

OTHER TRANSACTIONS

There are still other situations where the sale or exchange requirement is an important consideration. For example, foreclosure, condemnation, and other involuntary events are treated as sales even though they may not qualify as such for state law purposes. Similarly, as discussed in greater detail later in this chapter, the collection of the face value of a corporate bond (i.e., bond redemption) at maturity is treated as a sale or exchange.

Holding Period

LO.4

Explain the holding period rules for classifying a capital asset transaction as either short-term or long-term.

The exact treatment of a capital gain or loss depends primarily on how long the taxpayer held the asset or what is technically referred to as the taxpayer's *holding period*. The holding period is a critical element in determining which of the various tax rates will apply. As might be expected, the longer the holding period is, the lower the applicable tax rate will be. A *short term* gain or loss is one resulting from the sale or disposition of an asset held *one year or less*.[21] A *long-term* gain or loss occurs when an asset is held for *more than one year*.

In computing the holding period, the day of acquisition is not counted but the day of sale is. The holding period is based on calendar months and fractions of calendar months, rather than on the number of days.[22] The fact that different months contain different numbers of days (i.e., 28, 30, or 31) is disregarded.

> ### Example 7
>
> P purchased 10 shares of EX, Inc. on March 16, 2016. Her gain or loss on the sale is short-term if the stock is sold on or before March 16, 2017, but long-term if sold on or after March 17, 2017.

> ### Example 8
>
> T purchased 100 shares of FMC Corp. stock on February 28, 2016. His gain or loss will be long-term if he sells the stock on or after March 1, 2017.

The holding period runs from the time property is acquired until the time of its disposition. Property is generally considered *acquired* or *disposed* of when title passes from one party to another. State law usually controls the passage of title and must be consulted when questions arise.

STOCK EXCHANGE TRANSACTIONS

The holding period for securities traded on a stock exchange is determined in the same manner as for other property. The trade dates, rather than the settlement dates, are used as the dates of acquisition and sale.

Generally, both cash and accrual basis taxpayers must report (recognize) gains and losses on stock or security sales in the tax year of the trade, even though cash payment

---

[21] § 1222.   [22] Rev. Rul. 66-7, 1966-1 C.B.188.

(settlement) may not be received until the following year. This requirement is imposed because the installment method of reporting gains is not allowed for sales of stock or securities that are traded on an established securities market.[23]

Example 9

C, a cash basis calendar year taxpayer, sold 300 shares of ARA stock at a gain of $5,000 on December 29, 2017. The settlement date was January 3, 2018. C must report the gain in 2017 (the year of trade).

SPECIAL RULES AND EXCEPTIONS

Section 1223 contains a number of special provisions that must be used for determining the holding period of certain properties. The rules address the holding period of property acquired (1) in a tax-deferred exchange; (2) by gift; (3) by inheritance; (4) in a wash sale; (5) as a stock dividend; or (6) by exercising stock rights or options.

Property Acquired in Tax-Deferred Transaction

The holding period of property received in an exchange *includes* the holding period of the property given up in the exchange if the basis of the property is determined by reference, in whole or in part, to the basis in that property given up (e.g., a substituted basis in a like-kind exchange).[24] This rule applies only if the property exchanged is a capital asset or a § 1231 asset (e.g., real or depreciable property used in a trade or business) at the time of the exchange. For this purpose, an involuntary conversion–where the taxpayer normally purchases replacement property for that which was involuntarily converted—is treated as an exchange.[25]

As suggested above, this rule commonly can be found operating when there is a like-kind exchange. For example, if a taxpayer purchased land on May 16, 1981 and swapped it for other land in 2017, the taxpayer's holding period for the new land would begin in 1981 since the basis of the replacement land is the same as that for the old land, $50,000, (i.e., the basis of the new land was "determined by reference" to the property given up). Normally, if any gain or loss is deferred, the holding period of the replacement property includes the holding period of the property that was converted or exchanged.

Example 10

In 2015, the city of Milwaukee condemned 10 acres of M's farm land (a § 1231 asset) in order to build an exit for an interstate highway. M had acquired the land on May 1, 1998 for $20,000. M received $120,000 for the land and therefore realized a gain of $100,000. On July 7, 2017, M replaced the property by purchasing new land for $120,000. As a result, he was able to defer all of the realized gain, producing a basis for the new property of $20,000 ($120,000 cost less $100,000 deferred gain). Since an involuntary conversion is treated as an exchange, M's holding period begins on the date that he acquired the original property, May 1, 1998.

Property Acquired by Gift

Another exception provides that if a taxpayer's basis in property is the same basis as another taxpayer had in that property, in whole or in part, the holding period will include that of the other person.[26] Therefore, the holding period of property acquired by gift generally will include the holding period of the donor. This will not be true, however, if the property is sold at a loss and the basis in the property for determining the loss is fair market value on the date of the gift. If the donee's basis is fair market at the date of the gift, the donee's holding period begins on the date of the gift.

---

[23] § 453(k)(2). See Chapter 14 for a detailed discussion of the installment sale method.

[24] § 1223(1).

[25] § 1223(1)(A).

[26] § 1223(2).

Example 11

G received a gold necklace from her elderly grandmother as a birthday gift on August 31, 2017. The necklace was worth $5,200 at that time and had a basis to the grandmother of $1,300. Grandmother had bought the necklace in 1998. Contrary to her grandmother's wishes, G sold the family heirloom for $5,000 on December 13, 2017. G will recognize a gain of $3,700 ($5,000 − $1,300). Her holding period began in 1978 since her $1,300 basis is determined (under § 1015) by reference to her grandmother's basis, *and* her holding period includes the time the necklace was held by her grandmother.

Example 12

If G's grandmother had a basis in the necklace of $6,000, G's basis for determining loss would be $5,200, the fair market value at the date of the gift (see discussion in Chapter 14). Because G's basis is *not* determined by reference to her grandmother's basis, the grandmother's holding period is not added to G's holding period and the holding period begins on the date of the gift. Since G only held the necklace for three months, she will have a $200 short-term capital loss ($5,200 basis − $5,000 sales price).

Property Acquired from a Decedent

A special rule is provided for the holding period of property acquired from a decedent. The holding period formally begins on the date of death. However, the Code provides that, if the heir's basis in the property is its fair market value under § 1014 and the property is subsequently sold after the decedent's death, the property is deemed to have a long-term holding period.[27]

Example 13

P sold 50 shares of Xero Corp. stock for $11,200 on July 27, 2017. The stock was inherited from P's uncle who died on May 16, 2017, and it was included in the uncle's Federal estate tax return at a fair market value of $12,000. Since P's basis in the stock ($12,000) is determined under § 1014, the $800 loss on the sale will be a capital loss from property deemed to be held more than 12 months. This would be the case even if P's uncle had purchased the stock within days of his death. The decedent's prior holding period is irrelevant.

Other Holding Period Rules

There are various other provisions that contain special rules for determining holding periods. The holding period of stock acquired in a transaction in which a loss was disallowed under the "wash sale" provisions (§ 1091) is added to the holding period of the replacement stock.[28] Also, when a shareholder receives stock dividends or stock rights as a result of owning stock in a corporation, the holding period of the stock or stock rights includes the holding period of the stock already owned in the corporation.[29] The holding period of any stock acquired by exercising stock rights, however, begins on the date of exercise.[30]

The holding period of property acquired by exercise of an option begins on the day after the option is exercised.[31] If a taxpayer sells the property acquired by option within one year after exercising the option, then he or she will have a short-term gain or loss.

---

[27] § 1223(9).

[28] § 1223(3); Reg. § 1.1223-1(d).

[29] § 1223(5); Reg. § 1.1223-1(e).

[30] § 1223(6); Reg. § 1.1223-1(f).

[31] See, for example, *Helvering v. San Joaquin Fruit & Inv. Co.*, 36-1 USTC ¶9144, 17 AFTR 470, 297 U.S. 496 (USSC, 1936), and *E.T. Weir*, 49-1 USTC ¶9190, 37 AFTR 1022, 173 F.2d 222 (CA-3, 1949).

> ### Example 14
>
> N owned an option to purchase ten acres of land. She had owned the option more than one year when she exercised it and purchased the property. Her holding period for the property begins on the day after she exercises the option. Had she sold the option, her gain or loss would have been long-term. If she had sold the property immediately, her gain or loss would have been short-term.

The holding period of a commodity acquired in satisfaction of a commodity futures contract includes the holding period of the futures contract. However, the futures contract must have been a capital asset in the hands of the taxpayer.[32]

Treatment of Capital Gains and Losses

The Taxpayer Relief Act of 1997 and the amendments of the Jobs and Growth Tax Relief Reconciliation Act of 2003 significantly cut the tax rates on capital gains but not without introducing an inordinate amount of complexity. The adventure begins below.

LO.5

Apply the capital gain and loss netting process to a taxpayer's capital asset transactions and explain their treatment.

THE PROCESS IN GENERAL

The first step in determining the treatment of a taxpayer's capital gain or loss is identifying the applicable holding period. Once the holding period is determined, the gain or loss can normally be assigned to an appropriate group to determine its taxation. Historically, there have only been two groups: short-term and long-term. However, beginning in 1997, the law made the classification process a bit more cumbersome, producing the following groups for individual taxpayers.

- *Short-Term Group.* Gains and losses from properties held not more than one year.

- *Long-Term Group.* Generally gains and losses from properties held more than one year. However, individual taxpayers must subdivide the long-term group into additional subgroups according to the rate at which they are to be taxed. The long-term group includes:

  1. The 28% group (28CG and 28CL).
     - Capital gains and losses from collectibles (e.g., works of art, antiques, gold and silver bullion, etc.).[33]
     - Capital gains from qualified small business stock (taxable portion of § 1202 gains discussed below).

  2. The 25% group (25CG).
     - Capital *gains* (and only gains) from the sales of depreciable real estate (e.g., office buildings, warehouses, apartment buildings) that are held for more than 12 months but only to the extent of any unrecaptured straight-line depreciation on such property. (See Chapter 17 for discussion of depreciation recapture.)

  3. The 15% group (15CG and 15CL).
     - Capital gains and losses from the dispositions of other capital assets held more than 12 months. Note that the gains in this group potentially could be taxed at a rate of 0% (if the taxpayer's rate is below the 25% bracket) or a rate of 20% (if the taxpayer is in the 39.6% bracket). For purposes of discussion in this book, all of these gains are referred to as 15% gains.

The effect of the rules is to require taxpayers to assign their capital gains and losses into one of four different groups and net the amounts to determine the net gain or loss in each group as shown below.

---

[32] § 1223(8); Reg. § 1.1223-1(h).   [33] § 1(h)(1)(C) and (h)(4).

Holding Period (months)	Short-Term	Long-Term		
	≤ 12 Ordinary Rate	Collectibles & § 1202 Stock > 12 28%	Realty > 12 25%	> 12 15% *
Gains...............	$xx,xxx	$ x,xxx	Gains only	$xx,xxx
Losses	(xxx)	(x,xxx)	—	(x,xxx)
Net gain or loss	????	????	Gains only	????

* Note that such gains could be taxed at either 0% or 20%, depending on the taxpayer's tax bracket for ordinary income.

The capital gains of most individuals arise from sales of stocks and bonds and mutual fund transactions. Rarely do individuals have gains from collectibles, § 1202 stock, or depreciable realty. Consequently, for most individuals, the classification and netting process is much easier. In the vast majority of cases, there would only be two groups: (1) short-term and (2) long-term gains taxed at 15 percent.

NETTING PROCESS

Generalizations about the treatment of capital gains and losses are difficult because the actual treatment can be determined only after the various groups (i.e., the four groups above) are combined, or netted, to determine the overall net gain or loss during the year. This process is described below.[34]

Netting within Groups

The first step in the netting process is to combine the gains and losses within each group to produce one of the following:

1. Net short-term capital gain or net short-term capital loss (NSTCG or NSTCL).
2. Net 28% capital gain or net 28% capital loss (N28CG or N28CL).
3. Net 15% capital gain or net 15% capital loss (N15CG or N15CL).

Note that the first step requires no netting in the 25% group since this group initially contains only gains.

Netting between Groups

The second step requires the combination of the net capital loss positions in any particular group against any net capital gain positions. The treatment of these different groups is explained below.

1. *Short-Term Capital Gains and Losses.* A NSTCG receives no special treatment and is taxed as ordinary income. If a NSTCL results, it may be used to offset net gains of the long-term group in the following order: (1) the net 28% gain; (2) any 25% gain; and (3) the net 15% gain. Any remaining NSTCL not absorbed by the capital gains in the groups above is deductible subject to limitations on the deduction of capital losses discussed below.

2. *28% Group.* A N28CG is taxed at a maximum 28 percent.[35] Any net loss in the 28% group (N28CL) is applied in the following order: (1) 25% gain; (2) net 15% gain; and (3) NSTCG. Any remaining N28CL that is not absorbed is deductible subject to limitations on the deduction of capital losses discussed below.

3. *25% Group.* The 25% group generally includes *only* capital *gains* from the sales of depreciable real estate held for more than 12 months. Such gains are only included to the extent of any unrecaptured straight-line depreciation on such property. The net 25% capital gain (N25CG) is taxed at a maximum rate of 25 percent.[36] Note that there can be no net loss in the 25% group.

4. *15% Group.* A N15CG is taxed at a maximum of 15 percent. However, if the taxpayer's tax bracket (determined by *including* the N15CG) is only 10 or 15 percent, the net

---

[34] § 1(h)(1).

[35] § 1(h)(1)(C). Note that 28% gains are taxed at the lower rates (10, 15, and 25 percent), if such brackets are not filled by the taxpayer's other taxable income.

[36] § 1(h)(1)(B). Note that 25% gains are taxed at the lower rates (10% or 15%) if such brackets are not filled by the taxpayer's other taxable income.

gain falling into these brackets is taxed at 0 percent.[37] Similarly, if the taxpayer's tax bracket is 39.6 percent, the rate is 20 percent. Any N15CL is applied in the following order: (1) the net 28% gain; (2) any 25% gain; and (3) any NSTCG. Any remaining N15CL not absorbed is deductible subject to limitations on the deduction of capital losses discussed below.

It should be noted that the three *long-term* groups (the 28, 25, and 15 percent groups) are always netted together before taking into accounting any short-term items. Also observe that Congress has generally given taxpayers the best possible treatment of net capital losses in that a NSTCL offsets the net capital gain from the highest taxed group, then the next highest taxed and so on.

Example 15

During the year, T, who is in the 35% tax bracket, reported the following capital gains and losses.

	Short-Term	Long-Term 28%	Long-Term 15%
Gains.......	$10,000	$5,000	$8,000
Losses	(4,000)	(1,000)	(1,000)
Net	$ 6,000	$4,000	$7,000

In this case, T first nets the items within each group. She nets the $10,000 STCG and $4,000 STCL to arrive at a NSTCG of $6,000; she nets a $5,000 28CG and a $1,000 28CL to produce a N28CG of $4,000; and she nets the $8,000 15CG and the $1,000 15CL, resulting in a N15CG of $7,000. No further netting of these groups can occur since each group contains a positive amount. T's NSTCG of $6,000 receives no special treatment and is taxed as ordinary income. T's N28CG is taxed at 28% while her N15CG is taxed at 15 percent.

Example 16

This year, L, who is in the 28% tax bracket, reported the following capital gains and losses:

	Short-Term	Long-Term 28%	Long-Term 15%
Gains.......	$10,000	$5,000	$8,000
Losses	(15,000)	(1,000)	(1,000)
Net	$ (5,000)	$4,000	$7,000
Netting......	5,000	(4,000)	(1,000)
Net.........	$ 0	$ 0	$6,000

Here L has a NSTCL of $5,000 which is netted *first* against N28CG of $4,000, reducing it to zero. The remaining NSTCL of $1,000 would next be offset against N25CG, if any. In this case, there is no N25CG, therefore the remaining NSTCL of $1,000 is offset against the N15CG of $7,000, reducing it to $6,000 which would be taxed at a rate of 15 percent.

---

[37] § 1(h)(1)(D) and (E). The 0% rate for 15% gains falling in the 10% or 15% ordinary income tax brackets was made permanent by the American Taxpayer Relief Act of 2012.

Note that 25% and 28% gains, falling in the 10% or 15% brackets will be taxed at the normal 10% or 15% rate.

Example 17

This year, X, who is in the 35% tax bracket, reported the following capital gains and losses:

	Short-Term	Long-Term 28%	Long-Term 25%	Long-Term 15%
Gains.......	$14,000	$ 1,000	$1,000	$6,000
Losses	(4,000)	(9,000)	—	(1,000)
Net	$10,000	$(8,000)	$1,000	$5,000
Netting	(2,000)	8,000	(1,000)	(5,000)
Net	$ 8,000	$ 0	$ 0	$ 0

Here X has a N28CL of $8,000 which is netted first against the 25CGs of $1,000, reducing this group to zero. X next uses the remaining $7,000 N28CL to offset his $5,000 N15CG, reducing it to zero. The remaining N28CL of $2,000 ($7,000 − $5,000) is offset against NSTCG, producing a NSTCG of $8,000 which is treated as ordinary income. Note that the effect of the rules is to net the long-term groups before considering any short-term items. Absent these rules, X would prefer to use the N28CL loss against the NSTCG which would leave $5,000 to be taxed at 15% and $2,000 to be taxed as ordinary income, a far more beneficial result. X must net the long-term groups first.

Treatment of Capital Losses

While capital gains receive favorable treatment, such is not the case with capital losses. As can be seen above, capital losses are first netted with capital gains within the same group (rather than reducing ordinary income). A net capital loss from a particular group can then be combined with net capital gains from the other groups. If after netting all of the groups together, the taxpayer has an overall net capital loss, the loss is deductible against ordinary income. This deduction is limited to the lesser of (1) $3,000 ($1,500 in the case of a married individual filing a separate return) or (2) the net capital loss. In either case, the capital loss deduction cannot exceed taxable income before the deduction.[38] The deductible capital loss is a deduction *for* adjusted gross income. Any losses in excess of the annual $3,000 limitation are carried forward to the following year where they are treated as if they actually occurred in such year. In effect, an unused capital loss can be carried over for an indefinite period.[39] However, should the taxpayer die, any unused capital loss is normally lost.

If the netting process results in a NSTCL and either a N28CL or N15CL or both, the NSTCL is applied first toward the maximum $3,000 limit. For example, if the taxpayer has a NSTCL of $5,000 and a N15CL of $4,000, the NSTCL is used first. Any NSTCL in excess of the $3,000 limit along with any other unused losses may be carried forward to subsequent years indefinitely. In this case, the NSTCL carryover retains its character to be treated just as if it had occurred in the subsequent year. The N15CL or N28CL are both carried over as N28CLs. In other words, any long-term capital loss carryover is carried over as a 28CL. In the example above, $3,000 of the $5,000 NSTCL would be used first against ordinary income and the $2,000 remaining would be carried over as a STCL while the $4,000 N15CL would be carried over as a 28CL. In the absence of a NSTCL or, if after deducting any existing NSTCL, the taxpayer has not reached the annual $3,000 limit for the capital loss deduction, the taxpayer uses any other net capital losses (e.g., the excess of N15CL over N28CG and N25CG or the excess of N28CL over 25 CG and N15CG) to reduce ordinary income up to the $3,000 limit.[40] In this regard, the order in which the remaining net capital losses are used is irrelevant since any remaining losses (i.e., the long-term losses) are carried over as a N28CL which is treated as if it occurred in the subsequent year.

---

[38] § 1212(b).

[39] Reg. § 1.211-1(b)(4)(i).

[40] § 1211(a).

Example 18

During the year, B reported the capital gains and losses revealed below. B's only other taxable income included his salary of $50,000. He had no other deductions for AGI. The combination of gains, losses, and ordinary income is shown in the following table.

	Short-Term	Long-Term 28%	Long-Term 15%
Gains	$10,000	$ 5,000	$9,000
Losses.	(18,000)	(7,000)	(6,000)
Net.	$ (8,000)	$(2,000)	$3,000
Netting (long-term against long-term)		2,000	(2,000)
		$ 0	$1,000
Netting (long-term against short-term).	1,000		(1,000)
	$ (7,000)		$ 0
Deduction.	3,000		
Carryover	$ (4,000)		

B first nets the long-term items, that is, the N28CL of $2,000 is netted against the N15CG of $3,000. This produces a N15CG of $1,000 ($3,000 – $2,000). B then combines the $8,000 NSTCL and the remaining N15CG of $1,000, leaving a NSTCL of $7,000. In determining his AGI, B may deduct only $3,000 of the NSTCL. Therefore his AGI is $47,000 ($50,000 – $3,000). The unused NSTCL of $4,000 ($7,000 – $3,000) is carried forward to future years as a STCL where it is treated as if it arose in the subsequent year.

Example 19

This year, Q reported the capital gains and losses as shown below. He had no other deductions for AGI. The combination of gains, losses, and ordinary income is revealed in the following table.

	Short-Term	Long-Term 28%	Long-Term 15%
Gains	$ 1,000	$5,000	$ 4,000
Losses.	(2,000)	(3,000)	(9,000)
Net.	$(1,000)	$2,000	$(5,000)
Netting (long-term against long-term)	0	(2,000)	2,000
Net.	$(1,000)	$ 0	$(3,000)
Deduction.	1,000		2,000
Carryover	$ 0		$(1,000)

Here Q has a NSTCL of $1,000 and a net $5,000 N15CL. He first combines the long-term groups, using $2,000 of the $5,000 N15CL to offset the N28CG of $2,000, reducing it to zero. The remaining $3,000 normally would be netted against 25CG if there were any. No further netting is allowed. Therefore, J first uses the NSTCL of

$1,000 and then $2,000 of the $3,000 N15CG remaining toward the $3,000 offset against ordinary income. The remaining N15CL of $1,000 is carried over and is treated as a *28CL*. It should be emphasized that the N15CL of $1,000 does not retain its character but becomes a capital loss in the 28% group. Note that the carryover rule is quite favorable. If next year J had $1,000 of N28CG and $1,000 of N15CG, the carryover would wipe out the N28CG, leaving the most favorable gain to be taxed.

Example 20

W's records for 2016 and 2017 revealed substantial ordinary income and the following capital gains and losses:

		Long-Term	
	Short-Term	28%	15%
2016 gains	$ 1,000	$ 5,000	$ 4,000
2016 losses	(2,000)	(9,000)	(9,000)
	$ (1,000)	$ (4,000)	$ (5,000)
2017	$ 10,000	$ 12,000	$ 15,000

In 2016, there can be no further netting. Therefore, W first uses the NSTCL of $1,000 against ordinary income and then uses $2,000 of the $9,000 in long-term losses, leaving a long-term capital loss carryover of $7,000. Note that it makes no difference which long-term loss is used (i.e., the 28% loss or the 15% loss) since all long-term capital loss carryovers are treated as 28CLs.

   In 2017, W treats the $7,000 long-term capital loss carryover as a N28CL. As a result, W would report a N28CG of $5,000 ($12,000 – the $7,000 loss carryover), N15CG of $15,000 and a NSTCG of $10,000.

DIVIDENDS TAXED AT CAPITAL GAIN RATES

In negotiations related to the *Jobs and Growth Tax Relief Reconciliation Act of 2003,* Congress and the Bush administration considered a number of alternative statutory schemes to reduce or eliminate the double taxation of corporate dividends. In the end, Congress opted to reduce the tax on dividends as well as capital gains. Since 2003 the taxation of dividends has followed that for capital gains.

   Currently (2013 and beyond), qualifying dividends are taxed at capital gains rates:[41] generally 15% but 0% for those in the 15% bracket or lower and 20% for those in the 39.6% bracket. 0% for dividends that would otherwise be taxed at an ordinary rate of 15% or lower. Qualified dividends are not included in the capital gain and loss netting process but are simply added to the net capital gain for purposes of computing the tax. As a result, the dividends are taxed at capital gains rates regardless of whether the taxpayer has other capital gains or losses.[42] In 2017, the higher 20% rate applies for taxpayers with taxable incomes exceeding $470,700 for joint filers and surviving spouses; $444,550 for heads of household; $418,400 for single filers; and $235,350 for married taxpayers filing separately. For details, see the discussion below regarding the calculation of the capital gains tax.

---

[41] § 1(h)(11). The 0% rate was made permanent by the American Taxpayer Relief Act of 2012.

[42] Like other long-term capital gains, dividends qualifying for capital gain treatment are not investment income for purposes of the investment interest limitation. However, a taxpayer can elect to treat the dividends as investment income and forego the capital gain treatment. See § 1(h)(11)(D)(i).

Qualified dividends are dividends from domestic corporations or qualified foreign corporations but only if the stock meets a holding period requirement.[43] *Qualified foreign corporations* generally include those that are incorporated in possessions of the United States, those subject to a treaty with the U.S. (involving the exchange of tax information by the governments) and others, the stocks of which are traded on a U.S. stock exchange (certain foreign corporations that are not subject to U.S. tax are not included). The holding period test requires the taxpayer to hold the stock for more than 60 days during a 120 day window that begins 60 days before the stock goes ex-dividend. This requirement helps prevent taxpayers from exploiting the preferential treatment for dividends. To illustrate the possible injustice, consider a taxpayer who buys a stock a few days before the ex-dividend date, receives a $1,000 dividend and then sells the stock. Assuming the value of the stock drops in direct proportion to the amount of the dividend, a sale immediately after the ex-dividend date would produce a $1,000 short-term capital loss. It appears that the $1,000 dividend is offset by the $1,000 loss and the net effect is zero. However, the dividend is taxed at 15% and the loss may offset ordinary income that is taxed at 39.6 percent. In such case, the taxpayer is better-off by $246 ($396 – $150). The holding period rule requires taxpayers to be at risk for at least 61 days if they want to use this scheme.[44]

CORPORATE TAXPAYERS

The capital gains and losses of corporate taxpayers are treated a bit differently from those of individual taxpayers. Corporations separate all of their capital gains and losses into only two groups: short-term and long-term (holding period of more than one year). Unlike individuals, there is no further subdividing of the long-term group. Items within the groups are then netted, producing one of the following: NLTCG, NLTCL, NSTCG, or NSTCL. If the taxpayer has a NSTCG and a NLTCG, no further netting is allowed. However, if the taxpayer has either a NSTCL and NLTCG or a NSTCG and a NLTCL, these results can be combined to produce a final position. This can be illustrated as follows:

> **LO.6**
>
> Explain the differences in tax treatment of the capital gains and losses of a corporate taxpayer versus those of an individual taxpayer.

	Short-Term	Long-Term	Result
Holding period (months)	≤12	>12	
Gains.	$xx,xxx	$xx,xxx	
Losses	(xxx)	(x,xxx)	
Net gain or loss	????	????	
Possibilities	NSTCG	NLTCG	No further netting
	NSTCG	NLTCL	NLTCL or NSTCG
	NSTCL	NLTCG	NSTCL or NLTCG
	NSTCL	NLTCL	No further netting

A corporate taxpayer receives no special treatment for either a NSTCG or NLTCG.[45] They are treated just like ordinary income. If after netting, the corporation has a NSTCL or a NLTCL, such losses receive special treatment. Unlike an individual taxpayer, a corporation is not allowed to offset capital losses against ordinary income. A corporate taxpayer's capital losses can be used only to reduce its capital gains.[46] Any excess losses are first carried back to the three prior years as *short-term capital losses* and offset against any net short-term capital gains and then any net long-term capital gains. Absent any capital gains in the three prior years, or if the loss carried back exceeds any capital gains, the excess may be carried forward for five years.[47] If the loss is not used at the end of the five-year period, it is lost.

---

[43] § 1(h)(11)(B).

[44] The holding period is extended for preferred stock. For other special rules see § 1(h)(11).

[45] For tax years ending after May 22, 2008 and beginning before May 22, 2009, NLTCGs from the sale of certain

timber by a C Corporation are taxed at a maximum rate of 15 percent. See § 1201(b).

[46] § 1212(a).

[47] *Ibid.*

Example 21

An examination of C Corporation's records for 2017 revealed $200,000 of net ordinary taxable income, a long-term capital loss of $9,000 and a short-term capital gain of $2,000. The corporation nets the loss against the gain to produce a NLTCL of $7,000. The corporation cannot offset the loss against ordinary income and, therefore, reports $200,000 of taxable income (undiminished by the NLTCL). Instead the NLTCL is carried back to the third prior year, 2014, as a STCL where it can be used to first offset any NSTCG and then any NLTCG. If there are no capital gains in 2014, the corporation would carryover the loss, now a STCL of $7,000, to 2015 to use against capital gains. This process would continue until the loss is entirely used or it expires at the end of 2022. Note that when the loss is used in prior years, an immediate refund can be obtained.

CALCULATING THE TAX

Section 1(h) provides a special tax calculation to ensure that an individual's capital gains will not be taxed at a rate greater than the applicable preferred rate (i.e., in 2017 the 28, 25, 20, 15, 10, or 0 percent rate). This calculation can only reduce the tax, not increase it.

Example 22

H and W are married. For 2017, their sole source of income was a 15CG of $97,000 from the sale of assets held four years. Their taxable income is computed as follows:

15CG.	$97,000
Standard deduction	(12,700)
Exemption deduction (2 × $4,050)	(8,100)
Taxable income	$76,200

The 10% and 15% tax brackets for taxpayers filing jointly in 2017 extend to $75,900 at which point any dollar of income in excess of that amount is taxed at a rate of 25 percent. The effect of the special capital gains calculation is to tax the portion of the N15CG that falls into the 10% and 15% bracket, $75,900, at a 0% rate and the portion that falls into the 25% bracket at 15 percent. Therefore, $75,900 of the N15CG is taxed at 0% and the remaining $300 ($76,200 − $75,900) is taxed at 15 percent. The total tax is $45 ([$75,900 × 0% = $0] + [$300 × 15% = $45]).

It may be clear from the above example that whenever an individual's *ordinary* taxable income exceeds the amount that would be taxed at 10 or 15 percent (e.g., $75,900 in 2017 for a joint return, $50,800 for head of household and $37,950 for single), none of the N15CG is taxed at 0 percent. In such case, the taxpayer computes the tax liability by first calculating the regular tax on ordinary taxable income and adding to that a tax of 15% on the N15CG. If ordinary taxable income puts the taxpayer in the 39.6% bracket, the 20% rate would be applied instead of the 15% rate. On the other hand, if ordinary taxable income does not exceed the amount that is taxed at 10 or 15 percent, a portion of the N15CG is taxed at the 0% rate until the 10 and 15 percent brackets are exhausted. Similarly, if ordinary taxable income partially fills up the 35% bracket, a portion of the gain is taxed at 15% until the 35% bracket is full and the preferential 20% rate applies to the balance. A similar approach applies for N25CGs and N28CGs.

Before proceeding, it is important to understand some statutory terms. The first term is *net capital gain*—the excess of the net long-term capital gain over the net short-term capital loss for a year. If there is no net short-term capital loss, the net capital gain is simply the net gain from the 15% group, the 25% group, and the 28% group combined. If there is a short-term loss, it is the excess of the combined long-term gains minus the net short-term capital loss. The second term is *adjusted net capital gain*—the net capital gain reduced (but not below zero) by the 25% gain and the net 28% gain (reduced by any net short-term capital loss).

The actual steps to compute the capital gains tax are built into worksheets in the instructions for Schedule D of Form 1040. They are also summarized in Exhibit 16-1.

EXHIBIT 16-1	Tax Computation Involving Capital Gains

Step 1:   Calculate the regular income tax using the regular rates on the taxpayer's taxable income.

Step 2:   Determine the tax on the *ordinary income*.

    a. Select the greater of:

- Ordinary taxable income (taxable income – net capital gain), or
- The lesser of:
  - The maximum amount that would be taxed at 15 percent, or
  - Taxable income – the adjusted net capital gain

    b. Compute the regular income tax on this amount

Step 3:   Determine the tax on the *net capital* gain by adding the following together.

    a. *Tax on 0% Gains*: 0% of the portion of the adjusted net capital gain that would have been taxed at 10 or 15 percent when added to ordinary income [i.e., the lesser of (1) the adjusted net capital gain or (2) the maximum amount that would normally be taxed at 10 or 15 percent minus the amount of ordinary income].

    b. *Tax on 15% Gains*: 15% of (the adjusted net capital gain minus any 0% gains)

    c. *Tax on 25% Gains*: The lesser of:

- 25% of the 25% gains, or
- If less, (1) 10 or 15 percent (respectively) of the amount of the 25% gains that, when added to ordinary income and any 0% gains, would be taxed at 10 or 15 percent,* plus (2) 25% of any remaining 25% gains.

    d. *Tax on 28% Gains*: The lesser of:

- 28% of the 28% gains, or
- If less, (1) 10 or 15 percent (respectively) of the amount of the 28% gains that, when added to ordinary income, any 0% gains, and any 25% gains, would be taxed at 10 or 15 percent,** plus (2) 28% of any remaining 28% gains.

Step 4:   Add the tax on the ordinary income (Step 2) to the tax on the net capital gain (Step 3) to get the total capital gains tax.

Step 5:   The final tax is the lesser of the taxes computed in Step 1 and Step 4.

* This is the amount that would otherwise be taxed at 10 or 15 percent when added to ordinary income and any 0% gains (or stated differently, it is the maximum amount that would be taxed at 10 or 15 percent minus the amount of ordinary income and the amount of 0% gains).

** This is the amount that would otherwise be taxed at 10 or 15 percent when added to ordinary income, any 0% gains, and any 25% gains (or, stated differently, it is the maximum amount that would be taxed at 15% minus the amount of ordinary income and the amount of 0% gains).

Example 23

J and K are married and file a joint return for 2017. They have taxable income of $93,600, including a N15CG of $15,000. Thus they have ordinary taxable income of $78,600. Their tax is computed as follows:

Step 1: Regular tax on $93,600 = $14,988 as computed below

Tax on $75,900 (10% and 15% brackets)	$10,453
Plus: Tax on excess at 25%	
([$93,600 − $75,900] × 25%)	+ 4,425
Equals: Total tax	$14,878

Step 2: **a.** Ordinary income = $78,600 ($93,600 − $15,000)
   b. Regular tax on ordinary income of $78,600 = $11,128

Step 3: Tax on the net capital gain = $2,250 as computed below

   a. Tax on 0% Gains = 0% of zero (All of the net capital gain would have been taxed at a rate exceeding 15% since V's ordinary income plus 25% gains and 28% gains equaled or exceeded $73,800—the limit of the 15% bracket)
   b. Tax on 15% gains = 15% × $15,000 = $2,250
   c. Tax on 25% gains = 25% of zero
   d. Tax on 28% gains = 28% of zero

Step 4: Total capital gains tax = $13,378 ($11,128 + $2,250)

Step 5: The final tax is $13,378. The savings is $1,500 ($14,878 − $13,378). Note that this $1,500 is the 10% tax rate difference (25% − 15%) on the $15,000 gain.

Example 24

V, single, had taxable income for 2017 of $100,000, including the following:

Loss from stock held for investment 11 months.	$ (2,000)
Gain from stamps held for investment 3 years.	3,000
Gain from land held for investment 9 years.	16,000
Loss from stock held for investment 2 years.	(3,000)

V would summarize his gains and losses as follows:

		Long-Term	
	Short-Term	28%	15%
	$(2,000)	$3,000	$16,000
	0	0	(3,000)
	$(2,000)	$3,000	$13,000
Netting	2,000	(2,000)	
	$ 0	$1,000	$13,000

The loss is a STCL since it was held for not more than 12 months. The gain on the sale of the stamps is treated as a 28CG since it is a collectible. Gains from collectibles are treated as 28CGs if they were held more than 12 months. The gain and loss from the land and stock are both classified as 15% items since they were held more than 12 months. Thus V's overall capital gain is $14,000, consisting of a N28CG of $1,000 and a N15CG of $13,000. V's tax is computed as follows:

Step 1:   Regular tax on $100,000 = $20,982 as computed below

Tax on $91,900 (10, 15, and 25 percent bracket)	$18,714
Plus: Tax on excess at 28% ([$100,000 − $91,900] × 28%)	2,268
Equals: Total tax	$20,982

Step 2:   **a.** Ordinary income = $86,000 ($100,000 − $14,000)

   b. Regular tax on ordinary income of $86,000 = $17,294

Tax on $37,950	$ 5,226
Plus: Tax on excess at 25% ([$86,000 − $37,950] × 25%)	12,013
Equals: Total tax	$17,239

Step 3:   Tax on the net capital gain = $2,230 ($280 + $1,950)

   a. Tax on 0% gains = 0% of zero (All of the net capital gain would have been taxed at a rate exceeding 15% since V's ordinary income exceeded $37,950—the limit of the 15% bracket.)

   b. Tax on 15% gains = 15% × $13,000 = $1,950

   c. Tax on 25% gains = 25% of zero

   d. Tax on 28% gains = 28% × $1,000 = $280

Step 4:   Total capital gains tax = $19,469 ($17,239 + $2,230)

Step 5:   The final tax is $19,469 (the lesser of *Step 1* or *Step 4*). The difference between the regular tax and the capital gains tax is $1,513 ($20,982 − $19,469). There is no capital gain difference on the 28% gain since the ordinary rate and the capital gain rate are the same.

Example 25

Same as *Example 24,* except V's total taxable income is $40,000.

Step 1:	Regular tax on $40,000 = $5,739		
	Tax on $37,950		$5,226
	Plus: Tax on excess at 25% ([$40,000 − $37,950] × 25%)		513
	Equals: Total tax		$5,739

Step 2:   **a.** Ordinary income = $26,000 ($40,000 − $14,000)
b. Regular tax on $26,000 = $3,434 ($9,325 × 10% + $16,675 × 15%)

Step 3:   Tax on the net capital gain = $408 ($0 + $158 + $250)

a. Tax on 0% gains = $0 ($11,950 × 0%—The N15CG is taxed at 0% to the extent the limit on the 15% tax bracket exceeds the ordinary income [$37,950 − $26,000 = $11,950])

b. Tax on 15% gains = $158 ([$13,000 − $11,950 = $1,050] × 15%— The adjusted net capital gain reduced by the portion taxed at 0% multiplied by 15%)

c. Tax on 25% gains = 25% of zero

d. Tax on 28% gains = 25% × $1,000 = $250 [Since ordinary income plus the 0% gains, 15% gains, and 25% gains are more than the limit on the 15% tax bracket ($26,000 + $13,000 + $1,000 > $37,950) but less than the top of the 25% bracket amounts, the 28% gains are taxed at 25 percent.]

Step 4:   Total capital gains tax = $3,842 ($3,434 + $408)

Step 5:   The final tax is $3,842 (the lesser of *Step 1* or *Step 4*). The difference between the regular tax and the capital gains tax is $1,897 ($5,739 − $3,842). Observe that there is no difference on the 28% gain that was taxed at the ordinary income rate.

TAX REFORM

For tax years beginning after 2012, the Taxpayer Relief Act of 2012 provides that the top rate for capital gains and dividends will rise permanently to 20% (up from 15%). This increase is simultaneous with the ordinary rate increase to 39.6% for taxpayers with taxable incomes exceeding $470,700 for joint filers and surviving spouses; $444,550 for heads of household; $418,400 for single filers; and $235,350 for married taxpayers filing separately. These thresholds are to be increased annually for inflation after 2014.

In addition, as mentioned earlier, the § 1411 surtax on net investment income could increase the rate on long-term capital gains and dividends of high income taxpayers (i.e., those with modified adjusted gross income over $250,000 for joint filers or surviving spouses, $125,000 for a married individual filing a separate return, and $200,000 in any other case). Recall that § 1411 imposes a 3.8% surtax on investment-type income and gains for tax years beginning after 2012. When this surtax applies, the overall rate for 15% gains might be 18.8% (15% + 3.8%), and for those with taxable incomes over $413,350 ($466,900 for joint filers) could rise to 23.8% (20% + 3.8%).

Example 26

J and K are married and file jointly. For 2017, they have taxable income of exactly $500,000, including a 15% capital gain of $100,000, making their ordinary income $400,000. Ignoring the net investment income tax, their tax is calculated below. Note that a portion of the capital gain is taxed at 15 percent and a portion at 20 percent.

Tax on ordinary income of 400,000 = $107,217

Tax on $233,350 from tax schedule		$ 52,223
Tax on excess ($400,000 – $233,350) × 0.33		54,994
Total tax on ordinary income		$107,217

Tax on net capital gain = $17,500

Tax from $400,000 to $470,700 at 15%	$10,605	
Tax from $470,700 to $500,000 at 20%	5,860	16,465
Gross income tax		$123,682

REPORTING CAPITAL GAINS AND LOSSES

Individual taxpayers report any capital gains or losses on Schedule D of Form 1040.[48] This form is designed to facilitate the netting process, with one part used for reporting short-term gains and losses and another part used to report long-term transactions. A third part of the form is available for the second step of the netting process in the event the taxpayer has either NSTCGs and NLTCLs *or* NLTCGs and NSTCLs.

Regular corporations must report capital gains and losses on Schedule D of Form 1120 in much the same manner as individual taxpayers. Partnerships and S corporations must also report capital gains and losses on a separate schedule (Schedule D of Form 1065 for partnerships and Schedule D of Form 1120S for S corporations). However, these conduit entities are limited to the *first* step of the netting process. Each owner (partner or S corporation shareholder) must include his or her share of the results from the entity with the appropriate capital transactions being netted on the owner's Schedule D, Form 1040.

CHECK YOUR KNOWLEDGE

Review Question 1

For 2017, Ms. Reyes earned a salary of $70,000 from her job as an art curator. In addition, she sold stock, realizing the following capital gains and losses:

15CG	$10,000
15CL	(7,000)
STCL.	(11,000)

In 2018, she changed jobs, becoming a tax accountant and earning a salary of $300,000. In addition, she realized a 15CG of $12,000. Compute Ms. Reyes's adjusted gross income for 2017 and 2018 and indicate the amount, if any, that is eligible for preferential treatment as long-term capital gain.

Her adjusted gross incomes for 2017 and 2018 are $67,000 and $307,000, respectively. After netting her capital gains and losses in 2017, Ms. Reyes has a net capital loss of $8,000, all of which is short-term. The deduction for capital losses of an individual is generally limited to $3,000. As a result, her adjusted gross income is $67,000 ($70,000 – $3,000). She is entitled to carry over the remainder of her short-term loss of $5,000. In 2018, she nets the $5,000 short-term capital loss against her $12,000 15CG to produce a N15CG of $7,000. The $7,000 is combined with her other $300,000 of salary income to produce an adjusted gross income of $307,000. Of this amount, her N15CG of $7,000 is taxed at a preferred rate of 15 percent.

---

[48] See Appendix for a sample of this form.

Review Question 2

True-False. This year Mr. and Mrs. Simpson retired. The couple's only income was a capital gain from the sale of stock held three years. Assuming the Simpsons file a joint return, all $100,000 of their taxable income is taxed at a rate of 15 percent.

False. The tax computation operates to ensure that the 15CG is taxed at 0% to the extent that ordinary income does not absorb the 10 and 15 percent brackets. For 2017 the 15% bracket for a joint return extends to taxable income of $75,300. Therefore, $75,300 is taxed at a 0% rate and the remaining $24,700 is taxed at a 15% rate.

The Simpsons should have considered making the sales in two separate years (perhaps 2017 and 2018) if they have no other income in either year. That would allow them to double the benefit of the 0% rate, plus take advantage of two standard deductions and two sets of personal exemptions.

Review Question 3

True-False. An individual taxpayer is generally entitled to deduct any capital loss recognized during the current year to the extent of any capital gains recognized plus $3,000. Any capital loss in excess of this amount retains its character and may be used in subsequent years until it is exhausted.

True.

Capital Gain Treatment Extended to Certain Transactions

LO.7

Identify various transactions to which capital gain or loss treatment has been extended.

The Internal Revenue Code contains several special provisions related to capital asset treatment. In some instances the concept of capital asset is expanded and in others it is limited. Some of the provisions merely clarify the tax treatment of certain transactions.

PATENTS

Section 1235 provides that certain transfers of patents shall be treated as transfers of capital assets held for more than one year. This virtually assures that a long-term capital gain will result if the patent is transferred in a taxable transaction, because the patent will have little, if any, basis since the costs of creating it are usually deducted under § 174 (research and experimental expenditures) in the tax year in which such costs are incurred. Any transfer, other than by gift, inheritance, or devise, will qualify as long as *all substantial rights* to the patent are transferred. All substantial rights have been described as all rights that have value at the time of the transfer. For example, the transfer must not limit the geographical coverage within the country of issuance or limit the time application to less than the remaining term of the patent.[49]

The transferor must be a *holder* as defined in § 1235(b). The term *holder* refers to the creator of the patented property or to an individual who purchased such property from its creator if such individual is neither the employer of the creator nor related to such creator.[50]

The sale of a patent will qualify for § 1235 treatment even if payments are made over a period that ends when the purchaser's use of the patent ceases or if payments are contingent on the productivity, use, or disposition of the patent.[51] It also is important to note that §§ 483 and 1274, which require interest to be imputed on certain sales contracts, do not apply to amounts received in exchange for patents qualifying under § 1235 that are contingent on the productivity, use, or disposition of the patent transferred.[52]

Example 27

K, a successful inventor, sold a patent (in which she had a basis of zero) to Bell Corp. The sale agreement called for K to receive a percentage of the sales of the property covered by the patent. All of K's payments received in consideration for this patent will be long-term capital gain regardless of her holding period.

---

[49] Reg. § 1.1235-2(b).

[50] For definition of "relative," see § 1235(d).

[51] § 1235(a).

[52] §§ 483(d)(4) and 1274(c)(4)(E). See Chapter 14 for a discussion of the imputed interest rules.

LEASE CANCELLATION PAYMENTS

Section 1241 allows the treatment of payments received in cancellation of a lease or in cancellation of a distributorship agreement as having been received in a sale or exchange. Therefore, the gains or losses will be treated as capital gains or losses if the underlying assets are capital assets.[53]

Incentives for Investments in Small Businesses

Congress has frequently provided incentives for investment in general or for specific investments. The Subchapter S election, for example, was intended to remove any impediment for small business owners who were not incorporating because they believed there was a double tax on corporate profits. Other incentives provide special treatment upon the disposition of certain business interests. The following sections deal with various prominent examples.

LOSSES ON SMALL BUSINESS STOCK: § 1244

Losses on dispositions (e.g., sale or worthlessness) of corporate stock are generally classified as capital losses. For a year in which a taxpayer has no capital gains, the deduction for capital losses would be limited to $3,000 annually. In contrast, a loss on the disposition of a sole proprietorship would be recognized upon the disposition of the assets used in the business. Losses on the sale of many (if not most) of the assets would be treated as ordinary losses, thereby avoiding (or partially avoiding) the $3,000 limit. Similarly, proper planning could result in ordinary loss treatment upon the disposition of interests in businesses operated in the partnership form.

Without special rules, the limitation on deductions for capital losses might discourage investment in new corporations. For example, if an individual invested $90,000 in stock of a new corporate venture, deductions for any loss from the investment, absent offsetting gains, would be limited to $3,000 annually.[54] Thus, where the stock becomes worthless it could take the investor as long as 30 years to recover the investment. This restriction on losses also is inconsistent with the treatment of losses resulting from investments by an individual in his or her sole proprietorship or in a partnership. In the case of a sole proprietorship or a partnership, losses generally may be used to offset the taxpayer's other income without limitation. For example, assume a sole proprietor sank $150,000 into a purchase of pet rocks that he ultimately sold for only $100,000. In such case, he would have an ordinary loss of $50,000, all of which could be used to offset other ordinary income. Assume the same individual invested $150,000 in a corporation that had the same luck. If the taxpayer could at best sell the stock for $100,000, he would realize a capital loss of $50,000. Obviously the sole proprietor is in a much better position. To eliminate these problems and encourage taxpayers to invest in small corporations, Congress enacted § 1244 in 1958.

Under § 1244, losses on "Section 1244 stock" generally are treated as ordinary rather than capital losses.[55] Ordinary loss treatment normally is available *only to individuals* who are the original holders of the stock. If these individuals sell the stock at a loss or the stock becomes worthless, they may deduct up to $50,000 annually as an ordinary loss. Taxpayers who file a joint return may deduct up to $100,000 regardless of how the stock is owned (e.g., separately or jointly). When the loss in any one year exceeds the $50,000 or $100,000 limitation, the excess is considered a capital loss.

Example 28

T, married, is one of the original purchasers of RST Corporation's stock, which qualifies as § 1244 stock. She separately purchased the stock two years ago for $150,000. During the year, she sold all of the stock for $30,000, resulting in a $120,000 loss. On a joint return for the current year, she may deduct $100,000 as an ordinary loss. The portion of the loss exceeding the limitation, $20,000 ($120,000 – $100,000), is treated as a long-term capital loss.

---

[53] See Chapter 17 for treatment if the asset is a § 1231 asset.

[54] A taxpayer can offset any capital losses against capital gains, if any.

[55] § 1244(a).

Stock issued by a corporation (including preferred stock issued after July 18, 1984) qualifies as § 1244 stock only if the issuing corporation meets certain requirements. The most important condition is that the corporation's total capitalization (amounts received for stock issued, contributions to capital, and paid-in surplus) must not exceed $1 million at the time the stock is issued.[56] This requirement effectively limits § 1244 treatment to those individuals who originally invest the first $1 million in money and property in the corporation.

Example 29

In 2015, F provided the initial capitalization for MNO Corporation by purchasing 700 shares at a cost of $1,000 a share for a total cost of $700,000. In 2017, G purchased 500 shares at a cost of $1,000 per share or a total of $500,000. All of F's shares otherwise qualify as § 1244 stock. Only 300 of G's new shares qualify for § 1244 treatment, however, since 200 of the 500 purchased caused the corporation's total capitalization to exceed $1 million.

QUALIFIED SMALL BUSINESS STOCK (§ 1202 STOCK)

As part of the *Revenue Reconciliation Act of 1993,* Congress created a new tax incentive to stimulate investment in small business. By virtue of this special rule, individuals who start their own C corporations or who are original investors in C corporations (e.g., initial public offerings) may be richly rewarded for taking the risk of investing in such enterprises.

Exclusion

Under § 1202, noncorporate investors (i.e., individuals, partnerships, estates, and trusts) are allowed to exclude up to $10 million (or if greater, 10 times the invested capital) of the gain on the sale of *qualified small business stock* held for more than five years.[57] The exclusion is 50% of the gain. The balance of this gain is treated as a 28% gain. The effect of this provision is to impose a maximum effective tax of 14% (50% × 28% maximum capital gain rate), or 7 percent, or 0% on the gains from such investments (depending on when the stock was purchased),[58] a far lower rate than the 39.6% that may apply to other types of income received by the taxpayer. However, the exclusion amount is increased to 75% for stock acquired after February 17, 2009 and before September 28, 2010; and amazingly, 100% for gain related to stock acquired after September 27, 2010 and before January 1, 2015. The table below summarizes the treatment.

Qualified Small Business Stock: Exclusion of Gain

Acquisition Period	Exclusion	Tax Preference Add-Back
Before 2/18/2009	50%	7% (3.5% of gain)
2/18/2009–9/27/2010	75%	7% (3.5% of gain)
After 9/27/2010.	100%	0%

---

[56] § 1244(c)(3)(A).

[57] Special rules apply for computing the exclusion on the sale of stock in a specialized small business investment company (see following discussion). The latest change was made by

the *Tax Relief, Unemployment Insurance Reauthorization, and Job Creation Act of 2010.*

[58] § 1h. Recall that the § 1202 gain on the sale of qualified small business stock is excluded from the adjusted net capital gain. Therefore, the 15% rate does not apply.

Example 30

On October 31, 2007, N purchased 1,000 shares of Boston Cod Corporation for $10,000. The stock was part of an initial public offering of the company's stock that was designed to raise $30 million to open another 200 fast fish restaurants. On December 20, 2017, N sold all of her shares for $50,000. As a result, she realized a capital gain of $40,000, her only gain or loss during the year. Since N was one of the original investors and the stock qualified as § 1202 stock at the time of its issue (assets at that time were less than $50 million), she is entitled to exclude 50% of her gain, or $20,000. The maximum tax on the $20,000 gain is $5,600 ($20,000 × 28%). Note that if the taxpayer is in an ordinary bracket lower than 28% (e.g., 25, 15, or 10 percent), the gain would be taxed at that lower rate.

In the netting process, only the § 1202 gain remaining after the exclusion is taken into account.

Example 31

Assume the same facts as above, but assume that in addition to the $40,000 gain on § 1202 stock, N also has other long-term capital gains of $10,000 and short-term capital losses of $5,000. N first applies the 50% exclusion and then nets the remainder with the other capital gains and losses. Therefore, N's net capital gain for the year is $25,000 ([$40,000 − $20,000 = $20,000] + $10,000 − $5,000).

Example 32

Assume N has a gain on § 1202 stock of $40,000 and a short-term capital loss of $23,000. N first applies the 50% exclusion and then nets the remaining gain with the capital loss. As a result, N has a net capital loss of $3,000 ($20,000 − $23,000).

Rollover Provision

An individual who realizes a gain on the sale of QSB stock held for more than six months can defer recognition of the gain by reinvesting in other QSB stock within 60 days of the sale. Note that the stock qualifies for the rollover provision if it is held more than six months (not five years). The individual must recognize gain to the extent that the amount reinvested is less than the sales price of the original stock. If the taxpayer uses the rollover provision, the basis in the newly acquired QSB stock is reduced by the deferred gain. The holding period of the new QSB stock includes the holding period of the old QSB stock.

Example 33

D purchased Netbrowser stock two years ago, for $10,000. The stock qualified as § 1202 stock. After rising dramatically, the stock started to fall so D sold it for $14,000 before he lost all of his profit. He realized a $4,000 gain on the sale. D wanted to preserve the special treatment for § 1202 stock so 45 days after the sale, he reinvested in MMX Inc., another issue of § 1202 stock, for $15,000. D recognizes no gain on the sale since his holding period of two years exceeded the required six months and he reinvested all $10,000 received from the sale of § 1202 stock. His basis in the replacement stock is $11,000 ($15,000 − $4,000) and the two-year holding period of the old stock attaches to the new. Had D reinvested only $13,000, he would have recognized a gain of $1,000 ($14,000 − $13,000) and have a basis in the replacement stock of $10,000 ($13,000 − deferred gain of $3,000). Note that this rollover provision enables the taxpayer to move in and out of positions in QSB stock so long as QSB is repurchased.

Section 1202 Requirements

Stock qualifies as § 1202 stock if it is issued after August 10, 1993 and meets a long list of requirements.

1. At the time the stock is issued, the corporation issuing the stock must be a *qualified small business.* A corporation is a qualified small business if

   - The corporation is a domestic C corporation.
   - The corporation's gross assets do not exceed $50 million at the time the stock was issued (i.e., cash plus the fair market value of contributed property measured at the time of contribution plus the adjusted basis of other assets).

2. The seller is the original owner of the stock (i.e., the stock was acquired directly from the corporation or through an underwriter at its original issue).

3. During substantially all of the seller's holding period of the stock, the corporation was engaged in an active trade or business other than the following:

   - A business involving the performance of providing services in the fields of health, law, engineering, architecture, accounting, actuarial science, performing arts, consulting, athletics, financial services, brokerage services, or any other business where the principal asset is the reputation or skill of one or more of its employees.
   - Banking, insurance, financing, leasing, or investing.
   - Farming.
   - Businesses involving the production or extraction of products eligible for depletion.
   - Business of operating a hotel, motel, or restaurant.

4. The corporation generally cannot own

   - Real property with a value that exceeds 10% of its total assets unless such property is used in the active conduct of a trade or business (e.g., rental real estate is not an active trade or business).
   - Portfolio stock or securities with a value that exceeds 10% of the corporation's total assets in excess of its liabilities.

Note that the active trade or business requirement and the prohibition on real estate holdings severely limit the exclusion. These conditions effectively grant the exclusion to corporations engaged in manufacturing, retailing, or wholesaling businesses.

The new provision also imposes a restriction, albeit a liberal one, on the amount of gain eligible to be excluded on the sale of a particular corporation's stock. The maximum amount of gain that may be excluded on the sale of one corporation's stock is the *larger* of

1. $10 million, reduced by previously excluded gain on the sale of such corporation's stock; or

2. 10 times the adjusted basis of all qualified stock of the corporation that the taxpayer sold during the tax year.

This exclusion is extremely attractive, but it should be remembered that whatever Congress gives it can also take away. And that is exactly what Congress has done with § 1202 stock. For purposes of the alternative minimum tax, § 57 provides that 7% of the amount excluded from gross income under § 1202 (i.e., 3.5% of the total gain) is a tax preference item. In addition, the excluded gain is generally not considered investment income for purposes of determining the investment interest limitation.

ROLLOVER OF GAIN ON CERTAIN PUBLICLY TRADED SECURITIES

Another creature of the 1993 Act encourages investment in small businesses owned by disadvantaged taxpayers. Individuals and C corporations that recognize gain on the sale of publicly traded securities are allowed to defer recognition of such gain if they reinvest the proceeds from the sale in common stock or a partnership interest in a *specialized small business investment company* (SSBIC).[59] The reinvestment must occur within 60 days of the sale. An SSBIC is generally any corporation or partnership licensed by the Small Business Administration under § 301 of the Small Business Investment Act of 1958 (as in effect on May 13, 1993). This typically includes investment companies that finance small businesses owned by disadvantaged taxpayers.

The maximum amount of gain that a taxpayer may exclude per year is generally limited to $50,000 (or, if smaller, $500,000 reduced by any previously excluded gain). These limits are increased to $250,000 and $1 million, respectively, for C corporations. Note that the special deferral privilege is not available for partnerships, S corporations, estates, or trusts.

The operation of the deferral provision is virtually identical to the rollover rules for gains on the sale of a residence and involuntary conversions. As a general rule, the taxpayer must recognize gain to the extent that the sales proceeds are not properly reinvested. Any gain deferred reduces the basis of the stock acquired.

Example 34

G sold 4,000 shares of IBM stock for $200,000, realizing a long-term capital gain of $40,000. Less than a week later, G used the entire $200,000 plus additional cash of $15,000 to purchase an interest in the P Partnership, an SSBIC. G may exclude the gain of $40,000 since she reinvested at least $200,000 in qualified property within 60 days. Her basis in the partnership interest would be $175,000 ($215,000 cost − $40,000 deferred gain).

Dealers and Developers

Since property held primarily for sale to customers in the ordinary course of a trade or business (or inventory) is generally excluded from the definition of a capital asset, any gain or loss on the sale of inventory is generally treated as ordinary gain or loss. For taxpayers who would otherwise benefit from capital gain treatment, this is an obstacle. In certain instances, Congress has provided special relief.

DEALERS, INVESTORS, AND TRADERS OF SECURITIES

With the arrival of the Internet and the ease in which individuals can buy and sell securities (e.g., computerized trading, day traders), the need for taxpayers and practitioners to understand the potential problems has significantly increased. Important differences in the tax treatment exist, depending on whether the taxpayer is an investor, trader or dealer.[60]

Dealers

A dealer is a taxpayer who purchases securities from customers or sells securities to customers in the ordinary course of business. The securities held by a dealer represent inventory held primarily for resale. Dealers are distinguished from traders in two ways: (1) they have customers and (2) their income is primarily based on a mark-up on the buying and selling of securities, rather than obtaining profit from price fluctuations. Dealers report ordinary income or ordinary loss from their business transactions, using the mark-to-market provisions discussed below.

---

[59] § 1202(g).

[60] For an excellent discussion, see Robison and Mark, "On-Line Transactions Intensify Trader vs. Investor Question," *Practical Tax Strategies* (February, 2001).

The difficulty with the tax treatment of dealers is that they not only hold stocks and bonds for sale to customers as part of their regular business operations, but they also invest in stocks and bonds for their own account. As may be apparent, the potential for abuse is great. Since long-term capital gain and ordinary loss are generally preferred, securities dealers have the natural tendency to classify the assets to provide the greatest tax benefit. On the other hand, the IRS wants to do just the opposite. To eliminate the potential controversy and prohibit taxpayers from using their hindsight, Congress enacted § 1236. This provision simply requires the dealer to indicate that a particular security is held for investment (and is therefore a capital asset) by the end of the day on which it was acquired. If the security is not properly identified on a timely basis, the dealer must characterize any gain or loss as ordinary.

Investors

In contrast to dealers, investors are not conducting a trade or business. Their income is normally derived from the price movement of the securities as well as dividends and interest. Most individuals are investors. The basic rules discussed in this chapter concerning capital gains and losses (including the wash sales provisions) apply to investors. Investors report their gains and losses on Schedule D. On the expense side, because investors are not carrying on a trade or business, their expenses may be restricted in some way. For example, the investment interest provisions of § 163(d) limit the deduction of investment interest to investment income. Similarly, the home office deduction is not extended to investors since it is allowed only for those carrying on a trade or business. Likewise, § 179 concerning limited expensing is allowed only for property used in a business. Moreover, any expenses that are deductible are treated as investment expenses and characterized as miscellaneous itemized deductions subject to the 2% limitation as well as the 2% cutback rule. And perhaps the most significant problem for investors is the elimination of the deduction of these expenses for purposes of the alternative minimum tax (AMT).

Traders

The tax treatment of a trader's transactions can differ significantly from those of an investor. For this reason, it is important to draw the distinction. Unfortunately, there is not a clear line of demarcation between the two. A trader is one whose and security transactions are so regular and continuous as to rise to the level of a trade or business. In this regard, the distinguishing factors are the individual's intent and the frequency or regularity of trades.

Although traders are treated as conducting a business, they do not have inventory and do not have clients. Therefore, their gains and losses on the sales of securities are still treated as capital gains and capital losses and reported on Schedule D, the same as an investor. Similarly, dividend and interest income are still treated as investment income, reported on Schedule B. But expenses are treated much differently. Traders may deduct their expenses such as margin account interest, management fees, home office expenses and others as deductions for AGI on Schedule C. This solves the limitations associated with miscellaneous itemized deductions, the 2% cutback rule and the AMT. Notwithstanding the fact that traders are in a trade or business they are not subject to self-employment tax. Dividends, interest from securities and gain or loss from the sale of capital assets, are not considered self-employment income. In addition to these rules, traders are entitled to special treatment not extended to investors: the use of the mark-to-market rules.

Traders and Mark-to-Market Provisions

Traders are given an important option unavailable to investors. Taxpayers who are considered traders (but not investors) may take advantage of the mark-to-market (MTM) rules of § 475. Under the MTM rules, traders who make the § 475(f) election are deemed to have sold all of their stocks and securities for their fair market value on the last business day of the taxable year. As a result, traders must recognize all gains and losses as of that date. Traders report their gains and losses on Schedule C. Due to the deemed sale, the basis of the securities is increased to fair market value and used as the basis for subsequent transactions. Although making the MTM election eliminates the opportunity to defer income beyond year end, it offers at least one huge advantage. Section 475(d)(3) provides that the gains and losses recognized on the deemed sales are treated as ordinary income or ordinary losses.

This rule is extremely important since it allows traders (who make the election) to avoid the limitation on the deduction of capital losses.[61] By making the election, losses can be used to offset all other taxable income without limitation. Moreover, as business losses, they could add to or create a net operating loss that can be carried back two years and forward for twenty years. Also, the wash sales rules do not apply.

Although the MTM election converts capital losses to ordinary losses, it also converts capital gains to ordinary income. As a practical matter, this is of little significance since the income of most traders would be short-term capital gain which is treated as ordinary income. However, traders who want to preserve the possibility of long-term capital gain treatment for certain securities may do so by taking advantage of another special rule. Section 475(f)(1)(B) permits a trader to segregate trader transactions from investor transactions by using separate accounts for each.

For the § 475(f) election to be effective for a particular tax year, a statement must be filed with the IRS no later than the due date (without extensions) for the tax return for the immediately preceding year. Thus, an election for 2017 must be filed no later than the due date of the 2016 return, April 15, 2017. The election is a change in accounting method so those rules (see Chapter 5) must be observed.

SUBDIVIDED REAL ESTATE

The dealer versus investor debate also raises its ugly head for taxpayers selling land. Is the land held for investment or primarily for resale?

It is not uncommon for a taxpayer to hold land for investment for many years and then subdivide or improve it just before selling it. If the subdivision and improvements are significant, the property will probably be deemed to be held primarily for sale to customers in a trade or business. If the activities are minor, the land probably retains its character as a capital asset. As was pointed out earlier in this chapter, the determination usually is made based on the frequency, continuity, and volume of sales, but development activities are also very important.

In an attempt to prevent disputes, Congress created a safe harbor that guarantees capital gain treatment where there is a limited amount of subdivision activity. This rule allows the taxpayer, as someone once said, to subdivide and conquer the ordinary income problem. Under § 1237, real estate is not treated as held primarily for sale if all of the following conditions are met:[62]

1. The tract of land has been held at least five years prior to the sale (except in the case of inheritance).

2. The taxpayer has made no substantial improvements to the property that increase the value of the lots sold while the property was owned.

3. The parcel sold, or any part thereof, had not previously been held by the taxpayer primarily for resale.

4. No other real property was held by the taxpayer primarily for sale during the year of the sale.

Even if the requirements are met, the taxpayer may still be required to report a portion of the gain as ordinary income. If five or fewer lots are sold from the same tract of land, the entire gain is capital gain. However, in the year that the sixth lot is sold, all lots sold in that year and later years become the target of § 1237(b). This special rule provides that 5% of the sales price (not gain) is ordinary income.[63] In addition, any selling expenses reduce the ordinary income portion of the gain (limited to the amount of ordinary income), rather than the amount treated as capital gain.[64]

---

[61] To appreciate the mark-to-market election, see *L.S. Vines* 126 T.C. 279 (2006).

[62] § 1237(a).

[63] § 1237(b)(1).

[64] § 1237(b)(2).

> **Example 35**
>
> Twenty years ago X bought 100 acres 20 miles south of Tulsa for $100,000. This year he retired and decided to sell the land. In order to sell the property, he subdivided it into 10 lots of 10 acres each. This year X sold five lots for $310,000 and paid a real estate commission of $10,000. As a result, he recognized a gain of $250,000 ($310,000 − $10,000 − $50,000 basis). Since he sold only five lots, the gain on each sale is treated as long-term capital gain. Had X sold six lots for the same total price, 5% of his selling price, $15,500 (5% × $310,000), would be considered ordinary income and he could reduce this amount by the selling expenses of $10,000, for net ordinary income on the sale of $5,500.

Note that § 1237 applies to property that has been subdivided, but it is of no help where significant improvements have been made to the property.

Other Related Provisions

NONBUSINESS BAD DEBTS

Bad debt losses from nonbusiness debts are deductible as short-term capital losses. Nonbusiness bad debts are deductible only in the year they become totally worthless since no deduction is allowed for partially worthless debts.[65] These rules and others related to the allowable deduction for bad debts were discussed in Chapter 10.

FRANCHISE AGREEMENTS, TRADEMARKS, AND TRADE NAMES

Section 1253 includes specific guidelines for the treatment of both the transferee and the transferor of payments with respect to franchise, trademark, and trade name agreements. The transfer of such rights is *not* treated as the sale or exchange of a capital asset by the transferor *if* he or she retains significant power, right, or continuing interest with respect to the property.[66] Capital gain and loss treatment also is denied for periodic payments that are contingent on the productivity, use, or sale of the property.[67]

"Significant power, right, or continuing interest" is defined in the Code by example. Some of the characteristics listed in the Code as indicative of such power, right, or interest retained by the transferor of the franchise are as follows:[68]

1. The right to terminate the franchise at will;
2. The right to disapprove any assignment;
3. The right to prescribe quality standards;
4. The right to require that the transferee advertise only products of the transferor;
5. The right to require that the transferee acquire substantially all of his or her supplies or equipment from the transferor; and
6. The right to require payments based on the productivity, use, or sale of the property.

The transferee is allowed current deductions for amounts paid or accrued that are contingent on the productivity, use, or sale of the property transferred.[69] Other payments must be at least partially deferred. They generally are amortized over 15 years.[70]

---

[65] See § 166(d) and related discussion in Chapter 10.

[66] § 1253(a).

[67] § 1253(c).

[68] § 1253(b)(2).

[69] § 1253(d)(1).

[70] § 197(d)(1)(F).

Example 36

M, Inc. and R enter into a franchise agreement that allows R to operate a hamburger establishment using the trade name and products of M, Inc. According to the contract, M, Inc. has retained all six rights that are listed above. R is required to pay M $50,000 upon entering the contract and 2% of all sales. The term of the contract is 25 years with provision for renewals. R must also pay for any supplies provided by M. Both the $50,000 payment and the percentage royalty payment are ordinary income to M, Inc.

R may treat the royalty payments to M, Inc. as ordinary deductions incurred in his trade or business. The initial fee of $50,000 is amortized equally over 10 years beginning with the year in which the payment is made.

SHORT SALES

Investors who believe that the price of a security will fall rather than rise may bank on their belief by using short sales. Selling short essentially means selling shares that are not actually owned. To accomplish this, the seller typically borrows shares from a broker, sells such shares, and agrees to return an equivalent number of substantially identical shares to the broker within a certain period of time. For example, an investor may sell 100 shares of borrowed stock for $100 per share, or $10,000. If the stock price falls to $80 per share, the investor can purchase 100 shares in the market for $8,000, replace the 100 borrowed shares, and have a tidy profit of $2,000. Of course, if the price goes up to $110, it costs the investor $11,000 to *cover* the short position and a loss is realized.

The tax consequences of short sales are triggered at the time the seller replaces the borrowed shares (i.e., the short position is closed or covered). No gain or loss is recognized until this time.[71] The character of the gain or loss realized depends on whether the asset involved (normally stock) is a capital asset. Determination of the holding period is more confusing. If the replacement securities have been held for a year or less before the *short sale* or are acquired after the sale, the gain or loss realized on closing the position is short term.[72] Moreover, if the taxpayer does not use such stock to replace the borrowed shares, the holding period of such securities starts again, beginning on the date the short position was closed.[73] If the replacement property has been held for more than a year prior to the short sale, the gain or loss recognized on closing is long-term, regardless of the holding period of the actual shares used to close the short position.

Example 37

On March 15, 2016, T purchased 100 shares of S stock for $4,000. On February 15, 2017, T sold 100 shares of S stock short for $5,000. On June 15, 2017, T closed out her short position by delivering the March 15, 2016 shares. Because T held the replacement shares less than one year before she shorted the stock (March 15, 2016 to February 15, 2017), she reports a $1,000 short-term capital gain.

---

[71] Reg. § 1.1233-1(a)(1).

[72] § 1233(b).

[73] *Ibid.*

> ### Example 38
>
> Same facts as *Example 35,* except T closed out her position by purchasing 100 new shares on June 15, 2017 for $6,500. In addition, she sold the original shares on August 15, 2017 for $7,000. T reports a capital loss of $1,500 ($5,000 – $6,500) upon covering her short position, and it is short-term since she held substantially identical stock less than a year before she shorted the stock (March 15, 2016 to February 15, 2017). In addition, T reports a *short-term* capital gain on the sale of the original stock of $3,000 ($7,000 – $4,000) even though she has held the stock for more than one year (March 1, 2016 to August 15, 2017). The holding period for the original stock begins again on the date the short sale was closed by virtue of the fact that she owned such stock less than one year before the short sale.

Constructive Sale Treatment for Appreciated Financial Positions

For many years, investors often wanted to lock in their gain positions without having to recognize them for tax purposes. To accomplish this, an investor would sell stock short and close out the position at a later time. This was referred to as selling short against the box. The tax benefit of this technique was eliminated in 1997. Now, if a taxpayer undertakes a short sale or similar disposition of property that he or she owns, the taxpayer must treat the short sale as the disposition of the underlying property and recognize gain as if the underlying property had been sold.[74]

> ### Example 39
>
> P owns 200 shares of BDF Corporation that was purchased at a cost of $24 per share. On November 14 of the current year, P sold 50 shares of BDF short for $50 per share. P is treated as selling the shares for $2,500 on November 14 and must recognize a gain of $1,300 ($2,500 – $1,200).

This rule does not apply if the transaction is closed within 30 days after the close of the year of the short sale or similar disposition.

OPTIONS

Options of one variety or another have become commonplace in the business and investment world. They can be used in a variety of ways (e.g., an option to buy a house or buy land), but they are probably best known as a technique—sometimes a speculative one—to invest in the stock and commodities markets. The popularity of options has skyrocketed since the Chicago Board Options Exchange began organized trading in listed options in 1973. Currently, listed options on hundreds of securities can be bought and sold just like the securities themselves. One need only glance at the daily quotes in the *Wall Street Journal* or similar financial resource on the Internet to appreciate this everyday phenomenon. This growth in the use of options requires tax advisers to have some appreciation of how they work and how they are taxed.

For some, however, options are shrouded in a cloud of mystery, an esoteric investment tool too sophisticated for the common investor. In reality, the basic operation of options is not that complicated. An option simply gives the holder the right to buy or sell a specific asset at a certain price by a specified date. A taxpayer who owns an option may either exercise the option, sell the option, or allow it to expire. The tax treatment of these actions is just as straightforward as the operation of the option itself.

---

[74] § 1259.

Treatment of Option Buyer

If the taxpayer exercises the option, the amount paid for the option is treated as a capital expenditure and added to the taxpayer's basis for the property. If the taxpayer sells the option or allows it to expire, the tax treatment depends on the nature of the underlying property.[75] In other words, if the taxpayer sells the option, the sale is treated as a sale of the option property. Therefore, any gain or loss recognized is a capital gain or loss only if the option property is a capital asset.

Example 40

On May 1, J purchased for $500 an option to buy 100 shares of Wells Fargo common stock at a price of $100 per share at any time before August 2nd. On August 1, when Wells Fargo was trading at $130 per share, J exercised his option and bought 100 shares for $10,000. Although J is immediately better from his purchase, he has no income. The basis of his stock is $10,500 (the $500 cost of the option + the $10,000 cost of the stock) and the holding period begins on August 2nd.

Example 41

On January 2, Compaq common stock was trading at what K thought was a bargain price of $65 per share. Consequently, K purchased for $700 an option to buy 100 shares of Compaq at a price of $80 on or before March 15. After the corporation reported its earnings, the stock value jumped, and by March 1 the price was bouncing between $95 and $100 per share. The value of K's option had also increased, and he sold it for $3,000. Since the option property, the stock, is a capital asset, K reports a short-term capital gain of $2,300 ($3,000 – $700).

Example 42

Same facts as *Example 39,* except Compaq's earnings were disappointing and the value of the stock as well as the value of K's option decreased. On March 15, the stock was trading at $60 per share and K decided to let the option expire. K recognizes a short-term capital loss of $700.

Options are generally billed as a way to secure a potentially large profit from a relatively small investment with a known risk. The option buyer knows in advance that the most that can be lost is the amount paid for the option. There are generally two types of options: puts and calls. A *call* is simply the shorthand term given to an option that gives the holder the right to purchase a particular security at a fixed price. All of the discussion and examples above deal with call options. For example, if an individual believes the price of IBM will rise from $50 to $70 over the next several months, she might purchase a call that enables her to buy 1,000 shares at a price far lower than the $50,000 that would be required to actually buy the stock. The ultimate tax treatment of the call depends, as explained above, on whether the taxpayer sells or exercises the option or allows it to lapse.

Treatment of Option Writer (Seller)

In any option agreement, there are two parties, the party who buys the option and the person who "writes," or sells, the option. Individuals who write, or sell, call options obligate themselves to deliver a certain number of shares at a particular price in exchange for the payment of some amount referred to as the call premium. If the call is written by a person

---

[75] § 1234(a). Note that the lapse of an option is treated as a sale or exchange [§ 1234(b)].

who owns the underlying stock (a "covered" call), the individual can deliver such stock if the call is exercised. If the writer does not own the stock (a "naked" call), the stock must be purchased to meet the obligation—a very risky situation. Writers of covered calls generally view the call premium as an additional source of income or as a hedge against a possible decline in the value of the stock. If the buyer exercises the call, the writer of the option adds the premium to the amount realized in determining the gain or loss realized on the stock sold. The gain or loss is long-term or short-term depending on the holding period of the underlying stock. If the buyer allows the call to expire, the writer of the call treats the premium received for the option as a short-term capital gain regardless of the actual holding period.[76] The gain is reported at the time the option expires.

Example 43

After discussing it with her broker, W decided to write call options on her 100 shares of Colgate that she bought several years ago for $3,000. She deposited the stock with her broker and instructed him to write a call that allows an investor to purchase 100 shares of Colgate at $40 per share at a premium of $5 per share. Within a few business days, W's account was credited with $500 for writing the call. If the call is not exercised, W has a $500 short-term capital gain. If the call is exercised, W sells her stock and realizes a long-term capital gain of $1,500 ($4,000 + $500 − $3,000).

Puts

To understand puts, one has to mentally shift gears. Puts are the exact opposites of calls. Whereas a buyer of a call buys the right to purchase stock at a fixed price, a buyer of a put buys the right to sell stock at a fixed price. As in short sales, the buyer of a put typically believes that the price of the underlying stock will drop. If the put is sold, the taxpayer reports a short-term capital gain or loss regardless of the holding period. If the put is exercised (i.e., the taxpayer does in fact sell the underlying stock), the amount realized on the sale is decreased by the premium paid for the put. If the put lapses, a loss is allowable as of the date the option expires. As a practical matter, most puts are bought with the intention of selling them.

Example 44

After seeing reports on television that the airline industry was falling on hard times, P believed the current $47 price on Boeing stock would fall. He immediately called his broker and bought a put at a price of $200 on March 4. The put enables him to sell 100 shares of the stock at a price of $45 per share before August 24. The price did in fact fall and bottomed at $40 per share. As a result, his put, that is, his right to sell the stock at $45, became more valuable, and he sold the put for $500. P must report a short-term capital gain of $300 ($500 − $200).

---

[76] If the writer of the call is in the trade or business of granting options, the gain would be ordinary rather than capital gain. § 1234(b).

Corporate Bonds and Other Indebtedness

Investments in corporate bonds and other forms of indebtedness present several unique problems that must be considered by taxpayers who choose this form of investment. Under the general rules, mere collection of principal payments does not constitute a sale or exchange and, therefore, a capital gain or capital loss cannot result. However, the Code creates an exception for certain forms of debt. This special rule provides that any amounts received by the holder on retirement of any debt are considered as amounts received in exchange for the debt.[77] Consequently, capital gain or loss is normally recognized when the debt is redeemed or sold for more or less than the taxpayer's basis in the debt.

LO.8

Discuss the tax treatment of investments in corporate bonds and other forms of indebtedness.

Example 45

B purchased a $1,000, 10% bond issued by Z Corporation for $990. Assuming the bond is held to maturity and redeemed by the corporation, B will recognize a capital gain of $10. If B had sold the bond prior to redemption for $995, he would recognize a capital gain of $5.

A second and more difficult problem to be considered concerns the *interest element* that may be inherent in the purchase price of a corporate bond. For example, if the rate at which a bond pays interest—the stated rate—is less than the current market rate, the bond will sell for less than its face value, or at a discount. In this case, the *discount* effectively functions as a substitute for interest income. Conversely, if the stated rate exceeds the market rate, the bond will sell for more than its face value, or at a premium. Here, the *premium* essentially reduces the amount of interest income. Without special rules, the proper amount of interest income would not be captured and reported in a timely manner.

Example 46

Several years ago when interest rates were 10 percent, T purchased a $10,000, 8% corporate bond for $8,000, or a $2,000 discount. This year the bond matured and T redeemed the bond for its par value of $10,000. Under normal accounting procedures, the redemption is treated as an exchange and the taxpayer would recognize a long-term capital gain of $2,000 ($10,000 − $8,000). In this case, the taxpayer would have converted the discount of $2,000, which from an economic view is ordinary interest income, to capital gain. Moreover, this income would be deferred until T sold the bond.

The example above illustrates the problems that the special tax rules governing bond transactions address. The provisions ensure that any premium or discount is not treated as part of the capital gain or loss realized on disposition of the bond, but rather is treated as an *adjustment* to the taxpayer's interest income received from the bond. In addition, the Code provides rules for determining how much of the premium or discount will affect interest income and *when* the additional interest income (in the case of discount) or the interest expense (in the case of premium) will be reported.

The Code provides a separate set of rules governing the treatment of premium and discount. In the case of discount, the rules differ depending on when the discount arises. One set applies when the bonds were *originally issued* at a discount (the "original issue discount" provisions) and another set applies if the discount arises when the bonds are purchased later in the open market (the "market discount" rules). The rules governing premium are the same regardless of when the premium arises.

---

[77] § 1271.

ORIGINAL ISSUE DISCOUNT

When corporate bonds are *issued* at a price less than the stated redemption price at maturity (i.e., the bond's face value), the resulting discount is referred to as *original issue discount,* or more commonly OID. The amount of OID is easily computed as follows:

	Redemption price (face value)	$x,xxx
−	Issue price	− xxx
=	Original issue discount	$x,xxx

The OID provisions generally require the holder of the bond to amortize the discount and include it in income during the period the bond is held.[78] For purposes of computing the gain or loss on disposition of the bond, the holder must increase the basis of the bond by the amount of any amortized discount. Any gain or loss on the disposition of the bond normally is capital gain. However, if at the time of issue there was an intention to call the bond before maturity, any gain on the bond is treated as ordinary income to the extent of any unamortized discount.[79]

Before examining the amortization methods, it should be emphasized that the Code furnishes a de minimis rule that may exempt the debt from the OID amortization requirements. OID is considered to be zero when the bond discount is less than one-fourth of one percent of the redemption price at maturity multiplied by the number of complete years to maturity.[80] This may be expressed as follows:

	Redemption price at maturity	$ x,xxx
×	Percentage	× 0.25%
×	Number of complete years to maturity	xx
=	*De minimis* amount	$ x,xxx

In most cases, new bond issues do not create OID because the stated interest rate is set near the market rate so that the amount of discount that arises, if any, does not exceed the de minimis amount. As a result, no amortization is required.

For bonds issued after July 1, 1982, the discount is amortized into income using a technique similar to the effective interest method used in financial accounting.[81] To determine the includible OID, the OID attributable to an accrual period must be computed. This is done by multiplying the *adjusted issue price* at the beginning of the *accrual period* by the *yield to maturity* and reducing this amount by any interest payable on the bond during the period. The adjusted issue price is the bond's original issue price as increased for previously amortized OID. The accrual period is generally the six-month period ending on the anniversary date of the bond (date of original issue) and six months before such date. The yield to maturity must be determined using present value techniques or may be found in bond tables designed specifically for this purpose.[82]

Once the OID attributable to the entire bond period is computed, this amount is allocated ratably to each day in the bond period. The bondholder's includible OID is the sum of the daily portions of OID for each day during the taxable year that the owner held the bond.

---

[78] §§ 1271 through 1275.

[79] § 1271(a)(2).

[80] § 1273(a)(3).

[81] § 1272(a). For bonds issued after July 1, 1982, and before January 1, 1985, the accrual period is one year.

[82] Given the issue price, the redemption price, and the number of periods to maturity, the yield to maturity may be approximated by reference to appropriate present-value tables.

Example 47

On July 1, 2017, R purchased 100 newly issued 30-year, 8% bonds with a face value of $1,000 for $800 each or $80,000. The bonds pay interest semiannually on July 1 and December 31. The OID rules apply since the $200 discount per bond exceeds the de minimis amount of $75.

	Redemption price at maturity	$ 1,000
×	Percentage	× 0.25%
×	Number of complete years to maturity	× 30
=	*De minimis* amount	$ 75

Using present value calculations, the annual yield to maturity for this bond is 10.14% (or 5.07% semiannually). The OID that R must include in income in 2017 and 2018 for all of the bonds is computed in the aggregate as follows:

	7/1–12/31 2017	1/1–6/30 2018	10/1–12/31 2018
Adjusted issue price	$ 80,000	$ 80,056**	$ 80,115
Semiannual yield.	× 5.07%	× 5.07%	× 5.07%
Total effective interest.	$ 4,056	$ 4,059	$ 4,062
Less: Interest received	– 4,000*	– 4,000	– 4,000
Includible OID	$ 56	$ 59	$ 62

* $100,000 × 4% = $4,000

** $80,000 + $56 = $80,056

R would include the amount of OID in income in addition to the interest income actually received. Note that the issuer of the bond would include in its annual deduction for interest expense the amount of OID that must be amortized.

Example 48

Assume the same facts as above, except that R sells all of the bonds for $85,000 on July 1, 2018. Assuming there was no intention to call the bonds when issued, R will report a capital gain of $4,885 ($85,000 – $80,115).

Additional computations are required when the purchase price exceeds the original issue price as increased by OID amortized by previous holders. As a practical matter, the issuer of the bond is obligated to provide the taxpayer a Form 1099-OID, Statement of Original Issue Discount, disclosing the amount of interest income to be reported annually. For those who do not receive such a form, the IRS provides a special publication with the necessary information.

For bonds issued before July 2, 1982, the OID is generally included in the income of the holder ratably over the term of the bond (i.e., a straight-line method is used).[83]

Example 49

Assume the bond in *Example 48* was issued prior to July 2, 1982. The original issue discount included annually would be $667 ($20,000 ÷ 30).

---

[83] § 1272(a); for bonds issued before May 28, 1969, special rules apply. See § 1272(b).

Although the OID rules are to apply to virtually all debt instruments, there are several notable exceptions:[84]

1. U.S. Savings Bonds (which are treated as discussed in Chapter 5).

2. Tax-exempt state and local obligations (although the discount income is not included as taxable income, the taxpayer increases the basis of the instrument).

3. Debt instruments that have a fixed maturity date not exceeding one year [unless held by certain parties identified in § 1281(b), including accrual basis taxpayers].

4. Obligations issued by individuals before March 2, 1984.

5. Nonbusiness loans between individuals of $10,000 or less.

In 1984, the coverage of the OID rules was substantially extended to help curb abuses that occurred when a taxpayer sold property and received a note in exchange. The application of the OID rules in this area was discussed in Chapter 14 in conjunction with unstated interest.

MARKET DISCOUNT

As previously noted, without special rules, amortization of discount would not be required where the security was treated as having no OID (e.g., where the discount on the bond when originally issued was small). For example, if a bond having a $10,000 face value bearing 10% interest over a 30-year term was issued for $9,500, there would be no OID since the discount is less than $750 (0.25% × 30 × $10,000). In subsequent years, however, interest rates might rise, causing the bond to sell at a substantially greater discount (i.e., lower value), say $8,000 (e.g., if rates rose to 14% the bond's price might fall to $8,000). In such case, an investor could purchase the bond and ultimately report the built-in appreciation as capital gain—the $2,000 rise from the discounted price to face value at maturity—notwithstanding the fact that a portion of the increase in value actually represents interest income. Moreover, the investor could borrow amounts to purchase the investment and obtain an immediate deduction for interest on the debt, although the income from the bond was deferred until it was redeemed or sold. This highly publicized and extremely popular investment technique was foreclosed by the Deficit Reduction Act of 1984 for newly issued bonds.

Changes made in 1993 make the rules applicable to *all* bonds purchased after April 30, 1993. Code § 1276 provides that any gain on the disposition of a bond is treated as ordinary income to the extent of any accrued *market discount*. Market discount, in contrast to OID, is measured at the time the purchaser acquires the bond. Hence, market discount is the excess of the stated redemption price over the basis of the bond immediately after *acquisition*.[85] Like OID, market discount is considered to be zero if it is less than one-fourth of one percent of the stated redemption price multiplied by the number of complete years to maturity after acquisition. The portion of market discount that is considered ordinary income upon disposition of the bond is computed assuming the discount accrues ratably over the number of days from the purchase of the bond to the bond's maturity date.

Example 50

On January 1, 2016, T purchased a bond issued in 2015 having a face value of $10,000 for $8,000. The bond matures four years later on January 1, 2020. The market discount on the bond is $2,000, the difference between the stated redemption price of $10,000 and the taxpayer's $8,000 basis in the bond immediately after acquisition (assuming there was no OID). The $2,000 is deemed to accrue on a daily basis over the 1,460 days remaining on the bond's term. Assuming T sells the bond for $9,000 on January 2, 2017, her gain is $1,000, of $500 of which is ordinary interest income ($2,000 × [365 ÷ 1,460]) and the remaining $500 is long-term capital gain.

---

[84] §§ 1272(a)(2) and 1274(c)(2).

[85] § 1277(a)(2). If the bond also has OID, the market discount is reduced by the amortized portion of OID.

In lieu of using the daily method of computing the accrued market discount, the taxpayer may use the effective interest method similar to that used for amortizing OID. In addition, the taxpayer may elect to report accrued market discount in taxable income annually rather than at the date of disposition. If this election is made, the taxpayer increases the basis of the bond by the amount of market discount included in income.

Congress also enacted provisions limiting the taxpayer's interest deduction on loans to purchase market discount bonds. Section 1277 requires the taxpayer to defer the deduction for interest expense until that time when income from the bond is reported.

CONVERSION TRANSACTIONS

The original issue discount and market discount provisions exist in order to prevent taxpayers from converting ordinary interest income into capital gain when the interest element is in the form of a discount. In certain instances, taxpayers may still be able to avoid this treatment by structuring the transactions somewhat differently. Congress refers to these as *conversion transactions.*

Conversion transactions are certain investments on which the return is attributable to the time value of money, or for which the sales price of the investment is known at the time the investment is made. Upon the sale or disposition of such investments, any gain is treated as ordinary income, rather than capital gain, to the extent of a return on the investment calculated at 120% of the applicable federal rate.[86] Any gain in excess of the ordinary income or any loss realized on the investment is treated as capital gain or loss, assuming the contract is a capital asset to the taxpayer.

BOND PREMIUM

The treatment of premium depends in part on whether the interest income on the bond is taxable.[87] When the interest income is taxable, the taxpayer *may* elect to amortize and deduct the premium as interest expense and concomitantly reduce the basis in the bond. The interest expense in this case is considered investment interest and is, therefore, deductible as an itemized deduction to the extent of net investment income. If the taxpayer does not elect to amortize the premium, the unamortized premium is simply included as part of the taxpayer's basis in the bond and thus decreases the gain or increases the loss on disposition of the bond.

If the interest income on the bond is tax-exempt, the premium *must* be amortized and the bond's basis decreased. No deduction is allowed for the amortized premium since it merely represents an adjustment in the amount of nontaxable income received by the holder. In other words, no deduction for the premium is allowed since it represents interest expense related to producing tax-exempt income. Note that by requiring amortization of the premium, the taxpayer is prohibited from securing a deduction for the premium in the form of a capital loss or a reduced gain on the disposition of the bond.

Example 51

V purchased a $1,000 tax-exempt bond for $1,100. If V holds the bond to maturity, all of the premium will be amortized and his basis in the bond will be $1,000. Therefore, on redemption of the bond for $1,000, no gain or loss is recognized. However, if amortization of the premium was not required, V would report a capital loss of $100 on redemption of the bond.

The method to be used for amortizing premium depends on when the bond was issued. If the bond was issued before September 28, 1985, the premium is amortized using the straight-line method over the number of months to maturity. Premium on bonds issued on or after that date must be amortized based on the bond's yield to maturity determined when the bond was issued.

---

[86] § 1258. [87] § 171.

TIMING OF CAPITAL ASSET TRANSACTIONS

A taxpayer with investments that he or she may wish to sell should pay careful attention to the timing of those sales, particularly near the end of a year. Since the netting process takes into consideration only the sales for the year under consideration plus any capital loss carryovers, the year into which a particular transaction falls may have significant impact on the total amount of taxes paid. The taxpayer must also consider market conditions, since he or she may believe that waiting to sell a particular asset may cost more than paying any additional tax.

Strictly from a tax planning perspective, a taxpayer should consider timing the recognition of year-end capital gains and losses using the following strategy:

1. *No Capital Gains or Losses Currently*—recognize up to $3,000 STCL or LTCL to take advantage of the annual capital loss deduction.

2. *Currently Have STCG*—recognize either STCL or LTCL to offset the STCG and more, if possible, to take advantage of the capital loss deduction.

3. *Currently Have LTCG*—recognize either LTCL or STCL to offset the LTCG and more, if possible, to take advantage of the capital loss deduction.

4. *Currently Have STCL*—if less than $3,000, recognize more STCL or LTCL to take advantage of the capital loss deduction. If more than $3,000, recognize either STCG or LTCG to offset the STCL in excess of $3,000.

5. *Currently Have LTCL*—if less than $3,000, recognize more LTCL or STCL to take advantage of the capital loss deduction. If more than $3,000, recognize either STCG or LTCG to offset the LTCL in excess of $3,000.

The current tax rate differential between ordinary income and capital gains for noncorporate taxpayers (including flow-through entities) makes it far more important to distinguish between ordinary income and capital gain. Taxpayers should carefully plan in order to secure the benefit of this rate differential, which can be as great as 20% (35% − 15%).

SECTION 1244 STOCK

The importance of § 1244 should not be overlooked when making an investment.

Example 52

Dr. G is extremely successful and consequently is often approached by friends, promoters, and others asking her to make an investment in one deal or another. If G loans $30,000 to a friend to start a business which ultimately fails, the loss would be governed by the worthless-security rules and thus treated as a capital loss. In such case, Dr. G's annual loss deduction is limited to the extent of her capital gains plus $3,000. If G has no capital gains (which are not necessarily easily found), it could take her as long as ten years to deduct her loss. However, if the investment had been in the form of § 1244 stock, the entire $30,000 loss would be deductible in the year incurred.

Under § 1244, the taxpayer is allowed to deduct up to $50,000 ($100,000 in the case of a joint return) of loss *annually*. Any loss in excess of this amount is treated as a capital loss and is subject to limitation. In light of these rules, a taxpayer who anticipates a loss on § 1244 stock that exceeds the annual limitation should attempt to limit the loss recognized in any one year to $50,000 (or $100,000).

Example 53

C, a bachelor, invested $200,000 in Risky Corporation several years ago, receiving 1,000 shares of § 1244 stock. It now appears that Risky, true to its name, will fail and that C will receive at best $100,000 for his investment. If C sells all of his shares this year, $50,000 of the loss is completely deductible as an ordinary loss under § 1244, while the remaining $50,000 of the loss would be a capital loss of which only $3,000 could be deducted (assuming he has no capital gains). C should sell half of his shares this year and half of his shares next year. By so doing, his loss for each year will be $50,000. In such case, neither loss would exceed the annual limitation, and therefore both would be deductible in full.

Problem Materials

DISCUSSION QUESTIONS

16-1 *Capital Asset Defined.* Define a capital asset. How would you describe the way a capital asset is defined?

16-2 *Sale of a Business.* How is the sale of an operating business treated? Discuss the sale of sole proprietorships, partnerships, and corporations in general.

16-3 *Holding Period.* Explain the holding period requirements that must be met to secure favorable capital gain treatment. How does one determine the holding period for purchased property?

16-4 *Holding Period.* What is the rule for determining the holding period for property acquired by gift?

16-5 *Holding Period.* What is the holding period of property acquired from a decedent?

16-6 *Holding Period—Stock Exchange Transactions.* T placed an order with her stock broker to sell 100 shares of Kent Electronics, Inc. stock on December 23, 2017. Because the sale order was received after the close of the market on the 23rd, the sale was executed at 9:00 a.m. on December 30, 2017. T received a settlement check from the brokerage house on January 5, 2018. What is the date of sale and what is the last date of T's holding period?

16-7 *Holding Period—Worthless Securities.* D purchased 1,000 shares of H, Inc. for $4,450 in a speculative investment on October 25, 2016. Weeks later, on January 5, 2017, D received notice that the H, Inc. stock was worthless. What are the amount and character of D's loss in 2017?

16-8 *Capital Gain and Loss Netting Process.* Describe the three possible results of the capital gain and loss netting process. How are the gains treated for tax purposes?

16-9 *Capital Gains Tax.* D is single and has taxable income for the current year of $72,000, including a $7,000 capital gain on the sale of stock held for two years. Describe how D will determine the tax on his income for the year.

16-10 *Capital Loss Deduction: Individuals.* How is the capital loss deduction limited for individual taxpayers?

16-11 *Capital Gains and Losses: Corporations.* The tax rules governing a corporation's capital gains and losses differ somewhat from those for an individual.
   a. Explain how a corporation treats capital gains and losses and how this treatment differs from that of an individual.
   b. Some commentators are fond of saying that corporations rarely have capital gains and losses to worry about. Why might this be true?

16-12 *Capital Loss Carryover.* Capital losses in excess of the annual limit can be carried forward to the subsequent year. How long may losses be carried forward by individual taxpayers? What is the character of the loss carryover and what happens if net losses from each of the groups (short-term, 28 percent, and 15 percent) are carried forward?

16-13 *Patents.* What is necessary for a patent to qualify for capital gain or loss treatment under § 1235?

16-14 *Ordinary versus Capital Loss Treatment.* What are the tax consequences to P, a bachelor, of a $70,000 loss occurring on June 1 of the current year attributable to the following:

  a. An uncollectible nonbusiness loan to XYZ Corporation.

  b. Worthless bonds of XYZ Corporation acquired on November 30 of the prior year.

  c. The sale of XYZ stock qualifying as § 1244 stock when acquired two years ago.

16-15 *Section 1244 Stock.* When is a taxpayer's stock considered § 1244 stock? Why is the designation significant?

16-16 *Section 1202 Exclusion.* S purchased qualified small business stock in U Corp. on October 27, 2017 for $35,000 with hopes to later qualify for the § 1202 exclusion.

  a. What two major requirements must U Corp. meet throughout S's holding period?

  b. What is the first day on which S may sell the stock and qualify for the § 1202 exclusion?

  c. What is the rollover provision and why is it important?

16-17 *Rollover of Gain on Sales of Publicly Traded Securities.* Q sold common stock in K Corp., a publicly traded corporation, for $140,000, realizing a gain of $60,000.

  a. How much must Q reinvest in a corporation or partnership that is licensed by the Small Business Administration under § 301(d) of the Small Business Investment Act of 1958 (as in effect on May 13, 1994) in order to defer all of the $60,000 gain?

  b. By what day must Q reinvest to qualify for this gain rollover (deferral)?

16-18 *Dealers, Traders, and Investors.* In September 2017, R decided to try his luck in the stock market. Using a recent inheritance and borrowing funds on margin, he started investing. On a tip, one of his purchases was 10,000 shares of Overpriced Corp. He paid $70 per share at a total cost of $700,000. By December, 2017, the stock price had slipped to $30 per share. The prices of his other investments also were falling. All of this was happening and he was paying interest on his margin account as well.

  a. Would R be considered a dealer? Why or why not?

  b. If R is a dealer, how could R guaranteed that a particular investment will not be subject to capital gain or loss treatment?

  c. If R is an investor, how will his gains or losses be treated for tax purposes? His expenses?

  d. If R is a trader, how will his gains or losses be treated for tax purposes? His expenses?

  e. What is the mark-to-market election? Is R eligible for the mark-to-market election?

  f. If R can make the election, when must it be made and what effect will it have? Explain the effect of the election on any unrealized gains and losses he may have, expenses that he may incur such as margin interest and home office costs, and other concerns such as self-employment taxes and the alternative minimum tax.

16-19 *Dealers in Securities.* How does a dealer in securities guarantee that a particular "investment" will qualify for capital gain or loss treatment?

16-20 *Original Issue Discount—Deep Discount Bonds.* Financial consulting services often advise investment in so-called *deep discount bonds* (e.g., a $1,000 par value bond maturing in 10 years with coupon rate of 6% that sells at a discounted price of $400). Explain how such an investment could provide any tax savings in light of the original issue discount rules.

16-21 *Bond Premium.* This year, G purchased a $1,000 bond for $1,100. The bond matures in 2021 and pays interest at a rate of 10 percent. Interest is paid semiannually on February 1 and August 1. Explain the treatment of the premium on the bond if the bond was issued by

  a. General Motors

  b. City of Sacramento

PROBLEMS

16-22 *Identifying Capital Assets.* Which of the following items are capital assets?

  a. An automobile held for sale to customers by Midtown Motors, Inc.
  b. An automobile owned and used by Sherry Hartman to run household errands.
  c. An automobile owned and used by Windowwashers, Inc.
  d. The private residence of Robert Hamilton.
  e. Letters from a famous U.S. President written to Jane Doe. (Jane Doe has the letters.)
  f. A warehouse owned and used by Holt Packing Company.
  g. Gold bullion.
  h. A country and western ballad written by W. Nelson.

16-23 *Identifying Capital Assets.* Which of the following properties are capital assets? Briefly explain your answers.

  a. A house built by a home-building contractor and used by her as her principal residence.
  b. A house, 80% of which is used as a residence and 20% of which is used to store business inventory.
  c. The same house in (b) above, used as stated for 10 years, and now used exclusively as a residence.
  d. Undeveloped land held for investment by a real estate broker.
  e. Stock held for investment by a stock broker.

16-24 *Capital Gain Netting Process.* D sold the following capital assets during 2017:

Description	Date Acquired	Date Sold	Sales Price	Adjusted Basis
100 shares XY Corp.	1/10/95	1/12/17	$14,000	$1,000
50 shares LM Inc	9/14/16	1/12/17	1,900	4,000
140 shares CH Corp.	11/20/16	4/10/17	3,400	3,000
Gold necklace	4/22/03	6/30/17	5,000	1,300
Personal auto	5/10/11	8/31/17	4,000	6,500

Explain the effects of the transactions above on D's taxable income and final tax liability.

16-25 *Calculation of Capital Gains Tax.* Refer to the facts in *Problem 16-24* above. Assuming D, single, has taxable income of $87,000 that is accurately calculated (net of her standard deduction and exemption), compute her tax liability.

16-26 *Capital Gain Netting Process.* Each of the following situations deals with capital gains and losses occurring during the current year for an individual taxpayer. For each case, determine the change in adjusted gross income and the maximum tax to be imposed on any gain.

Note: N15CG(L) = Net 15% capital gain or (loss)
      NSTCG(L) = Net short-term capital gain or (loss)

Case	N15CG(L)	NSTCG(L)
A	$1,200	$1,200
B	1,600	(1,000)
C	(1,200)	1,800
D	4,500	(800)
E	2,400	1,800

16-27 *Gain and Losses on Property Acquired by Gift.* In each of the following independent situations, assume that the taxpayer received the capital asset as a gift on March 19, 2017, that the donor had held the property since 2011, and that the property was sold during 2017. No gift taxes were payable on the transfer. Determine the gain or loss recognized in each case.

Case	Date of Sale	Sales Price	Donor's Basis	FMV Date of Gift
A	4/19	$1,000	$ 400	$ 600
B	6/3	1,000	1,400	1,200
C	11/20	1,000	900	1,100

16-28 *Capital Gains and Losses.* K, a single individual, earned salaries and wages of $66,000 and interest $2,000 and dividends of $1,700 for the current year. In addition, K sold the following capital assets:

100 shares of GHJ common stock, held 14 months	$3,400 gain
1955 Ford pickup, used five years for personal purposes	4,500 gain
30 acres of land, held three years for investment	6,200 loss

   a. Compute K's net capital gain or loss.
   b. Compute K's adjusted gross income.

16-29 *Capital Gains and Losses.* L, a single individual, earned salaries and wages of $64,000 and interest of $3,000 and dividends of $3,700 for the current year. In addition, L sold the following capital assets:

10 shares LMN common stock, held ten months	$1,400 gain
1990 Dodge sedan, used four years for personal purposes . . .	2,600 loss
10 acres of land, held six years for investment	9,200 loss

   a. Compute L's overall capital gain or loss.
   b. Compute L's adjusted gross income.

16-30 *Capital Gains Tax.* During her calendar year 2017, G, a single individual with no dependents, had the following capital gains and losses:

Asset	Gain/Loss	Holding Period
200 shares of Western Airlines	$ 1,400 loss	11 months
Land held for appreciation	12,300 gain	8 years
Silver vases held for appreciation	1,800 loss	15 months

   a. Assuming G's taxable income (properly calculated) is $37,000, calculate G's gross tax.
   b. Same as above, except G's taxable income is $95,000.

16-31 *Capital Gains Tax.* R is a single, calendar year taxpayer. During 2017, R recognized a $10,000 15% capital gain from the sale of stock held for three years. Calculate R's tax liability (before credits and prepayments) for each of the following levels of taxable income, assuming that the net capital gains have been included in the taxable income numbers.
   a. $37,950
   b. $40,950
   c. $124,000
   d. $600,000

16-32 *Capital Gains Tax.* H and J are married, calendar year taxpayers who elect to file jointly. They have no dependents and do not itemize their deductions. Their income and deductions for 2017 are summarized below.

Salaries and wages	$107,500
Interest income	16,900
Qualifying dividends received	4,600
Short-term capital loss	5,000
Long-term capital gains (held > 12 months)	20,000

Determine H and J's tax liability (before credits and prepayments).

16-33 *Effective Tax Rate on Net Capital Gains.* T is an unmarried, calendar year taxpayer. He provides more than one-half the support of his elderly mother, who is living in a nearby nursing home. T's income and deductions for 2017 are summarized below.

Salary	$154,950
Interest income	14,550
Itemized deductions	12,800
Personal and dependency exemptions	2

a. Calculate T's taxable income and income tax liability (before credits and prepayments) for the year.
b. How would your answers to (a) above change if T also had a $20,000 capital gain during the year from the sale of stock held 15 months?
c. Is the additional income tax from the capital gain limited to $3,000 ($20,000 × 15%)? If not, explain why.

16-34 *Tax Treatment of Dividends as Capital Gain.* P and H, married, cash basis, calendar year taxpayers who file a joint return have the following income and expenses for 2017:

Salaries and wages	$91,900
Qualifying dividends	4,000
Long-term capital gains (15% gains)	5,000
Short-term capital gains or (losses)	0
Itemized deductions	31,700
Dependents—None	

a. Calculate the federal income tax for P and H for the year.
b. How would your answer differ if P and H also had short-term capital losses of $10,000?

16-35 *Netting Process and Capital Losses.* T, an unmarried taxpayer, sold the following capital assets during her calendar year 2017:

	Date Acquired	Date Sold	Sales Price	Adjusted Basis
100 shares CZ Corp.	1/10/17	9/17/17	$14,000	$18,000
75 shares PC, Inc.	7/6/17	9/17/17	5,200	4,300
Silver coins (held as a collector)	12/2/12	11/20/17	2,000	5,000

Complete each of the following requirements based on T's taxable income of $47,200 before capital gains and losses:
a. T's net 15% capital gain or loss.
b. T's net 28% capital gain or loss.
c. T's net short-term capital gain or loss.
d. T's capital loss deduction in arriving at adjusted gross income.
e. T's capital loss carryover to 2018 (describe amount and character).
f. How would your answers to (d) and (e) differ if T's basis in the PC stock had been $1,000?

16-36 *Capital Loss and Carryover.* N, a single individual with no dependents, earned a salary of $59,000 and interest and dividends of $6,500 for the current year. N also has the following capital gains and losses for the current year:

1990 Dodge sedan, used four years for personal purposes...	$ 2,600 loss
30 shares MNO common stock, held ten months..........	400 gain
50 shares NOP common stock, held four years............	3,600 loss
Long-term capital loss carryforward from prior year........	11,600 loss
10 acres of land, held six years for investment	9,200 gain

    a. Compute L's overall capital gain.
    b. Compute L's adjusted gross income.

16-37 *Capital Gains and Losses.* Each of the following independent cases involves capital gains and losses occurring during the calendar year for an unmarried individual taxpayer.

Note: N15CG(L) = Net 15% capital gain or (loss)
NSTCG(L) = Net short-term capital gain or (loss)

Case	N15CG(L)	NSTCG(L)
A	$1,200	$(4,300)
B	(5,000)	200
C	(1,200)	(2,300)
D	(7,000)	200
E	(5,000)	(200)

    a. Determine the amount deductible in arriving at adjusted gross income in each case for the current year.
    b. Which, if any, of the above case(s) generate(s) a capital loss carryover to the following year? Give the amount and character.

16-38 *Capital Loss Deduction and Capital Loss Carryover.* W, an unmarried calendar year individual, had numerous capital asset transactions during the years listed. Determine the amount deductible in each year and the amount and character of any carryover.

Year	N15CG(L)	NSTCG(L)
2017	$(8,000)	$1,000
2018	(1,500)	(2,000)
2019	0	(4,000)
2020	2,000	(3,000)

16-39 *Capital Loss Deduction and Capital Loss Carryover.* M, an unmarried calendar year individual, had numerous capital asset transactions during the years listed. Determine the amount deductible in each year and the amount and character of any carryover.

Year	N15CG(L)	NSTCG(L)
2017	$1,000	$(5,000)
2018	(6,000)	0
2019	3,000	(3,000)
2020	(3,000)	(3,000)

16-40 *Capital Loss Carryovers.* For her calendar year 2016, H, a single individual with no dependents, had unused short-term capital losses of $10,000. For 2017, her gains and losses were as follows:

Asset	Amount	Holding Period
Corporate stock	$ 1,400 loss	11 months
Land held for appreciation	14,300 gain	8 years
Miniature dolls held as a collector....................	1,800 gain	25 months

After completing the netting process, how much are H's 15% gains and 28% gains?

16-41 *Requirements for § 1244 Stock.* During the year, X, who is single, sold stock and realized a loss. For each of the following situations, indicate whether § 1244 would apply to the taxpayer's stock loss. Unless otherwise indicated, Code § 1244 applies.
  a. The stock was that issued to X when she incorporated her business several years ago.
  b. The stock was that of General Motors Corporation and was purchased last year.
  c. X inherited the stock from her grandfather, who had started the company ten years ago.
  d. X is a corporate taxpayer.
  e. X acquired her stock interest in 2009. The other four owners had acquired their interest for $250,000 each in 2004.
  f. The loss was $60,000.

16-42 *Section 1244 Stock Computation.* S is a bachelor. During the year, he sold stock in X Corporation that qualifies as § 1244 stock at a loss of $70,000. In addition, S sold stock in Y Corporation, realizing a $4,000 15% capital gain. Compute the effect of these transactions on S's AGI.

16-43 *Short Sales.* K purchased 400 shares of Intel common five years ago for $7,000. During the current year, she sold short 200 shares for $17,500. Her plan is to either buy new shares to cover the short sale or deliver 200 of the original shares in one year. Assuming the stock drops, and as planned, K purchases 200 shares for $16,000 to cover the short sale, how are these transactions treated for tax purposes?

16-44 *Worthless Securities.* Several years ago, T was persuaded by his good friend W to invest in her new venture, Wobbly Corporation. T purchased 100 shares of Wobbly stock from W for $60,000. He also purchased Wobbly bonds, which had a face value of $20,000 for $18,000. This year, Wobbly declared bankruptcy and T's investment in Wobbly became worthless. What are the tax consequences to T?

16-45 *Sale of Stock.* B owned 50% of the stock in a small incorporated dress shop. The business was successful for several years until a new freeway diverted nearly all of the traffic away from the location. The shop was moved, but to no avail, and the stock continued to quickly decline in value. Other than small interest payments, the income of the business came exclusively from sales of women's apparel.
  The total paid-in capital of the corporation was $250,000, all in the form of cash. B's basis in the stock was always $125,000. In an attempt to prevent further losses, the shop was sold to a larger competitor during 2015. B received $50,000 for all of her stock.
  a. How will B report the loss on the joint return she files with her husband for 2017?
  b. How would your answer to (a) differ if the stock became totally worthless in 2015 rather than being sold?

16-46 *Worthless Securities.* Y purchased 30 shares of BCD Corporation common stock on March 2, 2016, for $2,475. On February 26, 2017, Y was notified by her broker that the stock was worthless.
  a. What are the amount and character of Y's loss?
  b. Could this loss qualify as an ordinary deduction under § 1244? Explain.

16-47 *Section 1202 Exclusion.* E purchased qualified small business stock in P, Inc. on October 27, 2010 for $75,000. The stock continued to qualify until E sold it for $400,000 on December 15, 2017.
  a. How much is E's gain realized upon this sale?
  b. How much of this gain may E exclude from gross income?
  c. What is the maximum amount of tax that E could pay on this gain (assuming no change in tax rates)?
  d. How could E avoid recognizing the gain realized?

16-48 *Rollover of Gain on Sale of Publicly Traded Securities.* R sold common stock in L Corp., a publicly traded corporation, on March 13, 2017 for $160,000, realizing a gain of $40,000. On April 1, 2017, R reinvested $200,000 in M Partnership, a partnership licensed by the Small Business Administration under § 301(d) of the Small Business Investment Act of 1958 (as in effect on May 13, 1993).
  a. How much gain must R recognize on the sale of the L Corp. stock?
  b. What is R's basis in his interest in M Partnership?

16-49 *Combining the Exclusion and Rollover.* Y sold common stock in X Corp., a publicly traded corporation, on October 1, 2009 for $200,000, realizing a gain of $35,000. On October 15, 2009, Y reinvested $250,000 in N, Inc., a corporation licensed by the Small Business Administration under § 301(d) of the Small Business Investment Act of 1958 (as in effect on May 13, 1993), the stock of which is qualified small business stock. On December 1, 2017, Y sold all of the N, Inc. stock for $625,000.

    a. How much is Y's gain realized on the sale of the N, Inc. stock?

    b. How much of this gain is excludable from gross income?

16-50 *Lease Cancellation Payment.* L rents a house to T for $450 per month under a two year lease. When T is transferred, he offers L $675 to terminate the lease. If L accepts, what is the tax treatment of the transaction to L and T?

16-51 *Franchise Agreements.* J entered into a franchise agreement with Box, Inc. under which J will operate a fast food restaurant bearing the trademark and using the products of Box. Box retained "significant power, right and continuing interest" related to the franchise agreement.

    J made an initial payment under the contract of $40,000, which entitles him to the rights under the contract for 15 years with indefinite extensions at the agreement of both parties. J also is required to pay for all supplies used plus a royalty of 1.5% of gross sales. J's sales were $112,000 during the first year. All of the payments described, totaling $41,680, were made during the current year.

    a. How will J report these payments on his cash basis tax return for the current year?

    b. How would Box, Inc. treat the payments from J on its return for the current year? The corporation reports on the cash basis.

16-52 *Original Issue Discount.* On January 1, 2016, B purchased from XYZ Corporation a newly issued, $1 million, 30-year, 4% bond for $300,000. The bond produces a semiannual yield to maturity of 7 percent. Interest is paid semiannually on January 1 and July 1. What is B's income with respect to the bond in 2016 and 2017?

16-53 *Market Discount.* D purchased a $10,000, 7% bond, for $6,350, on January 1, 2016. The bond was issued at par on January 1, 2015 and matures January 1, 2020. On January 1, 2017, D sold the bond for $8,000. What is D's income from the sale?

16-54 *Conversion Transaction.* J purchased a non-interest-bearing financial instrument on June 1, 2016 for $60,000. It was purchased subject to a contract that allows J to redeem the instrument for $66,000 on May 31, 2017, but it may not be redeemed early. The applicable federal rate is 5% throughout J's holding period. What are the amount and character of J's gain recognized in 2017?

16-55 *Comprehensive Capital Gain Problem.* P is an unmarried full-time investor with no dependents. Her income for the year 2017 is as follows:

Taxable interest income	$25,900
Excludable municipal bond interest	8,600
Qualifying dividends	11,650
Consulting fees	6,400
Social Security benefits	8,400

Although P does not have sufficient deductions to itemize, her records reveal the following:

Investment expenses	$ 850
Expenses related to consulting	1,200

In addition to the above, P recognized the following gains and losses during the year:

Loss on sale of 100 shares of A, Inc., held three years	$(1,200)
Loss on sale of personal automobile.	(1,800)
Sales price of 100 shares of B Corp., sold short	8,200
(This short sale was closed the following year with newly purchased shares costing $9,600. P owned no B Corp. stock at the time of the short sale.)	
Gain on sale of unimproved land held as an investment for six years	45,000

Calculate P's adjusted gross income, taxable income, and gross income tax based on the above for 2017. Begin by calculating P's self-employment tax.

16-56 *Investors versus Traders.* M has a large portfolio of stocks. It seems that she is always buying and selling one stock or another. During the year, she realized gains of $300,000 and losses of $500,000 on sales of stocks that she held for less than a year. At the end of the year, she had unrealized gains of $150,000 and unrealized losses of $375,000. In managing her portfolio, she paid $12,000 of investment expenses. She also has paid $10,000 in margin interest. She conducts all of these activities online in her home office. This year she purchased a new computer for $3,000. Explain the tax treatment of her income and expenses (including how they would be reported) (e.g., forms) as well as any related effects (e.g., self-employment taxes, alternative minimum tax) if she is considered:

   a. An investor.

   b. A trader who has not made the § 475(f) mark-to-market election.

   c. A trader who has made the § 475(f) mark-to-market election.

TAX RESEARCH PROBLEMS

16-57 *Transfer of Patents.* G has just completed a successful invention of a new automotive fuel conservation device. He is willing to sell his patent rights for all areas of the United States east of the Rocky Mountains.

   In the current year, G entered into an agreement with a marketing firm, giving it exclusive rights to market his invention anywhere east of the Rockies. In exchange, he received a principal sum and is to receive royalties based on sales volume.

   Is G entitled to capital gain treatment on this sale under § 1235? Would it make any difference if the transferee of the patent was given exclusive rights to the patent and was given the right to "sublease" the patent?

   Research aids:

      Kueneman v. Comm., 80-2 USTC ¶9616, 46 AFTR2d 80-5677, 628 F.2d 1196 (CA-9, 1980).

      Klein Est. v. Comm., 75-1 USTC ¶9127, 35 AFTR2d 75-457, 507 F.2d 617 (CA-7, 1974).

      Rouverol v. Comm., 42 T.C. 186 (1964), non. acq., 1965-2 C.B. 7.

16-58 *Sale of Subdivided and Improved Real Property.* D, a full-time physician, has owned 15 acres of unimproved suburban real estate for 10 years. The property was originally purchased for $30,000 and has been held solely for investment. D is now interested in selling the property and has several alternatives. She has come to you for advice concerning the tax treatment of these alternatives. What is the proper tax treatment of each of the following?

   a. A sale of the entire acreage to an unrelated party in a single transaction for $150,000.

   b. Recording the property with the county as 30 single residential lots, adding roads and improvements at a cost of $100,000, and selling the lots for $25,000 each.

   c. Recording the property with the county as 30 single residential lots, and then selling them to an unrelated developer in a single transaction for $190,000.

   d. Recording the property with the county as 30 single residential lots and then selling them for $190,000 in a single transaction to a partnership in which D is a 40% partner. The partnership then adds roads and improvements at a cost of $100,000 and sells the lots for $25,000 each.

17

Property Transactions: Dispositions of Trade or Business Property

Learning Objectives

Upon completion of this chapter you will be able to:

LO.1 Trace the historical development of the special tax treatment allowed for dispositions of trade or business property.

LO.2 Define § 1231 property.

LO.3 Apply the § 1231 gain and loss netting process to a taxpayer's § 1231 asset transactions.

LO.4 Explain the purpose of the depreciation recapture rules.

LO.5 Compute depreciation recapture under § 1245.

LO.6 Compute depreciation recapture under § 1250.

LO.7 Explain the additional recapture rule applicable only to corporate taxpayers.

LO.8 Identify tax planning opportunities related to sales or other dispositions of trade or business property.

Chapter Outline

Introduction

As is no doubt clear by now, the treatment of property transactions is a complex story that seeks to answer three questions: (1) What is the gain or loss realized? (2) How much is recognized? and (3) What is its character? This chapter, the final act in the property transaction trilogy, addresses the problems in determining the character of gains or losses on the dispositions of *property used in a trade or business.*

In an uncomplicated world, it might seem logical to assume that gains or losses from property dispositions—be it stock, equipment, buildings, or whatever—would be treated just like any other type of income or deduction. But, as shown in the previous chapter, treating all items alike apparently was not part of the grand plan. Congress forever changed the process with the institution of preferential treatment for capital gains in 1921. Since that time taxpayers have been required to determine not only the gain or loss realized and recognized but also whether a disposition involved a capital asset. It is important to understand that these rules did not simply tip the scales in favor of capital gain. In the interest of fairness and equity, they also established a less than friendly environment for capital losses. The limitations on the deductibility of capital losses is clearly a major disadvantage, particularly considering that ordinary losses are fully deductible. The end result of Congress's handiwork was the creation of a system in which the preferred result is capital gain treatment for gains and ordinary treatment for losses. This chapter contains the saga of what happens when Congress attempts to provide taxpayers with the best of both worlds.

Section 1231

The road to tax heaven—capital gain and ordinary loss—begins at § 1231 (in tax parlance properly pronounced as "twelve thirty-one"). While § 1231 can be a completely bewildering provision, its basic operation is relatively simple. At the close of the taxable year, the taxpayer nets all gains and losses from so-called § 1231 property (e.g., land and depreciable property used in a trade or business). If there is a net gain, it is treated as a long-term capital gain. If there is a net loss, it is treated as an ordinary loss. In short, § 1231 allows taxpayers to have their cake and eat it, too. Unfortunately, this is accomplished only with a great deal of complexity, much of which makes sense only if the historical events that shaped § 1231 are considered.

HISTORICAL PERSPECTIVE

LO.1

Trace the historical development of the special tax treatment allowed for dispositions of trade or business property.

At first glance, it seems that the productive assets of a business—its property, plant, and equipment—would be perfect candidates for capital gain treatment and would therefore be considered capital assets. Indeed, that was exactly the case initially. From 1921 to 1938, real or depreciable property used in business was in fact treated as a capital asset. At that time, the classification of such property as a capital asset seemed not only appropriate but desirable—particularly as the economy grew during the early 1920s and taxpayers were realizing gains. However, the opposite became true with the onset of the Great Depression. As the economy deteriorated, businesses that had purchased assets at inflated prices during the booming 1920s found themselves selling such properties at huge losses during the depression-plagued 1930s. To make matters worse, the tax law treated such losses as capital losses, severely limiting their deduction. But Congress apparently had a sympathetic ear for these concerns. Hoping that a change would help stimulate the economy, Congress enacted legislation that removed business properties from the list of capital assets. The legislative history to the Revenue Act of 1938 provides some insight into Congressional thinking, explaining that "corporations will not, as formerly, be deterred from disposing of partially obsolescent property, such as machinery or equipment, because of the limitations imposed … upon the deduction of capital losses."[1] With the 1938 changes in place, business got the ordinary loss treatment it wanted but at the same time was saddled with ordinary income treatments for its gains.

---

[1] House Ways and Means Committee, H.R. Rep. 1860, 75th Cong., 3d Sess. (1938).

Although these rules worked well during the Depression years as businesses were reporting losses, they produced some unduly harsh results once the country moved to a wartime economy. By 1942, the build-up for World War II had the economy humming and inflation had once again set in. Businesses that earlier had sold assets for 10 cents on the dollar now found themselves realizing gains. Of course, under the 1938 changes these gains no longer benefited from preferential treatment but were taxed at extraordinarily high tax rates (88% for individuals and 40% for corporations). The shipping industry was particularly hard hit by the new treatment. Shippers not only had gains as the enemy destroyed their insured ships but also profited when they were forced to sell their property to the government for use in the war. Other businesses that had their factories and equipment condemned and requisitioned also felt the sting of higher ordinary rates. Although these companies could have deferred their gains had they replaced the property under the involuntary conversion rules of § 1033, qualified reinvestment property was in short supply, making § 1033 virtually useless. Understanding the plight of business, Congress once again came to the rescue. In 1942, Congress enacted legislation generally reinstating capital gain treatment but preserving ordinary loss treatment.

The changes in 1942 stemmed primarily from a need to provide relief for those whose property was condemned for the war effort. But in the end they went much further. For consistency, capital gain treatment was extended not only to condemnations of a business property but to other types of involuntary conversions as well. Under the new rules, casualty and theft gains from business property and capital assets also received capital gain treatment. In addition, the new legislation unexpectedly extended capital gain treatment to regular sales of property, plant, and equipment. Apparently, Congress felt that capital gain treatment was also appropriate for taxpayers who were selling out in anticipation of condemnation or simply because wartime conditions had made operations difficult. While Congress thought capital gain treatment was warranted for these gains, it also knew that other businesses had not profited from the war and were still suffering losses from their property transactions. Accordingly, it acted to preserve ordinary loss treatment. The end result of these maneuvers was the enactment of § 1231, an extremely complex provision that provides taxpayers with the best of all possible tax worlds: capital gain and ordinary loss.

The product of Congressional tinkering in 1942 still remains today. To summarize, real and depreciable property used in a trade or business is specifically denied capital asset status. But this does not necessarily mean that such property will be denied capital gain treatment. As explained at the outset, § 1231 generally extends capital gain treatment to gains and losses from these assets if the taxpayer realizes a net gain from all § 1231 transactions. On the other hand, if there is a net loss, ordinary loss treatment applies. But this summary lacks a great deal of precision. The specific rules of § 1231 are described below.

SECTION 1231 PROPERTY

The special treatment of § 1231 is generally granted only to certain transactions involving assets normally referred to as *§ 1231 property*.[2] Section 1231 property includes a variety of assets, but among them the most important is *real or depreciable property that is used in the taxpayer's trade or business* and that is held for more than one year.[3] This definition takes in most items commonly identified as a business's fixed assets, normally referred to as its property, plant, and equipment. For example, the reach of § 1231 includes depreciable personal property used in business, such as machinery, equipment, office furniture, and business automobiles. Similarly, realty used in a business, such as office buildings, warehouses, factories, and farmland, is also considered § 1231 property.

> **LO.2**
> Define § 1231 property.

---

[2] As explained below, § 1231 also applies to involuntary conversions of pure capital assets held more than one year that are used in a trade or business or held for investment. Involuntary conversions by theft or casualty of personal assets are not included under § 1231 but are subject to a special computation.

[3] The holding period is determined in the same manner as it is for capital assets. See § 1223 discussed in Chapter 16.

The Code specifically excludes the following assets from § 1231 treatment:

1. Property held primarily for sale to customers in the ordinary course of a trade or business, or includible in inventory, if on hand at the close of the tax year;

2. A copyright; a literary, musical, or artistic composition; a letter or memorandum; or similar property held by a taxpayer whose personal efforts created such property or by certain other persons; or

3. A publication of the United States Government received from the government other than by purchase at the price at which the publication is offered to the general public.[4]

Note that the excluded assets are also excluded from the definition of a capital asset. As a result, gains or losses on the disposition of inventory, property held primarily for resale, literary compositions, and certain government publications always yield ordinary income or ordinary loss.

One of the critical conditions for § 1231 treatment requires that the property be used in a trade or business. Although this test normally presents little difficulty, from time to time it has created problems, particularly for those with rental property. As an illustration, consider the common situation of a taxpayer who sells rental property such as a house, duplex, or apartment complex. Is the property sold a capital asset or § 1231 property? If a taxpayer sells rental property at a gain, the gain would normally receive capital gain treatment regardless of whether the property is a capital asset or § 1231 property. On the other hand, if the taxpayer sells the rental property at a loss, § 1231 treatment is usually far more desirable. Although the Code does not provide any clear guidance on the issue, the courts have generally held that property used for rental purposes is considered as used in a trade or business and is therefore eligible for § 1231 treatment.[5]

OTHER § 1231 PROPERTY

From time to time, Congress has been convinced that particular industries deserve special tax relief. As a result, it has added a number of other properties to the § 1231 basket. Those eligible for capital gain and ordinary loss are

1. Timber, coal, and iron ore to which § 631 applies;[6]

2. Unharvested crops on land used in a trade or business and held for more than one year;[7] and

3. Certain livestock.[8]

Timber

Under § 631, the mere cutting of timber by the owner of the timber, or by a person who has the right to cut the timber and has held the timber or right more than one year, is to be treated, at his or her election, as a sale or exchange of the timber that is cut during the year. The timber must be cut for sale or for use in the taxpayer's trade or business. In such case, the taxpayer would report a § 1231 gain or loss and potentially receive capital gain treatment for what otherwise might be considered the taxpayer's inventory—a very favorable result. It may appear that the timber industry has secured an unfair advantage, but timber's eligibility is arguably justified on the grounds that the value of timber normally accrues incrementally as it grows over a long period of time.

The amount of gain or loss on the "sale" of the timber is the fair market value of the timber on the first day of the taxable year minus the timber's adjusted basis for depletion. For all subsequent purposes (i.e., the sale of the cut timber), the fair market value of the timber as of the beginning of the year will be treated as the cost of the timber. The term *timber* not only includes trees used for lumber and other wood products, but also includes evergreen trees that are more than six years old when cut and are sold for ornamental purposes (e.g., Christmas trees).[9]

---

[4] § 1231(b)(1).

[5] See, for example, *Mary Crawford,* 16 T.C. 678 (1951) A. 1951-2 C.B. 2, and *Gilford v. Comm.,* 53-1 USTC ¶9201, 43 AFTR 221, 201 F.2d 735 (CA-2, 1953).

[6] § 1231(b)(2).

[7] § 1231(b)(4).

[8] § 1231(b)(3).

[9] § 631(a).

Example 1

B owned standing timber that he had purchased for $250,000 three years earlier. The timber was cut and sold to a lumber mill for $410,000 during 2017. The fair market value of the standing timber as of January 1, 2017 was $320,000. B has a § 1231 gain of $70,000 if he makes an election under § 631 ($320,000 fair market value of the timber on the first day of the taxable year less its $250,000 adjusted basis for depletion). The remainder of his gain on the *actual* sale of the timber, $90,000 ($410,000 selling price − $320,000 new "cost" of the timber), is ordinary income. Any expenses incurred by B in cutting the timber would be deductible as ordinary deductions.

An election under § 631 with respect to timber is binding on all timber owned by the taxpayer during the year of the election *and* in all subsequent years. The IRS may permit revocation of such election because of significant hardship. However, once the election is revoked, IRS consent must be obtained to make a new election.[10]

Section 631 also applies to the sale of timber under a contract providing a retained economic interest (i.e., a taxpayer sells the timber, but keeps the right to receive a royalty from its later sale) for the taxpayer in the timber. In such a case, the transfer is considered a sale or exchange. The gain or loss is recognized on the date the timber is cut, or when payment is received, if earlier, at the election of the taxpayer.[11]

Coal and Iron Ore

When an owner disposes of coal or domestic iron ore under a contract that calls for a retained economic interest in the property, the disposition is treated as a sale or exchange of the coal or iron ore. The date the coal or ore is mined is considered the date of sale and since the property is § 1231 property, the gain or loss will be treated under § 1231.[12]

The taxpayer may not be a co-adventurer, partner, or principal in the mining of the coal or iron ore. Furthermore, the coal or iron ore may not be sold to certain related taxpayers.[13]

Unharvested Crops

Section 1231 also addresses the special situation where a farmer sells land with unharvested crops sitting upon the land. In this case, it seems logical that the farmer should allocate the sales price between the crops and the land to ensure ordinary income or loss for the sale of the farmer's inventory and capital gain or ordinary loss on the sale of the land. While this may be the theoretically correct result, Congress wanted to eliminate potential controversy over the allocation. Accordingly, for administrative convenience it brought the entire transaction into the § 1231 fold in 1951. Currently, whenever land used in a trade or business and unharvested crops on that land are sold at the same time to the same buyer, the gain or loss is subject to § 1231 treatment as long as the land has been held for more than a year.[14] It is worth noting that the benefits of § 1231 were not extended to farmers free of charge. At the same time, Congress eliminated the current deduction for production expenses. The law now provides that any expenses related to the production of crops cannot be deducted currently but must be capitalized as part of the basis of the crops.[15] Such treatment, in a year when land and crops are sold, reduces the farmer's capital gain on the sale rather than any other ordinary income.

---

[10] *Ibid.*

[11] § 631(b).

[12] § 631(c).

[13] § 631(c)(1) and (2).

[14] § 1231(b)(4).

[15] § 268.

Example 2

F sold 100 acres of land used in his farming business just days before the corn on the land was harvested. For the "package" deal, he received $600,000, including an estimated $70,000 for the unharvested crops that he figured had cost $20,000 to produce. F had purchased the land in 2000 for $200,000. In determining the character of his gain, F is not required to allocate the sales price between the crops and the land since he sold both at the same time to the same buyer, therefore qualifying for § 1231 treatment. He will recognize a § 1231 gain of $380,000 computed as follows:

Sales price.	$600,000
Adjusted basis ($200,000 + $20,000).	−220,000
Section 1231 gain.	$380,000

Note that F has effectively turned the $50,000 ($70,000 − $20,000) profit from the sale of his crops from ordinary income into potential capital gain.

Livestock

Livestock that are used for breeding and other income producing purposes are depreciable assets much like machinery and thus qualify for § 1231 treatment. In many situations, however, livestock are used for these purposes for only a short period of time and then sold. If this is the farmer's or rancher's normal practice, the IRS is inclined to argue that the animals are held primarily for resale, in which case the law specifically denies § 1231 treatment. To help end this controversy, Congress specifically made all livestock (other than poultry) used for draft, breeding, dairy, or sporting purposes eligible for § 1231 treatment if they are held for over a year.[16] In the case of cattle and horses, the holding period is extended to two years. Note that this treatment is extremely beneficial since the taxpayer effectively gets capital gain from animals pulled out of the breeding process and sold. Moreover, the farmer or rancher is allowed to deduct the costs of raising such animals currently against ordinary income. The extension of the holding period for cattle and horses was in part, an attempt to cut back on the benefits of this favorable treatment.

SECTION 1231 NETTING PROCESS

LO.3

Apply the § 1231 gain and loss netting process to a taxpayer's § 1231 asset transactions.

The treatment of § 1231 gains or losses ultimately depends on the outcome of a netting process that is far more complicated than outlined earlier.[17] As can be seen from the flowchart in Exhibit 17-1, the taxpayer must first identify all of the gains and losses that enter into the netting process. These include gains and losses from what has been described above as § 1231 property. Also, the § 1231 "bucket" includes *involuntary conversions* of certain *capital assets*. Surprisingly, gains or losses recognized from casualties, thefts, or condemnations of capital assets that are used in a trade or business or held for investment are part of the § 1231 netting process. Involuntary conversions of capital assets that are held for *personal use* are not considered under § 1231 but are subject to special rules.

After identifying all of the § 1231 transactions, the taxpayer must segregate the § 1231 gains and losses arising from casualty and theft from those attributable to sale, exchange, and condemnation. The end result is that there are two sets of § 1231 transactions:

1. Involuntary conversions due to casualty and theft of
   - Section 1231 property.
     - Real and depreciable property used in business and held more than one year.
     - Timber, coal, iron ore, unharvested crops, and livestock.
   - Capital assets.
     - Used in a trade or business or held for investment in connection with business and held more than one year.

---

[16] § 1231(b)(3). [17] § 1231(a).

2. Sales and exchanges of:
   - Section 1231 property.
     - Real and depreciable property used in business.
     - Timber, coal, iron ore, unharvested crops, and livestock.

Involuntary conversion due to condemnation of:
   - Section 1231 property.
     - Real and depreciable property used in business and held more than one year.
     - Timber, coal, iron ore, unharvested crops, and livestock.
   - Capital assets.
     - Used in a trade or business or held for investment in connection with business and held more than one year.

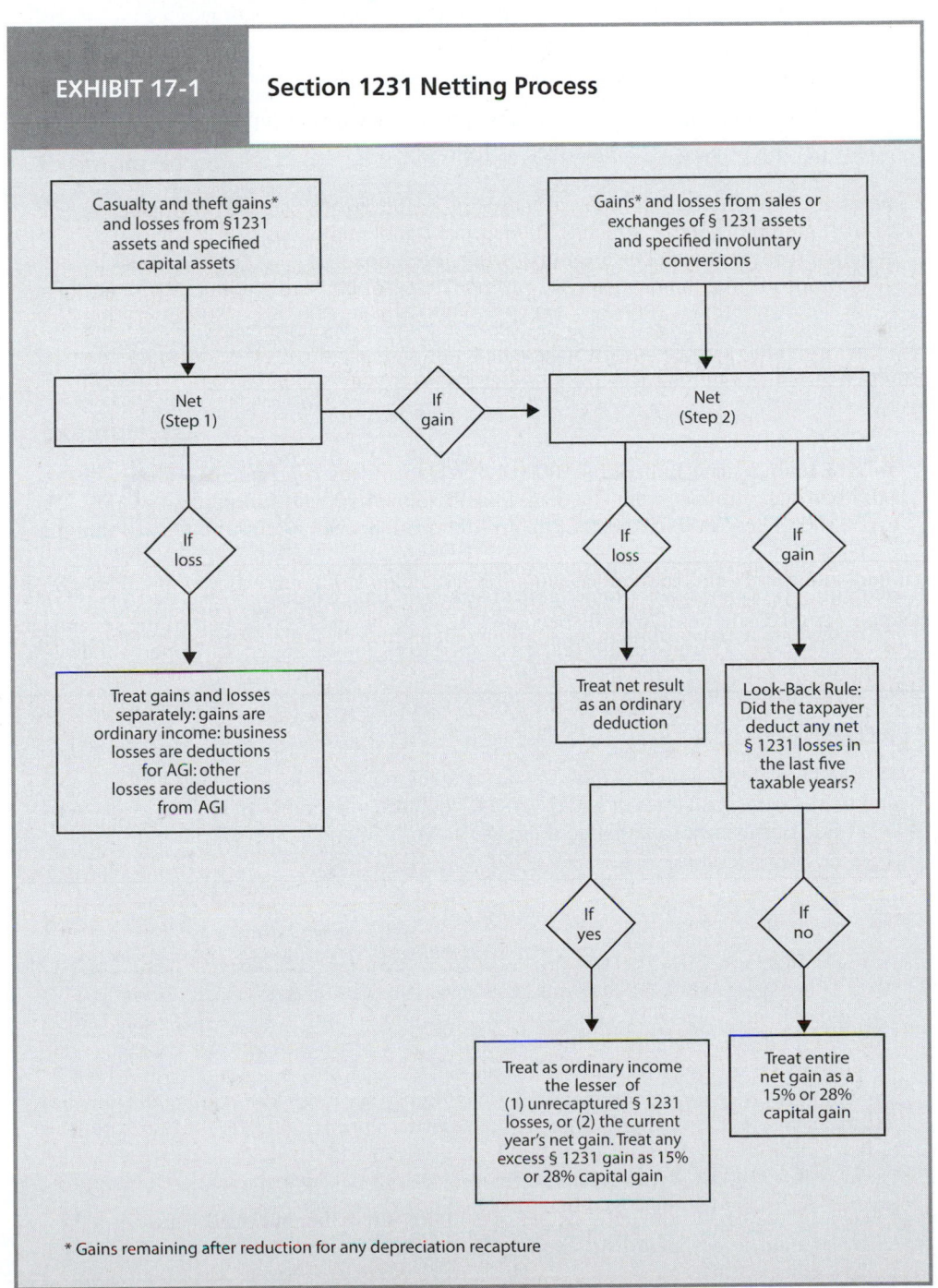

EXHIBIT 17-1   Section 1231 Netting Process

* Gains remaining after reduction for any depreciation recapture

Within each of these two categories, each gain and loss is assigned to one of the three *potential* long-term capital gain groups and netted just as if they had been 28, 25, or 15 percent capital gains or losses (see Chapter 16). This means that each § 1231 gain or loss is assigned to one of the following categories: (1) 15% group for § 1231 gains and losses (15G or 15L); (2) 25% group for unrecaptured § 1250 depreciation on gains from § 1231 assets (25G discussed below); and (3) 28% group for gains and losses from collectibles (28G or 28L). Once all of the appropriate transactions have been poured into the § 1231 process, the netting process can begin. There are three steps:

1. First, all of the gains and losses in the first category of § 1231 transactions (casualties and thefts) are netted. Specifically, gains and losses within the 15% and 28% groups are netted to arrive at one of the following: (1) a net gain or loss on 15% § 1231 assets (N15G or N15L); and (2) a net gain or loss on 28% § 1231 assets (N28G or N28L). Any net loss positions are then combined with the net gain positions using the rules discussed for netting the three groups for capital asset transactions:

   - A N28L first offsets 25G, then N15G.

   - A N15L first offsets a N28G, then 25G.

   - There can be no net loss in the 25G group since this group contains only gains.

   This netting process is summarized as follows:

Section 1231 Gains and Losses from Casualty and Theft

	Collectibles	Unrecaptured Depreciation	Other
	28%	25%	15%
Gains	$x,xxx	Gains only	$xx,xxx
Losses	(x,xxx)	–	(x,xxx)
Net gain or loss	????	Gain only	????
Possibilities:			
1	N28G	25G	N15G
2	N28G	25G	N15L
3	N28L	25G	N15G
4	N28L	25G	N15L

If the netting process results in a net gain position(s) (e.g., a N28G, N25G, and a N15G) the net gains from casualties and thefts become § 1231 gains and become part of the second category of other § 1231 transactions (each assigned to either the 28, 25, or 15 percent groups).

Example 3

During the year, T, who is in the 35% tax bracket, reported the following § 1231 gains and losses from casualties of § 1231 assets (including casualties of capital assets used in a trade or business) and netted them as shown below.

Section 1231 Gains and Losses

	Collectibles	Unrecaptured Depreciation	Other
	28%	25%	15%
Gains	$10,000	$4,000	$ 2,000
Losses	(4,000)	0	(7,000)
Net gain or loss	$ 6,000	$4,000	$(5,000)
Netting	(5,000)	0	5,000
To § 1231 other	$ 1,000	$4,000	$ 0

T has a N28G of $1,000 and a N25G of $4,000. Since the end results are net gains, each net gain is assigned to its appropriate group in the second category of other § 1231 transactions.

If a net loss results, the casualty and theft gains and losses are removed from the § 1231 process and treated separately. The gains are treated as ordinary income, and the losses on business use assets are deductible for AGI. Any other casualty and theft losses are deductible from AGI.

2. The second step of the process is to combine any net casualty or theft gains from the first step with the gains or losses in the second set of § 1231 transactions. In this regard, the net casualty and theft gains must be assigned to the appropriate group (15, 25, or 28 percent group) in the second category of § 1231 transactions (sales and exchanges of § 1231 assets and certain condemnations). For example, if the taxpayer had a net 15% gain from § 1231 casualties, this gain would become a 15% gain in the second category of § 1231 transactions. These transactions are then netted just as if they had been 28, 25, or 15 percent capital gains or losses to determine if there is a net gain or loss.

3. The final step in the § 1231 netting process is to characterize the gain or loss resulting from netting the transactions in the second step. If the net result is a loss, the net loss is treated as an ordinary deduction for AGI. It is not treated as a capital loss. If the net result is a gain (e.g., a N25G and a N15G), these gains are normally treated as capital gains and become part of the capital gain and loss netting process.

The § 1231 netting process is illustrated in Exhibit 17-1 above and the following examples.

Example 4

During the current year, D sold real estate used in her business for $45,000. She had purchased the property several years ago for $36,000. D also sold a business car (held for more than 15 months) at a loss of $1,200. D's gain on the real estate is computed as follows:

Selling price	$ 45,000
Less: Adjusted basis	(36,000)
Gain realized and recognized	$ 9,000

D nets the gain and loss as follows:

15% gain from sale of § 1231 asset	$ 9,000
15% loss from sale of § 1231 asset	(1,200)
Net 15% § 1231 gain for year	$ 7,800

D's net 15% § 1231 gain of $7,800 is treated as a 15% capital gain. If she had other capital gains or losses during the year, they will be subject to the capital gain and loss netting process discussed in Chapter 16.

Example 5

During the year R, a sole proprietor, sold a business computer for $32,000. His basis at the time of the sale was $44,000. He also sold land used in his business at a gain of $1,400 and had an uninsured theft loss of works of art used to decorate his business offices (i.e., capital assets held in connection with a trade or business). R had purchased the artwork for $1,500 and it was valued at $5,000 before the burglary. All of the assets were acquired more than 12 months ago.

R nets his gains and losses as follows:

Step 1: The net loss from the casualty is $1,500 (adjusted basis). Since R has a net 15% casualty loss, it is not treated as a § 1231 loss. Instead, the loss is treated as an ordinary loss (which is fully deductible for AGI since the art works were business property).

Step 2: Combine gains and losses from sales of § 1231 assets:

15% loss from sale of business computer	$(12,000)
15% gain from sale of business land	1,400
Net § 1231 loss for year	$(10,600)

Step 3: A net § 1231 loss is treated as an ordinary deduction. Thus, R's $10,600 loss can be used to offset other ordinary income.

Note that the theft loss of the works of art is included in the first step of the netting process even though these items are capital assets. This loss would have offset, dollar for dollar, any casualty or theft gains (net of depreciation recapture) from § 1231 assets as well as any casualty or theft gains from other capital assets held in connection with R's business. Also note that the current year's deductible § 1231 loss may result in a change in the character of any net § 1231 gains in the next five years due to the look-back rule.

LOOK-BACK RULE

For many years, taxpayers took advantage of the § 1231 netting process. For example, assume a taxpayer in the 35% tax bracket currently owns two § 1231 assets, both held for 15 months. One asset has a built-in gain of $10,000 and the other has a built-in loss of $9,000. If both assets are sold during the year, the loss offsets the gain and the taxpayer pays a capital gain tax of $150 ([$10,000 − $9,000 = $1,000] × 15%). If the taxpayer had sold the assets in different years, the loss would *not* have reduced the gain, and the tax after both transactions would have been $1,500 in one year ($10,000 × 15%) and $3,150 ($9,000 × 35%) of savings in the other year, for a net tax savings of $1,650 ($3,150 − $1,500). As might be imagined, taxpayers carefully planned their transactions to maximize their tax savings.

In an effort to prevent taxpayers from cleverly timing their § 1231 gains and losses to ensure that § 1231 losses reduced ordinary income and not potential capital gain, Congress enacted the so-called *look-back* rule in 1984. Under this rule, a taxpayer with a net § 1231 gain in the current year must report the gain as ordinary income to the extent of any *unrecaptured net* § 1231 losses reported in the past five taxable years.[18] In recapturing the § 1231 gains, recapture occurs in the following order: 28% gains, 25% gains, and 15% gains. Unrecaptured net § 1231 losses are simply the *net* § 1231 losses that have occurred during the past five years that have not been previously recaptured (i.e., the excess of net § 1231 losses of the five preceding years over the amount of such loss that has been recaptured in the five prior years).

Example 6

Assume the same facts in *Example 5* and that R's 2016 net § 1231 loss of $10,600 is the only loss he has deducted in the past five years. In 2017 (the current year), R has a net 15% § 1231 gain of $15,000. R is subject to the look-back rule since in the prior year he reported a § 1231 loss of $10,600 that has not been recaptured. He must report $10,600 of ordinary income and $4,400 of net 15% § 1231 gain. Should R have a § 1231 gain in the following year, he will not be subject to the look-back rule again since he has recaptured all prior year's net § 1231 losses.

---

[18] § 1231(c).

APPLICABILITY OF LOWER RATES

Five potential tax rates apply to long-term capital gains while six rates can apply to ordinary income, which includes short-term capital gains.

To ensure that the appropriate rate is applied, the following process should be followed:

- The first step is to complete the § 1231 netting process.
  - If there is a net § 1231 loss, that loss must be treated as an ordinary loss and it is left out of the capital gain and loss netting process entirely.
  - If there is a net § 1231 gain, it is treated as a long-term capital gain and is entered into the capital gain and loss netting process in the next step. In order to do this, a determination must be made as to which part of the gain, if any, is 25% gain, and which part, if any, is 15% gain.
- Netting of capital gains and losses occurs in each of the various groups of assets.
  - Short-term gains are netted against short-term losses and long-term gains are netted against long-term losses.
  - Within the long-term netting process, gains and losses are further broken down in the various sub-groups with 15% gains and losses, and 28% gains and losses being netted. Since there are no 25% losses, the 25% gains are not reduced.
  - The net gains and losses from these three groups are netted against one another as prescribed in Chapter 16 (e.g., 28% losses are first offset against 25% gains, then 15% gains, and 15% losses are first offset against 28% gains, then 25% gains).
- Short-term gains and losses are netted/combined with long-term gains and losses. Short-term losses are first netted against 28% gains, then 25% gains, and finally 15% gains. Net long-term losses are netted against short-term gains.
- The net results are subject to the capital gains tax.
  - Short-term gains are treated like ordinary income.
  - Long-term gains are subject to tax at the appropriate specified capital gains rates (0, 10, 15, 25, and 28 percent).
  - Losses are subject to the $3,000 annual limit with the excess being carried forward.

Numerous possibilities exist, therefore, for any net § 1231 gain. Perhaps, the gain would be offset by capital losses, receiving no favorable treatment at all. However, if the § 1231 gain survives the netting process to be included in a net capital gain, it is subject to the preferred rates right along with any other long-term capital gains with surviving unrecaptured § 1250 gain being treated as 25% gain and any other surviving gain treated as 15% gain.

 CHECK YOUR KNOWLEDGE

Review Question 1

Indicate whether the following gains and losses are § 1231 gains or losses or capital gains and losses or neither. Make your determination prior to the § 1231 netting process and assume any holding period requirement has been met.

- **a.** Gain on the sale of General Motors stock held as a temporary investment by Consolidated Brands Corporation.
- **b.** Gain on the sale of a four-unit apartment complex owned by Lorena Smith. This was her only rental property.
- **c.** Loss on the sale of welding machinery used by Arco Welding in its business.
- **d.** Loss on theft of welding machinery used by Arco Welding in its business.
- **e.** Gain on sale of diamond bracelet by Nancy Jones.
- **f.** Income from sale of electric razors by Razor Corporation, which manufactures them.
- **g.** Gain on condemnation of land on which Tonya Smith's personal residence is built.
- **h.** Gain on condemnation of land owned by Tonya Smith's business.
- **i.** Loss on sale of personal automobile.

Answer. The § 1231 hodgepodge contains not only gains and losses from § 1231 property but also those from involuntary conversions by casualty, theft, or condemnation of capital assets that are used in a trade or business or held as an investment in connection with a trade or business.

a. The sale of the GM stock is not included in the § 1231 pot since it is a sale of a capital asset and not an involuntary conversion.

b. The rental property is generally considered property used in a trade or business and thus § 1231 property even if the owner owns only a single property.

c. The welding machinery is depreciable property used in a business and is therefore considered § 1231 property.

d. The theft of the welding machinery is also a § 1231 transaction. Note, however, that in processing the § 1231 gains and losses, the casualties must be segregated from the sales.

e. The sale of the diamond bracelet produces capital gain since it is a pure capital asset and not trade or business property.

f. The razors are inventory and are therefore neither capital assets nor § 1231 property.

g. The condemnation of the land near the residence is considered a personal involuntary conversion gain. Since the land is not held in connection with a trade or business, it does not qualify as § 1231 property, but it is a capital asset.

h. The condemnation of the land held for business does enter into the § 1231 hodge-podge as a regular § 1231 gain.

i. Although the personal automobile is a capital asset, no loss is allowed from the sale.

Review Question 2

During his senior year at the University of Virginia, Bill decided that he never wanted to leave Charlottesville. After some thought, he opened his own hamburger joint, Billy's Burgers. That was 20 years ago and Bill has had great success, owning a number of businesses all over Virginia and North Carolina. Not believing in corporations, Bill and his wife, Betty, operate all of these as partnerships.

a. Information from the partnerships and his own personal records revealed the following transactions during the current year:

1. Sale of one of 50 apartment buildings that one of their partnerships owns: $50,000 gain (ignore depreciation).

2. Sale of restaurant equipment: $20,000 loss.

Assuming both assets have been held for several years, how should Bill and Betty report these transactions on their current year return?

Answer. Under § 1231, the taxpayer generally nets gains and losses from the sale of § 1231 property. If a net gain results, the gain is treated as a long-term capital gain, while a net loss is treated as an ordinary loss. For this purpose, § 1231 property generally includes real or depreciable property used in a trade or business. In this case, both the apartment complex and the restaurant equipment are § 1231 property and both are in the 15% group. As a result, the couple should net the gain and loss and report a 15% capital gain of $30,000.

b. The couple's records for the following year revealed several gains and losses:

1. Office building burned down: $20,000 loss.

2. Crane for bungee jumping business stolen: $35,000 gain (assume no depreciation had been claimed).

3. Parking lot sold: $14,000 loss.

4. Exxon stock sold: long-term capital loss of $10,000.

5. Condemnation of Greensboro land held for use in the business: $15,000 gain.

Assuming each of the assets was held for several years, determine how much 15% capital gain or loss as well as the amount of ordinary income or loss that Bill and Betty will report for the year.

Answer. The § 1231 netting process requires the taxpayer to separate § 1231 casualty gains and losses from other § 1231 transactions (sometimes referred to as regular § 1231 items). The casualty loss on the office building and the casualty gain on the crane are both considered § 1231 15% casualties since they involve § 1231 property (i.e., real or depreciable property used in business). Note that the condemnation—even though it is an involuntary conversion—is not treated as a § 1231 casualty. The casualty items are netted to determine whether there is a net gain or loss. Here, there is a net casualty 15% gain of $15,000 ($35,000 – $20,000). This net gain is then combined with any "regular" § 1231 items, in this case the $14,000 loss on the sale of the parking lot (real property used in a business) and the $15,000 gain on the condemnation of the land (a capital asset). Note that both "regular" § 1231 items are also in the 15% group. After netting these items, the partnership has a net gain of $16,000. This $16,000 net § 1231 gain is treated as a 15% capital gain and is combined with $10,000 15% capital loss on the sale of the stock. The end result is a $6,000 15% capital gain. This process can be summarized as follows (see also Exhibit 17-3):

| | | | Capital Gains and Losses | |
Transaction	15% § 1231 Casualties	15% § 1231 Regular	Short-Term	15%
1. Office burned.............	$(20,000)			
2. Crane stolen..............	35,000			
3. Parking lot sold...........		$(14,000)		
4. Exxon stock sold...........				$(10,000)
5. Condemnation of land	0	15,000		
Net casualty	$ 15,000 ⟶	15,000		
Net § 1231 gain............		$ 16,000 ⟶		16,000
Net 15% capital gain				$ 6,000

c. Same as in (b), except Bill and Betty reported a net § 1231 loss of $3,000 in the previous year.

Answer. In this case, the look-back rule applies, causing $3,000 of the net 15% § 1231 gain to be treated as ordinary income. As a result, the couple's 15% capital gain from the § 1231 netting process is $13,000 and their net 15% capital gain is only $3,000.

Depreciation Recapture

HISTORICAL PERSPECTIVE

For many years, taxpayers have taken advantage of the interaction of § 1231 and the depreciation rules to secure significant tax savings. Prior to 1962 there were no substantial statutory restrictions on the depreciation methods that could be adopted. Consequently, a taxpayer could quickly recover the basis of a depreciable asset by selecting a rapid depreciation method such as declining balance and using a short useful life. If the property's value did not decline as quickly as its basis was being reduced by depreciation deductions, a gain was ensured if the property was disposed of at a later date. The end result could be quite beneficial.

Example 7

During the current year, T purchased equipment for $1 million. After two years, T, using favorable depreciation rules, had claimed and deducted $600,000 of depreciation, leaving a basis of $400,000. Assume that the property did not truly depreciate in value and T was able to sell it in the third year for its original cost of $1 million. In such case T would report a gain of $600,000 ($1,000,000 − $400,000). Except for time value of money considerations, it appears that the $600,000 gain and the $600,000 of depreciation are simply a wash. However, the depreciation reduced ordinary income that would be taxed at ordinary rates while the gain would be a § 1231 gain and likely taxed at capital gain rates. As an illustration of the savings that could be achieved, assume that the law at this time provided for a top capital gain rate of 20% and the taxpayer's ordinary income was taxed at a 40% rate. In this case the depreciation would offset ordinary income and provide tax savings of $240,000, but the $600,000 gain on the sale would be treated as a capital gain and produce a tax of only $120,000. Thus, even though the taxpayer has had no economic gain or loss with respect to the property—he bought and sold the equipment for $1,000,000—he was able to secure a tax benefit of $120,000 ($240,000 − $120,000).

The above example clearly illustrates how taxpayers used rapid depreciation and the favorable treatment of § 1231 gains to effectively convert ordinary income into capital gain. In fact, this strategy—deferring taxes with quick depreciation write-offs at ordinary rates and giving them back later at capital gains rates—was the foundation of many tax shelter schemes.

LO.4

Explain the purpose of the depreciation recapture rules.

Legislation to limit these benefits came in a number of forms, but the most important was the enactment of the so-called *depreciation recapture* rules. These rules strike right at the heart of the problem, generally treating all or some portion of any gain recognized as ordinary income, based on the amount of depreciation previously deducted. Thus, in the above example, the taxpayer's $600,000 gain, which was initially characterized as a § 1231 gain, is treated as ordinary income because of the $600,000 of depreciation previously claimed. In this way, all of the tax savings initially given away by virtue of the ordinary depreciation deductions are recaptured. In this regard, it may be useful to think of a gain as consisting of two parts: the gain attributable to depreciation and the gain attributable to holding the asset (resulting from appreciation and inflation). "Depreciation gains" normally are treated as ordinary income while "holding gains" are § 1231 gains and potentially taxed as long-term capital gains. Unfortunately, much like § 1231 in general, the recapture rules can become quite complex. The operations of the specific provisions are discussed below.

WHEN APPLICABLE

Before specific recapture rules are examined, there are two very important points to keep in mind. First, depreciable assets held for one year or less do not qualify for § 1231 treatment. Thus, any gain from the disposition of such assets is always reported as ordinary income. Second, the depreciation recapture rules *do not apply* if property is disposed of at a *loss*. Remember that losses from the sale or exchange of depreciable assets are treated as § 1231 losses if the property is held more than a year. In addition, casualty or theft losses of such property are included in the § 1231 netting process. Any loss from a depreciable asset held one year or less is an ordinary loss regardless of whether it was sold, exchanged, stolen, or destroyed.

TYPES OF DEPRECIATION RECAPTURE

There are essentially *three* depreciation recapture provisions in the Code. These are

1. Section 1245 Recapture—commonly called the *full recapture rule,* and applicable primarily to depreciable personalty (rather than realty).

2. Section 1250 Recapture—commonly called the *partial recapture rule,* and applicable to most depreciable realty if a method of depreciation other than straight-line was used.

3. Section 291 Recapture—commonly called the *additional recapture rule,* and applicable *only* to corporate taxpayers.

These depreciation recapture provisions affect the character—not the amount—of the gain. Losses are not affected. Each of these recapture rules is discussed below.

FULL RECAPTURE—§ 1245

The recapture concept was first introduced with the enactment of § 1245 by the Revenue Act of 1962. Section 1245 generally requires any gain recognized to be reported as ordinary income to the extent of *any* depreciation allowed on § 1245 property after 1961.

> **LO.5**
> Compute depreciation recapture under § 1245.

Definition of § 1245 Property

The recapture of depreciation under § 1245 applies only to *§ 1245 property,* normally *depreciable personal property.*[19] Because the definition of personal property itself is so broad, § 1245 generally covers a wide variety of depreciable assets such as

- Machinery and equipment used in production of goods and services.

- Office furniture and equipment.

- Automobiles, vans, trucks, and other transportation equipment.

- Livestock used for breeding or production.

- Intangibles such as patents, copyrights, trademarks, and goodwill that have been amortized under § 197 or otherwise.

Essentially the amortization is treated the same as depreciation, just like any portion of the cost of a depreciable asset that is expensed under § 179 is treated as depreciation allowed.[20] It is important to understand that § 1245 applies only if the property is depreciable or amortizable. Consequently, it pertains only to property that is used in a trade or business and property held for the production of income. For example, livestock that are considered inventory are not subject to depreciation and are therefore not § 1245 property, although any gain or loss from the disposition of inventory is ordinary income.

Although the above definition is usually sufficient, § 1245 property actually includes a number of other assets besides depreciable personalty, including the following:[21]

1. Property used as an integral part of manufacturing, production, or extraction, or in furnishing transportation, communications, electrical energy, gas, water, or sewage disposal services.
   a. However, any portion of a building or its structural components is not included.
   b. A research facility or a facility for the bulk storage of commodities related to an activity listed above is included.

2. A single-purpose agricultural or horticultural structure (e.g., greenhouses).

3. A storage structure used in connection with the distribution of petroleum or any primary product of petroleum (e.g., oil tank).

4. Any railroad grading or tunnel bore.

5. Certain other property that is subject to a special provision allowing current deductibility or rapid amortization (e.g., pollution control facilities and railroad rolling stock).

---

[19] § 1245(a)(3).

[20] See § 197(f)(7) for intangibles and § 1245(a)(3)(D) for expensed property and certain other properties subject to unique expensing rules.

[21] The definition parallels that of § 38 property, which qualified for the investment tax credit. § 48(a)(1).

Operation of § 1245

Section 1245 generally requires any gain recognized to be treated as ordinary income to the extent of *any* depreciation allowed.[22] To state the rule in another way: Any gain on the disposition of § 1245 property is ordinary income to the extent of the *lesser* of the gain recognized or the § 1245 recapture potential, generally the depreciation claimed and deducted. Although both statements say the same thing, the latter helps focus attention on two points and eliminates some misconceptions. First, a taxpayer is never required to report more income than the amount of gain realized regardless of the amount of depreciation claimed and deducted (i.e., regardless of the amount of recapture potential). For example, if the taxpayer realizes a gain of $10,000 and has deducted depreciation of $15,000, the taxpayer reports only $10,000 of income, all of which would be ordinary. Note that the depreciation recapture rules do not affect the amount of gain or loss, only the character of any gain to be recognized. Second, using the term *recapture potential* helps emphasize that sometimes the amount that must be recaptured may include more than mere depreciation.

Section 1245 *recapture potential* includes *all* depreciation or amortization allowed (or allowable) with respect to a given property—regardless of the method of depreciation used. This is why § 1245 is often called the full recapture rule. Recapture potential also includes adjustments to basis related to items that are expensed (e.g., under § 179 expense election) or where tax credits have been allowed under various sections of the Code.[23]

To summarize, determining the character of gain on the disposition of § 1245 property is generally a three-step process:

1. Determine the amount of gain to be recognized, if any.

2. The gain is ordinary income to the extent of the *lesser* of the gain recognized or the § 1245 recapture potential (all depreciation allowed or allowable).

3. Any recognized gain in excess of the recapture potential retains its original character, usually § 1231 gain.

Recall that there is no § 1245 depreciation recapture when a property is sold at a loss, so any loss is normally a § 1231 loss.

Example 8

T owned a printing press that he used in his business. Its cost was $6,800 and T deducted depreciation in the amount of $3,200 during the three years he owned the press. T sold the press for $4,000 and his realized and recognized gain is $400 ($4,000 sales price − $3,600 adjusted basis). T's recapture potential is $3,200, the amount of depreciation taken on the property. Thus, the entire $400 gain is ordinary income under § 1245.

Example 9

Assume the same facts as in *Example 8*, except that T sold his press for $7,000. In this case, T's realized and recognized gain would be $3,400 ($7,000 − $3,600). The ordinary income portion under § 1245 would be $3,200 (the amount of the recapture potential), and the remaining $200 of the gain is a § 1231 gain. Note that in order for any § 1231 gain to occur, the property must be sold for more than its original cost since all of the depreciation is treated as ordinary income.

---

[22] § 1245(a).

[23] See § 1245(a)(2) for a listing of these adjustments and their related Code sections, including the basis adjustment related to the earned portion of any investment credit.

> ### Example 10
>
> Assume the same facts as in *Example 8*, except that the printing press is sold for $3,000 instead of $4,000. In this case, T has a loss from the sale of $600 ($3,000 − $3,600 adjusted basis). Because there is a loss, there is no depreciation recapture. All of T's loss is a § 1231 loss.

Exceptions and Limitations

In many ways, § 1245 operates much like the proverbial troll under the bridge. It sits ready to spring on its victim whenever the proper moment arises. Section 1245 generally applies whenever there is a transfer of property. However, § 1245 does identify certain situations where it does not apply, most of which are nontaxable events. For example, there is no recapture on a transfer by gift or bequest since both of these are nontaxable transfers.[24]

In involuntary conversions and like-kind exchanges, the depreciation recapture under § 1245 is limited to the *gain recognized.*[25] Similarly, in nontaxable business adjustments such as the formation of partnerships, transfers to controlled corporations, and certain corporate reorganizations, § 1245 recapture is limited to the gain recognized under the controlling provisions.[26] In any situation where recapture is not triggered, it is generally not lost but carried over in some fashion.

PARTIAL RECAPTURE—§ 1250

As originally enacted in 1961, the concept of recapture as set forth in § 1245 generally applied only to personalty. Gains derived from dealing in realty were not subject to recapture. In 1963, however, Congress eliminated this omission by enacting § 1250, a special recapture provision that applied to most buildings. Since 1963, § 1245 has generally been associated with depreciation recapture for personal property while § 1250 served that role for buildings. Although the two provisions are similar, § 1250 is far less damaging. Specifically, § 1250 calls for the recapture of only a *portion* of any *accelerated* depreciation allowed with respect to *§ 1250 property.* Note that while §§ 1250 and 1245 are essentially the same—they both convert potential capital gain into ordinary income—§ 1250 differs from § 1245 in several important ways: (1) it applies only if an accelerated method is used; (2) it does not require recapture of all the depreciation deducted but only a portion—generally only the *excess of accelerated depreciation over what straight-line would have been;* and (3) it applies to a different type of property, *buildings and their components,* rather than personal property. These basic concepts are illustrated in the following example and discussed further below.

LO.6

Compute depreciation recapture under § 1250.

> ### Example 11
>
> T purchased an office building in 1979 for $600,000. In 1979, depreciation generally was computed using either the straight-line or accelerated method based on the estimated useful life of the property and estimated salvage value, all determined by the taxpayer. T depreciated the building over its estimated useful life of 40 years, using an accelerated method and no salvage value. This year, T sold the building for $900,000. At the time of sale, accelerated depreciation actually deducted was $500,000. Straight-line depreciation using the same facts would have been $300,000. The building is § 1250 property since it is realty acquired after 1969. As determined below, T recognizes a gain of $800,000, $200,000 is recaptured as ordinary income under § 1250 and the $600,000 balance is § 1231 gain.

---

[24] §§ 1245(b)(1) and (2). Recapture of depreciation under § 1245 is required, however, to the extent § 691 applies (relating to income in respect to a decedent).

[25] § 1245(b)(4).

[26] § 1245(b)(3). See Chapter 19 for further discussion of nontaxable business adjustments.

Amount realized		$ 900,000*
Adjusted basis:		
Cost	$600,000	
Depreciation (accelerated)	(500,000)	
Adjusted basis		(100,000)
Gain on sale		$ 800,000
Depreciation recapture under § 1250:		
Accelerated depreciation actually deducted	$500,000	
Hypothetical straight-line depreciation	(300,000)	
Section 1250 recapture reported as ordinary income		$ 200,000
Section 1231 gain		$ 600,000

* A separate allocation and calculation would be required to determine any gain or loss on the land and is ignored here for simplicity.

Note that under the partial recapture rule of § 1250 only the excess of the actual amount of accelerated depreciation deducted ($500,000) over what the straight-line depreciation would have been ($300,000), a difference of $200,000, is recaptured. This excess is treated as ordinary income. Had the property been § 1245 property, all $500,000 would have been recaptured. Also observe that under § 1250 none of the straight-line depreciation, $300,000 is recaptured. However, this unrecaptured depreciation on § 1250 property is taxed at a maximum rate of 25% as discussed below.

As noted in the example, § 1250 does not recapture the straight-line depreciation. In enacting § 1250 Congress wanted to ensure that ordinary income treatment would be applied only to what were truly excess depreciation deductions. Gain not attributable to excess depreciation was considered attributable to a rise in price levels and was eligible for relief provided for capital gains and not subject to recapture.

Section 1250 Property

Section 1250 property is generally any real property that is depreciable and is not covered by § 1245.[27] For the most part, § 1250 applies to all of the common forms of real estate such as office buildings, warehouses, apartment complexes, and low-income housing. As a practical matter, sales of these properties rarely produce recapture because the law has required the straight-line method for depreciation since 1986. However, § 1250 property also includes 15- and 20-year realty which is depreciated using the 150% declining balance and, therefore, is capable of creating excess depreciation. This category includes such assets as multi-purpose agricultural structures (e.g., barns), land improvements (e.g., roads, sidewalks, fences, landscaping, shrubbery, docks), gas stations, convenience stores, and more. As explained earlier, nonresidential real estate (e.g., warehouses and office buildings) placed in service after 1980 and before 1987 for which an accelerated method was used is covered by the full recapture rule of § 1245.[28]

Depreciation of Real Property

Section 1250 applies only if an accelerated method of depreciation is used. If the straight-line depreciation method is used, § 1250 does not apply and there is no depreciation recapture for noncorporate taxpayers.[29] For this reason, a critical first step in determining the relevance of § 1250 is determining how the taxpayer has depreciated the realty.

Realty Placed in Service before 1987. Prior to 1987, taxpayers could choose to use either an accelerated or straight-line method to compute depreciation for realty. This was an extremely important decision. It affected not only the amount of depreciation the taxpayer claimed but also the character of any gain on a subsequent disposition of the property.

---

[27] § 1250(c).

[28] It is important to note, however, that such properties are § 1250 property if the optional straight-line method is used. § 1245(a)(5).

[29] As explained within, corporate taxpayers are still required to recapture 20% of any straight-line depreciation under § 291. Also, any unrecaptured straight-line depreciation is taxed at a maximum rate of 25 percent.

For example, a taxpayer could accelerate depreciation deductions but only at the possible expense of recapture. Alternatively, the taxpayer could accept the slower-paced straight-line method and avoid the § 1250 recapture rules. But the Tax Reform Act of 1986 ended this flexibility and at the same time simplified the law. Taxpayers who place realty in service *after 1986* must use the straight-line method for residential and nonresidential realty. As a result, the recapture rules of § 1250 do not apply to residential and nonresidential realty acquired after 1986. However, much of the existing inventory of real property was acquired before 1987 and may therefore be subject to § 1250, depending on the depreciation method used.

Realty Placed in Service from 1981 through 1986. For real property acquired between the beginning of 1981 and the end of 1986, the taxpayer could either use the accelerated depreciation method allowed under ACRS or elect an optional straight-line method. In most cases, a taxpayer would select the accelerated method. If an accelerated method is used for *residential* realty acquired during 1981 through 1986, § 1250 applies, requiring recapture of the excess depreciation. However, as noted earlier, if an accelerated method is used for *nonresidential* realty acquired during 1981 through 1986, the property is considered § 1245 and the full recapture rule applies.

By the close of 2005, realty acquired during 1981 through 1986 became fully depreciated since the lives were 15, 18, or 19 years during this time. As a result, there is no § 1250 recapture for residential realty since there is no excess depreciation (i.e., total accelerated depreciation would be identical to total straight-line depreciation). Similarly, there is no § 1250 recapture for nonresidential realty if the straight-line method was used. However, to reiterate, if the accelerated method was used in depreciating nonresidential realty acquired during these tainted years, 1981–1986, § 1245 applies and all of the accelerated depreciation is recaptured.

Realty Placed in Service before 1981. All depreciable real property acquired before 1981 is classified as § 1250 property. For such property acquired before 1981 (non-ACRS property), taxpayers were required to estimate useful lives and salvage values. Although various methods could be used, there were restrictions.[30] In those situations where an accelerated method was used, § 1250 applies subject to certain limitations. As discussed further below, none of the excess depreciation produced by realty for years after 1963 and before 1970 is subject to recapture. In the case of *low-income housing* and other *residential* real estate, excess depreciation resulting after 1969 and before 1976 is no longer recaptured. After 1975, excess depreciation on low-income housing is exempt from recapture if the property is held more than 16⅔ years.

Summary of § 1250 Application

The significance of § 1250 has declined considerably over the years. Subject to certain unusual situations (e.g., certain low-income housing, certain Liberty Zone property, etc.), the following general observations can be made about the current status of § 1250:

- For residential and nonresidential realty acquired after 1986, there is no § 1250 recapture because the straight-line method must be used for such property and no excess depreciation results.

- For *residential* realty acquired during 1981–1986 there is no § 1250 recapture since these assets are fully depreciated and there is no excess depreciation.

- For *nonresidential* realty acquired during 1981–1986 for which the straight-line method was used, there is no recapture under § 1250, but § 1245 requires full-recapture if an accelerated method was used for the property.

- The reach of § 1250 is usually limited to realty acquired during 1970–1980. And much of this property, which at this point is 27–37 years old, has turned over and in the hands of the new buyer § 1250 does not apply.

Although the traditional recapture rules of § 1250 may not apply, gains on § 1250 property are not guaranteed the benefits of favorable capital gain rates. As explained further below, such gains may be taxed at a rate of up to 25% to the extent of any unrecaptured straight-line depreciation.

---

[30] § 167(j).

Operation of § 1250

The two critical factors in determining the amount, if any, of *§ 1250 recapture* are the gain realized *and* the amount of *excess depreciation*. Excess depreciation refers to depreciation deductions in excess of that which would be deductible using the straight-line method. For property held one year or less, all depreciation is considered excess depreciation.[31]

As a general rule, § 1250 requires recapture of the excess depreciation, that is, the excess of accelerated over straight-line. Consequently, even if the taxpayer uses an accelerated method to compute the amount of depreciation deducted on the return, the hypothetical amount of straight-line depreciation must still be computed in order to determine the excess of accelerated over straight-line when the property is sold. In determining the hypothetical amount of straight-line depreciation, the taxpayer uses the same life and salvage value, if any, that were used in computing accelerated depreciation.[32] Because of this approach, a taxpayer who uses the straight-line method would have no excess depreciation and no recapture. Because the § 1250 recapture rule applies only to any excess depreciation claimed by a taxpayer, it is sometimes referred to as the partial recapture rule. However, it should be emphasized that beginning in 1997, the unrecaptured § 1250 depreciation (e.g., the straight-line depreciation) on § 1250 property held more than 12 months is subject to a special 25% tax rate (assuming it survives the § 1231 netting process).

Determining the taxation of any gain recognized on the disposition of § 1250 property is a four-step process:

1. Determine the amount of gain to be recognized, if any.
2. The gain is ordinary income to the extent of the *lesser* of the gain recognized or the § 1250 recapture potential (generally the excess depreciation allowed).[33]
3. Any recognized gain in excess of the recapture potential is usually treated as § 1231 gain.
4. Any gain recognized on § 1250 property held more than 12 months that is due to depreciation that is not recaptured and which survives the applicable netting processes is taxed at a maximum rate of 25% to the extent of any unrecaptured depreciation. Any additional gain is generally 15% gain.

Two other considerations should be noted. If § 1250 property is held for a year or less, all depreciation (not just the excess) is recaptured.[34] In addition, there is no § 1250 depreciation recapture when a property is sold at a loss, so any loss is normally a § 1231 loss.

Unrecaptured § 1250 Gain

As may be apparent from Step 3 above, under § 1250, taxpayers are required to recapture depreciation only if an accelerated method is used to depreciate the property. Consequently, individual taxpayers never recapture depreciation on § 1250 property if the method is used. Without some special rule, any gain attributable to straight-line depreciation for § 1250 property held more than 12 months would normally qualify for taxation at a 15% rate. Congress felt this treatment was too generous and created a special rule for *unrecaptured § 1250 gain*. The unrecaptured § 1250 gain is the lesser of (1) the gain recognized, or (2) the depreciation allowed after each (the gain recognized and the depreciation allowed) is reduced by any § 1250 recapture. The resulting amount will equal the amount of straight-line depreciation that was claimed or would have been claimed had the straight-line method been used (or, if less, the gain recognized minus the § 1250 recapture).

---

[31] § 1250(b).

[32] § 1250(b)(5).

[33] See § 1250(a) and discussion following dealing with recapture of only a portion of the excess depreciation for certain properties.

[34] § 1250(b)(1).

Example 12

About 10 years ago, F purchased some residential rental property for $100,000. This year he sold the property for $110,000. He had claimed straight-line depreciation of $30,000 over this time, resulting in a basis of $70,000 (do not attempt to verify this amount). As a result, F recognized a gain of $40,000. Since the property is realty and a straight-line depreciation method was used there is no § 1250 recapture. Consequently, the entire gain is a § 1231 gain. However, the § 1231 gain will be treated as a 25% gain to the extent of any straight-line depreciation claimed. Therefore, $30,000 of the gain is a 25% § 1231 gain while $10,000 is a 15% § 1231 gain (i.e., in the capital gain netting process these will be 15% and 25% long-term gains, respectively). If F had sold the property for $90,000, he would have had a gain of $20,000, all of which would have been a 25% gain (i.e., the lesser of the gain realized, $20,000, or the unrecaptured straight-line depreciation, $30,000).

Example 13

Same facts and $110,000 sales price from *Example 12* above, except that F also has a $400 gain on the sale of K Corporation stock held 26 months. F is single and has taxable income, excluding these transactions, of $90,000. F's tax would be computed as follows (using the 2017 tax rates for single taxpayers):

Regular tax on $90,000:

Tax on $37,950.	$ 5,226	
Tax on excess at 15% ([$90,000 − $37,950 = $52,050] × 25%).	13,031	
		$18,239
Tax on 15% gains (15% × $10,400).		1,560
Tax on 25% gains (25% × $30,000).		7,500
Total tax		$27,299

Combined Results

The net gain from the disposition of § 1250 property can be treated as ordinary income subject to the regular tax rate, 15% capital gain, and/or 25% capital gain (and rarely 28% capital gain). Each step in the netting and tax calculation processes has been covered. *Examples 14* through *17* and *Comprehensive Example 19* illustrate how they work in combination.

Example 14

During the current year, L sold a small office building for $38,000. The building cost $22,000 in 1980, and she had deducted depreciation of $12,000 using an accelerated method ($10,000 was assigned to the land and was not depreciable). Straight-line depreciation would have been $10,600. L's gain recognized on the sale is $28,000 ($38,000 amount realized − $10,000 adjusted basis). Of that amount, $1,400 ($12,000 − $10,600 = $1,400 excess depreciation) is ordinary income under § 1250 and the remainder, $26,600, is § 1231 gain. Of the $26,600 § 1231 gain, the unrecaptured depreciation of $10,600 ($12,000 − $1,400) is a 25% gain. The $16,000 excess of the amount realized over the original basis is 15% gain.

Example 15

M purchased a rental duplex during 1986 for $60,000 (not including any value assigned to land). He deducted $60,000 depreciation using the 19-year realty ACRS tables. Depreciation using the straight-line recovery percentages for 19-year realty would have resulted in total depreciation of $60,000 (the duplex is fully depreciated under each method). This year, on May 3, M sold the property for $87,000. His gain is reported as follows:

Sales price.		$ 87,000
Less: Adjusted basis		
Cost	$60,000	
Depreciation allowed	(60,000)	0
Gain to be recognized.		$ 87,000
Accelerated depreciation claimed and deducted		$ 60,000
Straight-line depreciation (hypothetical)		(60,000)
Excess depreciation subject to recapture		$ 0
Character of gain:		
Ordinary income (partial recapture)		$ 0
Section 1231 gain subject to 25% rate		60,000
Section 1231 gain subject to 15% rate		27,000
Total gain recognized		$ 87,000

First, observe that the property is residential property (rather than nonresidential property) so it is subject to § 1250 that requires recapture of the excess of accelerated depreciation over straight line. In this case, however, there is no excess depreciation since the rental property is fully depreciated. Thus, without a special rule, the gain not recaptured under § 1250 might be subject to the 15% capital gains rate. However, the depreciation that has not been recaptured, $60,000, is carved out and is considered a 25% § 1231 gain. Also observe that the $60,000 of 25% § 1231 gain is the amount of straight-line depreciation. The remaining gain (i.e., the amount above the original cost) of $27,000 is a 15% § 1231 gain.

Example 16

Assume the same facts as in *Example 15,* except that M elected to recover his basis in the duplex using the 19-year straight-line method. Consequently she still recognizes gain of $87,000 computed as follows:

Sales price.		$ 87,000
Less: Adjusted basis:		
Cost	$60,000	
Depreciation (straight-line)	(60,000)	
		0
Gain		$(87,000)

None of the gain is subject to § 1250 recapture since M used straight-line depreciation (a requirement after 1986). However, the amount representing the unrecaptured depreciation (i.e., the straight-line depreciation) of $60,000 is considered a 25% § 1231 gain and the $27,000 balance is considered a 15% § 1231 gain.

> ### Example 17
>
> Assume the same facts as in *Example 15,* except that the property is an office building rather than a duplex. In this case, because the property is nonresidential real property and the accelerated method was used, the asset is treated as § 1245 property rather than § 1250 property. Thus, M is subject to full rather than partial depreciation recapture. All of the $60,000 depreciation is recaptured and treated as ordinary income. The balance of the gain, $27,000 is treated as a 15% § 1231 gain.

History of § 1250

Over the years, § 1250 has been changed frequently, with a general trend toward an expanded scope. The rules explained above apply only to depreciation allowed on nonresidential property after 1969 and residential property (other than low-income housing) after 1975. Only a *portion* of any other excess depreciation on § 1250 property is included in the recapture potential. The following percentages are applied to the gain realized in the transaction or the excess depreciation taken during the particular period, whichever is less:

1. For all excess depreciation taken after 1963 and before 1970, 100% less 1% for each full month over 20 months the property is held.[35] Any sales after 1979 would result in no recapture of pre-1970 excess depreciation since this percentage, when calculated, is zero.

2. For all excess depreciation taken after 1969 and before 1976, as follows:

   a. In the case of low-income housing, 100% less 1% for each full month the property is held over 20 months.

   b. In the case of other residential rental property (e.g., an apartment building) and property that has been rehabilitated [for purposes of § 167(k)], 100% less 1% for each full month the property is held over 100 months.[36]

All sales from this group of real property after August 1992 will have no recapture of excess depreciation claimed before 1976.

3. For excess depreciation taken after 1975 on low-income housing and property that has been rehabilitated [for purposes of § 167(k)], 100% less 1% for each full month the property is held over 100 months.[37]

In summary, 100% of the excess depreciation allowed with respect to § 1250 property after 1975 is subject to recapture unless it falls into one of the above categories. Any gain recognized to the extent of any unrecaptured depreciation will be considered 25% gain. The rules for the various categories are set forth in § 1250(a).

Exceptions and Limitations under § 1250

Generally, the exceptions and limitations that apply under § 1245 also apply under § 1250. Thus, gifts, inheritances, and most nontaxable exchanges are allowed to occur without triggering recapture.[38] This exception is extended to any property to the extent it qualifies as a principal residence and is subject to deferral of gain under § 1034 or nonrecognition of gain under § 121.[39] In such nontaxable exchanges, the excess depreciation (that is not recaptured) taken prior to the nontaxable exchange on the property transferred carries over to the property received or purchased.[40] Similarly, in the case of gifts and certain nontaxable transfers in which the property is transferred to a new owner with a carryover basis, the excess depreciation carries over to the new owner.[41] In the case of inheritances in which basis to the successor in interest is determined under § 1014, no carryover of excess depreciation occurs.[42]

---

[35] § 1250(a)(3).

[36] § 1250(a)(2).

[37] § 1250(a)(1).

[38] § 1250(d)(1) through (d)(4).

[39] § 1250(d)(7).

[40] Reg. §§ 1.1250-3(d)(5) and (h)(4).

[41] Reg. §§ 1.1250-3(a), (c), and (f).

[42] Reg. § 1.1250-3(b).

Certain like-kind exchanges and involuntary conversions may result in the recognition of gain solely because of § 1250 if insufficient § 1250 property is acquired. Since not all real property is depreciable, it is possible that the replacement property would not be § 1250 property and would still qualify for nonrecognition under the appropriate rules of §§ 1033 or 1034. In such situations, gain will be recognized to the extent the amount that would be recaptured exceeds the fair market value of the § 1250 property received (property purchased in the case of an involuntary conversion).[43]

Example 18

D completed a like-kind exchange in the current year in which he transferred an apartment complex (§ 1250 property) for rural farmland (not § 1250 property). The apartment had cost D $175,000 in 1980 and depreciation of $89,000 has been taken under the 200% declining-balance method. D would have deducted $62,000 under the straight-line method.

The farm land was worth $200,000 at the time of the exchange. There were no improvements on the farm property. D's realized gain on the exchange is $114,000 ($200,000 amount realized − $86,000 adjusted basis in property given up). If there had been no § 1250 recapture, then D would have had no recognized gain. Because the property acquired was not § 1250 property, § 1250 supersedes (overrides) § 1031. D has a recognized gain of $27,000 ([$89,000 − $62,000], the amount of excess depreciation), which is all ordinary income under § 1250.

Exhibit 17-2 provides an overview of the handling of sales and exchanges of business property. Exhibit 17-3 provides a chart that may be useful in summarizing property transactions. Note that for purposes of this Exhibit 17-3, no distinction is made between 15, 25, and 28 percent § 1231 gains and losses or 15, 25, and 28 percent capital gains and losses. A comprehensive example of sales and exchanges of trade or business property is presented below.

EXHIBIT 17-2	**Stepwise Approach to Sales or Exchange of Trade or Business Property—An Overview**

Step 1: Determine the amount of gain to be recognized, if any. There is no recapture in the case of losses.

Step 2: Calculate any depreciation recapture on the disposition of § 1245 property and § 1250 property sold or exchanged at a taxable *gain* during the year.

Step 3: For any remaining gain (after recapture) on depreciable property held for more than one year, add to other § 1231 gains and losses and complete the § 1231 netting process.
  • *The § 1231 gain must be broken down into the portions that qualify as 15%CG and 25%CG (and rarely 28%CG).*

Step 4: Complete the netting process for capital assets, taking into consideration the net § 1231 gain, if any.
  • *The § 1231 gain is combined with other long-term capital gains and losses (with separate netting for 15%CG, 25%CG, and 28%CG). Then the long-term capital gain or loss is combined with the short-term capital gain or loss.*

---

[43] § 1250(d)(4)(C). A similar rule is provided for rollovers
(deferral) of gains from low-income housing under § 1039
[See § 1250(d)(8)].

EXHIBIT 17-3	**Summary of Property Transactions**

Recognized Gains (losses)	Depreciation Recapture	Section 1231 Casualty and Theft*	Section 1231 Other*	Capital Gains/Losses Long-Term* Short-Term		Ordinary Income (loss)
	Section 1245 Full recapture personalty Section 1250 Partial recapture realty Section 291 Corporations only 20% straight-line	<u>Casualty and Theft</u> 1. Section 1231 property Real or depreciable property used in business Timber, coal, iron ore, livestock, unharvested crops 2. Capital assets used in trade or business or held for investment in connection with business more than a year	<u>Sale or Exchange</u> Section 1231 property Real or depreciable property used in business Timber, coal, iron ore, livestock, unharvested crops <u>Condemnation</u> 1. Section 1231 property 2. Capital assets used in trade or business or held for investment in connection with business more than a year	<u>Sale or Exchange</u> Capital assets All property except inventory, property held for resale, real and depreciable property used in trade or business, literary compositions, and government publications		
	$x,xxx					→ $ x,xxx
		$ x,xxx $(x,xxx)	$ x,xxx $(x,xxx)	$ x,xxx $(x,xxx)	$ x,xxx $(x,xxx)	
		<u>Net loss</u>				→ $(x,xxx)
		<u>Net gain</u>	$ x,xxx			
			<u>Net loss</u>			→ $(x,xxx)
			<u>Net gain</u>			
			Look-back rule: Recaptured gains Unrecaptured gains →	$ x,xxx	$ x,xxx	$ x,xxx
				$ x,xxx	$ x,xxx	
				$x,xxx Overall CG or NCL		

* These categories must be subdivided into 15, 25, and 28 percent groups.

Example 19

Ted and Carol Smith sold the following assets during 2016.

Description	Holding Period	Selling Price	Adjusted Basis	Recognized Gain (Loss)
Land and building (straight-line depreciation)......	3 years	$14,000	$9,000	$5,000
Cost, $13,000				
Depreciation allowed, $4,000				
Photocopier................	14 months	2,600	2,000	600
Cost, $2,500				
Depreciation allowed, $500				
Business auto...............	2 years	1,800	1,920	(120)
Cost, $4,000				
Depreciation allowed, $2,080				

In determining the tax consequences of these sales, the Smiths must start with gains and losses from § 1231 transactions. The ultimate treatment of the gains, the character of the gain and any possible depreciation recapture must be considered.

- On the sale of the land and the building, there is no depreciation recapture for the building since straight-line depreciation was used. However, there is unrecaptured depreciation of $4,000 which is accounted for as a 25% § 1231 gain. The balance of the gain on the land and building, $1,000, is a 15% § 1231 gain.

- On the sale of the photocopier, $500 of the § 1231 gain of $600 is recaptured under § 1245 and treated as ordinary income. The balance of the gain, $100, is a 15% § 1231 gain.

- On the sale of the automobile, there is no recapture since it is sold at a loss. The $120 loss is treated as a 15% § 1231 loss. This information is summarized below.

	Section 1231 Gains and Losses		
	Collectibles	Unrecaptured Depreciation	Other
	28%	25%	15%
Land and building..............		$4,000	$1,000
Photocopier			100
Automobile....................			(120)
Capital gains from § 1231	$0	$4,000	$ 980

In this situation, the Smiths net the various groups, resulting in net gains in each of the groups as shown above. These amounts are then combined with the appropriate capital gain groups to determine the final treatment. Note that if the Smiths had unrecaptured § 1231 losses, they would first offset the 28% gains, then 25% gains, and finally 15% gains. The information is summarized in Exhibit 17-3.

Example 20

Assume that the Smiths, from the previous example, had the following capital asset transactions during the same year:

Description	Holding Period	Selling Price	Adjusted Basis	Description of Gain or (Loss)
100 shares XY Corp..........	4 months	$ 3,200	$4,200	$(1,000) STCL
100 shares GB Corp..........	3 years	3,200	4,600	(1,400) LTCL
1 acre vacant land	5 years	12,000	5,000	7,000 LTCG

Taking into consideration the § 1231 gains from *Example 19*, the Smith's summarize their transactions as follows.

| | Short-Term | Capital Gains and Losses | | |
		Collectibles	Unrecaptured Depreciation	Other
	Ordinary	28%	25%	15%
Capital gains from § 1231		$0	$4,000	$ 980
XY stock loss..............	(1,000)			
GB stock loss				(1,400)
Vacant land gain............				7,000
	$(1,000)	$0	$4,000	$6,580
Netting.................	1,000		(1,000)	
Total	$ 0	$0	$3,000	$6,580

Ted and Carol Smith would report a $3,000 N25CG and a $6,580 N15CG.

A Form 4797, Schedule D and Schedule D Tax Worksheet containing the information from Examples 19 and 20 are included in Exhibit 17-4 that follows. Note that neither the Form 4797 nor Schedule D Parts I or II require the taxpayer to distinguish the 25% gains from the 28% or 15% gains. These distinctions come into view on Schedule D, Part III Summary where Line 18 refers to the 28% Rate Gain Worksheet and Line 19 requires identification of the amount of unrecaptured § 1250 Gain Worksheet (i.e., the 25% gain). The actual tax is computed on the Schedule D Tax Worksheet that can be found in the instructions for Form 1040 for Schedule D. On the Schedule D Tax Worksheet, the rates are more apparent (line 24–15 percent, line 30–25 percent, and line 33–28 percent). The tax for the taxpayers in Examples 19 and 20 is computed on the Schedule D Tax Worksheet, assuming the taxpayers have taxable income of $126,830 as computed below. Note that the taxable income includes the capital gains and recapture.

Wages...		$137,350
Section 1245 recapture		500
Capital gains:		
N15CG	$6,580	
N25CG	3,000	
		9,580
Adjusted gross income.................................		$147,430
Standard deduction for 2016............................		(12,600)
Exemptions for 2016 (2 × $4,050).......................		(8,100)
Taxable income		$126,730
Tax per Schedule D Tax Worksheet		$ 21,827

EXHIBIT 17-4	Completed Form 4797

Form 4797

Sales of Business Property
(Also Involuntary Conversions and Recapture Amounts
Under Sections 179 and 280F(b)(2))
► Attach to your tax return.
► Information about Form 4797 and its separate instructions is at *www.irs.gov/form4797.*

OMB No. 1545-0184

2016

Department of the Treasury
Internal Revenue Service

Attachment
Sequence No. **27**

Name(s) shown on return
Ted & Carol Smith

Identifying number
123 – 45 – 6789

1 Enter the gross proceeds from sales or exchanges reported to you for 2016 on Form(s) 1099-B or 1099-S (or substitute statement) that you are including on line 2, 10, or 20. See instructions . . . . | **1** |

Part I **Sales or Exchanges of Property Used in a Trade or Business and Involuntary Conversions From Other Than Casualty or Theft—Most Property Held More Than 1 Year** (see instructions)

2	(a) Description of property	(b) Date acquired (mo., day, yr.)	(c) Date sold (mo., day, yr.)	(d) Gross sales price	(e) Depreciation allowed or allowable since acquisition	(f) Cost or other basis, plus improvements and expense of sale	(g) Gain or (loss) Subtract (f) from the sum of (d) and (e)
	Auto	03/09/10	10/02/15	1,800	2,080	4,000	–120

3	Gain, if any, from Form 4684, line 39	**3**	
4	Section 1231 gain from installment sales from Form 6252, line 26 or 37	**4**	
5	Section 1231 gain or (loss) from like-kind exchanges from Form 8824	**5**	
6	Gain, if any, from line 32, from other than casualty or theft	**6**	5,100
7	Combine lines 2 through 6. Enter the gain or (loss) here and on the appropriate line as follows:	**7**	4,980

Partnerships (except electing large partnerships) and S corporations. Report the gain or (loss) following the instructions for Form 1065, Schedule K, line 10, or Form 1120S, Schedule K, line 9. Skip lines 8, 9, 11, and 12 below.

Individuals, partners, S corporation shareholders, and all others. If line 7 is zero or a loss, enter the amount from line 7 on line 11 below and skip lines 8 and 9. If line 7 is a gain and you didn't have any prior year section 1231 losses, or they were recaptured in an earlier year, enter the gain from line 7 as a long-term capital gain on the Schedule D filed with your return and skip lines 8, 9, 11, and 12 below.

| **8** | Nonrecaptured net section 1231 losses from prior years. See instructions . . . . | **8** | |
| **9** | Subtract line 8 from line 7. If zero or less, enter -0-. If line 9 is zero, enter the gain from line 7 on line 12 below. If line 9 is more than zero, enter the amount from line 8 on line 12 below and enter the gain from line 9 as a long-term capital gain on the Schedule D filed with your return. See instructions . . . . | **9** | |

Part II **Ordinary Gains and Losses** (see instructions)

10	Ordinary gains and losses not included on lines 11 through 16 (include property held 1 year or less):		

11	Loss, if any, from line 7	**11**	( )
12	Gain, if any, from line 7 or amount from line 8, if applicable	**12**	
13	Gain, if any, from line 31	**13**	500
14	Net gain or (loss) from Form 4684, lines 31 and 38a	**14**	
15	Ordinary gain from installment sales from Form 6252, line 25 or 36	**15**	
16	Ordinary gain or (loss) from like-kind exchanges from Form 8824.	**16**	
17	Combine lines 10 through 16	**17**	500

18 For all except individual returns, enter the amount from line 17 on the appropriate line of your return and skip lines a and b below. For individual returns, complete lines a and b below:

a If the loss on line 11 includes a loss from Form 4684, line 35, column (b)(ii), enter that part of the loss here. Enter the part of the loss from income-producing property on Schedule A (Form 1040), line 28, and the part of the loss from property used as an employee on Schedule A (Form 1040), line 23. Identify as from "Form 4797, line 18a." See instructions . . | **18a** | |
b Redetermine the gain or (loss) on line 17 excluding the loss, if any, on line 18a. Enter here and on Form 1040, line 14 | **18b** | 500 |

For Paperwork Reduction Act Notice, see separate instructions. Cat. No. 13086I Form **4797** (2016)

EXHIBIT 17-4   Continued

Form 4797 (2016)   Ted & Carol Smith   123 – 45 – 6789   Page **2**

Part III   Gain From Disposition of Property Under Sections 1245, 1250, 1252, 1254, and 1255
(see instructions)

19	(a) Description of section 1245, 1250, 1252, 1254, or 1255 property:		(b) Date acquired (mo., day, yr.)	(c) Date sold (mo., day, yr.)
A	Land and Building		07/14/03	11/21/15
B	Photocopier		06/12/04	08/31/15
C				
D				

	These columns relate to the properties on lines 19A through 19D. ▶		Property A	Property B	Property C	Property D
20	Gross sales price (**Note:** *See line 1 before completing.*) . .	20	14,000	2,600		
21	Cost or other basis plus expense of sale	21	13,000	2,500		
22	Depreciation (or depletion) allowed or allowable . . .	22	4,000	500		
23	Adjusted basis. Subtract line 22 from line 21	23	9,000	2,000		
24	Total gain. Subtract line 23 from line 20	24	5,000	600		
25	**If section 1245 property:**					
a	Depreciation allowed or allowable from line 22 . . .	25a		500		
b	Enter the **smaller** of line 24 or 25a	25b		500		
26	**If section 1250 property:** If straight line depreciation was used, enter -0- on line 26g, except for a corporation subject to section 291.					
a	Additional depreciation after 1975. See instructions .	26a	0			
b	Applicable percentage multiplied by the **smaller** of line 24 or line 26a. See instructions	26b	0			
c	Subtract line 26a from line 24. If residential rental property **or** line 24 isn't more than line 26a, skip lines 26d and 26e	26c	5,000			
d	Additional depreciation after 1969 and before 1976 . .	26d				
e	Enter the **smaller** of line 26c or 26d	26e				
f	Section 291 amount (corporations only)	26f				
g	Add lines 26b, 26e, and 26f.	26g	0			
27	**If section 1252 property:** Skip this section if you didn't dispose of farmland or if this form is being completed for a partnership (other than an electing large partnership).					
a	Soil, water, and land clearing expenses	27a				
b	Line 27a multiplied by applicable percentage. See instructions	27b				
c	Enter the **smaller** of line 24 or 27b	27c				
28	**If section 1254 property:**					
a	Intangible drilling and development costs, expenditures for development of mines and other natural deposits, mining exploration costs, and depletion. See instructions	28a				
b	Enter the **smaller** of line 24 or 28a	28b				
29	**If section 1255 property:**					
a	Applicable percentage of payments excluded from income under section 126. See instructions	29a				
b	Enter the **smaller** of line 24 or 29a. See instructions .	29b				

Summary of Part III Gains. Complete property columns A through D through line 29b before going to line 30.

30	Total gains for all properties. Add property columns A through D, line 24	30	5,600
31	Add property columns A through D, lines 25b, 26g, 27c, 28b, and 29b. Enter here and on line 13	31	500
32	Subtract line 31 from line 30. Enter the portion from casualty or theft on Form 4684, line 33. Enter the portion from other than casualty or theft on Form 4797, line 6	32	5,100

Part IV   Recapture Amounts Under Sections 179 and 280F(b)(2) When Business Use Drops to 50% or Less
(see instructions)

			(a) Section 179	(b) Section 280F(b)(2)
33	Section 179 expense deduction or depreciation allowable in prior years.	33		
34	Recomputed depreciation. See instructions	34		
35	Recapture amount. Subtract line 34 from line 33. See the instructions for where to report . .	35		

Form **4797** (2016)

EXHIBIT 17-5 | **Completed Schedule D**

SCHEDULE D
(Form 1040)

Department of the Treasury
Internal Revenue Service (99)

Capital Gains and Losses

▶ Attach to Form 1040 or Form 1040NR.
▶ Information about Schedule D and its separate instructions is at *www.irs.gov/scheduled*.
▶ Use Form 8949 to list your transactions for lines 1b, 2, 3, 8b, 9, and 10.

OMB No. 1545-0074

2016

Attachment
Sequence No. **12**

Name(s) shown on return	Your social security number
Ted & Carol Smith	123 – 45 – 6789

Part I — **Short-Term Capital Gains and Losses—Assets Held One Year or Less**

See instructions for how to figure the amounts to enter on the lines below. This form may be easier to complete if you round off cents to whole dollars.	**(d)** Proceeds (sales price)	**(e)** Cost (or other basis)	**(g)** Adjustments to gain or loss from Form(s) 8949, Part I, line 2, column (g)	**(h) Gain or (loss)** Subtract column (e) from column (d) and combine the result with column (g)
1a Totals for all short-term transactions reported on Form 1099-B for which basis was reported to the IRS and for which you have no adjustments (see instructions). However, if you choose to report all these transactions on Form 8949, leave this line blank and go to line 1b .				
1b Totals for all transactions reported on Form(s) 8949 with **Box A** checked	3,200	4,200		–1,000
2 Totals for all transactions reported on Form(s) 8949 with **Box B** checked				
3 Totals for all transactions reported on Form(s) 8949 with **Box C** checked				

4 Short-term gain from Form 6252 and short-term gain or (loss) from Forms 4684, 6781, and 8824 .	**4**	
5 Net short-term gain or (loss) from partnerships, S corporations, estates, and trusts from Schedule(s) K-1	**5**	
6 Short-term capital loss carryover. Enter the amount, if any, from line 8 of your **Capital Loss Carryover Worksheet** in the instructions	**6**	( )
7 **Net short-term capital gain or (loss).** Combine lines 1a through 6 in column (h). If you have any long-term capital gains or losses, go to Part II below. Otherwise, go to Part III on the back	**7**	–1,000

Part II — **Long-Term Capital Gains and Losses—Assets Held More Than One Year**

See instructions for how to figure the amounts to enter on the lines below. This form may be easier to complete if you round off cents to whole dollars.	**(d)** Proceeds (sales price)	**(e)** Cost (or other basis)	**(g)** Adjustments to gain or loss from Form(s) 8949, Part II, line 2, column (g)	**(h) Gain or (loss)** Subtract column (e) from column (d) and combine the result with column (g)
8a Totals for all long-term transactions reported on Form 1099-B for which basis was reported to the IRS and for which you have no adjustments (see instructions). However, if you choose to report all these transactions on Form 8949, leave this line blank and go to line 8b .				
8b Totals for all transactions reported on Form(s) 8949 with **Box D** checked	15,200	9,600		5,600
9 Totals for all transactions reported on Form(s) 8949 with **Box E** checked				
10 Totals for all transactions reported on Form(s) 8949 with **Box F** checked.				

11 Gain from Form 4797, Part I; long-term gain from Forms 2439 and 6252; and long-term gain or (loss) from Forms 4684, 6781, and 8824	**11**	4,980
12 Net long-term gain or (loss) from partnerships, S corporations, estates, and trusts from Schedule(s) K-1	**12**	
13 Capital gain distributions. See the instructions	**13**	
14 Long-term capital loss carryover. Enter the amount, if any, from line 13 of your **Capital Loss Carryover Worksheet** in the instructions	**14**	( )
15 **Net long-term capital gain or (loss).** Combine lines 8a through 14 in column (h). Then go to Part III on the back	**15**	10,580

For Paperwork Reduction Act Notice, see your tax return instructions.   Cat. No. 11338H   **Schedule D (Form 1040) 2016**

EXHIBIT 17-5	Continued

Schedule D (Form 1040) 2016　Ted & Carol Smith　　　　　　　　　　123 – 45 – 6789　Page **2**

Part III　**Summary**

16 Combine lines 7 and 15 and enter the result . . . . **16** | 9,580

- If line 16 is a **gain,** enter the amount from line 16 on Form 1040, line 13, or Form 1040NR, line 14. Then go to line 17 below.
- If line 16 is a **loss,** skip lines 17 through 20 below. Then go to line 21. Also be sure to complete line 22.
- If line 16 is **zero,** skip lines 17 through 21 below and enter -0- on Form 1040, line 13, or Form 1040NR, line 14. Then go to line 22.

17 Are lines 15 and 16 **both** gains?
☒ **Yes.** Go to line 18.
☐ **No.** Skip lines 18 through 21, and go to line 22.

18 Enter the amount, if any, from line 7 of the **28% Rate Gain Worksheet** in the instructions . . ▶ | **18**

19 Enter the amount, if any, from line 18 of the **Unrecaptured Section 1250 Gain Worksheet** in the instructions . . . . ▶ | **19** | 3,000

20 Are lines 18 and 19 **both** zero or blank?
☐ **Yes.** Complete the **Qualified Dividends and Capital Gain Tax Worksheet** in the instructions for Form 1040, line 44 (or in the instructions for Form 1040NR, line 42). **Don't** complete lines 21 and 22 below.

☒ **No.** Complete the **Schedule D Tax Worksheet** in the instructions. **Don't** complete lines 21 and 22 below.

21 If line 16 is a loss, enter here and on Form 1040, line 13, or Form 1040NR, line 14, the **smaller** of:

- The loss on line 16 or
- ($3,000), or if married filing separately, ($1,500) } . . . . **21** | (|)

Note: When figuring which amount is smaller, treat both amounts as positive numbers.

22 Do you have qualified dividends on Form 1040, line 9b, or Form 1040NR, line 10b?

☐ **Yes.** Complete the **Qualified Dividends and Capital Gain Tax Worksheet** in the instructions for Form 1040, line 44 (or in the instructions for Form 1040NR, line 42).

☐ **No.** Complete the rest of Form 1040 or Form 1040NR.

Schedule D (Form 1040) 2016

EXHIBIT 17-5   Continued

Form **8949**	**Sales and Other Dispositions of Capital Assets**	OMB No. 1545-0074
Department of the Treasury Internal Revenue Service	▶ Information about Form 8949 and its separate instructions is at *www.irs.gov/form8949*. ▶ File with your Schedule D to list your transactions for lines 1b, 2, 3, 8b, 9, and 10 of Schedule D.	**2016** Attachment Sequence No. **12A**

Name(s) shown on return	Social security number or taxpayer identification number
Ted & Carol Smith	123 – 45 – 6789

Before you check Box A, B, or C below, see whether you received any Form(s) 1099-B or substitute statement(s) from your broker. A substitute statement will have the same information as Form 1099-B. Either will show whether your basis (usually your cost) was reported to the IRS by your broker and may even tell you which box to check.

Part I   **Short-Term.** Transactions involving capital assets you held 1 year or less are short term. For long-term transactions, see page 2.

Note: You may aggregate all short-term transactions reported on Form(s) 1099-B showing basis was reported to the IRS and for which no adjustments or codes are required. Enter the totals directly on Schedule D, line 1a; you aren't required to report these transactions on Form 8949 (see instructions).

You *must* check Box A, B, *or* C below. Check only one box. If more than one box applies for your short-term transactions, complete a separate Form 8949, page 1, for each applicable box. If you have more short-term transactions than will fit on this page for one or more of the boxes, complete as many forms with the same box checked as you need.

- [X] **(A)** Short-term transactions reported on Form(s) 1099-B showing basis was reported to the IRS (see **Note** above)
- [ ] **(B)** Short-term transactions reported on Form(s) 1099-B showing basis **wasn't** reported to the IRS
- [ ] **(C)** Short-term transactions not reported to you on Form 1099-B

1	**(a)** Description of property (Example: 100 sh. XYZ Co.)	**(b)** Date acquired (Mo., day, yr.)	**(c)** Date sold or disposed of (Mo., day, yr.)	**(d)** Proceeds (sales price) (see instructions)	**(e)** Cost or other basis. See the **Note** below and see *Column (e)* in the separate instructions	**(f)** Code(s) from instructions	**(g)** Amount of adjustment	**(h)** Gain or (loss). Subtract column (e) from column (d) and combine the result with column (g)
						Adjustment, if any, to gain or loss. If you enter an amount in column (g), enter a code in column (f). See the separate instructions.		
	10000 sh. XY Corp.	08/01/13	12/01/15	3,200	4,200			–1,000
2 Totals. Add the amounts in columns (d), (e), (g), and (h) (subtract negative amounts). Enter each total here and include on your Schedule D, **line 1b** (if **Box A** above is checked), **line 2** (if **Box B** above is checked), or **line 3** (if **Box C** above is checked) ▶				3,200	4,200			–1,000

Note: If you checked Box A above but the basis reported to the IRS was incorrect, enter in column (e) the basis as reported to the IRS, and enter an adjustment in column (g) to correct the basis. See *Column (g)* in the separate instructions for how to figure the amount of the adjustment.

For Paperwork Reduction Act Notice, see your tax return instructions.	Cat. No. 37768Z	Form **8949** (2016)

EXHIBIT 17-5   Continued

Form 8949 (2016)   Attachment Sequence No. **12A**   Page **2**

Name(s) shown on return. Name and SSN or taxpayer identification no. not required if shown on other side	Social security number or taxpayer identification number
Ted & Carol Smith	123 – 45 – 6789

Before you check Box D, E, or F below, see whether you received any Form(s) 1099-B or substitute statement(s) from your broker. A substitute statement will have the same information as Form 1099-B. Either will show whether your basis (usually your cost) was reported to the IRS by your broker and may even tell you which box to check.

Part II   **Long-Term.** Transactions involving capital assets you held more than 1 year are long term. For short-term transactions, see page 1.

Note: You may aggregate all long-term transactions reported on Form(s) 1099-B showing basis was reported to the IRS and for which no adjustments or codes are required. Enter the totals directly on Schedule D, line 8a; you aren't required to report these transactions on Form 8949 (see instructions).

You *must* **check Box D, E,** *or* **F below. Check only one box.** If more than one box applies for your long-term transactions, complete a separate Form 8949, page 2, for each applicable box. If you have more long-term transactions than will fit on this page for one or more of the boxes, complete as many forms with the same box checked as you need.

- [X] **(D)** Long-term transactions reported on Form(s) 1099-B showing basis was reported to the IRS (see **Note** above)
- [ ] **(E)** Long-term transactions reported on Form(s) 1099-B showing basis **wasn't** reported to the IRS
- [ ] **(F)** Long-term transactions not reported to you on Form 1099-B

1 (a) Description of property (Example: 100 sh. XYZ Co.)	(b) Date acquired (Mo., day, yr.)	(c) Date sold or disposed of (Mo., day, yr.)	(d) Proceeds (sales price) (see instructions)	(e) Cost or other basis. See the **Note** below and see *Column (e)* in the separate instructions	(f) Code(s) from instructions	(g) Amount of adjustment	(h) Gain or (loss). Subtract column (e) from column (d) and combine the result with column (g)
10000 sh. GB Corp.	12/01/10	12/01/15	3,200	4,600			−1,400
Vacant Land	12/01/08	12/01/15	12,000	5,000			7,000
2 Totals. Add the amounts in columns (d), (e), (g), and (h) (subtract negative amounts). Enter each total here and include on your Schedule D, **line 8b** (if **Box D** above is checked), **line 9** (if **Box E** above is checked), or **line 10** (if **Box F** above is checked) ▶			15,200	9,600			5,600

Note: If you checked Box D above but the basis reported to the IRS was incorrect, enter in column (e) the basis as reported to the IRS, and enter an adjustment in column (g) to correct the basis. See *Column (g)* in the separate instructions for how to figure the amount of the adjustment.

Form **8949** (2016)

EXHIBIT 17-5 | **Continued**

Schedule D Tax Worksheet

Keep for Your Records

Complete this worksheet only if line 18 or line 19 of Schedule D is more than zero. Otherwise, complete the Qualified Dividends and Capital Gain Tax Worksheet in the Instructions for Form 1040, line 44 (or in the Instructions for Form 1040NR, line 42) to figure your tax. Before completing this worksheet, complete Form 1040 through line 43 (or Form 1040NR through line 41).

Exception: Do not use the Qualified Dividends and Capital Gain Tax Worksheet **or** this worksheet to figure your tax if:

- Line 15 or line 16 of Schedule D is zero or less **and** you have no qualified dividends on Form 1040, line 9b (or Form 1040NR, line 10b); **or**
- Form 1040, line 43 (or Form 1040NR, line 41) is zero or less.

Instead, see the instructions for Form 1040, line 44 (or Form 1040NR, line 42).

Ted & Carol Smith   123 – 45 – 6789

#	Description		Amount
1.	Enter your taxable income from Form 1040, line 43 (or Form 1040NR, line 41). (However, if you are filing Form 2555 or 2555-EZ (relating to foreign earned income), enter instead the amount from line 3 of the Foreign Earned Income Tax Worksheet in the Instructions for Form 1040, line 44)	1.	126,730
2.	Enter your qualified dividends from Form 1040, line 9b (or Form 1040NR, line 10b)	2.	
3.	Enter the amount from Form 4952 (used to figure investment interest expense deduction), line 4g	3.	
4.	Enter the amount from Form 4952, line 4e*	4.	
5.	Subtract line 4 from line 3. If zero or less, enter -0-	5.	
6.	Subtract line 5 from line 2. If zero or less, enter -0-**	6.	
7.	Enter the **smaller** of line 15 or line 16 of Schedule D	7.	9,580
8.	Enter the **smaller** of line 3 or line 4	8.	
9.	Subtract line 8 from line 7. If zero or less, enter -0-**	9.	9,580
10.	Add lines 6 and 9	10.	9,580
11.	Add lines 18 and 19 of Schedule D**	11.	3,000
12.	Enter the **smaller** of line 9 or line 11	12.	3,000
13.	Subtract line 12 from line 10	13.	6,580
14.	Subtract line 13 from line 1. If zero or less, enter -0-	14.	120,150
15.	Enter: • $36,250 if single or married filing separately; • $75,300 if married filing jointly or qualifying widow(er); or • $48,600 if head of household	15.	75,300
16.	Enter the **smaller** of line 1 or line 15	16.	75,300
17.	Enter the **smaller** of line 14 or line 16	17.	75,300
18.	Subtract line 10 from line 1. If zero or less, enter -0-	18.	117,150
19.	Enter the **larger** of line 17 or line 18	19.	117,150
20.	Subtract line 17 from line 16. This amount is taxed at 0%.	20.	0

If lines 1 and 16 are the same, skip lines 21 through 41 and go to line 42. Otherwise, go to line 21.

#	Description		Amount
21.	Enter the **smaller** of line 1 or line 13	21.	6,580
22.	Enter the amount from line 20 (if line 20 is blank, enter -0-)	22.	0
23.	Subtract line 22 from line 21. If zero or less, enter -0-	23.	6,580
24.	Enter: • $400,000 if single; • $225,000 if married filing separately; • $450,000 if married filing jointly or qualifying widow(er); or • $425,000 if head of household	24.	470,700
25.	Enter the smaller of line 1 or line 24	25.	126,730
26.	Add lines 19 and 20	26.	117,150
27.	Subtract line 26 from line 25. If zero or less, enter -0-	27.	9,580
28.	Enter the **smaller** of line 23 or line 27	28.	6,580
29.	Multiply line 28 by 15% (.15)	29.	987
30.	Add lines 22 and 28	30.	6,580

If lines 1 and 30 are the same, skip lines 31 through 41 and go to line 42. Otherwise, go to line 31.

EXHIBIT 17-5	Continued

Schedule D Tax Worksheet—*Continued*   Ted & Carol Smith   123 – 45 – 6789

31.	Subtract line 30 from line 21	**31.**	0
32.	Multiply line 31 by 20% (.20)	**32.**	0
	If Schedule D, line 19, is zero or blank, skip lines 33 through 38 and go to line 39. Otherwise, go to line 33.		
33.	Enter the **smaller** of line 9 above or Schedule D, line 19 . . . . **33.**		3,000
34.	Add lines 10 and 19 . . . . **34.** 126,730		
35.	Enter the amount from line 1 above **35.** 126,730		
36.	Subtract line 35 from line 34. If zero or less, enter -0- . . . . **36.**		0
37.	Subtract line 36 from line 33. If zero or less, enter -0- **37.**		3,000
38.	Multiply line 37 by 25% (.25)	**38.**	750
	If Schedule D, line 18, is zero or blank, skip lines 39 through 41 and go to line 42. Otherwise, go to line 39.		
39.	Add lines 19, 20, 28, 31, and 37 . . . . **39.** 126,730		
40.	Subtract line 39 from line 1 . . . . **40.**		0
41.	Multiply line 40 by 28% (.28)	**41.**	0
42.	Figure the tax on the amount on **line 19.** If the amount on line 19 is less than $100,000, use the Tax Table to figure the tax. If the amount on line 19 is $100,000 or more, use the Tax Computation Worksheet	**42.**	20,830
43.	Add lines 29, 32, 38, 41, and 42	**43.**	22,567
44.	Figure the tax on the amount on **line 1.** If the amount on line 1 is less than $100,000, use the Tax Table to figure the tax. If the amount on line 1 is $100,000 or more, use the Tax Computation Worksheet	**44.**	23,225
45.	**Tax on all taxable income (including capital gains and qualified dividends).** Enter the **smaller** of line 43 or line 44. Also include this amount on Form 1040, line 44 (or Form 1040NR, line 42). (If you are filing Form 2555 or 2555-EZ, do not enter this amount on Form 1040, line 44. Instead, enter it on line 4 of the Foreign Earned Income Tax Worksheet in the Form 1040 instructions)	**45.**	22,567

*If applicable, enter instead the smaller amount you entered on the dotted line next to line 4e of Form 4952.

**If you are filing Form 2555 or 2555-EZ, see the footnote in the Foreign Earned Income Tax Worksheet in the Instructions for Form 1040, line 44, before completing this line.

ADDITIONAL RECAPTURE—CORPORATIONS

Corporations generally compute the amount of § 1245 and § 1250 ordinary income recapture on the sales of depreciable assets in the same manner as do individuals. However, Congress added Code § 291 to the tax law in 1982 with the intent of reducing the tax benefits of the accelerated cost recovery of depreciable § 1250 property available to corporate taxpayers. For sales or other taxable dispositions of § 1250 property, corporations must treat as ordinary income 20% of any § 1231 gain *that would have been* ordinary income if § 1245 rather than § 1250 had applied to the transaction.[44] The effect of this provision is to require the taxpayer to recapture 20% of any straight-line depreciation that has not been recaptured under some other provision. Technically, the amount that is treated as ordinary income under § 291 is computed in the following manner:

LO.7

Explain the additional recapture rule applicable only to corporate taxpayers.

Amount that would be treated as ordinary income under § 1245	$xx,xxx
Less: Amount that would be treated as ordinary income § 1250	(x,xxx)
Equals: Difference between recapture amounts	$xx,xxx
Times: Rate specified in § 291	× 20%
Equals: Amount that is treated as ordinary income	$xx,xxx

---

[44] § 291(a)(1).

Example 21

This year K Corporation sold residential rental property for $500,000. The property was purchased for $400,000 in 1986. Assume that K claimed ACRS depreciation of $140,000 (i.e., do not attempt to verify this estimate). Straight-line depreciation would have been $105,000. K's depreciation recapture and § 1231 gain are computed as follows:

Step 1:	Compute realized gain:			
	Sales price			$500,000
	Less: Adjusted basis:			
	Cost	$400,000		
	ACRS depreciation	(140,000)	(260,000)	
	Realized gain			$240,000
Step 2:	Compute *excess depreciation:*			
	Actual depreciation			$140,000
	Straight-line depreciation			(105,000)
	Excess depreciation			$ 35,000
Step 3:	Compute § 1250 depreciation recapture:			
	Lesser of: the realized gain of $240,000 or excess depreciation			$ 35,000
	Section 1250 depreciation recapture			$ 35,000
Step 4:	Compute depreciation recapture if § 1245 applied:			
	Lesser of: the realized gain of $240,000 or actual depreciation $140,000			
	Depreciation recapture if § 1245 applied			$140,000
Step 5:	Compute § 291 ordinary income:			
	Depreciation recapture if § 1245 applied			$140,000
	Section 1250 depreciation recapture			(35,000)
	Excess recapture potential			$105,000
	Times: Section 291 rate			× 20%
	Section 291 ordinary income			$ 21,000
Step 6:	Characterize recognized gain:			
	Section 1250 depreciation recapture			$ 35,000
	Plus: Section 291 ordinary income			21,000
	Ordinary income			$ 56,000
	Realized gain			$240,000
	Less: Ordinary income			(56,000)
	Section 1231 gain			$184,000

Note that without the additional recapture required under § 291, K Corporation would have reported a § 1231 gain of $205,000 ($240,000 total gain – $35,000 § 1250 recapture). If the property had been subject to § 1245 recapture, K Corporation would have only a $100,000 § 1231 gain ($240,000 – $140,000 § 1245 recapture). Section 291 requires that the corporation report 20% of this difference ($205,000 – $100,000 = $105,000 × 20%), or $21,000, as *additional* recapture. Note that this is 20% of the straight-line depreciation that is normally not recaptured on the disposition of non-residential or residential real estate.

> ### Example 22
>
> Assume the same facts as in *Example 21,* except that the property is an office build-ing rather than residential realty *and* straight-line depreciation was elected. An individual taxpayer would report the entire gain of $205,000 ($500,000 – [$400,000 basis – $105,000 straight-line depreciation]) as a § 1231 gain. However, the corporate taxpayer must recapture $21,000 (20% × $105,000 depreciation) as ordinary income under § 291. The remaining $184,000 ($205,000 – $21,000) would be a § 1231 gain.

OTHER RECAPTURE PROVISIONS

There are several other recapture provisions that exist. They include the recapture of farm-land expenditures,[45] recapture of intangible drilling costs,[46] and recapture of gain from the disposition of § 126 property (relating to government cost-sharing program payments for conservation purposes).[47] Another type of recapture is investment credit recapture.[48] This is discussed in detail in Chapter 13.

 ## CHECK YOUR KNOWLEDGE

Review Question 1

True-False. This year T sold equipment for $6,000 (cost $15,000, depreciation $10,000), recognizing a gain of $1,000 ($6,000 – $5,000). To ensure that all of the ordinary deduc-tions obtained from depreciation are recaptured, T must report ordinary income of $10,000 and a capital loss of $9,000, ultimately producing net income of $1,000.

False. This novel approach may seem consistent with Congressional intent, but it is incor-rect. Under § 1245 any gain realized is treated as ordinary income to the extent of any depreciation allowed. As a result, the entire $1,000 is ordinary income. It may be use-ful to think of the depreciation recapture as an adjustment to the depreciation claimed. Depreciation of $10,000 was claimed, but the value of the equipment dropped by $9,000 ($15,000 cost – $6,000 sales price). T claimed an ordinary depreciation deduction of $10,000, and recognized ordinary income of $1,000, for a net ordinary deduction of $9,000.

Review Question 2

True-False. This year L sold a machine and recognized a small gain. Assuming L claimed straight-line depreciation, there is no depreciation recapture.

False. The machine is § 1245 property since it is depreciable personalty. Under the full re-capture rule of § 1245, all depreciation is subject to recapture regardless of the method used.

---

[45] § 1252. [47] § 1255.

[46] § 1254. [48] § 47.

Review Question 3

Several years ago Harry purchased equipment at a cost of $10,000. Over the past three years he claimed and deducted depreciation of $6,000. Assuming that Harry sold the equipment for (1) $7,000, (2) $13,000, or (3) $1,000, determine the amount of gain or loss realized and its character (i.e., ordinary income or § 1231 potential capital gain).

	1	2	3
Amount realized.	$ 7,000	$13,000	$ 1,000
Adjusted basis ($10,000 – $6,000).	– 4,000	– 4,000	– 4,000
Gain (loss) recognized.	$ 3,000	$ 9,000	$ (3,000)

The equipment is § 1245 property since it is depreciable personalty. As a result, the full recapture rule operates and any gain recognized is ordinary income to the extent of any depreciation deducted. In the first case, the entire $3,000 is ordinary income (the lesser of the gain recognized, $3,000, or the recapture potential, $6,000). In the second situation, $6,000 is ordinary income (the lesser of the gain recognized, $9,000, or the recapture potential, $6,000) and $3,000 is § 1231 gain. In the final case, § 1245 does not apply because the property is sold at a loss. Therefore, Harry has a § 1231 loss that is potentially an ordinary loss. Its ultimate treatment depends on the outcome of the § 1231 netting process.

Review Question 4

True-False. In 1990, Sal purchased an office building to rent out. This year she sold the building, recognizing a large gain. The entire gain is a § 1231 gain since there is no recapture under either § 1245 or § 1250.

True. The office build is § 1250 property. The recapture rules of § 1250 apply only when the taxpayer uses an accelerated method, in which case the excess of accelerated depreciation over straight-line is treated as ordinary income. However, since 1987 taxpayers have been required to use the straight-line method in computing depreciation on real estate. As a result, § 1250 is inapplicable and Sal's gain retains its original § 1231 character. Nevertheless, the gain will not be treated as a 15% gain to the extent of any unrecaptured § 1250 depreciation (i.e., all of the straight-line depreciation) but rather 25% gain.

Review Question 5

True-False. In 1997, Z Corporation purchased an office building to rent out. This year the corporation sold the building, recognizing a large gain. The entire gain is a § 1231 gain since there is no recapture under either § 1245 or § 1250.

False. There is no recapture under § 1245 or § 1250. However, under § 291, corporate taxpayers are required to recapture up to 20% of any straight-line depreciation. The 25% rate does not apply to corporate taxpayers.

Review Question 6

True-False. In 1986, the Rose Partnership purchased a new office building to use as its headquarters. This year the partnership sold the building, recognizing a gain of $100,000. The partnership claimed and deducted accelerated depreciation of $40,000. Straight-line depreciation would have been $40,000. The partnership will report ordinary income of zero and § 1231 gain of $100,000.

False. This would be true if the building were § 1250 property, but § 1250 does not apply. Nonresidential real estate such as this office building that was acquired from 1981 through 1986 is treated as § 1245 property and is subject to the full recapture rule if accelerated depreciation was used. In this case, the taxpayer opted for accelerated depreciation, so $40,000 is ordinary income and the remaining $60,000 is a 15% § 1231 gain.

Review Question 7

True-False. In 1984, the Daisy Partnership purchased a new apartment complex to rent out. This year the partnership sold the building, recognizing a gain of $100,000. The partnership claimed and deducted straight-line depreciation of $35,000. Accelerated depreciation would have been $40,000. The partnership will report ordinary income of $35,000 and § 1231 gain of $65,000.

False. In contrast to *Question 6,* the property is residential real estate and is consequently treated as § 1250 property. The partial recapture rule of § 1250 applies only if the taxpayer actually uses an accelerated method. In this case the taxpayer used straight-line, so the recapture rules of § 1250 are not triggered. As a result, the entire $100,000 gain is a § 1231 gain. However, the gain will be a 25% gain to the extent of any unrecaptured § 1250 gain (i.e., the $35,000 straight-line depreciation).

Related Business Issues

INSTALLMENT SALES OF TRADE OR BUSINESS PROPERTY

As discussed in Chapter 14, gains on sales of trade or business property may be deferred using the installment sale method. However, depreciation recapture does not qualify for installment sale treatment. Thus, ordinary income from depreciation recapture must be reported in the year of sale—*regardless* of whether the seller received any payment in that year.[49] Consequently, only the § 1231 gain from such sales will qualify for installment gain deferral.

Example 23

During the year, K sold a rental house for $90,000. According to the terms of the sale, K received $30,000 down and the balance in two equal installments of $30,000 over the next two years. K had purchased the house in 1986 for $60,000 and deducted $20,000 of accelerated depreciation. Had she used the straight-line method, the straight-line depreciation would have been $15,000. K realizes a gain of $50,000 and has $5,000 of § 1250 recapture, computed as follows:

Amount realized	$90,000
Adjusted basis ($60,000 – $20,000)	–40,000
Gain realized	$50,000
Accelerated depreciation on residential real estate acquired before 1987	$20,000
Hypothetical straight-line depreciation.	–15,000
Excess depreciation	$ 5,000

K must report all of the depreciation recapture, $5,000, as ordinary income in the year of the sale. In addition, she must report $15,000 of the remaining gain of $45,000 as a § 1231 gain under the installment sale rules for the year of sale, computed as follows:

$$\frac{\text{Remaining gain, \$45,000}}{\text{Contract price, \$90,000}} \times \text{Payment received \$30,000} = \text{Gain recognized \$15,000}$$

Note that in computing the gross profit ratio, only the remaining gain is used in the numerator and not the entire $50,000 gain realized, as would normally be the case.

---

[49] § 453(i). See Chapter 14 for a detailed discussion of installment reporting.

INTANGIBLE BUSINESS ASSETS

Historically, many purchased intangible assets were not subject to amortization for tax purposes. This was because the life of the assets was indefinite and the amortization deduction was indeterminable. However, § 197 currently allows the amortization (over 15 years) of most *purchased* intangibles acquired after August 11, 1993. No amortization is allowed, of course, for intangibles *developed* by the taxpayer.

For years, conventional thinking was that goodwill and similar intangibles were capital assets. A taxpayer who purchased or developed goodwill and similar intangibles generally recognized capital gain (or loss) to the extent the proceeds of the sale of a business were allocated to them.

All this became much more complex with the passage of § 197. Section 197(e) stipulates that upon the sale or disposition of § 197 assets, they are to be treated as depreciable property.

Private Letter Ruling 200243002 brought clarity to this change. Under this ruling, intangible assets that are not subject to amortization are still treated as capital assets. This applies to assets placed in service on or before August 11, 1993, and any self developed goodwill and other intangibles (with no basis). However, intangibles purchased after August 11, 1993 (i.e., amortizable "§ 197 intangibles") are to be treated as depreciable assets and upon sale they are subject to § 1245 and § 1231 treatment.

Under § 1245, any gain recognized will be ordinary income to the extent of amortization allowed. Any remaining gain or loss will be subject to the netting process under § 1231 and whatever treatment is required after the netting process.

DISPOSITIONS OF BUSINESS ASSETS AND THE SELF-EMPLOYMENT TAX

Gains and losses on the disposition of business assets do not increase or decrease self-employment income. So, even though gains are ordinary income for income tax purposes to the extent of depreciation recapture under § 1245 and § 1250, these amounts are not included in self-employment income.

Tax Planning Considerations

TIMING OF SALES AND OTHER DISPOSITIONS

LO.8

Identify tax planning opportunities related to sales or other dispositions of trade or business property.

Timing the sale of trade or business properties is very important and, from a tax perspective, can be critical. In the simplest case, if a taxpayer has a tax loss or is in a lower tax bracket, any contemplated sales at a gain should be considered to take advantage of the favorable tax result under § 1231. If tax rates are particularly high in the current year, loss transactions should be considered. Any net § 1231 loss is treated as an ordinary deduction for AGI and avoids the $3,000 deduction limit imposed on net capital losses.

In addition, a net § 1231 gain qualifies as a long-term capital gain. For high-income taxpayers with no capital asset transactions or with a net capital gain in the current year, the net § 1231 gain qualifies for the maximum capital gains tax rate of 15 percent. The benefit can be even greater for a taxpayer with substantial capital losses for the year. Because the losses in excess of $3,000 would otherwise be suspended, any net § 1231 gain that would be offset by these losses can be currently recognized at no additional tax cost.

If a taxpayer has recognized or could recognize a § 1231 gain for the year and benefit from § 1231 treatment, additional sales of § 1231 property at a loss should be avoided. Because such losses must be netted against the gains, the favorable treatment of the gains is lost.

The look-back rule must be considered whenever a taxpayer is contemplating the timing of sales of § 1231 gain and loss assets. If no § 1231 losses have been recognized in the past five years, the gain assets should be sold in the current year to receive the favorable treatment of net § 1231 gains. The loss assets can then be sold in the next year and be treated as ordinary losses. This plan will not work, however, if the loss assets are sold first.

Finally, the timing of casualty and theft gains and losses should be considered. Obviously, a taxpayer cannot control the timing of such losses—not legally, anyway. However, the § 1033 gain deferral rules discussed in Chapter 15 may offer some tax planning opportunity.

Because this deferral provision is generally elective, the taxpayer should consider existing § 1231 gains or losses before making a decision to defer gain. For example, a taxpayer with substantial capital losses may decide not to defer a capital gain or § 1231 gain under § 1033 even though the involuntarily converted asset is to be replaced. Immediate recognition of the gain will not have any negative tax consequences because it can be offset by the existing capital losses. The replacement property will have a higher (cost) basis for future depreciation. This plan is much more important to corporate taxpayers because excess capital losses can be carried forward only five years.

SELECTING DEPRECIATION METHODS

The accelerated cost recovery system provides taxpayers with several choices of depreciation methods and conventions. For example, a taxpayer with depreciable personalty may elect to use the straight-line method and either the class life or a longer alternative life. For real estate, an alternative 40-year life may be used.

Effect of Recapture

Generally, a taxpayer should adopt the most rapid method of depreciation available because this results in a deferral of income taxes. Unless tax rates are expected to change significantly in the near future, the tax benefits produced by large depreciation deductions currently allow the taxpayer the use of the money that would otherwise have been used to pay income taxes. In addition, the availability of the like-kind exchange and involuntary conversion provisions eliminates the risk of depreciation recapture when the taxpayer plans to continue in business. It is also important to remember that, for noncorporate taxpayers, there is no depreciation recapture possibility for real estate placed in service after 1986. Because only the straight-line depreciation method can be used, there will be no excess depreciation. However, the unrecaptured § 1250 depreciation is taxed at 25 percent.

Section 179

As discussed in Chapter 9, any § 179 expense amount is treated as depreciation allowed. As a result, the comments above may also apply in deciding whether to claim the option to expense the cost of qualifying property. If more than one qualifying asset is placed in service during the year and their total cost exceeds the annual limit (or reduced limit), the taxpayer must select the assets to be expensed. Obviously, only the assets not expected to be sold should be considered for this option. Given the time value of money, however, it seems unlikely that any taxpayer should forgo the § 179 expense option—unless the additional record keeping is considered to outweigh the current tax benefit.

INSTALLMENT SALES

Installment sales provide an excellent tax deferral possibility. Caution must be exercised, however, if trade or business property is to be sold under a deferred-payment arrangement. Because any depreciation recapture must be reported as income in the year of sale regardless of the amount of money received, taxpayers should require a cash down payment sufficient to pay any income taxes resulting from the depreciation recapture.

SALES OF BUSINESSES

The sale of a business typically involves some recognition of intangible assets, whether it be goodwill, or some similar asset, or other assets such as customer lists. The buyer is generally entitled to amortize the intangibles over 15 years. The seller may have ordinary income, capital gain, and/or § 1231 gain.

The IRS generally is required to recognize agreements between the buyer and the seller as to the value of the various assets in the sale of a business so long as they are reasonable. Thus in negotiating the value of the underlying assets, the buyer should consider the possible deductions related to the purchased assets. For depreciable assets and purchased intangibles, the deductions come in the form of depreciation and amortization. With respect to these assets, the buyer should also evaluate the effects of the depreciation recapture of the assets if they are to be sold in a short period of time.

DISPOSITIONS OF BUSINESS ASSETS AND THE SELF-EMPLOYMENT TAX

Gains on the disposition of business assets do not increase self-employment income. Similarly, losses do not reduce self-employment income. Generally speaking, foregoing allowable depreciation is not really optional since the basis of the depreciable assets must be reduced by depreciation allowed or allowable. So a taxpayer who does not feel like he or she needs the deduction, and realizes that the resulting gain if the asset is sold at a gain will be depreciation recapture, should claim it anyway!

Example 24

D purchased a machine for $4,000 in the current year. The machine qualifies for expensing under § 197. D is uncertain as to whether she should claim the entire $4,000 since she expects to sell the machine for $3,200 the next tax year. Her dilemma involves the fact that the $4,000 is an ordinary deduction and the $3,200 is an ordinary gain. Why not just depreciate the machine? The reason is that by claiming the entire amount, she defers the tax on $3,200 for a year—assuming no change in her marginal tax rate.

Taxpayers paying self-employment tax should normally depreciate assets as rapidly as possible since the depreciation allowed will reduce the self-employment tax, but the future gain on the disposition of the asset is not includible in self-employment income.

Example 25

D, in the prior example, can deduct the full $4,000, reducing her income tax and her self-employment tax. However, when she sells the machine the next year, the gain is subject only to income tax (as ordinary income).

Problem Materials

DISCUSSION QUESTIONS

17-1 *Section 1231 Assets.* What are § 1231 assets? What is the required holding period? Does the § 1231 category of assets include § 1245 and § 1250 assets as well? Elaborate.

17-2 *Excluded Assets.* What type of property is excluded from § 1231 treatment?

17-3 *Section 1231 Netting Process.* Briefly describe the § 1231 netting process. Are personal use assets included in this process?

17-4 *Net § 1231 Gains.* What is the appropriate tax treatment of net § 1231 gains? Are they offset by short-term capital losses? Can they be offset by capital loss carryovers from prior years?

17-5 *Net § 1231 Losses.* What is the appropriate tax treatment of net § 1231 losses? Are they subject to any annual limitation? Can they be used to create or increase a net operating loss for the year?

17-6 *Certain Casualty or Theft Gains and Losses.* Which casualty or theft gains and losses are included in the § 1231 netting process? What is the proper treatment of a net casualty or theft gain? What is the proper treatment of a net casualty or theft loss?

17-7 *Section 1231 Look-Back Rule.* Describe how the § 1231 look-back rule operates. Why do you think Congress enacted such a rule?

17-8 *Section 1245 Property.* What category of trade or business property is subject to § 1245? What depreciable real property has been included in this category?

17-9 *Full Depreciation Recapture—§ 1245.* What is meant by § 1245 recapture potential? Why is this rule sometimes called the full recapture rule? What is the lower limit of § 1245 recapture?

17-10 *Section 1245 Recapture Potential.* During the current year Z sold a vacuum used in his pool-cleaning business. The vacuum had cost $3,600 three years ago, and he had expensed the entire amount under § 179.
a. How much is the § 1245 recapture potential with respect to this vacuum?
b. If the vacuum was sold for $900, what is the character of the gain?

17-11 *Asset Classification.* When will the sale or other disposition of depreciable equipment be subject to both § 1231 and § 1245? What is the appropriate treatment of any loss from the sale of such equipment?

17-12 *Section 1245 Property.* F gave property with § 1245 recapture potential to his daughter, D. Will F be required to recapture any of the depreciation previously claimed? How must D characterize any gain she might recognize on a subsequent disposition of the property?

17-13 *Section 1245 Recapture Potential.* What happens to the § 1245 recapture potential when property is disposed of in a like-kind exchange?

17-14 *Section 179 Expense Treatment.* Explain the proper tax treatment of any gain recognized on the disposition of an asset that the taxpayer had earlier elected to expense under § 179. Does this mean that any amounts ever deducted under § 179 will always be subject to recapture? Explain.

17-15 *Section 1250 Property.* Is land included in the definition of § 1250 property? Is any real property depreciated under the straight-line method included in this definition?

17-16 *Section 1250 Property.* Is nonresidential real estate acquired after 1980 always § 1250 property? Explain.

17-17 *Section 1250 Property.* Why will depreciable real property placed in service after 1986 never be subject to § 1250 recapture? How is the un-recaptured depreciation treated?

17-18 *Section 1250 Recapture Potential.* Why is § 1250 sometimes called the partial recapture rule? Will the § 1250 recapture potential ever simply disappear? Explain.

17-19 *Section 1250 Recapture Potential.* This year Y sold a duplex that she had rented out for several years. The house had cost $40,000 20 years earlier and depreciation expense of $27,000 has been claimed. Straight-line depreciation would have been $24,500.
a. How much is the § 1250 recapture potential with respect to the duplex?
b. If the duplex was sold for $75,000, what is the character of Y's gain and how is it taxed?

17-20 *Additional Recapture—§ 291.* Briefly describe the additional depreciation recapture rule of § 291.
a. Which taxpayers are subject to this rule?
b. Compare this to the special rate for un-recaptured depreciation on § 1250 property for individual taxpayers.

17-21 *Section 291 Recapture.* Can a corporation that has always elected to use the straight-line depreciation method for all real property ever be subject to additional recapture under § 291? Explain.

17-22 *Reporting § 1231 Transactions.* What tax form does a taxpayer use to report the results of § 1231 transactions? How is any depreciation recapture reported on this form?

17-23 *Planning § 1231 Transactions.* Under what circumstances should a taxpayer with an involuntary conversion gain from business property consider not electing to defer the gain under § 1033?

17-24 *Planning § 1231 Transactions.* A taxpayer plans to trade in depreciable property in order to acquire new property but is quite disappointed to find that his old equipment is worth less than its unrecovered cost basis. He is currently in the top marginal tax bracket and has no capital gains or losses or other § 1231 transactions for the year. What tax advice would you offer this taxpayer concerning the planned exchange?

17-25 *Installment Sales and Depreciation Recapture.* Briefly describe how recapture is reported when either § 1245 property or § 1250 property is disposed of in an installment sale. What tax planning should a taxpayer undertake concerning such sales?

PROBLEMS

17-26 *Characterizing Assets.* Indicate whether the following gains and losses are § 1231 gains or losses or capital gains and losses or neither. Make your determination prior to the § 1231 netting process.

a. Printing press used in A's business; held for three years and sold at a loss.
b. Goodwill sold as part of the sale of B's business.
c. Vacant lot used five years as a parking lot in C's business; sold at a gain.
d. House, 80% of which is D's home and 20% of which is used as a place of business; held 15 years and sold at a gain.
e. Camera used in E's business; held for 10 months and sold at a gain.
f. Land used by F for 10 years as a farm and sold at a loss.
g. Personal residence sold at a loss.

17-27 *Section 1231.* During the year H sold the following assets, both of which had been held for several years:

Asset	Gain (loss)
Vacant land held for investment	$52,000
Equipment used in his business.	(12,000)

Determine how much capital gain or loss and the amount of ordinary income or loss that H will report for the year. At what rate will the gain, if any, be taxed?

17-28 *Section 1231 Netting.* G operates the Corner Bar and Grill as a sole proprietorship. During the year he sold the following assets, all of which had been held for several years:

Asset	Gain (loss)
IBM stock.	$(12,000)
Land and building used in the business. . .	34,000
Equipment used in the business	(3,000)

The building had been acquired in 1993. Straight-line depreciation claimed and deducted with respect to the building was $8,000. Straight-line depreciation on the equipment was $4,000. Determine how much capital gain or loss as well as the amount of ordinary income or loss that G will report for the year and explain how they will be taxed.

17-29 *Involuntary Conversions and § 1231.* Assume the same facts as in *Problem 17-28.* In addition, G's records revealed the following information:
- A portion of the grill's parking lot was condemned by the city when it decided to expand the adjacent street. G pocketed the cash and recognized a gain of $5,000.
- A pool table was destroyed as part of a barroom brawl. G realized a casualty loss of $2,000.

Determine how much capital gain or loss as well as the amount of ordinary income or loss that G will report for the year. At what rate will the recognized gain, if any, be taxed?

17-30 *Section 1231 Hodgepodge.* For 30 years Rae has operated The General Store, a hardware store in Columbus. Rae runs the business as a sole proprietorship. During the year, she recognized the following gains and losses from assets held several years:

1. Uninsured warehouse burned down: $10,000 loss.
2. Equipment stolen $190,000 gain (ignore depreciation).
3. Parking lot sold: $120,000 gain.
4. IBM stock sold capital loss of $70,000.
5. Condemnation of land: $1,000 gain.

Determine how much capital gain or loss as well as the amount of ordinary income or loss that Rae will report for the year. At what rate will the gain, if any, be taxed?

17-31 *Section 1231 Lookback.* J has recognized the following § 1231 gains and losses in the current year (2017) and since the inception of his business:

Year	Net § 1231 Gain (Loss)
2017	$50,000
2016	12,000
2015	(35,000)
2014	0
2013	65,000
2012	(13,000)

How will J treat the $50,000 gain for the current year?

17-32 *Section 1231—Timber.* A owns timber land that she purchased in 1991. During the current calendar tax year, the timber was cut and A elected § 631 treatment for the gain. Her cost assignable to the timber was $25,000 and its fair market value on January 1 of this year was $40,000. The actual sales price of the cut timber when it was sold was $55,000.
   a. How much is A's gain or loss recognized and what is its character?
   b. Can A deduct the costs of cutting the timber?

17-33 *Section 1231—Unharvested Crops.* This year L sold her farmland, which she had owned for 20 years. L had made minor improvements to the farm and had used straightline depreciation to depreciate them. No personal property was sold with the farm. The sales price was $80,000 and L's adjusted basis was $36,000. The unharvested crops on the land represented $8,000 of the sales price, and L had spent $3,200 in producing the crop to the point of sale.
   a. How does L report the gain or loss from the sale of the farm?
   b. If L has no other sales of trade or business property or of capital assets, how much of the gain is included in her taxable income?

17-34 *Section 1245 Recapture.* During the current year, D sold a drill press he had used in his wood shop business for three years. D had purchased the press for $820 and had deducted depreciation of $476. Straight-line depreciation would have been $410. Determine the amount and character of gain or loss to D under each of the following circumstances below:
   a. The press is sold for $500.
   b. The press is sold for $100.
   c. The press is sold for $900.

17-35 *Section 1245 Recapture.* This year N sold three different pieces of equipment used in her business:

Description	Holding Period	Sales Price	Cost	Depreciation Allowed
Processing machine	3 years	$1,200	$1,400	$600
Work table	4 years	1,600	1,300	500
Automatic stapler	2 years	500	900	300

What are the amount and character of N's gain or loss from these transactions?

17-36 *Section 1245 Recapture.* Fill in the missing information for each of the three independent sales of § 1245 assets identified below. Enter a dollar amount or n/a (for not applicable) in each blank space.

	Assets		
	A	B	C
Sales price...	$105	$ 90	$____
Cost...	100	125	100
Depreciation allowed	30	____	30
Depreciation recapture.................................	____	____	20
Section 1231 gain or (loss)	____	(10)	____

17-37 *Basis Reductions.* Dr. T purchased a treadmill for use in his cardiology practice for $13,000 on August 14, 2015. T claimed § 179 expense of $10,000 and depreciation of $429 in 2014. The depreciation for 2016 and 2017 is $735 and $524, respectively. T sold the treadmill on January 13, 2017 for $3,500,

a. What are the amount and character of T's gain on the sale?

b. What would be your answer if the unit had been sold for $13,500?

17-38 *Section 1250 Recapture.* Fill in the missing information for each of the three independent sales of § 1250 assets identified below. Enter a dollar amount or n/a (for not applicable) in each blank space.

	Assets		
	X	Y	Z
Sales price.	$100	$___	$200
Cost	135	100	100
Depreciation allowed	55	___	30
Straight-line depreciation	___	20	___
Depreciation recapture	0	10	___
Section 1231 gain or (loss)	___	30	120

17-39 *Real Property Acquired after 1986.* V sold an office building in the current year that she had purchased for $60,000 two years earlier. Depreciation of $4,127 was claimed before the building was sold for $75,000. Determine V's gain, its character and the rate at which it will be taxed?

17-40 *Depreciation Recapture.* K purchased a warehouse on January 18, 1986 for $50,000 ($10,000 allocable to the land and $40,000 allocable to the building). The property was 19-year realty and was depreciated using the 175% declining balance method and mid-month convention. The unit was sold on January 15 of the current year for $120,000 ($30,000 allocable to the land and $90,000 allocable to the building). At the time the property was sold, the building was fully depreciated (i.e., K deducted depreciation of $40,000 while holding the property).

a. Determine K's gain, its character and the rate at which it will be taxed.

b. If K had used the straight-line method and a 19-year life under ACRS, the depreciation deductions would have been the same, $40,000. Determine K's gain, its character and the rate at which it will be taxed.

c. What would be your answer to (b) if K were a corporation?

17-41 *Depreciation Recapture.* Happy Acres operates a small organic farm. In the current year, it sold some of its land including a barn for $500,000. The company purchased the property seven years earlier for $300,000. The barn is used for multiple purposes (e.g., storage of hay, tractors, equipment, animals). For MACRS, multi-purpose agricultural buildings are considered 20-year property and are depreciated using the 150% declining balance method (§ 168(b)(2)(A)). Assume accelerated depreciation deducted was $125,000 and straight-line depreciation would have been $105,000. For the following questions, ignore the land.

a. Compute the amount of gain realized and its character.

b. What amount of the gain, if any, is taxed at 25 percent?

c. What would your answer to (a) be if the company is a corporation?

17-42 *Depreciation Recapture.* JWP Development, an LLC, built a hotel in downtown Chicago in 1980 at a cost of $700,000. It depreciated the building using an accelerated method over a useful life of 40 years. This year it sold the building for $1,000,000. At the time of the sale, the company had deducted accelerated depreciation of $400,000. Straight-line depreciation on the building would have been $150,000. (Do not try to verify these amounts.)

a. What is the amount of the company's gain and what is its character?

b. What amount of the gain, if any, will be taxed at a 25% rate?

c. If the company had used the straight-line method, what would be the amount and character of the gain? At what rate would the gain be treated?

d. What would be your answer to (a) if JWP were a corporation?

17-43 *Installment Sales and Recapture.* Assume the same facts as in *Problem 17-42* except that Z sold the property under an installment contract with $100,000 down and $100,000 in each of the next nine years along with reasonable interest. How much gain would Z report in the year of sale and the following year and what is its character?

17-44 *Unrecaptured § 1250 Gain.* B purchased a small warehouse for $45,000 in 2013. This year he sold the property for $62,000. He had deducted straight-line depreciation of $6,500 on the property prior to the sale. What is the amount of gain, if any, and how will it be taxed?

17-45 *Twenty-Five Percent Gains.* V had the following gains and losses for the current year:

Section 1250 recapture	$2,000
Net § 1231 gains.	6,000
Net short-term capital loss.	(3,000)

V's § 1231 gain was from a building that was held 15 years. The total depreciation allowed was $5,000. How much are V's *15% gains* and *25% gains,* respectively?

17-46 *Section 1231 Gain and Look-Back Rule.* R sold land and a building used in farming for many years at a gain of $30,000 during 2017. No other sales or dispositions of § 1231 assets were made during the year. The § 1250 depreciation recapture for the building was zero and the unrecaptured depreciation was $1,000.
   a.   How is R's gain to be reported if he had a net § 1231 gain of $10,000 in 2014, a net § 1231 loss of $12,000 in 2015, and no § 1231 transactions in 2016?
   b.   How would your answer to (a) differ if the sale of the property had resulted in a loss of $7,500?

17-47 *Section 1231 and Depreciation Recapture.* Fill in the missing information for each of the separate sales of § 1231 assets indicated below. Enter a dollar amount or n/a (for not applicable) in each blank space.

	Land	Building	Machine	Machine
Sales price.	$100	$ ___	$ 90	$ ___
Cost	140	100	125	100
Depreciation allowed	0	30	___	30
Straight-line depreciation	0	20	___	___
Depreciation recapture	___	___	___	___
Section 1231 gain or (loss)	___	30	(10)	5

17-48 *Depreciation Recapture and the § 1231 Netting Process.* T had three § 1231 transactions during the current year. All of the assets were held for several years.
   a.   Theft of electric cart used on business premises. The cart was worth $600, originally cost $800, and had an adjusted basis of $425.
   b.   Sale of equipment used in manufacturing. The equipment sold for $5,500, originally cost $8,000, and had an adjusted basis of $4,250.
   c.   Sale of land and a small building used for storage. The property was sold for $60,000, originally cost $56,000, and had an adjusted basis of $42,500. Straightline depreciation was claimed on the building.

Determine the amount of ordinary income or loss and capital gain or loss that T must report from these transactions for the current year.

17-49 *Section 1231 Transactions.* K has the following business assets that she is interested in selling in either 2017 or 2018.

	Fair Market Value	Basis
Manufacturing equipment	$220,000	$400,000
Factory building	350,000	220,000
Land used for factory	450,000	120,000

Straight-line depreciation of $60,000 was claimed on the factory. K has never sold any other § 1231 assets.

a.   What are the tax results if K sells the land and building in 2017 and the equipment in 2018?
b.   What are the tax results if K sells the equipment in 2017 and the land and building in 2018?
c.   What are the tax results if K sells all the assets in 2017?

17-50 *Comprehensive Problem for Capital Asset and Trade or Business Property Transactions.* T owned a number of apartment units and sold several properties related to that trade or business during the current year as follows:

Description	Holding Period	Sales Price	Cost	Depreciation Allowed	Method
Apartment unit, including land (straight-line depreciation = $2,400)...	3 years	$65,000	$24,000	$3,000	DB
Lawn tractor......................	5 years	1,000	3,000	2,600	SL
Spray painter	2 years	500	1,400	600	SL

During a severe winter storm, T also lost a depreciable motor scooter used in his business. The scooter, which was owned by T for two years and used exclusively in the business, had cost $2,600 and had an adjusted basis of $1,750.

In addition, T sold several capital assets during the current year as follows:

Description	Holding Period	Sales Price	Adjusted Basis
100 shares LM Corp.	16 months	$2,000	$1,000
75 shares PL, Inc.	8 months	1,600	6,000
Silver ingots	6 years	2,600	6,000

Assuming T has never deducted § 1231 losses before, calculate the following amounts based on the above information:

a.   The amount of § 1245 recapture and § 1250 recapture, if any.
b.   The net § 1231 gain or loss.
c.   The capital gain or loss and the rate at which it is taxed.
d.   The net short-term capital gain or loss.
e.   The overall impact of the above transactions on T's adjusted gross income.

17-51 *Netting Gains and Losses.* G had the following gains and losses for the current calendar year:

DFG Corporation stock held 3 years..................	$4,000
Gold held 6 years.................................	(5,000)
Sale of business building:	
Section 1250 recapture.........................	1,500
Section 1231 gain.............................	7,000

Depreciation of $7,500 had been claimed on the building. What is the character of these gains in calculating the capital gains tax?

17-52 *Capital Gains Tax.* C, an unmarried head of household, has the following gains and losses for the current taxable year:

GHJ, Inc. stock held 16 months	$(3,000)
Land held for investment 15 years	4,000
Sale of business real estate held 15 years:	
Section 1250 recapture	1,800
Net § 1231 gain	7,250

Depreciation claimed on the real estate was $7,800. C's taxable income (properly calculated and including the information above) is $121,900. How much is C's income tax for the current calendar year?

17-53 *Comprehensive Problem with Sales of Business Use Assets.* O and P are married. They have no dependents and elect to file jointly for the current year. They recently decided to retire, sell their home, and try renting for a while. Their income and related transactions for the year follow:

Ordinary income from business	$ 45,200
Interest income	10,100
Sale of personal residence of 20 years:	
Sales price	$760,000
Selling costs	43,000
Adjusted basis	195,000
Sale of business:	
Section 1245 recapture	15,000
Section 1250 recapture	26,000
Section 1231 gain	90,000
Gain on sale of stock held five years	16,000
Itemized deductions (after 2% cutback)	23,400

O and P had claimed depreciation on the § 1245 property and the § 1250 property in the amount of $25,000 and $56,000, respectively. Calculate O and P's adjusted gross income, taxable income, and gross income tax for the current year.

17-54 *Sections 1231 and 1245 Property.* The terms § 1231 property and § 1245 property are often used interchangeably. However, there are times when a specific asset can be classified as (1) *both* § 1231 and § 1245 property; (2) only § 1231 property; or (3) only § 1245 property. Based on the values assigned to the letters below, indicate the appropriate classification for each of the following mathematical expressions.

> Let: X = asset's original cost
>   Y = depreciation claimed
>   Z = asset's adjusted basis
>   T = amount realized on sale

  a. If T Z, asset is § _____ property.
  b. If T > X, asset is § _____ property.
  c. If X > T < Z, asset is § _____ property.
  d. If Y > T > Z, asset is § _____ property.

17-55 *Sections 1231 and 1250 Property.* It is possible that (1) *both* § 1231 and § 1250 apply to the sale of depreciable real property, (2) only § 1250 applies, or (3) only § 1231 applies. Based on the values assigned to the letters below, indicate which Code sections apply for each of the following mathematical expressions.

> Let: X = asset's original cost
>   Y = depreciation claimed
>   Z = asset's adjusted basis
>   T = amount realized on sale
>   S = amount of straight-line depreciation

  a. If Y > S and T Z, § _____ applies.
  b. If Y > S and T > X, § _____ applies.
  c. If Y = S, § _____ applies.
  d. If Y > S and (T − Z) (Y − S), § _____ applies.

17-56   *Sale of Property Converted from Personal Use—Comprehensive Problem.* L owned and used a house as her personal residence since she purchased it in 2012 for $110,000. On February 11, 2015, when it was worth $85,000, L moved out and converted the property into a rental property. She rented the house until December 15, 2017, when it was sold for $104,500.

    a. Determine L's depreciation deductions for the rental property from the time it was converted in 2015 until it was sold in 2017. Ignore land value.

    b. What are the amount and character of L's gain or loss to be recognized from the sale?

17-57   *Sale of Property Converted to Personal Use—Comprehensive Problem.* Z purchased a computer system with peripherals for $14,500 on August 12, 2014. The system was used exclusively in his business. In October 2017, when the computer was worth $8,200, Z closed the business and began using the unit for personal purposes.

    a. Determine Z's depreciation deductions for the computer system from the time it was purchased until it was converted to personal use, assuming that he elected the maximum § 179 expensing option for other assets placed into service in 2014.

    b. Assume the computer system was sold for $5,400 on May 15, 2017 rather than being converted to personal use. What are the amount and character of Z's loss?

TAX RESEARCH PROBLEMS

17-58   *Capital Assets versus § 1231 Assets.* R inherited a residence that had been used exclusively by her grandmother as a principal residence for 30 years. Upon receiving the property, R immediately offered the property for rent and rented to several tenants. After several months, R encountered an interesting potential business venture that would require a substantial capital investment. After an agonizing decision, she proceeded to sell her inherited rental unit. The unit was sold at a loss and R deducted the loss under § 1231. Since she had no § 1231 gains, the loss was deducted as an ordinary deduction. Is the treatment R chose the appropriate treatment for the loss? Does the character of the property to her grandmother carry over to R, resulting in disallowance of the loss or capital loss treatment?

    Research aids:

        Campbell v. Comm., 5 T.C. 272 (1945).

        Mary E. Crawford, 16 T.C. 678 (1951), acq. 1951-2 C.B. 2.

17-59   *Business Use of Personal Residence.* J purchased a home in March 1999 for $120,000. Twenty percent of its cost was attributable to the land. From the date of purchase until March 2012, 20% of the house was used as a home-office, the costs of which were properly deducted annually (including depreciation). The home was used exclusively as J's residence from April 2012 until the house was sold for $325,000 on November 15, 2017.

    a. J used the straight-line method and the normal useful life of 32.5 years (applicable at the time, it would be 39 years for property placed in service currently). What amount of depreciation did he claim over the 15-year period that the property was used as a home-office?

    b. Is there any depreciation recapture to be reported if gain is reported on the sale?

    c. Is there depreciation recapture to be reported if all or part of the gain is excluded?

Employee Compensation and Taxation of Business Forms

18

Employee Compensation and Retirement Plans

Learning Objectives

Upon completion of this chapter you will be able to:

LO.1 Distinguish between taxable and nontaxable employee fringe benefits.

LO.2 Explain the tax treatment of the receipt of property for services.

LO.3 Explain the advantages and disadvantages of qualified retirement plans.

LO.4 Distinguish between a defined benefit plan and a defined contribution plan.

LO.5 Explain the requirements associated with qualified retirement plans.

LO.6 Explain the special qualified plans available for self-employed individuals.

LO.7 Describe various qualified plans for employees such as § 401(k) plans and individual retirement accounts.

LO.8 Describe nonqualified deferred compensation plans.

LO.9 Determine the tax consequences of the issuance and exercise of both nonqualified and qualified stock options.

Chapter Outline

Introduction

For a large majority of individual taxpayers, compensation received for services rendered as an employee is the most significant, if not the only, source of taxable income. Because of this significance, the topic of taxation of employee compensation is of primary interest to the tax-paying public. Employee compensation consists not only of cash wage and salary payments but an incredible variety of compensation "packages" designed to accommodate the needs and desires of employer and employee alike.

The tax consequences to both the employer and employee of various types of employment compensation are examined in this chapter. Because the concept of compensation includes provisions for employee retirement income, the chapter also includes a discussion of the numerous types of retirement income plans available to both employees and self-employed taxpayers.

Taxation of Current Compensation

Under the broad authority of § 61, a taxpayer's gross income includes all compensation for services rendered including wages, salaries, fees, fringe benefits, sales commissions, customer tips, and bonuses. Compensatory payments may be made in a medium other than cash. For example, payment for services rendered may be made with property, such as marketable securities. In such cases, the fair market value of the property is the measure of the gross compensation income received.[1]

Payment for services performed by Taxpayer A for Taxpayer B could consist of services performed by Taxpayer B for Taxpayer A. For example, a lawyer might agree to draft a will for a carpenter, who in turn agrees to repair the lawyer's roof. As a result of such a *service swap,* both taxpayers must recognize gross income equal to the value of the services received.[2]

STATUTORY FRINGE BENEFITS

LO.1

Distinguish between taxable and nontaxable employee fringe benefits.

As a general rule, any economic benefit bestowed on an employee by his or her employer that is intended to compensate the employee for services rendered represents gross income. This is true whether the benefit is in the form of a direct cash payment or an indirect noncash benefit that nonetheless improves the recipient's economic position.

Certain indirect or *fringe benefits,* however, are excludable from gross income under specific statutory authority. The following is a list of nontaxable fringe benefits and the authority for their exclusion from income. The details of these exclusions are discussed in Chapter 6.

---

[1] Reg. § 1.61-2(d).   [2] *Ibid.*

1. Employer payment of employee group-term life insurance premiums (up to $50,000 of coverage)—§ 79.

2. Employer contributions to employee accident or health plans—§ 106.

3. Amounts paid to an employee under an employer's medical expense reimbursement plan—§ 105(b).

4. Employee meals or lodging furnished for the convenience of the employer—§ 119.

5. Amounts received under an employer's group legal services program—§ 120.

6. Amounts received under an employer's educational assistance program—§ 127.

7. Amounts received under an employer's dependent care assistance program—§ 129.

8. No-additional-cost services, qualified employee discounts, working condition fringes, and *de minimis* fringes—§ 132.

The length of the above list demonstrates Congressional tolerance for the use of innovative fringe benefits to attract employees. Employers who want to design the most flexible compensation package for employees who have differing compensation needs may use a *cafeteria plan* of employee benefits. Under a cafeteria plan, an employee is allowed to choose among two or more benefits consisting of both cash and statutory nontaxable benefits.[3]

Deferred Compensation

Deferral of compensation can be accomplished under a variety of methods that includes both "qualified" and "nonqualified" plans. A qualified plan is one that meets the requirements of Code § 401(a) and offers the employer a current deduction for money set aside for the eventual benefit of the employee. In this manner, the employees are not taxed on the amount set aside until it is distributed to them, and the income earned on the funds is exempt from tax. A nonqualified plan, on the other hand, does not possess all the specialized tax benefits, but offers a plan that is easier to administer and allows for discrimination among employees. Some of the more popular types of each of these plans are listed in Exhibit 18-1.

The purpose of deferred compensation plans is to allow employees to receive income at a later date when, presumably, they will have much less income. The employee's tax objective in participating in such an arrangement is to ensure that they will be taxed only when payments are received under the plan or agreement. The employer's tax objective is to offer a vehicle that will attract and compensate key personnel while obtaining a current tax deduction for any funds set aside for these employees.

Changes in the tax law, specifically the 1986 Tax Reform Act, reduced some of the glamour of deferred arrangements through its repeal of the capital gains differential and compression of the individual-corporate tax rate structure. However, subsequent legislation has reinstated a modest resurgence in plan activity due to the prospects of a widening capital gain differential and a probable increase in tax rates. Nevertheless, while the 1986 Act reduced the tax benefits of qualified plans, it is still possible to achieve both deferral of taxation and capital gains treatment on the eventual distribution of funds to the employee. However, most deferred compensation arrangements are not ordinarily utilized as vehicles to recharacterize the form of income.

While numerous deferred compensation arrangements focus on tax benefits, most qualified plans are flexible and have a wide range of purposes other than reducing an employee's tax liability. For example, a retirement benefit program can have a substantial psychological impact on an employee's morale because it offers an effortless program of saving for the future. In addition, a nonqualified deferred compensation arrangement can be tailored to attract and compensate new executives for benefits they may have forfeited when they left their former employer. Finally, both qualified and nonqualified deferred compensation plans can provide other benefits, such as disability guarantees, death benefits, income security, and plan loans, to safeguard and preserve the well-being of the company's most valued asset—its employees.

[3] § 125.

EXHIBIT 18-1	Types of Deferred Compensation Plans

Qualified Plans:
      Defined contribution plans
      Defined benefit plans
      Money purchase plans
      Stock bonus plans
      Employee stock ownership plans
      Cash or deferred arrangements [§ 401(k)]
      Simplified employee plans
      Individual retirement accounts
      Incentive stock options
      SIMPLE plans

Nonqualified Plans:
      Restricted stock
      Deferred payments
      Rabbi trusts
      Secular trusts
      Nonqualified stock options

Receipt of Property for Services

LO.2

Explain the tax treatment of the receipt of property for services.

From a corporate employer's point of view, any form of employee compensation that somehow strengthens that employee's commitment to the corporation is highly desirable. One such type of compensation is a payment made in the capital stock of the corporation itself. Such payment converts the employee into a stockholder and gives him or her an equity interest in the future prosperity of the corporation.

When stock in the corporate employer is used to compensate employees, it is typical for the employment contract to provide that the employee must continue to work for the corporation for some stated time period before he or she is given unrestricted ownership of the stock. If the employee leaves the job before the period expires, the stock received will be forfeited. In this situation, the tax consequences of the compensatory payment to both employee and employer are governed by § 83.

GENERAL RULE OF § 83

If in connection with the performance of services, property of any type is transferred to any person other than the person for whom such services are performed, § 83(a) provides that the fair market value of such property shall be included in the gross income of the person performing such services. If the recipient made any payment for the property, only the excess of the property's value over the amount of such payment is includible gross income. Such inclusion shall occur in the first taxable year in which the rights of the person having the beneficial interest in such property are *transferable* or are not subject to a *substantial risk of forfeiture,* whichever is applicable. If the property received for services is not immediately transferable by the recipient or is subject to risk of forfeiture, it is referred to as *restricted property.*

Regulation § 1.83-3(c)(1) explains that a substantial risk of forfeiture exists when the ownership of the transferred property is conditioned, directly or indirectly, upon the future performance (or refraining from performance) of substantial services by the recipient. The Regulation also states that the existence of a substantial risk of forfeiture can only be determined by examining the facts and circumstances of the specific situation.

Under § 83(h), a taxpayer that pays for services using property is entitled to a deduction equal to the fair market value of the property. The deduction must be taken in the taxable year in which (or with which) ends the taxable year in which the value of the property is recognized as gross income to the recipient.

Example 1

Corporation M is on a fiscal year ending June 30. On November 1, 2013, the corporation gave employee E, a calendar year taxpayer, 100 shares of its own stock worth $100 per share as compensation for E's services to Corporation M. If E leaves M's employ for any reason during the three-year period beginning on November 1, 2013, he must return the shares. On November 2, 2016, E is still employed and the risk of forfeiture of the stock lapses. On this date the stock is worth $120 per share. For his taxable year 2016, E must include $12,000 in gross income; his tax basis in his shares will also be $12,000. Corporation M has a deduction of $12,000 for its fiscal year ending June 30, 2017.

The Regulations make it clear that a deduction is available to the transferor of the property only if the transfer is an expense meeting the deductibility requirements of § 162 or § 212. If the transfer constitutes a capital expenditure, it must be capitalized rather than deducted.[4]

Example 2

Refer to the facts in *Example 1*. If the shares were transferred to E because E performed organizational services for Corporation M, the corporation must capitalize the $12,000 amount included in E's gross income.

THE § 83(b) ELECTION

Section 83(b) gives a taxpayer who has performed services for *restricted* property an interesting option. Within 30 days of the receipt of the property, the taxpayer may choose to include its fair market value in his or her current year's gross income. This election accelerates the recognition of gross income to the taxpayer. However, the election could be beneficial if the property were rapidly appreciating in value and consequently would have a higher fair market value on the date the risk of forfeiture or other restrictions are scheduled to lapse.

Example 3

In 2014, employee Z receives property worth $10,000 as payment for services rendered. The property is subject to a substantial risk of forfeiture, but Z elects to include the $10,000 value in her 2014 gross income. In 2016, when the risk of forfeiture lapses, the property is worth $25,000. However, Z has no gross income attributable to the property in 2016. Z will have a $10,000 basis in her stock, and Z's employer has a $10,000 deduction for its taxable year that includes December 31, 2014.

The election is not without risk. If the property depreciates during the forfeiture period, the election leads to a larger gross income inclusion as well as acceleration of tax recognition. And more costly still, if the property is in fact forfeited, the taxpayer receives no deduction for the original gross income inclusion.[5] Obviously, the decision to use the § 83(b) election requires a careful analysis of both the current and expected future value of the property, current and future marginal tax rates, and the nature of the restriction involved.

---

[4] Reg. § 1.83-6(a)(4). [5] § 83(b)(1).

Qualified Retirement Plans for Corporations

LO.3

Explain the advantages and disadvantages of qualified retirement plans.

Historically, Congress has viewed with favor the establishment of employer retirement plans as part of a total compensation package offered to employees. The existence of an employer designed and administered plan encourages the young employee to think seriously about his or her retirement years and offers the employee a most convenient way to provide financially for such retirement.

Congress provided an extremely attractive set of tax benefits available to *qualified* employer retirement plans as part of the Internal Revenue Code of 1954. Since the enactment of the 1954 Code, the scope of the benefits has been periodically expanded, and Congress has made different forms of qualified plans available to an ever-increasing number of individual taxpayers. Before examining the various types of qualified plans and the specific features of each, it will be useful to analyze the two basic tax benefits associated with qualified plans for employees—the tax-free nature of employer contributions and the tax-free growth of these contributions.

TAX BENEFITS OF QUALIFIED PLANS

When an employer makes a current contribution to a *qualified* retirement plan on behalf of an employee, §§ 402(a) and 403(a) provide that the value of the contribution is not includible gross income to the employee, even though the employee has obviously received additional compensation in the form of the contribution. In contrast, if the contribution was made by the employer to a *nonqualified* retirement plan in which the employee had a vested interest, the employee would have additional gross income equal to the value of the contribution. As a result, the net amount saved toward retirement by the employee participating in a nonqualified plan is less than the amount saved by the employee participating in a qualified plan.

The second major benefit of qualified retirement plans is that the earnings generated by employer contributions are nontaxable. Sections 401(a) and 501(a) provide that a trust created to manage and invest employer contributions to a qualified retirement plan is exempt from tax.

EXHIBIT 18-2	Comparison of Nonqualified versus Qualified Retirement Plans' Year-End Values of Employer Contributions	
	Nonqualified Plan A	Qualified Plan B
Year 1..	$ 7,500	$ 10,000
Year 2..	15,675	21,200
Year 15...	220,208*	372,800**

  * $7,500 × 29.361 (factor for the sum of an annuity of $1.00 at 9% for 15 years)
** $10,000 × 37.280 (factor for the sum of an annuity of $1.00 at 12% for 15 years)

The effect of these two benefits on the total amount of savings available to an employee at retirement is illustrated in Exhibit 18-2. The exhibit compares two retirement plans, A and B. The plans are identical in every respect but one—A is a nonqualified personal savings plan while B is a qualified employer's trust. The exhibit is based on the following assumptions:

1. The employer will make an annual $10,000 contribution to the plan on behalf of the employee.

2. The employee has a 25% marginal tax rate. Therefore, the net amount saved by the employee in Plan A is only $7,500 ($10,000 − $2,500 tax on the current compensation represented by the contribution). The net amount saved in Plan B is $10,000.

3. Funds invested in both plans can earn a 12% before-tax return. The earnings from Plan A are taxable to the employee so that the plan's after-tax rate of return is 9 percent. Plan B is in the form of a qualified trust and therefore its earnings are tax-exempt.

The difference in the amounts available to an employee after 15 years of participation in either plan is dramatic. It is not difficult to understand why qualified retirement plans have become such an attractive fringe benefit to employees concerned with providing for their retirement years. However, before the analysis presented in Exhibit 18-2 is complete, it is necessary to examine the general rule as to the taxability of benefits paid out of a qualified plan upon an employee's retirement.

When an employee begins to withdraw funds from a nonqualified retirement savings plan, such funds represent *after-tax* dollars, and he or she will not be taxed on these funds a second time. In comparison, benefits received by an employee out of a qualified plan funded solely by employer contributions are fully taxable to the employee. It is important to understand that the retirement dollars available under Plan A of Exhibit 18-2 are excludable (as a return of capital), while the retirement dollars available under Plan B are fully includible in the recipient's gross income.

TAXABILITY OF QUALIFIED PLAN LUMP-SUM DISTRIBUTIONS

If an employee who has made no contributions to the employer's qualified retirement plan receives a distribution from the plan, the employee has no investment in the distribution and therefore must include the entire amount in adjusted gross income.[6] When the distribution is made by a series of payments (i.e., an annuity), the taxability of the distribution is spread over a number of years.[7] If the distribution is made in a lump sum, all the retirement income is taxed in one year.[8] Given the progressive rate structure of the Federal income tax, the normal tax on a large lump sum distribution could be prohibitive.

To mitigate this problem, Congress provided two relief provisions that benefit the recipient of a lump-sum distribution from a qualified retirement plan. First, an employee could treat the portion of a distribution attributable to the employee's participation in the retirement plan prior to 1974 as long-term capital gain.[9] The Tax Reform Act of 1986 generally repealed such capital gain treatment. However, a taxpayer who was age 50 before January 1, 1986 (or a person who receives it on his or her behalf) may elect to utilize this relief provision. In such case, the long-term capital gain portion of a distribution will be taxed at a flat 20% rate.[10] Note that in 2017, individuals who turned 50 before 1986 would be 80 years old at this point.

A second relief provision is a special procedure for computing the amount of current tax on a lump sum distribution.[11] A taxpayer who was age 50 before January 1, 1986 may elect to use a 10-year forward averaging computation based on 1986 income tax rates for distributions received after 1986.[12] The calculation is made on Form 4792 (2016).

Under pre-2000 law, the averaging computation could be elected only for lump sum distributions received on or after the taxpayer had reached 59½ years of age, and a taxpayer could only make one such election.[13] Note that those who were born before 1936 continue to be eligible for ten-year averaging even after the five-year averaging is repealed.

---

[6] If the employee has made contributions to the plan, he or she will have an investment in the plan, which may be recovered tax-free under the rules of § 72.

[7] § 402(a).

[8] § 402(e)(1).

[9] § 402(a)(2), repealed by the Tax Reform Act of 1986.

[10] Tax Reform Act of 1986, Act § 1122(h)(3).

[11] § 402(e).

[12] Tax Reform Act of 1986, Act § 1122(h)(5) A special five-year averaging rule was repealed for tax years after 1999.

[13] § 402(e)(4)(B).

ADDITIONAL TAXES ON PREMATURE OR EXCESS DISTRIBUTIONS

Congress intended for the tax-favored status of qualified plans to serve as an inducement for taxpayers to provide for a source of retirement income. Therefore, if a taxpayer makes a premature withdrawal from a qualified plan, a 10% penalty tax is imposed on the amount of the distribution included in the taxpayer's gross income.[14] However, the Code does permit penalty-free withdrawal from IRAs before age 59½ if any of the distributions are

- On account of death or permanent disability.

- In the form of annuity payments over the taxpayer's lifetime.

- For medical expenses of the individual, his or her spouse and dependents that exceed 7.5% of AGI.

- For medical insurance of the individual, his or her spouse and dependents (without regard to the 7.5% of AGI floor) if the individual has received unemployment compensation for at least 12 weeks, and the withdrawal is made in the year such unemployment compensation is received or the following year.

- For qualified education expenses. For this purpose, the term qualified higher education expenses is defined in § 529(e)(3) and generally means tuition, fees, books, supplies, and equipment required for enrollment or attendance at an eligible educational institution. It also includes the reasonable costs of room and board. In order to qualify, the expenses must be for education furnished to the taxpayer, the taxpayer's spouse, or any child or grandchild of the taxpayer or the taxpayer's spouse at an eligible education institution. Such expenses are reduced by amounts excluded from gross income that are used for such education.

- For first-time homebuyer expenses. The penalty waiver applies only to the first $10,000 withdrawn during the taxpayer's lifetime. The withdrawals must be used within 120 days of withdrawal to acquire, construct, or reconstruct a home that is the principal residence of the individual, his or her spouse, or any child, grandchild, or ancestor of the individual or spouse. Acquisition costs include any usual settlement, financing, or other closing costs. Although the name of the law suggests that it applies only to the purchase of a taxpayer's first home (and therefore is a once-in-a-lifetime opportunity), such is not the case. A first time homebuyer is defined as an individual (or if married, such individual's spouse) who had no present ownership interest in a principal residence during the two-year period ending on the date of acquisition. Thus, as long as the taxpayer has not owned a home in the past two years, withdrawals may be made from an IRA to help pay for the "new" home even though it is not the taxpayer's first home.

- To reservists called to active duty for at least 179 days.

ROLLOVER CONTRIBUTION

There are many situations in which taxpayers receive lump-sum distributions from qualified plans prior to retirement. For example, a taxpayer who quits his job with his current employer to accept a position with a new employer may have a right to a distribution from his current employer's qualified plan. Any taxpayer who receives a qualified plan distribution but does not need additional disposable income can exclude the distribution from gross income (and thus avoid both the income tax and any penalty tax on the distribution) by making a *rollover contribution* of the distributed funds. A rollover contribution must be made into another qualified employer plan, a Keogh plan, or an IRA, and it must be made within 60 days of the receipt of the distribution.[15] Note that in the case of a withdrawal, an employer is normally required to withhold 20% of the distribution as an estimated tax payment. However, withholding can be avoided if the amount is rolled directly into another qualified retirement plan, Keogh plan, or an IRA on a timely basis.[16] Failure to observe these rules can create a severe hardship and may lead to a penalty.

---

[14] § 72(t).

[15] § 402(a)(5).

[16] § 3405(c)(2).

> **Example 4**
>
> T is 45 years old. This year his employer laid-off 200 employees and, unfortunately, T lost his job. T decided to take a lump-sum distribution from his retirement plan of $200,000. Absent a direct rollover, T's employer will withhold $40,000 (20% × $200,000) and T will receive $160,000. Note that in order to avoid taxation on the $200,000 as well as the 10% early withdrawal penalty, T must rollover the entire $200,000 to a qualified plan, even though he only received $160,000. Consequently, he would have to find an additional $40,000 to go along with the $160,000 to avert a catastrophe!

Plan Loans

Plan participants can avoid making taxable withdrawals from qualified plans while indirectly utilizing their retirement funds by borrowing money from their qualified plans. There is a very complex limit on the amount of a plan loan. In very general terms, a plan loan to a participant is limited to the lesser of (1) one-half the participant's vested accrued benefit (but not less than $10,000) or (2) $50,000. Any amount of a loan in excess of this limit is considered a taxable distribution.[17] Currently, owners of any small business (those with fewer than 100 employees) are generally permitted to make participant loans.

> **Example 5**
>
> R and S are members of P's small business qualified plan. R has accrued vested benefits of $14,000, and S has accrued vested benefits of $80,000. R can borrow up to $10,000 even though this amount exceeds 50% of his vested benefits. If S, on the other hand, borrows $62,000 from the fund, $22,000 will be treated as a taxable distribution to her because this exceeds 50% of her benefits (which is more severe than the $50,000 ceiling violation).

In order to avoid being treated as a taxable distribution, a loan must be repaid in quarterly installments with interest within five years of the loan. However, if a taxpayer uses the loan to purchase a principal residence, any reasonable repayment period is allowed. The treatment of the interest expense depends on how the loan proceeds were used and whether the taxpayer is a key employee. If the plan loan is secured by the residence, the interest is qualified residence interest and is fully deductible as an itemized deduction. If the loan is used for investment purposes, the interest is considered investment interest and is normally deductible to the extent of any investment income. Unlike regular employees, key employees are not allowed to deduct any interest on plan loans.

---

[17] § 72(p).

TYPES OF QUALIFIED PLANS

LO.4

Distinguish between a defined benefit plan and a defined contribution plan.

Qualified plans fall into two basic categories, defined benefit plans and defined contribution plans. A *defined benefit plan* is one designed to systematically provide for the payment of definitely determinable benefits to retired employees for a period of years or for life. The focus of the plan is on the eventual retirement benefit to be provided. The amount of the benefit is usually based on both an employee's compensation level and years of service to the company. Defined benefit plans are commonly referred to as pension plans. The current amount of employer contributions that are required to fund future pension benefits under a given plan must be determined actuarially.[18]

Defined contribution plans provide for annual contributions to each participating employee's retirement account. Upon retirement, an employee will be entitled to the balance accumulated in his or her account. Defined contribution plans are designed to allow employees to participate in the current profitability of the business. Generally, in profitable years, an employer will make a contribution to a qualified trust and such contribution will be allocated to each employee's retirement account. However, contributions may be made to a qualified profit sharing plan without regard to current or accumulated profits of the employer corporation.[19] Although the employer may have the discretion as to the dollar amount of an annual contribution, such contributions must be recurring and substantial if the plan is to be qualified.[20]

While most defined contribution plans constitute "profit sharing plans," other types of defined contribution arrangements exist. These arrangements include *money purchase plans, stock bonus plans, and employee stock ownership plans.* Each of these is briefly discussed below.

Money Purchase Plans

A money purchase plan is a defined contribution plan that is treated like a defined benefit plan. The employer's annual contribution is determined by a specific formula that involves either a percentage of compensation of covered employees or a flat dollar amount. Under a money purchase plan, unlike a defined benefit plan, a definite pension amount is not guaranteed. Rather, a participant's retirement benefit will be determined by his or her vested account balance at retirement.

Because an employee's account balance will be fashioned according to a definite formula under a money purchase plan, a certain amount of flexibility is permitted in structuring the plan's contribution formula.

Example 6

Under a company's money purchase plan formula, an employer is required to contribute to the plan 3% of an employee's compensation plus an extra 1% for each year of prior service up to a maximum of 10 percent. Thus, an employee with 12 years of service would receive a contribution equal to 13% (3 + [12 limited to 10]) of his covered compensation. A new employee would receive only 3 percent.

Note that under a money purchase plan an employer is required to make a contribution. If an employer fails to make these required contributions under the plan, the employer will be subject to certain excise taxes. This minimum funding standard does not apply to stock bonus or profit-sharing plans.[21]

Stock Bonus Plans

A stock bonus plan is another type of deferred compensation arrangement in which the employer establishes a plan in order to contribute shares of the company's stock. A stock bonus plan is subject to the same requirements as a profit sharing plan; therefore, a stock

---

[18] Reg. § 1.401-1(b)(1)(i).   [20] Reg. § 1.401-1(b)(1)(ii).

[19] § 401(a)(27).   [21] § 412(h)(1).

bonus plan must have a predetermined formula for allocating and distributing the stock among the employees. All benefits paid from the plan must be distributed in the form of the employer company's stock. An exception is made for fractional shares distributed from the plan, which may be paid in the form of cash.[22]

Employee Stock Ownership Plans

Another variety of qualified plans is the Employee Stock Ownership Plan (ESOP). As the name suggests, the major purpose of the ESOP legislation was to encourage stock ownership by all employees by giving employers and employees a host of tax incentives. Supporters of ESOPs believe in the fundamental principle that ownership of a business by its employees can help cure many of the ills of a market-based economy. A major proponent of this principle, former Senator Russell Long, now deceased, endlessly extolled the virtues of ESOPs, saying that they could eliminate all of what is wrong with capitalism. According to Long and his followers, ESOPs increase worker productivity, improve labor relations, promote economic justice, provide a source of low-cost capital and are basically a savior for our economic system. On the other hand, critics of ESOPs say such claims are merely snake oil. Regardless of the view, ESOPs are now plentiful and have been a part of the system for more than 25 years.

Technically, an ESOP is a defined contribution plan. Like other qualified plans, a company that wants an ESOP first establishes a trust to which it makes annual contributions. The employer contributes either cash or its own stock. If the employer contributes cash, the ESOP uses the cash to purchase stock or securities of the sponsoring employer (rather than stocks or bonds of other companies). Regardless of how the stock or securities are obtained, they are then allocated to individual employee accounts within the trust using some type of formula. For example, the allocation may be in proportion to the employee's compensation or according to years of service or some combination of compensation and years of service. As a result, the company's employees—rather than outsiders—wind up owning a portion or all of the company. Any income earned by the ESOP is treated like that in other plans; that is, the income is completely tax-exempt. When the employee retires, he or she typically sells his or her shares of stock back to the trust and receives cash.

The tax benefits of this arrangement, once huge, have been whittled back by Congress over the years. Nevertheless, ESOPs still offer significant advantages. If the employer contributes stock, it receives a deduction for the value of the stock contributed.[23] Since it costs the employer little or nothing to issue the stock, the employer increases its cash flow by the taxes saved from the deduction. If the employer contributes cash that is subsequently used by the ESOP to purchase stock from the employer, the same benefit is obtained.

Example 7

This year P Corporation established an ESOP. Under the terms of the plan, P transferred 30,000 shares of unissued stock valued at $90,000 to the trust. Under § 1032, the issuance of the stock is nontaxable to P. However, P is entitled to a deduction for the value of the stock contributed, $90,000. Assuming P's marginal rate is 34 percent, the contribution provides tax savings of $30,600 ($90,000 × 34%) with little or no cash drain.

The deductibility of contributions to an ESOP becomes even more attractive in the case of a *leveraged* ESOP. In a leveraged ESOP, the ESOP typically borrows money from a lender (e.g., a bank) and uses the cash to purchase the sponsoring corporation's stock. In subsequent years, the company makes contributions to the ESOP that are used to repay the

---

[22] Reg. § 1.401-1(b)(1)(iii).   [23] § 1032.

interest and principal on the loan. When the contributions are used to pay the loan, such contributions are deductible. Observe that the effect is to allow the company to deduct the payments of not only the interest but also the principal. This feature makes the ESOP a very attractive form of debt financing for the employer. Similarly, the Code allows the company to deduct any dividends paid on ESOP stock which are used to repay the loan or which are passed through to the employees (a special feature of ESOPs).

Another significant benefit of the ESOP—no doubt the one that attracts the most attention—is the tax-free rollover permitted by § 1042. If the conditions of this provision are met, a shareholder who sells stock to an ESOP and who has owned the stock for at least three years may defer recognition of any gain realized on the sale by reinvesting in other stocks or bonds. This enables a retiring owner to get out of the business at the cost of one capital gains tax (rather than two taxes in most cases) that is deferred until the replacement property is sold.

SIMPLE Plans

As a general rule, retirement plan coverage is lower for small employers than among medium and larger employers. Congress believed that one of the reasons for this result stemmed from the complexity of the rules relating to establishment of tax-qualified retirement plans as well as the high costs associated with complying with those rules. In an effort to encourage small employers to adopt retirement plans for its employees, Congress created a simplified retirement plan option known as SIMPLE (the Savings Incentive Match Plan for Employees).[24]

Under a SIMPLE plan, employers with 100 or fewer employees and no other employer-sponsored retirement plan are permitted to establish a savings incentive match plan for their employees. Deductible contributions may be made either to individual IRA accounts established for each employee or to accounts established as part of a § 401(k) plan. One of the key benefits of adopting a SIMPLE plan is that those plans which satisfy the SIMPLE plan contribution requirements are not required to satisfy the nondiscrimination and top-heavy requirements that other qualified plans must continue to meet.

Under a SIMPLE plan, an employer generally must either match elective employee contributions dollar-for-dollar up to 3% of compensation or make a 2% of compensation contribution on behalf of each eligible employee. The limitation on employee contributions is reflected in the table below. Contributions to a SIMPLE account are deductible by the employer and excluded from the employee's income. Distributions are generally taxed under the rules applicable to IRAs. All employees with W-2 income of at least $5,000 annually must be allowed to participate.

The annual contribution limit to a SIMPLE plan is as follows:

Year	Amount
2009–12	11,500
2013–14	12,000
2015 and thereafter.	12,500

Catch-Up Contributions

A SIMPLE plan can permit participants who are age 50 or over at the end of the calendar year to make catch-up contributions. The catch-up contribution limit for 2009 thru 2017 is $2,500. The amount of a catch-up contribution that a participant can make for a year cannot exceed the lesser of the following amounts:

- The catch-up contribution limit; or

- The excess of the participant's compensation over the salary reduction contributions that are not catch-up contribution.

---

[24] §§ 1421 and 1422 of the Small Business Job Protection Act of 1996 amending § 401(k) and § 408(p).

In order for a retirement plan to be *qualified* and therefore eligible for preferential tax treatment, it first must comply with a long list of requirements set forth in §§ 401 through 415. These requirements are extremely complex and can prove burdensome to the employer wishing to establish a qualified plan for his or her employees. The rigorous requirements are intended to ensure that a qualified retirement plan operates to benefit a company's employees in an impartial and nondiscriminatory manner.

> **LO.5**
> Explain the requirements associated with qualified retirement plans.

The current requirements for plan qualification came into the law in 1974 with the enactment of the Employees Retirement Income Security Act (ERISA). Prior to ERISA, many qualified plans were designed to benefit only those employees who were officers of the company, shareholders, or highly compensated executives. Since the passage of ERISA, such discriminatory plans are no longer qualified.

EXISTENCE OF A QUALIFIED TRUST

Under § 401 and the accompanying Treasury Regulations, contributions made as part of a qualified plan must be paid into a domestic (U.S.) trust, administered by a trustee for the exclusive benefit of a company's employees. The plan must be in written form and its provisions must be communicated to all employees. The plan must be established by the employer. Any type of employer—sole proprietor, partnership, trust, or corporation—may establish a plan.

ANTI-DISCRIMINATION RULES

A retirement plan will not qualify if the contributions to or benefits from the plan discriminate in favor of the *prohibited group*. The prohibited group is defined as employees who are highly compensated or who are officers or shareholders of the company. If a plan provides for contributions or benefits to be determined under an equitable and reasonable formula, the fact that the prohibited group receives a greater dollar amount of contributions or benefits than employees in the nonprohibited group will not constitute discrimination.[25]

The Small Business Job and Protection Act of 1996 substantially simplified the definition of a "highly compensated employee." Currently, a highly compensated employee is a 5% owner during the current or prior year, or an employee with compensation during the prior year over $120,000 (2017). Employers may also elect to limit the pool of highly compensated employees to anyone who satisfies the basic definition and is in the top 20% of employees by compensation.[26]

An important aspect of the statutory antidiscrimination rules for qualified plans is the fact that such plans may be integrated with public retirement benefits.[27] Under the integration rules, the calculation of plan benefits may take into account the extent to which an employee is covered by Social Security or a state retirement program. In effect, an employer can credit a portion of its Social Security contribution toward the amount it is required to contribute to the qualified plan. Without any limitations, integration could be used to pay substantially more benefits to a highly compensated employee. For example, assume H owns a corporation that has two employees, H who earns $150,000 and L who earns $20,000. Also assume that the corporation's qualified plan contribution rate was 6.2% of compensation. Using integration and ignoring current limitations, the corporation would not be required to contribute any amounts for L since all of its required contribution is met by its payment for L's Social Security. On the other hand, it would contribute 6.2% for H for every dollar above the Social Security wage base, $127,200 in 2017. As might be expected, special rules exist to prohibit such abuse. Nevertheless, integration can be used in a limited fashion to increase the benefits to highly compensated employees at the expense of other employees.

---

[25] §§ 401(a)(4) and (5).   [27] § 401(a)(5).

[26] § 414(q).

SCOPE OF PLAN PARTICIPATION AND COVERAGE

A qualified retirement plan must provide that a substantial portion of a company's employees are eligible to participate in the plan. Specifically, any employee who has reached age 21 must be eligible to participate after completing one year of service for the employer.[28] The plan may not exclude an employee from participation on the basis of a maximum age.[29]

In addition to these *minimum* and *maximum* age and service conditions, a qualified plan must meet complex minimum coverage requirements. A qualified plan must satisfy one of the following three minimum coverage tests: the *percentage test,* the *ratio test,* or the *average benefits test.*[30]

Under the percentage test, a plan must benefit 70% or more of all of the employer's non-highly compensated employees. For this test, all eligible employees are considered to benefit under the plan. A plan that has no coverage requirements or highly compensated employees will automatically satisfy this test.

Example 8

P Corporation has two divisions, R and S. P Corporation adopts a plan that covers only the employees of division S. If R division has 2 highly compensated and 20 non-highly compensated employees and S division has 18 highly compensated and 80 non-highly compensated employees, P satisfies the percentage test. This is because the plan covers 80% (80% of [20 + 80]) of the nonhighly paid employees.

The ratio test requires that the plan benefit a classification of employees that does not allow more than a reasonable difference between the percentage of an employer's highly compensated employees who are covered and a similarly computed percentage for non-highly compensated employees. In other words, the ratio test allows the percentage test to be proportionately reduced.

Example 9

Assume the same facts as *Example 8.* Because only 90% of the highly compensated employees are covered (18 of 20), only 90% of the percentage test must be met. Thus, the plan would meet the ratio test if as few as 63% of the non-highly compensated employees are covered (90% of 70%).

A plan will satisfy the average benefits test if (1) it benefits employees under a classification that the IRS finds does not discriminate and (2) the average benefit percentage for non-highly compensated employees is at least 70% of the average benefit percentage for highly compensated employees. The average benefit percentage, with respect to any group of employees, is the sum of all employer contributions and benefits under the plan provided to the group, expressed as a percentage of pay for all group members. An employer may compute the average benefit percentage based on either the current plan year or on a rolling average of three plan years that includes the current year. Once the employer makes this choice, it must obtain IRS consent to revoke it.[31]

---

[28] § 410(a)(1). The plan may defer participation for two years if it provides immediate 100% vesting.

[29] § 410(a)(2).

[30] § 410(b)(1).

[31] § 410(b)(2)(C).

The 50/40 Rule

While this rule is not a separate coverage rule, the 50/40 rule deserves attention because of the significance of the law involved. Basically, a plan will lose its qualification unless on each day of the plan year, it benefits the lesser of (1) 50 employees or (2) 40% of all employees of the employer. The 50/40 requirement applies separately to each qualified plan, and the Regulations exempt certain plans from this rule.[32]

VESTING REQUIREMENTS AND FORFEITURES

Once an employee is participating in an employer-sponsored retirement plan, he or she may not be entitled to any benefits under the plan for a certain period of time. After the requisite period of time, the employee's benefits *vest* and become nonforfeitable regardless of his or her continued employee status.

Under a qualified plan, vesting for non-top heavy employees must occur according to one of two statutory schedules designed to guarantee that an employee obtains a right to plan benefits within a reasonable time.[33] These two schedules are often referred to as "Cliff" vesting and "Graded" vesting.

Cliff Vesting

This schedule derived its name from the tendency, before ERISA, of some employers to push off the employment "cliff" (terminate) those employees just about to become vested in the retirement plan. Beginning in 2002, the cliff vesting must be complete within three years. Under three-year cliff vesting, an employee would not be entitled to any vesting before completing three years of service. At the end of the third year, the employer would have to vest the employee 100% in his or her accrued benefit attributable to employer contributions.[34]

Graded Vesting

The second permissible non-top heavy vesting schedule is graded vesting. Under such a schedule, employees must become proportionately vested over a two- to six-year vesting period. Under six-year graded vesting, a plan must provide at a minimum the following:

20%	vesting after two years service;
40%	vesting after three years service;
60%	vesting after four years service;
80%	vesting after five years service; and
100%	vesting after six years service.

Under this schedule, the potential for discrimination diminishes because vesting occurs at a more gradual rate and, after three years of service, all employees are entitled to some vesting.[35]

If an employee leaves the job before some or all of the retirement benefits have vested, he or she forfeits the right to such benefits. Previous employee contributions toward these forfeited benefits are not returned to the employer, but instead transfer to remaining plan participants in a nondiscriminatory manner.[36]

FUNDING AND CONTRIBUTION LIMITATIONS

Qualified retirement plans must be *funded*. Consequently, an employer is required to make current payments into a qualified trust. For a defined benefit plan, an actuarially determined minimum current contribution is required by statute.[37] For a defined contribution plan, the annually determined contribution must be *paid* to the trustee. Because of these rules, an employer must back up its promises to the employees with actual plan contributions.

---

[32] § 401(a)(26) and Prop. Regs. § 1.401(a)(26)-2.

[33] § 411(a)(2).

[34] § 411(a)(2)(A).

[35] § 411(a)(2)(B).

[36] Rev. Rul. 71-149, 1971-1 C.B. 118.

[37] § 412.

The Code limits the amount of contributions or benefits that are provided for employees. If these amounts should be exceeded, the plan will terminate.[38] In addition, § 404 establishes a limit on the amount that an employer may deduct. Sometimes the deductibility issue may have an impact on the amount that an employer may contribute on behalf of an employee. The maximum amounts that can be contributed to various plans are shown in Exhibit 18-3 below.

EXHIBIT 18-3	Maximum Annual Inflation-Adjusted Dollar Amounts	
Plan Type	*2016*	*2017*
Defined Benefit Plan	$210,000	$215,000
Defined Contribution Plan	53,000	54,000
Annual Compensation Limit.	265,000	270,000
Cash or Deferred [§ 401(k)].	18,000	18,000
Highly Compensated Employees	120,000	120,000
SIMPLE Contribution Limit.	12,500	12,500

Defined Contribution Plans

Under a defined contribution plan, the maximum contribution that can be made to the account of an employee is limited to the lesser of the following:

1. $54,000 (in 2017); or
2. 100% of the employee's compensation (subject to limits described in Exhibit 18-3 above).

Example 10

S is a participant in Summa Inc.'s qualified profit sharing plan. If S's annual salary is $275,000, her employer can make a maximum annual contribution for 2017 on her behalf of $54,000 (the *lesser* of $54,000 or 100% of S's first $270,000 of compensation).

Example 11

If S's current salary is $35,000, the annual contribution is limited to $35,000 (the *lesser* of $54,000 or 100% of S's compensation).

Defined Benefit Plans

Under a defined benefit plan, the maximum annual benefit that can accrue to a participant is limited to the lesser of the following:[39]

1. $215,000 for 2017; or
2. 100% of the participant's average compensation for his or her three most highly compensated consecutive years of service with the employer.

Section 401(a)(17) was amended in 1993 to reduce the annual compensation limit to $150,000. Proposed regulations provide illustrations of how these new compensation limits affect *average compensation* for defined benefit plans.[40]

---

[38] §§ 415(a) and (b).

[39] § 415(b)(1)(A).

[40] Prop. Reg. § 1.401(a)(17)-1(b).

The limit is indexed annually for inflation, and adjustments to this figure are to be made if benefit payments are to begin before or after Social Security retirement age. Adjustments will be downward if payments begin before Social Security retirement age and upward if they begin after that age. The amount of the adjustment is determined actuarially based upon a straight-life annuity.[41] The current limitation is $215,000 for 2017.

TOP HEAVY PLANS

Section 416 contains additional requirements for qualified status of retirement plans that are deemed to be "top heavy." A *top heavy plan* is one in which more than 60% of the cumulative benefits provided by the plan are payable to *key employees*. Key employees include officers of the employer and highly compensated owner-employees. If a top heavy plan exists, § 416 provides an extra measure of assurance that the plan does not discriminate against non-key employees. To maintain qualified status a top heavy plan *must provide* a more rapid vesting schedule (generally 100% vesting after three years of service) and a minimum benefit to *all* employees regardless of Social Security or similar public retirement benefits.

DEDUCTIBILITY OF CONTRIBUTIONS BY EMPLOYER

Section 404(a) allows a deduction for employer contributions to qualified retirement plans if the contributions represent an ordinary and necessary business expense. In addition, § 404 contains complex rules that limit the dollar amount of the annual deduction. (Note that the statutory limitations on employer deductions are independent of the previously discussed limitations on the amount of contributions.) For example, the deduction for an employer's contribution to a qualified profit sharing plan is subject to a general limitation of 25% of total annual compensation paid to participating employees.[42] If an employer makes a contribution that exceeds this percentage limitation, the excess may be carried forward and deducted in succeeding years (subject to the percentage limitation for each succeeding year).[43]

DETERMINATION LETTERS

At this point, it should be obvious to the beginning tax student that the qualification rules for employer-sponsored plans are many and complex. As a result, employers are well advised to request a determination letter from the IRS before a plan is put into effect. Such determination letter is a *written approval* of the plan verifying that the plan, as described to the IRS, complies with all requirements for qualified status. If a plan treated by an employer as qualified is disqualified in an IRS audit, the employer could be liable for a considerable amount of unwithheld income and payroll taxes on employer contributions.

Qualified Plans for Self-Employed Individuals

Unincorporated taxpayers who earn money through self-employment are often precluded from retirement benefits afforded employees. To mitigate this result, Keogh (H.R. 10) plans were developed whereby contributions to such a plan are tax deductible, earnings accrue tax-free, and the self-employed individual is not taxed on any of the benefits until retirement. While Keogh plans provide substantial benefits, there are specific requirements that must be followed.

LO.6
Explain the special qualified plans available for self-employed individuals.

A self-employed individual who establishes an employer qualified retirement plan for his employees is not an employee eligible for participation in the plan. Self-employed individuals include sole proprietors and the partners in a business partnership. These taxpayers, however, may use the *Keogh* rules to obtain the tax benefits of a qualified plan.[44] A Keogh

---

[41] § 415(b)(2)(B).

[42] § 404(a)(3).

[43] *Ibid.*

[44] See § 410(c)(1). It is interesting to note that retirement plans for self-employed individuals often are referred to as Keogh *or* H.R. 10 plans. Actually, the descriptions are interchangeable since H.R. 10 designated the legislative bill introduced by Congressman Keogh and passed by Congress in 1962.

plan must benefit both the self-employed taxpayer and his or her employees in a nondiscriminatory manner under the wide range of rules for qualified plans previously discussed. In addition, the top heavy rules of § 416 apply to Keogh plans.[45]

To be eligible for a Keogh plan, the sole proprietor or partner must be an individual who satisfies one of the following conditions:[46]

1. Has "earned income" for the taxable year;

2. Would have had "earned income" for the year, but the trade or business being carried on had no net profits; or

3. Has been self-employed for any prior taxable year.

Generally, net earnings from self-employment will be the gross income from the trade or business less any related deductions; plus any distributive share of income or loss (if any) from a partnership. More specific definitions that are required for the tax computations are found in Exhibit 18-4.

EXHIBIT 18-4	Special Definitions for Keogh Plans
Earned income	Self-employment income reduced by the self-employment tax deduction and the amount of the allowable Keogh deduction
Net earnings from self-employment	Earnings from self-employment without regard to the self-employment tax deduction or the allowable Keogh deduction
Modified net earnings from self-employment	Net earnings from self-employment reduced by the self-employment tax deduction
Self-employment tax deduction	One-half of the self-employment taxes due for the year

CONTRIBUTION LIMITATIONS

Annual contributions to Keogh plans are generally subject to the same limitations that apply to employer plans. For a defined contribution plan, the annual contribution by a self-employed taxpayer is limited to the lesser of $54,000 (2017) or 100% of *earned income*.[47] As seen in Exhibit 18-4, earned income is net earnings from self-employment as reduced by the deduction for self-employment taxes as well as the deduction for the allowable Keogh contribution, so the computation is a circular one.[48] The computation of the allowable contribution can best be expressed in the following formula:

$$
\begin{array}{rl}
& \text{Net earnings from self-employment (NE)} \\
- & \underline{\text{Self-employment tax deduction}} \\
& \text{Modified net earnings from self-employment (MNE)} \\
- & \underline{\text{Allowable contribution (AC)}} \\
& \text{Earned income (EI)} \\
\times & 100\% \\
= & \underline{\underline{\text{Allowable contribution (AC)}}}
\end{array}
$$

The results of this formula can now be restated in the form of the equation found in Exhibit 18-5. Notice that the solution to this equation demonstrates that the actual limit on a self-employed taxpayer's annual contribution to a defined contribution Keogh plan is just 50% of *modified net earnings*. For individuals who have self-employment income but no liability for employment taxes (e.g., they have exceeded the maximum FICA through other employment), the allowable contribution will be 50% of their *net earnings* from self-employment not to exceed the dollar limit for the year.

---

[45] § 416(i)(3).

[46] § 415(c)(1)(B).

[47] §§ 415(c)(1) and (3)(B).

[48] § 401(c)(2).

EXHIBIT 18-5	Circular Computation of Allowable Keogh Contribution

$$AC = 1.00(EI) = 1.00(MNE - AC) = 1.00MNE - 1.00AC$$

or

$$2.00AC = MNE$$

thus

$$AC = (MNE/2.00 = 0.50MNE \; [50\% \; of \; MNE])$$

Example 12

During the current year, Mr. T earned $75,924 and paid $7,848 in self-employment taxes. The maximum contribution T can make to his defined contribution plan is 100% of $72,000 ($75,924 − [½ of $7,848]) less the contribution itself. Therefore, the maximum contribution is $36,000 (100% of [$75,924 − $3,924 − $36,000]). Note that this contribution is actually 50% of the modified net earnings of $72,000.

A different limitation applies to a Keogh plan if it is purely a discretionary profit sharing plan as opposed to the defined contribution plan discussed above. In this case, § 404(a)(3) limits the deductible contribution to only 15% of *modified net earnings* from self-employment. Once again, because the computation is a circular one, a calculation similar to Exhibit 18-5 would be necessary. While the computation is not illustrated, the results of such a determination indicate that the actual limit is 13.043% of *modified net earnings* (net earnings if no self-employment taxes are paid) from self-employment.

Many individuals do not want to be locked into maximum contributions of 50% of modified net earnings that are required annually by a defined contribution plan. To provide some flexibility, most individuals have a combination of plans:

1. A purely discretionary profit sharing plan; and
2. A defined contribution plan.

The sum of the two contributions would be the maximum allowable but the portion to be contributed to the profit sharing plan would be optional each year.

Qualified Plans for Employees

Since the establishment of employer-qualified plans as part of the Internal Revenue Code of 1954, Congress has expanded the scope of the law to provide similar plans for individual taxpayers who are not covered by an employer plan or who wish to supplement their employer plan.

LO.7

Describe various qualified plans for employees such as § 401(k) plans and individual retirement accounts.

CASH OR DEFERRED ARRANGEMENTS [§ 401(k) PLANS]

Cash or deferred arrangements (CODAs), also known as salary reduction plans or § 401(k) plans, have attained enormous popularity because these plans offer all the tax advantages of a qualified retirement plan and allow employees to exclude from their taxable wages or salaries the amount contributed to the plan. However, such amounts are still subject to FICA and Medicare taxes. Contributions made on behalf of the employee can come in the form of bonuses paid to the employee, additional salary, or an agreement by the employee to reduce his or her normal salary.[49]

---

[49] Reg. § 1.401(k)-1(a).

One of the major benefits of a § 401(k) plan is the flexibility it offers an employee. For example, a plan may be designed to allow an employee to defer up to 6% of his or her compensation. If the employee elects, he can defer 6 percent, or any smaller amount such as 1, 2, or 3 percent. This gives employees greater control of their taxable income in as much as they may choose annually how much they want in salary and how much they want to defer in trust. In addition, loans from the trust are available to the plan participants.

The amount that an employee may elect to defer under a § 401(k) plan may not exceed $18,000 for 2017 as shown in the table below.[50] While this figure is adjusted annually for inflation, it must be reduced by contributions to other retirement plans such as tax sheltered annuities and simplified employee plans. Any amounts in excess of this limit must be included in the individual's gross income. Furthermore, the limitations apply to the plan year and not to the calendar year of the individual. Thus, a CODA on a noncalendar year (e.g., 2016 and 2017) could theoretically allow an employee on a calendar year to defer up to $36,000 ($18,000 + $18,000), for example, in a single year.

Section 401(k) Plan Contributions Limitations

Year	Amount
2012	17,000
2013–14	17,500
2015–17	18,000

Employer Contributions

One of the major benefits of a § 401(k) plan to an employer is that it provides a low-cost method of financing retirement benefits to the employee. Thus, amounts that would have been paid in salaries or wages can now be directed toward the retirement plan. The offsetting administrative expenses of initiating and operating the plan should be relatively low so that they do not detract from its overall benefits. When establishing a § 401(k), contributions made to the trust should be treated as employer contributions as opposed to employee contributions. This is necessary to ensure the exclusion from income that is available only to contributions made by the employer.[51]

Example 13

An employee's election form to fund a § 401(k) plan should not state that she elects to contribute $5,000 of her salary to a § 401(k) plan. Instead, the election should request that the employer reduce her salary by $5,000 in exchange for the employer's agreement to fund a § 401(k) plan by the amount of $5,000.

An employer is entitled to take a deduction for a contribution to a CODA of up to 25% of an employee's compensation. This 25% limit is reduced by the employee's actual contribution. Compensation for this purpose is net compensation after considering the employee's contribution.

---

[50] § 402(g)(5). [51] § 414(h)(1).

Example 14

E, an employee of Z Corporation, desires to make an elective contribution of $8,000 to a qualified CODA. If E's compensation for the year is $110,000, the available contribution that Z Corporation can make for the year is determined as follows:

Compensation	$110,000
Less: E's contribution	(8,000)
Net Compensation	$102,000
Employer limit.	× 25%
Maximum Contribution	$ 25,500
Less: E's contribution	(8,000)
Available Contribution	$ 17,500

Catch-Up Adjustment for Individuals Over Age 50

The Pension Protection Act of 2006 made permanent a provision that allows taxpayers over the age of 50 to make additional elective deferrals in excess of the otherwise permissible limits. These additional amounts—commonly called catch-up contributions—can be contributed to § 401(k) plans, § 403(b) plans, SEPs, and SIMPLE plans. These additional deferrals may be made without regard to the qualification requirements or limitations that usually apply to these provisions. The amount of the catch-up adjustments (by year) are illustrated in the table below:

Year	§ 401(k)	§ 403(b)	SEPs	SIMPLE	IRAs
2015–17 . . .	6,000	6,000	6,000	3,000	1,000

Plan Requirements

In order to secure the benefits of a CODA, specific requirements must be satisfied. While a detailed explanation is beyond the scope of this coverage, a synopsis of these rules summarizes their features.[52]

1. A CODA must meet the qualification requirements of a profit sharing or stock bonus plan including its participation and coverage requirements.

2. A CODA must provide for an election by each eligible participant to have their employer make payments to a qualified trust or directly to them in cash.

3. Amounts held under a qualified CODA are restricted as to when the funds may be distributed to the employee, and the employee's right to those benefits must be nonforfeitable.

4. Under complicated rules, amounts available for tax deferral may not discriminate in favor of highly compensated employees.[53]

Roth § 401(k) Plans

Beginning in 2006, taxpayers may create a Roth § 401(k), § 403(b) or similar plans. Amounts contributed to such plans (i.e., salary reductions), like those to Roth IRAs, would not be deferred but would be reported on a participant's Form W-2. For most purposes, these Roth § 401(k) plans are identical to Roth IRAs with certain limited differences. For example distributions for first-time home-buyers before age 59½ are not permitted tax-free. In addition, there is no income limitation imposed on a Roth § 401(k). Taxpayers may establish Roth § 401(k) plans regardless of their adjusted gross income.

---

[52] § 401(k)(2) and (3).   [53] Reg. § 1.401(k)-1(a)(4)(iv).

INDIVIDUAL RETIREMENT ACCOUNTS

Prior to 1974, the benefits of qualified retirement plans were generally limited to employees of companies that opted to incur the expense of establishing plans. In 1974, however, Congress decided to provide an incentive for retirement savings in situations where there was no employer-provided plan and created the Individual Retirement Account (IRA). Since their creation, IRAs have been immensely popular.

The basic operation of a conventional IRA then and now mirrors that for employer-provided plans. Under the IRA provisions, an individual is generally entitled to make an annual tax-deductible contribution to the IRA. The contribution is a deduction for AGI, making it available to those who do not itemize deductions as well as those who do. Contributions are then invested and the income earned on such investments is not taxable currently. However, when amounts are withdrawn from the IRA they are fully taxable (both the earnings and the amounts representing the contributions). From an investment perspective, the tremendous advantages of the IRA relative to a traditional savings arrangement are the same as discussed earlier for employer-provided retirement plans. As explained above, the benefits of an IRA can be traced to two key factors: (1) the amounts invested are before-tax, providing a greater initial investment and (2) the tax is deferred until the amounts are withdrawn, resulting in greater earnings over the life of the investment.

The popularity of the IRA and the need to stimulate savings for retirement has caused Congress to expand the IRA concept over the years. Currently, there are three types of savings arrangements that bear the IRA name. They are

1. The traditional or conventional IRA (discussed above).
2. The Roth IRA.
3. The Educational IRA.

Unfortunately, even though each of these savings vehicles is called an IRA, their treatment can be quite different.

TRADITIONAL IRA

The traditional IRA is currently the most common type of IRA since they have been in existence since 1974. Individuals are permitted to make three types of contributions to a traditional IRA.

1. Deductible contributions.
2. Nondeductible contributions.
3. Rollover contributions (i.e., contributions of amounts withdrawn from other qualified retirement plans).

Deductible Contributions to a Traditional IRA

As a general rule, an individual who is not covered by an employer-sponsored retirement plan can deduct contributions to a traditional IRA. Only contributions of money are allowed. Contributions of property cannot be made. The maximum contribution for 2017 is $5,500. However, the deduction cannot exceed the taxpayer's compensation for the year.[54] In addition, taxpayers over 70½ cannot make contributions to a traditional IRA.

IRA Contribution Limit	
Year	Amount
2008–12	5,000
2013 and thereafter.	5,500

Similar to the § 401(k) rules discussed earlier, individuals age 50 and over are permitted to make additional annual IRA contributions. The catch-up contribution is limited to $1,000 for 2006 and thereafter. This catch-up amount is not inflation adjusted.

---

[54] § 219(b)(1).

Example 15

H and W are married with two kids, Z and K. H's mom, M, also lives with the family. This year, Z, 14, received $500 of interest income from a savings account and earned $1,500 from sacking groceries at the local supermarket. K, 17, earned $5,000 delivering pizzas. M, age 75, earned $7,000 from a part-time job at a fast-food restaurant and had $40,000 of interest and dividends. Since Z's earned income is only $1,500, the maximum amount that he can deduct for contributions to an IRA is limited to $1,500 (his compensation). In contrast, K is able to contribute and deduct the maximum amount of $5,500 (2017) since she has compensation of at least $5,500. On the other hand, M cannot make contributions to an IRA since she is more than 70½ years old.

Example 16

Assume the same facts as *Example 15* except that M is 55 years old. In this case, her contribution to an IRA is limited to $6,500 for 2017. This includes the $5,500 that was available because of her compensation, as well as the $1,000 additional *catch-up adjustment* due to her age.

Deduction Phase-Out Rules for Plan Participants

If a taxpayer or his or her spouse is an active participant in an employer-sponsored retirement plan *and* has AGI in excess of a specified *applicable dollar amount*, the maximum deductible amount is phased out.[55] The applicable dollar amounts differ depending on which of following four categories the taxpayer is in:

1. Files jointly and is an active participant in an employer-sponsored plan.
2. Files jointly, is not active in another employer-sponsored plan but has a spouse that is active in an employer-sponsored plan.
3. Files married filing separately and is active in an employer-sponsored plan.
4. Files as a single or head of household taxpayer and is active in another employer-sponsored plan.

EXHIBIT 18-6	**Applicable Dollar Amount Phase-Out Ranges for Individual Retirement Accounts**			
	Joint Filer Who Is Active Participant	*Single or Head of Household Who Is Active Participant*	*Joint Filer Who Is Inactive but Active Spouse*	*Married Separate Who Is Active Participant*
2016	$98,000–$118,000	$61,000–$71,000	$184,000–$194,000	$0–$10,000
2017	$99,000–$119,000	$62,000–$72,000	$186,000–$196,000	$0–$10,000

The applicable dollar amounts at which the phase-out begins and the IRA deduction ends are shown for each group in Exhibit 18-6. Note that the applicable dollar amounts increase over the next several years (except in the latter two cases). Also observe that if AGI exceeds the applicable dollar amount by more than $10,000, none of the contribution is deductible.

---

[55] § 219(g) and (g)(3)(B).

For excess AGI amounts between $0 and $10,000, the phase-out is proportional. For example, if the excess AGI is $4,000, the taxpayer loses 40% of the $5,000 deduction or $2,000. The amount of the phase-out can be computed using the following formula:

$$\frac{\text{AGI} - \text{Applicable dollar amount}}{\$10,000} \times \text{IRA deduction} = \text{Reduction in deductible allowance}$$

Example 17

Q, a single taxpayer, is a salesperson for C Corporation. She actively participates in her employer's qualified retirement plan. In 2016, her compensation and AGI were $28,000. Even though she participates in her employer's plan, she may make a contribution to an IRA. Her maximum deductible contribution is $5,500 (2016) since her AGI did not exceed the applicable dollar amount of $62,000 (2016). In 2017, her compensation and AGI increased to $66,000. Since she participates in an employer plan and her AGI exceeds the applicable dollar amount of $62,000 (2017), the amount that she can deduct is subject to the phase-out rules. Her maximum deductible IRA contribution for 2017 is $3,300 ($5,500 [2017 maximum contribution amount] − $2,200 phase-out as calculated below).

$$\frac{\$66,000 \text{ AGI} - \$62,000 \text{ applicable dollar amount}}{\$10,000} = 40\% \times \$5,500 \text{ (2017 amount)}$$

= Reduction in deductible allowance in the amount of $2,200

Example 18

T, who works as an accountant for a small corporation is single and age 38. He received compensation of $73,500 in 2017. T's employer does not maintain a retirement plan. Since T is not an active participant in a qualified plan, he is not subject to the phase-out rules and can deduct contributions to a traditional IRA of up to $5,500.

Special Rules for Married Couples

Traditional IRAs provide a special rule for married couples where one spouse is the major breadwinner. Each spouse may make a deductible IRA contribution of up to $5,500 (2017) provided the couple's *combined* compensation exceeds the amount of the contributions. In effect, this allows a married couple to contribute up to $11,000 even though only one spouse works (assuming the working spouse has AGI of at least $11,000).

Example 19

H and W are married. H had compensation income of $22,000 while W had no compensation and stayed at home taking care of the family's children. Although W had no compensation for the year, she may make a deductible IRA contribution of $5,500 to her own account in addition to H's contribution to his account since their combined compensation of $22,000 exceeded their total contributions for the year of $11,000.

As noted above, if one spouse is an active participant in an employer-provided plan but the other spouse is not, the nonworking spouse may still contribute to a traditional deductible IRA but the nonworking spouse's contribution is subject to phase-out if the couple's AGI exceeds $186,000 in 2017. The active participant's phase-out begins at $99,000 for 2017.

Example 20

H and W are married. W is covered by a qualified plan sponsored by her employer. H is not employed. The couple files a joint return for 2017 reporting AGI of $135,000. Even though H is married to an active participant in a qualified plan, he may make a deductible IRA contribution of $5,500 since the applicable dollar amount for the spouse of an active participant begins at $186,000. On the other hand, W may not make a deductible IRA contribution since the couple's AGI exceeds the $99,000 applicable dollar amount for married plan participants in 2017 by more than $10,000.

Example 21

Assume the same facts as the *Example 20* above except that the couple's AGI is $205,000. In this case, neither spouse could make a deductible contribution because their AGI exceeds the applicable dollar amounts ($186,000 and $99,000) by more than $10,000 for each spouse.

Nondeductible IRA Contributions to a Traditional IRA

Individuals are permitted to make *nondeductible* contributions to their IRAs. These contributions can be made only to the extent that the maximum deduction for IRA contributions is not claimed (i.e., $5,500 or 100% of compensation).[56] Note that there is no phase-out or compensation income limitation that applies to nondeductible contributions.

Example 22

G, single, had compensation and AGI for 2017 of $71,000. G is covered by his employer's qualified plan. Since G's AGI exceeds the threshold by $9,000 ($71,000 − $62,000) his maximum deductible contribution is $550 ($5,500 − [90% × $5,500]). However, he is still permitted to make nondeductible contributions of $4,950 ($5,500 − $550).

Excess Contributions

Since the earnings generated by contributions into an IRA are tax deferred, taxpayers might be tempted to contribute amounts in excess of the contribution limit. To prohibit this possibility, a 6% penalty tax is imposed on any excess contribution left in an IRA after the close of the taxable year.

Rollover Contributions

As alluded to earlier, one reason for establishing an IRA is for the purpose of *rolling over* a lump-sum distribution from a qualified retirement plan. In addition, individuals who receive distributions from an IRA may also make rollovers of distributions into another IRA. By rolling over a distribution to an IRA, the taxpayer avoids taxation as well as any early withdrawal penalty.

Rollovers generally take one of two forms: (1) The distribution is paid to the plan participant who then must roll the distribution into an IRA within 60 days; or (2) the distribution is paid directly to the IRA. Failure to transfer the funds to an IRA within the 60-day period makes the distribution taxable and also subject to the early withdrawal penalty. Note that by having the distribution paid directly to the IRA, the participant avoids the provision that requires the employer to withhold 20% of the distribution as an estimated tax payment. It should also be noted that taxpayers who choose to roll over a lump-sum distribution forego the right to use any beneficial capital gain or forward averaging rules for computing the tax on the distribution when it is ultimately withdrawn from the IRA.

---

[56] § 408(o).

Due Date for Contributions

An IRA can be established during the year or after year-end. Contributions can be made to a traditional IRA at any time during the year or by the due date for filing a return for that year, not including extensions. For most people, this means contributions for 2017 must be made by April 15, 2018. In addition, if a contribution is made between January 1 and April 15, 2018 the taxpayer should designate the year targeted for that contribution (2017 or 2018). As discussed below, the due date for creating and contributing to a SEP-IRA is the extended due date.

Withdrawals from a Traditional IRA

Income earned in an IRA is tax-exempt, regardless of the deductibility of the contributions to the IRA.[57] When funds are withdrawn from an IRA, an amount of the withdrawal proportionate to any unrecovered nondeductible contributions in the account is not subject to tax; the balance of the withdrawal is fully includible in gross income.[58]

Example 23

In the current year, taxpayer A, age 61, withdrew $9,000 from his IRA, after which the account balance was $26,000. A has made $1,500 of unrecovered nondeductible contributions to the IRA. The nontaxable portion of the withdrawal is $386, computed as follows:

$$\frac{\text{(Nondeductible contributions of } \$1,500)}{\text{(Account balance before withdrawal } \$26,000 + \$9,000)} \times \$9,000 \text{ withdrawal} = \$386$$

For subsequent years, A's unrecovered nondeductible contribution balance is $1,114 ($1,500 − $386).

Taxpayers, age 70½ or older, can take advantage of a special rule for withdrawals that are contributed to charities. These individuals can withdraw and donate up to $100,000 per year from their IRAs to qualifying charitable organizations and exclude such amounts from gross income. Consistent with the exclusion, no deduction is allowed for the contribution. Without the rule, the amount withdrawn could be taxable and there might not be an offsetting contribution deduction (e.g., the taxpayer does not itemize).

Distribution Requirements

Without special rules, IRA owners might postpone distributions for as long as possible, hoping to take advantage of tax deferral to build their estate. However, the law requires taxpayers to take the entire IRA balance or start taking periodic distributions from their IRAs no later than April 1 of the year following the year in which the taxpayer reaches age 70½. The minimum distribution is generally based on either the life expectancy of the taxpayer or the joint life expectancies of the taxpayer and his or her spouse or another designated beneficiary. If a taxpayer has multiple IRA accounts, the minimum distribution amount is computed for each account but can be satisfied from a single account. The actual calculation of the required distribution is somewhat complex and beyond the scope of this text. However, it is important to note that if the distributions received are less than the required distribution amount, a penalty equal to 50% of the shortage may apply. Special rules apply to IRAs that are inherited. Note that Roth IRAs are not subject to these distribution requirements while the individual is alive; however, those who inherit a Roth IRA are subject to minimum distribution rules.

---

[57] § 408(c).   [58] § 408(d).

Roth IRAs

The 1997 Tax Act created a nondeductible IRA called the Roth IRA. Under this plan honoring Senator Roth of Delaware, individuals may make nondeductible contributions of up to $5,500 annually. However, the $5,500 maximum contribution limit is reduced to the extent of any contributions to another IRA in the same taxable year. In addition, the maximum annual contribution that can be made to a Roth IRA is phased out for single individuals with AGI between $116,000 and $131,000 and for joint filers with AGI between $183,000 and $193,000. The increase in contribution limits for the Roth IRA closely follows the traditional IRA over the next several years.

A Roth IRA is an IRA which is designated at the time of establishment as a Roth IRA. The major benefits of a Roth IRA are that distributions from a Roth IRA are generally not taxable, and unlike a deductible or nondeductible IRA, contributions to a Roth IRA may be made even after the individual for whom the account is established reaches the age of 70½.

Technically, only qualified distributions are nontaxable. A qualified distribution is any distribution that

- Is made after the taxable five-year period beginning with the first taxable year in which the individual made a contribution to a Roth IRA, and

- Meets *one* of the following conditions:
    1. Is made on or after the date on which the individual attains age 59½.
    2. Is made to a beneficiary (or to the individual's estate) on or after the death of the individual.
    3. Is attributable to the individual being disabled.
    4. Is a distribution for first-time homebuyer expenses (see earlier discussion).
    5. Is used for certain education expenses.

Note that there are no minimum distribution rules for Roth IRAs while an individual is alive. However, those who inherit a Roth IRA are required to take minimum distributions.

Distributions from a Roth IRA that are *not* qualified distributions are includible in income to the extent they are not attributable to contributions. In addition, these distributions are subject to the 10% early withdrawal tax that also applies to other IRAs. An ordering rule applies for purposes of determining what portion of a distribution is not a qualified distribution and is includible in income. Under the ordering rule, distributions from a Roth IRA are treated as made from contributions *first*. For purposes of determining the amount of contributions, all of an individual's Roth IRAs are treated as a single Roth IRA. Thus, no portion of a distribution from a Roth IRA is treated as attributable to earnings until the total of all distributions from a Roth IRA exceeds the sum of all contributions as well as rollover contributions. In effect, a taxpayer can make withdrawals of previous *contributions* without penalty or tax at any time—even within the mandatory five-year holding period.

Example 24

L first opened a Roth IRA at his bank on November 1, 2013, making a contribution of $5,000. He continued to make $5,000 contributions in 2014, 2015, 2016, and 2017. On May 1, 2017, L celebrated his 65th birthday, retired and took a distribution of $11,000 from his Roth IRA to take a trip to Europe. Under the ordering rule, the $11,000 withdrawal represents his contributions in 2013 ($5,000), 2014 ($5,000), and 2015 ($1,000) and, therefore, is neither taxable nor subject to the 10% penalty that otherwise applies to distributions during the five-year holding period. Note that he can begin withdrawing distributions in excess of previous contributions (without penalty) once the five-year holding period requirement is met in 2018. Observe that the five-year holding period begins in 2013, the first taxable year that L contributed to the Roth IRA.

Conversion of Traditional IRA to Roth IRA

The lure of tax-free earnings and tax-free distributions forever is so strong that individuals who have traditional IRAs may want to convert them to Roth IRAs. Graciously, Congress has blessed such conversions. The law permits individuals to convert traditional IRAs to Roth IRAs if certain requirements are met.

All individuals are entitled to convert their traditional IRAs to Roth IRAs. Technically, the conversion is accomplished by transferring the assets from a traditional IRA and reinvesting them (within 60 days) in a Roth IRA. This is normally referred to as a "conversion contribution." There is no minimum or maximum amount that must be converted. Most importantly, on conversion any previously untaxed amounts in the traditional IRA are taxable as ordinary income. The 10% penalty for withdrawal before age 59½ does not apply. After conversion, the taxpayer's AGI includes the taxable portion of the conversion for all purposes (e.g., 2% floor on miscellaneous itemized deductions, 7.5% floor on medical expenses). The conversion must be completed by December 31 of the year in question.

Example 25

C, single, age 48, has an AGI of $70,000 for 2017. As of May 1, he had accumulated $200,000 in his traditional IRA that he wants to convert. C's AGI for conversion purposes is $70,000, the amount of his AGI before considering any taxable income resulting from the conversion. The amounts in the IRA represent deductible contributions, nontaxable earnings and funds from a prior rollover from his § 401(k) plan. Assuming C converts the traditional IRA, he will have taxable income of $70,000. There is no penalty for early withdrawal.

CREDIT FOR CONTRIBUTIONS TO PLANS BY LOW-INCOME INDIVIDUALS

To encourage low and middle-income taxpayers to save for their retirement, the 2001 Tax Act created a nonrefundable credit for contributions to certain retirement saving plans (§ 25B). The saver's credit is available for contributions to § 401(k) plans, § 403(b) plans, § 457 state and local government plans, SIMPLE plans, SEP plans, traditional IRAs, and Roth IRAs. The credit is in addition to the deduction to which the taxpayer is normally entitled. The amount of the saver's credit is generally equal to 50% of the individual's retirement savings contributions not to exceed $2,000. Thus the maximum credit is $1,000 (50% × $2,000). On a joint return, the maximum credit would be $2,000, however, the credit decreases as the taxpayer's income increases. The allowable credit percentage is a function of the taxpayer's modified adjusted gross as follows:

Modified Adjusted Gross Income Savings Credit Determination (2017)

Joint Return		Head of Household		All Others		
Over	Not Over	Over	Not Over	Over	Not Over	Percentage
$ 0	$37,000	$ 0	$27,750	$ 0	$18,500	50%
37,000	40,000	27,750	30,000	18,500	20,000	20%
40,000	62,000	30,000	46,500	20,000	31,000	10%
62,000		46,500		31,000		0%

The credit is *not* available to the following individuals:

1. Individuals who have not attained the age of 18 by the close of the tax year;
2. Individuals for whom a dependency exemption my be claimed; and
3. Full-time students.

Example 26

T, single, graduated from college last year and took a job with a national accounting firm. His adjusted gross income for the year was $26,000. If T contributes $5,500 to a Roth IRA, he may claim a credit of $200 for 2017 (10% credit percentage × $2,000 ceiling amount). Had T been a full-time college student for the year, he would not have been eligible for the credit.

EDUCATION IRAS (COVERDELL EDUCATION SAVINGS ACCOUNTS)

In an effort to encourage savings and provide a vehicle to promote higher education, the Tax Reform Act of 1997 created a special type of IRA formerly known as an education IRA but now referred to as a Coverdell Education Savings Account (CESA).[59] Although the creation of such an account has nothing to do with retirement planning, as the name might suggest, the tax treatment of this arrangement is very similar to that for nondeductible contributions to traditional or Roth IRAs—thus its classification as an IRA.

Currently, taxpayers may make *nondeductible* contributions of up to $2,000 in cash per year into a CESA for certain qualified beneficiaries. The 2012 American Taxpayer Relief Act extended these rules on a permanent basis. A CESA is a trust account that is created for the purpose of paying *qualifying higher education* expenses. A qualified beneficiary is any individual under the age of 18 years, or any special needs child regardless of age. Qualifying higher education expenses include tuition, fees, books, supplies, and equipment required for enrollment that are incurred during the taxable year for a student who attends an eligible education institution. The term also includes amounts contributed to a prepaid tuition plan. In certain circumstances, *room and board* are also included in these expenses. An eligible educational institution means any post-secondary education courses (e.g., undergraduate or graduate courses) as well as the cost of elementary, secondary, private, and parochial schools.

Similar to retirement IRAs, earnings on the amounts contributed to a CESA are not taxed as they accumulate. Withdrawals from a CESA are totally nontaxable to the extent that they are used exclusively for the purpose of paying qualifying higher education expenses. Furthermore, no contribution may be made during a taxable year in which a contribution is made by *anyone* to a qualified prepaid tuition program on behalf of the same beneficiary. Note also that for any year in which an exclusion from gross income is claimed with respect to distribution from an education IRA, neither a American Opportunity Tax Credit nor a Lifetime Learning credit may be claimed with respect to education expenses incurred during that year on behalf of the same beneficiary.

Contribution Limit

The $2,000 annual contribution limit, computed at the donor level, is phased out ratably for contributors with AGI (computed with certain modifications) between $95,000 and $110,000 ($190,000 and $220,000 for contributors filing joint returns). The term "Modified AGI" means AGI increased by income earned outside the U.S. that normally is excluded under § 911. Individuals with modified AGI greater than the upper phase-out range are not allowed to make contributions to an education IRA established on behalf of any other individual. The contribution phase-out computation is shown in Exhibit 18-7.

---

[59] § 530.

EXHIBIT 18-7	Phase-Out for CESAs

$$\text{Reduction of the } \$2{,}000 = \$2{,}000 \text{ Contribution} \times \frac{\text{Modified AGI} - \text{Threshold}}{\text{Income range}}$$

	Modified AGI Phase-Out Begins	Modified AGI Phase-Out Complete
Married filing jointly ..	$190,000	$220,000
Other taxpayers.	$ 95,000	$110,000

Multiple CESAs for a Single Beneficiary

Taxpayers contributing more than $2,000 per year to an a CESA for a single beneficiary are subject to a penalty. Section 4973 imposes a six percent excise tax on excess contributions. An excess contribution consists of two parts:

1. The amount by which contributions to all CESAs for a single beneficiary exceed $2,000, plus

2. The amount contributed during the year to a qualified tuition plan.

Note that this rule prohibits a taxpayer from contributing to both a qualified tuition plan and a CESA without penalty. These rules do not appear to prohibit parents from contributing $2,000 to a CESA for one child while the grandparents contribute to a prepaid tuition plan. Moreover, there is no rule requiring that the person contributing be related to the beneficiary. Similarly, there is no restriction on the number of CESAs an individual may establish as long as each has a different beneficiary.

Distributions

Distributions from a CESA that are used to pay qualifying education expenses are generally nontaxable. In reality, this general rule is a bit more complex. Technically, distributions from a CESA are deemed to consist of a proportionate part of both the original contributions and the earnings on such contributions. Distributions representing contributions are always nontaxable. Distributions of earnings are excludable from gross income only to the extent that the distribution does not exceed qualified higher education expenses incurred by the beneficiary during the year the distribution is made. In effect, all of the earnings on a CESA are nontaxable as long as they are used for qualified education expenses. Distributions of earnings in excess of qualified expenses cause a ratable portion of the entire distribution to be taxable. In addition, an excise tax of 10% is imposed on the portion not used for education.

Rollovers

If any balance remains in a CESA at the time a beneficiary becomes 30 years old, such amount *must* be distributed, and the amount representing the account's earnings will be taxable. In addition, the distribution will be subject to a 10% penalty tax because the distribution was not for educational purposes. Prior to the time the beneficiary reaches 30, the 1997 Act allows tax-free (and penalty-free) transfers and rollovers of account balances from one CESA benefiting one beneficiary to another education IRA benefiting a different beneficiary (as well as redesignations of the named beneficiary), provided that the new beneficiary is a member of the family of the old beneficiary. For this purpose, a family member includes the beneficiary's spouse or a familial relative described in the rules governing dependency exemptions. These would include a child, sibling, parent and certain other individuals. For example, if the taxpayer's son did not fully utilize the amount in the CESA, the unused balance could be converted to an account for his daughter or his grandchild.

Gift and Estate Tax Treatment

Contributions made to CESAs are considered completed gifts and qualify for the annual exclusion. Distributions are not treated as gifts nor is a rollover to another beneficiary and, therefore, not subject to gift tax. Amounts in a CESA are not includible in the estate of any individual. If a beneficiary dies and the interest passes to a spouse, the spouse simply becomes the beneficiary of the CESA. If the interest passes to someone other than a spouse, the CESA terminates at death and the account balance is includible in the beneficiary's income (e.g., a child).

SIMPLIFIED EMPLOYEE PENSIONS

The concept of a Simplified Employee Pension (SEP) was added to the law in 1978 to provide employers with a way to avoid the fearsome complexities involved in establishing and maintaining a qualified retirement plan. By following the relatively simple rules of § 408(k), which are designed to prevent discrimination in favor of the prohibited group, an employer may establish a SEP. This qualified plan allows the employer to make contributions directly into an employee's existing IRA, thereby avoiding the necessity of a qualified trust.

The annual limit on SEP contributions is the lesser of 25% of employee compensation (subject to compensation limits) or $54,000 (2017). Employer contributions to a SEP are excludable from an employee's gross income.[60]

SEPs are not available just to employees. An individuals with earnings from self-employment also may create a SEP-IRA, even if he or she is an employee elsewhere and covered by an employer's retirement plan. Like other IRAs, a SEP-IRA can be created after the end of the year. Unlike traditional IRAs, the SEP-IRA may be created by the *extended* due date of the tax return. For example, if a self-employed person extends his or her return until October 15, he or she has until October 15 to create and fund a SEP. Observe that this rule differs significantly from Keogh plans. A Keogh plan must be established before the close of the tax year while SEPs can be established after year-end. Thus SEPs, like other IRAs, are one of the few tax planning tools that can be implemented after the tax year has come to a close.

The computation of the maximum amount that a self-employed person can contribute is—like Keogh plans—a bit complicated. The 25% limit is applied to net profit reduced by the deduction for half of the self-employment tax as well as the deduction for the SEP-IRA contribution itself. Thus, the calculation is circular. Ignoring the deduction for self-employment taxes, the maximum deduction would be 20% of self-employment income.

Retirement Planning Using Nonqualified Deferred Compensation

For many years employers have designed total compensation packages for valued employees that combined both a current compensation element and a *deferred* compensation element. A *nonqualified* deferred compensation arrangement typically is one in which the employee is compensated for current services rendered by the employer's promise to pay a certain amount at some future date. Although nonqualified deferred compensation plans do not receive the favorable tax treatment given to qualified plans, such arrangements are often attractive to employers because of their flexibility. Many employers find that what may be lost in tax benefits is more than made up in the savings derived from not having to comply with restrictive rules concerning the discrimination, participation, vesting, and funding that apply to qualified plans. The two questions that must be answered about a deferred compensation arrangement are:

LO.8
Describe nonqualified deferred compensation plans.

1. When is the employee taxed on deferred compensation that is earned currently but will be received in a later year?

2. When is the employer entitled to a business deduction for deferred compensation that will be paid in a later year?

Note that if a plan is a qualified plan, an employer is entitled to a current deduction for contributions and the employee is taxed on such contributions only when they are distributed. For nonqualified plans, however, the timing of the deduction and income is not quite as clear.

In order to completely answer the first question, an examination of the constructive receipt doctrine is necessary. To thoroughly answer the second, an examination of funded and unfunded plans is required.

---

[60] § 402(h).

CONSTRUCTIVE RECEIPT

The Regulations state that income (both current and deferred) is to be included in gross income for the taxable year in which it is actually or constructively received by the taxpayer.[61] Thus for a cash basis taxpayer, all items that constitute gross income (whether in the form of cash, property, or services) are to be included for the taxable year in which they are actually or constructively received. Consequently, the question to be resolved is whether deferred compensation is constructively received in the taxable year when it is authorized or in the year of actual receipt.

A mere promise to pay, not represented by notes or secured in any way, is not regarded as a receipt of income under the cash receipts and disbursements method. This should not be construed to mean that under the cash receipts and disbursements method income may be taxed only when realized in cash. Income, although not actually received, is constructively received by an individual in the taxable year during which it is credited to his account or set aside for him so that he may draw upon it at a later date.[62] Thus, under the doctrine of constructive receipt, a taxpayer may not deliberately turn his back upon income, nor may a taxpayer, by a private agreement, postpone receipt of income from one year to another.

Income is not constructively received if the taxpayer's control of its receipt is subject to substantial limitations or restrictions. Consequently, if a corporation credits its employees with bonus stock, but the stock is not available to those employees until some future date, the mere crediting on the books of the corporation does not constitute constructive receipt. In most cases, speculating whether an employer would have been willing to relinquish a payment earlier or determining a taxpayer's control over funds is not an easy task. As a result, in each case involving a deferral of compensation (especially nonqualified plans), the determination of whether the constructive receipt doctrine is applicable must be made on a fact-and-circumstances basis.

Example 27

T, a football player, entered into a two-year contract to play football for the California Cauliflowers. In addition to his salary, as an inducement for signing the contract, T would be paid a signing bonus of $150,000. Although T could have demanded and received his bonus at the time of signing the contract, T's attorneys suggested that the $150,000 be transferred to an escrow agent to be held for five years and then paid to T over the next five years as an annuity. If T should die, the escrow account would become part of his estate. Because the bonus is set aside for T, the $150,000 bonus must be included in T's gross income in the year in which the club unconditionally paid the amount to the escrow agent. The employer's obligation for payment terminated when the amount of the bonus was fixed at $150,000 and irrevocably set aside for T's sole benefit.[63]

TREATMENT OF NONQUALIFIED DEFERRED COMPENSATION PLANS

Persuaded by corporate scandals at companies such as Enron, the *American Jobs Creation Act of 2004* imposes new restrictions and limitations on the design of nonqualified deferred compensation plans.[64] Under the new law, in order for deferred compensation to be excluded from gross income, the deferred compensation plan must meet specific guidelines. These guidelines include: (1) a distribution requirement, (2) an acceleration of benefits requirement, and (3) certain election requirements.

Restrictions on Distributions

Under Code § 409A(a)(2)(A), a nonqualified deferred compensation plan may not permit distributions from the plan earlier than

- The participant's separation from service, as determined by the IRS, subject to a special rule for separation from service of any "specified employee";

- The date the participant becomes "disabled";

---

[61] Reg. § 1.451-1(a).

[62] Reg. § 1.451-2(a).

[63] Rev. Rul. 55-527, 1955-2 C.B. 25.

[64] § 409A.

- The participant's death;

- A time specified, or a schedule fixed, under the plan at the date of the deferral of the compensation;

- To the extent allowed by the IRS, a change in the ownership or effective control of the corporation, or in the ownership of a substantial portion of the corporation's assets; or

- The occurrence of an "unforeseeable emergency" as defined in § 409A(a)(2)(B)(ii).

Additionally, specified employees (referred to as "key employees") of publicly traded corporations generally may not receive their distributions earlier than six months after separation. A key employee is defined as an officer with compensation greater than $175,000 in 2017 (adjusted for inflation and limited to 50 employees); 5% owners; and 1% owners with compensation greater than $175,000. Furthermore, taking a distribution with a "haircut" (i.e., forfeiture of a portion of the account balance in exchange for access to the plan account) is no longer a distribution option.

Acceleration of Benefits

Section 409A does not permit a plan to allow for the acceleration of benefits. However, under the anticipated IRS regulations, a nonqualified deferred compensation plan would not violate the prohibition on accelerations in certain limited situations. For example, a plan could provide that upon separation from service of a participant, account balances less than $10,000 will be automatically distributed (except in the case of specified key employees).

Election Requirements

Under the new law, the flexibility of a participant to change his or her deferral elections generally must be made in the tax year preceding the year in which the services are performed, or within 30 days of becoming eligible for plan participation. If the award is performance-based (e.g., an incentive bonus), the election must be made no later than six months before the end of the performance period.

In addition to the above rules, a deferred compensation plan may not provide that the deterioration in the financial status of the employer will trigger payment of the deferred compensation. Offshore Rabbi trusts and Rabbi trusts that are convertible into Secular trusts (protecting the assets from general creditors) are also prohibited under the new law.

Effective Date of New Rules

The new rules generally apply to amounts deferred after December 31, 2004. If a plan fails to meet the requirements, or is not operated in accordance with any of these three requirements, all compensation earned and deferred must be included in income for the first tax year that the nonqualified deferred compensation plan fails to meet the requirements, to the extent not subject to a "substantial risk of forfeiture" and not previously included in gross income.[65] A 20% penalty will also be imposed on the amount required to be included in income. Interest will also be assessed on the underpayment, at the underpayment rate plus one percentage point. Any compensation that becomes taxable will be subject to income tax withholding.

UNFUNDED DEFERRED COMPENSATION PLANS

If an employer contractually promises to pay deferred compensation to an employee and does not set aside current funds in some type of trust arrangement, the employee is put in the position of an unsecured creditor of the employer. If the employee is a cash basis taxpayer and does not have any current right to payment under the deferred compensation plan, there is no constructive receipt of the compensation and thus no current taxable income to the employee. The employee will not be taxed until the year in which the deferred compensation is actually paid.[66]

From the employer's point of view, such unfunded arrangements are attractive because they do not require any current cash outflow from the business. However, neither a cash basis nor an accrual basis employer may take a deduction for deferred compensation until the deferred amount is includible in the employee's gross income.[67]

---

[65] § 409A(a)(1)(A)(i).

[66] Rev. Rul. 69-649, 1969-2 C.B. 106.

[67] Rev. Rul. 69-650, 1969-2 C.B. 106.

FUNDED DEFERRED COMPENSATION PLANS

Employees who agree to a nonqualified deferred compensation arrangement normally prefer that their employers secure the promise of future compensation by transferring current funds into an independent trust for the employee's benefit. While these employees desire the protection of a funded plan, they do not wish to subject those funds to current taxation. Therefore, innovative methods have been devised to allow deferral of an employee's income under a funded method by making the employee's interest in those funds forfeitable. To this end, an employer can establish one of many types of trusts. Two of the more common nonqualified arrangements are the *Rabbi trust* and the *Secular trust.* The rules of § 83, discussed earlier in the chapter, apply to these funded deferred compensation plans.[68]

Rabbi Trusts

Rabbi trusts are so named because the first IRS ruling that approved this arrangement involved a fund established by a congregation for its rabbi. In the typical Rabbi trust arrangement, the rights of employees are forfeitable, so an employee will not recognize taxable income until he or she actually receives a distribution from the trust. If a deferred compensation arrangement provides that employees' rights in the retirement fund eventually become nonforfeitable (i.e., vested), an employee must recognize taxable income in the year his or her rights vest. In both cases, the employer will receive a deduction only in the taxable year in which the deferred compensation is includible in the gross income of the employee.[69]

Example 28

As part of a deferred compensation arrangement, employer X agrees to place $10,000 annually into a trust account for employee Y. Y's rights to the trust funds are forfeitable until he completes 10 years of service for X. In the year in which Y's risk of forfeiture lapses, the value of the trust funds is included in Y's gross income. Subsequent payments into the fund by X are fully taxable to Y.[70]

A disadvantage of the Rabbi trust is that if the employer gets into financial difficulty, the trust assets are subject to the claims of the employer's creditors. In addition, any income that is generated by the trust will be taxable to the employer.

Secular Trusts

Designed in 1988, the Secular trust is a variation of the Rabbi trust.[71] Under a Secular trust, the employee receives a vested interest in the full amount of the transfer to the trust. Because the employee has a nonforfeitable interest, the employee is taxed immediately on the transfer of funds to the trust even though he or she has not actually received the funds. In return for the transfer, the employer receives an immediate deduction. The advantage of this arrangement is that the trust assets are not subject to the claims of the employer's creditors. The disadvantage, of course, is that the funds are immediately taxable to the employee. A Secular trust differs from a Rabbi trust, because the assets of the Rabbi trust will not be protected from the creditors of the employer in the event of bankruptcy.

Stock Options

LO.9

Determine the tax consequences of the issuance and exercise of both nonqualified and qualified stock options.

As an alternative to the payment of compensation in the form of corporate stock, corporate employers may issue *options* to purchase stock at a specified price to employees whom the company wants to retain. As a general rule, stock options have no value on the date they are issued because the option price is equal to or greater than the market price of the stock. Consequently, the options will have value to the recipient (and become a cost to the employer) *only if* the market price of the shares increases.

---

[68] § 402(b).

[69] § 404(a)(5).

[70] Reg. § 1.402(b)-1(b).

[71] PLR8841023.

If an option has no value upon date of grant to an employee, the employee obviously has not received taxable income. However, in certain unusual cases options may have a value at date of grant. If such value can be determined with reasonable accuracy under criteria provided in Regulation § 1.83-7(b)(2), the value represents compensation income to the recipient of the option. If an option is actively traded on an established market, it is deemed to have an ascertainable value at date of grant.[72]

Example 29

Corporation C grants employee D an option to purchase 100 shares of C common stock for $11 a share at any time over the next ten years. If C stock is selling at $9 per share, D's option has no readily ascertainable value. Therefore, D has no taxable income at date of grant, and a zero-tax basis in the option. If, however, D's option is actively traded on an established market and as a result can be valued at $5, D has received taxable compensation of that amount, and will have a $5 basis in the option.

OPTION EXERCISE

When the owner of a stock option that had no ascertainable value at date of grant exercises the option, the difference between the option price and the market price (bargain element) of the stock purchased represents ordinary income to the owner. If the option had an ascertainable value at date of grant, so that the recipient recognized taxable income upon receipt of the option, no additional income is recognized when the option is exercised.[73]

Example 30

In 2014, employee M received certain stock options as part of her compensation from Corporation Q. At date of grant, the options had no ascertainable value. However, in 2017 M exercised the options and purchased 1,000 shares of Q stock, market value $90 per share, for the option price of $60 per share. In 2017 M must recognize $30,000 of ordinary income ($30 per share bargain element × 1,000 shares). M's tax basis in her shares is $90,000.

From the employer's point of view, the value of a stock option can be taken as a deduction under the previously discussed rule of § 83(h). Generally, an employer will receive a deduction at date of grant if the option has a readily ascertainable value. If the option has no value at date of grant, the deduction will equal the income recognized by the owner of the option when the option is exercised.

Incentive Stock Options

In the past, Congress has experimented with a variety of *qualified stock options*—options afforded preferential tax treatment under § 421. Currently there is only a single type of qualified option, the Incentive Stock Option (ISO) of § 422A.[74]

Under § 421(a), the exercise of an ISO will not result in any income recognition to the owner. Correspondingly, the corporate employer who issued the option will never receive any deduction for the spread between option and market price at date of exercise. If and when the stock received upon exercise is sold, the employee will realize capital gain equal to the difference between the option price and selling price. The difference in tax consequences between a nonqualified stock option and an ISO is presented in the example below.

---

[72] Reg. § 1.83-7(b)(1).

[73] Reg. § 1.83-7(a).

[74] The rules of § 422A apply to options granted on or after January 1, 1976 and outstanding on January 1, 1981.

Example 31

Employee T was granted an option in 2011 to purchase one share of his corporate employer's stock at any time within the two succeeding calendar years. At the time the option was granted, the option price was $150 and the market price was $140. Assume that T exercised the option in 2013 when the stock had a market price of $200, and the stock acquired was sold in 2017 for $375. The tax consequences for each tax year would be as follows:

	Nonqualified Stock Option	*Incentive Stock Option*
2011	None	None
2013	Market price of $200 − $150 option price = $50 ordinary income and $200 basis in purchased stock ($150 cost + $50 income recognized). Employer deduction = $50	No income and $150 basis in purchased stock
2017	Sale price of $375 − $200 basis = $175 capital gain	Sale price of $375 − $150 basis = $225 capital gain

---

It should be noted that § 83 will apply to a tax-free transfer of an incentive stock option in determining a taxpayer's AMTI. Under § 83(a), the taxpayer will include in AMTI the excess of the stock's fair market value at the first time it is transferable over the amount paid for the stock under the option. See Chapter 13 for a discussion of the alternative minimum tax (AMT).

HOLDING PERIOD REQUIREMENTS

For the beneficial rule of § 421(a) to apply, an individual may not dispose of the stock purchased upon exercise of the ISO within two years from the date of the granting of the option and within one year from the date of exercise.[75] Additionally, the individual must be an employee of either the corporation granting the ISO or a parent, subsidiary, or successor corporation from the date of grant until the day three months before the date of exercise.[76]

If an individual violates the holding period requirement by disposing of his or her stock too quickly after purchase, § 421(b) provides that the *compensation income* (ordinary income) the individual did not recognize at date of exercise must be recognized in the year of disposition. Any gain so recognized increases the cost basis of the stock.[77] In such a situation the employer will be entitled to a corresponding deduction.

Example 32

Beta Corporation grants an ISO to employee Z on November 1, 2011. The option allows Z to purchase 500 shares of Beta stock at $3 per share. Z exercises the option on December 1, 2016, when Beta stock is selling for $7 per share. Z sells his 500 shares on March 1, 2017 for $9 per share. Because of the premature disposition (less than one year from date of exercise), Z must recognize $2,000 ordinary income (500 shares × $4 bargain price [$7 market price − $3 option price]) and a $1,000 capital gain in 2017. Additionally, Beta Corporation may claim a $2,000 deduction in 2017.

If the amount realized on a premature sale is less than the value of the stock at date of exercise, only the excess of the amount realized over the option price is recognized as ordinary income.[78]

---

[75] § 422A(a)(1).

[76] § 422A(a)(2).

[77] Reg. § 1.421-5(b)(2).

[78] § 422A(c)(2).

> ### Example 33
>
> Refer to the facts in *Example 32*. If Z sold his Beta stock for $6 rather than $9 a share, his ordinary income (and Beta's deduction) would be limited to $1,500 (500 shares × $3 bargain price [$6 selling price − $3 option price]).

QUALIFICATION REQUIREMENTS

An employee stock option must meet a number of statutory requirements set forth in § 422A(b) to qualify as an ISO. The primary requirements are as follows:

1. The option is granted pursuant to a plan that specifies the total number of shares that may be issued under options and the class of employees eligible to receive the options. The shareholders of the corporation must approve the plan within 12 months before or after the date the plan is adopted.

2. The options are granted within ten years of the date of adoption or the date of shareholder approval, whichever is earlier.

3. The option price is not less than the market value of the stock at date of grant.

4. The option must be exercised within ten years of date of grant.

5. The option can only be exercised by the recipient employee during his or her lifetime and can only be transferred at the employee's death.

6. The recipient of the option does not own stock possessing more than 10% of the total combined voting power of all classes of stock of the employer corporation or of its parent or subsidiary corporation.[79]

A major restriction on the use of ISOs is the statutory requirement that the value of stock with respect to which ISOs are *exercisable* shall not exceed $100,000 per calendar year per employee. For purposes of this requirement, the value of the stock is determined at date of grant.[80]

> ### Example 34
>
> In calendar year 2016, Corporation Q granted Employee F an ISO to purchase 1,000 shares of Q stock with a current aggregate value of $200,000. In calendar year 2017, Corporation Q granted Employee F a second ISO to purchase 1,200 shares of Q stock with a current aggregate value of $300,000. If Employee F decides to exercise any of her ISOs in 2017, she may only purchase 500 (500/1,000 × $200,000 = $100,000 limit) shares through exercise of her 2016 option or 400 shares through exercise of her 2017 option (400/1,200 × $300,000 = $100,000 limit).

Exclusion from Wages

The *American Jobs Creation Act of 2004* eliminated the uncertainty as to employer withholding obligations upon the exercise of statutory stock options. The Act provides a specific exclusion from the FICA/FUTA payroll tax withholding obligations for remuneration on account of the transfer of stock pursuant to the exercise of an incentive stock option or under an employee stock purchase plan, or any disposition of such stock.[81] The new law also provides that federal income tax withholding is not required on a disqualifying disposition of stock acquired from ISO and employee stock purchase plans (ESPP), nor when compensation is recognized in connection with an ESPP discount.

---

[79] § 422A(c)(6) waives this requirement in certain cases.

[80] § 422A(b)(7).

[81] §§ 3121(a)(22), 3306(b)(19), 421(b), and 423(c).

NONQUALIFIED STOCK OPTIONS

A Nonqualified Stock Option (NQSO), also referred to as a nonstatutory stock option, is generally any option that does not meet the statutory requirements in the Code to be treated as an Incentive Stock Option (ISO). NQSOs are often used as implements of deferred compensation because the corporation can avail itself of a tax deduction without a cash outlay and the options themselves can be issued with more flexible terms than ISOs. The only major disadvantage of using an NQSO is the potential for income recognition to the employee. That potential is, in turn, dependent upon whether the option has a readily ascertainable fair market value.

Readily Ascertainable Fair Market Value

If an option is actively traded on an established exchange (e.g., American Stock Exchange or Chicago Board of Options Exchange), it is deemed to have a readily ascertainable fair market value. An option that is not traded on an established exchange will not have a readily ascertainable fair market value unless it can be measured with reasonable accuracy. The Regulations support this presumption with detailed conditions for determining value.[82]

Determining value is important because, if the option has a readily ascertainable fair market value at the time of grant, the employee will be taxed immediately. Any gain or loss that accrues after the time of the grant will be recognized as capital gain or loss on the disposition of the underlying stock. When gain is recognized, the employee's basis in the stock includes any amounts paid for the stock plus the amount that was recognized as ordinary income at the time of the grant. The corporate employer takes a deduction in the same year (and for the same amount) income is recognized by the employee.[83] It is important to notice that the result of these options is conditioned on establishing a value for the option and not establishing a value for the stock of the corporation.

No Readily Ascertainable Fair Market Value

If an option does not have a readily ascertainable fair market value, the transaction will remain "open," and the employee will not be taxed when the option is granted. Instead, the employee recognizes ordinary income when the option is exercised. The amount of income to be recognized is the spread between the value of the stock purchased and the price paid at the date of exercise. Any appreciation in the stock after the exercise date will be recognized as capital gain. The corporate employer takes a corresponding tax deduction in the same year and to the extent of ordinary income recognized by the employee.

Example 35

On January 1, 2017, R Corporation grants S, an employee, the option to purchase 1,000 shares for $12 per share on or before August 15, 2018. At the time of the grant, R stock is valued at $20 per share. On June 3, 2018, when the value of R stock is $35, S exercises the option and acquires the stock for $12,000 (1,000 × $12). On November 1, 2018, S sells the stock for $48,000 (1,000 × $48). If the option granted has no readily ascertainable fair market value, S will recognize $23,000 ($35,000 – $12,000) of ordinary income and a $13,000 ($48,000 – $35,000) capital gain, both in 2018. R takes a deduction of $23,000 in 2018. If on the other hand, the option has a readily ascertainable value (for example $8 per share), S must recognize $8,000 of ordinary income in 2017 (the grant date) and a capital gain of $28,000 in 2018 (the sale date). R will take an $8,000 deduction in 2017.

STOCK APPRECIATION RIGHTS

Occasionally, NQSOs can create a problem for employees when they generate taxable income without providing resources to pay the tax. Unfortunately, when this occurs, some employees find it necessary to sell the stock to raise the capital, and this defeats the purpose of providing equity compensation. To ameliorate this dilemma, some employers wrap an NQSO with a Stock Appreciation Right (SAR).

---

[82] Reg. § 1.83-7(b)(2). [83] Reg. § 1.421-6(c), (d), (e), and (f).

An SAR is a type of right (similar to an option) that entitles the employee to a cash payment equal to the difference between the fair market value of one share of the common stock of the corporation on the date of the *exercise* of the SAR over its fair market value on the date it was *granted.* An employee need not own any stock of the corporation to receive an SAR, and SARs are granted without cost to the employee. An SAR cannot be exercised before one year after it was granted and must be exercised by the fifth year, or the SAR will be deemed exercised and cash will be paid to the employee. An SAR is not included in taxable income until the year the right is exercised. The IRS has ruled that an employee who receives an SAR will not be in constructive receipt of income in the year it was granted.[84]

Tax Planning Considerations

The area of employment compensation and retirement planning offers tremendous opportunity for creative tax planning. During a taxpayer's productive years, he or she needs to be able to analyze and appreciate the tax consequences of the various types of compensation alternatives that may be offered. The taxpayer must be aware of the tradeoff between types of compensation that will be taxed currently and fringe benefits that may not be taxable upon receipt. Sophisticated forms of compensation such as § 83 property and incentive stock options should be considered in designing a specialized compensation package.

Taxpayers should also appreciate the necessity for long-range retirement planning. An understanding of the different tax consequences of qualified and nonqualified retirement plans is essential to effective planning for post-employment years. Exhibit 18-8 contains a comparison of the plans discussed in this chapter.

PLANNING FOR RETIREMENT INCOME

One of the central features of an individual's financial plan should be a provision for some source of retirement income. As the life span of the average American lengthens, the number of prospective retirement years increases. As a result, many individuals realize that some amount of current investment is necessary in order to ensure that their retirement years can be a period of financial security.

In analyzing a particular retirement plan, two basic questions must be answered:

1. Are payments into the plan deductible for Federal income tax purposes by the taxpayer?

2. To what extent are retirement benefits received from a plan includible in the recipient taxpayer's gross income?

EXHIBIT 18-8	IRA Deductions for Active Participants in Qualified Plans for 2017		
AGI before IRA Deduction	Single or Head of Household	Filing Jointly or Widower	Married, Filing Separately
$ 0 – $ 10,000	Full	Full	Partial
$ 10,000 – $ 62,000	Full	Full	None
$ 62,000 – $ 72,000	Partial	Full	None
$ 72,000 – $196,000	None	Partial	None
$196,000 +	None	None	None

Locate income and filing status. If the word *Full* appears, a $5,500 deduction is available in 2017; if *None* appears, no deduction is available; and if *Partial* appears, a prorated amount is deductible.

---

[84] Rev. Rul. 80-300. 1980-2 C.B. 165.

ADVANTAGES OF IRAs

IRAs used to be among the best retirement saving plans around until Congress clipped some of their more generous features in 1986. Today they are still a useful part of many retirement portfolios; however, some limitations will apply.

Prior to 1987, IRAs were available to anyone who had not reached the age of 70½. Contributions were allowable up to the $3,000 annual limit and were fully tax deductible. Today, these rules apply to only two types of people:

- Those who are not eligible for an employer-sponsored retirement plan; or

- Those whose incomes fall below specified levels.

For individuals with company retirement plans, deductible IRAs are still available, provided certain tests can be satisfied. The first test of IRA deductibility is income. A taxpayer may still make a fully deductible IRA contribution as long as AGI does not exceed certain levels. Exhibit 18-8 provides a list of eligible individuals and the limitations on IRA deductions.

Example 36

H and W have AGI of $193,000 and file a joint tax return. Their table amount indicates they are entitled to a partial deduction. To determine their deduction, subtract their AGI from the limit for that particular row for 2017 ($193,000 − $186,000 to get $7,000). Next, divide that amount ($7,000) by $10,000 to get a percentage ($7,000/$10,000 = 70%). This is the percentage of the IRA base, $5,500, that may be deducted. Accordingly, H and W may deduct $3,850.

Note: The taxpayers may still *contribute* the full $5,500 (2017), but cannot deduct the extra $1,650.

SPOUSAL IRAs

Holding a job is not a prerequisite to opening and deducting an IRA. A nonworking spouse may start a *spousal IRA*, as long as both taxpayers file jointly and the combined total of both spouse's earned income equals $11,000 (2017). When these two requirements are met, each spouse may make contributions to an IRA. Together, they may contribute as much as $11,000 ($13,000 if the couple is at least 50) in any single year. No more than $5,500 (2017) of that amount, however, may go to either account. If the combined total earned income is less than $11,000, the deduction is not lost. The combined total of the IRA's is limited to the amount of combined income (limited to $5,500 (2017) per spouse).

WHAT IS AN ACTIVE PARTICIPANT?

As discussed earlier, an individual may not be eligible for a deductible IRA if he or she is an active participant or eligible to participate in a pension or profit sharing plan. As a general rule, the IRS considers a taxpayer an active participant in a defined plan if the plan's guidelines state that the taxpayer is covered, even if they decline to participate. As a result, just being eligible for a plan makes the taxpayer an active participant.

If an individual is not sure if he is an active participant, he can look at his W-2 form, provided by his employer. It provides a box for the taxpayer's employer to check. If this box is blank, additional research may be necessary. Exhibit 18-9 provides aid in determining whether a taxpayer is eligible to participate.

MAKING A NONDEDUCTIBLE CONTRIBUTION TO AN IRA

Even if a taxpayer is not eligible, for whatever reason, to make deductible contributions to an IRA, a nondeductible contribution is available. Whether a taxpayer should make a nondeductible IRA contribution depends on the circumstances. Some of the following pros and cons should be considered before a taxpayer makes a decision.

The most obvious pro is that even though a taxpayer may not deduct his or her annual IRA contribution, the earnings from IRA investments accumulate and compound tax-deferred. This means a faster fund build-up compared to a taxable savings account. (See Exhibit 18-10 for a similar comparison.)

EXHIBIT 18-9	Active Participation

Participation in any of the following plans can make a taxpayer an active participant and not eligible to deduct IRA contributions.

- Qualified pension, profit sharing, or stock bonus plans, including Keogh plans
- Qualified annuity plans simplified employee pension plans (SEPs)
- Retirement plans for Federal, state, or local government employees
- Certain union plans [so-called § 501(c)(18) plans]
- Tax-sheltered annuities for pubic school teachers and employees of charitable organizations.
- Section 401(k) plans

EXHIBIT 18-10	Comparison of Corporate Retirement Plans

Description	Corporate Plan	Keogh [HR 10]	Roth or Traditional IRA	SEP	CODA (§ 401(k))	Funded Rabbi	Funded Secular
Qualified	Yes	Yes	Yes	Yes	Yes	No	No
Participation	21 years old or > 1 year = 100% vested	21 years old or > 1 year = 100% vested	Limited by AGI	21 years old or 3 out of 5 year's service	1 year's service	No requirements	
Limitations	100% I $54,000 or 100% of $270,000 I 100% average.	100% I $54,000 or 13.043% of $270,000 I 100% average.	$5,500 or 100% Earned Income	$54,000 or 15% Earned Income	$18,000 (for 2017)	No limitations if paid as reasonable compensation	
Vesting	3 years Cliff or 6 years Graded	3 years Cliff or 6 years Graded	100%	100%	100% of employee's contribution	Subject to claims of creditors	100%
Premature Distributions	Rollover or 10% penalty	Rollover or 10% penalty	Rollover or 10% penalty	Rollover or 10% penalty	Rollover or 10% penalty	Taxable only if not previously taxed	
Lump-Sum 10-Year Averaging Available If Born before 1936	Yes	Yes	No, taxed as ordinary income or tax free	No, taxed as ordinary income	Yes	Not available: in some cases funds previously taxed	
Date Plan Must Be Established	By last day of plan year	By last day of plan year	Regular tax due date	Regular tax due date	By last day of plan year	By last day of plan year	
Required Date to Contribute	Extended due date	Extended due date	Regular due date	Regular due date	Extended due date	Year end	
Employee Loans from the Plan	Yes	None: owner-employees	None	None	Limited	Yes, but very risky	Yes

The most obvious con is that once money is put into an IRA, it is locked in until the taxpayer attains the age 59½. Otherwise, the taxpayer is subject to pay a 10% penalty for early withdrawal. The penalty applies to the deductible portion of the IRA contribution and to any earnings that may have accumulated tax-deferred in the account. However, no penalty applies when nondeductible contributions are withdrawn.

Many investment counselors suggest tax-free bonds as a reasonable alternative to making a nondeductible IRA contribution. The earnings from the bonds are tax-free and are not subject to a penalty if the taxpayer needs to withdraw any of the money. Moreover, a taxpayer is not limited to investing $5,500 ($11,000 for spousal IRAs).

Bonds, however, come with two potential drawbacks. First, a taxpayer can possibly get locked into the bonds until maturity. If interest rates rise, the value of the bonds generally declines, and a taxpayer would potentially have to sell the bonds at a loss. Second, depending on the market, the yields on bonds are sometimes low compared to the after-tax yields of other securities. So, potentially, bonds can be a very poor investment.

Problem Materials

DISCUSSION QUESTIONS

18-1 *Taxation of Barter Transactions.* Your friend who is a practicing dentist tells you that he filled a tooth for a friend's child "for no payment" because the friend had prepared the dentist's income tax return for the previous year. Must the dentist recognize taxable income because of this arrangement? Explain.

18-2 *Taxation of Fringe Benefits.* Define the term *fringe benefit.* As a general rule are fringe benefits taxable?

18-3 *Taxation of Fringe Benefits.* Every year, Employer E gives each employee the choice of a turkey or ham as a Christmas "gift." Is the value of this fringe benefit taxable to the employees? Would your answer be different if each employee received a Christmas bonus of $500 cash?

18-4 *Fringe Benefits—Cafeteria Plans.* What is a cafeteria plan of employee benefits?

18-5 *Reasons for Stock Options.* How does a corporation benefit from compensating valuable employees with shares of stock in the corporation rather than a cash wage or salary?

18-6 *Receipt of Restricted Property for Services.* What factors should a taxpayer consider when deciding to make an election under § 83(b) with regard to restricted property?

18-7 *ISO Plans.* An ISO (incentive stock option) allows the recipient both a deferral of income and a conversion of ordinary income into capital gain. Explain.

18-8 *Funded versus Unfunded Deferred Compensation Arrangements.* Why would an employee normally prefer a funded rather than an unfunded deferred compensation arrangement? Which would the employer normally prefer?

18-9 *Deferred Compensation and the Constructive Receipt Doctrine.* Explain the doctrine of constructive receipt as it relates to a cash basis employee who has a deferred compensation arrangement with his or her employer.

18-10 *Tax Advantages of Qualified Retirement Plans.* Discuss the tax advantages granted to qualified retirement plans.

18-11 *Defined Benefit versus Defined Contribution Plans.* Differentiate between a defined benefit retirement plan and a defined contribution retirement plan.

18-12 *Retirement Plan Qualification Requirements.* Any employee of Trion Ltd. Partnership can participate in the company's pension plan after they have been employed by Trion for 36 consecutive months. Can Trion's plan be a qualified retirement plan? Discuss.

18-13 *The Meaning of Vested Benefits.* Explain the concept of vesting as it relates to qualified retirement plans. How does it differ from the concept of participation?

18-14 *Profit-Sharing Plans versus Pension Plans.* Many small, developing companies will choose to establish a qualified profit-sharing plan rather than a pension plan. Why?

18-15 *Spousal IRAs.* Discuss the purpose of a spousal IRA (individual retirement account).

18-16 *Lump-Sum Distribution Rollovers.* Why might an employee who receives a lump sum distribution from a qualified retirement plan choose to roll over the distribution into an IRA? What are the negative tax consequences of doing so?

18-17 *Roth IRAs versus Traditional IRAs.* In 1998, Congress provided taxpayers wanting to establish an IRA a choice. Taxpayers may now use either a Roth IRA or a traditional IRA or both.
   a. Identify the major differences between Roth IRAs and traditional IRAs.
   b. Identify circumstances when a Roth IRA may be preferred over a traditional IRA and vice versa.

18-18 *Education (Coverdell) IRAs.* One of the tax incentives created for higher education in 1998 was the Education IRA.
   a. Explain how an education IRA works.
   b. Compare an education IRA to a qualified prepaid tuition and how it relates to the Hope and Lifetime Learning credits.

PROBLEMS

18-19 *Receipt of Restricted Property for Services.* D, a calendar year taxpayer, is an employee of M Corporation, also on a calendar year for tax purposes. In 2017, M Corporation transfers 100 shares of its own common stock to D as a bonus for his outstanding work during the year. If D quits his job with M within the next three years, he must return the shares to the corporation. At date of transfer, the shares are selling on the open market at $35 per share. Three years later, when the risk of forfeiture lapses, the stock is selling at $100 per share.
   a. Assume D does not make the election under § 83(b). How much income must he recognize in 2017 because of his receipt of the stock? In 2020 when his restriction lapses?
   b. Assume D does elect under § 83(b). How much income must he recognize in 2017? In 2020?
   c. Refer to questions (a) and (b). In each case how much of a deduction may M Corporation claim and in which year should the deduction be taken?

18-20 *Tax Consequences of a Nonqualified Stock Option Plan.* In 2017, Z Corporation grants a nonqualified stock option to employee M. The option allows M to purchase 100 shares of Z Corporation stock for $20 per share at any time during the next four years. Because the current market value of Z stock is $22 per share, the option has a readily ascertainable value of $200 ($2 per share bargain element X 100 shares) at date of grant. M exercises the option in 2017 when the market value of the Z stock has increased to $28 per share.
   a. How much income does M recognize in 2017 because of the receipt of the option?
   b. How much income does M recognize in 2018 upon exercise of the option?
   c. What amount of deduction is available to Corporation Z because of the option granted to M? In what year is the deduction claimed?

18-21 *Tax Consequences of a Nonqualified Stock Option Plan.* In 2017, X Corporation grants a nonqualified stock option to E, a valued employee, as additional compensation. The option has no value at date of grant, but entitles E to purchase 1,000 shares of X stock for $20 per share at any time during the next five years. E exercises the option in 2018, when X Corporation's stock is selling on the open market at $48 per share.
   a. How much income does E recognize in 2017 because of her receipt of the option?
   b. How much income does E recognize in 2018 upon exercise of the option?
   c. What amount of deduction is available to X Corporation because of the option granted to E? In what year is the deduction claimed?

18-22 *Nonqualified Stock Option Plans.* Refer to the facts in *Problems 18-20* and *18-21*. In each case, what tax basis does the employee have in the purchased corporate stock?

18-23 *Incentive Stock Options (ISO) versus Nonqualified Stock Options.* Refer to the facts in *Problem 18-21*. If the stock option issued by X corporation had been an ISO rather than a nonqualified option, how much income would E recognize in 2018 upon option exercise?

18-24 *Incentive Stock Option Plans.* In May 2016, employee N exercised an ISO that entitled him to purchase 50 shares of Clay Corporation common stock for $120 a share. The stock was selling on the open market for $210 per share. N sold the 50 shares in 2019 for $390 per share.
  a. How much income must N recognize in 2016 upon exercise of the option?
  b. How much income must N recognize in 2019 upon sale of the Clay stock?

18-25 *Incentive Stock Options—Early Disposition of Stock.* Refer to the facts in *Problem 18-24*. What would be the tax consequences if N sold the Clay stock in August 2016 for $250 per share? For $190 per share?

18-26 *Tax Computation on Lump Sum Distributions.* T participated in his employer's qualified profit sharing plan from 1981 until his retirement at age 64 in the current year. T made no contributions to the plan. In the current year, T received a lump sum distribution of $75,000 from the plan.
  a. How much of the distribution is taxable to T in the current year?
  b. As far as the tax treatment is concerned, what options are available?

18-27 *Tax Computation on Lump-Sum Distributions.* In the current year, Mrs. Z, age 61, retired after a 35-year career with the same corporate employer. She received her entire $51,000 account balance from her employer's qualified profit sharing plan. In the current year, Mrs. Z and her husband will file a joint return on which they will report $21,000 of other taxable income (net of all deductions and exemptions). As far as the tax treatment is concerned, what options are available?

18-28 *Qualified Pension Plan—Maximum Annual Benefits.* During his last three years as president of R Corporation, G was paid $200,000 in 2015, $230,000 in 2016, and $280,000 in 2017 as total compensation for his services. These were the three highest compensation years of his employment. What is the maximum retirement benefit payable to G from the corporation's qualified pension plan (a defined benefit plan)?

18-29 *Qualified Profit Sharing Plans—Maximum Annual Contribution.* In the current year, Mr. W, a corporate vice president, earned a base salary of $350,000. His corporate employer maintains a qualified retirement plan that provides for an annual contribution equal to 10% of each employee's base level of compensation. Based on these facts, compute the maximum current-year contribution to Mr. W's retirement account.

18-30 *Additional Taxes on Plan Distributions.* In the current year, Mr. L, age 51 and in perfect health, resigns as President of Meta Industries, Inc. Mr. L receives a $300,000 lump sum distribution from Meta's qualified retirement plan. Before consideration of this distribution, Mr. L's taxable income for the year is over $200,000. If Mr. L decides not to "roll over" the contribution into another qualified plan or IRA, compute the net after-tax amount of the distribution that Mr. L will be able to spend.

18-31 *Maximum Annual Contributions to Keogh Plans.* H is a self-employed business person with several employees. He has established a profit-sharing plan for himself and his employees. The annual net earned income from his business is $132,000. What is the maximum amount of a deduction available to H for his contribution to the plan for the year?

18-32 *Maximum Annual Contributions to IRAs.* H and W file a joint tax return. W is a lawyer with current-year earned income of $180,000. H works part-time as a landscape architect and earned $22,000 in the current year.

    a. Assume that W is an active participant in the firm's qualified profit-sharing plan. How much may W and H contribute to their IRAs for the current year? How much of the contribution is deductible?

    b. Assume neither H nor W is an active participant in a qualified retirement plan. How does this assumption change your answers to (a) above?

18-33 *Maximum Deductible Contributions to IRAs.* In the current year, Ms. A, a single taxpayer, contributed $1,400 to her IRA. She also is an active participant in her employer's qualified money purchase pension plan. Ms. A's adjusted gross income (before any deduction for her IRA contribution) is $29,640. How much of the IRA contribution is deductible in 2017?

18-34 *Taxability of IRA Distributions.* Taxpayer B, age 66, makes his first withdrawal of $8,800 from his IRA in the current year and uses the money to make a down payment on a sailboat. At the end of the year, B's IRA balance is $36,555. During previous years, B had made nondeductible contributions to the IRA totaling $13,400. Based on these facts, what amount of the $8,800 withdrawal must B include in current-year gross income?

18-35 *Simplified Employee Pensions.* Z is an employee of a company that has established a SEP. Z's current-year salary is $18,000.

    a. How much may Z's employer contribute to her IRA during 2017?

    b. May Z make any additional deductible contribution herself to her IRA?

TAX RESEARCH PROBLEMS

18-36 *Current versus Deferred Compensation.* Roy Hartman is a 55-year-old executive of the Robco Oil Tool Corporation. The corporation does not have any type of qualified pension or profit-sharing plan, nor does it intend to adopt one in the near future. However, in an effort to ensure the continuing services of Mr. Hartman, Robco Corporation has offered him a choice between two different compensation arrangements. One pays $40,000 additional annual salary; and the other provides for $50,000 a year deferred compensation for 10 years beginning when Roy retires at age 65. Currently, Hartman's marginal tax rate is 31 percent. Roy does not expect to be in a lower tax bracket within his last 10 years of employment or after retirement. Since he does not need the $28,800 which would remain after paying current taxes on the $40,000 additional annual salary, Mr. Hartman asks you to evaluate his alternative compensation proposals. Assuming a 10% pre-tax return on savings will prevail over the entire 20-year period (10 years before and 10 years after retirement), and assuming that he would save the entire $28,800 annual after-tax salary under the $40,000 additional annual compensation arrangement, which alternative would you recommend? Why?

18-37 *Qualified Retirement Plans.* Shelly Carol is the sole shareholder of Gills Corporation. The corporation has been in business since 1989 manufacturing dog food. Profits have averaged about $300,000 per year for the past five years. Shelly projects that with the purchase of additional manufacturing equipment costing $700,000, he can double his production of dog food, resulting in additional profits of $200,000. Unfortunately, Shelly does not have the funds readily available to make the additional capital purchases, so in order to implement the plan she intends to borrow the entire $700,000.

Required:

1. How can Gills Corporation achieve its goal of financing the capital improvements while providing an incentive benefit to its employees?

2. Assume that Gills Corporation's payroll is approximately $600,000 and that Shelly intends to set aside $100,000 for the benefit of the employees. Compare the plan selected in (1) above with an ordinary pension or profit-sharing plan.

3. What are some of the disadvantages that Shelly should consider in using the plan established in (1)?

Research aids:

Section 401(a)(28)(C).

Section 404(a)(3).

Section 404(a)(9).

Section 409(h).

Section 4975(e)(7).

19

Taxation of Business Forms and Their Owners

Learning Objectives

Upon completion of this chapter you will be able to:

LO.1 Understand the basic rules governing the taxation of the four business forms: sole proprietorships, partnerships, S corporations, and C corporations.

LO.2 Compute the net taxable income or loss for the four types of business organizations.

LO.3 Explain the basic tax consequences of forming a new business.

Chapter Outline

Introduction

For most people, their only encounter with the income tax is the annual filing of their own personal income tax returns. It is clearly an experience that few enjoy. Having endured the filing of an individual income tax return, it would seem to most that the taxation of business must be exceedingly complex since businesses are usually involved in far more complicated transactions than individuals. While this may be the case in some instances, the truth is that the basic computation of the taxable income of a business differs little from that of an individual. In this sense, whatever one knows about individual taxation generally serves them well when trying to understand business taxation. Many are quite surprised to find that most of the general rules that apply to individuals also apply to businesses. For example, the basic tax formula used to compute taxable income is identical for each: gross income minus deductions equals taxable income. And the elements of that formula, gross income and deductions, are defined in the same manner for businesses as they are for individuals. Nevertheless, despite the similarities of individual and business taxation, there are differences. This chapter examines the tax rules that apply to the basic forms of organizations used to carry on business in the United States: sole proprietorships, partnerships, limited liability companies, and corporations. The chapter initially focuses on the taxation of routine operations and concludes with a brief overview of the tax consequences of forming a particular type of business organization. For an in-depth discussion of these organizational forms, consult the second volume of this two-volume series, *Corporate, Partnership, Estate and Gift Taxation.*

Sole Proprietorships

LO.1

Understand the basic rules governing the taxation of the four business forms: sole proprietorships, partnerships, S corporations, and C corporations.

More businesses are operated as sole proprietorships than any other form. This is a reflection, in part, of our entrepreneurial society. But it also is due to the fact that sole proprietorships are the simplest form of business—personally, legally, and for tax purposes. In this regard, it should be noted that the term "sole proprietorship" includes all individuals who perform services as an independent contractor. Thus all individuals who receive a Form 1099 reporting service income are considered sole proprietors. In addition, the sole proprietorship has increased in popularity with the advent of the single member limited liability company (SMLLC).[1]

For tax purposes, SMLLCs are simply ignored, a tax "nothing" as many say.[2] What this means is that when the owner of the SMLLC is an individual, the SMLLC is simply treated as a sole proprietorship. As a result, an individual can now obtain the protection of limited liability for his or her sole proprietorship without having to incorporate. More importantly, this new entity enables one-owner businesses to obtain limited liability without the need for the additional complexity that incorporation brings (e.g., an additional tax and a corporate tax return).

The tax treatment of a sole proprietorship differs somewhat from the treatment used in financial accounting. For financial accounting purposes, sole proprietorships are treated as entities separate and distinct from their owners. For tax purposes, however, the sole proprietorship is not a separate taxable entity. The sole proprietorship does not file a separate tax return. Instead, the relevant information of the sole proprietorship is reported on the individual's personal income tax return along with the individual's other items of income and deduction. The proprietorship's income and deductions are not merely thrown together with all of the other items, however. They are segregated—at least somewhat. All of the *ordinary* income and deductions relating to the proprietorship's operations are captured on a separate schedule, Schedule C (or Schedule F for farming operations), which accompanies the individual's Form 1040 (see Exhibit 19-1).[3] Note that the net income or loss of the proprietorship reported on line 31 of Schedule C is transferred to line 12 on page 1 of Form 1040 to become part of the individual's total adjusted gross income. All items subject to special tax treatment, such as capital gains and losses, charitable contributions, and dividend income are reported on the appropriate tax return schedule (e.g., Schedule D for capital gains and Schedule A for charitable contributions) as though the owner engaged in the transactions rather than the proprietorship.

---

[1] Creation of SMLLCs have been permitted in all states since Hawaii's law went into effect on April 1, 1997.

[2] Reg. § 301.7701-3(b)(1).

[3] §§ 61(a) and 162.

EXHIBIT 19-1   Schedule C (Form 1040)

SCHEDULE C	**Profit or Loss From Business**	OMB No. 1545-0074
(Form 1040)	(Sole Proprietorship)	**2016**
Department of the Treasury	▶ Information about Schedule C and its separate instructions is at *www.irs.gov/schedulec*.	Attachment
Internal Revenue Service (99)	▶ **Attach to Form 1040, 1040NR, or 1041; partnerships generally must file Form 1065.**	Sequence No. **09**

Name of proprietor	Social security number (SSN)
Mary A Smith	123 – 45 – 6789

A Principal business or profession, including product or service (see instructions)
Retail Apparel

B Enter code from instructions
G ▶ 4 4 8 1 3 0

C Business name. If no separate business name, leave blank.
Mary's Proprietorship

D Employer ID number (EIN), (see instr.)

E Business address (including suite or room no.) ▶ 1710 North Shore Street
City, town or post office, state, and ZIP code   Tampa, FL 33260

F Accounting method: (1) [x] Cash   (2) ☐ Accrual   (3) ☐ Other (specify) ▶

G Did you "materially participate" in the operation of this business during 2016? If "No," see instructions for limit on losses   [x] Yes   ☐ No

H If you started or acquired this business during 2016, check here   ▶ ☐

I Did you make any payments in 2016 that would require you to file Form(s) 1099? (see instructions)   ☐ Yes [x] No

J If "Yes," did you or will you file required Forms 1099?   ☐ Yes   ☐ No

Part I Income

1	Gross receipts or sales. See instructions for line 1 and check the box if this income was reported to you on Form W-2 and the "Statutory employee" box on that form was checked ▶ ☐	1	150,000	00
2	Returns and allowances	2		
3	Subtract line 2 from line 1	3	150,000	00
4	Cost of goods sold (from line 42)	4	60,000	00
5	**Gross profit.** Subtract line 4 from line 3	5	90,000	00
6	Other income, including federal and state gasoline or fuel tax credit or refund (see instructions)	6		
7	**Gross income.** Add lines 5 and 6 ▶	7	90,000	00

Part II Expenses. Enter expenses for business use of your home **only** on line 30.

8	Advertising	8			18	Office expense (see instructions)	18		
9	Car and truck expenses (see instructions)	9			19	Pension and profit-sharing plans	19		
10	Commissions and fees	10			20	Rent or lease (see instructions):			
11	Contract labor (see instructions)	11			a	Vehicles, machinery, and equipment	20a		
12	Depletion	12			b	Other business property	20b	4,900	00
13	Depreciation and section 179 expense deduction (not included in Part III) (see instructions)	13	12,000	00	21	Repairs and maintenance	21	1,800	00
					22	Supplies (not included in Part III)	22		
					23	Taxes and licenses	23	3,200	00
					24	Travel, meals, and entertainment:			
14	Employee benefit programs (other than on line 19)	14			a	Travel	24a		
15	Insurance (other than health)	15			b	Deductible meals and entertainment (see instructions)	24b		
16	Interest:				25	Utilities	25		
a	Mortgage (paid to banks, etc.)	16a			26	Wages (less employment credits)	26	30,000	00
b	Other	16b			27a	Other expenses (from line 48)	27a		
17	Legal and professional services	17			b	**Reserved for future use**	27b		

28	**Total expenses** before expenses for business use of home. Add lines 8 through 27a ▶	28	51,900	00
29	Tentative profit or (loss). Subtract line 28 from line 7	29	38,100	00
30	Expenses for business use of your home. Do not report these expenses elsewhere. Attach Form 8829 unless using the simplified method (see instructions). **Simplified method filers only:** enter the total square footage of: (a) your home: _____ and (b) the part of your home used for business: _____. Use the Simplified Method Worksheet in the instructions to figure the amount to enter on line 30	30		
31	**Net profit or (loss).** Subtract line 30 from line 29. • If a profit, enter on both **Form 1040, line 12** (or **Form 1040NR, line 13**) and on **Schedule SE, line 2.** (If you checked the box on line 1, see instructions). Estates and trusts, enter on **Form 1041, line 3.** • If a loss, you **must** go to line 32.	31	38,100	00
32	If you have a loss, check the box that describes your investment in this activity (see instructions). • If you checked 32a, enter the loss on both **Form 1040, line 12,** (or **Form 1040NR, line 13**) and on **Schedule SE, line 2.** (If you checked the box on line 1, see the line 31 instructions). Estates and trusts, enter on **Form 1041, line 3.** • If you checked 32b, you **must** attach **Form 6198.** Your loss may be limited.	32a ☐ All investment is at risk. 32b ☐ Some investment is not at risk.		

For Paperwork Reduction Act Notice, see the separate instructions.   Cat. No. 11334P   Schedule C (Form 1040) 2016

LO.2

Compute the net taxable income or loss for the four types of business organizations.

Actual determination of a sole proprietorship's income simply requires the application of the basic rules that apply to an individual. Like other businesses, the net income of the proprietorship is generally the gross income from operations less the costs of doing business. The net income or loss of the proprietorship is reported on Schedule C of Form 1040 and flows through to page 1, line 12. The major difference between the taxation of proprietorships and other forms of business lies in its lack of uniqueness. Because the sole proprietorship is not treated as a separate entity, the owner cannot enter into taxable transactions with the proprietorship as a creditor, an employee, a customer, or in any other role. For example, a sole proprietor does not receive a salary from the proprietorship. His or her "compensation" is simply the net income of the business. As a result, a sole proprietor is not subject to normal payroll taxes. Instead, a sole proprietorship's net ordinary income is subject to self-employment tax.[4] This requirement is reflected in line 31 of Schedule C, which requires the net profit of the proprietorship to be entered on Schedule SE for computing the self-employment tax.

Example 1

The records of a proprietorship owned by Mary Smith show the following information for the year:

Sales	$150,000
Cost of goods sold	60,000
Operating expenses:	
Depreciation	12,000
Rent	4,900
Repairs	1,800
Payroll and property taxes	3,200
Employee salaries	30,000
Mary's compensation	25,000
Capital gain	2,000

All of the amounts shown above are recorded on Schedule C (Exhibit 19-1) except for the last two. Thus, gross income is $90,000 ($150,000 − $60,000) and *net ordinary income* is $38,100 ($90,000 − $12,000 − $3,000 − $1,100 − $1,800 − $3,200 − $800 − $30,000). Note that line 31 of Schedule C requires the net income to be reported on Form 1040, increasing Mary's adjusted gross income (AGI), and on Schedule SE to determine any *self-employment tax*. The amount listed above as "Mary's compensation" does not qualify as salary since an owner cannot be an employee of his or her own proprietorship. The $25,000 is neither deductible by the proprietorship nor includible income to Mary. It is simply a nontaxable withdrawal. The capital gain is reported on Mary's Schedule D with all her other capital gains and losses.

Example 2

Assume the same facts in *Example 1*, except that cost of goods sold is $100,000 instead of $60,000. The proprietorship now has a *net ordinary loss* of $1,900. The $1,900 loss is reported on Form 1040, reducing AGI, and on Schedule SE, reducing self-employment income from Mary's other sources (if any). The fact that the proprietorship has a net loss does not change the treatment of any other item listed in *Example 1*. If the $1,900 proprietorship loss is not offset by Mary's other income, she is eligible for the net operating loss (NOL) two-year carryback and/or 20-year carryforward computation (discussed in Chapter 10).[5]

The fact that a sole proprietor cannot be an employee has important implications regarding fringe benefits. Several of the fringe benefits, such as group-term life insurance, and employer-provided meals and lodging, are not available to sole proprietors since they are not considered employees. As discussed in Chapter 6, businesses are normally allowed to deduct the costs of fringe benefits for their employees and they are nontaxable to the employees. However, when a proprietorship pays for these items, the payment is treated as if the owner made the payment directly.

---

[4] § 6017. See Chapter 1. [5] § 172(c).

The problem is easily seen with the cost of the owner's medical insurance. For example, if the proprietorship pays the medical insurance premium for the owner, it is treated as if the owner paid the premium. The expense is not reported on Schedule C but is reported as part of the taxpayer's total medical expenses. Consequently, the expense would be subject to the treatment reserved for medical expenses, which are generally not deductible unless total medical expenses exceed 10% of the taxpayer's AGI. Had the owner been considered an employee, the payment would have been deductible by the proprietorship and nontaxable to the owner. Without employee status, the proprietor is denied such favorable treatment. Depending on the taxpayer's situation, the loss of the special treatment for certain fringe benefits may cause him or her to opt for another form of business organization (e.g., a regular C corporation) where employee status and, therefore, favorable fringe benefit treatment is available. Interestingly, because health insurance is such an important fringe benefit, Congress decided to address this particular inequity.

To put sole proprietors (as well as partners and owners of S corporations) on equal footing with shareholder-employees of C corporations, special treatment for health insurance is provided in § 162(l). As explained in Chapter 11, self-employed individuals (i.e., sole proprietorships, partners, LLC members, and more than 2% S shareholders) are allowed to deduct 100% of the amounts paid for health insurance on behalf of a self-employed individual, his or her spouse, and dependents as a deductible business expense. The deduction for health insurance is allowed in determining adjusted gross income (i.e., a deduction *for* AGI) rather than being treated as an itemized medical expense deduction subject to the 10% floor. No deduction is allowable to the extent it exceeds the taxpayer's net earnings from self-employment. Thus the deduction cannot create a loss. More important, the deduction *does not reduce* the income base for which the taxpayer is liable for self-employment taxes.

Partnerships

LO.1 Understand the basic rules governing the taxation of the four business forms: sole proprietorships, partnerships, S corporations, and C corporations.

When two or more parties agree to go into business together, they often choose to operate as a partnership. Partnerships are quite common due in part to the fact that they are easy to form. The parties simply need to agree to do business together. Unlike the formation of a corporation, no special forms need to be filed, and there is no formal registration with the state. Perhaps surprisingly, there is no requirement that the partnership agreement be in writing. An oral agreement will suffice, although reflecting the terms of the arrangement in a written document is obviously more prudent.

There are two types of partnerships: general partnerships and limited partnerships. General partnerships are owned solely by general partners while limited partnerships have at least one general partner and one limited partner. The two differ primarily in the rights and obligations of the partners. As their title suggests, limited partners are liable for partnership debts only to the extent of their contribution and have no voice in management. In contrast, general partners have unlimited liability for partnership obligations but may participate in the management and control of the partnership.

As mentioned in Chapter 3, all 50 states have enacted legislation authorizing the formation of limited liability companies (LLCs). LLCs are unique, borrowing characteristics from both corporations and partnerships. For example, as in the case of a corporation, owners of an LLC (or members, as they are normally called) are liable for obligations of the LLC only to the extent of their investment. Beyond this, however, LLCs are normally more like partnerships (e.g., interests are normally not freely transferable, the LLC dissolves upon certain events, and most LLCs lack centralized management). Technically, the Internal Revenue Code does not recognize LLCs. However, regulations provide that an LLC that has at least two members will be treated as a partnership unless it elects to be treated as a corporation. For this reason, all of the rules that apply to the taxation of partnerships also apply to LLCs with only a few modifications.

TAXATION OF PARTNERSHIP OPERATIONS

LO.2 Compute the net taxable income or loss for the four types of business organizations.

In many respects, partnerships are taxed like proprietorships. Neither are separate taxable entities. The partnership is merely a conduit through which income, deductions, credits, and other items flow to the individual partners, who report them on their own returns.[6]

[6] §§ 701 and 702(b).

The amount of each item allocated to a partner is normally based on the partner's capital interest in the partnership or some other allocation method adopted by the partners.[7] Consistent with this pass-through approach, the items normally retain their character when they are allocated to the partners. For example, tax-exempt income received by the partnership flows through and is reported as tax-exempt income by the partners. To accomplish this pass-through, the partnership must file an annual information return, Form 1065 (see Exhibit 19-2). The return is simply a compilation of the items of tax consequence to the partnership and its partners. It not only reports information about the partnership's income or loss for the year but also how the income or loss must be allocated among the partners.

The various items of income, deduction, and credit that flow through to each partner are reported in one of two ways. Any item that may receive special treatment by a partner, such as capital gains, dividends, or charitable contributions, must be separately stated on Schedule B of Form 1065 (see Exhibit 19-3). In this way, the character of the item is preserved and the special treatment that the item deserves is not lost. To illustrate, consider dividends. Although dividends are treated as ordinary income by individual taxpayers, they must be separately stated since corporate taxpayers are entitled to the dividends-received deduction. Similarly, charitable contributions must be separately stated since the limitations on the deduction differ between corporations and individuals and, moreover, the limitation for each partner may differ. All other items of income and expense—those that do not receive any special treatment—are netted to arrive at the partnership's *ordinary income* (or *loss*). They are summarized on page 1 of Form 1065 (see line 22 on page 1 of Form 1065). Each partner's *share* of the partnership's net ordinary income and separately stated items are reported on Schedule K-1 (see Exhibit 19-4). When the partners file their own returns, they must incorporate the partnership information from Schedule K-1. For example, individual taxpayers report their share of ordinary income from the partnership on Schedule E of Form 1040 while all other items are reported on the partner's appropriate schedule as if the partner had received the income or paid the expense.[8] For instance, if the partnership reported a long-term capital gain, or long-term capital loss the individual partner would report his share on his own Schedule D.

Another similarity between proprietorships and partnerships concerns employment taxes.[9] A *general* partner's share of the partnership's ordinary income (after removal of certain passive income items such as depreciation recapture income) is subject to self-employment tax. In contrast, a *limited* partner's share of partnership ordinary income is not subject to self-employment tax since it represents investment income to a limited partner. While the treatment of LLC members for this purpose is not clear, it would appear that members of a limited liability company who are considered managers, that is, who have authority to make business decisions, would be treated as general partners, and consequently their distributive share would be subject to self-employment tax. In contrast, nonmanagers would be treated like limited partners.

It is important to understand that the flow-through aspect of partnership taxation is just one of part of a complete system that ensures that partnership income is taxed once and only once. While the intricacies of this system are beyond this overview, the thrust of the system is easily illustrated. Consider a typical situation in which two individuals form a partnership, each contributing $10,000 to the partnership in exchange for a 50% interest. Assume the partnership immediately takes the money and purchases stock for $20,000 that it subsequently sells for $22,000. In this case, the partnership has income of $2,000 ($22,000 − $20,000), and each partner reports his $1,000 share. Note that the partners report their share of partnership income even if they receive no distributions from the partnership, However, to ensure that the partnership's income is not taxed again when it is distributed, each partner must keep track of his investment, that is, the adjusted basis for his or her partnership interest. In this case, each partner has an original basis equal to the amount that he contributed to the partnership, $10,000. Upon reporting partnership income, each partner adjusts his basis in his partnership interest for his share of income, increasing it from $10,000 to $11,000. When a partner actually receives his $1,000 share of the income, the distribution is treated as tax-free to the extent of his basis. Each partner would then reduce his basis by $1,000, back to his original basis of $10,000. The end result is that the partners have reported and received income that has been subject to only *one* tax.

---

[7] §§ 702(a) and (c), and 704(a) and (b).

[8] Under § 704(d), the deduction for losses and separately stated expenses allocated to the partner generally cannot exceed the partner's basis in the partnership.

[9] § 1402, Reg. § 1.707-1(c), and Prop. Reg. § 1.1402(a)-18.

EXHIBIT 19-2   **Form 1065**

Form **1065**
Department of the Treasury
Internal Revenue Service

U.S. Return of Partnership Income

For calendar year 2016, or tax year beginning _____ , 2016, ending _____ , 20 ___.

▶ Information about Form 1065 and its separate instructions is at *www.irs.gov/form1065.*

OMB No. 1545-0123

2016

A Principal business activity Retail Trade	Name of partnership H and L Partnership	**D** Employer identification number 66 – 0770333
B Principal product or service Apparel	**Type or Print** Number, street, and room or suite no. If a P.O. box, see the instructions. 3109 State Street	**E** Date business started 1 – 1 – 93
C Business code number 448110	City or town, state or province, country, and ZIP or foreign postal code State College, PA 16801	**F** Total assets (see the instructions) $ 120,000 00

G   Check applicable boxes: **(1)** ☐ Initial return   **(2)** ☐ Final return   **(3)** ☐ Name change   **(4)** ☐ Address change   **(5)** ☐ Amended return
       (6) ☐ Technical termination - also check (1) or (2)

H   Check accounting method: **(1)** ☐ Cash   **(2)** ☒ Accrual   **(3)** ☐ Other (specify) ▶ _____

I   Number of Schedules K-1. Attach one for each person who was a partner at any time during the tax year ▶ 2

J   Check if Schedules C and M-3 are attached . . . . ☐

Caution. *Include **only** trade or business income and expenses on lines 1a through 22 below. See the instructions for more information.*

Income	**1a**	Gross receipts or sales	**1a** 150,000 00	
	b	Returns and allowances	**1b**	
	c	Balance. Subtract line 1b from line 1a	**1c**	150,000 00
	2	Cost of goods sold (attach Form 1125-A)	**2**	60,000 00
	3	Gross profit. Subtract line 2 from line 1c	**3**	90,000 00
	4	Ordinary income (loss) from other partnerships, estates, and trusts (attach statement) . .	**4**	
	5	Net farm profit (loss) (attach Schedule F (Form 1040))	**5**	
	6	Net gain (loss) from Form 4797, Part II, line 17 (attach Form 4797)	**6**	
	7	Other income (loss) (attach statement)	**7**	
	8	**Total income (loss).** Combine lines 3 through 7	**8**	90,000 00
Deductions (see the instructions for limitations)	**9**	Salaries and wages (other than to partners) (less employment credits)	**9**	30,000 00
	10	Guaranteed payments to partners	**10**	25,000 00
	11	Repairs and maintenance	**11**	1,800 00
	12	Bad debts	**12**	
	13	Rent	**13**	4,900 00
	14	Taxes and licenses	**14**	3,200 00
	15	Interest	**15**	
	16a	Depreciation (if required, attach Form 4562)	**16a** 12,000 00	
	b	Less depreciation reported on Form 1125-A and elsewhere on return	**16b** **16c**	12,000 00
	17	Depletion **(Do not deduct oil and gas depletion.)**	**17**	
	18	Retirement plans, etc.	**18**	
	19	Employee benefit programs	**19**	
	20	Other deductions (attach statement)	**20**	
	21	**Total deductions.** Add the amounts shown in the far right column for lines 9 through 20 .	**21**	76,900 00
	22	**Ordinary business income (loss).** Subtract line 21 from line 8	**22**	13,100 00

Sign Here

Under penalties of perjury, I declare that I have examined this return, including accompanying schedules and statements, and to the best of my knowledge and belief, it is true, correct, and complete. Declaration of preparer (other than general partner or limited liability company member manager) is based on all information of which preparer has any knowledge.

▶ _____   ▶ _____
    Signature of general partner or limited liability company member manager   Date

May the IRS discuss this return with the preparer shown below (see instructions)? ☐ **Yes**   ☐ **No**

Paid Preparer Use Only

Print/Type preparer's name	Preparer's signature	Date	Check ☐ if self-employed	PTIN
Firm's name ▶			Firm's EIN ▶	
Firm's address ▶			Phone no.	

For Paperwork Reduction Act Notice, see separate instructions.   Cat. No. 11390Z   Form **1065** (2016)

EXHIBIT 19-3   **Schedule B (Form 1065)**

Form 1065 (2016)   Page **2**

Schedule B   **Other Information**

		Yes	No
1	What type of entity is filing this return? Check the applicable box:		

a [X] Domestic general partnership   b [ ] Domestic limited partnership
c [ ] Domestic limited liability company   d [ ] Domestic limited liability partnership
e [ ] Foreign partnership   f [ ] Other ▶

		Yes	No
2	At any time during the tax year, was any partner in the partnership a disregarded entity, a partnership (including an entity treated as a partnership), a trust, an S corporation, an estate (other than an estate of a deceased partner), or a nominee or similar person?		X
3	At the end of the tax year:		
a	Did any foreign or domestic corporation, partnership (including any entity treated as a partnership), trust, or tax-exempt organization, or any foreign government own, directly or indirectly, an interest of 50% or more in the profit, loss, or capital of the partnership? For rules of constructive ownership, see instructions. If "Yes," attach Schedule B-1, Information on Partners Owning 50% or More of the Partnership		X
b	Did any individual or estate own, directly or indirectly, an interest of 50% or more in the profit, loss, or capital of the partnership? For rules of constructive ownership, see instructions. If "Yes," attach Schedule B-1, Information on Partners Owning 50% or More of the Partnership		X
4	At the end of the tax year, did the partnership:		
a	Own directly 20% or more, or own, directly or indirectly, 50% or more of the total voting power of all classes of stock entitled to vote of any foreign or domestic corporation? For rules of constructive ownership, see instructions. If "Yes," complete (i) through (iv) below		

(i) Name of Corporation	(ii) Employer Identification Number (if any)	(iii) Country of Incorporation	(iv) Percentage Owned in Voting Stock

		Yes	No
b	Own directly an interest of 20% or more, or own, directly or indirectly, an interest of 50% or more in the profit, loss, or capital in any foreign or domestic partnership (including an entity treated as a partnership) or in the beneficial interest of a trust? For rules of constructive ownership, see instructions. If "Yes," complete (i) through (v) below		X

(i) Name of Entity	(ii) Employer Identification Number (if any)	(iii) Type of Entity	(iv) Country of Organization	(v) Maximum Percentage Owned in Profit, Loss, or Capital

		Yes	No
5	Did the partnership file Form 8893, Election of Partnership Level Tax Treatment, or an election statement under section 6231(a)(1)(B)(ii) for partnership-level tax treatment, that is in effect for this tax year? See Form 8893 for more details		X
6	Does the partnership satisfy **all four** of the following conditions?		
a	The partnership's total receipts for the tax year were less than $250,000.		
b	The partnership's total assets at the end of the tax year were less than $1 million.		
c	Schedules K-1 are filed with the return and furnished to the partners on or before the due date (including extensions) for the partnership return.		
d	The partnership is not filing and is not required to file Schedule M-3		X
	If "Yes," the partnership is not required to complete Schedules L, M-1, and M-2; Item F on page 1 of Form 1065; or Item L on Schedule K-1.		
7	Is this partnership a publicly traded partnership as defined in section 469(k)(2)?		X
8	During the tax year, did the partnership have any debt that was cancelled, was forgiven, or had the terms modified so as to reduce the principal amount of the debt?		X
9	Has this partnership filed, or is it required to file, Form 8918, Material Advisor Disclosure Statement, to provide information on any reportable transaction?		X
10	At any time during calendar year 2016, did the partnership have an interest in or a signature or other authority over a financial account in a foreign country (such as a bank account, securities account, or other financial account)? See the instructions for exceptions and filing requirements for FinCEN Form 114, Report of Foreign Bank and Financial Accounts (FBAR). If "Yes," enter the name of the foreign country. ▶		X

Form **1065** (2016)

EXHIBIT 19-4   **Schedule K-1 (Form 1065)**

b51113

☐ Final K-1   ☐ Amended K-1   OMB No. 1545-0123

Schedule K-1
(Form 1065)

2016

Department of the Treasury
Internal Revenue Service

For calendar year 2016, or tax

year beginning _____ , 2016

ending _____ , 20 _____

Partner's Share of Income, Deductions,
Credits, etc.   ▶ See back of form and separate instructions.

Part I	**Information About the Partnership**

A Partnership's employer identification number
66 – 00770333

B Partnership's name, address, city, state, and ZIP code

H and L Partnership
3109 State Street
State College, PA 16801

C IRS Center where partnership filed return
Cincinnati, OH

D ☐ Check if this is a publicly traded partnership (PTP)

Part II	**Information About the Partner**

E Partner's identifying number
454 – 52 – 6467

F Partner's name, address, city, state, and ZIP code

H Partner
1615 Salem Drive
Lancaster, PA 17604

G ☒ General partner or LLC member-manager   ☐ Limited partner or other LLC member

H ☒ Domestic partner   ☐ Foreign partner

I1 What type of entity is this partner?   Individual

I2 If this partner is a retirement plan (IRA/SEP/Keogh/etc.), check here . . . .   ☐

J Partner's share of profit, loss, and capital (see instructions):

	Beginning	Ending
Profit	50.0 %	50.0 %
Loss	50.0 %	50.0 %
Capital	50.0 %	50.0 %

K Partner's share of liabilities at year end:

Nonrecourse . . . . $ _____
Qualified nonrecourse financing . $ _____
Recourse . . . . $ _____

L Partner's capital account analysis:

Beginning capital account . . . $ _____
Capital contributed during the year $ _____
Current year increase (decrease) . $ _____
Withdrawals & distributions . . $ (_____)
Ending capital account . . . . $ _____

☐ Tax basis   ☐ GAAP   ☒ Section 704(b) book
☐ Other (explain)

M Did the partner contribute property with a built-in gain or loss?
☐ Yes   ☒ No
If "Yes," attach statement (see instructions)

Part III	**Partner's Share of Current Year Income, Deductions, Credits, and Other Items**

#	Description		#	Description
1	Ordinary business income (loss) 6,550		15	Credits
2	Net rental real estate income (loss)			
3	Other net rental income (loss)		16	Foreign transactions
4	Guaranteed payments 25,000			
5	Interest income			
6a	Ordinary dividends			
6b	Qualified dividends			
7	Royalties			
8	Net short-term capital gain (loss)			
9a	Net long-term capital gain (loss) 1,000		17	Alternative minimum tax (AMT) items
9b	Collectibles (28%) gain (loss)			
9c	Unrecaptured section 1250 gain			
10	Net section 1231 gain (loss)		18	Tax-exempt income and nondeductible expenses
11	Other income (loss)			
			19	Distributions
12	Section 179 deduction			
13	Other deductions		20	Other information
14	Self-employment earnings (loss) A 31,550 C 45,000			

*See attached statement for additional information.

For IRS Use Only

For Paperwork Reduction Act Notice, see Instructions for Form 1065.   IRS.gov/form1065   Cat. No. 11394R   **Schedule K-1 (Form 1065) 2016**

The importance of the flow-through or conduit concept cannot be overemphasized. Not only does the flow-through system ensure a single level of tax, it also enables the losses of the partnership to flow-through to the partners who—subject to certain limitations—can use the losses to offset other income that they may have. As will become apparent, this treatment is quite advantageous when compared to that given to C corporations where income may be taxed twice and losses cannot be used unless the corporation itself has income.

TRANSACTIONS BETWEEN PARTNERSHIP AND PARTNERS

Unlike sole proprietors, whose profit from the business is simply what's left after paying all the expenses, partners may also receive compensation for services performed for the partnership. While it may seem logical in this situation to treat the partner as an employee and the compensation as salary, the courts have taken a different approach, and the Code reflects their view. If the amount of the compensation is independent of how well the partnership fares during the year, that is, the compensation does not depend on the partnership's income, the compensation is referred to as a *guaranteed payment*.[10] In most cases, the partnership deducts the guaranteed payment to the partner just as it would a salary payment to an employee, and the partner reports the amount as income. There are several critical differences, however. Perhaps the most important of these is that a guaranteed payment, unlike a salary, is not subject to withholding. There are no income taxes withheld, no W-2 is completed, and the amount is not subject to employment taxes at the partnership or partner level. Instead, the amount of the guaranteed payment is reported on Schedule K (and deducted on page 1 in computing net income) and is treated as self-employment income subject to self-employment taxes. A guaranteed payment is treated as self-employment income whether it is received by a general or limited partner.

Partners, like proprietors, also are not considered employees for purposes of several of the fringe benefit rules. As noted above, employers can normally deduct the costs of providing their employees with certain benefits, yet the employee has no taxable income. For partnerships, however, the amount of the benefit is generally treated like a guaranteed payment, deductible by the partnership but taxable income to the partner. Such benefits are also subject to employment taxes. Similarly, partners are not entitled to participate with other employees in a qualified pension plan. Instead, each partner may establish his or her own Keogh plan. Although a Keogh plan provides benefits very similar to typical qualified plans, they are not identical. For example, the amount of contribution that can be made is more limited, and loans from the plan are normally prohibited.

Unlike the proprietorship, most other transactions between the partnership and its partners are treated as if each were dealing with a third party. For example, partners may lend money, rent property, or sell assets to their partnership and, with few exceptions, the partners will include interest income, rent income and gain, and perhaps loss just as if they were not dealing with their own partnership. Meanwhile, the partnership is normally allowed a deduction for the interest, rent, or depreciation expense as the case may be. Exceptions do exist, however. As discussed in Chapter 7, losses on sales between a partnership and a partner who owns more than 50% of the partnership are generally disallowed under § 267. The same rule applies to C and S corporations. In a similar fashion, § 267 provides that an accrual basis partnership is allowed to deduct accrued expenses payable to a related cash basis taxpayer only in the period in which the payment is included in the recipient's income. This matching rule also applies to C corporations and their more-than-50-percent shareholders as well as S corporations and *any* of their shareholders.

---

[10] § 707(c).

Example 3

The records of a partnership owned and operated equally by H and L show the following information for the year:

Sales	$150,000
Cost of goods sold	60,000
Operating expenses:	
Depreciation	12,000
Rent	4,900
Repairs	1,800
Payroll and property taxes	3,200
Employee salaries	30,000
Guaranteed payments to H	25,000
Capital gain	2,000

Note that the above information is identical to *Example 1* except the business is a partnership with two owners. Page 1 of Form 1065 (Exhibit 19-2) is similar to Schedule C (Exhibit 19-1). The major difference is that the guaranteed payments are deductible in determining net ordinary income or loss. Thus, *gross income* is the same at $90,000 but *net ordinary income* is $13,100, which is $25,000 less than it is for the proprietorship because of the guaranteed payments. Each partner's share is $6,550 (50% × $13,100). In addition to the $13,100 net ordinary income, information relevant to the partners includes guaranteed payments of $25,000, net capital gain of $2,000, and earnings from self-employment of $38,100 ($13,100 + $25,000). The total ordinary income of the partnership and each of the separately stated items is reported on Schedule K (Exhibit 19-3). The amount of each one of these items that is allocated to a partner for reporting on his or her personal return is detailed on Schedule K-1 (Exhibit 19-4). Since the Schedule K-1s are the same for H and L except for the guaranteed payments, only H's information is illustrated, showing $6,550 ordinary income, $25,000 guaranteed payments, $1,000 net capital gain, and $31,550 ($6,550 + $25,000) net earnings from self-employment. In contrast, L's Schedule K-1 has no amount for guaranteed payments and his self-employment income is only $6,550. Each partner reports the amounts from Schedule K-1 as follows: net ordinary income and guaranteed payments on page 2 of Schedule E, self-employment income on Schedule SE, and capital gain on Schedule D. Thus, the treatment of the partnership items by H and L together is the same as the treatment of the proprietorship items by Mary in *Example 1*.

Example 4

Assume the same facts as in *Example 3*, except that cost of goods sold is $100,000 instead of $60,000. The partnership now has a *net ordinary loss* of $26,900. Each partner's share is $13,450 (50% × $26,900). H reports total ordinary income and self-employment income of $11,550 ($25,000 guaranteed payments − $13,450 ordinary loss) while L reports a net ordinary loss of $13,450, assuming his basis in the partnership equals or exceeds that amount. Again, the combined treatment for H and L is the same as it is for proprietor Mary in *Example 2*. If L's income from other sources does not exceed his loss from the partnership, he is eligible for the NOL carryback and carryforward.

Example 5

During the year, K received the following amounts from a partnership in which she has a 30% capital interest:

1. $2,750 interest on a $25,000 loan made to the partnership
2. $3,600 rental income from a storage building rented to the partnership
3. $6,000 for special tools sold to the partnership (the tools were acquired for personal use two years ago for $5,500)

Assume the partnership's net ordinary income, excluding the above items, is $40,000, and the depreciation deduction for the tools is $1,200. Thus, net income for the partnership and includible income for K, after the above three items are considered, are

	Partnership				*Partner K*
Net income before	$40,000				
Interest on loan	(2,750)				$2,750 interest income
Rental of building.	(3,600)				3,600 rental income
Tools:					
Sale.	0				500 capital gain
Depreciation	(1,200)				0
Net income after.	$32,450	×	30%	=	$9,735 partnership income

Special rules also govern the treatment of gains on sales of property between a partner and a partnership. Under § 707(b)(2), a sale of property to a partnership that normally would result in capital gain is transformed into ordinary income if the partner controls the partnership and the property would not be a capital asset in the hands of the partnership. For example, if a more-than-50-percent partner sold investment land to a partnership that subdivides the land and sells it as inventory, any gain that the partner recognizes would be ordinary income and not capital gain. As discussed below, a similar rule applies to C and S corporations. However, the rule is not identical and creates some interesting planning opportunities.

S Corporations

LO.1

Understand the basic rules governing the taxation of the four business forms: sole proprietorships, partnerships, S corporations, and C corporations.

The final form of business organization to be considered is the corporation. A corporation, unlike a partnership, is normally viewed as an entity separate and distinct from its owners. Historically, this has been its principal advantage. The owners of the corporation, the shareholders, are insulated from the liabilities of the corporation. Shareholders are liable only to the extent of their investment in the corporation. For years, it has been this attribute, limited liability, that caused many businesses to choose the corporate form for conducting their operations.

Until 1958, all corporations were taxed in the same manner. Consistent with their treatment as separate legal entities, they were also treated as separate entities for tax purposes. Unfortunately, this treatment created the possibility for the corporation's income to be taxed *twice:* once when the corporation receives the income and again when the income is distributed as a dividend to its shareholders. Double taxation can occur because the corporation is not allowed to deduct any dividend payments to its shareholders. To the regret of many small business owners who could not easily shift the burden of double taxation to customers or employees, the risk of double taxation was the price to be paid for limited liability. Then, in 1958, bowing to pressure from small business, the Eisenhower administration proposed special rules to eliminate the trade-off between double taxation and limited liability. Congress responded to the president's wishes and made an important new addition to the

Code: Subchapter S. Subchapter S allows certain closely held corporations to elect to be taxed like partnerships.[11]

Since the enactment of Subchapter S, there have been two types of corporations for Federal *tax* purposes: "S" corporations, so-called because they are governed by Subchapter S of the Internal Revenue Code, and all other corporations, referred to as regular, or "C," corporations. The latter are governed, as might be expected, by Subchapter C. For all other purposes, the law recognizes no distinction between C and S corporations—both are simply corporations, separate legal entities that provide limited liability to their shareholders. While C and S corporations are identical for *nontax* purposes, their tax treatment, as explained above, differs significantly. S corporations are generally taxed like partnerships and do not risk the possibility of double taxation, whereas C corporations are treated as separate taxable entities and may have their income taxed twice.

ELECTION OF S CORPORATION STATUS

The special tax treatment provided for S corporations is available only if the corporation qualifies for S treatment and all of the shareholders consent to the corporation's election to be taxed under Subchapter S. While there are several requirements that a corporation must satisfy in order to qualify for the election, the most important concerns its shareholders.[12] The corporation can have no more than 100 *eligible* shareholders. For this purpose, only individuals, estates, and certain trusts are eligible to own the stock. Regular C corporations and partnerships cannot own the stock of an S corporation. Nonresident aliens (individuals who are not U.S. citizens and who do not live in the U.S.) are also barred from owning stock in an S corporation. In counting the number of shareholders, members of a single family (six generations of descendants and ancestors) generally are treated as a single shareholder. An S corporation may own stock of another S corporation only if it owns all of the stock. The S election is terminated if any of these conditions are violated or a majority of the shareholders revoke the election. When either of these events occurs, the S election terminates, and the corporation becomes a C corporation and normally cannot reelect S status for five years.

MAKING THE S ELECTION

The S election is made by filing Form 2553, to which all shareholders must consent. For the election to be effective for the current year, the election must be filed within two months and 15 days after the corporation's taxable year begins. If the S election is not made within this period, the election is effective for the corporation's following taxable year. It should be noted, particularly for newly formed corporations, that a failure to obtain S status for the corporation's first taxable year means that it will be treated as a C corporation until the S election becomes effective. While the consequences of this are beyond the scope of this overview, suffice it to say that numerous problems can arise when a C corporation converts to S status. These difficulties are ignored in the discussion below, but the reader should be forewarned that these converted corporations may be subject to special rules.

TAXATION OF S CORPORATION OPERATIONS

Like a partnership, an S corporation is normally treated as a conduit. Consequently, the method of reporting the amount of S corporation income that flows through to the shareholders is virtually identical to that for a partnership.[13] The various nonseparately stated items that make up the S corporation's ordinary income are summarized on page 1 of Form 1120S (see Exhibit 19-5). The separately stated items are reported on Schedule K (see Exhibit 19-6). Each shareholder's *share* of the S corporation's ordinary income and separately stated items are reported on Schedule K-1 (see Exhibit 19-7). Like partners, when S corporation shareholders file their own returns, they must incorporate the information on Schedule K-1. As a result, *Example 3* and *Example 4,* which illustrate how a partnership's income is summarized and passed through to its partners, are equally applicable to S corporations and their shareholders (other than the treatment of the owner's compensation discussed below). Exhibits 19-5, 19-6, and 19-7 contain a completed Form 1120S, including Schedules K and K-1, using the facts of *Example 3*. Note the similarity in the forms and the reporting.

LO.2

Compute the net taxable income or loss for the four types of business organizations.

---

[11] §§ 1361 and 1362. Some states do not recognize S corporations and treat them as C corporations for state tax purposes.

[12] §§ 1361(b) and (c).

[13] §§ 1363 and 1366.

EXHIBIT 19-5 **Form 1120S**

Form **1120S**	**U.S. Income Tax Return for an S Corporation**	OMB No. 1545-0123
Department of the Treasury Internal Revenue Service	▶ Do not file this form unless the corporation has filed or is attaching Form 2553 to elect to be an S corporation. ▶ Information about Form 1120S and its separate instructions is at *www.irs.gov/form1120s*.	20**16**

For calendar year 2016 or tax year beginning _____ , 2016, ending _____ , 20____

A S election effective date 1-1-1993	TYPE OR PRINT	Name **H and L Corporation**	**D** Employer identification number 66 – 0770333
B Business activity code number (see instructions) 448110		Number, street, and room or suite no. If a P.O. box, see instructions. **3109 South Street**	**E** Date incorporated 1-1-1993
C Check if Sch. M-3 attached ☐		City or town, state or province, country, and ZIP or foreign postal code **State College, PA 16801**	**F** Total assets (see instructions) $ 15,100 00

G Is the corporation electing to be an S corporation beginning with this tax year? ☐ Yes ☒ No   If "Yes," attach Form 2553 if not already filed

H Check if: **(1)** ☐ Final return **(2)** ☐ Name change **(3)** ☐ Address change **(4)** ☐ Amended return **(5)** ☐ S election termination or revocation

I Enter the number of shareholders who were shareholders during any part of the tax year . . . . ▶ 2

Caution: Include **only** trade or business income and expenses on lines 1a through 21. See the instructions for more information.

Income	**1a**	Gross receipts or sales	**1a** 150,000 00	
	b	Returns and allowances	**1b**	
	c	Balance. Subtract line 1b from line 1a	**1c**	150,000 00
	2	Cost of goods sold (attach Form 1125-A)	**2**	60,000 00
	3	Gross profit. Subtract line 2 from line 1c	**3**	90,000 00
	4	Net gain (loss) from Form 4797, line 17 (attach Form 4797)	**4**	
	5	Other income (loss) (see instructions—attach statement)	**5**	
	6	**Total income (loss).** Add lines 3 through 5 . . . . ▶	**6**	90,000 00
Deductions (see instructions for limitations)	**7**	Compensation of officers (see instructions—attach Form 1125-E)	**7**	25,000 00
	8	Salaries and wages (less employment credits)	**8**	30,000 00
	9	Repairs and maintenance	**9**	1,800 00
	10	Bad debts	**10**	
	11	Rents	**11**	4,900 00
	12	Taxes and licenses	**12**	3,200 00
	13	Interest	**13**	
	14	Depreciation not claimed on Form 1125-A or elsewhere on return (attach Form 4562)	**14**	12,000 00
	15	Depletion **(Do not deduct oil and gas depletion.)**	**15**	
	16	Advertising	**16**	
	17	Pension, profit-sharing, etc., plans	**17**	
	18	Employee benefit programs	**18**	
	19	Other deductions (attach statement)	**19**	
	20	**Total deductions.** Add lines 7 through 19 . . . . ▶	**20**	76,900 00
	21	**Ordinary business income (loss).** Subtract line 20 from line 6	**21**	13,100 00
Tax and Payments	**22a**	Excess net passive income or LIFO recapture tax (see instructions) . .	**22a**	
	b	Tax from Schedule D (Form 1120S)	**22b**	
	c	Add lines 22a and 22b (see instructions for additional taxes) . . .	**22c**	
	23a	2016 estimated tax payments and 2015 overpayment credited to 2016	**23a**	
	b	Tax deposited with Form 7004	**23b**	
	c	Credit for federal tax paid on fuels (attach Form 4136)	**23c**	
	d	Add lines 23a through 23c	**23d**	
	24	Estimated tax penalty (see instructions). Check if Form 2220 is attached . . . . ▶ ☐	**24**	
	25	**Amount owed.** If line 23d is smaller than the total of lines 22c and 24, enter amount owed . .	**25**	
	26	**Overpayment.** If line 23d is larger than the total of lines 22c and 24, enter amount overpaid . .	**26**	
	27	Enter amount from line 26 **Credited to 2017 estimated tax** ▶ _____ Refunded ▶	**27**	

Sign Here

Under penalties of perjury, I declare that I have examined this return, including accompanying schedules and statements, and to the best of my knowledge and belief, it is true, correct, and complete. Declaration of preparer (other than taxpayer) is based on all information of which preparer has any knowledge.

▶ _____ Signature of officer   Date   ▶ _____ Title

May the IRS discuss this return with the preparer shown below (see instructions)? ☐ Yes ☐ No

Paid Preparer Use Only

Print/Type preparer's name	Preparer's signature	Date	Check ☐ if self-employed	PTIN
Firm's name ▶			Firm's EIN ▶	
Firm's address ▶			Phone no.	

For Paperwork Reduction Act Notice, see separate instructions.   Cat. No. 11510H   Form **1120S** (2016)

EXHIBIT 19-6	Schedule K (Form 1120S)

Schedule K		Shareholders' Pro Rata Share Items		Total amount	
Income (Loss)	**1**	Ordinary business income (loss) (page 1, line 21)	**1**	13,100	00
	2	Net rental real estate income (loss) (attach Form 8825)	**2**		
	3a	Other gross rental income (loss)	3a		
	b	Expenses from other rental activities (attach statement) . .	3b		
	c	Other net rental income (loss). Subtract line 3b from line 3a	**3c**		
	4	Interest income	**4**		
	5	Dividends: **a** Ordinary dividends	**5a**		
		b Qualified dividends	5b		
	6	Royalties	**6**		
	7	Net short-term capital gain (loss) (attach Schedule D (Form 1120S))	**7**		
	8a	Net long-term capital gain (loss) (attach Schedule D (Form 1120S))	**8a**	2,000	00
	b	Collectibles (28%) gain (loss)	8b		
	c	Unrecaptured section 1250 gain (attach statement)	8c		
	9	Net section 1231 gain (loss) (attach Form 4797)	**9**		
	10	Other income (loss) (see instructions) . . . Type ▶	**10**		
Deductions	**11**	Section 179 deduction (attach Form 4562)	**11**		
	12a	Charitable contributions	**12a**		
	b	Investment interest expense	**12b**		
	c	Section 59(e)(2) expenditures **(1)** Type ▶ _____ **(2)** Amount ▶	**12c(2)**		
	d	Other deductions (see instructions) . . . Type ▶	**12d**		
Credits	**13a**	Low-income housing credit (section 42(j)(5))	**13a**		
	b	Low-income housing credit (other)	**13b**		
	c	Qualified rehabilitation expenditures (rental real estate) (attach Form 3468, if applicable) . .	**13c**		
	d	Other rental real estate credits (see instructions) Type ▶	**13d**		
	e	Other rental credits (see instructions) . . . Type ▶	**13e**		
	f	Biofuel producer credit (attach Form 6478)	**13f**		
	g	Other credits (see instructions) . . . . . Type ▶	**13g**		
Foreign Transactions	**14a**	Name of country or U.S. possession ▶			
	b	Gross income from all sources	**14b**		
	c	Gross income sourced at shareholder level	**14c**		
		Foreign gross income sourced at corporate level			
	d	Passive category	**14d**		
	e	General category	**14e**		
	f	Other (attach statement)	**14f**		
		Deductions allocated and apportioned at shareholder level			
	g	Interest expense	**14g**		
	h	Other	**14h**		
		Deductions allocated and apportioned at corporate level to foreign source income			
	i	Passive category	**14i**		
	j	General category	**14j**		
	k	Other (attach statement)	**14k**		
		Other information			
	l	Total foreign taxes (check one): ▶ ☐ Paid ☐ Accrued	**14l**		
	m	Reduction in taxes available for credit (attach statement)	**14m**		
	n	Other foreign tax information (attach statement)			
Alternative Minimum Tax (AMT) Items	**15a**	Post-1986 depreciation adjustment	**15a**		
	b	Adjusted gain or loss	**15b**		
	c	Depletion (other than oil and gas)	**15c**		
	d	Oil, gas, and geothermal properties—gross income	**15d**		
	e	Oil, gas, and geothermal properties—deductions	**15e**		
	f	Other AMT items (attach statement)	**15f**		
Items Affecting Shareholder Basis	**16a**	Tax-exempt interest income	**16a**		
	b	Other tax-exempt income	**16b**		
	c	Nondeductible expenses	**16c**		
	d	Distributions (attach statement if required) (see instructions)	**16d**		
	e	Repayment of loans from shareholders	**16e**		

Form **1120S** (2016)

EXHIBIT 19-7   **Schedule K-1 (Form 1120S)**

671113

☐ Final K-1   ☐ Amended K-1   OMB No. 1545-0123

Schedule K-1
(Form 1120S)
Department of the Treasury
Internal Revenue Service

20**16**

For calendar year 2016, or tax
year beginning _____ , 2016
ending _____ , 20 _____

Shareholder's Share of Income, Deductions, Credits, etc.   ▶ See back of form and separate instructions.

Part III	**Shareholder's Share of Current Year Income, Deductions, Credits, and Other Items**		
1 Ordinary business income (loss) 6,550		**13** Credits	
2 Net rental real estate income (loss)			
3 Other net rental income (loss)			
4 Interest income			
5a Ordinary dividends			
5b Qualified dividends		**14** Foreign transactions	
6 Royalties			
7 Net short-term capital gain (loss)			
8a Net long-term capital gain (loss) 1,000			
8b Collectibles (28%) gain (loss)			
8c Unrecaptured section 1250 gain			
9 Net section 1231 gain (loss)			
10 Other income (loss)		**15** Alternative minimum tax (AMT) items	
11 Section 179 deduction		**16** Items affecting shareholder basis	
12 Other deductions			
		17 Other information	

Part I   **Information About the Corporation**

A Corporation's employer identification number
66 – 00770333

B Corporation's name, address, city, state, and ZIP code

H and L Corporation
3109 State Street
State College, PA 16801

C IRS Center where corporation filed return
Cincinnati, OH

Part II   **Information About the Shareholder**

D Shareholder's identifying number
454 – 52 – 6467

E Shareholder's name, address, city, state, and ZIP code

H Shareholder
1615 Salem Drive
Lancaster, PA 17604

F Shareholder's percentage of stock
ownership for tax year . . . . _____ 50 %

For IRS Use Only

* See attached statement for additional information.

For Paperwork Reduction Act Notice, see Instructions for Form 1120S.   IRS.gov/form1120s   Cat. No. 11520D   **Schedule K-1 (Form 1120S) 2016**

TRANSACTIONS BETWEEN AN S CORPORATION AND ITS SHAREHOLDERS

Although the taxation of routine operations of an S corporation and that of a partnership are virtually identical, there are differences. The most important of these concerns the treatment of the owners' compensation, including employment taxes. In the discussion of partnerships, it was observed that partners are not considered "employees" of the partnership. As a result, they were not eligible for many nontaxable fringe benefits. In addition, any compensation paid to them was generally treated as a guaranteed payment that was not reported on a Form W-2 but on Schedule K-1 and was subject to self-employment tax. In contrast, shareholders of an S corporation may be "employees" of the S corporation. Consequently, salaries paid to S shareholders in their capacity as employees are subject to withholding, including Social Security and Medicare taxes, and, therefore, the salary does not qualify as self-employment income. A shareholder-employee of an S corporation receives a W-2, reporting all of this information. Also in contrast to partnerships, the shareholder's share of the S corporation's ordinary income is *not* considered self-employment income. Thus, the S corporation's Schedules K and K-1 do not contain a line for self-employment income.

Despite these differences, the treatment of the fringe benefits of S shareholders closely resembles that for partners. For purposes of fringe benefits, any shareholder owning more than 2% of the stock is treated in the same manner as a partner. Consequently, the benefits are treated as compensation that is included on the shareholder-employee's W-2 and that the S corporation can deduct. Such benefits are not subject to employment taxes, however. The net effect for those who own more than a 2% share is that they are denied several nontaxable fringe benefits.

Most other transactions between the S corporation and its shareholders are treated as if they each were dealing with a third party, again like a partnership. For instance, losses on sales between an S corporation and a shareholder who owns more than 50% of the stock are generally disallowed. Gains on sales of property by a more than 50% shareholder to a corporation (either an S or a C corporation) are treated a bit differently than what occurs in similar situations for partnerships. Under § 1239, such gains are treated as ordinary income only if the property is depreciable in the hands of the transferee (i.e., buyer). For example, if a more-than-50-percent S shareholder sold a warehouse to an S corporation that would depreciate the building, the portion of the gain allocable to the sale of the building would be ordinary income while the gain attributable to the sale of the land that is not depreciable would be capital gain.

C Corporations

Of the four business forms discussed in this chapter, only the C corporation is a separate taxable entity. And, as the only separate taxable entity, it is the only form of business for which the income may be taxed twice. The possibility of double taxation became a virtual certainty for owners of closely held businesses after 1986, and, consequently, most businesses that were eligible to elect the S corporate form usually did. There are many corporations, however, for which the S corporation election was not an alternative, and these corporations continue to operate as C corporations. As a practical matter, although the number of S corporations may be greater than the number of C corporations, the vast majority of business conducted in the United States is conducted by C corporations (e.g., publicly traded corporations).

LO.1

Understand the basic rules governing the taxation of the four business forms: sole proprietorships, partnerships, S corporations, and C corporations.

TAXATION OF CORPORATE OPERATIONS IN GENERAL

The overall taxation of a corporation closely resembles that for an individual. Nevertheless, differences do exist. This section looks at the basic rules for computing the corporation's tax liability, identifying the similarities and differences between corporate and individual taxation.

Tax Formula

The basic formula for computing the corporation's taxable income, although similar to that for an individual, is really far simpler. A quick comparison of the two formulas (given in Chapter 3 in Exhibits 3-1 and 3-2 and on the inside back cover of this text) reveals that taxable income for both entities is computed in the same manner—total income less

LO.2

Compute the net taxable income or loss for the four types of business organizations.

exclusions and deductions. Note, however, that the corporate formula is not confused with such items as adjusted gross income, itemized deductions, and exemptions. These latter items, as discussed below, are all unique to individual taxation.

Accounting Periods and Methods

Before determining the taxable income of any entity, the entity must select a reporting period and the accounting methods used to allocate items between periods. Corporations, like individuals, can use the calendar year or a fiscal year. In this regard, corporations have far greater flexibility than partnerships and S corporations, which are generally restricted to using the calendar year for reporting purposes.

With respect to accounting methods, individuals, partnerships, and S corporations have somewhat greater flexibility than C corporations. As discussed in Chapter 5, individuals, partnerships, and S corporations may use the cash or accrual method. In contrast, corporations generally are required to use the accrual method. However, there are several broad exceptions. Personal service corporations and corporations whose average annual gross receipts do not exceed $5 million are allowed to use the cash method. Recall, however, that both individuals and corporations must use the accrual method in determining sales and costs of goods sold if they maintain an inventory of items to sell to customers.

Income

The all-inclusive definition of income in § 61 applies to all taxpayers. Section 61 simply states that "gross income means all income from whatever source derived …." It makes no distinction between individuals or corporations. Thus, the determination of a corporation's or an individual's income is based on the same definition. All of the concepts underlying that definition are equally applicable to both individuals and corporations.

Exclusions

Both individuals and corporations are entitled to exclude certain types of income. For example, both entities are entitled to exclude interest on municipal bonds. Similarly, both are normally allowed to exclude life insurance proceeds, although such proceeds are received in a different context. Corporations often receive proceeds on the death of an insured officer or shareholder, and individuals receive amounts upon the death of a family member. Most of the other exclusions, such as those for scholarships and child support, are obviously personal in nature and unique to individuals. The exclusion rules for gifts and inheritances do apply to both individuals and corporations; but corporations rarely receive gifts or inheritances. However, corporations may receive contributions to their capital from both shareholders and nonshareholders (e.g., a city gives a corporation land on which to build a plant), in which case they may exclude such contributions. Many of the exclusions for individuals are those for employee benefits, such as Social Security, meals and lodging, group-term life insurance, health insurance, disability insurance, educational assistance, child and dependent care, tuition reduction, qualified employee discounts, and working condition fringe benefits. Once again, these exclusions are unique to individuals and are not a concern when determining a corporation's income.

Deductions in General

Section 162 provides the general rule governing deductions, allowing taxpayers to deduct all the ordinary and necessary expenses incurred in carrying on a trade or business. Like its counterpart in the income area, this provision applies to both individuals and corporations. Both are allowed to deduct business expenses. The critical feature of corporate taxation is that all activities of a corporation are considered business. Therefore, corporations normally do not have the often exasperating problem that individuals do in determining whether an expense is a business or personal expense. Because all of a corporation's expenses are business related, the complexity in the individual tax formula attributable to personal expenses cannot be found in the corporate tax formula. Corporations have no AGI so there is no need to classify deductions as *for* AGI or as itemized deductions. All expenditures are either deductible or not deductible. Similarly, corporations are not entitled to such personal deductions as the standard deduction or the deduction for personal and dependency exemptions.

The treatment of salaries and fringe benefits to owners deserves special mention, given the differing treatment of these items in the partnership and S corporation area. Salaries and fringe benefits of *shareholders* who are *employees* of their C corporations normally are treated the same as salaries and fringe benefits paid to any other employee. Salaries are deductible corporate expenses, subject to withholding and regular employment taxes (not self-employment taxes). This is the same treatment that applies to salaries paid to shareholders of an S corporation. Fringe benefits are deductible by the corporation and nontaxable to the shareholder-employees. This treatment of fringe benefits allows shareholders in a C corporation to obtain their advantages while more-than-2-percent shareholders in S corporations and partners cannot.

There are several deductions that corporations have that individuals do not have. In addition, there are often differences in the manner in which certain deductions are computed. The most important of these are considered below.

Credits

Many of the tax credits available to individuals are also available to corporations. For example, corporations may claim the credits for rehabilitation of buildings, building and improving low-income housing, investment in solar and geothermal property, hiring certain targeted persons, research and experimentation, providing access for the disabled, and the use of alcohol as fuel. Certain credits that are personal in nature are obviously not available to corporations. These include the child and dependent care credit, the education credits, the credit for the elderly and permanently disabled, and the earned income credit.

Tax Rates

Corporations have their own unique tax rate schedule. The rates for corporations are on the inside-back cover of the text. The rates for individuals and corporations can be easily compared by turning to the inside front cover of this text. As seen in the corporate tax rate schedule, the tax rates for corporations are progressive, increasing from a low of 15% on the first $50,000 of income to a high of 35% on incomes more than $10 million. To restrict the tax benefit of the lower graduated rates to small corporate businesses with taxable income of $100,000 or less, a 5% surtax is imposed on corporate taxable income in excess of $100,000, up to a maximum surtax of $11,750—the net "savings" of having the first $100,000 of corporate income taxed at the lower rates rather than 34 percent. The effect is to create a 39% bracket for incomes from $100,000 to $335,000. In a similar fashion, the tax rate increases by 3 percentage points from 35 to 38% when income exceeds $15 million. The 3% surtax from $15 million to $18,333,333 wipes out the 1% benefit derived from the lower 34% bracket on the first $10 million of taxable income ($100,000 surtax [$3\% \times \$3,333,333$] eliminates $100,000 benefit [$(35\% - 34\% = 1\%) \times \$10,000,000$]).

Reporting

A corporation reports all of its relevant tax information on Form 1120. The return is due on the 15th day of the third month after the close of its taxable year. An automatic extension of six months is available.

Example 6

The records of a C corporation owned equally by D and E show the following information for the year:

Sales	$150,000
Cost of goods sold	60,000
Operating expenses:	
Depreciation	12,000
Rent	4,900
Repairs	1,800
Payroll and property taxes	3,200
Employee salaries	30,000
D's salary	25,000
Capital gain	2,000

This information is the same as that for the proprietorship *(Example 1)*, the partnership *(Example 3)*, and the S corporation (Exhibit 19-5). Page 1 of Form 1120 (Exhibit 19-8) is similar to Forms 1065 (Exhibit 19-2) and 1120S (Exhibit 19-5). There are two differences. First, the computation is for *taxable income*, not net ordinary income. As a result, *gross income* is $92,000 ($150,000 − $60,000 + $2,000), which is $2,000 greater than it is for the partnership and S corporation because of the net capital gain. *Taxable income* of $15,100 also is $2,000 greater than the net ordinary income for the partnership and S corporation. The second difference is that the C corporation has a *tax liability* of $2,265 ($15,100 × 15%), which is calculated on Schedule J (Exhibit 19-9) of Form 1120. D has includible salary income of $25,000 but the corporate activities have no effect on E's tax return.

DIFFERENCES BETWEEN CORPORATE AND INDIVIDUAL TAXATION

As may be apparent from the discussion above, the *basic* rules to determine a corporation's taxable income are essentially the same as those applied to determine the taxable income of individuals, sole proprietors, partnerships, and S corporations. The organizational form simply does not affect the tax treatment of most transactions that occur during the ordinary course of business. For example, the computations related to sales, costs of goods sold, and numerous operating expenses such as those for salaries and wages paid to nonowner employees, repairs and maintenance, utilities, insurance, rent, supplies, travel, entertainment, interest, repairs, bad debts, and advertising are all the same regardless of the form of business. However, despite all of these similarities, there are differences. The most significant of these are covered below. Note that while the following discussion is couched in terms of the differences between corporate and individual taxation, it effectively includes a comparison of corporate taxation to the taxation of partnerships and S corporations as well since they are merely conduits.

Dividend Income

Dividend income received by an individual receives no special treatment and is simply included along with other items in the taxpayer's gross income. As explained earlier, this treatment results in double taxation since the income is also taxed at the corporate level and is not deductible by the corporation when distributed to the shareholders. Note that if the shareholder is a corporation, *triple* taxation or more could result. To prevent this, Congress provided corporations with a deduction for dividends received.

The amount of the deduction for dividends received normally is 70% of the amount of the dividend.[14] However, this may be increased to 80 or 100 percent depending on the corporate shareholder's ownership in the dividend-paying corporation as summarized below:

Relationship to Dividend-Paying Corporation	Dividends-Received Deduction
Owns 20% or less	70%
Owns more than 20%, but less than 80%	80%
Is an affiliated group member (80% of stock is owned by other members of the group)	100%

The 70 and 80 percent dividends-received deductions may be limited to 70 and 80 percent of taxable income, respectively. For this purpose, taxable income is computed before the dividends-received deduction, net operating loss (NOL) carryovers and carrybacks, and capital loss carrybacks. By ignoring the carrybacks, the dividends-received deduction is not affected when a corporation subsequently incurs a capital loss or an NOL and carries either back.

The taxable income limitation does not always apply. The taxable income limitation is ignored if the dividends-received deduction when subtracted from taxable income either creates an NOL or adds to an existing NOL.

---

[14] § 243 through 246.

Example 7

This year, three corporations—R, S, and T—each received $40,000 of dividends from less than 20% owned corporations. Consequently, the tentative dividends-received deduction of each corporation is $28,000 (70% × $40,000). However, to determine the amount of the dividends received deduction actually allowed, each corporation must compute its taxable income limitation and determine if it is applicable. The computation of the taxable income limitation is shown below.

	R	S	T
Dividends received	$40,000	$40,000	$40,000
Sales	60,000	20,000	10,000
Costs of goods sold and other operating expenses	−30,000	−30,000	−30,000
Taxable income before the dividends-received deduction	$70,000	$30,000	$20,000
Taxable income before the dividends-received deduction	$70,000	$30,000	$20,000
	× 70%	× 70%	× 70%
Taxable income limitation	$49,000	$21,000	$14,000

R may claim a dividends-received deduction of $28,000 since it is less than its taxable income limitation of $49,000. In S's situation, however, the dividends-received deduction is limited to $21,000 *unless* the tentative dividends-received deduction of $28,000 *adds to or creates a net operating loss.* In this case, subtracting the tentative dividends-received deduction of $28,000 from $30,000 does not add to or create a loss, so S's dividends-received deduction is limited to $21,000. T's situation presents the third possibility. Similar to S's, T's dividends-received deduction is limited to $14,000 *unless* the tentative dividends-received deduction of $28,000 *adds to or creates a net operating loss.* In this case, subtracting the tentative dividends-received deduction of $28,000 from $20,000 creates an NOL of $8,000. Consequently, T is allowed to deduct the normal dividends-received deduction of $28,000.

Capital Gains and Losses

The world of capital gains and capital losses is very similar for corporations and individuals. The definition of capital gains and losses is identical for both individuals and corporations. The determination of the holding period is also identical.[15] Short-term refers to holding periods of one year or less while long-term refers to holding periods of more than one year. For corporate taxpayers, there is no special treatment of long-term gains and losses from collectibles (i.e., no 28% rate), qualified small business stock (i.e., no 50% exclusion) or gain from unrecaptured depreciation on § 1250 property (i.e., no 25% rate). Consequently, there is no need to distinguish between these items and other long-term gains or losses. As a result, the netting process is much simpler. All short-term items are placed in a separate group and netted together to determine the net short-term capital gain (NSTCG) or loss (NSTCL). Similarly, all long-term items (including mid-term items) are placed in a separate group and netted to determine the net long-term capital gain (NLTCG) or loss (NLTCL). The final step concerns the netting of NSTCG or NSTCL with NLTCL and NLTCG. There are six possible combinations as shown in Exhibit 19-10.

---

[15] §§ 1222(5), (6), (7), and (8).

EXHIBIT 19-8   Form 1120

Form **1120**		**U.S. Corporation Income Tax Return**			OMB No. 1545-0123

Department of the Treasury
Internal Revenue Service

For calendar year 2016 or tax year beginning _____, 2016, ending _____, 20 _____

► Information about Form 1120 and its separate instructions is at *www.irs.gov/form1120.*

2016

A Check if:
1a Consolidated return (attach Form 851) ☐
b Life/nonlife consolidated return ☐
2 Personal holding co. (attach Sch. PH) ☐
3 Personal service corp. (see instructions) ☐
4 Schedule M-3 attached ☐

TYPE OR PRINT

Name
H and L Corporation

Number, street, and room or suite no. If a P.O. box, see instructions.
3109 State Street

City or town, state, or province, country, and ZIP or foreign postal code
State College, PA 16801

B Employer identification number
66 – 0770333

C Date incorporated
1 – 1 – 1993

D Total assets (see instructions)
$ 120,000 00

E Check if: (1) ☐ Initial return (2) ☐ Final return (3) ☐ Name change (4) ☐ Address change

Income

1a	Gross receipts or sales	1a	150,000 00		
b	Returns and allowances	1b			
c	Balance. Subtract line 1b from line 1a			1c	150,000 00
2	Cost of goods sold (attach Form 1125-A)			2	60,000 00
3	Gross profit. Subtract line 2 from line 1c			3	90,000 00
4	Dividends (Schedule C, line 19)			4	
5	Interest			5	
6	Gross rents			6	
7	Gross royalties			7	
8	Capital gain net income (attach Schedule D (Form 1120))			8	2,000 00
9	Net gain or (loss) from Form 4797, Part II, line 17 (attach Form 4797)			9	
10	Other income (see instructions—attach statement)			10	
11	**Total income.** Add lines 3 through 10		►	11	92,000 00

Deductions (See instructions for limitations on deductions.)

12	Compensation of officers (see instructions—attach Form 1125-E)		►	12	25,000 00
13	Salaries and wages (less employment credits)			13	30,000 00
14	Repairs and maintenance			14	1,800 00
15	Bad debts			15	
16	Rents			16	4,900 00
17	Taxes and licenses			17	3,200 00
18	Interest			18	
19	Charitable contributions			19	
20	Depreciation from Form 4562 not claimed on Form 1125-A or elsewhere on return (attach Form 4562)			20	12,000 00
21	Depletion			21	
22	Advertising			22	
23	Pension, profit-sharing, etc., plans			23	
24	Employee benefit programs			24	
25	Domestic production activities deduction (attach Form 8903)			25	
26	Other deductions (attach statement)			26	
27	**Total deductions.** Add lines 12 through 26		►	27	76,900 00
28	Taxable income before net operating loss deduction and special deductions. Subtract line 27 from line 11.			28	15,100 00
29a	Net operating loss deduction (see instructions)	29a			
b	Special deductions (Schedule C, line 20)	29b			
c	Add lines 29a and 29b			29c	

Tax, Refundable Credits, and Payments

30	**Taxable income.** Subtract line 29c from line 28. See instructions			30	15,100 00
31	Total tax (Schedule J, Part I, line 11)			31	2,265 00
32	Total payments and refundable credits (Schedule J, Part II, line 21)			32	
33	Estimated tax penalty. See instructions. Check if Form 2220 is attached		► ☒	33	0 00
34	**Amount owed.** If line 32 is smaller than the total of lines 31 and 33, enter amount owed			34	2,265 00
35	**Overpayment.** If line 32 is larger than the total of lines 31 and 33, enter amount overpaid			35	
36	Enter amount from line 35 you want: **Credited to 2017 estimated tax ►**		Refunded ►	36	

Sign Here

Under penalties of perjury, I declare that I have examined this return, including accompanying schedules and statements, and to the best of my knowledge and belief, it is true, correct, and complete. Declaration of preparer (other than taxpayer) is based on all information of which preparer has any knowledge.

► _____   _____   _____
Signature of officer   Date   Title

May the IRS discuss this return with the preparer shown below? See instructions. ☐ Yes ☐ No

Paid Preparer Use Only

Print/Type preparer's name	Preparer's signature	Date	Check ☐ if self-employed	PTIN

Firm's name ► _____   Firm's EIN ► _____

Firm's address ► _____   Phone no. _____

For Paperwork Reduction Act Notice, see separate instructions.   Cat. No. 11450Q   Form **1120** (2016)

EXHIBIT 19-9 Schedule J (Form 1120)

Form 1120 (2016)	H and L Corporation	66 – 0770333	Page **3**

Schedule J Tax Computation and Payment (see instructions)

Part I–Tax Computation

1	Check if the corporation is a member of a controlled group (attach Schedule O (Form 1120)). See instructions ▶ ☐		
2	Income tax. Check if a qualified personal service corporation. See instructions . . . . ▶ ☐	**2**	2,265 00
3	Alternative minimum tax (attach Form 4626)	**3**	
4	Add lines 2 and 3	**4**	2,265 00
5a	Foreign tax credit (attach Form 1118) **5a**		
b	Credit from Form 8834 (see instructions) **5b**		
c	General business credit (attach Form 3800) **5c**		
d	Credit for prior year minimum tax (attach Form 8827) **5d**		
e	Bond credits from Form 8912 . . . . **5e**		
6	**Total credits.** Add lines 5a through 5e	**6**	
7	Subtract line 6 from line 4	**7**	2,265 00
8	Personal holding company tax (attach Schedule PH (Form 1120))	**8**	
9a	Recapture of investment credit (attach Form 4255) **9a**		
b	Recapture of low-income housing credit (attach Form 8611) **9b**		
c	Interest due under the look-back method—completed long-term contracts (attach Form 8697) **9c**		
d	Interest due under the look-back method—income forecast method (attach Form 8866) **9d**		
e	Alternative tax on qualifying shipping activities (attach Form 8902) **9e**		
f	Other (see instructions—attach statement) **9f**		
10	**Total.** Add lines 9a through 9f	**10**	
11	**Total tax.** Add lines 7, 8, and 10. Enter here and on page 1, line 31	**11**	2,265 00

Part II–Payments and Refundable Credits

12	2015 overpayment credited to 2016	**12**	
13	2016 estimated tax payments	**13**	
14	2016 refund applied for on Form 4466	**14**	( )
15	Combine lines 12, 13, and 14	**15**	
16	Tax deposited with Form 7004	**16**	
17	Withholding (see instructions)	**17**	
18	**Total payments.** Add lines 15, 16, and 17	**18**	
19	Refundable credits from:		
a	Form 2439 . . . . **19a**		
b	Form 4136 . . . . **19b**		
c	Form 8827, line 8c **19c**		
d	Other (attach statement—see instructions). **19d**		
20	**Total credits.** Add lines 19a through 19d	**20**	
21	**Total payments and credits.** Add lines 18 and 20. Enter here and on page 1, line 32 . . .	**21**	

Schedule K Other Information (see instructions)

		Yes	No
1	Check accounting method: **a** ☐ Cash **b** ☒ Accrual **c** ☐ Other (specify) ▶ _____		
2	See the instructions and enter the:		
a	Business activity code no. ▶ _____		
b	Business activity ▶ _____		
c	Product or service ▶ _____		
3	Is the corporation a subsidiary in an affiliated group or a parent-subsidiary controlled group?		X
	If "Yes," enter name and EIN of the parent corporation ▶ _____		
4	At the end of the tax year:		
a	Did any foreign or domestic corporation, partnership (including any entity treated as a partnership), trust, or tax-exempt organization own directly 20% or more, or own, directly or indirectly, 50% or more of the total voting power of all classes of the corporation's stock entitled to vote? If "Yes," complete Part I of Schedule G (Form 1120) (attach Schedule G)		X
b	Did any individual or estate own directly 20% or more, or own, directly or indirectly, 50% or more of the total voting power of all classes of the corporation's stock entitled to vote? If "Yes," complete Part II of Schedule G (Form 1120) (attach Schedule G) .		X

Form **1120** (2016)

EXHIBIT 19-10	**Capital Gain Netting Process for Regular Corporations**

Case 1:	NLTCG and NSTCG cannot be combined
Case 2:	NSTCG > NLTCL = Overall NSTCG
Case 3:	NLTCG > NSTCL = Overall NLTCG
Case 4:	NLTCL > NSTCG = Overall NLTCL
Case 5:	NSTCL > NLTCG = Overall NSTCL
Case 6:	NSTCL and NLTCL cannot be combined

The treatment of a corporation's capital gains and losses varies somewhat from that of an individual. They both treat short-term capital gains as ordinary income. If an individual has a NLTCG (including any gains on collectibles), a special tax calculation results in the gain being taxed at a favorable rate, depending on the taxpayer's regular tax rate on ordinary income. The rate normally is 0, 15, or 20 percent. In addition, taxpayers in the 39.5% bracket pay the net investment income tax on their captial gains of 3.8 percent. In contrast, a corporation receives no favorable treatment for long-term capital gains. Corporations simply include both net long-term capital gains and net short-term capital gains along with other ordinary income and compute the tax liability using the current rates. Thus, a corporation's capital gains could be taxed at a rate as high as 39% (34% plus a 5% surcharge).

The treatment of a net capital loss of a corporation differs significantly from that for an individual. As a general rule, individuals are allowed to offset capital losses against capital gains and up to $3,000 of ordinary income annually.[16] In contrast, capital losses of a corporation offset *only* capital gains.[17] A corporation is *never* permitted to reduce ordinary income by a capital loss. As a result, corporations cannot deduct their excess capital losses for the year. Instead, a corporation must carry the excess capital losses *back* for three years and *forward* for five years, to use them to offset capital gains in those years. The losses are first carried back three years. All of the losses, whether short-term or long-term, are carried back as short-term capital losses. They are treated as if they occurred in the prior year and reduce the amount of capital gains reported in the earliest year. Any amount not used to offset gain in the third previous year can offset gain in the second previous year and then the first previous year. If the sum of the capital gains reported in the three previous years is less than the capital loss, the excess is carried forward. Losses carried forward may be used to offset capital gains recognized in the succeeding five tax years. Losses unused at the end of the five-year carryforward period expire.

Example 8

B Corporation has income, gains, and losses as follows:

	2014	2015	2016	2017
Ordinary income.	$100,000	$100,000	$100,000	$100,000
Net capital gain or (loss).	4,000	3,000	2,000	(10,000)
Total income.	$104,000	$103,000	$102,000	$ 90,000

B reported taxable income in years 2014, 2015, and 2016 of $104,000, $103,000, and $102,000, respectively, since net capital gains are added into taxable income. In 2017, B must report $100,000 taxable income because capital losses are deductible only to the extent of capital gains. However, B is entitled to carry the net capital loss back to years 2014, 2015, and 2016 and file a claim for refund for the taxes paid on the capital gains for each year. Because the 2017 capital loss carryback ($10,000) exceeds

[16] § 1211(b)(1) and Reg. §§ 1.1211-1(b)(2) and (6).   [17] §§ 1211(a) and 1212(a).

the sum of the capital gains in the prior three years ($9,000), B has a $1,000 capital loss carryforward. This loss carryforward can be used to offset the first $1,000 of capital gains recognized in the next five years 2018 through 2022.

Corporations treat all capital loss carrybacks and carryovers as short-term losses. At present, this has no effect on the tax due and it is often immaterial whether the carryover is considered long-term or short-term. However, if Congress ever reinstates special treatment for long-term capital gains, keeping short-term and long-term carryovers separate will once again have meaning.

Sales of Depreciable Property and Recapture

Corporations, like individuals, must recapture depreciation on the sales of most depreciable property under the normal recapture provisions of §§ 1245 and 1250. Unlike the other entities, however, C corporations (and in certain cases S corporations) are subject to the special recapture rules of § 291. These rules, explained in detail in Chapter 17, require the corporation to recapture 20% of any straight-line depreciation that normally is not recaptured on the sale of depreciable realty.

Example 9

Business T sells a shopping center for $800,000; $200,000 allocated to land and $600,000 to buildings. The basis for the land is $125,000 and for the building is $120,000 ($450,000 cost − $330,000 accumulated depreciation, based on the straight-line method). T's § 1231 gain on the land is $75,000 ($200,000 − $125,000), regardless of whether T is an S or C corporation, a proprietorship, or a partnership. T's gain on the buildings is $480,000 ($600,000 − $120,000). Since only straight-line depreciation was used, all gain on the buildings is § 1231 gain for a proprietorship or a partnership. However, if T is a C corporation (or an S corporation that was a C corporation at any time during the three prior years), $66,000 of the $480,000 gain is ordinary income, computed as follows:

Amount that would have been recaptured under § 1245 (lesser of accumulated depreciation or gain)	$330,000
Less § 1250 gain	− 0
	$330,000
Multiplied by the statutory rate	× 20%
§ 291(a)(1) ordinary income	$ 66,000

The C or S corporation has ordinary income of $66,000 and § 1231 gain of $489,000 ($75,000 + [$480,000 − $66,000]).

Charitable Contributions

A corporation's charitable contribution deduction, although similar to that for individuals, differs in several important respects. The first difference concerns timing of the deduction. Normally, charitable contributions can be deducted only in the year in which payment is actually made. However, accrual basis corporations are permitted to deduct the contribution prior to the year of payment—in effect, accrue the deduction—if all of the following requirements are met:

- The corporation is an accrual basis taxpayer.

- The charitable contribution is authorized during the year by the board of directors.

- The contribution is paid to the charity by the 15th day of the third month following the close of the tax year (March 15 for calendar year corporations).

The second difference between corporate and individual contribution deduction rules concerns the limitation on the amount of the annual deduction. An individual's charitable contributions are generally limited to 50% of AGI, although the limitation can be 30 or 20 percent in certain cases. In contrast, the corporation's deduction is limited to 10% of taxable income before the contribution deduction, the dividends-received deduction, the domestic production activities deduction, any capital loss carryback to the tax year and any NOL carrybacks.[18] Any amount in excess of this limitation may be carried forward and deducted in any of the five succeeding years. In any year in which there are both *current* contributions and carryforwards, the current contributions are deducted first. If any portion of the 10% limitation is still available, the carryforwards are used on a first-in, first-out basis.[19] At the end of the five-year period, any carryover not deducted expires.

Example 10

W Inc. has the following information for its 2017, 2018, and 2019 tax years:

	2017	*2018*	*2019*
Taxable income before charitable deductions	$50,000	$57,000	$65,000
Charitable contributions	6,200	6,000	5,100

Assume W did not have dividend income in any of the three years. Taxable income and carryforwards are computed as follows:

	2017	*2018*	*2019*
Taxable income before charitable deductions	$50,000	$57,000	$65,000
Less charitable contributions:			
Current year	5,000	5,700	5,100
Carryforward from 2017			1,200
Carryforward from 2018			200
Taxable income	$45,000	$51,300	$58,500
Charitable contributions:			
Carryforward from 2017	$ 1,200	$ 1,200	$ 0
Carryforward from 2018		300	100
Carryforward from 2019			0

A third difference between the C corporation and individual contribution rules concerns inventory donations. Normally, the amount of a contribution of inventory is limited to the basis of the property. However, certain exceptions allow a C corporation to deduct its basis plus one-half of the unrealized appreciation in value (the deduction cannot exceed twice the basis). For example, this rule applies to any inventory item donated to a qualifying charity that is used solely for the care of the ill, the needy, or infants as well contributions of computer technology to schools.[20]

Net Operating Losses

Section 172 allows corporations, like individuals, to deduct net operating losses occurring in other years. Fortunately, the NOL for a corporation is much simpler to compute. The difficulty in computing the NOL of an individual stems from trying to isolate the individual's true business loss. Consider an individual's tax return that after all is said and done reveals a negative number on the line for taxable income. This negative number on an individual's return is not simply attributable to the fact that business expenses exceeded business revenues. The number also reflects many nonbusiness items as well as artificial deductions (e.g., mortgage interest, medical expenses, and exemptions). Consequently, a

---

[18] § 170(b)(2).   [20] § 170(e)(3).

[19] § 170(d)(2).

series of complex adjustments are required to determine the loss attributable solely to business activities. For example, no deduction is allowed for personal exemptions, nonbusiness expenses can be deducted only to the extent of nonbusiness income, and special rules exist for capital gains and losses. The calculation of a corporation's NOL is far easier since a corporation's negative taxable income is also its business loss. The only modification in computing the NOL of a corporation concerns NOLs from other years.[21] Any NOL from another year is omitted from the computation of the current year's NOL. Note also that the dividends-received deduction, although artificial in nature, is not limited if, as explained above, it either creates an NOL or adds to an existing NOL.[22]

The carryover period for a corporate NOL is the same as that for individuals. The corporation normally carries the NOL back 2 years and forward 20 years.[23] A corporation may elect not to carry the loss back. If this election is made, the loss would be carried forward for 20 years.[24] This election is irrevocable.

Example 11

A corporation's records show the following:

	2015	2016	2017
Net operating income (loss)	$25,000	$28,000	$(45,000)

Assume the corporation has never had dividend income and its only NOL occurred in 2017. The $45,000 NOL is carried back to offset the entire ordinary income in 2015 ($25,000). The remaining $20,000 ($45,000 − $25,000) of NOL is deducted in 2016, leaving $8,000 ($28,000 − $20,000) ordinary income in 2016. Tax refunds are obtained for these years based on decreases in taxable income due to the 2016 NOL. Thus, all of the tax paid in 2015 and a portion of the tax paid in 2016 are refunded. An election may be made, however, to carry the 2017 NOL forward instead of back. This may be advisable if the corporate marginal tax rates in 2018 (or later years if applicable) are expected to exceed those in the past two years. Of course, the present value of receiving a current refund for a carryback compared with paying a reduced tax in the future for the carryforward election *must* be included in the decision.

Alternative Minimum Tax

While the AMT for corporations and individuals is quite similar, there are many important differences relating to the rate, exemptions, and adjustments. These differences are explained in detail in Chapter 13. As also explained there, the most important distinction is that certain small corporations are completely exempt from the AMT. As a general rule, a corporation is exempt from the AMT for a particular year if its average annual gross receipts for all three-taxable-year periods ending before such tax year do not exceed $7,500,000. However, special provisions apply to the corporation's first three taxable years that generally drop this threshold to $5,000,000.

Formation of a Business

The formation of a business normally requires the transfer of assets from the owner to the business in exchange for an interest in the business. For example, when two individuals decide to incorporate, they typically transfer property to the corporation in exchange for stock. If the individuals were to form a partnership, they would contribute property in exchange for an interest in the partnership. Without special rules, these exchanges would be taxable events and, consequently, could deter the owners from using the corporate or

LO.3
Explain the basic tax consequences of forming a new business.

---

[21] § 172(d)(1).

[22] § 172(d)(5).

[23] § 172(b)(1).

[24] § 172(b)(3)(C). This is the same carryover available to individuals (see Chapter 10).

partnership form where otherwise it is perfectly appropriate. However, Congress recognized this problem early on and created special rules. These rules generally provide that any gain or loss realized on the transfer of property to a corporation or partnership in exchange for an interest in the entity is not recognized. The treatment is very similar to that for like-kind exchanges (discussed in Chapter 15). This section provides a brief overview of the specific tax consequences of forming a sole proprietorship, a partnership, or a corporation.

FORMATION OF A SOLE PROPRIETORSHIP

When an individual starts a business and decides to operate it as a sole proprietorship, the transfer of assets from the owner to the business is not a taxable event. In the eyes of the tax law, there is nothing to tax. No exchange has occurred since the owner still legally owns the assets and the sole proprietorship is not considered a separate taxable entity. Consequently, there are no tax consequences. The primary tax consideration is the property's basis for depreciation, any depreciation recapture potential, and the holding period. In those situations when the individual uses assets from another business activity in the new operation, the assets retain all of these tax attributes (basis, potential recapture, and holding period). This is not necessarily the case if personal assets are converted to business use. In this situation, the property's basis is the *lesser* of its value or basis. This rule ensures that the owner is not allowed a deduction for any decline in value that occurred while the property was held for personal use.

Example 12

T operates a proprietorship. During the year, T transfers the following assets from personal to business use:

Asset	Cost	Market Value
Automobile	$10,100	$ 5,200
Land	8,200	15,300

This is a nontaxable transfer. The assets are recorded on the proprietorship's *tax* books at the lower of (1) T's basis, which is the cost of the assets, or (2) market value on the transfer date. Thus, the automobile is recorded at $5,200 and the land at $8,200.

Example 13

V operates a proprietorship. After using the following equipment for two years of its five-year MACRS life, V transfers it from business to personal use (numbers are rounded for convenience):

Asset	Cost	Accumulated Depreciation	Basis	Market Value
Equipment	$10,000	$5,200	$4,800	$6,300

This is a nontaxable transfer. The market value of $6,300 is not considered when assets are transferred from the proprietorship to the owner. V records the equipment at its $4,800 basis and the potential § 1245 recapture of $5,200 transfers to him. If V sells the equipment, the first $5,200 of gain is § 1245 ordinary gain (see Chapter 17). This same treatment generally applies if the equipment is transferred to another business in a tax-free exchange.

FORMATION OF PARTNERSHIPS

A partnership is formed by contributions of cash, property, or services in exchange for an interest in the partnership. While most exchanges are taxable events, as suggested above, special rules provide that the transfer of *property* to a partnership in exchange for an interest in the partnership is nontaxable for both the partner and the partnership.[25] Any gain or loss realized is normally not recognized. This rule only applies to contributions of property. If the partner receives an interest in exchange for past services or services to be performed in the future, the receipt of the interest is treated as compensation and the partner normally reports income equal to the value of the interest. In this instance, additional special rules apply to the partnership and the remaining partners.

Although the partner and the partnership do not recognize any of the gain or loss realized on the exchange, such gain or loss does not escape tax. The gain or loss is preserved in the basis assigned to the partnership's basis in the assets received and the partner's basis in the partnership interest. The partner's initial basis in the partnership is generally the sum of the amount of cash contributed plus the adjusted basis of any property contributed.[26] The partnership's basis for the property received is generally the same as it was in the hands of the contributing partner.[27] In other words, the partner's basis for the property normally carries over to the partnership and becomes the partnership's basis for the property. As noted above, however, if the contributed property was formerly used for personal purposes, the lesser of the property's basis or fair market value is used in computing the partner's basis for the interest received as well as the partnership's basis for the property.

Example 14

This year T contributed the following assets to the ST partnership in exchange for a 50% interest worth $26,000.

Asset	Cost	Accumulated Depreciation	Basis	FMV
Property used in proprietorship:				
Equipment.	$10,000	$5,200	$ 4,800	$ 6,000
Converted personal assets:				
Automobile.	10,000		10,000	5,000
Land	8,000		8,000	15,000
Total.			$22,800	$26,000

Although T has realized a gain on the exchange of $3,200 ($26,000 − $4,800 − $10,000 − $8,000), the gain is not recognized. T's basis in his partnership interest is $17,800 ($4,800 + $5,000 + $8,000). The partnership's bases for the assets received are $4,800 for the equipment, $5,000 or the automobile, and $8,000 for the land. Note that when the property contributed is being converted from personal use, the lower of the property's value or basis is used in computing both the partner's basis for his interest and the partnership's bases for the assets. The result is identical to that found in *Example 12* and *Example 13* for a sole proprietor. It is important to note that for financial accounting purposes, the treatment of the partner and partnership is quite different than it is for tax purposes. For financial accounting, the assets are recorded at their fair market value and the contributing partner's capital account reflects the total fair market value of the property contributed. For example, in *Example 14* above, the partnership's financial accounting records would show the assets at a total value of $26,000 rather than their tax basis of $17,800. Similarly, the partner's capital account would reflect the value of his interest, $26,000, rather than his tax basis of $17,800. This obviously creates some interesting and difficult problems that must be considered when accounting for partnership transactions.

---

[25] § 721.

[26] § 722.

[27] § 723.

FORMATION OF CORPORATIONS

Like the formation of a partnership, the transfer of assets to a corporation in exchange for stock is normally a nontaxable transaction. Section 351 provides nonrecognition of any gain or loss realized on the exchange if the following requirements are met:

- The transferors of property, as a group, must control the corporation immediately after the exchange. Control is generally defined as ownership of at least 80% of the stock outstanding.

- The transferors must receive solely stock on the exchange. If a shareholder receives any other property—so-called boot—the shareholder must recognize any realized gain to the extent of the boot received. Losses are not recognized. Special rules apply when the transferor contributes liabilities to a corporation.

If these conditions are met, the transferors of property do not recognize any gain or loss realized. Note, however, that shareholders who contribute services in exchange for stock are not covered by § 351 and must recognize gain equal to the value of services. Service shareholders are treated as if they were paid cash for their services and then used such cash to purchase an interest in the corporation.

Any gain or loss not recognized is merely postponed and, as with a partnership, is preserved in the basis of the assets to the corporation and the basis of the stock to the shareholders. As a general rule, the basis of the shareholder's stock is the same as the basis of the property transferred increased by any gain recognized on the exchange and reduced by the value of the boot received.[28] This basis is generally referred to as a substituted basis and may be expressed as follows:

	Transferor's adjusted basis for the property transferred
+	Gain recognized
–	Boot received
=	Adjusted basis in stock received

The corporation's basis for the assets received is the same as it was in the hands of the transferor increased by any gain recognized by the transferor.[29] The corporation's basis in the property received is referred to as a *carryover basis* and may be expressed as follows:

	Transferor's adjusted basis for the property transferred
+	Gain recognized by the shareholder
=	Corporation's adjusted basis for property received

Example 15

This year R and S formed T Corporation. R transferred land worth $70,000 (basis $20,000) for 70 shares of stock worth $70,000. S transferred cash of $40,000 for 40 shares of stock. R has realized a gain of $50,000 computed as follows:

Amount realized:	
Fair market value of stock received	$70,000
Adjusted basis of property transferred	(20,000)
Gain realized	$50,000

Although R has realized a gain of $50,000, none of it is recognized since the transaction meets the conditions of § 351. In this case, the transferors of property, R and S, together own 100% of the stock immediately after the exchange, thus satisfying the 80% control test. R's basis in her stock is a substituted basis of $20,000, whereas S's basis is $40,000. The corporation would have a carryover basis in the land contributed by R of $20,000. The basis calculations are shown below.

---

[28] § 358.   [29] § 362.

	R	S
Transferor's adjusted basis for the property transferred................	$20,000	$40,000
+ Gain recognized	0	0
− Boot received	0	0
Shareholder's adjusted basis in stock received	$20,000	$40,000
Transferor's adjusted basis for the property transferred................	$20,000	$40,000
+ Gain recognized by the shareholder	0	0
Corporation's adjusted basis for property received	$20,000	$40,000

Note that if R were to sell her stock immediately for its value of $70,000, she would recognize the gain deferred on the exchange of $50,000 ($70,000 − $20,000).

Example 16

Same facts as in *Example 15,* except R receives 65 shares of stock worth $65,000 and cash of $5,000. In this case, the requirements of § 351 are still satisfied but because R received boot of $5,000 she must recognize $5,000 of her $50,000 realized gain. The basis calculations for R and the corporation are shown below.

Transferor's adjusted basis for the property transferred...........................	$20,000
+ Gain recognized	5,000
− Boot received	(5,000)
Shareholder's adjusted basis in stock received	$20,000
Transferor's adjusted basis for the property transferred...........................	$20,000
+ Gain recognized by the shareholder	5,000
Corporation's adjusted basis for property received	$25,000

Formation of an S Corporation

While the taxation of ordinary operations of an S corporation mirrors that for a partnership, other transactions in which an S corporation engages are often governed by the rules applying to C corporations, sometimes modified to reflect the fact that an S corporation is a conduit. This is true for the tax consequences of forming an S corporation where the rules for C corporations and S corporations are identical. For this reason, the rules governing formation of an S corporation are identical to those discussed above for C corporations.

Problem Materials

DISCUSSION QUESTIONS

19-1 *Basic Comparison.* List the tax advantages of each of the following:
    a. Proprietorship
    b. Partnership
    c. S corporation
    d. C corporation

19-2 *Transactions between Owners and the Business.* An owner leases a building to his business at the market value of $500 per month. Is this a deductible expense for any of the organizational forms? Is this includible gross income to the owner?

19-3 *Assets Exchanged for a Capital Interest.* When must an owner recognize gain on appreciated assets exchanged solely for an ownership interest?

19-4   *Losses on Sale.* May an owner sell equipment ($4,000 basis and $3,200 market value) to her business and recognize the loss?

19-5   *Compensation Paid to Owner.* Which organizational forms treat compensation paid to owners in the following manner?
   a.   The compensation is a deductible business expense.
   b.   The compensation is subject to FICA withholding.

19-6   *Business Deductions.* How are the following items treated by each of the four organizational forms?
   a.   Property insurance expense
   b.   Medical insurance premiums (that qualify as employee benefits) paid for employees who are owners
   c.   Medical insurance premiums (that qualify as employee benefits) paid for employees who are *not* owners
   d.   Net capital loss
   e.   Charitable contributions of $5,000 when taxable income before this deduction is $40,000

19-7   *Entity Losses.* Taxpayers with substantial income from investments are establishing a new retail business. They expect the business to have net losses for the first three to four years and continually increasing net income after that. They plan to withdraw very little cash from the business other than compensation for their services.
   a.   Which organizational form should they choose now? Why?
   b.   Will this form be appropriate if the business begins to have net income? Why? What should they do then?

19-8   *Limited Liability Companies and Limited Partnerships.* When are limited liability companies or limited partnerships preferable to general partnerships? Why?

19-9   *Partnership versus S Corporation.* List the tax advantages of each of the following:
   a.   A partnership when compared with an S corporation
   b.   An S corporation when compared with a partnership
   c.   A limited liability company when compared to a partnership and an S corporation

19-10   *Schedule K-1.* Why must each partner and each S corporate shareholder be provided with a Schedule K-1 or the information that would appear on it?

19-11   *Business Income.* How are the following items treated by each of the four organizational forms?
   a.   Dividend income of $5,000
   b.   Net capital gain of $2,000
   c.   Tax-exempt interest income of $1,100

19-12   *Accrued Expenses.* At the end of its taxable year, the accrual basis business accrues $800 interest expense owed to a cash basis owner on a long-term note. In which year is the $800 deductible by the business and includible by the owner for each of the four organizational forms if the interest is paid one month after the business year?

PROBLEMS

19-13   *Dividends-Received Deduction.* K Corporation has the following items of revenue and expense for the current year:

Sales revenue, net of returns	$100,000
Cost of sales	30,000
Operating expenses	40,000
Dividends (from less than 20% owned corporation)	20,000

   a   What is K Corporation's dividends-received deduction for the current year?
   b.   Assuming that K Corporation's operating expenses were $72,000 instead of $40,000, compute its dividends-received deduction for the current year.

19-14 *Dividends-Received Deduction.* This year R Corporation (a cash method, calendar year taxpayer) has the following income and expenses:

Sales revenue, net of returns	$100,000
Revenues from operations	$170,000
Operating expenses	178,000
Dividends (from less than 20% owned corporation)	40,000

   a   What is R Corporation's dividends-received deduction?

   b. Assuming R Corporation's tax year has not yet closed, compute the effect on its dividends-received deduction if R accelerated $5,000 of operating expenses to this year that were planned for next year.

19-15 *Contributions.* L transfers the following assets in exchange for an ownership interest in a business that has been owned and operated for several years by three of his friends.

Asset	Cost	Accumulated Depreciation	Basis	Market Value
Land	$12,000	$ 0	$12,000	$18,000
Building	80,000	18,000	62,000	95,000
Van	15,000	0	15,000	10,000

The land and building were rented to an unrelated person in the past and the van was used as a nonbusiness family vehicle. All of the accumulated depreciation is recapturable. Determine (1) L's recognized gain or loss, (2) L's basis in the business, (3) the business' basis in each asset, and (4) any potential depreciation recapture that is transferred to the business. Assume L receives the following ownership interest:

   a. 20% of a partnership;

   b. 30% of an S corporation;

   c. 85% of an S corporation; or

   d. 40% of a C corporation.

19-16 *Net Income.* A calendar year business has the following information for the current taxable year:

Sales	$180,000
Cost of goods sold	70,000
Dividend income	5,000
Net capital loss	(4,000)
Compensation to Z	12,000
Other operating expenses	40,000

Assume Z is single and her only other income is $30,000 salary from an unrelated employer.

   a. Assume the business is a proprietorship. Calculate its net ordinary income and Z's adjusted gross income.

   b. Assume the business is a partnership. Calculate its net ordinary income and Z's adjusted gross income if Z is a 20% owner and no special allocations are made.

   c. Assume the business is an S corporation. Calculate its net ordinary income and Z's adjusted gross income if Z is a 20% owner.

   d. Assume the business is a C corporation. Calculate its *taxable income* and Z's adjusted gross income if Z is a 25% owner.

19-17 *Owner/Employee Benefits.* A business pays medical insurance premiums of $3,200 during the year for its 60% owner, J. Net income before this expense is considered is $36,000. FICA taxes are 7.65 percent. Calculate the business' net income for the year and all tax effects on J, after the premium payments are considered if the business is each of the following:

   a. A proprietorship

   b. A partnership

   c. A S corporation

   d. A C corporation

19-18 *Net Losses.* A calendar year business has the following information for the current taxable year:

Sales..	$180,000
Cost of goods sold................................	130,000
Net capital gain	6,000
Compensation to Z................................	18,000
Charitable contributions...........................	1,000
Other operating expenses	65,000

Assume Z is single and her only other income is $30,000 salary from an unrelated employer.

a. Assume the business is a proprietorship. Calculate its net ordinary loss and Z's adjusted gross income.

b. Assume the business is a partnership. Calculate its net ordinary loss and Z's adjusted gross income if Z is a 20% owner and no special allocations are made.

c. Assume the business is an S corporation. Calculate its net ordinary loss and Z's adjusted gross income if Z is a 20% owner.

d. Assume the business is a C corporation. Calculate its *taxable loss* and Z's adjusted gross income if Z is a 20% owner.

19-19 *Self-Employment Income.* G Enterprises has the following information:

Net ordinary income before the items below are considered....	$40,000
Compensation to Y.................................	12,000
Dividend income	2,000
Net capital gain	5,000

Y performs services for business and receives $1,000 per month whether the business has net income or net losses. Determine Y's self-employment income for each of the following assumptions.

a. G is a proprietorship and Y is its proprietor.

b. G is a general partnership and Y is a 40% partner.

c. G is a limited partnership and Y is a 40% limited partner.

d. G is an S corporation and Y is a 40% shareholder.

e. G is a C corporation and Y is a 40% shareholder.

19-20 *Transactions.* V purchased land as an investment in 1980 for $25,000. She sells the land to a business for its $100,000 market value. The business will develop, subdivide, and sell the land in one-acre plots. Determine the amount and character of the gain (ordinary or capital) in each of the following situations:

a. The business is a partnership and V is a 40% owner.

b. The business is a partnership and V is a 90% owner.

c. The business is an S corporation and V is a 90% owner.

d. The business is a C corporation and V is a 90% owner.

19-21 *Gains and Losses.* E, Inc. has operated as a regular C corporation for many years. The corporation is owned equally by P and J. In 2004, the corporation purchased an office building for a total of $1,000,000. Appraisals indicated that the building was worth $900,000 and the land was worth $100,000. This year the corporation sold the apartment building for $1,500,000 (including the land valued at $300,000). Assume the corporation deducted straight-line depreciation of $230,000.

a. How much gain does the corporation recognize and what is its character?

b. How would your answer to (a) change if the business had been a partnership instead of a corporation?

19-22 *Charitable Contributions.* XYZ, Inc. is a regular C corporation and has no dividends received deduction or other loss carrybacks. The corporation reported the following items:

	2016	2017
Net income (before contributions)	$100,000	$200,000
Charitable contributions	22,000	15,000

How much net income will the corporation report in 2016 and 2017 and what are the consequences of any carryovers that may exist?

19-23 *Gains on Sales of Property to an Entity.* H and W, husband and wife, each own a 50% interest in Landco. H is a land developer. Typically H buys land, holds it for a while, and then sells it to Landco. In 2013, H bought 100 acres north of town for $100,000. He did nothing except hold the land until 2017 when he sold it to Landco for $400,000, realizing a $300,000 gain. After obtaining the land, Landco engages in the normal development activities (sought zoning variances, street plans, utility plans, etc.) necessary to subdivide the land. Landco then sold the lots to builders.

a. What is H trying to accomplish?

b. Assuming H wants to minimize his ultimately tax liability, should Landco be a partnership or an S corporation? Explain your answer.

19-24 *Owner/Employee Relationships.* X and Y are doctors who have been operating as a partnership but are considering incorporating. They want to pay themselves salaries of $150,000 each. In addition, since they will now be employees, they wish to establish a group life insurance plan to pay their yearly (1) life insurance premiums of $15,000 each and (2) medical insurance premiums of $4,000 each. The other employees are covered under a life insurance plan. A typical year for the doctors is as follows:

Revenue.	$550,000
Operating expense.	190,000
Owner compensation.	300,000
Life insurance premiums.	30,000

a Calculate the business' ordinary net income if the partnership is incorporated and S status is elected. An employer's share of FICA taxes is 6.2% of the first $127,200 (2017) *and* 1.45% of each person's salary, and unemployment taxes are 6.2% of the first $7,000 of each person's salary. The employee must also pay the same FICA tax as the employer.

b. Ignoring limited liability considerations, should the partners incorporate and elect S status? A self-employed person must pay 12.4% of the first $127,200 (2017) and 2.9% of self-employment income. However, one-half of the self-employment tax is a deductible business expense. Assume X and Y have no other includible income, have total itemized deductions and exemptions of $20,000 each, and file as single taxpayers.

19-25 *Comprehensive Comparison.* A service business has the following information for the current calendar year:

Revenues from services	$300,000
Operating expenses:	
Depreciation	22,000
Insurance	1,400
Office supplies	1,800
Repairs	2,300
Salary (or compensation) to owner/employee W.	25,000
Payroll taxes for W	*
Salary to nonowner employees	50,000
Payroll taxes for nonowner employees	4,600
Group-term life insurance premiums:	
For W	750
For nonowner employees	1,320
Utilities and telephone	7,900
Charitable contributions.	1,100
Rent expense	4,800 **
Other items:	
Capital gain.	2,000
Capital loss	5,000 ***
Dividend income (from 10% owned corporation)	6,000
Rehabilitation credit	3,000

* Payroll taxes for W are $2,300 ($25,000 × 7.65% = $1,912.50 FICA + $434 FUTA = $2,346.50, rounded to $2,300 for simplicity) if the business is an S or C corporation.

** The rent expense is for a building rented from W. $400 of the rent expense was accrued at the end of the year but not paid until January of the next year.

*** There have been no capital gains in prior years.

W is a 90% owner. W has no other includible income, files a married joint return, has four exemptions, and has other itemized deductions of $8,500 (including no medical expenses and no miscellaneous deductions).

a. Calculate the net business income for the partnership and the S corporation, and the taxable income and tax liability for the C corporation.

b. Calculate W's Federal income tax liability and self-employment tax liability for each of the three organizational forms.

TAX RESEARCH PROBLEMS

19-26 *Family Business.* B operates a proprietorship that manufactures and sells utility tables. Net ordinary income has been increasing approximately 20% each year. Last year, net ordinary income was $60,000 on net assets of $225,000. B needs $75,000 to expand the business. Although B's daughter is only 11 years old, she plans to join her father in the business at some point in the future. B is considering forming either a partnership or corporation with his daughter. His ownership interest would be 75% and hers would be 25 percent. If the daughter's interest is held in trust until she reaches age 18, can B serve as the trustee without disqualifying the joint ownership arrangement?

19-27 *Incorporating a Proprietorship or Partnership.* E and F have operated competing businesses for several years. Recently, they agreed to combine their assets and form a corporation. They plan to transfer appreciated property to the newly organized corporation in exchange for stock and notes. The assets have a market value of $320,000 and a basis to the owners of $175,000. After the exchange, each of them will own stock valued at $100,000 and long-term notes with a face value of $60,000 and an annual interest rate of 10 percent. The term of the notes has not been established yet but E and F are considering making a third of them ($20,000 to E and $20,000 to F) payable at the end of three years, a third payable at the end of five years, and the remainder payable at the end of 10 years. Based on their present plans, will the transfer of appreciated property to the corporation for stock and notes qualify as a nontaxable exchange?

Research aids:

Section 351 and accompanying Regulations.

Pinellas Ice & Cold Storage Co. v. Comm., 3 USTC ¶1023, 11 AFTR 1112, 287 U.S. 462 (1933).

Camp Wolters Enterprises, Inc., 22 T.C. 737 (1955) aff'd in 56-1 USTC ¶9314, 49 AFTR 283, 230 F2d 555 (CA-5, 1956).

Robert W. Adams, 58 T.C. 4 (1972).

Appendices

Tax Rate Schedules and Tables

A

Appendix Outline

A-1 2016 Income Tax Rate Schedules

2016 Tax Rate Schedules

 The Tax Rate Schedules are shown so you can see the tax rate that applies to all levels of taxable income. Do not use them to figure your tax. Instead, see chapter 30.

Schedule X—If your filing status is **Single**

If your taxable income is: Over—	But not over—	The tax is:	of the amount over—
$0	$9,275	10%	$0
9,275	37,650	$927.50 + 15%	9,275
37,650	91,150	5,183.75 + 25%	37,650
91,150	190,150	18,558.75 + 28%	91,150
190,150	413,350	46,278.75 + 33%	190,150
413,350	415,050	119,934.75 + 35%	413,350
415,050	....	120,529.75 + 39.6%	415,050

Schedule Y-1—If your filing status is **Married filing jointly** or **Qualifying widow(er)**

If your taxable income is: Over—	But not over—	The tax is:	of the amount over—
$0	$18,550	10%	$0
18,550	75,300	$1,855.00 + 15%	18,550
75,300	151,900	10,367.50 + 25%	75,300
151,900	231,450	29,517.50 + 28%	151,900
231,450	413,350	51,791.50 + 33%	231,450
413,350	466,950	111,818.50 + 35%	413,350
466,950	....	130,578.50 + 39.6%	466,950

Schedule Y-2—If your filing status is **Married filing separately**

If your taxable income is: Over—	But not over—	The tax is:	of the amount over—
$0	$9,275	10%	$0
9,275	37,650	$927.50 + 15%	9,275
37,650	75,950	5,183.75 + 25%	37,650
75,950	115,725	14,758.75 + 28%	75,950
115,725	206,675	25,895.75 + 33%	115,725
206,675	233,475	55,909.25 + 35%	206,675
233,475	....	65,289.25 + 39.6%	233,475

Schedule Z—If your filing status is **Head of household**

If your taxable income is: Over—	But not over—	The tax is:	of the amount over—
$0	$13,250	10%	$0
13,250	50,400	$1,325.00 + 15%	13,250
50,400	130,150	6,897.50 + 25%	50,400
130,150	210,800	26,835.00 + 28%	130,150
210,800	413,350	49,417.00 + 33%	210,800
413,350	441,000	116,258.50 + 35%	413,350
441,000	....	125,936.00 + 39.6%	441,000

2016 Tax Table

See the instructions for line 44 in the Instructions for Form 1040 to see if you must use the Tax Table below to figure your tax.

Example. Mr. and Mrs. Brown are filing a joint return. Their taxable income on Form 1040, line 43, is $25,300. First, they find the $25,300–25,350 taxable income line. Next, they find the column for married filing jointly and read down the column. The amount shown where the taxable income line and filing status column meet is $2,871. This is the tax amount they should enter on Form 1040, line 44.

Sample Table

At least	But less than	Single	Married filing jointly*	Married filing separately	Head of a household
			Your tax is—		
25,200	25,250	3,320	2,856	3,320	3,121
25,250	25,300	3,328	2,864	3,328	3,129
25,300	25,350	3,335	(2,871)	3,335	3,136
25,350	25,400	3,343	2,879	3,343	3,144

If line 43 (taxable income) is— At least	But less than	Single	Married filing jointly *	Married filing separately	Head of a household
			Your tax is—		
0	5	0	0	0	0
5	15	1	1	1	1
15	25	2	2	2	2
25	50	4	4	4	4
50	75	6	6	6	6
75	100	9	9	9	9
100	125	11	11	11	11
125	150	14	14	14	14
150	175	16	16	16	16
175	200	19	19	19	19
200	225	21	21	21	21
225	250	24	24	24	24
250	275	26	26	26	26
275	300	29	29	29	29
300	325	31	31	31	31
325	350	34	34	34	34
350	375	36	36	36	36
375	400	39	39	39	39
400	425	41	41	41	41
425	450	44	44	44	44
450	475	46	46	46	46
475	500	49	49	49	49
500	525	51	51	51	51
525	550	54	54	54	54
550	575	56	56	56	56
575	600	59	59	59	59
600	625	61	61	61	61
625	650	64	64	64	64
650	675	66	66	66	66
675	700	69	69	69	69
700	725	71	71	71	71
725	750	74	74	74	74
750	775	76	76	76	76
775	800	79	79	79	79
800	825	81	81	81	81
825	850	84	84	84	84
850	875	86	86	86	86
875	900	89	89	89	89
900	925	91	91	91	91
925	950	94	94	94	94
950	975	96	96	96	96
975	1,000	99	99	99	99

1,000

If line 43 (taxable income) is— At least	But less than	Single	Married filing jointly *	Married filing separately	Head of a household
			Your tax is—		
1,000	1,025	101	101	101	101
1,025	1,050	104	104	104	104
1,050	1,075	106	106	106	106
1,075	1,100	109	109	109	109
1,100	1,125	111	111	111	111
1,125	1,150	114	114	114	114
1,150	1,175	116	116	116	116
1,175	1,200	119	119	119	119
1,200	1,225	121	121	121	121
1,225	1,250	124	124	124	124
1,250	1,275	126	126	126	126
1,275	1,300	129	129	129	129
1,300	1,325	131	131	131	131
1,325	1,350	134	134	134	134
1,350	1,375	136	136	136	136
1,375	1,400	139	139	139	139
1,400	1,425	141	141	141	141
1,425	1,450	144	144	144	144
1,450	1,475	146	146	146	146
1,475	1,500	149	149	149	149
1,500	1,525	151	151	151	151
1,525	1,550	154	154	154	154
1,550	1,575	156	156	156	156
1,575	1,600	159	159	159	159
1,600	1,625	161	161	161	161
1,625	1,650	164	164	164	164
1,650	1,675	166	166	166	166
1,675	1,700	169	169	169	169
1,700	1,725	171	171	171	171
1,725	1,750	174	174	174	174
1,750	1,775	176	176	176	176
1,775	1,800	179	179	179	179
1,800	1,825	181	181	181	181
1,825	1,850	184	184	184	184
1,850	1,875	186	186	186	186
1,875	1,900	189	189	189	189
1,900	1,925	191	191	191	191
1,925	1,950	194	194	194	194
1,950	1,975	196	196	196	196
1,975	2,000	199	199	199	199

2,000

If line 43 (taxable income) is— At least	But less than	Single	Married filing jointly *	Married filing separately	Head of a household
			Your tax is—		
2,000	2,025	201	201	201	201
2,025	2,050	204	204	204	204
2,050	2,075	206	206	206	206
2,075	2,100	209	209	209	209
2,100	2,125	211	211	211	211
2,125	2,150	214	214	214	214
2,150	2,175	216	216	216	216
2,175	2,200	219	219	219	219
2,200	2,225	221	221	221	221
2,225	2,250	224	224	224	224
2,250	2,275	226	226	226	226
2,275	2,300	229	229	229	229
2,300	2,325	231	231	231	231
2,325	2,350	234	234	234	234
2,350	2,375	236	236	236	236
2,375	2,400	239	239	239	239
2,400	2,425	241	241	241	241
2,425	2,450	244	244	244	244
2,450	2,475	246	246	246	246
2,475	2,500	249	249	249	249
2,500	2,525	251	251	251	251
2,525	2,550	254	254	254	254
2,550	2,575	256	256	256	256
2,575	2,600	259	259	259	259
2,600	2,625	261	261	261	261
2,625	2,650	264	264	264	264
2,650	2,675	266	266	266	266
2,675	2,700	269	269	269	269
2,700	2,725	271	271	271	271
2,725	2,750	274	274	274	274
2,750	2,775	276	276	276	276
2,775	2,800	279	279	279	279
2,800	2,825	281	281	281	281
2,825	2,850	284	284	284	284
2,850	2,875	286	286	286	286
2,875	2,900	289	289	289	289
2,900	2,925	291	291	291	291
2,925	2,950	294	294	294	294
2,950	2,975	296	296	296	296
2,975	3,000	299	299	299	299

(Continued)

* This column must also be used by a qualifying widow(er).

2016 Tax Table — *Continued*

If line 43 (taxable income) is—		And you are—				If line 43 (taxable income) is—		And you are—				If line 43 (taxable income) is—		And you are—			
At least	But less than	Single	Married filing jointly *	Married filing separately	Head of a household	At least	But less than	Single	Married filing jointly *	Married filing separately	Head of a household	At least	But less than	Single	Married filing jointly *	Married filing separately	Head of a household
		Your tax is—						Your tax is—						Your tax is—			
3,000						**6,000**						**9,000**					
3,000	3,050	303	303	303	303	6,000	6,050	603	603	603	603	9,000	9,050	903	903	903	903
3,050	3,100	308	308	308	308	6,050	6,100	608	608	608	608	9,050	9,100	908	908	908	908
3,100	3,150	313	313	313	313	6,100	6,150	613	613	613	613	9,100	9,150	913	913	913	913
3,150	3,200	318	318	318	318	6,150	6,200	618	618	618	618	9,150	9,200	918	918	918	918
3,200	3,250	323	323	323	323	6,200	6,250	623	623	623	623	9,200	9,250	923	923	923	923
3,250	3,300	328	328	328	328	6,250	6,300	628	628	628	628	9,250	9,300	928	928	928	928
3,300	3,350	333	333	333	333	6,300	6,350	633	633	633	633	9,300	9,350	935	933	935	933
3,350	3,400	338	338	338	338	6,350	6,400	638	638	638	638	9,350	9,400	943	938	943	938
3,400	3,450	343	343	343	343	6,400	6,450	643	643	643	643	9,400	9,450	950	943	950	943
3,450	3,500	348	348	348	348	6,450	6,500	648	648	648	648	9,450	9,500	958	948	958	948
3,500	3,550	353	353	353	353	6,500	6,550	653	653	653	653	9,500	9,550	965	953	965	953
3,550	3,600	358	358	358	358	6,550	6,600	658	658	658	658	9,550	9,600	973	958	973	958
3,600	3,650	363	363	363	363	6,600	6,650	663	663	663	663	9,600	9,650	980	963	980	963
3,650	3,700	368	368	368	368	6,650	6,700	668	668	668	668	9,650	9,700	988	968	988	968
3,700	3,750	373	373	373	373	6,700	6,750	673	673	673	673	9,700	9,750	995	973	995	973
3,750	3,800	378	378	378	378	6,750	6,800	678	678	678	678	9,750	9,800	1,003	978	1,003	978
3,800	3,850	383	383	383	383	6,800	6,850	683	683	683	683	9,800	9,850	1,010	983	1,010	983
3,850	3,900	388	388	388	388	6,850	6,900	688	688	688	688	9,850	9,900	1,018	988	1,018	988
3,900	3,950	393	393	393	393	6,900	6,950	693	693	693	693	9,900	9,950	1,025	993	1,025	993
3,950	4,000	398	398	398	398	6,950	7,000	698	698	698	698	9,950	10,000	1,033	998	1,033	998
4,000						**7,000**						**10,000**					
4,000	4,050	403	403	403	403	7,000	7,050	703	703	703	703	10,000	10,050	1,040	1,003	1,040	1,003
4,050	4,100	408	408	408	408	7,050	7,100	708	708	708	708	10,050	10,100	1,048	1,008	1,048	1,008
4,100	4,150	413	413	413	413	7,100	7,150	713	713	713	713	10,100	10,150	1,055	1,013	1,055	1,013
4,150	4,200	418	418	418	418	7,150	7,200	718	718	718	718	10,150	10,200	1,063	1,018	1,063	1,018
4,200	4,250	423	423	423	423	7,200	7,250	723	723	723	723	10,200	10,250	1,070	1,023	1,070	1,023
4,250	4,300	428	428	428	428	7,250	7,300	728	728	728	728	10,250	10,300	1,078	1,028	1,078	1,028
4,300	4,350	433	433	433	433	7,300	7,350	733	733	733	733	10,300	10,350	1,085	1,033	1,085	1,033
4,350	4,400	438	438	438	438	7,350	7,400	738	738	738	738	10,350	10,400	1,093	1,038	1,093	1,038
4,400	4,450	443	443	443	443	7,400	7,450	743	743	743	743	10,400	10,450	1,100	1,043	1,100	1,043
4,450	4,500	448	448	448	448	7,450	7,500	748	748	748	748	10,450	10,500	1,108	1,048	1,108	1,048
4,500	4,550	453	453	453	453	7,500	7,550	753	753	753	753	10,500	10,550	1,115	1,053	1,115	1,053
4,550	4,600	458	458	458	458	7,550	7,600	758	758	758	758	10,550	10,600	1,123	1,058	1,123	1,058
4,600	4,650	463	463	463	463	7,600	7,650	763	763	763	763	10,600	10,650	1,130	1,063	1,130	1,063
4,650	4,700	468	468	468	468	7,650	7,700	768	768	768	768	10,650	10,700	1,138	1,068	1,138	1,068
4,700	4,750	473	473	473	473	7,700	7,750	773	773	773	773	10,700	10,750	1,145	1,073	1,145	1,073
4,750	4,800	478	478	478	478	7,750	7,800	778	778	778	778	10,750	10,800	1,153	1,078	1,153	1,078
4,800	4,850	483	483	483	483	7,800	7,850	783	783	783	783	10,800	10,850	1,160	1,083	1,160	1,083
4,850	4,900	488	488	488	488	7,850	7,900	788	788	788	788	10,850	10,900	1,168	1,088	1,168	1,088
4,900	4,950	493	493	493	493	7,900	7,950	793	793	793	793	10,900	10,950	1,175	1,093	1,175	1,093
4,950	5,000	498	498	498	498	7,950	8,000	798	798	798	798	10,950	11,000	1,183	1,098	1,183	1,098
5,000						**8,000**						**11,000**					
5,000	5,050	503	503	503	503	8,000	8,050	803	803	803	803	11,000	11,050	1,190	1,103	1,190	1,103
5,050	5,100	508	508	508	508	8,050	8,100	808	808	808	808	11,050	11,100	1,198	1,108	1,198	1,108
5,100	5,150	513	513	513	513	8,100	8,150	813	813	813	813	11,100	11,150	1,205	1,113	1,205	1,113
5,150	5,200	518	518	518	518	8,150	8,200	818	818	818	818	11,150	11,200	1,213	1,118	1,213	1,118
5,200	5,250	523	523	523	523	8,200	8,250	823	823	823	823	11,200	11,250	1,220	1,123	1,220	1,123
5,250	5,300	528	528	528	528	8,250	8,300	828	828	828	828	11,250	11,300	1,228	1,128	1,228	1,128
5,300	5,350	533	533	533	533	8,300	8,350	833	833	833	833	11,300	11,350	1,235	1,133	1,235	1,133
5,350	5,400	538	538	538	538	8,350	8,400	838	838	838	838	11,350	11,400	1,243	1,138	1,243	1,138
5,400	5,450	543	543	543	543	8,400	8,450	843	843	843	843	11,400	11,450	1,250	1,143	1,250	1,143
5,450	5,500	548	548	548	548	8,450	8,500	848	848	848	848	11,450	11,500	1,258	1,148	1,258	1,148
5,500	5,550	553	553	553	553	8,500	8,550	853	853	853	853	11,500	11,550	1,265	1,153	1,265	1,153
5,550	5,600	558	558	558	558	8,550	8,600	858	858	858	858	11,550	11,600	1,273	1,158	1,273	1,158
5,600	5,650	563	563	563	563	8,600	8,650	863	863	863	863	11,600	11,650	1,280	1,163	1,280	1,163
5,650	5,700	568	568	568	568	8,650	8,700	868	868	868	868	11,650	11,700	1,288	1,168	1,288	1,168
5,700	5,750	573	573	573	573	8,700	8,750	873	873	873	873	11,700	11,750	1,295	1,173	1,295	1,173
5,750	5,800	578	578	578	578	8,750	8,800	878	878	878	878	11,750	11,800	1,303	1,178	1,303	1,178
5,800	5,850	583	583	583	583	8,800	8,850	883	883	883	883	11,800	11,850	1,310	1,183	1,310	1,183
5,850	5,900	588	588	588	588	8,850	8,900	888	888	888	888	11,850	11,900	1,318	1,188	1,318	1,188
5,900	5,950	593	593	593	593	8,900	8,950	893	893	893	893	11,900	11,950	1,325	1,193	1,325	1,193
5,950	6,000	598	598	598	598	8,950	9,000	898	898	898	898	11,950	12,000	1,333	1,198	1,333	1,198

(Continued)

* This column must also be used by a qualifying widow(er).

2016 Tax Table — *Continued*

12,000

If line 43 (taxable income) is— At least	But less than	Single	Married filing jointly *	Married filing separately	Head of a household
12,000	12,050	1,340	1,203	1,340	1,203
12,050	12,100	1,348	1,208	1,348	1,208
12,100	12,150	1,355	1,213	1,355	1,213
12,150	12,200	1,363	1,218	1,363	1,218
12,200	12,250	1,370	1,223	1,370	1,223
12,250	12,300	1,378	1,228	1,378	1,228
12,300	12,350	1,385	1,233	1,385	1,233
12,350	12,400	1,393	1,238	1,393	1,238
12,400	12,450	1,400	1,243	1,400	1,243
12,450	12,500	1,408	1,248	1,408	1,248
12,500	12,550	1,415	1,253	1,415	1,253
12,550	12,600	1,423	1,258	1,423	1,258
12,600	12,650	1,430	1,263	1,430	1,263
12,650	12,700	1,438	1,268	1,438	1,268
12,700	12,750	1,445	1,273	1,445	1,273
12,750	12,800	1,453	1,278	1,453	1,278
12,800	12,850	1,460	1,283	1,460	1,283
12,850	12,900	1,468	1,288	1,468	1,288
12,900	12,950	1,475	1,293	1,475	1,293
12,950	13,000	1,483	1,298	1,483	1,298

13,000

At least	But less than	Single	Married filing jointly *	Married filing separately	Head of a household
13,000	13,050	1,490	1,303	1,490	1,303
13,050	13,100	1,498	1,308	1,498	1,308
13,100	13,150	1,505	1,313	1,505	1,313
13,150	13,200	1,513	1,318	1,513	1,318
13,200	13,250	1,520	1,323	1,520	1,323
13,250	13,300	1,528	1,328	1,528	1,329
13,300	13,350	1,535	1,333	1,535	1,336
13,350	13,400	1,543	1,338	1,543	1,344
13,400	13,450	1,550	1,343	1,550	1,351
13,450	13,500	1,558	1,348	1,558	1,359
13,500	13,550	1,565	1,353	1,565	1,366
13,550	13,600	1,573	1,358	1,573	1,374
13,600	13,650	1,580	1,363	1,580	1,381
13,650	13,700	1,588	1,368	1,588	1,389
13,700	13,750	1,595	1,373	1,595	1,396
13,750	13,800	1,603	1,378	1,603	1,404
13,800	13,850	1,610	1,383	1,610	1,411
13,850	13,900	1,618	1,388	1,618	1,419
13,900	13,950	1,625	1,393	1,625	1,426
13,950	14,000	1,633	1,398	1,633	1,434

14,000

At least	But less than	Single	Married filing jointly *	Married filing separately	Head of a household
14,000	14,050	1,640	1,403	1,640	1,441
14,050	14,100	1,648	1,408	1,648	1,449
14,100	14,150	1,655	1,413	1,655	1,456
14,150	14,200	1,663	1,418	1,663	1,464
14,200	14,250	1,670	1,423	1,670	1,471
14,250	14,300	1,678	1,428	1,678	1,479
14,300	14,350	1,685	1,433	1,685	1,486
14,350	14,400	1,693	1,438	1,693	1,494
14,400	14,450	1,700	1,443	1,700	1,501
14,450	14,500	1,708	1,448	1,708	1,509
14,500	14,550	1,715	1,453	1,715	1,516
14,550	14,600	1,723	1,458	1,723	1,524
14,600	14,650	1,730	1,463	1,730	1,531
14,650	14,700	1,738	1,468	1,738	1,539
14,700	14,750	1,745	1,473	1,745	1,546
14,750	14,800	1,753	1,478	1,753	1,554
14,800	14,850	1,760	1,483	1,760	1,561
14,850	14,900	1,768	1,488	1,768	1,569
14,900	14,950	1,775	1,493	1,775	1,576
14,950	15,000	1,783	1,498	1,783	1,584

15,000

At least	But less than	Single	Married filing jointly *	Married filing separately	Head of a household
15,000	15,050	1,790	1,503	1,790	1,591
15,050	15,100	1,798	1,508	1,798	1,599
15,100	15,150	1,805	1,513	1,805	1,606
15,150	15,200	1,813	1,518	1,813	1,614
15,200	15,250	1,820	1,523	1,820	1,621
15,250	15,300	1,828	1,528	1,828	1,629
15,300	15,350	1,835	1,533	1,835	1,636
15,350	15,400	1,843	1,538	1,843	1,644
15,400	15,450	1,850	1,543	1,850	1,651
15,450	15,500	1,858	1,548	1,858	1,659
15,500	15,550	1,865	1,553	1,865	1,666
15,550	15,600	1,873	1,558	1,873	1,674
15,600	15,650	1,880	1,563	1,880	1,681
15,650	15,700	1,888	1,568	1,888	1,689
15,700	15,750	1,895	1,573	1,895	1,696
15,750	15,800	1,903	1,578	1,903	1,704
15,800	15,850	1,910	1,583	1,910	1,711
15,850	15,900	1,918	1,588	1,918	1,719
15,900	15,950	1,925	1,593	1,925	1,726
15,950	16,000	1,933	1,598	1,933	1,734

16,000

At least	But less than	Single	Married filing jointly *	Married filing separately	Head of a household
16,000	16,050	1,940	1,603	1,940	1,741
16,050	16,100	1,948	1,608	1,948	1,749
16,100	16,150	1,955	1,613	1,955	1,756
16,150	16,200	1,963	1,618	1,963	1,764
16,200	16,250	1,970	1,623	1,970	1,771
16,250	16,300	1,978	1,628	1,978	1,779
16,300	16,350	1,985	1,633	1,985	1,786
16,350	16,400	1,993	1,638	1,993	1,794
16,400	16,450	2,000	1,643	2,000	1,801
16,450	16,500	2,008	1,648	2,008	1,809
16,500	16,550	2,015	1,653	2,015	1,816
16,550	16,600	2,023	1,658	2,023	1,824
16,600	16,650	2,030	1,663	2,030	1,831
16,650	16,700	2,038	1,668	2,038	1,839
16,700	16,750	2,045	1,673	2,045	1,846
16,750	16,800	2,053	1,678	2,053	1,854
16,800	16,850	2,060	1,683	2,060	1,861
16,850	16,900	2,068	1,688	2,068	1,869
16,900	16,950	2,075	1,693	2,075	1,876
16,950	17,000	2,083	1,698	2,083	1,884

17,000

At least	But less than	Single	Married filing jointly *	Married filing separately	Head of a household
17,000	17,050	2,090	1,703	2,090	1,891
17,050	17,100	2,098	1,708	2,098	1,899
17,100	17,150	2,105	1,713	2,105	1,906
17,150	17,200	2,113	1,718	2,113	1,914
17,200	17,250	2,120	1,723	2,120	1,921
17,250	17,300	2,128	1,728	2,128	1,929
17,300	17,350	2,135	1,733	2,135	1,936
17,350	17,400	2,143	1,738	2,143	1,944
17,400	17,450	2,150	1,743	2,150	1,951
17,450	17,500	2,158	1,748	2,158	1,959
17,500	17,550	2,165	1,753	2,165	1,966
17,550	17,600	2,173	1,758	2,173	1,974
17,600	17,650	2,180	1,763	2,180	1,981
17,650	17,700	2,188	1,768	2,188	1,989
17,700	17,750	2,195	1,773	2,195	1,996
17,750	17,800	2,203	1,778	2,203	2,004
17,800	17,850	2,210	1,783	2,210	2,011
17,850	17,900	2,218	1,788	2,218	2,019
17,900	17,950	2,225	1,793	2,225	2,026
17,950	18,000	2,233	1,798	2,233	2,034

18,000

At least	But less than	Single	Married filing jointly *	Married filing separately	Head of a household
18,000	18,050	2,240	1,803	2,240	2,041
18,050	18,100	2,248	1,808	2,248	2,049
18,100	18,150	2,255	1,813	2,255	2,056
18,150	18,200	2,263	1,818	2,263	2,064
18,200	18,250	2,270	1,823	2,270	2,071
18,250	18,300	2,278	1,828	2,278	2,079
18,300	18,350	2,285	1,833	2,285	2,086
18,350	18,400	2,293	1,838	2,293	2,094
18,400	18,450	2,300	1,843	2,300	2,101
18,450	18,500	2,308	1,848	2,308	2,109
18,500	18,550	2,315	1,853	2,315	2,116
18,550	18,600	2,323	1,859	2,323	2,124
18,600	18,650	2,330	1,866	2,330	2,131
18,650	18,700	2,338	1,874	2,338	2,139
18,700	18,750	2,345	1,881	2,345	2,146
18,750	18,800	2,353	1,889	2,353	2,154
18,800	18,850	2,360	1,896	2,360	2,161
18,850	18,900	2,368	1,904	2,368	2,169
18,900	18,950	2,375	1,911	2,375	2,176
18,950	19,000	2,383	1,919	2,383	2,184

19,000

At least	But less than	Single	Married filing jointly *	Married filing separately	Head of a household
19,000	19,050	2,390	1,926	2,390	2,191
19,050	19,100	2,398	1,934	2,398	2,199
19,100	19,150	2,405	1,941	2,405	2,206
19,150	19,200	2,413	1,949	2,413	2,214
19,200	19,250	2,420	1,956	2,420	2,221
19,250	19,300	2,428	1,964	2,428	2,229
19,300	19,350	2,435	1,971	2,435	2,236
19,350	19,400	2,443	1,979	2,443	2,244
19,400	19,450	2,450	1,986	2,450	2,251
19,450	19,500	2,458	1,994	2,458	2,259
19,500	19,550	2,465	2,001	2,465	2,266
19,550	19,600	2,473	2,009	2,473	2,274
19,600	19,650	2,480	2,016	2,480	2,281
19,650	19,700	2,488	2,024	2,488	2,289
19,700	19,750	2,495	2,031	2,495	2,296
19,750	19,800	2,503	2,039	2,503	2,304
19,800	19,850	2,510	2,046	2,510	2,311
19,850	19,900	2,518	2,054	2,518	2,319
19,900	19,950	2,525	2,061	2,525	2,326
19,950	20,000	2,533	2,069	2,533	2,334

20,000

At least	But less than	Single	Married filing jointly *	Married filing separately	Head of a household
20,000	20,050	2,540	2,076	2,540	2,341
20,050	20,100	2,548	2,084	2,548	2,349
20,100	20,150	2,555	2,091	2,555	2,356
20,150	20,200	2,563	2,099	2,563	2,364
20,200	20,250	2,570	2,106	2,570	2,371
20,250	20,300	2,578	2,114	2,578	2,379
20,300	20,350	2,585	2,121	2,585	2,386
20,350	20,400	2,593	2,129	2,593	2,394
20,400	20,450	2,600	2,136	2,600	2,401
20,450	20,500	2,608	2,144	2,608	2,409
20,500	20,550	2,615	2,151	2,615	2,416
20,550	20,600	2,623	2,159	2,623	2,424
20,600	20,650	2,630	2,166	2,630	2,431
20,650	20,700	2,638	2,174	2,638	2,439
20,700	20,750	2,645	2,181	2,645	2,446
20,750	20,800	2,653	2,189	2,653	2,454
20,800	20,850	2,660	2,196	2,660	2,461
20,850	20,900	2,668	2,204	2,668	2,469
20,900	20,950	2,675	2,211	2,675	2,476
20,950	21,000	2,683	2,219	2,683	2,484

(Continued)

* This column must also be used by a qualifying widow(er).

2016 Tax Table — *Continued*

If line 43 (taxable income) is— At least	But less than	And you are— Single	Married filing jointly *	Married filing separately	Head of a household
		Your tax is—			
21,000					
21,000	21,050	2,690	2,226	2,690	2,491
21,050	21,100	2,698	2,234	2,698	2,499
21,100	21,150	2,705	2,241	2,705	2,506
21,150	21,200	2,713	2,249	2,713	2,514
21,200	21,250	2,720	2,256	2,720	2,521
21,250	21,300	2,728	2,264	2,728	2,529
21,300	21,350	2,735	2,271	2,735	2,536
21,350	21,400	2,743	2,279	2,743	2,544
21,400	21,450	2,750	2,286	2,750	2,551
21,450	21,500	2,758	2,294	2,758	2,559
21,500	21,550	2,765	2,301	2,765	2,566
21,550	21,600	2,773	2,309	2,773	2,574
21,600	21,650	2,780	2,316	2,780	2,581
21,650	21,700	2,788	2,324	2,788	2,589
21,700	21,750	2,795	2,331	2,795	2,596
21,750	21,800	2,803	2,339	2,803	2,604
21,800	21,850	2,810	2,346	2,810	2,611
21,850	21,900	2,818	2,354	2,818	2,619
21,900	21,950	2,825	2,361	2,825	2,626
21,950	22,000	2,833	2,369	2,833	2,634
22,000					
22,000	22,050	2,840	2,376	2,840	2,641
22,050	22,100	2,848	2,384	2,848	2,649
22,100	22,150	2,855	2,391	2,855	2,656
22,150	22,200	2,863	2,399	2,863	2,664
22,200	22,250	2,870	2,406	2,870	2,671
22,250	22,300	2,878	2,414	2,878	2,679
22,300	22,350	2,885	2,421	2,885	2,686
22,350	22,400	2,893	2,429	2,893	2,694
22,400	22,450	2,900	2,436	2,900	2,701
22,450	22,500	2,908	2,444	2,908	2,709
22,500	22,550	2,915	2,451	2,915	2,716
22,550	22,600	2,923	2,459	2,923	2,724
22,600	22,650	2,930	2,466	2,930	2,731
22,650	22,700	2,938	2,474	2,938	2,739
22,700	22,750	2,945	2,481	2,945	2,746
22,750	22,800	2,953	2,489	2,953	2,754
22,800	22,850	2,960	2,496	2,960	2,761
22,850	22,900	2,968	2,504	2,968	2,769
22,900	22,950	2,975	2,511	2,975	2,776
22,950	23,000	2,983	2,519	2,983	2,784
23,000					
23,000	23,050	2,990	2,526	2,990	2,791
23,050	23,100	2,998	2,534	2,998	2,799
23,100	23,150	3,005	2,541	3,005	2,806
23,150	23,200	3,013	2,549	3,013	2,814
23,200	23,250	3,020	2,556	3,020	2,821
23,250	23,300	3,028	2,564	3,028	2,829
23,300	23,350	3,035	2,571	3,035	2,836
23,350	23,400	3,043	2,579	3,043	2,844
23,400	23,450	3,050	2,586	3,050	2,851
23,450	23,500	3,058	2,594	3,058	2,859
23,500	23,550	3,065	2,601	3,065	2,866
23,550	23,600	3,073	2,609	3,073	2,874
23,600	23,650	3,080	2,616	3,080	2,881
23,650	23,700	3,088	2,624	3,088	2,889
23,700	23,750	3,095	2,631	3,095	2,896
23,750	23,800	3,103	2,639	3,103	2,904
23,800	23,850	3,110	2,646	3,110	2,911
23,850	23,900	3,118	2,654	3,118	2,919
23,900	23,950	3,125	2,661	3,125	2,926
23,950	24,000	3,133	2,669	3,133	2,934

If line 43 (taxable income) is— At least	But less than	And you are— Single	Married filing jointly *	Married filing separately	Head of a household
		Your tax is—			
24,000					
24,000	24,050	3,140	2,676	3,140	2,941
24,050	24,100	3,148	2,684	3,148	2,949
24,100	24,150	3,155	2,691	3,155	2,956
24,150	24,200	3,163	2,699	3,163	2,964
24,200	24,250	3,170	2,706	3,170	2,971
24,250	24,300	3,178	2,714	3,178	2,979
24,300	24,350	3,185	2,721	3,185	2,986
24,350	24,400	3,193	2,729	3,193	2,994
24,400	24,450	3,200	2,736	3,200	3,001
24,450	24,500	3,208	2,744	3,208	3,009
24,500	24,550	3,215	2,751	3,215	3,016
24,550	24,600	3,223	2,759	3,223	3,024
24,600	24,650	3,230	2,766	3,230	3,031
24,650	24,700	3,238	2,774	3,238	3,039
24,700	24,750	3,245	2,781	3,245	3,046
24,750	24,800	3,253	2,789	3,253	3,054
24,800	24,850	3,260	2,796	3,260	3,061
24,850	24,900	3,268	2,804	3,268	3,069
24,900	24,950	3,275	2,811	3,275	3,076
24,950	25,000	3,283	2,819	3,283	3,084
25,000					
25,000	25,050	3,290	2,826	3,290	3,091
25,050	25,100	3,298	2,834	3,298	3,099
25,100	25,150	3,305	2,841	3,305	3,106
25,150	25,200	3,313	2,849	3,313	3,114
25,200	25,250	3,320	2,856	3,320	3,121
25,250	25,300	3,328	2,864	3,328	3,129
25,300	25,350	3,335	2,871	3,335	3,136
25,350	25,400	3,343	2,879	3,343	3,144
25,400	25,450	3,350	2,886	3,350	3,151
25,450	25,500	3,358	2,894	3,358	3,159
25,500	25,550	3,365	2,901	3,365	3,166
25,550	25,600	3,373	2,909	3,373	3,174
25,600	25,650	3,380	2,916	3,380	3,181
25,650	25,700	3,388	2,924	3,388	3,189
25,700	25,750	3,395	2,931	3,395	3,196
25,750	25,800	3,403	2,939	3,403	3,204
25,800	25,850	3,410	2,946	3,410	3,211
25,850	25,900	3,418	2,954	3,418	3,219
25,900	25,950	3,425	2,961	3,425	3,226
25,950	26,000	3,433	2,969	3,433	3,234
26,000					
26,000	26,050	3,440	2,976	3,440	3,241
26,050	26,100	3,448	2,984	3,448	3,249
26,100	26,150	3,455	2,991	3,455	3,256
26,150	26,200	3,463	2,999	3,463	3,264
26,200	26,250	3,470	3,006	3,470	3,271
26,250	26,300	3,478	3,014	3,478	3,279
26,300	26,350	3,485	3,021	3,485	3,286
26,350	26,400	3,493	3,029	3,493	3,294
26,400	26,450	3,500	3,036	3,500	3,301
26,450	26,500	3,508	3,044	3,508	3,309
26,500	26,550	3,515	3,051	3,515	3,316
26,550	26,600	3,523	3,059	3,523	3,324
26,600	26,650	3,530	3,066	3,530	3,331
26,650	26,700	3,538	3,074	3,538	3,339
26,700	26,750	3,545	3,081	3,545	3,346
26,750	26,800	3,553	3,089	3,553	3,354
26,800	26,850	3,560	3,096	3,560	3,361
26,850	26,900	3,568	3,104	3,568	3,369
26,900	26,950	3,575	3,111	3,575	3,376
26,950	27,000	3,583	3,119	3,583	3,384

If line 43 (taxable income) is— At least	But less than	And you are— Single	Married filing jointly *	Married filing separately	Head of a household
		Your tax is—			
27,000					
27,000	27,050	3,590	3,126	3,590	3,391
27,050	27,100	3,598	3,134	3,598	3,399
27,100	27,150	3,605	3,141	3,605	3,406
27,150	27,200	3,613	3,149	3,613	3,414
27,200	27,250	3,620	3,156	3,620	3,421
27,250	27,300	3,628	3,164	3,628	3,429
27,300	27,350	3,635	3,171	3,635	3,436
27,350	27,400	3,643	3,179	3,643	3,444
27,400	27,450	3,650	3,186	3,650	3,451
27,450	27,500	3,658	3,194	3,658	3,459
27,500	27,550	3,665	3,201	3,665	3,466
27,550	27,600	3,673	3,209	3,673	3,474
27,600	27,650	3,680	3,216	3,680	3,481
27,650	27,700	3,688	3,224	3,688	3,489
27,700	27,750	3,695	3,231	3,695	3,496
27,750	27,800	3,703	3,239	3,703	3,504
27,800	27,850	3,710	3,246	3,710	3,511
27,850	27,900	3,718	3,254	3,718	3,519
27,900	27,950	3,725	3,261	3,725	3,526
27,950	28,000	3,733	3,269	3,733	3,534
28,000					
28,000	28,050	3,740	3,276	3,740	3,541
28,050	28,100	3,748	3,284	3,748	3,549
28,100	28,150	3,755	3,291	3,755	3,556
28,150	28,200	3,763	3,299	3,763	3,564
28,200	28,250	3,770	3,306	3,770	3,571
28,250	28,300	3,778	3,314	3,778	3,579
28,300	28,350	3,785	3,321	3,785	3,586
28,350	28,400	3,793	3,329	3,793	3,594
28,400	28,450	3,800	3,336	3,800	3,601
28,450	28,500	3,808	3,344	3,808	3,609
28,500	28,550	3,815	3,351	3,815	3,616
28,550	28,600	3,823	3,359	3,823	3,624
28,600	28,650	3,830	3,366	3,830	3,631
28,650	28,700	3,838	3,374	3,838	3,639
28,700	28,750	3,845	3,381	3,845	3,646
28,750	28,800	3,853	3,389	3,853	3,654
28,800	28,850	3,860	3,396	3,860	3,661
28,850	28,900	3,868	3,404	3,868	3,669
28,900	28,950	3,875	3,411	3,875	3,676
28,950	29,000	3,883	3,419	3,883	3,684
29,000					
29,000	29,050	3,890	3,426	3,890	3,691
29,050	29,100	3,898	3,434	3,898	3,699
29,100	29,150	3,905	3,441	3,905	3,706
29,150	29,200	3,913	3,449	3,913	3,714
29,200	29,250	3,920	3,456	3,920	3,721
29,250	29,300	3,928	3,464	3,928	3,729
29,300	29,350	3,935	3,471	3,935	3,736
29,350	29,400	3,943	3,479	3,943	3,744
29,400	29,450	3,950	3,486	3,950	3,751
29,450	29,500	3,958	3,494	3,958	3,759
29,500	29,550	3,965	3,501	3,965	3,766
29,550	29,600	3,973	3,509	3,973	3,774
29,600	29,650	3,980	3,516	3,980	3,781
29,650	29,700	3,988	3,524	3,988	3,789
29,700	29,750	3,995	3,531	3,995	3,796
29,750	29,800	4,003	3,539	4,003	3,804
29,800	29,850	4,010	3,546	4,010	3,811
29,850	29,900	4,018	3,554	4,018	3,819
29,900	29,950	4,025	3,561	4,025	3,826
29,950	30,000	4,033	3,569	4,033	3,834

(Continued)

* This column must also be used by a qualifying widow(er).

2016 Tax Table — Continued

30,000

If line 43 (taxable income) is— At least	But less than	Single	Married filing jointly *	Married filing separately	Head of a household
30,000	30,050	4,040	3,576	4,040	3,841
30,050	30,100	4,048	3,584	4,048	3,849
30,100	30,150	4,055	3,591	4,055	3,856
30,150	30,200	4,063	3,599	4,063	3,864
30,200	30,250	4,070	3,606	4,070	3,871
30,250	30,300	4,078	3,614	4,078	3,879
30,300	30,350	4,085	3,621	4,085	3,886
30,350	30,400	4,093	3,629	4,093	3,894
30,400	30,450	4,100	3,636	4,100	3,901
30,450	30,500	4,108	3,644	4,108	3,909
30,500	30,550	4,115	3,651	4,115	3,916
30,550	30,600	4,123	3,659	4,123	3,924
30,600	30,650	4,130	3,666	4,130	3,931
30,650	30,700	4,138	3,674	4,138	3,939
30,700	30,750	4,145	3,681	4,145	3,946
30,750	30,800	4,153	3,689	4,153	3,954
30,800	30,850	4,160	3,696	4,160	3,961
30,850	30,900	4,168	3,704	4,168	3,969
30,900	30,950	4,175	3,711	4,175	3,976
30,950	31,000	4,183	3,719	4,183	3,984

31,000

At least	But less than	Single	Married filing jointly *	Married filing separately	Head of a household
31,000	31,050	4,190	3,726	4,190	3,991
31,050	31,100	4,198	3,734	4,198	3,999
31,100	31,150	4,205	3,741	4,205	4,006
31,150	31,200	4,213	3,749	4,213	4,014
31,200	31,250	4,220	3,756	4,220	4,021
31,250	31,300	4,228	3,764	4,228	4,029
31,300	31,350	4,235	3,771	4,235	4,036
31,350	31,400	4,243	3,779	4,243	4,044
31,400	31,450	4,250	3,786	4,250	4,051
31,450	31,500	4,258	3,794	4,258	4,059
31,500	31,550	4,265	3,801	4,265	4,066
31,550	31,600	4,273	3,809	4,273	4,074
31,600	31,650	4,280	3,816	4,280	4,081
31,650	31,700	4,288	3,824	4,288	4,089
31,700	31,750	4,295	3,831	4,295	4,096
31,750	31,800	4,303	3,839	4,303	4,104
31,800	31,850	4,310	3,846	4,310	4,111
31,850	31,900	4,318	3,854	4,318	4,119
31,900	31,950	4,325	3,861	4,325	4,126
31,950	32,000	4,333	3,869	4,333	4,134

32,000

At least	But less than	Single	Married filing jointly *	Married filing separately	Head of a household
32,000	32,050	4,340	3,876	4,340	4,141
32,050	32,100	4,348	3,884	4,348	4,149
32,100	32,150	4,355	3,891	4,355	4,156
32,150	32,200	4,363	3,899	4,363	4,164
32,200	32,250	4,370	3,906	4,370	4,171
32,250	32,300	4,378	3,914	4,378	4,179
32,300	32,350	4,385	3,921	4,385	4,186
32,350	32,400	4,393	3,929	4,393	4,194
32,400	32,450	4,400	3,936	4,400	4,201
32,450	32,500	4,408	3,944	4,408	4,209
32,500	32,550	4,415	3,951	4,415	4,216
32,550	32,600	4,423	3,959	4,423	4,224
32,600	32,650	4,430	3,966	4,430	4,231
32,650	32,700	4,438	3,974	4,438	4,239
32,700	32,750	4,445	3,981	4,445	4,246
32,750	32,800	4,453	3,989	4,453	4,254
32,800	32,850	4,460	3,996	4,460	4,261
32,850	32,900	4,468	4,004	4,468	4,269
32,900	32,950	4,475	4,011	4,475	4,276
32,950	33,000	4,483	4,019	4,483	4,284

33,000

At least	But less than	Single	Married filing jointly *	Married filing separately	Head of a household
33,000	33,050	4,490	4,026	4,490	4,291
33,050	33,100	4,498	4,034	4,498	4,299
33,100	33,150	4,505	4,041	4,505	4,306
33,150	33,200	4,513	4,049	4,513	4,314
33,200	33,250	4,520	4,056	4,520	4,321
33,250	33,300	4,528	4,064	4,528	4,329
33,300	33,350	4,535	4,071	4,535	4,336
33,350	33,400	4,543	4,079	4,543	4,344
33,400	33,450	4,550	4,086	4,550	4,351
33,450	33,500	4,558	4,094	4,558	4,359
33,500	33,550	4,565	4,101	4,565	4,366
33,550	33,600	4,573	4,109	4,573	4,374
33,600	33,650	4,580	4,116	4,580	4,381
33,650	33,700	4,588	4,124	4,588	4,389
33,700	33,750	4,595	4,131	4,595	4,396
33,750	33,800	4,603	4,139	4,603	4,404
33,800	33,850	4,610	4,146	4,610	4,411
33,850	33,900	4,618	4,154	4,618	4,419
33,900	33,950	4,625	4,161	4,625	4,426
33,950	34,000	4,633	4,169	4,633	4,434

34,000

At least	But less than	Single	Married filing jointly *	Married filing separately	Head of a household
34,000	34,050	4,640	4,176	4,640	4,441
34,050	34,100	4,648	4,184	4,648	4,449
34,100	34,150	4,655	4,191	4,655	4,456
34,150	34,200	4,663	4,199	4,663	4,464
34,200	34,250	4,670	4,206	4,670	4,471
34,250	34,300	4,678	4,214	4,678	4,479
34,300	34,350	4,685	4,221	4,685	4,486
34,350	34,400	4,693	4,229	4,693	4,494
34,400	34,450	4,700	4,236	4,700	4,501
34,450	34,500	4,708	4,244	4,708	4,509
34,500	34,550	4,715	4,251	4,715	4,516
34,550	34,600	4,723	4,259	4,723	4,524
34,600	34,650	4,730	4,266	4,730	4,531
34,650	34,700	4,738	4,274	4,738	4,539
34,700	34,750	4,745	4,281	4,745	4,546
34,750	34,800	4,753	4,289	4,753	4,554
34,800	34,850	4,760	4,296	4,760	4,561
34,850	34,900	4,768	4,304	4,768	4,569
34,900	34,950	4,775	4,311	4,775	4,576
34,950	35,000	4,783	4,319	4,783	4,584

35,000

At least	But less than	Single	Married filing jointly *	Married filing separately	Head of a household
35,000	35,050	4,790	4,326	4,790	4,591
35,050	35,100	4,798	4,334	4,798	4,599
35,100	35,150	4,805	4,341	4,805	4,606
35,150	35,200	4,813	4,349	4,813	4,614
35,200	35,250	4,820	4,356	4,820	4,621
35,250	35,300	4,828	4,364	4,828	4,629
35,300	35,350	4,835	4,371	4,835	4,636
35,350	35,400	4,843	4,379	4,843	4,644
35,400	35,450	4,850	4,386	4,850	4,651
35,450	35,500	4,858	4,394	4,858	4,659
35,500	35,550	4,865	4,401	4,865	4,666
35,550	35,600	4,873	4,409	4,873	4,674
35,600	35,650	4,880	4,416	4,880	4,681
35,650	35,700	4,888	4,424	4,888	4,689
35,700	35,750	4,895	4,431	4,895	4,696
35,750	35,800	4,903	4,439	4,903	4,704
35,800	35,850	4,910	4,446	4,910	4,711
35,850	35,900	4,918	4,454	4,918	4,719
35,900	35,950	4,925	4,461	4,925	4,726
35,950	36,000	4,933	4,469	4,933	4,734

36,000

At least	But less than	Single	Married filing jointly *	Married filing separately	Head of a household
36,000	36,050	4,940	4,476	4,940	4,741
36,050	36,100	4,948	4,484	4,948	4,749
36,100	36,150	4,955	4,491	4,955	4,756
36,150	36,200	4,963	4,499	4,963	4,764
36,200	36,250	4,970	4,506	4,970	4,771
36,250	36,300	4,978	4,514	4,978	4,779
36,300	36,350	4,985	4,521	4,985	4,786
36,350	36,400	4,993	4,529	4,993	4,794
36,400	36,450	5,000	4,536	5,000	4,801
36,450	36,500	5,008	4,544	5,008	4,809
36,500	36,550	5,015	4,551	5,015	4,816
36,550	36,600	5,023	4,559	5,023	4,824
36,600	36,650	5,030	4,566	5,030	4,831
36,650	36,700	5,038	4,574	5,038	4,839
36,700	36,750	5,045	4,581	5,045	4,846
36,750	36,800	5,053	4,589	5,053	4,854
36,800	36,850	5,060	4,596	5,060	4,861
36,850	36,900	5,068	4,604	5,068	4,869
36,900	36,950	5,075	4,611	5,075	4,876
36,950	37,000	5,083	4,619	5,083	4,884

37,000

At least	But less than	Single	Married filing jointly *	Married filing separately	Head of a household
37,000	37,050	5,090	4,626	5,090	4,891
37,050	37,100	5,098	4,634	5,098	4,899
37,100	37,150	5,105	4,641	5,105	4,906
37,150	37,200	5,113	4,649	5,113	4,914
37,200	37,250	5,120	4,656	5,120	4,921
37,250	37,300	5,128	4,664	5,128	4,929
37,300	37,350	5,135	4,671	5,135	4,936
37,350	37,400	5,143	4,679	5,143	4,944
37,400	37,450	5,150	4,686	5,150	4,951
37,450	37,500	5,158	4,694	5,158	4,959
37,500	37,550	5,165	4,701	5,165	4,966
37,550	37,600	5,173	4,709	5,173	4,974
37,600	37,650	5,180	4,716	5,180	4,981
37,650	37,700	5,190	4,724	5,190	4,989
37,700	37,750	5,203	4,731	5,203	4,996
37,750	37,800	5,215	4,739	5,215	5,004
37,800	37,850	5,228	4,746	5,228	5,011
37,850	37,900	5,240	4,754	5,240	5,019
37,900	37,950	5,253	4,761	5,253	5,026
37,950	38,000	5,265	4,769	5,265	5,034

38,000

At least	But less than	Single	Married filing jointly *	Married filing separately	Head of a household
38,000	38,050	5,278	4,776	5,278	5,041
38,050	38,100	5,290	4,784	5,290	5,049
38,100	38,150	5,303	4,791	5,303	5,056
38,150	38,200	5,315	4,799	5,315	5,064
38,200	38,250	5,328	4,806	5,328	5,071
38,250	38,300	5,340	4,814	5,340	5,079
38,300	38,350	5,353	4,821	5,353	5,086
38,350	38,400	5,365	4,829	5,365	5,094
38,400	38,450	5,378	4,836	5,378	5,101
38,450	38,500	5,390	4,844	5,390	5,109
38,500	38,550	5,403	4,851	5,403	5,116
38,550	38,600	5,415	4,859	5,415	5,124
38,600	38,650	5,428	4,866	5,428	5,131
38,650	38,700	5,440	4,874	5,440	5,139
38,700	38,750	5,453	4,881	5,453	5,146
38,750	38,800	5,465	4,889	5,465	5,154
38,800	38,850	5,478	4,896	5,478	5,161
38,850	38,900	5,490	4,904	5,490	5,169
38,900	38,950	5,503	4,911	5,503	5,176
38,950	39,000	5,515	4,919	5,515	5,184

(Continued)

* This column must also be used by a qualifying widow(er).

39,000

At least	But less than	Single	Married filing jointly *	Married filing separately	Head of a household
39,000	39,050	5,528	4,926	5,528	5,191
39,050	39,100	5,540	4,934	5,540	5,199
39,100	39,150	5,553	4,941	5,553	5,206
39,150	39,200	5,565	4,949	5,565	5,214
39,200	39,250	5,578	4,956	5,578	5,221
39,250	39,300	5,590	4,964	5,590	5,229
39,300	39,350	5,603	4,971	5,603	5,236
39,350	39,400	5,615	4,979	5,615	5,244
39,400	39,450	5,628	4,986	5,628	5,251
39,450	39,500	5,640	4,994	5,640	5,259
39,500	39,550	5,653	5,001	5,653	5,266
39,550	39,600	5,665	5,009	5,665	5,274
39,600	39,650	5,678	5,016	5,678	5,281
39,650	39,700	5,690	5,024	5,690	5,289
39,700	39,750	5,703	5,031	5,703	5,296
39,750	39,800	5,715	5,039	5,715	5,304
39,800	39,850	5,728	5,046	5,728	5,311
39,850	39,900	5,740	5,054	5,740	5,319
39,900	39,950	5,753	5,061	5,753	5,326
39,950	40,000	5,765	5,069	5,765	5,334

40,000

At least	But less than	Single	Married filing jointly *	Married filing separately	Head of a household
40,000	40,050	5,778	5,076	5,778	5,341
40,050	40,100	5,790	5,084	5,790	5,349
40,100	40,150	5,803	5,091	5,803	5,356
40,150	40,200	5,815	5,099	5,815	5,364
40,200	40,250	5,828	5,106	5,828	5,371
40,250	40,300	5,840	5,114	5,840	5,379
40,300	40,350	5,853	5,121	5,853	5,386
40,350	40,400	5,865	5,129	5,865	5,394
40,400	40,450	5,878	5,136	5,878	5,401
40,450	40,500	5,890	5,144	5,890	5,409
40,500	40,550	5,903	5,151	5,903	5,416
40,550	40,600	5,915	5,159	5,915	5,424
40,600	40,650	5,928	5,166	5,928	5,431
40,650	40,700	5,940	5,174	5,940	5,439
40,700	40,750	5,953	5,181	5,953	5,446
40,750	40,800	5,965	5,189	5,965	5,454
40,800	40,850	5,978	5,196	5,978	5,461
40,850	40,900	5,990	5,204	5,990	5,469
40,900	40,950	6,003	5,211	6,003	5,476
40,950	41,000	6,015	5,219	6,015	5,484

41,000

At least	But less than	Single	Married filing jointly *	Married filing separately	Head of a household
41,000	41,050	6,028	5,226	6,028	5,491
41,050	41,100	6,040	5,234	6,040	5,499
41,100	41,150	6,053	5,241	6,053	5,506
41,150	41,200	6,065	5,249	6,065	5,514
41,200	41,250	6,078	5,256	6,078	5,521
41,250	41,300	6,090	5,264	6,090	5,529
41,300	41,350	6,103	5,271	6,103	5,536
41,350	41,400	6,115	5,279	6,115	5,544
41,400	41,450	6,128	5,286	6,128	5,551
41,450	41,500	6,140	5,294	6,140	5,559
41,500	41,550	6,153	5,301	6,153	5,566
41,550	41,600	6,165	5,309	6,165	5,574
41,600	41,650	6,178	5,316	6,178	5,581
41,650	41,700	6,190	5,324	6,190	5,589
41,700	41,750	6,203	5,331	6,203	5,596
41,750	41,800	6,215	5,339	6,215	5,604
41,800	41,850	6,228	5,346	6,228	5,611
41,850	41,900	6,240	5,354	6,240	5,619
41,900	41,950	6,253	5,361	6,253	5,626
41,950	42,000	6,265	5,369	6,265	5,634

42,000

At least	But less than	Single	Married filing jointly *	Married filing separately	Head of a household
42,000	42,050	6,278	5,376	6,278	5,641
42,050	42,100	6,290	5,384	6,290	5,649
42,100	42,150	6,303	5,391	6,303	5,656
42,150	42,200	6,315	5,399	6,315	5,664
42,200	42,250	6,328	5,406	6,328	5,671
42,250	42,300	6,340	5,414	6,340	5,679
42,300	42,350	6,353	5,421	6,353	5,686
42,350	42,400	6,365	5,429	6,365	5,694
42,400	42,450	6,378	5,436	6,378	5,701
42,450	42,500	6,390	5,444	6,390	5,709
42,500	42,550	6,403	5,451	6,403	5,716
42,550	42,600	6,415	5,459	6,415	5,724
42,600	42,650	6,428	5,466	6,428	5,731
42,650	42,700	6,440	5,474	6,440	5,739
42,700	42,750	6,453	5,481	6,453	5,746
42,750	42,800	6,465	5,489	6,465	5,754
42,800	42,850	6,478	5,496	6,478	5,761
42,850	42,900	6,490	5,504	6,490	5,769
42,900	42,950	6,503	5,511	6,503	5,776
42,950	43,000	6,515	5,519	6,515	5,784

43,000

At least	But less than	Single	Married filing jointly *	Married filing separately	Head of a household
43,000	43,050	6,528	5,526	6,528	5,791
43,050	43,100	6,540	5,534	6,540	5,799
43,100	43,150	6,553	5,541	6,553	5,806
43,150	43,200	6,565	5,549	6,565	5,814
43,200	43,250	6,578	5,556	6,578	5,821
43,250	43,300	6,590	5,564	6,590	5,829
43,300	43,350	6,603	5,571	6,603	5,836
43,350	43,400	6,615	5,579	6,615	5,844
43,400	43,450	6,628	5,586	6,628	5,851
43,450	43,500	6,640	5,594	6,640	5,859
43,500	43,550	6,653	5,601	6,653	5,866
43,550	43,600	6,665	5,609	6,665	5,874
43,600	43,650	6,678	5,616	6,678	5,881
43,650	43,700	6,690	5,624	6,690	5,889
43,700	43,750	6,703	5,631	6,703	5,896
43,750	43,800	6,715	5,639	6,715	5,904
43,800	43,850	6,728	5,646	6,728	5,911
43,850	43,900	6,740	5,654	6,740	5,919
43,900	43,950	6,753	5,661	6,753	5,926
43,950	44,000	6,765	5,669	6,765	5,934

44,000

At least	But less than	Single	Married filing jointly *	Married filing separately	Head of a household
44,000	44,050	6,778	5,676	6,778	5,941
44,050	44,100	6,790	5,684	6,790	5,949
44,100	44,150	6,803	5,691	6,803	5,956
44,150	44,200	6,815	5,699	6,815	5,964
44,200	44,250	6,828	5,706	6,828	5,971
44,250	44,300	6,840	5,714	6,840	5,979
44,300	44,350	6,853	5,721	6,853	5,986
44,350	44,400	6,865	5,729	6,865	5,994
44,400	44,450	6,878	5,736	6,878	6,001
44,450	44,500	6,890	5,744	6,890	6,009
44,500	44,550	6,903	5,751	6,903	6,016
44,550	44,600	6,915	5,759	6,915	6,024
44,600	44,650	6,928	5,766	6,928	6,031
44,650	44,700	6,940	5,774	6,940	6,039
44,700	44,750	6,953	5,781	6,953	6,046
44,750	44,800	6,965	5,789	6,965	6,054
44,800	44,850	6,978	5,796	6,978	6,061
44,850	44,900	6,990	5,804	6,990	6,069
44,900	44,950	7,003	5,811	7,003	6,076
44,950	45,000	7,015	5,819	7,015	6,084

45,000

At least	But less than	Single	Married filing jointly *	Married filing separately	Head of a household
45,000	45,050	7,028	5,826	7,028	6,091
45,050	45,100	7,040	5,834	7,040	6,099
45,100	45,150	7,053	5,841	7,053	6,106
45,150	45,200	7,065	5,849	7,065	6,114
45,200	45,250	7,078	5,856	7,078	6,121
45,250	45,300	7,090	5,864	7,090	6,129
45,300	45,350	7,103	5,871	7,103	6,136
45,350	45,400	7,115	5,879	7,115	6,144
45,400	45,450	7,128	5,886	7,128	6,151
45,450	45,500	7,140	5,894	7,140	6,159
45,500	45,550	7,153	5,901	7,153	6,166
45,550	45,600	7,165	5,909	7,165	6,174
45,600	45,650	7,178	5,916	7,178	6,181
45,650	45,700	7,190	5,924	7,190	6,189
45,700	45,750	7,203	5,931	7,203	6,196
45,750	45,800	7,215	5,939	7,215	6,204
45,800	45,850	7,228	5,946	7,228	6,211
45,850	45,900	7,240	5,954	7,240	6,219
45,900	45,950	7,253	5,961	7,253	6,226
45,950	46,000	7,265	5,969	7,265	6,234

46,000

At least	But less than	Single	Married filing jointly *	Married filing separately	Head of a household
46,000	46,050	7,278	5,976	7,278	6,241
46,050	46,100	7,290	5,984	7,290	6,249
46,100	46,150	7,303	5,991	7,303	6,256
46,150	46,200	7,315	5,999	7,315	6,264
46,200	46,250	7,328	6,006	7,328	6,271
46,250	46,300	7,340	6,014	7,340	6,279
46,300	46,350	7,353	6,021	7,353	6,286
46,350	46,400	7,365	6,029	7,365	6,294
46,400	46,450	7,378	6,036	7,378	6,301
46,450	46,500	7,390	6,044	7,390	6,309
46,500	46,550	7,403	6,051	7,403	6,316
46,550	46,600	7,415	6,059	7,415	6,324
46,600	46,650	7,428	6,066	7,428	6,331
46,650	46,700	7,440	6,074	7,440	6,339
46,700	46,750	7,453	6,081	7,453	6,346
46,750	46,800	7,465	6,089	7,465	6,354
46,800	46,850	7,478	6,096	7,478	6,361
46,850	46,900	7,490	6,104	7,490	6,369
46,900	46,950	7,503	6,111	7,503	6,376
46,950	47,000	7,515	6,119	7,515	6,384

47,000

At least	But less than	Single	Married filing jointly *	Married filing separately	Head of a household
47,000	47,050	7,528	6,126	7,528	6,391
47,050	47,100	7,540	6,134	7,540	6,399
47,100	47,150	7,553	6,141	7,553	6,406
47,150	47,200	7,565	6,149	7,565	6,414
47,200	47,250	7,578	6,156	7,578	6,421
47,250	47,300	7,590	6,164	7,590	6,429
47,300	47,350	7,603	6,171	7,603	6,436
47,350	47,400	7,615	6,179	7,615	6,444
47,400	47,450	7,628	6,186	7,628	6,451
47,450	47,500	7,640	6,194	7,640	6,459
47,500	47,550	7,653	6,201	7,653	6,466
47,550	47,600	7,665	6,209	7,665	6,474
47,600	47,650	7,678	6,216	7,678	6,481
47,650	47,700	7,690	6,224	7,690	6,489
47,700	47,750	7,703	6,231	7,703	6,496
47,750	47,800	7,715	6,239	7,715	6,504
47,800	47,850	7,728	6,246	7,728	6,511
47,850	47,900	7,740	6,254	7,740	6,519
47,900	47,950	7,753	6,261	7,753	6,526
47,950	48,000	7,765	6,269	7,765	6,534

* This column must also be used by a qualifying widow(er).

(Continued)

2016 Tax Table — Continued

48,000

At least	But less than	Single	Married filing jointly *	Married filing separately	Head of a household
48,000	48,050	7,778	6,276	7,778	6,541
48,050	48,100	7,790	6,284	7,790	6,549
48,100	48,150	7,803	6,291	7,803	6,556
48,150	48,200	7,815	6,299	7,815	6,564
48,200	48,250	7,828	6,306	7,828	6,571
48,250	48,300	7,840	6,314	7,840	6,579
48,300	48,350	7,853	6,321	7,853	6,586
48,350	48,400	7,865	6,329	7,865	6,594
48,400	48,450	7,878	6,336	7,878	6,601
48,450	48,500	7,890	6,344	7,890	6,609
48,500	48,550	7,903	6,351	7,903	6,616
48,550	48,600	7,915	6,359	7,915	6,624
48,600	48,650	7,928	6,366	7,928	6,631
48,650	48,700	7,940	6,374	7,940	6,639
48,700	48,750	7,953	6,381	7,953	6,646
48,750	48,800	7,965	6,389	7,965	6,654
48,800	48,850	7,978	6,396	7,978	6,661
48,850	48,900	7,990	6,404	7,990	6,669
48,900	48,950	8,003	6,411	8,003	6,676
48,950	49,000	8,015	6,419	8,015	6,684

49,000

At least	But less than	Single	Married filing jointly *	Married filing separately	Head of a household
49,000	49,050	8,028	6,426	8,028	6,691
49,050	49,100	8,040	6,434	8,040	6,699
49,100	49,150	8,053	6,441	8,053	6,706
49,150	49,200	8,065	6,449	8,065	6,714
49,200	49,250	8,078	6,456	8,078	6,721
49,250	49,300	8,090	6,464	8,090	6,729
49,300	49,350	8,103	6,471	8,103	6,736
49,350	49,400	8,115	6,479	8,115	6,744
49,400	49,450	8,128	6,486	8,128	6,751
49,450	49,500	8,140	6,494	8,140	6,759
49,500	49,550	8,153	6,501	8,153	6,766
49,550	49,600	8,165	6,509	8,165	6,774
49,600	49,650	8,178	6,516	8,178	6,781
49,650	49,700	8,190	6,524	8,190	6,789
49,700	49,750	8,203	6,531	8,203	6,796
49,750	49,800	8,215	6,539	8,215	6,804
49,800	49,850	8,228	6,546	8,228	6,811
49,850	49,900	8,240	6,554	8,240	6,819
49,900	49,950	8,253	6,561	8,253	6,826
49,950	50,000	8,265	6,569	8,265	6,834

50,000

At least	But less than	Single	Married filing jointly *	Married filing separately	Head of a household
50,000	50,050	8,278	6,576	8,278	6,841
50,050	50,100	8,290	6,584	8,290	6,849
50,100	50,150	8,303	6,591	8,303	6,856
50,150	50,200	8,315	6,599	8,315	6,864
50,200	50,250	8,328	6,606	8,328	6,871
50,250	50,300	8,340	6,614	8,340	6,879
50,300	50,350	8,353	6,621	8,353	6,886
50,350	50,400	8,365	6,629	8,365	6,894
50,400	50,450	8,378	6,636	8,378	6,904
50,450	50,500	8,390	6,644	8,390	6,916
50,500	50,550	8,403	6,651	8,403	6,929
50,550	50,600	8,415	6,659	8,415	6,941
50,600	50,650	8,428	6,666	8,428	6,954
50,650	50,700	8,440	6,674	8,440	6,966
50,700	50,750	8,453	6,681	8,453	6,979
50,750	50,800	8,465	6,689	8,465	6,991
50,800	50,850	8,478	6,696	8,478	7,004
50,850	50,900	8,490	6,704	8,490	7,016
50,900	50,950	8,503	6,711	8,503	7,029
50,950	51,000	8,515	6,719	8,515	7,041

51,000

At least	But less than	Single	Married filing jointly *	Married filing separately	Head of a household
51,000	51,050	8,528	6,726	8,528	7,054
51,050	51,100	8,540	6,734	8,540	7,066
51,100	51,150	8,553	6,741	8,553	7,079
51,150	51,200	8,565	6,749	8,565	7,091
51,200	51,250	8,578	6,756	8,578	7,104
51,250	51,300	8,590	6,764	8,590	7,116
51,300	51,350	8,603	6,771	8,603	7,129
51,350	51,400	8,615	6,779	8,615	7,141
51,400	51,450	8,628	6,786	8,628	7,154
51,450	51,500	8,640	6,794	8,640	7,166
51,500	51,550	8,653	6,801	8,653	7,179
51,550	51,600	8,665	6,809	8,665	7,191
51,600	51,650	8,678	6,816	8,678	7,204
51,650	51,700	8,690	6,824	8,690	7,216
51,700	51,750	8,703	6,831	8,703	7,229
51,750	51,800	8,715	6,839	8,715	7,241
51,800	51,850	8,728	6,846	8,728	7,254
51,850	51,900	8,740	6,854	8,740	7,266
51,900	51,950	8,753	6,861	8,753	7,279
51,950	52,000	8,765	6,869	8,765	7,291

52,000

At least	But less than	Single	Married filing jointly *	Married filing separately	Head of a household
52,000	52,050	8,778	6,876	8,778	7,304
52,050	52,100	8,790	6,884	8,790	7,316
52,100	52,150	8,803	6,891	8,803	7,329
52,150	52,200	8,815	6,899	8,815	7,341
52,200	52,250	8,828	6,906	8,828	7,354
52,250	52,300	8,840	6,914	8,840	7,366
52,300	52,350	8,853	6,921	8,853	7,379
52,350	52,400	8,865	6,929	8,865	7,391
52,400	52,450	8,878	6,936	8,878	7,404
52,450	52,500	8,890	6,944	8,890	7,416
52,500	52,550	8,903	6,951	8,903	7,429
52,550	52,600	8,915	6,959	8,915	7,441
52,600	52,650	8,928	6,966	8,928	7,454
52,650	52,700	8,940	6,974	8,940	7,466
52,700	52,750	8,953	6,981	8,953	7,479
52,750	52,800	8,965	6,989	8,965	7,491
52,800	52,850	8,978	6,996	8,978	7,504
52,850	52,900	8,990	7,004	8,990	7,516
52,900	52,950	9,003	7,011	9,003	7,529
52,950	53,000	9,015	7,019	9,015	7,541

53,000

At least	But less than	Single	Married filing jointly *	Married filing separately	Head of a household
53,000	53,050	9,028	7,026	9,028	7,554
53,050	53,100	9,040	7,034	9,040	7,566
53,100	53,150	9,053	7,041	9,053	7,579
53,150	53,200	9,065	7,049	9,065	7,591
53,200	53,250	9,078	7,056	9,078	7,604
53,250	53,300	9,090	7,064	9,090	7,616
53,300	53,350	9,103	7,071	9,103	7,629
53,350	53,400	9,115	7,079	9,115	7,641
53,400	53,450	9,128	7,086	9,128	7,654
53,450	53,500	9,140	7,094	9,140	7,666
53,500	53,550	9,153	7,101	9,153	7,679
53,550	53,600	9,165	7,109	9,165	7,691
53,600	53,650	9,178	7,116	9,178	7,704
53,650	53,700	9,190	7,124	9,190	7,716
53,700	53,750	9,203	7,131	9,203	7,729
53,750	53,800	9,215	7,139	9,215	7,741
53,800	53,850	9,228	7,146	9,228	7,754
53,850	53,900	9,240	7,154	9,240	7,766
53,900	53,950	9,253	7,161	9,253	7,779
53,950	54,000	9,265	7,169	9,265	7,791

54,000

At least	But less than	Single	Married filing jointly *	Married filing separately	Head of a household
54,000	54,050	9,278	7,176	9,278	7,804
54,050	54,100	9,290	7,184	9,290	7,816
54,100	54,150	9,303	7,191	9,303	7,829
54,150	54,200	9,315	7,199	9,315	7,841
54,200	54,250	9,328	7,206	9,328	7,854
54,250	54,300	9,340	7,214	9,340	7,866
54,300	54,350	9,353	7,221	9,353	7,879
54,350	54,400	9,365	7,229	9,365	7,891
54,400	54,450	9,378	7,236	9,378	7,904
54,450	54,500	9,390	7,244	9,390	7,916
54,500	54,550	9,403	7,251	9,403	7,929
54,550	54,600	9,415	7,259	9,415	7,941
54,600	54,650	9,428	7,266	9,428	7,954
54,650	54,700	9,440	7,274	9,440	7,966
54,700	54,750	9,453	7,281	9,453	7,979
54,750	54,800	9,465	7,289	9,465	7,991
54,800	54,850	9,478	7,296	9,478	8,004
54,850	54,900	9,490	7,304	9,490	8,016
54,900	54,950	9,503	7,311	9,503	8,029
54,950	55,000	9,515	7,319	9,515	8,041

55,000

At least	But less than	Single	Married filing jointly *	Married filing separately	Head of a household
55,000	55,050	9,528	7,326	9,528	8,054
55,050	55,100	9,540	7,334	9,540	8,066
55,100	55,150	9,553	7,341	9,553	8,079
55,150	55,200	9,565	7,349	9,565	8,091
55,200	55,250	9,578	7,356	9,578	8,104
55,250	55,300	9,590	7,364	9,590	8,116
55,300	55,350	9,603	7,371	9,603	8,129
55,350	55,400	9,615	7,379	9,615	8,141
55,400	55,450	9,628	7,386	9,628	8,154
55,450	55,500	9,640	7,394	9,640	8,166
55,500	55,550	9,653	7,401	9,653	8,179
55,550	55,600	9,665	7,409	9,665	8,191
55,600	55,650	9,678	7,416	9,678	8,204
55,650	55,700	9,690	7,424	9,690	8,216
55,700	55,750	9,703	7,431	9,703	8,229
55,750	55,800	9,715	7,439	9,715	8,241
55,800	55,850	9,728	7,446	9,728	8,254
55,850	55,900	9,740	7,454	9,740	8,266
55,900	55,950	9,753	7,461	9,753	8,279
55,950	56,000	9,765	7,469	9,765	8,291

56,000

At least	But less than	Single	Married filing jointly *	Married filing separately	Head of a household
56,000	56,050	9,778	7,476	9,778	8,304
56,050	56,100	9,790	7,484	9,790	8,316
56,100	56,150	9,803	7,491	9,803	8,329
56,150	56,200	9,815	7,499	9,815	8,341
56,200	56,250	9,828	7,506	9,828	8,354
56,250	56,300	9,840	7,514	9,840	8,366
56,300	56,350	9,853	7,521	9,853	8,379
56,350	56,400	9,865	7,529	9,865	8,391
56,400	56,450	9,878	7,536	9,878	8,404
56,450	56,500	9,890	7,544	9,890	8,416
56,500	56,550	9,903	7,551	9,903	8,429
56,550	56,600	9,915	7,559	9,915	8,441
56,600	56,650	9,928	7,566	9,928	8,454
56,650	56,700	9,940	7,574	9,940	8,466
56,700	56,750	9,953	7,581	9,953	8,479
56,750	56,800	9,965	7,589	9,965	8,491
56,800	56,850	9,978	7,596	9,978	8,504
56,850	56,900	9,990	7,604	9,990	8,516
56,900	56,950	10,003	7,611	10,003	8,529
56,950	57,000	10,015	7,619	10,015	8,541

(Continued)

* This column must also be used by a qualifying widow(er).

2016 Tax Table — *Continued*

57,000

At least	But less than	Single	Married filing jointly *	Married filing separately	Head of a household
57,000	57,050	10,028	7,626	10,028	8,554
57,050	57,100	10,040	7,634	10,040	8,566
57,100	57,150	10,053	7,641	10,053	8,579
57,150	57,200	10,065	7,649	10,065	8,591
57,200	57,250	10,078	7,656	10,078	8,604
57,250	57,300	10,090	7,664	10,090	8,616
57,300	57,350	10,103	7,671	10,103	8,629
57,350	57,400	10,115	7,679	10,115	8,641
57,400	57,450	10,128	7,686	10,128	8,654
57,450	57,500	10,140	7,694	10,140	8,666
57,500	57,550	10,153	7,701	10,153	8,679
57,550	57,600	10,165	7,709	10,165	8,691
57,600	57,650	10,178	7,716	10,178	8,704
57,650	57,700	10,190	7,724	10,190	8,716
57,700	57,750	10,203	7,731	10,203	8,729
57,750	57,800	10,215	7,739	10,215	8,741
57,800	57,850	10,228	7,746	10,228	8,754
57,850	57,900	10,240	7,754	10,240	8,766
57,900	57,950	10,253	7,761	10,253	8,779
57,950	58,000	10,265	7,769	10,265	8,791

58,000

At least	But less than	Single	Married filing jointly *	Married filing separately	Head of a household
58,000	58,050	10,278	7,776	10,278	8,804
58,050	58,100	10,290	7,784	10,290	8,816
58,100	58,150	10,303	7,791	10,303	8,829
58,150	58,200	10,315	7,799	10,315	8,841
58,200	58,250	10,328	7,806	10,328	8,854
58,250	58,300	10,340	7,814	10,340	8,866
58,300	58,350	10,353	7,821	10,353	8,879
58,350	58,400	10,365	7,829	10,365	8,891
58,400	58,450	10,378	7,836	10,378	8,904
58,450	58,500	10,390	7,844	10,390	8,916
58,500	58,550	10,403	7,851	10,403	8,929
58,550	58,600	10,415	7,859	10,415	8,941
58,600	58,650	10,428	7,866	10,428	8,954
58,650	58,700	10,440	7,874	10,440	8,966
58,700	58,750	10,453	7,881	10,453	8,979
58,750	58,800	10,465	7,889	10,465	8,991
58,800	58,850	10,478	7,896	10,478	9,004
58,850	58,900	10,490	7,904	10,490	9,016
58,900	58,950	10,503	7,911	10,503	9,029
58,950	59,000	10,515	7,919	10,515	9,041

59,000

At least	But less than	Single	Married filing jointly *	Married filing separately	Head of a household
59,000	59,050	10,528	7,926	10,528	9,054
59,050	59,100	10,540	7,934	10,540	9,066
59,100	59,150	10,553	7,941	10,553	9,079
59,150	59,200	10,565	7,949	10,565	9,091
59,200	59,250	10,578	7,956	10,578	9,104
59,250	59,300	10,590	7,964	10,590	9,116
59,300	59,350	10,603	7,971	10,603	9,129
59,350	59,400	10,615	7,979	10,615	9,141
59,400	59,450	10,628	7,986	10,628	9,154
59,450	59,500	10,640	7,994	10,640	9,166
59,500	59,550	10,653	8,001	10,653	9,179
59,550	59,600	10,665	8,009	10,665	9,191
59,600	59,650	10,678	8,016	10,678	9,204
59,650	59,700	10,690	8,024	10,690	9,216
59,700	59,750	10,703	8,031	10,703	9,229
59,750	59,800	10,715	8,039	10,715	9,241
59,800	59,850	10,728	8,046	10,728	9,254
59,850	59,900	10,740	8,054	10,740	9,266
59,900	59,950	10,753	8,061	10,753	9,279
59,950	60,000	10,765	8,069	10,765	9,291

60,000

At least	But less than	Single	Married filing jointly *	Married filing separately	Head of a household
60,000	60,050	10,778	8,076	10,778	9,304
60,050	60,100	10,790	8,084	10,790	9,316
60,100	60,150	10,803	8,091	10,803	9,329
60,150	60,200	10,815	8,099	10,815	9,341
60,200	60,250	10,828	8,106	10,828	9,354
60,250	60,300	10,840	8,114	10,840	9,366
60,300	60,350	10,853	8,121	10,853	9,379
60,350	60,400	10,865	8,129	10,865	9,391
60,400	60,450	10,878	8,136	10,878	9,404
60,450	60,500	10,890	8,144	10,890	9,416
60,500	60,550	10,903	8,151	10,903	9,429
60,550	60,600	10,915	8,159	10,915	9,441
60,600	60,650	10,928	8,166	10,928	9,454
60,650	60,700	10,940	8,174	10,940	9,466
60,700	60,750	10,953	8,181	10,953	9,479
60,750	60,800	10,965	8,189	10,965	9,491
60,800	60,850	10,978	8,196	10,978	9,504
60,850	60,900	10,990	8,204	10,990	9,516
60,900	60,950	11,003	8,211	11,003	9,529
60,950	61,000	11,015	8,219	11,015	9,541

61,000

At least	But less than	Single	Married filing jointly *	Married filing separately	Head of a household
61,000	61,050	11,028	8,226	11,028	9,554
61,050	61,100	11,040	8,234	11,040	9,566
61,100	61,150	11,053	8,241	11,053	9,579
61,150	61,200	11,065	8,249	11,065	9,591
61,200	61,250	11,078	8,256	11,078	9,604
61,250	61,300	11,090	8,264	11,090	9,616
61,300	61,350	11,103	8,271	11,103	9,629
61,350	61,400	11,115	8,279	11,115	9,641
61,400	61,450	11,128	8,286	11,128	9,654
61,450	61,500	11,140	8,294	11,140	9,666
61,500	61,550	11,153	8,301	11,153	9,679
61,550	61,600	11,165	8,309	11,165	9,691
61,600	61,650	11,178	8,316	11,178	9,704
61,650	61,700	11,190	8,324	11,190	9,716
61,700	61,750	11,203	8,331	11,203	9,729
61,750	61,800	11,215	8,339	11,215	9,741
61,800	61,850	11,228	8,346	11,228	9,754
61,850	61,900	11,240	8,354	11,240	9,766
61,900	61,950	11,253	8,361	11,253	9,779
61,950	62,000	11,265	8,369	11,265	9,791

62,000

At least	But less than	Single	Married filing jointly *	Married filing separately	Head of a household
62,000	62,050	11,278	8,376	11,278	9,804
62,050	62,100	11,290	8,384	11,290	9,816
62,100	62,150	11,303	8,391	11,303	9,829
62,150	62,200	11,315	8,399	11,315	9,841
62,200	62,250	11,328	8,406	11,328	9,854
62,250	62,300	11,340	8,414	11,340	9,866
62,300	62,350	11,353	8,421	11,353	9,879
62,350	62,400	11,365	8,429	11,365	9,891
62,400	62,450	11,378	8,436	11,378	9,904
62,450	62,500	11,390	8,444	11,390	9,916
62,500	62,550	11,403	8,451	11,403	9,929
62,550	62,600	11,415	8,459	11,415	9,941
62,600	62,650	11,428	8,466	11,428	9,954
62,650	62,700	11,440	8,474	11,440	9,966
62,700	62,750	11,453	8,481	11,453	9,979
62,750	62,800	11,465	8,489	11,465	9,991
62,800	62,850	11,478	8,496	11,478	10,004
62,850	62,900	11,490	8,504	11,490	10,016
62,900	62,950	11,503	8,511	11,503	10,029
62,950	63,000	11,515	8,519	11,515	10,041

63,000

At least	But less than	Single	Married filing jointly *	Married filing separately	Head of a household
63,000	63,050	11,528	8,526	11,528	10,054
63,050	63,100	11,540	8,534	11,540	10,066
63,100	63,150	11,553	8,541	11,553	10,079
63,150	63,200	11,565	8,549	11,565	10,091
63,200	63,250	11,578	8,556	11,578	10,104
63,250	63,300	11,590	8,564	11,590	10,116
63,300	63,350	11,603	8,571	11,603	10,129
63,350	63,400	11,615	8,579	11,615	10,141
63,400	63,450	11,628	8,586	11,628	10,154
63,450	63,500	11,640	8,594	11,640	10,166
63,500	63,550	11,653	8,601	11,653	10,179
63,550	63,600	11,665	8,609	11,665	10,191
63,600	63,650	11,678	8,616	11,678	10,204
63,650	63,700	11,690	8,624	11,690	10,216
63,700	63,750	11,703	8,631	11,703	10,229
63,750	63,800	11,715	8,639	11,715	10,241
63,800	63,850	11,728	8,646	11,728	10,254
63,850	63,900	11,740	8,654	11,740	10,266
63,900	63,950	11,753	8,661	11,753	10,279
63,950	64,000	11,765	8,669	11,765	10,291

64,000

At least	But less than	Single	Married filing jointly *	Married filing separately	Head of a household
64,000	64,050	11,778	8,676	11,778	10,304
64,050	64,100	11,790	8,684	11,790	10,316
64,100	64,150	11,803	8,691	11,803	10,329
64,150	64,200	11,815	8,699	11,815	10,341
64,200	64,250	11,828	8,706	11,828	10,354
64,250	64,300	11,840	8,714	11,840	10,366
64,300	64,350	11,853	8,721	11,853	10,379
64,350	64,400	11,865	8,729	11,865	10,391
64,400	64,450	11,878	8,736	11,878	10,404
64,450	64,500	11,890	8,744	11,890	10,416
64,500	64,550	11,903	8,751	11,903	10,429
64,550	64,600	11,915	8,759	11,915	10,441
64,600	64,650	11,928	8,766	11,928	10,454
64,650	64,700	11,940	8,774	11,940	10,466
64,700	64,750	11,953	8,781	11,953	10,479
64,750	64,800	11,965	8,789	11,965	10,491
64,800	64,850	11,978	8,796	11,978	10,504
64,850	64,900	11,990	8,804	11,990	10,516
64,900	64,950	12,003	8,811	12,003	10,529
64,950	65,000	12,015	8,819	12,015	10,541

65,000

At least	But less than	Single	Married filing jointly *	Married filing separately	Head of a household
65,000	65,050	12,028	8,826	12,028	10,554
65,050	65,100	12,040	8,834	12,040	10,566
65,100	65,150	12,053	8,841	12,053	10,579
65,150	65,200	12,065	8,849	12,065	10,591
65,200	65,250	12,078	8,856	12,078	10,604
65,250	65,300	12,090	8,864	12,090	10,616
65,300	65,350	12,103	8,871	12,103	10,629
65,350	65,400	12,115	8,879	12,115	10,641
65,400	65,450	12,128	8,886	12,128	10,654
65,450	65,500	12,140	8,894	12,140	10,666
65,500	65,550	12,153	8,901	12,153	10,679
65,550	65,600	12,165	8,909	12,165	10,691
65,600	65,650	12,178	8,916	12,178	10,704
65,650	65,700	12,190	8,924	12,190	10,716
65,700	65,750	12,203	8,931	12,203	10,729
65,750	65,800	12,215	8,939	12,215	10,741
65,800	65,850	12,228	8,946	12,228	10,754
65,850	65,900	12,240	8,954	12,240	10,766
65,900	65,950	12,253	8,961	12,253	10,779
65,950	66,000	12,265	8,969	12,265	10,791

(Continued)

* This column must also be used by a qualifying widow(er).

2016 Tax Table — Continued

If line 43 (taxable income) is—		And you are—			
At least	But less than	Single	Married filing jointly *	Married filing separately	Head of a household
		Your tax is—			

66,000

At least	But less than	Single	MFJ *	MFS	HoH
66,000	66,050	12,278	8,976	12,278	10,804
66,050	66,100	12,290	8,984	12,290	10,816
66,100	66,150	12,303	8,991	12,303	10,829
66,150	66,200	12,315	8,999	12,315	10,841
66,200	66,250	12,328	9,006	12,328	10,854
66,250	66,300	12,340	9,014	12,340	10,866
66,300	66,350	12,353	9,021	12,353	10,879
66,350	66,400	12,365	9,029	12,365	10,891
66,400	66,450	12,378	9,036	12,378	10,904
66,450	66,500	12,390	9,044	12,390	10,916
66,500	66,550	12,403	9,051	12,403	10,929
66,550	66,600	12,415	9,059	12,415	10,941
66,600	66,650	12,428	9,066	12,428	10,954
66,650	66,700	12,440	9,074	12,440	10,966
66,700	66,750	12,453	9,081	12,453	10,979
66,750	66,800	12,465	9,089	12,465	10,991
66,800	66,850	12,478	9,096	12,478	11,004
66,850	66,900	12,490	9,104	12,490	11,016
66,900	66,950	12,503	9,111	12,503	11,029
66,950	67,000	12,515	9,119	12,515	11,041

67,000

At least	But less than	Single	MFJ *	MFS	HoH
67,000	67,050	12,528	9,126	12,528	11,054
67,050	67,100	12,540	9,134	12,540	11,066
67,100	67,150	12,553	9,141	12,553	11,079
67,150	67,200	12,565	9,149	12,565	11,091
67,200	67,250	12,578	9,156	12,578	11,104
67,250	67,300	12,590	9,164	12,590	11,116
67,300	67,350	12,603	9,171	12,603	11,129
67,350	67,400	12,615	9,179	12,615	11,141
67,400	67,450	12,628	9,186	12,628	11,154
67,450	67,500	12,640	9,194	12,640	11,166
67,500	67,550	12,653	9,201	12,653	11,179
67,550	67,600	12,665	9,209	12,665	11,191
67,600	67,650	12,678	9,216	12,678	11,204
67,650	67,700	12,690	9,224	12,690	11,216
67,700	67,750	12,703	9,231	12,703	11,229
67,750	67,800	12,715	9,239	12,715	11,241
67,800	67,850	12,728	9,246	12,728	11,254
67,850	67,900	12,740	9,254	12,740	11,266
67,900	67,950	12,753	9,261	12,753	11,279
67,950	68,000	12,765	9,269	12,765	11,291

68,000

At least	But less than	Single	MFJ *	MFS	HoH
68,000	68,050	12,778	9,276	12,778	11,304
68,050	68,100	12,790	9,284	12,790	11,316
68,100	68,150	12,803	9,291	12,803	11,329
68,150	68,200	12,815	9,299	12,815	11,341
68,200	68,250	12,828	9,306	12,828	11,354
68,250	68,300	12,840	9,314	12,840	11,366
68,300	68,350	12,853	9,321	12,853	11,379
68,350	68,400	12,865	9,329	12,865	11,391
68,400	68,450	12,878	9,336	12,878	11,404
68,450	68,500	12,890	9,344	12,890	11,416
68,500	68,550	12,903	9,351	12,903	11,429
68,550	68,600	12,915	9,359	12,915	11,441
68,600	68,650	12,928	9,366	12,928	11,454
68,650	68,700	12,940	9,374	12,940	11,466
68,700	68,750	12,953	9,381	12,953	11,479
68,750	68,800	12,965	9,389	12,965	11,491
68,800	68,850	12,978	9,396	12,978	11,504
68,850	68,900	12,990	9,404	12,990	11,516
68,900	68,950	13,003	9,411	13,003	11,529
68,950	69,000	13,015	9,419	13,015	11,541

69,000

At least	But less than	Single	MFJ *	MFS	HoH
69,000	69,050	13,028	9,426	13,028	11,554
69,050	69,100	13,040	9,434	13,040	11,566
69,100	69,150	13,053	9,441	13,053	11,579
69,150	69,200	13,065	9,449	13,065	11,591
69,200	69,250	13,078	9,456	13,078	11,604
69,250	69,300	13,090	9,464	13,090	11,616
69,300	69,350	13,103	9,471	13,103	11,629
69,350	69,400	13,115	9,479	13,115	11,641
69,400	69,450	13,128	9,486	13,128	11,654
69,450	69,500	13,140	9,494	13,140	11,666
69,500	69,550	13,153	9,501	13,153	11,679
69,550	69,600	13,165	9,509	13,165	11,691
69,600	69,650	13,178	9,516	13,178	11,704
69,650	69,700	13,190	9,524	13,190	11,716
69,700	69,750	13,203	9,531	13,203	11,729
69,750	69,800	13,215	9,539	13,215	11,741
69,800	69,850	13,228	9,546	13,228	11,754
69,850	69,900	13,240	9,554	13,240	11,766
69,900	69,950	13,253	9,561	13,253	11,779
69,950	70,000	13,265	9,569	13,265	11,791

70,000

At least	But less than	Single	MFJ *	MFS	HoH
70,000	70,050	13,278	9,576	13,278	11,804
70,050	70,100	13,290	9,584	13,290	11,816
70,100	70,150	13,303	9,591	13,303	11,829
70,150	70,200	13,315	9,599	13,315	11,841
70,200	70,250	13,328	9,606	13,328	11,854
70,250	70,300	13,340	9,614	13,340	11,866
70,300	70,350	13,353	9,621	13,353	11,879
70,350	70,400	13,365	9,629	13,365	11,891
70,400	70,450	13,378	9,636	13,378	11,904
70,450	70,500	13,390	9,644	13,390	11,916
70,500	70,550	13,403	9,651	13,403	11,929
70,550	70,600	13,415	9,659	13,415	11,941
70,600	70,650	13,428	9,666	13,428	11,954
70,650	70,700	13,440	9,674	13,440	11,966
70,700	70,750	13,453	9,681	13,453	11,979
70,750	70,800	13,465	9,689	13,465	11,991
70,800	70,850	13,478	9,696	13,478	12,004
70,850	70,900	13,490	9,704	13,490	12,016
70,900	70,950	13,503	9,711	13,503	12,029
70,950	71,000	13,515	9,719	13,515	12,041

71,000

At least	But less than	Single	MFJ *	MFS	HoH
71,000	71,050	13,528	9,726	13,528	12,054
71,050	71,100	13,540	9,734	13,540	12,066
71,100	71,150	13,553	9,741	13,553	12,079
71,150	71,200	13,565	9,749	13,565	12,091
71,200	71,250	13,578	9,756	13,578	12,104
71,250	71,300	13,590	9,764	13,590	12,116
71,300	71,350	13,603	9,771	13,603	12,129
71,350	71,400	13,615	9,779	13,615	12,141
71,400	71,450	13,628	9,786	13,628	12,154
71,450	71,500	13,640	9,794	13,640	12,166
71,500	71,550	13,653	9,801	13,653	12,179
71,550	71,600	13,665	9,809	13,665	12,191
71,600	71,650	13,678	9,816	13,678	12,204
71,650	71,700	13,690	9,824	13,690	12,216
71,700	71,750	13,703	9,831	13,703	12,229
71,750	71,800	13,715	9,839	13,715	12,241
71,800	71,850	13,728	9,846	13,728	12,254
71,850	71,900	13,740	9,854	13,740	12,266
71,900	71,950	13,753	9,861	13,753	12,279
71,950	72,000	13,765	9,869	13,765	12,291

72,000

At least	But less than	Single	MFJ *	MFS	HoH
72,000	72,050	13,778	9,876	13,778	12,304
72,050	72,100	13,790	9,884	13,790	12,316
72,100	72,150	13,803	9,891	13,803	12,329
72,150	72,200	13,815	9,899	13,815	12,341
72,200	72,250	13,828	9,906	13,828	12,354
72,250	72,300	13,840	9,914	13,840	12,366
72,300	72,350	13,853	9,921	13,853	12,379
72,350	72,400	13,865	9,929	13,865	12,391
72,400	72,450	13,878	9,936	13,878	12,404
72,450	72,500	13,890	9,944	13,890	12,416
72,500	72,550	13,903	9,951	13,903	12,429
72,550	72,600	13,915	9,959	13,915	12,441
72,600	72,650	13,928	9,966	13,928	12,454
72,650	72,700	13,940	9,974	13,940	12,466
72,700	72,750	13,953	9,981	13,953	12,479
72,750	72,800	13,965	9,989	13,965	12,491
72,800	72,850	13,978	9,996	13,978	12,504
72,850	72,900	13,990	10,004	13,990	12,516
72,900	72,950	14,003	10,011	14,003	12,529
72,950	73,000	14,015	10,019	14,015	12,541

73,000

At least	But less than	Single	MFJ *	MFS	HoH
73,000	73,050	14,028	10,026	14,028	12,554
73,050	73,100	14,040	10,034	14,040	12,566
73,100	73,150	14,053	10,041	14,053	12,579
73,150	73,200	14,065	10,049	14,065	12,591
73,200	73,250	14,078	10,056	14,078	12,604
73,250	73,300	14,090	10,064	14,090	12,616
73,300	73,350	14,103	10,071	14,103	12,629
73,350	73,400	14,115	10,079	14,115	12,641
73,400	73,450	14,128	10,086	14,128	12,654
73,450	73,500	14,140	10,094	14,140	12,666
73,500	73,550	14,153	10,101	14,153	12,679
73,550	73,600	14,165	10,109	14,165	12,691
73,600	73,650	14,178	10,116	14,178	12,704
73,650	73,700	14,190	10,124	14,190	12,716
73,700	73,750	14,203	10,131	14,203	12,729
73,750	73,800	14,215	10,139	14,215	12,741
73,800	73,850	14,228	10,146	14,228	12,754
73,850	73,900	14,240	10,154	14,240	12,766
73,900	73,950	14,253	10,161	14,253	12,779
73,950	74,000	14,265	10,169	14,265	12,791

74,000

At least	But less than	Single	MFJ *	MFS	HoH
74,000	74,050	14,278	10,176	14,278	12,804
74,050	74,100	14,290	10,184	14,290	12,816
74,100	74,150	14,303	10,191	14,303	12,829
74,150	74,200	14,315	10,199	14,315	12,841
74,200	74,250	14,328	10,206	14,328	12,854
74,250	74,300	14,340	10,214	14,340	12,866
74,300	74,350	14,353	10,221	14,353	12,879
74,350	74,400	14,365	10,229	14,365	12,891
74,400	74,450	14,378	10,236	14,378	12,904
74,450	74,500	14,390	10,244	14,390	12,916
74,500	74,550	14,403	10,251	14,403	12,929
74,550	74,600	14,415	10,259	14,415	12,941
74,600	74,650	14,428	10,266	14,428	12,954
74,650	74,700	14,440	10,274	14,440	12,966
74,700	74,750	14,453	10,281	14,453	12,979
74,750	74,800	14,465	10,289	14,465	12,991
74,800	74,850	14,478	10,296	14,478	13,004
74,850	74,900	14,490	10,304	14,490	13,016
74,900	74,950	14,503	10,311	14,503	13,029
74,950	75,000	14,515	10,319	14,515	13,041

(Continued)

* This column must also be used by a qualifying widow(er).

2016 Tax Table — Continued

If line 43 (taxable income) is—		And you are—				If line 43 (taxable income) is—		And you are—				If line 43 (taxable income) is—		And you are—			
At least	But less than	Single	Married filing jointly *	Married filing separately	Head of a household	At least	But less than	Single	Married filing jointly *	Married filing separately	Head of a household	At least	But less than	Single	Married filing jointly *	Married filing separately	Head of a household
		Your tax is—						Your tax is—						Your tax is—			
75,000						**78,000**						**81,000**					
75,000	75,050	14,528	10,326	14,528	13,054	78,000	78,050	15,278	11,049	15,340	13,804	81,000	81,050	16,028	11,799	16,180	14,554
75,050	75,100	14,540	10,334	14,540	13,066	78,050	78,100	15,290	11,061	15,354	13,816	81,050	81,100	16,040	11,811	16,194	14,566
75,100	75,150	14,553	10,341	14,553	13,079	78,100	78,150	15,303	11,074	15,368	13,829	81,100	81,150	16,053	11,824	16,208	14,579
75,150	75,200	14,565	10,349	14,565	13,091	78,150	78,200	15,315	11,086	15,382	13,841	81,150	81,200	16,065	11,836	16,222	14,591
75,200	75,250	14,578	10,356	14,578	13,104	78,200	78,250	15,328	11,099	15,396	13,854	81,200	81,250	16,078	11,849	16,236	14,604
75,250	75,300	14,590	10,364	14,590	13,116	78,250	78,300	15,340	11,111	15,410	13,866	81,250	81,300	16,090	11,861	16,250	14,616
75,300	75,350	14,603	10,374	14,603	13,129	78,300	78,350	15,353	11,124	15,424	13,879	81,300	81,350	16,103	11,874	16,264	14,629
75,350	75,400	14,615	10,386	14,615	13,141	78,350	78,400	15,365	11,136	15,438	13,891	81,350	81,400	16,115	11,886	16,278	14,641
75,400	75,450	14,628	10,399	14,628	13,154	78,400	78,450	15,378	11,149	15,452	13,904	81,400	81,450	16,128	11,899	16,292	14,654
75,450	75,500	14,640	10,411	14,640	13,166	78,450	78,500	15,390	11,161	15,466	13,916	81,450	81,500	16,140	11,911	16,306	14,666
75,500	75,550	14,653	10,424	14,653	13,179	78,500	78,550	15,403	11,174	15,480	13,929	81,500	81,550	16,153	11,924	16,320	14,679
75,550	75,600	14,665	10,436	14,665	13,191	78,550	78,600	15,415	11,186	15,494	13,941	81,550	81,600	16,165	11,936	16,334	14,691
75,600	75,650	14,678	10,449	14,678	13,204	78,600	78,650	15,428	11,199	15,508	13,954	81,600	81,650	16,178	11,949	16,348	14,704
75,650	75,700	14,690	10,461	14,690	13,216	78,650	78,700	15,440	11,211	15,522	13,966	81,650	81,700	16,190	11,961	16,362	14,716
75,700	75,750	14,703	10,474	14,703	13,229	78,700	78,750	15,453	11,224	15,536	13,979	81,700	81,750	16,203	11,974	16,376	14,729
75,750	75,800	14,715	10,486	14,715	13,241	78,750	78,800	15,465	11,236	15,550	13,991	81,750	81,800	16,215	11,986	16,390	14,741
75,800	75,850	14,728	10,499	14,728	13,254	78,800	78,850	15,478	11,249	15,564	14,004	81,800	81,850	16,228	11,999	16,404	14,754
75,850	75,900	14,740	10,511	14,740	13,266	78,850	78,900	15,490	11,261	15,578	14,016	81,850	81,900	16,240	12,011	16,418	14,766
75,900	75,950	14,753	10,524	14,753	13,279	78,900	78,950	15,503	11,274	15,592	14,029	81,900	81,950	16,253	12,024	16,432	14,779
75,950	76,000	14,765	10,536	14,766	13,291	78,950	79,000	15,515	11,286	15,606	14,041	81,950	82,000	16,265	12,036	16,446	14,791
76,000						**79,000**						**82,000**					
76,000	76,050	14,778	10,549	14,780	13,304	79,000	79,050	15,528	11,299	15,620	14,054	82,000	82,050	16,278	12,049	16,460	14,804
76,050	76,100	14,790	10,561	14,794	13,316	79,050	79,100	15,540	11,311	15,634	14,066	82,050	82,100	16,290	12,061	16,474	14,816
76,100	76,150	14,803	10,574	14,808	13,329	79,100	79,150	15,553	11,324	15,648	14,079	82,100	82,150	16,303	12,074	16,488	14,829
76,150	76,200	14,815	10,586	14,822	13,341	79,150	79,200	15,565	11,336	15,662	14,091	82,150	82,200	16,315	12,086	16,502	14,841
76,200	76,250	14,828	10,599	14,836	13,354	79,200	79,250	15,578	11,349	15,676	14,104	82,200	82,250	16,328	12,099	16,516	14,854
76,250	76,300	14,840	10,611	14,850	13,366	79,250	79,300	15,590	11,361	15,690	14,116	82,250	82,300	16,340	12,111	16,530	14,866
76,300	76,350	14,853	10,624	14,864	13,379	79,300	79,350	15,603	11,374	15,704	14,129	82,300	82,350	16,353	12,124	16,544	14,879
76,350	76,400	14,865	10,636	14,878	13,391	79,350	79,400	15,615	11,386	15,718	14,141	82,350	82,400	16,365	12,136	16,558	14,891
76,400	76,450	14,878	10,649	14,892	13,404	79,400	79,450	15,628	11,399	15,732	14,154	82,400	82,450	16,378	12,149	16,572	14,904
76,450	76,500	14,890	10,661	14,906	13,416	79,450	79,500	15,640	11,411	15,746	14,166	82,450	82,500	16,390	12,161	16,586	14,916
76,500	76,550	14,903	10,674	14,920	13,429	79,500	79,550	15,653	11,424	15,760	14,179	82,500	82,550	16,403	12,174	16,600	14,929
76,550	76,600	14,915	10,686	14,934	13,441	79,550	79,600	15,665	11,436	15,774	14,191	82,550	82,600	16,415	12,186	16,614	14,941
76,600	76,650	14,928	10,699	14,948	13,454	79,600	79,650	15,678	11,449	15,788	14,204	82,600	82,650	16,428	12,199	16,628	14,954
76,650	76,700	14,940	10,711	14,962	13,466	79,650	79,700	15,690	11,461	15,802	14,216	82,650	82,700	16,440	12,211	16,642	14,966
76,700	76,750	14,953	10,724	14,976	13,479	79,700	79,750	15,703	11,474	15,816	14,229	82,700	82,750	16,453	12,224	16,656	14,979
76,750	76,800	14,965	10,736	14,990	13,491	79,750	79,800	15,715	11,486	15,830	14,241	82,750	82,800	16,465	12,236	16,670	14,991
76,800	76,850	14,978	10,749	15,004	13,504	79,800	79,850	15,728	11,499	15,844	14,254	82,800	82,850	16,478	12,249	16,684	15,004
76,850	76,900	14,990	10,761	15,018	13,516	79,850	79,900	15,740	11,511	15,858	14,266	82,850	82,900	16,490	12,261	16,698	15,016
76,900	76,950	15,003	10,774	15,032	13,529	79,900	79,950	15,753	11,524	15,872	14,279	82,900	82,950	16,503	12,274	16,712	15,029
76,950	77,000	15,015	10,786	15,046	13,541	79,950	80,000	15,765	11,536	15,886	14,291	82,950	83,000	16,515	12,286	16,726	15,041
77,000						**80,000**						**83,000**					
77,000	77,050	15,028	10,799	15,060	13,554	80,000	80,050	15,778	11,549	15,900	14,304	83,000	83,050	16,528	12,299	16,740	15,054
77,050	77,100	15,040	10,811	15,074	13,566	80,050	80,100	15,790	11,561	15,914	14,316	83,050	83,100	16,540	12,311	16,754	15,066
77,100	77,150	15,053	10,824	15,088	13,579	80,100	80,150	15,803	11,574	15,928	14,329	83,100	83,150	16,553	12,324	16,768	15,079
77,150	77,200	15,065	10,836	15,102	13,591	80,150	80,200	15,815	11,586	15,942	14,341	83,150	83,200	16,565	12,336	16,782	15,091
77,200	77,250	15,078	10,849	15,116	13,604	80,200	80,250	15,828	11,599	15,956	14,354	83,200	83,250	16,578	12,349	16,796	15,104
77,250	77,300	15,090	10,861	15,130	13,616	80,250	80,300	15,840	11,611	15,970	14,366	83,250	83,300	16,590	12,361	16,810	15,116
77,300	77,350	15,103	10,874	15,144	13,629	80,300	80,350	15,853	11,624	15,984	14,379	83,300	83,350	16,603	12,374	16,824	15,129
77,350	77,400	15,115	10,886	15,158	13,641	80,350	80,400	15,865	11,636	15,998	14,391	83,350	83,400	16,615	12,386	16,838	15,141
77,400	77,450	15,128	10,899	15,172	13,654	80,400	80,450	15,878	11,649	16,012	14,404	83,400	83,450	16,628	12,399	16,852	15,154
77,450	77,500	15,140	10,911	15,186	13,666	80,450	80,500	15,890	11,661	16,026	14,416	83,450	83,500	16,640	12,411	16,866	15,166
77,500	77,550	15,153	10,924	15,200	13,679	80,500	80,550	15,903	11,674	16,040	14,429	83,500	83,550	16,653	12,424	16,880	15,179
77,550	77,600	15,165	10,936	15,214	13,691	80,550	80,600	15,915	11,686	16,054	14,441	83,550	83,600	16,665	12,436	16,894	15,191
77,600	77,650	15,178	10,949	15,228	13,704	80,600	80,650	15,928	11,699	16,068	14,454	83,600	83,650	16,678	12,449	16,908	15,204
77,650	77,700	15,190	10,961	15,242	13,716	80,650	80,700	15,940	11,711	16,082	14,466	83,650	83,700	16,690	12,461	16,922	15,216
77,700	77,750	15,203	10,974	15,256	13,729	80,700	80,750	15,953	11,724	16,096	14,479	83,700	83,750	16,703	12,474	16,936	15,229
77,750	77,800	15,215	10,986	15,270	13,741	80,750	80,800	15,965	11,736	16,110	14,491	83,750	83,800	16,715	12,486	16,950	15,241
77,800	77,850	15,228	10,999	15,284	13,754	80,800	80,850	15,978	11,749	16,124	14,504	83,800	83,850	16,728	12,499	16,964	15,254
77,850	77,900	15,240	11,011	15,298	13,766	80,850	80,900	15,990	11,761	16,138	14,516	83,850	83,900	16,740	12,511	16,978	15,266
77,900	77,950	15,253	11,024	15,312	13,779	80,900	80,950	16,003	11,774	16,152	14,529	83,900	83,950	16,753	12,524	16,992	15,279
77,950	78,000	15,265	11,036	15,326	13,791	80,950	81,000	16,015	11,786	16,166	14,541	83,950	84,000	16,765	12,536	17,006	15,291

(Continued)

* This column must also be used by a qualifying widow(er).

2016 Tax Table — Continued

84,000

At least	But less than	Single	Married filing jointly *	Married filing separately	Head of a household
84,000	84,050	16,778	12,549	17,020	15,304
84,050	84,100	16,790	12,561	17,034	15,316
84,100	84,150	16,803	12,574	17,048	15,329
84,150	84,200	16,815	12,586	17,062	15,341
84,200	84,250	16,828	12,599	17,076	15,354
84,250	84,300	16,840	12,611	17,090	15,366
84,300	84,350	16,853	12,624	17,104	15,379
84,350	84,400	16,865	12,636	17,118	15,391
84,400	84,450	16,878	12,649	17,132	15,404
84,450	84,500	16,890	12,661	17,146	15,416
84,500	84,550	16,903	12,674	17,160	15,429
84,550	84,600	16,915	12,686	17,174	15,441
84,600	84,650	16,928	12,699	17,188	15,454
84,650	84,700	16,940	12,711	17,202	15,466
84,700	84,750	16,953	12,724	17,216	15,479
84,750	84,800	16,965	12,736	17,230	15,491
84,800	84,850	16,978	12,749	17,244	15,504
84,850	84,900	16,990	12,761	17,258	15,516
84,900	84,950	17,003	12,774	17,272	15,529
84,950	85,000	17,015	12,786	17,286	15,541

85,000

At least	But less than	Single	Married filing jointly *	Married filing separately	Head of a household
85,000	85,050	17,028	12,799	17,300	15,554
85,050	85,100	17,040	12,811	17,314	15,566
85,100	85,150	17,053	12,824	17,328	15,579
85,150	85,200	17,065	12,836	17,342	15,591
85,200	85,250	17,078	12,849	17,356	15,604
85,250	85,300	17,090	12,861	17,370	15,616
85,300	85,350	17,103	12,874	17,384	15,629
85,350	85,400	17,115	12,886	17,398	15,641
85,400	85,450	17,128	12,899	17,412	15,654
85,450	85,500	17,140	12,911	17,426	15,666
85,500	85,550	17,153	12,924	17,440	15,679
85,550	85,600	17,165	12,936	17,454	15,691
85,600	85,650	17,178	12,949	17,468	15,704
85,650	85,700	17,190	12,961	17,482	15,716
85,700	85,750	17,203	12,974	17,496	15,729
85,750	85,800	17,215	12,986	17,510	15,741
85,800	85,850	17,228	12,999	17,524	15,754
85,850	85,900	17,240	13,011	17,538	15,766
85,900	85,950	17,253	13,024	17,552	15,779
85,950	86,000	17,265	13,036	17,566	15,791

86,000

At least	But less than	Single	Married filing jointly *	Married filing separately	Head of a household
86,000	86,050	17,278	13,049	17,580	15,804
86,050	86,100	17,290	13,061	17,594	15,816
86,100	86,150	17,303	13,074	17,608	15,829
86,150	86,200	17,315	13,086	17,622	15,841
86,200	86,250	17,328	13,099	17,636	15,854
86,250	86,300	17,340	13,111	17,650	15,866
86,300	86,350	17,353	13,124	17,664	15,879
86,350	86,400	17,365	13,136	17,678	15,891
86,400	86,450	17,378	13,149	17,692	15,904
86,450	86,500	17,390	13,161	17,706	15,916
86,500	86,550	17,403	13,174	17,720	15,929
86,550	86,600	17,415	13,186	17,734	15,941
86,600	86,650	17,428	13,199	17,748	15,954
86,650	86,700	17,440	13,211	17,762	15,966
86,700	86,750	17,453	13,224	17,776	15,979
86,750	86,800	17,465	13,236	17,790	15,991
86,800	86,850	17,478	13,249	17,804	16,004
86,850	86,900	17,490	13,261	17,818	16,016
86,900	86,950	17,503	13,274	17,832	16,029
86,950	87,000	17,515	13,286	17,846	16,041

87,000

At least	But less than	Single	Married filing jointly *	Married filing separately	Head of a household
87,000	87,050	17,528	13,299	17,860	16,054
87,050	87,100	17,540	13,311	17,874	16,066
87,100	87,150	17,553	13,324	17,888	16,079
87,150	87,200	17,565	13,336	17,902	16,091
87,200	87,250	17,578	13,349	17,916	16,104
87,250	87,300	17,590	13,361	17,930	16,116
87,300	87,350	17,603	13,374	17,944	16,129
87,350	87,400	17,615	13,386	17,958	16,141
87,400	87,450	17,628	13,399	17,972	16,154
87,450	87,500	17,640	13,411	17,986	16,166
87,500	87,550	17,653	13,424	18,000	16,179
87,550	87,600	17,665	13,436	18,014	16,191
87,600	87,650	17,678	13,449	18,028	16,204
87,650	87,700	17,690	13,461	18,042	16,216
87,700	87,750	17,703	13,474	18,056	16,229
87,750	87,800	17,715	13,486	18,070	16,241
87,800	87,850	17,728	13,499	18,084	16,254
87,850	87,900	17,740	13,511	18,098	16,266
87,900	87,950	17,753	13,524	18,112	16,279
87,950	88,000	17,765	13,536	18,126	16,291

88,000

At least	But less than	Single	Married filing jointly *	Married filing separately	Head of a household
88,000	88,050	17,778	13,549	18,140	16,304
88,050	88,100	17,790	13,561	18,154	16,316
88,100	88,150	17,803	13,574	18,168	16,329
88,150	88,200	17,815	13,586	18,182	16,341
88,200	88,250	17,828	13,599	18,196	16,354
88,250	88,300	17,840	13,611	18,210	16,366
88,300	88,350	17,853	13,624	18,224	16,379
88,350	88,400	17,865	13,636	18,238	16,391
88,400	88,450	17,878	13,649	18,252	16,404
88,450	88,500	17,890	13,661	18,266	16,416
88,500	88,550	17,903	13,674	18,280	16,429
88,550	88,600	17,915	13,686	18,294	16,441
88,600	88,650	17,928	13,699	18,308	16,454
88,650	88,700	17,940	13,711	18,322	16,466
88,700	88,750	17,953	13,724	18,336	16,479
88,750	88,800	17,965	13,736	18,350	16,491
88,800	88,850	17,978	13,749	18,364	16,504
88,850	88,900	17,990	13,761	18,378	16,516
88,900	88,950	18,003	13,774	18,392	16,529
88,950	89,000	18,015	13,786	18,406	16,541

89,000

At least	But less than	Single	Married filing jointly *	Married filing separately	Head of a household
89,000	89,050	18,028	13,799	18,420	16,554
89,050	89,100	18,040	13,811	18,434	16,566
89,100	89,150	18,053	13,824	18,448	16,579
89,150	89,200	18,065	13,836	18,462	16,591
89,200	89,250	18,078	13,849	18,476	16,604
89,250	89,300	18,090	13,861	18,490	16,616
89,300	89,350	18,103	13,874	18,504	16,629
89,350	89,400	18,115	13,886	18,518	16,641
89,400	89,450	18,128	13,899	18,532	16,654
89,450	89,500	18,140	13,911	18,546	16,666
89,500	89,550	18,153	13,924	18,560	16,679
89,550	89,600	18,165	13,936	18,574	16,691
89,600	89,650	18,178	13,949	18,588	16,704
89,650	89,700	18,190	13,961	18,602	16,716
89,700	89,750	18,203	13,974	18,616	16,729
89,750	89,800	18,215	13,986	18,630	16,741
89,800	89,850	18,228	13,999	18,644	16,754
89,850	89,900	18,240	14,011	18,658	16,766
89,900	89,950	18,253	14,024	18,672	16,779
89,950	90,000	18,265	14,036	18,686	16,791

90,000

At least	But less than	Single	Married filing jointly *	Married filing separately	Head of a household
90,000	90,050	18,278	14,049	18,700	16,804
90,050	90,100	18,290	14,061	18,714	16,816
90,100	90,150	18,303	14,074	18,728	16,829
90,150	90,200	18,315	14,086	18,742	16,841
90,200	90,250	18,328	14,099	18,756	16,854
90,250	90,300	18,340	14,111	18,770	16,866
90,300	90,350	18,353	14,124	18,784	16,879
90,350	90,400	18,365	14,136	18,798	16,891
90,400	90,450	18,378	14,149	18,812	16,904
90,450	90,500	18,390	14,161	18,826	16,916
90,500	90,550	18,403	14,174	18,840	16,929
90,550	90,600	18,415	14,186	18,854	16,941
90,600	90,650	18,428	14,199	18,868	16,954
90,650	90,700	18,440	14,211	18,882	16,966
90,700	90,750	18,453	14,224	18,896	16,979
90,750	90,800	18,465	14,236	18,910	16,991
90,800	90,850	18,478	14,249	18,924	17,004
90,850	90,900	18,490	14,261	18,938	17,016
90,900	90,950	18,503	14,274	18,952	17,029
90,950	91,000	18,515	14,286	18,966	17,041

91,000

At least	But less than	Single	Married filing jointly *	Married filing separately	Head of a household
91,000	91,050	18,528	14,299	18,980	17,054
91,050	91,100	18,540	14,311	18,994	17,066
91,100	91,150	18,553	14,324	19,008	17,079
91,150	91,200	18,566	14,336	19,022	17,091
91,200	91,250	18,580	14,349	19,036	17,104
91,250	91,300	18,594	14,361	19,050	17,116
91,300	91,350	18,608	14,374	19,064	17,129
91,350	91,400	18,622	14,386	19,078	17,141
91,400	91,450	18,636	14,399	19,092	17,154
91,450	91,500	18,650	14,411	19,106	17,166
91,500	91,550	18,664	14,424	19,120	17,179
91,550	91,600	18,678	14,436	19,134	17,191
91,600	91,650	18,692	14,449	19,148	17,204
91,650	91,700	18,706	14,461	19,162	17,216
91,700	91,750	18,720	14,474	19,176	17,229
91,750	91,800	18,734	14,486	19,190	17,241
91,800	91,850	18,748	14,499	19,204	17,254
91,850	91,900	18,762	14,511	19,218	17,266
91,900	91,950	18,776	14,524	19,232	17,279
91,950	92,000	18,790	14,536	19,246	17,291

92,000

At least	But less than	Single	Married filing jointly *	Married filing separately	Head of a household
92,000	92,050	18,804	14,549	19,260	17,304
92,050	92,100	18,818	14,561	19,274	17,316
92,100	92,150	18,832	14,574	19,288	17,329
92,150	92,200	18,846	14,586	19,302	17,341
92,200	92,250	18,860	14,599	19,316	17,354
92,250	92,300	18,874	14,611	19,330	17,366
92,300	92,350	18,888	14,624	19,344	17,379
92,350	92,400	18,902	14,636	19,358	17,391
92,400	92,450	18,916	14,649	19,372	17,404
92,450	92,500	18,930	14,661	19,386	17,416
92,500	92,550	18,944	14,674	19,400	17,429
92,550	92,600	18,958	14,686	19,414	17,441
92,600	92,650	18,972	14,699	19,428	17,454
92,650	92,700	18,986	14,711	19,442	17,466
92,700	92,750	19,000	14,724	19,456	17,479
92,750	92,800	19,014	14,736	19,470	17,491
92,800	92,850	19,028	14,749	19,484	17,504
92,850	92,900	19,042	14,761	19,498	17,516
92,900	92,950	19,056	14,774	19,512	17,529
92,950	93,000	19,070	14,786	19,526	17,541

* This column must also be used by a qualifying widow(er).

(Continued)

2016 Tax Table — *Continued*

93,000

If line 43 (taxable income) is—		And you are—			
At least	But less than	Single	Married filing jointly *	Married filing separately	Head of a household
		Your tax is—			
93,000	93,050	19,084	14,799	19,540	17,554
93,050	93,100	19,098	14,811	19,554	17,566
93,100	93,150	19,112	14,824	19,568	17,579
93,150	93,200	19,126	14,836	19,582	17,591
93,200	93,250	19,140	14,849	19,596	17,604
93,250	93,300	19,154	14,861	19,610	17,616
93,300	93,350	19,168	14,874	19,624	17,629
93,350	93,400	19,182	14,886	19,638	17,641
93,400	93,450	19,196	14,899	19,652	17,654
93,450	93,500	19,210	14,911	19,666	17,666
93,500	93,550	19,224	14,924	19,680	17,679
93,550	93,600	19,238	14,936	19,694	17,691
93,600	93,650	19,252	14,949	19,708	17,704
93,650	93,700	19,266	14,961	19,722	17,716
93,700	93,750	19,280	14,974	19,736	17,729
93,750	93,800	19,294	14,986	19,750	17,741
93,800	93,850	19,308	14,999	19,764	17,754
93,850	93,900	19,322	15,011	19,778	17,766
93,900	93,950	19,336	15,024	19,792	17,779
93,950	94,000	19,350	15,036	19,806	17,791

94,000

At least	But less than	Single	Married filing jointly *	Married filing separately	Head of a household
94,000	94,050	19,364	15,049	19,820	17,804
94,050	94,100	19,378	15,061	19,834	17,816
94,100	94,150	19,392	15,074	19,848	17,829
94,150	94,200	19,406	15,086	19,862	17,841
94,200	94,250	19,420	15,099	19,876	17,854
94,250	94,300	19,434	15,111	19,890	17,866
94,300	94,350	19,448	15,124	19,904	17,879
94,350	94,400	19,462	15,136	19,918	17,891
94,400	94,450	19,476	15,149	19,932	17,904
94,450	94,500	19,490	15,161	19,946	17,916
94,500	94,550	19,504	15,174	19,960	17,929
94,550	94,600	19,518	15,186	19,974	17,941
94,600	94,650	19,532	15,199	19,988	17,954
94,650	94,700	19,546	15,211	20,002	17,966
94,700	94,750	19,560	15,224	20,016	17,979
94,750	94,800	19,574	15,236	20,030	17,991
94,800	94,850	19,588	15,249	20,044	18,004
94,850	94,900	19,602	15,261	20,058	18,016
94,900	94,950	19,616	15,274	20,072	18,029
94,950	95,000	19,630	15,286	20,086	18,041

95,000

At least	But less than	Single	Married filing jointly *	Married filing separately	Head of a household
95,000	95,050	19,644	15,299	20,100	18,054
95,050	95,100	19,658	15,311	20,114	18,066
95,100	95,150	19,672	15,324	20,128	18,079
95,150	95,200	19,686	15,336	20,142	18,091
95,200	95,250	19,700	15,349	20,156	18,104
95,250	95,300	19,714	15,361	20,170	18,116
95,300	95,350	19,728	15,374	20,184	18,129
95,350	95,400	19,742	15,386	20,198	18,141
95,400	95,450	19,756	15,399	20,212	18,154
95,450	95,500	19,770	15,411	20,226	18,166
95,500	95,550	19,784	15,424	20,240	18,179
95,550	95,600	19,798	15,436	20,254	18,191
95,600	95,650	19,812	15,449	20,268	18,204
95,650	95,700	19,826	15,461	20,282	18,216
95,700	95,750	19,840	15,474	20,296	18,229
95,750	95,800	19,854	15,486	20,310	18,241
95,800	95,850	19,868	15,499	20,324	18,254
95,850	95,900	19,882	15,511	20,338	18,266
95,900	95,950	19,896	15,524	20,352	18,279
95,950	96,000	19,910	15,536	20,366	18,291

96,000

If line 43 (taxable income) is—		And you are—			
At least	But less than	Single	Married filing jointly *	Married filing separately	Head of a household
		Your tax is—			
96,000	96,050	19,924	15,549	20,380	18,304
96,050	96,100	19,938	15,561	20,394	18,316
96,100	96,150	19,952	15,574	20,408	18,329
96,150	96,200	19,966	15,586	20,422	18,341
96,200	96,250	19,980	15,599	20,436	18,354
96,250	96,300	19,994	15,611	20,450	18,366
96,300	96,350	20,008	15,624	20,464	18,379
96,350	96,400	20,022	15,636	20,478	18,391
96,400	96,450	20,036	15,649	20,492	18,404
96,450	96,500	20,050	15,661	20,506	18,416
96,500	96,550	20,064	15,674	20,520	18,429
96,550	96,600	20,078	15,686	20,534	18,441
96,600	96,650	20,092	15,699	20,548	18,454
96,650	96,700	20,106	15,711	20,562	18,466
96,700	96,750	20,120	15,724	20,576	18,479
96,750	96,800	20,134	15,736	20,590	18,491
96,800	96,850	20,148	15,749	20,604	18,504
96,850	96,900	20,162	15,761	20,618	18,516
96,900	96,950	20,176	15,774	20,632	18,529
96,950	97,000	20,190	15,786	20,646	18,541

97,000

At least	But less than	Single	Married filing jointly *	Married filing separately	Head of a household
97,000	97,050	20,204	15,799	20,660	18,554
97,050	97,100	20,218	15,811	20,674	18,566
97,100	97,150	20,232	15,824	20,688	18,579
97,150	97,200	20,246	15,836	20,702	18,591
97,200	97,250	20,260	15,849	20,716	18,604
97,250	97,300	20,274	15,861	20,730	18,616
97,300	97,350	20,288	15,874	20,744	18,629
97,350	97,400	20,302	15,886	20,758	18,641
97,400	97,450	20,316	15,899	20,772	18,654
97,450	97,500	20,330	15,911	20,786	18,666
97,500	97,550	20,344	15,924	20,800	18,679
97,550	97,600	20,358	15,936	20,814	18,691
97,600	97,650	20,372	15,949	20,828	18,704
97,650	97,700	20,386	15,961	20,842	18,716
97,700	97,750	20,400	15,974	20,856	18,729
97,750	97,800	20,414	15,986	20,870	18,741
97,800	97,850	20,428	15,999	20,884	18,754
97,850	97,900	20,442	16,011	20,898	18,766
97,900	97,950	20,456	16,024	20,912	18,779
97,950	98,000	20,470	16,036	20,926	18,791

98,000

At least	But less than	Single	Married filing jointly *	Married filing separately	Head of a household
98,000	98,050	20,484	16,049	20,940	18,804
98,050	98,100	20,498	16,061	20,954	18,816
98,100	98,150	20,512	16,074	20,968	18,829
98,150	98,200	20,526	16,086	20,982	18,841
98,200	98,250	20,540	16,099	20,996	18,854
98,250	98,300	20,554	16,111	21,010	18,866
98,300	98,350	20,568	16,124	21,024	18,879
98,350	98,400	20,582	16,136	21,038	18,891
98,400	98,450	20,596	16,149	21,052	18,904
98,450	98,500	20,610	16,161	21,066	18,916
98,500	98,550	20,624	16,174	21,080	18,929
98,550	98,600	20,638	16,186	21,094	18,941
98,600	98,650	20,652	16,199	21,108	18,954
98,650	98,700	20,666	16,211	21,122	18,966
98,700	98,750	20,680	16,224	21,136	18,979
98,750	98,800	20,694	16,236	21,150	18,991
98,800	98,850	20,708	16,249	21,164	19,004
98,850	98,900	20,722	16,261	21,178	19,016
98,900	98,950	20,736	16,274	21,192	19,029
98,950	99,000	20,750	16,286	21,206	19,041

99,000

If line 43 (taxable income) is—		And you are—			
At least	But less than	Single	Married filing jointly *	Married filing separately	Head of a household
		Your tax is—			
99,000	99,050	20,764	16,299	21,220	19,054
99,050	99,100	20,778	16,311	21,234	19,066
99,100	99,150	20,792	16,324	21,248	19,079
99,150	99,200	20,806	16,336	21,262	19,091
99,200	99,250	20,820	16,349	21,276	19,104
99,250	99,300	20,834	16,361	21,290	19,116
99,300	99,350	20,848	16,374	21,304	19,129
99,350	99,400	20,862	16,386	21,318	19,141
99,400	99,450	20,876	16,399	21,332	19,154
99,450	99,500	20,890	16,411	21,346	19,166
99,500	99,550	20,904	16,424	21,360	19,179
99,550	99,600	20,918	16,436	21,374	19,191
99,600	99,650	20,932	16,449	21,388	19,204
99,650	99,700	20,946	16,461	21,402	19,216
99,700	99,750	20,960	16,474	21,416	19,229
99,750	99,800	20,974	16,486	21,430	19,241
99,800	99,850	20,988	16,499	21,444	19,254
99,850	99,900	21,002	16,511	21,458	19,266
99,900	99,950	21,016	16,524	21,472	19,279
99,950	100,000	21,030	16,536	21,486	19,291

$100,000 or over use the Tax Computation Worksheet

* This column must also be used by a qualifying widow(er).

2017 Estate and Gift Tax Rates

If Taxable Transfer is

Over	But Not Over	Tax Liability	Of the Amount Over
$ 0	$ 10,000	18%	$ 0
10,000	20,000	$ 1,800 + 20%	10,000
20,000	40,000	3,800 + 22%	20,000
40,000	60,000	8,200 + 24%	40,000
60,000	80,000	13,000 + 26%	60,000
80,000	100,000	18,200 + 28%	80,000
100,000	150,000	23,800 + 30%	100,000
150,000	250,000	38,800 + 32%	150,000
250,000	500,000	70,800 + 34%	250,000
500,000	750,000	155,800 + 35%	500,000
750,000	1,000,000	248,300 + 39%	750,000
1,000,000	—	345,800 + 40%	1,000,000

A-4 Estate and Gift Tax Valuation Tables

Section 1

Table S (4.4)
Single Life Factors Based on Life Table 2000CM
Interest at 4.4 Percent

Age	Annuity	Life Estate	Remainder	Age	Annuity	Life Estate	Remainder
0	21.4812	0.94517	0.05483	55	14.3029	0.62933	0.37067
1	21.5798	0.94951	0.05049	56	14.0285	0.61725	0.38275
2	21.5405	0.94778	0.05222	57	13.7495	0.60498	0.39502
3	21.4955	0.94580	0.05420	58	13.4666	0.59253	0.40747
4	21.4469	0.94366	0.05634	59	13.1793	0.57989	0.42011
5	21.3952	0.94139	0.05861	60	12.8873	0.56704	0.43296
6	21.3405	0.93898	0.06102	61	12.5909	0.55400	0.44600
7	21.2835	0.93647	0.06353	62	12.2910	0.54080	0.45920
8	21.2234	0.93383	0.06617	63	11.9879	0.52747	0.47253
9	21.1603	0.93105	0.06895	64	11.6816	0.51399	0.48601
10	21.0942	0.92815	0.07185	65	11.3721	0.50037	0.49963
11	21.0250	0.92510	0.07490	66	11.0563	0.48648	0.51352
12	20.9527	0.92192	0.07808	67	10.7352	0.47235	0.52765
13	20.8780	0.91863	0.08137	68	10.4101	0.45804	0.54196
14	20.8018	0.91528	0.08472	69	10.0818	0.44360	0.55640
15	20.7246	0.91188	0.08812	70	9.7511	0.42905	0.57095
16	20.6468	0.90846	0.09154	71	9.4179	0.41439	0.58561
17	20.5678	0.90498	0.09502	72	9.0829	0.39965	0.60035
18	20.4874	0.90145	0.09855	73	8.7474	0.38488	0.61512
19	20.4051	0.89783	0.10217	74	8.4129	0.37017	0.62983
20	20.3200	0.89408	0.10592	75	8.0808	0.35556	0.64444
21	20.2324	0.89023	0.10977	76	7.7521	0.34109	0.65891
22	20.1419	0.88624	0.11376	77	7.4270	0.32679	0.67321
23	20.0480	0.88211	0.11789	78	7.1061	0.31267	0.68733
24	19.9498	0.87779	0.12221	79	6.7900	0.29876	0.70124
25	19.8469	0.87326	0.12674	80	6.4795	0.28510	0.71490
26	19.7389	0.86851	0.13149	81	6.1751	0.27170	0.72830
27	19.6256	0.86353	0.13647	82	5.8772	0.25860	0.74140
28	19.5071	0.85831	0.14169	83	5.5866	0.24581	0.75419
29	19.3837	0.85288	0.14712	84	5.3036	0.23336	0.76664
30	19.2556	0.84725	0.15275	85	5.0288	0.22127	0.77873
31	19.1225	0.84139	0.15861	86	4.7626	0.20956	0.79044
32	18.9844	0.83532	0.16468	87	4.5055	0.19824	0.80176
33	18.8412	0.82901	0.17099	88	4.2573	0.18732	0.81268
34	18.6932	0.82250	0.17750	89	4.0188	0.17683	0.82317
35	18.5402	0.81577	0.18423	90	3.7900	0.16676	0.83324
36	18.3820	0.80881	0.19119	91	3.5710	0.15712	0.84288
37	18.2186	0.80162	0.19838	92	3.3619	0.14792	0.85208
38	18.0496	0.79418	0.20582	93	3.1630	0.13917	0.86083
39	17.8755	0.78652	0.21348	94	2.9739	0.13085	0.86915
40	17.6962	0.77863	0.22137	95	2.7943	0.12295	0.87705
41	17.5114	0.77050	0.22950	96	2.6249	0.11549	0.88451
42	17.3214	0.76214	0.23786	97	2.4650	0.10846	0.89154
43	17.1253	0.75352	0.24648	98	2.3142	0.10182	0.89818
44	16.9238	0.74465	0.25535	99	2.1717	0.09556	0.90444
45	16.7166	0.73553	0.26447	100	2.0391	0.08972	0.91028
46	16.5033	0.72615	0.27385	101	1.9130	0.08417	0.91583
47	16.2844	0.71651	0.28349	102	1.7964	0.07904	0.92096
48	16.0595	0.70662	0.29338	103	1.6806	0.07395	0.92605
49	15.8285	0.69645	0.30355	104	1.5740	0.06926	0.93074
50	15.5907	0.68599	0.31401	105	1.4689	0.06463	0.93537
51	15.3462	0.67523	0.32477	106	1.3375	0.05885	0.94115
52	15.0949	0.66418	0.33582	107	1.1884	0.05229	0.94771
53	14.8370	0.65283	0.34717	108	0.9478	0.04170	0.95830
54	14.5728	0.64120	0.35880	109	0.4789	0.02107	0.97893

Table S (4.6)   Section 1
Single Life Factors Based on Life Table 2000CM
Interest at 4.6 Percent

Age	Annuity	Life Estate	Remainder	Age	Annuity	Life Estate	Remainder
0	20.6611	0.95041	0.04959	55	13.9887	0.64348	0.35652
1	20.7593	0.95493	0.04507	56	13.7264	0.63141	0.36859
2	20.7249	0.95335	0.04665	57	13.4595	0.61914	0.38086
3	20.6853	0.95152	0.04848	58	13.1885	0.60667	0.39333
4	20.6421	0.94954	0.05046	59	12.9130	0.59400	0.40600
5	20.5961	0.94742	0.05258	60	12.6327	0.58110	0.41890
6	20.5474	0.94518	0.05482	61	12.3478	0.56800	0.43200
7	20.4964	0.94283	0.05717	62	12.0593	0.55473	0.44527
8	20.4426	0.94036	0.05964	63	11.7673	0.54130	0.45870
9	20.3859	0.93775	0.06225	64	11.4720	0.52771	0.47229
10	20.3264	0.93501	0.06499	65	11.1733	0.51397	0.48603
11	20.2639	0.93214	0.06786	66	10.8681	0.49993	0.50007
12	20.1986	0.92913	0.07087	67	10.5574	0.48564	0.51436
13	20.1310	0.92603	0.07397	68	10.2425	0.47115	0.52885
14	20.0620	0.92285	0.07715	69	9.9241	0.45651	0.54349
15	19.9921	0.91964	0.08036	70	9.6030	0.44174	0.55826
16	19.9217	0.91640	0.08360	71	9.2792	0.42684	0.57316
17	19.8502	0.91311	0.08689	72	8.9533	0.41185	0.58815
18	19.7775	0.90976	0.09024	73	8.6265	0.39682	0.60318
19	19.7030	0.90634	0.09366	74	8.3004	0.38182	0.61818
20	19.6258	0.90279	0.09721	75	7.9763	0.36691	0.63309
21	19.5463	0.89913	0.10087	76	7.6553	0.35214	0.64786
22	19.4640	0.89535	0.10465	77	7.3375	0.33752	0.66248
23	19.3786	0.89141	0.10859	78	7.0235	0.32308	0.67692
24	19.2891	0.88730	0.11270	79	6.7139	0.30884	0.69116
25	19.1950	0.88297	0.11703	80	6.4096	0.29484	0.70516
26	19.0961	0.87842	0.12158	81	6.1109	0.28110	0.71890
27	18.9922	0.87364	0.12636	82	5.8185	0.26765	0.73235
28	18.8833	0.86863	0.13137	83	5.5330	0.25452	0.74548
29	18.7696	0.86340	0.13660	84	5.2548	0.24172	0.75828
30	18.6514	0.85797	0.14203	85	4.9844	0.22928	0.77072
31	18.5285	0.85231	0.14769	86	4.7223	0.21722	0.78278
32	18.4007	0.84643	0.15357	87	4.4689	0.20557	0.79443
33	18.2679	0.84032	0.15968	88	4.2242	0.19431	0.80569
34	18.1306	0.83401	0.16599	89	3.9889	0.18349	0.81651
35	17.9884	0.82747	0.17253	90	3.7630	0.17310	0.82690
36	17.8411	0.82069	0.17931	91	3.5467	0.16315	0.83685
37	17.6888	0.81369	0.18631	92	3.3400	0.15364	0.84636
38	17.5311	0.80643	0.19357	93	3.1433	0.14459	0.85541
39	17.3684	0.79895	0.20105	94	2.9562	0.13598	0.86402
40	17.2005	0.79122	0.20878	95	2.7784	0.12781	0.87219
41	17.0274	0.78326	0.21674	96	2.6106	0.12009	0.87991
42	16.8490	0.77506	0.22494	97	2.4522	0.11280	0.88720
43	16.6649	0.76658	0.23342	98	2.3027	0.10592	0.89408
44	16.4752	0.75786	0.24214	99	2.1614	0.09943	0.90057
45	16.2800	0.74888	0.25112	100	2.0298	0.09337	0.90663
46	16.0788	0.73962	0.26038	101	1.9047	0.08762	0.91238
47	15.8720	0.73011	0.26989	102	1.7890	0.08229	0.91771
48	15.6593	0.72033	0.27967	103	1.6740	0.07700	0.92300
49	15.4405	0.71026	0.28974	104	1.5682	0.07214	0.92786
50	15.2150	0.69989	0.30011	105	1.4638	0.06734	0.93266
51	14.9828	0.68921	0.31079	106	1.3332	0.06133	0.93867
52	14.7439	0.67822	0.32178	107	1.1851	0.05451	0.94549
53	14.4983	0.66692	0.33308	108	0.9455	0.04349	0.95651
54	14.2464	0.65533	0.34467	109	0.4780	0.02199	0.97801

Section 1

Table S (4.8)
Single Life Factors Based on Life Table 2000CM
Interest at 4.8 Percent

Age	Annuity	Life Estate	Remainder	Age	Annuity	Life Estate	Remainder
0	19.8956	0.95499	0.04501	55	13.6857	0.65692	0.34308
1	19.9930	0.95966	0.04034	56	13.4349	0.64488	0.35512
2	19.9630	0.95822	0.04178	57	13.1795	0.63261	0.36739
3	19.9280	0.95654	0.04346	58	12.9198	0.62015	0.37985
4	19.8897	0.95470	0.04530	59	12.6555	0.60747	0.39253
5	19.8487	0.95274	0.04726	60	12.3863	0.59454	0.40546
6	19.8051	0.95065	0.04935	61	12.1124	0.58140	0.41860
7	19.7594	0.94845	0.05155	62	11.8347	0.56806	0.43194
8	19.7112	0.94614	0.05386	63	11.5534	0.55456	0.44544
9	19.6601	0.94369	0.05631	64	11.2686	0.54089	0.45911
10	19.6065	0.94111	0.05889	65	10.9802	0.52705	0.47295
11	19.5500	0.93840	0.06160	66	10.6852	0.51289	0.48711
12	19.4908	0.93556	0.06444	67	10.3845	0.49846	0.50154
13	19.4296	0.93262	0.06738	68	10.0793	0.48381	0.51619
14	19.3670	0.92962	0.07038	69	9.7705	0.46898	0.53102
15	19.3037	0.92658	0.07342	70	9.4587	0.45402	0.54598
16	19.2398	0.92351	0.07649	71	9.1439	0.43891	0.56109
17	19.1750	0.92040	0.07960	72	8.8267	0.42368	0.57632
18	19.1091	0.91724	0.08276	73	8.5084	0.40840	0.59160
19	19.0416	0.91400	0.08600	74	8.1904	0.39314	0.60686
20	18.9716	0.91063	0.08937	75	7.8741	0.37796	0.62204
21	18.8993	0.90717	0.09283	76	7.5605	0.36290	0.63710
22	18.8245	0.90358	0.09642	77	7.2498	0.34799	0.65201
23	18.7466	0.89984	0.10016	78	6.9425	0.33324	0.66676
24	18.6650	0.89592	0.10408	79	6.6393	0.31868	0.68132
25	18.5790	0.89179	0.10821	80	6.3409	0.30437	0.69563
26	18.4883	0.88744	0.11256	81	6.0480	0.29030	0.70970
27	18.3929	0.88286	0.11714	82	5.7608	0.27652	0.72348
28	18.2927	0.87805	0.12195	83	5.4803	0.26305	0.73695
29	18.1879	0.87302	0.12698	84	5.2067	0.24992	0.75008
30	18.0787	0.86778	0.13222	85	4.9407	0.23715	0.76285
31	17.9650	0.86232	0.13768	86	4.6825	0.22476	0.77524
32	17.8467	0.85664	0.14336	87	4.4328	0.21278	0.78722
33	17.7235	0.85073	0.14927	88	4.1916	0.20120	0.79880
34	17.5960	0.84461	0.15539	89	3.9594	0.19005	0.80995
35	17.4637	0.83826	0.16174	90	3.7364	0.17935	0.82065
36	17.3265	0.83167	0.16833	91	3.5226	0.16909	0.83091
37	17.1844	0.82485	0.17515	92	3.3183	0.15928	0.84072
38	17.0371	0.81778	0.18222	93	3.1238	0.14994	0.85006
39	16.8849	0.81048	0.18952	94	2.9387	0.14106	0.85894
40	16.7277	0.80293	0.19707	95	2.7626	0.13261	0.86739
41	16.5653	0.79513	0.20487	96	2.5965	0.12463	0.87537
42	16.3978	0.78710	0.21290	97	2.4395	0.11710	0.88290
43	16.2246	0.77878	0.22122	98	2.2913	0.10998	0.89002
44	16.0461	0.77021	0.22979	99	2.1512	0.10326	0.89674
45	15.8620	0.76138	0.23862	100	2.0207	0.09699	0.90301
46	15.6721	0.75226	0.24774	101	1.8965	0.09103	0.90897
47	15.4767	0.74288	0.25712	102	1.7816	0.08552	0.91448
48	15.2754	0.73322	0.26678	103	1.6674	0.08004	0.91996
49	15.0680	0.72326	0.27674	104	1.5624	0.07499	0.92501
50	14.8540	0.71299	0.28701	105	1.4588	0.07002	0.92998
51	14.6335	0.70241	0.29759	106	1.3290	0.06379	0.93621
52	14.4061	0.69149	0.30851	107	1.1817	0.05672	0.94328
53	14.1721	0.68026	0.31974	108	0.9433	0.04528	0.95472
54	13.9318	0.66873	0.33127	109	0.4771	0.02290	0.97710

Table S (5.0)   **Section 1**
Single Life Factors Based on Life Table 2000CM
Interest at 5.0 Percent

Age	Annuity	Life Estate	Remainder	Age	Annuity	Life Estate	Remainder
0	19.1799	0.95899	0.04101	55	13.3935	0.66968	0.33032
1	19.2763	0.96382	0.03618	56	13.1536	0.65768	0.34232
2	19.2501	0.96250	0.03750	57	12.9089	0.64545	0.35455
3	19.2192	0.96096	0.03904	58	12.6600	0.63300	0.36700
4	19.1851	0.95925	0.04075	59	12.4064	0.62032	0.37968
5	19.1485	0.95742	0.04258	60	12.1477	0.60739	0.39261
6	19.1095	0.95547	0.04453	61	11.8844	0.59422	0.40578
7	19.0685	0.95342	0.04658	62	11.6170	0.58085	0.41915
8	19.0251	0.95125	0.04875	63	11.3459	0.56729	0.43271
9	18.9791	0.94895	0.05105	64	11.0711	0.55355	0.44645
10	18.9306	0.94653	0.05347	65	10.7925	0.53963	0.46037
11	18.8795	0.94397	0.05603	66	10.5073	0.52536	0.47464
12	18.8258	0.94129	0.05871	67	10.2162	0.51081	0.48919
13	18.7702	0.93851	0.06149	68	9.9204	0.49602	0.50398
14	18.7133	0.93567	0.06433	69	9.6208	0.48104	0.51896
15	18.6558	0.93279	0.06721	70	9.3180	0.46590	0.53410
16	18.5978	0.92989	0.07011	71	9.0119	0.45060	0.54940
17	18.5391	0.92695	0.07305	72	8.7032	0.43516	0.56484
18	18.4793	0.92396	0.07604	73	8.3930	0.41965	0.58035
19	18.4180	0.92090	0.07910	74	8.0829	0.40414	0.59586
20	18.3543	0.91772	0.08228	75	7.7742	0.38871	0.61129
21	18.2886	0.91443	0.08557	76	7.4677	0.37339	0.62661
22	18.2205	0.91103	0.08897	77	7.1639	0.35819	0.64181
23	18.1495	0.90748	0.09252	78	6.8631	0.34316	0.65684
24	18.0749	0.90375	0.09625	79	6.5660	0.32830	0.67170
25	17.9962	0.89981	0.10019	80	6.2736	0.31368	0.68632
26	17.9131	0.89565	0.10435	81	5.9861	0.29931	0.70069
27	17.8253	0.89127	0.10873	82	5.7042	0.28521	0.71479
28	17.7330	0.88665	0.11335	83	5.4285	0.27142	0.72858
29	17.6363	0.88181	0.11819	84	5.1594	0.25797	0.74203
30	17.5354	0.87677	0.12323	85	4.8976	0.24488	0.75512
31	17.4302	0.87151	0.12849	86	4.6433	0.23217	0.76783
32	17.3205	0.86602	0.13398	87	4.3973	0.21986	0.78014
33	17.2061	0.86030	0.13970	88	4.1594	0.20797	0.79203
34	17.0875	0.85438	0.14562	89	3.9302	0.19651	0.80349
35	16.9643	0.84822	0.15178	90	3.7101	0.18550	0.81450
36	16.8364	0.84182	0.15818	91	3.4989	0.17495	0.82505
37	16.7038	0.83519	0.16481	92	3.2969	0.16485	0.83515
38	16.5661	0.82830	0.17170	93	3.1046	0.15523	0.84477
39	16.4236	0.82118	0.17882	94	2.9213	0.14607	0.85393
40	16.2762	0.81381	0.18619	95	2.7471	0.13735	0.86265
41	16.1238	0.80619	0.19381	96	2.5825	0.12912	0.87088
42	15.9665	0.79832	0.20168	97	2.4270	0.12135	0.87865
43	15.8035	0.79018	0.20982	98	2.2800	0.11400	0.88600
44	15.6353	0.78176	0.21824	99	2.1411	0.10706	0.89294
45	15.4617	0.77308	0.22692	100	2.0116	0.10058	0.89942
46	15.2823	0.76411	0.23589	101	1.8884	0.09442	0.90558
47	15.0975	0.75487	0.24513	102	1.7743	0.08872	0.91128
48	14.9069	0.74534	0.25466	103	1.6609	0.08305	0.91695
49	14.7103	0.73551	0.26449	104	1.5566	0.07783	0.92217
50	14.5071	0.72535	0.27465	105	1.4537	0.07269	0.92731
51	14.2974	0.71487	0.28513	106	1.3247	0.06624	0.93376
52	14.0810	0.70405	0.29595	107	1.1784	0.05892	0.94108
53	13.8580	0.69290	0.30710	108	0.9410	0.04705	0.95295
54	13.6286	0.68143	0.31857	109	0.4762	0.02381	0.97619

Section 3

Table B
Annuity, Income, and Remainder Interests For a Term Certain

	5.0%			Interest Rates		5.2%	
Years	Annuity	Income Interest	Remainder	Years	Annuity	Income Interest	Remainder
1	0.9524	.047619	.952381	1	0.9506	.045430	.950570
2	1.8594	.092971	.907029	2	1.8542	.096416	.903584
3	2.7232	.136162	.863838	3	2.7131	.141080	.858920
4	3.5460	.177298	.822702	4	3.5295	.183536	.816464
5	4.3295	.216474	.783526	5	4.3056	.223894	.776106
6	5.0757	.253785	.746215	6	5.0434	.262256	.737744
7	5.7864	.289319	.710681	7	5.7447	.298723	.701277
8	6.4632	.323161	.676839	8	6.4113	.333387	.666613
9	7.1078	.355391	.644609	9	7.0449	.366337	.633663
10	7.7217	.386087	.613913	10	7.6473	.397659	.602341
11	8.3064	.415321	.584679	11	8.2199	.427432	.572568
12	8.8633	.443163	.556837	12	8.7641	.455734	.544266
13	9.3936	.469679	.530321	13	9.2815	.482637	.517363
14	9.8986	.494932	.505068	14	9.7733	.508210	.491790
15	10.3797	.518983	.481017	15	10.2408	.532519	.467481
16	10.8378	.541888	.458112	16	10.6851	.555628	.444374
17	11.2741	.563703	.436297	17	11.1075	.577592	.422408
18	11.6896	.584479	.415521	18	11.5091	.598471	.401529
19	12.0853	.604266	.395734	19	11.8907	.618319	.381681
20	12.4622	.623111	.376889	20	12.2536	.637185	.362815
21	12.8212	.641058	.358942	21	12.5984	.655119	.344881
22	13.1630	.658150	.341850	22	12.9263	.672166	.327834
23	13.4886	.674429	.325571	23	13.2379	.688371	.311629
24	13.7986	.689932	.310068	24	13.5341	.703775	.296225
25	14.0939	.704697	.295303	25	13.8157	.718417	.281583
26	14.3752	.716759	.281241	26	14.0834	.732336	.267664
27	14.6430	.732152	.267848	27	14.3378	.745566	.254434
28	14.8981	.744906	.255094	28	14.5797	.758143	.241357
29	15.1411	.757054	.242946	29	14.8096	.770098	.229902
30	15.3725	.768623	.231377	30	15.0281	.781462	.218538
31	15.5928	.779641	.220359	31	15.2358	.792264	.207736
32	15.8027	.790134	.209666	32	15.4333	.802532	.197468
33	16.0025	.800127	.199873	33	15.6210	.812293	.187707
34	16.1929	.809645	.190355	34	15.7994	.821571	.178429
35	16.3742	.818710	.181290	35	15.9691	.830391	.169609
36	16.5469	.827343	.172657	36	16.1303	.838775	.161225
37	16.7113	.835564	.164436	37	16.2835	.846744	.153256
38	16.8679	.843395	.156605	38	16.4292	.854319	.145681
39	17.0170	.850852	.149148	39	16.5677	.861520	.138480
40	17.1591	.857954	.142046	40	16.6993	.868365	.131635
41	17.2944	.864718	.135282	41	16.6245	.874872	.125128
42	17.4232	.871160	.128840	42	16.9434	.881057	.118943
43	17.5459	.877296	.122704	43	17.0565	.886936	.113064
44	17.6628	.883139	.116861	44	17.1639	.892525	.107475
45	17.7741	.888703	.111297	45	17.2661	.897837	.102163
46	17.8801	.894003	.105997	46	17.3632	.902887	.097113
47	17.9810	.899051	.100949	47	17.4555	.907688	.092312
48	18.0772	.903858	.096142	48	17.5433	.912251	.087749
49	18.1687	.908436	.091564	49	17.6267	.916588	.083412
50	18.2559	.912796	.087204	50	17.7060	.920711	.079289
51	18.3390	.916949	.083051	51	17.7814	.924630	.075370
52	18.4181	.920904	.079096	52	17.8530	.928356	.071644
53	18.4934	.924670	.075330	53	17.9211	.931897	.068103
54	18.5651	.928257	.071743	54	17.9858	.935263	.064737
55	18.6335	.931674	.068326	55	18.0474	.938463	.061537
56	18.6985	.934927	.065073	56	18.1059	.941505	.058495
57	18.7605	.938026	.061974	57	18.1615	.944396	.055604
58	18.8195	.940977	.059023	58	18.2143	.947145	.052855
59	18.8758	.943788	.056212	59	18.2646	.949757	.050243
60	18.9293	.946464	.053536	60	18.3123	.952241	.047759

A-5 2016 Optional State Sales Tax Tables

2016 Optional State Sales Tax Tables

Alabama (1, 4.0000%) · Arizona (2, 5.6000%) · Arkansas (2, 6.5000%)

Income At least	But less than	AL 1	2	3	4	5	Over 5	AZ 1	2	3	4	5	Over 5	AR 1	2	3	4	5	Over 5
$0	$20,000	223	255	277	294	309	329	231	250	262	271	279	290	314	344	364	378	391	407
$20,000	$30,000	337	384	416	441	462	492	378	408	428	444	456	473	500	549	580	604	624	651
$30,000	$40,000	397	452	489	518	543	577	460	496	520	538	553	574	602	660	698	727	751	783
$40,000	$50,000	449	510	552	584	611	650	532	573	601	622	640	664	690	757	801	834	862	899
$50,000	$60,000	496	562	608	643	673	715	598	644	675	699	718	745	771	846	895	932	962	1004
$60,000	$70,000	538	609	658	697	729	774	658	709	743	769	790	820	844	926	980	1021	1054	1100
$70,000	$80,000	577	653	705	746	780	828	715	770	806	834	857	889	912	1001	1059	1104	1140	1189
$80,000	$90,000	613	693	748	792	827	878	768	827	866	896	921	955	976	1072	1134	1181	1220	1273
$90,000	$100,000	647	732	789	835	872	925	818	881	923	955	981	1017	1037	1138	1204	1255	1296	1352
$100,000	$120,000	693	782	844	892	932	988	887	954	999	1034	1062	1101	1118	1228	1299	1353	1398	1459
$120,000	$140,000	753	849	915	966	1009	1070	977	1051	1100	1138	1169	1212	1225	1345	1423	1483	1532	1599
$140,000	$160,000	808	910	980	1036	1081	1146	1062	1142	1195	1236	1270	1317	1325	1455	1540	1605	1657	1730
$160,000	$180,000	860	967	1041	1100	1148	1217	1141	1227	1284	1328	1364	1414	1418	1558	1649	1718	1774	1852
$180,000	$200,000	908	1021	1099	1160	1211	1283	1217	1308	1369	1416	1454	1507	1507	1656	1752	1826	1886	1969
$200,000	$225,000	959	1077	1159	1223	1277	1352	1297	1394	1458	1508	1549	1605	1600	1758	1861	1939	2003	2091
$225,000	$250,000	1014	1138	1223	1291	1347	1426	1383	1486	1555	1608	1651	1712	1701	1868	1978	2061	2129	2223
$250,000	$275,000	1065	1195	1284	1355	1413	1496	1465	1574	1647	1703	1749	1812	1796	1973	2089	2177	2249	2348
$275,000	$300,000	1114	1249	1342	1415	1477	1563	1545	1659	1736	1794	1843	1910	1887	2074	2196	2288	2364	2468
$300,000	or more	1409	1573	1687	1777	1852	1958	2027	2176	2275	2351	2413	2500	2439	2681	2839	2959	3057	3192

California (3, 7.5000%) · Colorado (2, 2.9000%) · Connecticut (4, 6.3500%)

Income At least	But less than	CA 1	2	3	4	5	Over 5	CO 1	2	3	4	5	Over 5	CT 1	2	3	4	5	Over 5
$0	$20,000	292	312	326	336	345	357	113	121	127	131	134	138	272	293	307	317	325	337
$20,000	$30,000	481	514	536	553	567	586	183	195	203	209	214	221	440	475	497	514	528	547
$30,000	$40,000	585	626	653	673	690	713	220	235	245	252	258	266	532	574	602	622	639	662
$40,000	$50,000	678	725	756	779	799	825	253	270	281	290	296	306	613	662	694	718	737	763
$50,000	$60,000	763	815	850	876	898	928	284	302	314	324	331	342	687	742	778	804	826	856
$60,000	$70,000	841	899	936	966	989	1022	311	331	345	355	363	375	754	815	854	884	908	941
$70,000	$80,000	915	976	1018	1049	1075	1110	337	359	373	384	393	405	817	884	926	958	984	1020
$80,000	$90,000	984	1050	1094	1128	1155	1194	361	384	399	411	421	434	877	948	994	1028	1056	1095
$90,000	$100,000	1049	1120	1166	1202	1232	1273	384	408	425	437	447	461	933	1009	1058	1094	1124	1165
$100,000	$120,000	1137	1214	1264	1303	1335	1379	415	441	458	472	483	498	1008	1091	1144	1184	1216	1260
$120,000	$140,000	1254	1338	1394	1436	1471	1520	456	484	503	517	529	546	1108	1199	1257	1301	1337	1386
$140,000	$160,000	1365	1455	1516	1562	1600	1652	494	524	545	560	573	591	1202	1300	1364	1412	1451	1504
$160,000	$180,000	1468	1565	1630	1679	1720	1776	530	562	584	600	614	633	1289	1395	1464	1515	1557	1614
$180,000	$200,000	1567	1670	1739	1792	1835	1895	564	598	621	639	653	673	1373	1486	1559	1614	1658	1719
$200,000	$225,000	1671	1781	1854	1910	1956	2020	600	636	660	679	694	715	1461	1581	1659	1717	1765	1830
$225,000	$250,000	1783	1900	1978	2038	2087	2155	638	676	702	722	738	761	1555	1684	1767	1829	1880	1949
$250,000	$275,000	1891	2015	2097	2160	2212	2284	675	715	742	763	780	804	1645	1782	1870	1936	1989	2063
$275,000	$300,000	1994	2125	2211	2278	2332	2408	710	752	781	802	820	845	1732	1876	1969	2038	2095	2172
$300,000	or more	2626	2795	2907	2994	3065	3164	924	977	1013	1041	1064	1095	2258	2447	2568	2660	2734	2836

District of Columbia (4, 5.7500%) · Florida (1, 6.0000%) · Georgia (2, 4.0000%)

Income At least	But less than	DC 1	2	3	4	5	Over 5	FL 1	2	3	4	5	Over 5	GA 1	2	3	4	5	Over 5
$0	$20,000	171	184	194	201	207	216	254	272	284	293	301	311	155	167	175	181	186	193
$20,000	$30,000	284	307	323	335	345	360	418	447	467	482	494	510	251	270	282	292	299	310
$30,000	$40,000	348	376	395	410	422	440	509	544	568	586	600	621	304	326	341	352	361	374
$40,000	$50,000	404	437	459	476	491	511	589	630	657	678	695	718	350	375	392	405	415	430
$50,000	$60,000	456	493	518	537	553	576	662	708	739	762	781	807	392	420	439	453	465	481
$60,000	$70,000	504	544	572	593	611	637	730	780	814	839	860	889	431	461	482	497	510	528
$70,000	$80,000	549	592	622	646	666	693	793	848	884	912	934	966	467	500	521	538	552	571
$80,000	$90,000	591	638	670	696	717	747	852	911	950	980	1004	1038	501	536	559	577	592	612
$90,000	$100,000	631	681	716	743	766	797	909	972	1013	1045	1071	1106	533	570	595	614	629	651
$100,000	$120,000	686	740	778	807	832	866	985	1053	1098	1132	1160	1199	576	616	642	663	680	703
$120,000	$140,000	758	818	859	892	919	957	1085	1160	1210	1247	1278	1321	633	676	705	728	746	771
$140,000	$160,000	826	891	936	972	1001	1043	1180	1261	1315	1356	1390	1436	687	733	765	789	808	836
$160,000	$180,000	889	960	1009	1047	1079	1123	1269	1356	1414	1458	1494	1543	737	786	820	845	867	896
$180,000	$200,000	951	1026	1078	1119	1153	1200	1354	1447	1508	1555	1593	1646	784	837	872	900	922	953
$200,000	$225,000	1015	1095	1151	1195	1231	1282	1443	1542	1607	1657	1698	1755	835	890	928	957	980	1013
$225,000	$250,000	1085	1171	1230	1277	1315	1370	1540	1645	1715	1768	1812	1872	889	948	988	1018	1043	1078
$250,000	$275,000	1152	1243	1306	1355	1396	1454	1632	1743	1817	1873	1920	1983	940	1003	1044	1077	1103	1140
$275,000	$300,000	1216	1312	1379	1431	1474	1535	1721	1838	1916	1975	2024	2091	990	1055	1099	1133	1161	1199
$300,000	or more	1610	1737	1825	1894	1951	2032	2261	2415	2516	2594	2657	2745	1291	1374	1430	1473	1509	1558

Hawaii (1,6, 4.0000%) · Idaho (1, 6.0000%) · Illinois (2, 6.2500%)

Income At least	But less than	HI 1	2	3	4	5	Over 5	ID 1	2	3	4	5	Over 5	IL 1	2	3	4	5	Over 5
$0	$20,000	263	298	322	340	355	376	338	385	417	442	463	493	241	262	276	287	296	309
$20,000	$30,000	402	456	492	520	543	575	514	584	631	668	699	742	386	418	440	457	471	490
$30,000	$40,000	476	540	582	615	642	680	607	688	743	787	822	873	466	503	529	549	566	589
$40,000	$50,000	540	612	660	697	728	770	688	778	840	889	929	985	535	578	607	630	649	675
$50,000	$60,000	597	677	730	770	804	851	760	859	927	980	1024	1086	599	646	678	703	724	753
$60,000	$70,000	649	735	793	837	873	924	826	932	1005	1062	1110	1177	657	708	743	770	793	825
$70,000	$80,000	696	789	851	898	937	992	886	1000	1078	1139	1189	1260	711	766	803	833	857	891
$80,000	$90,000	741	839	905	956	997	1055	943	1063	1145	1210	1263	1338	762	820	860	891	917	953
$90,000	$100,000	783	887	956	1009	1053	1115	996	1122	1209	1276	1332	1411	810	871	913	946	974	1012
$100,000	$120,000	838	950	1024	1081	1128	1194	1067	1201	1293	1365	1425	1509	874	940	985	1021	1050	1091
$120,000	$140,000	911	1032	1113	1175	1226	1297	1160	1304	1403	1481	1545	1636	959	1031	1080	1118	1150	1195
$140,000	$160,000	979	1109	1195	1262	1317	1393	1246	1401	1506	1589	1658	1754	1040	1116	1169	1210	1245	1293
$160,000	$180,000	1042	1180	1272	1342	1401	1482	1327	1490	1601	1689	1761	1864	1114	1196	1252	1296	1332	1384
$180,000	$200,000	1101	1247	1344	1419	1480	1566	1403	1574	1691	1783	1859	1967	1186	1271	1331	1377	1416	1470
$200,000	$225,000	1163	1317	1419	1498	1563	1654	1482	1662	1785	1881	1962	2075	1260	1351	1414	1463	1504	1561
$225,000	$250,000	1230	1392	1500	1584	1652	1748	1567	1756	1885	1987	2071	2190	1341	1437	1503	1555	1598	1659
$250,000	$275,000	1293	1463	1577	1664	1736	1837	1648	1845	1980	2086	2175	2299	1418	1518	1588	1642	1688	1752
$275,000	$300,000	1353	1531	1650	1741	1817	1922	1725	1930	2071	2182	2274	2403	1492	1597	1669	1727	1774	1841
$300,000	or more	1710	1934	2083	2199	2294	2426	2186	2438	2611	2747	2861	3021	1940	2071	2162	2234	2295	2379

Income		Indiana — 4 — 7.0000%						Iowa — 1 — 6.0000%						Kansas — 1 — 6.5000%					
At least	But less than	1	2	3	4	5	Over 5	1	2	3	4	5	Over 5	1	2	3	4	5	Over 5
$0	$20,000	294	318	334	345	355	368	268	292	308	320	330	343	394	454	494	525	551	588
$20,000	$30,000	464	502	526	544	559	580	433	473	499	518	534	557	597	686	747	793	832	887
$30,000	$40,000	555	600	630	651	669	694	523	572	603	627	646	673	703	808	879	934	979	1044
$40,000	$50,000	635	687	720	745	765	793	602	658	695	723	745	776	795	913	992	1054	1106	1178
$50,000	$60,000	707	764	802	830	852	883	675	738	778	810	835	870	877	1006	1094	1162	1219	1298
$60,000	$70,000	773	835	876	906	931	965	741	810	855	889	917	955	951	1091	1186	1260	1321	1407
$70,000	$80,000	834	901	945	978	1005	1041	802	878	926	964	994	1036	1019	1169	1270	1349	1415	1507
$80,000	$90,000	891	963	1010	1045	1073	1113	860	941	994	1034	1066	1111	1082	1241	1349	1433	1502	1600
$90,000	$100,000	944	1021	1071	1108	1138	1180	915	1001	1057	1100	1134	1182	1142	1309	1423	1511	1584	1687
$100,000	$120,000	1016	1099	1152	1193	1225	1270	989	1082	1143	1189	1227	1278	1221	1400	1521	1615	1694	1803
$120,000	$140,000	1111	1201	1260	1304	1339	1388	1086	1189	1256	1307	1348	1405	1324	1518	1649	1751	1836	1955
$140,000	$160,000	1200	1297	1360	1408	1446	1499	1178	1289	1362	1417	1462	1524	1420	1628	1768	1877	1968	2095
$160,000	$180,000	1282	1386	1453	1504	1545	1602	1263	1383	1461	1520	1569	1635	1509	1729	1878	1994	2090	2225
$180,000	$200,000	1360	1471	1542	1596	1640	1700	1344	1473	1556	1619	1670	1741	1593	1825	1982	2104	2205	2348
$200,000	$225,000	1442	1559	1635	1692	1739	1802	1430	1566	1655	1722	1777	1853	1680	1925	2090	2219	2325	2475
$225,000	$250,000	1530	1655	1735	1796	1845	1913	1522	1668	1763	1834	1893	1973	1774	2031	2206	2341	2454	2612
$250,000	$275,000	1614	1745	1830	1894	1946	2017	1610	1764	1865	1941	2003	2088	1862	2132	2315	2457	2575	2741
$275,000	$300,000	1694	1832	1921	1988	2042	2117	1695	1857	1963	2043	2108	2198	1947	2228	2419	2568	2691	2864
$300,000	or more	2175	2352	2466	2552	2622	2719	2206	2419	2558	2663	2748	2866	2446	2798	3036	3221	3375	3592

Income		Kentucky — 4 — 6.0000%						Louisiana — 2 — 4.7514%						Maine — 4 — 5.5000%					
At least	But less than	1	2	3	4	5	Over 5	1	2	3	4	5	Over 5	1	2	3	4	5	Over 5
$0	$20,000	237	255	267	276	284	295	204	219	229	236	243	251	181	194	203	209	215	223
$20,000	$30,000	384	413	432	447	459	476	333	358	374	386	397	411	296	316	330	341	350	362
$30,000	$40,000	465	499	522	540	555	575	405	435	454	469	481	498	359	383	400	413	423	438
$40,000	$50,000	536	576	602	622	639	662	468	502	525	542	556	576	415	443	462	477	489	506
$50,000	$60,000	601	645	674	697	715	741	526	564	590	609	625	647	466	497	518	535	548	567
$60,000	$70,000	661	709	741	765	786	814	579	621	649	670	687	711	512	547	570	588	603	623
$70,000	$80,000	716	768	803	829	851	881	629	674	704	727	746	772	556	593	618	637	653	676
$80,000	$90,000	768	824	861	889	913	945	676	724	757	781	801	829	597	637	663	684	701	725
$90,000	$100,000	818	877	916	946	971	1005	720	772	806	832	854	883	636	678	707	729	747	772
$100,000	$120,000	885	948	990	1023	1049	1086	780	836	873	901	924	956	689	734	765	788	808	835
$120,000	$140,000	973	1042	1088	1123	1153	1193	859	920	961	992	1018	1053	759	808	841	867	889	918
$140,000	$160,000	1056	1130	1180	1218	1250	1294	933	1000	1044	1078	1105	1144	824	877	913	941	965	997
$160,000	$180,000	1133	1213	1266	1307	1341	1387	1003	1074	1122	1158	1187	1229	886	942	981	1011	1035	1070
$180,000	$200,000	1207	1292	1348	1391	1427	1477	1069	1145	1196	1234	1266	1310	944	1004	1045	1077	1103	1140
$200,000	$225,000	1285	1374	1434	1480	1518	1571	1139	1220	1274	1315	1348	1395	1006	1069	1113	1147	1174	1213
$225,000	$250,000	1369	1464	1527	1576	1616	1672	1215	1301	1358	1402	1438	1487	1072	1140	1186	1222	1251	1293
$250,000	$275,000	1449	1549	1616	1667	1710	1769	1287	1378	1438	1485	1523	1575	1136	1207	1256	1293	1325	1368
$275,000	$300,000	1526	1631	1701	1755	1800	1861	1356	1452	1516	1564	1604	1659	1197	1272	1323	1362	1395	1441
$300,000	or more	1994	2127	2217	2287	2344	2423	1778	1903	1986	2049	2101	2173	1581	1665	1730	1781	1823	1883

Income		Maryland — 4 — 6.0000%						Massachusetts — 4 — 6.2500%						Michigan — 4 — 6.0000%					
At least	But less than	1	2	3	4	5	Over 5	1	2	3	4	5	Over 5	1	2	3	4	5	Over 5
$0	$20,000	218	238	251	261	270	282	210	222	229	235	240	247	228	245	257	265	272	282
$20,000	$30,000	358	389	410	426	440	459	336	354	365	374	382	392	367	394	412	426	437	453
$30,000	$40,000	436	472	498	517	534	557	404	425	439	450	459	471	444	476	497	513	527	545
$40,000	$50,000	504	546	575	598	616	643	464	488	503	516	526	540	511	547	571	590	605	627
$50,000	$60,000	566	613	646	671	692	721	519	544	562	576	587	602	572	612	639	660	677	700
$60,000	$70,000	624	675	711	738	761	793	568	596	615	630	642	659	628	672	701	724	742	768
$70,000	$80,000	678	733	771	801	826	861	614	645	665	681	694	712	680	727	759	783	803	831
$80,000	$90,000	728	787	828	860	887	924	658	690	712	728	742	762	729	780	813	839	860	890
$90,000	$100,000	776	839	883	916	945	984	699	733	756	773	788	809	776	829	865	892	915	946
$100,000	$120,000	841	909	956	992	1023	1065	754	790	815	834	850	872	838	895	934	963	987	1021
$120,000	$140,000	927	1001	1052	1092	1125	1172	827	866	893	913	930	954	921	983	1025	1057	1083	1120
$140,000	$160,000	1008	1088	1143	1186	1222	1273	895	937	966	988	1006	1032	998	1065	1110	1145	1173	1213
$160,000	$180,000	1083	1169	1228	1274	1313	1367	958	1003	1034	1057	1077	1104	1071	1142	1190	1227	1257	1299
$180,000	$200,000	1156	1246	1309	1358	1399	1457	1019	1066	1098	1123	1144	1173	1140	1215	1266	1305	1337	1382
$200,000	$225,000	1232	1328	1394	1447	1490	1552	1082	1132	1166	1193	1214	1245	1212	1292	1346	1387	1421	1469
$225,000	$250,000	1314	1416	1487	1542	1589	1654	1151	1203	1239	1267	1290	1323	1291	1375	1432	1476	1512	1562
$250,000	$275,000	1393	1500	1575	1634	1682	1751	1216	1271	1309	1338	1362	1396	1365	1454	1514	1560	1598	1651
$275,000	$300,000	1468	1581	1660	1721	1773	1845	1278	1336	1375	1406	1432	1467	1437	1530	1593	1641	1681	1736
$300,000	or more	1929	2074	2175	2255	2321	2414	1655	1728	1778	1816	1849	1894	1872	1990	2069	2131	2182	2253

Income		Minnesota — 1 — 6.8750%						Mississippi — 2 — 7.0000%						Missouri — 2 — 4.2250%					
At least	But less than	1	2	3	4	5	Over 5	1	2	3	4	5	Over 5	1	2	3	4	5	Over 5
$0	$20,000	271	285	294	301	306	314	438	496	536	566	591	625	174	192	204	214	221	232
$20,000	$30,000	440	464	479	491	500	512	669	758	817	863	901	953	281	309	328	343	355	372
$30,000	$40,000	533	562	581	595	606	622	790	895	965	1019	1064	1126	340	373	396	413	427	448
$40,000	$50,000	615	649	671	687	701	719	895	1014	1093	1154	1205	1275	391	429	455	475	491	514
$50,000	$60,000	690	729	753	772	787	807	989	1120	1208	1275	1330	1408	438	480	509	531	549	575
$60,000	$70,000	759	801	829	849	865	888	1074	1216	1311	1384	1444	1528	481	527	558	582	602	630
$70,000	$80,000	823	869	899	921	939	964	1153	1305	1407	1485	1550	1640	520	570	604	630	652	682
$80,000	$90,000	883	933	965	989	1009	1035	1226	1388	1496	1579	1648	1743	558	611	647	675	698	730
$90,000	$100,000	940	994	1028	1054	1075	1103	1295	1466	1579	1667	1740	1840	594	650	688	717	742	776
$100,000	$120,000	1017	1076	1113	1141	1163	1194	1387	1569	1691	1785	1862	1970	641	702	743	774	801	837
$120,000	$140,000	1119	1184	1225	1256	1281	1315	1506	1704	1837	1938	2022	2139	704	770	815	850	878	918
$140,000	$160,000	1215	1286	1331	1364	1391	1428	1618	1830	1972	2081	2171	2297	764	835	883	920	951	995
$160,000	$180,000	1305	1381	1429	1465	1495	1534	1721	1947	2097	2213	2309	2442	819	895	946	986	1019	1065
$180,000	$200,000	1390	1472	1523	1562	1593	1636	1818	2057	2216	2338	2439	2580	872	952	1007	1049	1084	1133
$200,000	$225,000	1480	1567	1622	1664	1697	1743	1920	2172	2339	2469	2575	2724	927	1012	1070	1115	1152	1204
$225,000	$250,000	1577	1670	1730	1774	1810	1858	2029	2295	2472	2608	2721	2878	987	1077	1138	1186	1225	1281
$250,000	$275,000	1670	1769	1832	1879	1917	1968	2132	2411	2597	2740	2858	3023	1044	1139	1203	1254	1295	1353
$275,000	$300,000	1759	1864	1930	1980	2020	2074	2231	2522	2716	2866	2989	3162	1099	1198	1266	1319	1362	1423
$300,000	or more	2301	2439	2528	2593	2647	2719	2815	3181	3425	3613	3769	3985	1430	1557	1644	1711	1767	1845

Income At least	Income But less than	Exemptions 1	2	3	4	5	Over 5
Nebraska					1	5.5000%	
$0	$20,000	247	268	282	292	301	312
$20,000	$30,000	398	433	456	473	486	506
$30,000	$40,000	481	523	551	571	588	611
$40,000	$50,000	554	603	634	658	678	704
$50,000	$60,000	620	675	710	737	759	789
$60,000	$70,000	681	741	780	809	833	866
$70,000	$80,000	737	802	845	877	903	939
$80,000	$90,000	790	860	906	940	968	1007
$90,000	$100,000	840	915	964	1000	1030	1071
$100,000	$120,000	908	989	1042	1081	1114	1158
$120,000	$140,000	997	1086	1144	1188	1223	1272
$140,000	$160,000	1081	1178	1240	1288	1327	1380
$160,000	$180,000	1159	1263	1330	1381	1423	1480
$180,000	$200,000	1233	1344	1416	1471	1515	1576
$200,000	$225,000	1311	1430	1506	1564	1611	1676
$225,000	$250,000	1396	1522	1604	1666	1716	1785
$250,000	$275,000	1476	1610	1696	1762	1815	1888
$275,000	$300,000	1553	1694	1785	1854	1911	1988
$300,000	or more	2020	2205	2325	2415	2488	2589

Income At least	Income But less than	Exemptions 1	2	3	4	5	Over 5
Nevada					5	6.8500%	
$0	$20,000	261	281	294	304	312	323
$20,000	$30,000	421	451	472	487	500	518
$30,000	$40,000	508	544	569	587	602	624
$40,000	$50,000	585	626	654	675	692	716
$50,000	$60,000	655	701	731	755	774	801
$60,000	$70,000	719	769	802	828	849	878
$70,000	$80,000	779	832	868	896	918	950
$80,000	$90,000	835	892	930	960	984	1017
$90,000	$100,000	888	948	989	1020	1046	1081
$100,000	$120,000	960	1024	1068	1101	1129	1167
$120,000	$140,000	1054	1125	1172	1208	1238	1280
$140,000	$160,000	1143	1219	1270	1309	1341	1386
$160,000	$180,000	1226	1306	1361	1403	1437	1485
$180,000	$200,000	1305	1390	1448	1492	1529	1579
$200,000	$225,000	1388	1478	1539	1586	1625	1678
$225,000	$250,000	1477	1573	1637	1687	1728	1785
$250,000	$275,000	1562	1663	1731	1783	1827	1887
$275,000	$300,000	1645	1750	1821	1876	1921	1984
$300,000	or more	2141	2275	2366	2435	2493	2573

Income At least	Income But less than	Exemptions 1	2	3	4	5	Over 5
New Jersey					4	7.0000%	
$0	$20,000	273	285	293	299	304	311
$20,000	$30,000	448	468	482	492	500	512
$30,000	$40,000	545	570	586	598	608	622
$40,000	$50,000	631	659	678	693	704	721
$50,000	$60,000	709	741	763	779	792	810
$60,000	$70,000	781	817	840	858	872	892
$70,000	$80,000	849	887	912	932	948	969
$80,000	$90,000	912	954	981	1002	1019	1042
$90,000	$100,000	972	1017	1046	1068	1086	1111
$100,000	$120,000	1054	1102	1133	1157	1177	1204
$120,000	$140,000	1161	1214	1249	1275	1297	1327
$140,000	$160,000	1262	1320	1358	1386	1410	1443
$160,000	$180,000	1357	1419	1460	1491	1516	1551
$180,000	$200,000	1448	1514	1557	1590	1617	1654
$200,000	$225,000	1543	1613	1660	1695	1724	1763
$225,000	$250,000	1646	1721	1771	1808	1839	1881
$250,000	$275,000	1745	1824	1876	1916	1949	1994
$275,000	$300,000	1839	1923	1978	2020	2055	2102
$300,000	or more	2416	2526	2598	2654	2699	2761

Income At least	Income But less than	Exemptions 1	2	3	4	5	Over 5
New Mexico					1	5.1250%	
$0	$20,000	257	276	289	298	306	316
$20,000	$30,000	409	441	461	476	488	505
$30,000	$40,000	492	530	554	572	587	607
$40,000	$50,000	564	608	636	657	673	697
$50,000	$60,000	630	678	710	733	752	778
$60,000	$70,000	689	743	777	803	823	852
$70,000	$80,000	745	803	840	868	890	921
$80,000	$90,000	797	859	899	929	953	985
$90,000	$100,000	847	912	955	986	1012	1047
$100,000	$120,000	913	984	1029	1064	1091	1129
$120,000	$140,000	1000	1078	1128	1165	1195	1237
$140,000	$160,000	1081	1166	1220	1260	1293	1338
$160,000	$180,000	1157	1248	1306	1349	1384	1432
$180,000	$200,000	1230	1326	1388	1434	1471	1522
$200,000	$225,000	1306	1408	1473	1522	1562	1616
$225,000	$250,000	1387	1496	1566	1618	1660	1718
$250,000	$275,000	1465	1580	1653	1709	1753	1814
$275,000	$300,000	1539	1660	1738	1796	1843	1907
$300,000	or more	1988	2145	2245	2320	2381	2464

Income At least	Income But less than	Exemptions 1	2	3	4	5	Over 5
New York					2	4.0000%	
$0	$20,000	159	167	173	177	180	185
$20,000	$30,000	260	273	282	289	294	301
$30,000	$40,000	316	332	342	350	357	366
$40,000	$50,000	365	383	395	404	412	422
$50,000	$60,000	409	430	444	454	462	474
$60,000	$70,000	450	473	488	499	509	522
$70,000	$80,000	489	513	529	542	552	566
$80,000	$90,000	525	551	569	582	593	608
$90,000	$100,000	559	587	606	620	631	647
$100,000	$120,000	605	635	656	671	683	701
$120,000	$140,000	666	699	721	738	752	771
$140,000	$160,000	723	760	783	802	817	837
$160,000	$180,000	777	816	841	861	877	899
$180,000	$200,000	828	869	897	918	935	958
$200,000	$225,000	882	926	955	977	996	1021
$225,000	$250,000	940	987	1018	1042	1061	1088
$250,000	$275,000	995	1045	1078	1103	1124	1152
$275,000	$300,000	1049	1101	1136	1162	1184	1214
$300,000	or more	1373	1441	1486	1521	1549	1588

Income At least	Income But less than	Exemptions 1	2	3	4	5	Over 5
North Carolina					2	4.7500%	
$0	$20,000	247	274	292	306	317	333
$20,000	$30,000	385	427	455	477	494	518
$30,000	$40,000	459	509	542	568	588	617
$40,000	$50,000	523	580	618	647	670	703
$50,000	$60,000	580	644	686	718	744	781
$60,000	$70,000	633	702	748	783	811	851
$70,000	$80,000	681	756	805	843	874	916
$80,000	$90,000	727	806	859	899	932	977
$90,000	$100,000	769	854	909	952	987	1035
$100,000	$120,000	827	917	977	1023	1060	1112
$120,000	$140,000	901	1000	1065	1115	1156	1212
$140,000	$160,000	971	1078	1148	1202	1245	1306
$160,000	$180,000	1036	1150	1225	1282	1329	1393
$180,000	$200,000	1098	1218	1297	1358	1407	1476
$200,000	$225,000	1162	1290	1373	1437	1490	1562
$225,000	$250,000	1231	1366	1455	1523	1578	1655
$250,000	$275,000	1297	1439	1532	1604	1662	1743
$275,000	$300,000	1360	1509	1606	1681	1743	1828
$300,000	or more	1735	1924	2049	2145	2223	2331

Income At least	Income But less than	Exemptions 1	2	3	4	5	Over 5
North Dakota					1	5.0000%	
$0	$20,000	183	200	212	221	229	239
$20,000	$30,000	295	322	340	355	367	383
$30,000	$40,000	357	389	411	428	442	462
$40,000	$50,000	411	447	472	492	508	531
$50,000	$60,000	461	501	528	550	568	593
$60,000	$70,000	506	549	580	603	623	650
$70,000	$80,000	548	595	627	653	674	704
$80,000	$90,000	588	638	672	699	722	754
$90,000	$100,000	626	678	715	743	767	801
$100,000	$120,000	676	733	772	803	828	864
$120,000	$140,000	743	805	847	881	909	948
$140,000	$160,000	806	872	918	954	984	1027
$160,000	$180,000	865	935	984	1023	1055	1100
$180,000	$200,000	921	995	1047	1088	1122	1170
$200,000	$225,000	980	1059	1113	1156	1192	1243
$225,000	$250,000	1044	1127	1185	1230	1269	1322
$250,000	$275,000	1104	1192	1253	1301	1341	1397
$275,000	$300,000	1163	1254	1318	1368	1410	1470
$300,000	or more	1516	1632	1713	1777	1831	1907

Income At least	Income But less than	Exemptions 1	2	3	4	5	Over 5
Ohio					1	5.7500%	
$0	$20,000	248	266	278	287	294	304
$20,000	$30,000	403	432	451	466	477	494
$30,000	$40,000	488	523	546	564	578	598
$40,000	$50,000	564	604	630	650	667	690
$50,000	$60,000	632	677	707	729	748	773
$60,000	$70,000	695	744	777	801	822	849
$70,000	$80,000	754	807	842	869	891	921
$80,000	$90,000	810	866	904	932	956	988
$90,000	$100,000	862	922	962	992	1017	1052
$100,000	$120,000	933	998	1041	1073	1100	1137
$120,000	$140,000	1026	1097	1144	1180	1209	1250
$140,000	$160,000	1114	1191	1242	1281	1312	1357
$160,000	$180,000	1196	1278	1333	1374	1409	1456
$180,000	$200,000	1274	1362	1420	1464	1500	1551
$200,000	$225,000	1356	1449	1511	1558	1597	1650
$225,000	$250,000	1445	1544	1610	1660	1701	1758
$250,000	$275,000	1530	1635	1704	1757	1800	1860
$275,000	$300,000	1612	1721	1794	1850	1895	1958
$300,000	or more	2106	2248	2343	2415	2474	2555

Income At least	Income But less than	Exemptions 1	2	3	4	5	Over 5
Oklahoma					1	4.5000%	
$0	$20,000	252	285	308	326	341	362
$20,000	$30,000	392	443	478	505	528	559
$30,000	$40,000	468	528	568	600	627	664
$40,000	$50,000	533	601	647	683	713	755
$50,000	$60,000	592	667	718	757	790	837
$60,000	$70,000	646	727	782	825	861	911
$70,000	$80,000	696	782	841	887	926	980
$80,000	$90,000	743	834	897	946	987	1044
$90,000	$100,000	787	883	949	1001	1044	1104
$100,000	$120,000	846	949	1020	1075	1121	1185
$120,000	$140,000	924	1035	1111	1171	1221	1291
$140,000	$160,000	996	1115	1197	1261	1315	1390
$160,000	$180,000	1064	1190	1277	1345	1402	1481
$180,000	$200,000	1128	1261	1353	1424	1484	1568
$200,000	$225,000	1195	1335	1432	1507	1570	1659
$225,000	$250,000	1267	1415	1517	1596	1663	1756
$250,000	$275,000	1335	1490	1597	1681	1750	1849
$275,000	$300,000	1401	1563	1674	1762	1834	1937
$300,000	or more	1794	1996	2136	2245	2336	2465

Income At least	Income But less than	Exemptions 1	2	3	4	5	Over 5
Pennsylvania					1	6.0000%	
$0	$20,000	214	228	237	244	250	258
$20,000	$30,000	346	368	383	394	404	417
$30,000	$40,000	419	445	463	476	487	503
$40,000	$50,000	482	512	533	548	561	579
$50,000	$60,000	540	574	596	614	628	648
$60,000	$70,000	593	630	654	674	689	711
$70,000	$80,000	642	682	709	730	747	770
$80,000	$90,000	688	731	760	782	800	826
$90,000	$100,000	732	778	808	832	851	878
$100,000	$120,000	792	840	873	899	920	949
$120,000	$140,000	869	923	959	987	1010	1042
$140,000	$160,000	943	1000	1039	1069	1094	1129
$160,000	$180,000	1011	1073	1114	1147	1173	1210
$180,000	$200,000	1076	1142	1186	1220	1249	1288
$200,000	$225,000	1144	1214	1261	1298	1328	1369
$225,000	$250,000	1218	1292	1342	1381	1413	1457
$250,000	$275,000	1289	1367	1420	1460	1494	1541
$275,000	$300,000	1356	1438	1494	1537	1572	1621
$300,000	or more	1765	1871	1943	1998	2044	2108

Income At least	Income But less than	Exemptions 1	2	3	4	5	Over 5
Rhode Island					4	7.0000%	
$0	$20,000	283	301	312	321	328	337
$20,000	$30,000	448	477	495	509	520	535
$30,000	$40,000	538	572	594	610	624	642
$40,000	$50,000	616	655	680	699	715	736
$50,000	$60,000	686	730	759	780	797	821
$60,000	$70,000	751	799	830	853	872	898
$70,000	$80,000	810	863	896	921	942	970
$80,000	$90,000	866	922	958	985	1007	1037
$90,000	$100,000	919	979	1017	1046	1069	1101
$100,000	$120,000	990	1055	1096	1127	1152	1187
$120,000	$140,000	1084	1154	1199	1233	1261	1299
$140,000	$160,000	1171	1247	1296	1333	1363	1404
$160,000	$180,000	1252	1334	1387	1426	1458	1502
$180,000	$200,000	1329	1416	1472	1514	1548	1595
$200,000	$225,000	1410	1503	1562	1607	1643	1693
$225,000	$250,000	1498	1596	1659	1707	1745	1798
$250,000	$275,000	1580	1684	1751	1801	1842	1898
$275,000	$300,000	1660	1769	1839	1892	1935	1994
$300,000	or more	2137	2279	2370	2439	2494	2570

Income At least	Income But less than	Exemptions 1	2	3	4	5	Over 5
South Carolina					2	6.0000%	
$0	$20,000	263	283	296	306	314	324
$20,000	$30,000	421	454	475	490	503	520
$30,000	$40,000	507	546	572	591	606	627
$40,000	$50,000	583	628	657	679	696	721
$50,000	$60,000	651	702	734	759	778	806
$60,000	$70,000	713	769	805	832	853	883
$70,000	$80,000	772	832	871	900	923	956
$80,000	$90,000	826	891	932	964	989	1023
$90,000	$100,000	878	947	991	1024	1051	1088
$100,000	$120,000	948	1022	1070	1105	1134	1174
$120,000	$140,000	1039	1120	1173	1212	1244	1288
$140,000	$160,000	1125	1213	1270	1313	1347	1394
$160,000	$180,000	1205	1299	1360	1406	1443	1494
$180,000	$200,000	1281	1382	1447	1495	1535	1589
$200,000	$225,000	1361	1468	1537	1589	1631	1688
$225,000	$250,000	1447	1561	1634	1690	1734	1795
$250,000	$275,000	1529	1650	1727	1785	1833	1897
$275,000	$300,000	1607	1734	1816	1877	1927	1995
$300,000	or more	2082	2247	2353	2433	2498	2586

South Dakota (1, 4.2923%) · Tennessee (2, 7.0000%) · Texas (1, 6.2500%)

Income At least	But less than	SD 1	SD 2	SD 3	SD 4	SD 5	SD Over 5	TN 1	TN 2	TN 3	TN 4	TN 5	TN Over 5	TX 1	TX 2	TX 3	TX 4	TX 5	TX Over 5
$0	$20,000	269	307	332	352	368	391	384	429	459	483	502	529	276	303	321	334	345	360
$20,000	$30,000	412	469	508	537	562	596	602	671	718	754	784	826	445	489	518	540	558	583
$30,000	$40,000	487	555	600	635	664	704	719	801	857	899	935	984	537	590	625	652	674	704
$40,000	$50,000	552	628	679	719	752	797	821	915	977	1026	1066	1122	618	680	720	751	777	812
$50,000	$60,000	610	694	751	794	830	881	914	1017	1086	1140	1184	1246	691	761	806	841	870	909
$60,000	$70,000	663	754	815	863	902	956	998	1110	1185	1243	1291	1359	759	835	885	924	955	998
$70,000	$80,000	711	809	875	926	967	1026	1076	1196	1277	1339	1391	1463	821	905	959	1001	1035	1082
$80,000	$90,000	757	861	930	984	1029	1091	1149	1277	1363	1429	1484	1561	881	970	1028	1073	1109	1160
$90,000	$100,000	799	909	983	1039	1086	1152	1218	1353	1444	1514	1572	1653	936	1032	1094	1141	1180	1234
$100,000	$120,000	856	973	1052	1113	1163	1233	1310	1455	1552	1628	1690	1777	1012	1115	1182	1234	1276	1334
$120,000	$140,000	930	1057	1143	1209	1263	1340	1431	1588	1694	1776	1844	1939	1111	1224	1298	1355	1401	1465
$140,000	$160,000	999	1136	1227	1298	1357	1438	1545	1714	1827	1915	1988	2090	1204	1327	1408	1469	1519	1589
$160,000	$180,000	1063	1208	1305	1381	1443	1530	1650	1830	1951	2044	2122	2230	1291	1423	1510	1576	1630	1704
$180,000	$200,000	1123	1277	1379	1459	1524	1616	1751	1940	2068	2167	2249	2363	1373	1514	1607	1677	1735	1815
$200,000	$225,000	1186	1348	1456	1540	1609	1706	1856	2056	2191	2295	2382	2503	1460	1610	1709	1784	1845	1930
$225,000	$250,000	1254	1425	1539	1628	1701	1803	1969	2180	2323	2433	2525	2653	1554	1714	1819	1899	1965	2055
$250,000	$275,000	1318	1497	1617	1710	1787	1894	2076	2298	2448	2564	2660	2794	1643	1813	1924	2009	2078	2174
$275,000	$300,000	1379	1566	1692	1789	1869	1981	2178	2411	2568	2689	2790	2930	1729	1908	2025	2114	2187	2288
$300,000	or more	1741	1976	2134	2256	2357	2498	2795	3088	3286	3440	3567	3745	2248	2482	2636	2753	2848	2980

Utah (2, 4.7000%) · Vermont (1, 6.0000%) · Virginia (2, 4.3000%)

Income At least	But less than	UT 1	UT 2	UT 3	UT 4	UT 5	UT Over 5	VT 1	VT 2	VT 3	VT 4	VT 5	VT Over 5	VA 1	VA 2	VA 3	VA 4	VA 5	VA Over 5
$0	$20,000	249	277	296	311	323	340	163	169	173	175	178	181	181	199	211	221	228	239
$20,000	$30,000	392	436	466	489	507	533	259	269	275	280	284	289	287	314	333	348	360	376
$30,000	$40,000	470	522	557	584	606	637	312	323	331	336	341	348	344	377	399	416	430	450
$40,000	$50,000	537	596	636	667	692	728	357	371	379	386	392	399	394	431	457	476	492	515
$50,000	$60,000	599	664	708	742	770	809	399	414	424	431	437	446	440	481	509	530	548	573
$60,000	$70,000	654	725	773	810	841	883	436	453	464	472	479	488	481	526	556	579	599	626
$70,000	$80,000	706	782	834	874	906	952	472	490	502	511	518	528	520	568	600	625	646	675
$80,000	$90,000	754	836	891	933	968	1017	504	524	537	546	554	565	556	607	641	668	690	721
$90,000	$100,000	800	886	944	989	1026	1078	536	557	570	580	589	600	590	644	680	709	732	765
$100,000	$120,000	862	954	1016	1064	1104	1159	577	600	615	626	635	648	636	694	733	763	788	823
$120,000	$140,000	942	1043	1110	1162	1206	1266	632	657	674	686	696	710	697	759	802	834	862	900
$140,000	$160,000	1018	1126	1198	1255	1301	1366	684	711	729	742	753	768	754	821	866	901	931	972
$160,000	$180,000	1088	1203	1280	1340	1390	1459	732	761	780	795	806	822	806	878	926	964	995	1038
$180,000	$200,000	1155	1276	1358	1421	1474	1547	778	809	829	845	857	874	857	932	983	1023	1056	1102
$200,000	$225,000	1225	1353	1440	1507	1562	1639	826	859	881	897	910	928	910	989	1043	1085	1120	1168
$225,000	$250,000	1300	1436	1527	1598	1657	1739	877	913	936	953	968	987	967	1050	1107	1152	1188	1240
$250,000	$275,000	1372	1514	1611	1685	1747	1833	926	964	988	1007	1022	1043	1021	1109	1168	1215	1254	1308
$275,000	$300,000	1440	1590	1690	1768	1833	1923	973	1013	1039	1058	1074	1096	1073	1165	1227	1276	1316	1373
$300,000	or more	1853	2042	2170	2268	2350	2465	1257	1309	1343	1369	1390	1418	1369	1484	1501	1580	1642	1764

Washington (1, 6.5000%) · West Virginia (1, 6.0000%) · Wisconsin (1, 5.0000%)

Income At least	But less than	WA 1	WA 2	WA 3	WA 4	WA 5	WA Over 5	WV 1	WV 2	WV 3	WV 4	WV 5	WV Over 5	WI 1	WI 2	WI 3	WI 4	WI 5	WI Over 5
$0	$20,000	280	304	320	333	343	357	269	293	309	321	331	345	228	246	258	266	274	283
$20,000	$30,000	457	496	523	543	559	582	434	474	501	520	537	559	367	396	416	430	442	458
$30,000	$40,000	554	602	634	658	678	706	525	573	605	630	649	676	443	479	502	520	534	553
$40,000	$50,000	641	695	732	760	783	815	604	661	698	726	748	780	509	551	578	598	615	637
$50,000	$60,000	719	781	821	853	879	915	677	740	782	813	839	874	570	617	647	670	688	714
$60,000	$70,000	791	859	904	938	966	1006	743	813	859	893	921	960	625	677	710	735	756	784
$70,000	$80,000	859	932	980	1018	1048	1091	805	881	930	968	999	1041	677	733	769	797	819	849
$80,000	$90,000	922	1000	1052	1093	1125	1171	863	945	998	1038	1071	1117	726	786	825	854	878	910
$90,000	$100,000	983	1066	1121	1164	1199	1247	918	1005	1062	1105	1140	1188	772	836	877	908	934	968
$100,000	$120,000	1064	1153	1213	1259	1297	1350	992	1087	1148	1195	1233	1285	834	903	948	982	1009	1046
$120,000	$140,000	1171	1269	1335	1385	1427	1485	1090	1194	1261	1313	1355	1412	915	992	1041	1078	1108	1149
$140,000	$160,000	1272	1379	1450	1504	1550	1612	1182	1295	1368	1424	1470	1532	992	1075	1128	1169	1201	1246
$160,000	$180,000	1366	1480	1557	1616	1664	1731	1268	1389	1468	1528	1577	1644	1064	1153	1210	1253	1288	1336
$180,000	$200,000	1456	1578	1659	1722	1773	1845	1349	1479	1563	1627	1679	1751	1132	1227	1288	1334	1371	1423
$200,000	$225,000	1551	1680	1767	1833	1888	1964	1435	1573	1663	1731	1787	1863	1203	1304	1370	1419	1458	1513
$225,000	$250,000	1654	1791	1883	1954	2012	2093	1528	1675	1771	1844	1903	1985	1281	1388	1458	1510	1553	1611
$250,000	$275,000	1751	1897	1994	2069	2130	2216	1616	1772	1874	1951	2013	2100	1354	1468	1542	1597	1642	1704
$275,000	$300,000	1845	1998	2101	2179	2244	2334	1701	1865	1972	2053	2120	2211	1425	1545	1622	1681	1728	1793
$300,000	or more	2416	2615	2748	2850	2934	3052	2215	2430	2571	2677	2764	2884	1852	2009	2111	2187	2249	2334

Wyoming (1, 4.0000%)

Income At least	But less than	1	2	3	4	5	Over 5
$0	$20,000	171	183	192	198	203	210
$20,000	$30,000	280	300	313	323	332	343
$30,000	$40,000	340	364	380	392	402	416
$40,000	$50,000	393	421	439	453	465	481
$50,000	$60,000	441	472	493	509	522	540
$60,000	$70,000	485	520	543	560	574	594
$70,000	$80,000	527	564	589	608	623	645
$80,000	$90,000	566	606	633	653	669	692
$90,000	$100,000	603	646	674	695	713	737
$100,000	$120,000	653	699	730	753	772	798
$120,000	$140,000	719	770	803	829	850	879
$140,000	$160,000	781	836	872	900	923	954
$160,000	$180,000	839	898	937	967	991	1025
$180,000	$200,000	895	957	999	1031	1057	1092
$200,000	$225,000	953	1020	1064	1098	1125	1163
$225,000	$250,000	1017	1087	1134	1170	1200	1240
$250,000	$275,000	1077	1152	1201	1239	1270	1313
$275,000	$300,000	1135	1214	1266	1306	1338	1384
$300,000	or more	1487	1590	1658	1710	1752	1811

Note: Residents of **Alaska** do not have a state sales tax, but should follow the instructions on the next page to determine their local sales tax amount.

---

1 Use the Ratio Method to determine your local sales tax deduction, then add that to the appropriate amount in the state table. Your state sales tax rate is provided next to the state name.

2 Follow the instructions on the next page to determine your local sales tax deduction, then add that to the appropriate amount in the state table.

3 The California table includes the 1.25% uniform local sales tax rate in addition to the 6.25% state sales tax rate for a total of 7.50%. Some California localities impose a larger local sales tax. Taxpayers who reside in those jurisdictions should use the Ratio Method to determine their local sales tax deduction, then add that to the appropriate amount in the state table. The denominator of the correct ratio is 7.50%, and the numerator is the total sales tax rate minus 7.50%.

4 This state does not have a local general sales tax, so the amount in the state table is the only amount to be deducted.

5 The Nevada table includes the 2.25% uniform local sales tax rate in addition to the 4.6000% state sales tax rate for a total of 6.85%. Some Nevada localities impose a larger local sales tax. Taxpayers who reside in those jurisdictions should use the Ratio Method to determine their local sales tax deduction, then add that to the appropriate amount in the state table. The denominator of the correct ratio is 6.85%, and the numerator is the total sales tax rate minus 6.85%.

6 The 4.0% rate for Hawaii is actually an excise tax but is treated as a sales tax for purpose of this deduction.

Which Optional Local Sales Tax Table Should I Use?

IF you live in the state of...	AND you live in...	THEN use Local Table...
Alaska	Any locality	C
Arizona	Mesa, Phoenix	A
	Chandler, Glendale, Gilbert, Peoria, Scottsdale, Tempe, Tucson, Yuma, or any other locality	B
Arkansas	Any Locality	B
Colorado	Adams County, Arapahoe County, Boulder County, Centennial, Colorado Springs, Denver City/Denver County, El Paso County, Larimer County, Pueblo County, or any other locality	A
	Aurora, Boulder, Fort Collins, Greeley, Jefferson County, Lakewood, Longmont, or Pueblo City	B
	Arvada, Thornton, or Westminster	C
Georgia	Any locality	B
Illinois	Aurora, Elgin, or Waukegan	B
	Arlington Heights, Bloomington, Champaign, Chicago, Cicero, Decatur, Evanston, Joliet, Palatine, Peoria, Schaumburg, Skokie, Springfield, or any other locality	A
Louisiana	Ascension Parish, Bossier Parish, Caddo Parish, East Baton Rouge Parish, Iberia Parish, Jefferson Parish, Lafayette Parish, Lafourche Parish, Livingston Parish, Orleans Parish, Ouachita Parish, Rapides Parish, St. Bernard Parish, St. Landry Parish, St Tammany Parish, Tangipahoa Parish, or Terrebonne Parish	C
	Calcasieu Parish or any other locality	B
Mississippi	City of Jackson only	A
	City of Tupelo only	B
Missouri	Any locality	B
New York	Counties: Albany, Allegany, Broome, Cattaraugus, Cayuga, Chemung, Clinton, Cortland, Dutchess, Erie, Essex, Franklin, Fulton, Genesee, Herkimer, Jefferson, Lewis, Livingston, Madison, Monroe, Montgomery, Nassau, Niagara, Oneida, Onondaga, Ontario, Orange, Orleans, Oswego, Otsego, Putnam, Rensselaer, Rockland, St. Lawrence, Saratoga, Schenectady, Schoharie, Schuyler, Seneca, Steuben, Suffolk, Sullivan, Tompkins, Ulster, Warren, Washington, Westchester, Wyoming, or Yates Cities: Olean, Salamanca, Auburn, Gloversville, Johnstown, Oneida (Madison County), Rome, Utica, Oswego, Saratoga Springs, Ithaca, Glens Falls, Mount Vernon, New Rochelle, White Plains, Yonkers	B
	Counties: Chautauqua, Chenango, Columbia, Columbia, Delaware, Greene, Hamilton, Tioga, Wayne Cities: New York or Norwich (Chenango County)	A
	Any other locality	D*
North Carolina	Any locality	A
South Carolina	Aiken County, Andersonn County, Bamberg County, Charleston County, Cherokee County, Chesterfield County, Colleton County, Darlington County, Dillon County, Florence County, Georgetown County, Hampton County, Horry County, Jasper County, Lee County, Lexington County, Marion County, Marlboro County, Newberry County, Orangeburg County, York County, or any other locality	B
Tennessee	Any locality	B
Utah	Any locality	A
Virginia	Any locality	B

* Note: Local Table D is just 25% of the NY State table.

2016 Optional Local Sales Tax Tables

Income		Exemptions						Exemptions						Exemptions						Exemptions					
At least	But less than	1	2	3	4	5	Over 5	1	2	3	4	5	Over 5	1	2	3	4	5	Over 5	1	2	3	4	5	Over 5
		Local Table A						Local Table B						Local Table C						Local Table D					
$0	$20,000	37	40	42	43	44	46	48	54	58	61	63	67	60	68	73	77	80	85	40	42	43	44	45	46
20,000	30,000	60	64	67	69	71	73	75	83	89	94	98	103	92	104	112	118	123	130	65	68	71	72	74	75
30,000	40,000	72	77	81	83	86	88	89	99	106	111	116	122	110	123	132	140	145	154	79	83	86	88	89	92
40,000	50,000	83	89	93	96	98	102	101	113	121	127	132	139	124	140	150	158	165	174	91	96	99	101	103	106
50,000	60,000	93	100	104	107	110	114	112	125	134	140	146	153	138	155	166	175	182	193	102	108	111	114	116	119
60,000	70,000	103	110	114	118	121	125	123	136	146	153	159	167	150	168	181	190	198	209	113	118	122	125	127	131
70,000	80,000	111	119	124	127	131	135	132	147	157	164	171	180	161	181	194	204	213	225	122	128	132	136	138	142
80,000	90,000	119	127	133	137	140	145	141	156	167	175	182	191	172	193	207	218	227	239	131	138	142	146	148	152
90,000	100,000	127	135	141	145	149	154	149	165	177	185	192	202	182	204	218	230	239	253	140	147	152	155	158	162
100,000	120,000	137	146	152	157	161	166	160	178	190	199	206	217	195	218	234	246	256	271	151	159	164	168	171	175
120,000	140,000	151	160	167	172	176	182	174	194	206	216	225	236	212	238	255	268	279	294	167	175	180	185	188	193
140,000	160,000	163	174	181	187	191	198	188	208	222	233	242	254	228	255	274	288	300	316	181	190	196	201	204	209
160,000	180,000	175	187	194	200	205	212	200	222	237	248	258	271	243	272	291	307	319	336	194	204	210	215	219	225
180,000	200,000	187	199	207	213	218	225	212	235	251	263	273	287	257	288	308	324	337	356	207	217	224	230	234	240
200,000	225,000	198	211	220	226	232	239	225	249	265	278	289	303	272	304	326	343	356	376	221	232	239	244	249	255
225,000	250,000	211	225	234	241	247	255	238	264	281	294	305	321	288	322	345	362	377	397	235	247	255	261	265	272
250,000	275,000	224	238	247	255	261	269	251	278	296	310	321	338	303	338	362	381	396	418	249	261	270	276	281	288
275,000	300,000	235	250	260	268	274	283	263	291	310	325	337	354	317	354	379	399	415	437	262	275	284	291	296	304
300,000	or more	307	325	338	348	356	368	336	371	394	413	428	449	403	449	481	505	525	553	343	360	372	380	387	397

B

Tax Forms

Appendix Outline

Form **1040A**	Department of the Treasury—Internal Revenue Service **U.S. Individual Income Tax Return** (99)	**2016**	IRS Use Only—Do not write or staple in this space.

Your first name and initial	Last name	OMB No. 1545-0074
		Your social security number

If a joint return, spouse's first name and initial	Last name	**Spouse's social security number**

Home address (number and street). If you have a P.O. box, see instructions.	Apt. no.	▲ Make sure the SSN(s) above and on line 6c are correct.

City, town or post office, state, and ZIP code. If you have a foreign address, also complete spaces below (see instructions).

Presidential Election Campaign
Check here if you, or your spouse if filing jointly, want $3 to go to this fund. Checking a box below will not change your tax or refund. ☐ You ☐ Spouse

Foreign country name	Foreign province/state/county	Foreign postal code

Filing status
Check only one box.

1 ☐ Single
2 ☐ Married filing jointly (even if only one had income)
3 ☐ Married filing separately. Enter spouse's SSN above and full name here. ▶
4 ☐ Head of household (with qualifying person). (See instructions.) If the qualifying person is a child but not your dependent, enter this child's name here. ▶
5 ☐ Qualifying widow(er) with dependent child (see instructions)

Exemptions

If more than six dependents, see instructions.

6a ☐ **Yourself.** If someone can claim you as a dependent, **do not** check box 6a.
b ☐ **Spouse**

c **Dependents:**

(1) First name Last name	(2) Dependent's social security number	(3) Dependent's relationship to you	(4) ✔ if child under age 17 qualifying for child tax credit (see instructions)
			☐
			☐
			☐
			☐
			☐
			☐

Boxes checked on 6a and 6b ___

No. of children on 6c who:
• lived with you ___
• did not live with you due to divorce or separation (see instructions) ___

Dependents on 6c not entered above ___

Add numbers on lines above ▶ ___

d Total number of exemptions claimed.

Income

Attach Form(s) W-2 here. Also attach Form(s) 1099-R if tax was withheld.

If you did not get a W-2, see instructions.

7	Wages, salaries, tips, etc. Attach Form(s) W-2.		7
8a	**Taxable** interest. Attach Schedule B if required.		8a
b	**Tax-exempt** interest. **Do not** include on line 8a.	8b	
9a	Ordinary dividends. Attach Schedule B if required.		9a
b	Qualified dividends (see instructions).	9b	
10	Capital gain distributions (see instructions).		10
11a	IRA distributions. 11a	11b Taxable amount (see instructions).	11b
12a	Pensions and annuities. 12a	12b Taxable amount (see instructions).	12b
13	Unemployment compensation and Alaska Permanent Fund dividends.		13
14a	Social security benefits. 14a	14b Taxable amount (see instructions).	14b
15	Add lines 7 through 14b (far right column). This is your **total income.** ▶		15

Adjusted gross income

16	Educator expenses (see instructions).	16	
17	IRA deduction (see instructions).	17	
18	Student loan interest deduction (see instructions).	18	
19	Tuition and fees. Attach Form 8917.	19	
20	Add lines 16 through 19. These are your **total adjustments.**		20
21	Subtract line 20 from line 15. This is your **adjusted gross income.** ▶		21

For Disclosure, Privacy Act, and Paperwork Reduction Act Notice, see separate instructions. Cat. No. 11327A   Form **1040A** (2016)

Form 1040A (2016)   Page **2**

Tax, credits, and payments	22	Enter the amount from line 21 (adjusted gross income).	22	

23a Check if: □ **You** were born before January 2, 1952, □ Blind □ **Spouse** was born before January 2, 1952, □ Blind **Total boxes checked ▶ 23a** □

b If you are married filing separately and your spouse itemizes deductions, check here ▶ 23b □

Standard Deduction for—
- People who check any box on line 23a or 23b or who can be claimed as a dependent, see instructions.
- All others:
Single or Married filing separately, $6,300
Married filing jointly or Qualifying widow(er), $12,600
Head of household, $9,300

24	Enter your **standard deduction**.	24
25	Subtract line 24 from line 22. If line 24 is more than line 22, enter -0-.	25
26	**Exemptions.** Multiply $4,050 by the number on line 6d.	26
27	Subtract line 26 from line 25. If line 26 is more than line 25, enter -0-. This is your **taxable income.** ▶ 27	
28	**Tax,** including any alternative minimum tax (see instructions). 28	
29	Excess advance premium tax credit repayment. Attach Form 8962. 29	
30	Add lines 28 and 29. 30	
31	Credit for child and dependent care expenses. Attach Form 2441. 31	
32	Credit for the elderly or the disabled. Attach Schedule R. 32	
33	Education credits from Form 8863, line 19. 33	
34	Retirement savings contributions credit. Attach Form 8880. 34	
35	Child tax credit. Attach Schedule 8812, if required. 35	
36	Add lines 31 through 35. These are your **total credits.** 36	
37	Subtract line 36 from line 30. If line 36 is more than line 30, enter -0-. 37	
38	Health care: individual responsibility (see instructions). Full-year coverage □ 38	
39	Add line 37 and line 38. This is your **total tax.** 39	

If you have a qualifying child, attach Schedule EIC.

40	Federal income tax withheld from Forms W-2 and 1099. 40	
41	2016 estimated tax payments and amount applied from 2015 return. 41	
42a	**Earned income credit (EIC).** 42a	
b	Nontaxable combat pay election. 42b	
43	Additional child tax credit. Attach Schedule 8812. 43	
44	American opportunity credit from Form 8863, line 8. 44	
45	Net premium tax credit. Attach Form 8962. 45	
46	Add lines 40, 41, 42a, 43, 44, and 45. These are your **total payments.** ▶ 46	

Refund

Direct deposit? See instructions and fill in 48b, 48c, and 48d or Form 8888.

47	If line 46 is more than line 39, subtract line 39 from line 46. This is the amount you **overpaid.** 47	
48a	Amount of line 47 you want **refunded to you.** If Form 8888 is attached, check here ▶ □ 48a	

▶ **b** Routing number □□□□□□□□□   ▶ **c** Type: □ Checking □ Savings

▶ **d** Account number □□□□□□□□□□□□□□□□□

49	Amount of line 47 you want **applied to your 2017 estimated tax.** 49	

Amount you owe

50	**Amount you owe.** Subtract line 46 from line 39. For details on how to pay, see instructions. ▶ 50	
51	Estimated tax penalty (see instructions). 51	

Third party designee

Do you want to allow another person to discuss this return with the IRS (see instructions)? □ **Yes.** Complete the following. □ **No**

Designee's name ▶   Phone no. ▶   Personal identification number (PIN) □□□□□

Sign here

Joint return? See instructions. Keep a copy for your records.

Under penalties of perjury, I declare that I have examined this return and accompanying schedules and statements, and to the best of my knowledge and belief, they are true, correct, and accurately list all amounts and sources of income I received during the tax year. Declaration of preparer (other than the taxpayer) is based on all information of which the preparer has any knowledge.

Your signature   Date   Your occupation   Daytime phone number

Spouse's signature. If a joint return, **both** must sign.   Date   Spouse's occupation   If the IRS sent you an Identity Protection PIN, enter it here (see inst.) □□□□□□

Paid preparer use only

Print/type preparer's name   Preparer's signature   Date   Check ▶ □ if self-employed   PTIN

Firm's name ▶   Firm's EIN ▶

Firm's address ▶   Phone no.

Form **1040A** (2016)

Department of the Treasury—Internal Revenue Service

Form 1040EZ

Income Tax Return for Single and Joint Filers With No Dependents (99)

2016

OMB No. 1545-0074

Your first name and initial | Last name | Your social security number

If a joint return, spouse's first name and initial | Last name | Spouse's social security number

Home address (number and street). If you have a P.O. box, see instructions. | Apt. no. | ▲ Make sure the SSN(s) above are correct.

City, town or post office, state, and ZIP code. If you have a foreign address, also complete spaces below (see instructions).

Presidential Election Campaign
Check here if you, or your spouse if filing jointly, want $3 to go to this fund. Checking a box below will not change your tax or refund.
☐ You   ☐ Spouse

Foreign country name | Foreign province/state/county | Foreign postal code

Income

Attach Form(s) W-2 here.

Enclose, but do not attach, any payment.

1   Wages, salaries, and tips. This should be shown in box 1 of your Form(s) W-2. Attach your Form(s) W-2.   **1**

2   Taxable interest. If the total is over $1,500, you cannot use Form 1040EZ.   **2**

3   Unemployment compensation and Alaska Permanent Fund dividends (see instructions).   **3**

4   Add lines 1, 2, and 3. This is your **adjusted gross income.**   **4**

5   If someone can claim you (or your spouse if a joint return) as a dependent, check the applicable box(es) below and enter the amount from the worksheet on back.
☐ You   ☐ Spouse
If no one can claim you (or your spouse if a joint return), enter $10,350 if **single;** $20,700 if **married filing jointly.** See back for explanation.   **5**

6   Subtract line 5 from line 4. If line 5 is larger than line 4, enter -0-. This is your **taxable income.**   ▶ **6**

Payments, Credits, and Tax

7   Federal income tax withheld from Form(s) W-2 and 1099.   **7**

8a   **Earned income credit (EIC)** (see instructions)   **8a**

b   Nontaxable combat pay election.   8b

9   Add lines 7 and 8a. These are your **total payments and credits.**   ▶ **9**

10   **Tax.** Use the amount on **line 6 above** to find your tax in the tax table in the instructions. Then, enter the tax from the table on this line.   **10**

11   Health care: individual responsibility (see instructions)   Full-year coverage ☐   **11**

12   Add lines 10 and 11. This is your **total tax.**   **12**

Refund

Have it directly deposited! See instructions and fill in 13b, 13c, and 13d, or Form 8888.

13a   If line 9 is larger than line 12, subtract line 12 from line 9. This is your **refund.**
If Form 8888 is attached, check here ▶ ☐   **13a**

▶ b   Routing number   ▶ c Type: ☐ Checking   ☐ Savings

▶ d   Account number

Amount You Owe

14   If line 12 is larger than line 9, subtract line 9 from line 12. This is the **amount you owe.** For details on how to pay, see instructions.   ▶ **14**

Third Party Designee

Do you want to allow another person to discuss this return with the IRS (see instructions)?   ☐ **Yes.** Complete below.   ☐ **No**

Designee's name ▶ | Phone no. ▶ | Personal identification number (PIN) ▶

Sign Here

Joint return? See instructions.

Keep a copy for your records.

Under penalties of perjury, I declare that I have examined this return and, to the best of my knowledge and belief, it is true, correct, and accurately lists all amounts and sources of income I received during the tax year. Declaration of preparer (other than the taxpayer) is based on all information of which the preparer has any knowledge.

Your signature | Date | Your occupation | Daytime phone number

Spouse's signature. If a joint return, **both** must sign. | Date | Spouse's occupation | If the IRS sent you an Identity Protection PIN, enter it here (see inst.)

Paid Preparer Use Only

Print/Type preparer's name | Preparer's signature | Date | Check ☐ if self-employed | PTIN

Firm's name ▶ | Firm's EIN ▶

Firm's address ▶ | Phone no.

For Disclosure, Privacy Act, and Paperwork Reduction Act Notice, see instructions.   Cat. No. 11329W   Form **1040EZ** (2016)

Form 1040EZ (2016)   Page **2**

Use this form if

- Your filing status is single or married filing jointly. If you are not sure about your filing status, see instructions.
- You (and your spouse if married filing jointly) were under age 65 and not blind at the end of 2016. If you were born on January 1, 1952, you are considered to be age 65 at the end of 2016.
- You do not claim any dependents. For information on dependents, see Pub. 501.
- Your taxable income (line 6) is less than $100,000.
- You do not claim any adjustments to income. For information on adjustments to income, use the Tax Topics listed under *Adjustments to Income* at *www.irs.gov/taxtopics* (see instructions).
- The only tax credit you can claim is the earned income credit (EIC). The credit may give you a refund even if you do not owe any tax. You do not need a qualifying child to claim the EIC. For information on credits, use the Tax Topics listed under *Tax Credits* at *www.irs.gov/taxtopics* (see instructions). If you received a Form 1098-T or paid higher education expenses, you may be eligible for a tax credit or deduction that you must claim on Form 1040A or Form 1040. For more information on tax benefits for education, see Pub. 970.

  Caution: If you can claim the premium tax credit or you received any advance payment of the premium tax credit in 2016, you must use Form 1040A or Form 1040.
- You had only wages, salaries, tips, taxable scholarship or fellowship grants, unemployment compensation, or Alaska Permanent Fund dividends, and your taxable interest was not over $1,500. But if you earned tips, including allocated tips, that are not included in box 5 and box 7 of your Form W-2, you may not be able to use Form 1040EZ (see instructions). If you are planning to use Form 1040EZ for a child who received Alaska Permanent Fund dividends, see instructions.

Filling in your return

If you received a scholarship or fellowship grant or tax-exempt interest income, such as on municipal bonds, see the instructions before filling in the form. Also, see the instructions if you received a Form 1099-INT showing federal income tax withheld or if federal income tax was withheld from your unemployment compensation or Alaska Permanent Fund dividends.

For tips on how to avoid common mistakes, see instructions.

Remember, you must report all wages, salaries, and tips even if you do not get a Form W-2 from your employer. You must also report all your taxable interest, including interest from banks, savings and loans, credit unions, etc., even if you do not get a Form 1099-INT.

Worksheet for Line 5 — Dependents Who Checked One or Both Boxes

Use this worksheet to figure the amount to enter on line 5 if someone can claim you (or your spouse if married filing jointly) as a dependent, even if that person chooses not to do so. To find out if someone can claim you as a dependent, see Pub. 501.

A. Amount, if any, from line 1 on front . . . .
     `+ _____ 350.00` Enter total ▶   A. _____

B. Minimum standard deduction . . . .   B. _____ 1,050

C. Enter the **larger** of line A or line B here . . . .   C. _____

D. Maximum standard deduction. If **single,** enter $6,300; if **married filing jointly,** enter $12,600 .   D. _____

E. Enter the **smaller** of line C or line D here. This is your standard deduction . . . .   E. _____

F. Exemption amount.
   - If single, enter -0-.
   - If married filing jointly and —
     —both you and your spouse can be claimed as dependents, enter -0-.
     —only one of you can be claimed as a dependent, enter $4,050.
   }   F. _____

G. Add lines E and F. Enter the total here and on line 5 on the front . . . .   G. _____

(keep a copy for your records)

If you did not check any boxes on line 5, enter on line 5 the amount shown below that applies to you.
- Single, enter $10,350. This is the total of your standard deduction ($6,300) and your exemption ($4,050).
- Married filing jointly, enter $20,700. This is the total of your standard deduction ($12,600), your exemption ($4,050), and your spouse's exemption ($4,050).

Mailing Return

Mail your return by **April 18, 2017.** Mail it to the address shown on the last page of the instructions.

---

www.irs.gov/form1040ez   Form **1040EZ** (2016)

Form **1040** Department of the Treasury—Internal Revenue Service   (99)   **2016**   OMB No. 1545-0074   IRS Use Only—Do not write or staple in this space.

U.S. Individual Income Tax Return

For the year Jan. 1–Dec. 31, 2016, or other tax year beginning _____ , 2016, ending _____ , 20 ____   See separate instructions.

Your first name and initial	Last name		Your social security number
If a joint return, spouse's first name and initial	Last name		Spouse's social security number

Home address (number and street). If you have a P.O. box, see instructions.   Apt. no.

▲ Make sure the SSN(s) above and on line 6c are correct.

City, town or post office, state, and ZIP code. If you have a foreign address, also complete spaces below (see instructions).

Presidential Election Campaign
Check here if you, or your spouse if filing jointly, want $3 to go to this fund. Checking a box below will not change your tax or refund.   ☐ You   ☐ Spouse

Foreign country name	Foreign province/state/county	Foreign postal code

Filing Status

Check only one box.

1. ☐ Single
2. ☐ Married filing jointly (even if only one had income)
3. ☐ Married filing separately. Enter spouse's SSN above and full name here. ▶
4. ☐ Head of household (with qualifying person). (See instructions.) If the qualifying person is a child but not your dependent, enter this child's name here. ▶
5. ☐ Qualifying widow(er) with dependent child

Exemptions

6a ☐ **Yourself.** If someone can claim you as a dependent, **do not** check box 6a . . . . .

b ☐ **Spouse** . . . .

c **Dependents:**		(2) Dependent's social security number	(3) Dependent's relationship to you	(4) ✓ if child under age 17 qualifying for child tax credit (see instructions)
(1) First name	Last name			
				☐
				☐
				☐
				☐

If more than four dependents, see instructions and check here ▶ ☐

Boxes checked on 6a and 6b ____
No. of children on 6c who:
• lived with you ____
• did not live with you due to divorce or separation (see instructions) ____
Dependents on 6c not entered above ____
Add numbers on lines above ▶ ____

d   Total number of exemptions claimed . . . .

Income

Attach Form(s) W-2 here. Also attach Forms W-2G and 1099-R if tax was withheld.

If you did not get a W-2, see instructions.

7	Wages, salaries, tips, etc. Attach Form(s) W-2	**7**	
8a	**Taxable** interest. Attach Schedule B if required	**8a**	
b	**Tax-exempt** interest. **Do not** include on line 8a . . .	8b		
9a	Ordinary dividends. Attach Schedule B if required	**9a**	
b	Qualified dividends	9b		
10	Taxable refunds, credits, or offsets of state and local income taxes	**10**	
11	Alimony received	**11**	
12	Business income or (loss). Attach Schedule C or C-EZ	**12**	
13	Capital gain or (loss). Attach Schedule D if required. If not required, check here ▶ ☐	**13**	
14	Other gains or (losses). Attach Form 4797	**14**	
15a	IRA distributions .	15a		**b** Taxable amount . . .	**15b**	
16a	Pensions and annuities	16a		**b** Taxable amount . . .	**16b**	
17	Rental real estate, royalties, partnerships, S corporations, trusts, etc. Attach Schedule E	**17**	
18	Farm income or (loss). Attach Schedule F	**18**	
19	Unemployment compensation	**19**	
20a	Social security benefits	20a		**b** Taxable amount . . .	**20b**	
21	Other income. List type and amount _____	**21**	
22	Combine the amounts in the far right column for lines 7 through 21. This is your **total income** ▶	**22**	

Adjusted Gross Income

23	Educator expenses	23	
24	Certain business expenses of reservists, performing artists, and fee-basis government officials. Attach Form 2106 or 2106-EZ	24	
25	Health savings account deduction. Attach Form 8889 .	25	
26	Moving expenses. Attach Form 3903	26	
27	Deductible part of self-employment tax. Attach Schedule SE .	27	
28	Self-employed SEP, SIMPLE, and qualified plans . .	28	
29	Self-employed health insurance deduction	29	
30	Penalty on early withdrawal of savings	30	
31a	Alimony paid **b** Recipient's SSN ▶	31a	
32	IRA deduction	32	
33	Student loan interest deduction	33	
34	Tuition and fees. Attach Form 8917	34	
35	Domestic production activities deduction. Attach Form 8903	35	
36	Add lines 23 through 35	36	
37	Subtract line 36 from line 22. This is your **adjusted gross income** . . . . . ▶	37	

For Disclosure, Privacy Act, and Paperwork Reduction Act Notice, see separate instructions.   Cat. No. 11320B   Form **1040** (2016)

Form 1040 (2016)   Page **2**

Tax and Credits	38	Amount from line 37 (adjusted gross income)	38
	39a	Check if: ☐ **You** were born before January 2, 1952, ☐ Blind. **Total boxes** ☐ **Spouse** was born before January 2, 1952, ☐ Blind. **checked** ▶ 39a	
	b	If your spouse itemizes on a separate return or you were a dual-status alien, check here ▶ 39b ☐	

Standard Deduction for—
• People who check any box on line 39a or 39b **or** who can be claimed as a dependent, see instructions.
• All others:
Single or Married filing separately, $6,300
Married filing jointly or Qualifying widow(er), $12,600
Head of household, $9,300

40	**Itemized deductions** (from Schedule A) **or** your **standard deduction** (see left margin) . .	40
41	Subtract line 40 from line 38	41
42	**Exemptions.** If line 38 is $155,650 or less, multiply $4,050 by the number on line 6d. Otherwise, see instructions	42
43	**Taxable income.** Subtract line 42 from line 41. If line 42 is more than line 41, enter -0- . .	43
44	**Tax** (see instructions). Check if any from: **a** ☐ Form(s) 8814 **b** ☐ Form 4972 **c** ☐	44
45	**Alternative minimum tax** (see instructions). Attach Form 6251	45
46	Excess advance premium tax credit repayment. Attach Form 8962	46
47	Add lines 44, 45, and 46 . . . . ▶	47
48	Foreign tax credit. Attach Form 1116 if required	48	
49	Credit for child and dependent care expenses. Attach Form 2441	49	
50	Education credits from Form 8863, line 19	50	
51	Retirement savings contributions credit. Attach Form 8880	51	
52	Child tax credit. Attach Schedule 8812, if required . . .	52	
53	Residential energy credits. Attach Form 5695	53	
54	Other credits from Form: **a** ☐ 3800 **b** ☐ 8801 **c** ☐	54	
55	Add lines 48 through 54. These are your **total credits**	55
56	Subtract line 55 from line 47. If line 55 is more than line 47, enter -0- . . . . . . ▶	56

Other Taxes	57	Self-employment tax. Attach Schedule SE	57
	58	Unreported social security and Medicare tax from Form: **a** ☐ 4137 **b** ☐ 8919 . .	58
	59	Additional tax on IRAs, other qualified retirement plans, etc. Attach Form 5329 if required	59
	60a	Household employment taxes from Schedule H	60a
	b	First-time homebuyer credit repayment. Attach Form 5405 if required	60b
	61	Health care: individual responsibility (see instructions) Full-year coverage ☐	61
	62	Taxes from: **a** ☐ Form 8959 **b** ☐ Form 8960 **c** ☐ Instructions; enter code(s)	62
	63	Add lines 56 through 62. This is your **total tax** . . . . ▶	63

Payments	64	Federal income tax withheld from Forms W-2 and 1099 . .	64	
If you have a qualifying child, attach Schedule EIC.	65	2016 estimated tax payments and amount applied from 2015 return	65	
	66a	**Earned income credit (EIC)**	66a	
	b	Nontaxable combat pay election	66b	
	67	Additional child tax credit. Attach Schedule 8812 . . .	67	
	68	American opportunity credit from Form 8863, line 8 . . .	68	
	69	Net premium tax credit. Attach Form 8962	69	
	70	Amount paid with request for extension to file	70	
	71	Excess social security and tier 1 RRTA tax withheld . . .	71	
	72	Credit for federal tax on fuels. Attach Form 4136 . . .	72	
	73	Credits from Form: **a** ☐ 2439 **b** ☐ Reserved **c** ☐ 8885 **d** ☐	73	
	74	Add lines 64, 65, 66a, and 67 through 73. These are your **total payments** . . . . . ▶	74	

Refund	75	If line 74 is more than line 63, subtract line 63 from line 74. This is the amount you **overpaid**	75
	76a	Amount of line 75 you want **refunded to you**. If Form 8888 is attached, check here . ▶ ☐	76a
Direct deposit? See instructions.	▶ b	Routing number ☐☐☐☐☐☐☐☐☐ ▶ **c** Type: ☐ Checking ☐ Savings	
	▶ d	Account number ☐☐☐☐☐☐☐☐☐☐☐☐☐☐☐☐☐	
	77	Amount of line 75 you want **applied to your 2017 estimated tax** ▶ 77	

Amount You Owe	78	**Amount you owe.** Subtract line 74 from line 63. For details on how to pay, see instructions ▶	78
	79	Estimated tax penalty (see instructions) 79	

Third Party Designee	Do you want to allow another person to discuss this return with the IRS (see instructions)? ☐ **Yes.** Complete below. ☐ **No**
	Designee's name ▶ Phone no. ▶ Personal identification number (PIN) ▶ ☐☐☐☐☐

Sign Here
Joint return? See instructions. Keep a copy for your records.

Under penalties of perjury, I declare that I have examined this return and accompanying schedules and statements, and to the best of my knowledge and belief, they are true, correct, and accurately list all amounts and sources of income I received during the tax year. Declaration of preparer (other than taxpayer) is based on all information of which preparer has any knowledge.

Your signature	Date	Your occupation	Daytime phone number
Spouse's signature. If a joint return, **both** must sign.	Date	Spouse's occupation	If the IRS sent you an Identity Protection PIN, enter it here (see inst.) ☐☐☐☐☐☐

Paid Preparer Use Only	Print/Type preparer's name	Preparer's signature	Date	Check ☐ if self-employed	PTIN
	Firm's name ▶			Firm's EIN ▶	
	Firm's address ▶			Phone no.	

SCHEDULE A
(Form 1040)

Department of the Treasury
Internal Revenue Service (99)

Itemized Deductions

► Information about Schedule A and its separate instructions is at *www.irs.gov/schedulea*.
► **Attach to Form 1040.**

OMB No. 1545-0074

2016

Attachment
Sequence No. **07**

Name(s) shown on Form 1040

Your social security number

Medical and Dental Expenses	**Caution:** Do not include expenses reimbursed or paid by others.		
	1 Medical and dental expenses (see instructions)	**1**	
	2 Enter amount from Form 1040, line 38 **2**		
	3 Multiply line 2 by 10% (0.10). But if either you or your spouse was born before January 2, 1952, multiply line 2 by 7.5% (0.075) instead	**3**	
	4 Subtract line 3 from line 1. If line 3 is more than line 1, enter -0-		**4**
Taxes You Paid	5 State and local **(check only one box):**		
	a ☐ Income taxes, **or**	**5**	
	b ☐ General sales taxes		
	6 Real estate taxes (see instructions)	**6**	
	7 Personal property taxes	**7**	
	8 Other taxes. List type and amount ► _____	**8**	
	9 Add lines 5 through 8		**9**
Interest You Paid	10 Home mortgage interest and points reported to you on Form 1098	**10**	
	11 Home mortgage interest not reported to you on Form 1098. If paid to the person from whom you bought the home, **see instructions** and show that person's name, identifying no., and address ►		
Note: Your mortgage interest deduction may be limited (see instructions).	_____ _____	**11**	
	12 Points not reported to you on Form 1098. See instructions for special rules	**12**	
	13 Mortgage insurance premiums (see instructions)	**13**	
	14 Investment interest. Attach Form 4952 if required. (See instructions.)	**14**	
	15 Add lines 10 through 14		**15**
Gifts to Charity	16 Gifts by cash or check. If you made any gift of $250 or more, see instructions	**16**	
If you made a gift and got a benefit for it, see instructions.	17 Other than by cash or check. If any gift of $250 or more, see instructions. You **must** attach Form 8283 if over $500 . . .	**17**	
	18 Carryover from prior year	**18**	
	19 Add lines 16 through 18		**19**
Casualty and Theft Losses	20 Casualty or theft loss(es). Attach Form 4684. (See instructions.)		**20**
Job Expenses and Certain Miscellaneous Deductions	21 Unreimbursed employee expenses—job travel, union dues, job education, etc. Attach Form 2106 or 2106-EZ if required. (See instructions.) ► _____	**21**	
	22 Tax preparation fees	**22**	
	23 Other expenses—investment, safe deposit box, etc. List type and amount ► _____	**23**	
	24 Add lines 21 through 23	**24**	
	25 Enter amount from Form 1040, line 38 **25**		
	26 Multiply line 25 by 2% (0.02)	**26**	
	27 Subtract line 26 from line 24. If line 26 is more than line 24, enter -0-		**27**
Other Miscellaneous Deductions	28 Other—from list in instructions. List type and amount ► _____		
	_____		**28**
Total Itemized Deductions	29 Is Form 1040, line 38, over $155,650?		
	☐ **No.** Your deduction is not limited. Add the amounts in the far right column for lines 4 through 28. Also, enter this amount on Form 1040, line 40.	}	**29**
	☐ **Yes.** Your deduction may be limited. See the Itemized Deductions Worksheet in the instructions to figure the amount to enter.		
	30 If you elect to itemize deductions even though they are less than your standard deduction, check here . . . . ► ☐		

For Paperwork Reduction Act Notice, see Form 1040 instructions.

Cat. No. 17145C

Schedule A (Form 1040) 2016

SCHEDULE B		OMB No. 1545-0074

SCHEDULE B
(Form 1040A or 1040)

Department of the Treasury
Internal Revenue Service (99)

Interest and Ordinary Dividends

▶ Attach to Form 1040A or 1040.
▶ Information about Schedule B and its instructions is at *www.irs.gov/scheduleb.*

OMB No. 1545-0074

2016

Attachment
Sequence No. **08**

Name(s) shown on return

Your social security number

Part I

Interest

(See instructions on back and the instructions for Form 1040A, or Form 1040, line 8a.)

Note: If you received a Form 1099-INT, Form 1099-OID, or substitute statement from a brokerage firm, list the firm's name as the payer and enter the total interest shown on that form.

		Amount
1	List name of payer. If any interest is from a seller-financed mortgage and the buyer used the property as a personal residence, see instructions on back and list this interest first. Also, show that buyer's social security number and address ▶	
1		
2	Add the amounts on line 1 . . . . **2**	
3	Excludable interest on series EE and I U.S. savings bonds issued after 1989. Attach Form 8815 . . . . **3**	
4	Subtract line 3 from line 2. Enter the result here and on Form 1040A, or Form 1040, line 8a . . . . ▶ **4**	

Note: If line 4 is over $1,500, you must complete Part III.

Part II

Ordinary Dividends

(See instructions on back and the instructions for Form 1040A, or Form 1040, line 9a.)

Note: If you received a Form 1099-DIV or substitute statement from a brokerage firm, list the firm's name as the payer and enter the ordinary dividends shown on that form.

		Amount
5	List name of payer ▶	
5		
6	Add the amounts on line 5. Enter the total here and on Form 1040A, or Form 1040, line 9a . . . . ▶ **6**	

Note: If line 6 is over $1,500, you must complete Part III.

Part III

Foreign Accounts and Trusts

(See instructions on back.)

You must complete this part if you **(a)** had over $1,500 of taxable interest or ordinary dividends; **(b)** had a foreign account; or **(c)** received a distribution from, or were a grantor of, or a transferor to, a foreign trust.

		Yes	No
7a	At any time during 2016, did you have a financial interest in or signature authority over a financial account (such as a bank account, securities account, or brokerage account) located in a foreign country? See instructions		
	If "Yes," are you required to file FinCEN Form 114, Report of Foreign Bank and Financial Accounts (FBAR), to report that financial interest or signature authority? See FinCEN Form 114 and its instructions for filing requirements and exceptions to those requirements		
b	If you are required to file FinCEN Form 114, enter the name of the foreign country where the financial account is located ▶		
8	During 2016, did you receive a distribution from, or were you the grantor of, or transferor to, a foreign trust? If "Yes," you may have to file Form 3520. See instructions on back		

For Paperwork Reduction Act Notice, see your tax return instructions.   Cat. No. 17146N   Schedule B (Form 1040A or 1040) 2016

SCHEDULE C
(Form 1040)

Department of the Treasury
Internal Revenue Service (99)

Profit or Loss From Business
(Sole Proprietorship)

▶ Information about Schedule C and its separate instructions is at *www.irs.gov/schedulec.*
▶ **Attach to Form 1040, 1040NR, or 1041; partnerships generally must file Form 1065.**

OMB No. 1545-0074

2016

Attachment
Sequence No. **09**

Name of proprietor

Social security number (SSN)

A	Principal business or profession, including product or service (see instructions)	**B** Enter code from instructions ▶
C	Business name. If no separate business name, leave blank.	**D** Employer ID number (EIN), (see instr.)

E   Business address (including suite or room no.) ▶
City, town or post office, state, and ZIP code

F   Accounting method: **(1)** ☐ Cash   **(2)** ☐ Accrual   **(3)** ☐ Other (specify) ▶

G   Did you "materially participate" in the operation of this business during 2016? If "No," see instructions for limit on losses   ☐ Yes   ☐ No

H   If you started or acquired this business during 2016, check here   .   .   .   .   ▶ ☐

I   Did you make any payments in 2016 that would require you to file Form(s) 1099? (see instructions)   .   .   .   .   ☐ Yes   ☐ No

J   If "Yes," did you or will you file required Forms 1099?   .   .   .   .   ☐ Yes   ☐ No

Part I   Income

1	Gross receipts or sales. See instructions for line 1 and check the box if this income was reported to you on Form W-2 and the "Statutory employee" box on that form was checked . . . . . ▶ ☐	**1**
2	Returns and allowances	**2**
3	Subtract line 2 from line 1	**3**
4	Cost of goods sold (from line 42)	**4**
5	**Gross profit.** Subtract line 4 from line 3	**5**
6	Other income, including federal and state gasoline or fuel tax credit or refund (see instructions) . . .	**6**
7	**Gross income.** Add lines 5 and 6 . . . . ▶	**7**

Part II   Expenses. Enter expenses for business use of your home **only** on line 30.

8	Advertising	**8**	18	Office expense (see instructions)	**18**
9	Car and truck expenses (see instructions).	**9**	19	Pension and profit-sharing plans .	**19**
10	Commissions and fees .	**10**	20	Rent or lease (see instructions):	
11	Contract labor (see instructions)	**11**	a	Vehicles, machinery, and equipment	**20a**
12	Depletion	**12**	b	Other business property . . .	**20b**
13	Depreciation and section 179 expense deduction (not included in Part III) (see instructions).	**13**	21	Repairs and maintenance . . .	**21**
			22	Supplies (not included in Part III) .	**22**
			23	Taxes and licenses	**23**
			24	Travel, meals, and entertainment:	
14	Employee benefit programs (other than on line 19) . .	**14**	a	Travel	**24a**
15	Insurance (other than health) .	**15**	b	Deductible meals and entertainment (see instructions) .	**24b**
16	Interest:		25	Utilities	**25**
a	Mortgage (paid to banks, etc.)	**16a**	26	Wages (less employment credits) .	**26**
b	Other	**16b**	27a	Other expenses (from line 48) . .	**27a**
17	Legal and professional services	**17**	b	**Reserved for future use** . . .	**27b**

28	**Total expenses** before expenses for business use of home. Add lines 8 through 27a . . . ▶	**28**
29	Tentative profit or (loss). Subtract line 28 from line 7	**29**
30	Expenses for business use of your home. Do not report these expenses elsewhere. Attach Form 8829 unless using the simplified method (see instructions). **Simplified method filers only:** enter the total square footage of: (a) your home: _____ and (b) the part of your home used for business: _____. Use the Simplified Method Worksheet in the instructions to figure the amount to enter on line 30	**30**
31	**Net profit or (loss).** Subtract line 30 from line 29. • If a profit, enter on both **Form 1040, line 12** (or **Form 1040NR, line 13**) and on **Schedule SE, line 2.** (If you checked the box on line 1, see instructions). Estates and trusts, enter on **Form 1041, line 3.** • If a loss, you **must** go to line 32.	**31**
32	If you have a loss, check the box that describes your investment in this activity (see instructions). • If you checked 32a, enter the loss on both **Form 1040, line 12,** (or **Form 1040NR, line 13**) and on **Schedule SE, line 2.** (If you checked the box on line 1, see the line 31 instructions). Estates and trusts, enter on **Form 1041, line 3.** • If you checked 32b, you **must** attach **Form 6198.** Your loss may be limited.	**32a** ☐ All investment is at risk. **32b** ☐ Some investment is not at risk.

For Paperwork Reduction Act Notice, see the separate instructions.   Cat. No. 11334P   **Schedule C (Form 1040) 2016**

Schedule C (Form 1040) 2016   Page **2**

Part III	**Cost of Goods Sold** (see instructions)

33 Method(s) used to
value closing inventory: **a** ☐ Cost   **b** ☐ Lower of cost or market   **c** ☐ Other (attach explanation)

34 Was there any change in determining quantities, costs, or valuations between opening and closing inventory?
If "Yes," attach explanation . . . .   ☐ **Yes**   ☐ **No**

35	Inventory at beginning of year. If different from last year's closing inventory, attach explanation . . .	**35**
36	Purchases less cost of items withdrawn for personal use	**36**
37	Cost of labor. Do not include any amounts paid to yourself	**37**
38	Materials and supplies	**38**
39	Other costs	**39**
40	Add lines 35 through 39	**40**
41	Inventory at end of year	**41**
42	**Cost of goods sold.** Subtract line 41 from line 40. Enter the result here and on line 4	**42**

Part IV	**Information on Your Vehicle.** Complete this part **only** if you are claiming car or truck expenses on line 9 and are not required to file Form 4562 for this business. See the instructions for line 13 to find out if you must file Form 4562.

43 When did you place your vehicle in service for business purposes? (month, day, year) ▶ _____ / _____ / _____

44 Of the total number of miles you drove your vehicle during 2016, enter the number of miles you used your vehicle for:

a Business _____   **b** Commuting (see instructions) _____   **c** Other _____

45 Was your vehicle available for personal use during off-duty hours? . . . .   ☐ **Yes**   ☐ **No**

46 Do you (or your spouse) have another vehicle available for personal use?. . . . .   ☐ **Yes**   ☐ **No**

47a Do you have evidence to support your deduction? . . . .   ☐ **Yes**   ☐ **No**

  b If "Yes," is the evidence written? . . . .   ☐ **Yes**   ☐ **No**

Part V	**Other Expenses.** List below business expenses not included on lines 8–26 or line 30.

------------------------	
48 **Total other expenses.** Enter here and on line 27a	**48**

Schedule C (Form 1040) 2016

SCHEDULE D
(Form 1040)

Department of the Treasury
Internal Revenue Service (99)

Capital Gains and Losses

► **Attach to Form 1040 or Form 1040NR.**
► **Information about Schedule D and its separate instructions is at** *www.irs.gov/scheduled.*
► **Use Form 8949 to list your transactions for lines 1b, 2, 3, 8b, 9, and 10.**

OMB No. 1545-0074

2016

Attachment
Sequence No. **12**

Name(s) shown on return

Your social security number

Part I Short-Term Capital Gains and Losses—Assets Held One Year or Less

See instructions for how to figure the amounts to enter on the lines below. This form may be easier to complete if you round off cents to whole dollars.	**(d)** Proceeds (sales price)	**(e)** Cost (or other basis)	**(g)** Adjustments to gain or loss from Form(s) 8949, Part I, line 2, column (g)	**(h) Gain or (loss)** Subtract column (e) from column (d) and combine the result with column (g)
1a Totals for all short-term transactions reported on Form 1099-B for which basis was reported to the IRS and for which you have no adjustments (see instructions). However, if you choose to report all these transactions on Form 8949, leave this line blank and go to line 1b .				
1b Totals for all transactions reported on Form(s) 8949 with **Box A** checked				
2 Totals for all transactions reported on Form(s) 8949 with **Box B** checked				
3 Totals for all transactions reported on Form(s) 8949 with **Box C** checked				

4 Short-term gain from Form 6252 and short-term gain or (loss) from Forms 4684, 6781, and 8824 .	**4**	
5 Net short-term gain or (loss) from partnerships, S corporations, estates, and trusts from Schedule(s) K-1	**5**	
6 Short-term capital loss carryover. Enter the amount, if any, from line 8 of your **Capital Loss Carryover Worksheet** in the instructions	**6** (	)
7 **Net short-term capital gain or (loss).** Combine lines 1a through 6 in column (h). If you have any long-term capital gains or losses, go to Part II below. Otherwise, go to Part III on the back	**7**	

Part II Long-Term Capital Gains and Losses—Assets Held More Than One Year

See instructions for how to figure the amounts to enter on the lines below. This form may be easier to complete if you round off cents to whole dollars.	**(d)** Proceeds (sales price)	**(e)** Cost (or other basis)	**(g)** Adjustments to gain or loss from Form(s) 8949, Part II, line 2, column (g)	**(h) Gain or (loss)** Subtract column (e) from column (d) and combine the result with column (g)
8a Totals for all long-term transactions reported on Form 1099-B for which basis was reported to the IRS and for which you have no adjustments (see instructions). However, if you choose to report all these transactions on Form 8949, leave this line blank and go to line 8b .				
8b Totals for all transactions reported on Form(s) 8949 with **Box D** checked				
9 Totals for all transactions reported on Form(s) 8949 with **Box E** checked				
10 Totals for all transactions reported on Form(s) 8949 with **Box F** checked.				

11 Gain from Form 4797, Part I; long-term gain from Forms 2439 and 6252; and long-term gain or (loss) from Forms 4684, 6781, and 8824	**11**	
12 Net long-term gain or (loss) from partnerships, S corporations, estates, and trusts from Schedule(s) K-1	**12**	
13 Capital gain distributions. See the instructions	**13**	
14 Long-term capital loss carryover. Enter the amount, if any, from line 13 of your **Capital Loss Carryover Worksheet** in the instructions	**14** (	)
15 **Net long-term capital gain or (loss).** Combine lines 8a through 14 in column (h). Then go to Part III on the back	**15**	

For Paperwork Reduction Act Notice, see your tax return instructions.   Cat. No. 11338H   Schedule D (Form 1040) 2016

Schedule D (Form 1040) 2016   Page **2**

Part III	**Summary**

16 Combine lines 7 and 15 and enter the result **16**

- If line 16 is a **gain,** enter the amount from line 16 on Form 1040, line 13, or Form 1040NR, line 14. Then go to line 17 below.
- If line 16 is a **loss,** skip lines 17 through 20 below. Then go to line 21. Also be sure to complete line 22.
- If line 16 is **zero,** skip lines 17 through 21 below and enter -0- on Form 1040, line 13, or Form 1040NR, line 14. Then go to line 22.

17 Are lines 15 and 16 **both** gains?
☐ **Yes.** Go to line 18.
☐ **No.** Skip lines 18 through 21, and go to line 22.

18 Enter the amount, if any, from line 7 of the **28% Rate Gain Worksheet** in the instructions . . ▶ **18**

19 Enter the amount, if any, from line 18 of the **Unrecaptured Section 1250 Gain Worksheet** in the instructions . . . . ▶ **19**

20 Are lines 18 and 19 **both** zero or blank?
☐ **Yes.** Complete the **Qualified Dividends and Capital Gain Tax Worksheet** in the instructions for Form 1040, line 44 (or in the instructions for Form 1040NR, line 42). **Don't** complete lines 21 and 22 below.

☐ **No.** Complete the **Schedule D Tax Worksheet** in the instructions. **Don't** complete lines 21 and 22 below.

21 If line 16 is a loss, enter here and on Form 1040, line 13, or Form 1040NR, line 14, the **smaller** of:

- The loss on line 16 or
- ($3,000), or if married filing separately, ($1,500) } . . . . **21** ( )

Note: When figuring which amount is smaller, treat both amounts as positive numbers.

22 Do you have qualified dividends on Form 1040, line 9b, or Form 1040NR, line 10b?

☐ **Yes.** Complete the **Qualified Dividends and Capital Gain Tax Worksheet** in the instructions for Form 1040, line 44 (or in the instructions for Form 1040NR, line 42).

☐ **No.** Complete the rest of Form 1040 or Form 1040NR.

Schedule D (Form 1040) 2016

SCHEDULE E (Form 1040) Department of the Treasury Internal Revenue Service (99)	**Supplemental Income and Loss** (From rental real estate, royalties, partnerships, S corporations, estates, trusts, REMICs, etc.) ▶ Attach to Form 1040, 1040NR, or Form 1041. ▶ Information about Schedule E and its separate instructions is at *www.irs.gov/schedulee.*	OMB No. 1545-0074 20**16** Attachment Sequence No. **13**

Name(s) shown on return | Your social security number

Part I   **Income or Loss From Rental Real Estate and Royalties**   **Note:** If you are in the business of renting personal property, use **Schedule C** or **C-EZ** (see instructions). If you are an individual, report farm rental income or loss from **Form 4835** on page 2, line 40.

A Did you make any payments in 2016 that would require you to file Form(s) 1099? (see instructions)   ☐ Yes   ☐ No

B If "Yes," did you or will you file required Forms 1099?   ☐ Yes   ☐ No

1a Physical address of each property (street, city, state, ZIP code)

A

B

C

1b	Type of Property (from list below)	**2**	For each rental real estate property listed above, report the number of fair rental and personal use days. Check the **QJV** box only if you meet the requirements to file as a qualified joint venture. See instructions.		Fair Rental Days	Personal Use Days	QJV
A				A			☐
B				B			☐
C				C			☐

Type of Property:

1 Single Family Residence   3 Vacation/Short-Term Rental   5 Land   7 Self-Rental

2 Multi-Family Residence   4 Commercial   6 Royalties   8 Other (describe)

Income:	**Properties:**		A	B	C
3 Rents received	**3**				
4 Royalties received	**4**				
Expenses:					
5 Advertising	**5**				
6 Auto and travel (see instructions)	**6**				
7 Cleaning and maintenance	**7**				
8 Commissions.	**8**				
9 Insurance	**9**				
10 Legal and other professional fees	**10**				
11 Management fees	**11**				
12 Mortgage interest paid to banks, etc. (see instructions)	**12**				
13 Other interest.	**13**				
14 Repairs.	**14**				
15 Supplies	**15**				
16 Taxes	**16**				
17 Utilities	**17**				
18 Depreciation expense or depletion	**18**				
19 Other (list) ▶ _____	**19**				
20 Total expenses. Add lines 5 through 19	**20**				
21 Subtract line 20 from line 3 (rents) and/or 4 (royalties). If result is a (loss), see instructions to find out if you must file **Form 6198**	**21**				
22 Deductible rental real estate loss after limitation, if any, on **Form 8582** (see instructions)	**22**	(	)(	)(	)

23a	Total of all amounts reported on line 3 for all rental properties	**23a**	
b	Total of all amounts reported on line 4 for all royalty properties	**23b**	
c	Total of all amounts reported on line 12 for all properties	**23c**	
d	Total of all amounts reported on line 18 for all properties	**23d**	
e	Total of all amounts reported on line 20 for all properties	**23e**	

24   **Income.** Add positive amounts shown on line 21. **Do not** include any losses . . . . | **24** | |

25   **Losses.** Add royalty losses from line 21 and rental real estate losses from line 22. Enter total losses here | **25** (|) |

26   **Total rental real estate and royalty income or (loss).** Combine lines 24 and 25. Enter the result here. If Parts II, III, IV, and line 40 on page 2 do not apply to you, also enter this amount on Form 1040, line 17, or Form 1040NR, line 18. Otherwise, include this amount in the total on line 41 on page 2 . . . | **26** | |

For Paperwork Reduction Act Notice, see the separate instructions.   Cat. No. 11344L   Schedule E (Form 1040) 2016

Schedule E (Form 1040) 2016

Attachment Sequence No. **13**   Page **2**

Name(s) shown on return. Do not enter name and social security number if shown on other side.	Your social security number

Caution: The IRS compares amounts reported on your tax return with amounts shown on Schedule(s) K-1.

Part II   **Income or Loss From Partnerships and S Corporations**   **Note:** If you report a loss from an at-risk activity for which **any** amount is **not** at risk, you **must** check the box in column **(e)** on line 28 and attach **Form 6198.** See instructions.

27   Are you reporting any loss not allowed in a prior year due to the at-risk, excess farm loss, or basis limitations, a prior year unallowed loss from a passive activity (if that loss was not reported on Form 8582), or unreimbursed partnership expenses? If you answered "Yes," see instructions before completing this section.   ☐ **Yes**   ☐ **No**

28	**(a)** Name	**(b)** Enter **P** for partnership; **S** for S corporation	**(c)** Check if foreign partnership	**(d)** Employer identification number	**(e)** Check if any amount is not at risk
A			☐		☐
B			☐		☐
C			☐		☐
D			☐		☐

	Passive Income and Loss		Nonpassive Income and Loss		
	(f) Passive loss allowed (attach **Form 8582** if required)	**(g)** Passive income from **Schedule K-1**	**(h)** Nonpassive loss from **Schedule K-1**	**(i)** Section 179 expense deduction from **Form 4562**	**(j)** Nonpassive income from **Schedule K-1**
A					
B					
C					
D					
29a Totals					
b Totals					

30	Add columns (g) and (j) of line 29a	30	
31	Add columns (f), (h), and (i) of line 29b	31	( )
32	**Total partnership and S corporation income or (loss).** Combine lines 30 and 31. Enter the result here and include in the total on line 41 below	32	

Part III   **Income or Loss From Estates and Trusts**

33	**(a)** Name	**(b)** Employer identification number
A		
B		

	Passive Income and Loss		Nonpassive Income and Loss	
	(c) Passive deduction or loss allowed (attach **Form 8582** if required)	**(d)** Passive income from **Schedule K-1**	**(e)** Deduction or loss from **Schedule K-1**	**(f)** Other income from **Schedule K-1**
A				
B				
34a Totals				
b Totals				

35	Add columns (d) and (f) of line 34a	35	
36	Add columns (c) and (e) of line 34b	36	( )
37	**Total estate and trust income or (loss).** Combine lines 35 and 36. Enter the result here and include in the total on line 41 below	37	

Part IV   **Income or Loss From Real Estate Mortgage Investment Conduits (REMICs)—Residual Holder**

38	**(a)** Name	**(b)** Employer identification number	**(c)** Excess inclusion from **Schedules Q,** line 2c (see instructions)	**(d)** Taxable income (net loss) from **Schedules Q,** line 1b	**(e)** Income from **Schedules Q,** line 3b

| 39 | Combine columns (d) and (e) only. Enter the result here and include in the total on line 41 below | 39 | |

Part V   **Summary**

| 40 | Net farm rental income or (loss) from **Form 4835.** Also, complete line 42 below . . . . . . | 40 | |
| 41 | **Total income or (loss).** Combine lines 26, 32, 37, 39, and 40. Enter the result here and on Form 1040, line 17, or Form 1040NR, line 18 ▶ | 41 | |

42   **Reconciliation of farming and fishing income.** Enter your **gross** farming and fishing income reported on Form 4835, line 7; Schedule K-1 (Form 1065), box 14, code B; Schedule K-1 (Form 1120S), box 17, code V; and Schedule K-1 (Form 1041), box 14, code F (see instructions) . .   **42**

43   **Reconciliation for real estate professionals.** If you were a real estate professional (see instructions), enter the net income or (loss) you reported anywhere on Form 1040 or Form 1040NR from all rental real estate activities in which you materially participated under the passive activity loss rules . .   **43**

Schedule E (Form 1040) 2016

| SCHEDULE F
(Form 1040)

Department of the Treasury
Internal Revenue Service (99) | **Profit or Loss From Farming**

▶ Attach to Form 1040, Form 1040NR, Form 1041, Form 1065, or Form 1065-B.
▶ Information about Schedule F and its separate instructions is at *www.irs.gov/schedulef*. | OMB No. 1545-0074
2016
Attachment
Sequence No. **14** |

| Name of proprietor | Social security number (SSN) |

| **A** Principal crop or activity | **B** Enter code from Part IV
▶ | **C** Accounting method:
☐ Cash ☐ Accrual | **D** Employer ID number (EIN), (see instr) |

E Did you "materially participate" in the operation of this business during 2016? If "No," see instructions for limit on passive losses ☐ Yes ☐ No

F Did you make any payments in 2016 that would require you to file Form(s) 1099 (see instructions)? . . . . ☐ Yes ☐ No

G If "Yes," did you or will you file required Forms 1099? . . . . ☐ Yes ☐ No

Part I — Farm Income—Cash Method. Complete Parts I and II (Accrual method. Complete Parts II and III, and Part I, line 9.)

1a	Sales of livestock and other resale items (see instructions)	**1a**		
b	Cost or other basis of livestock or other items reported on line 1a . . .	**1b**		
c	Subtract line 1b from line 1a		**1c**	
2	Sales of livestock, produce, grains, and other products you raised		**2**	
3a	Cooperative distributions (Form(s) 1099-PATR) .	**3a**	**3b** Taxable amount	**3b**	
4a	Agricultural program payments (see instructions) .	**4a**	**4b** Taxable amount	**4b**	
5a	Commodity Credit Corporation (CCC) loans reported under election		**5a**	
b	CCC loans forfeited	**5b**	**5c** Taxable amount	**5c**	
6	Crop insurance proceeds and federal crop disaster payments (see instructions)			
a	Amount received in 2016	**6a**	**6b** Taxable amount	**6b**	
c	If election to defer to 2017 is attached, check here ▶ ☐	**6d** Amount deferred from 2015	**6d**	
7	Custom hire (machine work) income		**7**	
8	Other income, including federal and state gasoline or fuel tax credit or refund (see instructions)		**8**	
9	**Gross income.** Add amounts in the right column (lines 1c, 2, 3b, 4b, 5a, 5c, 6b, 6d, 7, and 8). If you use the accrual method, enter the amount from Part III, line 50 (see instructions) . . . . ▶		**9**	

Part II — Farm Expenses—Cash and Accrual Method. Do not include personal or living expenses (see instructions).

10	Car and truck expenses (see instructions). Also attach **Form 4562**	**10**		**23**	Pension and profit-sharing plans	**23**	
11	Chemicals	**11**		**24**	Rent or lease (see instructions):		
12	Conservation expenses (see instructions)	**12**		**a**	Vehicles, machinery, equipment	**24a**	
13	Custom hire (machine work) .	**13**		**b**	Other (land, animals, etc.) . .	**24b**	
14	Depreciation and section 179 expense (see instructions) .	**14**		**25**	Repairs and maintenance . .	**25**	
				26	Seeds and plants	**26**	
15	Employee benefit programs other than on line 23 . . .	**15**		**27**	Storage and warehousing . .	**27**	
16	Feed	**16**		**28**	Supplies	**28**	
17	Fertilizers and lime . . .	**17**		**29**	Taxes	**29**	
18	Freight and trucking . . .	**18**		**30**	Utilities	**30**	
19	Gasoline, fuel, and oil . . .	**19**		**31**	Veterinary, breeding, and medicine	**31**	
20	Insurance (other than health) .	**20**		**32**	Other expenses (specify):		
21	Interest:			**a**	_____	**32a**	
a	Mortgage (paid to banks, etc.) .	**21a**		**b**	_____	**32b**	
b	Other	**21b**		**c**	_____	**32c**	
22	Labor hired (less employment credits)	**22**		**d**	_____	**32d**	
				e	_____	**32e**	
				f	_____	**32f**	

33	**Total expenses.** Add lines 10 through 32f. If line 32f is negative, see instructions . . . . ▶	**33**	
34	**Net farm profit or (loss).** Subtract line 33 from line 9	**34**	

If a profit, stop here and see instructions for where to report. If a loss, complete lines 35 and 36.

35 Did you receive an applicable subsidy in 2016? (see instructions) . . . . ☐ Yes ☐ No

36 Check the box that describes your investment in this activity and see instructions for where to report your loss.

a ☐ All investment is at risk. **b** ☐ Some investment is not at risk.

For Paperwork Reduction Act Notice, see the separate instructions.   Cat. No. 11346H   Schedule F (Form 1040) 2016

Schedule F (Form 1040) 2016   Page **2**

Part III   Farm Income—Accrual Method (see instructions).

37	Sales of livestock, produce, grains, and other products (see instructions)	**37**	
38a	Cooperative distributions (Form(s) 1099-PATR) .	**38a** [____] **38b** Taxable amount	**38b**	
39a	Agricultural program payments	**39a** [____] **39b** Taxable amount	**39b**	
40	Commodity Credit Corporation (CCC) loans:		
a	CCC loans reported under election	**40a**	
b	CCC loans forfeited	**40b** [____] **40c** Taxable amount	**40c**	
41	Crop insurance proceeds	**41**	
42	Custom hire (machine work) income	**42**	
43	Other income (see instructions)	**43**	
44	Add amounts in the right column for lines 37 through 43 (lines 37, 38b, 39b, 40a, 40c, 41, 42, and 43) . .	**44**	
45	Inventory of livestock, produce, grains, and other products at beginning of the year. Do not include sales reported on Form 4797	**45**		
46	Cost of livestock, produce, grains, and other products purchased during the year	**46**		
47	Add lines 45 and 46	**47**		
48	Inventory of livestock, produce, grains, and other products at end of year .	**48**		
49	Cost of livestock, produce, grains, and other products sold. Subtract line 48 from line 47*	**49**	
50	**Gross income.** Subtract line 49 from line 44. Enter the result here and on Part I, line 9 . . . . . ▶	**50**	

*If you use the unit-livestock-price method or the farm-price method of valuing inventory and the amount on line 48 is larger than the amount on line 47, subtract line 47 from line 48. Enter the result on line 49. Add lines 44 and 49. Enter the total on line 50 and on Part I, line 9.

Part IV   Principal Agricultural Activity Codes

⚠ CAUTION

Do not file Schedule F (Form 1040) to report the following.

• *Income from providing agricultural services such as soil preparation, veterinary, farm labor, horticultural, or management for a fee or on a contract basis. Instead file Schedule C (Form 1040) or Schedule C-EZ (Form 1040).*

• *Income from breeding, raising, or caring for dogs, cats, or other pet animals. Instead file Schedule C (Form 1040) or Schedule C-EZ (Form 1040).*

• *Sales of livestock held for draft, breeding, sport, or dairy purposes. Instead file Form 4797.*

These codes for the Principal Agricultural Activity classify farms by their primary activity to facilitate the administration of the Internal Revenue Code. These six-digit codes are based on the North American Industry Classification System (NAICS).

Select the code that best identifies your primary farming activity and enter the six-digit number on line B.

Crop Production
111100   Oilseed and grain farming
111210   Vegetable and melon farming
111300   Fruit and tree nut farming
111400   Greenhouse, nursery, and floriculture production
111900   Other crop farming

Animal Production
112111   Beef cattle ranching and farming
112112   Cattle feedlots
112120   Dairy cattle and milk production
112210   Hog and pig farming
112300   Poultry and egg production
112400   Sheep and goat farming
112510   Aquaculture
112900   Other animal production

Forestry and Logging
113000   Forestry and logging (including forest nurseries and timber tracts)

Schedule F (Form 1040) 2016

**Schedule R
(Form 1040A
or 1040)**

Department of the Treasury
Internal Revenue Service (99)

Credit for the Elderly or the Disabled

▶ Complete and attach to **Form 1040A or 1040.**
▶ Information about Schedule R and its separate instructions is at
www.irs.gov/scheduler.

OMB No. 1545-0074

20**16**

Attachment
Sequence No. **16**

Name(s) shown on Form 1040A or 1040

Your social security number

You may be able to take this credit and reduce your tax if by the end of 2016:
- You were age 65 or older **or** • You were under age 65, you retired on **permanent and total** disability, and you received taxable disability income.

But you must also meet other tests. See instructions.

TIP In most cases, the IRS can figure the credit for you. See instructions.

Part I	**Check the Box for Your Filing Status and Age**		
If your filing status is:	**And by the end of 2016:**		**Check only one box:**

Single, Head of household, or Qualifying widow(er)	**1** You were 65 or older	**1**	☐
	2 You were under 65 and you retired on permanent and total disability . .	**2**	☐
Married filing jointly	**3** Both spouses were 65 or older	**3**	☐
	4 Both spouses were under 65, but only one spouse retired on permanent and total disability	**4**	☐
	5 Both spouses were under 65, and both retired on permanent and total disability	**5**	☐
	6 One spouse was 65 or older, and the other spouse was under 65 and retired on permanent and total disability	**6**	☐
	7 One spouse was 65 or older, and the other spouse was under 65 and **not** retired on permanent and total disability	**7**	☐
Married filing separately	**8** You were 65 or older and you lived apart from your spouse for all of 2016 .	**8**	☐
	9 You were under 65, you retired on permanent and total disability, and you lived apart from your spouse for all of 2016	**9**	☐

Did you check box 1, 3, 7, or 8? ──── **Yes** ──▶ Skip Part II and complete Part III on the back.
──── **No** ──▶ Complete Parts II and III.

Part II	**Statement of Permanent and Total Disability** (Complete **only** if you checked box 2, 4, 5, 6, or 9 above.)

If: **1** You filed a physician's statement for this disability for 1983 or an earlier year, or you filed or got a statement for tax years after 1983 and your physician signed line B on the statement, **and**

2 Due to your continued disabled condition, you were unable to engage in any substantial gainful activity in 2016, check this box . . . . ▶ ☐

- If you checked this box, you don't have to get another statement for 2016.

- If you **didn't** check this box, have your physician complete the statement in the instructions. You **must** keep the statement for your records.

For Paperwork Reduction Act Notice, see your tax return instructions. Cat. No. 11359K **Schedule R (Form 1040A or 1040) 2016**

Schedule R (Form 1040A or 1040) 2016   Page **2**

Part III	Figure Your Credit	

10 If you checked (in Part I):   Enter:
  Box 1, 2, 4, or 7 . . . .$5,000
  Box 3, 5, or 6 . . . .$7,500 } **10**
  Box 8 or 9 . . . .$3,750

> | Did you check box 2, 4, 5, 6, or 9 in Part I? | → Yes → | You **must** complete line 11. |
> | | → No → | Enter the amount from line 10 on line 12 and go to line 13. |

11 If you checked (in Part I):
  • Box 6, add $5,000 to the taxable disability income of the spouse who was under age 65. Enter the total.
  • Box 2, 4, or 9, enter your taxable disability income.   } **11**
  • Box 5, add your taxable disability income to your spouse's taxable disability income. Enter the total.

(TIP) For more details on what to include on line 11, see *Figure Your Credit* in the instructions.

12 If you completed line 11, enter the **smaller** of line 10 or line 11. **All others,** enter the amount from line 10 . . . .   **12**

13 Enter the following pensions, annuities, or disability income that you (and your spouse if filing jointly) received in 2016.

  a Nontaxable part of social security benefits and nontaxable part of railroad retirement benefits treated as social security (see instructions). **13a**

  b Nontaxable veterans' pensions and any other pension, annuity, or disability benefit that is excluded from income under any other provision of law (see instructions). **13b**

  c Add lines 13a and 13b. (Even though these income items aren't taxable, they **must** be included here to figure your credit.) If you didn't receive any of the types of nontaxable income listed on line 13a or 13b, enter -0- on line 13c **13c**

14 Enter the amount from Form 1040A, line 22, or Form 1040, line 38 . . . . .   **14**

15 If you checked (in Part I):   Enter:
  Box 1 or 2 . . . . . . $7,500
  Box 3, 4, 5, 6, or 7 . . . $10,000 }   **15**
  Box 8 or 9 . . . . . . $5,000

16 Subtract line 15 from line 14. If zero or less, enter -0- **16**

17 Enter one-half of line 16 . . . .   **17**

18 Add lines 13c and 17 . . . .   **18**

19 Subtract line 18 from line 12. If zero or less, **stop;** you **can't** take the credit. Otherwise, go to line 20 . . . .   **19**

20 Multiply line 19 by 15% (0.15) **20**

21 Tax liability limit. Enter the amount from the Credit Limit Worksheet in the instructions .   **21**

22 **Credit for the elderly or the disabled.** Enter the **smaller** of line 20 or line 21. Also enter this amount on Form 1040A, line 32, or include on Form 1040, line 54 (check box **c** and enter "Sch R" on the line next to that box) **22**

                                                                    Schedule R (Form 1040A or 1040) 2016

SCHEDULE SE (Form 1040)	Self-Employment Tax	OMB No. 1545-0074
Department of the Treasury Internal Revenue Service (99)	▶ Information about Schedule SE and its separate instructions is at *www.irs.gov/schedulese*. ▶ **Attach to Form 1040 or Form 1040NR.**	20**16** Attachment Sequence No. **17**

Name of person with **self-employment** income (as shown on Form 1040 or Form 1040NR)	Social security number of person with **self-employment** income ▶

Before you begin: To determine if you must file Schedule SE, see the instructions.

May I Use Short Schedule SE or Must I Use Long Schedule SE?

Note. Use this flowchart **only if** you must file Schedule SE. If unsure, see *Who Must File Schedule SE* in the instructions.

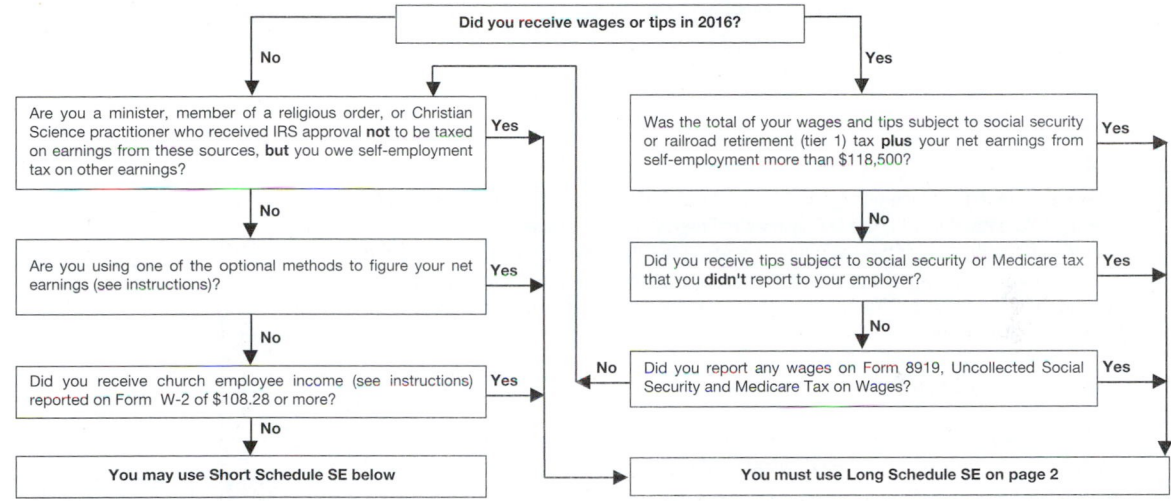

Section A—Short Schedule SE. **Caution.** Read above to see if you can use Short Schedule SE.

1a	Net farm profit or (loss) from Schedule F, line 34, and farm partnerships, Schedule K-1 (Form 1065), box 14, code A	**1a**
b	If you received social security retirement or disability benefits, enter the amount of Conservation Reserve Program payments included on Schedule F, line 4b, or listed on Schedule K-1 (Form 1065), box 20, code Z	**1b** ( )
2	Net profit or (loss) from Schedule C, line 31; Schedule C-EZ, line 3; Schedule K-1 (Form 1065), box 14, code A (other than farming); and Schedule K-1 (Form 1065-B), box 9, code J1. Ministers and members of religious orders, see instructions for types of income to report on this line. See instructions for other income to report	**2**
3	Combine lines 1a, 1b, and 2	**3**
4	Multiply line 3 by 92.35% (0.9235). If less than $400, you don't owe self-employment tax; **don't** file this schedule unless you have an amount on line 1b . . . . ▶	**4**
	Note. If line 4 is less than $400 due to Conservation Reserve Program payments on line 1b, see instructions.	
5	**Self-employment tax.** If the amount on line 4 is: • $118,500 or less, multiply line 4 by 15.3% (0.153). Enter the result here and on **Form 1040, line 57,** or **Form 1040NR, line 55** • More than $118,500, multiply line 4 by 2.9% (0.029). Then, add $14,694 to the result. Enter the total here and on **Form 1040, line 57,** or **Form 1040NR, line 55**	**5**
6	**Deduction for one-half of self-employment tax.** Multiply line 5 by 50% (0.50). Enter the result here and on **Form 1040, line 27,** or **Form 1040NR, line 27**	**6**	

For Paperwork Reduction Act Notice, see your tax return instructions.   Cat. No. 11358Z   Schedule SE (Form 1040) 2016

Schedule SE (Form 1040) 2016   Attachment Sequence No. **17**   Page **2**

Name of person with **self-employment** income (as shown on Form 1040 or Form 1040NR)	Social security number of person with **self-employment** income ▶

Section B—Long Schedule SE

Part I Self-Employment Tax

Note. If your only income subject to self-employment tax is **church employee income,** see instructions. Also see instructions for the definition of church employee income.

A If you are a minister, member of a religious order, or Christian Science practitioner **and** you filed Form 4361, but you had $400 or more of **other** net earnings from self-employment, check here and continue with Part I . . . . ▶ ☐

1a	Net farm profit or (loss) from Schedule F, line 34, and farm partnerships, Schedule K-1 (Form 1065), box 14, code A. **Note.** Skip lines 1a and 1b if you use the farm optional method (see instructions)	**1a**	
b	If you received social security retirement or disability benefits, enter the amount of Conservation Reserve Program payments included on Schedule F, line 4b, or listed on Schedule K-1 (Form 1065), box 20, code Z	**1b** (	)
2	Net profit or (loss) from Schedule C, line 31; Schedule C-EZ, line 3; Schedule K-1 (Form 1065), box 14, code A (other than farming); and Schedule K-1 (Form 1065-B), box 9, code J1. Ministers and members of religious orders, see instructions for types of income to report on this line. See instructions for other income to report. **Note.** Skip this line if you use the nonfarm optional method (see instructions)	**2**	
3	Combine lines 1a, 1b, and 2	**3**	
4a	If line 3 is more than zero, multiply line 3 by 92.35% (0.9235). Otherwise, enter amount from line 3	**4a**	
	Note. If line 4a is less than $400 due to Conservation Reserve Program payments on line 1b, see instructions.		
b	If you elect one or both of the optional methods, enter the total of lines 15 and 17 here . .	**4b**	
c	Combine lines 4a and 4b. If less than $400, **stop;** you do not owe self-employment tax. **Exception.** If less than $400 and you had **church employee income,** enter -0- and continue ▶	**4c**	
5a	Enter your **church employee income** from Form W-2. See instructions for definition of church employee income . . .	**5a**		
b	Multiply line 5a by 92.35% (0.9235). If less than $100, enter -0-	**5b**	
6	Add lines 4c and 5b	**6**	
7	Maximum amount of combined wages and self-employment earnings subject to social security tax or the 6.2% portion of the 7.65% railroad retirement (tier 1) tax for 2016	**7**	118,500 00
8a	Total social security wages and tips (total of boxes 3 and 7 on Form(s) W-2) and railroad retirement (tier 1) compensation. If $118,500 or more, skip lines 8b through 10, and go to line 11	**8a**	
b	Unreported tips subject to social security tax (from Form 4137, line 10)	**8b**	
c	Wages subject to social security tax (from Form 8919, line 10)	**8c**	
d	Add lines 8a, 8b, and 8c	**8d**	
9	Subtract line 8d from line 7. If zero or less, enter -0- here and on line 10 and go to line 11 . ▶	**9**	
10	Multiply the **smaller** of line 6 or line 9 by 12.4% (0.124)	**10**	
11	Multiply line 6 by 2.9% (0.029)	**11**	
12	**Self-employment tax.** Add lines 10 and 11. Enter here and on **Form 1040, line 57,** or **Form 1040NR, line 55**	**12**	
13	**Deduction for one-half of self-employment tax.** Multiply line 12 by 50% (0.50). Enter the result here and on **Form 1040, line 27,** or **Form 1040NR, line 27**	**13**	

Part II Optional Methods To Figure Net Earnings (see instructions)

Farm Optional Method. You may use this method **only** if **(a)** your gross farm income[1] was not more than $7,560, **or (b)** your net farm profits[2] were less than $5,457.

14	Maximum income for optional methods	**14**	5,040 00
15	Enter the **smaller** of: two-thirds (2/3) of gross farm income[1] (not less than zero) **or** $5,040. Also include this amount on line 4b above	**15**	

Nonfarm Optional Method. You may use this method **only** if **(a)** your net nonfarm profits[3] were less than $5,457 and also less than 72.189% of your gross nonfarm income,[4] **and (b)** you had net earnings from self-employment of at least $400 in 2 of the prior 3 years. **Caution.** You may use this method no more than five times.

16	Subtract line 15 from line 14	**16**	
17	Enter the **smaller** of: two-thirds (2/3) of gross nonfarm income[4] (not less than zero) **or** the amount on line 16. Also include this amount on line 4b above	**17**	

[1] From Sch. F, line 9, and Sch. K-1 (Form 1065), box 14, code B.
[2] From Sch. F, line 34, and Sch. K-1 (Form 1065), box 14, code A—minus the amount you would have entered on line 1b had you not used the optional method.
[3] From Sch. C, line 31; Sch. C-EZ, line 3; Sch. K-1 (Form 1065), box 14, code A; and Sch. K-1 (Form 1065-B), box 9, code J1.
[4] From Sch. C, line 7; Sch. C-EZ, line 1; Sch. K-1 (Form 1065), box 14, code C; and Sch. K-1 (Form 1065-B), box 9, code J2.

Schedule SE (Form 1040) 2016

SCHEDULE EIC
(Form 1040A or 1040)

Department of the Treasury
Internal Revenue Service (99)

Earned Income Credit

Qualifying Child Information

1040A
1040
EIC

▶ Complete and attach to Form 1040A or 1040 only if you have a qualifying child.
▶ Information about Schedule EIC (Form 1040A or 1040) and its instructions is at *www.irs.gov/scheduleeic.*

OMB No. 1545-0074

2016

Attachment
Sequence No. **43**

Name(s) shown on return

Your social security number

Before you begin:
- See the instructions for Form 1040A, lines 42a and 42b, or Form 1040, lines 66a and 66b, to make sure that **(a)** you can take the EIC, and **(b)** you have a qualifying child.
- Be sure the child's name on line 1 and social security number (SSN) on line 2 agree with the child's social security card. Otherwise, at the time we process your return, we may reduce or disallow your EIC. If the name or SSN on the child's social security card is not correct, call the Social Security Administration at 1-800-772-1213.

! CAUTION
- *You can't claim the EIC for a child who didn't live with you for more than half of the year.*
- *If you take the EIC even though you are not eligible, you may not be allowed to take the credit for up to 10 years. See the instructions for details.*
- *It will take us longer to process your return and issue your refund if you do not fill in all lines that apply for each qualifying child.*

Qualifying Child Information	Child 1		Child 2		Child 3	
1 Child's name If you have more than three qualifying children, you have to list only three to get the maximum credit.	First name	Last name	First name	Last name	First name	Last name
2 Child's SSN The child must have an SSN as defined in the instructions for Form 1040A, lines 42a and 42b, or Form 1040, lines 66a and 66b, unless the child was born and died in 2016. If your child was born and died in 2016 and did not have an SSN, enter "Died" on this line and attach a copy of the child's birth certificate, death certificate, or hospital medical records.						
3 Child's year of birth	Year ___ ___ ___ *If born after 1997 **and** the child is younger than you (or your spouse, if filing jointly), skip lines 4a and 4b; go to line 5.*		Year ___ ___ ___ *If born after 1997 **and** the child is younger than you (or your spouse, if filing jointly), skip lines 4a and 4b; go to line 5.*		Year ___ ___ ___ *If born after 1997 **and** the child is younger than you (or your spouse, if filing jointly), skip lines 4a and 4b; go to line 5.*	
4 a Was the child under age 24 at the end of 2016, a student, and younger than you (or your spouse, if filing jointly)?	☐ **Yes.** *Go to line 5.*	☐ **No.** *Go to line 4b.*	☐ **Yes.** *Go to line 5.*	☐ **No.** *Go to line 4b.*	☐ **Yes.** *Go to line 5.*	☐ **No.** *Go to line 4b.*
b Was the child permanently and totally disabled during any part of 2016?	☐ **Yes.** *Go to line 5.*	☐ **No.** The child is not a qualifying child.	☐ **Yes.** *Go to line 5.*	☐ **No.** The child is not a qualifying child.	☐ **Yes.** *Go to line 5.*	☐ **No.** The child is not a qualifying child.
5 Child's relationship to you (for example, son, daughter, grandchild, niece, nephew, foster child, etc.)						
6 Number of months child lived with you in the United States during 2016 • If the child lived with you for more than half of 2016 but less than 7 months, enter "7." • If the child was born or died in 2016 and your home was the child's home for more than half the time he or she was alive during 2016, enter "12."	_____ months *Do not enter more than 12 months.*		_____ months *Do not enter more than 12 months.*		_____ months *Do not enter more than 12 months.*	

For Paperwork Reduction Act Notice, see your tax return instructions.

Cat. No. 13339M

Schedule EIC (Form 1040A or 1040) 2016

Purpose of Schedule

After you have figured your earned income credit (EIC), use Schedule EIC to give the IRS information about your qualifying child(ren).

To figure the amount of your credit or to have the IRS figure it for you, see the instructions for Form 1040A, lines 42a and 42b, or Form 1040, lines 66a and 66b.

Taking the EIC when not eligible. If you take the EIC even though you are not eligible and it is determined that your error is due to reckless or intentional disregard of the EIC rules, you will not be allowed to take the credit for 2 years even if you are otherwise eligible to do so. If you fraudulently take the EIC, you will not be allowed to take the credit for 10 years. You may also have to pay penalties.

Future developments. For the latest information about developments related to Schedule EIC (Form 1040A or 1040) and its instructions, such as legislation enacted after they were published, go to *www.irs.gov/scheduleeic*.

 You may also be able to take the additional child tax credit if your child was your dependent and under age 17 at the end of 2016. For more details, see the instructions for line 43 of Form 1040A or line 67 of Form 1040.

Qualifying Child

A qualifying child for the EIC is a child who is your . . .

Son, daughter, stepchild, foster child, brother, sister, stepbrother, stepsister, half brother, half sister, or a descendant of any of them (for example, your grandchild, niece, or nephew)

was . . .

Under age 19 at the end of 2016 and younger than you (or your spouse, if filing jointly)

or

Under age 24 at the end of 2016, a student, and younger than you (or your spouse, if filing jointly)

or

Any age and permanently and totally disabled

Who is not filing a joint return for 2016
or is filing a joint return for 2016 only to claim
a refund of withheld income tax or estimated tax paid

Who lived with you in the United States for more than half of 2016.

 You can't claim the EIC for a child who didn't live with you for more than half of the year, even if you paid most of the child's living expenses. The IRS may ask you for documents to show you lived with each qualifying child. Documents you might want to keep for this purpose include school and child care records and other records that show your child's address.

 If the child didn't live with you for more than half of the year because of a temporary absence, birth, death, or kidnapping, see Exception to time lived with you *in the instructions for Form 1040A, lines 42a and 42b, or Form 1040, lines 66a and 66b.*

 If the child was married or meets the conditions to be a qualifying child of another person (other than your spouse if filing a joint return), special rules apply. For details, see Married child *or* Qualifying child of more than one person *in the instructions for Form 1040A, lines 42a and 42b, or Form 1040, lines 66a and 66b.*

Form **1040X**
(Rev. January 2016)

Department of the Treasury—Internal Revenue Service

Amended U.S. Individual Income Tax Return

▶ Information about Form 1040X and its separate instructions is at *www.irs.gov/form1040x.*

OMB No. 1545-0074

This return is for calendar year ☐ 2015 ☐ 2014 ☐ 2013 ☐ 2012
Other year. Enter one: calendar year _____ **or** fiscal year (month and year ended): _____

Your first name and initial	Last name	Your social security number
If a joint return, spouse's first name and initial	Last name	Spouse's social security number

Current home address (number and street). If you have a P.O. box, see instructions.	Apt. no.	Your phone number

City, town or post office, state, and ZIP code. If you have a foreign address, also complete spaces below (see instructions).

Foreign country name	Foreign province/state/county	Foreign postal code

Amended return filing status. You **must** check one box even if you are not changing your filing status. **Caution:** In general, you cannot change your filing status from joint to separate returns after the due date.

☐ Single
☐ Married filing jointly
☐ Married filing separately
☐ Head of household (If the qualifying person is a child but not your dependent, see instructions.)
☐ Qualifying widow(er)

Full-year coverage.
If all members of your household have full-year minimal essential health care coverage, check "Yes." Otherwise, check "No." (See instructions.)
☐ Yes ☐ No

Use Part III on the back to explain any changes

			A. Original amount or as previously adjusted (see instructions)	B. Net change— amount of increase or (decrease)— explain in Part III	C. Correct amount
Income and Deductions					
1	Adjusted gross income. If net operating loss (NOL) carryback is included, check here . . . . ▶☐	1			
2	Itemized deductions or standard deduction	2			
3	Subtract line 2 from line 1	3			
4	Exemptions. **If changing, complete Part I on page 2 and enter the amount from line 29**	4			
5	Taxable income. Subtract line 4 from line 3	5			
Tax Liability					
6	Tax. Enter method(s) used to figure tax (see instructions): _____	6			
7	Credits. If general business credit carryback is included, check here . . . . ▶☐	7			
8	Subtract line 7 from line 6. If the result is zero or less, enter -0- . . .	8			
9	Health care: individual responsibility (see instructions)	9			
10	Other taxes	10			
11	Total tax. Add lines 8, 9, and 10	11			
Payments					
12	Federal income tax withheld and excess social security and tier 1 RRTA tax withheld (**If changing**, see instructions.)	12			
13	Estimated tax payments, including amount applied from prior year's return	13			
14	Earned income credit (EIC)	14			
15	Refundable credits from: ☐ Schedule 8812 Form(s) ☐ 2439 ☐ 4136 ☐ 8801 ☐ 8863 ☐ 8885 ☐ 8962 or ☐ other (specify): _____	15			
16	Total amount paid with request for extension of time to file, tax paid with original return, and additional tax paid after return was filed			16	
17	Total payments. Add lines 12 through 16			17	
Refund or Amount You Owe					
18	Overpayment, if any, as shown on original return or as previously adjusted by the IRS			18	
19	Subtract line 18 from line 17 (If less than zero, see instructions.)			19	
20	**Amount you owe.** If line 11, column C, is more than line 19, enter the difference			20	
21	If line 11, column C, is less than line 19, enter the difference. This is the amount **overpaid** on this return			21	
22	Amount of line 21 you want **refunded to you**			22	
23	Amount of line 21 you want **applied to your** (enter year): _____ estimated tax .	23			

Complete and sign this form on Page 2.

For Paperwork Reduction Act Notice, see instructions.   Cat. No. 11360L   Form **1040X** (Rev. 1-2016)

Form 1040X (Rev. 1-2016)   Page **2**

Part I   Exemptions

Complete this part **only** if you are increasing or decreasing the number of exemptions (personal and dependents) claimed on line 6d of the return you are amending.

See *Form 1040* or *Form 1040A instructions* and *Form 1040X instructions*.

			A. Original number of exemptions or amount reported or as previously adjusted	B. Net change	C. Correct number or amount
24	Yourself and spouse. **Caution:** If someone can claim you as a dependent, you cannot claim an exemption for yourself	24			
25	Your dependent children who lived with you	25			
26	Your dependent children who did not live with you due to divorce or separation	26			
27	Other dependents	27			
28	Total number of exemptions. Add lines 24 through 27	28			
29	Multiply the number of exemptions claimed on line 28 by the exemption amount shown in the instructions for line 29 for the year you are amending. Enter the result here and on line 4 on page 1 of this form . .	29			

30   List **ALL** dependents (children and others) claimed on this amended return. If more than 4 dependents, see instructions.

(a) First name Last name	(b) Dependent's social security number	(c) Dependent's relationship to you	(d) Check box if qualifying child for child tax credit (see instructions)
			☐
			☐
			☐
			☐

Part II   Presidential Election Campaign Fund

Checking below will not increase your tax or reduce your refund.

☐   Check here if you did not previously want $3 to go to the fund, but now do.

☐   Check here if this is a joint return and your spouse did not previously want $3 to go to the fund, but now does.

Part III   Explanation of changes. In the space provided below, tell us why you are filing Form 1040X.

▶ Attach any supporting documents and new or changed forms and schedules.

Sign Here
Remember to keep a copy of this form for your records.

Under penalties of perjury, I declare that I have filed an original return and that I have examined this amended return, including accompanying schedules and statements, and to the best of my knowledge and belief, this amended return is true, correct, and complete. Declaration of preparer (other than taxpayer) is based on all information about which the preparer has any knowledge.

▶ _____   _____   ▶ _____   _____
Your signature   Date   Spouse's signature. If a joint return, **both** must sign.   Date

Paid Preparer Use Only

▶ _____   _____   _____
Preparer's signature   Date   Firm's name (or yours if self-employed)

_____   _____
Print/type preparer's name   Firm's address and ZIP code
                           ☐ Check if self-employed

_____   _____   _____
PTIN   Phone number   EIN

For forms and publications, visit IRS.gov.   Form **1040X** (Rev. 1-2016)

Form 1120X
(Rev. November 2016)
Department of the Treasury
Internal Revenue Service

Amended U.S. Corporation Income Tax Return

► Information about Form 1120X and its instructions is at *www.irs.gov/form1120x*.

OMB No. 1545-0123

For tax year ending
►

(Enter month and year.)

Please Type or Print	Name		Employer identification number
	Number, street, and room or suite no. If a P.O. box, see instructions.		
	City or town, state, and ZIP code		Telephone number (optional)

Enter name and address used on original return. If same as above, write "Same."

Internal Revenue Service Center
where original return was filed ►

Fill in applicable items and use Part II on the back to explain any changes

Part I Income and Deductions (see instructions)		(a) As originally reported or as previously adjusted	(b) Net change — increase or (decrease) — explain in Part II	(c) Correct amount
1	Total income	1			
2	Total deductions	2			
3	Taxable income. Subtract line 2 from line 1	3			
4	Total tax	4			

Payments and Credits (see instructions)

5a	Overpayment in prior year allowed as a credit . . .	5a			
b	Estimated tax payments	5b			
c	Refund applied for on Form 4466	5c			
d	Subtract line 5c from the sum of lines 5a and 5b . .	5d			
e	Tax deposited with Form 7004	5e			
f	Credit from Form 2439	5f			
g	Credit for federal tax on fuels and other refundable credits	5g			
6	Tax deposited or paid with (or after) the filing of the original return			6	
7	Add lines 5d through 6, column (c)			7	
8	Overpayment, if any, as shown on original return or as later adjusted			8	
9	Subtract line 8 from line 7			9	

Tax Due or Overpayment (see instructions)

10	**Tax due.** Subtract line 9 from line 4, column (c). If paying by check, make it payable to the "**United States Treasury**" . . . . ►	10	
11	**Overpayment.** Subtract line 4, column (c), from line 9 . . . . ►	11	
12	Enter the amount of line 11 you want: **Credited to 20** Estimated tax ► Refunded ►	12	

Sign Here

Under penalties of perjury, I declare that I have filed an original return and that I have examined this amended return, including accompanying schedules and statements, and to the best of my knowledge and belief, this amended return is true, correct, and complete. Declaration of preparer (other than taxpayer) is based on all information of which preparer has any knowledge.

► _____   _____ ► _____
   Signature of officer   Date   Title

Paid Preparer Use Only	Print/Type preparer's name	Preparer's signature	Date	Check ☐ if self-employed	PTIN
	Firm's name ►			Firm's EIN ►	
	Firm's address ►			Phone no.	

For Paperwork Reduction Act Notice, see instructions.   Cat. No. 11530Z   Form **1120X** (Rev. 11-2016)

Form 1120X (Rev. 11-2016)   Page **2**

Part II   **Explanation of Changes to Items in Part I** (Enter the line number from Part I for the items you are changing, and give the reason for each change. Show any computation in detail. Also, see **What To Attach** in the instructions.)

If the change is due to a net operating loss carryback, a capital loss carryback, or a general business credit carryback, see **Carryback Claims** in the instructions, and check here . . . . ▶ ☐

Form **1120X** (Rev. 11-2016)

B-5 Application for Extension of Time to File Income Tax Returns

Form **4868**

Department of the Treasury
Internal Revenue Service (99)

Application for Automatic Extension of Time To File U.S. Individual Income Tax Return

▶ Information about Form 4868 and its instructions is available at *www.irs.gov/form4868.*

OMB No. 1545-0074

20**16**

There are three ways to request an automatic extension of time to file a U.S. individual income tax return.

1. You can pay all or part of your estimated income tax due and indicate that the payment is for an extension using Direct Pay, the Electronic Federal Tax Payment System, or using a credit or debit card. See *How To Make a Payment,* on page 3.

2. You can file Form 4868 electronically by accessing IRS *e-file* using your home computer or by using a tax professional who uses *e-file.*

3. You can file a paper Form 4868 and enclose payment of your estimate of tax due.

 **It's Convenient, Safe, and Secure**

IRS *e-file* is the IRS's electronic filing program. You can get an automatic extension of time to file your tax return by filing Form 4868 electronically. You'll receive an electronic acknowledgment once you complete the transaction. Keep it with your records. Don't mail in Form 4868 if you file electronically, unless you're making a payment with a check or money order (see page 3).

Complete Form 4868 to use as a worksheet. If you think you may owe tax when you file your return, you'll need to estimate your total tax liability and subtract how much you've already paid (lines 4, 5, and 6 below).

Several companies offer free e-filing of Form 4868 through the Free File program. For more details, go to IRS.gov and click on *freefile.*

 Pay Electronically

You **don't** need to file Form 4868 if you make a payment using our electronic payment options. Your extension will be automatically processed when you pay part or all of your estimated income tax electronically. You can pay online or by phone (see page 3).

 ***E-file* Using Your Personal Computer or Through a Tax Professional**

Refer to your tax software package or tax preparer for ways to file electronically. Be sure to have a copy of your 2015 tax return— you'll be asked to provide information from the return for taxpayer verification. If you wish to make a payment, you can pay by electronic funds withdrawal or send your check or money order to the address shown in the middle column under *Where To File a Paper Form 4868* (see page 4).

 File a Paper Form 4868

If you wish to file on paper instead of electronically, fill in the Form 4868 below and mail it to the address shown on page 4.

For information on using a private delivery service, see page 4.

Note: If you're a fiscal year taxpayer, you must file a paper Form 4868.

General Instructions

Purpose of Form

Use Form 4868 to apply for 6 more months (4 if "out of the country" (defined on page 2) and a U.S. citizen or resident) to file Form 1040, 1040A, 1040EZ, 1040NR, 1040NR-EZ, 1040-PR, or 1040-SS.

Gift and generation-skipping transfer (GST) tax return (Form 709). An extension of time to file your 2016 calendar year income tax return also extends the time to file Form 709 for 2016. However, it doesn't extend the time to pay any gift and GST tax you may owe for 2016. To make a payment of gift and GST tax, see Form 8892. If you don't pay the amount due by the regular due date for Form 709, you'll owe interest and may also be charged penalties. If the donor died during 2016, see the instructions for Forms 709 and 8892.

Qualifying for the Extension

To get the extra time you must:

1. Properly estimate your 2016 tax liability using the information available to you,

2. Enter your total tax liability on line 4 of Form 4868, and

3. File Form 4868 by the regular due date of your return.

 Although you aren't required to make a payment of the tax you estimate as due, Form 4868 doesn't extend the time to pay taxes. If you don't pay the amount due by the regular due date, you'll owe interest. You may also be charged penalties. For more details, see Interest *and* Late Payment Penalty *on page 2. Any remittance you make with your application for extension will be treated as a payment of tax.*

You don't have to explain why you're asking for the extension. We'll contact you only if your request is denied.

Don't file Form 4868 if you want the IRS to figure your tax or you're under a court order to file your return by the regular due date.

▼ DETACH HERE ▼

Form **4868**

Department of the Treasury
Internal Revenue Service (99)

Application for Automatic Extension of Time To File U.S. Individual Income Tax Return

For calendar year 2016, or other tax year beginning   , 2016, ending   , 20   .

OMB No. 1545-0074

20**16**

Part I Identification	**Part II** Individual Income Tax
1 Your name(s) (see instructions)	**4** Estimate of total tax liability for 2016 . . $
	5 Total 2016 payments . . . .
Address (see instructions)	**6** **Balance due.** Subtract line 5 from line 4 (see instructions) . . . .
	7 Amount you're paying (see instructions) . . ▶
City, town, or post office State ZIP Code	**8** Check here if you're "out of the country" and a U.S. citizen or resident (see instructions) . . . . . . ▶ ☐
2 Your social security number **3** Spouse's social security number	**9** Check here if you file Form 1040NR or 1040NR-EZ and didn't receive wages as an employee subject to U.S. income tax withholding . . . . ▶ ☐

For Privacy Act and Paperwork Reduction Act Notice, see page 4.   Cat. No. 13141W   Form **4868** (2016)

B-6 Underpayment of Estimated Tax

Form **2210**	**Underpayment of Estimated Tax by Individuals, Estates, and Trusts** ▶ Information about Form 2210 and its separate instructions is at *www.irs.gov/form2210*. ▶ **Attach to Form 1040, 1040A, 1040NR, 1040NR-EZ, or 1041.**	OMB No. 1545-0074 **2016** Attachment Sequence No. **06**

Department of the Treasury
Internal Revenue Service

Name(s) shown on tax return | Identifying number

Do You Have To File Form 2210?

Complete lines 1 through 7 below. Is line 7 less than $1,000? → **Yes** → **Don't file Form 2210.** You don't owe a penalty.

↓ **No**

Complete lines 8 and 9 below. Is line 6 equal to or more than line 9? → **Yes** → You don't owe a penalty. **Don't file Form 2210** (but if box **E** in Part II applies, you must file page 1 of Form 2210).

↓ **No**

You may owe a penalty. Does any box in Part II below apply? → **Yes** → You **must** file Form 2210. Does box **B, C,** or **D** in Part II apply?

↓ **No**   **No** / **Yes** → You must figure your penalty.

Don't file Form 2210. You aren't required to figure your penalty because the IRS will figure it and send you a bill for any unpaid amount. If you want to figure it, you may use Part III or Part IV as a worksheet and enter your penalty amount on your tax return, but **don't file Form 2210.**

You **aren't** required to figure your penalty because the IRS will figure it and send you a bill for any unpaid amount. If you want to figure it, you may use Part III or Part IV as a worksheet and enter your penalty amount on your tax return, but **file only page 1 of Form 2210.**

Part I Required Annual Payment

1	Enter your 2016 tax after credits from Form 1040, line 56 (see instructions if not filing Form 1040)	1
2	Other taxes, including self-employment tax and, if applicable, Additional Medicare Tax and/or Net Investment Income Tax (see instructions)	2
3	Refundable credits, including the premium tax credit (see instructions)	3 ( )
4	Current year tax. Combine lines 1, 2, and 3. If less than $1,000, **stop;** you don't owe a penalty. **Don't** file Form 2210	4
5	Multiply line 4 by 90% (0.90) 5	
6	Withholding taxes. **Don't** include estimated tax payments (see instructions)	6
7	Subtract line 6 from line 4. If less than $1,000, **stop;** you don't owe a penalty. **Don't** file Form 2210	7
8	Maximum required annual payment based on prior year's tax (see instructions)	8
9	**Required annual payment.** Enter the **smaller** of line 5 or line 8	9

Next: Is line 9 more than line 6?

☐ **No.** You **don't** owe a penalty. **Don't** file Form 2210 unless box **E** below applies.

☐ **Yes.** You may owe a penalty, but **don't** file Form 2210 unless one or more boxes in Part II below applies.

• If box **B, C,** or **D** applies, you must figure your penalty and file Form 2210.

• If box **A** or **E** applies (but not **B, C,** or **D**) file only page 1 of Form 2210. You **aren't** required to figure your penalty; the IRS will figure it and send you a bill for any unpaid amount. If you want to figure your penalty, you may use Part III or IV as a worksheet and enter your penalty on your tax return, but **file only page 1 of Form 2210.**

Part II Reasons for Filing. Check applicable boxes. If none apply, **don't** file Form 2210.

A ☐ You request a **waiver** (see instructions) of your entire penalty. You must check this box and file page 1 of Form 2210, but you aren't required to figure your penalty.

B ☐ You request a **waiver** (see instructions) of part of your penalty. You must figure your penalty and waiver amount and file Form 2210.

C ☐ Your income varied during the year and your penalty is reduced or eliminated when figured using the **annualized income installment method.** You must figure the penalty using Schedule AI and file Form 2210.

D ☐ Your penalty is lower when figured by treating the federal income tax withheld from your income as paid on the dates it was actually withheld, instead of in equal amounts on the payment due dates. You must figure your penalty and file Form 2210.

E ☐ You filed or are filing a joint return for either 2015 or 2016, but not for both years, and line 8 above is smaller than line 5 above. You must file page 1 of Form 2210, but you **aren't** required to figure your penalty (unless box **B, C,** or **D** applies).

For Paperwork Reduction Act Notice, see separate instructions.   Cat. No. 11744P   Form **2210** (2016)

Form 2210 (2016)   Page **2**

Part III	**Short Method**

Can You Use the Short Method?	You can use the short method if: • You made no estimated tax payments (or your only payments were withheld federal income tax), **or** • You paid the same amount of estimated tax on each of the four payment due dates.
Must You Use the Regular Method?	You must use the regular method (Part IV) instead of the short method if: • You made any estimated tax payments late, • You checked box **C** or **D** in Part II, **or** • You are filing Form 1040NR or 1040NR-EZ and you didn't receive wages as an employee subject to U.S. income tax withholding.

Note: *If any payment was made earlier than the due date, you can use the short method, but using it may cause you to pay a larger penalty than the regular method. If the payment was only a few days early, the difference is likely to be small.*

10	Enter the amount from Form 2210, line 9	**10**	
11	Enter the amount, if any, from Form 2210, line 6 . . . . **11**		
12	Enter the total amount, if any, of estimated tax payments you made . **12**		
13	Add lines 11 and 12	**13**	
14	**Total underpayment for year.** Subtract line 13 from line 10. If zero or less, **stop;** you don't owe a penalty. **Don't file Form 2210 unless you checked box E in Part II**	**14**	
15	Multiply line 14 by 0.02656	**15**	
16	• If the amount on line 14 was paid **on or after** 4/15/17, enter -0-. • If the amount on line 14 was paid **before** 4/15/17, make the following computation to find the amount to enter on line 16.		
	Amount on Number of days paid line 14 × before 4/15/17 × 0.00011	**16**	
17	**Penalty.** Subtract line 16 from line 15. Enter the result here and on Form 1040, line 79; Form 1040A, line 51; Form 1040NR, line 76; Form 1040NR-EZ, line 26; or Form 1041, line 26. **Don't file Form 2210 unless you checked a box in Part II** . . . . ▶	**17**	

Form **2210** (2016)

Form 2210 (2016)   Page **3**

Part IV **Regular Method** (See the instructions if you are filing Form 1040NR or 1040NR-EZ.)

		Payment Due Dates			
Section A—Figure Your Underpayment		(a) 4/15/16	(b) 6/15/16	(c) 9/15/16	(d) 1/15/17
18 **Required installments.** If box C in Part II applies, enter the amounts from Schedule AI, line 25. Otherwise, enter 25% (0.25) of line 9, Form 2210, in each column	**18**				
19 Estimated tax paid and tax withheld (see the instructions). For column (a) only, also enter the amount from line 19 on line 23. If line 19 is equal to or more than line 18 for all payment periods, stop here; you don't owe a penalty. **Don't file Form 2210 unless you checked a box in Part II**	**19**				
Complete lines 20 through 26 of one column before going to line 20 of the next column.					
20 Enter the amount, if any, from line 26 in the previous column	**20**				
21 Add lines 19 and 20	**21**				
22 Add the amounts on lines 24 and 25 in the previous column	**22**				
23 Subtract line 22 from line 21. If zero or less, enter -0-. For column (a) only, enter the amount from line 19	**23**				
24 If line 23 is zero, subtract line 21 from line 22. Otherwise, enter -0-	**24**				
25 **Underpayment.** If line 18 is equal to or more than line 23, subtract line 23 from line 18. Then go to line 20 of the next column. Otherwise, go to line 26 . ▶	**25**				
26 Overpayment. If line 23 is more than line 18, subtract line 18 from line 23. Then go to line 20 of the next column	**26**				

Section B—Figure the Penalty (Use the Worksheet for Form 2210, Part IV, Section B—Figure the Penalty in the instructions.)

27 **Penalty.** Enter the total penalty from line 14 of the Worksheet for Form 2210, Part IV, Section B—Figure the Penalty. Also include this amount on Form 1040, line 79; Form 1040A, line 51; Form 1040NR, line 76; Form 1040NR-EZ, line 26; or Form 1041, line 26. **Don't file Form 2210 unless you checked a box in Part II** . . . . ▶	**27**	

Form **2210** (2016)

Form **2220**

Department of the Treasury
Internal Revenue Service

Underpayment of Estimated Tax by Corporations

► Attach to the corporation's tax return.
► Information about Form 2220 and its separate instructions is at *www.irs.gov/form2220.*

OMB No. 1545-0123

2016

Name	Employer identification number

Note: Generally, the corporation isn't required to file Form 2220 (see Part II below for exceptions) because the IRS will figure any penalty owed and bill the corporation. However, the corporation may still use Form 2220 to figure the penalty. If so, enter the amount from page 2, line 38 on the estimated tax penalty line of the corporation's income tax return, but **do not** attach Form 2220.

Part I   Required Annual Payment

1 Total tax (see instructions) **1**

2a Personal holding company tax (Schedule PH (Form 1120), line 26) included on line 1   **2a**

b Look-back interest included on line 1 under section 460(b)(2) for completed long-term contracts or section 167(g) for depreciation under the income forecast method . .   **2b**

c Credit for federal tax paid on fuels (see instructions) **2c**

d **Total.** Add lines 2a through 2c **2d**

3 Subtract line 2d from line 1. If the result is less than $500, **do not** complete or file this form. The corporation doesn't owe the penalty **3**

4 Enter the tax shown on the corporation's 2015 income tax return. See instructions. **Caution: If the tax is zero or the tax year was for less than 12 months, skip this line and enter the amount from line 3 on line 5** . .   **4**

5 **Required annual payment.** Enter the **smaller** of line 3 or line 4. If the corporation is required to skip line 4, enter the amount from line 3 . . . .   **5**

Part II   Reasons for Filing—Check the boxes below that apply. If any boxes are checked, the corporation **must** file Form 2220 even if it doesn't owe a penalty. See instructions.

6 ☐ The corporation is using the adjusted seasonal installment method.

7 ☐ The corporation is using the annualized income installment method.

8 ☐ The corporation is a "large corporation" figuring its first required installment based on the prior year's tax.

Part III   Figuring the Underpayment

			(a)	(b)	(c)	(d)
9	Installment due dates. Enter in columns (a) through (d) the 15th day of the 4th (**Form 990-PF filers:** Use 5th month), 6th, 9th, and 12th months of the corporation's tax year	**9**				
10	Required installments. If the box on line 6 and/or line 7 above is checked, enter the amounts from Schedule A, line 38. If the box on line 8 (but not 6 or 7) is checked, see instructions for the amounts to enter. If none of these boxes are checked, enter 25% (0.25) of line 5 above in each column	**10**				
11	Estimated tax paid or credited for each period. For column (a) only, enter the amount from line 11 on line 15. See instructions.	**11**				
	Complete lines 12 through 18 of one column before going to the next column.					
12	Enter amount, if any, from line 18 of the preceding column	**12**				
13	Add lines 11 and 12	**13**				
14	Add amounts on lines 16 and 17 of the preceding column	**14**				
15	Subtract line 14 from line 13. If zero or less, enter -0-	**15**				
16	If the amount on line 15 is zero, subtract line 13 from line 14. Otherwise, enter -0-	**16**				
17	**Underpayment.** If line 15 is less than or equal to line 10, subtract line 15 from line 10. Then go to line 12 of the next column. Otherwise, go to line 18	**17**				
18	**Overpayment.** If line 10 is less than line 15, subtract line 10 from line 15. Then go to line 12 of the next column	**18**				

Go to Part IV on page 2 to figure the penalty. Do not go to Part IV if there are no entries on line 17—no penalty is owed.

For Paperwork Reduction Act Notice, see separate instructions.   Cat. No. 11746L   Form **2220** (2016)

Form 2220 (2016)   Page **2**

Part IV	**Figuring the Penalty**		(a)	(b)	(c)	(d)

			(a)	(b)	(c)	(d)
19	Enter the date of payment or the 15th day of the 4th month after the close of the tax year, whichever is earlier. *(C Corporations with tax years ending June 30 and S corporations:* Use 3rd month instead of 4th month. *Form 990-PF and Form 990-T filers:* Use 5th month instead of 4th month.) See instructions	**19**				
20	Number of days from due date of installment on line 9 to the date shown on line 19	**20**				
21	Number of days on line 20 after 4/15/2016 and before 7/1/2016	**21**				
22	Underpayment on line 17 × $\frac{\text{Number of days on line 21}}{366}$ × 4% (0.04)	**22**	$	$	$	$
23	Number of days on line 20 after 6/30/2016 and before 10/1/2016	**23**				
24	Underpayment on line 17 × $\frac{\text{Number of days on line 23}}{366}$ × 4% (0.04)	**24**	$	$	$	$
25	Number of days on line 20 after 9/30/2016 and before 1/1/2017	**25**				
26	Underpayment on line 17 × $\frac{\text{Number of days on line 25}}{366}$ × 4% (0.04)	**26**	$	$	$	$
27	Number of days on line 20 after 12/31/2016 and before 4/1/2017	**27**				
28	Underpayment on line 17 × $\frac{\text{Number of days on line 27}}{365}$ × 4% (0.04)	**28**	$	$	$	$
29	Number of days on line 20 after 3/31/2017 and before 7/1/2017	**29**				
30	Underpayment on line 17 × $\frac{\text{Number of days on line 29}}{365}$ × *%	**30**	$	$	$	$
31	Number of days on line 20 after 6/30/2017 and before 10/1/2017	**31**				
32	Underpayment on line 17 × $\frac{\text{Number of days on line 31}}{365}$ × *%	**32**	$	$	$	$
33	Number of days on line 20 after 9/30/2017 and before 1/1/2018	**33**				
34	Underpayment on line 17 × $\frac{\text{Number of days on line 33}}{365}$ × *%	**34**	$	$	$	$
35	Number of days on line 20 after 12/31/2017 and before 3/16/2018	**35**				
36	Underpayment on line 17 × $\frac{\text{Number of days on line 35}}{365}$ × *%	**36**	$	$	$	$
37	Add lines 22, 24, 26, 28, 30, 32, 34, and 36	**37**	$	$	$	$
38	**Penalty.** Add columns (a) through (d) of line 37. Enter the total here and on Form 1120, line 33; or the comparable line for other income tax returns	**38**	$			

*Use the penalty interest rate for each calendar quarter, which the IRS will determine during the first month in the preceding quarter. These rates are published quarterly in an IRS News Release and in a revenue ruling in the Internal Revenue Bulletin. To obtain this information on the Internet, access the IRS website at *www.irs.gov.* You can also call 1-800-829-4933 to get interest rate information.

Form **2220** (2016)

Form **4626**	**Alternative Minimum Tax—Corporations**	OMB No. 1545-0123
Department of the Treasury Internal Revenue Service	▶ Attach to the corporation's tax return. ▶ Information about Form 4626 and its separate instructions is at *www.irs.gov/form4626*.	20**16**

Name		Employer identification number

Note: *See the instructions to find out if the corporation is a small corporation exempt from the alternative minimum tax (AMT) under section 55(e).*

1	Taxable income or (loss) before net operating loss deduction	**1**
2	**Adjustments and preferences:**	
a	Depreciation of post-1986 property	**2a**
b	Amortization of certified pollution control facilities.	**2b**
c	Amortization of mining exploration and development costs	**2c**
d	Amortization of circulation expenditures (personal holding companies only)	**2d**
e	Adjusted gain or loss	**2e**
f	Long-term contracts	**2f**
g	Merchant marine capital construction funds.	**2g**
h	Section 833(b) deduction (Blue Cross, Blue Shield, and similar type organizations only)	**2h**
i	Tax shelter farm activities (personal service corporations only)	**2i**
j	Passive activities (closely held corporations and personal service corporations only)	**2j**
k	Loss limitations	**2k**
l	Depletion	**2l**
m	Tax-exempt interest income from specified private activity bonds	**2m**
n	Intangible drilling costs	**2n**
o	Other adjustments and preferences	**2o**
3	Pre-adjustment alternative minimum taxable income (AMTI). Combine lines 1 through 2o.	**3**
4	**Adjusted current earnings (ACE) adjustment:**	
a	ACE from line 10 of the ACE worksheet in the instructions **4a**	
b	Subtract line 3 from line 4a. If line 3 exceeds line 4a, enter the difference as a negative amount. See instructions **4b**	
c	Multiply line 4b by 75% (0.75). Enter the result as a positive amount. **4c**	
d	Enter the excess, if any, of the corporation's total increases in AMTI from prior year ACE adjustments over its total reductions in AMTI from prior year ACE adjustments. See instructions. **Note:** *You **must** enter an amount on line 4d (even if line 4b is positive).* **4d**	
e	ACE adjustment.	
	• If line 4b is zero or more, enter the amount from line 4c	**4e**
	• If line 4b is less than zero, enter the **smaller** of line 4c or line 4d as a negative amount	
5	Combine lines 3 and 4e. If zero or less, stop here; the corporation does not owe any AMT	**5**
6	Alternative tax net operating loss deduction. See instructions	**6**
7	**Alternative minimum taxable income.** Subtract line 6 from line 5. If the corporation held a residual interest in a REMIC, see instructions	**7**
8	**Exemption phase-out** (if line 7 is $310,000 or more, skip lines 8a and 8b and enter -0- on line 8c):	
a	Subtract $150,000 from line 7 (if completing this line for a member of a controlled group, see instructions). If zero or less, enter -0- **8a**	
b	Multiply line 8a by 25% (0.25) **8b**	
c	Exemption. Subtract line 8b from $40,000 (if completing this line for a member of a controlled group, see instructions). If zero or less, enter -0-	**8c**
9	Subtract line 8c from line 7. If zero or less, enter -0-	**9**
10	Multiply line 9 by 20% (0.20)	**10**
11	Alternative minimum tax foreign tax credit (AMTFTC). See instructions	**11**
12	Tentative minimum tax. Subtract line 11 from line 10	**12**
13	Regular tax liability before applying all credits except the foreign tax credit	**13**
14	**Alternative minimum tax.** Subtract line 13 from line 12. If zero or less, enter -0-. Enter here and on Form 1120, Schedule J, line 3, or the appropriate line of the corporation's income tax return . . .	**14**

For Paperwork Reduction Act Notice, see separate instructions.   Cat. No. 12955I   Form **4626** (2016)

Form **6251**	**Alternative Minimum Tax—Individuals**	OMB No. 1545-0074
Department of the Treasury Internal Revenue Service (99)	▶ Information about Form 6251 and its separate instructions is at *www.irs.gov/form6251*. ▶ Attach to Form 1040 or Form 1040NR.	20**16** Attachment Sequence No. **32**

Name(s) shown on Form 1040 or Form 1040NR | Your social security number

Part I Alternative Minimum Taxable Income (See instructions for how to complete each line.)

1	If filing Schedule A (Form 1040), enter the amount from Form 1040, line 41, and go to line 2. Otherwise, enter the amount from Form 1040, line 38, and go to line 7. (If less than zero, enter as a negative amount.)	**1**	
2	Medical and dental. If you or your spouse was 65 or older, enter the **smaller** of Schedule A (Form 1040), line 4, **or** 2.5% (0.025) of Form 1040, line 38. If zero or less, enter -0-	**2**	
3	Taxes from Schedule A (Form 1040), line 9	**3**	
4	Enter the home mortgage interest adjustment, if any, from line 6 of the worksheet in the instructions for this line	**4**	
5	Miscellaneous deductions from Schedule A (Form 1040), line 27.	**5**	
6	If Form 1040, line 38, is $155,650 or less, enter -0-. Otherwise, see instructions	**6**	( )
7	Tax refund from Form 1040, line 10 or line 21	**7**	( )
8	Investment interest expense (difference between regular tax and AMT).	**8**	
9	Depletion (difference between regular tax and AMT)	**9**	
10	Net operating loss deduction from Form 1040, line 21. Enter as a positive amount	**10**	
11	Alternative tax net operating loss deduction	**11**	( )
12	Interest from specified private activity bonds exempt from the regular tax	**12**	
13	Qualified small business stock, see instructions	**13**	
14	Exercise of incentive stock options (excess of AMT income over regular tax income)	**14**	
15	Estates and trusts (amount from Schedule K-1 (Form 1041), box 12, code A)	**15**	
16	Electing large partnerships (amount from Schedule K-1 (Form 1065-B), box 6)	**16**	
17	Disposition of property (difference between AMT and regular tax gain or loss)	**17**	
18	Depreciation on assets placed in service after 1986 (difference between regular tax and AMT)	**18**	
19	Passive activities (difference between AMT and regular tax income or loss)	**19**	
20	Loss limitations (difference between AMT and regular tax income or loss)	**20**	
21	Circulation costs (difference between regular tax and AMT)	**21**	
22	Long-term contracts (difference between AMT and regular tax income)	**22**	
23	Mining costs (difference between regular tax and AMT)	**23**	
24	Research and experimental costs (difference between regular tax and AMT)	**24**	
25	Income from certain installment sales before January 1, 1987	**25**	( )
26	Intangible drilling costs preference	**26**	
27	Other adjustments, including income-based related adjustments	**27**	
28	**Alternative minimum taxable income.** Combine lines 1 through 27. (If married filing separately and line 28 is more than $247,450, see instructions.)	**28**	

Part II Alternative Minimum Tax (AMT)

29	Exemption. (If you were under age 24 at the end of 2016, see instructions.)

IF your filing status is . . .	AND line 28 is not over . . .	THEN enter on line 29 . . .		
Single or head of household	$119,700	$53,900	}	
Married filing jointly or qualifying widow(er)	159,700	83,800		**29**
Married filing separately	79,850	41,900		

If line 28 is **over** the amount shown above for your filing status, see instructions.

30	Subtract line 29 from line 28. If more than zero, go to line 31. If zero or less, enter -0- here and on lines 31, 33, and 35, and go to line 34	**30**	
31	• If you are filing Form 2555 or 2555-EZ, see instructions for the amount to enter. • If you reported capital gain distributions directly on Form 1040, line 13; you reported qualified dividends on Form 1040, line 9b; **or** you had a gain on both lines 15 and 16 of Schedule D (Form 1040) (as refigured for the AMT, if necessary), complete Part III on the back and enter the amount from line 64 here. • **All others:** If line 30 is $186,300 or less ($93,150 or less if married filing separately), multiply line 30 by 26% (0.26). Otherwise, multiply line 30 by 28% (0.28) and subtract $3,726 ($1,863 if married filing separately) from the result.	**31**	
32	Alternative minimum tax foreign tax credit (see instructions)	**32**	
33	Tentative minimum tax. Subtract line 32 from line 31	**33**	
34	Add Form 1040, line 44 (minus any tax from Form 4972), and Form 1040, line 46. Subtract from the result any foreign tax credit from Form 1040, line 48. If you used Schedule J to figure your tax on Form 1040, line 44, refigure that tax without using Schedule J before completing this line (see instructions)	**34**	
35	**AMT.** Subtract line 34 from line 33. If zero or less, enter -0-. Enter here and on Form 1040, line 45	**35**	

For Paperwork Reduction Act Notice, see your tax return instructions. Cat. No. 13600G Form **6251** (2016)

Form 6251 (2016)   Page **2**

Part III   **Tax Computation Using Maximum Capital Gains Rates**

Complete Part III only if you are required to do so by line 31 or by the Foreign Earned Income Tax Worksheet in the instructions.

36 Enter the amount from Form 6251, line 30. If you are filing Form 2555 or 2555-EZ, enter the amount from line 3 of the worksheet in the instructions for line 31	**36**	
37 Enter the amount from line 6 of the Qualified Dividends and Capital Gain Tax Worksheet in the instructions for Form 1040, line 44, or the amount from line 13 of the Schedule D Tax Worksheet in the instructions for Schedule D (Form 1040), whichever applies (as refigured for the AMT, if necessary) (see instructions). If you are filing Form 2555 or 2555-EZ, see instructions for the amount to enter	**37**	
38 Enter the amount from Schedule D (Form 1040), line 19 (as refigured for the AMT, if necessary) (see instructions). If you are filing Form 2555 or 2555-EZ, see instructions for the amount to enter	**38**	
39 If you did not complete a Schedule D Tax Worksheet for the regular tax or the AMT, enter the amount from line 37. Otherwise, add lines 37 and 38, and enter the **smaller** of that result or the amount from line 10 of the Schedule D Tax Worksheet (as refigured for the AMT, if necessary). If you are filing Form 2555 or 2555-EZ, see instructions for the amount to enter	**39**	
40 Enter the **smaller** of line 36 or line 39	**40**	
41 Subtract line 40 from line 36	**41**	
42 If line 41 is $186,300 or less ($93,150 or less if married filing separately), multiply line 41 by 26% (0.26). Otherwise, multiply line 41 by 28% (0.28) and subtract $3,726 ($1,863 if married filing separately) from the result . . ▶	**42**	

43 Enter:
  • $75,300 if married filing jointly or qualifying widow(er),
  • $37,650 if single or married filing separately, or
  • $50,400 if head of household.   }   .   .   .   .   .
	43	

44 Enter the amount from line 7 of the Qualified Dividends and Capital Gain Tax Worksheet in the instructions for Form 1040, line 44, or the amount from line 14 of the Schedule D Tax Worksheet in the instructions for Schedule D (Form 1040), whichever applies (as figured for the regular tax). If you did not complete either worksheet for the regular tax, enter the amount from Form 1040, line 43; if zero or less, enter -0-. If you are filing Form 2555 or 2555-EZ, see instructions for the amount to enter	**44**	
45 Subtract line 44 from line 43. If zero or less, enter -0-	**45**	
46 Enter the **smaller** of line 36 or line 37	**46**	
47 Enter the **smaller** of line 45 or line 46. This amount is taxed at 0%	**47**	
48 Subtract line 47 from line 46	**48**	

49 Enter:
  • $415,050 if single
  • $233,475 if married filing separately
  • $466,950 if married filing jointly or qualifying widow(er)
  • $441,000 if head of household   }   .   .   .   .
	49	

50 Enter the amount from line 45	**50**	
51 Enter the amount from line 7 of the Qualified Dividends and Capital Gain Tax Worksheet in the instructions for Form 1040, line 44, or the amount from line 19 of the Schedule D Tax Worksheet, whichever applies (as figured for the regular tax). If you did not complete either worksheet for the regular tax, enter the amount from Form 1040, line 43; if zero or less, enter -0-. If you are filing Form 2555 or Form 2555-EZ, see instructions for the amount to enter	**51**	
52 Add line 50 and line 51	**52**	
53 Subtract line 52 from line 49. If zero or less, enter -0-	**53**	
54 Enter the smaller of line 48 or line 53	**54**	
55 Multiply line 54 by 15% (0.15) . . . . ▶	**55**	
56 Add lines 47 and 54	**56**	
If lines 56 and 36 are the same, skip lines 57 through 61 and go to line 62. Otherwise, go to line 57.		
57 Subtract line 56 from line 46	**57**	
58 Multiply line 57 by 20% (0.20) . . . . ▶	**58**	
If line 38 is zero or blank, skip lines 59 through 61 and go to line 62. Otherwise, go to line 59.		
59 Add lines 41, 56, and 57	**59**	
60 Subtract line 59 from line 36	**60**	
61 Multiply line 60 by 25% (0.25) . . . . ▶	**61**	
62 Add lines 42, 55, 58, and 61	**62**	
63 If line 36 is $186,300 or less ($93,150 or less if married filing separately), multiply line 36 by 26% (0.26). Otherwise, multiply line 36 by 28% (0.28) and subtract $3,726 ($1,863 if married filing separately) from the result	**63**	
64 Enter the **smaller** of line 62 or line 63 here and on line 31. If you are filing Form 2555 or 2555-EZ, do not enter this amount on line 31. Instead, enter it on line 4 of the worksheet in the instructions for line 31 . .	**64**	

Form **6251** (2016)

B-8 Forms for Tax Credits

Form **2441**	**Child and Dependent Care Expenses**		OMB No. 1545-0074

Form **2441**

Department of the Treasury
Internal Revenue Service (99)

► **Attach to Form 1040, Form 1040A, or Form 1040NR.**

► **Information about Form 2441 and its separate instructions is at** *www.irs.gov/form2441.*

1040
1040A
1040NR
2441

OMB No. 1545-0074

20**16**

Attachment
Sequence No. **21**

Name(s) shown on return

Your social security number

Part I   Persons or Organizations Who Provided the Care—You **must** complete this part.
(If you have more than two care providers, see the instructions.)

1	(a) Care provider's name	(b) Address (number, street, apt. no., city, state, and ZIP code)	(c) Identifying number (SSN or EIN)	(d) Amount paid (see instructions)

Did you receive dependent care benefits?	→	**No** →	Complete only Part II below.
	→	**Yes** →	Complete Part III on the back next.

Caution: If the care was provided in your home, you may owe employment taxes. If you do, you cannot file Form 1040A. For details, see the instructions for Form 1040, line 60a, or Form 1040NR, line 59a.

Part II   Credit for Child and Dependent Care Expenses

2   Information about your **qualifying person(s).** If you have more than two qualifying persons, see the instructions.

(a) Qualifying person's name		(b) Qualifying person's social security number	(c) **Qualified expenses** you incurred and paid in 2016 for the person listed in column (a)
First	Last		

3	Add the amounts in column (c) of line 2. **Do not** enter more than $3,000 for one qualifying person or $6,000 for two or more persons. If you completed Part III, enter the amount from line 31	**3**	
4	Enter your **earned income.** See instructions	**4**	
5	If married filing jointly, enter your spouse's earned income (if you or your spouse was a student or was disabled, see the instructions); **all others,** enter the amount from line 4 .	**5**	
6	Enter the **smallest** of line 3, 4, or 5	**6**	
7	Enter the amount from Form 1040, line 38; Form 1040A, line 22; or Form 1040NR, line 37 . . . . . [**7**]		

8   Enter on line 8 the decimal amount shown below that applies to the amount on line 7

If line 7 is:				If line 7 is:		
Over	**But not over**	**Decimal amount is**		**Over**	**But not over**	**Decimal amount is**
$0—15,000		.35		$29,000—31,000		.27
15,000—17,000		.34		31,000—33,000		.26
17,000—19,000		.33		33,000—35,000		.25
19,000—21,000		.32		35,000—37,000		.24
21,000—23,000		.31		37,000—39,000		.23
23,000—25,000		.30		39,000—41,000		.22
25,000—27,000		.29		41,000—43,000		.21
27,000—29,000		.28		43,000—No limit		.20

8   X.

9	Multiply line 6 by the decimal amount on line 8. If you paid 2015 expenses in 2016, see the instructions	**9**	
10	Tax liability limit. Enter the amount from the Credit Limit Worksheet in the instructions. . . . . . . [**10**]		
11	**Credit for child and dependent care expenses.** Enter the **smaller** of line 9 or line 10 here and on Form 1040, line 49; Form 1040A, line 31; or Form 1040NR, line 47	**11**	

For Paperwork Reduction Act Notice, see your tax return instructions.   Cat. No. 11862M   Form **2441** (2016)

Form 2441 (2016)   Page **2**

Part III	**Dependent Care Benefits**		

12 Enter the total amount of **dependent care benefits** you received in 2016. Amounts you received as an employee should be shown in box 10 of your Form(s) W-2. **Do not** include amounts reported as wages in box 1 of Form(s) W-2. If you were self-employed or a partner, include amounts you received under a dependent care assistance program from your sole proprietorship or partnership **12**

13 Enter the amount, if any, you carried over from 2015 and used in 2016 during the grace period. See instructions **13**

14 Enter the amount, if any, you forfeited or carried forward to 2017. See instructions . . . **14** ( )

15 Combine lines 12 through 14. See instructions **15**

16 Enter the total amount of **qualified expenses** incurred in 2016 for the care of the **qualifying person(s)** . . . **16**

17 Enter the **smaller** of line 15 or 16 . . . . **17**

18 Enter your **earned income.** See instructions **18**

19 Enter the amount shown below that applies to you.

   • If married filing jointly, enter your spouse's earned income (if you or your spouse was a student or was disabled, see the instructions for line 5).

   • If married filing separately, see instructions.   **19**

   • All others, enter the amount from line 18.

20 Enter the **smallest** of line 17, 18, or 19 . . . . . . **20**

21 Enter $5,000 ($2,500 if married filing separately **and** you were required to enter your spouse's earned income on line 19). **21**

22 Is any amount on line 12 from your sole proprietorship or partnership? (Form 1040A filers go to line 25.)

   ☐ **No.** Enter -0-.

   ☐ **Yes.** Enter the amount here **22**

23 Subtract line 22 from line 15 . . . . **23**

24 **Deductible benefits.** Enter the **smallest** of line 20, 21, or 22. Also, include this amount on the appropriate line(s) of your return. See instructions **24**

25 **Excluded benefits. Form 1040 and 1040NR filers:** If you checked "No" on line 22, enter the smaller of line 20 or 21. Otherwise, subtract line 24 from the smaller of line 20 or line 21. If zero or less, enter -0-. **Form 1040A filers:** Enter the **smaller** of line 20 or line 21 . . **25**

26 **Taxable benefits. Form 1040 and 1040NR filers:** Subtract line 25 from line 23. If zero or less, enter -0-. Also, include this amount on Form 1040, line 7, or Form 1040NR, line 8. On the dotted line next to Form 1040, line 7, or Form 1040NR, line 8, enter "DCB." **Form 1040A filers:** Subtract line 25 from line 15. Also, include this amount on Form 1040A, line 7. In the space to the left of line 7, enter "DCB". **26**

To claim the child and dependent care credit, complete lines 27 through 31 below.

27 Enter $3,000 ($6,000 if two or more qualifying persons) **27**

28 **Form 1040 and 1040NR filers:** Add lines 24 and 25. **Form 1040A filers:** Enter the amount from line 25 . . . . **28**

29 Subtract line 28 from line 27. If zero or less, **stop.** You cannot take the credit. **Exception.** If you paid 2015 expenses in 2016, see the instructions for line 9 . . . . . **29**

30 Complete line 2 on the front of this form. **Do not** include in column (c) any benefits shown on line 28 above. Then, add the amounts in column (c) and enter the total here. **30**

31 Enter the **smaller** of line 29 or 30. Also, enter this amount on line 3 on the front of this form and complete lines 4 through 11 . . . . **31**

Form **2441** (2016)

Form **3468**

Department of the Treasury
Internal Revenue Service (99)

Investment Credit

▶ Attach to your tax return.
▶ Information about Form 3468 and its separate instructions is at *www.irs.gov/form3468*.

OMB No. 1545-0155

20**16**

Attachment
Sequence No. **174**

Name(s) shown on return

Identifying number

Part I   **Information Regarding the Election To Treat the Lessee as the Purchaser of Investment Credit Property**

If you are claiming the investment credit as a lessee based on a section 48(d) (as in effect on November 4, 1990) election, provide the following information. If you acquired more than one property as a lessee, attach a statement showing the information below.

1   Name of lessor

2   Address of lessor

3   Description of property

4   Amount for which you were treated as having acquired the property   . . . .   ▶ $

Part II   **Qualifying Advanced Coal Project Credit, Qualifying Gasification Project Credit, and Qualifying Advanced Energy Project Credit**

5   Qualifying advanced coal project credit (see instructions):

a   Qualified investment in integrated gasification combined cycle property placed in service during the tax year for projects described in section 48A(d)(3)(B)(i)   . . . . $ _____ × 20% (0.20)   **5a**

b   Qualified investment in advanced coal-based generation technology property placed in service during the tax year for projects described in section 48A(d)(3)(B)(ii) .   . . . . $ _____ × 15% (0.15)   **5b**

c   Qualified investment in advanced coal-based generation technology property placed in service during the tax year for projects described in section 48A(d)(3)(B)(iii) .   . . . . . $ _____ × 30% (0.30)   **5c**

d   Total. Add lines 5a, 5b, and 5c **5d**

6   Qualifying gasification project credit (see instructions):

a   Qualified investment in qualified gasification property placed in service during the tax year for which credits were allocated or reallocated after October 3, 2008, and that includes equipment that separates and sequesters at least 75% of the project's carbon dioxide emissions . . . . $ _____ × 30% (0.30)   **6a**

b   Qualified investment in property other than in **a** above placed in service during the tax year . . . . . . $ _____ × 20% (0.20)   **6b**

c   Total. Add lines 6a and 6b **6c**

7   Qualifying advanced energy project credit (see instructions):
Qualified investment in advanced energy project property placed in service during the tax year . . . . $ _____ × 30% (0.30)   **7**

8   Reserved **8**

9   Enter the applicable unused investment credit from cooperatives (see instructions) **9**

10   Add lines 5d, 6c, 7, and 9. Report this amount on Form 3800, Part III, line 1a **10**

For Paperwork Reduction Act Notice, see separate instructions.   Cat. No. 12276E   Form **3468** (2016)

Form 3468 (2016)   Page **2**

Part III	Rehabilitation Credit and Energy Credit

11 Rehabilitation credit (see instructions for requirements that must be met):

a Check this box if you are electing under section 47(d)(5) to take your qualified rehabilitation expenditures into account for the tax year in which paid (or, for self-rehabilitated property, when capitalized). See instructions. **Note:** This election applies to the current tax year and to all later tax years. You may not revoke this election without IRS consent . . . . ▶ ☐

b Enter the dates on which the 24- or 60-month measuring period begins _____
and ends _____

c Enter the adjusted basis of the building as of the beginning date above
(or the first day of your holding period, if later) . . . . $ _____

d Enter the amount of the qualified rehabilitation expenditures incurred, or
treated as incurred, during the period on line 11b above . . . . . $ _____

Enter the amount of qualified rehabilitation expenditures and multiply by the percentage shown:

e Pre-1936 buildings . . . . $ _____ × 10% (0.10) | **11e** |

f Certified historic structures . . . . $ _____ × 20% (0.20) | **11f** |

For properties identified on line 11f, complete lines 11g and 11h.

g Enter the assigned NPS project number or the pass-through entity's employer identification number (see instructions) . . . . _____

h Enter the date that the NPS approved the Request for Certification of Completed Work (see instructions) . . . . _____

i Rehabilitation credit from an electing large partnership (Schedule K-1 (Form 1065-B), box 9) . . | **11i** |

12 Energy credit:

a Basis of property using geothermal energy or solar energy (acquired before January 1, 2006, and the basis attributable to construction, reconstruction, or erection by the taxpayer before January 1, 2006) placed in service during the tax year (see instructions) $ _____ × 10% (0.10) | **12a** |

b Basis of property using solar illumination or solar energy placed in service during the tax year that was acquired after December 31, 2005, and the basis attributable to construction, reconstruction, or erection by the taxpayer after December 31, 2005 (see instructions) $ _____ × 30% (0.30) | **12b** |

Qualified fuel cell property (see instructions):

c Basis of property placed in service during the tax year that was acquired after December 31, 2005, and before October 4, 2008, and the basis attributable to construction, reconstruction, or erection by the taxpayer after December 31, 2005, and before October 4, 2008 $ _____ × 30% (0.30) | **12c** |

d Applicable kilowatt capacity of property on line 12c (see instructions) ▶ _____ × $1,000 | **12d** |

e Enter the lesser of line 12c or line 12d . . . . | **12e** |

f Basis of property placed in service during the tax year that was acquired after October 3, 2008, and the basis attributable to construction, reconstruction, or erection by the taxpayer after October 3, 2008 . . . . $ _____ × 30% (0.30) | **12f** |

g Applicable kilowatt capacity of property on line 12f (see instructions) ▶ _____ × $3,000 | **12g** |

h Enter the lesser of line 12f or line 12g . . . . | **12h** |

Qualified microturbine property (see instructions):

i Basis of property placed in service during the tax year that was acquired after December 31, 2005, and the basis attributable to construction, reconstruction, or erection by the taxpayer after December 31, 2005 . . . . $ _____ × 10% (0.10) | **12i** |

j Kilowatt capacity of property on line 12i . . . . ▶ _____ × $200 | **12j** |

k Enter the lesser of line 12i or line 12j . . . . | **12k** |

Form **3468** (2016)

Form 3468 (2016)   Page **3**

| Part III | Rehabilitation Credit and Energy Credit *(continued)* |

Combined heat and power system property (see instructions):

Caution: You cannot claim this credit if the electrical capacity of the property is more than 50 megawatts or 67,000 horsepower.

l Basis of property placed in service during the tax year that was acquired after October 3, 2008, and the basis attributable to construction, reconstruction, or erection by the taxpayer after October 3, 2008 . . . . $ _____ × 10% (0.10) | **12l** |

m If the electrical capacity of the property is measured in:

• Megawatts, divide 15 by the megawatt capacity. Enter 1.0 if the capacity is 15 megawatts or less.

• Horsepower, divide 20,000 by the horsepower. Enter 1.0 if the capacity is 20,000 horsepower or less . . . . | **12m** |

n Multiply line 12l by line 12m . . . . | **12n** |

Qualified small wind energy property (see instructions):

o Basis of property placed in service during the tax year that was acquired after October 3, 2008, and before January 1, 2009, and the basis attributable to the construction, reconstruction, or erection by the taxpayer after October 3, 2008, and before January 1, 2009 . . . . $ _____ × 30% (0.30) | **12o** |

p Enter the smaller of line 12o or $4,000 . . . . | **12p** |

q Basis of property placed in service during the tax year that was acquired after December 31, 2008, and the basis attributable to construction, reconstruction, or erection by the taxpayer after December 31, 2008 . . . . $ _____ × 30% (0.30) | **12q** |

Geothermal heat pump systems (see instructions):

r Basis of property placed in service during the tax year that was acquired after October 3, 2008, and the basis attributable to construction, reconstruction, or erection by the taxpayer after October 3, 2008 . . . . $ _____ × 10% (0.10) | **12r** |

Qualified investment credit facility property (see instructions):

s Basis of property (other than wind facility property and the construction of which began after 2016) placed in service during the tax year . . . . $ _____ × 30% (0.30) | **12s** |

t Basis of wind facility property placed in service during the tax year and the construction of which begins during 2017 . . . . $ _____ × 24% (0.24) | **12t** |

13 Enter the applicable unused investment credit from cooperatives (see instructions) . . . . . | **13** |

14 Add lines 11e, 11f, 11i, 12a, 12b, 12e, 12h, 12k, 12n, 12p, 12q, 12r, 12s, 12t, and 13. Report this amount on Form 3800, Part III, line 4a . . . . | **14** |

Form **3468** (2016)

Form **3800**	**General Business Credit**	OMB No. 1545-0895
Department of the Treasury Internal Revenue Service (99)	▶ Information about Form 3800 and its separate instructions is at *www.irs.gov/form3800*. ▶ You must attach all pages of Form 3800, pages 1, 2, and 3, to your tax return.	**2016** Attachment Sequence No. **22**

Name(s) shown on return | Identifying number

Part I   Current Year Credit for Credits Not Allowed Against Tentative Minimum Tax (TMT)
(See instructions and complete Part(s) III before Parts I and II)

1 General business credit from line 2 of all Parts III with box A checked **1**

2 Passive activity credits from line 2 of all Parts III with box B checked **2**

3 Enter the applicable passive activity credits allowed for 2016 (see instructions) **3**

4 Carryforward of general business credit to 2016. Enter the amount from line 2 of Part III with box C checked. See instructions for statement to attach **4**

5 Carryback of general business credit from 2017. Enter the amount from line 2 of Part III with box D checked (see instructions) **5**

6 Add lines 1, 3, 4, and 5 . . . . **6**

Part II   Allowable Credit

7 Regular tax before credits:
• Individuals. Enter the sum of the amounts from Form 1040, lines 44 and 46, or the sum of the amounts from Form 1040NR, lines 42 and 44 . . . .
• Corporations. Enter the amount from Form 1120, Schedule J, Part I, line 2; or the applicable line of your return **7**
• Estates and trusts. Enter the sum of the amounts from Form 1041, Schedule G, lines 1a and 1b; or the amount from the applicable line of your return . . . .

8 Alternative minimum tax:
• Individuals. Enter the amount from Form 6251, line 35 . . . .
• Corporations. Enter the amount from Form 4626, line 14 . . . . **8**
• Estates and trusts. Enter the amount from Schedule I (Form 1041), line 56 . . .

9 Add lines 7 and 8 . . . . **9**

10a Foreign tax credit **10a**
b Certain allowable credits (see instructions) **10b**
c Add lines 10a and 10b **10c**

11 **Net income tax.** Subtract line 10c from line 9. If zero, skip lines 12 through 15 and enter -0- on line 16 **11**

12 **Net regular tax.** Subtract line 10c from line 7. If zero or less, enter -0- **12**

13 Enter 25% (.25) of the excess, if any, of line 12 over $25,000 (see instructions) **13**

14 Tentative minimum tax:
• Individuals. Enter the amount from Form 6251, line 33 . . .
• Corporations. Enter the amount from Form 4626, line 12 . . . **14**
• Estates and trusts. Enter the amount from Schedule I (Form 1041), line 54 . . . .

15 Enter the greater of line 13 or line 14 . . . . **15**
16 Subtract line 15 from line 11. If zero or less, enter -0- **16**
17 Enter the **smaller** of line 6 or line 16 . . . . **17**
C corporations: See the line 17 instructions if there has been an ownership change, acquisition, or reorganization.

For Paperwork Reduction Act Notice, see separate instructions.   Cat. No. 12392F   Form **3800** (2016)

Form 3800 (2016)   Page **2**

Part II   **Allowable Credit** *(Continued)*

Note: If you are not required to report any amounts on lines 22 or 24 below, skip lines 18 through 25 and enter -0- on line 26.

18	Multiply line 14 by 75% (.75) (see instructions)	**18**	
19	Enter the greater of line 13 or line 18	**19**	
20	Subtract line 19 from line 11. If zero or less, enter -0-	**20**	
21	Subtract line 17 from line 20. If zero or less, enter -0-	**21**	
22	Combine the amounts from line 3 of all Parts III with box A, C, or D checked	**22**	
23	Passive activity credit from line 3 of all Parts III with box B checked **23**		
24	Enter the applicable passive activity credit allowed for 2016 (see instructions)	**24**	
25	Add lines 22 and 24	**25**	
26	Empowerment zone and renewal community employment credit allowed. Enter the smaller of line 21 or line 25	**26**	
27	Subtract line 13 from line 11. If zero or less, enter -0-	**27**	
28	Add lines 17 and 26	**28**	
29	Subtract line 28 from line 27. If zero or less, enter -0-	**29**	
30	Enter the general business credit from line 5 of all Parts III with box A checked	**30**	
31	Reserved	**31**	
32	Passive activity credits from line 5 of all Parts III with box B checked **32**		
33	Enter the applicable passive activity credits allowed for 2016 (see instructions)	**33**	
34	Carryforward of business credit to 2016. Enter the amount from line 5 of Part III with box C checked and line 6 of Part III with box G checked. See instructions for statement to attach . .	**34**	
35	Carryback of business credit from 2017. Enter the amount from line 5 of Part III with box D checked (see instructions)	**35**	
36	Add lines 30, 33, 34, and 35	**36**	
37	Enter the **smaller** of line 29 or line 36	**37**	
38	**Credit allowed for the current year.** Add lines 28 and 37. Report the amount from line 38 (if smaller than the sum of Part I, line 6, and Part II, lines 25 and 36, see instructions) as indicated below or on the applicable line of your return. • Individuals. Form 1040, line 54, or Form 1040NR, line 51 . . . . • Corporations. Form 1120, Schedule J, Part I, line 5c . . . . • Estates and trusts. Form 1041, Schedule G, line 2b	**38**	

Form **3800** (2016)

Form 3800 (2016)   Page **3**

Name(s) shown on return	Identifying number

Part III   General Business Credits or Eligible Small Business Credits (see instructions)

Complete a separate Part III for each box checked below (see instructions).

A ☐ General Business Credit From a Non-Passive Activity   E ▨ Reserved

B ☐ General Business Credit From a Passive Activity   F ▨ Reserved

C ☐ General Business Credit Carryforwards   G ☐ Eligible Small Business Credit Carryforwards

D ☐ General Business Credit Carrybacks   H ▨ Reserved

I   If you are filing more than one Part III with box A or B checked, complete and attach first an additional Part III combining amounts from all Parts III with box A or B checked. Check here if this is the consolidated Part III .   .   .   . ▶ ☐

(a) Description of credit		(b) If claiming the credit from a pass-through entity, enter the EIN	(c) Enter the appropriate amount	
Note: On any line where the credit is from more than one source, a separate Part III is needed for each pass-through entity.				
1a	Investment (Form 3468, Part II only) (attach Form 3468)	1a		
b	Reserved	1b	▨	▨
c	Increasing research activities (Form 6765)	1c		
d	Low-income housing (Form 8586, Part I only)	1d		
e	Disabled access (Form 8826) (see instructions for limitation)	1e		
f	Renewable electricity, refined coal, and Indian coal production (Form 8835)	1f		
g	Indian employment (Form 8845)	1g		
h	Orphan drug (Form 8820)	1h		
i	New markets (Form 8874)	1i		
j	Small employer pension plan startup costs (Form 8881) (see instructions for limitation)	1j		
k	Employer-provided child care facilities and services (Form 8882) (see instructions for limitation)	1k		
l	Biodiesel and renewable diesel fuels (attach Form 8864)	1l		
m	Low sulfur diesel fuel production (Form 8896)	1m		
n	Distilled spirits (Form 8906)	1n		
o	Nonconventional source fuel (carryforward only)	1o		
p	Energy efficient home (Form 8908)	1p		
q	Energy efficient appliance (carryforward only)	1q		
r	Alternative motor vehicle (Form 8910)	1r		
s	Alternative fuel vehicle refueling property (Form 8911)	1s		
t	Reserved	1t	▨	▨
u	Mine rescue team training (Form 8923)	1u		
v	Agricultural chemicals security (carryforward only)	1v		
w	Employer differential wage payments (Form 8932)	1w		
x	Carbon dioxide sequestration (Form 8933)	1x		
y	Qualified plug-in electric drive motor vehicle (Form 8936)	1y		
z	Qualified plug-in electric vehicle (carryforward only)	1z		
aa	New hire retention (carryforward only)	1aa		
bb	General credits from an electing large partnership (Schedule K-1 (Form 1065-B))	1bb		
zz	Other. Enhanced oil recovery (Form 8830) and certain other credits . . .	1zz		
2	Add lines 1a through 1zz and enter here and on the applicable line of Part I	2	▨	
3	Enter the amount from Form 8844 here and on the applicable line of Part II .	3		
4a	Investment (Form 3468, Part III) (attach Form 3468)	4a		
b	Work opportunity (Form 5884)	4b		
c	Biofuel producer (Form 6478)	4c		
d	Low-income housing (Form 8586, Part II)	4d		
e	Renewable electricity, refined coal, and Indian coal production (Form 8835)	4e		
f	Employer social security and Medicare taxes paid on certain employee tips (Form 8846)	4f		
g	Qualified railroad track maintenance (Form 8900)	4g		
h	Small employer health insurance premiums (Form 8941)	4h		
i	Increasing research activities (Form 6765).	4i		
j	Reserved	4j	▨	▨
z	Other	4z		
5	Add lines 4a through 4z and enter here and on the applicable line of Part II .	5	▨	
6	Add lines 2, 3, and 5 and enter here and on the applicable line of Part II . .	6	▨	

Form **3800** (2016)

Form **2106**	Employee Business Expenses	OMB No. 1545-0074

Department of the Treasury
Internal Revenue Service (99)

▶ Attach to Form 1040 or Form 1040NR.

▶ Information about Form 2106 and its separate instructions is available at *www.irs.gov/form2106.*

20**16**

Attachment
Sequence No. **129**

Your name	Occupation in which you incurred expenses	Social security number

Part I   Employee Business Expenses and Reimbursements

Step 1 Enter Your Expenses

		Column A Other Than Meals and Entertainment		Column B Meals and Entertainment
1	Vehicle expense from line 22 or line 29. (Rural mail carriers: See instructions.)			
2	Parking fees, tolls, and transportation, including train, bus, etc., that **didn't** involve overnight travel or commuting to and from work			
3	Travel expense while away from home overnight, including lodging, airplane, car rental, etc. **Don't** include meals and entertainment.			
4	Business expenses not included on lines 1 through 3. **Don't** include meals and entertainment			
5	Meals and entertainment expenses (see instructions)			
6	**Total expenses.** In Column A, add lines 1 through 4 and enter the result. In Column B, enter the amount from line 5			

Note: *If you weren't reimbursed for any expenses in Step 1, skip line 7 and enter the amount from line 6 on line 8.*

Step 2 Enter Reimbursements Received From Your Employer for Expenses Listed in Step 1

7	Enter reimbursements received from your employer that **weren't** reported to you in box 1 of Form W-2. Include any reimbursements reported under code "L" in box 12 of your Form W-2 (see instructions).		

Step 3 Figure Expenses To Deduct on Schedule A (Form 1040 or Form 1040NR)

8	Subtract line 7 from line 6. If zero or less, enter -0-. However, if line 7 is greater than line 6 in Column A, report the excess as income on Form 1040, line 7 (or on Form 1040NR, line 8)		

Note: *If **both columns** of line 8 are zero, you can't deduct employee business expenses. Stop here and attach Form 2106 to your return.*

9	In Column A, enter the amount from line 8. In Column B, multiply line 8 by 50% (0.50). (Employees subject to Department of Transportation (DOT) hours of service limits: Multiply meal expenses incurred while away from home on business by 80% (0.80) instead of 50%. For details, see instructions.)		
10	Add the amounts on line 9 of both columns and enter the total here. **Also, enter the total on Schedule A (Form 1040), line 21** (or on **Schedule A (Form 1040NR), line 7**). (Armed Forces reservists, qualified performing artists, fee-basis state or local government officials, and individuals with disabilities: See the instructions for special rules on where to enter the total.) ▶		10

For Paperwork Reduction Act Notice, see your tax return instructions.   Cat. No. 11700N   Form **2106** (2016)

Form 2106 (2016)   Page **2**

Part II   Vehicle Expenses

Section A—General Information (You must complete this section if you are claiming vehicle expenses.)

			(a) Vehicle 1	(b) Vehicle 2
11	Enter the date the vehicle was placed in service	11	/ /	/ /
12	Total miles the vehicle was driven during 2016	12	miles	miles
13	Business miles included on line 12	13	miles	miles
14	Percent of business use. Divide line 13 by line 12	14	%	%
15	Average daily roundtrip commuting distance	15	miles	miles
16	Commuting miles included on line 12	16	miles	miles
17	Other miles. Add lines 13 and 16 and subtract the total from line 12 . .	17	miles	miles

18	Was your vehicle available for personal use during off-duty hours?	☐ Yes ☐ No
19	Do you (or your spouse) have another vehicle available for personal use?	☐ Yes ☐ No
20	Do you have evidence to support your deduction?	☐ Yes ☐ No
21	If "Yes," is the evidence written?	☐ Yes ☐ No

Section B—Standard Mileage Rate (See the instructions for Part II to find out whether to complete this section or Section C.)

22	Multiply line 13 by 54¢ (0.54). Enter the result here and on line 1	22	

Section C—Actual Expenses

			(a) Vehicle 1	(b) Vehicle 2
23	Gasoline, oil, repairs, vehicle insurance, etc.	23		
24a	Vehicle rentals	24a		
b	Inclusion amount (see instructions) .	24b		
c	Subtract line 24b from line 24a .	24c		
25	Value of employer-provided vehicle (applies only if 100% of annual lease value was included on Form W-2—see instructions)	25		
26	Add lines 23, 24c, and 25. . .	26		
27	Multiply line 26 by the percentage on line 14	27		
28	Depreciation (see instructions) .	28		
29	Add lines 27 and 28. Enter total here and on line 1	29		

Section D—Depreciation of Vehicles (Use this section only if you owned the vehicle and are completing Section C for the vehicle.)

			(a) Vehicle 1	(b) Vehicle 2
30	Enter cost or other basis (see instructions)	30		
31	Enter section 179 deduction and special allowance (see instructions)	31		
32	Multiply line 30 by line 14 (see instructions if you claimed the section 179 deduction or special allowance).	32		
33	Enter depreciation method and percentage (see instructions) .	33		
34	Multiply line 32 by the percentage on line 33 (see instructions) . .	34		
35	Add lines 31 and 34	35		
36	Enter the applicable limit explained in the line 36 instructions . . .	36		
37	Multiply line 36 by the percentage on line 14	37		
38	Enter the **smaller** of line 35 or line 37. If you skipped lines 36 and 37, enter the amount from line 35. Also enter this amount on line 28 above	38		

Form **2106** (2016)

Form **2120** (Rev. October 2005) Department of the Treasury Internal Revenue Service	**Multiple Support Declaration** ▶ Attach to Form 1040 or Form 1040A.	OMB No. 1545-0074 Attachment Sequence No. **114**

Name(s) shown on return

Your social security number

During the calendar year .... , the eligible persons listed below each paid over 10% of the support of:

Name of your qualifying relative

I have a signed statement from each eligible person waiving his or her right to claim this person as a dependent for any tax year that began in the above calendar year.

Eligible person's name

Social security number

Address (number, street, apt. no., city, state, and ZIP code)

Eligible person's name

Social security number

Address (number, street, apt. no., city, state, and ZIP code)

Eligible person's name

Social security number

Address (number, street, apt. no., city, state, and ZIP code)

Eligible person's name

Social security number

Address (number, street, apt. no., city, state, and ZIP code)

Instructions

What's New

The rules for multiple support agreements still apply to claiming an exemption for a qualifying relative, but they no longer apply to claiming an exemption for a qualifying child. For the definitions of "qualifying relative" and "qualifying child," see your tax return instruction booklet.

Purpose of Form

Use Form 2120 to:

● Identify each other eligible person (see below) who paid over 10% of the support of your qualifying relative whom you are claiming as a dependent, and

● Indicate that you have a signed statement from each other eligible person waiving his or her right to claim that person as a dependent.

An eligible person is someone who could have claimed a person as a dependent except that he or she did not pay over half of that person's support.

If there are more than four other eligible persons, attach a statement to your return with the required information.

Claiming a Qualifying Relative

Generally, to claim a person as a qualifying relative, you must pay over half of that person's support. However, even if you did not meet this support test, you may be able to claim him or her as a dependent if all five of the following apply.

1. You and one or more other eligible person(s) (see above) together paid over half of that person's support.

2. You paid over 10% of the support.

3. No one alone paid over half of that person's support.

4. The other dependency tests are met. See *Step 4, Is Your Qualifying Relative Your Dependent?* in the Form 1040 or Form 1040A instructions.

5. Each other eligible person who paid over 10% of the support agrees not to claim that person as a dependent by giving you a signed statement. See *Signed Statement* on this page.

Note. To find out what is included in support, see Pub. 501, Exemptions, Standard Deduction, and Filing Information.

Signed Statement

You must have received, from each other eligible person listed above, a signed statement waiving his or her right to claim the person as a dependent for the calendar year indicated on this form. The statement must include:

● The calendar year the waiver applies to,

● The name of your qualifying relative the eligible person helped to support, and

● The eligible person's name, address, and social security number.

Do not file the signed statement with your return. But you must keep it for your records and be prepared to furnish it and any other information necessary to show that you qualify to claim the person as your dependent.

Additional Information

See Pub. 501 for details.

Paperwork Reduction Act Notice. We ask for the information on this form to carry out the Internal Revenue laws of the United States. You are required to give us the information. We need it to ensure that you are complying with these laws and to allow us to figure and collect the right amount of tax.

You are not required to provide the information requested on a form that is subject to the Paperwork Reduction Act unless the form displays a valid OMB control number. Books or records relating to a form or its instructions must be retained as long as their contents may become material in the administration of any Internal Revenue law. Generally, tax returns and return information are confidential, as required by Internal Revenue Code section 6103.

The average time and expenses required to complete and file this form will vary depending on individual circumstances. For the estimated averages, see the instructions for your income tax return.

If you have suggestions for making this form simpler, we would be happy to hear from you. See the instructions for your income tax return.

Cat. No. 11712F

Form **2120** (Rev. 10-2005)

Form **3903**	**Moving Expenses**	OMB No. 1545-0074

Department of the Treasury
Internal Revenue Service (99)

► Information about Form 3903 and its instructions is available at *www.irs.gov/form3903.*
► **Attach to Form 1040 or Form 1040NR.**

2016
Attachment
Sequence No. **170**

Name(s) shown on return

Your social security number

Before you begin: ✓ See the **Distance Test** and **Time Test** in the instructions to find out if you can deduct your moving expenses.

✓ See **Members of the Armed Forces** in the instructions, if applicable.

1	Transportation and storage of household goods and personal effects (see instructions) . . .	1
2	Travel (including lodging) from your old home to your new home (see instructions). **Do not** include the cost of meals	2
3	Add lines 1 and 2	3
4	Enter the total amount your employer paid you for the expenses listed on lines 1 and 2 that is **not** included in box 1 of your Form W-2 (wages). This amount should be shown in box 12 of your Form W-2 with code **P**	4
5	Is line 3 **more than** line 4?	
	☐ **No.** You **cannot** deduct your moving expenses. If line 3 is less than line 4, subtract line 3 from line 4 and include the result on Form 1040, line 7, or Form 1040NR, line 8.	
	☐ **Yes.** Subtract line 4 from line 3. Enter the result here and on Form 1040, line 26, or Form 1040NR, line 26. This is your **moving expense deduction**	5

For Paperwork Reduction Act Notice, see your tax return instructions.   Cat. No. 12490K   Form **3903** (2016)

Form **4562**	**Depreciation and Amortization** (Including Information on Listed Property) ▶ Attach to your tax return. ▶ Information about Form 4562 and its separate instructions is at *www.irs.gov/form4562*.	OMB No. 1545-0172
Department of the Treasury Internal Revenue Service (99)		**2016** Attachment Sequence No. **179**
Name(s) shown on return	Business or activity to which this form relates	Identifying number

Part I   **Election To Expense Certain Property Under Section 179**
Note: If you have any listed property, complete Part V before you complete Part I.

1	Maximum amount (see instructions)	**1**
2	Total cost of section 179 property placed in service (see instructions)	**2**
3	Threshold cost of section 179 property before reduction in limitation (see instructions)	**3**
4	Reduction in limitation. Subtract line 3 from line 2. If zero or less, enter -0-	**4**
5	Dollar limitation for tax year. Subtract line 4 from line 1. If zero or less, enter -0-. If married filing separately, see instructions	**5**

6	**(a)** Description of property	**(b)** Cost (business use only)	**(c)** Elected cost	

7	Listed property. Enter the amount from line 29	**7**
8	Total elected cost of section 179 property. Add amounts in column (c), lines 6 and 7	**8**
9	Tentative deduction. Enter the **smaller** of line 5 or line 8	**9**
10	Carryover of disallowed deduction from line 13 of your 2015 Form 4562 . .	**10**
11	Business income limitation. Enter the smaller of business income (not less than zero) or line 5 (see instructions)	**11**
12	Section 179 expense deduction. Add lines 9 and 10, but don't enter more than line 11	**12**
13	Carryover of disallowed deduction to 2017. Add lines 9 and 10, less line 12 ▶	**13**

Note: Don't use Part II or Part III below for listed property. Instead, use Part V.

Part II   **Special Depreciation Allowance and Other Depreciation (Don't** include listed property.**)** (See instructions.)

14	Special depreciation allowance for qualified property (other than listed property) placed in service during the tax year (see instructions)	**14**
15	Property subject to section 168(f)(1) election	**15**
16	Other depreciation (including ACRS)	**16**

Part III   **MACRS Depreciation (Don't** include listed property.**)** (See instructions.)

Section A

17	MACRS deductions for assets placed in service in tax years beginning before 2016	**17**
18	If you are electing to group any assets placed in service during the tax year into one or more general asset accounts, check here . . . . ▶ ☐	

Section B—Assets Placed in Service During 2016 Tax Year Using the General Depreciation System

(a) Classification of property	(b) Month and year placed in service	(c) Basis for depreciation (business/investment use only—see instructions)	(d) Recovery period	(e) Convention	(f) Method	(g) Depreciation deduction
19a 3-year property						
b 5-year property						
c 7-year property						
d 10-year property						
e 15-year property						
f 20-year property						
g 25-year property			25 yrs.		S/L	
h Residential rental property			27.5 yrs.	MM	S/L	
			27.5 yrs.	MM	S/L	
i Nonresidential real property			39 yrs.	MM	S/L	
				MM	S/L	

Section C—Assets Placed in Service During 2016 Tax Year Using the Alternative Depreciation System

20a Class life					S/L	
b 12-year			12 yrs.		S/L	
c 40-year			40 yrs.	MM	S/L	

Part IV   **Summary** (See instructions.)

21	Listed property. Enter amount from line 28	**21**
22	**Total.** Add amounts from line 12, lines 14 through 17, lines 19 and 20 in column (g), and line 21. Enter here and on the appropriate lines of your return. Partnerships and S corporations—see instructions .	**22**
23	For assets shown above and placed in service during the current year, enter the portion of the basis attributable to section 263A costs	**23**

For Paperwork Reduction Act Notice, see separate instructions.   Cat. No. 12906N   Form **4562** (2016)

Form 4562 (2016)   Page **2**

Part V   **Listed Property** (Include automobiles, certain other vehicles, certain aircraft, certain computers, and property used for entertainment, recreation, or amusement.)

Note: For any vehicle for which you are using the standard mileage rate or deducting lease expense, complete **only** 24a, 24b, columns (a) through (c) of Section A, all of Section B, and Section C if applicable.

Section A—Depreciation and Other Information (Caution: See the instructions for limits for passenger automobiles.**)**

24a Do you have evidence to support the business/investment use claimed? ☐ Yes ☐ No   **24b** If "Yes," is the evidence written? ☐ Yes ☐ No

(a) Type of property (list vehicles first)	(b) Date placed in service	(c) Business/ investment use percentage	(d) Cost or other basis	(e) Basis for depreciation (business/investment use only)	(f) Recovery period	(g) Method/ Convention	(h) Depreciation deduction	(i) Elected section 179 cost
25 Special depreciation allowance for qualified listed property placed in service during the tax year and used more than 50% in a qualified business use (see instructions) . **25**								
26 Property used more than 50% in a qualified business use:								
		%						
		%						
		%						
27 Property used 50% or less in a qualified business use:								
		%				S/L –		
		%				S/L –		
		%				S/L –		

28 Add amounts in column (h), lines 25 through 27. Enter here and on line 21, page 1 .   **28**

29 Add amounts in column (i), line 26. Enter here and on line 7, page 1 . . . .   **29**

Section B—Information on Use of Vehicles

Complete this section for vehicles used by a sole proprietor, partner, or other "more than 5% owner," or related person. If you provided vehicles to your employees, first answer the questions in Section C to see if you meet an exception to completing this section for those vehicles.

	(a) Vehicle 1		(b) Vehicle 2		(c) Vehicle 3		(d) Vehicle 4		(e) Vehicle 5		(f) Vehicle 6	
30 Total business/investment miles driven during the year (**don't** include commuting miles) .												
31 Total commuting miles driven during the year												
32 Total other personal (noncommuting) miles driven												
33 Total miles driven during the year. Add lines 30 through 32												
34 Was the vehicle available for personal use during off-duty hours?	Yes	No	Yes	No	Yes	No	Yes	No	Yes	No	Yes	No
35 Was the vehicle used primarily by a more than 5% owner or related person? . .												
36 Is another vehicle available for personal use?												

Section C—Questions for Employers Who Provide Vehicles for Use by Their Employees

Answer these questions to determine if you meet an exception to completing Section B for vehicles used by employees who **aren't** more than 5% owners or related persons (see instructions).

	Yes	No
37 Do you maintain a written policy statement that prohibits all personal use of vehicles, including commuting, by your employees?		
38 Do you maintain a written policy statement that prohibits personal use of vehicles, except commuting, by your employees? See the instructions for vehicles used by corporate officers, directors, or 1% or more owners . .		
39 Do you treat all use of vehicles by employees as personal use?		
40 Do you provide more than five vehicles to your employees, obtain information from your employees about the use of the vehicles, and retain the information received?		
41 Do you meet the requirements concerning qualified automobile demonstration use? (See instructions.) . . .		

Note: If your answer to 37, 38, 39, 40, or 41 is "Yes," don't complete Section B for the covered vehicles.

Part VI   **Amortization**

(a) Description of costs	(b) Date amortization begins	(c) Amortizable amount	(d) Code section	(e) Amortization period or percentage	(f) Amortization for this year
42 Amortization of costs that begins during your 2016 tax year (see instructions):					

43 Amortization of costs that began before your 2016 tax year **43**

44 Total. Add amounts in column (f). See the instructions for where to report **44**

Form **4562** (2016)

Form **4684**	**Casualties and Thefts**	OMB No. 1545-0177
Department of the Treasury Internal Revenue Service	► Information about Form 4684 and its separate instructions is at *www.irs.gov/form4684*. ► **Attach to your tax return.** ► **Use a separate Form 4684 for each casualty or theft.**	20**16** Attachment Sequence No. **26**

Name(s) shown on tax return	Identifying number

SECTION A—Personal Use Property (Use this section to report casualties and thefts of property **not** used in a trade or business or for income-producing purposes.)

1 Description of properties (show type, location, and date acquired for each property). Use a separate line for each property lost or damaged from the same casualty or theft.

Property **A** _____

Property **B** _____

Property **C** _____

Property **D** _____

		Properties			
		A	**B**	**C**	**D**
2 Cost or other basis of each property	**2**				
3 Insurance or other reimbursement (whether or not you filed a claim) (see instructions)	**3**				
Note: *If line 2 is **more** than line 3, skip line 4.*					
4 Gain from casualty or theft. If line 3 is **more** than line 2, enter the difference here and skip lines 5 through 9 for that column. See instructions if line 3 includes insurance or other reimbursement you did not claim, or you received payment for your loss in a later tax year . .	**4**				
5 Fair market value **before** casualty or theft	**5**				
6 Fair market value **after** casualty or theft	**6**				
7 Subtract line 6 from line 5	**7**				
8 Enter the **smaller** of line 2 or line 7	**8**				
9 Subtract line 3 from line 8. If zero or less, enter -0- . .	**9**				

10 Casualty or theft loss. Add the amounts on line 9 in columns A through D	**10**	
11 Enter the **smaller** of line 10 or $100	**11**	
12 Subtract line 11 from line 10	**12**	
Caution: *Use only one Form 4684 for lines 13 through 18.*		
13 Add the amounts on line 12 of all Forms 4684	**13**	
14 Add the amounts on line 4 of all Forms 4684.	**14**	
15 • If line 14 is **more** than line 13, enter the difference here and on Schedule D. **Do not** complete the rest of this section (see instructions). • If line 14 is **less** than line 13, enter -0- here and go to line 16. • If line 14 is **equal** to line 13, enter -0- here. **Do not** complete the rest of this section.	**15**	
16 If line 14 is **less** than line 13, enter the difference	**16**	
17 Enter 10% of your adjusted gross income from Form 1040, line 38, or Form 1040NR, line 37. Estates and trusts, see instructions	**17**	
18 Subtract line 17 from line 16. If zero or less, enter -0-. Also enter the result on Schedule A (Form 1040), line 20, or Form 1040NR, Schedule A, line 6. Estates and trusts, enter the result on the "Other deductions" line of your tax return	**18**	

For Paperwork Reduction Act Notice, see instructions.	Cat. No. 12997O	Form **4684** (2016)

Form 4684 (2016)   Attachment Sequence No. **26**   Page **2**

Name(s) shown on tax return. Do not enter name and identifying number if shown on other side.	Identifying number

SECTION B—Business and Income-Producing Property

Part I   **Casualty or Theft Gain or Loss**   (Use a separate Part I for each casualty or theft.)

19 Description of properties (show type, location, and date acquired for each property). Use a separate line for each property lost or damaged from the same casualty or theft. **See instructions if claiming a loss due to a Ponzi-type investment scheme and Section C is not completed.**

Property **A** _____

Property **B** _____

Property **C** _____

Property **D** _____

		Properties			
		A	**B**	**C**	**D**
20 Cost or adjusted basis of each property	**20**				
21 Insurance or other reimbursement (whether or not you filed a claim). See the instructions for line 3	**21**				
Note: *If line 20 is **more** than line 21, skip line 22.*					
22 Gain from casualty or theft. If line 21 is **more** than line 20, enter the difference here and on line 29 or line 34, column (c), except as provided in the instructions for line 33. Also, skip lines 23 through 27 for that column. See the instructions for line 4 if line 21 includes insurance or other reimbursement you did not claim, or you received payment for your loss in a later tax year	**22**				
23 Fair market value **before** casualty or theft	**23**				
24 Fair market value **after** casualty or theft	**24**				
25 Subtract line 24 from line 23	**25**				
26 Enter the **smaller** of line 20 or line 25	**26**				
Note: *If the property was totally destroyed by casualty or lost from theft, enter on line 26 the amount from line 20.*					
27 Subtract line 21 from line 26. If zero or less, enter -0-	**27**				
28 Casualty or theft loss. Add the amounts on line 27. Enter the total here and on line 29 **or** line 34 (see instructions)				**28**	

Part II   **Summary of Gains and Losses**   (from separate Parts I)

(a) Identify casualty or theft	**(b)** Losses from casualties or thefts		**(c)** Gains from casualties or thefts includible in income
	(i) Trade, business, rental or royalty property	*(ii)* Income-producing and employee property	

Casualty or Theft of Property Held One Year or Less

29 _____	( )	( )	
_____	( )	( )	
30 Totals. Add the amounts on line 29 . . . . **30**	( )	( )	

31 Combine line 30, columns (b)(i) and (c). Enter the net gain or (loss) here and on Form 4797, line 14. If Form 4797 is not otherwise required, see instructions **31**

32 Enter the amount from line 30, column (b)(ii) here. Individuals, enter the amount from income-producing property on Schedule A (Form 1040), line 28, or Form 1040NR, Schedule A, line 14, and enter the amount from property used as an employee on Schedule A (Form 1040), line 23, or Form 1040NR, Schedule A, line 9. Estates and trusts, partnerships, and S corporations, see instructions **32**

Casualty or Theft of Property Held More Than One Year

33 Casualty or theft gains from Form 4797, line 32 . . . . **33**

34 _____	( )	( )	
_____	( )	( )	
35 Total losses. Add amounts on line 34, columns (b)(i) and (b)(ii) **35**	( )	( )	

36 Total gains. Add lines 33 and 34, column (c) **36**

37 Add amounts on line 35, columns (b)(i) and (b)(ii) **37**

38 If the loss on line 37 is **more** than the gain on line 36:

   a Combine line 35, column (b)(i) and line 36, and enter the net **gain** or (loss) here. Partnerships (except electing large partnerships) and S corporations, see the note below. All others, enter this amount on Form 4797, line 14. If Form 4797 is not otherwise required, see instructions **38a**

   b Enter the amount from line 35, column (b)(ii) here. Individuals, enter the amount from income-producing property on Schedule A (Form 1040), line 28, or Form 1040NR, Schedule A, line 14, and enter the amount from property used as an employee on Schedule A (Form 1040), line 23, or Form 1040NR, Schedule A, line 9. Estates and trusts, enter on the "Other deductions" line of your tax return. Partnerships (except electing large partnerships) and S corporations, see the note below. Electing large partnerships, enter on Form 1065-B, Part II, line 11 . . . . **38b**

39 If the loss on line 37 is **less** than or **equal** to the gain on line 36, combine lines 36 and 37 and enter here. Partnerships (except electing large partnerships), see the note below. All others, enter this amount on Form 4797, line 3 . . . . **39**

Note: *Partnerships, enter the amount from line 38a, 38b, or line 39 on Form 1065, Schedule K, line 11. S corporations, enter the amount from line 38a or 38b on Form 1120S, Schedule K, line 10.*

Form **4684** (2016)

Form 4684 (2016)   Page **3**

Name(s) shown on tax return	Identifying number

SECTION C—Theft Loss Deduction for Ponzi-Type Investment Scheme Using the Procedures in Revenue Procedure 2009-20 (Complete this section in lieu of Appendix A in Revenue Procedure 2009-20. See instructions.)

Part I   Computation of Deduction

40	Initial investment	40		
41	Subsequent investments (see instructions)	41		
42	Income reported on your tax returns for tax years prior to the discovery year (see instructions).	42		
43	Add lines 40, 41, and 42	43		
44	Withdrawals for all years (see instructions)	44		
45	Subtract line 44 from line 43. This is your total qualified investment	45		
46	Enter .95 (95%) if you have no potential third-party recovery. Enter .75 (75%) if you have potential third-party recovery	46	.	
47	Multiply line 46 by line 45	47		
48	Actual recovery	48		
49	Potential insurance/Securities Investor Protection Corporation (SIPC) recovery . .	49		
50	Add lines 48 and 49. This is your total recovery	50		
51	Subtract line 50 from line 47. This is your deductible theft loss. Include this amount on line 28 of Section B, Part I. Do not complete lines 19-27 for this loss. Then complete Section B, Part II.	51		

Part II   Required Statements and Declarations (See instructions.)

- I am claiming a theft loss deduction pursuant to Revenue Procedure 2009-20 from a specified fraudulent arrangement conducted by the following individual or entity.

  Name of individual or entity _____

  Taxpayer identification number (if known) _____

  Address _____

- I have written documentation to support the amounts reported in Part I of this Section C.

- I am a qualified investor as defined in section 4.03 of Revenue Procedure 2009-20.

- If I have determined the amount of my theft loss deduction using .95 on line 46 above, I declare that I have not pursued and do not intend to pursue any potential third-party recovery, as that term is defined in section 4.10 of Revenue Procedure 2009-20.

- I agree to comply with the conditions and agreements set forth in Revenue Procedure 2009-20 and this Section C.

- If I have already filed a return or amended return that does not satisfy the conditions in section 6.02 of Revenue Procedure 2009-20, I agree to all adjustments or actions that are necessary to comply with those conditions. The tax year(s) for which I filed the return(s) or amended return(s) and the date(s) on which they were filed are as follows:

  _____
  _____
  _____

Form **4684** (2016)

Form **4797**	**Sales of Business Property**	OMB No. 1545-0184
Department of the Treasury Internal Revenue Service	(Also Involuntary Conversions and Recapture Amounts Under Sections 179 and 280F(b)(2)) ▶ Attach to your tax return. ▶ Information about Form 4797 and its separate instructions is at *www.irs.gov/form4797*.	**2016** Attachment Sequence No. **27**

Name(s) shown on return | Identifying number

1 Enter the gross proceeds from sales or exchanges reported to you for 2016 on Form(s) 1099-B or 1099-S (or substitute statement) that you are including on line 2, 10, or 20. See instructions . . . . | **1**

Part I **Sales or Exchanges of Property Used in a Trade or Business and Involuntary Conversions From Other Than Casualty or Theft—Most Property Held More Than 1 Year** (see instructions)

2	(a) Description of property	(b) Date acquired (mo., day, yr.)	(c) Date sold (mo., day, yr.)	(d) Gross sales price	(e) Depreciation allowed or allowable since acquisition	(f) Cost or other basis, plus improvements and expense of sale	(g) Gain or (loss) Subtract (f) from the sum of (d) and (e)

3	Gain, if any, from Form 4684, line 39	**3**
4	Section 1231 gain from installment sales from Form 6252, line 26 or 37	**4**
5	Section 1231 gain or (loss) from like-kind exchanges from Form 8824	**5**
6	Gain, if any, from line 32, from other than casualty or theft	**6**
7	Combine lines 2 through 6. Enter the gain or (loss) here and on the appropriate line as follows:	**7**

Partnerships (except electing large partnerships) and S corporations. Report the gain or (loss) following the instructions for Form 1065, Schedule K, line 10, or Form 1120S, Schedule K, line 9. Skip lines 8, 9, 11, and 12 below.

Individuals, partners, S corporation shareholders, and all others. If line 7 is zero or a loss, enter the amount from line 7 on line 11 below and skip lines 8 and 9. If line 7 is a gain and you didn't have any prior year section 1231 losses, or they were recaptured in an earlier year, enter the gain from line 7 as a long-term capital gain on the Schedule D filed with your return and skip lines 8, 9, 11, and 12 below.

8	Nonrecaptured net section 1231 losses from prior years. See instructions	**8**
9	Subtract line 8 from line 7. If zero or less, enter -0-. If line 9 is zero, enter the gain from line 7 on line 12 below. If line 9 is more than zero, enter the amount from line 8 on line 12 below and enter the gain from line 9 as a long-term capital gain on the Schedule D filed with your return. See instructions	**9**

Part II **Ordinary Gains and Losses** (see instructions)

10 Ordinary gains and losses not included on lines 11 through 16 (include property held 1 year or less):

11	Loss, if any, from line 7	**11** ( )
12	Gain, if any, from line 7 or amount from line 8, if applicable	**12**
13	Gain, if any, from line 31	**13**
14	Net gain or (loss) from Form 4684, lines 31 and 38a	**14**
15	Ordinary gain from installment sales from Form 6252, line 25 or 36	**15**
16	Ordinary gain or (loss) from like-kind exchanges from Form 8824.	**16**
17	Combine lines 10 through 16	**17**

18 For all except individual returns, enter the amount from line 17 on the appropriate line of your return and skip lines a and b below. For individual returns, complete lines a and b below:

a If the loss on line 11 includes a loss from Form 4684, line 35, column (b)(ii), enter that part of the loss here. Enter the part of the loss from income-producing property on Schedule A (Form 1040), line 28, and the part of the loss from property used as an employee on Schedule A (Form 1040), line 23. Identify as from "Form 4797, line 18a." See instructions . . | **18a**

b Redetermine the gain or (loss) on line 17 excluding the loss, if any, on line 18a. Enter here and on Form 1040, line 14 | **18b**

For Paperwork Reduction Act Notice, see separate instructions.   Cat. No. 13086I   Form **4797** (2016)

Form 4797 (2016)   Page **2**

Part III   Gain From Disposition of Property Under Sections 1245, 1250, 1252, 1254, and 1255
(see instructions)

19	(a) Description of section 1245, 1250, 1252, 1254, or 1255 property:	(b) Date acquired (mo., day, yr.)	(c) Date sold (mo., day, yr.)
A			
B			
C			
D			

These columns relate to the properties on lines 19A through 19D. ▶		Property A	Property B	Property C	Property D
20 Gross sales price (**Note:** *See line 1 before completing.*)	20				
21 Cost or other basis plus expense of sale	21				
22 Depreciation (or depletion) allowed or allowable	22				
23 Adjusted basis. Subtract line 22 from line 21	23				
24 Total gain. Subtract line 23 from line 20	24				
25 **If section 1245 property:**					
a Depreciation allowed or allowable from line 22	25a				
b Enter the **smaller** of line 24 or 25a	25b				
26 **If section 1250 property:** If straight line depreciation was used, enter -0- on line 26g, except for a corporation subject to section 291.					
a Additional depreciation after 1975. See instructions	26a				
b Applicable percentage multiplied by the **smaller** of line 24 or line 26a. See instructions	26b				
c Subtract line 26a from line 24. If residential rental property **or** line 24 isn't more than line 26a, skip lines 26d and 26e	26c				
d Additional depreciation after 1969 and before 1976	26d				
e Enter the **smaller** of line 26c or 26d	26e				
f Section 291 amount (corporations only)	26f				
g Add lines 26b, 26e, and 26f	26g				
27 **If section 1252 property:** Skip this section if you didn't dispose of farmland or if this form is being completed for a partnership (other than an electing large partnership).					
a Soil, water, and land clearing expenses	27a				
b Line 27a multiplied by applicable percentage. See instructions	27b				
c Enter the **smaller** of line 24 or 27b	27c				
28 **If section 1254 property:**					
a Intangible drilling and development costs, expenditures for development of mines and other natural deposits, mining exploration costs, and depletion. See instructions	28a				
b Enter the **smaller** of line 24 or 28a	28b				
29 **If section 1255 property:**					
a Applicable percentage of payments excluded from income under section 126. See instructions	29a				
b Enter the **smaller** of line 24 or 29a. See instructions	29b				

Summary of Part III Gains. Complete property columns A through D through line 29b before going to line 30.

30	Total gains for all properties. Add property columns A through D, line 24	30	
31	Add property columns A through D, lines 25b, 26g, 27c, 28b, and 29b. Enter here and on line 13	31	
32	Subtract line 31 from line 30. Enter the portion from casualty or theft on Form 4684, line 33. Enter the portion from other than casualty or theft on Form 4797, line 6	32	

Part IV   Recapture Amounts Under Sections 179 and 280F(b)(2) When Business Use Drops to 50% or Less
(see instructions)

		(a) Section 179	(b) Section 280F(b)(2)
33	Section 179 expense deduction or depreciation allowable in prior years	33		
34	Recomputed depreciation. See instructions	34		
35	Recapture amount. Subtract line 34 from line 33. See the instructions for where to report	35		

Form **4797** (2016)

Form **4952**	**Investment Interest Expense Deduction**	OMB No. 1545-0191
Department of the Treasury Internal Revenue Service (99)	▶ Information about Form 4952 and its instructions is at *www.irs.gov/form4952.* ▶ **Attach to your tax return.**	20**16** Attachment Sequence No. **51**

Name(s) shown on return	Identifying number

Part I	**Total Investment Interest Expense**		
1	Investment interest expense paid or accrued in 2016 (see instructions)	**1**	
2	Disallowed investment interest expense from 2015 Form 4952, line 7	**2**	
3	**Total investment interest expense.** Add lines 1 and 2	**3**	

Part II	**Net Investment Income**				
4a	Gross income from property held for investment (excluding any net gain from the disposition of property held for investment)	**4a**			
b	Qualified dividends included on line 4a	**4b**			
c	Subtract line 4b from line 4a			**4c**	
d	Net gain from the disposition of property held for investment	**4d**			
e	Enter the **smaller** of line 4d or your net capital gain from the disposition of property held for investment (see instructions)	**4e**			
f	Subtract line 4e from line 4d			**4f**	
g	Enter the amount from lines 4b and 4e that you elect to include in investment income (see instructions)			**4g**	
h	Investment income. Add lines 4c, 4f, and 4g			**4h**	
5	Investment expenses (see instructions)			**5**	
6	**Net investment income.** Subtract line 5 from line 4h. If zero or less, enter -0-			**6**	

Part III	**Investment Interest Expense Deduction**		
7	Disallowed investment interest expense to be carried forward to 2017. Subtract line 6 from line 3. If zero or less, enter -0-	**7**	
8	**Investment interest expense deduction.** Enter the **smaller** of line 3 or 6. See instructions	**8**	

For Paperwork Reduction Act Notice, see page 4.   Cat. No. 13177Y   Form **4952** (2016)

Form **6252**

Department of the Treasury
Internal Revenue Service

Installment Sale Income

▶ Attach to your tax return.
▶ Use a separate form for each sale or other disposition of property on the installment method.
▶ Information about Form 6252 and its instructions is at *www.irs.gov/form6252.*

OMB No. 1545-0228

2016

Attachment
Sequence No. **79**

Name(s) shown on return

Identifying number

1	Description of property ▶	
2a	Date acquired (mm/dd/yyyy) ▶ _____ **b** Date sold (mm/dd/yyyy) ▶ _____	
3	Was the property sold to a related party (see instructions) after May 14, 1980? If "No," skip line 4	☐ Yes ☐ No
4	Was the property you sold to a related party a marketable security? If "Yes," complete Part III. If "No," complete Part III for the year of sale and the 2 years after the year of sale	☐ Yes ☐ No

Part I   Gross Profit and Contract Price. Complete this part for the year of sale only.

5	Selling price including mortgages and other debts. **Don't** include interest, whether stated or unstated		**5**	
6	Mortgages, debts, and other liabilities the buyer assumed or took the property subject to (see instructions)	**6**		
7	Subtract line 6 from line 5	**7**		
8	Cost or other basis of property sold	**8**		
9	Depreciation allowed or allowable	**9**		
10	Adjusted basis. Subtract line 9 from line 8	**10**		
11	Commissions and other expenses of sale	**11**		
12	Income recapture from Form 4797, Part III (see instructions) . . .	**12**		
13	Add lines 10, 11, and 12		**13**	
14	Subtract line 13 from line 5. If zero or less, **don't** complete the rest of this form (see instructions)		**14**	
15	If the property described on line 1 above was your main home, enter the amount of your excluded gain (see instructions). Otherwise, enter -0-		**15**	
16	**Gross profit.** Subtract line 15 from line 14		**16**	
17	Subtract line 13 from line 6. If zero or less, enter -0-		**17**	
18	**Contract price.** Add line 7 and line 17		**18**	

Part II   Installment Sale Income. Complete this part for the year of sale **and** any year you receive a payment or have certain debts you must treat as a payment on installment obligations.

19	Gross profit percentage (expressed as a decimal amount). Divide line 16 by line 18. For years after the year of sale, see instructions		**19**	
20	If this is the year of sale, enter the amount from line 17. Otherwise, enter -0-		**20**	
21	Payments received during year (see instructions). **Don't** include interest, whether stated or unstated .		**21**	
22	Add lines 20 and 21		**22**	
23	Payments received in prior years (see instructions). **Don't** include interest, whether stated or unstated	**23**		
24	**Installment sale income.** Multiply line 22 by line 19		**24**	
25	Enter the part of line 24 that is ordinary income under the recapture rules (see instructions) . . .		**25**	
26	Subtract line 25 from line 24. Enter here and on Schedule D or Form 4797 (see instructions) . . .		**26**	

Part III   Related Party Installment Sale Income. Don't complete if you received the final payment this tax year.

27	Name, address, and taxpayer identifying number of related party

28	Did the related party resell or dispose of the property ("second disposition") during this tax year?	☐ Yes ☐ No
29	If the answer to question 28 is "Yes," complete lines 30 through 37 below unless one of the following conditions is met. Check the box that applies.	
a	☐ The second disposition was more than 2 years after the first disposition (other than dispositions of marketable securities). If this box is checked, enter the date of disposition (mm/dd/yyyy). . . ▶ _____	
b	☐ The first disposition was a sale or exchange of stock to the issuing corporation.	
c	☐ The second disposition was an involuntary conversion and the threat of conversion occurred after the first disposition.	
d	☐ The second disposition occurred after the death of the original seller or buyer.	
e	☐ It can be established to the satisfaction of the IRS that tax avoidance wasn't a principal purpose for either of the dispositions. If this box is checked, attach an explanation (see instructions).	

30	Selling price of property sold by related party (see instructions)	**30**	
31	Enter contract price from line 18 for year of first sale	**31**	
32	Enter the **smaller** of line 30 or line 31	**32**	
33	Total payments received by the end of your 2016 tax year (see instructions)	**33**	
34	Subtract line 33 from line 32. If zero or less, enter -0-	**34**	
35	Multiply line 34 by the gross profit percentage on line 19 for year of first sale	**35**	
36	Enter the part of line 35 that is ordinary income under the recapture rules (see instructions) . . .	**36**	
37	Subtract line 36 from line 35. Enter here and on Schedule D or Form 4797 (see instructions). . .	**37**	

For Paperwork Reduction Act Notice, see page 4.   Cat. No. 13601R   Form **6252** (2016)

Form **8283**	**Noncash Charitable Contributions**	OMB No. 1545-0908
(Rev. December 2014) Department of the Treasury Internal Revenue Service	▶ Attach to your tax return if you claimed a total deduction of over $500 for all contributed property. ▶ Information about Form 8283 and its separate instructions is at *www.irs.gov/form8283*.	Attachment Sequence No. **155**
Name(s) shown on your income tax return		Identifying number

Note. Figure the amount of your contribution deduction before completing this form. See your tax return instructions.

Section A. Donated Property of $5,000 or Less and Publicly Traded Securities—List in this section **only** items (or groups of similar items) for which you claimed a deduction of $5,000 or less. Also list publicly traded securities even if the deduction is more than $5,000 (see instructions).

Part I **Information on Donated Property**—If you need more space, attach a statement.

1	(a) Name and address of the donee organization	(b) If donated property is a vehicle (see instructions), check the box. Also enter the vehicle identification number (unless Form 1098-C is attached).	(c) Description of donated property (For a vehicle, enter the year, make, model, and mileage. For securities, enter the company name and the number of shares.)
A			
B			
C			
D			
E			

Note. If the amount you claimed as a deduction for an item is $500 or less, you do not have to complete columns (e), (f), and (g).

	(d) Date of the contribution	(e) Date acquired by donor (mo., yr.)	(f) How acquired by donor	(g) Donor's cost or adjusted basis	(h) Fair market value (see instructions)	(i) Method used to determine the fair market value
A						
B						
C						
D						
E						

Part II **Partial Interests and Restricted Use Property**—Complete lines 2a through 2e if you gave less than an entire interest in a property listed in Part I. Complete lines 3a through 3c if conditions were placed on a contribution listed in Part I; also attach the required statement (see instructions).

2a Enter the letter from Part I that identifies the property for which you gave less than an entire interest ▶ _____
If Part II applies to more than one property, attach a separate statement.

b Total amount claimed as a deduction for the property listed in Part I: **(1)** For this tax year ▶ _____
(2) For any prior tax years ▶ _____

c Name and address of each organization to which any such contribution was made in a prior year (complete only if different from the donee organization above):
Name of charitable organization (donee)
_____
Address (number, street, and room or suite no.)
_____
City or town, state, and ZIP code
_____

d For tangible property, enter the place where the property is located or kept ▶ _____
e Name of any person, other than the donee organization, having actual possession of the property ▶ _____

		Yes	No
3a	Is there a restriction, either temporary or permanent, on the donee's right to use or dispose of the donated property?		
b	Did you give to anyone (other than the donee organization or another organization participating with the donee organization in cooperative fundraising) the right to the income from the donated property or to the possession of the property, including the right to vote donated securities, to acquire the property by purchase or otherwise, or to designate the person having such income, possession, or right to acquire?		
c	Is there a restriction limiting the donated property for a particular use?		

For Paperwork Reduction Act Notice, see separate instructions. Cat. No. 62299J Form **8283** (Rev. 12-2014)

Form 8283 (Rev. 12-2014) | Page **2**

Name(s) shown on your income tax return	Identifying number

Section B. Donated Property Over $5,000 (Except Publicly Traded Securities)—Complete this section for one item (or one group of similar items) for which you claimed a deduction of more than $5,000 per item or group (except contributions of publicly traded securities reported in Section A). Provide a separate form for each property donated unless it is part of a group of similar items. An appraisal is generally required for property listed in Section B. See instructions.

Part I **Information on Donated Property**—To be completed by the taxpayer and/or the appraiser.

4 Check the box that describes the type of property donated:

a ☐ Art* (contribution of $20,000 or more) **d** ☐ Art* (contribution of less than $20,000) **g** ☐ Collectibles** **j** ☐ Other
b ☐ Qualified Conservation Contribution **e** ☐ Other Real Estate **h** ☐ Intellectual Property
c ☐ Equipment **f** ☐ Securities **i** ☐ Vehicles

*Art includes paintings, sculptures, watercolors, prints, drawings, ceramics, antiques, decorative arts, textiles, carpets, silver, rare manuscripts, historical memorabilia, and other similar objects.

**Collectibles include coins, stamps, books, gems, jewelry, sports memorabilia, dolls, etc., but not art as defined above.

Note. In certain cases, you must attach a qualified appraisal of the property. See instructions.

5	(a) Description of donated property (if you need more space, attach a separate statement)	(b) If tangible property was donated, give a brief summary of the overall physical condition of the property at the time of the gift	(c) Appraised fair market value
A			
B			
C			
D			

	(d) Date acquired by donor (mo., yr.)	(e) How acquired by donor	(f) Donor's cost or adjusted basis	(g) For bargain sales, enter amount received	See instructions	
					(h) Amount claimed as a deduction	(i) Date of contribution
A						
B						
C						
D						

Part II **Taxpayer (Donor) Statement**—List each item included in Part I above that the appraisal identifies as having a value of $500 or less. See instructions.

I declare that the following item(s) included in Part I above has to the best of my knowledge and belief an appraised value of not more than $500 (per item). Enter identifying letter from Part I and describe the specific item. See instructions. ▶ _____

Signature of taxpayer (donor) ▶ _____ Date ▶ _____

Part III **Declaration of Appraiser**

I declare that I am not the donor, the donee, a party to the transaction in which the donor acquired the property, employed by, or related to any of the foregoing persons, or married to any person who is related to any of the foregoing persons. And, if regularly used by the donor, donee, or party to the transaction, I performed the majority of my appraisals during my tax year for other persons.

Also, I declare that I perform appraisals on a regular basis; and that because of my qualifications as described in the appraisal, I am qualified to make appraisals of the type of property being valued. I certify that the appraisal fees were not based on a percentage of the appraised property value. Furthermore, I understand that a false or fraudulent overstatement of the property value as described in the qualified appraisal or this Form 8283 may subject me to the penalty under section 6701(a) (aiding and abetting the understatement of tax liability). In addition, I understand that I may be subject to a penalty under section 6695A if I know, or reasonably should know, that my appraisal is to be used in connection with a return or claim for refund and a substantial or gross valuation misstatement results from my appraisal. I affirm that I have not been barred from presenting evidence or testimony by the Office of Professional Responsibility.

Sign Here Signature ▶ _____ Title ▶ _____ Date ▶ _____

Business address (including room or suite no.)	Identifying number
City or town, state, and ZIP code	

Part IV **Donee Acknowledgment**—To be completed by the charitable organization.

This charitable organization acknowledges that it is a qualified organization under section 170(c) and that it received the donated property as described in Section B, Part I, above on the following date ▶ _____

Furthermore, this organization affirms that in the event it sells, exchanges, or otherwise disposes of the property described in Section B, Part I (or any portion thereof) within 3 years after the date of receipt, it will file **Form 8282,** Donee Information Return, with the IRS and give the donor a copy of that form. This acknowledgment does not represent agreement with the claimed fair market value.

Does the organization intend to use the property for an unrelated use? . . . . ▶ ☐ Yes ☐ No

Name of charitable organization (donee)	Employer identification number
Address (number, street, and room or suite no.)	City or town, state, and ZIP code
Authorized signature	Title	Date

Form **8283** (Rev. 12-2014)

Form **8582**

Department of the Treasury
Internal Revenue Service (99)

Passive Activity Loss Limitations

▶ See separate instructions.

▶ Attach to Form 1040 or Form 1041.

▶ Information about Form 8582 and its instructions is available at *www.irs.gov/form8582*.

OMB No. 1545-1008

2016

Attachment
Sequence No. **88**

Name(s) shown on return

Identifying number

Part I	**2016 Passive Activity Loss**		

Caution: *Complete Worksheets 1, 2, and 3 before completing Part I.*

Rental Real Estate Activities With Active Participation (For the definition of active participation, see **Special Allowance for Rental Real Estate Activities** in the instructions.)

1a	Activities with net income (enter the amount from Worksheet 1, column (a))	1a	
b	Activities with net loss (enter the amount from Worksheet 1, column (b))	1b (	)
c	Prior years unallowed losses (enter the amount from Worksheet 1, column (c))	1c (	)
d	Combine lines 1a, 1b, and 1c	1d	

Commercial Revitalization Deductions From Rental Real Estate Activities

2a	Commercial revitalization deductions from Worksheet 2, column (a) .	2a (	)
b	Prior year unallowed commercial revitalization deductions from Worksheet 2, column (b)	2b (	)
c	Add lines 2a and 2b	2c (	)

All Other Passive Activities

3a	Activities with net income (enter the amount from Worksheet 3, column (a))	3a	
b	Activities with net loss (enter the amount from Worksheet 3, column (b))	3b (	)
c	Prior years unallowed losses (enter the amount from Worksheet 3, column (c))	3c (	)
d	Combine lines 3a, 3b, and 3c	3d	

4 Combine lines 1d, 2c, and 3d. If this line is zero or more, stop here and include this form with your return; all losses are allowed, including any prior year unallowed losses entered on line 1c, 2b, or 3c. Report the losses on the forms and schedules normally used . . . . | 4 |

If line 4 is a loss and: • Line 1d is a loss, go to Part II.

• Line 2c is a loss (and line 1d is zero or more), skip Part II and go to Part III.

• Line 3d is a loss (and lines 1d and 2c are zero or more), skip Parts II and III and go to line 15.

Caution: *If your filing status is married filing separately and you lived with your spouse at any time during the year,* **do not** *complete Part II or Part III. Instead, go to line 15.*

Part II	**Special Allowance for Rental Real Estate Activities With Active Participation**		

Note: *Enter all numbers in Part II as positive amounts. See instructions for an example.*

5	Enter the **smaller** of the loss on line 1d or the loss on line 4	5	
6	Enter $150,000. If married filing separately, see instructions . .	6	
7	Enter modified adjusted gross income, but not less than zero (see instructions)	7	
	Note: *If line 7 is greater than or equal to line 6, skip lines 8 and 9, enter -0- on line 10. Otherwise, go to line 8.*		
8	Subtract line 7 from line 6	8	
9	Multiply line 8 by 50% (0.5). **Do not** enter more than $25,000. If married filing separately, see instructions	9	
10	Enter the **smaller** of line 5 or line 9	10	

If line 2c is a loss, go to Part III. Otherwise, go to line 15.

Part III	**Special Allowance for Commercial Revitalization Deductions From Rental Real Estate Activities**		

Note: *Enter all numbers in Part III as positive amounts. See the example for Part II in the instructions.*

11	Enter $25,000 reduced by the amount, if any, on line 10. If married filing separately, see instructions	11	
12	Enter the loss from line 4	12	
13	Reduce line 12 by the amount on line 10	13	
14	Enter the **smallest** of line 2c (treated as a positive amount), line 11, or line 13	14	

Part IV	**Total Losses Allowed**		

15	Add the income, if any, on lines 1a and 3a and enter the total	15	
16	**Total losses allowed from all passive activities for 2016.** Add lines 10, 14, and 15. See instructions to find out how to report the losses on your tax return	16	

For Paperwork Reduction Act Notice, see instructions.   Cat. No. 63704F   Form **8582** (2016)

Form 8582 (2016)   Page **2**

Caution: *The worksheets must be filed with your tax return. Keep a copy for your records.*

Worksheet 1—For Form 8582, Lines 1a, 1b, and 1c (See instructions.)

Name of activity	Current year		Prior years	Overall gain or loss	
	(a) Net income (line 1a)	(b) Net loss (line 1b)	(c) Unallowed loss (line 1c)	(d) Gain	(e) Loss
Total. Enter on Form 8582, lines 1a, 1b, and 1c . . . . ▶					

Worksheet 2—For Form 8582, Lines 2a and 2b (See instructions.)

Name of activity	(a) Current year deductions (line 2a)	(b) Prior year unallowed deductions (line 2b)	(c) Overall loss
Total. Enter on Form 8582, lines 2a and 2b . . . . ▶			

Worksheet 3—For Form 8582, Lines 3a, 3b, and 3c (See instructions.)

Name of activity	Current year		Prior years	Overall gain or loss	
	(a) Net income (line 3a)	(b) Net loss (line 3b)	(c) Unallowed loss (line 3c)	(d) Gain	(e) Loss
Total. Enter on Form 8582, lines 3a, 3b, and 3c . . . . ▶					

Worksheet 4—Use this worksheet if an amount is shown on Form 8582, line 10 or 14 (See instructions.)

Name of activity	Form or schedule and line number to be reported on (see instructions)	(a) Loss	(b) Ratio	(c) Special allowance	(d) Subtract column (c) from column (a)
Total . . . . ▶			1.00		

Worksheet 5—Allocation of Unallowed Losses (See instructions.)

Name of activity	Form or schedule and line number to be reported on (see instructions)	(a) Loss	(b) Ratio	(c) Unallowed loss
Total . . . . ▶			1.00	

Form **8582** (2016)

Worksheet 6—Allowed Losses (See instructions.)

Name of activity	Form or schedule and line number to be reported on (see instructions)	(a) Loss	(b) Unallowed loss	(c) Allowed loss
Total . . . . ▶				

Worksheet 7—Activities With Losses Reported on Two or More Forms or Schedules (See instructions.)

Name of activity:	(a)	(b)	(c) Ratio	(d) Unallowed loss	(e) Allowed loss
Form or schedule and line number to be reported on (see instructions): ------------------					
1a Net loss plus prior year unallowed loss from form or schedule . ▶					
b Net income from form or schedule . . . . ▶					
c Subtract line 1b from line 1a. If zero or less, enter -0- ▶					
Form or schedule and line number to be reported on (see instructions): ------------------					
1a Net loss plus prior year unallowed loss from form or schedule . ▶					
b Net income from form or schedule . . . . ▶					
c Subtract line 1b from line 1a. If zero or less, enter -0- ▶					
Form or schedule and line number to be reported on (see instructions): ------------------					
1a Net loss plus prior year unallowed loss from form or schedule . ▶					
b Net income from form or schedule . . . . ▶					
c Subtract line 1b from line 1a. If zero or less, enter -0- ▶					
Total . . . . ▶			1.00		

Form **8582** (2016)

Form **8615**	**Tax for Certain Children Who Have Unearned Income**	OMB No. 1545-0074

Form **8615**

Department of the Treasury
Internal Revenue Service (99)

Tax for Certain Children Who Have Unearned Income

▶ Attach only to the child's Form 1040, Form 1040A, or Form 1040NR.
▶ Information about Form 8615 and its separate instructions is at *www.irs.gov/form8615.*

OMB No. 1545-0074

20**16**

Attachment
Sequence No. **33**

Child's name shown on return

Child's social security number

Before you begin: If the child, the parent, or any of the parent's other children for whom Form 8615 must be filed must use the Schedule D Tax Worksheet or has income from farming or fishing, see **Pub. 929,** Tax Rules for Children and Dependents. It explains how to figure the child's tax using the **Schedule D Tax Worksheet** or **Schedule J** (Form 1040).

A Parent's name (first, initial, and last). **Caution:** *See instructions before completing.*

B Parent's social security number

C Parent's filing status (check one):

☐ Single   ☐ Married filing jointly   ☐ Married filing separately   ☐ Head of household   ☐ Qualifying widow(er)

Part I   Child's Net Unearned Income

1	Enter the child's unearned income (see instructions)	**1**	
2	If the child **did not** itemize deductions on **Schedule A** (Form 1040 or Form 1040NR), enter $2,100. Otherwise, see instructions	**2**	
3	Subtract line 2 from line 1. If zero or less, **stop;** do not complete the rest of this form but **do** attach it to the child's return	**3**	
4	Enter the child's **taxable income** from Form 1040, line 43; Form 1040A, line 27; or Form 1040NR, line 41. If the child files Form 2555 or 2555-EZ, see the instructions	**4**	
5	Enter the **smaller** of line 3 or line 4. If zero, **stop;** do not complete the rest of this form but **do** attach it to the child's return	**5**	

Part II   Tentative Tax Based on the Tax Rate of the Parent

6	Enter the parent's **taxable income** from Form 1040, line 43; Form 1040A, line 27; Form 1040EZ, line 6; Form 1040NR, line 41; or Form 1040NR-EZ, line 14. If zero or less, enter -0-. If the parent files Form 2555 or 2555-EZ, see the instructions	**6**	
7	Enter the total, if any, from Forms 8615, line 5, of **all other** children of the parent named above. **Do not** include the amount from line 5 above	**7**	
8	Add lines 5, 6, and 7 (see instructions)	**8**	
9	Enter the tax on the amount on line 8 based on the **parent's** filing status above (see instructions). If the Qualified Dividends and Capital Gain Tax Worksheet, Schedule D Tax Worksheet, or Schedule J (Form 1040) is used to figure the tax, check here . . . . ▶ ☐	**9**	
10	Enter the parent's tax from Form 1040, line 44; Form 1040A, line 28, minus any alternative minimum tax; Form 1040EZ, line 10; Form 1040NR, line 42; or Form 1040NR-EZ, line 15. **Do not** include any tax from **Form 4972, 8814,** or **8885** or any tax from recapture of an education credit. If the parent files Form 2555 or 2555-EZ, see the instructions. If the Qualified Dividends and Capital Gain Tax Worksheet, Schedule D Tax Worksheet, or Schedule J (Form 1040) was used to figure the tax, check here . . . . ▶ ☐	**10**	
11	Subtract line 10 from line 9 and enter the result. If line 7 is blank, also enter this amount on line 13 and go to **Part III**	**11**	
12a	Add lines 5 and 7 . . . . **12a**		
b	Divide line 5 by line 12a. Enter the result as a decimal (rounded to at least three places)	**12b**	× .
13	Multiply line 11 by line 12b	**13**	

Part III   Child's Tax—If lines 4 and 5 above are the same, enter -0- on line 15 and go to line 16.

14	Subtract line 5 from line 4 . . . . **14**		
15	Enter the tax on the amount on line 14 based on the **child's** filing status (see instructions). If the Qualified Dividends and Capital Gain Tax Worksheet, Schedule D Tax Worksheet, or Schedule J (Form 1040) is used to figure the tax, check here . . . . ▶ ☐	**15**	
16	Add lines 13 and 15	**16**	
17	Enter the tax on the amount on line 4 based on the **child's** filing status (see instructions). If the Qualified Dividends and Capital Gain Tax Worksheet, Schedule D Tax Worksheet, or Schedule J (Form 1040) is used to figure the tax, check here . . . . ▶ ☐	**17**	
18	Enter the **larger** of line 16 or line 17 here and on the **child's** Form 1040, line 44; Form 1040A, line 28; or Form 1040NR, line 42. If the child files Form 2555 or 2555-EZ, see the instructions . .	**18**	

For Paperwork Reduction Act Notice, see your tax return instructions.   Cat. No. 64113U   Form **8615** (2016)

Form **8814**

Department of the Treasury
Internal Revenue Service (99)

**Parents' Election To Report
Child's Interest and Dividends**

▶ Information about Form 8814 and its instructions is at *www.irs.gov/form8814.*
▶ Attach to parents' Form 1040 or Form 1040NR.

OMB No. 1545-0074

20**16**

Attachment
Sequence No. **40**

Name(s) shown on your return

Your social security number

Caution: The federal income tax on your child's income, including qualified dividends and capital gain distributions, may be less if you file a separate tax return for the child instead of making this election. This is because you cannot take certain tax benefits that your child could take on his or her own return. For details, see *Tax benefits you cannot take* in the instructions.

A Child's name (first, initial, and last)

B Child's social security number

C If more than one Form 8814 is attached, check here . . . . ▶ ☐

Part I	Child's Interest and Dividends To Report on Your Return

1a	Enter your child's **taxable** interest. If this amount is different from the amounts shown on the child's Forms 1099-INT and 1099-OID, see the instructions	**1a**	
b	Enter your child's **tax-exempt** interest. **Do not** include this amount on line 1a **1b**		
2a	Enter your child's ordinary dividends, including any Alaska Permanent Fund dividends. If your child received any ordinary dividends as a nominee, see the instructions	**2a**	
b	Enter your child's qualified dividends included on line 2a. See the instructions **2b**		
3	Enter your child's capital gain distributions. If your child received any capital gain distributions as a nominee, see the instructions	**3**	
4	Add lines 1a, 2a, and 3. If the total is $2,100 or less, skip lines 5 through 12 and go to line 13. If the total is $10,500 or more, **do not** file this form. Your child **must** file his or her own return to report the income	**4**	
5	Base amount	**5**	2,100 00
6	Subtract line 5 from line 4	**6**	
	If both lines 2b and 3 are zero or blank, skip lines 7 through 10, enter -0- on line 11, and go to line 12. Otherwise, go to line 7.		
7	Divide line 2b by line 4. Enter the result as a decimal (rounded to at least three places) . . . . **7** .		
8	Divide line 3 by line 4. Enter the result as a decimal (rounded to at least three places) . . . . **8** .		
9	Multiply line 6 by line 7. Enter the result here. See the instructions for where to report this amount on your return **9**		
10	Multiply line 6 by line 8. Enter the result here. See the instructions for where to report this amount on your return **10**		
11	Add lines 9 and 10	**11**	
12	Subtract line 11 from line 6. Include this amount in the total on Form 1040, line 21, or Form 1040NR, line 21. In the space next to line 21, enter "Form 8814" and show the amount. If you checked the box on line C above, see the instructions. Go to line 13 below	**12**	

Part II	Tax on the First $2,100 of Child's Interest and Dividends

13	Amount not taxed	**13**	1,050 00
14	Subtract line 13 from line 4. If the result is zero or less, enter -0-	**14**	
15	**Tax.** Is the amount on line 14 less than $1,050?		
	☐ **No.** Enter $105 here and see the **Note** below.	} . . .	**15**
	☐ **Yes.** Multiply line 14 by 10% (.10). Enter the result here and see the **Note** below.		

Note: If you checked the box on line C above, see the instructions. Otherwise, include the amount from line 15 in the tax you enter on Form 1040, line 44, or Form 1040NR, line 42. Be sure to check box **a** on Form 1040, line 44, or Form 1040NR, line 42.

For Paperwork Reduction Act Notice, see your tax return instructions.   Cat. No. 10750J   Form **8814** (2016)

Form **8829**	**Expenses for Business Use of Your Home**	OMB No. 1545-0074
Department of the Treasury Internal Revenue Service (99)	▶ File only with Schedule C (Form 1040). Use a separate Form 8829 for each home you used for business during the year. ▶ Information about Form 8829 and its separate instructions is at *www.irs.gov/form8829*.	**2016** Attachment Sequence No. **176**

Name(s) of proprietor(s)	Your social security number

Part I   Part of Your Home Used for Business

1	Area used regularly and exclusively for business, regularly for daycare, or for storage of inventory or product samples (see instructions)	1	
2	Total area of home	2	
3	Divide line 1 by line 2. Enter the result as a percentage	3	%

For daycare facilities not used exclusively for business, go to line 4. All others, go to line 7.

4	Multiply days used for daycare during year by hours used per day	4		hr.
5	Total hours available for use during the year (366 days x 24 hours) (see instructions)	5	8,784	hr.
6	Divide line 4 by line 5. Enter the result as a decimal amount . . .	6	.	

7	Business percentage. For daycare facilities not used exclusively for business, multiply line 6 by line 3 (enter the result as a percentage). All others, enter the amount from line 3 . . . . . ▶	7	%

Part II   Figure Your Allowable Deduction

8	Enter the amount from Schedule C, line 29, **plus** any gain derived from the business use of your home, **minus** any loss from the trade or business not derived from the business use of your home (see instructions)			8	

See instructions for columns **(a)** and **(b)** before completing lines 9–21.

			(a) Direct expenses	(b) Indirect expenses		
9	Casualty losses (see instructions).	9				
10	Deductible mortgage interest (see instructions)	10				
11	Real estate taxes (see instructions)	11				
12	Add lines 9, 10, and 11	12				
13	Multiply line 12, column (b) by line 7		13			
14	Add line 12, column (a) and line 13				14	
15	Subtract line 14 from line 8. If zero or less, enter -0-				15	
16	Excess mortgage interest (see instructions) .	16				
17	Insurance	17				
18	Rent	18				
19	Repairs and maintenance	19				
20	Utilities	20				
21	Other expenses (see instructions).	21				
22	Add lines 16 through 21	22				
23	Multiply line 22, column (b) by line 7		23			
24	Carryover of prior year operating expenses (see instructions) . .		24			
25	Add line 22, column (a), line 23, and line 24				25	
26	Allowable operating expenses. Enter the **smaller** of line 15 or line 25				26	
27	Limit on excess casualty losses and depreciation. Subtract line 26 from line 15				27	
28	Excess casualty losses (see instructions)		28			
29	Depreciation of your home from line 41 below		29			
30	Carryover of prior year excess casualty losses and depreciation (see instructions)		30			
31	Add lines 28 through 30				31	
32	Allowable excess casualty losses and depreciation. Enter the **smaller** of line 27 or line 31 . .				32	
33	Add lines 14, 26, and 32				33	
34	Casualty loss portion, if any, from lines 14 and 32. Carry amount to **Form 4684** (see instructions)				34	
35	**Allowable expenses for business use of your home.** Subtract line 34 from line 33. Enter here and on Schedule C, line 30. If your home was used for more than one business, see instructions ▶				35	

Part III   Depreciation of Your Home

36	Enter the **smaller** of your home's adjusted basis or its fair market value (see instructions) . .	36	
37	Value of land included on line 36	37	
38	Basis of building. Subtract line 37 from line 36	38	
39	Business basis of building. Multiply line 38 by line 7	39	
40	Depreciation percentage (see instructions).	40	%
41	Depreciation allowable (see instructions). Multiply line 39 by line 40. Enter here and on line 29 above	41	

Part IV   Carryover of Unallowed Expenses to 2017

42	Operating expenses. Subtract line 26 from line 25. If less than zero, enter -0-	42	
43	Excess casualty losses and depreciation. Subtract line 32 from line 31. If less than zero, enter -0-	43	

For Paperwork Reduction Act Notice, see your tax return instructions.	Cat. No. 13232M	Form **8829** (2016)

Form **8863**

Department of the Treasury
Internal Revenue Service (99)

Education Credits
(American Opportunity and Lifetime Learning Credits)
▶ Attach to Form 1040 or Form 1040A.
▶ Information about Form 8863 and its separate instructions is at *www.irs.gov/form8863.*

OMB No. 1545-0074

20**16**

Attachment Sequence No. **50**

Name(s) shown on return

Your social security number

⚠ **CAUTION** *Complete a separate Part III on page 2 for each student for whom you're claiming either credit before you complete Parts I and II.*

Part I   Refundable American Opportunity Credit

1 After completing Part III for each student, enter the total of all amounts from all Parts III, line 30 . | **1** |

2 Enter: $180,000 if married filing jointly; $90,000 if single, head of household, or qualifying widow(er) . . . . | **2** |

3 Enter the amount from Form 1040, line 38, or Form 1040A, line 22. If you're filing Form 2555, 2555-EZ, or 4563, or you're excluding income from Puerto Rico, see Pub. 970 for the amount to enter . . . . . | **3** |

4 Subtract line 3 from line 2. If zero or less, **stop**; you can't take any education credit . . . . | **4** |

5 Enter: $20,000 if married filing jointly; $10,000 if single, head of household, or qualifying widow(er) . . . . | **5** |

6 If line 4 is:
• Equal to or more than line 5, enter 1.000 on line 6 . . . .
• Less than line 5, divide line 4 by line 5. Enter the result as a decimal (rounded to at least three places) . . . . | **6** |

7 Multiply line 1 by line 6. **Caution:** If you were under age 24 at the end of the year **and** meet the conditions described in the instructions, you **can't** take the refundable American opportunity credit; skip line 8, enter the amount from line 7 on line 9, and check this box . . . . ▶ ☐ | **7** |

8 **Refundable American opportunity credit.** Multiply line 7 by 40% (0.40). Enter the amount here and on Form 1040, line 68, or Form 1040A, line 44. Then go to line 9 below. . . . . | **8** |

Part II   Nonrefundable Education Credits

9 Subtract line 8 from line 7. Enter here and on line 2 of the Credit Limit Worksheet (see instructions) | **9** |

10 After completing Part III for each student, enter the total of all amounts from all Parts III, line 31. If zero, skip lines 11 through 17, enter -0- on line 18, and go to line 19 . . . . | **10** |

11 Enter the smaller of line 10 or $10,000 . . . . | **11** |

12 Multiply line 11 by 20% (0.20) . . . . | **12** |

13 Enter: $131,000 if married filing jointly; $65,000 if single, head of household, or qualifying widow(er) . . . . | **13** |

14 Enter the amount from Form 1040, line 38, or Form 1040A, line 22. If you're filing Form 2555, 2555-EZ, or 4563, or you're excluding income from Puerto Rico, see Pub. 970 for the amount to enter . . . . | **14** |

15 Subtract line 14 from line 13. If zero or less, skip lines 16 and 17, enter -0- on line 18, and go to line 19 . . . . | **15** |

16 Enter: $20,000 if married filing jointly; $10,000 if single, head of household, or qualifying widow(er) . . . . | **16** |

17 If line 15 is:
• Equal to or more than line 16, enter 1.000 on line 17 and go to line 18
• Less than line 16, divide line 15 by line 16. Enter the result as a decimal (rounded to at least three places) . . . . | **17** |

18 Multiply line 12 by line 17. Enter here and on line 1 of the Credit Limit Worksheet (see instructions) ▶ | **18** |

19 **Nonrefundable education credits.** Enter the amount from line 7 of the Credit Limit Worksheet (see instructions) here and on Form 1040, line 50, or Form 1040A, line 33 . . . . | **19** |

For Paperwork Reduction Act Notice, see your tax return instructions.   Cat. No. 25379M   Form **8863** (2016)

Form 8863 (2016)				Page **2**
Name(s) shown on return			Your social security number	

⚠ **CAUTION**   *Complete Part III for each student for whom you're claiming either the American opportunity credit or lifetime learning credit. Use additional copies of page 2 as needed for each student.*

Part III   Student and Educational Institution Information
See instructions.

20 Student name (as shown on page 1 of your tax return)	**21** Student social security number (as shown on page 1 of your tax return)

22   Educational institution information (see instructions)

a. Name of first educational institution	**b.** Name of second educational institution (if any)
(1) Address. Number and street (or P.O. box). City, town or post office, state, and ZIP code. If a foreign address, see instructions.	**(1)** Address. Number and street (or P.O. box). City, town or post office, state, and ZIP code. If a foreign address, see instructions.
(2) Did the student receive Form 1098-T from this institution for 2016? ☐ Yes ☐ No	**(2)** Did the student receive Form 1098-T from this institution for 2016? ☐ Yes ☐ No
(3) Did the student receive Form 1098-T from this institution for 2015 with box 2 filled in and box 7 checked? ☐ Yes ☐ No	**(3)** Did the student receive Form 1098-T from this institution for 2015 with box 2 filled in and box 7 checked? ☐ Yes ☐ No
If you checked "No" in **both (2) and (3)**, skip **(4)**.	If you checked "No" in **both (2) and (3)**, skip **(4)**.
(4) If you checked "Yes" in **(2) or (3)**, enter the institution's federal identification number (from Form 1098-T). — __ __ — __ __ __ __ __ __	**(4)** If you checked "Yes" in **(2) or (3)**, enter the institution's federal identification number (from Form 1098-T). — __ __ — __ __ __ __ __ __

23	Has the Hope Scholarship Credit or American opportunity credit been claimed for this student for any 4 tax years before 2016?	☐ Yes — **Stop!** Go to line 31 for this student. ☐ No — Go to line 24.
24	Was the student enrolled at least half-time for at least one academic period that began or is treated as having begun in 2016 at an eligible educational institution in a program leading towards a postsecondary degree, certificate, or other recognized postsecondary educational credential? See instructions.	☐ Yes — Go to line 25. ☐ No — **Stop!** Go to line 31 for this student.
25	Did the student complete the first 4 years of postsecondary education before 2016? See instructions.	☐ Yes — **Stop!** Go to line 31 for this student. ☐ No — Go to line 26.
26	Was the student convicted, before the end of 2016, of a felony for possession or distribution of a controlled substance?	☐ Yes — **Stop!** Go to line 31 for this student. ☐ No — Complete lines 27 through 30 for this student.

⚠ **CAUTION**   *You can't take the American opportunity credit and the lifetime learning credit for the **same student** in the same year. If you complete lines 27 through 30 for this student, don't complete line 31.*

American Opportunity Credit

27	Adjusted qualified education expenses (see instructions). **Don't enter more than $4,000**	27	
28	Subtract $2,000 from line 27. If zero or less, enter -0-.	28	
29	Multiply line 28 by 25% (0.25)	29	
30	If line 28 is zero, enter the amount from line 27. Otherwise, add $2,000 to the amount on line 29 and enter the result. Skip line 31. Include the total of all amounts from all Parts III, line 30, on Part I, line 1 .	30	

Lifetime Learning Credit

31	Adjusted qualified education expenses (see instructions). Include the total of all amounts from all Parts III, line 31, on Part II, line 10	31	

Form **8863** (2016)

Form **8917**	**Tuition and Fees Deduction**	OMB No. 1545-0074
Department of the Treasury Internal Revenue Service	▶ Attach to Form 1040 or Form 1040A. ▶ Information about Form 8917 and its instructions is at *www.irs.gov/form8917*.	20**16** Attachment Sequence No. **60**

Name(s) shown on return | **Your social security number**

⚠ **CAUTION** You **cannot** take both an education credit from Form 8863 and the tuition and fees deduction from this form for the **same student** for the same tax year.

Before you begin:

✔ To see if you qualify for this deduction, see *Who Can Take the Deduction* in the instructions below.

✔ If you file Form 1040, figure any write-in adjustments to be entered on the dotted line next to Form 1040, line 36. See the 2016 Form 1040 instructions for line 36.

1

(a) Student's name (as shown on page 1 of your tax return)		(b) Student's social security number (as shown on page 1 of your tax return)	(c) Adjusted qualified expenses (see instructions)
First name	Last name		

2 Add the amounts on line 1, column (c), and enter the total . . . . | **2** |

3 Enter the amount from Form 1040, line 22, or Form 1040A, line 15 | **3** |

4 Enter the total from either:

• Form 1040, lines 23 through 33, plus any write-in adjustments entered on the dotted line next to Form 1040, line 36, **or**

• Form 1040A, lines 16 through 18. . . . . | **4** |

5 Subtract line 4 from line 3.* If the result is more than $80,000 ($160,000 if married filing jointly), **stop**; you cannot take the deduction for tuition and fees . . . . | **5** |

*If you are filing Form 2555, 2555-EZ, or 4563, or you are excluding income from Puerto Rico, see *Effect of the Amount of Your Income on the Amount of Your Deduction* in Pub. 970, chapter 6, to figure the amount to enter on line 5.

6 **Tuition and fees deduction.** Is the amount on line 5 more than $65,000 ($130,000 if married filing jointly)?

☐ **Yes.** Enter the smaller of line 2, or $2,000. ⎫

☐ **No.** Enter the smaller of line 2, or $4,000. ⎭ . . . . | **6** |

Also enter this amount on Form 1040, line 34, or Form 1040A, line 19.

For Paperwork Reduction Act Notice, see your tax return instructions.   Cat. No. 37728P   Form **8917** (2016)

Form **8949**	**Sales and Other Dispositions of Capital Assets**	OMB No. 1545-0074

Form **8949**

Department of the Treasury
Internal Revenue Service

▶ Information about Form 8949 and its separate instructions is at *www.irs.gov/form8949*.
▶ File with your Schedule D to list your transactions for lines 1b, 2, 3, 8b, 9, and 10 of Schedule D.

2016

Attachment
Sequence No. **12A**

Name(s) shown on return	Social security number or taxpayer identification number

Before you check Box A, B, or C below, see whether you received any Form(s) 1099-B or substitute statement(s) from your broker. A substitute statement will have the same information as Form 1099-B. Either will show whether your basis (usually your cost) was reported to the IRS by your broker and may even tell you which box to check.

Part I   **Short-Term.** Transactions involving capital assets you held 1 year or less are short term. For long-term transactions, see page 2.

Note: You may aggregate all short-term transactions reported on Form(s) 1099-B showing basis was reported to the IRS and for which no adjustments or codes are required. Enter the totals directly on Schedule D, line 1a; you aren't required to report these transactions on Form 8949 (see instructions).

You *must* check Box A, B, *or* C below. **Check only one box.** If more than one box applies for your short-term transactions, complete a separate Form 8949, page 1, for each applicable box. If you have more short-term transactions than will fit on this page for one or more of the boxes, complete as many forms with the same box checked as you need.

- ☐ **(A)** Short-term transactions reported on Form(s) 1099-B showing basis was reported to the IRS (see **Note** above)
- ☐ **(B)** Short-term transactions reported on Form(s) 1099-B showing basis **wasn't** reported to the IRS
- ☐ **(C)** Short-term transactions not reported to you on Form 1099-B

1 **(a)** Description of property (Example: 100 sh. XYZ Co.)	**(b)** Date acquired (Mo., day, yr.)	**(c)** Date sold or disposed of (Mo., day, yr.)	**(d)** Proceeds (sales price) (see instructions)	**(e)** Cost or other basis. See the **Note** below and see *Column (e)* in the separate instructions	**Adjustment, if any, to gain or loss.** If you enter an amount in column (g), enter a code in column (f). **See the separate instructions.**		**(h)** Gain or (loss). Subtract column (e) from column (d) and combine the result with column (g)
					(f) Code(s) from instructions	**(g)** Amount of adjustment	
2 Totals. Add the amounts in columns (d), (e), (g), and (h) (subtract negative amounts). Enter each total here and include on your Schedule D, **line 1b** (if **Box A** above is checked), **line 2** (if **Box B** above is checked), or **line 3** (if **Box C** above is checked) ▶							

Note: If you checked Box A above but the basis reported to the IRS was incorrect, enter in column (e) the basis as reported to the IRS, and enter an adjustment in column (g) to correct the basis. See *Column (g)* in the separate instructions for how to figure the amount of the adjustment.

For Paperwork Reduction Act Notice, see your tax return instructions.   Cat. No. 37768Z   Form **8949** (2016)

Form 8949 (2016)   Attachment Sequence No. **12A**   Page **2**

Name(s) shown on return. Name and SSN or taxpayer identification no. not required if shown on other side	Social security number or taxpayer identification number

Before you check Box D, E, or F below, see whether you received any Form(s) 1099-B or substitute statement(s) from your broker. A substitute statement will have the same information as Form 1099-B. Either will show whether your basis (usually your cost) was reported to the IRS by your broker and may even tell you which box to check.

Part II **Long-Term.** Transactions involving capital assets you held more than 1 year are long term. For short-term transactions, see page 1.

Note: You may aggregate all long-term transactions reported on Form(s) 1099-B showing basis was reported to the IRS and for which no adjustments or codes are required. Enter the totals directly on Schedule D, line 8a; you aren't required to report these transactions on Form 8949 (see instructions).

You *must* check Box D, E, *or* F below. Check only one box. If more than one box applies for your long-term transactions, complete a separate Form 8949, page 2, for each applicable box. If you have more long-term transactions than will fit on this page for one or more of the boxes, complete as many forms with the same box checked as you need.

- ☐ **(D)** Long-term transactions reported on Form(s) 1099-B showing basis was reported to the IRS (see **Note** above)
- ☐ **(E)** Long-term transactions reported on Form(s) 1099-B showing basis **wasn't** reported to the IRS
- ☐ **(F)** Long-term transactions not reported to you on Form 1099-B

1 **(a)** Description of property (Example: 100 sh. XYZ Co.)	**(b)** Date acquired (Mo., day, yr.)	**(c)** Date sold or disposed of (Mo., day, yr.)	**(d)** Proceeds (sales price) (see instructions)	**(e)** Cost or other basis. See the **Note** below and see *Column (e)* in the separate instructions	**(f)** Code(s) from instructions	**(g)** Amount of adjustment	**(h)** Gain or (loss). Subtract column (e) from column (d) and combine the result with column (g)

2 Totals. Add the amounts in columns (d), (e), (g), and (h) (subtract negative amounts). Enter each total here and include on your Schedule D, **line 8b** (if **Box D** above is checked), **line 9** (if **Box E** above is checked), or **line 10** (if **Box F** above is checked) ▶

Note: If you checked Box D above but the basis reported to the IRS was incorrect, enter in column (e) the basis as reported to the IRS, and enter an adjustment in column (g) to correct the basis. See *Column (g)* in the separate instructions for how to figure the amount of the adjustment.

Form **8949** (2016)

Form **8959**	**Additional Medicare Tax**	OMB No. 1545-0074

Department of the Treasury
Internal Revenue Service

▶ If any line does not apply to you, leave it blank. See separate instructions.
▶ Attach to Form 1040, 1040NR, 1040-PR, or 1040-SS.
▶ Information about Form 8959 and its instructions is at *www.irs.gov/form8959*.

2016
Attachment Sequence No. **71**

Name(s) shown on return

Your social security number

Part I   **Additional Medicare Tax on Medicare Wages**

1 Medicare wages and tips from Form W-2, box 5. If you have more than one Form W-2, enter the total of the amounts from box 5 . . . . **1**

2 Unreported tips from Form 4137, line 6 . . . . **2**

3 Wages from Form 8919, line 6 . . . . **3**

4 Add lines 1 through 3 . . . . **4**

5 Enter the following amount for your filing status:
Married filing jointly $250,000
Married filing separately $125,000
Single, Head of household, or Qualifying widow(er) $200,000   **5**

6 Subtract line 5 from line 4. If zero or less, enter -0- **6**

7 Additional Medicare Tax on Medicare wages. Multiply line 6 by 0.9% (0.009). Enter here and go to Part II **7**

Part II   **Additional Medicare Tax on Self-Employment Income**

8 Self-employment income from Schedule SE (Form 1040), Section A, line 4, or Section B, line 6. If you had a loss, enter -0- (Form 1040-PR and Form 1040-SS filers, see instructions.)   **8**

9 Enter the following amount for your filing status:
Married filing jointly $250,000
Married filing separately $125,000
Single, Head of household, or Qualifying widow(er) $200,000   **9**

10 Enter the amount from line 4 . . . . **10**

11 Subtract line 10 from line 9. If zero or less, enter -0- . . . **11**

12 Subtract line 11 from line 8. If zero or less, enter -0- **12**

13 Additional Medicare Tax on self-employment income. Multiply line 12 by 0.9% (0.009). Enter here and go to Part III **13**

Part III   **Additional Medicare Tax on Railroad Retirement Tax Act (RRTA) Compensation**

14 Railroad retirement (RRTA) compensation and tips from Form(s) W-2, box 14 (see instructions) **14**

15 Enter the following amount for your filing status:
Married filing jointly $250,000
Married filing separately $125,000
Single, Head of household, or Qualifying widow(er) $200,000   **15**

16 Subtract line 15 from line 14. If zero or less, enter -0- **16**

17 Additional Medicare Tax on railroad retirement (RRTA) compensation. Multiply line 16 by 0.9% (0.009). Enter here and go to Part IV **17**

Part IV   **Total Additional Medicare Tax**

18 Add lines 7, 13, and 17. Also include this amount on Form 1040, line 62, (Form 1040NR, 1040-PR, and 1040-SS filers, see instructions) and go to Part V **18**

Part V   **Withholding Reconciliation**

19 Medicare tax withheld from Form W-2, box 6. If you have more than one Form W-2, enter the total of the amounts from box 6 . . . . **19**

20 Enter the amount from line 1 . . . . **20**

21 Multiply line 20 by 1.45% (0.0145). This is your regular Medicare tax withholding on Medicare wages **21**

22 Subtract line 21 from line 19. If zero or less, enter -0-. This is your Additional Medicare Tax withholding on Medicare wages **22**

23 Additional Medicare Tax withholding on railroad retirement (RRTA) compensation from Form W-2, box 14 (see instructions) **23**

24 **Total Additional Medicare Tax withholding.** Add lines 22 and 23. Also include this amount with federal income tax withholding on Form 1040, line 64 (Form 1040NR, 1040-PR, and 1040-SS filers, see instructions) **24**

For Paperwork Reduction Act Notice, see your tax return instructions.   Cat. No. 59475X   Form **8959** (2016)

Form **8960**	**Net Investment Income Tax—Individuals, Estates, and Trusts**	OMB No. 1545-2227

Department of the Treasury
Internal Revenue Service (99)

▶ Attach to your tax return.
▶ Information about Form 8960 and its separate instructions is at *www.irs.gov/form8960*.

2016
Attachment Sequence No. **72**

Name(s) shown on your tax return

Your social security number or EIN

Part I Investment Income

☐ Section 6013(g) election (see instructions)
☐ Section 6013(h) election (see instructions)
☐ Regulations section 1.1411-10(g) election (see instructions)

1	Taxable interest (see instructions)	1
2	Ordinary dividends (see instructions)	2
3	Annuities (see instructions)	3
4a	Rental real estate, royalties, partnerships, S corporations, trusts, etc. (see instructions)	4a
b	Adjustment for net income or loss derived in the ordinary course of a non-section 1411 trade or business (see instructions)	4b
c	Combine lines 4a and 4b	4c
5a	Net gain or loss from disposition of property (see instructions)	5a
b	Net gain or loss from disposition of property that is not subject to net investment income tax (see instructions)	5b
c	Adjustment from disposition of partnership interest or S corporation stock (see instructions)	5c
d	Combine lines 5a through 5c	5d
6	Adjustments to investment income for certain CFCs and PFICs (see instructions)	6
7	Other modifications to investment income (see instructions)	7
8	Total investment income. Combine lines 1, 2, 3, 4c, 5d, 6, and 7	8

Part II Investment Expenses Allocable to Investment Income and Modifications

9a	Investment interest expenses (see instructions)	9a
b	State, local, and foreign income tax (see instructions)	9b
c	Miscellaneous investment expenses (see instructions)	9c
d	Add lines 9a, 9b, and 9c	9d
10	Additional modifications (see instructions)	10
11	Total deductions and modifications. Add lines 9d and 10	11

Part III Tax Computation

12	Net investment income. Subtract Part II, line 11 from Part I, line 8. Individuals complete lines 13–17. Estates and trusts complete lines 18a–21. If zero or less, enter -0-	12
	Individuals:	
13	Modified adjusted gross income (see instructions)	13
14	Threshold based on filing status (see instructions)	14
15	Subtract line 14 from line 13. If zero or less, enter -0-	15
16	Enter the smaller of line 12 or line 15	16
17	Net investment income tax for individuals. Multiply line 16 by 3.8% (.038). **Enter here and include on your tax return** (see instructions)	17
	Estates and Trusts:	
18a	Net investment income (line 12 above)	18a
b	Deductions for distributions of net investment income and deductions under section 642(c) (see instructions)	18b
c	Undistributed net investment income. Subtract line 18b from 18a (see instructions). If zero or less, enter -0-	18c
19a	Adjusted gross income (see instructions)	19a
b	Highest tax bracket for estates and trusts for the year (see instructions)	19b
c	Subtract line 19b from line 19a. If zero or less, enter -0-	19c
20	Enter the smaller of line 18c or line 19c	20
21	Net investment income tax for estates and trusts. Multiply line 20 by 3.8% (.038). **Enter here and include on your tax return** (see instructions)	21

For Paperwork Reduction Act Notice, see your tax return instructions.   Cat. No. 59474M   Form **8960** (2016)

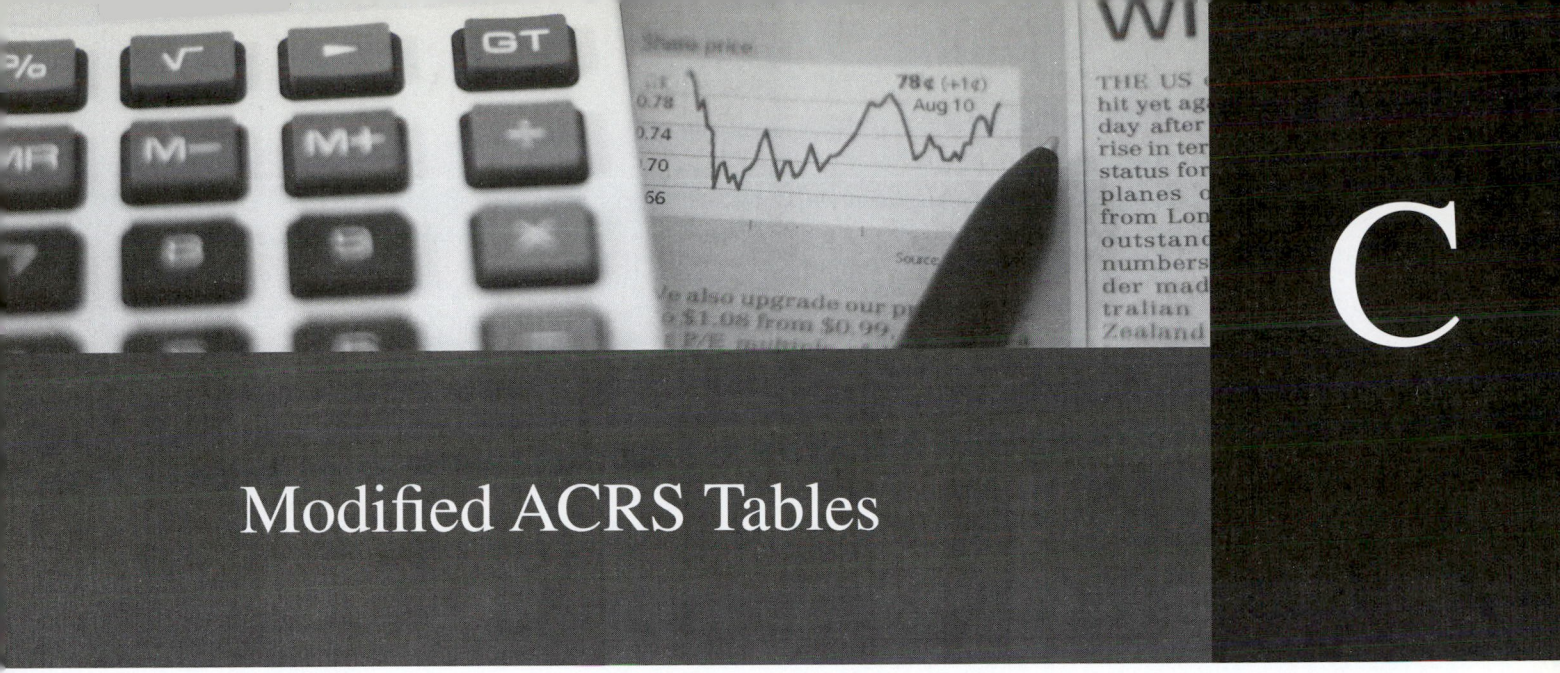

C

Modified ACRS Tables

Appendix Outline

Modified ACRS Accelerated Depreciation Percentages Using the Half-Year Convention for 3-, 5-, 7-, 10-, 15-, and 20-Year Property Placed in Service after December 31, 1986

Recovery Year	Property Class					
	3-Year	5-Year	7-Year	10-Year	15-Year	20-Year
1	33.33	20.00	14.29	10.00	5.00	3.750
2	44.45	32.00	24.49	18.00	9.50	7.219
3	14.81	19.20	17.49	14.40	8.55	6.677
4	7.41	11.52	12.49	11.52	7.70	6.177
5		11.52	8.93	9.22	6.93	5.713
6		5.76	8.92	7.37	6.23	5.285
7			8.93	6.55	5.90	4.888
8			4.46	6.55	5.90	4.522
9				6.56	5.91	4.462
10				6.55	5.90	4.461
11				3.28	5.91	4.462
12					5.90	4.461
13					5.91	4.462
14					5.90	4.461
15					5.91	4.462
16					2.95	4.461
17						4.462
18						4.461
19						4.462
20						4.461
21						2.231

Modified ACRS Depreciation Rates for Residential Rental Property Placed in Service after December 31, 1986

Recovery Year	Month Placed in Service					
	1	2	3	4	5	6
1	3.485	3.182	2.879	2.576	2.273	1.970
2	3.636	3.636	3.636	3.636	3.636	3.636
3	3.636	3.636	3.636	3.636	3.636	3.636
4	3.636	3.636	3.636	3.636	3.636	3.636
5	3.636	3.636	3.636	3.636	3.636	3.636
6	3.636	3.636	3.636	3.636	3.636	3.636
7	3.636	3.636	3.636	3.636	3.636	3.636
8	3.636	3.636	3.636	3.636	3.636	3.636
9	3.636	3.636	3.636	3.636	3.636	3.636
10	3.637	3.637	3.637	3.637	3.637	3.637
11	3.636	3.636	3.636	3.636	3.636	3.636
12	3.637	3.637	3.637	3.637	3.637	3.637
13	3.636	3.636	3.636	3.636	3.636	3.636
14	3.637	3.637	3.637	3.637	3.637	3.637
15	3.636	3.636	3.636	3.636	3.636	3.636
16	3.637	3.637	3.637	3.637	3.637	3.637
17	3.636	3.636	3.636	3.636	3.636	3.636
18	3.637	3.637	3.637	3.637	3.637	3.637
19	3.636	3.636	3.636	3.636	3.636	3.636
20	3.637	3.637	3.637	3.637	3.637	3.636
21	3.636	3.636	3.636	3.636	3.636	3.636
22	3.637	3.637	3.637	3.637	3.637	3.637
23	3.636	3.636	3.636	3.636	3.636	3.636
24	3.637	3.637	3.637	3.637	3.637	3.637
25	3.636	3.636	3.636	3.636	3.636	3.636
26	3.637	3.637	3.637	3.637	3.637	3.637
27	3.636	3.636	3.636	3.636	3.636	3.636
28	1.970	2.273	2.576	2.879	3.182	3.485
29	0.000	0.000	0.000	0.000	0.000	0.000

Modified ACRS Depreciation Rates for Residential Rental Property Placed in Service after December 31, 1986 (continued)

Recovery Year	Month Placed in Service					
	7	8	9	10	11	12
1	1.667	1.364	1.061	0.758	0.455	0.152
2	3.636	3.636	3.636	3.636	3.636	3.636
3	3.636	3.636	3.636	3.636	3.636	3.636
4	3.636	3.636	3.636	3.636	3.636	3.636
5	3.636	3.636	3.636	3.636	3.636	3.636
6	3.636	3.636	3.636	3.636	3.636	3.636
7	3.636	3.636	3.636	3.636	3.636	3.636
8	3.636	3.636	3.636	3.636	3.636	3.636
9	3.636	3.636	3.636	3.636	3.636	3.636
10	3.636	3.636	3.636	3.636	3.636	3.636
11	3.637	3.637	3.637	3.637	3.637	3.637
12	3.636	3.636	3.636	3.636	3.636	3.636
13	3.637	3.637	3.637	3.637	3.637	3.637
14	3.636	3.636	3.636	3.636	3.636	3.636
15	3.637	3.637	3.637	3.637	3.637	3.637
16	3.636	3.636	3.636	3.636	3.636	3.636
17	3.637	3.637	3.637	3.637	3.637	3.637
18	3.636	3.636	3.636	3.636	3.636	3.636
19	3.637	3.637	3.637	3.637	3.637	3.637
20	3.636	3.636	3.636	3.636	3.636	3.636
21	3.637	3.637	3.637	3.637	3.637	3.637
22	3.636	3.636	3.636	3.636	3.636	3.636
23	3.637	3.637	3.637	3.637	3.637	3.637
24	3.636	3.636	3.636	3.636	3.636	3.636
25	3.637	3.637	3.637	3.637	3.637	3.637
26	3.636	3.636	3.636	3.636	3.636	3.636
27	3.637	3.637	3.637	3.637	3.637	3.637
28	3.636	3.636	3.636	3.636	3.636	3.636
29	0.152	0.455	0.758	1.061	1.364	1.667

Modified ACRS Depreciation Percentages for Nonresidential Real Property Placed in Service after December 31, 1986 and before May 13, 1993

Recovery Year	Month Placed in Service					
	1	2	3	4	5	6
1	3.042	2.778	2.513	2.249	1.984	1.720
2	3.175	3.175	3.175	3.175	3.175	3.175
3	3.175	3.175	3.175	3.175	3.175	3.175
4	3.175	3.175	3.175	3.175	3.175	3.175
5	3.175	3.175	3.175	3.175	3.175	3.175
6	3.175	3.175	3.175	3.175	3.175	3.175
7	3.175	3.175	3.175	3.175	3.175	3.175
8	3.175	3.174	3.175	3.174	3.175	3.174
9	3.174	3.175	3.174	3.175	3.174	3.175
10	3.175	3.174	3.175	3.174	3.175	3.174
11	3.174	3.175	3.174	3.175	3.174	3.175
12	3.175	3.174	3.175	3.174	3.175	3.174
13	3.174	3.175	3.174	3.175	3.174	3.175
14	3.175	3.174	3.175	3.174	3.175	3.174
15	3.174	3.175	3.174	3.175	3.174	3.175
16	3.175	3.174	3.175	3.174	3.175	3.174
17	3.174	3.175	3.174	3.175	3.174	3.175
18	3.175	3.174	3.175	3.174	3.175	3.174
19	3.174	3.175	3.174	3.175	3.174	3.175
20	3.175	3.174	3.175	3.174	3.175	3.174
21	3.174	3.175	3.174	3.175	3.174	3.175
22	3.175	3.174	3.175	3.174	3.175	3.174
23	3.174	3.175	3.174	3.175	3.174	3.175
24	3.175	3.174	3.175	3.174	3.175	3.174
25	3.174	3.175	3.174	3.175	3.174	3.175
26	3.175	3.174	3.175	3.174	3.175	3.174
27	3.174	3.175	3.174	3.175	3.174	3.175
28	3.175	3.174	3.175	3.174	3.175	3.174
29	3.174	3.175	3.174	3.175	3.174	3.175
30	3.175	3.174	3.175	3.174	3.175	3.174
31	3.174	3.175	3.174	3.175	3.174	3.175
32	1.720	1.984	2.249	2.513	2.778	3.042
33	0.000	0.000	0.000	0.000	0.000	0.000

**Modified ACRS Depreciation Percentages for
Nonresidential Real Property Placed in Service after
December 31, 1986 and before May 13, 1993 (continued)**

Recovery Year	Month Placed in Service					
	7	8	9	10	11	12
1	1.455	1.190	0.926	0.661	0.397	0.132
2	3.175	3.175	3.175	3.175	3.175	3.175
3	3.175	3.175	3.175	3.175	3.175	3.175
4	3.175	3.175	3.175	3.175	3.175	3.175
5	3.175	3.175	3.175	3.175	3.175	3.175
6	3.175	3.175	3.175	3.175	3.175	3.175
7	3.175	3.175	3.175	3.175	3.175	3.175
8	3.175	3.175	3.175	3.175	3.175	3.175
9	3.174	3.175	3.175	3.175	3.174	3.175
10	3.175	3.174	3.175	3.174	3.175	3.174
11	3.174	3.175	3.174	3.175	3.174	3.175
12	3.175	3.174	3.175	3.174	3.175	3.174
13	3.174	3.175	3.174	3.175	3.174	3.175
14	3.175	3.174	3.175	3.174	3.175	3.174
15	3.174	3.175	3.174	3.175	3.174	3.175
16	3.175	3.174	3.175	3.174	3.175	3.174
17	3.174	3.175	3.174	3.175	3.174	3.175
18	3.175	3.174	3.175	3.174	3.175	3.174
19	3.174	3.175	3.174	3.175	3.174	3.175
20	3.175	3.174	3.175	3.174	3.175	3.174
21	3.174	3.175	3.174	3.175	3.174	3.175
22	3.175	3.174	3.175	3.174	3.175	3.174
23	3.174	3.175	3.174	3.175	3.174	3.175
24	3.175	3.174	3.175	3.174	3.175	3.174
25	3.174	3.175	3.174	3.175	3.174	3.175
26	3.175	3.174	3.175	3.174	3.175	3.174
27	3.174	3.175	3.174	3.175	3.174	3.175
28	3.175	3.174	3.175	3.174	3.175	3.174
29	3.174	3.175	3.174	3.175	3.174	3.175
30	3.175	3.174	3.175	3.174	3.175	3.174
31	3.174	3.175	3.174	3.175	3.174	3.175
32	3.175	3.174	3.175	3.174	3.175	3.174
33	0.132	0.397	0.661	0.926	1.190	1.455

Modified ACRS Depreciation Percentages for Nonresidential Real Property Placed in Service after May 12, 1993

Month Placed in Service	Recovery Year				
	1	2	...	39	40
1	2.461%	2.564%		2.564%	0.107%
2	2.247	2.564		2.564	0.321
3	2.033	2.564		2.564	0.535
4	1.819	2.564		2.564	0.749
5	1.605	2.564		2.564	0.963
6	1.391	2.564		2.564	1.177
7	1.177	2.564		2.564	1.391
8	0.963	2.564		2.564	1.605
9	0.749	2.564		2.564	1.819
10	0.535	2.564		2.564	2.033
11	0.321	2.564		2.564	2.247
12	0.107	2.564		2.564	2.461

Modified ACRS Accelerated Depreciation Percentages Using the Mid-Quarter Convention for 3-, 5-, 7-, 10-, 15-, and 20-Year Property Placed in Service after December 31, 1986

	Quarter Placed in Service			
Recovery Year	1	2	3	4
3-Year Property:				
1	58.33	41.67	25.00	8.33
2	27.78	38.89	50.00	61.11
3	12.35	14.14	16.67	20.37
4	1.54	5.30	8.33	10.19
5-Year Property:				
1	35.00	25.00	15.00	5.00
2	26.00	30.00	34.00	38.00
3	15.60	18.00	20.40	22.80
4	11.01	11.37	12.24	13.68
5	11.01	11.37	11.30	10.94
6	1.38	4.26	7.06	9.58
7-Year Property:				
1	25.00	17.85	10.71	3.57
2	21.43	23.47	25.51	27.55
3	15.31	16.76	18.22	19.68
4	10.93	11.37	13.02	14.06
5	8.75	8.87	9.30	10.04
6	8.74	8.87	8.85	8.73
7	8.75	8.87	8.86	8.73
8	1.09	3.33	5.53	7.64
10-Year Property:				
1	17.50	12.50	7.50	2.50
2	16.50	17.50	18.50	19.50
3	13.20	14.00	14.80	15.60
4	10.56	11.20	11.84	12.48
5	8.45	8.96	9.47	9.98
6	6.76	7.17	7.58	7.99
7	6.55	6.55	6.55	6.55
8	6.55	6.55	6.55	6.55
9	6.56	6.56	6.56	6.56
10	0.82	6.55	6.55	6.55
11		2.46	4.10	5.74

**Modified ACRS Accelerated Depreciation Percentages
Using the Mid-Quarter Convention for 3-, 5-, 7-, 10-,
15-, and 20-Year Property Placed in Service after
December 31, 1986 (continued)**

Recovery Year	Quarter Placed in Service			
	1	2	3	4
15-Year Property:				
1	8.75	6.25	3.75	1.25
2	9.13	9.38	9.63	9.88
3	8.21	8.44	8.66	8.89
4	7.39	7.59	7.80	8.00
5	6.65	6.83	7.02	7.20
6	5.99	6.15	6.31	6.48
7	5.90	5.91	5.90	5.90
8	5.91	5.90	5.90	5.90
9	5.90	5.91	5.91	5.90
10	5.91	5.90	5.90	5.91
11	5.90	5.91	5.91	5.90
12	5.91	5.90	5.90	5.91
13	5.90	5.91	5.91	5.90
14	5.91	5.90	5.90	5.91
15	5.90	5.91	5.91	5.90
16	0.74	2.21	3.69	5.17
20-Year Property:				
1	6.563	4.688	2.813	0.938
2	7.000	7.148	7.289	7.430
3	6.482	6.612	6.742	6.872
4	5.996	6.116	6.237	6.357
5	5.546	5.658	5.769	5.880
6	5.130	5.233	5.336	5.439
7	4.746	4.841	4.936	5.031
8	4.459	4.478	4.566	4.654
9	4.459	4.463	4.460	4.458
10	4.459	4.463	4.460	4.458
11	4.459	4.463	4.460	4.458
12	4.460	4.463	4.460	4.458
13	4.459	4.463	4.461	4.458
14	4.460	4.463	4.460	4.458
15	4.459	4.462	4.461	4.458
16	4.460	4.463	4.460	4.458
17	4.459	4.462	4.461	4.458
18	4.460	4.463	4.460	4.459
19	4.459	4.462	4.461	4.458
20	4.460	4.463	4.460	4.459
21	0.557	1.673	2.788	3.901

Alternative Depreciation System
Recovery Periods

General Rule: Recovery period is the property's class life unless:
1. There is no class life (see below), or
2. A special class life has been designated (see below).

Type of Property	*Recovery Period*
Personal property with no class life	12 years
Nonresidential real property with no class life	40 years
Residential rental property with no class life	40 years
Cars, light general purpose trucks, certain technological equipment, and semiconductor manufacturing equipment	5 years
Computer-based telephone central office switching equipment	9.5 years
Railroad track	10 years
Single purpose agricultural or horticultural structures	15 years
Municipal waste water treatment plants, telephone distribution plants	24 years
Low-income housing financed by tax-exempt bonds	27.5 years
Municipal sewers	50 years

Modified ACRS and ADS Straight-Line Depreciation Percentages Using the Half-Year Convention for 3-, 5-, 7-, 10-, 15-, and 20-Year Property Placed in Service after December 31, 1986

Recovery Year	Property Class					
	3-Year	5-Year	7-Year	10-Year	15-Year	20-Year
1	16.67	10.00	7.14	5.00	3.33	2.50
2	33.33	20.00	14.29	10.00	6.67	5.00
3	33.33	20.00	14.29	10.00	6.67	5.00
4	16.67	20.00	14.28	10.00	6.67	5.00
5		20.00	14.29	10.00	6.67	5.00
6		10.00	14.28	10.00	6.67	5.00
7			14.29	10.00	6.67	5.00
8			7.14	10.00	6.66	5.00
9				10.00	6.67	5.00
10				10.00	6.66	5.00
11				5.00	6.67	5.00
12					6.66	5.00
13					6.67	5.00
14					6.66	5.00
15					6.67	5.00
16					3.33	5.00
17						5.00
18						5.00
19						5.00
20						5.00
21						2.50

ADS Straight-Line Depreciation Percentages for Real Property Using the Mid-Month Convention for Property Placed in Service after December 31, 1986

Month Placed in Service	Recovery Year		
	1	2–40	41
1	2.396	2.500	0.104
2	2.188	2.500	0.312
3	1.979	2.500	0.521
4	1.771	2.500	0.729
5	1.563	2.500	0.937
6	1.354	2.500	1.146
7	1.146	2.500	1.354
8	0.938	2.500	1.562
9	0.729	2.500	1.771
10	0.521	2.500	1.979
11	0.313	2.500	2.187
12	0.104	2.500	2.396

Table of Cases Cited

Table of Code Sections Cited

Table of Regulations Cited

Regulations

Table of Revenue Procedures and Revenue Rulings Cited

Glossary of Tax Terms

—A—

A. (*see* Acquiescence).

Accelerated Cost Recovery System (ACRS). An alternate form of depreciation enacted by the Economic Recovery Tax Act of 1981 and significantly modified by the Tax Reform Act of 1986. The modified cost recovery system applies to assets placed into service after 1986 and is referred to as MACRS. Under both systems, the cost of a qualifying asset is recovered over a set period of time. Salvage value is ignored. § 168.

Accelerated Depreciation. Various depreciation methods that produce larger depreciation deductions in the earlier years of an asset's life than straight-line depreciation. Examples: double-declining balance method (200% declining balance) and sum-of-the-years'-digits method. § 167 (*see* Depreciation).

Accounting Method. A method by which an entity's income and expenses are determined. The primary accounting methods used are the accrual method and the cash method. Other accounting methods include the installment method, the percentage-of-completion method (for construction), and various methods for valuing inventories, such as FIFO and LIFO. §§ 446 and 447 (*see also Specific Accounting Methods*).

Accounting Period. A period of time used by a taxpayer in determining his or her income, expenses, and tax liability. An accounting period is generally a year for tax purposes, either a calendar year, a fiscal year, or a 52–53 week year. §§ 441 and 443.

Accrual Method of Accounting. The method of accounting that reflects the income earned and the expenses incurred during a given tax period. However, unearned income of an accrual basis taxpayer must generally be included in an entity's income in the year in which it is received, even if it is not actually earned by the entity until a later tax period. § 446.

Acquiescence. The public endorsement of a regular Tax Court decision by the Commissioner of the Internal Revenue Service. When the Commissioner acquiesces to a regular Tax Court decision, the IRS generally will not dispute the result in cases involving substantially similar facts (*see* Nonacquiescence).

Ad Valorem Tax. A tax based on the value of property.

Adjusted Basis. The basis (i.e., cost or other basis) of property plus capital improvements minus depreciation allowed or allowable. See § 1016 for other adjustments to basis. § 1016 (*see* Basis).

Adjusted Gross Income. A term used with reference to individual taxpayers. Adjusted gross income consists of an individual's gross income less certain deductions and business expenses. § 62.

AFTR (American Federal Tax Reports). These volumes contain the Federal tax decisions issued by the U.S. District Courts, U.S. Court of Federal Claims, U.S. Circuit Courts of Appeals, and the U.S. Supreme Court (*see* AFTR2d).

AFTR2d (American Federal Tax Reports, Second Series). The second series of the American Federal Tax Reports. These volumes contain the Federal tax decisions issued by the U.S. District Courts, U.S. Court of Federal Claims, U.S. Circuit Courts of Appeals, and the U.S. Supreme Court (*see* AFTR).

Alternate Valuation Date. The property contained in a decedent's gross estate must be valued at either the decedent's date of death or the alternate valuation date. The alternate valuation date is six months after the decedent's date of death, or, if the property is disposed of prior to that date, the particular property disposed of is valued as of the date of its disposition. § 2032.

Alternative Minimum Tax. A tax imposed on taxpayers only if it exceeds the "regular" tax of the taxpayer. Regular taxable income is adjusted by certain timing differences, then increased by tax preferences to arrive at alternative minimum taxable income.

Amortization. The systematic write-off (deduction) of the cost or other basis of an intangible asset over its estimated useful life. The concept is similar to depreciation (used for tangible assets) and depletion (used for natural resources) (*see* Goodwill; Intangible Asset).

Amount Realized. Any money received, plus the fair market value of any other property or services received, plus any liabilities discharged on the sale or other disposition of property. The determination of the amount realized is the first step in determining realized gain or loss. § 1001(b).

Annual Exclusion. The amount each year that a donor may exclude from Federal gift tax for each donee. Currently, the annual exclusion is $12,000 per donee (2007 and 2008). The annual exclusion does not generally apply to gifts of future interests. § 2503(b).

Annuity. A fixed amount of money payable to a person at specific intervals for either a specific period of time or for life.

Appellate Court. A court to which other court decisions are appealed. The appellate courts for Federal tax purposes include the Courts of Appeals and the Supreme Court.

Arm's-Length Transaction. A transaction entered into by unrelated parties, all acting in their own best interests. It is presumed that in an arm's-length transaction the prices used are the fair market values of the properties or services being transferred in the transaction.

Assessment of Tax. The imposition of an additional tax liability by the Internal Revenue Service (i.e., as the result of an audit).

Assignment of Income. A situation in which a taxpayer assigns income or income-producing property to another person or entity in an attempt to avoid paying taxes on that income. An assignment of income or income-producing property is generally not recognized for tax purposes, and the income is taxable to the assignor.

Attribution. (*see* Constructive Ownership).

Audit. The examination of a taxpayer's return or other taxable transactions by the Internal Revenue Service in order to determine the correct tax liability. Types of audits include correspondence audits, office audits, and field audits (*see also* Correspondence Audit; Office Audit; Field Audit).

—B—

Bad Debt. An uncollectible debt. A bad debt may be classified either as a business bad debt or a nonbusiness bad debt. A business bad debt is one that has arisen in the course of the taxpayer's business (with a business purpose). Nonbusiness bad debts are treated as short-term capital losses rather than as ordinary losses. § 166.

Bargain Sale, Rental, or Purchase. A sale, rental, or purchase of property for less than its fair market value. The difference between the sale, rental, or purchase price and the property's fair market value may have its own tax consequences, such as consideration as a constructive dividend or a gift.

Bartering. The exchange of goods and services without using money.

Basis. The starting point in determining the gain or loss from the sale or other disposition of an asset, or the depreciation (or depletion or amortization) on an asset. For example, if an asset is purchased for cash, the basis of that asset is the cash paid. §§ 1012, 1014, 1015, 334, 359, and 362.

Beneficiary. Someone who will benefit from an act of another, such as the beneficiary of a life insurance contract, the beneficiary of a trust (i.e., income beneficiary), or the beneficiary of an estate.

Bequest. A testamentary transfer (by will) of personal property (personalty).

Board of Tax Appeals (B.T.A.). The predecessor of the United States Tax Court, in existence from 1924 to 1942.

Bona Fide. Real; in good faith.

Bonus Depreciation. Depreciation that taxpayers can take in addition to normal depreciation and expensing for certain newly acquired property.

Boot. Cash or property that is not included in the definition of a particular type of nontaxable exchange (*see* §§ 351(b) and 1031(b)). In these nontaxable exchanges, a taxpayer who receives boot must recognize gain to the extent of the boot received or the realized gain, whichever is less.

Burden of Proof. The weight of evidence in a legal case or in a tax proceeding. Generally, the burden of proof is on the taxpayer in a tax case. However, the burden of proof is on the government in fraud cases. § 7454.

Business Purpose. An actual business reason for following a course of action. Tax avoidance alone is not considered to be a business purpose. In areas such as corporate formation and corporate reorganizations, business purpose is especially important.

Business Purpose Doctrine. A judicial theory used by courts to deny the tax benefits of a transaction that otherwise meets statutory and administrative requirements if the transaction did not have a business purpose—i.e., it was only motivated by tax considerations (*see also* Economic Substance Doctrine).

—C—

C Corporation. A so-called regular corporation that is a separate tax-paying entity and is subject to the tax rules contained in Subchapter C of the Internal Revenue Code (as opposed to an S corporation, which is subject to the tax rules of Subchapter S of the Code).

Capital Asset. All property held by a taxpayer (e.g., house, car, clothing) except for certain assets that are specifically excluded from the definition of a capital asset, such as inventory and depreciable and real property used in a trade or business.

Capital Contribution. Cash, services, or property contributed by a partner to a partnership or by a shareholder to a corporation. Capital contributions are not income to the recipient partnership or corporation. §§ 721 and 118.

Capital Expenditure. Any amount paid for new buildings or for permanent improvements; any expenditures that add to the value or prolong the life of property or adapt the property to a new or different use. Capital expenditures should be added to the basis of the property improved. § 263.

Capital Gain. A gain from the sale or other disposition of a capital asset. § 1222.

Capital Loss. A loss from the sale or other disposition of a capital asset. § 1222.

Cash Method of Accounting. The method of accounting that reflects the income received (or constructively received) and the expenses paid during a given period. However, prepaid expenses of a cash basis taxpayer that benefit more than one year may be required to be deducted only in the periods benefited (e.g., a premium for a three-year insurance policy may have to be spread over three years).

CCH. (*see* Commerce Clearing House).

Certiorari. A Writ of Certiorari is the form used to appeal a lower court (U.S. Court of Appeals) decision to the Supreme Court. The Supreme Court then decides, by reviewing the Writ of Certiorari, whether it will accept the appeal or not. The Supreme Court generally does not accept the appeal unless a constitutional issue is involved or the lower courts are in conflict. If the Supreme Court refuses to accept the appeal, then the certiorari is denied (cert. den.).

Claim of Right Doctrine. If a taxpayer has an unrestricted claim to income, the income is included in that taxpayer's income when it is received or constructively received, even if there is a possibility that all or part of the income may have to be returned to another party.

Closely Held Corporation. A corporation whose voting stock is owned by one or a few shareholders and is operated by this person or closely knit group.

Commerce Clearing House. A publisher of tax materials, including a multivolume tax service, volumes that contain the Federal courts' decisions on tax matters (USTC) and the Tax Court regular (T.C.) and memorandum (TCM) decisions.

Community Property. Property that is owned together by husband and wife, where each has an undivided one-half interest in the property due to their marital status. The ten community property states are Alaska, Arizona, California, Idaho, Louisiana, Nevada, New Mexico, Texas, Washington, and Wisconsin.

Condemnation. The taking of private property for a public use by a public authority, an exercise of the power of eminent domain. The public authority compensates the owner of the property taken in a condemnation (*see also* Involuntary Conversion).

Conduit Principle. The provisions in the tax law that allow specific tax characteristics to be passed through certain entities to the owners of the entity without losing their identity. For example, the short-term capital gains of a partnership would be passed through to the partners and retain their character as short-term capital gains on the tax returns of the partners. This principle applies in varying degrees to partnerships, S corporations, estates, and trusts.

Constructive Dividends. The constructive receipt of a dividend. Even though a taxable benefit was not designated as a dividend by the distributing corporation, a shareholder may be designated by the IRS as having received a dividend if the benefit has the appearance of a dividend. For example, if a shareholder uses corporate property for personal purposes rent-free, he or she will have a constructive dividend equal to the fair rental value of the corporate property.

Constructive Ownership. In certain situations, the tax law attributes the ownership of stock to persons "related" to the person or entity that actually owns the stock. The related party is said to constructively own the stock of that person. For example, under § 267(c) a father is considered to constructively own all stock actually owned by his son. §§ 267, 318, and 544(a).

Constructive Receipt. When income is available to a taxpayer, even though it is not actually received by the taxpayer, the amount is considered to be constructively received by the taxpayer and should be included in income (e.g., accrued interest on a savings account). However, if there are restrictions on the availability of the income, it is generally not considered to be constructively received until the restrictions are removed (e.g., interest on a 6-month certificate of deposit is not constructively received until the end of the 6-month period if early withdrawal would result in loss of interest or principal).

Contributions to the Capital of a Corporation. (*see* Capital Contributions).

Corpus. The principal of a trust, as opposed to the income of the trust. Also called the *res* of the trust.

Correspondence Audit. An IRS audit conducted through the mail. Generally, verification or substantiation for specified items is requested by the IRS, and the taxpayer mails the requested information to the IRS (*see* Field Audit; Office Audit).

Cost Depletion. (*see* Depletion).

Court of Appeals. The U.S. Federal court system has 13 circuit Courts of Appeals, which consider cases appealed from the U.S. Court of Federal Claims, the U.S. Tax Court, and the U.S. District Courts. A writ of certiorari is used to appeal a case from a Court of Appeals to the U.S. Supreme Court (*see* Appellate Court).

Creditor. A person or entity to whom money is owed. The person or entity who owes the money is called the debtor.

—D—

Death Tax. A tax imposed on property upon the death of the owner, such as an estate tax or inheritance tax.

Debtor. A person or entity who owes money to another. The person or entity to whom the money is owed is called the creditor.

Decedent. A deceased person.

Deficiency. An additional tax liability owed to the IRS by a taxpayer. A deficiency is generally proposed by the IRS through the use of a Revenue Agent's Report.

Deficit. A negative balance in retained earnings or in earnings and profits.

Dependent. A person who derives his or her primary support from another. In order for a taxpayer to claim a dependency exemption for a person, there are five tests that must be met: support test, gross income test, citizenship or residency test, relationship or member of household test, and joint return test. § 152.

Depletion. As natural resources are extracted and sold, the cost or other basis of the resource is recovered by the use of depletion. Depletion may be either cost or percentage (statutory) depletion. Cost depletion has to do with the recovery of the cost of natural resources based on the units of the resource sold. Percentage depletion uses percentages given in the Internal Revenue Code multiplied by the gross income from the interest, subject to limitations. §§ 613 and 613A.

Depreciation. The systematic write-off of the basis of a tangible asset over the asset's estimated useful life. Depreciation is intended to reflect the wear, tear, and obsolescence of the asset (*see* Amortization; Depletion).

Depreciation Recapture. The situation in which all or part of the realized gain from the sale or other disposition of depreciable business property could be treated as ordinary income. See text for discussion of §§ 291, 1245, and 1250.

Determination Letter. A written statement regarding the tax consequences of a transaction issued by an IRS District Director in response to a written inquiry by a taxpayer that applies to a particular set of facts. Determination letters are frequently used to state whether a pension or profit-sharing plan is qualified or not, to determine the tax-exempt status of nonprofit organizations, and to clarify employee status.

Discriminant Function System (DIF). The computerized system used by the Internal Revenue Service in identifying and selecting returns for examination. This system uses secret mathematical formulas to select those returns that have a probability of tax errors.

Dissent. A disagreement with the majority opinion. The term is generally used to mean the explicit disagreement of one or more judges in a court with the majority decision on a particular case.

District Court. A trial court in which Federal tax matters can be litigated; the only trial court in which a jury trial can be obtained.

Dividend. A payment by a corporation to its shareholders authorized by the corporation's board of directors to be distributed pro rata among the outstanding shares. However, a constructive dividend does not need to be authorized by the shareholders (*see also* Constructive Dividend).

Donee. The person or entity to whom a gift is made.

Donor. The person or entity who makes a gift.

Double Taxation. A situation in which income is taxed twice. For example, a regular corporation pays tax on its taxable income, and when this income is distributed to the corporation's shareholders, the shareholders are taxed on the dividend income.

—E—

Earned Income. Income from personal services. § 911(d)(2). To be distinguished from income from a passive investment such as dividends, rents, or interest.

Earnings and Profits (E&P). The measure of a corporation's ability to pay dividends to its shareholders. Distributions made by a corporation to its shareholders are dividends to the extent of the corporation's earnings and profits. §§ 312 and 316.

Economic Substance Doctrine. A judicial theory used by courts to deny the tax benefits of a transaction if the transaction did not result in a meaningful change to the taxpayer's economic position other than reducing federal income taxes. The theory operates to deny tax benefits notwithstanding that it meets statutory and administrative requirements.

Eminent Domain. (*see* Condemnation).

Employee. A person in the service of another, where the employer has the power to specify how the work is to be performed (*see* Independent Contractor).

Employee Achievement Award. An award of tangible personalty that is made for length of service achievement or safety achievement. § 274(j).

Encumbrance. A liability.

Entity. For tax purposes, an organization that is considered to have a separate existence, such as a partnership, corporation, estate, or trust.

Escrow. Cash or other property that is held by a third party as security for an obligation.

Estate. All of the property owned by a decedent at the time of his or her death.

Estate Tax. A tax imposed on the transfer of a decedent's taxable estate. The estate, not the heirs, is liable for the estate tax. §§ 2001–2209 (*see* Inheritance Tax).

Estoppel. A bar or impediment preventing a party from asserting a fact or a claim in court that is inconsistent with a position he or she had previously taken.

Excise Tax. A tax imposed on the sale, manufacture, or use of a commodity or on the conduct of an occupation or activity; considered to include every Internal Revenue Tax except the income tax.

Executor. A person appointed in a will to carry out the provisions in the will and to administer the estate of the decedent. (Feminine of executor is executrix.)

Exempt Organization. An organization (such as a charitable organization) that is exempt from Federal income taxes. §§ 501–528.

Exemption. A deduction allowed in computing taxable income. Personal exemptions are available for the taxpayer and his or her spouse. Dependency exemptions are available for the taxpayer's dependents. §§ 151–154 (*see* Dependent).

—F—

F. Supp. (Federal Supplement). Volumes in which the decisions of the U.S. District Courts are published.

F.2d (Federal Reporter, Second Series). Volumes in which the decisions of the U.S. Court of Federal Claims and the U.S. Courts of Appeals are published.

Fair Market Value. The amount that a willing buyer would pay a willing seller in an arm's-length transaction.

Fed. (Federal Reporter). Volumes in which the decisions of the U.S. Court of Federal Claims and the U.S. Courts of Appeals are published.

FICA (Federal Insurance Contributions Act). The law dealing with social security taxes and benefits. §§ 3101-3126.

Fiduciary. A person or institution who holds and manages property for another, such as a guardian, trustee, executor, or administrator. § 7701(a)(6).

Field Audit. An audit conducted by the IRS at the taxpayer's place of business or at the place of business of the taxpayer's representative. Field audits are generally conducted by Revenue Agents (*see* Correspondence Audit; Office Audit).

FIFO (First-In, First-Out). A method of determining the cost of an inventory. The first inventory units acquired are considered to be the first sold. Therefore, the cost of the inventory would consist of the most recently acquired inventory.

Filing Status. The filing status of an individual taxpayer determines the tax rates that are applicable to that taxpayer. The filing statuses include Single, Head of Household, Married Filing Jointly, Married Filing Separately, and Surviving Spouse (Qualifying Widow or Widower).

Fiscal Year. A period of 12 consecutive months, other than a calendar year, used as the accounting period of a business. § 7701(a)(24).

Foreign Corporation. A corporation that is not organized under U.S. laws, other than a domestic corporation. § 7701(a)(5).

Fraud. A willful intent to evade tax. For tax purposes, fraud is divided into civil fraud and criminal fraud. The IRS has the burden of proof of proving fraud. Civil fraud has a penalty of 75% of the underpayment (§ 6653(b)). Criminal fraud requires a greater degree of willful intent to evade tax (§§ 7201–7207).

Freedom of Information Act. The means by which the public may obtain information held by Federal agencies.

Fringe Benefits. Benefits received by an employee in addition to his or her salary or wages, such as insurance and recreational facilities.

FUTA (Federal Unemployment Tax Act). A tax imposed on the employer on the wages of the employees. A credit is generally given for amounts contributed to state unemployment tax funds. §§ 3301–3311.

Future Interest. An interest, the possession or enjoyment of which will come into being at some point in the future. The annual exclusion for gifts applies only to gifts of present interests, as opposed to future interests.

—G—

General Partner. A partner who is jointly and severally liable for the debts of the partnership. A general partner has no limited liability (*see* Limited Partner).

Gift. A transfer of property or money given for less than adequate consideration in money or money's worth.

Gift-Splitting. A tax provision that allows a married person who makes a gift of his or her property to elect, with the consent of his or her spouse, to treat the gift as being made one-half by each the taxpayer and his or her spouse. The effect of gift-splitting is to take advantage of the annual gift tax exclusions for both the taxpayer and his or her spouse. § 2513.

Goodwill. An intangible that has an indefinite useful life, arising from the difference between the purchase price and the value of the assets of an acquired business. Goodwill is amortizable over a 15-year period. § 197.

Grantor. The person who creates a trust.

Gross Estate. The value of all property, real or personal, tangible or intangible, owned by a decedent at the time of his or her death. §§ 2031–2046.

Gross Income. Income that is subject to Federal income tax. All income from whatever source derived, unless it is specifically excluded from income (e.g., interest on state and local bonds). § 61.

Guaranteed Payment. A payment made by a partnership to a partner for services or the use of capital, without regard to the income of the partnership. The payment generally is deductible by the partnership and taxable to the partner. § 707(c).

—H—

Half-Year Convention. When a taxpayer is using MACRS, personalty placed in service at any time during the year is treated as placed in service in the middle of the year, and personalty disposed of or retired at any time during the year is treated as disposed of in the middle of the year. However, if more than 40% of all personalty placed in service during the year is placed in service during the last three months of the year, the mid-quarter convention applies. § 168(d)(4)(A).

Heir. One who inherits property from a decedent.

Hobby. An activity not engaged in for profit. § 183.

Holding Period. The period of time that property is held. Holding period is used to determine whether a gain or loss is short-term or long-term. §§ 1222 and 1223.

H.R. 10 Plans. (*see* Keogh Plans).

—I—

Income Beneficiary. The person or entity entitled to receive the income from property. Generally used in reference to trusts.

Income in Respect of a Decedent (IRD). Income that had been earned by a decedent at the time of his or her death, but is not included on the final tax return because of the decedent's method of accounting. Income in respect of a decedent is included in the decedent's gross estate and also on the tax return of the person who receives the income. § 691.

Independent Contractor. One who contracts to do a job according to his or her own methods and skills. The employer has control over the independent contractor only as to the final result of his or her work (*see* Employee).

Indirect Method. A method used by the IRS in order to determine whether a taxpayer's income is correctly reported when adequate records do not exist. Indirect methods include the Source and Applications of Funds Method and the Net Worth Method.

Information Return. A return that must be filed with the Internal Revenue Service even though no tax is imposed, such as a partnership return (Form 1065), Form W-2, and Form 1099.

Inheritance Tax. A tax imposed on the privilege of receiving property of a decedent. The tax is imposed on the heir.

Installment Method. A method of accounting under which a taxpayer spreads the recognition of his or her gain ratably over time as the payments are received. §§ 453, 453A, and 453B.

Intangible Asset. A nonphysical asset, such as goodwill, copyrights, franchises, or trademarks.

Inter Vivos Transfer. A property transfer during the life of the owner.

Internal Revenue Service. Part of the Treasury Department, it is responsible for administering and enforcing the Federal tax laws.

Intestate. No will existing at the time of death.

Investment Credit Recapture. When property on which an investment credit has been taken is disposed of prior to the full time period required under the law to earn the credit, then the amount of unearned credit must be added back to the taxpayer's tax liability—this is called recapture of the investment credit. § 47.

Investment Tax Credit. A credit against tax that was allowed for investing in depreciable tangible personalty before 1986. The credit was equal to 10% of the qualified investment. §§ 38 and 46–48.

Involuntary Conversion. The complete or partial destruction, theft, seizure, requisition, or condemnation of property. § 1033.

Itemized Deductions. Certain expenditures of a personal nature that are specifically allowed to be deductible from an individual taxpayer's adjusted gross income. Itemized deductions (e.g., medical expenses, charitable contributions, interest, taxes, and miscellaneous itemized deductions) are deductible if they exceed the taxpayer's standard deduction.

—J—

Jeopardy Assessment. If the IRS has reason to believe that the collection or assessment of a tax would be jeopardized by delay, the IRS may assess and collect the tax immediately. §§ 6861–6864.

Joint and Several Liability. The creditor has the ability to sue one or more of the parties who have a liability, or all of the liable persons together. General partners are jointly and severally liable for the debts of the partnership. Also, if a husband and wife file a joint return, they are jointly and severally liable to the IRS for the taxes due.

Joint Tenancy. Property held by two or more owners, where each has an undivided interest in the property. Joint tenancy includes the right of survivorship, which means that upon the death of an owner, his or her share passes to the surviving owner(s).

Joint Venture. A joining together of two or more persons in order to undertake a specific business project. A joint venture is not a continuing relationship like a partnership, but may be treated as a partnership for Federal income tax purposes. § 761(a).

—K—

Keogh Plans. A retirement plan available for self-employed taxpayers. § 401.

Kiddie Tax. Unearned income of a child under age 19 (or age 24 if a full-time student) is taxed at the child's parents' marginal tax rate. § 1(i).

—L—

Leaseback. A transaction in which a taxpayer sells property and then leases back the property.

Leasehold Acquisition Expenses. Costs related to acquiring a lease such as legal and brokerage fees.

Leasehold Improvement. An alteration of property rented to a third party. Typically the alteration increases the value of or improves the property. Examples of leasehold improvements are new carpeting, cabinetry, lighting, and walls. The improvement could be made and paid for by the lessor or the lessee. A tenant may want to invest in leasehold improvements in order to customize the space to suit its specific needs.

Lessee. A person or entity who rents or leases property from another.

Lessor. A person or entity who rents or leases property to another.

Life Insurance. A form of insurance that will pay the beneficiary of the policy a fixed amount upon the death of the insured person.

LIFO (Last-In, First-Out). A method of determining the cost of an inventory. The last inventory units acquired are considered to be the first sold. Therefore, the cost of the inventory would consist of the earliest acquired inventory.

Like-Kind Exchange. The exchange of property held for productive use in a trade or business or for investment (but not inventory, stock, bonds, or notes) for property that is also held for productive use or for investment (i.e., realty for realty; personalty for personalty). No gain or loss is generally recognized by either party unless boot (other than qualifying property) is involved in the transaction. § 1031.

Limited Liability. The situation in which the liability of an owner of an organization for the organization's debts is limited to the owner's investment in the organization. Examples of taxpayers with limited liability are corporate shareholders and the limited partners in a limited partnership.

Limited Liability Company (LLC). A form of business entity permitted by all states in the U.S. under which the owners are treated as partners and the company is subject to the rules of partnership taxation for Federal tax purposes.

Limited Partner. A partner whose liability for partnership debts is limited to his or her investment in the partnership. A limited partner may take no active part in the management of the partnership according to the Uniform Limited Partnership Act (*see* General Partner).

Lump Sum Distribution. Payment at one time of an entire amount due, or the entire proceeds of a pension or profit-sharing plan, rather than installment payments.

—M—

Majority. Of legal age (*see* Minor).

Marital Deduction. Upon the transfer of property from one spouse to another, either by gift or at death, the Internal Revenue Code allows a transfer tax deduction for the amount transferred.

Market Value. (*see* Fair Market Value).

Material Participation. Occurs when a taxpayer is involved in the operations of an activity on a regular, continuous, and substantial basis. § 469(h).

Mid-Month Convention. When a taxpayer is using ACRS or MACRS, realty placed in service at any time during a month is treated as placed in service in the middle of the month, and realty disposed of or retired at any time during a month is treated as disposed of in the middle of the month. § 168(d)(4)(B).

Mid-Quarter Convention. Used for all personalty placed in service during the year if more than 40% of all personalty placed in service during the year is placed in service during the last three months of the year. § 168(d)(4)(C).

Minimum Tax. (*see* Alternative Minimum Tax).

Minor. A person who has not yet reached the age of legal majority. In most states, a minor is a person under 18 years of age.

Mortgagee. The person or entity that holds the mortgage; the lender; the creditor.

Mortgagor. The person or entity that is mortgaging the property; the debtor.

—N—

NA. (*see* Nonacquiescence).

Negligence Penalty. A penalty imposed by the IRS on taxpayers who are negligent or intentionally disregard the rules or regulations (but are not fraudulent), in the determination of their tax liability. § 6662.

Net Investment Income Tax. Special 3.8% tax imposed by § 1411 on an individual's investment income net of related expenses. Applies only to high income individuals.

Net Operating Loss (NOL). The amount by which deductions exceed a taxpayer's gross income. § 172.

Net Worth Method. An indirect method of determining a taxpayer's income used by the IRS when adequate records do not exist. The net worth of the taxpayer is determined for the end of each year in question, and adjustments are made to the increase in net worth from year to year for nontaxable sources of income and nondeductible expenditures. This method is often used when a possibility of fraud exists.

Ninety-Day (90-Day) Letter. (*see* Statutory Notice of Deficiency).

Nonacquiescence. The public announcement that the Commissioner of the Internal Revenue Service disagrees with a regular Tax Court decision. When the Commissioner nonacquiesces to a regular Tax Court decision, the IRS generally will litigate cases involving similar facts (*see* Acquiescence).

Nonresident Alien. A person who is not a resident or citizen of the United States.

—O—

Office Audit. An audit conducted by the Internal Revenue Service on IRS premises. The person conducting the audit is generally referred to as an Office Auditor (*see* Correspondence Audit; Field Audit).

Office Auditor. An IRS employee who conducts primarily office audits, as opposed to a Revenue Agent, who conducts primarily field audits (*see also* Revenue Agent).

—P—

Partner. (*see* General Partner; Limited Partner).

Partnership. A syndicate, group, pool, joint venture, or other unincorporated organization, through or by means of which any business, financial operation, or venture is carried on, and which is not a trust, estate, or corporation. §§ 761(a) and 7701(a)(2).

Passive Activity. Any activity that involves the conduct of any trade or business in which the taxpayer does not materially participate. Losses from passive activities generally are deductible only to the extent of passive activity income. § 469.

Pecuniary Bequest. Monetary bequest (*see* Bequest).

Percentage Depletion. (*see* Depletion).

Percentage of Completion Method of Accounting. A method of accounting that may be used on certain long-term contracts in which the income is reported as the contract reaches various stages of completion.

Performing Artists. Individuals who work in the performing arts (e.g., actors, actresses, musicians, dancers) are allowed to deduct their business expenses for adjusted gross income if they meet restrictive standards, including (1) AGI not greater than $16,000; (2) at least two employers from which they earn at least $200 from each; (3) expenses exceeding 10% of their pay. See Chapter 7 and § 62(a)(2)(B).

Personal Property. All property that is not realty; personalty. This term is also often used to mean personal use property (*see* Personal Use Property; Personalty).

Personal Use Property. Any property used for personal, rather than business, purposes. Distinguished from "personal property."

Personalty. All property that is not realty (e.g., automobiles, trucks, machinery, and equipment).

Portability. An estate tax concept. Under the portability rules, the unused unified credit of a spouse may be used by the surviving spouse if the decedent spouse files an estate tax return and makes the appropriate election.

Portfolio Income. Interest and dividends. Portfolio income, annuities, and royalties are not considered to be income from a passive activity for purposes of the passive activity loss limitations. § 469(e).

Present Interest. An interest in which the donee has the present right to use, possess, or enjoy the donated property. The annual exclusion is available for gifts of present interests, but not for gifts of future interests (*see* Future Interest).

Private Letter Ruling. A written statement from the IRS to a taxpayer in response to a request by the taxpayer for the tax consequences of a specific set of facts. The taxpayer who receives the Private Letter Ruling is the only taxpayer that may rely on that specific ruling in case of litigation.

Pro Rata. Proportionately.

Probate. The court-directed administration of a decedent's estate.

Prop. Reg. (Proposed Regulation). Treasury (IRS) Regulations are generally issued first in a proposed form in order to obtain input from various sources before the regulations are changed (if necessary) and issued in final form.

—Q—

Qualified Pension or Profit-Sharing Plan. A pension or profit-sharing plan sponsored by an employer that meets the requirements set forth by Congress in § 401. §§ 401–404.

Qualified Residence Interest. Interest on indebtedness that is secured by the principal residence or one other residence of a taxpayer. §§ 162(h)(3) and (5)(A).

—R—

RAR. (*see* Revenue Agent's Report).

Real Property. (*see* Realty).

Realized Gain or Loss. The difference between the amount realized from the sale or other disposition of an asset and the adjusted basis of the asset. § 1001.

Realty. Real estate; land, including any objects attached thereto that are not readily movable (e.g., buildings, sidewalks, trees, and fences).

Recapture. The recovery of the tax benefit from a previously taken deduction or credit. The recapture of a deduction results in its inclusion in income, and the recapture of a credit results in its inclusion in tax (*see* Depreciation Recapture; Investment Credit Recapture).

Recognized Gain or Loss. The amount of the realized gain or loss that is subject to income tax. § 1001.

Reg. (*see* Regulations).

Regulations (Treasury Department Regulations). Interpretations of the Internal Revenue Code by the Internal Revenue Service.

Related Party. A person or entity that is related to another under the various code provisions for constructive ownership. §§ 267, 318, and 544(a).

Remand. The sending back of a case by an appellate court to a lower court for further action by the lower court. The abbreviation for "remanding" is "rem'g."

Research Institute of America (RIA). A publisher of tax materials, including a multi-volume tax service and volumes that contain the Federal courts' decisions on tax matters (AFTR, AFTR2d).

Resident Alien. A person who is not a citizen of the United States, and who is a resident of the United States or meets the substantial presence test. § 7701(b).

Rev. Proc. (*see* Revenue Procedure).

Rev. Rul. (*see* Revenue Ruling).

Revenue Agent. An employee of the Internal Revenue Service who performs primarily field audits.

Revenue Agent's Report (RAR). The report issued by a Revenue Agent in which adjustments to a taxpayer's tax liability are proposed. (IRS Form 4549; Form 1902 is used for office audits.)

Revenue Officer. An employee of the Internal Revenue Service whose primary duty is the collection of tax. (As opposed to a Revenue Agent, who audits returns.)

Revenue Procedure (Rev. Proc.). A procedure published by the Internal Revenue Service outlining various processes and methods of handling various matters of tax practice and administration. Revenue Procedures are published first in the Internal Revenue Bulletin and then compiled annually in the Cumulative Bulletin.

Revenue Ruling (Rev. Rul.). A published interpretation by the Internal Revenue Service of the tax law as applied to specific situations. Revenue Rulings are published first in the Internal Revenue Bulletin and then compiled annually in the Cumulative Bulletin.

Reversed (Rev'd). The reverse of a lower court's decision by a higher court.

Reversing (Rev'g). The reversing of a lower court's decision by a higher court.

Right of Survivorship. (*see* Joint Tenancy).

Royalty. Compensation for the use of property, such as natural resources or copyrighted material.

—S—

S Corporation. A corporation that qualifies as a small business corporation and elects to have §§ 1361–1379 apply. Once a Subchapter S election is made, the corporation is treated similarly to a partnership for tax purposes. An S corporation uses Form 1120S to report its income and expenses. (*see* C Corporation).

Section 38 Property. Property subject to the investment tax credit (*see* Investment Tax Credit).

Section 179 Election. Allows taxpayers to expense immediately a limited amount of the cost of an asset in lieu of depreciating such cost.

Section 199 Domestic Production Activity Deduction. Also referred to as DPAD. Special deduction generally granted to taxpayers who engage in domestic production and manufacturing activities.

Section 1231 Property. Depreciable property and real estate used in a trade or business held for more than one year. Section 1231 property may also include timber, coal, domestic iron ore, livestock, and unharvested crops.

Section 1244 Stock. Stock of a small business corporation issued pursuant to § 1244. A loss on § 1244 stock is treated as an ordinary loss (rather than a capital loss) within limitations. § 1244.

Section 1245 Property. Property that is subject to depreciation recapture under § 1245.

Section 1250 Property. Property that is subject to depreciation recapture under § 1250.

Securities. Evidences of debt or of property, such as stock, bonds, and notes.

Separate Property. Property that belongs separately to only one spouse (as contrasted with community property in a community property state). In a community property state, a spouse's separate property generally includes property acquired by the spouse prior to marriage, or property acquired after marriage by gift or inheritance.

Severance Tax. At the time they are severed or removed from the earth, a tax on minerals or timber.

Sham Transaction. A transaction with no substance or bona fide business purpose that may be ignored for tax purposes.

Simple Trust. A trust that is required to distribute all of its income currently and does not pay, set aside, or use any funds for charitable purposes. § 651(a).

Small Business Corporation. There are two separate definitions of a small business corporation, one relating to S corporations and one relating to § 1244. If small business corporation status is met under § 1361(b), a corporation may elect Subchapter S. If small business corporation status is met under § 1244(c)(3), losses on § 1244 stock may be deducted as ordinary (rather than capital) losses, within limitations.

Specific Bequest. A bequest made by a testator in his or her will giving an heir a particular piece of property or money.

Standard Deduction. A deduction that is available to most individual taxpayers. The standard deduction or total itemized deductions, whichever is larger, is subtracted in computing taxable income. §§ 63(c) and (f).

Statute of Limitations. Law provisions that limit the period of time in which action may be taken after an event occurs. The limitations on the IRS for assessments and collections are included in §§ 6501–6504, and the limitations on taxpayers for credits or refunds are included in §§ 6511–6515.

Statutory Depletion. (*see* Depletion).

Statutory Employee. Certain individuals considered employees under the law (§ 3121(d)) but who report their income from their occupations as well the related expenses on Schedule C, thus avoiding the need to itemize and the limitations on miscellaneous itemized deductions. Statutory employees receive a W-2 with box 13 checked. Payroll taxes are withheld from their W-2 wages but income tax withholding is optional. Their net income reported on Schedule C is not subject to self-employment taxes. Includes the following: life insurance salespersons who work full-time for a single life insurance company selling life insurance or annuity contracts; traveling salespersons who work full-time for one person to solicit orders for merchandise from customers for resale or supplies for use by the customers in their businesses; agent-drivers or commission-drivers that distribute meat, vegetable, fruit or bakery products, beverages (other than milk) or laundry or dry cleaning services (e.g., a delivery man that distributes bakery products); individuals who work off the premises of the person for whom the services are performed according to furnished specifications on material provided and the products are returned to the principal. See Chapter 8 for a complete discussion.

Stock Option. A right to purchase a specified amount of stock for a specified price at a given time or times.

Subchapter S. Sections 1361–1379 of the Internal Revenue Code (*see also* S Corporation).

Substance vs. Form. The essence of a transaction as opposed to the structure or form that the transaction takes. For example, a transaction may formally meet the requirements for a specific type of tax treatment, but if what the transaction is actually accomplishing is different from the form of the transaction, the form may be ignored.

—T—

Tangible Property. Property that can be touched (e.g., machinery, automobile, desk) as opposed to intangibles, which cannot (e.g., goodwill, copyrights, patents).

Tax Avoidance. Using the tax laws to avoid paying taxes or to reduce one's tax liability (*see* Tax Evasion).

Tax Benefit Rule. The doctrine by which the amount of income that a taxpayer must include in income when the taxpayer has recovered an amount previously deducted is limited to the amount of the previous deduction that produced a tax benefit.

Tax Court (United States Tax Court). One of the three trial courts that hears cases dealing with Federal tax matters. A taxpayer need not pay his or her tax deficiency in advance if he or she decides to litigate the case in Tax Court (as opposed to the District Court or Claims Court).

Tax Credits. An amount that is deducted directly from a taxpayer's tax liability, as opposed to a deduction, which reduces taxable income.

Tax Evasion. The illegal evasion of the tax laws. § 7201 (*see* Tax Avoidance).

Tax Preference Items. Those items specifically designated in § 57 that may be subject to a special tax (*see also* Alternative Minimum Tax).

Tax Shelter. A device or scheme used by taxpayers either to reduce taxes or defer the payment of taxes.

T.C. (Tax Court: United States Tax Court). This abbreviation is also used to cite the Tax Court's Regular Decisions (*see* Tax Court; T.C. Memo).

T.C. Memo. The term used to cite the Tax Court's Memorandum Decisions (*see* Tax Court; T.C.).

Tenancy by the Entirety. A form of ownership between a husband and wife wherein each has an undivided interest in the property, with the right of survivorship.

Tenancy in Common. A form of joint ownership wherein each owner has an undivided interest in the property, with no right of survivorship.

Testator. A person who makes or has made a will; one who dies and has left a will.

Treasury Regulations. (*see* Regulations).

Trial Court. The first court to consider a case, as opposed to an appellate court.

Trust. A right in property that is held by one person or entity for the benefit of another. §§ 641–683.

—U—

Uncertain Tax Position. Positions taken by a company on a tax issue in its tax return where it is not certain that the position will prevail on audit and appeals. Corporations that have $100 million in assets and that issue audited financial statements must complete Schedule UTP to report such positions and attach it to Form 1120. Under FASB FIN 48 (ASC 740), companies that have uncertain tax positions must set up a reserve for financial accounting purposes for any position that is more likely than not to fail upon audit and appeals.

Unearned Income. Income that is not earned or is not yet earned. The term is used to refer to both prepaid (not yet earned) income and to passive (not earned) income.

Unearned Income of a Minor Child. (*see* Kiddie tax).

Unified Credit. A credit available to reduce an individual's estate and gift tax. Also referred to as an exemption or applicable exclusion.

Uniform Gift to Minors Act. An Act that provides a way to transfer property to minors. A custodian manages the property on behalf of the minor, and the custodianship terminates when the minor achieves majority.

U.S. Tax Court. (*see* Tax Court).

USSC (U.S. Supreme Court). This abbreviation is used to cite U.S. Supreme Court cases.

USTC (U.S. Tax Cases). Published by Commerce Clearing House. These volumes contain all the Federal tax-related decisions of the U.S. District Courts, the U.S. Court of Federal Claims, the U.S. Courts of Appeals, and the U.S. Supreme Court.

—V—

Valuation. (*see* Fair Market Value).

Vested. Fixed or settled; having the right to absolute ownership, even if ownership will not come into being until some time in the future.

Continuous Individual Tax Return Problems and Three Comprehensive Individual Tax Return Problems for 2016

I

General Instructions. Information is provided below for a continuous tax return problem. The tax return begins by providing a basic fact pattern, covering the topics found in Chapter 3. Additional facts are added to the facts for Chapter 3 in order to cover the topics discussed in Chapters 4, 5, 6, 7, and 8. In addition to the tax returns that must be prepared, questions relating to such returns are included.

CHAPTER 3: CONTINUOUS TAX RETURN PROBLEMS

3-1 **Problem Facts.** Larry K. and Cathy L. Zepp have been married 18 years. Larry is 62 years old (Social Security number 123-45-6789) while Cathy is 47 years old (Social Security number 123-45-6788). They live at 1234 Elm Dr. in Indianapolis, Indiana 46202. The couple uses the cash method of accounting and files their return on a calendar-year basis. They are tired of politics and do not want to contribute to the presidential election campaign.

a. Larry is a salesman employed by DSK Industries. This year he earned $111,500. Federal and state income taxes withheld were $17,000 and $6,000 respectively. Social Security tax withheld was $6,913 and Medicare tax withheld was $1,617.

b. Cathy recently completed a graduate degree in computer technology. She freelances as an independent contractor in computer graphics. She uses her own name as the name of her business. Her earnings received from various engagements were $12,000. Her only expenses paid during the year were for miscellaneous office supplies of $3,000. She paid estimated federal taxes during the year of $1,000 ($250 on each due date). Her business uses the cash method of accounting.

c. Other income earned by the couple included interest income of $4,000 from a certificate of deposit issued by Highland National Bank and $975 of interest from tax-exempt bonds issued by the State of Indiana.

d. The couple paid moving expenses of $2,000 that are fully deductible.

e. The couple has adequate health insurance coverage for the entire year.

f. The couple owns a duplex that it rents out. It is located at 111 Nowhere Ave., Indianapolis, Indiana. Their rental records reveal the following information for the year.

Rental income	$12,000
Rental expenses	
Insurance	400
Mortgage interest	8,000
Repairs	1,000
Real property taxes on rental property	600

g. Other expenses paid during the year included:

Unreimbursed medical expenses	$ 9,000
Interest on home mortgage	12,000
Real property taxes on home	1,900
State income taxes withheld (see above)	6,000
Charitable contributions.	1,000
Rental of safety deposit box to hold gold coins	
held for investment	100
Unreimbursed employee business expenses of Larry	3,000

Prepare the 2016 individual income tax return for the Zepps. Complete Form 1040 and Schedules A, B, C, E, and SE. Assume that all of the expenses except their business expenses are incurred jointly.

3-2   Continuous Tax Return: Additional Questions. Answer the following questions relating to the continuous tax return problem for Chapter 3 above:

a. What is the Zepp's marginal tax rate? Average tax rate?

b. The Zepps recently heard that making a contribution to an individual retirement account (IRA) may be a wise tax move. It is their understanding that contributions to a traditional or conventional IRA are deductible and the earnings on the accounts are not taxable until withdrawn (see Chapter 18 for more information). Assuming both Larry and Cathy make a deductible contribution of $4,000 each for a total of $8,000, compute the exact amount of tax the couple will save. Show computations illustrating how the savings are derived.

c. This question relates to the income tax of your state and may or may not be applicable. Check with your instructor for further instructions.

Larry incurred $3,000 of expenses related to his employment while Cathy incurred $3,000 related to her freelancing activity (i.e., self-employment). Which of the following statements is (are) true regarding the treatment of the expenses for state income tax purposes?

1. Both expenses were deductible in full.

2. Neither of the expenses was deductible.

3. The employment related expenses were deductible but the expenses related to self-employment were not deductible.

4. The expenses related to self-employment were deductible but the employment related expenses were not deductible.

d. Assume that Larry (instead of Cathy) had the self-employment income of $9,000. Which of the following statements is true?

1. Larry paid 15.3% self-employment tax on self-employment income of $9,000.

2. Larry paid 15.3% self-employment tax on self-employment income of $8,312.

3. Larry paid the same amount of self-employment tax that Cathy would have paid had she earned the income.

4. Larry pays less than the amount of self-employment tax that Cathy would have paid had she earned the income.

CHAPTER 4: CONTINUOUS TAX RETURN PROBLEMS

4-1 **Problem Facts.** This is a continuation of the tax return problem beginning in Chapter 3. See previous facts above.

New Facts: Larry and Cathy Zepp just called and after a quick discussion the following additional information was obtained:

a. Larry received a corrected W-2 in the mail. The corrected W-2 (see below) reveals that his wages increased to $120,000 (rather than $111,500) and federal income taxes withheld were $7,000 (rather than $17,000). Social Security and Medicare taxes also were revised.

b. Last year's federal tax liability before prepayments was $10,000.

c. They forgot to note on their tax organizer that they had two children, a son and a daughter: Zachary W. Zepp (111-33-4444, date of birth 12/1/2005) and Jennifer A. Zepp (111-33-4445, 1/4/2007). Both children live with them the entire year. Zachary is a full-time student. Jennifer is considered legally blind.

d. Larry explained that he was formerly married to Sue Gottaway (443-44-1234) who currently has custody of their son Sam A. Gottaway (447-93-9444, 4/14/1995). Sue has agreed to surrender the exemption for Sam to Larry and has provided Larry the necessary form. Sue provides all of Sam's support. Sam is a full-time student at the University of Texas.

Prepare the 2016 individual income tax return for the Zepps. Complete Forms 1040, 2210, Schedules A, B, C, E, SE, and any other forms required. Assume that all of the expenses except their business expenses are incurred jointly.

22222	a Employee's social security number 123 – 45 – 6789	OMB No. 1545-0008		
b Employer identification number (EIN) 25 – 2222345			1 Wages, tips, other compensation $120,000.00	2 Federal income tax withheld $7,000.00
c Employer's name, address, and ZIP code DSK Industries 1635 Longest Drive Indianapolis, Indiana 46202			3 Social security wages $118,500.00	4 Social security tax withheld $7,347.00
			5 Medicare wages and tips $120,000.00	6 Medicare tax withheld $1,740.00
			7 Social security tips	8 Allocated tips
d Control number 0068251111		9		10 Dependent care benefits
e Employee's first name and initial Last name Suff. Larry K. Zepp 1234 Elm Drive Indianapolis, Indiana 46202		11 Nonqualified plans	12a
		13 Statutory employee / Retirement plan / Third-party sick pay	12b
		14 Other	12c
			12d
f Employee's address and ZIP code				

15 State Employer's state ID number IN	16 State wages, tips, etc.	17 State income tax $6,000.00	18 Local wages, tips, etc.	19 Local income tax	20 Locality name

Form W-2 Wage and Tax Statement **2016** Department of the Treasury—Internal Revenue Service
Copy 1—For State, City, or Local Tax Department

4-2 Continuous Tax Return: Additional Questions. Refer to the facts for the continuous tax return problem (Chapters 3 and 4 above). The Zepp's tax organizer indicated that their daughter, Jennifer Zepp, received $3,000 of interest income from a savings account at Chase National Bank. Using this additional information and the facts above, prepare a separate Form 1040 for Jennifer Zepp. Do not include Jennifer's income on her parents' return.

4-3 Continuous Tax Return: Additional Questions. Answer the following question relating to the continuous tax return problem above. The Zepps generally could have avoided the estimated tax penalty by paying estimated taxes or by relying on their prior year's tax liability. Ignoring their prior year liability, how much should the couple have paid on each installment date to avoid the penalty? Alternatively, what would the amount of last year's tax liability have to be to avoid the penalty?

4-4 Continuous Tax Return: Additional Questions. Answer the following questions relating to the continuous tax return problem above. If Cathy had hired Jennifer as an employee and paid her $4,000 to help her on certain business-related projects, what effect would it have on the family's tax liability? Provide an explanation that shows precisely why the family's total tax liability increased or decreased. For simplicity, assume that Jennifer had no other income.

4-5 Continuous Tax Return: Additional Questions. Answer the following questions relating to the continuous tax return problem above. For purpose of the questions below, assume Cathy was also an employee and received wages of $50,000 in addition to her self-employment income. Ignore *Problems 4-2, 4-3,* and *4-4* above.
  a. Does the couple's taxable income increase by $50,000, more than $50,000 or less than $50,000? Explain specifically what accounts for the change in taxable income and tax liability, if any.
  b. What would the Zepp's marginal tax rate be on the next $1,000 of income? For this question, use the actual change in tax to determine the marginal rate and compare it to the marginal rate in the tax rate schedule.

CHAPTER 5: CONTINUOUS TAX RETURN PROBLEMS

5-1 Problem Facts. This is a continuation of the tax return problem covering Chapters 3 and 4. See previous facts above.

New Facts: This morning's mail contained a note from Larry Zepp, including the following information:
  a. Cathy forgot to explain several things about her consulting income. First, $2,400 of the $12,000 she received was for services to be performed in 2017. Second, she performed consulting services in December but was not paid until January when she received $475. She had sent the client a bill for $475 in December and the amount was included in the $12,000 she reported earlier.
  b. Larry paid federal estimated income taxes of $12,000 ($3,000 on each of the due dates). He made no state estimated tax payments.
  c. A Schedule K-1 from a calendar-year partnership in which Larry is a small investor was included. The relevant portions of the Schedule K-1 are shown below. In addition, Larry received a $775 distribution from the partnership during the year.

Prepare the 2016 individual income tax return for the Zepps. Complete Forms 1040, 2210, Schedules A, B, C, E, and SE. Assume that all of the expenses except their business expenses are incurred jointly.

651113

| Final K-1 | Amended K-1 | OMB No. 1545-0123 |

Schedule K-1
(Form 1065)

2016

Department of the Treasury
Internal Revenue Service

For calendar year 2016, or tax

year beginning _____ , 2016

ending _____ , 20 _____

Partner's Share of Income, Deductions, Credits, etc.

▶ See back of form and separate instructions.

| **Part I** | **Information About the Partnership** |

A Partnership's employer identification number
75 – 1234567

B Partnership's name, address, city, state, and ZIP code

KLM Associates
3214 Memorial
Houston, TX 77452

C IRS Center where partnership filed return

D ☐ Check if this is a publicly traded partnership (PTP)

| **Part II** | **Information About the Partner** |

E Partner's identifying number
123 – 45 – 6789

F Partner's name, address, city, state, and ZIP code

Larry K. Zepp
1234 Elm Drive
Indianapolis, IN 46202

G ☐ General partner or LLC member-manager   ☒ Limited partner or other LLC member

H ☐ Domestic partner   ☐ Foreign partner

I1 What type of entity is this partner? _____

I2 If this partner is a retirement plan (IRA/SEP/Keogh/etc.), check here ☐

J Partner's share of profit, loss, and capital (see instructions):

	Beginning	Ending
Profit	%	%
Loss	%	%
Capital	%	%

K Partner's share of liabilities at year end:

Nonrecourse . . . . $ _____
Qualified nonrecourse financing . $ _____
Recourse . . . . $ _____

L Partner's capital account analysis:

Beginning capital account . . . $ _____
Capital contributed during the year $ _____
Current year increase (decrease) . $ _____
Withdrawals & distributions . . $ (_____)
Ending capital account . . . . $ _____

☐ Tax basis   ☐ GAAP   ☐ Section 704(b) book
☐ Other (explain)

M Did the partner contribute property with a built-in gain or loss?
☐ Yes   ☐ No
If "Yes," attach statement (see instructions)

| **Part III** | **Partner's Share of Current Year Income, Deductions, Credits, and Other Items** |

1	Ordinary business income (loss)	15	Credits
	200		
2	Net rental real estate income (loss)		
3	Other net rental income (loss)	16	Foreign transactions
4	Guaranteed payments		
5	Interest income		
	150		
6a	Ordinary dividends		
6b	Qualified dividends		
7	Royalties		
8	Net short-term capital gain (loss)		
9a	Net long-term capital gain (loss)	17	Alternative minimum tax (AMT) items
9b	Collectibles (28%) gain (loss)		
9c	Unrecaptured section 1250 gain		
10	Net section 1231 gain (loss)	18	Tax-exempt income and nondeductible expenses
11	Other income (loss)		
		19	Distributions
12	Section 179 deduction		775
13	Other deductions	20	Other information
14	Self-employment earnings (loss)		

*See attached statement for additional information.

For IRS Use Only

For Paperwork Reduction Act Notice, see Instructions for Form 1065.   IRS.gov/form1065   Cat. No. 11394R   **Schedule K-1 (Form 1065) 2016**

5-2 **Continuous Tax Return Problem. Additional Questions.** Refer to the facts for the continuous tax return problem (Chapters 3, 4, and 5 above).

  a. According to the Schedule K-1, Larry Zepp received $775 of distributions from the partnership. How do the distributions impact the couple's individual income tax return? Explain.

  b. Is the partnership income considered self-employment income of Larry Zepp for purposes of computing any self-employment tax he might owe? Explain.

  c. Assume Cathy reached an agreement with a local fitness center to prepare various flyers, advertisements, and do some work on the company's website. In exchange, she received an annual membership to the center worth $500. Explain the tax consequences to Cathy.

CHAPTER 6: CONTINUOUS TAX RETURN PROBLEMS

6-1 **Problem Facts.** This is a continuation of the tax return problem covering Chapters 3, 4, and 5. See previous facts above.

New Facts:

  a. This year Larry began receiving Social Security benefits. For the year, he received $12,000.

  b. The couple received a Form 1099 from National Funds (see below) regarding an investment in a mutual fund.

  c. Cathy was unemployed for a short period and received unemployment compensation of $800 reported on the Form 1099-G (see below).

  d. Cathy received $2,000 of alimony from her first husband.

  e. Cathy inherited $100,000 from her rich uncle.

  f. The Zepps overpaid their income taxes for the prior year and received both a federal and state refund. The federal refund was $1,700. They received a Form 1099-G from the state of Indiana reporting the state refund of $925. Last year, the Zepps' total itemized deductions were $19,000, including a deduction for state income taxes of $2,598.

  g. Larry's father died this year and Larry was the beneficiary of his father's life insurance policy. Larry received life insurance proceeds of $25,000.

  h. In June, DSK honored Larry for his 25 years of service. He received a plaque and a gift certificate for $400 at The Golf Shop, which he intends to use to buy a new driver.

  i. Cathy's father had loaned her $5,000 to help her complete school and start her business. This year he told her that she did not have to repay him.

Prepare the 2016 individual income tax return for the Zepps. Complete Forms 1040, 2210, Schedules A, B, C, E, and SE. Assume that all of the expenses except their business expenses are incurred jointly.

☐ CORRECTED (if checked)

PAYER'S name, street address, city or town, state or province, country, ZIP or foreign postal code, and telephone no. National Funds 888 Toobad Drive Boston, MA 02104	**1a** Total ordinary dividends $ 3,000.00	OMB No. 1545-0110 20**16** Form **1099-DIV**	**Dividends and Distributions**
	1b Qualified dividends $ 3,000.00		
	2a Total capital gain distr. $ 1,400.00	**2b** Unrecap. Sec. 1250 gain $	**Copy B** **For Recipient**
PAYER'S federal identification number RECIPIENT'S identification number 123 – 45 – 6789	**2c** Section 1202 gain $	**2d** Collectibles (28%) gain $	
RECIPIENT'S name Larry K. Zepp	**3** Nondividend distributions $	**4** Federal income tax withheld $	This is important tax information and is being furnished to the Internal Revenue Service. If you are required to file a return, a negligence penalty or other sanction may be imposed on you if this income is taxable and the IRS determines that it has not been reported.
		5 Investment expenses $	
Street address (including apt. no.) 1234 Elm Drive	**6** Foreign tax paid $ 70.00	**7** Foreign country or U.S. possession	
City or town, state or province, country, and ZIP or foreign postal code Indianapolis, Indiana 46202	**8** Cash liquidation distributions $	**9** Noncash liquidation distributions $	
FATCA filing requirement ☐	**10** Exempt-interest dividends $	**11** Specified private activity bond interest dividends $	
Account number (see instructions)	**12** State **13** State identification no. ---------------------------------- 	**14** State tax withheld $ $	

Form **1099-DIV**   (keep for your records)   www.irs.gov/form1099div   Department of the Treasury - Internal Revenue Service

---

☐ CORRECTED (if checked)

PAYER'S name, street address, city or town, state or province, country, ZIP or foreign postal code, and telephone no. Indiana Department of Revenue 100 N. Senate Ave. Indianapolis, IN 46204-2254	**1** Unemployment compensation $ 800.00	OMB No. 1545-0120 20**16** Form **1099-G**	**Certain Government Payments**
	2 State or local income tax refunds, credits, or offsets $ 925.00		
PAYER'S federal identification number RECIPIENT'S identification number 123 – 45 – 6789	**3** Box 2 amount is for tax year	**4** Federal income tax withheld $	**Copy B** **For Recipient**
RECIPIENT'S name Cathy L. Zepp	**5** RTAA payments $	**6** Taxable grants $	This is important tax information and is being furnished to the Internal Revenue Service. If you are required to file a return, a negligence penalty or other sanction may be imposed on you if this income is taxable and the IRS determines that it has not been reported.
Street address (including apt. no.) 1234 Elm Drive	**7** Agriculture payments $	**8** If checked, box 2 is trade or business income ▶ ☐	
City or town, state or province, country, and ZIP or foreign postal code Indianapolis, Indiana 46202	**9** Market gain $		
Account number (see instructions)	**10a** State **10b** State identification no. --------------------------------	**11** State income tax withheld $ $	

Form **1099-G**   (keep for your records)   www.irs.gov/form1099g   Department of the Treasury - Internal Revenue Service

6-2 **Continuous Tax Return Problem. Additional Questions.** Refer to the facts for the continuous tax return problem (Chapters 3, 4, 5, and 6 above).

    a. What is the Zepp's marginal tax rate?

    b. At what rate were the dividends taxed?

    c. Which of the following statements is true regarding the tax treatment of Larry's Social Security benefits?

        1. None of the Social Security payments was taxable.

        2. 50% of the Social Security payments was taxable.

        3. 85% of the Social Security payment was taxable.

        4. None of the above.

CHAPTER 7: CONTINUOUS TAX RETURN PROBLEMS

7-1 **Problem Facts.** This is a continuation of the tax return problem covering Chapters 3, 4, 5, and 6. See previous facts above.

New Facts:

    a. The $400 paid in 2016 for the insurance coverage related to the rental property was for a one-year term that begins on February 1, 2017.

    b. On September 1, the couple refinanced the mortgage on the rental property to get a lower interest rate. They paid points of $1,800. The term of the new loan was 15 years.

    c. Cathy paid medical insurance premiums of $4,000.

    d. In early January, Cathy billed a customer $627 for setting up a website. The customer left town and Cathy indicates that the receivable is now worthless.

    e. During the year, Larry explored the possibility of selling for a new employer. However, after some interviewing, he decided to stay with DSK. He paid $30 to have new resumes printed and another $20 to register his name on an employment website.

    f. Larry paid several parking tickets during the year while calling on customers. Total cost was $48.

    g. Larry contributed $250 to the Democratic National Party and Cathy contributed $250 to the Republican National Party.

    h. The couple paid $3,000 premium for a $1,000,000 life insurance policy on Larry's life. Cathy was the beneficiary.

    i. Cathy continued her hobby of breeding and selling terriers. This year she sold 10 puppies for $6,000. Her expenses for raising the dogs (food, shots, etc.) were $2,000.

Prepare the 2016 individual income tax return for the Zepps. Complete Forms 1040, 2210, Schedules A, B, C, E, and SE. Assume that all of the expenses except their business expenses are incurred jointly.

7-2 Continuous Tax Return: Additional Questions. Refer to the facts for the continuous tax return problem (Chapters 3, 4, 5, and 6 above).

    a. Larry incurred $3,000 of expenses related to his employment while Cathy incurred $3,000 related to her freelancing activity (i.e., self-employment). Which of the following statements is true regarding the treatment of the expenses for federal income tax purposes?

        1. The expenses of both Larry and Cathy were subject to the 2% limitation.

        2. The expenses of both Larry and Cathy were fully deductible as deductions for AGI (i.e., deductible in arriving at adjusted gross income).

        3. The expenses of both Larry and Cathy were considered itemized deductions but only the employment expenses were subject to the 2% limitation.

        4. The expenses of Cathy affected the amount of Larry's expenses that are deductible.

        5. None of the above is correct.

    b. Assume Larry is considered a statutory employee (see Box 13 of his W-2 in an earlier chapter). Indicate the amount, if any, by which the couple's taxable income increases or decreases.

    c. Did Cathy's payment for medical insurance affect her self-employment tax?

    d. The couple paid $1,000 for tax preparation of last year's return. Before last year, Larry did the return but since last year's return involved filing a Schedule C for Cathy he decided to get professional tax help. The accountant's fee was $400. Explain the treatment of the tax preparation fee.

CHAPTER 8: CONTINUOUS TAX RETURN PROBLEMS

8-1 Problem Facts. This is a continuation of the tax return problem covering Chapters 3, 4, 5, 6, and 7. See previous facts above.

New Facts:

    a. Cathy paid $1,000 of tuition for a course that she took at the local university. The course related to her to computer graphics business.

    b. Cathy worked out of her home. According to her records, she drove 8,000 miles from her home to her clients and back during the year. She does not have a qualifying home office. She has records of her mileage but nothing for gas, oil, or related expenses.

    c. Cathy took a client to lunch and they discussed some of the work she was doing for the client. Cathy paid for her meal, $16, and the client's meal, $20. She kept the receipts.

    d. The couple provided additional information regarding their moving expenses. On May 1, the couple moved downtown to try downtown living and reduce Larry's commute. Before the move, Larry's roundtrip commute from home was 60 miles and after the move the commute was only five miles. The cost of the move was $2,000 as previously reported.

Prepare the 2016 individual income tax return for the Zepps. Complete Forms 1040, 2210, Schedules A, B, C, E, and SE. Assume that all of the expenses except their business expenses are incurred jointly.

8-2 Continuous Tax Return: Additional Questions. Refer to the facts for the continuous tax return problem (Chapters 3, 4, 5, 6, and 7 above).

    a. Cathy had several options regarding the treatment of her educational expenses related to her job. Explain these options and demonstrate with calculations why one is better than another.

    b. Were the moving expenses deductible? Why or why not? Explain.

Part 2: Comprehensive Tax Return Problems

COMPREHENSIVE TAX RETURN PROBLEM I

1. **David R. and Susan L. Holman**

   a. David and Susan Holman are married and file a joint return. David is 38 years of age and Susan is 36. David is a self-employed certified real estate appraiser (C.R.E.), and Susan is employed by Wells Fargo Bank as a trust officer. They have two children: Richard Lawrence, age seven, and Karen Ann, age four. The Holmans currently live at 5901 W. 75th Street, Los Angeles, California 90034, in a home they purchased and occupied on September 6, 2016.

   Until August 12, 2016 the Holman family lived at 3085 Windmill Lane in Dallas, Texas, where David was employed by Vestpar Company, a real estate appraisal company and Susan was a bank officer for First National Bank. They sold their home in Dallas and moved to Los Angeles so that Susan could assume her new job as a trust officer and David could become self-employed.

   b. David and Susan sold their home in Dallas for $515,000 and incurred the following expenses:

Sales commission	$18,900
Attorney's fee	1,800
Title insurance	2,650
Document preparation fee	90
Recording fee	30
Pest inspection fee	190
Prepayment penalty for early retirement of home mortgage (3 points)	1,500

   The Holmans had purchased the Dallas home on August 4, 2008 and never held it for rent or used it for business purposes. The home originally cost $177,500, and they had paid $6,200 for a cedar fence and $7,900 for landscaping. Within seven weeks of receiving a contract of sale on their house, the Holmans paid $8,500 for interior and exterior painting and $600 for steam-cleaning of the carpets. The sale was closed on August 1, 2016 and the Holmans were required to move out of the home by August 15, 2016.

   c. In moving from Dallas to Los Angeles, the Holmans incurred the following expenses, none of which were reimbursed:

Cost of moving household goods	$9,250
Meals	295
Lodging	350
House-hunting expenses (including $150 for meals)	1,000
Temporary living expenses (20 days; including meals costing $400)	1,700

   Not included in any of the above expenses are the costs for driving two automobiles from Dallas to Los Angeles. David and Susan each drove a car, taking turns driving with the children. Although neither one of them kept receipts, Susan noted that her auto mileage was 1,500 miles. In addition, David noted that the number of miles from their old home to their old workplace was 24 miles, and the number of miles from their old home to their new workplace is 1,514 miles.

   d. The Holmans purchased their new home for $525,000 by making a $125,000 down payment and financing the remaining balance with a 30-year, 6% conventional mortgage loan from California Federal Savings and Loan. They were required to prepay two points ($8,000) in return for the favorable mortgage terms. New furniture and drapes cost an additional $27,500.

e. The Holmans received the following Forms W-2, reporting their salaries for 2016:

1. David R. Holman, Social Security No. 452-64-5837:

Gross salary from Vestpar, Inc.	$95,000
Federal income taxes withheld	9,050
F.I.C.A. taxes withheld:	
Social Security	4,650
Medicare	1,088
California income taxes withheld	3,000

2. Susan L. Holman, Social Security No. 467-32-5452:

	First National Bank	Wells Fargo Bank	Total
Gross salary	$17,500	$34,000	$51,500
Federal income taxes withheld	1,100	4,150	5,250
F.I.C.A. taxes withheld:			
Social Security	1,085	2,108	3,193
Medicare	254	493	747

	First National Bank	Wells Fargo Bank	Total
California income taxes withheld	—	2,950	2,950

f. On October 1, 2016 David rented office space at 5510 Wacker Drive, Los Angeles, California 90025. The terms of the one-year lease agreement called for a monthly rent of $800, with the first and last month's rent paid in advance.

David decided to operate his business in the name of "David R. Holman, Certified Real Estate Appraiser," and he elected to use the cash method of accounting for his revenues and expenses. The following items relate to his business for 2016:

Gross receipts	$85,000
Expenses:	
Advertising	250
Bank service charges	50
Dues and publications	450
Insurance	600*
Interest	275
Professional services	525
Office rent	3,200**
Office supplies	700
Meals and entertainment	500
Miscellaneous expenses	75

* Three months of coverage
** Includes prepayment of last month's rent for September, 2017

David drove his personal automobile, a 2013 Buick Verano, 5,000 miles for business purposes from October 1 through December 31. Rather than keeping receipts, he elected to use the automatic mileage method for determining his auto expenses. David's total auto mileage for the year was 20,000 miles.

On October 3, 2016 David purchased the following furniture and equipment for use in his business:

Office furniture	$17,000
Copying machine	5,800
Computers	6,500
Laser printers	2,500
Telephone system	3,100

David elects to expense the maximum amount allowed under the optional expensing rules of § 179. He also elects to compute the maximum depreciation allowance using the appropriate MACRS percentages.

g. The Holmans received interest income during 2016 from the following:

U.S. Treasury bills	$1,475
First National Bank, Dallas	625
Wells Fargo Bank	400
Tarrant County municipal bonds	800

h. David and Susan received the following dividends during 2016:

Ford Motor Company	$ 300
Eastman Kodak Company	575
IBM Corporation	125
Apple stock dividend (20 new shares of stock valued at $60 per share, received March 9, 2016)	1,200

i. The Holmans have never maintained foreign bank accounts or created foreign trusts.

j. The Holmans report the following stock transactions for 2016:
1. Sold 100 shares of IBM stock for $120 per share on August 1, 2016. David had inherited 500 shares of IBM stock from his uncle on July 18, 2012, and the stock was valued at $170 per share on the date of his uncle's death.
2. Sold 400 shares of Apple stock for $78 per share on July 20, 2016. Susan had received 1,000 shares of Apple stock as a birthday present from her grandfather on June 3, 2007. Her grandfather had purchased the stock for $35 per share on May 7, 2003, and the stock was valued at $60 per share on the date of the gift. Susan's grandfather paid gift taxes of $10,000 as a result of the gift. **Note:** The amount of the annual exclusion taken into account in determining the taxable gift was $10,000.
3. Sold 300 shares of Intel stock for $40 per share on December 28, 2016, but did not receive the sales proceeds until January 3, 2017. The Holmans had paid $25 per share for the stock on May 21, 2013.

k. Susan has summarized the following cash expenditures for 2016 from canceled checks, mortgage company statements, and other documents:

Prescription medicines and drugs	$ 982
Medical insurance premiums (paid by Susan)	2,830
Doctors' and hospital bills (net of reimbursements)	1,535
Contact lenses for David	218
Real estate taxes paid on:	
Dallas residence	3,400
Los Angeles residence	5,600
Sales taxes paid on Susan's new auto	1,485
Ad valorem taxes paid on both autos	350
Interest paid for:	
Dallas home mortgage	5,250*
Los Angeles home mortgage	10,200**
Credit card interest	480
Personal car loan	1,720
Cash contributions to:	
United Methodist Church	5,200
Salvation Army	1,500
Barack Obama Campaign Fund	250
Susan's unreimbursed employee expenses	470***
David's unreimbursed employee expenses	360
Tax return preparation fee	375

*Does not include the mortgage prepayment penalty identified in item (b) above.

**Does not include the interest points charged for the new mortgage identified in item (d) above.

***Does not include any costs for meals or entertainment.

Susan also noted that she and David had driven their personal automobiles 500 miles to receive medical treatment for themselves and their children. She also has a receipt for 100 shares of Apple stock that she gave to her alma mater, Southern Methodist University, on November 12, 2016. The stock was valued at $70 per share on the date of the gift and was from the block of Apple stock Susan had received as a wedding present from her grandfather (see item (j)(2) above for details).

l. The Holmans paid the following child care expenses during 2016:

1. Kindergarten Daycare School $2,800
   1177 Valley View
   Dallas, Texas 75210
   EIN: 74-0186254

2. Happy Trails Day Center.   2,200
   3692 Airport Blvd.
   Los Angeles, California 90034
   EIN: 78-0593676

Of the $5,000 total child care expenses, $3,000 was for Karen, and the remaining $2,000 was for Richard.

m. Social Security numbers for the Holman children are provided below:

Richard L. Holman, Social Security No. 582-60-4732
Karen A. Holman, Social Security No. 582-60-5840

n. David and Susan made estimated Federal income tax payments of $1,750 each quarter, on 4/15/16, 6/15/16, 9/15/16, and 1/15/17.

o. The Holmans have always directed that $6 go to the Presidential Election Campaign by checking the "yes" boxes on their Form 1040.

Required:
Complete the Holmans' Federal income tax return for 2016. If they have a refund due, they would prefer having it credited against their 2017 taxes.

Comprehensive Tax Return Problem 2

2. **Richard M. and Anna K. Wilson**

   a. Richard and Anna Wilson are married and file a joint return. Richard is 47 years of age and Anna is 46. Richard is employed by Telstar Corporation as its controller and Anna is self-employed as a travel agent. They have three children: Michael, age 22; Lisa, age 17; and Laura, age 14. Michael is a full-time student at Rutgers University. Lisa and Laura both live at home and attend school full-time. The Wilsons currently live at 3721 Chestnut Ridge Road, Montvale, New Jersey 07645, in a home they have owned since July 2004.

   Richard and Anna provided over half of the support of Anna's mother, who currently lives in a nursing home in Mahwah, New Jersey. They also provided over half of the support of their son, Michael, who earned $4,750 during the summer as an accounting student intern for a national accounting firm.

   b. Richard received a Form W-2 from his employer reporting the following information for 2016:

   Richard M. Wilson, Social Security No. 294-38-6249:

Gross wages and taxable benefits.	$63,000
Federal income taxes withheld	11,400
F.I.C.A. taxes withheld:	
Social Security.	3,906
Medicare	914
State income taxes withheld.	1,850

   The taxable benefits reported on his W-2 Form include $2,700 (based on the currently deductible standard auto mileage rate) for Richard's personal use of the company car provided by his employer.

   c. Anna operates her business under the name "Wilson's Travel Agency," located at 7200 Treeline Drive, Montvale, NJ 07645. Anna has one full-time employee, and her Federal employer identification number is 74-2638596.

   Anna uses the cash method of accounting for her business, and her records for 2016 show the following:

Fees and commissions	$134,000
Expenses:	
Advertising	1,425
Bank service charges	75
Dues and subscriptions	560
Insurance.	1,100
Interest on furniture loan.	960
Professional services	700
Office rent.	6,000
Office supplies.	470
Meals and entertainment.	1,000
Payroll taxes	2,170
Utilities and telephone.	3,480
Wages paid to full-time employee.	22,800
Miscellaneous expenses.	20

   Automobile expenses and amounts paid to her children are not included in the above expenses. Anna paid her daughters Lisa and Laura $750 and $450, respectively, for working part-time during the summer. Since she did not withhold or pay any Federal income or employment taxes on these amounts, Anna is not certain that she is allowed a deduction. She does feel that the amounts paid to her children were reasonable, however.

   Anna purchased a new 2015 Honda Accord on November 20 of last year, and her tax accountant used the actual cost method in determining the deductible business expenses for her 2015 Federal tax return. Because the deductible amount seemed so small, she is not certain whether she should claim actual expenses (including depreciation), or simply use the automatic mileage method. She has the following records relating to the business auto:

Original cost	$26,000
Depreciation claimed in 2015	
($26,000 × 5% = $1,300 × 80% business use).	1,040
Gas, oil, and repairs in 2016.	1,790
Parking and tolls directly related to her work paid in 2016	410
Insurance for 2016.	650
Interest on car loan for 2016	750

Anna drove the auto 20,000 miles for business purposes and 5,000 miles for personal purposes during the year. The above expenses for 2016 have not been reduced to reflect her personal use of the vehicle.

On January 7, 2016 Anna purchased the following items for use in her business:

Office furniture	$8,900
Copying machine.	5,700
Dell notebook computer.	1,500
Printer	1,600
Fax machine.	300

Anna wishes to claim the maximum amount of depreciation deductions or other cost recovery allowed on the office furniture and equipment.

d. Richard attended an accounting convention in Washington, D.C. for three days in October. He incurred the following unreimbursed expenses related to the trip:

Air fare (round-trip)	$470
Registration fee for meeting.	225
Hotel cost	375
Meals.	130
Taxis.	20
Airport parking.	18
Road tolls.	2

e. Richard and Anna received Forms 1099-INT reporting interest income earned during 2016 from the following:

Citibank of Mahwah	$845
Montvale National Bank.	900
Telstar Employees' Credit Union.	755

f. The Wilsons received the following dividends during 2016:

Telstar Corporation	$300
Chevron Corporation.	200

These dividends were labeled as "qualified dividends" on the respective Forms 1099-DIV.

g. The Wilsons have never had a foreign bank account or created a foreign trust.

h. The Wilsons had the following property transactions for 2016:

1. Anna sold 300 shares of Chevron Corporation stock on September 9, 2016 in order to pay for Michael's fall semester of college. She received a check in the amount of $14,950 from Merrill Lynch on September 16, 2016. The stock was from a block of 1,000 shares that Richard and Anna had purchased for $35 per share on February 1, 2003.

2. They gave each of the children 100 shares of Chevron stock on December 30, 2016, when the stock was valued at $62.50 per share. The stock was from the same block of stock purchased for $35 per share in February, 2003. No gift taxes were paid on these gifts.

3. They gave 100 shares of Chevron stock to Richard's alma mater, Rider University, on December 29, 2016. The average trading price of Chevron stock on that day was $61.25. This stock was also from the original block of 1,000 shares the Wilsons had purchased for $35 per share in 2003. The address of Rider University is 2083 Lawrenceville Road, Lawrenceville, New Jersey 08648.

4. On May 17, 2016, Richard and Anna were notified by the bankruptcy judge handling the affairs of Bubbling Crude Oil Company in Houston, Texas that the company's shareholders would not receive anything for their stock ownership because all of the assets were used to satisfy claims of creditors. Richard had purchased 2,000 shares of the stock for $6 per share on April 1, 2007. Unfortunately, the stock did not meet the requirements of § 1244.

i. Richard and Anna own a rental condominium located at 7777 Boardwalk in Atlantic City, New Jersey. The unit was purchased on July 29, 2015 for $25,000 cash and a $175,000 mortgage. Of the purchase price, $50,000 was allocated to the land. The following items relate to the rental unit for 2016:

Gross rents.	$16,400
Expenses:	
Management fee.	2,460
Cleaning and maintenance	1,200
Insurance.	840
Property taxes	2,750
Interest paid on mortgage	13,675
Utilities	850

Although the unfurnished unit was vacant for 11 weeks during the year, the Wilsons never used the property for personal purposes. When the property is rented, the tenant is required to pay for all utilities, and the Wilsons are charged a management fee equal to 15% of the rents collected.

j. The Wilsons have prepared the following summary of their other expenditures for 2016:

Prescription medicines and drugs	$ 425
Medical insurance premiums (paid by Richard).	1,595
Doctors' and hospital bills (net of reimbursements)	805 [1]
Dentist.	2,750 [2]
Real estate taxes paid on home	1,625
State income taxes paid during 2016	2,100 [3]
Interest paid for	
Original home mortgage	8,690
Home equity loan (secured by home)	410 [4]
Credit card interest	275
Personal car loan	725
Cash contributions to First Presbyterian Church	1,200
Fee for preparation of 2015 tax return	650 [5]

(1) Does not include $11,485 of doctor bills paid by Richard and Anna for medical treatment provided to Anna's mother at the nursing home. Also not included is $115 that Anna paid for a new pair of eyeglasses for her mother.

(2) $2,350 of this amount represents a prepayment of Laura's braces. The dentist required the prepayment before he would begin the two-year dental program involved.

(3) Does not include amounts withheld from Richard's wages.

(4) Represents interest paid on a $25,000 home equity loan obtained by the Wilsons in 2016 to obtain a new boat.

(5) $200 is related to preparation of Schedule C.

k. Anna made an $11,500 deductible contribution to her Keogh plan on December 15, 2016.

l. Richard paid the following unreimbursed employee business expenses:

Professional dues	$450
Professional journals.	385
Office gifts to subordinates (none over $25)	115

m. During the year, the Wilsons paid tuition of $9,350 and spent $1,875 on books and supplies for Michael's senior year of college.

n. The Wilsons received a state income tax refund of $130 in 2016. They had $18,750 of itemized deductions for 2015, and their 2015 taxable income was $52,825.

o. Richard and Anna made timely estimated Federal income tax payments of $2,250 each quarter on 4/15/16, 6/15/16, 9/15/16, and 1/15/17.

p. Social Security numbers for Anna, the children, and Anna's mother are provided below:

	Number
Anna K. Wilson.	296-48-2385
Michael D. Wilson	256-83-4421
Lisa M. Wilson	257-64-7573
Laura D. Wilson	258-34-2894
Ruth Knapp	451-38-3790

q. The Wilsons have always checked the "no" boxes on their Form 1040 regarding the Presidential Election Campaign fund contribution.

Required:
Complete the Wilsons' Federal income tax return for 2016. If they have a refund due, they would prefer having it credited against their 2017 taxes.

COMPREHENSIVE TAX RETURN PROBLEM 3

1. **Jane Doe**

   a. Jane Elizabeth Doe, age 64, is single and files as an unmarried taxpayer. Her Social Security Number is 447-45-6789. She does not have any dependents and claims the standard deduction. Her address is 4321 Somewhere Dr., Indianapolis, IN, 46202. Jane is a florist and owns a chain of highly successful flower shops called Jane's Flowers. She has been in business since 1979.

   b. Her florist business is operated as a single-member LLC and is treated as a sole proprietorship for tax purposes. Revenues and expenses from operations for 2016 (exclusive of certain transactions discussed below) were:

Sales...	$1,800,000
Cost of goods sold	(600,000)
Other operating expenses.............................	(20,000)
Net income from operations...........................	$1,180,000

   In addition to the information above, Jane was involved in the following transactions related to her flower business.

   c. May 7, 2016: Purchased used refrigeration equipment (7-year property) for use in her business. The total cost was $800,000. Jane wants to maximize her deductions with respect to the purchase.

   d. June 3, 2016: Sold machinery (7-year property) used in her business for $160,000. She had purchased the machinery for $100,000 on May 4, 2014. She did not elect § 179 limited expensing on this asset. MACRS depreciation for 2014 was $14,286 and for 2015 was $24,490. **Note:** Depreciation must be computed for the current year.

   e. August 1, 2016: Sold the building that formerly housed the business (prior to leasing space at another location). She had purchased the building on June 15, 1986 for $120,000 ($20,000 of the purchase price was allocated to the land). She sold the building for $180,000. Of the sales price, $30,000 was allocable to the land while the remaining $150,000 was allocable to the building. The building was depreciated using the ACRS rules in effect in 1986 (accelerated method using 175% declining balance, a mid-month convention in the year of acquisition and disposition, and a 19-year life). The building was fully depreciated.

   f. August 1, 2016: As part of the sale of her building on August 1, she sold a barn that served primarily as a storage shed behind her building. She purchased the barn for $50,000 on February 9, 2008. The barn is considered a multi-purpose agricultural structure (20-year property under MACRS). It was depreciated using 150% declining balance and the half-year convention. The sales price of the barn was $80,000. For purposes of computing the gain or loss, ignore the land since it is included in part (e) above. The company provided a partial depreciation schedule as shown below. Depreciation for the year of disposition must be computed.

	Accelerated Depreciation Claimed and Deducted	Hypothetical Straight-Line Depreciation
2008.....................	$1,875	$1,250
2009.....................	3,610	2,500
2010.....................	3,339	2,500
2011.....................	3,089	2,500
2012.....................	2,857	2,500
2013.....................	2,643	2,500
2014.....................	2,444	2,500
2015.....................	2,261	2,500
Sold August 1, 2016.........	????	????

g. Besides operating her business, Jane also owned an apartment building until she sold it this year. The address of the building was 4321 Fair Street, Indianapolis, IN 46202. Her rental income and expenses from the apartment prior to the sale and excluding any depreciation on the property for 2016 are shown below. Note that depreciation for the current year must be computed.

Rental income.	$80,000
Other operating expenses.	(20,000)

She sold the building on December 1, 2016 for $600,000 ($500,000 allocated to the building and $100,000 allocated to the land). She purchased the property on May 1, 2008 for $215,000 ($200,000 allocated to the building and $15,000 allocated to the land). She had depreciated it using the appropriate MACRS straight-line rates. Note that depreciation for the current and prior years must be computed.

h. On December 4, 2016, Jane sold 500 shares of Microsoft stock for $27,000. She originally purchased 100 shares on March 7, 2003 for $7,000. That original purchase of 100 shares grew to 1,000 shares after a number of stock splits.

i. Jane has paid estimated taxes throughout the year of $500,000 ($125,000 on each installment due date).

Required:
Complete the federal income tax return of Jane Doe for 2016. Ignore the alternative minimum tax but include the net investment income tax as well as the additional Medicare tax. If she has a refund due, she would prefer having it credited against her 2017 taxes. Forms and instructions to obtain are Form 1040, including Schedules C, D, E, and SE; Form 4562, Form 4797, Form 8959, and Form 8960.

Index

S

Quick References for Form 1040

Use the page numbers on the following form for a quick reference to where this item is discussed in the text.

Form **1040** Department of the Treasury—Internal Revenue Service (99) **20 16** OMB No. 1545-0074 IRS Use Only—Do not write or staple in this space.

U.S. Individual Income Tax Return

For the year Jan. 1–Dec. 31, 2016, or other tax year beginning _____ , 2016, ending _____ , 20 _____   See separate instructions.

Your first name and initial   Last name   Your social security number

If a joint return, spouse's first name and initial   Last name   Spouse's social security number

Home address (number and street). If you have a P.O. box, see instructions.   Apt. no.   ▲ Make sure the SSN(s) above and on line 6c are correct.

City, town or post office, state, and ZIP code. If you have a foreign address, also complete spaces below (see instructions).

Presidential Election Campaign
Check here if you, or your spouse if filing jointly, want $3 to go to this fund. Checking a box below will not change your tax or refund.   ☐ You ☐ Spouse

Foreign country name   Foreign province/state/county   Foreign postal code

Filing Status
Check only one box.

1 ☐ Single   4-15 through 4-22; Exhibit 4-4
2 ☐ Married filing jointly (even if only one had income)
3 ☐ Married filing separately. Enter spouse's SSN above and full name here. ▶
4 ☐ Head of household (with qualifying person). (See instructions.) If the qualifying person is a child but not your dependent, enter this child's name here. ▶
5 ☐ Qualifying widow(er) with dependent child

Exemptions

6a ☐ **Yourself.** If someone can claim you as a dependent, **do not** check box 6a . . . . .
b ☐ **Spouse** . . . .

Boxes checked on 6a and 6b   **4-2**
No. of children on 6c who:
• lived with you
• did not live with you due to divorce or separation (see instructions)
Dependents on 6c not entered above
Add numbers on lines above ▶

c **Dependents:**		(2) Dependent's social security number	(3) Dependent's relationship to you	(4) ✓ if child under age 17 qualifying for child tax credit (see instructions)
(1) First name Last name				
4-2 through 4-22;				☐
Exhibit 4-4				☐
				☐
				☐

If more than four dependents, see instructions and check here ▶ ☐

d   Total number of exemptions claimed . . . .

Income

Attach Form(s) W-2 here. Also attach Forms W-2G and 1099-R if tax was withheld.

If you did not get a W-2, see instructions.

7	Wages, salaries, tips, etc. Attach Form(s) W-2	7	6-19
8a	**Taxable** interest. Attach Schedule B if required	8a	6-6
b	**Tax-exempt** interest. **Do not** include on line 8a . . .	8b	6-7
9a	Ordinary dividends. Attach Schedule B if required	9a	6-3
b	Qualified dividends	9b	6-4
10	Taxable refunds, credits, or offsets of state and local income taxes . . .	10	6-55
11	Alimony received	11	6-39
12	Business income or (loss). Attach Schedule C or C-EZ	12	3-8, 19-2
13	Capital gain or (loss). Attach Schedule D if required. If not required, check here ▶ ☐	13	3-32, 3-33, 16-3
14	Other gains or (losses). Attach Form 4797	14	17-28
15a	IRA distributions . 15a 18-26 b Taxable amount . . .	15b	18-26
16a	Pensions and annuities 16a 18-7 b Taxable amount . . .	16b	6-10
17	Rental real estate, royalties, partnerships, S corporations, trusts, etc. Attach Schedule E	17	3-9, 3-11, 19-5, 19-12
18	Farm income or (loss). Attach Schedule F	18	
19	Unemployment compensation	19	6-24
20a	Social security benefits 20a b Taxable amount . . .	20b	6-22
21	Other income. List type and amount _____	21	6-54
22	Combine the amounts in the far right column for lines 7 through 21. This is your **total income** ▶	22	

Adjusted Gross Income

3-18

23	Educator expenses	23	8-8		
24	Certain business expenses of reservists, performing artists, and fee-basis government officials. Attach Form 2106 or 2106-EZ	24	7-23		
25	Health savings account deduction. Attach Form 8889 .	25	11-13		
26	Moving expenses. Attach Form 3903	26	8-9		
27	Deductible part of self-employment tax. Attach Schedule SE .	27	1-25		
28	Self-employed SEP, SIMPLE, and qualified plans .	28	18-17, 18-31		
29	Self-employed health insurance deduction	29	11-16		
30	Penalty on early withdrawal of savings	30	7-20		
31a	Alimony paid b Recipient's SSN ▶ _____	31a	6-40		
32	IRA deduction	32	18-22		
33	Student loan interest deduction	33	11-31		
34	Tuition and fees. Attach Form 8917	34	8-5		
35	Domestic production activities deduction. Attach Form 8903	35	10-30		
36	Add lines 23 through 35	36			
37	Subtract line 36 from line 22. This is your **adjusted gross income** . . . . . ▶	37	3-18		

For Disclosure, Privacy Act, and Paperwork Reduction Act Notice, see separate instructions.   Cat. No. 11320B   Form **1040** (2016)

Form 1040 (2016) Page **2**

Tax and Credits	38	Amount from line 37 (adjusted gross income)	38	3-18
	39a	Check if: ☐ **You** were born before January 2, 1952, ☐ Blind. ☐ **Spouse** was born before January 2, 1952, ☐ Blind. Total boxes checked ▶ 39a		
	b	If your spouse itemizes on a separate return or you were a dual-status alien, check here▶ 39b☐		
Standard Deduction for— • People who check any box on line 39a or 39b **or** who can be claimed as a dependent, see instructions. • All others: Single or Married filing separately, $6,300 Married filing jointly or Qualifying widow(er), $12,600 Head of household, $9,300	40	**Itemized deductions** (from Schedule A) **or** your **standard deduction** (see left margin)	40	3-19, 11-2
	41	Subtract line 40 from line 38	41	
	42	**Exemptions.** If line 38 is $155,650 or less, multiply $4,050 by the number on line 6d. Otherwise, see instructions	42	4-2
	43	**Taxable income.** Subtract line 42 from line 41. If line 42 is more than line 41, enter -0-	43	3-6; Exhibit 3-3
	44	**Tax** (see instructions). Check if any from: **a** ☐ Form(s) 8814 **b** ☐ Form 4972 **c** ☐	44	4-23
	45	**Alternative minimum tax** (see instructions). Attach Form 6251	45	3-24, 13-3; Exhibit 13-1
	46	Excess advance premium tax credit repayment. Attach Form 8962	46	
	47	Add lines 44, 45, and 46 ▶	47	
	48	Foreign tax credit. Attach Form 1116 if required ... 48	13-41	
	49	Credit for child and dependent care expenses. Attach Form 2441 49	13-44	
	50	Education credits from Form 8863, line 19 ... 50	13-48	
	51	Retirement savings contributions credit. Attach Form 8880 51	18-28	
	52	Child tax credit. Attach Schedule 8812, if required . 52	4-13, 3-42	
	53	Residential energy credits. Attach Form 5695 ... 53	13-56	
	54	Other credits from Form: **a** ☐ 3800 **b** ☐ 8801 **c** ☐ 54	13-27	
	55	Add lines 48 through 54. These are your **total credits**	55	
	56	Subtract line 55 from line 47. If line 55 is more than line 47, enter -0- ▶	56	
Other Taxes	57	Self-employment tax. Attach Schedule SE	57	1-24
	58	Unreported social security and Medicare tax from Form: **a** ☐ 4137 **b** ☐ 8919	58	
	59	Additional tax on IRAs, other qualified retirement plans, etc. Attach Form 5329 if required	59	18-8
	60a	Household employment taxes from Schedule H	60a	
	b	First-time homebuyer credit repayment. Attach Form 5405 if required	60b	
	61	Health care: individual responsibility (see instructions) Full-year coverage ☐	61	
	62	Taxes from: **a** ☐ Form 8959 **b** ☐ Form 8960 **c** ☐ Instructions; enter code(s)	62	1-21, 1-22, 3-26
	63	Add lines 56 through 62. This is your **total tax** ▶	63	
Payments If you have a qualifying child, attach Schedule EIC.	64	Federal income tax withheld from Forms W-2 and 1099 64	3-24	
	65	2016 estimated tax payments and amount applied from 2015 return 65	3-24, 4-40	
	66a	**Earned income credit (EIC)** 66a	13-57	
	b	Nontaxable combat pay election 66b		
	67	Additional child tax credit. Attach Schedule 8812 67	13-60	
	68	American opportunity credit from Form 8863, line 8 68	13-49	
	69	Net premium tax credit. Attach Form 8962 69		
	70	Amount paid with request for extension to file 70	4-37	
	71	Excess social security and tier 1 RRTA tax withheld 71	1-23	
	72	Credit for federal tax on fuels. Attach Form 4136 72		
	73	Credits from Form: **a** ☐ 2439 **b** ☐ Reserved **c** ☐ 8885 **d** ☐ 73		
	74	Add lines 64, 65, 66a, and 67 through 73. These are your **total payments** ▶	74	
Refund Direct deposit? See instructions.	75	If line 74 is more than line 63, subtract line 63 from line 74. This is the amount you **overpaid**	75	
	76a	Amount of line 75 you want **refunded to you.** If Form 8888 is attached, check here ▶☐	76a	
	b	Routing number ▶c Type: ☐ Checking ☐ Savings		
	d	Account number		
	77	Amount of line 75 you want **applied to your 2017 estimated tax** ▶ 77		
Amount You Owe	78	**Amount you owe.** Subtract line 74 from line 63. For details on how to pay, see instructions ▶	78	
	79	Estimated tax penalty (see instructions) 79	4-40	

Third Party Designee Do you want to allow another person to discuss this return with the IRS (see instructions)? ☐ **Yes.** Complete below. ☐ **No**
Designee's name ▶　　Phone no. ▶　　Personal identification number (PIN) ▶

Sign Here Joint return? See instructions. Keep a copy for your records.
Under penalties of perjury, I declare that I have examined this return and accompanying schedules and statements, and to the best of my knowledge and belief, they are true, correct, and accurately list all amounts and sources of income I received during the tax year. Declaration of preparer (other than taxpayer) is based on all information of which preparer has any knowledge.
Your signature | Date | Your occupation | Daytime phone number
Spouse's signature. If a joint return, **both** must sign. | Date | Spouse's occupation | If the IRS sent you an Identity Protection PIN, enter it here (see inst.)

Paid Preparer Use Only
Print/Type preparer's name | Preparer's signature | Date | Check ☐ if self-employed | PTIN 2-2
Firm's name ▶ | Firm's EIN ▶
Firm's address ▶ | Phone no.

www.irs.gov/form1040　Form **1040** (2016)

Tax Formula for Corporate Taxpayers

Total income (from whatever source)	$ xxx,xxx
Less: Exclusions from gross income	− xx,xxx
Gross income	$ xxx,xxx
Less: Deductions	− xx,xxx
Taxable income	$ xxx,xxx
Applicable tax rates	× xx%
Gross tax	$ xx,xxx
Less: Tax credits and prepayments	− x,xxx
Tax due (or refund)	$ xx,xxx

Tax Formula for Individual Taxpayers

Total income (from whatever source)			$ xxx,xxx
Less: Exclusions from gross income			− xx,xxx
Gross income			$ xxx,xxx
Less: Deductions *for* adjusted gross income			− xx,xxx
Adjusted gross income			$ xxx,xxx
Less: 1. The larger of:			
a. Standard deduction	$ x,xxx		
or		or	− x,xxx
b. Total itemized deduction	$ x,xxx		
2. Number of personal and dependency exemptions × exemption amount . .			− x,xxx
Taxable income			$ xxx,xxx
Applicable tax rates (from tables or Schedules X, Y, or Z)			× xx%
Gross income tax			$ xx,xxx
Plus: Additional taxes (e.g., self-employment taxes and recapture of tax credits)			+ x,xxx
Less: Tax credits and prepayments			− x,xxx
Tax due (or refund)			$ xx,xxx

Standard Deductions and Exemptions

	Standard Deduction Amount	
Filing Status	2016	2017
Single	$ 6,300	$ 6,350
Unmarried head of household	9,300	9,350
Married persons filing a joint return (and surviving spouse)	12,600	12,700
Married persons filing a separate return	6,300	6,350
Additional for unmarried persons 65 and/or blind	1,550	1,550
Additional for married persons 65 and/or blind	1,250	1,250
Dependent (increase for earned income)	1,050 ($350)	1,050 ($350)

	Exemption Amount	
Filing Status	2016	2017
Personal and Dependency Exemption	$ 4,000	$ 4,050

Phase-Out Levels: Exemptions and Itemized Deductions

Filing Status	2017 Threshold AGI
Single individuals (not surviving spouse nor head of household)	$261,500
Married filing jointly or surviving spouse	313,800
Head of household	287,650
Married filing separately	156,900